DICTIONARY
OF
AMERICAN BIOGRAPHY

DICTIONARY OF American Biography

Supplement Nine

1971–1975

Kenneth T. Jackson
Editor in Chief

Karen E. Markoe
General Editor

Arnold Markoe
Associate Editor

WITH AN INDEX GUIDE TO THE SUPPLEMENTS

Charles Scribner's Sons / NEW YORK

Maxwell Macmillan Canada / TORONTO

Maxwell Macmillan International / NEW YORK OXFORD SINGAPORE SYDNEY

Copyright © 1994 by Charles Scribner's Sons

Charles Scribner's Sons
Macmillan Publishing Company
866 Third Avenue
New York, NY 10022

Maxwell Macmillan Canada, Inc.
1200 Eglinton Avenue East
Suite 200
Don Mills, Ontario M3C 3N1

Library of Congress Cataloging-in-Publication Data
(Revised for suppl. 9)

Dictionary of American biography. Supplement three–

    Supplement 9–   editor-in-chief: Kenneth T.
Jackson.
    Supplement 9 has imprint: New York : Scribner's ;
Toronto : Maxwell Macmillan Canada ; New York :
Maxwell Macmillan International.
    Supplements 1–2 comprise v. 11 of the edition of the
main work published in 10 v., 1946–1958.
    Includes bibliographical references and index.
    Contents: —3. 1941–1945.   [etc.]—
9. 1971–1975.
    1. United States—Biography—Dictionaries.
I. Garraty, John Arthur, 1920–   . II. Jackson,
Kenneth T.
E176.D563 Suppl.   920.073   77–2942
ISBN 0-684-15054-9 (suppl. 3)

ISBN 0-684-19398-1

1 3 5 7 9 11 13 15 17 19 V/C 20 18 16 14 12 10 8 6 4 2

Printed in the United States of America

∞ The paper used in this publication meets the minimum requirements of the American National Standard
for Information Sciences—Permanence of Paper for Printed Library Materials, ANSI Z39.48-1984.

Acknowledgment is gratefully made to those publishers and individuals who have permitted the use of the
following materials in copyright.

OGDEN NASH

2 lines from "Columbus," Copyright © 1935 by Ogden Nash; 2 lines from "England Expects," Copyright ©
1935 by Ogden Nash; 4 lines from "Lather As You Go," Copyright © 1942 by Ogden Nash; 2 lines from "Let's
Not Climb the Washington Monument Tonight," Copyright © 1947 by Ogden Nash; and 4 lines from "Song
to Be Sung by the Father of Infant Female Children" (also published as "Song to Be Sung by the Father of
Six-months Old Female Children"), Copyright © 1963, 1936 by Ogden Nash. From VERSES FROM 1929
ON by Ogden Nash. Copyright © 1933, 1935, 1936, 1942, 1947 by Ogden Nash. Copyright © renewed 1961,
1975 by Frances Nash, Isabel Nash Eberstadt, and Linell Nash Smith. "Columbus" and "Let's Not Climb the
Washington Monument Tonight" first appeared in the *Saturday Evening Post*. Reprinted by permission of
Little, Brown and Company and Curtis Brown, Ltd.
    1 line from "A Man Can Complain, Can't He?" Copyright © 1963, 1936 by Ogden Nash. From
THERE'S ALWAYS ANOTHER WINDMILL by Ogden Nash. First appeared in the *New Yorker*. Reprinted
by permission of Little, Brown and Company and Curtis Brown, Ltd.
    4 lines from "Invocation," Copyright © 1931 by Ogden Nash; 8 lines from "The Pulpiteers Have Hairy
Ears," Copyright © 1931 by Ogden Nash; 2 lines from "Reflections on Veracity," Copyright © 1931 by Ogden
Nash; and 2 lines from "Spring Comes to Murray Hill," Copyright © 1931 by Ogden Nash. From HARD
LINES by Ogden Nash. Copyright © 1930, 1931 by Ogden Nash. Reprinted by permission of Little, Brown
and Company and Curtis Brown, Ltd.

MARGARET LEECH PULITZER

4 lines from quotation by Margaret Leech Pulitzer as reprinted in *New York Times Book Review*, Nov. 1, 1959.
Copyright © 1959 by The New York Times Company. Reprinted by permission.

ALLAN SHERMAN

6 lines from "Sarah Jackman," Copyright © 1962 by Allan Sherman, and 4 lines from "Hello Muddah, Hello
Faddah," Copyright © 1963 by Allan Sherman. Reprinted by permission of Curtain Call Productions, Inc.

PREFACE

The *Dictionary of American Biography* traces its origins to Feb. 14, 1920, when Frederick Jackson Turner, a Harvard professor already famous for the "frontier" thesis, proposed that the new American Council of Learned Societies sponsor a reference work similar to the British *Dictionary of National Biography*. After much discussion the project began in 1925, and the first volume in the long-awaited effort was published on Nov. 8, 1928.

Sixty-six years have now elapsed since the initial appearance of the *DAB*. During its long and distinguished publishing history, it has continued to maintain the highest standards of accuracy, balanced judgment in interpretation, and a consistent focus on "just portraiture," and it has continued to rank as the standard reference work on persons of significance in the American past. With this supplement, which contains the biographies of 544 persons, written by more than 300 authors, the *DAB* extends its coverage through 1975 and reaches a total of 18,654 sketches.

Following previous *DAB* procedure, Supplement 9 covers Americans who died in the five-year period between Jan. 1, 1971, and Dec. 31, 1975. In general, the editors have included persons who made major professional or artistic contributions while living in the United States and who contributed notably to its history, whether or not they ever actually became citizens. Similarly, we have generally not included persons, such as Eamon de Valera, who were born in the United States but who left at a very young age and whose major achievements took place in other countries.

Although this is the first supplement produced independently of the American Council of Learned Societies, in selecting a few hundred persons from the more than nine million Americans who died in those years, the editors followed the practice established by their predecessors for generations. First, they compiled a substantial list of candidates from a variety of sources. Second, they classified the names according to profession or occupation. Third, they submitted the lists to specialists or groups of specialists who helped to rank the potential biographies. Finally, an advisory board, consisting of Professors Stuart W. Bruchey of the University of Maine, Joshua Lederberg of Rockefeller University, and Arthur M. Schlesinger of the City University of New York, reviewed the final list and made recommendations for additions and deletions.

Although this volume includes several organized crime figures and one notorious bank robber, most of the persons profiled in these pages were chosen because of substantial positive achievements. The initial volumes of the *DAB* stressed the lives of soldiers, elected officials, writers, and clergymen. This supplement, following a trend that began several decades ago, gives a more balanced coverage of fields, with significant representation in the performing arts, entertainment, sports, music, reform, and both the natural and the social sciences. No reference book can change the fact that white, affluent males have been disproportionately numbered among the leaders of American society. But we can recognize the first persons to overcome racial and gender barriers and to open the way for others. Thus, this volume includes more women and minorities than previous volumes, among them pioneers like Kenny Washington, who integrated post–World War II professional football, and Jackie Robinson, who integrated major-league baseball. Similarly, we have chosen to include many persons, such as Anne Sexton and Jane Bowles, who became better known after their deaths.

Contributors were asked not only to appraise the circumstances and influences that shaped careers, but to provide basic biographical data, including the full dates of birth and death, the full names and occupations of parents, the number of siblings, the educational institutions

Preface

attended and degrees granted, the names of spouses and the dates of marriages and divorces, and the number of children. Wherever appropriate, we have also included information on residences, cause and place of death, and place of burial. The length of articles has been determined both by the relative significance of the subject and by the completeness of the biographical information available.

Any large-scale research effort depends on the cooperation and enthusiasm of hundreds of persons, and this project is no exception. Irving Dilliard of Collinsville, Ill., however, merits special recognition because he has been associated with the *DAB* for more than sixty years and his two entries in Supplement 9 bring to ninety-nine the number of biographies he has written. Additionally, we are grateful for the advice and counsel of Richard H. Gentile and William M. Gargan, whose contributions went far beyond their individual entries. On the staff of the reference division of Charles Scribner's Sons, we wish especially to thank Leland S. Lowther, who compiled the initial lists of potential biographees; John Fitzpatrick, who shared with us his matchless experience in producing previous *DAB* supplements; Ann Leslie Tuttle and Richard Fumosa, the project's assistant editors; Sylvia K. Miller, who directed the entire effort with professionalism and efficiency; and Timothy J. DeWerff, who as associate project editor for two years has always been a model of grace and good judgment. Finally, Karen Day, the head of the Scribner reference division, had confidence in this project from its inception in 1989, and she has ever since been a source of encouragement and support.

Kenneth T. Jackson
Karen E. Markoe
Arnold Markoe
January 5, 1994

A

ABBOTT, WILLIAM A. ("BUD") (Oct. 2, 1896–Apr. 25, 1974), comedian and actor best known as the straight man in the comedy team of Abbott and Costello, was born in Asbury Park, N.J., the son of Rae Abbott, a bareback rider, and Harry Abbott, Sr., an advance man for the Barnum and Bailey Circus. Dropping out of school after the fourth grade, Bud began his real education at the Coney Island amusement park, where his father got him a job selling candy. He went on to have considerable success serving as a shill for the park's concessions. By age sixteen he had graduated from the carnival world into the world of burlesque, where he worked his way up the ladder of off-stage jobs, beginning as a ticket seller and eventually producing his own shows. Bud spent as much time as he could backstage, where by carefully observing such stars as W. C. Fields and Bert Lahr he eventually absorbed a deep knowledge of the slapstick, gags, crosstalk, and other burlesque forms of humor that made people laugh. By the 1930's, Bud was a very successful comedy straight man, earning top dollar at Minsky's Republic Theatre in Times Square.

In 1936, he teamed up with Lou Costello, and the two began a meteoric rise that would make them successively headliners in vaudeville, radio stars, and the most successful comedy team in the movies during the 1940's.

Their characters remained the same throughout their long collaboration; Bud was the selfish, shifty, fast-talking, scheming city slicker, and Lou was the naïf, the innocent, incompetent put-upon with the high squeaky voice whom Bud constantly manipulated.

Abbott and Costello appeared regularly on the radio for thirteen years. They began to do a regular comedy segment on the "Kate Smith Show" in 1938. Listeners wrote in to complain that they could not tell who was speaking and who was answering during the routines because Abbott's and Costello's voices sounded so much alike. To solve this problem, Costello created the high-pitched voice for which he eventually became famous. The team's success with Kate Smith led to appearances on the "Edgar Bergen and Charlie McCarthy Show," and eventually to their own "Abbott and Costello Program," which began on Oct. 8, 1941, and was one of radio's top fifteen programs for the next six years.

Their routines in the 1939 musical-comedy revue *The Streets of Paris*, their only Broadway show, attracted the attention of Universal Pictures film studio, which brought them to Hollywood to appear in the movie *One Night in the Tropics* (1940). Although their job was merely to provide comic interludes in a romance plot that featured two pairs of lovers, critics agreed that Abbott and Costello had stolen the picture. Universal executives realized they had a potential box office bonanza in their midst, immediately signed the comedy team to a multipicture contract, and set about crafting a tailor-made vehicle for Abbott and Costello. Their next film, *Buck Privates* (1941), established the model for all subsequent Abbott and Costello films. Here the pair are drafted into the army, where Abbott does his best to conform, but is constantly thwarted by Costello, for whom he has been made responsible. After many mishaps the two incompetents become heroes. The audience's sympathy switches from one to the other throughout the picture, though never really concerned with what happens to either of them. *Buck Privates* was a huge commercial success, earning more than $4 million at the box office, more than any previous Universal picture, and enough to make it the third-highest-grossing picture of 1941.

Their third film, *In the Navy* (1941), had the same plot but a different service environment, as did their fifth film, *Keep 'Em Flying* (also 1941), which put the team in the army air corps. Eventually the team was sent out West, to the South Seas, to a harem, to Africa, to Alaska, and even to Mars. They also made a series of comedy-horror pictures: *Abbott and Costello Meet Frankenstein* (1948), . . . *Boris Karloff* (1949), . . . *The Invisible Man* (1951), . . . *The Mummy* (1955), and so on. Altogether, the team made thirty-six films in seventeen years, their last being *Dance with Me, Henry*, a 1956 flop that marked the end of their association.

The plots of these films were simplistic for their time, and seem even more so now. One film may parody jungle adventure movies, another murder mysteries, and still another Foreign Legion adventure films, but there is a remarkable lack of real variety in the team's output. Indeed, the modern viewer is hard-pressed to understand what made the team and their films so popular in the 1940's. Perhaps it was the very predictability of their films that made them so successful. An audience made anxious by a war and its uncertain aftermath took comfort in going to an Abbott and Costello film because they knew what to expect. Or perhaps the team's success can be attributed to their devoted maintenance of the slapstick tradition; certainly, their many comedy routines in the films were polished by many years of burlesque, vaudeville, and radio performance.

The most famous of these routines, one that epitomizes the team's comic style, is the dialogue "Who's on first?," performed hundreds of times by the team before it became part of their film *The Naughty Nineties* (1945). Abbott is the tormentor who begins this baseball dialogue in which all the players' names are homonyms for common expressions: one player is named "Who," another is "What," and a third is "I don't know." Costello plays the increasingly frustrated and exasperated questioner who simply wants to know what the names and positions of the various players are. When Costello asks "Who's on first?," Abbott simply replies, "Who." Each of Costello's questions seems, to him at least, to be answered by another question, and each tormenting answer that appears

not to be an answer drives him to higher and higher levels of excitement. Simple in design, brilliant in execution, "Who's on first?" is one of the sublime routines in American comic history.

As the comedy team's film career wound down, they managed to hold onto fame for a while by taking their act onto television. Just as their movie career had recycled comedy routines from their burlesque and vaudeville years, their television career recycled film bits as television sketches. They frequently hosted and performed on the "Colgate Comedy Hour" from 1951 to 1954, and in 1952 and 1953 they had their own program, the "Abbott and Costello Show," for which they filmed fifty-two half-hour episodes. Although the critics hated their show and it quickly passed from the scene, it has had an immortal afterlife in reruns ever since it went off the air.

After breaking up with Costello in the mid-1950's, Abbott tried a solo act in Las Vegas, but it was unsuccessful and he retired from show business.

Bud Abbott married Jenny Mae Pratt on Sept. 17, 1918; they had two children.

Bud Abbott was an intensely patriotic man who devoted large amounts of his time and energy to entertaining U.S. servicemen and promoting the sale of war bonds during World War II. He entertained troops at more than three hundred army and navy camps, and at one point sold more than $78 million worth of war bonds during a thirty-one day tour.

Although he made millions during his career, Abbott died a relatively poor man in Woodland Hills, Calif. He was a compulsive gambler and a dramatically unsuccessful investor who got himself into serious trouble with the Internal Revenue Service for failure to pay his taxes.

[Bob Thomas, *Bud and Lou: The Abbott and Costello Story* (1977), gives a good account of their lives. Jim Mulholland, *The Abbott and Costello Book* (1975), offers discussion of the various phases of the comedy team's career, and Leonard Maltin, *Movie Comedy Teams* (1970), focuses on their films. An obituary is in the *New York Times*, Apr. 25, 1974.]

P. M. W. THODY

ABEL, RUDOLF IVANOVICH (1903–Nov. 15, 1971), also known as Emil R. Goldfus, Martin Collins, Andrew Kayotis, and "Mark," was a colonel in the Soviet Union's KGB-operated undercover intelligence networks in the United States for nine years, before his apprehension and exchange for American spy-plane pilot Francis Gary Powers in 1962.

Abel was born in St. Petersburg; his father (whose surname was Fischer) was a politically active factory worker who inspired his son. In 1927, Abel joined the Red Army and was assigned to intelligence work. It is believed that he managed to penetrate the Abwehr (the German Secret Service) during World War II.

As he admitted later during his trial for espionage, Abel entered the United States illegally in 1948. He rented an artist's studio in Brooklyn, N.Y., under the name Emil R. Goldfus, and lived fairly openly as a painter and photographer who had interests in music and radio. Abel formed relationships with some prominent intellectual and cultural figures of the Brooklyn Heights section of New York City. He impressed those who befriended him with his gift for languages. After his famous repatriation to the Soviet Union in 1962, Abel admitted that it was his instinctive linguistic skills that persuaded him to pursue a career in intelligence work.

The discovery of Abel's espionage activities came about through the defection of his assistant, Reino Hayhanen, who refused to return to Moscow when ordered back by his superiors. Hayhanen was a desperate alcoholic and presumably was considered unreliable by Abel and his Communist superiors in Moscow. In testimony at Abel's trial, Hayhanen claimed that he was an espionage agent, with the rank of lieutenant colonel in the KGB, who worked under Abel's direction. Hayhanen came to the United States in 1952 with a passport issued in Finland. He knew Abel by his code name, "Mark," and knew Abel's cover identity as that of a photographer.

When questioned by the FBI, Abel admitted to nothing beyond his illegal entry into the United States. The indictment against him made three charges: that he conspired to transmit to the Soviet Union information relating to American national defense, particularly with regard to arms, equipment, and dispositions of American armed forces and its atomic energy programs; that he sought actively to gather such information; and that he had remained in the United States without registering as a foreign agent.

At the time of his arrest on June 21, 1957, Allen W. Dulles, director of the CIA, referred to Colonel Abel as the most important foreign operative ever caught, the master spy of Soviet intelligence functions in America. During his trial, no defense witnesses were presented; Abel was found guilty and sentenced to more than thirty years in prison. Appeals failed; on Mar. 28, 1960, the United States Supreme Court upheld his conviction.

Although convicted and imprisoned, Abel was set free under extraordinary circumstances. In June 1960, the father of Francis Gary Powers wrote to Colonel Abel in the Atlanta (Ga.) Federal Penitentiary, urging him to engineer an exchange for his son, who had been shot down over the Soviet Union while flying an American reconnaissance plane. He was subsequently found guilty of espionage against the Soviet Union. Abel's lawyer, James Donovan, sought to arrange contacts between President Eisenhower's office, the Soviets, and the families of the convicted spies. At first, the Soviet government—which had made no "official" move on his behalf throughout his arrest, trial, and imprisonment—was not expected to agree to a trade of spies because doing so would mean acknowledging that Abel was indeed a Soviet espionage agent.

A dramatic exchange was worked out and made in Berlin on Feb. 10, 1962. The release of Abel required that President Kennedy commute Abel's sentence in order to effect the transfer.

Abel left no trace of his spy activities. He never confessed to anything except to being Rudolf Abel, which may in fact have been a pseudonym. His capture seemed a triumph for American counterintelligence, but no one in Abel's "ring" was ever uncovered except the defector Hayhanen, who volunteered his cooperation. It is more than possible that Abel never obtained any secret information vital to American security interests.

In an interview published in *Molodoi Kommunist* (Young Communist) in February 1966, four years after his return to the Soviet Union, the mysterious KGB colonel was characterized as a dedicated patriot who served his country for more than thirty years in dangerous jobs. Abel's decorations included the Order of Lenin and the Order of the Red Banner. Abel described his vocation in mundane terms: it was not the adventurous, exciting life depicted in films; being a spy was rather "arduous, painstaking work that calls for intense effort, stamina, perseverance, fortitude, willpower, serious knowledge and great mastery." And in March 1966, before the Moscow Press Club, Abel spoke again about his role as a KGB agent in the United States. He claimed that he was "not the great master spy they [American prosecutors] made me out to be. I was only a radio operator."

While little is known of his personal life (his friends and acquaintances in the United States attempted but failed to contact him in the Soviet Union) it is assumed that he had a wife, Helen, and a daughter, Lidiya. After his return to the Soviet Union both women published a letter in the government newspaper *Izvestia*, openly thanking Premier Nikita Khrushchev for making the exchange possible.

Abel died of lung cancer.

[On Abel's life in the United States, see Louise Bernikow, *Abel* (1970); the majority opinion of Supreme Court Justice Felix Frankfurter in *Abel* v. *United States*, 362 U.S. 217 (1960); and an interview with Abel, which appeared in *Molodoi Kommunist* (Young Communist) in 1966. An obituary appears in the *New York Times*, Nov. 17, 1971.]
                                        ROBERT J. KELLY

ABRAMS, CREIGHTON WILLIAMS, JR. (Sept. 15, 1914–Sept. 4, 1974), army officer, was born in Springfield, Mass., the oldest of three children of Creighton Abrams, Sr., a repairman on the Boston and Albany Railroad, and Nellie Randall. When he was a boy, his family settled in nearby Feeding Hills, where he gardened and raised calves in 4-H clubs, trapped animals for their pelts, repaired a Model-T, and learned to shoot. He was captain of an undefeated football team as a senior at Agawam High School, edited the school paper, and was valedictorian and senior class president.

Of average height, stocky, and muscular, Abrams was appointed in 1932 to the United States Military Academy, where his record was unremarkable except for frequent violations of discipline and in his final year a letter in football. When he graduated in 1936 he married Julia Harvey, a Vassar student whom he had met on a blind date. They had six children. Abrams was commissioned a second lieutenant and assigned to the First Cavalry Division. His promotions in World War II were rapid. As a lieutenant colonel he commanded the Thirty-

seventh Tank Battalion in the Fourth Armored Division when it landed in France in June 1944. His battalion participated in the breakout from the Normandy beachhead in late July 1944 and the sweep into the Brittany peninsula and the advance to the Seine in August. In September the battalion was the spearhead of General George Patton's drive toward Metz, capturing Sainte Genevieve in an action that permitted the Fourth Armored Division's crossing of the Moselle and its capture of Nancy on September 15. When the Germans broke through in the Battle of the Bulge in December 1944, Abrams led the task force that raised the siege of Bastogne.

After the war Abrams served as director of tactics at the Armor School at Fort Knox, Ky. (1946–1948), revised the army's manual on armored tactics, and graduated from the Command and General Staff College (1949) and the Army War College (1953). He commanded armored units in Europe from 1949 to 1952 and served as chief of staff of three corps in succession in Korea in 1953 and 1954. After serving two years as chief of staff of the Armor Center at Fort Knox (1954–1956), he was appointed assistant deputy chief of staff for Reserve Components (1956–1959). Abrams was promoted to brigadier general in 1956 and to major general in 1960.

Abrams was placed in positions of great responsibility during some of the most dramatic crises faced by the Kennedy administration. As assistant commander and then commander of the Third Armored Division (1959–1962) he played an important role in the Berlin crisis of 1962, and when he returned to the United States he commanded federal troops during rioting at the University of Mississippi in 1962 and at Tuscaloosa and Birmingham, Ala., in 1963. Later that year he was promoted to lieutenant general and assigned to command of V Corps in Europe. In 1964 he was promoted to full general and became vice–chief of staff of the United States Army.

In 1967, President Lyndon Johnson sent Abrams to Vietnam as deputy commander of U.S. Military Assistance Command, Vietnam (MACV), subordinate to General William Westmoreland. Abrams worked to improve the army of the Republic of Vietnam (ARVN), which performed well when it bore the brunt of the enemy's offensive, which began on Jan. 30, 1968 (Tet).

Abrams assumed command of MACV in the summer of 1968, in the wake of an announcement that peace talks would begin in Paris. President Johnson's Manila communiqué of October 1966 had promised a total American withdrawal within six months of a cease-fire. Abrams feared that this six-month deadline would impair his program for the modernization of the ARVN. In the latter half of 1968, Abrams committed a major share of his resources to a pacification campaign that was designed to clear the countryside of enemy forces and establish security for the local population before a cease-fire could take effect early in 1969. In fact, the Paris negotiations continued far beyond that year, and the campaign was abandoned as Abrams was forced to commit his diminishing forces to defensive operations.

Abrams knew that both the Paris peace talks and increasing antiwar sentiment in the United States required the prevention of a repetition of the Tet offensive. He gave top priority, therefore, to securing population centers, particularly Saigon, against attack, and by October 1969 had virtually ended major field operations by American forces, abandoning "search and destroy" missions for the sake of long-range reconnaissance patrols designed to locate enemy staging areas, ammunition dumps, communication centers, and rest camps, which could be attacked by his superior artillery and airpower. This strategy was not designed to win the war but only to prevent the South Vietnamese from losing it.

At the same time, General Abrams, in spite of private reservations, was responsible for implementing the Nixon administration's policy of "Vietnamization" of the war, which sought to upgrade the ARVN by improving the training of its younger officers and arming and equipping its units with American matériel as American units were withdrawn. By the spring of 1972 American forces had been reduced from an April 1969 peak of 543,400 to about 90,000.

In June 1972 President Nixon nominated General Abrams army chief of staff. Abrams took command of a large army demoralized by its Vietnam experience, plagued by racial tension and drug use in the ranks, and to a large extent dependent on conscription. He was able to devote only two years to the creation of a smaller, more professional volunteer army before his death from lung cancer in Washington, D.C. He is buried in Arlington National Cemetery.

Abrams, whom Patton considered his peer in armored warfare, earned a reputation in World War II as a hard-driving master of the offensive who believed that he could reduce his own casualties by striking the enemy with maximum violence. Ironically, his command of a rearguard action in Vietnam precluded offensive operations, while his defensive measures were hampered by diminishing resources.

[The Abrams papers, consisting of messages sent and received during his service in Vietnam, 1967–1972, are in the Historical Records Branch, Center of Military History, Washington, D.C. For biographical information see Lewis Sorley, *Thunderbolt* (1993). See also Will Lang, "Colonel Abe," *Life*, Apr. 23, 1945; Kenneth Koyen, *The Fourth Armored Division* (1946); "This Is the Army," *Time*, Oct. 13, 1961; Kevin P. Buckley, "General Abrams Deserves a Better War," *New York Times Magazine*, Oct. 5, 1969; and Jeffrey J. Clarke, *Advice and Support: The Final Years* (1988). An obituary is in the *New York Times*, Sept. 4, 1974.]

ROBERT L. BERNER

ACE, JANE (Oct. 12, 1905–Nov. 11, 1974), radio comedienne known for her malapropisms, was born in Kansas City, Mo., daughter of Jacob Epstein, a retail clothing merchant. She attended Central High School in Kansas City, where she was a few years behind her future husband, Goodman Ace, whom she married in 1922. Epstein, wanting to ensure his attractive, blonde, blue-eyed daughter's financial security, was not impressed with Goodman's suit. When Goodman told him that he worked for the *Kansas City Post*, Epstein replied, "Oh, really, where's your newsstand?" Despite her father's misgivings, the marriage was very successful and ended only with Jane's death fifty-two years later.

The comedy team of Jane and Goodman Ace was created by accident. Goodman was supplementing his income from newspaper writing by broadcasting "The Movie Man," a fifteen-minute weekly radio program devoted to reviews about the film world. One evening in 1929, after his own show had ended, Goodman was asked to improvise on air to mask a small emergency. Since Jane was waiting for him in the studio, Goodman called her in to chat with him. They talked about the bridge game they had played the night before and about a sordid murder committed a few days earlier, and then Jane quipped, "You care to shoot a game of bridge, dear?" Their improvisation was particularly enjoyed by a local advertising executive who offered to sponsor them on their own radio show. The Aces created "Easy Aces," a fifteen-minute program that aired twice a week in Missouri during 1930.

After the Aces went to Chicago for a trial run on CBS in October 1931, the "Easy Aces" became a national network feature for the next fifteen years. Jane and Goodman moved to New York City to continue the show for NBC in 1933; again using a fifteen-minute format, they broadcast three evenings a week. The show returned to CBS in 1948 for a half hour on Wednesdays.

"Easy Aces" was an urbane situation comedy throughout its history. Jane played a scatter-brained housewife and Goodman a breadwinner. Other regulars included Mary Hunter as Jane's friend Marge (gifted with a memorable laugh), Ethel Blume as Betty, Jane's friend, and Helene Dumas as Laura, their maid. A typical program might feature Jane's scheme to borrow money for a pet project from a businessman whom Goodman is trying to impress; another might involve Jane's manipulations for a mink coat. Her efforts to outwit her husband led to complication resolved by the end of the show. She delivered the laugh lines to Goodman's "straight-man" feeding, punctuated by his response, "Isn't that awful." Because Goodman wanted to stress the apparent spontaneity of the show, the couple talked over a card table with a built-in microphone, a prop retained from their early days when it had been used to remedy Jane's "mike fright."

Goodman wrote all the scripts for "Easy Aces" and eventually became one of radio's and television's most renowned comedy writers. Jane, however, with her gift for presenting overlapping dialogue delivered in her characteristic midwestern nasal twang and with her hilarious malapropisms, was the star of the show. Goodman defined the term *malapropism*, named for a Mrs. Malaprop, a character in Sir Richard Brinsley Sheridan's play, *The Rivals*, who confused and misused words that sounded similar, as "an actual word with a meaning of its own, even though the meaning is out of context." He went on to distinguish a malapropism from "a verbal boner that confuses things that don't contain similar-sounding words," as in Jane's "Love makes the world go round together." Goodman's lines for Jane blurred the distinction between the true malapropism and a verbal boner and were labeled "janeaceisms" by Goodman. Jane thus delivered malapropisms that made a point, such as: "I got up at the crank of dawn"; "Living in a squander"; "The food in that restaurant is abdominal." She is especially remembered for the phrases "Time wounds all heels," "words of one cylinder," "He's a ragged individualist," "The fly in the oatmeal," "You could have knocked me down with a feather," "thumb-nose description," "Congress is still in season," and "insufferable friends." While Gracie Allen and others were also adept at delivering malapropisms, it was Jane Ace who pioneered their use in radio comedy and linked them indelibly with her name in the public's mind.

The show was canceled in 1945 after Goodman's dispute with the sponsor; it was revived as "mr. ace and JANE" in February 1948, when it aired before a live audience. The half-hour show was again canceled in May 1949 because of low ratings. Removed from the comfort and informality of the closed studio, the revived show lacked the charm and apparent effortlessness of the original. However, during the 1945–1948 hiatus, transcripts of the original show were edited and sold to independent local stations, giving the Aces a larger audience than had heard the original broadcasts. Fees from these rebroadcasts allowed the Aces to retire from radio, which was particularly appealing to Jane who never regarded herself as an actress.

Between May 10 and June 14, 1950, an attempt to re-create the show on television was a failure. The dialogue was tailored to radio; the Aces's humor depended on the audience hearing the lines, not watching the actors delivering them. Television camera close-ups ruined the apparent spontaneity of the dialogue and highlighted the show's lack of visual effects. The Aces happily returned to private life at their Ritz Tower apartment in New York City, enjoying visits to the racetrack, the baseball park, and Miami. Goodman continued his comedy-writing career, especially for the "Perry Como Show," answering all requests for news of Jane with, "She's all right . . . if you like Jane." Jane lived in privacy until her death.

[For further information, see *Time*, Sept. 8, 1947; John Dunning, *Tune in Yesterday* (1976); Mark Singer, Profile, "Goody," *New Yorker*, Apr. 4, 1977; and Arthur Frank Wertheim, *Radio Comedy* (1979).

Obituaries appear in the *New York Times* and the *Washington Post*, both Nov. 12, 1974.]
ELIZABETH R. NELSON

ACHESON, DEAN GOODERHAM (Apr. 11, 1893–Oct. 12, 1971), statesman, lawyer, and author, was born in Middletown, Conn., the son of Edward Campion Acheson, Episcopal bishop of Connecticut, and Eleanor Gertrude Gooderham. As a high State Department official (1941–1947) and secretary of state (1949–1953), Acheson was one of the most influential individuals in the history of American foreign relations. He was more than "present at the creation" (to use the title of his memoirs); he was a principal author and implementor of the basic policies that guided the United States throughout the Cold War.

Acheson had an Anglo-Canadian heritage. His father served briefly in the British army in Canada before entering the ministry. His mother was a member of a Toronto family prominent in the whiskey distillery business. Acheson graduated in 1911 from Groton School. The austerity of that famed training ground for sons of the American aristocracy was not to his taste. Yale, however, was enjoyable for Acheson. He rowed on the crew and was more interested in social life than scholarship. He graduated in the class of 1915 and thence to Harvard Law School and serious use of his great intellectual power, graduating in 1918. He benefited especially from the teaching and friendship of Professor Felix Frankfurter. On May 5, 1917, he married Alice Stanley, who graduated that year from Wellesley College. They had three children.

After brief noncombat service in the United States Navy during World War I, Acheson went to Washington for a two-year clerkship with Supreme Court Justice Louis D. Brandeis. In 1921, at a time when most distinguished legal careers were to be made in New York, Acheson entered the firm of Covington and Burling in Washington. Throughout his life he would return to that firm after periods of public service.

In May 1933 Acheson joined the administration of President Franklin D. Roosevelt as under secretary of the Treasury, but resigned in November because he believed the president's monetary policy, leading to the devaluation of the dollar, lacked sufficient legal justification. Returning to the practice of law, he remained a conservative Democrat but declined invitations to join a revolt against Roosevelt.

With the outbreak of war in Europe in 1939 and the extension of Japanese conquests in Asia, Acheson became an articulate public advocate of military preparedness and a foe of isolationism. In a November 1939 speech he simultaneously spoke to the needs of the moment and set forth a philosophy of American foreign policy that would guide him later in high office: "I think it clear that with a nation, as with a boxer, one of the greatest assurances of safety is to add reach to power." Were the totalitarian nations to prevail, the result would be "our internment on this continent and such portion of the one to the south as we can physically control. Here, surrounded by armed and hostile camps, we will have to conduct our economy as best we can and attempt to preserve the security and dignity of human life and the freedom of the human spirit."

With other interventionists he helped persuade Roosevelt to conclude the destroyer-bases deal of September 1940 with Great Britain, whereby the United States gave old American warships to Britain in return for lease rights to establish American bases on British colonial islands from Newfoundland to the Caribbean. In January 1941 Roosevelt brought Acheson back into government as assistant secretary of state for economic affairs. For the next four years he dealt with both wartime economic measures and postwar planning. He played a major role at the Bretton Woods (N.H.) conference in creating the International Monetary Fund and the International Bank for Reconstruction and Development (World Bank), the basic institutions of a new international economic system.

Following the appointment of James F. Byrnes as secretary of state by President Harry S. Truman in 1945, Acheson was promoted to under secretary of state. He served in that capacity under Byrnes and his successor, George C. Marshall, until June 30, 1947. During this period, when the conflict between the Soviet Union and the West began, Acheson was frequently the acting secretary of state while Byrnes or Marshall were abroad. He directed much of the day-to-day activity of the Department of State, and contributed to the intellectual foundations of the Truman Doctrine (March 1947) and the Marshall Plan (June 1947). Acheson advocated strong support for Iran and Turkey against Soviet pressure in 1946, and in 1947 was the principal articulator of the concept that the ultimate well-being of the

United States depended on the economic reconstruction of Western Europe and Japan. With David E. Lilienthal, he presented the plan for the international control of atomic weapons which, in altered form, became the public American proposal announced by Bernard Baruch (Baruch Plan) and summarily rejected by the Soviet Union in June 1946.

In July 1947 Acheson returned a second time to the practice of law, but only for eighteen months. In January 1949 he was nominated by President Truman as secretary of state and confirmed by the Senate to succeed Marshall, who had resigned for health reasons. The close daily collaboration of the sophisticated and haughty eastern secretary of state and the homespun midwestern president was the heart of foreign policy for the next four years. Acheson strove with great effectiveness to protect and enhance the president's authority. At the same time Acheson gave his subordinates in the State Department great responsibility and respect. For many a Foreign Service professional, the Acheson years were a golden age.

Acheson advocated the calculation of national interest uncluttered by considerations of personal ambition, domestic politics, or moralistic generalities. The nation's fundamental international objective, he believed, was the acquisition and preservation of power sufficient, with a margin of safety, to contain the expansion of the Soviet Union and Communism, and to prevail in war should containment fail. Political, economic, and military power were for Acheson equally important and mutually dependent. Political power at home required educating the public concerning national purpose; abroad, it meant making allies and supporting their needs. Economic power meant reconstruction and a high level of trade within the non-Communist world. Military power meant perfection of a nuclear deterrent, large conventional forces, overseas bases, and rearmament of allies. Acheson judged every action in terms of its efficacy in the struggle against the Soviet Union. That which strengthened the West and weakened the Soviet Union was always to be sought and its reverse avoided.

The first months of Acheson's secretaryship, from January to July 1949, were filled with accomplishment. He completed the negotiation of the North Atlantic treaty and shepherded it through the Senate in the spring of 1949. In May the Soviets, having failed to prevent the establishment of the West German government, lifted the Berlin blockade. In the summer Congress approved an expensive military aid program for the North Atlantic allies. Then came two shocks: the Soviet detonation of an atomic bomb in August and the triumph of the Communists in China, formally marked by the proclamation of the People's Republic of China in October.

Acheson's response to the end of the American nuclear monopoly was to advocate the development of the thermonuclear, or hydrogen, bomb. President Truman agreed in January 1950 and the work began. Acheson also arranged for a comprehensive study, directed by the head of the State Department Policy Planning Staff, Paul Nitze, on the nature of the conflict with the Soviet Union. The result was a classified but widely leaked National Security Council memorandum, completed in April 1950. NSC-68, as it has been known ever since, was pure Acheson in its emphasis on the inseparable nature of political, economic, and military power and the total nature of the Soviet threat. The document called for a three- to fourfold increase in military spending, intensified covert action against the foe, and an accelerated nuclear buildup. It was skeptical of the utility of negotiations in solving differences with the Soviet Union, except under conditions of predominant Western power.

Acheson's response to the Communist victory in China was to continue an unsuccessful effort to persuade congressional and other critics that events in China were determined by the Chinese, and specifically by the corruption and political blundering of the Chinese Nationalists, and not by anything the American government did or failed to do. The most important part of this effort was the publication by the Department of State in August 1949 of a 1,000-page volume of narrative and original documents on U.S. policy known as the "China White Paper." Unfortunately for Acheson, the "White Paper" added fuel, not water, to the fires of controversy. Acheson went on to argue that China and the Soviet Union, regardless of ideology or leaders of the moment, were natural antagonists. The United States should stand aside and let that conflict develop, and not become China's enemy through a policy of intervention. The purpose of Acheson's Press Club speech of January 1950 was to make this argument. The speech was remembered, however, for an incidental description of the American defense perimeter in the Pacific as including Japan and the Philippines, but not South Korea—thereby, said Acheson's critics afterwards, inviting the North Korean attack of June 1950.

The Korean War was the pivotal event of Acheson's four years as secretary of state. He reinforced President Truman's determination that the North Korean aggression had to be turned back and orchestrated the diplomatic side of that endeavor: arranging UN Security Council action (possible only because the Soviets happened to be absent), reassuring allies and gathering their support, raising the issue of West German rearmament as a necessary element in defending Europe. By September 1950 American military intervention had routed the North Korean army. Here Acheson's judgment faltered. He agreed that all of Korea should be united by force, supported the crossing of the 38th parallel by the forces under command of General Douglas MacArthur and their drive north toward the border of China, and grossly underestimated the chances that the People's Republic of China, feeling threatened by the proximity of American forces on its border, would enter the war.

After the devastating Chinese attack of November 1950, Acheson struggled to stabilize American foreign policy. He reassured European allies fearful of the outbreak of nuclear war. As General Douglas MacArthur had repeatedly disobeyed orders in publicly criticizing the president's foreign policy, Acheson helped President Truman to dismiss MacArthur as commander of Korean operations. While he advocated strong military efforts to drive the Chinese back into North Korea, he was willing to accept an armistice that left Korea divided into two countries.

Meanwhile Acheson pressed ahead with the political and military strengthening of NATO through the appointment of General Dwight D. Eisenhower as its supreme commander, the stationing of additional American troops in Europe, assistance to the French in their war against the forces of Ho Chi Minh in Indochina (Vietnam), and a peace treaty and defense agreement with Japan (signed in 1951). Acheson's support of the French in Indochina had greater long-term consequences than he, or anyone, had imagined at the time. The support initially was part of a tacit bargain to persuade the French to accept the revival of West German economic and military power. "The French blackmailed us," Acheson said years later. By 1951, however, Acheson believed that preserving a non-Communist Indochina was a vital American interest, regardless of developments in Europe. In 1954, as a private citizen, Acheson deplored the decision of President Eisenhower not to use American military forces to save the French when the fortress of Dien Bien Phu was under siege.

In retrospect, Acheson believed that policies toward the Middle East during his tenure were the least successful. His purpose was to accommodate Middle Eastern nationalism without breaking completely with the British ally. This meant nudging an unwilling British government toward acceptance of Iran's nationalization of the British-owned oil industry, and later into making political concessions to Egypt. Acheson believed the United States should be evenhanded in dealing with the conflict between the new state of Israel and its Arab neighbors, but believed that Truman's quick recognition of Israel was ill-advised.

Acheson had little knowledge or interest in Latin America except for Brazil, whose vitality and frontier potential excited him. Africa was still largely in the colonial possession of the British, French, Portuguese, and Belgians, and Acheson believed it would and should so remain.

Few secretaries of state have received so much criticism as Acheson. The attacks came from the right wing of the Republican party and focused on the "loss" of China, the alleged green light for North Korean aggression, and false accusations that he had tolerated Communists within the State Department. Senator Joseph R. McCarthy was the most strident of the attackers, men whom Acheson dismissed as "primitives." His open disdain for people and arguments he considered contemptible drove his opponents into ever deeper rage. President Truman, however, stood by his secretary of state, saying Acheson's presence was vital to American security.

With the inauguration of Republican president Eisenhower in January 1953, Acheson returned a third time to private life and the practice of law. But he was too committed to foreign policy to confine himself to the problems of corporate clients. In the final eighteen years of his life he wrote six books, scores of articles, and maintained an extensive exchange of letters with friends around the world. Three of the books were political commentary: *A Democrat Looks at His Party* (1955), *A Citizen Looks at Congress* (1957), and *Power and Diplomacy* (1958); three were memoirs: *Sketches from Life of Men I Have Known* (1961), *Morning and Noon* (1965), and his major work, *Present at the Creation: My Years in the State Department* (1969). In addition, many of his essays and short pieces were collected in *Fragments of My Fleece* (1971), *Grapes from Thorns* (1972), and *This Vast External Realm* (1973).

In the final phase of his career Acheson enjoyed criticizing what he considered the follies of the Eisenhower administration and Secretary of State John Foster Dulles. He also lambasted the views of former diplomat George F. Kennan favoring the possibility of "disengaging" Soviet and American forces in Europe. Any diminution of American military strength in Europe was always anathema to Acheson.

With the inauguration of Democratic president John F. Kennedy in 1961, Acheson's advice was once again welcome in the White House. He advocated staunch resistance in 1961 to a Soviet effort to dislodge the Western allies from Berlin. Kennedy asked him to join a special circle of advisers during the Cuban missile crisis of October 1962. Although his recommendation that the United States bomb the missile installations first and negotiate second was rejected, he went as a special envoy to French president Charles de Gaulle. In 1965 he urged President Lyndon B. Johnson to press on to victory in Vietnam. His message on every issue through 1967 was vintage Cold War: be tough, be brave, and do not shrink from spending money or using military force. But when consulted by Johnson on Vietnam in 1968, and given access to cables and other documents, he said the president had been misled with poor information, that victory was no longer possible at acceptable cost, and that the United States should begin to disengage. Acheson's abandonment of the traditional hard line was a significant element in Johnson's decision, in March 1968, to seek a negotiated settlement of the war while renouncing his candidacy for reelection in November.

As a senator, Richard M. Nixon had been among Secretary of State Acheson's most strident critics, speaking on one occasion of "Acheson's College of Cowardly Communist Containment." But in 1969, on the advice of Henry Kissinger, his national security adviser, President Nixon invited Acheson to the White House. The two men became mutual admirers. Acheson was flattered that the Nixon-Kissinger worldview—with its emphasis on the importance of military power and realistic, nonmoralistic calculation—was so close to his own.

Acheson died suddenly of a stroke while working at his desk at his country home in Sandy Spring, Md. He had just completed a letter to his friend Anthony Eden, former British foreign secretary and prime minister.

[There are major collections of Acheson's letters and memoranda in the Harry S. Truman Library in Independence, Mo., and the Sterling Memorial Library of Yale University in New Haven, Conn. His official State Department work is documented in the National Archives, Washington, D.C., and much has been published in the many volumes of Department of State, *Foreign Relations of the United States*, covering the years of 1941–1947 and 1949–1952. Books written by Acheson are listed in the article above. See also Gaddis Smith, *Dean Acheson* (1972); David S. McLellan, *Dean Acheson: The State Department Years* (1976); David S. McLellan and David C. Acheson, eds., *Among Friends: Personal Letters of Dean Acheson* (1980); and Douglas Brinkley, *Dean Acheson: The Cold War Years, 1953–1971* (1992). An obituary appears in the *New York Times*, Oct. 13, 1971.]

GADDIS SMITH

ADDERLEY, JULIAN EDWIN ("CANNONBALL") (Sept. 15, 1928–Aug. 8, 1975), alto saxophonist, was born in Tampa, Fla., the son of Julian Carlyle Adderley, a former cornet player and high school teacher and guidance counselor, and Jessie Johnson, an elementary school teacher. Julian ("Cannonball") Adderley had a reputation as a hearty eater early in life; when he was going to school in Tallahassee, a fellow student wanted to call him a cannibal but mispronounced it as "cannibol." People not knowing the joke heard the name as "Cannonball."

Adderley began playing the alto saxophone in 1942 at the age of fourteen. He originally wanted to play tenor, but during World War II he bought an alto because it was the only saxophone available to him. Later he played the tenor saxophone solos of Lester Young and Coleman Hawkins, thus developing a hard, explosive style of playing the alto saxophone. About the same time, Adderley was influenced by Eddie ("Cleanhead") Vinson and Charlie Parker.

In 1948, Adderley graduated from Florida A&M University with a B.A. in music and became a high school music teacher and band leader at Dillard High School in Fort Lauderdale, Fla. During the years 1949–1950, Adderley concentrated on teaching; he rarely practiced his horn, playing only to demonstrate concepts for his students. In 1950, he went into the army where he met an alto saxophonist named Hafis and started playing again. Adderley joined the U.S. Army Band and spent most of his service life in Fort Knox, Ky. He was discharged from the army in 1953 and returned to Fort Lauderdale and teaching for two and a half more years. Now there were more playing opportunities and Adderley formed a small band that played jazz and rhythm and blues.

Enrolling in summer school at New York University for graduate study in 1955, Adderley immediately began playing with the Oscar Pettiford group at the Cafe Bohemia. His younger brother, Nat Adderley, cornetist and composer, was free-lancing in New York City after leaving Lionel Hampton's band. In 1956, Cannonball Adderley formed his first quintet. Nat and Cannonball recorded their first album together, "Bohemia After Dark" (Savoy 4514). This was the year that Charlie Parker died, and record companies and writers were looking for someone to call the "New Bird." Adderley was a new face in New York and promoters advertised him as Bird's replacement. He objected to this kind of advertisement because he wasn't playing Bird's way, but the publicity people insisted on packaging his album as the "New Bird."

Adderley broke up his band because they weren't doing well and joined the Miles Davis Sextet in late 1957 with John Coltrane, Red Garland, Paul Chambers, Philly Joe Jones, and Bill Evans. In an interview, Cannonball said about the Miles Davis Sextet, "I think I really began to grow there, because the band was such a classically good band; in fact the band was like a workshop; Miles really talked to everybody and told everybody not what to do, rather than what to do. . . . I think up to that point I never played so well." He continued to play with Miles Davis through 1959, leaving the band to start another quintet with his brother.

The Cannonball Adderley Quintet's first hit record featured Bobby Timmons's tune "Dis Here." Their fusion of gospel, soul, and jazz resulted in a very melodic style that bridged the gap between rock and jazz. Recording the Tim-

mons tune, Joe Zawinul's "Mercy, Mercy, Mercy," and "Walk Tall" created a new style of jazz referred to as "soul jazz." The Cannonball Adderley Quintet received wide recognition and success.

As bandleader, Adderley had a different rapport with his audience than Miles Davis, who played with his back to the audience. *Down Beat* critic John S. Wilson stated, "His unique ability to talk with his audience with intelligence, civility, and wit does a great deal toward establishing a warm, receptive atmosphere for his group." The warm atmosphere Adderley could create, combined with his teaching background, led his group through a series of concert appearances and lecture demonstrations on jazz at colleges.

In 1962, Julian Edwin Adderley married Olga James, an actress; they lived in Corona, Long Island. She recalls how Julian would not practice at home, but would think through the music. He would write and listen to music at home and would practice in the club or on the stand. Adderley was concerned with the kind of music he thought should be played; he would perform music that he thought promoted the art on the concert stage, but he would not play extended compositions in nightclubs.

Cannonball Adderley was an innovative improviser and a masterful alto saxophonist. He was a highly articulate man who communicated with his audience. Adderley had a strong commitment to fellow artists and an agreement with Riverside Records to promote new jazz talent. Under the name of "Cannonball Adderley Presentations," he was responsible for introducing Blue Mitchell, Wes Montgomery, and Nancy Wilson. He was the leader of his own group through the 1960's until his death in 1975. Cannonball Adderley died in Gary, Ind., after suffering a paralyzing stroke, at the age of forty-six.

[See the following articles in *Down Beat*: D. DeMichael, "The Responsibility of Success: Cannonball," 29, no. 13 (1962); B. Quinn, "The Well Rounded Ball," 34, no. 23 (1967); C. Albertson, "Cannonball the Communicator," 37, no. 1 (1970); and P. Wilson, "Conversing with Cannonball," 39, no. 12 (1972). See also J. Winter, "Julian Cannonball Adderley," *Coda* 186 (1982). An obituary is in the *New York Times*, Aug. 9, 1975.]

MATTHEW MARVUGLIO

ADONIS, JOE (Nov. 22, 1902–Nov. 26, 1971), racketeer, was born Giuseppe Antonio

11

Doto in the Italian town of Montemarano, east of Naples. Several years after his birth (sources differ regarding whether he was seven or thirteen) his family moved to the United States, where they settled in Brooklyn, N.Y. Adonis was twenty-three when he was arrested for the first time, but the charges, auto theft and gun possession, were dismissed, setting a pattern that was to endure for the next quarter century.

During Prohibition Adonis was the bootlegging partner of several other rising young gangsters—"Lucky" Luciano, Meyer Lansky, Frank Costello, and "Bugsy" Siegel—and he opened a speakeasy in Brooklyn called Joe's Italian Kitchen. It became popular with politicians as well as gangsters, and as such symbolized the easy relations between the two groups in Prohibition-era New York. Adonis further muddied the line between the legitimate and the illegitimate by claiming to be the champion of Italian Americans.

Adonis's bootlegging operation, which served some of Manhattan's most popular speakeasies, was termed the "Broadway Mob" by the press. He also owned several businesses, including auto dealerships. In 1932 Harry Bennett of the Ford Motor Company gave a contract to haul new cars to Adonis's Automotive Conveying Company of New Jersey.

Adonis joined the Mafia as a member of the crime family headed by "Joe the Boss" Masseria, who was killed in 1931 during a power struggle with another boss, Salvatore Maranzano. Adonis was rumored to have been one of the gunmen who shot Masseria at the Nuova Villa Tammaro restaurant in Coney Island, Brooklyn, on April 15. Whatever his role, Adonis and several other of Masseria's young followers, including Luciano, joined Maranzano's crime network. Tensions soon developed between Maranzano and the Luciano–Adonis camp, and the younger mobsters struck first. A group of gunmen posing as policemen shot Maranzano to death in his office in the Grand Central Building in Manhattan on Sept. 10, 1931. Mafia informer Joseph Valachi later testified that the murder was committed by Jewish gangsters hired by Luciano.

Luciano and his allies, including Adonis, became the most powerful racketeers on the East Coast. Adonis's criminal specialties included labor racketeering, political corruption, and gambling. His control of labor unions gave Adonis vast influence on Brooklyn's docks, and he was close to important politicians, such as William O'Dwyer, who eventually became Brooklyn district attorney and mayor of New York City. Adonis also had a string of illegal gambling parlors in greater New York and held an interest in several "carpet joints," or illegal seasonal gambling casinos, such as the Piping Rock in Saratoga, N.Y., and the Colonial Inn in Hallandale, Fla.

In the mid-1930's the election of reformer Fiorello La Guardia as mayor of New York City and the appointment of Thomas Dewey as an independent state prosecutor drove Adonis from the city. He and his family moved from Brooklyn into a mansion on Dearborn Road in Fort Lee, N.J., just across the Hudson River from New York City via the new George Washington Bridge.

Adonis did business from the back room of a restaurant he owned in the neighboring community of Cliffside Park. Duke's, at 73 Palisades Avenue, became a New Jersey version of Joe's Italian Kitchen. Adonis regularly played host to other members of the New York underworld, such as Albert Anastasia and Willie Moretti, a killer who told a Senate committee that Duke's was "like Lindy's on Broadway." Another mobster, Tony Bender, asserted his Fifth Amendment protection against self-incrimination when asked if he'd ever been in Duke's. A lifelong Democrat, Adonis turned Republican in GOP-dominated Bergen County and for a time received the kind of treatment from police and prosecutors he once enjoyed in Brooklyn. Federal and New York investigators who parked in front of Duke's to keep an eye on its denizens were sometimes told by local police to move on.

After the United States entered World War II, military planners searched desperately for details about the coastal areas of Sicily. A Navy intelligence officer contacted Meyer Lansky, who passed the request on to his Italian partners. Adonis, Lansky later recalled, "dug up some foreign Italians and we brought them down together to 90 Church Street," the headquarters of navy intelligence.

Adonis supposedly adopted his surname as a comment on his good looks, and he was known for his impeccable grooming and elaborate wardrobe. He had several glamourous girlfriends, including Virginia Hill, who later became famous as the paramour of Bugsy Siegel. He also traveled in style: When he eventually was forced to leave the country, he did so in one of the best suites aboard the Italian liner *Conte Biancamano.*

Although Adonis was commonly described as a social menace, Robert Lacey has argued convincingly in his Lansky biography that Adonis and his partners were primarily gaming entrepreneurs whose other crimes, from bribery to murder, usually were designed to protect and promote these gambling businesses. Adonis ran a club on the New Jersey Palisades, the Barn, which was famed for its high-stakes crap games. John Scarne, a professional gambling consultant, has called the Barn "the biggest moneymaker in [the] history of all illegal gambling casinos." He estimated the Barn's annual profits from craps at $10 million.

Adonis undoubtedly possessed many business skills. In 1946 he advised a young employee of the Colonial Inn to have fifty copies made of an off-color, black-market record. Adonis told the employee to sell the copies, which cost $4 each to press, for $50. This quickly produced a profit of more than $2,000. "You see?" Adonis told the man. "I'm a Mob guy—I'm a businessman. I want you to know about business."

With notoriety came danger. When Senator Estes Kefauver's committee on organized crime held hearings in New York in 1950, Adonis refused to testify and was indicted for contempt. Shortly thereafter, in 1951, he was convicted in New Jersey on gambling charges and, for the first time in his life, went to prison. In 1954 Adonis, who had never become a naturalized citizen, was convicted of perjury for twice having sworn under oath that he was born in Brooklyn.

To avoid jail, Adonis returned to Italy in 1956. After a brief stay in Naples he moved to Rome, but was expelled by the police there for being "socially undesirable." He moved into an elegant apartment in downtown Milan, but was expelled from that city in 1971 for alleged Mafia activity. "I'm just a poor old man," he complained to the court that banished him. "I don't understand what you've got against me." He was sent to Serra de Conti, a town near Ancona, and lived there under police surveillance until he died. He was survived by four children and his wife, who brought his body back to New Jersey for burial.

[See also Hank Messick, *Lansky* (1971); Howard Abadinsky, *Organized Crime* (1981); Carl Sifakis, *The Mafia Encyclopedia* (1988); and Robert Lacey, *Little Man: The Gangster Life of Meyer Lansky*

(1991). A detailed obituary appears in the *New York Times*, Nov. 27, 1971.]

RICK HAMPSON

AIKEN, CONRAD POTTER (Aug. 5, 1889–Aug 17, 1973), poet and author of short fiction, novels, and critical essays, was born in Savannah, Ga., the son of William Ford Aiken, an eye surgeon, and his cousin, Anna Potter. His maternal grandfather, Dr. William James Potter, was a radical New England Congregationalist minister who forsook the dogmas of organized religion for Darwinism and Unitarianism. The Reverend Potter often shared his New Bedford, Mass., pulpit with Ralph Waldo Emerson. Aiken's father was a Quaker.

Conrad often spent his days reading Edgar Allan Poe's horror stories among the ancient vaults and eroded tombstones of Savannah's Colonial Park, which had once been a burial ground. The two worlds of his Puritan ancestry and his southern childhood were later to merge in his fiction and verse.

When Conrad was eleven, his father, in a fit of jealous anger, shot and killed his wife and himself as Conrad lay in bed in the next room. In his "third person autobiography," *Ushant: An Essay* (1952), he recalled that "after the desultory early-morning quarrel, came the half-stifled scream," followed by "his father's voice counting three, and the two loud pistol shots," then tiptoeing "into the dark room, where the two bodies lay motionless and apart, and, finding them dead, found himself possessed of them forever." The tragedy is also recalled in his autobiographical poem "Obituary in Bitcherel."

Sent to live with his mother's relatives in New England, he attended the Middlesex School in Concord, Mass. There he edited the school paper and excelled at tennis and baseball. Aiken also became familiar with the Unitarian spirit of self-inquiry so obvious in the internal musings of the narrator "D." in *Blue Voyage* (1927) and *Ushant.*

From 1907 to 1911, he was a student at Harvard University; in his sophomore year, he was elected president of the *Harvard Advocate.* At Harvard, he read Spanish and Italian poets in their native languages, read Arthur Symons's book on the Symbolists, and became impressed by Walt Whitman, and by Harvard professor George Santayana's insistence on the philosophical content of poetry. Aiken began to practice verse forms on a regular schedule, not caring whether the poems made sense. Later, he would tell would-be poets that they should begin by mastering the forms of verse; the words would then fall into place.

He declined the honor of being class poet. His "undergraduate poem," *The Clerk's Journal: Being the Diary of a Queer Man*, was published in 1971 with the addition of a "brief memoir" of the school; of his favorite teacher; and of T. S. Eliot, a fellow student one year older than Aiken. They often "got drunk together," and Aiken later said that he and Eliot influenced each other, that "the juices flowed both ways." He likened their relationship to that of Melville and Hawthorne.

In his senior year, on probation for cutting classes to write a poem, Aiken toured Europe on a bicycle for six months, then returned to graduate with the class of 1912. Shortly after receiving his B.A. on Aug. 25, 1912, he married Jessie McDonald, a Radcliffe graduate student. They had three children.

Eliot moved to England in 1914. In 1921, the Aikens moved there also because they felt that British schools and culture were superior to their American counterparts. As time passed, Aiken alternately made his home in Rye, East Sussex, England; in New York City; and in Brewster, Mass., on Cape Cod.

At Harvard, Aiken had played on the tennis team; in England, he reported the Wimbledon tennis matches for the *New Yorker*, and, beginning in 1934, as Samuel Jeake, Jr., wrote the magazine's "London Letter." But when in January 1936 he reported the deaths of King George V and Rudyard Kipling under the title "Kiplings and Kings Depart," the magazine severed the connection for several years.

The Aikens were divorced in 1930, and the children remained with their mother. Later that year, Aiken married Clarisse Lorenz, a writer and the author of *Lorelei Two: My Life with Conrad Aiken* (1983); they were divorced in 1937. On July 7 of that year, Aiken married Mary Augusta Hoover, a painter, who survived him, and to whom, in part, he dedicated *Ushant*.

Aiken's numerous books never provided an adequate living for him, his wives, and his children. He earned some income by writing, sometimes anonymously, more than 250 reviews for the *New Republic*, *Poetry*, the *Chicago Daily News*, and *Poetry Journal*. One of the latter was a "scathing review" of his own *Nocturne of Remembered Spring* (1917). He was a contributing editor to *Dial* in 1917 and 1918, and wrote "Letters from America" for *Athenaeum* and the *London Mercury*. In the 1917–1918 academic year, he was a tutor in English at Harvard. One of his students was Nathan M. Pusey, president of Harvard from 1953 to 1971.

Aiken's first volume of verse, *Earth Triumphant and Other Tales in Verse*, was published in 1914. Beginning in 1916, he experimented with adapting musical forms to poetry in a series of "symphones," including *Senlin: A Biography* (1918). His first volume of short stories was *Bring! Bring!* (1925). In the 1930's, he began publishing "preludes," experimental poems, that he said were an "all-out effort at a probing of the self-in-relation-to-the-world, the formation of a new Weltanschauung." Two of these, "Preludes for Memnon" and "Time in the Rock," along with two stories, "The Coming Forth by Day of Osiris Jones," and "Landscape West of Eden," are generally considered central to Aiken's corpus.

Altogether he was to publish five novels and five volumes of short fiction, almost forty volumes of verse (including three for children), and a volume of more than 250 critical essays, *Collected Criticism* (1968), that he had written from 1916 on for the *New Republic*, the *Dial*, and the *Chicago Daily News*. He also wrote essays in foreign languages, and, in 1937, the essay "Literature" for the Federal Writers Project Massachusetts *Guide*.

Two of his best-known short stories, "Silent Snow, Secret Snow" (1934), a story of a boy who is losing contact with reality, and "Mr. Arcularis" (1934; dramatized in 1957), an account of a man's subconscious imagining that he is on an ocean voyage while he is actually dying during surgery, were filmed for television. Aiken edited and/or compiled six volumes of twentieth-century American verse. One of these, Emily Dickinson's *Selected Poems* (1924), was credited with establishing her reputation as a major poet. Aiken also made four recordings of his own verse. His widely acclaimed autobiography, *Ushant* (1952), an interior monologue reflecting the influence psychoanalytic thought had on Aiken's work, is narrated by "D." (Aiken). "D." always refers to himself in the third person; his mind moves back and forth in time, and he writes in a poetic style rather than in the factual narrative style of most autobiographies. In the book, Aiken's real-life friends have pseudonyms: Ezra Pound is "Rabbi Ben Ezra," T. S. Eliot is "the Tsetse," and Aiken's three wives are "Lorelei One, Two, and Three." His last composition, *Thee: A Poem by Conrad Aiken* (1967), was a long work presenting his philosophy of the universe.

Aiken received a Pulitzer Prize for his *Selected Poems*, and the Shelley Memorial Award, both in 1930; a Guggenheim Fellowship in 1934; the Gold Medal of the fifth annual National Book Award in 1954 for *Collected Poems*; the 1956 Bollingen Prize in Poetry from Yale University for A *Letter from Li and Other Poems*; the 1957 Academy of American Poets Fellowship; a 1958 Gold Medal of the National Institute of Arts and Letters; the 1961 Huntington Hartford Foundation Award; the Gold Medal of Achievement from the Brandeis University Creative Awards Commission in 1967; and the National Medal for Literature in 1969. From 1950 to 1952, he held the chair of poetry with the title of Poetry Consultant to the Library of Congress. In accepting the National Book Award, Aiken said that poetry was "again staking claim to its true province, nothing less than the kingdom of all knowledge, reconquering borderlands lost to drama and the novel, philosophy, religion and science as well."

But a decade and a half later, he was pessimistic. Described in a 1969 interview as "a large, rotund, paunchy man who resembles sculptures of Buddha," he told an interviewer that his work was rarely taught in colleges and that he was seldom thought of as a great poet. He complained that "American poetry had come to a temporary pause. . . . Wallace Stevens was our last great poet." Robert Lowell was "greatly overestimated," he didn't "terribly like" Archibald MacLeish's "later things," and Allen Ginsberg's poetry was a "howl." He did think that John Berryman, whose verse had won the National Book Award in 1969, was "one of the more hopeful younger poets." He liked John O'Hara's short stories, but in general he was uninspired by the status of American writing: "Everything is deteriorating."

For all his seriousness as a writer, Aiken also admired another genre: "I read all the comics I can lay my hands on. . . . They're so real that I actually find myself dreaming about them and becoming part of their tapestry."

In 1973, Governor James Carter of Georgia appointed Aiken as his state's poet laureate. Aiken died in Savannah.

[The Henry E. Huntington Library in San Marino, Calif., holds Aiken's manuscripts and other papers. For further biographical information see "Conrad Aiken," *New York Herald Tribune*, Sept. 24, 1950; Harvey Breit, "Talk with Conrad Aiken," *New York Times*, Dec. 24, 1950; Malcolm Cowley, "Biography with Letters," *Wake* 11 (1952); Frederick John Hoffman, *Conrad Aiken* (1962); and Jay Martin, *Conrad Aiken* (1962). An obituary is in the *New York Times*, Aug. 18, 1973.]

CLARENCE A. ANDREWS

ALBRIGHT, WILLIAM FOXWELL (May 24, 1891–Sept. 19, 1971), biblical archaeologist, was born in Coquimbo, Chile, the son of American missionaries from Iowa, Wilbur Finley Albright and Zephine Viola Foxwell. Already a voracious reader when he was ten years old, Albright earned money by running errands and sent $5 to the United States for R. W. Rodgers's *History of Babylonia and Assyria*, which he later said he memorized. His family returned to Iowa when he was in his teens, and after graduating from high school in Plainfield he worked his way through Upper Iowa University (UIU) at Fayette by doing chores on his grandfather's farm. At the age of sixteen, while enrolled in UIU's preparatory academy, he began teaching himself Hebrew and Akkadian using his father's textbooks.

He graduated from UIU with a B.A. in classics in 1912 and accepted a job as principal of a high school in Menno, S.Dak., a German-speaking town in the southeastern corner of the state. Much to his surprise, the next year he was awarded a fellowship to Johns Hopkins University in Baltimore. He was admitted to the Oriental Seminary of Johns Hopkins in 1913 and earned his doctorate in archaeology and linguistics under Professor Paul Haupt in 1916.

In 1919 he was awarded the Thayer Fellowship at the American School of Oriental Research in Jerusalem. Two years later, Albright was named director of the American School. During the next eight years he directed excavations in Palestine at Gibeah, Tell Beit Mirsim, Bethel, and Ader. Albright quickly earned a reputation as a master orientalist, an expert on the culture and history of the Near East. Albright knew some twenty-five languages.

He had met his wife, Ruth Norton, a Sanskrit doctoral candidate, while they were both studying at Johns Hopkins. After a two-year, long-distance courtship, they were married on Aug. 31, 1921, in Jerusalem. They had four children. Albright remained director of the American School in Jerusalem until 1929, when he joined the faculty at Johns Hopkins University as W. W. Spence Professor of Semitic Languages and became chairman of the Oriental Seminary.

Beginning with the February issue in 1931, Albright served as the editor of the *Bulletin of the American Schools of Oriental Research*, a position he held until he resigned in 1968 because of failing eyesight. Albright used the journal to publish the results of his numerous excavations and research. Nearly one-quarter of all his published work, which numbered over 800 articles, books, and lectures, appeared in the journal.

From 1933 to 1936 he was both professor at Johns Hopkins and director of the Jerusalem School. During this period he excavated Tell Beit Mirsim in southern Palestine and published the first of his findings in 1936. In his three-volume *Excavation of Tell Beit Mirsim*, to which he added volumes in 1938 and 1943, Albright established the fundamental chronology of the archaeology of Palestine. Another major work, *The Archaeology of Palestine and the Bible*, was published in 1932. He returned to the United States in 1939 and, with the exception of a few trips to the Near East, remained there for the rest of his life. The last major excavation in which he took part was in 1950 and 1951, when he was chief archaeologist for the South Arabian Expedition of the American Foundation for the Study of Man. Archaeologists praised Albright for his use of potsherd as a dating yardstick. He was credited with dating a number of Biblical cities, including Tirzah, the capital of Israel for half a century in the time of Jeroboam I.

In his most famous work, *From the Stone Age to Christianity*, published in 1940, he traced the synthesis of Near Eastern cultures and traditions. The *Baltimore Sun* stated: "Dr. Albright traces the growth of man's belief in God from prehistoric days to the time of Christ, analyzing its progress made against the historic backgrounds and changing philosophies of the periods covered." The book has been translated into German, French, Spanish, Italian, and Portuguese, among other languages.

In 1947, Albright was the first outside expert to declare that the Dead Sea scrolls were genuine. Albright called the finding "the most momentous discovery in modern time pertaining to the Bible." Beginning in 1956, he served as senior editor of the Anchor Bible series, in which each book of the Bible is translated with notes and commentaries from various scholars. His long association with Johns Hopkins culminated in his appointment as professor emeritus in 1958. His last major work, *Yahweh and the Gods of Canaan*, was published in 1968.

The following winter, when he visited Israel at the age of seventy-seven, Albright was the recipient of the *Yaqqir Yerusalayim* (Worthy Nobleman of Jerusalem) award. He was the first nonresident of Jerusalem and the first non-Jew to be chosen for the honor. The title is awarded to those who have contributed to the city and are past the age of seventy.

Albright died in Baltimore, Md. In a fitting tribute, the American School of Oriental Research in Jerusalem was renamed the W. F. Albright Institute of Archaeological Research in Jerusalem.

[Chief among Albright's many books, in addition to those cited in the text, are *Archaeology and the Religion of Israel* (1942), *The Biblical Period* (1950), *Recent Discoveries in the Bible Lands* (1955), *History, Archaeology, and Christian Humanism* (1964), *New Horizons in Biblical Research* (1966), and *The Book of Matthew* from the Anchor Series (1971). For bibliographies of Albright's writings see Harry M. Orlinsky, ed., *An Indexed Bibliography of the Writings of William Foxwell Albright* (1941); David Noel Freeman, "Bibliography of W. F. Albright," *Eretz Israel* (1958–1969) and *The Published Works of William Foxwell Albright* (1975); and G. Ernest Wright, ed., *The Bible and Ancient Near East* (1961). Albright's 350 articles in scholarly journals are indexed in the *Bulletin of American Schools of Oriental Research* (BASOR). A biography is Leona Glidden Running and David Noel Freeman, *William Foxwell Albright* (1975). An obituary is in the *New York Times*, Sept. 20, 1971.]

RICHARD G. DEITSCH

ALDRICH, WINTHROP WILLIAM (Nov. 2, 1885–Feb. 25, 1974), lawyer, financier, and diplomat, was born in Providence, R.I., the tenth of eleven children born to Abby Pierce Chapman Greene and Nelson Wilmarth Aldrich. Winthrop William Aldrich came from one of the bluest of blue bloodlines: his lineage included one of the original Pilgrims who came to America on the *Mayflower*; Roger Williams, religious dissident and founder of the Rhode Island colony; and General Nathaniel Greene, hero of the American Revolutionary War and a man whom many historians rank second only to George Washington for contributing to America's ultimate victory. His own father, after making his personal fortune in investments, served as a U.S. congressman from 1879 to 1881 and as a U.S. senator from 1881 to 1911. A conservative pillar of the Republican party, the senior Aldrich defended protective tariffs and the gold standard, opposed efforts to regulate American big business, and played a key role in weakening the reach of both the 1887 Interstate Commerce Act and the 1890 Sherman Antitrust Act.

Winthrop Aldrich attended the Hope Street High School in Providence, a private preparatory school; Harvard University, from which he graduated with a B.A. degree in 1907; and Harvard Law School, where he graduated tenth in his class in 1910. He joined the New York City law firm of Byrne, Cutcheon, and Taylor after graduation, and after successfully passing the New York State bar examination in 1912, he became a junior partner at his firm. In 1919, Aldrich left Byrne, Cutcheon, and Taylor to join the firm of Murray, Prentice, and Howland. For the next ten years he devoted most of his time and energy to handling legal business for the Equitable Trust Company, a finance institution in which his brother-in-law, John D. Rockefeller, Jr., held a major interest.

Meanwhile, on Dec. 7, 1916, Aldrich had married Harriet Alexander; the couple eventually had six children. In 1917, when the United States entered World War I, Aldrich—since boyhood a lover of the sea and an avid and skilled sailor—enlisted in the U.S. Naval Reserve. During the war he held a number of active assignments, including serving as a commander of patrol boats and a navigation officer on the cruiser *New Orleans*.

In 1929, Aldrich demonstrated his mastery of legal matters, negotiating skills, and financial affairs when he oversaw the merger of the Equitable Trust Company with Seaboard National. Later that same year, after the death of Chellis A. Austin, president of the combined organization, Aldrich was asked to take over as acting president. Although reluctant to switch from law to finance, Aldrich accepted this new responsibility. After overseeing another merger, this time with the Chase Bank of New York, in 1930, he became the official president of the expanded institution. In 1934 he became chair-

man of the board of directors, and thereafter was head of the Chase National Bank, the Chase Bank, and the Chase Safe Deposit Company (now the Chase Manhattan Bank) until 1953.

A leading member of the overlapping social, financial, and Republican party establishments, Aldrich angered many of his peers in March 1933, when he publicly demonstrated a willingness to support at least some of Democratic president Franklin D. Roosevelt's efforts to reform the American banking system. He declared in the *Literary Digest*, a popular conservative periodical, that "the spirit of speculation should be eradicated from the management of commercial banks." He suggested that banks should take no part in the selling of private financial instruments, and should limit themselves to underwriting federal, state, and municipal securities. Moreover, he expressed support for Roosevelt's proposed Federal Reserve System, under which the federal government would both regulate and insure private banks. Certainly, Aldrich's public support of parts of Roosevelt's reform plan contributed to its ultimate success.

After the outbreak of war in Europe in 1939, Aldrich assumed the presidencies of two related charitable organizations, the American Society for British Medical and Civilian Aid and the American Society for French Medical and Civilian Aid, and in June 1940 became president of the two combined societies, renamed the Allied Relief Fund. In its separate and combined identities, the charity raised funds to buy ambulances and supplies for hospitals. From 1940 to 1943 Aldrich also held the post of president of the British War Relief Society, America's largest charity effort for its British allies, and when all American efforts—excepting the Red Cross—to raise charitable funds for America's allies were combined into the National War Fund in January 1943, Aldrich became the head of this organization. After World War II, Aldrich supported American efforts for European reconstruction, including the Marshall Plan.

A wealthy man in his own right, connected to many other wealthy people by birth and marriage, and at the center of the highest levels of American finance, Aldrich—as his charitable activities indicate—was in a position to raise large sums of money for issues and people he supported. He worked actively to raise funds for the campaign of Eisenhower in 1952, reportedly raising some $2,500,000 in New York. Thus it came as no surprise when after Eisenhower's election, Aldrich was offered a diplomatic plum, the ambassadorship to the Court of St. James, which he accepted. The British, well aware of Aldrich's charitable work for Great Britain during World War II, welcomed his appointment. He served as a popular ambassador until the Suez crisis of 1957, after which he resigned his post.

Aldrich received many honors during his life. He was decorated by the governments of Belgium, France, Great Britain, Luxemburg, and the Netherlands for his charitable efforts on behalf of these countries during and after World War II. Pope Pius XII made him a Knight Commander of the Order of Pius IX. The United States government gave him its Medal of Merit. He was awarded numerous honorary degrees, including degress from Colgate, Northeastern, Brown, Lafayette, Columbia, and Georgetown.

A sailing enthusiast, Aldrich won the Astor Cup in 1923 in his schooner *Flying Cloud*. He helped to finance and build the *Enterprise*, the America's Cup defender that he himself navigated to victory against Sir Thomas Lipton's *Shamrock V* in 1930. Subsequently, he served as a commodore at the New York Yacht Club, which regulates America's Cup competition. He also liked to play golf and was an amateur watercolorist and musician.

Aldrich died in New York City.

[Aldrich's papers are held by the Baker Library at Harvard University. The Baker Library also contains an oral history conducted by Crawford Wheeler with Aldrich at the Chase National Bank in 1960 and 1961. Arthur M. Johnson, *Winthrop W. Aldrich: Lawyer, Banker, Diplomat* (1968), is the definitive biography. An obituary is in the *New York Times*, Feb. 26, 1974.]

PHILIP G. HOLTHAUS

ALINSKY, SAUL DAVID (Jan. 30, 1909–June 12, 1971), radical activist, community organizer, and author, was born in Chicago, the son of Benjamin Alinsky and Sarah Tannenbaum, recent Jewish immigrants from Russia. His father was a tailor and a landlord. Saul's younger brother died in childhood; he had two half brothers and a half sister from his father's earlier marriage. Following his parents' divorce, Saul spent most of his time with his mother in Chicago.

After graduation from Marshall High School, Saul attended the University of Chicago from 1926 to 1930, studying urban problems and field research with some of that institution's world-famous sociologists. He graduated with a Bachelor of Philosophy degree, and for the next two years he did graduate study in criminology at the University of Chicago. In June 1932, he married Helene Simon of Philadelphia, whom he had met while an undergraduate.

In the 1930's, Alinsky was a member of Clifford Shaw's staff in the Institute for Juvenile Research. Shaw argued that delinquency resulted from the disorganization of American urban society rather than from the disorganization of the individual. Alinsky also served as a criminologist at Joliet State Prison from 1933 to 1935.

After returning to Shaw's organization from Joliet in 1939, Alinsky became involved in organizing Chicago's notorious stockyards neighborhood the Back of the Yards. This led to an acrimonious break between the two men, as Shaw felt this was outside the work of his institute. With the assistance of Roman Catholic archbishop Bernard Sheil, Alinsky created the Industrial Areas Foundation to continue his organizing efforts and headed the foundation until his death.

Alinsky's philosophy was that many of the problems of urban slums resulted from the feeling of powerlessness among poor urban dwellers. The traditional social work approach did not work because people from outside the community dictated to the urban poor. Alinsky's goal was to create viable organizations through which people could take control of their own lives. He felt that a functioning group could be created in three years. This approach often brought him into conflict with the social work establishment, the traditional political power structure, and the upper class.

The Back of the Yards Council first exemplified the success of Alinsky's methods. Subsequent attempts to create similar organizations in Kansas City and South St. Paul were less successful because of a lack of funding and trained organizers. More might have been achieved, but the outbreak of World War II channeled Alinsky's activities into other areas. A childhood injury prevented any military service, and Alinsky spent the war years improving worker morale for the War Manpower Board.

From the late 1940's until the middle of

the next decade, Alinsky's professional and personal career reached its nadir. Helene Alinsky drowned in 1947, though she successfully rescued two children from Lake Michigan. As he was recovering from this loss, another close friend died suddenly of polio. These two tragedies sapped his enthusiasm for work. Moreover, the beginning of the McCarthy era made support difficult for one who called himself a radical. Despite such problems, Alinsky's Industrial Areas Foundation had some success organizing Mexican Americans in California.

In 1952, Alinsky married Jean Graham, who soon manifested symptoms of multiple sclerosis. They divorced in 1969, and he married Irene McGinnis in 1971. In 1949, Alinsky authored a laudatory biography of labor leader John L. Lewis. Funding from the Schartzhaupt Foundation kept the Industrial Areas Foundation a viable, though small and personal, organization. Another major source of support was Monsignor John O'Grady of Catholic Charities.

Alinsky continued organizing, with varying degrees of success, in several California cities; Lackawanna, N.Y.; and New York City. Lack of experienced organizers, inadequate funding, the hostility of the social work establishment, and Alinsky's penchant for personal control prevented expansion of his work. When, because of other involvements, he did not take personal control, organization was indifferent and not always successful. Moreover, a weakness in the Alinsky approach was his tenet that organizations should be self-sustaining in three years. Some of his groups, upon maturing, became new establishments whose ultimate aims were not what Alinsky would have wished. One example was that the Back of the Yards Council worked assiduously to prevent integration of that area.

In 1961, Alinsky broke new ground when he took on the City of Chicago and his alma mater with the creation of the Temporary Woodlawn Organization. The normal problems of a run-down urban area were exacerbated by the university's expansion plans. This was one of the first attempts to organize a northern urban black community. A number of Alinsky's new tactics were pioneered in this struggle. Because urban blacks lacked political muscle, a caravan of buses delivered citizens to City Hall to register to vote. Other tactics aimed at legally embarrassing the establishment were tested or threatened.

Following serious race rioting in Rochester, N.Y., in the summer of 1964, Alinsky was invited to that city to organize the black community. FIGHT (Freedom, Integration, God, Honor—Today), the Rochester organization, successfully pressed its demands against both the city and the Eastman Kodak Corporation. Again, there was emphasis on using embarrassment and ridicule as organizing methods. While these unified Alinsky's clients, they led others to question Alinsky's good taste. In the struggle with Eastman Kodak, Alinsky also successfully used stock proxies as a major weapon.

The last years of Alinsky's life were spent in trying to shift emphasis from direct organization to creating an institute that would train larger numbers of organizers for urban communities. Aware of his own mortality, he wanted to ensure that others would continue his work. While visiting Carmel, Calif., Alinsky died of a heart attack on June 12, 1972.

Although variously called a Marxist, a fascist, a conservative, a cynic, and a tool of the Roman Catholic church, Alinsky was none of these. He was arrogant and eloquent; he could be smooth or abrasive to achieve what he felt were desirable goals. None who met him were neutral or indifferent. Alinsky was loved, hated, and feared. Despite his immigrant roots, Alinsky was a home-grown radical firmly rooted in American traditions. James Madison of the *Federalist Papers* and, to a lesser extent, Thomas Jefferson as a populist were his sources of inspiration. His lifelong goal was to help the poor and unorganized gain control over their own destinies and to help the urban underclass fully participate in American democracy. He firmly believed that neither government nor an elite should determine the fate of the urban poor.

[The best source of Alinsky materials is the Industrial Areas Foundation. Though a prolific lecturer in his later years, and the author of some articles and papers, books written by Saul Alinsky are relatively few. These include *Reveille for Radicals* (1946); *John L. Lewis: An Unauthorized Biography* (1949); and *Rules for Radicals* (1971). There are two useful biographies of Alinsky: P. David Finks, *The Radical Vision of Saul Alinsky* (1984); and Sanford Horwitt, *Let Them Call Me Rebel* (1989). Donald Reitzes, *The Alinsky Legacy* (1987), is an episodic and anecdotal account of Alinsky and his work; it may be the most readable.]

ART BARBEAU

ALLEN, FORREST CLARE ("PHOG") (Nov. 18, 1885–Sept. 16, 1974), basketball coach, athletic director, and osteopath, was born in Jamesport, Mo., the fourth of the six sons of William T. Allen, a salesman, and Alexine Perry. When Forrest Allen was two years old, the family moved to Independence, Mo. Throughout their school years, the Allen boys played football, basketball, and baseball.

Basketball became Forrest Allen's favorite sport. In 1902 he played for the Modern Woodmen of America basketball squad in Kansas City. In 1903 he played basketball for the Kansas City Athletic Club. The Allen brothers' basketball team, organized in 1904, lost only one game in four seasons and easily defeated teams from the universities of Missouri and Kansas. While playing for the Kansas City Athletic Club, Allen met James Naismith, the inventor of basketball, who had been employed by the University of Kansas since 1898 as the chapel director, athletic director, physical education chairman, and basketball coach.

Forrest Allen enrolled in Kansas University in Lawrence in 1904, partly because one of his brothers played football, baseball, and basketball there. At Kansas, which Allen attended for two years, he played football and basketball. He coached basketball at Baker University in nearby Baldwin, Kans., in 1907 and 1908. When Naismith talked to Allen about the Baker job, Naismith laughed, "You can't coach basketball! You just play it." Allen responded: "I certainly can teach free-throwing. I can teach the boys to pass at angles and run in curves."

In 1908 and 1909, Allen coached basketball, part time, at the University of Kansas, winning the Missouri Valley championship both years. In addition, he took a position coaching basketball at Haskell Indian School in Lawrence in 1909. During his college days, Allen also umpired baseball games, calling the strikes, balls, and outs in a deep voice. The sobriquet "Foghorn" became "Fog," and finally "Phog."

Allen married Elizabeth ("Bessie") Milton, a graduate of the State Teachers College, Warrensburg, Mo., in June 1908. The Allens had six children. Two sons, Milton and Robert, became basketball All-Americans at Kansas University under their father's coaching.

In 1909 Allen enrolled in the Kansas City School of Osteopathy, believing that study there would aid him in coaching and treating athletic injuries. He received his Doctor of Osteopathy degree in 1912. Between 1912 and 1919, Allen coached all sports and served as athletic director at Central Missouri State Teachers College, Warrensburg, Mo. He compiled an 84–31 basketball win-loss record there.

In 1919 the University of Kansas invited him to be director of athletics, in which role he served until 1937, and freshman basketball coach. He assumed the duties of head basketball coach in 1920, a year in which he also served as football coach. He was often accused of emphasizing basketball at the expense of other sports at Kansas. Yet Allen was a major force behind obtaining a 38,000-seat football stadium for the university. In 1923 Allen inaugurated the Kansas Relays, an annual track and field carnival that became one of the nation's premier collegiate meets. From 1924 to 1946, in addition to his other duties, Allen served as head of the physical education department.

Allen also joined with other American college coaches on issues affecting the game of basketball. When the Joint Basketball Rules Committee arbitrarily drafted rules in 1927 that would have virtually eliminated the dribble, Allen called a meeting of college basketball coaches to oppose, successfully, a rule they feared would kill the game. Allen was one of the founders of this National Association of Basketball Coaches of the United States, serving as president for its first two years, 1928 and 1929; he chaired the association's research committee for eight years. Allen also was vice-president and a member of the National Collegiate Basketball Rules Committee, as well as chairman of its research committee for thirteen years. Starting in the late 1920's, he campaigned vigorously to include basketball in the Olympic Games, which occurred for the first time in 1936 in Berlin. Allen helped establish the National Collegiate Athletic Association (NCAA) basketball tournament beginning in 1939.

Allen's basketball coaching record was impressive. When he retired at Kansas in 1956, his teams had won 590 and lost 219 games in thirty-nine seasons. As of 1991, he was still ranked fourth in total victories among the NCAA Division I coaches, with 746 victories. It is not likely that anyone will top Allen's total of forty-eight years in coaching college basketball.

During his thirty-nine years at K.U., Allen coached fourteen All-American players. His Kansas teams won or shared twenty-four conference championships; they won the 1923 national title and the 1952 NCAA championship. After the NCAA win, seven members of the Kansas team combined with the American Athletic Union (AAU) champions, the Peoria Caterpillars, to represent the United States in the Olympic Games in Helsinki, Finland, where they defeated the Soviet Union in the finals. Allen accompanied them as the assistant coach.

With the editorial assistance of his wife Elizabeth, Allen wrote three books: *My Basketball Bible* (1924), *Better Basketball* (1936), and *Coach "Phog" Allen's Sport Stories for You and Youth* (1947). He was a popular speaker throughout Kansas. His caustic comments and feuds with sports personalities and the AAU made lively news items. The feud between Allen and the AAU dated back to the time when Allen wanted to have basketball played in the 1932 Olympic Games. The AAU refused in 1932, but then relented and allowed basketball to be played in the 1936 Olympics. Allen was chosen to coach the first team, but resigned in disgust over AAU policies. He called the AAU "a clique of a few eastern toadying, self-sophisticated, hypocritical, sanctimonious athletic politicians who activate themselves on their own ego."

After 1956, Allen practiced osteopathy in Lawrence, Kans. Through the years, professional athletes such as baseball players Johnny Mize, Ted Williams, and Mickey Mantle consulted Dr. Allen regarding their injuries. He once said he "won more games on the treating table than I ever won on the athletic field."

What made Phog Allen a successful coach? He wanted his players to believe that they were better for having played basketball. Oklahoma State coach Hank Iba called Allen a fierce competitor, whose ball teams "really went after you." Adolph Rupp remembered: "He taught me it took three basic things to be a successful basketball coach . . . discipline, sound fundamentals and teamwork."

Allen was honored many times, including being named Coach of the Year by the National Association of Basketball Coaches. In 1955 the University of Kansas named its newly constructed, 17,000-seat fieldhouse (then the second largest in the United States) after him.

Allen, called the "Father of Basketball Coaching" by James Naismith, died in Lawrence.

[Scrapbooks and articles focusing on Forrest Allen and records concerning his administrative duties are in the University of Kansas Archives, Lawrence, Kans. Memorabilia are in the Naismith Basketball Hall of Fame in Springfield, Mass. In addition to the publications mentioned in the text, Allen wrote *Basketball* with Harold Foster and Edward Hickey (1965). For a biography of Forrest Allen, see Donald Elston, "A Biography of Forrest C. 'Phog' Allen" (Master of Science thesis, University of Kansas, 1967). See also Neil D. Isaacs, *All the Moves: A History of College Basketball* (1975); and John Hendel, *Kansas Jayhawk Basketball* (1991). Statistics on Allen's coaching career are from *Official 1992 NCAA Basketball*. Articles include Theodore M. O'Leary, "Dr. Forrest C. Allen, Basketball Wizard," *The Jayhawker*, 1934/35; " 'Phog' Allen completes 25th Year as Coach," *The* (Kansas University) *Graduate Magazine*, Feb. 1942; and Jim Hathaway, "The End of an Era," *The Jayhawker* (1956). An obituary appears in the *New York Times*, Sept. 17, 1974.]

SONDRA VAN METER McCOY

ALLEN, GEORGE EDWARD (Feb. 29, 1896–Apr. 23, 1973), lawyer and businessman, was born and raised in Booneville, Miss., the son of Samuel P. Allen and Mollie Plaxico. His uncle, John Allen, who served as a private in the Confederate army, was elected to Congress for eight terms. In 1912, Allen was appointed an alternate to the Democratic National Convention in Baltimore, replacing the Booneville delegate, who was unable to attend.

After attending several southern colleges for short periods, Allen earned the LL.B. degree from Cumberland College of Tennessee in Lebanon (1917), finishing second from last in a class of 178. He then began a law practice in the small town of Okolona, Miss. His legal career was interrupted in 1918 by his service in France as a first lieutenant in a machine-gun battalion. Allen later said that he was "one of the first officers sent home after the Armistice." Upon returning to civilian life, Allen resumed his law practice but gave it up in 1919 to become secretary of the Indiana State Chamber of Commerce. After a brief period Allen went to Louisville, Ky., as director of the Louisville Convention and Publicity League. Next, he moved to Chicago, where he became a partner in several hotel ventures and pyramided a relatively small cash investment into a share of a syndicate that controlled more than twenty hotels. As a sideline, he sold jokes to luncheon-club speakers.

Allen entered the hotel business in Washington, D.C., in 1929, when Harry Wardman, a Washington builder, asked Allen to manage his hotels and apartment buildings, known as the Washington Properties. They included the Wardman Park Hotel (now the Sheraton Park); Allen lived there until shortly before his death, dividing his time between Washington and California. As manager of several large hotels in Washington, he became friendly with many New Deal politicians and businessmen who liked him for his geniality and story-telling abilities. In 1930, he married Mary Keane; they had no children.

Byron Patton ("Pat") Harrison of Mississippi took Allen to the 1932 Democratic National Convention and worked to secure Allen's appointment by President Roosevelt in 1933 as one of the three commissioners of the District of Columbia. He was the youngest commissioner on record and held that position until 1938. According to *United States News* (Feb. 1, 1946), Allen "excelled at gladhandling visiting notables and making speeches, humorous or otherwise, on ceremonial occasions." He obtained improved municipal services for Washington by putting through an income tax for the District of Columbia. He supervised the preparation of a liquor law for the District, and then proposed an election within its Takoma Park section to permit its residents to vote on granting of liquor licenses in their community; the election was blocked by a court order instigated by the "drys." Allen also liked to make surprise visits to District institutions and startled senators by appearing on the Senate floor during consideration of District legislation. He had found a provision, seldom if ever used, giving District commissioners floor privileges.

An enthusiastic worker for District suffrage, Allen was also the relief administrator for the District of Columbia. Because of his interest in unemployment, Allen dressed like one of the jobless, posed as an unemployed waiter, and traveled throughout the Midwest, sleeping in flophouses and tourist camps and applying unsuccessfully for more than twenty-five jobs. He returned to Washington with recommendations for drastic changes in administrative methods. One of Allen's memorandums to Roosevelt from this report became the basis of the president's work-relief program of 1935, which gave real work instead of doles to all employable unemployed at a cost of $4.8 billion.

In 1938, after his term as commissioner expired, Allen became vice-president for public relations of the Home Insurance Company of New York and was a member of the board of the War Damage Corporation. Among his other important financial connections that followed were the directorships of the Republic Steel Corporation, Consolidated Vultee, Aviation Corporation, Steel Rock Iron Mines, Penn Mutual Life Insurance, and General Aniline and Film Corporation. Nevertheless, politics continued to hold his attention.

Allen was reappointed District commissioner by the president in May 1939; he resigned in April 1940. He then became secretary of the Democratic National Committee in 1943 and was one of the circle who advised Roosevelt to choose Truman as his 1944 running mate. Allen planned Truman's first speech in Detroit and managed much of his presidential campaign. After Truman assumed the presidency, Allen frequently visited the White House. As a member of Truman's informal cabinet, with no official title or position, he offered advice, helped in the preparation of Truman's speeches, and served as liaison between the White House and Congress.

President Truman assigned Allen to study extant war agencies and suggest how best to close them down. Allen's "The Liquidation of Federal War Agencies: A Study" proposed that the bulk of such offices be "reconverted" by June 30, 1946, in "a democratic and a decent manner" under an experienced administrator. He excluded agencies that grappled with prices and other reconversion problems and research bureaus that were "vital to our national welfare." He also recommended that experts be assigned the task of finding new jobs for employees discharged in the process.

In January 1946, Allen was nominated to the Reconstruction Finance Corporation (RFC). The agency, originally created to extend financial assistance to agriculture, commerce, and industry by direct loans to banks, other credit agencies, and, with approval of the Interstate Commerce Commission, to railroads or to receivers of railroads, had been designated by the Surplus Property Board as disposal agent for the government's postwar surplus of capital and producer goods. Allen's nomination caused an uproar of protest both in the media and in Congress, where both liberals and conservatives felt that Truman was "passing jobs around." Many were skeptical of the nominee's administrative and banking abilities and his ties to the White House. Appearing before the Senate

Committee on Banking and Currency, Allen rebutted all questions with his usual openness and his replies elicited much laughter. He was recommended for Senate approval by a vote of fourteen to five. Senator Robert A. Taft, Republican of Ohio, who doubted Allen's ability but not his integrity for the RFC post, carried his opposition onto the Senate floor but failed to prevent a voice vote of approval on February 18. The *United States News* considered Allen a "conservative" influence on the president, but some close to Truman asserted the reverse. Allen was sworn in as a RFC member on Mar. 25, 1946, after resigning from the Home Insurance Company, which had paid him $29,000 per year, but he continued to hold other corporate posts that yielded him an estimated $50,000 per year. Allen's only instructions from Truman were to operate the RFC honestly and effectively and to make loans where they would do the national economy the most good.

Under Allen, an economic mission of twelve members went to Germany. The group included representatives from the major cabinet departments and was to put the American occupation zone on a self-sustaining basis; to work out an Anglo-American plan to balance German exports and imports out of and into American and British zones; to study the export potential of postwar Germany; and to review American reparations policy. While in Germany he negotiated agreements granting loans to the nation for procurement of raw materials to be used by German industry to produce exports. The loans were made by the U.S. Commercial Corporation, an RFC subsidiary.

Upon his return to the United States, Allen entered Anglo-American talks on the economic unification of the British- and American-occupied zones in Germany. Late in 1946 he suggested that the RFC Act be amended to divest the agency of its war powers. He resigned from his RFC post in January 1947.

Allen played an important role in gaining Truman the Democratic presidential nomination in 1948. According to the *St. Louis Post Dispatch*, in July 1948 Allen stopped a movement to draft his friend Dwight D. Eisenhower as a presidential candidate by asking Eisenhower to issue a statement saying he would not run if nominated and would not serve if elected. Allen's friendship with Eisenhower had begun in London during World War II, when Eisenhower was commander in chief of Allied forces.

Allen had many interests. He served as special assistant to Norman H. Davis, chairman of the American Red Cross, and in 1943 was chosen by Davis to be chairman of the newly created Committee on American and United Nations Prisoners of War. Allen also did work on behalf of the Warm Springs Foundation, the March of Dimes, and the Boy Scouts of America. He was also president of the Franklin D. Roosevelt Memorial Foundation. In Washington he was a deacon in the Negro Universal Church of God and a trustee of the Columbia Hospital for Women. In 1952 he produced his own television show, "Man of the Week." In 1964, Allen was listed by *Poor's Register of Corporations, Directors and Executives* as the person sitting on the most boards of directors (thirty-two) in the United States; by 1967 he was in fourth place on that list.

Although often a White House guest of Roosevelt and Truman, Allen was perhaps closest to Eisenhower, whom Allen frequently visited in the executive mansion. He was the president's bridge partner and a neighbor in Gettysburg, Pa., where Eisenhower had a farm. Allen was numbered among the small group of industrialists and financiers, or "Ike's millionaires," as they were known, who vacationed with the president at various locations.

During the 1950's, Allen became a business executive. He also made money in the stock market using his "Law of Politico-Market Cycles." In one of the many articles that he wrote for the *New York Times* business section ("Politics Determines Which Way Stocks Will Go," Jan. 10, 1971), Allen explained that "the stock market is a political thermometer. It measures the hot or cold state of mind of literally millions of shareholders. They either have confidence enough to invest their money in the future of various companies or they don't. . . . A look at the charts will show that third years of every recent Administration have been periods of rising stock prices." In a *New York Times Magazine* interview (Aug. 21, 1960), Allen noted that his fortune resulted from knowing how to read the newspapers for significant trends and from knowing how to parlay shrewd business and political-social contacts into a money-making combination.

In 1950, Allen published an autobiography, *Presidents Who Have Known Me* (revised 1960), a critical and commercial success that was not appreciated by Truman. In April 1960, Truman called Allen "a fixer" who "would do anything to suck in." Truman noted that he had had no contact with his former friend since leaving the White House, but the coolness was "not on my part." The former president also noted that during his administration Allen was called "one of my palace guard" and a "poker-playing crony." In the Eisenhower administration, Allen was referred to as "an industrialist and statesman and bridge partner" of the president. Allen remarked that "friendship with a President is a very delicate business" and that his friendship with Eisenhower was purely personal, since "there is all the difference in the world between personal friendship and political friendship." He practiced "companionship without involvement," since any advice he gave to a president had "no motive of personal advantage, betterment or profit."

While the secret of his success was not explicitly revealed, Allen seemed to be that rare individual who could leave presidents, by occupation a brooding and tense group, feeling just a little better. He was a warm, humorous man and a witty raconteur. Profiles often mentioned his generous girth and grin. Contemporaries described his "Irvin Cobb chin" on a 6-foot, 212-pound frame and his penchant for detective stories, for an occasional poker game, and for $2 bets at the racetrack. Allen died in Palm Desert, Calif.

[The William D. McCain Library and Archives, University of Southern Mississippi, Hattiesburg, has Allen's 1972 oral history. The Harry S. Truman Library, Independence, Mo., has a 1969 oral history. The Dwight D. Eisenhower Library, Abilene, Kans., has photocopies of his papers (1942–1969) and some of Allen's correspondence.
Allen's autobiography should still be considered the best source about his life. He also wrote "My Two Years with Truman," *Saturday Evening Post*, June 21, 1947.
Information on Allen's closed confirmation hearings before the Senate Committee on Banking and Commerce is in the 1946 *Congressional Record*. The National Archives, Washington, D.C., houses records of the RFC, the government of the District of Columbia, and the director of liquidation and the Liquidation Advisory Committee, Bureau of the Budget. In addition, the Washingtonia Division, District of Columbia Public Library, has three clipping files on Allen.
Major articles on Allen include Kenneth Crawford, "Mysterious Mr. Allen." *Saturday Evening Post*, Jan. 5, 1946; Cabell Phillips, "The 'Inner Circle' at the White House," *New York Times Magazine*, Feb. 24, 1946; Roger Butterfield, "What's Funny About George Allen," *Life*, Sept. 9, 1946; Andrew Tully, "The Extraordinary Story of George E. Allen," *Washington Daily News*, Nov. 3–6, 1959; and Merriman Smith, " '. . . and His Friend, George E. Allen,' " *New York Times Magazine*, Aug. 21, 1960. An obituary is in the *New York Times*, April 24, 1973.]

MARTIN J. MANNING

ALLEN, JAMES EDWARD, JR. (Apr. 25, 1911–Oct. 16, 1971), educator, was born in Elkins, W.Va., the first child of James E. Allen, the president of Davis and Elkins College, and Susan Garrott, the college librarian. The local newspaper proclaimed: "There is an addition to the faculty of Davis and Elkins College in the person of James E. Allen, Jr." It was an appropriate welcome for one who would rise to become commissioner of education, first of New York State, then of the United States.

Early in his life, Allen absorbed the dedication to hard work, sympathy for the underprivileged, and sense of moral responsibility characteristic of his strongly religious parents. He graduated from Davis and Elkins in 1932 (after failing one class, a Latin course taught by his father), intending to pursue a business career in Charleston. The following year, however, he was hired by the West Virginia State Department of Education, where he compiled statistical data on school finance. On Apr. 23, 1938, Allen married Florence Pell Miller, like him a West Virginian from a small town. The newly married couple left their native state in 1939 for Princeton, N.J., where Allen became research associate with the Princeton (University) Surveys, studying educational finance in New Jersey and Massachusetts.

The move to Princeton would be the first of many between 1939 and 1947. As a result of his work, Allen came to know Alfred Simpson, a professor at Harvard University's School of Education, who encouraged him to pursue graduate study there. He enrolled in Harvard in 1941, earning a master's of education in 1942. That year the Allens became parents of twins, a boy and a girl. Their three-room apartment in Cambridge, Mass., was suddenly noisier and more crowded. Nevertheless, Allen managed to receive an Ed.D. in 1945. While at Harvard, he became acquainted with James Conant, Francis Keppel, and John Gardner, men who served as models of the educational statesmanship Allen himself would later epitomize.

After a brief stint as a civilian operations analyst for the Air Force in Tampa during the period 1944–1945, Allen accepted an appointment as assistant professor of education at Syracuse University. While on the Syracuse faculty he spent several months in Washington, D.C., as a staffer for President Truman's Commission on Higher Education, which was to make recommendations on the role the federal government would play in meeting the country's postwar higher education needs. Shortly after Allen returned to Syracuse in 1947, Francis Spaulding, New York State Commissioner of Education and former dean of the Harvard School of Education, offered Allen the position of executive assistant to the commissioner. The gypsy phase of Allen's career was over.

When Spaulding died in 1950, the New York State Board of Regents appointed Allen deputy commissioner. In 1955 he assumed the commissionership upon the retirement of Lewis Wilson. At age forty-four he held what was arguably the most important education job in the nation. Allen's fourteen-year tenure as Commissioner of Education in New York, from Sept. 1, 1955, to May 1, 1969, was marked by immense growth of the state's education system and, in the later years, considerable turmoil over school desegregation. During Allen's term the number of public school students rose from 2,300,000 to 3,400,000 and annual educational expenditures climbed from $1 billion to $4.1 billion. At the same time, Allen succeeded in reducing the number of school districts by more than half, thus strengthening the remaining consolidated districts.

This simultaneous expansion and contraction called upon all of Allen's well-developed skills as an educational planner, manager, and politician. He favored local control of schools, and endorsed a decentralization of New York City's school system. The debate over control of the schools in the Ocean Hill–Brownsville School District touched off a series of disturbances there, which in turn resulted in a citywide teachers' strike. Although a supporter of local control, he pressed local boards to maintain standards. Unhappy with the lack of clarity and precision in much education goal-setting, he advocated greater accountability: "Broadly generalized statements of goals will not satisfy the increasingly intense scrutiny of the public, of legislative bodies, hard-headed businessmen, and taxpayers." He wanted "well-defined, pre-

cise presentations of goals that can be understood clearly and appraised accurately."

One of Allen's clearest goals as New York's Education Commissioner was equal educational opportunity. Because he used the powers of his office to champion racial equality and civil rights throughout the 1960's, Allen placed himself at the center of a heated fight over racial imbalance in the schools. A number of school districts brought suits against Allen's integration orders. In a decision on one of these suits, with significant implications for educational policy across New York State and beyond, a New York appellate court upheld "the judgment of the Commissioner that correction of racial imbalance is an educational aid to a minority group in attaining the skills and level of education which others have had for generations and that compulsory education should be designed for the greatest good of all."

By 1969 the era of education growth in New York was drawing to a close. The previous year, Allen had been approached by the Nixon administration about the post of United States Commissioner of Education. He took the job in 1969 in part because Robert Finch, the newly nominated Secretary of Health, Education, and Welfare, and a liberal on education matters, assured him that education would have high priority in the Nixon White House. Accepting Nixon's overture proved to be the largest mistake Allen made in his professional life.

On May 1, 1969, Allen became assistant secretary for education and United States Commissioner of Education. He had been a champion of the preeminence of the states in education. In 1966 he had helped found the Education Commission of the States to give them a collective national voice. On the other hand, he had welcomed the federal government into education financing when many states sought to block federal involvement. He had also helped launch the National Assessment of Educational Progress to provide comparative data on student learning outcomes nationwide. So in one sense the post of chief education officer for the federal government seemed a natural capstone to a career that had increasingly been concerned with charting a vigorous national education policy.

But President Nixon had been elected in part as a reaction against the "Great Society" view of government as a benevolent social force. Consequently, Allen found that he was not consulted on major decisions affecting education. His choices for top positions in the Office of Education were rejected by the White House, and the Office's budget was cut by $370 million. Allen continued to advocate racial integration in the schools and student rights, and to propose new research and social action ventures such as the National Institute of Education and the Right to Read program, at a time when the Nixon administration was playing to the conservatism of "the silent majority" and devoting considerable resources to the war in Vietnam. On June 10, 1970, after barely more than a year in office, Robert Finch asked for Allen's resignation.

Shortly thereafter Allen returned to Princeton to accept a visiting lectureship at the Woodrow Wilson School of Public and International Affairs, a position he held when Allen and his wife were flying on a small charter plane from Las Vegas, Nev., to the Grand Canyon in Arizona on Oct. 16, 1971. The plane flew into a severe storm and crashed in a heavily wooded area called Pine Mountain, sixty miles east of the Arizona-Nevada border. Six other passengers and the two crewmen were killed in addition to the Allens.

Those who have written about or known James Allen have tended to refer to him as an educational statesman and a practical visionary. His speeches on equal opportunity, environmental education, and multiculturalism leave no doubt that he had a vision of the future of American education and society. In pursuing this vision, for all his balance and diplomacy, he was resolute, tough-minded, and fearless.

[Allen's papers pertaining to his post in New York are held by the New York State Library, which has published A Guide to the Papers of James E. Allen, Jr. (1970). See also Louis Leonard Tucker, James E. Allen, Jr.: From Elkins to Washington (1969); and David E. Koontz, James E. Allen, Jr.: Educational Statesman (1981). An obituary is in the New York Times, Oct. 18, 1971.]

KEVIN P. REILLY

ALSOP, STEWART JOHONNOT OLIVER (May 17, 1914–May 26, 1974), journalist, was born in Avon, Conn., the son of Joseph Wright Alsop, Sr., an insurance executive and public official, and Corinne Douglas Robinson, a legislator. Raised on a genteel farm where his father wore black tie at dinner, Alsop graduated from Groton School in 1932 and from Yale with a B.A. four years later. He then worked as an editor at the publishing house of Doubleday Doran in New York.

Although his parents were Republicans, Alsop admired both President Franklin Roosevelt and Eleanor Roosevelt, his mother's cousin. Embracing Roosevelt's interventionist foreign policy, young Alsop rooted for Britain during World War II and tried to enlist in the American military before the Japanese attacked Pearl Harbor, but was rejected for boyhood asthma.

Alsop went to England in 1942 to join the Sixtieth Regiment, King's Royal Rifle Corps. Commissioned in the British Army in 1943, he saw action in North Africa and Italy, for which he was commended. On June 20, 1944, Alsop married Patricia Hankey in London. Only later did Alsop learn that his wife was in the British intelligence. They had six children.

In 1944 Alsop transferred to U.S. Army intelligence with General William ("Wild Bill") Donovan's elite Office of Strategic Services (OSS). Shortly after D day Alsop parachuted behind German lines and successfully contacted the French underground. This dangerous work earned Alsop the French croix de guerre with palm. Alsop and Thomas Braden described OSS methods and operations in Sub Rosa (1946).

The quiet, contemplative Alsop resigned his commission in 1945 to join his gregarious older brother, Joseph W. Alsop, Jr. (1910–1989), already an established journalist, in writing a political column called "Matter of Fact" for the New York Herald Tribune. Their first joint effort appeared on Dec. 31, 1945, and the column was soon widely syndicated. Basing themselves in Washington, the brothers became near neighbors in Georgetown, and each hosted memorable dinner parties that helped make the neighborhood fashionable.

The Alsops shamelessly exploited family ties, including cousin Alice Roosevelt Longworth. Joe's ability to uncover a political story matched Stew's capacity for analysis. Each traveled extensively, refusing to write about any country or its leaders without a visit. Both wrote lucidly, with Joe's bite complementing Stew's wit.

Their column helped shape the political landscape at the beginning of the Cold War in the late 1940's. They correctly and shrewdly predicted the Communist coup in Czechoslovakia, the Soviet Union's Berlin blockade, and the vulnerability of South Korea to attack. By 1950 their column appeared in 137 papers, and the brothers won Overseas Press Club awards in 1950 and 1952.

The Alsops, like President Harry Truman, wanted a vigorous federal government that would pursue reform at home while containing communism abroad. They favored both the Marshall Plan's massive economic assistance to Europe and military alliances such as the North Atlantic Treaty Organization.

At the same time the Alsops defended Dean Acheson and Henry A. Wallace against Senator Joseph R. McCarthy's repeated charges that Communists occupied high places in the government. The brothers found no evidence to support such claims. Incensed by the Atomic Energy Commission's humiliation of the nuclear physicist J. Robert Oppenheimer, they published a rebuttal entitled *We Accuse!* (1954).

In the mid-1950's the Alsops drifted apart. While Joe remained a fervent anti-Communist and, amid the prosperity of the 1950's, lost interest in Roosevelt-style reforms, Stew, the restless intellectual, found anti-Communism sterile, feared nuclear holocaust, and worried about the public's desire to ignore domestic issues. In 1958 the brothers ended their joint column. Neither ever exerted as much influence alone as the two had together.

In 1958, Stewart became a contributing editor at the *Saturday Evening Post.* He eventually wrote a popular column on a regular basis, but the *Post* was dying, and in 1968 Alsop moved his column to the more liberal *Newsweek,* where it remained a biweekly fixture until near his death.

Alsop's columns often packed a punch. Having abandoned anti-Communism, Alsop in 1964 warned against an American war in Vietnam, but he did not oppose President Lyndon Johnson's troop escalation in 1965 because he believed that differences over foreign policy were best aired in private. Like others, Alsop later rued his failure to speak out and believed that his silence had served Johnson poorly.

When he did attack the war, he traced its inconclusiveness to Vietnamese disdain for American culture and to military mismanagement, noting that only one-seventh of American soldiers in Vietnam served in combat, that 88 percent of combat soldiers were draftees, and that draftees died at twice the rate of regular army personnel. His factural observations sidestepped the debate over the war, and even those who disagreed with his conclusions, like his hawkish brother Joe, found his information instructive.

In 1969 he pointed out how student deferments had both muffled protest by protecting the influential middle class from the draft and created fear and resentment on college campuses. By 1970 he argued that only the abolition of the draft could restore prestige and morale to the army.

In 1973 the Watergate scandal alarmed Alsop, who stated that if the corruption and cover-up involved Richard Nixon, then the president would have to resign. Readers found this attack of Yankee conscience startling, and Nixon grew nervous, but Alsop was merely stating a political reality, that a discredited president could no longer govern. Alsop always combined rare political insight with ruthless integrity and hard-boiled factual analysis.

Nor should one forget his wit. In 1971 Alsop suddenly took ill and was diagnosed with a rare, incurable leukemia. Through experimental treatments at the National Institutes of Health in Bethesda, Md., where he died, his cancer went into remission for a time. He wrote his last book, *Stay of Execution* (1973), about that experience. In 1974, as a powerful treatment overwhelmed him, Alsop one day found himself in a dream. He was on a train, and the conductor called out "Baltimore," but Alsop decided not to get off. When he woke up, he realized that he had consciously decided not to die. Ever the loyal Washingtonian, he knew that Baltimore symbolized death.

Alsop was buried in Middletown, Conn.

[The Alsop brothers' professional papers are at the Library of Congress. A smaller collection of Stewart's papers are at Boston University. Alsop wrote six books: *Sub Rosa* (1946) (with Thomas Braden); *We Accuse!* (1954) (with Joseph Alsop); *The Reporter's Trade* (1958), a collection of columns (with Joseph Alsop); *Nixon and Rockefeller* (1960); *The Center* (1968), a best-seller on the political middle ground; and *Stay of Execution* (1973). Material may also be found in Joseph Alsop, *I've Seen the Best of It* (1992). Obituaries are in the *Washington Post* and the *New York Times,* both May 27, 1974.]

W. J. RORABAUGH

ALTMEYER, ARTHUR JOSEPH (May 8, 1891–Oct. 16, 1972), Social Security administrator and government official, was born to Carrie A. Smith and John G. Altmeyer in De Pere, Wis. As an adult, Altmeyer did not talk of his early life; thus, little is known of his parents other than that his father was of German descent and his mother of Dutch heritage. After his parents divorced when Arthur was fourteen, he went to live with grandparents, working as an office boy in the law office of a grandfather and uncle to pay for his support. He did not complete high school until he was nineteen years old and then worked a year to save toward college expenses. In 1911 he read a pamphlet on workmen's compensation that motivated him to enroll at the University of Wisconsin to study under John R. Commons. He completed the undergraduate program in three years, working as Commons's research assistant and graduating in 1914 with Phi Beta Kappa honors.

For three years Altmeyer taught in the Minnesota iron range district, where he became a school principal. On July 3, 1916, he married a teacher, Ethel May Thomas of Superior, also a University of Wisconsin graduate. In 1918 he returned to the university and received the M.A. in 1921 and the Ph.D. in 1931, both under Commons. During his years as a graduate student, he worked in the offices of the Wisconsin State Tax and Industrial commissions. In 1920 he began a long and productive career in the administration of various forms of social insurance. For two years he was the chief statistician to the Wisconsin Industrial Commission and then secretary of the commission from 1922 to 1933. In that capacity he was involved with deliberations that led to the Wisconsin Unemployment Reserves and Compensation Act, the first such act passed in the United States to provide for both workmen's and unemployment compensation. In 1931, when the Wisconsin Industrial Commission was given the responsibility to administer unemployment relief throughout the state, Altmeyer pioneered in yet another field of social welfare.

In 1933 Secretary of Labor Frances Perkins asked Altmeyer to come to Washington to direct the Labor Compliance Division of the National Recovery Administration; in June 1934 he became the Second Assistant Secretary of Labor, serving until November 1935. Within a month of becoming Perkins's assistant, he was named chairman of the technical board President Franklin Roosevelt created to assist the new Committee on Economic Security. In 1935, after Congress passed the Social Security Act

drafted by the Committee, Roosevelt appointed Altmeyer a member of the new three-member Social Security Board. He was board chairman from 1937 until its abolition in July 1946. At that time, as Commissioner for Social Security under the new Federal Security Agency (FSA), he assumed most of the powers of the former board.

During seventeen years as head of the vast Social Security program, Altmeyer was responsible for Old Age, Survivors and Disability Insurance; Unemployment Compensation; Old Age Assistance; Aid to the Blind; Aid to the Permanently and Totally Disabled; Aid to Dependent Children; and child health and welfare services. As the leading champion of expanded coverage for farmers, domestic workers, and other groups, Altmeyer directed the successful efforts to have Congress broaden the program by major amendments in 1939 and 1950, and he indicated the new directions that would be taken after he had left the agency. Associates credited to Altmeyer's tactical skills the generally favorable reaction of Congress and the public to the administration of Social Security in the early years.

During World War II, Altmeyer was for seven months in 1942 the executive director of the War Manpower Commission. In the postwar period he was the United States representative on the Social Commission of the United Nations, one of several appointments he held in the administration of international social insurance and labor welfare. He assiduously lobbied for a worldwide charter of social security principles. In April 1953, executive reorganization under President Dwight Eisenhower replaced the FSA with the Department of Health, Education and Welfare and forced Altmeyer into an early retirement.

During his many years of federal service, Altmeyer was widely known as "Mr. Social Security" and as one of the nation's most respected leaders in the field of public welfare. In 1953, he returned to Madison, where he lived for nineteen years except for two years he spent in Washington, D.C. (1964–1966), in an advisory capacity for private pension funds. He was president of the National Conference of Social Work (1954–1955), was a consultant to many social planners, both in the United States and abroad, and was a visiting lecturer at five universities. In 1958 Wisconsin Democratic leaders urged him to run for the U.S. Senate, but he declined to seek elective office. He did, however, chair the Social Security Committee of the Democratic Advisory Council during the 1960 presidential campaign. After 1966, unstable health caused Altmeyer gradually to reduce his activities, although he maintained close contact with many associates from his lifetime of social welfare endeavors, and he was an occasional consultant to Near Eastern and Latin American governments seeking to establish social security systems. He died in Madison and was survived by his wife; they had no children.

Altmeyer was studious, serious, and reticent. He was not noted for personal magnetism or humor, but co-workers revered him for his humanitarianism, his knowledge of the field of social insurance, and his calm, impartial administration of his offices. With Edwin E. Witte and Wilbur J. Cohen, he formed a trio of John R. Commons–trained social economists whose intellectual prowess and administrative skills had a profound influence upon the acceptance by the federal government of the responsibility to provide economic and social security to a broad range of citizens.

[The Altmeyer Papers are at the State Historical Society of Wisconsin in Madison, as are the papers of Wilbur Cohen. A memoir is in the Columbia Oral History Collection. At the National Archives are the extensive official records of the Social Security Administration (RG 47). See also Altmeyer's books, *The Industrial Commission of Wisconsin—A Case Study in Labor Law Administration* (1932) and *The Formative Years of Social Security* (1966). Extensive material on Altmeyer is in Edwin E. Witte, *The Development of the Social Security Act* (1962); Martha Derthick, *Policymaking for Social Security* (1979); and Carolyn L. Weaver, *The Real Crisis in Social Security* (1982). A sketch can be found in *Biographical Dictionary of Social Welfare in America* (1986). Obituaries are in the *New York Times*, Oct. 18, 1972, and *Social Security Bulletin*, Dec. 1972.]
MARTHA H. SWAIN

AMLIE, THOMAS RYUM (Apr. 17, 1897– Aug. 22, 1973), lawyer and congressman, was born near Binford, Griggs County, N.Dak., the son of Paul William Amlie, a farmer, and Julia Ryum. The family farm never prospered, and following his mother's death in 1912 Amlie lived with an aunt in nearby Cooperstown, graduating from the local high school in 1916. From 1916 to 1918, he studied at the University of North Dakota, leaving for military service.

He attended the University of Minnesota in 1919, then worked as an organizer for the agrarian Non-Partisan League. He entered the University of Wisconsin in 1921 to study law, received his degree in 1923, and became a practicing attorney in the Wisconsin towns of Beloit and then Elkhorn. On Feb. 21, 1925, Amlie married Marian Caldwell Strong, who died in 1930 following an extended illness. He married Gehrta Farkasch Beyer on May 7, 1932. Together they raised three sons from his first marriage, a son from her first marriage, and a daughter.

For several decades politics in Wisconsin had been played out largely in Republican party primaries in contests between the party's conservative wing and the progressive wing, headed by Robert M. La Follette and then by his sons Robert M., Jr., and Philip. Following the death of the long-time incumbent in Wisconsin's First Congressional District, Amlie ran in the 1931 Republican primary for the vacant congressional seat as a La Follette progressive, defeated his conservative rival, and served as United States Representative from 1931 to 1933.

The most significant phase of Amlie's career followed his 1932 Republican primary loss for renomination to Congress. Increasingly radicalized by the Great Depression, Amlie attended the September 1933 conference called by the League for Independent Political Action, which led to the creation of the Farmer-Labor Political Federation (FLPF). Amlie galvanized the conference with his speech, and he was selected as chairman of the new organization. Joined by radical *Common Sense* editor Alfred M. Bingham as executive secretary, with philosopher John Dewey serving as honorary chairman, Amlie strove to make the FLPF, which in 1935 was renamed the American Commonwealth Political Federation (ACPF), a viable third-party alternative by the election year of 1936.

Amlie's radicalism was of a distinctly American kind. He agreed with the Marxist proposition that capitalism was doomed, and he believed in the 1933–1936 period that President Franklin D. Roosevelt's New Deal reforms could at best postpone the inevitable collapse. But he also believed that the Marxist concept of class struggle was ill-suited to American traditions. His intellectual hero was not Karl Marx but rather the American economist Thorstein Veblen. In a country that had known prosperity and opportunity, Amlie held, people did not think in terms of rigid class lines. Only an appeal couched in such American terms as abundance and efficiency could persuade voters to turn to a publicly owned and operated "production for use" economic system, an American "cooperative commonwealth."

Amlie looked to Wisconsin and Minnesota to provide the foundation stones for a national third party. In Wisconsin he hoped to persuade the La Follette Republicans to form a new state party; in Minnesota he hoped to build upon the existing state Farmer-Labor party. Amlie helped convince Philip and Robert M. La Follette, Jr., to launch the Wisconsin Progressive party in 1934, and he was elected as a Progressive to his former congressional seat in 1934 and 1936. But under the La Follettes the Wisconsin Progressive party did not move in the more radical direction desired by Amlie. Nor did the Minnesota Farmer-Labor party commit itself to serve as a nucleus for a national ACPF effort. In the country at large, third-party sentiment tended rather toward what Amlie considered the superficial and simplistic panaceas of Senator Huey P. Long's "Share Our Wealth" movement and Representative William Lemke's 1936 Union party presidential bid.

Given the failure of the ACPF to attract a significant following, Amlie concluded that the only politically realistic course would be to try to push the New Deal in the direction of more fundamental change. Amlie thus abandoned his national third-party crusade after 1936, joining with other like-minded congressmen in an unsuccessful endeavor to pass legislation designed to graft a form of economic planning onto the existing economic system. In 1938, Amlie ran for the Progressive party nomination for United States senator from Wisconsin, losing the primary election to Herman Ekern, a veteran associate of "Old Bob" La Follette. His tenure in the House of Representatives now over, Amlie was nominated by President Roosevelt in 1939 to serve on the Interstate Commerce Commission, but Amlie withdrew his name in the face of heated opposition. Amlie ran again for Wisconsin's First Congressional District seat in 1941, this time as a Democrat supporting Roosevelt's foreign policy and attacking isolationism, but he was defeated by his Republican opponent. Following his defeat, he moved his family from Elkhorn to Madison, Wis.

Amlie worked in 1942 for the liberal Union for Democratic Action political organization and advised the Political Action Committee of the Congress of Industrial Organizations in the 1944 campaign. He now believed that the Democratic party was the only viable instrument to achieve the limited reform to which the American people had proven agreeable and that third parties in Wisconsin and Minnesota would only divide the reform vote and result in the election of conservatives. In 1950, Amlie published *Let's Look at the Record*, a comparative study and compilation of Democratic and Republican voting records in Congress. He remained active in Wisconsin state politics in the post–World War II era. His last try for elective office came in 1958 in a losing bid for the Democratic nomination in Wisconsin's Second Congressional District. Of an intellectual bent, he characteristically thought in terms of systematic concepts, patterns, and trends. As a speaker, his presentation was crafted and his style serious and substantive rather than flamboyant or emotional. Amlie's basic historical significance was as a leader during the mid-1930's of the intellectually spirited but politically futile effort to create an indigenous American radical movement bolder than New Deal liberalism yet not dependent on European Marxist ideology. Forced into retirement by Parkinson's disease, Amlie died in Madison.

[The Thomas R. Amlie Papers are deposited in the State Historical Society of Wisconsin in Madison. Amlie's views in the mid-1930's are outlined in his *The Forgotten Man's Handbook* (1936). The fullest account of his career is Robert E. Long, "Thomas Amlie: A Political Biography" (Ph.D. diss., University of Wisconsin, 1969). More specialized studies are Theodore Rosenof, "The Political Education of an American Radical: Thomas R. Amlie in the 1930's," *Wisconsin Magazine of History*, Autumn 1974; Stuart Weiss, "Thomas Amlie and the New Deal," *Mid-America*, Jan. 1977; and Hugh T. Lovin, "Thomas R. Amlie's Crusade and the Dissonant Farmers—A New Deal Windfall," *North Dakota Quarterly*, Winter 1981. An obituary is in the Madison *Capital Times*, Aug. 22, 1973.]

THEODORE ROSENOF

ANDERSON, CLINTON PRESBA (Oct. 23, 1895–Nov. 11, 1975), U.S. secretary of agriculture, representative, and senator from New Mexico, was born in Centerville, S.Dak., the son of Andrew Jay Anderson, a storekeeper and farmer, and Hattie Belle Presba. He attended public schools in Parker and Mitchell, S.Dak., and studied at Dakota Wesleyan University (1913–1915) and the University of Michigan (1915–1916), but did not complete a degree. In 1917, while working as a newspaper reporter in South Dakota, he became ill with tuberculosis and traveled west to a sanatorium in Albuquerque, N.Mex. Within nine months he had recovered sufficiently to join the staff of the *Albuquerque Evening Herald*, a position that introduced him to the turbulent world of New Mexico politics. In 1921 he became managing editor and chief investigative reporter for the *Albuquerque Journal*. In that capacity, he helped uncover shady dealings in the leasing of American naval oil reserves, a situation that emerged as the "Teapot Dome" scandal. On June 22, 1921, Anderson married Henrietta McCartney, with whom he subsequently had two children.

The following year, Anderson cashed in his financial holdings in the *Journal* and purchased the insurance division of a local bank, which in 1923 became the Clinton P. Anderson Agency. At a time of rapid expansion in the state's highway construction, Anderson offered road contractors a local source of modestly priced workman's compensation insurance. This broadened his contacts with the state's business and political communities. From the mid-1920's to 1932, his dealings quickly transcended the local scene as demonstrated by his rise from the presidency of the Albuquerque Rotary Club to the presidency of that organization's international body from 1932 to 1933.

In 1933 and 1934 Anderson served as New Mexico state treasurer and in 1935 and 1936 as a field representative of the New Deal's Federal Emergency Relief Administration. Also in 1936 he began a two-year term as chairman of the Unemployment Compensation Commission of New Mexico. While in that post he established the Mountain States Mutual Casualty Company to take on the business of larger insurance companies that were cutting back on their workman's compensation policies due to a dramatic growth in claim volume. The success of Anderson's insurance ventures guaranteed his subsequent financial independence.

In 1940, Anderson concluded two years as executive director of the United States Coronado Exposition, a celebration commemorating Spanish exploration in the Southwest, and won a tight Democratic primary race for New Mexico's single seat in the U.S. House of Representatives. He went on to win the general election easily. In the House, Anderson received committee assignments pertinent to his constituency's interests, including Indian Affairs, Irrigation and Reclamation, and Public Lands.

Despite chronic health problems, Anderson easily secured reelection in 1942 and 1944. Earning the respect of Speaker of the House Sam Rayburn, he was awarded a valued seat on the Appropriations Committee in 1943 and subsequently was appointed chair of special committees to investigate campaign spending irregularities and wartime food shortages. In the latter post, during early 1945, he conducted a well-publicized series of hearings across the nation and produced reform proposals that impressed newly installed President Harry Truman. In May 1945 Truman selected Anderson as his secretary of agriculture. Having operated a dairy farm in Albuquerque, he became the first person from an irrigation farming region to hold that cabinet post.

Anderson's three years in the Truman administration proved to be stormy. His credentials as a successful businessman and presidential poker partner were stronger than his agricultural policy expertise or his skills for administering a sprawling bureaucracy. Early in 1948 Senator Carl Hatch decided not to seek reelection and recommended Anderson as his successor. Anderson easily won the primary and general elections and entered the Senate in January 1949. He was reelected in 1954, 1960, and 1966 and served until his retirement in January 1973.

Anderson found the Senate's legislative environment more agreeable than that of the cabinet. In the upper house of Congress he was able to choose issues that interested him and pursue them at his own pace. Although he would survive to the age of eighty, serious health problems (including diabetes, heart ailments, a stroke, and Parkinson's disease) frequently sidelined him.

Anderson's primary interests in the Senate reflected those of New Mexico, and he channeled sizable federal appropriations to his adopted state in support of land reclamation, river basin management, water desalinization, outdoor recreation, defense and space installations, and nuclear power development. He twice chaired the Joint Committee on Atomic

Energy (1955–1956; 1959–1960); and the Senate committees on Interior and Insular Affairs (1961–1963); and Aeronautical and Space Sciences (1963–1972). Anderson also served on the Senate Agriculture Committee, where he championed flexible price supports, and then on the Senate Finance Committee, a post that allowed him to advance legislation for health care and social security support for the aged, including early versions of the Medicare program, enacted in 1965.

From 1955 through the mid-1960's Anderson provided important legislative leadership in natural resources policy, merging his early role as regional spokesman for the water-deficient West with that of advocate for a broad national conservation strategy. He successfully tied proposals for solving western resources problems to nationally based programs for natural resources protection and development. More than that of any other single legislator or policy-maker, his imprint lay on the Wilderness Act of 1964.

Anderson was widely respected for his intellect and legislative style. A difficult taskmaster to those who worked for him, he displayed great charm and finesse to friends, political colleagues, and business associates. His six-foot, two-inch frame, broad smile, and friendly manner allowed him to command the attention of virtually any audience, until his health problems eroded his stamina during his final Senate term. On the Senate floor, he exercised his effectiveness through careful preparation and quiet conversation with potential adversaries, rather than with frequent and long-winded speeches. A master legislative mechanic, he displayed an inner confidence and an understanding of his range of options, permitting him to use available power constructively. As necessary, he relied on such legislative weapons as humor, logic, political IOU's, and intimidation.

When Anderson encountered those whom he believed were lying or trying to mislead him, a darker side of his character emerged, and he could become petty and vindictive—tenacious in pursuit of settling old scores. This facet of his personality became dramatically evident in his single-minded and successful 1959 campaign to defeat the nomination of former Atomic Energy Commission chief Lewis Strauss to be secretary of commerce—the only cabinet rejection between 1925 and 1989. Anderson died in Albuquerque, N.Mex.

[The Library of Congress holds an extensive and rich collection of papers of Anderson's Senate years; and the Truman Library has his cabinet papers. His autobiography, written with Milton Viorst, is *Outsider in the Senate: Senator Clinton Anderson's Memoirs* (1970). His cabinet service is detailed in James Lee Forsythe, "Clinton P. Anderson: Politician and Businessman as Truman's Secretary of Agriculture" (Ph.D. diss., Univ. of N.Mex., 1970), and his foreign policy views are set forth in J. Samuel Walker, "Confessions of a Cold Warrior: Clinton P. Anderson and American Foreign Policy, 1945–1972," *New Mexico Historical Review*, Apr. 1977. No full-scale biography of Anderson yet exists, but his career is explored from the perspective of his natural resources interests in Richard Allan Baker, *Conservation Politics: The Senate Career of Clinton P. Anderson* (1985). For an exploration of Anderson's campaign to defeat the nomination of Lewis Strauss, see Richard Allan Baker, "A Slap at the 'Hidden-Hand Presidency': The Senate and the Lewis Strauss Affair," *Congress and the Presidency*, Spring 1987. Obituaries appear in the *New York Times* and *Washington Star*, Nov. 12, 1975, and in the *Washington Post*, Nov. 13, 1975.]

RICHARD ALLAN BAKER

ANDERSON, MARGARET CAROLYN (Nov. 24, 1886–Oct.18, 1973), editor, writer, and publisher of the *Little Review*, was born in Indianapolis, Ind., the first of three daughters of Arthur Aubrey Anderson, a railroad executive, and Jesse Shortridge. Margaret and her two sisters grew up in Columbus, Ind., where Margaret developed a strong sense of independence, a thirst for beauty, and a complete disdain for the "higher joys of country clubs and bridge." In 1903, Anderson enrolled at the Western College for Women in Oxford, Ohio, where, for the next three years, she studied piano. After leaving school in 1906, she returned home and began a campaign to convince her parents to allow her to move to Chicago, a city then undergoing a renaissance in theater, music, and the arts.

Arriving in Chicago with her sister Lois in the fall of 1908, Anderson began conducting interviews and writing book reviews for the *Interior* (later the *Continent*), a religious magazine edited by Clara E. Laughlin. She also reviewed for Francis Hackett at the *Chicago Evening Post*. After losing her allowance because of her extravagant spending habits, she found a clerical position in Browne's Bookstore at eight dollars per week. Browne's, located in the Fine Arts Building, was connected with the

Dial, a literary review edited by Francis F. Browne. Recognizing Anderson's talent, Browne placed her on the magazine's staff. Anderson enjoyed her work as literary editor at the *Dial*, but continuing in her position became uncomfortable after Browne made an unwelcome advance towards her. Fortuitously, in the summer of 1913, Clara Laughlin suddenly resigned as editor of the *Continent*; Anderson readily agreed to fill her mentor's shoes. Anderson did well in Chicago both professionally and socially. Through Floyd Dell, Hackett's successor at the *Chicago Evening Post*, she met Theodore Dreiser, Sherwood Anderson, and other leading figures of the Chicago Renaissance. It was at one of Dell's parties that she announced her intention to publish the *Little Review*. The idea struck her as a cure for depression. She was depressed, she realized, because her life was uninspired. "I demand that life be inspired every moment," she declared. "The only way to guarantee this is to have inspired conversation every moment." Her solution was to publish a magazine filled with the best conversation the world had to offer.

Anderson found several financial supporters, including Eunice Tietjens and DeWitt Wing. Following Wing's advice, she went to New York to solicit publishers' advertisements. She returned to Chicago and in March 1914 launched the *Little Review*, "A Magazine of the Arts, Making No Compromise with the Public Taste." The inaugural issue included Vachel Lindsay's poem "How a Little Girl Danced," articles on Nietzsche and Gertrude Stein, and Anderson's own essay on Jan Paderewski. It was an auspicious beginning. Anderson, however, soon encountered trouble, when an editorial celebrating anarchism in the May issue cost her Wing's support. Fiercely independent, she continued publishing even though her lack of finances forced her, along with her sister Lois and a *Little Review* staff member, to pitch a tent on the shores of Lake Michigan, where they lived rent-free from May through November.

In 1916, Anderson met Jane Heap, a graduate of the Chicago Art Institute and the daughter of a midwestern psychiatrist. Heap, the most interesting conversationalist Anderson had ever known, joined the staff of the *Little Review* and lived and worked closely with Anderson for the next eight years. They briefly moved to Muir Woods, Calif., where they published the September 1916 issue, famous for its "want ad"—

twelve blank pages expressing the editors' dismay with the lack of "real art" being offered them.

The paucity of suitable material, however, was short-lived. Upon returning to Chicago, Anderson received the first of many letters from Ezra Pound. After the *Little Review* moved to New York in 1917, Pound became its foreign editor. Under his auspices, the *Little Review* was to receive contributions from such modern literary giants as T. S. Eliot, Gertrude Stein, Ernest Hemingway, and James Joyce. In the March 1918 issue, Anderson began the serialization of Joyce's *Ulysses*, the deed on which the *Little Review*'s reputation would forever rest. During the three years Joyce's novel ran, issues would be seized by the United States Post Office, declared obscene, and burned in four separate incidents. In October 1920, the Society for the Suppression of Vice prosecuted the *Little Review* after the Washington Square Bookshop in New York sold a copy of the July–August issue—containing Joyce's Nausicaa episode—to a minor. In December of that year, the editors were placed on trial. They were represented by noted Tammany Hall lawyer and patron of the arts, John Quinn. Quinn lost the case, and on Feb. 21, 1921, the editors were found guilty, fingerprinted, and fined $50 each. More important, they were enjoined from printing further excerpts of *Ulysses*. After the verdict, Anderson began to lose interest in the magazine, which became a quarterly in the fall. It then suspended publication between 1927 and the final issue in 1929.

In 1922, Anderson met Georgette Leblanc, the French singer and former lover of Maurice Maeterlinck. Leblanc soon replaced Heap in Anderson's affections. Around the same time, Anderson also met Alfred Richard Orage, who introduced her to the works of the mystic philosopher George I. Gurdjieff. Anderson, Heap, and Leblanc soon became Gurdjieff's loyal disciples. Leaving Jane Heap in charge of the *Little Review*, Anderson and Leblanc left for France in 1923. There they would share their lives together until Leblanc's death in 1941. They made plans for Leblanc to perform in concert with Anderson as her accompanist. At the last minute, however, Leblanc's backer withdrew, leaving the women stranded. They stayed first at Leblanc's sister's Château de Tancarville. Leblanc's relatives were wealthy, but they practiced a parsimony that made life at the château unpleasant. In 1924, and again in 1935, Anderson and Leblanc spent time studying with Gurdjieff at Fontainebleau-Avon. Although Anderson and Leblanc returned to the château when funds were low, they escaped to more congenial quarters whenever possible. Traveling in France from Paris to the Pyrenees, they stayed in small hotels, chalets, and even a lighthouse. They lived quietly, supporting themselves primarily on royalties from Anderson's *My Thirty Years' War* (1930) and Leblanc's *Souvenirs* (1932).

Anderson never married, and although she never declared herself a lesbian, scholars have considered her in the company of lesbian writers. In *My Thirty Years' War*, she proudly proclaimed, "I am no man's wife, no man's delightful mistress, and I will never, never, never be a mother."

In June 1939, after Leblanc was diagnosed with cancer, Anderson and Leblanc fled Paris for the relative safety of Le Cannet in southern France, where they remained until Leblanc's death in 1941. Only then did Anderson agree to return home. In June 1942, with a $400 gift from Ernest Hemingway, Anderson bought a ticket for New York on the *Drotingholm*. On board ship she met Dorothy Caruso, the widow of Enrico Caruso, the famous tenor. They formed a fast friendship and lived together until Dorothy's death in 1955. During her years with Dorothy, Anderson compiled *The Little Review Anthology* (1953) and wrote the second volume of her autobiography, *The Fiery Fountains* (1951). In 1956, she returned to Le Cannet, where she lived and wrote in seclusion. Here she completed *The Unknowable Gurdjieff* (1962) and *The Strange Necessity* (1970), the final volume of her autobiography. She died in a hospital in Cannes and was buried in Notre Dames des Anges Cemetery alongside Georgette Leblanc.

[The largest assemblage of Anderson's papers is in the *Little Review* collection at the University of Wisconsin, Milwaukee. Additional material can be found in the Janet Flanner–Solita Solano Collection at the Library of Congress and at the Houghton Library of Harvard University. Anderson's autobiographical writings are the most comprehensive sources for material on her life.

There is no full-length biography. See Janet Flanner's *New Yorker* profile, June 3, 1974; Morril Cody and Hugh Ford, *The Women of Montparnasse* (1984); and Hugh Ford, *Four Lives in Paris* (1987).

Jane Rule, *Lesbian Images* (1975), discusses Anderson's sexuality. For biographical sketches, see Mathilda M. Hills's thoroughly researched article in Barbara Sicherman, et al., eds., *Notable American Women: The Modern Period* (1980), and the entries in the *Dictionary of Literary Biography*, vols. 4 and 91. An obituary is in the *New York Times*, Oct. 20, 1973.]

WILLIAM M. GARGAN

ANGELI, PIER (June 19, 1932–Sept. 10, 1971), actress, was born Anna Maria Pierangeli in Cagliari, Sardinia, Italy, the daughter of Luigi Pierangeli, a construction engineer, and his wife Enrica. When she was three, her family moved to Rome. They lived a prosperous life there, and Anna Maria was remembered for her devotion to animals and her indifference to school.

Although the family suffered tremendous hardships during World War II, Anna Maria continued to go to school. Afterward, she attended art school in Rome. Her acting debut arose from meeting the French director Leonide Moguy at a party. He was trying to cast the lead actress role for a film called *Domani e Troppo Tardi* (released in America in 1952 as *Tomorrow Is Too Late*). The eighteen-year-old Anna Maria was by then a wide-eyed beauty with an ethereal demeanor, and although she had never taken acting lessons, Moguy thought she would be perfect for the role of Mirella, a naïve teenager who is destroyed by wrongful sexual allegations. She was an overnight success, winning the best actress award at the Venice Film Festival.

Angeli also attracted the attention of Stewart Stern from Metro-Goldwyn-Mayer, who had co-written a script for *Teresa* (1951), the story of an Italian girl who marries an American soldier, then has to deal with living in the U.S. with a husband who is a mother-dominated weakling, rather than the hero she had imagined. She won the title role, even though she knew only a few words of English at the time. For this and later films in America, her name was changed to Pier Angeli. The film was a success, and Angeli garnered particularly good notices when the film was released: critics compared her to a young Greta Garbo. Along with her mother and her twin sister Marissa, also an actress, Angeli moved to Hollywood. Her father had died in 1950, just before her acting career started.

Part of her success in *Teresa* was because she

was very much like the immature character that she played. During the filming, she was extremely reluctant to play scenes in which she hugged or kissed John Ericson, her on-screen husband. Her room was filled with dozens of stuffed animals. This childlike quality actually endeared her to her fellow actors, and the Italian director Vittorio de Sica, who acted with her in *Teresa*, praised her for her purity of soul.

She was also effective in her second American film, *The Light Touch* (1951), as an innocent girl who reforms a jewel thief played by Stewart Granger. Her star was already beginning to dim somewhat, though, by the time her third film, *The Devil Makes Three*, was released in 1952. She played an embittered German B-girl opposite Gene Kelly, but she was losing both momentum and her reputation as an up-and-coming star.

During the next few years, Angeli's career was noted for good roles that got away and bad roles that did not. She had been announced to make *Romeo and Juliet* with Marlon Brando, but the movie fell through when there was a British-Italian production of the same play. She lost the ingénue role in *The Rose Tattoo* (1955) to her sister. During the filming of *Story of Three Loves* (1953), she broke her wrist doing her own stunts on a trapeze. This delayed production, forcing the studio to substitute Kirk Douglas for Ricardo Montalban. *Sombrero* (1953) and *The Flame and the Flesh* (1954), with Lana Turner, brought her stock even lower. She was loaned to Columbia for the 1955 release *Port Afrique*, a melodrama in which she played a Spanish café singer.

Angeli's mother kept such a tight control over her daughters that the actress was not allowed to go out on an unchaperoned date until she had been in Hollywood for two years. In 1954, Angeli met James Dean, who was scheduled to star with her in the film *Somebody Up There Likes Me* (1956). The two had an intense romance that was well hidden from the press. She broke off with Dean, probably yielding to parental pressure, and married singer Vic Damone later that year; they had one son and were divorced only four years later.

Angeli retained her role in *Somebody Up There Likes Me*, ultimately released in 1956. After James Dean's sudden death, Paul Newman was brought in to play the part of boxer Rocky Marciano. Angeli turned in a sensitive performance as his wife. It was to be the only

film that would live up to the promise that she showed in *Teresa*. The film was a critical and financial success.

Angeli finished her MGM contract with *The Vintage* (1957), in which she starred with Mel Ferrer, and *Merry Andrew* (1958), in which she teamed with Danny Kaye. This would also be the substantial end to her career in Hollywood.

In 1958 her divorce from Vic Damone put her in the headlines. This included a bitter child custody dispute. She was granted full custody in 1960, but Damone kept the case alive, claiming that the boy was not being raised as an American. In 1965, the order was modified to joint custody that still allowed the child to go to school in Rome. Afterward, she resumed acting in England, but this move did not turn her career around.

In 1962 she married Italian bandleader Armando Trovajoli. This union produced another son, and by 1966 a second divorce and another child custody battle, which she lost.

By this time, she was continuing her film career in Europe, playing roles in low-budget films with "international casts" that often included American leading men whose Hollywood careers had dried up. She reverted to her original name. Although she did get a small but effective part in *The Battle of the Bulge* (1965), most of the 1960's saw her working in everything from low-budget spy films to sexploitation films such as *Love Me, Love My Wife* (1970), which included her in protracted nude scenes. Few of her films from this period were ever shown in the United States.

By 1971, she was back in Hollywood, trying for a career rebirth. She did get a role in a minor film, *Octaman* (1972), but there seemed little chance that she could ever recapture her past glory. She died of a barbiturate overdose on Sept. 10, 1971. One newspaper reported that she was about to be offered a starring role in an episode of the television series "Bonanza" at the time of her death.

[See David Shipman, *Great Movie Stars: The International Years* (rev. ed., 1980); and Kerry Segrave and Linda Martin, *The Continental Actress: European Film Stars of the Postwar Era* (1990). An obituary appears in the *New York Times*, Sept. 11, 1971.]

TERRY BALLARD

ANGELL, ERNEST (June 1, 1889–Jan. 11, 1973), chairman of the American Civil Liberties Union, was born in Cleveland, Ohio, one of two children born to Elgin Adelbert Angell, a lawyer, and Lily Curtis. He attended University School in Cleveland, and after graduating in 1907, he attended Harvard College, where he was elected to Phi Beta Kappa. He graduated in 1911 and two years later received an LL.B. degree from Harvard Law School. After service in World War I as a captain of infantry, Angell returned to Cleveland and resumed the practice of law. He was appointed New York regional director of the Securities and Exchange Commission in 1936, serving under Joseph P. Kennedy, who was then its chairman. He had a principal role in the criminal investigation of Richard Whitney, president of the New York Stock Exchange. Two years later he resumed the practice of corporate and litigation law with the New York firm of Harden, Hess and Eder. His main association during his long career was as a partner in the Wall Street firm of Spence, Windels, Walser and Hotchkiss.

As a Republican with strong establishment, Wall Street, and social connections, Angell was an unusual figure in the leadership of the American Civil Liberties Union, which he had joined in the 1920's. He saw the ACLU as an instrument for the protection and expansion of civil liberties through the formal pursuit of legal remedies in court, and he opposed efforts to involve the ACLU in political, public relations, and lobbying efforts in behalf of a wide range of controversial causes. He believed that the ACLU's prestige, influence, and success lay in the fervent appeal to principle, not partisanship, and he resisted identification of the organization as an appendage of the Democratic party. As a lawyer with fundamentally conservative personal values and moderate political views, Angell believed that the ACLU should champion only causes involving conventional constitutional doctrine derived from the First and Fourteenth Amendments.

Roger Baldwin, the founder and preeminent figure in the history of the ACLU, selected Angell for membership on its board in the late 1930's, at a decisive point in the fortunes of the organization. The Hitler-Stalin pact had caused a division in the ranks, and Corliss Lamont, an avowed Marxist and the most leftist of the members of the board, aggressively opposed a resolution barring anyone holding totalitarian views from membership in the ACLU. The resolution carried, effectively expelling members of the Communist party. The elevation of Angell to the chairmanship in 1950 blunted conservative attacks on the ACLU.

The ACLU had a strong record in support of pacifism, dating back to World War I. Angell, who was a member of the American Legion, argued that the ACLU should not oppose the draft, and it did not, although it sought to broaden the definition of conscientious objector status, beyond conventional religious conviction and belief, to include political grounds as a basis for excuse from service. Angell was welcomed to the White House by President Franklin Roosevelt, who heard his views on the matter but declined to alter government policy. The ACLU did not pursue the matter, and far greater numbers, proportionally, of asserted pacifists went to prison in World War II for refusing induction than had gone in World War I.

In 1941, when the director of Selective Service, Lewis Hershey, ordered local boards to draft wildcat strikers employed in defense plants, on the ground that the strikes had been instigated by Communists to undermine national security, Angell informally persuaded the attorney general to modify the government's program. Angell also sought to convince officials in the War Department of the profound inequity and offensiveness of segregation in the armed services, efforts that were unavailing. The ACLU publicly urged an end to segregation in the services, but the war crisis was not conducive to confronting the issue in other than the most limited and technical of lawsuits.

In 1940, Congress had passed the Smith Act (the Alien Registration Act), which authorized criminal prosecution of members of the Communist party. After convictions under the act were upheld by the Supreme Court in the *Dennis* case (1951), Angell urged the attorney general to prosecute under the act only those who could be shown to have personally participated in a definitive criminal conspiracy rather than simply being members of the Communist party.

In the 1960's two events profoundly changed the ACLU. Angell adhered resolutely to his position that the ACLU should not involve itself in political matters, notably the debate relating to public policy and the Vietnam War. It was his view that the lack of a formal declaration of war and the anti–civil liberties consequences of the war, such as broad police intelligence intrusions and the breakup of antiwar demonstrations on campuses and elsewhere, were appropriate concerns of the ACLU. He opposed, however, direct intervention by the ACLU in the court defense of indicted opponents of the war, such as Dr. Benjamin Spock and others.

Angell instituted a major reform of the ACLU, over the violent opposition of the radical faction of the board. The board was enlarged to give voice to the affiliate civil liberties organizations in states and cities across the nation, thereby nationalizing and democratizing the organization and stabilizing the ACLU's policy council. It provided the basis for a dramatic increase in membership and financial support, and led to a new era of expanded national prestige.

Angell was the author of *Supreme Court Primer* (1937), a brief, general outline of the Court's functions, and *Les Aspects constitutionnels des libertés publiques aux États-Unis* (1964). He also edited *The Rule of Law in the United States*. He married Katharine Sergeant in 1915; they had two children and were divorced in 1929. (She later became the wife of *New Yorker* writer E. B. White and became the first editor of fiction at that magazine.) Elizabeth Brosius Higgins, whom he married in 1939, died in 1970; they had two children. Angell died in New York City.

[Comprehensive references to Angell's leadership of the ACLU and letters and papers that he wrote are in the archival materials of the organization maintained at the Seeley G. Mudd Library of Princeton University. Valuable for discussion of the controversies in which Angell was involved is Samuel Walker, *In Defense of American Liberties* (1990). An obituary is in the *New York Times*, Jan. 12, 1973.]

KENNETH CONBOY

ANGLE, PAUL McCLELLAND (Dec. 25, 1900–May 11, 1975), historian, author, and administrator, was born in Mansfield, Ohio, the son of John Elmer Angle, a grocer, and Nellie Laverne McClelland, a secretary and teacher. He had three brothers and two sisters. From the age of nine, he worked in his father's store and had a wide range of duties.

Angle attended Oberlin College (1918–1919) and Miami University, where he majored in history and political science; he graduated from the latter magna cum laude with Phi Beta Kappa honors in 1922. Two years later, he earned a master's degree at the University of Illinois.

To pay off accumulated debts, Angle was temporarily a steelworker, an insurance salesman, and a representative of the American Book Company. In 1925, when he was about to accept an assistant professorship at Miami University, he learned of an opening in Springfield, Ill., that attracted him. Leaders of the Lincoln Centennial Association, founded in 1909, were developing the group into a specialized society for research on Lincoln's life and career. The post of executive secretary was open, and Theodore C. Pease, a professor of history at the University of Illinois, recommended Angle for the post.

Angle was hired, and for the next twenty years he lived in Springfield. In 1932, he was appointed historian of the Illinois State Library, and he became secretary of the Illinois State Historical Society.

At the age of twenty-eight, Angle won national acclaim. In its December 1928 issue, the *Atlantic Monthly* printed the first of a three-part series entitled "Lincoln—the Lover," previously undisclosed letters between Lincoln and Ann Rutledge (1813–1835) that were announced as fully documenting the story of their romance. *Atlantic* editor Ellery Sedgwick declared that the handwriting had been authenticated and that the letters were on paper that had passed strict physical tests.

Angle declared the letters a colossal hoax. Sedgwick dismissed him as a publicity seeker and published the entire series. But as more and more scholars supported Angle's position, it was finally admitted that the letters had been fabricated. Angle's analysis was printed in the April 1929 issue of the *Atlantic Monthly*. Ruth Painter Randall summarized the controversy in her biography of Ann Rutledge in *Notable American Women*. She concluded that "the verdict of Lincoln scholars, after careful analysis, is that there is not a scrap of reliable evidence to support this long-lived legend."

Under Angle the Illinois State Historical Library assembled the largest collection of prepresidential Lincoln manuscripts, documents, and notes. It also acquired one of the five existing copies, in Lincoln's handwriting, of the Gettysburg Address. Angle revised the State Historical Society's *Journal* to make it readable, attractive, and respectable.

Angle moved the annual meetings of the society, until then always held in Springfield, to communities throughout the state. He arranged for historical tours of the areas by those attending the meetings. Another important contribution was the selection of historic sites for official marking and dedication. All of these activities led to a much greater interest in history statewide and a substantial increase in the society's membership.

In 1945, Angle accepted the invitation of the Chicago Historical Society to become its director and secretary. Virtually overnight he became active in Chicago's civic affairs. Angle's experience led the mayor of Chicago to put him in charge of a committee that was to decide what city records to preserve. He continued as secretary of the Chicago Historical Society until 1970 but resigned the directorship in 1965 to devote himself to research, editing, and writing.

Angle's impressive production of books and articles started in 1925 when, under the title *Lincoln in Springfield*, he prepared for the Lincoln Centennial Association a guide to the places in Springfield that were associated with Lincoln's life. A year later he brought out the seven-volume *Lincoln in the Year . . . , Lincoln's day-by-day activities during the years 1854–1860*.

Angle was still under thirty when Houghton Mifflin published *New Letters and Papers of Lincoln* (1930). Also in 1930, Angle edited a one-volume edition of William H. Herndon's *Life of Lincoln*, which since 1889 had been reprinted a dozen times in two volumes. Angle's introduction and notes added so much that Herndon's *Life* was republished in 1936.

Angle's publications came to the attention of Carl Sandburg, who asked Angle to help him with his *Mary Lincoln: Wife and Widow* (1932). More than half of that book consisted of the letters, documents, and appendix that Angle assembled and arranged.

The intimate association of Lincoln with Springfield so fascinated Angle that he researched and wrote a history of the Illinois state capital (1935). Bearing Lincoln's words *"Here I Have Lived"* as its title and dedicated to Angle's friend and benefactor, Logan Hay, it covers the period from the region's prehistoric times to Lincoln's departure for Washington, D.C. In the course of the book Lincoln recalls the Black Hawk war, Mormon troubles, the first railroads and their effects, and the Lincoln-Douglas debates.

The *New York Times* credited Angle with portraying "with liveliness, color and accuracy the rapidly developing life, growth, manners and customs, wealth and culture of the Illinois frontier town from its first log cabin in the proud little city that with cheers sent its most eminent citizen to the White House and in sorrow received his remains."

From the late 1930's to the early 1970's, Angle produced an outstanding number of books and articles, including *Handbook of Illinois History*, written with Richard L. Beyer (1943), *A Shelf of Lincoln Books* (1946), *The Lincoln Reader* (1947), *By These Words* (1954), *A Lincoln in Letters Portrait by His Oldest Sons* (1968), and *First in the Hearts of His Countrymen* (1970).

On several occasions Angle treated subjects other than Lincoln and related themes. In 1931, he made a detailed study of the Marine Bank of Springfield, distinguished as the "oldest bank in Illinois." A concern with violence led him to research the fighting in the southern Illinois coalfields; as a result, facts about the Herrin massacre stood out in his *Bloody Williamson* (1952), which publisher Alfred A. Knopf called "a hair-raising story of unparalleled violence." Twice he wrote on the Chicago Fire: *The Great Chicago Fire of 1871* (1969) and *The Great Chicago Fire, October 8–10, 1871* (1971).

Angle married Vesta Verne Magee on June 17, 1926; they had two children. In World War II he served the U.S. Army Air Force as a consultant in history. An athlete in his college years, he turned to gardening as an adult.

Angle died in Chicago and donated his body to medical research. The Chicago Historical Society arranged a tribute meeting at which the *Chicago Sun-Times* editorial director, Emmett Dedmon, said most fittingly: "With those of us who knew Paul Angle, his memory will be ever green, his books a bottomless harvest, and the glow of his friendship as rich as a prairie sunset over the land he loved."

[The libraries of the Illinois State Historical Society in Springfield and the Chicago Historical Society have large collections of Angle's works and articles about him. A broad-ranging account of his life and work is Irving Dilliard, "Paul M. Angle: Warm Recollections and Clear Impressions," *Journal of the Illinois State Historical Society*, Nov. 1975. See also Philip K. Wrigley, *A Memoir of a Modest Man* (1975). Obituaries are in the *Chicago Tribune* and

Chicago Sun-Times, both May 12, 1975, and in the *New York Times*, May 13, 1975.]
IRVING DILLIARD

APGAR, VIRGINIA (June 7, 1909–Aug. 7, 1974), physician, was born in Westfield, N.J., the daughter of Charles Emory Apgar, a businessman and automobile salesman, and Helen May. Her family, which included a brother, shared musical interests. Apgar studied violin from the age of six and joined in family concerts. She was a member of the Amateur Chamber Music Players and performed with the Teaneck (N.J.) Symphony. She also belonged to the Catgut Acoustical Society, where she learned the craft of building her own stringed instruments.

As early as high school Apgar set her sights on a medical career. Following graduation from Westfield High School in 1925, she enrolled in Mount Holyoke College, where she enrolled in a rigorous premedical curriculum. Apgar worked as a librarian and a waitress, earned letters in athletics, and was a violinist in the orchestra and a reporter for the college newspaper. She majored in zoology and graduated in 1929.

In 1933, Apgar was awarded a degree in medicine from Columbia University College of Physicians and Surgeons in New York City, and she became a surgical intern at Presbyterian Hospital, the fifth woman to be awarded that internship. After the two-year internship she was dissuaded by the professor of surgery from pursuing a specialty in surgery because of the obstacles posed to women in that field. She reluctantly switched to anesthesiology, a relatively new field in medicine. In 1937, she became the fiftieth physician to be certified as an anesthesiologist in the United States.

For the next twenty years, Apgar remained at Columbia Presbyterian Medical Center, where she was clinical director of the department of anesthesiology. Under her direction the department gained a national reputation for excellence. In 1949, she was appointed a full professor at the College of Physicians and Surgeons, where she remained until 1959. The delivery room held a particular fascination for Apgar. During her tenure at the hospital she assisted in the delivery of thousands of babies as attending anesthesiologist.

Apgar's work as an anesthesiologist in the delivery room ultimately prompted the development of the Apgar Score System. She noticed that newborn infants were largely ignored while medical attention focused on the mother's well-being. Infants were usually examined later in the nursery. This was hazardous for infants with medical problems because there were sometimes serious complications that needed prompt attention. Apgar believed that some type of health test that could alert medical staff to the infants' general condition at the time of delivery was needed. Her careful observations of the signs of newborn infants led to the publication of the Apgar Score System in 1952.

The Apgar Score System is designed to rate an infant on a scale of 0 to 2 on five infant signs, one minute and five minutes after birth. The five functions are heart rate, respiration, reflex irritability, muscle tone, and color. On each item a score of 0 shows no response, a 1 is marginal functioning, and a 2 represents the best response. Thus a baby's total score may range from 10 for best functioning to 0 for a baby in extreme jeopardy. Generally, Apgar scores of 7 and above indicate no risk for survival, while scores of 4 and below alert physicians to possible risk factors. The assessment is easy and quick to administer and has been adopted worldwide as a useful screening examination for neonates.

After thirty years at Columbia, teaching, mentoring, and assisting in delivering more than fifteen thousand babies, Apgar surprised her colleagues and friends by leaving her post to enter the Johns Hopkins University School of Hygiene and Public Health in Baltimore. There, while pursuing a master's degree in public health, she was offered the directorship of the division of clinical malformations in the March of Dimes Foundation.

The foundation was embarking on a program of research on birth defects. Apgar was not convinced that she knew enough about birth defects to lead the program. She said to an interviewer for the *New York World-Telegram and Sun*, "They . . . were looking for someone . . . who likes to travel and talk. I love to see new places and I certainly can chatter, and I definitely did not want to retire . . . but I had to tell . . . the truth. I knew very little about birth defects. They insisted I could learn." She obtained her master's in 1959 and was appointed to the March of Dimes Foundation the same year.

At the foundation in New York City, Apgar's work centered on birth defects and prenatal care. Her responsibilities as director included distributing more than $5 million annually in research grants. She remained with the foundation until her death. In 1967 she became vice-president and director of basic research, and in 1973 she became senior vice-president in charge of medical affairs. Her research and lectures focused on the dangers of drugs and radiation for the developing fetus. She was an outspoken advocate of early prenatal care. She published numerous articles and in 1972, with Joan Beck, the book *Is My Baby All Right?*

Throughout her career, Apgar, who never married, received national international honors. She was a sought-after medical consultant, and her addresses to medical meetings were enthusiastically received. Nevertheless, she remained modest and unassuming, and has been described as compassionate and warm. Apgar died in New York City.

[An obituary is in the *New York Times*, Aug. 8, 1974.]

M. VIRGINIA WYLY

ARENDT, HANNAH (Oct. 14, 1906–Dec. 4, 1975), political philosopher and historian, was born in Hannover, Germany, the only child of Paul and Martha Cohn Arendt, both of whom had grown up in Jewish families of Russian descent that had established themselves as entrepreneurs in Königsberg, the capital city of East Prussia. Paul Arendt, an engineer and amateur classical scholar, contracted syphilis before his marriage, and the disease recurred when his daughter was two and a half. The family then returned to Königsberg, where Arendt's childhood was overshadowed by her father's deterioration and, finally, his death in 1913 by paresis (syphilitic insanity) when she was seven. Martha Arendt was left to manage her grief and her precocious, energetic child through World War I, with episodic battles between the Germans and the Russians taking place on the nearby eastern front.

Arendt's parents were Social Democratic in their politics, and Martha Arendt supported the Left in the post–World War I political turmoil, instilling in her daughter an admiration for socialist leader Rosa Luxemburg. But Arendt was not inclined to activism. In the context of a second family—her mother remarried in 1920, and Arendt gained two older stepsisters—she cultivated literary and philosophical interests. After finishing her diploma, the *Abitur*, in Königsberg in 1924, she set out in the fall of

that year to study theology with Rudolf Bultmann at the University of Marburg. There she was drawn to the young philosopher Martin Heidegger, who had attracted a following with the lectures that eventually became *Being and Time*, the chief sourcebook for a mode of thought that had the name *Existenzphilosophie* in Germany and later *existentialisme* in France. Basically, this was a mode of thought that called for careful descriptive and analytical attention to the ways in which people exist in the world, act in situations, choose their company, make their destinies, and orient themselves toward history—a nontheistic, this-worldly mode.

Arendt had a brief, intense love affair with Heidegger in 1925, and then decided to finish her studies in the calmer arena of the seminars offered by Karl Jaspers, a fatherly psychiatrist turned philosopher, who taught in Heidelberg. There, in September 1929 she married Günther Stern, who later became a well-known writer under the pen name Gunther Anders. Arendt completed a dissertation on *The Concept of Love in St. Augustine* (1929) and received her Ph.D., but soon turned her attention to the current scene. Her concern was with the rising tide of anti-Semitism, and also with the complex history of German-Jewish relations, which she approached by studying a famous late-eighteenth-century moment of cultural rapprochement when Jewish salon hostesses dominated literary life in Berlin. She wrote a biographical study of one such hostess, Rahel Varnhagen, that focused on how Varnhagen repudiated her Jewishness only to find her way back to it near the end of her life; the book was not published until 1958.

Arendt began to associate with Kurt Blumenfeld, leader of the German Zionist Organization, and, after Hitler came to power in 1933, she worked actively for the Zionists, harboring fugitives and doing research to help Blumenfeld publicize abroad the plight of Hitler's enemies and victims. She was arrested by the Gestapo, and, after she was questioned and released, set out for the safety of Paris and the many opportunities there to work for the Zionist cause. In a number of administrative capacities with organizations like Youth Aliyah, she helped secure passage for Jewish children to Palestine.

While she was in Paris, Arendt also developed friendships with German émigré critics, poets, and artists who were Marxists. In 1936 she met a vigorous, self-educated working-class

Berliner named Heinrich Bluecher, a former associate of Rosa Luxemburg's Spartacus Group and a Communist activist. On Jan. 16, 1940, after both were divorced, they married. Both she and Bluecher became close to Walter Benjamin, a friend of the poet and playwright Bertolt Brecht, and the most talented literary critic of their generation. Benjamin had a profound influence on Arendt's sense of history, particularly of how the deep currents of the nineteenth century had contributed to the storm of war they all knew was coming.

When the German army smashed into France in 1940, Arendt and Bluecher were separated and sent with the other German exiles in Paris to an internment camp in the south of France. They escaped, were reunited with each other, and set out on a dangerous journey via Portugal to America, which they reached safely in May 1941 and where Arendt's mother later joined them. While they were living in New York City during the war, struggling to learn English and to make ends meet with journalistic and publishing jobs, Arendt and Bluecher also envisioned the work that eventually resulted in *The Origins of Totalitarianism* (1951), the book that would establish Arendt's American reputation as a political analyst and historian of major importance.

While Arendt was preparing *The Origins of Totalitarianism*, she published preliminary essays and studies in Jewish journals of opinion and in leftist liberal magazines like the *Partisan Review*, and through this connection she began to make American friends. She found American Jewish colleagues who supported her ideas that the Jews should have an army to fight Hitler and that the Jews living in Palestine should work toward a post-war state in conjunction with the Arabs of Palestine. She also found American colleagues who were, as she was, not easily located on the conventional left-to-right spectrum of political beliefs. The poet Randall Jarrell helped her find work from 1946 to 1948 as an editor at Schocken Books, where she produced an important edition of Franz Kafka's diaries, and it was during this time that she met the novelist Mary McCarthy who became a steadfast friend for the rest of Arendt's life. Dwight Macdonald brought Arendt to the editorial board of his magazine, *politics*, and Salo Baron of Columbia University affiliated her with various projects for postwar Jewish cultural reconstruction. These relationships gave Arendt an American intellectual context in which to tell the story of European totalitarianism.

In the three densely woven parts of *The Origins of Totalitarianism* Arendt tracked the histories of European anti-Semitism, overseas and continental imperialism, and totalitarianism, showing how nineteenth-century race theory turned into lethal racist ideology, how modern bureaucracies lent themselves to police-state operations, how nation-states disintegrated and class structures dissolved to produce masses of people characterized by their bitter resentment of economic chaos and their absence of any sense of political life or political freedom. But she also formulated many of the theoretical distinctions that undergirded her later work. She distinguished, for example, between social oppression and political discrimination; between socioeconomic forces and political action, a distinction that later grew into a triptych—labor, work, action; between nationalism and supranationalism; between authoritarianism and totalitarianism, which Arendt argued was a completely novel form of government. Her claim that Stalin's regime resembled Hitler's as a totalitarian form was controversial. In the context of the Cold War, her book appeared to support American anti-Communism; but Arendt herself was a courageous critic of McCarthyism and the fascistic forms American anti-Communism took. She was grateful to receive her citizenship the year her book was published, 1951, and she always praised America's republican traditions, but she was never hesitant to hold her new country to the high political standards she outlined in her subsequent books.

The Human Condition (1958), an essay collection entitled *Between Past and Future* (1961, expanded 1968), and *On Revolution* (1963) might all be described as antidotes to totalitarianism. Arendt had focused in her first book on the social and political factors that crystallized in Nazism and Stalinism, but in these subsequent books she emphasized how political spaces are founded and preserved, how political action is distinguished from labor and work, and how revolutions can prepare the way for constitutional protections. She was working to create what she once called "a new science of politics," one in which the best of the European, and especially Greco-Roman, political thought was recuperated, but in forms fit for modern conditions of nation-state political life.

Arendt never sought a science of politics that

could be laid down, gridlike, on events. She looked, rather, for large patterns in political life—such as the shift away from valuation of action to valuation of labor, which she thought marked the twentieth century—in the light of which particular events could be considered. Her technique was to explore the broad concepts that she felt defined "the human condition," such as life itself, existence with others or plurality, natality, mortality, existence in a cultural world and on the earth. She then analyzed these concepts in their interactions through history until the present day. Then Arendt invoked different dimensions of the dynamic network of her concepts and distinctions each time she felt compelled to comment on an event in Europe, like the Hungarian Revolution of 1956, or on America's internal political life. She was particularly active in commenting on American politics in the late 1960's and early 1970's, when she published the influential essays entitled "On Violence," "Civil Disobedience," and "Lying in Politics: Reflections on the Pentagon Papers," which were collected in *Crises of the Republic* (1972). The worldwide student revolt and anti–Vietnam War movement that exploded in 1968 seemed to Arendt a continuation of the ambiguous—freedom-loving and freedom-destroying—revolutionary traditions she had considered in *On Revolution*, just as the corruption and mendacity of American governmental structures in that period seemed to her ominously reminiscent of midcentury proto-totalitarian phenomena. She both celebrated the joy in political action she saw among the idealistic young and wrote cautionary tales for those making righteous claims for the necessity of revolutionary violence. She both celebrated the strength of American constitutionalism and rebuked the leaders who scorned the First Amendment and indulged dreams of American imperialism.

As her books were published one by one through the late 1950's, 1960's, and early 1970's, Arendt was offered many university appointments and lectureships, and she spent time at many colleges, including Princeton University, the University of California at Berkeley, the University of Chicago (1963–1967), and the New School for Social Research (1967–1975) in New York City, which she and Bluecher always called home and from which he commuted to a teaching post at Bard College. She was able to teach part-time most years, and was always able to go to Europe in the summers, where she carefully maintained her old friendships, particularly with Karl Jaspers (until his death in 1969). Even while she was itinerant, Arendt gave a great deal of her attention to the preservation of her friendships and her European past, and this habit also translated into her work in the form of a series of intellectual portraits of people with whom she carried on real or imaginary conversations. Many of these portraits, including ones of Jaspers, Walter Benjamin, and Rosa Luxemburg, were collected in a volume called *Men in Dark Times* (1968).

Arendt's prolific "life of the mind" (her favorite phrase for thinking) brought her invitations and prizes from many directions in America and, even more frequently, in Europe, where she allowed herself to do radio and TV interviews because she did not, then, have to suffer the loss of privacy that comes with living in the countries where one is a celebrity. But she was also often the subject of intellectual controversies, particularly for a book called *Eichmann in Jerusalem* (1963), published first as a series of articles in the *New Yorker*.

Two dimensions in particular of Arendt's report on Eichmann's trial in Jerusalem, which she attended, were debated in magazines and journals around the world. First, she had argued that the establishment by the Nazis of the "Jewish Councils" that participated in the Nazis' horrifying program of roundups and transportation to concentration camps had been crucial to the efficiency of the "Final Solution." This argument, which was meant to show how invidious and morale-destroying the Nazis' methods had been, was interpreted as a kind of blaming of the victims for their fate. Second, she concluded from Eichmann's testimony that he was not a psychopath, not a demonic creature, but, on the contrary, a banal man, a man who either could not or would not think what he was doing. Arendt recanted an argument she had made in *The Origins of Totalitarianism* about the "radical evil" of the Nazi regime and emphasized "the banality of evil." Many of her critics, however, read this conclusion as a form of absolution or as a terrifying underestimation of the Nazis' mentality.

For Hannah Arendt herself, the possibility that Eichmann was a man whose most important political characteristic was his thoughtlessness opened a line of inquiry that occupied her during the last decade of her life. She had often reflected on what relations can and ought to exist between thinking and action (or theory and praxis, to use more common technical terms), but she had not considered not-thinking and what behavior might flow from not-thinking. The inquiry, in turn, catalyzed an ambitious three-volume philosophical project that eventually was titled *The Life of the Mind* (1978).

The first volume of this work takes up the questions Eichmann's thoughtlessness had posed: Can thinking prevent evildoing? What is the difference between thinking and knowing or cognition, including the "knowing right from wrong" used to define mental competence legally? The general "what is thinking?" theme of the first volume then led to the obvious corollary, "what is acting?" or, in terms of action's source, "what is willing?" Arendt had argued in the first volume that thinking does not directly determine or direct action, but that thinking does, on the other hand, have a by-product, judging, which gives action its guiding terms—pleasure or displeasure, rightness or wrongness. As was her intellectual custom, Arendt tracked the philosophical history of each mental faculty as she tried to compass it and find images for its interrelations, and she thus tried to present thinking, willing, and judging interactively, dynamically.

By the fall of 1975 Arendt had completed drafts of the first two volumes of *The Life of the Mind*, but she had only lecture notes and sketches for the third. Her work schedule had been somewhat curtailed by her mourning the death of her husband in 1970 and then by her own declining health. She had had a heart attack while delivering parts of her book as the prestigious Gifford Lecturer in Aberdeen, Scotland, and this attack presaged the one from which she died in her New York City apartment; her ashes are buried at Bard College. Three years later, her last book appeared incomplete, but edited by Mary McCarthy into a powerfully coherent statement.

In the many obituaries and reflective articles that appeared after Arendt's death, as in the large shelf of studies published since then, her position in American and European intellectual life has been reaffirmed. Among female philosophers born at the beginning of the century and living through three quarters of its tumultuous history, she and Simone de Beauvoir are the major figures, although Arendt's work was not adopted by feminist theorists until later. Her work certainly takes a place of preeminence among the great twentieth-century contributions in all of the areas that she took up—the history of totalitarianism, theory of revolution, social criticism, modernist political philosophy, and philosophy of the mind.

[Most of Hannah Arendt's papers and correspondences are located in the Manuscript Division of the Library of Congress. Her correspondence with Jaspers has been published in German and English; these letters, and her correspondences with Heidegger (which are being prepared for publication), Blumenfeld, and others are in the German Literary Archive in Marbach, near Stuttgart. Bluecher's manuscripts are in the Bard College Library.

A full-length biography by Elisabeth Young-Bruehl, *Hannah Arendt: For Love of the World* (1982), contains a German and English bibliography and includes some of Arendt's youthful German poems as an appendix. Arendt's essays on Jewish topics have been collected in Ron H. Feldman, ed., *The Jew As Pariah* (1978); a collection of previously unpublished essays, edited by Jerome Kohn, is in preparation. Arendt has been the subject of book-length studies by Margaret Canovan (1974 and 1992), Bhikhu Parekh (1981), George Kateb (1983), and Patricia Bowen-Moore (1989), among others, and there are numerous doctoral dissertations, essays, essay collections, and special editions of journals dedicated to her and her work. An obituary appears in the *New York Times*, Dec. 6, 1975.]

ELISABETH YOUNG-BRUEHL

ARMSTRONG, HAMILTON FISH (Apr. 7, 1893–Apr. 24, 1973), a founder and editor of *Foreign Affairs* magazine, was born in New York City, the son of David Maitland Armstrong, an artist and stained-glass designer and onetime consul general to the Papal States, and Helen Neilson. He was a grandnephew of Hamilton Fish, secretary of state under President Grant. One of seven children, Armstrong achieved less public notice than his sister Margaret, a painter and author of *Fanny Kemble: A Passionate Victorian*. Yet his influence as editor and adviser was felt around the world.

Armstrong attended the Gilman Country School in Baltimore, Md. He celebrated his happy boyhood in *Those Days* (1963). He entered Princeton University in 1912, where he majored in English. He served four years on the *Daily Princetonian* and in his senior year edited the *Nassau Literary Magazine*. He also helped create the International Polity Club, and was its secretary and then president.

After receiving his B.A. in 1916, he spent a year in the publicity department at the *New Republic* magazine in New York City. A memento of his literary years was *Book of New York Verse* (1917). In the early 1920's he published poetry in literary magazines.

Armstrong played soccer and football at school. He joined the United States Army late in 1917 and was appointed military attaché to the Serbian War Commission in the United States. Late the next year he was assigned to the Military Intelligence Section of the United States General Staff. In December 1918, he became military attaché to the American Legation in Belgrade and remained there until he was demobilized in 1919. On Dec. 31, 1918, he married Helen McGregor Byrne. They had one child and divorced in 1938.

Armstrong joined the *New York Post* in 1919 and in 1921 and 1922 served the newspaper as special correspondent in eastern Europe. He was to make a specialty of the area in later studies. When the Council on Foreign Affairs founded the quarterly *Foreign Affairs* in 1922, Armstrong became its managing editor. On the death in January 1928 of the editor in chief, Archibald Cary Coolidge of Harvard, Armstrong became editor. He retained the post almost to his own death half a century later.

Armstrong and his colleagues at *Foreign Affairs* sought to provide readers at home and abroad with accurate information on politics and foreign concerns. Based in New York City, *Foreign Affairs* began with a circulation of 3,700. By the year of Armstrong's death, it had risen to 70,000, with subscribers all over the world.

Under Armstrong, *Foreign Affairs* provided a forum for political leaders and authoritative spokesmen at home and abroad, especially in Europe. Franklin D. Roosevelt, Henry Stimson, Anthony Eden, Leon Trotsky, Marshall Tito, V. I. Lenin, and Konrad Adenauer were among the formidable names whose views he solicited. Although their opinions were self-serving and possibly deceptive, it was possible for trained analysts to gain from their pronouncements.

Armstrong himself contributed many articles to his publication. He was the first American to interview Adolf Hitler after he assumed power in Germany. From this and his Berlin visit came *Hitler's Reich* (1933). It began with the somber words, "A people has disappeared."

Foreign Affairs itself leaped into the news in 1947 with its publication of "The Sources of Soviet Conduct," by an author identified only as "X." The author later was identified as George F. Kennan, the chief of State Department policy planning, who advocated containment of the Soviet Union in the Cold War era.

Armstrong's own writings multiplied with the years as he emphasized peace and the difficulties of achieving it. Although he wrote clearly, his emphasis on chronology and an overabundance of data tended to appeal to experts rather than to general readers. He was, however, able to reach firm conclusions at critical times. Presidents and others often solicited his advice. In 1923, he became a trustee to the Woodrow Wilson Foundation, and he later became its president. He served as director of the Council on Foreign Relations. Armstrong was thrice delegate to the International Studies Conference of the Institute of Intellectual Cooperation. He counseled diplomat John. G. Winant on the European Advisory Commission. In 1944, Armstrong was appointed special adviser to Secretary of State Edward R. Stettinius, Jr., and in 1945 served as adviser to the United States delegation to the United Nations Conference on International Organization in San Francisco.

Armstrong's authoritative book, *The New Balkans* (1926), contained warnings for the future regarding Germany and the Soviet Union. *Chronology of Failure: The Last Days of the French Republic* (1940) wrote *finis* to his warnings of the year before, in *When There Is No Peace*. In *The Calculated Risk* (1947), a fearful Armstrong demanded a plan for Europe similar to what would later become the Marshall Plan, one that would be equal to the emergency created by Stalin's warlike actions. In *Tito and Goliath* (1951), he took satisfaction in Tito's disruption of Stalin's Cominform.

A Republican while in college, Armstrong became a Democrat because he approved of President Franklin D. Roosevelt's policies. His entire life was spent in his boyhood home in New York City. On Dec. 27, 1945, he married Carman Barnes, a writer. They later divorced. In 1951, he married Christa von Tippelskirch. Armstrong retired in 1972. He died in New York City.

[An obituary appears in the *New York Times*, Apr. 25, 1973.]

LOUIS FILLER

ARMSTRONG, LOUIS ("SATCHMO") (Aug. 4, 1901–July 6, 1971), jazz musician and entertainer, was born in New Orleans, La., the son of Mary Ann and Willie Armstrong; his father was a day laborer. The date of his birth is questionable. He always claimed to have been born on July 4, 1900, a date he gave to a draft registrar in 1918. Recent research gives good documentation for the 1901 date. However, several of his early associates insist he was born about 1898, a date that squares better with events of his youth. Early chroniclers have given Daniel as his middle name, but Armstrong himself denied it.

His father, Willie, rose to become straw boss in a turpentine factory. Willie abandoned Armstrong's mother, probably about the time of his birth, and Armstrong remained bitter toward him until the end of his life. His mother (usually called Mayann) was about fifteen at the time of Armstrong's birth. She did domestic work and was probably a part-time prostitute as well. While Armstrong was still an infant, she moved into a rough vice district, leaving him in the care of his paternal grandmother, who worked as a laundress and domestic.

After the birth of his sister, when Armstrong was about five, he moved back in with his mother. Armstrong was raised in extreme deprivation, both emotionally and physically. Surrogate "stepfathers" came and went as Mayann changed boyfriends. Some were kind to Armstrong and some were not. At times he had to scavenge for food in garbage cans or eat remains of dinners scraped off restaurant plates by a stepfather who worked as a waiter. He went barefoot much of the time and owned little more than the shirt and pants he put on in the morning. Mayann was wayward and frequently left Armstrong to take care of himself and his baby sister.

Despite this rearing, Armstrong often spoke of his youth with fondness. He was apparently well liked, or made himself so, by the prostitutes, pimps, gamblers, and toughs of the neighborhood. He sang in a street-corner quartet for pennies, sold newspapers, ran errands, and apparently felt relatively secure in this rather vicious environment. It is worth noting, however, that he did not return to his hometown for nearly ten years after he left it and subsequently visited only for professional reasons.

Critically important to his career was the fact that the vice district was awash with honky-tonks featuring the new hot music aborning in New Orleans. The bands in the tonks were usually small, rough, two- to four-piece combinations, but Armstrong also heard the five- to seven-piece dixieland bands that were developing the classic New Orleans style. He became entranced by music and decided early to make it his career.

He was, however, far too poor to buy an instrument. Probably in January 1913, he was arrested for a minor offense and committed to a home for wayward boys, referred to in jazz literature as the "Waifs' Home." (There is evidence that he had served an earlier term in this institution.) Such institutions typically had bands, and here Armstrong learned the rudiments of brass technique. On his discharge, in about June 1914, he worked at day labor and sat in with local bands occasionally, especially in the neighborhood honky-tonks. At first he used borrowed horns, but eventually he acquired a battered instrument of his own, which allowed him to practice. In time he was hired to work regularly at various of the tonks.

Armstrong was shy about putting himself forward, and throughout his life compensated by putting himself in the hands of dominating men who could blaze trails for him. One of the first was cornetist Joseph ("King") Oliver, who became a leading figure in jazz. Armstrong later spoke in vague terms of Oliver as his mentor, but their playing styles were diametrically opposed, and it is doubtful that Oliver had much influence on Armstrong's approach to jazz. Oliver's principal contribution was emotional support and practical advice.

Oliver was coleader of a band organized by Edward ("Kid") Ory, accounted the best jazz band in New Orleans. For some years jazz musicians had been leaving the city, attracted by more money and better conditions in Chicago and the West Coast, and in 1918 Oliver left for Chicago. He arranged for Armstrong to replace him with the Ory group. Armstrong went on quickly to establish himself as a comer, playing on the famous riverboats and gigging around New Orleans with the better black bands, occasionally working at day labor to earn more money for the family, of which he was now the sole support.

In 1922 Oliver brought him to Chicago to work with the legendary Creole Jazz Band. Armstrong was only second cornetist, but the few solos he was allowed to play on the influential recordings made by this group, especially

"Froggie Moore," show a rhythmic spring beyond the somewhat stiffer two-beat rock of his fellow musicians.

In 1918 Armstrong had married a New Orleans prostitute named Daisy Parker. In Chicago he became involved with the Oliver group's pianist, Lillian Hardin. Armstrong divorced Daisy in 1923 and married Lillian the next year. She came from a middle-class background and had modest training in classical music. She recognized Armstrong's enormous musical gift and pressed him to move from under the shadow of Oliver. In 1924 Armstrong went to New York to join the talented band of Fletcher Henderson. Armstrong's solos with this group astounded musicians for the brilliance of his technique, the intensity of his swing, and the imaginative construction of his melodic line. Although largely unknown to the public, he was becoming an admired figure in the world of popular music.

In 1925 Armstrong returned to Chicago, again at his wife's urging, where it was arranged for him to make records under his own name, aimed at the black audience. In this casual fashion the famous "Hot Five" series of about five dozen sides was cut between 1925 and 1928. These records are considered by many critics to be the single most important body of work in jazz. They were rivaled in influence only by the early records of Charlie Parker and the boppers; hardly a musician in jazz was untouched by them.

At the beginning the Hot Fives group employed, in the main, New Orleans musicians and used the standard New Orleans format of cornet, clarinet, and trombone over a rhythm section. (Beginning in about 1926 Armstrong gradually switched from the mellower cornet to the more brilliant trumpet.) But as it became clear that Armstrong was the selling point, he was brought more and more to the fore. The last of the series of recordings are Armstrong showcases, with the other musicians merely supporting actors. Early in the series Armstrong began to sing. His success with the public, especially on "Heebie Jeebies," encouraged his recording directors to feature his singing.

Among the best of these performances are the ebullient blazing hot "Hotter Than That," the rather introspective "Big Butter and Egg Man," and "Cornet Chop Suey," which features a sequence of breaks that trumpeters everywhere learned. Perhaps the most admired of all are

three from 1928, "Tight Like This," "Muggles," and "West End Blues." "West End Blues," considered by many to be the greatest jazz record ever made, opens with a long, flawless cadenza and ends with a majestic solo, near tragic in feeling. In these recordings, Armstrong displayed an emotional range that no other jazz musician had ever possessed. The impact of these recordings on the jazz world was overpowering. Armstrong did not invent the jazz solo nor was he the first commanding soloist in the music. But so powerful a player was he that his method became the model for jazz.

Various business managers, recording directors, and music industry entrepreneurs into whose hands Armstrong put himself set out very quickly to move him into the commercial music business. He began to attract a substantial audience of white jazz fans, and the strategy was to move him from the black to the white market. Armstrong, who did not think of jazz as an art or of himself as an artist, was quite willing to reach out for fame and wealth. Under the guidance of his managers he began playing and singing popular tunes, some of them classic standards but more of them novelties and banal love tunes. He gave up the New Orleans small-band format entirely and fronted a standard big dance band, heavily featuring his playing and singing. Through the 1930's and much of the 1940's, Armstrong led a series of musically weak bands, attracting audiences as much for his singing as for his playing. He appeared in movies and on radio, and by the mid-1930's he was one of the most popular entertainers in America.

Questions remain about the quality of the music Armstrong made during this period. He was employing a much sparer line than he did when he played with the Hot Fives (in part to save his badly abused lip), and many of the recordings from this period, such as "Star Dust," "Struttin' with Some Barbecue," "E'vntide," and "Between the Devil and the Deep Blue Sea," contain masterly jazz solos, as good or better than all but the greatest of the Hot Five material. But on these records he had constant recourse to the upper register for showy effect, overused the half-valve, and too frequently relied on favorite phrases or musical figures that had become Armstrong clichés. Even so, there were few musicians in jazz who could equal Armstrong's work even at his weaker moments. It is simply that on the whole, his playing at this time did not come up to his earlier work standards.

By the late 1920's Armstrong's marriage to Lil Hardin was breaking up, and they separated around 1932. While they were still married, he had become involved with Alpha Smith. He married Smith in 1938. They divorced in about 1940. Shortly after his marriage to Smith he began courting a Cotton Club dancer named Lucille Wilson. They married in 1942 and were still married at the time of Armstrong's death. Armstrong had no children.

At the end of World War II the swing band movement collapsed, taking Armstrong down with it. The new bop movement was drawing away young jazz fans. Indeed, to many of the boppers and their followers Armstrong was the enemy—the very image of an Uncle Tom.

Fortunately for him, he was now in the hands of a tough, hard-talking manager with gangland connections, Joe Glaser, who had been important in structuring Armstrong's popular success in the big band era. Glaser had no interest in artistic concerts; he wanted only to make money.

There was at that time a revival of interest in dixieland jazz, which had been dormant for fifteen years. In 1947 Glaser put Armstrong in a group of jazz all-stars, playing a semblance of the old New Orleans style. Armstrong's personality and warmth were enough to attract a new generation of fans. Through the 1950's and 1960's his fame spread, until by the end of his life, he was a star. He had hits with "Blueberry Hill" and "Mack the Knife," among others, but it was the ordinary pop tune "Hello, Dolly!" that put him over the top. In 1964 his recording of the song pushed the Beatles out of the number-one spot on the *Billboard* chart.

As his success grew, Armstrong came under attack from militant blacks who wanted him to speak out against racial inequality. For years he avoided doing so; his audience was largely white, many of them southerners. Then, in the fall of 1957, angered by a television broadcast of whites howling at black children attending a newly integrated school, he made a scathing verbal attack on the American government for failing to take more action in the matter. His comments were widely published, and although Armstrong never became anything approaching militant in racial matters, he did thereafter occasionally take stands on racial issues.

By the late 1960's Armstrong was doing more singing than playing. It was what his audiences

wanted, and, in any case, years of abuse had badly damaged his lip. He stuck to tried and true material: his hits and such jazz standards as "Indiana" and "Muskrat Ramble." There is no doubt that on occasion he could still play brilliant jazz, as he did, for example, in "Satchmo: A Musical Autobiography of Louis Armstrong," issued in 1957. But for Armstrong, pleasing the public was his first concern, and artistic considerations came in a poor second.

The deprivations of Armstrong's childhood, particularly the absence of his father, left him with a need for approval. It must also be borne in mind that Armstrong grew up at a time in which show business was virtually the only escape from poverty for blacks, a culture that lacked the romantic European notion of the artist who sacrifices all for his art. To Armstrong, the whole point of being a musician was to please audiences. Nonetheless, his place in music history rests not on his popularity as an entertainer but on the body of jazz masterpieces made between 1924 and 1936, which in considerable measure shaped American jazz.

[The primary resource for scholars is the Louis Armstrong Archive in the Benjamin S. Rosenthal Library, Queens College, Flushing, N.Y. Much of the material is as yet uncatalogued, but it is estimated to contain six hundred and fifty reel-to-reel tapes, two hundred commercial broadcasts, one thousand disc recordings, scrapbooks, photographs, and letters and autobiographical writings. Also valuable for details of Armstrong's career and general background are the oral histories lodged in the Hogan Jazz Archive at Tulane and the Institute for Jazz Studies at Rutgers. The Hogan Jazz Archive also has material relevant to Armstrong's early years in New Orleans. Published autobiographies are *Swing That Music* (1936), *Satchmo* (1954), and an interview with Richard Meryman, *Louis Armstrong* (1971). Biographies include Albert McCarthy, *Louis Armstrong* (1960); Max Jones and John Chilton, *Louis* (1971); Hugues Panassié, *Louis Armstrong* (1971); James Lincoln Collier, *Louis Armstrong* (1983); and Gary Giddins, *Satchmo* (1988). An obituary is in the *New York Times*, July 7, 1971.]

JAMES LINCOLN COLLIER

ARQUETTE, CLIFFORD (Dec. 28, 1905– Sept. 23, 1974), comic actor on radio and television best known for his Charley Weaver character, was born in Toledo, Ohio. His parents were a vaudeville team of uneven quality who left the stage to settle down and raise a family in Toledo. His father worked as a barber.

The Arquette household continued to have loose ties to the world of show business and was home to itinerant musicians. At age six, Arquette dyed his hair black, affixed a tiny mustache, and won a Charlie Chaplin contest, besting 300 other children. Although Arquette had no formal training in music, he took up several instruments and left high school at age fourteen to become a professional musician. His band, Cliff Arquette and His Purple Derbies, found steady work for three years at Cleveland's Euclid Beach amusement park.

When he was seventeen, Arquette moved to Los Angeles, where he worked at a variety of odd jobs. After a stint in a band that played one-night stands throughout the South and West, Arquette formed several vaudeville acts, including Cliff and Lolly, the Nuts of Harmony, and the Three Public Enemies. By the early 1930's, Arquette's troupe had established itself as a successful attraction.

Vaudeville was in decline, however, and so in 1936 Arquette moved to radio, which was attracting many former vaudevillians. Here he found his medium, gaining notice for his comic renditions of old people. Arquette first appeared on a network radio show with Fred Astaire and Charlie Butterworth, where he was described as the "Grandpaw Sneed of the Fred Astaire programs." In the popular "Fibber McGee and Molly" show, he played the "Oldtimer," which became his best-known radio role. After the irrepressible Fibber spun an elaborate tall tale, the Oldtimer inevitably responded, "That's purty good, Johnny, but that ain't the way I heerd it." The rejoinder, delivered with impeccable timing, never failed to get a laugh from the audience. His other radio credits include "Hollywood Mardi Gras," "The Dick Haymes Show," "Lub and Abner," "Clamour Manor," and "Point Sublime."

The Oldtimer became the prototype of the character Charley Weaver, who was introduced to television audiences in the early 1950's on the comedy show "Dave 'n' Charley," which Arquette did with his friend Dave Willock. Dressed in a turned-up hat, fake mustache, skinny suspenders, low-slung trousers, gold-rimmed spectacles and white wig (Arquette himself was balding), Charley delivered corn-pone humor and caustic comebacks with folksy aplomb. The show aired for three years, but while it received high marks from critics, it had a limited audience. Don Page of the *Los Angeles Times* wrote, "The only trouble was Dave and Cliff were too advanced for television at that stage of its development." The duo eschewed a script, preferring instead to ad-lib bits that they had sketched out on the way to the studio. Arquette and Willock tried again in 1955 with "Do It Yourself." Ostensibly concerned with home improvements and other hobbies, the show gave the two the opportunity to exchange repartee while Arquette, as Charley, made a mess of a project. Between the two programs, Arquette kept busy with roles in the "RCA Victor Show" and "Dragnet." At one time, he even played Jack Benny's father.

Arquette took pains to establish Charley Weaver as a fellow audiences laughed with, rather than at. Charley was the "smart bumpkin" who always managed to get in the last word against more sophisticated people. Arquette often visited old-age homes, studying senior citizens in order to develop a sympathetic character. Seniors wrote to Arquette to commend his portrayal of older people.

In 1955, Arquette retired from his hectic life to run a commercial film firm while also engaging in his favorite hobby, woodworking. He was a military history aficionado, gourmet cook, photographer, artist, and collector of Americana. During his radio days, one writer described Arquette as a "cartoonist, song and radio script writer, pianist, tap dancer, character actor and makeup artist." Without his Charley Weaver getup, Arquette had the appearance of a genial businessman. Unrecognizable to his fans, Arquette could slip with ease into anonymity whenever he chose.

In 1957, Jack Paar, host of "The Tonight Show," offhandedly mused on the air one night, "Whatever happened to Cliff Arquette?" Arquette, who was watching at the time, had a sudden relapse of show-business fever. He got in touch with Paar, who several weeks later put Charley Weaver on the show. Arquette garnered so much acclaim that he was made a regular. Charley was the perfect foil for Paar's emotional high jinks. In the wake of a typical Paar outpouring, Arquette would slow the show to a crawl with a letter from "Mamma in Mt. Idy." This mythical town in Ohio supplied Charley with gossip about innumerable characters. Arquette also gained fame for matching (and outmatching) wits with Paar's guests. While adopting Charley's trademark slightly befuddled air, Arquette was usually one step ahead of his opponent in the verbal joust. "No one wants to insult an old man on the air," he told *Newsweek* magazine. "That means they can't bomb you. Also, I talk slow and think fast." Paar warned his guests, "Watch that old man. He'll let you have it."

Arquette's collaboration with Paar lasted until the volatile host was fired in 1962. During that time, Arquette launched a show of his own, "Charley Weaver's Hobby Lobby." The point of the show was for Arquette to interview famous guests about their favorite pastimes, but Charley Weaver's jokes about Mt. Idy were more interesting, and the hobbies were soon discarded. Renamed the "Charley Weaver Show," it never found a workable format and was soon canceled. Arquette's Mt. Idy books, *Charley Weaver's Letters from Mamma* (1959), *Charley Weaver's Family Album* (1960), and *Things Are Fine in Mt. Idy* (1960), were more successful. *Life* magazine called Charley "an antidote for too much civilization."

While on "The Tonight Show," Arquette bought a 125-year-old farmhouse in Gettysburg, Pa. Formerly a Civil War orphanage, it was converted into a Civil War museum for Arquette's Americana collection and wood carvings. Arquette dressed his wood soldiers in authentic scaled-down uniforms that he had been researching for the past twenty-five years. In an apartment above the museum, Arquette went into semiretirement in 1962, explaining, "People say to me that I owe it to the putlic to keep going. But I figure the public owes me a rest."

Arquette was twice married and divorced. He had one child.

For the next six years, Arquette remained outside the spotlight, while damping the occasional flare-up of show-biz fever through appearances on the "Roy Rogers and Dale Evans Show," and the "Jonathon Winters Show." In 1968, however, Charley Weaver became one of the two regular panelists on the popular "Hollywood Squares" game show, a perfect vehicle for Arquette. The stars were asked questions and gave responses that contestants were to judge true or false. Arquette's specialty was giving an answer that sounded absurd but was correct. The show gave him ample opportunity for wisecracking. Most of his fans had never known Cliff Arquette the radio and TV comedian and assumed Charley Weaver was a real person. In 1972, after a heart attack and debilitating stroke, it appeared that Arquette would retire perma-

nently. But his show-business blood got the better of him, and he returned to "Hollywood Squares" in 1973. He died in Los Angeles the following year.

[Features on Arquette during his heyday with "The Tonight Show" appear in *Newsweek*, July 28, 1958, *Look*, May 26, 1959, and *Life*, Aug. 10, 1959. Information on Arquette's radio appearances may be found in *Tune in Yesterday* (1976); his television work is listed in *The Complete Directory of Prime Time Network TV shows, 1946–Present* (1979). There is an obituary in the *New York Times*, Sept. 24, 1974.]
MICHAEL GOLDBERG

ATHENAGORAS I (Mar. 25, 1886–Jul. 6, 1972), ecumenical patriarch of the Eastern Orthodox church, was born Aristokles Spyrou in the village of Vassilikon (Tsaraplana) in the province of Epirus in present-day northern Greece. He was the son of Eleni Markarou and Matthaios Spyrou, a prominent local physician and civic leader. At the time of his birth, Epirus was still part of the Ottoman Empire, a factor that would have a later bearing on the future patriarch's relations with the Turks and his dealings with people of other cultures.

Athenagoras attended grammar school from 1895 to 1899 at the nearby town of Konitsa. Early on, he decided to dedicate his life to Orthodoxy, and in 1906, after completing secondary school in Yannina (the capital of Epirus), he studied at the Theological Seminary of the Ecumenical Patriarchate on the island of Halki, near Istanbul. In 1910, he was ordained a deacon, discarding his baptismal name and assuming the ecclesiastical name Athenagoras, meaning "one who speaks in Athens." That same year Athenagoras was also appointed archdeacon and superintendent of schools in Pelagonia in Ottoman-controlled Macedonia, and served in that capacity until 1918, when he retreated to one of the monasteries of Mount Athos for a year of study and meditation. In 1919, he was appointed archdeacon to the archbishop of Athens and first secretary of the Holy Synod, and later that year he was ordained a priest with the title archmandrite, a celibate priest. (Although Greek Orthodox priests are permitted to marry, bishops must remain celibate.)

In 1922, Athenagoras was elevated to the rank of bishop and named metropolitan of the island of Corfu (Kerkyra), a position he held until 1930. Athenagoras arrived on Corfu at a time of great upheaval in Greece. Following the forced exchange of populations of Greece and Asia Minor after World War I, Corfu was beset with extreme poverty, thousands of refugee families, and a large number of orphans. Athenagoras set out building orphanages and caring for the poor. He is particularly remembered during this period for single-handedly stopping the Italian navy's bombing of the island in 1923, by rowing out to the Italian flagship under heavy bombardment to intervene personally, demanding of the Italian admiral that he spare civilian lives. His ability to deal with difficult situations and different backgrounds, and his strong organizational skills, date to this early period.

Athenagoras's lifelong role as a conciliator had its beginnings in his office as archbishop of the Greek Orthodox church of North and South America, a position to which he was elected by the Holy Synod of the Ecumenical Patriarchate of Constantinople (Istanbul), and the seat of which is located in New York City. Athenagoras arrived in the United States in February 1931, at a time when the Greek immigrant community was politically divided—into Royalists, who supported the king of Greece, and Republicans, who favored a parliamentary form of government—and the Greek Orthodox church in America lacked organizational strength. The new archbishop muted these political squabblings, asking Greek Americans to "leave your arguments outside the church door. You will find them there when you come out." Athenagoras energetically sought to perpetuate Greek Americans' cultural and religious heritage through the archdiocese. He traveled widely in the United States, visiting three hundred churches and establishing an educational system unique among ethnic groups. It included the organization of the afternoon Greek schools and Sunday schools in every parish, and day schools in some of the larger communities; training for clergy, at the Holy Cross Greek Orthodox Theological School in Pomfret, Conn.; and the creation of the teacher's training school at Saint Basil's Academy in Garrison, N.Y.

Athenagoras championed the causes of charity and philanthropy in America. A deep love of children guided his creation of the Children's Home of Saint Basil's Academy, and he helped form the Greek Ladies Philoptochos Society, a national charitable organization. In February 1938, Athenagoras became a naturalized citizen of the United States, a country to which he

had become immensely devoted. During the period he spent in the United States, the archbishop developed personal relationships with Presidents Roosevelt and Truman, who saw him as a confidant and as a spokesman for the small but vocal Greek-American community.

After seventeen years in the United States, on Nov. 1, 1948, Athenagoras was elected, by a vote of the bishops of the Holy Synod in Istanbul, archbishop of Constantinople, New Rome, and the 286th ecumenical patriarch of the Holy Orthodox Catholic Apostolic Eastern church, continuing an unbroken line of ecumenical patriarchs that had begun in A.D. 381. Athenagoras's leadership role, as with those who had preceded him, was neither absolute nor supreme, but it had its origins in the historic patriarchate of Constantinople. (This forms one of the distinctions between the so-called Greek East and Latin West—Orthodox have never recognized the primacy of the pope.) His Holiness Patriarch Athenagoras assumed his role as the spiritual leader of more than 200 million Orthodox Christians at a time of immense physical suffering and spiritual void, following two destructive world wars and the start of the Cold War. Nevertheless he sought to bring about cooperation and unity not only among the Eastern Orthodox churches, but among all Christians. In particular, Athenagoras sought reconciliation and reunion with the Roman Catholic church, putting aside theological differences that had been made manifest by the Great Schism of 1054. The Great Schism had divided the two churches after nearly one thousand years of unity.

Patriarch Athenagoras approached the goal of Christian unity by first establishing order and discipline within the Eastern Orthodox churches, where ethnic and national antagonisms prevailed following the world wars. The Patriarchal Encyclical of Jan. 31, 1951, to all Orthodox patriarchates marked the fifteen hundredth anniversary of the Ecumenical Council of Chalcedon of A.D. 451, and it was followed by the sending of delegations of metropolitans to the patriarchates of Alexandria, Antioch, and Jerusalem. Athenagoras visited the patriarchates in 1959, and in 1961 the first Pan-Orthodox Conference was held on the Greek island of Rhodes, bringing together representatives of the world's Orthodox churches to discuss matters of doctrine and their relationship with other Christian churches. At the Second Pan-Orthodox

Conference (1963), Athenagoras used his considerable diplomatic skills to propose a "dialogue on equal terms" with the Roman Catholic church.

Athenagoras's efforts at reconciliation with the Roman Catholic church were symbolized by his three historic meetings with Pope Paul VI, the first of which occurred on the Mount of Olives in Jerusalem on Jan. 5 and 6, 1964. At the first meeting the ecumenical patriarch and the pope prayed together and exchanged the brotherly "kiss of love." Patriarchal delegates visited the Vatican in 1965, as well as the Archbishop Michael of Canterbury and the archbishop of Utrecht. A historic moment of reconciliation occurred on Dec. 7, 1965, when Patriarch Athenagoras in Istanbul and Pope Paul in the Vatican simultaneously presided over the annulment of the churches' mutual excommunication of 1054 between Constantinople and Rome. Personal visits by Pope Paul to Istanbul (July 25 and 26, 1967) and by Patriarch Athenagoras to Rome (October 28 and 29) followed. A few years earlier, the patriarch had further strengthened the Eastern Orthodox church's ties with the Anglican church by receiving the Archbishop of Canterbury in Istanbul (1962), a visit he repaid by traveling to London for a conference with the archbishop and a visit with Queen Elizabeth II. In 1967, Athenagoras journeyed to meet with Patriarch Justinian of Romania, Patriarch Germanos of Serbia, and Patriarch Kyrillos of Bulgaria.

From his quarters in the Phanar district of Istanbul, Patriarch Athenagoras greeted a steady flow of visitors until his death. Dressed in his black vestments and standing well over six feet tall, with a long white beard and penetrating eyes, to many who met him Patriarch Athenagoras had the appearance of a biblical prophet. Decades after his death, he continued to be revered by countless Greek Orthodox worldwide and remembered by many as the leader of an ecumenical movement that envisions the union of all Christians.

[Archives concerning the Greek Orthodox church in America and the role of Athenagoras as archbishop, consisting of correspondence and personal papers, are deposited at the Greek Orthodox Archdiocese in New York City. The archives of the patriarch are held at the Ecumenical Patriarchate, located in the Phanar, Istanbul, Turkey. See also Xenophon Diamond, *Athenagoras I: Our Great Patriarch* (1969); and Demetrios Gr. Tsakonas, *A Man Sent By God: The Life of Patriarch Athenagoras*, trans. from the Greek by George Angeloglou (1977). An obituary is in the *New York Times*, July 7, 1972.]

JONATHAN G. ARETAKIS

ATLAS, CHARLES S. (1893–Dec. 23, 1972), physical culturist and moralist, was born Angelo Siciliano. According to published accounts, Siciliano was born on Oct. 30, 1893, near Acri, in Calabria, Italy, and came to the United States in 1903 with his father, Santo Siciliano, a farmer, who soon returned to Italy. His mother, Teresa, a devout Roman Catholic, raised him in a waterfront section of Brooklyn, New York, while working as a seamstress in a sweatshop. However, Santo Siciliano's naturalization papers state that Angelo was born Apr. 20, 1893, in Brooklyn, N.Y., and they suggest that he lived much of his childhood with his father. Lacking interest in his studies, Angelo left high school in 1908, taking a job as a leather worker in a factory that made women's pocketbooks.

Frail and possibly anemic as a youth, Angelo was twice victimized in incidents that shaped his life and career. At age fifteen he was attacked and beaten on the streets. The following year, still the "ninety-seven-pound weakling" of future advertisements, he was humiliated when a Coney Island bully kicked sand in his face and he was unable to respond. That summer, while touring the Brooklyn Museum, Angelo learned that the muscles he had observed on the museum's statues of Greek and Roman gods were the result of "exercise." Determined to develop muscles of his own, Angelo joined the YMCA, where he worked on stretching machines, fashioned a set of homemade barbells, and began reading Bernarr Macfadden's *Physical Culture* magazine. Though disappointed by the results, Angelo nevertheless remained open to other solutions. At age seventeen, on his regular Sunday trip to the Prospect Park Zoo, he stopped to admire a muscular lion; its physique, he reasoned, must have developed in a more natural way, perhaps from the animal pitting one muscle against another.

Using a system of isotonic exercise that he derived from this observation, Siciliano transformed his body and, with it, his life. By age nineteen he earned a living by demonstrating a chest developer in a storefront on Broadway; his growing resemblance to a hotel (or bank) statue led his peers to start calling him Atlas—a name he took legally in 1922. Beginning in 1914, Siciliano performed feats of strength in vaudeville with Young Sampson, with Earle E. Lieberman in The Orpheum Models, and in the Coney Island Circus Side Show.

In 1916, while doing the Coney Island show, Siciliano was seen by an artist and introduced to New York City's community of sculptors, including Arthur Lee, Mrs. Harry Payne Whitney, and James Earle Fraser. In 1918 he married Margaret Cassano; they had two children. Until 1921, Siciliano was one of the nation's most popular male models, his physique serving as the basis for some forty-five statues, including one of George Washington in New York City's Washington Square and another of Alexander Hamilton at the Treasury Building in Washington, D.C.

Siciliano's career took another turn in 1921, when he won $1,000 as the victor in Macfadden's contest for the "World's Most Perfectly Developed Man." He won again the following year at Madison Square Garden—provoking Macfadden's lament, "What's the use of holding them? Atlas will win every time"—and, late in 1922, he used his prize money to open a mail-order body-building business to market his exercise methods. The Atlas course required no special equipment, stressed a holistic approach that included advice on diet, grooming, and personal behavior, and held out as an ideal a body that, like Atlas's own, was "perfect" in its symmetry and proportions (5′ 10″, 180 pounds; neck, 17″; chest, 47″; biceps, 17″; forearm 14″, waist, 32″; thigh, 23¾″; calf, 16¼″) rather than heavily muscled.

For several years the enterprise foundered, even while competitors thrived. The amicable and obliging Atlas—a poor businessman, by most accounts—spread himself too thin, opening and then closing a Manhattan gymnasium, and for two years serving without compensation as the physical director of a summer camp. The turnaround began in late 1928, when he hired Charles P. Roman, a young advertising executive whose firm had serviced the Atlas account. Charles Atlas Ltd. was incorporated in February 1929, with the two partners holding the stock in equal shares, an arrangement that held until 1970, when Atlas sold his interest to Roman and retired.

Under Roman's management, the Atlas company prospered. Atlas ran the addressing machine, bent thousands of railroad spikes and

removed his shirt for awestruck visitors, and, through a series of publicity stunts—in 1938 he pulled the observation car of the Broadway Limited along 112 feet of Pennsylvania Railroad track—became a celebrity. Roman coined the term "Dynamic Tension" to describe Atlas's methods, and in the 1930's wrote the famous ad depicting a young man who, having taken up the Atlas system, avenges his humiliation at the hands of a beach bully.

These and other advertisements appeared in *Popular Science, Moon Man*, and other pulp magazines aimed at lower- and middle-class males. The advertisements, which had great appeal for young men coming of age during the Great Depression, offered more than a thirty-dollar set of body-building exercises; Atlas embodied the nineteenth-century ideal of the self-made man, a dream of self-improvement and rapid transformation (not unlike the Clark Kent/Superman character who first appeared in 1938) that began with a strengthened, healthy body but also encompassed confidence, ambition, and worldly success. Moreover, the advertising copy reflected Atlas's own deeply held belief in the importance of bodily health to general well-being.

The company weathered investigations by the Federal Trade Commission in 1932, 1937, and 1938—the last for "misrepresentative advertising." A London branch opened in 1936, a Rio de Janeiro office in 1939. By 1942, when Atlas Ltd. received another stimulus from the predictable wartime enthusiasm for physical fitness, more than 400,000 copies of the Atlas program of self-development had been sold.

Despite continued financial success and international celebrity, for decades Atlas lived a private, simple, and patterned life, not unlike the one advocated in his course materials. His routine consisted of morning exercises, work at the office, an evening with the family, and more exercises. Atlas died of a heart attack in Long Beach, Long Island, not far from his home in Point Lookout.

[The only biography, thoughtful and richly illustrated, is Charles Gaines, *Yours in Perfect Manhood: Charles Atlas* (1982). Useful articles about Atlas include "Music Makers," *Time*, Feb. 22, 1937; "Muscle Business," *Fortune*, Jan. 1938; Maurice Zolotow, " 'You, Too, Can Be a New Man,' " *Saturday Evening Post*, Feb. 7, 1942; James Lincoln Collier, "Charles Atlas, Muscles and Me," *Boys' Life*, Oct. 1983; Joseph Gustaitis, "Charles Atlas: The World's

Most Perfectly Developed Man," *American History Illustrated*, Sept. 1986; and Peter Bushyeager, "The World of Atlas," *Men's Health*, Oct. 1991. An obituary is in the *New York Times*, Dec. 24, 1972.]

WILLIAM GRAEBNER

AUDEN, WYSTAN HUGH (Feb. 21, 1907–Sept. 28, 1973), poet, dramatist, librettist, and essayist, was born in York, England, the third and last son of Constance Rosalie Bicknell, a former nurse, and George Augustus Auden, a physician. Wystan had a relatively happy, comfortable childhood. He shared his father's interests in science and psychiatry, as well as in Saxon and Norse culture, which influenced his early poetry. Even more influential was his often-domineering mother, whose Christian faith and enthusiasm for music helped shape her son's adult sensibilities. When Auden was eight, he was sent away to school, first to St. Edmund's in Surrey (1915–1920), and later to Gresham's in Norfolk (1920–1925), where he lost his religious faith. At the age of fifteen, Auden decided to be a poet, although he still also vaguely planned a career in science.

At Christ Church College, Oxford (1925–1928), Auden initially studied natural sciences, but soon switch to English. "I am going to be a poet," Auden told his tutor, Nevill Coghill, and then added, after Coghill had offered some conventional advice, "I mean a great poet." Auden became well known in Oxford undergraduate literary life and met many young writers with whom he would become closely associated: Cecil Day-Lewis (later poet laureate), Louis Mac-Neice, Stephen Spender (who privately printed Auden's first chapbook of poems in 1928), and novelist Christopher Isherwood, a former Cambridge student who lived in Kensington. In Oxford's permissive atmosphere, Auden explored his homosexuality openly. His wide-ranging intellectual interests, unorthodox literary opinions, and casual attitude toward study, however, hurt his academic performance. He finished dismally with a third-class bachelor of arts degree in 1928.

After graduation Auden went to Berlin for eighteen months. There he learned German and became saturated with German culture, which exercised a lifelong influence on his poetry and ideas. He became particularly interested in the poems and plays of Bertolt Brecht and in the psychological theories of Georg Groddeck and Homer Lane, which held that all illnesses are psychosomatic and manifestations of the subconscious elements within us. Berlin's notoriously permissive nightlife, later celebrated in Isherwood's famous Sally Bowles stories (the basis of the musical and film *Cabaret*) also provided Auden with a laboratory for sexual experimentation. Returning to England in July 1929, Auden looked for work unsuccessfully. Eventually, in 1930, he replaced Day-Lewis as a schoolmaster at Larchfield Academy near Glasgow, Scotland, the first of several teaching jobs. At the same time, the poet T. S. Eliot, an editor at Faber and Faber, having rejected an earlier collection, accepted Auden's *Poems* for publication in 1930. Auden's premiere volume divided critics. Older reviewers found it obscure and eccentric; younger critics recognized Auden's clinical perspective, compressed lyricism, and versatile technique as a breakthrough in English poetry. His work immediately became the model for his contemporaries, the so-called Auden Generation.

Meanwhile, Auden had begun another imaginative venture that would prove equally influential—writing verse drama. Beginning with the publication of *Paid on Both Sides*, a tragic "charade," in the summer of 1928, Auden reinvented English-language poetic drama for the modern age. Having no living tradition on which to ground his plays, Auden borrowed from a variety of sources: Norse saga; music hall theater; pantomime; the thriller; as well as from the plays of Brecht, Jean Cocteau, and William Butler Yeats. Most notable among Auden's plays were *The Dance of Death* (1933) and his three collaborations with Isherwood, *The Dog beneath the Skin* (1935), *The Ascent of F6* (1936), and *On the Frontier* (1938), all of which were successfully produced in London by Rupert Doone's experimental Group Theatre. These plays helped foster a revival of verse drama on both sides of the Atlantic and influenced a number of poet-playwrights, including Eliot, MacNeice, Christopher Fry, Delmore Schwartz, and Archibald MacLeish. Auden also wrote poetic narration for cinema and radio, most notably for the documentary film *Night Mail* (1935) and BBC Radio's *Hadrian's Wall* (1937).

During the 1930's, Auden's political vision turned to the left, but unlike many of his associates, he never joined the Communist party. Believing contemporary society to be sick, Auden studied Marx, as he had Freud, more from a psychological than from a political perspective. In retrospect, his political views seem as much antifascist and anti-authoritarian as pro-Marxist. His experimental poem, *The Orators: An English Study* (1932), which mixes verse and prose in alternately lyric, dramatic, and quasi-narrative modes, was intended as "a critique of the fascist outlook." What neither Auden nor his staunchly leftist admirers realized was that the poet was slowly moving from a sociopolitical to a religious worldview.

In 1935, Auden left teaching to write for documentary films. At the same time, he agreed to marry Thomas Mann's daughter, Erika, whom he had never met, so that she could obtain a British passport and leave Nazi Germany. The marriage took place on June 15, 1935. The couple never lived together, nor did they ever divorce. Erika Mann was largely lesbian in her inclinations, and she and Auden remained lifelong friends. Auden traveled widely during this period. In the summer of 1936, he visited Iceland with MacNeice. They collaborated on the travel book *Letters from Iceland* (1937), which contained Auden's long satirical poem, "Letter to Lord Byron." More important, in January 1937, Auden went to Spain, which was then locked in civil war, to work for the Republican and Communist side. He returned home in March, secretly disillusioned by the repression, bureaucracy, and anticlericalism of the Communists, but he made no public criticism for fear of helping Franco's cause. Auden wrote the political poem *Spain* (1937), which was issued as a special fund-raising pamphlet by Faber. In January 1938, Auden and Isherwood traveled to China, which was resisting the Japanese invasion, and collaborated on *Journey to a War* (1939), a travel book that also included Auden's sonnet sequence "In Time of War."

After returning to England in September 1938, Auden and Isherwood decided to emigrate to America. Auden had grown increasingly unhappy with the stultifyingly close-knit British intellectual life. He wanted freedom to create his own life-style in a society that had fewer set patterns and restrictions than Britain's. They arrived in the United States on Jan. 26, 1939, and Auden's works immediately began appearing in the most influential journals. (Random House had already published six Auden volumes in the United States, and two more would appear before the end of 1939.) Auden's poetry continued to change and develop. *An-

other Time* (1940), his first "American" book of poems, displayed an extraordinary range of forms, from sonnets and ballads to poems modeled on blues and cabaret songs. Auden soon exercised almost as much influence on younger American poets as he had on his British contemporaries. Poets as diverse as Randall Jarrell, Anthony Hecht, William Jay Smith, James Merrill, Howard Moss, John Ashbery, Frank O'Hara, Donald Justice, and Weldon Kees all show Auden's influence in different ways. One young American poet, however, had an enduring personal influence on Auden; in April 1939, he met the eighteen-year-old Chester Kallman, and the two poets quickly fell in love. Although the relationship eventually presented difficulties, Kallman would remain Auden's lifelong companion.

Once he was settled in America, Auden underwent an all-important experience—a conversion to Christianity. His regained faith, influenced by the Danish existentialist theologian Søren Kierkegaard, shaped most of Auden's subsequent poetry. At about the same time, Auden began work on a remarkable series of long poems that explored the political, artistic, and spiritual issues of the war years and their aftermath. Each written in a different genre and form (or set of forms), these poems stand near the center of Auden's poetic achievement: *The Double Man* (1941), which contained both "New Year Letter" and the sonnet sequence, "The Quest"; *For the Time Being* (1944), which contained both the long title poem and "The Sea and the Mirror: A Commentary on Shakespeare's *The Tempest*" (1944); and *The Age of Anxiety* (1947), which later became the basis of Leonard Bernstein's second symphony. In May 1946, Auden became an American citizen. The literary world noted this event; in 1948, he was awarded the Pulitzer Prize in poetry for *The Age of Anxiety*, his first eligible volume.

By 1950, Auden stood unchallenged as the most highly regarded English-language poet of his generation. He received the Bollingen Prize in poetry for lifetime achievement in 1954. Having settled in New York City just before the outbreak of World War II, Auden faced significant resentment from British intellectuals who felt he had abandoned his homeland in a time of trouble. Auden's astonishing productivity in poetry, criticism, and opera, however, eventually created an oeuvre too significant for English critics to ignore. His election to the Oxford Professor of Poetry in 1956 signaled the thaw in his relations with the United Kingdom. His Oxford lectures were popular, and his British reputation regained its preeminence.

In his middle age, Auden's poetry gradually became more relaxed and public. Although he typically worked in an impressive variety of forms and styles, the "late" Auden manner is witty, discursive, and gently didactic. More than ever, Auden concerned himself with exploring the moral and spiritual dimensions of his material, though usually with irreverent humor and lyric charm. This later poetic style emerged in *Nones* (1951) and continued to evolve through his remaining collections, the most notable of which are *The Shield of Achilles* (1955), for which he received the National Book Award; *Homage to Clio* (1960); and *About the House* (1965). Many critics, enamored of his early work, rejected the late work as too digressive and didactic, but since Auden's death, its value has become clearer. Auden was the century's most prolific major poet in English, and his work constantly changed as his values and ideas developed. Not surprisingly, critics were often a decade or so behind in fully understanding new directions in his work.

Kallman fired Auden's taste for opera, an art form he had scarcely known in England. Auden became a permanent devotee, especially of the Italian bel canto period, not a fashionable taste at the time. He wrote influentially about opera, especially in *Secondary Worlds* (1968). More important, Auden, usually working in collaboration with Kallman, became the greatest English-language opera librettist of the century. Writing libretti was the logical extension of Auden's early interest in poetic drama. Auden's first libretto, *Paul Bunyan* (1941), was written for Benjamin Britten, who had previously set many Auden poems to music as well as composed scores for several of his plays and films. Auden and Kallman collaborated on the libretto for Igor Stravinsky's *The Rake's Progress* (1951). They wrote two libretti for Hans Werner Henze, *Elegy for Young Lovers* (1960) and *The Bassarids* (1966), as well as one for Nicolas Nabokov's *Love's Labour's Lost* (1973). Additionally, they translated several operas, including Mozart's *The Magic Flute* and *Don Giovanni*.

Auden was also a distinguished essayist and critic. His wide-ranging study, *The Enchafèd Flood* (1950), examined romanticism in relation to literary descriptions of the sea. *The Dyer's Hand* (1962) collected many of Auden's influential essays, including several studies of Shakespeare. *Forewords & Afterwords* (1973) gathered introductions he wrote for literary, historical, and theological volumes, as well as some of the long reviews he contributed to the *New York Review of Books* and the *New Yorker*.

On reaching sixty-five in 1972, Auden decided to leave New York and retire to a cottage provided by Christ Church College, Oxford. He planned to divide his time between Oxford and his house in Kirchstetten, Austria. His health had begun to fail, a condition aggravated by heavy drinking, smoking, and drugs (sleeping pills and benzedrine). He and Kallman now spent half the year apart. Auden hoped to find a supportive social community at Oxford, but he was generally unhappy there. The cozy social life he remembered had vanished. He spent the summer in Austria, planning to return to Oxford in October. On Sept. 28, 1973, Auden gave a poetry reading in Vienna to the Austrian Society of Literature. He was found dead of a heart attack in his hotel room the next morning and was buried in Kirchstetten. In 1974, a memorial stone was set up in the Poet's Corner of London's Westminster Abbey. Though he died an American citizen, England acknowledged its native son.

[Auden's papers are primarily in the Berg Collection of the New York Public Library and the Humanities Research Center of the University of Texas at Austin. There are also papers in the Bodleian Library at Oxford, the British Museum, and the Butler Library at Columbia University. Auden's complete works are being published by Princeton University Press; volumes issued to date are *Plays* (1988) and *Libretti* (1993), both edited by Edward Mendelson. The most comprehensive biography is Humphrey Carpenter's *W. H. Auden* (1981). Outstanding critical studies include Monroe K. Spears, *The Poetry of W. H. Auden* (1963); John Fuller, *A Reader's Guide to W. H. Auden* (1970); Samuel Hynes, *The Auden Generation* (1976); Edward Mendelson, *Early Auden* (1981); and Anthony Hecht, *The Hidden Law* (1993). *The W. H. Auden Newsletter* reports on new scholarly developments. An obituary is in the *New York Times*, Sept. 30, 1973.]

DANA GIOIA

B

BAILEY, JOHN MORAN (Nov. 23, 1904–
Apr. 10, 1975), Democratic national chairman,
was born in Hartford, Conn., the only child of
Michael A. Bailey and Louise A. Moran. His
father, a physician, was a founder of Hartford
Hospital and served for many years as a city
alderman. His mother owned and managed
considerable real estate holdings in Hartford and
was active in Catholic charities and Democratic
party politics.

Bailey attended Hartford Public High School
before entering the Catholic University of
America in 1922. A star athlete, he captained
the college baseball team and played basketball
and football with distinction. Although he was
a good student and graduated with a B.A. in
science in 1926, Bailey's athletic pursuits prevented him from obtaining high enough grades
in chemistry and other premed courses to enter
medical school. Instead, he went on to Harvard
Law School, where he received his LL.B. in
1929. Bailey returned to Hartford later in that
year, passed the Connecticut bar examination,
and opened a small practice. On Aug. 1, 1933,
he married Barbara Josephine Leary, a schoolteacher he had met while attending law school;
they had four children.

In 1929, Bailey backed a family friend's campaign for mayor and ran for Democratic precinct captain. Although he lost by thirty votes,
Bailey so enjoyed this first election experience
that he decided to pursue a political career. In
order to learn the fundamentals of his new profession, he joined the entourage of Thomas J.
Spellacy, the Democratic boss of Hartford. As
Spellacy's aide-de-camp and chauffeur, Bailey
gained appointment to the staff of Mayor
William J. Rankin in 1931 and election to the
Central Committee, the governing body of the

Connecticut Democratic party, in 1932. A year
later he became a judge of the Hartford police
court by means of a patronage deal made by
Spellacy with Republicans in the state legislature. In 1935, Spellacy's influence waned and
Bailey was forced to give up his judgeship for
the lesser post of clerk of the police court. He
returned to the police bench on the strength of
his own legislative contacts in 1939. At the same
time he functioned as a political factotum and
minor public official in Hartford during the
1930's, Bailey involved himself deeply in the
activities of the newly formed Young Democratic Club locally and nationally. A willing
speechmaker and recruiter, he traveled widely
in behalf of the Young Democrats and was
elected the group's national treasurer in 1937
and 1939.

His own modest success, and the prospect of
a smashing Democratic victory with President
Franklin Roosevelt at the top of the ticket, em-
boldened Bailey to seek election as probate
judge of Hartford County in 1940. However, a
newspaper story alleging a $1,000 discrepancy
in the account of the clerk of the police court
during Bailey's last term enabled Republicans
to block his bid. They posed the question: "Who
do you want handling your money after you are
dead?" and defeated Bailey by fifteen thousand
votes even as Democrats won the governorship
and other major offices on Roosevelt's coattails.
Though later cleared of wrongdoing, Bailey
never again sought elective office.

In 1941, Governor Robert Hurley appointed
Bailey to a four-year term as statute revision
commissioner. The job, which entailed checking and drafting bills that came up for consideration by the general assembly, enabled Bailey
to acquire an encyclopedic knowledge of the

legislative process. He also gained an unexpected opportunity to demonstrate his ability as a party tactician when Republican governor Raymond Baldwin waited until after the 1945 legislative session to appoint replacements for the statute revision commissioner and three other Democratic officeholders whose terms had expired. Bailey refused to vacate his office until his successor was confirmed by the state senate, as required by law, and urged his colleagues to stay in their positions. To Baldwin's chagrin, Bailey and the other Democrats held their patronage-rich offices jointly with the new Republican appointees until the general assembly returned; their stand was upheld by the Connecticut Supreme Court of Errors.

Although he accepted appointment as executive assistant to Democratic state chairman John McGuire in 1946, Bailey's ambition was for the top post. Toward that end, he forged alliances with dissident ethnic ward leaders and orchestrated the overthrow of his mentor, Spellacy, in Hartford. Controlling the city convention, he saw to it that members of his coalition won legislative nominations and state convention seats, and that Spellacy and his supporters were shut out. Bailey also proved to be the driving force at the 1946 state conclave, promoting the successful nomination of Wesleyan professor and poet Wilbert Snow for governor. Snow, in turn, delivered the state chairmanship to his benefactor.

Fortified by his family's wealth and income derived from the lucrative Hartford law firm he founded with political ally Alfred Wechsler in 1946, Bailey remained the unpaid, full-time head of the Connecticut Democratic party for the next twenty-nine years. Choosing high-quality gubernatorial candidates, fashioning ethnically and geographically balanced tickets, dispensing patronage deftly, and displaying brilliant generalship as the principal Democratic legislative leader, he was able to hold together the Roosevelt coalition and to guide his party toward majority status.

Bailey's first major success as state chairman came in 1948, when he engineered the nomination of left-leaning millionaire New Dealer Chester Bowles for governor. A political masterstroke, the Bowles candidacy pumped much-needed campaign money into Democratic coffers, deflated a third-party effort by Henry Wallace Progressives, and helped the Democrats eke out an election victory despite President Harry Truman's loss of Connecticut by fourteen thousand votes. Six years later, Bailey's handpicked candidate was moderate former Congressman Abraham Ribicoff, who upset Republican incumbent John Davis Lodge to become the first Jewish governor of the state. Ribicoff, who went on to win a landslide reelection in 1958, was appointed Secretary of Health, Education and Welfare in 1961, and captured a seat in the U.S. Senate in 1962. Irish-born John Dempsey, another Bailey protégé, kept the governorship in Democratic hands from 1961 to 1971.

Seeking a place in the national political limelight, Bailey asked Governor Bowles to name him to the U.S. Senate seat left vacant by Bowles's appointment of Republican Raymond Baldwin to the Supreme Court of Errors in 1949. However, the governor passed over Bailey in favor of William Benton, whom Bowles believed to be more electable in 1950. Bailey managed to get some national notoriety in 1956 as a booster of the vice-presidential campaign of Massachusetts Senator John F. Kennedy by circulating a sixteen-page memorandum prepared by Kennedy aide Theodore C. Sorensen that used statistics, quotations, and analyses to counter the widely held view that Kennedy's Catholicism was a liability to the Democratic ticket. In addition to launching the "Bailey Memorandum," he acted as a floor captain for the Kennedy bid, which was only narrowly defeated by that of Tennessee Senator Estes Kefauver, at the Democratic national convention in Chicago.

Following the defeat of Adlai Stevenson and Kefauver, Bailey enlisted in Kennedy's campaign for the presidency. An important cog in the successful 1960 operation, he did advance work in the critical primary states of Wisconsin and West Virginia, rounded up delegates in New England and upstate New York, and served as the intermediary between the young Kennedy campaign staff and the older generation of party power brokers that included Richard Daley, mayor of Chicago; Carmine De Sapio, Tammany Hall boss; and David Lawrence, governor of Pennsylvania. As a reward for his tireless effort, President Kennedy named Bailey Democratic national chairman in January 1961.

Although Bailey was given charge of all assistance provided to state and local candidates and the party's vital voter-registration effort, he had little real influence in the new administration. Attorney General Robert F. Kennedy controlled the staffing of the Democratic National Committee, and other important patronage was handled by the White House. Presidential assistant Lawrence F. O'Brien generally informed officeseekers when they received positions, and the national chairman was given the thankless task of telling them when they did not. Still, Bailey's skilled management of the party machinery helped Democrats gain four U.S. Senate seats and hold House losses down to four seats in the off-year election of 1962.

President Lyndon B. Johnson retained Bailey but reduced his role considerably. A White House aide, Clifton Carter, was assigned to oversee Democratic National Committee operations in 1964; following the president's landslide election in that year, the committee's budget was slashed and its voter registration operation closed down. Though little more than a figurehead, Bailey remained loyal to the president and kept his national post until August 1968.

By 1968, American intervention in Vietnam had changed the political landscape drastically, and Bailey found his leadership in Connecticut challenged by a determined band of middle-class amateurs linked to the antiwar presidential candidacy of Senator Eugene J. McCarthy of Minnesota. Running against what they termed the "old politics" of the Democratic party regulars, the McCarthy volunteers, led by the Reverend Joseph Duffey and housewife Anne Wexler, garnered 44 percent of the vote in the spring primaries. There followed a long series of negotiations during which Bailey's foes threatened to oppose the renomination of Senator Ribicoff if they were not given a fair share of the forty-four seats in the Connecticut delegation to the Democratic national convention in Chicago. Although Bailey ultimately granted them only nine seats, the insurgents succeeded in embarrassing the national chairman by preventing him from invoking the unit rule and delivering all of his state's convention votes to his chosen candidate and the eventual Democratic nominee, Vice-President Hubert H. Humphrey.

In 1970, Duffey's upset victory over the Connecticut Democratic convention's choice for the U.S. Senate in a primary contest and the nomination for governor of Congressman Emilio Daddario, who also was not in the Bailey camp, seemed to damage Bailey's reputation

further. But the election defeats of both Duffey and Daddario allowed Bailey to hold on to power, and he returned to form as party king-maker in 1974, convincing Attorney General Robert Killian to end his gubernatorial campaign and run for lieutenant governor on a ticket led by Congresswoman Ella T. Grasso. Grasso then became the first woman and first Italian-American governor of Connecticut, and the first woman elected as a state governor who did not succeed her husband. Bailey continued to advise Grasso on appointments and legislative strategy until his death in Hartford.

Theodore H. White described John Bailey as a "tall, cigar-smoking, baldheaded man who affects an exterior hardness of manner, talks in a high, rusty, confidential tone of voice, and effectively conceals the fact that he is a Harvard Law School graduate." While he often spoke in the manner of the earlier generation of party bosses ("I go with the bird who can fly, not with the pigeon who can't get off the ground"), Bailey did not adopt its autocratic style. He preferred a politics of subtle persuasion and compromise, if necessary, and he was known as a man who kept his word.

[Bailey's papers are in private hands. Some of the records of the Democratic National Committee under Bailey's chairmanship are at the John F. Kennedy Library in Boston and the Lyndon B. Johnson Library in Austin, Tex. Joseph I. Lieberman, *The Power Broker* (1966), is a useful biography up to 1966; Lieberman's *The Legacy* (1981) adds material on Bailey's later years. See also Duane Lockard, *New England State Politics* (1959); David S. Broder, "Strategists for '62 and '64," *New York Times Magazine*, Oct. 15, 1961, and "Practical Politics—As it Is in Connecticut," *U.S. News and World Report*, July 30, 1962; Theodore H. White, *The Making of the President 1960* (1961) and *The Making of the President 1964* (1965); Milton MacKaye, "The Party Chairmen: Democrat Bailey," *Saturday Evening Post*, Sept. 29, 1962; Theodore C. Sorensen, *Kennedy* (1965); and John W. Jeffries, *Testing the Roosevelt Coalition* (1979). Obituaries are in the *Hartford Courant* and the *New York Times*, both Apr. 1, 1975.]

RICHARD H. GENTILE

BAKER, JOSEPHINE (June 3, 1906–Apr. 12, 1975), entertainer, was born in St. Louis, Mo., the natural child of Carrie McDonald, a laundress, and Eddie Carson, a drummer. She grew up in humiliating poverty, scavenging for food in garbage cans in the Chestnut Valley, St.

Louis's notorious tenderloin district and the cradle of ragtime. Her formal education ended in the fourth grade when she left the Lincoln School and became a domestic worker.

On July 2, 1917, at age eleven she witnessed the East St. Louis race riot, one of the worst in American history. She later claimed that the massacre was a turning point in her life, convincing her that she was a black Joan of Arc, anointed by God to save her people from oppression.

When she was thirteen, Baker ran away from home to marry Willie Wells, but the marriage did not last. She found a job waiting on tables and performing with a ramshackle trio called the Jones Family Band. She then left St. Louis to join the Theatre Owners Booking Agency, who placed entertainers on the black vaudeville circuit extending from New York to Florida. Some performers nicknamed it TOBA for "Tough on Black Asses," because it paid so little money, except to headliners.

In September 1921, at age fifteen, she eloped in Camden, N.J., with a railroad porter, Willie Baker, whose name she kept throughout her career. Josephine and Willie Baker lived for a while in a theatrical boardinghouse in Philadelphia, but, at sixteen, leaving her husband behind, she begged and badgered her way into the road company of *Shuffle Along* (1922), the hit Broadway musical of the early 1920's. She became a protégée of Eubie Blake, one of the show's authors.

Her real success, however, came on Oct. 2, 1925, when she was nineteen, in Paris, on the opening night of a makeshift vaudeville production titled *La Revue Nègre* at the Théâtre des Champs-Élysées. She made her entry nude, except for a hot pink feather tucked between her legs; she was carried upside down and doing the split on the shoulders of a large black man named Joe Alex. Together, they performed a fiery pas de deux called *The Dance of the Savages*.

Her popularity was soon immense with both the general public and avant-garde intellectuals. She embodied the glamor, pain, and poignancy of the jazz age and Paris in the 1920's. An admirer gave her a real baby leopard that wore a Van Cleef and Arpels diamond choker. Pablo Picasso painted her, exulting, "She is the Nefertiti of now." Alexander Calder portrayed her in wire. And Colette wrote her fan letters. *New Yorker* correspondent Janet Flanner declared, "Her magnificent dark body, a new model to the French, proved for the first time that black was beautiful."

From 1926 to 1927, she appeared at the Folies Bergère in her most famous costume, a girdle of rhinestone-studded bananas. From 1927 to 1936, she remained an international celebrity, toured the world, acted in movies, took a range of lovers that included mystery writer George Simenon, architect Le Corbusier, and Pepito de Abatino, a former plasterer from Italy, who passed himself off as a Roman count.

Under Pepito de Abatino's tutelage, she was transformed from an untamed force of nature who "ate spaghetti with her hands" to a cosmopolitan woman of the world. He persuaded her to take singing, ballet, and French lessons, and also encouraged her to write a novel, fly a plane, and jockey in a horse race. He masterminded her change in professional style from zany comedy dancer to chanteuse. On Dec. 15, 1934, she starred in a revival of *La Créole*, an Offenbach operetta, in which she received laudatory reviews congratulating her on becoming a full-fledge French headliner.

Baker returned to New York City to appear in a Ziegfeld Follies show that opened at the Winter Garden Theatre on Jan. 31, 1936. Costars Fannie Brice, Bob Hope, Judy Canova, and Eve Arden dazzled the reviewers, who in turn had a field day trouncing "La Bakaire." Brooks Atkinson of the *New York Times* commented coldly, "Miss Baker has refined her art until there is nothing left in it." During this visit, she divorced her husband Willie Baker. She also cut ties with Pepito de Abatino, blaming him for her Ziegfeld failure. He died of cancer shortly thereafter.

On Nov. 30, 1937, Baker married French sugar broker Jean Lion and became a French citizen. She separated from him fourteen months later. They were divorced in 1942. The source of friction was Baker's career and her relentless need for attention. She had been so starved for love in her formative years that no single man could meet her emotional needs.

Josephine Baker possessed daunting courage and a talent for placing herself in the path of major events. These qualities marked her adventures as a spy during World War II. While performing in southern France, Portugal, and North Africa, she displayed "sang-froid extraordinaire" and allegedly secured secrets for the Free French. In December 1941, she delivered a stillborn child in a Casablanca clinic—the father is unknown. She let the Resistance fighters use her hospital room as a meeting place to trade secrets.

Soon after the liberation of Paris on Aug. 25, 1944, Josephine Baker returned to her beloved city. For her heroism, General Charles de Gaulle awarded her the Legion de Honneur and the Rosette de la Resistance.

On her forty-first birthday, June 3, 1947, she married her fourth husband, Jo Bouillon, a bisexual orchestra leader who had performed in Paris during the Occupation. The newlyweds resided at Les Milandes, Baker's fifteenth-century château in south-central France. They transformed the three-hundred-acre estate into a tourist center, a utopian community that was to serve as a model of harmony. To this end, she created her "rainbow tribe," adopting twelve children of different races and nationalities as an example of brotherhood.

Josephine Baker made a successful return trip to the United States in 1951. She championed civil rights causes during the McCarthy era, traveling anonymously through the American South to see what life under Jim Crow was like for the average African American. When a waiter ignored her dinner request at the Stork Club in New York City, she tried to sue the restaurant. In her well-publicized criticisms of the club she included Walter Winchell, who happened to be present but did not come to her rescue. He retaliated by attacking her in print, calling her "pro-Communist" as well as "a dangerous woman who hates colored people as much as she hates Jews."

She considered herself an astute political observer, lavished attention on dictator Juan Perón and his wife Evita, and praised Fidel Castro. Over the years, her name was also linked with Benito Mussolini, Marshal Tito, and the Pasha of Marrakesh.

Josephine Baker's financial affairs—always her weak point—were becoming increasingly disordered. Frustrated by her fiscal irresponsibility and her determination to continue adopting children, Jo Bouillon left Baker in 1960, and moved to Buenos Aires, where he opened a French restaurant. The couple never divorced.

After Baker went bankrupt and lost Les Milandes, Princess Grace of Monaco came to her rescue with the down payment on a house in Roquebrune, a town on the French Riviera. Princess Grace was also instrumental in getting

the Société des Bains de Mer, the company that runs the Monte Carlo casino, to assist Baker with her floundering career.

Josephine Baker died in Paris on Apr. 14, 1975, in the middle of a comeback and just four days after celebrating her fiftieth anniversary in French show business. Her funeral took place at the Church of the Madeleine, a massive model of a Greek temple built under Napoleon's regime. Baker was the only American to receive a twenty-one-gun salute and a military funeral in France (an honor reserved for kings and presidents).

Josephine Baker is mainly remembered as a supreme visual performer in the great tradition of the Parisian music hall. She also developed a remarkable voice, light and sweet, like that of a bird. Moreover, she was one of the most thrilling stage presences of the twentieth century, displaying powers of endurance that are granted only to a few. She was an affecting actress, although she never found the proper vehicle for her ability.

[Libraries housing collections of Baker's letters, programs, and magazine articles include the Performing Arts Research Center of the New York Public Library at Lincoln Center; the Schomburg Center of the New York Public Library; La Bibliothèque de l'Arsenal, Paris; La Bibliothèque Municipal in Perigeux; Sterling Library at Yale University; and the Missouri Historical Society. The Center for Jazz Studies at Rutgers University has taped interviews with Baker.

Baker recorded over a hundred songs during her career. Most of her output first appeared on four labels in France: Odeon, Columbia, Pacific, and RCA. Baker's film career includes *La Sirene des Tropiques* (1927); *Zou-zou* (1934); and *Princess Tam-Tam* (1935). In 1991, *The Josephine Baker Story* was aired by HBO.

Autobiographies and biographies include Josephine Baker and Marcel Sauvage, *Les mémoires de Joséphine Baker*, 3 vols. (1927–1947); Josephine Baker and Andre Rivollet, *Une vie de toutes les couleurs* (1926); Jacques Abtey, *La guerre secrète de Joséphine Baker* (1948); Stephen Papich, *Remembering Josephine* (1976); Lynn Haney, *Naked at the Feast* (1981); Bryan Hammond and Patrick O'Connor, *Josephine Baker* (1988); and Phyllis Rose, *Jazz Cleopatra: Josephine Baker in Her Time* (1989). An obituary appears in the *New York Times*, Apr. 13, 1975.]

LYNN HANEY

BALABAN, BARNEY (June 8, 1887–Mar. 7, 1971), motion-picture exhibitor and executive, was born in Chicago, the oldest of seven sons of Goldie Manderbursky and Israel Balaban, Russian immigrants who owned a grocery store. Balaban attended elementary school on Chicago's West Side but left at the age of twelve to work as a messenger for Western Union. In 1903 he became a clerk at the Western Cold Storage Company. In 1908, with his parents and his siblings, particularly his brother A. J., he rented a small movie theater. Balaban later attributed the idea of getting into film exhibition to his mother. According to the story as he told it, in 1907 Goldie Balaban accompanied her son to a nickelodeon. As they paid their admission, she exclaimed, "Why, Barney, the customers pay before they even see what they're paying for! There'll be money in that business!"

In 1912 the Balabans opened their second theater; in 1914, their third. In 1916, they formed a partnership with Sam Katz, another Chicago exhibitor, who married Balaban's sister. Balaban and Katz, as the new company was named, used the smaller businesses as collateral for a loan and in 1917 opened the Central Park Theatre, Chicago's first picture palace. Between 1919 and 1924 the partners expanded their chain of large, up-to-date movie theaters; by the end of this period the company dominated the Chicago film market and set an example that was followed by theater chains throughout the country.

Film historian Douglas Gomery suggests that Balaban and Katz revolutionized the film-exhibition business by concentrating on five factors. First, they carefully scouted for ideal locations for their theaters, accessible to middle-class filmgoers. Second, they indulged in lavish buildings, making the picture-going experience glamorous. Third, they emphasized service, carefully training personnel from ushers to baby-sitters. Fourth, knowing they could not entirely control the films they showed, they packaged their pictures with lavish stage shows designed to make every visit to the theater spectacular.

The fifth contribution was primarily Balaban's. His tenure at the Western Cold Storage Company had given him experience with air-conditioning. As the center of the nation's meat-packing industry, Chicago was also just about the only city in which the concept of air-cooling had been implemented. Early air-conditioning systems were massive and proved cost effective only when used in large spaces.

Balaban and Katz worked with the chief engineer of Kroeschell Bros. Ice Machine Company to adapt the technology to their movie palaces, and thus expanded film exhibition to a year-round business.

Balaban and Katz attracted the attention of Hollywood's film studios, anxious to ensure exhibition venues for their products. In 1926, Paramount Pictures purchased the chain. Sam Katz moved to the studio's New York office to supervise all of Paramount's theaters, renamed the Publix chain. Balaban remained in Chicago to run the Balaban and Katz subsidiary. In February 1929 he married Tillie Urkov; they had three children.

Paramount made more money than any other studio during the 1920's, but with the advent of the Great Depression the corporation's emphasis on theater acquisition turned briefly into a liability. Theater attendance went down with the economy. The company was reorganized several times in the early 1930's and went into receivership. In 1936, at the suggestion of adviser Joseph Kennedy, the presidency of Paramount was offered to Balaban, a major stockholder as a result of the Balaban and Katz purchase. He moved to New York City to take over the corporation and remained there for thirty years.

Within his first year, Balaban cut enough costs and streamlined enough departments to turn a profit for the company. He was known throughout his tenure at Paramount as a fiscal conservative who paid more attention to the bottom line than to stars or scripts. All major expenditures, either in the New York office or in the Los Angeles studios, had to meet with his approval. In terms of its film product, the studio played it safe, relying on stars who had established reputations in vaudeville, the stage, or radio.

Balaban was eager to expand technologically and to embrace the new medium of television. In 1939 Paramount invested in the DuMont video company, and in 1940 it purchased its first television station, through Balaban and Katz, in Chicago. Balaban also experimented with the concept of theater-based television in the late 1940's, although this technology finally proved uncompetitive.

In 1948 the Supreme Court ordered Paramount and the other vertically integrated motion-picture companies to divest themselves of their theater chains. In 1949 Balaban divided the corporation in two. Paramount Pictures, of which he remained president, kept the studio, the copyrights on the film library, and the distribution end of the business, while United Paramount Theaters took the exhibition end. Paramount was unable to expand its television-station chain because of an FCC ruling against the ownership of television stations by any company convicted of monopoly practices. In 1958, Balaban raised additional capital by selling the company's backlog of pre-1948 films to the Music Corporation of America for $50 million.

Balaban kept a low public profile throughout his time at Paramount. In the late 1940's he went on a State Department–sponsored tour of theaters abroad and came back a vocal advocate of motion-picture companies' cooperation in exporting films that would accurately and positively represent the United States to overseas viewers. He was intensely patriotic and proud to present the U.S. government with specimens of Americana he acquired—particularly the copy of the Bill of Rights that he donated to the Library of Congress in 1946. He was active in a number of charitable and religious organizations, including the United Jewish Appeal.

In 1964, Balaban moved from the presidency of Paramount to the chairmanship of the board. Two years later he was eased out, and Paramount was taken over by Gulf and Western. Balaban died in Byram, Conn.

[Douglas Gomery covers Balaban's work for Balaban and Katz in his *Shared Pleasures* (1992) and his Paramount period in *The Hollywood Studio System* (1986). Balaban is discussed in *Continuous Performance*, by his sister-in-law Carrie Balaban (1941). He was profiled in *Forbes*, Feb. 1, 1945. A clipping file is maintained at the Billy Rose Theatre Collection of the New York Public Library. Obituaries are in the *New York Times*, Mar. 8, 1971; and *Variety*, Mar. 10, 1971.]

TINKY ("DAKOTA") WEISBLAT

BALCHEN, BERNT (Oct. 23, 1899–Oct. 17, 1973), aviator and polar expert, was born in Tveit, Norway, the son of Lauritz Balchen, a physician, and Dagny Dietrichson. When Balchen was four years old, his mother divorced his father and left Tveit. Balchen was raised by his father, and then by other relatives after his father's death when Balchen was eight years old, in the small village in the Topdal valley, where he developed a lifelong love of the outdoors. At age 12, he went to live with his mother and stepfather in Kristiansand. An indifferent student but accomplished athlete, he graduated from high school in 1915, then spent a year at the forestry school in Moseby before finding employment in lumber camps.

In search of adventure, Balchen joined the French foreign legion in the summer of 1918. Soon recalled home to serve in the Norwegian army, he volunteered during the winter of 1918–1919 to fight with the White Army of Finland, which was battling for Finnish independence against the Russian Bolsheviks. After recovering from a severe bayonet wound received during a battle near Sortavala, he returned to duty with the Norwegian army. In 1921 he transferred to the Royal Norwegian Naval Air Force, where he learned to fly.

Balchen's first trip to the Arctic came in 1925, when he went to Spitsbergen on a planned search-and-rescue mission for Roald Amundsen, the famed Norwegian explorer who was reported lost while attempting a flight over the North Pole. Although the aerial rescue proved unnecessary when Amundsen was found by a Norwegian sealing ship, Balchen had time to form an attachment to the northern regions that would shape his life.

In 1926, Balchen returned to Spitsbergen as an engineer and standby crew member for the dirigible *Norge*, which Amundsen planned to use on another attempt to be the first to fly over the North Pole. On May 9, however, two days before Amundsen left (without Balchen) for a successful flight over the North Pole to Alaska, Richard E. Byrd and Floyd Bennett claimed the honor of the first polar flight in a trimotored Ford transport. Balchen, who helped Byrd redesign and rebuild the skis for the Ford, later had cause to doubt that Byrd actually had reached the Pole. Although the two men eventually became estranged, Byrd was instrumental in persuading Balchen to obtain a leave of absence from the Norwegian air force and go to the United States.

Balchen found employment with the Fokker Aircraft Company, an association that would last from 1926 until 1933. While employed by Fokker, Balchen took frequent leaves of absence for special assignments. In 1927, for example, he flew with Western Canada Airways, moving eight tons of equipment from Cache Lake to Fort Churchill on Hudson Bay, the planned terminus for the Hudson Bay Railways. A delighted Canadian government reported: "There has been no more brilliant operation in the history of commercial aviation." Also in 1927, Balchen flew as pilot for Byrd's transatlantic flight in the Ford trimotor *America*. When bad weather forced the aircraft down off Vers-sur-Mer on the coast of France, Balchen's airmanship enabled the crew to escape without injury.

Balchen went on to serve as chief pilot for Byrd's Antarctic expedition of 1928–1930. He was at the controls when the Ford trimotor *Floyd Bennett* carried Byrd over the South Pole for the first time on Nov. 29, 1929.

Balchen married Emmy Soerlie on Oct. 18, 1930. They had one son. They separated in 1941 and were divorced in 1948. Balchen became a naturalized citizen of the United States on Nov. 5, 1931.

After flying as chief pilot for the Ellsworth Antarctic Expedition from 1933 to 1935, Balchen returned to Norway and helped establish the country's first commercial airline, Det Norsk Luftfartselskap (DNL). In 1936, he negotiated the first bilateral air agreement between Norway and the United States. However, plans for a transatlantic service via Iceland in partnership with Pan American Airways failed to materialize after the British government pressured Pan American to cancel the arrangement with DNL.

Balchen was in the United States when Germany invaded Norway in April 1940. Called to duty with the Norwegian air force, he was assigned to the RAF Ferry Command. On Sept. 5, 1941, he was transferred to the United States Army Air Corps at the special request of General H. H. Arnold. Balchen headed Task Force Eight, charged with constructing an air base at Söndre Strömfjord, Greenland. Known as Bluie West-8, the base served as a key facility on the North Atlantic ferry route. In January 1944 Balchen was transferred to the United States Army Air Force in Europe as chief of the Allied Air Transport Command for Scandinavia, Finland, and the USSR. Stationed in the United Kingdom, he commanded a number of special projects under the code names of SONNIE, BALL, WHEN AND WHERE, and SEPALS that supported resistance groups in Scandinavia.

In February 1946 Balchen rejoined DNL and served as president and managing director of the airline. He played a major role in the negotiations that led to the formation of Scandinavian Airlines System (SAS). He also developed a polar air route between Scandinavia and the United States. At the same time, he assisted the American government by establishing intelligence networks along the Soviet border and by expanding facilities at Sola airport in Norway to be used by bombers of the United States Air Force's Strategic Air Command in the event of war.

On Feb. 28, 1948, Balchen married Inger Engelbrethsen. They had one son. The marriage ended in divorce in 1966.

Recalled to active duty as a colonel with the United States Air Force on Oct. 11, 1948, Balchen took command of the Tenth Rescue Squadron at Fort Richardson, Alaska, where he pioneered Arctic rescue techniques. In February 1951, he became project officer for Operation Blue Jay, engaged in the construction of a giant air base at Thule, Greenland, 930 miles from the North Pole. Failing to receive a promotion to brigadier general, which he blamed on the political machinations of Admiral Byrd, who was angry after Balchen challenged his claim to have flown over the North Pole in 1926, he retired from the air force on Oct. 31, 1956.

Balchen married Audrey Schipper on Nov. 30, 1966. As consultant to the United States Air Force, SAS, and several military contractors, he remained interested in national defense matters, especially as they related to the Arctic. Balchen also developed his talents as an artist, painting mainly in watercolors. In addition, he wrote a cookbook and his autobiography. He died in suburban Mt. Kisco, N.Y., and was buried at Arlington National Cemetery on his seventy-fourth birthday.

[The major collections of Balchen's papers are at the Library of Congress and the United States Air Force Historical Research Center, Maxwell Air Force Base, Ala. His autobiography is *Come North with Me* (1958). Clayton Knight and Robert C. Durham's biography, *Hitch Your Wagon: The Story of Bernt Balchen* (1950), was written with Balchen's assistance. An obituary appears in the *New York Times*, Oct. 18, 1973.]

WILLIAM M. LEARY

BARKER, ALEXANDER CRICHLOW ("LEX") (May 8, 1919–May 11, 1973), movie actor, was born in Rye, N.Y. His father was Alexander Crichlow Barker, a civil engineer, and his family was among the elite families listed in the New York Social Register, a fact that Barker's publicists used to good effect later in his career. Barker's education was meant to prepare him to continue in his father's footsteps. He attended the prestigious Phillips Exeter Academy in New Hampshire, where he starred in both football and track. After graduating from Exeter he advanced to Princeton University, but there the well-laid plans of the Barker family went awry; Lex, Jr., soon discovered that he had little interest in engineering. To avoid summer school, Barker took up with a summer stock company in Princeton, and soon "caught the acting bug." A year later, in 1942, Barker was spotted by a Twentieth Century–Fox talent scout and offered a screen test.

The audition won him a contract from the studio, but his film career was temporarily put on hold when he enlisted in the army after the outbreak of World War II. Barker rose to the rank of major and served as the aide-de-camp to General Mark Clark. In 1944, Barker received a head wound from artillery fire, was captured by the German Army, and then spent some time in a prisoner-of-war camp. With the end of the war in 1945, Barker returned to Hollywood, where he resumed his career. Although Fox re-signed him, the studio put him only into one bit part (in *Doll Face*) during his first year. He had little better luck at Warner Brothers, which he moved to in 1946. Because of his striking good lucks and impressive physique, Barker was too noticeable to play supporting roles, yet Warner Brothers wasn't ready to give him a shot at a leading role.

Barker's career was on the decline when RKO rescued him in 1948. The studio, having failed to re-sign Johnny Weissmuller to its successful Tarzan series, was looking for a new Ape Man, and Barker's build and looks gained him the role. RKO was anxious about finding a worthy successor to the hugely popular Weissmuller, an Olympic gold medalist in swimming who had come to personify the Tarzan character. Although Barker, the tenth actor to play the role, adequately portrayed Tarzan, he never reached Weissmuller's popularity.

Barker's first Tarzan movie, *Tarzan's Magic Fountain* (1949), received generally favorable reviews from the critics. Some still appeared brokenhearted at losing Weissmuller, but at least one reviewer commented, "Barker's handsome physique fits the Burroughs description, and he is actor enough to make the jungle man

a more animated person than he has been." Barker, in noting RKO's attempt to increase Tarzan's basic intelligence, noted wryly, "Tarzan is progressing. I have more dialogue than my predecessors. Two-syllable words, too."

One problem with the Tarzan series after Weissmuller—more apparent to critics than to fans, who continued to flock to each new release—was that the writers were simply running out of steam. Plots tended increasingly toward mechanical action picture models, with roaming elephants and threatening "natives" thrown in to satisfy audiences. Barker's next film, *Tarzan and the Slave Girl* (1950), was given a lukewarm reception by the critics, who ridiculed the plot and were generally unenthusiastic about the new Jane, Vanessa Brown. *Tarzan's Peril*, released the following year, was perhaps the most successful of Barker's Ape Man films, but the following efforts, *Tarzan's Savage Fury* (1952), and *Tarzan and the She-Devil* (1954), were generally panned, and each saw a dip in box office receipts. Barker, however, was generally credited with performing well despite the limitations of the role.

These limitations, including the often inane plotting, shallow characterization, and limited vocabulary—Barker spoke just eighty-three lines in one film—had helped drive Weissmuller away from the role. Barker believed RKO was ready to develop the series further, but director/producer Sol Lessor, who owned the film rights to the Tarzan series, refused to go beyond the tested (and profitable) formula. Lessor, in fact, claimed that *Tarzan's Savage Fury* was fatally flawed by its excessive dialogue. "Tarzan had 137 lines in that one," he complained. "Nearly talked himself to death." Barker's Tarzan never did get beyond the two-syllable stage, and by the fourth film Barker was looking for a way out.

In 1952, Barker announced to the press, "My career has reached a crisis. It's time for a change. I'm definitely determined to get out of the jungle. . . . Actually, I don't regret having taken the role of Tarzan, because with it I've achieved a sort of stardom which I couldn't have gained any other way." Barker soon discovered, however, that the "sort of stardom" Tarzan conferred was not easily transferable to other roles. His opportunities were generally low-budget Westerns, the most satisfying being *The Deerslayer* (1956). To the public and the studios, Barker and Tarzan were interchangeable. As

Barker later related, "I was all set to play Sherlock Holmes' brother in Billy Wilder's *The Adventures of Sherlock Holmes*, and then the [producers] in Hollywood cabled back that I had the 'aura' of Tarzan about me. So they hired Christopher Lee, who is noted for playing Dracula. How's that for an aura!" In 1953, when Barker married his third wife, film star Lana Turner, one headline screamed, "Tarzan and Turner to Marry!"

Barker became increasingly frustrated with what he perceived as Hollywood's narrowmindedness. His perilous financial condition added to his resentment. Besides Turner, he had married and divorced Constance Thurlow (1942–1949; they had two children) and Arlene Dahl (1951–1952), and he had mounting alimony payments. His marriage to Turner lasted until 1957. That year, he finally turned his back on Hollywood and moved to Europe in search of new opportunities.

In Europe, Barker's Tarzan legacy opened many doors. Although most of the roles he took were for adventure films, they offered more complexity of character than his American roles. His career got an extra boost when the internationally recognized Italian director, Frederico Fellini, cast him in a pivotal role in the classic *La Dolce Vita* (1960). "No producer would have handed me the break Fellini did when he cast me in the sensational *La Dolce Vita*," Barker reported, "which started me on an acting career in Europe."

By the mid-1960's, Barker had achieved the kind of stardom in Europe he had yearned for in the United States. He was among the highest-grossing stars in Germany and Italy, known particularly for his depiction of "Old Shatterhand" in a series of movies based on the frontier sagas of German writer Karl May. In 1966, he won the German equivalent of the Oscar for best foreign actor. By this time, Barker had begun to produce films as well. Now fluent in French, Italian, Spanish, and German, he had become a sort of movie ambassador to the world, helping to coordinate numerous film collaborations between different countries. He was especially fond of shooting pictures in Yugoslavia, which combined dramatic scenery with low expenses, and in 1966 was honored by the Yugoslavian government for his work there.

Barker's marriages also became international affairs. His fourth wife, Irene Lambert, was Swiss; she died in 1962, shortly after giving birth

to a son. In 1965, Barker wed for the last time, marrying Maria del Carmen Cervera, a former Spanish beauty queen. In 1966, Barker became a Swiss citizen.

By 1970, Barker had made over sixty films outside of the United States. Because the European film industry was experiencing a slowdown, Barker turned back to America for work. Hollywood was no more impressed with his European credentials than with his Tarzan work, however, and Barker received few offers before his death of a heart attack three years later.

[Barker, whose Tarzan association and complicated love life made him the focus of numerous features in the Hollywood press, is well represented in the clippings file at the Academy for Motion Pictures library in Los Angeles. An obituary appears in the *New York Times*, May 12, 1973.]

MICHAEL GOLDBERG

BATES, THEODORE LEWIS ("TED") (Sept. 11, 1901–May 30, 1972), advertising executive, was born in New Haven, Conn., the son of Vernal Warner Bates and Elizabeth H. Hailes. He graduated from Andover Academy in 1920 and from Yale University in 1924 with a B.A.

Bates's first job after graduation from college was with the Chase National Bank, where he worked for six months as a courier. He then became manager of advertising. After a short period with the bank, he worked in advertising at the George Batten Company and rose to be vice-president of their successor firm, Batten, Barton, Durstine, and Osborn. He married Elizabeth Turull on Aug. 4, 1934; the couple had two children.

From 1935 to 1940, Bates was vice-president of the firm of Benton and Bowles. He then founded his own advertising agency, Ted Bates and Company. The new firm enjoyed a modest success at first. But as its sales and billings grew rapidly following World War II, the Ted Bates firm became one of the leading advertising agencies in the world utilizing the new medium of television.

Bates was self-effacing and modest, never seeking for himself the same publicity that he sought for the products his company represented. The television commercials that he and his company developed were loud, often raucous, and filled with repetitive sounds and action. Although many observers decried these commercial messages, they were extremely successful. Bates is credited with establishing modern advertising with his efforts in television. He and his firm were responsible for path-breaking advertising, including a campaign to promote the analgesic Anacin that featured hammers pounding the heads of headache sufferers. Among the Bates agency's most noted clients was the Colgate-Palmolive Company. Bates developed some very lucrative campaigns for this group, including the Palmolive Fourteen-Day Beauty Plan. The products and the plan were extolled on the "Colgate Comedy Hour," an early and very successful television series. He was also responsible for the campaign that claimed that Wonder Bread "Builds Strong Bodies Twelve Ways," which was investigated for truth in advertising. The campaign was permitted to continue.

Bates assumed the title of honorary chairman of his firm in the late 1950's, and some thought that this meant that he was retiring. In fact, the move was only a ploy to provide him with anonymity. He continued to be very active in the firm's affairs. The flamboyant Rosser Reeves served as chairman, chief executive officer, and head of the company. Reeves and Bates worked together on new advertising campaigns. Bates continued to supply ideas and contributed to the growing success of the firm. At the time of his death, annual billings for the firm were estimated to be $425 million.

Bates focused his efforts on extending the firm's work into Europe, Australia, and Southeast Asia. Although he again adopted the title of chief executive officer for a time in the early 1960's, he continued to shun personal publicity. He told interviewers that he had never had a martini lunch, given a speech, attended a convention, or signed a publicity release. His advertising techniques consisted of the wide use of repetitive slogans, presented in a simple, straightforward way, always putting the attributes of the product ahead of the presentation or the location of the presentation. This method, described in 1963 as the "unique selling proposition," has been found to be the most successful technique available in recent studies of commercials and advertising techniques.

Bates served as director of the Advertising Council, which monitors ethical standards in the industry and supervises charitable work for the members. He was an important figure in this body for most of his later life.

Bates, an avid and skillful angler, died in New York City.

[Rosser Reeves, *Realty in Advertising* (1961), outlines the Bates advertising techniques. See also Charles Anthony Wainwright, *Television Commercials* (1965), which includes Clinton S. Ferris, "What Goes into a Good Selling Commercial?" An obituary is in the *New York Times*, June 1, 1972.]
                                                    DAVID SMITH

BATTLE, JOHN STEWART (July 11, 1890– Apr. 9, 1972), governor of Virginia, was born in New Bern, N.C., the son of the Reverend Dr. Henry Wilson Battle and Margaret Stewart.

His father became pastor of the First Baptist Church in Petersburg, Va., where the family moved in 1893, and his grandfather was General Cullen A. Battle of the Confederate Army. He attended public schools in Petersburg before entering Wake Forest College in North Carolina in 1908. In 1910, he transferred to the law school of the University of Virginia in Charlottesville.

Upon receiving his law degree in 1913, Battle began to practice law in Charlottesville in association with Lemuel F. Smith. He served briefly as a private in the United States Army during World War I. On June 12, 1918, he married Mary Jane Lipscomb of Charlottesville; they had two children.

Battle's political career began when he was elected in 1929 to the House of Delegates to represent the Charlottesville area in Virginia's general assembly. From 1934 to 1949, he was a member of the Virginia senate, with a special interest in issues of taxation and budget. He was chairman of the Senate's finance committee during his final four years in the legislature, and from 1940 to 1950 he served as a member of the Governor's Advisory Committee on the Budget. Among the measures Battle sponsored in the general assembly were the establishment of the unemployment compensation system in Virginia, the establishment of the probation and parole system, and the abolition of the sheriff's fee system in counties and cities.

Not until he ran for the office of governor as the Democratic candidate in 1949 did Battle face opposition in a political campaign. Endorsed by Senator Harry F. Byrd and his supporters, Battle's most serious competition in the primary came from Francis Pickens Miller, a former Army officer who had the support of labor and African Americans. After winning the primary, Battle defeated the Republican candidate, Walter O. Johnson, in the general election, with the votes of farmers, businessmen, and white-collar workers. He stressed in the campaign the need for money to build schools and the continuation of the financial programs already in place. On election day, Battle culled five times the number of votes of his nearest opponent.

In his inaugural address on Jan. 18, 1950, Battle called for increasing school building expenditures. The $45-million-dollar "Battle Fund" represented the first time that Virginia had made direct grants to localities for building public schools. By the end of his term, more than four hundred new schools had been built. Also in his inaugural address was a request for the power to seize coal mines for state operation in an emergency. One week later the newly activated Virginia Fuel Commission took over and operated all unionized coal mines in Virginia until a strike was settled.

In 1952, Battle won acclaim for his leadership of the Virginia delegation in defiance of the loyalty oath required of delegates to the Democratic National Convention in Chicago, where Adlai E. Stevenson was the nominee for president. As head of the delegation, Battle had concerns with regard to the pro–civil rights course that the Democratic party had been taking. Under the terms of the loyalty oath, no delegate could take part in the convention unless he pledged to support the convention nominees for president and vice-president, ensuring that they would appear on the ballot in the delegate's home state under the Democratic party heading. This measure was a response to the formation in 1948 of the splinter Dixiecrat party that had run Strom Thurmond for president. The loyalty oath requirement led the Virginia delegation, along with those from Louisiana and South Carolina, to revolt and refuse to file their pledges with the credentials committee. On the verge of the expulsion of these delegations, Battle took the lead. The southern governor spoke for a mere three minutes on the podium, but his words altered the course of the convention. Invoking the Jeffersonian ideal of freedom of thought and action, he persuaded the convention to overrule the requirement and seat the delegations.

Although he believed strongly in segregation, Battle refused Senator Byrd's call for "massive resistance" to school desegregation. This stand was noted by President Dwight D. Eisenhower, who appointed Battle in 1958 to serve on the six-member Civil Rights Commission that had been created to investigate voting rights violations. During public hearings of the commission, Battle fought Montgomery, Ala., officials who were attempting to impede the commission's work. He dissented from the commission's first report to Congress, which offered legislation to ensure equal voting, educational, and housing rights. He contended that the commission's report was not impartial or factual but, in fact, reinforced "preconceived [antisegregation] ideas in race relations."

At the end of his two-year term, Battle refused Eisenhower's request that he stay on and returned to his private law practice with the firm of McGuire, Woods and Battle, which he had joined upon leaving the governorship in 1954, continuing there until his retirement in 1969. He also served as director of the American Gas and Electric Company, the Fredericksburg and Potomac Railroad Company, and the National Bank and Trust Company. He received an honorary LL.D. from Hampden-Sydney College, Virginia, in 1950 and also from the University of Richmond in 1952. For relaxation he was an avid golfer and fisherman. Battle died in Albermarle County, Va.

[For details of his political career see Virginius Dabney, *Virginia* (1971); Ralph Eisenberg, *Virginia Votes, 1924–1968* (1971); Eleanora W. Schoenbaum, ed., *Political Profiles* (1977); and Robert Sobel and John Raimo, eds., *Biographical Directory of the Governors of the United States, 1789–1978* (1978). An obituary is in the *New York Times*, Apr. 10, 1972.]

CAROL R. BERKIN

BEALL, JAMES GLENN (June 5, 1894–Jan. 14, 1971), U.S. representative and senator, was born in Frostburg, Md., the son of Olin Beall (pronounced "Bell") and Florence B. Glenn. As a child, Beall suffered from polio and had several operations before age twelve. His left arm and leg were withered permanently, but he remained active, later playing golf regularly. Beall attended public schools in Frostburg, Md., and Gettysburg College (1916–1917) in Gettysburg, Pa. He later received honorary degrees from Gettysburg College and Mount St. Mary's College. He served in the Ordnance

Corps of the U.S. Army from 1918 to 1919, attaining the rank of sergeant. Afterward, he worked in his father's insurance and real estate business in Frostburg. Beall wed Mary Margaret Schwarzenbach on Sept. 15, 1926, and they had three sons, including John Glenn Beall, Jr., who later held his father's U.S. Senate seat, and George Beall, U.S. attorney for Maryland.

Beall's political career began when he became a member of the Allegany County Road Commission, a position he held from 1923 to 1930. For the next four years, he represented Allegany County as a state representative. He was a member and later head of the Maryland State Roads Commission in 1938 and 1939. Beall's political career in Washington began when he defeated Walter ("Big Train") Johnson, the former major league pitcher, in the 1942 Republican primary and easily defeated the Democratic candidate for a U.S. House seat. The voters of the Sixth District (which included Allegany, Frederick, Garrett, Montgomery, and Washington counties in Maryland) elected Beall as their U.S. Representative from 1943 to 1953 for a total of five terms. As a capstone, he served two terms in the U.S. Senate from 1953 to 1965.

An emphasis on service gave Beall a broad base of support and a forty-one year career as a Republican politician in Maryland; he enjoyed calling himself "the service Senator." He was a mild-mannered, friendly man who had a reputation for taking a personal interest in people's problems.

Marylanders could count on Beall to promote their interests. He voted against building Dulles Airport and the St. Lawrence Seaway because these projects would hurt Friendship Airport, located near Baltimore, and Baltimore's port. To recognize the past economic importance of western Maryland, Beall sought to convert the Chesapeake and Ohio Canal between Washington, D.C., and Cumberland, Md., into a national historical park. His dream became reality one year after his death, and the U.S. Senate honored Beall in 1985 by naming the Cumberland terminus for him. On the lighter side, Beall once arranged to have 100 pounds of backfin crabmeat and a Baltimore chef sent to the Senate restaurant so his fellow legislators might learn the difference between the restaurant's so-called Maryland crabcakes and real Maryland crabcakes.

Because Beall believed Maryland and the District of Columbia had common problems, he sat on the U.S. House and U.S. Senate District Committees. He frequently sponsored home rule legislation for the District, worked for teacher pay raises, introduced slum clearance and urban renewal bills, and sought increases in the federal payment to the District. Early in his career, Beall consistently supported anti-Communist activities to such an extent that the Americans for Democratic Action called him "reactionary." Beall voted to establish a permanent Committee on Un-American Activities (1945), to control subversive activities (1948), and to penalize countries trading with the Soviet Union (1952). In 1949, Beall opposed legislation to supply arms to Western Europe for fear the area would fall to Communism. He won a U.S. Senate seat in 1952 by stressing the need to root out Communism and corruption as practiced by the "parlor pinks" and liberals in the Truman administration. He sat on the Senate Armed Services Committee and was a vocal supporter of Senator Joseph McCarthy. Yet, when the Senate voted to censure McCarthy in August 1954, Beall supported the disciplinary action. That same month Beall also opposed an amendment to make membership in the Communist party a crime. Beall was willing to revise the rigidity of his postwar views to meet changing realities.

Similarly, though regularly voting for bills to cut spending, Beall cosponsored a 1959 bill for $380 million in grants to redevelop chronically depressed areas, and he supported federal aid to education and an Appalachian aid program. Beall sat on the flood control as well as the roads and public works committees in the House, and he was a member of the banking and currency and commerce committees in the Senate. He opposed labor unions and supported legislation such as opening gas and oil resources to private development. Even so, Beall believed private industry should not harm the public. He sponsored hearings in 1958 to investigate potentially fraudulent activities of a savings and loan association in Maryland. The hearings revealed irregularities, but the problem was out of the federal government's jurisdiction. Three years later, the State of Maryland arrested the president of the investigated savings and loan and established new banking regulations.

Beall consistently voted for all civil rights legislation. In the 1930's, he introduced bills in the Maryland legislature to repeal the state's Jim

Crow laws. As a U.S. representative, he voted to abolish poll taxes, to create a permanent Fair Employment Practices Commission, and to establish legal rights for African Americans. He supported civil rights long before it became fashionable or politically expedient to do so. For Beall, civil rights was not a political issue; it was a moral issue.

After losing reelection in 1964 for a third term in the U.S. Senate, Beall returned to Frostburg, Md., to work in the insurance and real estate business his father had started. He continued to be involved with the Episcopal church, the Elks, Eagles, the American Legion, and the Shriners. He directed the First National Bank of Western Maryland and headed the Cumberland Fair Board. Beall showed special interest in, and acted as president for, the League for Crippled Children of Allegany County. This special interest came from his experience with polio as a child. He died of a heart ailment in his Frostburg home.

[Little information exists on Beall because his papers were destroyed when he left office. See Elsie Carper, "Beall Talks of 22 Years Service," *Washington Post*, Dec. 6, 1964, and *Congressional Record* 131 (137) (Oct. 16, 1985). Obituaries are in the *Washington Star*, Jan. 14, 1971; and in the *Baltimore Sun*, *New York Times*, and *Washington Post*, all Jan. 15, 1971.]

BRUCE A. THOMPSON

BEHRMAN, SAMUEL NATHANIEL ("S.N.") (1893–Sept. 9, 1973), playwright and essayist, was born in Worcester, Mass., the son of Joseph Behrman and Zelda Feingold, who had immigrated from Lithuania shortly before his birth. Lacking official records, he later chose June 9 to celebrate his birthday. His father was a devout Bible scholar who supported his family as a grocer and teacher in an immigrant section of Worcester. Behrman attended Clark University in Worcester from 1912 to 1914 and then transferred to Harvard University, where he enrolled in George Pierce Baker's renowned "47 Workshop" for drama students. He received a bachelor's degree in 1916. Two years later he earned a master's from Columbia University and settled in New York City to earn his living as a writer.

Behrman published essays and short stories in the *Smart Set*, the *New Republic*, and other magazines and secured a position at the *New York Times* writing classified ads and reviews. He collaborated with playwright J. Kenyon Nicholsan and veteran writer Owen Davis on some unsuccessful plays before finally persuading the Theatre Guild to produce a dramatization of his short story "The Second Man" in 1927. This production began Behrman's long association with the guild and its stars, Alfred Lunt and Lynn Fontanne. It also revealed Behrman's gift for creating witty and iconoclastic characters struggling for self-realization in the pursuit of marriage and money. It was a landscape that would occupy him for four decades and generate numerous theatrical productions.

Following the success of "The Second Man," Behrman embarked upon a decade of enormous productivity. At the urging of Harold Ross, he wrote profiles for the *New Yorker* and, like many of his contemporaries, was lured to Hollywood, where his screenplay credits included *Lilliom* (1930), *Sea Wolf* (1930), *Daddy Long Legs* (1931), *Anna Karenina* (1935), and A *Tale of Two Cities* (1935). But it was on Broadway that Behrman distinguished himself with a stream of sophisticated comedies, including *Meteor* (1929), *Serena Blandish* (1929), and his masterpieces, *Biography* (1932) and *End of Summer* (1936).

Behrman's comic talent was not in writing gags but in recording the foibles of people in their efforts to acquire power and money. His most interesting protagonists are women who refuse to conform to conventional attitudes and who wreak havoc among the men in their lives as a result. Marion Froude of *Biography* throws her social circle into an uproar when she begins her memoirs because her ex-lover is afraid of being compromised. Although she is encouraged in her enterprise (and courted) by a young, radical publisher, Marion eventually rejects all her suitors, destroys the manuscript, and resumes her career as a successful and independent painter. Similarly, Leonie in *End of Summer* presides over a house of fashionable people but rejects Kenneth's marriage proposal, preferring independence to social conformity.

Shortly after the opening of *End of Summer* in 1936, Behrman married Elza Heifetz Stone, sister of the famous violinist Jascha Heifetz. She had two children by a previous marriage. Their only child was born a year later. Behrman was guarded about his private life, although he did eventually publish several essays about his youth in *The Worcester Account* (1954). As a youngster he was deeply influenced by Daniel Asher, a Worcester friend who was eight years Behrman's senior and who informed his thinking and encouraged his writing. Asher's suicide in 1929 shocked Behrman, who eulogized him in the play *The Cold Wind and the Warm* (1958).

In 1938 Behrman was invited by Maxwell Anderson, Elmer Rice, and Robert Sherwood to join the Playwrights' Company. Weary of what they perceived to be constant tampering with their plays by the Theatre Guild and other producers, the group incorporated to produce their own work. Although Behrman was reluctant at first because of his association with the Guild, he did become an active member of the company. *No Time for Comedy* (1939), his premiere work, is a witty urban study of a middle-age dramatist who has writer's block and marital problems.

Behrman wrote four more plays for the Playwrights' Company, including an adaptation of Franz Werfel's *Jacobowsky and the Colonel* (1944), which won a New York Drama Critics' Award. He accumulated other honors, among them, membership in the National Institute of Arts and Letters and the Creative Arts Award for theater from Brandeis. He also continued writing screenplays for Hollywood, among the most notable, *Waterloo Bridge* (1940) and *Quo Vadis* (1954), and collaborated on the musical *Fanny* (1954). Adapted from Marcel Pagnol, with music and lyrics by Harold Rome, *Fanny* was Behrman's longest-running New York production, with 888 performances.

Behrman's final play, *But for Whom Charlie* (1964), is significant because it illustrates the regard with which he was held in the American theater. In 1964, the highly publicized Lincoln Center Repertory Company gave its premiere season at the American National Theatre and Academy (ANTA) Washington Square Theatre. This splendid company, which included Jason Robards, Faye Dunaway, Hal Holbrook, David Wayne, and director Elia Kazan, selected Arthur Miller's play *After the Fall*, along with Eugene O'Neill's *Marco Millions* and Behrman's *But for Whom Charlie*. Unfortunately, the production did not capture Behrman's drawing-room spirit, and much of the writing recalled but did not match the wit of his earlier plays. Behrman's celebrated emancipated woman, Gilian Prosper, for example, seems almost vulgar in comparison with her delightful predecessors. The play received mixed notices, but Behrman was disappointed with the production and the press.

He withdrew from the theater but not from writing. In the next few years he published a delightful collection of essays, *The Suspended Drawing Room* (1965), drawn largely from his *New Yorker* writings; a semiautobiographical novel, *The Burning Glass* (1968); and, at the age of 79, his memoir, *People in a Diary* (1972). Behrman proved to be remarkably resilient and prolific, prospering in one of America's most fickle enterprises: the professional theater. He died in New York City.

[The largest collection of Behrman's plays and papers is at the Wisconsin State Historical Society in Madison. Other manuscripts and letters are on file at the Humanities Research Center of the University of Texas. Useful secondary sources include Kenneth T. Reed, *S. N. Behrman* (1975); and Robert R. Jorge, entry in *Twentieth-Century American Dramatists* (1981). An obituary is in the *New York Times*, Sept. 10, 1973.]

BARRY B. WITHAM

BÉKÉSY, GEORG VON (June 3, 1899–June 13, 1972), physicist, aural physiologist, and art collector, was born in Budapest, the son of Alexandor von Békésy, an Austro-Hungarian diplomat, and Paula Mazaly. As a child he lived in Munich, Budapest, Constantinople, and Zurich. Békésy studied and loved music, developing enough skill on the piano to contemplate a concert career, but he soon came to prefer studying the plastic arts, especially sculpture. As early as his teens he had accumulated an estimable collection of objets d'art. After completing his secondary school education in Zurich and Budapest, he matriculated in 1916 at the University of Bern, where he received his baccalaureate in chemistry in 1920.

At the end of World War I, the Békésy family finances and prospects were in ruins. Békésy returned to Budapest and served briefly in the military. Still with no particular career goals in mind, he entered the University of Budapest in 1920 and emerged in 1923 with a Ph.D. in physics, specializing in optics and interference microscopy. His dissertation was on fluid dynamics.

Unable to find a job in optics, Békésy accepted a government position in the laboratory of the Hungarian Postal, Telephone, and Telegraph System. Its notoriously poor telephone service, plagued by internal engineering problems, was causing numerous malfunctions throughout Europe. Békésy was assigned to determine which of the three major components—sending equipment, transmitting lines and switches, or receiving equipment—was most responsible for the faults. Using a line-monitoring test that he had devised, he soon determined that the earphones of telephone receiving sets were the weakest link in the chain. He began to consider ways to reduce the unacceptable levels of distortion they created. This research naturally and quickly led to the study of the human ear.

In the 1920's, the official view of the mechanism and physiology of the human ear was the one that Hermann von Helmholtz had formulated in the 1860's. Békésy was able to proceed beyond Helmholtz by inventing revolutionary techniques of dissection and microscopy in which the specimen was immersed in fluid. These techniques kept the middle and inner ear in a lifelike state longer after death, and thus permitted more accurate and detailed observations.

Except for the period 1926–1927, spent at the Siemens and Halske Laboratories in Berlin, Békésy worked for Hungarian Telephone for twenty-three years. He began teaching at the University of Budapest in 1932, becoming professor of experimental physics in 1940. He continued his research unperturbed throughout the Nazi period, but he found that the Soviet occupation after World War II brought an intolerable climate for further study and emigrated to Sweden in 1946, resuming his work at the Karolinska Institutet. The following year he went to Harvard University, where in 1949 he was appointed senior research fellow in psychophysics. While at Harvard he was naturalized as an American citizen.

Békésy won the 1961 Nobel Prize in Physiology or Medicine mainly because he was regarded as a helper of the deaf. His discoveries about the mechanics, acoustics, and physiology of hearing had enabled physicians to identify, diagnose, and treat many different kinds of deafness. Later he acknowledged and returned this honor by bequeathing his greatest treasure, his collection of art works and rare books, to the Nobel Prize Foundation.

Békésy's attraction to the study of the ear was originally, and remained primarily, aesthetic. He appreciated not only the beauty of sound but also the beauty of the physical structure of the ear, especially the inner ear. He was so awestruck by the organum spirale the first time he saw it under a microscope, that he decided to stay the course of investigating the ear. Art also contributed to Békésy's laboratory method and scientific achievements. He said that learning to distinguish among art objects—genuine from fake, one period or genre from another, high quality from kitsch—had given him habits of scrutiny that helped him to analyze problems in physics.

In 1966, Békésy retired from Harvard and assumed a chair endowed by the Hawaiian Telephone Company as professor of sensory sciences at the University of Hawaii. He remained in this position until his death in Honolulu.

Békésy was quiet and reserved but friendly and charming, with an excellent sense of humor. He was so absorbed in art and the ear that he claimed to prefer the lonely scholar's existence. He never married and had no children.

[The largest collection of Békésy's manuscripts, movies, and photographs is at the Library of Congress. His books are at the University of Hawaii. His only monograph was *Sensory Inhibition* (1967); E.G. Wever translated many of his pre-Harvard articles from German and published them, together with some pre-1958 English articles, as *Experiments in Hearing* (1960). A brief autobiographical sketch that he completed two months before his death, "Some Biophysical Experiments from Fifty Years Ago," was published in *Annual Review of Physiology* (1974). Short biographies are in the Nobel Foundation's catalog of Békésy's art collection; J. Wirgin, ed., *The Georg von Békésy Collection* (1974); *Biographical Memoirs. National Academy of Sciences* 48 (1976); Tyler Wasson, ed., *Nobel Prize Winners* (1987); and Frank N. Magill, ed., *The Nobel Prize Winners: Physiology or Medicine*, vol. 2, 1944–1969 (1991). Obituaries are in the *New York Times* and the *Washington Post*, both June 16, 1972.]

ERIC V. D. LUFT

BEMIS, SAMUEL FLAGG (Oct. 20, 1891–Sept. 26, 1973), historian, was born in Worcester, Mass., the son of Charles Harris Bemis, a journalist, and Flora M. Bemis. Considered the dean of American diplomatic historians in the years before his death, Bemis had a long and distinguished career as a scholar and teacher, principally at Yale University, in the middle third of the twentieth century. A prolific writer, he twice won the Pulitzer Prize for his books.

He was educated at Clark University in Worcester, where he earned a B.A. in 1912 and an M.A. in 1913, and at Harvard, where he completed a second M.A. in 1915 and a Ph.D. in 1916.

Bemis began his teaching career in 1917 as an instructor in history at Colorado College. His first book, an expanded version of his doctoral dissertation, *The United States and the Abortive Armed Neutrality of 1794*, appeared the next year. On June 20, 1919, he married Ruth M. Steele, with whom he had one child. In 1920 he moved on to Whitman College in Walla Walla, Wash., as a full professor. Three years later, his second book, *Jay's Treaty*, brought him a Knights of Columbus award of the then princely sum of $3,000, given annually to the college teacher who produces the best book on American history.

After a year as research associate at the Carnegie Institution in Washington, D.C., Bemis was appointed professor of history at George Washington University in 1924, remaining there for a decade. From 1927 to 1929 he directed the European Mission for the Library of Congress, an assignment designed to improve the library's collections. The job took him to the national archives of western and central Europe, where he arranged for the photocopying of documents relating to American diplomacy and, to a lesser extent, general American history. He was especially proud of this work, which as part of a larger effort mounted by Herbert Putnam and Worthington C. Ford after Word War I, at last made the Library of Congress, Bemis wrote, a "national library, [and] certainly the best place in the world to write about the diplomatic history of the United States." His own books were suffused with the archival research he conducted during summer vacations and on sabbatical in the great libraries and archives of England, France, Spain, and Latin America.

In 1927 Bemis won the Pulitzer Prize in history for *Pinckney's Treaty*. Over the next two years he directed the publication of the landmark, ten-volume series *The American Secretaries of State and Their Diplomacy*, acting both as editor and contributor, a role he repeated nearly forty years later when volumes XI–XV brought the series up to date (1963–1966). *The Hussey-Cumberland Mission and American Independence* was published in 1931. Four years later, Bemis collaborated with the bibliographer

Grace Gardner Griffin on *Guide to the Diplomatic History of the United States, 1775–1921*, which immediately became the standard reference in the field.

Bemis left George Washington University in 1934, first for a visiting lectureship at Harvard and then for Yale in 1935, where he taught for the next quarter century, ending his career as Sterling Professor of Diplomatic History and Inter-American Relations in 1960. During his first two years in New Haven he wrote two books, each of which extended his reputation for readability, stylistic clarity, and solid scholarship. *The Diplomacy of the American Revolution* addressed historical problems that had been virtually ignored since 1852 and quickly became the standard diplomatic monograph in colonial history courses nationwide. A *Diplomatic History of the United States*, published in 1936, went through multiple editions in the next thirty years as the course text in hundreds of colleges and secondary schools.

In the 1940's, Bemis turned his attention south of the border and wrote several works on Latin America, including *The Latin American Policy of the United States* (1943), a book that reflected both his careful research and his unbridled nationalism, particularly in his recurring emphasis on the "forbearance" of the American government in the face of what he believed was ineptitude or corruption on the part of particular Latin American regimes. Like many professional historians of his era, Bemis was unabashedly patriotic, with strong ties to the nation's past and especially to its values of democracy, constitutionalism, and justice. In assessing the motives of the American government in foreign affairs, he usually gave unqualified acceptance to the premise that they were generally good. Known affectionately as "Flaggwaver" or "American Flagg" Bemis, he defended himself by saying, "I wouldn't want to be called by any other flag."

He was a careful writer, whose graceful prose appealed to both an academic and a popular audience. *John Quincy Adams and the Foundations of American Foreign Policy* brought him the Pulitzer Prize for biography in 1950. Its successor volume, *John Quincy Adams and the Union*, found a wide readership and critical praise in 1956. In all, Bemis wrote or edited nearly thirty volumes. He was, an admiring colleague wrote, a "historians' historian."

On his mandatory retirement in 1960 at age

sixty-eight, under faculty policies then in force at Yale, he was given emeritus status but was asked to continue as a graduate school lecturer in foreign policy for another year. In 1961 he served as president of the American Historical Association and simultaneously held a Guggenheim Fellowship. Two years later, Yale made him a doctor of humane letters and in its citation acknowledged his "perdurable wisdom" and "Worcester County wit" as hallmarks of his teaching. Although he once told an interviewer that he was "as cold as potato salad," he was a highly respected figure on the New Haven campus. On his retirement, the undergraduate paper, the *Yale Daily News*, praised both his warmth and the concern he had shown for his students over the years. Bemis died at his home in Bridgeport, Conn.

[Bemis's papers and research library were purchased by the Harry S. Truman Library and Institute in Independence, Mo. His last book, *American Foreign Policy and the Blessings of Liberty, and Other Essays*, was published in 1962. There is no biography. An obituary appears in the *New York Times*, Sept. 28, 1973.]

ALLAN L. DAMON

BENNETT, EARL W. (Jan. 18, 1880–Sept. 18, 1973), industrialist, was born in White Cloud, Mich. His father was superintendent of supplies for a lumber company in Grand Rapids, Mich. The family moved to North Carolina in 1896 when the father was transferred to a mining operation in that state. Bennett took a job as a lumber camp cook at $50 per month for ten months in order to earn money for business school. He attended the Bryant and Stratton School in Chicago and finished its two-year program in nine months. He went to work at the mail-order department of Marshall Field in Chicago at $5 per week, gaining experience in all of the company's departments over a three-year period by threatening to resign if he were not transferred.

In 1900, homesick and unable to afford a trip to North Carolina, Bennett visited his grandmother in Midland, Mich. While there, he applied for a position with the three-year-old Dow Chemical Company and was hired by the company's founder, Herbert Dow, as an apprentice bookkeeper and office boy. His responsibilities included bookkeeping, picking up mail, and occasionally sweeping out the office. In 1902, he

was named company auditor, and by 1907 he had risen to the post of assistant treasurer and assistant secretary, earning $1,800. In 1905, he married Eva Barclay; they had eight children.

At Dow, Bennett became one of a senior management team of four executives under Herbert Dow. Dow ran the company informally, spending much of his time in its laboratories and supervising production. Bennett became, in effect, the chief financial officer of the corporation. In 1915, the board of directors of Dow Chemical arranged to sell the company to a syndicate of buyers. Before Christmas, Dow and his four senior executives traveled to Cleveland to discuss the offer. Dow told his management team that he would not oppose the sale but would not remain associated with the company. Bennett was the first to announce that he, too, would leave the company and follow Dow. The other three followed suit. With the prospect of losing the five top people in the company, the syndicate abandoned its plan to acquire Dow Chemical.

Dow prospered during World War I, but peace brought unique problems, among them the settlement of claims against the government for production facilities that had been built to meet war needs. Bennett convinced Dow that the company should settle the claims quickly, even if it received less money, in order to close down unnecessary operations and return to peacetime production. His instincts proved correct, and after the war Dow Chemical prospered.

Elected to the Dow board of directors in 1925, Bennett held all of the responsibilities of the corporate treasurer, although the title was held by J. C. Crider, a stockholder. Bennett was named a vice-president of the company in 1931 and became treasurer in 1934.

During the mid-1930's, Bennett perceived that Dow Chemical would one day require more financing than was available to the company from Cleveland banks. He began visiting New York City in order to introduce himself to bankers and investment houses. Although many ignored this small man from the Midwest—he was five feet, six inches tall and weighed 110 pounds—he began a relationship with the investment banking firm of Smith, Barney that would last for years.

Bennett had a profound impact on the development of styrene, a material that was used in making synthetic rubber during World War II.

Willard Dow, son of the founder, who became the head of Dow following the death of his father in 1930, decided in the mid-1930's to end research on styrene, believing it would remain a fruitless quest. The chemists working on the project approached Bennett, who told them he would set up a special account for them if they renamed the project, permitting research to continue until the Dow chemists were successful.

In 1941, Bennett, other executives, and the company were accused by the federal government of a conspiracy to control magnesium production. Willard Dow freely acknowledged that his company had a monopoly, but contended that it was the company's production methods, not a conspiracy, that had led to its monopoly position. The case was never brought to trial.

The next year, Dow Chemical embarked on its first foreign venture, working with the Canadian government to manufacture synthetic rubber. Bennett was named to the board of directors of Dow Chemical of Canada.

Bennett was instrumental in providing the capital that enabled Dow to continue to expand following World War II. In 1947, he arranged $105 million in financing through debentures, preferred stock, and private financing. Five years later he devised a financing plan to raise $100 million in subordinated debentures, in effect unsecured loans. The sale of the debentures was handled by Smith, Barney.

Following the death of Willard Dow in 1949, Bennett was elected chairman of the board of Dow Chemical, a position he held until 1960. At that time, he was named honorary chairman for life. (In 1959, his son, Robert, was named treasurer of Dow Chemical.) Bennett stepped down from the company's executive committee in the summer of 1962 and left the board in 1969. He had been associated with the company for sixty-nine years. He died in Midland, Mich.

[Bennett's papers are in the archives of Dow Chemical, Post Street Archives, Midland, Mich. Details of his career are included in Don Whitehead, *The Dow Story* (1968). Obituaries are in the *Midland* (Mich.) *Journal*, Sept. 19, 1973; and the *New York Times*, Sept. 20, 1973.]

RICHARD CONIGLIONE

BENNY, JACK (Feb. 14, 1894–Dec. 26, 1974), comedian and actor, was born Benjamin

Kubelsky in Chicago, Ill., the son of Meyer Kubelsky and Emma Sachs. The family lived in suburban Waukegan, Ill., north of Chicago, where his father was at various times a peddler of household goods, the owner of a tavern, and finally a haberdasher. Benny had one sister.

Never a good student—he was expelled from Central High School in Waukegan after attending for only one term—Benny demonstrated an early interest in show business. For a while, as a very young child, he was considered something of a violin prodigy. At age seventeen, he was a violinist in the pit orchestra at Waukegan's leading vaudeville house. In 1912, with his parents' consent, he left home to become half of a touring piano-and-violin act with Cora Salisbury, a forty-five-year-old widow. After two seasons he joined another musical act, touring vaudeville houses across the country for five years.

The name "Jack Benny" evolved after several false starts. When an established violinist named Jan Kubelik claimed that a violinist named Kubelsky might be mistaken for him, Benny decided to call himself Ben K. Benny. Later, he was obliged to change his name once again, this time to Jack Benny, when entertainer Ben Bernie claimed that the names were too similar.

In 1917, Benny and his partner, Lyman Woods, brought their act to the prestigious Palace Theater in New York City, but they were indifferently received. After one year in the U.S. Navy, during which time he began adding jokes to his musical performance, Benny went solo, at first offering what he called "Fiddle Funology" and then, as he phased out his violin-playing, billing himself as the "Aristocrat of Humor." By the end of the 1920's he had established a national reputation as a master of ceremonies and monologist.

On Jan. 14, 1927, Benny married Sadie Marks, a young woman he had met six years earlier but scarcely remembered from that time. Later she changed her name to Mary Livingstone and became an integral part of his radio family. They had one child.

In 1928, Benny made a one-reel comedy called *Bright Moments*, in which he appeared with his wife, who was billed as Marie Marsh. The following year, he signed a contract with Metro-Goldwyn-Mayer (MGM) and starred in several musical films. He was the master of ceremonies for MGM's lavish, all-star *Hollywood Revue of 1929*. Benny's other movies made at the time, some for studios other than MGM, were inconsequential. He also returned briefly to the theater to star in a new edition of Earl Carroll's *Vanities* (1930).

It was in radio that Benny made his most indelible mark. After appearing as a guest on Ed Sullivan's radio program in 1931, he was given his first network show, which premiered on May 2, 1932, under the sponsorship of Canada Dry Ginger Ale. From that point on, although his sponsors changed—Jell-O held the franchise for eight consecutive seasons, beginning in 1934— Benny built a solid career as one of the country's most popular radio comedians. Aided by a team of talented writers, including Bill Morrow, Ed Beloin, Milt Josefsberg, and Hilliard Marks, and a group of expert supporting players, he created the character Jack Benny who endured for decades.

Amazingly, this character was constructed almost entirely of negative qualities. The Benny whom radio audiences came to know and love was a vain, stingy, overconfident man who was the target of everyone's jokes and quips. Perennially aged thirty-nine, he fancied himself a ladies' man and bon vivant, yet he was constantly mocked or snubbed by women. On the show he cultivated the friendship of such distinguished actors as Ronald Colman and James Stewart, who disliked him and tried to avoid him. (In real life they were good friends.) His parsimony was legendary—he insisted on driving an antique Maxwell car and kept his money in a vault deep in the subbasement of his house. Nevertheless, he won the affection and loyalty of his listeners, who recognized many of the same qualities in themselves. In the days before television, Benny could, with a pause, an inflection, or a single line, evoke gales of laughter and waves of sympathy for this foolish, self-important, but lovable man. "Timing," he wrote, "is not so much knowing when to speak, but when to pause." In perhaps his most memorable routine, a thief approached him with a gun and demanded his money or his life. After a lengthy pause that generated spiraling laughter, Benny replied, "I'm thinking it over!"

Benny was especially fortunate in the actors who made up his radio family. Genial announcer Don Wilson joined early in the run, and on another early show, his wife, Sadie, became Mary Livingstone, a friend of Benny's whose wry, sarcastic comments on his shortcomings delighted listeners and kept her a permanent fixture on the show for twenty years. Bandleader Phil Harris joined the cast in 1936, playing the hard-drinking, happy-go-lucky braggart and know-it-all in charge of an equally disreputable group of musicians. Black actor Eddie Anderson turned up the following year as Benny's long-suffering but wily valet, Rochester. Ill-paid and overworked, but never ill-treated, Rochester became one of the show's most endearing characters, slyly managing to beat or put down his employer on many occasions. (After 1945, at a time when America was becoming more socially conscious, jokes about Rochester that might be construed as racist were eliminated.)

A permanent feature of Benny's radio show was the young singer who performed at least one song on each program. Tenors Frank Parker, James Melton, Kenny Baker, and Dennis Day were among those who filled this role at various times, but it was Day who had the longest engagement, not only singing but also playing the naive, none-too-bright "kid" whose domineering mother, in the voice of Verna Felton, always had something disparaging to say about Benny.

Over the years, Benny hired a number of talented actors who created characters that are now part of radio folklore. Among them was Mel Blanc, whose repertoire of voices and accents included such characters as Benny's put-upon violin teacher, Professor LeBlanc, and a monosyllabic Mexican named Sy. (He also voiced Benny's sputtering Maxwell.) Other favorite performers included Frank Nelson, who, whatever the character, always greeted Benny with a supercilious "Yes-s-s-s?"; Artie Auerbach, creator of Mr. Kitzel, a peddler who, among other things, hawked frankfurters in his Yiddish-flavored dialect ("de peekle een de meedle and de mustard on top!"), and Sheldon Leonard as the racetrack tout, ready to offer Benny advice or odds on anything. Many other actors, including Sam Hearn, Bea Benaderet, Elliot Lewis, and Sandra Gould, contributed to the show over its long run.

One of the best-remembered features of Benny's radio shows was his long-standing "feud" with comedian Fred Allen. The "feud," in which the two traded angry barbs and insults, began in 1936 and attracted such attention that it continued for ten weeks and resurfaced periodically for many more years. Allen, noted for his biting wit, enjoyed feigning hostility toward a friend he admired greatly. The "feud" was even the basis for a 1940 movie called *Love Thy Neighbor*, starring Benny and Allen.

Benny worked assiduously on each of his radio programs, broadcast on Sunday night at 7 P.M. for many years. During World War II, he spent his summers away from the show touring military bases all over the world. In 1948, he moved from NBC to CBS. Two years later, on Oct. 28, 1950, the inevitable occurred: Benny launched his show on television, bringing with him most of the performers who had served him so well on radio. His appearance matched his radio persona: tall and handsome, with a bemused or exasperated expression on his face, he would stride onstage in an assured, slightly effeminate manner that was popular with impressionists. No longer needing to rely on pauses and vocal inflections, he could now use such visual devices as the pained look directly into the camera or the hand-to-cheek pose to express exasperation. The character of Jack Benny was as vain and stingy as ever, and now that he was visible, viewers were no less generous in their affection for him. The true-life Benny was, in fact, a philanthropic, self-effacing man, widely loved by everyone; but audiences continued to believe in his radio-television persona. His radio program continued until 1955, and his television show appeared on a regular basis until 1965.

Although his screechy violin playing was the target of innumerable jokes, Benny was actually a competent violinist. In October 1956, he gave a violin concert at Carnegie Hall in New York City, performing with the New York Philharmonic Orchestra at the suggestion of violinist Isaac Stern. From then on, he played at benefit concerts with nearly every major symphony orchestra in the United States and Canada, as well as abroad. In all his concerts, he balanced comedy and music in felicitous proportions.

Benny's career was dominated by his work in radio and television, yet he also made a number of films over the years. In the 1930's he appeared in such musicals as *Broadway Melody of 1936* (1935), *The Big Broadcast of 1937* (1936), and *College Holiday* (1936). A peak came in 1942 when he costarred with Carole Lombard in Ernst Lubitsch's stinging black comedy *To Be or Not to Be*. As a vain Polish actor whose theater troupe is put out of business by invading Nazis, Benny gave a richly comic performance. Other of his 1940's movies include *Charley's*

Aunt (1941), *George Washington Slept Here* (1942), and *The Horn Blows at Midnight* (1945), which he mocked repeatedly as the nadir of his film career. His movie appearances in subsequent decades were sporadic—most often he was a guest star or unbilled walk-on in films throughout the 1950's and 1960's.

Benny remained active until the end of his life, performing at music-and-comedy concerts or appearing as a guest on television talk shows. In 1959, a junior high school in Waukegan was named in his honor, and in 1968 he donated all of his memorabilia to the University of California at Los Angeles. He died in Holmby Hills, Calif., and was buried in Hillside Cemetery in Los Angeles. He retained to the end his persona of a man who, for all of his human frailties, was dearly loved by the American people.

[*Sunday Nights at Seven*, Benny's autobiography, published posthumously (1990), includes extensive personal material contributed by his daughter, Joan. Books on Benny include Irving Fein, *Jack Benny* (1976); Milt Josefsberg, *The Jack Benny Show* (1977); and Mary Livingstone Benny and Hilliard Marks, with Marcia Borie, *Jack Benny* (1978). An obituary is in the *New York Times*, Dec. 27, 1974.]

TED SENNETT

BENSON, SALLY (Sept. 3, 1900–July 19, 1972), writer, was born Sara Mahala Redway Smith in St. Louis, Mo., the daughter of Alonzo Redway Smith, a cotton broker, and Anna Prophater. The family moved to New York City when she was eleven, and she graduated from Horace Mann High School in the Bronx six years later. She was not a good student and had no interest in college, so she began working at National City Bank, first "singing into dictaphones" and then as a foreign exchange bank teller. At age nineteen, she met and married Reynolds Benson, athletics manager at Columbia University. They had one child and were later divorced.

Her writing career began with a job interviewing minor celebrities in the arts for the *New York Morning Telegraph*. She also reviewed books and movies, often at a rate of one per day. In 1930, Benson wrote her first piece of fiction, a short story called "Apartment Hotel." Starting at the top, she sold it to the *New Yorker*, which asked for more stories. From that beginning, the magazine accepted all but one of the stories she submitted. The one they refused, "The

Overcoat," was published by *American Mercury* and became an O. Henry prize story for 1935. Her long association with the *New Yorker* was due in part to the editor's appreciation of her writing style, with its sophisticated wit and "venomous satire on human foibles," and to her claim that she hadn't tried other markets. "My style fits here and it wouldn't most places," she said.

She also wrote stories under the pseudonym "Esther Evarts" and specialized in reviews of mystery stories for the *New Yorker*. Her preference for mysteries, she once explained, arose from her liking for "straight history over historical novels" as well as her dislike for certain authors. "Why must all the men novelists get so damned virile, so chest-out, shoulders back, here-we-come, girls, as soon as they hit a success? Why must they go trucking all over the world and slaver with delight at wars?" In this conversation with interviewer Robert Van Gelner, Benson did not specify which novelists she was indicting, but she did exclude William Faulkner and W. Somerset Maugham from the blanket criticism.

As for Benson's own work, her stories have been characterized as pithy, concise, ruthless satire, "revealing the mediocrity of self-deluded and self-indulgent characters," and "exposing a society which fosters useless lives by its role expectations," yet with a warmth and compassion that tempers the sharp edges. A rapid writer (her first draft was her final draft), Benson wrote many of her stories in less than three hours.

Her first short-story collection, *People Are Fascinating*, was published in 1936, followed by *Emily* in 1938. A retelling of Greek mythology, *Stories of the Gods and Heroes*, came out in 1940. In 1941, her most famous group of stories, *Junior Miss*, about the "troubles, trials and foibles" of twelve-year-old Judy Graves, was a Book-of-the-Month Club selection, acclaimed as a fine example of a young girl's "rites of passage" and recommended for young readers everywhere. Yet the book is filled with the wry anguish of growing up and despite its title is a rewarding work to read for adults. It was dramatized for Broadway by Jerome Chodorov and Joseph Fields and later became a national radio series, with scripts written by Benson. Subsequently, *Junior Miss* was also made into a movie and a television musical.

Meet Me in St. Louis, a selection of stories that appeared in the *New Yorker* as "5135 Kens-

ington," was based on Benson's sister's diary about family life in St. Louis at the time of the World's Fair in 1904. These largely autobiographical sketches were picked up by Metro-Goldwyn-Mayer to be made into a charming musical box-office hit starring Judy Garland. While Benson was at the studio working on the screen treatment, she assembled the stories into novel form, and the book was published in 1942, followed quickly by *Shadow of a Doubt* (1942) and *Women and Children First* (1943).

Following the success of *Meet Me in St. Louis*, Benson wrote scripts for a number of films, including *Shadow of a Doubt* (1943), *Experiment Perilous* (1944), *National Velvet* (1944), *Anna and the King of Siam* (1946), *Come to the Stable* (1949), *No Man of Her Own* (1950), *Conspirator* (1950), *The Belle of New York* (1952), *The Farmer Takes a Wife* (1953), *The Adventures of Huckleberry Finn* (1960), *Bus Stop* (1961), *Summer Magic* (1962), *Viva Las Vegas* (1963), *Signpost to Murder* (1963), and *The Singing Nun* (1966). Her screenplay for *Anna and the King of Siam* was nominated for an Academy Award in 1946.

Benson's playwrighting credits include *Seventeen* (adapted from the novel by Booth Tarkington, 1954) and *The Young and the Beautiful* (based on F. Scott Fitzgerald's "Josephine" stories in the *Saturday Evening Post*, 1956). She also wrote scripts for television, including a "DuPont Show of the Month" episode in 1957 and an adaptation of *Hans Brinker* for "Hallmark Hall of Fame."

Benson died in Woodland Hills, Calif.

[For biographical information see the interview with Robert Van Gelder, *Writers and Writing* (1946). See also Mary Anne Ferguson, "Sally Benson," in Lina Mainiero, ed., *American Women Writers* (1979); and Hugh Fordin, *The Movies' Greatest Musicals* (1984). Obituaries appear in the *New York Times*, July 22, 1972; and *Newsweek*, July 31, 1972.]

DOROTHY S. ("DOREY") SCHMIDT

BENTON, THOMAS HART (Apr. 15, 1889–Jan. 19, 1975), artist and author, was born in Neosho, Mo., the eldest son of Maecenas E. Benton, a lawyer, and Elizabeth Wise. His namesake and great-uncle was Thomas Hart Benton, renowned U.S. senator and writer. Benton's father was a Confederate army veteran who served five terms in the U.S. House of

Representatives. Young Benton attended grade school in Washington, D.C., but returned to Missouri when his father was defeated for re-election; he graduated from Neosho High School in 1905.

His father was determined that Benton should follow family tradition and become a lawyer, but Benton—who had been sketching locomotives and Indians from his earliest years— persuaded his family to accept his desired career in art. A chance encounter led to a job as staff artist for the *Joplin* (Mo.) *American*, a position he left to study at the Chicago Art Institute for more than a year with his father's consent and financial support.

Impatient and uncertain of his artistic abilities, Benton left America in August 1908 for study at the Académie Julien in Paris. There he met many other aspiring artists and sculptors, among them Diego Rivera, Jacob Epstein, Jo Davidson, and Leon Kroll. Benton was influenced by the work of Cézanne and Manet, and he was fascinated by the work of El Greco, but he sold few paintings. In his free time he read a great deal; he was particularly influenced by Hippolyte Taine's *Philosophie de l'Art*. He left France after three years, still lacking a distinctive painting style. Back home in Missouri, Benton missed the pace of city life, though, and he soon moved to New York City, where he found cramped living quarters. There, from 1912 until 1916, he experimented with color styling and was attracted to synchromist ("with color and sound") theories.

In the spring of 1916 he began work at a film studio at Fort Lee, N.J., where he earned a living painting posters and designing sets for motion picture companies; he also tried his hand as a film actor. He taught art for a New York City neighborhood association in 1917, when he met Rita Piacenza, whom he would marry in 1922; the couple had two children. After a brief stint in the navy during World War I, Benton continued teaching and developed a friendship with Thomas Craven, an outspoken critic of contemporary art. Craven encouraged Benton to drop European ideas and styles in favor of American themes that would accentuate local experiences. Benton visited Martha's Vineyard, Mass., in 1920; the island became his summer retreat, where he began to paint with more confidence and vigor. There Benton began to develop his realistic style and to experiment with the role of colors in convey-

ing artistic ideas. Benton's painting, *The Lord Is My Shepherd*, completed in 1926, marked his emerging vibrant style, at the center of which were images of ordinary people farming, loving, and praying.

The 1920's were a busy time for Benton. Besides the annual summer trek to his seaside studio, Benton undertook long journeys by bus, train, and car that carried him, sketchbook in hand, to steel mills, cotton gins, oil fields, and grain elevators. Thereafter his work glorified simple themes depicting Americans hard at work and play, and it linked Benton with fellow artists Grant Wood and John Steuart Curry as American folk painters of an emerging "regional" school. He also flirted with Communism and became something of an iconoclast, with subjects ranging from southwestern boomtowns to cotton bales aboard steamboats on the Mississippi River.

Benton experimented while he taught at the Art Students League in New York City (where Jackson Pollock was his student), and the heroic-sized murals he devoted himself to had an innovative, three-dimensional character melding an energetic style with popular themes. His mural at the New School for Social Research in New York City, *Modern America* (1931), was the first large-scale mural executed with egg tempera in the United States. More mural commissions followed, ranging from the Whitney Museum to the Missouri State Capitol, usually with historical and sometimes unconventional themes.

He began teaching at the Kansas City Art Institute in 1935; while there, he found time to write his autobiography, *An Artist in America*, in 1937. Two paintings of nudes (*Susanna and the Elders* and *Persephone*) provoked critical free-for-alls in 1938–1939. Undaunted by critics, Benton shocked art patrons by saying he wanted his works displayed not in museums but "in privies or anywhere anybody had time to look at 'em." After a furor in art circles, Benton was dismissed from the staff of the Kansas City Art Institute in 1941, but he continued to live in Kansas City.

By this time, though, Benton had become a thoroughly established artist, and he was able to choose from a variety of commissions, including even book illustrations. With the advent of World War II his subject matter became decidedly grim, and his realism came under increasing attack from critics of the regional school.

Benton, mellowed by age, nevertheless kept busy with important commissions; at the age of seventy-one, he undertook a mural for the Harry S. Truman Library. He then painted a portrait of President Truman that showed he had lost none of his artistic talent (Truman called Benton "the best damned painter in America"). His productivity slowed after a heart attack in 1966. He was working on a mural depicting the sources of country music when he died in Kansas City.

[A number of paintings by Benton are held by the Benton Testamentary Trust, United Missouri Bank of Kansas City. His autobiography, *An Artist in America* (4th ed., 1983), is full of zest and tells a romanticized history down to 1937 with additional chapters added to later editions. Many of his writings appear in Matthew Baigell, ed., *A Thomas Hart Benton Miscellany* (1971). See also Polly Burroughs, *Thomas Hart Benton: A Portrait* (1981); R. D. Hurt and Mary K. Dains, eds., *Thomas Hart Benton: Artist, Writer and Intellectual* (1989); and Erika Doss, *Benton, Pollock, and the Politics of Modernism* (1991). An obituary is in the *New York Times*, Jan. 21, 1975.]

ROBERT A. RUTLAND

BENTON, WILLIAM BURNETT (Apr. 1, 1900–Mar. 18, 1973), advertising executive, publisher, and United States senator, was born in Minneapolis, the son of Charles William Benton and Elma Caroline Hixson. His family had a tradition of intellectual achievement; ancestors on both sides had been New England clergymen and teachers. After the death of his father in 1913 Benton received a scholarship to the Shattuck Military Academy in Faribault, Minn., from which he graduated in 1917. He studied at Carleton College the following year, served in the Student Army Training Corps during World War I, then entered Yale University, where he became chairman of the board of the *Yale Record*, a humor periodical. He graduated in 1921 and was awarded a Rhodes Scholarship, which he declined in order to pursue a business career.

Drawn to the world of advertising after having worked little more than a year at the National Cash Register Company, he found employment first at the New York City office of Lord and Thomas and soon thereafter at the George Batten Company. Assigned to the trade paper branch, he transformed what was then considered a dull and largely unprofitable mar-

ket into a lucrative field. Because he insistently and astutely urged that the Batten agency merge with Barton, Durstine, and Osborne, uniting their respective strengths in copywriting and client solicitation, he was fired, precipitating a crisis that brought about the merger two months later. For more than a year he again worked for Lord and Thomas, this time in Chicago, earning a salary of $25,000 when he resigned to open his own firm in 1929.

With Chester Bowles, a fellow Yale graduate and future governor of Connecticut, he opened the Benton and Bowles agency in July 1929. The young partners brought fresh ideas to the advertising world, including introduction of consumer research and use of the new medium of radio advertising. Concentrating on food and drug accounts such as General Foods and Bristol Myers, the agency prospered; by 1935 Benton's income had risen to $250,000. At the end of the year he retired, he said, "to search after that ever elusive perspective on oneself."

University of Chicago president Robert Maynard Hutchins, a Yale classmate, persuaded the young retiree to join the university to work on public relations and fund-raising. The university's innovative atmosphere under Hutchins's leadership captured Benton's imagination. From 1937 to 1945 he was part-time vice-president, becoming a trustee in 1946 after he left the institution. Benton placated two influential critics of the university, Charles Walgreen, the drug store magnate, and Robert McCormick, publisher of the *Chicago Tribune*. Each had leveled charges of radicalism against the faculty.

Widening the university's reach through radio, motion pictures, and publication engaged Benton's attention. He transformed the University of Chicago Round Table, a Sunday program of academic discussion, into a highly popular radio broadcast. He persuaded reluctant university trustees to acquire the *Encyclopaedia Britannica* only after he agreed to invest $100,000 of his own money as working capital, the university to own all the preferred stock, Benton the common. In 1943 he became owner, publisher, and chairman of the board of the *Britannica*. He established its first board of editors and set about making the work a means of education as well as a reference set. For years he had believed educational films to be "perhaps the most striking opportunity for public service in the field of education today." As owner of the *Britannica* he bought ERPI, a faltering educational film project of Eastman Kodak Company, and converted it into Encyclopaedia Britannica Films, Inc., the largest producer and distributor of educational films. In 1939 he acquired the Muzak Corporation, presciently envisioning expansion of its musical programs beyond restaurants and hotels to offices, department stores, hospitals and other markets. Nearly twenty years later Benton sold Muzak at a net profit to himself of over $4 million.

Public affairs and politics from his early years held Benton's interest. In 1942 he helped found the Committee for Economic Development (CED), a nonprofit organization; and as vice-president insisted that it, in addition to preparing businessmen for postwar opportunities, develop a research base. His work with the CED enlarged an already broad acquaintance with business leaders and his understanding of foreign relations. In September 1945 President Truman appointed him assistant secretary of state for public affairs, with duties involving consolidating wartime information agencies under the State Department and starting a peacetime information program.

In his new public role Benton struggled with foreign service bureaucrats to win passage of the Foreign Service Act of 1946. He worked with Congress and newspaper networks to maintain a postwar information service and strengthen the Voice of America, which broadcast news of the United States to foreign countries. He helped push through the Fulbright Act and was instrumental in establishing the United Nations Educational, Scientific, and Cultural Organization (UNESCO). In September 1947, following enactment of the Smith-Mundt bill giving legislative sanction to his program, he resigned.

During the next two years Benton rescued the *Britannica* from financial troubles and headed State Department delegations to the UNESCO conference in Mexico City and a conference on freedom of information and the press in Geneva. Following the resignation of Raymond Baldwin from the United States Senate, Chester Bowles, now governor of Connecticut, in 1949 appointed Benton to fill the vacancy, which involved standing for election in 1950 to complete the unexpired term. That year he defeated the Republican candidate, Prescott Bush, by a margin of 1,102 votes.

In the Senate Benton was assigned to the Committee on Government Operations and the Rules Committee. He ordinarily supported President Truman, except for a vote he later deeply regretted in favor of the McCarran Internal Security Act. The next year he vigorously opposed the McCarran-Walter immigration act. On Aug. 6, 1951, in a climate of national hysteria following Senator Joseph McCarthy's charges of Communist influence in the State Department, he called for McCarthy's resignation from the Senate.

Early in life Benton had identified himself as an independent in politics; now a Democrat he sought to persuade General Dwight D. Eisenhower to run for president on the Democratic ticket. Eisenhower's eventual race on the Republican ticket, perhaps more than McCarthy's intervention in the Connecticut campaign, in 1952 cost Benton election to a full term. Benton was a member of the platform committee in 1952 and every subsequent election year except 1960 until his death.

Out of public office at the age of fifty-two, Benton devoted himself to publication of the "Great Books of the Western World," expansion of *Britannica* interests including purchase of Compton's Pictured Encyclopedia, the G. C. Merriam Company, publisher of Webster's dictionaries, and Frederick B. Praeger, Inc. He participated in numerous public interest groups, serving on boards and winning many honors. He wrote three insightful books following visits abroad: *This Is the Challenge* (1958), published shortly after the public's discovery of Soviet expertise in science and technology; *The Voice of Latin America* (1961), urging inter-American cooperation; and *The Teachers and the Taught* (1966), describing Soviet continuing progress in education. From 1963 to 1968 he served as ambassador to UNESCO in Paris.

Benton died in New York City, survived by his wife, Helen Hemingway, whom he had married June 12, 1928, and four children.

[The offices of the *Encyclopaedia Britannica* and D'Arcy Masius Benton & Bowles have biographical material. Sidney Hyman, *The Lives of William Benton* (1969), is a full account up to the time of its writing. An obituary is in the *New York Times*, Mar. 19, 1973.]

JAMES A. RAWLEY

BERG, MORRIS ("MOE") (Mar. 2, 1902– May 30, 1972), baseball player, espionage agent, and linguist, was born in New York City and raised in Newark, N.J., the son of Bernard Berg, a pharmacist, and Rose Tashker. His brother, Dr. Samuel Berg, on military assignment in Nagasaki six weeks after the dropping of the atomic bomb, authored the first study of the effects of radioactive fallout on humans.

Moe Berg played with five major league baseball teams over a sixteen-year period (1923, 1926–1939). His baseball talents were not of the first rank; he was considered a strong defensive player as a catcher, a modestly effective batter, and a woefully slow base runner. He played a utility role throughout most of his career (only once, in 1929, did he appear in more than one hundred games). He was ideally suited to function as a late-inning defensive replacement, an occasional pinch hitter, and a brainy presence in the dugout and the bullpen. A consummate team player, Berg understood that his prime contribution had to do with preparing younger, more gifted teammates for on-the-field successes. Berg, a contemporary of many of baseball's greatest and larger-than-life performers, was described by no less an authority than Casey Stengel as the "strangest fellah who ever put on a uniform."

Berg's background was atypical for a baseball player. A magna cum laude graduate of Princeton University in 1923, he demonstrated facility in French, German, Italian, Latin, classical Greek, and Sanskrit. (It was humorously said of him that he was fluent in a dozen languages but couldn't hit in any of them.) A star shortstop on the Princeton baseball team, Berg attracted the attention of major league scouts and upon graduation faced an intriguing dilemma: should he sign a contract to play for the Brooklyn Dodgers, attend the Sorbonne to study experimental phonetics and philosophy, or accept a teaching position at Princeton? He opted for the former and made his major league debut in 1923. Early success was followed by a disappointing lack of hitting, and Berg was demoted to the minor leagues. He resurfaced with the Chicago White Sox in 1926. Within a year, he was made a catcher; this move enabled him to have a steady, if unspectacular, major league career.

Berg's academic bent did not prevent him from reveling in the camaraderie of the dugout, the bullpen, and the clubhouse. One teammate commented, "We'd all sit around and listen to him discuss the Greeks, Romans, Japanese, anything. Hell, we didn't know what he was talking about, but it sure sounded good." Ted Lyons, Hall of Fame pitcher and frequent batterymate of Berg's, said, "He was different because he was different. He made up for all the bores in the world. He did it softly, stepping on no one." Berg made it clear throughout his life that his commitment to baseball, which some considered a waste of his other considerable talents, was absolutely correct for him. "It's my theater," he would say.

Berg pursued his academic interests diligently. He attended Columbia Law School in the off-seasons, was admitted to the New York State Bar in 1929, and practiced law in the off-seasons in New York City. He voraciously read newspapers from around the world and accumulated a large personal library. He numbered scholars, diplomats, and entertainers among his acquaintances. (Will Rogers, the humorist, would greet his old friend by saying, "Moe, let's paint the town pink. Let's step out tonight with two exciting verbs.") In 1938 when Berg appeared on the nationally syndicated radio program "Information Please," his stunning breadth of knowledge resulted in the National Broadcasting Company receiving 10,000 phone calls from listeners wanting to know more about him. He became one of baseball's finest ambassadors and wrote a superb article for the *Atlantic Monthly* in September 1941 titled "Pitchers and Catchers," which delineates the cat-and-mouse game played out by pitcher, catcher, and batter. Berg described the catcher as "the Cerberus of baseball."

Berg was interested in foreign cultures and spent several off-seasons traveling in Europe and Asia. He was deeply interested in the Japanese and taught himself the language. He visited Japan twice, in 1932 and 1934, with fellow major leaguers to promote baseball via instruction and exhibition games. Berg carried with him a letter of introduction to the American embassy signed by Cordell Hull, secretary of state under Franklin D. Roosevelt. Evidently, Berg took some opportunities to film the sites of Japanese factories, munitions plants, harbors, refineries, and railroad yards. The film was used during the planning for 1942 bombing raids on Tokyo led by General Jimmy Doolittle.

With the outbreak of World War II, Berg actively solicited his friend, Nelson Rockefeller, the coordinator of the Office of Inter-American Affairs, to get him a position with that office. Berg retired from baseball and spent 1941 to

1943 as a roving goodwill ambassador in Latin America. He also reported on pro-Axis sentiment in Central and South America. Thus, when General William Donovan began recruiting operatives for the Office of Strategic Services, Berg was a natural choice given his proficiency with foreign languages, his excellent physical condition, his prior dealings in espionage, and his poise in high-pressure situations.

Documents released after World War II reveal that Berg was an operative of major importance in the European theater. He completed missions in France, Italy, Norway, Sweden, Switzerland, and Yugoslavia. The major thrust of his work had to do with determining what progress German scientists were making toward the successful manufacture of atomic weapons. Using a variety of disguises, including those of a German officer and a graduate student of physics, he also arranged for prominent European scientists to escape to the United States (about this, President Roosevelt said, "I see Berg is still catching pretty well."). In 1946, he was awarded the Medal of Merit, the highest honor given to civilians during wartime; he refused the award because he felt he was doing a citizen's duty and should not receive special recognition.

The postwar years did not treat Berg well. A failed business venture and difficulties with the Internal Revenue Service embittered him. Although he continued to perform occasional, minor espionage activity, he struck friends and acquaintances as increasingly eccentric. Never one to seek the stability of home (he shuttled between his brother's home and his sister's home, both in Newark, N.J.), marriage (he was a lifelong bachelor), or job, Berg seemed to rely for survival on a Gatsbyesque celebrity of anonymity: appearing out of nowhere at social, athletic, and academic events, dropping in on friends unannounced and staying on as a guest for weeks, reading and note-taking obsessively, and then vanishing for periods of time.

Baseball remained the sole anchor for Berg and he was a frequent presence at major league parks. In 1972, Berg aggravated an internal injury and entered a hospital. His last words were reported to have been, "How did the Mets do today?"

[Memorabilia, newspaper clippings, and correspondence are in the archives of the National Baseball Hall of Fame, Cooperstown, N.Y. A biography written by Louis Kaufman, Barbara Fitzgerald, and Tom Sewell, is *Moe Berg: Athlete, Scholar, Spy* (1975). See also Ethel Berg, *My Brother, Morris Berg* (1976); and Nicholas Dawidoff, "Scholar, Lawyer, Catcher, Spy," *Sports Illustrated*, Mar. 23, 1992. Berg's baseball statistics are in *The Baseball Encyclopedia*. An obituary appears in the *New York Times*, June 1, 1972.]

MICHAEL GILMARTIN

BERLE, ADOLF AUGUSTUS, JR. (Jan. 29, 1895–Feb. 17, 1971), public official and author, was born in Boston, Mass., the second of four children of Adolf Augustus Berle, a Congregational minister and author, and Mary Augusta Wright, a former missionary among the Sioux. Strongly influenced by his father's rigorous, innovative educational ideas, published as *The School in the Home* (1912), he graduated high school at age twelve, then had to wait two years before matriculating at Harvard. He graduated cum laude (1913). After earning an M.A. (1914), he obtained an LL.B. from the Harvard Law School (1916), becoming, according to his biographer, "the youngest graduate in its history."

Berle joined Louis D. Brandeis's law firm as an apprentice in 1916, enlisted in the army as a private the following year, and within two weeks became a second lieutenant. After a stint at the Army War College in Washington, D.C., he was assigned to the Dominican Republic on inactive duty in order to work for the New York law firm of Rounds, Hatch, Dillingham, and Debevoise, straightening out Dominican landholding laws. He also worked for army intelligence. In the fall of 1918, Berle was assigned to the Russian Section of the American delegation to the Paris Peace Conference.

Dissatisfied with the conference's anti-Bolshevik stance and with the peace treaty's harsh treatment of Germany, he resigned from the delegation in May 1919 but, as an army officer, had to wait a month to be demobilized.

Upon returning to New York, Berle joined the Rounds firm. In 1924 he and a friend established their own practice, Lippitt and Berle, and in 1933 he joined with his brother, Rudolf, to form the firm with which he practiced until his death. His specialties and those of the firms he helped organize were corporate law and Latin American affairs. Interested in teaching, the multifaceted Berle taught one day per week at the Harvard Business School (1925–1928). In 1927, he joined the faculty of Columbia

University's law school, which remained his "intellectual home" until he retired in 1966. Even while in government service he continued to hold classes there.

On Dec. 11, 1927, after a two-year courtship, Berle married Beatrice Bend Bishop, daughter of the elegant, tough-minded investor and book collector Cortlandt Field Bishop. Strongly opposed to the marriage, Bishop disinherited his daughter in 1928; ten years later she obtained her rightful portion of the estate through a lawsuit. She was a perfect consort for Berle: an intelligent, dynamic woman, she graduated from Vassar (1923), received an M.A. in history from Columbia (1924), earned an M.D. from New York University (1938), and practiced medicine for many years. The Berles had three children.

A prolific, innovative writer, Berle throughout his life produced a flood of articles, pamphlets, and reviews, many dealing with the changing nature of America's economy and power structure. His first article in the *Harvard Law Review* (1917) dealt with the then-new concept of administrative law. His first of more than a dozen works, *Studies in the Law of Corporation Finance* (1928), anthologized some of his work on aspects of the corporation. *The Modern Corporation and Private Property* (1932), written with the economist Gardiner C. Means, has been called "one of the most influential books of the twentieth century." At a time when the Great Depression had brought America's economy to a virtual standstill, Berle and Means argued cogently that the changed meaning of corporate ownership had resulted in a concentration of wealth and power divorced from stockholder or public control, and that to deal with large corporations, the American economy needed increased federal oversight and intervention.

Berle's espousal of increased state control made him a natural choice for the "brain trust" Franklin D. Roosevelt asked to advise him during the 1932 presidential election campaign. Berle—whose commitment to public service had involved him during the 1920's with New York City's Henry Street Settlement House and with the American Indian Aid Association, in an effort to restore their lands to the Navajos in New Mexico—became a close associate of Roosevelt. He drafted Roosevelt's 1932 Commonwealth Club speech, which historian Richard Hofstadter has described as "the most momentous of the campaign" because it indicated the drastic innovations the New Deal would undertake. The aggressive, arrogant, overbearing Berle's personal shortcomings were overlooked because of his brilliance and creativity. After Roosevelt's victory, Berle took no official post but did offer advice and comment on various pieces of legislation. He also served briefly as financial adviser to the American embassy in Havana, on Cuba's financial crisis.

Although without formal appointment, the contentious Berle remained a close adviser to the president, who cherished his "adventurous mind." Berle also advised Fiorello La Guardia in his successful bid for the mayoralty of New York City in 1933, subsequently serving (1934–1937) as city chamberlain. Characterized as "a brilliant prime minister without portfolio," Berle was involved in the rehabilitation of the city's finances, helping to draft the plan that ultimately would unify under public ownership New York's rapid-transit system, sketching out many of the mayor's speeches, assisting La Guardia's successful reelection campaign (made possible by the support of the New York–based, newly created American Labor party), and furthering the writing of a new city charter that, on adoption in 1937, abolished his office.

Finally succumbing to Roosevelt's blandishments, Berle in 1938 became assistant secretary of state for Latin American affairs. Initially the appointment had implications for domestic policy: a strong advocate of planning had been appointed at a time when antitrust sentiment was growing. But Berle concentrated on foreign affairs. Participating in various inter-American conferences, he took an active role in implementing the Good Neighbor policy and, after World War II broke out in 1939, successfully promoted "collective security in the hemisphere." He also laid the groundwork for the postwar development of the St. Lawrence Seaway, negotiated with Allied governments in exile, penned drafts of government statements on the international situation, and in 1944 chaired an international conference that helped set the course of postwar civil aviation worldwide. As administrator of State Department intelligence, Berle met with former Communist agent Whittaker Chambers (1939); the anti-Soviet Berle, however, did not react to Chambers's tales of subversion by Alger Hiss and others; indeed, he did not turn over Chambers's information to the FBI until 1941.

Berle did not escape the bitter internal strife that rent the State Department in the early 1940's. Moreover, his ties with Roosevelt grew weaker as the president made increased use of other advisers. Berle had been valued for his superior intellect and superb analytical skills, but in 1944 he was forced to resign, having used up his political capital. He then served as ambassador to Brazil (1945–1946).

Berle returned to his law practice and teaching, with various forays into public service. As chairman (1947–1955) of New York's newly organized Liberal party (a breakaway from the now Communist-dominated American Labor party), Berle was an effective spokesman, but policy generally was set by the garment unions, which financially supported the new party. The staunchly anti-Soviet Berle was in contact with the Central Intelligence Agency, and while his influence was limited, during the early 1950's he was active in such agency "fronts" as Radio Free Europe and the National Committee for a Free Europe. He chaired the board of trustees of the Twentieth Century Fund (1951–1971), seeking "to influence American development toward a more effectively just civilization."

Berle's writing commanded respect and attention until his death in New York City, but his impact lessened over time. His continuing interest in hemispheric problems and involvement with democratic Latin American intellectuals and political figures led to service as chairman of President John F. Kennedy's Interdepartmental Task Force on Latin America (January–July 1961). Its recommendations resulted in the Alliance for Progress, an ultimately unsuccessful program designed to advance economic and political democracy in Central and South America through cooperative efforts. Berle's strong disapproval of Cuba's pro-Soviet head, Fidel Castro, led him to support the ill-fated Bay of Pigs incursion, which failed to rouse anti-Castro Cubans.

Berle was a child prodigy who lived up to his promise. With his lively, keen intellect and tremendous capacity for work, he carried on a number of careers simultaneously and successfully. He was not humble. Even Roosevelt wondered whether Berle was worth the trouble. But as a critic once conceded, Berle was "a public servant and political economist extraordinary." Much of his writing, especially his book with Means, was prescient in its treatment of the changing corporation. Unlike many of his fellow New Dealers, Berle did not wish to break up the corporation but to tame it. A man of influence for much of his life, he had the misfortune to peak early. His variegated government career notwithstanding, he probably will be best remembered for his efforts as a member of the brain trust in 1932. Despite a commitment to social progress, Berle was in his writings and activities mainly concerned with stability and order.

[An extensive collection of Berle's papers, including his diary, is at the Franklin D. Roosevelt Library, Hyde Park, N.Y. The diary for the years 1937–1971 has been published in microform (1978). A small Berle file is at the Baker Library, Harvard Business School. A selection of Berle's papers is Beatrice Bishop Berle and Travis B. Jacobs, eds., *Navigating the Rapids, 1918–1971* (1973). A bibliography of Berle's published work to 1964 is in *Columbia Law Review*, Dec. 1964, an issue dedicated to him. His other major publications include *New Directions in the New World* (1940); *Power Without Property* (1959); *Latin America* (1962); and *Leaning Against the Dawn* (1969).

A detailed biography is Jordan A. Schwartz, *Liberal* (1987). See also Elliott A. Rosen, *Hoover, Roosevelt, and the Brains Trust* (1977). An obituary is in *The New York Times*, Feb. 18, 1971. The Oral History Project, Columbia University, has extensive interviews with Berle that were published on microform (1978).]

DANIEL J. LEAB

BERRYMAN, JOHN (Oct. 25, 1914–Jan. 7, 1972), poet, was born in McAlester, Okla., the son of John Allyn Smith, a bank clerk, and Martha Little. A winner of the Bollingen Prize, the Pulitzer Prize, and the National Book Award for his poetry, Berryman belongs to the generation of American poets that includes Delmore Schwartz, Robert Lowell, and Randall Jarrell. His poems, especially *Homage to Mistress Bradstreet* and *The Dream Songs*, the two works on which his reputation rests, are intricate, introspective, difficult, and compelling, marked by nervous, jagged rhythms and an idiosyncratic use of idioms. Sometimes called a "confessional" poet, Berryman refused to accept easy labeling, preferring, he said, to let his poetry speak for itself.

He began life as John Allyn Smith, Jr., in a family that moved every two or three years through a succession of small Oklahoma towns, where his father found employment in local banks and briefly as an assistant fish and game warden for the state. In 1925 the family settled in Tampa, Fla., and opened a restaurant, which was sold within the year to cover the crippling losses Smith sustained in land speculations. The parents soon separated and shortly after divorce papers were filed in June 1926, Smith committed suicide. Young John was eleven; he bore the scars of this loss for the rest of his life. In September his mother married John Angus McAlpin Berryman, a bond broker in New York City, and young John assumed the Berryman surname (legally adopting it in 1936).

In 1928 he entered South Kent School, an English-style boarding school in Connecticut that prized academic performance and athletic prowess. Berryman could deliver academically, ranking at the top of his class through four years, but lacked the requisite physical skills for sports. Called "Blears" because of his thick glasses, he was often bullied and generally thought of himself as a beleaguered outsider.

In 1932 he entered Columbia College, where he became a protégé of the teacher and poet Mark Van Doren. Commuting from his parents' Manhattan home during his freshman year, Berryman remained under the dominating influence of his mother, who kept a close watch over his activities and associations, even after a scholarship allowed him to move onto campus. Berryman's time at Columbia was satisfying on many levels. Socially active, admired by women for his skill as a dancer, he wrote poems and reviews for campus publications, won several university poetry prizes and, in 1935, while still an undergraduate, was published in *The Nation*. After graduating Phi Beta Kappa with an English major, he received a fellowship to Clare College, Cambridge, where he met or corresponded with William Butler Yeats, T. S. Eliot, I. A. Richards, W. H. Auden, F. R. Leavis, Dylan Thomas, and Stephen Spender, and where he won the Oldham Shakespeare Prize. By 1937 he had begun to think of himself as a poet, particularly after Robert Penn Warren agreed to publish some of his poems in *The Southern Review*.

In 1938 Berryman returned to New York City and after a year's search, found employment as part-time poetry editor for *The Nation*, and then as an instructor in English at Wayne State University in Detroit. Early in December 1939 he suffered his first bout of physical and nervous exhaustion, which was misdiagnosed as petit mal and which, combined with his poor eye-sight, exempted him from the World War II draft.

Harvard gave him a three-year appointment as an English instructor in 1940, the year his work was featured in *Five Young American Poets*, an anthology that included Randall Jarrell. His first individual collection, *Poems*, was published in 1942. On October 24 of that year, he married Eileen Patricia Mulligan in New York. In 1943 he secured a lectureship at Princeton, and in 1944–1946, he held a Rockefeller Foundation research fellowship for a critical edition of *King Lear* (not published). In 1946 Berryman returned to Princeton as first an associate and then a resident fellow in creative writing.

During this period, he published regularly in academic journals, recorded his poetry for the Library of Congress, and began a series of marital infidelities (recording the first of them in "Sonnets to Chris," published as *Berryman's Sonnets* in 1967), which increased in frequency and number over the next several years. In 1948 he published *The Dispossessed*, a major work that earned him the Poetry Society of America's Shelley Memorial Award, and two years later his critical biography, *Stephen Crane*.

Between 1950 and 1953 Berryman lectured at Princeton, the University of Washington, the University of Cincinnati, and Harvard. He separated from his wife and began to exhibit the first signs of alcoholism, losing an appointment at the University of Iowa after an arrest for public intoxication. "Homage to Mistress Bradstreet" was published in *Partisan Review* in 1953 and three years later as a book; Edmund Wilson called it the most important American poem since Eliot's *The Wasteland*. Nominated for a Pulitzer, it received the Harriet Monroe Poetry Prize from the University of Chicago in 1957.

In 1955 Berryman joined the faculty of the University of Minnesota in Minneapolis, where he remained until his death. He was named Regents' Professor of Humanities in 1969. Divorced from his first wife on Dec. 19, 1956, he married Elizabeth Ann Levine six days later; they had a son in 1957. That summer Berryman was sent by the State Department on a two-month lecture tour to fourteen universities in India. He published *His Thought Made Pockets and the Plane Buckt* in 1958 and suffered yet another nervous collapse. Thereafter he was hospitalized annually, for increasingly longer periods each time, for alcoholism and physical exhaustion. Divorced from his second wife in 1959, Berryman married Kathleen ("Kate") Donahue on Sept. 1, 1961; they had two children.

A warm and generous but demanding teacher, Berryman was a visiting professor in 1959–1963 at the University of Utah, the University of California at Berkeley, the Bread Loaf School in Vermont, and a writer in residence at Brown University. In 1964 he published 77 Dream Songs, for which he won the Pulitzer Prize in Poetry. In 1966 he was granted a Guggenheim Fellowship to finish Dream Songs, and spent the year in Dublin. On his return to the United States, he published Berryman's Sonnets and Short Poems and received prizes from the Academy of American Poets and the National Endowment for the Arts for "distinguished service to American letters." Suffering from acute alcoholism, he was again hospitalized, but completed the concluding four sections of The Dream Songs under the title His Toy, His Dream, His Rest, for which he was given the National Book Award in 1969. That same year, he shared the Bollingen Prize with Karl Shapiro.

In mid-1970, after having been admitted twice in a five-month span to an alcohol detoxification unit, he claimed full recovery and a religious conversion. Readmitted to treatment late in October, he joined Alcoholics Anonymous and began writing a novel, a thinly disguised account of his rehabilitation, published posthumously in 1973 as Recovery. Despite such efforts, he returned to heavy drinking in the last months of 1971. In December he won a senior fellowship from the National Endowment for the Humanities to complete his biography of Shakespeare, which he had begun twenty years earlier. Berryman ended his life by leaping from the Washington Avenue Bridge in Minneapolis, landing on the western embankment of the Mississippi. He is buried in St. Paul, Minn.

[Berryman's papers are at the University of Minnesota in Minneapolis. Posthumous publications include his essays and short stories, The Freedom of the Poet, edited by Robert Giroux (1976); Henry's Fate, selected and introduced by John Haffenden (1977); and We Dream of Honour: John Berryman's Letters to His Mother, selected and introduced by Richard J. Kelly (1988). A convenient guide to manuscripts, critical literature, and the poetry is Berryman's Collected Poems 1937–1971, edited and introduced by Charles Thornbury (1989). See also John Haffenden, The Life of John Barryman (1982); Eileen Simpson, Poets in Their Youth (1982); and E. M. Halliday, John Berryman and the Thirties; A Memoir (1987).]

ALLAN L. DAMON

BICKEL, ALEXANDER MORDECAI (Dec. 17, 1924–Nov. 7, 1974), educator and lawyer, was born in Bucharest, Rumania, the son of Solomon Bickel, a writer, and Yetta Schafer. He immigrated to the United States in 1939 and was naturalized in 1943. During World War II he saw action as a machine gunner in Italy and France. In 1947 he graduated from City College of New York, where he was a member of Phi Beta Kappa, and two years later earned an LL.B., summa cum laude, at Harvard Law School.

For the next several years Bickel served in a variety of judicial clerkships and public policy roles, beginning in 1949–1950 as law clerk to Chief Judge Calvert Magruder on the U.S. Court of Appeals for the First Circuit, in Boston, Mass. In 1950 he became a law officer in the U.S. State Department and in 1952 began a one-year term as law clerk to Supreme Court Justice Felix Frankfurter. Bickel returned to the State Department in 1953 as a special assistant to the director of the policy planning staff. The next year he returned to Harvard University as a research associate in the law school and began work on his first book, The Unpublished Opinions of Mr. Justice Brandeis, which was published in 1957.

In 1956 he began a distinguished career as a professor of law at Yale University. Described by his students as "mesmeric," "bright, witty, and off-putting, all at the same time," Bickel was as much admired for his energetic and urbane lecturing style as he was for the intellectual subtlety of his case analysis. By 1960 he was a full professor. Six years later he was named Chancellor Kent Professor of Law and Legal History. From 1971 to 1974 he was William C. DeVane Professor and, in 1974, became Sterling Professor of Law. Honored by Yale with an M.A. in 1960, Bickel was a member of the American Academy of Arts and Sciences and a Guggenheim fellow. He delivered the Oliver Wendell Holmes lectures at Harvard in 1969 and spent the next academic year as a fellow at the Center for Advanced Study in Behavioral Sciences in California. On Oct. 17, 1959, Bickel married Josephine Ann Napolino, with whom he had two children.

Often mentioned as a possible candidate for the Supreme Court, Bickel was a man of strong and often contradictory opinions, who defied easy labeling or definition. As a leading constitutional authority, his lectures, books, and law journal articles helped shape the national legal debate on such issues as the nature and reach of the Supreme Court's power, the powers of Congress in relation to the courts, the war powers of the president, and national policies of school integration and open housing. A constitutional conservative, he rejected absolutist doctrines as dangerously confining and as conducive to tyranny. In his years at Yale, he moved steadily toward a rejection of judicial activism in establishing social policy on the ground that any such exercise of judicial power was both unworkable and intolerable. His scholarly writing was directed toward both a historical analysis of the Supreme Court and an assessment of its present-day role in American life. His books include *The Least Dangerous Branch* (1962), *Politics and the Warren Court* (1965), and *Reform and Continuity* (1971). He died before completing a two-volume history of the Court in the early twentieth century. *The Morality of Consent*, seen by some critics as a preliminary summary of his legal philosophy, was published posthumously in 1975.

A contributing editor of *The New Republic* from 1957 until his death, and a commentator for magazines such as *Commentary*, Bickel most often reflected a liberal Democratic viewpoint, but he was far from doctrinaire. In 1961 he bitterly attacked John F. Kennedy's appointment of Robert F. Kennedy to the post of attorney general, declaring that RFK was not fit for the office. In 1968, however, in the midst of the Vietnam War, he traveled across the country speaking in behalf of RFK's insurgent campaign for the Democratic presidential nomination. In a wry aside to a reporter who had called attention to his earlier statement, Bickel said he was considering publishing a list of good presidents who were "not fit to be Attorney General."

As a public man and policymaker, appearing on television broadcasts, at national gatherings, and in congressional hearings in the 1960's, he was a fervent supporter of civil rights activism and a forceful advocate of integration in education, housing, recreation, and employment. He was frequently at odds with the Kennedy administration, which he otherwise generally approved, because of its appointment of segre-

gationist judges to the federal courts in the South. A decade later Bickel concluded that programs leading to integration and assimilation were not working, and were perhaps unlikely to work in the near future. In the Holmes lectures at Harvard in 1969, later expanded and published as *The Supreme Court and the Idea of Progress*, he argued that the key to improving the condition of blacks and other minorities in the United States was not to be found in court doctrines or intervention by the federal government. Relief, he said, lay in local autonomy, in community participation, and in quality education controlled by parents, even if that education was delivered in segregated schools or the political involvement of minorities was achieved through weighted voting in violation of the established principle of one person, one vote.

Bickel's role as a lawyer (as distinct from his academic role as an authority on the Constitution) was equally complex because he often took unexpected positions in the cases he helped to litigate as lead lawyer or consultant. In his best-known court appearance, he successfully defended the *New York Times* against the Nixon White House in the Pentagon Papers case of 1971, in which the administration had sought, through prior restraint, to prevent publication of documents and memos relating to the government's policies in Vietnam on the ground that publication threatened national security. To the dismay of some civil libertarians, Bickel ignored the doctrine that the First Amendment provided absolute freedom of the press and pursued instead the more pragmatic argument that publication of the papers did not represent a clear and present danger to the nation. He told the Supreme Court that if the president should possess the inherent power to exercise prior restraint, he could do so only when there was a "direct, immediate, and visible" result that threatened the nation's very existence. No such result, he said, would flow from printing the Pentagon Papers as the *New York Times* proposed to do. The Court agreed by a vote of six to three.

Bickel was well established as one of the preeminent legal scholars of his generation when he succumbed to cancer in New Haven, Conn., at the age of forty-nine.

[Bickel's thought is best found in *The Supreme Court and the Idea of Progress* (1970) and *The Morality of Consent* (1975). The latter is reviewed in the

New York Times Book Review, Sept. 21, 1975. In the same issue, see Victor S. Navasky's brief profile of Bickel. An obituary is in the *New York Times*, Nov. 8, 1974.]

ALLAN L. DAMON

BICKEL, KARL AUGUST (Jan. 20, 1882–Dec. 11, 1972), president of United Press Associations (UP) from 1923 to 1935, was born in Geneseo, Ill., one of six children of William August Bickel, a general store merchandiser, and Emily Anderson. War dispatches from Richard Harding Davis so inspired young Bickel that he took a job with the two-page *Geneseo Daily Arena* while still in high school. After high school graduation, Bickel became editor of the Rock Island edition of the *Davenport* (Iowa) *Times* and later was managing editor of the *Davenport Republican*. In 1903, he began studying history at Stanford University and supported himself by working as a correspondent for the *San Francisco Examiner*. As a result of his efforts in covering the San Francisco earthquake in 1906, the *Examiner* made him a city editor in the newspaper's emergency headquarters. Briefly in 1907, Bickel was city editor of the *San Francisco Daily News*. He became manager of the UP's bureau in Portland, Oreg., in 1908 and married Helen Madira Davis there later that year; the couple had no children.

The president of UP, Roy Howard, was not impressed with the Portland bureau's productivity and was on the verge of firing Bickel, who first quit to become editor and publisher of *The Daily News* in Grand Junction, Colo. Bickel nearly made himself seriously ill working every day in a desperate attempt to make the newspaper turn a profit. In 1912, he took a leave of absence and went to Florida, then New York, in search of a new job. A friend strongly advised Bickel to approach Howard. Although the two men had a stiff initial reunion, Howard asked Bickel to take over the Connecticut bureau. Howard wanted to stop Hearst International News Service from taking away UP customers. So on Apr. 6, 1913, Bickel became UP's first business manager/sales representative. Not a natural salesman, he had to learn by reading numerous books on salescraft.

In 1915, at the height of World War I, Bickel set up headquarters in Chicago and traveled from Minnesota to Texas promoting the wire service. He was named business manager of United Press in 1916. Bickel's close relation-

ships with newspaper clients proved vital to the wire service in 1919 when, because of inaccurate information provided by a U.S. Navy admiral, the United Press wrongly announced that an armistice ending World War I had been signed. Bickel managed to retain nearly all the newspaper clients despite the controversy.

That year, Bickel played a part in establishing a nighttime wire service called United News. This made United Press a twenty-four-hour news operation, intensifying its competition with the larger Associated Press. Bickel also was instrumental in starting the United Feature Syndicate, which offered book serials, the memoirs of the exiled Crown Prince of Germany in 1920, the flapper-girl drawings of John Held, Jr., tennis advice from Helen Wills, and opinions from Benito Mussolini, among others.

Howard resigned as president of United Press in 1922 to become general business director of the Scripps-McRae League. Bickel became UP's general news manager and was named its president one year later. The decade that followed was marked by frantic growth and change for the wire service. By 1928, United Press claimed 952 member newspapers in the United States and Canada and a total of 1,150 clients worldwide. The wire service boasted fifty-one domestic and twenty-eight foreign bureaus, and it leased more than 105,000 miles of telegraphic wire for news transmissions.

Bickel built on Howard's work while president, expanding coverage in eastern Europe and Latin America. In 1923, Bickel and his wife went to Moscow at the request of the newly created Russian news agency, Rosta. He helped design Rosta's telephone circuits and newsroom layout and also ordered its teleprinter machines, some of which were still in use thirty years later.

The Bickels' decision to return home from Russia by way of Japan created an inroad for the United Press in Eastern Asia. Japan had just suffered a devastating earthquake. The owners of the *Osaka Mainichi* and the *Tokyo Nichi Nichi* were determined to rebuild and bought the United Press's special-report service on world economic affairs. Later, in an effort to gain better access across the Pacific, Bickel successfully campaigned to reduce the commercial cable rates between Asia and San Francisco. By the end of the decade, United Press dispatches were received across China, Japan, Hong Kong, the Philippines, and what was then the Malay

Peninsula: Indo-China, Manchukuo, and Siam.

However, government-based news agencies from other countries were allowed a lower government cable rate than American agencies. Bickel protested, claiming that this higher rate for private companies reduced the free flow of news. Throughout his tenure as president of United Press, Bickel insisted that government and corporate information cartels dangerously inhibited the free flow of news around the globe. He presented these views while attending two international press conferences at the League of Nations in Geneva during the late 1920's. At the second conference, Bickel secured a resolution calling for world leaders to guarantee press freedom and unbiased international reporting. Of the sixty-four nations represented, only Turkey voted against the resolution. Gradually, many international monopolies began to break apart, including those involving the Associated Press.

Bickel also campaigned for cooperation between newspapers and a budding new medium, radio. His book, *New Empires: The Newspaper and the Radio* (1930), chronicles his enthusiasm. He believed radio could sell advertising in newspapers by providing basic news bulletins then cuing the public to the more in-depth stories available in print. In 1924, Bickel arranged for United Press bulletins on general election returns to be broadcast over the first-ever news hookup of radio stations. Despite that success, many newspaper publishers, including Roy Howard, believed radio was a competitor for advertising revenue. As late as 1931, Scripps-Howard Newspapers agreed to sell United Press reports to radio stations only if the news was embargoed for twenty-four hours. Bickel argued that radio was the perfect medium for boosting newspaper circulation. The disagreement contributed to Bickel's already poor health. Howard finally relented, and negotiations with radio stations for twenty-four-hour news access began.

At age fifty-three, Bickel retired from UP, saying that "the press association business is a young man's business." His last official act in 1935 was to authorize the selling of news bulletins to radio stations. The next year, Bickel headed Scripps-Howard Radio, Inc. He consolidated all Scripps-Howard stations into the Continental Radio Company and purchased existing stations in smaller markets, such as WCPO in Cincinnati and WNOX in Knoxville. Bickel

wrote W. W. Hawkins in 1936, "Newspapers in the future will be handicapped without radio as if they tried to compete without trucks, leased wire and effective presses."

The Bickels moved to Sarasota, Fla., and in 1942 Bickel published a history of the region, *The Mangrove Coast*. The energy he once devoted to international press affairs was poured into philanthropic work. He was called Sarasota's "one-man chamber of commerce" for his service as a trustee for the Ringling Museums and numerous other civic organizations. The Bickels contributed the Russian icons and Japanese prints they collected in their travels to the Ringling Museum. Bickel died in Sarasota.

[Bickel's books include: *New Empires: The Newspaper and the Radio* (1930) and *The Mangrove Coast* (1942). An extensive biography, as well as information on the Bickel Collection, is available at the Ringling Museum in Sarasota, Fla. Obituaries are in the *New York Times*, the *Washington Post*, the *St. Petersburg Times*, and the *Sarasota Herald Tribune*, all Dec. 12. 1972.]

VIRGINIA WHITEHOUSE

BIDDLE, GEORGE (Jan. 24, 1885–Nov. 6, 1973), artist, was born in Philadelphia, Pa., the son of Algernon Sydney Biddle and Frances Robinson. Through his lawyer father, he was descended from one of Pennsylvania's oldest and most distinguished Quaker families. On the maternal side, he could claim kinship with such notables as Thomas Jefferson, Edmund Randolph, and Robert E. Lee.

Left fatherless at the age of seven, Biddle passed his early childhood just outside of Philadelphia. Among his closest boyhood companions was his brother Francis, who later became attorney general of the United States. In 1892, following a tour of Europe, he entered Haverford School, and in 1898 he was sent off to boarding school at the Groton School in Groton, Mass. A breakdown in health, however, forced Biddle to drop out of Groton in 1901, and he did not complete his secondary education there until the spring of 1904. The following fall he went to Harvard, where he completed his undergraduate degree in 1908, receiving a law degree there three years later.

By then, however, Biddle knew that he would never practice law. Thanks largely to his tour of some of the great European art collections, his interest in drawing and painting, which had periodically manifested itself since his childhood, had become a full-blown passion. As a result, shortly after earning his law degree, he began a year of study at the Julien Academy in Paris, which was followed by a year at the Pennsylvania Academy of Fine Arts. Returning to Europe in 1913, he worked under the tutelage of the American impressionist Frederick Frieseke in France. While there, he also became friendly with Mary Cassatt, whose works, along with those of Edgar Degas, had a marked influence on Biddle's early style.

In 1916 Biddle returned to Philadelphia, and shortly after the United States' entry into World War I, he enlisted in the army. In August 1917 he was commissioned a lieutenant. That same month he married Anne (Nancy) Coleman, and by fall he was on his way to Europe, where his fluency in German led to his assignment with the army's enemy intelligence section. Leaving the service as a captain, he returned to the United States early in 1919. Three years later Biddle and his wife were divorced.

Seeking escape from both his domestic difficulties and the painful memories of war, Biddle spent a large portion of the years 1920 through 1922 in Tahiti, where he painted and engaged in printmaking. The tropical Polynesian environment had much the same effect on Biddle that it had had on Paul Gauguin many years earlier. Thus, the shift in Biddle's work toward more exuberant color, flattened perspectives, and greater concern for overall pattern bore striking similarity to Gauguin's stylistic evolution in Tahiti.

Biddle's works from Tahiti won considerable praise and sold well when they were shown in New York. But this first substantial success of his career did not allay the artist's own uneasiness with his progress. In 1923 he went to Paris, where he spent much of the next three years. There, largely under the influence of the painter Jules Pascin, he began evolving a style that was fundamentally realistic but also contained strong elements of expressive distortion and caricature. In the process the design of his works became looser and more fluid.

He married Jane Belo in 1925; they divorced four years later. In the spring of 1929, Biddle began building a residence and studio in suburban Croton-on-Hudson, N.Y., which was to be his home base for the rest of his life. On Apr. 17, 1931, he married sculptor Helene Sardeau, with whom he had a son.

By 1930 Biddle was firmly entrenched in the New York art community and known primarily as an easel painter and printmaker whose subjects included portraiture, landscape, and figurative genre. By then, however, inspired in large part by the Mexican renaissance in mural art, he was becoming interested in that branch of his profession as well, and in 1933 he completed a mural on agriculture for Chicago's Century of Progress exposition.

That same year, motivated by concern for the social problems of the Great Depression and a conviction that art could help in alleviating those problems, he approached President Franklin D. Roosevelt, whom he had known at Groton and Harvard, with a proposal for a federal program for producing murals promoting American ideals. Eventually this lobbying effort gave birth to the Works Progress Administration's Federal Arts Program, through which many artists, impoverished by the depression, found gainful employment. For Biddle himself, it led to a commission for a mural at the Department of Justice in Washington, D.C.

Completed in 1936, this multipaneled work depicts the contrasts between an exploitative social order and one founded on principles of equality and justice. At its unveiling, one critic said it was an "example of the poisonous pattern of Moscow that is being shoved down the American throat." Several years later Biddle defended himself against such criticism, at least indirectly, in his autobiography, *An American Artist's Story* (1939), where he argued for the artist's obligation to involve himself in bettering society according to his political lights.

In 1942 Biddle went to Brazil, where he collaborated with his wife on murals and bas reliefs for Rio de Janeiro's National Library. Upon returning to the United States, he went to Washington, D.C., where he spearheaded the organization of an army-sponsored group of artists assigned to chronicling the military operations of World War II. Congress ultimately cut the program, however, and many of the artists involved ended up working as correspondents for *Life*. Among those enlisted by *Life* was Biddle, who covered the war in North Africa and Italy. Shortly after completing these assignments he published *Artist at War* (1944), a diary account of his combat artist's experience.

Appointed to the federal Fine Arts Commission in 1950, Biddle continued to pursue his painting and printmaking endeavors. The once favorable critical attention given his work, however, ebbed in the face of American art's new preoccupations with abstractionism. Labeling the abstractionists "narcissistic," he was unwilling to explore the nonrepresentational possibilities in his own work and came to be viewed in some quarters as a reactionary. Among his last works was a series of lithographs recording his impressions of India from a visit in 1959. He died at his home in Croton-on-Hudson.

[Biddle's papers, including his diaries, are at the Library of Congress and the Archives of American Art, Smithsonian Institution, both in Washington, D.C. His publications include *George Biddle's War Drawings* (1944); *The Yes and No of Contemporary Art* (1957); *Indian Impressions* (1960); and *Tahitian Journal* (1968). Among the writings on Biddle are Zakaria Ali, "George Biddle in Tahiti," an unpublished manuscript on file at the Smithsonian Institution's National Portrait Gallery–National Museum of American Art Library, Washington, D.C.; and Martha Pennigar, *The Graphic Work of George Biddle* (1979). An obituary appears in the *New York Times*, Nov. 8, 1973.]

FREDERICK S. VOSS

BIGGERS, JOHN DAVID (Dec. 19, 1888–Dec. 31, 1973), glass manufacturer, was born in St. Louis, Mo., the son of William David Biggers, a businessman, and Emma Melvina Fisse. He attended Smith Academy in St. Louis, studied for a year at the University of Washington in St. Louis (1905–1906), and graduated from the University of Michigan in Ann Arbor in 1909. While in college he worked for the Continental Screen Company of Detroit, where his father was general manager. On Oct. 22, 1912, he married Mary Isobel Kelsey; they had three children.

In 1909, Biggers joined Larned, Carter and Company, overalls manufacturers, and by 1910 he had become the company's advertising manager. He then entered chamber of commerce work, first as an assistant secretary of the Detroit Board of Commerce (1910–1911) and later as secretary of the Toledo (Ohio) Commerce Club (1911–1914). His service in the latter position began what he later called a "romance with Toledo."

In 1914, Biggers joined the Owens Bottle Company in Toledo, where he rose to vice-president in charge of sales, became closely associated with Edward D. Libbey, a leader in the glass industry, and began a career in glass man-

ufacturing that, with the exception of the years 1926–1930, lasted until his retirement. During this four-year interval he became affiliated with the Graham brothers (Joseph, Robert, and Ray) and their ventures in the automobile industry. In 1926 and 1927, he was managing director of Dodge Brothers in London and subsequently served as an official of the Graham Brothers Corporation, the Graham-Paige Corporation, and the Graham-Paige International Corporation.

In 1930, Biggers became president and chief executive officer of the Libbey-Owens-Ford Glass Company, which under his direction grew to become the nation's leading producer of window and safety glass and its second-largest producer of plate glass. Libbey-Owens-Ford owed its success partly to a contract signed in 1931 with General Motors, under the terms of which it bought GM's glass-making facilities and became its exclusive supplier of automotive glass.

Other factors played a part, among them, a policy of promoting the usage of glass by manufacturers, the successful exploitation of a new technique for drawing glass from furnaces in sheets, a pioneering role in securing the adoption of safety glass by automobile manufacturers, and the addition of such new product lines as Tuf-flex (a heat-tempered plate glass), thermopanes (glass insulating units), Vitrolite (colored structural glass for use in construction), and Plaskon plastics (for use in automobiles and household products). Under Biggers, the company acquired a reputation as one of the nation's most progressive companies and one of its most profitable during the Great Depression. It was considered a leader in combining price stability with an enlightened labor outlook.

Biggers was a Republican critical of Franklin Roosevelt's New Deal. But he was also a strong advocate of business-government teamwork and was on friendly terms with Roosevelt personally. In 1937, he accepted an appointment to the Commerce Department's Business Advisory Council and agreed to head the recently authorized U.S. Census of Partial Employment, Unemployment, and Occupations. This task earned him praise both for the thoroughness of the undertaking and for spending less than $2 million of his $5 million appropriation. In 1940, Biggers became a deputy commissioner on the Defense Advisory Commission, where he worked primarily as an assistant to William

Knudsen in efforts to foster defense production.

In 1941, he served both as chief of production for the Office of Production Management and as head of an OPM commodity section responsible for steel, aluminum, magnesium, paper, pulp, and chemicals. And in September 1941, Biggers was sent to London as a special minister in charge of coordinating British and American war production and speeding deliveries under the Lend-Lease Act. In late 1941, Biggers returned to Libbey-Owens-Ford, where he continued as chief executive officer until his retirement in 1960. His first wife died in 1942, and on June 24, 1944, he married Frances Morrison Kline Doyle; they had no children.

For his contributions to America's "miracle of production" during World War II, Biggers received the President's Medal for Merit, and after the war he won further honors as an internationally recognized "industrial statesman" and a "builder of enterprise." *Forbes* named him one of the "fifty foremost business leaders" in 1948. During his career he saw Libbey-Owens-Ford grow from $12 million in sales and 2,607 employees in 1930 to more than $300 million in sales and 12,692 employees in 1960.

Biggers also helped form the Toledo Labor-Management-Citizens Committee, which became a model for organizing industrial peace in other cities and reflected his strong faith in collective bargaining, community action, and labor returns geared to gains in industrial productivity. Such views marked him as a member of the "enlightened" wing of America's corporate elite in the 1950's, as did his selection as chairman of the Business Advisory Council in 1953 and his close affiliation with such groups as the Committee for Economic Development and the Council on Foreign Relations.

After his retirement, Biggers continued to hold directorships in several major corporations and to play an important role in Toledo's economic and civic development, especially as the principal organizer of the Toledo Area Development Corporation and as a prominent supporter of the Toledo Museum of Art, the Toledo Hospital, the University of Toledo, and the Toledo Boys club.

Biggers is remembered chiefly for his contributions to the growth of the glass industry and for his industrial statesmanship in trying to build bridges between business and government, find a basis for labor-management cooperation, and develop a corporate citizenship imbued with a sense of community responsibility. He was a handsome, courtly, even-tempered individual who always retained some of the "boosterism" associated with the "Chamber of Commerce" style, but who was also a master of business management, a commanding presence in the boardroom and administrative conference, and an articulate and emphatic spokesman for the positions he held. He died at his home in Perrysburg, Ohio.

[There is no biography, but substantial biographical sketches can be found in B. C. Forbes, ed., *America's Fifty Foremost Business Leaders* (1948); New York University School of Commerce, Accounts, and Finance, *Builders of Enterprise* (1950); and articles in *Business Week*, Sept. 25, 1937; and *Glass Industry*, May 1960. An obituary is in the *New York Times*, Jan 1, 1974.]

ELLIS W. HAWLEY

BLACK, ELI (1922–Feb. 3, 1975), business executive, claimed to be a descendant of a line of rabbis and scholars that went back to the seventeenth century, although his early life and lineage are shrouded in mystery. After graduation in 1940 from Yeshiva University, where he received rabbinical training, he served for four years as rabbi of a congregation in Woodmere, N.Y. Black then left the religious life for one in business. He married Shirley Lubell in 1946; they had two children.

Black's initial position in the business world was at Lehman Brothers. After a few years he joined American Securities Corporation, where he handled financing of several deals, one of which was for American Seal-Kap, a $5 million, Long Island–based operation that he considered "a small company with huge problems." American Seal-Kap was the leading manufacturer of seals for milk bottles at a time when that container was being phased out.

In 1954, Black joined American Seal-Kap as its chairman and chief executive officer. Immediately he started restructuring the company, selling off unprofitable and soon-to-be-obsolete lines of business and purchasing promising properties. In 1965, he renamed the company AMK, and two years later purchased John Morrell and Company, which was twenty times its size, creating an $840 million giant.

In 1970, Black merged his firm with United Fruit, one of the nation's best-known companies and the largest single firm in the banana

business. Its prime product was Chiquita bananas, but it also had oil palm plantations and
lettuce and melon farms. The company was
renamed United Brands. United Fruit generated a substantial cash flow, which Black put to
work in additional investments: A&W (root beer
and drive-in restaurants), which Black tried to
expand into fast foods, and Baskin-Robbins, a
highly successful ice cream producer.

Black also acted to mend United Fruit's reputation. He erected modest but clean houses for
banana plantation workers and provided them
with schools and hospitals at which they received free education and medical care. American supervisors were replaced by natives.
Wages and benefits were increased. United's
Inter-Harvest lettuce subsidiary was one of the
first to sign a labor agreement with the United
Farm Workers (1970).

Although large and dominant in some of its
product areas, United Brands ran into trouble
from the start. In 1973, the banana countries in
Central America formed the Union of Banana
Exporting Countries and demanded a $1 tax on
each forty-pound box of bananas. The plan
failed, but in 1974 Honduras passed a fifty-
cents-per-box tax, which it subsequently reduced to twenty-five cents.

In September 1974, Hurricane Fifi ravaged
more than half the company's Honduras plantations, resulting in a $20 million loss. Simul-
taneously Panama enacted an export tax on
bananas that cost an additional $11 million.
John Morrell turned in a bad year, losing $6
million. A cash crunch obliged the company to
omit dividends on its preferred stock, and it attempted to sell subsidiaries to raise needed
funds.

Even before the hurricane struck, Black was
selling off assets. In 1973, he sold United
Brands' 83-percent share in Baskin-Robbins to
J. Lyons (U.K.) for $37.6 million. In early
1974, its money-losing Revere (Mass.) sugar refinery was sold to Sucrest, a transaction on
which United Brands took an $8.2 million loss.
In early 1975, Black sold United Brands' majority ownership of Foster Grant, a profitable
manufacturer of plastics and sunglasses, to West
Germany's Hoechst AG for $70 million.

Part of the reason for Black's failure was his
unfamiliarity with the business. He recognized
this, and in 1974 asked Edward Gelsthorpe, a
former Gillette president, to assist him. In November 1974, Gelsthorpe became executive

vice-president and chief operating officer.
Gelsthorpe believed United's problems could
not be solved while Black was at the helm, and
a few months later he attempted to organize
other executives in a move to replace Black.

On Feb. 3, 1975, Black broke open one of
the windows in his office on the forty-fourth
floor of New York's Pan Am Building and
leaped to his death. For the next few days newspaper stories attributed his action to overwork
and the pressures of taking United Brands out of
debt. Then the Securities and Exchange Commission learned that Black had authorized a
$1.25 million bribe of Honduran government
officials to obtain a reduction in the country's
banana tax, which was to have been followed by
an additional $1.25 million. Another $750,000
in bribes was later uncovered, these to Italian
officials.

[There is no biography of Eli Black, nor a recent
history of United Brands or United Fruit. The only
sources are journalistic accounts of the times. See
"Bold Start of AMK and United Fruit," *Business
Week*, July 4, 1970; "United Brands Trades More
Assets for Cash," *Business Week*, Jan. 13, 1975; Mary
Bralove, "Was Eli Black's Suicide Caused by Ten-
sions of Conflicting Worlds?" *Wall Street Journal*,
Feb. 14, 1975; "The Great Banana Bribe," *News-
week*, Apr. 21, 1975; and "On a Clear Day . . . ,"
Nation, Apr. 26, 1975. Obituaries appear in the *New
York Times* and the *Wall Street Journal*, both Feb. 4,
1975.]

ROBERT SOBEL

BLACK, HUGO LAFAYETTE (Feb. 27,
1886–Sept. 25, 1971), lawyer, senator, and Supreme Court justice, was born in the north Alabama hill country of Clay County. Black was
the last of eight children of a rural storekeeper,
William Lafayette Black, and his wife, Martha
Ardellah Toland, a postmistress. He was educated in public and private schools and then
undertook a year's study at Birmingham Medical College (now the University of Alabama
School of Medicine) in 1903. He transferred to
the University of Alabama Law School in Tuscaloosa the next year. After graduation in 1906,
he opened a law office in his hometown of Ash-
land, Ala. Shortly thereafter he moved to Birmingham, where his law practice was heavily
involved in personal injury litigation and similar concerns of that industrial city's marginal-
ized working-class whites; he united social
activity with promoting his practice by joining

the Freemasons, Odd Fellows, Knights of Pythias, Loyal Order of Moose, Ku Klux Klan, and various veteran and lawyer groups. Black never apologized for his Klan membership, which he variously explained as an effort to be a moderating influence from within the group, and to be "even-up" with corporate attorneys who used such memberships to their advantage before white working-class juries.

His Birmingham practice was complemented by part-time service as police court judge and public prosecutor. In his role as the latter, two incidents reflected his concerns for civil liberties and foreshadowed views he later manifested on the U.S. Supreme Court. The first was his exposure of a torturous jail in Bessemer, Ala., where confessions were obtained through ruthless flogging; the second was his abolishment of a corrupt fee system in Birmingham, which compensated law enforcement personnel on the basis of number of arrests and incarcerations. After artillery service in World War I that did not take him out of the country, Black returned to Birmingham, where his practice burgeoned. However, he regretfully saw large personal injury verdicts that he had won at trial frequently reduced on appeal because of excessiveness. Two events were significant in this part of his life: one was his first marriage to Josephine Foster, Junior Leaguer, member of a prominent southern family, and later the mother of the couple's three children, on Feb. 21, 1921; the other was the previously mentioned Klan affiliation, which commenced on Sept. 11, 1923.

Black's prospering law practice occasioned his entry in the 1925 race to succeed the retiring Oscar Underwood in the U.S. Senate. In a whirlwind grass-roots campaign in which he wore out two motor cars, Black scored an upset victory in the Democratic primary, a de facto electoral triumph in the Alabama of those days.

Black's first Senate term was that of a conventional southern Democrat, that is, generally supportive of New Deal reforms, save civil rights, and especially antilynching legislation; it was also devoted to a self-improvement reading program of great books.

The self-improvement reclusion ended with his reelection to a second term in 1932 and the coming of the New Deal. By skillful use of bombshell press releases and exploitation of witnesses, Black developed the legislative hearing into a thrilling event and won the attention of a hostile press. He emerged as the New Deal's grand inquisitor, successfully pillorying Washington lobbyists as well as the executives of corrupt and corruptive public utilities. These dramatic disclosures, plus his support of questionable seizures of private papers (including law firm–client correspondence), overshadowed his more substantial legislative accomplishments: the Fair Labor Standards (Minimum Wage) Act, originally the Black-Connery bill, which became law in 1938, and virtual coauthorship of the prototype New Deal statute, the Public Utility Holding Company Act of 1935, as well as the Tennessee Valley Authority.

Not all events of his second term were legislative successes; Black was deeply involved with President Franklin Roosevelt's ill-starred cancellation of air-mail contracts with private airline carriers and transference of that function to the unprepared and disaster-beset Army Air Corps. Black also was numbered among the last-ditch defenders of Roosevelt's abortive court-packing plan of 1937. Both services helped make him Roosevelt's first and surprise nomination to the Supreme Court in August 1937. Partly because Black permitted charges of his Klan membership to be denied on the Senate floor, the nomination was easily approved and Black took his seat on the Court on Aug. 19, 1937. Shortly thereafter, Ray Sprigle, an investigative reporter with the *Pittsburgh Post-Gazette*, produced incontrovertible proof of Black's Klan membership. Sprigle won a Pulitzer Prize for the series of articles. Fortunately for Black, he was supported by admirers as diverse as Cardinal Mundelein of Chicago and NAACP executive secretary Walter White. Indeed, the issue eventually became the subject of cocktail party jokes that asserted (at the time of his appointment) that the newest member of the court need only dye, rather than buy, his robe, and many years later found expression in a quip that an old age spent in a black robe frightening white people was poetic justice for younger years spent in a white robe frightening black people.

The storm of controversy eventually petered out, aided by Black's nationwide radio address on Oct. 1, 1937, in which he forthrightly admitted the obvious and declared the subject closed. Black settled into routine service on what was becoming a New Deal Court. His move from the Senate—where his lightning-fast mind and razor tongue made him a loner with few friends and many enemies—to the Supreme Court lent an especial focus to his dominant will and forceful personality. A judicial colleague complained, "You can't just disagree with him—you've got to go to war with him." Notable disagreements in Black's early service were his insistence that business corporations lay outside the protection of the Constitution and his repudiation of the contrived formulas that the Court had developed to test the legality of rate regulation of public utilities.

Any doubt as to Black's commitment to fundamental American freedoms were dissolved on Lincoln's Birthday, 1940, when he wrote the opinion in *Chambers* v. *Florida*, 309 U.S. 227, reversing the death sentences visited upon six black tenant farmers as a result of coerced confessions: "No higher duty, no more solemn responsibility rests upon this court than that of translating into living law and maintaining this constitutional shield deliberately planned and inscribed for the benefit of every human being subject to our Constitution—of whatever race, creed or persuasion."

Notwithstanding the lyric eloquence of his opinion in the *Chambers* case, a few years later Black also wrote *Korematsu* v. *United States*, 323 U.S. 214 (1944), validating the wartime removal and detention of over one hundred thousand Japanese-American citizens and their relatives, solely on the basis of race. Despite the condemnation of the opinion in the ensuing postwar years, Black never regretted having written the opinion, remarking once, "I would do precisely the same thing today." His jurisprudential fundamentalism insisted that a war could not be fought with the courts in control.

Black repeatedly asserted during his judicial career that the First Amendment left both state and federal governments utterly powerless to restrict expression ("make no law means *make no law* not make some laws"). Such reductionism also provides a telling insight into his love-hate relationship with Justice Felix Frankfurter over a second point of jurisprudence—Black's belief that the Fourteenth Amendment, as originally understood by those who framed and ratified it, fastened the constraints of the first eight amendments upon the states. Black never retreated from his efforts to have this "incorporation" theory adopted by the Court, but one by one most of the provisions of the first eight amendments were gradually assimilated, case by case, into the due process clause of the Fourteenth Amendment. Both justices persisted in opposition until the end of their lives. The duel between the two also encompassed the thrust of the commerce clause upon local taxation and regulation on interstate activity. Sometimes the confrontation achieved seemingly perverse results, as in *Bridges* v. *California*, 314 U.S. 252 (1941), in which Black, inveterate enemy of corporations, defended the right of newspapers to comment on pending cases, and Frankfurter, longtime opponent of constructive (that is, out-of-court) contempt, denounced it. Black and Frankfurter were also divided over the character and consequences of picket line violence. A counterweight association was provided by Justice William Douglas, whose ideas on government business regulation and personal liberties were substantially parallel to Black's.

The Black-Douglas association went back to the early New Deal when Black was the Senate paladin of the Public Utility Holding Company Act, and Douglas Securities and Exchange Commissioner. The two met when Douglas protested a perceived flaw, quickly remedied in an amendment, in pending legislation. Douglas also applauded Black's attempted exclusion of corporations from constitutional protection. It was essentially an ideological partnership rooted in shared political values rather than personal friendship. Indeed, strains of disagreement came from Black's disapproval of Douglas's multiple marriages and antipathy over what the latter called his "salty" jokes. Ever the personal puritan, Black forcefully asserted his personal detestation of pornography in the very act of asserting, with equal conviction, the right of a pornographer to ply his trade without governmental repression.

Black's equanimity and courtliness were particularly tested in the years following World War II, when a combination of the death of his beloved Josephine on Dec. 7, 1951, and widespread concern with Communist subversion and Soviet imperialism produced a climate of opinion at considerable variance to Black's convictions about free speech and free association. Also exacerbating the milieu was the Court's criminal justice decisions, which, Richard Nixon forcefully asserted, weakened the "peace forces" against the "criminal forces."

As the 1950's passed, the reactive criticism abated, and Black settled into his remaining years with a felicitous second marriage, on Sept. 11, 1957, to Elizabeth Seay DeMeritte, an admiral's sister who was his secretary. Moreover, changing public opinion implicitly accepted and approved the bitter legislative dissents of his earlier opinions. A discordant note was suggested by Black's irate response to the sit-ins, and "smash-ins," of the civil rights movement (*Tinker* v. *Des Moines School District*, 343 U.S. 501, 525 [1968]). Related to this response was his formidable dissent to a judicially fabricated right of privacy (*Griswold* v. *Connecticut*, 381 U.S. 479 [1965]), which could not be located in the constitutional text. Further, Black's position on the First Amendment's separation of church and state, where he validated state subsidization of transportation expenses of parochial school students while insisting that governmental support could not be afforded either a favored sect individually or all religions together, was elusive at best (*Everson* v. *Board of Education*, 330 U.S. 1 [1947]). Equally iconoclastic were his unyielding antitrust beliefs that commercial competition was an almost Darwinian process affording no shelter to collusive or anticompetitive arrangements.

Black was involved in a well-publicized feud with Justice Robert Jackson over the successor to Chief Justice Stone in the period 1945–1946. Ostensibly triggered by Black's failure to recuse himself from a case argued by a former partner, the disagreement, which ended with a handshake, was actually the end product of deep personal and philosophical differences.

There is no question that Black was an elemental force who left his mark on the Constitution and his times. Like the man himself, his jurisprudence was a collection of paradoxes. His uncompromising absolutes regarding the literality of constitutional constraints on governmental repression were combined with almost an indifference to economic regulation ("Whether the legislature takes Adam Smith or Lord Keynes as its textbook is no concern of ours," *Ferguson* v. *Skrupa*, 372 U.S. at 732 [1968]). Nonetheless, Black exhibited a particular fidelity to his absolutes, even when they were in conflict. Thus, by assenting in *Eastern Railroads' Presidents' Conference* v. *Noerrs Motor Freight Corp.*, 365 U.S. 27 (1961), which held that the First Amendment right of legislative petition overruled a possible Sherman Act constraint of trade, Black withheld his personal antipathy of the lobbying process and put aside his deep appreciation of the Sherman Act as a charter of economic liberty comparable to the First Amendment in the political sphere. Similarly, his dissent from the Court's invalidation

of a state contraceptive prohibition (*Griswold* v. *Connecticut*), rested on his insistence that constitutional rights be spelled out in that document rather than fabricated judicially under the rubric of due process. In a shorter and more immediate sense, an especially significant impact attended his stay (later affirmed by the Supreme Court) of a federal injunction barring Lyndon Johnson from the ballot in the 1948 Texas senatorial election following a primary victory (by 87 votes in over 1,000,000 cast) stained by widespread reports of flagrant fraud (*Johnson* v. *Stevenson*, 335 U.S. 801 [1948]).

Black's last opinion, *New York Times* v. *U.S.*, 403 U.S. 714 (1970), came shortly before his death and stirringly proclaimed his faith in freedom of the press by denying the government's injunction to suppress publication of damaging disclosures on the Vietnam War that had been purloined by a Pentagon consultant. In it, he cited and rejected Solicitor General Griswold's rebuttal of Black's view that the words "no law" in the First Amendment meant precisely that.

Blessed with remarkably good health, Black continued playing tennis and bridge well into his eighties. A minor stroke suffered while returning from conference signaled the beginning of the end. After a series of strokes he died at Bethesda Naval Hospital, and is buried in Arlington National Cemetery along with his two wives. Unfortunately but typically, Black had ordered the destruction of his bench and conference notes, resources of major importance, upon his death; the order was reluctantly carried out by his son.

[Black and his wife Elizabeth wrote a memoir, *Mr. Justice and Mrs. Black: The Memoirs of Hugo L. Black and Elizabeth Black* (1986). Biographies include John P. Frank, *Mr. Justice Black, The Man and His Opinions* (1949); Virginia van der Veer Hamilton, *Hugo Black: The Alabama Years* (1972); Daniel Meador, *Mr. Justice Black and His Books* (1974); Howard Ball, *The Vision and the Dream of Justice Hugo L. Black; An Examination of a Judicial Philosophy* (1975); Hugo L. Black, Jr., *My Father: A Remembrance* (1975); Gerald T. Dunne, *Hugo Black and the Judicial Revolution* (1977); James J. Magee, *Mr. Justice Black: Absolutist on the Court* (1980); and Tony Freyer, ed., *Justice Hugo Black and Modern America* (1990). An obituary appears in the *New York Times*, Sept. 26, 1972.]

GERALD T. DUNNE

BLACKMER, SYDNEY ALDERMAN (July 13, 1895–Oct. 5, 1973), actor, producer, and director, was born to Walter Steele and Clara De Roulhac on July 13, 1895, in Salisbury, N.C. He excelled both as a student and an athlete. He and his family originally planned that he would follow in his father's footsteps and become a lawyer. To this end, he attended the University of North Carolina at Chapel Hill, where he was a star player on the football team. In 1914 he went to Europe and tried to enlist in the British Commonwealth forces; he failed to gain entry, though, and returned to North Carolina to complete his B.A. in 1915 and, a year later, his LL.B. Decades later, in 1964, he would also receive an LL.D. from North Carolina and a Litt.D. from Catawba College, North Carolina.

After a brief stint as an artillery officer in World War I, he soon decided that his courtroom skills would stand him in good stead on the New York stage. He debuted in *The Morris Dance* in February 1917. Later that same year, he premiered his rendition of President Theodore Roosevelt in what proved to be an insignificant play; his brief appearance was its only memorable moment. Throughout his long career he would go on to play Teddy Roosevelt—to whom, with the right pair of glasses and a little bit of makeup, he bore a startling resemblance—in no fewer than ten plays and movies, the two most unforgettable being *This Is My Affair* and *Rough Riders*. After seeing his performance of *Rough Riders*, Roosevelt's daughter, Alice Roosevelt Longworth, remarked, "It *was* my father."

Over the span of the next fifty-five years he appeared in over two hundred feature films and television serials, as well as forty stage plays. His film debut came in 1917 opposite Pearl White in serial features known collectively as *The Perils of Pauline*. In the fall of 1924 he had his first Broadway lead, in the long-running play *Mountain Man*. To prepare for the part, he spent the summer of 1921 alone, roughing it in the hills of northern Georgia.

No doubt his greatest role came as Shirley Booth's alcoholic husband, Doc, in William Inge's *Come Back, Little Sheba* (1950). He played this role so convincingly and with such passion that he suffered a severely sprained ankle, broken nose, two cracked ribs, and bruises, cuts, and abrasions over 90 percent of his body. Years later Miss Booth admitted that there were times she was so frightened by Blackmer's drunken scenes she forgot they were acting. For this role Blackmer received both the 1950 Donaldson Award and the Antoinette Perry ("Tony") Award.

Over the years, Blackmer starred opposite several other famous actresses. In the 1930's version of *Heidi* he played Shirley Temple's adoptive father. Later he played opposite Helen Hayes, Eva Le Gallienne, and Tallulah Bankhead. Among his other famous movie appearances were: *People Will Talk* (1951), with Cary Grant and Jeanne Crane; *Tammy and the Bachelor* (1957), with Debbie Reynolds and Leslie Nielsen; *The High and the Mighty* (1956), with John Wayne and Robert Stack; *How to Murder Your Wife* (1967), with Jack Lemmon; and *Rosemary's Baby* (1969), with Mia Farrow.

Blackmer also appeared in several TV movies and on such famous TV series as "Bonanza" and "Big Valley." His voice alone was so elegant and powerful that he narrated over two dozen films and TV documentaries. In his later years, he also became a respected producer and director.

However, Blackmer was more than just a suave and handsome celluloid image. He was a man who never forgot his roots. Although in later life he and his second wife, actress Suzanne Kaaren, whom he married in 1942, lived with their sons at 100 Central Park South in New York City, Blackmer never gave up his family home at 112 South Fulton Street in Salisbury, North Carolina; he and the family spent many happy days there.

Blackmer, very much a leader in his profession, always spent freely of his time and money on behalf of worthy causes. During the infamous and bitter actor-manager struggle in the New York theater in 1919, he used his legal talents to protect actors' financial and contractual rights vis-à-vis long- and short-term film rights and profits. Subsequently, he was a founder of the Actor's Equity Association and a member of the National Executive Board of the American Federation of Television and Radio Artists and president of the Theater Authority—the clearinghouse for benefit performances.

In 1928, Blackmer's marriage to the glamorous movie starlet Lenore Ulric became the theatrical social event of that year. Their tempestuous marriage lasted until 1939, when their divorce also caused a great sensation in Hollywood and New York and made headlines not only in the tabloids but also in reputable newspapers.

A lifelong political activist, Blackmer spent

much of his later life working for the Democratic party nationally and especially in North
Carolina. One of his closest friends was Governor, later Senator, Terry Sanford.

In the 1960's Blackmer also found time to
serve as a national vice-president of the Muscular Dystrophy Association (MDA) of America. In 1973, even as Blackmer discovered he
had cancer, he helped Jerry Lewis initiate the
first of his now famous annual Labor Day MDA
Telethons, which have raised countless millions
of dollars for children over the last two decades.

On Oct. 5, 1973, Sydney A. Blackmer lost
his struggle with cancer, dying at the Sloan-
Kettering Institute for Cancer Research at the
age of seventy-eight. He was survived by his
wife and two sons, who returned his body to his
beloved North Carolina, where he is buried in
a small Episcopal Cemetery near Salisbury.

[Biographical information is dispersed but can be
found in David Quinlan, *The Illustrated Encyclopedia of Movie Character Actors* (1985); and Evelyn
Mack Truitt, ed., *Who Was Who on Screen* (1983).
Obituaries appear in the *New York Times*, Oct. 6,
1973; and *Variety*, Oct. 10, 1973.]

WILLIAM HEAD

BLANCHFIELD, FLORENCE ABY (Apr. 1,
1882–May 12, 1971), commander of the Army
Nurse Corps during World War II and the first
woman commissioned into the regular U.S.
Army, was born in the Shenandoah Valley of
northern Virginia, the daughter of Joseph Plun-
kett Blanchfield, a stonemason and railroad employee, and Mary Louvenia Anderson, a
practical nurse. She consistently listed her birthplace as Sheperdstown, W.Va., and the year as
1884, although birth records show that she was
actually born in Warren County, Va., in 1882.
Blanchfield presumably adjusted these data during World War I to allow an older sister to
appear younger than she was, so that both
women could meet the age requirements of the
Army Nurse Corps.

Blanchfield was educated in the public
schools of Walnut Springs, Va. (1889–1898),
and at a private boarding school in Oranda, Va.
(1898–1899). After nursing her terminally ill
brother, Blanchfield moved to Pittsburgh,
where her mother's family lived, and enrolled
at South Side Hospital Training School for
Nurses, from which she graduated in 1906. The
following year, she did postgraduate work at Dr.

Howard Kelly's Sanitorium in Baltimore and at
the Johns Hopkins University Hospital. From
1915 to 1933, Blanchfield studied various
nonnursing subjects at the Martin School of
Business in Pittsburgh, the University of California, and, by correspondence, Columbia
University. While stationed at Fort McPherson, Ga., in 1928, she studied chemistry.

Blanchfield had a lengthy career as a civilian
nurse prior to her military experience, holding
supervisory positions at Montefiore Hospital in
Pittsburgh, Suburban General Hospital in Bellevue, Pa., and the United States Steel Corporation in Bessemer, Pa. She also worked as a civil
service employee at Ancon Hospital in Panama
in 1913, during the construction of the canal.

Blanchfield enlisted in the Army Nurse Corps
(ANC) when the United States entered World
War I. She served briefly at an Ellis Island hospital before going on to three hospitals in France
(1917–1919). A lieutenant in the relative rank
that the army assigned to the Nurse Corps,
which held women to lower rank and benefit
levels, she was briefly deactivated at the war's
end and nursed again in Pittsburgh before returning to the ANC in January 1920. Blanchfield never married, instead devoting the rest of
her life to the ANC—which, for most of her
career, required that its women be single.

Blanchfield moved through more than a
dozen assignments prior to World War II, serving at army posts in eight states, the Philippines,
and China; in 1925, she did special-duty nursing for the secretary of war. In July 1935, she
was assigned to the Office of the Superintendent
of the ANC, which was within the Office of the
Surgeon General. In 1939, after more than two
decades of service, she was promoted to the relative rank of captain.

From then until 1943, Blanchfield served as
chief assistant to Julia Flikke, who headed the
ANC at the war's beginning. Flikke was increasingly ill, however, and much of the responsibility fell to Blanchfield even prior to Flikke's
retirement in May 1943. Promoted to the relative rank of colonel in June 1943, Blanchfield
headed a corps of some fifty-seven thousand
women by the end of the war; male colonels
sometimes commanded as few as five hundred.
Both she and Flikke received pay that was one
rank lower than the one they ostensibly held.

Rank was only one of the ways in which the
ANC was treated differently from other army
corps. Perhaps most bothersome was the mari-

tal status of nurses. Unlike the women of the WAC, WAVES, and other new branches, and unlike men of any service, nurses who married were discharged. Blanchfield probably expended more energy on recruitment of nurses than on any other task. To do this, she also had to cope with a traditional requirement to work closely with the Red Cross and other civilian bodies not subject to her command.

In 1940, there were only seven hundred nurses in the ANC. By April 1941, it was taking in nearly that many in a single month. After Pearl Harbor, the growth was exponential, and by the end of the war, Blanchfield commanded women from Alaska to Australia and hundreds of points between—a situation unparalleled by any male of her limited rank. She made a number of inspection tours overseas.

Among Blanchfield's wartime accomplishments was the establishment of basic training schools in the nine continental service commands and in all overseas theaters; nurses in these schools learned survival techniques that included crawling through an obstacle course while under fire. She also modernized uniforms, implemented combat-line surgical teams, began programs in air evacuation and psychiatric nursing, launched publication of *The Army Nurse*, and inaugurated a publicity program to acquaint the public with the achievements of wartime nurses. Blanchfield soon developed a reputation for effective administration, great energy, and diplomatic skill.

These characteristics served her well when Congress almost drafted nurses late in 1945. She privately opposed the move, believing that there was no genuine shortage, but her superiors thought differently. The surgeon general testified in favor of the draft in the congressional hearings that were held after President Roosevelt proposed drafting nurses in his 1945 State of the Union speech. With the secretary of war also supporting the bill, it passed the House in March and was reported favorably by the Senate Military Affairs Committee in April. With victory in Europe in early May, however, Blanchfield's view that it was unnecessary prevailed.

On June 14, 1945, she was awarded the Distinguished Service Medal for "exceptional . . . executive ability [that] contributed materially to the brilliant record achieved by the Army Nurse Corps during the war." After demobilization, Blanchfield's highest priority became the regularization of nurses within the army's structure.

With her close congressional ally, Frances Payne Bolton, she worked for comparable rank and other benefits. The Army-Navy Nurse Act, passed on July 18, 1947, ended the practice of relative rank; the next day, General Dwight D. Eisenhower gave Blanchfield her commission, the first for a woman in the regular army. She was honored with the service number of N1 but was demoted from full colonel to lieutenant colonel. She later won retroactive compensation through special legislation.

Although considered a paragon of executive ability, Blanchfield can perhaps be faulted for an excessive modesty that limited her value as a role model. She also insisted that the records of nurses dismissed for pregnancy not reveal the real reason for their leaving the service. Moreover, in military tradition, she was protective of her bureaucratic turf, which made her less than supportive of the new women's military units. Her records reflect more interaction with civilian nurses than with her military colleagues; in more than one thousand pages of the ANC histories that she wrote, there is virtually no mention of the Navy Nurse Corps.

Finally, Blanchfield must bear some of the criticism for the ANC's slow rate of racial integration. While the Women's Army Corps made a point of including blacks from the beginning, the ANC did not accept significant numbers until pressured to do so by civil rights organizations and Congress. Indeed, Congress forced acceptance not only of blacks but also of married women, male nurses, and female physicians. When demobilization began in July 1945, there were only 512 black nurses in the ANC, less than 1 percent of the total.

Blanchfield retired in September 1947, after almost thirty years of service, but continued to devote herself to the ANC by writing two unpublished histories of it. In retirement she spent her time on hobbies that ranged from dressmaking to auto mechanics. She died in Washington, D.C., and was buried at Arlington National Cemetery with full military honors. In 1982, when the Defense Department named its first medical facility for a woman, a Fort Campbell, Ky., hospital was dedicated to Florence Blanchfield.

[A Blanchfield Collection is in the Nursing Archives of Mugar Library at Boston University, and there are materials in the National Archives within the records of the Office of the Surgeon General.

The collection in the army's Center of Military History in Washington includes short biographies by Doris W. Egge (1974); Maj. Cindy Gurney (1986); and Col. Charles F. Bombard, Capt. Wynona Bice-Stephens, and Maj. Karen Ferguson. Blanchfield's histories of the ANC, written with "technical preparation by Mary W. Standlee," are *The Army Nurse Corps in World War II* (1948) and *Organized Nursing and the Army in Three Wars* (1950). Standlee presented the carbon typescripts, with many original photographs, to the University of Texas in Austin, where they are available as bound books. Blanchfield also wrote articles for *American Journal of Nursing:* "The Needs of the Army Nurse Corps," Nov. 1943 and "New Status in Military Nursing," Sept. 1947. Books discussing Blanchfield include Mary M. Roberts, *The Army Nurse Corps Yesterday and Today* (1957); and Edith A. Aynes, *From Nightingale to Eagle: An Army Nurse's History* (1973). Aynes also wrote a feature article on her in *Nursing Outlook,* Feb. 1959. Other significant coverage is in *Current Biography Yearbook* 1943. An obituary is in the *New York Times,* May 13, 1971.]

DORIS WEATHERFORD

BLOCKER, DAN (Dec. 10, 1928–May 13, 1972), actor, was born in DeKalb, Tex., the son of Ora Shack Blocker and Mary Davis. At nearly fourteen pounds, reportedly the largest baby ever born in Bowie County, Blocker was listed as "Bobby Don" on the birth certificate belatedly filed in March 1929. When Dan was six, the family moved to the small West Texas town of O'Donnell, southwest of Lubbock, where the family business was a general store. By the time he was twelve, Blocker was six feet tall and weighed 200 pounds. He was often challenged to fight by older boys and later boasted that he was never beaten.

After grade school he was sent to Texas Military Academy, a prestigious prep school in San Antonio, Tex., where he participated in Golden Gloves boxing. After graduation Blocker enrolled in Hardin-Simmons University in Abilene, and then in 1947 transferred to Sul Ross State College in Alpine, where he graduated in 1950 with a degree in speech and drama.

Blocker, an athlete valuable for both skill and size (at six feet, four inches and weighing 275 pounds), played college football, racking up an undefeated season and conference championship that earned the Lobos a postconference invitation to the Florida Tangerine Bowl. Despite pro offers in boxing and football, Blocker's increasing interest in drama took him to Boston, where he acted in summer stock.

Drafted into the U.S. Army in 1950, he saw combat in Korea with the Forty-fifth Infantry Division, rising to the rank of sergeant. Upon his discharge in 1952, he returned to Sul Ross to work on his master's degree in English and drama. That same year, on August 25, he married his college sweetheart, Dolphia Lee Parker, an Oklahoma native whose family raised quarterhorses; they had four children.

Blocker taught school in Sonora, Tex., and Carlsbad, N.Mex., before moving to California in 1956 to pursue a Ph.D. at UCLA. That move soon brought professional acting opportunities as well, and the year 1957 saw both his first film (*Outer Space Jitters*, a short) and his first major TV appearance on "Restless Gun," a Western, in a December 23 episode entitled "The Child." During the next two years, Blocker appeared in many of the episodes of this series, as well as numerous others. His first feature film, *The Young Captives*, was released in 1959, the same year NBC launched the Western series "Bonanza" (1959–1973).

Blocker's role in "Bonanza," a series depicting the life of a widower with three sons on the mythical Ponderosa Ranch, was that of the middle son, Eric ("Hoss") Cartwright. Despite popular belief, the nickname was not derived from the character's resemblance to his equine companions, but was given him by his Scandinavian mother; in her native tongue, *hoss* meant "good luck." As Hoss, Blocker was the gentle giant, sweet-natured, somewhat gullible, wearing the ten-gallon hat of an earlier West. That high-domed hat became his trademark for the thirteen years "Bonanza" was one of the top ten television programs, as each Sunday at 9:00 P.M. the thundering beat of the theme music brought the four Cartwrights, Ben and his boys, riding into American households. Blocker rode a Morgan horse, since his size could not be supported by the quarterhorses the others rode. An article in *Look* in January 1962 quoted Blocker as joking that he had "the only horse in TV with fallen arches."

The success of "Bonanza," the longest-running Western on television after "Gunsmoke," was credited to the ensemble roles portrayed by Lorne Greene, Pernell Roberts, Blocker, and Michael Landon, who performed both on TV and in road shows, capitalizing on their widespread popularity. Jack Gould, TV critic for the *New York Times*, suggested that the series' popularity was in no small part due to the "remarkably consistent performance of a huge hulk of a man not afraid to use his strength but also invoking gentleness and humor."

Blocker's sometimes sophisticated wit was rarely evident in the roles he played. In the *Look* article, he mused, "Most people think big men are slobs. They aren't. They're just cast that way." Blocker was cast in several films during his tenure with "Bonanza": *The Errand Boy* (1961), *Come Blow Your Horn* (1963), *Lady in Cement* (1968), and *The Cockeyed Cowboys of Calico County* (1970).

Well known and admired throughout the country, Blocker was singled out for honors by his native state. He was named Texan of the Year in 1963 by the Texas Press Association and served as honorary chairman of the Texas Cancer Crusade in 1966. A Democrat, Blocker appeared publicly in support of that party's candidates.

Enormously popular among adults and children alike, Blocker, unlike many successful actors, was also a competent businessman. As part-owner, he helped launch a successful nationwide chain of still-popular steak houses, appropriately named "Bonanza," offering western-style food.

Dan Blocker died in Los Angeles of a pulmonary embolism several weeks after undergoing gall bladder surgery. He is buried in Woodman Cemetery in DeKalb, Tex.

[Blocker's biographical file is in the Barker Texas History Center, University of Texas at Austin. See the relevant entry in *The Handbook of Texas*, III (1976). Articles about Blocker include "TV's Gentle Giant," *Look*, Jan. 30, 1962; and "Bonanza," *Saturday Evening Post*, Dec. 4, 1965. See also Vincent Terrace, *The Complete Encyclopedia of Television Programs, 1947–1976* (1976); and Alex McNeil, *Total Television: A Comprehensive Guide to Programming from 1948 to 1980* (1980). An obituary is in the *New York Times*, May 15, 1972.]

DOROTHY S. ("DOREY") SCHMIDT

BLUE, BEN (Sept. 12, 1901–Mar. 7, 1975), actor and comedian, was born Samuel Bernstein in Montreal, Canada, the son of David A. Bernstein and Sadie Goldberg. (Blue later changed his name when told that a marquee could only accommodate seven letters.) Blue and his father, an art dealer, moved to Baltimore in 1911 after his parents' divorce; shortly thereafter Blue began his career as an entertainer, dancing for coins in the streets.

In 1914, at age thirteen, Blue dropped out of school to make his own living as a window dresser in a haberdashery in Baltimore. The store window became a stage for Ben Blue. As he did his work he would dance and make faces for passersby, often gathering large crowds that would wildly applaud his antics. Later that year Blue landed a job imitating Charlie Chaplin outside Baltimore movie houses to promote Chaplin films.

In 1916, Blue determined that his future was on the stage, and he gave up his last dollar to buy a train ticket to New York. For seven months he struggled as a window dresser at the huge Macy's store on Herald Square until he landed a job on Broadway in the chorus of George M. Cohan's *Married*. The show lasted one year, after which Blue endured a long period off the stage.

His big break came in 1917 when he landed another chorus job in Cohan's *Irene*. Blue was also named as an understudy, and when the show's regular comedian became ill, Blue stepped in. The *New York Post* reported his three performances to be "a riot."

Blue did not immediately parlay his brief Broadway success into stardom. At age nineteen, he and some partners opened a string of dancing schools in Minnesota. Although the business failed within three years, Blue married one of his dance instructors, Mary, in 1922.

The couple set out for Hollywood, where Blue honed his pantomime skills in nightclubs and cafés, devising the routines—notably "The Skating Dance," and "The Dying Swan," which was first performed in Oakland—that would take him back to New York as well as to London, Paris, Budapest, and other European dance capitals. In London alone he gave twenty-seven command performances before members of the royal family.

These routines gave Ben Blue name recognition. He now had opportunities in other areas of show business including shorts and two-reel comedy films. Additionally, he made radio appearances (though his art was mostly visual) and became a headline act on the vaudeville circuit.

Shorts and two-reelers led to feature films in 1936. Blue worked steadily through 1948, first with Paramount, then with MGM. Among his films were *College Holiday* (1936), *High, Wide and Handsome* (1937), *The Big Broadcast of 1938* (1938), *College Swing* (1938), *Paris Hon-*

eymoon (1939), *Panama Hattie* (1942), and *My Wild Irish Rose* (1947).

Meanwhile, Blue continued to take his act on the road. In New York he was a regular in *George White's Scandals* in the late 1930's and early 1940's. He also performed in other American cities and toured with the USO during World War II.

In 1937, Mary Blue sued for divorce, claiming that her husband spent large sums on gambling and escorted other women to social functions; she was given custody of their only child. In 1940, Blue married Axie Dunlap, a player with him in *George White's Scandals*. They had two children.

By the early 1950's, with vaudeville dead, Blue turned to television to practice his craft. His visual comedy was a perfect fit for TV's early years. Dancing, miming, and making faces, Blue often portrayed the poor soul trying to make good in a cruel world. The critic Pauline Kael, when comparing comics in *Reeling* (1976), wrote that the mere thought of Blue made her smile.

Blue was a regular on "The Frank Sinatra Show" from 1949 to 1951. In 1954 he hosted alternate weeks of NBC's "Saturday Night Revue." Of this show, a New York *Herald Tribune* review said, "It will remind you of real, old time Burlesque. . . . It's so terrible it's funny."

Blue also made numerous guest appearances on "The Jack Benny Show," "The Ed Sullivan Show," "The Colgate Comedy Hour," "The Ed Wynn Show," "All Star Review," and "The Milton Berle Show." From 1967 to 1968 he played a farm handyman on the situation comedy show *Accidental Family*.

In 1963, after a fifteen-year hiatus from the movies, Blue returned to the big screen in the star-studded comedy *It's a Mad Mad Mad Mad World*, playing an old, broken-down World War I flying ace with a plane of the same description. Sid Caesar's character hires Blue to transport him in the race for buried treasure, but once in the air, Caesar realizes that the cars below are going faster than Blue's plane.

Three years later, in the successful comedy film *The Russians Are Coming, the Russians Are Coming*, Blue played a classic routine of trying and failing to catch a horse.

Three more films, *A Guide for the Married Man* (1967), *The Busy Body* (1967), and *Where Were You When the Lights Went Out?* (1968), wound up Blue's film career.

In addition to his dancing schools of the early 1920's, Blue owned a Santa Monica supper club during the 1950's, where he often performed. He also owned clubs in London and Paris, and was the proprietor of Slapsie Maxies, one of Hollywood's most popular restaurants. In 1969 Blue was indicated on six counts of tax evasion, but was required to pay only a $1,000 fine.

Most of Blue's remaining years were spent in retirement in Westlake Village, a suburb of Los Angeles, where he died.

[Material on Ben Blue is in the New York Public Library's Performing Arts Research Center at Lincoln Center. Early profiles are in the *New York Post*, Apr. 9, 1938 and Feb. 11, 1939. See also Joe Franklin, *Encyclopedia of Comedians* (1979); and Larry Langman, *Encyclopedia of American Film Comedy* (1987). For information on Blue's television career, see Tim Brooks and Earl Marsh, *The Complete Dictionary to Prime Time Network TV Shows* (1979). Obituaries are in the *Los Angeles Times* and the *New York Times*, both Mar. 9, 1975.]

STEPHEN MCKAY

BOGGS, THOMAS HALE (Feb. 15, 1914– Oct. 16, 1972?), congressman, was born in Long Beach, Miss., one of six children of William Robertson Boggs, a bank cashier, and Claire Josephine Hale. When he was five his family moved to the New Orleans suburb of Gretna, where he was educated in the public and parochial schools of Jefferson Parish. Entering Tulane University on an honor scholarship in 1931, he worked part-time with a local newspaper while pursuing his studies in journalism. After receiving his B.A. degree with Phi Beta Kappa honors in 1935, he entered Tulane Law School, from which he received his LL.B. degree in 1937. Soon afterward, on Jan. 22, 1938, he married Corinne ("Lindy") Morrison Claiborne, daughter of a wealthy Louisiana sugar planter. They had three children.

Admitted to the Louisiana bar in 1937, Boggs began practicing civil law in New Orleans, specializing in gas and oil matters. In 1939, when the "Louisiana Hayride" scandals were shaking state government, he became leader of a small reform organization, the People's League, that temporarily broke the power of the old Huey P. Long political machine. In 1940 Boggs declared himself a Democratic candidate for Congress from the Second Louisiana District, which included most of New Orleans and four adjacent parishes. In a hard-hitting campaign in which he employed a booming oratory that became his political hallmark, Boggs linked the incumbent candidate to the corrupt Long machine and became, at age twenty-six, the youngest member of Congress. In 1942 the machine rallied and defeated Boggs in his bid for reelection. He returned to private practice, enlisted in the naval reserve, was commissioned an officer, and served with the Potomac River Naval Command and the United States Maritime Service until 1946. Returning to politics after World War II, Boggs won back his congressional seat, this time for keeps.

Befriended in Washington by powerful House Speaker Sam Rayburn of Texas, Boggs received choice committee appointments, first to Banking and Currency and, after 1949, to the key Ways and Means Committee. From the outset of his career the witty and urbane Boggs, more liberal at heart than most of his southern congressional colleagues, evinced a strong interest in international affairs. In 1947 he sponsored a resolution calling for a united Europe under the United Nations. He supported the Marshall Plan and backed the Truman administration on Greek-Turkish aid. On Ways and Means, where he chaired subcommittees on tariffs and trade, he developed a scholar's understanding of the complex field of trade legislation and was an articulate and bipartisan spokesman for liberal foreign trade policies. In the period 1957–1958, amid rising protectionist sentiment, he ably led the Eisenhower administration's efforts in the House to reduce tariffs and renew the expiring Reciprocal Trade Agreements Act.

After an unsuccessful 1951 bid to become governor of Louisiana, Boggs concentrated on national politics. He rose steadily in the ranks of House leadership. In 1955 he became deputy whip, and from that post he rose to majority whip in 1962 and to majority leader in 1971. In the latter role he was next in line for the position of House Speaker. While Rayburn's friendship was important, merit and hard work were major factors in Boggs's rise to leadership. A masterful politician, he was an articulate and forceful debater, a skillful parliamentarian, a hardworking and competent commiteeeman, and an adroit compromiser.

A close friend of Lyndon B. Johnson, Boggs was instrumental in persuading the Texan to join the John F. Kennedy ticket as vice-president in 1960. Boggs was a member of the Warren Commission, which investigated the assassination of President Kennedy, and served in 1968 on the President's Commission on the Causes and Prevention of Violence. He worked behind the lines for the New Frontier and the Great Society domestic programs and helped to guide through Congress social legislation improving housing, education, and health care, including Medicare. He tried unsuccessfully to bring his more conservative southern colleagues into the mainstream of national politics, where he had clearly placed himself.

A committed party loyalist, Boggs was chairman of the Democratic National Committee between 1958 and 1972. In 1964 he was parliamentarian and in 1968 chairman of the Democratic National Convention in Chicago, where he presided over the drafting of an unusually liberal platform, one that alienated many white southerners, including many of his own constituents, and led to rioting in the streets.

Although Boggs joined other southern congressmen in signing the 1956 "Southern Manifesto" opposing the Supreme Court's 1954 *Brown* v. *Board of Education of Topeka* decision and its 1955 sequel, *Brown II*, over time he moderated his stand on racial issues. Indeed, his rise in the Democratic party's national leadership was dependent on his willingness to do so. In 1965, urged on by his wife, Lindy, he broke with the conservative southern congressional bloc and supported the Voting Rights Act. He favored the bill, he said, "because I believe the fundamental right to vote must be a part of this great experiment in human progress under freedom which is America." Three years later he voted for the Open Housing Act. His support of these measures very nearly cost him his seat in 1968, when his Republican opponent, appealing to a conservative middle-class electorate, polled 49 percent of the Second District vote.

Despite this narrow victory, Boggs was a great campaigner, a powerful orator and crowd pleaser whose ability to win over an audience made him popular with fellow Democrats facing tough reelections. In 1972 Boggs, a sternly partisan Democrat who had his eye on the House speakership and who was unopposed at home, volunteered to campaign for colleagues in need of help. The plane Boggs was flying in from Anchorage to Juneau, Alaska, on a campaign trip to assist Congressman Nick Begich in his reelection bid, disappeared over Portage Pass on Oct. 16, 1972. The plane was never found, and Boggs, Begich, and two others were lost. Boggs officially served until Jan. 3, 1973, when he was presumed dead pursuant to House Resolution 1 of the Ninety-third Congress.

Boggs's wife, Lindy, who had long served ably as a key member of his staff, was elected to succeed him and was regularly reelected until her resignation in 1991. The Boggs's children became active in public life: Barbara Sigmund, until her death in 1990, was mayor of Princeton, N.J.; Thomas Hale Boggs, Jr., became a Washington lawyer and lobbyist; and Corinne ("Cokie") Roberts became a correspondent for National Public Radio and ABC.

[Boggs's political and personal papers are at the Howard-Tilton Memorial Library, Tulane University. Boggs was author of "Executive Impoundment of Congressionally Appropriated Funds," *University of Florida Law Review*, Winter 1972; and coauthor with Gerald Ford of "Impressions of New China: Joint Report to the United States House of Representatives," House Document 92–237 (1972). A four-part series, "The Life and Career of Hale Boggs," by Bruce Eggler, was published in the New Orleans newspaper *The States-Item*, Jan. 4–9, 1973. Other articles about Boggs include Richard L. Engstrom, "The Hale Boggs Gerrymander: Congressional Redistricting, 1969," *Louisiana History*, Winter 1980; and "New Majority Leader: Thomas Hale Boggs," *New York Times*, Jan. 20, 1971. A 1983 undergraduate honors thesis by Mark Jonathan Doherty, "Hale Boggs and Civil Rights: a Case Study of a Southern Moderate," is at Tulane University. Scott Bailus is author of a 1992 Tulane University M.A. thesis entitled "The Courage of His Convictions: Hale Boggs and Civil Rights." An oral history interview with Lindy Boggs, July 23, 1992, is in the John C. Stennis Oral History Collection, Mississippi State University. Obituaries are in the *New York Times*, Nov. 25, 1972, and *Time*, Oct. 30, 1972.]
CHARLES D. LOWERY

BOHLEN, CHARLES EUSTIS ("CHIP") (Aug. 30, 1904–Jan. 1, 1974), Foreign Service officer, was born in Clayton, N.Y., the son of Charles Bohlen, a banker and sportsman, and Celestine Eustis. The second of three sons, he grew up in Aiken, S.C., and Ipswich, Mass. After extensive private tutoring, he graduated from St. Paul's School in Concord, N.H., in 1923 and received his B.A. in modern European history from Harvard in 1927.

Following a worldwide tramp steamer trip,

he entered the Foreign Service in March 1929. His initial training included four months at the Foreign Service School in Washington, D.C.; experience in Prague as vice-consul; Russian-language studies at the École Nationale des Langues Orientales Vivantes, during much of his time while stationed in Paris; and two summers in Estonia. Along with George F. Kennan, Bohlen belonged to the original small group of Foreign Service officers who received almost exclusive training on Russia and its language. William C. Bullitt, America's first ambassador to the Soviet Union, chose Bohlen to serve as one of the embassy's three Russian-language officers.

Arriving in Moscow on Mar. 8, 1934, Bohlen was reintroduced to Avis Howard Thayer, who was there visiting her brother Charles, an embassy clerk. Bohlen married Avis on Aug. 29, 1935, at her family home at Villanova, Pa.; they had three children.

In Washington, Bohlen worked with Under Secretary William Phillips, and in the summer of 1936 resumed his Russian-area concentration in the Division of Eastern European Affairs. On Jan. 4, 1938, he returned to Moscow as second secretary and consul, after duties the previous year as American delegation secretary at the International Sugar Conference in London and the Conference of the Nine Powers in Brussels. He interpreted for Ambassador Joseph E. Davies at the last of Stalin's three great purge trials, and served under Davies's successor, Laurence Steinhardt. By the end of 1940, Bohlen became second secretary under Ambassador Joseph C. Grew in Tokyo; after the attack on Pearl Harbor, Bohlen and the others were interned on the embassy grounds until their release in June 1942. The return home marked the end of what Bohlen termed his "apprenticeship," for he now became assistant chief of the Russian section of the Division of European Affairs.

He met President Franklin D. Roosevelt's chief assistant, Harry Hopkins, and in January 1944 became chief of the Division of European Affairs, the first of the original six Russian specialists to head a State Department division. Bohlen accompanied Secretary of State Cordell Hull to the Moscow Conference of Foreign Ministers in 1943. While taking notes and advising Hull, Bohlen successfully tested his interpretation skills for the upcoming Teheran Conference.

At Teheran, Bohlen was presidential interpreter and recorder of American delegation minutes. He attended certain sessions and informal discussions at the Dumbarton Oaks conferences in 1944. As special assistant to the secretary of state from 1945 to 1947, he contributed to several of the president's speeches. Bohlen worked closely with Hopkins on the pre-Yalta missions abroad and functioned at Yalta as both interpreter and adviser; later, he would express some criticism of Roosevelt's Yalta dealings.

In May 1945, President Harry S. Truman allowed Bohlen and Hopkins to instigate lengthy discussions in Moscow with Stalin. Bohlen's prime activity at the San Francisco Conference was translating the United Nations Charter from English into Russian. At the Potsdam Conference, he assisted Secretary of State James F. Byrnes.

During the immediate postwar years, Bohlen carried out advisory functions to the secretary, attended most of the Councils of Foreign Ministers, and the initial United Nations Security Council meetings. Particularly pleased to serve under Secretary of State George C. Marshall, Bohlen (who was confirmed by the Senate as counselor in the Department of State in 1947) served as interpreter for Marshall on numerous foreign missions and contributed to the first draft of Marshall's famed Harvard University commencement address in June 1947.

Under Secretary of State Dean Acheson, Bohlen served as minister to France in 1949 and 1950, and was later the senior State representative on the National Security Council's Planning Staff. Shortly after hostilities broke out in Korea, Bohlen (again a counselor to the State Department) experienced his first observation of actual warfare as he accompanied General Omar Bradley; in Tokyo, General Matthew Ridgway briefed Bohlen, whose primary involvement subsequently concerned aspects of the prisoner-of-war situation. According to Bohlen, the Korean War marked diplomatically the decisive departure of the United States from isolationism.

Although a Democrat who disagreed with aspects of Secretary of State John Foster Dulles's foreign policy, Bohlen accepted the Moscow ambassadorial post in 1953. Baffled by the highly publicized vindictive treatment of his nomination by certain Republicans both in the Foreign Relations Committee and on the Senate floor, Bohlen won committee approval of his nomination (15–0) and Senate confirmation (74–13). In retrospect, he considered this victory a turning point of public opinion against McCarthyism.

The Bohlens remained in Moscow from Apr. 11, 1953, until Apr. 17, 1957. During those years, Bohlen attended the 1955 Geneva Conference, assisted in alerting officials at home to the implications of Nikita Khrushchev's secret speech of Feb. 25, 1956, and attended meetings in London during the 1956 Suez crisis. Despite rumors that Bohlen was displeased with Dulles's decision to remove him from Moscow in 1957, Bohlen reaffirmed his determination to remain with the Foreign Service. Though he rejected the ambassadorial post in Pakistan, he accepted that in the Philippines (a country which he had visited only for one week in 1928); there, he dealt with military base agreements and unsuccessfully attempted to increase Filipino jurisdiction over crimes committed by American servicemen. After Christian A. Herter became secretary of state, Bohlen returned to Washington and accompanied President Eisenhower to Paris for the December 1959 NATO meeting and the short-lived May 1960 summit.

During the transition period before John F. Kennedy's inauguration, Bohlen agreed to remain as special assistant to the secretary of state for Soviet affairs. He also served on a special task force overseeing the situation in Laos. He attended President Kennedy's Key West and Nassau discussions with Prime Minister Harold Macmillan, assisted at Kennedy's meetings in France and his first June 1961 meetings with Khrushchev in Vienna, joined Vice-President Lyndon B. Johnson and General Lucius D. Clay's mission to Berlin in August 1961, and accompanied Secretary of State Dean Rusk to the March 1962 Geneva conference.

On October 17, only days before Bohlen's departure for France to his new ambassadorial post there (where his mother had served as hostess to her father, the United States ambassador from 1893 to 1897), President Kennedy showed him reconnaissance photographs of the Soviet missile bases being installed in Cuba and appointed him to an emergency committee headed by Rusk to discuss the removal of the bases. The next day, after another conversation with the President, Bohlen submitted a handwritten top secret memorandum in which he advised applying initial diplomatic, rather than outright military, means to assess Khrushchev's true intent.

Several years later, when President Charles de Gaulle demanded the withdrawal of NATO forces from French soil, Bohlen convinced President Johnson to have the Pentagon comply promptly with the April 1967 deadline. De Gaulle honored Bohlen with the Grand Cross of the Legion of Honor and hosted a farewell luncheon on Jan. 30, 1968. Bohlen had rejected in 1966 the suggestion that he return as ambassador in Moscow; in July 1968, while deputy under secretary for political affairs, he headed the American delegation to the Soviet Union during the inauguration of Pan American Airways's New York–Moscow route.

After forty years with the Foreign Service, Bohlen retired in 1969; as its highest ranking career officer upon Rusk's resignation, Bohlen's final assignment was to serve two days as acting secretary of state until William Rogers was sworn in on January 22. That year Bohlen began his presidency of Italamerica, an investment company. During the Vietnam War, Bohlen lamented such a situation that demonstrated that, no matter how powerful its diplomatic and military structures, a nation must have the total support of public opinion to solidify successful military operations. He died of cancer in Washington, D.C.

During the postwar atomic age, Bohlen advised the West not to appear too anxious to ingratiate itself with the Soviets but at the same time neither to disregard diplomatic conversations nor fear to react forcefully to Soviet divide-and-conquer tactics. As long as statesmen and nations would remain rational and continue working together within the diplomatic spheres, he remained cautiously hopeful about the ultimate outcome of the lengthy Cold War. For Bohlen, that frequently intense conflict was always a dangerous reality, because it had been created by the Soviet Union's Bolshevik ideology, which perceived postwar America as its archenemy and operated within a framework where violence could be an instrument of policy and where there was no differentiation between good and evil or right and wrong.

[Bohlen's papers and oral histories are held at Princeton University, the Library of Congress, Columbia University, and the John F. Kennedy Library. Bohlen published some of his diplomatic reminiscences and analyses in *Witness to History*, *1929–1969* (1973). An elaboration on a series of lectures presented at Columbia University in April 1969 appears in *The Transformation of American Foreign Policy* (1969). See the detailed bibliography in T. Michael Ruddy, *The Cautious Diplomat* (1986). The several confirmation hearings may be found in Congressional publications; a brief summary of the 1953 hearing appears in James N. Rosenau, *The Nomination of "Chip" Bohlen*, Cases in Practical Politics, Eagleton Institute of Politics (1958). See Edward Bliss, Jr., ed., *In Search of Light* (1967), for Edward R. Murrow's Mar. 27, 1953, commentary on Bohlen's successful nomination. Obituaries are in the *New York Times*, Jan. 2, 1974; and the *Times* (London), Jan. 3, 1974.]

MADELINE SAPIENZA

BONTEMPS, ARNA WENDELL (Oct. 13, 1902–June 4, 1973), author, critic, and educator, was born Arnaud Bontemps in Alexandria, La., to Creole parents, Marie Carolina Pembrooke and Paul Bismark Bontemps. His relationship with his father, a stonemason turned lay minister in the Seventh Day Adventist church, was complicated by his attachment to his mother, a former schoolteacher, who died when Bontemps was twelve but not before she had instilled in her son a love for the world of books and imagination stretching beyond his father's view that life consisted of practical concerns.

Several racially motivated incidents led the strong-willed Paul Bontemps to relocate his family to Los Angeles when Arna was three. He and the more exuberant Uncle Buddy, younger brother of the grandmother with whom Arna went to live in the California countryside, proved to be contradictory influences upon Arna after his mother's death. As the older of two children, Arna disappointed his father by choosing a life of writing over following four generations of Bontemps into the stonemason's trade. It was the warm, humorous Uncle Buddy who became for his great-nephew a resource for, as well as support of, the art of storytelling. While Paul Bontemps respected Uncle Buddy's ability to spell and read, he disapproved of his alcoholism, his association with the lower classes, and his fondness for minstrel shows, black dialect, preacher and ghost stories, signs, charms, and mumbo jumbo. Through Buddy, however, Arna Bontemps was able to embrace the black folk culture that would form the basis for much of his writing.

To counter what he perceived as the pernicious effects of Uncle Buddy's attitudes, the elder Bontemps sent his son to San Fernando Academy, a predominantly white boarding school, from 1917 to 1920, with the admonition, "Now don't go up there acting colored." As Arna grew older, he found his parents' antipathy to their own blackness echoed by educators and intellectuals sympathetic to the philosophy of assimilationism. He later pronounced such views efforts to "miseducate" him. He began to understand the opposing responses of his great-uncle and his father toward their racial roots as symbolizing the conflict facing American blacks to "embrac[e] the riches of the folk heritage" or to make a clean break with the past and all that it signified. He concluded that American education reduced the Negro experience to "two short paragraphs: a statement about jungle people in Africa and an equally brief account of the slavery issue in American history." He would devote his life to reinstating the omissions.

Bontemps's diverse occupations were unified by the common goal of forwarding a social and intellectual atmosphere in which African-American history, culture, and sense of self could flourish. Having graduated from Pacific Union College in 1923, he moved from California to New York City to teach at the Harlem Academy and to write. Bontemps became fast friends with Langston Hughes, a physical look-alike as well as an intellectual twin, evidenced by Hughes's 1926 manifesto on black art which became Bontemps's as well: "We younger Negro artists who create now intend to express our individual dark skinned selves without fear or shame."

In the summer of 1924, at age twenty-one, Bontemps published a poem, "Hope," in *Crisis*, a journal instrumental in advancing the careers of most of the young writers associated with the Harlem Renaissance. Recognition thereafter came quickly with his poems "Golgotha Is a Mountain" and "The Return," which in 1926 and 1927, respectively, won the Alexander Pushkin Award for Poetry offered by *Opportunity: Journal of Negro Life*, and "Nocturne at Bethesda," which in 1927 won a first prize for poetry from *Crisis*. Both the *Opportunity* pieces are atavistic poems connecting Bontemps to other Harlem Renaissance poets who express a longing for their roots in Africa. They synthesize racial consciousness and personal emotion, rendering the theme of alienation central to so much of Renaissance poetry as well as suggesting through images of jungles, rain, and the throbbing of drums the attempt to return to original sources, to unleash racial memory by moving back to a more primitive, more sensuous time. Bontemps asserts the archetypal black consciousness as a suffering but indomitable self, a symbol of endurance. In "Nocturne for Bethesda," as in many other poems, he juxtaposes racial consciousness with the traditional Christianity of his youth, lamenting in this poem the inability of religious teachings to make the suffering of the black race meaningful; only through the power of racial memory can blacks find solace. But while the poet recognizes the sustenance gained from such a return in consciousness, he also acknowledges that only a moment of intense insight is possible before the vision fades in the harsh light of reality. Although his stay in Harlem spanned barely seven years, Bontemps interacted with a chorus of new voices who made the Harlem Renaissance a golden age of black art. In addition to Hughes, these included Jean Toomer, Claude McKay, James Weldon Johnson, Countée Cullen, and Zora Neale Hurston.

Although Bontemps harbored plans of pursuing a Ph.D. in English, the Great Depression, family responsibilities, and the demands of his writing contracts with publishing houses stifled such hopes as well as the spirit of optimism that pervaded his early verse. Having married Alberta Johnson on Aug. 26, 1926, Bontemps was now a family man already supporting two of the six children he would eventually father. Forced by economic necessity to leave the Harlem Academy in 1931 to teach at Oakwood Junior College, a black Seventh Day Adventist school in Huntsville, Ala., Bontemps's situation there mirrored the working conditions of much of his career: he was typically short on funds and rarely had a comfortable place to work. His persistence paid off, however, particularly when he turned to writing children's books in the belief that a younger audience was more receptive to the positive images of blacks he wished to instill. Over the next forty years he wrote and edited such books for children and adolescents as *Popo and Fifina* (1932), *You Can't Pet a Possum* (1934), *We Have Tomorrow* (1945), *Frederick Douglass: Slave-Fighter-Freeman* (1959) and its sequel *Free at Last: The Life of Frederick Douglass* (1971), and *Young Booker: Booker T. Washington's Early Days* (1972).

His first novel, *God Sends Sunday*, the story of the most successful black jockey in St. Louis, was published in 1931. Most critics were receptive to the book, and Bontemps himself liked the story well enough to collaborate with Countée Cullen to turn it into a play, *St. Louis Woman* (1939). It premiered in New York on Mar. 30, 1946, and ran for 113 performances. Bontemps's efforts to alter the perception of blacks in American literature ultimately proved disadvantageous to his teaching career: the administration of Oakwood Junior College accused him of promoting subversive racial propaganda and allegedly ordered him to burn his books. He resigned in 1934 and took his family to California, much as his father had done years before. While "temporarily and uncomfortably quartered" with his father and stepmother, Bontemps produced *Black Thunder*, his best and most popular novel. Published in 1936, it offers a fictional version of an 1800 slave rebellion led by Gabriel Prosser. Rendering the theme of revolution through the device of the slave narrative, the novel has become one of the great historical novels in the American tradition.

In 1935 Bontemps accepted a teaching assignment at the Shiloh Academy in Chicago, resigning in 1937 to work for the Illinois Writer's Project. The Caribbean flavor of some of his writing may be traced to a study tour in the Caribbean subsidized by a Rosenwald Fellowship for creative writing received in 1938 and renewed in 1942. His third novel, *Drums at Dusk*, appeared in 1939; continuing his interest in slave history, it depicts the revolt of blacks in Haiti occurring simultaneously with the French Revolution.

After receiving a master's degree in library science from the University of Chicago in 1943, Bontemps was appointed head librarian at Fisk University in Nashville, Tenn., where he remained until 1965. During this period he received two Guggenheim Fellowships for creative writing (1949, 1954). Using his friendship with Hughes to establish at Fisk University Library a Langston Hughes collection, securing as well the papers of such Harlem Renaissance figures as Jean Toomer, James Weldon Johnson, and Countée Cullen, and establishing a collection to honor George Gershwin, Bontemps made the library an important resource for the study of African-American culture.

While his poetry, fiction, and histories have been widely recognized, perhaps Bontemps's most enduring contribution to African-American literary history lies in the scholarly anthologies he compiled and edited, alone or in collaboration with Hughes. Appealing primarily to high school and college undergraduate students, they include *Golden Slippers* (1941), a collection of poems by black writers suitable for young readers; *The Book of Negro Folklore* (1958), a collection of animal tales and rhymes, slave narratives, ghost stories, sermons, and folk songs as well as essays on folklore by Sterling Brown and Zora Neale Hurston; *Hold Fast to Dreams: Poems Old and New* (1969), an anthology of poems blending without chronological or biographical data works by blacks and whites, English and American authors; *Great Slave Narratives* (1969); and *The Harlem Renaissance Remembered* (1972), a collection of eyewitness descriptions of the period accompanied by a memoir by Bontemps.

Bontemps's series of anthologies was capped with a collection of his own poetry in 1963. *Personals*, consisting of twenty-three poems of the 1920's, remains a moving record of a young black artist exercising his imagination for the first time amid Harlem's turbulent literary and social excitement; it also contains an introductory comment describing the goals of the writers of the period and Bontemps's 1940's reaction to the Harlem milieu of the 1920's. Appropriately titled, the collection reveals the personal wonder of a young man whose consciousness is expanding with the enormous possibilities of self-definition and self-acceptance through art while simultaneously acknowledging a brooding sense of homelessness. This expression of the black self makes *Personals* a mirror for the development of black American literature during the 1920's. Bontemps captured the significance of the poetry of the period to all black artists in his 1963 introduction to *American Negro Poetry*: "In the Harlem Renaissance of the twenties poetry led the way for the other arts. It touched off the awakening that brought novelists, painters, sculptors, dancers, dramatists, and scholars of many kinds to the notice of a nation that had nearly forgotten about the gifts of its Negro people."

In 1966 Bontemps renewed his ties with Chicago by teaching black studies at the University of Illinois at Chicago Circle. In 1969 he became curator of the James Weldon Johnson Memorial Collection at Yale University, an important repository of original materials from the Harlem Renaissance. By 1971 he was back at Fisk as writer in residence, working on an autobiography he would not live to complete. He died in Nashville of a heart attack on June 4, 1973.

Though his accomplishments as librarian, historian, editor, poet, critic, and novelist were stunning, Arna Bontemps was perhaps as overshadowed by Langston Hughes as Zora Neale Hurston was by Richard Wright. Epitomizing, however, in his own steady production the quiet, understated endurance celebrated in his poems, contributing in ways large and small to the perpetuation of what, in his early years, was a limited interest in African-American life and culture, Bontemps paved the way for subsequent scholars and writers to find easier access to research materials as well as public recognition. He takes his place as a pioneer who, as Arthur P. Davis asserts, "kept flowing that trickle of interest in Negro American literature—that trickle which is now a torrent."

[A collection of Bontemps's papers is held at the George Arents Research Library, Syracuse University. Several oral history audiotapes, photographs, correspondence, interviews, and manuscripts are available in the Fisk University Library Special Collections. The Bontemps–Hughes letters are located in the James Weldon Johnson Collection at Yale University.

The *Arna Bontemps–Langston Hughes Letters, 1925–1967* have been edited by Charles Nichols (1980). Bibliographies of material on Bontemps include James A. Page, *Selected Black American Authors: An Illustrated Bio-Bibliography* (1977); and Robert E. Fleming, *James Weldon Johnson and Arna Wendell Bontemps: A Reference Guide* (1978). Other useful references are Sterling Brown, *The Negro in American Fiction* (1937); Hugh M. Gloster, *Negro Voices in American Fiction* (1948); Robert A. Bone, *The Negro Novel in America* (1958); Darwin T. Turner, *Black American Literature: Poetry* (1969); Houston A. Baker, Jr., *Black Literature in America* (1971); Roger Whitlow, *Black American Literature: A Critical History* (1973); James D. Young, *Black Writers in the Thirties* (1973); Jack Conroy, "Memories of Arna Bontemps: Friend and Collaborator," *American Libraries*, Dec. 1974; and Arthur P. Davis, "Arna Bontemps," in *From the Dark Tower: Afro-American Writers, 1900–1960* (1974). An obituary is in the *New York Times*, June 6, 1973.]

SUSAN NEAL MAYBERRY

BOURKE-WHITE, MARGARET (June 14, 1904–Aug. 27, 1971), commercial photogra-

pher and photojournalist, was born in New York City, the second of three children, and grew up in Bound Brook, N.J., where she completed her primary and secondary education. Her parents were Joseph White and Minnie Bourke. From her father, who made a modest living as an industrial engineer in the printing industry, she acquired a fascination with modern technology, which was to be the main subject matter of her early work as a professional photographer. Her mother was a perfectionist, and it was from her that Bourke-White derived a lifelong drive to excel at whatever she did.

In 1921, Bourke-White enrolled at Columbia University with an eye to becoming a herpetologist. While there, she began studying photography with Clarence H. White, a noted member of Alfred Stieglitz's Photo-Secession movement. Under White's influence, the art of picture taking became a major preoccupation, and although Bourke-White continued to pursue her academic studies in the biological sciences, her career ambitions following her training with White were focused increasingly on photography.

In 1922, following the death of her father, Bourke-White transferred to the University of Michigan where she met Everett Chapman, an engineering student whom she married June 13, 1924. In the fall she followed her husband to Purdue University, where he had a teaching position and she became a student. Largely because of Chapman's emotional instability, the marriage was fraught with problems from the start, and the couple divorced in 1926; they had no children.

Bourke-White later continued her undergraduate studies in Cleveland at Western Reserve University. In the fall of 1926, she enrolled at Cornell University, where she received her bachelor's degree in biology the following spring. Supporting herself at Cornell by taking pictures of the campus and selling them to students and alumni, she developed a considerable expertise in architectural photography. By the time she graduated in 1927, she was firmly committed to making photography her profession.

Later that year, Bourke-White returned to Cleveland and there established herself as an industrial and architectural photographer. Fearless when it came to mounting high scaffolding or scaling roofs in order to achieve a good angle in her pictures, she soon had a reputation as an emerging talent in the photography business. Early in 1929, her work came to the appreciative attention of magazine publisher Henry Luce. Several months later, his newly founded business magazine, *Fortune*, offered her a photographer's position on its staff. Bourke-White readily accepted and moved to New York City the following year, where she established a studio in the Chrysler Building. For the next several years she divided her time between commercial free-lance work and assignments for *Fortune*.

In 1930, *Fortune* sent Bourke-White to the Soviet Union to do a story on Russian industrialization. Out of this assignment she produced her first book, *Eyes on Russia* (1931), the most extensive photographic account published to that point on the Soviet Union. With that, Bourke-White's reputation escalated rapidly; in 1932, Alfred Stieglitz declared her to be "one of the world's great artists."

A few years later, Bourke-White's work began undergoing a significant change in emphasis. While covering the severe drought and Dust Bowl conditions of the Plains States for *Fortune* in 1934, she became less interested in recording the mechanical aspects of modern life and more concerned with photographing its human elements. Shortly after meeting writer Erskine Caldwell in 1936, that newly awakened interest led to a collaboration with Caldwell that resulted in *You Have Seen Their Faces* (1937), a picture and word chronicle of the life of southern sharecroppers. The book was widely praised at its publication and is considered to be one of Bourke-White's finest accomplishments.

This first success with Caldwell led to two other collaborations with the writer, *North of the Danube* (1939) and *Say, Is This the U.S.A.* (1941). It also led to Bourke-White's marriage to him, Feb. 27, 1939, and their settling down in Darien, Conn. However, the union ended in divorce three years later; they had no children.

While pursuing her projects with Caldwell, Bourke-White also worked as a photographer for *Life*, whose staff she had joined in 1936. Among her most memorable early picture stories for that magazine were pieces about a New Deal dam project in Montana and the community life of Muncie, Ind.

As a *Life* correspondent during World War II, Bourke-White was in the Soviet Union when the Germans invaded that country on June 22, 1941. As the only Western photojournalist there

at the time, she obtained a scoop that most reporters could only dream of, and through the summer and fall of 1941, her exclusives on the Soviet war received prominent treatment in the pages of *Life*. This, however, was but the first of several journalistic distinctions earned by Bourke-White during the war. Unwilling to accept the discriminatory constraints that army press officers were inclined to place on women reporters, she became the first female allowed to accompany and record an Army Air Force bombing mission. Toward the war's end in Europe, she also produced one of the most noteworthy picture chronicles of German concentration camps.

Behind Bourke-White's many successes in news photography was an unrelenting aggressiveness, which in combination with her feminine charm and physical attractiveness, enabled her to penetrate into places that might otherwise have been closed to her. In the postwar years, that aggressiveness contributed to a number of other professional triumphs that further solidified her place as one of the most admired photojournalists of her time. Not the least of those achievements was her coverage of India's emergence as an independent nation, which in addition to her photo stories on the subject for *Life*, also yielded a book, *Halfway to Freedom* (1949).

Following the completion of an assignment to cover the Korean conflict in 1952, Bourke-White began suffering from the early symptoms of Parkinson's Disease. As this illness took an increasing toll, her photographic output diminished, and after submitting her last story to *Life* in 1957, she turned to finishing her autobiography, *Portrait of Myself* (1963). Confined in her later years mostly to her house in Darien, Conn., she died in 1971.

[Bourke-White's papers, along with photographic proofs of her work, are housed at the Syracuse University Library, Syracuse, New York. Publications authored by the subject include *They Called It "Purple Heart Valley"* (1944) and *"Dear Fatherland, Rest Quietly"* (1946). Chief among the books on Bourke-White's work are Sean Callahan, ed., *The Photographs of Margaret Bourke-White* (1972); Theodore M. Brown, *Margaret Bourke-White, Photojournalist* (1972); and Jonathan Silverman, *For the World to See: The Life of Margaret Bourke-White* (1983). For a full-dress biography see Vicki Goldberg, *Margaret Bourke-White: A Biography* (1986). An obituary appears in the *New York Times*, Aug. 28, 1971.]
FREDERICK S. VOSS

BOWEN, CATHERINE DRINKER (Jan. 1, 1897–Nov. 1, 1973), biographer, was born in Haverford, Pa., the youngest of six children of Henry Sturgis Drinker, an attorney, and Aimee Ernesta Beaux. Her ancestors were among the first English settlers in Philadelphia. Drinker grew up in a household of extraordinary drive and competitiveness. She recalled that her four brothers looked over her shoulder, "seldom approving but always challenging." Henry, Jr., the oldest brother, was a prominent Philadelphia lawyer and a talented musician. Another brother, Philip, invented the iron lung; and her brother Cecil was a renowned medical scholar and dean of the Harvard School of Public Health.

In her early youth, Drinker and her family lived on the Haverford College campus outside Philadelphia. When her father left his law practice to become president of Lehigh University in 1905, the family moved to Bethlehem, Pa. Drinker received private tutoring at home; attended Bishopthorpe Manor, a finishing school, and the Moravian Seminary in Bethlehem; then entered St. Timothy's School in Catonsville, Md., from which she graduated in 1916.

In her formative years, Drinker discovered her passion and skill for writing when she began keeping diaries of the family's travels to Europe, Asia, and the Middle East. From the age of eight, she said, she "possessed . . . an unremitting curiosity." Music was her greatest love, and she became an accomplished violinist.

Drinker studied music at the Peabody Conservatory in Baltimore and the Institute of Musical Art (now the Juilliard School) in New York City, earning a teacher's certificate. In 1919 she gave up a career as a professional violinist to marry Ezra Bowen. In 1920 the Bowens settled in Easton, Pa., where Ezra chaired the economics department at Lafayette College. They had two children.

As a young mother, Bowen began a career as a free-lance writer. She produced articles for yachting magazines and in 1923 and 1924 wrote a daily column for the *Easton Express*. In 1924, her first two books were published: *A History of Lehigh University* and *The Story of an Oak Tree*, a book for children. Her only novel, *Rufus Starbuck's Wife* (1932), about a troubled marriage, was partly autobiographical, for her own marriage was unraveling. After a long separation, the Bowens were divorced in 1936. She married Dr. Thomas McKean Downs in 1939.

Bowen, a tall, long-jawed woman with aristocratic features and bearing, gained critical acclaim and national popularity for her writing in the 1930's. *Friends and Fiddlers* (1935), in collaboration with Barbara von Meck, was an engaging collection of essays that blended her passions for music and writing. It was music that led her into the field of biography. *Beloved Friend: The Story of Tchaikovsky and Nadejda von Meck* (1937), also written in collaboration with Barbara von Meck, was a fresh and revealing study of the Russian composer and his patron. The book was based on exhaustive research, but Bowen did not go to Russia.

For her next project, a dual biography of Tchaikovsky's mentors, Bowen spent months in the libraries of Paris, Berlin, Leningrad, and Moscow. *Free Artist: The Story of Anton and Nicholas Rubinstein* (1939), authoritative and vividly written, placed Bowen in the front rank of biographers. She wanted to follow this work with a portrait of Felix Mendelssohn but was cut off from access to primary source material by the outbreak of World War II.

During the war, Bowen applied herself to an American subject: Justice Oliver Wendell Holmes. She was drawn to Holmes because of her interest in the Constitution and American government. "Whenever I get interested in a subject, I always find it easier to study it through a person than deal with it in the abstract," she said. Though denied access to the justice's unpublished writings, Bowen was a skilled and indefatigable archivist who found voluminous new materials and interviewed dozens of Holmes associates. "If the significance of his life lay wholly in his legal achievements," wrote Bowen, "there would be no place for a biography written by a layman. If its significance lay wholly in his written words, there would be no place for a biography at all. But Holmes's greatness lay most of all in his manner of meeting life. He had a genius for living, a genius for finding himself wholly, using himself wholly. He loved life and believed in it. . . . For him, the act of learning was always an adventure."

Bowen, who wrote in a rich, evocative style, approached her subjects with enthusiasm and excitement. Her gift was an ability to take major historical figures out of the pantheon and to bring them vividly to life. She passionately believed that good biography was also good literature.

"Writing biography is exciting business,"

Bowen wrote. "Like courtship, it has its moments of gratification and its days of despair when history closes her doors and will not show her face. . . . To recreate the past is no less a task artistically, than to write a novel or an epic poem."

Yankee from Olympus: Justice Holmes and His Family (1944) was a triumphant success. "It is not a portrait of a judge, but of a man, warm, intimate, sympathetic, penetrating," Henry Steele Commager wrote in a review for the *New York Herald Tribune*. "If Holmes had his choice, we may well believe that it is rather by this portrait that he would prefer to be known."

Bowen next wrote about John Adams because she wanted to explore Holmes's New England heritage and the origins of American government. *John Adams and the American Revolution* (1950) was another biographical masterpiece. She next focused on Sir Edward Coke (1552–1634), the English attorney general and author of the Petition of Right that was used as a model by leaders of the American Revolution. For six years, Bowen researched Coke's life at libraries in England and the United States. *The Lion and the Throne: The Life and Times of Sir Edward Coke* (1957) won critical acclaim on both sides of the Atlantic and earned Bowen the National Book Award for nonfiction.

In *Francis Bacon: The Temper of a Man* (1963), Bowen illuminated the life of Coke's great rival. A. L. Rowse, the British historian, wrote in the *New York Times Book Review* that Bowen, who had produced the best study of Coke, also painted the most perceptive and insightful Bacon portrait.

Miracle at Philadelphia: The Story of the Constitutional Convention (1966) was Bowen's most ambitious work, a masterful study that captured the drama and conflict in the shaping of American government. *Family Portrait* (1970), a memoir of Bowen's family, was described by the author as "a celebration and a mourning." In it Bowen revealed more about other family members than herself.

Bowen died in Haverford, Pa. She was then working on a study of Benjamin Franklin, which was published as *The Most Dangerous Man in America: Scenes from the Life of Benjamin Franklin* (1974). At the time of her death, Bowen was widely viewed as America's premier biographer.

[Bowen's papers are in the Library of Congress. She wrote about her approach to biography in *The Writing of Biography* (1951); *Adventures of a Biographer* (1959); and *Biography: The Craft and the Calling* (1969). Her son, Ezra Bowen, provides reminiscences of Bowen in *Henry and Other Heroes* (1974). There are interviews with Bowen in the *New York Times Book Review*, July 2, 1950, and Mar. 10, 1957; and *Women's Wear Daily*, June 2, 1970. Obituaries are in the *Philadelphia Inquirer*, Nov. 2, 1973; and the *New York Times*, Nov. 3, 1973.]

STEVE NEAL

BOWEN, IRA SPRAGUE (Dec. 21, 1898–Feb. 6, 1973), astronomer and physicist, was born in Seneca Falls, N.Y. His father, James Henry Bowen, was a Methodist minister and later business agent for the Methodist church. The family, including an older brother and Ira, moved often in New York State, so Ira received his first schooling from his mother, Philinda May Sprague, a licensed teacher. After her husband's death in 1908, Mrs. Bowen taught at Houghton Wesleyan Methodist Seminary, where Ira completed high school. He continued in the college course at the seminary for three years, where he was keenly interested in the courses in mathematics, physics, and astronomy. Then he entered Oberlin College for his senior year and received the B.A. in 1919.

Bowen took graduate studies at the University of Chicago, where he became assistant to Nobel laureate Robert A. Millikan, and transferred with him when Millikan moved to the California Institute of Technology in 1921. There, while teaching and publishing research papers, Bowen was persuaded by his colleagues to complete the requirements for the Ph.D., which he received in 1926. He then became assistant professor at Caltech and advanced to professor in 1931. Bowen married Mary Jane Howard in 1929; they had no children. She pursued a career as child psychologist, and was a warm hostess to her husband's colleagues.

In their first year at Caltech, Bowen and Millikan obtained the highest records of cosmic rays to that time by using unmanned sounding balloons launched from San Antonio, Tex. Bowen also measured cosmic-ray intensity in mountain lakes in California. From these field experiences, he began a lifelong avocation of hiking western mountains and deserts. His dissertation presented a formula for the ratio of heat lost by evaporation and by conduction to the air from any water surface, which came to be known as the Bowen ratio.

Using advanced equipment available at Mount Wilson Observatory, Bowen analyzed the more complex spectra of the first twenty elements of the periodic table. He went on to solve the problem of anomalous green lines, called "nebulium lines" in the spectra of galactic nebulae. These lines had been considered a hypothetical element found only in outer space. Bowen's careful analysis proved that the lines were due to supposedly "forbidden" transitions between energy levels of ionized atoms of ordinary elements, such as oxygen, that could prevail only under the unusually low density in gaseous nebulae.

In 1938 Bowen was invited to visit the University of California's Lick Observatory on Mount Hamilton, where he worked with Arthur B. Wyse. Using newly available photographic emulsions, they were able to determine that the relative abundance of elements in gaseous nebulae is about the same as that of the sun and stars, with hydrogen as the most abundant element.

Bowen developed a procedure of baking photographic plates at high temperature before their exposure, which considerably increased the speed at which long exposures of distant objects could be taken. He also designed an image slicer, which came to be called Bowen's device; it consists of an array of narrow reflecting mirrors that reduces the loss of light onto the photographic image of distant stars and nebulae.

During World War II Bowen organized and guided the photographic section for a major Caltech program on solid-fuel rockets supported by the Office of Scientific Research and Development. He developed very high-speed cameras that took successive very short exposures of projectives in early flight. Separately, he collaborated in studies of the transparency of seawater.

In 1946 Bowen was appointed director of the Mount Wilson Observatory by the Carnegie Institution of Washington, D.C. He closely directed the completion of the Hale 200-inch telescope that had been under construction at Caltech from 1930, but was delayed by World War II. He assumed the task of testing the mirror on stars and of guiding the final steps of its polishing. The largest reflecting telescope in the world at that time was installed on Palomar Mountain in southern California in 1948. The Mount Wilson and Palomar Observatories

(later named Hale Observatories), jointly owned by Caltech and the Carnegie Institution, were under Bowen's direction from that year until 1964. He formalized the agreement between the two organizations and was an effective administrator of this unique joint endeavor. Caltech enlarged its teaching program in astronomy, and several professors there held joint appointments.

As soon as a forty-eight-inch Schmidt telescope was also installed at Palomar Observatory in 1948, it was used first, at Bowen's insistence, to create a detailed survey of the entire sky within its range. The Palomar Sky Survey from 1948 to 1957 created a series of nine hundred photographic plates of the sky from the North Pole to declination − 30 degrees, and copies of it were distributed to observatories worldwide. Bowen always encouraged use of the facilities under his direction by astronomers elsewhere, especially those not located at major observatories. As astronomy advanced during the 1950's, he promoted the construction of more large telescopes at various locations throughout the world, and he generously provided advice to other astronomers and telescope designers.

Bowen organized the Carnegie Image Tube Committee, which eventually developed an effective device for amplifying star records. He retired as director of the two observatories in 1964, but continued his own researches. He did not often make astronomical observations himself. However, over the years he became an expert on the optical design of telescopes to provide exceptionally large fields of excellent definition. He also designed ingenious cameras for use with telescopes. He offered his engineering plans and drawings to other observatories and to commercial companies for production.

Bowen was elected to the National Academy of Sciences in 1936. He received distinguished awards from several astronomical societies. His hobbies included numismatics and collecting early books on physics and astronomy.

[Bowen's papers are at Henry E. Huntington Library, Pasadena, Calif. Among his significant publications are "The Chemical Composition of the Nebulae," *Publications of Astronomical Society of the Pacific* 1934; "New Lines in the Spectra of the Gaseous Nebulae," *Publications of Astronomical Society of the Pacific* 1938 (with A. B. Wyse); and "Wavelengths of Forbidden Nebular Lines," *Astronomical Journal* 1955. Biographies of him are Caryl P. Haskins, "Ira Sprague Bowen," *Yearbook for 1973,*

American Philosophical Society, Philadelphia; Laurence H. Aller, "Ira Sprague Bowen," *Quarterly Journal of Royal Astronomical Society of London* 1974; and Horace W. Babcock, "Ira Sprague Bowen," *Biographical Memoirs. National Academy of Sciences* 53 (with bibliography). An obituary is in the *New York Times*, Feb. 8, 1973.]

ELIZABETH NOBLE SHOR

BOWLES, JANE AUER (Feb. 22, 1917–May 4, 1973), writer, was born in New York City, the only child of Sidney Major Auer, a native of Cincinnati, and Claire Stajer of New York City. Both parents were second-generation Austro-Hungarian Jews, and the family lived on West Eighty-ninth Street after Jane was born. Claire had been a teacher before she married; Sidney owned a garment company that failed and was eventually reduced to working as an insurance agent, as his unschooled father had done. Her father died of a hypertension attack in his living room in 1930 at their home in Woodmere, Long Island. Jane once said that her father's death left her alone with her mother, this being the worst thing that could ever have happened to her. Jane also never forgot her father's criticisms that she was a procrastinator and overly dramatic. These characteristics would haunt her in later life.

Jane was privately tutored and attended Madame Tisnée's, a French school for children in Manhattan; she later attended public school in Woodmere after the family moved to this middle-class Jewish community (her parents were nonpracticing Jews). Claire was passionately devoted to Jane, especially after Sidney's death, pampering her "million-dollar baby" with expensive clothes and much attention. First encouraged to write at public high school in 1930, Jane shortly moved on to a private boarding school, the Stoneleigh School in Greenfield, Conn., an institution that she later claimed had anti-Semitic housing policies. In her first winter term at Stoneleigh, Jane fell from a horse and broke her right leg; the injury never healed correctly and, after a diagnosis of tuberculosis of the knee, Jane was sent by her mother to a clinic in Leysin, Switzerland, for treatment.

In Switzerland Jane learned French and studied French literature as well as reportedly writing a novel in French (*Le Phaéton Hypocrite*, now lost). When she returned to the United States in 1934 following an unsuccessful recuperation,

surgeons decided to fuse the knee joint, alleviating her chronic pain but causing an irreparable limp. Jane's temperament at this time was characterized by both flamboyance and severe self-doubt, and her distinctive appearance of red-hennaed hair and casual male clothing caused her mother to dismay. Her lesbian attractions and affairs were evident to friends and to her mother; Jane openly frequented the lesbian bars of Manhattan and developed passionate crushes, especially on torch singers of the period such as Helen Morgan and Libby Holman (who became an intimate of hers).

However, Jane's most significant union was with the writer and composer Paul Bowles, whom she married on Feb. 21, 1938. Paul wrote scores for ballets and incidental music for the stage works of Philip Barry, Tennessee Williams, and Lillian Hellman. Upon meeting Bowles at a party in the Plaza Hotel in New York City, Jane was struck with this distinguished-looking young artist whose reserved character was a strong contrast to her impetuous, impulsive nature. When Jane introduced Paul to her mother, Claire Auer breathed a sigh of relief that Jane was perhaps smitten by a male and would give up her lesbianism. Although it has been strongly argued that Jane and Paul never had sexual relations, even after marriage vows, Jane's biographer gives a different account. Paul himself was an open homosexual who circulated with Jane in the gay literati circles of playwright Tennessee Williams and his lover, Frank Merlo; the composer Virgil Thomson; poets and lovers Gregory Corso and Allen Ginsberg; novelist William Burroughs; and Gertrude Stein and Alice B. Toklas.

The Bowleses' travels through Europe, North Africa, Central America, and Mexico—frequently undertaken with one other guest—creating the dynamic of a trio—and their expatriate sensibilities figured in the prose and plays of each Bowles, as in Paul's most celebrated work, *The Sheltering Sky* (1949). Some critics have suggested that in writing this novel Paul was greatly influenced by Jane's only completed novel, *Two Serious Ladies* (1943), a work about two eccentric women that draws upon periods when Jane lived with Paul on Staten Island and in Central America, among other locations. Writer Alan Sillitoe called *Ladies* "a landmark in twentieth century American literature," but it only gained a cult following and is still considered to be a "novelist's novel."

Jane was clearly the more autobiographical writer. The puppet play *A Quarreling Pair* was written during her early 1940's difficult love affair in Mexico with the American Helvetia Perkins; Perkins tried to wrestle Jane away from her husband—and briefly succeeded. While Jane was staying with Perkins in the Chelsea Hotel in New York City, she finished *Two Serious Ladies*; she also attempted suicide by slitting her wrists after a difficult time with Perkins (Jane would later claim that the attempt was not serious).

Paul, in an interview in 1993, offered a description of Jane's writing: "I am not certain whether it is sufficiently realized that Jane was above all a dealer in comedy. For life to be bearable, it must be made absurd. Her characters find themselves in situations which necessitate being understood as basically ridiculous. They are serious and laughable." He added, "Some days I would see her behavior in a peculiar fashion, not like her usual self. If I seemed confused by this, she would smile crookedly and explain: 'I'm a character today.' "

At one point the Bowleses lived in a Brooklyn boardinghouse with poet W. H. Auden, composer Benjamin Britten, novelist Carson McCullers, and Oliver Smith, a theater producer who later commissioned Jane's only completed full-length play, *In the Summer House*, which Jane began in 1947. The play has challenged critics and audiences alike since its first Broadway staging in 1953, directed by José Quintero and starring Mildred Dunnock and Judith Anderson. Negative reviews resulted in the play's closing after a run of two months. The play concerns the relationship between an eccentric and histrionic mother and her brooding, enigmatic daughter; the latter character is possibly responsible for the mysterious offstage death of another young girl. In the play, mother berates daughter; the former even believes her capable of murder. It is not difficult to see an autobiographical tint to the play, considering Jane's own dysfunctional relationship with her doting mother. The play was included in the anthology edited by Louis Kronenberger, *Best Plays of 1953–54* (1954).

In July 1947, Paul Bowles moved to Morocco. Jane, apprehensive about leaving her lesbian circle in New York, was unsure that she would find female companionship in their future home base of Tangier. Nonetheless, Jane followed in 1948 and, there, became entangled with a lesbian Arab marketplace vendor, Cherifa, who caused her innumerable financial and domestic problems. After this point, Jane no longer lived exclusively with her husband and found it increasingly difficult to write. With the exception of a few short stories for American magazines, she did not publish new work. Once when she was asked to devise a short biography of herself for *World Authors*, she wrote, "I started to 'write' when I was about fifteen and was obliged to do composition in school. I always thought it the most loathsome of all activities, and still do. At the same time I felt even then that I had to do it."

In 1957, Jane Bowles suffered a stroke resulting in aphasia and vision loss, which made it impossible for her to continue as a writer. She drank and took pills indiscriminately for various psychiatric conditions and finally became a vagrant, a nuisance in the streets and bars of Tangier. Paul reluctantly had her institutionalized for a latent occurrence of manic-depressive psychosis, aggravated by seizures, more strokes, and alcohol. After nearly six years of hospitalization in Spain, broken up by short periods of returning to her husband in Tangier, Jane fell into a comatose condition and died in Malaga, Spain.

[Jane Bowles's letters and eighteen notebooks are at the Humanities Research Center at the University of Texas in Austin. Also see *Out in the World: Selected Letters of Jane Bowles, 1935–1990*, edited by Millicent Dillon (1985). Her few complete writings are as follows: *Two Serious Ladies* (1943); the short stories, "A Guatemalan Idyll," *Cross Section*, 1944, edited by Edwin Seaver; "A Day in the Open," *Cross Section*, 1945, edited by Edwin Seaver; "Plain Pleasures," *Harper's Bazaar* (Feb. 1946); "Camp Cataract," *Harper's Bazaar* (Sept. 1949); and "A Stick of Green Candy," *Vogue*, Feb. 15, 1957. Jane did publish one nonfiction piece on her experiences in Tangier, "East Side: North Africa," *Mademoiselle* (Apr. 1951). *The Collected Works of Jane Bowles* (1966), with an introduction by Truman Capote, and an expanded version of the collected works, *My Sister's Hand in Mine* (1978), are the definitive American collections of her work (separate British collections, gathered and somewhat altered by her husband, who changed the nonfiction piece to fiction, were published under the title *Plain Pleasures* in 1966). Act I of *In the Summer House* was first published in *Harper's Bazaar* (Apr. 1947); the play was published in book form in 1954. For biography see Millicent Dillon, *A Little Original Sin* (1981); and Christopher Sawyer-Lauçanno, *An Invisible Spectator: A Biography of Paul Bowles* (1989). An obituary is in the *New York Times*, May 31, 1973.]

RICHARD FUMOSA

BOYD, LOUISE ARNER (Sept. 16, 1887–
Sept. 14, 1972), arctic explorer and geographer,
was born in San Rafael, Calif., the third child
of John Franklin Boyd, a mining operator and
investor, and Louise Cook Arner. Boyd was
taught by a governess, then attended Miss Stewart's School in San Rafael and, later, Miss
Murison's School in San Francisco. At an early
age she became a skilled marksman and equestrian. She did not attend college.

Shortly after the deaths of two of her brothers, both in their teens, Boyd was brought by
her father into the family business, an investment company. After the death of her mother
in 1919 and of her father a year later, she was
heiress to a vast fortune (garnered during the
gold rush), as well as the family's San Rafael
estate, Maple Lawn.

Boyd toured Europe in 1928, keeping a
record of her travels and a diary of her impressions. With curiosity aroused through reading
about arctic exploration and polar travel, she
returned to Europe in the summer of 1924 and
cruised from Norway to Spitsbergen, a chain of
islands located in the Arctic Ocean between
Norway and East Greenland. On that trip Boyd
discovered the Arctic, "a land of extraordinary
grandeur," which became the guiding passion
of her life. She returned to the Arctic in 1926
and organized her own expedition aboard the
MS *Hobby*, a Norwegian sealer, to hunt polar
bears with friends in Franz Josef Land, an ar-
chipelago in the Arctic Ocean north of Novaya
Zemlya. This expedition was the first of seven
that Boyd personally organized, headed, and
financed, and the one on which her lifelong
interest in photography began. (Boyd was reported to have shot and killed twenty-nine polar
bears, a claim that she herself never made and
one that she vigorously denied in later years.
The trip did, however, yield many photographs
of live bears.)

Boyd quickly became a celebrity in the tabloids and the subject of derision among scientists who considered the wealthy woman a
nonscientist dabbling in what was then considered a man's field. Despite these obstacles to
being taken seriously, she returned to the Arctic
in 1928, her interest sparked by stories of the
wild coast of East Greenland. About to set off
on the *Hobby* when word came of the missing
Norwegian explorer Roald Amundsen, Boyd
placed ship, crew, and equipment at the service
of the Norwegian government. The *Hobby* set

off from Tromsø, Norway, on what proved to be
an unsuccessful search; Boyd documented the
journey extensively in photographs. For her efforts Norway awarded her the Order of Saint
Olaf. Still determined to explore the coast of
East Greenland, Boyd meticulously planned a
scientific journey for the summer of 1931 with
the goal of further mapping the fjords there.

The 1931 expedition, aboard the Norwegian
vessel SS *Veslekari*, laid the groundwork for in-
depth research in the voyages of 1933, 1937,
and 1938. More important, the scientific significance of this and subsequent expeditions became apparent. Boyd photographed the Franz
Josef and King Oscar fjord region extensively,
using state-of-the-art equipment and the latest
photogrammetric mapping techniques to correct earlier errors. Dr. Isaiah Bowman and others at the American Geographical Society
(AGS) had introduced Boyd to the emerging
scientific method that utilized an interdisciplinary approach. With the 1931 trip, Boyd began
a lifelong relationship with the AGS, which
sponsored all subsequent expeditions and published her reports, photos, and maps. The Danish government honored her by naming the area
around Greenland's De Geer glacier Miss Boyd
Land, a designation that has remained to the
present.

The second *Veslekari* expedition set out on
June 28, 1933, to study the botany, animal life,
archaeology, and glacial features of the Franz
Josef and King Oscar fjord region, utilizing the
latest in ultrasonic depth-measuring tools. On
the return from the interior of Franz Josef
Fjord, the *Veslekari* ran aground. With the approaching pack ice of winter, it became imper-
ative to free the ship, or risk wintering over.
Boyd's diaries record the harrowing experience—a passing iceberg was used to free the
ship—and the AGS published her observations
as *The Fiord Region of East Greenland* (1935).

In August 1934, Boyd attended the International Geographical Congress in Warsaw; her
travels through the Danzig Free State, East
Prussia, and the Polish corridor were documented in *Polish Countrysides* (1937). The goal
of Boyd's 1937 expedition was to travel as far up
the East Greenland coast as weather would permit. With a scientific team that included pa-
leogeologists, surveyors, a hydrographer, and a
botanist, Boyd discovered a previously undocu-
mented ocean bank (named the Louise A. Boyd
Bank). The *Veslekari* escaped from a complex

maze of ice floes by means of dynamite and ice anchors.

The Boyd expedition of 1938 landed at a point on East Greenland (77°48' north latitude) farther north on that island than any ship had previously reached; it was the second highest latitude reached by any ship, and Boyd spent a few hours on shore, just south of Cape Montpensier, making observations and photographing the forbidding environment. For this undertaking she received the AGS's Cullum Award, the first time it had been presented to a woman. Publication of her study, *The Coast of Northeast Greenland* (1948), was delayed because of the important strategic information it might contain for the enemy during the approaching war. During World War II, Boyd was consultant to the National Bureau of Standards, conducting research concerning long-distance radio transmission. In 1941, she joined Captain Robert Abram Bartlett, who had accompanied Robert E. Peary on his 1897 North Pole expedition, for scientific research in the Canadian Arctic.

Boyd made available to the War Department and other agencies her many photographs, maps, and scientific findings. In her eighth and final expedition, on June 16, 1955, at the age of sixty-seven, she achieved a lifetime dream of flying over the North Pole and photographing the area.

Boyd dressed fashionably when she was not exploring the Arctic. "I like the pleasant things most women enjoy," she was quoted as saying, "even if I do wear breeches and boots on an expedition, even sleep in them at times. . . . but I powder my nose before going on deck, no matter how rough the sea is." Boyd was an avid gardener and a civic leader in the San Francisco area. She donated a portion of her estate to the city of San Rafael (now known as Boyd Park), and her library of arctic and Scandinavian books to the universities of California and Alaska. Her honors include election to the Council of Fellows of the American Geographical Society and being named a chevalier of the French Legion of Honor. Boyd, who never married, died in a San Francisco convalescent home, her personal fortune depleted from her expeditions.

[The Marin County Historical Association, located on the grounds of Maple Lawn in San Rafael, has an archive of Boyd's papers. A large collection of her photographs and maps is in the Golda Meir Library at the University of Wisconsin, Milwaukee. Among her articles are "Fiords of East Greenland: A Photographic Reconnaissance Throughout the Franz Josef and King Oscar Fiords," *Geographical Review*, Oct. 1932; and "The Louise A. Boyd Seven Arctic Expeditions," *Photogrammetric Engineering*, Dec. 1950. Biographical information is available in Elizabeth F. Olds, *Women of the Four Winds* (1985); and Marion Tinling, *Women into the Unknown* (1989). Obituaries are in the *New York Times*, Sept. 17, 1972; and *Geographic Review*, Apr. 1973.]

JONATHAN G. ARETAKIS

BOYD, WILLIAM (June 5, 1898–Sept. 12, 1972), actor, was born in Cambridge, Ohio, the son of Charles W. Boyd, a farm worker, and Lida Alberta Wilkins. The family moved to Tulsa, Okla., where he attended public school. Upon the death of his parents, he left school at an early age and worked in the Oklahoma oil fields. He held a variety of jobs, including tool dresser and surveyor. In 1919, he went to Hollywood and appeared as an extra in Cecil B. DeMille's production, *Why Change Your Wife?* (1919). His first important role was in another DeMille motion picture, *The Volga Boatman* (1926). During the 1920's, the well-built young man, five feet, eleven inches in height, with platinum hair, blue eyes, and an easygoing manner, became an attractive leading man. Among his better-known pictures of this period were *King of Kings* (1927), *Dress Parade* (1927), and *Two Arabian Knights* (1928), which established him as a well-paid star earning about $100,000 a year. When the transition from silent films to talking pictures took place, Boyd was among the fortunate screen actors with a good speaking voice. In keeping with the free spending spirit of the times among Hollywood actors, he acquired an impressive home in Beverly Hills, a beach house at Malibu, and a ranch. He also developed a reputation as a playboy.

In the depression year of 1931, Boyd's high style of living came to an end when Radio Pictures canceled his contract. Contributing to his downfall was bad publicity that he received in a case of mistaken identity and publication of his picture in newspapers across the country for someone else's crime. The guilty person was another well-known actor with the same name. He was a William Boyd who had notably played Sergeant Quirt in the stage play, *What Price Glory?* He had been arrested for the possession of illegal whiskey and gambling equipment.

For the next three years, Boyd, now frequently referred to as Bill Boyd, accepted subordinate parts in B movies, usually as a villain in Westerns or as a gangster. Among his gangster films were *The Wiser Sex* (1932) with Melvyn Douglas and Claudette Colbert and *State's Attorney* (1932) with John Barrymore and Helen Twelvetrees. In 1934, he received the part of Hopalong Cassidy for a series of low-budget movies produced by Harry Sherman and distributed by Paramount. The fictional character of the friendly, soft-spoken cowboy had been created by the pulp writer, Clarence E. Mulford, who wrote twenty-five books about this Western hero who walked with a limp caused by a knee injury in a gunfight. In motion pictures, some of the rougher aspects of the character were eliminated and Hopalong, with his devoted horse Topper, became a symbol of virtue who never smoked, drank, or used profane language. The success of this screen cowboy, particularly but not exclusively with children, led to the production of fifty-four pictures in the series. Eventually, Hopalong Cassidy became the longest-running role in Hollywood history. By 1936, a critic wrote, "Not knowing Hopalong is about as bad as not knowing Terry and the Pirates or Buck Rogers." Among these films were *Three on the Trail* (1936), *Partners of the Plains* (1938), and *Heart of Arizona* (1938). Although critics referred to Hopalong Cassidy films as another of the many "horse operas" that appeared, they also commented that these cattle-rustling, hard-riding, and fast-shooting films were above average for low-budget productions for the family trade. They were polished presentations with competent casts and excellent photography.

By 1943, rising costs forced Sherman to stop production, but Boyd produced twelve more films in partnership with Benedict Bogeaus and Lewis Rachmil. Originally, each picture had a budget of $10,000 and a ninety-hour shooting schedule. By 1947, Boyd found costs prohibitive and discontinued production. Boyd, however, had both the imagination to see the intrinsic value of Hopalong Cassidy and the determination to gain television rights to the character. At great risk and sacrifice to himself, he sold many of his assets, including his ranch, to purchase the television rights for about $350,000 and form Hopalong Cassidy Productions. The negotiations were a complex matter that took years of bargaining and reportedly it was necessary to sign 1,500 separate contracts. All of this was done in the early days of television when the prospects for success of such a product were highly speculative.

The old Hopalong films were shown on almost every television station in the nation and they proved to be a financial bonanza. This success led to the production of twenty-six half-hour shows for television. The first, *The Knife of Carlos Valero* appeared in October 1950. During this same year, there was also an adaptation for radio which was broadcast on the Mutual Network to 496 stations with an estimated audience of twenty-five million, mainly children between the ages of four to thirteen. In competition with Roy Rogers and Buck Jones, Hopalong Cassidy was promoted on radio as "the most famous hero of them all." In addition, a Hopalong Cassidy comic strip appeared in 155 newspapers and there were comic books distributed in the millions.

Boyd, an able businessman, took advantage of licensing products associated with the popular character. Shirts, pants, bicycles, and about fifty other products had a wide appeal for children. Boyd wisely licensed quality products at reasonable prices and refused to merchandise products that did not meet his high standards. It was reported in 1950 that 108 licensed manufacturers turned out products at the rate of seventy million dollars a year.

Boyd married Ruth Miller in 1921. They had one son who lived nine months and were divorced. In 1926, he married Elinor Fair and divorced her in 1929. He married Dorothy Sebastian in 1930, and they were divorced in 1936. In 1937 he married Grace Bradley, to whom he attributed much of his success. He retired in 1953, invested in real estate, and lived quietly. During his later years, he engaged in philanthropic activities, especially for children's hospitals and homes because children had made his success possible.

[Material on Boyd is in the New York Public Library's Performing Arts Research Center at Lincoln Center. See also the cover story on Boyd in *Time*, Nov. 27, 1950. An obituary is in the *New York Times*, Sept. 14, 1972.]

ERNEST A. MCKAY

BOYLE, HAROLD VINCENT ("HAL") (Feb. 21, 1911–Apr. 1, 1974), journalist referred to as the "Poor Man's Plato" by the Associated Press (AP), was born in Kansas City, Mo., one of four children of Peter E. Boyle and Margaret Mary Gavaghan, a self-educated Irish immigrant.

As a youngster Boyle had initially aspired to become a civil engineer, but because he did not excel in mathematics, he redirected his secondary school education toward a career in teaching. After graduating from high school in Kansas City in 1928, he attended Kansas City Junior College for two years. During his first year as a college student Boyle began his association with the Associated Press. He worked as an office boy at night in its Kansas City office, and had his first story—on a triple hanging—published in 1928.

In 1930, Boyle enrolled at the University of Missouri in Columbia, from which he graduated with a degree in journalism and distinction in English in 1932. While completing one year of graduate study in English, he worked as an AP correspondent in Columbia. For two years he reported on intercollegiate sports and campus news. He next advanced his journalistic career by becoming a night editor in St. Louis (1935–1936) and a feature editor in Kansas City (1936–1937).

On Nov. 6, 1937, Boyle married Mary Frances Young; they had one child before her death in 1968. Also in 1937, Boyle was reassigned to the New York City bureau of the AP, where he worked as night editor for five years. In 1942, he received his first overseas assignment, to cover the American Expeditionary Force as a war correspondent.

Upon his arrival on the shores of North Africa in November 1942, Boyle was immediately thrust into battle. Landing with the invasion forces amid fighting, he had to dodge enemy cross fire by swimming to the Moroccan shore. His eyewitness accounts as a correspondent continued; a year later he wrote his first human-interest column in Salerno, Italy, while under fire. Although his environment was less than conducive to writing, Boyle wrote prolifically, sometimes completing five to twelve "on the spot" stories daily. According to other reporters, he wrote "thousands of words daily."

As the troops entered and captured cities during the European campaign, Boyle was not far behind, composing stories about the soldiers and the war. Exhibiting his characteristic drive, he once hitchhiked four hundred miles for a story. Among the events he covered during the war were George S. Patton's landings at Casablanca and Sicily, Mark Clark's landing at Salerno, the First Army's campaign to the Elbe, the North Africa campaign, and the Battle of the Bulge.

In 1942 Boyle's column, "Leaves from a War Correspondent's Notebook," first appeared, and eventually was featured in more than four hundred newspapers that subscribed to AP. Boyle was lauded by colleagues for "depicting soldiers with neither embellishment or deprecation," and his stories were "made to read like poetry." He became the AP's first human-interest columnist, displaying a gift for words, unceasing curiosity, an interest in both the individual human and in humanity, a humorous approach, and a light touch. His column was read eagerly by mothers and wives nationwide, eager to hear news of their men fighting abroad.

In 1945, Boyle was awarded the Pulitzer Prize for distinguished reporting. When he learned of the award, he responded with typical self-effacing modesty: "They must have made a mistake."

After hostilities in Europe had ceased, Boyle went to the Pacific Theater and became one of the first correspondents to reach Tokyo after V-J Day. Five years later he began to write on the Korean War. According to one of his AP colleagues in Korea, "He filed more copy than anyone else." Boyle also covered the conflict in Vietnam. On America's longest war, he echoed the frustrations of an entire generation: "You may be wondering what's going on. So do I. When I was here 48 hours, I thought I knew for sure what the truth was here. Now that I've been here toward 48 days, I'm not sure what is untrue."

At the end of the Korean War, Boyle returned to the United States, and in the late 1950's he continued his human-interest column, which featured interviews with celebrities and public figures.

In 1968, after twenty-five years of distinguished reporting with the AP, Boyle had published close to six thousand columns. A year later, *Help, Help! Another Day*, a volume of his selected works, was published.

Although he was described by colleagues as "warm-hearted, articulate; of blithe spirit; one of the finest journalists of our time," Boyle harbored fears of inadequacy. When asked about his biggest fear, he responded, "The biggest thing I have to fight is a feeling of insufficiency

—that I won't be able to muster the talent to do the work the way I'd like."

In 1973 Boyle announced that he was suffering from amyotrophic lateral sclerosis, commonly known as Lou Gehrig's disease. He died of a massive heart attack in New York City.

[Boyle wrote *Help! Help! Another Day* (1969). See "500 By-lines a Day," *Newsweek*, Nov. 18, 1957; Don Maley, " 'Every Human Being Has a Story' and Boyle's Been Telling Them," *Editor and Publisher*, Sept. 14, 1968, and " 'I Never Met a Man I Didn't Feel Sorry For': Boyle a 40 Year AP Vet," *Editor and Publisher*, Sept. 21, 1968; and "Boyle Stories," in "Talk of the Town," *The New Yorker*, Apr. 15, 1974. An obituary is in the *New York Times*, Apr. 2, 1974.]

LaRose Parris

BRADDOCK, JAMES J. (Dec., 6, 1905–Nov. 29, 1974), heavyweight boxing champion, was born in a Hell's Kitchen tenement in New York City. When Braddock was less than a year old, his family moved across the Hudson River to West New York, N.J. His father was a security guard, pier watchman, and furniture mover. Braddock grew up in northern New Jersey. He dropped out of school at fourteen to work in a New York City print shop.

Growing up in an era when the best-known Irish Americans were boxing champions, Braddock was inspired to take up prizefighting by the examples of John L. Sullivan, Jack Dempsey, and Mickey Walker. An older brother, Joseph, had nineteen professional fights and encouraged his brother to take up the sport. With his brother as his trainer, Braddock launched his amateur career at seventeen and had more than one hundred amateur fights, winning the New Jersey light-heavyweight and then the heavyweight amateur championships.

After turning professional as a middleweight (160 pounds) in 1926, Braddock went undefeated in his first thirty-eight fights. Braddock, who wore a green robe with a white shamrock as he entered the ring, was about six feet, three inches tall and was quick and tough, a puncher and a boxer. As he got stronger, Braddock moved into the light-heavyweight division (175 pounds) and gained recognition as a title contender. The *Ring* magazine rated Braddock as the fourteenth-ranked light-heavyweight in the world in 1927, then as the number one challenger in 1928.

Braddock won in a decision over former wel-terweight champion Pete Latzo in 1928 and knocked out former light-heavyweight champion Jimmy Slattery in 1929. On July 18, 1929, Braddock challenged light-heavyweight champion Tommy Loughran at Yankee Stadium. Loughran easily outpointed Braddock in fifteen rounds. Braddock, frustrated by Loughran's elusive style, was kept off balance by the champion's left jab. After losing to Loughran, Braddock's career went into a tailspin. He lost four of his next five fights, including a ten-round decision to future champion Maxie Rosenbloom. Between 1929 and 1933, Braddock lost more fights than he won and his name disappeared from the world rankings. After breaking his hand in a fight with Abe Feldman on Sept. 25, 1933, Braddock had to produce medical evidence of his injury to get paid for the fight. Braddock, who couldn't afford an operation for his hand, quit boxing.

In 1930, Braddock married Mae Fox; they had three children. To support his family after he quit the ring, Braddock worked as a long-shoreman, bartender, and laborer. When he failed to get work, Braddock went on relief. As his hand healed, Braddock attempted a boxing comeback.

Braddock's manager, Joe Gould, arranged a fight with heavyweight contender Corn Griffin in a preliminary bout to the June 14, 1934, Primo Carnera–Max Baer heavyweight title fight. Braddock outboxed and outpunched the heavily favored Griffin, stunning the crowd and the boxing world with a third-round knockout.

Braddock moved back into the top rankings with successive decisions over contenders John Henry Lewis and Art Lasky. In return, he was awarded a title shot on June 13, 1935, against Max Baer, a ten-to-one favorite. The hard-hitting Baer, who viewed the fight as a mismatch, trained very little. The challenger respected Baer's power but thought that the champion could be beaten. Three years earlier, Braddock had watched Loughran outpoint Baer by using the left jab to keep him on the defensive. Braddock followed a similar strategy: "When I boxed Baer, I kept sticking him like Loughran did," he recalled years later.

Braddock, who was in better condition, patiently outboxed Baer to win the heavyweight championship. It was the most astonishing upset in the history of the heavyweight division. Braddock became a Depression folk hero, nick-named the "Cinderella Man" by Damon Runyon. He was the prototypical boxing hero in a decade in which Hollywood produced such films as *Golden Boy, City for Conquest,* and *Kid Galahad.* W. C. Heinz, the boxing writer, wrote of Braddock: "In no list that you will ever see will he be listed among the ten greatest, but that is as it should be. . . . He may, however, in the sense that others see themselves in him and read their own struggles into his, have belonged to more people than any other champion who ever lived."

After two years without a fight, Braddock signed to defend his championship against former champion Max Schmeling in June 1937 at Madison Square Garden. Braddock's manager broke the contract with Schmeling in the face of opposition from Jewish organizations because Schmeling was a citizen of Nazi Germany. Instead, Braddock signed to fight Joe Louis, the sport's biggest attraction, in Chicago's Comiskey Park. It was far from certain that Braddock could have defeated Schmeling, who had knocked out Louis in 1936. By fighting Louis, Braddock was guaranteed $500,000 and 10 percent of the net profits from heavyweight title promotions over the next decade if Braddock lost the fight.

On June 22, 1937, the underdog Braddock defended his title against Louis. He knocked Louis down in the first round with a short, right uppercut. Louis took command in the second round, scoring with left-right combinations. In the eighth round, Louis knocked out Braddock. "When he knocked me down, I could have stayed there for three weeks," Braddock told Peter Heller. Braddock said that he had endured more punishment between the fourth and eighth rounds than he ever had in his boxing career. Dan Parker of the *New York Daily Mirror* wrote of Braddock: "The exhibition of courage the gallant Anglo-Irishman gave before that final bolt of lightning struck him on the side of the jaw awakened admiration and compassion for him in the heart of everyone in that vast crowd." Braddock's reputation was enhanced by the Louis fight.

On Jan. 21, 1938, Braddock finished strongly in the last three rounds to win a decision over heavyweight contender Tommy Farr. At the urging of his wife, Braddock retired with a record of fifty-two victories in eighty-four bouts, including twenty-eight knockouts and twenty-one defeats. He was elected to the Boxing Hall of Fame in 1964.

In the first decade of his retirement, Braddock received $150,000 from promoter Mike Jacobs as his percentage of the net profits from Louis title fights. Braddock served in World War II as a stevedore in the merchant marine. He later opened a marine-army surplus business in New Jersey and was a member of the Operating Engineers Union, running generators and welding equipment. Braddock was among boxing's more popular figures, even in retirement. He died at his home in North Bergen, N.J.

[Braddock was interviewed at length about his career by Peter Heller, *In This Corner . . . ! Forty World Champions Tell Their Stories: The Candid View of the Champion's Corner* (1973). He is profiled in John D. McCallum, *The World Heavyweight Boxing Championship: A History* (1974), and his career is analyzed in Chris Mead, *Champion: Joe Louis, Black Hero in White America* (1985). An obituary is in the *New York Times,* Nov. 30, 1974.]

STEVE NEAL

BRENNAN, WALTER (July 25, 1894–Sept. 21, 1974), television and film actor, was born in Lynn, Mass., to William John Brennan and Margaret Elizabeth Flanagan. Of his father, an engineer and inventor, Brennan later recalled, "He was one of the most wonderful men in the world, but he didn't know how to make money." The younger Brennan knocked around with traveling vaudeville acts before earning his high school diploma from Swampscott (Mass.) High School at the age of twenty.

After serving in World War I, Brennan had many occupations, including stints as an investment banker, a financial reporter, and—upon moving to Los Angeles—a real estate agent, land speculator (at which he failed miserably), insurance agent, and stapler salesman. He occasionally picked up bit parts in undistinguished movies, but rejected the idea of a career in the movies because movie acting had "no class or respectability." Brennan married his high school sweetheart, Ruth Wells, in 1920; they had three children.

Brennan's career changed markedly after Howard Hawks cast him in the role of "Old Atrocity" in the rollicking period piece on 1850's San Francisco, *Barbary Coast* (1935). The role set three important precedents for Brennan: it established him as a talented character actor, it debuted Brennan's cantankerous old-timer character who would become his bread and butter (although he was only forty-one at the time), and it brought him together with Howard Hawks, who would use Brennan in some of the famed director's best work. After *Barbary Coast*, Brennan appeared in ten pictures, including a meaty supporting part in King Vidor's *The Wedding Night*.

Brennan gained a reputation among top directors as a dependable, hardworking, and talented actor. In 1936, he appeared in William Wyler's *These Three* and Fritz Lang's *Fury* before playing the role of Edward Arnold's sidekick in Hawks's and Wyler's *Come and Get It*. According to one critic, Brennan "acts as a coalescing force" in this sprawling drama about an avaricious lumber tycoon, and he won his first Oscar for Best Supporting Actor for his "senti-mentally crude" role. Brennan repeated this feat in 1938 for his performance in *Kentucky* as a vengeful family patriarch who stokes the long-burning feud between his and a rival horse-racing family.

Brennan became the first actor to earn three Oscars when, in 1940, the Academy voted him Best Supporting Actor for his role as Judge Roy Bean in Wyler's *The Westerner*. Although his good friend Gary Cooper was the nominal star, Brennan had the choice role as the crusty, corrupt, and idiosyncratic Western legend. Wyler's emphasis on character development—a new twist for a Western—enabled Brennan to milk the part for all it was worth. The successful chemistry between Cooper and Brennan was reprised in Hawkes's *Sergeant York* (1941), which earned Cooper an Academy Award for Best Actor and Brennan a nomination as best supporting actor. That year, he also played a supporting role in Frank Capra's *Meet John Doe*. Since *Barbary Coast*, he had appeared in over forty-two feature films.

Brennan became in the 1940's and 1950's the premier character actor in Hollywood although he won no more awards. He appeared in a wide range of film genres and was comfortable in both dramatic and comedic roles, but Brennan was most strongly identified as the crusty old-timer in some of the most important Westerns of the era. (Brennan easily transplanted this character to non-Westerns as well, including his role as Humphrey Bogart's drunken sidekick in Hawks's *To Have and Have Not* [1945].) This character was not a static one, however. In John Ford's *My Darling Clementine* (1946), Bren-

nan played the greedy, sadistic Pa Clanton, who gets his final comeuppance from the pure-hearted Wyatt Earp, played by Henry Fonda. In Hawks's classic *Red River* (1948), Brennan played Groot Nadine, the loyal, tough-minded sidekick to the self-made, ruthless cattle baron Tom Dunston (John Wayne). Brennan is by turns the voice of comedy (helped by a running gag that had him constantly removing his false teeth, a bit of shtick that Hawks had initiated) and the voice of wisdom. In John Sturges's modern Western, *Bad Day at Black Rock* (1955), starring Spencer Tracy and Robert Ryan, Brennan appeared as the good-hearted but cowardly Doc Velie. In what was perhaps his most memorable role—and certainly his funniest—Brennan was again John Wayne's sidekick, this time as Stumpy, the gimpy, toothless, and wise-cracking deputy to Wayne's straight-arrow Sheriff John Chance in Hawks's *Rio Bravo* (1959). Brennan's last significant Hollywood Western was as the vile-hearted river pirate Colonel Hawkins in the multidirected (John Ford, George Marshall, and Henry Hathaway) epic, *How the West Was Won* (1962), with a star-studded cast featuring Henry Fonda, John Wayne, Jimmy Stewart, Gregory Peck, Eli Wallach, Harry Morgan, and Robert Preston.

How the West Was Won was the swan song of the "classic" Western. Brennan did not mourn its passing, however, because he was now kept busy with a hit television show, "The Real McCoys," which ran from 1957 to 1963. Brennan at first had no interest in television, which he considered inferior to films. But after producers Norman and Irving Pincus hounded Brennan for several months, he agreed to film a pilot, certain that no network would buy the show. Many industry experts agreed, since "The Real McCoys" would have been the first television situation comedy that took place in a rural area. Audiences, however, were tiring of urban settings, and the popularity of "The Real McCoys" paved the way for "The Andy Griffith Show," "Petticoat Junction," and "The Beverly Hillbillies." Brennan was a large part of the show's success, bringing equal parts of Stumpy and Groot Nadine to the portrayal of a cantankerous codger who heads a clan of West Virginia mountain folk newly moved to a ranch in California's San Fernando Valley.

When "The Real McCoys" finished its successful run, Brennan decided television's five-day-a-week work schedule and steady employment suited the New England work ethic that had always been his trademark. As he once admitted, "Ruth [his wife] says I'm much more fun to live with when I have a job." Thus although he had amassed a small fortune through careful investment, he continued to work until a few years before his death, at the age of eighty. His work during this time included a final, farcical reprise of his old-timer cowboy role in the TV movies *The Over-the-Hill Gang* (1969) and *The Over-the-Hill-Gang Rides Again* (1970). Brennan once told a reporter, "Heck, I never wanted anything out of this business except a good living. Never wanted to be a star or a glamorous figure. Just wanted to be good at what I was doing." In over 250 films for over forty-five years, Walter Brennan was one of the best.

[For a complete listing of Walter Brennan's feature films, as well as critical commentary, see Christopher Lyon, ed., *The International Dictionary of Films and Filmmakers*, vol. 3 (1984). Biographical information may be found in *Celebrity Register* (1961); and David Thomson, *A Biographical Dictionary of Film* (1981). Useful information may also be found in Brennan's clippings files at the Academy of Motion Picture Arts and Sciences Library in Los Angeles, Calif. For Brennan's television work, see *The Complete Directory of Prime Time Network TV Shows, 1946–Present* (1979). For commentary on Brennan's work in specific films, see Jay Robert Nash and Stanley Ralph Ross, *The Motion Picture Guide*, vols. 1–10 (1986). There is an obituary in the *New York Times*, Sept. 23, 1974.]

MICHAEL GOLDBERG

BRONK, DETLEV WULF (Aug. 13, 1897– Nov. 17, 1975), university president and scientist, was born in New York City to Mitchell Bronk and Marie Wulf. He left the city at the age of three when his father, pastor of the Ascension Baptist Church at 160th Street and Park Avenue, was transferred to Bayonne, N.J., where the family resided from 1900 to 1912. During his high school years the family lived in Troy, N.Y. This was "homeland" for the patrilineal side of Bronk's family, descendants of Mattheus Brunck, who settled in West Camp on the Hudson River in 1710.

After graduating from high school in Troy in 1915, Bronk enrolled in Swarthmore College. However, in 1918 he left Swarthmore and became an aviation cadet at the United States Na-

vel Aviation Corps, learning to fly warplanes at Pensacola Airbase in Florida. In December 1918, he was commissioned an ensign and for the next nine months was on leave but also on call for active service. Bronk returned to college in September 1919. He was never called for active duty and graduated from Swarthmore in June 1920 with a B.S. in electrical engineering. Bronk was appointed as a graduate student and instructor in physics at the University of Pennsylvania in January 1921, a prelude to his enrollment in the physics department at the University of Michigan later that same year.

During this period he met and courted Helen Alexander Ramsey, a student at Swarthmore. They were married on Sept. 10, 1921, in a ceremony performed by Bronk's father. A year later they were living in Ann Arbor, Mich., where Bronk began graduate studies in physics at the University of Michigan. This was the first of their several homes, including one on Penzance Point, Mass., on Cape Cod, which facilitated recreational sailing along the Atlantic coast from Chesapeake Bay to the Bay of Fundy, and provided proximity to the Marine Biological Laboratories in Woods Hole, Mass., where Bronk did research. Bronk was a physically vigorous person whose wiry five-foot, nine-inch frame was well suited to the skiing, mountain climbing, and sailing that he enjoyed. The Bronks had three sons.

In June 1926, Bronk was granted a Ph.D. in physics and physiology by the University of Michigan. He was a pioneer in the emerging discipline of biophysics. His first academic position was at Swarthmore College, where he taught for two years. Simultaneously, he was a part-time instructor of physiology in the medical school of the University of Pennsylvania, continuing his interests in physics and physiology. In 1928, he received a National Research Council Fellowship, which enabled him to go to England for a year of research with Edgar Douglas Adrian and Archibald Vivian Hill. Adrian, a professor of physiology at Cambridge University, was doing pioneer studies of the activity in single nerve fibers, and Hill, a biophysicist at the University of London, was studying heat production in nerve and muscle. Bronk chose his mentors well. Both became Nobel laureates, Hill in 1922 and Adrian in 1932. In 1929, he returned to Swarthmore as professor of biophysics and dean of men, but within the year he accepted an appointment at the medical school of the University of Pennsylvania as Johnson Professor of Biophysics and director of the Eldridge Reaves Johnson Foundation for Medical Physics. At last he could devote full time to research and teaching graduate students. From its inception, the Johnson Foundation offered graduate students the opportunity for advanced study of physics and biology, leading to a Ph.D. in biophysics.

After his year with Adrian and Hill, he initiated a prolonged investigation of neuronal mechanisms, including neural regulation of the cardiovascular system. He and his collaborators studied the sensory receptors that monitor blood pressure and its reflex control via the sympathetic nervous system. The latter studies led to extensive investigations of transmission of signals through the sympathetic ganglion, contributing to our understanding of how the action potential in presynaptic nerves causes release of acetylcholine, which excites action potentials in postsynaptic nerves. Concomitantly, a major set of studies concerned the functioning of individual neurons, including heat production, oxygen utilization, and recovery from electrical activity. He worked actively in the laboratory with many collaborators from 1923 to about 1950.

As director of the Johnson Foundation for Medical Physics at the University of Pennsylvania, Bronk became involved in reorganizing the Institute of Neurology, which he headed for several years. His motivation was the integration of knowledge derived from basic research in neurophysiology with that derived from medical studies of neurological diseases. Later, as chairman of the National Research Council and president of the National Academy of Science, Bronk was involved in the establishment of several organizations promoting the integration of biological and/or physical sciences, an idea commensurate with his choice of studies at the University of Michigan in physics and physiology.

In 1940, Bronk became head of the Department of Physiology in Cornell Medical School in New York City, taking many of his colleagues with him. However, in 1941 he and they returned to the University of Pennsylvania and the Johnson Foundation, becoming involved in war-related research.

World War II focused the attention of scientists on immediate practical problems. In 1942, Bronk became coordinator of research in the Office of the Air Surgeon, a post very different from that of an aviation cadet in World War I, but in the same branch of the armed services. He organized a corps of physiologists who, serving at air bases at home and abroad, developed the Army Air Force (AAF) altitude training and night vision training programs for pilots. During this period he remained director of the Johnson Foundation at the University of Pennsylvania and was involved in studies of the effects of low oxygen pressure on human performance. From 1942 to 1946, he also spent much time in Washington, D.C., and was directly involved in the work of the National Research Council, an organization of scientists supervised by the National Academy of Sciences. Bronk was elected to the membership of this organization in 1939.

In 1949, Bronk became president of the Johns Hopkins University. There he drafted the "Hopkins plan," which promoted attitudes and conditions that favored self-directed study and scholarship. He blurred the distinction between college and graduate school by encouraging competent undergraduates to participate in graduate studies. At the same time, Bronk emphasized that scientists and other scholars were morally bound to improve and assist in the development of a strong democratic nation, and to promote the welfare of all its citizens. Soon, however, an exceptional opportunity to develop his views of the ideal university was offered, and in 1953 he became the first president of the Rockefeller Institute for Medical Research. The Institute, concerned solely with research in the biological and medical sciences, was transformed into the Rockefeller University, offering advanced study and research in biology, medical sciences, physics, mathematics, and philosophy. Initially, all of the students worked toward a Ph.D. At present, the university offers the Ph.D. and, in collaboration with Cornell Medical School, an M.D.-Ph.D. degree for graduate students interested primarily in medical research.

Bronk's scientific publications testify to about thirty years of hands-on laboratory research. However, he was also involved in a wide range of problems having to do with science, such as promoting the creation of the National Science Foundation and the Presidential Science Advisory Committee. He spoke and wrote often about the role of science in modern society and the associated responsibilities of scientists. His activities included the postwar reorganization, as chairman, of the National Research Council in Washington, D.C. (1946–1950), and service as foreign secretary (1945–1950) and then president of the National Academy of Sciences (1950–1962). Concomitantly, he was a member of the board of the National Science Foundation (1950–1964) and its chairman (1955–1964). His research contributions and his role in promoting science as a national asset were recognized internationally. He was elected a foreign associate of the Royal Society of Great Britain (1948), of the French National Academy of Science (1953), and of the Russian Academy (1958).

He was a rare individual, a scientist, educator, and humanist, as stated on a plaque in front of the Detlev Wulf Bronk Laboratory on the campus of the Rockefeller University in New York City. Bronk died in New York City.

[Bronk's collected papers are available for study at the Rockefeller University Archives at the Rockefeller Archive Center in North Tarrytown, N.Y. Other relevant material is part of the archives at the National Academy of Sciences in Washington, D.C. A complete list of Bronk's published works is available in Frank Brink, Jr., "Detlev Wulf Bronk," *Biographical Memoirs* 50 (1979). Eulogies, memoirs, and recollections are available in the records of the National Science Foundation, Washington, D.C.; the Philosophical Society, Philadelphia; and in "Recollections of Detlev Bronk by Colleagues and Friends, February 18, 1976." An obituary is in the *New York Times*, Nov. 18, 1975.]

FRANK BRINK, JR.

BROWDER, EARL RUSSELL (May 20, 1891–June 27, 1973), general secretary of the Communist party, author, and lecturer, was born in Wichita, Kans., the son of William Browder, a farmer and clerk, and Martha Hankins. The descendant of an old American family whose forebears had migrated from England to America a century before the American Revolution, Browder became executive secretary of the American Communist party and its candidate for the presidency of the United States in 1936 and 1940. One of the twentieth century's most prominent radicals, Browder was forced to leave school in the third grade to help support his family, when his father became an invalid. His going to work as an errand boy for a wholesale drug firm marked the end of his formal education, although he continued to

read widely and in 1914 completed a law school correspondence course.

His political career began in 1907 at the age of sixteen, when he joined the Socialist party. He was, he once said, a "promising young executive" on working days, but an ardent radical on all other occasions. Browder was eventually engaged in most of the reform and labor movements of his time. He attributed his politics in part to the influence of his father, who had lost the family farm in the 1880's and who had known mostly hard times after he moved to Wichita in search of steadier employment. An active Populist before his illness, the father had encouraged wide-ranging discussions at table among his seven children, four of whom eventually joined the Communist movement.

In 1912, Browder, now a Kansas City accountant, abandoned the Socialists when the party expelled "Big Bill" Haywood, the leader of the Left. He did not join Haywood in the Industrial Workers of the World, but chose instead an association with William Z. Foster's Syndicalist League of North America, which was based on the belief that labor reform could be achieved through the American Federation of Labor.

Over the next two years, Browder served as coeditor of the League's Kansas City paper, *The Toiler*, but late in 1914 abandoned syndicalism for trade unionism, becoming president of his local chapter in the Bookkeepers, Stenographers, and Accountants Union. By 1916 he had given up trade unionism to manage a farmers' cooperative near Kansas City and to serve on the advisory board of the Cooperative League of America.

He openly opposed America's entry into World War I and in 1917 was arrested and found guilty both of conspiracy to prevent the enforcement of the draft law and of nonregistration. Browder was imprisoned for a year on the second charge, while appealing his conviction on the first. He emerged from jail as the Bolshevik Revolution was capturing the imagination of radicals everywhere. Prepared to support its principles in the United States, Browder rejoined the Socialist party and went to work as the first editor of *The Worker's World*, a pro-Communist paper based in Kansas. But in mid-1919, the appeal of his conspiracy conviction was denied, and he was sent to the federal prison at Fort Leavenworth, Kans., where he served a sixteen-month sentence. In 1933, President

Franklin Roosevelt granted him a full pardon.

Browder's time in prison coincided with the formation of the Communist party in the United States, and although he took no part in the early stages of the party's development, he was given honorary charter membership because his radical sympathies were well known. After his release from Leavenworth, he left Kansas for employment as head bookkeeper in a New York wholesale company; in January 1921 he began his active association with Communism. By spring he was traveling about the country recruiting non-Communist trade unionists for the American delegation to the Profintern, the first Congress of the Red International of Labor Unions, which met in Moscow in July. Serving as the delegation's secretary and using the pseudonym Joseph Dixon, Browder met Lenin and immediately declared himself a follower.

In the early 1920's Browder worked tirelessly but covertly to expand the party's membership despite the legal obstacles that state and federal law had erected in the aftermath of the "Great Red Scare" of 1919–1920. In 1926, he married Russian-born Raissa Berkman, and headed off to China on behalf of the Profintern. He remained there for three years, first in Hankow and then Shanghai, as general secretary of the Pan-Pacific Trade Union Secretariat. Returning to the United States in 1929, he began a fifteen-year tenure as head of the Communist party, taking control of the organization—with Stalin's blessing—in the aftermath of an internecine struggle that had threatened the party's existence and which, in the opinion of Moscow, demanded a change in leadership. As party chief, Browder was responsible for repairing the damage.

Throughout the next decade he moved about the country speaking wherever he could find an audience and doing whatever was necessary to convince the public that "Communism is twentieth-century Americanism." He wrote for the Communist press and published a half-dozen books, nearly all of them ideological expositions of the party line on domestic and foreign issues. After 1935, under his leadership, the party pursued a united front policy designed to create a coalition of reform groups to bring about social change. Conciliatory moves were directed toward such anti-Communist elements as the Roman Catholic and Protestant clergy, the Socialists, trade unionists like John L.

Lewis, and the newly formed Congress of Industrial Organizations. Browder's efforts eventually attracted many native-born Americans to a political party that previously had been identified principally with ethnic groups. In the years just before World War II, Communist party membership swelled to a high of 100,000.

During this period, Browder openly supported the New Deal, but he quickly repudiated Roosevelt when the President reacted negatively to the Nazi-Soviet pact of 1939. Over the next two years, party membership declined dramatically, and in 1940 Browder was arrested, tried, and found guilty of unlawful use of his passport. While his conviction was on appeal, he was his party's candidate for the Presidency in that year's election. His appeals denied, he entered prison in 1941, serving fourteen months of a four-year term in Atlanta's federal prison, before Roosevelt commuted the sentence.

Despite the wartime alliance between the United States and the Soviet Union, the American Communists never again achieved the influence they had exercised in the 1930's. In 1946, Browder was removed from his leadership position and expelled from the Communist party as a deviationist. Except for an occasional lecture and the appearance of *Keynes, Foster, and Marx*, his thirteenth and final book in 1950, Browder's public career was over. After the death of his wife in 1955, he lived in virtual obscurity until his death at the home of his son, William, chairman of Princeton University's mathematics department. His other sons, Felix and Andrew, were also mathematicians.

[Browder assisted Theodore Draper with interviews and documents in Draper's history of Communism, the first volume of which, *The Roots of American Communism* (1957), contains a biographical sketch of Browder. An obituary is in the *New York Times*, June 28, 1973.]

ALLAN L. DAMON

BROWN, JOHNNY MACK (Sept. 1, 1904– Nov. 14, 1974), Western movie actor and athlete, was born in Dothan, Ala., one of nine children of Hattie McGillaray and John Henry Brown, a merchant who sold shoes. As a child Brown enjoyed hunting, fishing, and many team sports. His aptitude for physical activities garnered him an athletic scholarship to the University of Alabama, where he played as halfback and was captain of the football team. In 1926, during his senior year, he caught two clinching touchdown passes in the Rose Bowl game against the University of Washington. The game brought him national prominence—in part, he later claimed, because it represented the first time a southern team had participated in that championship. He was named to the 1927 All-America football team.

While in college, the tall, good-looking Brown caught the attention of character actor George Fawcett, who suggested he try for a career in films. Brown opted to finish college instead. Upon graduation he married his college sweetheart, Cornelia ("Connie") Foster; they had four children.

For a few months after college, Brown worked as assistant coach for the Alabama football team. While traveling with the team in California in January 1927, he visited Fawcett and arranged to take a screen test at Metro-Goldwyn-Mayer (MGM). He made his film debut almost immediately, playing a bit part in the baseball comedy *Slide, Kelly Slide*. Before the year was out, he had graduated to leading-man status, playing opposite Marion Davies in *The Fair Co-ed*. This film led to a long-term contract with MGM.

For the next few years, Brown was a leading juvenile player for MGM and was loaned to other studios, appearing with such notable stars as Greta Garbo, Norma Shearer, and Mary Pickford. Despite a strong Southern accent, he made a smooth transition to talking pictures. He made his singing debut in *Montana Moon* (1930), playing a simple cowboy whose serenades win the heart of Joan Crawford. The part in which he was best received, and for which he is perhaps best remembered, was the title role in *Billy the Kid* (1930), directed by King Vidor. Silent Western star William S. Hart reputedly coached Brown for the role, sharing his knowledge of guns and horses with the young actor. Despite this success, Brown's career at MGM was on the wane. With the advent of the 1930's, the studio looked for a harder edge in its juvenile actors and began to cultivate the talents of Clark Gable. Playing a newspaperman, Brown was shot halfway through *The Secret Six* (1931); his friend Gable avenged his death and got his girl. Brown was cut out of his next film, *Laughing Sinners*, entirely, and his scenes were reshot with Gable.

MGM terminated Brown's contract, and for a few years Brown experimented with a variety of parts, many of them athletes or light juveniles. By the mid-1930's, however, he had settled into the saddle as a star of Westerns produced by a succession of studios, principally "Poverty Row" institutions like Republic and Monogram Pictures. Brown remained a Western star until 1952, performing in hundreds of films with his horse, Reno. He had less financial security and status than he had enjoyed at MGM, but he later maintained that he had never liked appearing in that studio's drawing-room comedies and much preferred being a B-picture star.

The Browns raised four children of their own as well as Johnny's youngest brother during their years in Hollywood and maintained an active social and athletic life in the film capital. The family was known for its musical evenings. Brown also socialized by hunting, polo playing, and dancing.

In addition to performing in feature films, Brown made serials and hosted a radio show, "Under Western Skies." His appeal as a Western star was mainly to children, and his multimedia exposure included a series of Dell comics chronicling his adventures as a hero of the frontier, *Johnny Mack Brown Western Comics*, that was published well into the 1950's.

As early as the late 1940's, however, Brown's career was faltering, in part because of a weight problem that rendered his rugged Western persona difficult to maintain. Both his film and football careers were remembered, however, and he was elected to the College Football Hall of Fame in 1957. He graduated to character roles in the 1950's and eventually had spot parts on such television programs as "Perry Mason" and "Wells Fargo." By the early 1960's, with their children grown, Johnny and Connie Brown had moved from their Hollywood mansion to a modest apartment.

In 1961 Brown was hired as host/manager for a restaurant owned by a friend. He told syndicated columnist Bob Thomas, "It's hard work, but I find I like it. I figure it's much the same as acting—I'm dealing with people. . . . Besides, it gives me something to do. . . . You can't sit at home waiting for the phone to ring." Brown returned to films briefly in the mid-1960's, appearing in *Requiem for a Gunfighter* (1965), *The Bounty Killer* (1965), and *Apache Uprising* (1966). In the last he played his first and last villain, a craven sheriff. In April 1970 an *Esquire* retrospective titled "Big Jocks" found

Brown in "sort of semi-like retirement." Despite remarks about his considerable weight, the magazine's writers paid tribute to the affable actor, noting that he had been "as big a gun as Gene Autry or Hopalong Cassidy." Brown died in Woodland Hills, Calif.

[The Billy Rose Theatre Collection of the New York Public Library maintains clipping files on Brown and has a bound, privately published book about him from the early 1960's by Mario De Marco, *The All-American Cowboy.* An extensive file on Brown is also maintained at the University of Alabama's Paul W. Bryant Museum. *Film Fan Monthly* ran John Cocchi's "Johnny Mack Brown," a survey of the actor's life and film career, in June 1970. In the following month the magazine began a chronological list of Brown's films. An obituary appears in the *New York Times,* Nov. 16, 1974.]

TINKY ("DAKOTA") WEISBLAT

BROWN, PRENTISS MARSH (June 18, 1889–Dec. 19, 1973), congressman and senator, was born in St. Ignace, Mich., the son of James John Brown, a lawyer, and Minnie Gagnon. His father served as city attorney of Detroit and prosecuting attorney of Cheboygan and Mackinac Counties in northern Michigan. Brown attended St. Ignace public schools and graduated from high school in 1906. He earned a bachelor of arts degree with Phi Beta Kappa honors in 1911 from Albion College, where he played baseball. After studying political economy for one year at the University of Illinois on a scholarship, he was admitted to the Michigan bar in 1914 and practiced law with his father at St. Ignace.

A Democrat, Brown served as prosecuting attorney of Mackinac County from 1914 to 1926 and city attorney of St. Ignace from 1916 to 1928. Brown, who chaired the Democratic party state convention five times, lost bids for election in 1924 to the U.S. House of Representatives and in 1928 for justice of the Michigan Supreme Court. He also belonged to the state board of law examiners from 1930 to 1942 and presided over the St. Ignace school board.

In 1932 Brown became the first Democrat ever elected to the U.S. House of Representatives from Michigan's Eleventh Congressional District, encompassing the northern tip of lower Michigan and parts of the Upper Peninsula. As a congressman from March 1933 until November 1936, he served on the Banking and Currency Committee and helped draft the Home Owners Loan Act and the Banking Acts of 1933 and 1935. His efforts also facilitated House enactment of legislation amending the Reconstruction Finance Corporation and creating Federal Deposit Insurance, the Federal Housing Administration, the Rural Electrification Administration, the Civilian Conservation Corps, and several farm credit agencies.

Michigan voters elected Brown to the U.S. Senate in November 1936. A few days later Governor Frank D. Fitzgerald named Brown to complete the Senate term of Republican James Couzens, thereby giving Brown seniority rights over other first-time senators not taking office until January 1937. Brown, who had developed an interest in economic issues in college, specialized in monetary legislation as a senator. Brown's committees included finance, banking and currency, and commerce and manufacturing. He chaired the Democratic Senatorial Campaign Committee in 1938, the Special Committee on Taxation of Governmental Securities and Salaries from 1938 to 1940, the Claims Committee, and the Democratic Steering Committee in 1941 and 1942. The Steering Committee determined the Senate legislative process and filled vacancies on all other committees. Although normally a liberal/progressive politically, Brown acted independently of Franklin D. Roosevelt when he disagreed with the president's positions. For example, he opposed Roosevelt's Supreme Court reorganization plan in 1937 and led a Senate group advising the president to withdraw it. He also rejected Roosevelt's 1938 proposal to reorganize executive branch agencies and his 1940 plan to place the independent Civil Aeronautics Authority under control of the Commerce Department. During World War II the Selective Service Act of 1940 and the 1941 act to extend the service of trainees beyond the one-year limitation likewise dismayed Brown.

But Brown generally supported Roosevelt's domestic and international programs. He backed the Neutrality Act of 1939 that repealed the arms embargo and in 1940 sponsored legislation advancing a $20 million credit to Finland, victim of an attack by the Soviet Union. Brown, who represented numerous Scandinavian constituents, stressed the Finns' desperate need for food, clothing, shelter, transportation, and other nonmilitary products. Brown amended the Excess Profits Tax Act, subjecting federal and state employees to the same rates as all other Americans and also making government securities taxable. His attempts to tax future state, county, and municipal bonds failed. Other Brown legislation continued or broadened the lending authority of the Reconstruction Finance Corporation and the Federal Housing Authority. In 1941, he supported the Lend-Lease Act and secured Senate approval of legislation authorizing the issuance of defense bonds.

The farm bloc disagreed with Brown over agricultural price ceilings. In December 1941 Brown framed a bill setting limits on farm prices. The farm bloc protested Brown's plan to sell government crop surpluses below parity prices. Parity involves a system of regulating prices of farm commodities, usually by government supports, to provide farmers with the same purchasing power they had in the 1909–1914 period. Brown predicted that such action would add a billion dollars per year to the country's cost of living and claimed that the average of all farm prices was actually 102 percent of parity when government farm benefit payments were taken into account. In September 1942, the Senate approved Brown's measure, authorizing President Roosevelt to stabilize wages and salaries and to set farm prices at or above the 1909–1914 level as compared with the prices of nonfarm commodities. Farm lobbyists persuaded the House to raise the ceiling to 112 percent of parity, but the Senate retained Brown's version. Republican Homer Ferguson defeated Senator Brown in his bid for reelection in 1942. Brown's resistance to the farm bloc contributed to his defeat.

President Roosevelt then appointed Brown director of the Office of Price Administration (OPA), where he served from January to October 1943. Brown vowed to keep price increases to one-half of 1 percent per month. Organized labor and consumers favored stricter price controls, while the food industry protested rollbacks in meat, butter, and canned vegetable prices. Congress rejected Brown's requests for increased federal subsidies to control prices and for more OPA investigators, and slashed his budget considerably. Lou Maxon, his deputy, resigned in July, sharply criticizing OPA policies. Chester Bowles, Maxon's replacement, reorganized the OPA, consulted with business about price controls, and simplified pricing and rationing regulations. Nevertheless, the OPA largely controlled rising prices and inflation during

Brown's tenure. Consumer prices increased only 12 percent, while farm income jumped 90 percent, worker wages 33 percent, and corporate profits after taxes 15 percent.

In December 1943, Brown entered a law partnership with Edward Fallon, Mackinac County prosecuting attorney, and Wendell Lund, War Production Board special assistant, with offices in Detroit and Washington, D.C. Besides chairing the board of the Detroit Edison Company from 1944 to 1954, Brown headed the First National Bank of St. Ignace, the Arnold Transit Company, and several utility companies and served on the board of directors of several corporations. His most satisfying personal achievement came as chairman of the Mackinac Bridge Authority, when he secured financial backing to construct the five-mile-long Mackinac Bridge. The structure had the world's longest total suspension span (8,344 feet) when it was completed in 1957. It crosses the Mackinac Straits, where Lakes Huron and Michigan meet, and connects Michigan's upper and lower peninsulas.

Brown, a Methodist and an ardent baseball fan, married Marion Elizabeth Walker of St. Ignace, Mich., on June 16, 1916, and had seven children. An inveterate doodler, Brown shunned the Washington social life and often attended Detroit Tigers baseball games. He resided in St. Ignace, where he died.

[The Prentiss M. Brown papers are located at the University of Michigan at Ann Arbor. There is no biography of Brown. The best source remains *Current Biography* (1943), pp. 78–81. *Who Was Who in America 1974–1976* contains personal data. My own interview with Prentiss M. Brown, conducted in St. Ignace, Michigan, Aug. 22, 1972, provided invaluable background information. For Brown's role in aiding Finland, see David L. Porter, *The Seventy-sixth Congress and World War II, 1939–1940* (1979). An obituary is in the *New York Times*, Dec. 20, 1973.]

DAVID L. PORTER

BRUNDAGE, AVERY (Sept. 28, 1887–May 8, 1975), businessman and Olympic leader, was born in Detroit, Mich., the son of Charles Brundage, a stonecutter, and Amelia Lloyd, a seamstress. His father left soon after his birth, and the child was raised by relatives in Chicago. A high school honor student, Brundage worked his way through the University of Illinois, graduating in 1909 with a bachelor's degree in civil engineering. In college he was a basketball player and the leading point scorer on the track team; he was also the editor of the college magazine and a member of several honorary fraternities. He was part of the 1912 United States Olympic team, finishing fifth in the pentathlon and fourteenth in the decathlon. In 1914, 1916, and 1918, he was the national champion in the "all-round," a series of ten track and field events completed in one day with only five minutes' rest between events. After the 1912 games, he worked as a construction superintendent on a Chicago skyscraper, and in 1915 he founded the Avery Brundage Company, a general construction firm.

He continued to participate in the all-around into the 1920's, but then took up handball and became one of the country's leading players. He also joined the Amateur Athletic Union (AAU) and played a leading role in the founding of the American Olympic Association. On Dec. 22, 1927, he married Elizabeth Dunlap; they had no children. In 1929 he succeeded General Douglas MacArthur as president of the American Olympic Association and chairman of the American Olympic Committee, a post he was to hold until 1953. He also served seven terms as president of the AAU beginning in 1928, and from 1930 to 1952 he was vice-president of the International Amateur Athletic Federation. He was a vice-president of the International Olympic Committee (IOC) from 1945 to 1952, at which time he assumed the presidency, a post he held for twenty years.

Brundage was, by far, the most powerful figure in the history of the Olympic movement and amateur athletics. He was an insistent defender of amateurism, fighting a determined battle against commercialization and professionalism. In response to a 1946 demand on the part of the Scandinavian countries that athletes be paid for the work time they lost while competing, Brundage rammed through an explicit definition of "amateur." An amateur, the new rule said, was "one whose connection with sport is and has been solely for pleasure . . . without financial gain of any kind, direct or indirect." In 1956 Brundage even wanted to exclude any competitors who intended to turn pro after the games, and considered eliminating sports like figure skating and basketball because they led participants too easily into the professional ranks.

Brundage equated the Olympic spirit with his definition of amateurism and his belief that politics should never intrude on sport. "In an imperfect world," he said in 1956, "if participation in sport is to be stopped every time the laws of humanity are violated, there will never be any international contests." He received no pay himself, but because his construction and real estate businesses in Chicago proved so lucrative, he was able to finance his own activities on behalf of sport. He was abrasive and unbending, "like Oliver Cromwell's idea of God," one critic insisted, "righteous and inflexible." He was so sure of his philosophy that he ignored criticism and generally had his own way.

During the 1930's his attitude toward Nazi Germany caused him particular trouble. Many Americans thought that the 1936 games should not proceed in Berlin because Hitler had banned Jewish athletes. Brundage reacted by blaming the protest on "alien agitators," "Communists," and "certain Jews." He forced the participation of the American team. He always insisted that Adolf Hitler never snubbed Jesse Owens, that he greeted no athlete because the IOC had told him not to do it. On his return to the United States after the games, Brundage appeared at a Madison Square Garden rally of the German-American Bund and praised Germany as the best exemplar of the Olympic spirit since the Greeks. German anti-Communism and patriotism could teach the United States a great deal, he said. Brundage also supported the Keep America Out of War Committee and the America First Committee. He resigned from both the day after Pearl Harbor.

After the war, Brundage was convinced that athletes could teach nations how to get along without further conflict. He temporarily unified the West Germans and East Germans into one Olympic team, forced a promise (though unfulfilled) of an integrated team from the South Africans, and tried but failed to solve the Taiwan–Red China problem. He oversaw the entry of the Soviet Union into the Olympics, praising its nationwide physical education program and choosing to ignore the conflict between amateurism and state subsidy of athletes.

His determination to exclude professionalism from world athletics embroiled him in constant controversy. In 1932, he suspended the amateur status of the leading American sportswoman, Mildred ("Babe") Didrikson, because her picture appeared in an automobile advertisement. In 1947 he refused to allow Barbara

Ann Scott, a Canadian figure skater, to keep an automobile she received after winning the world championship. In 1948 he protested the role of the American Hockey Association in selecting the American Olympic hockey team because the AHA was supported by professional hockey owners.

In addition to his work on behalf of amateur athletics, Brundage accumulated what was probably the world's best private collection of Oriental art. He later donated these treasures to the Center of Asian Art and Culture in San Francisco, Calif. His wife died in 1971. On June 20, 1973, at the age of eighty-five, Brundage married Mariann von Reuss, a German princess half his age, and spent most of his considerable wealth. After his death, information on his lifelong extramarital sex life, including the existence of two illegitimate children by former Olympic gymnast Lilian Dresden, became public.

Brundage was a powerful man. Six feet tall and weighing around two hundred pounds, he looked years younger than his true age because of a lifetime of vigorous exercise and regular but sparse eating habits. Every morning he walked four-and-a-half miles from his home on Lake Shore Drive in Chicago to his office in the La-Salle Hotel. His only physical problem was poor eyesight—he wore glasses from the age of ten. He died in Garmisch-Partenkirchen, Germany.

[Brundage's papers, including his unpublished autobiography, "The Olympic Story," are deposited at the University of Illinois in Urbana, Ill. See also Archives of the International Amateur Athletic Federation, London, and Archives of the International Olympic Committee, Lausanne. Books include René Yvon Lefebvre d'Argencé, *Chinese Treasures from the Avery Brundage Collection* (1968); and Allan Guttman, *The Games Must Go On* (1984). See also Roger Butterfield, "Avery Brundage," *Life*, June 14, 1948; Robert Shaplen, "Profiles: Amateur," *New Yorker*, July 23, 1960; and William Oscar Johnson, "Avery Brundage, The Man Behind the Mask," *Sports Illustrated*, Aug. 4, 1980. An obituary appears in the *New York Times*, May 9, 1975.]

JOHN F. MARSZALEK

BUCK, PEARL COMFORT SYDEN-STRICKER (June 26, 1892–Mar. 6, 1973), writer and philanthropist, was born in Hillsboro, W.Va., to Absolom Sydenstricker and Caroline Stulting, who were on furlough from a Presbyterian mission in China. She was the

third of four daughters and fifth of seven children, three of whom reached maturity.

Taken to Chinkiang (Zhenjiang), China, when three months old, Buck learned to speak Chinese before English. Her father was so dedicated that the family lived with, and dressed like, the local peasants. Her primary education included her nurse's Chinese legends, her father's Bible readings, basic instruction from her mother, and her own reading of Victorian novelists. Her first published writing appeared in *The Shanghai Mercury* when she was seven.

Buck received private tutoring until 1905, then attended missionary and boarding schools until 1910. In the latter year she enrolled at Randolph-Macon Women's College in Virginia, where she was elected to Phi Beta Kappa. After obtaining her B.A. in 1914, she held a teaching assistantship in psychology at Randolph-Macon until she returned to China to care for her critically ill mother.

In 1917 she met John Lossing Buck, an American agricultural missionary. After a brief courtship she married him on May 30, and they moved to Nanshuchow, in northern China. Their daughter, Carol, was born in 1921, and in 1922 the family moved to the University of Nanking, where John taught agriculture and Pearl taught English literature.

In 1922, Buck began writing articles and short stories about China for U.S. magazines. During their 1924–1925 leave the Bucks learned that Carol was retarded. Buck decided to care for the child at home while she completed a master's degree in English at Cornell University. In early 1925 she wrote an essay, "China and the West," that won the $200 Laura Messenger Prize in History. In July, 1925, the Bucks adopted a daughter they named Janice.

After returning to China in the summer of 1925, Buck taught at Southeastern University until 1927, at Chung Yung University from 1928 to 1930, and at the University of Nanking during 1931. Her need to earn more money compelled her to write longer works. Her first novel was lost in the 1927 Nanking uprising, during which the Bucks narrowly escaped death; a peasant woman hid them in her hut.

In 1929, after placing Carol in the Vineland Training School in New Jersey, Buck returned to China and devoted herself to writing an expanded short story set in China. After several rejections, the manuscript was published in 1930 as *East Wind: West Wind*. The publication of her next novel, *The Good Earth* (1931), transformed her life. The novel's exotic topic, its focus on the eternal human struggle with life, and its lucid, flowing style appealed to readers throughout the world.

Heading the best-seller lists for months, *The Good Earth* sold nearly two million copies, was translated into more than thirty languages, inspired a 1932 Broadway play, and won the 1932 Pulitzer Prize for fiction. In 1937, Paul Muni and Luise Rainer starred in the film version of the book. In later years the movies *Dragon Seed* (1944) and *Satan Never Sleeps* (1962) also reached the screen.

Buck's subsequent books, such as *The House of Earth* trilogy, published in 1935, were well received. During the 1930's she also published a two-volume translation of the Chinese saga *Shui Hu Chuan, All Men are Brothers* (1933), *The Mother* (1934), and biographies of her parents, *The Exile* and *The Fighting Angel* (both 1936).

During the early 1930's, the Bucks' marriage deteriorated while Buck and Richard Walsh, her publisher, grew closer. In mid-1934, the Bucks legally separated. In 1935, Walsh and Buck obtained divorces in Nevada and were married on June 11, 1935. For the remainder of her life she continued to be a prolific writer and raised nine adopted children from various racial backgrounds. Her 1938 book, *The Proud Heart*, dramatized her inner conflict between a career and marriage. In 1938, Buck became the first American woman to win the Nobel Prize for literature, awarded for her earlier portrayals of China and for her parents' biographies.

When the United States entered World War II, Buck devoted her talents to supporting United China Relief, providing data for servicemen's Asian guidebooks, and writing radio scripts for broadcast in China. She published three books—of which *Dragon Seed* (1942) remains the best known. Her other two books from this era were *Of Men and Women* (1941) and *American Unity and Asia* (1942). During this time Buck tried to impart knowledge of Asia through the East and West Association, which she founded in 1941 to bring Asian cultural figures to the United States. She also directed the publication of *Asia* magazine from 1941 to 1946.

As the war came to an end, the changes in Asia provided Buck with material for novels such as *Pavilion of Women* (1946) and *Imperial*

Woman (1956). Her study of an interracial marriage in *The Hidden Flower* (1952) and her ambitious history of Korea, *The Living Reed* (1963), lacked the quality of her earlier works but were popular successes.

In the postwar era, Buck wrote novels about America, many drawing on her family's nineteenth-century experiences. Between 1945 and 1953, she issued five volumes under the pseudonym John Sedges. The first of these works, *The Townsman*, won both popular and scholarly acclaim for its accurate depiction of Kansas in the 1850's.

Buck disbanded the East and West Association in 1951, because any kind of interest in Asia was seen by many as sympathy for Communist China. She focused her efforts on helping poor children by establishing Welcome House in 1949. It was designed to be an adoption agency for Amerasian children. In 1964, she published two books based on her experiences with this effort: *Children for Adoption* and *Welcome Child*.

In the late 1950's, Buck became very concerned with the potential for nuclear war. In 1959 she published the novel *Command the Morning* and a less-than-successful play, *Desert Incident*. From 1958 to 1965, Buck served as president of the Authors Guild.

Long engaged in work on mental retardation, Buck gallantly publicized her experiences with her daughter Carol in *The Child Who Never Grew* (1950). These activities and a deepening relationship with Harvard philosopher William Ernest Hocking buoyed her during the difficult years of her husband's illness (beginning in 1953; he died in 1960). She later recounted this traumatic time in her life in *A Bridge for Passing* (1962) and *The Goddess Abides* (1972).

In 1964, Buck established the Pearl S. Buck Foundation to assist fatherless, half-American children throughout Asia. As chair, she appointed a young former dance instructor, Theodore F. Harris, whose background in organizing charity events proved invaluable to fund-raising. Harris and Buck published a joint work, *For Spacious Skies*, in 1966.

In 1969, a *Philadelphia* magazine article accused Harris of misusing Foundation funds. In spite of Buck's support, there was enough truth to the charges to force him to resign. In 1970, Buck and Harris moved to Danby, Vt., where Harris established Creativity, Inc., a firm that managed most of Buck's later projects, such as

Pearl Buck's America (1965) and *Pearl Buck's Oriental Cookbook* (1966).

In 1972, as Western travel to the People's Republic of China opened up, Buck requested one last trip to her beloved China. However, PRC officials refused, stating that "her writings had displayed 'an attitude of distortion, smear and vilification' toward Communist China." A few months later, Buck died at Danby of lung cancer. At the time of her death she was working on a book entitled *The Red Earth*, which was to be a story of the descendants of the characters from *The Good Earth*.

Buck left a contested estate and twenty-nine manuscripts, twenty-five of which were issued posthumously. The bulk of her estate, totaling over $7 million, eventually went to the Pearl S. Buck Foundation, as did 90 percent of her property. The rest went to her children.

Despite her controversy-filled last years, Buck's prolific production as a writer and her humanitarian efforts made her a preeminent international figure. She produced over one hundred books, speeches, and plays. Eighty-five of the books were published in her lifetime, and she remains one of America's most popular writers. She proclaimed her own epitaph in 1972: "Of course, one pays the price for being prolific . . . Heaven knows the literary Establishment can't forgive me for it, nor for the fact that my books sell."

[Biographies are Theodore Harris, *Pearl S. Buck*, 2 vols. (1969–1971); and Nora Stirling, *Pearl Buck* (1983). See also Michael Hunt, "Pearl Buck—Popular Expert on China, 1931–1949," *Modern China*, Jan. 1977; and Mary Lee Welliver, "Pearl S. Buck's Manuscripts" (M.A. thesis, West Virginia University, 1977). An obituary is in the *New York Times*, Mar. 7, 1973, and an account of her funeral, *New York Times*, Mar. 10, 1973.]

WILLIAM HEAD

BUDENZ, LOUIS FRANCIS (July 17, 1891–Apr. 27, 1972), labor leader, educator, and star anti-Communist witness for Senator Joseph R. McCarthy, was born in Indianapolis, Ind., to Henry Joseph Budenz, a bank teller, and Mary Gertrude Sullivan. His father was a devout Catholic and a third-generation Indianan. Louis attended St. John's High School in Indianapolis; St. Xavier College in Cincinnati, Ohio; and St. Mary's College in Kansas, before receiving his LL.B. from the Indianapolis Law School in 1912.

As a young man, Louis was excommunicated from the Catholic church because he married a divorced woman. Her name and the dates of their relationship, however, do not appear in any of the accounts of Budenz's life. His second wife was Margaret Rodgers; they had four children.

Budenz joined the labor movement because he was appalled by the sight of workers unable to live decently on their earnings. In 1913 he became associate editor of *The Carpenter*, the official publication of the Brotherhood of Carpenters and Joiners. In 1914, he became assistant director of the Central Catholic Verein in St. Louis. Between 1914 and 1919 he worked as the secretary of the St. Louis Civic League, and in 1920 he was a franchise expert to the Federal Electric Railways Commission. He then served as a publicity director for the American Civil Liberties Union for about a year. Returning to labor circles at the age of thirty, he served for ten years (1921–1931) as editor of *The Labor Age* and helped organize strikes by hosiery mill workers in Kenosha, Wis., in 1928; silk workers in Paterson, N.J., in 1930; and auto workers in Toledo, Ohio, in 1934. In the course of these activities, he was arrested and acquitted twenty-one times.

In 1924, Budenz was the New Jersey campaign manager for Senator Robert M. La Follette of Wisconsin, the Progressive party candidate for president. Budenz drifted further to the left as a member of a group known as the "Muste Trotzkyites" before openly joining the Communist party in October 1935, when Earl Browder, leader of the Party in the United States, asked Budenz to go public with his affiliation. Accordingly, Budenz announced his allegiance to the Communist International in the columns of *The Daily Worker* in 1935 and soon became its labor editor. Transferred to Chicago by the Communist party in 1937, Budenz became editor of another leftist publication, the *Midwest Daily Record*. Later, while appearing as a witness at the McCarthy hearings, Budenz related that the Hitler-Stalin nonaggression pact, signed in 1939, dealt the death blow to the *Midwest Daily Record*. Returning to New York City in 1940, Budenz became managing editor of *The Daily Worker* and president of its publishing house, Freedom of the Press Company. He also served on the national committee of the Communist party of the United States.

Budenz's much-publicized resignation from

the party and return to the Roman Catholic church came about through the efforts of Monsignor Fulton J. Sheen, an American prelate known for his regular radio broadcasts, who in 1940 issued a pamphlet, *Communism: Answers to a Communist*, directed largely as a response to Budenz's Communist writings. The monsignor later invited Budenz to his home to discuss Communism and Catholicism. An announcement of the former Communist's return to the Church was made to the Associated Press on Oct. 10, 1945, by Sheen. In Bishop Sheen's autobiography, he writes about secretly giving the family religious instruction at their home in suburban Westchester County, N.Y. Along with his wife and children, Budenz, who said he was returning to "the faith of my fathers," was received into the Church at a ceremony at St. Patrick's Cathedral on Fifth Avenue, in New York City. "Reason and faith have led us to this happy step," stated Budenz. Soon thereafter, he joined the economics department at Notre Dame University and moved his family to South Bend, Ind. Within a year, he returned to New York City to join the faculty of Fordham University, another Catholic institution whose 1950 class voted Budenz "its favorite personality in the news."

Beginning in 1946, Budenz made numerous public accusations against the Communist party and its members, becoming an almost professional anti-Communist witness and speaker. Testifying before the House Un-American Activities Committee, he identified Gerhardt Eisler as the secret head of the Communist party in the United States. Budenz then became a principal witness in several sensational trials against Communists, and he repeatedly supplied the FBI with so-called secret information. He served as a government witness in deportation proceedings against Rumanian-born labor leader John Santo (1947), and in the trial in New York City of eleven leading Communists in 1949. In Washington, he testified in August 1948 before the House Un-American Activities Committee as it investigated charges against Alger Hiss. In April 1950, he appeared before the Senate Foreign Relations subcommittee to examine charges by Senator Joseph McCarthy that Communists had infiltrated the Department of State. He alleged that Owen Lattimore, who was then an adviser to the State Department on Far Eastern Affairs, was a member of a Communist cell. In August 1950, Budenz prepared

for the House Un-American Activities Committee a list of 380 purported Communists in the United States. Besides revealing the names of alleged party members, Budenz was concerned with exposing the militant character of Communism and its goal of world domination.

In 1947, Budenz published an autobiographical account of his spiritual and political experiences, *This Is My Story*. *New York World-Telegram* critic Harry Hansen pronounced it to be "the most damaging evidence of the conspiratorial character of the American Communist party every published." Lewis Gannett of the *New York Herald Tribune* thought the book lacked "perspective," but that it had "sociopsychological significance and, at times, suspense" in its portrayal of a "troubled, genuinely altruistic if also ambitious man."

In 1950, Budenz published *Men Without Faces*, another exposé of the alleged international Communist conspiracy. The book was called "disturbing" by the *Christian Science Monitor* review, "because it reveals the extent to which supposedly intelligent citizens have become mouthpieces of communism."

A self-proclaimed authority on Communism in the United States, Budenz contributed articles to *Collier's*, the *American Legion Magazine*, and other periodicals. In a series of nationwide lecture tours, he spoke before Catholic organizations, college audiences, and dozens of civic groups. In August 1947, he gave five radio talks on "The Catholic Hour" on the subject of the Catholic church and labor, and in September of the same year, he lectured in Chicago at a rally of the Polish-American Congress. Budenz profited handsomely from his anti-Communist efforts, at one point admitting that he averaged more than $10,000 annually in lecture fees alone.

Budenz was of medium height, of slight build, with thinning reddish hair, and was described as having a "crusader's gleam in his blue eyes" and "a machine-gun, staccato voice."

As the anti-Communist craze waned in the 1960's, Budenz faded from public view. He suffered a heart attack in 1962, and retired from the Fordham University faculty at about the same time. He spent the final decade of his life in relative obscurity at 196 Allison Avenue in Middletown, R.I. His final book, *The Bolshevik Invasion of the West*, was published in 1965. He died in Newport Hospital of a heart ailment after a long illness.

[Books by Budenz include *This Is My Story* (1941); *Men Without Faces* (1950); *The Cry Is Peace* (1952); *The Techniques of Communism* (textbook, 1953); and *The Bolshevik Invasion of the West* (1965). An obituary is in the *New York Times*, Apr. 28, 1972.]

NANCY V. FLOOD

BUNCHE, RALPH JOHNSON (Aug. 7, 1904–Dec. 9, 1971), scholar, educator, civil rights advocate, and world statesman, was born in Detroit, Mich., the son of Fred Bunch, a barber, and Olive Agnes Johnson. Ralph changed the spelling of his last name to Bunche in 1917. Bunche achieved international renown as the first person of color to receive the Nobel Peace Prize. The award was made in recognition of his successful mediation in 1948 and 1949 of the first war between Israel and its neighboring Arab states. His distinguished career encompassed pioneering work in the cause of civil rights and racial equality in the United States; in the development of American governmental and public understanding of Africa; in the establishment of the United Nations; and in the evolution of its innovative programs for decolonization, international mediation, and the containment of armed conflict through international peacekeeping operations.

Bunche attended elementary school in Detroit, Mich.; Toledo, Ohio; and Knoxville, Tenn., between 1910 and 1914. His family then moved to Albuquerque, N.Mex., because of his mother's ill health. There he continued his schooling and had his first encounter with racial discrimination: while attending a performance at the local nickelodeon, Bunche, his mother, and sister were told to move to the rear of the theater. Orphaned in 1917, he moved to Los Angeles to live with his maternal grandmother, Lucy Taylor Johnson, and his mother's sisters and brother. He graduated with honors from the Los Angeles 30th Street Intermediate School where he was assigned to "practical" courses because he was an African American. But his grandmother insisted that he be given an academic course to prepare him for college. Throughout his life Bunche proudly acknowledged his grandmother's influence, instilling in him pride and a determination to succeed.

In 1922, he graduated first in his class and as valedictorian from Jefferson High School. Because of his race, he was denied election to the citywide scholarship honor society. While in high school he worked as a newsboy for the *Los Angeles Times* and in his last year as a carpet layer. The same year he entered the southern branch of the University of California (later to become UCLA) on an academic scholarship, which he augmented by working at a variety of jobs, including summers on a coastwise merchant ship. At UCLA, in addition to being an outstanding student in philosophy and political science, he was president of the debating society and a student council leader, and he excelled in football, basketball, and baseball. In 1927, after graduating summa cum laude and serving as class valedictorian, he entered Harvard University which awarded him a scholarship to study political science. He received additional financial support from a black women's organization in Los Angeles, which established The Ralph Bunche Scholarship Fund. According to a fellow graduate student, Robert C. Weaver, Secretary of Housing and Urban Development under Lyndon Johnson, "Bunche was extremely attractive, quite vocal, articulate . . . [He had] an uncanny ability to produce stupendous amounts of work over long sustained periods of application . . . [which] maximized the impact of his knowledge, the brilliance of his personality, and was . . . the chief factor in his spectacular career."

After completing his M.A. at Harvard in 1928, Bunche joined the faculty of Howard University in Washington, D.C., a predominantly black institution. He was awarded the Ozias Goodwin Fellowship to return to Harvard the following year to complete his courses for the Ph.D. in government and international relations. Over the next five years, Bunche alternated between teaching and working for his Ph.D. A Julius Rosenwald Fellowship in 1932 enabled him to undertake research in West Africa for his dissertation comparing French colonial administration in Dahomey and the neighboring mandated territory, Togoland. In 1934, he was awarded the Toppan Prize for the year's best dissertation in political science at Harvard University, and he became the first African American to earn the Ph.D. in Government and International Relations there.

On June 23, 1930, Bunche married Ruth Ethel Harris, a first-grade teacher in Washington, originally from Montgomery, Ala.; they had three children.

At Howard University, Bunche established and chaired the Political Science Department, and served for a time as an assistant to President

Mordecai Johnson. Howard University in the 1930's was the intellectual center of young black scholar-activists, and Bunche was a leading member of this group; his home on the Howard University campus served as a gathering place. In 1931, he organized a protest against the presentation of *Porgy and Bess* at Washington's National Theater because of its segregation policy. He succeeded in having the theater desegregated during the run of the play. In 1935, he helped organize a conference at Howard University assessing the impact of the New Deal on the economic condition of Negroes and at which he presented the subsequently published (1936) paper, "A Critique of New Deal Social Planning as It Affects Negroes."

In 1936, Bunche helped found the National Negro Congress. That year also saw the publication of *A World View of Race*, in which he expounded his views on the pervasive and perverse manifestations of class and race.

Bunche pursued postdoctoral training in anthropology and undertook field research in Africa, all in 1936 and 1937. A grant from the Social Science Research Council enabled him to study at the London School of Economics and the University of Capetown in South Africa, and to conduct research in East and South Africa. His inquiries brought him face to face with the problems confronting Africa and deepened his understanding of the continent. While in London, he studied Swahili privately with Jomo Kenyatta, who later became the first president of independent Kenya.

In the United States, Bunche became increasingly involved in efforts to understand and ameliorate conditions of the black population. In 1934 he was codirector of the summer Institute on Race Relations at Swarthmore College. In 1939 he joined Gunnar Myrdal, the eminent Swedish sociologist, in collecting data for the seminal study *An American Dilemma: The Negro Problem and Modern Democracy*, published in 1944. Bunche prepared four monographs on various aspects of black political life that were used and quoted by Myrdal as the bases of the chapters on politics. One of the monographs was published posthumously in 1973 as *The Political Status of the Negro in the Age of FDR*. In February 1939, at the request of the program committee of the Republican party, Bunche prepared a study on why blacks had abandoned the GOP in the 1932 and 1936 national elections. Bunche's report emphasized that despite the long-standing loyalty to the party of Lincoln, blacks defected from it because of "bread and butter" considerations and the failure of the party to address their "fundamental political objectives . . . namely, enfranchisement in the South, protection of civil liberties, antilynching legislation, and appointment of members of the Race to policy-forming and other responsible positions."

World War II gave Bunche the opportunity to shift his focus to the international arena. In 1941, he joined the Office of the Coordinator of Information for the Armed Forces as a specialist on colonialism and race relations. This office became the Office of Strategic Services in 1942, at which time Bunche became head of the Africa Section in the Research and Analysis Branch. Outside the government, as a member of the Committee on Africa, the War, and Peace Aims—an influential group of academics and practitioners with African expertise—he helped prepare the 1942 publication, *The Atlantic Charter and Africa from an American Standpoint*.

Two years later, he transferred to the State Department's postwar planning group on the future of the colonial world. He served as a counselor on the American delegation at Dumbarton Oaks (1944) and the San Francisco Conference (1945), which drafted the United Nations Charter. Bunche played a key role in drawing up Chapters XI, XII, and XIII of the UN Charter, which deal with the UN regime for colonial territories. In the fall of 1945, he was an American member of the Preparatory Commission that put the United Nations into operation, and in January 1946 he was a member of the American delegation to the first session of the UN General Assembly. Shortly thereafter, Bunche joined the UN Secretariat as head of the Trusteeship Department.

In 1946, the future of Palestine was among the leading issues on the United Nations agenda. Bunche's service on the United Nations Committee on Palestine (UNSCOP) gained him a reputation within the UN as a keen analyst of this thorny issue. When war broke out between the newly created state of Israel and its neighboring Arab states in May 1948, Bunche was designated by Secretary-General Trygve Lie as his representative in Palestine; Bunche also headed the Secretariat support staff of the UN mediator, Count Folke Bernadotte of Sweden. Bernadotte was assassinated in Jerusalem in September and Bunche was appointed acting mediator. Through his perseverance and diplomatic skill during the next six months, Bunche succeeded in negotiating individual armistice agreements between Israel and four Arab states: Egypt, Jordan, Syria, and Lebanon.

The success brought Bunche the Nobel Peace Prize in 1950. In the United States he was widely hailed as the first black to receive recognition by the world for his extraordinary achievement. Bunche's picture was on the cover of most of the leading magazines of the day. He was in constant demand as a speaker and recipient of awards and honorary degrees. In 1949, he was awarded the Spingarn Medal of the National Association of Colored People (NAACP), and became one of its directors, a position he held until his death. That same year he received an honorary Doctor of Laws degree from Harvard University. All told, he received sixty-nine honorary degrees. Many elementary and high schools were named after him throughout the country, as was a small park opposite United Nations headquarters in New York. Bunche Hall at UCLA is named for the famous alumnus. President Harry Truman offered him the position of assistant secretary of state, which Bunche declined, saying that he did not wish to go back to live in Washington because it was a "Jim Crow" town.

Bunche almost left the United Nations in 1950, when he accepted appointment as professor of government at Harvard University. Although he always expressed his desire to return to academia, he changed his mind and chose to remain with the United Nations, where he became an indispensable top-level adviser and troubleshooter to Secretary-General Lie and his successors, Dag Hammarskjöld and U Thant. Elevated to the position of under-secretary-general without portfolio, he eventually became under-secretary-general for special political affairs, where he was instrumental in developing and administering the various UN peacekeeping and truce observation activities that came into being during his years of service: Sinai, 1956; Congo, 1960; Cyprus, 1962; Yemen, 1963; and India-Pakistan, 1965. He also played an important role in establishing the International Atomic Energy Agency and the United Nations Development Program (UNDP). Throughout his diplomatic career, first in the State Department and subsequently in the United Nations, Bunche focused his attention on the colonial world, and he can properly be considered to be one of the architects of decolonization.

Bunche's international renown did not insulate him from U.S. Senator Joseph McCarthy's obsession with Communists. Bunche, whose views on race, class, and antisegregation activities in the 1930's were considered radical and "Marxist," was accused of associating with known Communists and belonging to such Communist-dominated organizations as the National Negro Congress. In truth, Bunche had broken with this group before the outbreak of World War II because its leadership had been coopted by the American Communist party. In a twelve-hour hearing before the International Organizations Employee Loyalty Board in May 1954, Bunche denied the Communist accusation, and the board rendered a "favorable loyalty determination." In 1963, President Lyndon Johnson presented Bunche with the Medal of Freedom, which he had been designated to receive by President John F. Kennedy.

Bunche's career falls into two distinct parts, domestic and international, that really comprised a single commitment. As a scholar and activist, he strove to improve the human condition, particularly the state of people of color. For Bunche, civil rights in the United States and human rights in the international arena were part of one continuum.

When Bunche achieved the status of *diplomat extraordinaire*, the embodiment of the UN ideals and super-international civil servant, he also became the most noted and admired black person of his time in the United States. Although barred by UN rules from becoming involved in domestic politics, Bunche had an understanding with three secretaries-general under whom he served that he could speak his mind on racism in the United States, which he did often.

His international position did not deter him in 1965 from marching alongside the Reverend Martin Luther King, Jr., in Selma, Ala., even though his body was racked with pain from phlebitis and diabetes. Nor did it deter him from privately and publicly expressing his sometimes critical views of aspects of the civil rights movement as well as his support for its aims. Most noted at the time (1967) was Bunche's opposition to Dr. King's efforts to amalgamate the civil rights and anti–Vietnam War movements as "a serious tactical error . . . bound to alienate many friends and supporters of the civil rights movement and greatly weaken it."

Bunche retired from the United Nations early in 1971 because of ill health; he died on December 9 of that year. His life was one of great personal achievement and lasting importance for the United States and the world. Ralph Bunche rose from very modest origins to become one of the world's foremost and admired figures, acclaimed both in his own country and the world at large. As A. Philip Randolph noted: "Important as Dr. Bunche's work in the United Nations has been, I remember him best for his early commitment to the civil rights campaigns during the 1930's and 1940's. Our movement was young then, and it was totally committed young people like Ralph Bunche whose spirit and resilience, in the face of overwhelming odds, gave strength to the rest of us." U Thant, a secretary-general of the United Nations under whom Bunche served, described Bunche as "an international institution in his own right, transcending both nationality and race in a way that is achieved by very few."

[Bunche's papers are in the Library of the University of California at Los Angeles and in the Schomburg Library of the New York Public Library. Publications by Bunche include A *World View of Race* (1936); Dewey W. Grantham, ed., *The Political Status of the Negro in the Age of FDR* (1973); and Robert R. Edgar, ed., *An African American in South Africa* (1992). Biographies of Bunche are Peggy Mann, *Ralph Bunche: UN Peacemaker* (1975); Benjamin Rivlin, ed., *Ralph Bunche: The Man and His Times* (1990); and Brian Urquhart, *Ralph Bunche: An American Life* (1993). An obituary appears in the *New York Times*, Dec. 10, 1971.]

BENJAMIN RIVLIN

BURNETT, LEO (Oct. 21, 1891–June 7, 1971), advertising executive, was born in St. Johns, Mich., to Noble Burnett and Rose Clark. He painted signs at his father's dry-goods store as a young boy. He was attracted to journalism and so in 1914 received a degree in that subject from the University of Michigan. He worked for a year with the *Peoria Journal* as a crime reporter and was editor and advertising director for the Cadillac Motor Company in-house magazine. He became acquainted with Theodore F. MacManus, who had led Cadillac in its effort to surpass Packard as the luxury car choice. On May 29, 1918, he married Naomi Geddes; they had three children. After World War I, Burnett moved to Indianapolis to work for the Lafayette car company but soon began working for a local advertising firm.

Seeking greater opportunities in advertising, Burnett moved to Chicago. After a short stint with the local office of a New York firm, Homer M. Kee, he opened his own advertising firm on Aug. 5, 1935, with the help of some colleagues from Indiana. The Leo Burnett Company, Inc., soon attracted the clients Hoover Vacuum Company and the Minnesota Valley Canning Company, the predecessor of the Green Giant Company, a large food processor.

Burnett was a short man who barely spoke above a whisper. His strength was the ability to understand his client's business and to create memorable advertising characters. Charlie the Star-Kist Tuna, the Pillsbury Doughboy, the Jolly Green Giant, Tony the Tiger, and Morris the Cat were all Burnett inventions. Tony the Tiger created the brand identity of Kellogg's Frosted Flakes, and an off-color parody of the Pillsbury Doughboy led to major litigation in which Pillsbury successfully restrained a pornographic magazine from depicting Burnett's Doughboy engaged in various sex acts; the case remains an important precedent on the limits of parody as applied to advertisements.

Burnett's working style emphasized intensive commitment to a few clients (around thirty), but Burnett would make up for the intensity of this work by taking larger commissions. He helped develop new products, such as plastic food-storage bags and "his and hers" diapers. He also worked closely with Ray Kroc in developing the spectacularly successful McDonald's fast-food chain.

Burnett excelled at taking familiar images and recycling them in a commercial context. The Jolly Green Giant was created for a food processor located in the lumbering country of Minnesota. Burnett used this to create a "giant" who was an amalgam of Paul Bunyan, Frankenstein's monster, and the giant of the Jack and the Beanstalk legend. At his Lake Zurich, Ill., farm in the 1950's, Burnett hit upon another American icon, the cowboy, as the basis for the Marlboro Man. This tattooed individual, usually seen roping cattle, became the symbol of the tobacco industry's emphasis on masculinity in the face of danger. The success of this campaign probably played a role in the 1969 congressional decision to ban tobacco advertising on television and radio.

Burnett centralized his operations in a Wacker Drive office (in a commercial area near the Loop), which conducted virtually all American operations for the Leo Burnett Agency. He led the "Chicago school" of advertising, emphasizing "simple language and warm appeal," in the words of the *Chicago Sun-Times*.

Burnett was a director of the Advertising Council, the industry's public-service organization from 1941 to 1971, and chairman from 1962 to 1963. He was also a trustee of the American Heritage Foundation and a trustee of Chicago's Adler Planetarium. His interest in astronomy is reflected in his firm's logo of a hand reaching for five stars. In 1964, Burnett created the slogan "In your heart, you know he's right," for Barry Goldwater's successful bid for the Republican presidential nomination, but he was dropped for another agency during Goldwater's fall campaign for the presidency.

Burnett urged his employees to make ads for the fun of it. Money, he always reasoned, would follow. He died at his Lake Zurich farm. The advertising firm of Lee Burnett continued as one of the largest in the world.

[Burnett edited and compiled *Good Citizen* (1947). His staff at Leo Burnett edited *Communications of an Advertising Man* (1961), based on his memos and speeches. Stephen Fox, *The Mirror Makers* (1984), places Burnett's work in its historical context. A review of an exhibit of Burnett's advertising work is in the Chicago *Sun-Times*, Oct. 21, 1991. An obituary appears in the *New York Times*, June 9, 1971.]

JOHN DAVID HEALY

BUSCH, HERMANN (June 24, 1897–June 3, 1975), cellist, was born in Siegen, Westphalia, Germany, to Wilhelm Busch and Henriette Schmidt, the fifth child in a family of musical children that included eminent conductor Fritz Busch and celebrated violinist Adolf Busch. Busch's father, a violin maker and owner of a musical instrument shop, had hoped to be a concert musician himself, but was forced by circumstances to settle for the founding and conducting of a small orchestra that played in taverns and at various social events. Busch's mother operated her own embroidery business in addition to playing the piano in her husband's orchestra on weekends and raising five children.

Busch's father encouraged his children to study music and learn to play at least one instrument. Fritz and Adolf Busch were already playing with their father's "Salonkapelle" orchestra in the villages of the Siegerland when their brother Hermann was born in 1897. When Hermann was six years old he took up the violin, much to the chagrin of his brothers, who felt that the family orchestra needed a cellist, not another violinist. Under pressure to switch instruments, Busch began to study the cello, taking his first lessons from his father at the age of nine. When his father decided that he needed a professional music teacher, the family moved from Siegen to Siegburg, a little city in the Rhineland not far from Cologne. In Siegburg, the family would be closer to brother Adolf, who was then studying at the Cologne Conservatory. It was hoped that Hermann would also study there.

In Cologne, Busch attended the Conservatory and studied the cello under the guidance of Friedrich Grützmacher. He also intermittently studied with Jacques Rendsburg in Bonn during this time. In 1913, he transferred to the Vienna Academy of Music, where he studied with Paul Grümmer, whom he replaced years later as the principal cellist in the Busch Quartet.

In 1914, Busch volunteered for the army, but World War I did not prevent him from being involved in music. It was during the war that Busch became a member of the Brussels Symphony Orchestra. After the war, he was engaged as a solo cellist for the city of Bochum's orchestra. Busch's four years in Bochum had a great impact on the rest of his life as it was there that on May 18, 1924, he married Charlotte Ising, the daughter of a Bochum businessman. They had one child, a daughter.

From 1923 to 1927 Busch was a member of the Vienna Symphony Orchestra, where he was first cellist. In the years following, he performed as a soloist in a number of major cities in Europe, including Vienna, Rome, Milan, and London. He was also a member of the faculty of the Folkswangschule in Essen from 1927 to 1930. In 1926, he began to play regularly with his brother Adolf and pianist Rudolf Serkin in the Busch Trio. The Busch Trio, which toured extensively in Europe prior to World War II, gained a great deal of recognition and acclaim for their concert performances. Occasionally, his brother Fritz directed these concerts.

In 1930, Busch became a member of the Busch Quartet, founded by his brother Adolf in

1919. The quartet was composed of Hermann Busch, cello; Adolf Busch and Gösta Andresson, violins; and Karl Doktor, viola. The Busch Quartet achieved international fame as a string ensemble, touring widely in Europe and eventually in North America. Busch remained a member of both the Busch Trio and the Busch Quartet until his brother Adolf's death in 1952.

When Hitler assumed power in 1933, the Busch Quartet immediately canceled all of their concerts in Germany. Busch, though not Jewish, renounced his German citizenship and moved his family to Basel, Switzerland, where his brother Adolf and Rudolf Serkin had already established themselves in 1927. From Basel, the Busch Quartet undertook many concert trips to England, France, and Italy, as well as other European countries. With the outbreak of World War II these concert trips became impossible. In 1940, Busch emigrated to New York City, following by one year the emigration to America of his brother Adolf and Rudolf Serkin.

When the war came to an end, the Busch Quartet again embarked on a series of concert tours in Europe. In 1951, the Busch Quartet played in Germany again for the first time. While in America, Busch continued to appear as a soloist and play with several orchestras and string ensembles—especially in New York City, where he made his home.

In 1950, Busch and his brother Adolf, along with Rudolf Serkin and others, founded the Marlboro School of Music in Marlboro, Vt. The three musicians directed the school and performed in the school's summer music festivals. With the founding of the Marlboro School, Busch hoped to enhance the opportunities for the study and performance of chamber music in America. In 1954, Busch was appointed professor of music at the University of Miami in Coral Gables, Fla. Busch continued to teach the cello there until his retirement in 1964.

Busch was greatly admired as a soloist and as a member of the Busch Trio and the Busch Quartet, both of which have had a lasting impact on chamber music in Europe and the United States. In addition to his reputation as an artist and performing musician, Busch is also remembered as both a devoted teacher of the cello and as a founder of the Marlboro School of Music and its summer music festivals.

Hermann Busch gave his last public concert in Dahlbruch, Germany, on June 5, 1966, a matinee performance, which took place on the occasion of the seventy-fifth birthday of Adolf Busch. He played his brother's piano trio in A-minor, Opus 15, with Pina Carmirelli and Rudolf Serkin. He died in Bryn Mawr, Pa., and was survived by his wife, his daughter, and four grandchildren.

[See Fritz Busch, *Pages from a Musician's Life,* translated by Marjorie Strachey (1953) and *Festkonzert Program zum 75. Geburtstag Hermann Buschs. Bruder Busch Gesellschaft e.V.* (Program to a special concert held to celebrate Hermann Busch's 75th birthday, June 1975). An obituary is in the *New York Times,* June 5, 1975.]

RICHARD STRINGER-HYE

BUSH, PRESCOTT SHELDON (May 15, 1895–Oct. 8, 1972), United States senator and banker, was born in Columbus, Ohio, the son of Samuel Prescott Bush, a steel company president, and Flora Sheldon. After attending the Douglas School in Columbus and St. George's School, Newport, R.I. (1908–1913), Bush entered Yale. A superb athlete, he played varsity golf, football, and baseball. He was also president of the Yale Glee Club, a Whiffenpoof (second bass), and the best close-harmony man in the class of 1917. His devotion to singing at Yale would remain strong his entire life, evidenced in part by his founding of the Yale Glee Club Associates, an alumni group, in 1937.

After graduation, Bush served in the American Expeditionary Forces (1917–1919) as a captain in the field artillery during World War I. He received training in intelligence at Verdun and was briefly assigned to a staff of French officers. Alternating between intelligence and artillery, Bush was under fire in the Meuse-Argonne offensive.

After his discharge in 1919, Bush went to work for the Simmons Hardware Company in St. Louis, Mo. On Aug. 6, 1921, Bush married Dorothy Walker. They had five children; one of them, George Herbert Walker Bush, would become the forty-first president of the United States.

The Bushes moved to Columbus, Ohio, in 1923, where Bush worked for the Hupp Products Company. He left in November 1923 to become president of sales for Stedman Products of South Braintree, Mass. In 1925, he joined the United States Rubber Company in New

York City as manager of its foreign division and moved to Greenwich, Conn.

Bush became vice-president at the investment banking firm of W. A. Harriman and Company in 1926 and, when it merged with Brown Brothers in 1931, became a partner in the new firm of Brown Brothers, Harriman. Bush called it "my good fortune" to work with close friends, including Yale classmates E. Roland Harriman, Knight Woolley, and Ellery James, as well as Robert A. Lovett and Thomas McCance.

In 1935, Bush was president of the United States Golf Association, and from then until 1952 was moderator of the Greenwich Representative Town Meeting. Six-foot-four and very strong, Bush looked imposing. With a reputation for integrity and administrative ability, he was a director of many corporations: Columbia Broadcasting System, Dresser Manufacturing Company, Union Banking Corporation, Simmons Company, Massachusetts Investors Second Fund, Rockbestos Products Corporation, United States Guarantee Company, Commercial Pacific Cable Company. He also served as chairman of the board of Pennsylvania Water and Power Company.

President Franklin D. Roosevelt asked Bush and three other businessmen to organize the United Service Organizations (USO) at the beginning of the Second World War. Bush served as National Campaign chairman in 1942, raising a record $32 million. In 1943 and 1944, he was chairman of the National War Fund Campaign.

From 1944 to 1956, Bush was a member of the Yale Corporation, the principal governing body of Yale University. His involvement in politics deepened. From 1947 to 1950 he served as Connecticut Republican finance chairman, and was the Republican candidate for the United States Senate in 1950, losing to Senator William Benton by only 1,000 votes. The following year, Bush was Connecticut chairman of the United Negro College Fund. One of the UNCF's earliest supporters, he believed in the American dream for everyone, black or white.

In 1952, Bush won election to the Senate, defeating Abraham Ribicoff for the vacancy caused by the death of James O'Brien McMahon. A friend of Dwight D. Eisenhower, Bush often played golf with the president. He served on the Banking and Currency Committee and was chairman of its Subcommittee on

Securities. Appearing on CBS-TV's "Face the Nation" on Feb. 13, 1955, Bush talked about "prosperity with peace, which incidentally is another contribution of the Eisenhower Administration." Recognized as an expert on the economy and government finance, Bush's Senate speeches were sometimes widely published.

In a speech on Nathan Hale given June 6, 1955, in New London, Conn., Bush shared reflections on the Cold War. "We must maintain strong defenses, military and spiritual," Bush said, predicting, "It is our conduct, our patriotism and belief in our American way of life, our courage that will win the final battle." As his wife noted in Yale's "The Observation Post" (November 1972), Bush had "an innate sense of right from wrong," and often saw issues—including foreign policy—in terms of morality. He did not believe public and private morality could be separated.

In 1956, Bush was chairman of the Republican National Platform Committee, and that November he was reelected to the Senate, defeating Thomas Dodd by more than 128,000 votes. He served on the Armed Services and Public Works Committees. His commitment to civil rights was captured by a photograph that appeared in the *New York Times* on Mar. 2, 1960; he is catching some sleep in his clothes on his office couch during an all-night filibuster in the Senate.

During the Kennedy administration, Bush usually voted against President John F. Kennedy, but he supported the Peace Corps and the administration's plan to buy $100 million worth of United Nations bonds in 1962. A hard-working senator, Bush often flew to Hartford to speak to constituents, returning to Washington by night train. In poor health at sixty-seven, he did not seek reelection in 1962. The head of the Connecticut AFL-CIO later told Prescott Bush, Jr., that if his father had run, he would have had the support of labor for the first time.

Bush worked again at Brown Brothers, Harriman but spent half the year in Hobe Sound, Fla., where he sang in church every Sunday. In 1966, Bush wrote, "Wherever I found myself in war or peace, in business or politics, in sports or social life, always the fact of Yale seemed to be there." In *Looking Forward* (1987), then–Vice-President George Bush called his parents the greatest influence on his life and said, "Dad taught us about duty and service." The autobiography is dedicated "To my mother and father, whose values lit the way." In 1988, Bush became the first senator's son to be elected president. Prescott Bush died in New York City.

[The Prescott Bush Papers are at the University of Connecticut, Storrs. The Greenwich Library Oral History Project has interviews with Prescott Bush, Jr., and Mary Walker. Bush's articles include "Timely Monetary Policy," *Banking*, June 1954 and July 1954; "To Preserve Peace Let's *Show* the Russians How Strong We Are!" *Reader's Digest*, July 1959; "Politics Is Your Business," Chamber of Commerce, State of New York, *Bulletin*, May 1960. There is material by and about Bush in the *History of the Class of 1917 Yale College* (1919) and the supplementary class albums; see also Dorothy Bush's column, "Washington Life as Seen by a Senator's Wife," which appeared in Connecticut newspapers, including the *Hartford Courant* and the *Greenwich Time*; and *Looking Forward* (1987) by George Bush, with Victor Gold.

For Bush's business career, see John Atlee Kouwenhoven, *Partners in Banking: An Historical Portrait of a Great Private Bank, Brown Brothers, Harriman* (1968). Obituaries are in the *Washington Post*, Oct. 9, 1972; the *New York Times*, Oct. 9, 1972; the *Hartford Courant*, Oct. 9, 1972; and *Yale Alumni Magazine*, Dec. 1972.]

RALPH KIRSHNER

BUSH, VANNEVAR ("VAN") (Mar. 11, 1890–June 28, 1974), government science administrator, was born in Everett, Mass., the son of Richard Perry Bush and Emma Linwood Paine. His father had studied at Tufts College and was a liberal Universalist minister in Chelsea, Mass., where Vannevar attended public school. Vannevar worked his way through Tufts College by tutoring mathematics. He received both a B.S. and an M.S. degree from Tufts in 1913. In 1916 he obtained a doctorate of engineering degree (D.Eng.) in a joint program through Harvard and the Massachusetts Institute of Technology (MIT) while an instructor of mathematics at Tufts; he became an assistant professor of electrical engineering at Tufts in 1916. On Sept. 5, 1916, Bush married Phoebe Davis, the daughter of a prosperous Chelsea grocer. They had two children.

During World War I, Bush worked for the United States Navy, developing a magnetic device that would allow surface ships to determine the precise location of area submarines. Bush found that the technical problems of wartime scientific pursuits were nothing compared with the organizational and human problems involved in such work. Because the navy had no development funds, Bush took his unfinished device to New York financier J. P. Morgan's American Research and Development Company (AMRAD), presenting it to the navy after resolving its technical problems. But the bureaucratic obstacles of the armed forces seemed daunting. Bush had perfected his sub-tracking instrument for use on wooden subchasers; the navy brass insisted the device be put on iron subchasers. Bush spent six months trying to adapt the device to iron ships before the navy reversed itself and permitted the instrument's use on wooden ships. Of the one hundred devices put into production at AMRAD, only three got to the North Sea before the armistice. No German U-boat was ever detected by Bush's instrument.

Bush thus saw the lack of coordination between science and the armed forces as potentially dangerous. Because of security concerns, the navy disallowed cooperation among their researchers, some of whom were working on similar or compatible projects. Bush learned of the existence of one such group after the war and later reminisced that if he had been able to join forces with this group, a more effective sub-tracking device, less expensive and easier to build, would have been produced and put to great use during the war.

He emerged from his World War I experience fully committed to new organizational principles, ones that were just coming into fashion in American culture. Disparate elements of any large enterprise, Bush believed, had to be coordinated in their efforts to achieve a common goal; without such horizontal as well as vertical integration, chaos ensued. Bush recognized the need for a centralizing body to bring the technical and the political together, to harness engineers and decision makers to the same goals. Indeed, Bush defined an engineer as someone who had not just technical knowledge about the problems to be solved, but also knowledge of how the world worked and how scientific advancements affected that world; otherwise, the aspiring engineer was a mere scientist.

In 1919 Bush became associate professor of electrical power transmission at MIT; in 1923 he was promoted to full professor, and nine years later, in 1932, he became vice-president and dean of engineering, a position he held until 1938. During the interwar years Bush pursued the dual threads of his career as an academic and an entrepreneur with dazzling success. He quickly won popularity among his students for his stimulating teaching and his crusty insistence that even engineers learn how to write clear English sentences. He also promoted graduate work in electrical engineering, a pioneering effort in the 1920's and 1930's, and MIT rapidly became a major center of graduate training in the field. As a researcher at MIT, Bush proved to be something of a technical genius. In his work involving the mathematical analysis of power circuits, Bush invented a successful, if primitive, mechanical computer and, with the assistance of junior colleagues and students, pushed the device's metamorphosis into a sophisticated differential analyzer that weighed one hundred tons and could solve differential equations with as many as eighteen variables. Mechanically speaking, this machine was a direct antecedent of the electronic analogue computer of the post–World War II era. The differential analyzer was put to many uses in research and in industry; it brought Bush and MIT special recognition.

Bush also proved himself an effective, if abrasive, academic administrator at MIT; he had wide-ranging intellectual curiosity, was sufficiently self-confident to countenance originality in others, and possessed impressive talents as an executive. Thus, when Karl T. Compton became MIT's president in 1932, he used the efficient Bush as his right-hand man (and his lightning rod). As an inventor and entrepreneur, Bush liked to say that he never patented a device, much preferring to be creative than commercial. Yet he did turn over his more useful gadgets to companies he helped found, and in this way became a wealthy man. He and his associates in the Boston area founded half a dozen or so manufacturing companies. Two became very profitable. One of them Bush established in 1922 with his former college roommate, Laurence K. Marshall, to market the S-tube, a device invented by C. G. Smith that greatly improved the delivery of electricity to radios. Initially known as the American Appliance Company and run out of a workshop near the MIT campus in Cambridge, the firm soon turned handsome profits and was eventually redubbed the Raytheon Manufacturing Company. When Bush died in 1974, Raytheon was a diversified electronics company with fifty-five plants, fifty-two thousand employees, and approximately $1 billion in annual sales.

Bush also established the Spencer Thermostat Company, which sold a new kind of metal thermostat. These efforts gave him financial security and considerable experience as a business executive.

In 1939, Bush moved to the nation's capital as president of the Carnegie Institution of Washington, a general purpose scientific research organization. This set the stage for the most important period of Bush's life, at least from the standpoint of national history. His work at Carnegie made him a major player in the harnessing of the resources of science and technology on the one hand, and of government and the military on the other, and proved instrumental in the winning of the war against the Axis powers in World War II. Bush had participated in the politics of American national science in the 1930's, when he served on President Roosevelt's Science Advisory Board and the National Advisory Committee for Aeronautics with Karl Compton. Like Compton, Bush believed that technological and scientific research would have large-scale economic benefits and consequences, and that it was the job of the scientist-administrator to cultivate said research in the right channels.

In Washington, Bush was increasingly drawn into high-level governmental discussions of national defense. The discovery by German scientists of nuclear fission in 1939 alarmed the American scientific community and, as the United States prepared for war, Bush pressed the White House into creating precisely that large centralized coordinating committee he had so hungered for in World War I. His efforts led one newspaper reporter to call Bush the czar of American war research. The first step was taken when President Roosevelt appointed Bush head of the National Defense Research Committee in 1940. Bush appointed four leading scientists to the committee: Compton, president of MIT; James B. Conant, president of Harvard; Frank B. Jewett, president of the National Academy of Sciences; and Richard C. Tolman, dean of engineering at the California Institute of Technology. Each man was responsible for a general area of defense research, but all four acted as an advisory committee with Bush in deciding matters of general scientific and technological defense policy. American military technology was hopelessly outclassed by the Axis powers and, in some respects, by almost all of the major belligerents in the war. Bush

turned the old model of government-run factories and laboratories into a new blueprint in
which federal contracts were awarded to business firms and academic institutions for development and research. Time was essential; hence
he promoted a tradition of cooperation among
disparate units.

In May 1941, President Roosevelt finally created the office of Scientific Research and Development (OSRD) and placed Bush in charge.
Bush in turn subsumed the National Defense
Research Committee within the OSRD, thus
ending any possibility of bureaucratic infighting
or inefficiency. Known as an effective, slash-
and-burn administrator, Bush soon brought the
entire defense research and development establishment under his control and even oversaw
cooperative projects with the Allies (as with the
British on radar). It would be difficult to name
any military innovation from this period, ranging from radar to sulfa drugs, from target control devices for artillery to the atom bomb itself,
that was not managed under Bush's general supervision. During the war, perhaps two-thirds
of America's physicists worked under Bush's direction.

After the Allied victory in 1945, Bush returned to his post as president of the Carnegie
Institution and promoted a new form of national politics of American science. In a constant stream of articles and speeches, and above
all, in *Science, The Endless Frontier* (1945), a
report on the lessons of wartime mobilization
for peace he wrote at the president's behest,
Bush argued for substantial federal investment
in basic scientific research along the lines of the
bid and contract system he had invented for
ORSD. This became the model for all postwar
federal scientific agencies, including the National Science Foundation, established in 1950.
In the Cold War era, Bush became known as an
elder statesman of the concept that a strong national defense would preserve freedom, just as
technological innovation in commerce and industry would bring about prosperity. In 1955,
he retired from the Carnegie Institution and
returned to Cambridge and MIT. He was made
chairman of the MIT Corporation in 1957,
and, subsequently, honorary chairman for life.
He surrendered this position in 1971 to James
R. Killian, who had been President Dwight
Eisenhower's science adviser.

Bush lived in retirement in a large home in
Belmont, Mass., and a summer house in Cape
Cod. He died at his Belmont home at the age of
eighty-four; his health had been poor for a year
and a half, and he developed pneumonia after
suffering a stroke.

[Bush's papers are located at the Library of Congress, in Washington, D.C. An oral history memoir
of his experiences at the Carnegie Institution of
Washington is in the Oral History Research Office,
Columbia University; a microfilm copy is available
for purchase or interlibrary loan. Among his books
are *Principles of Electrical Engineering*, with William
H. Timbie (1922); *Operational Circuit Analysis*
(1929); *Scientists Face the World of 1942*, with Karl
T. Compton and Robert W. Trullinger (1942); *Science, The Endless Frontier* (1945); *Endless Horizons*
(1946); *Modern Arms and Free Men* (1949); *Science
Is Not Enough* (1967); and his autobiography, *Pieces
of the Action* (1970). As for secondary accounts, and
further guides to sources, an indispensable book is
Daniel J. Kevles, *The Physicists* (1977). See also
James Phinney Baxter III, *Scientists Against Time*
(1946); and Alan I. Marcus and Howard P. Segal,
Technology in America (1989). An obituary is in the
New York Times, June 30, 1974.]

HAMILTON CRAVENS

BUTTERWORTH, WILLIAM WALTON
("WALT") (Sept. 7, 1903–Mar. 31, 1975),
career diplomat and ambassador to Sweden and
Canada, was born in New Orleans, La., the son
of William Walton Butterworth, a physician,
and Maude Revencamp Campbell. He was educated at the New Orleans Academy from 1909
to 1916. From 1916 to 1921 he attended
Lawrenceville Preparatory School. In 1921 he
entered Princeton University, graduating with
honors in 1925. From 1925 to 1927, he was a
Rhodes Scholar at Worcester College of Oxford
University, where he studied American and English literature.

In May 1928, Butterworth joined the United
States Foreign Service. On November 10 of the
same year he married Virginia Parker; they had
two children. After a year of service and training
at the State Department in Washington, D.C.,
he was posted to Singapore as vice-consul. He
returned to Washington, D.C., in the summer
of 1931. After a year he was assigned as third
secretary to the American Legation in Ottawa,
Canada. He remained there from 1932 to 1934
before being promoted to second secretary and
then being reassigned to the American embassy
in London. He acted as financial attaché working on trade policy relations for the Lend-Lease
Program, which began in January 1941.

From late 1941 to late 1942 he was in Washington, D.C., again, on temporary assignment as a special assistant to the under secretary of commerce. His next appointment was as a member of the Advisory Commission of Trade Policy in Relation to Lend-Lease. From 1942 to 1944 he served as first secretary of the American Legation in Lisbon, Portugal, and then as first secretary for the American embassy in Madrid, Spain. He simultaneously worked on the Iberian peninsula as director general for operations of the U.S. Commercial Company, a government-owned corporation engaged in preclusive buying of strategic materials.

In 1944, Butterworth began a twenty-month stint as consul of the American embassy in Madrid. He held the same position with the rank of minister in Nanking, China, from 1946 to 1947. There he served with General of the Army George C. Marshall, who had been dispatched to China by President Harry S. Truman to attempt a rapprochement between Chiang Kai-shek and his Nationalists and Mao Tse-tung and his Communists.

Six months after Marshall left his impossible and failed China mission in January 1947 to become secretary of state, Butterworth returned to Washington, D.C., to become assistant secretary of state for Far Eastern affairs. Having agreed with many of the viewpoints of the foreign service officers in China known as the China Hands (such as John S. Service, John Emerson, John King Fairbank, John Patton Davies, and John Carter Vincent), Butterworth ran afoul of Chiang Kai-shek, T. V. Soong, Representative Walter Judd of Minnesota, and the "China Lobby." During Butterworth's arduous confirmation hearings, one senator denounced the Marshall Mission and declared that Butterworth was a "symbol of American failure in China."

Despite being passed over fourteen times as assistant secretary of state for Far Eastern affairs, his confirmation was finally approved, and Butterworth served in this position until 1950. In the spring of 1949, he rejected pleas from the Chinese Nationalists for a multimillion-dollar loan to bolster their crumbling regime, supporting instead the Truman administration's stand not to "pour more U.S. aid down the bottomless 'rat hole' of China."

Among those who worked with him on Asian issues were the preeminent Harvard scholar and dean of Asian Studies in the United States, John King Fairbank, who said of Butterworth: "He's outgoing but in a dignified sort of way." Another former foreign service colleague, Oliver Edmund Clubb, added "Mr. Butterworth was honest, capable, and courageous."

In 1950, as Senator Joseph McCarthy and others began their Communist witch-hunts of branches of the government—especially the State Department—Butterworth was posted to Sweden as American ambassador. At a time when many of his colleagues, among them, Davies, Vincent, and Service, had their careers ruined by accusations and innuendo of communist sympathies, President Truman sent Butterworth to Stockholm to remove him from harm's way. After three years in Sweden, he returned to London as minister and deputy chief of the U.S. Economic and Aid Mission; he served in this capacity from 1954 to 1955. With the humiliation of Senator McCarthy, Butterworth's career finally became secure again. In early 1956 he became the American representative to the European Coal and Steel Community with the rank of ambassador. In 1958 he simultaneously took on the job of American representative to the European Economic Community for the European Atomic Energy Commission.

Both assignments came to an end in 1962, when Butterworth was posted to Ottawa, Canada, as American ambassador. It was a pleasant and fruitful experience for Butterworth, despite the controversies of the Vietnam war, which hardened U.S.-Canadian relations. In his six years in Ottawa, Butterworth calmed tensions over tariffs, Vietnam, the stationing of U.S. nuclear warheads in Canada, and the Cuban missile crisis. When he retired in 1968, one Canadian cabinet minister declared that all Canadians were grateful to Mr. Butterworth for "forthrightly speaking Washington's mind."

After forty-one illustrious years in the State Department, he retired to Princeton. From 1969 to 1974 he traveled, lectured at Princeton, and spoke to many conferences and scholarly meetings. After a brief illness he died at Roosevelt Hospital in New York City.

[Butterworth's papers are at Princeton University and in the National Archives. For information on Butterworth's political career, see William Head, *America's China Sojourn* (1983). An obituary appears in the *New York Times*, Apr. 2, 1975.]

WILLIAM HEAD

BUTTS, JAMES WALLACE ("WALLY") (Feb. 7, 1905–Dec. 17, 1973), football coach and athletic director, was born near Milledgeville, Ga., the only child of James Wallace Butts, who ran a dray service (moving business), and Anna Lousetta Hutchinson. His mother died when he was only three years old, whereupon his father moved to Atlanta, and he was subsequently raised by a grandmother, aunts, and uncles. He attended Milledgeville's Georgia Military College, a prep school, where he became a standout athlete, starring in baseball, basketball, and football, and serving as captain of the latter two teams. In 1924, Butts entered Mercer University in Macon, Ga., where he competed in the same three sports and was particularly outstanding in football: he captained his college team and was named an All Southern Collegiate Athlete during his senior season in 1927.

Graduating with a B.A. in 1928, Butts made the transition from athlete to coach. He began his coaching career at Madison A&M University, serving there until 1932. He next coached at his alma mater, Georgia Military College, from 1932 to 1934. He rounded out his apprenticeship to the coaching profession at Male High in Louisville, Ky., where in the years 1934 to 1937 he had the distinction of leading his team to three consecutive undefeated championship seasons.

Meanwhile, in 1929, Butts married Winifred Faye Taylor; the couple eventually had three children.

In 1938, Butts moved up to the college level of coaching when Joel Hunt, a former star player at Texas A&M and head coach at the University of Georgia, hired him as an assistant. When Hunt quit the following year, Butts was named head coach and began the remarkable twenty-two-year career at the University of Georgia that would make him a Georgia icon and a college football coaching legend.

A motivator, an innovator, and a master field tactician, Butts built the University of Georgia into a national football power, making the college's "Bulldogs" one of the most celebrated teams in the United States. Between 1939 and 1960, he led his team to 140 victories and 9 ties, against only 86 losses. His teams claimed four Southeastern Conference championships and appeared in eight bowl games (winning five). In 1942 his Bulldogs won eleven games and lost one, and in 1946 the team won eleven games

and lost none; in both these years Georgia's team was ranked number one in the nation by at least one poll.

Butts often said that most winning coaches had something going for them beyond their own ability, by which he meant quality players around which to build and maintain a program. He coached some of the best players in football, including 1942 Heisman Trophy winner Frank Sinkwich, 1946 Maxwell Award recipient Charley Trippi, and Fran Tarkenton, who went on to become the leading passer in the history of the National Football League. Butts instilled discipline and a sense of values in all the young men who passed through his football program.

Butts was a master tactician with the passing game. He brought Sinkwich, Trippi, and 1948 All-American Johnny Rauch to Georgia from the North and used these talented players to establish the Bulldogs as the aerial masters of southern football. Winning conference championships in 1942, 1946, and 1948 by means of his powerful offensive blend of running and passing, Butts's teams hastened the end of one-dimensional football in the South. The 1940's ended with Butts perceived as perhaps America's top collegiate football coach.

Since football began at the University of Georgia in 1892, no decade was so unkind to the Bulldogs as the 1950's, however. Five seasons ended with more losses than wins. Even more humiliating, the Bulldogs lost eight consecutive games to their archrival Georgia Tech from 1949 to 1956. Influential University of Georgia alumni and faculty members launched several attempts to oust Butts during these dark days, but he survived and rebuilt the program by bringing in such new stars as Tarkenton and Pat Dye, who went on to become a famous coach at Auburn.

Perhaps Butts's finest moment came when All-Americans Tarkenton and Dye led Georgia to the 1959 Southeastern Conference championship, proving that the game had not passed Butts by. He coached one last season, finishing with a 6–4 record and closing out his career in dramatic style with a 7–6 win over Georgia Tech before his hometown fans in Athens, Ga.

Butts gave up coaching to become athletic director at the University of Georgia in 1960, a position he held for three years. During this time he found himself in the midst of one of the biggest controversies ever to shake southern football. The *Saturday Evening Post* published a sensationalized article that accused Butts of colluding with Paul ("Bear") Bryant, legendary coach of the University of Alabama football team, to throw a football game. The article reported that Butts had shared information about Georgia's formations with Bryant before the Bulldogs and Bryant's "Crimson Tide" met to open the 1962 season. Both Butts and Bryant sued the *Saturday Evening Post*, and Butts's case made it to court. He won a $3 million libel suit; a later Supreme Court decision whittled the judgment down to $460,000.

After leaving the University of Georgia in 1963, Butts launched a new career in insurance that eventually made him a millionaire. He owned and operated his own company in Athens, which thrived on the business of University of Georgia alumni.

Forever the athlete, Butts suffered a fatal heart attack after jogging several miles along an Athens street. He is memorialized by a $12-million, state-of-the-art, glass-covered office and practice facility at the University of Georgia. The Butts-Mehre Building (Mehre coached the Bulldogs from 1929 to 1937), was funded through private donations from Bulldog boosters and dedicated in 1987, earning immediate recognition as perhaps the finest facility of its kind in all of college athletics.

[Memorabilia, newspaper clippings, programs, and the like related to Butts's career are held by the University of Georgia's athletic museum in the Butts-Mehre Building of the Athens campus. The Butts-Bryant scandal is covered in detail in James Kirby, *Fumble: Bear Bryant, Wally Butts, and the Great Football Scandal* (1986). Obituaries are in the *Atlanta Journal* and the *Athens Banner-Herald*, both Dec. 18, 1973.]

JEFF DANTZLER

BYINGTON, SPRING (Oct. 17, 1893–Sept. 7, 1971), actress, was born in Colorado Springs, Colo., the daughter of Edwin Lee Byington, an English instructor, and Helene Cleghorn, a physician. Named after a family friend, Byington attended public schools in Colorado.

Byington began her acting career at the age of fourteen. Through her mother's friendship with Mrs. Elitch Long, she became associated with the famous Elitch Garden Stock Company in Denver, Colo., for three years beginning in 1907. She then went on tour with other stock companies in Toledo, Ohio; Cincinnati, Ohio;

and Indianapolis, Ind. Her pre-Broadway experience also included trips with acting companies to Canada, Argentina, and Brazil. The manager of the acting troupe that toured Brazil was Roy Carey Chandler, whom Byington married. They had two daughters before their divorce. It was Byington's only marriage.

In 1924 Byington made her Broadway debut in a small part in George Kaufman and Marc Connelly's satirical comedy, *Beggar on Horseback*. Between 1924 and 1934 she acted on the Broadway stage in twenty plays, always in a supporting role. Some of her more notable performances were in *Weak Sisters* (1925), *Puppy Love* (1926), *The Merchant of Venice* (1928), *Tonight at Twelve* (1928), and *Ladies Don't Lie* (1929). She was praised for her comedic performances in *When Ladies Meet* (1932), and *Once in a Lifetime* (1930), the Kaufman and Hart satire in which she portrayed a Louella Parsons–prototype columnist. Brooks Atkinson in the *New York Times* lauded her performance as Janet Cannot in *The Great Adventure* (1926) as "simple, attractive, dignified, and illuminating, without any of the superfluous scroll work which is often confused with acting."

In 1933 Byington began her movie career in *Little Women*, playing the role of the motherly Marmee. She worked without interruption for thirty-seven years, acting in almost one hundred films, while never being signed by any studio. She was the quintessential supporting actress, both in the roles she was given to portray and the manner in which she portrayed them.

Most of her film appearances were in light domestic comedies, and her characters were usually motherly types. She played the mother in three 1935 films, *Mutiny on the Bounty*, *Way Down East*, and *Ah! Wilderness*. During the 1930's she was also Mother Jones in the series of seventeen low-budget, popular, and profitable *The Jones Family* feature films for Twentieth Century–Fox. She continued as Mickey Rooney's mother in *A Family Affair* (1937), the first of the Andy Hardy pictures. Other notable performances in mother roles were in *I'll Be Seeing You* (1944) and *My Brother Talks to Horses* (1946). Her only Academy Award nomination came in 1938 for her impressive portrayal of the eccentric playwriting mother in *You Can't Take It With You*.

She depicted other sympathetic and supportive characters in *The Story of Alexander Graham Bell* (1939), *Meet John Doe* (1941), and

When Ladies Meet (1941), where she recreated her Broadway role as the heroine's confidant. She also played Judy Garland's co-worker at the music shop in *In the Good Old Summertime* (1949), the wife of a general in Mario Lanza's *Because You're Mine* (1957), and a nun in *Angels in the Outfield* (1951).

Byington was successful at playing motherly types because she looked and acted like everyone's ideal mother. The small actress exuded warmth and understanding and also possessed a twinkling eye that hinted at mischief. Byington expressed her attitude toward motherhood in these words, "Mothers scheme and plan and love with all the versatility of a three-ring circus." Her characterizations were described as warm, whimsical, amusing, darling, sparkling, impishly chic, fluttery, young-in-spirit, pixilated, and dithery. Sometimes her portrayals exhibited mischief but never malice. When asked why she favored light-hearted comedic roles to more heavy substantive ones, she replied, "Lady Macbeth and I aren't friends."

An exception to her wholesome pleasant screen image came when she played a demented housekeeper in *Dragonwyck* (1946). Her only leading role, and her favorite, was as Louisa in the 1950 comedy of the same name, in which she impersonated a crotchety widow who became transformed when she discovered new love. She ended her film career in the way she knew best, as the slightly addled mother of Doris Day in *Please Don't Eat the Daisies* (1960).

During the 1950's Byington's successful career of playing everyone's mother was transferred to radio and television. She achieved her greatest popularity on television as the star of the weekly situation comedy, "December Bride." The series began in June 1952 on CBS radio. It became a CBS-TV series in October 1954 and ran for five seasons on Monday evening after "I Love Lucy." Byington played Lily Ruskin, an aging, young-at-heart, mischievous mother who moved in with her daughter Frances Rafferty and her son-in-law. Each episode had Lily, along with her neighbor and cohort, Verna Felton, disrupting the domestic bliss of the household. *Look* magazine called the two "TV's happiest outlaws."

In 1956, at the height of its popularity, "December Bride" was the third highest-rated program on television, and Byington received more fan mail for her television role than the total of her stage and film work. She loved the part of Lily, a type of role she had perfected over the years in the theater and on film. Byington was in her sixties when she starred on "December Bride"; she credited it with keeping her young and alert because "Lily is a kid all the way." The series ran in syndication after 1959, including in several foreign countries.

Byington later played the cook in the television program "Laramie" and made guest appearances in other shows such as "I Dream of Jeannie," "Batman," and the television movie, *The Money Maker*. In 1956 she extended her motherly role to print when she began writing an advice column, "What Shall I Do?" for the monthly publication *Photoplay*.

Byington lived a quiet life alone in a small house in Hollywood Hills, Calif. Even at the height of her popularity, she rarely participated in the entertainment social scene. She preferred time with her daughters' families, reading (especially science fiction), cooking, and attending plays and movies. She died of cancer at her home.

[See Richard Lamparski, *Whatever Became of . . . ? Third Series* (1970); a chronological list of her stage performances appears in *Who Was Who in the Theater* (1978); a compilation of her movies is in James Robert Parish and Ronald L. Bowers, *The MGM Stock Company: The Golden Era* (1973). An obituary is in the *New York Times*, Sept. 9, 1971.]

FRANCES T. GIGLIO

BYRNES, JAMES FRANCIS (May 2, 1879– Apr. 9, 1972), politician and Supreme Court justice, was born in Charleston, S.C., to Elizabeth E. McSweeney Byrnes, a dressmaker, Irish immigrant, and widow of James Francis Byrnes, a municipal clerk, who died at twenty-six of tuberculosis only months before his son's birth. Supported by his mother, Byrnes attended parochial school and learned shorthand. At the age of fourteen he left school to become a law clerk in the firm of Mordecai and Gadsden under the personal tutelage of a partner, Benjamin H. Rutledge. At twenty-one Byrnes won the position of court stenographer in the Second Circuit Court of South Carolina, requiring him to move to Aiken, S.C. At the direction of the presiding circuit court judge, James H. Aldrich, Byrnes studied law and was admitted to the bar three years later. Then he bought the *Aiken Journal and Review*, which he edited and published for four years. He won his first public office in 1908, solicitor (prosecutor) for the South Carolina Second Judicial Circuit. In 1910 he announced his candidacy for the U.S. Congress, later recalling, "I campaigned on nothing but gall and gall won by 57 votes."

Byrnes was a superb legislator because he knew his constituents' needs, and was incessantly seeking conciliation of adverse positions and counting votes. "The art of legislating is the art of intelligent compromise," he later reflected. "In my experience there were really few bills in which a great principle was involved; the issues were really a matter of policy, not principle." He began his career by calling for the formation of the House Committee on Roads, which put Washington into the business of building the federal highway system. "We fellows in Congress have mostly got to promise our people something from the Treasury, and in the old days in the South and West we generally used to promise Federal roads," he explained. He also became a member of the powerful Banking and Currency Committee and took part in the famous Pujo investigation of J. P. Morgan and Company. Following reelection he won appointment to the House Appropriations Committee.

An important part of Byrnes's political career was determined when, in 1906, he left the Roman Catholic religion in which he had been baptized to marry Maude Perkins Busch of Aiken; the couple had no children. He always put Southern political and social norms—including white supremacy—above Catholicism or even the Democratic party. Yet, although Byrnes became Episcopalian, that did not protect him from being occasionally assailed in South Carolina as a renegade Catholic or as a Catholic apostate in the urban North. He knew that his political career would be threatened if South Carolinians viewed him as a pariah from their traditions.

Enormously ambitious, vain and restless, Byrnes enjoyed a promising career in the House and rose in its hierarchy. But his interest in foreign affairs and the greater prestige of the Senate made him decide to run against Cole L. Blease in 1924, in a four-way race for the Democratic Senate nomination. Blease had been in statewide politics for over three decades, and as a top vote-getter was known to stir prejudices by denouncing "niggers" and "aristocrats." This rhetoric appealed to both low-country farmers and industrial workers in the Piedmont region.

Byrnes finished second to Blease in the primary, but in the runoff he threatened to pull an upset. Blease's supporters—including the Ku Klux Klan, which Byrnes had eschewed—circulated an alleged endorsement by ten former classmates at Charleston's St. Patrick's Roman Catholic School that mentioned Byrnes's former Catholicism; this was a political kiss-of-death in Protestant South Carolina. Byrnes's supporters frantically trumpeted his membership in the Episcopal church, but Blease defeated Byrnes by 2,200 votes out of 200,000.

Byrnes then moved from Aiken to Spartanburg, where for the next six years he practiced law, became a director of the Spartanburg Chamber of Commerce, and cultivated the Piedmont industrial vote. The Great Depression presented him with an opportunity in 1930 for a comeback against Blease as the representative of those who espoused economic development over racism. At one point in the campaign, Blease used a recent lynching as an occasion to denounce black rapists, telling a frenetic crowd, "When you catch the brute who assaulted a white woman wait until the next morning to notify me," and "I say the hell with the Constitution." During his House career, Byrnes had espoused white supremacy, opposed the women's suffrage amendment because it might lead to black enfranchisement in the South, and opposed an antilynching bill as outside the jurisdiction of the federal government. Now, Byrnes took the high road by declaring, "We've had enough talk about lynching. My speech today is about conditions in our factories." With the Depression as an issue, Byrnes won election to the Senate by 4,500 votes.

Known by leading Democrats in the Senate from his years in the House, Byrnes moved into the Senate hierarchy almost immediately. The election of Franklin D. Roosevelt to the presidency in 1932 further enhanced Byrnes's power. Byrnes and FDR had been early supporters of Woodrow Wilson for the presidency in 1912, and they knew each other well during Roosevelt's days as assistant secretary of the Navy. FDR liked Byrnes enormously and used him as a Senate whip during the New Deal. He was prominent among Democratic party leaders, chaired a few select committees, and had memberships on the powerful Appropriations, Banking and Currency, and Foreign Relations Committees. Although he later asserted that he had been a Democrat and not a New Dealer,

Byrnes gave Roosevelt unflinching loyalty during his first term and won a landslide reelection in 1936, declaring, "I admit I am a New Dealer, and if [the New Deal] takes money from the few who have controlled the country and gives it back to the average man, I am going to Washington to help the President work for the people of South Carolina and the country."

But after 1936, Byrnes, anticipating that he would be senator longer than Roosevelt would be president, turned against the administration. Although he had endorsed the Wagner National Labor Relations Act of 1935, he voted against the Wages and Hours Act of 1938. He endorsed the "court-packing" plan of 1937 to reform the judiciary by adding justices, but he opposed FDR's "purge" of conservatives, including Senator "Cotton Ed" Smith of South Carolina in 1938. He fought Roosevelt's fiscal policies during the economic debates of 1938, explaining that he had supported them earlier only because of the Great Depression. On the other hand, he supported FDR's foreign policy by spearheading repeal of the Neutrality Act, supporting defense preparedness, and pushing for the Lend-Lease bill.

In the words of journalists Joseph Alsop and Robert Kintner, Byrnes was "a small, wiry, neatly made man, with an odd, sharply angular face from which his sharp eyes peer out with an expression of quizzical geniality." Standing five feet, eight inches tall and weighing about 150 pounds, Byrnes was a dapper man who claimed only simple tastes for "two tailor-made suits a year, three meals a day, and a reasonable amount of good liquor." His friends saw him as an adroit, gregarious, and charming politician; his critics thought him "sly." While he engendered few animosities, his political demands sometimes left hard feelings. "When I see Jimmy Byrnes coming toward me," Republican leader Charles McNary declared, "I put one hand on my watch and one on my wallet and wish to goodness I knew how to protect my conscience." A fellow Democrat, John Bankhead of Alabama, once told a New Deal official, "I would rather have any twelve other Senators opposing me than Jimmy Byrnes opposing me. He's tireless, he's shrewd, and he's vindictive."

Also, he was restless again. Plagued by occasionally poor health and feeling that a Supreme Court appointment would be better for his health—and give the South a seat it deserved

there—Byrnes began to campaign for nomination to the Court in 1939. He backed Roosevelt for a third term in 1940, but it was said that he lusted for vice-president until FDR disappointed him by taking Henry Wallace. Nevertheless, Roosevelt consoled Byrnes with a Supreme Court nomination to succeed the retiring Justice James C. McReynolds in June 1941.

But Byrnes was unhappy there. "I've got ants in my pants," he remarked in 1942. "I've been listening all day to some fellows here arguing about something that happened 15 years ago and, frankly, I don't give a damn about what happened then. My country's at war and I want to be in it. I don't think I can stand the abstraction of jurisprudence at a time like this." With enormous uncertainty surrounding markets on the home front, Roosevelt offered Byrnes the post of director of economic stabilization, with responsibility for controlling prices and formulating a fair-minded tax program. It was a political hot potato, but his stabilization policies won public approval and on May 28, 1943, Roosevelt added total industrial mobilization to Byrnes's portfolio by making him chairman of the new War Mobilization Board. He now virtually ran the economy of the country and the press tagged him the "assistant president."

Byrnes wanted to be president and, given the poor state of Roosevelt's health, most of official Washington anticipated that FDR's running mate in the fourth-term campaign of 1944 would succeed him before a completed term. Byrnes thought he had FDR's support, but the president indicated that Wallace, Harry Truman, and William O. Douglas were also "acceptable" to him. Wallace proved too liberal for the increasingly conservative electorate, and Byrnes was too conservative for the unions and blacks who composed the Democratic party's urban strength. Byrnes was the South's choice for vice-president, but Edward Flynn, the political boss of the Bronx, N.Y., Democratic party, wanted no part of a Catholic apostate and warned that Byrnes would drive Catholic and Negro votes away from the Democratic party in urban America. Thus, the Democratic party selected a "Missouri compromise" in Senator Harry Truman. FDR had disappointed Byrnes again.

Byrnes had promised to lead the Office of War Mobilization and Reconversion until the invasion of Germany. In February 1945, FDR took Byrnes with him to the Yalta Conference where Byrnes took shorthand notes on what he observed. However, he was not included in key negotiations. When Roosevelt died and Truman became president, what transpired at Yalta loomed as critically important and so did Byrnes's notes. Truman brought Byrnes in as secretary of state in June on the erroneous assumption that Byrnes knew and understood Roosevelt's plans for postwar peace.

Thus, Byrnes became a major figure in the early Cold War years. He accompanied Truman to the Potsdam meeting; he also represented the United States at the London Conference of Foreign Ministers in September, the December Big Three foreign ministers' conference in Moscow which created the United Nations Atomic Energy Commission, and the United Nations organizational meetings in December 1945 and January 1946. At first thought to be "soft" on the Soviets, Byrnes displayed a hard line toward Soviet efforts to expand its hegemony, compelling Soviet evacuation of Iran in 1946. Although Truman already had decided to remove Byrnes in favor of General George C. Marshall, Byrnes continued to act as foreign policy spokesman through 1946, espousing both the formation of an autonomous German democratic state as vital to a reconstructed western economy, and American determination to play an active role in European and world affairs.

When Byrnes resigned on Jan. 10, 1947, he gave poor health as the reason, but it was evident that he and Truman had personal differences. Byrnes kept public silence from the 1948 election campaign until June 1949, when he began to attack Truman's domestic policies.

Ever ambitious, he had decided that the capstone of his career would be the governorship of South Carolina. In 1950 he won 85 percent of the vote in a campaign in which he assailed both the Ku Klux Klan and Truman's "socialistic experimentation." As governor he upheld racial segregation of public schools and urged Truman to end the Korean War by bombing China. In 1952 he supported Dwight Eisenhower for president, and he never endorsed a Democrat for president again. Prevented by law from serving a second gubernatorial term, he retired in 1955.

Always a staunch segregationist, Byrnes abhorred the advocacy of civil rights by northern Democrats. During his Senate career he had blocked antilynching bills via parliamentary maneuvers. He had opposed the Wages and Hours bill of 1938 because the same wage "would have to be paid to every negro working in any store as well as to white employees." In reference to the Democratic party's ending in 1936 of the rule requiring a vote of two-thirds of convention delegates to nominate a presidential candidate, he said on the Senate floor, "The Negro has not only come into the Democratic party, but the Negro has come into control of the Democratic party." No longer would the South have veto on a Democratic candidate.

Byrnes feared for white supremacy, which he called "the very soul of the South." When Senator Barry Goldwater of Arizona voted against the Civil Rights bill of 1964, Byrnes called it the Republican presidential nominee's "finest hour." In large measure his career was a harbinger of the South's flight to the Republican party. Byrnes died in Columbia, S.C.

[Byrnes wrote about his role in foreign affairs in *Speaking Frankly* (1947) and his careers in *All in One Lifetime* (1958). Useful works about him are Winfred Bobo Moore, Jr., "New South Statesman: The Political Career of James Francis Byrnes, 1911–1941" (Ph.D. diss., Duke University, 1976) and John W. Partin, " 'Assistant President' for the Home Front" (Ph.D. diss., University of Florida, 1977). Articles about him include Joseph Alsop and Robert Kintner, "Sly and Able: The Real Leader of the Senate, Jimmy Byrnes," *Saturday Evening Post*, July 20, 1940; Delbert Clark, "Our No. 1 Stabilizer," *New York Times Magazine*, Oct. 18, 1942; Turner Catledge, "Commander in Chief for the Home Front," *New York Times Magazine*, June 6, 1943; and George Curry, "James F. Byrnes," in Robert H. Ferrell and Samuel Flagg Bemis, eds., *The American Secretaries of State and Their Diplomacy*, vol. 14 (1965).

Byrnes's tenure as secretary of state is discussed in Richard D. Burns, "James F. Byrnes," in Norman Graebner, ed., *An Uncertain Tradition: American Secretaries of State in the Twentieth Century* (1961); Denise O. Conover, "James F. Byrnes, Germany, and the Cold War, 1946" (Ph.D. diss., Washington State University, 1978); Patricia Dawson Ward, *The Threat of Peace: James F. Byrnes and the Council of Foreign Ministers, 1945–1946* (1979); and Robert L. Messer, *The End of an Alliance: James F. Byrnes, Roosevelt, Truman, and the Origins of the Cold War* (1982). An obituary is in the *New York Times*, Apr. 10, 1972.]

JORDAN A. SCHWARZ

C

CAFFERY, JEFFERSON (Dec. 1, 1886–Apr. 13, 1974), diplomat, was born in Lafayette, La., the son of Charles Duval Caffery, a well-to-do lawyer who was elected to three terms as mayor of Lafayette, and Mary Catherine Parkerson. He grew up on the "mansion block" of the city.

Lafayette at the turn of the century was still a village. Like most of their neighbors, the Cafferys had a barn behind the house. There were plenty of chores for a boy to do. In later years family friends recalled having seen the future ambassador drive the cows home for milking in the evening. "Jeff," as he was known to the family, also attended a small private school and read voraciously in his father's library. Riding horseback was his principal recreation, for he was something of a loner.

Enrolled in the local "industrial institute" at the age of fourteen, Jefferson transferred to Tulane University a year later. After graduating with a B.A. in 1906, he read law with his father for three years and was admitted to the bar. Returning from a trip to England in the summer of 1908, however, he determined to be a professional diplomat and travel all over the world.

Although admission to the diplomatic service was by examination, traces of the old spoils system lingered. The hurdle facing a college graduate was not so much the examination as the designation to take it. On the recommendation of a senator and two congressmen from Louisiana, Secretary of State Philander Knox designated Caffery to take the examination. After passing the test in January 1911, Caffery became secretary of the American legation at Caracas, Venezuela.

For the next eight years Caffery served as secretary of legation or embassy at a series of posts in Venezuela, Sweden, Persia, and France. From 1920 to 1925 he was second in command or acting chief of mission in Madrid, Athens, and Tokyo. In Athens he had to administer relief to Greek refugees from Turkey. In Tokyo he was responsible for American aid to the victims of the great earthquake of 1923. Philanthropy of this sort characterized the American engagement in European and Asian affairs in the isolationist period following World War I.

The situation in Latin America, where Caffery was posted from 1926 to 1944, was different. There isolationism did not apply and United States diplomats did not cease to be activists. Caffery, who defined diplomacy as "getting things done," was particularly adept at finding accommodation with local leaders. He developed a pragmatic and aggressive style, that was largely devoid of political idealism. In the process he acquired a reputation as a trouble-shooter, which clung to him until the end.

Caffery was promoted to be minister to El Salvador in 1926. Some of his contemporaries refused these promotions because they entailed a loss of tenure under the Rogers Act. Caffery, however, welcomed the opportunity and endured as chief of mission, either minister or ambassador, for the next twenty-nine years, a record in American history, as President Eisenhower pointed out on Caffery's retirement in 1955.

In El Salvador, Caffery recalled, he "did not have enough work to do." His subsequent assignments to Colombia, Cuba, and Brazil were more challenging. In Colombia he obtained the restoration of the Barco concession to the Gulf Oil Company by helping the president collect a loan from banks in New York and Boston. In Cuba Caffery contrived the overthrow of a revolutionary president opposed to the United States by winning over the leader of the Cuban army.

As ambassador to Brazil from July 1937 to September 1944, Caffery fostered the paradoxical partnership between the Brazilian dictator, Getulio Vargas, and Franklin Delano Roosevelt; he helped arrange an encounter between the two presidents aboard a United States destroyer at Natal, Brazil, on Jan. 28, 1943. In March of the previous year Brazil had still been technically neutral. Caffery had nonetheless been able to persuade Vargas to allow the United States to use an air corridor along Brazil's northeast coast for flights to Africa. Airborne supplies thus reached British forces in Egypt in time to help turn back the German thrust from Tripoli. Vargas, who seized power by a coup on Nov. 10, 1937, was expected to align himself with the Axis. Caffery deterred him from this course by threatening to restrict American imports of Brazilian coffee.

In 1937 Caffery was married to Gertrude McCarthy, an heiress from Chicago eight years younger than he. The marriage, which remained childless, lasted thirty-six years until Mrs. Caffery's death. More gregarious and communicative than her husband, Mrs. Caffery provided the means and the management necessary for entertainment on the grand scale.

From November 1944 to May 1949, Caffery served as ambassador to France, a post usually filled by a political appointee. In the political and economic shambles of World War II, however, a trouble-shooter was needed. In Paris, Caffery gained recognition as a "diplomat's diplomat," a title given him in the citation accompanying the Foreign Service Cup he received in 1971. A manual for diplomats published in 1948 described the Paris embassy under Caffery as the "showcase of American diplomacy."

During Caffery's assignment to Paris, the principal objective of American foreign policy was to prevent a Communist takeover of the western European democracies by promoting their economic recovery. The focus of Franco-American relations consequently was on aid programs. Caffery's contribution consisted principally in publicizing American aid and in combating Communism within the French government and in the labor unions. In so doing he enlarged the traditional role of the embassy. The "diplomat's diplomat" was anticipating the missions of the USIS and CIA. At the close of his mission to France in

May 1949, Caffery was awarded the Grand Cross of the Legion of Honor by the French government. In October 1950 he received the U.S. State Department's Distinguished Service Award. His career had reached a pinnacle. It continued at a high level of effectiveness until his retirement.

In Egypt from 1949 to 1955, Caffery reverted to classical diplomacy, mediating between the British and the Egyptians in their protracted negotiations under a treaty that allowed a British garrison to occupy the Suez Canal zone in peacetime. Unwilling to evacuate the zone unconditionally, the British were seeking somehow to internationalize their presence in Egypt. To the dismay of both Winston Churchill and Anthony Eden, Caffery refused to sit in on the negotiations as their ally. Preserving American evenhandedness, he helped shape the compromises that both sides accepted in October 1954. The British agreed to withdraw their troops within twenty months on condition that they might return if Turkey or an Arab nation were attacked by an "outside" power during the next seven years.

Caffery's mission to Egypt ended with the signing of the agreement. In order to arrive at this settlement, Eisenhower had permitted Caffery to extend his term as ambassador three years beyond the statutory retirement age of sixty-five. Egypt had, in the meantime, undergone a revolution. In July 1952, Colonel Gamal Abdel Nasser replaced King Farouk as head of the government. While carefully refraining from any offer of American intervention, Caffery had stood by the king until his departure into exile.

Impressed by this display of trustworthiness, Nasser reached out to the embassy. Prospects of drawing Egypt into alignment with the West looked bright for a while. They faded, however, when it became obvious that Nasser wanted arms without conditions. As Caffery later explained to the Senate Foreign Relations Committee, "we had conditions." Because the Soviet Union was willing to supply weapons to a country at war with Israel, Nasser turned his back on the West. It was left to Secretary of State Kissinger some twenty years later to restore U.S.-Egyptian relations to the degree of cordiality existing in Caffery's time.

Departing Cairo in January 1955, the Cafferys lived in retirement mostly in Rome until they returned to Lafayette in 1973. Caffery died in Lafayette the following year.

[Caffery's papers are at the University of Southwestern Louisiana (USL) in Lafayette, La. The collection includes three volumes of his unpublished memoirs, entitled "Adventure in Diplomacy." The only outline of Caffery's entire career in print is contained in a booklet published by the USL Libraries, Philip F. Dur, *Jefferson Caffery of Louisiana: Ambassador of Revolutions* (1982). See also Philip F. Dur, "Jefferson Caffery of Louisiana: Highlights of His Career", Part 1, 1911–1933," *Louisiana History*, Winter 1974; Part 2, 1933–1944, *ibid.*, Fall 1974; Steven S. Sapp, "Jefferson Caffery: Cold War Diplomat," *Louisiana History*, Spring 1982; and Philip F. Dur, "Ambassador Caffery and the French Alliance," *ibid.*, Summer 1986. An obituary is in the *New York Times* Apr. 15, 1974.]

PHILIP F. DUR

CAMPBELL, JOHN WOOD, JR. (June 8, 1910–July 11, 1971), author and editor, was born in Newark, N.J. His father, an electrical engineer for Bell Telephone Laboratories, influenced and encouraged his son's early interest in the sciences.

After receiving his secondary education at Blair Academy, a boys' school in Blairstown, N.J., Campbell entered the Massachusetts Institute of Technology. There he met Norbert Weiner, one of the pioneers in computer science. The knowledge of computers he gained from this association added authenticity to Campbell's writing and helped make him second only to E. E. ("Doc") Smith in the popularity of his work during the early 1930's.

His first published science fiction story, "When the Atoms Failed," appeared in 1930 in *Amazing Stories*, the world's first science fiction magazine, while he was still an undergraduate at M.I.T. Encouraged by this early success, he published seven short stories and three novels in the next two years.

He met Dona Stuart while attending M.I.T. and the two were married in 1931. They had four children before they were divorced in the late 1940's. In 1950 Campbell married Margaret ("Peg") Winter, the widow of J. A. Winter who, with L. Ron Hubbard, was one of the founders of dianetics, a movement that Campbell embraced for a time.

Although he did well in most of his classes, he did not graduate from M.I.T. because he failed to complete the foreign language requirement. He then transferred to Duke University, where he earned his B.S. in 1932 in the midst of the Great Depression. Quickly discovering

that there was no demand for his physics degree, he supported his family working for the research laboratory of Mack Trucks, for Hoboken Pioneer Instruments, and also selling cars, electric fans, and gas heaters while continuing to write science fiction.

Campbell's career can be divided into three phases. The first phase coincides roughly with his attendance at M.I.T. During this period he used his own name and wrote galactic epics in which super scientists used super science to save the universe. He moved into the second phase of his career with the publication, in the November 1934 issue of *Astounding Stories*, of "Twilight," his first story written as Don A. Stuart, a pen name he invented by dividing his wife's name into three parts. Campbell wrote sixteen stories during the next four years, using the Stuart pseudonym. In these stories he departed from the established formula by allowing his scientists to be human, to have feelings, and even to make mistakes. He was one of the first science fiction writers to incorporate human emotion and human foibles into his narrative. Among his best-known stories of this phase is "Who Goes There?" which appeared in 1938 and dealt with the problem of identifying the true enemy when an alien that can change its shape can perfectly mimic anyone or anything in its desire to destroy all human life on earth. The 1951 motion picture "The Thing from Outer Space" was loosely based on this story.

In September 1937 Campbell joined the firm of Street and Smith, in New York City, which at that time published *Astounding Stories*. In May 1938 he took over as its editor and embarked on the third, longest, and most productive phase of his career. When later asked by Isaac Asimov why he abandoned his writing career to be an editor, he smilingly answered that as an author he wrote only his own stories but as an editor he wrote the stories a hundred people wrote—a simple statement of fact in the case of Campbell as editor.

When he assumed the position of editor of *Astounding Stories* (a name he would change to *Astounding Science Fiction* and finally to *Analog Science Fact-Science Fiction*), he had no experience as an editor. What he did have was a keen analytical mind and a clear idea of the direction in which he wanted to move the magazine. Science fiction written in 1938 was only to be found in the "pulp" magazines of the day. The majority of the stories frankly deserved little more. By insisting that any story that appeared in his magazine be well written, detailed, integrated, and internally consistent, Campbell led science fiction into its "Golden Age." As an editor Campbell was exigent, an attitude that has earned him a reputation for being dogmatic and hard to please. He personally read every story submitted and no story was rejected without detailed suggestions as to how it might be improved enough to be published.

Campbell was eager to launch new writers and openly solicited stories from unpublished authors. He was also generous with ideas for new stories. New writers with no credits but with a wealth of new ideas flocked to his door. Campbell's publication was soon filled with literate, well-thought-out, tightly plotted stories and dominated the field well into the 1950's. In addition to editing *Astounding*, Campbell edited the fantasy magazine *Unknown* from its inception in 1939 until its demise in 1943.

In his thirty-four years of editing magazines, Campbell discovered and launched the careers of more budding young authors than any other science fiction editor. Authors such as Isaac Asimov, Robert A. Heinlein, L. Ron Hubbard, and A. E. van Vogt, have acknowledged their debt to Campbell not only for publishing their early stories but also for supplying the ideas for some of these stories. Asimov stated flatly that "everything in my writing career I owed to him," a sweeping statement from a man who wrote hundreds of books on a wide range of topics.

Campbell's editorials generated his greatest controversy. Over the years he used this platform to expound on and sometimes advocate such causes as extreme right-wing political ideals and what many viewed as pseudoscientific crackpot philosophies. The most notorious of the latter was his championing of L. Ron Hubbard's dianetics.

Although critics are divided concerning Campbell's abilities as a writer, he was one of the most important and influential editors of the century. Even his detractors admit that he shaped modern science fiction into a respected genre of adult literature. Under his leadership *Astounding Stories* and *Analog* won nine Hugos (the highest award for science fiction). In 1970, Campbell was elected to the Science Fiction Hall of Fame. After his death two awards were founded bearing his name and a number of memorial anthologies were published.

Campbell died from heart disease at his home in Mountainside, N.J.

[Campbell's correspondence is reprinted in Perry A. Chapdelaine, Sr., Tony Chapdelaine, and George Hay, *The John W. Campbell Letters*, vol. 1 (1985). Some of his major works are *The Mightiest Machine* (1947); *Who Goes There?* (1948); *The Incredible Planet* (1949); *The Moon Is Hell* (1951); *Cloak of Aesir* (1952); *Islands of Space* (1956); *Collected Editorials from Analog* (1966); and *The Space Beyond* (1976). Also see his colleected works in the *Best of John W. Campbell* (1976), edited by Curtis C. Smith. Biographical sketches appear in Peter Nicholls, John Clute, and Carolyn Eardley, *The Science Fiction Encyclopedia* (1979); Isaac Asimov, *Asimov on Science Fiction* (1981); E. F. Bleiler, ed., *Science Fiction Writers* (1982); Curtis C. Smith, ed., *Twentieth-Century Science-Fiction Writers* (1986); James Guinn, *The New Encyclopedia of Science Fiction* (1988); and Marilyn P. Fletcher and James L. Thorson, *Reader's Guide to Twentieth-Century Science Fiction* (1988). An obituary is in the *New York Times*, July 13, 1971.]

ANNA B. PERRY

CANNON, JAMES THOMAS (Apr. 10, 1910–Dec. 5, 1973), writer, was born in the Greenwich Village section of New York City, the son of Thomas J. Cannon and Loretta Monahan. His father was a local political official who was part of the Democratic party organization that in Manhattan was called Tammany Hall. After one year at Regis High School, he dropped out to work for the *New York Evening World* in its classified advertising department. He then moved to the *New York Daily News* in 1926 as a copy boy. "I worked from midnight to 8 A.M.," he said. "I was sorry for anybody else who didn't work those hours because I thought it was the best of all possible lives." Soon he was promoted to general-assignment reporter.

Influenced by Ernest Hemingway and the Broadway columnists Damon Runyon and Mark Hellinger, Cannon was hired by the *New York Evening Journal* as a police reporter, by the *New York World-Telegram* as a radio columnist, by International News Service as a Washington political columnist, and in 1936 by the *New York American* as a sportswriter. Drafted into the army during World War II, he was a combat correspondent for *Stars and Stripes*, the army newspaper. His dispatches to the newspaper *PM* were reprinted in a book, *The Sergeant Says* (1943).

In 1946 Cannon joined the *New York Post* as a sports columnist. Except for a brief return to combat reporting during the Korean War, he remained a *Post* sportswriter until 1959, when he joined the *New York Journal-American* as America's highest-paid sports columnist, at a reported salary of $1,000 per week.

When the *Journal-American* merged with the *New York Herald-Tribune* and the *World-Telegram and Sun* in 1966 to create the *World Journal Tribune*, Cannon's column appeared there until the paper ceased publication in 1967. Although his column resumed on the Hearst Headline Service newswire, it did not appear in a New York newspaper until the *Post* hired him in 1972, after he had had a stroke. After a relapse in October 1973, he died in New York City.

Cannon's columns were hailed by *Newsweek* magazine book critic Jack Kroll as "verbal Irish coffee of toughness laced with sentimentality, that Hemingway rhythm of stoic lyricism. It was Cannon who brought the Hemingway tone into sports writing, crossing it with Damon Runyon. And behind the mask of the New Journalism, you can still detect the old Cannon blend of hard nose and soft heart."

Cannon was described by the author Wilfred Sheed as "tough, but fastidious, because he had found the words himself and he valued them, like a gangster's jewelry." Ernest Hemingway called Cannon "an excellent sportswriter and . . . also a very good writer aside from sports. I don't know anybody who takes his job more seriously or with more confidence. He's able to convey the quality of the athlete and the feeling, the excitement, of the event."

In addition to commentary and interviews, Cannon occasionally wrote what were known as his "You're . . ." columns. "You're Ted Williams, who never wanted partners." "You're Rocky Marciano, who bled for your fame." "You're Roger Maris, who isn't Babe Ruth." He also wrote one-sentence opinions prefaced by the phrase "Nobody Asked Me, But . . ." that also surveyed the world beyond sports: "Guys who address me as 'friend' have a hard time making me one." "Shoeshine guys never miss flicking my corn with their brushes." "Only lions should be asked to eat hamburgers that aren't well done."

Cannon's columns were collected in three books: *Nobody Asked Me* (1951), *Who Struck John?* (1956), and a volume edited by his broth-

ers Jack and Tom, *Nobody Asked Me, But . . . the World of Jimmy Cannon* (1978).

Cannon was more aware than most sportswriters of his era of the sociological impact of the black athlete. Of Joe Louis, the world heavyweight champion, he wrote, "He's a credit to his race—the human race." Of all his assignments, he appeared to enjoy boxing the most, even though he labeled it "the red-light district of sports."

Some editors deride the sports pages as the "toy department" of the newspaper, but Cannon was fulfilled by his career. "My beat," he said, "is those spots to which people have come to be entertained, where the violence and dissent is all part of the joy."

Short and chunky, Cannon was not athletic. His primary exercise was walking. To gather thoughts for his "Nobody Asked Me, But . . ." columns, he often strolled the streets of Manhattan to observe people and events. A lifelong bachelor, Cannon frequented Toots Shor's, then a popular sports hangout, as well as various New York nightclubs. He developed friendships with several entertainers, notably Frank Sinatra and the comedian Joe E. Lewis. When a book publisher asked Sinatra to select a writer to collaborate on the singer's autobiography, he chose Cannon, who demanded that Sinatra "tell everything." Sinatra declined. The book was never written. Despite their disagreement, Cannon remained friendly with Sinatra, as he did with several of his sports subjects. "It all comes down," he once wrote of quarterback Joe Namath, "to a man being great at something." To those who enjoyed Jimmy Cannon's writing, he could have applied that phrase to himself.

[Most of Cannon's columns are on microfilm of the *New York Post* and the *New York Journal-American*. An obituary is in the *New York Times*, Dec. 6, 1973.]

DAVE ANDERSON

CARROLL, LEO GRATTAN (Oct. 25, 1886– Oct. 16, 1972), actor and director, was the youngest of six children born to Catherine Jane Calnan and Captain William Carroll, both Irish, in the village of Weedon, Northamptonshire. Captain Carroll, whose voice and mannerisms became part of his son's professional technique, was an Ordnance officer in the British army. As a child Leo felt extreme self-consciousness from which the stage was his escape. "I became interested in the theatre as a youngster because I never like to be me. I've always been shy—it is very hard for me to walk down the aisle of a church if it is full of people."

After attending grammar school in York, he was apprenticed at fifteen to a wine merchant. Then, attracted by performances of Gilbert and Sullivan, he took an amateur part in Dibdin's comic opera *Liberty Hall*. In July 1911, he made his professional debut at Scarborough: a walk-on in *The Prisoner of Zenda*. Untrained in theater, he studied professional actors in London while working as an assistant stage manager. Taking over a small part, he made his first London appearance in *The Blindness of Virtue* (1912). In July, he was engaged to play the juvenile lead in the American company of *Rutherford and Son*, making his New York debut on Christmas eve.

With the outbreak of World War I, Carroll joined the British infantry, fighting in the French trenches and later at Salonica. He was posted to the Egyptian Expeditionary Force in Palestine, where, on Oct. 30, 1916, he suffered a lung wound that hospitalized him for two years.

Returning to England, he toured extensively with provincial stock companies. He was in New York in 1920 for a brief run of *Hedda Gabler*, and from 1921 to 1924 between tours he made ten brief London appearances acting in and directing new plays for the Repertory Theatre Players. In 1923, Carroll had a featured role in *Love in Pawn*, a successful West End comedy, and later that year he won a prestigious part as General Jeb Stuart in John Drinkwater's *Robert E. Lee*. A turning point in Carroll's career was the role of Roddy Dunton in Harry Wall's war drama *Havoc* (1924). Carroll had directed a theater society performance of the play the previous November and was now engaged as director of the New York company. He spent most of the rest of his professional life in the United States.

Following the New York run of *Havoc* and an appearance as Matyas Oez in Molnar's *Carnival* (1924), Carroll directed an English repertory season in Montreal. On his return he played Pawnie, an amusing "elderly maiden gentleman," in Noël Coward's *The Vortex* (1925) and the following year appeared in Margaret Kennedy's equally popular *The Constant Nymph*. In the next five years Carroll appeared in ten plays, including A. A. Milne's *The Per-*

fect Alibi; *The Novice and the Duke*, an adaptation of *Measure for Measure* with Carroll as the villain, Angelo; Shaw's *Too True to Be Good*; and Shakespeare's *Troilus and Cressida*. On July 15, 1926, he married Edith Nancy de Silva, a Liverpool actress; they had one son.

On Oct. 20, 1933, Carroll opened with Laurence Olivier in *The Green Bay Tree*, playing the comically immaculate but sinister butler, Trump. The play brought Carroll a contract from Metro-Goldwyn-Mayer, where in 1934 he had an almost identical part in Clarence Brown's *Sadie McKee*. Typecast as the polished, imperturbable Briton, he had small parts in several films, including *What Every Woman Knows* and *The Barretts of Wimpole Street*, productions that displayed Carroll's technique to advantage. In 1935 he appeared in three Broadway comedies and four films, including *Clive of India* with Ronald Coleman.

From 1936 through 1940, Carroll performed in nine Broadway plays, one of which he directed, and ten films. The productions included historical dramas, romantic comedies, classical works (notably the film *Wuthering Heights* in 1939, again with Olivier), sensational thrillers, even light opera. These added to Carroll's reputation as a versatile supporting actor from whom, as the *New York Post* critic wrote, "an intelligent performance can always be expected."

In 1940 he played in *Rebecca*, the first of six films with director Alfred Hitchcock—he appeared in more Hitchcock films than any other actor. In *Spellbound* (1945), drawing on the sinister note in Carroll's amiability, Hitchcock gave the actor his best film role as Dr. Murchison, the director of a psychiatric sanatorium. The same ambiguity lent strength to his roles as Senator Morton in *Strangers on a Train* (1951) and as "the Professor," chief of counterintelligence, in *North by Northwest* (1959).

Although he made fifteen pictures in the 1940's, Carroll's greatest success was on Broadway. *Angel Street* (1941) ran for three years and, as Burns Mantle predicted, made "a star of Leo G. Carroll." As Detective Inspector Rough, he rescued the heroine from Vincent Price. In 1944 he had the title role in *The Late George Apley*. His lightly ironic portrayal of the proper Bostonian received unqualified praise as Carroll's best work. In later seasons he played an emotionally brutal professor in *The Druid Circle* (1947); the outspoken waiter in Shaw's *You Never Can Tell*

(1948); and a match-making priest in *Jenny Kissed Me* (1948). In 1949 Carroll began a television career with six dramatic productions, chiefly for "Philco Television Playhouse," playing in Walter Hampden's production of *Macbeth* and recreating his own stage roles.

In 1951, with characteristic energy he appeared in four plays, three films, and a broadcast drama, but thereafter Carroll took fewer jobs and turned increasingly to television. From 1953 to 1955 he was popular in the *Topper* series, playing a staid investment banker agreeably haunted by the ghosts of a glamorous couple and their dog. He appeared in plays in San Francisco in 1953, New York in 1954, and Puerto Rico in 1959. His last stage work was a production of *The Pleasure of His Company* in 1961. Carroll worked regularly in pictures, notably in Molnar's *The Swan* (1956) and Hitchcock's *North by Northwest* (1959). On television he was a priest in "Going My Way" (1963), a series with Gene Kelly.

In 1964, his career accelerated unexpectedly with a television role in "The Man from U.N.C.L.E." Carroll became popular as Mr. Waverly, a kindlier version of the spy master he played in *North by Northwest*. The series ran four years and produced a sequel. Independently, in 1966 Carroll appeared in three espionage adventure movies. Versatile to the last, he made a country music picture in 1969 and ended his career on Apr. 2, 1970, with an episode of a television police show. He died in Hollywood.

In more than three hundred stage plays, aside from films and television, Leo G. Carroll developed a technical polish that raised even small parts to distinction. The austerity of his appearance, in contrast with his avuncular and slightly mischievous manner, gave him a magnetic presence. He loved to attend plays as well as act in them, and said of his sixty-year career: "It has brought me much pleasure of the mind and heart. I owe the theatre a great deal. It owes me nothing."

[The Margaret Herrick Library of the Academy of Motion Picture Arts and Sciences, Beverly Hills, Calif., maintains a file on Carroll. Articles include W. L. Gresham, "Mama and Papa," *Theatre Arts*, Apr. 1945; and Henry Harding, "U.N.C.L.E.'s Uncle," *TV Guide*, July 31, 1965. See also *Biographical Encyclopedia and Who's Who of American Theatre* (1966). An obituary is in the *New York Times*, Oct. 19, 1972.)

ALAN BUSTER

CARTER, WILLIAM HODDING, JR. (Feb. 3, 1907–Apr. 4, 1972), editor, publisher, and author, was born in Hammond, La., the son of William Hodding Carter, a locally prominent farmer and businessman in Tangipahoa Parish, and Irma Dutartre. Carter, named for his father, went by Hodding rather than Will, although he shared his father's sense of noblesse oblige, love for the land, and hatred of demagoguery. According to Carter, his youth formed many of his basic values. He learned Confederate and Ku Klux Klan lore as well as Christian humility from his Bible-quoting grandmother, and he learned common humanity from a black boyhood friend. The wrenching sight of a burned, hanging body of a lynch mob's victim that young Carter stumbled upon in the woods haunted him for the rest of his life.

In 1923 Carter entered Bowdoin College, where, feeling isolated and defensive as the only southerner, he discovered that taking on prejudices was "good for the spirit." He contributed essays, stories, and poems to campus publications and edited the college annual, the *Bugle*. After graduating with a B.A. in 1927, he studied journalism at Columbia University (1927–1928) and then taught English at Tulane University (1928–1929). While in New Orleans, he met Betty Werlein, then a young college student, who shared his political and writing interests. They married on Oct. 14, 1931, and collaborated as publishers and authors thereafter. The couple had three sons.

Carter worked as a reporter for the New Orleans *Item* in 1929, as night bureau manager for United Press in New Orleans in 1930, and then as bureau chief for Associated Press in Jackson, Miss., from 1931 to 1932. In 1932 he was fired by the AP for "insubordination"; his former boss predicted Carter "would never make a newspaperman." Carter returned to Hammond, La., to prove otherwise. With the support of his father and help of his wife, Carter converted a throwaway mimeograph advertiser into a four-page tabloid daily known as the Hammond *Daily Courier*. The Carters kept the paper alive by trading advertising for rent, supplies, and even food. Carter fed his readers a steady diet of editorials attacking Senator Huey Long, whom Carter dubbed the "Crawfish" and likened to a corrupt carpetbagger of Reconstruction days. Carter also mobilized local political resistance to the Long political machine and support for Roosevelt's New Deal, which Long opposed.

Carter's district was unique in never sending a Long supporter to Congress. By writing anti-Long articles for national magazines and newspapers, Carter gained widespread attention, but repeated physical threats and boycotts, a failed bid for the state legislature in 1935, and especially the loss of a state printing contract dispirited Carter, and Long's assassination in 1935 chastened him. It was time to leave Hammond.

In 1936 he accepted an invitation from David Cohn and William Alexander Percy to set up and edit an independent newspaper in Greenville, Miss., a Delta community that Carter came to love as an oasis of toleration and freedom. The Delta and the town became the axis of Carter's identity and interest. He wrote two novels (*The Winds of Fear* [1944] and *Flood Crest* [1947]) set in the Delta world he knew so intimately, as well as three histories (*Lower Mississippi* [1942], *Gulf Coast Country* [1951], and *Man and the River: The Mississippi* [1970]), a collection of poems (*The Ballad of Catfood Grimes and Other Verse* [1964]), and hundreds of articles from his stance as loving critic of the region and its people.

With money from the sale of the *Courier* and $16,000 from Percy, Cohn, and others, the Carters launched the *Delta Star* in 1936. Two years later Carter bought out his principal rival and formed the *Delta Democrat-Times*, his journalistic home until his death. In spring 1940 Carter went to Harvard as a Nieman Fellow, and in summer 1940 he took a leave of absence from the *Delta Democrat-Times* to become an editor of the experimental paper *PM* in New York. Uncomfortable with *PM's* left-leaning politics and angry with its antisouthern tone, Carter gladly left big-city journalism. In late 1940 his National Guard unit was called into federal service but while on maneuvers in Florida shortly before the war, he injured his right eye. The injury kept him from combat and eventually cost him sight in that eye. During the war, therefore, he edited a Guard divisional paper before being transferred to the War Department's Public Relations Bureau and then to military intelligence in Washington. In Washington Carter coauthored *Civilian Defense of the United States* (1942) for the government and finished *Lower Mississippi*. In 1943 he helped to start and edit the Middle East editions of *Yank* and *Stars and Stripes* in Cairo, Egypt, but he was reassigned to Washington in 1944 to work on psychological warfare. He remained

there until his honorable discharge as a major in 1945.

The years away from his native South and his involvement in selling the war against fascism led Carter to rethink some of the basic assumptions of southern culture. He came home committed to identifying "things wrong with the South," none more so than race relations. Carter had already assayed the consequences of racial injustice in his novel, *The Winds of Fear* (1944). Set in a contemporary small southern town, the book reveals the consuming "hate and suspicion and intolerance" that lead to murder, rape, and riot following the death of a black soldier. Only the intervention of a moderate newspaperman and a minority of concerned citizens save the town from destruction. The novel's characters and themes seemed to predict Carter's own future.

Carter regularly wrote editorials condemning racial, religious, and economic intolerance. He railed especially against Senator Theodore G. Bilbo, who personified demagoguery and racial prejudice and who was the thinly disguised subject of Carter's angry novel, *Flood Crest*, about Red- and race-baiting, the convict-lease system, and political abuses. In 1946 Carter won the Pulitzer Prize for twelve editorials on state and local issues. The prize committee cited Carter's Aug. 27, 1945, editorial, "Go for Broke," arguing for fairness for returning Nisei soldiers, in particular. In the editorial Carter delivered what became his lifelong motto: "An active minority can have its way against an apathetic majority." The growing reputation that followed the award, along with his own writing for national periodicals, imbued Carter with a strong sense of responsibility to speak *for* as well as *to* the South. In his autobiographical musings *Southern Legacy* (1950) and *Where Main Street Meets the River* (1953), and later in his collection of essays, *First Person Rural* (1963), he both defended the region's distinctive clannish unity, individualism, personalism, sense of history and place, religiosity, and good manners, while he simultaneously scored it for the sins of racism and intolerance and the corruption of one-party politics. He also warned against federal government interference with southern folkways and institutions. Any such action would excite the subconsciously "guilt-ridden" white South to invoke the ghosts of Reconstruction to prevent any change from within or without. That the enduring myths of Reconstruction were real and powerful Carter had no doubt, as his own angry history of Reconstruction, *The Angry Scar* (1959), attested. The South, Carter repeatedly wrote, was a tangle of contradictions—individualist in rights and conformist in social thinking, hospitable to yet suspicious of strangers, gentle in manner but violent in action—that demanded patience from outsiders yet honest, immediate attention from southerners.

Caught between his concern for maintaining the integrity of southern distinctiveness and his desire to end social injustice, Carter consistently distanced himself from national civil rights organizations. His emphasis on Christian brotherhood and the moral as well as legal obligations to blacks brought him close to condemning segregation, but almost alone among southern "liberals," Carter opposed *court-ordered* desegregation. The Supreme Court's desegregation decision in 1954 was a personal as well as a national watershed. Although fearing its compulsory implications, Carter endorsed the decision itself as morally right. He urged southern legislatures to comply with the "equal" part of the separate-but-equal doctrine by bringing black facilities up to white standards and to eliminate the poll tax and other discriminatory practices that kept blacks from protecting themselves. He also decried southern "massive resistance" and lawlessness. In 1955 the Mississippi legislature censured Carter for an article he had published in *Look* attacking the White Citizens' Council, Carter's bête noire. Still, the civil rights movement rushed past Carter. His distrust of national civil rights organizations and his desire to have southerners settle racial matters themselves made Carter uncomfortable with the direct action of boycotts, freedom rides, and sitdown strikes that invited federal involvement.

By the mid-1960's Carter was retiring into historical and popular writing. In 1962 he turned over effective control of the *Delta Democrat-Times* to his son Hodding Carter III and became writer-in-residence at Tulane University. He wrote often for the *New York Times Magazine*, finished the third of three military history books for the Landmark series for young readers, among other works, and continued to write editorials and essays on southern themes, including a growing number of warnings not to let industrial development destroy the South's land and heritage. The murder of Medgar Evers in 1963 and the violence of "Freedom Summer" 1964 shocked Carter, as did the subsequent "Black Power" movement. With moderation seemingly in retreat everywhere, Carter wrote *So the Heffners Left McComb* (1965), deploring the intimidation that drove a "moderate" family from a Mississippi town. Carter remained much in demand as a speaker and writer about the South, but failing eyesight and the death of his youngest son Thomas in 1964 drew him inward. In 1968 the assassination of Robert Kennedy, for whom Carter had particular affection, plunged Carter further into a deep depression from which he never fully recovered. He left Tulane in 1970 because of poor health. His final significant work (and nineteenth book), *Their Words Were Bullets: The Southern Press in War, Reconstruction, and Peace* (1969), allowed Carter to reflect on the importance of editorial moderation during times of crisis and to restate his lifelong credo of loving the South enough to criticize it. Carter died of a heart attack in Greenville.

[The Hodding and Betty Werlein Carter Papers in the Manuscripts Division of Mississippi State University contain biographical material, scrapbooks, and most of Carter's publications. Runs of the Hammond *Daily Courier* and the Greenville *Delta Democrat-Times* are in the Louisiana State University Library and Mississippi Department of Archives and History, respectively. The only biographies are James E. Robinson, "Hodding Carter: Southern Liberal, 1907–1972" (Ph.D. diss., Mississippi State University, 1974); and Ann Waldron, *Hodding Carter: The Reconstruction of a Racist* (1993). See also William C. Havard, "The Journalist as Interpreter of the South," *Virginia Quarterly Review*, Winter 1983; and *Southern Liberal Journalists and the Issue of Race, 1920–1944* (1985) and "Liberal on the Levee: Hodding Carter, 1944–1954," *Journal of Mississippi History*, May 1987, both by John T. Kneebone. Obituaries are in the *New York Times* and the *Washington Post*, both Apr. 5, 1972.]

RANDALL M. MILLER

CASADESUS, ROBERT MARCEL (Apr. 7, 1899–Sept. 19, 1972), pianist, composer, and teacher, was born in Paris, France, the son of Robert Guillaume Casadesus, a composer and actor. His mother, Marie Varnay, died giving birth to Robert, and he was raised by his grandparents in a renowned French musical family. An uncle, François Louis, was a conductor and composer who founded the American Conservatory at Fontainebleau in 1918. Another uncle, Marius, was a violinist who later performed with his nephew in violin-piano concerts for many years. An aunt, Rose, a concert pianist, gave Robert his first lessons and early training. He entered the Paris Conservatory at age ten, studying solfège for two years and earning a first medal.

Casadesus studied piano with Louis Diémer and in 1913, after only nine months of study with him, won first prize in piano. In 1914, Casadesus began the study of harmony with Xavier Leroux, but his education was interrupted when his father entered military service in World War I, making it necessary for Robert to find employment. He played celesta and other percussion instruments at the Opéra Comique while continuing his piano studies at the conservatory. His formal debut as a pianist occurred in 1917. He was drafted into the French army in 1918, but the war ended before he saw action. In 1919 he returned to the conservatory and his studies with Leroux, and won a first prize in harmony. In 1921 he received the Diémer Prize in piano.

Casadesus married Gabrielle ("Gaby") L'Hôte, a talented student at the conservatory, on July 16, 1921. They had three children, of whom only the older son, Jean, pursued a career in music, as a concert pianist.

Immediately after his marriage, Casadesus began a busy professional life, composing, teaching, and performing. In 1922 he befriended composer Maurice Ravel, and they toured Europe in two-piano concerts throughout the 1920's. In 1929, Casadesus gave fifteen concerts in Russia. He toured South America in 1931, and Africa and the Middle East in 1933.

On Jan. 20, 1935, Casadesus made his American debut, playing Mozart's Piano Concerto in D Major, "The Coronation" (K537), with Hans Lange and the New York Philharmonic Orchestra at Carnegie Hall. In 1936 he performed Brahms's Piano Concerto in B Flat Major with the same orchestra, conducted by Arturo Toscanini. *New York American* critic Grena Bennett proclaimed him the most brilliant and proficient pianist heard that season, his playing "an adroit blend of brilliancy, facility, and artistry" (Jan. 31, 1936).

Casadesus and his wife gave their first concert for two pianos and four hands in 1928. The *New York Times* (May 27, 1943) characterized their performance of Mozart's Concerto for Two Pianos (K 448) as "a perfection of ensemble rarely heard in two-piano teams." On occasion Casadesus composed works for two pianos to enlarge the slender repertory of dual-piano showpieces. He and Gaby premiered his Concerto for Two Pianos and Orchestra (opus 17) in Warsaw in 1935.

In 1940, the Casadesus family, on tour in the United States, established residence in Princeton, N.J., where Casadesus continued to teach, compose, and perform. *Time* (June 4, 1945) described the ménage in New Jersey: "Robert and Gaby rehearse continually on two Steinways in the first floor living room. Jean (17) and Guy (13) do their practising there, too. A fuzzy-haired neighbor, Albert Einstein, sometimes drops in with his violin."

Casadesus began recording for Columbia in Europe in 1928, and in the United States in 1941. With the violinist Zino Francescatti he recorded the complete sonatas for violin and piano by Beethoven in the 1950's. Recordings of Mozart piano concertos with George Szell, the five piano concertos of Beethoven, the complete piano works of Debussy, his own compositions, and many other works in the piano repertory constitute his extensive discography. His recordings of Ravel's complete piano music won the Grand Prix du Disque in 1955.

Teaching was an important aspect of Casadesus's professional life. He began in 1922, at the American Conservatory in Fontainebleau, and maintained his association with this school throughout his life. In 1934, he succeeded Isidor Phillipp as head of the piano department there. During the war, the Fontainebleau school was reestablished in the United States, first at Newport, R.I., and, in 1942, at Great Barrington, Mass. The school reopened in France in 1946, with Casadesus as director. He ceased teaching in 1952, in order to devote more time to composition, performance, and administration, and became general director in 1955. Among his pupils were Monique Haas, Grant Johannsen, Ross Pratt, and Charles Rosen.

Casadesus earned many awards. In 1937 he received a gold medal for his Concerto for Two Pianos (opus 17) at the Paris Exposition. In 1959, he received the Brahms Medal and the gold medal of the city of Paris. In 1964 he was named commander of the Legion of Honor by the French government.

David Ewen, in *Musicians Since 1900*

(1978), describes Casadesus as a specialist in the classical, Romantic, and modern repertory, especially effective in the music of Mozart and the French masters. "He was extolled for the sensitivity of his musical perception, the subtlety of his colorations, the consummate mastery of his technique."

Casadesus wrote songs, chamber works, works for soloists and orchestra, seven symphonies—more than fifty works altogether—characterized in a *New York Times* review (Nov. 17, 1969) of his Sonata for Strings (opus 64) as "carefully proportioned, very civilized, and autocratically aloof."

In 1969, Casadesus made his one hundredth concert appearance with the New York Philharmonic, celebrating his fiftieth year as a performer. Over his long career he gave about three thousand concerts and made more than one hundred recordings. He died in Paris.

[Casadesus's papers are in the Robert and Gaby Casadesus Collection of the International Piano Archives at Maryland, Music Library, University of Maryland, College Park. Biographical works include Regina Casadesus-Patorni, *Ma Famille Casadesus* (1962); and Gaby Casadesus, *Mes Noces musicales* (1989). Sasha Stookes, *The Art of Robert Casadesus* (1960), lists and describes his musical compositions through 1960. See also "A Family Affair," *Time*, Dec. 4, 1950; Abram Chasins, "Paris to Princeton," *Saturday Review*, Aug. 27, 1955; and Irving Kolodin, "Casadesus Chez Szell," *Saturday Review*, Dec. 13, 1969. An obituary is in the *New York Times*, Sept. 20, 1972.]

JOHN C. REINERS

CASALS, PABLO (Dec. 29, 1876–Oct. 22, 1973), cellist, conductor, and composer, born Pablo Carlos Salvador Casals y Defilló, the second of eleven children, in Vendrell, Spain, a province of Catalan. His father, Carlos Casals y Ribas, was an organist and choirmaster at the church of Santa Ana and was also interested in politics. Pablo's mother, Pilar Ursula Defilló y Amiguet, encouraged Pablo to pursue a career in music. By age five Pablo was singing in the Vendrell church choir and studying piano, organ, and violin; by six years of age he was attending the calle Montserrat community school. He began to study cello when he was ten.

Pablo and his mother went to Barcelona in 1888 so that Pablo could study at the Municipal School of Music. He graduated in 1893 with a first prize in cello, piano, and composition. Be-

tween 1894 and 1897 he studied at the Royal Conservatory of Music in Madrid. He and his mother then went to Brussels for a short time before moving on to Paris, France. Financial burdens forced Pablo to return to Barcelona, where he was appointed to the faculty of the Municipal School of Music. His first appearance as a soloist with an orchestra was with the Madrid Symphony.

In 1899 Casals returned to Paris, making the city the base of his musical activity for the next several years. In addition to his concerts throughout Europe, he made his first solo tour in the United States in 1904 at the Metropolitan Opera in New York City. Prior to this debut he had been touring with the famed singer Emma Nevada.

In 1904 he took up residence in the Auteuil district outside of Paris. In addition to giving private lessons, he established friendships with many artists of the time. One such collaboration was with pianist Alfred Cortot and violinist Jacques Thibaud. Together they formed a trio that toured every year until the 1930's.

In 1906 Casals married cellist Guilhermina Suggia, a student twelve years his junior. Their marriage ended in 1912, but during that six-year period they toured together giving concerts, including his debut as a conductor in Paris in 1908.

In 1914 Casals returned to the United States and married the concert singer Susan Scott Metcalfe on April 4. They had met in 1904 when appearing on the same program in New York. When World War I began they remained in the United States, where he established his reputation as a great artist.

In 1920 he returned to Barcelona and formed an orchestra, which he conducted for seventeen years. In 1928 he gave his last solo performance in the United States. He separated from Metcalfe in 1929; they divorced in 1956.

After the Spanish Civil War Casals went to France; he did not return to Spain as long as Franco was in power. Indeed, he refused to tour any country under dictatorship, spurning the Soviet Union, Hitler's Germany, and Mussolini's Italy. Instead, he spent much of his time in Prades, France, helping exiled Catalans. This tradition was finally broken in 1950 when he performed at a Bach festival in East Germany.

In 1954 Martita Angélica ("Marta") Montañez, an eighteen-year-old cellist from Puerto Rico, began to study with Casals. She soon became his lover and traveled with him wherever he taught. One such trip was to Puerto Rico in 1956; Casals decided to make it his home. In 1957 he suffered a heart attack. After his recovery, he and Marta were married on Aug. 3, 1957.

In the period 1957–1958 Casals began the first of several seasons as conductor of the Puerto Rico Symphony Orchestra and as president of the Conservatory of Music of Puerto Rico.

In 1961 he performed for President John F. Kennedy at the White House. He traveled to Japan and Israel to teach and perform.

In 1962, at the age of eighty-five, he established the Pablo Casals Foundation to ensure that all proceeds from the performances of his oratorio *El Pessebre* (*The Manger*), which he had begun in 1943, would go to charitable organizations and peace efforts. The work became the centerpiece of a series of concerts Casals conducted in the 1960's to promote world peace, beginning with a presentation in San Francisco in April 1962. Seventy performances of the work all over the world had been given by 1969. Casals died in Rio Piedras, P.R.

[On Casal's life and work see H. L. Kirk, *Pablo Casals* (1974), which includes a complete list of his published compositions and a discography catalog; and Alden Whitman, *Come to Judgment* (1980). David Blum, *Casals and the Art of Interpretation* (1977), details several compositions from a musical standpoint, according to Casals's interpretation. Obituaries appear in the *New York Times*, Oct. 24, 1973, and *Time*, Nov. 5, 1973.]

CHARLES CASSARA

CERF, BENNETT ALFRED (May 25, 1898–Aug. 27, 1971), publisher, was born in New York City, the only child of Gustave Cerf, a lithographer and elocution teacher, and Frederika Wise. Cerf attended Public School 10, where one of his friends was the future playwright Howard Dietz. When Cerf was fifteen, his mother died, leaving him $125,000 that had been placed in trust for Cerf by his maternal grandfather. His uncle Herbert Wise moved into the Cerf home; Cerf would later call him "the greatest influence on my young life."

After attending Townsend Harris High School and Packard Commercial School (while working part-time for an accountant), Cerf entered Columbia University's School of Journalism (then an undergraduate program), in 1915.

In his freshman year, he wrote a column, "The Stroller," for the *Daily Spectator*, the student newspaper. In his sophomore year, he was editor in chief of *The Jester*, the student humor magazine, to which he added a book-review column. During World War I, Cerf served in the army at Camp Lee, Va., returning to Columbia after the war. At Columbia, Cerf's Pi Lambda Phi fraternity brothers included Richard Rogers and Oscar Hammerstein II. Cerf acknowledged the influence of professors Raymond Weaver and Benjamin Kendrick, and a number of years later published a mystery by another professor, Harrison Steeves, titled *Good Night, Sheriff* (1941). Cerf received a B.A. from Columbia College (1919) and a B.Litt. from the School of Journalism (1920).

Cerf then joined the Wall Street brokerage firm of Sartorius, Smith and Lowei and at the same time was hired by Merryle Stanley Rukeyser to write a column called "Advice to Investors" for the *New York Tribune*. But Cerf was soon fired for telling a reader she would be insane to invest in a bankrupt company (which threatened to sue the newspaper). He continued to work at the brokerage house but did not always find the work interesting.

In 1923, Richard L. Simon, a Columbia classmate of Cerf's who was leaving Boni and Liveright to start his own publishing company with Max Schuster, recommended that Cerf replace him. Agreeing to Horace Liveright's request for a loan of $25,000, Cerf entered publishing as a vice-president. Two years later, Cerf and his closest friend, Donald S. Klopfer, bought the Modern Library from Liveright for $165,000 (in addition to the $50,000 Cerf had already loaned Boni and Liveright). The Modern Library, with 109 titles in 1925, published inexpensive editions of classics, including American authors (which Everyman's Library, on which it was modeled, did not have).

Cerf and Klopfer, equal partners, expanded the Modern Library from their office at 73 West Forty-fifth Street, with Cerf handling editorial matters and Klopfer dealing with business and production issues. They complemented each other in many ways, including personality. Cerf was exuberant; Klopfer, calm and sympathetic. Cerf recalled that when employees had personal problems, they went to Klopfer. The partners shared one secretary, first Pauline Kreiswirth and then Mary Barber.

Modern Library Books, redesigned by Elmer

Adler (who replaced the imitation-leather binding), Lucien Bernhardt (who drew a new colophon), and Rockwell Kent (who did the endpapers), sold for ninety-five cents. The college market was especially lucrative because there were no paperbacks at that time. Cerf was also interested in fine press books, and in 1927 he became the American agent for Francis Meynell's Nonesuch Press, based in England. The partners also wanted to publish their own books. While talking to Klopfer and Kent, Cerf said, "I've got the name for our publishing house. We just said we were going to publish a few books on the side at random. Let's call it Random House." Rockwell Kent drew the colophon.

In 1928, a magnificent edition of Voltaire's *Candide* was the first book published by Random House. The stock market crash of 1929 destroyed the market for luxury editions, so Random House concentrated on trade publishing. The inexpensive Modern Library books helped the firm, now at 20 East Fifth-seventh Street, get through the Great Depression profitably.

In 1933, Eugene O'Neill—who had known Cerf when Liveright had been his publisher—and Robinson Jeffers came to Random House. Cerf remembered, "One of the conditions made by Eugene O'Neill was that I give a job to his old friend Saxe Commins." Richard Simon recalled, "Cerf considers O'Neill's insistence on the job for Commins as the luckiest break in the life of Random House." Commins's editorial judgment and fierce dedication to his authors played a large part in the success of Random House.

In 1933, a censorship case gave Random House enormous publicity and greatly enhanced its prestige in the literary world. James Joyce's *Ulysses* had not been permitted into the United States on the ground that it was obscene. Cerf asked Morris Ernst to handle the case, offering him a royalty on *Ulysses* if he won. Federal Judge John M. Woolsey, who had been a founder of the *Columbia Law Review* and an editor of *Revue de droit maritime comparé*, ruled that *Ulysses* was not obscene in a decision of Dec. 6, 1933, that was also a favorable book review: "*Ulysses* is an amazing tour de force when one considers the success which has been in the main achieved with such a difficult objective as Joyce set for himself." Cerf published Judge Woolsey's decision as an introduc-

tion to *Ulysses* (1934). Also included in the book was a letter of Apr. 2, 1932, from James Joyce to Cerf: "I wish you all possible success in your courageous venture both as regards the legislation of *Ulysses* as well as its publication."

Random House also published Marcel Proust, Gertrude Stein, W. H. Auden, and Stephen Spender. Cerf called publishing plays his "secret love," even though they rarely made any money. The exception was Eugene O'Neill, whose plays became best-sellers. Cerf also published plays by his friends George Kaufman and Moss Hart.

In 1936, Haas and Smith merged with Random House. Harrison Smith was soon bought out; and Cerf, Klopfer, and Robert Haas each owned one-third of the company (until 1956, when Haas sold his stock to his partners). With Haas came William Faulkner, Robert Graves, Edgar Snow, Isak Dinesen, and André Malraux. Smith and Haas had also published Jean de Brunhoff's *Babar the Elephant*, which Haas's wife, Merele Haas, had translated from the French. Haas's secretary, Louise Bonino, was an excellent editor of juvenile books who later headed that department at Random House.

Cerf was proud of publishing *The Public Papers and Addresses of Franklin D. Roosevelt* (1938), but the five-volume set had disappointing sales. Cerf recalled, "a lot of booksellers hated Roosevelt, too, and wouldn't order any copies." The president, Cerf noted, "was a rich man, but he took his full royalty. . . . But I don't regret our loss on our venture one bit. I had a couple of weekends at Hyde Park with F.D.R. and one at the White House." The following year, senior editor Harry Maule came to Random House, bringing with him Sinclair Lewis, Vincent Sheehan, Mignon Eberhart, and William McFee. In 1940, Cerf edited the Allied Relief Ball souvenir program, which included articles by Thomas Mann, Klaus Mann, and Somerset Maughan, poems by W. H. Auden and Duff Cooper, and a drawing by Jean Cocteau.

Cerf married Phyllis Fraser, Ginger Rogers's cousin, who had been a child actress and was now editing two daytime radio serials, in a ceremony performed by New York mayor Fiorello La Guardia on Sept. 17, 1940. They had two sons. (Cerf's first marriage, to Sylvia Sidney on Oct. 2, 1935, had ended in divorce.)

Cerf's partner Donald Klopfer joined the U.S. Air Force in 1942, and Cerf had to take on more publishing assignments. During World War II, Random House published war books by Quentin Reynolds, William L. Shirer, Robert Considine, and John Gunther. In 1943, Ray Freiman became production manager and art director, raising the already high standards. During the war, Random House was building a brilliant staff of editors. Cerf himself edited *The Pocketbook of War Humor* (1943) and the extremely successful *Try and Stop Me: A Collection of Anecdotes and Stories, Mostly Humorous* (1944). Although his books of jokes and anecdotes sold millions of copies, he gave a modest explanation of his success: "I've always said I've learned how to exploit a very small talent to the ultimate degree, and mine is very small compared to the people that I really admire."

At the request of Norman Cousins, Cerf wrote a column on publishing, "Trade Winds," for the *Saturday Review of Literature* (1942–1957). King Features had bought the serialization rights to *Try and Stop Me*, which several hundred newspapers were carrying, and Cerf was asked to do a daily humor column that had the same name. In 1950, he started writing "The Cerf Board" for *This Week*, a Sunday supplement that went to newspapers having a combined circulation of over ten million. But it was Cerf's role as a panelist from 1951 to 1967 on the CBS television program "What's My Line?," hosted by John Daly and including Arlene Francis, Dorothy Kilgallen, and Fred Allen, that made him most famous. Cerf enjoyed appearing on television every week and being recognized wherever he went in the country. Many of his closest friends were in show business, including Kitty Carlisle Hart and Claudette Colbert. Cerf received humor awards from the *Harvard Lampoon* and the *Yale Record*.

Phyllis Cerf made a large contribution to Random House. She thought they should publish better children's books, and her husband agreed with her after he started reading to their two young sons. As a result Random House began Landmark Books, an extremely successful series on American history for older children written by first-rate authors. Dorothy Canfield Fisher wrote *Paul Revere and the Minute Men* (1950); for example. Phyllis Cerf asked Theodor Geisel (Dr. Seuss) and his wife, Helen, to join her in starting a company that would publish books for children just beginning to read. They became the editors and publishers of Beginner

Books, with Random House as the distributor. The new firm became so profitable that Random House bought it. Phyllis Cerf also started two other series: Take-Along Books and Step-Up Books. Her work was not limited to children's books. Cerf said, "I began to rely more and more on what she would say about manuscripts."

Random House bought the mansion at 457 Madison Avenue—built by Henry Villard and designed by Stanford White—in 1946 and remained there until 1969. In 1947, Random House published the *American College Dictionary*. Cerf published a book he knew would infuriate his friends—Whittaker Chambers's *Witness* (1952), an account of the Alger Hiss controversy—that had been brought to him by a new editor. "If it hadn't been for David McDowell," Cerf later remarked, "I would have refused to see Chambers, which would have been entirely wrong of me."

In the 1950's, Random House published John O'Hara, Karl Shapiro, Ralph Ellison, Truman Capote, Irwin Shaw, James Michener, and Ayn Rand. Cerf recalled the pleasure of working with Robert Penn Warren: "He knows how good he is as a writer, but he is reticent about it." The last time Cerf saw William Faulkner, "he talked to me about Albert Erskine, who became his editor after Saxe Commins died. Faulkner said, 'You know, I think Albert is the best book editor I know.' " Robert Loomis and Jason Epstein also edited at Random House.

Thirty percent of Random House stock was sold to the public on Oct. 2, 1959. In 1960, Random House acquired Alfred A. Knopf, the publisher Cerf said he most admired. Alfred and Blanche Knopf joined the board of directors of Random House, and the Knopf imprint retained its autonomy. In 1961, Random House bought Pantheon Books, whose authors included Boris Pasternak, Anne Morrow Lindbergh, Günter Grass, and Jan Myrdal. Pasternak's *Dr. Zhivago* became a film, which led to an enormous increase in book sales. Random House authors in the 1960's included William Styron and Philip Roth, as well as Shelby Foote, who wrote a brilliant and "monumental history of the Civil War."

Cerf never tried to hide his love of publicity or how much he enjoyed his life. He had come to publishing from Wall Street, and almost everything he did made business sense. Hiram

Haydn, an editor in chief, noted in his *Words and Faces* (1974), "The vast spiral staircase between the first and second floors of Random House must have persuaded as many courted authors to join the firm's list as the partners or any editor." Cerf sold Random House to RCA, and his own account of the negotiations in December 1965 makes it clear that he struck the other participants as frivolous, an impression he did nothing to discourage. He was negotiating with David Sarnoff, the head of RCA, who had offered three-fifths of a share of RCA for each share of Random House; Cerf wanted sixty-two hundredths. The difference amounted to about $1 million dollars and would bring the price of Random House to $40 million. Sarnoff suggested continuing the negotiations the next day. Cerf amazed Sarnoff (and the bankers of Lehman Brothers and Lazard Frères) by announcing that he and his wife intended to keep their plans for a vacation with Frank Sinatra. Cerf's experience in a brokerage house as a young man enabled him to size up everyone correctly when he sold his life's work. He received exactly what he wanted for his publishing house, which included total editorial independence.

After Cerf's death in Mount Kisco, N.Y., the *Saturday Review* gave this assessment of Cerf: "He gave full measure to his profession. Everyone connected with the world of books is in his debt."

[The Bennett Cerf/Random House papers are at the Rare Book and Manuscript Library, Columbia University. *At Random: The Reminiscences of Bennett Cerf* (1977), edited by Phyllis Cerf Wagner and Albert Erskine, is based on over a thousand pages of transcripts of tape-recorded interviews at the Columbia University Oral History Research Office. Among the many books edited by Cerf is *Modern American Short Stories* (1945), which contains brief biographical sketches by Cerf of authors. Cerf's columns are supplemented by his articles, which include "Horace Liveright," *Publisher's Weekly*, Oct. 7, 1933. For Cerf on Richard Simon, see *Saturday Review*, Sept. 10, 1960; for Simon on Cerf, see "Try and Stop Them," *Saturday Review*, Dec. 23, 1950. Michael Moscato and Leslie LeBlanc, eds., *The United States of America v. One Book Entitled Ulysses by James Joyce* (1984) contains Cerf's correspondence about the case. Donald Hall, ed., *The Oxford Book of American Literary Anecdotes* (1981) includes four by Cerf. See also Mrs. Bennett Cerf, "My Husband Is No Joke to Live With," *Good Housekeeping*, June 1954. There is material on Cerf in Charles A. Madison, *Book Publishing in America* (1966); Hiram Haydn, *Words & Faces* (1974); and John W. Tebbel, *A History of Book Publishing in the United States*, vol. 3 (1978) and vol. 4 (1981). See also Geoffrey Hellmann, "Publisher," *New Yorker*, May 9 and May 16, 1959; and Murray Kempton, *New York Post*, Aug. 2, 1958. Obituaries are in the *New York Times*, Aug. 29, 1971; *Publishers Weekly*, Sept. 6, 1971; and *Saturday Review*, Sept. 11, 1971.]

RALPH KIRSHNER

CHANDLER, NORMAN (Sept. 14, 1899–Oct. 20, 1973), newspaper publisher, was born in Los Angeles, Calif., one of eight children of Harry Chandler, a newspaper publisher, and Marian Otis. After attending the local elementary school and Hollywood High School, Chandler entered Stanford University in 1918 and graduated in 1922. He was then hired as secretary to his father at the *Los Angeles Times*, a newspaper his grandfather, Harrison Grey Otis, had owned and published from 1881 to 1917. In 1920, he married Dorothy Buffum, whose family owned and managed a large department store. They had two children.

There was never any doubt that Chandler would follow his father into the newspaper business. He worked at the paper part-time while a student, doing everything from sweeping floors to apprenticing in the stereotype and composing rooms. In 1929, he was elevated to assistant to the publisher. Five years later Chandler was named to the board of directors of the Times-Mirror Company, which controlled the newspaper, and became assistant to the general manager of the corporation. In 1938, he became vice-president and general manager, and in 1941 he became president when his father moved into the post of board chairman. Upon the death of his father in 1944, Chandler was named publisher of the newspaper, a post he held until 1960. He was assisted in the management of the newspaper by his brothers, Harrison and Philip.

In the mid-1940's, when the Chandler children left home to attend school, Dorothy Buffum Chandler completed her college education and then went to work at the newspaper. She became administrative assistant to the president of the Times-Mirror Corporation in 1948. She also contributed to the management of the women's department at the *Times*.

In 1942, the *Times* won its first Pulitzer Prize for "the most disinterested and meritorious service" and emerged as a national newspaper, reflecting both Chandler's effort and the growth of

California. By then, Chandler had become active in civic improvement. He sponsored the Great Los Angeles Plans, dedicated to the betterment of the city, and in 1945 helped plan an opera house and an auditorium, and later, the Hollywood Bowl. The Times Charities, founded in 1944, became a multimillion-dollar operation supporting summer camps, urban public swimming pools, and many related youth activities. Chandler became a trustee of both the University of Southern California and the California Institute of Technology.

In 1948, the Times-Mirror Corporation established an afternoon newspaper, the *Los Angeles Mirror*, with Virgil Pinkley, a former United Press manager, as publisher. "Los Angeles had grown into an industrial and manufacturing community during wartime," explained Chandler, "and a tabloid paper of the *Mirror*'s type might appeal to the new elements of our population more than the *Times*." The *Mirror* was successful; by 1956, it had a circulation of more than three hundred thousand.

Chandler expanded the *Times*'s coverage of national and foreign news, transforming what many considered a narrow, parochial newspaper into one with influence far beyond Los Angeles. His accession coincided with a major spurt in the growth of the *Times*'s readership area. When Chandler took over, the *Times* ranked thirty-fourth in advertising lineage among the nation's newspapers. Within a year it was third. By 1955, on most days it had more pages than even the *New York Times*.

Chandler's father and grandfather considered themselves moderate Republicans and for decades battled the *Los Angeles Herald*, founded in 1904 by William Randolph Hearst, which was the city's liberal newspaper. At first Chandler, too, was quite conservative, but in time he changed. Nevertheless, he remained a moderate Republican while allowing the *Mirror* to espouse a more liberal editorial policy. In 1952, for example, the *Times* supported Senator Robert Taft of Ohio for the Republican presidential nomination while the *Mirror* came out for Dwight Eisenhower. "We were kind of lopsided in those days," he recalled. "If we gave the Republicans a big story, we'd give the Democrats a small one. And we only gave management's side in labor disputes."

In the 1950's, Chandler expanded Times-Mirror into other media. It began in 1956, when he acquired television station KTTV,

which he sold to Metromedia in 1963. He also became vice-president and director of the Tejon Ranch Company and Chandler-Sherman Corporation, as well as several local businesses, including Merchants National Bank and Buffum's Department Store (owned by his wife's family).

In 1956, on the occasion of the *Times*'s seventy-fifth anniversary, the California legislature commended the newspaper as one of the world's leading journals and praised Chandler as a major contributor to journalism and the well-being of Los Angeles.

In the years that followed, Chandler purchased other newspapers, including *Newsday*, a Long Island–based tabloid; the *Dallas Times Herald*; and some smaller ones. He also entered book publishing, cable television, and public relations. By the early 1960's the Times-Mirror Corporation had become one of the nation's largest and most powerful media conglomerates.

In 1960, Chandler stepped down and turned operations over to his son. Eight years later, he became chairman of the Times-Mirror Executive Committee, relinquishing all other responsibilities at the company. He died in Los Angeles.

[There is no biography of Chandler, nor is there a history of the Times-Mirror Corporation. Obituaries are in the *Los Angeles Times* and the *New York Times*, both Oct. 21, 1973.]

Robert Sobel

CHANEY, LON, JR. (Feb. 10, 1906–July 13, 1973), television and movie actor, was born Creighton Tull Chaney in Oklahoma City, Okla. His parents, Lon Chaney and Frances Cleveland Bush, began their careers as small-time vaudevillians. The Chaneys spent many years following the vaudeville circuit across the country while Creighton Chaney was growing up. Eventually, Lon Chaney, Sr., became well established in Hollywood, starring in a number of films that required heavy use of makeup, such as *The Hunchback of Notre Dame* and *The Phantom of the Opera*. His many roles in horror films earned him the title "The Man of a Thousand Faces." Before Lon Chaney could make the transition to the talkies, he died of throat cancer in 1933.

Although Lon Chaney, Sr., actively dissuaded his son from entering show business, Creighton Chaney began to seek work in Hollywood even before his father's death. He later recalled that his father had warned him, "I've taken my bumps, I know." Thanks in part to the elder Chaney's established name in Hollywood, Creighton Chaney soon found work. Although he began as a stunt man, he earned his first film credit within a year, appearing in *Bird of Paradise*. RKO then put him on contract, casting him for a role in the serial *The Last Frontier*. Because of his height and build—he stood over six feet four with broad shoulders, craggy features, and a wide back—he was cast as the "heavy" in a number of minor films during the 1930's, including *Road Demon* (1938) and *Jesse James* (1939). Married for the first time in 1933, he was divorced three years later after having two children. Chaney then married Patsy Beck, a model, in 1937, and they remained together until his death.

Chaney finally found a role that was perfectly suited to him as the tragic, half-witted Lenny in the film version of John Steinbeck's *Of Mice and Men*. Chaney premiered the role in a theater production that toured the Pacific Coast, and then gained the part in the Hal Roach–directed film. Opposite Burgess Meridith, who played George, Lenny's friend, protector, and ultimate executioner, Chaney infused his role with humanity and sympathy. Critics lauded Chaney's performance in a role that allowed him to escape his father's long shadow.

Of Mice and Men should have given Chaney an entrée into other high-quality productions. Chaney instead turned to horror films that capitalized on his father's name, but were much inferior to the classics that had featured the elder Chaney. Creighton Chaney went so far as to change his name to Lon Chaney, Jr. This "piece of showmanship," as *Variety* reported it, pleased theater owners and movie executives who stood to gain by Lon Chaney's continued marquee value. Others were less appreciative, however, seeing Chaney's new moniker as a crass attempt to cash in on his father's legitimate career that had been ended by a premature death.

Man-Made Monster, released in 1940, did little to mollify Chaney's critics. Chaney regained some credibility with his next performance, however. Universal Pictures, despite the miserable box office results of *The Werewolf of London* in 1935, revamped the trite werewolf genre with *The Wolf Man* (1941) and chose Chaney for the lead. While the casting of

Chaney was calculated to connect the film to the elder Chaney, both the film's high production quality and Chaney's sympathetic performance received critical acclaim. Chaney played Larry Talbot, an American college student who visits Wales and suffers the inevitable bite from a werewolf "during a midnight stroll on the moors. *The Wolf Man* was noted for its graphic transformation scenes, which used tightly focused shots of Chaney reverting from human to werewolf. Shooting these scenes required twenty-two hours to produce a few minutes of finished film. The movie also featured a strong supporting cast, including Bela Lugosi as the werewolf and Claude Rains as Talbot's father.

At this point in his career, Chaney took roles in a series of third-rate productions, slipping ever deeper into his father's shadow. While he lost the chance of gaining legitimacy in his own right, he never had to look very hard for work. He eventually appeared in over eighty movies.

Chaney's Wolf Man character made the rounds in a number of horror films in the 1940's, usually as the sidekick monster. In *Frankenstein Meets the Wolf Man* (1943), Chaney played the werewolf to Boris Karloff's monster. This gaudy exploitation of past triumphs in the genre had none of the breakthrough qualities of *The Wolf Man* and lacked the earlier film's strong supporting cast. Standards slipped a bit more with *House of Frankenstein*, in which Universal was "inspired to add more fiends to its predictable witch's brew." Gene Wright, in the retrospective *Horrorshows*, called the film "flimsy and predictable," but wrote, "It's an enjoyable monster mash, and if the creatures aren't very frightening, it's because by now they had begun to assume the familiarity of old friends." Other critics were less forgiving. Frank Mankel, in *Terrors of the Screen*, saw Chaney's roles in *House of Frankenstein* and similar vehicles such as *The Mummy's Tomb* (1942), *The Ghost of Frankenstein* (1942), *The Son of Dracula* (1943), and *The House of Dracula* (1945) as shams: "When these relatively cheap, crude movies failed to attract audiences, [Chaney] joined with Bud Abbott and Lou Costello in spoofing the very roles he had helped to downgrade [in] *Abbott and Costello Meet Frankenstein* (1948)."

During the 1950's and 1960's, Chaney mostly gave his monsters a rest, but the quality of his roles did not improve. His film credits during this period included *Casanova's Big Night*

(1953), *Not as a Stranger* (1955), *The Black Sleep* (1956), *The Defiant Ones* (1958), *Apache Uprising* (1966), and *Buckskin* (1968), among many others. He occasionally appeared in horror films, including *Manfish* (1956), *Cyclops* (1957), *The Haunted Palace* (1963), and *Hillbillies in a Haunted House* (1967). He also starred as the Indian Chingachgook in the television series based on James Fenimore Cooper's *Last of the Mohicans* (1956). Chaney's sole demanding part came in *High Noon* (1952), where he played the retired sheriff to Gary Cooper's heroic Marshal Kane.

Chaney's last years were difficult, as he suffered from numerous ailments, including gout, cataracts, liver disorders, and beriberi. He withdrew from public view, and when he died in 1973, his last wish "was that his death receive no publicity." Most of his obituaries referred to him as the "son of one of the giants of the silver screen," or made similar references to his father. In 1978, rock star Warren Zevon paid tribute to the Chaneys in his Top Ten hit "Werewolves of London."

[For information on horror movies of Lon Chaney, Jr., see Frank Mankel, *Terrors of the Screen* (1970); and Gene Wright, *Horrorshows: Horror in Film, Television, and Radio* (1986). For general information and analysis of Chaney's films, see Scott and Barbara Siegel, *The Encyclopedia of Hollywood* (1979). There are few published features on Chaney, but various items are collected in the clippings files at the Academy of Motion Pictures Library in Los Angeles. Obituaries appear in the *New York Times* and the *Los Angeles Times*, both July 14, 1973.]

MICHAEL GOLDBERG

CHAPMAN, JOHN ARTHUR (June 25, 1900–Jan. 19, 1972), journalist, drama critic, and author, was born in Denver, Colo., the son of Arthur Chapman and Lillian Mathewson Eddy. He was the oldest child. Two brothers survived to adulthood and a sister died in childhood. His father was a journalist, managing editor of the *Denver Times*, and author of the popular poem "Out Where the West Begins" as well as histories of the pony express and the state of Colorado.

Chapman attended public schools and graduated in 1916 from East Denver High School, where he was editor of the yearbook. He studied at the University of Colorado for a year and from 1917 to 1919 worked as a reporter for the *Denver Times*. In 1919, he moved with his family to New York City and attended Columbia University. He joined the fledgling tabloid newspaper, the New York *Daily News*, in 1920. Joseph Medill Patterson, founder and publisher of the paper, hired him on the strength of his striking photograph of the funeral of William Frederick Cody, the frontiersman known as "Buffalo Bill." On July 31, 1923, Chapman married Georgia Anderson. They had one child.

The *Daily News* called Chapman a "jack-of-all-newspaper trades and a master of all of them." From 1924 to 1926, he managed Pacific and Atlantic Photos, a bureau that transported photographic plates from Europe to the United States. Returning to the *Daily News* as a reporter, he became drama editor in 1929. During the 1930's he wrote a daily column, "Mainly about Manhattan," which combined shrewd observations and witty commentary on various aspects of life in New York City. In 1940 he succeeded Ed Sullivan as the paper's Hollywood columnist, but he disdained writing gossip and returned to New York in 1942. With the resignation of Burns Mantle as drama critic in 1943, Chapman succeeded him and spent the next twenty-eight years "on the aisle."

During these years he wrote candid reviews for the New York *Daily News* as well as the *Saturday Evening Post*. He also contributed to the magazine *Theater Arts*, using the pseudonym George Spelvin. These theatrical columns won him wide renown. His writing was characterized by straightforward prose, polished phrases, and witty epigrams. His reviews consistently reflected a basic fairness, integrity, and droll sense of humor. When Mae West appeared in the Broadway play *Catherine Was Great*, Chapman wrote, "I'm afraid *Catherine Was Great* will be a bust, which is one more than Mae West needs." He was affectionately called "Old Frost Face," "The Curmudgeon," and "Mr. Theater" by colleagues and friends.

During his career with the *Daily News* the paper's circulation increased to over 2 million, but Chapman always insisted that he wrote to a small audience, "a tough one: me." He held himself to high and exacting standards and was especially proud of his spelling and correct grammar. His reviews were composed very rapidly and went straight to the printer without clearing the copy desk. An editor at the newspaper recalled a permanent wager requiring the drama critic to pay a certain sum of money if he made an orthographic error. Chapman never lost the wager.

While he did not earn a college degree, Chapman taught a course on the theater at New York University in 1956–1957 and received an honorary doctor of humanities degree from the University of Denver in 1963. He was a member of the Silurians, an organization of veteran newspapermen, and served as president of the New York Drama Critics Circle, a professional awards-giving group. He edited the annual *Best Plays and Year Book of Drama in America* from 1947 to 1953 and *Broadway's Best* from 1957 to 1960. He also wrote *Tell It to Sweeney: An Informal History of the New York Daily News* (1961), which covered the story of the newspaper from its inception through the 1950's. "Tell It to Sweeney" was an advertising slogan of the *Daily News* and suggested Chapman's theme of the consistent appeal of the paper to the "man in the street."

Chapman's contributions to the American theater were significant. His output of reviews and criticisms was noteworthy and formidable, numbering in the thousands. As a member of the board of governors of the American Theater Wing, he labored to maintain the Tony Awards as a vital force in the American theater. He was devoted to talented professionals and promoted hitherto unknown actors and actresses, such as Helen Hayes and Mary Martin. His editions of *Best Plays and Year Book of Drama in America* are essential reference works, invaluable to theater lovers and scholars.

Chapman lived in Westport, Conn., with his family although he maintained close ties with his native Colorado. He was an accomplished cook and enjoyed fly-fishing, photography, and carpentry. He retired from the *Daily News* in August 1973 and died the following January in Westport. His body was cremated and his ashes scattered in the mountains of Colorado.

[There are obituaries in the *New York Times*, Jan. 20, 1972; and the New York *Daily News*, Jan. 20, 1972.]

KEVIN J. O'KEEFE

CHARLES, EZZARD MACK (July 7, 1921–May 28, 1975), heavyweight boxing champion, was born in Lawrenceville, Ga., the only son of William and Alberta Charles. His father worked as a janitor. When his parents divorced, Charles relocated with his mother to Cincinnati, which became his adopted hometown.

Charles's boxing career began at age sixteen. He completed two years of high school before dropping out to make the ring his career. Lightning hand speed and deadly accuracy quickly earned him the nicknames the "Cincinnati cobra" and "the hawk." A sparkling amateur career resulted in a 42–0 mark, with two national Amateur Atheletic Union middleweight titles in four years. Charles never lost an amateur tournament, capturing two Golden Glove titles and two Cincinnati city titles, and knocking out Canada's amateur champion in two rounds.

Charles turned professional in 1940. He won twenty straight fights over the first eighteen months of the decade before dropping a ten-round decision to ex–middleweight champion Ken Overlin. His early career was interrupted by World War II, when Charles enlisted in the U.S. Army, serving from 1943 to 1945.

Charles was arguably the best light-heavyweight ever. He defeated future light-heavyweight champions Archie Moore (three times), Joey Maxim (twice), and Anton Christoforidis (once). But when Charles became the premier light-heavyweight contender, champion Gus Lesnevich ducked a title bout with him. Unfazed, Charles moved up in weight class and eventually became the heavyweight champion, holding the title from 1949 through 1951.

As a light-heavyweight, Charles was known as a knockout artist—a style of fighting that he changed after Feb. 28, 1948, when Charles beat challenger Sam Baroudi so badly that the other fighter died; after this Charles became more of a ring technician than a power puncher. Charles was so shaken by this death that he initially considered retirement, but Baroudi's father convinced the fighter to continue. Charles returned to the ring but donated the purse from his next fight to the late boxer's family. In later years critics complained that Charles lacked the "killer instinct" needed to put fighters away, which was a particularly painful criticism for him to accept.

Charles never moved very far into the heavyweight class: in ten of his thirteen title fights, he was outweighed. The six-footer generally weighed in the 180's for his bouts. The most he ever weighed for a title fight was 192 pounds; the least was 180, just five pounds above the heavyweight minimum. He routinely fought and beat men who outweighed him by as much as fifty pounds.

After winning twenty-eight of twenty-nine

postwar fights, Charles won the National Boxing Association heavyweight crown, a title left vacant by the retirement of Joe Louis, with a fifteen-round decision over Jersey Joe Walcott on June 22, 1949. When Louis mounted a comeback, Charles captured the title on Sept. 27, 1950, from the ex-champ. However, the victory wound up as a split decision for Charles, whose career was defined by his opponent. "Instead of being hailed as the heavyweight champion of the world, [he] became known merely as the man who beat Joe Louis, destined forever to become an antihero to one of the most popular names in all of sports," commented boxing historian Bert Randolph Sugar. "Nobody gave any credit to Ezzard. . . . People just didn't want to see Louis lose. It wasn't Ezzard's fault," observed Rocky Marciano.

Charles went on to fight Walcott three more times for the title, defending his title in 1951 and losing the belt and a rematch in 1951 and 1952. Charles fought twice more to regain the heavyweight championship, but he came up short both times against the only undefeated champion in heavyweight history, Rocky Marciano. Marciano "decisioned" Charles in fifteen rounds on June 6, 1954, and knocked Charles out in the eighth round three months later. Marciano, who took on all comers in winning forty-seven straight fights, later said these were two of his toughest victories.

Charles was among the busiest of heavyweight champions: only Joe Louis, Muhammad Ali, and Larry Holmes won more title fights; only Floyd Patterson and Jersey Joe Walcott lost more title fights. The four showdowns with Walcott make the record, which still holds, for the most heavyweight title fights to have been fought by the same two men.

Charles, whose skills had clearly eroded, kept fighting until 1959. He lost thirteen of his last twenty-three fights, winding up his career with a mark of 96–25–1, with fifty-eight knockouts. Charles retired briefly in 1956, but came back within two years. His final bout was a defeat at the hands of an unknown, Alvin Green, on Sept. 1, 1959. Twenty-one years later, an ailing Charles was elected to the Boxing Hall of Fame.

Charles continued to live in Cincinnati. Outside the ring, he sat in with the orchestra at the Cincinnati Conservatory of Music during rehearsals. He played both the bass violin and the saxophone. He was a regular churchgoer and a golf aficionado.

After leaving boxing, Charles fell on hard times. Two years after his retirement in 1959, Charles announced he had no money left from the $2 million in purses he had collected in the ring. "I was saving for a rainy day, and . . . it's a flood," said Charles, who was married with three children.

Charles returned to the ring as a professional wrestler, and later worked as a greeter at a nightclub and a coordinator of youth boxing in Chicago. But in February 1966 he was struck with Lou Gehrig's disease. His health deteriorated slowly until he was eventually bound to a wheelchair. He died in a Veterans Administration Hospital in Chicago.

[See *Our World*, Apr. 1949; and Bert Randolph Sugar, *The 100 Greatest Fighters of All Time* (1954). An obituary is in the *New York Times*, May 29, 1975.]

LARRY McSHANE

CHASE, MARY ELLEN (Feb. 24, 1887–July 28, 1973), author, educator, and lecturer, the second of the eight children of Edward Everett Chase, a lawyer and judge, and Edith Lord, a schoolteacher, was born in Blue Hill, Maine, a maritime area where her ancestors had settled 200 years earlier. Her education began in a rural two-room school, where inadequate funds limited the school term to twenty-five weeks per year; she notes, however, that her mother, whom she describes as her first and best teacher, ably supplemented her children's instruction.

At age thirteen Chase entered Blue Hill Academy, a school with a predominantly classical curriculum and, upon graduation at seventeen, she enrolled in the University of Maine to major in Greek and history. In the spring of her sophomore year, responding to her father's insistence about the need for practical experience, she took a leave from her studies to teach three terms in rural schools and then returned to complete study for her bachelor's degree. Following her graduation in 1909, cum laude with Phi Beta Kappa membership, Chase taught various subjects in private boarding schools, first in Wisconsin and then in Chicago, until a prolonged illness necessitated a lengthy convalescence in Montana. Her decision to enroll in a graduate program in English came during the enforced idleness of this period, when her extensive reading resulted in a fascination for words and an intense desire to teach English prose rather than history.

With the attainment of her Ph.D. in 1922, she realized her wish when she became an assistant professor in the University of Minnesota's English Department, as well as an evening instructor in the Extension Division and a part-time instructor at the nearby College of St. Catherine. Her career as a lecturer also started at this time. Initially a source of supplemental income, her speaking assignments, which ranged from literary analyses for women's clubs to high school commencement addresses, became a source of pleasure, for Chase found enchantment in unfamiliar places and chance acquaintanceships. So greatly did she enjoy her lecture tours that she continued them throughout her professional life. In 1926, motivated partly by her wish to spend her days as a teacher in what she called her own part of the country, she accepted an invitation to join the faculty of Smith College, where she remained for twenty-nine years.

Chase did not marry; she devoted her life to study, teaching, and writing. Her dedication bore fruitful returns. As a teacher—she disliked the word "educator"—she not only achieved her personal goal of a full professorship, an uncommon accomplishment for a woman of that period, but also found complete satisfaction in her work. Smith College, she said, fulfilled all her expectations and desires; moreover, she regarded teaching English literature as "more fun to do than anything else in the world." That her classes consistently filled to capacity attests to her popularity as a teacher.

She also enjoyed success as a writer, whose diverse range of publications included *Thomas Hardy from Serial to Novel* (1927), an adaptation of her doctoral dissertation; an English textbook, *Constructive Theme Writing* (1957), designed to aid the college student in mastering what Chase called the "formidable problem" of learning to use language well; and several biblical analyses and interpretations, inspired by her teaching of courses in the literature of the Bible. Her intention in the first of these studies, *The Bible and the Common Reader* (1944), was to enhance reader enjoyment through a better understanding of the various literary forms of poetry and prose to be found in the Bible as a whole. The popularity of this work led to a sequel with a narrower focus, *Life and Language of the Old Testament* (1955); followed by *The Psalms for the Common Reader* (1962).

In addition to these scholarly works, Chase wrote numerous novels and autobiographical works. In one of the most appealing of the autobiographies, appropriately called A *Goodly Heritage* (1932), she fondly re-created the joyous days of simple pleasures during her childhood and early youth in a Maine seacoast town. She again recaptured the impressions of a child living in a distant, uncomplicated era in the charming story *The White Gate* (1954).

The memories of the areas Chase loved so well as a child materialized as the settings of many of her novels. Her most impressive works, however, are those that chronicle the economic and cultural transformation of New England villages in the late nineteenth and early twentieth centuries brought about by the decay of shipping activities and the intrusion of summer visitors. Her *Silas Crockett* (1935), for example, traces the fortunes of four generations of the seafaring Crockett family, from the prosperous days when Saturday Cove served as a vibrant shipbuilding center for the entire coast to its decline into a herring-packing factory town. The title figure of *Mary Peters* (1934) also lives through periods of upheaval and change. Although these stories reflect Chase's sadness concerning the decay of the maritime life of New England, she countered her disappointment by emphasizing the enduring heroism of those who survived the changes.

Though she is primarily remembered for regional fiction about the Maine seacoast and its inhabitants, Chase moved beyond the boundaries of Maine in a number of her works. The early part of *The Lovely Ambition* (1960) is set in rural England, another of her favorite places, which she again highlighted in *This England* (1936), a collection of delightful essays about her summer vacations abroad. In A *Journey to Boston* (1965) she wrote with warmth and admiration of a different type of New Englander, the hardworking Polish immigrant who had settled in the Connecticut River Valley, and she made a complete departure from her other works in the novella *Dawn in Lyonesse* (1938), a modern version of the Tristan and Isolde tale.

Whatever her subject or setting, however, Chase's enduring love of words emerges in vivid images and vibrant, gracefully flowing sentences. As for her characterizations, her own abiding affection for and intense interest in "all sorts of people" endows her fictional people with a refreshing, lifelike quality that has assured their timeless appeal.

For several years after her retirement from Smith in 1955, Chase maintained her active pace of life. She wrote several books, including three for children, and pursued her hobbies of bird-watching and gardening at Windswept, her summer home in Maine. She also traveled to England to study Hebrew at Cambridge University. Eventually, she was confined to a Northampton, Mass., nursing home where she spent the remainder of her life. She was buried in Blue Hills, Maine.

[The most comprehensive account of Chase's professional life appears in the autobiographical *A Goodly Fellowship* (1939). Short biographical sketches are included in Max J. Herzberg, *The Reader's Encyclopedia of American Literature* (1962); and *American Women Writers*, vol. 1 (1979). An obituary appears in the *Springfield Union*, July 30, 1973.]

DOROTHY KISH

CLAPP, MARGARET ANTOINETTE (Apr. 11, 1910–May 3, 1974), educator and author, was born in East Orange, N.J., the daughter of Alfred Chapin Clapp and Anna Roth. She attended East Orange High School, where she was known for her scholarly interests and language skills and was vice-president of the school's athletic association. After graduation in 1926 she attended Wellesley College, where she majored in economics and played varsity basketball. In her senior year, she won academic distinction as a Wellesley College Scholar and served as the head of College Government, a faculty-student body. In an oral interview almost a half-century later, she recalled her efforts on behalf of "more liberal rules" and "more places to smoke." She was awarded a B.A. in 1930.

Clapp began teaching English literature and history at the Todhunter School for Girls in New York City in 1930. She also started graduate work in history at Columbia University, earning an M.A. in 1937. When Todhunter amalgamated with the Dalton School in 1939, she remained on the faculty as an English teacher until 1941. Female scholars seeking careers in higher education faced serious obstacles in the 1940's. During and immediately after World War II, Clapp combined doctoral studies at Columbia with various, often part-time, positions. In 1942 and 1943 she was a research analyst in the New York City office of the British Broadcasting Corporation; until 1945 she

did similar work at the American Red Cross (ARC), helping to write the administrative history of ARC Wartime Services. From 1942 to 1944 she taught in the history department of the Business School of City College of New York, the first woman to do so. In 1945 and 1946 she was at the New Jersey College for Women; the following year she taught at Columbia University. In 1946, she received a Ph.D. from Columbia and was appointed assistant professor at Brooklyn College for the 1947–1949 school years. Her special fields were late-nineteenth- and early-twentieth-century American history.

Clapp's career path changed dramatically with the publication of her doctoral dissertation in 1947. Entitled *Forgotten First Citizen*, it was a biography of John Bigelow, a prominent New Yorker whose active life as editor, writer, diplomat, and civic leader spanned almost a century of political and social history, from pre–Civil War times to shortly before the outbreak of World War I. The book was widely praised for its wealth of information, vivid style, and balanced judgment. In Clapp's view, a good biography had to have "some of the elements of a novel," to "re-create the complexities of man," and to be "readable as well as accurate." Her success as a biographer was confirmed when Columbia University awarded her the Pulitzer Prize in 1948.

Clapp was still an assistant professor at Brooklyn College when she was chosen to become Wellesley College's eighth president, an office she held from 1949 until her resignation in July 1966. Her overriding priority during these years was academic excellence. Inadequate salaries and too little support for faculty scholarship were twin evils she successfully combated throughout her tenure, during which the average faculty salary increased 133 percent.

Clapp realized as well that the diverse backgrounds of the students demanded both curricular and student-life adaptations to meet new needs, including a more flexible curriculum and wide opportunities for self-pacing and, for the best-prepared students, independent research. Although she was conservative in many respects, she was a persistent feminist, convinced that women should plan their lives for "marriage plus something" and that many more should persevere through graduate education. She was a realist about economic and other barriers: scholarships more than tripled during her presidency.

In addition, Clapp campaigned tirelessly for endowment growth and continuing improvement of campus facilities. The book value of Wellesley's endowment more than doubled under her aegis, while the campus benefited from expansion of the library (renamed the Margaret Clapp Library in 1974), new residence halls, an arts center, and a faculty-alumnae center. In addition, Clapp served on the Problems and Policies Committee of the American Council of Education, on the U.S. State Department's Board of Foreign Scholarships, and as a trustee of several independent schools and of the Carnegie Endowment for International Peace.

After resigning from Wellesley, Clapp went to India to head the Lady Doak School, a primarily undergraduate liberal arts college for women in Madurai, Madras. Lady Doak, founded in 1948, was a nondenominational Christian college; about 60 percent of its students were Hindus and Muslims. Clapp saw that the school, which had recently become part of the newly established University of Madurai, would be facing "a yeasty year," and she was eager to help. The first Westerner to serve as Lady Doak's principal, she impressed the community during her brief tenure (1967–1968) by her clear comprehension of the complexities of the school's situation. Her accomplishments included the establishment of a new constitution for the college's governing council and the selection of a strong Indian successor as principal.

Except for occasional visits home, Clapp remained in India until 1971. For three years she served as the first female chief cultural officer of the United States Information Service in New Delhi and chaired the U.S. Educational Foundation there. Her responsibilities included coordinating American educational efforts, serving as cultural attaché at the embassy, editing the *American Review*, and supervising educational and cultural programs. In 1971 she returned to the United States, settling in Tyringham, Mass., where she died. She never married or had children.

[Margaret Clapp's papers are in the Wellesley College Archives. In addition to the Bigelow biography, Clapp contributed a chapter, "The Social and Cultural Scene," to A. Nevins and J. Kraut, eds., *The Greater City* (1948), and edited *The Modern University* (1950), which includes her essay, "Contemporary Universities." See also *Wellesley Alumnae Magazine* articles from Mar. 1958, Nov. 1961, and July 1966. Obituaries appear in the *Washington Post* and the *New York Times*, both May 4, 1974.]

URSULA SYBILLE COLBY

CLARK, JOSEPH JAMES ("JOCKO") (Nov. 12, 1893–July 13, 1971), naval flag officer, was born in Pryor, Okla., the son of William A. Clark and Lillie B. Berry. His father was a rancher and cattleman in rural Oklahoma, where Clark attended public school. In 1907 he enrolled at Willie Halsell College in Vinita, Okla., and in 1909 he transferred to the Oklahoma Agricultural and Mechanical College at Stillwater, entering the military training program. He was promoted to corporal during his first year and became sergeant in 1910. Convinced that the army was his calling, Clark persuaded his father to speak to family friend Congressman James S. Davenport about an appointment to West Point. Davenport instead offered him an appointment to the Naval Academy at Annapolis, Md.

Clark entered the Naval Academy in 1914, where he maintained an adequate academic standing (he graduated forty-seventh in a class of 199) and played lacrosse and soccer. His predilection for hazing almost cost him his career. As punishment for excesses, Clark was turned back one year, and the incident made evident to him the need for discipline in his career. The outbreak of World War I and the accompanying demand for naval officers led to the accelerated graduation of his class in June 1917, however, rendering his punishment superfluous.

Clark reported aboard the cruiser *North Carolina*, which from July 1917 until December 1918 was engaged in escorting convoy troops across the Atlantic. In July 1918, Clark suffered a serious leg wound and was transferred to the Naval Hospital at Portsmouth, N.H. He remained there until Feb. 1, 1919, when he began a period of service (1919–1922) on destroyers in Atlantic, European, and Mediterranean waters. In 1921, as executive officer of the USS *Bulmer*, Clark worked with the American Relief Administration and Near East Relief. Following a brief assignment (1923–1924) at the Naval Academy as an instructor of navigation, Clark was ordered to the U.S. Naval Air Station at Pensacola, Fla., for instruction in flying. It proved to be a turning point in his career.

After qualifying as a naval aviator on Mar.

16, 1925, Clark joined the Battle Fleet attached to the aircraft squadrons, where he served as navigational aide to Commander John Rodgers and developed navigation data for the first flight from the West Coast to Honolulu. Beginning in 1926 Clark served successively in several aviation assignments. First he joined the battleship USS *Mississippi* as senior aviator, then moved to the battleship USS *Pennsylvania* as aviation aide to Rear Admiral Montgomery M. Taylor, commander of Battleship Division Three. He ended the decade as executive officer of the U.S. Naval Air Station at Anacostia, in Washington, D.C.

In the 1930's, Clark was given a series of command assignments in the Navy's air arm. From 1931 to 1933 he commanded Fighting Squadron Two-B stationed aboard the USS *Lexington*, and after a brief interlude as aeronautical member of the Board of Inspection and Survey, Clark returned to fleet aviation operations as air officer on the *Lexington* (1936–1937). Before Japan's attack on Pearl Harbor, Clark had a variety of assignments that included temporary command of Patrol Wing Two of Fleet Air Base in Pearl Harbor (1937–1939), inspector of naval aircraft at the Curtiss-Wright Corporation in Buffalo, N.Y. (1940), and routine land assignments at naval air facilities in the United States. On May 18, 1941, Clark reported aboard the USS *Yorktown* as executive officer and remained on that carrier during the early stages of World War II. In January 1942, soon after the attack on Pearl Harbor, the *Yorktown*, docked in Norfolk, Va., sailed to the Pacific in time to be the only carrier participating in the raid on Marcus and Gilbert islands.

Following service on the *Yorktown*, Clark worked briefly in the Bureau of Aeronautics in Washington, D.C., before assuming command of the new escort carrier *Suwannee* in the spring of 1942. He skippered her from the time she was commissioned through the assault on and occupation of French Morocco in November 1942. Clark had a reputation as a hard taskmaster—he was known as the "Patton of the Pacific." It was said of him that he could "make more noise on the bridge than a 5-inch gun." After Morocco, Clark was promoted to captain.

In early February 1943, Clark assumed command of the new carrier USS *Yorktown*, bringing the vessel into commission in Apr. 1, 1943, and commanding her during operations against Marcus, Wake, Jaluit, Makin, Kwajalein, and Wotje islands in the fall of 1943. On Aug. 31, 1943, the *Yorktown* launched her planes in combat and achieved complete surprise in attacking Japanese facilities at Marcus Island. All enemy aircraft on the ground were destroyed. Throughout the remainder of 1943, Clark directed successful air operations against Japanese shore installations, shipping, and aircraft and received a letter of commendation and the Silver Star for his efforts.

On Jan. 31, 1944, Clark became a rear admiral and served as a task group commander operating alternately with the First and Second Fast Carrier Task Groups of the U.S. Pacific Fleet, with the USS *Hornet* as his flagship. During this period his ships attacked Truk, the Carolines, Palau, the Marianas, the Bonins, Tokyo, the Ryukyus, and Okinawa. For these actions, the Navy awarded Clark the Navy Cross, the Distinguished Service Medal with Gold Star, and the Legion of Merit.

After the war, Clark held a series of administrative posts before taking command of Carrier Division Four and Carrier Task Force 87 on two cruises to the Mediterranean between 1948 and 1950. Promoted to vice-admiral during the Korean War, Clark commanded Carrier Division Three and Carrier Task Force Seventy-seven and perfected close air-support techniques that gained fame as the "Cherokee strikes," a name derived from his Indian heritage.

Clark retired in 1953 with the rank of admiral and began a successful business career in New York City. His last post was chairman of the board of Hegeman Harris, a New York investment firm.

Clark was married four times. In 1932 he married Mary Catherine Wilson; they had two children. His other wives were Shannon Kelley, China Robbins, and Olga Choubaroff. Clark died at the Naval Hospital at St. Albans, N.Y.

[Numerous biographical sketches, service jacket entries, newspaper clippings, obituaries, and other press releases are in the Biographical Z Files, Naval Historical Center, Washington, D.C. Clark's autobiography, written with Clark G. Reynolds, is *Carrier Admiral* (1967). See also Joseph J. Clark, "The Marianas Turkey Shoot," *American Heritage*, Oct. 1967; and Clark G. Reynolds, *Famous American Admirals* (1978). An obituary is in the *New York Times*, July 14, 1971.]

VERNON L. WILLIAMS

CLARK, WALTER VAN TILBURG (Aug. 3, 1909–Nov. 10, 1971), poet, writer of short stories, novelist, critic, and educator, was born to Walter Ernest Clark and Euphemia Abrams in a log cabin in the woods near East Orland, Maine, where his parents spent their summers. His father was a professor of political science and chairman of the department at City College, New York; his mother had studied music at Cornell and Columbia. When Walter Clark became president of the University of Nevada in 1917, his son's environment became the American West, which was to become the background for his writing. There he first learned about western history from his grammar school principal, who as a bride of sixteen had helped fight off Indians who attacked a wagon train and killed her husband.

At high school in Reno, Nev., Clark drew cartoons, began writing verse, took part in dramatics and debating, and played basketball and tennis. Climbing and camping in the Sierras and hiking in the desert, he came to know and love the West's spaciousness. He further developed his athletic skills by swimming in the not-too-distant Pacific Ocean. An early interest in fishing and hunting waned as he came to feel that living creatures were more attractive than dead ones.

Odd jobs helped defray the costs of his education both in high school and at the University of Nevada. There from 1926 to 1932, while earning bachelor's and master's degrees in English with minors in philosophy and psychology and continuing to write verse, he took part in dramatics and played tennis and basketball. As a graduate student, he taught undergraduates and wrote his master's thesis on the Irish legend of Tristam and Iseult. Later in life he would comment that *Who's Who in America* listed him as a teacher first and an author second, a ranking with which he agreed.

From 1931 to 1934, he was a teaching assistant at the University of Vermont while he worked on his Ph.D. degree, concentrating on Greek and American philosophers. In 1932, his father paid the publishing costs of Clark's first volume of verse, *Ten Women in Gale's House and Shorter Poems*. His doctoral thesis, completed in 1934, was on the poetry of Robinson Jeffers. On Oct. 14, 1933, at Elmira, N.Y., he married Barbara Frances Morse, daughter of a Presbyterian minister in Pennsylvania; the couple had met at the University of Nevada. Al-though the marriage was to endure until her death from cancer on Nov. 12, 1969, there were many periods of separation. In the 1951–1952 school year, for instance, when he taught at the University of Iowa Writers' Workshop, his wife did not accompany him. However, fellow teachers said later that Clark talked about her a lot.

From 1936 to 1941, and again from 1942 to 1945, he taught English, coached tennis and basketball, and directed dramatics at the Cazenovia, N.Y., High School in the Finger Lakes Area. (In 1941 and 1942, the Clarks lived at Indian Springs north of Las Vegas.) Their two children were born at Cazenovia.

Evenings and weekends he was "writing constantly," at first publishing only a few poems. By 1938, he had completed a number of short stories. "The Hook" (1940), a story about a hawk, was the first of his works to draw public attention.

The Ox-Bow Incident (1940), a novel about the lynching of three innocent men believed to be cattle rustlers, was the second, immediately attracting attention as a Western novel with true literary merit, quite unlike the stories of cowboy life with which the American public had become saturated. A 1943 film version, which followed the novel's story line faithfully, also received highly favorable reviews.

Rejected for military service because of a hernia, Clark wrote short stories for the *Atlantic Monthly*, the *Saturday Evening Post*, and the *New Yorker*. One of the best, "The Portable Phonograph," a tale of five men who are the last survivors of the human race, was published in the *Yale Review* in 1941. One of his stories was selected each year from 1941 to 1945 for the *O. Henry Memorial Award Prize Stories*. "Hook" (1941); "The Portable Phonograph" (1942); "The Ascent of Ariel Goodbody," (1943); and "The Buck in the Hills," (1944). "The Wind and the Snow of Winter" was the 1945 O. Henry Award winner.

Clark's second novel, *The City of Trembling Leaves* (1945), with a rites-of-passage theme, disappointed reviewers, some of whom thought the novel had been written before *The Ox-Bow Incident*, had been rejected by publishers, and was now being published because of the reputation of the first book.

In the fall of 1945, Clark taught briefly at a high school in Rye, N.Y.; a physical disability forced him to resign. The Clarks then moved to the artists' and writers' colony sponsored by Mabel Dodge Luhan in Taos, N.Mex. In September 1946, they moved again to a ranch in Washoe Valley between Reno and Carson City, Nev. There Clark wrote two novellas with chess and academic themes, then turned to *The Track of the Cat* (1949), a novel about a hunt for a black panther that has been killing range cattle. This moral parable has been called the "finest Western story ever written," and Clark's best novel.

Moving to Virginia City, Nev., he wrote *The Watchful Gods and Other Stories* (1950). During the 1950–1951 school year, he taught part-time at the Virginia City High School; during the 1951–1952 school year he taught at the University of Iowa's Writer's Workshop, but turned down an offer to remain there. The next school year, he held a part-time position in the Department of English at the University of Nevada, but he resigned in protest over university policy regarding faculty tenure.

From 1954 to 1956, he was at the University of Montana, teaching English classes and developing a creative-writing program. From 1956 to 1960, he helped develop the creative writing program at San Francisco State University. In 1957, he testified for the defense in the censorship trial of *Howl*, a book of poetry by Allen Ginsberg. In June 1958, he received an honorary doctorate from Colgate University.

During the 1960–1961 school year, he was a resident at the Center for Advanced Studies at Wesleyan University in Connecticut. He then returned to San Francisco State to resume his directorship of the creative writing program.

In his remaining years he published one chapter of a proposed biography of Alfred Doten, a pioneer Nevada journalist and publisher, and taught at the University of Nevada on a part-time basis. Clark, after receiving an honorary doctorate from the University of Nevada, died of cancer and is buried in Masonic Cemetery in Virginia City, Nev.

[See Charlton Laird, *Walter Van Tilburg Clark: Critiques* (1983), particularly the pieces "Credo" and "Autobiographical Information" by Clark himself, and the "Chronology" contributed by his son, Robert M. Clark. Max Westbrook, *Walter Van Tilburg Clark* (1969), includes a bibliography of Clark's writings, a listing of reviews of his books, and a listing of scholarly essays about Clark and his work. L. L. Lee, *Walter Van Tilburg Clark* (1973), is also useful. An obituary appears in the *New York Times*, Nov. 12, 1971.]

CLARENCE A. ANDREWS

CLEMENTE, ROBERTO (Aug. 18, 1934– Dec. 31, 1972), baseball player, was born Roberto Clemente y Walker to Melchor Clemente and Luisa Walker in Carolina, P.R., where his father worked as a sugarcane cutter and, later, joined his wife in running a grocery store. Although he was an all-around athlete, Clemente's passion was always baseball. His idol was the great Negro League batter Monte Irvin. At the age of fourteen, Clemente was picked to play for the Sello Rojo Rice Company team by Roberto Marin, who remained his lifelong friend and mentor. In 1952, Clemente signed with the Santurce Cangrejeros, a professional baseball team. His .356 batting average attracted the notice of major league scouts in 1953, and he accepted the Brooklyn Dodgers' offer of a $10,000 bonus plus a salary of $5,000 per year, the highest amount the team had yet offered to a Hispanic player.

Clemente was sent to Montreal for the 1954 season to play on the Dodger International League farm team (the Montreal Royals) but saw limited action. The Dodgers reportedly wanted to hide Clemente from other scouts who, at that time, could have legally drafted him. The $10,000 salary was considered a small sacrifice to make in order to prevent the rival Giants from hiring him. Dodgers vice-president Buzzy Bavasi later said, "We didn't want the Giants to have Clemente and Willy Mays in the same outfield. It was a cheap deal for us." Clemente spent a miserable year wondering where his career was going. Ready to quit, he was urged by Marin to stick it out so that he would be eligible for the draft at the end of the season.

The Pittsburgh Pirates had not won a World Series since 1930. Their scout, Clyde Sukeforth, discovered Clemente in Montreal, and the Pirates chose him in the first round of the minor league draft on Nov. 22, 1954—promising him that he would play every day. Clemente started slowly, tailoring his batting, which always looked awkward, to Forbes Field, where the high scoreboard and the depth of the field made it ideal for hitting triples. "Clemente's unorthodox hitting style . . . contradicted every known hitting technique," said veteran manager Lou Boudreau, who also called him "one of the worst-looking great hitters I've seen."

Clemente became the Pirates' permanent and spectacular right fielder, winning the Gold Glove award twelve straight times. His batting averages for the first five years averaged about .281. In 1960, the year the Pirates won the World Series against the New York Yankees, Clemente batted .314. That year he hit sixteen home runs, scored eighty-nine runs, and batted in ninety-four runs—a team high. Most of his runs batted in came at crucial points in big games. In the World Series he had nine hits in twenty-nine times at bat for a .310 average. Clemente expected to be named Most Valuable Player in 1960; when he placed eighth, he was angry and remained bitter about it for the rest of his career. It was said that he never wore his World Series ring.

Clemente's feud with sportswriters, who called his pride and outspokenness "arrogance," began at this time. He felt they used his problems with the English language to make him look stupid and foolish and believed that their criticism was motivated by racism and prejudice. He claimed that Hispanic players were treated worse than the African-American players and were denied lucrative endorsements. He also resented the press for labeling his injuries and illnesses as "malingering" and "hypochrondria."

He led the National League in batting in 1961, with .351, and the major leagues as a whole in 1964, 1965, and 1967. Clemente was invited to play in the All-Star Game in 1961, receiving the second-highest number of votes on the National League squad. Each year between 1961 and 1966, he played between 144 and 155 games and batted over .310. He won two more National League batting titles, with a .339 average in 1964 and .329 in 1965. He reached double figures in both outfield assists and home runs each season. In these same years, he also won six Gold Glove awards and played in every All-Star Game. In all, Clemente played in a dozen All-Star Games in his eighteen-season career.

Clemente was a hero in his native Puerto Rico. He returned there and married Vera Cristina Zabala on Nov. 14, 1964, in San Juan, where they raised three children. In 1966, he was finally named Most Valuable Player in the National League. In 1967, his best year for slugging average, he won his fourth batting title (.357), hit 23 home runs, drove in 110 runs, and scored 103. After this banner year, age and persistent injuries began to take their toll. He remained an All-Star player and Gold Glove winner in right field, but his batting declined. About this time Clemente set for himself the

goal of reaching 3,000 hits. In 1967, he led the National League with 209 hits, raising his total to 2,238. The following year he was plagued by injuries that affected him into June of the 1969 season. The team was doing well in the pennant race, and in spite of his injuries, Clemente banged out ten hits in two games against his favorite opponents, the Dodgers, a feat not previously accomplished in the twentieth century. The Pirates won division titles in the next two years and beat the Baltimore Orioles in a seven-game World Series in 1971.

Even so, Clemente was 118 hits short of his goal as the 1972 season began. He limped through the season with a bad ankle, severely bruised heels, persistent stomach problems, and general exhaustion. By September he was still 25 hits short of 3,000. The Pirates were doing so well that attention focused on Clemente's batting goal. He chipped away at it, raising his average to .310. The Pirates returned home at the end of September with Clemente set to hit 3,000. Anticlimactically for Clemente and his fans, a credited hit turned into an error—he had it, then he didn't. But September 30, in a game against the New York Mets, Clemente whacked a Jon Matlack curveball off the wall in left-center field for a double and had his 3,000th— the eleventh player in baseball history to reach this goal. After the game Clemente said, "I give this hit to the fans of Pittsburgh and to the people of Puerto Rico and the man who made me play baseball, Roberto Marin."

It was to be Clemente's last hit. He returned home to Puerto Rico after the playoffs with the Cincinnati Reds to celebrate the holiday season. On Dec. 23, 1972, Managua, Nicaragua, was hit by a severe earthquake. Clemente organized and chaired the Puerto Rican relief effort, even going door to door in his neighborhood asking for donations. Against the pleas of family and friends, on New Year's Eve he boarded a rickety old DC-7 that had been donated to the relief effort. The plane developed engine trouble upon takeoff and plummeted into the ocean near Carolina. No bodies were ever retrieved from the shark-infested waters. At his funeral the new governor of Puerto Rico, Rafael Hernandez Colon, said, "Our people have lost one of their great glories."

Three months after his death, in an unprecedented move, Clemente was inducted into the Baseball Hall of Fame on Mar. 20, 1973, an honor normally withheld for at least five years after the player's last game. In April, at their opening game, the Pirates retired Clemente's number, 21. Clemente had long worked toward a dream of opening a sports center in San Juan that would provide free sports activities for poor children. His death spurred an outpouring of money. Schoolchildren in Pittsburgh, baseball players, and fans made contributions in his memory, and Carolina Sports City was finally completed in 1987.

[Clemente's papers and additional information about his career are available at the Baseball Hall of Fame Library in Cooperstown, N.Y. Biographical information can be found in Arnold Hano, *Roberto Clemente, Batting King* (1968); Kal Wagenheim, *Clemente!* (1973); Jerry Brondfield, *Roberto Clemente, Pride of the Pirates* (1976); and Thomas Gilbert, *Roberto Clemente* (1991). Statistical data and basic career information can be found in Mike Shatzkin, ed., *The Ballplayers* (1990). An obituary appears in the *New York Times*, Jan. 2, 1973.]

PAMELA LAKIN

CLYDE, GEORGE DEWEY (July 21, 1898– Apr. 2, 1972), educator, irrigation engineer, and governor of Utah, was born in Springville, Utah, to Hyrum Smith Clyde and Elenore Jane Johnson Clyde. His parents, pioneer settlers in Utah, were members of the Church of Jesus Christ of Latter-day Saints. Clyde's father, a farmer on one of the area's first reclamation projects, helped foster his son's early interest in irrigation and agriculture.

Clyde graduated as valedictorian from Springville High School in 1917. He served briefly in the U.S. Army but saw no war action. In 1921 he received his B.S. in agricultural engineering from Utah State Agricultural College (now Utah State University) and again was valedictorian of his class. He married Ora Packard on Sept. 19, 1919; they had five children. In 1923 he received an M.S. in civil engineering from the University of California at Berkeley, where he was a Thompson Scholar.

Upon returning to Utah, Clyde established a practice as a consulting engineer in irrigation and joined the faculty at Utah State Agricultural College in Logan. In 1928 he was promoted from assistant professor of irrigation and water supply to associate professor. He became professor of irrigation engineering in 1930. Before resigning in 1945, Clyde served ten years (1935–1945) at Utah State Agricultural College as dean of the School of Engineering and Tech-

nology, and six years (1939–1945) as director of the school's engineering experiment station. After his resignation Clyde became chief of the division of irrigation engineering and water conservation research in the Soil Conservation Service of the U.S. Department of Agriculture. In 1953, he was named chief of engineers in the Soil Conservation Service.

The public interest focused on Clyde when Governor J. Bracken Lee named him director of the Utah Water and Power Board, a nonpartisan position (1953). As a result of this appointment, Clyde emerged as a regional leader and spokesman in the successful battle for authorization of the Upper Colorado River Basin Storage Project. His dedication to resource development played a large part in his decision to seek political office.

Ironically, incumbent Governor Lee lost the Republican nomination to Clyde in the gubernatorial primary in September 1956. Clyde was one of the three candidates opposing Lee. *Newsweek* (Sept. 14, 1956) pronounced that Lee had been "undeniably a good administrator," but a "critic of the Eisenhower Administration's foreign policy." Among Clyde's supporters was Utah's U.S. senator Arthur V. Watkins, a fellow champion of water reclamation. In the November election, Clyde ran against Democratic nominee Lorenzo C. Romney, and Lee ran as an independent. Clyde defeated Romney by 127,654 votes to 110,511, with Lee finishing third.

Inheriting a general fund surplus of about $9 million, Clyde spoke of need for this surplus to be spent on education, public works and highways, and salary increases. Following his inauguration on Jan. 7, 1957, he submitted to the legislature recommendations for greater aid to school districts. With a comfortable Republican majority in both houses of the legislature, he asked to create an office of legislative auditor, and coordinating committees on higher education and highway safety, and demanded that the legislature reorganize the Finance Department.

Clyde was reelected in 1960, defeating William A. Barlocker, the mayor of St. George, Utah. His second term is perhaps best remembered for a feud with public school teachers over Utah's education program. The dispute came to a head in a statewide teachers' strike, culminating in a two-day "recess" in May 1964. Clyde refused to give more money to schools, claiming the state could not afford more funding. He came under strong criticism from many fellow Republicans for his stand against the teachers.

In 1965, Clyde stepped down from the governorship and returned to engineering, working as a consultant with the firm of Clyde, Criddle, and Woodward. He retired in 1970. Clyde never fully recovered from a severe stroke suffered in 1971. He died in Salt Lake City.

Clyde's legacy lies in his campaign for the Upper Colorado River Storage Project. This legislation, enacted by the U.S. Congress in March 1956, was designed to provide water for an area covering 100,000 square miles. Clyde believed that water was the most valuable fuel in the West, bringing power to the region. Well-versed in natural resource education, he spoke as an agent of natural resource reclamation. The Upper Colorado River Storage Project embodied his concern for the West, the environment, and conservation.

Clyde's rise to the governorship was unique in Utah politics. Unlike his predecessors, he had little experience in partisan politics. He was brought to politics through the attention he gained as an advocate of water development in the West, particularly Utah and the surrounding region.

[Clyde's personal papers are in the Utah State Archives, Salt Lake City. On his governorship, see the *New York Times*, Apr. 12, 1958. Obituaries are in the *Salt Lake Tribune* and the *New York Times*, both Apr. 3, 1972.]

F. ROSS PETERSON

COLUM, PADRAIC (Dec. 8, 1881–Jan. 11, 1972), an associate of the founders of Ireland's famed Abbey and the *Irish Review*, and for some sixty-five years a poet, dramatist, essayist, historian, novelist, and author of books for children, was born by the River Comlin in Longford, County Longford, in central Ireland. His father, also named Padraic Colum (pronounced "pahdric column"), was the master of a workhouse. His mother was Susan MacCormack.

Colum later said that he was born where "waifs, strays and tramps congregated . . . and was entertained by the gossip and history of old women and old men who were survivors of an Ireland that had disappeared" and by the " 'casuals,' itinerants who stayed only for a night or so, men and women who were genuine wayfarers and nomads." While he was yet a boy, the Colums moved to a grandmother's farm in nearby County Cavan. There in the evening the family gathered around a peat fire and listened to storytellers recount the legends and history of Ireland, tell folktales, sing old Irish songs, and recite scraps of Irish poetry. Colum later attributed much of his own story-telling ability to his childhood experiences, and he used some of these materials in his novel *The Flying Swans* (1969).

Colum attended local public schools and then worked as a railroad clerk for a short time. But he spent more time jotting down verses on the backs of railway schedules than he did attending to his clerical duties. To inquiries about the beginnings of his career as a poet, Colum would reply that such questions were "stupid . . . a poet's first poem is always a few lines written about somebody's cat." By age eighteen, however, he first saw his verses published in *The Irish Independent* and *The United Irishman*, the latter a weekly journal published by Arthur Griffith, founder of the Sinn Fein ["Ourselves Alone"] society whose aim was to renew Irish culture and promote independence from Great Britain. Colum reported his experiences with Griffith in *Ourselves Alone* (1959), the "story of the origins of the Irish Free State."

Those were the years of the Irish Renaissance—the years when William Butler Yeats, James Joyce, Lady Isabella Augusta Gregory, AE (George W. Russell), Sean O'Casey, John Millington Synge, James Stephens, and the Fay brothers were writing. Colum, who moved to Dublin after the death of his parents, became a friend, admirer, or acquaintance of them all, a critic of their works, and a biographer of several, acquiring, as one consequence, the title "Joyce's Boswell." For his part, Joyce once angrily called Colum "Patrick What-do-you-Colum" in a broadside, but later, in a friendlier mood in *Ulysses*, said that Colum had "that strange thing called genius," adding that to some extent the author, playwright, and "whimsical teller of tales for children," was unfairly overshadowed by those around him.

Colum's first play was produced in 1901 when he was a mere twenty-year-old. *The Saxon Shillin'* (1903) was written to discourage young Irishmen from joining the British army. *Broken Soil* (1903), revised as *The Fiddler's House* (1907), was produced by the new National Irish Theater Society at the Abbey Theater. *The Land* (1905) was the first critical success of the Abbey. Colum continued to write plays even though they were not box-office successes. "You can make a fortune writing plays," he said, "but not a living."

In 1911, Colum, David James Stephens, and Thomas MacDonagh (one of the leaders of the 1916 Irish Revolution) founded the *Irish Review*, a literary journal. Colum's first volume of poems, *Wild Earth: A Book of Verse*, was published in 1907; a revised and augmented text was published as *Wild Earth and Other Poems* in 1916.

In 1909, Colum met Mary Gunning Maguire, a graduate of Ireland's National University and an author and teacher. Colum nicknamed her "Molly Maguire" after the 1840's Irish secret society that terrorized law officers attempting to evict tenants unable to pay their rents. They were married in 1912. In 1914, they came to the United States where they became American citizens and remained for the rest of their lives. Both were to have equally distinguished careers as authors and sometime university teachers. "I got jobs to do in the United States," Colum said. "I found publishers." Mary Colum became a reviewer of poetry for the *New York Times Book Review*.

Colum wrote more than sixty volumes: poetry, plays, a novel, a biography, several books in the Irish language, two books of Hawaiian legends, and *A Treasury of Irish Folklore* (1954). Despite all his books, he insisted that "poems were made to be said. They are for our voices, not just our eyes." Poetry "is the deepest creation of the imagination."

Although the Colums were childless, Colum wrote many of his books, romances, tales and legends for children. Some of these were illustrated by Ukrainian-born Boris Artzybasheff, others by Hungarian-born William Andrew ("Willy") Pogány.

In 1923, at the invitation of the Hawaiian government, the Colums lived in a grass hut near the Bishop Museum while Colum, the "Lakumele mai Ilelani" (the poet from Ireland), wrote his collections of tales: *At the Gateway of the Day* (1924) and *The Bright Islands* (1925).

The Colums maintained a lifelong friendship with James Joyce. In 1928, Joyce asked Colum to write the introduction to *Anna Livia Plurabelle*.

Colum was awarded the 1952 fellowship of the American Academy of Poets, and he was a member of the American Academy of Arts and Letters. In 1953, he received the Gregory Medal of the Irish Academy of Letters, and in 1961 the Regina Medal for distinguished contributions to children's literature. In 1958, Columbia University awarded him an honorary doctor of letters degree, and Trinity College, Dublin, also awarded him an honorary degree that year. In 1964, Georgetown University presented him with its 175th Anniversary Medal of Honor

Mary Colum's first book, *From These Roots: The Ideas That Have Made Modern Literature* was published in 1937. Her autobiography, *Life and the Dream* (1947), telling of the exciting years in Dublin and the poets the Colums came to know in America—among them Carl Sandburg, Vachel Lindsay, Hart Crane, and Eleanor Wylie—was published in 1947. She received two Guggenheim Fellowships in literary criticism, and in 1934 Georgetown University awarded her its John Ryder Randall gold medal for distinction in literature. She was elected to the National Institute of Arts and Letters in 1953. From 1952 to 1956 she was a guest professor of comparative literature at Columbia University.

With her husband she was writing *Our Friend James Joyce* at the time of her death on Oct. 23, 1957. The book, both a biography and an account of the relationships among the three, was published in 1958. Padraic Colum continued to be a moving spirit in the James Joyce Society which met regularly at a New York City bookstore. He lived to be ninety years old, finally dying at a nursing home in Enfield, Conn., where he had resided since suffering a stroke in the summer of 1970. Both the Colums were interred in Dublin, Ireland.

[Colum's papers and documents—notebooks, manuscripts, galley proofs, and letters are at the State University of New York at Binghamton. Mary Colum, *Life and the Dream* (1947); and Mary and Padraic Colum, *Our Friend James Joyce* (1958), are rich with details of both Colums' careers. *The Dictionary of Literary Biography*, vol. 19, includes a biography, two photographs, and a bibliography of primary and secondary sources. Stanley J. Kunitz and Howard Haycroft, *Junior Book of Authors* (1934), has excellent brief statements. *Something About the Author*, vol. 15, is also an excellent source with many personal statements from the Colums, and a list of secondary sources. An obituary is in the *New York Times*, Jan. 12, 1972.]

CLARENCE A. ANDREWS

CONDON, ALBERT EDWIN ("EDDIE") (Nov. 16, 1905–Aug. 4, 1973), jazz guitarist and entrepreneur, was born in Goodland, Ind., the ninth and last child of John Condon and Margaret McGrath. His father was a saloon keeper and then a policeman. The family later moved to Chicago Heights, Ill.

Music was an important part of family life. Condon's father played the violin, and seven brothers and sisters also played musical instruments. Condon was picking out melodies on the piano when he was nine years old. When he was in the seventh grade he began playing ukulele. By his first year at Bloom Township High School he was playing tenor banjo.

In the spring of 1922, at the age of sixteen, Condon went on the road with Hollis Peavey's Jazz Bandits. In the fall Condon left the band to work with the legendary cornet player Bix Beiderbecke at the Alhambra Ballroom in Syracuse, N.Y. In January 1923 Condon, billed as "the world's youngest banjo player," rejoined Peavey's Jazz Bandits. But by the end of the year he moved to Chicago.

Condon, a handsome, well-dressed, quickwitted, sharp-tongued young man aptly nicknamed "Slick," began associating with young Chicago musicians, many of whom were to become famous jazz players: Bud Freeman, Jimmy McPartland, Dave Tough, Benny Goodman, Muggsy Spanier, George Wettling, Joe Sullivan, and Frank Teschemacher. At night, after their own musical jobs were over, Condon and friends would go to speakeasies on the South Side and hear the music of such African-American masters as King Oliver, Louis Armstrong, and Bessie Smith.

Bandleader Red McKenzie was so impressed after hearing Condon and six of his friends (including McPartland, Freeman, Sullivan, and Gene Krupa) that he set up a recording session with Okeh Records (1927). The band was called the McKenzie-Condon Chicagoans. The recording was successful, and a second one quickly followed. These sessions introduced and defined a new kind of jazz, called "Chicago style," defined by the rich contrapuntal textures of New Orleans and Dixieland jazz with an emphasis on individual improvised solos.

McKenzie persuaded Condon to go to the capital of the jazz world, New York City. He arrived in May 1928 and in a few days thought that he had found a job for himself and his friends. He encouraged Krupa, Sullivan, and Teschemacher to quit their bands and join him, but the job never materialized. Condon talked his way

into another recording session at Okeh. The $150 he and his friends made was only enough to pay an overdue hotel bill, with enough left over to buy a round of hamburgers so small and thin that Condon called them "transparent." He found little work for the rest of the year.

On Feb. 8, 1929, Condon organized the first interracial recording session on a national label, Victor. The band was called Eddie's Hot Shots. Later that year he participated in other interracial recordings with Fats Waller and Louis Armstrong. In November he joined the Mound City Blue Blowers. Red McKenzie played comb and tissue paper and sang. The rest of the novel instrumentation was suitcase with whisk broom and two lutes (Condon played one). He played with this band until 1933. In that year he began playing the four-string guitar, which he tuned like a banjo.

In 1937 Condon began an eight-year engagement at Nick's, a Greenwich Village nightclub owned by Nick Rongetti. But Condon was repeatedly fired from his job because he would engage in conversations with the customers— often important journalists, critics, and media people—and take them out to talk and drink in another club down the street. Frequently he did not return in time to play the next set.

In 1942, with the help of advertising executive Ernest Anderson, Condon began a series of jazz concerts, first at Carnegie Hall and then at Town Hall, which continued until 1946. In the same year he presented one of the first jazz programs on television, again with a racially mixed group. At the end of the year he took first place as best guitarist in *Downbeat* magazine's readers' poll. He won the poll again in 1943. Condon married Phyllis Smith on Nov. 16, 1942. They had two children.

In 1945 Condon opened a nightclub in Greenwich Village at 47 West Third Street that featured his own brand of Chicago style jazz. In 1958 the club moved to the Sutton Hotel on East Fifty-sixth Street; it finally closed in 1967.

In 1948 and 1949 he again brought jazz to television. The program was called "The Eddie Condon Floor Show." In the early 1950's he wrote a record review column, often very humorous, for the New York–based newspaper *Journal-American*. In 1957 he toured Great Britain and in 1964 went to Japan, Australia, and New Zealand. His last public appearance was on July 5, 1973, at Carnegie Hall as part of the Newport in New York Jazz Festival.

Throughout his career Condon played hundreds of recording sessions and thousands of engagements. Because he never took solos, being content to function only as a rhythm player, he was often overlooked by critics. But his playing was purposefully subtle in volume, harmonically inventive, and rhythmically driving. He promoted and organized some of America's finest jazz groups. He helped bring recognition and respectability to jazz, winning serious critical acclaim and building concert audiences for the music. He died in New York City.

[Condon's autobiography, prepared with the assistance of Thomas Sugrue, is *We Called It Music* (1947). With Richard Gehman, he edited an anthology, *Eddie Condon's Treasury of Jazz* (1956), and, with Hank O'Neal, a photographic autobiography, *The Eddie Condon Scrapbook of Jazz* (1973). The definitive discography is Giorgio Lombardi, *Eddie Condon on Record 1927–1971* (1987). See also Paul Smith, "Eddie Condon," *Guitar Player*, Nov. 1975; and W. Howland Kenny, "He Played Rhythm: Eddie Condon the Musician," *Journal of Jazz Studies*, Spring/Summer 1977. An obituary is in the *New York Times*, Aug. 5, 1973.]

JOHN VOIGT

CONDON, EDWARD UHLER (Mar. 2, 1902–Mar. 26, 1974), physicist, was born in Alamogordo, N.Mex., the son of William Edward Condon, a civil engineer who developed sites for railroad expansion, and Caroline Barr Uhler, a sometime grocer.

After graduating from a high school in Oakland, Calif., in 1918, Condon worked as a newspaper reporter in Oakland and San Francisco before entering the University of California at Berkeley in 1921. Initially an astronomy major, Condon continued his newspaper reporting. He married Emilie Honzik on Nov. 9, 1922; they had three children. Condon switched to physics, was elected to Phi Beta Kappa and Sigma Xi, and received a B.A. with highest honors in 1924.

Condon continued as a graduate student at Berkeley, receiving his Ph.D. in 1926. His thesis extended the work of James Franck. Condon's research on subatomic particles led to a fundamental and widely applicable concept known as the Franck-Condon principle.

This was a period of lively ferment and rapid growth in theoretical physics. Max Planck had introduced the concept of quantum mechanics in 1900. Werner Heisenberg and Max Born developed nuclear physics at the University of Göttingen. Condon received an International Education Board Fellowship to study at Göttingen in 1926, then in Munich with Professor Arnold Sommerfeld.

Returning to the United States in 1927, Condon worked in public relations for Bell Telephone Laboratories, combining his newspaper experience and knowledge of scientific research. Theoretical physics exercised a greater attraction, however, and he lectured in physics at Columbia University in the spring of 1928.

In the fall of 1928, Condon became assistant professor of physics at Princeton University. He left in 1929 and returned in 1930 as an associate professor, remaining until 1937. His 1929 book *Quantum Mechanics*, coauthored with P. M. Morse, was the first English-language text on the subject. In 1935, Condon published, with George Shortly, *The Theory of Atomic Spectra*, which remained for decades the authoritative volume in its field. Condon's research in molecular and nuclear physics led to many published papers on such topics as infrared spectroscopy as well as optical rotatory power and the interaction of subatomic particles in relation to electromagnetic charge. Condon's investigation of the wave mechanics of radioactive decay established a major concept explaining nuclear fission.

Condon's research did not detract from his success as a teacher of both graduate students and undergraduates. He inspired and nurtured many who became successful physicists and many others who appreciated his enthusiasm, clarity, and wit.

In 1937, Condon moved to Pittsburgh and became associate director of research at Westinghouse Electric Corporation. He established research fellowships that enabled ten scholars annually to pursue research projects of their own choosing. He also collaborated with the University of Pittsburgh to build the first industrial cyclotron in the United States. Condon then turned his attention to a mathematical game called "nim," which was played by many mathematicians and engineers at Westinghouse. Under his supervision they built the world's first electronic digital computer to play the game against human challengers. The computer, called the Nimatron, beat all comers at the New York World's Fair.

In the 1940's, government-sponsored defense research began to dominate programs at Westinghouse and elsewhere. Condon's research focused on the development of airborne microwave radar, and he was a key consultant on many projects. He joined the National Defense Research Committee (NDRC) in 1941 and served on its secret S-1 committee to study the control of nuclear fission. Condon was also one of the founding group of the Radiation Laboratory at MIT. J. Robert Oppenheimer, director of the Los Alamos Scientific Laboratory, appointed Condon associate director in 1943 to further the Manhattan District Project, which was developing the atomic bomb. At its Los Alamos, N.Mex., facility, Condon contributed to staffing and organizational needs, and he solved an important isotope separation problem by applying electromagnetic principles.

The power and importance of nuclear energy held the world's attention in 1945, and Condon publicly expressed his opinion that nuclear energy should remain under civilian control. This position was vigorously opposed by certain military and political factions. When Condon was nominated as director of the National Bureau of Standards (NBS) he was confirmed by a comfortable margin, but the debates that surfaced hinted at the developing bitter controversy.

Condon also became adviser to the Senate Committee on Atomic Energy that year. The committee was considering bills to establish a national system for the control of civilian and military uses of nuclear energy. Condon and Senator Brien McMahon supported legislation that established civilian control under the Atomic Energy Commission. The following year, Condon became president of the American Physical Society.

In 1948, the House Un-American Activities Committee chaired by J. Parnell Thomas released a report calling Condon a security risk. Administration hearings found no basis for doubts about Condon's loyalty but congressional enemies of the administration did not retract their accusations. Condon's requests for a congressional hearing to reply to accusations against him went unanswered.

When President Harry Truman addressed the American Association for the Advancement of Science (AAAS) in September 1948, he defended the role of independent scientists in shaping government policy and decried the current atmosphere of suspicion and vilification. Condon survived the challenges of his loyalty and re-

mained at the NBS. While there, he established an applied mathematics division that worked on the development of electronic digital computers.

Condon became Director of Research at Corning Glass Works in 1951 and served as president of the AAAS in 1953. Corning Glass Works held contracts for government defense research, and the issue of Condon's security clearance resurfaced, perhaps because of administration changes in Washington. After Condon's clearance was renewed in 1954 by the Eastern Industrial Security Board, Secretary of the Navy Charles Thomas requested that the decision be reconsidered. Thomas reportedly acted on the request of Vice-President Richard Nixon. Condon, doubting the possibility of fair treatment, withdrew his application for clearance, resigned his position at Corning and sought work free of political controversy.

After teaching at Oberlin College and the University of Pennsylvania Condon became, in 1956, professor and chairman of physics at Washington University in St. Louis. He was editor of the *Reviews of Modern Physics* from 1957 to 1968. Condon edited, with Hugh Odishaw, the *Handbook of Physics* in 1958. In 1963, he moved to the University of Colorado as professor of physics and fellow of the Joint Institute for Laboratory Astrophysics.

In 1966, the University of Colorado named Condon head of a project for the U.S. Air Force to study unidentified flying objects. The final report in 1969 concluded that there was insufficient objective evidence to justify further effort and expense on investigating phenomena that were largely explained by natural causes and by fraud.

Condon was elected president of the American Association of Physics Teachers in 1964 and president of the Society for Social Responsibility in Science in 1968 and 1969. He retired in 1970 and died in Boulder, Colo.

[See Grace Marmor Spruch, "Reporter Edward Condon," *Saturday Review*, Feb. 1, 1969; and Wesley E. Brittin and Halis Odabasi, eds., *Topics in Modern Physics: A Tribute to Edward U. Condon* (1971). Obituaries appear in the *New York Times*, Mar. 27, 1974; and *Physics Today*, June 1974.]

MICHAEL F. HAINES

CONNOR, THEOPHILUS ("BULL") EUGENE (July 11, 1897–Mar. 10, 1973), police commissioner and politician, was born in

Selma, Ala., the son of Molly Godwin and King Edward Connor, a railroad dispatcher. Because his father's work required travel, the family moved in 1905 to Atlanta, Ga., where his mother died four months after giving birth to the family's fifth child. Although Connor traveled widely with his father, he lived with relatives in Birmingham, where he attended school and where he lost the sight of one eye in a boyhood accident. He never completed high school.

In 1916 he met Beara Levens in Plantersville, Ala.; the two were married in 1920. Connor took a job as a railroad telegrapher, and he and his wife moved frequently as he sought better employment. In Dallas, Tex., in 1921, he successfully filled in for a sick announcer to do a "baseball matinee," the re-creation of a baseball game transmitted over the telegraph wires. He was a hit, and in 1922 he returned to Birmingham and began re-creating the games of the Birmingham Barons in the Southern League. His powerful voice earned him the nickname "Bull."

In 1934 he won election to the Alabama legislature and earned a reputation as a fierce debater and reformer, gaining the friendship and support of the county's most important Democrat, State Senator James A. Simpson. In 1937 he was elected commissioner of public safety in Birmingham. He was most interested in crime control, and he firmly enforced segregation laws. In 1938 he prevented the integrated meeting of the Southern Conference for Human Welfare in Birmingham despite the fact that First Lady Eleanor Roosevelt was among the attendees. He told the meeting: "Negroes and whites would not segregate together" in Birmingham.

In 1948 he became a delegate to the Democratic National Convention, at first supporting Harry Truman, but then changing his mind because of the president's civil rights position. At the convention he was part of the Dixiecrat walkout, carrying the Alabama state standard on his way out of the hall. When the Progressive party candidate, Senator Glen H. Taylor of Idaho, ignored a city ordinance and attempted to address an integrated audience in Birmingham, Connor had him arrested.

In 1950 Connor ran in the Democratic primary for governor. He came in sixth in a field of fifteen, running on an anti-Communist, anti–civil rights platform. In 1951 he was found in a hotel room with his secretary and was convicted on a morals charge, which was later overturned on appeal by the Alabama Supreme Court. The scandal convinced him not to run for reelection as police commissioner in 1953, however, and he departed the office after having served sixteen years.

For a year Connor was proprietor of a service station. In 1954 he ran against a popular incumbent for county sheriff and lost badly. In 1956 he lost the race for Birmingham commissioner of public improvements. He was again a delegate to the Democratic National Convention, and this time he supported the ticket. In 1957 he was reelected to the post of commissioner of public safety, emphasizing a position he would espouse the rest of his career. He promised to protect the city from outside agitators creating racial unrest. In 1960 he was elected national Democratic party committeeman from Alabama.

In the late 1950's the activism of Birmingham blacks led by Fred L. Shuttlesworth, Jr., resulted in a stern response from Connor against demonstrators but little protection for blacks from bombings and other violence. During the 1960's Connor attempted to enforce Birmingham's antiblack code and in the process became the individual who most symbolized diehard southern opposition to integration. In 1961 Connor was reelected commissioner of public safety by the widest margin of his career.

On May 14, 1961, a mob attacked freedom riders in the Birmingham bus station. The police response was tepid, and the resulting negative national publicity began to cause city leaders to back off from their support of Connor. As community moderates sought to avoid racial confrontation, Connor grew increasingly inflexible. In 1962 he ran for governor and came in fifth out of seven candidates, but this defeat did not moderate his tough antisegregationist stance. Neither did the replacement of the commission form of government by a new mayor-council format. Despite his active campaigning for the old system, Connor ran for mayor in the new government. He was defeated again. He remained as police commissioner, however, until court action could determine exactly when the new mayor-council form of government was to take effect.

When demonstrators protested, from April to May of 1963, against segregation and the imprisonment of Martin Luther King, Jr., in Birmingham, Connor used fire hoses and police dogs against them to the horror of a nationwide television audience. On May 23, 1963, the Alabama Supreme Court ruled that the mayor-council form of government was valid and ordered Connor and the other commissioners to vacate office immediately. Under a new administrator, lunch counters were desegregated by July 30, 1963, as the city attempted to moderate its harsh image.

Connor continued to speak out against integration while a private citizen. He condemned the September 1965 bombing of a church that killed four black girls, but he continued to defend his record and tactics. In 1964 he ran for the Alabama Public Service Commission and won a narrow victory in a runoff. In December 1966 he suffered a crippling stroke but ran again successfully for reelection in 1968 and attended the 1968 Democratic National Convention. He lost reelection to the Public Service Commission in 1972.

At the height of Connor's anti–civil rights activities, the Apr. 15, 1963, issue of *Newsweek* reported Connor to be "as much a giant in Birmingham as the cast iron statue of Vulcan, god of the forge, atop Red Mountain just outside town. Both are monuments—Vulcan to the city's steel economy and Connor to her standing as the biggest, toughest citadel of segregation left in the Deep South." Referring to the galvanizing effect that Connor's resistance to integration had on the nation, President John F. Kennedy said of him, "The Civil Rights movement should thank God for Bull Connor. He's helped it as much as Abraham Lincoln." Connor died in Birmingham.

[Connor's papers are located in the Birmingham Public Library. There is a vertical file on Connor in the Alabama Department of Archives and History in Montgomery. A thorough and readable biography is William A. Nunnelley, *Bull Connor* (1991). Obituaries appear in the *New York Times*, Mar. 11, 1973; the *Montgomery Advertiser*, Mar. 11, 1973; and the *Washington Post*, Mar. 12, 1973.]

JOHN F. MARSZALEK

CONSIDINE, ROBERT ("BOB") BERNARD (Nov. 4, 1906–Sept. 25, 1975), newspaper columnist, writer, and radio and television personality, was born in Washington, D.C., the son of James Considine, a tinsmith, and Sophie Small. He attended Gonzaga High School, but did not graduate. He went on to work as a messenger for the Census Bureau and then the Bureau of Public Health. Later he became a typist in the Treasury Department and, in 1927, a clerk in the Department of State. During these years he took evening courses in journalism and short-story writing at George Washington University in order to pursue a career as a writer.

It was through an early enthusiasm for tennis that Considine began his career as a newspaperman. When in 1927 his name was misspelled in the *Washington Herald's* account of a tennis match, he went to the sports editor to complain and was hired to contribute occasional tennis articles. In 1929 he began to write a weekly tennis column for the *Washington Post*. Four years later Considine joined the *Washington Herald*, where he was sports editor briefly before being discharged and told to "stick to writing." On July 21, 1931, Considine married Mildred Anderson; they had four children. During the mid-1930's he covered the Washington Senators baseball team for the *Herald*, wrote some editorials, and did a series of daily short stories on government clerks entitled "Uncle Sam's Children." In 1933 Considine started what was to become a well-known sports column, "On the Line."

In 1937 William Randolph Hearst hired Considine to work for the *American*, but later that year he was transferred to another Hearst newspaper, the *New York Daily Mirror*. At that time, International News Service (INS), a Hearst syndicate, took over half of Considine's contract and distributed his column nationally. "On the Line" often appeared in the *American* in the space formerly occupied by a column written by Damon Runyon, who had been transferred to another position. Considine believed that the placement of "On the Line" in Runyon's spot got his column "off to a start" in New York. Soon he was assigned to cover stories other than sporting events, including the trial in 1938 of New York politician James J. Hines, who had allegedly sabotaged and intimidated members of the National Electrical Manufacturers Association. By 1942 Considine was writing exclusively for INS.

During World War II, Considine was assigned to England, where he reported on the preparations for the Normandy invasion and on the activities of the Eighth Air Force. He also covered the North Africa campaign and after V-E Day was assigned to the China-Burma-

India theater. In later years, Considine reported on both the Korean and Vietnam wars. During the postwar years, Considine covered many important domestic and international events. He accompanied Presidents Eisenhower, Kennedy, Johnson, and Nixon on their international travels, including Nixon's historic trips to China and the Soviet Union. Among Considine's other notable assignments were the execution of Julius and Ethel Rosenberg, the trial of Jack Ruby, the death and funeral of Pope Pius XII, and the Bikini Island hydrogen bomb tests. One of Considine's most heralded achievements was gaining an exclusive interview with Soviet Premier Nikita Khrushchev in 1957. Along with "Hearst Task Force" members William R. Hearst, Jr., and Frank Conniff, he interviewed the Russian leader for four hours and then worked thirteen hours at his typewriter without a break, producing forty pages of copy.

In the course of his career, Considine wrote, coauthored, or edited more than twenty-five books. During World War II, he coauthored with Ted W. Lawson the best-selling book *Thirty Seconds Over Tokyo* (1943), an account of Lt. Col. James Doolittle's 1942 air raid on Japan. He also wrote a wartime biography of General Douglas MacArthur, *MacArthur the Magnificent* (1942). Considine's writing interests ranged from sports (*The Babe Ruth Story*, 1948), written with Babe Ruth; to crime (*The Men Who Robbed Brink's*, 1961); to fire insurance (*Man Against Fire*, 1955); to anti-Communism (*The Red Plot Against America*, 1949), written with Robert E. Stripling. In 1967 he wrote his autobiography, *It's All News to Me*.

Considine also found time to produce a number of screenplays, which were made into Hollywood films. Among the most successful were *Ladies Day* (1942), *Thirty Seconds Over Tokyo* (1944), *The Beginning of the End* (1947), *The Babe Ruth Story* (1948), and *Hoodlum Empire* (1952). Considine was also active in radio and television broadcasting, beginning as the *Washington Post*'s first nightly newscaster in 1932. For many years he did a fifteen-minute widely syndicated weekly radio show for NBC, "On the Line with Bob Considine." He was also a regular participant on the television news show "America After Dark."

Considine's speed, accuracy, and concentration as a writer and his seemingly inexhaustible energy were legendary in the newspaper profes-

sion. He was known to work at two typewriters at one time, writing a news story on one and a column or book on the other. His colleagues at the *Washington Post* recalled that he wrote a column on the 1942 World Series in nine minutes—on a train with his typewriter on a baggage car and the conductor shouting, "All aboard." During his career he received numerous awards and honors, including two awards from the Overseas Press Club, for his interview with Khrushchev (1957) and for coverage of the death and funeral of Pope Pius XII (1959). In his final column in 1975, Considine wrote: "I'll croak in the newspaper business. Is there any better way to go?" He died in New York City.

[In addition to the books cited in the text, Considine wrote *Innocents at Home* (1950), *The Maryknoll Story* (1950), *The Panama Canal* (1951), *It's the Irish* (1961), and *The Remarkable Life of Armand Hammer* (1975). For biographical information see *Saturday Review of Literature*, Jan. 21, 1950; *New York Times*, May 15, 1960; *Saturday Review*, Oct. 28, 1961; and *Variety*, Oct. 29, 1969. Obituaries are in the *New York Times* and the *Washington Post*, both Sept. 26, 1975.]

JOHN M. CARROLL

CONTE, RICHARD (Mar. 24, 1916–Apr. 15, 1975), film and television actor, was born Nicholas Peter Conte in Jersey City, N.J., the son of Pasquale Conte, a barber, and Julia Fina, a homemaker. Conte was educated in public schools and graduated from Dickinson High School. After graduation, he worked at a number of jobs, including Wall Street messenger and pianist in a swing band. In the summer of 1935, Conte was waiting tables at a Connecticut resort when his employer insisted that he take part in the resort's amateur stage production. Reluctantly, Conte agreed to take the acting assignment in order to keep his job. It was a choice that changed his life. Attending one of the performances were several leaders of the renowned Group Theater in New York City, including Elia Kazan and Robert Lewis, who immediately offered Conte a scholarship to attend their acting workshops at the Neighborhood Playhouse in Manhattan. Conte laughed off the offer, saying he had little interest in the theater. His curiosity piqued, however, he attended the Group Theater's now-legendary performance of Clifford Odets's *Waiting for Lefty*—the first professional play he had ever seen—and was immediately transformed. "I don't know what happened to me," he later told the *New York Times*, "but I cried, and all of a sudden I wanted to be an actor more than anything else. I rushed backstage and asked them to give me another chance at the scholarship." Lewis happily complied, and Conte was on his way.

Conte became deeply committed to his newfound goal in life, gaining a reputation for taking the craft of acting seriously, which earned him high marks with theater directors and producers. After several years at the Neighborhood Playhouse in New York, he began to get roles off and on Broadway. His big break came with a significant part in the Broadway hit *Jason* (1942). Critic George Jean Nathan called Conte the outstanding young actor of the year, and other notices were equally glowing. He followed that success with a widely praised performance in another Broadway production, *The Family* (1943).

As his career was picking up speed, World War II began, and Conte was drafted into the army. His military duty consisted largely of serving in the entertainment corps, and he was released after less than a year because of medical problems. Twentieth Century–Fox signed him to a contract in 1943 and required only that he change his name to Conty, which was more clearly pronounceable and less ethnic. Conte compromised by changing his first name to Richard. He had his own reasons for changing his name—he hoped to avoid being typecast as a "Mediterranean type." His classic Italian features betrayed him, however, and Hollywood producers cast him accordingly. Conte did not complain; the roles were usually challenging, and the films were generally high-quality productions. Indeed, Conte rarely complained about anything. He gained a reputation as a hardworking, well-focused actor and was rewarded for his dependability. Only after he signed the lucrative Fox contract did he marry his sweetheart of several years, Ruth Strohm, a New York actress. They had one child.

Having started his film career during World War II, he found himself in a number of war films during his first years in Hollywood. His first major film, *Guadalcanal Diary* (1943), was well received and is considered to be several cuts above the usual World War II action movie; Conte's performance as Captain Davis received many plaudits. He next appeared in *A Bell for Adano* (1945), a film about Americans who capture an Italian town and make peace with the inhabitants. This well-crafted picture was immediately embraced by the American public because its uplifting end-of-the-war message.

A Walk in the Sun (1945), another war picture with an ensemble cast, had quite a different message. Lewis Milestone, who had directed the fiercely antiwar *All Quiet on the Western Front* (1930), delivered a less polemical view in *Walk in the Sun*, but the film directly challenged the celebratory view of war common in American cinematography. Conte played a wisecracking Italian-American soldier participating in the liberation of Italy. Unlike *Adano*, however, the film does not end in reconciliation: all that the Allies have won is a small farmhouse housing an assortment of Nazis, and the casualties on both sides are substantial. Although the critics praised the film's somber message, the public was more interested in healing the wounds of war than in circumspection.

After Conte turned in yet another effective and understated performance in Joseph Mankiewicz's crime thriller, *Somewhere in the Night* (1946), the studio heads at Fox decided to try him in more challenging roles. Their enthusiasm for Conte's work was no doubt heightened by the ever-increasing fan mail he was receiving as well as the generally successful track record of the films in which he appeared. In *Cry of the City* (1948), a gritty film noir directed by Robert Siodmak, Conte gave what was described as "a blood-chilling performance" in the role of a cynical, heartless criminal who is chased down by a police lieutenant, played by Victor Mature. The role gave Conte a chance to stretch beyond the generally upbeat characters he had played in the past.

Following the success of *Cry of the City*, Conte's status as a leading man was assured. For the next few years he continued to star in very good, although not quite great movies, most of which were successful at the box office. In *Call Northside 777* (1948), another crime thriller, Conte played a Polish American wrongly accused of murdering a policeman. In this film he turned in a performance that became his trademark—intensely focused with complex character shadings. Over the next few years Conte continued to appear in tough-minded, well-crafted crime films such as *Thieves' Highway* (1949), *The Sleeping City* (1950), *The Blue Gardenia* (1953), and *New York Confidential*

(1955). In all of them he played characters caught within moral dilemmas, whichever side of the law they happened to walk on.

In 1956, Conte asked for a change of pace and was given a part in the lighthearted domestic comedy *Full of Life*. Although he once again played an Italian, he was glad to have the opportunity to prove his skills as a comic actor. Appearing opposite Judy Holliday, he received wide praise for his effort, and the film was a box office smash. *Full of Life* marks both the pinnacle of Conte's career and its decline. Although he continued to take leading roles into the 1960's, none of the parts he was given matched the quality of those he had enjoyed in the past. In part, the fading of the crime drama left him without the roles for which he was noted, and he was not able to go much farther in comedy.

Just as Conte's career was slowing down, he and his wife divorced in 1963. During the 1960's, he picked up television parts, none of them very memorable. He also appeared in supporting roles in such films as *Who's Been Sleeping in My Bed* (1963), *Synanon* (1965), and *Hotel* (1967). Once, in 1969, he tried his hand at directing in the uninspiring *Operation Crossbow*. Fittingly, Francis Ford Coppola paid tribute to Conte's legacy in crime drama by casting him in the role of the mobster Don Barzini in *The Godfather* (1972). Conte married actress Shirley Colleen Garner in 1972. He died in Los Angeles.

[The Academy of Motion Pictures Library in Los Angeles maintains a substantial file on Conte. An extended interview, portraying him as a rising star, appears in the *New York Times*, Mar. 3, 1946. An obituary is in the *New York Times*, Apr. 16, 1975.]

MICHAEL GOLDBERG

COOLEY, HAROLD DUNBAR (July 26, 1897–Jan. 15, 1974), congressman, was born in Nashville, N.C., the son of Hattie Gertrude Davis and Roger Atkinson Pryor Cooley. His father, a lawyer, died when Cooley was nine and his mother when he was sixteen. The five orphaned Cooley children developed strong family ties, made even stronger after one of them, Hubert, died in an automobile accident. Cooley attended public schools in Nash County and, at age eighteen, decided to follow his father's footsteps by studying law. He attended the University of North Carolina Law School at

Chapel Hill for two years and was admitted to the bar in 1918.

Cooley enlisted in the United States Navy and was in ground training with the Naval Aviation Flying Corps in Massachusetts at the end of World War I. In 1919, he attended the Yale Law School as a special student and studied constitutional law under William Howard Taft. He then returned to Nashville and opened a law office. On June 30, 1923, he married Madeline Matilda Strickland, whom he had known since childhood. She was a graduate of the New England Conservatory and an accomplished pianist. They had two children. Until 1934, Cooley practiced law in Nashville and nearby counties. He was politically active on behalf of candidates of the Democratic party and served as a presidential elector in 1932.

Cooley was elected to Congress as a Democrat by special election in 1934 to fill the vacancy caused by the death of Edward W. Pou, who had represented North Carolina's Fourth District for thirty years. Cooley won a majority on the first primary ballot, even though there were five other Democratic contenders. He served in Congress from 1934 until January 1967.

As a freshman member of Congress, Cooley was appointed to the House Committee on Agriculture, and it is his service on this committee for which he is most remembered. He joined the committee during the development of the New Deal agricultural program and remained a lifelong advocate of its policies. Cooley became chairman of the committee in 1949, and except during the Eighty-third Congress (1953–1954), when a Republican majority controlled the House, he held this influential position for the remainder of his congressional career.

Cooley served on congressional subcommittees that studied world agricultural problems after World War II and led a six-week fact-finding mission to Europe in 1945. He was also a delegate to the Interparliamentary Union conferences held in Cairo (1947), Rome (1948), Stockholm (1949), and Dublin (1950), and he served as an adviser to the United Nations Education, Scientific and Cultural Organization.

In 1956, Cooley refused to sign the so-called Southern Manifesto criticizing the Supreme Court's school desegregation decision. The manifesto was endorsed by more than one hundred senators and representatives from eleven southern states, but Cooley explained that he thought the document would aggravate an already dangerous situation. Of the three North Carolina Democrats who refused to sign the manifesto, only Cooley survived the primary election, and he won after making strong segregationist statements. He responded to his critics by saying, "It hardly seems necessary for me to tell you that I am and always have been opposed to mixing of the races in the public schools." He was still defending his stand on the manifesto ten years later in the 1966 campaign.

Early in the 1960's, Cooley used his influence to win approval of the Food for Freedom Program, which authorized the sale of surplus farm commodities in other countries. Cooley believed this would help people in poorer nations while providing an additional market for American agricultural goods.

Cooley was known for his oratorical ability and his political success was attributed partly to his friendly and courteous manner. He was also known as a fierce and partisan debater. As chairman of the House Agriculture Committee he was often embroiled in controversy. His opposition to proposals that threatened the New Deal farm-price-support program brought him into conflict with secretaries of agriculture in both the Truman and the Eisenhower administrations.

Cooley was also involved in controversy over import quotas for foreign sugar producers. In 1960, in a fierce battle between the House and Senate, Cooley was forced to retreat from his opposition to reductions in the Cuban sugar quota, but succeeded in limiting the reductions his opponents pushed through.

A front-page story in the New York Times in 1962 charged that Cooley was mentioned "again and again" in the "secret papers" of the late dictator of the Dominican Republic, Generalissimo Rafael Leónidas Trujillo Molina. The newspaper reported that Dominican agents said Cooley assured them he would support Dominican sugar interests and gave them advice about their lobbying activities. Cooley issued a lengthy statement denying that his conduct had been in any way improper or that he had shown any special favors to the Dominicans.

Cooley was especially known as a friend to tobacco farmers. The tobacco-farm program developed under Cooley's leadership of the House Agriculture Committee won him praise in his district and in other tobacco-growing areas. When the Federal Trade Commission pub-

lished its plan to require cigarette advertisements to carry warnings on the health dangers of tobacco in 1964, Cooley responded angrily, saying, "I think someone in the FTC must be emotionally disturbed."

Cooley was defeated for reelection in 1966, at age sixty-nine, resulting from changes in the demographic makeup of his district, which had shifted from primarily rural to primarily urban; a strong anti–Johnson administration backlash, revolving around civil rights issues, inflation, and the Vietnam War; and the youthfulness of his opponent, James C. Gardner. The Raleigh News and Observer noted that Cooley's defeat had reduced North Carolina's Democratic influence in Washington to its lowest point in the twentieth century. Cooley was the seventh-ranking House member in terms of seniority at the time of his defeat.

After leaving Congress, Cooley resumed the practice of law in Nashville, N.C. He died at age seventy-six in Wilson, N.C., after having been hospitalized for several months with emphysema; he is buried in Nashville, N.C.

[Cooley's papers, comprising some 140,000 items, are in the Southern Historical Collection, University of North Carolina at Chapel Hill. An article written by Cooley (" 'I Can See Farm Bankruptcy' if Price Supports Are Removed") is in the U.S. News and World Report, Aug. 30, 1957. For information on the 1956 primary and 1966 general elections see The News and Observer, Raleigh, N.C., May 1956 and Nov. 1966, various issues, and "The South Tips Its Hand," U.S. News and World Report, June 8, 1956. Cooley's career is chronicled in numerous articles in the New York Times from 1934 to 1966; see particularly Apr. 9, 1956; July 4, 1960; July 3–4, 1962; and Nov. 9–10, 1966. From The Reporter see Douglas Cater and Walter Pincus, "Our Sugar Diplomacy," Apr. 13, 1961; "Sweet Talk," Sept. 9, 1965; and Julius Duscha, "Bailing out the Cotton Industry," May 5, 1966. See also Rowland Evans and Robert Novak, "The Yarmolinsky Affair," Esquire, Feb. 1965. Obituaries are in the New York Times and The News and Observer, both Jan. 16, 1974.]

ROBYN BURNETT

CORDIER, ANDREW WELLINGTON (Mar. 3, 1901–July 11, 1975), diplomat, educator, and university president, was born on a farm near Canton, Ohio, to Wellington J. Cordier and Ida Mae Anstine. After graduating from Hartville high school as both varsity quarterback and valedictorian, Cordier enrolled at Manchester College in Indiana. While working toward his B.A. degree (1922), he taught history, Latin, and math at Greentown High School. He then entered the University of Chicago, where he obtained both his M.A. (1923) and his Ph.D. (1926) in history. While associate professor of history at Manchester from 1923 to 1927, he married Dorothy Elizabeth Butterbough on May 23, 1926; they had two children. In 1927 Cordier became chairman of the department of history and political science at Manchester, a position he held until 1944. During his academic career he served as a Republican county leader and built a reputation as a foreign affairs expert who traveled widely to investigate crises as varied as the Chaco Wars in Paraguay and the Sudetenland crisis.

Although Cordier earlier participated in federal educational adult programs and the Office of Price Administration, his major government service began when he joined the U.S. State Department in 1944 as adviser on international security. He drafted preliminary versions of the United Nations Charter, served on the delegation to the San Francisco Conference (April 1945), and joined the Preparatory Commission for the United Nations in London; he also advised Senator Arthur Vandenberg on UN issues. In March 1946 Cordier accepted the position of executive assistant to UN secretary-general Trygve Lie with the rank of undersecretary. Cordier believed firmly that the $100 million spent to establish the world organization was the "best investment humanity has made" and as "chef de cabinet" for two secretaries-general became the model of the committed international civil servant. From 1946 to 1962 he was "the man to the left of the president," successively advising sixteen General Assembly leaders on procedure and precedents. Characterized as a "demon parliamentarian," Cordier also scheduled meetings, prepared the agenda, supervised UN staff, and mediated delegate disputes. Brian Urquhart remembered a great bear of a man, a "tough, bumbling figure who was always prepared to dive in, no matter how shallow the water." Beyond the Assembly, Cordier served Lie as special representative to Korea (1950–1952), and acted as Dag Hammarskjöld's envoy in the Mount Scopus affair (1958). During the period 1955–1957, he implemented Hammarskjöld's vision of a nonviolent international force to police Middle East battle zones (UNEF), and was instrumental in negotiating the agreement to clear the Suez Canal (1956). As the UN's rep-

resentative in the Congo in 1960, Cordier's strong action in closing airports remains controversial since it appeared to place the UN on one side of the murky conflict. He was a major player in the cadre that kept the UN functioning after Hammarskjöld's death, and later said that working for the secretary was his "richest personal experience."

In February 1962 Cordier left the UN to become dean of the School of International Affairs at Columbia University. He presided over a great expansion of SIA's faculty and students, and built an acclaimed fifteen-story building. Cordier's interest in architectural design and interior decoration allowed him to participate in modeling the structure, even as he had contributed to the shaping of the UN Secretariat. Late in the 1960's, student anger against the Vietnam War and a controversial gymnasium in a public park swept the Columbia campus and forced President Grayson Kirk into retirement. On Aug. 23, 1968, the university trustees asked the sixty-seven-year-old Cordier to become acting president while they searched for a successor. Over the next year, Cordier's diplomatic skills found a new arena as he worked twenty-hour days, proclaimed an open-door policy, isolated Columbia's radical fringe, allied himself with liberal reformers, and drew up plans for a university senate. He consulted all factions, noting that "it is almost impossible to listen to someone talk for two hours without finding something you can agree with," negotiated compromises, and after agreements were won "his word was always good." He told the graduates of 1969 that a university that "stands still is moving backwards" and pledged that a reemphasis on teaching combined with "freedom from disruptive tactics" would allow Columbia to prosper. The "Old Man" was cheered by all factions, the university senate declared he had "restored our faith in ourselves and the institution we cherish," and on Aug. 20, 1969, a grateful board of trustees made him Columbia's fifteenth president. He served only until September 1970 but continued to emphasize educational reform at Columbia while widening ties to the surrounding community. He dominated the new senate, often acting as "his own rule maker," but brought stability and calm after the tumult of 1968. In September 1970, he became president and trustee emeritus and returned to his deanship at the School of International Affairs.

Cordier's last years were full of accomplishment. As dean, he withstood a radical charge that SIA had ties to the CIA, and later offered a "Marshall Plan" of aid to Vietnam (1972). He chaired the UN Panel on a World University whose proposals were implemented by the General Assembly in December 1973. He edited two volumes on Hammarskjöld's career and led the team that issued eight volumes of Public Papers of the secretaries-general. Formally retired after June 1972, he nevertheless served as Director of Development for SIA and in the 1973–1974 academic year was Regents Professor at the University of California, Berkeley. At the time of his death, the workaholic Cordier was living in Great Neck, Long Island, working on his memoirs.

[Cordier's papers covering the period 1918–1975 are at Columbia University. Included is the draft of an unpublished biography by Doreen Geary, "Death of a Stalwart." A taste of Cordier's style is available in four videotapes he did for the USA–UNA, "World Without Borders," and his oral history at Columbia. An obituary is in the *New York Times*, July 13, 1975.]

GEORGE J. LANKEVICH

CORDINER, RALPH JARRON (Mar. 20, 1900–Dec. 5, 1973), industrialist and business executive, was born on a 1,280-acre wheat farm near Walla Walla, Wash., the son of George M. Cordiner and Mary Jarron. After attending local public schools, he entered the U.S. Navy and served for one year during World War I. Cordiner then enrolled in Whitman College in Walla Walla, where he majored in economics. He graduated with honors in 1922. While there he worked part time as a salesman of electrical appliances for Pacific Power and Light, which introduced him to both selling and the electric industry. Cordiner showed an aptitude for both, and upon graduation he sought and obtained a post as commercial manager for Pacific Power and Light in Walla Walla.

Shortly thereafter Cordiner married Gwyneth A. Lewis; they had four children.

Later in 1922, Cordiner went to work for the Edison General Electric Appliance Company, a General Electric affiliate, in Portland. In 1927, he became the company's manager for the Northwest region, and in 1930, the Pacific Coast manager (in San Francisco). In 1932, he moved to Bridgeport, Conn., where he was manager of the heating device section of the Appliance and Merchandise Division of General Electric and chairman of the Management Committee.

Cordiner became a protégé of Charles E. Wilson, a GE vice-president a few years his senior. His successes resulted in promotion to assistant manager of appliance sales in 1934. In 1935, Cordiner became manager of the Radio Division, and the following year returned to the Appliance and Merchandise Division, as assistant manager under Wilson.

In 1938, Wilson became executive vice-president of General Electric and heir apparent to President Gerard Swope. Cordiner then succeeded Wilson as head of the Appliance and Merchandise Division. Realizing that he would be destined to remain in Wilson's shadow, Cordiner in 1939 accepted the presidency of Schick, where he spent the next three years.

In December 1942, Wilson became vice-president of the War Production Board (WPB) and asked Cordiner to join him there. Cordiner became director general of war production scheduling and a year later advanced to the executive vice-chairmanship of the WPB. He remained in that post until June 1943. Rather than return to Schick, he became assistant to Wilson at General Electric and in 1945 was named vice-president. Among his duties was heading a task force to revamp the corporation to meet postwar requirements.

In 1949, Cordiner was elevated to the board of directors and was named executive vice-president, which placed him in line to succeed Wilson. In 1950, when Wilson was named by President Harry S. Truman to become director of the Office of Defense Mobilization, he was succeeded by Philip Reed, not Cordiner. In 1958, Reed stepped down, and Cordiner was elected chairman of the board and chief executive officer. He also served as president in 1961, until Gerald L. Philippe was elected to that office in August.

As CEO, Cordiner drew up a plan to decentralize management, out of which came the structure that served the company well until the 1980's, when it was reshaped by CEO Jack Welsh. More autonomy was granted to division managers, and in time to plant managers as well. Greater efficiencies were realized, but less direct control by headquarters had dire results in some areas.

One of Cordiner's less successful ventures involved a computer business acquired by Reed.

At the time General Electric was considered the most computerized company in the world and was one of IBM's major customers. Computers seemed a logical extension of General Electric's business, so in the early 1950's it produced some military items but hesitated to move into the civilian area. Cordiner believed the market for large mainframes was limited, that they were unprofitable, and that the product was bound to suffer when the country entered a recession he expected to hit in the late 1950's. He rejected the Computer Division's pleas for funding, used earnings to reduce debt, and as a result handed the company over to his successor, Frederick Broch, in fine financial shape. The end of General Electric's venture into computers came in 1970, when the operation was sold to Honeywell.

In 1960, the *Saturday Review* named Cordiner its "Businessman of the Year." In accepting the award, he spoke of the responsibilities of business, which of course included earning money to continue operations. But there were other considerations. "A company is likely to grow and earn profits if it recognizes the reality of the ethical and social demands of society, and considers them as valid elements in the economic decisions of business."

However, General Electric was involved in unethical practices of which Cordiner was unaware. In 1961, the government accused the firm and other electrical manufacturers of price fixing and market splitting through the use of rigged bids for contracts. Three General Electric managers were sent to jail, and the company had to pay fines of $437,000. "We were diligent in the light of the facts as we then knew them," said Cordiner, conceding that he should have known more of what was going on. "Why and how we failed has nothing to do with decentralization, in my opinion." He promised to take steps to ensure more monitoring. Nonetheless, there were calls for his resignation. Cordiner retired in 1963 and died in Clearwater, Fla.

[Some of Cordiner's views can be found in his book, *New Frontiers for Professional Managers* (1956). See "Cordiner Rides Out the Storm," *Business Week*, Apr. 29, 1961. Obituaries are in the *New York Times* and the *Washington Post*, both Dec. 6, 1973.]

ROBERT SOBEL

CORNELL, KATHARINE (Feb. 16, 1893– June 12, 1974), actress, producer, and theatrical manager, was born prematurely in Berlin, Germany, the only child of Peter Cortelyn Cornell, a physician, and Alice Gardner Plimpton, socially prominent residents of Buffalo, N.Y. They returned there in July 1893.

In 1901, Dr. Cornell ceased practicing medicine to co-own and manage a local theater. Young Katharine's desire to devote her life to the stage came after seeing Maude Adams fly as Peter Pan in 1907 and watching, "day in and day out," actress/manager Jessie Bonstelle's rehearsals for summer-stock seasons at her father's theater. Bonstelle encouraged her and later offered Cornell her first acting opportunities.

Sent to Oaksmere finishing school, in Mamaroneck, N.Y., fifteen-year-old Katharine was an active athlete and wrote, directed, and acted in school plays. In her final year, Oaksmere presented a new play every two weeks, coached by professionals from New York. Director Edward Goodman of the Washington Square Players invited Cornell to contact him in Manhattan. Shy and insecure, she was slow to pick up the cue.

Graduating in 1911, Cornell toured Europe with an aunt, returning to Oaksmere to coach drama and athletics for five years. Financially independent at her mother's death in 1915, she moved to New York City with her aunt, attending rehearsals and understudying at the Washington Square Players. In her New York "debut" at twenty-three (in November 1916), substituting for a sick actress, she spoke four words in *Bushido*. She acted minor roles for two years, the Players paying her $40 for the 1917–1918 season. Then Jessie Bonstelle offered thirty-two weeks of stock, acting small parts at $50 per week, the first of three seasons doing a new play every week in Detroit and Buffalo that Cornell later credited with giving her discipline and teaching her the business.

After the first summer, Bonstelle got Cornell an audition as a replacement in the third road company of *The Man Who Came Back*. Always poor at sight-reading, she was allowed a week's rehearsal with the stage manager, but after auditioning, was asked to play the same day's matinee (Jan. 1, 1919); the sudden assignment may have overcome the extreme nervousness before a performance that plagued Cornell all her life; in any case, she "loved" her first touring experience.

Following a second stock season, Bonstelle cast her as Jo in a British production of *Little*

Women: Cornell's much-praised London debut was Nov. 20, 1919. Then back to Detroit, alternating with Bonstelle as leading woman in her third stock season, for which Guthrie McClintic had been hired as director. He replaced Bonstelle as Cornell's artistic mentor, and they fell in love.

Cornell attracted good notices in her first Broadway role in Rachel Crothers's *Nice People* (Mar. 2, 1921). She married Guthrie McClintic on Sept. 8, 1921, five days after she left *Nice People* and one day before beginning rehearsals as Sydney Fairfield in A *Bill of Divorcement* (opened on Oct. 10, 1921), which brought her rave reviews and her first long run.

Barred from stereotypical ingénue roles by dark exotic looks and a strong stage presence, Cornell was cast as unconventional, passionate women, often in shocking or sordid stories, beginning as a degraded drug addict in *The Man Who Came Back*. In 1923, she played hoydenish Mary Fitton, the "dark lady" in *Will Shakespeare* (January 1), inhibited Laura Pennington in *The Enchanted Cottage* (March 31), and both the libertine's mistress and her own daughter in *Casanova* (September 26). In 1924, she portrayed a "pathological psychology" in *The Way Things Happen* directed by McClintic (January 28), then a painfully crippled girl and "a horrible woman" in other brief runs. Meantime, with the noncommercial Actor's Theatre, she revealed a lighter side as Shaw's *Candida* (December 12). The special matinees drew critical acclaim and popular demand, prompting a five-month commercial run. Eugene Speicher painted her famous portrait in this role she would later revive.

"Carnal, doomed" Iris March in Michael Arlen's sensational *The Green Hat* (1925) returned her to the "tarnished ladies" in "trash of a violent kind" who brought her early fame and popularity; similar sensations followed in *The Letter* (1927), *The Age of Innocence* (1928), and *Dishonored Lady* (1930).

In 1930, as a directing gift for McClintic, Cornell acquired Rudolf Besier's *The Barretts of Wimpole Street*, profoundly altering their lives. Her longtime friend Stanton Griffis decided that Cornell should produce *Barretts* herself. With fellow-admirer A. Conger Goodyear, Griffis, who was a stockbroker, invested $27,000 to form Cornell and McClintic Productions, Inc., asking only for this original amount if *Barretts* succeeded, but requiring all profits to be used

exclusively for future C. & M.C. productions. Cornell's personal factotum Gertrude Macy, named General Manager, bought 10 percent of the company for $3,000. Cornell's Elizabeth Barrett was universally praised, Brooks Atkinson noting that "the disciplined fury that she has been squandering on catch-penny plays [here] becomes the vibrant beauty of finely-wrought character."

Cornell, directed by McClintic, began a new career as the last great actress/manager in the American theater. Over twenty-nine years, a span exceeded only by the Theatre Guild and the Shuberts, Cornell and McClintic mounted twenty-four productions in New York City and revived "the road" through nationwide tours. The McClintics lived at Beekman Place in New York City, later moving across the Hudson to the New Jersey Palisades.

Cornell's most extraordinary tour came in 1933 and 1934: covering more than 16,000 miles, playing to half a million people in seventy-seven cities, giving 225 performances in twenty-nine weeks, divided among *The Barretts*, *Candida*, and *Romeo and Juliet*. Then, in New York (from Dec. 20, 1934), each play was given a limited run; *Saint Joan* (from Mar. 9, 1936) completed this remarkable sequence.

Cornell often toured either after Broadway runs or before opening in New York. Among the memorable roles she played were the tragic Oparre in *The Wingless Victory* (1936), Linda Esterbrook in *No Time for Comedy* (1939), Jennifer Dubedat in *The Doctor's Dilemma* (1941), and Masha in *The Three Sisters* (1942). She toured *The Barretts* for U.S. troops in World War II (August 1944–February 1945), bringing it back to Broadway in March. She starred in Anouilh's modern *Antigone* (1946), *Antony and Cleopatra* (1947), *The Prescott Proposals* (1953), and *The Dark Is Light Enough* (1955). Cornell made two television appearances: in *The Barretts of Wimpole Street* (Producers Showcase, NBC, 1956) and *There Shall Be No Night* (Hallmark Hall of Fame, NBC, 1957). On film, she appeared briefly in *Stage Door Canteen* (1943) and narrated the documentary *Helen Keller in Her Story* (1954). She recorded *Sonnets from the Portuguese* and *The Barretts of Wimpole Street* for Caedmon Records. Her awards include the New York Drama League Medal (1935) and the AWTA Award (1974).

After the 1951 Broadway revival and tour of *The Constant Wife*, its highest-grossing and last success, the corporation's money was exhausted by a series of box-office failures. Cornell last appeared as Mrs. Patrick Campbell in *Dear Liar* (two tours and Broadway, 1959 and 1960). Guthrie McClintic died on Oct. 29, 1961, and Cornell never returned to work. She died at age eighty-one at her home, "Chip Chop," on Martha's Vineyard.

Of several actresses dubbed "First Lady of the American Theater," Katharine Cornell most clearly earned and deserved the title, first bestowed on her by Alexander Woollcott.

[The Cornell/McClintic archives are in the Billy Rose Theatre Collection in the New York Public Library for the Performing Arts, located at Lincoln Center for the Performing Arts; some manuscripts are at Smith College and SUNY, Buffalo. Cornell published two autobiographies: *I Wanted To Be an Actress*, as told to Ruth Sedgewick (1938); and *Curtain Going Up*, as told to Gladys Malvern (1943). Guthrie McClintic, *Me and Kit* (1955), gives alternative versions of many events. The most detailed biography is Tad Mosel, *Leading Lady* (1978), written with Gertrude Macy; a scholarly study is offered by Lynda T. Moss, *A Historical Study of Katharine Cornell as an Actress and Manager, 1931–1960* (Ph.D. diss., University of Southern California, 1974). Lewis Funke and J. E. Booth, *Actors Talk About Acting* (1961), contains an interview with Cornell and McClintic.

An obituary appears in the *New York Times*, June 10, 1974.]

DANIEL S. KREMPEL

CORRELL, CHARLES JAMES (Feb. 2, 1890–Sept. 26, 1972), radio comedian and creator with Freeman Gosden of "Amos 'n' Andy," was born in Peoria, Ill., the son of Joseph Boland Correll, a bricklayer, and Julia A. Fiss (there are some inconsistencies about his mother's first name). He grew up in a stable, working-class family, and while still in school he worked as an usher in a local vaudeville house and developed an interest in show business. After graduating from public high school in Peoria in 1907, he entered his father's trade. In his spare time, he played piano in Peoria's silent movie houses and sang, danced, and took small parts in local shows.

In 1918, after being noticed by the director of a local show, Correll was offered a job with the Joe Bren Producing Company of Chicago. Bren specialized in producing minstrel shows as fund-raisers for charitable groups in small cit-

ies. For the next six years, Correll traveled the country, directing productions for Bren. In 1920, in Durham, N.C., he met Freeman Gosden, who had just been hired by Bren and was to be trained by Correll. The two became friends, often sharing an apartment during summers when both were in Chicago, preparing for the next season. In 1924, both were brought to Bren's home office in Chicago, Gosden to manage Bren's new circus division and Correll to manage the shows division.

Once again sharing an apartment, Correll and Gosden began to write musical reviews together, and they worked up a "song and chatter" act. In March 1925, they began eight months of weekly appearances on radio station WEBH in Chicago. Soon they were appearing in shows and on radio programs in St. Louis; Columbus, Ohio; and other cities in the Midwest. During the summer of 1925, they resigned from the Bren Company and began concentrating on a career in vaudeville. However, the *Chicago Tribune*'s radio station offered them $200 per week, and in November 1925, they began a series of nightly broadcasts on WGN.

At the suggestion of the station's management, Correll and Gosden used their experiences with minstrel shows to work up a "radio comic strip" about two African Americans and on Jan. 12, 1926, "Sam 'n' Henry" began nightly ten-minute broadcasts on WGN. The show was an immediate hit. In 1928, however, the *Chicago Daily News* lured Correll and Gosden away from WGN, although the *Chicago Tribune* retained all rights to "Sam 'n' Henry" and continued broadcasting the show with two new men.

On Mar. 19, 1928, Correll and Gosden began broadcasting on the *Chicago Daily News*'s radio station, WMAQ. Six nights a week they presented a fifteen-minute show about two African-American men living in Harlem. "Amos 'n' Andy" focused on the misadventures of Amos Jones, played by Freeman Gosden as energetic, enterprising, and honest, and Andrew H. Brown, played by Correll as indolent but good-hearted. Gradually the team added characters, but until the 1940's all the writing and voices were done by Correll and Gosden. No one seems to have been bothered by having two white men performing all the parts in a story line with all African-American characters.

The show was a huge success, and with the help of the *Tribune*'s publicity staff, in 1929

Correll and Gosden wrote a book (*All About Amos 'n' Andy and Their Creators Correll and Gosden*) to satisfy listeners' curiosity. Within a short time NBC offered Correll and Gosden $100,000 per year, and on Aug. 19, 1929, Pepsodent toothpaste began sponsoring "Amos 'n' Andy" on the NBC Red network.

"Amos 'n' Andy" was network radio's first huge success. Within a few years, Correll and Gosden moved to California, where they appeared in movies (*Check and Double Check* in 1930 and *The Big Broadcast of 1936*), published books of "Amos 'n' Andy" dialogue, and lived the life of Hollywood stars. Despite protests about the racial stereotyping of "Amos 'n' Andy," especially from the African-American press, Correll and Gosden's show remained popular throughout the Great Depression and into the 1940's. Short, stocky, and dark-haired (later gray-haired), Correll became the relaxed, gregarious half of the partnership, balancing Freeman Gosden's more temperamental, difficult, and creative personality.

Correll enjoyed his success. He bought a large, lavish home in Beverly Hills; he indulged in expensive and stylish clothes, and became an enthusiastic golfer. After a divorce from Marie Janes, whom he had married in 1927, he married Alyce Mercedes McLaughlin, a dancer, in 1937. They had four children.

With the advent of World War II, listenership began to drop. In February 1943, after changing networks and sponsors several times, "Amos 'n' Andy" left the air. In October it returned as a half-hour weekly variety program featuring guest stars, an orchestra, outside writers, and a studio audience. This show continued on NBC until 1948, when Correll and Gosden, along with Jack Benny and other stars, left NBC. For $2.5 million Correll and Gosden sold CBS all the rights to Amos and Andy for the next twenty years; they also received star salaries to play the chief parts.

Within a few years, television ended the success of their variety show, but from 1954 to 1960, Correll and Gosden stayed on CBS radio with a new show, "The Amos and Andy Music Hall," mixing skits with popular records. On Nov. 25, 1960, they left the air permanently.

In the mid-1950's, CBS developed a television situation comedy based on the Amos and Andy characters. Correll and Gosden were creative consultants, but the cast was entirely African American. The show had modest success

with audiences, but it was embroiled in constant racial controversy. The National Association for the Advancement of Colored People protested the show vehemently, and the cast had frequent problems with the scripts. Neither Correll nor Gosden was prepared for the bitterness that the television show engendered, and both men, especially Gosden, felt deeply wounded by some accusations.

After the television series ended and their last radio show was over, Correll and Gosden remained friends, living near each other in Beverly Hills, Calif. Correll continued to maintain his midwestern roots and returned to Chicago, where he died.

[The bulk of Correll's papers are in the Cinema-Television Library and Archives of Performing Arts at the Doheny Library, University of Southern California. The authoritative study of Correll, Gosden, Amos, and Andy is Melvin Patrick Ely, *The Adventure of Amos 'n' Andy* (1991). Gosden, Correll, and "Amos and Andy" have been the subjects of much scholarly and popular interest. There is an excellent brief survey of that literature, especially concerning racial controversies, in Thomas Allen Greenfield, *Radio: A Reference Guide* (1989).
See also John Dunning, *Tune in Yesterday* (1976); and Arthur Frank Wertheim, *Radio Comedy* (1979). An obituary is in the *New York Times*, Sept. 27, 1972.]

NICHOLAS A. SHARP

COSTELLO, FRANK (Jan. 26, 1891–Feb. 18, 1973), racketeer, was born Francesco Castiglia in the hill town of Lauropoli in the Italian province of Calabria. His family immigrated to the United States when he was four and settled in East Harlem, one of New York City's poorest and most crowded sections. Frank quit school in the fifth grade. As a teenager he was arrested several times for robbery and assault; his first conviction came at the age of twenty-two, when he was sentenced to one year for carrying a concealed firearm; he served ten months of the sentence. In 1914 Costello met and married Loretta ("Bobbie") Geigerman; they did not have any children.

By the mid-1920's he was a successful bootlegger, bringing liquor into the United States from Canada across the Great Lakes. After Prohibition he developed a slot machine empire that won him the title King of the Slots. When New York City mayor Fiorello La Guardia ordered a crackdown on the machines, Costello moved his operation to New Orleans. He also owned one of Manhattan's most famous nightclubs, the Copacabana, and was a partner in several seasonal gambling casinos known as "carpet joints" in Saratoga, N.Y.; Hot Springs, Ark.; greater New Orleans; and southern Florida. His partners included Meyer Lansky and Charles ("Lucky") Luciano. When the latter went to prison in 1936, Costello's importance in the Luciano crime network expanded.

Newspapers called Costello the prime minister of the underworld because his criminal specialty was political influence. His role in New York's Democratic organization became apparent in 1943, when investigators working for Manhattan District Attorney Frank S. Hogan wiretapped Costello's telephone and heard him talking to Thomas A. Aurelio, a candidate for the Democratic nomination for a judgeship. "When I tell you something is in the bag, you can rest assured," Costello told him. Aurelio responded: "I want to assure you of my loyalty for all you have done; it's undying." Aurelio did obtain the nomination and, despite the disclosure of his conversation with Costello, became a judge.

The following year Costello left $27,200 in cash in a New York taxi and created a sensation when he sent his lawyer to retrieve it from the police. Mayor La Guardia tried to block the money's return, and litigation ensued. Costello was able to prove legal title to the money, but the Internal Revenue Service intervened and he recovered only a fraction.

Costello was largely successful in using cash from his rackets to buy political influence, which he used in turn to nurture his rackets, because he disdained drug dealing and unnecessary violence. His name frequently appeared in newspaper gossip columns, and his daily routine was well known: mornings holding court in the barbershop of the Waldorf-Astoria Hotel; afternoons in the steam room of the Biltmore Hotel; evenings dining out with his wife at a number of better midtown restaurants. A clothes horse, he resisted his lawyer's entreaties to dress modestly when appearing in court.

In 1949 he organized a dinner at the Copacabana that raised $10,000 for the Salvation Army. Guests included a congressman, eight judges, and the Manhattan borough president.

By 1950 Costello was one of the nation's most notorious gangsters. *Time* magazine reported that millions of Americans considered him to be "a kind of master criminal, shadowy as a ghost, and cunning as Satan, who ruled a vast, mysterious and malevolent underworld, and laughed lazily at the law." In 1951 Costello was subpoenaed to appear before Senator Estes Kefauver's Senate committee on organized crime, which described him as "a political boss and an underworld emperor." The hearings were televised, but at the insistence of Costello's lawyer, the mobster's face was not shown. Instead the camera focused on his hands, which twisted nervously as he evaded questions or denied insinuations. Equally memorable was his voice, a gravelly rumble that resulted from a throat operation years earlier. He was found guilty of contempt of the Senate for refusing to answer questions and served fourteen months in prison.

In 1954 Costello was sentenced to five years for tax evasion after IRS agents found a $51,095 discrepancy between expenditures and reported income over a four-year period. Costello served eleven months in the federal penitentiary in Atlanta, but the conviction was eventually overturned in 1956 on the grounds that it was based on illegal wiretaps.

Meanwhile, Costello was being challenged by Vito Genovese for primacy in Luciano's crime family. Several organized crime historians have speculated that Costello's fortunes declined along with the health of Willie Moretti, a Costello ally who commanded a squad of thugs. On the evening of May 2, 1957, Costello was walking through the lobby of his New York City apartment building, the Majestic, when a man wearing a large hat approached him, said, "This is for you, Frank," and fired a revolver at Costello's face from a distance of less than ten feet. The bullet hit Costello in the head, but caused only a superficial wound. Asked later who shot him, Costello replied, "I didn't see nothin'. I haven't an enemy in the world." Joseph Valachi and other police informers later said the gunman was Vincent ("The Chin") Gigante, a former boxer who later became one of the most powerful gangsters in New York.

Police detectives who searched Costello's pockets found a cryptic note containing a figure that corresponded with the house take at the new Tropicana Casino in Las Vegas for a week in April. It was the first solid evidence of mob interest in casinos there.

Organized crime investigators decided that Genovese had sent Costello a message, and that it had been understood. Shortly thereafter Costello retired from active participation in organized crime, and Genovese became the dominant figure in Luciano's crime family.

Costello continued to have trouble with the IRS, however. In October 1958 a final ruling was handed down in his tax case and he returned to prison until June 1961. An effort was made to deport him, but the Italian government said Italy "should not be expected to carry the burden of a man who . . . lived here only a short time."

Costello spent the last decade of his life quietly, dividing his time between his New York apartment and his estate at Sands Point on Long Island. He died in a Manhattan hospital, eleven days after suffering a heart attack at home.

[See Leonard Katz, *Uncle Frank* (1973); George Wolf with Joseph DiMona, *Frank Costello* (1974); David Hanna, *Frank Costello* (1974); and Robert Lacey, *Little Man: Meyer Lansky and the Gangster Life* (1991). An obituary is in the *New York Times*, Feb. 19, 1973.]

RICK HAMPSON

COUDERT, FREDERIC RENE, JR. (May 7, 1898–May 21, 1972), congressman and lawyer, was born in New York City, the son of Frederic René Coudert, Sr., and Alice Tracy Wilmerding. He was a member of a prominent American family, and his father was a distinguished international lawyer. He attended the Browning School in New York City and the Morristown School in New Jersey. He graduated from Columbia University with a B.A. in 1918 and from Columbia Law School with an LL.B. in 1922. From 1917 to 1918, he served as a first lieutenant in the Twenty-seventh Division of the 105th United States Infantry.

Admitted to the bar in 1923, Coudert first joined the New York City firm of Cravath and Henderson. In 1924, he entered his family's international law firm, Coudert Brothers. In the period 1924–1925 he served as assistant United States attorney for the Southern District of New York and in 1929 was the Republican candidate for district attorney of New York County. His first marriage, to Mary K. Callery, a sculptor, took place on June 23, 1923. They had one child and divorced in 1931. He married Paula Murray in October 1931; they had two children.

Coudert was elected to the New York State Senate in 1938, representing New York City's seventeenth congressional district until 1946.

He served as chairman of the Military Affairs Committee and the Committee on General Laws. He sponsored legislation establishing faculty tenure at the city colleges (1938) and a law prohibiting multiple jobs in the schools intended to broaden the employment base (1939). He also sponsored bills to remove notarization of income tax returns, to repeal the one-cent city cigarette tax, and to reorganize the city's health department pension fund.

Coudert received most attention as the head of a subcommittee investigating Communism in New York City schools. The Joint Legislative Committee to Investigate Procedures and Methods of Allocating State Moneys for Public School Purposes and Subversive Activities, which was established by a legislative resolution of Mar. 29, 1940, consisted of a subcommittee on allocation of state funds chaired by Assemblyman Herbert Rapp, and a subcommittee on subversive activity, chaired by Coudert.

In September 1940, the Coudert subcommittee began interviewing or interrogating nearly 1,000 individuals in private sessions. The text of these sessions was never made public. Fewer than one hundred witnesses testified at public hearings beginning Dec. 2, 1940. When the subcommittee released names of individuals, it insisted that it was citing only those who had been identified as Communists by at least two persons, generally former party members. Students were not asked to testify in public. The Coudert subcommittee publicly identified as Communists sixty-nine public school or college teachers, primarily at Brooklyn and City Colleges, and stated that it had information on more than four hundred others who had been identified by one individual during the private sessions. Coudert pointed out that the subcommittee's investigation affected only a small percentage of teachers. The subcommittee sought to subpoena the membership list of the New York Teachers Union of the American Federation of Teachers, but the union refused until forced to do so by the courts. The teachers union itself came under suspicion. Although the list was never released to the public after being turned over to the subcommittee in January 1941, witnesses were directed to review it prior to their testimony.

The subcommittee's work was supported by the boards of education and higher education, but when the subcommittee refused to provide more information on its findings, several officials, including the presidents of the board of education and Brooklyn College, were provoked. The subcommittee concluded that neither of the boards had really faced the issue, nor had they properly disciplined the officer of the Teachers Union who had withheld the membership list. As reported in the *New York Times* (Apr. 27, 1942), board of education president James Marshall wrote in a letter to the editor that the subcommittee's report had "done far more to break down American morale and the confidence of our people in American institutions than the handful of Communists in a system of more than 30,000 loyal teachers." Of the sixty-nine publicly named teachers, eleven resigned, the contracts of six who never had tenure were not renewed, nine were dismissed, and twenty underwent trials at City College. The cases of a number of the remaining accused individuals were reopened by the United States Senate Internal Security Subcommittee in the early 1950's.

Along with the subcommittee counsel, Coudert was the only subcommittee member to attend the hearings on a regular basis. When he was invited to run for Congress after a member's death, he declined because of the hearings. He then was elected to Congress in 1946. Representing the traditionally Republican seventeenth ("Silk Stocking") congressional district located on Manhattan's Upper East Side, Coudert compiled a conservative record. While serving on the Appropriations Committee, one of the key House committees, Coudert was able to focus particular attention on limiting federal spending.

Winning reelection by increasingly smaller majorities, Coudert retired in 1958 after his sixth term. He then served as a member of Governor Nelson Rockefeller's Temporary State Commission on Governmental Operations of the City of New York from 1959 to 1961. He was chairman of William F. Buckley, Jr.'s New York City mayoral campaign in 1965. Coudert retired from Coudert Brothers in 1972 due to declining health.

Coudert was an active racing yachtsman. He received the Chevalier Legion of Honor and served as president of the Federation of French Alliances in the United States from 1965 to 1972. He died in New York City.

[See New York State, Joint Legislative Committee to Investigate Procedures and Methods of Allocating State Moneys for Public School Purposes and Subversive Activities, "Report of the Subcommittee Relative to the Public Educational System of the City of New York," *Legislative Document*, no. 49 (1942); New York State, Joint Legislative Committee on the State Education System, "Report of the New York City Subcommittee Concerning Administration and Financing of the Public Education System of the City of New York under the Control of that City's Board of Education and the Board of Higher Education," *Legislative Document*, no. 60 (1944); Robert W. Iversen, *The Communists and the Schools* (1959); and Paula M. Coudert, Paul B. Jones, and Lawrence Klepp, *Frederic R. Coudert, Jr.: A Biography* (1985). An obituary is in the *New York Times*, May 23, 1972.]

MARGARET LATIMER

COURANT, RICHARD (Jan. 8, 1888–Jan. 27, 1972), mathematician, was born in Lublinitz, Upper Silesia, then a German city, the son of Martha Freund and Siegmund Courant, a small businessman. In 1897 his family moved to Breslau, the capital of Silesia. There Courant attended the König-Wilhelms Gymnasium, where he excelled in arithmetic. During this time, Courant's parents endured a string of financial setbacks, and his father declared bankruptcy in 1902. Two years later, the family moved to Berlin. Courant remained in Breslau, alone, to attend school.

Courant's career as an educator started when, at age fourteen, alarmed by escalating money problems at home, he answered an advertisement in a local newspaper for a tutor "qualified in all subjects." Although he soon lost that job through bullying his pupil, he succeeded in building up a lucrative sideline tutoring other students in mathematics, acquiring patience and other necessary pedagogical skills in a hurry. He later said that he supported himself from the time he was fourteen. During his last year of high school, in 1905, Courant stopped going to class and started attending lectures in mathematics and physics at the local university. The following spring he took and passed the *Abitur*, the final examination of high school. He officially enrolled in the University of Breslau in 1906.

Courant intended to study physics, but since the quality of instruction in this subject was so poor at Breslau, he switched to mathematics. Still dissatisfied, he entered the University of Zurich.

In the fall of 1907, after one semester, Courant left Zurich and transferred to Göttingen, where he worked as David Hilbert's assistant and attended his lectures, also taking Edmund Husserl's courses in philosophy and Woldemar Voigt's in physics. Among his other professors at Göttingen were Hermann Minkowski, Felix Klein, and Ernst Zermelo, mathematicians with a strong interest in physics. He was invited to join Hilbert and Minkowski's joint seminar on mathematical physics. He later recalled, "I had wanted to be a physicist, but the physicists at that time were very uninspiring people, and the attraction that Hilbert and Minkowski exercised was overwhelming." Fascinated by the interplay of concepts and proofs in their physics seminar, Courant wrote his dissertation under Hilbert's direction, for which he received a doctor's degree in 1910. Hilbert's interest in the applications of mathematics exerted a lasting influence on Courant.

After a year of required military service in the German army, in 1911 Courant returned to Göttingen to continue work on the topic he had treated in his dissertation. With this work he qualified to teach at the University of Göttingen; there he delivered the *Habilitation* thesis "Über die Anwendung des Dirichletschen Prinzipes" early in 1912. He married twice; his first wife, Nelly Neumann, was a mathematics teacher. They were married in 1912, separated in 1915, and divorced in 1916. On Jan. 22, 1919, he married Nerina Runge, the daughter of Carl Runge, professor of applied mathematics at Göttingen; they had four children.

After six years as *Privatdozent* at Göttingen (1912–1918), interrupted by army service (1914–1918), and a short time as professor of mathematics at the University of Münster (1920), Courant became full professor at Göttingen in 1921 and director of his own new Mathematical Institute, built with funds from the Rockefeller Foundation. Under his leadership and great organizing skill, it became the mecca of mathematics. True to his philosophy, Courant's institute made no distinction between pure and applied mathematics.

Courant, fundamentally interested in mathematical physics, used mathematics to make the underpinnings of physics more rigorous. In lectures on this subject, he discussed mathematical problems that had their roots in classical physics. The algebra and analysis in the 1924 textbook *Methoden der mathematischen Physik*, by Courant "and D. Hilbert" (the coauthorship was symbolic, Courant's tribute to his teacher), later provided physicists with tools for further developing quantum mechanics, despite the book's classical physics origins.

Hitler's rise to power forced Courant, who was Jewish, from Göttingen in 1933; after a year at Cambridge University, he accepted a visiting professorship at New York University (NYU). It was not an easy decision. He once said, "There was really nothing scientifically at NYU." In 1936, after two years in New York, he received a permanent appointment, becoming head of the graduate department of mathematics. Courant was a great believer in the application of mathematics to the solution of practical problems. Starting with a pool of "not ungifted but extraordinarily poorly prepared" students of immigrant parents, he was instrumental in establishing the Institute of Mathematical Sciences (now the Courant Institute) at NYU and served as its director from 1953 until his retirement in 1958.

Courant became an American citizen in 1940. As a patriotic gesture, in 1941 he conceived and wrote (with Herbert Robbins of Columbia University) *What Is Mathematics?*, a nontechnical book that enjoyed a huge success and was translated into a number of languages. During World War II, Courant served as a member of Warren Weaver's Applied Mathematics Panel. He also organized a large team of scientists to work on military projects for the government, which led to continued large-scale government support for applied mathematics at NYU's institute after the war ended.

Courant died in New Rochelle, N.Y.

[Courant's papers are in the Courant Institute of Mathematical Sciences archives at NYU. A list of his publications is in P. S. Aleksandrov and O. A. Oleinik, "In Memory of Richard Courant," *Russian Mathematical Surveys*, July–Aug. 1975. Major publications include *Differential and Integral Calculus*, 2 vols. (1927–1929); *Supersonic Flow and Shock Waves*, written with Kurt Otto Friedrichs (1948); *Dirichlet's Principle, Conformal Mapping, and Minimal Surfaces* (1950); and *Introduction to Calculus and Analysis*, written with Fritz John, 2 vols. (1965–1974). On the role of Hilbert in Courant's career, see Courant's "Reminiscences from Hilbert's Göttingen," *Mathematical Intelligencer*, 1981. The most complete and compelling account of his life is Constance Reid, *Courant in Göttingen and New York* (1976). An obituary is in the *New York Times*, Jan. 29, 1972.]

JUDITH R. GOODSTEIN

COX, JAMES MIDDLETON, JR. (June 27, 1903–Oct. 27, 1974), publisher, was born in Dayton, Ohio, the son of James M. Cox, the Democratic party candidate for the presidency in 1920 and publisher of Ohio, Georgia, and Florida newspapers, and Mary Simpson Harding. Named at birth James McMahon, he accepted his father's preference to call himself James M. Cox, Jr.

Cox studied at Culver Military Academy in Indiana (1917–1920) and Cheshire (Conn.) Academy (1922–1924) before entering Yale University, from which he graduated with a Ph.B. degree in 1928. He began a newspaper career in 1929 as a police reporter on the *Dayton Daily News*, which was owned by his father. During the next several years he held positions of increasing importance at the *News*, serving as general manager (1931–1938), assistant publisher (1938–1939), and assistant publisher and vice president (1939–1949). He was on active duty in the United States Navy from 1942 to 1945, becoming a lieutenant commander.

Meanwhile, his father extended the family's newspapers outside Ohio; the first such venture was the acquisition of the *Miami* (Fla.) *News* in 1931, followed by the purchase of the *Atlanta Journal* in 1939. The Cox newspaper interests in the course of the years embraced twelve papers: the *Atlanta Journal* and the *Atlanta Constitution*, the *Dayton Daily News* and the *Dayton Journal Herald*, the *Miami News*, the *Palm Beach* (Fla.) *News*, the *West Palm Beach Post* and the *West Palm Beach Times*, the *Delray Beach News Journal*, the *Boynton Beach News Journal*, the *Springfield* (Ohio) *Daily News*, and the *Springfield Daily Sun*.

The Cox communications empire moved into radio in 1934 with the purchase of an Erie, Pa., station whose license was then transferred to Dayton. Cox assumed responsibility for setting up the radio station, using the call letters WHIO, and hiring as manager J. Leonard Reinsch, later the head of all Cox broadcasting business. The station operated from downtown studios next door to the *Dayton Daily News*. Cox radio holdings widened to include five AM and four FM stations at the time of Cox's death.

After his return from military duty, Cox not only actively managed newspaper and radio operations but also persuaded his father to enter the television field. The senior Cox first acquired stations in Dayton, Atlanta, and Miami. At the time of the junior Cox's death, the Cox empire comprised five television and thirty-four wholly or partially owned cable TV systems.

After the death of his father in 1957, Cox was responsible for seven newspapers, three radio stations, and two television stations. His father's will named him one of four trustees to operate the Cox newspapers, and Atlanta Newspapers, Inc., named him board chairman. On the foundation that his father and he had already built, he developed the Cox interests into a giant media empire and conglomerate.

Cox brought vision, foresight, and business acumen to his entrepreneurship. Possessed of a quick mind, he had a knack for selecting able executives and giving them great latitude. A particularly masterful choice was J. Leonard Reinsch, who became president of Cox Broadcasting Corporation, of which Cox was board chairman. Cox and Reinsch shared similar views as to the huge potential of the communications industry; against the opposition of numerous stations, they envisioned great growth for the community antenna systems.

A conservative Democrat, Cox hired liberal editors. He conducted business over lunch with his editors, individually and frequently. Only once did he encroach on editorial independence. In 1972, believing the Democratic party candidate, George McGovern, "just won't do," he ordered his editors to endorse Richard M. Nixon. Exposed by the *New York Times*, the order created a flap in the media; Cox later acknowledged it might have been wiser if the newspapers had "taken a walk" instead of supporting Nixon. One editor resigned, and another gave official endorsement to Nixon while making his personal endorsement of McGovern in his regular column.

Ultimately, the Cox media empire became nationwide, with television stations in Pittsburgh, Pa., Charlotte, N.C., and the San Francisco–Oakland area; radio stations in Los Angeles, Dayton, Atlanta, and Miami and additional newspapers and a monthly magazine in Florida. CATV systems were organized in fifteen states.

The conglomerate grew as Cox interests absorbed the Atlanta franchise for the American Football League; United Technical Publications, involving a dozen magazines; a truck line and a steel warehouse in Georgia; eleven automobile auction houses; and a movie company,

Bing Crosby Productions. Radio, television, and affiliated holdings were brought together as the aforementioned Cox Broadcasting Corporation. Its stock was admitted to the New York Stock Exchange in 1964; earnings the previous year had been $2.4 million. In 1968, Cox became chairman of a second major company, Cox Enterprises, Inc., publisher of newspapers. In 1973, the last full year before Cox's death, the net income of Cox Broadcasting Corp. exceeded $10.1 million, and that of Cox Cable Communications, Inc. approached $1.7 million.

A golfer, yachtsman, naturalist, and philanthropist, Cox headed a $20-million fund drive for Wittenberg University in Springfield, Ohio. With family members, he gave over a million dollars to the University of Miami (Florida), of which he was a trustee, and where the science building is named for him. He also established the James M. Cox, Jr., Arboretum in Dayton. In addition to his home in Dayton, he maintained apartments in Atlanta and Miami. Cox married three times; first to Helen Rumsey on Nov. 21, 1930; they were divorced in 1950. His second marriage, to Jan Streate in 1951, also ended in divorce. His third marriage was to Mrs. Devereaux Haigh Lippit, Jr. (née Betty Gage), of Atlanta, in 1958. He died in Atlanta, survived by his third wife; he had no children.

[The *New York Times* of Aug. 23, 1964, has a profile on Cox and Leonard Reinsch. The files of the *Wall Street Journal* and the *New York Times* have invaluable material on the Cox business interests. Obituaries appear in the *New York Times*, the *Atlanta Journal*, and the *Atlanta Constitution*, all Oct. 28, 1974.]

JAMES A. RAWLEY

COX, WALLACE MAYNARD ("WALLY") (Dec. 6, 1924–Feb. 15, 1973), television and movie actor, was born in Detroit, Mich. His father, George Wallace Cox, was an advertising copywriter; his mother, Eleanor Frances Atkinson, was a mystery writer who used the pseudonym Eleanor Blake. Cox's parents divorced when he was young, and he moved with his mother and sister, Eleanor, to New York City. A shy youth, he did well in school while suffering the usual bullying accorded to socially and physically awkward students. He planned to study botany at City College of New York, but instead he quit school in 1942 in order to

work to support his family when his mother became ill and was partially paralyzed. After a number of odd jobs, he was drafted into the army, serving a short stint in Fort Walters, Tex. He then entered New York University to study handicrafts. Upon graduating in 1946, he set up shop as a silversmith, making accessories for New York haberdashers.

There was little about Cox's life that pointed to a career in show business. While at a party, however, he delivered a comic monologue based on an imitation of a soldier he knew in the army. Cox met with such success that he took his act to other parties, building a reputation along the way. Besides encouragement from his sister, Cox also received advice and praise from actor Marlon Brando, his close friend. Although the pair may have seemed to be an odd couple—Brando was then emerging as the symbol of hip macho—their friendship remained strong throughout Cox's life.

Cox was soon circulating among the theater crowd and joined the American Creative Theater Group. At one theater party, a well-connected guest heard Cox and persuaded Max Gordon, owner of the famous New York nightclub, the Village Vanguard, to audition the aspiring comic. Gordon put Cox to work on the night of the audition. The audience responded so enthusiastically that Cox went on to complete a two-month engagement, and his entertainment career was assured. He spent two years on the nightclub circuit, during which time a *New York Herald Tribune* reviewer wrote, "His night club monologues were . . . full of elaborate, stuffy detail which was terribly important in the lives of small, unimportant people . . . and he invested these small facts with such great earnestness that he was hilarious and curiously poignant."

Cox got his next break when theatrical producer Dwight Deere Wiman chose him for a role in the musical revue *Dance Me a Song*. Although the revue was largely panned, Cox was a hit. The *New York Post* declared, "Just put him down as the humorous find of the year." Cox was soon inundated with offers from nightclubs, Broadway, television, and radio. He accepted several offers and spent the next few years moving from engagements at the Plaza Hotel in New York to appearances on the variety shows of Perry Como, Ed Sullivan, Garry Moore, and Arthur Godfrey.

In 1951 Cox starred in a "Philco Television

Playhouse" production, playing a man who was continually and unintentionally the cause of an involved commotion. From this role came the seed of "Mr. Peepers," a situation comedy on NBC starring Cox as high school science teacher Robinson Peepers, whose earnest efforts to help out always ended in a mess. The show began inauspiciously in July 1952, intended to be an eight-week series to fill a gap in the summer replacement schedule. At the end of the summer, however, more than 8,000 letters poured into NBC in support of the show, spurred on in part by a glowing review in *Time* magazine. When an unlucky NBC series called "Doc Corkle" was canceled after three episodes, Cox's show was tapped to fill the slot. Wally Cox had been in the right place at the right time.

If Cox's early life gave little hint of his show business future, it at least provided him with the basic material for his most important role. "There's a lot of Mr. Peepers in me," Cox conceded. "When I was a kid in the Midwest, I got straight A's in school, and I spent thirteen years on the psychiatrist's couch paying for it." The erstwhile botany major relished the role of science teacher, recalling, "I was a flower-watcher. I still am, for that matter." In his classic lecture "Wake Up Your Sluggish Soil," Mr. Peepers concludes, "Spare the leaf mold, spoil the hepatica. Remember, your dirt is the restaurant where your flowers dine." Mr. Peepers was known for the "thoughtful absurdities" that constituted his rapport with students: "Yes, I think tonsils are useful to some people"; "No, I don't think we know just how fast a dinosaur can run."

Cox's unaffected personality made the silly goings-on in Mr. Peepers's classroom a treat for millions of watchers. In April 1953, the show was given the Peabody Award for excellence in television broadcasting. After the series went off the air in 1954, Cox and writer William Redfield pieced together material from the series to produce *Mr. Peepers: A Sort of Novel* (1955).

"Mr. Peepers" was Cox's greatest triumph, but it also circumscribed his future career. His roles afterward were largely an attempt to recreate this formula, with little success. In 1956, Cox starred in "The Adventures of Hiram Holliday," in which a meek, mild-mannered proofreader from a New York newspaper was found to possess amazing skills, including fencing, scuba diving, art forgery, and piloting. The show was canceled in six months.

If Cox had difficulty recapturing the glint of stardom, he had no problem finding work. During the 1960's he turned to the movies, taking roles in such films as *State Fair* (1962), *Spencer's Mountain* (1963), *The Bedford Incident* (1965), *A Guide for the Married Man* (1967), *The One and Only Genuine Original Family Band* (1968), *The Cockeyed Cowboys of Calico County* (1970), and *The Barefoot Executive* (1971), none of which garnered much critical acclaim. He also kept busy in television, mostly appearing in single episodes of well-known series, including "The Adventures of Ozzie and Harriet" (1961), "Car 54, Where Are You?" (1962), "The Lucy Show" (1963), "The Twilight Zone" (1964), "Mission: Impossible" (1966), and "Ironside" (1967).

Cox always had an urge to write, and during this time he published several books. In 1961, he wrote *My Life As a Small Boy*, a semiautobiographical account that he also illustrated. *Kirkus Reviews* praised the book, noting that "like its author, this collection of short pieces via small town Americana is quietly funny, quietly touching, and quietly slick." The *New York Times* also praised it, commenting that "after reading the compassionate and uncomplaining accounts of his past tribulations, one is inclined to subject Mr. Cox to no more bullying." Cox's next effort, *Ralph Makes Good*, appears to have gone largely unreviewed by major publications. *The Tenth Life of Osiris Oaks*, a children's book that Cox wrote with Everett Greenbaum in 1972, gained mixed attention. While the *New York Review of Books* praised the "cheerful, light-hearted" nature of the book, the *New York Times* panned it.

Cox's big comeback came in 1968, when he became one of the two permanent panelists on the popular game show, "Hollywood Squares." Once again, Cox took on the role of Mr. Peepers, delivering his lines in the shy, diffident, and slyly comic style that had become his trademark. Cox died in Los Angeles.

[Magazine and newspaper features on Cox are in *Time*, July 28, 1952; *Newsweek*, Nov. 10, 1952; the *New York Times*, Jan. 11, 1953; *New York World-Telegram Magazine*, Feb. 21, 1953; *American Magazine*, Oct. 1953; and *Good Housekeeping*, Nov. 1953. Reviews of Cox's books appear in *Kirkus Reviews*, Aug. 15, 1951; the *New York Times*, Apr. 16, 1972; and *New York Review of Books*, Dec. 14, 1972. There is an obituary in the *New York Times*, Feb. 16, 1973.]

MICHAEL GOLDBERG

CRISP, DONALD (July 27, 1880–May 25, 1974), actor and director, was born in Aberfeddy, Scotland, and was educated at the exclusive Eton school and at Oxford University. Little is known of Crisp's family or his early life. He volunteered for the Boer War at the age of nineteen. He saw combat at the sieges of Ladysmith and Mafeking and was wounded during his three years of service. In later years, he enjoyed telling about his wartime friendship with a young journalist named Winston Churchill. After leaving the British army in 1902, Crisp acted on the stage in Great Britain before emigrating to the United States in 1906. John C. Fisher heard him sing at a ship's concert during the crossing, and offered him a job as handyman and as a tenor in the chorus of New York's Fisher-Reilly Opera Company. Crisp returned home from the company's tour of Mexico and Cuba determined to work in the theater. He soon went to work as a stage manager on Broadway for Cohan & Harris.

Crisp's career virtually traces the first half-century of the movies as a commercial entertainment medium. He was involved in over four hundred films as an assistant director, director, or actor over a span of fifty-five years. His first movie was a mutascope for the old Biograph Studio in New York City, entitled *The French Maid* (1907). He later described a mutascope as a viewing machine "where you put a penny in the slot and turned a handle." Soon after, he joined the company of actors associated with director D. W. Griffith, first at Biograph and later at Reliance-Majestic, and appeared in one of Griffith's masterpieces, *Birth of a Nation* (1915).

Griffith also gave Crisp the opportunity to direct. Before Griffith, Crisp explained to an interviewer, "There was no such thing as a director. He was merely the man that shouted the instructions through a megaphone." In addition to acting the role of General Grant, Crisp served as Griffith's assistant director on *Birth of a Nation*, in charge of battle scenes. Just how much Crisp actually did is open to some debate, however. Crisp said he did the film's outdoor shooting, though Anthony Slide calls this claim a "villainous" attack on Griffith's integrity. Slide concludes that Crisp shot no scenes of any importance and attributes his claim to youthful boastfulness. Between 1914 and 1921, Crisp directed more than fifty films even though he spent World War I as an officer in British Intelligence whose responsibility was gathering information on conditions in Russia as the tsarist regime fell.

Crisp continued to act in and direct motion pictures despite the common attitudes toward movie actors. In a 1949 interview, he recalled that on one occasion he had held a coat over Mary Pickford's face as she was entering the studio because of the low esteem in which movie actors were held.

As the industry advanced, Crisp moved with it. In 1919, he acted in *Broken Blossoms* with Lillian Gish, and once again served as Griffith's assistant director. This film is one of the first in which Crisp portrayed a father, but his character was unusually brutal. *Broken Blossoms* also marked his first mention in a review. Mordaunt Hall of the *New York Times* called him "violently realistic."

In 1919, Crisp divorced his first wife, Marie Stark, and went to work for Famous Players Lasky. Impressed by his business acumen, studio head Adolph Zukor assigned him to help establish the company in London, Paris, and Berlin. Crisp also spent time on Zukor's behalf in Bombay, India.

After his return, Crisp worked at a hectic pace through the 1920's. He directed a number of films in Great Britain, then returned to Hollywood to act in several dozen more in support of such stars as Douglas Fairbanks and Vilma Banky, and to direct such popular epics as *Don Q, Son of Zorro* (1925), starring Fairbanks and Mary Astor. In addition to directing, Crisp played the supporting role of Don Sebastian. Mordaunt Hall wrote that *Don Q* was "a swift film with plenty of action." Of Crisp's direction, he wrote that he "has lost none of his cunning since he took to directing." Two years later, Crisp directed William Boyd and Bessie Love in *Dress Parade*, the first movie filmed at West Point.

An astute businessman, Crisp also began to serve The Bank of Italy (later The Bank of America) as an adviser on loans to studios and producers. He was involved in many of the large movie loans granted from the 1920's through the 1950's. He accumulated substantial real estate holdings on the West Coast. With the advent of sound near the end of the 1920's, Crisp gave up directing to concentrate on acting. He told an interviewer he stopped directing because "so many studio heads wanted their nieces and nephews in starring roles."

Crisp's last directed film, from 1930, is a long-forgotten trifle entitled *The Runaway Bride*. Two years later, he married its writer, Jane Murfin. They were divorced in 1944, and she died in 1957. They had no children. Initially a playwright in New York, Murfin is best known for her work at MGM, including the screenplays to *Pride and Prejudice*, *Dragon Seed*, *The Women* (with Anita Loos), and *Andy Hardy's Private Secretary*.

Crisp made the shift from silent films to "talkies" easily, thanks to a resilient but naturally restrained acting style and a pleasing voice. His amiability came through on the screen, and he was soon in demand as one of the most versatile of all Hollywood's character actors. While he had often played villains in silent films (as with Fairbanks in *The Black Pirate* in 1926), he now began to create a series of largely sympathetic characters.

Though he portrayed Katharine Hepburn's icy father in *A Woman Rebels* (1936), and a stuffy military officer opposite Kay Francis as Florence Nightingale in *The White Angel* (1936), he also fought alongside Erroll Flynn in *The Charge of the Light Brigade* (1936) and *The Sea Hawk* (1940), and he portrayed Francis Bacon in *The Private Lives of Elizabeth and Essex* (1939).

Because he was approaching age sixty, and because he possessed a natural dignity, Crisp was often cast as a judge (*The Oklahoma Kid*, 1939), a physician (*Wuthering Heights*, 1939), or a clergyman (*Dr. Ehrlich's Magic Bullet* and *Knute Rockne—All-American*; both 1940). Reviews generally mentioned him in passing though almost always admiringly. In his review of *National Velvet* in 1944, for example, James Agee wrote that Crisp's performance is one of the "good things" about the movie.

Crisp's years of greatest activity correspond to the decades when the "studio system" dominated Hollywood. Actors and directors were under contract to all-powerful studios that virtually controlled their professional lives. As a result of studio assignments, Crisp worked with such stars as Bette Davis, Merle Oberon, Jean Harlow, Spencer Tracy, Clark Gable, and Laurence Olivier. He also worked with such diverse directors as Howard Hawks, Michael Curtiz, William Wyler, and Busby Berkeley.

Crisp was under contract at several different studios. Among his more important assignments were *Red Dust* (1932), *What Every Woman Knows* (1934), and *Dr. Jekyll and Mr. Hyde* (1941) for MGM; *Jezebel* (1938) for Warner Brothers; and *Laddie* (1935) and *A Woman Rebels* (1936) for RKO. He had his greatest triumph in Twentieth Century–Fox's adaptation of Richard Llewellyn's popular novel *How Green Was My Valley*. Crisp won the 1941 Oscar for best supporting actor for his portrayal of Gwilym Morgan, the strong but gentle patriarch in a story of family breakdown and individual survival in a Welsh mining town. Film critic Bosley Crowther wrote of his performance, "No one that we can think of could bring more strength and character to the difficult role of Gwilym Morgan than Donald Crisp." Six months before Pearl Harbor, Crisp turned up to receive his Oscar dressed in a military officer's uniform. *How Green Was My Valley* also won Oscars for best film, best director (John Ford), and best cinematography.

Crisp's portrayal of Morgan was so successful that he never quite escaped from it. Although he played a megomaniacal ranger in *The Man from Laramie* (1955), the rest of his career consisted mainly of benevolent old codgers in a series of family stories at MGM, including *National Velvet* and the first three Lassie movies. He created the character a final time in *Pollyanna* (1960), when he was eighty.

Though he played similar characters in many of these films, he made each role fresh, his choice of manner and gesture never merely repeated. Unwilling to retire, Crisp made several dozen movies in the 1950's and 1960's. His last film was *Spencer's Mountain* (1963). He died in Van Nuys, Calif.

[For one of Crisp's publications, see "We Lost So Much Dignity as We Came of Age," in *Films and Filming*, Dec. 1960. Also of value are John Douglas Eames, *The MGM Story* (1976); Richard B. Jewell and Vernon Harbin, *The RKO Story* (1982); and Clive Hirschhorn, *The Columbia Story* (1989). Anthony Slide considers Crisp's role as an associate of D. W. Griffith in "The Other Griffith Actors," *Films in Review* 1975. For considerations of *How Green Was My Valley*, see Robert Gressner, *The Moving Image* (1968); and Janey Ann Place, *The Non-Western Films of John Ford* (1979). An obituary is in the *New York Times*, May 27, 1974.]

MICHAEL LASSER

CROSS, MILTON JOHN (Apr. 16, 1897–Jan. 3, 1975), radio announcer and opera commentator, was born on the West Side of New York

City, the son of Robert Cross, an employee of the American Bible Society, and Margaret Lockhard. He graduated from the De Witt Clinton High School in 1915 and was enrolled from 1921 to 1923 in a certificate program at the Damrosch Institute of Music (later incorporated into the Juilliard School of Music) with the object of becoming an educational supervisor. The school sought to produce teachers who would instruct the general public in how to play music for their own enjoyment; at the same time, it fostered competent musicians. Cross became a tenor and sang in local churches and temples. He also performed in minor nonsinging roles with the Metropolitan Opera Company in New York. In 1921 a friend who was an early radio enthusiast interested Cross with his duties at WJZ in Newark, N.J., the second commercial radio station in the country. Cross soon found himself as the station's full-time announcer, but he also sang songs, read stockmarket reports, played the piano, and read the comics. He concentrated on classical music; a rival station that stressed popular music was driven off the air for want of suitable material.

Although Cross had announced opera intermittently since 1923, his serious entrance into opera broadcasting was as the voice of the Chicago Civic Opera for the NBC Network (WJZ was then on that company's Blue Network). Cross received a baptism by fire one day when the network was ready to air *Il Trovatore*. Suddenly local utility magnate Samuel Insull decided to read the opera company's financial report to the live audience in Chicago, an event that was not to go over the air. Insull droned on for thirty-five minutes to the live audience, while radio listeners heard Cross describe the opera, the cast, Verdi's life, the hall, and even the Pullman cars carrying the cast. Cross was soon thereafter chosen to narrate the first live broadcast of Metropolitan Opera in New York City; thus on Christmas Day 1933, Cross described *Hansel and Gretel* to the radio audience. He would continue opera broadcasts for more than thirty years; in fact, the next day he returned with a broadcast of *Norma*, featuring Metropolitan standouts Rosa Ponselle and Giacomo Lauri-Volpe. By 1933 the performances were always aired complete, but Cross would handle the entire broadcast himself, including lengthy intermissions.

Meanwhile, Cross's career as a studio announcer blossomed. In the late 1930's he be-

came connected with a quiz-style program entitled *Information, Please*, which had a long radio and short television run.

On Dec. 7, 1940, the Texaco gasoline company took on its long-standing sponsorship of the Metropolitan broadcasts. The first broadcast under Texaco sponsorship starred Ezio Pinza as Mozart's Figaro. The music was no longer interrupted by commentary, and musicologist Olin Downes gave Cross a chance to rest during intermission breaks. The popularity of the broadcasts was enormous. *Current Biography* featured Cross in its very second issue in 1940—the article termed Cross the man with the most famous voice in the United States, excepting only Franklin Roosevelt and Charlie McCarthy. When World War II began, Cross stayed at the studio microphones while Edward R. Murrow and others made their reputations as war correspondents. Cross remained a calm voice for the arts during this period, arguing against a ban on performances of Richard Wagner, the putative cultural icon of the Third Reich. V-E Day found Cross at the studio talking to a delirious Parisian reporter.

In the meantime Cross continued to bring opera broadcasts to the public, eventually describing every opera the Metropolitan performed during the years 1931–1974. To present the names of the performers on those broadcasts is to repeat the recent history of opera—Melchior, Peerce, Hines, Nilsson, Uppman, Stevens, Siepi, Reiner, Bernstein, Boehm, and von Karajan would certainly head the list. Cross would describe artistic performances in diplomatic language, but he was known to give more direct advice at rehearsals, which he attended to prepare for the broadcasts. In later years, he worked from a script provided by a broadcast producer.

The broadcasts were described in Cross's time as the foremost regularly scheduled cultural event in the United States. Certainly they brought not only the music but also the visual artistry (through Cross's voice) and the ideas of opera to the hinterlands. Opera became well known across the nation and many of America's future best voices would come from small towns that knew opera only through the broadcasts and local college productions.

Cross also served from time to time as voice of the New York Philharmonic Orchestra. In November 1963 it fell on Cross to describe the concert given in memory of the just-assassinated

John Kennedy; Cross quoted movingly from Lincoln's second inaugural address. But the Philharmonic always saw Cross as a Met personality.

Cross married Lillian Ellegood in 1925. They had one daughter who died at a young age. His wife was an accomplished church organist; when she died in February 1973 he missed two Saturday afternoon broadcasts for the first time in his career. In the last few years, his studio announcing decreased, although audiences could still hear his distinctive voice from time to time between ABC shows. (The American Broadcasting Company was formed from NBC's Blue Network.) One Christmas, Cross told audiences it would be "shingles all the way," because he was suffering from the ailment. Cross died in his home in Manhattan on the night before the Jan. 4, 1975, broadcast of *The Italian Girl in Algiers*. Peter Allen immediately took over as host.

[Cross's broadcasts are preserved at the New York Public Library for the Performing Arts. Cross wrote several works on music aimed at laypersons wishing basic dates, plot outlines, and so forth. These works include *New Milton Cross' Complete Stories of the Great Operas* (1955) and *More Stories of the Great Operas* (1971), which are classics in their field. Paul Jackson, *Saturday Afternoons at the Old Metropolitan Opera Broadcasts, 1931–1950* (1992) extensively describes those broadcasts, but contains relatively little on Cross. An obituary is in the *New York Times*, Jan. 4, 1975, and commemorations are in *Opera News*, Feb. 8, 1975.]

JOHN DAVID HEALY

CROWLEY, LEO THOMAS (Aug. 15, 1889– Apr. 15, 1972), banker, industrialist, and corporate and federal official, was born in Milton Junction, Wis., the son of Thomas Franklin Crowley and Catherine Elizabeth Ryan. Working as a delivery boy for a grocery store, he helped to support his eight brothers and sisters after his father's death in 1901. He attended the public schools in Milton Junction and Madison, Wis., and worked as a grocer while studying at the University of Wisconsin, where he was elected to Phi Beta Kappa. He owned his own grocery store by the time he graduated. He went to work for the General Paper and Supply Company of Madison and became the company's president in 1917, at the age of twenty-eight.

Crowley rose rapidly in Wisconsin business circles. In 1928 he became president and direc-

tor of the State Bank of Wisconsin. In the early 1930's, he bought several banks and became chairman of the Wisconsin Banking Review Board. In 1933 Governor Albert G. Schmedman appointed Crowley chairman of the Wisconsin Advisory Committee. He was also chairman of the executive council and state director of the National Recovery Administration. The possibility of Crowley's running for United States senator from Wisconsin was discussed, but he never held elective public office.

In 1934, President Franklin D. Roosevelt appointed Crowley chairman of the Federal Deposit Insurance Corporation. The FDIC, authorized under the Glass-Steagall Act of 1933, insured deposits up to $5,000 in participating banks. The agency also served as receiver during the reorganization of failing banks. In his capacity as chairman, Crowley participated in the crafting of the Banking Act of 1935, together with Marriner Eccles of the Federal Reserve Board and Comptroller of the Currency J. F. T. O'Connor. But the final legislation bore Eccles's stamp much more than that of Crowley and other administration conservatives, such as O'Connor, Jesse Jones of the Reconstruction Finance Corporation, and Senator Carter Glass of Virginia. The new law moved further toward monetary management, credit control, and federal supervision than Crowley would have liked. Crowley also believed that legislation regarding the FDIC should be separate and take priority over other banking laws, while Eccles successfully championed an omnibus law that made significant changes in the Federal Reserve System.

In 1939 Crowley also became chairman of the board of the Standard Gas and Electric Company of Chicago, a holding company controlling utilities in twenty states and Mexico. The following year he became president of Standard Gas and Electric as well. He had been supported for these posts by Jesse Jones and apparently had the concurrence of President Roosevelt in assuming his multiple private and public roles. Crowley remained chairman of the FDIC until 1945.

Crowley also held numerous corporate directorships, including those of National Guardian Life Insurance Company, Pan American Airways, Lehman Corporation, and several utility companies. In addition, he was a trustee of St. Mary's Hospital in Madison, Wis.

Although rumors named Crowley as a possible successor to Postmaster General James A. Farley in 1940, ostensibly to keep a Roman Catholic in the Roosevelt Cabinet, the president instead named Frank Walker, also a Catholic.

In March 1942, President Roosevelt named Crowley (still head of the FDIC) to head the newly created Office of the Foreign Economic Administration, which included the function of Alien Property Custodian. In the latter capacity Crowley could seize and dispose of enemy-owned or controlled businesses in the United States, foreign-owned patents, copyrights, and trademarks, and foreign ships. Rather than sell off the properties, Crowley administered at least $3 billion of seized assets, including thousands of patents that he licensed to American manufacturers for a fee of $50. Many of the patents involved chemical processes developed by German firms. Crowley also ensured republication of foreign scientific and technical works when the United States acquired copyright jurisdiction.

When Secretary of Commerce Jesse Jones and Vice-President Henry Wallace engaged in a well-publicized feud over the Bureau of Economic Warfare in June 1943, Roosevelt defused the conflict by abolishing the BEW and replacing it with the Office of Economic Warfare on July 15, 1943. The President named Crowley, long rumored to be a Jones protégé, to head the new agency. Roosevelt also moved the Export-Import Bank, the rubber and petroleum agencies, and other similar enterprises into the OEW, making OEW directly responsible to the State Department. Crowley resigned from his $50,000-per-year job as head of Standard Gas and Electric to accept the post. Refusing even the token "dollar-a-year" which usually came with such service, Crowley became a "nothing-a-year" man to suport the war effort. Liberals and sympathizers of Vice-President Wallace soon left the agency, and Crowley dismissed one economist, allegedly to placate Representative Martin Dies, who suspected the offending staff member of Communist sympathies.

In less than a year, President Roosevelt centralized all foreign economic operations by merging the Office of Economic Warfare, the Office of Lend-Lease Administration, and the Office of Foreign Relief and Rehabilitation into the Foreign Economic Administration in September 1943. Crowley, whom FDR regarded as "one of the best administrators in or out of Government," headed the new agency until 1945, when he resigned from all his federal posts.

After he left government service, Crowley maintained a number of business associations, including acting as chairman of the Chicago, Milwaukee, St. Paul and Pacific Railroad from 1945 to 1963. A lifelong Roman Catholic, Crowley was a member of the Knights of Columbus. Pope Pius XI decorated him with the Order of St. Gregory the Great and in 1946 Pope Pius XII named him a Knight Commander with Star of the Order of Pius IX for his services to his church. Crowley never married.

[The State Historical Society of Wisconsin has interviews with Crowley conducted by the *Milwaukee Journal*. His role in the Banking Act of 1935 is documented in Helen M. Burns, *The American Banking Community and New Deal Banking Reforms, 1933–1935* (1974); and in Sidney Hyman, *Marriner S. Eccles: Private Entrepreneur and Public Servant* (1976). His wartime work is mentioned in passing in James MacGregor Burns, *Roosevelt: The Soldier of Freedom, 1940–1945* (1970). An obituary is in the *New York Times*, Apr. 16, 1972.]

SUSAN ESTABROOK KENNEDY

CUTLER, ROBERT (June 12, 1895–May 8, 1974), banker, lawyer, and government official, was born in Brookline, Mass., the son of George Chalmers Cutler, a lumber manufacturer, and Mary Franklin Wilson. The youngest of five brothers from a close-knit, affluent old New England family, Cutler attended the Volkmann School in Boston. At Harvard, where he received a B.A. in 1916, Cutler was chosen class poet and commencement orator and was elected to Phi Beta Kappa. After graduation, he taught freshman English at Harvard and Radcliffe for a year, wrote short literary pieces for *The Nation*, and published a novel, *Louisburg Square*. Cutler's love story of an ill-fated debutante ably depicted the manners and morals of the proper Boston the author knew best and won praise from the critics. He had all but decided to make writing his life's work when World War I intervened.

Cutler enlisted in the army in 1917 but did not reach France until 1918. He saw no significant action as a first lieutenant with the Seventy-sixth Division of the American Expeditionary Force before the Armistice and was subsequently assigned to the Army of Occupation in Germany. Serving as adjutant to the Third Army Military Police Battalion in Coblenz, Cutler handled the administrative duties at headquarters with aplomb and efficiency.

When he returned to civilian life in 1919, his father and author Owen Wister urged him to attend Harvard Law School. Somewhat to his surprise, Cutler found the subject matter to his liking and decided upon law as a career. After receiving an LL.B. in 1922, he was so eager to begin practice that he spurned an offer to become private secretary to Supreme Court Justice Oliver Wendell Holmes, Jr. Instead, he joined his brother George at the Boston law firm of Herrick, Smith, Donald & Farley. Before he immersed himself in his new profession, however, Cutler turned out one last novel. *The Speckled Bird*, published in 1923, chronicled the sad life of another wealthy young woman and received only mixed reviews.

As an associate with Herrick, Smith, Cutler found a home in corporate law. He drafted by-laws, wrote records, and handled rate regulation cases for numerous subsidiary companies during the 1920's. Having been made a full partner in his firm in 1929, he graduated to the role of corporate counsel for some of the largest enterprises in New England. Soon after the inauguration of President Franklin D. Roosevelt in 1933, Cutler became an expert on the finer points of the National Industrial Recovery Act and the Securities Act and was often called upon to represent industrial and financial clients before federal agencies.

Because of his professional standing, capacity for hard work, and skill as an after-dinner speaker, Cutler was in demand for the charitable and political fund-raising chores of the Great Depression decade. He volunteered his services to the Greater Boston Community Fund (GBCF), a coalition of private welfare groups, for four years (1936–1940), chaired the GBCF's successful drive in 1937, and went on to the presidency of a national charitable association, Community Chests and Councils (1940–1942). In politics he served as finance chairman of the campaign of his friend, Henry Cabot Lodge, Jr., who defeated the roguish Democratic governor, James Michael Curley, for the United States Senate in 1936. Cutler also was an enthusiastic backer of reform Democrat Maurice J. Tobin, who bested Curley in the Boston mayoral elections of 1937 and 1941. In 1940 Tobin prevailed upon the nominally Republican Cutler to join his administration as city corporation counsel. His responsibilities in

this position included issuing opinions on a wide range of city business, drafting enabling bills for consideration by the state legislature, and commanding a battery of lawyers who argued Boston's cases in the trial courts.

In 1942, Cutler left Boston and the practice of law to become a colonel and assistant deputy director of the Army Specialist Corps (ASC), which had been created to recruit noncombatant officers with special skills, such as lawyers, scientists, and technicians. In short order, he recognized that the ASC was competing needlessly with the regular Army Procurement Service and prepared a memorandum proposing that the two personnel operations be merged for greater efficiency. It naturally followed that he would become a senior colonel of the Officer Procurement Service, the agency created as a result of his memo, which commissioned nearly 30,000 new officers in twelve months.

In the fall of 1943, Secretary of War Henry L. Stimson sought to make further use of Cutler's legal and organizational skills. He made Cutler a special assistant in the War Department and put him in charge of the knotty problem of accommodating voting by members of the armed services in wartime. Cutler influenced the course of service voting legislation in Congress and then, upon passage of a complex compromise bill, functioned in the dual role of coordinator of soldier voting for the army and executive officer of the newly formed War Ballot Commission. As a result of his efforts, a full 35 percent of the 9.2 million American servicemen at war around the globe had their marked ballots delivered by priority mail to the United States in 1944. For most of the next year Cutler carried out special assignments for Stimson, Army Chief of Staff General George C. Marshall, and other War Department officials. In December 1945 he was awarded the Distinguished Service Medal and the Legion of Merit and left the army with the rank of brigadier general.

Upon his return from Washington, Cutler moved up in the Brahmin establishment of Boston. He was elected president of the Old Colony Trust Company (1946) and chairman of the board of Peter Bent Brigham Hospital (1949). He headed the Committee of Citizens to Survey Metropolitan Boston (1947–1949), a large-scale effort to gather and publish accurate data on the health and welfare facilities and services available in the region. Rejoining government intermittently during the postwar years, Cutler managed the military's successful presentation of the case for a supplementary defense budget at U.S. Senate hearings in 1948 as a special assistant to Secretary of Defense James V. Forrestal. He also served briefly as deputy director of the Psychological Strategy Board, part of the country's new Cold War planning apparatus, in 1951.

In 1952, he joined Senator Lodge in the movement that drafted General Dwight D. Eisenhower to run for president and, at the Republican National Convention in Chicago, played a key role in the successful credentials fight for disputed seats in the Texas delegation which led to Eisenhower's nomination on the first ballot. Eisenhower had known Cutler since the 1948 defense budget hearings, and in the fall asked his Bostonian friend to serve as his personal companion and principal factotum on a climactic campaign train trip across the country. After his landslide victory, president-elect Eisenhower tapped Cutler to do a study of the National Security Council, the advisory body established in 1947 to bring together the various elements of national security policy, and to make recommendations toward its overhaul and improvement. Among Cutler's proposals was the creation of the new post of special assistant to the President for National Security Affairs, which he assumed at Eisenhower's request in 1953.

Through Cutler, Eisenhower established and maintained a military-style planning operation in his administration and gave the NSC a more central role in the formulation of Cold War defense and foreign policy than it had under Harry Truman. Working up to seventy hours a week, the special assistant chaired the Policy Planning Board of experts from the various departments and agencies, briefed the president on the papers produced by the planners, and prepared the agenda for weekly NSC meetings at which he was moderator. After the NSC meetings, where policy options were discussed fully and debated, Eisenhower informed Cutler of the decision he had reached and the latter recorded it and oversaw its implementation. Unlike the special assistants in succeeding administrations, Cutler was not a national security "adviser." Although he did express himself on matters of policy, his role was more that of a coordinator or "custodian" of the process leading to a presidential decision. "My job," Cutler later wrote, "was to administer, to serve, to get things done, and to be trusted."

Cutler was present at the creation of Eisenhower foreign policy for nearly four years (January 1953–April 1955 and January 1957–July 1958) and received the presidential Medal of Freedom in 1955. He was instrumental in the deliberations that resulted in the termination of the Korean War (1953); CIA-engineered coups in Iran (1953) and Guatemala (1954); the avoidance of war in Indochina after the fall of the French at Dien Bien Phu (1954); the innovative but ill-fated "Atoms for Peace" (1953) and "Open Skies" (1955) arms control initiatives; the anti-Communist "Eisenhower Doctrine" for the Middle East (1957), and the subsequent landing of Marines in Lebanon (1958). Within the administration, Cutler made an unsuccessful attempt to convince the president to speak out against Wisconsin senator Joseph R. McCarthy. Although he himself was a tough-minded opponent of Communism who saw the leaders of the Soviet Union as an "implacable gang dedicated to ruling the world," Cutler believed McCarthy's hyperbolic red-baiting to be indecent and damaging to America's prestige.

In 1959, Eisenhower lured Cutler away from private banking to serve as both special assistant to the Secretary of the Treasury and the United States member of the eight-man board of executive directors of the Inter-American Development Bank, a precursor to John F. Kennedy's Alliance for Progress, which supplemented private capital with government loans in order to promote economic development and modernization in Latin America. He left this last government post in 1962.

Outside of his beloved Boston, Robert Cutler was probably the least-known member of President Eisenhower's inner circle. To friends and those with whom he worked closely, he was the highly efficient but always affable "Bobby," a raconteur with a ready supply of ribald stories. However, because he held that decision making should be left solely to the president and that those entrusted with government secrets had an obligation to "keep their traps shut," journalists and others seeking a glimpse inside the corridors of power viewed him as something of a glib and shadowy mandarin.

Cutler, who never married, spent his remaining years writing and raising money for the Harvard Medical Center, other institutions affiliated with his alma mater, and St. Paul's Episcopal Cathedral in Boston. *No Time for Rest*, his engaging autobiography, was published in 1966. Cutler died in Concord, Mass.

[Records pertaining to Robert Cutler's government service are in the files of the War and Defense Departments in the National Archives and in the papers of the Special Assistant to the President for National Security Affairs and other collections in the Dwight D. Eisenhower Library. Some of Cutler's work with the National Security Council is revealed in the documents included in the volumes of *Papers Relating to the Foreign Relations of the United States, 1952–1960*. His testimony on the role and operation of the National Security Council before the Subcommittee on National Policy Machinery of the United States Senate Committee on Government Operations is in the subcommittee's report, *Organizing for National Security*, vol. 1 (1961), and in Henry M. Jackson,

ed., *The National Security Council* (1965). In addition to works cited in the text, Cutler wrote *Whereof We Are Made* (1965), a memoir printed privately for family members and friends. His articles include "The Development of the National Security Council," *Foreign Affairs*, Apr. 1956; and "I Shall Vote for Eisenhower," *Atlantic Monthly*, Oct. 1956. Articles on Cutler are Samuel Lubell, "Mystery Man of the White House," *Saturday Evening Post*, Feb. 6, 1954; and Anthony Leviero, "Untouchable, Unreachable and Unquotable," *New York Times Magazine*, Jan. 30, 1955. See also Anna Kasten Nelson, " 'The Top of the Hill': President Eisenhower and the National Security Council," *Diplomatic History*, Fall 1983; and John Prados, *Keepers of the Keys* (1991). Obituaries are in the *Boston Globe*, May 9, 1974; and in the *New York Times* and the *Washington Post*, both May 10, 1974.]

RICHARD H. GENTILE

D

DALE, CHARLES MARKS (Sept. 6, 1881–Nov. 16, 1971), comedian and performer in vaudeville, movies, and television, was born on the Lower East Side of Manhattan into a Jewish working-class family. The little schooling he obtained was at P.S. 20, alma mater of Edward G. Robinson, Paul Muni, George and Ira Gershwin, and Jacob Javits. He never graduated, but he was awarded honorary alumnus status in 1963. In 1898 Dale was working as a printer's apprentice when he was involved in a bicycle accident with Joseph Seltzer on the corner of Eldridge and Delancey streets. The resulting argument led to a ride on a tandem bike with Seltzer and initiated a partnership that lasted seventy-three years.

Seltzer and Marks's first engagement was a stag party on Mar. 15, 1899, which netted them $3. They performed regularly at saloons in the Bowery or on Coney Island, working at Childs' Cafeteria between engagements. A quarter's investment provided them with business cards refused by another act, and thus Seltzer and Marks became known as Smith and Dale in 1900. That December, they joined the Imperial Vaudeville and Comedy Company in Roundout, New York—they worked the "Borscht Belt" before it was named—and developed their first classic routine, "The Schoolroom." Returning to New York, they joined with pianist Will Lester and tenor John Coleman to form the Avon Comedy Four, the most successful of more than 300 quartets then touring the vaudeville circuit. Personnel in the quartet changed many times over the next forty years, but Smith (the tough) and Dale (the "Dutchman") were constants. Exactly which partner contributed more to their skits can never be known; both agree they worked together for the good of the act.

In 1902 the Avon Four were booked into the Atlantic Garden in the Bowery at a splendid salary of $60 per week. Rarely out of work afterward, they were headliners who in 1904 introduced the "New Schoolteacher" skit to audiences; the *Clipper* reported "there are no dull moments." Their famous "Dr. Kronkhite" skit first appeared in 1906 on the stage of Hammerstein's Victoria Theatre on Forty-second street; it went on to become the most performed comedy act of all time. From the moment Dale, as Dr. Kronkhite, encouraged Smith to "take off dee coat, my boy" the laughs were unending. Smith, told by a pirouetting Dale that he is indeed the doctor, professes himself dubious. "How are you, Mr. Dubious," replies Dale most politely. After ten minutes of broad misunderstanding and bodily probing, Dale finally decides Smith needs glasses. As simple as it sounds, the act still got roars when performed on Ed Sullivan's television show sixty years later.

In 1908 the first Avons broke up when Lester left and was replaced by Irving Kaufman. That year Dale married Molly Cahill; their childless union lasted sixty years, surviving endless tours and three wars. After several national tours on vaudeville circuits, the Avons in 1909 took on New York's "blue laws" prohibiting Sunday performances. A judge, confused by a description of their routine, decided "they have no act," and dismissed the case; as a consequence the ban on Sunday performances ended. The troupe then became the first major American vaudeville group to tour England and soon anticipated yet another cultural change by recording their skits and songs. In 1914 they headlined the first all-American show at London's Finsbury Park Empire Theatre. The fame of the group spread as classic skits including "Hungarian Rhapsody," "Venetian Nights," and "The Realestaters" were added to their repertoire.

As a vaudeville headliner, the Avons were successful even as smaller theater chains (Keith-Albee) were supplanted by larger ones (Shubert/Erlanger). When Smith and Dale began their Broadway career in *The Passing Show* (1919), they created sub-Avon Fours who continued to tour. To support the Actors' Equity strike of August 1919 against the Shuberts, they left the Winter Garden and performed at a rival Keith theater. For many years Dale served on the Board of the American Guild of Variety Artists, where he fought for better wages and conditions for all actors. On Broadway, the team performed in additional *Passing Shows*, Earl Carroll's *Vanities*; *The Sidewalks of New York*; *Crazy Quilt*; *Mendel, Inc.*; and *The Sky's the Limit*, among others. As late as 1962 the octogenarian duo appeared in *Old Bucks and New Wings*, but legitimate theater was never their true milieu.

Even during the 1920's, the theater world marveled at the team's longevity and understood that the partners never had a serious quarrel. One memorable day in 1922 they performed before President Warren Harding in the afternoon and ex-president Woodrow Wilson in the evening. Another president, Harry Truman, remembered seeing the team perform while he was working as a theater usher in Kansas City in 1905. Dale lived quietly with his wife in Worcester, Mass., when not performing, but the team's professional success continued even after the Avons disbanded for good in the 1920's. Dale lost track of how many times he and Smith "played the Palace" in New York, and the team led the bill at London's Palladium in 1929, helped open Radio City Music Hall in 1932, and constantly appeared on radio. One of their skits, "From the Battery to the Bronx," was filmed as a Paramount short in 1929, and a brief movie career followed; they appeared in *Manhattan Parade* in 1931 and *Heart of New York* in 1932. They made many slapstick shorts, but Dale vetoed additional films, preferring Broadway to Hollywood. For their fortieth anniversary, Smith and Dale appeared in Frank Fay's vaudeville show at the Alvin Theatre on Mar. 15, 1939.

Almost as amazing as the duo's longevity was the fact that their act never really changed. Whether it was belligerent patter, exquisite tim-

ing, sight gags, or the very familiarity of the route is debatable—but the inevitable result was hilarity. Smith and Dale appeared on Milton Berle's first "Texaco Star Theatre" television show only a month before the Lamb's Club honored their fiftieth anniversary in 1948. Brooks Atkinson praised the comic pair with these words: "They are professional performers, acting two low comedy parts with style, authority and abandon. Don't change your act for at least 50 years." By then the Dales resided on West Fifty-fifth street, so it was easy for the team to reopen vaudeville at the Palace with Judy Garland in October 1951, to appear with Ed Sullivan, and to enjoy a sixtieth anniversary fete attended by Mayor Robert Wagner in 1958. Shortly before the team's seventieth anniversary party in 1968, Molly Dale died. Charlie subsequently joined Smith in residence at the Actor's Fund Home in Englewood, N.J. The duo's last professional appearance was on Ed Sullivan's show in November 1969. The career of Smith and Dale was the subject of Neil Simon's *The Sunshine Boys*, an acerbic comedy which bore little relation to the calm tenor of the team's historic partnership—it "Simonized" it! After Dale died in 1971 and was buried in Woodlawn Cemetery, show business folk said that God greeted him with "Take off dee coat, my boy," and asked him to stay forever.

[Charles Dale's accomplishments are cited in virtually all histories of vaudeville and Broadway as part of Smith and Dale. The Lincoln Center Library, New York, has clipping files on Dale, as well as clippings on the Avon Four and Joseph Smith. A planned biography by Aaron Fishman never appeared, but one chapter was published; see Abel Green, ed., *The Spice of Variety* (1952). An obituary appears in the *New York Times*, Nov. 17, 1971.]

GEORGE J. LANKEVICH

DALEY, ARTHUR JOHN (July 31, 1904–Jan. 3, 1974), sportswriter and author, was born in New York City, one of two children born to Daniel M. Daley, a sales executive, and Mary Greene. He attended Fordham Preparatory School, and in 1922 he entered Fordham University, where he participated in baseball, basketball, football, track, and swimming. After breaking his left arm in a football pileup, he joined the student newspaper and eventually became its sports editor.

After graduation in 1926, Daley joined the

New York Times as a sports reporter. One year later he reported on the heavyweight boxing match between Jack Dempsey and Gene Tunney. In 1932 he was sent to Los Angeles for his first Olympic games, and four years later he covered the games in Berlin. In 1942, he succeeded John Kieran in producing the daily column "Sports of the Times." He wrote thousands of columns on all sports, but baseball remained his favorite. Daley's writing was characterized by fairness, intelligence, and wit; he soon became one of the most noted and quoted columnists in the United States. He was the recipient of the Grantland Rice award in 1961; the Sportswriter of the Year award in 1963; and the Professional Football Writers' Distinguished Writing award in 1970. On May 8, 1956, he won the Pulitzer prize "for local reporting under conditions not usually subject to a deadline." The awarding of this prize to a sports reporter was very rare. The columns cited by the Pulitzer committee were on boxing, baseball, horse racing, and track.

One of Arthur Daley's columns concerned a talented baseball player's betrayal of his principles and was turned into a book, *The Natural*, by Bernard Malamud. Daley himself authored and coauthored several books, including *Times at Bat: A Half Century of Baseball* (1950), considered at the time of its publication "the most comprehensive book on baseball ever published." He collaborated with his *New York Times* colleague, John Kieran, on *The Story of the Olympic Games*, an authoritative history of the games from the first Olympiad held in Greece in 776 B.C. through modern times.

Daley was a modest and diffident man who won the respect and confidence of those he covered. Joe DiMaggio once said, "I knew I could trust him from the first day I met him." Daley married Betty Blake on Nov. 28, 1928. Their home was in suburban Greenwich, Conn., and they had four children. Daley never retired, and he died while on his way to the office to write his column.

[There are obituaries with photographs in the *New York Times*, Jan. 4, 1974; *Time*, Jan. 14, 1974; and *Newsweek*, Jan. 14, 1974.]

KEVIN J. O'KEEFE

DALEY, CASS (July 17, 1915–Mar. 22, 1975), singer, dancer, and comedienne, was born Catherine Dailey in Philadelphia, Pa., the daughter of Frank Dailey, a streetcar conductor, and his wife Catherine, a homemaker. She spent her childhood in Philadelphia, where she attended the local public schools. At the age of ten she began singing and dancing on an empty bread crate in front of a neighbor's store. Daley moved with her family to Camden, N.J., just across the Delaware River from Philadelphia, where she went to high school. At age seventeen she began working at a local nightclub, combining singing with her job as hatcheck girl and electrician. The next year, Daley began performing in amateur acts and in local theaters and cabarets. In 1932, she met and married her theatrical agent, Frank Kinsella.

An enthusiastic singer and dancer, Daley was not physically beautiful and thus was an easy mark for hecklers. She learned to ad-lib comic retorts and to poke fun at herself in self-defense. Her husband soon persuaded her to turn to comedy. From this beginning she developed an hilarious comic song-and-dance act that featured numerous rambunctious sight-gags. In 1946 one magazine's theater critic described her act: "When she comes on stage she looks like a nice, terribly shy girl in a long white gown. After a moment's pause and a demure curtsy, she suddenly chases the announcer, swings on the velvet curtain, howls a snatch of some unrefined ditty, walks on the side of her heels, pops her teeth and straddles the mike."

Her unabashed clowning soon caught the eye of New York entertainment impresario Florenz Ziegfeld. Having previously incorporated the raucous comedy of stage star Fanny Brice in his famous Follies, Ziegfeld was convinced Daley could follow in Brice's footsteps. At the age of twenty, she signed a contract to star in the 1936–1937 Ziegfeld Follies at Manhattan's Paramount Theater. She also changed her name to Cass Daley so it would fit on the theater marquee.

Her talents were soon in great demand. Over the next four years she proved in several Broadway shows and on radio that her funny face and physical behavior were not her only talent. In particular, her numerous appearances on "Fitch Bandwagon," a radio show, highlighted her uncanny sense of timing. She soon became America's most popular comedienne.

In 1941, Daley got her big break in movies when she signed a long-term contract with Paramount Pictures to do a series of lighthearted musical comedy films in which she was usually featured in several boisterous and acrobatic song-and-dance numbers. In each number she would cut up and go through numerous slap-stick contortions. All together she made a dozen full-length films and shorts between 1941 and 1954, among them, *The Fleet's In* (1941), *Star-Spangled Rhythm* (1942), *Crazy House* (1943), *Out of This World* (1945), *Ladies' Man* (1947), *Here Comes the Groom* (1951) (produced and directed by Frank Capra), and *Red Garters* (1954).

While none of her films received critical ac-claim, many were popular, especially those made during World War II. Moreover, many enduring songs debuted in these films, among them, the big band favorite "Tangerine" from *The Fleet's In*, the Harold Arlen and Johnny Mercer hit "That Old Black Magic" from *Star-Spangled Rhythm*, and Johnny Mercer and Hoagy Carmichael's "In the Cool, Cool, Cool of the Evening" from *Here Comes the Groom*.

Early in 1948, at the height of her career, she decided to cut back on taking film roles and have a family. Her only child, a son named Dale, was born in late 1948. In 1951, she nearly lost the light of her life when the brakes of the family car (parked on an incline near the family home) failed and rolled toward three-year-old Dale. The boy's elderly nurse managed to push him out of the way but was herself fatally injured.

After making *Red Garters* in 1954, Daley again retired to New York to raise her son. Her twenty-year marriage to Kinsella came to an end in 1955. Not until 1967 did she decide to attempt a comeback. She noted in 1973: "No-body ever gets out of show business. I made a horrible mistake when I decided to marry and raise my son and forgot about my career 25 years ago."

By mid-1967, she had remarried, this time to Hollywood businessman Robert Williamson. When her son entered college, she returned to the movies, playing a supporting role in Para-mount's *The Spirit Is Willing* (1968) and in 1969 in the moderately successful Hal B. Wal-lis comedy *Norwood: The Phynx*. In 1972, she returned to Broadway in a vaudeville revue re-vival named *The Big Show of 1936*. At the height of her comeback, she died in an accident at her home in Hollywood.

[An obituary appears in the *New York Times*, Mar. 24, 1975.]

WILLIAM HEAD

DANA, CHARLES ANDERSON (Apr. 25, 1881–Nov. 27, 1975), lawyer, financier, indus-trialist, and philanthropist, was born in the Gramercy Park neighborhood of New York City, the son of Charles A. Dana, a banker, and Laura Parkin. Scion of an old New England family, his forebears included author Richard H. Dana (*Two Years Before the Mast*) and Charles A. Dana, Abraham Lincoln's assistant secretary of war and longtime editor of the *New York Tribune*.

Dana received his B.A. from Columbia Uni-versity in 1902 and his law degree from Colum-bia in 1904. During college, he joined Squadron A, the famous silk-stocking New York City National Guard cavalry unit. He began work as a lawyer for the Pennsylvania Railroad before becoming an assistant prosecutor for New York County (Manhattan). In 1907, Dana gained national attention for his part in the pros-ecution of Harry Thaw for the murder of Stan-ford White, the world-famous architect. (Thaw was found not guilty by reason of insanity.) In 1908 Dana secured the Republican nomination for the New York State Assembly's 27th district and won three consecutive elections. He an-gered suffragettes by opposing revision of the New York State constitution to allow women to vote. He left Albany in 1914.

In the same year, Dana entered the business world when investment brokers at Spencer Trask and Company alerted him to the poten-tial of the struggling Spicer Manufacturing Company. Spicer made drive shafts and univer-sal joints for trucks and automobiles. Clarence Spicer was a superior mechanic but was unsuc-cessful as an industrial executive. Dana refi-nanced Spicer in return for a controlling interest in the company. He took over as president in 1916 and later became chief executive officer. He made the company a leading automotive parts concern even while he maintained a busy law practice for several years. During World War I, the company made drive shafts for thou-sands of army trucks.

After the war, Dana began to expand the product line and to acquire new companies. Demand for parts grew rapidly in the 1920's as car production more than doubled in the de-cade. Dana bought Chadwick Engine Works in Pottstown, Pa., to expand production of univer-sal joints. Then he added Parish Pressed Steel Company of Reading, Pa., for automobile and truck frames. Two axle manufacturers were acquired in the early 1920's. His last acquisition of the decade was Hayes Wheels and Forgings, Limited, of Ontario, Canada, then the world's largest manufacturer of automobile wheels. As automobile production shifted toward Detroit, Dana engineered the move of the Spicer corporation westward to Toledo, Ohio. Despite the Great Depression, Spicer's sales rose from $3.5 million in 1930 to $19 million in 1940. Before World War II, Spicer went international with sales to English manufacturers and other firms on the Continent.

Dana was an unconventional executive. He kept his "office" in his wallet and conducted business on trains, automobiles, and lake steamers. He once purchased a manufacturing plant for $3 million by writing a contract in the margin of a newspaper page. Although he was somewhat authoritarian, he learned to negotiate with organized labor and even sent coal and hot coffee out to his workers while they walked a picket line in subzero weather. During World War II, Spicer quintupled production for the war effort, and every one of Dana's plants flew the coveted Army-Navy "E" Award for excellent production of war materials. In 1946 Spicer was officially renamed the Dana Corporation in honor of its dynamic chief executive. In 1948, Dana was elected chairman of the board and turned the presidency over to a younger man.

To ensure that Washington would not waste his money, the industrial entrepreneur set up the Dana Foundation in 1950 to continue his philanthropic work in cooperation with local interests. Said Dana in 1959 to *Time*, "I found myself with all this money. If you wait until you're dead, it often doesn't get used the way you want it to." At first, Dana gave money to hospitals. Then in 1956, he began to endow liberal arts colleges. He donated entire buildings to Bucknell, Colgate, Dartmouth, Dickenson, and many small institutions in the South. He said that he favored small colleges over larger ones because he preferred the intimacy, companionship, and collegiality that these schools provided to the impersonal bureaucratic structure of large universities. His favorite tactic was to offer institutions a challenge grant—one-third to two-thirds of the money needed to finance a capital project. Thus inspired, schools almost always found donors willing to make up the difference. His maxim was "I'll do it if you will."

During his life, Dana served as officer or director of twenty companies, including Fisk Rubber, Manufacturers Trust, and the Curtiss-Wright Corporation. He married Agnes Ladson, and together they had four children. They divorced in 1938, and he married Eleanor Naylor in 1940. He retired from active business in 1967, remaining as honorary chairman of the board of Dana Corporation for the rest of his life. He spent his last years raising Shropshire and Merino sheep on his estate in Connecticut. He died in Wilton, Conn.

[For further biographical information see Rene McPherson, *Dana: Toward the Year 2000* (1973). An obituary is in the *New York Times*, Nov. 29, 1975.]

DAVID M. ESPOSITO

DANIELS, FARRINGTON (Mar. 8, 1889–June 23, 1972), educator, author, chemist, and solar energy proponent, was born in Minneapolis, Minn., the eldest of three children of Franc Birchard Daniels, a district superintendent for the American Express Company, and Florence Louise Farrington. Daniels attended public schools in Minneapolis. His teachers were struck by his intensity, maturity, and immense concentration, traits he carried into adulthood. At an early age, he showed an interest in science; he experimented with making explosives and acid batteries for running electric motors. He especially enjoyed chemistry and physics at East Side High School and decided to choose chemistry as his major in college. From 1906 to 1911 he attended the University of Minnesota, receiving a B.S. and an M.S. in chemistry. In 1911, Daniels elected to attend Harvard University for a doctoral study. He worked under Theodore W. Richards, who later became the first American to win the Nobel Prize in chemistry.

Daniels received a Ph.D. in physical chemistry from Harvard in 1914 and was awarded a Parker Fellowship to study in Europe. He was accepted by Fritz Haber to study at the Kaiser Wilhelm Laboratory for Physical Chemistry Research in Berlin. The beginning of World War I prevented him from going, so he instead took a post as an instructor in chemistry at Worcester Polytechnic Institute (WPI) in Worcester, Mass. His first paper, "An Adiabatic Calorimeter," published in the *Journal of the American Chemical Society*, was based on research done at WPI. It was in this period that he began work on nitrogen fixation.

In 1918, while still teaching at WPI, Daniels decided to join the army. He received a commission as first lieutenant in the Chemical Warfare Service. During the war Daniels worked with Charles A. Krause to improve gas masks at Clark University in Worcester. Their model was later approved for use in World War II. Daniels was discharged from the army December 31, 1918. His teaching contract was not renewed at WPI.

In 1919, Daniels was employed in Washington, D.C., by the Bureau of Soils (later the U.S. Fixed Nitrogen Research Laboratory) to study nitrogen fixation by a low-temperature electrochemical technique. Additionally, he studied the decomposition of nitrogen pentoxide and wrote a paper establishing that the rate process was first order independent of the concentration. This was an important finding because it helped debunk the radiation theory of reaction rates, which held that the minimum energy required for reaction (or activation energy) was proportional to the frequency of radiation, and to advance the study of chemical kinetics.

In 1920, Daniels joined the chemistry department at the University of Wisconsin, Madison, as an assistant professor. He became associate professor in 1924 and full professor in 1928, continuing in this position until his retirement as professor emeritus in 1959. From 1952 to 1959, he served as department chair. During his tenure as chair, he was instrumental in the construction of two chemistry buildings, one of which was named for him in 1972.

In 1944, Daniels was appointed associate director of the chemistry division of the Metallurgical Laboratory (Met Lab) of the Manhattan Project at the University of Chicago and then director in 1945. He thus played a major role in the development of the atomic bomb and in eventually converting the Met Lab to Argonne National Laboratory (ANL), a facility housed in nearby Dupage County, dedicated to exploring peaceful uses of atomic energy and other basic research. Daniels served as chair of Argonne's board of governors (1946–1948). Later, he was a consultant at both ANL and Oak Ridge National Laboratory in Tennessee. Daniels also served as chair of an advisory committee on isotopes for the Atomic Energy Commission (AEC). Daniels was one of the first scientists to design a nuclear reactor for peacetime use of nuclear

energy. His design—the "Daniels pile"—was unique in that it used helium as a heat exchanger; though never built, it was patented by the AEC in 1957.

Daniels had a fertile mind and made original contributions in the fields of nitrogen fixation, nitrogen oxides, chemical kinetics, photochemistry and photosynthesis, dry cell, thermoluminescence, radioisotopes, and the use of solar, wind, and atomic energy to produce electricity. He also did seminal work on the decomposition of organic halides; he contributed to applications of natural thermoluminescence in geochemistry and to thermoluminescence dosimetry and induced thermoluminescence as a way of measuring exposure to ionizing radiation. In the 1940's, with support from the Cottrell Foundation, he contributed to the development of what became known as the Wisconsin process for converting atmospheric nitrogen into chemicals for producing such varied products as fertilizers and explosives. He published more than three hundred papers and was granted seven patents in diverse areas.

Daniels was the author or coauthor of scientific texts on diverse topics, among them *Experimental Physical Chemistry* (1929), *Outlines of Theoretical Chemistry* (with Frederick Getman, 5th ed., 1931), *Physical Chemistry* (with R. A. Alberty, 1955), and *Outlines of Physical Chemistry* (with Frederick Getman, 7th ed., 1943), and coeditor of *Solar Energy Research* (1955), among others. From 1932 to 1942, Daniels was an associate editor of the *Journal of the American Chemical Society*.

Daniels was also the recipient of the highest American awards in the field of chemistry, given by the American Chemical Society: the Willard Gibbs Medal (1955), the Priestley Medal (1957), and the James Flack Norris Award for Excellence in Teaching Chemistry (1957). He received numerous other awards, citations, and honorary degrees nationally and internationally throughout his life. Daniels married Olive Miriam Bell in 1917. They had four children. Daniels died in Madison, Wis.

[Daniels's letters and papers are in the University of Wisconsin archives in Madison. His unpublished biography, written by his wife, is "Farrington Daniels, Chemist and Prophet of the Solar Age" (1978). An obituary appears in the *New York Times*, June 24, 1972.]

SAMUEL VON WINBUSH

DARIN, BOBBY (May 14, 1936–Dec. 20, 1973), singer and actor, was born Walden Robert Cassotto in the Italian neighborhood of East Harlem in New York City, the son of Vanina ("Nina") Cassotto. His father is unknown. The boy's mother and grandmother, Vivian Ferne (Walden) Cassotto, conspired to keep the unwanted pregnancy a secret and led Darin to believe that he was the son, rather than the grandson, of Vivian and her husband, Saverio Cassotto, recently deceased. Not until Darin was in his thirties did he learn that Nina, who had pretended to be his older sister, was really his mother. Nina subsequently met and married Charles Maffia, a clerk and truck driver. With government assistance supplementing Maffia's modest income, the two women and Maffia moved to the Bronx and raised Darin together.

Darin exhibited an early interest in show business by appearing in elementary school productions and by learning to imitate such popular entertainers as Al Jolson and Donald O'Connor. Darin's grandmother had been a vaudeville singer and dancer and encouraged him to develop his talents. Between the ages of eight and twelve Darin suffered repeated attacks of rheumatic fever, which left him bedridden for extended periods. Although his condition gradually improved, his physician told his family that he had little chance of surviving past the age of twenty-one. Darin remained on medication and continued to have related health problems for the rest of his life.

Darin was a gifted student and met the rigorous academic requirements for admittance to the Bronx High School of Science, where he learned to play the drums and started a band with four of his classmates. He honed his skills by performing at school dances and by singing and dancing before summer vacationers at New York's Catskill mountain resorts. After graduating from high school in 1953, Darin attended Hunter College in the Bronx (now Lehman College), where he took theater courses and appeared in a number of stage productions.

After less than a year at Hunter, Darin left college and scratched out a living for the next few years by writing songs and commercial jingles. By that time he had learned to play the piano and guitar as well as the drums and had chosen a new name, Darin, supposedly from a telephone directory. In 1956, Darin auditioned for Decca Records and was given a one-year contract. He made several unsuccessful records for Decca before moving on to Atco Records, a subsidiary of Atlantic Records, in 1957. In 1958, Atco released Darin's recording of "Splish Splash." The song, which Darin reportedly wrote in twelve minutes, was an instant hit and sold more than 100,000 copies in three weeks.

"Splish Splash" and other hit records, including "Early in the Morning" and "Queen of the Hop" made Darin an idol among teenagers at the age of twenty-two and led to appearances on the "Ed Sullivan Show," Dick Clark's "American Bandstand," and many other television programs. Darin, however, aspired to reach an older and wider audience and in 1959 released an album of old favorites called *That's All*. One of the twelve songs on the album was a new arrangement of "Mack the Knife," from Kurt Weill and Bertolt Brecht's *Threepenny Opera*. "Mack the Knife" was released as a single later that year and sold more than two million copies. Not surprisingly, the National Academy of Recording Arts and Sciences awarded Darin Grammys for the best single record and as best new performer of 1959.

Although his voice was considered to be only average by some critics and although the press faulted him for his arrogance and ambition, Darin was an irresistible showman. He developed a physically expressive style that was very much his own. He quickly won over audiences with his finger-snapping and flashy dance steps. Darin began working the nightclub circuit in Las Vegas by opening for comedian George Burns, who became a father figure to him. Soon he was headlining at the Copacabana and other clubs in New York City and had established himself as one of the most popular and highest-paid nightclub performers in the country.

In 1960, Darin had his first featured acting role in the movie *Come September* (for which he also wrote the title song), starring Rock Hudson, Gina Lollabrigida, and Sandra Dee. At the age of eighteen, Dee was already an established Hollywood star when she met Darin on the set. The two were married on Dec. 1, 1960, and settled in the Bel Air section of Los Angeles. Their marriage ended in divorce in 1966. They had one child.

Unlike many other entertainers who crossed over to film, Darin took his acting career very seriously and often chose challenging dramatic roles. He appeared in more than a dozen movies and was nominated for an Academy Award in 1964 as best actor in a supporting role for his portrayal of Corporal Jim Tompkins in *Captain Newman, M.D.*

Darin continued to perform in Las Vegas and on television for the rest of his life despite heart ailments that hospitalized him and increasingly threatened his career. In June 1973, he married Andrea Joy Yeager, a legal secretary. They separated several months later. Darin died in Los Angeles of heart failure.

[For a biography of Darin and a catalog of his recordings and films, see Al DiOrio, *Borrowed Time: The 37 Years of Bobby Darin.* Darin's obituary appears in the *New York Times*, Dec. 21, 1973.]

RICHARD DAVIDMAN

DAVIDOFF, LEO MAX (Jan. 16, 1898–Dec. 24, 1975), neurosurgeon, was born in Talsen, Latvia, one of nine children of Israel Davidoff, a cobbler and butcher, and Liebe Lemkus, a homemaker. The family came to Boston, Mass., in 1905. Davidoff attended several Massachusetts public schools, finishing high school in Salem. He graduated from Harvard College in 1920 and from Harvard's medical school with an M.D. in 1922.

His postgraduate training began with six months in pediatrics (1922) at the Boston City Hospital and a year in internal medicine (1922–1923) in Connecticut at New Haven Hospital. He received his training in surgery and neurosurgery at Peter Bent Brigham Hospital, Boston (1923–1926). Here he became the protégé of the legendary neurosurgeon, Harvey Cushing, who engaged only one resident at a time. Davidoff later emulated many of Cushing's diacritic inflections. When Cushing was asked whom he would have operate on him if he had a brain tumor, after reluctantly admitting that he could not operate on himself, he is reported to have replied, "Well, I guess I would have Davy do it." (Davy was Cushing's nickname for Davidoff.)

Between June and October 1925, Davidoff took leave from his residency to serve as surgeon on the schooners *Peary* and *Bowdein* for the Byrd-MacMillan Arctic Expedition to Greenland and Labrador. Although plagued by a recurrently squeamish stomach, he carried out his medical duties and read extensively, mostly about neurology. In his detailed and literate diary, *Trip to North*, he described Lt. Commander Byrd as "a Virginian F.F.V., a soldier,

short of speech, handsome, chivalrous, brave to the point of foolhardiness." Davidoff dedicated the volume to "My most beloved Idatchka who was my unexpected reward for my labors, hazards and heartaches." He married Ida Alice Fisher on Oct. 3, 1926; she became an active family therapist, and they had four children.

A Peter Bent Brigham Travelling Fellowship (1926–1927) took Davidoff to Europe, then the mecca of progressive, scientific medicine. He received further training in neurology under Dr. Gordon Holmes of National Hospital, London, and under Dr. Alfons Jakob at the Staatskrankenanstalt in Hamburg. He returned to the United States to become research assistant at the New York State Psychiatric Institute (1927–1929). From then on his professional career was spent entirely in New York City. He served as neurosurgeon at the Neurological Institute of New York (1929–1937), the Jewish Hospital of Brooklyn (1937–1945), and Montefiore Hospital, while simultaneously holding the post of professor of clinical neurological surgery at Columbia University's College of Physicians and Surgeons (1945–1949). He then was director of neurological surgery at Beth Israel Hospital and concomitantly was clinical professor of neurosurgery at New York University College of Medicine (Postgraduate) (1949–1954). Davidoff held the post of neurosurgeon at Mount Sinai Hospital (1951–1956) before assuming his seminal academic roles as a founding faculty member of the Albert Einstein College of Medicine of Yeshiva University, where he was first professor and chairman of surgery (1954–1958) and then of neurological surgery (1959–1966). He played a leadership role in the development of the college's clinical training programs, where he was also associate dean (1961–1966). He became professor emeritus in 1966. He was director of surgery (1954–1958) and director of neurological surgery at the affiliated Bronx Municipal Hospital Center (1959–1966), and attending neurosurgeon again at Montefiore Hospital.

After World War II, Davidoff participated in highly successful teaching missions to raise the standards of medical education and practice in Czechoslovakia in 1946 (he was a member of the Unitarian Service Committee Medical Mission, and awarded Order of the White Lion, Fourth Class, from Charles University); Poland; and Finland (where he was chairman of the Unitarian Service Committee and World

Health Organization Medical Mission). He was the first participant in the Exchange Professorship Program between the Albert Einstein College of Medicine and the Government Hospital in Tel-Hashomer, Israel (1960), was a special guest of the University of Teheran and the Government of Iran (1963), and served as chairman of the Overseas Medical Advisory Committee to the Tel-Aviv University Medical School.

Among Davidoff's many distinctions were founding member of the American Board of Neurological Surgery, charter member and president (1956–1957) of the Harvey Cushing Society, and honorary member of the American Society of Neuroradiology (1963), a unique distinction given for his major contributions to this discipline. In 1966, he was named the first honorary alumnus of the Einstein College of Medicine. In 1976, the department he founded was designated the Leo M. Davidoff Department of Neurological Surgery, and the Leo M. Davidoff Society was established to recognize excellent teaching in undergraduate medical education.

Davidoff performed 2,000 operations and made extensive studies of acromegaly; the treatment of brain tumors with surgery and radiotherapy; Parkinsonism; and the influence of the nervous system on the intestine. His contributions to medical literature include approximately 200 articles and 12 books, including the multivolume *Neuroradiology Workshop* (with Harold Jacobson and Harry Zimmerman; 1961), *The Normal Pneumoencephalogram* (with Cornelius G. Dyke; 1937), and *The Abnormal Pneumoencephalogram* (with Bernard S. Epstein; 1950).

His credo may be summarized by the prayer of Maimonides (the twelfth-century physician and philosopher), which he read at each of the Einstein commencements he attended: "Grant that I may be filled with love for my art and for my fellow men." A characteristic and self-sacrificing contribution was his offer to try the then-experimental medicine L-dopa, for the Parkinsonism that ended his active neurosurgical career. Relaxing distraction was provided by sculpting and gardening. He abhorred all forms of totalitarianism; human dignity was sacrosanct to him. He was a strict disciplinarian and demanding taskmaster when it came to the care of patients. Away from the hospital, this austere facade vanished, and he was charming, humorous, and graciously convivial with skills as a raconteur.

Davidoff died in his daughter's home in Wivenhoe (Essex), England.

[Biographical articles on Davidoff include H.M. Zimmerman, "In Memoriam: Leo M. Davidoff, M.D., 1898–1975," *Surgical Neurology*, July 1976; and Harold G. Jacobson, "A Revisit with Leo M. Davidoff, M.D.—A Titan of His Time," *Neurosurgery*, Nov. 1983. Obituaries appear in the *New York Times*, Dec. 25, 1975, and the *Harvard Medical School Alumni Bulletin*, Mar./Apr. 1976.]

ERNST R. JAFFÉ

DAVIS, ADELLE (Feb. 25, 1904–May 31, 1974), nutritionist and author, was born Daisie Adelle Davis in Lizton, Ind., the daughter of Charles Eugene Davis, a farmer, and Harriette McBroom. After her mother's death, when she was seventeen months old, she was raised by her father and an elderly aunt on the farm in Indiana. She is said to have attributed her lifelong interest in nutrition to the malnourishment she suffered as an infant, when after the death of her mother she was fed with a medicine dropper.

Davis began her college education at Purdue University in Lafayette in 1923, but after two years transferred to the University of California at Berkeley, where she received a B.A. degree in dietetics in 1927. In 1939, she received a master's degree in biochemistry from the University of Southern California School of Medicine. In the interim, Davis received dietetic training at Fordham and Bellevue hospitals in New York City and did graduate work in dietetics and nutrition at Columbia University and at UCLA. She also served as supervisor of nutrition in the Yonkers, N.Y., school system from 1928 to 1930. She was a nutritional consultant to physicians and health clinics in Oakland, Calif. (1931–1933), Los Angeles (1934–1938), and Palos Verdes, Calif., where she resided after 1948.

Davis married George Edward Leisey, an engineer, in 1943 and they later adopted two children. This marriage ended in divorce in 1953. She married Frank Vernon Sieglinger, a retired accountant, in 1960. An advocate of physical fitness, Adelle Davis played tennis regularly and enjoyed swimming.

Davis published her first two books, *Optimum Health* and *You Can Stay Well*, privately. As her popularity grew, she was noticed by major publishers, and eventually Macmillan published *Vitality Through Planned Nutrition* (1942, rev. 1949). *Let's Cook It Right* (1947, rev. 1972), *Let's Have Healthy Children* (1951), *Let's Eat Right To Keep Fit* (1954), and *Let's Get Well* (1965) followed, all published by Harcourt. Her most controversial book was *Exploring Inner Space: Personal Experiences Under LSD-25*, written under the pseudonym of Jane Dunlap and published in 1961. The descriptions of her mind-expanding experiences under the influence of LSD seemed to conflict with her views regarding the unhealthful effects of chemicals in food. Davis also wrote countless articles on health and nutrition for numerous periodicals. It is estimated that her books have sold nearly seven million copies worldwide.

Davis's views on health and nutrition were controversial and often put her at odds with the medical establishment and the refined food industry. She believed that most human illness, including mental depression and addiction, could be attributed to overly processed commercial foods and food additives. Her outspoken statements, such as, "Mass advertising of refined foods has exploited health for money to the extent that it amounts to mass murder," did not endear her to American food producers. She advocated organically grown foods, whole wheat baked goods, and brewer's yeast as healthful dietary elements. While she believed that a proper diet did not require vitamin supplementation, she also felt that the processed food diet of most Americans was so poor that added vitamins were essential. She held controversial views regarding the role of calcium as a pain-killer, the effect of vitamin E deficiency on premature infants, and skim milk consumption during pregnancy as a cause of cataracts in babies. Her emphasis on the value of raw milk, eggs, and cheese led to criticism by medical authorities that adoption of her dietary recommendations could lead to obesity and heart disease. While medical research has demonstrated that her views on cholesterol-rich dairy foods are extreme and perhaps dangerous, vitamin E deficiency as a cause of anemia in premature infants is now a well-recognized condition.

Davis often decried the lack of nutritional training in most medical school curricula, which led to frequent attacks by members of the medical educational community who felt that her teachings and writings were sensational, anecdotal, and filled with errors of fact and interpretation, a claim that Davis steadfastly denied.

Davis was in demand as a lecturer and nutritional consultant throughout her career and received numerous awards and honors. She provided individual nutritional consultation to such celebrities as W. C. Fields and Charles Laughton.

Many who have read the works of Adelle Davis and have adopted the culinary style she advocated claim to have increased energy and a sense of good health. As John Poppy wrote in an article in *Look* (Dec. 15, 1970), "an Adelle Davis reader tends to become a True Believer."

Adelle Davis died in Palos Verdes Estates, Calif. She will be remembered as a believer in good health and good nutrition despite ridicule and disdain from the processed food industry and the medical establishment, which she in turn accused of misguiding the American population. From a dietary point of view, Davis believed that "we are watching the fall of Rome."

[Additional biographical information is in *Look*, Dec. 1970; *Vogue*, May 1971; *McCall's*, Aug. 1971; *Life*, Oct. 22, 1971; *Harper's Bazaar*, June 1972; and *Time*, Dec. 18, 1972. An obituary is in the *New York Times*, June 1, 1974]

PHILLIP THARP SWENDER

DAVIS, BERNARD GEORGE (Dec. 11, 1906–Aug. 27, 1972), magazine publisher, was born in Pittsburgh, Pa., the son of Charles Davis, a scrap-metal broker, and Sarah Alice Harris. The youngest of six children, he grew up in a comfortable atmosphere of prosperity and achievement. After graduating from Peabody High School in Pittsburgh in 1923, he enrolled at the University of Pennsylvania for one year, attended Columbia University for a summer session (1926), and completed his undergraduate studies at the University of Pittsburgh, where he earned a B.S. in 1927. On Nov. 20, 1930, he married Sylvia Friedman; they had two children.

As the student editor of the University of Pittsburgh's humor magazine, the *Pitt Panther*, Davis was active in the Association of College Comics of the East, serving as secretary-treasurer his senior year. At the association's convention that year, he met William B. Ziff, the twenty-nine-year-old president of a small Chicago firm that published comic books and specialized magazines such as *Popular Aviation* and that sold advertising for a network of forty

African-American newspapers. Offered a job as an editorial assistant, Davis joined the William B. Ziff Company in 1927 and soon became an editor on Ziff's *America's Humor* magazine. A photography enthusiast, he later was the founding editor of the successful magazine that became *Popular Photography*.

Though their ensuing twenty-five-year relationship was always more professional than personal, Ziff, a widely traveled author active in public affairs and a prominent participant in the American Zionist movement, clearly valued Davis's evident magazine-publication management skills. In 1936, Davis was appointed vice-president and director, and the name of the firm was changed to the Ziff-Davis Publishing Company. He was also given a substantial minority equity position in the company, and when the enterprise moved from Chicago to New York City in 1946, he was named president. By the early 1950's, Davis was directing the publishing operations of a number of profitable Ziff-Davis magazines in such emerging special-interest fields as aviation, photography, and electronics.

After Ziff's death in 1953, Davis offered to buy the company from the Ziff family. The family, however, declined his offer, and Ziff's son, William B. Ziff, Jr., assumed control of the firm. In 1957, Davis sold his interests in Ziff-Davis Publishing to the family and, with his son, Joel, founded Davis Publications. The company eventually published thirty-four specialized magazines, annuals, and directories; its two best-known titles were *Ellery Queen's Mystery Magazine*, acquired with the purchase of Mercury Publications in 1957; and *Science and Mechanics*, acquired from the Curtis Publishing Company in 1959. Other publications included *Boat Builder, Camping Journal, Car Repair, Electronics Hobbyist, Elementary Electronics, Furniture, Hi-Fi Stereo Buyers Guide, Home Workshop, Income Opportunities, 101 Home Plans, Radio-TV Repair,* and *Woodworker*.

Davis continued as president of Davis Publications until 1967, when he became chairman of the board and named his son, Joel, to succeed him as president. He was also active in professional associations, serving as a member of the board of directors (1955–1968) and treasurer (1959–1967) of the Magazine Publishers Association, and as the magazine publishing representative on the American Council on Education for Journalism (1960–1966).

After a heart attack in 1968, Davis moved from New York City to Palm Beach, Fla. He retained the title of chairman but turned over most of the management responsibilities for Davis Publications to his son. Though semi-retired, an interest in foreign travel led him to accept a position with the University of Palm Beach as director of international programs in 1969. During a business trip to Seoul, Republic of Korea, he suffered another heart attack and died; in accordance with his wishes, the body was cremated in Korea.

As one of the publishing professionals who understood that the growing American interest in leisure activities, particularly after World War II, would present unique opportunities for the magazine industry, Davis proved adept both as senior executive during his thirty-year career at Ziff-Davis Publishing and later as the entrepreneurial founder of his own publishing firm. His forte was specialized publications, and the magazines, buyer's guides, and directories he published played a significant supporting role in defining the popular culture, as well as the avocational ideal of "the good life," in mid-twentieth-century America.

[An obituary is in the *New York Times*, Aug. 29, 1972.]

DAVID ABRAHAMSON

DEAN, JAY HANNA ("DIZZY") (Jan. 16, 1911–July 17, 1974), baseball player, was born in Lucas, Ark., the son of Albert Dean, an itinerant sharecropper who had played semiprofessional baseball as a young man, and Alma Nelson, who died when he was very young. Dean had very little formal schooling; he attended primary school through the second grade in Chickalah, Ark. From the age of ten he and his father and two brothers worked as migrant cotton pickers. Dean enlisted in the U.S. Army at the age of sixteen and was stationed at Fort Sam Houston in Texas for three years. A natural athlete, he was a star pitcher for the Twelfth Field Artillery team. On his discharge he joined a semiprofessional team in San Antonio, where he was discovered by a baseball scout.

In 1929, Dean signed a contract to play for the minor league St. Joseph, Mo., team; he then moved up to the Houston team in the Texas League. In 1930, he was called up to the St. Louis Cardinals. His brother Paul Dee ("Daffy") Dean also played for St. Louis from

1934 to 1940. On June 10, 1931, Dizzy married Patricia Nash, a Houston store clerk, who had to lend her husband-to-be the two dollars for the marriage license. Dizzy wanted to be married in the ballpark at home plate, but Nash refused. They had no children.

Dizzy Dean became, by some estimates, the greatest pitcher of his era. Pitching in the major leagues for the St. Louis Cardinals from 1930 to 1937, and for the Chicago Cubs from 1938 to 1941 (with one sad attempt at a belated comeback in 1947 with the St. Louis Browns, where he appeared in one more game), Dizzy won 150 games, lost 83, and finished with 1,115 strikeouts and an earned-run-average of 3.03. During that span, Dizzy turned in some amazing seasons. At the beginning of the 1934 season, for example, Dizzy predicted, "Me and Paul are going to win 45 games." He was almost right. In 1934, Dizzy and Daffy won 49 games between them—of course, Dizzy won 30 of them, leading the league with most victories, while he lost only 7, compiling a league-leading won-lost percentage of .811. That year he also led his league with 24 complete games. Dean's nickname is explained on the back of card 6 of the 1934 series of Big League Baseball Cards published by Goudey Gum Co. of Boston: "Dean made the White Sox dizzy trying to bat against him several years ago and so they dubbed him 'Dizzy.' He's been making them dizzy ever since."

On Sept. 24, 1934, Dizzy, in the first game of a double-header, pitched a one-hitter against the Dodgers. In the second game, his brother Paul pitched a no-hitter. When reporters talked to Dizzy after the game about the no-hitter, Ol' Diz told them, "If I had known what Paul was going to do, I would have pitched one too."

In 1935, Dean experienced a slight dropping off. He won only 28 games that year (once again leading the league with most victories) and lost 12. However, 29 of those decisions were complete games. From 1933 through 1936, Cardinal relief pitchers had little work when Dizzy was on the mound.

If Dizzy's exploits made his manager thank his lucky stars, Dizzy's practical jokes off the field were enough to cause his manager to pull out his hair. Not for nothing were the St. Louis Cardinals, with Leo Durocher, Daffy and Dizzy Dean, Frankie Frish, Ducky Medwick, Wild Bill Hallahan, and Pepper Martin dubbed the Gashouse Gang.

Dizzy's lifetime achievements in the big leagues no doubt would have been more impressive if his career had not been cut short by injury. During the 1937 All Star Game, the twenty-six-year-old pitcher broke his toe. To compensate for the injury, Dizzy began to experiment with his pitching style, and soon he damaged his throwing arm. The decline was swift and painful. From 1938 until the end of his career, Dizzy won only 16 more big league games.

After retiring from the game, Dizzy played golf and took up broadcasting. Because he handled (or mishandled) the English language with the same degree of humor and nonchalance that had characterized his days in a Cardinal uniform, Dizzy soon became a radio and (eventually) a television legend; he called himself a "commulater." "And now the players have gone back to their respectable positions," he would announce, describing a player's brow as covered with "pressperation."

On radio, when a listener wrote in to complain that Dizzy did not know the King's English, Dizzy responded: "Ol' Diz knows the King's English. And not only that. I also know the Queen's English."

When listeners protested that he should not use the word *ain't* over the airwaves, Dizzy defended himself in his own inimitable style. "Why, shore I say ain't," he told his critics, "but a lot of people who don't say ain't, ain't eating." Dean went on to ask: "What's wrong with ain't? And as for saying 'Rizzuto slid into second' it just ain't natural. Sounds silly to me. Slud is something more than slid. It means sliding with great effort."

In 1952, Hollywood released a movie about Dean's life. *The Pride of St. Louis* featured Dan Dailey playing the role of the pitching star.

Dizzy died in Reno, Nev. The epitaph he composed for himself reads: "There'll never be another like me."

[Dean's take on baseball can be found in Jerome Herman Dean, *Dizzy Baseball. A Gay and Amusing Glossary of Baseball Terms* (1952). For additional biographical information see Lee Allen, *Dizzy Dean: His Story in Baseball* (1967); M. Shapiro, *The Dizzy Dean Story* (1968); Curt Smith, *America's Dizzy Dean* (1978); and Jack Kavanaugh, *Dizzy Dean* (1991), a biography for young readers. An obituary is in the *New York Times*, July 18, 1974.]

LOUIS PHILLIPS

DE KRUIF, PAUL HENRY (Mar. 2, 1890–Feb. 28, 1971), bacteriologist and scientific writer, was born in Zeeland, Mich., the son of Hendrik de Kruif and Hendrika J. Kremer. His father, a self-made man, ran a prosperous farm implements business, but he was determined his son would make something greater of himself and escape small-town life. De Kruif entered the University of Michigan in 1907, as his father directed, to study a profession, either law, medicine, or engineering. In his sophomore year de Kruif settled on medicine after reading an article about Dr. Paul Ehrlich, the German scientist. After earning his B.S. in 1912, however, he decided that he preferred research to practicing medicine and graduate school to medical school. A Rockefeller research fellowship enabled him to study bacteriology under Professor Frederick G. Novy, a pioneer in the field, at the University of Michigan. De Kruif's dissertation demonstrated that healthy rat serum quickly and easily became toxic under certain conditions. He earned his doctorate in 1916 and was immediately hired by the University of Michigan as an assistant professor of bacteriology.

His teaching career was interrupted by World War I, though; in 1917 he entered the U.S. Army Sanitary Corps, where he became part of a research team that discovered the antitoxin for gangrene resulting from poison gas. His work earned him a promotion from lieutenant to captain.

At war's end de Kruif returned to the University of Michigan where he taught in both the medical school and the college. He married and had two sons. His wife, Mary, was also a professor, but de Kruif said little about her in interviews or in his memoirs, perhaps because of subsequent events. After only a few years of marriage, he fell in love with a laboratory assistant, Rhea Elizabeth Barbarin. Torn by conflicting feelings—love for Rhea, responsibility for his children, and guilt toward his wife—he decided the best solution was to augment his salary so that he could afford a divorce and remarriage. A scientific paper he presented in 1918 at the Society for Experimental Biology in Cincinnati, Ohio, resulted in a job offer two years later in the greener pastures of the Rockefeller Institute for Medical Research (now Rockefeller University) in New York City. A letter de Kruif had written to H. L. Mencken, an author he much admired, led to advice that launched him on a new and profitable career, scientific writing. Mencken introduced de Kruif into the New York literary scene, and soon de Kruif had his first commission.

The key year in de Kruif's transformation was 1922. He married Rhea Barbarin on December 11 and his first published piece of writing appeared, an essay on the state of American medicine in Harold Stearn's *Civilization in the United States* (1922). He earned fifty dollars for the assignment. Initially de Kruif expected to write in his spare time, but a series of articles he published on the medical profession for *Century* magazine (later reprinted as *Our Medicine Men* [1922]) forced him to write full-time: some of the unflattering portraits included in the articles resembled his colleagues at the Rockefeller Institute quite closely, and de Kruif was compelled to resign.

Another series of investigative articles on the medical profession led de Kruif to Sinclair Lewis, and the two began to collaborate on what would become *Arrowsmith* (1925). Although their relations were stormy Lewis nevertheless acknowledged de Kruif's assistance, and de Kruif earned 25 percent of the book's profits. *Arrowsmith* was awarded a Pulitzer Prize in 1926, which Lewis turned down without consulting his collaborator. Afterward de Kruif used to say that he got "one quarter" of a Pulitzer but turned it down.

De Kruif's most famous work was *The Microbe Hunters* (1926) a study of early microbiologists which sold over a million copies and was translated into eighteen languages. In the late 1920's and early 1930's, de Kruif wrote several books—*Hunger Fighters* (1928), *Seven Iron Men* (1929), and *Men Against Death* (1932)—and, with playwright Sidney Howard, *Yellow Jacket* (1934), which was made into a motion picture in 1938.

A letter de Kruif received from the poet Ezra Pound in 1934, in the midst of the Great Depression, sharpened his social conscience and helped turn his efforts in a more overtly political direction. Pound asked him if he had thought about the impact of poverty on health. The result was *Why Keep Them Alive?* (1936), written with his wife Rhea, an exposé of the effects of poverty on children, which made a plea for a more equitable distribution of wealth. The book was not well received, especially by the medical community. A work more flattering to the profession, *The Fight for Life* (1938), was more popular; it was adapted by Pare Lorentz as a documentary film. In 1939, de Kruif met with President Franklin Roosevelt to discuss public health issues. As a result, Roosevelt appointed him to several committees charged with investigating public health concerns, particularly polio, which had disabled the president more than a decade before. *Health Is Wealth* (1940) argued that expanded public health facilities offering preventive medical care might improve America's health. Like his 1936 study, it angered medical professionals with its critical portrayal of doctors.

Over the 1930's, de Kruif returned to his first love, bacteriological research, to help develop a pre-penicillin treatment for syphilis.

In the 1940's and 1950's, de Kruif wrote some two hundred articles, primarily for *Reader's Digest* and other magazines in the Curtis Publishing Company empire. He also continued to write books on scientific and medical topics: *Kaiser Wakes the Doctors* (1943), *Male Hormone* (1945), *Life Among the Doctors* (1949), and *A Man Against Insanity* (1957). He never lost his commitments to preventive medicine and a strong public health movement to help those living in poverty.

The death of his second wife in 1957 slowed de Kruif's prolific efforts. He was married for a third time, to Eleanor Lappage, in September 1959, and published his memoirs, *The Sweeping Wind*, in 1962, but his work on scientific subjects flagged. He traveled a great deal and enjoyed exercising—jogging in his younger days and walking as he got older. No matter where he lived in pursuit of a story, he always considered Holland, Mich., his home. He died there just four days shy of his eighty-first birthday.

[In addition to his memoirs, a portrait of de Kruif may be found in Albert Q. Maisel, "Fighter for the Right to Live," *Reader's Digest*, Dec. 1946 and Jan. 1947. An obituary appears in the *New York Times*, Mar. 2, 1971.]

JUDY KUTULAS

DENFELD, LOUIS EMIL (Apr. 13, 1891– Mar. 28, 1972), naval officer, was born in Westborough, Mass., the son of Louis Denfeld, an attorney, and Etta May Kelley. Denfeld attended high school in Duluth, Minn., where he had gone to live with his uncle Robert Denfeld, a retired navy officer. He graduated from the Naval Academy in 1912. Denfeld then had

sea duty in battleships *Virginia* and *Arkansas* and in *Paducah*, a gunboat. On June 5, 1915, he married Rachel Metcalf.

In 1916 Denfeld began several years of service in destroyers: in *Ammen*, which was based at Queenstown, Ireland, during World War I; as executive officer of *Lamberton* (1918–1919); and then as commanding officer of *McCall* in 1919. He had by this time become a lieutenant and in 1918 received the temporary rank of lieutenant commander; that rank was made permanent in 1922. Between 1919 and 1921 Denfeld was in Boston as assistant recruiting inspector and then inspector of the navy's New England division. During the remainder of the 1920's Denfeld had additional sea duty in *Wadsworth* (1921–1922), as commanding officer of submarine S-24 (1923–1924), and finally as commander of destroyer *Brooks* (1926–1928). He had two periods of service in Washington, D.C.: the first in the Ship Movements Division of the Office of the Chief of Naval Operations (1924–1926), and the second as aide to the chief of the Bureau of Navigation (1929–1931).

Denfeld advanced steadily, earning promotions to commander in 1933, to captain in 1939, and to rear admiral in 1942. He grew familiar with the higher workings of the navy while serving, from 1931–1933, as aide and flag secretary to Admiral Richard Henry Leigh, who commanded the Battle Force (1931–1932) and then the United States Fleet itself (1932–1933). Denfeld later served as aide to Chief of Naval Operations William D. Leahy (1937–1939). Between these tours he served in the Bureau of Navigation (1933–1935) and as commander of Destroyer Division Eleven (1935–1937). In 1939 and 1940 he assumed command of Destroyer Division Eighteen. After duty as commander of Destroyer Squadron One (1940–1941), Denfeld reported to London in February 1941 as a special naval observer to consult on antisubmarine warfare and to assess sites for future American bases. In April of that year he became chief of staff to the commander of the Atlantic Fleet Support Force. Denfeld was charged with developing a task force organization to escort the convoys that would be carrying Lend-Lease supplies to Great Britain. His efforts earned him a Legion of Merit.

In 1942 Denfeld began a three-year tour as assistant chief of the Bureau of Navigation, soon renamed the Bureau of Naval Personnel. In 1945 Denfeld took command of Battleship Division Nine, consisting of three of the world's mightiest warships: *Wisconsin*, *New Jersey*, and *Missouri*. His battleships provided antiaircraft gunfire support to a carrier task force during the Okinawan campaign, and also functioned independently of the carriers to bombard targets on shore.

With the end of World War II Denfeld returned to Washington to head the Bureau of Naval Personnel. Advanced in rank to vice-admiral, he had the tasks of supervising the orderly demobilization of the wartime navy and of developing recruitment and personnel policies for the postwar years. In early 1947 he was named commander in chief, Pacific, and promoted to full admiral. In addition to the normal duties of this position, Denfeld also administered on a military basis the Pacific islands formerly under Japanese rule, as per the United Nations agreement on American trusteeship of that area. Later that year he succeeded Fleet Admiral Chester Nimitz as chief of naval operations.

Despite his affable nature and years of experience in Washington, Denfeld had a stormy tenure. Much of the discord Denfeld encountered revolved around defining the missions of the army, navy, and newly independent air force in the event of conflict between the United States and the Soviet Union, the only likely great-power adversary. The disputes over missions inevitably involved budgetary matters, for military spending was being slashed in this uncertain period after the Second World War. The missions a service received would bear substantially upon its share of the budget. If, for instance, the air force monopolized the mission of strategic nuclear bombing, it would benefit immensely in the ongoing budget warfare.

The austere budget for fiscal year 1949 led Denfeld and Secretary of the Navy John L. Sullivan to halt construction of thirteen other ships in order to build a supercarrier, the *United States*. The first carrier designed since the end of the Second World War, it would be able to operate the newest jet planes, which in turn could handle atomic bombs. Although a dissenting vote was cast by the air force chief of staff, the supercarrier received the approval of the Joint Chiefs of Staff and of President Truman. Denfeld had not opposed the air force's call for funds for its prime new weapons system, the B-36 bomber.

By 1949 the air force had strengthened its position. During the Berlin airlift it had received forward bases in Great Britain for its bombers, and with the North Atlantic Treaty Organization (NATO) becoming a reality, it could expect additional European bases. New Secretary of Defense Louis A. Johnson cancelled construction of the *United States* and made other cuts in funds allocated to navy and marine aviation.

Tensions between the navy and the air force and their respective partisans in Congress and among the press erupted during the summer of 1949 into the highly publicized "revolt of the admirals," which took place in prolonged hearings on defense policy held before the House Armed Services Committee. For much of that time Denfeld was in Europe on NATO affairs. By the time he returned, the dispute had split the defense establishment and the navy itself. For instance, advances in the navy's capabilities in antisubmarine warfare were used by resentful air admirals to buttress their contention that Denfeld was indifferent to their need for better carriers and planes.

In September, Denfeld endorsed a letter by a subordinate claiming that morale within the navy was at its lowest point since 1916. When the letter was leaked to the press, Denfeld claimed that his endorsement did not mean that he concurred with all the opinions expressed in the letter. Pressured by Johnson to keep Denfeld "in line," the new secretary of the navy, Francis P. Matthews, felt that Denfeld should be relieved of his command for endorsing the letter in the first place. Matters came to a head when the navy's most respected air admiral, Arthur W. Radford, who was commander in chief of the Pacific Fleet, testified before the committee in October that the B-36 was a "billion-dollar blunder," and asserted that strategic bombing alone could not win a war. As he prepared to testify, Denfeld was under pressure to back either his superior, Matthews, or subordinates like Radford who had made clear their displeasure with defense policies. Denfeld stood with his service colleagues. However, in the opinion of historian Paolo E. Coletta, he had waited too long to define his position.

President Truman then acquiesced in the relief of Denfeld, who was informed on Oct. 28, 1949, that he would be replaced as chief of naval operations. Rather than accept the position in Europe that the secretary of the navy offered him, Denfeld took accrued leave and retired early in 1950. He then made clear in three articles written for the popular magazine *Collier's* the extent of his dissatisfaction with the defense policies of Matthews and Johnson. Denfeld, who became a consultant to a major oil company, then refrained from further embroilment in defense issues. Ironically, Denfeld's final actions as chief of naval operations brought him more respect from his fellow officers than anything else he had accomplished in his tenure. He died in Westborough, Mass., and was buried in Arlington National Cemetery.

[Photographs and other miscellaneous items relating to Denfeld are in the Westborough Public Library. See Louis E. Denfeld, "Reprisal: Why I Was Fired," *Collier's*, Mar. 18, 1950; Denfeld, "The Only Carrier the Air Force Ever Sank," *Collier's*, Mar. 25, 1950; "The Nation Needs the Navy," *Collier's*, Apr. 1, 1950. See also Robert S. Allen, "The Navy's Uncle Louie," *Collier's*, July 23, 1949; Vincent Davis, *The Admirals Lobby* (1967); Paolo E. Coletta, "Louis Emil Denfeld," in Robert William Love, Jr., ed., *The Chiefs of Naval Operations* (1980); Michael A. Palmer, *Origins of the Maritime Strategy: American Naval Strategy in the First Postwar Decade* (1989); and E. B. Potter, *Admiral Arleigh Burke: A Biography* (1990). An obituary is in the *New York Times*, Mar. 30, 1972.]

LLOYD J. GRAYBAR

DE SEVERSKY, ALEXANDER PROCOFIEFF (June 7, 1894–Aug. 24, 1974), aviator and military theorist, was born in Tiflis, Russia, the son of Nicholas Seversky, a pioneer Russian pilot, and Vera Vasilieff Procofieff. As a boy he displayed an interest in aviation, building model aircraft. His parents enrolled him in the Imperial Naval Academy of Russia, from which he graduated in 1914. He then undertook postgraduate work at the Russian Military School of Aeronautics. At this time de Seversky began work on a combination ski and pontoon system to enable Russian naval aircraft to operate during the winter.

During World War I, de Seversky was a Russian naval aviator. In July 1915, his plane was shot down, and he suffered the loss of his right leg when his own bombs exploded. De Seversky spent the next year recovering, and he eventually returned to active duty with a special decree from Tsar Nicholas II. After several attempts, he finally received permission to fly combat missions again. Despite the loss of his leg, he downed thirteen German aircraft and became

one of the most decorated men in Tsar Nicholas II's armed forces.

When the Russian Revolution erupted in 1917, de Seversky was in the United States as a member of the Russian Naval Aviation Mission. His Russian passport had been issued in French, the "de" appearing in front of "Seversky" for the first time. De Seversky liked the change—and kept it.

Deciding to stay in the United States in 1918, he found work as a test pilot, and soon afterward as a consulting engineer to the United States Air Service. In 1921, Brigadier General William Mitchell named de Seversky his special assistant. For the next three years, de Seversky worked to develop the first fully automatic synchronous bomb sight. The new device worked well, and General Mitchell arranged a government purchase of de Seversky's 364 patent claims for $50,000 in 1922. De Seversky used this money to start the Seversky Aero Corporation.

De Seversky began work intensively on a variety of engineering problems. He labored on retractable landing gears to be used on ice, water, or land. He concentrated on modifying and inventing a variety of structural designs. Wing flaps were the focus of yet other projects. During these years de Seversky made two important transitions in his personal life. On June 23, 1925, he married an American, Evelyn Olliphant, in New Orleans. Two years later he became a naturalized citizen. By this time he had also joined the United States Army Air Corps Specialists Reserve, and was commissioned a major.

In 1931, de Seversky founded the Seversky Aircraft Corporation and focused on the production of long-range pursuit planes, with himself as test pilot and chief designer. His experimentation through 1934 yielded a government contract for thirty-five amphibious airplanes. The company soon sold eighty-five "P35" pursuit planes, incorporating a number of efficiency mechanisms that had by then been perfected.

Unfortunately, these developments were accompanied by his company's growing financial distress. By 1938, the Seversky Aircraft Corporation averaged annual losses amounting to approximately $1 million. In 1938, de Seversky urged that a director of the corporation, W. Wallace Kellett, be named vice-president. Within five months, because of disagreements between board directors and de Seversky over company policy, the directors of the company named Kellett president and demoted de Seversky to director. By the following October, the name of the company was changed to the Republic Aviation Corporation and by May 1940, de Seversky was removed from the company's board entirely. The resulting litigation by de Seversky was eventually settled out of court.

When World War II began in Europe, de Seversky committed himself to enlightening the general public to the crucial factor of air power in modern war. In the 1942 publication of *Victory Through Air Power*, de Seversky argued for the absolute importance of a strategic air force with a wide radius of operational capability. He rejected the idea of advance bases and extensive ground organization. In de Seversky's construct, air power was clearly the critical factor in modern war. Made into a film produced by Walt Disney in 1943, the book played a pivotal role in persuading the Pentagon to give air power the necessary priorities to secure control of the air before launching a European invasion.

In March 1945, Secretary of War Robert Patterson named de Seversky his special consultant. De Seversky traveled to Japan and in 1946 to the Bikini atomic test site in order to analyze the effects of nuclear bombing. Through the late 1940's he lectured at a variety of military war colleges, such as Air University in Montgomery, Ala.; the Royal Canadian Air Staff College; the National Defence College in Canada; and the Strategic Intelligence School in Washington, D.C. In 1950, he published *Air Power: Key to Survival*, and in 1961, *America: Too Young to Die!*. In both of these works, and indeed, throughout his lectures in the 1950's, de Seversky focused on a myriad of strategic nuclear concerns. He continued his advocacy of air power's crucial role—especially in the nuclear age. In 1955, he argued that the "whole military philosophy must be changed," which meant, as expressed in *America: Too Young to Die!*, that the "organization plan of our Department of Defense . . . is fallacious to the point of absurdity."

De Seversky lived his final years at Asharoken Beach in Northport, Long Island, N.Y., and in New York City at Central Park South. He died at Memorial Hospital in New York City.

[See the biographical introduction in the 1950 edition of *Air Power: Key to Survival*. See also Edward Warner, "Douhet, Mitchell, Seversky: Theories of Air Warfare," in Edward M. Earle, ed., *Makers of Modern Strategy: Military Thought from Machiavelli to Hitler* (1944). An obituary is in the *New York Times*, Aug. 26, 1974.]

MICHAEL J. EULA

DEWEY, THOMAS EDMUND (Mar. 24, 1902–Mar. 16, 1971), public official, was born in Owosso, Mich., the son of George Martin Dewey, Jr., a newspaper editor, local Republican activist, and postmaster, and Annie Louise Thomas. An only child, young Dewey was reared, especially by his strong-willed mother, to respect hard work and methodicalness. At age nine, in addition to performing household chores, he sold newspapers and magazines; throughout his precollege years he never was absent from nor late for classes.

As a youngster Dewey acquired a strong interest in music, especially in song. During his years at the University of Michigan (1919–1923), Dewey's musical interests intensified into passion and his vocal talents bloomed. The young baritone won a statewide contest in 1923 and placed third in the national finals. He enrolled in the University of Michigan Law School in the spring of his senior year. In the summer following graduation Dewey worked in a Chicago law office and took voice training. While in Chicago he met another aspiring singer, Frances Eileen Hutt. That fall Dewey moved to New York, where he pursued voice lessons, legal studies at Columbia University Law School, and Hutt, not necessarily in that order. By 1924, Dewey had abandoned any serious plans for a concert career, as had Hutt.

After graduation from law school in 1925, Dewey began work at the law firm of Larkin, Rathbone and Perry, from which he was fired two years later. Subsequent employment at McNamara and Seymour proved more congenial. On June 28, 1928, Dewey and Hutt were married; they had two children. As the result of a salary cut necessitated by the exigencies of the Great Depression, Dewey in 1931 launched his public career. He accepted the position of chief assistant to George Z. Medalie, the United States attorney for the Southern District of New York, and was briefly Medalie's handpicked successor in late 1933. During these years of the celebrated probe by Judge Samuel Seabury into New York's legendary municipal corruption, Dewey built a reputation for painstaking investigation that led, most notably, to the conviction and incarceration of the notorious bootlegger Waxey Gordon.

Dewey returned to private practice in January 1934, but in the summer of 1935 he accepted an invitation from a somewhat reluctant Governor Herbert Lehman to become a special prosecutor. The current district attorney was a minion of Tammany Hall, and hence part of the overall problem of New York's civic corruption. Despite a limited staff and budget, Dewey enjoyed extraordinary success. Over the next few years the special prosecutor obtained convictions in all but one of seventy-three cases that came to trial. Most prominent among them was the conviction of Charles ("Lucky") Luciano, organized crime kingpin, on charges of abetting prostitution. The downfall of the mobster, hitherto considered virtually untouchable, at the hands of a crusading young lawyer became grist for Hollywood's mill, which transmuted the saga onto the screen as *Marked Woman* (1937), starring Humphrey Bogart and Bette Davis.

More significantly, the fight against crime ignited a political career. Despite limited financial resources, Dewey turned down a lucrative offer to join the prestigious law firm of Sullivan and Cromwell in order to run for Manhattan district attorney on Mayor Fiorello H. La Guardia's anti-Tammany Fusion ticket. He won a resounding victory, eliciting predictions that higher office awaited him. His four-year tenure as district attorney established Dewey's reputation as, with the exception of J. Edgar Hoover, the nation's foremost crime buster. He prosecuted the sinister gangster Louis (Lepke) Buchalter; the suave, well-connected former head of the Securities and Exchange Commission, Richard Whitney; and Tammany powerhouse James J. Hines. In 1938, Dewey narrowly lost the gubernatorial race against Lehman, the popular, highly respected incumbent, but immediately found himself, according to polls, the front-runner for the Republican presidential nomination in 1940.

Reports of the demise of the Republican party after the 1936 elections, like that of Mark Twain much earlier, had been greatly exaggerated. The failure of President Franklin Roosevelt's court-packing scheme, the economic downturn in 1937, Roosevelt's largely unsuccessful purge of political enemies in 1938 with accompanying strong Republican electoral gains, and the controversial decision to seek a third term

pointed to the president's vulnerability. Declaring himself a candidate, Dewey pronounced the New Deal a "failure." In foreign policy, under the tutelage of John Foster Dulles, he avoided the isolationism embraced by his two chief rivals for the nomination, Senators Arthur Vandenberg and Robert A. Taft, and avoided the outspoken internationalism voiced by Roosevelt. The 1940 Republican presidential nomination, however, went to dark-horse candidate Wendell Willkie. Dewey completed his term as district attorney at the end of 1941 and the following year was elected governor of New York, defeating James J. Bennett by nearly 650,000 votes. During his first term as governor he welded fiscal conservatism to liberal social policies, an amalgam that also characterized his subsequent two terms. His administration substantially added to the budgetary surplus, and by the end of his third term the state's income tax was 10 percent lower than when he entered office. Dewey also persuaded the legislature to raise wages for lower-level state employees and to bring an additional four hundred thousand persons under minimum-wage laws.

Dewey emerged as the Republican presidential standard-bearer in 1944. During the campaign he assailed the federal government's inefficient economic policies and pointed to the wasteful squabbling within its swollen bureaucracy. He did not, however, deny all the achievements of the New Deal: indeed, he called for an extension of Social Security. Dewey endorsed his party's strong civil rights stance, which urged an end to the poll tax, the passage of an antilynching measure, and an investigation into racial discrimination within the military. A call for continued bipartisan support for the war effort and a system of postwar collective security highlighted his foreign policy stance. Dewey won only twelve states and ninety-nine electoral votes.

Dewey was elected to a second term as governor in 1946, defeating James Mead in a landslide victory. Education received high priority during his second term. The state established a university that was largely decentralized. On the other hand, after a teachers' strike in Buffalo, Dewey strongly supported the Condon-Wadlin Bill, which made strikes by public employees illegal.

Whatever Dewey accomplished in fighting crime and corruption and in governing what at the time was the nation's most populous state, he may be best remembered as the candidate who lost a seemingly unlosable election. Republicans had gained control of Congress in 1946 for the first time since the Great Depression. Moreover, the pronounced unpopularity of President Harry S. Truman was apparent. The defections of left-wing and southern Democrats over issues of the Cold War and race, respectively, made Truman's defeat seem a foregone conclusion. Having once more defeated Robert A. Taft for the presidential nomination, a confident Dewey ran on a platform that promised progressive but fiscally sound domestic programs along with continued bipartisan support for foreign policy.

The staid Dewey, who firmly believed that a public official should always act with dignity, campaigned dispassionately and, in the words of Clare Booth Luce, looked like "the bridegroom on a wedding cake." Truman, in contrast, ran a "give 'em hell" campaign in which he denounced the Republicans as antilabor, anti–displaced persons, and anti–average small American. Worse for Dewey's prospects, a drop in farm prices convinced numerous farmers to vote Democratic. Nor did the Progressive party candidacy of Henry A. Wallace divert as much support from Truman as Republicans had hoped and assumed. Truman scored one of the greatest upset victories in the history of presidential elections, defeating Dewey by some two million popular votes and by a margin of 303–189 in the electoral college.

The astonishing upset quashed Dewey's presidential hopes but not his political power within the party. Shortly after his defeat he quietly began a movement to make Dwight Eisenhower, then president of Columbia University, the Republican standard-bearer in 1952. Ultimately, after a bruising convention fight in Chicago during which the Taft forces denounced Dewey as the man who twice had led the party to defeat, Eisenhower won the nomination. With Dewey's blessing Eisenhower selected as his running mate Richard M. Nixon, the junior California senator noted for his fervid anti-Communism and particularly for his role in the conviction of Alger Hiss for perjury.

Following his victory over Adlai E. Stevenson, Eisenhower brought into his administration members of Dewey's political circle, notably John Foster Dulles as secretary of state and Herbert Brownell as attorney general. Upon the death of Chief Justice Fred Vinson in 1953,

Dewey may have received (but declined) an invitation to succeed Vinson. Both Dewey and Eisenhower came to deplore the liberal views of Earl Warren, Dewey's running mate in 1948 and Vinson's ultimate replacement; but when President Nixon offered him the opportunity to succeed Warren, Dewey declined.

After his failure to win the presidency Dewey served one more term as governor, winning reelection in 1950 by a margin of victory of more than 570,000 votes over Congressman Walter J. Lynch. Scandals involving the state's harness racing commission sullied his last administration. Nevertheless, the creation of the New York Transit Authority, the Niagara Power Project, and the opening of the state's thruway system (later named for Dewey) insured Dewey's reputation as one of New York's most successful governors.

After his retirement from public life in 1954, Dewey reentered private law practice. He enjoyed both the preeminence of his law firm (which had been founded by Elihu Root but which now became Dewey, Ballantine, Bushby, Palmer, and Wood) and his assorted duties within the legal profession. He also continued during his postgubernatorial years in an unofficial capacity as an adviser to the Republican party. Frances Dewey died on July 17, 1970; Dewey died at Bal Harbour, Fla., and was buried in Pawling, N.Y.

[The Rush Rhees Library of the University of Rochester holds Dewey's papers. Other pertinent manuscript materials are scattered in various collections, most notably in the Library of Congress. See also *The Public Papers of Thomas E. Dewey*, 12 vols. (1944–1957); Dewey's *The Case Against the New Deal* (1940), a series of campaign speeches; *Journey to the Far Pacific* (1952), an account of a two-month trip; *Thomas E. Dewey on the Two-Party System*, ed. John E. Wells (1966), lectures delivered at Princeton University in 1950; and Rodney Campbell, ed., *Twenty Against the Underworld* (1974), uncompleted memoirs. Richard Norton Smith, *Thomas E. Dewey and His Times* (1982), is the only complete biography. See also Rupert Hughes, *Attorney for the People* (1940); and Stanley Walker, *Dewey, an American of This Century* (1944), an early campaign biography that contains twenty-one of Dewey's speeches. An obituary is in the *New York Times*, Mar. 17, 1971.]

ROBERT MUCCIGROSSO

DE WILDE, BRANDON (Apr. 9, 1942–July 6, 1972), actor, was born André Brandon de

231

Wilde in Brooklyn, N.Y., the son of Frederic de Wilde, a New York City stage manager, actor, and director, and Eugenia Wilson, a former actress who received commendations for her role in *Tobacco Road*. De Wilde attended Lenox School in Baldwin, Long Island, where he lived. Here he received instruction in acting; later, he attended the New Lincoln and the Professional Children's schools, and graduated from Searing School, New York City, in 1960. He furthered his education at Columbia University and the New School for Social Research.

De Wilde was exposed from his early years to the theater. By what may be regarded as chance, Theresa Fay, a casting director, visited the de Wilde family in Baldwin in 1949 and mentioned that producer Robert Whitehead was looking for a young boy for an important role in a new play, Carson McCullers's *The Member of the Wedding*. Fay suggested that Brandon read for the part. At first, Frederic and Eugenia de Wilde dissented: they wanted their only son to have a normal life. After much persuasion on the part of Fay, the young de Wilde was cast for the role of John Henry West and, under Harold Clurman's direction, alongside Julie Harris and Ethel Waters, he made his first appearance on the Broadway stage at the Empire Theatre on Jan. 5, 1950. His sensitive portrayal won for him the prestigious Donaldson Award for the outstanding debut performance of the 1949–1950 season, the youngest person ever to receive it. De Wilde also received the *Look* magazine Golden Globe Award for his role in *The Member of the Wedding*. He played the role of John Henry for 492 performances, never missing one, and Brooks Atkinson lauded his "air of personal indomitability," remarking that he had the magnetic personality of a real performer.

De Wilde subsequently appeared as Howay in *Mrs. McThing*, with Helen Hayes as leading lady in 1952, as Ferike in *The Emperor's Clothes* in 1953, and as C. D. Lewton in *Comes a Day* in 1958. He also performed in Stanley Kramer's successful film version of *The Member of the Wedding* in 1952.

Director George Stevens, impressed by theatrical skills in one so young, cast de Wilde as Joey in the film *Shane*, joining a superb cast that included Alan Ladd, Jean Arthur, and Van Heflin. As the wide-eyed, hero-worshiping young Joey, de Wilde exhibited resourcefulness beyond his years, and *Shane*, now considered a

classic, became the most financially successful Western up to that time, earning Paramount $9 million. It received six Academy Award nominations, including de Wilde's as Best Supporting Actor. He also won the *Photoplay* magazine Award, and Filmdom's Famous Fives. He was given a special *Look* magazine award as the year's best child actor. After *Shane*, he rejoined the cast of *The Member of the Wedding* (1952), this time on the road. Regarding the film *Goodbye, My Lady* (1956), de Wilde complained that he had the role of a tearjerker because he felt it lacked the quiet emotional restraint of his previous films; he also expressed dissatisfaction with *Night Passage* (1957) because he felt it was a cliché-filled picture. He had roles in *The Missouri Traveler* (1958), *Blue Denim* (1959), *All Fall Down* (1962), and in *Hud* (1963), which starred Paul Newman. But de Wilde was beginning to lose his youthful appeal and many felt he failed to make the grade as an adult actor. *Hud* was followed by *Those Calloways; In Harm's Way; God Bless You, Uncle Sam; The Deserter;* and some others that only a few saw and to which no one gave recognition. De Wilde also performed on radio's Theater Guild of the Air (NBC) and in such plays as *Fallen Idol* and *Sea Gull's Cry*.

De Wilde was his own best critic, realizing weaknesses or imperfections in his character portrayals. Reflecting on his later roles, he thought that his acting was not quite good enough. With few exceptions, de Wilde was coached for most roles by his father, and the son attributed much of his theatrical success to his guidance. De Wilde preferred roles with emotional depth. The professionals he worked with always praised his unpretentiousness, notwithstanding his early triumphs and the rave reviews from critics which experienced actors yearn to achieve.

De Wilde accepted several parts on NBC's "Philco Television Playhouse." For more than a year, he did "Jaimie," a live television series written especially for him (1954–1955). Other popular TV performances included "Climax!," "Playhouse 90," "Alfred Hitchcock Presents," "The Virginian," "The Greatest Show on Earth," and "The Nurses." He was a four-time winner of the Milky Way Award, given for outstanding television appearances.

De Wilde served in the U.S. Army in the period 1962–1963 and became a member of the U.S. Army Reserve. He was a member of the American Equity Association, the Screen Actors Guild, and the American Federation of Television and Radio Artists.

On Dec. 20, 1963, de Wilde was married to socialite and freelance writer Susan Maw at St. Bartholomew's Church in Manhattan. In 1969, his wife sued him for divorce on grounds of cruelty. She requested custody of their son, Jesse, aged two, property division, and reasonable support.

While costarring with Maureen O'Sullivan in a stage production of *Butterflies Are Free* at an amusement park theatre in Denver, de Wilde was killed in a traffic accident. He reportedly was driving in a heavy rainstorm when his van slammed into a flatbed truck parked beside the road. He died four hours later in a Denver hospital. He was survived by his second wife, Janice, to whom he had been married only a few months, and his five-year-old son.

[Newspaper clippings and photos are in the New York Public Library for the Performing Arts. See also "Double Life of Brandon de Wilde," *New York Times Magazine*, May 24, 1953; and Ted Sennett, *Great Hollywood Westerns* (1990). Obituaries are in the *Denver Post*, the *New York Times*, and the *Baldwin Citizen*, all July 7, 1972.]

CHARLOTTE MCGRATH

DIES, MARTIN (Nov. 5, 1900–Nov. 14, 1972), Congressman, was born in Colorado, Tex., the son of Olive M. Cline and Martin Dies, a legislator. Shortly after Dies's birth, he and his family moved to east Texas, where, in 1908, the elder Dies was elected to the U.S. House of Representatives.

Dies's parents were divorced during his father's first term in Congress. Dies spent time with both his mother and his father, attending public schools in Beaumont, Tex.; Washington, D.C.; and Greenville, Tex. He studied at Cluster Springs Academy, in Cluster Springs, Va., from 1914 to 1917, and completed his secondary education at Beaumont High School the following year. He briefly attended Wesley College in Greenville, the University of Texas in Austin, and the Hickman School of Speech and Expression in Washington, D.C. He received a Bachelor of Laws degree from National University in Washington in 1920.

On July 3, 1920, Dies married Myrtle McAdams; they had three sons. He practiced law in Orange, Tex., with his father and Kemper W.

Stephenson. In 1930 he was elected as a Democrat to the U.S. House of Representatives from Texas's Second Congressional District, the same district his father had represented.

Although he would later be known as one of the most conservative members of the House, the big, blond, broad-faced Texan gave little indication of this early in his political career. In his 1930 campaign he sounded almost like a late-nineteenth-century rural radical, condemning "capitalistic tyranny" and the evils of monopoly, and calling for lower tariff rates and inflation of the currency through a wider use of silver. When Franklin D. Roosevelt entered the White House in 1933, Dies initially supported most New Deal economic reforms.

By 1935, however, Dies began to abandon liberalism. He fought the administration on coal-industry regulation and minimum-wage legislation. Like his friend and mentor, Vice-President John Nance Garner of Uvalde, Tex., Dies was disturbed by sit-down strikes in the auto industry in late 1936, and he tried unsuccessfully to initiate a congressional investigation of the situation. His antipathy toward the new Congress of Industrial Organizations (CIKO), many members of which were involved in the sit-down strikes, also revealed his increasing distance from New Deal liberal positions.

Dies emulated his father's nativist sentiments, and during his first years in Congress, the younger Dies claimed that immigrants were taking jobs away from native-born Americans during the depression. Dies also believed that immigrants were particularly susceptible to the influence of radical philosophies. As Dies moved rightward, this element of his nativism dominated. By the late 1930's, the concepts of foreignness, un-Americanism, and radicalism had merged in Dies's thinking. The same emotional energy that had earlier invigorated his nativism began to propel his developing crusade against Communist subversion in America.

This crusade took shape early in 1938 when, at the urging of Vice-President Garner, Dies proposed the establishment of a special committee to investigate un-American activities. Dies's resolution received support not only from conservatives concerned about Communist subversion, but also from liberals who hoped that the committee would investigate the fascist organizations that had begun to appear in America. Dies's resolution passed in May 1938, creating the House Special Committee on Un-

American Activities (also known as HUAC, or, for the period from 1938 to 1945, the Dies Committee). The committee began its investigations immediately, with Dies as its chairman.

The committee's most famous investigations, such as the one of former State Department official Alger Hiss, took place after Dies left Congress and the chairmanship of the committee in 1944. Still, from the beginning, the committee gained headlines as it heard witnesses describing Communist influences in labor organizations such as the CIO, government agencies such as the Federal Theatre and Writers' Project, and various other groups and organizations. The committee did conduct some investigations of the German-American Bund and other fascist groups, but most of its hearings focused upon threats from the Left, rather than from the Right. Despite persistent questions about the fairness of the committee's procedures and the accuracy of the testimony it collected and reports it issued, the House of Representatives continued to reauthorize it.

A skilled political orator, Dies had speaking engagements all over the country. His name also appeared as the author of a book published during this period, *The Trojan Horse in America: A Report to the Nation* (1940). Though actually written by J. B. Matthews, a former Communist sympathizer who was serving on the Dies Committee staff, the book reflected Dies's views upon the threat of Communism and fascism to America.

Martin Dies's anti-Communist career reached its peak from 1938 to 1941, during the early years of the Dies Committee's existence. Starting in 1941, Dies faced a string of personal and political difficulties. In 1941, he made an unsuccessful attempt to win a U.S. Senate seat, and was shaken when he came in fourth. The United States' wartime alliance with the Communist regime in the Soviet Union complicated his task of conducting anti-Communist investigations, and his committee held no public hearings for a two-year period. In 1944, suffering from ill health, Dies announced that he would not run for another term in the House.

Dies and his wife then moved to the east Texas town of Lufkin, where he soon regained his health. He kept himself in the public eye through frequent lectures, usually opting to speak on anti-Communist themes that were regaining popularity because of the Cold War. When a position for a congressman-at-large

from Texas opened up in 1952, Dies returned to the House and remained there until 1959, when redistricting eliminated the position.

Unable to regain a seat on his old committee, Dies maintained a relatively low profile during his second stint in Congress. He compiled a conservative voting record, opposing civil rights initiatives, and proposing legislation aimed at crippling domestic Communists. He refused to support foreign aid, even when supporters justified it as necessary to hinder the spread of international Communism. Before he left Congress, he made one more unsuccessful bid for the Senate in a special election held in 1957 to fill the seat vacated by Price Daniel.

After he retired from the House, Dies resided in Lufkin until his death. He continued to give speeches, but also occupied himself with writing an account of his anti-Communist activities, *Martin Dies' Story* (1963). From 1964 to 1967, he wrote for the conservative periodical *American Opinion*. Although he covered a variety of topics ranging from the assassination of John F. Kennedy to the United States' involvement in Vietnam, most of the thirty articles expressed the anti-Communist themes upon which Dies had built his political career.

[Dies's papers are located at the Sam Houston Regional Library and Research Center in Liberty, Tex. The most thorough treatment of Dies is Dennis Kay McDaniel, "Martin Dies of Un-American Activities: His Life and Times" (Ph.D. diss., University of Houston, 1988). See also William Gellerman, *Martin Dies* (1944). For accounts of the workings of the House Un-American Activities Committee, see August Raymond Ogden, *The Dies Committee: A Study of the Special House Committee for the Investigation of Un-American Activities, 1938–1944* (1945); and Walter Goodman, *The Committee: The Extraordinary Career of the House Committee on Un-American Activities* (1968). The University of North Texas Oral History Collection holds the transcript of an interview with Dies conducted in 1966. An obituary appears in the *New York Times*, Nov. 15, 1972.]

J. KAAZ DOYLE

DILWORTH, RICHARDSON (Aug. 29, 1898–Jan. 23, 1974), mayor of Philadelphia, was born in Pittsburgh, Pa., the son of Joseph R. Dilworth, the owner of an iron factory, and Annie H. Wood, the daughter of the founder of the first sheet steel mill in the United States. When Dilworth was eight, illness forced his father to retire from the factory that he owned, and the family moved to New York City. Though born into privilege, Dilworth was always a tough competitor. He attended St. Mark's school in Southboro, Mass., where he captained the baseball team, starred on the football team, and was a leading member of the debate team. Dilworth graduated from prep school in 1917. He entered Yale for a short time and then quit the university and joined the U.S. Marine Corps as a private. Serving on the western front, Dilworth was hit by a high-explosive shell that shattered his left arm. Awarded a Purple Heart, Dilworth underwent a half dozen operations to save his arm. Though he never regained full use of the arm, Dilworth recovered well enough to be a starting end on Yale's 1920 varsity football team. On his return to Yale, Dilworth became interested in politics as a supporter of Woodrow Wilson's proposals for a League of Nations.

Despite his father's threat to cut off funding for his education if he got married, Dilworth and Elizabeth Brockie were married on June 2, 1922; they had three children. Dilworth took a job at the open hearths of the U.S. Steel Co. plant in Pittsburgh and then worked on a construction crew building an oil refinery in Ponca City, Okla. The Dilworths then moved to New York City, and he took a job with a real estate firm. His father relented and agreed to fund Dilworth's studies at Yale Law School. He was an editor of the law review and graduated cum laude in 1926.

Dilworth moved to Philadelphia, passed the bar, and worked briefly as an assistant city solicitor, which gave him an education in graft and corruption at city hall. He joined the law firm of Evans, Bayard, and Frick, whose clients included the Philadelphia Transit Company. In 1928, Dilworth helped conduct the Philadelphia Bar Association's probe into the corrupt relationship between law firms handling personal-injury cases and the police department. After a dozen years with the Evans law firm, Dilworth joined Murdoch, Paxson, Kalish, and Green, where he would become the senior partner. Dilworth was the counsel for the *Philadelphia Inquirer*. He gained national recognition as a libel lawyer, representing Time Inc., Curtis Publishing, and Triangle Publications. Dilworth and his first wife were divorced in August 1935. That same month, he married Anne Kaufman Hill, who was also newly divorced; they had two children.

After the United States entered World War II, the forty-three-year-old Dilworth volunteered for active duty with the marines. "I thought everybody who had the means to do their part should get into it," Dilworth said of his decision to serve. He was commissioned a captain and saw action on Guadalcanal and in the Russell Islands landings, earning a Silver Star. The Presidential Unit Citation referred to Dilworth's "gallantry and intrepidity in action" and his "unflagging zeal, heroic determination, and a courageous attitude in his desire to thwart the enemy." Discharged as a major, Dilworth returned to Philadelphia with political ambitions. "All of these people coming back from the war realized how backward we were in Philadelphia," Dilworth told the *Philadelphia Inquirer* in 1972.

Dilworth and another returning veteran, Joseph S. Clark, led a postwar reform movement that produced a new city charter in 1951 and ended the Republican organization's seventy-year control of city government. Clark and Dilworth had been allies in Democratic reform politics since the late 1920's, and they sensed that Philadelphia was ready for change. As the Democratic nominee for mayor in 1947, Dilworth exposed graft, waste, and corruption. He lost to Republican Mayor Bernard Samuels by 92,000 votes, but Dilworth's allegations sparked a grand-jury probe. Many officials were indicted in the next two years and nine committed suicide. Dilworth was elected city treasurer in 1949, leaving office in 1950 to become the Democratic nominee for governor of Pennsylvania. He narrowly lost to Republican John Fine. In 1951, Clark was elected mayor of Philadelphia, and Dilworth was elected district attorney.

As district attorney, Dilworth brought a new sense of purpose and direction to the office, cutting the backlog of cases and targeting organized crime. He successfully prosecuted seven top figures in the numbers racket. Dilworth also vigorously prosecuted policemen for using excessive force. During the Korean War, the former marine supported the appeal of Quaker peace demonstrators who had been harassed by police and convicted of disorderly conduct. Dilworth helped the Quakers win their appeal by arguing in court for the constitutional right to assembly.

Tall and handsome with patrician features and silver hair, Dilworth had style and charisma. Witty, urbane, and cultivated, Dilworth also had the toughness of a marine. One of the best-dressed public figures of his era, he was nicknamed "the man in the double-breasted suit." Dilworth was the most dynamic politician to emerge in Philadelphia in more than a half century, attacking political rivals as "crum bums," "crooks," and "fakers." Though usually unflappable, Dilworth had a sharp temper that he would sometimes display in public.

Elected mayor of Philadelphia in 1955, Dilworth did much more than clean out city hall. More than any chief executive in Philadelphia history, he changed the face of America's founding city and restored a sense of civic pride. "Philadelphia has done what other cities have merely talked about," Robert Futterman wrote in *The Future of Our Cities.* "Both in concept and execution, it leads the march of our major metropolitan areas."

Dilworth's goal was to "build for the future in developing the city." Early in his term, he outlined a master plan for the restoration of Philadelphia. A massive stone causeway that held sixteen railroad tracks and ran through Center City was torn down, making possible the development of plazas and parkways and a new complex of glass-encased office buildings, apartment towers, and a hotel. A four-hundred-acre Food Distribution Center was built on land provided by the city. Dilworth formed the Old Philadelphia Development Corporation with a mandate to revive Center City and the historic areas around Independence Hall and Society Hill. The Dilworths showed their commitment to urban renewal by building a home in a neighborhood that had been a slum.

The Dilworths were among the survivors of the sinking of the Italian luxury liner *Andrea Doria* in 1956. Crew members said that Dilworth calmed some passengers who were about to panic and guided them to lifeboats. "He told us all what to do," said Italian passenger Chiarmonti Miriello. Dilworth was on the last lifeboat sent by the liner *Ile de France.*

Dilworth wanted to seek the Pennsylvania governorship in 1958. John F. Kennedy said that Dilworth would have been a formidable contender for the presidency in 1960 had he been elected governor. But Dilworth made the political mistake of saying that the People's Republic of China should be recognized by the United States and admitted to the United Nations. His critics in the Philadelphia Democratic organization used the remark against Dilworth, and he chose not to run. In 1962, Dilworth resigned as mayor to run for governor, but he lost to Republican William W. Scranton.

In 1965, Mayor James H. J. Tate appointed Dilworth to a six-year term as president of the Philadelphia board of education. Dilworth played a role in integrating the school system and strived to improve the city's schools. A 1967 federally funded report said that the Philadelphia public schools were undergoing "the most dramatic reform in urban education since World War II." But the gains were short-lived. Tate and Dilworth had a falling out over school funding. Dilworth had even sharper differences with Tate's successor, Frank L. Rizzo, and resigned before Rizzo took office in 1971. He died in Philadelphia.

[Dilworth's papers are at the Pennsylvania Historical Society. His life is chronicled in Joe Alex Morris, *The Richardson Dilworth Story* (1962). Dilworth's administration is analyzed in Kirk R. Petshek, *The Challenge of Urban Reform: The Policies and Programs in Philadelphia* (1973). Edmund N. Bacon, director of the Philadelphia planning commission in the Clark-Dilworth era, writes about Philadelphia's urban renewal efforts in *Design of Cities* (1974). Obituaries are in the *Philadelphia Inquirer* and the *New York Times*, both Jan. 24, 1974.]

STEVE NEAL

DISNEY, ROY OLIVER (June 24, 1893–Dec. 20, 1971), motion-picture executive, was born in Chicago. His father, Elias Disney, who was at that time a building contractor, had received several lucrative commissions to build furniture for the Columbian Exposition that year, and wanted to name the baby Columbus. His mother, Flora Call, prevailed, however, and gave their third son the sensible name of Roy. In 1901, Roy Disney's younger brother, Walt, was born.

In 1906, dismayed by the increased rowdiness of their Chicago neighborhood, the Disneys moved to a farm in Marceline, Mo., where Roy attended high school. The farm failed, however, and in 1910 the family moved to Kansas City, Mo. Elias had a circulation franchise there for the local newspapers; Roy and Walt delivered them, and Elias invested their pay. When Roy demanded his money and Elias said it was tied up, Roy went to live with his uncle Will Disney in Ellis, Kans. In 1913 he began working as a clerk in a Kansas City bank for $19 per week. Four years later, he volunteered for the U.S. Navy and was sent to the Great Lakes Training Camp, north of Chicago. Disney served on a destroyer convoying merchant ships to Europe in the Atlantic Ocean until he was invalided out of the service in the fall of 1918.

He returned to Kansas City to live with his brother Herbert in the old family home (Elias, Flora, and their youngest child, Ruth, were then living in Chicago). Walt Disney joined them upon returning from his own tour of World War I European duty. Walt was intent upon being an artist, and Roy believed in his talent. Roy subsidized Walt and helped him obtain a job drawing at a small ad agency.

In 1920, Roy was diagnosed with tuberculosis and went to a veterans hospital in Tucson, Ariz., and then to Sawtelle Veterans Hospital in West Los Angeles. Out of his $85-per-month disability pension, he sent money to help Walt make his first films. When Walt got a commission in 1923 for six "Alice Comedies"—combined live action/animated films—Roy left the Sawtelle hospital to produce the films. He put $250 into the new business, the Disney Brothers Studio. Walt put in $40, and their uncle Robert Disney, who lived in Los Angeles, put up $500. Roy ran the camera and kept the books while Walt designed. Two years later, the studio was doing well enough that Roy married his fiancée of six years, Edna Francis, on Apr. 11, 1925; they had one son. Walt married three months later and began to rely on his brother less completely.

The studio moved to new offices on Hyperion Avenue, in Hollywood's Silver Lake District, and Walt renamed the company Walt Disney Studio. Roy remained in charge of finances and much of the business, since he was shrewder and less trusting than his brother. In 1932, Walt Disney Studio moved its distribution business to United Artists and in May 1933 issued *Three Little Pigs*, its first great success. Soon Mickey Mouse, Donald Duck, and other characters became popular, and the studio started making money.

Uncomfortable with the increasing size of the business, Roy entrusted the merchandising of Disney memorabilia to Kay Kamen, who made both Disney and himself millions of dollars. After Kamen's death in 1949, however, Roy realized that Disney would have done better to handle its own merchandising and keep all the

profits, which the company then did. In the meantime, the Hyperion Avenue quarters were too cramped. Roy selected a site in Burbank and began construction on Buena Vista Street in 1938.

Roy was the cautious Disney brother. While serving as president of the company, he forced Walt to think projects through completely before Roy would support them. Roy preferred to spend studio resources on proven money makers. Indeed, he was reluctant to change the successful Mickey Mouse short film format when Walt proposed a feature-length, $500,000 film in 1934. That film, *Snow White and the Seven Dwarfs*, eventually cost more than $1.75 million but was a commercial success. Thereafter, Roy advised Walt to steer away from short cartoons—indeed, to kill off Mickey Mouse; feature films made more money. This, of course, the sentimental Walt refused to do, and Mickey starred in *The Sorcerer's Apprentice*, later part of *Fantasia* (1940), a project Roy vehemently opposed on financial grounds.

Walt Disney Studio generally had a good track record, but in the late 1930's and early 1940's, it made three box-office flops—*Bambi* (1942), *Pinocchio* (1940), and *Fantasia*—and the outbreak of war in 1939 destroyed Roy's European distribution opportunities. At the same time, the loans for construction of the Burbank offices (occupied in late 1939) were coming due. Because of the debt load the studio carried (around $4.5 million), Roy convinced Walt to take the company public. The April 1940 offering raised $8 million and still left Walt, Roy, and their wives with large blocks of stock.

Partly to appear fiscally responsible to the new shareholders and partly in response to the financial scare he had had, Roy told employees that the studio was in financial straits and staff needed to be reduced. It was a miscalculation because the staff then unionized as part of the American Federation of Labor. Walt Disney refused to recognize the union, so they struck in 1941. Because of Walt Disney Studio's symbolic and economic importance, the federal government was instrumental in resolving the strike; Disney became a union studio in the end.

As time went on, the brothers argued more about money, but there was no serious rift until Walt wanted to build a theme park in Anaheim, Calif. Roy believed that Walt Disney Studios should stick with movies, and he refused to convince lenders and shareholders to back the enterprise. Indeed, he threatened to sue Walt if he used the Disney name to raise funds for the project. Walt raised much of the money for Disneyland by agreeing to produce a television series, "Zorro," for the struggling ABC network. It turned out to be a profitable deal for both parties. Once ground was broken in 1954, Roy arranged for Walt Disney Productions (as the studio by now was known) to buy a majority share in Disneyland.

After Walt's death in 1966, Roy oversaw completion of Walt Disney World near Orlando, Fla. He ignored Walt's plans for EPCOT, and that part of the complex was built only after Roy's death. He died in Burbank, Calif.

In addition to serving as the president (to 1966) and later chairman of Walt Disney Productions, Roy at the time of his death was a trustee of the California Institute of the Arts, which the Disneys had helped develop and where Disney artists trained.

[The Walt Disney Archives in Burbank, Calif., has a brief official biography of Disney in addition to corporate papers and correspondence. Leonard Mosley, *Disney's World* (1985), though a biography of Walt, is also a biography of the company and contains much useful information about Roy Disney. Roy's contributions to the company are acknowledged in Lynn Gartley and Elizabeth Leebron, *Walt Disney: A Guide to References and Resources* (1979). An obituary is in the *New York Times*, Dec. 22, 1971.]

ALANA J. ERICKSON

DOBZHANSKY, THEODOSIUS GRIGORIEVICH (Jan. 25, 1900–Dec. 18, 1975), zoologist, was born in Nemirov, Russia, the son of Gregory Dobzhansky, a teacher, and Sofia Voinarsky. He grew up and attended secondary school in Kiev. In his youth he collected butterflies as a hobby, and he also read Charles Darwin's *On the Origin of Species* (1859). In 1916, he decided to become a biologist and to study systematically only ladybird beetles of the family *Coccinellidae*. After graduating from Kiev University in 1921, he won appointment as an assistant in the faculty of agriculture at the Polytechnic Institute of Kiev, where he taught general biology and its cultural implications. From 1924 to 1927 he was lecturer in genetics at Leningrad University. He began studying genetics in 1921, and within a year he was doing fundamental Mendelian-style genetics experiments on the famous fruit fly *Drosophila*.

Since reading Darwin, Dobzhansky had been interested in human evolution, social arrangements, and cultures. But he believed that he first had to resolve matters at the microevolutionary level, including questions of geographical distribution and variability among populations, individual variability within populations, and the inheritance of variation. Unlike many of his Anglo-American colleagues, Dobzhansky based his research on both wild and laboratory species, but it was not until the 1930's that he began to stitch this research program together. On Aug. 8, 1924, he married Natalia ("Natasha") Sivertzev. They had one daughter.

At Leningrad he continued his work on *Coccinellidae* in the field and *Drosophila* in the laboratory. As early as 1924 he was arguing that every gene probably acted on all parts of the body. He brought his field and laboratory work together when he speculated that the gene complexes by which geographical races differed were harmoniously related, which he attributed to natural selection. This foreshadowed his later role as a major architect of the new Darwinian evolutionary synthesis of the 1940's and 1950's. By 1927, Dobzhansky was at a difficult juncture. He understood the systematics of natural strains of *Coccinellidae*, but little of its complicated, intractable genetics, and he knew something of the genetics of the laboratory populations of *Drosophila*, but nothing of it in the wild. He spent two summers in central Asia attempting to work out the genetics of domesticated animals (chiefly horses, cattle, and yaks), but produced no useful information for understanding the evolution of wild populations.

In 1927, Dobzhansky became a fellow of the Rockefeller Foundation's International Education Board at Columbia University in New York City, where he worked with the American Mendelian geneticist, Thomas Hunt Morgan. But it was Alfred H. Sturtevant, one of Morgan's top doctoral graduates, who became Dobzhansky's most useful collaborator. Under Sturtevant's guidance, he produced thirteen *Drosophila* papers between 1928 and 1932, mostly based on a soon-to-be-outmoded method of cytological analysis. When Morgan moved to the California Institute of Technology in the fall of 1928 to create a new division of biology, he took Sturtevant as a faculty colleague and Dobzhansky as a fellow of the Rockefeller International Board. Dobzhansky joined the faculty the next year. He stayed in America because he refused to live under Stalinist rule. In 1933, Dobzhansky published in *The American Naturalist* a classic article on geographical variation and evolution in ladybird beetles, in which he argued that it was environmental isolation, not genetic action per se, that caused speciation, and that populations became species as the result of being reproductively isolated from other populations. He was on his way to becoming a major architect of the modern evolutionary synthesis of the 1940's and 1950's. But Dobzhansky sought a strain of the fruit fly that could produce fertile hybrids with enough traits to be studied, yet not too many to manage in an experimental situation at one time. The answer was *Drosophila pseudoobscura*, which he studied for the next decade. By the mid-1930's he was combining the study of structure with that of genetic variation and change in evolution, which were the two major threads of biological science. In 1936 he was promoted to full professor at Cal Tech, and in 1937 he became a naturalized American citizen. His future as an American scientist working on an international stage was now secure.

In 1940, Dobzhansky moved to Columbia University as professor of zoology. His *Genetics and the Origin of Species* (1937) was a major contribution to the resuscitation of Darwinian selectionism. Dobzhansky modeled much of this work after Darwin's *On the Origin of Species*. Dobzhansky was not alone in this effort, even though his partnership with Sturtevant was disintegrating. From Sewall Wright, a mathematical geneticist at the University of Chicago, he learned much about the evolution of wild populations. Dobzhansky argued that both natural selection and random genetic drift played major roles in evolution and the making of species, thus answering the objections of critics of selection that selection could not explain the appearance of traits that random drift could easily explain. Behind Dobzhansky's conception of evolution was a holistic model of natural and social reality prevalent from the 1920's to the 1950's, in which the whole was seen as greater than or different from the sum of its parts. This holistic model was a very different blueprint of reality from the reductionist models of the late nineteenth and early twentieth centuries. The

holistic view, in which species and populations were statistical aggregates of individuals who varied around a common mean (which is what allowed them to interbreed and produce fertile hybrids), was both an extension of the implications of Darwinian selectionism as initially articulated in 1859 and a new departure. The novelty rested primarily in the conception of a population as a dynamic rather than a static entity; contingency had, to some extent, replaced traditional positivistic determinism in modern biological theory. The symmetry of all individuals in the population to one another was not considered a problem. Symmetry was simply a given, which made it possible to think of models of evolutionary change in which there were dynamic changes within a population (or group) and linear changes with regard to the direction that this network, or system of biological systems, might be said to be evolving.

Dobzhansky was perhaps the most formidable evolutionary biologist of his time. His contributions to the modern understanding of variation and evolution were as significant to his era as Darwin's were in an earlier time. Dobzhansky was no mathematician, yet his science required considerable mathematical and statistical reasoning. Fortunately, Wright supplied him with most of the mathematical expertise he required.

After World War II, Dobzhansky became a major spokesman of the biological sciences. He helped draft the famous 1951 UNESCO statement on racial equality. In 1953, at an international conference in Hamburg, Germany, he denounced the doctrines of the Soviet animal breeder T. D. Lysenko, who argued, following Stalinist ideology, that inherited characteristics could be changed by the environment and then genetically transmitted to succeeding generations. This modern form of Lamarckianism had become a test of doctrinal orthodoxy in the USSR. Dobzhansky paid homage to those scientists who refused to hew the party line. In the 1950's and 1960's, Dobzhansky's interests turned from demanding technical work on the evolutionary genetics of fruit flies to larger questions of the meaning of evolution and culture for humankind. In such works as *Evolution, Genetics, and Man* (1955) and *Mankind Evolving* (1962), he set those larger questions within the intellectual framework of the new evolutionary synthesis and of the holistic models of biological and cultural networks. As the civil rights movement of the 1960's and 1970's intensified, Dobzhansky spoke out in a variety of forums against racism. In 1962 he retired from Columbia University and became professor of population genetics at Rockefeller University (until 1971), and then he became adjunct professor of genetics at the University of California, Davis. Dobzhansky received many international honors for his work. Blessed with an impressive physical countenance and quick mind, he was a talented linguist, horseman, traveler, philosopher, and author. He died of congestive heart failure in Davis, Calif.

[Much of Dobzhansky's correspondence is at the American Philosophical Society in Philadelphia, Pa. Professor William B. Provine of Cornell University has a large collection of correspondence between Dobzhansky and Sewall Wright. There is a large oral history memoir of Dobzhansky (1962) at the Columbia Oral History Research Office, Columbia University, which is available on microfilm. A bibliography of his work appears following Francisco J. Ayala's memoir in *Biographical Memoirs. National Academy of Sciences* 105 (1985). His most important technical papers may be found in R. C. Lewontin, ed., *Dobzhansky's Genetics of Natural Populations I-XLIII* (1981). Works about Dobzhansky include Garland E. Allen, *Life Science in the Twentieth Century* (1975), and *Thomas Hunt Morgan* (1978); Hamilton Cravens, *The Triumph of Evolution* (1978); Ernst Mayr, *The Growth of Biological Thought* (1982); and William B. Provine, *Sewall Wright and Evolutionary Biology* (1986). An obituary is in the *New York Times*, Dec. 19, 1975.]

HAMILTON CRAVENS

DODD, THOMAS JOSEPH (May 15, 1907–May 24, 1971), U.S. senator, was born in Norwich, Conn., to Abigail Margaret O'Sullivan and Thomas Joseph Dodd, a Connecticut contractor. He attended Norwich Free Academy and St. Anselm's Academy and graduated from Providence College in 1930, where he majored in philosophy. Dodd earned his law degree in 1933 from Yale University.

Upon his Yale graduation, Dodd worked as a field agent for the Federal Bureau of Investigation. In 1935, he left the FBI to serve as Connecticut's state director of the National Youth Administration under President Roosevelt's New Deal until 1938. Dodd served in the U.S. Justice Department from 1938 to 1945 as a special assistant to five successive attorneys general in the newly formed civil rights division and specialized in prosecuting cases against the Ku Klux Klan and acts of industrial espionage during World War II. At the close of the war, Dodd was named chief assistant prosecutor to Supreme Court Justice Robert H. Jackson at the Nuremberg War Crimes Tribunal in Germany. Dodd played a substantial role in securing the conviction of major Nazi leaders for crimes against humanity and was awarded a Presidential Certificate of Merit and Medal of Freedom by President Truman in 1946.

He returned to America in 1946 and entered private law practice with the Hartford firm of Pelgrift, Dodd, Blumenfeld, & Nair. He also returned to his wife, Grace Murphy, whom he had married on May 19, 1934, and his family, which would eventually be comprised of six children, including a future U.S. senator from Connecticut, Christopher J. Dodd. He became active in Connecticut state politics and held several positions within the Democratic party. After unsuccessful attempts for the state's gubernatorial nomination in 1948 and 1952, Dodd was elected to the U.S. House of Representatives from Hartford and reelected in 1954. In 1956, he lost in his bid to unseat the incumbent Republican, Prescott Bush, from the U.S. Senate. Two years later, he defeated Republican William Purtell in the 1958 race for the U.S. Senate from Connecticut.

Dodd served as Connecticut's U.S. senator from 1959 to 1970. As a senator, Dodd earned a reputation as a liberal in domestic policy and as a militant anti-Communist in foreign policy. He proved a staunch supporter of President Kennedy's domestic agenda; was an outspoken champion for President Johnson's Great Society programs such as Medicare, Civil Rights, and the war on poverty; and in 1970 was a leader in expanding the Voting Rights Act of 1965. During Nixon's presidency, Dodd joined with liberal Democrats in defeating the nominations of Clement Haynsworth and Harrold Carswell to the Supreme Court. As Chairman of the Senate Juvenile Delinquency Subcommittee, Dodd led a 1962 investigation into the effects of television violence on youth and criticized the television industry for its lack of responsibility for the general welfare. In 1965, Dodd used his subcommittee to conduct hearings calling for gun control legislation, but had his strict proposals watered down in the 1968 Omnibus Crime Control Act. In 1970, Dodd sponsored the Drug-Abuse Prevention Act, which reduced criminal penalties for minor drug violations, but allowed police the right to search for suspected drugs without a search warrant or a warning through the act's controversial "no knock" provisions.

In foreign affairs, Senator Dodd used his seats on the Foreign Relations Committee and the Internal Security Subcommittee to promote his hawkish anti-Communist beliefs. He was a steadfast supporter of U.S. military efforts in South Vietnam throughout the 1960's and voted in full support of the Johnson and Nixon administrations to escalate the conflict in Southeast Asia. He vigorously denounced the Cooper-Church Amendment in 1970 as cowardly appeasement of the enemy even though the proposal would become the War Powers Resolution Act of 1973, which sought to restrict presidential authority to use U.S. combat forces. As a militant anti-Communist, Dodd led the fight to keep mainland China from United Nations membership, opposed efforts to reduce military aid to American allies, and supported measures in the late 1960's that would have granted the U.S. Attorney General broad discretionary powers to use wiretaps and other surveillance techniques in cases of suspected espionage and treason against American citizens.

In June 1966 the Senate Select Committee on Standards and Conduct began formal hearings on charges against Senator Dodd for official misconduct in office. Dodd had been the subject of a lengthy series of newspaper articles by investigative journalists Drew Pearson and Jack Anderson, alleging that he had misappropriated campaign funds for his private use, peddled his influence in the U.S. Senate for prominent businessmen, and falsified his travel records for monetary gain. The Committee hearings concluded in April 1967 and found Dodd at fault in these areas by unanimous vote; he was, however, formally acquitted of the charge of falsifying travel expenses. On June 23, 1967, the full Senate formally censured Dodd for his misconduct by a vote of ninety-two to five in a highly emotional debate. Dodd's censure was only the seventh in the Senate's history. Nevertheless, Dodd, proclaiming his innocence from all wrongdoing, continued to serve in the Senate until his term of office expired in 1970.

Undaunted, Dodd sought reelection to his Senate seat in 1970 as an independent after the Connecticut Democratic party opposed his candidacy. He lost in his bid for reelection in a three-way race to Republican Lowell Weicker. Dodd died of a heart attack at his home in Old Lyme, Conn.

[For additional information on the political career of Senator Dodd, see Frank Milburn's series of three articles, "Thomas J. Dodd," in Nelson Lichtenstein, ed., *Political Profiles: The Kennedy Years* (1974); *The Johnson Years* (1976); and *The Nixon-Ford Years* (1979). For two insightful treatments of the Connecticut political arena during Dodd's career, see John Jeffries, *Testing the Roosevelt Coalition* (1979); and Joseph Lieberman, *The Legacy: Connecticut Politics, 1930 to 1980* (1981). Additional biographical materials can be found in profiles of Dodd in the *New York Herald Tribune*, Nov. 5, 1958; and the *New York Times*, Nov. 6, 1958. An obituary appears in the *New York Times*, May 25, 1971.]

RONALD LETTIERI

DONLEVY, BRIAN (Feb. 9, 1901–Apr. 5, 1972), actor, was born Grosson Brian Donlevy in Portadown in County Armagh, Ireland. His father was a whiskey distiller. When Donlevy was ten months old, his family emigrated to America, settling in Sheboygan Falls, Wis. His father took a job in the woolen industry. In 1916, Donlevy ran away from home to join General Pershing's forces fighting Pancho Villa in Mexico. After he was mustered out, he enrolled briefly at St. John's Military Academy in Delafield, Wis. When America entered World War I, he ran away again, this time allegedly to join the famed group of American volunteer aviators known as the Lafayette Escadrille. Many years later, studio press releases stressed this adventurous episode; his name does not appear on the roster, however.

After the war, Donlevy was appointed to the U.S. Naval Academy at Annapolis, entering in the summer of 1921. There he participated in school theatricals and dabbled in writing poetry and fiction. Once again his restlessness intervened, and deciding that he was not suited for life as a navy officer, he resigned on Mar. 8, 1922. Assembling his writings, he headed for New York City.

For a time, he could find no work, then he met commercial artist Frank Leyendecker, who was so impressed by his handsome features that he asked him to pose for an Arrow Collar ad. Donlevy became a model, later using this experience to win roles as an extra in several films being shot in New York City. He also appeared on a few early radio shows.

In 1924, a chance meeting with actor Louis Wolheim led to Donlevy's career as a stage actor. In a generous mood after a bout of drinking, Wolheim promised to find him a role in his play, *What Price Glory?* To Wolheim's surprise, Donlevy turned up the next day and was given the role of Corporal Gowdy in the acclaimed World War I drama. For the next ten years, he appeared in many stage musicals and comedies, including *Hit the Deck!* (1927), *Up Pops the Devil* (1930), and *Three-Cornered Moon* (1933). In 1934, he had important roles in two Broadway successes, the comedy *The Milky Way* and the musical revue *Life Begins at 8:40*. The following year, he decided it was time to try for a new career in films.

In Hollywood, after a bleak beginning, he finally won a part in *Barbary Coast* (1935), playing a black-shirted bouncer who works for tyrannical gambling kingpin Edward G. Robinson in this rowdy melodrama of San Francisco in the 1850's. Following several gangster roles, Donlevy was awarded a term contract at Twentieth Century–Fox, where he was cast as either the hero in the studio's second-string movies (*Human Cargo*, 1936; *Born Reckless*, 1937), or as the principal villain in such major productions as *In Old Chicago* (1938) and *Jesse James* (1939). On loan to Paramount, he appeared as a nasty sort in Cecil B. DeMille's epic *Union Pacific* (1939) and as the brutal Sergeant Markoff in a remake of the Foreign Legion adventure *Beau Geste* (1939). His performance in the latter film earned him an Oscar nomination as best supporting actor.

On Dec. 22, 1936, Donlevy married singer Marjorie Lane; they had one child. His marriage to Ziegfeld Follies showgirl Yvonne Grey, whom he married in 1929, had ended in divorce earlier that year.

Donlevy was now regarded as a solid character actor specializing in villains. In 1940, he won the starring role that gave a substantial boost to his career. As the hobo who rises to become mayor and then governor in Preston Sturges's slyly amusing political satire *The Great McGinty*, he revealed a genial side to his acting ability that impressed critics. From then on, although he still played villainous types, he was often cast in more sympathetic roles: as a tough air force flight instructor in *I Wanted Wings* (1941), as Major Caton, a character based on Major James P. Devereaux, in *Wake Island* (1942), and as President Andrew Jackson in the comedy-fantasy *The Remarkable Andrew* (1942).

Throughout the 1940's, Donlevy was steadily employed in supporting or leading roles. He played a political boss in *The Glass Key* (1942), the revenge-minded Czech patriot Dr. Svoboda in *Hangmen Also Die* (1943), and an assistant district attorney in *Kiss of Death* (1947). In King Vidor's *An American Romance* (1944), he replaced Spencer Tracy in the starring role of an immigrant who becomes a powerful industrialist. He also played important parts in *Canyon Passage* (1946), *Two Years Before the Mast* (1946), and *The Beginning or the End* (1947), which was an early drama on the testing of the atomic bomb. Also in 1947, Donlevy's second marriage ended in divorce.

Donlevy continued to make films in the 1950's, but his roles were fewer, and he supplemented his work with regular appearances on television and occasionally in the theater. He starred as Steve Mitchell, an investigator of espionage, in the 1952 television series "Dangerous Assignment." In the 1960's, he appeared in some forgettable films, as well as in sporadic television assignments. In 1966, he married Lillian Lugosi, the former wife of horror-film star Bela Lugosi.

In the late 1960's, Donlevy retired to Palm Springs, Calif. He died in Woodland Hills, Calif.

[Additional information on Donlevy is in Gregory Mank, "Brian Donlevy," *Films in Review*, Apr. 1975; and James Robert Parish and William T. Leonard, *Hollywood Players—The Thirties* (1976). Obituaries are in the *New York Times*, Apr. 6, 1972, and *Variety*, Apr. 12, 1972.]

TED SENNETT

DOUGLAS, LEWIS WILLIAMS (July 2, 1894–Mar. 7, 1974), diplomat, congressman, and World War II shipping czar, was born in Bisbee, Ariz., the son of James Stuart Douglas and Josephine Leah Williams. As president of the United Verde Extension Mining Company, James Douglas, a Canadian immigrant, built a copper empire and accumulated enormous wealth. His son, educated initially in private schools in New York and New Jersey, graduated from Montclair Academy, N.J., and from Amherst College in Amherst, Mass., in 1916 with a degree in history and economics. Douglas pursued graduate study at the Massachusetts Institute of Technology in geology and metallurgy. When the United States entered World War I in 1917, Douglas was commissioned as a second lieutenant and fought with distinction with the Ninety-first Division in the Meuse-Argonne and Flanders campaigns. He was awarded the Belgian croix de guerre for heroism. Following the war, Douglas taught history and economics at Hatchley Preparatory School in New York State and at Amherst College; he also taught law briefly at Harvard. Douglas married Margaret ("Peggy") Zinsser on June 19, 1921; they had three children. They soon returned to Arizona, where Douglas was elected to the state legislature in 1923. In 1926, he captured an at-large Arizona seat in the United States House of Representatives.

Douglas was a rugged individualist who put principle before party. His principles were emphatically conservative, and although he won office as a Democrat, he was not supportive of that party's embracement of an emerging twentieth-century American liberalism emphasizing increased government responsibility and a sensitivity to the growing urban working classes. Instead, Douglas relentlessly resisted federal public works projects, government welfare programs, and the organization of labor. This position expressed his determination to defend individual and states rights and his concern that the consequences of big government would be unbalanced budgets, inflation, and the sapping of individual initiatives.

In other areas, Douglas advocated immigration restriction and despite his personal abhorrence of Prohibition, did not resist it publicly. While Douglas strongly espoused his party's commitment to lower tariffs and reciprocal agreements, his domestic philosophy was identifiably that of both Herbert Hoover and the Republican party. Nevertheless, Doublas supported Democrats Alfred E. Smith and Franklin D. Roosevelt for president in 1928 and 1932, respectively.

Douglas's endorsement of Roosevelt was short-lived. Initially, Roosevelt's campaign commitment to fiscal austerity attracted Douglas, and Roosevelt, impressed by Douglas's reputation for integrity and courage, appointed him the nation's first budget director in February 1933. But Roosevelt's subsequent move away from balanced budgets to a program favoring massive federal expenditure, deficit spending, and large-scale public works projects to relieve

unemployment alienated Douglas. Finally, when Roosevelt proved unwilling to take the lead in stabilizing world markets, Douglas resigned in August 1934.

For the remainder of the 1930's, Douglas continued to be one of the New Deal's most vociferous critics, attacking Keynesian economics, applauding the Supreme Court's invalidation of the National Industrial Recovery Act, and supporting the presidential candidacies of Republicans Alfred M. Landon and Wendell L. Willkie. In the meantime, Douglas had become vice-president of the chemical firm of American Cyanamid Company. Then, in 1937, he became the first American principal and vice-chancellor of McGill University in Montreal. Three years later he accepted the presidency of Mutual Life Insurance Company in New York City.

Douglas's return to the United States coincided with the outbreak of World War II. As a committed internationalist and Anglophile, he labored to push the nation toward war preparedness and support of the Allies. To Douglas, Anglo-American amity was the key to postwar peace and stability, and just before the Japanese attack on Pearl Harbor, he was chairman of the national policy board of the Committee to Defend America by Aiding the Allies. Although Douglas had not supported Roosevelt in the 1940 election, the president valued his capabilities, his strident anti-isolationism, and his strong support for a postwar world based on the principles of free trade and global cooperation.

Accordingly, in February 1942, Roosevelt appointed Douglas deputy administrator of the War Shipping Administration (WSA). Under his direction, the WSA established a scientifically managed and balanced pool of merchant ships for American war and civilian cargoes, for aid to the Allies, and for European civil relief and rehabilitation programs, thereby contributing significantly not only to the defeat of the Axis powers but also to the stabilization and recovery of the liberated nations. Douglas left the WSA in March 1944; the WSA disbanded in 1946.

In 1945, Douglas served three months as a special economic adviser to the deputy military governor in Germany, General Lucius Clay. He resigned when it appeared that leaders in Washington favored a punitive peace for Germany, a policy Douglas feared would launch Europe into economic and social anarchy. In

1947 President Harry Truman appointed him ambassador to Great Britain. During his three years at the Court of St. James's Douglas successfully strengthened Anglo-American ties, supported the Marshall Plan to revitalize the war-torn economies of Western Europe, helped rebuild Germany economically and politically, and played a vital role in the establishment of the North Atlantic Treaty Organization.

At the time, it was acknowledged that Douglas was America's most influential diplomat, its strongest link with Great Britain, and one of the most significant architects of the regeneration of Western European stability as a bulwark against Soviet Communism. In recognition of his service, Great Britain awarded him the Honorable Knight Grand Cross of the Most Excellent Order of the British Empire, the highest honor that Britain gives to foreigners.

In 1950 Douglas resigned his ambassadorship. The loss of an eye in a fishing mishap precipitated his resignation, but he had been ill for several years. While banking became his main business, he provided counsel to the Eisenhower administration, continued to express his nineteenth-century Jeffersonian and conservative ideals, and served as director for a number of Wall Street corporations. Always attached to England, Douglas was president of the Winston Churchill Foundation at the time of his death in Tucson.

[Douglas's papers are at the Arizona Historical Society in Tucson. The Columbia University Oral History Collection has the transcript of an interview with Douglas recorded in 1972. Douglas's *The Liberal Tradition* (1935) contains four of his anti–New Deal speeches. Biographical information can be found in Robert Paul Browder and Thomas G. Smith, *Independent: A Biography of Lewis W. Douglas* (1986). An obituary is in the *New York Times*, Mar. 8, 1974.]
JEFFREY J. SAFFORD

DRISCOLL, ALFRED EASTLACK (Oct. 25, 1902–March 9, 1975), governor of New Jersey, was born in Pittsburgh, Pa., the son of Alfred Robie Driscoll and Mattie Eastlack. Driscoll's family moved to New Jersey shortly after he was born. He attended Haddonfield public schools and graduated from Williams College in 1925 and Harvard Law School in 1928. Driscoll, an avid outdoorsman, said he went to law school after his wealthy father told him that he would not subsidize his avocations of mountain climb-

ing, canoeing, and wilderness hiking. As a law student, Driscoll explored northern Canada near the Arctic Circle looking for new oil fields. He and his colleagues found oil deposits but concluded that transportation costs from the remote area would prohibit further development.

Admitted to the New Jersey bar in 1929, Driscoll joined the law firm of Starr, Summerill, and Lloyd in Camden, where he practiced for eighteen years. Driscoll once told the *New York Times* that his favorite case was his "least successful." In the 1930's, he sought to establish that Franklin D. Roosevelt's National Recovery Administration was unconstitutional. But another lawyer succeeded first and received the credit for the legal milestone.

In May 1932, Driscoll married Antoinette Ware Tatem, the daughter of a wealthy and socially prominent New Jersey family. They had three children. In 1929, he was elected to the Haddonfield Board of Education in opposition to a group he suspected had more interest in patronage and building contracts than education. Driscoll served on the school board for nine years and was its president in 1937. Driscoll was also elected to the Haddonfield Borough Commission, on which he served as director of revenues and finances. He was a deacon and Sunday school teacher at the First Presbyterian Church.

Throughout his long political career, Driscoll never lost his earnestness and zeal. Soft-spoken, with a self-deprecating wit, Driscoll was a good public speaker. With his energy and vitality, he was also a highly effective campaigner. Elected to the state senate from Camden County in 1938 as a "good government" candidate, he advanced quickly in Trenton. Driscoll wrote and successfully pushed through the legislature a housing law protecting tenants against fire and accidents, civil rights laws, and additional funding for children with disabilities. In 1940, Driscoll was elected senate majority leader.

At the end of Driscoll's three-year senate term, he was appointed state alcoholic beverage commissioner. Even his critics acknowledged that Driscoll was impartial and fair in running a commission that had been previously tarnished by favoritism to political insiders. He announced his candidacy for governor in 1946. He was an underdog, but his reputation as an able and honest administrator helped him defeat former governor Harold G. Hoffman by a decisive margin in the Republican primary, then win the general election by a record plurality.

Driscoll was an innovative governor. When he took office, he sought to revise the century-old constitution, which allowed governors a single three-year term, permitted vetoes to be overridden by simple legislative majorities, provided one-year terms for members of the assembly, and defined a clumsy, top-heavy court system. Driscoll built public support for a new constitutional convention, which was approved by the legislature and a statewide referendum.

New Jersey's 1947 constitution, which was shaped by Driscoll and approved by referendum, established a bill of rights and extended the governor's term to four years. It further specified that the governor was the only statewide elected official, and that other constitutional offices, including attorney general, secretary of state, and treasurer, were to be filled by gubernatorial appointment. The governor's veto power was strengthened, and he was given the power to call legislative sessions at will.

Under Driscoll's constitution, legislative terms were extended and the more than one hundred independent state agencies created by the legislature were consolidated into not more than twenty. The overlapping court system was reorganized into a unified court system. Driscoll named the members of a state supreme court that was viewed as the finest of its era. It included Chief Justice William Vanderbilt and Justice William Brennan.

Driscoll once said that his only claim to political fame was that he twice defeated Jersey City Democratic boss Frank Hague, who had dominated the state's politics since the 1920's. During the 1947 constitutional convention, Hague threatened to sabotage Driscoll's new constitution. Hague, who controlled Democratic delegates, was still a force to be reckoned with. Driscoll convinced Hague to soften his opposition by guaranteeing $5 million in state revenues for Jersey City. Hague announced his retirement from politics after Driscoll's reelection in 1949.

When Driscoll proposed the New Jersey Turnpike in 1947, there were no multilane, high-speed roads in New Jersey. The state's main highways stretched through small towns and were badly congested. He secured federal aid and sold bonds to finance the turnpike. He was also responsible for the Garden State Parkway and the Walt Whitman Bridge linking Camden and Philadelphia. From 1970 until his death, Driscoll was chairman of the New Jersey Turnpike Authority.

A progressive in civil rights, Driscoll pushed through antidiscrimination laws, signed an order that desegregated the New Jersey National Guard, and refused to extradite an African American who had escaped from a South Carolina prison camp because, he argued, the prisoner had "amply paid his debt to society."

Driscoll was New Jersey's favorite-son presidential candidate at the 1948 Republican national convention. In 1952 he was among Dwight D. Eisenhower's key political allies. Senator Robert A. Taft, Eisenhower's rival for the nomination, said that Driscoll's support of Eisenhower was decisive in the outcome of the close contest for the Republican nomination.

Though eligible to seek reelection in 1953, Driscoll retired from politics to become president of the Warner-Lambert Pharmaceutical Company, a position he held until 1967. Driscoll increased funding for research and development, expanded the company's foreign operations, and boosted profits.

Driscoll died at Birdwood, his home in Haddonfield.

[Driscoll's gubernatorial papers are in the New Jersey archives. Neil R. Peirce and Michael Barone assess his record in *The Mid-Atlantic States of America* (1977). There are profiles in *Fortune*, Aug. 1959, and the *New York Times*, Mar. 21, 1965. An obituary is in the *Philadelphia Inquirer*, Mar. 10, 1975.]

STEVE NEAL

DUNCAN, DONALD FRANKLIN (June 6, 1891–May 15, 1971), merchandiser, was born in Rome, Ohio, the first of two sons born to James Duncan and Ann Virginia McCaffry. The family lived just south of Rome, in Huntington, W.Va. Donald left school after the eighth grade, probably to support the family after the death of his father.

Duncan first distinguished himself in the business world in 1919 with the Brach Candy Company. As sales manager, he sold miniature cedar chests of the sweets as sentimental keepsakes, a notion he successfully promoted nationwide. Duncan teamed up with Donald O. Scott, an engineer who had invented the four-wheel hydraulic brake. Duncan bought the patent from Scott but could not sell the idea to the automakers, so he sold the patent and moved on. The invention would become an automobile industry standard around 1925.

Duncan next went to work as a consultant for a fledgling ice cream company that was manufacturing a product called "ice cream on a stick." He developed a whole new marketing plan for the company, which included sending vendors out on bicycles. He also gave the company its new name, Good Humor. He introduced the idea of franchises by allowing ice cream makers to buy a license to manufacture Good Humor ice cream products.

In 1927 or 1928, while in San Francisco, a man brought him a fixed-string yo-yo. "It looked like nothing," he recalled. But Duncan was enticed by the slip-string yo-yo that was devised and manufactured by Pedro Flores. The slip-string allowed the yo-yo to continue spinning until given a return tug. After briefly manufacturing Flores's yo-yos in Chicago, Duncan bought the company in 1929, rounded the toy's edges for comfort, and developed a better slip-string. The improved model became the first Duncan yo-yo, trademarked the O-Boy Top.

Duncan masterminded the transformation of the public's disposition toward the yo-yo, from tepid interest to red-hot craze. He convinced newspaper magnate William Randolph Hearst of a plan to boost circulation while promoting Duncan's new "whirling tops." Duncan proposed holding contests in various cities. Contestants would be judged on how well they performed yo-yo tricks like "walking the dog" or "looping the loop." To receive a prize, winners had to sign up three newspaper subscribers.

Duncan received free publicity, and the contests brought in fifty thousand new subscribers in Chicago alone. Duncan had similar success in towns all over America. Photographers provided by Hearst captured celebrities like movie star Douglas Fairbanks, baseball player Hack Wilson, boxer Jack Dempsey, and entertainer Jack Benny with yo-yos. Bing Crosby even recorded some yo-yo songs for Duncan.

In 1935, with money from his yo-yo fortune, Duncan purchased the rights to the parking meter. He quickly convinced city governments of the value of the parking meter as a revenue raiser. Duncan sold his parking meter concern in 1959. During his time as chief executive officer, the Duncan Parking Meter Corporation manufactured 80 percent of the meters in use worldwide.

Duncan married Janet Ives on Mar. 1, 1923,

in Detroit, Mich. They had two children. They separated in 1946 and were divorced in 1948. He remarried shortly thereafter.

Meanwhile, the yo-yo surged and sputtered as World War II came and went. Duncan retired from the yo-yo business in 1957, selling the firm to family members, who later sold it to another company. Under Duncan the firm sold twenty to thirty million yo-yos per year, grossing as much as $7 million annually. Duncan died in Los Angeles.

[Duncan is quoted at great length about his business endeavors, especially the yo-yo, in George Malko, *The One and Only Yo-Yo Book* (1978). For a brief and humorous tribute to Duncan and the yo-yo, see Abbie Hoffman, "Yo-Yo Power," *Esquire*, Oct. 1971. An obituary is in the *New York Times*, May 16, 1971.]

DAVID S. KELLER

DUNN, MICHAEL (Oct. 20, 1934–Aug. 29, 1973), actor and singer, was born Gary Neil Miller in Shattuck, Okla. Of Scots-Irish and Native American ancestry, he was an exceptionally bright child. But early in his life his parents became concerned about his fragile health. At age four he dislocated both hips and thereafter suffered pain just from the everyday act of walking. Doctors eventually determined that he was suffering from nonhereditary dwarfism caused by a chemical imbalance during gestation. Though he refused to view his dwarfism as a handicap, the malady caused him continuous health problems; the deformity and associated pain in his hands and arms forced him to abandon a budding career as a concert pianist and eventually shortened his life.

Even though he grew to be only three feet, ten inches tall and weighed a mere seventy-eight pounds, his extraordinary intelligence enabled him to graduate from high school in Shattuck in 1949 at age fourteen. He enrolled at the University of Michigan in the fall of 1949 but transferred in 1950 to the University of Miami, Fla., in hopes that a warmer climate would soothe his aching body. There he edited the college's newspaper and theater magazine, was a cheerleader, acted in theater department productions, and sang in local nightclubs to help pay his tuition and other expenses. During his college years he changed his name to Michael Dunn to honor his Irish ancestry.

He graduated in June 1953. He had long

since decided he would seek a career in show business. In a 1966 *New York Times* interview he declared, "Frankly I knew there wouldn't be too much competition for roles. There are a great many professional midgets but there aren't a lot of dwarfs who can act." While seeking his big break in acting, he worked as a sports rewrite man for a newspaper, a hotel detective in Los Angeles, and eventually as a singer in nightclubs around the country. Despite his diminutive size, his booming, resonant voice soon gained him recognition for singing acts at clubs like Mister Kelly's in Chicago and the Hungry I in San Francisco.

He settled in New York in the early 1960s and thereafter obtained a series of roles as clowns, fools, and old men in off-Broadway productions. The most famous of these plays was *How to Make a Man*, in which he stole the show while acting as the insides of a robot. In 1963 he acted in two one-act plays offered under the title *Two by Saroyan* and received great critical acclaim. His costar, four-foot-tall, ninety-two-pound Phoebe Dorin and he became close friends and confidants, forming a loving relationship that lasted the remainder of Dunn's life.

Late in the same year director Edward Albee gave Dunn his long awaited break when he cast him as Cousin Lymon in Albee's Broadway adaptation of Carson McCuller's *Ballad of the Sad Cafe*. Both Dunn and the play enjoyed rave reviews. The play had a long and profitable run, and Dunn was subsequently nominated for a Tony Award for best supporting actor.

In 1965 he and Ms. Dorin began a nightclub act at the Plaza Fountain. The two entertainers developed the show from their extemporaneous after-hours singing sessions at the Plaza. Actor Roddy McDowell saw one such ad-lib performance, took photographs of it (they were subsequently published in the June 1965 issue of *Life* magazine), and urged the two friends to make their casual performance into a professional show. The locally popular cabaret show lasted for over two years.

About this time Dunn began an active television career by playing the evil Dr. Miguelito Loveless of the 1960's hit Western "The Wild Wild West," starring Robert Conrad and Ross Martin; he made seven appearances in this role. During the decade Dunn appeared on numerous other TV shows including "Bonanza," "Star Trek," "Get Smart," and "The Big Valley." For

his performances in the "The Wild Wild West" and "Bonanza" he was nominated three times for an Emmy for best guest appearance in a weekly drama.

In late 1965 he secured his first big movie role, playing the evil hunchback dwarf Karl Glocken in *Ship of Fools*; his performance was singled out for critical acclaim, and Dunn was nominated for an Academy Award as best supporting actor.

He appeared in a number of other movies, including *You're a Big Boy Now* (1967), *Without Each Other* (1967), *Madigan* (1968), *No Way to Treat a Lady* (1968), *Boom!* (1968), *Murders in the Rue Morgue* (1971), and *House of Freaks* (1973).

Despite his success in films and television, he remained active in the New York theater. He drew rave reviews in the late 1960's in such plays as *Here Come the Clowns*, *Shinbone Alley*, *Jamaica*, and *Malcolm*. One of his most famous performances was his 1969 role in *The Inner Journey* performed at the Lincoln Center for the Performing Arts. Of this latter performance, *New York Times* drama critic Clive Barnes declared: "Michael Dunn as the dwarf is so good that the play may be worth seeing merely for him. Controlled, with his heart turned inward, his mind is a pattern of pain. Mr. Dunn's Antaeus deserves all the praise it can be given."

Indeed, Barnes may have been describing Dunn's entire life. Despite almost constant pain from the degenerative childhood disease that eventually took his life, he never gave in to his suffering. During his brief life he taught himself to drive a car, ice skate, swim, fly a plane, and skydive. Whether acting on TV, in movies, or on stage; whether singing and dancing at a nightclub or relaxing after midnight at his favorite haunt, Downing's Irish Steakhouse on Eighth Avenue in New York, with his sweetheart Phoebe Dorin, he always met life with zest and bravado, enjoying all it had to offer.

Even as his health went into serious decline, he continued to work. He died in London during the filming of another movie, *The Abdication*, in which he appeared with Peter Finch and Liv Ullmann. He was survived by no immediate family. Director Anthony Harvey spoke for those who knew and admired him when he said, "Michael was a very talented and noble man. It was an honor to have worked with him." It was a sentiment that all the theatrical world echoed, especially his beloved "Pheeb."

[Materials concerning Dunn's life are sparse. Patricia Bosworth, "Just an Ordinary Guy, All Three Feet Ten of Him," *New York Times*, Sept. 20, 1966, offers a profile, and Evelyn Mack Truitt, "Dunn, Michael," in *Who Was Who on Screen*, 3d ed. (1983), provides information about his film career. John S. Wilson, "Dwarf in 'Sad Cafe' and Actress Team in Unusual Cabaret Act," *New York Times*, June 30, 1965, offers a brief discussion of his cabaret show. Obituaries appear in the *New York Times* and the *Washington Post*, Aug. 31, 1973, and in *Time* and *Newsweek*, Sept 10, 1973.]

WILLIAM HEAD

DUNNING, JOHN RAY (Sept. 24, 1907–Aug. 25, 1975), physicist, was born in Shelby, Nebr., the son of Josephine Thelen and Albert Chester Dunning, a grain merchant and amateur radio engineer. Encouraged by his family to enter the ministry or the law, Dunning was more interested in scientific endeavors and built his first radio set, reportedly the first in his part of the country, when he was twelve years old. In 1925, he graduated from Shelby High School and enrolled in Nebraska Wesleyan University, where he received a B.A. degree with highest honors in 1929. From 1929 to 1933, Dunning was a graduate student in physics at Columbia University. He married Esther Laura Blevins on Aug. 28, 1930; they had two children.

Dunning's entire academic career was spent at Columbia University, where he was appointed to the physics faculty as an instructor in 1933. His principal subject of research was the neutron. His collaboration with George B. Pegram produced twenty-four papers on neutrons between 1933 and 1936 and formed the basis for his Ph.D. dissertation (1935) on the emission and scattering of neutrons. In 1935, he was promoted to assistant professor, and in the 1935–1936 academic year was granted a Cutting Traveling Fellowship, which gave him the opportunity to meet many of the great nuclear physicists of his time, including Enrico Fermi in Rome, Ernest Rutherford and James Chadwick at Cambridge, Werner Heisenberg at the University of Leipzig, and Niels Bohr at the University of Copenhagen.

Upon his return to Columbia, Dunning brought his considerable talents, energy, and enthusiasm to developing a leading laboratory for neutron research. He had followed the development of the cyclotron at Berkeley and was determined, despite a lack of government funding, to build a cyclotron at Columbia. Foundation and industry gifts helped Dunning and his colleagues establish, in the basement of Pupin, Columbia University's first cyclotron, which is now part of the permanent collection of the Smithsonian Institution.

In 1938, Dunning was promoted to associate professor of physics. At this time startling developments were being announced from the laboratories of Enrico Fermi, who first fired neutron bullets into uranium, and Otto Hahn, who announced that uranium, when bombarded by neutrons, splits into elements weighing about half as much, implying the release of large amounts of energy. Dunning was working with his colleague and long-time collaborator, Eugene T. Booth, when on the evening of Jan. 25, 1939, he recorded a historic measurement of energy released from the fission of natural uranium, a moment of great importance. It was engagingly reported in the *New Yorker* (Aug. 19, 1945) and more formally in "The Fission of Uranium" (*Physical Review*, Mar. 1, 1939).

Dunning initiated and directed the original experiments at Columbia on the separation of uranium 235 from other isotopes by the gaseous diffusion method. During the Manhattan Project to build the atomic bomb, Dunning was the director of research for Division I SAM (Substitute Alloy Materials) Laboratories, the code name for the nuclear laboratory at Columbia University where the development of the gaseous diffusion process was carried out.

After World War II, Dunning served as scientific director for the construction of the 385 MEV synchrocyclotron at the Nevis Laboratories, a joint project of the Atomic Energy Commission, the Office of Naval Research, and Columbia University, located at Irvington-on-the-Hudson, N.Y. In 1946, President Harry S. Truman presented Dunning the highest award that could be granted by a president to a civilian, the Medal of Merit. The award reads, in part, ". . . for exceptionally meritorious conduct in the performance of outstanding service to the War Department, in accomplishments involving great responsibility and scientific distinction in connection with the development of the greatest military weapon of all time, the atomic bomb."

Dunning was promoted to full professor in 1946 and was appointed Thayer Lindsley professor of applied science. From 1950 to 1969, he served as dean of the School of Engineering and Applied Science at Columbia. Throughout his career he remained committed to informing and educating not only his colleagues and students, but the general public as well, about the nature and challenges of atomic energy. In 1941, he published, with Hugh Campbell Paxton, *Matter, Energy, and Radiation*. He delivered the Sigma Xi National Lectures in 1948: "The Future of Atomic Energy" and "Atomic Structure and Energy." These lectures were published in *American Scientist* (October 1949 and December 1950). Dunning was elected to the National Academy of Sciences in 1948. He retired to Florida in 1969 and died in Key Biscayne, Fla.

[The archives of the University of Chicago has a notebook of Dunning's recollections of his first observations of fission pulses. A biography is in *Biographical Memoirs. National Academy of Sciences* (1989). An obituary is in the *New York Times*, Aug. 28, 1975.]

NANCY J. HERRINGTON

DYER, ROLLA EUGENE (Nov. 4, 1886– June 2, 1971), pathologist, epidemiologist, and public health administrator, was born in Delaware County, Ohio, the son of the Reverend Rolla Dyer and Nettie Ryant. In 1903, he entered Kenyon College, which awarded him the B.A. in 1907. From then until 1911 he taught ancient and modern languages at various secondary schools, and from 1908 to 1909 took courses at Cumberland College in Lebanon, Tenn. He enrolled in 1911 at the University of Texas Medical Branch at Galveston, where he received his M.D. in 1915.

Dyer met Esther Gibney during his internship at Philadelphia General Hospital. They were married on June 24, 1916, and had three children.

When he returned later that year to Marlin, Tex., where his parents then lived, they helped to set him up in medical practice there with Dr. Walter H. Allen. This partnership had just begun when Allen had to accompany a patient to the Mayo Clinic, leaving Dyer in charge. The first patient he saw was a farmer who reported that Allen had treated him recently with intravenous quinine and that he needed a second dose. Dyer did not know the man was allergic to quinine. The dose sent the patient into respiratory failure that would have proved fatal if Dyer

had not reacted quickly. Allen, upon returning from Minnesota, just shrugged off the incident: "Oh, I forgot to tell you about that. He pretty near died on me too."

Nevertheless, Dyer remained distraught at having nearly killed his first patient. The stress caused him to lose eighteen pounds in just a few weeks. When his wife suggested that he had neither aptitude nor taste for the practice of medicine, he agreed, and asked Dr. Wilbur Carter, his former dean at Galveston, for advice. Carter suggested that he try the U.S. Public Health Service.

The USPHS immediately sent him to New Orleans in October 1916 to help contain the bubonic plague that had broken out there in 1914. His duties mostly involved quarantine enforcement rather than research. A flurry of transfers ensued in the next few years. He investigated pellagra in Spartanburg, S.C., from February to September 1917, then influenza in eastern Massachusetts until November 1918. After June 1919, his attention was directed primarily toward epidemiology. He did field work in Arkansas from August 1919 to June 1920, fought bubonic plague in Galveston and Beaumont, Tex., from August 1920 to June 1921, and served as an epidemiological aid to the New Jersey State Board of Health for a few months in 1921 until he was reassigned in June to the U.S. Hygienic Laboratory (now the National Institutes of Health, or NIH) in Washington, D.C. He became assistant director of the Hygienic Laboratory in August 1922 and held this post until 1942.

Dyer's first six papers, published between 1925 and 1929, all dealt with scarlet fever. His research in the 1920's led to the development of new skin tests and antitoxins for that disease. During this period he also determined that Rocky Mountain spotted fever was transmitted in the eastern United States by ticks

In 1929, Dr. George W. McCoy, director of the Hygienic Laboratory, assigned Dyer to join a group of five researchers to continue the work begun by Dr. Kenneth F. Maxcy on the etiology of typhus. Dyer suspected that fleas, rather than lice, were the vector of the American strains of typhus, and he directed his experiments accordingly. His nineteen papers on endemic or murine typhus published between 1931 and 1934, mostly in *Public Health Reports*, show how this disease is transmitted from rats to fleas to humans. This record of Dyer's research is his single most significant contribution to medical science, and laid the foundation for the development of the typhus vaccine during World War II.

Dyer was fearless as a researcher. Some of his colleagues had died from typhus and other rickettsial diseases they had contracted on the job, but that threat never seemed to bother him. In 1932, he contracted a severe case of murine typhus while pulverizing infected fleas for analysis. Even during his delirium, he did not abandon his dedication to research; he called for lice and fleas to be brought to his bed and instructed that a color film be made of the entire course of his illness. On another occasion, after he had almost succumbed to another poorly understood rickettsial fever in 1938, he used samples of his own blood to demonstrate that this disease had given him immunity to the deadly Australian Q fever. In 1940, he was able to prove that his illness had in fact been Q fever, rather than some "new" rickettsial disease. Altogether Dyer was attacked four times by the diseases he studied.

Having gained renown as an expert on rickettsial diseases, Dyer served from 1936 to 1942 as chief of the NIH Division of Infectious Diseases. From 1942 until his retirement in 1950, he was the medical research director of NIH and assistant surgeon general of the USPHS. Under his tenure, the annual budget of the NIH Research Grants and Fellowships Division, which he founded, grew from $85,000 to more than $50 million.

Dyer can in large measure be credited with launching the official campaign against smoking, insofar as he was on the team of seven scientists from four government agencies who first concluded in 1957 that cigarette smoking is linked to lung cancer.

After his retirement from NIH, Dyer served the Emory University School of Medicine as director of research at the Robert Winship Clinic until 1957, then as clinical professor of medicine. He died in Atlanta, Ga.

[Self-provided biographical source materials are on file in the Alumni Office of Kenyon College. Among the information on Dyer in the History of Medicine Division, National Library of Medicine, is a transcript of Harlan Phillips's interview with him on Nov. 13, 1962, as part of an oral history project that is included in the George Rosen Collection. Materials are also available at Emory University. Obituaries are in the (Baton Rouge, La.) *Morning Advocate* and the *New York Times*, both June 3, 1971, and in *Tropical Medicine and Hygiene News*, Aug. 1971.]

ERIC V. D. LUFT

DYETT, THOMAS BEN (1886–Nov. 2, 1971), lawyer, was born in Monserrat, West Indies. In search of a better life, he journeyed with his family to the United States at the age of seventeen. Dyett entered Howard University in Washington, D.C., in 1913 to take college preparatory courses. His education took a back seat to his stint in the segregated armed forces during World War I, but he later returned to receive both the B.A. degree in 1918 and the LL.B. degree in 1920. One of the few blacks during this period to accomplish this feat, Dyett won academic distinction for both degrees. He continued his graduate studies at Boston University, receiving his LL.M. degree in 1921. He was later admitted to the New York bar. It was also during this period that he met and married young Lily B. Ransom of Boston, Mass., who died in 1951. The couple had no children.

A competent lawyer and a committed veteran, Dyett worked to strengthen community ties. His efforts were reflected in his roles as chairman of the Legal Committee for the American Legion; executive member and judge advocate of Colonel Charles Young Post 398; member of the Board of Appeals No. 3 of Selective Service from 1941 to 1946, becoming chairman from 1943 to 1946; and member of the Executive Committee of the Army and Navy Committee of the YMCA, in charge of USO operations during World War II. He would spend more than fifty years dedicated to racial justice and equality.

Dyett was an assistant district attorney in Manhattan from 1927 to 1937. He represented New York as a Democratic delegate to the Constitutional Convention in 1938. Aware that a Republican reapportionment bill would create one additional senate and three additional assembly districts in Harlem, Dyett broke from the Democrats to support the legislation. Always on the cutting edge of reform, he was appointed in 1940 by Governor Herbert H. Lehman to succeed Henrietta Additon on the state correction commission, thus becoming its first black member. Serving on the commission from 1940 to 1946, he gained a reputation as a public-spirited attorney who recognized social problems and worked actively to implement solutions. He spent long hours in meeting sessions as a member of the Mayor's Committee on Unity.

In 1952 he became the first black appointee to the Municipal Civil Service Commission. Mayor Vincent R. Impelliteri chose him to fill the position made vacant by the death of Judge James S. Watson. However, the laws requiring majority nomination and vote precluded Dyett from assuming Watson's presidency. As a member of the New York County Lawyers' Association, the largest lawyers group in America, Dyett served on a wide range of committees dealing with such matters as membership, criminal court, and legal education. In 1955, he became the first black member of the board of directors in the organization's forty-seven-year existence. In 1958, he was also appointed to the Character and Fitness Committee of the Appellate Division, First Department, to screen applicants for admission as lawyers in Manhattan and the Bronx.

As one of the founders of the Harlem Lawyers Association, Dyett was nicknamed the "Dean of Black Lawyers." Personally humble, he sponsored admission to the Bar for hundreds of lawyers, black and white alike. Also to his credit are the accomplishments of his two young former law partners in Dyett, Alexander and Dinkins. Fritz W. Alexander 2d became the first black judge on the Court of Appeals, the state's highest court, and David N. Dinkins became the first black mayor of New York City.

Concerned about the economic, social, and educational conditions in Harlem, he joined a group of influential black men, organized by Professor Kenneth B. Clark of City College, who met to discuss issues and laws that affected the black community. In 1949, they founded the Carver Federal Savings and Loan Association, the first black-owned and -managed banking institution in the State of New York. Dyett served as the bank's first general counsel. In 1958, he cofounded the Allied Federal Savings and Loan Association in Jamaica, N.Y. Dyett was for many years general counsel to the United Mutual Life Insurance Company, the only one organized, managed, and controlled by blacks in New York State. Recognized as one of the city's leading blacks, he worked closely with Mayor La Guardia to reestablish racial harmony during the Harlem riots of 1943. In 1961, during the controversy over integrating the city school system, he and Kenneth B. Clark, A. Philip Randolph, president of the Sleeping Car

Porters, and Jackie Robinson, former baseball player and then president of Chock Full O'Nuts, wrote an open letter in defense of Superintendent John J. Theobald's efforts. His background on the board of directors of the NAACP Legal Defense and Educational Fund enabled him to understand the questions surrounding the issue.

While chairman of the New York Public Library's Citizen Committee, Dyett also served on a nineteen-member citizens' committee specially appointed by leaders of the Democratic, Republican, and Liberal parties to screen potential nominees for seventeen supreme court posts in two counties. It was the first time in New York history that both major political parties had consented to be bound by a citizens' committee on judicial selection.

Often honored for his contributions, Dyett died at the age of eighty-five. His death was announced on the front page of the *Amsterdam News*, the leading black newspaper in New York City.

[Obituaries are in the *Amsterdam News*, Nov. 3, 1971; the *New York Times*, Nov. 3, 1971; and *Alumni News* (Howard University), Dec. 1971.]

GLORIA GRANT ROBERSON

DYKSTRA, JOHN (Apr. 6, 1898–Mar. 2, 1972), automobile industry executive, was born on the outskirts of Stiens in the Dutch province of Friesland, one of four sons of Theodore Dykstra and Nellie DeVries. His father was a coppersmith who emigrated to the United States in 1902 and worked for the Hudson Motor Car Company in Detroit.

Dykstra left school in 1914 to become an apprentice diemaker, later attending night classes in mechanical engineering at the Cass Technical School (1915–1917). (He took correspondence courses in foremanship and related subjects at the LaSalle Extension University from 1921 to 1926.) From 1917 to 1919, Dykstra served in the U.S. Army, and in the latter year became an American citizen. He married Marion S. Hyde on Mar. 2, 1918; they had two children.

After the war, Dykstra was a diemaker at Layton and Lambert, which soon was taken over by Hudson. There he entered the administrative ranks, helping to organize body plant management and supervising production. He rose to plant manager for sheet metal and body fabrication.

In 1934, Dykstra left Hudson to join the Oldsmobile Division of the General Motors Corporation, where after serving in various managerial capacities he became general superintendent in 1939 and manufacturing manager in 1941. In 1947, he joined the Ford Motors Company as general production assistant to D. S. Harder, vice-president for manufacturing.

When automobile manufacture ceased in 1942 and Ford converted to military production, Dykstra began supervising the manufacture of a variety of armed carriers.

After World War II, Dykstra played a key role in the conversion of Ford to automobile manufacturing. He served as general manager at several Ford factories and in 1948 became manager of the general manufacturing division. Two years later he was named vice-president in charge of the aircraft engine, tractor, and machined products group and a director of Ford Motors.

Dykstra was known as one of the industry's foremost production executives with a mania for quality control, which he insisted began with the workers. "Inspectors cannot 'inspect' quality into products," he said. "The best guarantee of quality is pride of workmanship—regardless of the advances that have been made in automatic machinery and plant equipment." Under his leadership quality improved markedly; in 1960, Ford offered a twelve-month or twelve-thousand-mile guarantee, at the time the highest and most inclusive in the industry, obliging the other manufacturers to follow its lead in both quality control and warranties.

In November 1960, Henry Ford II relinquished the company presidency to Robert Strange McNamara, one of the "whiz kids" who came to Ford from the U.S. Army Air Forces after World War II and helped modernize the company. A month later McNamara accepted the post of Secretary of Defense in the Kennedy administration. Ford resumed the presidency, but on Apr. 12, 1961, yielded it to Dykstra.

Dykstra was sixty-three years old at the time, only two years away from Ford's mandatory retirement age, but there was a provision whereby his tenure might be extended by three years with board approval.

Dykstra inherited a company in the midst of an industrywide slump. Sales and profits were down for 1961, but then, despite a strike at the company's stamping plant that halted assembly operations for two weeks, rose to a record high the following year. Under Dykstra's leadership Ford entered the electronics industry through the acquisition of Philco Corporation, which had long been a force in radio and television set production. Philco was also a defense company, and received a contract to construct the first-stage booster for the Saturn rocket. The acquisition proved a disappointment. Philco could not compete effectively in the home entertainment field, and it was unable to win additional large defense contracts. The division eventually was disbanded, and in the end Philco's primary contribution to Ford was in the area of electronic components for automobiles.

Henry Ford decided not to extend Dykstra's contract, and let the public know in an unceremonious fashion. In April 1963, Dykstra's retirement was announced between innings of a Detroit Tigers baseball game. His successor was Arjay Miller, another "whiz kid." In time the Dykstra regime came to be looked upon as the transitional between those of McNamara and Miller.

Dykstra remained on the Ford board until 1965. He maintained an office at the company, and continued to live in suburban Birmingham, less than twenty miles from Ford headquarters. He died in Southfield, Mich.

[There are fleeting references to John Dykstra in the several histories of Ford Motors; see, for example, Victor Lasky, *Never Complain, Never Explain* (1981). An obituary is in the *New York Times*, Mar. 3, 1972.]

ROBERT SOBEL

E

EARLE, GEORGE HOWARD, III (Dec. 5, 1890–Dec. 30, 1974), governor of Pennsylvania, was born in Devon, Pa., the son of George Howard Earle, Jr., and Catherine Hansell French. His father's self-made fortune was the basis for his wealthy style of living, with houses and estate holdings in the Philadelphia Main Line suburbs. George graduated from the Delancey School in Philadelphia. He then spent two years at Harvard before entering his father's sugar business, first in Philadelphia and then in Chicago. On Jan. 20, 1916, he married Huberta Frances Potter of Bowling Green, Ky.; they had three children. Later that year he volunteered for the army expedition to the Mexican border. In 1917, he entered the navy and commanded a motor patrol boat, built with family funds, which patrolled the mouth of the Delaware Bay. When the boat caught fire he led the effort to save the ship and crew, for which he was awarded the Navy Cross. After World War I, Earle founded Flamingo Sugar Mills in Philadelphia. He was recognized as an outstanding polo player and sportsman.

Although previously a Republican, in 1932 Earle met Franklin D. Roosevelt through William C. Bullitt and contributed to Roosevelt's campaign. In 1933 and 1934, he was United States minister to Austria, where he reported home incidents of anti-Semitism and fascist activities. He resigned to become Democratic candidate for governor of Pennsylvania, with the backing of Joseph F. Guffey and David L. Lawrence, Pittsburgh Democratic leaders. The old Philadelphia Democratic organization was toppled by new leadership, which supported Earle. Earle's campaign was linked to Guffey's campaign for the United States Senate, and both won decisively.

The first Democratic governor of Pennsylvania in forty-four years, Earle was favored with a majority in the house of representatives. But Republicans held thirty-one of the fifty senate seats, thwarting his major reforms for the first two years of his term. Lawrence, appointed secretary of the commonwealth, manipulated all the administration's operations in the general assembly. Eight Republican senators bolted their leadership and agreed to give Earle a majority for one year to appropriate $5 million per month, an amount the Federal Emergency Relief Administration required Pennsylvania to contribute if federal relief was to continue. Higher state taxes accompanied the combined federal-state relief program. The rest of what was now being called the Little New Deal, however, was blocked in the senate until the November 1936 elections created overwhelming Democratic majorities in both houses.

The 1937 legislative session truly produced a New Deal at the state level. Laws favorable to labor proliferated, including a Little Wagner Act; abolition of employer funding of police and sheriffs' deputies; minimum wage, maximum hour, and working conditions measures; a labor relations board; occupational disease compensation; and machinery for an unemployment compensation system. Public works projects and centralized control of all welfare disbursements were instituted. The General State Authority was created to finance public works outside the government's mandatory debt limits. Cutthroat competition was curtailed through milk control, the Fair Trade Practices Act, and bank reforms. The Public Utilities Commission replaced the Public Service Commission and was given enlarged power to protect consumers. Earle's plan for a graduated personal income tax was held unconstitutional, however, and the electorate rejected his pleas for constitutional reform.

Earle was his own spokesman, augmenting traditional speech making with frequent radio talks. He learned to pilot small planes in order to move quickly about the state, but he had several accidents. Earle held a belief that the Depression's economic imbalance stemmed from the expanded efficiency of machinery. Welfare measures were necessary until consumption could catch up with the scale of production that was now possible. Both he and the public assumed he would be the Democratic candidate for the United States Senate in 1938, and he had some hopes for the presidency.

Catastrophic floods in March 1936 were handled efficiently by the state, and the labor unrest of that year was accompanied by little violence. Hunger marchers received sympathy from the governor. It was Earle's policy to minimize intervention by either the National Guard or the state police in labor disputes. In refusing to allow state police to stop bootleg coal-mining, he alienated legitimate mine operators as well as the miners they employed.

In 1938, Earle ran for the United States Senate. It was his downfall. Lawrence and Guffey made brief attempts at the gubernatorial candidacy, but both withdrew, alienating each other in the process. Claiming Works Progress Administration patronage, Guffey advanced the CIO's favorite, Lieutenant Governor Thomas Kennedy, who was also the secretary-treasurer of the UMW. Lawrence, with Earle's approval, chose the little-known Charles A. Jones of Pittsburgh, who prevailed in the primary. Earle's attorney general, Charles J. Margiotti, a former Republican who had been rejected as a gubernatorial candidate in the Democratic primary, charged key members of the Earle administration, including Lawrence, with many corrupt acts including contract kickbacks and acceptance of bribes. Although Margiotti was not able to give many specifics supporting his grandiose charges, his actions nonetheless led to investigations by a county grand jury and by the state house of representatives.

Earle was so angry that he briefly considered martial law in order to terminate both investigative processes, but instead defended his administration through public addresses. He had to explain a $95,000 loan from Matthew H. McCloskey, Jr., director of the General State Authority and an associate. Earle's rep-

utation was also damaged by affinity with his own appointees and party supporters who were under investigation. Furthermore, it appeared that the house investigation and other moves by Earle to thwart the grand jury were a cover-up. The state supreme court ruled that the legislative inquiry did not vitiate the powers of the grand jury. Both investigations were left pending through election day, giving voters an unfavorable impression. Earle and Jones both lost, and the Republican party won control. Three weeks later, the house dismissed all the corruption charges, but grand-jury indictment trials began in March 1939. Most of the accused parties, including Lawrence, were acquitted. Three officials were found guilty of relatively minor matters. The major programs of the Little New Deal, however, remained as permanent components of Pennsylvania state government.

Earle never became an elder statesman. He was appointed United States minister to Bulgaria in 1940, then was commissioned in the navy, rising to commander. He served as a naval attaché in Turkey in 1943 and in 1945 as assistant governor of Samoa. In 1945 he obtained a divorce and married Jacqueline Germaine M. Sacre of Belgium. They had two children. In 1949, he returned to the Republican party.

In the first administration of President Truman, Earle broke with the Democratic party and supported Thomas E. Dewey's candidacy in 1948. Moving to Boca Raton, Fla., he served as the finance chairman of Floridians for Eisenhower. Later he supported Richard M. Nixon and other Republican candidates, although he endorsed David Lawrence's Pennsylvania gubernatorial campaign in 1958. He eventually resumed his Pennsylvania residency and died in Bryn Mawr.

Earle's lasting influence as governor was summed up in 1968 by Pennsylvania state historian S. K. Stevens, who wrote, "The true worth of the Earle administration rest upon its social and welfare legislation and bringing a 'little New Deal' to Pennsylvania."

[Governor Earle's official papers are in the Pennsylvania State Archives; relevant materials on his Austrian and Bulgarian periods, his governance of American Samoa, and his naval service are in the National Archives. Richard C. Keller, *Pennsylvania's Little New Deal* (1982), is a study of the gubernatorial years. See also Sylvester K. Stevens, *Pennsylvania* (1968); and Michael P. Weber, *Don't*

Call Me Boss (1988). An obituary is in the *Philadelphia Evening Bulletin*, Dec. 31, 1974.]

LOUIS M. WADDELL

EGTVEDT, CLAIRMONT ("CLAIRE") LEROY (Oct. 18, 1892–Oct. 19, 1975), aeronautical engineer, was born in Stoughton, Wis., the son of Sever Peter Egtvedt and Mary E. Rublee. His father was a farmer and his mother a homemaker. Claire, as he was known, graduated from the local county high school in 1911. That same year he moved with his family to Seattle, Wash., where he enrolled in the Engineering School at the University of Washington in 1912. Egtvedt graduated with a B.S. in June 1917.

Upon graduation he went to work for the Boeing Airplane Company of Seattle, which William Boeing had founded the year before. In 1918 Boeing promoted Egtvedt to chief engineer, and in 1926 to vice-president and general manager. In 1933 Egtvedt became the company's president. The next year he became president of the newly reorganized Boeing Aircraft Company, which had subsidiaries in Wichita, Kans., and Vancouver, Canada. He remained president until 1939 when Philip Johnson took over and Egtvedt was named chairman of the board. However, when Johnson died on Sept. 14, 1944, Egtvedt reassumed the Boeing presidency until the end of World War II. In 1939 he again became chairman, a position he held until Apr. 25, 1966.

Although he spent almost fifty years with Boeing, Egtvedt's greatest contribution to the company, and to the nation, was his decision to build a new four-engine bomber—the Model 299. During the 1920's and early 1930's he publicly argued that European nations were moving ahead of the United States in the development of military aircraft, thus threatening the security of the nation. After discussions with military experts in the early 1930's, Egtvedt and Boeing's eastern representative, James E. Murray, began to conceptualize the creation of what Egtvedt called a "Dreadnought of the air."

Financial difficulties brought on by the Depression delayed the construction of the bomber. Instead, in February 1933, Boeing began production of the Model 247 commercial airliner in competition with Douglas's DC-2/3's. Later that year Boeing sold sixty of these sleek new aircraft to United Airlines.

In October 1933 Egtvedt made a daring decision to put the company's entire resources into modifying the Model 247 into the Model 299 bomber. Planning began in early 1934 and the first prototype, dubbed the Y1B-17 by the Army Air Corps, rolled out of Boeing's Seattle factory in July 1935.

On Aug. 20, 1935, Boeing senior test pilot Leslie Tower flew the plane from Seattle to Wright Field, Ohio, for competitive tests versus the twin-engine B-18 "Bollo." During the flight the new bomber shattered all existing altitude and speed records in its class.

On the morning of Oct. 30, 1935, the tests began. With Egtvedt, U.S. Army Air Corps Materiel Division Commander A. W. Robins, Boeing project engineer Robert Wells, and other interested parties looking on, the big silver plane taxied to the runway for takeoff. At the controls were U.S. Army Air Corps Materiel Division's chief test-pilot Major Ployer ("Pete") Hill and copilot First Lieutenant Donald L. Putt, a future war ace. Also on the plane were Tower, Pratt, and Whitney flight engineer Henry Igo and C. B. Benton of Boeing.

In a matter of seconds after takeoff the plane lay at the end of the runway in flames. Although many observers rushed to the crash site and pulled all five men from the wreckage, Hill died that afternoon and Tower a few days later. The other three, although seriously injured, survived. The failure of Hill to unlock the rudder lock had caused the crash. The lock, a new device developed especially for this large plane, was to prevent wind damage to the wings while on the ground. Hill and Putt, not used to such a device, forgot to check it, and Tower forgot to remind them.

Despite the disaster, pretest flights had convinced men like Air Corps Deputy Brigadier General Henry H. ("Hap") Arnold, General Headquarters Air Force Chief Brigadier General Frank Andrews, and General Robins of the value of the aircraft. Even though the B-18 won the 1935 contract, these men convinced the War Department to purchase thirteen experimental B-17A's. Over the next two years bombers flew several spectacular missions, including the interception of the Italian oceanliner *Rex*. This event occurred on May 12, 1938, when three B-17's led by Colonel Robert Olds and navigated by First Lieutenant Curtis LeMay simulated an attack against an invasion fleet by contacting the great passenger ship 725 miles out at sea.

Such successes eventually led to the construction of new models and the purchase of more aircraft. In 1938 Boeing produced the B-17B, with the B-17C/D appearing in 1940, and the B-17E in 1941. Along with the B-24 "Liberator," and later the Boeing B-29 "Super Fortress," the B-17F/G's built between 1941 and 1944 were the backbone of U.S. strategic air power in World War II.

Dubbed the "Flying Fortress," the B-17's of the Eighth Air Force spearheaded America's precision daylight bombing raids against German war industry from 1943 to 1945. By the war's end, 12,731 B-17's had dropped 640,000 tons of bombs on Europe.

Although Egtvedt retired as Boeing's president in 1939, he continued to push Boeing to utilize the work of men like Phil Johnson to build the B-29. Based on design experiments with the XB-15 initiated by Egtvedt and air corps leaders at Wright Field in the 1930's, Boeing began construction of the B-29 in 1942. The deployment of 3,900 B-29's in the second half of World War II assured the greatness and solvency of Boeing.

Between 1946 and 1966 Egtvedt, as chairman of the board, continued to support the development of new commercial and military aircraft. These aircraft included the Boeing 707 jetliner, which revolutionized passenger travel in the 1960's and the B-52 "Strato Fortress," built in the mid-1950's, which remained the backbone of the American heavy bomber force through the 1980's.

Throughout his life the man called "the father of the Flying Fortress" proved to be a reluctant hero who shied away from the limelight. He died at his home in Seattle, survived by his wife, Evelyn S. (Wayland) Egtvedt, whom he had married on Oct. 14, 1926.

[See also "Family Album," *Boeing Magazine*, Apr. 1946; and William L. Worden, "The Sky Was No limit," *Boeing Magazine*, May 1966. Other references include Alwyn T. Lloyd and Terry D. Moore, *B-17: Flying Fortress in Detail and Scale* (1980); *Pedigree of Champions: Boeing Since 1916*, 6th ed. (1985); Lisa Fusch, ed., *Year By Year: Seventy-five Years of Boeing History, 1916–1991* (1991); and William Head, *The Father of Air Force Logistics: The Life and Times of Brigadier General Augustine Warner Robins*, USAF Monograph (1991). An obituary is in the *New York Times*, Oct. 21, 1975.]

WILLIAM HEAD

ELLENDER, ALLEN JOSEPH (Sept. 24, 1890–July 27, 1972), U.S. senator, was born on a sugar cane plantation near Montegut, La., the son of French-speaking parents. His father, Wallace Ellender, was a farmer; his mother was Victoria Jarveaux.

Educated initially in plantation schools, Ellender attended St. Aloysius (1905–1909), a Catholic school in New Orleans, before attending Tulane University (1909–1913), from which he graduated with a law degree in 1913.

He began his law practice in Houma, La., becoming city attorney in 1913 and district attorney in 1915. In 1917 he married Helen Calhoun Donnelly of New Orleans, whom he met at Tulane. His only child, Allen Jr., was born in 1921, the year Ellender was elected to serve as a delegate to write a new Louisiana state constitution. In 1924 he was elected to the state legislature and reelected in 1928 as an anti–Huey Long member. Converting to Longism in 1928, Ellender defended Long against impeachment charges. The next year he directed Long's election campaign to the Senate. After Long's assassination in 1935, Ellender was elected to fill the Senate seat in 1936. A lifelong Democrat, he took office in January 1937.

Although Long had been hostile to Roosevelt and the New Deal, Ellender became a loyal New Dealer, supporting President Roosevelt on welfare, agriculture, housing, public works, and his 1937 court-packing scheme. A segregationist all his life, Ellender voted against antilynching and anti–poll tax measures and educational programs calling for racial integration. He voted for the Social Security Act and for the Fair Labor Standards (minimum-wage) Act, but only after agriculture was exempted from the latter's provisions.

During World War II he endorsed Roosevelt's war measures but opposed the Fair Employment Practices Commission, which called for ending racial discrimination in war plants. Ellender favored the Marshall Plan and other postwar recovery programs, but he worried about their costs. He also wanted to limit the number of displaced persons allowed to enter the United States.

By the late 1940's Ellender had become a world traveler and a critic of foreign aid. A conservative on issues of labor (he voted for the Taft-Hartley Act of 1947 and against increasing the minimum wage), Ellender was surprisingly liberal in his views on détente and exchange programs with the Soviet Union and other Communist-bloc nations. Ellender also favored wheat sales to the USSR. Believing that anticommunist forces fomented Cold War incidents in order to increase military spending and foreign aid, he opposed McCarthyism and was one of the first legislators to criticize the Wisconsin senator for his scare tactics.

Ellender joined Senators Robert Taft of Ohio and Robert Wagner of New York in passing significant housing and education legislation during the Truman administration.

Ellender became chairman of the Senate Committee on Agriculture in 1951. As a member of the agricultural establishment he supported farmers and farm programs, but he criticized waste and high costs. He blamed Eisenhower's Soil Bank and flexible commodity price supports for a $10 billion farm deficit by 1960.

Ellender became an architect of farm policy in the 1960's. Supporting sugar, rice, and cotton constituents, he opposed placing a limit on benefit payments to wealthy landowners. An expert in the game of broker politics, he assiduously sheltered the sugar program.

As a member of the Senate Appropriations Committee, Ellender's worldwide inspection tours of foreign installations became more intensive. Instructing agents abroad to deceive Ellender whenever possible, Federal Bureau of Investigation Director J. Edgar Hoover and Central Intelligence Agency Director Allen Dulles concealed from him the extent of intelligence operations abroad. Ellender suspected the two agencies of deliberately sabotaging exchange programs with the USSR, which Ellender visited five times. When Ellender claimed in 1962 that African nations were incapable of self-government without the help of Europeans, his credibility among foreign policy observers evaporated.

An admirer of Lyndon Johnson, Ellender nonetheless opposed Johnson's civil rights legislation. President Johnson catered to Ellender and bestowed countless political favors on him in exchange for support for his Vietnam policy. Although Ellender criticized the Vietnam War and claimed frequently he had warned Presidents Eisenhower and Kennedy about becoming involved in that situation, he refused to vote for McGovern-Hatfield, Cooper-Church, or other end-the-war measures.

An early supporter of the food-stamp con-cept, Ellender later advocated spreading the idea to impoverished peoples abroad through Public Law 480, an agricultural export subsidy. Author of the Food Stamp Act of 1964, he voted against the domestic poverty program and granting loans to slum dwellers.

In 1971 Ellender became president pro tempore of the Senate and chairman of the Appropriations Committee. Short (five feet four) and gregarious, Ellender was never shy about expressing his opinion on a variety of subjects. Health conscious long before being physically fit became a national obsession, he appeared younger than he was. He also furthered an image that he was frugal and down to earth. Sometimes verbose, he rose to his toes when making a point, gesturing with his hands and speaking rapidly in a clipped Acadian accent. Noted for his Acadian cooking, he courted presidents and won countless projects for Louisiana.

Frequently reelected without serious opposition, Ellender in 1972 faced a strong challenger in J. Bennett Johnston. Some voters viewed Ellender, who was eighty-one, as too old for office. After campaigning in north Louisiana, he returned to Washington, D.C., on July 27, 1972, to vote on an agricultural appropriations bill. Several hours later he died of a coronary occlusion at Bethesda Naval Hospital. President Nixon, Vice-President Spiro Agnew, and a large Senate delegation attended his funeral in Houma on July 31.

[Ellender's senatorial papers are at Nicholls State University, Thibodaux, La. See Stephen S. Rosenfeld, "The Travels of Allen Ellender," *New Republic*, Sept. 27, 1969; Thomas A. Becnel, "Fulbright of Arkansas v. Ellender of Louisiana: The Politics of Sugar and Rice, 1937–1974," *Arkansas Historical Quarterly*, Winter 1984; and Thomas A. Becnel, "Allen J. Ellender, Consensus Politician," *Louisiana History*, Summer 1991.]

THOMAS A. BECNEL

ELLINGTON, EARL BUFORD (June 27, 1907–Apr. 3, 1972), governor of Tennessee, was born in rural Holmes County, Miss., near the town of Lexington, the son of Abner Earl Ellington, a farmer, and Cora Ophelia Grantham. After graduating from Holmes County Agricultural High School, he attended Millsaps College in Jackson, Miss., sporadically between 1926 and 1929. "I would go to school for a quarter, and then get out and work for a quarter," he later wrote. "I didn't get to finish college. Times were hard then, and I did a little of everything from picking up laundry to delivering papers."

Returning to his home county after leaving college for the last time, Ellington edited a weekly newspaper in Durant, Miss. There, on Dec. 20, 1929, he married Catherine Ann Cheek, a schoolteacher from Tennessee. They had two children.

In 1931, Ellington and his wife moved to Tennessee, the state in which he would build his political career. For eight years he sold farm equipment for International Harvester Company of Memphis. In 1939, he purchased a general store in Verona, Tenn., and began to acquire farmland in the surrounding area. Ellington became active in local politics, and in 1946 he served as campaign manager for Joe L. Evins, the successful Democratic candidate for the U.S. House of Representatives.

In 1948, Ellington ran for office for the first time, winning a two-year term as a representative from Marshall County in the Tennessee General Assembly. Simultaneously, he worked as a field representative for the Tennessee Farm Bureau Federation Service Program and as manager of the Tennessee Farm Bureau Insurance Service. In his jobs with the farm bureau, a powerful force in Tennessee politics, he traveled the state, organizing an insurance sales force. He also laid the groundwork for his emergence into the statewide political arena.

Managing the successful campaign of gubernatorial candidate Frank Clement in 1952, Ellington won the position of chairman of the Democratic State Executive Committee the same year. In 1953, Governor Clement named him state agriculture commissioner; he served in this office until 1958, when he began his own campaign for governor. The state constitution prohibited Clement, who had already served two terms, from serving a third consecutive term. He supported Ellington, despite their apparent disagreement on civil rights, one of the major issues of the day. After the U.S. Supreme Court had declared segregated schools unconstitutional in 1954, Clement, a moderate, had facilitated the end of racial segregation in some Tennessee school systems. Ellington, on the other hand, proclaimed himself "an old-fashioned segregationist and states' righter" and promised to close any public school forced to integrate. Ellington won the Democratic primary in August 1958 and was elected governor over weak Republican and independent opposition in November.

Despite his campaign rhetoric, as governor from Jan. 19, 1959, to Jan. 15, 1963, Ellington obstructed not school desegregation but rather the efforts of die-hard segregationists to adopt the extremist policies of some other southern states. And while few black children actually enrolled in formerly all-white schools, under the Ellington administration school desegregation continued in Tennessee without the violence that occurred elsewhere.

As governor, Ellington focused his attention on reorganizing the state government, maintaining a balanced budget without increasing taxes, and developing the state's industrial base. His Reorganization Act of 1959 reduced the number of state officials reporting to the governor from over seventy to a mere eighteen, primarily by bringing independent boards and commissions into the departments of state government. Ellington made numerous industry-recruiting trips in the North, and his efforts paid off in rapid industrialization, new jobs, and rising tax revenues without tax increases; in 1959, unemployment in Tennessee reached an all-time low.

Upon leaving the governor's mansion in 1963, Ellington was appointed to a vice-presidency in the Louisville and Nashville Railroad. In 1965 his old friend, President Lyndon Johnson, called him to Washington to be director of the Office of Emergency Planning and to serve informally as the president's liaison with the nation's governors.

On Jan. 15, 1966, Ellington resigned the federal post to return to Tennessee to run for a second term as governor. In an arrangement that some would call "leapfrog government," he would seek again to succeed his political associate Frank Clement, who had succeeded him in turn in the governor's mansion. Ellington easily won election to his second term, and he took office on Jan. 16, 1967.

Civil rights remained a focus of public attention in Ellington's second gubernatorial effort. During the 1966 campaign, Ellington recanted his previous support for segregation, and early in his term he appointed the first black to the Tennessee governor's cabinet. He also established the Tennessee Commission on Human Relations to work toward dismantling the racial policies of the past. When Dr. Martin Luther

King, Jr., was assassinated in Memphis on Apr. 4, 1968, Ellington mobilized the National Guard to maintain order and issued a statement praising Dr. King and his efforts to end discrimination.

Ellington's success in his second term was limited by a combination of his own ill health and political changes in Tennessee's political landscape. Traditionally, the governor had dominated the legislative process; but by the time Ellington began his second term, reapportionment of the legislature had transferred political power from rural areas, where Clement and Ellington were strong, to the cities. National events, furthermore, had turned the tide in favor of the Republican party to such an extent that—to Ellington's chagrin—1968 Democratic presidential candidate Hubert Humphrey won only 28 percent of the vote in Tennessee, despite Ellington's active support. Ellington himself was politically crippled in the same year when Republicans won control of the state's house of representatives. He was succeeded in 1971 by Winfield Dunn, Tennessee's first Republican governor in fifty years. Ellington reportedly advised his successor, "It's no fun the second time."

Ellington showed little interest in politics after his second term and spent most of his time thereafter in Florida. He died of an apparent heart attack on a golf course in Boca Raton.

[Ellington's public papers are in the Tennessee State Library and Archives in Nashville. See D. E. Sumner, "A Clash over Race: Tennessee Governor Ellington versus CBS, 1960," *Journalism Quarterly*, Autumn 1991. Obituaries appear in the *New York Times*, the *Nashville Tennessean*, and the *Nashville Banner*, all Apr. 4, 1972.]

VAGN K. HANSEN

ELLINGTON, EDWARD KENNEDY ("DUKE") (Apr. 29, 1899–May 24, 1974), composer, bandleader, and pianist, was born in Washington, D.C., the son of James Edward Ellington and Daisy Kennedy. His father moonlighted as a butler while working as a blueprint maker for the U.S. Department of the Navy, and his mother worked as a receptionist and housecleaner for an important Washington physician. Duke, who received his royal title from a schoolmate as a comment on his elegant manner and dress, was the only male offspring in his mother's family, and she and her sister

showered him with all of their attention. As he said, "My mother and aunt felt I was so perfect that my feet did not touch the ground until I was ten years old." The bond with his mother was unique. Her death in 1935 stunned Ellington, but the resulting grief produced one of his first great extended compositions, "Reminiscing in Tempo." Even toward the end of his life, he continually mentioned his mother. At a 1969 White House party in honor of his seventieth birthday, Ellington stated to President Richard Nixon, "There is no place I would rather be tonight, except in my mother's arms." Although there were many women associated with Ellington throughout his life, including his wife, Edna, and his longtime companion, Evie Ellis, there were really only two women in his life, his mother and his sister, Ruth. He saw Ruth as the image of his mother, and so she became the focus of his emotional attention after their mother's death.

Although Ellington began piano lessons at age seven, he was more interested in athletics and art than in music. His interest in art was strongly supported by his father, and was his main focus at Washington's Armstrong High School, which he attended from 1914 to 1917. While a student at Armstrong he won a poster design contest organized by the National Association for the Advancement of Colored People. (The experience influenced him to leave high school before graduation to start his own sign-painting business. The Pratt Institute of Fine Art offered him a scholarship, which he eventually turned down.) During high school years, art and athletics won most of Ellington's attention; however, upon hearing several local pianists and the young Philadelphian Harvey Brooks perform, he began to apply himself to piano study more seriously.

While in high school Duke began performing professionally at the Washington True Reformers' Hall, first as solo ragtime pianist and later as a member of various small groups. He soon began substituting for pianist Lester Dishman at the Poodle Dog Café where he wrote his first composition, "Soda Fountain Rag," in 1914. This was followed by his first song with lyrics, "What Are You Going To Do When the Bed Breaks Down?" Like most of his contemporaries, Ellington was influenced by the major ragtime pianists and composers of the day. He also received help, instruction, and inspiration from a variety of local musicians. However, he singled out Henry Lee Grant, with whom he studied, and "Doc" Perry, a well-known pianist, as his major influences.

Ellington's work at the Poodle Dog was followed by work as a relief pianist at the hotel Ebbitt House, theater work at the Oriental Theatre, and work with various Washington band leaders including Louis Thomas, Daniel Doyle, "Doc" Perry, and Elmer Snowden. He was also one of five pianists in the thirty-four-piece orchestra of Russell Wooding. Together with Otto Hardwick, Snowden, and Arthur Whetsol, he did a brief tour in Wisconsin before forming his first group, the Duke's Serenaders, in 1918.

On July 2, 1918, Ellington married Edna Thompson. Mercer Ellington, their only child, was born on Mar. 11, 1919.

Ellington first visited New York City in March 1923 for a week's engagement as a member of Wilbur Sweatman's band. Upon his return to Washington, he joined Snowden's five-piece combo, the Washingtonians. In the summer of 1923, this group performed at various clubs in Atlantic City, N.J., and in September 1923 began a residency at the Hollywood Club on Broadway and Forty-ninth Street in New York City. This combo included three of the later-to-be-famous instrumentalists of future Ellington groups, Otto Hardwick, alto sax; Sonny Greer, drums; and Whetsol, trumpet. In early 1924, under Ellington's leadership, the Washingtonians gradually began to enlarge to a ten-piece orchestra. Important additions to the group included Bubber Miley, trumpet; "Tricky" Sam Nanton, trombone; Harry Carney, baritone sax; and Fred Guy, banjo, as the replacement for Snowden. With Miley as a co-composer, the band recorded its first important works, "East St. Louis Toodle-oo" (1926), "Black and Tan Fantasy" (1927), and "Creole Love Call" (1927). Although the enlarged Washingtonian Orchestra toured New England regularly and performed at other New York nightclubs, it continued its residency at the Kentucky Club (the renamed Hollywood Club) until 1927. The group also appeared in various revues and New York theaters.

The growing visibility of Ellington and his orchestra attracted the attention of the owners of the Cotton Club, then the most prized jazz/show/revue room in New York City. During his years at the Cotton Club, from December 1927 to February 1931, Ellington began to share with Louis Armstrong the leading position in the jazz world. It was also at the Cotton Club that Ellington, with the help of Bubber Miley and Sam Nanton, created his "jungle style," which was characterized by growl trumpet and trombone sounds, frequently with plunger mutes reminiscent of the moaning of the human voices "in a jungle night." During the Cotton Club period, Ellington was required to perform in a variety of music genres, including music for dancing, jungle-style production numbers, popular songs, "blue" or "mood" pieces, and standard instrumental jazz compositions. This musical variety helped Ellington develop a unique relationship with and understanding of his orchestra as "his instrument" for creative expression, even more than the piano. The experimentation with timbral colors, tonal effects, and unusual instrumental grouping became the hallmark of his style, the "Ellington effect," as coined by Billy Strayhorn, who in 1939 joined the orchestra as Ellington's arranger and second pianist.

In 1930 Ellington separated from his wife and moved with his son to an apartment in the Sugar Hill section of Harlem. The following year his Cotton Club success enabled him to move his parents and sister from Washington to join him and Mercer in New York City. This provided him with the strong family environment that both he and his son needed.

Although the Cotton Club period produced some important musical compositions, the decade from 1932 to 1942 is considered Ellington's most creative. His band had been enlarged to fourteen musicians, hence the variety of timbral colors was greatly increased. Some of the more important works written and recorded during the Cotton Club period and the decade that followed were "Mood Indigo" and "Rockin' in Rhythm" (1930), "It Don't Mean a Thing" and "Sophisticated Lady" (1932), "Solitude" (1934), "Echoes of Harlem" and "In a Sentimental Mood" (1935), "Prelude to a Kiss" and "Black and Tan Fantasy" (1938), and "In a Mellotone" and "Ko-Ko" (1940). Although not one of his own compositions, Ellington's 1937 recording of trombonist Juan Tizol's composition "Caravan" paved the way for "Cuban Jazz" (now called "Latin Jazz"). The combining of Afro-Cuban rhythms with jazz melodies and harmonies was not completely new by this time, but its use by the Ellington band gave it more credibility and visibility. The band's 1941 recording of Strayhorn's "Take The 'A' Train" was the first of over twenty recordings of that composition, and it later became the band's theme song.

In the mid-1940's Ellington again enlarged his group, to eighteen members, in order to increase the tonal colors. In January 1943 Ellington initiated a series of annual concerts at Carnegie Hall with his large-scale work "Black, Brown and Beige," a "tone parallel" intended to portray through music the history of African Americans in the United States. These concerts continued until 1952 and included performances of other large-scale works such as "Harlem," "Night Creature," "Such Sweet Thunder," and "Liberian Suite." The 1940's also witnessed his first full-length stage production, *Jump for Joy*.

From the 1950's until his death, Ellington continued to expand the scope of his compositions and his activities as a bandleader. His foreign tours, begun in the 1930's, became increasingly frequent and successful, and many of them inspired him to compose more large-scale works. In 1959 he composed his first film score, for Otto Preminger's *Anatomy of a Murder*. He also began writing for and recording with musicians other than those in his orchestra, such as John Coltrane, Max Roach, and Charles Mingus.

Strongly religious, Ellington was an avid student of the Bible, and he paid specific attention to the words of Solomon. Beginning in 1965 with the performance of "In the Beginning God" at Grace Episcopal Cathedral in San Francisco, he dedicated his time to composing music for "sacred services."

During the 1960's and 1970's, Ellington's achievements were recognized by many prestigious institutions. He received honorary doctorates from Howard University in 1963, Yale University in 1967, Morgan State University in 1968, and Berklee College of Music in 1971, as well as the Presidential Medal of Freedom in 1969. In 1970 Ellington was made a member of the National Institute of Arts and Letters and in 1971 became the only jazz musician to be made a member of the Royal Swedish Academy of Music in Stockholm. After his death in New York City, part of West 106th St. in Manhattan was named for him.

Duke Ellington is generally considered to be the most important and prolific composer in jazz history. Although most of his works were recorded by his orchestra, their exact number is unknown. Estimates suggest some two thousand compositions, including hundreds of instrumental pieces, popular songs, large-scale suites, several musical comedies, various film scores, and an unfinished opera, "Boola." Ellington the composer is inseparable from Ellington the bandleader because he used his orchestra as the vehicle for his creativity. Many of the musicians of the later Ellington band had been members of the Washingtonians and/or Cotton Club orchestra. Ellington therefore grew to know the individual musical personalities of all his players and wrote many works that featured the special talents of these artists. He consistently applied his genius to mix the players in unique combinations that produced the unique "Ellington effect."

[Ellington's papers and scores are held in the Yale University Library and in the Ellington Collection of the Smithsonian Museum. His autobiography, *Music Is My Mistress* (1973), was cowritten with Stanley Dance. Biographies include Barry Ulanov, *Duke Ellington* (1946); Peter Gammond, *Duke Ellington: His Life and Music* (1958); G. D. Lambert, *Duke Ellington* (1959); Stanley Dance, *The World of Duke Ellington* (1970); Derek Jewell, *Duke: A Portrait of Duke Ellington* (1977); and Mercer Ellington with Stanley Dance, *Duke Ellington in Person: An Intimate Memoir* (1979). An obituary is in the *New York Times*, May 25, 1974.]

WARRICK L. CARTER

ELLIOT, CASS ("MAMA") (Sept. 19, 1941–July 29, 1974), pop singer, was born Ellen Naomi Cohen in Baltimore, the daughter of Philip Cohen and Beth Levine, who were in the restaurant business.

She grew up in Baltimore and Arlington, Va., in homes that were always filled with music. Her father was an opera buff; her mother played the piano. Elliot loved listening to singers like Ella Fitzgerald, Judy Garland, and Blossom Dearie. She developed an interest in acting, especially musical comedy, and appeared in high school theater productions and sang with the choir. She left Forest Park High School in Baltimore shortly before graduating, however, and never got her diploma.

By seventeen, she had adopted the name Cassandra Elliot. Her father nicknamed her Cass, after the ill-fated prophetess of Greek mythology, as a girl; "Elliot," she said once, was in honor of a friend who had died in a car accident. At nineteen, Elliot moved to New York City to try for a stage career, winning a few small parts Off Broadway and a role in a touring company of *The Music Man*. She also directed at Café La Mama.

She soon became involved in the city's folk music scene. In 1963 she married James R. Hendricks and they sang with a short-lived group, the Big Three, which evolved into the Mugwumps with Denny Doherty and Zal Yanovsky. The group went electric and received some acclaim from critics, but little response from the public. When the Mugwumps broke up, Elliot fronted a jazz trio before moving to Los Angeles. In 1965 she joined up with Doherty and the husband-and-wife team of John and Michelle Phillips. They recorded backing vocals for records on Lou Adler's newly formed Dunhill label, then got their own contract with him as the Mamas and the Papas.

The foursome had immediate success. According to one account, "They were the right group at the right time, still redolent of nostalgia for the flower-power era, the last time pop music could be commercial and still appear to be innocent." The Mamas and the Papas had a hit in 1966 with their first single, "California Dreamin,' " which was rapidly followed by five more top five singles, including the number one hit, "Monday, Monday." The group was famous for its unique harmonies and warm melodic voices. Elliot sang contralto and, as the *New York Times* put it, "served as the large, homey foil to the ethereal beauty and the soprano of Michelle Phillips."

Mama Cass, as she was known to fans, was probably the most popular member of the group because of her earthy, often self-deprecating humor. Always overweight, she was living proof that one didn't have to be thin and beautiful to be a star. The five-foot-five-inch brunette said her weight, which swung wildly at times and reached 300 pounds, didn't hurt her career. "On the contrary, it's helpful," she once told an interviewer. "It sets me apart from the others. After all, you'd never mistake me for Jane Fonda, would you?" About her unpretentious style, she once remarked, "I didn't develop a sense of humor as a defense for being heavy. I've always had a weight problem. I simply learned that's the way I am and so I live with it."

Despite their commercial success, the Mamas and the Papas broke up in 1968 as the Phillips' marriage crumbled. Elliot embarked on a solo career, appearing at Caesar's Palace in Las Vegas for $40,000 per week in October 1968. The show was canceled after the first night because of illness. "I don't think there is a word in the English language to say what a disaster that was," she told the AP. "After that first night, I went into the hospital for eight weeks." After the Las Vegas debacle, Elliot said she gave up drugs and alcohol.

She scored her biggest solo hit single in 1968 with "Dream a Little Dream of Me," and recorded an album with British rock star Dave Mason. She became a familiar figure on television variety shows and specials.

In 1967 Elliot had a daughter outside of her marriage to Hendricks, whom she divorced in 1969. In 1972 she married a German nobleman, Baron Donald von Weidenman, but the marriage was annulled shortly thereafter.

Elliot died in her London apartment two days after the closing of a successful two-week show at the Palladium. She was about to begin a five-week tour of British night clubs. Initial reports stated that she had choked on a ham sandwich. That was later discounted by the British coroner, who listed a heart attack caused by obesity and stress as the cause of death. No traces of drugs or alcohol were found.

Her manager, Allan Carr, said she had slimmed down from 294 to 224 pounds in the months before her death, but the coroner's report said it was too little, too late.

[Two books by members of the Mamas and the Papas include reminiscences of Elliot: *California Dreamin': The True Story of the Mamas and the Papas*, by Michelle Phillips (1986); and *Papa John: an Autobiography*, by John Phillips (1986). An in-depth interview with her appears in the Oct. 26, 1968, issue of *Rolling Stone*. Good synopses of the history of the Mamas and the Papas appear in *The Rolling Stone Encyclopedia of Rock and Roll* (1983) and *The Penguin Encyclopedia of Popular Music* (1989), although both give Elliot's year of birth incorrectly as 1943. Complete obituaries by the *New York Times* and the Associated Press appear July 30, 1974, although the *Times* gives an incorrect birth date.]

PAUL GEITNER

ENGELHARD, CHARLES WILLIAM (Feb. 15, 1917–Mar. 2, 1971), industrialist and precious metals company executive, was born in New York City, the son of Charles W. Engelhard and Emy Marie Canthal. He attended St. Paul's School in Concord, N.H., and graduated from Princeton University in 1939 with a B.A. in history.

Engelhard was born to a well-to-do German family. His father, who emigrated to the United States near the turn of the nineteenth century, invested in several precious metal companies in the early 1900's. As a result, over the next few decades, the Engelhard fortune grew tremendously and by 1950, when the senior Engelhard died, the family was estimated to be worth between $10 million and $20 million.

Charles Engelhard had an odd sort of relationship with his father, who was autocratic and almost fifty years old when he was born. Unlike most father-son relationships, the relationship was very businesslike and lacked personal affection and warmth.

Armed with a college education, in 1940 Engelhard went to England to learn the family business. However, he returned home one year later and joined the Army Air Corps. While in the service, he was a bomber pilot and held the rank of captain by the end of World War II. After his discharge from the service, he resumed his work for his father's company and established a subsidiary in South Africa. On Aug. 18, 1947, he married Jane Reis-Brian, the widow of a Dutch banker. They had five children.

In 1950, after his father died, Engelhard, who had been groomed to run the company, assumed the leadership of the family's precious metal business in Newark, N.J. His business empire began to expand rapidly through a series of new domestic and international business and joint venture developments. For example, in the mid-1950's, while in South Africa, Engelhard met Harry Oppenheimer, a South African businessman with whom he developed a close friendship after discovering that they had a number of similar interests, which ranged from running businesses to racing thoroughbreds. Together they founded Rand American Investment Company in South Africa, the first of several such arrangements that linked the two international businessmen. During his travels abroad, Engelhard met Ian Fleming, the British writer and creator of British agent James Bond. Fleming's character, Auric Goldfinger, an international gold entrepreneur in his spy thriller, *Goldfinger*, was purportedly based on Engelhard.

While his businesses were thriving in the United States and abroad, Engelhard developed a keen interest in politics. His wealth enabled him to finance several political campaigns. In 1953, he backed Robert B. Meyner's successful campaign for governor of New Jersey. Then, in 1955, he himself was the Democratic candidate for Somerset County in the New Jersey senate race. This political race pitted him against Malcolm S. Forbes, the incumbent Republican candidate and the founder of *Forbes* magazine, a good friend, neighbor, and former classmate from Princeton. Because of the extreme wealth of both candidates, people called their senate race the "Battle of the Millionaires." In a hard-fought campaign, Engelhard lost the election by fewer than 360 votes. But in a sense, his political loss to Forbes was a victory for business. It forced him to devote more time to his intricate business empire. Interestingly enough, a few years later, it was his political rival, Forbes, who recommended Engelhard's appointment to New Jersey's State Planning and Development Council.

Engelhard continued to contribute to the state and national Democratic party financially. In 1957, he lent his support to the reelection of Governor Robert B. Meyner, by then a close friend. In 1960, he made financial contributions to the Kennedy-Johnson campaign, and in 1964 he contributed heavily to President Lyndon B. Johnson's presidential election campaign. For his support, the Kennedy and Johnson administrations selected Engelhard to represent the government at many international ceremonies. For example, he was a member of the American delegations to Gabon (1961), Algeria (1963), and Zambia (1964), and he was a member of Johnson's Special East-West Trade Committee (1965). He also represented the United States at the funeral of Pope John XXIII (1963) and at the coronation of Pope Paul VI (1963). In 1968, political circles speculated that Engelhard was to be nominated for the ambassadorship to France, but such an appointment never materialized.

In addition to his political activities, Engelhard was known for his philanthropy to many diverse causes. Two such examples were his 1968 donation of half a million dollars to Boystown and his 1969 donation of $1.25 million to Rutgers University's Graduate School of Business in Newark. This donation sparked a protest by blacks who believed that the Engelhard fortune and mining investments in South Africa had been made at the expense of black South

Africans. Engelhard also participated in community and business affairs through his appointments to public and private boards, such as the Newark Museum, Seton Hall University, the Prudential Insurance Company, Public Service Electric & Gas, and the Port Authority of New York.

Over the years, Engelhard, the international entrepreneurial business mogul, acquired several companies, and at one time was chairperson of six corporations. In 1967, Engelhard Industries merged with Minerals & Chemical Philipp to create a new billion-dollar corporation, Engelhard Minerals & Chemicals (EM & C). Engelhard, who was elected chairman of EM & C, also held financial interests in many international companies through a network of intricate legal and business arrangements.

Besides his business, political, and philanthropic interests, Engelhard acquired a passion for horses. In the late 1950's, he purchased his first race horse in South Africa. By 1970, he spent nearly $15 million on horses for his stables. His horses ran at international race tracks throughout Europe and Africa and paid off handsomely. In fact, several of them won derbies in the United States and abroad. All told, he owned more than 300 horses and several horse farms and stables in New Jersey and Kentucky.

Although he owned many extravagant residences throughout the world, Engelhard called Cragwood, a castle located on a 172-acre estate in Far Hills, N.J., his home. He also spent time at his other residences in Florida, New York, South Africa, England, and Canada, which were opulently decorated with Cézannes, Renoirs, and Monets. When traveling domestically and internationally, Engelhard was often accompanied by a retinue of employees and friends and had a private plane at his disposal.

In the twenty years during which he controlled numerous corporations worldwide, Engelhard's wealth grew to more than $250 million. He was an international entrepreneur, a philanthropist, a major financial contributor to the Democratic party, and a socialite and jetsetter whose own parties were the talk of the town, domestically and internationally. He lived one of the most illustrious life-styles of any American. Engelhard died at Pamplemousse, his Florida estate in Boca Grande.

[Articles about Engelhard include "The Engelhard Touch," *Forbes*, Aug. 1, 1965; "Time Begins to Run Out," *Forbes*, Sept. 1, 1967; "Merger as an Inflation Hedge," *Forbes*, June 15, 1969; "Our Man—Still in Africa," *Africa Today*, Sept.–Oct. 1970; and John A. Byrne, "Fathers and Sons," *Forbes*, Jan. 28, 1985. See also Newark (New Jersey) Public Library, biographical files. Obituaries are in the *New York Times*, the *Newark Evening News*, and the *Star-Ledger*, all Mar. 3, 1971.]

JOSEPH C. SANTORA

ERPF, ARMAND GROVER (Dec. 8, 1897–Feb. 2, 1971), investment banker, was born in New York City, the son of Bartholomew Erpf and Cornelia von Greiner. After graduating from Columbia University with a B.S. in 1917, he worked as assistant secretary and then assistant manager of the Suffren Company of New York and Brazil, importers of manganese ore. In 1919, he became an officer and part owner of C. E. Erpf and Company, his older brother Carl's crude-rubber brokerage. In 1923 he left the country to survey the textile industry in Saxony, Germany. Between 1924 and 1933, he was statistician, and later officer, director, and part owner, of Cornell, Linder, and Company of New York, a management engineering firm. He was married in 1928, but his marriage ended in divorce several years later.

In 1933, Erpf joined Carl M. Loeb, Rhoades, and Company (later Loeb, Rhoades, and Company). During his first three years at Loeb, Rhoades, he served as director of the statistical, research, and investment advisory departments. The company named him a general partner in 1936.

Erpf entered the United States Army as a lieutenant colonel in 1942. Promoted to colonel in 1944, he served in Washington with the General Staff Corps until 1945, then in the Western Pacific with army headquarters, and finally with the commanding general USAF, China Theater. He was awarded the Legion of Merit.

Erpf pioneered in many areas of the investment banking business. He possessed keen analytical abilities and, at the same time, was one of Wall Street's most idiosyncratic operatives. Erpf stated that in the mid-1950's he had been an investor in the establishment of Metromedia Inc., a television and outdoor advertising chain that included WNEW in New York City and WTTG in Washington, D.C., among its affiliates. As chairman of the executive committee of Crowell Collier, he promoted its acquisition of Macmillan Publishing Company in 1957. According to the *New York Times*, the company grew from sales of $27 million to sales of $225 million within a decade. Crowell Collier than acquired Brentano bookstores in 1962, and soon after that the Berlitz Schools of Languages and Berlitz Publications. In an interview with *Time*, Erpf acknowledged that he specifically liked the Brentano purchase because it could transform "publishing into a modern corporate enterprise to bring education to the masses." He predicted that if this happened, "we'll have a renaissance here that will make the Italian Renaissance look like a pond next to the ocean."

On Apr. 7, 1965, Erpf was married in Italy to Susan Stuart Mortimore, a New York artist, but Erpf did not publicly announce the marriage for three years. The couple had two children.

Erpf masterminded the financing of a new publication, *New York* magazine, an outgrowth of the Sunday magazine supplement of the *New York Herald Tribune* and its successor, the *World Journal Tribune*, which ceased publication in 1967. The first editor of *New York*, Clay Felker, credited Erpf with enabling the staff to maintain editorial control by having secured a broad array of financial backers rather than just one or several. Erpf also sat on the boards of numerous corporations and served as chairman of Aneid Equities.

Erpf was a strong supporter of education and the arts. He served as chairman of the council of Columbia University's Graduate School of Business, and in 1967, Loeb, Rhoades endowed the Armand G. Erpf chair in corporations at Columbia's business school at a testimonial seventieth birthday. He served on the boards of a number of cultural institutions, including the Chamber Music Society of Lincoln Center, the Whitney Museum of American Art, and the New York Cultural Center. Erpf was a serious art collector, with his eclectic tastes ranging from Chinese snuff bottles to avant-garde painting. According to *Fortune* magazine, he was a part owner of the Lone Ranger. Fascinated by mazes, he hired an English sculptor and known authority on mazes, Michael Ayrton, to build a brick maze on his five-hundred-acre estate in the Catskill Mountains. Erpf was quoted in *Time* magazine, proclaiming the 1,680-foot labyrinth with walls six to eight feet high as being symbolic of "a world so caught up with scientific rationalism, it doesn't know where it's going." Because its center was not reachable by traveling in a straight line but could only be ap-

proached by moving away from it, to Erpf the maze was "a spiritual truth."

Erpf was considered remote in his business affairs. He was often called on to predict the coming year's fiscal prospects, particularly as a strong proponent of capitalism. He cautioned his analysts not to get overly specialized. When one of his peers labeled him a "speculator" rather than an "analyst," Erpf responded to *Fortune*'s Charles E. Silberman that he considered speculation a "higher art" than analysis. The art was in recognizing the "less visible factors." *Time* considered him "elfinlike," with "an uncanny nose for investment opportunities." He believed in "large corporations" because only they could "bring solidity and stability into the market place of chaos." In another interview Erpf stressed that he found modern American capitalism most "exciting," because it was "moving into other areas than the mere production of commodities." He contended that it was in these areas that "more and more the human being is not a commodity, but must become an independent vital entity."

Erpf died of a heart attack at his office in New York City. Loeb, Rhoades was acquired in 1979 by Shearson Hayden Stone (later Shearson Lehman).

[See Charles E. Silberman, "Wall Street's Influential Analysts," *Fortune*, Jan. 1957; "The Renaissance Banker," *Time*, Apr. 13, 1962; Henry Raymont, "Chair at Columbia Established for Armand G. Erpf," *New York Times*, Dec. 15, 1967; and "Knossos in the Catskills," *Time*, Aug. 15, 1969. An obituary appears in the *New York Times*, Feb. 3, 1971.]

MARGARET LATIMER

EVANS, HERBERT McLEAN (Sept. 23, 1882–Mar. 6, 1971), anatomist and endocrinologist, was born in Modesto, Calif., the son of Clayburn Wayne Evans, a prominent physician and surgeon in Modesto and surgeon for the Pacific Railway, and Bessie McLean, whose father and brother both were medical doctors. Evans attended the University of California at Berkeley, where he studied with the noted paleontologist John C. Merriam and received a B.S. degree in 1904. After one year of graduate work at Berkeley, Evans married (against the advice of both sets of parents) his college sweetheart, Anabel Tulloch, on Sept. 15, 1905, and entered the Johns Hopkins University School of

Medicine in Baltimore. They had one child.

At Johns Hopkins, where he received his M.D. in 1908, Evans studied with one of the most influential anatomists in the country, Franklin P. Mall. Evans seemed to have little interest in clinical courses, preferring to work in the laboratory. Contrary to his father's hopes that he would join his practice in Modesto, Evans found research more interesting, and during the summers he traveled to Germany, where he began experiments on intravitam staining of animal tissues by acid azo dyes. One such dye is now called Evans blue.

In 1915, when Evans was only thirty-three years old, President Benjamin Ide Wheeler of the University of California offered him the chair of anatomy at Berkeley. Evans brought with him from Johns Hopkins two talented researchers, Katherine Scott (later Bishop) and George W. Corner. He seemed to feel that it was his mission to teach the very best students. His scholarship and idealism allowed him to challenge the boundaries of medical research, and he became a leading authority on the pituitary gland. Evans also became an indefatigable researcher on many aspects of reproductive physiology and was a prolific author, often publishing with his colleagues. In 1922, with Joseph A. Long of the Zoology Department at Berkeley, Evans published the classic monograph *The Oestrous Cycle in the Rat and Its Associated Phenomena*.

In 1923, Evans identified a dietary factor essential for reproduction by demonstrating that its lack caused a breakdown of the placenta and the reabsorption of fetuses in rats. This research, first published in the *Journal of the American Medical Association* (1923), is considered to be the first documentation of the alcohol- and ether-soluble dietary factor that would later come to be called Vitamin E. This article was republished, in an abbreviated form, in *Nutrition Reviews* (April 1990) as a Nutrition Classic.

In 1930, the Department of Anatomy and Evans's research laboratories were moved to the new Life Sciences Building on the Berkeley campus. In the same year, the University of California created the Institute of Experimental Biology, appointed Evans director, and named him Herzstein Professor of Biology. At this time Evans began his first collection of significant books in the history of science.

In 1932, Evans was forced to sell his collection of books during his divorce from Anabel. Over the years he collected and sold about twenty thousand books, many of them rare first editions that eventually became part of several university collections in the history of science.

After his divorce was final, Evans married Marjorie E. Sadler, a researcher in his laboratory, on June 28, 1932; they had one child. Also in 1932, Evans founded the History of Science Dinner Club on the Berkeley campus.

The Evanses were divorced in 1945, and on June 14 of that year he married Dorothy F. Atkinson, acting director of the English Department at Mills College in Oakland, Calif., who shared his interest in the history of science and his zeal for book collecting.

Between 1904 and 1959, Evans generated over five hundred publications. He and his associates Choh Hao Li and Miriam E. Simpson were the first to purify the sixth hormone of the anterior lobe of the pituitary, ACTH (adrenocorticotropic hormone), which was later used to treat rheumatoid arthritis and rheumatic fever. In 1959, a book of essays entitled *Men and Moments in the History of Science* was published in honor of Evans, who assembled the papers for this publication with assistance from a Ford Foundation grant.

In November 1967, Evans was interviewed by Alan S. Parkes of Christ's College, Cambridge, who called Evans "an almost legendary figure on the Berkeley campus." This interview, along with a curriculum vitae and a list of selected publications from 1907 to 1959, is in *Journal of Reproduction and Fertility* (1969).

In 1927, Evans was elected a member of the National Academy of Sciences and a foreign member of the Royal Society of London. He was the editor of *American Anatomical Memoirs* from 1918 to 1939, and of *Journal of Nutrition* from 1928 to 1930. He suffered a severe stroke in 1970 and died the following year in Berkeley, Calif.

[More than fifty cartons of Evans's papers and diaries, mostly uncataloged, are stored at the Bancroft Library of the University of California at Berkeley. His research is published in several volumes of *Memoirs of the University of California*. A memoir by George W. Corner, including a bibliography from 1904 to 1959, is in *Biographical Memoirs. National Academy of Sciences* 45 (1974). On his book collecting, see Jacob I. Zeitlin, "Herbert M. Evans, Pioneer Collector of Books in the History of Science," *ISIS*,

Winter 1971. An obituary is in the *New York Times*, Mar. 8, 1971.]

NANCY J. HERRINGTON

EVANS, WALKER (Nov. 3, 1903–Apr. 10, 1975), photographer, was born in St. Louis, Mo., the son of Walker Evans II and Jessie Crane. When he was two years old, the family moved to the exclusive suburb of Kenilworth, near Chicago, where his father worked very successfully as an advertising copywriter. In this formative period Evans grew up in comfortable circumstances. When he was twelve, the family moved again to Toledo, Ohio, where his father had been offered a more lucrative position in advertising.

Evans remembered his Kenilworth years as sheltered and privileged (his family kept a servant) and Toledo, with its industrial landscape and working-class population, as a rude shock. He attended high school for a year, then spent an unhappy year at the Loomis School in Windsor, Conn. After a summer working in an automobile factory at a job his father arranged, he moved to New York, where his sister was in school and his mother had taken an apartment. He next enrolled in Phillips Academy in Andover, Mass., where he studied literature. In 1922 he entered Williams College in Williamstown, Mass. Bored with the conventional curriculum, he left after one year, returning to his mother in New York, where he landed a night job in the map room of the New York Public Library.

In 1926, Evans accompanied his mother and sister to Europe and stayed on in Paris, where he attended classes briefly at the Sorbonne, read Baudelaire and Flaubert, and although feeling lonely and unhappy, absorbed the literary ferment of the time. Measuring his literary abilities against such figures as James Joyce, Evans began to despair of a writing career. While in Paris, he used a vest-pocket camera his father had given him, taking snapshots of friends and the city. After two years overseas he returned to New York and became part of the bohemian life of Greenwich Village and Brooklyn Heights.

In these years, while he worked at night at a Wall Street brokerage, he began to photograph seriously. With a small roll-film camera he undertook to explore the city, its people, architecture, signage, bridges, and street life. He experimented with abstract compositions, formalist designs, and high-vantage perspectives.

Encouraged by the poet Hart Crane, he produced a striking series of pictures of Brooklyn Bridge, three of which appeared in the first edition of Crane's poem *The Bridge* (1930). This was the first of several collaborations with writers. Evans developed significant friendships with Crane, the painter Ben Shahn, the photographer Ralph Steiner, and writers Lincoln Kirstein and James Agee.

Evans made his mark on the art of photography as a practitioner of what he called "documentary style." His reading of modern writers, including Walt Whitman and James Joyce, helped him cultivate a distinctive kind of photography: objective, detached, deceptively transparent, and understated. In an interview in 1971, Evans explained: "Flaubert's method I think I incorporated almost unconsciously, but anyway I used it in two ways: his realism and naturalism both, and his objectivity of treatment; the non-appearance of author, the non-subjectivity. That is literally applicable to the way I want to use the camera and do." Evans acknowledged several significant visual influences. One was a photograph by Paul Strand entitled "Blind Woman" (1915) that he saw in an old issue of Alfred Stieglitz's journal *Camera Work* at the New York Public Library. The image, he remembered, "charged me up." The wit, precision, and design of Ralph Steiner's photographs in the 1920's, especially of city signs, also inspired Evans toward urban subjects. Through his friend Berenice Abbott, he became familiar with the work of the French photographer Eugène Atget, whom he honored in an article, "Reappearance of Photography," which was published in Kirstein's magazine, *Hound and Horn* (1931). He praised Atget for a "lyrical understanding of the street," his fusion of "trained observation" and a personal poetry. Evans set about to produce a lyrical record of his own experience of New York and other American cities.

Several of Evans's photographs appeared in *Creative Art* and *Architectural Record* as well as *Hound and Horn*. He began to acquire a reputation as an original stylist in photography. In 1931 he collaborated with Kirstein and the poet John Brooks Wheelwright in documenting New England Victorian houses. In 1932, the Julien Levy Gallery in New York mounted a two-man exhibition of Evans's and George Platt Lynes's photographs. By this time Evans had begun to earn a living through his art; he published in small art periodicals, traveled on assignment, and undertook commercial projects. Disdaining the label of "art" photographer and the influence of Alfred Stieglitz, he developed a cool, elegant manner, a visual wit, and an eye for ironic juxtapositions. He was drawn especially to signs of craft and vernacular style in the social landscape.

Evans hit his stride during an assignment in Cuba in 1933. Hired to provide pictures for the book *The Crime of Cuba* (1933), by the journalist Carleton Beals, Evans was powerfully attracted to the vibrant life of the streets and plazas of Havana, with their promenaders, prostitutes, dockworkers, newsstands, and shop fronts. He further honed his eye for straightforward, uncluttered, descriptive photographs while recording a collection of African art for the Museum of Modern Art in 1934. The next year his photographs were included in a group show at the Julien Levy Gallery.

In 1935, Evans joined the staff of the historical section of the Farm Security Administration (FSA), headed by New Deal economist Roy Stryker. Evans worked in the northeastern and southern states and produced some of the most famous FSA pictures of Depression-era America. Working mainly with an 8-by-10-inch Deardorff camera, he avoided anecdotal or journalistic pictures. Evans emerged as the most celebrated FSA photographer, the most prominent exponent of the documentary style in the 1930's. His pictures of unpainted sharecroppers' shacks, row houses in New England factory towns, the interiors of West Virginia coal miners' dwellings, antebellum houses in the South, and portraits of down-and-out Americans, black and white, north and south, impressed themselves on the public as the very look of the Depression era. Kirstein wrote about Evans: "When you see certain sights, certain relics of American civilization past and present, in the countryside or on a city street, you feel they call for his camera, since he has already uniquely recorded their cognates or parallels."

In the summer of 1936 Evans took a leave from the FSA to join his friend James Agee on a *Fortune* magazine assignment on tenant farming in the South. They focused on three sharecropper families in Hale County, Ala., living among them for about a month. Their collaboration of picture and text, rejected for publication by *Fortune*, attracted little attention when it appeared in 1941 as *Let Us Now Praise*

Famous Men; reissued with additional pictures in 1962, the book has since been acclaimed as a classic work of the 1930's. In 1938 the Museum of Modern Art honored Evans with its first one-man show devoted to a photographer. The monograph *American Photographs* that accompanied the exhibition included an eloquent essay by Kirstein.

Evans left the FSA in 1938, the result of conflicts with Stryker. In that year he began a project that was to continue for several years, photographing New York subway riders with a hidden camera. The project revealed another side of Evans's experimentation with the medium and his gift for social observation. A selection of these candid, unconventional portraits was published in book form as *Many Are Called* (1966), with an essay by Agee.

In 1941, Evans married Jane Ninas, who had been his assistant on occasion in the South. They had no children. He held Guggenheim fellowships in 1940 and 1941, and again in 1959. From 1943 to 1945 he was a staff writer at *Time* magazine and then moved to *Fortune* as staff photographer and associate editor. There he remained for twenty years, publishing some forty portfolios and photographic essays, often providing his own accompanying texts. He was divorced from Ninas in 1955, and in 1960 he married Isabelle Boeschenstein von Steiger. They had no children and were divorced in 1972.

Evans retired from *Fortune* in 1965. In 1966 *Message from the Interior* appeared, a handsomely printed and artfully arranged selection from his pictures of interiors. In that year Evans joined the faculty of Yale University School of Art and Architecture as the first professor of graphic arts, where his aristocratic demeanor, ironic gentility, lucid and witty conversation, and wealth of experience attracted many students and admirers. He retired in 1972 and spent a year as artist-in-residence at Dartmouth College in Hanover, N.H. A high moment of Evans's career was a major retrospective in 1971 at the Museum of Modern Art. Here and abroad Evans was celebrated as one of the original artists of his generation in any medium. His example inspired a new generation of photographers of the social landscape. Exhibitions and publications since his death have revealed additional facets of his work, among them, early 1930's experiments in film and later work in color.

Although known best as a master of black-and-white photography, throughout his career Evans worked with color film and in the last few years of his life, while living in Old Lyme, Conn., he devoted himself entirely to polychromatic images. He became intrigued with the SX-70 Polaroid color camera and used it constantly, until a broken collarbone incurred by a fall in 1974 ended his active career. He died in New Haven, Conn.

[Surviving manuscripts, papers, letters, interviews, and memorabilia are held by the Walker Evans Estate; a selection appears in *Walker Evans at Work* (1982), with an essay by Jerry L. Thompson. See also the interviews with Paul Cummings, *Artists in Their Own Words* (1979); and Leslie Katz, *Art in America*, Mar./Apr. 1971. Unpublished transcripts of interviews can be found at the Archives of American Art. Evans's occasional essays on photography include "Photography," in Louis Kronenberger, ed., *Quality* (1969); "The Thing Itself Is Such a Secret and So Unapproachable," *Yale Alumni Magazine*, Feb. 1974; and "Walker Evans on Himself," the *New Republic*, Nov. 13, 1976. For studies of his work see John Szarkowski, *Walker Evans* (1971); and Gilles Mora, *Walker Evans* (1989). See also Alan Trachtenberg, "A Book Nearly Anonymous," *Reading American Photographs* (1989). Obituaries appear in the *New York Times*, Apr. 11, 1975; and the *British Journal of Photography*, Apr. 25, 1975. See also the film, *Walker Evans: His Time, His Presence, His Silence* (1969), directed by Sadat Pakay.]

ALAN TRACHTENBERG

EVOLA, NATALE ("JOE DIAMOND") (Feb. 22, 1907–Aug. 27, 1973), alleged boss of one of New York's five Mafia families, was born the second child of Francesca and Fillipo Evola. His parents, both immigrants from Italy, lived in New York City's Lower East Side tenement district; the boy's father described himself as a laborer on his son's birth certificate. Evola lived with his parents throughout his life, never marrying, and eventually bought a house in Brooklyn where he cared for his mother until his death.

Evola's association with the criminal underworld apparently began early. He was first arrested when he was twenty-three for possession of a gun, but the charge was dropped. In 1931 he appeared as an usher in the lavish wedding of Joseph Bonanno, who at this time was busy organizing localized bootlegging operations into a national crime syndicate which, over the next decades, became increasingly involved in gambling operations, loan sharking, extortion, and murder. A year after Bonanno's wedding, Evola was charged with coercion for using strong-arm tactics to settle a dispute in the New York Garment Truckers Association; the charges were subsequently dismissed. Evola spent the rest of his life consolidating his power within the Bonanno family and the garment district.

In the 1930's and 1940's, most Americans who were not directly affected by organized crime remained unaware of its existence. Then, in 1950, Senator Estes Kefauver of Tennessee chaired a dramatic series of televised congressional hearings. The American public watched as a colorful cast of underworld figures evaded questions and as Harry Anslinger of the Bureau of Narcotics and other officials described what was variously called the Syndicate, the Combination, or the Mafia. These hearings spurred law enforcement agencies, both federal and local, into action, and Evola was among the many caught in their slowly tightening net.

On Nov. 14, 1957, New York State troopers arrested sixty-two persons including Evola at what police claimed was a Mafia conference in Apalachin, N.Y. Just as people were settling in at the hilltop estate of Joseph Barbara, an alleged mobster, someone spotted a roadblock and the meeting broke up in a panic; men reputed to be underworld bosses, many middle-aged and older, in hand-tailored suits, fled through the woods in a desperate attempt to escape. Most were picked up by state police, bedraggled and exhausted, but carrying large amounts of cash—a suspicious total of more than $300,000. The majority refused to answer police questions; those who did, claimed that they had just dropped by to pay their respects to their friend Barbara, who had recently been ill. All were released after questioning.

Evola's troubles were compounded when just six months after the Apalachin incident, a small-time drug pusher, Nelson Cantellops, became a star witness for the federal government. Though some claimed that he had been coached by federal agents, Cantellops convinced a federal jury that he had witnessed Evola, Vito Genovese, and others plan to take over narcotics distribution in the East Bronx. Evola's lawyer, Maurice Edelbaum, defended his client as an innocent man, a devoted son, who had never in his fifty-two years been convicted of a crime; Edelbaum also gave proof that

Evola had been involved in legitimate businesses for the last sixteen years. Nevertheless, on Apr. 17, 1959, Evola was convicted of conspiring to violate federal narcotics laws, sentenced to ten years in prison and a fine of $20,000, and freed on $50,000 bail pending appeal. Then one month later, on May 21, 1959, Evola found himself posting an additional $2,500 bail after being indicted along with twenty-seven other men on charges of conspiring to obstruct justice by refusing to reveal the true purpose of the Apalachin conference. On December 18, a federal jury found each of the defendants guilty. Attorney General William P. Rogers hailed the convictions as a "landmark in the Government's fight against organized crime." In January, Judge Irving R. Kaufman sentenced Evola, whom he characterized as "a most important member of the underworld," to five years in prison and a $10,000 fine. On Nov. 28, 1960, the United States Court of Appeals overturned the lower court's verdict on the grounds that the government admittedly did not know the purpose of the meeting and thus could not prove that the defendants were lying about it; Chief Judge J. Edward Lumbard commented that the prosecution had never produced "a shred of legal evidence that the Apalachin gathering was illegal or even improper in either purpose or fact." Though freed of one conspiracy charge, Evola was not so lucky in appealing the narcotics case and his conviction was sustained. His time in prison was a lesson to some in the Mafia that dealing in narcotics should be avoided.

In the mid-1960's, the aging Joseph Bonanno failed in an attempt to have his rivals killed and was forced out of power by the Mafia National Commission, the loosely organized group of local bosses who together guided national policy. A violent battle known as the "Banana War" broke out between factions within the Bonanno organization. Around 1970, the Mafia National Commission appointed Evola as head of the Bonanno family after several other men had turned down the job or failed as effective leaders. From the Garment District offices of the Amity Trucking Company, owned by his brother Joseph, Evola allegedly rebuilt the Bonanno family's rackets and healed factional splits by pleasing both the elder Bonanno, now living as a recluse in Tucson, Ariz., and Carlo Gambino, Bonanno's traditional enemy who had become powerful in New York City. In 1970, the Joint

Legislative Committee on Crime summoned Evola, but he refused to answer any questions, including whether or not he had obtained control of legitimate businesses by loaning them money at rates they were unable to pay. At the time, Evola allegedly had an interest in at least eight garment and trucking companies. In 1972, after Mayor John Lindsay demanded that the mob be "run out of town," New York City police cracked down on truck parking in the garment district, accusing Evola, Gambino, and others of controlling business by monopolizing curb space. When Evola died of cancer at his Brooklyn home, the Mafia was being forced into a period of transition, squeezed from above by vigorous law enforcement and from below by the growing wealth of Latino and black gangs who dominated the narcotics trade. Evola's career spanned the development of organized crime from the bootlegging days of Prohibition, through the Mafia's rise to power in the middle decades of the century, until he successfully consolidated power during a period when the New York Mafia faced new challenges.

[The records of Evola's trials in federal courts, including full transcripts, are kept in the Federal Records Center in New York and can be accessed through the National Archives–Northeast Region in New York City. Evola is mentioned in Gay Talese, *Honor Thy Father* (1971); and Richard Hammer, *Playboy's Illustrated History of Organized Crime* (1975). Stephen Fox, *Blood and Power* (1989), provides useful background information on the Bonanno family. An obituary appears in the *New York Times*, Aug. 31, 1973.]

CORINNE T. FIELD

EWING, WILLIAM MAURICE (May 12, 1906–May 4, 1974), geophysicist, was born in Lockney, Tex., the fourth of ten children of Floyd Ford Ewing and Hope Hamilton. The eldest three children died very young, in New Mexico, before the family moved to the small town of Lockney. There Ewing's father was a farmer and a dealer in hardware and farm equipment. Both parents were intent upon their children acquiring a good education.

Ewing attended Rice Institute (now University) in Houston, Tex., on a scholarship after his first year. There he received a B.A. in physics in 1926, an M.A. in 1927, and a Ph.D. in 1931. In 1928 Ewing married fellow student Avarilla Hildenbrand; they had one son. During college summers Ewing worked for oil-prospecting companies, which provided field experience in seismic techniques in shallow lakes in Louisiana.

Ewing became instructor in physics at the University of Pittsburgh in 1929, and a year later he took a similar position at Lehigh University, where he was named associate professor in 1940. There he initiated the use at sea of explosives, called seismic refraction, to determine subsurface structure, a technique well established by then in exploration for oil on land. In 1935 he completed the first seismic-refraction lines across the continental shelf of the eastern United States and determined the sediment thickness. The next year he measured gravity at the Puerto Rico Trench. About 1939, with John Lamar Worzel and Allyn C. Vine, Ewing designed a prototype underwater camera; his photos were the first to show ripple marks on the ocean floor in deep water, suggesting previously unsuspected motion at such depths. Gradually, using ships of various agencies, Ewing extended his studies beyond the continental shelf to the deep ocean, modifying equipment and techniques.

On leave from Lehigh in 1940, Ewing, Vine, and Worzel went to Woods Hole Oceanographic Institution in Massachusetts to carry out basic oceanic studies for the U.S. Navy. An early report by Ewing, Worzel, and Columbus Iselin, "Sound Transmission in Sea Water" (1940), became a standard navy reference on the complex factors that affect underwater sound. Ewing, Worzel, and Vine also improved the bathythermograph, an oceanographic research device invented by Athelstan Spilhaus, so that it could instantly record ocean temperatures at depth from moving ships. Ewing discovered the low-velocity sound channel in the ocean called SOFAR, in which sound carries for unusually great distances.

Ewing was divorced in 1941, and in 1944 he married Margaret Kidder. They had four children. Apparently at the instigation of Walter H. Bucher, Ewing established a program in geophysics at Columbia University in 1946. He was named Higgins Professor of Geology at Columbia in 1947. When the 125-acre estate of Thomas Lamont was given to the university in 1948, Ewing's group, which required a quiet location for instruments, moved to that site, a few miles from the city campus, and the facility was named Lamont Geological Observatory. A major donation from the Doherty Foundation

in 1969 brought about a change in name to Lamont-Doherty Geological Observatory.

Ewing generated all programs at the observatory and participated in most of the publications by its staff from 1948 until 1972. Colleagues and students found him inexhaustible, on land or at sea, and an inspiring teacher through ideas and by example. He was a good improvisor of techniques to accomplish the task and thoroughly enjoyed research aboard ship.

In 1949 Ewing first used two research vessels for seismic-refraction studies, in order to gain the longer distances necessary for measurements of the thickness of the earth's crust through the ocean and its floor. At the same time, as another approach to determining subsurface structure, with Frank Press he began a network of seismographs to record the long, slow oscillations from earthquakes. These programs confirmed the universal difference in crustal thickness between the ocean floor and the continents.

Oceanography advanced greatly during the 1950's, especially with support from the Office of Naval Research. For Lamont, Ewing acquired his first ship in 1953, which made possible worldwide expeditions with multiple programs. He obtained a second research ship in 1962. Ewing and his colleagues improved the depth recorder for underway use, adapted the airborne magnetometer for its first use towed behind a ship, developed a technique for releasing deep-sea equipment free-fall for return by gasoline-filled balloons, and refined a method of measuring gravity from surface ships. As director of Lamont, Ewing required that his ships take continuous records of underway geophysical data and collect a great many deep-sea cores as well. He conducted seismic profiles to define the layers beneath the seafloor down to the Mohorovičić Discontinuity, which separates the crust of the earth from the mantle. He determined from seismic techniques that some features beneath the seafloor in the Gulf of Mexico are salt domes and thus petroleum traps. With Bruce C. Heezen he identified the effects of turbidity currents in deep water, and he participated in the definition of the Mid-Atlantic Ridge as part of a worldwide feature. Researchers and technicians at Lamont constantly developed and improved equipment for deep-sea use. The Lamont geophysical records contributed significantly to the understanding of seafloor spreading as proposed in the mid-

1960's that eventually led to understanding the movement of continents. Ewing was not an early believer in the revolutionary theory, but came to accept it. Ewing participated in the establishment in midcentury of a worldwide deep-ocean drilling program to define the earth's history. Ewing and Worzel led the first voyage on the drilling ship in 1968.

Ewing and his second wife were divorced in 1965, and he married Harriet Bassett that same year. After retiring as a professor at Columbia and as director of Lamont, in 1972 Ewing became a professor at the Marine Biomedical Institute of the University of Texas at Galveston. There he was provided with research facilities and a small ship, from which he began studying the subsurface structure of the Gulf of Mexico. He died in 1974 in Galveston. Among his many honors and awards were eleven honorary doctorates; election to the National Academy of Sciences (1948); the Arthur L. Day Medal of the Geological Society of America (1949); the Agassiz Medal (1955) and the John J. Carty Medal (1963) of the National Academy of Sciences; the William Bowie Medal (1957) and Walter H. Bucher Medal (1974) of the American Geophysical Union; the first Vetlesen Prize of Columbia University (1960); the Cullum Geographical Award of the American Geographical Society (1961); the Gold Medal of the (London) Royal Astronomical Society (1964); the Sidney Powers Memorial Medal of the American Association of Petroleum Geologists (1968); the Wollaston Medal of the Geological Society of London (1969); and the National Medal of Science (1973).

[Ewing's papers are at the University of Texas at Austin, in the History of Science Collections of the Humanities Research Center. Especially significant publications include two items with J. Lamar Worzel, "Explosion Sounds in Shallow Water" and "Long-Range Sound Transmission," in *Propagation of Sound in the Ocean* (1948); *Elastic Waves in Layered Media*, with Wenceslas S. Jardetzky, and Frank Press (1957); and "The Floors of the Oceans, vol. 1, The North Atlantic," with B. C. Heezen and M. Tharp, in *Special Papers of the Geological Society of America*, no. 65 (1959). Biographies include William Wertenbaker, "Profiles," *New Yorker*, Nov. 4, 11, 18, 1974; William Wertenbaker, *The Floor of the Sea: Maurice Ewing and the Search to Understand the Earth* (1974); J. Lamar Worzel, "Maurice Ewing 1906–1974," Geological Society of America Memorial (1975); Edward Bullard, "William Maurice Ewing 1906–1974," *Biographical Memoirs of Fellows of the Royal Society*, vol. 21 (Nov. 1975); and (very similar) Edward C. Bullard, "William Maurice Ewing," *Biographical Memoirs. National Academy of Sciences* 51 (1980).]

ELIZABETH NOBLE SHOR

F

FAIRCHILD, SHERMAN MILLS (Apr. 7, 1896–Mar. 28, 1971), inventor and entrepreneur, was born in Oneonta, N.Y., the only child of Josephine Mills Sherman and George Winthrop Fairchild. His father served in Congress from 1906 until 1919 and was involved in several business enterprises, including an important antecedent of International Business Machines (IBM), of which he was chairman from 1913 to 1923. George Fairchild died in December of 1924, little more than a year after his wife, leaving his son with a fortune of approximately $2 million and a seat on IBM's board of directors.

By then Sherman Fairchild had already established a reputation as an inventor. While a freshman at Harvard during the fall of 1915, he devised ways to take photographs in dim light and other difficult conditions. A tuberculosis epidemic at Harvard prompted a transfer to the University of Arizona, where Fairchild turned his interests toward aerial photography, which was being used extensively in World War I. He designed an electrical linkage that made it possible to take aerial photos using a camera with a between-the-lens shutter. In 1920 he returned to New York and set up the Fairchild Aerial Camera Corporation, with the help of $25,000 from his father and a contract for twenty cameras worth $114,000 from the Signal Corps. Though he later studied at Columbia University and received private tutoring from engineering professors at New York University, Fairchild never obtained a college degree.

In an effort to promote its products, Fairchild Camera conducted aerial surveys of several cities and states. Though these initially failed to earn a profit, they garnered praise for their unprecedented accuracy and established Fairchild as the industry standard-bearer. In an effort to obtain aircraft more suitable for photography, Fairchild in 1924 formed Fairchild Aviation Corporation. Its first product, the FC-1, was a high-winged monoplane that featured several technical innovations, including an enclosed cockpit. Sales of a revised model, made popular when Charles Lindbergh flew one around the country, helped boost Fairchild's net worth to $6 million by 1929. He then bought airplane production facilities and also purchased interests in two airlines that soon became part of Pan American Airways, which he served as a director until 1956. In March 1929, Fairchild joined William A. Harriman, Lehman Brothers, and other Wall Street investors as a principal shareholder in the Aviation Corporation (AVCO), a giant holding company, but two years later returned to his earlier aviation interests, which in 1936 were renamed Fairchild Engine and Aviation Corporation.

During his rise to prominence in aviation, Fairchild cultivated a wide range of personal interests and a flamboyant life-style. An avid entertainer and socialite who enjoyed popular music, especially jazz, he frequently invited performers to his home. He cooked for them, using techniques he had studied at Cordon Bleu, and played piano. His French château at Huntington, Long Island, built during the early 1930's, included an enclosed tennis court that cost $25,000 but boasted energy-saving features devised and later marketed by Fairchild. Tennis stars such as Alice Marble and Bill Tilden joined Fairchild for weekends at the estate, as did numerous young women, who helped sustain Fairchild's lifelong reputation as one of New York's most eligible bachelors.

During the late 1930's, with his aviation interests losing between $50,000 and $100,000 annually, Fairchild immersed himself in the design and construction of a Manhattan town house on East Sixty-fifth Street. Home for Fairchild and his maiden aunt May, it featured soaring glass walls, a central garden courtyard, and floating teak ramps instead of stairs. No walls met at right angles. Like his airplanes, the house was chock-full of gadgets, including remote-controlled window blinds and a climate-control system that cost $37,000. It contained a photographic darkroom and a basement workshop, and later Fairchild added a sound recording studio. Initially the inventor commuted to offices at Rockefeller Center, but gradually he came to use the house as an office as well. The distinctions between his personal interests and his business endeavors, which had never been great, grew ever narrower.

Wartime demand for aircraft and the phenomenal appreciation of his IBM stock following World War II helped make Fairchild easily one of the hundred richest Americans, with a net worth of at least $80 million in 1960. This mounting fortune, combined with the facilities of Fairchild Camera and Instrument Corporation and the Fairchild Recording Equipment Company (founded in 1948), gave Fairchild the means to experiment and develop devices related to his numerous hobbies, without much concern about whether they earned a profit. He produced a string of innovations, including the Scan-A-Graver for reproducing photographs in newspapers, a photographic typesetter, a camera capable of taking 16,000 exposures per second, safety fuses for missiles, a transistorized hearing aid for his aunt, and recording devices so numerous and effective that he was made president of the Audio Engineering Society. His tape recorder was widely considered the best available, though its $3,500 price tag kept it out of the hands of all but the most avid, and wealthy, audiophiles.

By his own admission, Fairchild was a poor manager. He preferred to place his companies in the hands of strong, autonomous managers vested with generous stock options while he himself functioned as a technical adviser. A voracious reader who subscribed to more than two hundred technical journals and periodicals, he peppered his employees with clippings and monitored their activities. Fairchild also kept an eye out for promising new enterprises, and in 1950 opened an investment office in New York

City. This venture achieved its most stunning success in 1957, when a group of engineers employed by the Shockley Semi-Conductor Company approached Fairchild in search of financing for their work on silicon transistors manufactured using the planar technique. Fairchild offered them stock in Fairchild Camera and set them up in a subsidiary, Fairchild Semi-Conductor, whose growth drove up the stock's value by eighteen times between 1958 and July 1960.

In 1960, Fairchild graced the covers of both *Time* and *Fortune*. Each profiled him, an eighteenth-century gentleman scientist blessed with a twentieth-century fortune, as the archetype of a new brand of entrepreneur who dealt in fast-growing, so-called glamour stocks. Fairchild died in New York City.

[Profiles of Fairchild include "Multifarious Sherman Fairchild," *Fortune*, May 1960, and "The Yankee Tinkerers," *Time*, July 25, 1960. On his activities in aviation, see John B. Rae, *Climb to Greatness* (1968). On Fairchild Semiconductor, see Dirk Hanson, *The New Alchemists* (1982). Obituaries are in the *New York Times*, Mar. 29, 1971; *Time*, Apr. 12, 1971; and *Newsweek*, Apr. 12, 1971.]

STEVEN W. USSELMAN

FARNSWORTH, PHILO TAYLOR (Aug. 19, 1906–Mar. 11, 1971), scientist and inventor, was born near Beaver, Utah, the son of Lewis Edwin Farnsworth, a farmer, and Serena Amanda Bastian, a homemaker. He was raised in a Mormon family of limited economic means. The family moved frequently throughout Utah and Idaho, and Farnsworth spent his youth working on the family farm and occasionally attending school. In 1922 the Farnsworths moved to Provo, Utah.

Farnsworth's career was devoted to the study of physics, particularly electronics. At an early age he took an interest in fixing farm machinery and understanding how it operated. In 1919, when the family moved to Rigby, Idaho, the new farmhouse contained back issues of science and technical journals, which Farnsworth avidly studied. He applied his knowledge to the farm's electric power system, and at the age of thirteen won a national electronics contest. He admired Thomas Edison, Henry Ford, and other inventors. He also learned of recent developments in electricity, particularly efforts to transmit visual images. By that time engineers had developed the means to transmit pictures mechanically, primarily through the use of spinning discs. Farnsworth became interested in developing an electrical means of transmitting pictures by dividing an image into parts whose light values could be restored to reproduce the image. In 1922, at the age of fifteen, he explained his ideas to Justin Tolman, his science teacher at Rigby High School. Subsequently, the desire to build an electric television system became Farnsworth's preoccupation.

He pursued that interest in an anachronistic fashion. Although the independent inventor still played a role in American technology, invention was becoming standardized through academic training and employment in industrial research laboratories. Farnsworth, because of economic hardship, had little chance to take advantage of such opportunities. In 1922, after completing his high school education, he earned an electrician's license. The following year he enrolled in courses at Brigham Young University, but for financial reasons soon had to withdraw. He married Elma Gardner, whom he had met at Brigham Young, on May 27, 1926; they had four children.

Working for the community chest in Salt Lake City, Farnsworth met two professional fund-raisers, George Everson and Leslie Gorrell. Impressed by Farnsworth's efforts, Everson and Gorrell learned of his ideas about television and decided to back his venture. In 1926, after creating a corporation, Everson, Farnsworth, and Gorrell, they moved to California to acquire financial backing for Farnsworth's work.

After obtaining financial support, Farnsworth established a laboratory in San Francisco in 1926. Within a year he succeeded in developing an image dissector or camera tube. It was the first operating electric camera tube, though not the first of its kind. In 1923 Vladimir Zworykin, a Russian emigré working for Westinghouse, had designed an electric television transmitter and in 1924 or 1925 demonstrated it for Westinghouse executives. Zworykin's system operated on different principles from that of Farnsworth's; in addition, Zworykin's demonstration did not consistently produce clear images, and Westinghouse executives chose not to pursue that line of research. Farnsworth's image dissector worked, however, and in 1927 he applied for and subsequently received patents for his image dissector and a cathode tube receiver.

During the next three years Farnsworth improved upon his early effort. The image dissector had low sensitivity to light and Farnsworth subsequently developed and patented several improvements to the camera tube. He likewise built an electric scanning generator, a device that gave him the first all-electric television system. The inventor and his backers also sought to promote his work. In 1928 Farnsworth held press conferences and in his laboratory produced television images of movie stars and prominent scientists. Through those efforts and published descriptions of his system, Farnsworth and his work received considerable attention. In 1929 Farnsworth and his associates formed a new company, Television Inc.

While promoting his achievements, Farnsworth sought to maintain his independence. General Electric and Radio Corporation of America offered to hire Farnsworth and purchase his inventions. He rejected both overtures, but by the early 1930's his corporation was in difficult financial straits and backers questioned his opposition to selling. In 1931 he signed a contract with Philco Corporation for financial support of his corporation and continued control of his patents in exchange for assisting Philco in developing television. Farnsworth moved to Philadelphia, and Philco was soon competing with RCA in experimental broadcasting. In 1934 Farnsworth quit Philco and with the help of his company, Television Inc., now sought to display the new medium to the public. In 1934 he presented the first public demonstrations of his system at Philadelphia's Franklin Institute, and the next year opened his own station, W3XPF, in Philadelphia. Two European firms began to use Farnsworth's system for broadcasting, and in 1937 a patent-sharing agreement with American Telephone and Telegraph considerably enhanced his status. In 1938 he established Farnsworth Radio and Television, and by 1939, equipped with a manufacturing plant in Fort Wayne, Ind., he was ready to make television a commercial reality.

Despite Farnsworth's success, the viability of his enterprise and of commercial television depended on developing agreements with RCA. David Sarnoff, the president of RCA, had sponsored research and experimentation on television throughout the 1930's. Although interested in the commercial development of television, Sarnoff was faced with the fact that Farnsworth still controlled crucial patents. Zworykin's iconoscope provided RCA with an improved television camera, but Farnsworth's camera tube, now enhanced by the use of low voltage electron beams, still possessed certain advantages. For several years Sarnoff convinced the Federal Communications Commission to delay the implementation of commercial television, but in 1939 RCA agreed to purchase Farnsworth's patents and to pay him continuing royalties for the use of his inventions.

Although the agreement with RCA was a personal and financial triumph for Farnsworth, it removed him from further active research in the field. With control of the Farnsworth patents, RCA became the leader in the development of television. Farnsworth Radio and Television began manufacturing television sets in 1949, but ran into financial problems and eventually became a division of International Telephone and Telegraph. Farnsworth, while receiving numerous awards for his work in television, then turned his attention to research on atomic fusion. Throughout the remainder of his life Farnsworth, an intense, high-strung individual, was beset by medical problems and spent much of his time on a family ranch in Maine. He died in Salt Lake City, Utah.

[Farnsworth's papers are in the Marriott Library at the University of Utah. Materials on his numerous patent applications and interferences are in the United States Patent Office, Department of Commerce, Washington, D.C. His principal published articles include "An Electron Scanning System for Television," *Radio-Craft* 2 (Dec. 1930); "Electron Multiplier Tubes and Their Uses," *Journal of the Franklin Institute* 218 (1934); and, with Harry R. Lubcke, "The Transmission of Television Images," *Radio* 11 (Dec. 1929). The principal biographical studies are George Everson, *The Story of Television: The Life of Philo T. Farnsworth* (1949); Stephen F. Hofer, "Philo Farnsworth: The Quiet Contributor to Television" (Ph.D. diss., Bowling Green University, 1977); and Elma G. Farnsworth, *Distant Vision: Romance and Discovery of an Invisible Frontier* (1990). The best discussion of Farnsworth's work in the context of the technical development of television is Albert Abramson, *The History of Television, 1880–1941* (1987). Obituaries are in the *New York Times*, Mar. 13, 1971; and *Newsweek* and *Time*, both Mar. 22, 1971.]

RONALD RAINGER

FARRAR, JOHN CHIPMAN (Feb. 25, 1896–Nov. 5, 1974), editor and publisher, was born in Burlington, Vt., the son of Edward D. Farrar and Sally Wright. He received his B.A. degree from Yale in 1919, a year later than his class of 1918 because of his absence from the campus while serving in the air corps during World War I. Farrar was a reporter on the *New York World* from 1919 to 1921, when he became editor of a new literary magazine published by George H. Doran, *The Bookman*. His first job in book publishing came in 1925, when Doran made him editor of his book company. On the merger of Doran with Doubleday in 1927, Farrar became a director of the combined firm of Doubleday, Doran, where he and Stanley Rinehart, a fellow editor, acquired *John Brown's Body*, the famous historical poem by Stephen Vincent Benét, who had been Farrar's classmate at Yale.

In 1929, Farrar launched the publishing house of Farrar and Rinehart, with the financial backing of a popular mystery writer and playwright, Mary Roberts Rinehart, and her sons, Stanley and Frederick. In 1933, Stephen Vincent Benét, the firm's principal reader, urged the publication of Hervey Allen's long historical novel, *Anthony Adverse*, which became a national best-seller despite its unprecedentedly high price of three dollars.

During World War II, while chairman of the board of Farrar and Rinehart, Farrar volunteered to take charge of the overseas publications for the Office of War Information. By the war's end he had broken with the Rinehart brothers. At that time Roger W. Straus was leaving the U.S. Navy to start a publishing firm and asked Farrar to join him as a partner in launching Farrar, Straus and Company. In the fall of 1946, the company (which in 1964 became Farrar, Straus and Giroux) issued as its first book, James Branch Cabell's *There Were Two Pirates*. Among the firm's early successes were Carlo Levi's *Christ Stopped at Eboli* (1947) and Shirley Jackson's *The Lottery* (1949). Perhaps Farrar's most notable acquisition was Madeleine L'Engle's *A Wrinkle in Time* (1962), a book previously rejected by twenty-six publishers. It won the coveted Newbery Award and has remained a perennial best-seller.

Farrar, who served as the firm's chairman of the board until 1970, died in New York City.

In addition to his long career as a book editor and publisher, Farrar was noted for his interest in and encouragement of new and promising writers. In 1926, he had helped to create and found, with Robert Frost, the Bread Loaf Writers' Conference at Middlebury College in Vermont. In the 1920's, he also helped to revive the New York center of the international PEN, a writers' advocacy group, becoming its president in 1951. In 1926, he married Margaret Petherbridge; they had three children. She was for decades the crossword-puzzle editor of the *New York Times* and also pioneered in the publication of crossword-puzzle books at Simon and Schuster.

Farrar's reputation endures as a publisher of integrity, as a friend of younger writers, as an enemy of censorship, and as a supporter of high literary standards in an era of increasing commercialism.

[See Charles A. Madison, *Book Publishing in America* (1966); Victor Weybright, "John Chipman Farrar," *The New Century Association Year-Book* (1975); and John W. Tebbel, *A History of Book Publishing in the United States*, vol. 3 (1978) and vol. 4 (1981). An obituary is in the *New York Times*, Nov. 6, 1974.]

ROBERT GIROUX

FEIS, HERBERT (June 7, 1893–Mar. 2, 1972), economist and historian, was born in New York City, the son of Louisa Waterman and Louis Jacob Feis. Educated in the public schools of his native city, where his father was a businessman, he received his B.A. degree from Harvard in 1916. During World War I he was a lieutenant in the United States Navy, serving with the Sixth Battle Squadron of the British Grand Fleet. After the war he returned to Harvard and in 1921 received a Ph.D. degree in economics. In the same year his first book, *The Settlement of Wage Disputes*, was published. On March 25 of the following year he married Ruth Stanley-Brown, a great-granddaughter of President James Garfield.

Feis spent the decade of the 1920's in academe, first at Harvard (1920–1921), where he was an instructor in economics; then at the University of Kansas (1922–1925), where he was associate professor of economics; and lastly at the University of Cincinnati (1926–1929), where he was professor and head of the department of economics. During these years he published numerous papers, pamphlets, and books on labor relations and also served as industrial relations adviser to the International Labor Office of the League of Nations in Geneva. The

publication in 1930 of his first major book, *Europe, the World's Banker, 1870–1914*, which he wrote while holding a Guggenheim research fellowship, impressed Secretary of State Henry L. Stimson, who recruited him to serve as economic adviser to the Department of State.

From 1931 to 1947 Feis lived in Washington, D.C., with his wife and only child. He spent twelve years in the State Department and three with the War Department. During this tenure he shifted the focus of his scholarly interest from labor relations to international economic affairs. As the Department of State's specialist in this area, he served as chief technical adviser to the U.S. delegation at many of the international conferences held during the 1930's. These included the important World Economic and Monetary Conference of 1933 in London and the various meetings of the Conference of American Republics held in Buenos Aires (1936), Lima (1938), and Panama (1939). While he was with the State Department Feis wrote *The Sinews of Peace* (1944), a perceptive and important analysis of the complex economic problems that awaited the nations of the world after World War II was over.

In 1947 Feis left government service and embarked on a new career as a historian. His years as a Washington insider, where he was witness to many of the events about which he wrote, gave him a sure grasp of his subject. His 1947 book, *Seen from E. A.: Three International Episodes*, inaugurated a series of eleven books published over the ensuing twenty-five years, which together offer a comprehensive history of American foreign policy from 1933 to 1950. Written from the distinctive perspective of an eyewitness, these volumes trace the tortuous course the United States followed in abandoning its traditional isolationism for a policy of global intervention.

Included among these eleven books was Feis's important five-volume diplomatic history of World War II published by Princeton University Press. The first volume, *The Road to Pearl Harbor: The Coming of the War Between the United States and Japan* (1950), utilized for the first time both Japanese and American government documents to describe events leading to the United States' entry into the war. The last of the volumes, *Japan Subdued: The Atomic Bomb and the End of the War in the Pacific* (1961), discussed the complex problems involved in the Truman administration's decision to use the atomic bomb. His fourth volume, *Between War and Peace: The Potsdam Conference* (1960), won the Pulitzer Prize in History in 1961. All of the volumes, including the second and third volumes, *The China Tangle: The American Effort in China from Pearl Harbor to the Marshall Mission* (1953), and *Churchill-Roosevelt-Stalin: The War They Waged and the Peace They Sought* (1957), were praised for meticulous scholarship. Despite his closeness to the events, Feis wrote objectively and analytically, often using State and War Department documents not yet examined by other scholars. As participant historian, he understood the limits of those documents. His experience told him when they distorted or concealed the truth, and suggested when he should find new sources and conduct new interviews. Feis's particular gift as a historian, said one critic, was his "careful and wide-ranging research" and his "lucid skill in disentangling highly confused situations." A perceptive analyst, he was able to cut through a welter of conflicting points of view and contradictory information to expose the essence of the matter.

Feis was not without his critics. Some charged that as a "court historian" he could not write objectively about the government policies and actions that he himself had helped to formulate. His close involvement with the people and events about which he wrote, they said, "shackled" him to an "establishment line." One English critic described his 1960 prize-winning study of the Potsdam Conference as "a State Department brief, translated into terms of historical scholarship." But the dominant view was that while Feis's participation in events animated his narrative, he wrote objective history characterized by reasonably dispassionate analysis. As an insider with access to government documents closed to other scholars, he had an unusual advantage, a fact of which he was well aware. Perhaps because of this, he devoted much time during the 1960's trying to persuade government officials that they could open government documents to research scholars much sooner than was customary without jeopardizing the national security. He wrote an article for the *New York Times*, for example, defending Daniel Ellsberg's release of the Pentagon Papers, the top-secret study of the Vietnam War ordered in 1967 by Secretary of Defense Robert McNamara.

After leaving government service in 1947,

Feis became a member of the Institute for Advanced Study at Princeton, where he worked intermittently over the next decade. He returned to the Department of State in 1950 to serve for a year on its policy planning staff. In 1951 he accepted an appointment as visiting professor of history at Harvard and over the next decade held several such appointments at other institutions, including Columbia University. This tall, slim man, his convivial face topped by a cascade of tousled snow-white hair, was a familiar figure on the campuses of American universities during the 1960's, where he was a popular lecturer and recipient of many awards and honorary degrees. He spent his last years at his farm in York, Maine, but usually wintered in Antigua, where his daughter lived, or in Florida. He died in Winter Park, Fla.

[Feis's professional and personal papers (28,000 items) are located at the Library of Congress. An extraordinarily prolific writer, he was author of more than 150 articles published in *Foreign Affairs*, *Yale Review*, the *New York Times Magazine*, and other periodicals. Major monographs and books, in addition to those mentioned in the text, include *The Diplomacy of the Dollar* (1950); *Foreign Aid and Foreign Policy* (1964); *The Birth of Israel: The Tangled Diplomatic Bed* (1969); and *From Trust to Terror: The Onset of the Cold War, 1945–1950* (1970). Obituaries are in the *New York Times*, Mar. 3, 1972; *The Washington Post*, Mar. 4, 1972; *Newsweek*, Mar. 13, 1972; *Time*, Mar. 13, 1972; and *The American Historical Review* 78, no. 2 (Apr. 1971).]

CHARLES D. LOWERY

FERNÓS ISERN, ANTONIO (May 10, 1895–Jan. 19, 1974), doctor, public health official, and politician, was born in San Lorenzo, P.R., to Buenaventura Fernós and Dolores Isern Aponte. He attended elementary and high schools in the town of Caguas before leaving the island to pursue premedical studies at the Pennsylvania State Normal School at Bloomsburg. In May 1915 Fernós Isern graduated from the University of Maryland College of Physicians and Surgeons and School of Medicine.

He soon returned to Puerto Rico, where he quickly established a lifelong pattern of alternating periods of private practice with public service. In 1916 he began a private practice in Caguas. After two years he entered the public health sector, first as a health officer in San Juan and then as assistant commissioner of health for all of Puerto Rico, a post he held from 1920 to 1931.

In April 1920 he married Gertrudis Delgado Jiménez; they had two sons and a daughter, all of whom became lawyers.

In 1931 Fernós Isern was named the island's commissioner of health. Two years later he resumed private practice, specializing in cardiology from 1934 to 1940. Meanwhile, he participated in other aspects of public life. Following a devastating cyclone that swept the neighboring Dominican Republic in 1935, he presided over a medical mission to aid that country.

During the Great Depression Fernós Isern grew increasingly concerned with resource-poor Puerto Rico's ability to sustain its population. The United States had to pump millions of dollars of aid into the island to prevent massive starvation in the 1930's. Fernós Isern was one of the early members of the Popular Democratic party (PDP), which dedicated itself to improving the welfare of the poor majority of Puerto Ricans; its motto was "Bread, land, and liberty." In 1940 Fernós Isern ran for the position of resident commissioner, Puerto Rico's nonvoting representative in the U.S. House of Representatives, but lost the election. In 1942 he expanded his public role by becoming executive director of the General Supply and Food Commission and president of the Insular Petroleum Board.

Though he was again named commissioner of health in 1943, Fernós Isern was by now clearly on a political path. He served as acting governor on several occasions over the next three years and in 1946 was sent to Washington, D.C., to continue the term of Resident Commissioner Jesús Piñero, whom President Truman had named governor of Puerto Rico.

Often appearing in a white suit with oval spectacles clipped to his nose, Fernós Isern worked to reform Puerto Rico's political status in relation to the United States. In 1947 he helped to guide a bill through the U.S. Congress that allowed Puerto Rico to elect its own governor. The following year Puerto Ricans elected their first governor, Luís Muñoz Marín, leader of the PDP, and gave Fernós Isern a full four-year term as resident commissioner.

In his role as liaison between the U.S. government and a Puerto Rico that was seeking greater autonomy, Fernós Isern became one of the architects of the Puerto Rican Commonwealth, known in Spanish as the Estado Libre Asociado (Free Associated State). He felt that the two traditional postcolonial options of statehood or independence were not suitable for Puerto Rico, given its economic problems and its unique relationship with the United States. Commonwealth status, a creative third alternative, would end the island's colonial identity and make it virtually self-governing in terms of its internal affairs. Puerto Rico would have its own flag as well as the right to make domestic laws and elect its own officials without Congress's approval, while the U.S. government would retain control over the island's foreign and military affairs. Puerto Rico's resident commissioner would not have a vote in the U.S. House of Representatives, but in accordance with the principle of "no taxation without representation," the island would be exempt from federal taxes. Fernós Isern preferred commonwealth status over statehood or independence because he felt that in this way Puerto Ricans could enjoy the benefits of U.S. citizenship and access to U.S. markets while still preserving their cultural integrity and fiscal autonomy.

In 1951 Fernós Isern published his book *Puerto Rico libre y asociado* (*The Commonwealth of Puerto Rico*) in which he described in depth the idea of a commonwealth nation. That year too he served as president of the Puerto Rican Constitution Convention. He had fought hard in the U.S. House of Representatives for the passage of Law 600, which extended to Puerto Rico the right to draft its own constitution. On July 25, 1952, the Puerto Rican people approved their new constitution and the commonwealth was created.

In 1952 Fernós Isern was reelected resident commissioner, and in 1953 he was named an alternative representative of the United States to the United Nations. In 1954 he received a standing ovation in the U.S. House of Representatives following a speech in which he expressed his profound disapproval of a recent attack on the House by Puerto Rican independence fanatics, who had sprayed the House chamber with bullets and wounded five representatives.

In 1956 Fernós Isern was reelected again to a third term. While resident commissioner, Fernós Isern simultaneously served as chairman of the Puerto Rican Red Cross, chairman of the Public Housing Authority, and as a professor of public health at Puerto Rico's School of Tropical Medicine.

His eighteen years of public service as resident commissioner are unprecedented. During this time, he guided more than eighty bills involving Puerto Rico's interests through the U.S. House of Representatives. His one major defeat occurred in 1959, when he saw the death, in the face of great House opposition, of the innovative Fernós-Murray Bill (H.R. 5926), which would have increased Puerto Rico's autonomy in certain areas of government.

In 1964 he left his post as resident commissioner and ran successfully on the Popular Democratic party ticket for a seat in Puerto Rico's senate, where he served from 1965 to 1969.

Fernós Isern had a creative side as well. He wrote poetry and translated poems from the French. Fernós Isern died in San Juan, P.R.

[For Fernós Isern's own views on Puerto Rico, see his *Puerto Rico libre y asociado* (1951) and *Estado Libre Asociado de Puerto Rico* (1974). Articles making reference to Fernós Isern's activities as resident commissioner appear in the *New York Times* (Nov. 7, 1940; Aug. 29, 1953; March 2–4, 1954; Aug. 27, 1956; and Dec. 6, 1959). The University of Puerto Rico's library has a short, unpublished manuscript by R. Santiago Sosa, describing some details of Fernós Isern's life. Obituaries appear in the *San Juan Star* and in *El Mundo*, both Jan. 21, 1974.]

ALISON GARDY

FIELDS, DOROTHY (July 15, 1905–Mar. 28, 1974), lyricist and librettist, was born in Allenhurst, N.J., the daughter of Lew M. Fields and Rose Harris. Her father, born Lewis Maurice Schoenfeld, was famous as a member of the comedy duo Weber and Fields, but left performing in the year of Dorothy's birth to become a successful Broadway impresario. Although Lew Fields cautioned his children against pursuing careers in the theater, Dorothy's two older brothers, Joseph and Herbert, also became successful on Broadway, the former as a writer and producer, and the latter as a writer and Dorothy's sometime collaborator.

Dorothy Fields graduated in 1923 from the Benjamin Franklin School for Girls in New York City, where she excelled at English, drama, and basketball, and had her poems published in the school's literary magazine. After her father quashed her attempt to land an acting job with a stock company in Yonkers, she worked as a teacher and laboratory assistant, while continuing to submit her verses to magazines.

In 1926 Fields met the popular song composer J. Fred Coots, who suggested that they write some songs together. Although nothing memorable came out of this brief association, Coots introduced Fields to another composer and song-plugger, Jimmy McHugh. Through McHugh she got a job as a lyricist at Mills Music, Inc., where one of her first assignments was to write the lyric for a tune commemorating aviator Ruth Elder's attempt to cross the Atlantic Ocean. Fields later referred to herself as "Mills' Music's fifty-dollars-a-night girl," because she was paid fifty dollars for each lyric she composed.

In 1927 Fields received sole billing as lyricist for a revue at Harlem's Cotton Club that featured Duke Ellington and his Orchestra. The following year she and McHugh wrote the song "I Can't Give You Anything but Love," which was dropped from the revue *Revels of 1928*, but found a home alongside another soon-to-be-popular Fields-McHugh number, "Diga Diga Doo," in the all-black hit, Lew Leslie's *Blackbirds of 1928*.

After this initial success, the Fields-McHugh team collaborated on *International Revue* (1930), a flop despite two enduring songs, "Exactly Like You" and "On The Sunny Side of the Street." The family of jazz pianist Thomas ("Fats") Waller maintained that Waller, not McHugh, actually composed the melodies to "On the Sunny Side of the Street," "I Can't Give You Anything but Love," and others, and sold them to McHugh for a nominal fee. In any case, however, it is undisputed that Fields is the lyricist.

From 1930 to 1939 Fields worked in Hollywood, first with McHugh, with whom she wrote songs such as "I'm in the Mood for Love" and "Dinner at Eight" for the movie musicals *Love in the Rough* (1930) and *Every Night at Eight* (1935), and then with Jerome Kern. Kern and Fields first worked together on *Roberta* in 1935, and subsequent collaborations included *I Dream Too Much* (1935), *Swing Time* (1936), and *Joy of Living* (1938). In 1936, Kern and Fields won the Academy Award for Best Song for "The Way You Look Tonight," from *Swing Time*. Other Kern-Fields songs from this period that have gone on to become standards include "Lovely to Look At" and "A Fine Romance."

On July 15, 1939, Fields married David Eli Lahm, a clothing manufacturer. They had two children before his death in 1958. The same year, she returned to New York to work with composer Arthur Schwartz on the musical *Stars in Your Eyes.* She then collaborated with her brother Herbert, with whom she had already worked on screenplays and the short-lived musical *Hello Daddy* (1928), and on the books for three Cole Porter hits: *Let's Face It* (1941), *Something for the Boys* (1943), and *Mexican Hayride* (1944). In 1945 Dorothy and Herbert Fields wrote the book for Sigmund Romberg's *Up in Central Park.* Her lyrics for the show included "Close as Pages in a Book."

In 1946, Fields approached Oscar Hammerstein with her idea for a musical based on the life of sharpshooter Annie Oakley. Hammerstein agreed to produce the show, and Kern and Fields were contracted to write the songs. When Kern died before they were able to begin work on the project, Irving Berlin was hired to replace him. Berlin wrote both music and lyrics for *Annie Get Your Gun*, but Dorothy and Herbert Fields contributed an excellent book. The finished product, starring Ethel Merman as Annie, ran 1,147 performances. It remains one of the most popular shows in the repertoire.

Fields's work habits were highly disciplined. Typically, she would spend eight weeks researching, discussing, and making notes on a project, before settling into an 8:30 A.M. to 4:00 P.M. daily work routine. She worked at a bridge table in her apartment on the Upper West Side of Manhattan, and preferred to write with pencil on a yellow legal pad. She kept notebooks in which she copied passages from Dryden, Shaw, and Thoreau; unusual synonyms for commonly used words; humorous proverbs; rhyming phrases; odd-sounding words; and anything else that might come in handy in writing a lyric. Tall, slender, and well dressed, with chestnut hair and hazel eyes, she spoke well and was active in charitable causes throughout her life.

Fields collaborated with her brother and composer Morton Gould on the lackluster *Arms and the Girl* in 1950. The following year, she wrote several fine lyrics to Arthur Schwartz's melodies for *A Tree Grows in Brooklyn.* She scored two films with composer Harold Arlen, *Mr. Imperium* (1951) and *The Farmer Takes a Wife* (1953), then returned to Broadway to work with Schwartz again on *By the Beautiful Sea* (1954). Herbert Fields died in 1959, while *Redhead*, the show they were working on with composer Albert Hague, was having its out-of-town tryout. Although not a great show, *Redhead*

captured the Tony Award for Best Musical in a lean year for Broadway theater.

Her penultimate musical, *Sweet Charity*, written with composer Cy Coleman and librettist Neil Simon, was the biggest hit of the 1965–1966 season. Songs such as "Big Spender" and "If My Friends Could See Me Now" proved that Fields, despite her advancing age, had not lost her knack for up-to-the-minute slang and phraseology. In 1971, Fields became the first woman inducted into the Songwriters Hall of Fame. Her last show, *Two for the Seesaw* (1973), also written with Coleman, was not a popular success, but her lyrics were praised for their evocation of modern life in New York. She died at home in New York City.

During her forty-eight year career Fields cowrote more than 400 songs and worked on 15 musicals and at least 26 movies. Her lyrics were noted for their strong characterization, clarity of language, and middlebrow humor. An amateur pianist and lifelong lover of classical music, she was highly conscious of the melodic line, and tailored her lyrics to float freely over it. Fields's professional longevity, rare for a songwriter in the popular field, may be attributed to her undimming imagination and her willingness to adapt to changing trends in the musical theater.

[Fields's papers and clippings, mostly from the latter half of her career, are in the theater collection of the New York Public Library. The most thorough account of her life is in Caryl Brahms and Ned Sherrin, *Song By Song* (1984). See also Lehman Engels, *Their Words Are Music* (1975); Philip Furia, *The Poets of Tin Pan Alley* (1990); and Thomas Hischak, *Word Crazy* (1991). An obituary is in the *New York Times*, Mar. 29, 1974.]

GREGORY ROBINSON

FINE, LARRY (Oct. 5, 1902–Jan. 24, 1975), charter member of the Three Stooges, was born Louis Feinberg on Philadelphia's South Side, the son of Joseph Feinberg and Fanny Lieberman. He was the first of four children.

His show business bent became clear at an early age; as a two-year-old he danced for relatives atop a jewelry display case at his parents' watch repair shop. However, his other childhood talents gave no warning of the lowbrow slapstick comedies in which he would later achieve fame with Moe Howard and Curly Howard, two brothers with whom he founded the Three Stooges' first lineup. Fine first took up the violin as therapy to rejuvenate an arm that was injured when his father accidentally spilled a bottle of acid on it. Fine became so proficient at playing that in his teens he won several amateur contests. He later played the violin in a number of Stooges shorts and remained a jazz buff through the years.

Fine was also a teenage boxer, fighting forty amateur bouts under the name "Kid Roth." However, it was when he went into vaudeville that he came up with the alias of his fame, Larry Fine. His professional show business debut came in 1921, when he played the violin and danced with the Gus Edwards' Newsboy Sextet. He went on the vaudeville circuit, where Fine met his wife, Mabel Haney. They had two children. Through his active years, his family would live in hotels in Atlantic City, N.J., and Hollywood, as his work dictated. However, the couple was "wed" professionally before they married legally, performing together with Mabel's sister Loretta as "the Haney Sisters and Fine" until 1925, when Fine was signed by Ted Healy, a vaudeville headliner with a two-man supporting cast called "the Laugh Racketeers." Fine later said, "I was hesitant before accepting Healy's offer. I had never done comedy before and was afraid of the outcome." Fine, who replaced the departing Shemp Howard, was paired with the remaining Howard brother, Moe. With an assortment of third men, Fine and Moe Howard remained a team for the next forty-five years, appearing together in hundreds of Broadway shows, film shorts, live shows, and feature films.

The frizzy-haired Fine earned ninety dollars per week with Healy, who worked off and on with Larry and Moe for the next nine years. During this time, they signed a deal with MGM Studios and appeared in five films with stars such as Jimmy Durante, Joan Crawford, Fred Astaire, and Clark Gable. An appearance in the 1929 Broadway revue "A Night in Venice" prompted the *New York Times* to describe the trio as "three of the frowziest numbskulls ever assembled."

A 1934 financial contract dispute led to the final split with Healy. The Three Stooges—now with Curly Howard, another of Moe's brothers—signed their own agreement with Columbia Pictures on Mar. 6, 1934, which led to the first of 190 film shorts. *Woman Haters* featured a cameo appearance by Walter Brennan, then unknown.

The Stooges quickly established the roles that would carry them through the next four decades: Moe as the dictatorial leader, Curly the jovial smart aleck, and Larry the pliable jack-of-all-trades caught in the middle.

The film shorts featured the same type of comedy the Stooges perfected in their vaudeville years: outrageous physical jokes with hilarious sound effects, bad puns, and sight gags. A typical exchange from *Men in Black*, in which the Stooges play aspiring doctors, had a hospital executive asking Larry, "What do you men know about medicine?" "We graduated with the highest temperatures in our class," replied Fine.

Over the course of their many films, the Stooges, always in character, adopted a wide range of roles—icemen, football players, doctors, plumbers, and professors, to name but a few.

In addition to their work in short films—which launched the careers of several prominent stars, including Lucille Ball, and Lloyd Bridges—they appeared in another Broadway show, *The George White Scandals of 1939*, and did brief bits in a half-dozen feature films. However, the Stooges suffered a crushing blow with the death of Curly in 1952. Shemp Howard returned and the reconstituted trio enjoyed some of their greatest successes. The Motion Pictures Exhibitors awarded them the Laurel Award as the most successful two-reel movie makers in 1950, 1951, 1953, 1954, and 1955.

This last year proved bittersweet, as Columbia—sensing a change in the business—ended its twenty-four-year association with the group. Shemp died in the same year, and Fine began to consider retiring. Instead, they added Joe Besser and pressed on. When Besser left after a short stay, Joe DeRita signed on, and the Stooges endured well into the 1960's, spurred in part by a revival of their old movie shorts on television.

Within a year of their debut on television in January 1958, the Stooges became the number-one children's show, knocking off "Popeye." With DeRita, they made seven feature films between 1959 and 1965. They also did cameos in the Stanley Kramer comedy *It's a Mad, Mad, Mad, Mad World* and in *Four for Texas*, a Dean Martin vehicle.

Fine's son was killed in a 1961 motorcycle crash; his wife died six years later while her husband was on the road with the Stooges. Fine spent his last years in the Motion Picture and

Television Country Home in Woodland Hills, Calif.

The group continued to work until Larry suffered a 1970 stroke, which left him paralyzed on the left side. In his final years, Fine made personal appearances on high school and college campuses. He suffered a second stroke in late 1975, and a fatal stroke four months later. He is buried in Glendale, Calif.

[Biographical information can be found in Moe Howard, *Moe Howard and the Three Stooges* (1977); Jeff Lenburg, Joan Howard Maurer, and Greg Lenburg, *The Three Stooges Scrapbook* (1982); and Ronald L. Smith, *The Stooge Fan's I.Q. Test* (1988). See also "Salute to the Stooges," a one-hour television special that aired on VH-1. An obituary appears in the *New York Times*, Jan. 25, 1975.]

LARRY McSHANE

FIRESTONE, HARVEY SAMUEL, JR. (Apr. 20, 1898–June 1, 1973) industrialist and philanthropist, was born in Chicago, Ill., the eldest of five sons and a daughter born to rubber magnate Harvey S. Firestone and Idabelle Smith, a musical composer and a member of the American Society of Composers, Authors and Publishers (ASCAP). When he was two, his father founded Firestone Tire and Rubber Co., in Akron, Ohio. As a child, his first ride in a car was in one that his father had bought to test new pneumatic tire designs. The young Firestone graduated the Asheville (N.C.) school in 1916 and entered Princeton that same year. He played polo and tennis while in college. Despite taking time off to get his pilot's license and joining the U.S. Naval Aviation Corps during World War I, he graduated with a B.A. in 1920. During the summers of 1916, 1918, 1919, and 1921, he accompanied his father, inventor Thomas Edison, car manufacturer Henry Ford, and naturalist John Burroughs on camping trips to the Adirondack Mountains in upstate New York. On June 25, 1921, he married art collector and socialite Elizabeth Parke; they had four children.

Firestone joined his father's corporation in 1919, and was actively involved in its management for almost half a century. He persuaded his father to establish an executive recruiting program aimed at bringing recent college graduates into the firm. He also did much to secure the company's international expansion. In 1926, as vice-president of Firestone Plantations

Company, he toured the Philippines, Malaysia, Singapore, Sumatra, Ceylon, and Liberia in order to determine the best new sites for rubber production. At the time, Great Britain and the Netherlands controlled over 98 percent of the world's supply of raw rubber. In the fall of 1926, the younger Firestone negotiated a ninety-nine-year lease of one million acres with the Liberian government—land that had been allocated previously to black nationalist Marcus Garvey's Universal Negro Improvement Association. Firestone even won federal approval to set up a radio transmitter to maintain contact between company headquarters in Akron and field offices in Liberia. In 1928, he was instrumental in opening the company's first overseas plant in England. He visited Argentina in 1930 and made arrangements for a Firestone factory there. In 1933, he opened a Firestone plant in Spain. He did the same in Switzerland in 1935, and the following year established another in South Africa.

Firestone operations in Liberia were complicated by charges of American imperialism and collusion with dishonest Liberian officials. In 1930, a special international commission appointed by the League of Nations issued a shocking report charging the Liberian government with perpetuating "slavery, forced labor, exploitation of the native tribes, and financial corruption." Liberian authorities disputed the findings and conducted protracted negotiations with the League. Firestone personally defended the family name and company record in Africa (and elsewhere) on "The Voice of Firestone" radio broadcasts Monday nights on NBC. In 1932, he published a compilation of his radio speeches entitled *The Romance and Drama of the Rubber Industry*. With company operations in the Black Republic seriously compromised, he and his father lobbied for American military intervention. Presidents Herbert Hoover and Franklin Roosevelt rejected their appeals. In 1935, Roosevelt "resolved" the dispute by extending American financial aid in return for cosmetic reforms. Continued tensions between the Americo-Liberian elite (descendants of freed slaves) and native Africans culminated in the Liberian civil war, which began in 1989.

Harvey S. Firestone, Sr., founder of the firm, died in 1938, although his son did not become president of Firestone Tire and Rubber Company until 1941. In 1940, when access to foreign markets was endangered by Japanese expansionism in Asia, Firestone helped develop synthetic rubber factories with assistance from the government's Reconstruction Finance Corporation. Production began in 1942. Already a huge conglomerate, the company tripled its size during the war. Firestone also created the company's Postwar Planning Division, which made plans for diversification even before the end of the war. In 1948, he took over as chairman of the board and company chief executive officer.

Firestone was a Republican, but not particularly partisan. Although his father had vigorously supported Herbert Hoover in 1932, the younger rubber tycoon made peace with Roosevelt—especially during the war years. He was considerably closer to Harry Truman, and even dined at the White House. A staunch internationalist, Firestone supported establishment of the United Nations, and served as director of the UN Association of the United States. In 1950, he accepted Truman's invitation to join the International Development Advisory Board. He was reappointed nine years later by President Dwight D. Eisenhower. When the Korean War broke out in 1950, Firestone offered to supply the military's rubber requirements. He was also offended by McCarthyism, and in 1951 accepted Truman's request to join the President's Commission on Internal Security and Individual Rights, chaired by Fleet Admiral Chester Nimitz. When Congress refused to remove legal impediments to allow the commission to operate, Firestone and the others resigned in protest.

Firestone ran the corporation his father founded until he stepped down in 1963 at the age of sixty-five. During his fifteen-year tenure, sales doubled, and the number of foreign plants grew from twenty-four to forty-one. He continued as chairman of the board for the next three years, and wrote a book: *Man on the Move* (1967) was a light-hearted, comprehensive history of human transportation, "from caveman to spaceman," on land, sea, and air. He retired from serving the company in 1969.

Firestone, who owned estates in Akron and Newport, R.I., was active in philanthropic, educational, and religious affairs throughout his long career. With his brothers, he established the Firestone Foundation in 1947. In 1983, it was dissolved into separate branch family foundations. He served on the national council of the United Negro College Fund; was a trustee at Princeton, where he donated money to support

the Harvey S. Firestone Library erected in his father's honor; was active in the National Conference of Christians and Jews; founded the American Association against Addiction in 1968; and was appointed to the governing board of the United Service Organization (USO) by every president from Harry Truman through Richard Nixon. In recognition of Firestone's contribution to the USO, the Department of Defense awarded him its Medal for Distinguished Public Service in 1966 and 1973. Firestone was also active in the "Nixon Foundation," and was supposedly making arrangements to buy the president's boyhood family home in order to turn it into a museum when he died at his estate in Akron.

[Firestone's papers are at the Firestone Tire and Rubber Company Archives, Akron, Ohio. See also Alfred Lief, *The Firestone Story* (1951); and I. K. Sundiata, *Black Scandal* (1980). An obituary is in the *New York Times*, June 2, 1973.]

DAVID M. ESPOSITO

FLEISCHER, NATHANIEL STANLEY ("NAT") (Nov. 3, 1887–June 25, 1972), sportswriter, publisher, and boxing authority, was one of nine surviving children of Jewish immigrants who settled in the Lower East Side of Manhattan in 1868. While attending P.S. 15 and Townsend Harris Hall, Fleischer was active in the neighborhood Oregon Athletic Club, becoming president and participating on the basketball, baseball, and boxing teams. At City College of New York Fleischer organized and managed its first basketball team while participating on the track squad and working part-time as a cub reporter for two city newspapers. Fleischer received a B.S. in 1908 and for a while taught sixth-grade botany at P.S. 7 during the day and worked as a reporter for the *New York Press* at night. Unhappy in the classroom, Fleischer enrolled in a graduate course in commercial chemistry at New York University and attended a summer course in forestry at Yale University.

In 1912 Nat became a full-time reporter for the *Press*, earning forty-five dollars per week. In four years he rose to the rank of sports editor. Fleischer was a favorite of Frank Munsey, owner of the *Press* and other New York newspapers. Except for a stint in the army in 1917 and 1918, Fleischer worked steadily as a sports editor on five of Munsey's papers from 1916 to

1929. Fleischer was working for the *New York Evening Telegram* when Munsey died in 1929; the Scripps-Howard syndicate bought the *Telegram* after Munsey's death and immediately fired Fleischer. His dismissal, it could be said, turned out to be the best thing that ever happened to him, for it changed the direction of his life.

In 1922 Fleischer and three partners had founded *The Ring*, a monthly magazine intended to promote boxing and combat efforts in New York State to curtail or outlaw the sport. After losing his newspaper job Fleischer began to devote his considerable energies to making *The Ring* a success. He bought out his partners and began to promote *The Ring* as boxing's authoritative publication. Working tirelessly to give boxing—a sport plagued by fixed fights, betting scandals, and other forms of corruption—greater legitimacy, Fleischer originated the definitive method of rating boxers from all over the world. By 1933, with the aid of more than 140 ring observers in the United States and boxing reports published in seventy-five overseas newspapers, Fleischer was issuing monthly boxer ratings in a largely successful attempt to end mismatches and regularize the sport's operations.

The Ring lost money in its first years, but Fleischer subsidized the magazine with some of his considerable earnings from book sales. *Training for Boxers*, published in 1929, sold close to one million copies at one dollar each. Over his lifetime Fleischer wrote almost sixty books on boxing and wrestling, including thirteen biographies of boxing titlists; *Black Dynamite*, a five-volume history of African-American boxers; and numerous "how-to" guides for boxers, referees, seconds, and managers. In 1942 he began to write and publish the annual *Ring Record Book and Boxing Encyclopedia*, which instantly became the sport's premier resource volume.

During World War II Fleischer was boxing's ambassador to the armed forces. He flew more than 150,000 miles to visit 168 hospitals and camps, where he entertained the troops with boxing stories and his collection of fight films. He donated $25,000 worth of boxing equipment to military facilities and presented the army with 13,000 free copies of *The Ring*, almost 25 percent of his government-restricted press run. He also sent copies of the *Ring Record Book* to 250 camp libraries. *The Ring* lost

money during the war years, but Fleischer reaped benefits from his wartime largesse when the magazine's 1946 circulation jumped by 30,000, thanks to demobilized veterans who took out subscriptions. In 1948 *The Ring* had a monthly circulation of about 160,000 copies in the United States and 90,000 copies elsewhere in the world.

Fleischer conducted a worldwide campaign to reform boxing. Appearing often before legislative committees examining the sport, he insisted that incompetent and corrupt officials in the various boxing organizations, not the sport itself, were the problem. Discontinuing the sport, Fleischer claimed, would only drive it underground. He was instrumental in securing standard padding in gloves and under ring canvasses; establishing physical exams and health protection for boxers; initiating a system for stopping contests before knockouts on the basis of cuts; and standardizing training sessions for officials, trainers, and managers. He worked to ensure that boxers officially banned in one state or country would be denied bouts elsewhere. To promote boxing internationally, Fleischer helped set up boxing commissions in Europe, South America, Cuba, the West Indies, Japan, the Philippines, and Southeast Asia. For his efforts in behalf of boxing Fleischer was awarded La Medaille d'Honneur by the French government, the Commandatore della Stella al Merito Sportivo from the Italian government, the Order of the White Elephant from the Thai government, and an American Red Cross citation. Fleischer estimated that he officiated at more than one thousand bouts worldwide.

Fleischer married Gertrude ("Trudie") Phillips on Oct. 22, 1922. They had one daughter.

Fleischer was unquestionably the world's leading boxing authority. In his office in Madison Square Garden he displayed the world's largest collection of boxing memorabilia complemented by the largest library of boxing and wrestling books; his collection and library are now *The Ring* Magazine Museum. Holding the honorary title of "Mr. Boxing," Fleischer directed the affairs of *The Ring* every day until his death in New York City.

[Fleischer's autobiography is *Fifty Years at Ringside* (1969). Profiles of Fleischer appear in Howard Cohn, "Boxing's Boswell," *Sportfolio*, Aug. 1948; Gilbert Rogin, "Mr. Boxing, Himself," *Sports Illustrated*, Aug. 6, 1962; and the *Biographical Dictio-*

nary of American Sports: Boxing (1989). Obituaries are in the *New York Times*, June 26, 1972; and *The Ring*, Oct. 1972.]

DAVID BERNSTEIN

FORD, JOHN (Feb. 1, 1894–Aug. 31, 1973), actor and movie director, was born John Martin Feeney in Cape Elizabeth, Maine, the son of Sean Feeney, a saloon-keeper, and Barbara ("Abby") Curran. The family later moved to Portland, Maine, where Ford developed his great love for sailing and the movies.

"As a kid I was fascinated by the nickelodeons of that period," he later said. "Any time I got a nickel or a dime I would go to the movies." Ford graduated from Portland High School in 1914. When his older brother Francis disappeared for ten years (he initially toured on the vaudeville circuit) and later resurfaced in California as Francis Ford, a motion-picture star and director with his own company on the lots of Universal Studios, Ford set out to follow in his brother's footsteps. He arrived in California in July 1914, and his brother promptly hired him, putting him to work as an actor and general factotum. He roomed with Edmund Richard Gibson, who would go on to achieve fame as the cowboy star "Hoot" Gibson. For the next few years, Ford kept acting regularly; he may even have appeared as one of the klansmen in D. W. Griffith's epic *The Birth of a Nation* (1915). Undoubtedly, Griffith, along with Francis Ford, exerted great influence upon Ford's early directorial style. On July 3, 1920, Ford married Mary McBride Smith, formerly a lieutenant in the army medical corps. They had two children.

After directing thirty-nine films at Universal, Ford moved on to Fox Studios, where, in 1923, he first used the name John Ford, as a credit on the movie *Cameo Kirby*. In 1924, *The Iron Horse*, the story of the transcontinental railroad, established Ford's greatness as a filmmaker and brought him international fame. Using some five thousand extras, 116 locomotives, ten thousand head of cattle, and thirteen hundred buffalo, the movie took in over $2 million at the box office and was among the top-grossing films of the 1920's. The advent of sound pictures brought greater scope to Ford's work. His first talking picture was *The Black Watch* (1929). In 1931 his adaptation of Sinclair Lewis's novel *Arrowsmith* brought four Academy Award nominations, including one for best picture. *The*

Informer (1935) is frequently included on lists honoring the greatest films of all time. *Stagecoach* (1939) established John Wayne as a screen star and won two Academy Awards. Thomas Mitchell received the Oscar for best supporting actor, Richard Hageman won for best score, and John Ford that year was voted the best director by the New York Film Critics.

Before America officially entered World War II, Ford began training a field photo unit. After the United States entered the war, he was named chief of the Field Photographic Branch of the Office of Strategic Services. From 1941 to 1945 Ford and his crew of highly trained technicians produced some of the finest documentaries ever made, most especially *The Battle of Midway* (1942). Ford himself was with the fleet during this most famous of World War II naval battles. He told interviewer Axel Madsen in *Cahiers du Cinéma*, "When the attack arrived I had only an Eyemo, a 16mm camera. I shot film and continued to change film magazines and to stuff them in my pockets. The image jumps a lot because the grenades were exploding right next to me." The film won an Oscar for best documentary.

After the war, Ford returned to Hollywood and took up where he had left off, creating a body of work unrivaled by directors of Westerns, including such films as *Fort Apache* (1948), *She Wore a Yellow Ribbon* (1949), and *Wagon Master* (1950). He brought so much work to the Navajo Indians of Monument Valley that he was inducted into the tribe and given the name Natani Nez ("Tall Soldier"). However, some of his better films were not Westerns at all, among them, *The Quiet Man* (1952), with John Wayne and Maureen O'Hara, and *What Price Glory* (1952), based on the classic American play by Maxwell Anderson and Lawrence Stallings. His 1965 feature *Seven Women*, starring Anne Bancroft, was Ford's last commercial film for a studio.

There may be as many Americas as there are Americans, but the portrait and history of America as presented in the movies directed by John Ford may well have a lasting influence on how we view ourselves. From his very first film as a director (*The Tornado*, a 1917 two-reeler about a man who needs money to buy a home for his mother) until his final screen credit (*Chesty*, a never-released 1976 documentary about Marine Corps Lieutenant General Lewis ["Chesty"] Puller, the military hero who won more medals for valor in combat than any other Marine in history) Ford's movies have provided a panorama of American life with emphasis on the settling of the West and the depiction of the hero as a loner who must fight other men to achieve self-respect.

On Mar. 31, 1973, Ford was given the American Film Institute's first Life Achievement Award. At that ceremony President Richard Nixon also presented Ford with the Medal of Freedom. The commendation on the Medal of Freedom read: "In the annals of American film, no name shines more brightly than that of John Ford. Director and filmmaker for more than half a century, he stands preeminent in his craft—not only as a creator of individual films of surpassing excellence, but as a master among those who transformed the early motion pictures into a compelling new art form that developed in America and swept the world. As an interpreter of the Nation's heritage, he left his personal stamp indelibly printed on the consciousness of whole generations both here and abroad. In his life and in his work, John Ford represents the best in American films and the best in America."

Ford died in Palm Desert, Calif.

[The John Ford Papers are housed in the Lilly Library at Indiana University. There are several biographies of Ford, among them Peter Bogdanovich, *John Ford* (1978); Dan Ford, *Pappy* (1979); Andrew Sinclair, *John Ford* (1979); and Tad Gallagher, *John Ford* (1986). See also Peter Bogdanovich, *Directed by John Ford* (1971). An obituary appears in the *New York Times*, Sept. 1, 1973.]

LOUIS PHILLIPS

FOSDICK, RAYMOND BLAINE (June 9, 1883–July 18, 1972), lawyer, was born in Buffalo, N.Y., to Frank ("Pop") Sheldon Fosdick, a liberal high school principal, and Amie Inez Weaver. His brother, Harry Emerson Fosdick, later a prominent Baptist minister, preceded him by five years. Fosdick grew up in a progressive home. Sunday dinner discussions centered around Darwinism, Spencerism, and other ideas that seemed to run counter to his Baptist upbringing. From these early discussions he learned that "the life of the spirit is not dependent upon the obscurantisms of orthodoxy, and that moral values and ideals do not require the abdication of intelligence and critical judgment." For a boy of fourteen, he later wrote,

this realization "was an amazing discovery."

Fosdick attended Colgate University from 1901 to 1903 and then transferred to Princeton, from which he received his B.A. degree in 1905 and his M.A. degree in 1906. While at Princeton, he began a warm and friendly relationship with Professor Woodrow Wilson. To the displeasure of the future American president, Fosdick resigned a doctoral fellowship and enrolled in New York Law School from which he graduated in 1908 with a LL.B. degree. While studying law he worked with Lillian Wald at the Henry Street Settlement in exchange for room and board. After being admitted to the bar, he became assistant corporation counsel for the City of New York under Mayor George B. McClellan (son of the Civil War general). In this capacity Fosdick investigated everything from overcrowding in motion-picture theaters to loan sharking. In 1910, after the election of William J. Gaynor as mayor, Fosdick became commissioner of accounts. During his time with the city he acquired a reputation as a reformer and a graft-buster. While investigating prostitution he made the acquaintance of John D. Rockefeller, who headed a grand jury investigation into the same matter. Though he did not know it at the time, he was destined to spend most of his life administering Rockefeller family projects and philanthropies.

In 1912, Fosdick accepted Woodrow Wilson's offer to become comptroller and auditor of the national Democratic party. After Wilson's election as president that year Rockefeller suggested that Fosdick undertake a comprehensive study of European police systems. The investigation took Fosdick to all the major European countries except Russia. He published the results of his cross-cultural study in 1914 as *European Police Systems*. He also began a study of the American police system but did not complete this work until 1920 because his research was interrupted by the events surrounding World War I. In 1916, he agreed to become Secretary of War Newton D. Baker's special representative to the expedition against Pancho Villa commanded by General John J. Pershing. Fosdick's efforts improved recreational services available to troops and rid the army camps of many prostitution and alcohol-related problems. The day after the United States declared war on Germany, Fosdick, now chairman of the Commission on Training Camp Activities of the War and Navy Departments, went to Canada to study and report on Canadian training methods. He also inspected practices in Britain and France. As a result, the committee improved ways of training U.S. military personnel. In 1918, in collaboration with E. F. Allen, he published *Keeping Our Fighters Fit*. Later that year he was sent as special representative of the War Department to France, where he served as the civilian aide to General Pershing.

President Wilson appointed Fosdick the first undersecretary of the League of Nations in 1919. Fosdick accepted the post without pay, for the United States was not yet a member of the international group. When the Senate refused to ratify the League of Nations Covenant, thereby keeping the United States out of the League, Fosdick resigned in disappointment. He returned to the United States to found the New York law firm of Curtis, Fosdick, and Belknap; John D. Rockefeller was his first client. Still an active supporter of the League, Fosdick founded the League of Nations Association. He was also very active in philanthropic work. By 1930 he served on the boards of seven public service organizations, most of which were associated with Rockefeller family philanthropies.

Fosdick had married Winifred Finlay on Dec. 2, 1910. On Apr. 3, 1932, his wife fatally shot herself and their two children. Fosdick later wrote of the tragedy, "It takes time to recover from such a blow . . . one lives with the eternal question, unanswered and unanswerable: *Why? Why?*"

Although he was not a teetotaler, Fosdick published *Toward Liquor Control* (1933), the result of a twelve-country study begun at the request of Rockefeller. Among other things, his study recommended establishment of state liquor authorities with a monopoly on the liquor trade and elimination of all but federal taxation.

On Apr. 21, 1936, he married Elizabeth R. Miner. That same year the Rockefeller Foundation elected him president as did the Rockefeller General Education Board. In this dual capacity he sought to keep the activities of the two from overlapping. As foundation president, Fosdick ran the organization with "a note of crispness and dispatch," according to *Time* magazine. Under Fosdick, the foundation funded a number of scientific programs, among them, halting the spread of the malaria-carrying *Anopheles gambiae* mosquito in Brazil, creating

a yellow fever vaccine, and supporting fundamental research that helped lead to the Manhattan Project. Fosdick actively traveled to foundation offices around the world until the outbreak of World War II. The General Education Board promoted medical education, helped to support a number of historically black colleges, and funded special education programs. Under Fosdick's direction the Rockefeller Foundation continued to fund scholarship and research in Allied and neutral countries during the war.

Throughout his life Fosdick was an internationalist who worked hard to promote the League of Nations, a world court, and the United Nations as vehicles for peace. In 1944 he wrote, "Must this always be a blood-drenched planet in which civilizations appear as intermittent gleams between periodic convulsions of barbarism?"

In 1948, Fosdick retired to devote his remaining years to writing. He was a prolific author, producing fourteen books and dozens of articles published in periodicals ranging from the *New York Times Magazine* to *Science*. Though a practicing attorney, he had spent most of his life involved in quasi-governmental, philanthropic, and other forms of service activities. He liked to mention that one of his law partners had joked that he "practiced the law only when there wasn't anything more interesting to do." One contemporary described Fosdick as "a good conversationalist, genial, witty, and generous," summing him up as a man "equally popular playing games with children or discussing international affairs with statesmen."

Fosdick died in Newton, Conn.

[Fosdick's papers are at the Princeton University Library. Among his many published works is an autobiography, *Chronicle of a Generation* (1948). An obituary is in the *New York Times*, July 19, 1972.]

DANIEL LIESTMANN

FOX, JACOB NELSON ("NELLIE") (Dec. 25, 1927–Dec. 1, 1975), baseball player, was born in St. Thomas, Pa., the youngest of three sons of Jacob and Mae Fox. His father, a carpenter, was also an amateur baseball player; baseball was an interest that the younger Fox quickly acquired. In 1944, after several indifferent years of playing both baseball and soccer, Fox convinced his parents to take him to the nearby spring-training camp of the Philadelphia

Athletics. His father hoped to convince him that it was too difficult to break into professional baseball. But given the wartime shortage of draft-proof young men, the ploy backfired and Connie Mack immediately signed Fox to a contract.

Thus, Fox dropped out of high school after completing only three of the four quarters of the tenth grade in order to play professional baseball. Fox played four years in the minors, except for a brief period of time after he was drafted in 1946, when he served in Korea driving a small landing craft in Ichon Harbor. Upon his return to the United States he resumed his baseball career in earnest. He also married his childhood friend, Joanne Statler, in June 1948. They had two daughters.

Fox began his baseball career playing first base, but was quickly converted to a second baseman. He played in the minors in 1947 and 1948, ending each season with the Athletics, with whom he played for all of 1949 until he was traded in October to the Chicago White Sox. There, he established himself in fourteen seasons (1950–1963) as the premier second baseman of the era. Ironically, at the outset he broke almost every rule while playing the position. But after some stern lessons from one of his coaches, he perfected the pivot at the bag in making double plays.

Fox's career remains an example of how players with relatively modest talents, by a combination of work, enthusiasm, and hustle, can make a significant impact on the sport. A durable athlete, he played in 798 consecutive games, which was a record for second basemen. He was third on the all-time list for total games played at this position (2,295). Although possessed of an indifferent throwing arm, he was one of the best fielders in major-league history, winning four Gold Glove awards for his accomplishments. At the end of the 1992 season he still held the major-league record for the most years leading second basemen in putouts (10) and the most years leading second basemen in total chances (9). He also still held the American League record for career double plays (1,568) and the American League record (tied with four others) for years leading in double plays (5).

Although Fox threw right-handed, he batted left-handed. At the plate he was consistent if not spectacular. His career batting average was .288 and he hit over .300 in six seasons. He holds the American League record for the most seasons with 600 or more at-bats (12). His principal characteristic was accuracy, however, not power. His bat itself, shaped like a milk bottle, not only set him apart from others but enabled him to scatter hits around the field. He led the American League 13 times for the fewest strikeouts in a season. Fox was a key contributor to the team in 1959, when the White Sox went to the World Series for the first time since the infamous Black Sox scandal of 1919. His accomplishments that year earned him the Most Valuable Player Award. In his career he also played in 15 All-Star games.

Extremely well liked in Chicago, Fox was easily recognizable on the field. He consistently had a red bandana in his pocket and a wad of chewing tobacco in his mouth, a habit that he developed in order to calm his nerves. Working in the days before superstar salaries, he reportedly earned $22,500 in 1955, plus product endorsements estimated at $4,000.

In 1964, Fox was traded to the Houston Astros, where he played two seasons before retiring to return home to his native Pennsylvania. He resumed his baseball service when he was hired late in 1965 as a coach with the Houston Astros. Ted Williams hired him as a coach of the Washington Senators for the 1968 season, and he remained with that club through its 1973 season after it had become the Texas Rangers. Thereafter, in retirement, Fox owned a bowling alley in Pennsylvania and lived quietly. He died in Baltimore of malignant melanoma, a skin cancer resulting from his many years in the sun. After his death the Chicago White Sox retired his jersey with its familiar number 2. It was only the second number to be retired by the club in its history to that time.

[Articles about Jacob Fox include W. B. Furlong, "He Ain't Big, but He's All Fire," *Saturday Evening Post*, May 14, 1955; and "Nellie's Needle," *Time*, Dec. 15, 1975. An obituary appears in the *New York Times*, Dec. 2, 1975; supplemental information can be found in the *New York Times*, May 2, 1976.]

CHARLES R. MIDDLETON

FRAZER, JOSEPH WASHINGTON (Mar. 4, 1892–Aug. 7, 1971), automobile pioneer, was born in Nashville, Tenn., the son of James S. Frazer, attorney for the Louisville-Nashville Railroad, and Mary Washington. After attending the Nashville Day School, Frazer went to the Hotchkiss Academy in Connecticut and then to the Sheffield Scientific School at Yale, from which he graduated in 1911. He then sought a position in Detroit as a mechanic's helper at the Packard Motor Car Company, for which his brother was a dealer. He began his career working on the shop floor, but almost from the first Frazer gravitated toward sales.

In November 1914, Frazer married Lucille Frost of Chicago; they had one child. That year he took a sales position at Packard's New York City agency, transferring to his brother's dealership in Nashville in 1915. By 1916, he had his own Saxon Motor dealership in Cleveland, Ohio. Sorely in need of executive talent, General Motors (GM) hired Frazer in 1919. He remained with the company until 1923, serving first in sales. Ultimately he became treasurer of General Motors Export Division, where he helped form General Motors Acceptance Corporation. In 1923, GM loaned Frazer to Pierce-Arrow in Buffalo, N.Y., in order to establish a credit agency for that auto company.

Walter Chrysler, engaged in resurrecting Maxwell-Chalmers Motors Company, hired Frazer to head Maxwell sales, and he stayed on when Chrysler absorbed the company into the Chrysler Corporation in 1925. As vice-president of the Chrysler sales division and vice-president of the Plymouth Division, Frazer became one of the industry's most prominent executives. In 1939, he resigned from Chrysler to become president and general manager of Willys-Overland Motors, Inc., in Toledo, Ohio, makers of low-price cars. He staved off bankruptcy, increasing sales by 60 percent in his first year there. When World War II began in Europe, Willys entered the competition to produce a general utility vehicle for the United States Army. Another company, American Bantam, won the contest, but Ford and Willys also built the vehicle, which became the famous Jeep. As a result of Jeep sales, Willys's sales rose from $9 million to $170 million during the war.

Frazer left Willys in 1944 to become president of the Warren City Tank and Boiler Co., in Ohio, a subsidiary of the Graham-Paige Motor Corp. He reformed the company into Warren City Manufacturing. Through an exchange of stock, Frazer and his associates became majority owners of Graham-Paige, and Frazer himself became chairman and president.

In 1945, Frazer was introduced to Henry Kaiser, one of the nation's premier industrialists,

who was considering entering the automobile business. Graham-Paige was strapped for cash, and Kaiser needed the help of people who understood the industry. The two businessmen quickly agreed to organize the Kaiser-Frazer Corporation, to be jointly owned by Henry J. Kaiser Company and Graham-Paige. They started with $5 million in capital, half contributed by each partner; the sale of Kaiser-Frazer stock fetched another $53 million. The company planned to produce two cars—the Kaiser and the Frazer.

Kaiser knew next to nothing about automobiles, though, and Frazer had never worked in production. In 1941, the last full year of American car production before the war, Graham-Paige had turned out only 544 cars, of an industry total of 3,779,600. Nonetheless they proceeded. With government help, the company purchased the huge Ford Willow Run plant in Michigan, which they planned to transform from a manufacturer of military aircraft to the world's largest automobile plant. The plan was to produce Kaisers at Willow Run and the more expensive Frazers at the Graham-Paige plant.

The Kaiser-Frazer strategy was to come to market as rapidly as possible with a revolutionary car. (The big three auto companies, by contrast, had to convert their military plants and produce virtually the same models they presented in 1941.) This approach gave Kaiser-Frazer a beachhead from which it could expand rapidly. The initial shipments were made in June 1946, and from the beginning, demand was high. The company produced fewer than 12,000 cars in 1946, but in 1947 it turned out 144,000, making it the industry's fourth-largest carmaker, ahead of such firms as Studebaker, Nash, and Hudson. But with only 4 percent of production, Kaiser-Frazer fell far short of General Motors, Ford, and Chrysler.

In 1948, as the manufacture of Kaisers and Frazers increased but as the big three began to come out with flashier vehicles, Kaiser-Frazer Corporation stumbled. In 1949, production was a mere 58,000. Undeterred, the company produced two entirely different cars for the 1951 model year. Long, low, and sleek, the Kaiser Deluxe was one of the most attractive cars of the era. The other car was the Henry J, a four-cylinder that in its design was a decade ahead of its time. Kaiser-Frazer was an industry innovator, bringing out a hatchback sedan and a hard-top long before anyone else. But sales nevertheless remained sluggish. In 1954, only 17,000 cars were produced. In 1955, the company's last year of business, production came to under 6,000.

Frazer left the organization in 1953, largely because of his feeling that Kaiser was shunting him aside to take a more active role in management. He spent most of his remaining years as a consultant. He also became interested in aeronautics and attempted to develop and import the British Allard Palm Beach roadster. He retired to Newport, R.I., in the early 1960's and died there.

[Biographical information can be found in Richard M. Langworth, *Kaiser-Frazer* (1975). For details about Frazer's career see also Jerry Flint, *The Dream Machine* (1976); Brock Yates, *The Decline and Fall of the American Automobile Industry* (1983); and Robert Sobel, *Car Wars* (1984). An obituary appears in the *New York Times*, Aug. 8, 1971.]

ROBERT SOBEL

FREED, ARTHUR (Sept. 9, 1894–Apr. 12, 1973), motion-picture producer and lyricist, was born in Charleston, S.C., one of eight children of Max Freed, an art dealer, and Rosa Grossman. Freed attended public schools in Seattle, Wash., and graduated from Phillips Exeter Academy, in Exeter, N.H., in 1914. He went to work in Tin Pan Alley and also performed in vaudeville. Freed joined the army and staged military shows during World War I. He then returned to vaudeville and wrote songs for nightclub revues. He married Renee Klein on Mar. 14, 1923, and the couple had one child.

In 1921, Freed began collaborating with composer Ignacio ("Nacio") Herb Brown. Their first recording, "When Buddah Smiles," sold more than one million copies. In 1927, Freed and Brown wrote "Singin' in the Rain" for a stage musical that Freed was producing in Los Angeles, *The Hollywood Music Box Revue*. Freed later recalled that he wrote the song in about an hour and a half, but it would eventually become the pair's best-known number.

Freed and Brown joined Metro-Goldwyn-Mayer studios (MGM) in 1929 as lyricist and composer, respectively, for MGM's first all-sound musical, *The Broadway Melody. Hollywood Revue* (1929) featured the motion-picture debut of "Singin' in the Rain." The song was later sung by Judy Garland in *Little Nellie Kelly* (1940) and was the title song for what many critics regard as the best movie musical of all time, *Singin' in the Rain* (1952). Freed and Brown wrote songs for more than two dozen other MGM films and many became popular standards, including "Temptation," "All I Do Is Dream of You," and "You Were Meant for Me."

In 1938, Freed persuaded MGM president Louis B. Mayer to acquire film rights to L. Frank Baum's novel *The Wizard of Oz* and asked to be the film's producer. Mayer instead offered Freed the opportunity to try out as the film's assistant producer. The role of Dorothy was given to newcomer Judy Garland, whom Freed had discovered and brought under contract to MGM. Before *The Wizard of Oz* was finished, Mayer allowed Freed to begin work as the producer of *Babes in Arms*. Freed selected Mickey Rooney and Judy Garland as the leads, and it became one of the studio's biggest-grossing films in 1939. Freed produced several other "backstage musicals" featuring Rooney and Garland, including *Strike Up the Band* (1940), *Babes on Broadway* (1941), and *Girl Crazy* (1943).

Freed led the movie musical into a new era when he persuaded Vincente Minnelli to join his musical production unit to direct *Cabin in the Sky* (1943) and *Meet Me in St. Louis* (1944). Thereafter, Minnelli or former choreographer Stanley Donen directed virtually all of Freed's greatest films: *Easter Parade* (1948); *On the Town* (1949); *Annie Get Your Gun* (1950); *An American in Paris* (1951), which won an Academy Award for best picture; *Show Boat* (1951); *Singin' in the Rain* (1952); *The Band Wagon* (1953); *Silk Stockings* (1957); and *Gigi* (1958), which also won an Academy Award for best picture. All were box-office successes as well as artistic masterpieces, and they defined "the MGM musical." They featured a much greater integration of song and dance into the story line than in previous films and a sumptuous display of color, costume, and stage design.

Freed and his assistant Roger Edens had no hesitation in reaching outside the Hollywood community to obtain the most talented writers, dancers, musicians, designers, and choreographers. The Freed Unit became a virtual ensemble company within MGM, with Freed presiding over Minnelli and Donen, writers Betty Comden and Adolph Green, dancers

Gene Kelly and Fred Astaire, choreographers Michael Kidd and Bob Fosse, composer André Previn, and numerous other top-notch talents.

But while the Freed Unit was perfecting the movie musical, MGM and the motion-picture industry were entering a period of turmoil and decline. Television caused movie audiences to dwindle, and MGM's profits decreased as musicals began to go out of fashion during the 1950's. MGM also began to experience frequent changes of top management, which made it difficult for Freed to produce more big-budget musicals.

As the number of Freed's projects decreased, he devoted more time to his hobby of growing orchids and to other activities more befitting an "elder statesman" of the motion-picture industry. Freed was president of the Motion Picture Academy of Arts and Sciences from 1963 to 1966, and he produced several Academy Award shows. In 1968 he received a special Academy Award for superlative and distinguished service.

Freed spent much of the 1960's attempting to develop a move entitled *Say It with Music*, based on the life and works of Irving Berlin. He resigned from MGM in 1970, shortly after the new studio head, former television executive James T. Aubrey, Jr., canceled work on the project. Shortly thereafter, MGM ceased motion-picture production entirely and concentrated on hotels and real-estate development. Dorothy's ruby-red shoes from *The Wizard of Oz*, the show boat from *Show Boat*, and all of the studio's other costumes and props were put up for auction. The music department's library was incinerated, and the MGM sound stages and back lots were razed and turned into a housing development. Freed died in Hollywood.

In 1974, MGM released *That's Entertainment*, composed of more than two hours of highlights from MGM musicals. It was so successful that MGM followed it with *That's Entertainment, Part II* (1976).

[The Arthur Freed Collection is located at the Doheny Library, University of Southern California, Los Angeles, Calif., which also has the Roger Edens Papers and the MGM Script Collection. Interviews with Freed and other MGM personnel are included in the Popular Arts Project of Columbia University's Oral History Program. Many of Freed's productions are available on videocassette. Hugh Fordin, *The World of Entertainment!* (1975), is a comprehensive study of all the movies Freed produced. The creation of two of Freed's productions is analyzed in Donald Knox, *The Magic Factory* (1973); and Aljean Harmetz, *The Making of the Wizard of Oz* (1977). An obituary is in the *New York Times*, Apr. 13, 1973.]

STEPHEN G. MARSHALL

FRIML, CHARLES RUDOLF (Dec. 7, 1879– Nov. 12, 1972), composer and pianist, was born in Prague, Austria-Hungary, the son of Frantisek Friml, a baker, and Marie Kremak. Rudolf's father, an amateur musician, watched over his son's musical development and purchased a small piano for him. At the age of ten Rudolf published his first composition, and at age fourteen he was admitted to the Prague Conservatory of Music, where he studied piano under Josef Jiranek, theory and composition under Josef Foerster, and advanced composition under Antonin Dvořák.

Shortly after his graduation in 1896, Friml was engaged by Jan Kubelik as piano accompanist for his violin recitals. The duo toured Europe with great success between 1897 and 1900; while they were performing in London, impresario Daniel Frohman "happened to attend their concert and signed them up" for an eighty-concert American tour in 1901.

After teaming with Kubelik for a decade, Friml decided to explore the possibility of a virtuoso career by engaging Walter Damrosch's New York Symphony Orchestra to accompany his American solo debut at New York's Carnegie Hall on Nov. 17, 1904. On this program Friml played a number of short pieces and two major works, the Grieg Piano Concerto and his own B Flat Major Piano Concerto, a piece that *New York Times* critic Richard Aldrich called "a thing of shreds and patches." Friml concluded his program by playing an improvisation of a theme submitted from the audience. Although this concert and two solo recitals in Mendelssohn Hall on Dec. 7 and 14, 1904, received mixed reviews, the majority of the critics praised Friml's unique improvisational skills.

In early 1905, Friml rejoined Kubelik for two more seasons before settling permanently in the United States in 1906 to launch his own career. For the next six years Friml gave piano lessons, composed, performed in solo recitals, and appeared on an occasional symphony program. During this time he was billed as "the greatest improvisateur since Mozart," and while admitting later that "it was very silly," his improvisational playing often gave him a competitive edge in the struggle for artistic survival.

In 1912, Friml obtained national recognition through a fortunate circumstance. Victor Herbert had been hired by producer Arthur Hammerstein to write an operetta expressly for soprano Emma Trentini. Before Herbert could write the music though, the temperamental and uncooperative diva so incensed Herbert that he vowed to have nothing further to do with her. A composer had to be found on short notice, and Friml was engaged by Hammerstein upon the recommendation of music publishers Max Dreyfus and Rudolph Schirmer.

The resulting *Firefly*, whose musical score Friml composed in less than a month, opened in New York on Dec. 12, 1912 for a 120-performance run. Its many popular tunes, such as "Giannina Mia" and "Sympathy," established Friml's reputation and launched a meteoric career in which he wrote thirty-three operettas between 1912 and 1934, eleven in conjunction with lyricist Otto Harbach.

Friml reached the pinnacle of success during the 1920's—he became an American citizen in 1925—with *Rose Marie*, which opened on Sept. 2, 1924, for a 557-performance run; *The Vagabond King*, on Sept. 21, 1925, for a 511-performance run; and *The Three Musketeers*, on March 13, 1928, for a 319-performance run.

Musical tastes soon changed though, and the depression years of the early 1930's ushered in the age of the musical comedy. Friml's compositional style, which utilized "a full-bodied libretto with luscious melody, rousing choruses and romantic passions," became passé. The public now preferred comedic plots in contemporary settings with ongoing stage action.

Friml refused to adjust to the times. To him a Broadway musical was "a play with a little music" which, instead of featuring "pure rich voices," employed "a lot of voiceless people" trying to "do everything in singing, dancing and talking." Consequently, after the failure of his last two operettas, *Luana* in 1930 and *Music Hath Charms* in 1934, Friml moved to Hollywood, where he spent the next decade adapting his operettas to the screen and composing music for *Music for Madame* (1937) and *Northwest Outpost* (1947). His two most successful film efforts were *Rose-Marie* (1936), starring Nelson Eddy and Jeanette MacDonald, and *Firefly* (1937), featuring tenor Allan Jones, whose re-cording of the movie's "Donkey Serenade" sold more than a million copies.

Friml devoted the post–World War II years to composing and performing his own music. During his lifetime he wrote thousands of pieces for, as Otto Harbach marveled, Friml "poured melody out of his sleeve." And although most of his concert music "was never performed or recorded," Friml published numerous classical works, including a song cycle, an Easter cantata, two piano concerti, three orchestral suites, and a "Round the World Symphony."

Friml performed and conducted throughout Europe in the 1950's and 1960's, including a U.S. State Department–sponsored tour in 1963, but he was "particularly in love with the Orient," and traveled there many times.

A short, dapper man with a pencil-thin mustache, Friml, through proper diet and exercise, retained his physical vigor to the end of his life. A charter member (1914) of ASCAP, his music has been recorded by RCA Victor, Columbia, and Decca. In 1971, he was elected to the Songwriters' Hall of Fame and in 1972 to the Theater Hall of Fame.

Friml was married four times. In 1909, he married Mathilde Baruch; they had two children and divorced in 1915. He then wed Blanche Betters, with whom he had no children and whom he divorced in 1919. He then married Elsie Lawson in 1919, with whom he had one child; they were divorced in the mid-1920's. Finally, he married his Chinese-born secretary, Kay Ling, in 1952; they had no children. Friml died in Los Angeles.

[Biographical sources include David Ewen, *Composers for the American Musical Theatre* (1968) and *American Songwriters* (1987); Stanley Green, *The World of Musical Comedy* (1974); *High Fidelity Magazine*, Nov. 1972. A 1958 Westminster recording, *Friml Plays Friml*, contains conversational recollections of his career, and he displays his improvisational skill in the recording *The Great Rudolf Friml*. Obituaries appear in the London *Times*, the *New York Times*, and the *Washington Post*, Nov. 14, 1972.]

LOUIS R. THOMAS

FRISCH, FRANK FRANCIS ("THE FORDHAM FLASH") (Sept. 9, 1898–Mar. 12, 1973), baseball player, was born in the Ozone Park neighborhood of Queens, N.Y., the son of Franz Frisch, a wealthy linen manufacturer, and Katherine Stahl. Born in Frankfurt, Germany, Franz Frisch was a hard-working immigrant who liked baseball and took young Frankie to the Polo Grounds when his own favorite player Honus Wagner appeared with the Pittsburgh Pirates. Frank had three brothers: Charles, who died from appendicitis in his early twenties; and Harold and George, who both joined Franz in the linen business.

Frankie Frisch was raised in the Bedford Park section of the Bronx, N.Y., and attended Fordham Prep and Fordham University for two years. At Fordham, he was the star of the varsity football team and a member of Walter Camp's second-team all-American squad in 1918. His nickname "The Flash" derived from his speed on the gridiron and the basepaths. A natural left-handed batter, Frisch learned to switch-hit at Fordham and batted .476 in his last season at Fordham (1919). While playing baseball, Frisch suffered a severe injury to the middle finger on his right hand, leaving him with a deformed finger. He nevertheless led Fordham to national prominence and under the tutelage of coach Art Devlin, a former third baseman of the New York Giants, signed a contract to play for the Giants in June 1919 at the age of twenty-one, without playing a single game in the minor leagues.

Frisch joined a Giants team managed by the autocratic, verbally abusive John J. McGraw, whose intense desire to win found a willing ear in the young player. Frisch, who always spoke his mind, developed a love-hate relationship with McGraw during his eight seasons with the Giants. McGraw named Frisch team captain in 1924, and Frisch blossomed into an accomplished defensive second baseman, and an outstanding hitter and base runner who regularly finished among the league leaders in batting average, hits, runs scored, and stolen bases.

Standing five feet, eleven inches tall and weighing 165 pounds, Frisch had a thick chest and powerful arms and legs. By 1923, he was an established star earning more than $12,500, a figure believed to be the highest salary in team history. That year he batted a career-high .348 with a league-leading 223 hits and 311 total bases that included thirty-two doubles, ten triples, a career-high twelve home runs and 111 runs batted in. Following that season he married his childhood sweetheart Ada Lucy and moved to New Rochelle, N.Y., in Westchester County. The couple had no children.

Although the Giants won the pennant every season from 1921 to 1924 and Frisch sparkled in each World Series, with a composite batting average of .376, McGraw became disenchanted with the "Fordham Flash." McGraw unleashed a torrent of abuse at Frisch throughout the team's mediocre 1926 season, calling him a "cement head" at one point and blaming him for the team's lackluster performance. The two men squabbled constantly, perhaps because they were so alike—aggressive and outspoken.

Frisch's anger exploded after a game in St. Louis in August 1926 when McGraw questioned his desire to win a game, even though he had played with a severe charley horse. The next day, Frisch left the team and returned to New York. Although McGraw reinstated Frankie, the two men did not speak to each other for many years. Following the season, McGraw traded Frisch to the St. Louis Cardinals for Rogers Hornsby, the six-time National League batting champion and player-manager of the world champions. It was unquestionably the most sensational trade in baseball history up to that time.

The trade shocked fans in St. Louis and provided Frisch with the greatest challenge of his career, but one that he passed with great success. Although Hornsby continued his offensive brilliance with the Giants, Frisch's overall excellence clearly tilted the trade in the Cardinals' favor. Indeed, Frisch finished second in the voting for the league's Most Valuable Player Award, and Hornsby lasted only one season with McGraw in New York before being traded to the Boston Braves.

In 1927, Frisch set a fielding record for assists by a second baseman with 641, a record that has stood for more than forty-five years. He was named the National League's most valuable player in 1931. The nickname Gashouse Gang caught hold in 1934 when *New York Sun* sportswriter Frank Graham overheard Leo Durocher, then the Cardinals' shortstop, say that American Leaguers regarded his teammates as a bunch of gashouse ballplayers because of their dirty uniforms. As leader of the rambunctious Gashouse Gang of Cardinals, Frisch was made a player-manager in 1933, and in the following season piloted the team to the championship in a spirited seven-game series versus the Detroit Tigers. Frisch called his game-winning hit in the decisive seventh game the greatest thrill of his major-league career. Frankie retired after the 1937 season with a .316 lifetime batting average. In seventeen full seasons, he batted over .300 thirteen times and struck out more than eighteen times in a single season only twice. He played in fifty World Series games, the most ever by a National Leaguer, and was elected to baseball's Hall of Fame in 1947.

Frisch's statistics, outstanding though they are, do not tell the complete story of his impact on the game. The "Old Flash," as he referred to himself in later years, drove himself to succeed at any cost. His fierce competitive instincts antagonized opponents and umpires alike while drawing a legion of admiring fans. During ballgames, he wore his emotions on the field.

Frisch's character changed dramatically off the playing field. At home in New Rochelle with his wife Ada, he was an accomplished horticulturist and a devotee of classical music, enjoying particularly the music of Artur Schnabel, the noted pianist, and Richard Wagner. He himself played the violin and the ukulele and liked to dance.

He also had a talent for mimicry that he used to bait umpires while managing the Cardinals (1933–1938), the Pittsburgh Pirates (1940–1946) and the Chicago Cubs (1949–1951). His wonderful sense of humor eased the pain of second-division finishes with the Pirates and Cubs. He once told Casey Stengel, then managing the woeful Boston Braves, "Don't room higher than the second floor on the road. You might want to jump." While managing, he sparred frequently with umpires Beans Reardon and Bill Klem, once carrying an open umbrella to the third base coaching box to remind the umpires that the game should be halted due to rain. Reardon called Frisch "Happy" because Frisch, a hypochondriac, constantly complained about his players or his health.

Frankie Frisch enjoyed a third baseball career, that of broadcast announcer. After leaving the Cardinals, he broadcast Boston Braves games in 1939 and later worked for the New York Giants in 1947–1948, and again after he was fired as manager of the Cubs in 1951. His humor while broadcasting made him extremely popular and his high-pitched nasal voice often lamented, "Oh, those bases on balls"—a Frisch trademark.

Frisch suffered a heart attack in 1956, retired to Quonochontaug on the Rhode Island seashore, and became baseball's unofficial master raconteur. After his heart attack, Frisch quit smoking but could not resist rich food and desserts. His wife Ada died in 1971 and he married Augusta Kass in 1972. While driving from Rhode Island to Florida to attend spring training in February 1973, Frisch suffered critical injuries in a car crash and died five weeks later in Wilmington, Del. He was buried in Woodlawn Cemetery in the Bronx, N.Y.

[The Baseball Hall of Fame Library, Cooperstown, N.Y., contains extensive files on Frisch's career, including his oral reminiscences. For further reading see Frisch's autobiography *Frankie Frisch: The Fordham Flash*, as told to J. Roy Stockton (1962); and a popular biography by St. Louis sportswriter Bob Broeg, *The Pilot Light and the Gas House Gang* (1980). Obituaries appear in the *Saint Louis Post-Dispatch*, Mar. 12, 1973; and in the *New York Times*, Mar. 13, 1973.]

STEPHEN WEINSTEIN

G

GAISMAN, HENRY JAQUES (Dec. 5, 1869–Aug. 6, 1974), inventor and business executive, was born in Memphis, Tenn., to Jaques Gaisman and Sarah Kaufman. The family soon moved to Cincinnati, where Henry received his only formal education in the public schools. He never went to college. Little is now known about his early or middle years. He first came to prominence in 1906 as founder and president of a small manufacturing business in New York, Auto-Strop Safety Razor Company. The clean-shaven look had become fashionable, and Gaisman recognized, as had King Gillette a few years earlier, the increasing demand for safety razors, a product that vastly facilitated shaving. Such razors replaced the old straight razor—essentially a knife honed to a very keen edge. Each time a man shaved, he had to sharpen the blade, which was done on a flexible length of leather or canvas—a strop. Shaving with a straight-edge razor was both tedious and slightly dangerous, so men frequently chose to use the professional services of a barber or did not shave. Gillette invented a razor with a double-edged, disposable blade. His design both eliminated the need for repeated stropping of the straight edge and provided a measure of safety; the blade was held in a housing, which minimized cuts and nicks.

Gaisman, a creative thinker who eventually patented eighty-four inventions, believed many men would prefer to avoid the inconvenience of replacing blades; he designed a single-edge blade that could be easily stropped with a built-in mechanism. Although no detailed information remains, Auto-Strop seems to have been a financially successful firm; in the early 1920's it was paying steady 6-percent dividends and held a small but solid share of the razor business dominated by Gillette.

Gaisman was a very active inventor. He developed a nonslip belt for men's trousers, designed a better carburetor for automobiles, improved cutlery designs and the machine tools to manufacture cutlery, and built specialized photographic devices. His most successful invention was a technique used to write captions on photographic film when a picture was taken; George Eastman of Eastman Kodak bought the technique, called Autographics, for $300,000 in 1914, reportedly the highest price yet paid in America for a single invention.

During these years, Gaisman served on the board of the New York State Reformatories (1911–1919), chaired the safety razor division of the War Industries Board, and served as an expert for both the chief of the Bureau of Research of the General Staff and the Port of New York War Board.

Under Gaisman's direction, Auto-Strop held to a steady if uneventful course. But the 1920's offered new opportunities, in the United States and overseas. Gaisman recognized these opportunities, and in the late 1920's Auto-Strop grew dramatically, expanding from its base of two factories in New York City and Newark, N.J., by adding manufacturing facilities in Toronto, London, and Rio de Janeiro. The company was said to have sales offices "in all principal cities of the world." Auto-Strop reported impressive profits of nearly $1.5 million in 1929.

The basic Gillette patents all expired by the mid-1920's, and Gaisman saw an opportunity to design a superior blade that would fit the millions of Gillette razor handles consumers had bought over the years. He designed such a blade and offered it to Gillette in 1928 for $5 million. Gillette's directors, whose company was more than ten times the size of Auto-Strop

297

and who had long been accustomed to unchallenged dominance of the safety-razor market, took no interest in Gaisman's idea. So Gaisman set himself the task of designing and building a production line for his Probak razor; it came on the market at the end of 1929. The blade had an added advantage: it would fit the standard Gillette handle, but Gillette blades would not fit the Probak handle.

Gillette management finally realized that Gaisman's design had merit. They set to work in 1929 to design their own version; the blade came on the market only months after the Probak. But the Probak was patented, and Gaisman immediately sued for patent infringement. By July 1929, Gillette had learned that the Probak patent would carry the day, and the company sought accommodation. Gaisman agreed to merge Auto-Strop with Gillette in exchange for 310,000 shares of Gillette common stock.

In an audit of each company's books, it was discovered that Gillette's long-standing practice of booking shipments to its foreign subsidiaries as completed sales had, in the declining markets of the previous five years, led to overstating profits by more than $11 million. In the face of such misrepresentation, Gaisman refused to go through with the merger as negotiated; he demanded much more. Gillette had no room to bargain; the company paid Gaisman specially created preferred shares, which paid a guaranteed dividend and came with full voting rights. Gaisman thus received $20 million instead of roughly $3 million, as originally agreed; more significant, he became Gillette's largest shareholder and joined its board of directors.

Within a few months, it was clear that Gillette needed new leadership; Gaisman was elected chairman of the board (1930–1938), and he recruited Gerard Lambert as president (Lambert was the man who made Listerine). Under their combined leadership, Gillette designed and introduced an improved handle (the Goodwill), in which only the Gillette and Probak blades properly fit.

In 1934, Gaisman founded the Inventors Foundation in New York. Its purpose was to give practical guidance to inventors, with particular emphasis on how to protect inventions through patents. Several colleges in the New York area offered the program, which consisted of classes and seminars, including one at New York University that included women.

Gaisman stepped down as chairman of Gillette's board in 1938, the same year Gillette introduced its first electric razor. In 1951, at age 82, he married Catherine Vance, a nursing supervisor at Mount Sinai Hospital who was forty-nine years his junior. Gaisman died in White Plains, N.Y.

[There is no biography of Gaisman, and he left no papers. Information on his life and career can be found in articles in *Business Week*, Nov. 26, 1930, and Apr. 7, 1934; *Fortune*, Oct. 1931; and the *New York Times*, Apr. 30, 1951. See also Russell Adams, *King C. Gillette* (1978). An obituary appears in the *New York Times*, Aug. 7, 1974.]

FRED CARSTENSEN
ELDON BERNSTEIN

GAMBRELL, MARY LATIMER (Jan. 14, 1898–Aug. 19, 1974), historian and college president, was born in Belton, S.C., the only daughter of Macie Amanda Latimer and Enoch Pepper Gambrell. The Gambrells had been prominent in South Carolina for several generations. Her father was a planter, banker, and businessman; two of her four brothers became banking executives in New York City, two of them leading lawyers in Atlanta. Mary Gambrell was educated at home and in the Belton public schools, and received a B.A. in 1917 from Greenville (S.C.) Women's College. (The College subsequently became part of Furman University, which awarded Gambrell a Litt.D. in 1951). From 1918 to 1925 she taught in the preparatory academy of the Women's College; from 1927 to 1930 she taught in the Belton High School. She then began graduate work in history at Columbia University, where Dixon Ryan Fox supervised her M.A. (1931). She received her Ph.D. in 1937, with a dissertation, "Ministerial Training in Eighteenth Century New England," directed by Evarts Greene and John Krout; it was published that year by Columbia University Press.

From 1932 to 1937 she was a popular instructor of History at New Haven State Teachers' College. Described by an administrator as "forceful, pleasing, dignified and charming," she was soon made department chairman. In 1942, she gave the commencement address at New Haven; published under the title of "Old Wine in New Bottles" in *Vital Speeches*, it foreshadowed her lifelong commitment to traditional cultural and educational values and practices.

When, in 1937, she learned of a faculty appointment to be made at New York's Hunter College, she determined to "do all that I can with dignity" to be appointed. In those years, few universities and almost no men's colleges appointed women to the faculty. Those women appointed to women's colleges (as Hunter was then) had little prospect of a subsequent appointment elsewhere. Gambrell remained at Hunter for thirty years until her retirement in 1967. As instructor in history (1937–1944), assistant professor (1944–1949), associate professor (1949–1953), and professor (1953–1967), she was an effective teacher; her most popular course was on American cultural history.

Like so many of the gifted female historians in the Northeast, she was a member of the Berkshire Conference of Women Historians and served as its president from 1947 to 1949. The group, she argued, was not "dedicated to any program"; it should not act like a "pressure group." Neither then nor later was she an outspoken feminist. But she greatly valued the friendships the conference promoted. On occasion she traveled in Europe with Margaret Judson of Douglass College, whom she had met at a Berkshire meeting.

Hunter College early recognized her administrative abilities. She served as chairman of the Department of History between 1948 and 1962. When her history department colleague, John Meng, was named president of Hunter, Gambrell assumed the "number two" role of dean of faculties from 1961 to 1966. A history department colleague remembered that "hers was a commanding presence. Innate dignity and a sense of authority and purposefulness evoked immediate recognition." She believed in orderly process. She put particular stress on the rights and obligations of the faculty, whom she regarded as "the embodiment of the college."

A defining moment for Gambrell occurred in 1967. Two years earlier, she had served as acting president during a short leave that Meng had secured. In the spring of 1966 Meng had resigned, and Gambrell was again asked to serve as acting president. When it became clear that the man chosen to succeed Meng would not be able to take office until the summer of 1967, Gambrell decided to be formally inaugurated president for the intervening months. The ceremony did not appreciably increase Gambrell's authority. But it reflected the appreciation of the college for thirty years of distinguished service, as other deans and presidents had come and gone. Furthermore, she was, Meng declared at the inauguration, the first woman to head a major coeducational college in the United States.

As department chairman, dean, acting president, and president, Gambrell helped Hunter adjust to the admission of male students; she lobbied for a dramatic expansion of space at the Park Avenue campus; planned for the Bronx campus to become Lehman College; arranged for a new building for social work—all the while remaining intimately involved in a college of over 25,000 students. She was unflappable; when a security guard called her in the early morning hours to report that a fire had broken out at Hunter, her response was: "put it out."

Gambrell retired in June 1967. That fall, the New York City chapter of the American Association of University Women named her Woman of the Year. In 1974 Furman University named the freshmen women's dormitory Gambrell Hall in recognition of her professional distinction, the contributions she and her brothers had made to Furman, and her service on the university's council. But her true monument was her career at Hunter College and its triumphant conclusion.

[There is a box of Gambrell's papers in the Archives of Hunter College, City University of New York. An obituary is in the *New York Times*, Aug. 21, 1974.]

ROBERT D. CROSS

GANZ, RUDOLPH (Feb. 24, 1877–Aug. 2, 1972), pianist, composer, conductor, and pedagogue, was born in Zurich, Switzerland, the son of Rudolf Ganz and Sophie Bartenfeld. His father was a photographer, as were his grandfather and great-grandfather; one of his three brothers became a prominent art historian.

Ganz attended the Zurich Conservatory from 1889 to 1893, studying cello with Friedrich Hegar and the piano with Robert Freund. He gave his first public performance as a cellist in 1889. From 1893 to 1896, he studied piano with his granduncle, Carl Eschmann-Dumur, and composition with Charles Blanchet at the Lausanne Conservatory. For his graduation performance he played Beethoven's Piano Concerto no. 3 with the Lausanne Municipal Orchestra.

Ganz then continued his studies at the Strasbourg Conservatory from 1896 to 1899, studying piano with Fritz Blumer and organ with Ernst Münch. In 1899, he traveled to Berlin to study piano with Ferruccio Busoni and composition with Heinrich Urban; on December 7 of that year he performed Beethoven's Emperor Concerto and Chopin's Piano Concerto no. 1 with the Berlin Philharmonic Orchestra. In 1900, he conducted the premiere of his own Symphony no. 1 in E with the Berlin Philharmonic. His multifaceted musical career as pianist, composer, and conductor was established at that time.

In 1900, Ganz was invited to join the piano department at Chicago Musical College. In July of that year he married Mary Forrest, an American singer who was studying in Berlin, and they moved to Chicago together in September. They had one child.

Ganz taught at Chicago Musical College until 1905. During these years he also performed frequently, presenting the American premieres of works by such contemporary European composers as d'Indy and Ravel. From 1905 to 1921, Ganz toured throughout Europe and North America. The Ganz family had moved to New York in 1905; from 1906 to 1914, they made their home in Berlin, moving back to New York in 1914 when World War I broke out.

In 1921, Ganz was appointed conductor and music director of the St. Louis Symphony Orchestra, a position he held until 1927. During these years he also performed as guest conductor with such orchestras as the Los Angeles Philharmonic and the New York Philharmonic. He became a naturalized American citizen in 1925.

In 1928, Ganz returned to Chicago, resuming his teaching activities at Chicago Musical College. He served as president of the college from 1934 to 1954, when it became part of Roosevelt University; he continued to serve there as professor emeritus from 1954 to 1972. Although he resided permanently in Chicago from 1928 on, Ganz continued to tour as a pianist and conductor. From 1939 to 1948, he was conductor of the New York Philharmonic's Young People's Concerts. In 1956, his wife died, and in 1959 he married Esther La Berge, a concert singer and member of the voice faculty at Roosevelt University.

Ganz was active in all areas of his musical career until his death. He composed several hundred musical works, including songs, solo piano pieces, and chamber and orchestral works. The orchestral arrangement of his work Animal Pictures was premiered by the Detroit Symphony Orchestra in 1933; his Piano Concerto in E-flat Major, op. 32, was commissioned and premiered by the Chicago Symphony Orchestra under Frederick Stock in 1941; "Laughter—Yet Love, Symphonic Overture to an Unwritten Comedy," was commissioned and premiered by the Cincinnati Symphony Orchestra in 1950.

As conductor and pianist, Ganz premiered and promoted the works of many of his contemporaries, including Ravel, Claude Debussy, Béla Bartók, Aaron Copland, Jacques Ibert, Alexander Tcherepnin, Arthur Honegger, and Louis Gruenberg. He was awarded the French Legion of Honor in 1923 in recognition of his efforts to introduce the works of Ravel and Debussy to American audiences. In 1962, he and his wife presented the world premiere of some early songs by Anton von Webern. Among the composers who dedicated works to Ganz were Busoni, Charles Tomlinson Griffes, Tcherepnin, and Arnold Schönberg.

Ganz edited numerous publications, including editions of the sonatas for violin and piano by Beethoven, Johannes Brahms, and Edvard Grieg (with violinist Leopold Auer), as well as works by Chopin, Liszt, Mendelssohn, Ravel, Schubert, and Webern. He authored *Rudolph Ganz Evaluates Modern Piano Music* (1968) and in 1964 contributed to a revision of Ernest Hutcheson's book *The Literature of the Piano*.

Ganz was the recipient of numerous honors and awards. His long association with Chicago Musical College was commemorated by the naming of the Rudolph Ganz Recital Hall at Roosevelt University in 1957, and his contribution to the musical life of Chicago was acknowledged by a special award from Mayor Richard S. Daley in 1964. He died in Chicago.

[Ganz's papers are housed in the Newberry Library in Chicago. An unpublished catalog, "The Musical Works of Rudolph Ganz" (1990), has been compiled by Donald Draganski, music librarian at Roosevelt University. Several volumes of his songs, including *A Season Cycle of Songs* and *Ten Songs*, op. 8, were reissued in 1986. Ganz made numerous recordings on the reproducing piano for Welte, Duo-Art, Triphonola, and other companies from about 1913 to the early 1920's. For a listing, see Larry Sitsky, *The Classical Reproducing Piano Roll* (1990). Some of the Welte piano roll recordings were reissued on the recording *Rudolph Ganz Performs in 1913* (Recorded Treasures, 1964). See also *A 90th Anniversary Trib-*

ute to Rudolph Ganz (Veritas, 1967), for his radio broadcasts from the 1950's.

A biography, *Rudolph Ganz*, by Jeanne Colette Collester (the daughter of Esther La Berge) is in press. See also Olga Kuehl and Dorothy Packard, "Remembering Rudolph Ganz," *Clavier*, Oct. 1972; and Elizabeth Weber Hornick, "The Songs of Rudolph Ganz" (Ph.D. diss., University of Illinois at Urbana-Champaign, 1980). An obituary appears in the *New York Times*, Aug. 3, 1974.]

JANE GOTTLIEB

GAYLORD, EDWARD KING (Mar. 5, 1873– May 31, 1974), newspaper publisher, was the son of George Lewis Gaylord and Eunice Edwards. He was born on a farm near Muscotah, Kans., but his father grew tired of fighting drought and grasshoppers and moved the family to Grand Junction, Colo., in 1879. After working at farm chores and as a store clerk, Gaylord enrolled at Colorado College, where he joined the debating society and was editor and business manager of the college newspaper. In his junior year, Gaylord joined his brother Lewis in the purchase of a local newspaper with a $6,000 loan from a Missouri banker who was impressed with the young man's business acumem. The venture was successful from the outset; the brothers sold the newspaper for a handsome profit and moved to St. Joseph, Mo., where they purchased another journal, for which Gaylord again served as business manager.

During the Christmas holidays in 1902, Gaylord read a newspaper article telling of opportunities in the Oklahoma Territory. Within days, he took a train to Oklahoma City, Okla., a small village that was trying to become capital of the prospective state over the claims of the territorial seat at Guthrie. With two partners he purchased an interest in the *Daily Oklahoman* (circulation 3,500) early in 1903, and the newspaper soon moved to new headquarters with a larger press. Gaylord used "extra" editions to build circulation as he campaigned for removal of the capital to Oklahoma City. The Indian and Oklahoma territories were combined in 1907, and Oklahoma was admitted to the Union—another reason for an "extra," as was the 1910 referendum that moved the capital to Oklahoma City.

Statehood found Gaylord in full control of his newspaper, with a new printing plant on North Broadway that would become the focus of financial and political power in Oklahoma for several generations. In 1911 he took control of the weekly *Farmer-Stockman*, and in 1916 he purchased the bankrupt *Times*, thus adding an afternoon newspaper to his profitable enterprises. On Dec. 29, 1914, he married Inez Kennedy, ending his membership in a bachelors' group of ten known as the Pickwick Club. In time, a son and two daughters were born to the couple.

Gaylord's conservative nature was reflected in his newspapers' policies. He was an energetic booster for his community and for the petroleum and cattle industries that were the mainstays of the state's economy. Gaylord invested in oil leases and livestock himself, and in 1928 he purchased radio station WKY, despite his advisers' warnings that linking a newspaper with a radio station would lose money for both. Within two years, the radio station was making a profit; in 1949, he obtained a license for the first Oklahoma television station, WKY-TV.

Gaylord was instrumental in bringing new sources of water to Oklahoma City when the dwindling supply from local wells hindered the town's growth. He led a group of business leaders who promoted a $1.5 million bond issue in 1916 that provided for a reservoir, and in 1959 he was a leading voice in the construction of Lake Atoka with a hundred-mile pipeline to carry water to his hometown. Early on, Gaylord saw the need for a meat-packing industry close to the sources of range cattle, and he urged the building of a large stockyard on the western edge of Oklahoma City. A link with railroads already existed, but he was also instrumental in bringing several railroads to Oklahoma City so that, in the 1920's, four competing lines offered both freight and passenger service to the state capital. When the presence of railroad tracks cut the downtown district into inconvenient sections, Gaylord spearheaded a drive to move the tracks eastward, and the present-day civic center in Oklahoma City was built on land vacated by the railroads.

While his business ventures flourished, Gaylord at times found himself at odds with organized labor and the state's voters. When William H. ("Alfalfa Bill") Murray ran for governor in 1930, Gaylord accused him of being "an unconscionable liar" unfit for office. Murray won and the two reconciled when the governor ordered the National Guard to occupy a toll bridge on the Texas-Oklahoma border. Gaylord became an opponent of Franklin D. Roosevelt's New Deal, and his editorials endorsed Republican candidates even as the Democrats' power in Oklahoma gradually eroded through elections in the years following World War II.

Along with his oil and cattle investments, Gaylord started a trucking company to carry his newspaper to the furthest reaches of the state. He also bought television stations in Texas, Florida, and Wisconsin.

In addition to gifts to Colorado College, Gaylord showed a personal interest in the education of his employees' children. Associates told of his announcing scholarships for staff members, or making loans to an employee and then raising the man's salary to match the loan. He also gave large sums to the Oklahoma Educational Television Authority as anonymous gifts, but the source was revealed at a Federal Communications Commission hearing regarding another matter. On his ninetieth birthday Gaylord became the first publisher to produce an American newspaper entirely by computerized typesetting, and in 1974 he predicted the demise of printing "as we now know it." On his one-hundredth birthday, Gaylord spoke to a joint session of the Oklahoma legislature.

His wife died in 1974. Gaylord continued to manage his many interests until, at the age of 101, he died at his home in Oklahoma City. He was buried there after a funeral that included eulogies from President Richard M. Nixon and the Oklahoma congressional delegation.

[Gaylord's business correspondence is kept at the Oklahoma Publishing Company headquarters in Oklahoma City, Okla. Obituaries appear in the *Oklahoma City Times*, May 31, 1974; *Daily Oklahoman*, May 31, 1974, and June 1, 1974; and the *New York Times*, June 1, 1974.]

ROBERT A. RUTLAND

GERBER, DANIEL FRANK (May 6, 1898–Mar. 16, 1974), industrialist, was born in Fremont, Mich., the son of Daniel Frank Gerber and Dora Pauline Pratt. He was known as Daniel, while his father was known as Frank. Frank Gerber helped to establish the Fremont Canning Company in 1901 and devoted his full energy to it after an earlier family business, a tannery in Douglas, Mich., closed in 1905. He had invested in the canning company in anticipation of a decline in tanning as Michigan's lumbering era drew to a close. Frank and his father simply shifted from tanning to food processing.

The Fremont Canning Company was a small-town business serving a local market and drawing on local farmers for produce. Beginning in 1914, during a brief recession that lowered the cost of construction, Frank expanded the plant and began year-round production rather than canning only after the harvest. In 1917, when Frank succeeded his father as president of the firm, its sales topped the million-dollar mark for the first time. Following a brief decline at the end of World War I, the firm entered a period of steady growth, still focused on canning the peas, beans, and small fruits of local farmers.

After graduating from St. John's Military Academy in Delafield, Wis., in 1916, Gerber entered the U.S. Army and served in Europe during World War I. He was awarded the croix de guerre. After his discharge he spent a year at the Babson Institute of Business Administration in Massachusetts. In 1920, he joined the Fremont Canning Company as a salesman, rising to first vice-president by 1928. He married Dorothy Marion Scott on Jan. 18, 1923; they had five children.

In 1928, Gerber added prepared baby food to the company's product line, and the firm's growth thereafter was rapid; within a few years the small-town, fruit-and-vegetable canning firm was a national enterprise. The genesis of the new product came to take on an almost legendary dimension in discussions of the firm's history. According to company lore and literature, the Gerbers were late getting ready for a social function, and Mr. Gerber was complaining about how long it was taking to strain and prepare the baby's food. Mrs. Gerber pointed out that he was the one in the food industry, and if he didn't like the situation, he should do something about it. He did. During the first year, sales of prepared strained baby food exceeded $300,000 and increased steadily thereafter.

The company approached its new product line cautiously, employing scientists in company laboratories to test the nutritional content of the foods and develop new products. The idea of strained food was neither new nor particularly difficult to implement; the obstacle was customer resistance. Since many pediatricians still believed that a liquid diet was preferable during a baby's first year, the market for strained foods had never developed. The work of Gerber's nutritionists was aimed largely at convincing the medical community that the new product was safe and healthful for babies.

Following market studies and testing the products with little Sally Gerber, the new line was introduced with an advertising barrage in *Good Housekeeping, Children,* and the *Journal of the American Medical Association.* The famous "Gerber Baby," a sketch by Dorothy Hope Smith, was introduced both to reassure mothers and to provide product identification. The company also published pamphlets on topics in home economics and nutrition to win people over to the new idea of prestrained, prepared baby foods. It also worked with farmers to improve the crops that went into the baby foods. Gerber's scientific and educational efforts won quick acceptance for its products.

Sales of baby food increased steadily through the Great Depression, and by 1941 Gerber's baby food sales exceeded its "adult" food sales. The name of the firm was changed to the Gerber Products Company in 1941, and in 1943 Gerber began producing baby food exclusively. As World War II ended and the baby boom began, Gerber was poised for growth. Demand for Gerber products soared, and branch plants were established in California, New York, and Ontario. In 1945, Daniel succeeded his father as president of the firm. Growth and expansion continued, and the family firm went public and was listed on the New York Stock Exchange in 1956. Baby clothing, toys, and other products were added in the 1960's. The firm's slogan was "Babies are our business, our only business."

Like his father, Daniel Gerber was active in state and national trade associations; he also served as administrator of the Fruit and Vegetable Section of the Office of Price Administration from 1942 to 1943. While Gerber Products became a national firm with operations in several states and Canada, its headquarters remained in the small, west-central Michigan community of Fremont. Gerber was active in local service clubs and community organizations. He also served as chairman of the Old State Bank of Fremont for many years and as a director of the Detroit Edison Company, the Corn Products Company, and Laoli Mills, Inc.

Daniel Gerber had an idea and developed it into a major corporation, but he remained committed to the small town where he was born in and where both he and his idea grew up. He died in Fremont.

[See Library of Michigan, Biographical Vertical File. An obituary is in the *New York Times,* May 18, 1974.]

WILLIAM H. MULLIGAN, JR.

GERMER, LESTER HALBERT (Oct. 10, 1896–Oct. 3, 1971), physicist, was born in Chicago to Herman Gustav Germer and Marcia Halbert, who were of German descent. Germer's father was a physician; his mother was the daughter of a physician. In 1898 the family moved to Canastota in upstate New York, a busy town on the Erie Canal. Germer's father became a prominent citizen there, serving as an elder in the Presbyterian church, on the board of education, and as mayor. Germer attended public schools, excelling in algebra, geometry, physics, and German, and won a four-year scholarship to Cornell University, graduating six weeks early due to the entry of the United states into World War I. At Cornell he and two fellow students, who had found themselves dissatisfied with the science curriculum, met independently to pursue a more advanced program.

Upon graduation in 1917 Germer obtained a position at the Western Electric Company in New York City, the engineering and research arm of the American Telephone and Telegraph Company (AT&T). Two months later he volunteered for the army as a pilot, serving in France, where he was officially credited with having brought down four German warplanes. Following his discharge of Feb. 5, 1919, Germer was given a medical examination and was treated for shock and nervous strain. On Mar. 1, 1919, Germer returned to his position at Western Electric and was assigned to work with Dr. Clinton J. Davisson, an electron physicist who was doing research on a reliable, distortionless repeater, or amplifier, for use in the long-distance telephone lines of AT&T. While studying the effect of positive ion bombardment on the efficiency of electron emission for oxide coated cathodes, Davisson and Germer noted that electrons directed at metal targets were reflected without loss of energy, a surprising result. To Davisson, who had earlier sought to add understanding to the new atomic theories then in vogue, the appearance of these "elastically scattered" electrons offered a unique opportunity to probe the nature of the atoms making up the metal targets.

While Davisson and a newly appointed colleague, Charles Kunsman, began to pursue studies with the elastically scattered electrons, Germer was assigned to a new project on thermionic emission. He and Davisson published important results on this topic in 1922, and in 1924 Germer published the results of further studies as his Ph.D. dissertation. Germer had used his years since joining Western Electric to pursue graduate studies in physics at Columbia University in New York City; he was awarded the M.A. degree in June 1922, and the Ph.D. in 1927. On Oct. 2, 1919, Germer had married Ruth Woodard of Glens Falls, N.Y.; they had two children. Germer's hectic schedule (work, graduate school, and raising a family) was interrupted from April 1923 to July 1924, during which time he was treated for a nervous breakdown probably linked to a severe, recurrent sinus infection that was aggravated by noxious gas overseas.

Shortly after Germer returned to work in 1924, he was reassigned to the electron scattering studies that had been assigned to Kunsman in 1920 but had been abandoned in late 1923, at which time Kunsman left the company. On Feb. 5, 1925, while the electron tube previously used by Davisson and Kunsman was being reactivated, an accident occurred that eventually changed the character of the investigation. The heated, evacuated tube cracked, the nickel target was damaged, and the experiments were halted. When the tube was repaired and the experiments resumed, a surprisingly different pattern of the scattered electrons was observed. Attempts to explain this new behavior on the basis of the altered crystal structure of the nickel target were inconclusive, and Davisson and Germer expanded their study. Two years later, after further experimentation and after Davisson had obtained new theoretical insights during a trip to England and attendance at the 1926 meeting of the British Association for the Advancement of Science, Davisson and Germer realized that the new behavior of the scattered electrons could best be understood by attributing wave properties to them. In a series of papers published by Davisson and Germer, both jointly and separately, during the period 1927–1929, they demonstrated conclusively that electrons, like light, have the physical characteristics of waves as well as particles.

Davisson and Germer realized that their discovery also had potential for yielding information about the structure of the material from which the electrons were scattered. Germer pursued these studies, using both the scattering method he and Davisson had developed, and also an electron transmission method developed by George P. Thomson in England, publishing over twenty papers in the field. At that time he developed an interest in the behavior of metal contacts under electrical discharge, another subject of interest to AT&T, which he pursued until 1957, publishing nearly twenty papers on this topic.

Having completed this long series of studies, Germer's interest in electron diffraction was rekindled when a colleague at Bell Telephone Laboratories (the name used by the research arm of the Western Electric Company after 1925, and commonly referred to as Bell Labs) asked him to assist in developing a modified form of the electron scattering apparatus he and Davisson had used thirty years earlier. This method, called the postacceleration technique because the electrons are accelerated to high energies after they have been scattered by the target, and hence have enough energy to activate a fluorescent screen, had been proposed by Wilhelm Ehrenberg in 1934, but never developed. After Germer and his colleagues perfected this method, it proved to be so fruitful for the investigation of surface structures that Germer, even after his retirement from Bell Labs in 1961, continued this work as a research associate at Cornell University. During this time, besides publishing the results of his own research, he traveled to locations all over the world, lecturing and giving advice on the technique and interpretation of low-energy electron diffraction studies (LEED), a technique that has become indispensable to many fields of research.

An avid outdoorsman, Germer divided his later years between his research program at Cornell, his busy lecture schedule, and his great love of mountain climbing and hiking. He died after a fall while climbing near Gardiner, N.Y.

[The C. J. Davisson papers at the Library of Congress and the Owen W. Richardson papers on microfilm at the American Institute of Physics, New York City, contain many references to Germer in the correspondence between Davisson and his wife, and between Davisson and Richardson. The records of Germer's research while at Bell Labs are in the notebooks of L. H. Germer, C. H. Kunsman, and C. J. Calbick at the Bell Telephone Laboratories, Murray Hill, N.J. A bibliography of his published papers, along with a brief autobiographical statement, is available at the American Institute of Physics. Germer's most important paper, written with C. J. Davisson, is "Diffraction of Electrons by a Crystal of Nickel," *Physical Review*, Dec. 1927. A comprehensive study of their discovery is Richard K. Gehrenbeck, "C. J. Davisson, L. H. Germer, and the Discovery of Electron Diffraction" (Ph.D. diss., University of Minnesota, 1973). An obituary appears in *Physics Today*, Jan. 1972.]

RICHARD K. GEHRENBECK

GETTY, GEORGE FRANKLIN, II (July 9, 1924–June 6, 1973), corporate executive, was born in Los Angeles, the firstborn son of J. Paul Getty, the oil billionaire once reputed to be the wealthiest man in the world, and Jeanette Demont. George Getty was regarded as the heir apparent to head the vast holdings of Getty Oil and associated corporations.

Getty's parents separated when he was only two months old and divorced several months later. Getty was raised by his mother and stepfather, a stockbroker from Los Angeles named Bill Jones, and he had relatively little contact with his natural father until he reached adulthood. After briefly attending Princeton University in 1941, Getty enlisted in the Army Reserve Corps in 1942 and was called up for active duty in February 1943. He was commissioned a second lieutenant in the infantry in 1944. He was later assigned as a war crimes investigator to the legal section of the Supreme Command for the Allied Powers and spent sixteen months in the Philippines, Malaya, and Japan.

Following his discharge in 1947, Getty returned to Princeton for a brief period but left when his father agreed to let him into the family business. According to his father, "He started at the bottom, but quickly demonstrated a flair for business in general and an affinity for the oil business in particular."

But relations between father and son were not always smooth, and the two occasionally clashed on business issues. The Getty family holdings were controlled through the Sarah Getty Trust with J. Paul Getty as sole trustee. In 1941, he resigned to have his interests represented by an attorney, Thomas Dockweiler, as trustee. In 1946, twenty-two-year old George Getty, seeking a more active role in the family business, was named as a second trustee. In January 1948, in direct opposition to his father, George Getty went into court in an attempt to change some of the conditions controlling the trust. The senior Getty countered with his own

legal action and convinced the court to reappoint him as sole trustee. His son accepted the defeat and the conflict apparently did not have any lasting effect on the father-son relationship. Not long after this, the senior Getty "began to view George as the one who would naturally succeed [him] at the head of the Getty Family business."

Soon thereafter the Getty interests, represented by the Pacific Western Oil Corporation, acquired drilling rights in the so-called neutral zone shared by Kuwait and Saudi Arabia. The senior Getty sent his son to the area as manager for the Pacific Western interest and as his personal representative. Transferred back to the United States in 1950, Getty became manager of the midcontinent division of Pacific Western. He subsequently held increasingly more responsible positions with Spartan Aircraft Corporation, the Skelly Oil Company, and Tidewater Oil, all firms associated with Getty Oil. He also served as an officer with Minnehoma Financial Company and the Minnehoma Insurance Company, both founded by his grandfather, George Franklin Getty. His grandfather, an attorney in Minneapolis, had made a small fortune before investing in an oil lease in 1903 in the Indian Territory that was to become Oklahoma. The name of the original Getty company, Minnehoma Oil, combined the two seats of the family fortune, Minneapolis and Oklahoma.

Getty married Gloria Gordon of Denver in 1951; they had three children. In 1955, Getty was named executive vice-president and director at Pacific Western Oil. He left the following year to join Tidewater Oil, and in 1960, at the age of thirty-six, he was named to the presidency of Tidewater.

However, George Getty was still held under a tight rein by his father. At no time did the senior Getty relinquish his control of the companies and subsidiaries that made up the Getty family holdings. In the mid-1960's, he moved to merge the larger and more integrated Tidewater Oil into the parent company, Getty Oil. The proposed merger was controversial and was difficult to accomplish. George Getty played a significant role in the merger and expected to assume the presidency of the merged firms. He was disappointed. His father assumed the presidency, and George Getty was made executive vice-president and chief operating officer.

The late 1960's and early 1970's were difficult times for George Getty. His wife divorced him in 1967. In addition, Getty Oil experienced a number of reverses and his management abilities came under fire, particularly from his father. Relations between the two men worsened.

In May 1971, Getty married Jacqueline Riordan, a beautiful young widow with a fortune of approximately $30 million. They had no children. By early 1973, this marriage was in serious trouble, and his relationship with his daughters and his father had deteriorated further. In the final months before his death in June 1973, Getty relied heavily on barbiturates and alcohol, and there was evidence that he engaged in other forms of self-destructive behavior. Getty died in Los Angeles of a lethal dose of barbiturates and alcohol on June 6, 1973, at the age of forty-eight. After a lengthy investigation the coroner of Los Angeles County ruled the death a probable suicide.

[Biographical material on George Getty is scarce. See J. Paul Getty, autobiography, *As I See It* (1976); and Lenzner, *The Great Getty: The Life and Loves of J. Paul Getty—The Richest Man in the World* (1985). An obituary appears in the *New York Times*, June 7, 1973.]

GEORGE P. ANTONE

GIANCANA, SAM ("MOONEY") (May 24, 1908–June 19, 1975), racketeer, was born Gilormo Giancana and baptized Momo Salvatore Giancana, the son of Antonino Giangana, a Sicilian immigrant street peddler, and Antonia DiSimone. The family lived in a tenement on South Aberdeen Street in a neighborhood known as "The Patch," west of downtown Chicago, Ill. By Giancana's late teens he was head of a violent street gang known as "The 42's," which carried out beatings and other tasks for more established gangsters. Giancana became a driver, or "wheelman," in the underworld wars that racked Chicago in the 1920's. His first arrest and conviction came in 1925, for auto theft. Before he was twenty he had been arrested in three murder investigations, one for the slaying of a black man who ran for committeeman in the largely Italian Twentieth Ward. By 1963 Giancana had been arrested sixty times and had served prison sentences for auto theft, burglary, and moonshining.

After his release from prison in 1932, he came to the attention of Paul ("The Waiter")

Ricca, a figure of growing importance in the organization of Al Capone. Giancana became Ricca's chauffeur, and when Ricca went to prison in 1944, Giancana became the driver for his successor, Anthony Accardo. He married Angeline DeTolve on Sept. 26, 1933; they would have three daughters.

Giancana was declared 4F (unfit for service) at the beginning of World War II, after a Selective Service interviewer concluded he was a "constitutional psychopath with an inadequate personality manifested by strong antisocial trends." Giancana's wartime businesses included the forging of rationing stamps, and by 1945 he had moved with his wife and daughters to the affluent suburb of Oak Park.

Giancana took over the illegal lottery gambling operation of a black man he had met in prison and led other Italian-American mobsters in the seizure of several numbers operations in Chicago's black neighborhoods. He attended the alleged Mafia conclave at Appalachin, N.Y., in 1957, but escaped through the woods before state police closed in.

When Anthony Accardo began stepping back from mob operations in the late 1950's, Giancana emerged as the most visible boss in "The Outfit," as the Chicago Mafia was known, and one of the most celebrated criminals in America. He personified the Mafia's emergence from the relatively minor rackets of Italian urban ghettos and its infiltration of labor unions, gambling casinos and legitimate businesses. The new mob often relied more on corrupt politicians and police than on its own thugs. Once, an FBI agent stopped Giancana at an airport and asked what he did for a living. "Easy," the gangster replied. "I own Chicago. I own Miami. I own Las Vegas." Specifically, he held a hidden interest in several gambling casinos, provided capital for loan sharks and bookmakers, settled underworld disputes, and extorted tribute from less powerful mobsters.

Although he was described by a former FBI agent in 1983 as "a tough, swaggering, flamboyant murderer," Giancana possessed what biographer William Brashler described as "a beguiling, lilting charm." After his wife's death in 1954, he became a notorious ladies' man. His most famous affair was with Phyllis McGuire, youngest member of the McGuire Sisters, whom he met in Las Vegas in 1960. Giancana also bragged of his friendship with singer Frank Sinatra, and he and McGuire were frequent guests at a Lake Tahoe casino, half of which was owned by Sinatra. Sinatra eventually sold his interest in the casino after being confronted by the Nevada State Gaming Commission.

Giancana became one of the most conspicuous targets of Attorney General Robert Kennedy's assault on organized crime in 1961, and two years later FBI agents began to follow him around the clock. When he sued the Justice Department to stop it, the attendant publicity made his Oak Park home a tourist attraction. He eventually lost the case.

Robert Kennedy's campaign against Giancana was somewhat ironic. His brother John had been elected president in 1960, thanks partially to massive vote fraud in sections of Chicago under the political sway of The Outfit. Judith Campbell Exner, who had affairs with John Kennedy and Giancana, said Giancana told her, "Listen honey, if it wasn't for me, (Kennedy) wouldn't . . . be in the White House." In her book, *My Story* (1977), Exner wrote that she was introduced to both Giancana and John Kennedy on separate occasions by Frank Sinatra, and that on several occasions she saw Giancana immediately before or after she was with the president. Exner subsequently went further in an interview published in *People* magazine, claiming that Giancana and Kennedy actually met on one occasion. Kennedy broke off his affair with Exner in 1962, apparently after being told of her relationship with Giancana by FBI Director J. Edgar Hoover. For the same reason, Kennedy declined an invitation to stay at Sinatra's home in Palm Springs, Calif.

In 1965 Giancana was sentenced to a year in jail for refusing to testify before a federal grand jury in Chicago. Upon his release, Giancana left the country and lived in Mexico until 1974. When he returned to Chicago he again was subpoenaed by a grand jury; he appeared on four occasions, but apparently said nothing of substance. He was also subpoenaed by a Senate committee that was looking into the various CIA-Mafia plots to assassinate Fidel Castro.

On the night of June 19, 1975, a few days before he was to testify before the Senate committee in Washington, Giancana was preparing a snack in the basement of his Oak Park home. Someone with a .22 caliber pistol killed him with a shot in the back of the head, and then pumped six more bullets into him. The Chi-cago Crime Commission later identified three possible motives: Giancana had tried to reclaim his old rackets in Chicago; he had refused to share profits from his foreign operations; or someone feared he would cooperate with the Senate committee. No arrest was ever made in his murder.

[See William Brashler, *The Don: The Life and Death of Sam Giancana* (1977); Judith Katherine Exner with Ovid Demaris, *My Story* (1977); G. Robert Blakey and Richard N. Billings, *The Plot to Kill the President* (1981); "Testimony of the Chicago Crime Commission before the U.S. Senate Permanent Subcommittee on Investigations," (1983); and Antoinette Giancana and Thomas C. Renner, *Mafia Princess* (1984). An account of his murder appears in the *New York Times*, June 21, 1975, along with supplemental information.]

RICK HAMPSON

GIBBONS, EUELL (Sept. 8, 1911–Dec. 29, 1975), author of best-selling books on natural foods, was born in Clarksville, Tex., one of four children of Laura Augusta Bowers and Ely Joseph Gibbons, a blacksmith, grocer, carpenter, and homesteader. Gibbons's mother, a Tennessee farm girl, taught him to hunt, trap, and identify edible wild greens and fruits. By the age of five, he had created his first wild-foods recipe.

Until he finished sixth grade, Gibbons lived in the Southern Baptist Red River Valley. His father, also raised in Clarksville, moved the family in 1922 to New Mexico's drought-ravaged Estancia Valley, where he traded the family automobile for livestock, farm tools, and a half-dugout home. When he failed at homesteading, his father left to look for work. Within a week the livestock died, and only pinto beans remained for food.

With his mother and siblings close to starvation, Gibbons foraged for familiar edible wild weeds and kept the family alive on dandelion crowns, Russian thistle, wild garlic, lamb's-quarters, wild potatoes, and small game. Upon his father's return five weeks later, the family moved to Albuquerque.

At age fifteen, Gibbons left home and became a range hand in northern New Mexico for six years, regularly sending part of his salary home. It was during this period that he acquired knowledge of the ethnobotany of the semiagricultural Navajo Indians. He became a hobo when he was twenty-one, traveling on freight trains to California and then to Seattle. He foraged at the side of roads, ditches, and streams, eating weeds because he had no money for food. In 1933, Gibbons went to his first Communist party hobo camp meeting in northern California and came to believe that only the Communists were interested in the starving homeless. Even after getting a job as a laborer for the Continental Can Company, Gibbons was active as a Communist party publicist and leaflet author.

Gibbons's social agitation continued after he was fired from Continental Can and obtained work at a federal work camp in San Luis Obispo, Calif. It was there that Gibbons fell in love with the sea and discovered the food-laden zone between high and low tides, which he later described in his book *Stalking the Blue-Eyed Scallop* (1964). Jailed for inciting labor unrest, Gibbons exchanged a suspended sentence for a promise to relocate. He went to Seattle.

At the age of twenty-three, Gibbons enlisted in the army and worked as a boat builder and carpenter during his two-year tour of duty. After being honorably discharged in Seattle in 1936, Gibbons married Ann Swanson; they had two children. He continued to work as a boat builder while also engaging in political activity. He protested Japanese haulage of American scrap metal because the metal was used for Japan's military buildup and formally assumed the post of Communist party district organizer. He resigned from the Communist party in 1939 after the Soviets attacked Finland.

Gibbons left his family in Seattle in 1941 and began building boats for the navy in Hawaii during World War II. After watching medical ships take three days to unload wounded servicemen, he resigned his job and became a hospital worker. That job soon ended when he protested the rough treatment of patients. In 1946 he was divorced by his wife. He continued to live in Hawaii as a beachcomber on Oahu, giving lavish foraged edible food luaus served on banana leaves, which he later described in *Euell Gibbons's Beachcomber's Handbook* (1967).

With only a night school equivalency diploma, Gibbons enrolled as an anthropology and creative writing student at the University of Hawaii in 1947. In 1948, he won the Banks Memorial Creative Writing Award and was hired by the Honolulu *Advertiser,* for which he made up crossword puzzles in Hawaiian. That year he also met Freda Fryer, a divorced schoolteacher from Philadelphia. They were married

in 1949, the same year Gibbons became a Quaker, won custody of his two sons by his first wife, and moved to Maui. While Fryer taught kindergarten, Gibbons taught crafts at the Maui Vocational School.

In 1953, Gibbons and his family moved first to a Friends' community in New Jersey, then to Greenfield, Ind., to cofound a cooperative community. After it failed, Gibbons moved to the Quaker study center cooperative at Pendle Hill, Wallingford, Pa. While his wife taught primary school, Gibbons did maintenance work and took courses. In 1960, they moved to Tanguy Homesteads, a cooperative community near Philadelphia. That year his wife challenged Gibbons to write full-time while she supported them by teaching. In 1961, he completed "Mr. Markel Retires," a novel about a teacher who goes native. A literary agent advised him to revise it as nonfiction, relying heavily on his own experiences.

Gibbons spent a year researching the journals of Lewis and Clark, George Vancouver, and Captain John Smith, reviewing Navajo ethnobotanies, and testing his foraged food recipes on his wife's students at Tanguy Homesteads. After adding his personal experiences and philosophical asides, he published his researches in his first book, *Stalking the Wild Asparagus* (1962), an instant best-seller. This success allowed Gibbons to move into a home in Troxelville, Pa., in 1963. He joined the Lewisburg Quakers, where his many contributions at meetings were variously considered to be "anarchistic" or full of an "amazing religious depth."

Gibbons published a new book almost every two years thereafter and became an editor and columnist for *Organic Gardening and Farming.* His other works include *Stalking the Healthful Herbs* (1966), *Feast on a Diabetic Diet* (coauthored with his brother Joseph Gibbons, 1969), *Stalking the Good Life: My Love Affair with Nature* (1971), and *Stalking the Faraway Places* (1973).

Although he was financially secure from book sales and writing magazine columns, Gibbons made television advertisements endorsing General Foods cereals while providing video instruction about wild edible foods. On July 4, 1975, the Federal Trade Commission decided that Gibbons's television ads were dangerous for children because they did not explicitly acknowledge the danger of eating look-alike poisonous plants, and he was dropped as spokesman by General Foods. He was working with Gordon Tucker on an encyclopedia-manual of edible plants (published posthumously as *Euell Gibbons's Handbook of Edible Wild Plants* in 1979), when he died in Beavertown, Pa.

[Boston University houses the Euell Gibbons Collection of his unpublished works. For biographical material, see John McPhee, "Profiles: A Forager," *New Yorker*, Apr. 6, 1968. For information on the FTC controversy, see J. Goldstein, "Blame It All on George's Mother," *Organic Gardening and Farming*, Oct., 1975. See also John McPhee, "The Forager," *New York Times*, Jan. 10, 1976. An obituary is in the *New York Times*, Dec. 30, 1975.]

MARY ELLEN SWEENEY PERRI

GILBRETH, LILLIAN EVELYN MOLLER

(May 24, 1878–Jan. 2, 1972), industrial engineer and management consultant, was born in Oakland, Calif. The oldest of eight surviving children, she was the daughter of William Moller and Annie Delger. Her mother came from a prosperous family that had made its money in Oakland real estate, and her father was the proprietor of a thriving hardware retail business. As a result of her family's comfortable circumstances, Gilbreth enjoyed many early advantages.

A shy child, Gilbreth received her earliest education from her mother. The home tutoring came to an end at the age of nine when she was enrolled in the Oakland public school system. On completing her high school education in 1896, her parents were reluctant to honor her desire for more education. But eventually they allowed her to attend the University of California at Berkeley, where she majored in English. After receiving her undergraduate degree in 1900, she began working toward a master's degree in literature at Columbia University. Her unhappiness there, however, prompted her to return to the University of California, Berkeley, where she completed the work for her degree in 1902. Shortly thereafter she began working toward a doctorate in psychology.

In the spring of 1903, she interrupted her studies to make a tour of Europe. During a stopover in Boston she met Frank Gilbreth, who at age thirty-five was one of the country's leading building contractors and was rapidly making a name for himself as an industrial efficiency expert. On Oct. 19, 1904, they were married.

They settled in New York City, where Frank Gilbreth had his business.

Lillian Gilbreth had taken an interest in her husband's work even before their marriage, and she was soon playing an active role in it. Of special interest to her was Frank Gilbreth's preoccupation with increasing productivity in the construction industry by streamlining the motions required of workers for the completion of given tasks. In the process of collaborating with him on several publications devoted to that subject, she increasingly believed that their joint quests for what would later be dubbed "the one best way" was of far greater importance than her husband's building ventures. It was thus due in large part to her quiet encouragement that Frank Gilbreth finally gave up his construction business in 1911 to establish himself as a full-time management engineering consultant. The maiden venture of this new enterprise was a contract with the New England Butt Company in Providence, R.I., where the Gilbreths lived until shortly after World War I, when they moved to Montclair, N.J.

While continuing to collaborate in her husband's business, Lillian Gilbreth began work on a doctorate in industrial psychology at Brown University, which she completed in 1915. At the same time, having given birth to her first child in 1906, she had the major responsibility for raising a growing brood of offspring. The Gilbreths had twelve children over a period of seventeen years, eleven of whom lived to adulthood, and their crowded household often served as a testing ground for their motion theories. Years later the story of this large family, headed by efficiency experts, became the subject of memoirs coauthored by two of the Gilbreth children, *Cheaper by the Dozen* (1948) and *Belles on Their Toes* (1950).

By the early 1920's the Gilbreths' business was a thriving enterprise, and Frank Gilbreth was numbered among the most highly paid industrial consultants in the world. After his sudden death in 1924, however, the prosperity came to an end. Though determined to carry on their business, the newly widowed Lillian Gilbreth quickly found that clients were distrustful of a female consultant, and most of the contracts that the Gilbreths had with various businesses were soon canceled.

To support her family, Gilbreth established in her home the Motion Study Institute, which offered instruction in promoting efficiency in the workplace; she ran the institute successfully for six years. At the same time, she began to apply motion theory to home management. Her work in this area eventually spawned many articles for women's magazines and two books, *The Home-Maker and Her Job* (1927) and, with Orpha Mae Thomas and Eleanor Clymer, *Management in the Home* (1954). It also led to her serving as a consultant to home economics departments of numerous colleges and universities and to contracts with companies such as General Electric, whose products catered to the needs of home-makers. Ironically, Gilbreth herself never fully mastered her teachings on home management. Left to her own devices, she was barely capable of preparing the simplest of meals.

A gifted and fluent speaker, Gilbreth became a professor of management at Purdue University in 1935. In that position, which she held until 1948, she helped to establish the school's time and motion laboratory, and as an adviser there on careers for women, she was credited with fostering a more positive attitude toward women in industry. She also taught at a number of other schools including the University of Wisconsin and Newark College of Engineering.

One of the hallmarks of Gilbreth's career was her abiding concern for human well-being, and among her greatest achievements were her efforts to find ways to help the physically handicapped. In the 1940's, she collaborated with Edna Yost on *Normal Lives for the Disabled* (1944), and as a consultant to the Institute of Rehabilitation at the New York University Medical Center, she helped to develop a kitchen for the handicapped. Gilbreth's work with the disabled represented a continuation of her husband's efforts to rehabilitate disabled veterans of World War II; in 1968, the couple's contributions to the rehabilitation field were hailed as "phenomenal."

Gilbreth's distinction won her many honorary degrees and awards from professional societies. The recipient in the early 1930's of the first Gilbreth Medal granted by the Society of Industrial Engineers in memory of her husband, she was also the first woman to receive the Herbert Hoover Medal for distinguished service by an engineer. Blessed with a robust constitution, she remained professionally active practically until her death. At age ninety, her public-speaking schedule sometimes included as many as five engagements per week. She died in Scottsdale, Ariz.

[The papers of Lillian Gilbreth, as well as those of her husband, are at the Purdue University Library, Lafayette, Ind. Gilbreth's own writings include *The Quest of the One Best Way* (1925), which contains some autobiographical material; *The Foreman of Manpower Management* (1947), with Alice Rice Cook; and "Women in Industry" in *American Women: The Changing Image*, edited by Beverly Benner Cassara (1962). The most comprehensive biographical treatments are Edna Yost, *Frank and Lillian Gilbreth: Partners for Life* (1949); and Frank Gilbreth, Jr., *Time Out for Happiness* (1970). An obituary appears in the *New York Times*, Jan. 3, 1972.]

FREDERICK S. VOSS

GILLETTE, GUY MARK (Feb. 3, 1879–Mar. 3, 1973), United States representative and senator, was born near Cherokee, Iowa, the son of Mark Dennis Gillette, a farmer, and Mary Hull. He attended public schools there until 1896. After serving as a sergeant in the United States Volunteer Infantry in the Spanish-American War, he earned a Bachelor of Laws degree from Drake University and in 1900 was admitted to the bar.

Gillette, noted for his innate geniality, outstanding oratorical skills, and independence of mind, married Rose Freeman, a Cherokee County schoolteacher, on June 17, 1907. They had one son. He practiced law in Cherokee, serving as city attorney in 1906 and 1907 and prosecuting attorney for Cherokee County from 1907 to 1909. He was narrowly elected as a Democrat to the state senate from a strong Republican district and served four years there. During World War I he spent five months in France as a United States Army captain. During his absence, he was defeated for state auditor. Gillette then operated a dairy farm near Cherokee from 1919 to 1933.

From 1933 to 1936, the tall, silver-haired, soldierly Gillette served in the United States House of Representatives from the predominantly Republican Iowa ninth district. His electoral margins were 10,000 votes in 1932 and 26,000 votes in 1934. Gillette usually supported President Franklin D. Roosevelt's New Deal programs, but opposed the National Recovery Act and the Agricultural Adjustment Act.

In November 1936, Iowans resoundingly elected Gillette to fill the remaining two years of Democrat Louis Murphy's United States Senate term. Gillette supported a majority of New Deal measures, but angered President Roosevelt by rejecting his Supreme Court reorganization plan. According to Gillette, Roosevelt's proposal was inopportune, untimely, and an attempt to control the Supreme Court politically. Several New Dealers, led by Works Progress Administration head Harry Hopkins, retaliated by backing liberal Congressman Otha D. Wearin against Gillette in Iowa's June 1938 Senate primary. State Democratic officials, most notably Senator Clyde L. Herring and Governor Nelson Kraschel, defended Gillette.

A shrewd, hardy campaigner and distinguished orator, Gillette portrayed himself as an independent legislator standing alone against organized outsiders from Washington. Although he refrained from attacking Roosevelt, he vowed not to be a rubber-stamp member of Congress. Gillette trounced Wearin by 38,000 votes and received more votes than his three primary opponents combined. He defeated Republican Lester J. Dickinson by only 6,000 votes in the November 1938 election and opposed President Roosevelt's run for a third term in 1940.

As a member of the Agriculture and Forestry Committee, Gillette sought to expose monopoly and profiteering by middlemen in the food industry. He led the fight against Roosevelt's food subsidy program and favored creation of a Missouri Valley Authority. In 1942, while chairman of the subcommittee seeking new uses for surplus agricultural commodities, he cosponsored legislation to produce synthetic rubber from grain alcohol. Arguing that powerful petroleum interests were monopolizing contracts for production of synthetic rubber, Gillette maintained that synthetic rubber could be produced faster and more cheaply from grain alcohol.

Gillette, who also served on the Foreign Relations and Naval Affairs Committees, held isolationist views at the outset of World War II. In 1941 he opposed lend-lease, the extension of selective service, and the revision of the Neutrality Act. After American entry into World War II, however, Gillette supported Roosevelt's policies. His resolution supporting the Atlantic Charter and advising Roosevelt to negotiate a postwar peace charter became part of the Connally resolution approving American participation in the United Nations. A bipartisan Senate group, including Gillette, helped draft the United Nations Charter and formulate the Food and Agricultural Organization program. Gil-

lette favored creation of the War Refugee Board and of a commission to save European Jews. He spoke at many rallies in behalf of European Jews and proposed that the United States help them resettle.

In domestic affairs, Gillette chaired a committee that investigated the 1940 national elections and found that both Democrats and Republicans had violated spending limitations. In 1944 he introduced legislation to reduce expenditures in presidential contests. A member of the Rules Committee, he endorsed the Smith-Connally antistrike bill and abolition of the Fair Employment Practices Commission.

In 1944 Gillette opposed Roosevelt's fourth-term renomination. Although Gillette easily won the 1944 Iowa Democratic primary, Republican Bourke Hickenlooper unseated him in the November election. Gillette then served from January to June 1945 as chairman of the Surplus Property Disposal Board, responsible for disposing of $100 billion in surplus war property. From August 1945 to 1948 he presided over the 130,000-member American League for a Free Palestine, which urged the establishment of a free, independent state with a democratic Arab-Jewish government.

Gillette returned to the United States Senate in the 1948 election, defeating Republican incumbent George Wilson by the largest majority yet accorded an Iowa senatorial candidate. He served on the Rules Committee, chairing the Subcommittee on Privileges and Elections from 1950 to 1952. His subcommittee heard charges by Democrat Millard Tydings of Maryland that Republican Joseph McCarthy of Wisconsin had engaged in unethical conduct in helping Republican Marshall Butler win the 1950 election in Maryland. Gillette opposed pressing the investigation further and even offered to resign as subcommittee chairman. However, in August 1951, Gillette's subcommittee condemned McCarthy's tactics in the Maryland election. It also urged the Rules Committee to formulate explicit ethical standards for Senate election contests and for disciplining any senator violating standards.

After the report was released, Democrat William Benton of Connecticut urged the Rules Committee to investigate whether Senator McCarthy should be expelled. Testifying before Gillette's subcommittee in September, he cited ten instances in which McCarthy had demonstrated unethical behavior. Gillette's subcommittee infuriated Benton by delaying action on the latter's charges until May 1952, when it found that the Lustron Corporation had improperly given McCarthy $10,000. McCarthy countered by demanding Senator Benton's ouster, picturing him as a propagandist for the Communist party. Gillette resigned as subcommittee chairman the day after Wisconsin voters renominated McCarthy overwhelmingly in the September 1952 Republican primary. According to Gillette, McCarthy and Benton were seeking to discredit the subcommittee and to attack him personally. In 1954 Gillette supported motions by Republican Ralph Flanders of Vermont to remove McCarthy as chairman of both the Committee on Government Operations and its Permanent Subcommittee on Investigations, and to censure him.

Simultaneously, Gillette sought to make a single agency responsible for all campaign spending by candidates. He favored stricter enforcement of the $3 million limitation on campaign expenditures by political committees and $5,000 limitation for individual contributions.

In 1954, Republican Representative Thomas Martin unseated Gillette by 35,000 votes and prevented the latter from becoming the first Democrat from Iowa to win consecutive six-year Senate terms. Gillette, the only Democratic Senate incumbent to lose, attributed his defeat to low voter turnout. His setback, however, came largely from sagging farm prices. He had opposed both the flexible farm price support program and increasing consumer farm prices, and had been the lone remaining Democrat in the Iowa congressional delegation.

Gillette served as counsel for the Senate Post Office and Civil Service Committee in 1955 and 1956 and the Senate Judiciary Committee from 1956 to 1961. A Presbyterian, he enjoyed softball and music and participated in numerous veterans groups. He returned in 1961 to his farm near Cherokee, where he resided until his death.

[Gillette's papers remain in possession of the family. See "Evils in Campaign Funds," *U.S. News and World Report*, Oct. 10, 1952; Robert Griffith, *The Politics of Fear: Joseph R. McCarthy and the Senate* (1970); and Jerry Harrington, "Senator Guy Gillette Foils the Execution Committee," *The Palimpsest* 62, Nov./Dec. 1981. An obituary is in the *New York Times*, Mar. 4, 1973.]

DAVID L. PORTER

GIPSON, FREDERICK BENJAMIN (Feb. 7, 1908–Aug. 14, 1973), novelist, journalist, and rancher, was born near Mason, Tex., the son of Beckton Gipson and Emma Mayberry Dieschler. The Gipsons earned a hard living farming corn and cotton. Family stories of frontier life emphasized endurance, humor, justice, love of land and animals, and, on occasion, violence.

Gipson attended public school in Mason, graduating in 1926. The high school annual published his first story, a tale about cattle rustlers, which was influenced by Gipson's love of pulp Western fiction. After completing a bookkeeping course in San Antonio, he returned to Mason to work for a local grocer. Yearning to be a cowboy, he signed on in late 1927 for a nightmarish ten-day goat drive through almost continuous rain. Daunted, Gipson turned to breaking and driving mules. At twenty, he had his own team on a county road-building gang.

In 1931, the Great Depression forced Gipson and his father to seek work as day laborers. That fall, Gipson's younger brother urged Fred to come with him to the University of Texas. In 1933, still unemployed, Gipson decided to try college.

In Austin his stories about Mason County life helped him receive top grades in English. He also took courses in journalism. His story "Hard-Pressed Sam" was published by the *Southwest Review*, and his columns began to appear in the university's *Daily Texan*. In 1936, he won a writing contest judged by author J. Frank Dobie and was elected president of the journalism society.

Gipson left college in 1937 to be a reporter for Hart-Hankes Newspapers at the *Corpus Christi Caller-Times*. The chain soon made him a roving reporter, publishing his articles in three papers.

In 1939, Gipson met Tommie Wynn of San Angelo. They were married Jan. 23, 1940, and had two children. That June, after a honeymoon in Mexico, Gipson was fired from his newspaper job and took his wife to live at the family homestead near Mason. This experience became the basis for his 1950 novel, *The Home Place*.

Early in 1941, Joe Small, a college friend who had become a literary agent, helped Gipson sell his Western stories to magazines, and by August 1942 he had earned enough to build a small dwelling on the family farm. In 1943,

Gipson sold a story to *Collier's* for $500, and in 1944 *Reader's Digest* reprinted "My Kind of Man."

That November, Donald Day, editor of the *Southwest Review*, arranged a meeting between Gipson and Colonel Zack Miller, former proprietor of the 101 Wild West Show in Ponca City, Okla. Gipson collected one thousand pages of notes for a biography. Though Gipson had little confidence in the completed book, Miller was delighted. *Fabulous Empire: Colonel Zack Miller's Story* was published by Houghton Mifflin in 1946. Gipson then returned to an earlier novel about Charlie Sanders, a hill country character with whom he had hunted as a boy. The manuscript went to Houghton, where it stayed nine months until the publisher suggested revisions, which Gipson refused.

Meanwhile, Day helped Gipson get a job on the *Rocky Mountain Empire* magazine. The Gipsons left for Colorado in February 1948, but by summer, unhappy with life in Durango, they returned to Texas. The Charlie Sanders novel was accepted by Harper in June and published as *Hound-Dog Man* (1949). The Book-of-the-Month Club guaranteed Gipson $25,000, then a princely sum.

Despite this success, Gipson was troubled by fears of inadequacy. A new novel was refused by Harper. In 1950, however, the publisher brought out *The Home Place*, which became a best-seller and brought Gipson $27,500 in film rights. In 1951, another novel was completed but rejected by Harper, and Gipson's doubts again grew. In 1952, despite publication of *Big Bend: A Homesteader's Story* by the University of Texas Press, Gipson found himself depressed about both his literary future and the drought that for the next five years frustrated his plans to replant his acreage. Many of his stories were rejected by publishers. In 1953, he and Joe Small started *True West*, a pulp magazine of nonfiction Western stories, which Gipson edited.

Gipson's fortunes rose again. In 1953, his biography of Ed ("Fat") Alford, *Cowhand*, was published to good reviews, and a children's novel, *The Trail-Driving Rooster*, was accepted by Harper. The following year, Harper also bought *Recollection Creek*, a novel based on several of Gipson's earlier stories. In 1955, the television sale of his story "Brush Roper" took Gipson to Los Angeles as screenwriter.

In October 1955, Gipson wrote to Harper suggesting a dog story based on an event in his grandfather's life, and by January he had completed a manuscript of *Old Yeller* (1956). Its popularity was immediate. Harper promised him $35,000, and in June, Walt Disney paid $50,000 for the film rights. Financially secure, Gipson now began to have health problems. In May he experienced intense back pain, which continued intermittently all his life. Later, in Los Angeles to write the screenplay for *Old Yeller*, he developed an ulcer, aggravated by drinking and his chronic unhappiness whenever he was away from the hill country of Mason.

He continued to write. His next published book was *The Cow Killers* (1956), a powerful work in a narrative style new for Gipson. It was about Mexican peasants facing the government's extermination of farm animals with hoof-and-mouth disease.

Despite the end of the drought in 1957 and the success of Disney's *Old Yeller* in 1958, Gipson was unhappy. Three of his stories had been turned down, and he angrily objected to plot changes Twentieth Century–Fox made in filming *Hound-Dog Man*. In the period 1959–1960, Gipson fell into such serious depression that he agreed to shock treatments. Recovering, he was named president of the Texas Institute of Letters in 1960 and that summer began a sequel to *Old Yeller*. *Savage Sam* (1962) was completed in May 1961, and in October, Gipson went once more to Hollywood to write the screenplay for Disney.

Some weeks after his return in April 1962, his dog, the model for Savage Sam, was found clubbed to death. Despondent over this and other disappointments, Gipson's elder son Mike committed suicide. Two years later, Fred and Tommie Gipson were divorced, chiefly because of his drinking.

In his last years Gipson, in poor health, wrote magazine pieces and worked on several manuscripts. He often traveled to Mexico in search of a secretary and companion. In 1967, he hired Angelina Torres, whom he married on December 17. They were divorced six months later. Popular as a speaker, Gipson was named a fellow of the Texas Institute of Letters in 1970. He died at his ranch near Mason. Among his papers were six manuscript novels, two of which, *Little Arliss* (1978) and *Curly and the Wild Boar* (1979), were published posthumously.

Gipson's twelve books, six screenplays, and some two hundred magazine articles are marked by their simplicity, by their love of the land and animals, and by their sympathy for characters who struggle to endure on the land. As a storyteller, he aimed for "a simple and honest tale," romantic in action, like the pulp Western stories he grew up on, but truthful about hardship and realistic in detail, like stories of the frontier told to him by his family. He ranks with major writers of the Southwest like J. Frank Dobie and Walter Prescott Webb. Webb himself even suggested that Gipson shared Mark Twain's universality of appeal, and that *Old Yeller* stood the best chance of any Texas novel then written to achieve immortality.

[Gipson's extensive papers and manuscripts are at the Humanities Research Center of the University of Texas at Austin. See also Earle F. Walbridge, "Fred Gipson," *Wilson Library Bulletin*, Oct. 1957; "Fred Gipson on Writing for Young People," *Library Journal*, Feb. 15, 1960; Sam H. Henderson, *Fred Gipson* (1967); Mike Cox, *Fred Gipson, Texas Storyteller* (1980); and Glen E. Lich, *Fred Gipson at Work* (1990). An obituary is in the *New York Times*, Aug. 15, 1973.]

ALAN BUSTER

GIPSON, LAWRENCE HENRY (Dec. 7, 1880–Sept. 26, 1971), historian of colonial America, was born in Greeley, Colo., to Albert Eugene Gipson and Lina Maria West. He grew up in Caldwell, Idaho, where his father was a newspaper editor. After attending public schools in Caldwell, he enrolled at the University of Idaho, where he studied for a career in journalism and competed in intercollegiate athletics as a distance runner. Upon receiving the B.A. degree in 1903, he attended Oxford University as a Rhodes Scholar, earning a second B.A. degree in 1907.

Gipson returned to the United States in 1907 and taught history for three years at the College of Idaho. On Oct. 8, 1909, he married Jeannette Reed and the following year began graduate study at Yale University, where he was a Farnam Fellow in history. In 1910 he was appointed to the history faculty of Wabash College in Indiana, where he remained until 1924. He took a leave of absence in 1917 to return to Yale to complete his Ph.D. degree, which he received in 1918. His thesis was published by Yale University Press in 1920 as *Jared Ingersoll: A Study of American Loyalism in Relation to*

British Colonial Government, a volume that won the American Historical Association's Justin Winsor Prize.

Gipson's mentor at Yale was the distinguished colonial historian Charles McLean Andrews. As student at Oxford Gipson had begun to question the Whig interpretation of the American Revolution that blamed King George III and his Tory associates for the rupture. He was receptive to the revisionist "Imperial" school of colonial history led by Andrews, who called for a more objective assessment of the Crown, Parliament, Ministry, and even Loyalists in the quarrel. A strong believer in the new "scientific" history, which focused on patterns and forces in history rather than on people, Andrews expected his students to study institutional and administrative history. If Gipson, in choosing to do a biographical study of Ingersoll, went against his mentor's advice, he did not ignore his historiographical point of view. *Jared Ingersoll* differed from typical patriotic studies in its sympathetic treatment of a Loyalist torn between conflicting loyalties to the Crown and to his native Connecticut. From this volume Gipson progressed to more ambitious studies that in time made him the foremost of the Imperial historians.

In 1924 Gipson moved to Lehigh University in Bethlehem, Pa., where he served as head of the history department until 1946, when he became research professor. Afterward he concentrated most of his efforts on completing the project he launched when he first came to Lehigh. The support he received from Lehigh during his forty-eight-year association with that institution enabled him to produce his magnum opus, *The British Empire Before the American Revolution*. Gipson described this monumental fifteen-volume study as an "attempt to describe the whole Empire in some detail during the critical years before the outbreak of the War for American Independence." Publication began in 1936 with the appearance of the first three volumes. Unable during the Great Depression to find a New York publisher, Gipson turned to Caxton Printers, a family enterprise, to issue these initial volumes, which Knopf later reissued with revisions and in a format consistent with the other volumes in the series. During the next thirty-four years Gipson worked steadily to bring out twelve more volumes.

No other historian of the Imperial school of

314

colonial history rivals Gipson for comprehensiveness. In his volumes Gipson described in considerable detail the political, economic, and military aspects of the British empire in the mideighteenth century. He was sympathetic to its imperial administrators, and he defended mercantilism because he thought it benefited all parties. Britain's wars with France in the New World, he argued, were motivated not by lust for empire but by a maternal instinct to protect her colonies from French rapacity. It was natural and proper that the American colonists, whose per capita tax burden was much lighter than that of their English counterparts, should pay for benefits received. By refusing to pay their fair share of the costs of administering the empire, Gipson suggested that the colonists acted selfishly and myopically. But in the final analysis he blamed neither American radicals nor wicked men in England for the rupture. Maturing American nationalism was the catalyst that touched off the Revolution. Following John Adams, he concluded that the real American Revolution was in the hearts and minds of the people, and that it was completed long before the first shots at Lexington and Concord were fired. By 1763, he said, the English-speaking community in the thirteen colonies had reached a stage of maturity "with a mind of its own and a future it considered peculiarly its own." Like his teacher Andrews, he acknowledged the superiority of impersonal forces over people as the determinants of the course of history.

Although Gipson was loath to permit anything to divert him from his work on *The British Empire Before the American Revolution*, he did accept the Harmsworth Chair in American History at Oxford University in 1951. He also wrote a volume for the New American Nation Series, which was published in 1954 as *The Coming of the Revolution, 1763–1775*. That volume did not measure up to his best work, and certainly not to the seventh volume of his series, *The Great War for the Empire: The Victorious Years, 1758–1760*, which won the Bancroft Prize, or the tenth volume, *The Triumphant Empire: Thunder Clouds Gather in the West, 1763–1766*, which was awarded the Pulitzer Prize in history in 1962. The author of more than 150 books, articles, and reviews, he was faulted by some critics for writing history from a Tory point of view and for a turgid prose style, but few historians can match the depth of Gipson's

understanding of colonial American history.

Described by acquaintances as a "warm-hearted and generous" though "modest and retiring" man, Gipson was a Republican in politics and a Congregationalist in religion. He had no children. He died in his sleep at his home near Lehigh University.

[The Lawrence Henry Gipson Institute for Eighteenth-Century Studies at Lehigh University holds Gipson's papers, which include personal and family correspondence as well as his professional papers. Appraisals of Gipson's work can be found in Richard B. Morris, "The Spacious Empire of Lawrence Henry Gipson," *William and Mary Quarterly*, 3d ser., vol. 24 (Apr. 1967); and Jackson Turner Main, "Lawrence Henry Gipson, Historian," *Pennsylvania History* 36, Jan. 1969. An obituary is in *The American Historical Review* 77, no. 1, Feb. 1972.]
CHARLES D. LOWERY

GITT, JOSIAH WILLIAMS ("JESS") (Mar. 28, 1884–Oct. 7, 1973), editor and publisher, was born in Hanover, Pa., the son of Clinton Jacob Gitt and Emma Koplin. He received a B.A. in 1904 from Franklin and Marshall College, Lancaster, Pa., where he excelled in football, baseball, and track. After studying law at the University of Pittsburgh, he was admitted to the York County bar in 1908. He practiced law in York, Pa., until 1915, when he and his associate, Allen C. Weist, purchased controlling interest in the *York Gazette*. Three years later they bought the *York Daily*, and their newspaper became known as the *York Gazette and Daily*. On June 12, 1913, Gitt married Elizabeth Glatfelter Moul. They had four children.

Under Gitt, who was editor and publisher, the *Gazette and Daily* became widely known. While he considered himself a Jeffersonian Democrat, Gitt never felt compelled to toe the party line. In 1924 he backed Robert M. La Follette for the White House. He lent support to Gifford Pinchot, the pioneer conservationist, who became a close personal friend. He also backed the New Deal of Franklin D. Roosevelt. In 1948 Gitt became chairman of the Progressive party of Pennsylvania, and his paper was the only non-Communist daily to endorse Henry A. Wallace for president. He was an early opponent of McCarthyism, which he considered contrary to American values, and he also took up women's causes.

Gitt said his views were shaped by the Declaration of Independence, the Bill of Rights, and the Sermon on the Mount. He advocated an international organization that would settle disputes peacefully. His paper was also unique in that cartoons (drawn by Walt Partymiller) appeared regularly on the front page rather than the editorial page.

An opponent of racism, Gitt practiced what he preached. He gave Robert C. Maynard, who was black, his first position. Maynard went on to become the owner and publisher of the *Oakland* (Calif.) *Tribune*. Gitt was a forerunner in the campaign against cigarette smoking. He opposed the use of tobacco personally and banned cigarette advertising from his newspaper. He also refused to carry advertising for alcoholic beverages, and in 1964 he printed no advertising for Barry Goldwater.

For many years Gitt was a trustee of Franklin and Marshall College. He and his newspaper also shared many awards. In 1971, Columbia University honored him as "a positive and effective voice" for moving toward progressive solutions to society's problems. The Emergency Civil Liberties Committee gave him its Tom Paine Award for "his ceaseless, unflinching fight for civil liberties." His crusading journalism brought him one Heywood Broun Award after another.

The *Gazette and Daily* received the N. W. Ayer certificate four times for typographic excellence among tabloid newspapers. The 1957 Ayer Cup credited it with the best makeup of any newspaper in the United States of any size or format. In an introduction to a collection of Gitt's writings, Morris Rubin, publisher of the *Progressive*, wrote, "The people of York had a newspaper that covered local, national, and world affairs in a manner that was unrivaled in much larger communities."

Gitt sold the *Gazette and Daily* in 1970 after operating it for fifty-five years. He requested that its name be changed, and it became the *York Daily Record*. Gitt was an active golfer. He died in Boston, Mass.

[Some of Gitt's writings between 1915 and 1970 are collected in McKinley C. Olson, ed., *J. W. Gitt's Sweet Land of Liberty* (1975). An obituary appears in the *New York Times*, Oct. 9, 1973.]

IRVING DILLIARD

GLEASON, RALPH JOSEPH (Mar. 1, 1917–June 3, 1975), jazz critic and journalist, was born in New York City, the son of Ralph A. Gleason and Mary Quinlisk. He grew up in suburban Chappaqua, N.Y., where as a student at Horace Greeley High School, and home sick with the measles, he first heard the music of Louis Armstrong, Fletcher Henderson, and other legendary jazz players on the radio. It was, he said, love at first hearing and one of the factors that led him to Columbia University, so close to New York City's entertainment world, as an undergraduate in 1934. Through the following four years, Gleason used his role as a writer and then features editor for the *Spectator*, the college newspaper, as an excuse to become a regular visitor to the jazz clubs on Fifty-second Street. A student prank in his senior year caused his expulsion from Columbia and he left the school without graduating. In 1939 he co-founded with Gene Williams *Jazz Information*, the first American magazine devoted entirely to jazz. A year later, on Oct. 12, 1940, he married Jean Rayburn; they would have three children.

Gleason's first magazine venture lasted for two years. In 1942, he left New York for service in wartime Washington and overseas as a writer and editor with the Office of War Information. On his return to postwar life, he moved his family to California in 1946, saying later that, even though the Big Apple was the center of the jazz world, California gave him a greater opportunity than New York to appreciate the music. "You can relax and listen in San Francisco," he wrote. "You can't in New York."

Gleason took up free-lance writing and, through the next three decades, contributed jazz and popular music criticism to *Esquire*, the *New Statesman*, *American Scholar*, *Saturday Review*, and other periodicals. In 1948 he began a twelve-year association with *Downbeat* as associate editor, columnist, critic, and eventually contributing editor. In the 1960's he was variously an editor of *Ramparts* and a contributing editor of *HiFi Stereo* and *Scholastic Roto*. He was an editor and columnist for *Rolling Stone* from 1967 until his death. He was, as well, a prolific writer of liner notes for record albums. In 1970, he became a vice-president of Fantasy-Prestige-Milestone Records, a producer of jazz recordings. He was a lecturer in music from 1960 to 1963 in the University of California, Extension Division, and from 1965 to 1967 at Sonoma State College.

Joining the *San Francisco Chronicle* as a music reviewer in 1950, Gleason almost immediately broke new ground by treating folk music, jazz, and other popular musical forms with the same seriousness and critical standards that other critics applied to classical music performances. By 1953 he had been given a daily column in which he explored both contemporary musical trends and examined the history of American popular music, especially jazz. He spun off some of this material into the first syndicated weekly jazz column that ran in papers across the United States and in Europe for nearly ten years. In 1957, Gleason again tried to publish a scholarly jazz magazine but was no more successful with this venture than he had been in 1939. *Jazz: A Quarterly of American Music* folded after two years.

By the late 1950's, Gleason's reputation and influence as America's best-known popular music critic were firmly established. He had spent the decade roaming the North Beach area of San Francisco and other cultural venues, where both young and old performers were experimenting with a variety of musical forms. He actively advanced the careers of innovative musicians like Miles Davis and Dizzy Gillespie. His early support of the Modern Jazz Quartet led Milt Jackson, the group's vibraharpist, to compose "Ralph's New Blues" in his honor.

Gleason was instrumental in bringing serious critical attention to the music of Duke Ellington and in 1958 was the first critic to write favorably of comic and social satirist Lenny Bruce. By the early 1960's many younger musicians and other performers looked on Gleason as a starmaker, so influential were his reviews in attracting audiences to concerts or to recordings.

His reviews were often generous. "I write about jazz because I want to share my enjoyment with other people," he explained, but he could be harsh and, at times, even cruel. He once dismissed Pat Boone, a popular figure of mainstream music in the mid-1950's, "as pallid, pretentious, and even a bit of a phony." One victim of a similar acerbic review sent Gleason a bag of sugar, knowing that he was diabetic. Sometimes accused of arrogance and coldness, Gleason once said, "I don't care if I make it with musicians. . . . The important thing is that I stay straight with myself."

He liked to say that his judgment had only failed him twice, once in the 1940's, when he denigrated swing as a prostitution of traditional New Orleans and Chicago jazz, and then in

1963 at the Monterey Folk Festival, when he initially dismissed a young folk singer, Bob Dylan, as boring and "oppressively mournful." By 1964, however, he reversed himself on Dylan, just as he had reversed himself on swing in his Ellington essays, and the two became fast friends. He compared Dylan to Shakespeare and predicted that he would be the voice of his generation. He then turned his attention to Dylan's associates, protest singers like Joan Baez, and devoted his column to favorable reviews of emerging rock groups like the Beatles and the Rolling Stones.

During the 1960's, Gleason was a disk jockey on KHIP and KMPX in San Francisco and in 1962 produced and hosted "Jazz Casual," a program featuring performers like John Coltrane, Wes Montgomery, and the MJQ for National Education Television. His television documentary on Ellington, also in 1962, was nominated for two Emmys. In 1967 he won the first of two Deems Taylor Awards from the American Society of Composers, Authors, and Publishers for his article, "Jazz: Black Art, Black Music." He won the second award in 1973 for a tribute to Louis Armstrong in *Rolling Stone*, the magazine he cofounded with Jann Wenner in 1967.

Gleason died of a heart attack in Berkeley, Calif.

[Gleason's books include *Jam Session: An Anthology of Jazz* (1958); *The Jefferson Airplane and the San Francisco Sound* (1969); and *Celebrating the Duke: And Louis, Bessie, Billie, Bird, Carmen, Miles, Dizzy, and Other Heroes* (1975). *Rolling Stone* published a commemorative issue on Gleason in July 1975. See also Robert Draper, *Rolling Stone Magazine: The Uncensored Story* (1990). An obituary appears in the *New York Times*, June 4, 1975.]

ALLAN L. DAMON

GLUECK, ELEANOR TOUROFF (Apr. 12, 1898–Sept. 25, 1972), social worker and criminologist, was born in Brooklyn, N.Y., the daughter of Polish immigrant Anna Wodzislawska and Russian immigrant Bernard Leo Touroff, a New York City realtor. She graduated from Hunter College High School in 1916, received a B.A. in English from Barnard College in 1920, and earned a diploma in community organization at the New York School of Social Work in 1921. Through the influence of one of her teachers, Bernard Glueck, a psychiatrist, she became a settlement house social worker in Boston from 1921 to 1922, whereupon she began graduate studies at Harvard University. On Apr. 16, 1922, she married Dr. Glueck's brother, Sheldon Glueck, a lawyer and fellow graduate student at Harvard. Glueck received her M.Ed. in 1923 and her Ed.D. in 1925 from Harvard.

She joined her husband on the faculty of Harvard's Department of Social Ethics in 1925, and they later both moved to the Harvard Law School Crime Survey in 1928. Sheldon became professor of criminology in 1931 and in 1950 was named Roscoe Pound Professor of Law. Eleanor worked with him as a research criminologist (1925–1928), research assistant (1930–1953), research associate (1953–1972), and codirector of the Harvard Law School program Research into the Causes, Treatment and Prevention of Juvenile Delinquency (1966–1972). Their various titles notwithstanding, Eleanor and Sheldon Glueck were a creative, prolific team pioneering in longitudinal field studies of American crime and delinquency for fifty years.

Eleanor's publications include her doctoral thesis, *The Community Use of Schools* (1927); *Extended Use of School Buildings* (1927); *Evaluative Research in Social Work* (1936); and more than one hundred articles, reports, and reviews. She and her husband were also coauthors of eighteen books, including *Five Hundred Criminal Careers* (1930); *Five Hundred Delinquent Women* (1934); *One Thousand Juvenile Delinquents* (1934); *Later Criminal Careers* (1937); *Juvenile Delinquents Grown Up* (1940); *Unraveling Juvenile Delinquency* (1950); *Delinquents in the Making* (1952); *Predicting Delinquency and Crime* (1959); and *Delinquents and Nondelinquents in Perspective* (1968).

Dr. Richard C. Cabot, the founder of medical social work in Boston, first recognized the value of the Gluecks' scientific approach to criminology in the 1920's. Dean Roscoe Pound and Professor Felix Frankfurter recruited them for the Harvard Law School Crime Survey. William Healy and Augusta Fox Bronner, directors of the Boston Juvenile Court Clinic and the Judge Baker Foundation, were also early influential supporters of the Gluecks' interdisciplinary approach to a multiple-factor theory of juvenile delinquency and crime. As a result, their work yielded new insights for public policy, law, and medicine because they demonstrated how ineffective educational, police,

penal, and social-welfare practices had been on youthful lawbreakers. In the United States and abroad, assumptions about the socioeconomic, somatic, intellectual, and emotional factors in juvenile delinquency and criminal behavior changed as a result of these painstaking, exhaustive research projects.

Although finding a method of early detection and prevention of juvenile delinquency remained an unfulfilled goal, one major contribution of Eleanor Glueck's work was statistical evidence that the quality of a child's family life was the most important factor in determining juvenile delinquency. Without a stable and supportive family life, recidivism rates remained high even among juvenile delinquents who received the careful attention of progressive juvenile courts, probation officers, psychologists, psychiatrists, social workers, hospitals, and schools. Furthermore, in each study her fieldwork and long-term follow-up casework demonstrated that reform schools and prisons did not rehabilitate inmates.

This was alarming and discouraging news in the Great Depression and postwar years, as national concern about juvenile delinquency and social problems created a new interest in criminology. Yet the implications of the Gluecks' research, that the roots of crime lie in the foundation of American society, were only slowly accepted in the New Deal and Great Society eras. By 1940, criticism of the Gluecks' methods and goals by prominent researchers such as Edwin H. Sutherland, a former admirer and influential criminologist, led most sociologists and criminologists to reject or ignore their research results. Postwar social scientists continued to define social-welfare problems in terms of individual or familial deviance rather than economic and social inequality.

As research criminologists, the Gluecks were professionally isolated at Harvard Law School and never received the attention their work may have won in academic circles. Eleanor also encountered some gender and religious biases (she was Jewish), but she proved to be as effective a fund-raiser as she was a researcher. This was necessary because much of the Gluecks' research was supported by private foundations rather than by Harvard University or public funds. Eleanor's warm and engaging manner also won her respect and friendship among social-welfare and juvenile-justice professionals.

Working outside the academic mainstream,

with no graduate students or close professional colleagues, the Gluecks persevered in their original empirical research. The interdisciplinary nature of their work, at a time when criminology was defining its own area of specialization, and Eleanor's background in social work and education contributed to her marginal position. An out-of-fashion moralistic attitude toward her research subjects, free of sociology's jargon, also obscured her most useful contributions. Despite a lifetime of scientific research, she retained her professional ties to social work and the casework method, and she was a trustee of the Judge Baker Guidance Center for forty years. As a result, the validity of Eleanor Glueck's long-term work with young lawbreakers has only recently been recognized by sociologists and criminologists.

The Gluecks had one child, a daughter, who predeceased her parents. Eleanor's Sunday afternoon teas for Harvard Law School students made her a memorable campus figure. In 1958, Sheldon and Eleanor became the first husband-and-wife team to receive the honorary degrees of Doctor of Science from Harvard. In 1961, the Gluecks received some belated recognition from the American Society of Criminology when they won the August Vollmer Award. Eleanor retired from Harvard Law School in 1964, but continued researching and writing with her husband until she died suddenly at her Cambridge, Mass., home.

[The papers of Eleanor Glueck and her husband are at the Harvard Law School Library. Sheldon Glueck's autobiography, *Lives of Labor, Lives of Love* (1977), contains much material on Eleanor Glueck and provides a complete bibliography of their work. A reassessment of her career is in John H. Laub and Robert J. Sampson, "The Sutherland–Glueck Debate," *American Journal of Sociology*, May 1991. Obituaries are in the *New York Times* and the *Boston Globe*, both Sept. 26, 1972.]

PETER C. HOLLORAN

GLUECK, NELSON (June 4, 1900–Feb. 12, 1971), archaeologist and college president, was born and raised in Cincinnati, Ohio, one of seven children of Morris Glueck, a merchant, and Anna Rubin. Glueck's parents instilled in him a profound devotion to his Jewish heritage, which would later inform his archaeological pursuits. He traced his fascination with artifacts to childhood explorations of a fossil site and an Indian burial ground in and around Cincinnati.

Glueck attended public high school, then entered Hebrew Union College in Cincinnati at the age of fifteen, taking a degree in Hebrew literature in 1918. He received a B.A. from the University of Cincinnati in 1920 and, complying with his parents' wishes, returned to Hebrew Union College for rabbinical training. After his ordination in 1923, Glueck traveled on a fellowship to Germany, studying Eastern lore, Assyrian, and Ethiopic at the University of Berlin and Heidelberg University. He received his Ph.D. in biblical studies from the University of Jena, Germany, in 1927. Glueck's dissertation, which was published in 1967 under the title *Hesed in the Bible*, marked his promise as a scholar of biblical ideas.

In 1927, Glueck took a study trip to the American School of Oriental Research in Jerusalem to pursue a growing interest in Palestinian archaeology. The school was then headed by American archaeologist William F. Albright, who had devised one of the first systems for dating ruins of the ancient Near East. Albright trained Glueck in this system, which relied on the classification of Palestinian potsherds, or pottery fragments, according to hundreds of variations.

Intermittently during the period 1927–1932, Glueck traveled on foot to all of Albright's excavations, becoming an expert in ceramic chronology while at the same time experiencing the biblical resonances of the Holy Land. Archaeology, he was coming to find, had a way of "burning the mist off the Bible," in that it revealed the cultural context in which biblical events took place. During his training under Albright, Glueck decided against the rabbinical pulpit for which he had been trained in favor of, in his words, "treading ground where the Patriarchs and the Prophets had lived." He saw the south Transjordanian desert and the Negev as a vast terra incognita that required exploration square mile by square mile; Glueck's topographical survey of these regions, undertaken between 1932 and 1967, resulted in the discovery of approximately 1,500 ancient sites and established him as one of the foremost Palestinian archaeologists of the twentieth century.

Glueck alternated his nomadic wanderings through Palestine with his career as an educator and administrator. His contributions to archaeology were made during numerous leaves of

319

absence from Hebrew Union College in Cincinnati, where he had become an instructor in 1928. Glueck advanced through the ranks to become professor of the Bible and biblical archaeology in 1936, a position he held until his death. His teaching career included a stint as lecturer in biblical literature at the University of Cincinnati in the 1935–1936 academic year. Glueck also served as director of the American School of Oriental Research in Jerusalem from 1932 to 1933 and 1936 to 1940. He was annual professor at the American School of Oriental Research in Baghdad, Iraq (1933–1934) and used his position as field director there (1942–1947) to gather military intelligence for the Office of Strategic Services during World War II. On Mar. 26, 1931, Glueck married Helen Ransohoff Iglauer, a medical student at the University of Cincinnati who went on to become a professor of medicine there. They had one child.

In March 1948, Glueck was appointed president of Hebrew Union College in Cincinnati; shortly after that institution merged with the Jewish Institute of Religion in New York in July 1948, Glueck became the first president of the Hebrew Union College–Jewish Institute of Religion, a post that designated him as the leader of Reform Judaism in the United States. As such, Glueck gave the benediction at the inauguration of President John F. Kennedy in 1961. Under Glueck, the college opened a Los Angeles campus in 1950 and in 1960 founded the Hebrew Union College Biblical and Archaeological School in Jerusalem (later the Nelson Glueck School of Biblical Archaeology), a postdoctoral research and excavation center. Glueck made it a requirement for rabbinical students of the American college to spend one year studying at the center in Israel, in order to facilitate their learning of Hebrew.

Glueck called himself a biblical archaeologist because he grounded his archaeological excavations on his reading of the Old Testament. He believed that the Bible was an "almost infallible divining rod, revealing to the expert the whereabouts and characteristics of lost cities and civilizations." Using the Old Testament as his guide, Glueck mapped out the biblical kingdoms of Edom, Moab, and Ammon, providing the first scientific insight into the dating of the biblical patriarchs. He uncovered historical evidence of the Nabataeans, an early Arab people. His most celebrated finding came in 1934,

when he discovered Khirbet Nahas, a ruin he identified as King Solomon's mines. Four years later, using a verse from the book of 1 Kings as his guide, he identified Tell el-Khaleifeh as biblical Ezion-Geber, a port city also dating to the time of Solomon, which Glueck established was an important metallurgical center. A restudy of Glueck's findings at Tell el-Khaleifeh, which was conducted in the 1980's, disproved this identification, however.

Glueck often stated that it was not the intention of biblical archaeology to prove the historical accuracy of the Bible, which "is based on belief in God, whose Being can be scientifically suggested but never scientifically demonstrated." He believed that the value of biblical archaeology was its validation of what he called the Bible's "historical memory."

Glueck wrote several books popularizing biblical archaeology, namely, *The Other Side of the Jordan* (1940), *The River Jordan* (1946), *Rivers of the Desert: A History of the Negev* (1959), and *Deities and Dolphins: The Story of the Nabataeans* (1965). He contributed numerous popular articles on his findings to *National Geographic* and the *New York Times Magazine*. His technical reports were published in *Explorations in Eastern Palestine*, the annual journal of the American School of Oriental Research. Glueck died of cancer in Cincinnati.

[Glueck's personal papers and the records of Hebrew Union College–Jewish Institute of Religion during his administration are in the American Jewish Archives in Cincinnati. See also "Why I Am a Biblical Archaeologist," *Cincinnati*, June 1968. A complete bibliography of Glueck's writings is in James A. Sanders, ed., *Near Eastern Archaeology in the Twentieth Century* (1970), a festschrift published on the occasion of Glueck's seventieth birthday. See also Fritz Bamberger, "The Mind of Nelson Glueck," and G. Ernest Wright, "The Phenomenon of American Archaeology in the Near East," in that volume. A cover story, "The Search for Man's Past," appears in *Time*, Dec. 13, 1963. A tribute by Edward F. Campbell, Jr., is in *Biblical Archaeologist*, Feb. 1971. An obituary appears in the *New York Times*, Feb. 14, 1971.]

MELISSA A. DOBSON

GOLD, HARRY ("RAYMOND") (Dec. 11, 1911–Aug. 28, 1972), atom-bomb spy and espionage agent, was born in Bern, Switzerland, to Russian Jewish parents. His father was Sam Gold, a cabinetmaker. Harry was their only child. The family came to the United States in 1913, and Harry grew up in Philadelphia. He attended the Drexel Institute of Technology, where he obtained a diploma in chemical engineering in 1936, and later received a B.S. from Xavier University in Cincinnati, Ohio. During World War II, he placed his knowledge and technical skills in the service of a nation he had never visited.

The espionage career of Harry Gold came to light during the investigations and trials of Soviet agents who passed sensitive and secret information about the American atomic bomb project to the Soviet Union during World War II. Harry Gold was named as a participant in the spy ring of Klaus Fuchs, a naturalized British subject trained in nuclear physics. When war broke out in Europe, Fuchs began working on atomic energy research at the University of Birmingham. Not known at the time was that Fuchs was a Communist and a Soviet spy. In 1943, Fuchs arrived in the United States to work in the Manhattan Project (the United States atom bomb construction program) at Los Alamos, N.Mex. The Soviets supplied Fuchs with a contact who would forward any secrets he could pass. The courier was Harry Gold.

Gold was sympathetic to socialist and Communist ideologies even in high school. Though raised in a Jewish home, he expressed not religious convictions but rather a faith in the political creeds for which he diligently worked. After his arrest in 1950, Gold willingly described his involvement with military espionage. His motives, he claimed, were highminded. He believed his industrial and military spying would assist the Soviet Union, an American ally, to catch up with more advanced capitalist nations; he also believed his activities would not only redress the prejudicial policies of the American government toward the Soviets but hasten the defeat of the Nazis as well.

At first, Gold's activities were relatively harmless. He provided his Soviet contacts with formulas for blending motor oils, solvents for synthetic detergents, and other industrial engineering data. In 1943, however, at the height of the war in Europe, Gold was told by his Soviet superiors in the espionage ring that he would be working with American scientists who were doing important war research. Curiously, throughout the war years Gold never faced any serious threat of exposure.

On May 22, 1950, Gold was apprehended by the FBI and he admitted that he was the American conduit for Fuchs. Another suspect came to light, a United States Army technician stationed in Los Alamos named David Greenglass, who was arrested in June 1950. The spy network collapsed. In August, Julius Rosenberg and his wife Ethel were arrested after being named by Greenglass as another link in the espionage apparatus that included Dr. Fuchs, Harry Gold, and Greenglass himself.

During Gold's trial, Fuchs gave damning testimony against Gold, who received a thirty-year prison sentence. Gold appeared as a government witness in the subsequent sensational trials of Greenglass, the Rosenbergs, and Morton Sobell.

Harry Gold was referred to in the press as the government's star witness and the necessary link in the case against the Rosenbergs and Sobell. What lent authority and plausibility to his testimony was the fact that Gold apparently had nothing to gain by cooperating with the government. His performance in court may have contributed to the government's successful prosecutions: Gold was a man of average height and weight who seemed in appearance more like a businessman than a spy; his precise, professorial diction and emotional detachment made a tremendous impression on jurors and spectators alike. Gold matter-of-factly and quite dispassionately spelled out the connection between the defendants and Soviet agents operating in the United States.

According to Gold, in the spring of 1945 his chief Soviet contact, Anatoly Yakovlev, told him to pick up information in New Mexico. On a sheet of paper was Greenglass's name and address in Albuquerque, and the words of the recognition signal, "I come from Julius." There was also a piece from a Jell-O cardboard box that Rosenberg used to identify the courier. The information that Gold obtained and transmitted to the Soviets included sketches and diagrams of high-explosive lens molds being used in the atom bomb.

All those named, accused and indicted on Gold's evidence were convicted. The Rosenbergs were electrocuted in June 1953, but the perfect chain of information and secrecy had a flawed link. Gold claimed to have been the man to whom Fuchs passed on atomic research data in their clandestine meetings. In the Rosenberg trial, Gold's believability as a key government witness rested on the assumption that Fuchs had indeed identified him as such. But Fuchs had twice failed to make a positive identification of Gold from FBI surveillance photos and film. In 1950, Fuchs provided British authorities with a written confession that still remains classified as secret information in England. Fuchs, who resided in Germany, never discussed the case afterward.

During his sixteen years in prison Harry Gold adapted very well to the rigors of incarceration. He worked in the prison's medical research laboratory, studied mathematics, and maintained a positive outlook on the future. Was he a government stooge? Did he commit perjury? Apart from a later trial in which his evidence was treated with suspicion, the record indicates that he never said anything on the witness stand that contradicted his initial statements to the FBI in 1960.

Gold died six years after he was released in 1966 from the federal penitentiary in Lewisburg, Pa., leaving behind a somewhat convoluted rebuttal of his numerous critics and detractors. Two of Gold's challengers, Miriam and Walter Schneir (who first published *Invitation to an Inquest* in 1965), claim that his testimony cannot stand careful scrutiny.

The other question of interest about Gold is whether he was truly repentant. As with many true believers, he had an overweening pride in his own rehabilitation, and whether his cooperation was based on a sense of patriotism or was only a new task on which to fix his zealotry—or a cool calculation that cooperation would mean fewer years of imprisonment, despite official positions—we shall never know.

[Only sparse biographical data on Gold are available. A large, contentious literature has emerged around the Rosenberg case and the atomic-bomb spy network. A major source for research and commentary is the trial transcript *United States* v. *Julius Rosenberg, Ethel Rosenberg, Anatoli A. Yakovlev, David Greenglass and Morton Sobell*, U.S. District Court, Southern District of New York, C.134–245, Mar. 6–Apr. 6, 1951. See also Louis Nizer, *The Implosion Conspiracy* (1973); and Ronald Radosh and Joyce Milton, *The Rosenberg File: A Search for the Truth* (1983).]

ROBERT J. KELLY

GOLDWYN, SAMUEL (July 1879–Jan. 31, 1974), pioneer movie producer, was born Schmuel Gelbfisz in the Jewish ghetto of Warsaw, Poland, oldest of six children of Aaron David Gelbfisz, a secondhand dealer, and Hannah Reban Jarecka. Later publicity confused the facts (he moved his birth date forward to Aug. 27, 1882, for example), but even a carefully researched version of his early life resembles an improbable movie script. At sixteen he fled Warsaw, walking five hundred miles to Hamburg, Germany, where he learned glovemaking; the Jewish community later paid his passage to England. After walking 120 miles from London to the home of relations in Birmingham, he learned English and anglicized his name to Samuel Goldfish; while in England he acquired a taste for British clothes, manners, and speech. In 1898, he embarked for the United States, arriving on Jan. 1, 1899.

Rejecting Manhattan's Lower East Side, Goldfish traveled to Gloversville, N.Y., where immigrant Jews had established a glove manufacturing center. After working long hours and improving his English at business college, he persuaded a high-fashion glove company to hire him as a foreman.

Goldfish became a U.S. citizen on May 2, 1904. That year he offered to prove himself as a traveling salesman in his company's toughest territory, New England and upstate New York. He was soon famous in the industry, earning fifteen thousand dollars per year. By 1907, Pittsburgh, Philadelphia, Baltimore, and Washington, D.C., were added to his territory, and he had sponsored his two younger brothers' immigration and employment.

Gloversville women thought Goldfish "full of fun" though unrefined and aggressive. One who rejected Goldfish's proposal later married Jesse Lasky, a vaudeville manager and producer, and when Goldfish became manager of his company's New York office, she introduced him to her sister-in-law. Against the advice of Lasky's friend, theater owner Louis B. Mayer, who knew Goldfish's reputation as a womanizer, Blanche Lasky married Goldfish on May 8, 1910; they had one child.

In 1913, Goldfish persuaded Jesse Lasky and lawyer Arthur S. Friend to join him in the nascent movie business. While they continued their careers, Goldfish guided the new Jesse L. Lasky Feature Play Company, boldly deciding to produce only quality films of "feature length"—telling complex stories like those in stage plays—when most films were still only ten to thirty minutes long.

The company's first film, a Western based on

a Broadway play, *The Squaw Man*, was director Cecil B. DeMille's maiden effort. Sent to film in Flagstaff, Ariz., he found it "too built up" and went on to Los Angeles, setting up a "studio" in a barn at the city's edge. Thus, *The Squaw Man* became the first feature film made in Hollywood and was a nationwide success after its release in February 1914. The new company was suddenly a major producer in an explosively expanding industry made up of on-the-job learners inventing a new art and business.

Finding Lasky and DeMille headlined and praised while he, invisible, ran the business, Goldfish began a lifelong policy of self-advertisement, planting his name in every press release. Other characteristic patterns appeared as he learned his new business, from the value of stars to the selling price of production values. When director DeMille answered his complaints about half-lit actors' faces with a flippant "tell him it's Rembrandt lighting," supersalesman Goldfish decreed, "For Rembrandt lighting, they pay double."

From the first, Goldfish paid handsomely for prestigious properties: in the summer of 1914, outflanking rival Adolph Zukor, he advanced $100,000 for film rights to ten plays by Broadway's David Belasco, knowing this coup would attract writers to the company. Goldfish again outbid Zukor in 1915, signing opera star Geraldine Farrar for silent films of her famous roles.

Goldfish's early partnerships brought ego problems and power conflicts, causing his ejection from three companies he built. He frequently quarreled with Jesse Lasky, especially after Blanche Lasky divorced him for adultery in 1916. Later that year, Adolph Zukor agreed to a merger suggested by Goldfish, who was bitterly disappointed to be made chairman of the board while Lasky became first vice president of Famous Players–Lasky Corporation. Goldfish's combative and aggressive assertions of authority provoked Zukor and Lasky to force his resignation in September 1916.

Using the nine hundred thousand dollar buyout of his stock and investments, Goldfish formed a new company with Broadway producers Archibald and Edgar Selwyn; Edgar's playwright wife, Margaret Mayo; and director-producer Arthur Hopkins. Combining the best-sounding syllables of the partners' names, Goldwyn Pictures was incorporated in November 1916, with a trademark designed by Howard Dietz: a lion's head framed by the motto Ars Gratia Artis. Spending lavishly on "quality" talent, Goldfish, as its president, supervised every operational detail of the company. Two years later he totally identified with it by legally adopting its name. In December 1919, Samuel Goldfish became Samuel Goldwyn.

Although it quickly built prestige with the industry and the public, Goldwyn Pictures had too few commercial successes to meet costs and was forced to seek additional investors. Goldwyn tried various devices to increase film quality and income, creating Eminent Authors to hire prestigious scriptwriters and importing select foreign films, such as *The Cabinet of Dr. Caligari* (1921), all to no avail. By 1922, Goldwyn Films was bankrupt and Goldwyn lost control to the board chairman, Frank Joseph Godsol, who had brought du Pont money into the company and immediately began maneuvers to oust Goldwyn. Within months, Goldwyn Pictures merged with Loew's Incorporated's Metro Pictures; the addition of Louis B. Mayer Productions brought in a long-hated rival. Before Metro-Goldwyn-Mayer was even incorporated in 1924, Samuel Goldwyn withdrew with a substantial financial settlement.

Metro-Goldwyn-Mayer (MGM) had taken the Goldwyn Pictures' logo and motto but had neglected Goldwyn's right to his own name. Learning that he was forming Samuel Goldwyn, Inc., MGM sued, maintaining that Goldwyn Pictures had prior title. In 1923 Federal Circuit Judge Learned Hand ruled that Goldwyn could use the phrase "Samuel Goldwyn Presents" on his films, commenting that "a self-made man may prefer a self-made name."

Though amused when popularly believed to be part of MGM, Goldwyn avoided further corporate entanglements. Thrice burned, shut out by partners who owed much of their success to him, Goldwyn determined to stay independent, holding 100 percent of his new company's stock. Despite recurring financial and distribution problems, he never again surrendered control. Of all the moguls of his generation, Goldwyn was the only one still owning his own studio at his death.

Goldwyn shared power only with his second wife and lifelong business confidante, actress Frances Howard McLaughlin, whom he married Apr. 23, 1925; they had one child. Goldwyn moved permanently to Hollywood, where his wife skillfully managed his household and social life. Able to make and maintain friendships with rivals and even detested personal enemies, such as Mayer, she helped Goldwyn attain stature and influence that he might never have had without her.

Goldwyn spoke out with great freedom on issues others were reluctant to discuss. He became "the voice of the industry," writing in the *New York Times* and other publications against such trends as double features and in favor of his ideas for improving the industry and its products.

A generous contributor to and worker for many charities, Goldwyn proposed and was founding chairman in 1940 of the Permanent Charities Committee of the Motion Picture Industry, which centralized support for Hollywood's wartime charity efforts. He served as president of the United Jewish Welfare Fund, and in the 1950's established a scholarship at the UCLA medical school.

In an atmosphere of fear and hysteria in which even his superpatriotic *The Best Years of Our Lives* (1946) was labeled as a "Red" film, Goldwyn was the only producer to condemn publicly the House Committee on Un-American Activities for its 1947 investigations of Hollywood, privately telling President Truman that the committee's tactics themselves were un-American.

A lifelong admirer of creative talent, Goldwyn funded annual awards for both creative writing and the best painting by a southern California artist. He was honored for these and other efforts. The Hollywood Foreign Correspondent's Association named its Golden Globe Award for best foreign film of the year after Goldwyn. In 1960, the emperor of Japan awarded him that nation's Order of the Rising Sun for promoting "cultural understanding" between the United States and Japan. The last of his many honors was the nation's highest civilian award, the Medal of Freedom, presented to the ailing Goldwyn at his home in 1971 by President Richard Nixon.

Goldwyn's contributions to film include the discovery and nurture of numerous film stars. He gave important opportunities to Ronald Colman, Vilma Banky, Miriam Hopkins, Merle Oberon, Eddie Cantor, David Niven, Teresa Wright, Dana Andrews, Paulette Goddard, Lucille Ball, Danny Kaye, Gary Cooper, and Laurence Olivier, among others.

Goldwyn revered, coddled, and rewarded tal-

ent. He publicly advocated and implemented profit-sharing schemes long before they became usual in the industry. Legendary cinematographer Gregg Toland, who shot thirty-seven Goldwyn films, was the first creative employee to receive stock shares. William Wyler directed eight Goldwyn films, including *The Best Years of Our Lives*. Other Goldwyn titles (from more than seventy) include *Street Scene* (1931), *Arrowsmith* (1931), *Nana* (1934), *Dodsworth* (1936), *Dead End* (1937), *Wuthering Heights* (1939), and *The Little Foxes* (1941). He alternated these "quality" films with popular melodramas, mysteries, comedies, and musicals: *Stella Dallas* (1925; remade 1937), *Bulldog Drummond* (1929), *Raffles* (1930; remade 1939), *Whoopee!* (1930), *Roman Scandals* (1933), *The Goldwyn Follies* (1938), *Ball of Fire* (1941), *Guys and Dolls* (1955), and his controversial last film, *Porgy and Bess* (1959).

Unable to find suitable properties, Goldwyn stopped producing after the failure of *Porgy and Bess* (many had objected to that film's portrayal of "low-life" blacks). He felt that Hollywood's product had become "trashy." During this period he rented his studios to television producers. He was disabled in March 1969 by the first of a series of strokes. He died in Los Angeles.

Goldwyn was the most publicly colorful of his generation of eastern European immigrants who shaped and dominated the first five decades of Hollywood filmmaking. Many popular films embodied their immigrants' version of the American Dream, forming America's vision of itself as well as the moviegoing world's vision of America. Of Goldwyn's contributions to this vision, *The Best Years of Our Lives* is the best and was his proudest achievement.

Goldwyn viewed his films as personal statements, insisting that every detail conform to his taste and perfectionist standards; this often brought bitter conflicts with directors and writers, some of whom refused to work with him again. The lasting appeal of many of his films testifies to his accurate feel for audience responses and to the success of the rule he professed to follow: "to please myself, and if I did that, there was a good chance I would please others."

[Alva Johnston, *The Great Goldwyn* (1937), is full of entertaining anecdotes. See also Carol Easton, *The Search for Sam Goldwyn* (1976); Arthur Marx, *Goldwyn* (1976); and A. Scott Berg, *Goldwyn* (1989).

Goldwyn's films are surveyed in Alvin H. Marill, *Samuel Goldwyn Presents* (1976). Lawrence J. Epstein, *Samuel Goldwyn* (1981), analyzes many of the same films as examples of Goldwyn's "auteurship" through total control of production. An obituary is in the *New York Times*, Feb. 1, 1974.]

DANIEL S. KREMPEL

GOODMAN, PAUL (Sept. 9, 1911–Aug. 2, 1972), man of letters, was born in New York City, the son of Barnett and Augusta Goodman. Business failure provoked his father to desert the family, forcing his wife and her three children to move from Greenwich Village to a cheap apartment on the Upper East Side. Paul Goodman attended Hebrew school as well as a public institution for the academically gifted, Townsend Harris High School, from which he graduated at the top of his class in 1927. Entering the City College of New York, he fell under the influence of the rigorous philosopher Morris Raphael Cohen and began to imbibe the anarchist writings of Peter Kropotkin. Graduating with honors in 1931, Goodman then attended classes in classics at Columbia University, without officially enrolling, before transferring to the University of Chicago. Although the impoverished graduate student completed his Ph.D. requirements by 1940, continued indigence helped prevent him from formally becoming Dr. Goodman until 1954, when the University of Chicago Press published his thesis on *The Structure of Literature*. By then he had built a minor reputation outside academia with his short stories, poems, and essays, which were published in a variety of mostly avant-garde periodicals.

A committed pacifist who avoided military service during World War II, Goodman subscribed throughout his adult life to an independent, nonviolent, communitarian anarchism. The moral passion with which he rejected social and political norms consigned him, however, to the periphery of American intellectual life; and the consequences, from the 1930's through the 1950's, were poverty, neglect, and estrangement. Yet he never stopped writing, even when unsympathetic editors and publishers denied him a forum. For much of this period, Goodman derived much of his livelihood from lay therapy, which he conducted for about twenty-five hours a week at the New York Institute for Gestalt Therapy. A champion of the theories of Wilhelm Reich, who claimed that

physical satisfaction is the basis of mental and emotional health, Goodman became successful enough as a practitioner to coauthor, with Frederick Perls and Ralph Hefferline, a textbook on *Gestalt Therapy* (1951).

Goodman was also an apostle of sexual liberation, and the urgency of desire and the frustration of homosexual yearnings are themes that haunt his fiction. The open assertion of his bisexuality—and especially the openness of his homosexual preferences—made many of his friends and acquaintances uncomfortable. Such candor also led to his dismissal from teaching positions at the Manumit School of Progressive Education in New York (1942) and the experimental Black Mountain College in North Carolina (1950). Yet most of his adulthood was spent in a couple of common-law marriages because, as Goodman explained, "I don't believe that people's sexual lives are any business of the state; to license sex is absurd." He was married to Virginia Miller from 1938 until 1943; they had one daughter. Sally Duchsten was married to him from 1945 until his death and was the mother of Goodman's son and another daughter.

He had managed to survive three decades of marginality and failure, when the publication of a loosely connected set of essays made the itinerant teacher and bohemian famous at the age of forty-nine. *Growing Up Absurd* (1960) had already been rejected by over a dozen publishers, including the firm that had commissioned it. But Goodman's flair for articulating what troubled so many of the young—his salvos against an America that "thwarts aptitude and creates stupidity" and that lacks "enough man's work" or "honest public speech" or "the opportunity to be useful"—helped reactivate the radical tradition. Such criticism not only helped encourage the political and social changes of the 1960's but also made them intelligible. First serialized in *Commentary*, *Growing Up Absurd* validated the disaffection of many young Americans, who could discern little purpose in what Goodman called the Organized System—the bureaucratic apparatus of the liberal state and of consumer capitalism. Believing that human nature is intrinsically creative, innocent, and loving, he argued that oversized institutions violated these generous impulses.

The acclaim bestowed upon *Growing Up Absurd* enabled its author to apply more widely his credo that "voluntary association has yielded most of the values of civilization." He was free to dip into a trunkful of his unpublished manuscripts, releasing five books in 1962, for instance, and showing so astonishing a range that his oeuvre had to be catalogued under twenty-one separate categories in the New York Public Library. But only one topic, he asserted, inspired him—"the human beings I know in their man-made environment." This approach was holistic, aiming at the ideal of harmony: "Everything I do has exactly the same subject—the organism and the environment," especially its urban version. Analyzing the excessive scale and psychic dysfunction of contemporary institutions, Goodman imagined solutions, animated by the "democratic faith . . . that everybody is really able to take care of himself, to get on with people, and to make a good society."

With his older brother, the architect Percival Goodman, he offered a utopian contribution to communitarian theory and urban planning, *Communitas* (1947, rev. ed. 1960), which argued for a two-tiered economy (subsistence and luxury) that would remedy the maldistribution of wealth. Goodman's libertarian politics, burnished by pragmatism and empiricism, influenced the Berkeley Free Speech Movement in 1964 and the nascent New Left, and inspired *Utopian Essays and Practical Proposals* (1962) and *Like a Conquered Province: The Moral Ambiguity of America* (1967). An editor of the pacifist journal *Liberation* from 1962 to 1969, Goodman sharply condemned militarism and statism and became a familiar speaker at protests against American intervention in Vietnam. But by the end of the decade, he diverged from his "crazy young allies," who seemed to repudiate the tradition of scientific inquiry and professional standards. *The New Reformation: Notes of a Neolithic Conservative* (1970) was a final sign of his intellectual independence even more than of his radical stance. But Goodman was perhaps best known for his indictment of education as among the most dispiriting manifestations of the Organized System. *Compulsory Mis-Education* (1964) argued for a series of ingenious experiments, from practical apprenticeships to voluntary schools designed to foster a sense of plenitude; and *The Community of Scholars* (1962) envisioned small settings of learning that harkened back to a medieval system of higher education largely bereft of administration.

Goodman himself frequently taught as well, in institutions as varied as New York University, the University of Wisconsin, Sarah Lawrence College, San Francisco State College, and the University of Hawaii.

Social criticism and political activism did not distract his own muse, however. His short stories fill four volumes; and his longer fiction includes the vibrant but self-indulgent tetralogy, *The Empire City* (1959). His five volumes of plays and even more of poetry have also found admirers, though not widespread critical or scholarly recognition. Interviewing him in 1966, journalist Richard Kostelanetz found Goodman "perceptibly melancholic . . . and remarkably relaxed for a man so active and productive. He talks easily and engagingly. . . . His graying brown hair is long, dry, stiff and unruly; his dress [is] generally as informal as his language and habits." Whether obscure or famous, Goodman honored his own distinctive code of anarchism, which never curdled into hostility to "our beautiful, pluralist and populist experiment" in self-government. He lived mostly on New York's Lower West Side but spent part of every year on a farm in North Stratford, N.H., where, five years after his son Matthew, a promising scientist, was killed in a fall while mountain climbing, Goodman died of a heart attack.

[Biographical information can be found in Kingsley Widmer, *Paul Goodman* (1980), and Peter Parisi, ed., *Artist of the Actual: Essays on Paul Goodman* (1986), the only full-length treatments. He is portrayed, at the height of his fame in 1966, in Richard Kostelanetz's *Master Minds* (1969). Among the keenest analyses of Goodman's writings are Theodore Roszak's *The Making of a Counter Culture: Reflections on the Technocratic Society and Its Youthful Opposition* (1969), and Richard King's *The Party of Eros: Radical Social Thought and the Realm of Freedom* (1972). An obituary appears in the *New York Times*, Aug. 4, 1972.]

STEPHEN J. WHITFIELD

GORE, ROBERT HAYES (May 24, 1886–Dec. 26, 1972), governor of Puerto Rico, was born in Knottsville, Ky., the son of Joseph Henry Gore and Mary Carrico. His childhood was not pleasant because his father's death required that he work to support his family. He attended school briefly in Owensborough, Ky., after which his mother tutored him at home. Despite his financial handicap, Gore attended

St. Mary's College in Notre Dame, Ind. He graduated with a B.A. in 1904, and three years later, on Oct. 2, 1907, he married Lorena Haury. They had nine children. Shortly after his wedding, Gore's career plans began to blossom when he became a reporter for the *Evansville* (Ind.) *Press.* He worked his way through the ranks and became managing editor of the *Evansville Press* in 1909. He served in this position until 1916, in which year he became the editor and publisher of the *Terre Haute* (Ind.) *Post,* remaining there until 1921.

Because of his interest in his family, Gore wrote two books geared toward children during his tenure at the *Post. Wampus Cat* was published in 1918, followed by *Newsboys' Mystery Novels* that same year. This second work was influenced by his involvement in the newspaper business and journalism.

Despite his love for journalism, Gore found he was also interested in insurance. In fact, Gore is credited with having introduced the idea of selling liability insurance through subscriptions in newspapers in the early years of his career. His interest developed to such an extent that he resigned from the newspaper business and devoted his energies full-time to his insurance business, which eventually amassed over $2 million. It was so profitable that Gore founded the R. H. Gore Company, Insurance, in Chicago in 1921.

Despite his success in the insurance business, Gore decided to retire because of poor health. In 1929, he moved to the Fort Lauderdale, Fla., area. There Gore bought a farm and returned to his first love, the newspaper business. In 1929, following a savage hurricane, Gore took advantage of lowered real estate values and bought three small local newspapers, including the *Fort Lauderdale News.*

In 1932, Gore supported the presidential candidacy of Franklin Delano Roosevelt and became a member of the National Democratic Committee. After Roosevelt was elected, Gore's influence in the newspaper industry assured him a position in the new president's entourage. During Roosevelt's first year in office, Gore served as the president's national finance chairman. When Puerto Rican Territorial Governor James Beverly stepped down because he was frustrated with the legislature, Gore pressed his own candidacy for the post, as did several influential members of Puerto Rico's upper class, including Donald Draughon of the

United Porto Rico Sugar Company and James Farley, Roosevelt's campaign manager. On Apr. 27, 1933, Gore got his wish and was nominated governor of Puerto Rico.

Gore's selection was viewed with some dismay by native Puerto Ricans. Because of his strong belief in Roosevelt's New Deal policies and his desire, in the words of Raymond Carr, to create a "local Democratic party by a judicious handout of jobs," the new governor ran afoul of several political opponents who did not share his views. For example, Puerto Rican journalist Ruby Black described Gore as a "gum-chewing, plump balding man with a salesman's persona."

Gore tried to make the best of the situation, but he angered many liberal upper-class Puerto Ricans by removing many of them from the territory's university. Key island officials then succeeded in making Gore look inept, especially in the eyes of Secretary of War George H. Dern.

Gore's housecleaning in the university stemmed from his unofficial policy, as dictated to him by the secretary of war, of keeping track of anti-American sentiment and trying to lessen its effects on the island. Gore overstepped his bounds, trying almost to colonize the island. These efforts were coolly received in Washington. Gore's own lack of political tact did not help the situation. Indeed, his actions helped the Puerto Rican legislature reduce the governor's position to a figurehead post. After several battles with the legislature over the university and over the teaching of the English language in the island's public schools—which led to student protests and civil unrest—Gore resigned as governor and returned to Florida.

Gore then resumed his interests in the newspaper business and insurance, but he also built hotels, including the Governor's Club Hotel and Sea Ranch Resort Hotel, both in Fort Lauderdale; the Park Hill Hotel in Hendersonville, N.C.; the Franklin Hotel in Brevard, N.C.; the Green Park Hotel in Blowing Rock, N.C.; and the Algren Hotel in Ashville, N.C. These hotels were built under Gore's direction between 1935 and 1939.

A devout Roman Catholic, Gore became benefactor of Notre Dame University and left many of his papers and personal effects to the institution. Gore also continued his activity in the newspaper business, starting the *Pompano Beach Sun Sentinel* in 1960 and holding the honorary chairmanship of the Gore Newspaper

Company from 1963 to 1972. Gore was also an avid collector of beer steins and books about rare orchids. Gore died in his adopted home, Fort Lauderdale.

[Many of Gore's papers are held at the University of Notre Dame, Notre Dame, Ind. See Paul A. Gore's biography of his grandfather, *Past the Edge of Poverty* (1990). Raymond Carr, *Puerto Rico: A Colonial Experiment* (1984), contains some interesting biographical material not found in any other source. Thomas G. Matthews, *Puerto Rican Politics and the New Deal* (1960), contains detailed information about Gore's term as territorial governor of Puerto Rico. Also see *New York Times* articles from Apr. 1933 through Jan. 1934 on this subject. An obituary is in the *New York Times*, Dec. 27, 1972.]

BRIAN CARPENTER

GOSLIN, LEON ALLEN ("GOOSE") (Oct. 16, 1900–May 15, 1971), baseball player, was born on a farm outside of Salem, N.J. His parents, James Goslin and Rachel Baker, had a dairy and vegetable farm, and Leon helped with the chores while he attended Mannington Township School. The young man often rode his bicycle into the town of Salem to play baseball. Goslin also made his own bat and wooden ball from the wood of a fallen tree with a circular saw and a penknife. His schooling was interrupted after the sixth grade by his father's illness.

Back in school in 1917 after his father sold the farm and moved into Salem, the teenage Goslin played semiprofessionally with the Salem team. When Goslin went to work the following year at the Du Pont munitions factory, he played in an industrial league for $3 per game. Umpire Bill McGowan, who was then working in the International League, recognized the quality of Goslin's play and recommended the right-hander to the Columbia, S.C., team in the South Atlantic (or "Sally") League in 1920.

By the next year, 1921, Goslin was a full-time outfielder, having been converted from a pitcher by manager Zinn Beck. Goslin used his left-handed batting skills and his speed to lead the league in four offensive categories. At the end of 1921, after he batted .390 in the Sally League, Goslin's contract was purchased for $7,000 by the American League's Washington Senators. Goslin was not the best fielder, and his errors each year were in the double digits, but he had a high number of assists. In 1922

Goslin fractured a wrist but still managed to hit .324 in more than one hundred games; the next year Goslin came to bat six hundred times and hit for a .300 average.

In 1924, Goslin won the runs batted in (RBI) championship with 129 and led the Senators to their first pennant. And in their first World Series that year, Goslin had eleven hits, including a double and three home runs. He batted .344 during the Series and made six consecutive hits, including four in one game, to aid the Senators' winning effort.

In 1925, the Senators were again champions of the American League, with Goslin leading the league in triples, but went on to lose to the Pirates in the World Series, although Goslin again struck three home runs and hit over .300 with eight hits.

Goslin continued his .300 seasons in both 1926 and 1927, and then, in 1928, he won the batting championship on the last day of the season by making three hits in four plate appearances. Equally remarkable, he struck out but nineteen times during the entire season. Ironically, he had begun the season by injuring his arm so severely he had wondered if he would ever play again. Goslin's average fell below the .300 level for the first time in 1929, and the next year he was traded to the Browns of St. Louis on June 14.

Goslin was under contract to the Browns, with whom he averaged 104 RBI, until he was traded back to the Senators on Dec. 14, 1932. The next year he hit .297, and again the Senators played in the World Series. The American League team lost the series, four games to one, to the powerful New York Giants. Traded a year after he returned to the Senators, Goslin had the distinction of playing in every World Series game in which the Senators ever participated.

The 1934 season found him with the Detroit Tigers. Goslin was then thirty-three years old, an age at which a player's most productive years are over. But he provided manager Mickey Cochrane with 106 runs scored and another 100 runs driven in. Goslin became one of the Detroit "G-men"—the other two G's being Hank Greenberg and Charley Gehringer. Additionally, he came to bat more times than he ever had in his career and batted .305. He also marked 1934 with two interesting batting feats: he grounded into four consecutive double plays on April 28, and he hit safely ten consecutive times. In the World Series that year, one marked by the throwing of vegetables at Joe Medwick of the Cardinals, Goslin quarreled with umpire Bill Klem, a man who was fond of reminding players he never erred, on an elevator. When Goslin tried to apologize in public the next day, Klem became angry and shouted epithets at Goslin. Klem was eventually fined $200 for the abuse he had directed at Goslin, not to mention his public misbehavior. Goslin's is one of the first cases in which a ballplayer won a battle with an umpire.

The next year, Goslin forever endeared himself to Tiger fans when, against pitcher Larry French of the Cubs, he drove in Mickey Cochrane with the run that won the World Series at the Tigers' home park, Navin Field. That was to be his last World Series. When he retired, he had hit more home runs in World Series than any other player before.

In the eighteen years Goslin played baseball, the Yankees won the pennant ten times, the Philadelphia Athletics won three times—those two teams being the powerhouses of the American League—and the other five pennants went to teams on which Goslin played.

Goslin had one more productive year, 1936, during which he had 180 hits and 125 RBI. But in 1937, assigned to play in but seventy-nine games, Goose hit almost 80 points below the .315 he had hit in the previous year.

Released by the Tigers in May 1938, he was brought back to the Senators and Griffith Stadium. He played in only thirty-eight games with the Senators, his last stop in the majors. During that time, he hit his fifth career home run as a pinch hitter, a record at the time. For two years he was with the Trenton team in the Inter-State League as player and manager. His last year in professional baseball was as a nonplaying manager in 1941.

Goslin married Marian Wallace, a social worker, in December 1940. She died in 1959. For many years he ran a boat rental business in Bayside, N.J. He loved to talk about hitting fastball pitchers and was especially fond of recounting his home run off a young Bob Feller. He spoke very warmly as well of his friendship with Babe Ruth.

In his career, Goslin assisted in 47 double plays from the outfield, averaged 194 hits per year, averaged 114 RBI per year, and scored more than 100 runs on average each season. He knocked in at least 100 runs and also hit .300 or higher for eleven seasons.

He was elected to the Baseball Hall of Fame in 1968. At the time he was inducted, Goslin, in comparison with other members of the Hall of Fame, ranked twenty-fourth in hits with 2,735, twenty-fourth in doubles with 500, and eighteenth in RBI with 1,609. His lifetime batting average after 2,287 games and 8,665 times at bat was .316. Bill James, the baseball historian, in 1986 ranked him fourth among all left fielders and thirty-third among all professional baseball players.

He died in Bridgeton, N.J., in a hospital near his home.

[The library at the National Baseball Hall of Fame in Cooperstown, N.Y., is the source of primary material. Goslin recounted his career in Lawrence S. Ritter, *The Glory of Their Times* (1966). Bill James, *The Bill James Historical Baseball Abstract* (1986); and *The Baseball Encyclopedia* (1987) are the best sources for statistics. A chronological recounting is given in Martin Appel and Burt Goldblatt, *Baseball's Best* (1977). An obituary is in the *New York Times*, May 16, 1971.]

THOMAS H. BARTHEL

GOTTSCHALK, LOUIS REICHENTHAL (Feb. 21, 1899–June 23, 1975), historian and educator, was born in Brooklyn, N.Y., the son of Morris Frank Gottschalk and Anna Krystall, both Jewish immigrants from Russian Poland. Gottschalk's father, a barber and small shopkeeper of modest means, raised his family in Albany and Brooklyn. After attending local public schools, where he displayed considerable intellectual promise, Gottschalk entered Cornell University at sixteen. He earned his B.A. (1919), M.A. (1920), and Ph.D. (1921) there and was strongly influenced by his teachers, the medievalist George Lincoln Burr, the Americanist George Hull, and the Europeanist Carl Lotus Becker.

Becker interested him in French history, instilling the conviction that historians should strive to incorporate the methodologies of other disciplines into their work. Under his direction Gottschalk completed his doctoral dissertation, "The Political Career and Theories of Jean Paul Marat." Expanded into a full-scale biography and published in 1927 as *Jean Paul Marat: A Study in Radicalism*, it bore all the traits that would mark his later writings: extensive use of primary sources, both manuscript and printed; critical scrutiny of all the available evidence; and a dispassionate, nonpartisan approach combined with a straightforward narrative style. This objective study of the French Revolutionary earned Gottschalk a favorable reputation on both sides of the Atlantic.

He married Laura Reichenthal, a young Cornell undergraduate, in 1920. Divorced five years later, Gottschalk nevertheless retained her maiden name, adopted in tribute to her father, as his own middle name. In 1930 he wed Fruma Kasdan; they had two sons.

After completing his graduate studies, Gottschalk taught first at the University of Illinois, Urbana (1921–1923), then at the University of Louisville (1923–1927). His career at Louisville ended when he and other faculty quarreled with the school's new president, George Coville, over curriculum and academic policy. Dismissed from his position in 1927, Gottschalk left for the University of Chicago, where he rose from associate professor to Gustavus F. and Ann M. Swift Distinguished Service Professor in 1959. After thirty-seven years at the University of Chicago, fifteen of which were spent chairing the history department, he formally retired in 1964, but continued to teach at the University of Illinois, Chicago Circle, until his death. Besides teaching, Gottschalk also served as assistant editor (1929–1943) and acting editor (1943–1945) of the *Journal of Modern History*, helping to make it a force in the profession.

He won eminence as a historian of the French Revolution because of his numerous publications in the field. His *Era of the French Revolution (1715–1815)* appeared in 1929. A comprehensive and balanced account, it long remained a standard text. He then undertook a biography of the Marquis de Lafayette, a project that would occupy him for some forty years. Conscientiously gathering and analyzing all the materials that could be discovered concerning the French patriot, Gottschalk produced a series of volumes that traced his career in detail: *Lafayette Comes to America* (1935), *Lafayette Joins the American Army* (1937), *Lafayette and the Close of the American Revolution* (1942), *Lafayette Between the American and the French Revolution (1783–1789)* (1950), *Lafayette in the French Revolution Through the October Days* (1969), and *Lafayette in the French Revolution from the October Days Through the Federation* (1973). He also published a critical edition of the general's correspondence with George Washington in 1944. Gottschalk determined that Lafayette was motivated to aid the Americans less by any liberal ideas than by his dissatisfaction with conditions in France, his thirst for glory, and a traditional French hatred for England. But as a result of his American experience, Lafayette became a symbol of liberty, the "hero of two worlds," who guided the French Revolution during its first years.

During World War II, Gottschalk served on the Committee of Historians to Analyze and Appraise Current Conditions and Prospective Developments in Germany. In late 1943 it produced a secret report providing the Army Air Force with an appraisal of the effects that strategic bombing had on the Third Reich.

From his wartime experience Gottschalk gained a better understanding of the need for historical synthesis. In collaboration he wrote *Europe and the Modern World* (2 vols., 1951–1954), which described how European culture had spread around the globe and bound it together. He also coauthored and edited *The Foundations of the Modern World, 1300–1775.* Published in 1969 under the auspices of UNESCO as volume four of the "History of Mankind: Cultural and Scientific Development," it incorporated contributions made by historians from numerous countries who held diverse political viewpoints. While not entirely satisfactory as universal history, it did set forth the latest research and interpretations of the time.

Refining the methodology that he had learned at Cornell and infused into his own scholarship, Gottschalk for many years taught a "laboratory course in historical method" along with colleagues at Chicago. He also offered seminars in European historiography where graduate students presented papers that were rigorously evaluated by their fellows and instructor alike, applying his techniques. In this manner he trained several generations of historians, many of whom became eminent scholars in their fields.

Gottschalk explained his methods in a "laboratory manual" written for college undergraduates: *Understanding History: A Primer of Historical Method* (1950; 2d ed., 1969). In it he defined history as a "three-dimensional" discipline, one that partook of science, art, and philosophy. He observed that "as a method, it follows strict rules for ascertaining verifiable facts; as exposition and narrative, it calls for imagination, literary taste, and critical standards; as interpretation of life, it demands the philosopher's insights and judgments."

But he was concerned not only with the mechanics of historical writing and contended that historians should serve a wider purpose. In a presidential address before the American Historical Association, he declared that those engaged in the profession should employ their training "for the guidance of an unmoored society seeking firmer anchorage." Through numerous public talks and newspaper articles, Gottschalk stressed that, while history taught no "lessons," it did provide useful understanding of contemporary events.

Gottschalk's numerous contributions to his discipline were recognized by his election as president of the American Historical Association (1953) and the American Society for Eighteenth Century Studies (1971). The French government in 1953 named him a chevalier of the Legion of Honor for his work.

Always conscious of his origins and concerned about antisemitism, especially in the academic world, Gottschalk involved himself with Jewish causes. During the 1940's he presided over the Chicago Board of Jewish Education and also became active in B'nai B'rith, especially its Hillel Commission, which he chaired from 1963 to 1969. Reflecting on his heritage and career, Gottschalk mused: "I often wonder what would have happened to me if my parents had remained in Poland." He died in Chicago.

[Gottschalk's papers are in the University of Chicago archives. The University of Louisville archives hold records concerning his troubled stay there. His quarrel with the school's administration is discussed by Dwayne Cox, "The Gottschalk-Colvin Case: A Study in Academic Purposes and Command," *Register of the Kentucky Historical Society*, Jan. 1987. Richard Herr and Harold Parker, eds., *Ideas in History* (1965), contains an extensive bibliography of his writings. Gottschalk paid tribute to his teacher in "Carl Becker: Skeptic or Humanist?" *Journal of Modern History*, June 1946. He discussed his own teaching in "A Professor of History in a Quandary," *American Historical Review*, Jan. 1954. See also John Hall Stewart, "Louis Gottschalk and Lafayette," *Journal of Modern History*, Dec. 1970. Obituaries are in the *New York Times*, June 25, 1975; *University of Chicago Record*, Nov. 26, 1975; and *American Historical Review*, Apr. 1976.]

JAMES FRIGUGLIETTI

GRABLE, BETTY (Dec. 18, 1916–July 2, 1973), film actress, was born Ruth Elizabeth Grable in St. Louis, Mo., the youngest daughter of Leon Grable, an accountant and stockbroker, and Lillian Hoffman, who was the driving force behind her career. Betty Grable was educated at the Mary Institute, an exclusive girl's school in St. Louis, and later at the Hollywood Professional School, which taught child actors on the movie set. At an early age, her mother arranged toe, tap, ballet, and acrobatic dancing lessons for her, as well as training in voice and saxophone.

When she was five, Grable danced and played the saxophone on a local stage in St. Louis, performing about the same time in public ballet. Her mother coached her on a small dance platform at home, enforcing practice sessions during vacations, and introduced her to theatrical folk on tour. The Grables visited Hollywood during their vacation in the summer of 1928. In the spring of 1929, at Lillian's insistence, they moved with their daughters to California seeking Betty's big break.

Grable's first opportunity came at Twentieth Century–Fox, where she was hired as a dancer and singer. She appeared in the film *Happy Days* (1929) at age thirteen, and in *Let's Go Places* (1930) while singing with orchestras and remaining a member of the Goldwyn Chorus girls. Her mother, always seeking publicity, enrolled Grable in amateur-night performances, booked her for private parties and benefits, secured bit parts for her under the name Frances Dean, and wooed directors for her. Grable gained visibility dancing in RKO's *The Gay Divorcee* (1934), performing a specialty dance number that landed her a studio contract.

In the period 1935–1936, she appeared in a series of Paramount movies featuring her as "Betty Coed" that included the films *Collegiate*, *Pigskin Parade*, *College Swing*, and *Campus Confessions*. She turned down parts she felt were not in keeping with her style or image, favoring lowbrow to highbrow films, light to heavy story lines, fanciful to realistic roles, and romantic to woeful scripts. Her trick, wrote contemporary journalist Pete Martin, was "the ability to portray a pocket-sized red-hot mama who at the same time possesses the kind-hearted camaraderie and unimpeachable morals of a Girl Scout." Her robust health and peaches-and-cream complexion made her perfect for the role of college sweetheart, even though she never graduated from high school herself. She was careful about interviews and preferred to be given the questions in advance. Upon turning twenty-one, she married former child-star Jackie Coogan; they divorced in 1940, shortly after Grable's career took off.

Her big break came when Darryl Zanuck noticed her photo in a Los Angeles newspaper in 1939. She was doing a show with Jack Haley at the San Francisco Exposition at the time, and this exposure led her to a part in the Broadway musical, *Du Barry Was a Lady* (1939) with Ethel Merman. Haley had arranged for some publicity shots of Grable to be taken which appeared in the paper. Zanuck re-signed her with Fox, and she had a job waiting for her when she finished the musical. Returning from Broadway with good reviews, Grable landed the lead in *Down Argentine Way* (1940) when the original lead, Alice Faye, became ill. The film was such a success, that Grable and Faye subsequently shared top billing in *Tin Pan Alley* (1940).

Betty Grable remained in good physical shape from the exercise that her dance routine gave her; her clear-eyed, carefully nurtured health and radiance were captured on screen and her platinum hair set off her rosy pink skin. When preparing to make a film, she was like a fighter in training, pruning away excess pounds, toning for the screen's magnification. The luscious costuming of her movies further enhanced both this gorgeous image and the robust vitality so necessary to the characters she dramatized. Her stamina allowed her to work long hours without visibly tiring and perform strenuous song-and-dance routines time and time again to create the one perfect take. Her pictures were financial successes, so studio producers felt no risk in filming in technicolor, which raised production costs by one-third. This allowed her hair and skin to shine, and her overall image to be *saftig*, (zaftig). In lower-budget black and white, said a contemporary director, Betty Grable appeared as any other girl from "a five-and-dime store basement." Technicolor musicals starring Grable included *Footlight Serenade* (1942), *Springtime in the Rockies* (1942), and *Four Jills in a Jeep* (1944).

During World War II she became the serviceman's favorite pinup girl and was being labeled "the world's most popular blonde." Perhaps best known for her saucy bathing-suit photo looking over her shoulder in high heels, she was the darling of American GI's who requested three million copies of her picture. Her publicity agents once sent out 60,000 photos in one week. There was one photo of Betty Grable in cheesecake pose for every twelve men in uniform. In 1941, she appeared in Manhattan wearing a sweater knitted for her by the British Royal Air Force. Each week she received more than 10,000 fan letters. Her famous legs were insured by Lloyd's of London for a million dollars and immortalized after being pressed into cement outside Grauman's Chinese theatre. Indeed, her legs became her trademark and were, according to Pete Martin writing in *Time* (1950), among the factors that "made her wealthy and consistently magnetic at the box office."

In 1943, she married bandleader-trumpeter Harry James; they had two daughters. She shared his passion for horses and racing, and they established a horse-breeding estate in Calabasas, Calif. Soldiers around the world, however, still mooned: "I want a girl just like the girl that married Harry James." The separate Grable and James fan clubs now merged as the James Family Fan Clubs. They were married for twenty-two years before divorcing in 1965.

Between 1942 and 1951 Betty Grable was among the ten top box-office draws, according to an annual poll of exhibitors conducted by both the *Fame Annual* and the *Motion Picture Herald*, and she drew an annual salary of between $200,000 and $300,000. In 1942, as a newcomer, Grable placed eighth among such idols as Abbott and Costello, Mickey Rooney, and Clark Gable. In 1947 Grable earned $208,000, less than in previous years, but still ahead of Henry Ford II, president of Ford Motor Company, who earned $200,000. In the 1940's she was Hollywood's highest-paid woman by far, judged *Time* in 1949, and although she was down from her pinnacle, she remained "the best paid woman in the U.S."

She was careful about her costars and dance partners: Victor Mature's masculine body matched Grable's feminine charms in the limited attire worn in *Song of the Islands* (1942); Dan Daily, her first dance partner who costarred with her in *Mother Wore Tights* (1947) and *My Blue Heaven* (1950), matched her spirited, intricate dance steps, toe-to-toe. *Time* said of *Song of the Islands*: "There is blonde Miss Grable, especially well organized for paradisal parts, who doffs the sweater she has lived in at school on the U.S. Mainland and resumes her role as the community's No. 1 lei girl. Victor Mature also sheds most of his clothes. After watching bountiful Betty shake her seaweed and sing half a dozen songs, he succumbs." The American public took a vicarious vacation to sun-filled Hawaii for the price of a theater ticket and listened to uplifting renditions offering "hearts are high when the moon is low." This type of romantic musical proved to be the mother lode for Fox, with Grable's movies making profits of more than $15 million during the period 1940–1948.

Nostalgia worked well in such Grable films as *Sweet Rosie O'Grady* (1943), an 1880's period piece costarring Robert Young, wherein she sang "My Heart Tells Me" (in a wooden bathtub) as well as "Rosie," "Waiting at the Church," and "Going to the Country Fair." Grable's movies were fun, offering escape and romance. Her film *Coney Island* (1943) received rave reviews.

In her starring roles, Betty Grable always got her man. The strong female characters she played talked back saucily to men, were not taken in by smoothies, and were both willful and determined. Both sexes admired her sense of independence. Americans sensed that Grable was working patriotically on the home front to buoy wartime spirits. Her image perfectly paralleled the decade in which she starred, calling for confidence, competence, hard work, and a competitive spirit. Her character was modeled by a flinty perseverance that paid off in stardom. Grable displayed a kind of selflessness on screen, giving of herself in animated dance gyrations, or in reassuring songs of love. She was the girl left behind that servicemen were fighting to protect, and the reason they longed to return home.

In 1945 she made *Billy Rose's Diamond Horseshoe* after the birth of her first child and demonstrated "that motherhood's extra pound or so of flesh can improve even the screen's most unimprovable body." Grable films by this time were big-budget, lavish, vividly colored, always good-humored, and often preposterous. Women enjoyed Betty Grable as much as men; both longed for romance, fun, happy endings, fulfillment of dreams. It was observed by *Time* in 1948 that ambitious stenographers or Hollywood-hungry mothers saw Betty Grable as a "daydream that might come true."

As the postwar period ended in the 1950's, Grable moved on to *Wabash Avenue* (1950) and *How to Marry a Millionaire* (1953), costarring with Marilyn Monroe and Lauren Bacall. Monroe's career was rising as Grable's was

diminishing. Her last film was *How to Be Very, Very Popular* (1955), and she revived her career temporarily with a nightclub act that starred her with Dan Dailey in Las Vegas in a brief version of *Guys and Dolls* (1962). She bought a home in Las Vegas, periodically returning to California to appear in TV-produced movies during the late 1950's and 1960's. Grable died of lung cancer in Santa Monica, Calif.

[Full-length biographies are Doug Warren, *The Reluctant Movie Queen* (1981); and Spiro Pastos, *Pin-Up* (1986). Biographical material can be found in G. Ringgold, "Betty Grable," *Screen Facts* 4, no. 1 (no date); Kyle Crichton, "Out on Two Limbs," *Collier's*, May 17, 1941; "Living the Daydream," *Time*, Aug. 23, 1948; Pete Martin, "The World's Most Popular Blonde," *Saturday Evening Post*, Apr. 15, 1950; "Ham and Legs," *Time*, Apr. 13, 1959; and Jeffrey Gorney, "Betty Grable, 1916–1973," *Films in Review*, Aug.–Sept. 1973. The Desoto Brown Collection of Honolulu contains photos of Grable filming *Song of the Islands* in Hawaii. An obituary appears in the *New York Times*, July 4, 1973.]

Barbara Bennett Peterson

GRAHAM, FRANK PORTER (Oct. 14, 1886–Feb. 16, 1972), educator, mediator, and senator from North Carolina, was born in Fayetteville, N.C., the son of Alexander Graham and Katherine Sloan. He was raised in a Scotch Presbyterian family that emphasized the importance of education. His father became the first superintendent of public schools at Fayetteville and later at Charlotte, N.C.

Frank attended the University of North Carolina at Chapel Hill and graduated with a B.A. in 1909. He attended the law school at the university and was admitted to the bar, but never practiced law. In 1914 he was invited to teach a history course at the university. Excited by this challenge he decided that college teaching would be his life's work. He went to New York City and received an M.A. in history from Columbia University in 1916. With the entry of the United States into World War I, he joined the Marines as a private; he was discharged as a lieutenant in 1919. He taught at Chapel Hill until 1922, when he decided to do further graduate work, first at the University of Chicago, then at the Brookings Institution in Washington, D.C., and finally at the London School of Economics. He never completed the dissertation requirement for the Ph.D.

When he returned to Chapel Hill in 1925 to take up an appointment in the history department, he brought with him an enthusiasm to teach the importance of democratic values. In order to reach beyond the classroom, he joined many organizations and participated in many conferences concerned with improving the lot of the weak and poor. He supported workman's compensation laws, trade unions, public welfare, and restrictions on conditions of work for women and children.

In 1929, in the course of a major labor dispute in Gastonia, N.C., violence broke out and several persons were shot, including the chief of police, who died. A number of strikers were indicted for murder, and public sentiment was inflamed. Graham became a leading figure among those pressing for a fair trial. "We owe it to the most despised of those accused in this case that they be tried by due process of law without regard to their economic or religious views." Later that year he published "An Economic Bill of Rights," which called for free speech and assembly, the right of labor to organize and bargain collectively, and for a reduction of the sixty-hour work week in the textile mills.

Elected president of the University of North Carolina in 1930, Graham spoke about academic freedom in his inaugural address. "It means freedom from the prejudices of section, race or creed; it means a free compassion of her sons for all people in need of justice and brotherhood. . . . In the university should be found the free voice not only for the unvoiced millions but also for the unpopular and even hated minorities."

In 1931 the legislature consolidated the university at Chapel Hill with the State College at Raleigh and the Woman's College at Greensboro, and the following year Graham was elected president of the Consolidated University.

On July 21, 1932, he married Marian Drane, the daughter of an Episcopal clergyman, in Edenton, N.C. They had no children.

He remained president of the university until he was appointed to the Senate in 1949. Throughout his career at the university, he was known not only for his liberal views, but also for his personal warmth and gentle, persuasive manner. His concern for his students was legendary. When a former student, a socialist, was arrested during a major textile strike in High Point, N.C., in 1934, Graham publicly offered him bail. His attachment to liberal causes and his membership in more than 150 political organizations was often criticized by those who believed that the president of the university should not be active in social causes, no matter how worthy their goals.

A strong supporter of the New Deal, he was called for public service by both President Franklin Roosevelt and President Harry Truman. He served as chairman of the Advisory Council on Economic Security (1934); he was appointed to the Advisory Committee on Education (1938) and to the Advisory Committee on Economic Conditions in the South (1938). In 1941 he was appointed to the National Defense Mediation Board and in 1942 to the War Labor Board. He worked sixty-hour weeks, spending weekdays in Washington with the WLB and weekends on university business in Chapel Hill. He remained with the War Labor Board until December 1945, when he returned to full-time duties as president of the university.

Late in 1946 President Truman appointed Graham to serve on the Committee on Civil Rights, which issued its historic report, *To Secure These Rights*, on Oct. 29, 1947. Graham, one of two southerners on the committee, supported the recommendations to eliminate segregation, the poll tax, the white primary, and other forms of discrimination, but he opposed a Fair Employment Practices Committee possessing compulsory authority. In a minority statement he wrote, "The best way ultimately to end segregation is to raise the educational level of the people of the states affected; and to inculcate both the teachings of religion regarding human brotherhood and the ideals of our democracy regarding freedom and equality."

In 1947 Secretary of State George Marshall asked Graham to serve on a three-man United Nations Committee to mediate a dispute between the Netherlands and the Republican forces in Indonesia. The committee was successful in its negotiations, and early in 1948 Graham was able to report to the United Nations the cessation of hostilities between the sovereign United States of Indonesia and the Kingdom of the Netherlands.

On Mar. 22, 1949, Graham was appointed by Governor W. Kerr Scott to the U.S. Senate to fill the vacancy created by the death of Senator J. Melville Broughton. In 1950 Graham failed to be nominated in a bitterly contested

Democratic runoff primary. His defeat was thought to be the result of the strong opposition in the state to the Truman civil rights program. Graham noted, in his "Farewell Statement" to the Senate (Sept. 22, 1950): "I have run the risk of taking sides in the midst of events which could not wait for certification and conformity while freedom was embattled. . . . I took sides in the South and in the nation for the fairer consideration of Jews, Catholics, Negroes, and the foreign born; for fairer consideration of children, teachers, industrial workers, farmers, little business people and consumers."

From 1951 to 1970 Graham was employed by the United Nations. He was appointed Representative for India and Pakistan to try to resolve their dispute over Kashmir. While he was unsuccessful in his efforts to negotiate a peaceful solution in the conflict over Kashmir, he became an effective spokesman for the UN. He gave hundreds of speeches in support of the UN throughout the United States. He resigned from the UN in 1970. He died in Chapel Hill.

[The Graham papers are in the Southern Historical Collection of the University of North Carolina, Chapel Hill, N.C. The University of North Carolina Collection, which also contains some of Graham's papers, is housed there as well.

His early U.N. activities are discussed in Alastair M. Taylor, *Indonesian Independence and the United Nations* (1960). For a description of his political campaigns, see Julian M. Pleasants and Augustus M. Burns, *Frank Porter Graham and the Senate Race in North Carolina* (1990). Warren Ashby, *Frank Porter Graham: A Southern Liberal* (1980), is the only full biography. The North Carolina Collection at the university contains oral and television interviews with Graham. There is an obituary in the *New York Times*, Feb. 17, 1972.]

ALAN P. GRIMES

GRANT, JANE COLE (May 29, 1892–Mar. 16, 1972), journalist, free-lance writer, and feminist, was born Jeanette Cole Grant in Joplin, Mo., the second daughter of Robert T. Grant and Sophrona Cole. Her father, a farmer and merchant of Scottish-Irish ancestry, had originally come from Canada. On her mother's side she claimed descent from the famous abolitionist John Brown. She was raised in Missouri and Kansas, attending public schools. At the age of sixteen she went to New York City to prepare for a musical career, but her real talent

turned out to be journalism. She worked briefly for *Collier's Weekly* and in 1912 joined the *New York Times*. Assured at first that "women were merely tolerated at the *Times*," she came to the attention of manager Carl V. Van Anda. She steadily advanced to become the paper's first woman general assignment reporter at the foremost news operation in the country.

After America entered World War I, Grant began working in Paris for the Young Men's Christian Association. She became acquainted with Harold W. Ross, an American soldier who had just become editor of a newly founded army newspaper, *Stars and Stripes*. Ross was a shy, ungainly Coloradan who planned to return to the West Coast after his discharge. Grant convinced him to consider New York City. After the war she returned to her job at the *New York Times* and, on Mar. 27, 1920, married Harold Ross. They had no children. They agreed to live on her salary and to save Ross's earnings for a new publication. "Our magazine would fill the metropolitan gap" she later wrote, "it would be . . . attractive, gay and informative." She approached Raoul Fleischmann, heir to a bread-baking fortune, for a commitment of $25,000 and, on Feb. 21, 1925, the first issue of the *New Yorker* appeared. Within a year, the humorous and sophisticated weekly was a success. Grant has been called "midwife" for the magazine. She described her time at the magazine in a book entitled *Ross, the New Yorker, and Me* (1968).

Grant helped administer the magazine for the next six years while continuing her work for the *New York Times*. She also wrote articles for the *Saturday Evening Post*, the *American Mercury*, and other periodicals. She became active in women's causes, describing the origins of her commitment in an essay, "Confessions of a Feminist." On the day of her wedding to Ross, she was "jolted" out of apathy when one of the witnesses called her "Mrs. Ross." She formed the Lucy Stone League in 1921, on behalf of married women who wanted to maintain their maiden names.

Jane Grant was known for her lively repartee. She was one of the wits who made up the famous "Round Table," a luncheon gathering at New York's Algonquin Hotel. She was divorced from Harold Ross in 1929, and married William B. Harris, an editor of *Fortune* magazine, on Dec. 8, 1939; they had no children.

In their final years, the couple operated

White Flower Farm, a retail plant and seed operation in Litchfield, Conn. Grant died of cancer in Litchfield.

[See Grant's memoir, *Ross, the New Yorker, and Me* (1968). Obituaries are in the *New York Times*, Mar. 17, 1972; *Time*, Mar. 27, 1972; and *Newsweek*, Mar. 27, 1972.]

KEVIN J. O'KEEFE

GRANT, WILLIAM THOMAS, JR. (June 27, 1876–Aug. 6, 1972), merchant, was born in Stevensville, Pa., the younger son of William Thomas Grant and Amanda Louise Bird. His father was a flour miller and, later, a tea-store owner in Fall River, Mass. Both businesses were unsuccessful; Grant noted later that "there was never a time when the family income was sufficient" to give his mother "any sense of security." Yet, his father was "always the radiant optimist" who believed "shining success was just around the corner." After the tea-store venture, the family moved to Malden, Mass., where Grant grew up and attended school.

Grant earned his first income at the age of seven by running errands. He also delivered papers, assisted the operator of a butter-and-egg wagon, sold flower seeds, and worked at a drugstore soda fountain. He left high school in the middle of his second year. Grant became an errand boy for a group of Boston lawyers and then worked for a wholesale shoe house in that city and in a warehouse for a whetstone manufacturer in Pike's Station, N.H. In 1895, he returned to Boston and entered retailing as a clerk in a boot and shoe company, followed by jobs selling shoes in a department store and managing a shoe store in Amesbury, Mass. As a sideline, he promoted prizefights.

As a shoe buyer for Almy, Bigelow and Washburn in Salem, Mass., he noticed that merchandise priced at twenty-five cents moved most briskly. "Gradually the idea dawned on me that 25 cents was a magic price," he said in his autobiography (1954). Also important was what Grant called "dramatizing merchandise in its arrangement and display so as to make it 'come alive' and have the greatest attention value for the customer." With his life savings of $1,000 and an additional $7,000 from three partners, including Almy general manager Louis K. Roskoff and W. E. Bigelow, Grant planned his first store incorporating the "magic" twenty-five-cent prices for all types of fast-moving merchandise.

Grant opened his first store on the ground floor of the Lynn, Mass., Young Men's Christian Association (YMCA) on Dec. 6, 1906. Gold block letters outlined in dark navy blue on an orange background soon became familiar on all Grant stores. "Follow me and you'll wear diamonds," he told his first employees. Grant worked long hours while handling all buying and merchandising functions; he later remarked that he "was too busy working hard to make his store succeed to realize that business conditions were so bad." Grant's formula for operating his stores included pleasing the customer, maintaining quick turnover of merchandise, encouraging strict economy, and establishing good social relations.

In October 1908, Grant opened a second store, this one in Waterbury, Conn. The success of the Waterbury store marked the beginning of the Grant chain, since it gave Grant the courage to open a third store in Bridgeport, a larger city in Connecticut, followed by stores in Lewiston, Maine, and New Bedford, Mass. In the first ten years, there were thirty-six stores, most located in less than the best business districts; they had to draw customers with unusual values and ingenious promotions. By 1918, the twenty-five-cent ceiling on merchandise was raised to $1. During the 1920's, the Grant chain expanded rapidly and became the most familiar name in discount retailing. In 1940, Grant instituted a no-price-limit policy, and eventually the stores, located in forty-four states, sold such big-ticket items as refrigerators, televisions, and home-workshop equipment.

The first W. T. Grant store in New York City, at Sixth Avenue and Eighteenth Street, opened in 1913. Although situated in one of the city's busiest shopping districts, the store was unable to compete and was not a success. A fire soon after its opening ended the company's venture into downtown Manhattan retailing, although it did maintain its national headquarters in New York City and established successful Grant stores in other sections of the city. His experience in New York convinced Grant that the opportunity for his type of store was not to be found in big cities but in the many smaller industrial cities of the United States.

The W. T. Grant Company offered stock to the public in 1928, but the William T. Grant Foundation, founded in 1936 to assist in the emotional development of the young, continued to control about 25 percent of the outstanding stock. Grant was president of the company until 1924 and thereafter chairman of the board until 1966, when he retired on his ninetieth birthday; he decided that the business needed professional managers rather than a merchant at the top. He remained as honorary board chairman until his death, although he was no longer involved in active management and drew no salary.

Grant was an amateur philosopher, a photographer, and a talented oil painter. During his active years with the company, he gave a big party at his home on Cape Cod in the fall and at his home in Miami in the winter. There, he and his top executives could play golf, go fishing, and talk shop.

Grant married Lena Blanche Brownell in 1907; they adopted two children. After she died, he married Beth Bradshaw on Sept. 3, 1930; they adopted one child. Grant died in Greenwich, Conn.

By 1972, Grant's chain operated 1,188 stores throughout the United States and employed more than sixty thousand people, placing it among the largest retailing companies in the United States, but in 1975 the W. T. Grant Company went bankrupt, the biggest bankruptcy in retailing history. The company, which had so successfully found a retailing niche during the early twentieth century, was unable to do so in the 1970's. Caught between the rapidly expanding Sears and Penney chains and several new discount houses, W. T. Grant was unable to decide on a retailing focus.

[Grant's papers are not available to the public. The company's bankruptcy dispersed many of its assets and holdings, including any of Grant's personal or professional correspondence, into competing chains. The New England Historic Genealogical Society has Grant's membership application on file; the personal data are scanty, but the information listed supports the known facts about Grant's life. Three oral histories (Jeffrey Andrew, Emily Mudd, Perrin Galpin) in the Oral History Collection, Columbia University, have remarks about him. Grant's brief autobiography, *The Story of W. T. Grant and the Early Days of the Business He Founded*, written with Guy L. Sumner (1954; enl. ed., 1962), provides information on his early life and on the establishment of his chain stores. Grant also wrote *The Basis of Chain Store Success* (1928).

See *Fortune*, Nov. 1934, which has a case study of the W. T. Grant stores; and Godfrey Lebhar, *Chain Stores in America 1859–1962* (1963). An obituary is in the *New York Times*, Aug. 7, 1972.]

MARTIN J. MANNING

GRAY, HAROLD EDWIN (Apr. 15, 1906–Dec. 23, 1972), airline executive, was born in Guttenberg, Iowa, the only son among three children of Otis Elmer Gray and Bertha Hagensick.

Gray graduated from Elkader High School in Elkader, Iowa, and in 1923 entered Iowa State University. He left in 1925 to join the U.S. Army Flying Cadet Corps and received flight training at Brooks and Kelly airfields, near San Antonio, Tex. The following year Gray entered the University of Detroit, where he studied aeronautical engineering, supporting himself by designing airplanes. He left without a degree in 1928.

Gray then went to work for Ford Motor Company, which had recently entered the airplane business with its famous trimotor. In the course of his duties he met several Ford customers then entering the airline business. One of these was Sky View Airlines, a Miami-based operation that offered pleasure and charter flights. Within a few months Gray left Ford to become a pilot for Sky View, flying vacationers and honeymooners over Niagara Falls for $5 each. He was later transferred to the company's headquarters, where most of his work involved charter flights.

While in Miami, Gray socialized with employees of the young Pan American Airways, which was led by Juan Trippe. At the time Pan American was flying two small Fokker passenger planes on a route from Miami to Key West and Havana. But Trippe, who was to become a leading figure in the American airline business, had much wider ambitions. Even then he planned to transform Pan American into the national flag carrier. In March 1928, Gray left Sky View to join Pan American, flying its new route between Brownsville, Tex., and Mexico City. The following year he married ExaBell Sublett. They had two children.

During the 1930's, Gray helped plan and establish routes between the United States and Central and South America. In 1934, he qualified as a pilot on the new transoceanic Clippers. From 1937 to 1939 he conducted survey flights to Bermuda, Ireland, England, the Azores, Portugal, and southern France. In 1939, Gray commanded the *Yankee Clipper* on its initial airmail flight between the United States and the United Kingdom. Two years later, he flew the *Capetown Clipper* nineteen thousand miles between New York and Leopoldville, Belgian Congo. By then he was a senior pilot who also trained newcomers. Trippe considered him too important to the organization to continue flying, and he informed Gray that he would soon be moved to management.

During World War II, Gray worked on projects with the army and navy, and served as operations manager for Pan American's Atlantic Division. He became manager of the Pacific-Alaska Division in 1949, and in 1952, vice-president of the Atlantic Division. The following year Gray was promoted to executive vice-president of that division, a post he held until 1960. When the Atlantic and Pacific-Alaska divisions were merged in 1960, Gray was named executive vice-president in charge of the Overseas Division.

In 1964, at the age of sixty-five, Trippe stepped down as president. He became board chairman and chief executive officer, and the board named Gray his successor as president. Gray had a reputation for being a capable administrator. He was efficient and cold; one associate called him "a man of a hundred and ten percent integrity—as a person who trusted a slide rule should be." In 1965, midway through a speech, he learned that his older son, Lieutenant Commander Harold Gray, Jr., had been killed in an air strike over North Vietnam. He finished the speech, without any sign of emotion.

Gray had his own agenda for Pan American that involved closer relations with the federal government than those sought by Trippe, who in his last years had clashed with the Kennedy administration. For instance, Trippe optioned three Concorde SST passenger planes from a British-French consortium in an attempt to force the United States to build SST's. Gray worked to prevent the resulting ill will between the Kennedy administration and Trippe but failed to do so.

Soon thereafter, Gray campaigned for a fourth jetport for the New York metropolitan area, to relieve congestion and alleviate jet noise. In 1965 Pan American instituted a global jet freighter program. In 1965 Gray placed the first orders for the new 747 airliners.

Despite his successes, Gray was constantly troubled by Trippe's second-guessing and the internecine bickering Trippe engendered. He once told an associate, "All we have to do is be good, and people will recognize it." His differences with Trippe continued, and rumors flew that he might be replaced as heir apparent by

Najeeb Halaby, Roger Lewis, or some other current or former Pan American executive. But in 1968, Trippe stepped down, announcing at a directors' meeting, "I plan to nominate President Harold Gray to succeed me as chairman and chief executive officer of our company."

At the time Gray was over sixty-two years old, and Pan American executives usually retired at the age of sixty-five. There would be no exception for Gray, who in any case was undergoing cobalt treatment for lymph gland cancer. Gray retired in 1970, after eighteen months as chairman, and was succeeded by Halaby. He died in New York City.

[There is information on Gray's career in Matthew Josephson, *Empire of the Air* (1944); Robert Daley, *An American Saga* (1980); and Marylin Bender and Selig Altschul, *The Chosen Instrument* (1982). On the early days of Pan American, see Wesley P. Newton, *The Perilous Sky* (1978). An obituary is in the *New York Times*, Dec. 24, 1972.]

ROBERT SOBEL

GREEN, CONSTANCE MCLAUGHLIN (Aug. 21, 1897–Dec. 5, 1975), historian, was born in Ann Arbor, Mich., to Andrew Cunningham McLaughlin and Lois Thompson Angell. Her father, a professor of American history at the University of Michigan and later at the University of Chicago, won a Pulitzer Prize in 1936 for his book A *Constitutional History of the United States*. She attended Fräulein von Heidenaber's Höhere Töchter Schule in Munich for a term. In 1914 she entered the University of Chicago, majoring in history; she transferred to Smith College at Northampton, Mass., two years later. After receiving a B.A. in history in 1919, she taught freshman English at the University of Chicago until 1920, and then taught at Smith.

On Feb. 14, 1921, Constance married Donald Ross Green, a textile manufacturer. Soon after they settled in Holyoke, Mass., she became interested in the industrial development of that area. Despite her later assertion—"I wasn't going to be a dreary graduate student like the ones who were hanging around my father in those days"—she enrolled at Mount Holyoke College in South Hadley, Mass. In 1925 she obtained an M.A. with a thesis on "The New England Confederation of 1643."

That same year she became an instructor in history at Mount Holyoke; while teaching part-time there, she had three children. One of her interests was reading thrillers, and she even tried writing detective stories, but was "unable to come up with a plot that had any validity." Meanwhile, she began pursuing a doctorate in history at Yale University.

In 1937 Green obtained her Ph.D. and was awarded Yale's Edward Eggleston Prize for her dissertation, "Holyoke, Massachusetts: A Case History of the Industrial Revolution in America," published by Yale University Press in 1939. Although some reviewers found flaws in her work because they felt she lacked a critical approach and did not compare, integrate, or successfully detail social development, Clifford K. Shipton found her style "readable," her "freedom from bias" rare, and her "willingness to leave conclusions to the reader" confidence-inspiring. The book has been hailed as a landmark in urban history. In 1938 she became an instructor in history at Smith, and the following year director of research for the Smith College Council of Industrial Studies, supervising graduate investigation into the industrial history of the Connecticut Valley, including the history of small-arms manufacturing. She held this part-time post until 1946.

After America entered World War II Green was named the U.S. Army Ordinance Department's historian at the Armory in Springfield, Mass.; she continued in that position until 1945. Her husband died in 1946, the same year her *The Role of Women as Production Workers in War Plants in the Connecticut Valley* was published. She also moved that year to Washington, D.C., to work as a consulting historian for the American National Red Cross until 1948, when she became chief historian with the U.S. Army Ordinance Corps Army Historical Division, Department of Defense, and headed a research team in writing a volume on the technical services of the army. During her stay there, Yale University Press published her *History of Naugatuck, Connecticut* (1949).

Green remained with the army until 1951, when she became a Commonwealth Fund lecturer in American history at University College, University of London, and later that same year served as a historian on the research and development board of the Secretary of Defense.

In 1954 Green began plans for a history of Washington, D.C. After acquiring a grant from the Rockefeller Foundation administered by the American University and the Chapelbrook

Foundation, she spent the next eight years heading the Washington history project. Meanwhile, her *Eli Whitney and the Birth of American Technology* (1956) and *American Cities in the Growth of the Nation* (1957) exhibited her growth as a historian of technology and urbanization. The culmination of her career was a two-volume history of Washington, D.C., published by Princeton University Press in 1962 and 1963; *Washington: Vol. I, Village and Capital, 1800–1878*, won her the Pulitzer Prize in 1963. The book was heralded by critics, including Arthur M. Schlesinger, Jr. After hearing about the award she immediately bought her grandson red suspenders. Her father had bought suspenders himself when he won the prize upon his wife's suggestion that he spend the money on "something he really wanted."

More books followed, including *The Secret City: A History of Race Relations in the Nation's Capital* (1967), an expansion of a previous study on Washington, D.C., that attacked the popular myth of black progress. In 1971 Green served as visiting professor of history at Dartmouth College.

The stern, stately face photographed for a *Washington Post* interview of November 1972 shortly after Green had suffered a heart attack betrayed the kind, wondering eyes of earlier photographs. Green strove to illuminate the present by understanding the past, and in the process became an authority on urban history. Direct and engaging, Green showed little patience for those who had not learned from history. "How did the heart attack affect her life?" she was asked. "I gave up smoking," she replied. She died three years later at her daughter's home in Annapolis, Md.

[Green's *Washington* papers are in the Library of Congress, Washington, D.C. In addition to works already cited, her books include *Washington, Vol. II: Capital City, 1879–1950* (1963); *The Rise of Urban America* (1965); *The Church on Lafayette Square: A History of St. John's Church, Washington, D.C., 1815–1970* (1970); and *Vanguard: A History* with Milton Lomask (1971). An interview is in the *Washington Post* (Nov. 7, 1972); and obituaries are in the *Washington Post*, Dec. 7, 1975; and the *New York Times*, Dec. 8, 1975.]

RAYMOND L. ADAMS

GROFÉ, FERDE (Mar. 27, 1892–Apr. 3, 1972), composer and arranger, was born Ferdinand Rudolf von Grofé in New York City to

Emil von Grofé, an actor and singer, and Elsa Johanna Bierlich, a cellist. The Grofés moved to Los Angeles in 1893. His mother taught Ferde to write music before he learned to write English. At five he began music lessons on piano and violin. At fourteen Ferde ran away from home because his mother had remarried after his father's death, and in his words, "There was too much stepfather and too many stepsisters and stepbrothers at home." His first job was as a bookbinder's assistant, and he later worked in Los Angeles as a truck driver, and as a steel foundry worker. In the evenings he practiced violin, piano, drums, and cornet. He began taking casual engagements at lodge dances, picnics and parades.

In 1908 Grofé joined "Professor" Albert Jerome. Barnstorming throughout California, they cleaned and pressed clothes by day. At night Jerome played the cornet and taught dancing, with Grofé accompanying on piano. In Winthrop, a mining town in northern California, Jerome disappeared, leaving Grofé with the unpaid boarding bills. The only job he could find was playing in a bordello in Winthrop for two dollars per night.

In 1909 Grofé returned home. In that year he wrote his first commissioned work, *The Elks Reunion March* for an Elks convention in Los Angeles, and with the help of his grandfather, Bernhardt Bierlich, principal cellist with the Los Angeles Symphony, he got a job with that orchestra as a viola player. For the next ten years he played in the string section. To augment his salary from the symphony he also played popular music in hotel bands, vaudeville houses, nickel-a-turn dance halls, and silent-movie theaters.

While leading a dance orchestra in Los Angeles in 1919, Grofé's arrangements caught the attention of a local bandleader, Paul Whiteman. At the end of the year he was hired to be Whiteman's arranger and piano player. Both men had the same goal: the creation of a popular music blending jazz syncopations with the orchestrated style of European symphonic music. Both jazz and classical music purists criticized this hybrid, known as "symphonic jazz," but the public loved it. One of Grofé's first arrangements was of the song *Whispering*; recorded on Victor in 1920, it sold a million and a half copies. Grofé's arrangements of *Japanese Sandman* and *Avalon* were also best-sellers. The Whiteman Orchestra became an international success largely on the strength of Grofé's

arrangements, and Whiteman became known as the "King of Jazz."

Grofé brought fame to himself and to George Gershwin when he orchestrated Gershwin's *Rhapsody in Blue* for a New York premiere by the Whiteman band on Feb. 12, 1924. Grofé retired from active playing with Whiteman in 1925, although he remained under contract as an arranger until the end of 1931. Grofé was now known as an outstanding arranger, but what he wanted to do was compose his own music. His *Broadway at Night* (1924) went unnoticed. But in 1926 his *Mississippi Suite*, introduced by Whiteman at Carnegie Hall in New York City, received favorable attention. On May 11, 1929, he married Ruth Harriet MacGloan; they had two children.

The most famous of Grofé's compositions is the *Grand Canyon Suite*, introduced by the Whiteman band in Chicago on Nov. 22, 1931. As with most of his pieces, here Grofé painted a vivid musical picture of a part of the United States. In his words, "The richness of the land and the rugged optimism of its people had fired my imagination. I was determined to put it all to music some day." The composition has five movements, "Sunrise," "Painted Desert," "On the Trail," "Sunset," and "Cloudburst."

During the next two decades Grofé conducted musical ensembles for many radio broadcasts. Most important was the Philip Morris cigarette company program (1933–34), where "On the Trail" became the opening theme and subsequently the musical background of the famous commercial portraying the bell hop "Johnny" making his "Call for Philip Morris."

Not only was Grofé a skilled composer and orchestrator, he also was a bold experimenter and innovator in the use of nontraditional sounds. *Free Air* (1929) was scored for piano and bicycle pump. *Tabloid Suite* (1933) was for orchestra and typewriter. *Symphony in Steel* (1935) utilized an orchestra and pneumatic drill, a locomotive bell, four pairs of shoes, two brooms, and a compressed-air tank. *Hollywood Ballet* (1935) used the shouting of directors and the hammering of carpenters working on a set. *Hudson River Suite* (1956) includes parts for a barking dog, a siren, and a set of bowling pins. In *San Francisco Suite* (1960) there was a cable-car bell, a foghorn, and, portraying the earthquake of 1906, simulated explosions by the percussion section.

Grofé was one of the first composers or musicians to use electronic instruments. A Meissner electric piano was featured in a 1937 Carnegie Hall concert of his music. At the New York World's Fair (1939–1940) his New World Ensemble was made up of four electronic keyboards, called Novachords, and a Hammond organ. His score for the movie *Rocket Ship XM* (1950) included the eerie-sounding theremin.

Most of Grofé's extensive musical knowledge was gained through his own studies. However, from 1922 to 1925 he studied orchestration with Pietro Floridia. Later Grofé taught that subject at the Juilliard School of Music during the summers between 1939 and 1942. On Jan. 12, 1952, the day after he divorced his first wife, he married Anna May Lempton. They appeared together in two-piano concerts beginning in 1954.

Partially paralyzed by a stroke in 1962, he continued composing throughout that decade. Grofé died in Santa Monica, Calif.

[Many of Grofé's musical manuscripts and personal papers are held in the Library of Congress. Musical manuscripts and printed orchestrations are held by the Southern Methodist University Library. A thesis by James Farrington titled "Ferde Grofé: An Investigation into His Musical Activities and Works" (1985) is held by the Florida State University Library, along with other biographical material. See also "Ferde Grofé: A Style Is Born!," *International Musician*, Aug. 1953; and David Ewen, *Popular American Composers* (1962). An obituary appears in the *New York Times*, Apr. 4, 1972.]

JOHN VOIGT

GROSSINGER, JENNIE (June 16, 1892– Nov. 20, 1972), resort owner, was the daughter of Asher Selig Grossinger, overseer of an estate, and Malke Grumet. She was born in the small village of Baligrod, Galicia, part of the Austro-Hungarian Empire; with her mother and sister she came to New York City in 1900. From the time she was a little girl she had done chores on the family's small farm. In America, she felt the need to contribute to her family's earnings. Grossinger completed the fourth grade at the age of thirteen. Although the law forbade anyone under fourteen to work, she decided not to continue her education and instead went to work making buttonholes for two cents each. In order to earn more money, she carried coats home with her, working them late into the night and straining her vision by the candlelight. After being publicly reprimanded by her foreman, she vowed that anyone who ever worked for her would never be publicly humiliated.

Grossinger enrolled in night school; because of her age she was put in the first year of high school, but a sympathetic teacher had her transferred to the fifth grade in a nearby elementary night school. Her new teacher advised her to purchase a dictionary and use it to look up unfamiliar words. Thus began a lifelong desire for and effort at self-education. One of Grossinger's biographers, Joel Pomerantz, states that "the influence these [elementary school] teachers had in Jennie's life was second only to her parents." Her father's health was failing, and before he could be fired from his factory job, he quit. Grossinger, according to Pomerantz, became "furious at a system that would work a man almost to death and then discard him when his usefulness was at an end." Later in life, she rarely dismissed a worker.

Grossinger married a cousin, Harry Grossinger, on May 25, 1912; they had three children, one of whom died in infancy. After Selig's abortive attempts to run a butcher shop and a dairy shop, the family opened a small restaurant in which Malke did the cooking, Selig was host and manager, and Jennie waited on tables. In 1914, her father suffered a physical and emotional breakdown, and the doctor recommended that he change his life-style and move out of the city. He bought a small, ramshackle farmhouse in the Catskill Mountains, near Ferndale, N.Y., where he hoped to raise crops.

When her parents moved to the farm in 1914, Grossinger, described as a "tall, blonde young woman, with . . . a quick smile and high spirits," went with them; her husband stayed at his job in the city's garment industry. The farm was not successful, so the Grossingers decided to take in a few boarders, using the four best rooms for the new business, Grossinger's Kosher Farm. In their first season they had nine boarders who paid a total of $81 (the going rate was $12 per week, but their little farmhouse did not have indoor plumbing, a telephone, or electricity, so they charged only $9). Harry and Selig Grossinger formed a lifetime partnership. Harry recruited guests in New York City and spent his weekends helping out on the farm. In 1915 the family added a six-room wing to the seven-room home, allowing them to accommodate additional guests. By 1916, the Grossinger family was solidly, if modestly, established in the hotel business, and Harry gave up his job in New York City to devote full time to the business. Selig Grossinger took care of the farm, did the marketing, and met guests at the railway station; Malke Grossinger took care of the kitchen; and Jennie looked after the bookkeeping and management.

Early in 1919, Grossinger arranged for the purchase of the more modern Terrace Hill House on a nearby estate. It had a real lobby, indoor plumbing, and electric lighting. The family moved from the small farmhouse to what became "the Big G," Grossinger's Hotel. In the same year they bought a lake and the surrounding sixty-three acres of woodland. Within the next decade the business expanded steadily and became known as Grossinger's Hotel and Country Club.

No longer was Grossinger a self-conscious, shy young woman. "Her exuberant good nature and uncanny ability to meet people and make immediate, warm contact were tangible assets to the hotel." By the time her father died in 1931, she was clearly in charge. Her mother lived until 1952.

Early in its history characteristics appeared that made the "Big G" famous. For instance, Harry encouraged customers to bring musical instruments to entertain fellow guests, and talent abounded in staff and guest shows. Grossinger added a three-piece band consisting of college students who played dance music during the peak season; a dining room for four hundred guests; a forty-five-room building, each room with a bath—revolutionary for its time and place; a lake with rowboats; a canteen (it and the boating operation were run by two cousins who later opened the 21 Restaurant in New York City); camp activities for children; winter sports such as ice skating; menu choices; uniformed bellmen; golf; and other amenities that came to be expected at all Catskill hotels.

Grossinger felt her lack of formal education acutely and took every opportunity to broaden her knowledge. A cousin, who taught English and speech in a New York City high school, instructed her in English and poetry and introduced her to Shakespeare and the French novelists. Guests were welcome to read Grossinger's varied collection of books: Jewish history, psychiatry, Kipling, and others. She took voice and diction lessons, and studied French and Spanish. On one of her vacations she took up art, and liked it so much that she brought her

teacher, Jon Gnagy (who later became a prominent television artist), to Grossinger's to instruct the guests. She once said, "I love learning and art, perhaps because I went to school such a short time."

In 1929, Grossinger hired a public relations man, Milton Blackstone, to advertise the hotel; he originated the idea of offering a free honeymoon to couples who met at Grossinger's. An estimated fifty marriages per year resulted from meetings at "the Big G." One of the most celebrated of the marriages performed at Grossinger's was that of Eddie Fisher (who had worked at Grossinger's as a $20-per-week boatboy, handing out oars and pushing off rowboats at the lake) and Debbie Reynolds in 1954.

Although not the largest Catskill hotel, Grossinger's became widely known for its guest takeover days, winter "reunions" of summer guests in New York City, the continental hostess (a widowed cousin by marriage, Karla Grossinger), vacations donated to charities for raffle and door prizes, convention facilities, and courses of all kinds.

During World War II, Grossinger's sent packages to servicemen (who had been guests or employees) overseas and sponsored bond drives (the first hotel to do so; so much was raised that a bomber was named *Grossinger Lake*). The hotel gave wounded servicemen free stays. Franklin Delano Roosevelt asked Grossinger if she would send food for a children's picnic to be held at Hyde Park, and she did. He liked the pickled herring so much that she sent him a hamper of Jewish delicacies whenever he was at Hyde Park.

Grossinger's pioneered the Catskill practice of offering different talent acts every night (and, out of respect for those who stayed the season, never booked the same act twice in any one season). As a result, a large number of celebrities got their start at Grossinger's: Milton Berle, Sid Caesar, Red Buttons, Eddie Fisher, Alan King, Jackie Gleason, Jackie Mason, Tony Bennett, Henny Youngman, Imogene Coca, Danny Thomas, Shelly Winters, Jan Peerce, Joel Grey, Buddy Hackett, Mel Brooks, Liberace, Pearl Bailey, Harry Belafonte, Zero Mostel, Sammy Davis, Jr., and opera stars Robert Merrill and Roberta Peters. Established notables like Eddie Cantor, Danny Kaye, George Jessel, Moss Hart, Irving Berlin, Connie Francis, Joey Adams, Ella Fitzgerald, and Lionel Hampton became regular entertainers and guests.

Barney Ross was the first boxer to train at Grossinger's. He was followed by Jack Dempsey, Rocky Marciano, Max Baer, Ingemar Johansson, Gene Fullmer, Joey Maxim, and Dick Tiger. As a result, Damon Runyon, visiting with some sportswriters, dubbed the hotel "Lindy's with trees." By hosting boxing training, the hotel stayed open far beyond the end of summer, and Grossinger quickly realized that if guests were to be attracted, the hotel had to have winter sports as well. A toboggan slide and an ice skating rink were added.

Grossinger's employed people who were to become famous in athletics, or were already famous: Babe Didriksen Zaharias and Joe Turnesa were resident golf professionals (among those who played the Grossinger's course as guests were Gene Sarazen, Sammy Snead, and Doug Ford); Don Budge, Pancho Gonzalez, Bobby Riggs, Bill Talbert, Pancho Segura, and Jack Kramer gave tennis exhibitions. Florence Chadwick, who swam the English Channel, trained in Grossinger Lake for her second successful crossing, and a few years later became the first full-time aquatic director. Basketball games on Friday nights attracted some of the best collegiate stars in the country.

At its height, Grossinger's, some ninety-five miles northwest of New York City, accommodated one thousand three hundred guests in six hundred rooms (its dining room seated one thousand seven hundred), and employed a staff of one thousand. There were two kitchens, one for meat dishes and the other for dairy dishes. There was a nightclub with two stages. Grossinger's had its own post office, newspaper, airport, ski slope, Olympic-size swimming pool, golf course, and riding academy, and accommodated some 150,000 guests annually. The playhouse-theater was also used as a synagogue, a Catholic church, a Methodist meeting hall, and a Seventh-Day Adventist prayer site. Its slogan, "Grossinger's Has Everything," came from a letter written by a soldier in Burma during World War II who had received a fruitcake from someone at the hotel: "The fruitcake reminds me of Grossinger's—it has everything."

In later years Grossinger's children, Paul and Elaine, shared in the management of the enterprise. Paul graduated from the Cornell University School of Hotel Administration, and upon his father's death in 1964, he became president and chief executive officer. Elaine was secretary-treasurer.

One of Grossinger's earliest memories was of her mother nailing a contribution box to the wall of their tenement apartment. "A life without sharing," her mother said, "is barren." It was a lesson Grossinger learned well. In December 1954, she was featured on Ralph Edwards's *This Is Your Life*; because her interfaith activities and charities had been emphasized on the program, she was deluged by requests for help. Over the years she received awards from the U.S. Coast Guard, the Red Cross, the March of Dimes, the Boy Scouts, and the Albert Einstein School of Medicine. In 1960, an audience of over fifteen hundred gathered in the grand ballroom of the Hotel Astor in New York City raised enough money to spearhead a drive to build the Jennie Grossinger Medical Center in Tel Aviv, Israel.

Gradually the hotel business began to decline in the Catskills. The prospect of returning to the same place each year lost its allure in an age of jet travel, when it was possible to fly to Miami or even the Caribbean in as much time as it used to take to drive to the "mountains." Prosperity enabled many former guests to purchase second homes. Diet-conscious Americans found resorts like Grossinger's, where "no one should go hungry," less attractive. The staff had become unionized by the 1970's, reducing profit margins. In 1986, Grossinger's closed.

Eddie Cantor recalled his first visit to Grossinger's and his meeting with Malke, Grossinger's mother: "When I asked if all this land belonged to her, she replied, 'No, it belongs to God. I'm just watching it for Him while I'm alive.'" The daughter surely learned from the mother. She concluded one holiday address by saying, "I love the hotel business, and I love all of you people. My only wish is that when I go to heaven, God will make me a hotelkeeper there. And there, I assure you, you'll never have trouble with reservations." According to her daughter, Grossinger was a "woman before her time," developing the hotel that bore her parents' name into what many considered to be the apotheosis of resorts.

Harry Grossinger died in 1964. Grossinger's younger brother, also named Harry, died in 1965, making her the only surviving member of the remarkable family that came to the New World at the turn of the century, poor in everything but hope, love, and humanity. After years of suffering from arthritis, headaches, high blood pressure, back ailments, and occasional depression, Grossinger died at Grossinger, N.Y., leaving a legacy of hospitality.

[There are no family papers extant. Grossinger wrote *The Art of Jewish Cooking* (1958). See also Harold J. Taub, *Waldorf-in-the-Catskills* (1952); Joel Pomerantz, *Jennie and the Story of Grossinger's* (1970); and Tania Grossinger, *Growing up at Grossinger's* (1975). An obituary is in the *New York Times*, Nov. 21, 1972.]

JOSEPH N. HANKIN

GROVE, ROBERT MOSES ("LEFTY") (Mar. 6, 1900–May 22, 1975), major-league baseball player and member of the Baseball Hall of Fame, was born in Lonaconing, Md., one of seven children of John Grove and Emma Beeman. His father was a coal miner, and Grove grew up in a hardscrabble rural community that limited his formal education to the eighth grade. Upon leaving the two-room Charlestown School, the thirteen-year old Grove went on to labor in coal mines, on railroad crews, and in local factories. A shy and sensitive youth, he developed an aloof and surly attitude that stemmed from a fear of meeting people.

Grove taught himself to pitch, often using homemade equipment. He became a local star and was playing with a factory team in 1919 when he was scouted and signed to a professional contract by the newly organized Martinsburg, W.Va., team of the Blue Ridge League. The six-foot, three-inch left-hander debuted as a Martinsburg pitcher in 1920 and was earning $125 a month when his prowess attracted the attention of Jack Dunn, owner of the International League's Baltimore Orioles. For $3,100 Dunn bought Grove's contract from the Martinsburg owner, who used the windfall to build a much-needed outfield fence.

Joining the powerful Orioles was a heady experience for the unsophisticated Grove. Shunned as a rookie by his teammates, he became a driven loner. But the hard-throwing Grove became a dominant pitcher, winning twelve games and losing two in his first season. That winter Grove married Ethel Gardner of Lonaconing; they had two children.

Over the next four seasons Grove won ninety-seven games and lost thirty-four as the pitching star of the perennial champion Orioles. During these years Grove led the league in strikeouts each year, but his wildness also showed as he thrice led the league in bases on balls. As the

best pitcher in this top-ranked minor league, Grove was much coveted by major league teams. But the $100,000 sale price demanded by Dunn delayed Grove's major-league debut until 1925, when owner Connie Mack of the American League's Philadelphia Athletics purchased his contract. The $100,600 sale price was the highest paid for a player since the New York Yankees acquired Babe Ruth from the Boston Red Sox in 1920.

Much was expected of Grove when he joined the Athletics in 1925, but his debut with this second place team was inauspicious. Although he led the league in strikeouts, he also led in bases on balls and his 10–12 won-loss record was Grove's only losing season of his seventeen-year major-league career. Improving in 1926, he compiled a 13–13 record while leading the league in strikeouts and earned run average. A driven perfectionist, he improved his control and intimidated batters with his speed and his meanness. As he later admitted, "I've thrown at guys, but never at their heads." Grove was equally intolerant of errant teammates whom he cowed with occasional temperamental displays, but he applauded his brilliant catcher, Mickey Cochrane, of whom he said, "He could read my mind."

Grove's greatness came to fruition in 1927 when he began a skein of seven consecutive seasons during which he won at least twenty games each season. During these years the Athletics won consecutive American League pennants in 1929–1931, with Grove winning seventy-nine games and losing only fifteen. During the 1930 season, when hitters posted their highest batting marks of the twentieth century, Grove's 28–5 pitching record led all American League pitchers. And in 1931, Grove's 31–4 performance, which included a record-tying string of sixteen straight victories, won him the American League's Most Valuable Player Award. In three World Series appearances during these years Grove pitched in eight of the eighteen games, winning four and losing two, with an earned run average (ERA) of 1.75. At the pinnacle of his career, Grove was reputed to be the fastest pitcher in the game. As the columnist Arthur ("Bugs") Baer quipped, Grove "could throw a lamb chop past a wolf." But Grove remained an aloof loner, an inveterate hotel-lobby sitter who punished himself by smoking ten-cent cigars when he lost but more often rewarding himself with twenty-five-cent perfectos when he notched a frequent victory.

Grove's nine seasons with the Athletics ended in 1933 when the financially straitened Mack sold him to the Boston Red Sox for $125,000, an astonishing sum for an aging ballplayer in a Great Depression year. But Grove's pitching prowess was unsurpassed by any contemporary. Indeed, his 24–8 record of 1933 was his seventh straight season of twenty or more victories, and in nine seasons with the Athletics he compiled a 195–79 won-loss record with an ERA of 2.87.

But Grove's Boston debut in 1934 was hampered by arm trouble and his 8–8 mark was disappointing. He rebounded in 1935 and posted his eighth and last twenty-victory season. By then, with age tolling on his vaunted fastball, Grove had become a finesse pitcher who learned to pace himself and to rely more on the mixed deliveries he had developed in later years. Thus he became one of the few left-handed pitchers to successfully cope with Boston's notoriously short left-field fence. In eight seasons with the Red Sox Grove led the American League in ERA four times and compiled a 105–62 record. Grove was forty-one years old when he won his three-hundredth major-league game by beating the Cleveland Indians on July 25, 1941. It was his last major-league victory and he was released at the end of the season.

In 1947 Grove was elected to the Baseball Hall of Fame. At the time his 300–141 record was the highest winning percentage by a left-handed pitcher. His 3.06 ERA, compiled during a hitter's era, was as remarkable as his feat of twice striking out the opposing side in one inning on nine pitches, which he accomplished in 1928. A durable pitcher, he started 456 games and completed 300, and also appeared as a relief pitcher in 160 games. During his career Grove led the majors in more pitching performance areas than any other pitcher.

In retirement Grove resided in Lonaconing, where he owned and operated a bowling alley and served terms as police commissioner and town councilman. Widowed in 1961, he moved to Norwalk, Ohio, where he lived with his son and daughter-in-law until his death. He is buried in Frostburg, Md.

[Although no biography of Grove exists, an extensive file of clippings and photos can be found in the National Baseball Library at Cooperstown, N.Y. An excellent survey of Grove's career, written by a lifelong friend, is Ruth Bear Levy's "Recollections of Lefty Grove: Baseball's Greatest Left-handed Pitcher," *Maryland Historical Magazine*, Summer 1987 and Summer 1988. See also J. K. Keatley, "From Maryland's Past: Lefty Grove," *Maryland Magazine*, Summer 1987. Other useful sources include John Thorn and John B. Holway, *The Pitcher* (1987); Gerald Astor, *The Baseball Hall of Fame 50th Anniversary Book* (1988); Kevin Kerrane, *The Hurlers* (1989); and John A. Mercurio, *Record Profiles of Baseball Hall of Famers* (1990). The statistical record of Grove's career is found in *The Baseball Encyclopedia* (1969) and the major-league era during which Grove played is covered in David Q. Voigt, *American Baseball*, vol. 2 (1983). Obituaries appear in *Sporting News*, June 14, 1975, and the *New York Times*, May 23, 1975.]

DAVID QUENTIN VOIGT

GRUENING, ERNEST (Feb. 6, 1887–June 26, 1974), senator, editor, and author, was born in New York City, the son of Emil Gruening, a German-born eye and ear surgeon, and Phebe Fridenberg. After studying in New York City schools and at the Hotchkiss School in Connecticut, Gruening enrolled at Harvard College, intending to become a physician. He received a B.A. in 1907. Work as a reporter for the *Boston American* while he was a medical student at Harvard determined him to follow a career in journalism. After taking his M.D. in 1912 he successively worked for the *Boston Evening Herald* and the *Boston Traveler*. In 1917, during World War I, he went to Washington where he assisted in organizing the War Trade Board's bureau of imports; the war ended while he was an officer candidate. Without taking a commission in the Field Artillery Reserve he returned to journalism and was managing editor of the *New York Tribune* from 1918 to 1919. From 1919 to 1920, he worked as general manager of *La Prensa*, and from 1920 to 1923 served as general manager of the *Nation*.

Gruening had changed jobs frequently because of his resistance to publishers' curbs on his freedom. At the *Nation* he assailed United States policy in Latin America, criticizing American financial exploitation and gunboat diplomacy there and urging independence for Haiti and Santo Domingo. He accompanied the Senate Select Committee of five senators who investigated U.S. military occupation of those two nations in 1921. From 1921 to 1922, he visited Mexico, writing articles for the *Nation* and *Collier's Weekly*. In 1928, his book, *Mexico and Its Heritage*, voiced Gruening's concerns about that troubled nation and his admiration of President Plutarco Elias Calles.

Gruening left the *Nation* in 1923, giving his time to his book and magazine articles, and in 1924 he acted as national director of publicity for Robert La Follette's presidential campaign on the Progressive party ticket. He returned to the newspaper world in 1927 as founding editor of the *Portland* (Maine) *Evening News*. His crusading spirit impelled him to attack the interests of Samuel Insull, a Chicago utilities magnate, in electricity, finance, and politics in Maine. He exposed the pyramid of holding companies that Insull had erected and explained why Maine electric rates were high and investors imperiled. Gruening was largely responsible for the defeat of Insull's efforts to export Maine's hydroelectric power to his utility empire. After the Federal Trade Commission began to issue its damning report on the power industry, Gruening summarized the results of the ongoing investigation in 1931 in his book, *The Public Pays*. In 1964, he updated and enlarged the book, which he called *The Public Pays . . . and Still Pays*.

Gruening returned to the *Nation* as editor late in 1932. He urged Fiorello La Guardia to run for mayor of New York and discussed Latin American policy with President Franklin D. Roosevelt, who appointed him as adviser to the United States delegation that attended the Seventh Inter-American Conference at Montevideo, Uruguay, in 1933. At the conference Secretary of State Cordell Hull, encouraged by Gruening, rejected the right of armed intervention.

In early 1934, Gruening accepted the editorship of the *New York Evening Post*, but he soon clashed with the publisher, and in the summer Roosevelt appointed him director of a new agency, the Division of Territories and Island Possessions of the U.S. Department of the Interior. For more than two years he also served as administrator of the Puerto Rican Reconstruction Administration, striving for land distribution, adequate housing, rural electrification, and other causes. He helped organize the 1939 government Antarctic expedition, commanded by Admiral Richard E. Byrd, which fostered scientific research and American claims to the region.

A visit to Alaska in 1936 inspired in Gruening a lifelong interest in the territory, dazzling in its scenery but an orphan of the New Deal. In 1939, President Roosevelt appointed him territorial governor of Alaska. Resisted at first by persons wanting an Alaskan as governor, Gruening in time became popular with citizens. One of the many victories he gained in Congress on behalf of Alaska was approval of the Alaska highway; however, he lost the battle over the western route he preferred.

During World War II Gruening ended federal censorship of Alaskans' mail, opposed racial discrimination (later securing passage of an antidiscrimination bill), and instigated election of the first Native Americans to the legislature. In the immediate postwar years he continued his reform efforts, including the implementation of tax measures strenuously opposed by the powerful salmon industry. After Alaskans in a referendum voted for statehood in 1946, Gruening bent his efforts to attain that goal. Not reappointed in 1953 by the new Eisenhower administration, he wrote a book, *The State of Alaska* (1954), and campaigned for statehood, which came in 1958. His reward was election to the United States Senate in 1958, though by the margin of 2,581 votes.

Taking his seat in January 1959, Gruening won assignments on the Committees on Interior and Insular Affairs, Public Works, and Government Operations. A part of the rising Democratic tide, he customarily voted against Eisenhower administration measures, believing they minimized federal aid to domestic needs and were lavish in foreign aid. Working closely with the Majority Leader Lyndon B. Johnson and also with the northern Democrats, he strongly supported his party and spoke at length for the Civil Rights Act of 1960.

Gruening rejoiced in John F. Kennedy's election in 1960 and found opportunity to promote legislation meeting the distinctive needs of his far-north state. He repeatedly voiced skepticism about how foreign aid was spent, and he secured passage of a law restricting military aid to Latin America. By a margin of some eight thousand votes Alaskans in November 1962 elected him to a second term, during which he engineered enactment of the Public Works and Development Act in 1965.

Senator Gruening was perhaps the first public official to call for withdrawal of American forces from Vietnam. On Mar. 10, 1964, he delivered a speech entitled "The United States Should Get Out of Vietnam," asserting that no vital American interest was at stake in that conflict, and that in spite of substantial American aid the situation in Vietnam was deteriorating. In August 1964, he and Senator Wayne Morse were the only two senators to vote against the Gulf of Tonkin Resolution invoked by the Johnson administration as justification for extending the war. Throughout the remainder of his Senate term, he denounced the protracted war as illegal and needless, decrying the draft and what he called the "military-industrial-labor-congressional complex."

Gruening early evinced an interest in federal action to curb population growth at home and abroad. He secured legislation in 1966 to provide two new subcabinet positions entitled Assistant Secretary for Population Planning, one in the State Department and the other in the Department of Health, Education, and Welfare. He elicited endorsement of his cause from former President Eisenhower and President Johnson and, over a period of three years, held thirty-two congressional hearings on its behalf. Finding little cooperation from the federal bureaucracy he came to look on his crusade as largely educational. He introduced the bill to create the National Foundation for the Arts and the Humanities, which became law in 1965.

In 1968, Gruening lost his senate seat by a margin of 1,694 votes. His autobiography, *Many Battles* (1973), details his struggle against the forces he believed to be corrupting democratic society. He married Dorothy E. Smith on Nov. 19, 1914; they had three children, two of whom predeceased their father, who died in Washington, D.C.

[Gruening conducted an extensive correspondence, which is held in widely scattered manuscript collections. *Many Battles: The Autobiography of Ernest Gruening* (1973) is a full and fine account. Obituaries are in the *Washington Post* and the *New York Times*, both June 27, 1974.]

JAMES A. RAWLEY

GUGGENHEIM, HARRY FRANK (Aug, 23, 1890–Jan. 22, 1971), industrialist, ambassador, and publisher, was born in West End, N.J., the son of Daniel Guggenheim, a mining magnate and philanthropist, and Florence Shloss, a strong supporter of women's rights. The family patriarch, Simon Meyer Guggenheim, a tailor, had emigrated from a Jewish ghetto in Lengnau, Switzerland, to America in 1848, settling in Philadelphia with his son Meyer. Meyer established the mineral industry in Colorado. A

generation later, Daniel Guggenheim became head of the family firm, Guggenheim Brothers, and expanded its mining and smelting operations, and by 1901, the Guggenheims dominated mining in the United States.

Harry Guggenheim attended the Columbia Grammar School in New York City. In 1907, after high school, he enrolled in the Sheffield Scientific School at Yale University to study mining but left in 1908, after one term, to learn the practical side of the mining business at the family-owned American Smelting and Refining Company works at Aguascalientes, Mexico. He married Helen Rosenberg in November 1910; they had two children and were divorced. His second marriage, to Caroline Morton in February 1923, ended in divorce in 1939. The couple had one child. In 1939, Guggenheim married Alicia Patterson, who died in 1963; they had no children.

With a push from his father, in 1910 Guggenheim resumed his studies in England at Pembroke College, Cambridge University. There he majored in economics and political science, minored in chemistry, and earned a B.A. in 1913 and an M.A. in 1918. He excelled at tennis, becoming a Cambridge tennis blue and the president of the Pembroke College Lawn Tennis Club.

Returning from Cambridge to the United States in 1913, Guggenheim's career shifted into high gear. He later said, "I was permitted for the first time to sit in on the daily conferences of the brothers in my father's office" at 120 Broadway in New York City. He plunged directly into his new mining responsibilities, first as director of several copper companies, including the Braden Copper Company, the Kennecott Copper Corporation, and the Utah Copper Company, and then as a partner (1916–1923) in Guggenheim Brothers.

Early in 1917, shortly before America's entry into World War I, Guggenheim began taking flight lessons at Lake Worth, near Palm Beach. He completed his training as a pilot on Long Island and, after receiving a commission in the U.S. Naval Reserve on Sept. 14, 1917, was sent overseas, where he earned his wings at the American bombing and gunnery school outside Bordeaux, France. A lieutenant commander at the end of the war, Guggenheim was recalled to active duty in 1942, served on the USS *Nehenta Bay* in the Pacific, and rose to the rank of captain in 1945.

Guggenheim's enthusiasm for the field of aviation influenced his father to earmark funds for this purpose. In 1925, he gave $500,000 to endow the Daniel Guggenheim School of Aeronautics at New York University. The following year, he set up a $2.5-million fund to start six more aeronautical schools in the United States. Harry Guggenheim served as president and a trustee of the Daniel Guggenheim Fund for the Promotion of Aeronautics from 1926 until it was terminated in 1930.

Appointed by President Herbert Hoover, Guggenheim served as ambassador to Cuba from September 1929 to April 1933, when he resigned. Instructed to follow a policy of noninterference in the internal affairs of Cuba, Guggenheim spent much of his time admonishing General Gerardo Machado y Morales, the island's dictator, "not to murder too many of his political enemies," as he once put it. Hoover also appointed him to the National Advisory Commission for Aeronautics, on which he served from 1929 to 1938.

Carrying on the family tradition, Guggenheim established his own foundation and also had jurisdiction over the Solomon R. Guggenheim Foundation, founded by his uncle, whom he succeeded as board chairman in 1949, until the office was abolished and he was elected president of the board in 1957. He guided to completion the Solomon R. Guggenheim Museum in New York City, which was designed by Frank Lloyd Wright.

In 1949, Guggenheim rejoined Guggenheim Brothers and in 1951 became president of the firm, which then revived its mining exploration. In 1951, he also became chairman of a family-controlled company, the Anglo-Lautaro Nitrate Corporation, with South American mines that produced more than half of the world's natural nitrate and iodine supply. A consummate businessman, Guggenheim also operated a thriving timber and cattle plantation at Cain Hoy, S.C., and bred and raced thoroughbred horses from a farm in Lexington, Ky. In later years, his principal business interest was *Newsday*, a tabloid daily newspaper serving suburban Long Island, N.Y., which he founded with his third wife in 1940. He sold it to Times-Mirror in 1970. Guggenheim died in Sands Point, Long Island.

[Guggenheim's papers are in the Library of Congress, Manuscript Division, Washington, D.C., and the archives of Guggenheim Brothers, New York City. The papers of the Daniel Guggenheim Fund for the Promotion of Aeronautics, also in the Library of Congress, provide information relating to Guggenheim's role in the growth of American aeronautics. See also the Robert A. Millikan papers and the Theodore von Karman collection, both in the California Institute of Technology Archives, Pasadena, Calif.

Guggenheim wrote two books: *The Seven Skies* (1930) and *The United States and Cuba* (1934). There is no full-length biography. For biographical information see Milton Lomask, *Seed Money* (1964); Richard P. Hallion, *Legacy of Flight* (1977); and John H. Davis, *The Guggenheims* (1978). An obituary is in the *New York Times*, Jan. 23, 1971.]

JUDITH R. GOODSTEIN

GUTHRIE, RAMON (Jan. 14, 1896–Nov. 22, 1973), poet and teacher, was born Raymon Hollister Guthrie in New York City, the son of Harry Young Guthrie and Ella May Hollister. About two years after his birth, his father abandoned the family. His mother moved to Hartford, Conn., where, beset by poor health, she raised her son and an older daughter in difficult economic circumstances.

Guthrie's formal education was limited by the family's poverty. He was to say that he was "privately tutored—by myself." After finishing grammar school, he started to work at a variety of jobs but managed to attend the Mount Hermon School in Northfield, Mass., for part of each year from 1912 to 1915.

In 1915, Guthrie's mother's health worsened, and she went to live with a sister near New Haven, Conn. Guthrie took a job with the Winchester Repeating Arms factory there. Early in 1916, his mother committed suicide in the charity ward of a New Haven hospital. That fall, deciding not to return to Mount Hermon, he volunteered for the American Field Service.

Arriving in France in December, Guthrie served as an ambulance driver, first on the western front and later in the Balkans. With the entry of the United States into the war, he joined the U.S. Army Signal Corps and trained as an observer. He saw considerable action during the period 1917–1918, participating in the St. Mihiel and Argonne offensives. Guthrie survived a crash serious enough for him to be awarded a disability pension, and he was credited with shooting down four enemy aircraft and received the Silver Star.

Guthrie was shipped back to the United States in the summer of 1919 for convalescence, and his first poems began to appear in Norman Fitts's little magazine *S4N*, which Guthrie had helped found. With his disability pension as a resource, he soon returned to France, living first in Paris, where he became well known in the American expatriate community, and then in Toulouse, where he entered the university, took two degrees in law, and pursued studies in Provençal language and literature. While in Toulouse, he married Marguerite Maurney, a Frenchwoman he had met during the war, on Apr. 8, 1922; they had no children.

Guthrie and his wife returned to America in 1923, the year in which his first collection of poems, *Trobar Clus*, was published. He soon became part of the New York City avant-garde literary scene, but his search for a job took him to the University of Arizona, where he taught French for five terms. In 1926, he returned to France, partially at the behest of Sinclair Lewis, with whom he had developed a close friendship, and tried to make his living by his pen. Guthrie published two novels, *Marcabrun* (1926), a historical romance on Provençal themes, and *Parachute* (1928), one of the first aviation novels. Both enjoyed modest critical successes. He also published a second collection of poems, *A World Too Old* (1927).

In 1929, probably for financial reasons, Guthrie returned to the United States; in 1930, with the help of Sinclair Lewis, he was appointed professor of French at Dartmouth College in Hanover, N.H. From then until his retirement in 1963, except for duty in 1944 and 1945 with the Office of Strategic Services in France and Algiers, Guthrie taught full-time at the rural college, specializing in modern French writers, particularly Proust.

A commanding figure, yet warm and approachable, his eyes twinkling with humor, Guthrie was an unusually gifted teacher, inspiring numerous Dartmouth students to pursue literary and scholarly careers. He was said to have an uncanny ability, perhaps reflective of his artistic nature, to get into the skin of the authors he discussed and to make their works, their heroes, their ideas, and their sense of art come alive in a unique fashion.

During his Dartmouth years, Guthrie returned to France during summer vacations and sabbaticals to maintain contact with French culture, to write, and to paint. A talented amateur painter, he exhibited in shows on the East Coast. He wrote occasional articles on literary topics, including an account of his relationship with Sinclair Lewis, and frequent reviews. He also published translations and textbook anthologies of modern French literature.

While teaching, Guthrie did not abandon poetry, although only a little chapbook, *Scherzo from a Poem To Be Entitled The Proud City* (1933), appeared in print. Numerous unpublished manuscripts attest to his continuous work. He participated in a weekly meeting of poets living in the Dartmouth area, among them Richard Eberhart, Bink Noll, and Dilys Laing. As retirement approached, he put together a rigorously chosen collection of the work of three decades, published in 1959 as *Graffiti*.

Guthrie's most significant achievements as a poet occurred during the closing years of his life, in the context of an unremitting battle against cancer, for which he had a first operation in 1966, and with the Vietnam War, of which he was a fierce opponent, as a backdrop. In 1968, he published *Asbestos Phoenix*, a collection of moving lyrics, a number of which are evocative of his grief and horror at American involvement in Vietnam.

In May 1970, Guthrie was awarded the Marjorie Peabody Waite Award of the National Institute of Arts and Letters as "a mature artist for continuing integrity and accomplishment in his art." In the fall of that year, his greatest work, *Maximum Security Ward, 1964–70*, was published. In this forty-nine-poem sequence, the speaker, an old and physically helpless patient in an intensive-care unit, uses the resources of imagination, memory, intellect, and humor in a stubborn struggle against extinction.

Guthrie died in Hanover, N.H. While each of his last three volumes was favorably received when published (*Maximum Security Ward* was hailed as "a work of major character . . . like nothing else in contemporary poetry"), they soon dropped from view. His work received little sustained critical recognition during his lifetime, perhaps because of his late flourishing. This situation was rectified a decade after his death when *Maximum Security Ward* was republished and became the object of scholarly study.

[Guthrie's papers, including a number of unpublished poems, are in the Library of Dartmouth College. A good deal of biographical material is contained in the festschrift published on the occasion of his retirement, George E. Diller, ed., *Ramon Guthrie Ka-*

leidoscope (1963). A chronology of his life by Sally M. Gall is found in her edition of Guthrie's *Maximum Security Ward and Other Poems* (1984). An obituary is in the *New York Times*, Nov. 23, 1973.]

ROBERT A. PICKEN

GUTHRIE, SIR TYRONE (July 2, 1900–May 15, 1971), stage director, was born in Tunbridge Wells, Kent, England, the son of Thomas Clement Guthrie, an upper-class physician dedicated to helping the needy, and Norah Power, granddaughter of the great nineteenth-century Irish actor Tyrone Power. Guthrie attended a prestigious boarding school, Wellington College, from 1914 to 1918. He then studied history at St. John's College, Oxford, earning his B.A. in 1923. He received his M.A. from Oxford in 1931.

Guthrie became active in student theatricals, but his height (six feet, five inches), large frame, and small head made him ungainly, an impediment to an acting career. However, he possessed a good speaking and singing voice. In 1924, James B. Fagan invited Guthrie to act professionally at the Playhouse in Oxford; Guthrie stayed only a few months.

In 1924, Guthrie was hired as a producer for the BBC in Belfast, Northern Ireland. There Guthrie discovered he could motivate others to create innovative radio programs. He established a reputation as an announcer and wrote original plays for broadcast. Guthrie's radio work drew the attention of the Scottish National Players, a group that hired Guthrie in 1926 as their artistic director. He directed a range of productions, most by Scottish playwrights, as the group toured Scotland, performing under makeshift conditions. Two years later, Guthrie returned to the radio as a producer for the BBC in London, where he wrote several "microphone plays" that were considered breakthroughs at the time.

Guthrie returned to the stage for good in 1929, as artistic director of the Anmer Hall Company in Cambridge's Festival Theatre. There he directed a blend of classics and contemporary plays. His *Iphigenia in Tauris* featured old friend Flora Robson, not yet a leading actress. Guthrie led the Anmer Hall Company's move to London's Westminster Theatre in 1931, making his London directing debut with James Bridie's *The Anatomist*. On Sept. 5, 1931, Guthrie wed his sister's childhood friend Judith Bretherton; they had no children.

Guthrie's directorial work caught the eye of Lilian Baylis, head of London's Old Vic Theatre, and in 1933 he joined the Old Vic. He assembled a company that included Charles Laughton and Flora Robson, and significantly raised the Old Vic's standards for costuming and production. That first season Guthrie directed eight productions, including five of Shakespeare.

Guthrie left the Old Vic in 1934 but returned in 1936. He directed Laurence Olivier in *Hamlet*, a production so successful it was later presented at Elsinore for Danish royalty. Rain forced the performance indoors, with actors playing before an audience seated haphazardly around them, rather than having audience face actors separated from them behind the traditional proscenium arch. Guthrie noted how the new arrangement gave the play greater vigor, encouraging audience participation. This spurred him to challenge traditional theater practice. In 1938, he directed the largely untried Alec Guinness as a modern-dress Hamlet. He also mounted a version of *A Midsummer Night's Dream* that mocked picture-book stage techniques.

Continuing to direct in London's commercial theater, Guthrie made his New York City debut in 1936. At Lilian Baylis's death in 1937, he took over the Old Vic, steering it through the war years, arranging touring companies to help citizen morale and to entertain troops. Guthrie's impressive 1944–1945 Old Vic included Laurence Olivier, Ralph Richardson, and Sybil Thorndike; in the same season he suffered his greatest administrative failure when the Old Vic's opera and ballet companies broke away. After the war Guthrie left the Old Vic. He helped run the Hammersmith Lyric Theatre, directed independently (including opera), then returned once more to the Old Vic in 1951.

Guthrie wanted to experiment artistically. Invited to direct at the 1948 Edinburgh Festival, he chose an obscure sixteenth-century play, *The Three Estates*. He staged it in the Assembly Hall of the Church of Scotland, forcing the audience to sit on three sides of the stage with actors coming and going in their midst. Guthrie's mature directing style took shape: fluid movement of onstage crowds, visual splendor, rapidly spoken dialogue, and classic plays revitalized by fresh, imaginative approaches. He began to view theater as community ritual and sought theaters where he could implement this vision.

In 1952, Guthrie agreed to support local efforts to establish a Shakespeare festival in Stratford, Ontario. He gave guidance but insisted that all initiative come from Stratford's citizens. The community responded with a theater built according to Guthrie's specifications by his favorite collaborator, designer Tanya Moiseiwitsch. It featured a fixed stage structure composed of a balcony, steps, and doors beneath. The audience of fifteen hundred sat on three sides, with no one more than sixty-five feet away. That first season Guthrie assembled an otherwise all-Canadian cast around star performers Alec Guinness and Irene Worth. Enthusiastic local support, strong tourist appeal, and a fine company combined with Guthrie's iconoclastic stagings of Shakespeare to make the Stratford Festival a rousing success. Guthrie stayed until 1956.

Guthrie worked all over the world (Finland, Israel, Australia) but directed mostly in England and America. He began an informal affiliation with New York's Phoenix Theatre in 1955. That same year his direction of Thornton Wilder's *The Matchmaker* earned him a Tony award. His New York productions of Shakespeare and of Marlowe's *Tamburlaine* (1956) brought commercial and critical acclaim. Guthrie staged Metropolitan Opera productions, and in 1956 he directed the premiere of Lillian Hellman's and Leonard Bernstein's *Candide*. In 1961, Guthrie was knighted by Queen Elizabeth II.

Inspired by Stratford's success, Guthrie selected Minneapolis, Minn., for a comparable American theater. The city responded favorably, and in 1963 Guthrie began a three-year tenure as head of the Guthrie Theatre, which was designed after the Stratford model. Guthrie assembled an all-American cast around Hume Cronyn, Jessica Tandy, and Zoe Caldwell. He produced a modern-dress *Hamlet*, with George Grizzard as the Danish prince, for the theater's premiere. Guthrie's unorthodox direction drew attention and won praise. The University of Minnesota made Guthrie a member of its theater faculty. In 1963, he was named chancellor of Queen's University, Belfast.

Guthrie's legacy includes his architectural ideas, which became the model for many important theaters, including Britain's National Theatre and the Royal Shakespeare Company's Barbican Theatre. His innovations in open staging inspired generations of directors worldwide. His advocacy for community art gave impetus to America's growing regional theater movement.

Guthrie made many actors stars, but once they were stars, he viewed them skeptically. He dressed informally, sometimes in threadbare clothes, and lived for years above a London law college in a cramped apartment cluttered by cats and laundry hanging from low beams.

When not in London, Guthrie lived at his family's ancestral Irish home, Annagh-ma-Kerrig House, located in Newbliss, County Monaghan. Concerned that Irish youth lacked job prospects, Guthrie began a jam and preserve factory on his estate in 1962. He traveled widely to promote the jams and to give talks in order to raise funds to support the enterprise. However, mismanagement and bad luck caused the firm to fail in 1971. Guthrie died at Annagh-ma-Kerrig House. He willed his mansion to the Irish government, on the condition it be used as a retreat for artists and writers.

[Guthrie's writings include the books *Theatre Prospect* (1932); *A New Theatre* (1964); *In Various Directions* (1966); and *Tyrone Guthrie on Acting* (1971). With Robertson Davies and Grant MacDonald he wrote *Renown at Stratford* (1953) and *Twice Have the Trumpets Sounded* (1954); and with Davies, *Thrice the Brinded Cat Hath Mew'd* (1955). His plays include the radio plays *The Squirrel's Cage* (1931); *The Flowers Are Not for You to Pick* (1931); and *Matrimonial News* (1931); his stage plays are *Follow Me* (1932) and *Top of the Ladder* (1950). His autobiography is *A Life in the Theatre* (1959). Books describing Guthrie's life and work include James Forsyth, *Tyrone Guthrie* (1976); J. L. Styan, *The Shakespeare Revolution* (1977); and Alfred Rossi, *Astonish Us in the Morning* (1980). See also Robert Hatch, "Tyrone Guthrie: The Artist as Man of the Theatre," *Horizon*, Nov. 1963; and Brian Friel, "The Giant of Monaghan," *Holiday*, May 1964. Obituaries are in the *New York Times*, May 16, 1971; *Times* (London), May 17, 1971; and *Variety*, May 17, 1971.]

STUART J. HECHT

GUTTMACHER, ALAN FRANK (May 19, 1898–Mar. 18, 1974), obstetrician and family planning advocate, was born in Baltimore, Md., one of identical twins who were the last of three children of Adolf Guttmacher, a Reform rabbi, and Laura Oppenheimer, a social worker. In 1915, when Adolf suddenly died, teachers at the Park School in Baltimore recognized the academic aptitudes of his twin sons and recommended that they attend Johns Hopkins University rather than begin business careers.

Under the influence of the science faculty at Johns Hopkins, both Alan and Manfred Guttmacher shifted their interests from history and English to medicine. After obtaining their B.A.'s in 1919, they entered the university's famed medical school, where they were much impressed by the anatomist George Corner, a key figure in elaborating the operations of hormones. Alan Guttmacher's first professional paper, coauthored with his brother in 1921, was on the graafian follicle of the sow, but after receiving their M.D.'s in 1923, Manfred pursued a specialty in psychiatry, while Alan worked with Corner as assistant in anatomy at Johns Hopkins (1923–1924) and at the University of Rochester (1924–1925). His marriage to Leonore Gidding on July 22, 1925, led him to turn from the relative penury of a research assistant to the practice of obstetrics in Baltimore; he nevertheless continued his academic career as a member of the medical faculty at Johns Hopkins, where he rose to associate professor before leaving to become chief of obstetrics and gynecology at New York's Mount Sinai Medical School in 1952. He retained this post until 1962.

Guttmacher regarded teaching as his primary vocation and was very interested in popularizing developments in reproductive science. His first book, *Life in the Making* (1933), predicted revolutionary advances in the management of human reproduction, and it was followed by well-received manuals for general readers, including *Into This Universe* (1937), *Pregnancy and Birth* (1957), *Babies by Choice or Chance* (1959), *Complete Book of Birth Control* (1961), *Planning Your Family* (1964), *Complications of Pregnancy* (1965), *Birth Control and Love* (1969), and *Understanding Sex* (1970).

Guttmacher was deeply affected by the deaths from septic-induced abortions that he witnessed in the wards of the Johns Hopkins Hospital, and he resented, in particular, the refusal of his mentor in obstetrics, J. Whitridge Williams, to allow him to perform an abortion for a thirteen-year-old incest victim. Appalled by the high fertility and morbidity of indigent women, who were unable to gain access to contraception and abortion, both of which were available to the wealthy, Guttmacher became an outspoken critic of what he regarded as medical hypocrisy in these matters and an advocate of the "democratization" of birth control.

In the early 1960's both the Population Council and the Planned Parenthood Federation of America recruited Guttmacher for executive positions. As a member of the Population Council's medical advisory committee, he was responsible primarily for the decision to organize an international conference that revived interest in intrauterine contraceptive devices and set the stage for the council's investment of millions of dollars in the clinical testing and distribution of this technology. The Population Council was dominated by social scientists and the fact that Guttmacher was a medical doctor limited his stature within the organization; he accepted the presidency of the Planned Parenthood Federation of America in 1962. When concern about the possible side effects of the anovulant pill mounted following the discovery that the steroid tranquilizer thalidomide caused birth defects, Guttmacher aggressively defended the safety of the pill and was one of the key figures in the successful effort to maintain U.S. Food and Drug Administration approval for oral contraceptives.

As president of Planned Parenthood, Guttmacher enjoyed enormous success in increasing both private support for the organization and public funding for contraceptive services. Both the staff and budget of Planned Parenthood tripled under his tenure, and his testimony before the U.S. House of Representatives Ways and Means Committee in 1967 contributed to Social Security amendments requiring that 6 percent of appropriated funds for maternal and child health services be available for family planning. These regulations marked the time when contraceptive services were firmly established as part of federal maternal health programs.

Guttmacher played a similarly important role in the campaign to liberalize the laws restricting the practice of abortion. While he was at Johns Hopkins, he expressed his concern that the unilateral power of the chief of the obstetrical department to approve all abortions resulted in unacceptably arbitrary decisions. When Guttmacher became chief of obstetrics at Baltimore's Sinai Hospital in 1942, he established a committee of five drawn from relevant medical departments to review applications for abortion, and this system became standard practice in leading U.S. hospitals. After his 1952 move to New York, Guttmacher continued his efforts to rationalize the institutional circumstances surrounding abortion by supporting an American Law Institute model penal code and as a member of Governor Nelson Rockefeller's 1968 commission on abortion law reform. Several states had liberalized their laws by 1968, but Guttmacher was deeply concerned by the fact that simply making it easier to qualify medically for permission to obtain an abortion actually increased the level of discrimination against the poor. In 1969, he reluctantly concluded that the removal of abortion from the penal codes was the only fair remedy to unequal access, and he became one of the more prominent medical advocates of "abortion on demand." In 1970 the New York state legislature passed such a law, and the U.S. Supreme Court established a similar national standard in its 1973 *Roe* v. *Wade* decision. By the time Guttmacher died of leukemia in New York City, he was convinced that changes in the law had saved lives, minimized socioeconomic discrimination, and reduced the incidence of illegal abortion.

A tall and imposing figure in the hospital and on the popular lecture circuit, Guttmacher enjoyed the apparent paradox that as one of the country's most prominent obstetricians he was also an aggressive champion of birth control. An agnostic since his father's death, Guttmacher's advice to the young favored abstinence before marriage and an ethic of responsibility in all sexual conduct. His own successful marriage and three daughters confirmed his personal commitment to the American gender system of his time. His professional prominence was matched by a commitment to liberal reform in those areas of public policy where he felt that his experience gave him special insight and authority, and, as president of Planned Parenthood, he presided over the most successful period in the history of the birth control movement in the United States.

[Guttmacher's personal papers are in the Countway Library of Medicine, Boston, including an autobiographical memoir that ends in 1924. The Sophia Smith Collection, Smith College, Northampton, Mass., houses the archives of the Planned Parenthood Federation of America. The Katharine Dexter McCormick Library of the Planned Parenthood Federation of America, New York City, has files of newspaper stories covering Guttmacher's speeches. For Guttmacher's views on abortion, see "The Genesis of Liberalized Abortion in New York: A Personal Insight," *Case Western Reserve Law Review*, Summer 1972.

See also David Dempsey, "Dr. Guttmacher Is the Evangelist of Birth Control," *New York Times Magazine*, Feb. 9, 1969; *The Mount Sinai Journal of Medicine*, July–Aug. 1975; and Leslie Jean Reagan, "When Abortion Was a Crime: The Legal and Medical Regulation of Abortion, Chicago, 1880–1973" (Ph.D. diss., University of Wisconsin, 1991). An obituary is in the *New York Times*, Mar. 19, 1974. James Reed's interview with Leonore Gidding Guttmacher for the Schlesinger-Rockefeller Oral History Project is in the Schlesinger Library, Radcliffe College, Cambridge, Mass.]

JAMES W. REED

H

HAMILTON, JOHN DANIEL MILLER, II (Mar. 2, 1892–Sept. 24, 1973), Republican party national chairman, lawyer, and political strategist, was born in Fort Madison, Iowa, the son of John Daniel Miller Hamilton, a lawyer, and Mary Rice. He was the grandson of John Hamilton, the first governor of the Kansas-Nebraska territories. At the age of seven, John moved with his family from Iowa to Topeka, Kans., where his father was a lawyer for the Santa Fe Railroad. Hamilton attended Phillips Academy, Andover, Mass., graduating in 1913. He then entered Northwestern University, where he graduated from the law school in 1916. Hamilton was married three times and divorced twice. He married Laura Hall on Dec. 28, 1915; they had two children and divorced on Dec. 29, 1937. Hamilton married Jane Kendall Mason in 1940; this marriage lasted five years, and Hamilton married Rosamond Kittle Jackson on Nov. 1, 1947.

Hamilton practiced law for two years in Kansas City and then enlisted in the army during World War I as a machine gunner. He was still in training at Camp Hancock, Ga., when the war ended. On his return to Kansas, Hamilton practiced law in Topeka with Ralph T. O'Neil, past commander of the American Legion, which emerged as a significant political force in the 1920's. When Hamilton wanted to run for probate judge in 1920, he sought the support of Kansas Republican leader David W. Mulvane. Mulvane suggested that Hamilton wait a few years, but Hamilton ran anyway. He waged an aggressive door-to-door campaign, with strong support from returning veterans, and won the election. Impressed with Hamilton's drive and political skills, Mulvane became his mentor and sponsor.

Hamilton quickly rose to power and prominence. Elected to the Kansas legislature in 1924, he was chosen Republican floor leader in his first term and House speaker in his second term. As speaker, Hamilton fought the Ku Klux Klan, which had strong support in parts of the state. But he was no liberal. He helped to defeat the Child Labor Amendment to the Constitution.

In 1928, Hamilton sought the Republican nomination for governor of Kansas. He had the support of Mulvane and the conservative wing of the party. Clyde M. Reed, Hamilton's major rival, was supported by Republican progressives, including the editor of the *Emporia Gazette*, William Allen White; Senator Arthur Capper; and Alfred M. Landon. Reed defeated Hamilton and won the governorship. Two years later, Hamilton managed the gubernatorial campaign of Frank Haucke, former American Legion state commander, who defeated Governor Reed for the Republican nomination. Democrat Harry Woodring, capitalizing on the Republican split, beat Haucke in the general election.

Hamilton was elected Kansas Republican party chairman in 1930. He supported Lacey Simpson for governor in 1932, but when Simpson lost the primary to Landon, Hamilton backed Landon in the general election. The day after Landon's victory, Mulvane died and Landon named Hamilton as the state's Republican national committeeman.

During the next two decades, Hamilton gained recognition as one of the more skillful strategists in national politics. With his frank manner and forceful speaking style, he was an eloquent spokesman for his party. There was a serious movement among western committeemen to make Hamilton national chairman in

1934. In recognition of his growing influence, in 1935 Republican national chairman Henry P. Fletcher named Hamilton as assistant chairman and general counsel. Hamilton was the Republican point man against Franklin D. Roosevelt's New Deal.

With Landon emerging as a contender for the 1936 Republican presidential nomination, Hamilton resigned his job with the national committee and became Landon's campaign manager. In paving the way for Landon's nomination, Hamilton toured the country, forging alliances with party chairmen and elected officials, as James A. Farley had done for Roosevelt in 1932. After Landon's first-ballot nomination, Hamilton was selected by Landon as the Republican national chairman. Hamilton's style was as flamboyant as Landon's was bland. "To bored political onlookers," *Time* magazine reported from the 1936 Republican convention, "not Alf Landon but John Hamilton was the young Lochinvar come out of the West."

It was an uneasy collaboration. Hamilton wanted Landon to take a hard line against the New Deal, but the Kansas governor echoed Roosevelt by endorsing Social Security and farm subsidies. In a speech, Hamilton held up a dog tag and asked his audience if they wanted to wear a metal Social Security number. "In European countries, people carry police cards and are subject to police surveillance," he declared. "So far, American citizens have not been subjected to these indignities." Landon viewed Hamilton's rhetoric as excessive. Hamilton was also rankled that Landon denied a meaningful campaign role for former President Hoover. Hamilton helped Landon win the endorsement of Alfred E. Smith, Hoover's 1928 Democratic presidential rival. In an October 1936 letter to *U.S. News* publisher David Lawrence, Hamilton predicted that Landon would carry five states (in fact, Landon only carried two). Hamilton said in an interview in 1972 that despite Landon's lopsided defeat, the 1936 campaign served a purpose. "If the Republican party hadn't contested the 1936 election," he said, "we might have entered an era of splintered parties."

From the ashes of the Republican party's worst defeat, Hamilton built new foundations. He traveled to London and conferred with leaders of the British Conservative and Labour parties about the maintenance of political institutions. Hamilton, using the British parties

as his model, returned to Washington, D.C., and opened the Republican party's first permanent headquarters. He also hired a team of scholars, headed by former University of Wisconsin president Glen Frank, to define the party's goals and provide research for Republican speakers. Hamilton became the party's first full-time, salaried chairman.

Hamilton developed working relationships with the Republican congressional leadership, sponsoring weekend seminars on Capitol Hill and providing research on topical issues. He helped Senate Minority Leader Charles L. McNary and Democratic senator Burton K. Wheeler plot strategy to block Roosevelt's 1937 attempt to enlarge the Supreme Court. Hamilton funded the travel of hostile witnesses to Senate hearings on the court plan. The Republican chairman aided conservative Democratic senators in making their case against Roosevelt's domestic policies and made a public plea for Republicans and "Jeffersonian Democrats" to work together. Hamilton ran the party's first coordinated campaign for a midterm election in 1938. He toured the country, recruiting candidates and visiting more than three thousand county chairmen. His efforts to rejuvenate the party were successful. In the 1938 midterm elections, Republicans gained eighty-one seats in the House, six in the Senate, and thirteen governorships.

At the 1940 Republican convention, Hamilton denounced Roosevelt's appointments of prominent Republicans Henry L. Stimson as secretary of war and Frank Knox as secretary of the navy, declaring that Stimson and Knox were "no longer qualified to speak as Republicans." His comments polarized the party's bipartisan internationalist wing. Though publicly neutral in the competition for the presidential nomination, Hamilton worked behind the scenes for dark horse Wendell L. Willkie. At the party's convention, Hamilton broke the deadlock for Willkie by obtaining the support on the sixth ballot of Michigan Republican leader Frank McKay. Willkie, who had pledged to retain Hamilton as chairman, replaced him with Joseph W. Martin at the urging of *New York Herald Tribune* publishers Odgen and Helen Rogers Reid and of William Allen White, who had been appalled by Hamilton's attack on Stimson and Knox.

"Willkie's refusal to accept me was ample evidence in my mind that the party would not accept the English theory of permanency of personnel in organizational activities," Hamilton wrote in his memoirs. Willkie appointed Hamilton as executive director of the Republican National Committee and as political director of Willkie's campaign. Hamilton worked for Willkie with little enthusiasm and resigned from the national committee after Willkie's defeat. In 1943, Hamilton organized a coalition of Republican politicians who helped to block Willkie's bid for the 1944 presidential nomination.

Hamilton was a strategist and adviser to Senator Robert A. Taft in his unsuccessful campaigns for the 1948 and 1952 Republican presidential nominations. Taft valued Hamilton's judgment and experience, though he later regretted following Hamilton's advice to enter the 1952 New Hampshire primary, which he lost to Dwight D. Eisenhower.

In 1941, Hamilton moved to Philadelphia and practiced law with former senator George Wharton Pepper. Their firm, Pepper, Hamilton, and Scheetz, was among Philadelphia's more respected and successful firms. Their clients included the *Saturday Evening Post* and the Sun Oil Co. In 1950, Hamilton was named by a federal judge as the defense attorney for Harry Gold, who was arrested as a courier for the Soviet spy ring that included Julius and Ethel Rosenberg. Gold, who had confessed following his arrest, asked the court for a defense lawyer with "no radical connections" who "would not make a show." The judge praised Hamilton's defense as brilliant. Gold, who was sentenced to a thirty-year term, was released after serving sixteen years.

Hamilton died in Clearwater, Fla., where he lived in retirement. A year before his death, Hamilton said that he would be remembered as the manager of two losing presidential campaigns. But he was also the Republican party's most resourceful national chairman since Mark Hanna.

[Hamilton's papers at the Library of Congress include his unpublished memoirs and extensive correspondence. His role in national politics is covered most fully in Donald R. McCoy, *Landon of Kansas* (1966); James T. Patterson, *Congressional Conservatism and the New Deal* (1967) and *Mr. Republican: A Biography of Robert A. Taft* (1972); and Steve Neal, *Dark Horse: A Biography of Wendell Willkie* (1984). An obituary is in the *New York Times*, Sept. 26, 1973.]

STEVE NEAL

HAMMOND, LAURENS (Nov. 11, 1895–July 1, 1973), inventor and manufacturer, was born in Evanston, Ill., the fourth child of William Andrew Hammond, a banker, and Idea Louise Strong, an amateur artist. After his father died in 1898, his mother moved the family to Europe in order to resume her art studies. The family, including three sisters, one the writer Eunice Tietjens, lived in Paris, but soon left for Geneva, and later Dresden, because of the turmoil over the Dreyfus affair. Fascinated by science, Hammond patented his first invention, an automobile transmission, while barely a teenager. After he returned to Evanston in 1909, he sold his idea for an inexpensive yet sensitive barometer.

He attended Evanston Township High School and then Cornell University from 1912 to 1916, graduating with a degree in mechanical engineering. In 1917, he enlisted as a second lieutenant in the Sixteenth Engineering Regiment of the American Expeditionary Force. After serving in France, he was discharged as a captain in May 1919. For two years, he served as the chief engineer of the Gray Motor Company, a manufacturer of marine engines. During this time, he designed a diesel car engine, but could not sell the idea. In 1920, he sold his design for a "tickless" clock and with the money set up a studio in New York City to work full time as an inventor.

Hammond developed a synchronous motor that was in phase with the sixty-cycle alternating current that was then becoming standard in the United States. This motor was the basis for many of his later inventions. Its first use, in 1922, was the Teleview, a device for creating three-dimensional movies using a special, dual-lens camera and an eyepiece similar to a stereoscope. One observer at the première of the device in New York City reported: "So perfect was the sensation of depth and volume produced that when objects came forward on the screen, they seemed to project out into the audience and the onlooker had an impulse to reach out and seize them." The Teleview, however, never gained popularity. Hammond later modified the 3-D device for use in the theater, selling the effect to the Ziegfeld Follies. Using the royalties from Ziegfeld, Hammond traveled to Europe.

Hammond married Mildred Anton-Smith on Sept. 1, 1924, in Washington, D.C. They had two daughters. Returning to the United States in 1925 after his royalties ran out, Hammond turned down a job with Western Union in favor of working independently. After merging his synchronous motor with the "tickless" clock, he formed the Hammond Clock Co. in 1928 with half a dozen workers in a room over a Chicago grocery store. The business went well until the onset of the Great Depression. Then the soured economic climate and increased competition caused the company to lose money in the period 1931–1935.

In 1932, he used the clock motor to produce an electric bridge table that dealt cards for players, an example of Hammond's belief that toys for adults were the most promising area for invention. The table sold moderately well, but not enough to extricate the company from its financial straits.

While working on an experimental phonograph turntable, Hammond heard the motor emit a flute-like tone. This prompted him to investigate the possibilities of creating music with electricity. Using the keyboard from a secondhand piano, he started work on what would become the Hammond Organ. Synthesizing sound through electricity was not a novel idea: the massive Cahill Telharmonium, intended to pipe music over telephone lines, had preceded Hammond's work. Hammond believed, however, in addressing a problem without being preoccupied with previous efforts. Hammond's acumen in manufacturing and marketing also helped him to develop a product that could be sold even in the Depression. He demonstrated the Hammond Organ, which used ninety-one silver-dollar-sized motors, in the basement of the United States Patent Office on Jan. 1, 1934. The patent was granted Apr. 24, 1934, and in Spring 1935 the organ was exhibited at the Industrial Arts Exposition in New York City. At a special preview, George Gershwin bought the first one. Other early buyers included Rudy Vallée and Henry Ford. In the first eight months, 807 organs were sold. The organ lifted what was now Hammond Instrument Co. out of the red.

Sales were helped by an aggressive advertising campaign that claimed the organ produced all the necessary tone colors needed "for the rendition, without sacrifice, of the great works of the classical organ literature." The organ, the advertisements claimed, was the equivalent of a $10,000 pipe organ. Besides stimulating sales, the advertisements also drew the ire of pipe organ makers. They told the Federal Trade Commission the advertisements were misleading. Hearings convened in Chicago in March 1937 and concluded in Washington, D.C., in April 1938. The testimony included a blind test in the University of Chicago chapel, in which nine renowned musicians, mostly organists, were asked to distinguish between the chapel's pipe organ and a Hammond organ. The panel guessed wrong a third of the time. Hammond testified for three and a half days, maintaining that the Hammond Organ was better than those used by Bach and more advanced than contemporary pipe organs because it was flexible enough to play popular as well as classical music. During a demonstration at the hearings, an organ reproduced the sound of a locomotive, a calliope, and an earthquake. These effects were possible because, instead of traditional organ stops, the organ was equipped with drawbars that let the player mix harmonics, with the resultant possibility of creating 253,000 different tonal combinations. In July 1938 the FTC ordered the company to cease making the contested claims. Hammond responded that the publicity from the trial more than made up for the trial's cost.

By 1937, Hammond had given up management of the company's daily operations to concentrate on research. Hammond took another step toward synthesized sound in 1939 with the Novachord, which used vacuum tubes rather than motors. The instrument was shown at the 1939 World's Fair in New York City and Eleanor Roosevelt gave one to President Roosevelt for his birthday, but the instrument failed to catch on. The Solovox, an electric organ attachment for a standard piano, which was introduced in 1940, also failed in the market.

After World War II, during which Hammond worked on technology for guided missiles, glide bombs, and aerial cameras, he directed his concentration back to the home organ market. In 1949, his company introduced a spinet organ and in 1950, the first chord organ, which allowed the novice to play a full chord by pressing only one key. These helped ensure a profit for the Hammond company into the 1960's.

On Feb. 19, 1954 Hammond's first wife committed suicide by jumping from the window of their third floor apartment in Chicago shortly after she and Hammond had returned from a six-week European vacation. Hammond said she had been despondent over her health.

The next year, Hammond stepped down as Hammond president, though he remained chairman of the board. On Oct. 25, 1955, he married Roxana Scoville in West Cornwall, Conn., and retired in March 1960.

After his retirement, Hammond withdrew from the company and the music industry. He divided his time between homes in France; Antigua; Montevideo, Uruguay; New York City; and Cornwall, Conn. A private person, he divulged little of his personal life other than interests in chess, poker, and yachting. His pride in his work is illustrated by an incident reported in the *Cornell Alumni Bulletin*. While at a college reunion, he heard someone playing a Hammond organ. He asked the individual how often he played the instrument. The man allowed he had been playing it for only the third time. "I thought so," commented Hammond. "I am Larry Hammond. I manufacture them. They can be played beautifully." Hammond died in Cornwall, Conn.

[Extensive coverage of the FTC proceedings can be found in *Diapason*, 1937–1938. Sterling North profiled Hammond in "The Story of an Inventor," *Atlantic*, Sept. 1940. An obituary appears in the *New York Times*, July 3, 1973, and a longer obituary by J. F. Majeski appears in *Music Trades*, Aug. 1973.]

DAVID DUPONT

HANDLEY, HAROLD WILLIS (Nov. 27, 1909–Aug. 30, 1972), governor of Indiana, was born in La Porte, Ind., one of three sons of Harold Lowell, owner of a furniture company, and Lottie Margaret Brackbill. He attended public schools in La Porte and in 1932 received a B.A. degree from Indiana University, Bloomington, where he majored in economics, minored in political science, and was involved in campus politics. A friend and roommate at the Delta Tau Delta fraternity house was William E. Jenner, later U.S. senator from Indiana.

Following graduation and a brief stay in Washington, D.C., Handley returned home to assist in the family business, the Rustic Hickory Furniture Company. The Great Depression took a toll on the enterprise, however, and he spent two years shoveling coal on a delivery truck to help make ends meet. Attempts to revive the company failed, and when the family was forced to close the business toward the end of the 1930's, Handley became a sales representative for a North Carolina furniture company.

Throughout these years Handley's interest in politics grew. He organized the La Porte County Young Republicans in 1932 and ran unsuccessfully for the state senate in 1936. He was elected four years later and attended the 1941 legislative session in Indianapolis. Following American entry into World War II, he resigned his state senate seat and entered the United States Army. Initially a second lieutenant because of college ROTC training, he was promoted to first lieutenant after further instruction at Fort Benning, Ga. He served with the Eighty-fifth Infantry Division as a company executive officer and battalion commander. While he was attending school at Fort Leavenworth, Kans., his unit was shipped overseas. Despite requests to join his outfit, Handley was given stateside commands training infantry replacements. He was discharged in 1946 with the rank of lieutenant colonel.

During the war, while stationed in the Mojave Desert, Handley met Barbara Jean Winterble, a Red Cross psychiatric social worker assigned to the field hospital there. They married on Feb. 17, 1944, and had two children.

After the war Handley returned to La Porte and resumed his career in furniture sales; he also became associated with commercial and industrial film studios in Chicago and Hollywood. In 1948, he was elected to the state senate, and four years later he was nominated as lieutenant governor on the ticket headed by George N. Craig. Handley defeated his Democratic opponent, E. Spencer Walton, by 230,000 votes.

As lieutenant governor Handley presided over the state senate and served as commissioner of agriculture and of commerce and industry. He viewed himself as Indiana's leading salesman and made presentations across the country to attract new industry to the state. Often joking that when he became commissioner of agriculture, he "didn't know a gilt from a quilt," he educated himself by becoming active with 4-H clubs and attending thirty to thirty-five county fairs each year. At the same time he was accumulating political IOU's and building name recognition that served him well when he ran for governor in 1956.

There had not been a major tax increase in Indiana since the 1930's, and Handley believed that the state faced a financial crisis. He thus campaigned on a platform of raising some state taxes, an unlikely position for an Indiana Republican. He won nevertheless, defeating Ralph Tucker, mayor of Terre Haute, by 227,000 votes. He later admitted that Dwight Eisenhower's presidential coattails were a help.

Handley convinced the 1957 legislature to enact 50-percent increases in gasoline and gross income taxes (the latter including a provision for payroll withholding), an action that won him the nickname "High Tax Harold." (He always resented the sobriquet, noting that the state was desperate for revenue and that he also oversaw the repeal of most of the state property tax.) He refused to take any position on a controversial right-to-work law, fearful that doing so would jeopardize his legislative program. When both houses of the general assembly (controlled by Republicans) passed the measure, Handley let it become law without his signature—thus earning the enmity of the state's labor unions. In 1959, when Democrats controlled the house of representatives, he proposed a more modest legislative program, referring to it later as a "flag-waving session." He underestimated the importance of a school reorganization act passed that year with his support, a law that rapidly transformed public education in the state by forcing consolidation of small township schools.

In addition to the tax increases, the right-to-work law, and school reorganization, Handley's administration was noted for constructing a state office building; inaugurating an expanded program of highway construction (aided by federal funding for the interstate system); establishing a state veterinary school; and strengthening the department of mental health. His administration also began acquiring land for a deep-water port on Lake Michigan; having grown up farther north than any other Indiana governor, before or since, Handley was its natural advocate.

In 1958, Handley ran for the U.S. Senate seat being vacated by his friend Jenner. The campaign was conducted amid controversy over whether the state constitution prohibited a sitting governor from seeking another office. Although the state supreme court upheld his candidacy, lingering resentment over the tax increases, the right-to-work law, and a highway department scandal related to the Craig administration in which he had served contributed to his sound defeat by Democratic candidate, Vance Hartke.

Returning to private life in early 1961, Handley cofounded a successful advertising and public relations firm in Indianapolis. A popular speaker, he remained in demand nationwide. He was, in the words of an editorial at the time of his death, "an extremely articulate spokesman for the conservative cause," and a sketch that appeared during his tenure as governor observed that he stood "squarely in the tradition of conservative Republican politics in his state."

Handley's political orientation manifested itself in his attitude toward federal aid. Although he did not oppose all such programs (matching funds for highways, for example), in general he took a dim view of federal "paternalism." He once told a U.S. Chamber of Commerce luncheon that Washington bureaucrats had "substituted the image of a mother hen for the American eagle," and in an interview with *Nation's Business* (May 1950) he complained that the ability of state and local officials to respond to their constituents' needs was being curtailed by a "supercentralized government now far beyond the effective control of American taxpayers."

An affable man whose sartorial trademark was a bow tie with white polka dots, Handley served on the boards of several philanthropic groups, most notably as chair of the Comprehensive Mental Health Committee for Central Indiana and as a director of the United Fund of Greater Indianapolis. He died at Rawlins, Wyo., while on vacation.

[The official papers of the Handley administration are in the Indiana State Archives, Indianapolis. The transcript of an oral history, dated Feb. 1971, is on deposit in the Indiana State Library, Indianapolis. Interviews with Handley appear in the *Indianapolis Times*, Feb. 2, 1958; and *Nation's Business*, May 1959. An obituary is in the *New York Times*, Aug. 31, 1972.]

ROBERT G. BARROWS

HANSBURG, GEORGE BERNARD (October 1887–Dec. 3, 1975), inventor of the pogo stick, the "Babee-Tenda," and other children's products, was born in Russia, the second son of Bernard and Celia Hansburg, German Jews who emigrated to Ukraine during Otto von Bismarck's unification wars. Bernard Hansburg was a merchant, who bought produce in Germany to sell in Russia. George was educated in Ukraine, then emigrated alone to New York City in 1906, arriving at Ellis Island at the age of eighteen. That same year, he married Sophie

Werner, an émigré from Vilna, Lithuania. They had five children. Hansburg put himself through night school and the Art Students League, learning English and acquiring the design and drafting skills that would support his later career as an inventor.

Hansburg settled his family in Brooklyn, N.Y., and worked as a salesman while developing his early inventions. Accounts differ, but the pogo stick was invented sometime between 1909 and 1919. It became a fad of the Roaring Twenties, and it was featured in a dance number in the "Ziegfeld Follies." He got the idea for his invention from a Burmese tale about a young bride whose father, hoping to spare her from soiling her wedding clothes in mud puddles, put a cross-piece on a post and had her jump across the street. Legend has it that the bride's name was Pogo. By developing an internal spring for the tubular stick, Hansburg devised the invention that would enable him to devote the rest of his life to designing and manufacturing his own creations.

There is no evidence that Hansburg patented his invention until 1957, but he is given undisputed credit for the pogo stick in a field of inventors who were straining to invent the array of jumping, bouncing, and leaping devices that fascinated society in the early twentieth century. Between the time of Hansburg's arrival in New York City and his patent of the pogo stick, more than forty patents were granted for pedocycles, springing stilts, grasshopper-shaped spring shoes and "exercise sticks" that attempted to duplicate the pogo stick's self-generated forward movement.

Hansburg's first patent, in 1919, was for a self-propelled wheel toy operated with an elastic bank and a propeller. This was followed by a child's tricycle with sidecar, patented in 1925. In his most productive years, from the 1930's to the 1950's, he invented a series of baby walkers, strollers, bathtubs, and high chairs whose stable designs ensured that an active child could not accidentally tip them over. The "Babee-Tenda" was an infant seat that permitted the child both safety and freedom of movement by placing the chair in the center of a table. The "Bathmaster" was a baby bath equipped with thermometers for water and room temperatures, and an infant scale. The "Gate-Yard" was a playpen with a swinging side gate for easy access. From the 1960's until his death, Hansburg invented several items for retirees, including a leg support, a

golf-putting guide, and an adaptation of the pogo stick for exercising, as well as a telescoping stilt device that allowed the stilts to be adjusted to the height of the user.

In the beginning, Hansburg assigned his designs to manufacturers who then employed him. His first such arrangement was with the Fort Mohansic Chair Company in Ohio, which produced the "Babee-Tenda" and hired Hansburg to train its sales force. After a short period of manufacturing his own baby walkers under the title of the Mama Car Corporation of Long Island, N.Y., Hansburg made an arrangement with the Ideal Toy Corporation, which gave him an entire floor of its Jamaica, N.Y., facility to develop and manufacture a baby walker.

Hansburg's first wife died in 1945. During his two years at Ideal, Hansburg met Frances Michtom, whom he married in 1947; they had no children. Working as a team, they set up Master Juvenile Products Corporation in Walker Valley, N.Y., to manufacture the pogo stick and all of Hansburg's infant furniture designs. The couple operated Master Juvenile Products from 1947 until his retirement in 1969, living and working on a 1,000-acre property that contained their factory and home. After retiring to Hallandale, Fla., Hansburg endowed the University of Miami with funds to develop his design for a hospital bed, but the final product did not materialize.

Hansburg was an intelligent and dignified man who spoke with a slight Russian accent. An agnostic, he did not raise his children with any formal religious training. Although somewhat secretive about his past, refusing to divulge or celebrate his birthday, he held a very high opinion of his native land, believing the Russians were superior in both intelligence and imagination.

He made several fortunes in the course of his lifetime but was not focused on business as a goal in itself. To him, money was strictly a tool used to develop his inventions. He had a special gift for persuading others to realize his designs, but many of his inventions were never patented because of his suspicion of business deals and contracts. He once advised his son to "never sign your right name to a contract" because of possible bad consequences.

Given his lifelong commitment to products for children, one might suppose that he had a particular fondness for them, but this was not the case. Though genuinely concerned for the safety of infants—he invented the "Babee-Tenda" after seeing his own granddaughter fall over in a high chair—he was not particularly interested in children or especially affectionate. He did not become a naturalized citizen of the United States until the age of eighty-two, and died in Miami, Fla.

[Little published biographical material on Hansburg is available. There are fifteen patents listed for Hansburg, dating from 1919 to 1974; however, these do not represent the full range of his inventions, many of which were not patented. Obituaries appear in the *New York Times*, Dec. 9, 1975; and the *Miami Herald*, Dec. 4, 1975.]

SHARON CUMBERLAND

HANSEN, ALVIN HARVEY (Aug. 23, 1887–June 6, 1975), economist, was born in a small farming community in Viborg, S.Dak., to Niels Hansen and the former Bergita Mary Nielson, immigrants from Denmark. In 1910, he graduated from Yankton College, S.Dak., and took up positions as high school principal and then school superintendent in South Dakota before embarking on graduate studies at the University of Wisconsin, where he received his Ph.D. in 1918. In 1916, he married Mabel Lewis, who remained his lifelong companion. They had two daughters.

Hansen was also influenced at Wisconsin by the "social concerns" embodied in the institutional school teaching and writing of John R. Commons. Hansen taught at Wisconsin and then at Brown before being appointed to the University of Minnesota faculty as associate professor in 1919 and full professor in 1923. In 1927 he published *Business Cycle Theory*, which was not very original for its time and contained none of the subsequent Keynesian "heresies" against the orthodox economies of the time.

In 1937, Hansen was appointed to the Lucius S. Littauer Professorship of Political Economy at Harvard University. John Maynard Keynes's ideas about the structure of macroeconomics appeared in print in 1936 as the *General Theory of Money, Interest, and Employment*. While at Harvard, Hansen seized the Keynesian analysis for its explanation of the source of the worldwide depression and for the policies to which it pointed as the way back to full employment. For his remaining years at Harvard, Hansen taught, worked on, modified, and published on the concepts and policies that sprang from the Keynesian framework. His efforts influenced the direction of economic discourse and policy for the next thirty years, in part because of his many activities on government committees, including membership in the Council on Social Security and his role as economic adviser to the Federal Reserve Board, and also because he had many able and articulate students, among them John Kenneth Galbraith and Nobel prize winners Paul Samuelson, James Tobin, and Robert Solow. (In the December 1976 *American Economic Review* memoria, it was pointed out that Professor Hansen surely would have been a Nobel laureate in economics in the 1940's or 1950's if the prize had existed then.) Hansen received the profession's prestigious Francis A. Walker Award in 1967.

Hansen's five most influential books, out of the 108 he authored, were *Full Recovery or Stagnation?* (1938); *Fiscal Policy and Business Cycles* (1941); *Economic Policy and Full Employment* (1947); *Monetary Theory and Fiscal Policy* (1949); and *A Guide to Keynes* (1953). In his presidential address to the 1937 convention of the American Economic Association and in the book *Full Recovery or Stagnation?* Hansen broached his controversial mature-economy or stagnation thesis. In essence, rich or mature economies such as that of the United States tended toward a relative decline in the percentage of consumption spending and an increase in savings out of total income. Because of the decline in population growth and the maturity of major capital-using industries such as the railroads, it was unlikely that private real capital investment would be sufficient to offset the level of savings that could be generated at the full-employment income level. The result would be a shortfall of aggregate demand, persistent deflationary pressures, nagging unemployment, and a slowdown of economic growth. The way out was to have government investment financed by debt, at the ready when needed to supplement private investment, and policies to reduce the need for savings by providing stabilizers to the income flow through generous measures of unemployment insurance and social-security provisions.

The actual postwar experience, which exhibited a high rate of growth, reasonable levels of unemployment, and bouts of inflation rather than deflation tended to diminish Hansen's reputation. But to be fair, many of Hansen's economic prescriptions had been enacted into policy and these may have acted as stabilizers. Moreover, Hansen had already noted the problem of achieving full employment by policies of demand expansion if the economy was subject to inflexible wage and price setting. Hansen's advocacy of generous attitudes toward trade, foreign aid, and foreign investment was more or less followed in the postwar period, and this had a stimulating effect on the world economy. Hansen failed as a prophet partly because some of his policy recommendations were more successful than he thought, and also because he underestimated the forces of technological progress and the ability of the economy to generate new products and to fill existing needs such as housing.

In the Sturm und Drang of policy debates, it is possible to overlook Hansen's contributions to economic theory and analysis. Thus his *Monetary Theory and Fiscal Policy*, an elaboration on Hicks's "Mr. Keynes and the Classics: A Suggested Interpretation" (*Econometrica*, April 1937), helped solidify constructs showing the interaction of investment and savings (the IS curve), demand for money (liquidity preference), interest rate levels, money supply, and level of economic activity. The model which found its way into most money and banking and macroeconomic texts is usually labeled the Hicks-Hansen synthesis. The Hicks-Hansen model theoretically tied together the complex of variables showing under what conditions neoclassical discretionary monetary policy (designed to influence the interest rate) would be effective and under what conditions (corresponding to Keynesian depression) such monetary policy would prove ineffective, thereby requiring an expansionary fiscal policy in order to restore full employment. It should be noted that the Hicks-Hansen model is anathema to conservative monetarist economists because it calls for intervention at various points; it relies on discretionary action by monetary-fiscal *authorities* and not on consistent *rules*.

Hansen's academic career in economics spanned an immensely creative period in the development of the discipline from the dominance of Marshallian neoclassical economics at the turn of the century to the emergence of Keynesian macroeconomics at its mid-point. It was in the latter period of his career, when Hansen was in his mid-fifties, that he was most productive and influential. He was the leading American exponent in arguing the import of the Keynesian model in justifying activist fiscal policy (deficit spending) for stabilizing the level of aggregate economic activity. To fully appreciate Hansen's powers of exposition it is necessary to read the *Guide to Keynes*, holding it open on one corner of the desk, while at the same time perusing the relevant chapter in Keynes. Suddenly Keynes becomes readily understandable, and much is revealed, including anomalies and problems that Keynes himself had not solved to his own satisfaction.

Hansen died in Alexandria, Va.

[Biographical information can be found in the retrospective papers by Walter S. Salant, Paul Samuelson, James Tobin, and Richard Musgrave, *Quarterly Journal of Economics*, Feb. 1976, and "Alvin H. Hansen" in William Breit and Ross L. Ransom, *Academic Scribblers* (1982). An obituary appears in the *New York Times*, June 7, 1975.]

ELI SCHWARTZ

HARLAN, JOHN MARSHALL (May 20, 1899–Dec. 29, 1971), Supreme Court justice, was born in Chicago to Elizabeth Palmer Flagg and John Maynard Harlan, an attorney, Chicago alderman, twice a nominee for Chicago mayor, an unsuccessful independent candidate for Illinois governor, and a member of the Interstate Commerce Commission. The young Harlan was named for his grandfather, John Marshall Harlan, an associate justice of the United States Supreme Court from 1877 to 1911, famous for his dissent in the segregationist *Plessy* v. *Ferguson* (1896) decision. (These two men are the only members from the same family ever to sit on the Supreme Court.) His great-grandfather, James Harlan, was a state attorney general and, from 1835 to 1839, a member of Congress from Kentucky.

The young Harlan attended the Appleby School in Ontario, Canada, and the Lake Placid School in New York. He enrolled at Princeton in 1916, graduating four years later after serving as class president for three years and as a staffer on the student newspaper where he met his lifelong friend, Adlai Stevenson. In his senior year, Harlan's classmates voted him "most respected." In the period 1917–1918, during World War I, he belonged to the Students Army Training Corps and was later a seaman at the Great Lakes Naval Training Station near Chicago. He received a Rhodes Scholarship and attended Balliol College, Oxford University, where he studied jurisprudence and law for three years. (He was the first Rhodes scholar on the Supreme Court.) In 1924 he received his law degree from New York Law School and was admitted to the New York bar in 1925.

After joining the prestigious New York City law firm of Root, Clark, Buckner and Howland, he served from 1925 to 1927 as chief of the Prohibition unit under Emory R. Buckner, the U.S. Attorney for the Southern District, New York, who was also Harlan's mentor and one of his law firm's partners. Because Buckner made Harlan and his fifty other young subordinates swear off drinking they were called "Buckner's Boy Scouts." On appointment by New York Governor Alfred E. Smith, he was a special assistant state attorney general of New York from 1928 to 1930, successfully investigating the sewer scandals in Queens County. He returned to the law firm and became a partner in 1931, soon developing a reputation as a leading trial lawyer. On Nov. 10, 1928, he married Ethel Andrews, with whom he had a daughter.

During World War II, Harlan, as a lieutenant colonel, was chief of the Operational Analysis Section of the Eighth Air Force. In 1944 he was promoted to colonel in the Air Division, United States Group Control Council for Germany. During the war he won the Legion of Merit and the Belgian and French croix de guerre. He was a member of the Post-War Planning Section of the Air Force.

Between 1951 and 1952 he was the unsalaried chief counsel of Thomas Dewey's newly established New York State Crime Commission, investigating waterfront and gambling corruption in New York City. During this same period he gained fame as one of the attorneys defending the du Pont family in an antitrust suit. After over a year of litigation the case was dismissed. In January 1954 President Dwight D. Eisenhower nominated him to the United States Court of Appeals for the Second District, where he began service on March 9. He was serving there when Eisenhower nominated him to the Supreme Court on November 9 to replace the late Robert H. Jackson. The legal profession was pleased, considering him, as one lawyer at the time put it, "a real pro."

His confirmation was delayed because some senators believed him to be a "one-worlder," an individual willing to give up American sovereignty to the United Nations. His Rhodes Scholarship and his later membership on the Council of the Atlantic Union Committee made him suspect. Others said his defense of the du Ponts might cause him to be prejudiced in antimonopoly matters that came before the Court. Some conservative Republicans castigated him as a Dewey man, while Senator William Langer of North Dakota insisted that the next justice should come from one of the seven states, including North Dakota, that had never previously produced a justice or cabinet member. The real delay seemed to be the determination of southern senators to delay implementation of the recently promulgated *Brown* v. *Board of Education* decision and the additional worry that, like his grandfather, he would support civil rights for blacks. Finally on Mar. 16, 1955, Harlan was confirmed by a vote of 77–11. Southern senators cast nine of the eleven nay votes.

During his sixteen-year term Harlan gained a reputation, also like his grandfather, of being the "Great Dissenter" and, with Hugo Black, of being one of the intellectual pillars of the court. Though more a logician than an ideologue, he believed in judicial restraint, in precedent, and in a limited judicial role within the tripartite federal system. In a 1963 speech to the American Bar Association he castigated the idea that "all deficiencies in our society which have failed of correction by other means should find a cure in the courts. . . . This is a compliment to the judiciary, but untrue to democratic principle." He did not believe, as did a majority on the activist Court headed by Chief Justice Earl Warren, that the Fourteenth Amendment applied the Bill of Rights to the states. Within this philosophy he opposed reapportioning state legislatures according to the "one man, one vote" concept. Similarly he dissented in the *Miranda* decision, which required police to explain to suspects their rights to legal representation before being questioned. He also opposed the idea of the federal courts intervening in state obscenity cases unless "prudish overzealousness" was involved. He supported capital punishment and opposed expanding suffrage to eighteen-year-olds. Although he agreed with the Court majority in striking down state and local laws enforcing racial segregation, Harlan believed that the Court could go too far. He refused to support a judicially mandated end to state poll taxes. "Freedom of the individual," he wrote in a sit-in arrest case, "to choose his associates or his neighbors, to use and dispose of his property as he sees fit, to be irrational, arbitrary, capricious, even unjust in his personal relations are things all entitled to a large measure of protection from governmental interference." In this vein he went beyond his more activist colleagues in the 1971 *Cohen* v. *California* case and argued that wearing a jacket with an anti–Vietnam War obscenity on it into a courtroom was constitutionally protected free speech.

Harlan wrote a large number of dissents during his career, averaging over twenty each year. As he told his law clerks to whom he was always very close, he thought the Warren Court's direction was wrong but that balance would be restored eventually.

Harlan was tall (six feet, one inch), with blue eyes, dark eyebrows, and thinning gray hair. He was in excellent physical shape and had a reserved personality. His voice, according to a reporter in the 1920's, was "bass, but soft, slightly nasal and with a humorous catch—a voice for shrewd argument." Although a social man with a dry wit, he had no close friends on the Court except for his mentor, Felix Frankfurter, and later Hugo Black, with whom he differed judicially. He enjoyed golf, fishing, and historical literature.

Near the end of his life, Harlan developed eye problems, but kept up his hard work habits by installing special lighting in his office and holding written material close to his eyes. Eventually he had to depend on his memory when his eyesight prevented him from being able to read at all. He retired on Sept. 23, 1971, six days after Hugo Black. He died in Washington, D.C. Even those who disagreed with him considered him "a judge's judge" because of the craftmanship of his opinions.

[Harlan's legal papers are located in the Princeton University Library. Biographies are Tinsley E. Yarbrough, *John Marshall Harlan: Great Dissenter of the Warren Court* (1992); and Loren Beth, *John Marshall Harlan: The Last Whig Justice* (1992). See also David L. Shapiro, ed., *The Evolution of a Judicial Philosophy: Selected Opinions and Papers of Justice John M. Harlan* (1969); *Time*, Nov. 22, 1954; "Family Job," *New Yorker*, Dec. 4, 1954; and Eugene Gressman, "The New Justice Harlan," *New Republic*, Apr. 4, 1955. An obituary appears in the *New York Times*, Dec. 30, 1971.]

JOHN F. MARSZALEK

HARRIDGE, WILLIAM ("WILL") (Oct. 16, 1885–Apr. 9, 1971), baseball executive, was born in Chicago, Ill., the son of British immigrants who had settled in Hyde Park in 1876. With no special trade, Harridge's father worked at various jobs to support the family. Harridge graduated from Hyde Park High School while working as an office boy for the Wabash Railroad. After mastering stenography and typing at night school, he was hired full-time and given the responsibility of setting itineraries for theatrical companies and sports groups. In June 1911, Harridge married Maude Hunter; they had one child.

In 1911, Ban Johnson, president of the American League of Baseball, noting Harridge's skills in arranging the league's traveling schedules, hired him as his personal secretary. Harridge had never seen a baseball game. His duties included keeping the league's financial books; recording information on purchases, trades, and releases of players; and reviewing contracts.

In 1927 Johnson's public criticism of the baseball commissioner persuaded the American League team owners to force Johnson to take a leave of absence. Vice-President Frank Navin, owner of the Detroit team, became acting president, and Harridge was named secretary-treasurer. When Johnson unexpectedly returned after two months, he locked Harridge out of the league office. Harridge promptly set up another office in the same building, where he conducted day-to-day business until Johnson's permanent resignation later that year. Ernest S. Barnard, president of the Cleveland Indians, was then chosen league president. Harridge continued as secretary-treasurer. Both men initially had three-year contracts, which were renewed in five-year increments from 1930 on. In March 1931, Barnard died, and Harridge was elected president of the American League in May. Ultimately, he served a record twenty-eight years as league chief executive, all without a written contract, before retiring on Feb. 1, 1959.

Harridge earned the team owners' longtime loyalty and respect by avoiding publicity, by handling controversy discreetly, by following good business practices, and by bringing dignity to his office. His cautious approach let club owners rule the league. Harridge conducted business in a mild, gentlemanly manner. He displayed a meticulousness that underscored his efficiency and political skill with the owners.

On occasion Harridge demonstrated a measured leadership presence. He responded to fights on the field with fines and suspensions of managers, players, and even an umpire. One suspension and fine against New York Yankees star catcher Bill Dickey raised the ire of powerful Yankees owner Jacob Ruppert. But Harridge stood firm. In 1933 his strong support of newspaper reporter Arch Wards's idea for an all-star game convinced the team owners of its value. Harridge created administrative divisions within the league office to handle promotions, publicity, motion picture newsreels, and supervision of umpires. During World War II he supported continuing major-league competition despite the loss of many players to the armed forces. In 1945 umpire Ernie Stewart, with the encouragement of Commissioner "Happy" Chandler, made efforts to organize the league umpires to obtain higher salaries and better benefits. Harridge then immediately forced Stewart to resign and reminded Chandler that umpires were the responsibility of each league office. Harridge presided over the American League's first franchise shifts in fifty-two years, first in 1954 when the St. Louis Browns became the Baltimore Orioles and then the next year as the Philadelphia Athletics moved to Kansas City.

When Harridge retired in 1959, the owners created for him the title of chairman of the board of the American League. He continued to visit his office almost daily until his health began to fail. He died in Evanston, Ill. In February 1972, Harridge was elected by the Veterans Committee to the Baseball Hall of Fame.

[There is a file on Harridge in the Baseball Hall of Fame Museum in Cooperstown, N.Y. A profile is available in Marty Appel and Burt Goldblatt, *Baseball's Best* (1981). See also Lee Allen, *The American League Story* (1965); and Eugene Murdock, *Ban Johnson* (1982). Obituaries are in the *New York Times*, Apr. 10, 1971; and the *Sporting News*, Apr. 10, 1971.]

DAVID BERNSTEIN

HARRIS, SEYMOUR EDWIN (Sept. 8, 1897–Oct. 27, 1974), economist, teacher, author, and public servant, was born in New York City, the son of Augusta Kulick and Henry Harris. He received his B.A. from Harvard in 1920 and his Ph.D. from Harvard in 1926. His doctoral dissertation was awarded the David A. Wells Prize in 1927.

Harris began his teaching career at Princeton

as an instructor in 1920. He left that post in 1922 to return to Harvard as an instructor and to pursue graduate work in economics. Upon receipt of his doctorate, Harvard promoted him to lecturer (1927); he became assistant professor in 1933, associate professor with tenure (belatedly) in 1936, and full professor in 1945. Harris was appointed Lucius N. Littauer professor of political economy on July 1, 1957, a post he held until 1963. Between 1955 and 1959, he chaired Harvard's economics department. When he retired from Harvard in 1963, he became chair of the economics department at the University of California, San Diego.

In the late 1930's along with Alvin Hansen, Paul Samuelson, and John Kenneth Galbraith, Harris popularized Keynesian theory in a nation philosophically distrustful of the federal government and committed to individualism and private enterprise. He was a prolific author, writing more than fifty books in his career. Not all his works were well received. For instance, one reviewer, professor Robert Lekachman, charged that in Harris's *Economics of the Kennedy Years and a Look Ahead* (1964), the exposition was unclear, the statistics undigested, and the text ill-organized, but laid these "disfiguring marks" to "hasty composition." That this explanation was probably correct and that the faults were not endemic may be inferred from the success of Harris's other books. Harris also served as editor of the *Review of Economics and Statistics* (1943–1964) and as associate editor of the *Quarterly Journal of Economics* (1947–1974), and was editor of the volumes *Postwar Economic Problems* (1943), *Saving American Capitalism* (1948), *Schumpeter, Social Scientist* (1951), and *The Dollar in Crisis* (1961).

Harris's books on health—*The Economics of American Medicine* (1964) and *The Economics of Health Care* (1975)—and on education— *How Shall We Pay for Education?* (1948), *The Market for College Graduates* (1949), *More Resources for Education* (1961), *Higher Education* (1962), *Economic Aspects of Higher Education* (1964), and *Challenge and Change in American Education* (1965)—were ahead of their time. In the mid-1990's, for example, the United States was the only large industrial nation without a national health plan, and its public educational system was underfinanced and under critical attack for teaching mathematics and science poorly and for trying to do too much, as in sex education.

Harris criticized physicians for their high earnings, claiming they were more interested in income and status than in public service. He did note, however, that their higher incomes reflected longer working hours (sixty hours per week was not uncommon) and the shifting of travel costs to consumers (most doctors had given up house calls by the 1960's). At the same time, he claimed that hospital services and drugs were overpriced; hospital daily charges had risen at two and a half times the rate of income growth over the period 1948–1963, with most gains going to salaries and wages of professional staffs. To fund future medical costs he favored private insurance plans, cautioning that cost containment was necessary to protect consumers.

In education Harris recommended more realistic financing by the federal and state governments to keep education abreast of inflationary price changes. Further, he suggested that public colleges charge tuition with heavy subvention for students from low-income families through long-term loans (as long as forty years). He wanted to substitute user fees for tax underwriting of public college costs. Harris, however, was not ideologically bound to the private market approach. In an article in a Catholic journal he endorsed the policy of federal aid to private colleges, including those with religious affiliations. On the other hand, he maintained on constitutional and economic grounds that private primary and secondary schools should not receive public aid.

Harris's public service included serving as chief consultant (1961–1967) to Secretary of the Treasury Douglas Dillion, for which he received the Treasury Department's highest honor, the Alexander Hamilton Award. Presidential candidate Adlai Stevenson, and presidents Lyndon B. Johnson and John F. Kennedy sought his advice. (Prior to his death, Kennedy had intended to appoint him to the Federal Reserve Board; Johnson did not appoint him to the vacancy, however, which was a major disappointment.) In the 1950's, when Japanese exports to the United States began to grow, Harris chaired the New England Governors' Textile Committee, a group that requested legislative help to stem the flood of Japanese textiles to the United States.

Sidney Hyman, reviewing Harris's The Economics of the Political Parties (1962) in the New York Times, wrote: "He [Harris] does not spend his time in theorizing about a perfect economic world where crabs will walk straight, moles will see and elephants will fly. He is a committed political economist, at grips with the problems of the here and the now as they present themselves in the context of concrete cases and controversies."

Two cases may be cited to support Hyman's contention. First is Harris's New York Times article "The Gap Between Economist and Politician" (Apr. 14, 1963), in which he professed that the major reason for the gap was "the economists' neglect of the powerful noneconomic factors involved in the making of public policy." He called for a closing of the gap through the reciprocal recognition of the integrity of each group. In this article he focused on four problem areas: fiscal policy, the dollar problem, the trade expansion program, and agricultural policy.

Second, in his Times article "Can We Prosper Without Arms?" (Nov. 6, 1959), Harris proposed a reduction in defense spending to provide a tax cut and direct government investment in health programs, education, and slum clearance, in order to sustain employment. In 1960, Harris and Nobel Laureate Polykarp Kusch cochaired a committee created by the Democratic party to plan the transition from "a defense to a peace economy in event of world disarmament."

Harris married Ruth Black on Sept. 3, 1923; they had no children. After her death, he married Dorothy Marshall on Apr. 27, 1968. He died in San Diego, Calif.

[Harris's books not mentioned in text include The Assignats (1930); Monetary Problems of the British Empire (1931); Twenty Years of Federal Reserve Policy (1933); The Economics of the Recovery Program (1934); Exchange Depreciation (1936); Economics of Social Security (1941); Economics of American Defense (1941); Economics of America at War (1943); Price and Related Controls (1945); Economic Problems of Latin America (1944); Economic Reconstruction (1945); Inflation and the American Economy (1945); National Debt and the New Economics (1947); Stabilization Subsidies (1948); Foreign Economic Policy for the United States (1948); The European Recovery Program (1948); Economics of Mobilization and Inflation (1951); The Economics of New England (1952); John Maynard Keynes (1955); Inflation and Anti-inflationary Policies of American States (1956); Interregional and International Economics (1957); Higher Education in the United States (1960); American Economic History (1961);

and *Economics of Harvard* (1970). There is no published biography of Harris. An obituary is in the *New York Times*, Oct. 29, 1974.]

HAROLD L. WATTEL

HARTNETT, CHARLES LEO ("GABBY") (Dec. 20, 1900–Dec. 20, 1972), baseball player, was born in Woonsocket, R.I., the eldest of fourteen children of Fred Hartnett, a mill worker and bus and streetcar conductor, and Ellen ("Nell") Tucker. In 1910, the family moved to Millville, Mass., where Hartnett attended school through the eighth grade. Leaving school to help support his family, Hartnett picked berries for fifteen cents per quart and worked in the U.S. Rubber Shop. He took jobs as a semiprofessional baseball catcher for a variety of local mill teams and town squads. In 1918, Hartnett was given a partial scholarship to play baseball for Dean Academy, a junior college in Franklin, Mass. He attended Dean for two years but did not graduate.

In 1921, while working in the shipping department of the American Steel and Wire mill in Worcester, Mass., the young backstop signed a professional contract with the Worcester Boosters in the Eastern League. Playing one hundred games and batting .264 in his first season, Hartnett was scouted by the Giants' Jesse Burkett who reported to manager John McGraw that Hartnett's small hands would be a liability in the major leagues. Chicago Cubs scout Jack Doyle disagreed, and the Cubs acquired Hartnett's contract for $2,500. Unsure and nervous, rookie Hartnett's quiet manner, as the team traveled from Chicago to California for spring training in 1922, earned him the nickname "Gabby" from newspaperman Eddie Sullivan, who jokingly called him the "gabbiest guy" on the team.

Hartnett's tenure with the Cubs began as backup catcher to Bob O'Farrell. He played his first major league game from behind the plate in the 1922 season opener, catching Grover Cleveland Alexander. The Cubs won, but Hartnett went hitless. During the year, he saw action mostly as Alexander's personal backstop, batting .194 in thirty-one games. Continuing a reserve role in 1923, he appeared in thirty-one games at first base and thirty-nine catching while batting .268 with eight home runs. He began a fifteen-year stint as the Cubs' regular catcher in 1924.

The next year, Hartnett became baseball's first slugging catcher, with twenty-four home runs accompanying a .238 average and sixty-seven runs batted in. Following a personally disastrous 1929, when a throwing-arm injury limited him to twenty-two times at bat for the year, Hartnett enjoyed his best individual season in 1930, establishing career highs of 141 games, thirty-seven home runs, 122 runs batted in, 172 hits and eighty-four runs scored. His .339 batting average that year was exceeded by .344 in 1935, when he was named the National League's Most Valuable Player. He went on to hit .354 in 1937.

The Cubs appeared in four World Series at three-year intervals beginning in 1929. Chicago lost them all as Hartnett batted .241 with two home runs in fifty-four at bats. In 1935, while losing in six games to Detroit, Hartnett hit his series best .292. His personal career highlight came in the next-to-last series of the 1938 season. Trailing the league-leading Pirates by half a game and with darkness descending on Wrigley Field, Hartnett propelled a ninth-inning home run, known as the "homer in the gloamin'," that carried the Cubs to the National League pennant. At the start of 1938, he was made a coach. Then, in July, with the Cubs six and a half games from first, Hartnett was promoted to manager. For the balance of the season, Chicago won forty-four and lost twenty-seven. Perhaps emotionally drained from the tense pennant race, the Cubs were shut down 4–0 by the Yankees in the fall classic.

Hartnett was named starting catcher for the National League in the first five all-star games of 1933–1937. He batted .200 and was involved in two famous incidents. In 1934 Hartnett was catching when New York Giant's ace Carl Hubbell struck out, in order, Babe Ruth, Lou Gehrig, Jimmy Foxx, Al Simmons, and Joe Cronin. Three years later St. Louis Cardinals pitcher Dizzy Dean, after shaking off a Hartnett signal, was hit by a line drive that broke his toe, thus shortening his career.

Hartnett's tenure as player-manager continued through the 1940 season; he accumulated a record of 203 wins and 176 losses. A slate of eighty-four wins and seventy losses in 1939 resulted in a fourth-place finish for the Cubs, one place higher than the 1940 season, with seventy-five wins and seventy-nine losses. That year Hartnett played in only thirty-seven games batting .266. In November, he was released by the Cubs as both player and manager. In 1941,

Hartnett joined the New York Giants as player-coach under manager Bill Terry. For his last year as an active player, the forty-year old catcher hit .300 in sixty-four games with forty-five hits producing five home runs and twenty-six runs batted in.

Upon his retirement as a player in 1941, Hartnett held career records for a catcher in home runs (236), games played (1,990), season batting average (.354), and lifetime hitting average (.298). A defensive standout, Hartnett caught one hundred or more games in twelve seasons, eight of them consecutively (1930–1937). Managing pitchers was his forte: over the 1933–1934 seasons he handled 452 chances without an error. Dizzy Dean marveled at Hartnett's expertise at setting a target, "like throwing a ball in a funnel." Chosen to the all-time Golden Glove team, he led National League catchers six times in fielding percentage and assists and four times in putouts, and in 1992, still ranked fourth in career double plays. Hartnett moved on to managerial jobs in the American Association with Indianapolis (1942) and in the International League with Jersey City (1943–1945) and Buffalo (1946). He returned to major league baseball as coach for the Kansas City Athletics in 1965 and as scout in 1966. He also worked in public relations.

On Jan. 18, 1929, Hartnett married Martha Henrietta Marshall of Chicago. They had two children. He lived in Chicago in the off-season, where he established a successful insurance company. In 1955, Hartnett was elected to the National Baseball Hall of Fame in Cooperstown, N.Y. From 1947 to 1964, he owned the Gabby Hartnett Recreation Center, including a bowling alley and sporting goods store, in Lincolnwood, Ill. Hartnett died in Park Ridge, Ill.

[A biography is James M. Murphy, *The Gabby Hartnett Story* (1983). Shorter profiles are in Jack Zanger, *Great Catchers of the Major League* (1970); and Martin Appel and Burt Goldblatt, *Baseball's Best* (1977). An obituary appears in the *New York Times*, Dec. 21, 1972.]

DAVID BERNSTEIN

HARTSFIELD, WILLIAM BERRY (Mar. 1, 1890–Feb. 22, 1971), mayor of Atlanta, Ga., was born in Atlanta, the youngest son of Charles Green Hartsfield, a tinsmith, and Victoria Dagnall. He attended public schools but left Boys High School in his senior year to take a night

secretarial course at Dixie Business College. He became a clerk, and while pursuing that occupation married Pearl Williams, a Western Union operator, on Aug. 2, 1913. They had two children.

In 1916, Hartsfield became a clerk in the prestigious law firm of Rosser, Slaton, Phillips and Hopkins, studying law through working in the firm. Simultaneously, he embarked upon a program of self-education through reading in the humanities and the sciences, especially in the public library, and in 1917 he passed the Georgia bar examination. For the remainder of his life, he would declare that the Atlanta Public Library was his alma mater.

Building a reputation as a successful lawyer, Hartsfield established friendships with the business leaders of Atlanta and won acceptance in the power circles of the city. His true loves were the city and aviation, in that order. His wife consistently was relegated to a tertiary role. In 1923, he was elected to the city council and was immediately appointed chairman of the council's new aviation committee. In that position he negotiated the acquisition of land for a municipal airport and federal designation of Atlanta as a terminal and transfer point on the first New York–Miami and Chicago-Jacksonville air routes.

Hartsfield left the city council to serve in the Georgia General Assembly (1933–1936). His heart was still in local government, however, and his brief legislative career in the rural-dominated assembly was characterized primarily by his advocacy, though with little effect, of measures to benefit cities.

In 1936, he entered the mayoral race in Atlanta. The campaign was brutal. Incumbent Mayor James L. Key accused Hartsfield of offering bribes, of engaging in dishonest business practices, and of failing to pay his debts. Nevertheless, Hartsfield won a close race after accusing Key of converting the police force into an instrument of political favoritism, of overseeing the construction of a jail so shoddy that it invited escape, and of insulting the memory of the Confederacy by vetoing a bill to make Confederate Memorial Day a city holiday.

Sworn into office on Jan. 4, 1937, Hartsfield took the reins of a city so deep in debt it was compensating its municipal employees with certificates promising to pay at a later date. The police department was dominated by a dishonest and inefficient administration, and Atlanta was notorious for gambling and prostitution. Hartsfield's initial actions as mayor were designed to place city finances on a firm foundation by budgeting realistically based on anticipated revenues, to gain control of the police department by appointing new leadership, and to clean up the city's night spots by cracking down on gambling. Through his close friendship with Robert W. Woodruff, the head of the Coca-Cola Company, Hartsfield won the support of the city's bankers for refinancing the municipal payroll, and he successfully reformed the police department and other city agencies.

Hartsfield loved the spotlight, and he was determined to bring favorable publicity to his city as well as to himself. His greatest opportunity arrived in 1939 with the release of David O. Selznick's epic film *Gone with the Wind*, based on the novel by Atlantan Margaret Mitchell. Through a vigorous campaign led by the mayor, Atlanta was selected as the site of the film's premiere, which ranked among the most spectacular of all such events in Hollywood's golden era. Newspapers, magazines, radio, and newsreel cameras focused national attention on Atlanta during several days and nights of parades, balls, and appearances by Hollywood's brightest stars. Through it all Mayor Hartsfield occupied center stage.

Coming off his triumph with *Gone with the Wind* and the successes of his municipal policies, Hartsfield sought a second term as mayor in 1940 but neglected to campaign seriously. He lost to challenger Roy LeCraw by eighty-three votes out of more than 22,000 cast. Analysts declared that the deciding factor had been Hartsfield's twenty-five-mile-per-hour citywide speed limit, which was too low for the city's voters, enforced by motorcycle officers hiding behind billboards.

However, Hartsfield was out of office for only sixteen months. World War II had broken out, and in the spring of 1942 LeCraw resigned to enter military service. In a special election held that May, the voters returned Hartsfield to city hall. He would hold the office of mayor for the next twenty years.

After World War II, Hartsfield led Atlanta to the forefront of southern cities. His close ties with business leaders guaranteed that policies at city hall would be conducive to business interests. For example, Hartsfield initiated and administered a vast program of infrastructure improvements while ending each fiscal year with a budget surplus. By 1959, Atlanta's metropolitan population had surpassed one million, and Hartsfield had expanded the territorial limits of the city from 35 to 118 square miles through a controversial annexation enacted by the state legislature that had been opposed by suburban homeowners who objected to paying city taxes.

Hartsfield put a high priority on developing the Atlanta Municipal Airport through improvements in runways, lighting, and approaches. During his administration, Atlanta emerged as the hub of air transportation in the Southeast, a crucial factor in the city's simultaneous emergence as the commercial and financial center of the region. As chairman of the airport committee of the American Municipal Association, Hartsfield was instrumental in winning the approval of the Eisenhower administration, which was less than enthusiastic for public-works projects, for a federal program of assistance to airports.

Hartsfield led Atlanta through changes in racial policies without the turmoil that characterized the civil rights era elsewhere in the South. Nothing in his early political career indicated a devotion to equal rights for black people; but after the U.S. Supreme Court declared in 1944 that black voters could no longer be excluded from Democratic primaries, Hartsfield began to court the black leadership of his city. Subsequently, African Americans became an important element of the coalition that kept him in office. He appointed Atlanta's first black police officers in 1948, welcomed the convention of the National Association for the Advancement of Colored People to the city in 1951, helped end segregation on buses and trolleys in 1957, and presided over the integration of city schools in 1961.

Atlanta's business leadership consistently supported Hartsfield's progressive racial policies. In a phrase that caught the spirit of the alliance between business people interested in economic progress and black leaders dedicated to the elimination of discrimination, Hartsfield declared Atlanta a city "too busy to hate."

Hartsfield's personal life was not as successful as his public life. He and his wife spent little time together. By 1961, he was in love with a young widow, and he recognized that in the atmosphere of the times it was unlikely that he could win another election if he divorced his wife to marry her. Reluctantly, he decided not to seek reelection, announcing the decision on June 7, 1961. He was granted a divorce on Feb. 20, 1962, and on July 11, 1962, he married Tollie Bedenbaugh Tolan. He subsequently adopted her young son.

In 1962, the former mayor became president of Atlanta's Southeastern Fair. He traveled abroad frequently and freely offered commentary to the press on the state of affairs in Atlanta and the world.

He died in Atlanta. Shortly after his death, the Atlanta Municipal Airport, which had become one of the busiest in the world, was renamed the William Berry Hartsfield International Airport.

[Hartsfield's papers are in Emory University's Robert W. Woodruff Library in Atlanta. See Harold H. Martin, *William Berry Hartsfield: Mayor of Atlanta* (1978). Obituaries are in the *New York Times*, Feb. 24, 1971; and the *Atlanta Constitution*, Feb. 23, 1971.]

VAGN K. HANSEN

HAYAKAWA, SESSUE (June 10, 1890–Nov. 23, 1973), actor, was born Kintaro Hayakawa in Chiba province on the island of Honshu, Japan, the son of Yoichiro and Kane Hayakawa. His father, the governor of Chiba province, took great pride in his aristocratic lineage and raised all his sons according to samurai ideals. Despite the family's well-to-do life-style, Yoichiro had his son complete such menial tasks as cleaning lamps so the child would not "grow up a soft man of a rich family."

"Kimbo," as the child was called, was educated at the Navy Preparatory School in Tokyo, graduating in 1908. He then entered the Naval Academy in Etajima but a ruptured eardrum resulted in his dismissal. In his shame, Hayakawa attempted hara-kiri, stabbing himself thirty times. His condition was critical for weeks.

Hayakawa secluded himself in a monastery to recuperate. There he learned Zen Buddhism. His seclusion ended in May 1909, when he rescued a group of Americans whose ship had crashed in Tokyo Bay. Speaking with the Americans sparked his interest in traveling to the United States. Overcoming his father's opposition, Hayakawa enrolled in the University of Chicago to study political science. A star football player, he was thrown off the team for using judo to overcome his opponents.

On his way home to Japan after graduating in 1913, Hayakawa stopped in Los Angeles to see a performance of the Japanese Theatre. Claiming he could do a better job, Hayakawa changed his first name to Sessue and embarked on an acting career. He made his Hollywood debut in 1914 when his staging of *Typhoon* caught the attention of producer Thomas Ince, who then filmed the play with Hayakawa as the lead. On May 1 of the same year, Hayakawa married actress Tsui Aoki. During their forty-seven-year-marriage (ended by Aoki's death), the couple had three children.

Hayakawa's career was firmly established in 1916 when he starred in *The Cheat*. It was years before he could share his success with his family, however, for they regarded acting as a drop in status. All told, Hayakawa appeared in more than 120 silent films, including *The Bottle Imp*, *The City of Dim Faces*, and *Hidden Pearls*. "Public acceptance of me in romantic roles was a blow of sorts against racial intolerance," he said, "even though I lost the girl in the last reel."

In 1918 Hayakawa began his own film company, Haworth Pictures Corporation, bankrolled by a million-dollar loan from the parents of a college friend. Two years later, Hayakawa had made more than $2 million and repaid the loan. His fame was so great that in 1921 he was invited to visit President Warren Harding.

On his salary of $7,500 per week, Hayakawa and his family lived in grand style in a thirty-two-room mansion on Argyle Avenue in Hollywood. Their lavish parties became the stuff of legend and earned their home the nickname "Argyle Castle." The family left Hollywood in 1922 after an attempt was made on Hayakawa's life.

Hayakawa then traveled throughout America and Europe, starring in various plays. In 1923 he played to a packed house in France; a few months later, he gave a command performance for King George V and Queen Mary of England. A high-roller, he calmly lost a considerable sum gambling one night in 1926. His gold-plated Pierce Arrow automobile was so large that he ended up donating it to a fire department.

Three years later, he returned to America to star in *The Love City* on Broadway. The following year he established a Zen study hall in New York. In 1931, Paramount released Hayakawa's first talking picture, *Daughter of the Dragon*, while he continued to appear in plays throughout the Far East and in Paris.

Hayakawa's travel was cut short by World War II, when his sympathy with the West precluded his return to Japan. He moved to Paris and for twelve years supported his family by painting on silk.

When the war ended, Hayakawa resumed his acting career, accepting Humphrey Bogart's invitation to appear in *Tokyo Joe* (1949). That same year, he returned to Japan and produced the play *The Life of the Buddha*. To honor his work, Hayakawa was selected for the Zen Buddhist priesthood, passed his examination, and was ordained. He believed the concentration and discipline of Zen greatly improved his acting as well as the quality of his life. In his 1960 autobiography *Zen Showed Me the Way*, Hayakawa wrote, "Through Zen I am able to empty my mind of all thoughts that may hinder my performance."

In 1956 Hayakawa was offered the role of Colonel Saito in the film version of *The Bridge on the River Kwai*. At his wife's urging he accepted the part. "From the conflict of two men—Nicholson, the English colonel, and Saito, the Japanese colonel—stems all the . . . futility of war," Hayakawa later wrote. His performance earned him the Golden Globe Award and an Oscar nomination.

After this dramatic comeback, Hayakawa enjoyed a brief resurgence of his earlier fame. When it faded at the end of the 1950's, he moved to a small bungalow in Tokyo and taught acting.

In addition to his skills as an actor and director and his religious devotion, Hayakawa spoke Japanese, English, French, Spanish, German, Chinese, East Indian, and Malay. "Destiny has brought me much," he wrote in his autobiography. "She has been kind. But it has been left to me to fashion the acumen of deeds in the pattern destiny has drawn, to solve the great *koan* of life for myself."

Hayakawa died in Japan.

[See Richard Hubler, "Honorable 'Bad Guy,' " *Coronet*, May 1961; as well as articles in the *Los Angeles Times*, Dec. 22, 1957; the *New York Times*, Mar. 9, 1958; the *New York Post Magazine*, Oct. 19, 1958; and the *New York Herald Tribune*, Apr. 5, 1959. An obituary appears in the *New York Times*, Nov. 25, 1973.]

LAURIE ROZAKIS

HAYDEN, CARL TRUMBULL (Oct. 2, 1877–Jan. 25, 1972), senator, was born in Hayden's Ferry (now Tempe), Ariz., the son of Charles Trumbull Hayden and Sallie Calvert Davis. A descendant on his father's side of seventeenth-century English colonists, Hayden grew up in the frontier world of Arizona when it was still a territory in the town named for his father, who had settled there just after the Civil War. Graduating from the Normal School of Arizona at Tempe in 1896, he went on to Stanford University. Later when he entered national political life, he became known for the intensity of his reelection campaigns, even in the years when he faced no serious challenger. The refusal to take anything for granted, he said, went back to his years at Stanford when, in a race for student body president, he lost the only election of his life. "It taught me a lesson," he told a reporter in 1950. "I've been running like a rabbit ever since."

After earning his B.A. from Stanford in 1900, Hayden returned to Tempe, where he entered the flour-milling business and successfully ran for town council (1902–1904). For two years he served as treasurer of Maricopa County and then in 1907 was elected county sheriff, holding that post for five years. On Feb. 15, 1908, he married Nan Downing, who died in 1962; they had no children.

In 1912, when Arizona entered the Union as the forty-eighth state, Hayden was chosen as its first representative to Congress. For the next fifty-six years, forty-two of them in the Senate, Hayden would be Arizona's "man in Washington." As a freshman in Congress, he announced his interests in irrigation and water rights, in the commercial use of public lands, and in federal policies affecting mining rights, three areas that would remain priorities on his political agenda for most of his legislative career because of their self-evident importance to the economy of the Southwest. In his fourteen years in the House, he served on both the Irrigation and Public Lands Committees, on the Flood Control Committee, and on the Committee for Indian Affairs.

He was a political moderate, whose votes at times reflected liberal policy, as when he supported the creation of the United States Children's Bureau in 1912 to assist state welfare agencies in caring for homeless and dependent children. He also supported woman suffrage and the prohibition of child labor. On other occasions, Hayden took a more conservative position, voting for immigration quotas and Prohibition, and against a bill that made lynching a federal crime. During World War I, Hayden, who had been a member of the First Arizona National Guard, was posted to Camp Lewis, Wash., as a major of infantry in the United States Army.

He was elected to the Senate in 1926 and would serve there until 1968, longer than any person before him. Unknown to the country at large for much of that time, Hayden remained inconspicuous in Washington as well. Nonetheless he came to wield great power in the Senate because of his attention to its traditions, his dedication to hard work, and his remarkable diplomatic skill in roaming the Senate corridors and cloak room in search of the votes that were needed for measures he supported. What made his influence all the more remarkable was his public reticence. He once said that he owed his longevity in Congress to the principle that if a man keeps his mouth shut, he can't put his foot in it. Between 1927 and 1947, he took the Senate floor only once: to mount a six-week filibuster against certain provisions in the bill creating Boulder Dam. Ironically his third Senate speech, given in 1949, called for time limits on filibustering, which in the postwar years had become a favorite weapon of the southern bloc. When he did speak, he rarely spoke for more than five minutes at a time, in a dry, clear monotone without embellishment.

In the 1930's Hayden generally supported the New Deal, voting in favor of such measures as the repeal of Prohibition, Social Security, and the Tennessee Valley Authority. He continued to press for irrigation and roads in the West. Asked by Franklin Roosevelt why he always mentioned roads when he came to the White House, whatever else might be under discussion, Hayden replied, "Because Arizona has two things people will drive thousands of miles to see—the Grand Canyon and the Petrified Forest. They can't get there without roads." In the 1950's he was the key figure in establishing the formulas for the vast federal highway aid program.

His legislative record continued to reflect a middle-ground approach to government. He supported the desegregation of the military after World War II but voted against Medicare in 1962. He voted in favor of the Marshall Plan but opposed portions of the North Atlantic Se-

curity Pact, which established NATO. From the 1950's on, he advocated equal rights for women, and in the 1960's he went on record in favor of President Kennedy's program for federal aid to education. President Johnson designated Sept. 30, 1968, Carl Hayden Day at the White House to mark the signing of the Lower Colorado River Basin bill. The measure, providing $1.3 billion for water development, was one Hayden had long championed and the passage of which he had finally secured.

In 1957, Hayden, as the longest-serving member, assumed the unofficial title of dean of the Senate. Because the Democrats controlled the chamber, he became president pro tempore, presiding in the absence of the vice-president. On the assassination of President Kennedy in November 1963, he stood second in line for the presidency by virtue of that position. He retired from the Senate five years later. Hayden died in Mesa, Ariz.

[There is no full-length biography. See *Congressional Directory* (1968). Hayden's legislative record can be found in *Congress and the Nation, 1945–1964* (1965). An obituary appears in the *New York Times*, Jan. 26, 1972.]

ALLAN L. DAMON

HAYNES, HENRY DOYLE ("HOMER") (July 29, 1920–Aug. 7, 1971), musician and comedian, was born in Knoxville, Tenn., the son of Laura Mae Hopkins and Henry Alfred Haynes, a cotton mill worker. He received his high school diploma from the Knoxville city school system.

Haynes was a natural musical talent, self-taught on the guitar at an early age. By the age of nine, he appeared on radio station WNOX in Knoxville. In 1932, he met his lifelong partner, mandolin player Kenneth Burns, another Knoxville native and three months Haynes's senior. They auditioned for the same WNOX amateur show, and both were disqualified for sounding too professional.

Haynes and Burns soon formed a guitar-mandolin duo, an instrumentation format that came to prominence in country music in the 1930's. Many of these groups were "brother" acts, such as the Louvin Brothers, the Delmore Brothers, the Monroe Brothers, and years later in early rock the Everly Brothers. They modeled their act after the Blue Sky Boys, Earl and Bill Bolick, two brothers who specialized in gentle arrangements of traditional, sentimental parlor songs and gospel music. The Blue Sky Boys also peppered their act with cornball humor and skits, inspiring Haynes and Burns to develop their comedic skills as well. They got their stage names, "Homer and Jethro," when a WNOX announcer forgot their real names during his introduction and made up two names on the spot. Their new characters, from "Hoot 'n Holler, Tennessee," were set for the rest of their careers. Both men intermingled freelance instrumental work with their new Homer and Jethro act until 1938, when they committed themselves to the group full-time.

Homer and Jethro appeared occasionally on WNOX's "Plantation Party" show until 1948, and they began touring and appearing on other prominent country radio programs in the late 1930's. One of the first of these radio shows was the "Renfro Valley Barn Dance" in Kentucky. It was during Haynes's tenure at Renfro Valley that he met his wife, Elizabeth Coleman. They had three children. The Homer and Jethro act was interrupted by World War II. Both men served in the military. Haynes was an army corporal serving as a clerk and medical technician. Burns was stationed in the South Pacific.

When the act resumed, Homer and Jethro did a stint on WLW, a clear-channel radio station in Cincinnati, Ohio, affiliated with the National Broadcasting Company. In 1946, they made their first recordings for the King label, also in Cincinnati. They later appeared on KWTO in Springfield, Mo. Their popularity as a comedy musical duo gained momentum, climaxing with their 1949 appearance on the "National Barn Dance," broadcast on clear-channel WLS in Chicago. They continued as a staple act on the show until 1960. They also made appearances on WSM's "Grand Ole Opry" in Nashville, Tenn. By 1950, they were making television appearances, such as on a Roy Rogers special on NBC and Eddy Arnold's variety show on ABC. Haynes and Burns eventually made their home in the Chicago area, Haynes settling in Lansing, Ill.

In 1949, Homer and Jethro signed with RCA Victor records, a move facilitated in part by their association with guitarist Chet Atkins, Ken Burns's brother-in-law, member of Homer and Jethro's band, and eventual executive at RCA's Nashville studio. The RCA contract initially led to a brief association (1950–1951) with Spike Jones's City Slickers, the widely known

musical comedy band known particularly for their parodies of classical and popular music. From this experience Homer and Jethro began using the parody idea in their own routines, satirizing material as diverse as "How Much Is That Doggy (Hound Dawg) in the Window" and "Vesti la giubba" from the opera *Pagliacci*. This material was blended with their existing "cornpone" repertoire of songs such as "I'm My Own Grandpaw" and "The Battle of Kookamonga." They also incorporated spoken dialogues and stories, including a country bumpkin's account of witnessing his first hockey game, very similar to Andy Griffith's famous "What It Was, Was Football" routine in the 1950's. A popularity contest in *Billboard* magazine named Homer and Jethro the Favorite Comedy Team of 1952.

Homer and Jethro continued recording comedy albums and making live appearances throughout the 1950's. By the 1960's, they were making more mainstream television appearances (outside of country-music programs), including an appearance on Johnny Carson's NBC "Tonight Show." Short, blond, and boyish looking, Haynes was famous for his relaxed demeanor and trademark gum chewing. When asked by Carson why he always chewed gum, Homer, unperturbed, replied simply, "What the hell else are you gonna do with it?" Homer and Jethro probably became best known to the general public when they appeared in a Kellogg's Corn Flakes commercial in the 1960's.

Similar in circumstance to pianist-comedian Thomas ("Fats") Waller, few of Homer and Jethro's fans ever realized or appreciated their instrumental abilities. In his youth Haynes had aspired to be a serious concert guitarist and, early on, was a respected studio session rhythm guitarist. Among professional musicians in jazz and country music, Ken Burns was acknowledged as one of the premier mandolin players. Haynes's and Burns's talents were best exhibited in the early 1960's when Chet Atkins produced the RCA album *Homer and Jethro Play It Straight*, an album of jazz and popular music instrumentals demonstrating their flawless musicianship.

In 1971, while preparing for a performance at the Great Midwest Fair in Crete, Ill., Haynes collapsed and was taken to a hospital in Hammond, Ind., where he died. Eulogies appeared in the newspapers of the many small towns where the two men had entertained. Burns canceled all appearances for a time, eventually trying to return as a solo act. In 1976, he added twenty-seven-year-old Ken Eidson as the "new Homer." The Homer and Jethro act was soon retired. Jethro finished out his career in the 1980's as Ken Burns, a mandolin virtuoso, appearing on American Public Radio's "A Prairie Home Companion" and other programs.

[Newspaper clippings, publicity photos, and press releases for Homer and Jethro are on file at the Country Music Foundation Library and Media Center, Nashville, Tenn. A biographical entry on Haynes can be found in Linnell Gentry, *A History and Encyclopedia of Country, Western, and Gospel Music*, 2d ed. (1969).

Exemplary RCA albums of Homer and Jethro include *Barefoot Ballads*, *Cornfucius Say*, *Life Can Be Miserable*, *Musical Madness*, and *The Humorous Side of Country Music*. An obituary appears in the *New York Times*, Aug. 8, 1971.]

DAVID L. JOYNER

HAYWARD, LELAND (Sept. 13, 1902–Mar. 18, 1971), theatrical and film producer, talent agent, pilot, and airline executive, was born in Nebraska City, Nebr., the only son of Colonel William Hayward, a prosperous attorney, and Sarah Ireland Tappin. Hayward was educated at the Hotchkiss School in Connecticut and attended Princeton University in 1920 before leaving for academic reasons in his freshman year.

Hayward got his start in show business by traveling the country as a press agent for United Artists, a job he was fired from when he began publishing free-lance articles about actors and actresses who were not affiliated with UA. He continued to broaden his contacts as a talent scout, general contract man, and press agent for other companies in New York and Hollywood. In 1927, fascinated by the release of the first talking picture, he sold a manuscript of struggling writer and friend Ben Hecht's to MGM, and used his commission to pay his travel expenses to a meeting with John W. Rumsey, president of the American Play Company, an established literary agency in Manhattan. Hayward went to work for Rumsey, taking only half the commission, and lobbied for the establishment of a motion-picture department. In 1929 Hayward was able to purchase a 33 percent interest in APC. In 1932 his partnership with the company was dissolved, and Hayward established his own agency at 654 Madison Avenue in New York, positioning himself, at the age of thirty, to represent an impressive list of writers and performers that would eventually include Fred Astaire, Ginger Rogers, Edna Ferber, Howard Lindsey, Russell Crouse, Myrna Loy, Charles MacArthur, James Stewart, Burgess Meredith, Katharine Hepburn, Miriam Hopkins, Greta Garbo, Charles Laughton, Judy Garland, Dorothy McGuire, and Gregory Peck. One of his clients, Henry Fonda, had once been married to Hayward's second wife, Margaret Sullavan, but that never detracted from the cordial friendship the two men shared.

Hayward's appetite for business was legendary. By habit, he juggled several telephone calls at once, without losing the thread of any conversation. He also enjoyed the company of attractive and intelligent women, marrying five times. He was married to Lola Gibbs twice (1921–1922 and 1930–1934). In 1936 he married the actress Margaret Sullavan; they had three children, Brooke, Bridget, and William. Bridget and William suffered intensely from emotional distress exacerbated by their parents' estrangement; both were committed for psychiatric treatment during their growing-up years. Bridget died, probably as a result of an epileptic attack, in 1960, but her two surviving siblings went on to distinguish themselves professionally, William as coproducer of *Easy Rider* (1969) and other films, and Brooke as the author of *Haywire* (1977), a memoir of her family that included markedly honest reminiscences about their tribulations as well as their gifts. Hayward's third wife was Nancy ("Slim") Hawks, who earlier had been married to the director Howard Hawks; that marriage lasted from 1949 to 1960. In 1960 Hayward married Pamela Digby Churchill.

As a producer, Hayward enjoyed extraordinary success. Between 1944 and 1971 his productions won two Pulitzer Prizes (*State of the Union* and *South Pacific*), thirty Tony's, thirteen Donaldson Awards, fourteen "bests" in *Variety*'s annual critics' poll, and a New York Drama Critics Circle Award.

Hayward's first professional success stemmed from his reading of John Hersey's *A Bell for Adano*. He was convinced the book would make a great play, but could interest no Broadway producer in the venture. His client and friend, the playwright Paul Osborn, agreed to dramatize the work if Hayward would personally produce it. He did so, and the play made its debut at the Cort Theater on Dec. 6, 1944, running for 296 performances. His producer's eye was famously discerning and yet oddly catholic; he refused to confine himself to the formulaic or to any one genre, instead championing excellence in whatever guise he encountered it. His theatrical productions included *Mister Roberts* (1948); *South Pacific* (1949, coproduced with Joshua Logan); *Gypsy* (1959, coproduced with David Merrick); *The Sound of Music* (1959, coproduced with Richard Rodgers, Oscar Hammerstein II, and Richard Halliday); and *A Shot in the Dark* (1961). His classic films included the cinematic version of *Mister Roberts* (1955), *The Spirit of St. Louis* (1957), and *The Old Man and the Sea* (1958). Hayward's forays into television were largely CBS "spectaculars" such as *The Fabulous Fifties* (1960) and *The Gershwin Years* (1961), though a series and subsequent special he developed for NBC, *That Was the Week That Was* (1964), became a classic update of the traditional variety show.

In addition to Hayward's distinguished contributions to the performing arts, he had a lifelong interest in aviation, piloting his own plane from coast to coast on business trips. During World War II, he operated Allied pilot training bases, including Thunderbird field in Arizona. In 1946 he organized and was chairman of Southwest Airways, Inc., later rechristened Pacific Airlines.

An expert photographer, Hayward captured sensitive images of nature and empathetic poses of his famous friends. Many of these remain in the archives of the Theater Collection of the New York Public Library, which honored him with a retrospective exhibition that opened on Sept. 18, 1974.

As a result of his frenetic life-style, Hayward was plagued with stress-related ailments, including alarming bouts of internal bleeding. In his late sixties, he suffered two strokes. He died at his home in suburban Yorktown Heights, N.Y.

[Biographical data are at the Lincoln Center Branch of the New York Public Library and Museum of the Performing Arts, including a complete list of productions. See also Brooke Hayward, *Haywire* (1977); *Presenting Leland Hayward*, catalog for 1974 exhibition at the Vincent Astor Gallery, the New York Public Library & Museum of the Performing Arts; and Nancy ("Slim") Keith with Annette Tapert, *Slim* (1990). Unpublished material by Kathleen Mal-

ley Kavanaugh was consulted. An obituary is in the *New York Times*, Mar. 19, 1971.]

DEBORAH AYDT

HAYWARD, SUSAN (June 30, 1919–Mar. 14, 1975), actress, was born Edythe Marrener in Brooklyn, N.Y., the daughter of Walter Marrener, a wireman for the Brooklyn Rapid Transit Co. who once worked as a Coney Island barker, and Ellen Pearson. There is some disagreement about Hayward's date of birth, some sources giving 1917 or 1918, though 1919 is generally considered to be correct.

After graduating from Girls' Commercial High School at eighteen, she worked as a model in Manhattan. Moviemaker George Cukor saw photos of her in the *Saturday Evening Post* when he and David O. Selznick were searching for a Scarlett O'Hara for *Gone With the Wind*. Selznick arranged for Hayward to go to Hollywood for a screen test. She did not get the part, and after six months, Selznick dropped his option on her. Hayward nonetheless decided to remain on the West Coast and pursue a film career.

A hazel-eyed redhead who stood just under five feet four inches, Hayward was not a beauty in the classic sense. "She'll never get anywhere with that bump on the end of her nose," director William Wellman once remarked. But she once told an interviewer she was proud of her sex appeal and knew how to enhance it. "I keep my head lowered and look up at a man," she said. "Sort of sideways. Out of the corner of my eyes. Especially when he's lighting my cigarette. That'll get him. A pouting lip helps, but then mine pout naturally."

She met her agent, Benny Medford, after a bicycle accident threw her onto his lawn. He changed her name to Susan Hayward and got her a six-month, $50-per-week contract with Warner Brothers. When the studio used her only in color publicity photographs, she worked hard to improve her speech by, among other things, attending Ronald Colman movies. "I must have gone to see *Prisoner of Zenda* a hundred times," she told an interviewer in 1951. "I'd memorize his speeches and then try to imitate them on the way home."

After Warner Brothers, she got a contract at Paramount that paid $250 per week. Her first motion picture appearance was in a 1939 remake of *Beau Geste*, starring Gary Cooper. Afterward, work came steadily. In the 1940's and

1950's, she appeared in forty-four films, starting with minor roles and becoming the world's top female box-office draw.

In 1944, she was given the leading-woman role in a Republic picture, *The Fighting Seabees*, with John Wayne, and began attracting favorable reviews. She met actor Jeffrey ("Jess") Thomas Barker in 1944 while both were volunteering at the Hollywood Canteen to entertain soldiers. They were married that year and in 1945 had twin sons. Also in 1945, she signed with independent producer Walter Wanger, whom she credited with giving her her real start in the business. She was nominated for an Academy Award for her portrayal of an alcoholic in *Smash-Up*, a 1947 Wanger production.

Twentieth Century–Fox signed Hayward in 1949 to a seven-year contract with a starting annual salary of $150,000. The studio bought out the two remaining years on her Wanger contract for a reported $200,000.

She won her second Oscar nomination playing a naïve college girl in the 1949 wartime romantic drama, *My Foolish Heart*. Her third nomination was for her portrayal of singer Jane Froman in 1952's *With a Song in My Heart*. Her fourth nomination came for her appearance in 1955 as Lillian Roth in *I'll Cry Tomorrow*. She finally won for *I Want to Live*, a 1958 film based on the story of Barbara Graham, a hard-boiled murderess who died in the gas chamber at San Quentin in 1955. One writer described her as "a miniature dynamo with the voltage output of a powerhouse." After she won the Oscar, a producer was quoted as saying, "Thank heavens, now she can relax. Susie got what she's been chasing for 20 years."

At her peak, Hayward was one of the most sought-after and highest-paid actors in Hollywood. She and John Wayne were named the most popular film stars of 1952 by the Foreign Press Association of Hollywood. She won the 1953 Photoplay award as the most popular screen actress. The American Beauticians Congress voted her "the most beautiful girl in the world." "I never dreamed this could happen to a girl from Brooklyn," she once said.

Her public triumph came at the expense of her marriage. She and Barker underwent a messy divorce in 1954, due in part to tensions arising from her success and his lack thereof. On Apr. 24, 1955, Barker visited his sons and fought with Hayward. Two days later, she took an overdose of sleeping pills at her Sherman Oaks, Calif., home, then made a hysterical telephone call to her mother in Brooklyn. Mrs. Marrener called the police, who broke down Hayward's door, found her unconscious and rushed her to the hospital, where she recovered. The resulting publicity had barely been forgotten when Jill Jarmyn, an actress, charged that Hayward attacked her when she caught Hayward in bed with actor Donald Barry. Hayward accused Jarmyn of being insulting.

In 1957 Hayward married Eaton Chalkley, a wealthy lawyer and businessman, and moved to his home on 200 acres in Carrollton, Ga. "I don't want this bit where I have to have the face lifted and the wrinkles painted out in order to play leading ladies," she told an interviewer shortly before her fortieth birthday in 1959. "I'd prefer to quit now and go home to Georgia. Then, if I felt like it, come back after a time and play character roles." After a short illness, Chalkley died in 1965 with his wife at his bedside. That same year, an old family friend, the Rev. Daniel McGuire, converted her to Catholicism.

In 1967 Hayward made *Valley of the Dolls*, her first Hollywood film in four years. She made two television movies in the early 1970s. Hayward, who suffered from a brain tumor, died after a seizure in her Beverly Hills, Calif., home. She was buried in Carrollton.

[Several books have been written about Hayward, including Doug McClelland, *The Complete Life Story of Susan Hayward* (1975); Eduardo Moreno, *The Films of Susan Hayward* (1979); Beverly Linet, *Susan Hayward, Portrait of a Survivor* (1980); Christopher P. Anderson, *A Star, Is a Star, Is a Star!* (1980); and Robert LaGuardia and Gene Arceri, *Red* (1985). An obituary appears in the *New York Times*, Mar. 15, 1975.]

PAUL GEITNER

HEALD, HENRY TOWNLEY (Nov. 8, 1904–Nov. 23, 1975), president of the Ford Foundation, was born in Lincoln, Nebr., the son of Frederick de Forest Heald, a botanist, and Nellie Townley. Frederick left his post at the University of Nebraska soon after Henry was born, moving his family first to Texas and then Pennsylvania as he conducted research into plant pathology for the Department of Agriculture. Finally, in 1915, the Heald family moved to Pullman, Wash., where Frederick accepted a teaching post at Washington State College and became the head of the Department of Plant Pathology in 1917. Henry's mother tutored him at home until he was ready for the ninth grade at Pullman High School.

At Washington State College, Heald majored in civil engineering and worked during three summers for the U.S. Geological Survey. He received a B.S. in 1923 and took a job for one year as an assistant engineer on the construction of the McKay Dam for the U.S. Bureau of Reclamation at Pendleton, Oreg. He then enrolled at the University of Illinois, receiving his M.Sc. in civil engineering in 1925.

Over the next two years, Heald designed bridges for the Illinois Central Railroad, then took a job as a structural engineer for the Chicago Board of Local Improvements. In September 1927, he accepted an assistant professorship of civil engineering at the Armour Institute of Technology, a small and financially struggling college on Chicago's South Side.

On one of his visits home to Pullman, Heald was told by his younger sister about Muriel Starcher, a pretty girl in her sorority. Heald called her and took her to lunch. One week later he proposed. They were married on Aug. 4, 1928; they had no children.

While teaching at the Armour Institute, Heald worked as an engineer for the Louisville Bridge and Iron Company during the summer of 1929, and for the Walter Bates Steel Company in 1930. In 1931, he was promoted to associate professor and assistant to the dean of Armour Institute, beginning a quick ascent from dean of freshmen in 1933, to professor and dean of the institute in 1934, to acting president in 1937. In May 1938, he was formally elected president of Armour Institute. Managing a rejuvenation of the institution, Heald convinced sixty top industrialists to join the board of trustees and, in 1940, merged with Armour Lewis Institute, a foundering liberal arts school on Chicago's West Side, to form the Illinois Institute of Technology. He hired Mies van der Rohe to construct a new campus and in fourteen years expanded the school's area from seven to eighty-five acres, boosted its assets from $2 million to almost $17 million, and raised enrollment from seven hundred to seven thousand students. Heald's influence spread to the city as a whole. He led a project to rebuild the slums surrounding the Illinois Institute of Technology, bringing together a staff of experts who

drew up a plan for redevelopment that became a national model for urban renewal. In 1946, Heald headed a special committee of college presidents that cleaned up Chicago's politics-ridden public school system.

In 1951, Heald was offered the chancellorship of New York University, the nation's largest private higher-education institute. Although he had turned down lucrative jobs in private industry and a Republican nomination for mayor of Chicago, he accepted the opportunity to restructure New York University. The university—with thirty-five thousand students spread over six campuses in Manhattan and the Bronx—lacked a coherent sense of purpose. Heald raised faculty salaries, tuition, and admissions standards while eliminating departmental duplication and bringing in $44 million in gifts. Less tangibly, he forged a belief in the future. While at New York University, Heald chaired the Temporary Commission on Educational Finance, whose recommendations for the restructuring of New York State's aid to education were enacted by the legislature despite criticism.

In June 1956, Heald called in his top staff and told them, "Gentlemen, they've offered me the presidency of the Ford Foundation and I don't see how anyone in education could turn it down." Giving away $100 million per year, the Ford Foundation was the largest foundation in the United States. Under Heald's direction, it launched a program to help sixty-nine private colleges and universities become "regional and national centers of excellence"; encouraged team teaching, programmed instruction, and other educational innovations; designed a $40-million program for development of the arts; and fostered the growth of noncommercial television. Heald believed that the function of a foundation is "to discriminate, to pioneer, to show by example, to be prudent but not afraid, to be risky but not foolhardy, to explain fully."

Heald's greatest pleasure was work—ten hours a day in the office and many more at home. When *Time* ran a cover story on Heald the magazine described him as "a man who thrives on problems. . . . His desk is clean, his decisions swift, his temper always even." In December 1965, Heald retired from the foundation. He went on to work as a consultant facilitating the merger of Case Institute of Technology and Western Reserve University in Cleveland. He died in Winter Park, Fla.

[Heald's papers are housed at the New York University archive and at the Ford Foundation. See also *New York Times Magazine*, Sept. 30, 1956; *Time*, June 10, 1957; and *Newsweek*, July 26, 1965. Obituaries are in the *New York Times*, Nov. 25, 1975; *Newsweek*, Dec. 8, 1975; and *Time*, Dec. 8, 1975.]

CORINNE T. FIELD

HEATTER, GABRIEL (Sept. 17, 1890–Mar. 30, 1972), radio commentator and journalist, was born in New York City, the son of Henry Heatter and Anna Fishman, immigrants from Austria-Hungary. When Gabriel was three, the family moved from Manhattan to Brooklyn. There he attended elementary school and completed four years at Brooklyn Boys' High School. Unable to pass the State Regents' test in mathematics, he did not formally graduate. He subsequently took a few courses at New York Law School but never pursued a career in law.

At the age of fifteen, Heatter played a modest role in William Randolph Hearst's mayoralty campaign. Young Heatter had acquired a local reputation as "the boy orator" after winning a medal at a Settlement House contest and was hired to give brief street-corner declamations for the candidate. After the unsuccessful campaign, he was given a part-time assignment writing human interest stories from Brooklyn for Hearst's *New York Journal*.

The next decade and a half in Heatter's life was a period of painful frustration and depression, which he described in his autobiography. He held various reporting jobs but none ever led to any long-term association. The one bright spot during his twenties was his marriage in 1915 to Saidie Hermalin, a schoolteacher and daughter of the editor of *The Day*, a Yiddish newspaper. They had two children, Basil, a published novelist, and Maida, who achieved a national reputation as "the Julia Child of desserts."

Heatter achieved greater employment stability in 1922 when he accepted a public relations position with three steel companies. His duties involved editing a four-page house organ and giving inspirational talks to employees and management. While in this position, two events helped propel him into his career as one of the best known radio commentators in the country. The first was the result of a "debate" on the future of the Socialist party. The "debate" did not involve personal confrontation but consisted of publication in *The Nation* of "An Open Letter to Norman Thomas" by Heatter, accompanied by a response from the Socialist leader. Heatter's subsequent solo presentation of his views in a broadcast impressed the manager of station WMCA in New York, who offered him a contract as a newscaster in 1933. Heatter's coverage in 1936 of the execution of Bruno Richard Hauptman for the kidnapping and murder of the Lindbergh baby had an even greater impact on his career. The execution was unexpectedly delayed, and Heatter, who was on the scene, ad libbed for more than half an hour until he received a prearranged signal that the execution had occurred. Pausing dramatically in his commentary, Heatter announced, a few seconds ahead of his competitors, "Bruno Richard Hauptman is dead." The performance was widely regarded as a tour de force and led NBC to invite him to become the host on its weekly program, "We, the People."

Heatter is remembered especially for his broadcasts in World War II. During the worst periods, he always confidently assured his listeners that Hitler, Mussolini, and Tojo (he invariably personalized the war) would be defeated, and he fastened upon any story of personal heroism or small success to demonstrate that victory was inevitable. The oft-used opening words of his broadcasts, "Ah, there's good news tonight!" (which he chose as the title of his autobiography) became an irresistible temptation for nightclub mimics. His personal vendetta against Nazi leaders appealed to cartoonists. Thus, following Hitler's suicide, the *New Yorker* showed one of Helen Hokinson's stereotypical club ladies declaring, "I'm so glad for Gabriel Heatter." After the war, Heatter's crusading zeal for particular causes such as increasing Social Security benefits or raising postal workers' salaries led some of his audience to believe that an appeal to Gabriel Heatter would always produce results, a belief parodied by comedienne Jean Arthur in a popular 1948 film, *A Foreign Affair*, when she vowed that if the President of the United States would not listen to her, she would bring her case to Gabriel Heatter.

Heatter's success as a broadcaster lay partly in his ability to dramatize events and to sentimentalize. Each night it was his goal to find some human (or animal) interest angle to uncover ("a Heatter story," as he put it). A dog's saving a boy would produce a full emotional response. A request to his audience to leave out bread crumbs in winter for hungry robins became a Heatter perennial. As social historian Dixon Wecter observed, "Heatter is really an exhorter, not an analyst. . . . His influence is good because his heart is in the right place, even though it is a considerably enlarged organ."

Heatter was a ruggedly handsome man slightly over six feet tall whose voice reminded some of his hearers of a clergyman's; he claimed that he was occasionally asked if he had been trained for the ministry. Some of his correspondents addressed him as the "Reverend Gabriel Heatter." His critics sometimes suggested that his emotionalism was contrived because he seemed to speak with equal fervor in describing the role of the United Nations in advancing collective security and in praising the role of his sponsor's toothpaste in preventing dreaded gingivitis.

As the television age dawned in the late 1940's, there was speculation that Heatter might do a program called Gabriel Heatter's Opportunity Show. Spokespersons for the Mutual Broadcasting System tentatively announced that he would be master of ceremonies in a program that would feature amateur and professional dancers. The program never materialized, however. Instead, Heatter in 1950 briefly narrated a half-hour dramatic radio program, "A Brighter Tomorrow," in which he described episodes of triumph over handicap and adversity.

In 1951, Heatter and his wife moved from New York City to a permanent residence in Miami Beach, where he continued to broadcast until 1965. He also wrote a daily column for the *Miami Beach Sun* until 1968. His political views, though nonpartisan, remained those of a mainstream liberal and ardent believer in collective security on the international level. He still liked human interest stories and also did an occasional humorous piece. His own favorite column in the latter category was a paean to the martini cocktail. Following his wife's death in 1966, he lived with his daughter and her family in Miami Beach until his death.

[Heatter's autobiography, *There's Good News Tonight* (1960), is largely anecdotal and leaves many gaps in describing his career. Three first-rate analyses of his personality and modus operandi as a commentator are Philip Hamburger, "The Crier," *New Yorker*, Jan. 20, 1945; Dixon Wecter, "Hearing Is Believing," *Atlantic*, July 1945; and Jack Alexander, "The Great Gabbo," *Saturday Evening Post*, Mar.

1947. An obituary is in the *New York Times*, Mar. 31, 1972.]

CHARLES E. LARSEN

HEFLIN, VAN (Dec. 13, 1910–July 23, 1971), actor, was born Emmet Evan Heflin, Jr., in Walters, Okla., the son of Emmet Evan Heflin, a dentist, and Fanny Bleeker Shippey. In early childhood he lived in Oklahoma City; when his parents separated, he moved to Long Beach, Calif., to live with his grandmother. He attended Long Beach Polytechnic High School and worked as a seaman on schooners during summer vacations. Upon graduation, he sailed to Liverpool, England, working on a tramp steamer. After attending the University of Oklahoma for two years, he shipped out again as a seaman and traveled to South America, the Far East, and other distant ports. Eventually, he earned a third mate's license.

His first appearance in the theater was in a small part on Broadway in Channing Pollock's, *Mr. Moneypenny* (1928). Although he received good notices, the play closed after eight weeks. In 1931 he completed his final two years of academic work and graduated from the University of Oklahoma. He then studied for a year at the Yale School of Drama under George Pierce Butler. After a season in a stock company in Denver, Colo., he was an understudy in the Broadway musical, *Sailor Beware* (1933). His first important role on the New York stage was in *The Bride of Torozko* (1934) with Jean Arthur and Sam Jaffe. The *New York Herald Tribune* critic Percy Hammond wrote, "Mr. Van Heflin is an unreasonably bad actor." Nevertheless, he appeared with Ina Claire and Osgood Perkins in a subordinate role as Dennis McCarthy in S. N. Behrman's *End of Summer* (1936), which established him as an able actor. Katharine Hepburn, impressed by his performance in this play, helped him receive a contract with RKO to appear with her in a supporting role in *A Woman Rebels* (1936). He followed this with appearances in such unimpressive films as *The Outcasts of Poker Flat* (1937) and *Flight from Glory* (1937) and at his request soon received release from his contract to return to New York City. While making calls at casting offices, he found work on a number of radio soap operas. In total he performed anonymously on radio about 2,000 times. His big break occurred when he appeared again with Katharine Hepburn, this time on the stage in the hugely successful *The

Philadelphia Story (1939). Brooks Atkinson, critic for the *New York Times*, wrote that it was "hard to improve upon Van Heflin's honest and solid description of a tough-minded writer." During the two-year run of the play, he continued to perform on radio without a name credit in such parts as Adam in *The Man I Married* and Bob in *Betty and Bob*.

When Heflin returned to Hollywood he appeared in a number of distinctly different roles that showed his versatility as an actor. Among his films were *Santa Fe Trail* (1940); *The Feminine Touch* (1941) with Rosalind Russell; *H. M. Pulham, Esq.* (1941), in which he played a cynical advertising man; and *Johnny Eager* (1942) with Robert Taylor and Lana Turner. In this last film he was in the supporting role of a literate alcoholic who served as the conscience of a sadistic gangster. He stole the show from the two luminous stars who appeared with him, and he received the Academy Award for best supporting actor. Since he did not believe that he was sufficiently handsome for motion pictures, he said he had to concentrate on good acting.

Heflin was six feet one and had sandy blond hair and gray eyes. He was known for his ability to get along with people. Frank Sinatra called him "an actor's actor." Promoted to lead roles, he played the role of a young scientist in a police laboratory in *Kid Glove Killer* (1942) and a romantic star in *Seven Sweethearts* (1942). His next release was *Tennessee Johnson* (1943) with Ruth Hussey, in which he portrayed the controversial president Andrew Johnson.

During World War II, Heflin served as a second lieutenant, first in the field artillery and then as a combat cameraman with the Ninth Air Force in Europe. After the war he divided his career into motion picture, stage, and television segments. Always independent by nature, he reached an agreement with MGM to alter his contract so that he might have time to devote to other forms of entertainment in addition to motion pictures. An avid outdoorsman, he enjoyed sailing, hunting, and fishing. Heflin achieved some of his greatest film successes in the 1950's. He costarred with Alan Ladd in the outstanding Western *Shane* (1953), and appeared with Lauren Bacall, Fred MacMurray, Cornel Wilde, June Allyson, and Arlene Dahl in *Woman's World* (1954). In *Battle Cry* (1955), a tribute to the United States Marine Corps, he played a tough colonel with a soft

heart. *Patterns* (1956), with Everett Sloane and Ed Begley, Sr., was the motion-picture adaptation of Rod Serling's highly acclaimed television drama about big business. Heflin appeared as Fred Staples, a young industrial engineer caught in the ruthless affairs of the corporate jungle.

On the stage Heflin toured the United States in the Pulitzer Prize–winning play, *The Shrike* (1952). On Broadway, he played Eddie, a tragic longshoreman in *A View From the Bridge* (1955). In *A Case of Libel* (1964) he acted the part of Louis Nizer, the real-life trial lawyer.

Heflin also narrated television shows because he liked the anonymity and did not want to become overexposed. He narrated a series of scientific specials for the ABC television network. The first was *The Way Out* (1965), produced by David Wolper. He appeared on the television screen in a Dick Powell Theatre drama and three Playhouse 90 productions. His best-known television performances were in Rod Serling's *Certain Honorable Men* and Reginald Rose's *The Cruel Days*. Among his later motion pictures was *Stagecoach* (1966), in which he played a rough marshal riding shotgun. His last film appearance was as a mad bomber in *Airport* (1970). In 1934, Heflin married Esther Ralston; they divorced in 1936. In 1942 he married actress Frances M. Neal. They lived in Brentwood, Calif., and had three children before their divorce in 1967.

[Archival material on Heflin is in the New York Public Library's Performing Arts Research Center at Lincoln Center. An obituary is in the *New York Times*, July 24, 1971.]

ERNEST A. MCKAY

HERRMANN, BERNARD (June 29, 1911– Dec. 24, 1975), composer and conductor, was born in New York City, the son of Russian Jewish immigrants, Abraham [Dardick] Herrmann, a successful optometrist, and Ida Gorenstein. He grew up on the Lower East Side, attending DeWitt Clinton High School and rapidly advancing to music studies at New York University and the Juilliard School. His teachers (except the Australian eccentric Percy Grainger) made little impression on the iconoclastic Herrmann, who never took a degree and left Juilliard in 1932.

The great influence on his life and music emerged with his discovery of the *114 Songs* by the maverick Connecticut composer Charles Ives. In the cranky Ives, Herrmann discovered a kindred spirit. Eventually a friendship developed between the two men; years later Herrmann conducted a number of important broadcast and concert premieres of Ives's works.

Herrmann's conducting debut came in 1932 as part of the Broadway revue *Americana*. The first significant performance of his own music followed in 1933, when the Young Composers Group premiered an impressionistic string quartet. By the next year Herrmann was leading the New Chamber Orchestra in difficult modern repertory, including the East Coast premiere of Darius Milhaud's *La Création du monde*.

Herrmann joined the new Columbia Broadcasting System (CBS) in 1934. His talent for arranging, conducting, and programming was recognized from the outset. By 1935 he was a staff conductor, and by 1940 the chief conductor of the CBS Symphony. He held this post until the radio orchestra was disbanded in 1951; introducing a tremendous range of modern works during the Golden Age of Radio.

From 1937 Herrmann contributed original musical scores for hundreds of radio dramas, earning recognition as a master of economical scene painting. According to the dramatist Lucille Fletcher, who became his wife in 1939 following a lengthy courtship, he could "wave a fountain pen and turn six notes and two chords into a mountain slide or a fog in no time at all." His most famous broadcast was a dramatization of H. G. Wells's *The War of the Worlds* produced by another rising CBS talent, Orson Welles, in 1938. So lifelike was this collage of dance music and news bulletins that fear of a real-life Martian invasion overtook much of the Northeast.

When Welles took his Mercury Theatre to Hollywood, he invited Herrmann to compose the music for their first picture. This turned out to be *Citizen Kane* (1941), which was eventually recognized as one of the screen's great classics. Herrmann's music adroitly mixed radio-like transitional cues, spirited rags, and brooding symphonic music to limn the multifaceted character of the film's protagonist. The *Kane* score, together with its similarly innovative successors, *All That Money Can Buy* (also 1941) and *The Magnificent Ambersons* (1942), helped to invigorate a medium in which a more conventionally romantic idiom had been the norm.

Herrmann's success with large-scale dramatic composition had not come overnight. He had been composing concert scores since 1929. Most of these remained unpublished or even uncompleted, but the dramatic cantata *Moby Dick*, dedicated to Ives, was premiered by John Barbirolli and the New York Philharmonic in 1939. A symphony followed in 1941. Herrmann's most ambitious work was the opera *Wuthering Heights* (1943–1951). Long and demanding, it was never produced during the composer's lifetime, to Herrmann's great frustration.

Wuthering Heights exemplifies Herrmann's brooding romanticism and his growing fascination with things English, including the music of Edward Elgar, Gustav Holst, and Ralph Vaughan Williams. Its librettist was Herrmann's wife, Lucille Fletcher. They had two children but were divorced in 1948, after Herrmann had fallen in love with Fletcher's cousin, Lucille Anderson. The years preceding this divorce were dominated by Herrmann's difficulties with the opera and his self-doubts regarding his musical career. In true romantic fashion, much of this pain is reflected in *Wuthering Heights* and in two related film scores, *Jane Eyre* (1943) and *The Ghost and Mrs. Muir* (1947). The former film inspired Herrmann's Brontean interest; the latter is a death-haunted romantic fantasy of impossible love that contains Herrmann's most lyrical score.

Herrmann married Lucy Anderson in 1949. He was still a New York–based conductor who accepted an occasional film assignment. Two years later, however, frustrated by the decline of broadcast concerts and his failure to win a symphony conducting post, he moved to Hollywood to concentrate on composing for the cinema. His famously irascible personality did not make his task easy. While capable of great tenderness, he was also a frequent strain to friends and producers, to whom he was capable of saying, "Why do you show me this garbage?" However, Alfred Newman, the music director of Twentieth Century–Fox, did engage Herrmann to score a number of minor films. He soon created a memorable series of exotic soundscapes, using electronics for *The Day the Earth Stood Still* (1951), nine harps for *Beneath the 12-Mile Reef*, and African percussion for *White Witch Doctor* (both 1953). In 1954 he enjoyed an unusual composing collaboration with Newman himself on *The Egyptian*.

Herrmann's greatest Hollywood success came through his long association with Alfred Hitchcock. He was involved with every Hitchcock production from 1954 to 1966: *The Trouble with Harry, The Man Who Knew Too Much, The Wrong Man, Vertigo, North by Northwest, Psycho, The Birds* (sound effects only), *Marnie,* and *Torn Curtain.* The obsessively haunting *Vertigo* has been hailed by Royal S. Brown and others as among the greatest of all film scores. *Psycho,* a violent thriller scored entirely with string instruments, has been widely imitated in countless "slasher" movies into the 1990's. Eventually, however, clashes of ego and studio pressure for pop-oriented scores ruptured the long Hitchcock-Herrmann collaboration. After Hitchcock discarded the *Torn Curtain* music, the two men never spoke again.

Despite parallel success as the leading composer of screen fantasy in *The Seventh Voyage of Sinbad* (1958), *Journey to the Center of the Earth* (1959), *The Three Worlds of Gulliver* (1960), *Mysterious Island* (1961), and *Jason and the Argonauts* (1963), the irascible and embittered Herrmann found himself nearly unemployable in the Hollywood of the late 1960's. Divorced from Anderson in 1965, he composed chamber music for the first time since the 1930's and began to spend time in England. A final move to London was postponed until 1971 out of consideration for a favorite dog. (Herrmann often related to animals better than to people.)

Herrmann's European film career was dominated by derivative thrillers and lessening musical inspiration. But he also enjoyed a new collaboration with the Hitchcock-worshiping French director François Truffaut on *Fahrenheit 451* (1966) and *The Bride Wore Black* (1968). Buoyed by a warm reception in England and his marriage to a young journalist, Norma Shepherd, in 1967, he began to make recordings of his key concert and film scores, including the opera *Wuthering Heights* in 1966. These albums in turn kept Herrmann's reputation alive in the United States, eventually leading to his rediscovery and employment by a younger generation of filmmakers, including Brian De Palma (*Sisters,* 1972; *Obsession,* 1976) and Martin Scorsese (*Taxi Driver,* 1976). Returning to Hollywood for this last film, Herrmann died hours after supervising the final recording session. His last two scores were nominated posthumously for the Academy

Award, an honor that Hollywood had denied him since his Oscar for *All That Money Can Buy* in 1941.

In all, Herrmann scored some fifty motion pictures plus innumerable radio and television productions, including the Christmas operas *A Christmas Carol* (1954) and *A Child Is Born* (1955) for CBS-TV. Though never a great melodist, he was brilliantly adept at harmony, orchestral color, and dramatic timing. For all of these traits he is universally recognized as one of the supreme masters of film scoring.

[Herrmann's papers are collected at the library of the University of California in Santa Barbara. Steven C. Smith, *A Heart at Fire's Center* (1991), is a thorough account of the life and works, with full bibliography. Important interviews include Ted Gilling, "The Colour of the Music," in *Sight and Sound* 41 (Winter 1971–1972); and Leslie T. Zador and Gregory Rose, "A Conversation with Bernard Herrmann," in *Film Music 1,* edited by Clifford McCarty (1989). See also Page Cook, "Bernard Herrmann," in *Films in Review* 18 (Aug.–Sept. 1967); Royal S. Brown, "Herrmann, Hitchcock, and the Music of the Irrational," in *Cinema Journal* 21 (1982); Graham Bruce, *Bernard Herrmann* (1985); and Christopher Palmer, *The Composer in Hollywood* (1990). An obituary is in the *New York Times,* Dec. 25, 1975.]

JOHN FITZPATRICK

HESCHEL, ABRAHAM JOSHUA (Jan. 11, 1907–Dec. 23, 1972), theologian, was born in Warsaw, Poland, the youngest of five children born to Moshe Mordecai Heschel and Rivke Reizel Perlow. Heschel's male ancestors had been Hasidic rabbis for seven generations. He descended on his father's side from Dov Baer ("the Maggid of Mezeritch"), the successor to the Baal Shem Tov, and from his own namesake, grandfather Avraham Yehoschua Heschel, "the Apter Rav." On his mother's side, Heschel could look back to the noted Hasidic rabbis Levi Yitzhak of Berditchev and Pinchas of Koretz. Related to Hasidic nobility throughout Europe, and displaying precocious piety and intelligence, Heschel could have easily continued the Hasidic rabbinic line. Instead, he turned from Hasidism to pursue a secular education. If the Hasidic community viewed Heschel's decision to study in Vilna and Berlin with disappointment, even concern, his mother, pious and learned, supported his decision to expand his horizons (his father had died in 1917).

While at Berlin's Humboldt University in the years 1929 to 1933, Heschel studied simultaneously at the Hochschule für die Wissenschaft des Judentums and at the orthodox Hildesheimer Seminar. He was one of the few young scholars completely comfortable in both the orthodox Jewish and secular worlds. Awarded a Ph.D. in philosophy and Semitics in February 1933, he began teaching Talmud at the Hochschule, where in 1937 he impressed Martin Buber, who persuaded Heschel to succeed him at the Mittelstelle für Jüdische Erwachsenenbildung and as director of the Freie Jüdische Lehrhaus in Frankfurt am Main. Deported to Poland by the Nazis in 1938, Heschel taught briefly at the Institute for Jewish Studies before emigrating to London, where he established the Institute for Jewish Learning. Hebrew Union College, in Cincinnati, Ohio, brought him to the United States in 1940; he served on the college's faculty as an associate professor of philosophy and rabbinics until 1945. The Cincinnati years were personally difficult for Heschel: his English was poor; he had no family; the college administration, faculty, and student body practiced Reformed Judaism, appreciating neither his orthodox diet nor his Hasidic piety; he agonized over the plight of European Jewry; and he grieved for his mother and sister, who died at the hands of the Nazis. The most significant developments of these years were becoming a naturalized citizen in 1945, and meeting concert pianist and philosopher Sylvia Straus, whom he married on Dec. 10, 1946. They had one child.

When New York's Jewish Theological Seminary invited Heschel to join its faculty in 1946, he gladly accepted, becoming its first professor of Jewish ethics and mysticism. It was only after marrying that Heschel began to write his theological works. Fluent in Polish, Yiddish, and Hebrew since his childhood, Heschel eventually mastered English. Indeed, by 1950 he had developed a lucid and elegant English prose in which he wrote prolifically for the next twenty years, establishing a worldwide reputation as one of the foremost Jewish theologians of the century. His theology reflected the inner tension he had felt since his youth, described in the posthumously published A Passion for Truth (1973). This scion of Hasidic nobility felt pulled in two mutually exclusive directions: he wished both to imitate the joyous warmth and world-affirming spiritual intoxication of the Baal Shem Tov, and, following the philosophy of Reb Menahem Mendl, "The Kotzker," to steel himself to a discipline of unsmiling militancy against everything unjust and fraudulent. Heschel's theological synthesis recognized Israel's God as one whose "divine pathos" makes him willing to involve himself in the history of man. Mankind's appropriate response to God is to bear witness to him in ethics and action.

Such witness-bearing inspired Heschel to take militant, public stands against injustice and falsehood. One result of this "passion for truth" was his successful crusade to persuade Pope Paul VI to use Vatican II to absolve Jewry of the charge of deicide in the Crucifixion of Jesus. Personal contacts with Augustin Cardinal Bea in November 1961 resulted in Heschel's thirteen-page memorandum to Bea, "On Improving Catholic-Jewish Relations." This 1962 document, as well as Heschel's personal contact with Pope Paul VI in 1964, provided the thesis and language for Vatican II's "Declaration on the Relation of the Church to Non-Christian Religions" (Nostra Aetate). By personally lobbying the cardinal and the pope, Heschel played a central if hidden role in bringing about the 1965 Vatican II decision. The publication of The Prophets in 1962 coincided with Heschel's emergence as a prophetic voice of conscience. At the National Conference on Religion and Race in 1963 he electrified a racially mixed audience, throwing the weight of the Jewish community behind the struggle of blacks for equal justice under law. In 1965, he risked injury from police dogs and fire hoses to march with Martin Luther King, Jr., from Selma to Montgomery, Ala., later remarking, "When I marched in Selma, my feet were praying." In the same year, before the rise of broad popular opposition to the Vietnam War, Heschel joined Protestant theologian Reinhold Niebuhr and Roman Catholic priest Daniel Berrigan to form "Clergy and Laity Concerned About Vietnam." He regarded such involvement not as political entanglement, but as moral militancy. At one antiwar rally he declaimed, "This is not a political demonstration. It is a moral convocation, a display of concern for human rights." He cast a righteously indignant eye on the Soviet Union as well, and was one of the first to urge world Jewry to come to the aid of Soviet Jews.

Heschel, who had suffered a heart attack in 1969, died unexpectedly in his sleep in his home in New York City on Sabbath evening,

Dec. 23, 1972, timing which an ancient Jewish metaphor calls "God's kiss on the soul." Heschel's thoughts and actions influenced theology, ethics, and politics far beyond the boundaries of his orthodox Jewish faith. He had touched the world, changing the way Jews, Protestants, and Catholics think and behave. Heschel was the first Jewish appointee to the Harry Emerson Fosdick Chair at New York's (Protestant) Union Theological Seminary in 1965. The Jesuit magazine *America* devoted its entire issue of Mar. 10, 1973, to his life and work. *Time* magazine called him a "militant mystic," a man whose very names were reminders of the mysticism of Abraham and the militancy of Joshua.

[A. J. Heschel's published books in German, English, and Hebrew not mentioned above include *Maimonides: Eine Biographie* (1935); *Die Prophetie* (1936); *Don Jizchak Abravanel* (1937); *The Quest for Certainty in Saaida's Philosophy* (1944); *The Earth Is the Lord's* (1950); *Man Is Not Alone* (1950); *The Sabbath: Its Meaning for Modern Man* (1951); *Man's Quest for God: Studies in Prayer and Symbolism* (1954); *God in Search of Man: A Philosophy of Judaism* (1955); *The Prophets* (1962); *Torah Min Shemayim* (1962–1971); *Who Is Man?* (1965); *The Insecurity of Freedom: Essays on Human Existence* (1966); *Israel—An Echo of Eternity* (1969); and published posthumously, *The Circle of the Baal Shem Tov* (1985).

Biographical treatments and evaluations of Heschel's theology include Franklin Sherman, *The Promise of Heschel* (1970); John C. Merkle, ed., *Abraham Joshua Heschel: Exploring His Life and Thought* (1985); John C. Merkle, *The Genesis of Faith: The Depth Theology of Abraham Joshua Heschel* (1985), which includes a list of Heschel's published writings; Maurice Friedman, *Abraham Joshua Heschel and Elie Wiesel: You Are My Witnesses* (1987); David J. Moore, S.J., *The Human and the Holy: The Spiritualism of Abraham Joshua Heschel* (1989); and Jacob Neusner, ed., with Noam M. M. Neusner, *To Grow in Wisdom: An Anthology of Abraham Joshua Heschel* (1989), which includes an intimate biographical article by Dr. Susannah Heschel, "Heschel as *Mensch*: Testimony of His Daughter." Obituaries appear in the *New York Times*, Dec. 24, 1972; *Newsweek*, Jan. 8, 1973; *Time*, Jan. 8, 1973; and *Christian Century*, Jan. 10, 1973.]

THEODORE N. THOMAS

HEWITT, HENRY KENT (Feb. 11, 1887– Sept. 15, 1972), naval officer, was born in Hackensack, N.J., the son of Robert Anderson Hewitt and Mary Kent. He attended local schools and graduated in the first section of the U.S. Navy Academy class of 1907. Prior to World War I, he served aboard the battleships *Missouri, Connecticut,* and *Florida* and participated in the round-the-world cruise of the U.S. Atlantic Fleet (Great White Fleet) from December 1907 to February 1909. He also was executive officer on the destroyer USS *Flusher* under Lieutenant William F. Halsey.

On Aug. 23, 1913, Hewitt married Floride Hunt, whom he had met in Monterey, Calif., during the Great White Fleet cruise; they had two children. Following his marriage, he was assigned to the U.S. Naval Academy as a mathematics instructor. In 1916, Lieutenant Hewitt assumed command of the converted yacht USS *Eagle,* for survey work in the Caribbean, where he was instrumental in protecting American lives and property during the Cuban revolution of 1917.

Following American entry into World War I, Lieutenant Commander Hewitt assumed command of another converted yacht, the USS *Dorothea.* After promotion to temporary commander in July 1918, he took command of the destroyer USS *Cummings,* which operated as a convoy escort in European waters. Hewitt ended the war in command of another destroyer, USS *Ludlow.*

Hewitt was promoted to permanent commander in 1922. In addition to further battleship tours and shore duty at the Naval Academy, he was a student and later instructor at the U.S. Naval War College in the late 1920's and early 1930's. Following his War College assignment, Hewitt was promoted to captain in June 1932 and went on to command the heavy cruiser *Indianapolis,* Destroyer Division Twelve, and to hold planning positions on the battle-fleet staffs. He developed a reputation for precision and for effectiveness and was rewarded with major commands both afloat and ashore. He was promoted to flag rank as a rear admiral in December 1939.

During World War II, Hewitt first commanded Task Force Seven, which conducted neutrality patrols and, as American entry into the war approached, shifted to troop convoy escort duties. In April 1942, he took charge of U.S. amphibious forces in Atlantic and European waters and went on to conduct the operations for which he is best-known: Torch (Morocco), Husky (Sicily), and Avalanche (Italy) in 1943, and Dragoon-Anvil (southern France) in 1944. His mathematical skills enabled him to solve the highly complex logistic and coordination problems associated with amphibious warfare, and his battleship gunnery expertise aided in naval gunfire support of amphibious landings. Hewitt's experiences operating ashore in Cuba gave him an understanding of problems that ground troops would face. In addition, his experience in command and on large staffs provided him with detailed insights into coordination of large fleets.

Hewitt's contribution as western naval task force commander and naval forces commander in Operation Torch was incalculable. While strategic decisions on the scope and general timing of this first Allied landing against German forces in the European theater had been taken at a series of conferences earlier in the year, the decision whether to proceed as scheduled on Nov. 8, 1942, was left to Hewitt as the on-scene naval task force commander. Hewitt had already accomplished the near-impossible by transporting seventy thousand American soldiers and sailors in one hundred ships across three thousand miles of the U-boat infested Atlantic Ocean when, just a few days before the landing, he was faced with deteriorating weather and uncertain forecasts. After consulting with the American ground forces commander, Major General George S. Patton, Hewitt decided on November 7 to proceed with landings the next day—a calculated gamble. If he was wrong, the landing would turn into a shambles and the effort to open a front in Europe would be delayed. On the other hand, if he waited for certainty of better weather, he would probably lose the element of surprise and would keep his ships and their cargoes of troops at risk from U-boat attack.

Admiral Lord Louis Mountbatten—the overall Allied commander for this operation—regarded Hewitt's willingness to risk landing as crucial: "This was one of the great acts, one of the great decisions. . . . It was asking a great deal of the man . . . it could have been a disaster. But he took the decision, which required not just judgement but an enormous amount of intelligence. . . . He was a really great man, a very modest man, and his very modesty has prevented his being recognized properly in his own country." The success of Torch laid the groundwork for the landings in Sicily, Italy, and southern France and provided valuable lessons for the Normandy landings. For his success at Torch, Hewitt was promoted to vice admiral November 1942 and was given command of the Eighth Fleet (American naval forces in the Mediterranean).

Hewitt retained command of the Eighth Fleet until April 1945, when he was promoted to admiral. The official U.S. Navy historian of World War II, Samuel Eliot Morison, described Hewitt as "a man of impressive port and massive character—never self-seeking but always generous in giving credit to others, firm but just to his subordinates, tactful and conciliatory with compeers in the other armed services—Admiral Hewitt inspired loyalty, confidence, and affection."

Following World War II and command of the Twelfth Fleet (American naval forces in European waters) from August 1945 to October 1946, Hewitt returned to the United States and was assigned to special duty at the Naval War College in Newport, R.I. Prior to his retirement from active service in 1949, he served as naval representative to the United Nations Military Staff Committee.

Hewitt retired to Orwell, Vt. In retirement he wrote numerous articles for the U.S. Naval Institute and other periodicals and also did charity work. His military decorations included the Navy Cross, the Distinguished Service Medal, the Legion of Honor and croix de guerre with palm (France), the Order of Kutuzov (Soviet Union), the Order of the Bath (England), the Order of the Southern Cross (Brazil), the Order of Abdon Calderon (Ecuador), the Order of Nichan Iftikhar (Tunisia), the Order of King George I (Greece), the Order of Sts. Maurizio and Lazare (Italy), the Order of Orange-Nassau (the Netherlands), the Order of Leopold and croix de guerre (Belgium), and numerous campaign medals.

Hewitt died in Middlebury, Vt. In 1973 the U.S. Navy named a new Spruance-class destroyer in his honor, and in 1976 the U.S. Naval War College named its newest academic building for him.

[Biographical material is in an official U.S. Navy biography outline (1972) and U.S. Naval War College biographical sketch (1976). Coverage of Operation Husky is in "Battle of Sicily," *Time*, July 26, 1943. John H. Claggett has written extensively on Hewitt: "Admiral H. Kent Hewitt, U.S. Navy—Part I, Preparing for High Command," U.S. *Naval War College Review*, Summer 1975; "Admiral H. Kent

Hewitt, U.S. Navy—Part II, High Command," *U.S. Naval War College Review*, Fall 1975; and "Skipper of the *Eagle*," *U.S. Naval Institute. Proceedings*, Apr. 1976. Hewitt's career is covered in Samuel Eliot Morison, *History of United States Naval Operations in World War II*, vols. 2, 9, and 11. An obituary is in the *New York Times*, Sept. 16, 1972.]

DONALD B. DISNEY, JR.

HICKENLOOPER, BOURKE BLAKE-MORE (July 21, 1896–Sept. 4, 1971), lawyer and politician, was born in Blockton, Iowa, the son of Nathan Oscar Hickenlooper, general merchandiser and farmer, and Margaret Amanda Blakemore. Hickenlooper graduated from Blockton High School in 1914 and entered Iowa State College (Iowa State University) that same fall. He enlisted in the United States Army in 1917 and served in France as a second lieutenant with the Third Battalion in the 339th Field Artillery. After the war Hickenlooper returned to Iowa State College, graduating in 1919 with a degree in industrial science. In 1922 Hickenlooper graduated from the University of Iowa's law school and joined the firm of Johnson, Donnelly, and Lynch in Cedar Rapids. He began his own practice in 1925. On Nov. 24, 1927, Hickenlooper married Verna Eileen Bensch; they had two children. In 1935 Hickenlooper entered into the firm of Hickenlooper and Mitvalsky in Cedar Rapids, which he left in 1942.

In 1934 Hickenlooper was elected as a Republican to the state legislature, where he took a special interest in education, public health, highway development, child welfare, and government reorganization. In 1938 Hickenlooper was elected lieutenant governor, and in 1942 he became governor, defeating former Democratic Governor Nelson G. Kraschel by almost 200,000 votes, a margin that reflected not only Hickenlooper's popularity but also Iowans' swing to conservative Republican views. Voters narrowly elected Hickenlooper in 1944 to replace incumbent Democrat Guy Gillette in the U.S. Senate. Hickenlooper eventually would defeat three other Democratic Senate candidates—Albert J. Loveland in 1950, R. M. Evans in 1956, and Albert B. Smith in 1962.

In the Senate, Hickenlooper was a conservative, who displayed moderate bipartisanship on foreign policy. Although previously holding isolationist views, he supported the United Nations and President Truman's policy of containment, voting for aid to Greece and Turkey (1947), the Marshall Plan (1948), and the North Atlantic Treaty Organization (1949).

Hickenlooper's cooperation with the Truman administration on international policy did not, however, mitigate his fear for national security. In particular, he gained recognition when he investigated the administration of David E. Lilienthal, chairman of the Atomic Energy Commission (AEC). As a member of the Joint Congressional Committee on Atomic Energy, Hickenlooper wanted the U.S. to retain a monopoly on nuclear weapons. Earlier, he had supported General Leslie R. Groves for chairman of the AEC, but ultimately voted to approve Lilienthal's appointment. By 1949, however, Hickenlooper and others worried over lax security by the AEC, hence the investigation.

In 1950 Senator Joseph R. McCarthy initiated his disputed allegations about Communists in the State Department, and Hickenlooper served on the Tydings Subcommittee that looked into McCarthy's charges. After having the State Department submit the loyalty files of those named by McCarthy, Hickenlooper would not sign the committee's report, which cleared the State Department and chastised McCarthy. Consequently, Hickenlooper gained a reputation as a "Cold War warrior," a distinction augmented by his defense of General Douglas MacArthur after President Truman dismissed him for insubordination and by his refusal to vote for the censure of Senator McCarthy.

Although Hickenlooper endorsed General Dwight D. Eisenhower for president in 1952 over conservative Senator Robert A. Taft, Hickenlooper chided Democratic presidential nominee Adlai E. Stevenson for calling for an end to testing atomic bombs. In 1954 he sponsored the Cole-Hickenlooper Atomic Energy Act, which allowed private utilities to develop nuclear power.

As a member of the Foreign Relations Committee, eventually the ranking Republican member, Hickenlooper consulted with presidents, traveled to many nations, met many heads of state, and served as U.S. representative to the United Nations in 1959 and 1960. In 1962, he sponsored a noted amendment to the Foreign Aid Act, which denied aid to nations that expropriated American property unless compensation was offered within six months.

And in 1963, adjusting to changing situations, he reversed his earlier view and voted for the Test Ban Treaty. Then, fearing the fall of Southeast Asia to Communism, Hickenlooper helped sponsor the Gulf of Tonkin Resolution in 1964, which allowed the president to increase American military involvement in Vietnam. With regard to U.S.-Soviet relations, he helped gain Senate approval of the 1967 consular treaty, the first treaty between the two nations.

Hickenlooper was liked and respected by fellow senators, who saw him as a knowledgeable "consummate skeptic," especially when assessing the monetary costs of proposed legislation. Moreover, by 1962 he was chairman of the important Senate Republican Policy Committee, besides serving with seniority on Senate committees on agriculture, aeronautical and space science, banking, and foreign relations, as well as the Joint Congressional Atomic Energy Committee.

In 1968, over seventy years old and with his wife ill, Hickenlooper did not run for reelection. The Hickenloopers remained in Chevy Chase, Md. Verna Hickenlooper died in 1970, and Bourke died of a heart attack in 1972 while visiting friends in Shelter Island, N.Y.

[Hickenlooper's papers are at the Herbert Hoover Presidential Library in West Branch, Iowa. See Edward L. Schapsmeier and Frederick H. Schapsmeier, "A Strong Voice for Keeping America Strong: A Profile of Senator Bourke Hickenlooper," *Annals of Iowa* (Spring 1984); and U.S. Congress, *Memorial Addresses and Other Tributes in the Congress of the United States on the Life and Contributions of Bourke B. Hickenlooper* (1972). Obituaries are in the *Des Moines Tribune*, Sept. 4, 1971, and the *Des Moines Register* and the *New York Times*, both Sept. 5, 1971.]

THOMAS BURNELL COLBERT

HILL, ARTHUR MIDDLETON (Mar. 23, 1892–Sept. 5, 1972), transportation executive and government official, was born in Charleston, W.Va., the son of Ellen Dickinson and Arthur E. Hill, founder of a chain of wholesale and retail dry goods establishments.

For much of his youth, Hill worked at a variety of jobs in the West, including a two-year stint in an Arizona mining camp. After two years at Central Missouri State Teachers College, he returned to Charleston and spent the next seven years in banking. At the outbreak of World War I, he was commissioned as a second

lieutenant, and rose through the ranks to captain, then assistant chief of staff for the Seventy-seventh Infantry Division. Hill also attended the Army General College at Langres, France.

After World War I, he married Caroline Quavier Staunton on June 6, 1918; they had two children. Hill's involvement in transportation began that year, when he became secretary-treasurer of the Charleston Interurban Railway Company. The firm was later renamed the Charleston Transit Company, and Hill became its president and chairman. In 1924, he organized the Midland Transit Company, a bus transit firm that later became the Atlantic Greyhound Corporation serving the southeastern United States. In 1927, Hill was elected president of the newly organized National Association of Motor Bus Operators.

By the late 1920's, Arthur M. Hill was the major spokesman for the bus industry in its rivalry with the railroads. A major advocate of both cargo and passenger operations in motor transit, Hill strongly supported efficient practices in motor transportation, including new bus designs, increased passenger comfort, streamlined operations, and lean management. His emphasis on training bus personnel and improving highways resulted in much improvement throughout the industry.

In 1933, President Roosevelt appointed Hill chairman of the National Recovery Administration's Motor Bus Code Authority. The authority was designed to establish codes limiting price competition, encouraging cooperation in marketing bus transit, and weakening cutthroat competition in general. However, the authority was put out of business as part of the Supreme Court's 1935 decision in *Schecter Corp.* v. *U.S.* Shortly before World War II began, the Roosevelt administration named him as consultant to the advisory council of the Commission for National Defense.

During World War II, Hill also served as consultant to the Office of Defense Transportation, special assistant in charge of transportation to the Secretary of the Navy, chairman of the Naval Secretary's Committee on Public Works project, and director of rubber procurement for the Navy. For his efforts, Hill was awarded the Medal for Merit by the Navy Department. By this time, he and his first wife had divorced, and on Dec. 4, 1944, he married Mary McDowell Ellis.

Hill's performance of his wartime duties had

brought him to the attention of then Senator Harry S. Truman, who was impressed with his efficient leadership. On Aug. 26, 1947, President Truman appointed him to head the new National Security Resources Board, which included seven members drawn from the president's Cabinet. This agency, created by the National Defense Act of 1947, advised the president on the coordination of military, industrial, and civilian mobilization in the event of war. An article in *Business Week* showcased Hill's sensible, low-key approach in organizing and running this government agency. Hill made no secret of his Republican affiliation, and many in the Truman administration regarded his appointment as an attempt to keep the planning and conduct of war a bipartisan activity.

Hill asserted that the best way to avoid yet another war was to keep America fully prepared, and to this end he supported universal military training. Prominent men were encouraged to serve, on a rotating basis, as part-time advisers to his agency. He coordinated economic mobilization and developed a plan for instantaneous mobilization of the country under an emergency powers act. Throughout the summer and fall of 1948, Hill and his associates drafted such legislation to be presented to the Eighty-first Congress.

Frustrated by the lack of enthusiasm with which Congress received his proposals, Hill resigned his chairmanship on Dec. 6, 1948, and returned to the Atlantic Greyhound Corporation. Shortly thereafter he was also named a director of the International Telephone and Telegraph Corporation.

Hill returned to Greyhound as chairman of the executive committee of Greyhound Corporation, the parent company of Atlantic Greyhound, and he devoted his energy to the expansion and promotion of motor transit. No stranger to the value of public relations, as a result of his government experience, Hill used massive advertising to promote Greyhound, emphasizing safety and reliability.

From the late 1940's through the early 1950's, Greyhound had its greatest financial success under Hill's leadership. Surely and systematically, Hill guided the company and the motor transit industry toward complete domination over the railroads in passenger service. Hill retired from Greyhound in 1957 but remained as chairman of the Association of Mo-

tor Bus Owners until shortly before his death in Clifton Forge, Va.

[See "Pentagon Businessman" and "For a Peacetime WPB," *Business Week*, Sept. 13, 1947; and "America's New Defense Planner," *New York Times Magazine*, Sept. 21, 1947. An obituary is in the *New York Times*, Sept. 6, 1972.]

HYMAN SARDY

HODGES, GILBERT RAY (Apr. 4, 1924– Apr. 2, 1972), baseball player, was born Gilbert Ray Hodge in Princeton, Ind., the son of Charles Hodge, a coal miner, and Irene Horstmeyer. His family moved to Petersburg, Ind., thirty miles north of Princeton when Hodges was seven. At Petersburg High School, Hodges lettered in baseball, football, basketball, and track. After graduating in 1941, he turned down an offer from the Detroit Tigers and accepted an athletic scholarship to nearby Saint Joseph's College, where his elder brother was studying. Hodges attended Saint Joseph's for two years and enrolled in the Reserve Officer's Training Corps before signing a contract to play professional baseball with the Brooklyn Dodgers in 1943. Pressed for players during World War II, the Dodgers put the inexperienced Hodges into the lineup at third base for the final game of the 1943 season. The following year the marines called Hodges for active service, and he spent eighteen months in the South Pacific, where he fought on Iwo Jima and Okinawa.

After the war, the Dodgers sent Hodges to its minor league team at Newport News, Va., to learn how to be a catcher. During the offseason, Hodges attended classes at Indiana's Oakland City College, where he also played varsity basketball. In 1947, he made the Dodgers major league roster as the team's third-string catcher but appeared in only twenty-eight games. The following year, Hodges became the regular first baseman. Hodges's breakthrough season came in 1949, when he belted twenty-three homers and knocked in 115 runs, the first of seven consecutive seasons in which he surpassed the century mark in runs batted in. For these seven seasons, Hodges averaged twenty-four doubles, thirty-two homers, and 112 runs batted in; his overall batting average was .284.

Hodges's defensive performance established him as the outstanding first baseman of his generation and one of the greatest of all time—a remarkable achievement for a right-handed thrower and a man with no previous experience at the position. His defensive prowess stemmed in good part from an enormous pair of hands that enabled him to scoop up low throws and from quick feet that gained him an extra step at first base.

Hodges was an integral member of "The Boys of Summer," the men that made up the Brooklyn Dodgers team from 1947 to 1957. Along with Roy Campanella and Duke Snider, he provided the power that fueled the National League's most dominating offense to six pennants and its only championship in 1955. Hodges's great physical strength notwithstanding, he had difficulty in hitting a right-handed pitcher's curveball and would frequently "step in the bucket," moving away from the plate to avoid the ball as he swung. This problem was magnified in the 1952 World Series when Hodges went hitless in twenty-one plate appearances. His slump continued into the following season, and he received messages of encouragement from fans around the country. One hot Sunday in May 1953, a Brooklyn priest reportedly advised his congregation, "It's too hot for a sermon today. Go home, keep the commandments, and say a prayer for Gil Hodges." The slump soon lifted, and Hodges went on to a strong season, batting .302 with thirty-one homers and 122 runs batted in.

When the Dodgers moved from Brooklyn to Los Angeles after the 1957 season, Hodges's career was winding down, but he enjoyed two more fine years. In 1959 he had a team-leading .391 average in the World Series. He joined the expansion New York Mets in 1962 and hit the team's first home run in its opening game at St. Louis before retiring early in 1963 because of chronic knee problems. In his career, Hodges accumulated 370 homers, 1,274 runs batted in, and maintained a .273 average. He played in seven World Series and on six National League all-star teams and hit fourteen grand-slam home runs (a league record since surpassed by Willie McCovey), at least twenty-two homers in each of eleven consecutive seasons, and four home runs in a single game in 1950 (the sixth player to accomplish the feat).

Gil Hodges was one of the most popular players of his generation. Fans appreciated his perseverance, teammates admired his integrity and inner strength, and opposition players respected his leadership qualities. Hodges was a devout Catholic who often said that his family, not baseball, was his first love. He married Joan Lombardi of Bay Ridge, Brooklyn, in 1948; they had four children. He spent most of his free time with his family or engaged in various interests such as the little league team in Brooklyn named in his honor and his local bowling alley. Hodges was a man who commanded respect. He never showed his emotions on the playing field, nor did he seek the limelight that ordinarily accompanies athletic success. In times of stress, he was calm and reassuring and during brawls on the baseball field, he acted as peacemaker.

Hodges's decision to manage the Washington Senators in 1963 surprised some of his former Dodgers teammates, who felt that his personality was ill-suited to the demands of managing. However, Hodges's ability to lead and to instill the confidence necessary for success made him an outstanding manager. Taking over a dispirited Senators team in only its third year of existence, Hodges improved the team's standing in each of his four years at the helm. In 1968, Hodges returned to New York to manage the Mets, another team with a history of incompetence. In his first year as Mets manager, he led the team to a team-record seventy-three victories. The following season the Mets astounded the baseball world by winning one hundred games and the World Series in five games against the heavily favored Baltimore Orioles. To a man, Mets players credited Hodges with molding the team's success. In Hodges's first two years as manager, the team's performance improved by thirty-nine games.

Toward the close of the 1968 season, Hodges suffered a mild heart attack, from which he recovered. After the Mets' success in 1969 and in light of the competitive quality of the team in 1970 and 1971, Hodges approached the 1972 season with optimism. During spring training in West Palm Beach, Fla., in 1972, as a league-wide players' strike loomed, Hodges died after playing twenty-seven holes of golf with his three coaches. Hodges's funeral service was conducted by Brooklyn's Archbishop Francis J. Mugavero, and more than thirty-five thousand people filed past his bier.

[The Baseball Hall of Fame Library, Cooperstown, New York, contains extensive files on Hodges's career. With the help of Frank Slocum, Hodges wrote *The Game of Baseball* (1968), a guide to how he thought baseball should be played. Marino Amoruso wrote his biography, *Gil Hodges* (1991). See also Roger Kahn, *The Boys of Summer* (1971). Obituaries appear in the *New York Times*, Apr. 3, 1972; and *Sporting News*, Apr. 22, 1972.]

STEPHEN WEINSTEIN

HODGES, LUTHER HARTWELL (Mar. 9, 1898–Oct. 6, 1974), textile executive, governor of North Carolina, and secretary of commerce, was born in Cascade, Va., the son of John James Hodges, a tenant farmer of modest means, and Lovicia Gammon. The family moved to Rockingham County, N.C., when Hodges was two years old. While attending public school, Hodges worked as an office helper and mill laborer in a local cotton mill. Using the money he saved from these and other jobs, he left home to enter the University of North Carolina in 1915 and received an undergraduate degree in 1919.

Hodges served briefly in the U.S. Army near the end of World War I, never leaving the country. He then returned to Rockingham County, where he assumed responsibility for training and personnel at a mill owned by Marshall Field and Company, the large Chicago-based retailer. On June 24, 1922, Hodges married Martha Elizabeth Blakeney; they had three children. By 1935, Hodges was production manager of fifteen textile mills. Within four years, Hodges became general manager of all Marshall Field's domestic and international mills. The company moved him to New York City in 1940, and he assumed the position of vice-president in charge of manufacturing in 1943. He returned to North Carolina in 1947.

During the 1930's and 1940's, Hodges had become interested in politics, serving as an advocate for the textile industry and as a member of various governmental advisory committees or commissions in North Carolina. Hodges's appointment in 1944 to head the textile-pricing program of the Office of Price Administration (OPA) during World War II, and his selection as a special consultant to the secretary of agriculture, reflected his growing influence on the national level. In his OPA position Hodges played an important role in establishing prices for his entire industry during a time of great inflationary pressure. As a result, he secured the gratitude of many significant business leaders, some beyond the textile industry, for whom he had the authority to grant or withhold favors as part of the wartime price-control system. By this time he also had expanded his involvement at the local and national levels of Rotary International, the men's business organization. Beyond government, his role as a national Rotary representative frequently provided him access to decision makers on both domestic and international issues, such as the formation of the United Nations and the postwar recovery of Europe.

In 1950, Hodges ended his long career with Marshall Field and Company to devote more time to government service. That same year, he took charge of the industry division of the Economic Cooperation Administration, part of the Marshall Plan for the restoration of the European capitalist economy. He also affiliated himself at the state level with the progressive wing of the Democratic party in North Carolina, which promoted economic development through transportation, improved education, and incentives for industry but held strongly to racial segregation. During his years with Marshall Field, Hodges had become familiar with many of these issues through his service on various state boards and commissions. Seeking to advance the private sector while promoting the proper role of government, he decided to run for lieutenant governor on an openly antipolitician platform. Many seasoned politicians expressed surprise when he won the Democratic primary in spring 1952, virtually assuring his election that fall in the overwhelmingly Democratic state. Hodges became governor when Governor William B. Umstead died on Nov. 7, 1952. Hodges ran for his own four-year term in 1956, winning every county in the state.

While he continued to emphasize economic development, the major issue with which Hodges was forced to contend during his governorship was imposed from elsewhere. In a series of court decisions, the most notable being *Brown* v. *Board of Education of Topeka* (1954), the United States Supreme Court overturned decades-old laws racially segregating publicly supported schools. The potential implications of the court ruling for the entire system of racial segregation were not lost on whites in the South. Southern politicians divided into several camps in responding to the *Brown* ruling. One faction promoted individual, group, and state governmental resistance; this included closing all public schools and establishing privately run, segregated white schools. Such extreme views might have led to racial violence and a major confrontation between state and national governments. Hodges recognized that interracial violence or closing down the public education system might discourage investment.

Nonetheless, as with many other moderates, Hodges recognized the strength of the segregationist tradition, including its impact in his own life. He tried to convince people that public money spent on education and other development efforts was not wasted and that alienating the federal government would prove counterproductive. Occasionally he called upon examples from his years in the textile industry to show that North Carolina needed to change. He hoped the Research Triangle Park, a public-private high-technology initiative he had founded in the region surrounding Raleigh, Durham, and Chapel Hill, would prove to be his greatest legacy.

However, with the civil rights movement emerging in both the courts and on the streets of the South, and white resistance becoming increasingly militant, Hodges had to deal with implementing *Brown*. At the time, he portrayed himself as a moderate, able to convince both blacks and whites of the need for compromise and to avoid the sort of agitation and strife experienced elsewhere. He accomplished this by privately drawing many potential antagonists into the problem-solving process, making it difficult for them to dissociate themselves from any action that became public. Behind the scenes Hodges exerted pressure on black leaders to agree to what was being worked out, threatening to blame them for any failure to reach a settlement. While he occasionally took symbolic steps such as publicly meeting with prominent blacks, he also warned blacks against following the influence of militant groups such as the NAACP. Mostly, he prevented the sort of state-federal confrontations that were occurring elsewhere in the South and that he believed could damage North Carolina's progressive reputation. Hodges's deep-set eyes and intense stare were among his most obvious personal characteristics, and his sincerity and public image of political fairness served him well in North Carolina during a turbulent political era.

As Hodges's tenure as governor drew to a close in 1960, he found himself courted by various candidates for the Democratic presidential nomination. He eventually endorsed John F. Kennedy, a candidate Hodges believed would commit himself to economic development and moderation on racial matters. He helped Kennedy round up delegates prior to the 1960 convention and then campaigned actively throughout the South for the Kennedy-Johnson ticket. Following the election, Hodges seemed guaranteed of a major appointment in the administration for several reasons. His regional background would solidify Kennedy's marginal standing in the South, his lengthy experience in industry would assist Kennedy in reassuring the business community that he would promote economic development, and his reputation as a consensus-builder on racial issues would demonstrate that he could navigate between increasingly alienated racial groups.

When Kennedy took office in January 1961, Hodges became his secretary of commerce, at age sixty-two the oldest member of the president's cabinet. From the start, more than age distinguished Hodges from the Kennedy inner circle. Although politically shrewd and persuasive, his style was much more like that of a promoter or a booster of the kind with whom he had rubbed shoulders for decades at innumerable Rotary conventions and luncheons. One of his first public statements came in the form of a how-to piece on personal business selling in the Sunday supplement to the *New York Herald Tribune* (June 18, 1961). He stood out as a publicist among the many intellectuals and would-be scholars among Kennedy's confidants.

But within the early months of the administration, Hodges already found himself frustrated; the president made business and economic decisions without involving his secretary of commerce. Hodges unsuccessfully sought full discussion at cabinet meetings and tried to increase his access to the Oval Office. In 1961, he attempted to reduce the influence of the long-standing Business Advisory Council (BAC), an informal group of leaders of large industries that boasted of having veto power over major governmental decisions affecting the economy. While functioning outside the usual pattern of congressional and executive oversight, the BAC appeared unaccountable and potentially damaging to any economic initiative taken by the administration. Hodges gained part of what he wanted in decreasing the autonomy of the BAC, but in working out the settlement, the president put Hodges in his place.

Hodges had no influence with Kennedy on race relations, either, but he was able to pursue his own position. He carried his background as a moderate segregationist into the cabinet, where he encouraged both caution in confronting segregationists and vigor in denouncing violation of the law by civil rights activists. At one point he refused to testify before a Senate committee considering a civil rights bill. Counter to Kennedy's administration policy, Hodges spoke to an all-white segregated meeting in the South.

To remedy his apparent lack of intellectual qualifications, and perhaps as a way of reasserting his political ambitions, Hodges wrote a self-reflective autobiography, *Businessman in the State House: Six Years As Governor of North Carolina* (1962), and the somewhat moralistic *The Business Conscience* (1963). Part of the royalties of the latter book were to go to the United Negro College Fund. As a businessman who had been used to controlling things, Hodges found himself powerless following Kennedy's assassination in November 1963. He agreed to finish his four years as secretary of commerce, resigning in January 1965.

As if to get his bearings after more than a decade in public life, Hodges retreated to some of his old interests, reestablishing his ties with the business community. He joined the board of Research Triangle Park, and devoted his time to many voluntary associations. In 1967, Rotary International selected him as president, a role in which he could travel promoting his strong belief in the work ethic and economic development without the burdens of governmental compromises and the criticisms of political adversaries. In 1968, he retired to Chapel Hill, N.C., where he lived the rest of his life. After his first wife died in 1969 in a fire at their home in Chapel Hill, he married Louisa Finlayson, his former secretary, on Feb. 28, 1970. His son, Luther Hartwell, Jr., became an executive in North Carolina National Bank and served in the administration of President Jimmy Carter. Luther Hartwell Hodges, Sr., died in Chapel Hill.

[The Southern Historical Collection at the University of North Carolina in Chapel Hill has substantial manuscript holdings from Hodges's years in public life. Columbia University's Oral History Collection contains an interview with Hodges taped in 1968. See James W. Patton, ed., *Messages, Addresses, and Public Papers of Luther Hartwell Hodges, Governor of North Carolina, 1954–1961* (1963). See also Alfred G. Ivey, *Luther Hodges, Practical Idealist*

(1968). An obituary is in the *New York Times*, Oct. 7, 1974.]

CHARLES K. PIEHL

HODGINS, ERIC FRANCIS (Mar. 2, 1899–Jan. 7, 1971), editor, journalist, and author, was born in Detroit, Mich., the son of the Reverend Frederic Brinkley Hodgins, an Episcopal clergyman and editor, and Edith Gertrude Bull. Because of his father's frequent shifting of church duties, the family moved often. In his autobiography, Hodgins described his father as a frustrated journalist, his mother as suffering from what appeared to be nervous disorders, and himself as a bright but whiny, only child. Through his father's brief forays into editing, the boy began to discover the fascination of publishing. While Dr. Hodgins served as religious editor of the *Philadelphia Evening Telegraph* in 1912, his son would sit next to the sports editor at Philadelphia Athletics baseball games, intrigued by the telegraphing of the plays back to the city room.

Hodgins credited his first political awakenings, which also occurred in Philadelphia, to the presidential election of 1912 and the conspicuous role of the local Republican leader, Boies Penrose. His first true intellectual awakenings came around 1913 when he was hired as a part-time office boy at the *Civil Engineer's Pocket Book*. The publisher, John C. Trautwine, Jr., inspired Hodgins's pursuit of knowledge. Hodgins attended the Protestant Episcopal Academy in Philadelphia through 1915 and then the Trinity School in New York City, where he received his high school diploma in 1917. While at Trinity he discovered the New York Public Library and the world of writing. When Hodgins told his father he had decided to become an engineer, his father admitted that he had wished him to become a journalist.

Hodgins wanted to go to the Massachusetts Institute of Technology but just missed meeting the entrance requirements. He was advised to attend Cornell for one year and then try to transfer, but lack of funds required him to work for a year. In 1918, he enrolled at Cornell and signed up for the Student Army Training Corps. He qualified for restricted duty due to medical reasons. In fall 1919, he transferred to MIT as a sophomore, receiving a partial scholarship. In his junior year some of his poetry was published in MIT's humor magazine, *VooDoo*, and in his senior year he became its editor-in-chief and wrote the winning libretto for the drama society's "Tech Show."

Upon graduation from MIT in 1922, Hodgins became managing editor of the school's alumni journal, the *Technology Review*. In 1926, he began working evenings for the *Youth's Companion* and became its managing editor in 1927 and editor in chief in 1928. In 1929, Little, Brown published his first book, *Sky High: The Story of Aviation*, coauthored with F. Alexander Magoun. Hodgins remained at *Youth's Companion* through 1929, when it was bought by *American Boy*. He then moved to New York City, first selling advertising for *Redbook* and then becoming its associate editor. At the same time he was contributing to the *New Yorker*, and in 1932 he and Magoun published *Behemoth: The Story of Power*, a history of power and mechanical engineering. On July 5, 1930, he married Catherine Cornforth Carlson, who had been an editorial assistant at *Youth's Companion*. She died in childbirth in early 1933. Their son survived.

Soon after Hodgins's wife's death, Henry R. Luce of Time, Inc., invited him to join his three-year-old business journal, *Fortune*, as associate editor under managing editor Ralph Ingersoll. His first major assignment, an exposé on the European munitions industry, "Arms and the Men," drew wide attention. Hodgins wrote that his wife's death, alcohol, and depression hit him all at once, and in October 1934 he attempted suicide. He returned to work in short order, however. When Luce named Ingersoll general manager of Time, Inc., in 1935, Hodgins moved into his place at *Fortune*. As the journal's managing editor, he was known to be an able administrator and responsible for substantial notable editorial material, with writers such as James Agee, Russell Davenport, Edward Kennedy, Archibald MacLeish, and Charles Wertenbaker on staff. On Oct. 31, 1936, Hodgins and Eleanor Treacy, the art editor at *Fortune*, were married. They had one child but eventually separated.

In 1937, with a reorganization at Time, Inc., Luce named Hodgins as publisher of *Fortune*. In the late 1930's, Luce became concerned that *Fortune* more openly disclose its bias toward capitalism, a stance that caused some consternation among several staff writers. Hodgins, who had warned Luce before being hired that he was by no means conservative, found himself in the middle, although he attempted to look for resolutions. While the magazine was not known to be unfriendly toward business, it wanted business to be accountable for its actions and more open about its activities. In another reorganization at Time, Inc., in 1940, Hodgins was named editor in chief as well as publisher. He remained publisher until 1941, when he returned to writing full time. He also served as a vice-president until 1946.

The April 1946 issue of *Fortune* included an article by Hodgins titled "Mr. Blandings Builds His Castle." The witty, fictional account of the trials and tribulations of an advertising executive (Hodgins in disguise) in building a house in New Milford, Conn., was reprinted in several other journals. Hodgins reshaped it into a book, *Mr. Blandings Builds His Dream House*, which was published that same year. In reviews, Orville Prescott called it "savagely satiric" (*New York Times*, Dec. 30, 1946), and Brooks Atkinson described it as a "wry" book by an author who was both "light and expert" (*New York Times*, Dec. 29, 1946). Hodgins confessed that the book was one of the easiest tasks of his life, and that he completed it in less than three months. The book resulted in an even more famous film, starring Cary Grant, Myrna Loy, and Melvyn Douglas. In 1950, Hodgins published the successor novel, *Blandings' Way*, which recounts Blandings's experiences while living in the dream house, and how he is nearly undone by accusations of having Communist leanings. Hodgins felt this was a better novel than his first. In his *New York Times* review (Oct. 8, 1950), Nathaniel Benchley called it "a cheerful portrayal of a man in anguish." Both books were Book-of-the-Month Club selections.

Hodgins remained a writer at Time, Inc., until the late 1950's. He served as a member of the President's Materials Policy Commission (the Paley Commission) between 1950 and 1952. He was supervisory editor of its five-volume report, *Resources for Freedom* (1952). In 1960, he suffered a severe stroke. His lengthy recovery, including a stay as a patient in a psychiatric clinic and further hospitalization for a hip fracture, were related in his book *Episode: Report on the Accident Inside My Skull* (1964). The book received the Howard W. Blakeslee Award from the American Heart Association.

Hodgins died in New York City. He left behind his uncompleted autobiography. In a foreword, John Kenneth Galbraith wrote of

Hodgins's enormous respect in the publishing world as an editor and writer.

[Hodgins's papers and one microfilm reel covering "Mr. Blandings Builds His Castle" and the television series and film based on the book are at the MIT Archives, Cambridge, Mass. See also *Trolley to the Moon: An Autobiography* (1973); and Robert T. Elson, *Time Inc.*, 2 vols. (1968–1973). There is also a 162-page "Reminiscences of Eric Hodgins" (1969) at the Columbia University Oral History Project, New York City. An obituary is in the *New York Times*, Jan. 8, 1971.]

MARGARET LATIMER

HOFFA, JAMES RIDDLE ("JIMMY") (Feb. 14, 1913–1975?), trade union leader, was born in Brazil, Ind., the third of the four children born to John Cleveland Hoffa and Viola Riddle. His father was a coal miner whose death in 1920 forced the Hoffa family to move from Brazil to Clinton, Ind., in 1922, then to Detroit in 1924. Hoffa dropped out of school by the time he reached the ninth grade in order to support his widowed mother and three siblings. Hoffa first took a job as a stock boy at Frank and Cedar's department store, later moving on to a job on a warehouse loading dock of the Kroger Grocery and Bakery Company in Detroit following the stock market crash of 1929. While working for Kroger, Hoffa helped form a union local of the International Brotherhood of Teamsters (IBT) following a short strike in 1931. In 1932, Hoffa accepted a job as a full-time organizer for Joint Council 43 of the IBT in Detroit, and in 1935 Hoffa was appointed to the post of business agent for IBT local 299.

Hoffa met Josephine Poszywak while working for the union. In September 1936, they were married in Bowling Green, Ohio. The Hoffas had two children.

In the rough-and-tumble atmosphere of Depression-era labor organizing in Detroit, Hoffa quickly developed a reputation as a dedicated activist and a brilliant tactician in the Teamsters' efforts to unionize truckers. But testimony later given before the U.S. Senate disclosed that early in his union career Hoffa built relationships with a cadre of strong-arm men, some of whom had connections to organized-crime activities. He relied on these underworld allies from time to time to aid him in conducting IBT business, suppressing factional fights, and enforcing strike discipline in the particularly violent field of transportation unionism.

Soon Hoffa ran afoul of the law; he was convicted of assault and battery in 1937 and pleaded nolo contendere to conspiracy in 1940. His successful organizing efforts, however, gained Hoffa the attention of IBT president Daniel J. Tobin. In 1941 Tobin called upon Hoffa for help in forcibly ousting several dissident left-wingers from the leadership of an IBT union local in Minneapolis, Minn. In return for Hoffa's loyalty, Tobin offered the rising union leader the post of vice-president of the IBT's strategically important Central States Drivers Council. In that post Hoffa functioned as the chief negotiator for organized interstate truck drivers in the midwestern states. As chief union negotiator Hoffa helped bring labor peace to the booming midwestern trucking industry in the years following World War II by consolidating collective bargaining into a master central states trucking agreement. The contracts Hoffa helped negotiate gained Teamster drivers high wages and generous benefits, earning Hoffa the enthusiastic support of many IBT members. Hoffa became the youngest man ever elected to the executive board of the IBT in 1952, serving under IBT president Dave Beck.

During his tenure as IBT vice-president, Hoffa helped negotiate the labor contract that provided for the creation of a huge central states Teamster pension fund in 1955, financed by weekly employer contributions of two dollars per Teamster driver. Within the first year of its inception, Hoffa gained virtual control over the board of trustees, which was created to oversee the investments made by the Central States Pension Fund. Hoffa reportedly strengthened connections with organized-crime figures by arranging loans from the pension funds for gangsters like Paul Dorfman of Detroit, and by investing heavily in Las Vegas and Reno casinos and in Miami and Cleveland real estate ventures.

The year 1957 provided a decisive turning point in Hoffa's life. That year both he and the Teamsters union began a long struggle with the federal government that would dominate the remainder of Hoffa's career and much of his union's energy for over a decade. In 1957 the U.S. Senate created the Select Committee on Improper Activities in the Labor or Management Field, headed by Senator John L. McClellan of Arkansas. Dave Beck and Hoffa became chief targets of the McClellan committee's probe into the links between trucking unionism and organized crime, which was spearheaded by the committee's chief counsel, Robert F. Kennedy. During a series of nationally televised committee hearings, spellbound viewers watched as Beck and Hoffa were grilled by chief counsel Kennedy and commitee member Senator John F. Kennedy. The hearings disclosed evidence of political chicanery and rampant corruption within the union. As a result of the investigation Beck was charged and convicted of grand larceny. Hoffa, meanwhile, was charged but found innocent of attempting to bribe a staff member of the McClellan committee. Hoffa was then elected to replace Beck as general president of the IBT in 1957, determined to keep his union free from federal interference. McClellan committee investigators, however, contended that Hoffa's election was rigged, and a group of rank-and-file union members contested the ballot in a lawsuit filed in federal court. As a result of the suit, federal district court judge F. Dickenson Letts appointed a board of monitors to oversee the union's operations temporarily. Hoffa and his lawyer, Edward Bennett Williams of Washington, successfully fought off the court's attempts to intervene in Teamster affairs, however, and Hoffa was reelected to his presidency in 1961. As a result of the Senate's investigation of corruption within the Teamsters and other unions, Congress passed the Labor-Management Reporting and Disclosure (Landrum-Griffin) Act in 1959. The act restricted the rights of unions to engage in secondary boycotts and provided for closer monitoring of labor relations practices. As a result of the Senate investigation the AFL-CIO expelled the Teamsters union from membership in the labor federation, contending that the union had not done enough to cleanse its ranks of criminals.

By 1960 Hoffa was arguably the best-known labor leader in the United States. His aggressive leadership of the Teamsters union during the early 1960's further cemented his image in the minds of the American people. During his presidency of the IBT, from 1957 through 1971, Hoffa recorded a string of collective bargaining successes even while he tightened the control of the office of general president over the union. Under Hoffa the IBT constitution was rewritten so that local union leaders would automatically be named as delegates to the conventions at which the IBT's president and other officers were elected. In general, Hoffa presided over

the increasing centralization and bureaucratization of the union as local leaders supported him in return for political favors.

Hoffa matched his drive for power within the union with success in the organizing field. The IBT trucking contracts negotiated in the Hoffa era were notable for their "open end" provision that allowed the union or management to resort to a strike or lockout if all other attempts at resolving a grievance failed. It was widely believed that this provision favored the union, which had organized nearly 90 percent of long-haul truckers by the early 1960's. A threatened IBT walkout usually forced employers to accede to the union's demands. Yet, because Hoffa helped to systematize labor relations in their industry, many trucking company executives appreciated the efforts of the Teamster leader. Hoffa consolidated the 150 labor contracts that governed Teamster drivers nationally in the early 1950's into only 20 by the 1960's. His ultimate goal was to achieve a master freight agreement, a comprehensive nationwide trucking labor contract covering all unionized drivers and removing labor costs as a variable in the intense competition between trucking companies in the highly decentralized industry. He never fully realized this goal.

In his quest to dominate the labor relations of America's transportation industry, Hoffa became as well known for his highly publicized legal problems as for his collective bargaining successes. During the course of the McClellan committee's investigation, an abiding animosity developed between Hoffa and counsel Robert F. Kennedy, which intensified when the latter was appointed attorney general of the United States in 1961. Hoffa's legal troubles, in turn, mounted during the Kennedy administration. In 1962 Hoffa was tried in Nashville, Tenn., on charges that he received illegal payments from a Detroit trucking company that he and an associate had set up in their wives' names. While the case resulted in a mistrial, allegations of jury tampering emerged from the trial. A federal grand jury subsequently indicted Hoffa on charges of jury tampering in June 1963. Hoffa was convicted on two counts of jury fixing on Mar. 4, 1964. Less than three months later, Hoffa was convicted on separate charges of conspiracy and mail fraud. As Hoffa battled with the Justice Department during these years, his enmity toward the Kennedy administration grew to legendary proportions. Upon the assassination of John F. Kennedy in 1963, Hoffa was reported to have rejoiced: "Bobby Kennedy is just another lawyer now." Indeed, Hoffa's well-known hatred of the Kennedys led congressional investigators in the 1970's to consider whether or not Hoffa may have had any connection with a plot to assassinate President Kennedy. No conclusive evidence of such a plot was ever uncovered.

Hoffa's jury-tampering conviction was ultimately upheld by the Supreme Court in 1966, and Hoffa entered federal prison on Mar. 7, 1967. Frank Fitzsimmons, a Hoffa loyalist, succeeded Hoffa as president of the IBT. On Dec. 23, 1971, Hoffa's sentence was commuted by President Richard M. Nixon with the unusual provision that the former Teamster leader refrain from engaging in union affairs for the remainder of his original thirteen-year sentence. Upon his release from prison, Hoffa contested the legality of this conditional commutation. At the same time, a significant number of Teamster members expressed interest in Hoffa's return to the union despite the opposition of Hoffa's erstwhile friend, Frank Fitzsimmons, who by then was determined to retain the IBT presidency. In the midst of his fight to regain control over the Teamsters, Jimmy Hoffa mysteriously disappeared. On July 30, 1975, Hoffa drove to meet with unnamed associates in a restaurant parking lot in Bloomfield Township, Mich., near his family's summer cottage. Hoffa never returned from the meeting, and he was never seen again.

Hoffa's disappearance occasioned a massive and highly publicized national investigation. Little of substance was turned up by investigators. Although some evidence suggested that a group of Teamsters from New Jersey, linked to Anthony ("Tony Pro") Provenzano, may have abducted and murdered Hoffa to protect their corrupt interests in the Teamsters union, no charges were ever filed in connection with Hoffa's disappearance.

Jimmy Hoffa left a lasting impression on post–World War II America. He was symbolic of the rise of organized labor to a position of national power and of the elevation of many working Americans to the ranks of the middle class, thanks in part to generous union labor contracts. However, Hoffa also came to symbolize the corruption associated with segments of the labor movement as many unions lost the élan and idealism that had characterized them

in the 1930's, when millions like the young Hoffa were first drawn to the labor movement.

[Hoffa's autobiography, *The Trials of Jimmy Hoffa* (1970), seeks to bolster his image. See also Clark R. Mollenhoff, *Tentacles of Power* (1965); Walter Sheridan, *The Fall and Rise of Jimmy Hoffa* (1972); Steven Brill, *The Teamsters* (1978); and Arthur A. Sloane, *Hoffa* (1991).]

JOSEPH A. McCARTIN

HOFFMAN, PAUL GRAY (Apr. 26, 1891– Oct. 8, 1974), automotive executive and foreign-aid administrator, was born in Chicago, the son of George Delos Hoffman, an inventor and businessman, and Eleanor Lott. Hoffman was educated in the public schools in suburban Western Springs, Ill., and left the University of Chicago after an unsuccessful freshman year. He moved with his family to Pasadena, Calif., in 1911 and worked closely with his entrepreneurial father in the manufacture of brass plumbing and heating parts.

Hoffman began selling Studebaker automobiles in Los Angeles and quickly became a star salesman. By 1915, he was sales manager for Los Angeles and Orange counties, and two years later for all southern California. After stateside service as an army lieutenant, Hoffman declined a promotion to New York and persuaded Studebaker to sell him the distributorship for southern California. He studied the market carefully, pioneered radio advertising, and played a significant part in developing the Los Angeles street plan of 1924. Hoffman soon became a millionaire, a major investor in radio station KNX, and a promising Republican candidate for mayor of Los Angeles.

In 1925, Hoffman accepted Albert Erskine's urgent invitation to move to South Bend, Ind., as the Studebaker Corporation's vice-president for sales. His responsibilities were advertising, dealer relations, and systematic training for salesmen. He also showed an early interest in traffic and safety studies and persuaded Erskine to finance a research bureau at Harvard. After Erskine's reckless policies took Studebaker into receivership in 1933, Hoffman and Harold S. Vance were named by the court to rescue the company. Vance looked after manufacturing while Hoffman handled finance, sales, and publicity. To the surprise of many bankers and industrialists, they returned Studebaker to profitability, and when it emerged from receivership in 1935, Hoffman was named president.

While Studebaker prospered with wartime defense contracts, Hoffman foresaw a postwar automotive boom and positioned the firm with new models in advance of its Big Three competitors. When he left in 1948, Studebaker appeared to be the most successful of the smaller automakers, although critics later blamed Hoffman and Vance for expensive concessions to the United Auto Workers.

Like many businessmen, Hoffman resented New Deal regulations, and spoke often for free enterprise. In 1942, he was a founder and then chairman of the Committee for Economic Development. After the war Hoffman showed increasing interest in foreign policy and became a leading business supporter of foreign aid. He was surprised, however, when President Truman asked him in 1948 to become the chief administrator for the Marshall Plan as director of the Economic Cooperation Administration.

At the age of fifty-seven, Hoffman entered a new career of public service. He was a skilled administrator and excelled in relations with difficult people, whether members of Congress or European officials. Hoffman had long enjoyed friendly relations with important journalists, and the Marshall Plan received highly favorable coverage. When he resigned in 1950 the Marshall Plan was a clear success in Europe, although Hoffman was disappointed by its limited efforts in Asia. He viewed foreign aid as the nation's best hope of encouraging democracy and capitalism abroad, and opposed efforts to link aid to military assistance.

The Ford Foundation had just emerged from control by the Ford family when Hoffman became its president in 1951. Recruited by Henry Ford II, Hoffman was soon disappointed by the refusal of the foundation trustees to allow him the discretion he believed he had been promised. Hoffman advocated socially active programs rather than research, and controversy soon arose. His vigorous advocacy of civil liberties and his public denunciation of Senator Joseph McCarthy soon made the foundation a target of vicious criticism and congressional investigation. Hoffman also played a prominent role in denying the 1952 Republican nomination to Senator Robert Taft and in promoting the candidacy of General Dwight Eisenhower and the cause of Republican moderation. Early in 1953, the foundation trustees forced Hoffman to resign, both because they disagreed with his administrative style and decisions and because they resented his well-publicized political activity.

Hoffman immediately accepted the chairmanship of the Studebaker Corporation, only to discover that the company was in desperate production, sales, and labor difficulties. After negotiating a merger with Packard as well as a bitterly contested labor contract, Hoffman yielded control to a new management team that soon rejected his ideas. During this same period, he served as chairman of the controversial Fund for the Republic, a civil-liberties organization financed by the Ford Foundation.

Upon leaving Studebaker in 1956, Hoffman sought a political appointment and President Eisenhower named him to the American delegation to the United Nations. Hoffman threw himself into UN activity, particularly the cause of economic development. After leaving the United Nations delegation, he became chairman of the American Committee on United Europe and spoke widely in favor of a generous international development program. Late in 1958, Secretary General Dag Hammarskjöld named Hoffman director of the UN Special Fund to aid poor and underdeveloped nations. A vigorous sixty-seven-year-old, Hoffman undertook a demanding full-time position and retired only at the age of eighty. He was chiefly an administrator and advocate for aid, and relied on his staff for technical advice. Hoffman held a strongly capitalist view of economic development, and in later years was sometimes vigorously criticized. He traveled extensively, visiting development projects and begging governments for contributions of $250 million per year for the Special Fund, known after 1966 as the UN Development Program.

Hoffman was always a salesman at heart, whether selling automobiles or international development. His private life was quiet, although from his early thirties he was wealthy enough to engage in any hobby or sport he wished. He married Dorothy Brown on Dec. 18, 1915; they had seven children. Dorothy died in 1961, and on July 19, 1962, Hoffman married Anna Rosenberg, a labor and public relations consultant he had known for twenty years. Hoffman was an effective and popular speaker, never afraid of controversy, bravely advocating automobile safety in the 1930's and civil liberties in the 1950's. He wrote several books, including *Marketing Used Cars* (1929), *Peace Can Be*

Won (1951), and *World Without Want* (1962). He died in New York City.

[Most of Hoffman's personal papers are at the Truman Library in Independence, Mo. There is an extensive but uncataloged collection of corporate records at the Studebaker National Museum in South Bend, Ind. See also Alan R. Raucher, *Paul G. Hoffman. An obituary is in the *New York Times*, Oct. 9, 1974.]

PATRICK J. FURLONG

HOGAN, FRANK SMITHWICK (Jan. 17, 1902–Apr. 2, 1974), lawyer and prosecutor, was born in Waterbury, Conn., the son of Michael F. Hogan, an Irish immigrant who worked in a watch factory, and Anne Smithwick. He entered Columbia College in 1920 and helped to pay for his education with summer jobs, including those of encyclopedia salesman and Pullman porter. He received a bachelor's degree in 1924, and four years later he graduated from the Columbia Law School. "I never liked law school," he later recalled. "The law didn't excite me at all." He even failed a course in criminal law.

In 1928 Hogan joined a law firm in Manhattan's financial district, but soon left to start his own practice, specializing in insurance and real estate law. In 1935 he changed course and joined the staff of Thomas E. Dewey, who had been appointed a special prosecutor to investigate organized crime. Dewey became famous for successfully prosecuting the notorious mobster Charles ("Lucky") Luciano on racketeering charges and the Democratic party leader, James Hines, for conspiracy to conduct a lottery. Dewey subsequently was elected Manhattan district attorney, and Hogan remained on his staff. When Dewey ran for governor in 1941, Hogan was the only Democrat among four assistants he listed as qualified to succeed him. After gaining the support of the powerful Tammany Hall Democratic organization, Hogan was endorsed by all the major parties and elected district attorney at the age of thirty-nine.

As district attorney, Hogan followed Dewey's innovative approach to prosecution. Bureaus that dealt with special areas such as fraud and organized crime were charged with investigating crimes and developing cases, rather than merely waiting for the police to take the initiative. The Hogan office, as it was generally called, soon became a national model of aggressive, nonpartisan prosecution. Hogan's rackets bureau became particularly well known. Its targets included such prominent gangsters as Joseph ("Socks") Lanza, Frank Erickson, Joe Adonis, and Frank Costello. Wiretaps requested by Hogan's office and approved by New York State judges "gave a vivid picture of [Costello] as a political boss and an underworld emperor," according to a report by Senator Estes Kefauver's Select Senate Committee on organized crime. Such eavesdropping made it clear that Costello's financial contributions had won him significant influence with Tammany Hall, Hogan's political ally. Other taps obtained by Hogan's office established links between Teamsters union leader Jimmy Hoffa and Midwestern mobsters. The office also handled the college basketball point-shaving scandal in the early 1950's, the television-quiz-shows scandal, and numerous celebrated murder cases.

Although Hogan appeared in court occasionally at the beginning of his career, for most of his thirty-two years as district attorney he was almost entirely an administrator. He stressed to his assistants the importance of making certain that a case was supported by solid evidence before bringing it to court. To some, this quasijudicial posture seemed prudent; others derided it as overly cautious.

Hogan was a shy, courteous men who lived simply with his wife, the former Mary Egan, in a four-room apartment on Riverside Drive on Manhattan's Upper West Side; the couple had no children. Hogan almost always ate lunch at his desk and almost always ate the same thing: a chicken salad sandwich, followed by an apple. On Fridays, Hogan, a Roman Catholic, substituted fish for chicken.

Although he was often referred to as the "New York district attorney," Hogan only had jurisdiction over New York County, which is Manhattan. But that island generated sufficient crime to occupy hundreds of assistant district attorneys, investigators, and clerks—the largest nonfederal prosecutor's office in the nation.

In 1958 Hogan ran for the U.S. Senate from New York, securing the Democratic nomination with the help of Tammany Hall leader Carmine DeSapio. Although Hogan's personal integrity was not an issue, his old links to the corrupt machine hurt him in upstate New York, and Republican Kenneth B. Keating won the general election.

Some of Hogan's prosecutions were controversial, including the obscenity case he brought against comedian Lenny Bruce in 1964. The conviction was later reversed by an appeals court that held that Bruce's nightclub material was not without social importance. In 1968 Hogan, a proud alumnus of Columbia and a leader in alumni affairs, insisted on prosecuting hundreds of students involved in protests at the university, even though his alma mater had dropped its complaints against most of them.

The darkest shadow on Hogan's record fell toward the end of his tenure, when the Knapp Commission exposed systematic corruption in the New York City Police Department. The commission blamed local prosecutors, including Hogan, for a lack of initiative and recommended the appointment of a special prosecutor for police corruption. Despite evidence that corruption had in fact been allowed to flourish, Hogan condemned the special prosecutor's appointment: "It is unwarranted. It is unfair. It is unnecessary."

In an effort to clear his office's reputation, Hogan ran for his ninth term in 1973, even though he had suffered a stroke that summer and had undergone surgery for removal of a lung tumor. He faced a serious opponent for the first time in years, William vanden Heuvel. In the Democratic primary, vanden Heuvel acknowledged that Hogan had been a great prosecutor but claimed his time had passed. The voters did not agree; even though illness had forced Hogan to turn the administration of his office over to aides, he was reelected by a two-to-one margin. The returns, a jubilant Hogan told supporters on election night, vindicated his office.

It was Hogan's last hurrah. He never returned to work after the stroke and finally resigned as district attorney on the day after Christmas, seven weeks after his reelection. He died in New York City. The *New York Times* obituary calls Hogan "a kind of conscience of his city and a monument of his profession."

[See also articles on Hogan in *Collier's*, July 7, 1951, and the *New Yorker*, Apr. 14, 1951. For the role of Hogan's office in exposing the significance of organized crime in the United States, see G. Robert Blakey and Richard N. Billings, "The Plot to Kill the President" (1981). A detailed obituary appears in the *New York Times*, Apr. 3, 1974.]

RICK HAMPSON

HOLLAND, SPESSARD LINDSEY (July 10, 1892–Nov. 6, 1971), senator and governor of Florida, was born in Bartow, Fla., the son of Benjamin Franklin Holland, a citrus grower, and Fanny Virginia Spessard, a teacher. Holland was raised in a relatively well-off family and attended Summerlin Institute, a private school in Bartow. Upon graduation he was recruited to play professional baseball for the Philadelphia Athletics, but he decided instead to attend Emory University in Atlanta, receiving his B.A. in 1912. He taught high school in Warrenton, Ga. (1912–1914), and then went to law school at the University of Florida, earning his law degree in 1916.

Following graduation he began a legal practice in Bartow but left it briefly for the military. During World War I he served in France as an aerial observer with the Twenty-fourth Flying Squadron and was awarded a Distinguished Service Cross in October 1918. After the war Holland returned to his law firm and in 1919 married Mary Agnes Groover. They had four children.

In the same year Holland became a Polk County prosecutor and in 1920, a county judge. He was elected to the Florida Senate in 1932 and became a powerful and well-known legislator before he left office in 1940 to run for the governorship. He won the Democratic gubernatorial primary in that year and went on to win the general election. The Republicans did not field a candidate against him.

Holland's years as governor (1941–1945) coincided with American involvement in World War II. The war had a major impact on his fiscal success. Federal money poured into the state for military bases and war production, ending its chronic budget deficit, and Holland was able to bequeath a surplus to his successor. He did not, however, reform the state's regressive tax system, which was based heavily on sales taxes. The war also brought labor shortages, and Holland dealt with these by calling for tougher state labor regulations, giving early parole to model prisoners, and blocking recruitment of Florida workers by northern business firms. In addition he had to cope with the problems of gasoline rationing, even to the point of helping irresponsible tourists who had ignored Federal rules and become stranded in the state without enough gas to get home.

In September 1946 Holland was chosen by Governor Millard Caldwell to fill the Senate seat left vacant by the death of Charles O. Andrews. Two months later he won the seat in the regularly scheduled election. He was reelected to the Senate in 1952, 1958, and 1964, each time with increased margins. Yet despite his longevity and growing seniority, Holland never became a major political force in the Senate, nor did he chair any of the high-profile committees. He tended to seek assignment to utilitarian committees, such as Public Works, that could aid his state while enhancing his own support. The clearest example of this was his ability to secure significant amounts of federal money for flood control projects in southern Florida.

Most people considered Holland to be a typically conservative southern politician, although he referred to himself as a "moderate conservative." He sponsored the Tidelands Act, which returned off-shore resource rights to the individual states, and cosponsored the creation of Everglades National Park. Unlike most southern senators, he favored statehood for Alaska and Hawaii as early as 1950. He consistently voted for anti-Communist measures and was particularly vocal in support of loyalty oaths for student-loan recipients. In 1954, however, he played a small but pivotal role in blocking Senator Joseph McCarthy's attempt to avoid a vote of censure. He was a faithful supporter of U.S. policies in Vietnam during the 1960's.

Holland's record on civil rights was ambiguous. His initial reaction to the 1954 Supreme Court's *Brown* v. *Board of Education* decision ending racial segregation in public schools was to counsel "patience and moderation." Yet in 1956 he signed the "Southern Manifesto" in Congress, calling for legal opposition to *Brown*. In the first Senate race in Florida after the Court's ruling, Holland campaigned on a platform of segregation and states' rights. He opposed all civil rights legislation.

In spite of this, Holland was a long-time advocate of abolishing the poll tax, a device that had been used in the South to limit black voting. He had been instrumental in ending the Florida poll tax while in the state senate during the 1930's and he continued his opposition to the tax in the U.S. Senate, thereby alienating some of his southern colleagues. On five separate occasions, beginning in 1953, Holland sponsored a constitutional amendment to end the poll tax for federal elections. In 1962, with the support of President Kennedy, he succeeded in having the amendment accepted by the Senate. In 1964, after the ratification process was completed, it became the Twenty-fourth Amendment to the Constitution and Holland's most positive legacy to the nation.

The reasons for Holland's long advocacy of this reform were not entirely clear. His stand was often met with dismay by Southern conservatives and with suspicion by Northern liberals. While there seemed to have been a good deal of personal conviction involved, it is nonetheless true that by 1962 most southern states had already abolished their poll tax and it was no longer the crucial issue it once had been. Furthermore, Holland believed the poll tax should be abolished only by means of a constitutional amendment. Any other form of federal legislation would set a dangerous precedent for undermining states' rights. Thus the amendment might have been a shrewd maneuver to placate liberals while forstalling federal intervention in more important areas of state jurisdiction.

Holland was usually described as being moral, bland, and aloof, possessing the courtly air of a "southern gentleman." He was a notoriously poor speaker with a monotonic delivery. One of his political opponents claimed that he was simply not a "warm person," which might have been a polite way of calling him a "cold fish." Nevertheless, he devoted his life to serving his state, and the voters of Florida responded by repeatedly returning him to office. He never lost a state election. He announced his retirement because of ill health in 1970. He died in Bartow.

[The Spessard Holland papers are located in the Robert Manning Strozier Library of Florida State University and the P. K. Yonge Library of the University of Florida. There is no biography of Holland but a brief overview of his career is provided by James Dunn's article in D. C. Roller and R. W. Twyan, eds., *Encyclopedia of Southern History* (1979). His governorship is examined in Charlton Tebeau, *A History of Florida* (1971); and David R. Colburn and Richard K. Scher, *Florida's Gubernatorial Politics in the Twentieth Century* (1980). For his role in civil rights and the poll tax see Carl M. Brauer, *John F. Kennedy and the Second Reconstruction* (1977). The Florida flood control issue is discussed in Nelson Blake, *Land into Water, and Water into Land: A History of Water Management in Florida* (1980). Critical assessment is in Claude Denson Pepper, with Hays Gorey, *Pepper: Eyewitness to History* (1987). An obituary is in the *New York Times*, Nov. 7, 1971.]

ERIC JARVIS

HOMER, ARTHUR BARTLETT (Apr. 14, 1896–June 18, 1972), business executive, was born in Belmont, Mass. Information on his parents and childhood is sparse. He was married to Sara Yocum; they had three children.

After attending local elementary schools and Providence Technical High School, Homer took courses in mechanical drawing and machine design at the Rhode Island School of Design, where his father was managing director. He next entered Brown University, where he majored in economics and engineering administration. After graduating from Brown in 1917, Homer attended the U.S. Naval Academy and the U.S. Navy Submarine School. He became a lieutenant in the Submarine Service as an engineering officer and was assigned to the Bethlehem Steel shipyard in Quincy, Mass. In 1919, after Homer left the navy, he obtained a post at the Quincy shipyard as assistant to the general superintendent. In 1921, he became manager of the diesel engineering and sales division, in Bethlehem, Pa. In 1931 Homer was named sales manager of the shipbuilding division, and in 1934, assistant vice-president of shipbuilding.

In 1939, President Franklin Roosevelt ordered large increases in the navy's capital budget, and Homer was placed in charge of readying Bethlehem for an influx of contracts. When these contracts were received, he headed the Liberty ship program at Bethlehem. In this new position Homer became a national figure. Newspapers reported that he was a workaholic, with few outside interests except sailing. "He sticks to the business at hand with a singlemindedness that overlooks no pertinent detail," said one observer. "People who do not like him call him ruthless. Those who like him call him determined." In fact, however, Homer possessed neither of these attributes: he was, for the most part, unimaginative and vacillating. He lacked the clear vision of Charles Schwab and Eugene Grace, his two immediate predecessors, who made Bethlehem the second-largest American steel company. For the most part he continued policies he inherited and had the approval of his fellow steel executives, most of whom were cut from the same pattern. Homer was among the steel men who failed to prepare for the global markets that eventually shrank the market for American steel and caused the industry to collapse in the 1970's and 1980's.

In 1945, Chairman Grace recommended that Homer be elevated to the Bethlehem presidency. In this capacity Homer acted to boost spending on research and development, but he held back on a much-needed modernization plan. Later he created the $10 million research complex at South Mountain, Pa., near Bethlehem, a major installation that later was named for him.

As president of the company at a time when the United States had the only intact economy in the developed world, Homer was optimistic regarding the future of the steel industry. He advocated large-scale expansion, and led Bethlehem in this direction. In 1955, the steel industry produced 117 ingot tons (11.7 million tons) of steel, a new record. In May of that year, Homer predicted further growth. Capacity would increase by 50 percent by 1970, he assured an audience at the annual meeting of the Iron and Steel Institute. "As someone has said, the American people are 'wanters.' Their wants are going to require a great deal of steel." During the period from 1945 to 1959, Bethlehem's production capacity rose from 12.9 million tons to 23 million tons.

At the same time, however, Homer refused to invest in new technologies then being developed in Europe and Japan. Seeking labor peace in order to avoid strikes, he agreed to large wage and benefits increases that obliged the major steel companies to raise prices at a time when the foreign steel companies had just begun to challenge their American counterparts. Frank Brugler, who was Bethlehem's comptroller during the latter part of Homer's leadership, spoke for him and others when he said, "We're not in business to make steel, we're not in business to build ships, we're not in business to erect buildings. We're in business to make money"—to which Vice-President James Slater added, "Unlike some [companies] who can't wait, we don't have to add to capital unless we are sure it will pay out." Homer put it somewhat differently: "We are not only entitled to make, but have an obligation to make, the earnings and profits sufficiently high as to attract investors, so that the supply of funds needed for the replacement and expansion of our facilities, including adequate standby capacity for national defense, may be forthcoming."

When Grace stepped down in 1957, Homer became Bethlehem's chief executive officer, and upon Grace's death in 1960 he was named chairman as well. There were other executives the board might have selected rather than Homer, who was sixty-one years old at the time and regarded by those within the industry as the weakest candidate. But the board considered him the least willing to disrupt the old order they so prized.

Homer figured peripherally in the showdown between President John Kennedy and the steel executives who, in 1962, attempted to boost the price of steel contrary to their earlier assurances that they would not do so. He assigned the task of stating Bethlehem's position in favor of the price hike to President Edmund F. Martin, who had privately stated his opposition. Also in 1962, Homer told a reporter that Bethlehem was rich enough not to innovate. All the plants were making money. "We have a nice business as it is," he boasted. He did what he could to pay a large dividend and obtain all the tax credits possible under federal and state laws. Homer did, however, oversee the construction of a major facility at Burns Harbor, Ind., on the southern shore of Lake Erie, and the expansion and renovation of existing plants.

Homer retired in 1964 and moved from Bethlehem Pa., to Otter Cove, Conn., where he engaged in his favorite sport of sailing. He was an honorary vice-president of the Society of Naval Architects and Marine Engineers and a trustee of the Rhode Island School of Design. He died in Hartford, Conn.

[Homer's papers are in the Bethlehem Steel Archives. There is no biography of Homer. He is discussed in two histories of Bethlehem Steel: John Strohmeyer, *Crisis in Bethlehem* (1986); and Mark Reutter, *Sparrows Point* (1988). An obituary appears in the *New York Times*, June 19, 1972.]

ROBERT SOBEL

HOOPER, HARRY BARTHOLOMEW (Aug. 24, 1887–Dec. 18, 1974), baseball player, manager, and coach, was born at Elephant Head Homestead, Calif., the son of Joseph Hooper, a farmer, and Kathleen Keller. He was the fourth child of German immigrants who had settled as sharecroppers in the Santa Clara Valley. His family farmed at Garrison Ranch in the San Joaquin Valley from 1889 to 1897, but economic difficulties forced the Hoopers to return to sharecropping in the Santa Clara Valley. Hooper performed well in several sports at Saint Mary's College in Oakland, where he earned a B.S. degree in civil engineering in 1907. That spring, Alameda of the "outlaw" California State League (outside baseball's national agree-

ment) signed the outfielder for a few games. In June 1907, Hooper was sold to Sacramento of the California State League. Hooper remained with Sacramento through the 1908 season and also worked as a surveyor for the Western Pacific Railroad. Hooper considered baseball to be a recreational pastime and viewed himself primarily as an engineer.

In August 1908, Sacramento manager Charles Graham persuaded Boston Red Sox owner John I. Taylor to scout Hooper. Hooper quit his surveying job and signed a contract with Boston for 1909. He began the 1909 season as a reserve outfielder with the Red Sox, making two hits in his debut against the Washington Senators in April.

Hooper married Esther Henchy on Nov. 26, 1912. They had three children.

A right fielder with Boston from 1909 to 1920, he combined with center fielder Tris Speaker and left fielder "Duffy" Lewis to make up one of baseball's most legendary outfields. No major league outfield performed better defensively, with each player demonstrating unusual speed and powerful throwing arms. Hooper frequently made spectacular catches after running considerable distances and introduced the "rump slide," sliding on one hip with feet forward and knees bent to catch or trap fly balls. Runners trying to advance from first base to third on balls hit to right field often were thrown out by Hooper. The Hooper-Speaker-Lewis trio recorded 455 assists with Boston.

Hooper remains the only Red Sox player to perform on four world championship teams. His club triumphed over the New York Giants in 1912, the Philadelphia Phillies in 1915, the Brooklyn Dodgers in 1916, and the Chicago Cubs in 1918. In the final contest of the 1912 world classic, his splendid bare-handed catch of a line drive by Larry Doyle of the Giants into the temporary right center field bleachers at Boston preserved the Red Sox victory. During the fifth game of the 1915 World Series against Philadelphia, Hooper became the first player to belt two home runs in one World Series contest. In his four World Series, Hooper made twenty-four hits for a .293 batting mark.

At the plate, Hooper was the leadoff batter. Although he never led the American League in any important offensive categories, he reached base more than 40 percent of the time for Boston. The left-handed batter walked often and batted over .300 in 1911 and 1912. No Red Sox batters have surpassed Hooper's 300 stolen bases and 130 triples. In 1910 Hooper stole a career-high forty bases. Red Sox career records once held by Hooper included most seasons, games played, at bats, hits, singles, extra base hits, total bases, runs scored, walks, and strikeouts. Hooper established a major league record for right fielders by making 344 career assists. No other Red Sox outfielder made more career assists (238) or double plays (54).

At Hooper's suggestion, Boston manager Ed Barrow started employing slugging pitcher Babe Ruth in the outfield. The Boston dynasty collapsed when Red Sox owner Harry Frazee sold or traded several players, including Ruth, to the New York Yankees. In 1921 Boston sent Hooper to the Chicago White Sox for two players and cash. The White Sox needed veteran leadership after the 1919 World Series scandal (when they were paid to throw the series).

Hooper enjoyed his best hitting seasons between 1921 and 1925 and improved his home run production. His batting averages were .327 in 1921, .304 in 1922, and a career-pinnacle .328 in 1923. The right fielder retired as a major league player in 1926. Hooper's 17-year major league career included a .281 batting average, 389 doubles, 160 triples, seventy-five home runs, 1,136 walks, 375 stolen bases, and 817 runs batted in in 2,308 games.

After his retirement from baseball, Hooper sold real estate in Santa Cruz, Calif., managed the San Francisco Missions of the Pacific Coast League in 1927, piloted the Princeton University baseball squad in 1931 and 1932, and served as postmaster of Capitola, Calif., from 1937 to 1952. In 1971 the National Baseball Hall of Fame enshrined Hooper, who had been the Boston team captain and one of the first college-educated major league stars. Hooper died in Santa Cruz.

[The Ellery Clark, Jr., Red Sox Analytical Letter Collection, Annapolis, Md., has the correspondence of Hooper and his sons. Hooper's diaries are located at St. Mary's College in Moraga, Calif. The definitive biography is Paul J. Zingg, *Harry Hooper: An American Baseball Life* (1993). Lawrence Ritter, *The Glory of Their Times* (1966), contains Hooper's personal reflections on his baseball career. The National Baseball Library, Cooperstown, N.Y., houses material on Hooper's life. See also Robert Smith, *Baseball's Hall of Fame* (1973); Martin Appel and Burt Goldblatt, *Baseball's Best* (1977); Lowell Reidenbaugh, *Cooperstown* (1983); and Mike Shatzkin, ed.,

The Ballplayers (1990). An obituary appears in the *New York Times*, Dec. 19, 1974.]

DAVID L. PORTER

HOOVER, JOHN EDGAR (Jan. 1, 1895–May 2, 1972), director of the Federal Bureau of Investigation for almost forty-eight years, was born in Washington, D.C., to Dickerson Naylor Hoover, Sr., a civil servant, and Annie Margaret Scheitlin. Edgar, as he was called since childhood, lived in his Capitol Hill birthplace until his mother died, caring for her after his father's death in 1921. In 1938, Edgar moved to northwest Washington, D.C., where he lived alone (save for a housekeeper) until his death.

A good student, Hoover captained prizewinning cadet drill squads and debating teams at Central High School. He decided to forgo a traditional college education and enrolled in the law school of George Washington University, where he earned an LL.B. (1916) and an LL.M. (1917). Attending classes at night, he worked days as a clerk at the Library of Congress (LC). On July 26, 1917, he joined the Department of Justice (DOJ). Both the LC and DOJ functioned in accordance with the prevailing Progressive era philosophy of scientific efficiency and professionalism. By inclination and upbringing, Hoover found Progressivism a congenial philosophy that influenced his approach to law enforcement.

Hoover's first major assignment at DOJ was administrator of alien enemy matters, recommending detention or parole for Germans and Austrians who violated the World War I Alien Enemy Act. After the war, he became an assistant to Attorney General A. Mitchell Palmer and effective head of the General Intelligence Division, where he collected publicly available information on radicals. Reading radical literature convinced him that Communists posed as much danger to the United States as they had to Russia in 1917. He never deviated from this opinion.

The public first learned about Hoover in 1919 as the person responsible for the successful roundup of Russian Workers Union members by the Bureau of Investigation (BOI) of the DOJ. As a result of this limited operation, numerous radicals were deported. A few weeks later, Hoover took charge of the infamous Palmer raids. BOI-directed local police illegally arrested hundreds of suspected Communists. Most were later released, and DOJ endured public and congressional criticism. Hoover, who later tried to deny his role, learned from the raids to avoid situations that engendered widespread controversy.

In 1921, William Burns, the Harding administration's BOI director, appointed Hoover as assistant director. Burns continued the BOI's Progressive tradition by hiring personnel with investigative skills. But he also made agents of his political cronies. President Calvin Coolidge's attorney general, reformer Harlan Fiske Stone, secured Burns's resignation and named Hoover as acting director on May 10, 1924. On Dec. 10, 1924, Stone appointed Hoover director; he was the fifth individual to lead the sixteen-year-old bureau.

As a Progressive, Hoover wanted the BOI to represent scientific, efficient, and professional law enforcement. He revived legal training as a requisite for special agents and required them to pass background checks, interviews, and physical tests. The Identification Division, started in 1924 to house the nation's central fingerprint collection, and the crime laboratory, started in 1932, exemplified the scientific side of bureau work and were often featured in newsreels and "G-man" films.

Until 1934, scientific advances were almost all the bureau could show off. Its authority was limited to investigating federal law violations, not given by statute to other federal agencies, such as the post office, but few federal criminal statutes existed. State and local authorities traditionally handled crime. With the Treasury Department investigating Prohibition violations through the Volstead Act, the BOI relied mostly on the Dyer Act (interstate travel in stolen cars) and the Mann Act (crossing state lines for immoral purposes) to catch crooks. Notorious gangsters easily evaded local laws and seemed to rob, kidnap, and murder at will. In movies from that time, the gangsters were often the heroes, and the Keystone Kops represented law enforcement.

American attitudes toward federal laws began to change after Charles Lindbergh's baby was kidnapped in 1932. Under public pressure, Congress gave the bureau limited jurisdiction in the area of kidnapping. The Depression and President Franklin Roosevelt also helped change attitudes toward federal power. In 1934, Congress expanded the bureau's criminal jurisdiction dramatically. At that time, the BOI and the virtually defunct Bureau of Prohibition

formed the Division of Investigation under Hoover's directorship. The Division of Investigation was terminated, and the bureau acquired the name Federal Bureau of Investigation in 1935. The FBI gained personnel along with its increased repronsibilities, from approximately 300 agents in 1933 to over 1,000 when the United States entered World War II.

For Hoover, the most effective way to deter crime, catch criminals, and squelch subversion was to make the public believe that if the FBI was involved, crime absolutely would not pay. The FBI, personified by its director, took credit, sometimes unearned, for wiping out or arresting all the major criminal gang members and for solving almost all the major kidnappings of the era. This apparent success bolstered public confidence in the bureau, but to continue to thwart criminals, the FBI required ongoing public support and cooperation. The best way to achieve and maintain public confidence, Hoover thought, was for the bureau and its director to have unblemished reputations. In movies, newsreels, comic strips, and radio shows, Hoover and his seemingly invincible G-men captured the imagination of a hero-hungry America. They maintained their hero status by cultivating reporters and controlling G-man programs and scripts.

For gangsters, as later for Communists, Hoover used his prestige to educate the public about threats to American society and how the FBI, with the help of a vigilant public, would triumph. Books and articles carrying Hoover's byline were researched and written in the FBI Crime Records Division. This division also analyzed criticism of the FBI and Hoover and refuted it either directly or through sympathetic commentators. The FBI's success in the field and its seemingly unassailable reputation had the effects Hoover wanted: the public cooperated, and criminals surrendered. Congress usually, but not always, gave Hoover whatever he requested, and the bureau attracted clean-cut college boys to its investigative divisions and Ph.D.'s to its crime laboratory.

College-educated agents contrasted with the typical peace officer of the 1930's, who lacked higher education and professional skills. Hoover sought to change this in 1935 by establishing the FBI National Police Academy, where FBI agents trained policemen to conduct investigations. Academy graduates then returned home to train their colleagues. The academy influenced the professionalization of law enforcement not only in the United States but also in friendly foreign countries.

Behind the crime-fighting G-men lurked another, secret FBI. Hoover's agents collected information and conducted investigations that had no basis in federal law. Every president from Herbert Hoover through Richard Nixon used the bureau for political purposes. Roosevelt was probably Hoover's strongest influence in this regard. He and his successors requested special investigations of their critics, and Hoover frequently complied. In addition to authorizing these special investigations, Hoover collected whatever negative or titillating information on government officials came to the FBI's attention. Personally or through his assistants, he informed each president about the "derogatory information" collected on administration officials.

Hoover also informed high officials when they were the subjects of defamatory material the FBI received, assuring them that the information would be closely held. All information coming into the FBI on public officials and others went into the files, often without any investigation regarding its truth. Files on prominent individuals stayed in Hoover's office in order to limit their accessibility. However, no conclusive evidence has surfaced that Hoover initiated surveillance of government officials.

Roosevelt also gave the FBI responsibility for noncriminal investigations of subversives. In 1936, the rise of fascism and Stalinism abroad prompted Roosevelt secretly to authorize FBI investigations of subversive groups in the United States. As World War II approached and Hoover could count on public support, the FBI received investigative authority publicly. Despite apparently contrary Supreme Court decisions, Roosevelt also secretly sanctioned FBI use of so-called special techniques, such as wiretapping, with little DOJ oversight. Hoover interpreted his authority broadly and, until 1966, when a Supreme Court case involving the FBI's unauthorized use of listening devices endangered his public standing and caused him to prohibit their future use, convinced succeeding administrations to ratify similar authorizations.

During the late 1930's, the FBI built confidence in its Nazi-fighting ability by breaking German spy rings. The FBI also prepared for war by investigating foreign nationals for possible detention. Within hours of the Japanese attack on Pearl Harbor of Dec. 7, 1941, which brought the United States into World War II, aliens who were perceived to be potential spies for Japan and Germany were arrested. Because he insisted that all potential spies and saboteurs were in custody, Hoover opposed interning Japanese Americans; Attorney General Francis Biddle and President Roosevelt overruled him, and Japanese internment camps were established throughout the West.

During World War II, the FBI maintained public support by arresting deserters and preventing espionage and sabotage. The FBI also secretly ran spies in Latin America through its Special Intelligence Service (SIS). Contrary to Hoover's wishes, President Harry Truman disbanded the SIS after the war, and the FBI's jurisdiction was again limited to the United States.

A smaller postwar FBI returned to investigating federal crimes. However, Soviet expansion in Europe and espionage in North America produced a public outcry against Communism. Hoover possessed evidence of Soviet-backed subversion and espionage, and he was convinced that if the FBI and the American people relaxed their guard, Communism would prevail. Hoover made the decimation of American Communism his personal crusade. FBI investigations led to the convictions of Communist party leaders and several former government workers, including a ring of atom bomb spies.

Congressional committees and local Red squads also exposed alleged Communists and their sympathizers. In contrast to the public name-calling sometimes indulged in by the committees, the FBI quietly investigated allegations of subversion, supposedly leaving conclusions and punishments to others. Hoover attributed criticism of the bureau to a Communist "smear campaign." By lending his prestige to the notion that government critics were Reds, Hoover was responsible in part for discouraging legitimate dissent.

The FBI, in reality, did more than conduct benign investigations of suspected Communists. Hoover authorized secret assistance to congressional committees and mounted a successful counterintelligence operation to disrupt the Communist party and discredit alleged Communists and fellow travelers. Had these operations been uncovered at the time, probably they would have received widespread endorsement. Made public in the 1970's, they were considered abuses of power.

Hoover's power in the postwar years seemed so great that his critics then and later insisted he could investigate what and how he pleased. They blamed him for the FBI's supposed failure to battle organized crime and support black civil rights. Hoover contended that the FBI lacked clear-cut authority in both these areas. He was correct. In the post–World War II years, presidential administrations, Congress, the courts, and the American public preferred local to federal action. When administration policy, law, and public opinion changed, FBI civil rights and organized crime investigations became more aggressive.

Since the 1920's, Hoover had recognized the existence of national crime syndicates. He also recognized the difficulties in developing prosecutable organized crime cases and the potential for corruption among agents, both of which could damage FBI credibility. Therefore, he discouraged the passage of federal organized crime legislation, insisting that national syndicates would collapse if local laws were enforced. When, in the 1960's, Congress passed and the DOJ supported laws aimed at organized crime, the FBI seriously investigated such criminal activity regardless of Hoover's personal preferences.

Similarly, influences other than personal preference governed Hoover's approach to black civil rights. Hoover shared the racism typical of his white contemporaries. Nevertheless, throughout his tenure as director, black agents carried firearms, investigated cases, and underwent periodic ratings identical to those of all other agents (including several Hispanics). Starting in the 1940's, federal law and court interpretations enabled the FBI to investigate certain voting rights and equal employment violations. Yet other Supreme Court decisions severely curtailed federal intervention in the most violent and egregious compromises of civil liberties. In 1946, Hoover testified in favor of modifying civil rights statutes to clarify federal jurisdiction. But the laws, originally passed in 1866, remained unchanged.

Administration policy also discouraged federal action even though black civil rights cases often failed in local courts. Hoover hesitated to compromise the bureau's reputation by pursuing controversial investigations that would almost surely end in acquittals. Even when instructed to the contrary, Hoover insisted that the FBI investigate only at the request of DOJ's Civil Rights Division (CRD). CRD established investigatory guidelines and assigned FBI agents to observe, not protect, civil rights activists and their opponents during demonstrations. Nevertheless, FBI agents conducted numerous investigations of bombings, voting rights violations, and mob violence, causing critical white Southerners to call Hoover a "pawn of the NAACP [National Association for the Advancement of Colored People]."

President Lyndon B. Johnson changed Hoover's attitude toward civil rights investigations. Johnson strongly supported federal intervention and insisted that Hoover use his prestige to enforce civil rights statutes. Presidential encouragement, new laws, court decisions, and a changing public opinion converged to give the FBI an active civil rights role during Hoover's last years.

The FBI's black civil rights successes were overshadowed by Hoover's personal vendetta against Martin Luther King. Hoover regarded King as a hypocrite who used alleged Communists as advisers, who was sexually immoral (because of his numerous extramarital affairs), and who made false accusations about the FBI. In a vain effort to destroy King's reputation, Hoover authorized a counterintelligence program (Cointelpro) against him. This disinformation campaign was designed to turn the press against King, force his abdication as a civil rights leader, and possibly encourage him to commit suicide. The King Cointelpro, exposed in the 1970's, probably did more to discredit Hoover than any other action.

Black civil rights was the first major arena of social unrest in Hoover's last years. By the late 1960's, black power advocates, feminists, and anti–Vietnam War activists were challenging the political and social status quo. More militant than the weak American Communists, the most radical of these New Left individuals inspired bombings and other violence. The FBI now had more than 8,000 agents to respond to these challenges. Because it considered all New Left organizations potentially dangerous, the FBI infiltrated them and conducted surveillance.

FBI infiltration and surveillance of organizations that peacefully exercised First Amendment rights, suspected by critics, was confirmed by documents stolen in 1971 from a local FBI office. The selectively released papers, which were not widely publicized until after Hoover's death, opened a Pandora's box of FBI secrets.

They permanently altered the public's opinion of Hoover. While he lived, however, his reputation remained solid.

Because Hoover served under a succession of attorneys general, theoretically any one of them could have fired him. By 1935, however, attorneys general were, for all practical purposes irrelevant to Hoover. He maintained cordial relations with most of them and obeyed orders if given. But he preferred dealing directly with presidents (as they also preferred dealing directly with him). The effective assistance he gave each administration stands with his unshakable public support to explain Hoover's longevity as director of the FBI.

Particularly in later years, the FBI often appeared to consume Hoover's whole life. However, he also had a personal side. He had friends, like movie star Dorothy Lamour and his neighbor Harry Duncan, and interests, like horse racing, that had little to do with the FBI. He also socialized with political colleagues like Richard Nixon and politically useful media figures like Walter Winchell. His constant companion from the 1930's until his death was FBI Associate Director Clyde Tolson. While their working relationship was very much boss and subordinate and they lived in separate homes, their closeness prompted allegations of a homosexual liaison. No verifiable evidence of such a relationship has surfaced.

Hoover died in his Washington, D.C., home presumably from natural causes; no autopsy was conducted. By this time, the national consensus, so crucial to his success, was dissolving. To those who supported the Vietnam War and feared antiestablishment challenges, Hoover remained a hero. These people stood in line for hours to pay their respects as Hoover's body lay in state in the Capitol rotunda, a rare honor. President Richard M. Nixon delivered the eulogy at Hoover's funeral. Hoover was buried in his family's plot in Congressional Cemetery in Washington, D.C.

For others, however, Hoover's reputation was already entering eclipse. Unlike the case during the early Cold War years, his critics found voices and allies among the media and Congress. FBI revelations and other government scandals fed the skepticism of the postwar generation and horrified many of its elders. Shadow overcame light, and despite Hoover's many achievements, his reputation has remained darkened twenty years after his death.

Perhaps no other American commanded so much power for so long and is as controversial. Hoover learned early in his career how crucial public support was to his success. Therefore, he created an unassailable reputation for himself and the FBI, effectively rebutting anyone with the temerity to challenge him. For most of his life, Hoover served an American public that shared values, goals, and enemies. When that consensus fractured, the unblemished picture of Hoover cracked as well. He is remembered as a destroyer of civil liberties, not a savior of American democracy. The myth of Hoover as hero was replaced by a different myth of Hoover as villain. While both myths contain factual elements, neither presents a true picture.

Yet Hoover's legacy remains. The professionalization of law enforcement owes much to his promotion of scientific investigations, and a professionalized local police traces its roots in large part to his National Academy. The FBI continues to command worldwide respect as a crime-fighting organization, a tribute to Hoover's vision and organizational genius.

[Hoover left no personal papers per se. His marginal notes on FBI documents are the closest substitute. The files in the FBI's Freedom of Information Act Reading Room, many of which are available on microfilm from Scholarly Resources, Inc., and University Publications of America, are a good source for this marginalia. Handwritten letters from Hoover to members of Congress, attorneys general, and presidents are scattered in the papers of their recipients. The National Archives holds a Hoover memorabilia collection that includes his scrapbooks, official photographs, and biographical material. Artifactual Hoover memorabilia are maintained in the House of the Temple, Scottish Rite Supreme Council (Masons), Washington, D.C. The best printed source of Hoover documentary material is Athan Theoharis, ed., *From the Secret Files of J. Edgar Hoover* (1993). The only biographies written by scholars are Richard Gid Powers, *Secrecy and Power* (1987); and Athan Theoharis and John Cox, *The Boss* (1988). See also Ovid Demaris, *The Director* (1975), and Eugene Lewis, *Public Entrepreneurship* (1980). An obituary is in the *New York Times*, May 3, 1972.]

SUSAN ROSENFELD

HOPKINS, MIRIAM (Oct. 18, 1902–Oct. 9, 1972), actress, was born Ellen Miriam Hopkins in Bainbridge, Ga. Interviews throughout her career pointedly omit any reference to her family and childhood. She attended Goddard Seminary in Barre, Vt., where she played her first stage lead; she graduated from Syracuse University, and later studied dancing in New York City. By the time she was twenty, she had given up her idea of a career as a classical dancer to become a dancer and actress on the New York stage.

Hopkins's professional stage debut in New York was in *The Music Box Revue* in 1921. In the decade that followed, she appeared in fourteen stage plays, including *Lysistrata* and *The Bachelor Father*. She scored a great critical success in Theodore Dreiser's *An American Tragedy* in 1926. The same year, Hopkins married Brandon Peters and divorced him soon after; she married Austin Parker in 1928.

In 1930, Hopkins signed a contract with Paramount, moved to Hollywood, and made her first film, *Fast and Loose*. This was the beginning of her professional persona: intelligent, sophisticated, and recognizably southern in manner. After her arrival Hopkins adopted her son, Michael, and was among Hollywood's first single parents. She continued to make films at Paramount, including *Two Kinds of Women* (1932), *The World and the Flesh* (1932), *The Story of Temple Drake* (1933), and *All of Me* (1934). Among her most memorable films in this period were those she made with director Ernst Lubitsch: *The Smiling Lieutenant* (1931); *Trouble in Paradise* (1932), a highly erotic view of crime and sex outside of marriage; and Noël Coward's *Design for Living* (1933).

In 1933, Hopkins was loaned to MGM to be directed by King Vidor in *Stranger's Return*; she also appeared on the New York stage, replacing Tallulah Bankhead in *Jezebel*. Soon after, she signed a contract with Samuel Goldwyn and made *The Richest Girl in the World* (1935); *Becky Sharp* (1935), an early Technicolor film; and, in the same year, *Barbary Coast* and *Splendor*. In 1936 she was directed by William Wyler in *These Three*, a watered-down version of Lillian Hellman's *The Children's Hour*. In 1937 she made *The Woman I Love*, directed by Anatole Litvak, whom she married that year and divorced in 1939.

In 1939, Hopkins moved to Warner Brothers and starred in *The Old Maid*, with Bette Davis. She stayed with the studio making three more films, the last of which was *Old Acquaintance* (1943), again with Bette Davis. Her legendary feud with Davis dated from these collaborations. After these films she returned to the stage, once again replacing Tallulah Bankhead, this time in

The Skin of Our Teeth (1943), and appeared in eight additional stage productions. In 1945, she married her fourth and last husband, Ray Brock, whom she divorced in 1951.

Back in Hollywood at the end of the 1940's, Hopkins returned to the screen as Aunt Penniman in William Wyler's *The Heiress* (1949). In the 1950's she appeared in character roles: in *The Mating Season* (1951), *The Outcasts of Poker Flat* (1952), and *Carrie* (1952). In 1952, she replaced Jo Van Fleet in the New York stage production of *Look Homeward, Angel*. She appeared on screen in a new version of *The Children's Hour* (1962) and, perhaps most notably, in Russ Myer's much publicized *Fanny Hill* (1964). Her last film was *Comeback* (1970). During this period she appeared in numerous television dramas.

Although Hopkins's progress from Broadway ingenue in the 1920's to Hollywood contract player in the four decades that followed paralleled the careers of many actresses of her generation, a highly personal aesthetic set her apart from others. Both her Hollywood home and her New York townhouse at 13 Sutton Place were great gathering places for artists and intellectuals of the day. John O'Hara noted that her guests were there "because Miriam knew them all, had read their work, had listened to their music, and had bought their paintings. They were not there because a secretary had given her a list of highbrows."

Shortly before her death, Hopkins had returned to New York to take part in the Museum of Modern Art's sixtieth anniversary retrospective of Paramount Pictures. She was represented in a screening of *The Story of Temple Drake*, based on William Faulkner's *Sanctuary*, in which she played the lead role.

[An obituary appears in the *New York Times*, Oct. 10, 1972.]

DAVID COREY

HOWARD, MOE (June 19, 1897–May 4, 1975), comedian and member of the Three Stooges, was born Moses Horwitz in the Bensonhurst area of Brooklyn, N.Y., the son of Solomon Horwitz (originally Gorovitz), a clothing cutter, and Jennie Horwitz, a real estate agent. He attended P.S. 163 in Brooklyn and then Erasmus High School for two months. Howard never completed his high school education. To please his parents, he took a class in electric shop at the Baron De Hirsch Trade School in New York. Show business was the magnet attracting Moe from his studies and he would skip school to frequent the local theaters. While in school he earned a reputation as a prankster.

He began to frequent the sets of the Vitagraph Studios in Brooklyn, where he ran errands and made himself useful just for the pleasure of being around actors. This led to small parts in silent films with comedians John Bunny and Flora Finch and with juvenile favorite, Earle Williams.

In 1909 Howard joined an aquatic act, the Annette Kellerman Divers, along with Ted Healy, the future vaudeville star, who would be of influence in his career. The aquatic act was followed by a brief singing debut with his older brother Samuel ("Shemp") Howard. Shemp and he then formed a comedy "clean up" act that was purposefully so bad it cleared out the old audience to make room for a new crowd. Moe, in 1914, took a job performing on Captain Billie Bryant's showboat, the *Sunflower*, on the Mississippi River. He did this successfully for two summers.

Moe returned to vaudeville with Shemp and performed on the RKO and Loew's circuit until Ted Healy hired him in 1922 as his stooge; Shemp and Larry Fine joined him in 1925 to make up the trio. During a ten-year relationship with Ted Healy, the Three Stooges developed the slapstick and physical mayhem that became their trademark. On June 7, 1925, Moe married Helen Blanche Schonberger. They had two children.

The film *Soup to Nuts*, produced in 1930 and starring Healy, marked the Stooges' entrance into a medium where Moe would perform until his last film in 1965. The Stooges, led by Moe, appeared in 190 two-reel comedies for Columbia Pictures and twenty-two feature films in which they starred in at least seven. In all of these, Moe was always the leader, setting the routines' stunts and attending to the team's finances.

In 1940 Moe and his wife bought a home in Hollywood. They lived there for fifteen years.

After *Soup to Nuts*, Shemp left the team to pursue his own career in entertainment. The youngest Howard brother, Jerome ("Curly"), became his replacement and was considered by critics to be the best comedian of the three Stooges. Illness in 1946 forced Curly to leave

the trio, and Shemp returned until his death in 1955. Joe Besser became his replacement.

Two years after Shemp's death Columbia refused to renew the Stooges' contract on the theory that their comedy no longer fitted the sophisticated tastes of the audiences. However, their fame rebounded, and they once again found themselves in feature films. Tours and appearances on television talk shows underscored the popularity of the Stooges with the public. The act was faltering, however. When Larry Fine died in 1975, Moe carried on by himself until his weakness from lung cancer brought his long career to an end.

The comedy of the Three Stooges has suffered from the snobbery of those who scorned it as mere slapstick. But with the passage of time, Moe Howard and his Stooges gained respect as people have better understood their audience and their time.

[Moe Howard's autobiography is *Moe Howard and the Three Stooges* (1977). Commentaries about the work of the Stooges include Leonard Maltin, *The Great Movie Shorts* (1972); Stephen E. Bowles, "The Three Stooges: A Brief Pathology," *Films in Review*, Aug. 1975; Leonard Maltin, *The Great Movie Comedians* (1978); Jeff Lenburg, Joan Maurer, and Greg Lenburg, *The Three Stooges Scrapbook* (1982); and Joan Howard Maurer, *The Three Stooges Book of Scripts* (1984). Bibliographies of Stooges' films are in Stephen E. Bowles, "The Three Stooges: A Brief Pathology" and Lenburg, Maurer, and Lenburg, *The Three Stooges Scrapbook*. An obituary is in the *New York Times*, May 6, 1975.]

RONALD H. RIDGLEY

HUNT, HAROLDSON LAFAYETTE (Feb. 17, 1889–Nov. 29, 1974), billionaire oilman, was born near Vandalia in Fayette County, Ill. His father, Haroldson Lafayette Hunt, Sr., fought for the Confederacy, and at the close of the Civil War moved to southern Illinois, where he married Ella Rose Myers, a schoolteacher. The elder Hunt's skill and hard work as a farmer and commodity dealer made the family prosperous. In later years, he served as county sheriff, owned a local bank, and was a prominent member of the local Republican party. Ella Rose Hunt had attended college and taught school. H. L. Hunt was the youngest of eight children, and unlike his siblings, his mother educated him at home. From early on, he displayed special aptitude in math, and worked with his father buying and selling agricultural commodities and speculating in the Chicago futures market.

Rather than work in his father's bank, in 1905, at age sixteen, Hunt left home. He worked at a variety of jobs in several western states and supplemented his income by playing cards. After attending Valparaiso University in Indiana in the 1906–1907 academic year, Hunt resumed wandering through the West. On the death of his father in 1911, he took a small inheritance and began to invest in cotton-growing land near the Mississippi River in Chicot County, Ark. When the weather turned bad and the price of cotton declined, Hunt returned to the poker tables for reliable income.

In 1921, Hunt opened a gambling hall in El Dorado, Ark., then the center of an oil boom. By the end of the year, he had begun to buy small leases and to drill for oil. He soon purchased larger leases and drilled several wells. In less than four years, his producing wells and leases were worth about $600,000, but Hunt was again ready to move on.

He sold out in 1925, and for a few months tried his hand investing in Florida real estate, but oil promised a safer game of chance and a surer route to wealth. By 1926, his company was drilling again in Louisiana and Arkansas. Hunt, typically dressed in a blue suit, seldom worked on the rigs. Although not a trained geologist, his specialty was securing leases. While others bore the costs and risks of drilling wells in new territory, Hunt kept a team of oil field informers busy supplying him with information on their progress. If the initial well in a new area held promise, Hunt purchased leases. Once the well came in, he quickly bought more.

Hunt followed this strategy in the fabled East Texas Field. In 1930, his informants relayed the information that C. M. ("Dad") Joiner might be close to a major discovery in Rusk County. Hunt arrived at the well site in time to be part of a famous photograph of Joiner and his drilling team celebrating a successful drill stem test. After Daisy Bradford No. 3 came in, Hunt purchased Joiner's five thousand acres of leases for about $1.34 million. Joiner sold because he faced legal challenges to many of his leases and was deep in debt. Besides, at the time of his negotiations with Hunt, several wells drilled to the east of the Daisy Bradford well had not produced oil. Hunt, however, suspected that the main field was to the west of the Daisy Bradford

well and kept close tabs on drilling in that vicinity. By the time he signed the deal with Joiner, he knew that core samples indicated that a well to the west would be a strong producer. About four thousand acres of Joiner's lease lay to the west of Daisy Bradford No. 3. Located in the most prolific part of the East Texas Field, those leases became the basis of Hunt's great wealth. In November 1932, Joiner sued Hunt for fraud, but withdrew the suit without compensation in January 1932. Despite this, many thought Hunt took unfair advantage of Joiner, that wealth brought him enmity as well as envy.

Hunt was chronically short of capital in the 1920's and early 1930's. To buy out Joiner, he depended on funds provided by his friend and business partner, Pete Lake. To drill his first wells, he turned to First National Bank of Dallas. The bank's president, Nathan Adams, was one of the first bankers in the country willing to lend on the basis of oil in the ground.

With financing secured, Hunt rapidly developed his East Texas leases. Besides drilling wells, he also organized the Panola Pipeline Company. He had begun the project before the purchase of the Joiner leases, and by the end of 1930 he had a gathering line in place that collected oil from individual wells and ran it to a nearby Missouri Pacific rail line.

Hunt's earlier experiences in Arkansas and Louisiana had convinced him of the need to limit the number of wells and the amount of oil pumped to extend the life of a field. Now that he was the only major independent operator and had secure financing, he was all the more inclined to support prorationing of the East Texas Field. Moreover, the discovery of the field coincided with the Great Depression. Limited demand and vast supply sent the price of oil plunging down. Hunt tried to convince producers to limit production voluntarily, but many of the smaller producers, lacking credit, needed steady income even at a reduced price. Frenzied drilling caused precipitous declines in the field's pressure and oil's price. Hunt turned to the state government in Austin for assistance. Hunt supported the imposition of martial law and the shutdown of the field by Governor Ross Sterling in August 1931. After reopening the field in September, the Texas Railroad Commission imposed production limits on each well and tried to impose spacing requirements as well. Small producers, however, continued to produce "hot oil" in excess of their allowable quotas, and state and federal court rulings in the early 1930's often came down in the anti-prorationists favor. With the state's efforts in shambles, Hunt supported federal intervention. President Franklin D. Roosevelt issued orders blocking interstate shipment of "hot oil" in 1934. Responding to more adverse court rulings in 1935, Congress passed the Connally Hot Oil Act. Hunt thus owed the security of his fortune to governmental intervention. By 1936, federally enforced proration maintained field pressure and price.

The year 1936 was a turning point for Hunt. In October, he bought out his longtime partner, Pete Lake. He then incorporated the Hunt Oil Company. Indulging his superstition that six-letter words beginning with P were lucky, Hunt organized three affiliated companies: Penrod Drilling Company, Placid Oil Company, and Parade Gasoline Company. These joined Panola Pipeline. By the end of 1936, Hunt was drilling for oil, producing oil, transporting oil, and refining oil. His net worth at the end of that year was approximately $20 million.

After 1936, Hunt expanded his activities in West Texas, Louisiana, and Arkansas. From 1930 to 1938, the headquarters of Hunt's companies and his family's home had been Tyler, Tex., in the midst of the East Texas Field. By 1938, however, Hunt's East Texas holdings no longer needed close supervision, and most of his drilling activity was elsewhere. Hunt moved his family and his companies to Dallas, which offered better transportation and communication linkups between his increasingly far-flung holdings.

East Texas, however, still commanded Hunt's attention. In 1937, Hunt purchased a seven-thousand-acre farm near Tyler. Its chief attraction was a large pecan grove; Hunt loved pecans and considered them healthful. He eventually entered the food business and in 1960 began marketing food and drug products under the HLH brand. In the late 1930's, Hunt also pioneered the use of salt injection wells in the East Texas Field. By pumping the salt water produced with the oil back into the ground, Hunt helped maintain the pressure of the oil field and neatly disposed of what had previously been a waste product.

Increasingly, however, Hunt's focus was national and even international. Between 1938 and 1941, he concentrated his drilling in northern Louisiana. He also traded oil to Germany and Japan for commodities. The United States' declaration of war against those countries ended Hunt's business with them but brought unparalleled profit to his firm because of high American military demand for petroleum products. During the war, Hunt's properties produced about sixty-thousand barrels of oil per day, and by 1946, he earned a gross income of about $1 million per week.

After World War II, Hunt expanded his drilling operations into other southern states, and began drilling about three hundred wells per year. He opened a refinery in Tuscaloosa, Ala., and began to sell gasoline directly to the consumer through his Parade service stations. He also continued to buy land. Among his purchases was a 250,000-acre ranch in Wyoming. In 1948, *Life* and *Fortune* magazines designated Hunt the richest man in the United States.

What *Life* and *Fortune* did not mention was that by 1948 Hunt had three separate families that could lay claim to his riches. Hunt and his first wife, Lyda Bunker Hunt, whom he had married on Nov. 26, 1914, had six children born between 1915 and 1932. Between 1926 and 1934, Hunt had four children with Frania Tye, whom he may have married under the name Franklin Hunt on Nov. 11, 1925, while in Florida. Between 1943 and 1950, Hunt had four children with Ruth Ray, a secretary at the Hunt Oil Company. Lyda Hunt died in 1955, and in 1957, Hunt married Ruth Ray and legally adopted her four children. Beginning in 1935, Hunt set up trust funds for each of his children. To complicate the situation further, Hunt's oldest son, H. L. Hunt, Jr., displayed both a gift for finding oil on his own and mental instability. By the time of Lyda Hunt's death, he was mentally incompetent and his considerable property was also in trust. By that time, Hunt also had transferred ownership of Penrod Drilling to his other sons with Lyda: Bunker, Herbert, and Lamar.

Life and *Fortune* also neglected to mention that Hunt bragged that he made about $1 million per year from gambling. To the high-stakes poker games that Hunt had played since his youth, he added betting on horse races and football games, and marathon gin rummy and dice games. He bet with the most famous gamblers in the country, some of them apparently linked to organized crime. Hunt probably exaggerated his winnings, but he won more than he lost and bet on a very large scale.

By 1948, Hunt also had entered the political arena. He supported General Douglas MacArthur for president in the 1940's and early 1950's and emerged as a vociferous opponent of Communism. Hunt also linked his attack on Communism to an attack on New Deal liberalism, despite the latter's role in securing his fortune. He joined the governor of Texas, Allan Shivers, in opposing federal intervention in civil rights matters and a host of other issues. Chief among these other issues was the question of who controlled the tidelands, the oil-producing shelf off the coast of Texas. State control meant easier access to oil for H. L. Hunt. As in the 1930's, Hunt linked politics to profits.

In 1951, Hunt organized Facts Forum as a tax-exempt foundation for educational purposes, and its main mouthpieces were a newsletter and a radio commentary show. Hunt propagandized for what he called the "constructive" point of view. The typical Facts Forum format presented two sides of every issue: the far-left view and the far-right, or constructive view. Writers and commentators, however, argued the constructive side with more emotion and vigor. Listeners and readers knew where Hunt stood. They did not always know, however, that he financed and oversaw Facts Forum. Hunt recruited conservative lawyers and ex-FBI men to staff Facts Forum. By the end of 1952, Facts Forum's programs ran on more than three hundred radio stations and twenty television stations. Public contributions came pouring in.

Facts Forum quickly became intertwined with the career of Senator Joseph McCarthy of Wisconsin. Former McCarthy aids went to work for Facts Forum, which promoted McCarthy's brand of anti-Communism, as well as racism and anti-Semitism. Facts Forum included a circulating library that mailed out free books with titles such as *Hitler Was a Liberal*. *Facts Forum News*, claiming a peak circulation of sixty thousand, also aided the dissemination of the constructive point of view. When McCarthyism's appeal faded, so did the fortunes of Facts Forum.

In 1958, Hunt replaced Facts Forum with a new tax-exempt organization he called LIFE LINE (Hunt always spelled it with capital letters). This time Hunt's organization did not attempt to present both sides. It tried to downplay racism and anti-Semitism, but also heavily promoted religious fundamentalism. Far-right-wing anti-Communism remained the basic leitmotif of the radio broadcasts, television shows, and printed material funded by LIFE LINE. This organization persisted until the early 1970's.

Hunt's association with McCarthyism and other right-wing causes brought conflict and condemnation. LIFE LINE's criticism of President John F. Kennedy on the day of his assassination stirred public approbation. Members of Hunt's family helped finance other attacks on Kennedy, and federal investigators questioned them after the assassination. Outraged citizens boycotted HLH Products, the primary sponsor of LIFE LINE. Hunt received death threats.

After the 1950's, Hunt devoted less and less time to the oil business. Instead, he wrote a novel called *Alpaca*, which he published in 1960. It promoted Hunt's own version of utopia, a place where those who paid the highest taxes got more votes than those in lower tax brackets. He also wrote two autobiographical works, *Hunt Heritage* and *H. L. Hunt: Early Days*, which were published in 1973. Hunt also wrote a series of newspapers columns, including "Hunt for Truth." After 1968, he promoted and sold aloe vera cosmetics. Hunt's last wife, Ruth, convinced him to give up gambling and to join the Baptist church. When he died in Dallas, he left most of his remaining estate to her. His children's complicated relationship and their various trusts made settling his estate highly contentious.

[See Tom Buckley, "Just Plain H. L. Hunt," *Esquire*, Jan. 1967; Stanley H. Brown, *H. L. Hunt* (1976); and Harry Hurt, *Texas Rich* (1981). An obituary is in the *New York Times*, Nov. 30, 1974.]

WALTER L. BUENGER

HUNTER, IVORY JOE (Oct. 10, 1911–Nov. 8, 1974), singer and composer of country, blues, and popular songs, was born in Kirbyville, Tex. His father was the guitarist Dave Hunter, and his mother sang gospel. Although little is known of his early career, his piano style suggests the obvious influence of Fats Waller and Duke Ellington. Hunter often said that as a child he had listened to their records, and he publicly acknowledged that Waller was his idol.

By the age of twenty, Hunter had formed his own band, and he soon became a well-known itinerant blues entertainer in Texas through his popular radio shows. He was first recorded by

Alan Lomax for the Library of Congress folk-music programs in 1933, under the name Ivory Joe White; but it was not until he moved to the West Coast and began recording what some call "urban blues" for professional labels in 1937 that his career flourished. For his first commercial recordings he formed Johnny Moore's Three Blazers—Charles Brown, Johnny Moore, and Oscar Moore—to perform with him. By 1945, he had organized his own Ivory record label and had a regional hit with "Blues at Sunrise," even though the wartime restrictions on shellac limited the number of pressings.

Hunter first reached the national audience on the King label with "Pretty Mama Blues," recorded with several members of the Duke Ellington orchestra. During this period he frequently recorded with sidemen from Ellington's orchestra as well as white country musicians out of Nashville. He also played piano for Lowell Fulson on several of Fulson's recordings. A string of hits, including "Landlord Blues," "Guess Who," and "Jealous Heart" helped land him a contract with MGM, a major accomplishment for a black artist in 1949.

In 1950, Hunter's monster hit "I Almost Lost My Mind" sold a million records and skyrocketed to the top of the R&B charts. In the same year, his "I Need You So" rose to the number-two spot. By now, Hunter had achieved major stature in the entertainment world. His smooth style and relaxed delivery appealed to many followers of traditional popular music as well as country and western fans. It was, however, in the newly emerging field of rhythm and blues—what was soon to be labeled "rock and roll"—that Ivory Joe's impact was most felt.

In 1954, Hunter signed on with Jerry Wexler's Atlantic label. Wexler and Ahmet Ertegun were making a concerted effort to cross black artists over to the white rock-and-roll market. Hunter's style suited the effort perfectly. He did smooth ballads ("Empty Arms," "A Tear Fell") as well as up-tempo material ("I Got to Learn to Do the Mambo," "You Can't Stop That Rocking and Rolling"), and soon turned out a series of hit songs.

While he was with Atlantic, Hunter wrote and recorded what proved to be his biggest hit, "Since I Met You, Baby" (1956), which shot to the top of the R&B category and climbed to number twelve on the national pop charts.

After leaving Atlantic in 1959, Hunter jumped from one record company to another, never staying with any single label long enough to complete an entire album. Consequently, many of his important works were re-released in album form after his death. Until then, however, he continued his prodigious songwriting career; conservative estimates place the number of songs he wrote at between two thousand and three thousand. Superstars like Elvis Presley, Pat Boone, and Nat King Cole all recorded big hits from Hunter's songs, which helps explain why his songs are perhaps better known than he is.

An extraordinarily talented and prolific artist, Hunter was equally adept with pop, ballad, or spiritual styles. He even broke into the country and western field—almost unheard of for a black R&B artist. Although there is not total agreement on who was the first black to record country music, it is generally recognized that Hunter predated Ray Charles's venture into the field by three years. So strong was his following that a benefit concert was held for him at Nashville's Grand Ole Opry shortly before his death.

Recording at a time when blacks were still excluded from the larger white audience—Pat Boone's "cover" of "I Almost Lost My Mind" (1956) for example, was a much greater commercial success than Hunter's—Ivory Joe nonetheless is an important transitional figure. In the words of British enthnomusicologist Charlie Gillett, Hunter "attracted the white audience, and yet stayed near enough to the blues for the Negro audience to care about him."

Hunter died in Memphis, Tenn.

[Literature on Hunter is scarce. A good summary article is Robin Grayden, "No Ordinary Joe," *Melody Maker*, Aug. 25, 1979. See also Charlie Gillet, *The Sound of the City* (1970); and Jerry Wexler and David Ritz, *Rhythm and the Blues* (1993). An obituary is in the *New York Times*, Nov. 10, 1974.]

LOUIS CANTOR

HUNTLEY, CHESTER ("CHET") ROBERT (Dec. 10, 1911–Mar. 20, 1974) radio and television journalist, was born in Caldwell, Mont., the son of Percy Adams ("Pat") Huntley, a rancher and railroad telegrapher, and Blanche Tatham. A descendant through his father of John Adams and John Quincy Adams, Huntley grew up in what was the last American frontier of cattlemen and miners. His earliest years were spent on a ranch, but hard times eventually brought his father to full-time employment as a telegrapher for the Northern Pacific railroad. Huntley's boyhood was spent along the railroad's right-of-way in a succession of small towns. Despite the frequent uprooting that his father's career entailed, Huntley gained a lifelong appreciation of outdoor life and a belief in what he took to be the frontier values of family, independence, hard work, and honesty. At the height of his celebrity in the 1960's, he furnished his New York office with the roll-top desk used by his father in Bozeman, Mont., a brass spittoon, and an 1870 Winchester rifle hanging on the wall.

Two prime influences on his life were his maternal grandfather, W. R. Tatum, a rancher who exemplified the rugged spirit of the West, and a high school English teacher, Callie Allison, who taught him "a love of language," at Whitehall High School, from which he graduated in 1929. Anderson encouraged Huntley to take up debating, and that, in turn, led him to a national contest and a college scholarship. He attended Montana State College (1929–1932) as a premedical student and, on the strength of another debating scholarship prize, the Cornish School of Allied Arts in Seattle (1932–1933). Huntley received a B.A. from the University of Washington, Seattle, in 1934.

While a senior at Washington, he began work at KPCB, a small radio station, where he performed every kind of job, from sweeping up to writing advertising copy to on-air reporting. After graduation, he became the station's program director for two years and then in 1936 transferred to KHQ radio in Spokane, Wash., as an announcer and newscaster. Over the next twenty years, Huntley served a variety of stations and three national networks as a radio newsman, analyst, and commentator, all in Los Angeles, first at KFI radio (1937–1939), then on CBS (1939–1951), followed by ABC (1951–1955). He moved to New York with NBC radio in 1955.

Huntley married Ingrid Rolin on Feb. 23, 1936. They had two daughters and were divorced in 1959. His second marriage to Tipton Stringer, a television weathercaster, took place on Mar. 7, 1959. They had no children.

In 1942, in the wake of the zoot-suit riots brought on by often virulent discrimination against Mexican-Americans, Huntley wrote and produced for CBS radio a series of half-hour programs, "These Are Americans," which condemned the prejudice and showed the contributions of Latinos to society. In other programs he spoke out strongly against the wartime internment of Japanese-Americans. The series won him a George Foster Peabody Award and citations from Ohio State and New York universities. He won a second Peabody Award in 1954 for his skill as an analyst and his "talent for mature commentary." Then with KABC, Huntley appeared three times daily in Los Angeles, twice on radio and once on television, and, according to *Newsweek*, had "the highest ratings on any ABC news show."

Because Huntley believed strongly that reporters had an obligation to place an issue in context and show its several sides, he was sometimes at odds with pressure groups, notably during the McCarthy era, when he was called a communist and a campaign was started to have him taken off the air. In 1954 he successfully sued the campaign's leader for slander, winning a $10,000 settlement and a public apology. Years later, he rebutted the Nixon administration's attacks on newsmen during the Vietnam War. In a signed article in *TV Guide*, then the most widely read magazine in America, Huntley wrote that the president was mistaken if he believed that journalists were supposed to be the "cheerleaders" of society. "Tragically," he said, "that is their function in authoritarian societies—but not in free countries." The 1970 article earned him placement on the White House "enemies list" that came to light during the Watergate hearings.

In 1956 NBC paired Huntley with David Brinkley to cover the national presidential conventions. The two were the network's third choice (John Hersey and Henry Cabot Lodge had each turned down NBC's offer of the job) and originally they were to alternate the assignment. But when they began their coverage they blended their presentations, serving as complements of each other: Huntley, the rugged, rangy Westerner, unfailingly serious and stern in his delivery; Brinkley, the eastern sophisticate, puckish and irreverent in his. By fall, the network knew it had a popular team to replace John Cameron Swayze. Their first newscast took place on Oct. 20, 1956. By the end of the decade, the "Huntley-Brinkley Report" was one of the crown jewels of broadcasting and a prime source of revenue for NBC. A consumer survey in 1965 reported that Huntley and Brinkley were recognized by more Americans than Cary

Grant, James Stewart, John Wayne, and the Beatles, all of whom were then at the height of their popularity. Their signature sign-off, "Good night, David—Good night, Chet" had become the object of gentle parody on television variety shows and was as familiar to millions of Americans as Edward R. Murrow's "Good night and good luck" had been earlier on CBS.

More important, industry sources credit them with changing the face of television news. Unlike many of their predecessors and some of their competitors for the national audience, Huntley and Brinkley wrote their own copy. They transformed reporting, at least at the national level, from the "rip and read" practices of the past (a reference to newscasters' use of wire-service copy) to a serious business that could simultaneously inform, entertain, and earn a profit for the networks. They were a prime influence in turning television into the primary source of news for a large percentage of the American people.

In July 1970, after fifteen years of telecasting, Huntley retired from the daily grind to pursue personal interests. He worked in television syndication as a commentator and became a partner in a New York advertising agency. He returned to Montana to head Big Sky, Inc., a multimillion-dollar resort complex, which generated considerable controversy over environmental issues before his death from cancer in Bozeman.

[Huntley's memoir of his childhood in Montana, *The Generous Years: Remembrance of a Frontier Boyhood*, was published in 1968. An obituary appears in the *New York Times*, Mar. 21, 1974.]

ALLAN L. DAMON

HURLEY, ROY T. (June 3, 1896–Oct. 31, 1971), industrialist and business executive, was born in New York City, the son of Edward H. Hurley and Phoebe King. Hurley only had a New York City grammar school education, but he nonetheless acquired a widespread knowledge of engineering and industrial management techniques. He once said, "I took all the correspondence courses and read all the textbooks."

Hurley began his career in 1916 as an aircraft engine mechanic with the B. F. Sturtevant Company, Hyde Park, Mass. On June 3, 1917, Hurley married Ruth Applebee, whom he later divorced. They had two children. During World War I, he was an inspector of airplanes and engines for the United States Army at the Wright-Martin Aircraft Corporation in New Brunswick, N.J.

Wright-Martin was reorganized in 1919 as the Wright Aeronautical Corporation, which later became the engine manufacturing division of the Curtiss-Wright Corporation. In 1921, Hurley became chief engineer of the B. G. Aircraft Spark Plug Company of New York City. He left that position in 1927 to become vice-president and general manager of the Moto-Meter Gauge and Equipment Company in Long Island.

In 1931, Hurley designed a new type of aircraft spark plug with an expanded copper tube through the center. A marked improvement over the older mica plugs, it prevented preignition and greatly reduced spark-plug fouling. Shortly thereafter, Hurley left Moto-Meter to form the Hurley-Townsend Company of New York. He joined the Bendix Corporation in 1935 as a staff executive on production matters when Bendix acquired Hurley-Townsend.

During World War II, Hurley was the deputy chief of ordnance and a civilian production adviser to the army chief of ordnance, Lieutenant General Levin H. Campbell, Jr. He also served as assistant to Major General Thomas H. Hayes, chief of the industrial division of ordnance and deputy to Brigadier General Rosswell E. Hardy, chief of the ammunition branch. Returning to Bendix, he was named vice-president of manufacturing on Sept. 14, 1944, responsible for determining plant and facility requirements together with factory layout and product tooling as the corporation began converting to a peacetime economy. In 1948, Hurley joined the Ford Motor Company as director of manufacturing engineering.

In 1949, Paul Shields, an investment banker who had recently taken control of the Curtiss-Wright Corporation, asked Henry Ford II, who owned a neighboring Long Island estate, to recommend someone who could improve Curtiss-Wright's production program. Ford recommended Hurley, who had made his reputation as an expert on production and cost cutting at Bendix and Ford. He was named president of Curtiss-Wright on Aug. 8, 1949, and became chairman of the board upon Paul Shields's retirement in October 1951.

Hurley's eleven years at Curtiss-Wright did little to enhance his reputation as a shrewd businessman. The aviation giant was in serious trouble when he took over. It had become overextended during World War II and was still struggling to regain its footing six years later. To revive its sagging fortunes, Hurley initiated an aggressive program of aircraft engine development within the Wright Aeronautical Corporation, Curtiss-Wright's engine manufacturing division. The timing was right. The Korean War had just begun, and the demand for military versions of Wright Aeronautical's reciprocating engines skyrocketed. Moreover, engine sales to the airlines remained strong, and Curtiss-Wright's profit picture improved significantly in the early 1950's.

This initial prosperity was deceptive, however, because the jet age had dawned and conventional piston engines would soon be obsolete. To his credit, Hurley brought Wright Aeronautical into the jet age by entering into a licensing agreement with Armstrong-Siddley of Great Britain to manufacture that company's Sapphire jet. It was produced in America as the Wright J-65. Nevertheless, Hurley remained committed to the piston engine, convinced that it could compete successfully with gas turbines for the indefinite future. He was wrong, and piston engine sales declined precipitously in the late 1950's, along with company income and profits.

Instead of moving aggressively into turbine engine development, however, Hurley chose to diversify. It proved to be his undoing, as he took Curtiss-Wright far beyond the limits of the aviation industry. He frantically scrambled for a product that would give a quick return, but his efforts only dissipated the company's energies and further weakened its position in the industry. It did nothing to alleviate the immediate cash-flow problems, which were acute. The company's fortunes continued to decline throughout the late 1950's, and Hurley was forced to resign in May 1960. At a stockholder's meeting shortly before his resignation, he said, "I'm called a bum and I'm called a genius, but I think I'm somewhere in between."

Hurley married Esther Sarchian, his administrative assistant at Curtiss-Wright, Oct. 3, 1953. They had two children.

In recognition of his earlier achievements, Hurley was given the Horatio Alger Award in 1956. That same year Pennsylvania governor George Leader gave him the state's highest honor, its meritorious medal. After leaving Curtiss-Wright, he retired and moved to Santa Barbara, Calif., where he pursued a favorite hobby, raising organic foods. He died in Santa Barbara.

[The National Air and Space Museum, Washington, D.C., has a small biographical file on Hurley. Details on his controversial years as president of Curtiss-Wright can be found in William B. Harris, "Curtiss-Wright Throws Away the Book," *Fortune*, Jan. 1958; and "Clash that Upset Curtiss-Wright," *Business Week*, June 11, 1960. An obituary is in the *New York Times*, Nov. 6, 1971.]

LOUIS R. ELTSCHER

HUROK, SOLOMON ISAIEVITCH (Apr. 9, 1888–Mar. 5, 1974), impresario, producer, and theatrical manager, was born in Pogar, the Ukraine, Russia, to Israel Hurok, a hardware dealer, and Naomi Schream. In 1906, sent by his father on business to nearby Kharkov with 500 rubles, he chose to use the money to finance his emigration to America. He had 3 rubles left when he landed at Ellis Island. After holding various odd jobs in Philadelphia, including bottle washer and streetcar conductor, he moved to New York City, where he peddled hardware. He had little formal education, but studied English at the Educational Alliance on the Lower East Side of Manhattan.

Although he could not read music, Hurok was a devoted music lover and attended the opera whenever possible. He first combined his business savvy with his musical passions in 1911, when he persuaded violin virtuoso Efrem Zimbalist to play for a Socialist party function in Brooklyn. In 1913, he organized the Van Hugo Musical Society to provide concert programs for New York labor clubs and workers' groups. In 1914, he became a naturalized citizen of the United States.

His reputation as an incipient impresario ballooned in 1915, when, after first producing concerts at Madison Square Garden, he booked the huge Hippodrome for a popular-priced "Music for the Masses" Sunday matinee series. Featuring such stars as Zimbalist, Mischa Elman, Alma Gluck, Tito Ruffo, Ernestine Schumann-Heink, and Eugene Ysaye, Hurok managed to draw an ethnically diverse audience by advertising in foreign-language newspapers; he not only filled the theater's 4,700 seats but sold 1,000 on-stage seats.

Eventually, "S. Hurok Presents" became a

trademark symbolizing his lifelong practice of guaranteeing first-class performers at affordable prices to the broadest audiences. He spared no expense, as when in 1933 he lost $88,000 to bring the then unknown Ballet Russe de Monte Carlo to America. This was one of several damaging financial setbacks, but despite frequent monumental gambles he usually earned robust sums. For example, he took a spectacular chance in 1957 when, against all warnings, he promoted a tour of the Massed Pipers and Regimental Band of the Scots Guard, but the tour made millions. Hurok was unique in the promotion business because he bankrolled his own programs, rather than depending on outside investors. By 1966, his mailing list went out to 50,000 faithful ticket buyers. Nevertheless, although his own career demonstrated that capitalism and the arts could flourish together, he was a strong proponent of government subsidy for the arts.

Hurok became renowned for the quality of his bookings, consisting mostly of foreign artists. Dance historians consider him instrumental in making classical dance widely popular in America, beginning with his great coup of the 1920's, the management of Russian ballerina Anna Pavlova, the artist of whom he had the fondest recollections. A sampling of the terpsichorean sensations presented by this "King of Ballet" includes Isadora Duncan, Argentinita, Vicente Escudero, Mary Wigman, Loie Fuller, Uday Shankar, the Ballet Russe, the Sadler's Wells Ballet, the Royal Ballet (starring Margot Fonteyn and Rudolf Nureyev), the Kirov Ballet, the Paris Opera Ballet, the Royal Danish Ballet, the Stuttgart Ballet, and the Bolshoi Ballet (starring Galina Ulanova), the last a masterstroke during the cold war atmosphere of 1959. Folk or ethnic companies such as the Ballet Folklórico de Mexico, the Azuma Kabuki Dancers, and the Moiseyev Dancers were also S. Hurok attractions, as were such homegrown products as the Martha Graham, Katherine Dunham, and Agnes de Mille troupes and Canada's Royal Winnipeg and National Ballet companies.

Hurok—dubbed a "Mahatma of Music"—was also famed for the singers and musicians he sponsored, among them African-American contralto Marian Anderson, whom he discovered in Paris in 1933 and revealed to her native United States as one of its greatest treasures. Other representative musical artists were Fyo-dor Chaliapin, Rudolf Serkin, the Kolisch String Quartet, the Moscow Cathedral Choir, the German Grand Opera Company, the Vienna Choir Boys, Andrés Segovia, Arthur Rubinstein, Luisa Tettrazini, Isaac Stern, Mischa Elman, Emil Gilels, David Oistrakh, Jan Peerce, Pattice Munsel, Roberta Peters, Pierre Boulez, Sviatoslav Richter, and numerous others, most of them making their American debuts under Hurok's management.

In addition to occasionally producing plays on Broadway, he was active in promoting foreign theatrical troupes, including both the London and Bristol Old Vic companies, the Théâtre de France, the Théâtre National Populaire, the Compagnie Marie Bell, the D'Oyly Carte Opera Company, the Moscow Art Theater, the Comèdie Française, the Habima Players, and the Compagnie Madeleine Renaud–Jean-Louis Barrault, among others.

Presentations of S. Hurok–sponsored dance companies on television helped raise that medium's cultural standards. Television honored Hurok in 1966 when CBS-TV produced a 90-minute special devoted to his career, on which a glittering array of Hurok stars appeared.

Hurok, a gourmet, bon vivant, and party giver, was an energetic, flamboyant figure. He was twice married, once to a Brooklyn woman (date unavailable), the mother of his only child, and once to singer Emma Runitch (1933), from whom he was later separated. He often spoke of himself in the third person and his Russian-accented speech was peppered with malapropisms. One of his most famous was, "I don't know exactly what makes box-office. But if people don't want to come, nothing will stop them." Bald, pear-shaped, and short, he wore black horn-rimmed spectacles and affected a black cape, a silver-tipped cane, and a soft, black fedora. On formal occasions he wore a "chest salad" of decorations. David Wayne, who played him in the 1953 film *Tonight We Sing* (based on one of Hurok's two autobiographies), looked nothing like him.

Hurok passionately supported his attractions, appearing nightly to clap loudly and question audience members. He spared no expense to ensure the comfort and promote the happiness of his stars. Hurok appreciated artistic temperament, but he himself was an even-tempered, canny, yet ethical businessman; he often preferred a handshake to a formal contract. Still, his was a cutthroat business, and he accumulated his share of enemies. He carefully differentiated between his own practices as an "impresario" and those of mere "managers." A relentless talent scout, he was forever in search of new attractions. He had a special predilection for Russians, and was respected by the Soviets for such deeds as convincing the U.S. State Department to stop fingerprinting visiting performers. Unfortunately, his offices were firebombed (causing one death and injuries to thirteen people, including Hurok) in 1972 by zealots angered by his support of Soviet artists while restrictions hampered Soviet Jewish emigration (Hurok was himself Jewish).

In 1973, 1,500 spectators and a star-studded array of Hurok attractions honored this "Barnum of the Arts" at the Metropolitan Opera House. The French government made him a chevalier of the Légion d'Honneur in 1953 for his efforts at promoting French culture. The British government named him a commander of the British Empire. He died in New York City.

[Hurok's autobiographies, *Impresario* (1946) and *S. Hurok Presents* (1953), are helpful if self-serving, ghosted works. See also John Bainbridge, "S. Hurok," *Life*, Aug. 28, 1944; Ward Morehouse, "S. Hurok," *Theatre Arts*, Feb. 1957; Gerald Goode, "S. Hurok Presents," *Reader's Digest*, Apr. 1958; Harold C. Schonberg, "Presenting S. Hurok, Impresario," *New York Times Magazine*, Apr. 26, 1959; Irving Kolodin, "S. Hurok, Adventurer in the Arts," *Saturday Review*, May 1959; Allene Talmey, "How to Be S. Hurok," *Vogue*, Sept. 15, 1962; *Dance Magazine*'s Mar. 1967 awards issue; and Olga Maynard, "Sol Hurok at 85," *Dance Magazine*, May 1973. Obituaries appear in the *New York Times*, Mar. 6, 1974; *Variety*, Mar. 13, 1974; and *Time*, Mar. 18, 1974.]

SAMUEL L. LEITER

I–J

INGE, WILLIAM MOTTER (May 3, 1913–June 10, 1973), playwright and novelist, was born in Independence, Kans., the son of Luther Clayton Inge, a traveling salesman, and Maude Sarah Gibson. Because his father was away so often, Inge, a shy and introspective child, and his four siblings were reared mainly by his domineering, puritanical mother, with whom he had a very close relationship.

Inge attended Montgomery County High School (1926–1930) and the University of Kansas in Lawrence, majoring in speech and drama. He wrote the script for an annual college musical, acted in touring Toby shows (a comic tent show featuring a farm boy named Toby) during the summers, and, after gaining his B.A. in 1935, began teaching at Culver Military Academy in Indiana. His wish to move to New York City and become an actor was diverted by financial problems, so he entered graduate school at George Peabody College for Teachers in Nashville, Tenn., on a scholarship, but left shortly before graduation when he suffered a nervous collapse. He subsequently completed his M.A. degree (1938) by writing a thesis on director-playwright David Belasco.

Upon regaining his health, Inge worked as a radio script writer and announcer in Wichita while acting in amateur theater companies. After a case of stage fright forced him to abandon acting, he turned to teaching English, first at a Kansas high school and then for five years (1938–1943) at Stephens College for Women in Columbia, Mo., where he also taught theater. From 1943 to 1946 he was the arts and literature critic for the *St. Louis Star-Times*, and from 1946 to 1949 he taught at Washington College in St. Louis.

During his stint as a journalist he interviewed playwright Tennessee Williams, with whom he became friendly and had a brief homosexual love affair. Williams's *Glass Menagerie* (1945) inspired Inge to write plays himself. Williams helped Inge get his first play, *Farther Off from Heaven* (1947), produced in Dallas. His initial success persuaded Inge to give up teaching, which he disliked, and become a professional dramatist. He moved to New York City in 1949.

A heavy drinker, Inge had joined Alcoholics Anonymous in 1948. This experience was transmuted into his first Broadway play, the gloomy *Come Back, Little Sheba* (1950; film version, 1952), with brilliant performances by Shirley Booth and Sidney Blackmer as Lola and Doc, a midwestern housewife and her alcoholic husband. Worry over the production, which ultimately ran for 190 performances after it received mostly good reviews, took a heavy toll on Inge, who had to be hospitalized for a serious nervous condition worsened by drinking.

His next Broadway play, *Picnic* (1953; film version, 1955), earlier called *Front Porch* and *Summer Brave*, concerned the impact of the arrival in a small town of a handsome, muscular newcomer on a group of sexually frustrated women leading rather circumscribed lives. *Picnic* ran for 477 performances, and won, among other awards, the Drama Critics Circle Award and the Pulitzer Prize. Yet Inge continued to endure depression stemming from a lack of self-confidence. A much-revised version of the play, retitled *Summer Brave*, was published in 1962.

Another hit followed. *Bus Stop* (1955; film version, 1956) was a comedy-drama concerning the romantic encounter of a saloon singer and rodeo cowpoke in a Kansas City diner during a snowstorm. This reworking of Inge's one-act play, *People in the Wind*, ran for 478 performances on Broadway and evidenced his ability to portray lonely and frustrated small-town characters (his women were Inge's finest creations), holding them together with a conventionally realistic plot focusing on life crises; plot was secondary to character depiction. Inge had a talent for composing authentic everyday dialogue that captured the flavor of the Midwest. He came to be considered the American theater's first important voice from the heartland.

Inge refashioned another early work, *Farther Off from Heaven*, into *The Dark at the Top of the Stairs* (1957; film version, 1960). This semi-autobiographical drama of domestic strife in an Oklahoma household in the 1920's, as viewed through the eyes of a young boy, was Inge's fourth straight hit. After this success, he experienced many severe setbacks.

A *Loss of Roses* (1959; film version, *The Stripper*, 1963), Inge's most explicit grappling with his relationship with his mother, failed after 25 performances. It was plagued with expensive preproduction problems, and Inge was prevented from making the needed revisions. Negative critical reviews deeply wounded him. He worked off some of his despair writing his first movie script, *Splendor in the Grass* (1961), for which he won an Oscar. This success—Inge's only one during these final years—prompted him to move to California. He wrote the film version of James Lepo Herlihy's *All Fall Down* (1962). Another film script remained unproduced, and he was so dissatisfied with *Bus Riley's Back in Town* (1965) that he used a pseudonym on the credits. At the same time, his Broadway plays *Natural Affection* (1963) and *Where's Daddy?* (1966) both flopped.

Inge hoped to avoid thematically loaded plays, trying instead to write in a way that would enrich people's lives via their encounters with the human experiences he depicted. R. Baird Shuman notes that Inge wrote about "love, and the highest expression of love as Inge sees it often comes when someone realizes that non-judgmental, accepting love is the only kind that really endures. It is this sort of love that brings the main characters in many of Inge's plays a sense of ultimate fulfillment."

In his later years, he taught playwriting at various colleges in California. His play *Overnight* (1969) was produced by a university group but was never published. He did publish several one-act plays and two novels, *Good Luck, Miss*

Wyckoff (1971) and *My Son Is a Splendid Driver* (1971), an autobiographical novel about an English professor recalling his early years.

Inge's experiences nurtured a deeply cynical attitude that pervaded his later writing. His depression—part of it stemming from his discomfort with his homosexuality—grew so intense and debilitating that later in his life, one of his sisters had to live with and care for him. In 1973, Inge was sure he would never write again. He grew so despondent over his failures that he killed himself by carbon monoxide poisoning in Los Angeles.

[The chief collections of Inge's manuscripts and other primary sources are in the William Inge Collection, Independence Community College, Independence, Kans.; the Kansas Collection Research Library, University of Kansas, Lawrence; and the Humanities Research Center, University of Texas, Austin. His best plays are collected in *Four Plays by William Inge* (1958). The sole biography is Ralph F. Voss, *A Life of William Inge* (1989). Arthur F. McClure compiled a bibliography, *William Inge* (1982); for a critical survey see R. Baird Shuman, *William Inge* (rev. ed., 1989). An obituary appears in the *New York Times*, June 10, 1973.]

SAMUEL L. LEITER

IRELAND, CHARLES THOMAS, JR. ("CHICK") (Apr. 14, 1921–June 7, 1971), lawyer and business executive, was born in Boston, Mass., the son of Charles T. Ireland, Sr., and Margaret Keough. His father was a chiropodist and moved the family to Portland, Maine, when Charles was a child. In 1938, Ireland graduated from Portland High School and was voted the most likely to succeed. He received a B.A. from Bowdoin College in 1942, where he majored in history and was an editor of the college newspaper and a member of the basketball and tennis teams.

After leaving college, he enlisted in the United States Marine Corps for service in World War II. Private Ireland fought in the vicious Pacific battles on Iwo Jima, Saipan, and Tinian, and he was awarded the Silver Star, the Bronze Star, and Purple Heart. He was a captain when he left the marines three years later.

Ireland entered Yale Law School in 1945, graduating in 1947. He joined the Wall Street law firm of White and Case as a research clerk and soon moved to the tax department. When one of the firm's clients, the Alleghany Corporation, mentioned that they were looking for a new general counsel, a senior White and Case partner suggested Ireland, who accepted the post.

By 1953, Ireland had married Dorothy Schwebel Gardner, who had two children from a previous marriage. The couple had two children.

Soon after joining Alleghany, Ireland found himself offering important advice and guidance during a bitter and complicated proxy fight to gain control of the New York Central Railroad. Once Alleghany assumed control of the railroad in 1954, Ireland became secretary of the New York Central and remained there until 1959. In 1939, Chick Ireland returned to Alleghany as executive vice-president. Two years later he was elected president of Alleghany.

Meanwhile, in 1959 Harold Geneen became head of the International Telephone and Telegraph Company (ITT) and proceeded to remold it as a conglomerate by purchasing scores of other companies that produced a variety of goods and services and made profits for the parent company. In 1965, Ireland joined the board of directors of ITT, and in 1968 he joined Geneen and ITT on a full-time basis. Before the year was out Ireland had convinced Geneen that ITT should acquire the Hartford Fire Insurance Company. Geneen followed Ireland's advice on that acquisition, and on others to follow, including Avis, Sheraton Corporation of America, and five mutual funds. Ireland had overall operations responsibility for these new ITT subsidiaries. By 1971, Ireland had risen to senior vice-president of ITT, but he was anxious to find a job where he would be in control.

On Sept. 10, 1971, Ireland was named president of CBS. His appointment took many by surprise, since Ireland knew little about the broadcasting industry and seldom watched television. But CBS head William S. Paley was attracted to Ireland's training under Harold Geneen and his ability to manage a diversified company.

Ireland shunned the spotlight while at CBS. He worked long hours but always made time to spend summer weekends and vacations at his farm in Maine. In the months after he joined the company, CBS acquired record stores and two sports magazines and announced plans to buy the piano manufacturer Steinway and Sons. But the CBS organization was different from any other Ireland had encountered. His no-nonsense style and focus on financial details

often was at odds with the unpredictable nature of the entertainment industry. He died at his home in Chappaqua, N.Y., and was buried on the family farm in West Bath, Maine.

[An obituary appears in the *New York Times*, June 9, 1971.]

TOBY WERTHEIM

JACKSON, MAHALIA (Oct. 26, 1911–Jan. 27, 1972), gospel singer, was born into poverty in New Orleans, the illegitimate daughter of Johnny Jackson and Charity Clark. Her father was a stevedore, barber, and sometime minister; her mother was a maid.

Originally named Mahala and nicknamed Halie, Jackson was born with severely bowed legs and eye problems. But under the loving care of her mother's family, she overcame these early handicaps. At age five she lost her mother; she was raised for the next ten years by a maternal aunt, Mahala Paul, known affectionately in the family as Aunt Duke.

Jackson had limited formal education, dropping out of McDonough School No. 24 in New Orleans in the eighth grade. She worked as a laundress and a nursemaid until 1928 when she left her hometown for Chicago. Rooming with another aunt, she hoped to study nursing, but financial difficulties, exacerbated by the onslaught of the Great Depression, forced her to take up her old trade of laundress.

Meanwhile, Jackson became active in the Greater Salem Baptist Church choir in Chicago. During her New Orleans youth her strong, soulful singing of gospel songs in church had attracted local attention. Now, in the larger, more middle-class black neighborhoods of Chicago, she gained a wider audience. Although some black churches were reluctant at first to accept her expressive singing style, Jackson became much in demand as a soloist.

Jackson became an admirer of black activist Marcus Garvey, who came to Chicago during the Depression to lead protests against mistreatment of blacks by landlords. She later recalled, "They said he was a red and a dangerous crackpot—and maybe he was, but he kept a lot of people from losing their homes in those days when there was no one else to turn to." Her observations of Garvey's work and her own experiences of poverty and prejudice against blacks would make it easy for her to embrace the civil rights movement of the 1950's and 1960's.

A turning point in her singing career came in 1929 when she formed the Johnson Gospel Singers, which performed in Chicago as well as elsewhere in Illinois and in Indiana. Singing with the Johnsons increased Jackson's professional exposure and gave her confidence to go solo outside the limited venue of Chicago's black neighborhoods. Her solo career progressed more slowly. She was forced to work in a factory and as a hotel maid to make ends meet. Her first husband, Isaac Hockenhull, whom she married in 1936, encouraged her to look beyond gospel music. He insisted that she take voice lessons and sing classical music. Hockenhull's attempt to manipulate his wife's career, plus his gambling habits, led to divorce in 1941.

Others tried to convince Jackson to add blues to her repertoire. She refused, commenting, "I'll never give up gospel songs for the blues. Blues are the songs of despair, but gospel songs are the songs of hope."

In 1937 Jackson jazzed up her first name by adding an "i," increased her touring and, by the end of the decade, was finally making her living by singing gospel songs. She performed at tent revivals, in store-front churches, and in ballrooms. She increased her popularity by often greeting fans and selling tickets herself. Her career got a boost in 1939 when she toured with Thomas A. Dorsey, writer of such gospel classics as "Precious Lord" and "Peace in the Valley." Also in 1939 she invested her earnings in "Mahalia's Beauty Salon" and "Mahalia's House of Flowers," businesses located in Chicago that soon thrived.

During World War II Jackson continued to tour, but she also accepted a position as choir director of Chicago's St. Luke's Baptist Church. The biggest breaks in her career came after the war. First she debuted in New York City's Golden Gate Ballroom. Then she cut a record on the Apollo label, *I'm Gonna Tell God All About It One of These Days*, that received enough air play to expose her voice to a much wider audience. Her recording breakthrough came with the release of *Move On Up a Little Higher* in 1947, a hit all across the country, ultimately selling a million copies. *Move On Up* opened the door for Mahalia Jackson to national and international audiences.

Jackson had to hire a manager to handle the many offers to perform. She made another important move when she hired Mildred Falls as her pianist. For the remainder of Jackson's career Falls was usually her only instrumental accompanist on stage.

Jackson continued to record for Apollo until 1954. Some of her more successful songs included "Even Me," "Dig a Little Deeper," "Silent Night," "How I Got Over," and "In the Upper Room." Her 1950 recording of *I Can Put My Trust in Jesus* won a French Academy Award, ironically for the best jazz record of the year.

The year 1950 proved to be especially big for Jackson. On October 1 she appeared at Carnegie Hall, thrilling her listeners with renditions of "Amazing Grace" and other gospel favorites. Her Carnegie Hall triumph led to an appearance at a jazz symposium in Massachusetts and an invitation to be official soloist for the National Baptist Convention.

In 1952 Jackson embarked on the first of many spectacularly successful tours of Europe. Adoring fans mobbed her at every stop. In the midst of her success, however, she became severely ill. Arriving home in Chicago, she was diagnosed as having cancer. Despite successful surgery, Jackson continued to have health problems for the remainder of her life.

After a lengthy recovery, Jackson resumed singing, first in local Chicago churches and then to a large crowd at Chicago Stadium. Next came appearances on Ed Sullivan's popular television show and a deal with Columbia, a recording industry giant. In 1954 Jackson hosted her own CBS radio show and in 1955 a television show, but both were broadcast only in Chicago: CBS refused to air her television show nationally because of feared hostile southern white reaction.

Jackson experienced racial barriers both in the North and in the South. In 1956 she was threatened with violence after purchasing a home in a white Chicago neighborhood, Chatham Village, and shots were fired into her house while she was away on tour. Between singing engagements in the South, Jackson frequently had to sleep in a car because blacks were barred from most hotels.

These experiences occurred in the milieu of the 1954 U.S. Supreme Court decision outlawing separate but equal schools, the 1955 Montgomery bus boycott, and the 1957 integration riot at Central High School in Little Rock, Ark. During this period two young black leaders, Martin Luther King, Jr., and Ralph David Abernathy, began to make their mark on the growing civil rights movement. Jackson met both men at the National Baptist Convention in 1956. She agreed to their request to come to Montgomery to raise money for the ongoing legal battles there.

Long a political activist, Jackson supported Harry Truman in 1948, sang at the White House in March 1956 for President Dwight D. Eisenhower, and performed at the 1956 Democratic National Convention in Chicago. In 1960 she supported John Kennedy and later sang at his inaugural party.

After meeting King and Abernathy, Jackson channeled her political energy into the civil rights movement. She sang in Montgomery in 1955, departing two days before a bomb wrecked the bedroom in Abernathy's home where she had been staying. She also performed benefit concerts at numerous locations to help King and his newly organized Southern Christian Leadership Conference.

A highlight of Jackson's career came on Aug. 28, 1963, when she participated in King's March on Washington. During the climactic program at the Lincoln Memorial she sang, at King's request, a memorable rendition of "I Been 'Buked and I Been Scorned." Jackson later recalled, "I sensed I had reached out and struck a chord."

Five years later a shaken Jackson sang at Martin Luther King's funeral. The assassination of King accented a decade of violence in which John F. Kennedy and Robert Kennedy were also murdered and in which many others died in racial violence across the South and in northern cities and during protests against the Vietnam War. Aside from straining her health with a continuously heavy schedule of personal appearances, Jackson underwent the stress of a second divorce in 1967, this time from Sigmund ("Minters") Galloway, a building contractor and musician whom she had married in 1964.

In the last few years of her life Jackson set up the Mahalia Jackson Foundation to support black education. Her appeal and popularity remained strong, and despite lingering illness, she kept touring at home and abroad. In April 1971 she serenaded Emperor Hirohito in Japan on his seventieth birthday.

In a trip to Europe that same year, Jackson fell seriously ill and was flown home by an American military plane. She rallied for a time, but soon had a fatal setback with her ravaged heart. She died on Jan. 27, 1972, at Little Company of Mary Hospital in Chicago. She is buried in New Orleans.

During her career Jackson brought her brand of gospel music into the forefront of American culture. She used her popularity to make forceful statements on behalf of black civil rights. Despite her political activism, and perhaps because of it, she had millions of fans around the world. As her friend Harry Belafonte noted in his eulogy, Jackson was "the single most powerful black woman in the United States."

[Mahalia Jackson wrote an autobiography (with Evan McLeod Wylie), *Movin' On Up* (1966). Jules Schwerin, *Got to Tell It: Mahalia Jackson, Queen of Gospel* (1992), offers a scholarly analysis of Jackson's life and work. Laurraine Goreau, *Just Mahalia, Baby* (1975), is an awkwardly written, though thorough, biography; and Charles K. Wolfe, *Mahalia Jackson* (1990); and Darlene Donloe, *Mahalia Jackson: Gospel Singer* (1992) are popular biographies. Obituaries appear in the *New York Times*, and the *Chicago Tribune*, both Jan. 28, 1972.]

MICHAEL B. BALLARD

JAMES, ARTHUR HORACE (July 14, 1883– Apr. 27, 1973), governor of Pennsylvania and judge, was born in Plymouth, Pa., the only son among three children of James David James, a coal miner, and Rachel Edwards, both of whom had immigrated from Wales. He worked as a breaker boy (slate picker) and underground mine laborer during school vacations, graduated in 1901 from Plymouth High School, and in 1904 from Dickinson Law School. In 1905, he began practice in Plymouth and Wilkes-Barre. Recognized as an outstanding speaker, James entered politics as the Republican committee chairman in his legislative district. In 1919, he reversed twenty years of Democratic control in Luzerne County when he was elected district attorney. He pledged to eliminate vice, using a crusading approach he often employed throughout his career. In 1923, he was reelected by an overwhelming majority. Older politicians of the region recommended him to the Vare brothers, Republican power brokers in Philadelphia, and in 1926 he was nominated as lieutenant governor on a ticket headed by John S. Fisher. The Republicans won, and he presided over state senate sessions in 1927 and 1929. In 1932, he was elected to a ten-year term in the superior court. His wife, Ada Morris, whom he had married in 1912, became seriously ill after the election and died in 1935. Her illness and his interest in the judicial process made him rebuff suggestions that he run for governor in 1934 and 1937.

However, in 1938, after Gifford Pinchot, a former Republican governor, had announced that he would run for a third term, James entered the primary. He characterized Pinchot as a tool of John L. Lewis, head of the United Mine Workers, and used a ventriloquist's dummy to illustrate the point. After winning the Republican nomination, James made campaign appearances in a miner's cap and sang mining ballads. He pledged to end the Democrats' wasteful spending and job favoritism. A split between Democratic labor advocates and Senator Joseph Guffey's faction helped James defeat the Democratic nominee, Charles A. Jones, but more telling were the unresolved legislative and grand jury investigations into alleged corruption in the administration of the Democratic governor, George Earle. These rival inquiries remained unresolved by election day, suggesting evils far greater than the final indictments confirmed. James won decisively.

As governor, James began a retrenchment program as soon as he took office, characterizing it as "housekeeping." He fired 2,104 state employees, thereby abolishing one-sixth of the positions directly under the governor. He reduced spending for highways, although by the end of James's term the Pennsylvania Turnpike had been extended to the Ohio border. James disliked the emergency style of Earle's "Little New Deal," and many of his vetoes stated that government machinery already existed for the purpose of the measure he vetoed. He created a department of commerce to coordinate economic recovery, and encouraged voluntary cooperation to replace the New Deal's style of mandatory regulation. A "give-a-job" program was devised to persuade private employers to expand their work force. Because the general assembly would not act to halt bootleg anthracite mining, James brought about the nongovernmental Anthracite Emergency Program, which convinced some mine operators to resume production voluntarily.

James insisted that the New Deal perpetuated Democratic patronage and favoritism. Despite the impact of retrenchment and the growth of defense-related employment, he had to call a special legislative session in 1940 to supplement

relief funds. Several times he persuaded the federal government to increase Works Progress Administration activities in the state, arguing that they should be awarded on a fair-share basis. By the end of his term the $71 million deficit inherited from Earle had been eliminated, the budget balanced, and a surplus created; but his goal of tax reduction was never achieved. In fact, the Earle administration's emergency taxes were perpetuated and passed on to subsequent administrations.

James continually criticized Democratic political methods. In May 1940, he advocated that Congress remain in session to prevent President Roosevelt from personally committing the nation to war. At the Republican convention in Philadelphia he was a presidential nominee on the first five ballots. He pleaded for the Pennsylvania delegation's support for one more ballot, reasoning that Wendell L. Willkie's Democratic origins would eliminate him, but Jay Cooke of Philadelphia and a national committeewoman, Mrs. Worthington Scranton, swung to Willkie. At the roll call the votes of the entire delegation were cast for Willkie.

James insisted that Pennsylvania's selective-service machinery, one of the nation's first and most efficient, be nonpartisan. The State Council of Defense, created in May 1941, controlled air raid defense, scrap metal collection, recycling of paper and fats, and child-care centers. James sought to have factory buildings that had been closed during the Great Depression considered as sites for defense industry.

James's son, Arthur, Jr., died of appendicitis in 1939. His daughter, Dorothy, served as hostess of the executive mansion until October 1941, when James married Emily Radcliffe Case, the widow of a longtime friend, Dr. Claude Case. James's often-voiced dissatisfaction with the antiquated governor's mansion convinced the state general assembly to authorize plans for a new mansion in 1941, but funding remained unavailable for many years.

James established a reputation for listening to and being concerned with average citizens—for instance, he sheltered protest marchers in Harrisburg's State Farm Show Building and found food for them. While criticizing New Deal methods, he nevertheless stated that no truly destitute person would be cut from relief rolls. He strengthened workers' compensation procedures, and seventy-five thousand more workers became eligible for coverage during his administration; occupational disease laws and mine safety also were improved. Despite his coal mining background, James considered labor organizations dangerous. He sought to give employers legal powers matching those of the unions, an attitude that labor advocates labeled reactionary. His amended Labor Relations Act of 1939 gave employers the right to start a Labor Relations Board investigation, revived the legality of injunctions, impeded dues deductions and closed shop status, and made sit-down strikes illegal. In 1942, he vetoed legislation that would have granted the Labor Relations Board litigant status.

In the 1941 legislative session James vetoed many spending measures, stating various reasons (although his original pledge of retrenchment lay behind his objections). Several measures involving public health were involved. James also rebuffed legislative measures under which state funds would have been used for the obligations of local government. He protected police power on the highways by vetoing an amended traffic code requiring speed patrol cars to be white and softening grounds for suspension of drivers' licenses. He prevented the sale of wine except in the state liquor stores.

In 1942, James called an extraordinary legislative session authorized to act only on seventeen subjects that he enumerated, but disagreements arose about the limits of the subjects. He vetoed measures that did not conform. His methods of fiscal calculation were questioned by Democrats, but he insisted they were the same as those used by his predecessor. On Sept. 16, 1942, Auditor General F. Clair Ross, the Democratic gubernatorial candidate, criticized James for impeding the war effort, for holding a treasury surplus, for thinking legalistically, and for stalling action by referring problems to committees. Ross even suggested that state Republicans had repudiated James, but the Republican nominee for governor, Edward Martin, specifically endorsed James's policies and principles. The basic pattern of the succeeding Martin administration was an extension of James's 1941 and 1942 programs. James's term ended Jan. 19, 1943.

After returning to law practice, James was named to the Superior Court in February 1944 and ran for election to a full term that November, but lost by a narrow margin in the landslide endorsement of Roosevelt's wartime policies. James was robust and engaged in outdoor activ-

ities until his later years, when he showed signs of Parkinson's disease. He died in Plymouth, Pa.

[James's papers, in the Pennsylvania State Archives in Harrisburg, include some biographical material. The Le Roy Vincent Greene Collection at the Historical Society of Pennsylvania contains important statements by James's press secretary. A file of newspaper clippings is in the Osterhout Library, Wilkes-Barre. The *Harrisburg Patriot*, Sept. 15 and 17, 1942, covers the criticisms made of his administration in the 1942 election campaign. An obituary is in *New York Times*, Apr. 28, 1973.]

LOUIS M. WADDELL

JOHNSON, ALVIN SAUNDERS (Dec. 18, 1874–June 9, 1971), educator and author, was the first son of Jens Jensen Deyrup (whose name was changed to Johnson by the immigration service when he emigrated to the United States from Denmark in 1849) and his third wife, Edel Maria Katrina Bille, also a Danish emigrant. Born in Homer, Nebr., Johnson was raised on his father's farm amid a sprawling family of eight brothers, sisters, and step-sisters. His mother, who came from a line of scholars, saw to it that he was well read by the time he entered the University of Nebraska in 1892. Although Johnson began as a premedical student, he soon changed majors and obtained both his B.A. in (1897) and M.A. (1898) in classics. Upon his graduation, Nebraska appointed him a teaching fellow in Greek. An accomplished linguist, throughout his life Johnson would read for pleasure books in their original Latin, Greek, French, German, Danish, and Norwegian.

The eruption of the Spanish-American War in 1898 interrupted his academic career; Johnson enlisted in the Second Nebraska regiment. He spent four months in service at a training camp in Georgia, where he fell ill amidst outbreaks of typhoid, dysentery, and malaria. Three of the six men in his tent died. When the war ended, he was mustered out of the army early, in time to enroll in the fall session at Columbia University. He chose economics for graduate study, though he had no background in the subject. In his autobiography, *Pioneer's Progress* (1952), he wrote with wry humor, "No question was raised as to my antecedent scholarly preparation." Though he survived on hardtack and tutoring stipends, Johnson made his mark with Columbia's excellent faculty, of which Edwin Seligman, John Burgess, Franz Boaz, Franklin Giddings, and

John Bates Clark—whom he idolized—were members. When he passed his doctoral examination in the spring of 1901 he was recommended for the post of reader at Bryn Mawr College, a job that allowed him sufficient time to complete his dissertation. In 1902 he was awarded his Ph.D.

At the end of his first year, Bryn Mawr offered him a promotion, but Johnson accepted a lower-ranking position to return to Columbia. In the ensuing four years there, in addition to his teaching duties, he served as assistant editor of the *Political Science Quarterly* from 1902 to 1906; assisted historian Charles A. Beard with his semiannual report, "Record of Political Events"; edited doctoral dissertations; and was a staff member for Dodd, Mead, and Company's *New International Encyclopaedia*.

He managed to fit courtship into his busy schedule. On Apr. 18, 1904, Johnson married Edith Henry, who held an advanced degree in philosophy. They had seven children, all educated at home. Johnson later wrote of his wife, "I speculate on the place in philosophy Edith would have achieved if she had not turned aside to rear and educate our seven children, all of whom she brought up to college entrance without a single day of school."

Being something of a maverick, Johnson at times clashed with his mentor, J. B. Clark. The latter criticized his article, "The Effect of Labor-Saving Devices Upon Wages," published in the *Quarterly Journal of Economics* (Nov. 1905) as giving aid and comfort to the socialists; perhaps it did.

Johnson's early revolutionary agenda called for government regulation of railroad rates, abolition of trusts, abolition of the sweatshop, a graduated income tax, pensions for the aged and disabled, bank deposit guarantees, and federal public works during economic depression—a program that could be traced to his rural upbringing, when he had read the leaflets of the Farmer's Alliance.

After Columbia, Johnson's highly successful teaching career led him from instructor to full professor at the following universities: Nebraska, Texas, Chicago, Stanford (twice), and Cornell. In 1917 he left academia temporarily for publishing, becoming associate editor of the *New Republic*, where he remained until 1923. He founded the New School's *Social Research* and edited the periodical for almost ten years.

Of all his publishing work, the *Encyclopedia of the Social Sciences* remains the lasting testimonial to his abilities. From 1928 to 1934 he served as chief working editor under Edwin Seligman, his former teacher and colleague at Columbia. Johnson planned the volumes, chose the contributors, recruited and trained the staff, and read, revised, and edited all submissions. Of this venture, published in 1935, it has been said that since Diderot's in the eighteenth century, no encyclopedia generated more excitement or had more influence on the social sciences. Though Johnson lamented that his output was modest, it was by objective standards phenomenal. He wrote some 1,000 articles, three works of fiction, and two works of nonfiction in addition to his editing tasks.

In the meantime, Johnson returned to the academic fold, finding his niche in the unorthodox New School for Social Research. The institution, founded in 1919 by such innovative thinkers as philosopher John Dewey and economist Thorstein Veblen, was designed to break the mold of adult education, which the founders deemed too formalistic.

Between 1930 and 1931 the New School constructed its unique and controversial building at 66 West Twelfth Street in New York City. The structure, designed by Joseph Urban and containing frescoes contributed by Jose Clement Orozco and Thomas Hart Benton, was something of an experiment. So too was the curriculum. The school pioneered courses in comparative music, modern painting and dance, public housing, and psychoanalysis.

In 1933 Johnson invited scholars dismissed from their posts in Germany and Italy and later from countries overrun by the Germans to become a "University in Exile" at the New School. Among the first twelve to accept were psychologist Max Wertheimer, economist Emil Lederer, finance expert Gerhard Colm, and labor economist Frieda Wunderlich. In 1941 this faculty was empowered to grant advanced degrees. French and Belgian scholars, similarly rescued, created the École Libre des Hautes Études in 1942 as part of the school. Displaced artists were also welcomed. In all, nearly two hundred scholars of repute were rescued through Johnson's efforts, with the help of the Rockefeller and other foundations. For these humanitarian efforts, Johnson was honored during his lifetime by the governments of Germany, Denmark, Belgium, and France.

The New School's by-laws contain a singular

bill of rights for the faculty, which includes a statement that a faculty member cannot be a member of any organization that "asserts the right to dictate in matters of science or scientific opinion." By taking a stand against propaganda by the political right or left, the faculty bill of rights reflected Johnson's lifelong commitment to academic freedom. He battled infringements on freedom in the political arena as well, as a member of the New York State Commission against Discrimination in Employment. During World War II, the commission sought equal opportunities for blacks and other minorities in the state's labor-short war industries. Its work culminated in 1945 in the passage of the first antidiscrimination law in the United States.

After retirement, Johnson characteristically kept busy, writing articles for scholarly journals and creating programs for retired professionals at the New School. He died in his family home in Upper Nyack, N.Y.

[Additional works by Johnson were *The Professor and the Petticoat* (1914); *John Stuyvesant Ancestor and Other Sketches* (1917); *Deliver Us from Dogma* (1934); *Spring Storm* (1936); *The Public Library—A People's University* (1938); *The Clock of History* (1946); and *A Touch of Color and Other Tales* (1961). On his life and work, see Max Lerner, "Title," *New School Bulletin*, Nov. 14, 1949; Benjamin Fine, "Title," *New York Times*, Dec. 18, 1949; "The Green Thumb," *Time*, Sept. 29, 1952; and Maxine Greene, "Learning for Those Deeply Involved in Life," *Saturday Review of Literature*, Jan. 2, 1960. Johnson's autobiography is rich in anecdotal information but shy on dates. An obituary appears in the *New York Times*, June 9, 1971.]

HAROLD L. WATTEL

JOHNSON, HOWARD DEERING (1896– June 20, 1972), entrepreneur, was born in Boston, Mass. He left elementary school to work in his father's cigar store and import business. He was a soldier in the American Expeditionary Force in France in World War I. His father died soon after Johnson returned to the United States and left him the business, which was heavily in debt. He continued to operate the establishment for three years, but sold it in 1924 after paying off the debts. He used the proceeds from the sale to purchase a run-down drugstore and soda fountain in Wollaston, Mass. (now part of Quincy).

During his time in the cigar business, Johnson had concentrated on sales. He traveled throughout eastern Massachusetts delivering the products. His father insisted that all aspects of the retail and the wholesale business should be carried on without the need for paper or files, utilizing only the brain of the delivery agent. Howard Johnson continued this approach in his own enterprises. He never employed a secretary or a personal office staff, relying entirely on his memory and instincts to coordinate his work. He turned the derelict store in Wollaston into a successful business, and he soon employed seventy-five boys to deliver and sell newspapers in the area. The lunch counter was also turned into a money-maker. During summers, Johnson sold food and ice cream at the beaches at Wollaston and Nantasket.

Johnson loved ice cream. He especially enjoyed one particular kind of ice cream, and he eventually purchased the recipe for $300 from the German immigrant who had perfected it. Using the recipe he began to make ice cream and to sell it in his retail outlets. The ice cream was immediately successful in his store, and he became well known in the local community for the confection. The secret of the ice cream was the use of more butterfat and natural flavors. Soon his ice cream was in great demand throughout the year in the area of Boston where the store was located. Eventually Johnson created twenty-eight flavors, which he claimed would always be available in any Howard Johnson restaurant. He was well known for maintaining strict quality control in his establishments.

In 1928 a local restaurant owner who purchased his ice cream supply from Johnson's drugstore asked him if he could use the Howard Johnson name for his restaurant. Johnson negotiated a contract with the restaurant proprietor to become the exclusive supply agent for the restaurant's food. That year he grossed a quarter million dollars.

The new restaurant was sheathed with clapboards and painted in distinctive colors, blue and orange. Soon, Johnson was selling franchises for his restaurants. The colors, the clapboards, and the cupola became landmarks for other Howard Johnson establishments. Selling plain, wholesome, simple food, the chain expanded rapidly in the eastern part of the United States. Johnson trained the managers of his restaurants himself. Amenities such as high chairs for infants were a feature of his establishments. Travelers who entered a Howard Johnson restaurant knew exactly what awaited them. As Americans began to use cars for extensive travel, they welcomed the familiarity of the chain.

The first Howard Johnson restaurant in New York was opened in New Rochelle in 1938. His restaurant at the New York City World's Fair in Flushing, Queens, gave his products good visibility, and by 1940, 140 Howard Johnson restaurants covered much of New England, New York, New Jersey, and Florida.

Gasoline rationing and reduced travel during the war created a problem for businesses that depended on travel, but the Howard Johnson firm survived by manufacturing candy and confections for the armed services and catering in war production plants. The chain grew rapidly once the war was over, adding new restaurants at the rate of twenty-five per year for the next decade. The firm also developed motor hotels connected with the restaurants. The motor lodges also offered good service and cleanliness, and they were an immediate success. By 1965 the chain encompassed 770 restaurants and 265 motor lodges.

The Howard Johnson company also developed a higher-priced network of restaurants and motor lodges called Red Coach Grills. Howard Johnson was able to obtain many exclusive locations for his restaurants on the growing network of limited-access highways that began to cross the country in the 1950's. By 1959, when the founder retired, the Howard Johnson firm was the third-largest distributor of food in the United States, exceeded only by the United States Army and the United States Navy.

Johnson continued to be very active in the affairs of the company, acting as advance scout in determining new locations for franchises. He also continued to monitor his restaurants for cleanliness and proper food preparation, often showing up for an unannounced inspection. He was married to Bernice Manley. Their son, Howard B. Johnson, became president and chief executive officer of the firm when his father retired. Howard D. Johnson died in New York City.

[An obituary is in the *New York Times*, June 21, 1972.]

DAVID SMITH

JOHNSON, LYNDON BAINES (Aug. 27, 1908–Jan. 22, 1973), thirty-sixth president of the United States, was born near Stonewall,

Tex., the son of Samuel Ealy Johnson, a businessman and state legislator, and Rebekah Baines. In 1913 the family left its country farm and moved to Johnson City. These were prosperous years for Sam Johnson, who dealt heavily in local real estate before resuming a career in the state legislature in 1918.

Johnson grew up amid conflicting pressures from his parents and financial instability, which fostered a striving to succeed and a pervasive personal insecurity. Sam Johnson often took his son with him to Austin to see state government at work, but when his economic fortunes declined during the 1920's, he drank heavily and took out his frustrations on his oldest child. The abrupt swings from prosperity to hard times in the family finances convinced Lyndon that he could never have enough money to avoid the sudden losses that his father encountered.

Johnson attended local schools and graduated from Johnson City High School in 1924. For three years he drifted through odd jobs, until he decided in the winter of 1927 to enter Southwest Texas State Teachers College in San Marcos. His academic record during the three and a half years that followed was undistinguished, but his college experience was important in other ways. He published editorials in the campus newspaper, some of them ghostwritten by his mother, and participated in campus politics, where his rough tactics foreshadowed techniques he would later use in Congress and the presidency. He also conciliated his defeated foes in a way that demonstrated his penchant for consensus and compromise.

The most significant episode of Johnson's college career occurred during 1928 and 1929. In order to earn money, he taught at a small school in the Rio Grande Valley town of Cotulla. His students were disadvantaged Hispanics. The poverty he saw made a deep impression on him. It was there that he gained a lifelong faith in the power of education to transform the lives of those on the fringes of American society. At about this time he decided that politics would be his profession.

After graduation from college in the summer of 1930, Johnson taught school in Houston and coached a debate team. Participation in political campaigns in central Texas brought him to the notice of several local leaders. Those connections led to his appointment as the legislative assistant to newly elected Congressman Richard Kleberg of the Fourteenth District.

Johnson arrived in Washington, D.C., in December 1931.

During four years as Kleberg's aide in the early days of the New Deal, Johnson received an intensive education in Washington's customs and procedures and came to believe that government could improve the lives of all citizens. He also learned about the importance of winning elections. In the spring of 1933, he became Speaker of the Little Congress, an organization of legislative aides.

Late in the summer of 1934, Johnson met Claudia Alta ("Lady Bird") Taylor, a recent graduate of the University of Texas and the daughter of a prosperous eastern Texas landowner and merchant. Lyndon proposed on their first date and began an intense courtship. He persuaded her to marry him in San Antonio on Nov. 17, 1934. Lady Bird Johnson proved to be an ideal wife for him. Although their marriage experienced strain, it endured, and they were effective political partners. They had two children.

Johnson was appointed Texas state director of the National Youth Administration (NYA) in August 1935. For eighteen months, he threw his energies into programs aimed at sustaining young Texans through the Depression. To put people to work, he initiated a system of roadside parks that became a permanent feature of the state's landscape. With less fanfare, Johnson also extended aid to African-American college students at the state's black colleges. He did not challenge the segregated system that dominated Texas, but he did demonstrate a willingness to help blacks which gained him enduring support in the African-American community. Johnson's record with the NYA won him praise in Washington as well.

In February 1937, Congressman James Buchanan of the Tenth Texas District died. Johnson became a candidate in the special election held in April. Virtually unknown in the district, he identified himself publicly with Franklin D. Roosevelt and the president's plan to enlarge the membership of the Supreme Court. His campaign was funded with contributions from his wife's father and from her mother's estate as well as money from local businessmen. Canvasing the district with tireless energy, Johnson faced eight opponents in a race that a simple plurality decided. He won 28 percent of the vote and the election.

During his first four years in Congress,

Johnson was an effective advocate for his district. Among other appropriations, he obtained funding for a series of dams on the Colorado River. His voting record supported the policies of President Roosevelt, and he became a close ally of House Speaker Sam Rayburn. When the Democrats faced the possible loss of the House during the election of 1940, Johnson chaired the Democratic Congressional Campaign Committee. The money he raised from Texas oil interests helped the party to maintain its majority. Throughout this period, Johnson worked to establish close ties with wealthy Texans.

After the death of Morris Sheppard in 1941, Johnson entered a special senatorial election as a supporter of Roosevelt. Fueled with funds from affluent contributors, he made a strong campaign but lost to the popular governor of the state, W. Lee ("Pappy") O'Daniel. Leading in early returns, Johnson watched his margin slip away when the O'Daniel forces had election judges in East Texas add votes to the governor's total. Challenging the result in the courts would have pitted Johnson against the Democratic party power structure. Johnson resolved not to allow a similar process to defeat him in the future.

On the outbreak of World War II in Europe, Johnson voiced support for Roosevelt's policies of aiding the Allies. Behind the scenes he also helped Jews and other refugees from Nazi Germany gain entrance into the United States. The events of this period made a great impression on Johnson, who believed that the Western democracies had not acted soon enough to stop aggression. Campaigning in 1941, he told Texas voters that if war came, he would join the military. After Pearl Harbor, he entered the navy as a lieutenant commander. During the first half of 1942, he inspected facilities on the West Coast and then made a tour of the South Pacific. He went on a single combat mission as an observer, during which Japanese planes attacked and crippled the plane he was flying on. After this incident, General Douglas MacArthur awarded him the Silver Star. Johnson wore the decoration proudly, but opponents called the medal a reward for his political position rather than his valor. He left active duty and returned to Washington when the president ordered members of Congress to stay at their jobs.

In 1943 the Johnsons purchased a radio station in Austin with money that Mrs. Johnson provided. Lady Bird oversaw the daily operations of the station; Johnson used his influence to ensure that the revenues from advertisements expanded. It was the start of a media empire that grew substantially during the postwar period. As his political power developed, his personal finances prospered. By the time he reached the United States Senate in 1949 he was a wealthy man.

The road to the Senate was not easy for Johnson. Texas became more conservative during the 1940's, and Johnson moved rightward with his constituents. He supported segregation, opposed repeal of the poll tax, and voted against laws to secure fair treatment of African Americans in seeking jobs. Despite this shift, he endorsed Roosevelt in 1944 and fought the "Texas Regulars," a conservative, often racist faction of the Democrats who opposed the president. Conservatives sponsored opponents against him in the 1944 and 1946 primaries. The race in 1946 against Hardy Holler was particularly bruising, and the charges of personal enrichment that began during that contest dogged Johnson thereafter.

An opportunity to gain a Senate seat came in 1948, when Pappy O'Daniel retired. Johnson's major opposition was popular former governor Coke Stevenson. A friend of the Texas Regulars and strong supporter of segregation, Stevenson campaigned in the old style of leisurely visits to small towns. Johnson innovatively used a helicopter tour to overcome his lack of statewide name recognition. The first round of the primaries left Stevenson only slightly ahead of Johnson, and the two faced a runoff for the Democratic nomination in late August.

The voting produced a very close contest. In a counting process that led to frequent lead changes, Johnson finally earned an eighty-seven-vote margin based on the returns from several southern Texas counties, where large leads for Johnson came in very late. Stevenson and his partisans charged that agents of Johnson in several counties in the Rio Grande Valley had created fraudulent vote totals for their candidate. Ballot box 13 from the town of Alice in Jim Wells County produced an additional 202 votes for Johnson. Stevenson and his supporters charged then that the election returns were rigged. Biographers agree that illegal votes gave Johnson the victory, but no evidence that he knew and supervised what was being done on his behalf has been found.

Stevenson contested the election before the State Democratic Executive Committee and in the federal courts. Legal advice from an old Washington friend, Abe Fortas, and the tacit support of the administration of President Harry S. Truman helped Johnson win official endorsement as the senatorial nominee of the Texas Democratic party. He had no difficulty in defeating his Republican opponent in the general election. Johnson wryly called himself "Landslide Lyndon" for his victory. The title stuck and came to symbolize his reputation as a political wheeler-dealer who would let nothing stand in the way of his advancement. He went to the United States Senate determined to prove his ability as a leader and to establish his political legitimacy.

The Senate proved to be an ideal setting for Johnson's political style. In its clubby atmosphere, his knowledge of each member's personal frailties and strengths blended well with his talent for intimate personal contact. For the first several years of his Senate service Johnson established himself as a productive lawmaker for Texas and did little to anger his increasingly conservative constituents. As a southerner, he opposed efforts to limit filibusters against civil rights legislation. He also attacked the reappointment of Leland Olds to the Federal Power Commission, partly on the ground that Olds had Communist ties.

Johnson concentrated on moving up within the Senate hierarchy. He was elected Democratic Whip in January 1951. During these years he also acquired what became the Johnson Ranch in Stonewall and used his contacts in the broadcasting industry and the government to obtain the only very high frequency (VHF) television station in Austin. When the Truman administration and the Democratic presidential candidate, Adlai Stevenson, came out for federal control of the oil-rich tidelands off the Texas coast, many Texas Democrats bolted to Dwight D. Eisenhower in 1952. Although Johnson wanted to have the tidelands, he supported Stevenson and the Democratic ticket to preserve his own changes at future party leadership. By early 1953 he was elected minority leader of the Democrats in the Senate and was on his way to national power.

Johnson followed a bipartisan strategy in dealing with the new administration of President Dwight D. Eisenhower and stressed his willingness to cooperate with the White House in foreign policy matters during 1953 and 1954. He signaled his moderating racial views when he did not attack the Supreme Court's decision in *Brown* v. *Board of Education* in 1954, a case that set in motion racial desegregation of schools. In the spring of 1954, he easily defeated the conservative opponent in the Democratic primary in Texas.

Johnson had watched warily the rise of Senator Joseph R. McCarthy (R.-Wis), who had gained notoriety with his charges of Communist influence in the government. Careful not to make McCarthyism a partisan issue, Johnson waited until the senator overstepped himself in 1954 during nationally televised hearings about alleged Communists in the military. When resolutions of censure were introduced against McCarthy, Johnson selected moderate and conservative Democrats for the committee to hear the charges. The strategy helped produce a decisive senatorial rebuke of McCarthy that set his career on a downward path.

When the Democrats regained control of the Senate in the elections of 1954 Johnson became majority leader, a role that brought out his best legislative talents. Although he had only a two-vote majority, he mobilized the Democrats as a united force in the Senate. He was able to do this because he avoided partisanship and collaborated with the Eisenhower administration on foreign policy.

His health faltered during the summer of 1955, when he had a serious heart attack. After a long convalescence he returned to active politics at the end of the year. His ambition for the presidency had reached the point where he could think seriously about entering the race for the Democratic nomination in 1956. He defeated the conservative governor of Texas, Allan Shivers, in a contest to control the state's delegation to the national convention in the spring, but that victory did not enable him to stop party sentiment to renominate Adlai Stevenson. Johnson was still regarded as a regional candidate whose civil rights record precluded consideration for the presidency.

To address that liability, Johnson threw his influence behind an effort to write a civil rights bill in 1957. There had been no such legislation since Reconstruction. As ultimately enacted, the Civil Rights Bill of 1957 was a toothless measure that contained little of substance to disturb segregationists. Johnson, however, regarded the precedent of enacting a civil rights law over the opposition of southerners as the key

result of the struggle. Once that barrier had been broken, he reasoned, other legislation with more significance would follow.

The 1958 elections increased Democratic strength in the Senate and undercut some of Johnson's power. With a large margin over the Republicans, liberal Democrats were less willing to defer to Johnson's bipartisan strategy. Facing potential challenges to his dominance, Johnson looked to 1960 as his year to run for the presidency. Mistaking power in the Senate for national influence, he delayed announcing his candidacy and worked to achieve an impressive legislative record. Meanwhile, Senator John F. Kennedy of Massachusetts was gathering the delegates needed for the nomination. By the time Johnson announced his bid for the White House just before the Democratic convention, the nomination was in Kennedy's hands.

The day after Kennedy's nomination, July 14, 1960, he offered Johnson the vice-presidency. Aware that men in his family rarely lived past their early sixties, anxious to establish himself as a national figure, and seeing the vice-presidency as the natural next step in his career, Johnson accepted and threw himself into the presidential campaign. With his support and tireless campaigning, the Democrats achieved the narrow victory in Texas that was indispensable to Kennedy's defeat of Richard Nixon and the Republicans.

His years as vice-president were difficult for Johnson. Democratic senators rebuffed his effort to retain influence in their deliberations. Within the White House, Attorney General Robert Kennedy and other staff members treated Johnson with contempt. President Kennedy was publicly courteous toward Johnson and gave him formal duties involving the space program and civil rights. For three years, however, Johnson was relegated to the margins of the Kennedy administration.

When political problems surfaced in Texas over the affairs of a confidence man named Billie Sol Estes and when the business dealings of Johnson's former aide Robert Baker came under legal and congressional scrutiny, talk grew in Washington that Johnson might be dumped from the presidential ticket in 1964. Whether these rumors stemmed from the White House or not, they gained wide circulation during 1963. What Kennedy's intentions were toward Johnson remains unclear, but it is unlikely that the president intended to drop the man who would be vital in consolidating the South against Republican challenges. The murder of Kennedy on Nov. 22, 1963, made Johnson the president of the United States. During the years that followed Kennedy's death, conspiracy theorists sometimes charged that Johnson had taken part in a plot to kill Kennedy. The charge has never been substantiated.

In the wake of the slaying of Kennedy, Johnson's public actions reassured a shocked nation. His initial statement on November 22 and his address to a joint session of Congress on November 27, in which he invoked Kennedy's memory to push for the martyred president's legislative agenda, established Johnson's authority as chief executive. The early days of his presidency were a whirlwind of activity as Johnson reached out to every segment of society to build a consensus.

At six feet, four inches, the new president towered over most of the people around him. Perennially on the telephone, he cajoled and persuaded. In person, he pressed himself close to the object of his attention in what was known as the "Johnson Treatment." With his mastery of how Congress worked, the president set about pushing John Kennedy's legislative program on Capitol Hill.

During the first months of his presidency, Johnson's less attractive qualities received fleeting attention. Reporters noted his habit of stretching the truth and his occasional overt deceptions. His formal speeches were often flat and uninspiring. He was sarcastic and demanding to aides and employees one moment, charming and indulgent the next. Obsessed with press coverage, he tried first to seduce reporters and then to confuse them. A lifelong penchant for secrecy meant that accurate leaks of information to the press often caused the president to abandon or modify a nomination or policy initiative.

The first year in the White House was marked by a striking series of political successes. Early on, Johnson indicated that enactment of a civil rights bill would be one of his main domestic priorities. His other goal was to gain passage of a cut in income taxes, which Kennedy had also proposed. Holding the total federal budget to under $100 billion helped secure enactment of the tax-cut legislation. During these early months, Johnson also declared that his administration would wage a "war on poverty."

On civil rights, Johnson made it clear that he would accept no compromise with southern senators. The administration worked effectively with the Republican leader in the Senate, Everett Dirksen of Illinois, to fashion the Civil Rights Act of 1964 and achieve its passage in June. Johnson signed the bill into law on July 2. He recognized that the civil rights law would cost him southern support, but he believed that the measure represented justice for African Americans and would gain him greater credibility as a national leader.

Johnson expanded the nation's domestic agenda during 1964. In a speech at the University of Michigan on May 22, 1964, he called for a "Great Society" that would eliminate poverty, improve the environment, provide security for the elderly, and rebuild the nation's cities. He believed that the United States was so prosperous that it could achieve an enhanced quality of life for all citizens without having to redistribute income or ask any sector of the country for tangible sacrifice. Through these programs, Johnson hoped to establish himself as one of the greatest presidents in American history.

The Cold War with the Soviet Union defined the main foreign policy problem that the new president confronted. Johnson endorsed the basic premises of the containment policy that the nation had followed since 1947.

As vice-president, he had gone to South Vietnam in 1961 on a fact-finding mission for Kennedy. The visit persuaded Johnson that the United States should support the existing regime in South Vietnam and resist Communist actions to prevent a loss of Southeast Asia. Moreover, he wanted to honor Kennedy's commitment to the survival of South Vietnam. Soon after he took office, Johnson decided that the United States would not leave South Vietnam despite the internal weaknesses of the country. While the military prepared contingency plans for greater American involvement during 1964, Johnson emphasized to the American public his unwillingness to expand the conflict.

A serious foreign policy crisis arose in Vietnam in August 1964, when a naval encounter allegedly occurred between American vessels and North Vietnamese naval forces in the Tonkin Gulf. Johnson used the episode to obtain congressional authorization for retaliatory bombing strikes against North Vietnam. The Tonkin Gulf Resolution that Congress passed with virtual unanimity indicated that the American people were behind the administration's commitment to assist South Vietnam with limited military means when necessary. Johnson did not explain the conflicting reports about the engagement in the Tonkin Gulf, nor did he tell Congress that he regarded the resolution as an open-ended authorization to expand the war if more American forces should be needed.

Johnson's political skill in 1964 left the Republican party in some confusion about how best to defeat him. Senator Barry Goldwater of Arizona, the champion of a resurgent Republican conservatism, won the party's nomination over several more moderate rivals. Since Johnson had preempted the mainstream of national politics, Goldwater came across as a conservative extremist who would be reckless in foreign policy and destructive of accepted social programs, such as Social Security.

Johnson staved off efforts to have Robert Kennedy become his running mate. He chose instead to select the liberal leader, Senator Hubert Humphrey of Minnesota, as his vice-president. During the campaign, Johnson assured voters that he had no plans to broaden the war in Vietnam while simultaneously emphasizing that he did not intend to withdraw either. The result was a sweeping victory for Johnson. He received 61.1 percent of the popular vote; the vote in the electoral college was 486 to 52. Goldwater did carry five southern states where antipathy to the Civil Rights Act was strongest. Nationally the Democrats secured large majorities in both houses of Congress.

During the year that followed, Johnson pushed relentlessly for his Great Society programs. Congress responded with a torrent of legislation. Funding for education was increased; the most successful policy was the Head Start program for preschool students. Health insurance was provided for the elderly through the Medicare Act, which along with the parallel Medicaid program, expanded medical services for an entire segment of the population. Housing, immigration, and poverty were also targeted for congressional action. Johnson's war on poverty was waged through such agencies as the Office of Economic Opportunity, which directed more funding to the poor of the nation via such programs as the job corps, community action programs, and neighborhood youth corps. The president also secured passage of more than three hundred pieces of conservation legislation, while his wife launched a beautifi-

cation program to improve the appearance of the nation's cities and highways.

The agitation for civil rights had not ended with the enactment of the 1964 law. Demonstrations for changes in voting regulations were led by Martin Luther King, Jr., in the South. Johnson threw his endorsement behind a voting rights law in a passionate speech to Congress on Mar. 15, 1965, and for an even greater commitment to African Americans in an address at Howard University in June. The result was the Voting Rights Act of 1965, which outlawed such restrictions on voting as literacy tests and provided for federal supervision of elections in the South. Participation by blacks in southern politics grew in the years that followed. The Democratic party, however, faced a loss of white voters in the South.

Johnson had pushed vigorously for his Great Society in 1965 because he knew that his mandate would not last long. By the end of the year, a resurgence of conservatism had taken place. Urban riots in such cities as Los Angeles reduced white support for African-American causes. The war on poverty seemed to threaten the existing power structure in large cities. Congress proved less hospitable to administration programs, such as home rule for the District of Columbia and greater power for labor unions. Beyond these domestic issues, there was the spreading discontent with the course of the war in South Vietnam.

Foreign policy problems had plagued the president from the beginning of 1965. When the United States used military intervention in the Dominican Republic to forestall what the White House claimed would be the installation of a pro-Communist government, critics in Congress charged that Johnson had overreacted.

The most serious crisis, however, was in Vietnam. Following the American presidential election, the South Vietnamese government had come under increasing military pressure from the Communists in the South and their North Vietnamese sponsors. To counter a likely collapse of the Saigon regime, the Johnson administration decided that bombing strikes in the North were necessary to stop the flow of supplies to the North Vietnamese troops in the South and to produce negotiations. Expanded use of ground troops to protect air bases followed during the spring of 1965. When these measures did not bring the enemy to the bargaining table, Johnson authorized more bombing and authorized an offensive strategy for American soldiers on the ground in South Vietnam. In a speech to the nation on July 28, he said that an Asia threatened "by Communist domination would imperil the security of the United States itself. . . ."

Johnson's strategy of gradually intensifying the military pressure on North Vietnam continued for the next two and a half years. Critics on the right charged at the time and for years afterward that a greater military effort would have won the war. They also alleged that Johnson interfered with the military conduct of the fighting. Mindful of the dangers of Chinese and Soviet intervention, Johnson was reluctant to give the military free rein to wage an all-out war on North Vietnam. Protesters on the left during the 1960's and since have said that the step-by-step escalation that Johnson pursued was a brutal and cruel intervention into what was an internal struggle of the Vietnamese people.

The problem for Johnson during his presidency was that he could neither achieve victory in the short run nor persuade the American people to endure a prolonged war. His failings as a political leader became apparent as the war continued. His obsession with secrecy led him into deceptions that undermined the confidence of his constituents. He proved incapable of providing a convincing rationale for the war in his public statements or television appearances.

Johnson's political base eroded during 1966 and 1967. Student protests against the war intensified, as did urban rioting. A general sense spread that the Johnson administration was too indulgent toward lawbreakers and criminals. These feelings had strong racial overtones on which the Republican party capitalized. Complicating Johnson's problems, the popularity in the South of Alabama governor George C. Wallace rose in response to his attacks on the White House for its encouragement of integration in the schools and expanded opportunities for African Americans.

In the 1966 elections, the Republicans, with former vice-president Richard M. Nixon as their prominent spokesman, made substantial advances at the expense of the Democrats. The GOP gained forty-seven seats in the House of Representatives and three in the Senate. Internal friction within the Democratic party led to talk of a challenge against Johnson in 1968. Under Johnson the financial and organizational structure of the Democrats had been severely weakened.

Despite his political difficulties, Johnson made strides in certain areas in 1967. During the summer he conducted a summit with Soviet leader Aleksey Kosygin at Glassboro State College in New Jersey, and he appointed the first African American, Thurgood Marshall, to the United States Supreme Court.

But the war in Vietnam remained the president's primary concern. Newspaper reports during late 1967 indicated that the war was stalemated in South Vietnam. The administration sought various formulas to induce the enemy to negotiate, but none worked. By the end of the year, Robert Kennedy had decided not to become a candidate for the presidency, but there was a challenger in the race, Senator Eugene McCarthy, a liberal Democrat from Minnesota.

Concerned about his health and his ability to survive another term in office, Johnson considered whether he should announce a withdrawal from politics in early 1968. He knew that a presidential campaign would be difficult for him because of the demonstrators that would confront him at every rally. He had not declared his intentions as the year began, but a campaign had been mounted on behalf of his renomination.

In late January the outbreak of the Tet Offensive in South Vietnam undermined the administration's claims that the war was being won. Although the North Vietnamese suffered a military defeat, they gained a psychological victory. A few weeks later, McCarthy ran a close second to Johnson in the New Hampshire primary. It was a significant political setback for an incumbent president. A few days later, Robert Kennedy entered the race for the Democratic nomination.

Faced with requests from the military to expand the American commitment to South Vietnam, Johnson called senior advisers to the White House to reappraise the situation. Their judgment was that the war could not be won without sacrifices that the American people would not support. The president prepared a speech for delivery to a nationwide audience on Mar. 31, 1968, in which he announced a reduction in the bombing campaign and a renewed call for negotiations. At the end of the televised address, he told a stunned nation, "I shall not seek, and I will not accept the nomination of my party for another term as your president." The decision arose from personal considerations about his health, a conviction that he could not achieve peace as an active candidate, and an awareness that his political base had collapsed.

Withdrawal from presidential politics did not end Johnson's problems as president. The assassination of Martin Luther King, Jr., on April 4 triggered urban riots in Washington, D.C., and elsewhere. Johnson took the occasion to persuade Congress to pass the Fair Housing Act of 1968. The murder of Senator Robert Kennedy two months later ensured the Democratic nomination for Humphrey. Johnson had serious reservations about Humphrey's ability to be president and about his commitment to administration policies on Vietnam. As a result, Johnson sometimes hinted that he would prefer to see Richard Nixon, the Republican nominee, win the 1968 race. Wallace ran as a third-party candidate in the contest.

In October, the negotiations with the North Vietnamese, begun after Johnson's withdrawal from the presidential race, produced the possibility of a breakthrough that might lead to serious peace discussions. Johnson was prepared to declare an end to American bombing in Vietnam in return for talks with Hanoi. With the election just days in the future, the South Vietnamese government, hoping to see Nixon victorious and pushed by operatives for the Republican candidate through illegal back-channel negotiations, declined to come to the peace negotiations. The announcement of the bombing halt helped Humphrey, whom Johnson now favored; the unwillingness of Saigon to take part in talks tipped the electoral balance toward Nixon and the Republicans. Humphrey lost a close election to his Republican rival.

Johnson retired to his ranch in January 1969 and worked on his memoirs. They were published as *The Vantage Point* (1971) and provide an official record of Johnson's political decisions. He died in San Antonio.

Lyndon Johnson was one of the most important political figures in the United States during the twentieth century. More than any other president, he identified his administration with the aspirations of African Americans. He also used his liberal nationalism in domestic affairs to conduct a wide-ranging campaign to improve the lives of Americans, particularly the disadvantaged minorities. While those programs brought tangible gains for society, they also provided a conservative response that repudiated Johnson's liberalism throughout the succeeding three decades. The Great Society represented the high point of a Democratic liberalism that went back to Franklin D. Roosevelt and Woodrow Wilson.

In foreign policy, Johnson will always be associated with the Vietnam War. Although he continued the foreign policy of three previous presidents, the manner in which he escalated the war in 1965 and fought the war until 1968 led to an unprecedented degree of social turmoil within the United States. The result was a questioning of the premises of the policy of containing the Soviet Union and a retreat from the global military and political involvements that had arisen from it.

Johnson passionately wanted to be a great president. To attain that goal, he acted in ways that were often crude and frequently unethical. In a few instances they verged on the illegal. Yet he could also display a streak of deep moralism and compassion for the unfortunate. He told friends that he hoped to outdo Abraham Lincoln as a racial emancipator and Franklin D. Roosevelt as an architect of the welfare state. The war in Vietnam and the social turmoil that marked the 1960's will keep Johnson out of the first rank of presidents. But because of the complexities of his character and the issues that his presidency confronted, he will continue to be one of the most written about and studied of all chief executives.

[Lyndon Johnson's personal papers about his public career are housed at the Lyndon Baines Johnson Library in Austin, Tex. Records relating to his health and finances are not open for inspection as of this writing. The papers of Lady Bird Johnson are also unavailable to researchers at this time. Other records relating to Johnson can be found at the Franklin D. Roosevelt Library, the Harry S. Truman Library, the Dwight D. Eisenhower Library, the John F. Kennedy Library, and the Richard Nixon Presidential Papers Project. The public records of Blanco, Gillespie, Hays, and Travis Counties in Texas contain valuable information on Johnson and his family. Most of Johnson's memoirs, speeches, and public statements were ghost-written. Public statements appear in *Public Papers of the Presidents of the United States* (1964–1969); *A Time for Action* (1964); *My Hope for America* (1964); and *The Choices We Face* (1969).

A number of biographies cover Johnson's early life and rise to the presidency, among them, Alfred Steinberg, *Sam Johnson's Boy* (1968); Doris Kearns Goodwin, *Lyndon Johnson and the American Dream* (1976); Ronnie Dugger, *The Politician* (1982); Robert

Caro, *The Years of Lyndon Johnson* (2 vols., 1982 and 1990); Paul Conkin, *Big Daddy from the Pedernales* (1986); and Robert Dallek, *Lone Star Rising* (1991).

Among the most useful memoirs by members of the Johnson family are Rebekah Baines Johnson, *A Family Album* (1965); Sam Houston Johnson, *My Brother, Lyndon* (1970); and Lady Bird Johnson, *A White House Diary* (1970), the best single source on the Johnson marriage and his personality. For memoirs by members of his administration, see Eric F. Goldman, *The Tragedy of Lyndon Johnson* (1969); Harry McPherson, *A Political Education* (1972); Walt W. Rostow, *The Diffusion of Power* (1972); Jack Valenti, *A Very Human President* (1975); George Ball, *The Past Has Another Pattern* (1982); Richard N. Goodwin, *Remembering America* (1988); Dean Rusk, *As I Saw It* (1990); Clark Clifford, *Counsel to the President* (1991); Joseph Califano, *The Triumph and Tragedy of Lyndon Johnson* (1991). Other biographies that contain important information on Johnson are Arthur Schlesinger, *Robert Kennedy and His Times* (1978); Carl Solberg, *Hubert Humphrey* (1984); Laura Kalman, *Abe Fortas* (1990); and Deborah Shapley, *Promise and Power* (1992).

On the Johnson administration in general, see Vaughn Davis Bornet, *The Presidency of Lyndon B. Johnson* (1983); Robert A. Divine, ed., *The Johnson Years* (2 vols., 1987); Emmette Redford and Richard T. McCulley, *White House Operations* (1986); Harry Middletown, *LBJ* (1990), a photographic history; and John Morton Blum, *Years of Discord* (1991). For domestic policy, see James T. Patterson, *America's Struggle Against Poverty* (1981); Allen Matusow, *The Unraveling of America* (1984); Steven F. Lawson, *In Pursuit of Power* (1985); Lewis L. Gould, *Lady Bird Johnson and the Environment* (1988); Hugh Davis Graham, *The Civil Rights Era* (1990); and Nicholas Lemann, *The Promised Land* (1991).

On foreign policy, see Philip Geyelin, *Lyndon B. Johnson and the World* (1966); Abraham Lowenthal, *The Dominican Intervention* (1972); McGeorge Bundy, *Danger and Survival* (1988). For the Johnson administration and Vietnam, see Townsend Hoopes, *The Limits of Intervention* (1969); Henry Graff, *The Tuesday Cabinet* (1970); David Halberstam, *The Best and the Brightest* (1972); Herbert Schandler, *The Unmaking of a President* (1977); Larry Berman, *Lyndon Johnson's War* (1989); George C. Herring, *America's Longest War* (1986); Marilyn B. Young, *The Vietnam Wars, 1945–1990* (1991); James S. Olson and Randy Roberts, *Where the Domino Fell* (1991); and Ronald Spector, *After Tet* (1993). Two excellent bibliographies are Lyndon Baines Johnson Library, *Lyndon Johnson* (1984); and Craig H. Roell, *Lyndon Johnson* (1988). David Grubin Productions, *LBJ* (1992), is an evocative film on Johnson's life. Obituaries appear in the *New York Times*, Jan. 22 and 23, 1973.]

LEWIS L. GOULD

JONES, ROBERT TYRE, JR. (Mar. 17, 1902–Dec. 18, 1971), amateur golfer and the founder of the Augusta National Golf Course and the Masters tournament, was born in Atlanta, Ga., the second son of Robert Purmedus Jones and Clara Merrick Thomas. He was a sickly child who could eat only egg whites, pabulum, and black-eyed peas when he was three. Golf became a physical outlet and eventually an avocation for him. Jones's father, a baseball player at the University of Georgia, became a prominent attorney in Atlanta. The family's home was located on the East Lake course of the Atlanta Athletic Club, where Jones played his early golf. Jones became a nationally competitive golfer at the age of fourteen, and in the next fourteen years he proved to be the greatest golfer in the history of the game. He retired in 1930 after completing the "Grand Slam" of golf, winning the U.S. Open and Amateur and the British Open and Amateur championships in the same year.

Know as "Bobby," Jones played golf with a mismatched set of clubs, the best-known being his putter, which he named "Calamity Jane." He was strong, hitting the ball farther than most of the competition. Although he was capable of long periods of extreme proficiency, he was also beset by periods of inconsistency. His preference to remain an amateur reflected his lifetime priorities. Even while in his golfing prime, he finished his education and began a family. His persistent amateur status made his competition in the U.S. and British Open championships all the more serious, as professionals made every effort to stop the amateur. He had great success against professionals. For example, he entered eleven U.S. Open championships, winning four, finishing second in four, and finishing fifth, eighth, and eleventh in the others.

During his peak years from 1923 through his Grand Slam tour of 1930, Jones won thirteen major championships, including U.S. Open championships in 1923, 1926, 1929, and 1930; U.S. Amateur championships in 1924, 1925, 1927, 1928, and 1930; British Open championships in 1926, 1927, and 1930; and the British Amateur championship in 1930.

Between 1916 and 1930, when he played nationally competitive golf, Jones received an engineering degree from Georgia Institute of Technology, a bachelor's degree in English literature from Harvard, and a law degree from Emory University in Atlanta. He took long breaks from the game and did not practice as much as other serious golfers. On June 17, 1924, he married Mary Malone, his high school sweetheart; they had three children.

Following the 1930 Grand Slam, Jones retired to his legal practice, investments, and other business interests. He became a vice-president of A. G. Spalding and Company, a sporting goods manufacturer, designing golf clubs for them. In 1931, he worked in Hollywood, doing a series of films featuring movie stars learning how to play golf from him. He and Alister Mackenzie designed the Augusta National golf course in Augusta, Ga., which in 1934 hosted the precursor to the Masters championship, a tournament that rapidly became the premier event in golf. Jones headed his father's law firm, Jones, Bird and Howell until his death.

Jones was part of a group of illustrious athletes in the 1920's. Like Jack Dempsey in boxing, Babe Ruth in baseball, William ("Big Bill") Tilden in tennis, and Red Grange in football, Jones held a heroic stature in golf in a decade when sports were filmed and shown in movie theaters as part of newsreels. With a flair for the dramatic, a handsome face, and a sense of humor, he symbolized golf in the American psyche.

Just as his early years were marked by ill health, Jones suffered through his last years. He played his last round of golf in 1948. For the rest of his life he suffered from syringomyelia, a rare neurological disease that gradually sapped his strength, eliminated his ability to walk, and caused severe pain. For years he used a cane, braces were eventually placed on both legs, and he spent his final years confined to a wheelchair, often under sedation. He died in Atlanta.

Jones was the most famous individual in American golf in the 1920's. He was given a ticker tape parade in New York City upon his arrival from victories in England that was said to rival the reception for General John J. Pershing after World War I. His popularity resulted in an expansion of golf as a popular recreation. Municipalities and counties built and bought golf courses throughout the late 1920's and early 1930's, opening the game further to a public who followed the exploits of Bobby Jones.

[Jones wrote *Bobby Jones on Golf* (1966). On his career, see Robert Cantwell, "The Reel Life of Bobby Jones," *Sports Illustrated*, Sept. 23, 1968; Frank Hannigan, "Open and Shut Case: It's Jones," *Sports Illustrated*, June 14, 1976; and Dick Miller, *Triumphant Journey* (1980). Obituaries are in the *New York Times*, Dec. 19, 1971; and in *Newsweek*, Dec. 27, 1971.]

HARRY JEBSEN, JR.

JORDAN, BENJAMIN EVERETT (Sept. 8, 1896–Mar. 15, 1974), United States senator and textile executive, was one of six children born to the Reverend Henry Harrison Jordan, a lawyer turned Methodist minister, and Annie Elizabeth Sellers. The Reverend Jordan's ministry took him to many North Carolina towns, and at the time of his son's birth the family was living in Ramseur, N.C. For a strict Methodist household, Jordan was considered rather unruly. He dropped out of Rutherford College Preparatory School in 1913 and then out of Trinity College (later Duke University) in 1915. While he never possessed much aptitude for schooling, his love for education endured. He later helped others pursue their goals through gifts and loans and served as trustee of a number of institutions of higher learning, including American University and Duke.

Jordan went to work as a clerk in an uncle's jewelry store in Wellington, Kans., and then went into the army, serving in the Tank Corps in 1918 and 1919 and with the Army of Occupation in Germany in 1919. He returned to his uncle's store in Kansas and in about 1922 moved to Gastonia, N.C., to work in a textile mill, advancing from floor sweeper to mill hand to superintendent. On Nov. 29, 1924, Jordan married Katherine Augusta McLean; they had three children.

In 1927, another uncle and other members of his mother's family bought an abandoned cotton mill in Saxapahaw, N.C. The uncle asked Jordan to manage it and eventually saw to it that Jordan had the controlling stock. Within a decade the mill, which produced yarn, had turned a sufficient profit. The business, known as the Sellers Manufacturing Company, expanded considerably with the purchase of two other mills in North Carolina, the Jordan Spinning Company in Cedar Falls in 1939 and the Royal Cotton Mill Company in Wake Forest in 1945. Jordan was an innovator in mercerized cotton yarns and combined yarns. According to his biographer, a long-time employee, his peers regarded him as an exceptional salesman. Although his product was not of the best quality available, he was able to convince prospective buyers that it was the best available for the price. He worked closely with clients, tailoring his products to their requirements. They recognized him to be skillfull at negotiating contracts as well being reliable and honest. Because his family had moved so much when he was a child, he had learned to make friends fast.

Jordan disapproved of unions in his mills, managing to remove one from one of his plants and preventing any efforts to organize in his others. He was known to pitch in when he was needed, whether it be repairing a piece of equipment or making a loan for the down payment on a worker's home.

Jordan became active in state Democratic politics in the mid-1930's. He was a vigorous fund-raiser and served as chairman of the state Democratic executive committee (1949–1954) and as a Democratic national committeeman from North Carolina (1954–1958). He gained the reputation as an experienced behind-the-scenes deal maker.

On Apr. 19, 1958, Luther Hodges, the Democratic governor of North Carolina, appointed Jordan to fill the unexpired Senate term of the late W. Kerr Scott. Because Jordan was known to have turned down a previous Senate seat, a number of his colleagues were surprised that he accepted this offer. He was then elected to the seat that November. Hodges was also rumored to have appointed Jordan on condition that he would relinquish the seat so that the governor himself could run for the Senate in 1960.

The new senator moved into Washington with considerable ease and was considered an insider almost immediately. He did not seek the limelight, preferring to do his work behind closed doors. Just as he had made a reputation as an accomplished and practical businessman and party operative, he became an accomplished and practical legislator. He served on the agricultural and forestry and the public works committees, and he chaired the Public Works Subcommittee on Flood Control and Rivers and Harbors, seeing to it that considerable funds reached North Carolina. He also chaired the Joint Congressional Committee on Inaugural Ceremonies, which made him a much sought-after senator. He became a confidant of powerful politicians, and according to his biographer and his fellow senator from North Carolina, Sam Ervin, Jr., this included the Senate Majority Leader, Lyndon Johnson.

Jordan voted for Alaskan statehood in 1958, which was not a popular move in the South since it was sure to guarantee an increase in pro–civil rights votes. When he voted for Hawaiian statehood the following year, more southerners joined him.

Jordan was reelected to the Senate in 1960 and 1966. His lack of a clear voting pattern, however, continued to leave his constituency unsettled. In 1962, for example, he voted for President Kennedy's trade bill that reduced tariffs, an unpopular move within the textile industry. But in his active involvement in agricultural affairs, he supported the tobacco industry in spite of declaring that he was loath to do so.

Jordan was chairman of the Senate Committee on Rules and Administration. He gained his greatest attention as a senator when the investigation of Bobby Baker fell to the Rules Committee. Baker, secretary to the Senate majority, was accused of extensive improper business dealings. He resigned his position on October 1963, and Jordan began public hearings in early 1964. Baker was indicted by a federal grand jury on nine counts, including income-tax evasion, larceny, fraud, and misappropriation of campaign funds. In January 1967, he was convicted on most counts, and he went to prison in January 1971. President Johnson, considered to have been Baker's mentor, was in the midst of a presidential campaign at the time of the hearings. Jordan received considerable criticism for having kept the linkage between the president and Baker out of the hearing room and the press. Jordan's biographer stated that after the affair was over, Johnson seemed to have dropped Jordan as a friend.

From time to time, Jordan continued to bewilder his colleagues. Having long supported American military activity in Vietnam, in June 1970 Jordan voted for the Cooper-Church amendment calling for immediate cessation of military activity. His close associates realized how hard this reversal must have been for him, for he was noted for never admitting he was wrong on any matter.

Tied up with his activities in the Senate, Jordan may have neglected the fact that he was losing touch with his constituency. In the 1972 Democratic primary, Jordan lost to a Durham lawyer and three-term congressman, Nick Galifiankis. Friends surmised that he had begun campaigning too late and that his Vietnam vote may have lost him votes. Also, his health had begun to decline while his opponent was a considerably younger man. Jordan's successor, Jesse Helms, claimed that if Jordan had won the primary, he would not have run. Jordan's health continued to decline, and he died in Saxapahaw, N.C.

[Everett's papers are at the William R. Perkins Library, Special Collections Department, Duke University, Durham, N.C. They cover 1936 to 1974, predominately his Senate years. See also *Tributes to the Honorable B. Everett Jordan of North Carolina in the United States Congress* (1972); and Ben F. Bulla, *Textiles and Politics: The Life of B. Everett Jordan* (1992). An obituary appears in the *New York Times*, Mar. 16, 1974.]

MARGARET LATIMER

JORDAN, LOUIS (July 8, 1908–Feb. 4, 1975), jazz and rhythm-and-blues musician, was born in Wheatley, Ark., the son of Jimmy Jordan, a bandleader and music teacher, and Lizzie Reed. His family moved to Brinkley, Ark., shortly after his birth and it is there that he developed his musical skills. At the age of seven, he began his musical training on clarinet with his father, who, in addition to teaching music, was the musical director of the Rabbit Foot Minstrels, which featured Ma Rainey and the young Bessie Smith. (Jordan was to tour with this group while still in high school.) When Jordan spotted a saxophone in a music store window, he was so drawn to it, he said, that he "ran errands all over Brinkley until my feet were sore and I saved until I could make a down payment on that shiny instrument." His father then started him on the saxophone.

Jordan played with several Little Rock groups while in high school and as a music major at Arkansas Baptist College. In 1929, he made his professional debut as a member of Jimmy Pryor's Imperial Serenaders, and he began to attract the attention of other area musicians. The resorts and nightlife in Hot Springs, Ark., necessitated the hiring of large numbers of musical groups and entertainers. With his growing reputation, Jordan became one of the most sought-after sidemen for Hot Springs performances. In 1930, he joined Rudy ("Tuna Boy") Williams's Belvedere Orchestra, one of the most successful groups working the Hot Springs circuit. This gig was followed by engagements with various other area bands before Jordan moved to Philadelphia in 1932 to join the band of tuba player Jim Winters.

His experiences in Philadelphia and the surrounding areas helped broaden his musical scope. This growing exposure led to his move to New York City with the Charlie Gaines band, where he and Gaines took part in Clarence Williams's recording session for "I Can't Dance" and other songs. This was Jordan's first recording, and it exposed him to a wider audience and made more influential bandleaders aware of his style and abilities. He became a member of the musician's Local 802 and finally settled in New York City in the summer of 1935, when he joined violinist Leroy Smith's orchestra. Like other "society bands" of the day, Smith's group specialized in popular and high classical music and frequently performed in New York, with side performances in Cleveland and Atlantic City. After leaving Smith a year later, Jordan played briefly with Fats Waller and Kaiser Marshall before beginning a two-year stay with Chick Webb's Savoy Ballroom Band. In addition to playing alto, soprano, and baritone saxophone, he was the featured vocalist. The exposure and recordings with the Webb band gave him the notoriety and visibility he sought.

Upon leaving Webb's band in the summer of 1938, he began leading his own ensemble at the Elks' Rendezvous in New York City. That December, his band—later named the Tympany Five, even though it always had seven or eight members—made its first recording. His big break came when his group served as the opening act for the Mills Brothers at the Capitol Lounge in Chicago. Starting with a ten-minute show, their set was eventually expanded to one-third of the show's format. With a Decca recording contract and a loyal following, Jordan and the group were on their way. Although he was occasionally featured as soloist in performances and recordings with Louis Armstrong, Bing Crosby, Ella Ftizgerald, and others, it was as the alto sax leader and vocal soloist of the Tympany Five that he became successful.

Drawing from his vast experiences in show, dance, jazz, and minstrel bands, Jordan possessed a combination of showmanship and musicianship that became the most influential force in the emerging rhythm-and-blues style of the late 1940's and early 1950's. This mix of styles with a new "shuffle boogie" beat provided the foundation for all pop music groups that have followed. His was the most popular and influential rhythm-and-blues group during the 1940's and 1950's, as many of their recordings sold more than one million copies each, among them "Is You Is, or Is You Ain't (Ma' Baby)?" (1943), "Choo Choo Ch' Boogie" (1946), and others.

The military and musician union's ban on recording from August 1942 to September 1943 interrupted Jordan's recording career, as it did everyone's. By this time, however, he was a well-established personality; hence, he was able to turn to film and continue spreading his popularity. Movies became the primary vehicle through which Jordan helped popularize rhythm and blues. Because few of his audiences had access to full-time television and radio programming—for "race" music was not established until 1948—the short musical film made by Jordan and others became the primary medium for this new music. Made by small, independent film companies, these musical "shorts" played in more than six hundred theaters, most of which were located in the black communities of the southern and border states. The presence of Jordan in a short guaranteed a packed house. As reported in the July 8, 1946, issue of *Newsweek*, "Last week, the Negro film industry reached a new high-water mark with the release of 'Beware,' an Astor Pictures production starring Louis Jordan, one of Decca's most lucrative recorders. . . . The picture cinches Jordan's reputation as a great melody maker. . . . The presence of Jordan, who has just made his third personal appearance at the Paramount Theater in New York, assures [its] box-office success. The most successful Negro film to date was *Caldonia*, another Astor production with Jordan and His Tympany Five." In all, Jordan appeared in more than twenty films. During his peak productive years, 1938 to 1946, Jordan sold more than five million records.

His popularity in musical shorts was matched by his popularity on Nickelodeon jukeboxes. Long before the advent of the MTV cable network, these jukeboxes included a large screen that showed a film loop featuring clips from popular music shorts. As with music videos, these shorts featured brief plots in which the artists performed their latest recordings.

During a period of strict racial separation in music, Jordan was equally enjoyed by both blacks and whites. He was the music industry's first pop crossover artist. Many critics thought of him as being in the same genre as Cab Calloway, who was also accepted by white audiences. During the early 1930's, Calloway and his band had alternated with Duke Ellington's orchestra as the house band at Harlem's famous Cotton Club. When this club closed, Calloway moved to other similar high-class jazz spots. Calloway was a jazzman, but he was even more a great showman, comic, and singer. Jordan decided to be less of a jazz performer and to follow more in the direction of Calloway, concluding that jazzmen "play mostly for themselves. . . . I want to play for the people." What separated Jordan from Calloway was Jordan's black-oriented material and subjects. His recordings of the blues standards "Early in the Morning" and "I'm Gonna Move to the Outskirts of Town" (1941–1942) reveal that he was well versed in the black southern blues tradition as well as the evolving urban pop music field.

The most interesting of Jordan's use of "color" vignettes was "Saturday Night Fish Fry" (1949). The lyrics of this song describe a social gathering that suddenly turns raucous and attracts the police. As a humorist and not a satirist, he does not treat the incident with anger but with amusement. This was precisely the stance and social outlook of rhythm and blues.

As a savvy businessman, Jordan seldom failed to retain his rights to receive fees or royalties. One exception to this was the hit song "Caldonia" and the events surrounding it. In an attempt to protect the copyright from an unscrupulous publisher, Jordan credited the composing of "Caldonia" to his first wife, Fleecie Moore, whom he had married in the early 1940's. However, both Jordan and his manager, who devised the scam, were outsmarted in the end when the Jordans divorced in 1951. As one of Jordan's most successful and frequently recorded compositions, "Caldonia" earned large sums of money for Moore.

Jordan recorded for Decca from 1938 to 1953 and toured throughout that time. As his health began to fail, he curtailed the touring. Many believed that the new rock-and-roll was the cause of his inactivity, but it was in fact his health. "I had two years of ill health. . . . I'd go out and play a couple of months and I'd get sick," said Jordan.

After 1955, Jordan briefly led a big jazz band but soon returned to small-group performing. He continued to perform into the 1970's, with a solo tour of England in 1962 and group tours of Asia in 1967 and 1968. After leaving New York City in 1954, he lived for eighteen years with his second wife in Phoenix, Ariz., before they settled in Los Angeles in 1972. In October 1974, while performing in Sparks, Nev., Jordan suffered a heart attack. After a short stay in a hospital in Reno, he returned to Los Angeles to recuperate. Four months later, while shopping with his wife, Jordan suffered another attack, this time fatal.

Jordan's achievements in American popular music are frequently overlooked, with credit being given to many of the white pop musicians who followed him. However, his innovative combining of jazz, blues, and showmanship helped create rock-and roll. In 1953, his shuffle-boogie style was adopted by Decca's recording artist Bill Haley. Although he performed the style faster than Jordan, Haley's use of the shuffle boogie laid the foundation for rock-and-roll.

[There are no collected papers of compositions of Jordan, and although he was a very successful and influential recording figure, his recordings have not been collected for reissue. Most material exists as magazine articles: see D. Boyce, "Here Comes Mr. Jordan," *New Beat*, Jan. 1950; and Leonard Feather, "Louis Jordan: The Good Times Still Roll," *Down Beat*, May 29, 1969. Also see Arnold Shaw, *Honkers and Shouters* (1978); D. Colebeck, *Louis Jordan Discography* (1982); and D. Garcon and J. Lubin, *Louis Jordan Discographie* (1987). An obituary is in the *New York Times*, Feb. 6, 1975.]

WARRICK L. CARTER

JULIAN, PERCY LAVON (Apr. 11, 1899–Apr. 19, 1975), organic chemist, was born in Montgomery, Ala., the son of James Sumner Julian, a railroad mail clerk, and Elizabeth Adams. In the Julian household, great emphasis was placed on the value of education. "Make it 100" was the expected goal of the Julian children in school.

Even at an early age Percy wanted to be a chemist, but his father implored him to be a doctor. He attended elementary school in Montgomery, and because there was no public high school for blacks in the city, he went to a private school for his secondary education. Percy graduated in 1916, head of his class.

After graduation he enrolled in DePauw University in Greencastle, Ind. The college officials judged his academic background to be so impoverished that for two years Percy was required to attend the local academy even while carrying a full college load and working to support himself.

Graduating from DePauw in 1920 with a major in chemistry, Julian was inducted into Phi Beta Kappa and was class valedictorian. He wanted to continue his education in graduate school. But several universities wrote DePauw that they rejected Julian because no industry or white university would hire a black Ph.D.

Bitterly disappointed, and with no other choice available, Julian accepted a position to teach chemistry at Fisk University in Nashville, Tenn. Though he worked hard at teaching, the burning desire to continue his education remained entrenched.

In 1922, with the help of an Austin Fellowship, Julian enrolled at Harvard University, where he studied under the great chemist, E. P. Kohler. He earned straight A's and in 1923, was awarded a master's degree in organic chemistry. Julian returned to teaching. He first taught at West Virginia State College, then was appointed head of the chemistry department at Howard University.

In 1929 Julian was awarded a General Education Fellowship sponsored by the Rockefeller Foundation. He applied for admission to the University of Vienna in Austria. Against stiff international competition for one of the few openings available, he was accepted into the doctoral program. Julian mastered German and spent the next two years with the noted authority on chemistry of natural products, Ernst Späth. In 1931 he was awarded the Ph.D. in organic chemistry.

Julian returned to DePauw in 1932. In 1935 he and his assistant Josef Pikl synthesized the drug physostigmine. An alkaloid of the Calabar bean (*Physostigma venenosum*), physostigmine is used to treat glaucoma. Julian succeeded where other reputable chemists had failed at a task some had pronounced impossible. Interestingly, Julian made this discovery at DePauw, where he had his first real course in chemistry. He had returned to DePauw through the intercession of his old teacher and friend, Dean William Blanchard, who provided support and facilities for Julian. When Blanchard nominated Julian for appointment to the faculty at DePauw, however, the board of trustees turned him down.

Despite this setback, Julian's work at DePauw

had not gone unnoticed. Indeed, his reputation as a chemist made itself felt against the wall of resolve erected by American universities and firms not to employ blacks in research facilities.

In 1936, Julian was hired by Glidden Paint Company in Chicago and made Director of Research of its Soya Products Division. This appointment came immediately after a firm in Wisconsin rescinded an offer to hire him when officials discovered that a local ordinance barred blacks from overnight stays within city limits.

In appointing a black to a position of such major responsibility, Glidden acted with pioneering courage and, as it developed, good judgment. Under Julian, the previously failing soybean component of the company prospered. Julian used the soybean to yield previously unimagined products. His syntheses of Reichstein's Substance S made possible the mass production of cortisone. Cortisone, hailed as a wonder drug in treating arthritis, became available in large quantities and at a cost that placed it within the reach of the general public. Julian and his team also synthesized the female sex hormone progesterone, the male hormone testosterone, and other hormones. They produced a fire-resistant foam credited with saving thousands of lives at sea. A variety of other products, including the food supplement "lecithin granules," paper-sizing materials, and scores of ingredients used in poultry and other animal feed, were among a few of the realizations of Julian's fertile imagination.

Julian was among the most versatile of scientists. He did not confine himself to applied chemistry. His publications clearly demonstrated his active interest in basic research. Among some 185 papers, his studies on indoles, sterols, steroids, and conjugated systems provided enlightening reading for students of organic chemistry and biochemistry.

Julian left Glidden in 1953 to form his own company. He founded the Julian Laboratories in Chicago, with subsidiaries in Mexico and Guatemala. Later he founded Julian Associates and the Julian Research Institute.

Percy Julian, a devoted family man, married Anna Johnson in 1935. She was a member of Phi Beta Kappa and the first black person to earn a Ph.D. in sociology from the University of Pennsylvania. The couple had two children.

Among numerous recognitions, Julian received the NAACP Spingarn Medal for "brilliant contributions in the field of chemical research" (1947), the Chicagoan of the Year (1950), the American Institute of Chemistry's Chemical Pioneer Award (1968), and Sigma Xi's Proctor Prize (1974).

Those who knew Julian, spoke of him as being urbane, a person of wit, charm, and good humor. He was as much at home in the humanities as in the sciences, and he had a passionate love for the opera. His musical preferences were for the classics, spirituals, and jazz.

Julian's life cannot be recounted without wonderment that he ever became a scientist. What was it that ignited an unquenchable flame of desire in a black youth in a small southern town at the turn of the century to become a chemist? What kept him going when he encountered a series of barriers and rejections, any one of which would have justified his despair? Even after brilliant scientific contributions, he experienced social humiliations, rejections, and acts of violence because of his race. Yet he was not deterred. Family and friends detected no hate in him, and found an almost complete absence of bitterness. It seems appropriate to attribute his tenacity to a strong family with lofty values, an uncommon intellect, a scholarship grounded in sciences and humanities, and an indomitable spirit. Credit also those rare men of vision, courage, and integrity who rose above the petty narrowness of race and opened doors to this pioneer of the chemistry of natural products.

Percy Lavon Julian died in Chicago on Apr. 11, 1975, after a courageous fight against cancer.

[The definitive biography on Julian is Bernard Witkop, *Percy Lavon Julian: April 11, 1899–April 19, 1974* (1980). Other biographical materials include Louis Haber, *Black Pioneers of Science and Invention* (1970); W. Montague Cobb, "Percy Lavon Julian, Ph.D., Sc.D., LL.D., L.H.D., 1899," *National Medical Association* (1971), and "Onward and Upward," Lecture at DePauw University, Apr. 28, 1977; and Donald Cook, *Chemistry and DePauw University, 1837–1987* (1987). See also Percy Julian, "The Chemist as Scholar and Humanist," *The Chemist*, Mar. 1965, and "The Engineering Scientist as Scholar and Humanitarian," *ChemTech*, Mar. 1974; Max Tishler, "Percy L. Julian, The Scientist," *The Chemist*, Mar. 1965; and Stanley Wormley and Lewis Fenderson, *Many Shades of Black* (1969). An obituary is in the *New York Times*, Apr. 21, 1975.]

EDWARD S. JENKINS

K

KAHN, LOUIS I. (Feb. 20, 1901–Mar. 17, 1974), architect, was born on the island of Saaremaa (Oesel), Estonia, and brought to the United States by his parents Leopold Kahn and Bertha Mendelsohn in 1905. A talented draftsman, Kahn was educated at Philadelphia's Central High School and Public Industrial Art School. After studying under the noted Beaux Arts architect Paul Philippe Cret at the University of Pennsylvania and earning a degree in architecture in 1924, he obtained employment in the office of John Molitor, city architect of Philadelphia.

In Molitor's office, Kahn acquired valuable experience in large-scale project design, culminating in work as chief designer of the Sesquicentennial Exposition held in Philadelphia in 1926 (he would also help design the Bicentennial Exposition fifty years later). He left for two years of study in Europe, returning to Philadelphia in 1929. Paul Philippe Cret, his old teacher, managed to give him some work, but the Great Depression devastated the profession. In 1931 he joined other unemployed architects and engineers to form the Architectural Research Group. His work there on town planning would serve him well in future commissions, from the Mill Creek Redevelopment Project in Philadelphia (1946–1954), his plan for the Gandhinagar Capital in Gujarat, India (1963–1964), and his plans for the new capital of Bangladesh at Dacca (1962–1974), to his project for Independence Mall in Philadelphia (1972–1974). From 1935 through 1947, Kahn's work was limited to consultancies with such organizations as the Philadelphia Housing Authority and the Philadelphia Planning Commission. However, Kahn made a number of lifelong associates during these seemingly unproductive years, notably George Howe, with whom he went into partnership in 1941; Oskar Stonorov, with whom he worked from 1942 to 1943; and the structural engineer August E. Komendant, who would provide him with essential assistance in designing structures over his last two decades. Working with Stonorov, Kahn finally gained credit for an architectural design, the Psychiatric Hospital of Philadelphia (1944–1946).

In 1947, after Kahn had been a practicing architect for more than twenty years, his friend and associate George Howe recommended him for a position as visiting critic at the Yale School of Architecture. The experience changed his life, and transformed the course of contemporary architecture. Energized by his contact with architecture's young radicals at Yale, and enlightened by a study of architecture's roots during a year spent as resident architect at the American Academy in Rome (1950–1951), Kahn developed a comprehensive theory of architecture, based on the heretical notion that the root of a design is not what the client wants the building to be, but "what the building wants to be." For the next two decades he would be famous among students of architecture as the man who preached about form, who attempted to develop in their designs a "harmony of systems," who urged them to distinguish between "served" and "servant" spaces, and who cared less about geometry or cost of construction than he did about the quality of light in the finished spaces.

The result was a series of magnificent designs, many of which stand as masterpieces of modern architecture. Perhaps the best of them, appropriately for a man who worried so about light, are his museums. Kahn's first major commission was a new art gallery for Yale (1953), in which he created a series of free-flowing spaces flooded with light from a glass curtain wall in the back, while integrating the gallery's brick facade into its academic and commercial environment. Most controversially, he left the deeply coffered concrete ceiling, with its mechanical ducts and electrical conduits, exposed to view; a common design feature today, it was a bold gamble then. Throughout his career Kahn loved to work with concrete, not only because of its strength and plasticity but because of its workable surface on which he could create a background pattern appropriate to the space it defined. More than twenty years later, in his last commission, Kahn was asked to design a center for British art directly across the street from his 1953 masterpiece. This time Kahn chose to bring the light into the building through large interior courtyards, echoing not the cathedral paradigm of his earlier building but the example of a Renaissance palazzo (the center and its paintings were the gift of a latter-day Medici, Paul Mellon). In keeping with the change, Kahn's later museum combines its concrete forms not with the cold brightness of glass but with the warmth of oak panels, or brushed stainless steel; Kahn explained that he wanted this museum to be a place where one could sit and have a cup of tea while contemplating the artworks.

The third of Kahn's great museums was the Kimbell Art Museum in Fort Worth, Texas (1966–1972). Here, under the harsh Texas sun, Kahn's task was not to bring light into the museum space but to keep it out, or at least to soften its effects. Again Kahn evolved a brilliant solution: a combination of glass-curtain walls that received light only indirectly, off a great lawn, with cycloidal vaults that scattered the light through longitudinal slits. The result joins what he called the "green light" of the garden windows to the "silver light" of the vaults, yielding an illumination that is at once a positive presence and a neutral backdrop. The Kimbell Art Museum succeeds not only in its manipulation of light but also creates a sense of space, Kahn's other life-long concern.

Kahn's theory of space involved two distinct aspects. First was his distinction between "served" and "servant" space, or what an amateur might call living space and mechanical space. Kahn's first demonstration of the beauty that derives from a just response to this distinction was the A. N. Richards Medical Research

Building at the University of Pennsylvania (1958–1961). Here the eye is caught by a series of tall towers, echoing Renaissance towns like San Gimignano. These are the "servant" spaces, housing both mechanical and ventilating equipment. Suspended among the towers are glass-walled bays, the "served" spaces, which house the actual laboratories; below them are brick-covered strips which conceal more "servant" spaces.

This design led to Kahn's commission to design the Salk Institute for Biological Studies at La Jolla, Calif. (1959–1965), which he took as an opportunity to demonstrate the second potentiality of space. Salk gave Kahn a practically free hand, telling him only that he wanted a place he "could invite Picasso to." Kahn responded by creating—or transforming—a New England town common. A series of buildings integrating living and working spaces were set around a large central courtyard. But in place of a church he left the west side of the common open to the Pacific Ocean and the setting sun. Kahn was also sensitive to questions of light at La Jolla; each Salk Institute building is either a square shell enclosing a round space, or a round shell enclosing a square, trapping excess light between the double walls. Kahn would apply this solution in a highly developed form in his National Assembly Building in Dacca, Bangladesh, where massive brick-curtain walls shield the inner corridors and meeting rooms from the fierce sun, and in turn these working rooms hide from view the huge domed assembly chamber itself, filled with twice-filtered light.

The final key term in Kahn's architectural vocabulary is "structure," the ideal form that a building "wants to be." One can see this idea at work in a modest project, a Bath House at the Jewish Community Center in Trenton, N.J. (1955–1956). Here the successive need of people to gather, to change, and to bathe dictated a sequential structure, articulated in a series of simple brick pavilions connected at their corners. A somewhat larger example is the Erdman Hall Dormitories at Bryn Mawr College, Pa. (1960–1965), where Kahn applied the same pattern of linked diamonds to the successive spaces of dormitory rooms, and communal areas for study and work, culminating in a light-filled central gathering place. And the last example is the Library at Philip Exeter Academy, N.H. (1967–1972), where, behind a traditional facade of brick walls and rectangular windows, Kahn hid an inner courtyard, flooded with light and framed by high arcs of concrete, demonstrating his understanding that readers need a place to read.

During these incredibly productive last two decades of his life, Kahn accepted a series of commissions for large-scale projects in Teheran, Iran; in Ahmedabad, India; and in Dacca. It is as if he sought the opportunity to discover order on the largest possible scale, or yearned to accomplish elsewhere what he never achieved with his successive plans for transforming Philadelphia; perhaps he simply needed to work at sites where there were no preexisting obstacles to the revelation of form. The result, in any case, was that barely half of Kahn's work during these years was ever realized; when he suffered a fatal heart attack in New York on Mar. 17, 1974—characteristically, on his way home to Philadelphia from work in Bangladesh and India—his architectural practice was in debt. His estate was able to escape insolvency only when the State of Pennsylvania intervened and purchased his sketches and drawings.

Kahn's personal life and habits were as quiet as the first decades of his career. He married Esther Virginia Israeli in 1930, shortly after his return from Europe, and they had one daughter. In part because his face was badly scarred by a childhood accident, he was not a man who worked well in large groups. Former students have talked of how he would stare into some unknown distance without speaking, or pronounce oracular sentences, such as "The university is my chapel," in a barely audible voice. Yet in his dedication to the potentiality of perfection—in his students, in his sketches and drawings, and in the gradual development of buildings from a client's first idea to full realization—Louis I. Kahn left a legacy of inspiration.

[Nearly all of Kahn's writings and lectures have been collected in Alessandra Latour, ed., *Louis I. Kahn: Writings, Lectures, Interviews* (1991). His professional designs are available in Eugene Feldman and Richard Wurman, eds., *The Notebooks and Drawings of Louis I. Kahn* (1973); his other art is found in Jan Hochstein, ed., *The Paintings and Sketches of Louis I. Kahn* (1991). Plans of all completed works are available in Heinz Ronner, Sharad Jhaveri, and Alejandro Vasella, eds., *Louis I. Kahn: The Complete Works, 1935–1974* (1977). The best place to start a secondary search is the catalogue of Kahn's memorial exhibition, David B. Brownlee and David G. DeLong, eds., *Louis I. Kahn: In the Realm of Architecture* (1991). An obituary is in the *New York Times*, Mar. 20, 1974.]

HARTLEY SPATT

KALLEN, HORACE MEYER (Aug. 11, 1882–Feb. 16, 1974), philosopher and educator, was born in Berenstadt, Silesia, in Germany, the son of Jacob David, an Orthodox rabbi, and Esther Rebecca Glazier. Their son came with them to Boston in 1887, entered Harvard College thirteen years later, and graduated magna cum laude in 1903. Two professors particularly influenced him: Barrett Wendell, a literary historian who underscored the Old Testament's impact on American civilization; and William James, the philosopher, who later directed Kallen's dissertation on the nature of truth and gave his protégé an unfinished volume of his own, *Some Problems in Philosophy* (1912), to edit. Having received his doctorate from Harvard in 1908, Kallen did postgraduate work at Princeton, Oxford, and the Sorbonne. He also lectured in philosophy at Harvard from 1908 until 1911, and for the next seven years served as an instructor of philosophy and of psychology at the University of Wisconsin in Madison.

Kallen married Rachel Oatman Van Arsdale in 1926; they had two children.

Kallen was most fully associated with the New School for Social Research, which he helped to found in New York City in 1919, and where he would teach for the next fifty-one years. Until officially retiring in 1970, he held the rank of research professor of social philosophy, and had also served as dean of the graduate faculty in political and social science from 1944 until 1946. The New School's focus was adult education, and one of Kallen's books, *The Education of Free Men* (1949), reflected his lifelong interest in this project. "People believe readily enough and can be taught anything by anybody who knows the technique," he argued. "What is difficult to teach them is to doubt. Doubt is the beginning of intelligence," which the scientific method can reinforce. Kallen's own standard contributions to the curriculum at the New School were on "Beauty and Use" and on "Dominant Ideals of Western Civilization." Having once considered becoming a novelist and poet, he was most consistently absorbed in problems of aesthetics. The two-volume *Art and Freedom* (1942) defined art in terms that were pragmatic and liberal, as "a new use of nature, or of other art, which liberates the spirit, if for an instant only, from the coercions and constraints which beset it."

The challenge to the very texture of American democracy that mass immigration posed at the dawn of the century heightened the theoretical as well as the practical effort to promote assimilation and "Americanization." In this context of national anxiety over the feasibility of the "melting pot," Kallen began the philosophic work that would establish his reputation. Despite the catholicity of interest exhibited in his more than two dozen books, he is indelibly associated with only one idea, "cultural pluralism," a phrase that he first used in 1924 in *Culture and Democracy in the United States.* Therein he stated the case against the amalgamation that patriots demanded of the "hyphenate American" (a term that Kallen also coined).

As a Jamesian, he was more eager to validate the Many than to envision the One, and called for a society bound into a federation of ethnic groups. Kallen argued that the most limited of all human choices—who one's grandparents are—could become the foundation for the enlargement of freedom. An irreversible fact could be converted into an opportunity for self-realization, in which ancestry would be honored as a way of revitalizing democratic possibility. No wonder then that Kallen was fond of the metaphor of the orchestra, in which "each ethnic group is the natural instrument" contributing to the overall harmony and balance of the symphony: each realizes itself more fully in the society than it can by "segregation and isolation." Ethnicity therefore need not be dismissed as parochial strutting or as an alibi for obscurantism, but could instead promote national loyalty and cohesiveness by anchoring the individual in a continuous and comforting fabric of institutions that also enriches the larger community.

Kallen's reverberant article in the *Nation,* "Democracy Versus the Melting Pot" (1915), argued for "a democracy of nationalities having for its aim the equal growth and the free development of all." He rejected both homogenization and subservience to Anglo-Saxon culture. "Since people have to live together," he asserted, "plurality is a basic condition of existence. The need is to bring differences together to make a union, not unity." In his defense of

minority rights, Kallen was not very explicit on the political arrangements and processes that would sanction such growth and development. But in an atmosphere of chauvinism and nativism that the Great War had intensified, he championed diversity rather than absorption, particularism rather than conformism. The right to be equal, which was promised in the birth certificates of the republic, meant for Kallen the right to be different. The boldness of his theory, according to historian John Higham, was its abolition of "any claims of white Protestants to constitute a rightful majority and defined us all as minorities and all minorities as equal." Kallen's version of cultural pluralism ignored blacks and the creativity of their potential contribution, although he defended blacks against discrimination. By 1924, his freshest work as a democratic idealist was largely completed. *Cultural Pluralism and the American Idea* (1956) broadened the notion of diversity and repudiated racialism. But otherwise his writing on the multiethnic idea mostly involved refinements.

Converted to Zionism in 1902, Kallen praised the movement of Jewish national restoration as a necessary modern expression of the mission of his own ethnic group, as a reinforcement of its own distinctive identity. Zionism represented a vibrant substitute for the religious faith that the acids of skepticism and pragmatism had eroded. An ardent secularist, Kallen opposed not only the provincial Orthodox Judaism into which he had been born but also Reform Judaism, because its roots in history were severed, he claimed, when rationalist dogmas displaced experience. He also rejected the notion of the Chosen People. Having promoted Jewish culture by helping to establish the Menorah Society at Harvard in 1906, Kallen was to devote many of his energies not only to reconciling the general phenomena of ethnicity with democracy, but also to showing the compatibility of Jewishness with citizenship, since both, he believed, placed a supreme value upon the ideal of freedom. In Kallen's work Judaism was collapsed into Hebraism, a modernized variant of the religious civilization that had become outmoded. A participant in Jewish communal life, Kallen served as national vice-president of the American Jewish Congress.

Although he had a home in Oneonta, N.Y., Kallen died in Palm Beach, Fla., at the age of ninety-one.

[Kallen's papers are located in the American Jewish Archives in Cincinnati. His major works include *Judaism at Bay* (1932), *Individualism: An American Way of Life* (1933), and *The Decline and Rise of the Consumer* (1936). Though no published biography is extant, Sarah L. Schmidt's doctoral dissertation on "Horace M. Kallen and the Americanization of Zionism" (University of Maryland, 1973) is useful on his Jewish interests, as is William Toll's *Women, Men and Ethnicity: Essays on the Structure and Thought of American Jewry* (1991). See also Milton R. Konvitz, ed., *The Legacy of Horace M. Kallen* (1987). Konvitz as well as Sidney Hook also edited a festschrift, *Freedom and Experience: Essays Presented to Horace M. Kallen* (1947). His thought is contextualized in John Higham, *Send These to Me: Jews and Other Immigrants in Urban America* (1975); and in David A. Hollinger, *In the American Province: Studies in the History and Historiography of Ideas* (1985). An obituary appears in the *New York Times*, Feb. 17, 1974.]

STEPHEN J. WHITFIELD

KEATING, KENNETH BARNARD (May 18, 1990–May 5, 1975), lawyer, ambassador, congressman, and senator, was born in Lima, N.Y., the son of Thomas Mosgrove Keating and Louise Barnard. He attended Genesee Wesleyan Seminary in New York State, earned a B.A. from the University of Rochester in 1919, and graduated from Harvard University with an LL.B. in 1923.

Keating returned to Rochester in 1923 and established a thriving law practice as a member of the firm of Harris, Beach, Keating, Wilcox, Dale and Linowitz, with which he was affiliated until 1948. In 1928 he married Louise Depuy; they had one child. Louise died in 1968, and in 1974 Keating married Mary Pitcairn Davis, the widow of one of his Harvard classmates.

During World War II Keating served in the China-Burma-India theater, first as a colonel and later a brigadier general in the U.S. Army. He earned the Legion of Merit with oak leaf cluster, three battle stars, and the Order of the British Empire.

Keating's long tenure in the political arena began in 1946 when he was elected as a Republican to the U.S. House of Representatives, where he served until 1958 representing first the Fortieth and later the Thirty-eighth New York districts. As a congressman Keating voted for both the Truman Doctrine and the Marshall Plan. He was a strong anti-Communist who opposed recognition of China, sponsored a 1956 bill to limit judicial appeals by aliens sentenced

to deportation, and introduced a bill in 1958 written by Secretary of State John Foster Dulles that would have given the president the power to deny a passport to anyone who might be considered dangerous to U.S. security. He also lobbied for the legalization of the use of wiretaps by the Federal Bureau of Investigation to gather evidence against "gangsters" and "traitors."

Congressman Keating was also a leader in efforts to reform the U.S. Immigration quota system and was a consistent and vigorous supporter of civil rights. He defended the Supreme Court's desegregation decisions when many congressmen hesitated to take a stand. As a member of the Judiciary Committee, he helped draft the 1957 Civil Rights Act, giving the federal government the right to seek injunctions against the obstruction of the right to vote of any citizen. He supported a number of social welfare measures and in 1955 introduced a bill that would have given eighteen-year-olds the right to vote.

In 1958 Keating defeated Democrat Frank Hogan, the Manhattan district attorney, in the race for the United States Senate, despite union opposition brought on by his votes against several trade union bills.

In the Senate Keating served on the Judiciary Committee and on the Joint Congressional Committee on Immigration. He remained a staunch supporter of civil rights and tended to be liberal on domestic issues. He attempted to strengthen the 1960 civil rights bill by adding an amendment that would have provided "technical assistance to areas desegregating their schools." He also proposed the Twenty-third Amendment to the Constitution, giving residents of the District of Columbia the right to vote in presidential elections. In the same year, 1960, Keating and seven other Republican senators proposed a voluntary federal-state health insurance program for people older than sixty-five. This plan, in which states would contract with private firms for coverage and subscribers would make payments based on income, was more liberal than the one proposed by the Kennedy administration. The plan finally adopted contained many of the Keating plan's basic features but required a means test and allowed each state to determine the type and extent of medical assistance it would provide.

Although Keating was one of John F. Kennedy's most consistent Republican supporters, he was critical of the administration's Cuba policy, accusing Kennedy of complacency in the face of Soviet military aid to Cuba. On Oct. 10, 1962, he charged that Russia was installing offensive missiles on the island but refused to disclose the source of his information. It was not until October 14 that the Central Intelligence Agency obtained photographic evidence supporting his claim. One week later President Kennedy announced the U.S. blockade of Cuba.

In 1964 Robert Kennedy announced that he would seek Keating's seat in the Senate. Keating responded by welcoming the newcomer to New York, saying that "as his senator I would be glad to furnish him a guidebook, road maps, and other useful literature about the Empire State which any sojourner would find helpful."

The hard-fought and, at times, stormy campaign ended on an almost comedic note. There had been frequent negotiations concerning a public meeting between the candidates but the two camps could never agree on a time and a place for the proposed debate. Finally, in a time-honored political ploy, Keating bought a half hour of television time for October 28. He announced that since Kennedy refused to appear, he would place an empty chair on the stage and direct his statements to it. The ploy backfired when Kennedy bought the following time slot for his own appearance. He arrived early and tried to enter the Keating sound stage saying that he was an invited guest. He was refused entry and the "debate" went on with an empty chair on-stage and Kennedy off-stage loudly demanding that he be allowed to participate. When the program ended, Keating had no desire to answer the waiting reporters' questions. In a classic Keystone Kops chase scene, he rushed out with aides overturning chairs and flower pots to delay the pursuing reporters. The evening was a disaster for Keating, and Kennedy won the Senate race by 800,000 votes.

After this defeat, Keating joined the New York law firm of Royall, Koegel and Rogers and continued to work for immigration reform. In 1965 he became president of the American Immigration and Citizenship Conference, an organization that was working to end the national origins quota system.

He was elected associate justice of the New York Court of Appeals in 1965 and served until 1969, when President Richard M. Nixon appointed him ambassador to India, a post he resigned in 1972. In 1973 he was appointed U.S.

Ambassador to Israel, a position he held until his death in 1975. This last appointment was particularly appropriate because he had always been one of Israel's most ardent congressional supporters and was very popular with the American Jewish community. In 1955 he had urged the U.S. to allow Israel to purchase $50 million in "defensive arms" and in 1960, when the United Arab Republic was blockading shipments to Israel, he sponsored a pro-Israeli amendment to the foreign aid bill that would deny aid to countries that "wage economic warfare against other nations . . . including such procedures as boycotts, blockades, and the restriction of the use of international waterways."

Secretary of State Henry Kissinger's trip to the Middle East in early 1975 to negotiate an agreement between Israel and Egypt concerning the Sinai prompted one correspondent to say that Ambassador Keating "never established a great rapport with the Israeli Government or people." This observation is suspect in light of Prime Minister Golda Meir's statement that he was "a very good friend to Israel for many years, both in the U.S. Senate and in Israel itself. He was a man I liked and trusted and . . . I was grateful to him for his assistance and understanding."

Keating returned to the United States in April 1975 to participate in President Gerald Ford's reassessment of Mideast policy. He died in New York City. In 1979 Congress honored him by changing the name of the federal building in Rochester to the Kenneth B. Keating Federal Building.

[Keating's papers are located at the University of Rochester, Rochester, N.Y. Profiles appear in Nelson Lichtenstein and Eleanora W. Schoenebaum, eds., *The Kennedy Years* (1976); and Eleanora W. Schoenebaum and Michael L. Levine, *The Eisenhower Years* (1977). See also Lester David and Irene David, *Bobby Kennedy* (1986); I. L. Kenen, *Israel's Defense Line* (1981); Golda Meir, *My Life* (repr. ed. 1975); and listings in *Congress and the Nation*, Congressional Quarterly Service, vol. 2 (1969). An obituary is in the *New York Times*, May 6, 1975.]

ANNA B. PERRY

KELLY, GEORGE EDWARD (Jan. 16, 1887–June 18, 1974), playwright, was born in Schuykill Falls, Pa., one of ten children of impoverished Irish immigrants. His father, John H. Kelly, worked sporadically in a variety of jobs in unskilled labor; his mother, Mary Costello, was the stronger parent whose love of reading and particularly of Shakespeare had a strong impact on her son's literary development. George was forced to leave school at an early age in order to work in the local mill. Deeply ashamed of his background and always intensely private about his personal life (Kelly had an intimate relationship with William Weagly that lasted almost fifty years), Kelly would later invent a biography in which he was born into a prosperous family and privately educated.

Two of the other Kelly children also had illustrious careers. George's older brother, Walter, was a headliner in vaudeville where he appeared as the "Virginia Judge." John B. Kelly, his younger brother, was a rowing champion who became an Olympic gold-medalist in 1924, and in 1929 became the father of Grace, future film star and Princess of Monaco.

Tall, slim, and imperially handsome, with a firm jaw, dark, penetrating eyes, and a beautifully modulated speaking voice from which he had erased all traces of his humble rural origins, Kelly began his career as an actor. From 1911 to 1914 he played the leading roles in the national touring companies of Broadway hits like *The Virginian*, *Live Wires*, and *The Common Law*. In 1915 he entered vaudeville as the star of a popular one-act play called *Woman Proposes*. The vaudeville of his day provided high-class family entertainment and great stars like Sarah Bernhardt, Eleonora Duse, and Ethel Barrymore were proud to appear on the major circuits.

The following season, after a fruitless search for another vaudeville sketch in which to star, Kelly decided to write a play himself. For nearly two years he acted in and directed his own *Finders Keepers* on the Keith-Orpheum circuit. In 1917 Kelly joined the army for a year; for the fastidious young man army life was a horror from which he could not wait to be released.

From 1918 to 1922 Kelly wrote, directed, and toured with a dozen of his own vaudeville sketches. His short pieces, on such topics as marital infidelity, superstition, and class differences, already contained the astute character studies, the sly satiric jabs at middle-class pretensions, the pitched battles between bossy wives and hen-pecked husbands, and the sexual and moral conservatism, of his later full-length plays. By working in the compressed form of the vaudeville sketch, Kelly learned the importance of split-second timing and steadily building ac-

tion to a climax that paid off for both the actors and the audience.

For his Broadway debut in 1922, Kelly turned one of his vaudeville pieces, *Mrs. Ritter Appears*, into *The Torch-Bearers*. It was his most purely comic work, a satire on the little theater movement of the time in which the playwright exposed the artistic and moral shortcomings of a group of small-town theatrical amateurs. As he was to do for all his work, Kelly directed, superbly choreographing a stageful of characters who often moved and talked all at the same time.

The Show-Off (1924), Kelly's most famous play, was another comedy of provincial manners. Aubrey Piper, the title character, is an unwelcome son-in-law in the home of a conservative South Philadelphia family, a ne'er-do-well whose social and business maneuvers invariably misfire. The show-off became a synonym for a national type and helped to earn Kelly his reputation as an American Molière, a playwright dedicated to revealing our national follies. Yet Kelly's portrait is so shrewd and balanced that it transcends type; for all his foolishness the show-off proves to be loyal, dependable in a crisis, and good-hearted, and in the end he makes the financial killing that has always eluded him. His antagonist, the tart, scolding, common-sensical mother-in-law, is right about everything but lacks Aubrey's warmth. Kelly reveals the strengths and shortcomings of each of his large characters.

A perennial in community and college theaters, and in summer stock, *The Show-Off* provided successes for Pat Carroll and Jean Stapleton; when it was revived on Broadway in 1967 it afforded Helen Hayes one of the richest roles in her career.

Kelly's next play, *Craig's Wife* (1925), which won the Pulitzer Prize, was *A Doll's House* in reverse, in which a husband grows wise to, and then leaves, his autocratic spouse. Like the show-off, Craig's wife became a synonym for a national type, a house-proud suburban matron more devoted to things than to people. At the end of the play she is left completely alone. In 1936, Rosalind Russell, in her first dramatic role, portrayed Mrs. Craig on film; and in 1950, in *Harriet Craig*, Joan Crawford etched an especially fearsome portrait of Kelly's domestic tyrant.

Kelly refused to become a slick popular entertainer or to repeat the laugh-winning formulas of *The Torch-Bearers* or *The Show-Off*. His work became increasingly austere and idiosyncratic, and the seven plays that followed his first three hits did not achieve the same popular or critical acclaim. *Behold the Bridegroom* (1927) was a romantic tragedy and Kelly's own favorite among his plays. *Philip Goes Forth* (1931) was a comedy-drama about a would-be playwright from the provinces who discovers that the theater is not his true calling. In contrast, *Reflected Glory* written in 1929 but not produced until 1936, was about an actress who had the goods. *The Deep Mrs. Sykes* (1945) and *The Fatal Weakness* (1946) were droll comedies of manners and a return to Kelly's favorite type: the fussy, interfering matron whose lack of self-awareness creates havoc.

After he directed a 1947 revival of *Craig's Wife* on Broadway, Kelly wrote four more plays that he did not produce because he felt they could not be properly cast. In retirement in Sun City, Calif., Kelly welcomed visits from students and aspiring playwrights.

Kelly is certainly not a modernist, and his brand of well-made drawing-room comedy represents a style that, unfortunately, has long since disappeared from the theater. But within his own modestly scaled range Kelly is a master. All his plays remain stageworthy. The seemingly dictaphonic dialogue Kelly used in all his work contains a music all its own. His characters grill and bait each other in a homely wit replete with alliteration and cadenced repetition. Kelly is deeper, more incisive, and more surprising than his usual designation as a minor local colorist would suggest. Behind the vernacular snap of his dialogue is a cunning theatrical craftsman whose work transcends the boundaries of realism. Kelly is a major figure of the American theater of the 1920's who can claim his own distinct place among a company of writers that includes Eugene O'Neill, Philip Barry, S. N. Behrman, Elmer Rice, Sidney Howard, George Kaufman, Marc Connelly, Maxwell Anderson, and George Abbot.

[See Foster Hirsch, *George Kelly* (1975); and Arthur H. Lewis, *Those Philadelphia Kellys* (1977). An obituary is in the *New York Times*, June 19, 1974.]

FOSTER HIRSCH

KELLY, WALTER ("WALT") CRAWFORD, JR. (Aug. 25, 1913–Oct. 18, 1973), cartoonist, was born in Philadelphia, Pa., the son of Walter Crawford Kelly, a theatrical scene painter, and Genevieve MacAnnulla. In 1915 the family moved to Bridgeport, Conn., where Kelly spent his youth, and where he learned to draw from his father. He attended Warren Harding High School and was editor and cartoonist for the school paper. After graduation he became a reporter and artist for the *Bridgeport Post* and worked briefly with the Bridgeport welfare department.

In 1935 Kelly moved to California and joined Walt Disney Studios as an animator. He left in 1941 because of an impending strike and returned to the East Coast to work for the Western Printing and Lithographing Company as an illustrator of children's books. As part of his work he created a comic book in 1943 that featured a black child named Bumbazine and his pet alligator, Albert. One of the minor characters was a "possum" named Pogo. Over the next few years Pogo emerged as the figure who would dominate all of Kelly's career.

In 1948, by then a resident of Darien, Conn., he joined the staff of the *New York Star* as art director and political cartoonist. It was in the *Star* that the first "Pogo" comic strips appeared, creating an animal-populated world set in Georgia's Okefenokee Swamp. The language used was a southern dialect that Kelly had become interested in while serving as a civilian with the army's foreign language unit during World War II. In January 1949 the *Star* ceased publication and Kelly joined the *New York Post*, bringing "Pogo" with him. The strip became syndicated by Post-Hall (later Publishers-Hall) Syndicate in May 1949. Kelly always retained a personal copyright—one of the few cartoonists who did.

At first newspaper editors were dubious about adding a whimsical strip with talking animals to their comic pages. Their doubts evaporated, however, when "Pogo" quickly became one of the most popular comics in the nation. Collections of the strip soon came out in book form with the publication of *Pogo* in 1951. A second book, *I Go Pogo* (1952), had the "possum" running for president, resulting in a fad on university campuses of wearing "I Go Pogo" buttons. Eventually, Kelly published more than thirty books, including an anthology, *Ten Ever-Lovin' Blue-Eyed Years with Pogo* (1959).

In 1952 Kelly received the Cartoonist of the Year Award from the National Cartoonist Society. In 1954 he was elected president of the society, pledging to work for a reduction of violence in comic strips. Also in that year he was the first artist invited to contribute his work to the newly opened Collection of American Cartoonists at the Library of Congress. Around this time he moved to New York City, where he would remain the rest of his life.

Kelly's "Pogo" was a combination of slapstick, doubletalk, and puns. He said that there was a bit of himself in each of the swamp creatures and described his technique as dropping the main characters into a new situation and then trying to figure out how he would react under those circumstances. Included within the strip were inside jokes, such as drawing the faces of colleagues on minor characters or the custom of putting friends' names on the sides of the strip's ubiquitous swamp boats. Kelly claimed in 1959 that his goal with "Pogo" was "to have fun and make money at the same time."

Not all of Kelly's work was lighthearted. Often it took on a satirical, political edge. He reflected on topical issues by drawing the faces of well-known people on new animal characters. In 1956 and 1962 he drew Nikita Khrushchev as a pig; in other years he depicted Fidel Castro as a goat, J. Edgar Hoover as a bulldog, Spiro Agnew as a hyena, and in 1968, Lyndon Johnson as a steer with vision problems. Perhaps his most famous caricature debuted in 1953 with the introduction of Simple J. Malarkey, an evil wildcat with the face of Senator Joseph McCarthy of Wisconsin. Kelly was one of the few cartoonists willing to criticize McCarthy during that era.

Such satirical commentary sometimes made editors anxious because what Kelly was doing was novel to the comic pages. In response he claimed that "a cartoonist is a commentator on the day's events. There is nothing outside his province." Nevertheless, many papers decided to drop the political segments until the regular characters returned. In 1952 newspapers in Tokyo and Toronto refused to publish the Khrushchev strips. In 1968 an Alabama paper would not run strips that mocked Governor George Wallace, and a number of papers banned the series on Lyndon Johnson. Kelly protested this censorship, but often supplied alternative, nonpolitical sets of strips to replace the offending ones. Later, however, the banned material would appear in one of his books and by the early 1970's he refused to supply any more replacements. Some newspapers decided to simply move "Pogo" to the editorial page, and Kelly

agreed with this policy. In addition, a number of Kelly's books used satire to examine such themes as modern science (G. O. *Fizzickle Pogo*, 1958), right-wing political groups (*The Jack Acid Society Black Book*, 1962), mindless consumerism and the trading stamp phenomenon (*Pogo Puce Stamp Catalog*, 1962), and the problems of pollution (*Pogo: We Have Met the Enemy and He Is Us*, 1972).

Kelly also gave lectures, illustrated other people's books, and helped in the production of a 1961 government pamphlet that was a primer for parents regarding their children's television habits. But his genius was always identified with Pogo, "the reasonable, patient, soft-hearted, naive, friendly little person we all think we are." His concern was to provide humor that, he believed, was not an escape but a relief. "Pogo" was a path-breaking strip that first introduced political and social commentary to the comics page, thus setting the stage for the editorializing strips of the 1980's and beyond.

Kelly was married three times and had six children. He married his last wife, Selby, in 1972. He was in failing health through much of 1972 and 1973 and during that time a group of younger artists brought out "Pogo" under his supervision. Finally, former strips from the 1950's had to be substituted. Kelly died in Hollywood, Calif. "Pogo" continued to be written by his wife and one of his sons until 1975.

[Many of Kelly's ideas and opinions can be found in the text of his books. Particularly useful are *Ten Ever-Lovin' Blue-Eyed Years with Pogo* (1959), *Pogo Sunday Brunch* (1959), *Instant Pogo* (1962), *Pogo Poop Book* (1966), and *Equal Time for Pogo* (1967). A short biography of his early life is in *Uncle Pogo So-So Stories* (1953). A brief analysis of Kelly's work can be found in "Comic Books" by M. Thomas Inge, an article in Charles Reagan Wilson and William Ferris, eds., *Encyclopedia of Southern Culture* (1989). A particularly poignant, personal view is in Joseph P. Mastrangelo, "Remembering Walt Kelly: A Last Hello from the Old Swamp Boat," *Washington Post*, Nov. 10, 1973. Obituaries are in the *New York Times* and the *Washington Post*, both Oct. 19, 1973.]

ERIC JARVIS

KENDALL, EDWARD CALVIN (Mar. 8, 1886–May 4, 1972), biochemist, was born in South Norwalk, Conn., to George Stanley Kendall, a dentist, and Eva Frances Abbott. After completing high school he attended Columbia

University where he took three degrees in chemistry, including a Ph.D. under the guidance of Henry C. Sherman, a food chemist who directed his research on pancreatic amylase.

In a position with the pharmaceutical firm Parke, Davis, and Company, in 1910 he sought to study the isolation of the active compound in the thyroid gland. He returned to New York City in 1911 to pursue similar work at St. Luke's Hospital in Manhattan. He left the latter position in 1913, feeling that his employer did not appreciate the role of a research chemist.

Early in 1914, Kendall joined the Mayo Clinic in Rochester, Minn., where there was considerable success in thyroid surgery. Kendall, the clinic's only research chemist, was charged with isolating and studying the properties of the active substance in the thyroid gland. By 1914, he had prepared crystalline thyroxin and sought to learn its formula. During the next several years the pure thyroxin, an iodine compound, also received clinical trials which were successful in treating certain goiters. In 1926, he submitted a paper reporting its formula and structure for publication in the *Journal of Biological Chemistry*. Before the paper could be published, he learned that this had already been reported by Charles R. Harington of University College in London, England. Harington reported that the molecule contained four iodine atoms, not three, and had a somewhat different molecular structure; he proved to be correct.

Kendall now turned to the study of biological oxidations, giving particular attention to glutathione, a peptide which had been discovered in England in 1921. Kendall prepared crystalline glutathione and established its composition and structure correctly as glutamyl-cysteinyl-glycine, but pursued no further work on it.

The two decades following 1930 at the Mayo Clinic were occupied with discovering the relation between the hormones in the adrenal cortex and the incurable Addison's disease. The first half of this period was spent in studying the nature of various fractions of the adrenal gland after epinephrine (trademarked as "adrenalin" by Parke Davis) was well known and in clinical use. The newly created Institute of Experimental Medicine was correlated with the clinic's objectives. Kendall's research group had now grown to substantial size with temporary fellowships and a flow of professional visitors.

The investigation of the hormones of the adrenal cortex included the weekly processing of 900 pounds of adrenal glands obtained from slaughtered beef. Over a fifteen-year period, the glands were shipped to Rochester, Minn., by Wilson Laboratories (subsidiary of the Wilson Packing Company) of Chicago. As part of the arrangement, epinephrine was separated from the medulla of the gland and sent free of charge to the Parke Davis company for processing and sale as adrenalin. The hormones processed from the cortex of the adrenal glands were used partly for clinical use in the Mayo Clinic, and partly for isolation and study of the several corticoid hormones by Kendall and his research associates.

Research groups at Princeton and Columbia Universities, and in Zurich, reported the separation of seven crystalline compounds in 1936. Tadeus Reichstein and his group at the Technische Hochschule in Zurich reported isolation of seven crystalline compounds in 1936. By then Kendall's group had obtained five crystalline substances from their corticoid fractionations. These were identified for the moment as A, B, C, D, and E.

The publication of Reichstein's work led to complications for both Zurich and the Mayo Clinic. Reichstein's laboratory was an academic research operation that had sufficient staff to concentrate on synthesis and proof of structure of the various crystalline compounds; however, he had poor connections with clinical facilities. Conversely, Kendall's laboratory was associated with a clinic eager to test his compounds even before their formulas were established—but he and his staff were not as skilled in proof of structure as Reichstein's.

By 1944, research on Compound A had enough negative effects in clinical tests that most studies on it were abandoned with respect to Addison's disease, and attention was focused on Compound E. In late 1944, Lewis H. Sarett of Merck and Company produced a few milligrams of E, and by 1945, the compound was being produced in amounts that encouraged clinical testing.

Dr. Philip Hench, a physician in the Mayo Clinic, began making tests on patients with rheumatoid arthritis. Late in 1948, he injected the compound—which he and Kendall would soon name "cortisone"—into a woman with rheumatoid arthritis who went into remission as long as cortisone was available. Further tests were begun on other patients as soon as larger supplies of cortisone became available to

Hench. The results appeared to be favorable, in that there was temporary remission of arthritic symptoms, and Hench and Kendall were in high spirits.

In October 1950, the Nobel Prize in medicine and physiology was awarded to Kendall and Hench at the Mayo Clinic and Tadeus Reichstein in Zurich, for their studies on hormones of the adrenal cortex. Many other honors followed. Cortisone received much publicity, and it soon became available in quantity as synthesis increased at Merck. It was hailed as a wonder drug and used not only for treatment of rheumatoid arthritis, but for a host of other ailments. The medical profession slowly came to realize that it had to be used in limited amounts and with great caution.

Dr. Kendall retired from the Mayo Clinic in 1951 and became a visiting professor at Princeton University in New Jersey. Soon thereafter he developed a new research program at the James Forrestal Research Center near Princeton, where he sought without success to produce new medicinal agents.

Edward Kendall married Rebecca Kennedy on Dec. 30, 1915, and they had four children. He led an active life to the end. The coronary failure which took his life occurred during a consulting trip to Merck and Company in May 1972. He died three days later.

[Kendall published two books: *Thyroxine* (1929) and an autobiography entitled *Cortisone* (1971) which deals with his life and career up to 1951, after he received the Nobel Prize. See also Dwight J. Ingle's entry in *Biographical Memoirs. National Academy of Science* 47 (1975). An obituary appears in the *New York Times*, May 5, 1972.]

AARON J. IHDE

KENNY, JOHN V. (Apr. 6, 1893–June 2, 1975), political boss, was born in Jersey City, N.J., one of six children of Edward Kenny and Katherine Ward. His father was a tavern owner in the city's second ward, known as the "horseshoe." Kenny attended St. Michael's Parochial School and then went to St. Peter's Prep, graduating in 1911. He considered becoming a writer or reporter, or even a lawyer, but he did nothing to achieve these goals beyond attending the New Jersey Law School for a year. Kenny then became a bookkeeper in the dining car department of the Erie Railroad Company. On Apr. 8, 1918, he married Margaret Smith; they had one daughter.

Kenny made his entrance into the Jersey City Democratic party, controlled by Frank Hague, when he became a committeeman in place of his brother, who was murdered in 1916. Through Hague he then received a number of jobs in the Jersey City and Hudson County governments, including secretary to the county treasurer in 1924 and Jersey City tax commissioner in 1931. Between 1932 and 1941, he served as a member of the Hudson County Board of Chosen Freeholders.

In 1931, Kenny was made leader of Jersey City's second ward. In this capacity he worked during the 1930's and 1940's to produce a following; he approached various industries in the area, such as Armour, Swift, and Kraft, to obtain jobs for the ward's residents. In addition, he developed ties with the International Longshoremen's local, since the second ward contained part of the Jersey City waterfront. Kenny also benefited as a businessman from his Hague connection: in 1931 he founded the Industrial Utilities Corporation to clean, maintain, and renovate railroad cars, and through Hague's influence the company received a contract from the Pennsylvania Railroad Company.

Hague retired in 1947, but Kenny, or "the little guy," as he was called, was displeased with the succession of Hague's nephew, Frank Hague Eggers, which seemed to thwart Kenny's ambition to become public safety director. His subsequent activities irritated the Hague machine, causing him to be thrown out of the organization in June 1948. The "little guy" responded by assembling a slate of candidates to challenge the Hague forces in the election of city commissioners the following May. Kenny's ticket was ethnically mixed in comparison to the Hague practice of presenting an all-Irish slate. Campaigning vigorously on an anti-Hague theme and using the label "Freedom Ticket" as well as Churchill's victory sign, his associates were victorious and he became mayor. Although the unity of the victors disintegrated during the following year, Kenny was nevertheless able to take charge of Hudson County by gaining the support of the eleven other mayors there; he continued to control the county until 1972, chiefly through patronage and operating as a broker-type boss, making concessions and settling disputes among rival factions. In the 1949 gubernatorial election he did not support the Hague-backed Democratic candidate, Elmer Wene, with the result that

Jersey City went Republican for the first time in twenty years.

For the 1953 City elections Kenny put up another ethnically mixed ticket. While he and three of his candidates won, the other two commissioners were his rival, Eggers, and a Republican, Joshua Ringle. In December Kenny resigned as mayor, preferring to wield power without holding office. He was able to induce Ringle to accept his replacement and choice for mayor by offering the Republican some spoils and patronage. This maneuver left Eggers isolated. In gaining Ringle's support Kenny demonstrated one of his principal tactics, namely to pit opposing forces against one another and then to persuade them to ally with him. Before retiring he played a crucial part in the choice and election of Robert B. Meyner as governor in 1953.

During the early 1950's, Kenny's name came up in the investigation of waterfront crime by various government agencies. In April 1952, the New York County District Attorney issued a report indicating that he had committed perjury when he denied meeting secretly with a racketeer, Anthony Strollo (alias Tony Bender). He later affirmed the meeting, stating it was held to keep peace on the waterfront. In December 1955, Samuel Larner, a court-appointed Newark lawyer, began a two-and-a-half-year probe into Jersey City finances, which was highly critical of the practices of city officials, including Kenny.

These revelations hurt the Kenny candidates in the 1957 city elections, and they were defeated by a "Victory ticket," although its leader, Thomas Gangemi, was not elected. By this time Kenny was getting ready to retire; when he noticed the disunity among the Victoryites, though, he made a deal with Gangemi to join their political machines and make Gangemi the candidate for county supervisor. In November 1957, Kenny's county slate won by forty thousand votes, and Governor Meyner won reelection.

In 1960, Jersey City voters had approved a strong mayor–council form of government, and in the 1961 election Kenny's mayoral candidate, Gangemi, and seven of his council candidates were elected. When Gangemi was forced to resign in 1963, Kenny got his choice, Thomas Whelan, accepted for mayor. At the state level the "little guy" supported and helped to elect Richard Hughes as governor in 1961

and 1965. However, in 1969 he opposed the candidacy of Robert Meyner, his old ally, and advised county voters to split their votes between county candidates and Republican William Cahill, who won.

In November 1970, Kenny and eleven of his Jersey City and Hudson County associates were indicted by a federal grand jury on charges of extortion bribery; in addition, Kenny was charged with income tax evasion. Because of ill health his trial was severed. In May 1972, he pleaded guilty to income tax evasion and was sentenced to eighteen years in prison, later reduced to eighteen months, and a $30,000 fine. However, because of his health, he was released in March 1973 and spent the remaining years of his life in a nursing home in Paramus, N.J., where he died of heart disease.

[The best work on John V. Kenny is William Lemmey, "Bossism in Jersey City: The Kenny Years, 1949–1972" (unpublished Ph.D. diss., City University of New York, 1978). In the Jersey City Library there is a scrapbook of newspaper clippings from the *Jersey Journal* entitled "49—The Wildest Election: Story of Kenny's Revolution in 1949 that Overthrew Hague . . . ," mostly written by Martin Gately, with an interesting foreword on Kenny, written by J. Owen Grundy in 1969. See also Paul Hoffman, *Tiger in the Court* (1973); and William Lemmey, "The Last Hurrah Reconsidered: The Kenny Era in Jersey City, 1949–1972," in Joel Schwartz and Daniel Prosser, eds., *Cities of the Garden State: Essays in the Urban and Suburban History of New Jersey* (1977). An obituary appears in the *New York Times*, June 3, 1975.]

ALLAN NELSON

KENT, ROCKWELL (June 21, 1882–Mar. 13, 1971), artist and social activist, was born in Tarrytown Heights, N.Y., to Rockwell Kent, Sr., a prosperous attorney and mining engineer, and Sara Ann Holgate, a homemaker. For the first five years of his life, Kent lived in luxury, wintering in New York City, summering on Long Island, and spending spring and fall in suburban Tarrytown. In 1887, however, his father died after contracting typhoid during a business trip to Honduras. Kent was not told of his death; but as the family quickly entered a period of straitened circumstances, he guessed what had happened and reacted with anger and, often, wild behavior.

In part because of his behavior, Kent was shipped off to a military boarding school at the age of ten, supported both by scholarships and by a great aunt. That same aunt, Josie Banker, was an artist who noticed Kent's talent while he was still quite young. During the summer of 1895, she took Kent to Europe with her. In Dresden she studied the art of ceramic making and painting. When they returned, she purchased a kiln and began producing china herself. Kent assisted with the painting to earn money for his now needy family. Although he eschewed the style of the china, he ably executed the delft windmills and cottages featured on the pieces. As Kent settled down somewhat, he was withdrawn from military school and became a day student at the Horace Mann School in New York City.

Kent very nearly did not graduate from Mann in time to enter Columbia University on a scholarship to study architecture. He failed French and had to pass a last-minute test at the end of the summer of 1900. He then spent two years at Columbia, participating in a number of outside activities, including the drama club, the humor magazine, and Phi Delta Gamma fraternity. Yet his studies were not nearly as interesting to him as his summer and evening art studies, first with William Merritt Chase and then with Robert Henri. Both opened up new worlds for Kent. In 1902 Kent dropped out of Columbia to become a regular student at the New York School of Art, which was associated at that time with the realist painters. In 1905 Kent moved to Maine to paint, supporting himself with odd jobs, and putting his architecture training to work by building his own house. His family regarded him as a failure, a dropout who earned money digging ditches and whose socialist politics and personal habits—vegetarianism, in particular—were quirky. Not until his first show of fourteen seascapes painted in Maine was exhibited in the spring of 1907 in Tarrytown did his family begin to accept his talents as an artist.

As Kent's artistic skill grew, so too did his interest in socialism. As an art student, he observed and painted urban scenes and explored the poorer sections of New York City. In his autobiography, Kent credited Henri with teaching him to use his heart as an artist, to attain an emotional connection with his subjects that sometimes resulted in politicized pictures. A family friend who was a Christian socialist introduced Kent to the ideals of the movement. Several years later, while living on Caritas Island, Conn., he met several of the more prominent socialists in the United States who were his neighbors, including Mary ("Mother") Jones, W. E. B. Du Bois, and Rose Strunsky.

Kent married Kathleen Whiting on Dec. 31, 1909. She was the niece of Abbott Thayer, a naturalist painter who influenced Kent, particularly as he began to paint seascapes. The couple had five children, but their marriage was not a happy one. Kent also had a mistress, identified in his memoirs only as "Janet," by whom he had a sixth child. Supporting Janet and her child forced the Kents to sell their Maine house, depleting most of their savings and some of the money given them as wedding presents. At one point Kent tried to move Janet and her son into the family circle, but both women balked. The Kents finally divorced in 1926.

Kent's wanderlust had put additional stress on his marriage. For long periods of time, he was away from the family, generally because he craved adventure and wanted to paint landscapes that were wild and raw. He visited Newfoundland three times to paint and planned to open an art school on a remote bay there, but he was expelled from Canada in 1914 because his friendship with local Germans and admiration for things German caused the government to suspect him of being a spy. In 1916 he took his oldest son with him to Alaska for the year. In 1923 he sailed around Cape Horn in a small sailboat named the *Kathleen* and spent time painting on Tierra del Fuego. In 1931 and 1934 he made lengthy trips to Greenland.

After each trip, Kent showed his canvases and also wrote of his experiences. He had himself incorporated as Rockwell Kent, Inc., in 1916, and sold shares in himself to finance the writing of *Wildnerness: A Journal of Quiet Adventure in Alaska* (1920). In 1924 he published *Voyaging: Southward from the Strait of Magellan*, and in 1935 he published *Salamina*, a narrative of his two Greenland trips.

Kent's popularity as an artist peaked in the 1920's and 1930's. He was extremely versatile, using different mediums and capturing different types of subjects. His early seascapes were particularly renowned, but his figure drawings and paintings were also much admired. Especially during the 1930's he did many etchings, some with political overtones. Some lithographs, including the 1937 *Workers of the World Unite!*, were influenced by the style of socialist realism common in the Soviet Union. His work was displayed in many museums, including the Metropolitan Museum of Art, the Chicago Art Institute, and the Whitney Museum of American Art.

Kent kept busy in other ways during these years. After a two-week courtship, he married Frances Lee of Virginia on Apr. 5, 1926. Lee was a young divorcée with a small boy. Kent first met her at a cocktail party on Long Island. In 1927, with money inherited from his mother's relatives, the Bankers, he bought a farm in the Adirondack Mountains near the small village of Au Sable Forks, building his own house and barn. Named Asgaard Farm, this was his home base for the rest of his life. In the 1930's, he found that publishers were interested in using his lithographs and woodcuts to illustrate classics. The best known of these was the 1930 edition of *Moby Dick*, but he also illustrated *Candide, Beowolf*, and many of Shakespeare's plays. Under the name of Hogarth, Jr., he did satirical and humorous drawings for *Vanity Fair*. Occasionally Kent also did paid illustrations for ads, including Rolls Royce, and unpaid illustrations for political causes.

Kent's most political phase began in the 1930's and continued until his death. He belonged to both the American Artists' Congress and the League of American Writers, two creative front groups. He tried to organize artists for the Congress of Industrial Organizations. Kent supported Communist party candidate Earl Browder for president in 1936, and when Browder was convicted in 1940 of providing false information on a passport application, he headed the New York state chapter of the Citizens Committee to Free Earl Browder in 1941. He also led the Soviet-American Friendship Society for a time.

In 1937, he made national headlines when, on a post office mural he painted in Washington, D.C., he lettered in minuscule script and using an obscure Innuit dialect a message supporting independence for Puerto Rico. The government resisted having to pay for his political statement, but Kent had a contract and collected his $3,000 fee. Once the Post Office Department officially owned the mural, the text of the message was expunged. Kent supported the Loyalists during the Spanish Civil War and became the foster parent of a Spanish refugee child. In 1939, former Communist party member Benjamin Gitlow identified Kent as a member of the party before the House Committee on Un-American Activities. Kent's first autobiography, *This Is My Own* (1940), defended the Nazi-Soviet Pact and the Soviet Union's invasions of Poland and Finland.

In part because of his politics, but also because of the rise of abstract expressionism as an artistic style after World War II, Kent's popularity as an artist declined after the 1930's. He was married for a third time in 1940 to Sally Johnstone, an English-born, Canadian-educated young woman Kent hired as his secretary. Her presence at Asgaard Farm, and Lee's absences, finally broke up his second marriage.

Kent never lost his taste for left-wing politics. He was vice-president of the International Workers Order, a left-wing fraternal benefits society, off and on during the 1930's and 1940's, and was its last president when the federal government rescinded its charter at the peak of the McCarthy era. He was named as a member of the Communist party before the Un-American Activities Committee again in 1949 when his name topped the list of Americans belonging to alledgedly subversive organizations. Kent belonged, the committee claimed, to at least eighty-five such communist front groups. In 1953 Senator Joseph McCarthy subpoenaed Kent, who refused to cooperate, pleading the Fifth Amendment. That same year, he was denied a passport after he refused to sign an affidavit swearing he did not belong to the Communist party. He sued to get a passport and, in a case that went to the Supreme Court (*Kent* v. *Dulles*, 1958), won. In his local community, Kent campaigned for Progressive party candidate Henry Wallace in 1948 and organized a district branch of the American Labor party (ALP). During World War II, Kent had begun to bottle and sell the milk produced on his New York farm. His political activities in that year prompted a local boycott of what he facetiously called "Russian milk." The boycott grew larger and larger until Wallace himself got wind of it; while Kent assured Wallace that it provided good publicity for the Progressive party ticket, he also admitted that the boycott had cost him $15,000. The boycott was so effective that he abandoned the idea of running the dairy any longer, gave the business to his employees, and advised them to change its name and move the dairy away from Asgaard Farm to avoid any negative political associations. That same year, Kent himself decided to go into politics, declaring his candidacy for the House of Representatives on the ALP ticket, which was more liberal and internationalist than the Democratic party. Kent was responsible for an ALP proposal advocating the creation of a Department of Culture. A third-party candidate stood little chance of getting elected under any circumstances, but Kent antagonized many in his own small party. His campaign was a disaster; he was heckled during many of his speeches, and attacked by the American Legion.

Kent never lost his determination to make a grand gesture in the name of his political beliefs. In 1967, the Soviet Union awarded him the Lenin Peace Prize, which carried a $28,000 award. Kent asked that $10,000 of the money be donated to the National Liberation Front in South Vietnam for medical supplies. In 1967 opposition to the war was not yet widespread, and Kent's decision was not at all popular. Nevertheless, he was an early and vocal opponent of American participation in the war.

As he grew older, Kent continued to paint, write, and follow politics. He traveled to Europe several times, both before and after his passport case was settled. In 1955 he completed his lengthy autobiography, *It's Me, O Lord*, taking the title from a spiritual. His politics made it difficult to publish and also difficult for him to place paintings in museums. In 1953, after Kent's testimony before McCarthy's committee, the Farnsworth Museum in Rockland, Maine, declined Kent's offer of paintings because the museum's trustees thought him too controversial. Thereafter no other museums expressed any interest in his works until the Soviet government mounted a traveling Kent exhibit in 1958 and bought paintings for the Hermitage and Pushkin museums. In 1960, Kent decided to distribute his growing collection of some eighty paintings and eight hundred prints to friends. Thus, when lightning struck his Asgaard farmhouse in 1969 and burned it to the ground, not all of his works were lost. Kent, his family, and friends rebuilt the house, where he died at the age of eighty-nine.

[Most of Kent's papers are in the Archives of American Art at the Smithsonian Institution, Washington, D.C. A smaller collection is at the Butler Library at Columbia University. David Traxel, *An American Saga* (1980) tells the story of Kent's life. Also see *American Book Collector*, summer 1964. An obituary appears in the *New York Times*, Mar. 14, 1971.]

JUDY KUTULAS

KING, RICHARD, JR. (Dec. 17, 1884–May 4, 1974), banker and rancher, was born on the La Puerta de Agua Dulce Ranch, in Nueces County, Tex., to Richard King II and Elizabeth Pearl Ashbrook. He was named for his grandfather, Captain Richard King, founder of the celebrated King Ranch, who died four months later. (The patriarch bore no middle initials, nor have any of his namesake progeny, resulting in a rotation of "Jr." and numerals that often hinders identification.) The La Puerta Ranch, some 40,000 "good and well-watered acres" given to Richard's parents as a wedding gift, was home, school, and playground for the boy, as he studied under private tutors until he reached high school age. At that time he went to West Texas Military Academy in San Antonio, as had his father before him, and graduated with honors in 1903.

King studied agriculture at the University of Missouri for two years, then returned to the ranch to participate with his father in farming and ranching activities. He married Minerva Pierpont Heaney, daughter of a prominent Corpus Christi physician, on Oct. 12, 1907. They had two children, and the family moved to Corpus Christi around 1911.

Under the terms of Captain King's will, his widow, Henrietta, was his sole heir to the nearly million-acre King Ranch located South of Corpus Christi, and their son-in-law, Robert J. Kleberg, assumed management of the vast cattle empire. After Henrietta King's death in 1924, and following a lengthy trusteeship by Kleberg, each surviving heir received additional acreage, but ranch operation remained centralized. Richard King, the grandson (whose father had died in 1922), shared ownership of the Santa Fe division, some 150,000 acres, with his two sisters.

The Captain had long said that his goal was "to buy land, and never sell it," but this soon jeopardized the financial operations of the ranch. Richard once remarked, "People talk about what we inherited, but in those days it was mostly debts and hard times." Richard's designated role was therefore to become the banking liaison, and in 1913 he was appointed to the board of directors of the Corpus Christi National Bank, where his grandmother was the principal stockholder. Much of his time was spent going from bank to bank generating credit extensions and additional loans to keep both bank and ranch solvent.

After his mother's death in 1924, he was one of the eight trustees and four executors named in her will to direct the ten-year trusteeship she set up. He became vice-president of the bank in 1924, president in 1929, and chairman of the board in 1950. When Corpus Christi National Bank and State National Bank merged in 1956, he became chairman of the board, a position he held until 1970, when he was named chairman emeritus.

Having been raised on the ranch at La Puerta and possessing early memories of being boosted onto a saddle in front of a vaquero for a daily ride, King was perhaps happiest directing farming and ranching activities. He told one reporter, "Sometimes I don't think I understand all I know about figures and finance, but when I'm at the ranch, then I know what I'm talking about. . . . Cattle are like poker," he said. "They get into a man's blood and there's no cure for it."

For several decades, King operated his ranches independently, using the historic "HK" brand Captain King had used before adopting the "Running W." He was honored for his lifetime contributions to ranching by the Texas and Southwest Cattle Raiser's Association, which he served as an honorary vice-president and active member for more than sixty years. King also continued the farming interests of his father, who admired the "more civilized" techniques and livestock of the Midwest: these included raising experimental crops, encouraging settlement by farmers, and even selling small portions of ranchland; Richard continued and expanded these practices.

In 1956, ownership of the Santa Fe Ranch was transferred to the King Ranch, Inc., in return for 10 percent mineral rights on 600,000 acres of King Ranch property. The La Puerta Ranch, along with the historic ranch house constructed by his father after the original house burned, was sold in 1974 to one of his nephews.

King's interests in commerce were almost all related to the enhancement of the agricultural and oil industries that formed the backbone of the Texas Coastal Bend economy. As chairman of the Nueces County Board of Navigation and Canal Commissioners, King guided the growth of the port of Corpus Christi from a small shallow-water turning basin into a deepwater facility nearly ten miles long, capable of handling modern tankers and freighters that are essential for moving oil, cotton, grain, and other agricultural products. Before port expansion, cotton was shipped by rail to the port at Galveston. A major dry cargo dock is named the Richard King Terminal in his honor.

An affable man, whose desk in the bank lobby was accessible to all, King served on the boards of directors of numerous other corporations and financial institutions, including chairman of the Texas Sanitary Livestock Commission, director of Frost National Bank, Central Power & Light, Texas-Mexican Railway, Southwestern Life Insurance Co. of Dallas, National Finance Credit Corporation in Fort Worth, and Regional Agricultural Credit Corporation, Houston. He was a Democrat, an Episcopalian, and belonged to Sigma Alpha Epsilon, the Elks, and the Masonic Lodge.

One measure of King's influence in the community is that, in 1965, a new high school in Corpus Christi was named Richard King High School in his honor.

More than 450 people attended the valedictory dinner at the Corpus Christi Country Club on June 25, 1971, honoring "The Builder of the Port," and upon hearing of his death, delegates to the Texas Constitutional Convention signed a resolution citing the lifelong accomplishments of Richard King, Jr.

[Papers concerning the King Ranch are contained in the King Ranch archives, Kingsville, Tex. See also Tom Lea, *The King Ranch*, 2 vols. (1957); and David Frost, *The King Ranch Papers* (1985). Relevant newspaper articles appear in the *Corpus Christi Caller*, July 12, 1953; Mar. 17, 1970; May 8, 1971; June 26, 1971; Apr. 9, 1974; and Oct. 14, 1979; and the *Los Angeles Times*, Dec. 11, 1977. Obituaries appear in the *Corpus Christi Caller* and the *Corpus Christi Times*, both Mar. 4, 1974.]

DOROTHY S. ("DOREY") SCHMIDT

KINKAID, THOMAS CASSIN (Apr. 3, 1888– Nov. 17, 1972), naval officer, was born in Hanover, N.H., the son of Thomas Wright Kinkaid, a naval officer who rose to the rank of rear admiral, and Virginia Lee Cassin. He was raised at various naval stations, graduated from a Washington, D.C., high school, and went on to excel in athletics at the U.S. Naval Academy, from which he graduated in the lower half of the Class of 1908. His initial three-year tour of sea duty was aboard the battleship *Nebraska*, including the global voyage of the Great White Fleet, on which he began a career in ordnance and gunnery, the main line for advancement in the battleship-centered navy. Kinkaid served on another battleship, the *Minnesota*, from 1910 to 1913, before he began studying ordnance engineering in the Washington-Annapolis area. In April 1911 he married Helen Sherbourne Ross of Philadelphia; they had no children. He interrupted his course of study for service aboard the gunboat *Machias* in the politically tense Caribbean region in 1914. Choice battleship duty followed on the *Pennsylvania* (1916–1917) and the *Arizona* as gunnery officer (1918–1919), between which assignments he had World War I liaison duty at the British Admiralty. He attained the rank of lieutenant commander early in 1918.

After being posted at the Bureau of Ordnance, from 1919 to 1922, Kinkaid served as assistant chief of staff (1922–1924) to Mark L. Bristol, commander of U.S. naval forces off Turkey, and as captain of the destroyer *Isherwood* for one year. Duty at the Naval Gun Factory in Washington preceded staff duty as gunnery officer to the commander in chief of the U.S. Fleet, Admiral Henry A. Wiley, from 1927 to 1929. He was, successively, a senior student at the Naval War College, secretary for the navy's General Board, and a technical adviser at abortive naval disarmament talks at Geneva. Key ordnance posts followed: executive officer of the battleship *Colorado* (1933–1934) and head of the officer detail section, Bureau of Navigation (1934–1937), during which he was promoted to captain. Kinkaid commanded the heavy cruiser *Indianapolis* before assignment as U.S. naval attaché in Mussolini's Italy from the end of 1938 until March 1941. In June of that year he began escorting Atlantic convoys as a destroyer squadron commander during the quasi war with Germany. In November 1941 he was promoted to rear admiral.

When Kinkaid assumed command of a cruiser division in Hawaii, one week after the Pearl Harbor disaster, he happened to be one of the few flag officers on hand to command U.S. forces in initial combat operations against the Japanese. His peacetime performance had been successful, if unexceptional, and he provided steady leadership of the cruiser screens for the first carrier raids in the South and Central Pacific and in the battles of the Coral Sea and Midway. In July 1942 he took command of a carrier task force, which he led in the Guadalcanal campaign. Although not a naval aviator

(he was turned down for flight training due to slightly impaired hearing in 1929), he performed well enough until the Battle of the Santa Cruz Islands, October 26–27, when both his carriers were put out of action—the *Hornet* sunk and the *Enterprise* forced to withdraw with heavy damage; his tactics were criticized as a contributing factor. After the naval battle of Guadalcanal in mid-November, he was reassigned to the cruisers.

In January 1943 Kinkaid became commander, North Pacific Force, at Kodiak, Alaska; he recaptured Attu in May, was promoted to vice admiral in June, and occupied Kiska in August. Because of his demonstrated ability in resolving interservice difficulties in the North Pacific, General Douglas MacArthur was pleased to accept him as commander of Allied naval forces and of the U.S. Seventh Fleet in the Southwest Pacific theater in November 1943. As such, he headed "MacArthur's navy" throughout the offensive in that quarter until the final victory.

During this period, Kinkaid, shore-based at Brisbane, Australia, labored successfully to overcome shortages in men and matériel and to satisfy the often difficult demands made by MacArthur during the drive up the New Guinea coast throughout the spring of 1944. Although this offensive cooperated with the Navy-led Central Pacific offensive under Admiral Chester W. Nimitz to liberate the Philippines that autumn, the divided command situation led to near-disaster at the Battle for Leyte Gulf in October. There, with Kinkaid at sea, the Japanese fleet surprised and sank some of Kinkaid's Seventh Fleet amphibious shipping. Although historians have ascribed blame in varying degrees to both these men for the failure to conduct necessary air searches from Kinkaid's escort carriers and from Admiral William F. Halsey, Jr.'s fast carriers, both succeeded in providing the necessary naval and air support for the recapture of Leyte and Luzon throughout the autumn and winter of 1944–1945. Promoted to full admiral in April 1945, Kinkaid used his forces to mop up the southern Philippines through the spring and summer and to land marines in China following the Japanese surrender until his relief in November. He briefly commanded the Eastern Sea Frontier in New York and the Atlantic Reserve Fleet from 1946 until his retirement in 1950. He was recalled to active duty to serve on the National Security

Training Commission (1951–1953, 1955–1960). He died of emphysema at Bethesda Naval Hospital in Washington, D.C., and was buried at Arlington National Cemetery.

An able officer who learned to curb a hot Irish temper and to become soft-spoken and tactful, Kinkaid rendered valuable service in many positions. But the accident of his timely availability accounted for most of his senior commands, for he was by no means as superior a performer as many of his World War II contemporaries, as evidenced by his losses at Santa Cruz and Leyte Gulf.

[Kinkaid's career, based on his papers at the Naval Historical Center, Washington, D.C., is the subject of Gerald E. Wheeler, *Kinkaid of the Seventh Fleet: A Biography of Admiral Thomas C. Kinkaid, U.S. Navy* (1994), from which is drawn "Thomas C. Kinkaid: MacArthur's Master of Naval Warfare," in William M. Leary, ed., *We Shall Return! MacArthur's Commanders and the Defeat of Japan, 1942–1945* (1988). A line biography is kept at the Naval Historical Center. His World War II campaigns are detailed in Samuel Eliot Morison's fifteen-volume *History of U.S. Naval Operations in World War II*. On the Leyte Gulf controversy, see the Wheeler biography and Clark G. Reynolds, *The Fast Carriers: The Forging of an Air Navy* (1968, 1992). An obituary is in the *New York Times*, Nov. 19, 1972.]

CLARK G. REYNOLDS

KIRBY, ALLAN PRICE (July 31, 1892–May 2, 1973), financier and corporation executive, was born in Wilkes-Barre, Pa., the son of Fred Morgan Kirby and Jessie Amelia Owen. His father was a retail merchant and cofounder of the F. W. Woolworth Company. Young Kirby attended the Harry Hillman Academy in Wilkes-Barre, the Wyoming Seminary in Kingston, Pa. (1906–1908), and the Lawrenceville School in Lawrenceville, N.J. (1908–1910). He then entered Lafayette College in Easton, Pa., but left in 1912. In 1914 he became office manager for the Bathurst Lumber Company in New Brunswick, Canada, beginning a period of approximately twenty-five years in which Kirby was involved in a number of business ventures. Between 1915 and 1922, he was treasurer of the Jenkins-Kirby Packing Company, then became president of the Kirby-Davis Company, a position he held until 1934, when he became president of the Imperial Motor Corporation until 1946. He also served as vice-president of the Second National Bank of

Wilkes-Barre from 1922 until 1934. During World War I, he entered the Naval Reserve as a seaman and served on a "reconverted yacht" that his father had leased to the government for one dollar per year. On Feb. 14, 1918, he married Marian G. Sutherland; they had four children.

Kirby's career as a financier and his long association with the Alleghany Corporation began after he was introduced by his father's lawyer to Robert R. Young in 1935. Young had left General Motors to go into financial management and, with a partner, had acquired a broker's seat on the New York Stock Exchange. In 1937, Young and Kirby obtained control of the Alleghany Corporation, a holding company established in 1929 that controlled seven sizable railroads with twenty-three thousand miles of track and assets of some $2 billion; among these only the Chesapeake and Ohio Railroad was profitable. Young put up $750,000; Kirby, using monies inherited from his father, invested $4 million. Kirby became president, and his partner served as chairman of the board and chief executive officer. The personalities and approaches of the two men differed greatly. Young was "flamboyant," very much in the public view, stressing the need for public relations. Kirby was cautious in financial matters and in effect was a silent partner, avoiding the limelight; he let Young lead but maintained the right to recommend or "veto."

During the next twenty years the partners improved the position of the Alleghany Corporation. Young, as head of the Chesapeake and Ohio, managed it well; the situation of two other railroads, the Nickel Plate and the Missouri Pacific, was improved during this period. In 1954, Young resigned as chairman of the Chesapeake and Ohio; in the same year, the Alleghany Corporation sold its holdings in this railroad and acquired control of the New York Central Railroad through a proxy fight. Kirby and Young used funds from the sale of the Chesapeake and Ohio, and from other Alleghany activities, to acquire control of Investors Diversified Services, a huge investment conglomerate. In their struggle to obtain the New York Central, they had received help from Clint Murchison, Sr., a Texas millionaire; and in 1955 Murchison's two sons, Clint, Jr., and John, acquired control of Investors Diversified Services from the Alleghany Corporation in a stock arrangement engineered by Young.

In January 1958, following Young's suicide,

Kirby shed his silent partner image and was elected chairman of the Alleghany Corporation while remaining president. During the next five years, he faced a number of crises and challenges to his leadership. In 1959, with the help of Charles T. Ireland, Jr., he thwarted the bid of Abraham M. Sonnabend, a financier from Boston, to take over the Alleghany Corporation. Ireland subsequently became president. At this time the holdings of the company included a controlling interest in the New York Central Railroad system as well as investments in the Missouri Pacific Railroad, Investors Diversified Services, and the Court House Square Development in Denver.

Also in 1959, as a result of a lawsuit, Alleghany regained control of Investors Diversified Services, but soon afterward trouble developed between Kirby and the Murchison brothers over its management. The two sides became involved in a proxy fight for control of the Alleghany Corporation, which was won by the Murchisons in May 1961. Kirby reportedly spent $40 million in an unsuccessful effort to keep control of the company. He did not, however, let his defeat force him into retirement, and began to work to regain Alleghany. He later stated that "pride" was the motivation. "As nearly as I can remember, until the proxy fight with the Murchisons in 1961, I never got licked. I was very upset." Two and a half years later Kirby achieved his goal with the help of several associates, including Ireland. Kirby once again became chairman and chief executive officer, and Ireland was again president.

When he regained control of the Alleghany Corporation, Kirby was one of the richest men in the United States, possessing a fortune, estimated in 1961 to be between $250 million and $300 million, that included major investments in F. W. Woolworth, International Phillips Petroleum, International Telephone and Telegraph, Manufacturers Hanover Trust, and the New York Central Railroad, as well as the Alleghany Corporation and Investors Diversified Services. Through his investments and his activities as a financier, he had substantially increased the $50 million fortune he had inherited. He owned a twenty-seven-room mansion on a sixty-four-acre estate in Harding Township, N.J.; a chateau in Easton, Pa.; a hunting lodge in South Carolina; and a fishing camp on the Gaspé Peninsula in Canada. Nevertheless, he was hesitant to buy a Rolls Royce because he felt it too much a display of wealth, and he sometimes expressed doubt that he would be permitted by a restaurant's management to open a charge account. He died in Harding Township.

[For additional information on Kirby's association with the Alleghany Corporation, see Robert R. *Young and Alleghany Corporation* (1957). Also see "The Quiet Man," *Forbes*, Feb. 15, 1958; "Management: A Diversified Storm," *Time*, Sept. 19, 1960; "Proxy Fighter by Proxy: Allan Price Kirby," *Time*, Dec. 12, 1960; "Proxy Fights: Power Play," *Newsweek*, April 17, 1961; "The Murchisons and Allan Kirby," *Life*, April 28, 1961; and "Proxy Fight: Ayes of Texas?" *Newsweek*, May 22, 1961. An obituary is in the *New York Times*, May 3, 1973.]

ALLAN NELSON

KLEBERG, ROBERT JUSTUS, JR. (Mar. 29, 1896–Oct. 13, 1974), rancher, was born in Corpus Christi, Tex., the son of Robert Justus Kleberg, a lawyer and rancher, and Alice Gertrudis King, the youngest daughter of Captain Richard King, founder of a south Texas cattle ranching empire known as the King Ranch. Kleberg, Jr., had three sisters and a brother, U.S. Congressman Richard M. Kleberg. He spent his childhood at the Santa Gertrudis headquarters of the ranch in Kingsville, Tex., which his father then operated. Kleberg was educated in local public schools, graduated from high school in Corpus Christi, then took special agricultural courses at the University of Wisconsin for two years, returning home to the Santa Gertrudis Ranch in 1916.

Although the vast King Ranch (nearly a million acres, roughly the size of Rhode Island) belonged to Kleberg's maternal grandmother, Henrietta M. King, Kleberg's father was the general manager, and young Robert was being groomed to take his place. As his father's health failed, Kleberg took over the management of the ranch, becoming trustee and general manager at the death of his grandmother in 1924. On Mar. 2, 1926, after a three-week courtship, Kleberg married Helen Mary Campbell, daughter of a congressman from Kansas. They had one child.

Applying his inventive mind and scientific training to the ranch, Kleberg experimented with cattle breeding, attempting to produce a breed that could withstand the often severe heat and drought conditions of the south Texas coastal plains. From those experiments, some twenty years later, Kleberg produced the first officially recognized American breed of cattle, the hardy, stocky, cherry-red Santa Gertrudis, which can "live and thrive in any climate. On awful real estate they merely thrive; on better real estate they absolutely flourish." Kleberg was also successful in developing the grass that sustained his new breed, and within one eight-year period, he not only doubled the carrying capacity (number of cows per acre) of the ranch, but also reduced the time needed to be on pasture by almost half, so that King Ranch became the largest producer of beef in the country, even though it was situated in a predominantly arid region.

Kleberg demonstrated his ingenuity and inventiveness by devising or adapting means to accomplish virtually any ranching task. His designs included giant machines that uprooted the ubiquitous and water-wasting mesquite brush, dipping vats for ticks, electric cattle prods, and extremely durable fences that use no nails. Many of these devices are still in use.

Under Kleberg's management, the King Ranch acquired adjoining ranches and holdings from other King heirs. After her husband's death in 1932, Kleberg's mother incorporated those holdings and named him president and chief executive officer, a position he held until his death. King Ranch, Inc., continued to expand, with acquisitions in Australia, Africa, Spain, South America, and California, Pennsylvania, Kentucky, and Florida, eventually bringing the total holdings to more than 13 million acres. As described by Charles Murphy in an article for *Fortune*, "[Kleberg] dramatically recast and vastly enhanced . . . the fortunes of an already proud and powerful family. . . . He has made it something of a world force, as distinct and productive in its speciality as I.B.M. and General Motors and Boeing are in theirs."

Much of this expansion was made possible through the development of oil and gas resources on the ranch, which began with a Humble Oil and Refining Company lease of the entire property in 1933, an arrangement that removed the burden of existing debt and opened the way to the empire building through which Kleberg showed his kinship to his maternal grandfather. Each of them was "an individualist of formidable proportions." Kleberg's sophistication and charisma are said to have made him and his wife the prototypes of Edna Ferber's novel of Texas ranching, *Giant*.

Horse breeding produced two equally remarkable accomplishments. Texas quarterhorses, known for their agility and speed, are used on working ranches around the world, but are not noted for their stamina. Kleberg crossbred them with thoroughbreds to produce King Ranch Quarterhorses, a strain coveted for their speed and agility as well as their endurance. In 1935 Kleberg entered thoroughbred racing as a Texas upstart. He produced champions such as Assault, a Triple Crown winner, and Kentucky Derby winners Bold Venture and Middleground, as well as a dozen others who carried the King Ranch racing silks to earnings of millions of dollars.

Kleberg, known widely as "Mr. Bob," also directed a number of enterprises in Kingsville, a small town established by his father on land donated by Mrs. King, and in Alice, a town named for his mother. These included a bank, a newspaper, a lumberyard, a department store, a leather shop (which produced boots and saddles for hundreds of *Kineños*—King Ranch cowboys of Mexican descent), and a dairy that boasted the finest herd of Jersey milk cows his skillful breeding could produce.

A Democrat who was powerful in Texas politics, Kleberg had close ties with President Lyndon Johnson, but considered himself a conservative. Although soft-spoken, he expressed his views "on everything from horses, to politics, to liquor, to how high a hawk flies," according to the writer of his obituary in the *New York Times*. Kleberg was on the board of directors of numerous corporations and associations, and he continued in the active management of the ranch until his death. He died of stomach cancer in Houston, Tex., and is buried at the King Ranch.

[Papers concerning the King Ranch are in the Ranch Archives, Kingsville, Tex. See also Charles J. V. Murphy, "The World's Biggest Ranch," *Fortune*, Dec. 1933; *Reader's Digest*, May 1938; *Time* (cover), Dec. 15, 1947; Tom Lea, *The King Ranch* (1957); Charles Murphy, "The Fabulous House of Kleberg," *Fortune*, June, July, Aug. 1969; Tom Lea, *In the Crucible of the Sun* (1974); Hugh Best, "The Royal Family of Ranching," *Debrett's Texas Peerage* 1983; and David Frost, *The King Ranch Papers* (1985). An obituary appears in the *New York Times*, Oct. 15, 1974.]

DOROTHY S. ("DOREY") SCHMIDT

KLEIN, ANNE (Aug. 3, 1923–Mar. 19, 1974), fashion designer, was born Hannah

Golofski in the borough of Brooklyn in New York City. She attended the Girls Commercial High School, where she displayed an outstanding talent in design. As a result, she won a scholarship to the Trapagen School of Fashion. Klein had, however, begun working as a freelance sketcher for a wholesale fashion house when she was fifteen, and she chose to work full-time. A year later she had a regular job at Varden Petites, where she was central in changing the firm's production from a line fitting short, plump women to the now familiar small, lean line of junior dress; her approach in fact created a new category of sizes in ready-to-wear women's clothes.

In 1948, she married Ben Klein. He recognized her talent, and the same year founded Junior Sophisticates, with Anne as the principal designer. Over the next few years she led designers away from traditional "buttons and bows frilliness" back to a sleek, sophisticated style for juniors. A woman of small physical stature, she appreciated the particular needs of smaller women and fundamentally transformed the design of clothing in petite sizes. Following Coco Chanel's example in France, she was the first American designer to introduce men's items into women's lines. Her impact was such that she won the prestigious Coty Fashion Award in 1955. She won it again in 1969, and was elected to the Coty Fashion Hall of Fame in 1971.

By the late 1950's, Klein was emphasizing separates, permitting women to buy an array of jackets, slacks, skirts, and blouses that could be mixed and matched. She emphasized simplicity and elegance and was admired for her sense of line and proportion. Klein was a leader in using new fabrics to make familiar casual styles elegant (for example, satin for jeans, soft leather and suede in sportswear). Over the next decade, her approach became the standard for the majority of women's fashion design, both in the United States and abroad.

Klein found working for husband and company president Ben Klein increasingly difficult by the late 1950's; she soon left Junior Sophisticates and divorced Ben in 1960. In 1963, she married Matthew ("Chip") Rubinstein and set up her own design studio. Because of her stature in the industry, she attracted a steady flow of clients, particularly those needing quick help to shore up faltering lines. Charles Revson came to her to edit weak Evan-Picone and Dynasty lines; he credited her work with restoring those

lines and paid her an unprecedented six-figure fee. Soon thereafter Sandy Smith and Gunther Oppenheim, who held the license for Pierre Cardin coats, came to her in desperate need of quick redesign of the line. The results were so successful that they offered to create a sportswear company under her direction and of which she would be half owner; they would provide all capital. In 1968, Anne Klein and Company began operation and was immediately successful. By the early 1970's, the Anne Klein label was one of the most successful in women's fashion, carried in more than eight hundred American department stores and specialty shops. Because of this striking success, in 1973 Takihyo Company of Japan bought a half interest in both Anne Klein and Company and Anne Klein Studio; it later bought the remaining half.

In 1973, Klein was the only woman, and one of five American designers, invited to share the stage with five leading French designers in a special fashion show to raise funds for the renovation of the Palace of Versailles. The Metropolitan Museum of Art exhibited the American designs in 1993.

Anne Klein was evidently good at identifying and developing design talent. At Junior Sophisticates, for instance, she had hired Bill Blass as a sketcher when he came home from military service. Her company's success can be attributed to the outstanding design talent she assembled and nurtured, particularly Donna Karan and Maurice Antaya. (Karan formed her own company in 1985; Antaya took control of the Anne Klein II line.)

Klein had an uncommon breadth of interest in design and innovation. Among other things, in the late 1960's she developed and patented a special girdle to wear with miniskirts; she originated the idea of using snaps on doll clothing because she recognized the difficulty small children had with buttons; she designed an airplane interior and worked with a leading automotive company on car design; she developed an inside-out raincoat for women that, with pockets and zippers on the inside, gave access to their personal items and kept everything dry. Even when she was near death from cancer in 1974, she drew designs for a hospital room and hospital bed that would improve patient comfort and access.

Klein died in New York City. Hundreds of fashion industry people crowded her funeral two days later, in recognition of the fact that she was, as Rudi Gernreich declared, "one of the great forces of fashion with a real American look."

[For further information, see *Fifty Years of American Women in Fashion* (1981), guide to show at Fashion Institute of Technology; Caroline Rennolds Milbank, *New York Fashion* (1988). An obituary is in the *New York Times*, March 20, 1974.]

FRED V. CARSTENSEN

KNIGHT, FRANK HYNEMAN (Nov. 7, 1885–Apr. 15, 1972), economist, was born in White Oak, McLean County, Ill., the oldest of the eleven children of Winton Cyrus Knight and Julia Ann Hyneman, farmers of Irish descent. His parents were members of the Disciples of Christ whose strict beliefs had a lifelong effect on their eldest son.

Knight received his early education at Buckeye School, a small rural school of eight grades and a limited curriculum. He studied physics and geometry on his own and entered Lexington High School in 1903 for a year and a half. From the beginning his school attendance was sporadic, for he and his brothers were required to work on the farm. He learned to read at every opportunity, even while plowing.

In 1905, Knight entered American University in the mountain town of Harriman, Tenn., a former temperance university with an ambitious curriculum but an ill-prepared faculty. Along with his Bible courses, he learned typing and shorthand, which he put to good use in the spring of 1907 when he worked as secretary to the director of the Division of Works at the Jamestown Exposition in Virginia. He remained there until 1908, when he enrolled in Milligan College, a militantly evangelical religious college operated by the Tennessee Christian Missionary Society. He received a Bachelor of Philosophy degree with honors in 1911; the same day he married Minerva Shelburne, a classmate. They had four children.

From 1911 to 1913, Knight studied year round at the University of Tennessee; in his second year he was an assistant in the chemistry department and held other jobs in order to make ends meet. His majors were German literature and chemistry; his minors, economics and philosophy. He received both a B.A. and an M.A. in 1913; his master's thesis was entitled "Gerhart Hauptmann, a Realist."

In the summer of 1913, Knight's father gave him the money for a trip to Europe that enabled him to visit schools to which he had applied for doctoral work and to explore holdings in various libraries. While in Europe he was awarded a fellowship for doctoral work in philosophy at Cornell University. Cornell required both a major and a minor subject; Knight's declared minor was economics. In the spring of his first year, the chairman of the philosophy department castigated Knight for his skepticism and argumentative attitude. As a result, Knight transferred to the economics department.

Through hard work and his freedom to be a skeptic, he found his lifelong career—teaching economic theory, thought, and history. Under the direction and influence of Alvin Johnson and Allyn Young, his dissertation, "A Theory of Business Profit," was presented in 1916. It received the second prize in the Hart, Schaffner and Marx essay competition. After receiving his Ph.D., Knight spent a year at Cornell as an instructor in economics and two years with the same rank at the University of Chicago. In 1919, Knight became an associate professor of economics at the University of Iowa, where he taught for nine years.

Knight's reputation as an economist began when he became a full professor of economics at the University of Chicago in 1928. In 1921, while at Iowa, his dissertation had been expanded, with two chapters of it forming a book entitled *Risk, Uncertainty and Profit*. This work, which became a classic in economic theory, clarified many of the ambiguities present in earlier neoclassical writings in economic organization. At Chicago, Knight was one of the founders of the "Chicago School," which believed that the bank failures and crash of the stock market was the fault of big government. The Great Depression of the 1930's angered and depressed Knight; he and his Chicago colleagues constantly spoke out in their classrooms, professional writings, and meetings against governmental regulation of the economy and in favor of a free-market economy. He believed that the regulations imposed by government through the Federal Reserve system contributed to inflation and recommended that they pursue open market operations that would provide necessary government finances and increase the liquidity of the banking structure. He would not have approved of the use of large and continuous deficit budgets to combat mass unemployment and deflation. In the classroom Knight, in his high voice, addressed a wide range of issues, often using the latest issue of the *New Republic*, to encourage his students to debate. His students would find him in his office, wearing a green eyeshade, smoking a cigarette down to its nub by using a toothpick (endangering his mustache), going over his notes for his next class.

Knight divorced his wife in 1928, and in 1929 he married Ethel Verry, who was for many years director of the Chicago Child Care Society. They had two children.

The strictness of his upbringing and early education caused Knight to rebel against organized religion. Near the end of his life, when he was suffering from insomnia, a friend suggested some remedies. Knight replied, "It's not the sleeping, it's the waking. I can't forget that damned religion." He had read and studied the beliefs of many religious groups, but he never ascribed himself to any particular religion.

Knight received many honors. In 1936 and 1937, he had refused nomination as president of the American Economic Association, but he accepted in 1950. He was awarded the Walker Medal in 1957. He served as Morton D. Hall distinguished professor of economics at Chicago from 1946 to 1951. Others schools, such as Harvard and Cornell, attempted to lure him away, but he remained at Chicago. He officially retired in 1960 but continued to teach periodically and to lecture.

Knight was a skeptic all his life and never hesitated to question, doubt, or criticize if he felt someone, no matter how important, was in error. One of his students remarked that should Gabriel's horn have needed tuning, Knight would not have hesitated to point it out. He died in Chicago.

[Knight's papers, writings, correspondence, and teaching notes are in the Knight/Shelburne papers of the archives at the University of Chicago. See J. Ronnie Davis, "Three Days with Knight," *Nebraska Journal of Economics and Business*, 1974; and D. Dewey, "Frank Knight Before Cornell: Some Light on the Dark Years," in *History of Economic Thought and Methodology*, vol. 4 (1986). An obituary is in the *New York Times*, Apr. 21, 1972.]

BETTY B. VINSON

KNOWLAND, WILLIAM FIFE (June 26, 1908–Feb. 23, 1974), newspaper publisher and U.S. senator, was born in Alameda, Calif., the youngest of three children of Ella J. Fife and

Joseph Russell Knowland. He spent part of his childhood in Washington, D.C., where his father served in the House of Representatives. In 1914, Joseph Knowland lost a race for the Senate and bought a half-interest in the *Oakland Tribune*, which he used to dominate the California Republican party and to promote his son's political career.

Knowland's idea of a childhood game was to stand on a box and make a speech. At age twelve, he spoke for Warren G. Harding's presidential election, and at sixteen was finance chairman of the local Coolidge-Dawes Club. "Appearance—politician," noted his school yearbook. "Besetting sin—politics." Knowland's family believed that as early as high school he determined to become president of the United States, which was also his father's ambition for him. As a student, Knowland served as a copy boy and held other jobs on the *Oakland Tribune*. On Dec. 31, 1926, while a sophomore at the University of California, Berkeley, he eloped with classmate Helen Davis Herrick; they had three children.

After graduating from Berkeley in 1929, Knowland worked for the *Tribune*, becoming assistant publisher in 1933. At age twenty-four, he survived the Democratic landslide of 1932 to win election as a Republican to the California State Assembly. He was elected to the state senate in 1934, named to the Republican National Committee in 1938, and became chairman of its executive committee in 1941. Drafted into the United States Army as a private during World War II, Knowland attended officers candidate school and rose to the rank of major; among his duties was the writing of combat histories. In August 1945, while at the army historical section in France, he learned via telegram that Governor Earl Warren of California had named him to fill the vacancy caused by the death of U.S. Senator Hiram W. Johnson—an appointment arranged by his father, one of Warren's chief supporters. He assumed office on Aug. 26, 1945.

In 1946, Knowland retained the seat by defeating a popular Democrat, Will Rogers, Jr. In 1952 he ran on both the Republican and Democratic tickets, amassing more votes (almost four million) than any previous California candidate. Initially perceived as a moderate Republican, Knowland joined a "Young Turk" insurgency that challenged the leadership of Senator Robert A. Taft. Moderates nominated

Knowland for Senate floor leader in 1948, but Taft's supporters defeated him, 24 to 14.

As a Pacific Coast senator, Knowland endorsed a bipartisan foreign policy in defense of Europe and argued that Asia was equally vital to American interests. After touring the Far East in 1946, he warned the Senate that "someday in this age of the airplane and the atom, a twentieth-century Genghis Khan may come forth to jeopardize . . . the security of this nation." As the Nationalist Chinese government collapsed, Knowland dismissed the State Department's white paper on China as a "white-wash" and denounced its Far Eastern Division as defeatist. In November 1949, he visited Chungking the day before Communist troops conquered the city. He returned obsessed with defeating Communism in Asia. Knowland's hard-line, Asia-oriented policies and passionate support for Chiang Kai-shek earned him the title "Senator from Formosa," and steered him into the Republican party's right wing.

At the Republican convention in 1952, Knowland chaired the California delegation, pledged to Earl Warren. When Robert Taft tempted Knowland with offers of the vice-presidential nomination in return for California's votes, he declined to break his commitment to Warren. Caught unaware when the state's junior senator, Richard M. Nixon (whom he considered his protégé), maneuvered in favor of Dwight D. Eisenhower, Knowland was relegated to nominating Nixon for vice-president. He never trusted Nixon again.

Eisenhower's election in 1952 carried Republican majorities into Congress. Taft became Senate majority leader and appointed Knowland chairman of the Republican Policy Committee. In June 1953, the terminally ill Taft made Knowland acting majority leader, explaining that "nobody can push him around." Although Knowland shared Taft's political integrity and personal decorum, he lacked his parliamentary skills. A ponderous speaker with little humor, burly and gruff, and "as subtle as a Sherman tank," Knowland was often compared to a football player for his muscular physique and unyielding positions.

As Republican majority leader from 1953 to 1955, and minority leader from 1955 to 1959, Knowland proved no match for his wily Democratic counterpart, Lyndon B. Johnson. Although they often joined forces, Johnson could not resist imitating Knowland's lumbering walk

or ridiculing his legislative ineptness. During the Eighty-third Congress, the parties were so nearly equal in numbers that replacements for deceased Senators at times gave Senate Democrats a numerical advantage. Once, after Johnson defeated him on a vote in 1954, Knowland lamented his predicament of "being majority leader in this body without having a majority."

Knowland struggled to maintain Republican unity behind Eisenhower's domestic policies, particularly in support of civil rights legislation. He set in motion the legislative machinery to bring down Senator Joseph R. McCarthy, although he voted against McCarthy's censure. But he absolutely refused to "rubber stamp" foreign policy. He advocated a naval blockade of China and opposed foreign aid to neutral nations. When Senator John Bricker sponsored a constitutional amendment requiring Senate approval of executive agreements, Knowland implored the Eisenhower administration to compromise. He temporarily vacated his seat as majority leader to endorse a milder substitute for the Bricker Amendment; the substitute failed by a single vote.

Knowland withdrew his name from several presidential primaries when Eisenhower decided to stand for reelection in 1956. Rather than run for reelection to the Senate in 1958, he announced that he would campaign instead for governor of California. As governor, he believed that he could better control the state's large delegation and prevent Nixon from gaining the Republican presidential nomination. Knowland planned to challenge California's liberal incumbent governor, Goodwin Knight, but Nixon's supporters convinced Knight to run for the Senate to avoid splitting the party. In his campaign against Edmund G. ("Pat") Brown, Knowland made "right to work" (opposition to closed union shops) his major issue, thereby alienating the labor vote that Warren and Knight had courted. An economic recession, grass-roots organizing of the Democrats through federated clubs, and the state's rapidly changing demographics contributed to crushing defeats for both Knowland and Knight.

Returning to Oakland, Knowland became editor and publisher of the *Oakland Tribune* when his father died in 1966. Through the paper's editorial influence, and as chairman of the Oakland Chamber of Commerce, he ran the city, whose mayor and city council were regarded as "Knowland's appointees." Concerned that poverty and unemployment were spawning such radical groups as the Black Panthers, Knowland promoted urban redevelopment, especially through federal funds from the Office of Economic Opportunity, and opened his paper to more extensive coverage of Oakland's black community.

In 1964, Knowland headed the California campaign committee for Senator Barry Goldwater of Arizona, whose victory in the state primary secured him the Republican presidential nomination. Knowland suspected radicals of using the Berkeley campus as a staging ground for demonstrations against Goldwater and the *Tribune.* By pressuring the university to restrict campus speakers, he inadvertently helped trigger Berkeley's "Free Speech Movement," which stimulated greater student activism. However, public reaction to campus turmoil helped to elect a conservative Republican, Ronald Reagan, governor two years later. In 1968, Knowland endorsed Governor Reagan in a last, unsuccessful attempt to block Nixon's presidential nomination.

Knowland dramatically altered his private life in his sixties. He and Helen divorced in 1972 after forty-five years of marriage, and he married Ann Dickson, twenty-five years his junior, on Apr. 29, 1972. Knowland soon cautioned his new wife that he was "not an Onassis or Hughes" and could not afford her lavish spending. He was deeply in debt when they separated in December 1972. By 1974, he owed more than $900,000 in personal loans, secured by his *Tribune* stock. When the loans came due, Knowland stepped onto a dock on the Russian River, at his weekend retreat near Monte Rio, in Sonoma County, and fatally shot himself in the head.

[Knowland's papers are at Bancroft Library, University of California, Berkeley; the Regional Oral History Office at Berkeley contains oral histories recorded by Knowland, his daughters, and the executor of his estate. See also Theodore H. White, "The Gentlemen from California," *Collier's*, Feb. 3, 1956; Hollis Alpert, "The Senator from California," *New Yorker*, July 7, 1956; William S. White, *Citadel* (1957); Sherman Adams, *Firsthand Report* (1961); David W. Reinhard, *The Republican Right Since 1945* (1983); and Duane Tananbaum, *The Bricker Amendment Controversy* (1988). Obituaries are in the *Oakland Tribune*, Feb. 24–25, 1974; the *Los Angeles Times*, Feb. 24–25, 1974; the *Washington Post*, Feb. 24, 1974; and the *New York Times*, Feb. 24–25, 1974.]

DONALD A. RITCHIE

KOLB, LAWRENCE (Feb. 20, 1881–Nov. 17, 1972), physician and pioneer in drug addiction research, was born in Galesville, Md., one of fifteen children of Caroline Kirchner and of John Kolb, a store clerk at the time of Lawrence's birth and later the store owner. The family name is pronounced "Cobb." Lawrence did not get along well with his father, who was stern, dictatorial, and generally disapproving of whatever his children wanted.

Despite being a middle child in a large, poor family, never attending either high school or college, and receiving almost no serious career guidance or encouragement from anyone, Kolb succeeded—mainly through his own hard work and singleness of purpose. In 1904, without any formal education beyond grammar school, he was admitted to the medical school of the University of Maryland, from which he received his M.D. in 1908, third in his class. His father had not wanted him to study medicine, and had been openly convinced that Kolb would fail in the attempt. It was an older brother, who later became one of two steamboat captains in the family, who suggested that Lawrence become a physician. Moreover this brother financed Lawrence's medical education with a $1,200 loan. While in medical school, Lawrence boarded with another brother in Baltimore.

After a year of internship at University Hospital, Baltimore, Kolb joined the U.S. Public Health Service as assistant surgeon in 1909. He was promoted to passed assistant surgeon in 1913, surgeon in 1921, and senior surgeon in 1930.

In 1910, Kolb married Lillian Coleman; they had three children. Their oldest child, Lawrence Coleman Kolb, became a well-known psychiatrist.

Kolb's first assignment in the Public Health Service was the Marine Hospital in Baltimore, but a few months later he was reassigned to Reedy Island Station in the Delaware River as a quarantine officer. From 1914 to 1919, he diagnosed mental disorders among the immigrants at Ellis Island in New York City. While at Ellis Island, he spent a year of postdoctoral study at the New York State Psychiatric Institute, an organization later headed by his son.

In 1919, Kolb was transferred to Waukesha,

Wis., to supervise the remodeling of an old hotel into a hospital that would specialize in battle fatigue and other mental trauma from World War I. There he began his fifty-year study of drug addiction, even though this facility housed only a few addicts. In 1923, he went to the National Institutes of Health (then called the National Hygienic Laboratory) in Washington, D.C., to conduct extensive research on drug addiction, including animal experiments with opiates and cocaine, as well as studies of the demographics of addiction, its relation to crime, its effects on personality and intelligence, and its potential for treatment. He visited, counseled, and interviewed nonincarcerated addicts from Maine to Alabama. Among his published conclusions was that opium and morphine caused less personal and social harm than alcohol.

From 1928 to 1931, Kolb lived in Dublin, Ireland, where his children attended Trinity College. During this period he served at U.S. consulates throughout Europe, examining the mental health of possible immigrants, investigating the effects of their environment on their intelligence-test scores, and scrutinizing various methods of measuring intelligence. He was especially critical of Stanford Binet tests.

After returning from Europe and spending a brief time in Washington, D.C., Kolb was assigned in 1932 to establish the U.S. Department of Justice Hospital for Defective Delinquents in Springfield, Mo. Two years later he opened the Public Health Service Hospital for drug addicts in Lexington, Ky., and was its superintendent for four years. This hospital, Kolb's brainchild, included a full-fledged addiction research center staffed by psychiatrists, chemists, pharmacologists, and other medical personnel. In 1938, he was back in Washington, D.C., now as assistant surgeon general, heading the Division of Mental Hygiene. In this office he founded the U.S. Neuropsychiatric Institute, which did not receive adequate funding until World War II. By that time Kolb had left.

When he retired from the Public Health Service in 1944, Kolb settled in California, where he served as medical consultant to the State Department of Corrections, then as medical deputy director of the Department of Mental Hygiene. Retiring from state service at the age of seventy, Kolb accepted an invitation to reorganize the mental-health facility at the Norris-town, Pa., State Hospital, where he was assistant superintendent from July 1951 to December 1952. Until 1954 he was executive secretary of the Philadelphia Mental Health Survey Committee, appointed by the governor. After 1959 he worked occasionally for the Public Health Service as special consultant on mental health.

In 1962, at the age of eighty-one, Kolb published his ground-breaking work, *Drug Addiction: A Medical Problem*. In it he argued against the idea that addiction causes crime, and for the thesis that addicts would likely be productive citizens, as they typically were in the nineteenth century, if the law would just leave them alone. Citing the British adage "Opium soothes, alcohol maddens," Kolb contended that alcohol impairs judgment, whereas opiates do not. Even though his research led him to believe that drug addicts and alcoholics alike were generally unstable people who had mental problems before they became addicted, he held firmly that opiates ought to be legalized and readily available, even more so than alcohol, not only because they cause less social damage than alcohol but also because, in some cases, opiates may help a person to become a productive member of society. Kolb distinguished marijuana from the opiates on the ground that, like alcohol, it causes users to commit crimes. Yet he considered marijuana better than alcohol because it does not seem to be physically addictive.

Above all, Kolb argued that drug addicts were not criminals, that they would commit fewer crimes than the nonaddicted population if they did not have to fight the law in order to procure drugs, and that their social difficulties should be addressed by physicians rather than by the courts. His view that addicts should be treated rather than jailed was based on his belief that mental disorders are chemical rather than psychological, and thus beyond the individual control of the sufferer. Kolb's views on this subject proved, as he predicted, less controversial in Europe than in America.

Kolb died in Washington, D.C.

[Kolb's post-1912 papers, in the National Library of Medicine, include several autobiographical statements. The George Rosen Collection contains a sixty-six-page transcript of Harlan Phillips's 1963 interview with him. An obituary is in the *New York Times*, Nov. 19, 1972.]

ERIC V. D. LUFT

KROCK, ARTHUR (Nov. 16, 1886–April 12, 1974), journalist, was born in Glasgow, Ky., the son of Joseph Krock, an accountant, and Caroline Morris. He became one of the most prominent and influential political columnists in the twentieth century, especially in the years between the New Deal and the Vietnam War. A leading spokesman for conservative views, he was a four-time winner of the Pulitzer Prize for his reporting skills and for the quality of his policy analysis. He reported the political fortunes of eleven presidents, from Theodore Roosevelt to Lyndon Johnson. Most of them, from Franklin Roosevelt on, gave him preferential treatment and, on occasion, exclusive interviews, in part because he represented the *New York Times*, the most powerful newspaper in the country, and in part because he was Arthur Krock. Although he came to be the ultimate Washington insider—he was an intimate of Cabinet officers, diplomats, highly ranked bureaucrats, well-placed military men, and leading congressmen—he managed to preserve his journalistic independence and his personal integrity. In his analysis of governmental policy or his assessments of political effectiveness, he pulled no punches because of personal friendship.

Krock entered Princeton in 1904, but dropped out in the middle of his freshman year for financial reasons. He nonetheless maintained a lifelong connection to the university, which awarded him an M.A. in 1937, and to which he left his papers. He completed his formal education at Lewis Institute, Chicago, earning an A.A. in 1906. He believed that the age of modern journalism was the "age of the specialist" and made it a lifelong habit to read long after midnight on a regular basis to keep himself informed or to prepare himself for some new area of inquiry or analysis.

Krock's career began as a general assignment reporter in 1907 for the *Louisville Herald*. Within a year, the paper faced financial troubles, and Krock resigned so that an older, married colleague with children would have a job. After a brief stint as a deputy sheriff in Jefferson County, Ky., he resumed his newspaper career with the Associated Press in Louisville. By 1910 he was in Washington as a correspondent for the *Louisville Times* and, after 1911, for the *Louisville Courier-Journal* as well. He married Marguerite Polleys on Apr. 22, 1911; they had one son. One year after Marguerite Krock's death in 1938, Krock married Martha Granger Blair, a reporter for the *Washington Times-Herald*.

In 1915 he returned to Louisville to become executive manager of both the *Times* and the *Courier-Journal*. In 1919 he was named editor-in-chief of the *Louisville Times*, and in that position attended the Versailles Peace Conference. In 1923, following a dispute with Robert W. Bingham, the newspaper's owner, over editorial policies, he resigned in protest at the publisher's support of Prohibition and woman suffrage. He immediately joined Ralph Pulitzer's *New York World* as an assistant to the president and then as an editorial writer. He left the *World* for the *New York Times* in 1927, becoming a member of its editorial board. In 1932, he went to Washington as the *Times's* Washington correspondent and bureau chief.

In the next thirty-five years, he would dominate the *New York Times's* coverage of the federal government. From 1932 to 1952 he wrote every lead story on the biennial elections, and although he supplied four opinion columns per week (and one on Sunday), he generally wrote the principal daily story out of Washington as well. As an editor, he shaped the Washington bureau into a powerful fiefdom that continually warred (usually successfully) with the home office in New York. A conservative among liberals, he avoided confrontations, according to James Reston, who succeeded him as bureau chief in 1953, but he commanded respect and often put his job on the line when his authority was challenged or the freedom of his reporters was threatened. As bureau chief, he was stern and demanding, but he abhorred meetings—he held only three staff conferences during his twenty-one years as the man in charge—and took the position that his reporters knew what they were doing, until proved otherwise. He always addressed them formally, never by their first names, and expected similar address from them. As *Times* lore has it, he was once asked by a newly hired reporter how long someone had to be in the bureau before he could be called by his first name, and Krock replied, "For as long as you care to remain here."

Coming to Washington as the New Deal was changing the role of government, he recognized that political reporting would also change. He deliberately hired specialists, looking for reporters with strong preparation in political science, history, and especially economics, the areas on which his own reading centered and which he believed were essential to understanding what was happening not only in Washington but everywhere in the world.

Fifteen months after he assumed control of the Washington bureau, Krock was asked to develop a signed column to appear on the editorial page, an innovation that represented a radical departure from the established practice of using only unsigned editorials to express the paper's opinion on current events. "In the Nation," as his column was titled, offered background information, critical analysis, and personal commentary until his retirement in 1966; along with similar columns by David Lawrence and Walter Lippmann, it provided the model for papers everywhere. Krock's voice became increasingly conservative as the years passed. Although he saw himself as a liberal democrat within the tradition of Jefferson and Wilson, he believed that the New Deal represented a sharp, even radical, and ultimately misguided break with the party's past. He was particularly apprehensive about the growth of presidential power. "I am," he once said, "a walking allergy to Presidents that soon becomes insufferable."

Krock won his first Pulitzer Prize in 1935 for "the general excellence" of his coverage of the New Deal. Two years later, he won a second for an exclusive interview with President Roosevelt that revealed, among other things, Roosevelt's ill-conceived plan to enlarge the size of the Supreme Court. He was voted a third Pulitzer for an exclusive interview with President Truman in 1950, but turned it down because, as a member of the Pulitzer Prize advisory board, he believed acceptance would constitute a conflict of interest. In 1955 he received a special Pulitzer citation honoring the quality of his work as a Washington correspondent; his four Pulitzers are unmatched by any other journalist. In 1967 the University of Alabama presented him with the John Peter Zenger Award for his defense of freedom of the press. He received the Presidential Medal of Freedom in 1970.

After his retirement from the *Times*, Krock produced several books, one of which, *Memoirs: 60 Years on the Firing Line*, became a best-seller in 1968. He died in Washington.

[Krock's papers are at Princeton University. In addition to his *Memoirs*, his books include *In the Nation, 1932–1966* (1966), a selection of his columns; *The Consent of the Governed and Other Deceits* (1971); *Reminiscences* (1972); and *Myself When Young: Growing Up in the 1890's* (1972). See also James Reston, *Deadline: A Memoir* (1991). An obituary appears in the *New York Times*, Apr. 12, 1974.]
ALLAN L. DAMON

KRUGER, OTTO (Sept. 6, 1886–Sept. 6, 1974), actor who performed successfully on stage, screen, radio, and television, was born in Toledo, Ohio, the son of Bernard Alvin Kruger, an accountant, and Elizabeth Winters. Although numerous press releases gave his birth year as 1885, his birth certificate is dated 1886. Otto's mother died when he was four. His father's second marriage to a woman from a musical family led to his being urged to pursue a musical career. Legend holds that Otto's music lessons stopped abruptly when his maternal uncle "discovered jazz creeping into young Otto's interpretation of Chopin."

Although he attended public schools in Toledo, he did not complete his high school education. During his late teens Kruger seems to have lived a roustabout existence. He earned a little money tuning pianos, working as a telephone lineman, and cow punching. He tramped around the country and even lived in Central America for a brief period.

Why and when Kruger turned to acting is unclear, but by his early twenties he was traveling around the country in repertory companies and vaudeville shows. He began as a kind of theatrical jack-of-all-trades with a small Kansas repertory company. He humorously reminisced that his duties included serving as "mimic, bit player, bell ringer and all-around performer" for the munificent wage of nine dollars per week. After rising to the role of leading man in the repertory company, Kruger felt that he was ready for the challenge of Broadway. After moving to New York City, he worked for several stock companies and eventually attracted the attention of major producers. His stage debut at star level occurred in *The Natural Law* (1915). His theatrical career was briefly interrupted in 1917 when he volunteered for service in the U. S. Navy. After the war, in 1919, he immediately returned to the New York stage. Later that year he participated in the Actors' Equity strike. While engaged in a benefit performance for fellow strikers, he met a young actress, Sue MacManamy, and conducted a whirlwind courtship to win her. They had one child, and their marriage lasted until his death fifty-five years later.

Kruger rose to top billing on the New York stage during the 1920's. His best-remembered performances included parts in *Young America, The Gypsy Trail, Adam and Eve, The Straw, Alias Jimmy Valentine,* and *The Royal Family.* As the 1930's began, he replaced Noel Coward in the part of Elyot Chase in the actor-playwright's *Private Lives* and replaced Paul Muni in the part of George Simon in *Counsellor-at-Law.* His success in the latter role he later considered a liability because he felt it doomed him to too many roles as a lawyer.

Although Kruger had appeared in a silent film, *Under the Red Robe,* in 1923, his career as a motion picture actor did not begin in earnest until he moved to Hollywood under contract to Metro-Goldwyn-Mayer in 1932. His career as a movie actor never brought him the same degree of recognition he had enjoyed during his stage career, yet he always received excellent reviews. Like his motion picture contemporaries Louis Calhern, Douglass Dumbrille, and Henry Daniell, he appeared in so many movies that everyone recognized him, but few other than true film buffs remembered his name. He was often stereotyped as a villain, but he was equally successful in roles of greater breadth. He fell short, however, of winning the status of leading man. Bad films early in his career probably prevented his rise to the first rank of movie stars. Certainly, *Turn Back the Clock* (1933), *Ever in My Heart* (1933), *Beauty for Sale* (1933), and *Gallant Lady* (1934) were eminently forgettable films. Although the films themselves were panned critics invariably praised Kruger's performances. An anonymous reviewer later observed aptly, "He was not a major star but his intelligent contribution in major supporting roles lessened the mediocrity of many unworthy films." In all fairness, it should be added that Kruger also gave first-rate performances in highly praised films such as *High Noon* (1952) where he played a craven sheriff, and *Magnificent Obsession* (1954) where he played a benign guru.

Despite a succession of short-term film contracts, Kruger was never out of work. In a period of just over thirty years, he was under contract to more than a dozen studios and often returned to one of his former studios after a short interval. His age, grayish hair, and sharp features suited him for a variety of character roles rather than romantic leads. In an interview he once wryly observed, "For a while I played sad hus-bands, then I got nothing but lawyers. Then I was a doctor, and during the war I played Nazis." The variety of his roles testified to his versatility in a wide range of parts, including a psychiatrist (in *Dracula's Daughter* [1936]), a Nobel Prize–winning scientist (in *Dr. Ehrlich's Magic Bullet* [1940]), and an Oxford University graduate who becomes a sinister Nazi (in *Hitler's Children* [1954]). A *New York Times* movie critic sardonically commented that *Counsel for Crime* (1937) was another setback to the "Get-Kruger-out-of-the-courtroom" movement.

Kruger appeared in more than seventy films during his Hollywood years, but he always retained his love for the stage, returning intermittently to New York to appear in leading roles and also playing in the legitimate theater in Los Angeles. On one occasion he expressed regret for having been passed over by Hollywood for roles that he had played with great success on the stage, including major parts in *Parnell, The Male Animal, Accent on Youth, Laura,* and *Advise and Consent.*

Kruger's suave and urbane manner, combined with his excellent diction, added a third dimension to his career when he added radio and television to his repertory. Already in his sixties, he became a popular television host and sometime guest star, acting as host of "Lux Video Theatre" and making guest appearances on "Pulitzer Prize Playhouse," "GE Theater," "Science Fiction Theater," "Philip Morris Playhouse," and the "Perry Mason" series.

Admired and respected by his colleagues, Kruger was active in such professional associations as The Lambs and the Motion Picture Relief Fund for retired actors and actresses, serving for many years as vice-president of the latter organization. Following a series of strokes, he died on his eighty-eighth birthday in Woodland Hills, Calif. He was buried in Forest Lawn Cemetery.

[A file on Kruger that includes studio press releases, reviews, unpublished biographical sketches, and photographs is in the Herrick Library of the Motion Picture Academy of Arts and Sciences in Beverly Hills, Calif. An obituary appears in the *New York Times,* Sept. 7, 1974).]

CHARLES E. LARSEN

KRUPA, EUGENE BERTRAM ("GENE") (Jan. 15, 1909–Oct. 16, 1973), drummer and bandleader, was born in Chicago, the son of Bartley Krupa, an alderman, and Ann Oslowska. His first instrument was the saxophone, but by the age of twelve he was taking jobs as a drummer. He dropped out of Immaculate Conception High School before graduating.

In 1925, Krupa's mother persuaded him to attend St. Joseph's College, a preparatory seminary, in Rensselaer, Ind. After a year Gene returned home and began playing, in his words, at "every joint and hole-in-the-wall around Chicago." At this time important influences on his musical development were drummers Tubby Hall, Zutty Singleton, and Baby Dodds of New Orleans.

Krupa's first recording took place on Dec. 9, 1927, for Okeh Records. The band was co-led by Red McKenzie and Eddie Condon. In April 1928 Krupa again recorded with McKenzie and Condon. These recordings announced a new development of jazz, called the "Chicago style," and establish Krupa's reputation as a jazz drummer.

To further his career, Krupa went to New York City, the jazz capital. Work was hard to find, but he did record with Eddie Condon (1928), Red Nichols (1929, 1930, and 1931), Fats Waller (1929), and Hoagy Carmichael (1930). The Carmichael session included Bix Biederbecke, Tommy and Jimmy Dorsey, and Benny Goodman. As he had done on the South Side of Chicago, Krupa often went to Harlem to listen to African-American musicians, especially drummers Chick Webb and Cuba Austin.

In 1930 Krupa worked in orchestras for two of George Gershwin's musicals, *Girl Crazy* and *Strike Up the Band*. In the same year he began dating the telephone operator of his hotel, Ethel Fawcett. They were married in June 1933.

In the early 1930's Krupa studied privately with Stanford Moeller, who taught him the full arm movements that gave Krupa's drumming a dramatic and flashy style, along with prodigious volume.

From 1931 to 1934 Krupa worked with non-jazz big bands. But at the urging of John Hammond, at the end of 1934 he joined the newly formed swing band of Benny Goodman. At first audience reaction was negative, but the band began a rapid rise to success, beginning with a job at the Palomar in Los Angeles in the summer of 1935.

Playing with Goodman's big band, quartet, and trio, the young, handsome, and musically uninhibited Krupa became a pop music star. By 1937 he was the best-paid drummer in the world, making $25,000 per year.

Krupa was the first jazz drummer to function as a major soloist. Before him, drummers provided a rhythmic foundation for the music and seldom took extended solos. Not only a fine musician, Krupa was also a consummate showman: when he played he exuded excitement, with a full range of facial expressions, hair falling in his face, and arms wildly flailing away at the drums.

The zenith of Krupa's stay with Goodman was reached on Jan. 16, 1938, at a concert at New York's Carnegie Hall, where the audience went wild over Krupa's thundering playing on "Sing, Sing, Sing." But problems soon surfaced between Krupa and Goodman. Musically, Krupa played too heavily on many of the arrangements, and more important, Krupa had become more popular with audiences than Goodman. In March 1938 Krupa left to form his own band.

Soon "Gene Krupa and His Orchestra" rivaled the popularity of the Goodman band, particularly when vocalist Anita O'Day and trumpeter Roy Eldridge joined the band in 1941. Important recordings from this period are *Drummin' Man* (1938), *Drum Boogie* (1941), and *Let Me Off Uptown* (1941). Krupa also appeared in several movies, including *Some Like It Hot*, with Bob Hope (1939), and *Ball of Fire* (1941).

In 1941, Krupa divorced his wife. In 1942, he was arrested by federal narcotics agents who found a small amount of marijuana, supposedly owned by Krupa, in the possession of Krupa's seventeen-year-old valet. On May 18, 1943, Krupa was found guilty of the misdemeanor of possession and sentenced to ninety days' imprisonment. On a second charge of contributing to the delinquency of a minor by inducing him to transport an illegal substance, Krupa was sentenced to San Quentin for one to six years. On Aug. 9, 1943, he was released pending an appeal.

Krupa believed his career was over, but Benny Goodman convinced him to join his band for a USO tour of army camps in the fall of 1943. All went well, but Krupa was still frightened about how the public would react. Without any publicity he joined Tommy Dorsey for an engagement at the Paramount Theatre in New York City. The audience gave Krupa a standing ovation. Continuing to play, Krupa stood and bowed, then burst into tears. He remained with Dorsey until he was found not guilty of contributing to the delinquency of a minor. On June 11, 1944, he left to form his own band.

Krupa's new big band reflected the changing developments in jazz, including the hiring of such modernists as Gerry Mulligan. But by 1951 it was economically too difficult to maintain. Krupa began leading trios and quartets, a format he would continue for the next two decades. Also, between 1951 and 1953 he appeared in Norman Granz's world-touring concert series, Jazz at the Philharmonic. In 1954, along with Cozy Cole, he founded a school for drummers in New York City.

He appeared in the films *The Glenn Miller Story* (1954) and *The Benny Goodman Story* (1955). *The Gene Krupa Story* (1959) is historically inaccurate, but does feature Krupa's drumming on the soundtrack.

In the latter part of 1946 Krupa married Ethel again, this time in Mexico. She had been very supportive of him in adversity: while visiting him in prison she had offered to return the hundred thousand dollars he had given her when they were divorced. She died on Dec. 8, 1955. They had no children. He married Patricia Bowler in 1959; they adopted two children. This marriage ended in divorce in 1968.

Krupa occasionally appeared with a reformed Benny Goodman Quartet in the 1960's. Krupa's last recording date in April 1972 was with the person responsible for his first one, Eddie Condon. The session was released by Chiaroscuro Records as *Jazz at the New School*. Krupa's last public appearance was with the Benny Goodman Quartet on Aug. 18, 1973. He died in Yonkers, N.Y., and is buried in Chicago.

[A good general biography is Bruce Crowther's *Gene Krupa* (1987). See also George T. Simon, *The Big Bands* (1967), and *The Best of the Music Makers* (1979); "Drummin' Man" in Rudi Blesh, *Combo: USA* (1971); G. Hall and S. Kramer, *Gene Krupa and His Orchestra* (1975); and Bruce H. Klauber, *World of Gene Krupa* (1990). An obituary is in the *New York Times*, Oct. 17, 1973.]

JOHN VOIGT

KUIPER, GERARD PETER (Dec. 7, 1905–Dec. 24, 1973), astronomer, was born in Harencarspel, the Netherlands, the son of Gerard Kuiper and Anna de Vries. Interested in science from an early age, Kuiper enrolled in the astronomy program at the University of Leiden, where his instructors included astronomer Ejnar Hertzsprung and physicist Paul Ehrenfest. He earned a B.S. in 1927 and became an assistant in the university observatory the following year, a position he held until he received his Ph.D. in 1933. He served as a member of the Dutch solar eclipse expedition to Sumatra in 1929.

Upon completing his doctorate, Kuiper went to the Lick Observatory on Mt. Hamilton, Calif., as a research fellow. Two years later, in 1935, he accepted an instructorship at Harvard University in Cambridge, Mass., and, in 1936, he became an assistant professor at the University of Chicago. On June 20 of that year, Kuiper married Sarah Parker Fuller; they had two children. In 1937 he became a naturalized citizen. Kuiper's duties at Chicago focused on the university's Yerkes Observatory in Williams Bay, Wisc., which he later directed in the periods 1947–1949 and 1957–1960. He continued research on double stars, which he had begun at Leiden, and on the luminosity-mass relationship of main-sequence stars, publishing a classic paper on the latter topic in 1938.

As one of the nation's leading scientists, Kuiper became involved in war-related research in 1943, the year he attained the rank of full professor. He joined Harvard's Radio Research Laboratory and later served as an operations analyst with Eighth Air Force headquarters in England. At the end of the war, he participated in the "Alsos" mission to survey German scientific developments. Kuiper continued to study astronomy as time permitted, although his interest was rapidly shifting from stellar to planetary research. During the winter of 1943–1944, he visited the McDonald Observatory in Texas to conduct spectrographic studies of the major planets and their satellites. The most dramatic result of this research was the discovery of methane on Titan, the largest moon of Saturn. Kuiper's discovery of an atmosphere on a satellite overturned the existing belief that only planets possessed atmospheres.

Following World War II Kuiper devoted himself to planetary research. He discovered the fifth satellite of Uranus (Miranda) in 1948 and the second moon of Neptune (Nereid) in 1949. Kuiper then entered the field of lunar studies, finding virtually no consensus on important questions and discovering a shortage of adequate maps and photographs. By the mid-1950's, he had begun planning a lunar atlas of large-scale high-resolution photographs, a proposal that led the National Science Foundation to award him a grant in 1957. The project progressed slowly, integrating photographs from several observatories, until April 1960, when the University of Chicago Press published the *Photographic Lunar Atlas*.

During the closing months of 1959, however, Kuiper had found himself burdened by administrative duties and clashes with Yerkes astronomers who resented the lunar and planetary focus of the observatory. He soon realized that the best solution to his various difficulties would be a separate institute for lunar and planetary studies. The Southwest appeared to be an ideal location for this facility, because of the region's clear, steady air and the recently announced selection of Kitt Peak in southern Arizona as the site for a national observatory. The anticipated growth of the astronomy program at the University of Arizona in Tucson provided an additional incentive. In January 1960, the university agreed to house Kuiper and his staff in the newly created Lunar and Planetary Laboratory.

As Kuiper directed the move to Arizona, another important chapter in his career began. In May 1960, he was asked to serve on the Planetary and Interplanetary Sciences Subcommittee of the National Aeronautics and Space Administration (NASA). This appointment began an association with the space agency that greatly benefited the Lunar and Planetary Laboratory. In 1961, NASA provided funding for staff expansion research projects, and instruments to propel the laboratory into a prominent position in the rapidly growing space program. Three years later Kuiper received a grant of more than one million dollars for a space sciences building on campus to house the laboratory and related programs.

Kuiper's active involvement with specific NASA missions began in 1961, when he joined the committees planning the Ranger and Surveyor lunar probes. The Ranger program had many early problems, leading to the failure of the first five probes and a major reorganization in 1963. Kuiper accepted the position of chief experimenter and directed the successful redesign of the spacecraft. Kuiper and the laboratory

also contributed to later NASA programs, including the Jupiter and Saturn fly-bys of Pioneers 10 and 11, the Lunar Orbiter missions, the Apollo program, and various probes to other planets. Having established the facility as a leading part of the American space program, Kuiper retired as director of the Lunar and Planetary Laboratory in July 1973.

Among his many other activities, Kuiper had long engaged in site surveys for new observatories. He conducted early surveys of Cerro Tololo in Chile and Mauna Kea in Hawaii, both of which became major observatories in the 1970's. In the week before Christmas in 1973, Kuiper traveled to Mexico to conduct an aerial survey of possible observatory sites around Guadalajara and to tape two television programs on astronomy. During the trip, Kuiper died in Mexico City.

Kuiper's achievements in astronomy led to various awards during his life, including the Janssen Medal of the French Astronomical Society. As a fitting tribute, craters have been named after Kuiper on the moon, Mars, and Mercury.

[There is an extensive Kuiper archive in the Special Collections Department of the University of Arizona Library in Tucson; primary sources are also housed in the Mary Lea Shane Archives of Lick Observatory at the University of California, Santa Cruz, and the Yerkes Archives of the University of Chicago. Kuiper edited *The Atmospheres of the Earth and Planets* (1949), *The Solar System* (1953), and *Telescopes* (1960). Although no complete biography of Kuiper exists, a survey of his career is Dale P. Cruikshank, "20th-Century Astronomer," *Sky and Telescope* (Mar. 1974). See also Ewen A. Whitaker, *The University of Arizona's Lunar and Planetary Laboratory* (1986). There is an obituary in the *New York Times*, Dec. 25. 1973.]

GEORGE E. WEBB

KYES, ROGER MARTIN (Mar. 6, 1906–Feb. 13, 1971), business executive, was born in East Palestine, Ohio, the only child of Lafayette Martin Kyes, solicitor and later mayor of that town, and Myra Eunice Rogers.

Kyes attended Culver (Indiana) Military Academy, then transferred to the Rayen School in Youngstown, Ohio, because his father disagreed with Culver's teachings about the Civil War. He graduated from Harvard University cum laude in 1928. While at Harvard, Kyes met Helen Jacoby on a blind date. They were married on June 5, 1931 and had four children.

After graduating from Harvard, Kyes worked for Glenn L. Martin Company, a manufacturer of aircraft, in Cleveland, Ohio (1929–1930), and then for Black and Decker Manufacturing Company, which produced electric tools, in Towson, Md. (1930–1932). He next was vice-president of the Empire Plow Company in Cleveland (1932–1941). During the rest of the 1940's Kyes worked for Ferguson-Sherman (later Harry Ferguson, Inc.), a manufacturer of tractors and farm implements, in Detroit, initially as an executive consultant (1940), then as executive vice-president (1941–1943), general manager (1941–1947), and finally president (1943–1947).

While heading Harry Ferguson, Kyes negotiated with the General Motors Corporation (GM) concerning the latter's construction of manufacturing facilities for his firm. He impressed GM president Charles E. Wilson and joined GM in 1948 as executive in charge of procurement and schedules staff. The following year he was named assistant general manager of GM's unprofitable Truck and Coach Division. Kyes reorganized the division, cut its costs, and made it profitable within a year. Kyes became GM general manager in 1950 and was elected a vice-president.

After the outbreak of the Korean War in 1950, Kyes worked closely with Wilson on the conversion of GM facilities to the production of jeeps and other war matériel. He became well acquainted with industrial mobilization policies and developed a critical attitude toward the Pentagon's estimations of military requirements and procurement of military goods.

After Dwight Eisenhower was elected president in 1952, he asked Wilson to become his secretary of defense; Wilson asked Kyes to come with him to Washington as his deputy secretary of defense. Kyes agreed to do so, but only for one year. He resigned from his $85,000-per-year position at GM to take the $20,000-per-year post at the Pentagon. Kyes was confirmed as deputy secretary in February 1953.

Pentagon officials greeted the appointments with apprehension, since Wilson and Kyes had reputations as corporate cost cutters, and the end of active hostilities in the Korean War would mean cutbacks in military spending. After meeting Kyes, one Pentagon official said, "He looks like the kind of guy who'd say, 'Lay off 40,000 men.' "

Kyes's reputation was enhanced by his intimidating personal appearance; his tall stature and craggy features were accentuated by protruding eyeballs resulting from a thyroid condition. At parties he would introduce himself to strangers as "the ugliest man in Washington since Abe Lincoln." Despite his self-deprecating humor, Pentagon officials had good reason to be worried, because Kyes believed that the American military establishment was characterized by "unrealistic requirements, poor planning and inefficient execution . . . waste of money, poor utilization of manpower, unnecessary drain of materials from the civilian economy, and the inefficient use of tools, equipment and facilities."

One journalist wrote that Kyes came to Washington with the attitude that "he didn't have any friends to bring in with him and didn't expect to make any while he was at the Pentagon." His job was to oversee the day-to-day operations of the Pentagon and to act as Wilson's "hatchet man" by implementing the military cutbacks determined by Wilson and President Eisenhower. During Kyes's tenure at the Pentagon, annual American military expenditures dropped from $50 billion to $40 million, and the size of the armed forces was reduced accordingly.

Kyes also helped to plan and implement a reorganization of the Department of Defense that strengthened the authority of the secretary of defense relative to the military service chiefs. He also assisted in obtaining congressional approval for the U.S. Air Force Academy.

Kyes resigned from his Pentagon post in May 1954 and was succeeded by Secretary of the Navy Robert Anderson. Kyes returned to GM as a director and group vice-president in charge of the Dayton and Household Appliance groups. He was appointed vice-president of GM's Accessory Group in September 1959, and in 1970 was named an executive vice-president of the company.

Kyes retired from GM on Sept. 30, 1970. On Feb. 1, 1971, he joined the investment firm of Lazard Frères as a general partner. He died in Columbus, Ohio.

Kyes was an able production executive who attained wide public notice because of his work as deputy secretary of defense. He implemented military cutbacks from the Korean War levels and helped develop Eisenhower's "New Look" mobilization policies for the arms race between the United States and the Soviet Union. As one of President Eisenhower's most prominent budget cutters, Kyes was subjected to much criticism from Democrats, military bureaucrats, and their allies in the press. President Eisenhower, however, demonstrated his esteem by awarding Kyes the Medal of Freedom, the nation's highest peacetime civilian award, in 1954.

[There is no central body of Kyes papers, although some correspondence and other papers are in the collections of two other GM executives: the Charles Stewart Mott papers at the Gennessee Historical Collections Center, University of Michigan, Flint; and the Donaldson Brown papers, Hagley Museum and Library, Greenville, Del. There is no biography of Kyes, but useful information may be found in Robert Coughlin, ". . . The Ugliest Man Since Abe Lincoln," *Life*, Aug. 10, 1953; and Hanson Baldwin, "Men Who Run the Pentagon," *New York Times Magazine*, Feb. 14, 1954. Kyes is also mentioned in two studies of the Eisenhower administration: Glenn H. Snyder, "The 'New Look' of 1953," in Warner R. Schilling, Paul Y. Hammond, and Glenn H. Snyder, *Strategy, Politics and Defense Budgets* (1962); and E. Bruce Geelhoed, *Charles E. Wilson and Controversy at the Pentagon, 1953 to 1957* (1979). An obituary is in the *New York Times*, Feb. 15, 1971.]

STEPHEN G. MARSHALL

L

LAKE, VERONICA (Nov. 14, 1922–July 7, 1973), actress, was born Constance Frances Marie Ockleman in Brooklyn, N.Y., the daughter of Harry Ockleman, a merchant marine officer, and Constance Charlotte Trimble. The year of her birth is sometimes erroneously given as 1919. At an early age, her family moved to Saranac Lake, N.Y., where she attended St. Angela's Elementary School.

She first appeared on stage in a school play, *Poor Little Rich Girl*, at the age of eight. After her father died in a work-related accident in 1932, she attended Villa Maria Convent School, a boarding school in Montreal, Quebec. This later led to publicity stories that falsely claimed she took a premedical course at McGill University in that city. In 1937, she left Montreal and attended Miami High School.

At age fifteen she won a beauty contest and became Miss Florida. She soon went to California and studied at the Bliss Hayden School of Acting. Her first screen appearances were in small parts. Her first full-length film was *All Women Have Secrets* (1939) which starred Jeanne Cagney and Peter Lind Hayes. In these early films she used the name Constance Keane. The last name came from her stepfather, Anthony Keane, a staff artist for the *New York Herald Tribune.*

In 1940, she married John Detlie, an art director at Metro-Goldwyn-Mayer. They had two children, one of whom died in infancy. She reached new heights in her professional career during the wartime years, when she was active in war-bond drives, helping to raise $12 million.

She first attracted considerable attention in *I Wanted Wings* (1941) with her husky voice and the blonde "peek-a-boo" hairstyle that swept over part of her face. This helped her add a touch of romance to the film, which starred Ray Milland and William Holden. It was also on this film that she first used the name Veronica Lake, which was given to her by producer Arthur Hornblow.

Lake subsequently showed her comedic talents in the Preston Sturges film *Sullivan's Travels* (1941), which costarred Joel McCrea. He had wanted Lake to be cast as his leading lady over the objections of Paramount studio executives. When it was discovered that she was pregnant, some of her scenes were rewritten and the movie turned out a success. Lake never took her work seriously, but this was one film she wanted to be remembered for. Later that year, she made *Hold Back the Dawn* with Charles Boyer, Olivia de Havilland, and Paulette Goddard. The film was later nominated for an Academy Award for Best Picture.

In *I Married A Witch* (1942), Lake was once again part of a cast of well-established actors, even though she herself was still a relative newcomer. Fredric March, Robert Benchley, and Susan Hayward starred in this spoof of ghost films in which Cecil Kellaway and Lake played seventeenth-century witches. Always independent, and sometimes described as tough, her relations with March got off to a bad start. He regarded her as an amateur. The director, Rene Clair, also had a low opinion of her, but producer Preston Sturges insisted on hiring her. By the conclusion of the film's production, Clair admitted that he was wrong and apologized to her.

She frequently appeared indifferent, aloof, or belligerent on the set, but she apparently did so to overcome her fears.

Also in 1942, she began a profitable associa-

479

tion with Alan Ladd. She was selected to play opposite him partly because he was only five feet, four inches tall, and she was five feet, two inches. Their first picture, *This Gun for Hire* (1942), made Ladd a superstar, and *Life* magazine named Lake the top box-office attraction in 1943. Among their other pictures were *The Glass Key* (1942), a story of political corruption and murder, and *The Blue Dahlia* (1946), one of the most absorbing crime films of the 1940's. The fine cast, which also included William Bendix, made the movie another box-office hit for Ladd and Lake.

Saigon (1948) marked the beginning of Lake's decline in Hollywood. The film had a weak plot and her public appeal was on the wane. In all, she starred in twenty-six pictures. During the Hollywood years she was romantically linked with such figures as Aristotle Onassis, Tommy Manville, and Howard Hughes. A difficult personal life complicated by emotional instability—she was quick to anger and often irresponsible—and alcoholism contributed to her downfall. In 1943, she divorced John Detlie, and she married Andre de Toth, a director, in 1944. They had two children.

During the 1940's, Lake appeared on such radio programs as "Lux Radio Theatre" and "The Burns and Allen Show." In the 1950's, she made television appearances on "Lux Video Theatre," "Saturday Night," "Texaco Theater," and "The Tonight Show," among others. In 1951, she and de Toth filed for bankruptcy, and they divorced in 1952. The following year, however, she rebounded in one of her most successful stage plays, *Voice of the Turtle*, which opened in Atlanta, Ga.

In 1955, she married Joseph McCarthy, a songwriter, and they were divorced in 1960. By 1961, her acting career was in a shambles. She worked in a factory and as a cocktail waitress and barmaid in New York City. When newspaper stories revealed her occupation, fans mailed her money which she proudly returned.

She showed remarkable resilience despite her turbulent life and within two years made something of a comeback. In 1963, she received good notices for her role as fading film star Gale Joy in an off-Broadway revival of *Best Foot Forward*. She continued to work in radio, television, low-budget films, and on the stage, mainly in summer stock.

In 1967, she resided in Freeport, the Bahamas, and then moved to England, where she appeared on a stage in *A Streetcar Named Desire*. In 1969, she toured the British provinces in *Madame Chairman*, a play in which she had invested. It never opened in the West End of London as intended. It drew small audiences and poor reviews as a play, but she received raves for her "star quality."

At forty-seven she was still trim and attractive with an intriguing voice. She married her fourth husband, Robert Carlton Munro, in Fort Lauderdale, Fla., in 1972. When she died from hepatitis in Burlington, Vt., the following year, she had been in the process of obtaining a divorce. Although plagued by personal problems, financial setbacks, and emotional difficulties, she was a highly productive performer throughout her stormy life.

[Biographical material on Lake is available in the New York Public Library's Performing Arts Research Center at Lincoln Center. Her autobiography is *Veronica* (1969), written with Donald Bain. See also Jeff Lenburg, *Peekaboo: The Story of Veronica Lake* (1983). An obituary is in the *New York Times*, July 8, 1973.]

ERNEST A. McKAY

LANDIS, JESSIE ROYCE (Nov. 25, 1904– Feb. 2, 1972), actress, was born Jessie Royce Medbury in Chicago, the only child of Ella Gill and Paul Royce Medbury, a musician and portrait painter. Hoping his daughter would follow in his footsteps, Paul Medbury enrolled her in music school at an early age to study the piano. She found her way into an elocution class instead and never again considered any career but acting.

At age fourteen Landis attended the Hinshaw Dramatic School in Chicago. At sixteen she spent the summer with the Evanston Stock Company in Evanston, Ill., and met a twenty-two-year-old businessman named Lester Landis. When she was seventeen, he persuaded her to marry him, despite her parents' fears that she was too young. She moved to Evanston to live with his family, and a year later their only child was born. Lester Landis's family fortunes dwindled, and his wife went back to acting—in part for love of the theater, in part to help support her family. The latter motivation grew stronger as the couple discovered that their son suffered from Down's syndrome and needed to be placed in a special school. Jessie Royce Landis moved quickly into professional engagements and coaching work.

In 1924, Joseph Schildkraut, scouting for an actress to play the Young Countess in his touring company of *The Highwayman*, saw her perform. He cast her in the play, which opened in Chicago in December of that year. She and her husband had been growing apart for some time. He suggested at this time that she choose between him and the theater. She chose the theater, although she remained married to him and continued to return to Evanston to visit his family for some years, particularly when their son was home from school on vacation.

After her engagement in *The Highwayman*, Landis moved to New York City, where she landed the lead role in a touring company performing *Wings of Chance*, a play by Hugh Stange with a short run. She spent a season with Jessie Bonstelle's repertory company in Detroit, where she debuted as Jo in *Little Women*, then one of the American theater's most coveted roles, to excellent reviews. Returning to New York City in 1926, Landis played opposite Otis Skinner in a revival, and later a tour, of *The Honor of the Family*. She went on to work with Laurette Taylor in *Delicate Justice*.

After her son's death in 1928, Landis cut her ties with Evanston and her husband, whom she divorced. She went back to Broadway two weeks after the funeral to replace Estelle Winwood in a comic role in *The Furies*. She spent the summer of 1929 at the Elitch's Gardens in Denver, Colo., and on her return to New York found herself an established presence on the stage. She made a brief foray into films in 1930 but did not become a recognized film actress for almost twenty years.

Jessie Royce Landis was not the first lady of the American theater, but she was a versatile and active star from the 1930's to the 1960's. She played comedy and tragedy, Shakespeare and contemporary fare, Broadway and summer stock. She loved to work and was seldom out of a job. Some of her most memorable roles were Althoa Royce in George S. Kaufman's and Moss Hart's *Merrily We Roll Along* in 1934; Mama in *Papa Is All* in 1942, for which she donned character makeup for the first time to play a middle-aged Mennonite; and Janet Archer in *Kiss and Tell* in 1943. This last play ran for over two years and brought Landis extra income because she had invested in it. She worked frequently with the Theatre Guild, in New York and on tour, directing as well as acting.

In 1937 Landis married journalist and playwright Rex Smith. According to a press release in one of her scrapbooks at the New York Public Library, while married to Smith she was "one of the best known hostesses in the literati set in New York, gathering around her table most of the leading playwrights, novelists, critics, and newspapermen." The marriage was marked by frequent quarrels. After four years the couple separated; in 1944 they divorced. Landis consoled herself with her work, her friends, and her volunteer activities for the American Theatre Wing.

One of the highlights of Landis's career was her sojourn on the London stage starting in 1950, when she starred in *Larger Than Life*, based on a novel by Somerset Maugham. She followed this part with her first full-fledged musical role, the part of Mistress Knight in *And So to Bed*.

From the late 1940's until her death, Landis enjoyed success in films, usually playing an aristocratic mother. She appeared as Grace Kelly's mother in *To Catch a Thief* (1955) and *The Swan* (1956); June Allyson's mother in *My Man Godfrey* (1957); and Cary Grant's mother in *North by Northwest* (1959), despite the fact that she and Grant were the same age. She made frequent radio and television appearances as well. Her last film was *Airport* (1970).

In 1956, Landis married Major General J. F. R. Seitz, chief of the U.S. military mission to Iran. Shortly before, she published her autobiography, *You Won't Be So Pretty (But You'll Know More)* (1954). She revealed herself as a pragmatist and an optimist: "I've never been ashamed of anything I have done; I have never knowingly caused unhappiness. Unhappiness is like a disease and it is contagious. I just try to be happy and I think that is catching too." Landis died in Danbury, Conn.

[Aside from her autobiography, the most comprehensive source of information on Landis is the group of notebooks in the Billy Rose Theater Collection of the New York Public Library. An obituary appears in the *New York Times*, Feb. 3, 1972.]

TINKY ("DAKOTA") WEISBLAT

LAWRENCE, DAVID (Dec. 25, 1888–Feb. 11, 1973), editor and publisher, was born near Independence Hall in Philadelphia, Pa., to Harris Lawrence, an immigrant tailor, and Dora Lawrence. His family moved to Buffalo, N.Y., when Lawrence was an infant. There, in

1903, while still in high school, he began what was to become a lifelong career in journalism by selling some photographs of local athletes to the *Buffalo Express*.

He attended Princeton during Woodrow Wilson's presidency there and became a campus correspondent for the Associated Press (AP) and several newspapers. As an undergraduate, in the spring of 1908 he traveled to nearby Lakewood, N.J., to report on the health of a gravely ill President Grover Cleveland. Before returning to Princeton he befriended Mrs. Cleveland, who promised to inform him of any changes in her husband's condition. On June 24, 1908, Mrs. Cleveland wired Lawrence news of the president's death that morning, and Lawrence immediately telephoned the AP. After receiving his B.A. from Princeton in 1910, the AP rewarded him for his scoop by hiring him for a night-shift position with its Washington, D.C., bureau.

In Washington, he covered the White House, and after a stint in Mexico covering the Madero (1911) and Orozco (1912) revolutions, returned to Washington to report on the McNamara trial, which resulted from a labor disturbance in Los Angeles. In 1912, he was assigned to Wilson's first presidential campaign. Although he was to support every Republican president from Herbert Hoover on, the young Lawrence admired Wilson's policies and later called himself a conservative liberal.

At the start of World War I, Lawrence covered war news related to Washington for the AP. In 1915, he was the first journalist to uncover the resignation of Secretary of State William Jennings Bryan, an advocate of neutrality who had continued to argue against American involvement in the war despite the sinking of the passenger liner *Lusitania* by a German submarine.

Lawrence left the AP in 1916 to join the *New York Evening Post* as its Washington correspondent. He gained a measure of renown when, against the prevailing wisdom, he predicted a second-term Wilson victory over Charles Evans Hughes. His syndicated dispatches became the first to be carried nationally by wire and his daily column began appearing in large newspapers across the country.

Realizing that he had to pay for eight hours of wire time daily even though his column required only half an hour to transmit, Lawrence's entrepreneurial bent led him in

1919 to create the Consolidated Press Association (CPA), of which he became president. His association filled the remaining wire time with news of sports, agriculture, the financial markets, and foreign affairs. The most popular information disseminated by CPA was its stock market quotations and closing prices. This enterprise lasted until 1933, but it faded after the crash of 1929 diminished the public's interest in the stock market and caused newspapers to cut back on financial news. Meanwhile, Lawrence had started a second news service, Current News Features.

In 1926 he launched *The United States Daily*, a newspaper reporting on governmental affairs and carrying full texts of official documents. This newspaper became something of a status symbol in Washington, although it was thought to have more subscribers than readers and was unable to develop sufficient advertising sponsorship.

When the *Daily* folded in 1933, Lawrence divided its contents into two new companies: the Bureau of National Affairs, which continued to deliver daily and weekly reports in specialized fields; and the *United States News*, which carried news, analysis, and interpretation of national affairs. Originally a newspaper, the *United States News* was made into a magazine in 1940. Lawrence also founded the internationally oriented *World Report* in 1946 and was its president. He edited *United States News* until he merged the two publications in *U.S. News and World Report* in 1947.

From 1948 to 1959, he was president and editor of the consolidated *U.S. News and World Report*. Thereafter, until his death he was board chairman as well as editor of the magazine. During this period, his dispatch on national and world affairs was syndicated to more than three hundred daily newspapers in the United States. By the early 1980's, the magazine had more than two million subscribers, and it was claiming more than thirteen million readers.

An admirer of American industrialists, Lawrence opposed limiting their salaries during World War II and in December 1941 supported antistrike legislation. He warned against government growth and criticized President Franklin D. Roosevelt, the New Deal, and the Supreme Court. Despite his personal views, he was scrupulous in separating fact and opinion in his magazine.

He hired highly competent staff to work on

U.S. News and World Report, paid them well, and eventually made it possible for them to assume ownership of the company he had founded. He ended his career as a salaried worker employed by his former employees.

Well known as a generous supporter of charitable causes, he donated widely to religious, educational, medical, and civic organizations. When American University was in trouble in 1943, he directed a reorganization of its administration and bylaws and helped it to secure accreditation. He also worked to reform the county government in Fairfax, Va., where he owned a farm.

In 1918, Lawrence married Ellanor Campbell Hayes; she died in 1969. They had four children. Lawrence died at his home in Sarasota, Fla.

[In addition to his numerous magazine articles, Lawrence authored several books: *The True Story of Woodrow Wilson* (1924); *The Other Side of Government* (1929); *Beyond the New Deal* (1934); *Stumbling into Socialism* (1935); *The Future of Our Political Parties* (1935); *Nine Honest Men* (1936); *Who Were the Eleven Million?* (1937); *Supreme Court or Political Puppets?* (1937); and *Diary of a Washington Correspondent* (1942). An obituary is in the *New York Times*, Feb. 12, 1973.]

RICHARD L. TINO

LAZARUS, FRED, JR. (Oct. 29, 1884–May 27, 1973), department store executive and civic leader, was born in Columbus, Ohio, the second son of Fred Lazarus, Sr. and Rose Eichberg. Lazarus was born to an established but not unusually successful merchant family. His grandfather opened a men's store in Columbus after emigrating from Prussia to escape its Jewish segregation laws. Lazarus's father and uncle, Ralph, expanded the business to include women's apparel, and incorporated the store as the F. & R. Lazarus Company. Young Fred entered the business in 1902, when the concurrent illnesses of his father and uncle forced him to drop out of Ohio State University to help his older brother with management and day-to-day operations. Lazarus later claimed that becoming immersed in the family business so early was the most important turning point in his career.

Lazarus married Meta Marx on Feb. 11, 1911. They had four children, three of whom eventually rose to prominent positions within the Lazarus and Federated chains. Marx died in 1932, and Lazarus married Celia Kahn Rosenthal on Sept. 17, 1935.

F. & R. Lazarus prospered under the "Lazari" as the family came to be known. In 1928, the brothers expanded outside Columbus with the purchase of Shillito's, a major Cincinnati department store. In 1929, the firm was one of the founding members of Federated Department Stores, a holding company made up of such retailing giants as Bloomingdale's and Filene's. All the brothers played important parts in the expansion of the family fortune, but during these years Fred, Jr., began to emerge as the first among equals. He served as president of Shillito's from 1928 to 1947 and his roles as the Lazarus firm's chief representative to Federated, as well as the brother in charge of overall store operations and finance, grew in influence during this time. In that capacity he earned a reputation as a merchandising innovator and financial conservative.

Lazarus's overall approach to merchandising was well suited to the era. The great department stores offered low prices, but their chief draw was the enormous variety of goods. Lazarus understood the main attraction of the department store and used it to dominate his market. F. & R. Lazarus became the leading store in its area by carrying a greater variety of clothes, housewares, and appliances than anyone else. As one of Lazarus's competitors later described it: "They want a bigger tent than anybody else, and more monkeys and elephants. The bigger the better—that's Fred!"

Lazarus also had an eye for operational details that combined showmanship with solid merchandising techniques. Believing that a successful store needed "to be a bit of three-ring circus," Lazarus supported crowd-drawing attractions, such as auto shows, along with innovations to make shopping more convenient. One example of the latter came in the late 1920's when he introduced "size selling," where items are grouped by size rather than by style or manufacturer.

Lazarus's search for ways to boost sales went beyond the store. In 1939 he was part of a group of instigators of a successful campaign to extend the Christmas shopping season by moving Thanksgiving from the last Thursday in November to the fourth Thursday of the month. The group hired a lobbyist to present the idea to President Franklin Roosevelt. Roosevelt finally agreed and issued a proclamation in 1939, which Congress passed into law in 1941.

Lazarus was one of the earliest advocates of cost accounting, standardizing record-keeping practices in the industry, and group buying. To help promote these practices, Lazarus helped organize the Associated Merchandising Corporation in 1921. The AMC had grown to be the nation's largest buying office by the time of his death.

Lazarus's greatest accomplishment came as president of Federated. He assumed its leadership in 1945, partly because of his proven ability, and partly because of his adamant position that Federated either be disbanded or turned into a chain with a head office capable of implementing its plans for growth. Prior to this time Federated was more a confederation of major stores than a true department store chain. Lazarus's disenchantment with this weakness of the system became all the more urgent during World War II, when he became convinced that peace would bring an enormous economic boom and that Federated would have a tremendous opportunity for expansion.

In much the same way that Robert E. Wood revitalized Sears, by anticipating the postwar boom and rise of the suburbs and by positioning his company to take advantage of it, Lazarus made the downtown department store a real competitor to the new suburban shopping malls by expanding aggressively in the postwar years. Between 1945 and 1965 Lazarus engineered Federated's growth from a chain of five major stores to one with thirteen divisions operating eighty-eight stores. During the same period, annual sales grew from $201 million to $1.3 billion. Lazarus expanded quickly by buying the leading stores in the high-growth regions of the South and West. To keep expansion costs low, Lazarus typically acquired new companies by exchanging their stock for Federated's.

By linking Federated's interests so closely to the old central business districts (not until 1966 did suburban branch sales exceed downtown sales), Lazarus also accepted a major role for himself and his stores in civic affairs. This was in keeping with both his personal philosophy that the department store had an obligation to its city, and his conviction that it was in a store's best interests to seek solutions to urban problems. Personally, Lazarus was active in local and national philanthropic, educational, and civic institutions for most of his career. The scope of his interests can perhaps best be judged from the three honorary doctorates, in business, humanities, and law, that were bestowed upon him.

Lazarus retired as chairman of Federated in late 1967, and was replaced by his son Ralph. He died at home in Cincinnati.

[The best available sources of information on Lazarus are "Mr. Fred of the Lazari," *Fortune*, Mar. 1948; and "Lessons of Leadership: Part XIV, Expanding With Confidence," *Nation's Business*, July 1966. An obituary appears in the *New York Times*, May 28, 1973.]

THOMAS S. DICKE

LEAHY, FRANCIS WILLIAM ("FRANK") (Aug. 27, 1908–June 21, 1973), football coach, was born in O'Neill, Nebr., the son of Frank Leahy, a freighter and produce dealer, and Mary Kane. The family of four boys and four girls moved frequently throughout the Plains states, but settled in Winner, S.Dak. There Leahy attended public school, graduating from high school in 1927.

Leahy was an experienced cattle herder and had many dealings with Indians from the nearby Rosebud reservation. He excelled in many sports but his real strengths lay in football and boxing. For a time he seriously considered becoming a professional boxer. Destiny deemed otherwise, however, when his high school football coach, himself an illustrious alumnus of Notre Dame, convinced Knute Rockne that young Frank was deserving of a football scholarship to the South Bend powerhouse.

Despite being plagued by injuries, Leahy was the starting right tack on Notre Dame's national championship team of 1929. His own athletic prowess was overshadowed by others, but he was second to none in determination and obsessive work on fundamentals. His dreams died just days before the first game of his senior year when a knee injury in practice ended his playing career. Calamity was transformed into opportunity, however, when Leahy realized that by scrutinizing Rockne's methods he could learn the trade from one of the greatest coaches of all time. His knowledge was further enhanced when he and Rockne spent two weeks together as roommates at the Mayo Clinic in Rochester, Minn., at the end of the season talking nothing but football. When Frank Leahy graduated in 1931 with a B.S. in physical education, he weighed about 180 pounds, had blue eyes, blond hair, and resembled the film star Jimmy Stewart.

On Rockne's recommendation Leahy was hired as line coach at Georgetown University for the 1931 season. The spirited play of the Hoya line caught the eye of Jim Crowley, head coach of Michigan State, and in 1932 Leahy became the line coach for the Spartans. When Crowley went to Fordham as head coach the following year, Leahy went along and remained there for six years. On July 4, 1935, he married Florence ("Floss") Reilly; they had eight children. Although unknown to fans during this period Leahy was gaining attention from the coaching fraternity because of his development of the "Seven Blocks of Granite." Fordham's front line earned this sobriquet by winning all but two games in three seasons without the benefit of an outstanding backfield. One of its members, Vince Lombardi, went on to achieve even greater fame as the head coach of the Green Bay Packers.

Leahy burst into national prominence when he became head football coach at the perennially weak Boston College in 1939. In a miraculous turnaround B.C. defeated nineteen of twenty regular-season opponents in the next two years. Topping that were two bowl invitations. The high point was the epic 19–13 1941 Sugar Bowl victory over highly favored Tennessee.

Frank Leahy returned to Notre Dame in 1941, but only after securing a release from a newly signed contract with a bitter Boston College. He considered his return a holy mission, a continuation of the quest begun by his old teacher; his teams would represent "Our Lady" in sacred combat. After leading the Irish through its first undefeated season since Rockne's last year (1930), Leahy was voted coach of the year in 1941.

Through constant innovation Leahy's teams continued to roll up the victories. He invented the "pocket" to protect his quarterback on pass plays. In 1942 he abandoned the Notre Dame box formation in favor of the T formation utilized by the professional Chicago Bears. This was heretical in the view of Notre Dame's staunch followers and was strongly criticized. Fortunately for Leahy he had two extremely gifted quarterbacks in Angelo Bertelli and Johnny Lujack and the transition was a success. For the 1946 season he had a thirty-foot-high tower constructed in the middle of the practice field complete with loudspeakers so that he could better oversee the various groups of players.

Leahy's coaching career was interrupted by World War II when he entered the navy in 1944 as a lieutenant commander in charge of recreation programs for submarine crews. Returning in 1946 he led the Fighting Irish to another undefeated season and the number one ranking in the country. Three more undefeated seasons followed before Notre Dame finally lost to Purdue in 1950 after thirty-nine consecutive unbeaten games, all against strong opponents. The next unbeaten season, 1953, proved to be most costly to Leahy. Physical exhaustion and emotional strain caused an attack of acute pancreatitis at halftime of the Georgia Tech game. Shortly after the end of the season Leahy resigned for health reasons. In thirteen years he recorded 107 wins, 13 losses, and 9 ties. He had seven undefeated seasons, four national champions, and produced four Heisman Trophy winners. In addition, he wrote two books: *Notre Dame: The T Formation* (1949) and *Defensive Football* (1951). In an age when the popularity of college football reigned supreme, Frank Leahy hobnobbed with Hollywood celebrities, corporate executives, and national politicians.

Poor health was not the only reason for Leahy's resignation. For a number of years, some Notre Dame priests felt that football preeminence was tarnishing the university's fine academic reputation. In 1949 this faction was able to reduce the number of annual football scholarships, greatly distressing Leahy. His cause was further damaged by ethically questionable late-game tactics. Subterfuges helped to secure one victory and one tie. First there was the "sucker shift" (motion by offensive linemen inducing an offsides infraction by the opponents) against Southern California. Perhaps more devious was an infamous faked injury to stop the clock with Iowa leading Notre Dame, thereby gaining time to plan another play. While both of these stunts were standard football fare, scorn was heaped upon Leahy and Notre Dame for utilizing them.

After his retirement, his business ventures met with indifferent success, although he was quite popular on the lecture circuit. In 1970 he was elected to the National Football Foundation Hall of Fame. He died in Portland, Oreg.

[Leahy's papers are at the University of Notre Dame Library and consist of correspondence, clippings, and press releases. Biographies include Archie Ward, *Frank Leahy and the Fighting Irish* (1953);

and Wells Twombly, *Shake Down the Thunder* (1974). An obituary is in the *New York Times*, June 22, 1973.]

FRANCIS R. MCBRIDE

LEE, BRUCE (Nov. 27, 1940–July 20, 1973), martial arts expert and actor, achieved fame so quickly and died so soon thereafter that information about his early life remains sketchy. His birth name is variously reported as Lee Hseio Ling, Lee Hsaio Loong, and Lee Yuan Kim. Most sources agree that his father was a Cantonese Chinese opera and vaudeville performer who emigrated to the United States, and that Bruce Lee was born in San Francisco.

Some sources indicate that he left the United States at an early age when his father found acting work in Chinese opera in Hong Kong. It has been reported that Bruce Lee was a child actor who appeared in about twenty Hong Kong–made films. It is certain, however, that Hong Kong's movie industry would be the catalyst for Lee's international fame.

While in Hong Kong, Lee reportedly studied the martial arts, demonstrating great skill. He returned to the United States to attend college at Seattle University. While there, legend has it, he took part in a karate festival, was noticed by a talent scout for Twentieth Century–Fox studios, and was eventually signed to play the part of Kato, the Oriental houseboy and chauffeur of the hero in "The Green Hornet," a television series based on the popular radio serial of the 1930's and 1940's that ran during the 1966–1967 season. Thereafter Lee found work playing bit parts, providing technical advice for martial-arts action sequences, and playing Asian villains in Hollywood movies.

This phase of his career culminated in his scene-stealing appearance in *Marlowe* (1969), in which he played a villain who in one memorable scene destroys James Garner's office by means of kick-boxing and karate moves; in another equally memorable scene, he falls to his death from a roof when he leaps into the air to strike a lethal kicking blow with his foot and Garner deftly sidesteps the blow. But his career really did not take off until he returned to Hong Kong to star in a series of martial-arts films whose action sequences featuring Lee's almost balletic approach to martial-arts fighting set a standard for all subsequent actors in this genre.

Starring in rapid succession in a handful of Hong Kong–produced martial arts films, Lee became an international film star, transformed the martial arts movie from a subgenre aimed at the Asian community to a mainstream genre with world audience appeal (in the process preparing the way for such martial arts action film stars as Chuck Norris, Jean-Claude Van Damme, and Steven Seagal), and provided the Hong Kong film industry with a new image, clout in the world movie-making community, and huge sums of money.

Fists of Fury (1972) launched Lee's phenomenal rise. In this film Lee plays a martial arts expert who seeks vengeance on those who killed his teacher. This hugely successful film was followed in 1973 by both *Enter the Dragon*, in which he plays a master of the martial arts who is enlisted by the British government to stop opium smuggling, and *Return of the Dragon*, in which the Lee character visits his Chinese relatives in Italy and fights gangsters who want to take over his relatives' restaurant. Each release pushed Lee's star a little higher; and then, with his death under mysterious circumstances in July 1973, Lee became a film legend on the order of Valentino and James Dean.

The release of Bruce Lee's films in the Western world coincided with a heightened interest in the Eastern world stimulated in popular culture by curiosity about Eastern philosophies, acupuncture, the Chairman Mao cult, Oriental foods and the Oriental diet, and much more, and stimulated at the higher levels of culture by President Nixon's decision to recognize China after twenty-one years of American-imposed diplomatic isolation and his subsequent state visit in February 1972. Each new Lee film attracted new viewers, whose word-of-mouth advertising ensured greater numbers of viewers for successive Lee films. And before the Lee phenomenon could cool down, Lee himself was dead, at age thirty-two, officially of a kidney infection, but rumors of a drug-related death or death engineered by Asian mobsters fueled—and continue to fuel—the Lee myth.

On Aug. 17, 1964, he married Linda Emery, who had been a student in one of his kung fu classes. Their son Brandon, also a film actor, was accidentally killed in 1993 during the filming of a movie, when a gun supposedly loaded with blanks—but actually loaded with live ammunition—was fired at him. The bizarre death of Brandon Lee will certainly contribute to the Bruce Lee legend and cult.

Lee's star continued to rise after his death.

The owners of Lee film footage continually tried to find ways to work it into profitable commodities. *Game of Death* (1979), the movie on which Lee was working when he died, was eventually completed by using Bruce Lee look-alikes to flesh out the plot and already filmed Bruce Lee action sequences to give the film punch. Bruce Lee footage from "The Green Hornet" series was recycled as *Kato and the Green Hornet* (1974). *Circle of Iron* (1979), starring David Carradine in a role that Lee had written for himself, was also promoted as a kind of Bruce Lee film.

Lee was a small man by Western standards, but his mastery of a variety of martial arts techniques, his athletic ability, his dancerlike graceful movements, and his explosive power enabled him to fill the screen. No one could move with the speed, energy, and precision of Bruce Lee. He became, in consequence, a kind of dream hero, a James Bond rooted in Asiatic culture, but sufficiently Westernized to appeal to American and European audiences.

Bruce Lee had that undefinable essence known as "star quality." He was an Asiatic version of what the French call *un beau ténébreux*: dark, intense, moody, sexy, with more than a touch of James Dean. *Bruce Lee—The Legend*, a biographical film hastily created and released within a year of Lee's death, suggested that Lee was as tough, and as good at fighting, in real life as he had been in his screen persona. This may have mattered to some of his fans, but true cinema buffs, who know that nothing is real except the cinema image itself, recognized Lee for what he was: the creator of a new art form. Although the movies in which he appeared usually contained a credit line saying something like "Fight sequences designed by Bruce Lee," a more accurate credit would have said "Fight sequences choreographed by Bruce Lee." Bruce Lee combined the great fighter's perfectly muscled body and power with the great dancer's sense of space, balance, and graceful movement—this was the source of his uniqueness and of his legend.

[Biographical material on Bruce Lee can be found in Alex Ben Block, "The Hong Kong Style: Part I," *Esquire*, Aug. 1973; *Bruce Lee: The Untold Story* (1980); Jack Vaughn and Mike Lee, eds., *The Legendary Bruce Lee* (1986); Edward Gross, *Bruce Lee: Fists of Fury* (1990); and Michael Jahn, *Dragon: The Bruce Lee Story* (1993). A brief obituary appears in the *New York Times*, July 21, 1973.]

P. M. W. THODY

LEE, MANFRED B. (Oct. 20, 1905–Apr. 3, 1971), writer, was born Emanuel B. Lepofsky in Brooklyn, N.Y., the son of Rose and Benjamin Lepofsky. His father, a garment-industry worker, later became one of the first members of the International Ladies' Garment Workers' Union. Lee graduated summa cum laude from New York University in 1925 with a degree in English.

Shortly after college, he changed his name to Manfred Bennington Lee. Reportedly, his mother had wanted to name him "Manford," but the presiding physician thought it wasn't sufficiently Jewish-sounding and wrote "Emmanuel" on the birth certificate instead. Lee chose "Manfred" as a way of anglicizing the name "Manford" and so he could keep his nickname, "Manny." His choice of the name "Manfred," which etymologically means "man of peace," allegedly was a reflection of his lifelong belief in nonviolence.

In 1928, Lee and his cousin Frederic Dannay (born Daniel Nathan) were working in advertising and public relations when they entered a contest *McClure's* magazine was sponsoring for the best original detective novel by a first-time novelist. The contest rules required a pseudonym, and "Ellery Queen" was born. The name "Ellery" was chosen in honor of a childhood friend of Dannay's and "Queen," because it sounded royal. Lee and Dannay were unofficially informed that they had won the contest, but *McClure's* went bankrupt and was purchased by a company who ultimately awarded the $7,500 prize to another author. Their entry was eventually published in 1929 by the Frederick A. Stokes Company as *The Roman Hat Mystery*, the first of some thirty-five Ellery Queen novels the cousins wrote.

The name "Ellery Queen" was unique in that it was both the authors' pseudonym *and* the name of their detective; this was intended to act as a mnemonic device so that the reader would only have to remember one name. The early Queen novels also featured the unique "Challenge to the Reader": in the interests of fair play, all the necessary clues were revealed during the course of the book, but just before the solution was revealed, Queen challenged the reader to deduce the murderer's identity himself.

In 1932, Lee and Dannay adopted a second pseudonym, "Barnaby Ross," and wrote four novels featuring detective Drury Lane under that name within approximately one year. At the same time, Ellery Queen was asked to lecture at the Columbia University School of Journalism. Lee and Dannay flipped a coin to see who would give the lecture; Lee lost and gave the lecture while wearing a black mask. Eventually, the two went on a lecture tour together, with Dannay posing as Barnaby Ross and Lee still posing as Ellery Queen—both masked. The lecture tours soon fell into a routine in which either Lee or Dannay would challenge the other's skill as a detective; one would fire off clues for an imaginary murder case and challenge the other to solve the crime on the spot.

Rumors eventually circulated that "Ellery Queen" was another pen name of fellow mystery writer S. S. Van Dine and that "Barnaby Ross" was actually Alexander Woolcott, author and member of the Algonquin Round Table. A 1936 article in *Publisher's Weekly* finally revealed Lee and Dannay as the true authors behind both Queen and Ross.

All together, publishers estimated that Lee and Dannay sold around 100 million volumes and had about 120 million readers. Lee and Dannay also collaborated on screenplays for MGM, Paramount, and Columbia Pictures, as well as on scripts for the "Adventures of Ellery Queen" radio series. Their first effort as editors began in 1933 with *Mystery League* magazine, which folded after only four issues. In 1939, they created a radio show called "Author! Author!" They were permanent panelists; Ogden Nash, and eventually S. J. Perelman, served as moderators. Guest panelists included the likes of Moss Hart, George S. Kaufman, Mark Van Doren, and Dorothy Parker. The programs presented a dramatization of an "inexplicable event," and the panelists were challenged to come up with a set of circumstances that would explain the event. It aired for six months, but was canceled for lack of a sponsor.

On June 18, 1939, "The Adventures of Ellery Queen" debuted on the CBS network. It was the first hour-long dramatic show in the history of radio. These shows featured a counterpart to the "Challenge to the Reader" in which a distinguished studio guest was given the opportunity to solve the mystery; Lillian Hellman purportedly solved one of the on-air mysteries. By April 1940, the series had been reduced to a half-hour format, and it finally ended on May 27, 1948. For most of those nine years, every script was written by Lee and Dannay; toward the end, the final scripts were written by Lee and several uncredited collaborators, including Anthony Boucher.

In 1941, the first issue of *Ellery Queen's Mystery Magazine* appeared, stating: "Queen has waged an unceasing battle . . . on two fronts to raise the sights of mystery writers generally to the target of a genuine and respected literary forum . . . and to encourage good writing among our colleagues by offering a practical market not otherwise available among American magazines of high or low stature, as well as to develop new writers seeking expression in the genre." Since its inception, this magazine has published stories by at least eight Nobel and twenty-seven Pulitzer Prize–winning authors.

Lee married twice, first to Betty Miller; they had two children and eventually divorced. On July 4, 1942, Lee married radio actress Catherine Fox Brinker; they had five children, and Lee also adopted his wife's daughter from a previous marriage.

Lee's son Rand has compared Queen to his creators. In analyzing the pilot of the "Ellery Queen" TV series that aired on NBC during the early 1970's, he said that "One can imagine the NBC Ellery being cornered at a party by an enthusiastic fan and falling asleep in his chair while she gushes at him; chopping up redwood patio furniture to use in bird cages; finally succumbing to the charms of some pretty girl but forgetting to formally propose to her until their wedding day. My father actually did all those things."

Lee moved to a sixty-three acre estate in Roxbury, Conn., in the early 1950's. He posted signs declaring his property to be a game preserve, with no hunting allowed. When obstinate hunters tore down the signs, he simply had new ones posted.

He served on the local library board with William Styron—he reportedly once beat Arthur Miller for election to that same board—and he also served as Roxbury's justice of the peace for a period of time. In his spare time, he collected stamps and was an avid baseball fan; he started as a New York Giants fan, but switched his allegiance to the Mets when the Giants "defected" to the West Coast.

Lee died of a heart attack at his home.

[See Francis M. Nevins, *Royal Bloodlines: Ellery Queen, Author and Detective* (1973). An obituary is in the *New York Times*, Apr. 4, 1971.]

CHERYL L. DAVIS

LEONARD, JACK E. (Apr. 24, 1911–May 11, 1973), comedian, was born Leonard Kibard Lebitsky in Chicago, Ill., the son of Kibard and Ethel Lebitsky; his father was a tailor. Years later he would joke, "You know Chicago, the city where kids play robbers and robbers." As a young man he worked as a lifeguard and planned to become a physical education instructor; about his youthful consideration of swimming competitively he once quipped, "I swam against Johnny Weismuller in 1929 and he was so fast I haven't seen him since."

Instead of swimming he became a dancer on the vaudeville circuit, where he soon became famous for his comic rendition of the Charleston. In fact, he competed in dozens of Charleston dancing contests, earning enough money to pay his bills so he could pursue a career in show business. While in vaudeville he also changed his name to Jack E. Leonard. He never told anyone what the "E" stood for; some say it was in honor of his mother.

Leonard soon parlayed his dancing into a comic routine in which he also told jokes. The funny steps of the rotund five-foot, five-inch comic dancer eventually caught the eye of a vaudeville impresario who promoted him to a single-star act. Jack not only danced but soon specialized in slapstick and stand-up routines. Years later, he said he had patterned his act after that of Jack Waldron, who once told a heckler, "Let's play horse—I'll be the front end, and you just be yourself."

Thus, Jack E. Leonard's trademark became the nightclub one-line insult. For forty years "Fat Jacky Leonard," as he called himself, bad-mouthed people, most of them friends, most often famous celebrities. His stock-in-trade one-line barbs were usually aimed at the ego of whatever movie or TV star happened to be standing or sitting closest to the stage at the time. For example, he once told singer Perry Como, "You have a very fine voice—too bad it's in Bing Crosby's throat." Once, while appearing on the Red Skelton show, he chided Red, after the latter had bombed with three straight jokes, "What was that, one of your silent routines?"

One of his favorite butts was his good friend, Ed Sullivan, on whose show he appeared several times in the 1950's and 1960's. On one show he declared, "Ed, there's nothing wrong with you that reincarnation won't cure."

Although Leonard was a hit from the start of his long career, his big break didn't come right away. After vaudeville he toured with several big bands, played nightclubs, and even toured with USO shows during World War II. It was after one of these USO performances that he met his first wife, Kay, an acrobat. They were married in 1945 and had three children; Kay died of cancer on Dec. 2, 1967.

Postwar, in the 1950's and 1960's, Leonard began to earn large salaries for his performances. However, his big chance came with his guest appearances on commercial TV. He made guest shots on panel and game shows, variety shows such as Ed Sullivan's, and late-night talk shows with such headliners as Steve Allen ("The Tonight Show") and Jack Paar. On the average, from 1955 to 1970, he made thirty appearances a year, topping out at fifty-four in one year.

According to Sullivan, Leonard had "fully absorbed his stage personality. He was always on." Said Sullivan, "He's identical with his image on camera. He's just a wonderfully amusing guy." Indeed, all his barbs and insults were delivered in an innocent manner. Leonard once declared, "An insult is only funny if it's really ridiculous and it's ridiculous if it's aimed at some really big shot."

Of course, Jack didn't spare the obscure and humble, if they happened to be heckling him. He once told a noisy audience in Boston, "If I were Paul Revere, I wouldn't warn you." He didn't spare himself, either. Weighing between 200 and 350 pounds, depending on the state of one of his many diets, he often poked fun at his short, squat stature.

Leonard not only did television spots and nightclub acts but also cut several comedy records for RCA Victor and made three movies. In 1953 he had his only starring role as Porky in *Three Sailors and a Girl*. He later described it as "strictly for drive-out theaters. They wouldn't even show it on British TV."

In 1964, he made an appearance with Jerry Lewis in Lewis's comedy movie *The Disorderly Orderly*, and in 1965 he appeared in a television documentary entitled *The World of Abbott and Costello*. In 1966, he had a major role in a TV movie called *The Fat Spy*. In 1968, Leonard was elected to the New York City Friar's Club, an honor he cherished.

In March 1973, Leonard, by then suffering from diabetes, collapsed on stage at New York's Rainbow Grill. He was hospitalized at Mt. Sinai Hospital. Two months later, Leonard died of diabetic complications. He was survived by his second wife, Gladys. His funeral and burial took place in New York City, where he had lived most of his life.

[Biographical information can be found in Evelyn Mack Truitt, *Who Was Who on Screen* (1983). Obituaries appear in the *New York Times*, May 11, 1973, and in the *Washington Post*, May 12, 1973.]

WILLIAM HEAD

LEOPOLD, NATHAN FREUDENTHAL, JR. (Nov. 19, 1904–Aug. 29, 1971), author and coperpetrator with Richard Loeb in May 1924 of the kidnapping and murder of Robert ("Bobby") Franks in the "crime of the century," was born in Chicago, Ill., the son of Florence Foreman and Nathan Leopold, Sr., a wealthy South Side manufacturer. He was educated at the private Harvard School and at the University of Chicago, graduating at the age of nineteen.

In November 1923, Leopold and Richard Loeb (the son of a recently deceased vice-president of Sears, Roebuck, and Company) began planning a "perfect crime." To them, "perfect" meant not only insoluble, but free from passion or motive, an act of pure will. The two young men, precocious students, were influenced by Friedrich Nietzsche's concept of the "superman," a human being superior to common codes of morality. At first it was believed that Leopold, an avid reader of Nietzsche, instigated the crime. But later scholars believe that Loeb was the leader and Leopold only his tool.

The pair planned to make the event seem like a kidnapping for ransom. On the afternoon of May 21, 1924, using a rented automobile, they picked up fourteen-year-old Bobby Franks, the son of one of Chicago's wealthiest families, bludgeoned him to death with a chisel wrapped in tape, and stuffed his body into a culvert near the Lake Michigan shore, eight miles south of his home. They then attempted to collect $10,000 in ransom from the Franks family; however, the boy's body was discovered before the ransom could be paid.

Unwittingly, Leopold had left clues to his identity during the crime: he had dropped his glasses in the marsh where the body was buried. When confronted with the glasses and with evidence that the ransom note had been typed on his portable typewriter, he and Loeb confessed.

Their horrified parents hired Clarence Darrow, "the Great Defender," as defense attorney. Convinced that any Chicago jury would find the pair guilty—a finding that in the city's heated atmosphere would automatically result in their execution—Darrow had them plead guilty with mitigating circumstances. He contended that, although not legally insane, the young men were "mentally diseased" and incapable of judging right from wrong. After five weeks of testimony, much of it by psychiatrists, their trial before a judge in an overcrowded courtroom led to sentences of life imprisonment on the murder charge and ninety-nine years on the kidnapping charge. Leopold and Loeb were at first incarcerated in separate prisons in Joliet, Illinois; they would later be moved to other prisons.

The murder, trial, and imprisonment received national attention, and through the years became the subjects of numerous newspapers and magazine articles, as well as the subjects of a novel, *Compulsion* (1965), and a play by the same title (1959), both by a fellow student at the University of Chicago, Meyer Levin. The book, a partly fictional representation of events leading to the crime, also presents a detailed record of the trial, with lengthy excerpts from Darrow's summation—a masterly plea for mercy that undoubtedly influenced the judge's decision not to impose a death sentence.

Leopold called *Compulsion* "at once a horrible, a fascinating . . . and a beautiful book, forty percent fact . . . and the rest of it pure moonshine." Concerned that the novel had damaged his chances for parole, Leopold sued Levin for defamation of character. In response, a chastened Levin wrote an article in *Coronet*, urging Leopold's release.

In prison, the fates of Leopold and Loeb diverged. The latter was murdered on Jan. 28, 1936, by another inmate reportedly angered by Loeb's homosexual advances. (In fact, the man was angry because Loeb did not give him some cigarettes, as he had promised.) Leopold, on the other hand, became a model prisoner and won the respect of guards and prison officials. He enrolled in correspondence courses from the University of Iowa in advanced mathematics, physics, and classical languages. His intelligence and the quality of his work impressed both professors and administrators.

Leopold next persuaded the faculty at Iowa to help in organizing correspondence courses for prisoners and in replacing textbooks for the prison library that had been burned in a riot. He also convinced the prison staff to make it easier for inmates to borrow and read books. During World War II, he volunteered for medical tests that would advance knowledge of the causes and treatment of malaria (the disease was of concern to the military fighting in the Pacific). As a consequence of these activities, Governor William Stratton commuted his ninety-nine-year sentence to eighty-five years, which improved the possibility for his ultimate parole.

In 1958, supporting a fifth plea for release, Carl Sandburg, a longtime correspondent, and University of Iowa professor Helen Williams spoke on his behalf.

Shortly before his subsequent release, he announced the formation of the Leopold Foundation to aid disturbed children. The foundation was funded in part with proceeds from his *Life Plus 99 Years*, an autobiography first serialized by the *Chicago Daily News*, then published in full in 1958, with an introduction by the crime novelist Erle Stanley Gardner. The book bypassed the murder of Bobby Franks but gave a detailed description of Leopold's life in prison. Most reviewers praised the book in lengthy reviews.

On Mar. 13, 1958, after thirty-three years in prison, Leopold was released to the custody of the Church of the Brethren, to which he had been converted while in prison. He worked for $10 per month in the church's medical mission at Castañer, in Puerto Rico's hill country, where he taught mathematics and helped raise funds for the church. He also took correspondence courses from the University of Puerto Rico, earning a Master of Science degree in June 1961. Six months earlier he had married Trudi Feldman Garcia de Quevedo.

After Leopold's death, his body was donated to the University of Puerto Rico's School of Medicine, and his eyes to the school's eye bank.

[Daily editions of the *Chicago Tribune* and the *New York Times* from May 21 to Aug. 27, 1924, give reports of the finding of Bobby Franks's body, the first detention of Leopold, his arrest and charge with murder, and trial. Other sources are "Nathan Leopold After Thirty-two Years," *Life*, Mar. 4, 1957; and Elmer Gertz, *A Handful of Clients* (1965). An obituary is in the *New York Times*, Aug. 31, 1971.]
CLARENCE A. ANDREWS

LEVANT, OSCAR (Dec. 27, 1906–Aug. 14, 1972), pianist, composer, author, and racon-

teur, was born in Pittsburgh, Pa., the youngest son of Max Levant, a watchmaker, and Annie Radin. Max Levant ran a jewelry store from their home; Annie encouraged their four sons to study music. Oscar first studied piano with his brother Benjamin, who was ten years his senior, and subsequently with Martin Miessler, who had attended the Leipzig Conservatory in Germany. When he was twelve he went to the theater to see *Ladies First*, conducted by his uncle Oscar Radin. The show's pianist, George Gershwin, would later become his close friend. Levant was an ardent fan of the Pittsburgh Pirates, Charles Chaplin, and Douglas Fairbanks; this was an early indication of his lifelong passion for sports and movies.

Upon his father's death, Levant, a young man of medium height and with curly black hair and large dark eyes, left high school at age fifteen to live in New York City, where he studied piano with Sigismund Stojowski. He earned money playing piano for dance classes and attended many concerts. His brother Harry, who was conducting a Shubert revue at the Winter Garden Theater, let him play in the pit orchestra, which led to work with various dance orchestras.

On Feb. 14, 1924, Paul Whiteman premiered George Gershwin's *Rhapsody in Blue*. It was the sensation of the season and a seminal inspiration for Levant, who immediately learned the piece and played it with Whiteman's orchestra on one occasion. He recorded it for Brunswick Records in 1925, the first pianist after Gershwin to do so. He persuaded a mutual friend to introduce him to Gershwin, whom he idolized, and thus began a close friendship that lasted until Gershwin's untimely death in 1937.

In 1926 Levant went to England as accompanist to Rudy Wiedoeft, a classical saxophonist; they made several recordings for British Columbia Records. In 1927 his role as a pianist in the Broadway hit *Burlesque* led to a part in Paramount's film version of the play, entitled *The Dance of Life* (1929). After returning to New York, he met Barbara Smith, a dancer, who was then appearing in *Ziegfeld Follies of 1931*. They married on Jan. 5, 1932, and divorced in 1933.

He studied composition with Joseph Schillinger, a Russian theorist living in New York, and for the next few years—except for a time in 1934 when he played in radio jazz bands—devoted himself to composition, writing popular songs, Broadway show music, a sonatina for piano, and a string quartet. He returned to Hollywood in 1935 to write film music, and studied with composer Arnold Schoenberg for two years, completing the string quartet and *Nocturne.*

After George Gershwin succumbed to a brain tumor in 1937, Levant played Gershwin's *Concerto in F* at the Gershwin Memorial Concert at the Hollywood Bowl. Recognized as the foremost interpreter of Gershwin's piano compositions, he recorded them all: *Concerto in F, Rhapsody in Blue, Second Rhapsody, "I Got Rhythm" Variations for Piano and Orchestra,* and the three Preludes.

He returned to New York City in 1938 to conduct two Broadway shows, *The Fabulous Invalid* and *The American Way,* and was invited to join panelists Clifton Fadiman, Franklin P. Adams, and John Kieran on the nationally broadcast radio quiz show "Information Please." Listeners tried to stump the panelists with questions on literature, sports, music, theater, and movies. Levant's remarkable memory of music, movies, and sports trivia, along with his acerbic wit, made him an instant celebrity and launched his career as a concert pianist. During this period he met June Gilmartin, then working on Broadway as June Gale, and on Dec. 1, 1939, they were married.

Then followed a decade of successful creative activity. In 1940 his best-selling book *A Smattering of Ignorance* was published. He appeared as a soloist with Pierre Monteux and the San Francisco Symphony, then resumed his film career with *Rhythm on the River* (1940) and *Kiss the Boys Goodbye* (1941). In 1942 he premiered his piano concerto with Alfred Wallenstein and the NBC Symphony, went on radio and toured as a solo pianist-raconteur with his "Program of Piano Music with Comments," and made three movies for Warner Brothers. *Rhapsody in Blue* (1944) was reviewed in the New York *Sun* by Eileen Creelman, who wrote, "His acid, smart-alecky remarks are one of the hits of the film." *Variety's* critic said Levant played Gershwin's music ". . . with virtuosity and authority as befits a real-life confidant of the late composer." *Humoresque* (1947) and *Romance on the High Seas* (1948) followed.

In 1947 he was invited to play for President Harry S. Truman at the White House. The same year he moved to Beverly Hills with his wife and three daughters, and he collaborated with Al Jolson on the "Kraft Music Hall" radio show for two years. His next movie was *The Barkleys of Broadway* (1948). Eileen Creelman's review stated: "His snarling comedy and his [piano] playing . . . are equally entertaining." By 1949 he was appearing regularly on NBC-TV's "Who Said That?"

In 1950 he again performed for President Truman, and played the Gershwin *Concerto in F* in the hit movie *An American in Paris* (1951), but his frenzied schedule—a concert tour, television appearances, a performance and recording of Rubinstein's *Concerto in D minor,* and work on another movie—led to an addiction to prescription drugs and he suffered a heart attack in 1952. For the next ten years he was plagued with addictions, hospitalizations, and shock treatments, which impaired his memory.

Between 1956 and 1958 he became, in his own words, the "verbal vampire of television," on his own shows—one was canceled because of a vulgar witticism he made—and as a guest on network television. Describing a movie actress who wore bangs and dressed in daring, extreme décolletage, he said, "I've seen every part of her anatomy except her forehead." After his appearances on "The Jack Paar Show" in 1961, where his witty barbs were often aimed at his own eccentricities, he became a recluse until his death.

His solo career included appearances with the New York Philharmonic, the Philadelphia Orchestra, and the NBC, Cleveland, Pittsburgh, and San Francisco symphonies, with such noted conductors as Eugene Ormandy, Arturo Toscanini, Dimitri Mitropoulos, and Sir Thomas Beecham. He recorded more than a hundred classical compositions by Khachaturian, Debussy, Chopin, Gershwin, Tchaikovsky, Beethoven, and Grieg.

Although June Levant filed for a legal separation (1947) and a divorce (1958), their stormy marriage endured until Levant's death in Beverly Hills.

[Levant's autobiographical reminiscences are helpful: *A Smattering of Ignorance* (1940), *Memoirs of an Amnesiac* (1965), and *The Unimportance of Being Oscar* (1968). A play about Levant, *At Wit's End,* written by Joel Kimmel, with help from June Levant, premiered at Michael's Pub in New York City in Oct. 1991. An obituary is in the *Boston Globe,* Aug. 15, 1972.]

SUSAN FLEET

LEWIS, JOHN HENRY (May 1, 1914–Apr. 18, 1974), boxer, was born in Los Angeles, the son of Mattie Foster and John E. Lewis, a well-known boxing trainer. Lewis was raised in Phoenix, Ariz., where he excelled at basketball, baseball, football, swimming, and tennis. His great-great-uncle was Tom Molineaux, a New York City black recognized as the United States' first boxing champion in 1809. Lewis's initial ambition was to be a Methodist minister, but after training in a Phoenix gym run by his father, he made his professional boxing debut in 1931 at age seventeen, knocking out his first nine opponents. One fighter, Sam Terrain, died shortly after a fourth-round knockout by Lewis in Prescott, Ariz.

Lewis won his first major fight when he beat future heavyweight champion James Braddock in San Francisco on Sept. 21, 1932. He remained undefeated until decisioned by Maxie Rosenbloom in San Francisco on Nov. 16, 1932. Despite occasional defeats, Pacific Coast boxing authorities regarded Lewis as an up-and-coming star. He acquired a manager, Gus Greenlee, a black numbers operator and owner of the Pittsburg Crawfords, a top Negro Baseball League team. In 1934, Madison Square Garden in New York City signed Lewis for three bouts within a month. The first was against Braddock on Nov. 16, 1934. At twenty-nine and with his upset of Max Baer for the heavyweight championship still eight months in the future, Braddock was considered too old and slow for the flashy Arizonian. But the veteran Braddock knocked Lewis down in the seventh round and hung on for a decision after ten blistering rounds. Lewis won the next two bouts at the Garden, then won nine more bouts in the next seven months before losing again to Rosenbloom in Oakland and Abe Feldman in New York City in July 1935.

Lewis took a 40–7 record into the ring on Oct. 31, 1935, in St. Louis, when he met Bob Olin for the light-heavyweight title. Lewis won the championship in a grueling fifteen-round slugfest, becoming the first black to hold the crown since Battling Siki in 1923. At twenty-one he was among the youngest champions ever. Lewis made very little money from the bout, however, and had to contribute $5,000 toward Olin's purse.

Lewis's schedule accelerated in the next two years. He lost a nontitle bout with Rosenbloom on Nov. 29, 1935, in San Francisco, then took a bum-a-week tour, fighting overmatched or faded professionals. Between his winning of the light-heavyweight title in October 1935 and his match with Joe Louis for the heavyweight championship on Jan. 25, 1939, Lewis boxed fifty-eight matches, winning fifty-two. In this thirty-nine-month period, Lewis entered the ring at least every three weeks. He defended his title successfully against Jock McAvoy, Len Harvey, Emilio Martinez, Al Gainer, and in a rematch with Olin. Only in the battle against Gainer, who was also black, did Lewis earn as much as $7,000. He then traveled to England where he received much larger purses. In London, in November 1936, Lewis outpointed the English fighter Len Harvey. Lewis used a two-fisted approach to batter his game opponent. Lewis's biggest problem was a bad eye, due to a cut suffered in training for which he wore a plaster.

Five feet, eleven inches tall, Lewis was a natural 175-pounder, but enjoyed consistent success against larger fighters. Greenlee hoped that some of Lewis's speed and cleverness would challenge Joe Louis for the heavyweight crown. Neither fighter was keen for the bout because they were close friends outside the ring. Their trainers, Jack Blackburn and Larry Amadee, often worked together. Louis was now the world champion, having devastated Max Schmeling in the first round of their famous rematch on June 22, 1938. At 180 pounds and suffering from declining eyesight, Lewis was not an equal opponent for the Brown Bomber. Lewis wanted to get out of boxing, but needed a big purse. The fight was scheduled for Jan. 25, 1939.

Mike Jacobs, promoter for Lewis, kept the Garden prices low, fearing that white boxing fans would avoid the all-black bill. In fact, it was the first meeting between blacks for the championship since Jack Johnson and Jim Johnson fought to an eight-round draw twenty-six years before. The Garden sold out despite odds of 8–1 favoring Louis. John Henry Lewis, weighing in at 180 pounds, was far more nervous on the scales than the champion Joe Louis, who weighed twenty pounds more. Jack Blackburn, a long time trainer for Louis, advised him to be merciful and end the fight quickly. Louis knocked his friend down three times in the first round before referee Arthur Donovan stopped the fight after two minutes, twenty-nine seconds. A check of the motion-picture record revealed that Louis connected with thirty-nine punches, mostly right-hand smashes, while Lewis was able to land but three feeble jabs.

After the fight, the New York State Athletic Commission stripped Lewis of his light-heavyweight championship for avoiding opponents. Despite his near-blindness, Lewis tried unsuccessfully for a rematch and repeatedly refused to defend his light-heavyweight crown against Tiger Jack Fox of Spokane, the number-one challenger. The New York State Athletic Commission declared the title vacant on July 27, 1939. Lewis failed a physical for a match in London after the fight physician declared his left eye nearly blind. The National Boxing Commission in America then forced Lewis to retire. Of 104 matches, Lewis won 91 with 12 losses. He knocked out fifty-four opponents. His loss to Louis was his only defeat by knockout.

After leaving boxing, Lewis lived in Berkeley, Calif., working on construction projects. He gained wide respect as a community spokesman and member of the Methodist church. He died in Berkeley, survived by his wife Florence Anita (Reid) Lewis and their two children.

[Lewis's complete boxing record may be found in Nat Fleischer, *Ring Record Book and Boxing Encyclopedia* (1963). Fleischer includes a good review of Lewis's career in *Black Dynamite*, vol. 5 (1947). Accounts of major fights appear in Fleischer, *The Heavyweight Championship* (1949) and Chris Mead, *Champion Joe Louis* (1985). Arcel's recollections are found in Dave Anderson, *In the Corner* (1991). Obituaries appear in the *San Francisco Chronicle*, Apr. 18, 1974; and the *New York Times*, Apr. 19, 1974.]

GRAHAM HODGES

LIMÓN, JOSÉ ARCADIO (Jan. 12, 1908–Dec. 2, 1972), modern dancer and choreographer, was born in Culiacán, Sinaloa, Mexico, the first of eleven children. His father, Florencio Limón, was an army bandmaster. His mother, Francisca Traslavina, gave birth to José when she was sixteen and died from repeated childbearing eighteen years later. When José was seven, the family fled the Mexican Revolution to Tucson, Ariz., and later settled in Los Angeles, where Limón attended public school and learned how to play the piano from his father. At nineteen he entered the University of California at Los Angeles as an art major.

After a year, Limón left UCLA for New York City to pursue a career in painting. Soon after his arrival in 1928, however, he became disillusioned because the contemporary artistic scene was dominated by imitators of modern French artists. Limón, a romantic, drew his inspiration from the Renaissance artists El Greco and Michelangelo. Alienated, he began questioning his devotion to art, and, at the same time, his Catholic faith, which had been strong in the early, difficult years of his life.

Limón's friends suggested he consider modern dance. But Limón, believing dance was effeminate and effete, rejected the idea. Then, one evening, he saw a performance by the German modern dancer Harald Kreutzberg called *Angel of Last Judgment*. Astounded by Kreutzberg's strong movements and great emotion, Limón declared, "My God, that's what I want to do." The next day, he enrolled in classes at an innovative modern dance studio run by Doris Humphrey and Charles Weidman.

Though Limón began dancing at the late age of twenty, he had several advantages, namely a strong six-foot-plus build, natural athletic ability, and boundless enthusiasm. Within a year, he earned a secondary role in the Humphrey-Weidman Company's production of *Lysistrata*, and by 1930 had choreographed *Etudes in D Flat Major* and *Bacchanale*, works of pure movement without dramatic story lines.

Humphrey was Limón's mentor until her death in 1958. She developed a technique that emphasized the use of breathing in such movements as "fall and recovery," "rebound," "suspension," and "tension and relaxation." Limón added his own innovations based on his idea of the body as an orchestra composed of separate instruments that had to be individually mastered before they could work in concert. He developed exercises that isolated each body part and focused on its weight and potentialities of movement.

From Weidman, Limón came to appreciate a lightheartedness and humor in dance, neither of which came easily to him. Limón was instead drawn to tragic, dramatic roles. He had a serious presence even off-stage, often greeting acquaintances with a bow. During this period, Limón also studied ballet and appeared in Broadway shows such as *Americana*, *As Thousands Cheer*, and *Roberta*, which financially supported him. He spent summers at the Bennington College Dance Festival.

Limón had been a member of the Humphrey-Weidman Company for twelve years when he left the company following a personal conflict with Weidman. He toured with dancer May O'Donnell and meanwhile developed a romantic correspondence with Pauline Lawrence, dancer and costume designer for the Humphrey-Weidman Company. Limón and Lawrence were married on Oct. 13, 1941, and from then on Lawrence devoted herself to Limón's career. She urged Limón to return to the Humphrey-Weidman Company, where he became the lead dancer and in 1942 created *Chaconne*, a solo work inspired by his favorite composer, Bach, which foreshadowed the dramatic, charged works Limón would later create.

World War II interrupted Limón's work. As a naturalized American citizen, he was drafted into the United States Army in 1943, where he directed and performed in entertainment units. Honorably discharged two years later, Limón formed his own company. Humphrey, whose arthritis kept her from dancing, choreographed for Limón works such as *Lament for Ignacio Sanchez Mejías* (1946), about the death of a bullfighter; *Felipe el loco* (1954); and *Ritmo jondo* (1953).

Limón often taught during summers at Connecticut College and Bennington College. In his own work, he choreographed for both men and women, but he was especially concerned with expanding the possibilities for the male dancer beyond the "partner" role that had constrained him in ballet. Limón stressed classic themes that were biblical (*The Exiles*, 1950; *The Traitor*, 1954, in which Limón played Judas; and *There Is a Time*, 1956); literary (*The Moor's Pavane*, 1949, based on Shakespeare's *Othello*; and *The Emperor Jones*, 1956, derived from a Eugene O'Neill play); mythical (*Orfeo*, 1972, about the legend of Orpheus and Eurydice); and historical (*Carlota*, 1972, the story of the crazed widow of Mexico's French emperor Maximilan; and *Danza de la muerte*, 1937, based on the Spanish Civil War). A number of works were inspired by his native country, such as *La Malinche* (1949), the tragic legend of revolt and betrayal during the conquest of Mexico, and *Danzas mexicanas* (1939).

In 1951, the Mexican government invited the Limón Company to perform and reside in Mexico City. There, Limón created large-scale works such as *Los cuatro soles* and *Redes*. In the same year, the Juilliard School of Music in New York City invited him to join its faculty, and Limón accepted.

In 1954, the Limón Company was the first to be sent abroad by the State Department as part of its cultural exchange program. On separate occasions, the company toured South America, Europe, the Far East, and Australia. The postwar devastation Limón saw in Poland inspired him to choreograph *Missa Brevis* (1958), an exploration of guilt and anger.

Following Humphrey's death, Limón paid homage to her with A *Choreographic Offering* (1964). In that same year, he won the prized Capezio Dance Award and the *Dance Magazine* Award, and perhaps most significantly, he became the artistic director of the American Dance Theater at Lincoln Center. He then began experimenting with works that used minimal or no music, such as *The Winged* (1966) and *The Unsung* (1970), a tribute to the American Indian.

In the later part of his life, Limón, who was struggling with prostate cancer, devoted himself solely to choreography. He created *Dances for Isadora* (1971), in honor of Isadora Duncan, whom he referred to as his "artistic mother," and finally the two works *Orfeo* and *Carlota*, which both reflected the loss he felt after his wife's death in 1971. Limón lived on a farm in Stockton, N.J., but died in a hospital in Flemington, while his company was performing in Honolulu, Hawaii.

[See also Marcia B. Siegel, "José Limón (1908–1972)," *Ballet Review* 4, no. 4 (1973); Louis Chapin, "José Limón: Rich Legacy of Dance Recalled," *Christian Science Monitor* (Apr. 20, 1973); Katharine S. Cunningham, "A Legacy of José Limón," *Dance Scope* (Spring/Summer 1973); Doris Hering, "José Limón: Midstream Vintage Years in Retrospect," *Dance Magazine* (Nov. 1973); and Daniel Lewis, *The Illustrated Dance Technique of José Limón* (1984). Obituaries are in the *New York Times*, Dec. 3, 1972; *Dance News* (Jan. 1973); and *Dance Magazine* (Jan. 1973).]

ALISON GARDY

LINDBERGH, CHARLES AUGUSTUS, JR. (Feb. 4, 1902–Aug. 26, 1974), aviator, was born in Detroit, Mich., the only son of Charles Augustus Lindbergh, a lawyer and five-term member of the United States House of Representatives (1907–1917), and Evangeline Land, a high school science teacher. Unhappily married, the Lindberghs increasingly lived apart, but their son seems to have acquired enduring personality traits, interests, and values from both. His father, a progressive Republican, bequeathed his maverick streak, remarkable physical courage, and abiding love for the outdoors. His mother, with whom Charles spent most of his youth living on the family farm in Little Falls, Minn., imparted an aloof temperament.

Although he wished to become an aviator, Lindbergh bowed to parental pressure in 1920 and enrolled in the University of Wisconsin at Madison. There he planned to study civil engineering, a natural consequence of his aptitude for grasping technical details. During his sophomore year, however, he withdrew from college to take flying instruction in Lincoln, Nebr. Lindbergh became a barnstormer, noted especially for his daredevil stunts. Sensing that the heyday of barnstorming was passing and that he needed further professional training, Lindbergh enlisted in the United States Army in March 1924. A year later he graduated first in his class at Brooks Air Force Base in San Antonio, Tex., earning a commission as second lieutenant.

As an experienced pilot Lindbergh now could command more substantial employment. The government had initiated airmail service in 1918 but was increasingly turning it over to private enterprise during the 1920's. Lindbergh accepted a position with the St. Louis–based Robertson Aircraft Corporation in 1925, planning and flying the St. Louis–Chicago route while also meeting his Army Reserve requirements. During this time "Lucky Lindy" experienced some narrow escapes from disaster.

While working as an airmail pilot, Lindbergh became intrigued by the possibility of a transatlantic flight. After two Englishmen had made the flight from Newfoundland to Ireland in 1919, Raymond Orteig, a Frenchman who managed hotels in New York, offered a prize of $25,000 to anyone who could complete a solo nonstop flight from New York to Paris or vice versa, a distance of 3,600 miles. The prize lapsed unawarded after five years, but Orteig renewed it in 1926. Their appetites rekindled, various aviators, including the American Richard E. Byrd, tried—and failed. A few perished.

Lindbergh, who by now had secured financial backing from several St. Louis businessmen, remained undaunted. After assorted delays a plane designed to his specifications was completed. On May 10, 1927, Lindbergh flew this Wright-engine monoplane, *The Spirit of St. Louis*, from San Diego to St. Louis at an astounding speed in excess of 100 miles per hour. Two days later he flew from St. Louis to

Curtiss Field, Long Island, just east of New York City. His twenty-two-hour transcontinental trip established a record.

For a week Lindbergh and several competitors for the Orteig Prize waited anxiously for satisfactory flying conditions. On May 20, Lindbergh, upon hearing that the weather was clearing over the ocean, rushed to Curtiss Field at 3:00 A.M. Towed to nearby Roosevelt Field, Lindbergh and the *Spirit of St. Louis* took off from a dangerously muddy runway into an adverse wind. For the next thirty-three and one-half hours Lindbergh, having previously gone without sleep for nearly twenty-four hours, battled storms, fog, and most of all, drowsiness. His monoplane, stripped to a minimum weight, flew over Long Island and followed the Great Circle course from Nova Scotia to Newfoundland, and then over Ireland, northern France, and Paris, before landing at Le Bourget Airport, 10:24 P.M., Paris time, Saturday, May 21.

As the first person to solo nonstop across the Atlantic, the "Lone Eagle" instantly became a worldwide hero. Alerted by ground observers who had seen the *Spirit of St. Louis* over Ireland, Great Britain, and the continent, as many as 100,000 people broke through police lines to mob him at Le Bourget. This was only the beginning of the wild adulation he was to receive. First in France and then in Belgium and England, dignitaries and commoners alike flocked to catch a glimpse of this tall, slender figure, who received his newly acquired fame with modesty and grace. Lindbergh wished to refly the Atlantic, but President Calvin Coolidge, acting as his commander in chief, ordered him and his plane conveyed back to the United States aboard the cruiser *Memphis*. Once back, the celebration continued. President Coolidge awarded him the Distinguished Flying Cross and promoted him to colonel in the Air Corps Reserve. In New York City, Lindbergh was driven down the "Canyon of Heroes" on lower Broadway, with a gargantuan ticker tape parade attended by four million cheering celebrants.

During the year after his historic flight, Lindbergh undertook a whirlwind of activities that included writing a series of articles for the *New York Times* and *We* (1927), a brief account of that flight. He donated the *Spirit of St. Louis* to the Smithsonian Institution, received the nation's highest award, the Medal of Honor, and became a consultant to both Pan American Airways and Transcontinental Air Transport. He visited all the nation's states, seventeen Latin American countries, and Mexico, where he courted Anne Spencer Morrow, daughter of Dwight L. Morrow, the newly appointed American ambassador who was a senior partner in the J. P. Morgan banking firm. Throughout all, "Lindy" remained the great national and international hero.

Lindbergh and Anne Morrow were quietly married on May 27, 1929, at the bride's family home in Englewood Cliffs, N.J. To their chagrin, however, relentless newspaper reporters besieged them on their honeymoon in Maine. The refusal of the press to respect their privacy would greatly intensify.

At first glance the couple seemed oddly paired—she was petite, well educated, and socially polished. But Anne Lindbergh was determined to share fully in her husband's life. She became an adept aviator in her own right and Charles's flying companion. Flying their new monoplane, the *Sirius*, from California to New York in April 1930, the couple broke Charles's speed record for a coast-to-coast flight by several hours, despite Anne's pregnant condition. Two months later and only a few weeks after the birth of their son Charles, the Lindberghs completed a dramatic and dangerous flight via the polar route to the Far East that Anne later detailed in *North to the Orient* (1935). In 1937 they undertook even more ambitious air travel that took them across the Atlantic Ocean to various European cities, along the western coast of Africa, and across the South Atlantic before returning home. Anne Lindbergh described this journey in *Listen! The Wind* (1938). Both these trips provided valuable information for establishing commercial flying routes and advancing aviation technology. Ever mindful of the latter, Charles Lindbergh had become convinced as early as 1928 that rocketry had an important future. To achieve this distant goal he helped a then-little-known professor of physics at Clark University, Robert H. Goddard, to secure badly needed funding from the Guggenheim Foundation to establish a laboratory in Roswell, N.Mex.

Their richly fulfilling activities notwithstanding, tragedy struck the Lindberghs in 1932. Sometime in mid-evening on February 29 they discovered that their twenty-month-old son had been kidnapped from his second-story bedroom of their new home in Hopewell, N.J. They also found a ladder, tools, and a ransom note written in awkward English and demanding $50,000. For more than two months law-enforcement officials, private individuals, and Lindbergh himself pursued a host of clues and false leads in a frenetic hunt for the missing child. Finally, on May 12 the baby, its skull fractured, was found buried in a wooded area not far from the Lindbergh home. More than two years later police arrested Bruno Richard Hauptmann, a German-born carpenter who was living in the Bronx. Extradited to New Jersey, Hauptmann was tried for murder, found guilty, and sentenced to death. He was executed in April 1936, following a series of unsuccessful legal appeals. Covered exhaustively by the media, the kidnapping and death of the Lindbergh baby and the subsequent trial of Hauptmann became and remains one of the most celebrated crimes of the twentieth century. It led directly to congressional enactment in 1932 of the so-called Lindbergh law that made kidnapping a federal offense. The crime continues to elicit controversy concerning the guilt of Hauptmann, who steadfastly maintained his innocence.

The tragedy, replete with ghoulish public photographs of the dead child, all but completely deprived the Lindberghs of their cherished privacy. This, coupled with grave fears for the safety of a second son, Jon, who was born just months after the kidnapping of his brother, convinced them to emigrate. After Jon, the Lindberghs had four more children: two sons, two daughters. They left the United States in early 1936 for England, where they initially resided in the Kentish home of Harold Nicolson, a diplomat and biographer of Anne's father.

The Lindberghs remained in Europe until the spring of 1939. During this sojourn Charles deepened his friendship and worked more closely with Dr. Alexis Carrel, a Nobel Prize laureate in medicine (1912) whom he had met in 1930 while the latter was working at the Rockefeller Institute for Medical Research (now Rockefeller University) in New York City. At that time the two developed a perfusion pump for keeping the heart and other organs alive. While in Europe, Lindbergh collaborated further with Carrel, coauthoring *The Culture of Organs* (1938).

But Lindbergh's greatest interest remained aviation. Between 1936 and his return to the United States he was able to observe firsthand the air forces of various European states. He was most impressed, perhaps inordinately so, with the *Luftwaffe*, and warned both public officials and private citizens in the West of Germany's current and potential air power. On a visit to Germany in October 1938, Lindbergh, at the request of the American ambassador, attended an official dinner where, to his surprise, Reichsmarshall Hermann Goering presented him with the Service Cross of the German Eagle, a prestigious decoration for civilians. Anne Lindbergh immediately referred to the award as "the Albatross," which indeed it quickly became. Appalled by Nazi ideology and practices that culminated in the notorious *Kristallnacht* orgy of Nov. 9, 1938, critics, including President Franklin D. Roosevelt, castigated Lindbergh for having accepted the tribute. While publicly deploring Nazism, the Lone Eagle defended his acceptance and refused to return the award. This action, along with his numerous laudatory statements concerning Germany tarnished his reputation.

Convinced that a European war was imminent, Lindbergh returned to the United States in the early spring of 1939. In the period that intervened between his homecoming and Japan's attack on Pearl Harbor, Lindbergh, in his role as an officer in the military and then as a private citizen after his resignation, pursued two objectives. On the one hand, he labored unswervingly to convince the nation that it must vastly upgrade its air power. On the other hand, he strove just as assiduously to preach noninvolvement in the European conflagration that became World War II. Lindbergh did not believe that the European democracies could withstand German military prowess, nor was he loath to have Germany defeat the Soviet Union and destroy Communism. He further reasoned that a sufficiently prepared America could guarantee its own security against any possible transatlantic aggressor. Like his father a generation earlier, he had become an ardent isolationist.

Because President Roosevelt was determined to thwart Nazi aggression even if it increased the possibilities of war, a clash between Lindbergh and the chief executive, who had previously disliked each other, was virtually inevitable. The aviator quietly declined a cooptative administration offer to head a proposed Department of the Air Force. When Lindbergh's opposition to administration foreign policy persisted, Roosevelt and his supporters virulently attacked him for the succor he was giving Germany, wittingly or not. Lindbergh consequently resigned his military commission in April 1941 and joined the America First Committee, the most powerful organization of isolationists in the country. He proved a forceful speaker for the committee until a disastrous speech given in Des Moines, Iowa, on Sept. 11, 1941. In that address he blamed Roosevelt, the British, and the Jews for inclining the United States toward war. Although he denounced Nazi anti-Semitism, Lindbergh was immediately tarred as an anti-Semite. His usefulness as an antiwar advocate having been hopelessly compromised, he resigned from the committee.

After the attack on Pearl Harbor, Lindbergh called on all Americans to unite and to support the war effort. His request to reenlist in the military having been denied, he contributed as a civilian to his nation's cause, even though a hostile administration unsuccessfully tried to foil his attempts to work for private firms that did war contracting. Among the benefits that resulted from his labors were an improved design for the B-24 bombers manufactured at Henry Ford's plant at Willow Run, Mich., and other assorted solutions to problems concerning high-altitude and long-distance flying. United Aircraft sent Lindbergh to the South Pacific theater of operations in the spring of 1944 to evaluate the performance of their aircraft. Over the next several months, and without the knowledge of the government, he flew combat missions, destroying an enemy fighter plane in the process. He later published his reminiscences of these experiences in his *Wartime Journals* (1970).

Lindbergh remained publicly active for most of his life after the war. He worked for Pan American World Airways nearly until his death and was a consultant for other aviation firms. President Dwight D. Eisenhower made him a brigadier general in the Air Force Reserve in 1954. Both before and after his reinstatement in the military, he continued to advise on rocketry and space flight. Present at Cape Kennedy for the Apollo moonshot in 1968, he was able to witness the fruition of a prediction that Robert H. Goddard had made to him nearly forty years earlier.

Lindbergh also continued to write. Most of his efforts took article form, but *The Spirit of St. Louis* (1953) won the Pulitzer Prize for autobiography in 1954 and three years later was made into a movie of the same name, starring Jimmy Stewart.

A trip to Africa in 1964 proved epiphanic for Lindbergh, who returned home a confirmed environmentalist. "If I had to choose," he remarked, "I would rather have birds than airplanes." Lindbergh remained optimistic that technology could help humanity, but increasingly he worried about its undesirable effects. To the surprise of many, the world's most famous aviator strongly opposed the use of supersonic planes, fearing that they would perilously pollute the atmosphere. As a member of or advocate for various environmental groups, he fought to protect endangered species and the planet's ecological system. Convinced that the simple and natural must survive alongside the complex and civilized, he persuaded the Philippine government to protect their primitive Tasaday people, who knew virtually nothing of modernity. When he realized in 1974 that he was dying from cancer of the lymphatic glands, Lindbergh quietly flew from his suburban Darien, Conn., home, where he had resided since shortly after World War II, to his retreat on the island of Maui, Hawaii, where he selected his simple gravesite.

[The Sterling Memorial Library of Yale University houses the largest (more than one million items) collection of Lindbergh primary materials. Assorted Library of Congress collections also contain pertinent manuscript sources, as do holdings at the Minnesota Historical Society and the Missouri Historical Society. Lindbergh's notebooks for the years 1935–1939 can be found in the John Vinton Dahlgren Library of Georgetown University. See also Lindbergh's *Autobiography of Values* (1978), a posthumously published collection of observations and opinions. Detailed biographies of Lindbergh include Kenneth S. Davis, *The Hero: Charles A. Lindbergh and the American Dream* (1959); Leonard Mosley, *Lindbergh* (1976); and Walter Ross, *The Last Hero: Charles A. Lindbergh* (1976). See also Perry D. Luckett, *Charles A. Lindbergh: A Bio-Bibliography* (1986); and Joyce Milton, *Loss of Eden* (1993). A good deal of audiovisual material concerning Lindbergh exists. Useful works include *Lindbergh Versus the Atlantic* (1964); and *Lindbergh* (1990). An obituary appears in the *New York Times*, Aug. 27, 1974.]

ROBERT MUCCIGROSSO

LINK, THEODORE CARL (Sept. 22, 1904–Feb. 14, 1974), journalist, was born in St. Louis, Mo., the son of Edwin Cary Link, an architect, and Virginia Eliot Cabanne. The second of four children, Link was the grandson and namesake of architect Theodore C. Link, a German immigrant who designed more than one hundred buildings in his career, including Union Station in St. Louis. As a young man Link wanted to emulate his grandfather, but aside from enrolling in a few night courses at Washington University he was never active in architecture.

On July 5, 1930, he married June DeVore who divorced him in October 1938, after a brief separation. In 1940, he married Ruth Ferguson; they had two children.

Link began his career as an investigative reporter in 1924 with the *St. Louis Star*, where he worked until 1933. From the beginning his stories focused on organized crime. He covered the Cuckoo Gang Wars, and the battles between the Ku Klux Klan and anti-Klan forces in southern Illinois. He likened the gunfights of the Klan war in "bloody Williamson County" to the shootout at the OK Corral, noting in his stories that each of the three Klan incidents claimed more lives than that famous showdown. In a city plagued by street violence, Link discovered the existence of a gang called the Green Ones, which was responsible for almost one killing per day in St. Louis in 1926 and 1927. When Link went to work for the National Lead Company, he investigated a $15 million racket in connection with silicosis claims in the Lead Belt. As a result of his work, many lawyers were suspended and disbarred by the Bar Association.

Link worked briefly for both the *Globe-Democrat* and the *Times* before joining the staff of the *Post-Dispatch* in 1938. This made him one of the few men to work for all four St. Louis papers.

Link joined the United States Marine Corps in 1942 and served as a war correspondent and as editor of *Chevron*. He saw action in the Pacific theater on Guadalcanal, New Georgia, and Guam, and he was wounded at Bougainville in November 1943. He was awarded the Purple Heart, cited for service by Fleet Admiral Chester W. Nimitz, and discharged in 1945.

Upon his return to the *Post-Dispatch* he resumed his criminal investigations. In the late 1940's, his investigation into gambling turned up the bribery of a prosecutor and sheriff and vote fraud in Kansas City, Mo., both of which he tied to the Pendergast political machine and the Capone gang.

Link's ties to the Shelton gang from his Klan reporting in the 1920's and 1930's led him to new reports on the gang's postwar operations and its links to the Capone gang. This inquiry resulted in an indictment against several Illinois politicians. The threat to politics-as-usual resulted in indictments against Link for intimidation, conspiracy, and kidnapping. The charges concerned his presence at the Shelton's questioning of a fellow gangster in Link's hotel room in Peoria. The *Post-Dispatch* lashed back with articles by Link detailing gang payoffs to politicians and an editorial claiming the indictment "was a brazen attempt to turn the law against itself."

The coverage of the corruption led to the defeat of the Illinois Republican political machine ten days after the indictments. Both Governor Dwight Green and the state's attorney general lost their bids for reelection, and Adlai Stevenson was elected governor to clean up the system. The indictments against Link were later dismissed by the attorney general. For his reporting on the Illinois corruption, Link was given a special award for distinguished public service by the American Newspaper Guild.

Link's underworld connections convinced him of ties between gangs across the country. In 1949, his reports exposed the connections between organized crime in St. Louis and groups in Kansas City, Los Angeles, and Louisiana. After a series of articles in 1950 on Miami as the capital of the nation's organized crime, Link was contacted by a Senate investigating committee chaired by Estes Kefauver of Tennessee. Later that year, the committee held hearings and questioned witnesses involved in underworld activities. Upon the conclusion of the hearings, Senator Kefauver praised Link, writing, "In numerous instances, the first leads on the connections among the underworld, conniving politicians and corrupt law-enforcement officials were supplied to the committee investigators out of Ted Link's voluminous files."

In continuing to investigate organized crime and public corruption, Link refused to play party favorites. While his target in the Illinois inquiry was a Republican organization, he soon earned the ire of Democrats as well. In a long series of articles in 1951, Link exposed corruption in the Internal Revenue Bureau (IRB), now the Internal Revenue Service (IRS). He disclosed that a St. Louis company that obtained more than $500,000 in government loans had made payments to the chairman of the Democratic National Committee, William Boyle, Jr.,

and to another public official. As a result Boyle resigned and the IRB was overhauled. These articles won the *St. Louis Post-Dispatch* a Pulitzer Prize in 1951.

Link continued his investigative reporting throughout the remainder of his life, exposing such incidents as Senator Richard Nixon's attempts to fix a financial supporter's gambling debts in Havana and President Dwight D. Eisenhower's battle against efforts by Republican senators and IRB officials to prevent reforms of the St. Louis Internal Revenue office. He wrote stories on renewed gang warfare and union corruption in the 1950's, conditions in the slums, and the Garrison investigation of the Kennedy assassination in the 1960's.

Link's reporting was overshadowed briefly in 1960 by stories about his indictment and trial for the shooting death of an intruder at his home. While the story was front-page news for some months and elicited an irate editorial in a suburban newspaper calling for Link to be "muzzled," the trial resulted in Link's acquittal. Upon his death the *Post-Dispatch* called him "persistent, incorruptible and unintimidated . . . a bold reporter but a quiet man." It is certain that his work had a profound impact on both local and national politics.

[No published index of Link's newspaper work exists, but the *Post-Dispatch* maintains a card file that indexes his writing for that paper. See also Carl Baldwin, "Underworld, Politics Were This Reporter's Beat," *St. Louis Post-Dispatch*, Feb. 28, 1974. Obituaries appear in the *New York Times* and the *St. Louis Post-Dispatch*, both Feb. 15, 1974.]

KEN LUEBBERING

LIPCHITZ, JACQUES (Aug. 22, 1891–May 26, 1973), sculptor, was born Chaim Jacob Lipschitz in Druskieniki, Lithuania (then under Russian rule), the eldest of six children of Rachael Krinsky and Abraham Lipschitz, a building contractor born of a wealthy banking family whose many business enterprises made him the most prominent Jewish entrepreneur of the area.

At age five, Jacob began instruction in the Torah, but he soon rebelled against religious instruction, and any hope of his becoming a Talmudic scholar quickly vanished. At age eight he was sent to a commercial school in neighboring Bialystok, but he did little better in more practical subjects. The boy had only one absorbing interest—modeling figures, first from bread dough and later from clay. To make tangible the forms he saw in his mind gave the child the wonder and power of creating life itself. His father scoffed at this childish interest as being unworthy of serious consideration. If the boy had no aptitude for scholarship or business, he must be directed toward a respectable profession, such as architecture or engineering. Thus, it was to his mother the boy turned for affection and support; she alone saw purpose and beauty in her son's creations. A bond of empathy was early established between mother and son, which would become a recurrent theme in the artist's future work.

In 1906, following a disastrous war with Japan and revolution at home, the Jews, as so often in the past, again became the scapegoat of Russia's woes. As pogroms erupted throughout the empire, Abraham feared for the safety of his son in Bialystok. Jacob was sent to a high school in Vilna, where he could safely prepare for a respectable career. For the first time in an urban environment, Jacob learned that what his father regarded as a strange aberration was instead the manifestation of an esteemed fine art. Jacob at last had a name for that which he wished to become—a sculptor.

In 1909, a noted Russian sculptor, Ilya Günzberg, visited Vilna, and Jacob dared to bring a few small figures to him for judgment. Günzberg at once saw promise in these crude figures and told Jacob to go to Paris for training. This endorsement convinced Rachael that her son was the genius she believed him to be. Knowing her husband would not agree, she secretly arranged for an uncle to smuggle her son out of Russia. In October 1909, Jacob arrived in Paris. When he applied for an identity card, the police official gallicized Jacob's given name and misspelled his surname. Thus it was as Jacques Lipchitz that he became a Parisian.

He enrolled in the École des Beaux-Arts, where he was hazed by the other students as an untrained country bumpkin. Soon thereafter, though, he received word that his father had forgiven him and would support his studies, so he at once transferred to a private school, the Académie Julian. His days were given over entirely to art: classroom studies, daily visits to museums, and haunting flea markets to collect beautiful objects his keen eye could spot amid the junk. He once said, "If you want to get from sculpture, you must give. Talent is not enough

. . . Work, *work!*" This was the precept that disciplined his life.

To the revolution exploding in the world of art in the first decade of the twentieth century, the academies gave slight heed. Classicism still ruled, and Lipchitz enthusiastically subscribed to this ideal. At his first exhibit in 1911, he presented a bronze head, *Little Italian*, which could have graced a second-century Roman atrium. When Rodin visited the exhibit and gave special attention to this piece, Lipchitz was not pleased; if Rodin approved, he thought, there must be something wrong with his work.

Shortly thereafter, Lipchitz received word that his father's business had failed; the family could no longer support him in Paris and wanted him to return home. He refused, insisting that he could fend for himself. When he received an order to report to the Russian army for service in 1912, however, he did return home. He was excused from service because of tuberculosis, which he had first contracted in 1911, and he at once hastened back to Paris. By now he had companions in poverty, first among them the poet Max Jacob, who introduced him to Diego Rivera; this led him into the exciting world of the modern artists, notably Juan Gris, Amedeo Modigliani, Chaim Soutine, and Pablo Picasso. Expatriates all, they would frequently meet in the salon of the American expatriate Gertrude Stein. The sterile ties of the academy had been broken.

Lipchitz had at first been as critical of Picasso's work as he had been of Rodin's, but now he began to understand what the Cubists sought in their paintings—three-dimensional solidity. Painting, however, was a two-dimensional art; like his neighbor Brancusi, Lipchitz believed sculpture alone could give to Cubism its true expression. Lipchitz became a pioneer in Cubist sculpture. Like Picasso, he was fascinated by entertainers: acrobats, musicians, and puppets. As he moved progressively toward the more abstract from his *Encounter* in 1913 to *Man with a Guitar* in 1916, though, he never totally renounced representational technique. He would later state as his philosophy of aesthetics that every great piece of art must incorporate the indivisible trinity of point of view, representation, and beauty of form. Mere representation without a point of view was photography without creativity; point of view without representation was abstraction carried to the absurd; and without beauty of form, art became a chaos of paint dribbled on a canvas or a rough-hewn stone without meaning. "In art we must see things in their totality or else these ideas are leading us to a dead end," he insisted.

The outbreak of World War I found Lipchitz in Spain with Rivera. Here he was greatly influenced by the sculptured architecture of Gaudi. Returning to Paris in December 1914, he fell in love with a Russian poet, Berthe Kitrosser, whom he married in 1924. Lipchitz's work attracted the attention of a major art dealer, Léonce Rosenberg, who provided a monthly allowance that lifted Lipchitz from penury. Rosenberg, however, would accept only Cubist sculpture, and Lipchitz had come to view Cubism as a prison. It stressed only the solid; he now saw open space as essential to the beauty of form. A chance meeting with the eccentric American collector Alfred Barnes in 1922 resulted in a series of commissions profitable enough for Lipchitz to break free of Rosenberg. This he celebrated with his charming *Pierrot Escapes* (1927). At last financially secure, he hired Le Corbusier to build for him a house and studio in Boulogne-sur-Seine. Here he could realize his idea of melding solid with space to produce what he called "transparents," among them *Joie de Vivre* (1927), *Harpist* (1928), *Chimène* (1930), *Elle* (1931), and the joyful *Song of the Vowels* (1932). He had not so much abandoned Cubism as aerated it and given it an intricate effervescence.

Lipchitz had been apolitical in his art in the 1920's. To the ever more threatening totalitarianism of the 1930's, however, Lipchitz felt compelled to express his opposition, with chisel as well as with tongue and pen. He had always been an outspoken defender of freedom in the arts. Although he despised Dadaism and later "nonobjective" art, he vigorously defended the right of all artists to express their point of view. To make graphic his protest against Nazism, he redid some of his earlier sculptures, freeing them from their literal faithfulness to classical myths. He now represented Europa not as overwhelmed by the bull but as stabbing her rapist, and Prometheus not as submissively awaiting the piercing beak but as strangling the vulture with one hand. As forcefully as possible he was saying, "Resist the barbarians."

With the defeat of France in 1940, he and Berthe fled to Toulouse in the unoccupied zone. At first he refused to heed warnings that he was no longer safe in Europe and must escape to America. Lipchitz knew nothing about the United States; he pictured it as a vast land of treeless plains and gross cities of sterile skyscrapers. The Lipchitzes finally yielded to friends' pleas, and fled through Portugal to New York. Lipchitz brought with him only a single sculpture, his recently finished *Flight*. When he arrived in New York in June 1941, he felt lost; he had no money, no English, and, he thought, no friends. But if Lipchitz did not know America, America knew him. His first exhibition in New York had taken place in 1935, and Alfred Barr, the director of the Museum of Modern Art, had purchased several of his pieces. With the help of Barr and Curt Valentin, a leading New York art dealer, he opened a studio and was ready to start anew. His work became ever more autobiographical. After *Flight* came *Arrival*, *The Pilgrim*, *Spring*, and *The Promise*. Titles had always been important to Lipchitz, and in the titles of this period's could be read not only his own but the world's exodus from slavery.

In 1946, he and Berthe returned to Paris. He was made a chevalier of the Légion of Honor; he most highly prized this of all his many awards. Paris, however, was not the same for him. The old communality of artists had dispersed and New York City had become his home. Not so for his wife, though; their five years in the United States had been for her years of hated exile. She refused to return, and they separated; the divorce became final in 1947.

Back in New York, Lipchitz pushed on to new frontiers—beyond Cubism and transparents to a new freedom of expression which he called the "semiautomatic," and finally to experimenting with the use of common objects such as chisels, baskets, bones, and flowers to transform them directly into metal objects—pushing, as he said, "à la limite du possible." Lipchitz would always be preoccupied with change, adaptation, and growth.

Never fond of portraiture, Lipchitz nevertheless throughout his career, partly to supplement his income but mainly because of his interest in the subject, sculpted memorable heads of Gertrude Stein, Jean Cocteau, and Marsden Hartley, among others. Here he perhaps best expressed his adherence to the sacred indivisible trinity of aesthetics; we continue to see Stein *et al.* as he has depicted them.

In 1947, Lipchitz married Yulla Halberstadt, a young refugee from Berlin. With the birth of his daughter Lolya in October 1948, Lipchitz at the age of fifty-seven became a father for the first time and the family moved to suburban Hastings-on-Hudson. He now undertook the most ambitious, monumental works of his career. The mother-child theme reappeared in new forms: *Pastorale* (1947), *Mother and Child* (1948 and 1949), *The Cradle* (1949) and *Hagar* (1948, 1969, and 1971). In 1946 he was asked by the Church of Notre Dame in Assy, France, to make a statue of the Virgin. The surprised Lipchitz agreed, provided he might inscribe on the sculpture, "Jacob Lipchitz, Jew, faithful to the religion of his ancestors, has made this Virgin to foster understanding between men on earth, that the life of the spirit may prevail."

Lipchitz had just finished his nearly nine-foot Virgin entitled *Notre Dame de Liesse* when, on the evening of January 5, 1952, a fire destroyed his Manhattan studio and most of his sculptures, including the Virgin. Only his indomitable will, bolstered by friends, gave him the strength to begin again. A new studio, near his home on the Hudson River was ready within eighteen months. His first sculpture after the fire was *The Virgin in Flames*, followed by a second *Notre Dame de Liesse*, faithful in every detail to the original.

In 1958, Lipchitz became an American citizen. In November of the same year he was stricken with cancer. He credited his recovery to the prayers of the leader of the Lubavitcher Hassidic sect. His strengthened devotion to his faith was reflected in such works as *The Cup of Atonement* and *The Prophet*. Important commissions came to him in the last years of his life: *Peace on Earth* for the Los Angeles Music Center (1967), *Bellerophon Taming Pegasus* for the Columbia Law School (1969), and *Government of the People* for the civic center in Philadelphia (1971).

In 1961 Lipchitz bought a second home, in Italy near Pietrasanta with its famed Tommasi foundry. Here he produced his *Images of Italy* series and made the model for his last great monument, *Our Tree of Life*, intended for the Hebrew University in Jerusalem. He died while on vacation in Capri, and as requested, was buried in Jerusalem.

[The major collection of papers still extant are in the possession of Lipchitz's brother Reuben Lipchitz and are not open to the public. Lipchitz's autobiography, a series of taped interviews given in 1968 to

H. H. Arnason, was published under the title *My Life in Sculpture* (1972). Irene Patai's biography *Encounters* (1961) is a romanticized but perceptive portrayal. See also Wayne Craven, *Sculpture in America* (1968); and A. M. Hammacher, *Jacques Lipchitz* (1970), which provides an excellent critique of Lipchitz's work, as well as plates of his sculptures and a useful bibliography. An obituary is in the *New York Times*, May 28, 1973.]

JOSEPH F. WALL

LIPPMANN, WALTER (Sept. 23, 1889–Dec. 14, 1974), journalist, was born in New York City, the only child of Jacob Lippmann, a clothing manufacturer, and Daisy Baum, whose inheritance of her father's real estate holdings enabled her husband to retire at an early age. The family traveled to Europe annually during Walter's childhood, and he attended the finest schools, thriving on the rigorous academics of the Sachs School for Boys and the Sachs Collegiate Institute in New York. After his graduation in June 1906, Lippmann entered Harvard College.

Lippmann's family was Jewish but of a decidedly assimilationist bent, a tendency Lippmann took even further than his parents. But at Harvard, he quickly realized that certain avenues to success—most notably membership in its clubs, which dominated student life—were closed to him because of his religious origins. He responded by channeling his energy into areas where he could make a mark. He wrote for several student publications, became the founding president of Harvard's Socialist Club, and distinguished himself scholastically. He also showed an early talent for bringing himself to the attention of notable thinkers and doers. His mentors at Harvard included William James and George Santayana. He completed his undergraduate course work in 1909 but stayed on an extra year as Santayana's assistant, graduating with his class in 1910.

After Harvard, Lippmann worked briefly for the *Boston Common*, a reform-minded weekly, then worked for a year as an assistant to journalist Lincoln Steffens, doing the legwork on a series of Steffens's articles on financial institutions for *Everybody's* magazine. After the series was published, Lippmann was rewarded with a low-level editorial position at *Everybody's*. He quit that in early 1912 to work for George Lunn, the newly elected socialist mayor of Schenectady, N.Y. Four months later, when Lunn turned out to be more of a mild reformer than a militant socialist, Lippmann left that job as well and devoted the summer of 1912 to writing *A Preface to Politics*, which was published in 1913 to favorable reviews. One of the people it impressed was Herbert Croly, the founding editor of *The New Republic*, who invited Lippmann to join the new magazine.

The New Republic debuted Nov. 7, 1914. By 1915, both Lippmann and the magazine were moving toward an interventionist position on World War I. An interview in 1916 with President Woodrow Wilson left Lippmann deeply impressed, and he was instrumental in delivering the endorsement of *The New Republic* to Wilson in the presidential campaign of 1916.

When the United States entered the war on Apr. 6, 1917, Lippmann volunteered his services to the Wilson administration. He was appointed as an assistant to Secretary of War Newton D. Baker. On May 24, 1917, Lippmann married Faye Albertson, the daughter of a minister active in reform politics with whom Lippmann had been friendly in Boston. In June, he and Faye left for Washington. They returned to New York in October when Lippmann was recruited by Wilson's confidant, Colonel Edward M. House, to serve as a member of a secret commission charged with gathering information and making recommendations for the eventual peace settlement. The work of the commission, called the Inquiry, formed the basis for several of Wilson's Fourteen Points.

In June 1918, Lippmann left the Inquiry commission to work as a military propagandist on the western front. Commissioned a captain in the U.S. Army, he was in Europe when, on Oct. 3, 1918, Germany requested an armistice on the basis of the Fourteen Points. The Allies, impatient with American idealism, balked, and Wilson dispatched Colonel House to Europe. Once there, Colonel House tapped Lippmann, because of his earlier work with the Inquiry commission, to write a precise explanation of each point. Lippmann's explanations were written in less than twenty-four hours and were quickly dispatched to and accepted by Wilson.

Lippmann's chances to contribute further ended, however, when Wilson decided to attend the Paris Peace Conference himself and arrived with a huge delegation. Realizing that he would not get a specific assignment because of the fading influence of Colonel House,

Lippmann resigned from the army and returned to New York City and *The New Republic*. Lippmann was not happy with the treaty that was eventually negotiated at Versailles, but he was initially inclined to support it for the sake of the League of Nations. His fellow editors felt differently. They argued him around to their point of view, and *The New Republic* enthusiastically enlisted in the battle against ratification. Editors of *The New Republic* expressed disgust over the punishing reparations demanded of Germany and the conviction that the new boundaries were an invitation to future conflict. Lippmann was later to regret his opposition to the treaty, becoming convinced that the United States did have a role to play in European politics, but at the time he entered the battle with zest, and he did not limit himself to writing vitriolic editorials. In fact, taking advantage of background knowledge gained via his work on the Inquiry commission, Lippmann furnished Senator William E. Borah of Idaho, leader of the "Irreconcilables" (who felt that the United States had a moral obligation to stay out of the quarrels of Europe and opposed U.S. membership in the League of Nations), with damning information about secret wartime treaties among the Allies, information that Borah used to good effect during the Senate hearings.

By 1920, the small band of Irreconcilables, aided by Wilson's stubborn refusal to compromise with the Senate's "Reservationists" (a group led by Senator Henry Cabot Lodge of Massachusetts who would have been willing to accept U.S. membership in the League of Nations if Wilson had accepted some relatively minor reservations), had clearly won: the Treaty of Versailles failed to win Senate ratification. The United States, and Lippmann, moved on to other things. He began to write a regular column for *Vanity Fair* magazine, a column he continued through 1934. In 1921, he took a leave of absence from *The New Republic* to work on *Public Opinion*, published in 1922 and perhaps the most influential of the ten major books that he would publish; in it he argued that in modern democracies the public was operating in a vacuum, being asked to make decisions it could not possibly make intelligently. In 1922, instead of returning to *The New Republic*, Lippmann joined the *New York World*, a crusading newspaper of liberal bent, as assistant director of the editorial page. Lippmann became acting director in 1923 when Frank Cobb, who headed the editorial page, was stricken with cancer. In March 1924, after Cobb's death, he became director, a position he held until 1931, when the *World* was bought out by the *New York Telegram*. Under Lippmann, the *World's* editorials were always well written and thoughtfully presented. But some critics felt that the page became a bit too cautious and lacked the punch it had shown under Cobb.

After the demise of the *World*, Lippmann moved to the *New York Herald Tribune*, where he agreed to write four signed editorials each week and was promised complete editorial freedom. (By 1943, the number was reduced to two.) His new column, "Today and Tomorrow," debuted Sept. 8, 1931, and was an immediate success; eventually, it was syndicated in more than two hundred newspapers. Although his books, in which he frequently grappled with the imperfections of democracy, earned him a reputation as a political philosopher, it was through his newspaper column that he was to have his strongest influence.

His politics defied classification. He took pride in basing his analyses on what was politically possible, yet there were traces of a latent idealism that he never completely excised. Although he was an opinion columnist, he sometimes seemed curiously reluctant to give his opinion. When he made endorsements, they frequently had more to do with who was in the best political position to accomplish what Lippmann felt needed to be accomplished than who he felt was the more qualified candidate. In domestic politics, he had a horror of disorder, yet in international politics he realized more fully than most that the world could be a very messy place and that not all messes could be put right by well-meaning Americans. He was known for his impassive exterior, yet his intimates felt that he used it to conceal a highly sensitive nature.

Lippmann was a strong supporter of Franklin D. Roosevelt during the early years of Roosevelt's first term, then he turned against him, supporting Alf Landon for president in 1936 and leading the attack against Roosevelt's proposal to expand the Supreme Court in 1937. That year, Lippmann's personal life took an unexpected turn when he fell in love with Helen Byrne Armstrong, the wife of his close friend Hamilton Fish Armstrong, the editor of *Foreign Affairs*. Their clandestine affair was exposed when Helen was vacationing and four of Lipp-

mann's letters to her were forwarded back to her husband in New York, rather than on to her subsequent vacation stop. Lippmann initially urged her to patch things up with her husband. Then he reconsidered and told her that he would seek a divorce from Faye. (He and Faye had no biological children, but they had a foster daughter who was by then an adult; she and Lippmann remained close until his death.) Lippmann's divorce came through on Dec. 9, 1937; he married Helen on Mar. 26, 1938. Finding New York City uncomfortable in the wake of the scandal, the Lippmanns moved to Washington, D.C., where they made their home until Lippmann's retirement.

By 1939, his opinion of Roosevelt began to soften as Lippmann, who was always acutely aware of what public opinion would and would not allow, watched the president skillfully maneuver to aid England without sacrificing his own political base. World War II cemented Lippmann's reputation as a specialist in international affairs, which his column now covered almost exclusively. In the postwar period, he developed a reputation as a tough-minded and independent critic of U.S. foreign policy. He found the globalism that followed World War II—and with it the notion that the United States had an interest in every corner of the world—as naive as the isolationism that had preceded World War II. He also felt that many of the Soviet Union's actions sprang from rational interests rather than a desire to spread world revolution.

He was a caustic critic of Harry S. Truman. He supported Thomas E. Dewey in 1948 and Dwight D. Eisenhower in 1952, believing it was time the Republicans were given a chance and that Eisenhower would be better able than any Democrat to end the Korean War and defend the State Department from the attacks of Senator Joseph R. McCarthy, whom Lippmann despised but refrained from attacking too vehemently himself. Even within his own column, he was acutely aware of what the public was willing to accept and usually refrained from taking a position until he felt his audience was ready for it.

Lippmann won Pulitzer Prizes in 1958 and 1962. A one-hour television interview with him in 1960 garnered such raves that CBS signed him to a five-year contact, and six more interviews eventually ran. In 1963, he switched papers, moving from the *Herald Tribune* to the *Washington Post*, and began writing a weekly column for *Newsweek* magazine. As he grew older, his politics seemed to come full circle, returning in a sense to the activism of his youth. He also began to take an interest in domestic issues, such as civil rights, that he had ignored for decades.

For a journalist, Lippmann kept unusually rigid schedules. Once or twice a year, he and Helen traveled to Europe, lining up appointments with world leaders, as well as prominent members of the opposition, military leaders, and political observers. In 1961, Soviet premier Nikita Khrushchev asked Lippmann if he could delay his visit for a few days. Lippmann told him it was impossible, and it was Khrushchev who rearranged his schedule in order to meet with the American pundit. Also in 1961, the Lippmanns were scheduled to leave France as one of the top stories of the year was breaking. Rebellious army officers were threatening to march on Paris and overthrow French president Charles de Gaulle. The Lippmanns left as scheduled, missing the dramatic denouement as French soldiers obeyed de Gaulle rather than their commanding officers. But then, Lippmann's column was never about breaking news. He specialized in sober afterthoughts and in putting the events of the day in perspective.

Although Lippmann was a supporter of John F. Kennedy, he was far more impressed with Kennedy's successor, Lyndon B. Johnson, who pushed Kennedy's entire legislative program through Congress and courted Lippmann assiduously, awarding him the Presidential Medal of Freedom in 1964 and seeking his advice on foreign policy. They had a bitter falling out, however, over the Vietnam War. Lippmann felt that Vietnam was of no strategic significance to the United States, that the war could not be won, and that it was an unconscionable drain on resources that ought to be devoted to domestic matters. He initially blamed Johnson's advisers; he eventually blamed Johnson himself. Lippmann attacked many presidents over the years, but never as bitterly and unrelentingly as he tore into Johnson. By the time he retired from "Today and Tomorrow" on May 25, 1967, at the age of seventy-seven, those attacks had made him an unlikely hero of the left. He and Helen returned to New York City, and Lippmann continued his *Newsweek* column until 1971. He died in New York City.

[Lippmann's papers are at Yale University, along with a comprehensive collection of all his writings.

Ronald Steel, *Walter Lippmann and the American Century* (1980), written with Lippmann's cooperation but published after his death, is the standard biography. Also valuable are Marquis Childs and James Reston, *Walter Lippmann and His Times* (1959); and John Morton Blum, ed., *Public Philosopher: Selected Letters of Walter Lippmann* (1985). An obituary is in the *New York Times*, Dec. 15, 1974.]

LYNN HOOGENBOOM

LISTON, CHARLES ("SONNY") (May 8, 1932–Jan. 5, 1971), heavyweight boxing champion, was born in a shack outside Forrest City, Ark., the son of tenant farmer Tobey Liston and his second wife, Helen. Liston was the twenty-fourth of his father's twenty-five children.

Along with his many siblings, Liston grew up working in the local cotton fields. His father was an abusive alcoholic, and Liston left at age thirteen to live with an aunt in St. Louis, Mo., after an argument with him. "We grew up with few clothes, no shoes, little to eat. My father worked me hard and whupped me hard," Liston said of his childhood.

In St. Louis, Liston quickly encountered problems with the local police. Standing six feet, one inch tall and weighing two hundred pounds at the age of sixteen, Liston became a menacing presence in his neighborhood, occasionally working as a strike-breaking labor goon. He was arrested more than twenty times, and a St. Louis police captain once warned him to get out of town before he wound up dead in an alley. However, Liston was convicted on Jan. 15, 1950, of two counts of larceny and two counts of first-degree robbery; he spent more than two years in the Missouri state penitentiary in Jefferson City.

While Liston was behind bars, prison athletic director Father Alois Stevens first put a pair of boxing gloves on the teenager, whose hands were so enormous that they measured fifteen inches in circumference when taped.

Paroled in 1952, Liston quickly captured the local Golden Gloves championship. He became a professional fighter on Sept. 2, 1953, when he knocked out Don Smith in a single round in St. Louis. Auspiciously, the massive man known as "The Bear" then won his first nine fights before dropping an eight-round decision to Marty Marshall, who broke Liston's jaw. Sonny was not a man to forget defeat; Marshall lost two rematches with him. Liston's career was interrupted for nine months beginning in December 1956, when he was sent to the St. Louis workhouse for assaulting a policeman and stealing the officer's gun. After completing his term, Liston relocated to Philadelphia, where his career quickly flourished again.

The Marshall beatings were merely two of twenty-six straight fights Liston won as he moved inexorably toward the heavyweight championship. Known for his scowling at opponents, whom he quickly knocked out, he combined an intimidating ring presence with awesome power. His mystique was augmented by the rumors of underworld connections that dogged him, prompting him once to observe wryly, "I got to get me a manager that's not hot—like Estes Kefauver." Liston had testified before the Tennessee senator's 1960 hearings into mob control of boxing.

Liston's heavyweight-title-winning victory on Sept. 25, 1962, was indicative of the new champion's powerful style. When reigning titlist Floyd Patterson was knocked out after two minutes, six seconds, it was the first time in history that a heavyweight champion was counted out in the first round.

As the top fighter in the world, Liston became an easy target for sports columnists who remarked frequently on not only his menacing demeanor and vicious punching power but also his criminal background.

"The world of sport now realizes it has gotten Charles (Sonny) Liston to keep," wrote Pulitzer Prize winner Jim Murray of the *Los Angeles Times* in 1963. "It is like finding a live bat on a string under your Christmas tree." Liston, who posted a career record of fifty wins to four losses with thirty-nine knockouts, reveled in this role of the fighter America loved to hate: "A prizefight is like a cowboy movie. There has to be a good guy and a bad guy. People pays their money to see me lose. Only in my cowboy movie, the bad guy always wins."

Liston scored another knockout in a rematch with Patterson, but his seventeen-month reign as heavyweight champion ended at the hands of a brash fighter named Cassius Clay. Liston, who was viewed as nearly invincible before the fight, was unable to answer the bell for the seventh round, and Clay—soon to take the name of Muhammad Ali—became champion on Feb. 25, 1964.

The rematch with Clay on May 25, 1965, included the infamous "Phantom Punch." Although it appeared that Liston had barely been grazed by a Clay right hand, Sonny went down after one minute, forty-five seconds of the first round and never got up.

His demeanor outside the ring was as unforgiving as his attitude inside. A reporter once challenged Liston on his age, suggesting the fighter was older than believed. "My mammy says I'm thirty-four. Are you calling my mammy a [expletive] liar?" Liston raged, ending the questions.

After the Clay defeat, Liston began a comeback in 1966. He won eleven straight fights by knockout through 1968 and added three more wins in 1969 before losing a brutal bout to Leotis Martin, who sent the ex-champion to the canvas. He climbed back in the ring against the "Bayonne Bleeder," Chuck Wepner, and registered a tenth-round technical knockout on June 29, 1970. Six months later, Liston died.

Liston, in his final months, wound up jobless and nearly broke in Las Vegas. According to a friend, he became involved in drugs: "I knew he was hanging around with the wrong people. And I knew he was in desperate need of cash."

His wife Geraldine and their seven-year-old son Danielle returned to their Nevada home on Jan. 5, 1971; she had been unable to reach Liston for twelve days while visiting her mother. She arrived at the house to find Liston's lifeless body in their bedroom.

The official cause of death was lung congestion and heart failure, although Liston had fresh needle marks on his arm and police discovered heroin and a syringe in the house.

Liston was buried in Paradise Memorial Gardens in Las Vegas, beneath a simple gravestone with the epitaph, "A Man." Liston might have summed things up better himself during an interview with the *New York Times*: "Ever since I was born, I've been fighting for my life."

[Biographical material can be found in Robert Lipsyte, "Sonny," the *New York Times*, Jan. 7, 1971; Bert Randolph Sugar, *The 100 Greatest Fighters of All Times* (1984); and William Nack, "O Unlucky Man," *Sports Illustrated*, Feb. 4, 1991. An obituary appears in the *New York Times*, Jan. 7, 1971.]

LARRY McSHANE

LLOYD, HAROLD CLAYTON (Apr. 20, 1893–Mar. 8, 1971), actor, was born in Burchard, Nebr., the younger son of James Darsie ("Foxy") Lloyd, a sometime salesman and would-be entrepreneur unable to earn a steady living, and Elizabeth Fraser. In his early, ghost-written autobiography, Lloyd invented an idyllic childhood; but instead of the middle-class boyhood he wished he had had, he moved over fifteen times within the first ten years of his life, his parents quarreled bitterly (they divorced in 1910), and young Harold had to take on a number of jobs just to survive.

After his father received $3,000 as a settlement for injuries received when a brewery truck collided with his sewing-machine van, Lloyd moved with his father to San Diego, Calif., where he attended high school and performed with a local stock company. In 1912 and 1913 he appeared in stage adaptions of the *Cricket on the Hearth, Dr. Jekyll and Mr. Hyde,* and *Tess of the D'Urbervilles.* When his father's luncheonette-cum-poolroom failed, Lloyd moved to Los Angeles, where, reluctantly, he took work as a movie extra for $5 per day—as a legitimate actor he had disdain for the new medium.

In the extras pool at Universal, Lloyd met Hal Roach, who had ambitions to produce and direct his own films. When Roach established his first company, Rolin, in 1915, Lloyd starred in a series of short, rough-and-tumble comedies. Willie Work and Lonesome Luke, the early characters he created, were imitations of Charlie Chaplin; as Luke, Lloyd simply inverted the elements of Chaplin's tramp costume—where Chaplin's clothes were baggy and oversized, Luke's were tight-fitting. Also conforming to period convention, Lloyd sprouted a mustache: two dabs of greasepaint. Like other early comedies, the Lonesome Luke series was improvised on the spot, just before the camera rolled; a location, a character conflict, or a basic situation set in motion a series of slapstick gags. Although the Lonesome Luke persona was successful, Lloyd was embarrassed by its derivative quality.

Lloyd claimed he created the character that changed his life when he saw a dramatic film in which a parson wearing horn-rimmed glasses revealed a heroic streak—Lloyd liked the contrast between the character's mild-mannered appearance and his assertive behavior. Hal Roach, however, insisted that it was he, rather than Lloyd, who discovered the "glasses" character; their conflicting accounts suggest the sparring, competitive nature of their relationship. Roach accused Lloyd of not being funny except when he was given a gag, and Lloyd said Roach was

an indifferent, often distracted director who frequently had to come to him for advice. When they split in 1923, Lloyd set up his own independent company. He supervised every element of his films, from initial concept to advertising and distribution. He did not claim or want directorial credit, but he did in fact direct the bulk of each of his films, which are noted for their clean location photography; their terse, vigorous editing; their expert construction of comic routines; and their daring stunts that look remarkably realistic.

Lloyd's glasses character, always called Harold, was a more down-to-earth, less exaggerated figure than either Chaplin's tramp or Buster Keaton's Great Stone Face. Lloyd later said that he had wanted to create a character audiences could easily identify with, and he liked to claim that "Harold" offered him greater variety than the personas of the other silent clowns. "Harold," typically, was either a bumbling young man eager for success or an indolent aristocrat who slips by chance into high adventure. Initially a fool or a coward or a ne'er-do-well, "Harold" proves he has pep, pluck, determination, and resourcefulness, exactly the qualities embraced by the postwar generation as distinctly American.

Unlike Chaplin or Keaton, whose small size made them vulnerable in the world of silent comedy, Lloyd was of average height and had an unremarkable—noncomic—physique. (At the height of his fame in the 1920's, Lloyd without his trademark glasses, was an anonymous American Everyman who went unrecognized in public.) He seemed to be slightly heavyset for a physical comedian, and unlike Chaplin and Keaton had no training as an acrobat or a mime; nevertheless he spoke a deft and fluent body English. Lloyd's extraordinary agility earned him the label "King of Daredevil Comedy," which he resented, but perilous-looking stunts provide the comic highlights in most of his work. Scaling tall buildings, dangling from a variety of high places, conducting chases on swerving trucks and buses, weaving across a football field, Lloyd's body was in hyperactive overdrive, receiving and returning blows, falling and then sprinting back into action with magical resilience and balletic grace.

But like those of Chaplin and Keaton, Lloyd's physical routines were fused to a carefully developed character; and like that of his contemporaries, though in a more muted way, Lloyd's comedy was edged with pathos. His eyes reflected the wounds of desire and the assaults to his dignity that "Harold" endures.

Lloyd's major films of the 1920's include *Grandma's Boy* (1922), *Safety Last* (1923), *Why Worry?* (1923), *The Freshman* (1925), and *Speedy* (1928). In *Grandma's Boy*, Lloyd's first major character comedy (as opposed to the gag comedies of the 1910's), he played a coward who becomes a lion when he is given what he believes is a charmed talisman. In a famous scene, "Harold" eats mothballs thinking they are candy, and keeps up the pretense that he is enjoying himself while covert glances toward the camera reveal how he truly feels. This technique of playing two scenes at once, in which he marks the division between his character's public and private selves, was one of the ways Lloyd, like Chaplin and Keaton, enlisted audience sympathy.

In *The Freshman*, his masterpiece, "Harold" copies the behavior of heroes in the movies and of the most popular man on campus. He is an outsider who desperately wants to be accepted. As he starts his college career, however, he is beset by mishaps that never let up: during football practice he becomes a live tackling dummy; at a dance his tuxedo comes apart bit by bit, until he is finally exposed in his underwear. But in the finale the hero in him leaps out at last, and he scores a victory.

Like the tramp and the Great Stone Face, "Harold" did not need to speak in order to communicate; talking pictures threatened the survival of Lloyd's art. In *Feet First* (1930), when Lloyd scales a downtown skyscraper in a reprise of the comic routine from *Safety Last*, the actor's grunts and groans inject a misplaced realism that undermines the timeless, mythic quality the same action had attained when it was wrapped in glorious silence.

Lloyd had a dry voice, gray and featureless, and speaking seemed to freeze or at least to diminish his athleticism. He had many lines in each of his sound pictures, but he did not deliver his dialogue with the flair and rapier timing of comedy newcomers like Cary Grant, Katharine Hepburn, and Carole Lombard. Playing an assortment of stuffy characters (a preacher's son in *The Cat's Paw* [1934] and an academic in *Professor Beware* [1938], for example), Lloyd in the 1930's began to look more and more out of date. His best sound feature, *The Milky Way* (1936), in which he played a

Brooklyn milkman who becomes a champion prizefighter, allowed him to act with his body.

With the failure of *Professor Beware*, Lloyd knew his career as a star was over, and his ego would not allow him to play the supporting roles in other people's films he surely could have gotten. Briefly, in the early 1940's, he was a producer at RKO. Working with Preston Sturges on *The Sin of Harold Diddlebock* in 1947, he made a disastrous comeback. With his satiric, sour edge and his dependence on dialogue, Sturges inevitably clashed with Lloyd, and their film was a collision course for their opposing comic styles. The feature had only limited distribution; its producer, Howard Hughes, reedited it, gave it a new title of *Mad Wednesday*, and rereleased it in 1951, with equally poor results.

Lloyd married his leading lady, Mildred Davis, on Feb. 10, 1923, and demanded her retirement. In 1929, the couple moved into a Beverly Hills mansion, Greenacres, that had been under construction for five years; like Pickfair, the showpiece residence of Mary Pickford and Douglas Fairbanks, Greenacres became a symbol of movie colony splendor. But the Lloyds were not a happy family. Mildred became an alcoholic; their daughters, Gloria, and Peggy, each had two failed marriages; and Harold Jr., a homosexual and an alcoholic, died only a few months after his father. None of the children could sustain a career in show business. Like its inhabitants, Greenacres lost its original luster; there were fewer and fewer visitors, and no more dinner parties.

Nevertheless, Lloyd continued his optimistic course, pursuing his hobbies—experimenting with stereo sound systems, collecting exotic cars, taking stereo photographs—with the same dedication he had brought to films. In 1949, he was elected imperial potentate of the Shriners. And although he had never had close friends, he did not become reclusive in his prolonged retirement; he continued to be accessible to writers and students, and as an enthusiastic speaker about the old days, he appeared frequently at film festivals and retrospectives. Despite an accident in 1919 with a prop bomb that tore off the thumb and forefinger of his right hand—a handicap Lloyd always tried to conceal—he was a lifelong athlete who never smoked or drank and remained in good physical condition until his death in Beverly Hills, Calif.

For many years the received opinion about

Lloyd was that he was a proficient gagster, good for a laugh—an expert technical comedian whose work lacked the emotional and existential quality of Chaplin's or Keaton's. Lloyd also was criticized for being a man of his times whose work did not transcend the boundaries of its original period. Fearing the judgment of posterity, Lloyd withheld his films until the 1960's, when he released two compilation pictures: *Harold Lloyd's World of Comedy* (1962) and *Harold Lloyd's Funny Side of Life* (1966). In the decades since then, his reputation has steadily risen. Countering the "mechanical" label that trailed him for years, many critics now praise Lloyd for the warmth and exuberance of his glasses character. Critical consensus places him a close third in the trio of great silent clowns—he has earned a permanent place in film history as the creator of character comedy with universal resonance.

[Lloyd's autobiography, *An American Comedy* (1928; repr. 1971), is spotty and often evasive, but good on how Lloyd constructed his favorite comic routines. Tom Dardis, *Harold Lloyd* (1983) is a reliable biography. See Richard Schickel, *The Shape of Laughter* (1974) for an overview of Lloyd's films. An obituary is in the *New York Times*, Mar. 9, 1971.]

FOSTER HIRSCH

LOEB, MILTON B. (Jan. 28, 1887–Jan. 27, 1972), lawyer and manufacturing executive, was born in Lafayette, Ind., the son of Solomon Loeb, a merchant and banker, and Carrie Baer. It is possible that his father was a member of a family of Jewish businessmen who immigrated to the United States from the village of Bechtheim, near the German city of Worms, in the 1850's. Loeb graduated with a degree in law from the University of Michigan in 1908.

Loeb is best known as the creator of the trade name Brillo for the well-known household cleanser product. He practiced as a lawyer after graduation and became one of the founders of the Brillo Manufacturing Company through an association with a client. The client's brother-in-law, who sold aluminum kitchenware, had found that homemakers were experiencing difficulties in cleaning the aluminum pots and pans. He explained his problem to Loeb's client, who was a manufacturer of costume jewelry and worked with many types of metals. The jeweler invented a method for cleaning aluminum using a combination of steel wool and a special reddish soap he had developed to clean thoroughly without harm to the utensils.

The new product appeared to have great potential. Loeb, who had observed the brilliant shine that the product produced, suggested the name Brillo. In April 1913 the Brillo Manufacturing Company was incorporated, with Loeb as treasurer. A factory was built in Brooklyn. Its first product consisted of a special cake of red soap and loose wads of metal wool.

The company grew steadily through World War I. In 1915 a new line of steel wool products for commercial and industrial use was developed and marketed under the trade name Supreme. While still practicing law, Loeb took an increasingly active role in the company before he enlisted in the United States Army in World War I.

On Sept. 12, 1917, he married Theresa Hilder. They had two children before her death on May 23, 1942. Loeb subsequently married the former Mrs. Ethel Strauss Steiner.

After the war Loeb found that the expanding scouring-pad business required all of his time. He soon decided to leave his law practice to become president of Brillo, a position he held until his death. Loeb believed strongly in the power of marketing and advertising, and he concentrated on product and sales development. In 1921 he registered the trade names Brillo and Supreme with the U.S. Patent Office. In order to further the expansion of the company Loeb enlisted the assistance of a talented engineer and inventor, Crosby Field. In 1923 Field invented a revolutionary method of manufacturing metal wool. He became the company's vice-president and secretary and was responsible for the invention of numerous other machines and processes at Brillo. By the second half of the 1920's Brillo manufactured about 60 percent of the steel wool produced in the United States.

Loeb also saw the potential for his products in foreign markets. In the late 1920's Canada became the first foreign market developed by Loeb. A Canadian subsidiary, Brillo Manufacturing Co. Ltd. was later established in Toronto during the 1950's. His products were also exported to the British Isles from 1928. By 1939 the exports had grown to such an extent that the main importer of his products was renamed Brillo Manufacturing Company of Great Britain, Ltd. It became Brillo's first subsidiary and built a factory in north London. The British business suffered badly during World War II when steel wool production for domestic consumption was temporarily halted.

At the beginning of the postwar period Loeb's main business in the United States employed some 450 people. By 1950 Loeb decided to invest $1 million to increase the capacity of his two plants in Brooklyn. In 1955 he acquired the Williams Co. of London, Ohio, a manufacturer of industrial and household steel wool. Loeb believed that the Williams company products, Sun Ray and Jex, would supplement the Brillo line, particularly in the commercial field. He also felt that the acquisition would bring him closer to important Midwestern marketing areas.

Loeb's business in the British Isles also underwent a substantial expansion after World War II. On Sept. 22, 1955, Brillo Pads were advertised on the first night of commercial television broadcasting in Great Britain. The modern Brillo Pad did not become popular in Great Britain until after the television advertising campaign. Under Loeb's direction the company continued to expand in the British Isles during the second half of the 1950's. In 1959 the Brillo Manufacturing Company of Ireland, Ltd., was founded, and a factory was built outside Dublin.

In the fall of 1963 Loeb agreed to the merger of Brillo with the Purex Corporation, Ltd., of Lakewood, Calif., with Purex as the surviving name. Brillo was subsequently operated as an autonomous division under its existing management. Loeb became a director and senior vice president of Purex, while continuing in charge of Brillo operations and as managing director and chairman of Brillo's British subsidiary. During his lifetime Loeb also served as a director of the Soap and Detergent Association and a director and vice-president of S. Loeb and Sons; Loeb and Hene Co.; Loeb's, Inc.; and the Loeb Realty Co. He remained active both in business and philanthropy until shortly before his death in New York City.

[For a summary of the early history of Brillo, see "Welcome to Brillo" in *Waxwords*; *Employees' Magazine of British and Irish Johnson Wax*, Oct. 1987. An obituary is in the *New York Times*, Jan. 28, 1972.]
RICHARD A. HAWKINS

LONG, EDWARD VAUGHN (July 18, 1908–Nov. 6, 1972), United States senator, banker, and lawyer, was born on his parents' farm in northern Missouri, the son of Leslie D. Long and Lillian Shields. He attended public elementary schools in Lincoln County and high school in nearby Eolia, Mo., graduating in 1925. He studied one year at the University of Missouri in Columbia (1925–1926), then three years at Culver-Stockton College (1927–1930) in Canton, Mo. Thereafter he worked in a law office and read law in Quincy, Ill., and passed the Missouri bar in 1932. He was a schoolteacher for three years before beginning to practice law in Bowling Green. On Aug. 11, 1935 he married Florence Adeline Secor; the couple had one daughter. He was a Baptist, a thirty-third-degree Mason, and a very active Rotarian. He frequently traveled abroad for Rotary International.

Long's public career began with his election as Pike County prosecuting attorney in 1937. Later he served as city attorney for Bowling Green, 1941–1945, then was elected to the state senate, where he served from 1946 to 1956. A shrewd and successful businessman, he grew increasingly wealthy, becoming president or major stockholder of several banks and small loan companies in towns in central Missouri. Although critics assailed his support for higher interest rates for loan companies and other measures as self-serving, his affable manner and loyalty to the Missouri Democratic party brought increasing recognition. In 1956 he was elected lieutenant-governor. When the sudden death of Thomas Hennings, Jr., vacated one of Missouri's U.S. Senate seats in September 1960, state Democrats deadlocked over choice of a successor and Long emerged as the compromise choice. Appointed to serve until the next election, he was elected in 1960 and then in 1962 for a full term.

As a U.S. senator, Long compiled a moderately liberal record, generally supporting the agenda of the Kennedy and Johnson administrations. He served as a floor captain in the bitter struggle to pass the Civil Rights Act of 1964. However, he usually opposed new government investigation or regulation of banking and business. He was, for example, active in helping defeat Senator Estes Kefauver's proposal to investigate price fixing by dairy companies in 1963. His principal committee assignments in the Senate were the Banking and Currency Committee and the Judiciary Committee. Long gained national prominence when, as chairman of the Judiciary Committee's Subcommittee on

Administrative Practice and Procedure, he launched a series of investigations into invasion of individuals' privacy by government agencies. He became something of a hero to civil libertarians for his efforts, especially concerning government wiretapping. Obsessed with the subject, he gave speeches and wrote articles for national magazines and then wrote a book, *The Intruders: The Invasion of Privacy by Government and Industry* (1967). Long's activity brought him national publicity that distinguished him from the famous Long of Louisiana.

The press, however, charged that Long treated IRS and Justice officials with undue severity in his hearings, and underworld figures with leniency. In 1967 *Life* magazine charged that Long was deliberately misusing the hearings to discredit evidence obtained by wiretapping that had helped convict Teamster President Jimmy Hoffa. *Life* accused Long of accepting $48,000 from Morris Shenker, his longtime friend and Hoffa's chief counsel. Long's defense was that he had accepted legal fees from a few clients he shared with Shenker. The Senate Ethics Committee investigated the charges and cleared Long, reported it could find "no facts" to show any connection between Shenker's payments and Long's "duties and activities as a member of the Senate." *Life*, nevertheless, pursued the matter and uncovered ties between Shenker, also the broker for the Teamsters' pension fund, and investments in Las Vegas gambling enterprises with alleged underworld ties. Long eventually admitted receiving nearly $160,000 from Shenker but insisted that the sum represented shared legal fees.

This affair damaged Long's public image irreparably although he was never convicted of any crime. He lost the 1968 Senate Democratic primary to Attorney-General Thomas Eagleton and then retired from public life to his farm near Eolia, Mo.

Events surrounding Long's personal affairs and death in 1972 proved as controversial as his Senate career. After his sudden death it was revealed he had revised his will after a family quarrel and had virtually cut off his wife and daughter. Instead, he left his $2.3 million estate to his five-year old granddaughter and named his longtime secretary, Helen Dunlop, to be sole trustee. A flurry of lawsuits followed, with his wife suing his secretary for alienation of affections and charging fraud in business transactions. The secretary countersued, alleging that Long had been murdered with poisoned candy. An exhumation of the body confirmed that he died of natural causes; the lawsuits were later settled quietly out of court.

Except for these controversies, Long's career was in the main rather typical for a successful midwestern businessman-lawyer in politics. Affable and gregarious, he used his business skills and political connections to become a millionaire. His loyalty to the Missouri Democratic party helped him win high public office. Although protective of business interests, he remained a party loyalist and proved moderately liberal in the Senate. His most significant achievement was to focus public attention on the invasion of privacy which new technology was making possible. The issues he raised have continuing significance for both government and the individual.

[Long's unprocessed papers are in 300 boxes at the State Historical Society of Missouri Library in Columbia. Family permission is required for use. In addition to his book, *The Intruders: The Invasion of Privacy by Government and Industry* (1967), see his articles: "Speaking out," *Saturday Evening Post*, Nov. 20, 1965; "You Ought to Be Left Alone," *Esquire*, May 1966; "Burgeoning Big Brotherism," *Christian Century*, May 18, 1966; and "Are You Safe from Electronic Snoopers?" *Popular Science*, May 1967. See also W. Lambert, "Strange Help—Hoffa Campaign of the U.S. Senator from Missouri," *Life*, May 26, 1967; W. Lambert, "Deeper Debt of Gratitude to the Mob," *Life*, Nov. 10, 1967; "Senator Cleared of Misconduct Charges," *U.S. News*, Nov. 6, 1967; and "X-Rated Wrangle," *Newsweek*, Apr. 30, 1973. An obituary appears in the *New York Times*, Nov. 8, 1972.]

WAYNE C. BARTEE

LOPEZ, VINCENT JOSEPH (Dec. 30, 1895–Sept. 20, 1975), bandleader, pianist, and song writer, was born in Brooklyn, N.Y., the son of Portuguese immigrant Antonio Lopez, a former jeweler and naval bandmaster turned music teacher, and the Baroness Virginia Gonsalves, who came from a Spanish aristocratic family. As a child, Lopez's father had him practice the piano three hours per day during the school year and six hours per day during vacations. Lopez once described himself as a "child without a childhood."

His father did not intend this rigorous musical training to prepare Lopez for a musical career, but rather for the discipline required of the priesthood. When Lopez was twelve, his father sent him to St. Mary's Passionist Monastery in Dunkirk, N.Y. There Lopez found solace not in religion, but in the singing of Gregorian chants and playing popular tunes on the piano during recreation.

After three years at St. Mary's, Lopez convinced his teacher's that he was meant for a life beyond the monastery walls. His father, disappointed, immediately enrolled Lopez in Kissick's Business College in Brooklyn. Upon graduating nine months later, Lopez began a day job as a secretary in a milk company. In addition, he found a job playing piano from 9 P.M. to 4 A.M. at Clayton's, a Brooklyn saloon, through a friend from St. Mary's whose brother was a singing waiter there. A rival pianist, Jimmy Durante, began calling seventeen-year-old Lopez "the pianner kid."

Eventually, lack of sleep caused Lopez to lose both his jobs. Ashamed to face his father, who never forgave him for abandoning the priesthood, Lopez moved out of his parents' home into the care of the singing waiter, Dick Harding, who almost immediately found work for Lopez at McLaughlin's saloon, a mile from Coney Island.

In 1913, Lopez was asked to play at the Pekin Restaurant near Times Square in Manhattan, which was famous for its five-piece orchestras. After performing a few solos, he was hired, and three months later he was put in charge when the bandleader failed to come to work one day. Lopez could not enlist in the U.S. Army during World War I because of gout, so he stayed at the Pekin and became one of the first bandleaders to turn to Dixieland music.

During the Prohibition era, Lopez was forced to leave the Pekin. He performed in several vaudeville shows, including the successful *Rings of Smoke* and the short-lived *Lovebirds*. Lopez started his first job as a hotel bandleader in 1921 at the Pennsylvania Hotel (later the Statler Hilton) in Manhattan, where he stayed for five years.

On Mar. 5, 1921, Lopez married May Kenny, who died seventeen years later; they had one child. Lopez would not remarry until Aug. 8, 1951, thirteen years after his first wife's death, to Bettye Long.

On Nov. 27, 1921, Lopez and his band traveled to the WJZ radio station in Newark, N.J., to broadcast live dance music for the first time over the radio. Intensely shy, when the microphone was placed in front of Lopez, all he could say was, "Hello, everybody—Lopez speaking." These words became his trademark and a familiar greeting to Americans across the country for the next forty-five years. A month after his debut, Lopez had his own regular show, radio's first "remote" pickup broadcast, from the Pennsylvania Hotel. His late-night dance band broadcasts were a major source of entertainment throughout the 1930's and 1940's until disk jockeys and, later, talk show hosts replaced them.

Lopez kept an active touring schedule. In a vaudeville program at the Palace on Aug. 7, 1922, he pioneered the use of scenic sets to go along with his band's performances. Two years later, he gave a concert at the Metropolitan Opera House, followed by a performance at President Calvin Coolidge's inaugural ball. Thomas A. Edison was an early fan of his.

The most famous song associated with Lopez was "Nola," written in 1922 by Felix Arndt, who named it for his wife. Lopez once estimated in a display of hyperbole that he had played the song hundreds of thousands of times, but said he never tired of it.

In 1925, Lopez brought American jazz to the London Hippodrome. In that same year, he opened the elegant Casa Lopez nightclub in Manhattan, which burned down only two years later. He then opened a second nightclub, but it was less sumptuous and failed to attract enough patrons to stay open.

Good news soon came to Lopez with the signing of a million-dollar, ten-year contract with the St. Regis Hotel, the first such contract signed by a bandleader. Lopez stayed at the St. Regis for seven years, before the Great Depression of the 1930's forced the hotel to let him go. Lopez then wandered around the country, playing in obscure nightclubs. Then, in 1941, Lopez landed his steadiest job yet at the Hotel Taft's Grill Room, where he would play for twenty-six years, until he was seventy-three years old.

In 1949, Lopez appeared on "The Ed Sullivan Show," after which he had his own fifteen-minute television program for more than two years. He set a telecasting first in 1950 with *Dinner Date with Lopez*, a remote telecast from the Taft Grill that became a regular television show. Over the years, Lopez proved himself adaptable to the popular musical tastes of the times, from ragtime to Dixieland, jazz, swing, Latin American rhythms, and rock and roll. At the age of eighty-one he led a band at the Riverboat in Manhattan.

Lopez had a second career in numerology, which he learned about through a friend. Numerology became his way of resolving his "vague discontent with the loose ends of life." He believed that numbers revealed the rhythms of the universe. Through numerology, Lopez began to make predictions, some of them startlingly accurate, such as the exact date Italy entered World War II and the exact year of India's independence. Others were wrong—for example, his prediction that the Russians would not fight Japan and that President Roosevelt would not run for a fourth term.

Lopez wrote regularly for *American Astrology* magazine and hosted a numerology game twice a week at the Taft. He also answered questions on his radio show for fans who sent in their initials and dates of birth. Lopez's prophecies seemed most accurate when they concerned his eye for talent. Xavier Cugat, Artie Shaw, Tony Pastor, Glenn Miller, Rudy Vallée, Betty Hutton, Red Nichols, and the Dorsey brothers all performed for Lopez at one time or another. Lopez made one prophetic mistake: he turned down Jimmy Durante because of his looks.

[See Lopez's autobiography, *Lopez Speaking; My Life and How I Changed It* (1960); and his other books, *What's Ahead?* (1944) and *Numerology* (1961). See also Edmund Leamy, "After Years on Radio, Lopez Conquers Video," the *New York Times,* Dec. 15, 1956; John S. Wilson, "Hello, Everybody: Lopez, 70, Speaking," the *New York Times,* Nov. 27, 1964; and "Lopez, at 81, Back on Bandstand Here," the *New York Times,* May 19, 1975. An obituary appears in the *New York Times,* Sept. 21, 1975.]

ALISON GARDY

LYNN, DIANA ("DOLLY") (Oct., 7, 1926–Dec. 18, 1971), actress and singer, was born Delores Loehr to Louis Loehr, an oil company executive, and his wife, a pianist, in Los Angeles. Her mother gave Lynn her first piano instruction while she attended Miss Grace, a private school. At eleven, she played with the Los Angeles Junior Symphony Orchestra; she was the accompanist for a young violinist auditioning for a movie role. Dolly was signed instead of the violinist and began her screen career at thirteen, appearing in *There's Magic in Music*

(1939), a film tribute to the Interlochen Music Camp in Michigan.

Signed to a long contract by Paramount, she continued her schooling on the studio lot. Although roles for the adolescent actress were scarce, she finally won a supporting part in *The Major and the Minor* (1942). Her height of five feet, six inches made her a good foil for Ginger Rogers, the star of the film, since the role required Rogers to pass for a teenager. Her name was changed at this point, since her surname was considered too hard to pronounce and "Dolly" seemed childish.

Lynn's performance won her similar roles in other films, often as an annoying younger sister. She appeared as Betty Hutton's sister in *The Miracle of Morgan's Creek* (1944) and was praised for her "saucy charm." She was cast in several Henry Aldrich features with Jimmy Lydon in the title role, notably *Henry Aldrich Plays Cupid* (1944). In *And the Angels Sing* (1944), she was one of a quartet of sisters called "Angel," with Betty Hutton, Dorothy Lamour, and Mimi Chandler. She finally escaped "teenage" casting when she played the leader of an all-girl band in *Out of This World* (1945) with Eddie Bracken; she was also featured in *Duffy's Tavern* (1945). But Lynn emerged as a star in the film adaptation of the Cornelia Otis Skinner–Emily Kimbrough recollection of a European tour made by two unchaperoned young ladies, *Our Hearts Were Young and Gay* (1944). Her madcap performance in the role of Emily contributed to the lighthearted charm of the film—which, unfortunately, did not transfer to the sequel *Our Hearts Were Growing Up* (1946).

Lynn established herself as a light comedienne in *The Bride Wore Boots* (1946) with Barbara Stanwyck; *Easy Come, Easy Go* (1947); *Every Girl Should Be Married* (1948); *My Friend Irma* (1949); *My Friend Irma Goes West* (1950); and *Bedtime for Bonzo* (1951). However, she began to win dramatic roles in such films as *Ruthless* (1948), in which she played dual roles; *Paid In Full* (1950); and *The People vs. O'Hara* (1951) with Spencer Tracy.

While maintaining her movie career, Lynn also resumed her music career with a concert debut as an adult performer in Los Angeles in 1943. During World War II, she performed in benefit concerts nationwide. In 1946, Capitol Records released a three-record album of Lynn's piano renditions of such light classics as

"Laura," "Body and Soul," "Slaughter on Tenth Avenue," and Mozart's "Rondo."

Lynn married architect John Lindsay on Dec. 18, 1948; the marriage lasted only until 1953. During the early 1950's, she began to concentrate on stage performances. Her summer stock performance in *Dear Ruth* and her work with the La Jolla (Calif.) Players in *The Voice of the Turtle*, *Ring Around the Moon*, and *The Moon Is Blue* prepared her for her 1953 performance in the London production of *The Moon Is Blue*, which received rave reviews. In 1952 she made her New York City debut as Hedwig in Ibsen's *The Wild Duck*, with Maurice Evans and Mildred Dunnock, at the City Center. She also appeared opposite Sir Cedric Hardwicke in *Horses in Midstream* (1953) and was praised for her "radiance." In 1963 she returned to Broadway to star in the title role of Jean Kerr's *Mary, Mary*.

In December 1956 she married Mortimer Hall, son of *New York Post* publisher Dorothy Schiff; he was then manager of radio station KLAC in California. They had four children—a son and three daughters. Lynn was converted to domesticity, insisting that she be addressed as Mrs. Hall and confining her acting career to New York, where her husband moved as an executive for the *Post*. Since several dramatic television series were located in New York, she was able to secure roles on such acclaimed series as "Playhouse 90" (five appearances), "Schlitz Playhouse of Stars," "Stage 7," "G. E. Theatre," and "U.S. Steel Hour." She also appeared in a musical version of *Junior Miss* with David Wayne (1957) and in a ninety-minute adaptation of *The Philadelphia Story*, (the Katharine Hepburn–Grace Kelly role) with Gig Young and Christopher Plummer.

Lynn also appeared in many movies, notably in *Track of the Cat* (1954) with Robert Mitchum, *An Annapolis Story* (1955) with John Derek and Kevin McCarthy, and *The Kentuckian* with Burt Lancaster (1955). She again revealed her penchant for comedy in a remake of *The Major and the Minor* entitled *You're Never Too Young* (1955) with Dean Martin and Jerry Lewis; in a role reversal, Lynn played Ray Milland's schoolteacher role.

In February 1970 Lynn attempted to balance her private domestic life with a business career when she accepted a position as director of GO!, Bonwit Teller's travel agency, operated by Diners Fugazy Travel. Supported by a staff of agents, she planned to give advice on such problems as traveling with children and selecting a wardrobe. She gained her expertise from experience—thirty-one years of coast-to-coast travel to keep up with her career commitments. She died suddenly from a stroke in New York City, leaving her husband, then treasurer of the *Post*, and her children. She was planning a film comeback in Didion's *Play It As It Lays* at the time of her death.

[For further information, see Lynn's clippings in the New York Public Library Theater Collection at Lincoln Center. An obituary appears in the *New York Times*, Dec. 19, 1971.]

ELIZABETH R. NELSON

M

MABLEY, JACKIE ("MOMS") (ca. 1894–
May 23, 1975), comedienne, was born Loretta
May Aiken in Brevard, N.C., one of twelve
children of Jim Aiken, owner of several grocery
stores. She was of mixed black, Cherokee, and
Irish ancestry. Little is known of her early life.
Mabley regarded the Anacostia section of Washington, D.C., as her home town and spent several years in Cleveland, Ohio. Her great-
grandmother, Harriet Smith, who had been a
slave, was her religious inspiration. Mabley recalled, "She always told me, 'Put God in front
and go ahead.'"

Mabley left home at an early age for obscure
reasons. In one interview she suggested that she
departed to avoid a forced marriage to a man so
old that "someone threw one grain of rice and it
knocked him out." Describing local marital customs to another interviewer, Mabley insisted,
"We didn't get married up in the mountains
. . . I did get engaged two or three times, but
they always wanted a free sample. That how I
got stuck." Still, Mabley treasured her family.
After a first marriage, she married Ernest
Scherer, from whom she later separated. She
had three daughters and a son.

Mabley entered show business at thirteen.
Her first performances were at church fund-
raising events. She then joined the TOBA (Theatre Owners Booking Agency, or "Tough on
Black Artists"). Her various reasons included an
unwanted pregnancy, a desire to avoid prostitution, and "I prayed and it came to me more in
a vision than a dream; go on the stage." Mabley
was first discovered by the dance team of But-
terbeans and Susie, who brought her to New
York to make her debut at Connie's Inn. She
took her name from a fellow comedian and boyfriend, Jack Mabley. Later she claimed "He
took a lot off me . . . the least I could do was
take his name." She honed her talent playing
on bills with Pigmeat Markham, Cootie
Williams, Tim ("Kingfish") Moore, Bill ("Bo-
jangles") Robinson, and Peg Leg Bates. Mabley
discovered and nurtured Pearl Bailey. Mabley
became a favorite at the Cotton Club in New
York and Club Harlem in Atlantic City; she
often appeared with orchestra leaders Louis
Armstrong, Cab Calloway, Duke Ellington,
and Count Basie.

From the beginning she adopted a raucous
yet maternal stage presence. She envisioned her
character as a "good woman, with an eye for
shady dealings. She was like my granny, the
most beautiful woman I ever knew." In addition to stand-up comedy, she danced and sang
in a frumpy wardrobe consisting of a garish
house dress, or smock, a knit floppy hat, droop-
ing argyle socks, and outsize, rundown shoes.
Her bulging eyes and toothless mouth set in a
rubbery face prepared the audience for mirth
before she let loose her "up-tempo bullfrog"
voice. In a thirty-five minutes routine, she sang
bawdy songs, made bald double-entendres, and
denounced "ugly men." Typical was her description of a man who "had a job in a doctor's
office, sitting by the door making people sick."
Her most famous line was, "The only thing an
old man can do for me is bring a message from
a young one."

Mabley made her first cinematic appearance
in *Boarding Blues* (1929), also distributed as
Jazz Heaven, and she had a small role in Paul
Robeson's *Emperor Jones* (1933). She received
her first lead role only decades later in 1974,
though, when she starred as Grace Teasdale
Grimes, a spunky reformer of City Hall in
Amazing Grace (1974). Despite some negative

criticism, the film did well at the box office. Recordings enabled her to cross over from black stage to white mainstream. Recording first for Chess Records in Chicago in 1960, she sold over a million copies of her first hit, *Moms Mabley—The Funniest Woman in the World*; later she signed with Mercury Records and cut the stag party classic, *Now Hear This*. Her television debut came in 1967 in "A Time for Laughter," an all-black comedy special produced by Harry Belafonte for ABC. Over the next several years, she then became a television regular on the Merv Griffin, Smothers Brothers, Mike Douglas, Bill Cosby, and Flip Wilson shows. She refused, however, to appear on the Ed Sullivan Show because he would only allow her four minutes; she responded, "Honey, it takes Moms four minutes just to get on stage." As her fame grew, she enlarged her act to include fictional arguments with President Lyndon B. Johnson, whom she referred to as "Boy!" In August 1972, she stunned a Kennedy Center audience of middle-class blacks with a serious moment, a eulogy for Adam Clayton Powell, John F. Kennedy, Robert F. Kennedy, and Martin Luther King, Jr.

Her conservative streak led her to denounce rioters after the assassination of King—"They ain't civil rights people, they're looting people using the least excuse for their own selfish use," she exclaimed—to oppose abortion, and generally to regard the 1960's as anarchic. In her private life, Mabley was a faithful member of Harlem's Abyssinian Baptist Church. At the funeral for the Reverend Adam Clayton Powell, Jr., she claimed that he had converted her to the Baptists in the early 1950's.

Mabley lived in suburban Hartsdale, N.Y., with a maid and nurse. She owned a Rolls Royce with a monogrammed license plate, driven by a chauffeur. Plagued by arthritis, she died in White Plains Hospital after a lengthy heart illness. After a funeral and interment at Ferndale Cemetery in Hartsdale, Pastor Samuel Proctor led a massive tribute at the Abyssinian Baptist Church, which was attended by many of her show business friends and fellow Harlem worshipers.

[An excellent review of Mabley's career can be found in *Current Biography Yearbook* (1975). An obituary appears in the *New York Times*, May 25, 1975, and an account of the funeral and tribute is in the *Amsterdam News*, June 4, 1975. The Schom-burg Center for Research in New York City has a portrait collection of Moms Mabley.]

GRAHAM HODGES

McAULIFFE, ANTHONY CLEMENT (July 2, 1898–Aug. 11, 1975), army officer, was born in Washington, D.C., the son of John Joseph McAuliffe, a government employee, and Alice Katharine Gannon. After attending public schools in Washington, McAuliffe went to West Virginia University in 1916 and was appointed to the United States Military Academy at West Point, entering in June 1917. He graduated twice: first on Nov. 1, 1918, after completing the War Emergency Course; having been recalled to West Point as an officer cadet after the end of World War I, he graduated again on June 11, 1919. He was 29th out of 284 in the class of 1919.

McAuliffe married Helen Willet Whitman on Aug. 23, 1920; they had two children. After graduating from the Field Artillery School, Camp Zachary Taylor, Ky., McAuliffe served in the field artillery at Fort Lewis, Wash., from 1920 to 1921. He was stationed at the Presidio in San Francisco (1921–1922) and at the Presidio in Monterey, Calif. (1922–1923). McAuliffe became first lieutenant in 1923 and was stationed at Schofield Barracks, Hawaii. In 1926 he went to Fort Riley, Kans., and in 1927, Fort Hoyle, Md. He served in Hawaii from 1932 to 1936 as a general's aide and was promoted to captain in 1935. McAuliffe said, "I always had the idea that it was a mistake to specialize. My ambition was to command troops in battle."

Long after attending the Command and General Staff School, Fort Leavenworth, Kans., in the 1936–1937 academic year, McAuliffe called it "one of the most valuable years that I ever put in" and spoke appreciatively of "the principles that were so thoroughly beaten into me." From 1937 to 1939 he was an instructor in the Artillery School, Fort Sill, Okla. At the Army War College in Carlisle Barracks, Pa., McAuliffe did a study of race relations, advocating integration in 1940. Promoted to major, he served on the general staff, becoming lieutenant colonel in 1941 and colonel in 1942.

Amid World War II, the 101st Airborne Division was formed in the summer of 1942, with Brigadier General McAuliffe as artillery commander. He parachuted into Normandy in June 1944 and also took part in Operation Market-Garden, the airborne assault on the Netherlands in September 1944. In December he was in temporary command of the division when the German counteroffensive struck the Ardennes, thus beginning the Battle of the Bulge. The 101st rushed by truck to the road center of Bastogne, Belgium. Non-airborne units also played a crucial role: the 705th Tank Destroyer Battalion; Combat Command B of the Tenth Armored Division and Combat Command R, Ninth Armored Division, together had about forty tanks; the 969th and 755th Field Artillery Battalions, manned by black troops, had 155-mm howitzers.

Bastogne was surrounded by the Wehrmacht's XLVII Panzer Corps on Dec. 20, 1944. Two days later, a demand for surrender arrived. McAuliffe later recalled, "I just said, 'Nuts,' and went about my business." A written answer was needed, and McAuliffe said, "I asked the staff . . . what the reply should be, and [Lieutenant Colonel Harry] Kinnard said, 'That first crack of yours would be just the ticket,' so I said, 'Go ahead and write it up.' " The reply stated, "To the German Commander. Nuts! The American Commander." McAuliffe later remarked, "We were all very surprised then and have been since that this made such a great stir. We thought this was just for internal consumption."

The day after the ultimatum, Dec. 23, 1944, the skies cleared from England to the Ardennes: cargo planes dropped supplies for the 101st, and fighter-bombers attacked the German ring around Bastogne.

The siege of Bastogne was broken on Dec. 26, 1944, when a relief column led by Lieutenant Colonel Creighton Abrams of the Fourth Armored Division, of George S. Patton's Third Army, fought through the German defenses. McAuliffe had demonstrated superb battlefield leadership, keeping his troops informed and maintaining morale while making the best use of what he had. His casual defiance contributed to the mystique of the 101st Airborne, and he said his "Screaming Eagles had no superiors on the battlefield." In January 1945 McAuliffe became commander of the 103d Infantry Division, which broke the Siegfried Line and captured Innsbruck and the Brenner Pass.

After the war McAuliffe briefly commanded the Seventy-ninth Infantry Division. In 1945 and 1946 he commanded the airborne center at Camp Mackall, N.C., and later Fort Bragg, N.C. He was army ground forces adviser for Operation Crossroads, the atomic bomb tests, at Bikini in July 1946. McAuliffe believed that until world peace was established the United States should stockpile atomic weapons. He served as army secretary of the Joint Research and Development Board from August 1946 to December 1947 and as deputy director for research and development, logistics division, army general staff, in the following two years. McAuliffe went to Japan in March 1949 as commander of the Twenty-fourth Infantry Division. He became chief of the chemical corps and permanent major general in October 1949. In a speech to the American Chemical Society on Apr. 17, 1950, McAuliffe discussed the potential of chemical and biological weapons and the need for preparedness.

In 1951 McAuliffe became assistant chief of staff for personnel and lieutenant general. He integrated combat units in Korea, knowing they would not be resegregated when they returned to the United States. In 1953 McAuliffe became deputy chief of staff for operations and later that year commander of the Seventh Army in Germany. He received a fourth star in 1955 and became commander in chief of the United States Army in Europe. The next year McAuliffe retired from the army to become a senior executive at the chemical firm American Cyanamid Company in New York City, from which he retired in 1963. He was chairman of the New York State Civil Defense Commission from 1959 to 1963, after which he moved to Chevy Chase, Md.

McAuliffe grew tired of the continued interest in his "Nuts!" remark, which the *New York Times* called "so typically American that it baffled the Germans and French." He was, however, proud of his work in integrating the army, work that was to have an influence on American civilian life. After Operation Desert Storm of 1991, some journalists praised the army as the most integrated meritocracy in the country, noting that officer clubs were more integrated than faculty clubs. McAuliffe died in Washington, D.C., and was buried at Arlington National Cemetery.

[The Oral History Collection of Columbia University contains the transcript of a tape-recorded autobiographical interview with McAuliffe. His article on war in the atomic age is "Out of Balance?" *The Field Artillery Journal*, Nov.–Dec. 1946; Leonard Rapport and Arthur Northwood, Jr., *Rendezvous with Destiny: A History of the 101st Airborne Divi-*

sion (1948; reprinted 1965) has a preface by Mc-Auliffe; and Fred MacKenzie, *The Men of Bastogne* (1968) has a foreword by McAuliffe. An interview on Bastogne appears in the *New York Times*, Jan. 3, 1945. See also Maynard Nichols, "The Answer Is 'Nuts,' " *New York Times Magazine*, Jan. 14, 1945. S. L. A. Marshall, *Bastogne* (1946), contains information from an interview of Jan. 1945 with Mc-Auliffe; there is a biographical sketch in *Chemical and Engineering News*, Sept. 26, 1949. For evaluations of McAuliffe as commander, see Hugh M. Cole, *The Ardennes: Battle of the Bulge* (1965); John S. D. Eisenhower, *The Bitter Woods* (1969); Gerard M. Devlin, *Paratrooper! The Saga of U.S. Army and Marine Parachute and Glider Combat Troops During World War II* (1979); and Ralph M. Mitchell, *The 101st Airborne Division's Defense of Bastogne* (1986). Obituaries are in the *New York Times*, the *Washington Post*, and the *Washington Star*, all Aug. 14, 1975.]

RALPH KIRSHNER

McCORMACK, BUREN HERBERT ("MAC") (Mar. 4, 1909–Feb. 28, 1972), newspaper executive, was born in Jamestown, Ind., the son of Kise R. McCormack and Louella May Cook. His father owned a tailoring and cleaning business in Indianapolis.

McCormack's contact with the newspaper business began early. As a five-year-old in Jamestown, he delivered bundles of the *Jamestown Press* from the printing plant to the post office for five cents per week. When his family moved to Crawfordsville, Ind., in 1917, he became a carrier for the *Crawfordsville Journal* and the *Indianapolis News*. In 1925, the family moved to Indianapolis; he graduated from Shortridge High School there one year later.

Having won a Rector scholarship based on his academic performance at Shortridge, Mc-Cormack entered DePauw University in 1926. An English major, he spent four years on the staff of the student newspaper, *The DePauw*, becoming news editor in his senior year. He also wrote for the *DePauw Magazine* and *The Yellow Crab*. A natural athlete, he played varsity tennis. (Years later, he concentrated on golf and curling.) In 1930, he received a B.A. degree with distinction.

Personal and institutional links helped Mc-Cormack become a reporter for the *Wall Street Journal* in 1931, although he had taken only one journalism course as an undergraduate. He knew Bernard ("Barney") Kilgore, another *Journal* reporter, who had been a coworker on *The*

DePauw. Both were hired by Kenneth Craven ("Casey") Hogate, another DePauw alumnus. McCormack became part of a group of DePauw University graduates who rose through the ranks and dominated the newspaper for the next four decades. Throughout his career, he followed Hogate, Kilgore, and William F. Kerby, a graduate of the University of Michigan, into positions of higher authority.

During the 1930's and 1940's, McCormack helped widen the *Journal*'s audience from members of the New York financial community to businesspersons nationwide. His clear and simple writing style fit well into the strategy that Hogate and Kilgore wished to adopt at the *Journal:* to produce financial news for the nonspecialist and specialist alike. Between 1931 and 1943, McCormack was a copy desk man, chief of the copy desk, feature writer, and banking and financial news editor. In 1934, he helped inaugurate, and became the first regular writer of, the "What's News" column, a front-page summary of nonbusiness news deemed important to business.

During the 1940's and early 1950's, McCormack accepted increased editorial responsibility. He became assistant managing editor in 1943 and managing editor in 1946. In April 1950, he was named senior associate editor in charge of editorials, and in June 1951 he became executive editor of Dow Jones news services and publications. Because he did not possess a flair for editorial management, he had limited success. His tendency toward meticulous writing provided a barrier to effective management of writers. Nevertheless, McCormack accomplished enough to deserve credit along with Hogate, Kilgore, and Kerby for making the *Wall Street Journal* a nationally prominent business daily.

McCormack had much greater success when he moved to the business side of publishing in 1955. He became treasurer of the *Journal* that year and added the title of business manager in 1956. He accepted responsibility for keeping track of worldwide innovations in printing and data transmission and incorporated some of them into the *Journal*'s reorganized production department. As a result of his efforts, in May 1962 the *Journal* placed in operation the nation's first newspaper plant designed for facsimile printing, at Riverside, Calif. This and other improvements enabled the paper to publish simultaneously in nine plants throughout the country. McCormack's talent for directing specialized projects greatly benefited the paper.

McCormack was involved in the inauguration, on Feb. 4, 1962, of the *National Observer*, a weekly news magazine targeted at young readers and published by Dow Jones, the firm that owned the *Journal*. In charge of circulation sales at the outset, he wholeheartedly supported this publication, most likely because of his interest in education.

Throughout the late 1950's and the 1960's, McCormack received numerous promotions, becoming vice-president in 1957, editorial director in 1958, and general manager in 1961. He was named a director of Dow Jones in 1965, and its executive vice-president in 1966. He held the last two posts until his death.

McCormack pursued a number of nonbusiness interests. Most notably, from February 1955 to October 1968 he served on the board of trustees of the Masters School in Dobbs Ferry, N.Y., and was chairman for twelve of those years. He was national president of Sigma Delta Chi, the professional journalistic society, during the period 1961–1962. He helped revitalize that organization, which had lost its focus during the 1950's. He became a trustee of DePauw University in October 1969.

On Oct. 20, 1933, McCormack married Kathryn Tofaute; they had three children. Kathryn died in 1965, and in 1966 McCormack married Edna Hanson Marshall.

McCormack was a tall, energetic man known for his grace under pressure, for his diligence and humility, and for his resounding laugh. He exemplified the post–World War II organization man who was a loyal and willing team member. He died in Irvington-on-Hudson, N.Y.

[The *DePauw Alumnus*, June–July 1961, and Martin L. McAuliffe, *Profiles of Excellence* (1971), include short reviews of McCormack's life. Lloyd Wendt, *The Wall Street Journal* (1982), includes information about McCormack. See also William Kerby, *A Proud Profession* (1981); and Jerry M. Rosenberg, *Inside the Wall Street Journal* (1982). Obituaries are in the *New York Times* and the *Wall Street Journal*, both Feb. 29, 1972.]

GLEN E. AVERY

McELROY, NEIL HOSLER (Oct. 30, 1904– Nov. 30, 1972), business executive and secretary of defense, was born in Berea, Ohio, the son of Malcolm Ross McElroy and Susan Harriet Hosler, both of whom were schoolteachers. In 1912, the family moved to Madisonville, Ohio, a suburb of Cincinnati; he attended Cincinnati public schools and graduated with honors in 1921. At six feet, four inches and 210 pounds, McElroy excelled in major sports. In September 1921, he entered Harvard University and graduated with a B.A. degree in June 1925.

McElroy immediately went to work as a junior clerk for the advertising department of Procter and Gamble in Cincinnati. After four years he was promoted to director of promotions. On June 29, 1929, he married Mary Camilla Fry; they had three children.

McElroy remained in charge of promotions until 1940, when he became general manager in charge of promotions and advertising. On Oct. 13, 1943, he was elected to the board of directors and made vice-president in charge of promotions and advertising. Three years later, he became general manager and vice-president of promotions and advertising. On Oct. 13, 1948, he was elected president of Procter and Gamble, a post he held until Aug. 7, 1957.

During these years, McElroy became well known as an innovative promoter and a successful administrator. He continued and expanded the company's enlightened labor policies, such as guaranteed year-round employment, uniform five-day work weeks, paid vacations, disability benefits, generous pensions, profit sharing, and employee input on company policy. In 1940, he was one of the first to conceive of the idea of fostering competition among the company's own products—at the time, a radical concept but today common practice. This concept led to the introduction of numerous new product lines, such as Prell shampoo, Cheer detergent, Joy dishwashing liquid, and Lilt home permanent, which competed with long-standing favorites such as Tide, Oxydol, Ivory Soap, and Spic & Span. All of these products continued to be successful into the 1990's.

In addition, McElroy expanded Procter and Gamble by opening new factories in the United States and overseas. During his tenure, the company's annual income exceeded $100 million for the first time. His own income grew to $285,000 by 1957. A colleague once declared that "he was a brilliant sales and advertising executive capable of quick decisions and with a mania for facts."

Over the years, McElroy had been a willing public servant, providing informal advice to President Eisenhower on foreign and defense policy during the 1950's. Thus it followed that on Aug. 7, 1957, President Eisenhower officially selected him to succeed Charles Erwin Wilson as his second secretary of defense. At the president's news conference, he proclaimed McElroy to be "one of the most capable men . . . I know." Eisenhower also noted that McElroy's service meant a great cut in salary because the secretary's job paid only $25,000.

McElroy served as secretary of defense for twenty-six months. During his tenure, he became the first official to raise the Cold War issue of a "missile gap" with the Soviet Union. The debate over whether there really was a gap dominated the last years of the second Eisenhower administration. Not only did McElroy preside over the Defense Department during an era of vast changes in U.S. military posture, but four months after his appointment the United States launched its first space satellite. When he resigned for financial reasons in December 1959, the rocket age and space race were well under way. He was replaced by Thomas S. Gates, Jr.

Immediately after his resignation, McElroy became chairman of the board of Procter and Gamble, the second chair to serve since the death of William Cooper Procter in 1934. He served in this capacity until 1972. In addition, he was on the boards of directors of General Electric and Chrysler.

In 1969, President Richard M. Nixon appointed McElroy chairman of an eighteen-member commission on school finance that was to conduct a two-year study on ways to improve funding for American education. The final report recommended that states take over funding to alleviate the disparity between rich and poor school districts. The same plan was resurrected by presidents Bush and Clinton in the 1990's.

After completing his assignment for President Nixon in late 1971, McElroy learned that he had cancer. He died in Cincinnati, Ohio.

[See *Fortune*, May 1949; *Pathfinder*, May 3, 1950; *Time*, May 8, 1950; *Business Week*, Nov. 4, 1950; *Facts on File*, Aug. 1–7, 1957; *The Eisenhower Diaries*, edited by Robert H. Ferrell (1961); and Stephen E. Ambrose, *Eisenhower*, vol. 2 (1984). Obituaries are in the *New York Times*, Dec. 1, 1972; *Newsweek*, Dec. 11, 1972; *Time*, Dec. 11, 1972; and *Facts on File*, Dec. 24–30, 1972.]

WILLIAM HEAD

McGRAW, DONALD CUSHING (May 21, 1897–Feb. 7, 1974), publisher, was born in Madison, N.J., the youngest son of James H. McGraw, founder of the McGraw Publishing Company, and Mildred Whittlesey. He graduated from the Lawrenceville School and attended Princeton University before joining the United States Navy during World War I as a teacher of mathematics.

In 1919, McGraw began a long and successful career with the McGraw-Hill Publishing Company, which was created two years before by the merger of his father's firm with the publishing company of John A. Hill. Young McGraw went to work in the advertising division of *Chemical and Metallurgical Engineering* (now called *Chemical Engineering*). In 1921, he was transferred to the firm's pressroom and composing room.

On July 9 of that year, McGraw married Elizabeth Bidgood. They had three children. Their sons, Donald Cushing, Jr., and John Louis, were, like their father, later to rise to the highest ranks of McGraw-Hill.

By 1924, McGraw was managing both the print shop and the building operations where the printing plant was housed. In 1933, when the company stopped doing its own printing, he was assigned to manage production, which included contracting for printing and binding, engraving, and paper supply.

Two years later, McGraw was elected secretary of McGraw-Hill and made a member of its board of directors. After the United States entered World War II, he added to his responsibilities by serving as a consultant to the Publishing and Printing Division of the War Production Board. In 1945, he became vice-president for manufacturing and purchasing of McGraw-Hill's book and magazine divisions. In 1950 he was made director both of the company's book division and of Newton Falls Paper Mill, Inc., in which McGraw-Hill had a half-share.

On Sept. 17, 1953, McGraw was elected president, picking up the reins of his older brother Curtis, who had died suddenly the week before. During his presidency McGraw-Hill grew enormously in both domestic and international sales.

The company was already ranked fourth among American magazine publishers, and it was the foremost trade publisher with twenty-six domestic and nine international trade magazines. During McGraw's presidency, McGraw-Hill expanded that number to sixty publications. Its book company, well established in the field of business and technical books, began to produce encyclopedias, art books, religious books, and language-instruction materials. A wide range of educational, financial, and construction information services were also offered.

Under McGraw's leadership, his company acquired Standard and Poor's Corporation, F. W. Dodge Corporation, Webster Publishing Company, California Test Bureau, Educational Developmental Laboratories, Shephard's Citations, National Radio Institute, Capitol Radio Engineering Institute, Opinion Research Corporation, American Heritage Publishing Company, and four television stations in Indianapolis, Denver, San Diego, and Bakersfield, Calif.

McGraw possessed unremitting determination and optimism in striving for the continuing success of McGraw-Hill. In a speech at the Associated Business Publications' annual spring conference on May 26, 1955, he referred to an employee who once said about his father: "Mr. McGraw has a very high standard of dissatisfaction." McGraw had recognized the truth of that statement when he joined the firm as a young man. As president he emphasized its continuing significance, advising his staff that "only by maintaining a high standard of dissatisfaction for our own performance shall we be able to avoid complacency and to make the most of the great opportunities that are open to us in the years ahead." However much McGraw encouraged and earnestly entreated his employees, he did not wield excessive authority. He was known as a low-key manager, and he gave the staff the freedom to explore new arenas.

To him, the possibilities were nearly boundless in the mid-1950's. He was buoyed chiefly by the nation's annual $4 billion expenditure on research, and he was convinced that this research would provide increasingly sophisticated methods of producing improved goods and services. It was, as he saw it, up to him and his company as business publishers to help American business take advantage of these methods.

Publishing technical periodicals and books in various fields had been the primary vocation of McGraw-Hill since the beginning of the century. McGraw stressed the need to satisfy specialized reading interests promptly and more economically than other sources. He empha-

sized accurate and thorough reporting of information, knowing it would attract subscriptions and advertising that would in turn foster McGraw's primary objective—the growth of McGraw-Hill.

Faced with a changing marketplace that included the looming possibilities of television, McGraw adapted. He employed task forces comprised of people from several divisions who studied and then reported on various problems and issues pertaining to the company as a whole. McGraw utilized the results of these and other studies to enact necessary changes. He was prepared to develop whatever means of communication the people chose, even if that meant focusing on the electronic media over reading materials. In the meantime, he continued to publish whatever technical books, college textbooks, encyclopedias, fiction and nonfiction, periodicals, films, newsletters, and catalogs the market required.

By 1960, revenues had increased to $117 million, compared to $67 million when he took office. But rising costs and a recession at the beginning of 1961 brought about a decline in advertising, which caused a drop in the net income of the publications division. Subscriptions, however, rose to about 1.5 million readers; of that figure, 65.5 percent were renewals, which set new records. The occasional downturn in any of the several McGraw-Hill divisions did not seriously hinder the overall performance of the company during McGraw's tenure. Revenues continued to increase by the tens of millions of dollars in the succeeding years. By the end of his presidency in 1965, revenues had exceeded $216 million.

On Jan. 1, 1966, McGraw became chairman of the board. He held that position until Feb. 1, 1968, when he assumed the chairmanship of the executive committee, a position he retained for the remainder of his life.

Although McGraw had opportunities he would not have had were he not born to the company's co-founder, he proved to be a conscientious and enterprising manager. He devoted his entire business career to advancing the work of his father and his brothers before him, and he achieved a scope of expansion they could have only imagined. He died of a stroke in Boynton Beach, Fla.

[Some biographical material on McGraw can be found in the Business Information Center at

McGraw-Hill headquarters in New York City. See also Roger Burlingame, *Endless Frontiers: The Story of McGraw-Hill* (1959); and *Imprint on an Era: The Story of the McGraw-Hill Book Company* (1963). An obituary is in the *New York Times*, Feb. 9, 1974.]

ELIZABETH MCKAY

McHUGH, KEITH STRATTON (Feb. 22, 1895–June 7, 1975), business executive and government official, was born in Fort Collins, Colo., the son of Peter Joseph McHugh, a physician, and Lerah Gilette Stratton.

McHugh attended public schools in Fort Collins and graduated from the University of Wisconsin with a B.S. in chemical engineering in 1917. On Aug. 16, 1917, he married Frances Brown; they had no children. After America entered World War I, McHugh joined the U.S. Army and served as a captain with the American Expeditionary Force in France.

In 1919, McHugh went to work for American Telephone and Telegraph Company (AT&T) as a clerk and advanced through various engineering positions. In 1921, he was made a general commercial engineer at an AT&T subsidiary, Chesapeake and Potomac Telephone, in Washington, D.C.

In 1925, McHugh transferred to New York Telephone Company, as commercial manager of its upstate region; in 1927, he was made commercial manager of its Long Island region. McHugh was appointed vice-president in charge of public relations in early 1929 and was transferred back to AT&T corporate headquarters in New York City later that year. He was a commercial engineer at AT&T until 1934, and then successively was assistant vice-president, vice-president in charge of administration (1938), vice-president in charge of public relations (1946), and vice-president in charge of accounts and finance.

In 1949, McHugh was elected to the New York Telephone Company board of directors; later that year he was appointed the company's president. McHugh was president through 1959, during which time he helped the company expand to serve the postwar demand for increased telephone service. During his tenure, its telephones increased from 4.7 million to 6.1 million. Frances McHugh died in 1956, and on Dec. 4, 1957, he married Dorothy Barbee Miller. They adopted one child.

McHugh served the Greater New York Fund and numerous other civic organizations.

Through this service he became a close friend of Nelson Rockefeller and strongly supported his bid to obtain the Republican nomination for governor of New York in 1958. Rockefeller made the state economy an issue in his campaign against Democratic Governor W. Averell Harriman, charging that the Democrats were hostile to business and promising to give business growth and the creation of new job opportunities a high priory if elected. Rockefeller upset the incumbent Harriman by 530,000 votes.

After Rockefeller was inaugurated, he appointed McHugh head of the New York State Department of Commerce. McHugh resigned from his $150,000-per-year post at New York Telephone to accept the cabinet position, which paid $85,000, and was inducted on May 2, 1959.

Rockefeller appointed a Wall Street lawyer, Oren L. Root, deputy secretary of commerce. Root had organized and headed the volunteer committees who supported Wendell Willkie's 1940 presidential campaign and had been active since then in Republican politics. Political observers believed McHugh and Root would use the Department of Commerce as a base from which to build support for Rockefeller's efforts to obtain the Republican presidential nomination.

McHugh first came to wide public attention after Rockefeller appointed him head of the New York State Committee on Fallout Protection in 1959. On Feb. 17, 1960, McHugh's committee recommended the enactment of legislation that would make fallout shelters mandatory in all residential and commercial buildings by 1963. Homeowners would have to spend from $60 to $500 to construct shelters, and the recommendations would cost nearly $1 billion to implement. Although McHugh's proposals were praised by the *New York Times*, they were criticized by virtually everyone in New York politics. Rockefeller tried to minimize criticism by modifying McHugh's recommendations. In March 1960, he submitted several bills proposing tax credits to promote voluntary, rather than mandatory, construction of fallout shelters. The New York legislature rejected the proposed legislation the following month.

In July 1960, shortly before the Republican National Convention, McHugh and Root helped L. Judson Morehouse, New York Republican party chairman, prepare and publicize a study alleging that Rockefeller would make a better presidential candidate than the front-runner, Vice-President Richard Nixon. Nixon had enough party support, however, to obtain the nomination on the first ballot, although he lost the general election to Democrat John F. Kennedy.

After the fallout shelter fiasco and Rockefeller's failure to obtain the 1960 presidential nomination, McHugh concentrated on New York State Department of Commerce matters. He set up a task force to streamline government operations regarding business regulation and to attract businesses to the state. He also established Department of Commerce branch offices in Los Angeles, Chicago, and Montreal, as well as a liaison office with the European Common Market in Brussels, and for Asian businesses in Tokyo. The opening of these offices furnished well-publicized speech-making opportunities for Rockefeller.

McHugh supported Rockefeller's 1962 campaign for reelection against the Democratic candidate, U.S. Attorney Robert Morgenthau. Rockefeller campaigned on a pledge of "no new taxes," which McHugh later came to regret, since this resulted in increased state borrowing to pay for Rockefeller's many new government programs.

McHugh resigned from his cabinet position in 1966, but he continued to remain active in other state posts. He held a total of fifty committee and board appointments. In 1968, Rockefeller appointed McHugh head of a task force to study problems concerning the reconversion of the state economy after the end of the Vietnam War. McHugh's Post Vietnam Planning Committee warned that one-quarter of the state's 280,000 defense-plant workers would be out of jobs after the Vietnam War ended and recommended the creation of new state agencies to facilitate postwar economic adjustment.

McHugh had little involvement in political matters after Rockefeller lost the 1968 Republican presidential nomination to Richard Nixon. He died in New York City.

McHugh was Nelson Rockefeller's liaison with the business community. He personified the leadership of the liberal-internationalist wing of the Republican party: he lived on the East Coast; he headed a giant corporation; he proposed an active government role in economic matters; and he supported Nelson Rockefeller's bids for the Republican presidential nomination. Although Rockefeller and McHugh claimed success in promoting New York State's economic growth during the late 1950's and 1960's, this success resulted mainly from national economic factors outside of their control. The recession of the later Eisenhower administration was succeeded by the economic growth (and inflation) of the Kennedy and Johnson administrations, which carried New York State along with the rest of the nation.

[Syracuse University's George Arents Research Library has McHugh's papers dating from 1959, largely consisting of press clippings and speeches. A much smaller number of documents are in the Nelson Rockefeller Gubernatorial Papers at the Rockefeller Archives in North Tarrytown, N.Y. There is no biography. Myron D. Hartman, *The New York Red Book* (annual) is the official state yearbook containing information about the New York Department of Commerce and other state agencies. McHugh is mentioned briefly in William H. Rodgers, *Rockefeller's Follies* (1966), which describes the fallout shelter fiasco; and in James Underwood and William J. Daniels, *Governor Rockefeller in New York* (1982). An obituary is in the *New York Times*, June 8, 1975.]

STEPHEN G. MARSHALL

MacKAYE, BENTON (Mar. 6, 1879–Dec. 11, 1975), forester and regional planner, was born in Stamford, Conn., the son of James Morrison Steel MacKaye, a dramatist and actor, and Mary Keith Medbery. Because of the peripatetic nature of his father's theatrical activities, Benton spent his early years in several different places: Stamford and Ridgefield, Conn.; Manhattan and Mt. Vernon, N.Y.; Dublin, N.H.; and Washington, D.C. During the late 1880's his family purchased a summer home in Shirley Center, Mass., where young Benton liked to visit and make exploratory jaunts to nearby woods, fields, and streams. Later his family wintered in Cambridge, Mass., where he completed in the Latin School his preparatory education for college.

In 1900 MacKaye received a B.A. from Harvard University, and in 1905 he received an M.A. from the Harvard Forest School. His study at Harvard was much influenced by courses with geologists William Morris Davis and Nathaniel Southgate Shaler. Apparently motivated by Gifford Pinchot's crusade for forest conservation, he joined the U.S. Forest Service in 1905 and remained with this agency as a research forester until 1918. In this position he made field examinations of timberlands and watershed investigations of areas considered for acquisition as national forests under the Weeks Act of 1910, especially areas in the southern Appalachian Mountains and the White Mountains of New Hampshire. By 1916 he had begun also to study forests as recreation grounds. This study led to his interest in the preservation and enjoyment of wilderness areas. He married Jessie Belle Hardy on June 1, 1915.

During the period 1918–1919 MacKaye was a specialist in land colonization for the U.S. Department of Labor. Soon thereafter he became an instructor in the Harvard Forest School and began to develop plans for the Appalachian Trail, which he described as "a project in regional planning" and which Lewis Mumford later called "a dramatic social idea." The proposed trail was a footpath linking wilderness areas suitable for recreation and readily accessible to residents in the metropolitan areas along the Atlantic Seaboard. With the assistance of the Appalachian Trail Conference and its constituent hiking clubs, MacKaye during the 1920's conducted a vigorous campaign for the trail, which was basically completed in 1937 and given federal-government protection in 1938. It then extended some 2,000 miles along the crestline of the Appalachian Range from Maine to Georgia. MacKaye was very proud of his role in the establishment of the trail and was pleased to be called "the father of the Appalachian Trail."

Meanwhile he became more widely engaged in regional planning activities. Beginning in 1923, he worked with Lewis Mumford, Clarence Stein, Stuart Chase, and other planners to organize the Regional Planning Association of America. He also met Patrick Geddes, the Scottish planner, and was impressed by his ideas on geotechnics. From 1924 to 1928 he collaborated with Mumford in the preparation of special reports for the newly formed New York State Housing and Regional Planning Commission, and in 1925 he worked with Mumford to develop for *Survey Graphic* a special issue on regional planning, a landmark publication in the thinking of regional planners. In 1928 he completed a statewide plan on park and forest development in Massachusetts for the Governor's Commission on Open Spaces. His early and essentially continuing ideas concerning regional planning were set forth in 1928 in *The New Exploration, A Philosophy of Regional Planning*, a book, declared Mumford, "that de-

serves a place on the same shelf that holds Henry Thoreau's *Walden* and George Perkins Marsh's *Man and Nature*." In this publication MacKaye described a conflict in values between the urban industrial society and rural communal life. He contended that the latter, an "indigenous" area of stable values, should be preserved for its own sake and as a refuge from the limitation and confusion of the city. The entire natural environment should be protected and managed with planning for society's best interests.

MacKaye made one of his most remarkable planning proposals in the *New Republic*, Mar. 12, 1930. In an article entitled "The Townless Highway" he proposed a "highway built for the motorist and kept free from every encroachment, except the filling stations and restaurants necessary for his convenience." This proposal, of course, represented an idea that developed into familiar beltways around municipalities of today.

In 1932 MacKaye resumed federal government service as a consultant for a planning study for the U.S. Indian Service on Indian reservations in South Dakota, New Mexico, and Arizona. From 1934 to 1936 he worked for the Division of Land Planning and Housing of the Tennessee Valley Authority in attempts to prepare a comprehensive regional plan for the Tennessee River basin. Two years later he was a planning consultant on flood control policies of the U.S. Forest Service. He ended federal government service in 1945 on the staff of the Rural Electrification Administration after preparing a study of possible regional development under a proposed Missouri Valley Authority.

Next to his promotion of the Appalachian Trail, MacKaye was probably most proud of his role in the founding of the Wilderness Society in 1935 and in its earliest activities. He joined Robert Marshall, Aldo Leopold, and other prominent conservationists in organizing the society and was its first vice-president and its second president from 1945 to 1950. He contributed importantly to formulation of its policies, which sought wider public support for the preservation of American wilderness areas. As honorary president from 1945 until his death, he lived to see the society become one of the most influential conservation organizations in the United States.

During much of the thirty-year period of his retirement MacKaye lived mainly at the Mac-

Kaye family home at Shirley Center, Mass., and often spent winters at the Cosmos Club in Washington, D.C. He devoted most of this time to writing a synthesis of his life and philosophy of regional planning, which he hoped to publish under the title *The Geotechnics of North America*. The enormity of the task and failing health, however, permitted him to complete only a summary published in 1972, entitled *A Two-Year Course in Geotechnics*. The larger product of his final writing, much of it autobiographical, remains in manuscript form at repositories mentioned below. In this effort, and during a long career as a perceptive conservationist and planner, MacKaye was impressive as one who viewed all parts of the environment in their relation to organic habitability and human development. His ecological perceptions always seemed to motivate a search for what he called "a habitable globe."

With a shock of hair framing a thin face, deep-set eyes, and a tall, lean figure, MacKaye had a considerably Lincolnesque appearance. His personal habits were simple and, in some respects, ascetic. He enjoyed solitude but cultivated friendships. He had a fine sense of humor and a gift for bold epithets. To persons who disagreed with his novel planning concepts, he admitted that he probably appeared "wild as a wolf and crazy as a loon." His life was remarkably long and full of activity. It ended in 1975 after a brief illness in his beloved boyhood community, Shirley Center, Mass.

[MacKaye's personal papers are in the Dartmouth College Library. Copies of the manuscript for his proposed publication, *The Geotechnics of North America*, are in that library and also in the Manuscript Division, Library of Congress; Harvard College Library; and the Wilderness Society Archives.

Paul T. Bryant has edited a published collection of major writings of MacKaye in *From Geography to Geotechnics* (1968). MacKaye wrote many articles and letters on planning and wilderness subjects for magazines and newspapers. A seven-part series of articles published in *The Survey*, 1950–1951, entitled "Geography to Geotechnics," presents many of his basic thoughts. In a memorial issue of January/March 1976, *Living Wilderness* published appraisals of MacKaye's work and ideas by Lewis Mumford, Stuart Chase, George Marshall, Frederick Gutheim, and five other persons. Highlights of MacKaye's work are summarized by Paul H. Oesher in *American Forests*, June 1976. An obituary is in the *New York Times*, Dec. 13, 1975.]

HAROLD T. PINKETT

McKELDIN, THEODORE ROOSEVELT (Nov. 20, 1900–Aug. 10, 1974), mayor of Baltimore and governor of Maryland, was born in Baltimore, the tenth of eleven children of James A. McKeldin and Dora Grief. His father, a Scotch-Irish immigrant from Belfast, was a stonemason and later a policeman. James McKeldin named his son for the newly elected Republican vice-president of the United States, who had recently campaigned in Baltimore. The McKeldin family was in straitened circumstances, and Theodore's father was overly fond of liquor, a fact that prompted his son to vow never to drink. In later years, despite his opposition to Prohibition, Theodore McKeldin would not permit any liquor in his own home.

At the age of fourteen, Theodore finished grammar school and took his first job as a $20-per-week office boy for Alexander Brown & Sons. He subsequently went to work for the Fidelity and Deposit Company of Baltimore. McKeldin early developed a bent for oratory; after completing a Dale Carnegie course in public speaking at the local YMCA, McKeldin discovered that he was a proficient public speaker. Thus, Fidelity and Deposit employed him to travel around the country encouraging its agents. During vacations, he earned $2.50 per day as a grave digger. On Oct. 17, 1924, he married a fellow bank employee, Honolulu Claire Manzer, who had taught him bookkeeping. The couple had two children.

McKeldin continued his education at night, first at Baltimore City College, and later at the University of Maryland Law School, where he earned his law degree in 1925. He began practicing law and was a partner in the firm of McKeldin and Moylan. In 1927, he campaigned for William F. Broening, the successful Republican candidate for mayor of Baltimore. Appointed the mayor's executive secretary that year, McKeldin returned to his law practice in 1931. In 1939, he made an unsuccessful run for mayor of Baltimore. In 1942, he lost again in his first bid for the governorship; he was the only Republican willing to challenge Democratic Governor Herbert R. O'Conor. Undiscouraged by these losses, he returned to the hustings in 1943 to run against Howard Jackson, the incumbent mayor of Baltimore who had defeated him four years earlier. This time McKeldin triumphed by more than twenty thousand votes, a record margin for a Republican in an overwhelmingly Democratic city.

During McKeldin's first administration, the city charter was overhauled; a slum clearance program was begun, as was the planning for a new municipal airport and civic center; and expansion of the city's water supply was initiated. Because of wartime conditions, however, McKeldin generally had to be satisfied with maintaining city services on a steady course. A liberal Republican, he appointed some Democrats to fill city jobs, angering some party regulars. In 1946, he made a second run for the governorship, defeating a more conservative primary opponent, but losing in the general election to the Democratic candidate, William P. Lane, Jr.

Leaving office in 1947, McKeldin returned to his law practice and also pursued graduate work in economics at Johns Hopkins University. However, in 1950, he once again won the Republican nomination for the governorship. Vigorously stumping the state, McKeldin won the general election by some ninety-four thousand votes over Lane, who had been responsible for legislative passage of an unpopular state sales tax. Upon entering office in January 1951, McKeldin discovered that the sales tax could not be repealed, and, in fact found it necessary to raise both it and the state income tax during his first term. At the Republican National Convention in Los Angeles in 1952, McKeldin received a tentative offer of the vice-presidential nomination from Senator Robert A. Taft, the leader of the conservative wing of the party. Ever the moderate, McKeldin instead made a memorable speech nominating Dwight D. Eisenhower; nevertheless, McKeldin continued to harbor dreams of the vice-presidency for some years afterward.

After a bruising campaign in 1954, McKeldin won a second term as governor by defeating the popular former president of the University of Maryland, Dr. Harry C. ("Curley") Byrd, by better than sixty-two thousand votes. During his eight years in office, McKeldin launched an ambitious state highway construction program; established a state port authority; and created the state Commission on Administrative Organization. He also ensured the state's budget procedures were reorganized and that new state office buildings were constructed. McKeldin augmented his very modest gubernatorial salary of $4,500 with a number of paid out-of-state speaking engagements.

Because of a 1947 amendment to the state constitution, McKeldin could not seek a third term as governor. He tried to persuade the state's junior U.S. senator, J. Glenn Beall, Sr., a fellow Republican, to run for the governorship so that he could make a bid for Beall's Senate seat, but Beall was not interested. McKeldin then decided to try for another term as mayor of Baltimore in 1959 but was soundly defeated by a Democratic newcomer.

He returned to his law practice, but ran for mayor again in 1963, this time in an unusual fusion ticket with a Democratic reform candidate for city comptroller. McKeldin won by a narrow margin of some forty-five hundred votes in an election that saw Democrats chosen for all other elective city posts. McKeldin helped to bring about approval of a new city charter in 1964, which entailed improvements in the budget process and creation of a department of hospitals. McKeldin was also a supporter of New York Governor Nelson A. Rockefeller in the latter's unsuccessful bid for the Republican presidential nomination in 1968. Offended by remarks about immigrants allegedly made by Representative William B. Miller, the party's vice-presidential nominee, in the general election McKeldin bolted his party and backed Lyndon B. Johnson. In acknowledgment of that backing, Johnson sent McKeldin to represent the United States at the inauguration of the president of the Philippines in 1965 and named him to a group of American observers of the South Vietnamese elections in 1967. McKeldin also was appointed to the U.S. Indian Claims Commission by Johnson, but was denied reappointment in 1969 because of pressure placed by Senator Barry Goldwater, whom McKeldin failed to endorse in the 1964 federal election, on the new Nixon administration. McKeldin maintained an active interest in his native city during his years as a private citizen. His successor as mayor appointed him to the board of municipal zoning appeals in 1971, in which post he served until his death.

McKeldin was a warm, compassionate, and ebullient man of firm convictions, who relished politics. During his career as mayor and governor, he named as many Democrats as Republicans to appointive office. He placed a number of blacks in state positions and created a state commission to deal with interracial issues. The overwhelming support that he generally received from voters in Baltimore's black and Jewish precincts was noteworthy and was one reflection of his vigorous and consistent advocacy of civil rights for minorities. Despite his own staunch anti-Communism, McKeldin opposed the controversial efforts of Wisconsin Senator Joseph McCarthy to identify and remove alleged Communist sympathizers from federal government service, long before it was politically popular to do so. McKeldin died in Baltimore.

[McKeldin's papers are held at the University of Baltimore. Further archival material can be found at the Maryland Historical Society; the Enoch Pratt Free Library in Baltimore; and the McKeldin Library at the University of Maryland. See also Frank F. White, *The Governors of Maryland, 1777–1970* (1970); Robert Sobel and John Raimo, eds., *Biographical Directory of the Governors of the United States, 1789–1978* (1978); Melvin G. Holli and Peter d'A. Jones, eds., *Biographical Dictionary of American Mayors, 1820–1980* (1981); and Robert J. Brugger, *Maryland: A Middle Temperament, 1634–1980* (1988). Obituaries are in the *Baltimore Sun,* the *Washington Post,* and the *New York Times,* all Aug. 11, 1974.]

KEIR B. STERLING

McKINNEY, FRANK EDWARD, SR. (June 16, 1904–Jan. 9, 1974) banker, politician, and baseball executive, was born and reared in Indianapolis, the son of Roscoe Anthony McKinney, a fireman who became chief of the Indianapolis department, and Anna Moss. McKinney, who briefly considered entering the priesthood, attended Sacred Heart High School, but quit in his sophomore year in 1919. He took a job as messenger for the Meyer-Kiser Bank in Indianapolis. In 1922 he joined the People's State Bank as a bookkeeper, becoming cashier in 1933. There he met Owen J. ("Donie") Bush, a former major league baseball player and then manager of the Indianapolis Indians minor league team. Bush would provide McKinney entree into both politics and baseball. In 1923 Bush turned over management of his finances to McKinney, whose foresight saved Bush substantial losses from a 1927 tornado in Indianapolis and cemented their association.

McKinney's success in the world of baseball began when he managed his former high school's semipro baseball team and led it to the city championship. In 1938 he and Bush purchased the Louisville Colonels, who three years later won the Little World Series. Selling that team in 1941 to the Boston Red Sox, they bought the Indianapolis Indians, who won the league pennant in 1948 and the Little World Series in 1949. In 1946 McKinney headed a group, including Bing Crosby, that bought the Pittsburgh Pirates for $2.25 million. In 1950 he sold his holdings in the Pirates, and in 1951 he sold his interest in the Indianapolis Indians.

With Owen Bush's support, McKinney became a leader in the Indiana Democratic party. In 1934 he won election as Marion County (Indianapolis) treasurer. This was the only public office he ever held, but it secured his business success. Delinquent property taxes were so common in the depression years that, as an incentive, the treasurer was awarded a percentage of all the back taxes he collected. With his potential earnings as collateral, McKinney borrowed $100,000 to purchase control of the Fidelity Trust Company. He thereby became the youngest president of a financial institution in the nation. The loan was retired by the time he completed his second two-year term as county treasurer.

From this foundation, McKinney acquired banks through sales and mergers. By 1959 the small Fidelity Trust Company had grown into American Fletcher National Bank, the largest bank in Indiana, and McKinney was its chairman. Meanwhile he had also become majority stockholder in the Universal Broadcasting Corporation, which operated radio stations in Indianapolis, South Bend, Fort Wayne, and Anderson, Ind., and also owned television station WISH in Indianapolis. Over the years, he served on several corporate boards, including that of the New York Central Railroad.

McKinney's work for the Indiana Democratic party included service as subtreasurer or treasurer of the Marion County Committee, the Indianapolis Committee, Indiana State Central Committee, and the National Committee for Indiana. In 1940, he received national recognition from his party when he was appointed vice-chairman of the Democratic National Committee.

In 1942, McKinney entered the U.S. Army with the rank of major, and continually rose to the rank of colonel in the Army Finance Division. After the war he served in two civilian posts for President Truman, one dealing with settlement of war contracts (1945), the other with military housing (1949). He later declined Truman's offers to be Secretary of the Army and to hold a seat on the Federal Reserve Board.

In October 1951, William M. Boyle, chairman of the Democratic National Committee, resigned over a conflict of interest controversy. President Harry Truman, on the recommendation of Frank M. McHale, a longtime associate of McKinney and a major figure in the Indiana Democratic party, appointed McKinney to succeed Boyle. Although he served in that post less than a year, McKinney had an immediate and salutary impact on the office of national chairman. He promptly relinquished his interest in the United States Pipeline Company, which was seeking a government contract, and he also announced that he would forego the $35,000 annual salary provided to the chairman of the party. Discovering that the staff of the national committee lacked direction and expertise, McKinney moved quickly to create an executive committee, a professional research division, and a liaison link with congressional Democrats. He also laid out a plan to raise funds for the 1952 presidential campaign. All this was achieved while cutting the operating budget of the national committee.

When Adlai Stevenson won the Democratic presidential nomination in 1952, he wanted his own man to serve as chairman of the party's national committee; McKinney was replaced by Stephen Mitchell in August 1952.

Although much of McKinney's program was later dropped, his brief tenure as national chairman was widely praised. Truman considered him to be the best he had seen in that office, and he never concealed his disappointment that McKinney had been replaced by a friend of Stevenson who lacked the party experience and skills that McKinney had so ably demonstrated.

President Lyndon Johnson nominated McKinney as ambassador to Spain in 1968. Although he was confirmed to that post, ill health forced him to forgo the appointment.

McKinney married Margaret K. Warner on Nov. 24, 1932. The couple had four children, including Frank, Jr., who became a medalist swimmer on two U.S. Olympic teams and succeeded his father as head of the family enterprises.

McKinney's career was a classic example of American achievement, both financially and in public service. He received honorary degrees from St. Francis College (Pa.) and Indiana University. He served as chairman of the board of trustees of the latter. During his lifetime he held prominent positions in numerous civic, veterans, Catholic, and sports organizations.

[There are a few items on McKinney at the Truman Presidential Library in Independence, Mo.; the most important is McKinney's final report as Democratic party national chairman. Obituaries appear in the *Indianapolis Star* and the *New York Times*, January 11, 1974.]

THOMAS P. WOLF

MacLEOD, COLIN MUNRO (Jan. 28, 1909–Feb. 11, 1972), medical scientist, was born in Port Hastings, Nova Scotia, Canada, the son of John Charles MacLeod and Lillian Munro. His father was a Scottish Presbyterian minister and his mother a schoolteacher. An outstanding student, he skipped three full grades to graduate from secondary school at St. Francis College in Richmond, Quebec, at the age of fifteen. As a result, he had to defer his entry into McGill College for one year, during which he taught sixth grade in a Richmond school. After two years of premedical preparation, he entered McGill University Medical School, which awarded him the M.D. degree in 1932.

MacLeod completed his medical training with two years on the house staff of the Montreal General Hospital and then received an appointment at the hospital of the Rockefeller Institute for Medical Research in New York City. This move initiated an extraordinary career in medical science that produced notable contributions in basic and clinical research, education, administration, and science policy at the governmental level. He married Elizabeth Randol on July 2, 1938; they had one child. MacLeod became a naturalized citizen in 1941.

On arriving at the Rockefeller Institute in 1934, MacLeod joined the laboratory of Dr. O. T. Avery, who for the past twenty years had been studying the pneumococcus, the most common cause of bacterial pneumonia. One of the areas of interest in Avery's laboratory at that time was a phenomenon known as the transformation of pneumococcal types, which had been discovered by an English bacteriologist, Fred Griffith, in 1928. MacLeod elected to direct his major research effort to this problem.

Initially, work on the phenomenon had been motivated by its possible relation to the virulence of the pneumococcus, but it became clear that it had broader implications and represented something akin to the transfer of genetic information between two different pneumococci.

Thus, the research focused on the nature of the substance found in extracts of pneumococci that was transferring the information. MacLeod made significant progress in many aspects of the problem, but the ultimate goal proved elusive. Not until 1944 was he able to report, in a paper written with Avery and Maclyn McCarty (who joined the project in 1941) that the transforming substance was DNA. In effect, his first research project had led to the landmark discovery that genes are made of DNA.

Although he continued his association with this research until it was published, MacLeod's full-time participation in the laboratory work ended in 1941, when he moved to New York University School of Medicine as chairman of the Department of Microbiology. Here he initiated his role as an educator by building an academic department of medical microbiology that was characterized by excellence and versatility and became a model for preclinical science departments. At the same time, he continued his research, both on other aspects of pneumococcal transformation and on new ventures.

MacLeod's activity as a government science adviser began at New York University when he was a consultant in military medicine. In 1946, he became president of the Army Epidemiological Board and served for several years in this capacity. Later, during the administration of Mayor Robert F. Wagner, he was a leader in the group that organized the Health Research Council in 1959, a notable experiment in the support of medical and health research by a municipal government. As its first chairman (1960–1970), MacLeod guided the council through its formative period. It was a successful enterprise that was a victim of the city's fiscal crisis in the mid-1970's.

MacLeod left New York City in 1956 to become the John Herr Musser Professor of Research Medicine at the University of Pennsylvania. There he continued the pattern of participating broadly in the functions of the medical school while pursuing his advisory and consulting activities. Four years later he returned to New York University as a professor of medicine with the specific purpose of developing a division of genetics. When this initiative was beginning to thrive in 1963, he accepted his first full-time position in government as deputy director of the Office of Science and Technology in the White House. He was primarily responsible for the biological sciences, and his interests in the national and international promotion of science deepened. A major international accomplishment was his development of the cooperative program between the United States and Japan in the medical sciences, and he continued to serve as chairman of the U.S. delegation to the program for the rest of his life.

On leaving Washington, D.C., in 1966, MacLeod became vice-president for medical affairs of the Commonwealth Fund in New York, directing its programs for the study of medical education and delivery of medical care. This activity proved to be less rewarding than he had expected, and he found a new challenge in 1970, as president of the Oklahoma Medical Research Foundation, an organization that had not yet achieved its full potential. During the remaining year and a half of his life, he worked to improve this institution's position in medical research. At the same time he continued his interest in international medical problems. He died in London while en route to Bangladesh on a mission concerning cholera for the U.S. Public Health Service.

MacLeod had tremendous energy that made it possible for him to engage in several different activities at the same time. The productivity of the boards and committees that he chaired depended in great part on his skill in winning the cooperation of his colleagues. He was widely respected and admired for his abilities as both scientist and administrator, and acquired a wide circle of friends throughout the world.

[An extensive biographical sketch by Walsh McDermott is in *Biographical Memoirs. National Academy of Sciences* 54 (1983). His famous DNA paper is O. T. Avery, C. MacLeod, and M. McCarty, "Studies on the Chemical Nature of the Substance Inducing Transformation of Pneumococcal Types. Induction of Transformation by a Deoxyribonucleic Acid Fraction Isolated from Pneumococcus Type III," *Journal of Experimental Medicine*, Feb. 1944. An obituary is in the *New York Times*, Feb. 13, 1972.]

MACLYN MCCARTY

MacPHAIL, LELAND STANFORD ("LARRY") (Feb. 3, 1890–Oct. 1, 1975), major-league-baseball executive, was born in Cass City, Mich., the son of Curtis McPhail, owner of a general store and later a banker, and Catherine Ann MacMurtrie. MacPhail was named for the railroad magnate Leland Stanford, whose wife was a close friend of his mother. In later years MacPhail changed the spelling of his surname to emphasize his Scottish ancestry. At age ten he entered the Staunton Military Academy in Virginia and graduated six years later. A precocious student, he qualified for admission to the U.S. Naval Academy but chose to enroll at Beloit College in Beloit, Wis., where he majored in liberal arts and played varsity baseball. A year later MacPhail enrolled in the University of Michigan Law School but then transferred to George Washington University in Washington, D.C., where he received his law degree in 1910. Upon graduating, MacPhail went to work for two Chicago law firms in succession. That same year he married Inez Frances Thompson of Oak Park, Ill. They had three children. In 1915 MacPhail accepted the presidency of a department store in Nashville, Tenn.

When America entered World War I, MacPhail joined a state artillery regiment commanded by former Senator Luke Lea of Tennessee. Nationalized as the 114th Field Artillery Regiment, the unit saw action in two battles. As Colonel Lea's adjutant, Captain MacPhail served as battery commander and was slightly wounded on the last day of the war. Early in 1919 he participated in Colonel Lea's quixotic attempt to kidnap Kaiser Wilhelm II from his sanctuary in the Netherlands. Although the mission failed, widespread publicity made folk heroes of the conspirators, who were reprimanded by General John J. Pershing. MacPhail's participation in this scheme typified the brash, erratic behavior that later marked his career as a baseball executive. During the 1920's MacPhail engaged in such lucrative enterprises as a glass manufactury, an auto agency, and a real estate venture. He also served as a college football official and organized a golf club.

From 1930, when he organized a syndicate that purchased the moribund Columbus Senators of the minor American Association for $100,000, until 1947, when he resigned as president of the New York Yankees, MacPhail was one of the most innovative executives in professional baseball. As president of the Columbus team, he recouped his initial investment by selling the club (renamed the Red Birds) to the major-league St. Louis Cardinals while retaining full control of club operations. Over the next three years MacPhail used his Cardinals connection to build a winning minor-league team, which he ensconced in a new stadium

equipped for night games. Although criticized as a financially risky venture during the Great Depression, the Red Birds attracted a record 310,000 fans in 1932. But MacPhail's unbridled individualism angered the owners, who fired him at the close of the 1933 season.

MacPhail's promotional acumen impressed the Cincinnati Reds, who made him the club's vice-president and general manager in 1934. This last-place National League team was in dire financial straits. MacPhail persuaded executive Powel Crosley, a manufacturer of appliances, to assume the club's presidency. With Crosley's financial support, MacPhail refurbished the Reds' ball park, which he renamed Crosley Field, hired Frank Lane to build a farm system to develop players, and introduced radio broadcasts of road games. In 1935 he scored his biggest coup when he inaugurated night baseball into the major leagues. The Reds' seven night games attracted 124,000 fans and helped double home attendance. The following year the Reds finished in fifth place, but MacPhail, whose flamboyant, brawling style clashed with that of the conservative Reds owner, was forced to resign. Nevertheless, his policies laid the groundwork for the team's championship seasons of 1939 and 1940.

After a year's hiatus MacPhail returned to baseball as chief executive of the Brooklyn Dodgers. When he took charge, the Dodgers were $1.2 million in debt to local banks, but MacPhail induced the lenders to advance funds to finance his ideas for park improvement, farm-system development, and night baseball. The Dodgers' first night game in 1938 was memorable; visiting pitcher Johnny Vander Meer of the Reds pitched his second consecutive no-hit game. That year attendance rose to 750,000, and in 1939 it topped one million. MacPhail added to revenues by selling radio rights to Dodgers games, and in 1939 he arranged for the first telecast of a major-league game. In 1941, by dint of several canny player trades, MacPhail assembled a group of veteran players who won the team's first National League championship in twenty-one seasons. Although they lost the World Series, the Dodgers gained national fame and drew more than one million spectators both at home and on the road. In 1942 MacPhail resigned to enter military service as special assistant to Undersecretary of War Robert Patterson.

MacPhail was still in uniform in the fall of 1944 when he maneuvered to purchase the New

York Yankees for $2.8 million, more than he could afford. To meet the price, he persuaded businessmen Dan Topping and Del Webb to join him as equal partners. As president of the team, he again applied his successful formula of instituting night baseball, refurbishing the stadium, and selling contracts to local radio stations. In 1947 a contract with a local television station fetched $75,000 for the rights to all Yankee home games. In 1946 MacPhail flew the team to Panama for spring training and exhibition games that netted $65,000. That year the Yankees attracted a record 2.3 million fans, and the following year the Yankees won the American League pennant and the World Series. It was MacPhail's only world championship and the capstone of his baseball career. In the wake of this triumph he resigned and sold his share of the Yankees for $2 million.

As a baseball innovator, MacPhail's impact was far-reaching. Besides pioneering night baseball, sales of radio and television rights to games, and air travel (prior to 1946, major-league teams traveled by train), he also built winning teams in three major-league cities and was the only club president to win pennants in each league. As a baseball executive he served on major-league committees that selected a commissioner and gave players their first pension plan, a minimum-salary concession, and spring-training money. But if MacPhail was an effective executive, he was also controversial. His feuds with commissioners, fellow owners, managers, and sportswriters were widely publicized. He came to be known as the "roaring redhead."

In 1945 MacPhail was divorced from his first wife. In May he married Jean Bennett Wanamaker. They had one child. During the 1950's MacPhail raised thoroughbred horses and Black Angus cattle at his Glenangus Farms in Bel Air, Md. He also headed a syndicate that purchased and restored the Bowie race track in Maryland. Still interested in baseball, he offered prophetic advice to major-league owners in a perceptive *Life* magazine article in which he called for continental expansion of the leagues, realignment into divisions, and new parks, all of which came to pass.

MacPhail died in Miami, Fla. In 1978, he was voted into the Baseball Hall of Fame in Cooperstown, N.Y.

[The National Baseball Library at Cooperstown, N.Y., has a file on MacPhail. A useful biography is Don Warfield, *The Roaring Redhead* (1987). For his career as a baseball executive see Harold Parrott, *The Lords of Baseball* (1975). See also Frank Eck, "Larry MacPhail, Master Promoter," the *Sporting News*, Oct. 24, 1970; David Q. Voigt, *American Baseball* (1983); and Nicholas Dawidoff, "Master of the Trade," *Sports Illustrated*, Mar. 30, 1992. Obituaries appear in the *New York Times*, Oct. 2, 1975; and the *Sporting News*, Oct. 18, 1975.]

DAVID QUENTIN VOIGT

MAESTRI, ROBERT SIDNEY (Dec. 11, 1889–May 6, 1974), businessman and politician, was born in New Orleans, the son of Francis Maestri and Angele Lacabe. He attended public and parochial elementary schools, but left school after the third grade to work in the family furniture business. He also took courses at a local business school. Possessed of a keen business sense, Maestri eventually took over the firm and added real estate and securities to his rapidly expanding financial interests. Unsubstantiated rumors that Maestri repeatedly denied linked him to local prostitution and gambling operations. During World War I he served in the U.S. Army.

Maestri became a wealthy man whose ambition drove him to seek political office. However, his blunt manner and laconic way of speaking seemingly stood in the way of political success. During the early 1920's Maestri tried to curry favor with the New Orleans Regular Democratic Organization (RDO), the local political machine, but it failed to satisfy his political ambitions. So in 1927 Maestri hitched his political fortunes to the rising star of Huey Pierce Long. Maestri provided major financial backing for Long's victorious gubernatorial campaign in 1928.

Maestri, by exhibiting total loyalty and exceptional fund-raising ability, quickly assumed a privileged position within the Long inner circle. He became a leader of the Louisiana Democratic Association, Long's political organization, and served admirably as Louisiana Conservation Commissioner from 1929 until 1936. In 1929 he helped Huey Long stave off impeachment proceedings with sizable and timely financial contributions to Long's camp, who distributed the money wisely.

In 1936, the year after Long's assassination, a struggle between the Long machine and the RDO led to the forced resignation of New Orleans mayor T. Semmes Walmsley. Maestri, now a major force in the state Democratic party organization, became the Longite choice for the office. He ran unopposed and immediately asserted powerful influence with both political groups. A state legislature compliant to the Long organization extended his mayoral term to 1942.

The new municipal chief executive took his post seriously. Maestri moved swiftly to rejuvenate and revamp the Crescent City's pitiful fiscal structure, a casualty of the lengthy feud between Walmsley, who headed the RDO, and the vindictive Long organization. Through a system of tax reform, scavenging, and the cajoling of local business leaders, within two years the mayor established financial stability in a city that had been virtually bankrupt. Despite his coarse demeanor and lack of formal education, the mayor excelled at head-to-head negotiations. Maestri maintained close ties with Longite Louisiana governor Richard Leche and used the financial support of the state administration to benefit the city. He also successfully tapped New Deal funds to finance municipal building projects.

During a visit by President Franklin D. Roosevelt to New Orleans in April 1937, Maestri experienced an unfortunate and mercifully brief brush with the national media. While Roosevelt dined on Oysters Rockefeller in Antoine's Restaurant in the French Quarter, the earthy host mayor blurted out, "How ya like dem ersters?" His comment drew nationwide attention and became a Crescent City legend.

Despite his lack of sophistication and blunt retorts, Maestri was a warm man who cared about his constituents. He personally toured the city each day to look for municipal problems and to develop work assignments for repair crews. He also met regularly with citizens to hear their grievances. He was a generous man who often helped those in need with gifts of money from his own pocket. He also possessed a sharp sense of humor. When associates advised him to respond to a critical newspaper story, Maestri replied, "How can I fight the newspapers? I buy ink by the bottle; the newspapers buy it by the carload."

On Aug. 18, 1937, Maestri married Hilda Bertonier, his secretary. They had one daughter, born in 1942. The family enjoyed weekends and vacations in the couple's second home in Mandeville, a small community on the north shore of Lake Pontchartrain.

There was a dark side to the Maestri administration. The mayor was a classical political boss who ran a powerful spoils machine. Maestri, moreover, did little to control vice and police corruption in the Crescent City. When police officers complained to the mayor about low salaries, Maestri reputedly exclaimed heatedly, "What do you mean you want more money? You have a badge and a gun. If you want more money, go get more money!" In 1939 he was a major figure in the "hot oil" scandals that rocked Louisiana, although he himself evaded conviction. Labor interests also suffered. Maestri also resisted Governor Sam Houston Jones's efforts to introduce a civil service system and voting machines to New Orleans, reforms that would have threatened his power and the influence of the urban machine.

In 1942, Maestri nonetheless easily won reelection over attorneys Herve Racivitch and Shirley Wimberly. In his second term, however, the positive aspects of his administration dissipated. Maestri stopped his daily tours of the city, met less frequently with citizens, and devoted more time to political maneuvering. Municipal building projects stalled. Many attributed the change to Maestri's differences with Governor Jones, a leader of the anti-Long faction in state politics, and the mayor's growing penchant for political manipulation. Others noted the demands that World War II placed upon municipal resources. Still others contended that Maestri had simply lost interest in the city government.

In late 1945 an internal dispute between the Louisiana Democratic Association and the RDO further weakened Maestri's political position. On Jan. 22, 1946, deLesseps Story Morrison, a youthful war veteran and state legislator, defeated Maestri in a close mayoral election.

When the RDO reorganized after the election, it had no place for the former mayor. In 1950 Maestri indicated a desire to run again for mayor. When he received no backing from either Governor Earl Long, a former ally, or the RDO, he withdrew from the mayoral race and retired from politics.

For the remainder of his life Maestri lived in the Roosevelt Hotel in New Orleans, managed his vast financial interests (his real estate holdings were reputedly the largest in the city), and occasionally engaged in quiet political maneuvering. Maestri died in the Crescent City, the source of his wealth and the seat of his political power.

[See "Robert S. Maestri," *Administrations of the Mayors of New Orleans, 1803–1936* (Typescript compiled and edited by the Works Progress Administration, New Orleans, 1940, New Orleans Public Library); Edward F. Haas, "New Orleans on the Half-Shell: The Maestri Era, 1936–1946," *Louisiana History* (Summer 1972), and *DeLesseps S. Morrison and the Image of Reform: New Orleans Politics, 1946–1961* (1974); and T. Harry Williams, *Huey Long* (1969). An obituary appears in the New Orleans *Times-Picayune*, May 7, 1974.]

EDWARD F. HAAS

MAIN, MARJORIE (Feb. 24, 1890–Apr. 10, 1975), actress, was born Mary Tomlinson near Acton, Ind., the daughter of Mary McGaughey and Samuel Joseph Tomlinson, a minister in the Church of Christ. She attended public school in Elkhart, Ind., and studied at Franklin College before enrolling in the Hamilton School of Dramatic Expression in Lexington, Ky. Although her father disapproved of the theater, he allowed Main to study at Hamilton because the school was endowed by the Church of Christ. She graduated from its three-year course in 1909. Some sources state that she studied acting in New York and Chicago briefly after attending Hamilton. Others suggest that she taught dramatics at Bourbon College in Paris, Ky., before practicing the craft herself.

Despite her parents' condemnation of the stage, they allowed Main to perform Shakespearean recitations on the Chautauqua circuit. Her first success came as Katherine in *The Taming of the Shrew*. While on the circuit, she met Stanley LeFevre Krebs, a psychologist who delivered Chautauqua lectures. He and Main were married Nov. 2, 1921; they had no children.

Main branched out into vaudeville touring but continued stage roles when possible, working for a while with a stock company in Fargo, N.Dak. Her first Broadway role was in *Cheating Cheaters* in 1916, supporting John Barrymore. She changed her name to Marjorie Main in order to avoid embarrassment for her parents, who had not relaxed their disapproval of the theater. Different versions of her biography attribute the name to a desire to appear ordinary ("There's a main street, main entrance, main event, main everything," she told Liza Wilson and David McClure for *Collier's*, Dec. 8, 1951) or to a love of Sinclair Lewis and his novel *Main Street*. Her husband is often given credit for inventing the name.

Main spent some years assisting her husband with his traveling lecture work. After his death in 1934 she threw herself back into acting, receiving her big break on Broadway playing Mrs. Martin (the killer's mother) in *Dead End* (1935). She left that role to play the overburdened, wisecracking Lucy, the Reno hotel maid, in Claire Boothe Luce's *The Women* (1936).

She had played minor roles in a few films in the early 1930's. Main's real Hollywood initiation came, however, when Samuel Goldwyn brought her to Hollywood to reprise her *Dead End* role in 1937. He also employed her to portray Barbara Stanwyck's mother in *Stella Dallas*. These film parts led to a number of others, including that of Lucy in the film version of *The Women* (1939). Metro-Goldwyn-Mayer (MGM), looking for a character actress to pair with Wallace Beery, signed her to the first of two seven-year contracts in 1940. She played opposite Beery (and received star billing) for the first time in *Wyoming* (1940), as a female blacksmith.

For the next fourteen years, Main was a staple of MGM comedies and dramas, usually portraying an eccentric woman of authority—a judge, a landlady, a frontier woman—or someone's mother. Her twangy voice and loping stride endeared her to audiences, who associated her with country practicality.

The role for which Main is perhaps best remembered was not at MGM, but on loan to Universal-International. In 1947, that studio filmed *The Egg and I*, based on the autobiographical book by Betty MacDonald. It starred Claudette Colbert and Fred MacMurray as a city couple who move to the country. The pair's neighbors, Ma and Pa Kettle, were portrayed by Main and Percy Kilbride. Despite their supporting status, the Kettles made a hit with preview audiences. The picture garnered Main an Academy Award nomination and made so much money for Universal that the studio decided to follow it up with a series of low-budget "Ma and Pa Kettle" films.

The Kettles, a poverty-stricken, slapstick farm couple with fifteen children, were particularly popular in the Midwest. According to press reports, Main composed much of her own dialogue as Ma Kettle, supervised her makeup, and chose her own costumes (as she had for many roles beginning with *Dead End*.) She told one reporter, "I have a feeling for costumes. I read a script, confer with the producer or director about what kind of woman it is, and then usually ask for the right to work out my own wardrobe. On the majority of my films I've done my own costumes, and for the Kettle series my motto was: 'If it's wrong, it's right.' "

Offscreen, Main cultivated the same sort of simplicity and eccentricity she often portrayed on screen. For years she claimed she rode the bus to work from her Hollywood home, although she eventually gave in and bought an automobile. She enjoyed gardening and made a point of eating healthily. She was known for her fastidiousness. She often wore gloves while dining in restaurants, and she showed up for filming with sprays and even gauze facial masks to ward off germs. A strong opposer of liquor, she seldom allowed the characters she portrayed to imbibe. A reporter for *Collier's* noted, "Her forthrightness in protecting her own interests has given her the reputation around Hollywood of being somewhat difficult."

Between appearances as Ma Kettle, Main continued to play character parts. She played Judy Garland's loving but assertive housekeeping in *Summer Stock* (1950), Fred Astaire's rich aunt in *The Belle of New York* (1952), an energetic hotelkeeper in *Rose Marie* (1954), and, memorably, a picturesque farmer in *Friendly Persuasion* (1956).

Percy Kilbride tired of "Ma and Pa Kettle" and left the series after *Ma and Pa Kettle at Waikiki* (1955). Universal attempted two more Kettle pictures after his retirement, but audiences failed to respond to them without Kilbride. The last, *The Kettles on Old Mac-Donald's Farm* (1957), barely broke even. It was Main's last film. She did television work but spent much of her remaining time at her desert home in Palm Springs, Calif. She died in Los Angeles.

[The Billy Rose Theatre Collection of the New York Public Library maintains clipping files on Main. She was profiled in the *New York Times*, Dec. 14, 1941. Her life and career are most closely examined in a profile by W. Franklyn Moshier in *Films in Review*, Feb. 1966. An obituary is in the *New York Times*, Apr. 11, 1975.]

TINKY ("DAKOTA") WEISBLAT

MANGRUM, LLOYD EUGENE (Aug. 1, 1914–Nov. 17, 1973), professional golfer, was born in Trenton, Tex., to James and Etta Mangrum. It was a golfing family, and Lloyd, with his older brother Ray, first played the game while working as a caddy at the Stevens Park municipal course. Unable to afford golf lessons, he later worked at Dallas's El Tivoli Country Club during the day as caddy master and assistant to pro Johnny Parnell, and at night as the club security officer. Mangrum learned the game from such luminaries as Ben Hogan, Byron Nelson, and Jimmy Demaret. In 1928, Lloyd and Ray went to California, where Lloyd caddied at the Lakeside and Los Angeles country clubs. The following year, Lloyd turned professional at the age of fifteen. In 1933, he played in his first Professional Golfers Association (PGA) tournament.

The 1930's began as lean years for the young professional, but toward the end of the decade he began to display the skills that would ultimately make him one of the period's greatest money winners. He won the Pennsylvania Open Championship in 1938 and in 1939 was runner-up in the Western Open. In 1940, he placed second to Jimmy Demaret in the Masters and sixth in the National Open Championship. Although he did not win on the tour until 1940, when he won the Thomasville Open, he amassed a total of 46 career victories, 36 of them in PGA tournaments. From 1934 through his retirement in 1962, Mangrum, in addition to his victories, had 28 second-place finishes, 43 thirds, 247 top-10 finishes, and 343 top-25 finishes.

World War II interrupted Mangrum's professional career. He was drafted in January 1944 and served as a staff sergeant in the Third Army. During the invasion of Normandy, his jeep overturned and his arm was broken in two places, and it looked as if he might never again play championship golf. Undaunted by that injury and by two shrapnel wounds to his chin and knee suffered in the Battle of the Bulge, Mangrum spent part of his convalescent period in St. Andrews, Scotland, where he won the British G.I. Championship. In 1945, with four battle stars and two Purple Hearts, Mangrum returned to the United States and rejoined the PGA Tour.

Prior to his military service, Mangrum showed signs of greatness; he was seventh on the money list in 1941, and he improved to fourth in 1942. The slender six-footer, who had a thin mustache and black hair, lost no time in reasserting himself on the tour. In 1946 he won his first and only major championship, the U.S. Open, played at Cleveland's Canterbury Golf Club. Mangrum had finished in a 72-hole tie at 284 strokes with Vic Ghezzi and Byron Nelson, and he defeated both of them in a 36-hole play-off. Mangrum's total of 428 strokes over 108 holes earned him a purse of $1,500, another $1,000 from the United States Golf Association, and a bonus of $5,000 from the Wilson Sporting Goods Company, which he represented. Additionally, Tam O'Shanter Country Club contracted Mangrum as its tour representative for an annual stipend of $10,000.

His greatest financial year on tour was 1948, when he won eight tournaments; his earnings of $45,898 were second only to those of Ben Hogan. In 1950 Mangrum came close to winning another major victory in the U.S. Open, but he lost in a playoff to Hogan.

Mangrum played on the U.S. Ryder Cup team in 1941, 1947, 1949, and 1951; he served as captain in 1953 and honorary captain in 1955.

In 1951, Mangrum was the PGA's leading money winner, and he twice won the Vardon Trophy—in 1951, with a stroke average of 70.05 for 104 rounds, and again in 1953, with a stroke average of 70.22.

Mangrum's instructional volume, Golf—A New Approach (1949), reveals the inspirations for the major components of his game: "I patterned my swing after Sam Snead's, my short shots after Johnny Revolta's, and my putting after Horton Smith's." This book was written in response to a challenge issued by Bing Crosby following Mangrum's victory in the 1948 Pebble Beach tournament, which Crosby sponsored. Crosby wrote the foreword to the volume.

Reputed to have been always of good humor, Mangrum was also noted for his strict adherence to the rules of golf, and for having at times penalized himself for infractions. He was honored by induction into the Citizens Savings Hall of Fame, the California Golf Hall of Fame, and the PGA Hall of Fame.

Mangrum suffered several heart attacks prior to his death in Apple Valley, Calif. He was survived by his wife Eleta and their three children.

Lloyd Mangrum was one of the pioneers of professional golf. When he turned professional, the sport was suffering during the Great Depression. Approximately one-third of all country clubs were converted to municipal or public fee courses, and prize money was not plentiful. Mangrum, along with Ben Hogan, Sam Snead, and Jimmy Demaret, was an integral part of the nucleus of outstanding players who initially made golf attractive, and whose impetus started the steady growth and prosperity of the tour. Although these men remain famous in the history of golf, they were not to reap the great financial benefits for which they were in large part responsible.

[Lloyd Mangrum's books include Golf—A New Approach (1949); How To Break 90 at Golf (1952); and How to Play Better Golf (1954). Further information can be found in Al Barkow, The History of the PGA Tour (1989). An obituary appears in the New York Times, Nov. 18, 1973.]

JIM CASTAÑEDA

MARCH, FREDRIC (Aug. 31, 1897–Apr. 14, 1975), actor, was christened Frederick McIntyre Bickel, the youngest of four children born to John F. Bickel, a successful Racine, Wis., manufacturer, and "pillar in the Presbyterian Church," and Cora Brown Marcher.

March remembered his family as "a conservative crew" who knew "the value of money." The youngster was "completely indistinguishable from any other boy in town" apart from an overripe love of reciting at church bazaars and school entertainments. "I was ungodly stuck up about it," he recalled. March staged performances in the family barn and finished with a flourish, sliding down a shoot in his wagon.

Outgoing and popular, March was president of his grammar school and high school class, finished third in a state oratorical contest while only a sophomore, and won the following year. March went regularly to the theater, saw Maude Adams play Peter Pan, but decided to take his older brother's advice and major in economics at the University of Wisconsin. He took up debate and amateur dramatics, managed the football team, was a member of the track team and was elected president of the senior class in the School of Commerce. When the United States entered World War I, he enlisted in the army, went to Officers Candidate School and, at twenty years of age, became a lieutenant in the artillery. Discharged in February 1919, he returned to Wisconsin torn between choosing a career in banking or acting.

March received a scholarship from the National City Bank in New York City to train for work in their overseas branch. But the program was suddenly suspended after March arrived in New York and left him a bored bank clerk. While recuperating from appendix surgery, March "devoured books on the history of the theatre" and decided on a career in acting "without the faintest idea of how to go about it." He had several cheap pictures made, peddled them at agents' offices and prepared for a career as "a great Shakespearean actor." Instead, he began as a $7.50-per-day extra for Paramount Studios in *Paying the Piper*. He "staved off starvation" in 1920 by appearing in mob scenes for several more Paramount productions, including the *The Devil*, starring George Arliss, *The Great Adventure* with Lionel Barrymore, and *The Education of Elizabeth*, a vehicle for Billie Burke.

March eagerly promoted himself to D. W. Griffith as a double and stand-in for Richard Barthelmess to no avail. But his good looks won him jobs with commercial artists "immortalizing cravats, shoes and shaving-cream." Rejected as a super for David Belasco's stage production of *Deburau*, he was later hired for the bit part of Victor Hugo. The play opened at the Belasco Theatre on Dec. 23, 1920, and March's only line was "the rope gave way and I can't think why; it had no extra strain." The energetic thespian was also made third assistant stage manager and understudy. The night he replaced a principal in the cast was the most gratifying experience of his 56-year career.

His "unconscious cheek" got him a job in the off-Broadway production of George M. Cohan's *The County Chairman* and a road company production of *Shavings* before he returned to Broadway for a minor part in Al Jolson's production of *Lei Aloha*. His first break came when *The Law Breaker* opened at New York's Booth Theatre on Feb. 1, 1922. Alexander Woollcott thought the young Bickel showed genuine promise. Percy Hammond of the *New York Herald Tribune* found Bickel's performance as the troubled son of a banker "remarkably unaffected." Under the sensitive direction of lifelong friend, John Cromwell, March thought he had arrived. However, seven long years of acting apprenticeship would follow. On New Year's Eve, Bickel took Cromwell's advice and changed his stage name to Fredric March, a shortened version of his mother's maiden name. He signed a personal contract with Cromwell "respecting his judgment and guidance."

March married actress Ellis Baker, niece of character actor Edward Ellis, sometime after January 1924. They were divorced in 1927.

While doing summer stock at the Elitch Gardens Theatre in Denver, March fell in love with Brooklyn-born Florence Eldridge, the leading lady of the company. They were married on May 30, 1927, and immediately embarked on a road tour with the Theatre Guild Repertory Company. The 132-city tour in "barns, gyms and saloons" helped perfect March's technique. It led to his portrayal of Tony Cavendish, a takeoff on John Barrymore, in *The Royal Family*, a play staged at the El Capitan Theatre in Los Angeles. The performance won March a five-year contract with Paramount and meant "Florence and I could live simply and quietly in one place for awhile."

March made twenty-nine films at Paramount and while on loan to other studios over the next five years. Most of the movies were so bad "it made us all miss the theatre." The first was *The Dummy*, one of Paramount's first talking pictures, released on Mar. 3, 1929, with March and Cromwell in support of Ruth Chatterton and child actor Mickey Bennett. March's resonant voice played well to the primitive microphone of early talkies and quickly made him Paramount's most versatile performer. He costarred with silent screen star Clara Bow, the "It" girl, in her first talkie, *The Wild Party*. Paramount's playbill chimed, "You've had an eyeful of 'it,' now get an earful," but *Variety* found it was March who "vocally reigned supreme." March's next film at Paramount, *The Studio Murder Mystery*, was also Eldridge's first film in Hollywood. *Jealousy* with Jeanne Eagles was the fifth of seven films he made in 1929 alone.

Laughter, the seventh film March made in 1930, was one of his favorites. A fine script by Donald Ogden Stewart, deftly played by March, Nancy Carroll, and Frank Morgan, was both a critical and a box office success. The actor's next film, *The Royal Family of Broadway*, allowed March to re-create the Barrymore role and led to his first of five Oscar nominations. He would win an Academy Award the following year for his double role in *Dr. Jekyll and Mr. Hyde*. The part gave March an opportunity to break from Paramount publicity, which was grooming him as "the next John Gilbert." Critics were uniform in praising March's "triumph of realized nightmare."

March wearied under the inferior material his contract forced on him. He and Florence became respected members of the Hollywood community, known for their unaffected geniality and quiet dignity. The couple adopted two children. March's happiest screen projects came opposite Norma Shearer at Metro-Goldwyn-Mayer in *Smilin' Through* (1932) and *The Barretts of Wimpole Street* (1934). March began free-lancing when his studio contract expired, leading to wise choices in *Les Misérables* (1935) and *Anna Karenina* (1935) but ponderous ones in *Mary of Scotland* (1936), costarring Eldridge, and *Anthony Adverse* (1936). March received $125,000 per picture in a two-picture deal with Selznick-International in 1937. Both *A Star Is Born* with Janet Gaynor and *Nothing Sacred* opposite Carole Lombard were huge critical and box office successes. March's third Oscar nomination for the role of Norman Maine in *A Star Is Born* helped place him in the first rank of Hollywood stars.

March, now Hollywood's highest paid performer, returned to Broadway in 1938 to costar with his wife in *Yr. Obedient Husband*, staged by Cromwell. It proved a serious career misjudgment. The play closed after only a week and March's subsequent screen work failed to restore his preeminence as a box office attraction. *Trade Winds* (1939); *Susan and God* (1940), opposite Joan Crawford; *One Foot in Heaven* (1941); and *I Married a Witch* (1942) brought March into middle age and presumably past his peak.

March's contribution to anti-fascist causes led to an investigation by the House Un-American Activities Committee. The committee concluded that out of "humanitarian impulses" March had permitted his name to be used by organizations backed by Communists. March's war years were spent traveling 33,000 miles entertaining American troops abroad. He also commuted between Hollywood and Broadway, appearing with his wife in three plays, *The American Way* (1939), *Hope for a Harvest* (1941), and Thornton Wilder's *The Skin of Our Teeth* (1942). His best-known film of the period was *The Adventures of Mark Twain* (1944).

March's Oscar for his stunning portrayal of a war-weary veteran in *The Best Years of Our Lives* (1946) led to a series of indifferent roles, including *Christopher Columbus* (1949), "a lifeless tableau" that helped demonstrate that March's name on the marquee was not enough to ensure a film's success. March had turned down the role of Willy Loman before *Death of a Salesman* opened on Broadway, but played the coveted part in the 1951 film. It led to mixed reviews and his fifth Oscar nomination. March received starring billing but played supporting roles in *Executive Suite* (1954) and *The Bridges at Toko-Ri* (1955). *The Desperate Hours* (1955), opposite Humphrey Bogart, was a critical success but a box office failure. His performance in Eugene O'Neill's *Long Day's Journey Into Night*, opposite Eldridge, was the sensation of Broadway's 1956 season and earned March the New York Critics Awards and a Tony.

March's work in the 1960's and 1970's was distinguished, if less frequent. He and Eldridge costarred with longtime friend Spencer Tracy in *Inherit the Wind* (1960) and March was more than a match for Burt Lancaster and Kirk Douglas in *Seven Days in May* (1964), Paul Newman in *Hombre* (1967), and Lee Marvin in *The Iceman Cometh* (1973). March cultivated his garden and read during years of semiretirement with Florence at their forty-acre farm near New Milford, Conn. A year before his death they sold the farm and moved into a condominium in Los Angeles.

Fredric March's death in Los Angeles marked the passing of a towering figure in the history of Hollywood and the American stage. Few actors could match March's protean range and versatility. Critics fondly remembered the "intelligence and integrity" of his greatest performances, an acting style as "direct and unaffected" as any seen on the screen. March modestly considered himself "just a ham" whose acting betrayed a childlike interest in the world. Younger actors continue to venerate his consummate and unsurpassed craftsmanship. Years after his death, film and theatergoers continue to affirm March's place as one of the most gifted and beloved actors of his generation.

[March's papers, the source of many of the quotations in this article, are at the State Historical Society of Wisconsin in Madison, Wis. Many of his film scripts, with annotations in March's handwriting, are included in the collection. Biographic materials can also be found at New York Public Library's Theater and Film Collection and at the Library and Museum of the Performing Arts at Lincoln Center in New York City. Biographies include Michael Burrows, *Charles Laughton and Fredric March* (1969); and Lawrence J. Quirk, *The Films of Fredric March* (1971). See also Richard Schickel, *The Stars: The*

Personalities Who Made the Movies (1962); David Shipman, *The Great Movie Stars* (1970); and Leslie Halliwell, *The Filmgoer's Companion* (1974). Obituaries appear in the *New York Times*, Apr. 15, 1975, and in the Apr. 28, 1975, issues of *Time* and *Newsweek*.]

BRUCE J. EVENSEN

MAXWELL, MARVEL MARILYN (Aug. 3, 1920–Mar. 20, 1972), singer and actress, was born in Clarinda, Iowa, the daughter of Hal Maxwell, an insurance salesman, and Anna Tomlinson. Christened Marvel Marilyn Maxwell, she dropped her first name early in her career. Entertainment sources erroneously cite her year of birth as 1921 or 1922. Her mother, a piano accompanist for dancer Ruth St. Denis, put her daughter on the entertainment career path early. At age three, Maxwell performed a butterfly dance at the Brandeis Theatre in Omaha, Nebr., under the auspices of Ruth St. Denis. When her parents divorced in 1926, she lived with her mother and completed her early education in Clarinda.

In 1935, she moved with her mother to Fort Wayne, Ind., where her older brother owned a radio station. This was to be a pivotal move for her as she was able to persuade her brother to let her sing on a broadcast. The station's bandleader, Amos Astot, then hired her to be a vocalist for his band for $35 per week while she was still in high school. She dropped out of school after Buddy Rogers signed her to sing with his orchestra in New York City in late 1937. She went to California on tour with Rogers in May 1938.

In 1939, after moving to the Hollywood, Calif., area, Maxwell joined Ted Weems's All-American Band and helped contribute to its popularity, sharing the singing with Perry Como and Mary Lee on radio and recordings. The band performed on the radio with Jack Benny, "Hildegarde's 'Beat the Band' Show," "The Fibber McGee and Molly Show," and other musical/variety shows. Weems encouraged Maxwell to study dramatic acting at the Pasadena Playhouse. She continued singing on radio while she studied and had screen tests. It was during this time that she dyed her dark brown hair blond. Even after she left the band for acting, she continued singing on radio and in nightclubs, notably with Frank Sinatra.

Metro-Goldwyn-Mayer offered her a contract in 1941, and in 1942 she made her film debut in *Stand By for Action*, a military action drama starring Robert Taylor. Her contract film credits include *Salute to the Marines* (1943); *Du Barry Was a Lady* (1943); *Presenting Lily Mars* (1943); *Swing Fever* (1943); *Thousands Cheer* (1943); *Pilot Number Five* (1943); *Best Foot Forward* (1943); *Lost in a Harem* (1944); *Between Two Women* (1945); *The Show Off* (1946); *High Barbaree* (1947); *Summer Holiday* (1948); *Race Street* (1948); and *Champion* (1949). She also appeared in roles on- and off-Broadway, in nightclubs, and in several "Dr. Gillespie" medical sagas with Lionel Barrymore and Van Johnson. Her MGM contract ended in 1950 with *Key to the City*.

Maxwell's roles during this period generally characterized her as the beautiful, voluptuous blonde. Bosley Crowther, movie critic for the *New York Times*, referred to her as "a routine blonde warbler" in *Swing Fever*. In 1948 she won his critical praise as Belle in *Summer Holiday* when she dressed in scarlet, sang "Weary Blues," and tried to seduce Mickey Rooney. Crowther called her "pictorial and sensuous." While the 1948 movie *Champion* won acclaim for its star, Kirk Douglas, as well as an Academy Award for its editing staff, Maxwell's role as Grace Diamond was noted as simply an "attractive addition to the cast." In her last contract film, *Key to the City*, Crowther found her "lushly attractive as the bubble dancer who inhabits convention hotels."

Beginning in the 1940's, Maxwell went on tour with Bob Hope, entertaining American servicemen during the Korean War. She was the first American female entertainer to join Hope on his tours in Korea. Her trademark song, "I Want to Love You," was frequently requested. Her association with Hope helped her land roles in his films with Paramount. In 1951, she costarred with him in *The Lemon Drop Kid* and in 1953 in *Off Limits*.

After 1953, her roles in films became more sporadic as she made the transition to television and nightclub acts. She was signed to the series "Bus Stop" in 1961 as Gracie, the proprietress of a roadside café. She left after only thirteen episodes because of disputes over her character's development.

In addition to episode roles on television drama, she put in many guest appearances on game and variety shows, including Red Skelton and Bob Hope specials. Her last television appearance was as an aging stripper in an episode of "O'Hara, U.S. Treasury" on Oct. 22, 1971. The role was ironic, for Maxwell had actually worked as a stripper in Queens, N.Y., in 1967.

Maxwell married actor John Conte in 1944; they divorced in 1946. On Jan. 1, 1950, she married Anders ("Andy") McIntyre, a restaurant owner of Beverly Hills. They divorced on Mar. 22, 1951. On Nov. 21, 1954, she married Warner Brothers writer-producer Jerome L. Davis; they had one child, and that marriage too ended in divorce on Dec. 21, 1960.

Maxwell, like so many actresses during the 1940's, remained an "almost big" star. She enjoyed a measure of success with her films, and was very popular and well liked in the Hollywood social scene. After her death in her Beverly Hills home, Bob Hope helped establish the Marilyn Maxwell Scholarship Fund through the Young Musicians Foundation, an organization to which she had devoted much time in the last few years of her life.

[Memorabilia and a clipping file on Maxwell are in the Nottaway Valley Historical Museum in Clarinda, Iowa. See also Cleveland Amory, ed., *International Celebrity Register*, U.S. ed. (1959); Paul Michael, ed., *The American Movies Reference Book: The Sound Era* (1969); James R. Parish and Ronald L. Bowers, *The MGM Stock Company: The Golden Era* (1973); Ephraim Katz, *The Film Encyclopedia* (1979); Clive Hirschhorn, *The Hollywood Musical* (1981); James R. Parish and Vincent Terrace, *The Complete Actors' Television Credits, 1948–1988*, 2d ed., II (1990); and David Quinlan, *Quinlan's Illustrated Registry of Film Stars* (1991). Obituaries are in the *New York Times*, Mar. 21, 1972; *Variety*, Mar. 22, 1972; *Newsweek*, Apr. 3, 1972; and *Time*, Apr. 3, 1972.]

PATRICIA PALMER

MAYER, MARIA GOEPPERT (June 28, 1906–Feb. 20, 1972), Nobel laureate physicist, was born in Kattowitz, Upper Silesia (now Katowice, Poland), the only child of Friedrich Goeppert, a professor of pediatrics at Georgia Augusta University in Göttingen, and Maria Wolff. Her father actively encouraged his daughter to develop her scientific curiosity. Mayer attended public school and a private preparatory school for girls before entering Georgia Augusta University in 1924 to study mathematics.

She switched from mathematics to physics under the influence of her first course in quantum mechanics, taught by one of the chief theorists of the subject, Max Born. Mayer developed a close relationship with Born, under whom she took her doctoral degree, and with whom she shared a preference for a strictly mathematical style of physics. Born later described Mayer as one of his most talented students. The thrust of her doctoral dissertation (1930) extended Paul A. M. Dirac's theory of radiation and matter to the case of two-photon processes, using second-order time-dependent perturbation theory.

While completing her work at Georgia Augusta, she met Joseph Edward Mayer, an American chemist who completed studies with Gilbert Newton Lewis at the University of California at Berkeley. After their marriage in January 1930, the Mayers moved to Baltimore, where Joseph Mayer accepted an associated professorship of chemistry at Johns Hopkins University. Maria Mayer became an American citizen in 1933. The Mayers had two children.

For the first thirty years of Maria Mayer's career, she had no regular paid appointment. Most of her research during the years 1930–1939 (at Johns Hopkins) was in chemical physics and physical chemistry. During this period, Mayer collaborated with her husband on several papers concerning the application of quantum mechanics to chemistry. This work gave Mayer a greater appreciation for the role of experimental data in the formulation of physical theory and taught her to apply her theoretical talents to a variety of specific experimental results.

Mayer also worked with Alfred Lee Sklar, a student of her colleague Karl Herzfeld, on calculating the energy levels of a complex molecule, benzene, from strictly theoretical principles; this pioneering work established her reputation as a specialist in the analysis of the spectra of complex systems. Mayer and her husband, in their final years at Johns Hopkins, completed the textbook *Statistical Mechanics* (1940), which became one of the standard texts. It had ten printings by 1963; in 1977 a second edition was published.

The Mayers moved to New York City in 1939, when Joseph Mayer took a position in the chemistry department at Columbia University. Maria Mayer gave occasional lectures in the same department (1939–1945) and took over Enrico Fermi's physics class in 1941 when he became involved in nuclear fission research in what would later become the Manhattan

Project. After the start of World War II, Mayer joined Harold Urey's group, the Substitute Alloy Materials Laboratory (SAM), which was working on the difficulties of isotope separation for the Manhattan Project. Mayer made significant contributions toward the theory of both photochemical and chemical separation before beginning work on gaseous diffusion, the method eventually used.

In 1945 the Mayers accepted posts at the University of Chicago, where she became voluntary associate professor. They both joined the new Institute for Nuclear Studies, and Maria Mayer also held a half-time position as a research physicist in the theoretical division of the new Argonne National Laboratory. Lacking a comprehensive background in nuclear physics, she developed her knowledge of the field through discussions with colleagues. Her lack of familiarity with many traditional beliefs proved to be an advantage and led to her most famous contribution to physics.

In 1945, Niels Bohr's compound-nucleus interpretation of nuclear reactions and the assumption that the nucleus behaves like a liquid drop prevailed, but early in 1947, Mayer found evidence that nuclei in some instances behave as collections of discrete particles. She noticed that nuclei with 2, 8, 20, 50, or 82 neutrons or protons or with 126 neutrons were particularly abundant and therefore unusually stable. This phenomenon could not be explained by the liquid-drop model.

Mayer interpreted these "magic numbers," as she called them, as providing evidence that individual nucleons have individual values of energy and angular momentum and that they can be viewed as occupying different energy levels, or "shells," like electrons in an atom. Quantum mechanics could not predict the magic numbers above twenty. Two years later, as a result of a suggestion by Fermi, Mayer realized that the answer lay in an effect called "spin-orbit coupling," in which the intrinsic spin of each nucleon, when coupled with its orbital angular momentum, can affect its total binding energy enough to move some nucleons into the next energy level. Mayer first published the theory of the nuclear shell model in 1949.

Mayer's shell model was of great value to experimental nuclear physicists because it could account for many values of nuclear spin and magnetic moment. The model was accepted readily by physicists who had previously believed that discrete particles could not exist in the nucleus, in part because the shell model was also proposed simultaneously and independently by Otto Haxel, J. Hans D. Jensen, and Hans Suess in Germany. Mayer and Jensen subsequently collaborated on various theoretical aspects of the shell model, culminating in the publication of *Elementary Theory of Nuclear Shell Structure* (1955).

Mayer continued her work at the University of Chicago and Argonne Laboratory until 1960. In 1959, the University of California at San Diego offered both Mayers full paid professorships and they moved to La Jolla, near San Diego, the following year. Within weeks of their arrival, Mayer suffered a stroke. Although she continued to work, she never recovered her health, channeling her diminished energies into teaching. She died in La Jolla.

Mayer's work is remarkable in that her early theories, although mathematically derived, had a strong physical basis and in several cases foreshadowed later discoveries. Her early work served as a solid theoretical basis for subsequent developments in laser spectroscopy, double-beta decay, the theory of rare-earth elements, and photochemical isotope separation. In 1963, Mayer received the Nobel Prize for physics for her work with Jensen on the nuclear shell model.

[Mayer's papers and correspondence, along with those of her husband, are deposited in the Special Collections of Mandeville Library, University of California at San Diego. The transcript of an interview by T. S. Kuhn (1962) can be found in the Archive for the History of Quantum Physics.

Biographical information and a bibliography of Mayer's published work is in Robert G. Sachs, "Maria Goeppert Mayer," *Biographical Memoirs. National Academy of Sciences* (1979). See also Joan Dash, A *Life of One's Own* (1973). For discussion of Mayer's scientific work, see "Maria Goeppert Mayer," *Physics Today* 39 (1986); and "Mayer, Maria Goeppert," *Dictionary of Scientific Biography*, suppl. 2 (1990). An obituary appears in the *New York Times*, Feb. 22, 1972.]

KAREN E. JOHNSON

MEDWICK, JOSEPH ("DUCKY") MICHAEL (Nov. 24, 1911–Mar. 21, 1975), baseball player, was born in Carteret, N.J., the son of Elizabeth and John Medwick. His parents were born and married in Hungary, and his father was a sawmill worker. Medwick graduated from Carteret High School in 1930. He participated in several sports, but he showed great promise in baseball. He had offers for athletic scholarships from twenty-one colleges.

Scouted by Pop Kelchner of the St. Louis Cardinals, he was signed by that National League team. Medwick began his career in the Middle Atlantic League in 1930. He played under the name of Mickey King, wishing to preserve his amateur status because he hoped to play football at Notre Dame. After a successful season at Scottsdale, Pa., Medwick decided to concentrate on baseball.

Medwick was sent up to the Texas League the next year, and while in Houston, he had a candy bar named after him. Also, he was given the nickname of "Ducky," which he always hated, preferring "Muscles" or "Mickey," his name from childhood. In a 139-game season in Houston, Medwick hit 26 home runs and had 111 runs batted in. His popularity in Houston was demonstrated when he was chosen to throw out the first ball at the first all-star game ever held in the Houston Astrodome in 1968.

Medwick joined the National League Cardinals in 1932 and played in their last twenty-six games that season. The following year, he became the regular left fielder for the team and joined a rowdy bunch that came to be called "the Gashouse Gang." Medwick was a fierce competitor who hated to strike out or take a base on balls and became adept at hitting bad pitches. A contemporary described his hitting as "like a man fighting with bumblebees." In his career he averaged only 36 walks and 30 strikeouts per year. His ferocity off the field was well known too, and he occasionally fought with teammates. Some referred to him as the "hot-tempered Hungarian." Baseball historian Bill James called Medwick "the most aggressive physical player of his time." He also belonged to a jug band called the Mudcatters, which included teammates Pepper Martin and the Dean brothers.

In his first complete season with the Cardinals, Medwick hit .306, and he continued to reach the .300 mark for the next ten seasons. He committed only 7 errors that year, which became his career average.

The Cardinals reached the World Series in 1934, and Medwick scored 110 runs and had 106 runs batted in. He led the league in triples and had his second year (of seven) with 40 or more doubles. In the last game of the Series,

Medwick caused a riot. He got into a fight in the sixth inning after a hard slide into the Tigers third baseman. Then, when he returned to his position in the outfield, the fans at Navin Field hurled newspapers, scorecards, fruit, and bottles at him for a half hour. Finally, Medwick was ordered out of the game after a conference with the commissioner of baseball, Judge Kenesaw Mountain Landis. It is the only time a player has been thrown out of a World Series game for fighting. The next year, Medwick scored 132 runs and led the league with 126 runs batted in.

On Aug. 24, 1936, Medwick married Isabelle Heutel; they had two children. In that year, Medwick hit a record-setting 64 doubles. He had hits on ten consecutive at-bats between July 19 and 21. He led the league in runs batted in that year and the following two. Only Rogers Hornsby had ever accomplished that feat before.

In 1937, Medwick hit a career high of .374 and led most other offensive categories as well. He led the league in fielding percentage, making only four errors, and he was named the most valuable player. He was the last National League player to win the Triple Crown.

In 1938, Medwick held out successfully for a $20,000 contract and then went on to lead the league in doubles and in runs batted in. He hit .322. That year, his friend and manager Frankie Frisch was fired. In 1939, his last full season with the St. Louis Cardinals, Medwick had over 200 hits for the fourth and last time.

In 1940, Medwick was hitting .304 through thirty-seven games, but the Cardinals traded him on June 12 to the Brooklyn Dodgers for $200,000 and four players. The Cardinals management often traded players it believed were past their peak. Less than a week after the trade, he was struck in the head by a pitch from Bob Bowman, his former teammate, and knocked unconscious. In just four days Medwick was playing again. It has been said he was a more timid hitter after that incident. Yet he hit .305 in the years following the beaning and averaged 44 doubles and 113 runs batted in. He also never struck out more than 36 times after 1940. The beaning incident and the beaning of young shortstop Pee Wee Reese led to the use of an insert in batting caps that eventually evolved into the batting helmet.

In 1941, the Dodgers went to the World Series. Medwick's power declined that year, but he was fifth in the league in batting. In July 1943, Medwick's contract was sold to the Giants. His batting average that year was .278. In 1944 his average rose to .337, behind only Dixie Walker and Stan Musial, and he had 165 hits and 85 runs batted in. In 1945 he was traded to the Boston Braves, who released him before spring training in 1946. He was also dismissed by the St. Louis Browns after a brief tryout. He signed with the Dodgers on June 28 and hit over .300 in 77 at-bats.

After an episode in 1947 when he was signed by the New York Yankees and released in spring training, Medwick finished his major-league career with the Cardinals, averaging .332 in his last three years in major-league baseball. He finished his career in the minor leagues as a player and a player-manager. His last season was 1952.

Medwick lived in St. Louis and ran his own insurance firm. He loved golf and was proud of the many trophies he won playing that game. He was appointed assistant baseball coach at St. Louis University and tutored there from 1961 to 1965. In 1968, he was appointed hitting instructor for the nine Cardinal minor-league teams.

In the opinions of Ted Williams and Pie Traynor, Medwick was the second-greatest right-handed hitter who ever played the game, trailing only Rogers Hornsby. Medwick was anything but polite to the baseball writers who cast the votes for the Hall of Fame. Consequently, he waited fifteen years until his induction on July 22, 1968. Baseball historian Bill James ranked him as the seventh-best left fielder who ever played. Medwick averaged 202 hits per season and had a .324 lifetime batting average. He died in St. Petersburg, Fla.

[Newspaper clippings relating to Medwick's career are at the library of the National Baseball Hall of Fame in Cooperstown, N.Y. For statistics, see Bill James, *The Bill James Historical Baseball Abstract* (1985); and *The Baseball Encyclopedia* (1987). See also Leo Durocher, *Nice Guys Finish Last* (1975); Martin Appel and Burt Goldblatt, *Baseball's Best* (1980); and Robert W. Creamer, *Baseball in '41* (1991). An obituary is in the *New York Times*, Mar. 22, 1975.]

THOMAS H. BARTHEL

MELCHIOR, LAURITZ LEBRECHT HOMMEL (Mar. 20, 1890–Mar. 18, 1973), operatic tenor, was born in Copenhagen, Denmark, the son of Jørgen Conradt Melchior, a schoolmaster, and Julie Sofie Møller, who died a month after his birth. After some ten years at the Melchior School, a family institution, he began private vocal studies at age eighteen, and then entered the Royal Opera School, Copenhagen, where he made his debut in the baritone role of Silvio in *Pagliacci* on Apr. 2, 1913. After several years in baritone roles with this company, Melchior began to study as a tenor on the advice of the distinguished contralto Mme Charles Cahier, who had noted the brilliance of his upper register. After a year with Vilhelm Herold, Melchior made his tenor debut as Tannhäuser at the Royal Opera in Copenhagen on Oct. 8, 1918, then sang in Oslo and London, where he came to the attention of the British author Hugh Walpole, whose financial and moral backing was an enormous help to Melchior in launching an international career.

In the period 1922–1923, Melchior created the foundation of a Wagnerian repertoire with Anna Bahr-Mildenburg, for it was increasingly apparent that his voice was that of a Wagnerian heldentenor. An audition for Wagner's widow Cosima and their son Siegfried led to a Bayreuth engagement in 1924; on the strength of this he was asked to sing in the first postwar German season at Covent Garden (Siegmund in *Die Walküre* on May 14, 1924, under Bruno Walter) with Frida Leider, Lotte Lehmann, and Maria Olczewska. At Bayreuth that July, he sang the roles of Parsifal and Siegmund, successes that led to guest appearances in Berlin and Prague.

In January 1926, Melchior sailed to America and made his New York City debut at the Metropolitan Opera on February 17 as Tannhäuser. His New York season was a success, although he was not received with the wild enthusiasm that marked his later American performances. Melchior spent the following season in Hamburg, on sabbatical from the Metropolitan. Ample rehearsals enabled him to polish the roles he already knew and to learn new ones—Lohengrin and two Verdi dramatic parts, Radames in *Aïda* and the title role in *Otello*. His solid success as *the* Wagnerian heldentenor in New York came with his Tristan in 1929. From then on, his career moved in a steadily ascending curve.

With the increasing influence of the Nazis in the early 1930's, Melchior severed his connections with Bayreuth and other German opera houses. He accepted additional engagements in

Paris, Brussels, Buenos Aires, London, and New York; Giulio Gatti-Casazza of the Metropolitan, however, refused his pleas to sing the greatest of Italian dramatic roles—Otello—and restricted him to the Wagnerian repertory. In those roles he was fortunate to be partnered over almost twenty years by three of the greatest dramatic sopranos of the century—Frida Leider, Kristen Flagstad, and Helen Traubel, all great singers and great artists, who stimulated Melchior's developing powers to even greater achievements. In these years, particularly the 1930's, the Metropolitan's German wing was preeminent in the world, with a roster of Wagnerian singers that no other opera house could equal. Wagner was the mainstay of the house's income, and Melchior and Flagstad were a "draw" comparable to Enrico Caruso and Geraldine Farrar a generation earlier.

For a German-oriented singer, World War II brought inevitable shocks and dislocations. While the Metropolitan Opera did not, as in World War I, discontinue presenting German operas, there were inevitable changes: valued colleagues were no longer available; the Melchiors lost an estate near Berlin; and Europe became increasingly remote and inaccessible. Melchior became an American citizen, though he waited until June 1947 for formal naturalization. New and talented artists like Helen Traubel, Astrid Varnay, Alexander Kipnis, and Herbert Janssen joined Melchior at the Metropolitan. He continued to sing, with little apparent wear, the most difficult roles of the operatic repertoire.

Melchior's career at the Metropolitan continued until 1950, when he sang his final performance, as Lohengrin, on February 2, after a difference with the incoming general manager, Rudolf Bing. Melchior had already begun to change his focus, making increasing numbers of radio appearances and such frothy films as *Thrill of a Romance* (1945) and *Luxury Liner* (1948). Probably the underlying reason that he and Bing were unable to reconcile their differences was the note of frivolity and clowning that increasingly crept into Melchior's nonoperatic work. Though many of his last years' performances were in nightclubs, he retained enough voice to sing Siegmund in act 1 of *Die Walküre* in March 1960 to celebrate his seventieth birthday.

Melchior was married three times, first to Inger Holst-Rasmussen on Nov. 2, 1913; they

had two children. They were divorced in 1925, and on May 26 of that year he married Maria Hacker, a German film actress who until her death in February 1963 did much to advance Melchior's career. Her acute supervision of fees and engagements was profitable, and she promoted Melchior in the American consciousness not as an austere and remote figure in Wagnerian music-drama but as the lovable, roly-poly "Great Dane" of his later career in radio, films, and nightclubs. In 1964, Melchior married his former secretary, Mary Markham; they were divorced in February 1965. He died in Santa Monica, Calif.

A great vocal technician, Melchior had mastered—more successfully than any dramatic tenor of the century—the art of moving from a solid baritonal sound through the difficult register transition into an upper range of unparalleled brilliance and power. This accomplishment was coupled with a lovely legato line, and his work was eminently qualified for the much overused and rarely deserved accolade of bel canto. He displayed occasional rhythmic inexactness, and he was notorious for avoiding rehearsals, but his status as a great vocal artist is documented by a recorded legacy of enormous scope and value.

Melchior's first records were made in his very early baritone years, before World War I; he continued to record prolifically as a tenor for German companies in the 1920's, for EMI–His Master's Voice and RCA-Victor in the 1930's, and for Columbia and MGM in the 1940's and 1950's. Amazingly, in the era of 78-rpm records, when a side was played in four minutes, he recorded Siegmund in *Die Walküre* and most of Siegfried in the later *Ring* operas at a time when these were herculean undertakings. There are generous representations of most of his other roles as well. The Melchior voice is solidly represented in a discography that proves him to have been the heldentenor of the century, possibly of all time.

[The largest collection of Melchior material is at Dana College, Blair, Nebr., which maintains a Melchior Museum. The most informative work on Melchior is the authorized biography by Shirlee Emmons, *Tristanissimo* (1990). Comments on Melchior's voice and art are in Irving Kolodin, *The Story of the Metropolitan Opera, 1883–1950* (1953); J. B. Steane, *The Grand Tradition* (1974); and Paul Jackson, *Saturday Afternoons at the Old Met* (1992). His performances during his long New York career were extensively reviewed in the press; appreciations in the *New York Times*, Mar. 25, 1973, and Feb. 24, 1974, are especially valuable. An obituary is in the *New York Times*, Mar. 19, 1973.]

THOMAS FURCRON

MESTA, PERLE REID SKIRVIN (Oct. 12, 1889–Mar. 16, 1975), political hostess, diplomat, and advocate of women's rights, was born in Sturgis, Mich., the daughter of Harriet Elizabeth Reid and William Balser Skirvin, a successful oil prospector, real estate investor, and hotel owner. (Mesta changed the spelling of her first name from "Pearl" to "Perle" in the 1920's, a change that was made legal in 1944.) Her elementary and secondary education took place in private schools in Galveston, Tex., where the Skirvins were residing. In 1906 the family moved to Oklahoma City, Okla., where, in 1911, William Skirvin built the luxury Skirvin Hotel that afterward served as the family's home. Aspiring to a career in music, Mesta studied voice and piano at the Sherwood School of Music in Chicago. In 1915, seeking work as a "dramatic soprano," she moved to New York City. There, on Feb. 12, 1917, she married George Mesta, a wealthy Pittsburgh steel-machinery manufacturer who was more than fifteen years her senior; they had no children. The Mestas made their home in Pittsburgh but traveled extensively, especially to Washington, D.C., where George Mesta was a steel consultant during World War I, and later to Europe, where he had business interests. In Washington, Mesta met current and future national leaders as well as the foremost political hostesses of the day, contacts that would have an influence on her political-social role in later years.

In 1925, George Mesta died, bequeathing to his wife the bulk of his fortune, primarily stock in the Mesta Machine Company. She became a director of the company and gradually learned the business. Since she was not actively involved in running the company, Mesta moved to Washington, D.C. During the next ten years, she also had residences at different times in Boston, New York City, and Newport, R.I., where she dedicated her time to musical and social interests, and to her beloved niece and nephews.

Although Mesta showed an occasional interest in politics in the 1920's, such as serving as state chairman of a 1928 presidential campaign organization called the Hoover-Curtis Junior League, she did not exhibit a sustained involvement in political issues and candidates until almost a decade later. In 1936, having maintained connections to Oklahoma through her frequent trips home, she helped organize the Oklahoma State Council of Republican Women for Alfred M. Landon's presidential candidacy. She also attended the Republican National Convention, where she found herself "suddenly filled with the political fever." In 1937, she was an Oklahoma representative to the Republican National Policy Committee. Mesta also joined the National Woman's Party (NWP) in 1938, becoming an advocate of the Equal Rights Amendment (ERA) and a member of the NWP's executive council and its public relations committee. That same year, she also helped organize the World Woman's Party and served as the international publicity chairman for the organization's first meeting in Geneva, Switzerland, in 1939. In 1940, Mesta continued her lobbying efforts for the ERA at the Republican National Convention, and she has been credited with getting the plank in the Republican platform that advocated a constitutional amendment guaranteeing equal rights for women. This was the first time a major party's platform had supported the issue. Mesta was also an ardent campaigner for the Republican presidential candidate, Wendell Willkie. After Willkie's defeat in 1940, Mesta left the Republican party to protest the lack of support given the candidate by the conservative wing of the party. Subsequently, as her interests and stands on issues became more closely aligned with those of the Democratic party, so did her commitment to that group. In the 1944 federal election campaign, Mesta attended the Democratic convention as a representative to the Platform and Resolutions Committee from Arizona, her official residence at the time, and for a second time played a role in getting a national party's platform to endorse a constitutional amendment for equal rights.

Through her lobbying efforts on behalf of the ERA, Mesta got to know many prominent politicians, including Senator Harry S. Truman in 1942. Truman was sympathetic to the equal rights issue and used his influence on its behalf. In response, Mesta organized a party for Truman during a Democratic rally in Oklahoma City in 1943. This gesture reflected a developing friendship with the Trumans and was the first of a number of parties she would give for the Truman family. As Truman's political fortunes rose, so did Mesta's importance as a Washington hostess.

Although Mesta inherited wealth from her husband, which was increased on the death of her father in 1944, she also expanded her fortune in the 1930's and 1940's through shrewd investments in oil, real estate, and her eighteen-thousand-acre Arizona cattle ranch. Her wealth, combined with hard work, a friendly personality, and a flair for entertaining, helped to make Perle Mesta a prominent and influential figure in official Washington circles for several decades. She earned a reputation as Washington's premier hostess. Her parties were known for being lavish, lively gatherings of the famous and powerful, the great and near-great, from the worlds of government, business, and entertainment. Mesta believed she was providing a political service by bringing important bipartisan individuals together so that they might informally discuss issues and perhaps work out problems.

Mesta was also an accomplished fund-raiser for Truman and the Democrats, and her personal appeals to wealthy friends in 1948 kept the party's campaign afloat. She served as chairman of the national Jefferson-Jackson Day dinners in 1948, and in 1949 she again assisted with the dinners, helping to raise hundreds of thousands of dollars for the Democrats. In January 1949, she was given the honor of serving as cochairman of the nation's biggest party, Truman's inaugural ball.

Later that year, President Truman appointed Mesta to the post of United States minister to the Grand Duchy of Luxembourg, an appointment generally regarded as a recognition of her past support of Truman and the Democratic party. She was the third woman in American history to be selected as a foreign minister and the first envoy ever appointed to Luxembourg. Although the career diplomatic corps and some of the press were somewhat critical of her appointment, she was well received by the people of Luxembourg, who seemed charmed by her style of diplomacy and the attention it brought to the country. Because of her experience with the steel industry, she demonstrated an informed interest in Luxembourg's position as a leading steel-producing nation, and she took time to visit mines and industrial plants throughout the country. She helped establish a scholarship fund for Luxembourg students to study in the United States, and during one two-week period in the summer of 1950, she helped arrange for food and lodging for several hundred American students visiting Luxembourg. As anticipated, she maintained her reputation for frequent, gracious entertaining, much of which was financed by her own funds. Besides hosting the usual affairs of state, she entertained orphans on several occasions, giving them gifts, and held an annual party for all of the mayors of Luxembourg. Once a month, she held a party for American servicemen and servicewomen stationed in the countries surrounding Luxembourg. These events were so popular that she is said to have hosted over twenty-five thousand members of the armed services during her four-year tenure. Before leaving Luxembourg in 1953, Mesta was awarded the country's highest honor, the Grand Cross of the Crown of Oak, a decoration never before given to a woman.

Because of her special style and prominence, Mesta, who was called "Madam Minister" by her staff, became the inspiration for the successful 1950 Broadway musical comedy, "Call Me Madam," a story about an American woman ambassador. The phrase "The Hostess with the Mostes'," from an Irving Berlin song in the show, provided a sobriquet that Mesta carried for the rest of her life.

After her diplomatic career ended, Mesta traveled extensively, wrote newspaper and magazine articles based on her experiences, continued to work for an equal rights amendment for American women, served as an accredited representative to the United Nations for the World Woman's Party and the National Woman's Party, helped start a dairy business in Nevada—and continued giving elaborate parties. During the last two decades of her life, she was a popular Washington hostess to all of the presidential administrations except that of Kennedy, although her political prominence never reached the same height as it did during the Truman era. Even though her legal residences in those years were often in places other than the capital, Mesta wrote that she was "never unconscious of the fact that my heart belongs and always will belong to Washington." Because of declining health, Mesta moved to Oklahoma City in early 1974. She died there, a year later, of hemolytic anemia. She was buried in Pittsburgh, Pa., next to her husband.

[The most complete source on Perle Mesta is her autobiography, *Perle: My Story* (1960), written with

Robert Cahn. Mesta authored several articles on her diplomatic, travel, and entertaining experiences, which were published in *Woman's Day* (1937), *Mc-Calls* (1950's–1960's), and the *New York Herald Tribune* (1950's). The best short biographical sketches are in Eleanor Roosevelt and Lorena A. Hickok, *Ladies of Courage* (1954); and Barbara Sicherman and Carol Hurd Green, eds., *Notable American Women* (1980). See also "Widow from Oklahoma," *Time*, Mar. 14, 1949; and Flora Lewis, "Madame Minister to Luxembourg," *New York Times Magazine*, Dec. 25, 1949. Obituaries are in the *Washington Post*, Mar. 18, 1975, and the *New York Times*, Mar. 17, 1975.]

MARILYNN WOOD HILL

MEYER, FRANK STRAUS (May 9, 1909– Apr. 1, 1972), writer and political activist, was born in Newark, N.J., the son of Jack F. Meyer and Helene Straus. His father was a lawyer whose family had immigrated to the United States in the aftermath of mid-nineteenth-century revolutions in Germany. Meyer spent two years (1926–1928) at Princeton University before transferring to Balliol College, Oxford University, where he earned a B.A. in 1932. While at Oxford, Meyer embraced the Communist party of Great Britain and served as director of its student bureau as well as being a member of its central committee. In 1932 he enrolled at the London School of Economics. There he won election as the Communist presidential candidate of the students' union and was subsequently expelled from England for his Communist activities. From 1934 through the end of World War II, he described himself as a "dedicated Communist," recruiting potential members at the University of Chicago and later doing related organizational activities. On Oct. 11, 1940, he married Elsie Bown; they had two children.

Along with many other erstwhile leftists, Meyer broke with the Communist movement in the mid-1940's. Earl Browder's dismissal as head of the American Communist party in 1946 disillusioned him, but so, too, did the burgeoning philosophy of antistatism. Friedrich A. Hayek's *The Road to Serfdom* (1944) had a profound influence on his ideological reorientation. By the end of the 1940's, Straus was engaged in anti-Communist activities and testified about the party before government committees—in 1949 at the conspiracy trial of members of the Communist party's national executive committee, in the 1954 federal hearings about the Jefferson School of Social Science, before a U.S. Senate investigating panel in 1957, and before the House Un-American Activities Committee in 1959.

By 1952, Meyer was a Republican and a regular contributor to right-wing periodicals such as the *American Mercury* and the *Freeman*, and by 1955 he was a founding editor of William F. Buckley, Jr.'s, *National Review*. From his mountainside home in Woodstock, N.Y., he worked throughout the night, writing and chatting by phone with other conservative leaders throughout the country. More than any other conservative intellectual, Meyer would play a vital role in shaping the postwar American Right.

Meyer acknowledged that Richard M. Weaver, a rhetorician at the University of Chicago, was the intellectual source of his revised convictions. "There is the particular personal debt I owe him from long before I met him," Meyer recalled, "the great influence on my personal development towards conservatism that his *Ideas Have Consequences* had when it appeared in 1948." Indeed, Meyer credited Weaver with delineating the indispensable concept of American conservatism, "that respect for the tradition of metaphysical truth does not contradict a politics based on individual liberty—is not a 'fusionism' of disparate European traditions (as its more extreme authoritarian and libertarian critics have insisted) but is rather born out of the most fundamental American experience."

In Defense of Freedom: A Conservative Credo appeared in 1962 and expanded on several themes in Meyer's *National Review*, *Freeman*, and *Modern Age* essays. To Russell Kirk, and other proponents of order and tradition, he insisted that the essence of political society is to enhance the freedom of the person and to enable the individual to use his freedom to pursue virtuous ends. His own thought aimed to reconcile libertarianism and traditionalism. Freedom needed to be rooted in a transcendent moral order, while the primacy of personal freedom had to be protected by constitutional guarantees. In Meyer's judgment, traditional conservatives, such as Russell Kirk, spoke only of authority, order, community, duty, and obedience. Freedom was a rare word in their social thought. "Truth withers when freedom dies," Meyer wrote, "however righteous the authority that kills it," and "the denial of the claims of freedom leads not to conservatism but to authoritarianism and theocracy." Meyer's aim was for "that fused position which recognizes at one and the same time the transcendent goal of human existence and primacy of the freedom of the person in the political order."

Many conservative intellectuals deplored Meyer's thinking. Willmoore Kendall criticized Meyer's overemphasis on the role of religious belief in conservativism and his "near-neurosis" about the leviathan state. Russell Kirk questioned his refusal to concede the limitations of reason, to ignore the perils of being "an ideologue of liberty." And for scholars of the conservative tradition in American history, such as Clinton Rossiter, Meyer's "ultra-conservatism" refused to grant the permanence of New Deal social reforms and aspired to a "restorationist conservatism."

Another influential ex-Communist, Whittaker Chambers, confided to William F. Buckley, Jr., in a 1958 letter, that Meyer's conservatism could render the movement sterile and strident. "It will become like one of those dark little shops which apparently never sell anything. If, for any reason, you go in, you find, at the back, an old man, fingering for his own pleasure some oddments of cloth (weave and design of 1850). Nobody wants to buy them, which is fine because the old man is not really interested in selling. He just likes to hold and to feel. As your eyes become accustomed to the dim kerosene light, you are only slightly surprised to see that the old man is Frank Meyer."

Meyer would prove Chambers wrong, because by insisting that conservative ideas had to have electoral consequences, Meyer was at the energizing center of such activist enterprises as the Young Americans for Freedom, the New York State Conservative party, and the American Conservative Union. From his "Principles and Heresies" column in *National Review*, Frank Meyer forged the salient themes in the repertoire of 1950's conservatism: intransigent anti-Communism, consensual constitutional traditionalism, economic libertarianism, and preference for "local" rather than "leviathan" government. Shortly before his death from cancer at his home in Woodstock, he converted to Roman Catholicism.

[Major published writings of Frank Meyer include *The Moulding of Communists* (1961); *In Defense of*

Freedom (1962); *The Conservative Mainstream* (1969); and, as editor, *What Is Conservatism?* (1964); and *The African Nettle* (1965). Assessments of Meyer's social thought can be found in Willmoore Kendall, *The Conservative Affirmation* (1963); Russell Kirk, "An Ideologue of Liberty," *Sewanee Review*, Apr.–June 1964; George H. Nash, *The Conservative Intellectual Movement in America* (1976); Murray N. Rothbord, "Frank S. Meyer: The Fusionist as Libertarian Manqué," *Modern Age*, Fall 1981; Louis Filler, *Dictionary of American Conservatism* (1987); Tracy F. Munsil, "The Moulding of a Conservative: The Political Thought of Frank S. Meyer" (M.A. thesis, Arizona State University, 1989); and Frank Annunziata, introduction to Richard C. Cornuelle, *Reclaiming the American Dream* (1993). Obituaries are in the *New York Times*, Apr. 3, 1972; and the *National Review*, Apr. 28, 1972, which also includes tributes by William F. Buckley, Jr., and other prominent conservatives.]

FRANK ANNUNZIATA

MIRSKY, ALFRED EZRA (Oct. 17, 1900– June 19, 1974), biochemist, was born in Flushing, Queens, in New York City, to Michael David Mirsky, a businessman who manufactured nurses' uniforms, and Frieda Ittleson, who were both Russian immigrants. He attended the Ethical Culture School in New York, graduating in 1918, and Harvard College, where he was elected to Phi Beta Kappa and received a B.A. degree in 1922.

Wishing to pursue further study of biology and physiology, Mirsky enrolled in the Columbia University College of Physicians and Surgeons. He received a fellowship in the academic year 1924–1925 for the study of biochemistry at Cambridge University (England) under Joseph Barcroft. There he began a study he eventually completed under Lawrence J. Henderson at Harvard. He was awarded the Ph.D. by Cambridge in 1926, after submitting his dissertation, "The Haemoglobin Molecule."

At Cambridge, Mirsky collaborated with the American scientist Mortimer L. Anson. The two continued to work together in the United States until 1935, studying the structure of proteins. This early stage of Mirsky's work took place at a time when the molecular specificity of living material was being established over the prevailing view that protoplasm was an unspecific, undefinable soup of dispersed colloidal aggregates. Mirsky studied the hemoglobin molecule because it is comprised of a relatively short protein chain from which it is possible to isolate pure fractions. He subsequently developed methods of investigating increasingly complex biochemical systems.

Mirsky married Reba Paeff, a musician and children's book author, on May 25, 1926. The couple had two children. Their daughter, Reba Mirsky Goodman, became a pathology professor at Columbia University's College of Physicians and Surgeons. Their son, Jonathan Mirsky, became a professor of Chinese studies at Dartmouth College and later a journalist.

In 1927 Mirsky was appointed an assistant in the laboratory of Alfred E. Cohn at the hospital of the Rockefeller Institute for Medical Research in New York City. He remained there for forty-five years, becoming a full professor in 1954 and retiring in 1972. His career yielded seminal discoveries regarding the structure and function of biological molecules.

During his first decade at Rockefeller, Mirsky studied molecules in a variety of biological systems. Subjects for his investigations included chick embryos, the enzyme trypsin, albumins, and muscle proteins. In 1936 he took a sabbatical year to study proteins with Linus Pauling at the California Institute of Technology. Together they researched the role of hydrogen bonds in stabilizing the configuration of coiled proteins.

In 1938 Mirsky isolated a structural protein complex containing large amounts of DNA, which could be traced to the cell nucleus. This and other studies led in 1944 to the conclusion by Oswald T. Avery, Colin MacLeod, and Maclyn McCarty that genetic information was carried in the DNA molecule. Mirsky established a research partnership with Arthur W. Pollister of Columbia University and throughout the 1940's they carried on successful studies into the workings of the cell nucleus. They isolated DNA from a variety of mammalian cells and speculated on the relationship of nucleoproteins to genes. Hans Ris at Rockefeller University joined Mirsky's efforts from 1946 to 1951 to isolate chromosomes. Other colleagues included Vincent G. Allfrey, Marie Daly, and Herbert Stern.

Mirsky and Ris found that cells from various tissues of the same species contained identical amounts of DNA. When reproductive cells are formed, the chromosomes are reduced by half. These reproductive cells were shown to contain half the amount of DNA. This led to the concept of DNA constancy and supported the conclusion that DNA was the genetic material. Demonstration of this fact in nonbacterial systems strength-

ened the growth of the science that was coming to be known as "molecular biology." Following 1950, Mirsky and his colleagues continued their studies of the role of nucleic acids and proteins in the function of cells. They investigated the differential effects of proteins on gene expression in embryonic systems and the role of RNA in protein synthesis.

Mirsky edited the *Journal of General Physiology* from 1951 to 1961. He also edited, together with Jean Brachet, a multivolume reference work entitled *The Cell*, to which he contributed several major articles. *The Cell*, published between 1959 and 1967, was an essential reference for those wishing to master the new molecular biology.

Mirsky also played a major role in the education of nonspecialists. In 1959 he founded the Rockefeller University Christmas lecture series for high school students, which now bears his name. He was a consultant to *Scientific American* and contributed three significant articles between 1953 and 1968 introducing many nonspecialists to the new knowledge concerning nucleic acids and protein synthesis.

Mirsky was elected to the National Academy of Sciences in 1954 and to the American Philosophical Society in 1964. The latter honor was awarded in recognition of his many published review articles, book reviews, and speeches and essays on a wide variety of scientific and social issues. Mirsky cautioned against the misinterpretations of the social implications of scientific knowledge. He refuted, in particular, the arguments of eugenicists on the grounds that science did not support their conclusions regarding racial differences.

During Mirsky's sabbatical year in California, he had taken the opportunity to travel to China. Art and archaeology were lifelong and serious interests. He was a discriminating collector of ancient Greek coins and Chinese ceramics. These interests shaped his choices in travel and use of leisure time. He was a frequent and critical visitor to galleries, museums, and auctions.

Mirsky served Rockefeller University as librarian from 1965 to 1972. After the death of his wife in 1966 he married Sonia Wohl, an associate librarian at Rockefeller, in 1967. Mirsky died at his Manhattan home.

[Mirsky's papers occupy thirty-six shelf feet at the Rockefeller University Archives in North Tarrytown,

N.Y. The *Dictionary of Scientific Biography*, suppl. 2, contains an article by Seymour S. Cohen. The 1976 *Yearbook* of the American Philosophical Society carries a eulogy by Bruce S. McEwen. An obituary is in the *New York Times*, June 21, 1974.]

MICHAEL F. HAINES

MITCHELL, STEPHEN ARNOLD (Mar. 3, 1903–Apr. 23, 1974), political reformer and lawyer, was born in Rock Valley, Iowa, the son of Stephen Arnold Mitchell, a dairy farmer and banker, and Dorothy Norton Higgins. A Catholic, Mitchell attended local parochial schools, Creighton University, and Georgetown University School of Law, where he received his LL.B. in 1928.

He married Evelyn Josephine Miller on Feb. 16, 1931. The Mitchells had three children.

After receiving his law degree Mitchell moved to New York City, when he worked in both legal and executive capacities for General Motors until 1932. In 1932 he moved again, this time to Chicago, where he was associated with the firm of Taylor, Miller, Busch, and Boydon. At the beginning of World War II Mitchell became chief of the French Division of the Lend-Lease Administration in Washington, D.C., a position he held from 1942 to 1944. He then served as an adviser to the State Department on French economic affairs in Washington and Paris.

After the war Mitchell returned to Chicago and resumed private practice. One of his most prominent clients was Samuel Cardinal Stritch of the Archdiocese of Chicago. Mitchell coveted the post of U.S. attorney for Chicago, a jealously guarded political plum controlled by the senior Democratic U.S. senator from Illinois. It has been alleged that Mitchell tried to bypass the party patronage by using his powerful church connection to get the post, an action that not only cost him the job he wanted but also earned him the undying enmity of Boss Jack Arvey, head of the Chicago Democratic machine. Arvey blocked Mitchell and gave the office he wanted to Otto Kerner, who would again frustrate Mitchell's ambition later in his life.

Mitchell was an early political backer of Adlai Stevenson. In 1947 he organized a Stevenson for Senator Committee that included in its membership many powerful Chicago figures but few machine politicians. Again Mitchell ran afoul of Boss Arvey, who had already decided to back Paul Douglas for senator. Mitchell's committee was then hastily recast as the "Stevenson for Governor Committee." Mitchell's new goal of putting Stevenson in the governor's chair was acceptable to both reformers and machine politicians, and Stevenson won the governorship of Illinois in 1948; thereafter he always counted Mitchell as one of his most trusted and loyal supporters.

A federal scandal during the last year of the Truman administration brought Mitchell a degree of national prominence. Allegations that tax lawyers who were defending cases before the Internal Revenue Bureau had given expensive gifts to officials in the Justice Department prompted Chairman Emanuel Celler of the House Judiciary Committee to ask Mitchell to act as special counsel to his committee during the investigation of the scandal. Mitchell was engaged in this activity when Adlai Stevenson was drafted in 1952 as the nominee for president by the Democratic party. Stevenson wanted a new chairman of the Democratic National Committee, someone who would put the Stevenson stamp on the party. Stevenson had been advised that he should appoint a Catholic to provide balance to the organization, but he also wanted someone whom he could trust and who would be loyal to him. Mitchell fit all these criteria. Moreover, Stevenson believed that the Republicans would use the recent Justice Department scandal as campaign ammunition, but that this attack would be blunted by the fact that Mitchell had been engaged in cleaning up this scandal.

Traditionally, the Democratic party chose a professional politician as its chairman. Thus Stevenson encountered opposition to Mitchell's appointment from the city bosses, including Jack Arvey of Chicago. Stevenson not only stood his ground but required Arvey to nominate Mitchell before the Democratic National Committee. The *New York Times* noted that "Stevenson had picked a political amateur as party chairman," and commented that the choice was "personal and a split with tradition."

Mitchell ran the unsuccessful Stevenson campaign in 1952. This experience, perhaps coupled with his earlier run-ins with Boss Arvey, convinced Mitchell that the Democratic party must rid itself of the domination of big city bosses and southern reactionaries. He stayed on as chairman until 1955 and helped to pay off the campaign debt of $830,000. He also worked out a plan to ensure the loyalty of party officials, requiring them either to support the party nominee or relinquish their posts. Mitchell had a hand in picking his successor, Paul Butler of Indiana, whose rise to the party chairmanship was regarded as a victory for clean politics. Although no longer a party official himself, Mitchell worked in the Stevenson presidential campaign of 1956.

Reflecting on his experience in politics, Mitchell came to regard the use of political clubs as a way to increase participation by the general public. He published a book entitled *Elm Street Politics* in 1959 in which he described how he had organized a club in his neighborhood and described ways in which ordinary citizens could get involved in politics. He wrote, "The trouble with politics is that it is too much of a spectator sport." Mitchell believed that more voter participation in party primaries was essential. He wrote that "Bosses are built by people who ignore primaries," and further noted, "For every five persons who vote in the general election, only one votes in the primary. This plays directly into the hands of the political boss. He can handpick his candidates and get his choice ratified by his own organized minority. By ignoring the primary those who call themselves independents . . . permit the political boss to select the only candidates for whom they will be allowed to vote."

In an effort to put his ideas into action, Mitchell entered the 1960 Illinois Democratic primary as a candidate for governor. The machine candidate that year was his old nemesis Otto Kerner. The race was complicated by the entry of Joseph Lohman, the state treasurer. In the three-way race Mitchell was defeated. Mitchell commented, "I knew I didn't have a chance but I did it to challenge the machine. I was badly beaten, even though I got over 200,000 votes."

In 1968 Mitchell joined the quixotic campaign of Senator Eugene McCarthy of Minnesota. McCarthy forced President Lyndon Johnson to withdraw from the presidential race, but seemed unable to sustain a campaign. Mitchell served as his floor manager at the violence-ridden Democratic National Convention in Chicago. After the failure of the McCarthy effort, Mitchell served as vice-chairman of the Humphrey-Muskie Citizens Committee. This was his last political campaign.

Mitchell returned to the practice of law in

Santa Fe and Taos in New Mexico, and also in Chicago. He died of an apparent heart attack in Taos.

[For Mitchell's own view of his life, see *Elm Street Politics* (1959); and *As We Knew Adlai* (1966). John Bartlow Martin, *Adlai Stevenson and the World* (1977), is somewhat hostile to Mitchell but contains many references to his relationship with Stevenson. Obituaries of Mitchell are in the *New York Times* and the *Chicago Tribune*, both Apr. 24, 1974.]

DONALD F. TINGLEY

MOLEY, RAYMOND CHARLES (Sept. 27, 1886–Feb. 18, 1975), professor of political science, presidential adviser, and journalist, was born in Berea, Ohio, the son of Felix James Moley, an immigrant storekeeper from Ireland, and Agnes Fairchild. The family moved to the nearby village of Olmsted Falls, Ohio, in 1893. Moley graduated from Baldwin-Wallace College in Berea in 1906 and for the next three years worked as a teacher and superintendent of schools in Olmsted Falls. The onset of tuberculosis in 1909 led to nearly three years of convalescence in Colorado and New Mexico. He returned to Ohio in 1912 to teach history at Cleveland's West High School, where he remained until 1914. Meanwhile he continued his studies at Oberlin College, where he received his master's degree in 1913.

In 1914 Moley enrolled as a graduate student in political science at Columbia University. His doctoral dissertation on state government reform in the Progressive Era was supervised by the famed historian Charles A. Beard. He received his Ph.D. in 1918, and in that same year became an assistant professor of politics at Western Reserve University in Cleveland. He married Eva Dall of Olmsted Falls on Aug. 14, 1916, with whom he had twin sons. Reflecting his persistent attraction to a more active public role, however, in 1919 Moley accepted appointment as director of the Cleveland Foundation. The nation's first community trust, the foundation promoted civic reform, research on urban issues, business-government cooperation, and local philanthropy. Moley left this position in 1923 to become an associate professor of public law at Columbia University.

Moley made a reputation as an expert on criminal justice, publishing two widely acclaimed works: *Politics and Criminal Prosecution* (1929) and *Our Criminal Courts* (1930).

His increasing prominence in this field brought him to the attention of Louis M. Howe, then a member of the National Crime Commission and a close associate of Franklin D. Roosevelt. Through this connection Moley played a small role in Roosevelt's 1928 New York gubernatorial campaign, and later advised Governor Roosevelt on criminal justice matters. In 1930 Moley served on a committee that drafted a model state parole system for Roosevelt, and in 1931 Roosevelt appointed him as his chief representative on the New York State Commission on Administration of Justice.

In early 1932, Samuel I. Rosenman, counsel to Governor Roosevelt, now a presidential candidate, asked Moley to join the informal group of academic advisers to Roosevelt that became known as the Brain Trust. Moley quickly emerged as the leader of the group, whose most conspicuous other members included his Columbia University colleagues Rexford G. Tugwell and Adolf A. Berle, Jr.

Moley had been raised in the Populist political tradition of William Jennings Bryan, with its hostility to Wall Street and suspicion of the special interest. But he was also a great admirer of the "single-tax" theorist Henry George and of Cleveland reform mayor Tom L. Johnson. From George's writings Moley learned the importance of transcending Bryan's simple Manichaeanism that pitted the virtuous people against the evil interests, and of thinking systemically about economic and social issues. Johnson provided him with a practical example of the complexities of applying reform theories to recalcitrant reality. Moley's own experience at the Cleveland Foundation no doubt also convinced him that cooperation between business and government was both viable and conducive to the public good. Yet in many ways, particularly in the realm of foreign policy, Moley remained faithful to the small-town, midwestern values that Bryan had championed.

This ideological heritage shaped Moley's contributions to the Brain Trust. Though the group never developed a formal philosophy or a comprehensive manifesto, its members broadly agreed that the causes of the Great Depression lay in the chaotic, disarticulated, wasteful practices of the American economy. Rejecting the laissez-faire theory of conservative classical economists, as well as the confiscatory doctrines of socialism and the antitrust nostrums of the populists, the Brain Trusters sought remedies for the catastrophe of the Depression in government-directed economic planning on a national scale, with government acting in close consultation and cooperation with private business. Specifically, the Brain Trusters advocated greatly expanded spending on public works; national policies governing wages, prices, and production levels; relief for the long-suffering agricultural sector; and better regulation of banking and securities markets. In broad outline, these ideas informed the major programs of the early New Deal, including the Public Works Administration, the National Recovery Administration, the Agricultural Adjustment Administration, and the banking and securities legislation of 1933 and 1934.

In the four intervening months between Roosevelt's election in November 1932 and his inauguration in March 1933, Moley emerged as a key policy adviser to Roosevelt. So pervasive did his influence appear that Democratic Congressman Sam Rayburn of Texas pointedly declared to Moley, "I hope we don't have any goddamned Rasputin in this administration." A current joke had an old friend asking the president-elect a favor: "Can you get me an appointment with Moley?"

Now at the height of his fame and influence, Moley was a middle-aged man of medium height, a bit portly, whose hair was thinning. Affable and engaging, he was also toughminded and coolly analytical. Though his posture of repudiating romantic idealism and facing the world without illusions distanced him from many of his academic colleagues, he always retained something of the professorial manner, including a fondness for smoking a pipe.

Moley accompanied President-elect Roosevelt to two tense White House meetings with Herbert Hoover, who tried to persuade Roosevelt to continue the defeated president's efforts to fight the Depression through international agreements lowering tariffs, stabilizing exchange rates, and preserving the gold standard. Buttressed by the intensely nationalistic Moley, who argued that the causes of the Depression were domestic and that recovery required disentanglement from the international economic system, Roosevelt turned these suggestions aside.

Moley became assistant secretary of state in the new Roosevelt administration, with the understanding that his portfolio would extend well beyond diplomatic matters. During the famous

"Hundred Days" in 1933, Moley played a major role in shaping banking and securities legislation.

Moley received what became his last major assignment from Roosevelt just after the adjournment of the Hundred Days session of Congress in June 1933, when he was dispatched as the president's personal representative to the World Economic and Monetary Conference in London, with instructions to negotiate a vague agreement on currency stabilization. This was a delicate mission for Moley, who had to contend in London with Secretary of State Cordell Hull, the official head of the American delegation. Hull resented both Moley's presence and Moley's nationalistic views, which were sharply at odds with the secretary's own internationalism. In the end, Moley succeeded in severely antagonizing Hull, but failed to rescue the conference. On July 3, 1933, Roosevelt sent his notorious "bombshell message" to London, effectively foreclosing the possibility of further American international economic cooperation. Press accounts of the episode dwelt upon Roosevelt's apparent repudiation and public humiliation of Moley. Hull seized the occasion to insist that Moley be removed from the State Department. Ironically, the nationalistic, even isolationist, sentiments of the "bombshell message" faithfully reflected the views that Moley himself had long urged upon Roosevelt.

Moley resigned his government position in 1933 to return to teaching at Columbia and to assume the editorship of *Today*, a periodical intended to be "concerned with public affairs, independent in its political affiliations, . . . liberal in outlook"; it was absorbed by *Newsweek* in 1937. As a private citizen, he held a series of "Moley dinners" in 1934, designed to build business confidence in the New Deal and to defang the nascent and ferociously anti-Roosevelt Liberty League. He continued as an occasional speechwriter for the president, collaborating on Roosevelt's 1936 acceptance speech.

But though he retained his respect and affection for Roosevelt's person, Moley grew increasingly disenchanted with what he regarded as the New Deal's growing hostility toward business. Moley openly broke with the New Deal in 1939 when he published *After Seven Years*, a scrupulously accurate, vividly written, and highly critical account of Roosevelt's policies. In 1940 he supported Wendell Willkie for president,

and gradually drifted still further rightward. He backed Barry Goldwater for president in 1964, and actively encouraged the career of Richard M. Nixon, who awarded him the Medal of Freedom in 1970.

A gifted literary stylist, Moley perhaps made his greatest contributions less to the New Deal itself than to the historical image of the Roosevelt years, especially the election and Hundred Days, in which he was a direct participant. In later life he wrote a regular column for *Newsweek*, a biography of the Irish nationalist Daniel O'Connell, and several books about federal water projects. After divorcing his first wife, he married Frances S. Hebard on Jan. 15, 1949, with whom he had one daughter. He died in Phoenix, Ariz.

[Moley's papers are in the Hoover Institution on War, Revolution, and Peace at Stanford University. His book *The First New Deal* (1966), written with the assistance of Elliot A. Rosen, provides a later perspective on many of the events covered in *After Seven Years* (1939). *Realities and Illusions, 1886–1931: The Autobiography of Raymond Moley* (1980), is a posthumously published, somewhat fragmentary, memoir of Moley's early life. An obituary is in the *New York Times*, Feb. 19, 1975.]

DAVID M. KENNEDY

MONROE, VAUGHN WILTON (Oct. 7, 1911–May 21, 1973), bandleader, trumpeter, and singing star, was born in Akron, Ohio, to Ira C. Monroe, an itinerant rubber tire industry worker, and Mabel Louisa Maahs. At age fifteen he won the Wisconsin state trumpet championship for his interpretation of "Pearl of the Ocean." He spent the last two years of high school at Jeannette, Penn., where he played the trumpet in the school band and in various local bands. There he joined the Methodist church choir, where he decided to pursue a singing career. In June 1929 he graduated with honors and in September he entered Carnegie Institute of Technology, where he completed two years of engineering and a number of music classes. He supported himself by playing the trumpet in several Pittsburgh bands. In 1931 he left Carnegie for lack of funds and went on the road with a dance band that played the eastern Pennsylvania circuit.

In 1935 Monroe moved to Boston, where he joined the Harry and Jack Marshard band, which played society galas and debutante balls. In Boston he attended the New England Conservatory of Music (1936–1938), where he was trained for classical opera roles. In 1938 he fronted the Marshard brothers' second six-piece unit as a trumpeter-vocalist-bandleader. He adapted his disciplined basso voice to the deep throaty baritone of a microphone crooner, which filled the big dance halls and large hotel rooms of the era as few crooners could. On Apr. 2, 1940, Monroe married his high school sweetheart, Marion Baughman, who graduated from Pennsylvania State University with a degree in business administration. They had two children and made their home in West Newton, a Boston suburb.

In 1940 Monroe left the Marshard brothers and formed his own orchestra, touring New England, New Jersey, Pennsylvania, and eastern Canada. Along the way he gained a near ecstatic following. In 1941 the RCA Victor company signed him to a contract and organized his first big-time theater engagement at the Paramount Theatre in New York City. It proved an unprecedented box-office success. Between 1941 and 1951 RCA Victor sold more than 20 million copies of his records. Monroe was given his own room in mid-Manhattan at the Hotel Commodore. The Camel cigarettes company hired him to replace Benny Goodman on their weekly "Camel Caravan" radio show (1945–1953). Monroe also produced and headlined Camel cigarettes' half-hour weekly television show (1950–1951), which was an elaborate extravaganza with the effect of a Radio City Music Hall spectacular and a quality Broadway revue. In addition, Monroe performed as the "Voice of RCA" on television for fifteen years (1955–1970). His standing-room-only engagements at the Strand Theatre in Manhattan were always box-office events. His appeal to the black-tie set brought him repeated invitations to appear at the Waldorf Astoria. Wherever he went on tour, attendance at his concerts was unparalleled. Monroe's record sales skyrocketed. His radio show theme song, "Racing with the Moon" (1941), sold 1,750,000 copies. Other hit songs were "Ghost Riders in the Night," "Cool Water," "Let It Snow, Let It Snow, Let It Snow," "Mule Train," "Riders in the Sky," "Ballerina," "Dreamy New England Moon," "High Up in the Midnight Blue," "And Then All Too Soon," and "It's Lost from View," as well as World War II best-sellers "Desolation," "The Very Thought of You," and "When the Lights Go Up Again All Over the World." *Variety*

called him the number-one vocalist. His songs were played more often than any other performers' on juke boxes and by disc jockeys, and many of his records were number one in store sales.

Republic Pictures Corporation in Hollywood hired Monroe to replace retiring western singing stars Roy Rogers and Gene Autry, their chief money-makers. They first cast Monroe in *Singing Guns* (1950), for which he sang his hit song "Mule Train." His second film for Republic was *The Toughest Man in Tombstone* (1952), for which he was paid $500,000. The film established him as one of Hollywood's highest-paid stars.

These activities made Monroe a multimillionaire whose investments were as varied and multiple as his artistic interests. He owned office buildings in downtown Boston, a fleet of taxicabs, and a successful theme restaurant outside Boston, The Meadows, which he operated with the Marshard brothers. He was president of Vaughn Monroe Productions, which collected more than $1 million annually from his six bands alone. Monroe also ran a publishing firm, which published several of his own songs including the best-selling U.S. Army anthem, "Men of the Army"; a recording company; a children's book and music publishing firm; and a toy manufacturing company.

In spite of his wealth, Monroe continued to perform 200 nights out of the year in clubs and cruise ships, traveling from his home in Stuart, Fla., where he lived from the early 1960's. After a performance in Louisville, Ky., Monroe collapsed from an internal hemorrhage, a result of a long stomach ailment. He was operated on at the Martin County Memorial Hospital in Fla., where he died two weeks later.

[There is no biographical volume dedicated to Vaughn Monroe. Each of the following books contains a chapter on his music and life: Bruce Crowther, Mike Pinfold, and Franklin S. Driggs, *The Big Band Years* (1988), the most recent and best known of the three; Gene Fernell, *Thousand Golden Hours: The Exciting Age of America's Dance Bands* (1966); and George T. Simon, *The Big Bands* (1967), which has an introduction by Frank Sinatra, are no longer in print.

Biographical sketches of Monroe appeared in several newspaper entertainment sections: the *New York World Telegram*, July 4, 1947; the *San Francisco Chronicle*, May 21, 1950; the *Los Angeles News*, Mar. 14, 1951, Dec. 3, 1951, and Apr. 4, 1952; the *Los Angeles Times*, May 4, 1952; and the *Sunday Pictorial Review*, May 18, 1952.

Profiles of Monroe are in *Look*, Aug. 16, 1949; *Collier's*, Aug. 20, 1949; *American Magazine*, Jan. 1951; and *Coronet*, Dec. 1951. An obituary is in the *New York Times*, May 22, 1973.]

SHOSHANA KLEBANOFF

MOORE, HUGH EVERETT (Apr. 27, 1887– Nov. 25, 1972), cofounder of the Dixie Cup Corporation and population-control advocate, was born in Fort Scott, Kans., the youngest of six children of Alice Elizabeth Harbison and John James Moore. Hugh began making his own way at the age of twelve, when his father died.

Moore was a good student, graduating with honors and awards from Central High School in Kansas City, Mo., in 1905. While in high school, he worked for various local newspapers. He then worked on *The Reform*, a Kansas City newspaper, and next *The Packer*, a national fruit-and-produce trade newspaper. Moore was admitted to Harvard twice as a special student, in 1906 and again in 1908, but soon left to enter into a business venture with his brother-in-law, Lawrence Luellen, who had conceived the idea of a disposable drinking cup.

Despite resistance to this unique idea, Moore and Luellen were able to raise $200,000 to establish the paper cup business. They used a shock technique ("Did you know it is very dangerous to drink from the common drinking cup?"), substantiated by research, to capture the attention and money of those able to help him. Moore knew that contemporary studies showed public drinking glasses were a health menace— they were forbidden in many states. Therefore, Dixie Cups (at first called Health Kups) were developed at precisely the right time. To market his product, Moore edited a small magazine called *The Cup Campaigner*. With characteristic singleness of purpose he continued to build the firm even after his partner left for other ventures. In 1920, Moore moved the business to Easton, Pa., where he spent the rest of his life.

Moore served as a captain in Army Intelligence during World War I. He was chief salesman of the Dixie Cup Corporation until after World War II, raising sales to more than $50 million per year. When the company merged with the American Can Company in 1957, it had eight plants valued at $53 million. Moore continued his association with Dixie, serving as a consultant until shortly before his death.

Long before Moore sold the Dixie Cup business, he had begun to turn his attention to public service with the same intensity he had brought to the business world. In the late 1930's, as the threat of world war again loomed, he began to think of a role businessmen could play in the peace movement. Moore recalled, "I thought if there was anything I could do so that my grandsons and their generation would not face a third World War, I should do that." (His sons, Craig and Hugh, Jr., served in World War II, and his grandson, Scott Moore, served in Vietnam.) In 1939, Moore became chairman of the Executive Committee of the League of Nations Association, which advocated American entry into the League. He also was cofounder of the Committee to Defend America by Aiding the Allies and served as chairman of its Executive Committee. Moore was appointed by the National Peace Conference (comprised of forty American peace organizations) to convince President Franklin Roosevelt to hold a conference of Western nations to avert war.

In 1944, with money he had made from Dixie Cups, Moore established the Hugh Moore Fund, a nonprofit educational foundation to promote peace. He also formed Americans United for World Organization. In 1945, Moore was one of those representing the United States at the historic San Francisco conference to establish the United Nations. In 1948, he was treasurer of the Committee for the Marshall Plan.

Moore's efforts for world peace began to center on the population problem in the early 1950's. He continued to use the techniques of a hardheaded businessman, as well as sheer determination, to proclaim the message that overpopulation was at the very heart of many environmental and social problems. Moore wrote a pamphlet entitled *The Population Bomb* (1955), using the expression "population explosion" to describe the increasing numbers of people in the world. He wrote: "Today the population bomb threatens to create an explosion as disruptive and dangerous as the explosion of the atom, and with as much influence on prospects for progress or disaster, war or peace." Population experts had understood the danger for many years but had confined their warnings to scholarly areas. Moore brought the crisis to the public eye in a dramatic manner. The title of this pamphlet was lent to Paul Ehrlich, with Moore's permission, for his bestselling book (1969).

Until his death, Moore concentrated on the population problem, gaining support and funds from influential Americans and demanding government attention and funds as well. He distributed his pamphlet to more than fifty thousand American leaders, picked from *Who's Who in America*. He paid for numerous full-page ads in the *New York Times* that graphically described the population problem (for instance, "Whatever your cause, it's a lost cause unless we control population"). These ads were also signed by prominent politicians and businesspeople.

Former U.S. senator Kenneth Keating said of Moore, "He is a man with a mission . . . a forceful man whose enthusiasm rubs off on everyone around him." By late 1969, Moore had captured the attention of the government and had received a personal letter from President Richard Nixon: "Your dedication to easing the problem of world population growth has led to a significant public service and the people of the world are in your debt."

Moore was married on Sept. 15, 1917, to Berenice Brown. They had two children and were divorced in 1946. In 1947 he married Louise Wilde; they had no children. Moore died in New York City.

[The Harvard Library archives has information regarding Moore's acceptance to Harvard as a special student. The Sophia Smith Collection at Smith College has letters and other material regarding Planned Parenthood, Moore's work with population control, and the Hugh Moore Fund. Lawrence Lader, *Breeding Ourselves to Death* (1971), documents the work of Moore and the Hugh Moore Fund. An obituary is in the *New York Times*, Nov. 26, 1972.]

ELIZABETH A. ELKINS

MOORE, MARIANNE CRAIG (Nov. 15, 1887–Feb. 5, 1972), poet, was born in Kirkwood, Mo., a suburb of St. Louis, the daughter of John Moore and Mary Warner. Her father was an engineer whose scheme for a smokeless furnace failed; this failure left him mentally unstable. Marianne was born after her father had been placed in an asylum, and she never knew him. Mrs. Moore returned to the home of her father, a Presbyterian pastor in Kirkwood, and there raised her two children. The three Moores were forced to leave Kirkwood upon the death of Marianne's grandfather, and shortly thereafter settled in Carlisle, Pa. The family became

very closely bonded. Marianne's mother was watchful, loving, but domineering, and she pushed her children to excel in intellectual and cultural pursuits. In Carlisle, Mrs. Moore took a teaching job, and Marianne attended a private, church-affiliated school until she entered Bryn Mawr College, a short distance away, in 1905.

At Bryn Mawr, Marianne proceeded with the highly literate and moral education begun and encouraged by her mother. She chose to major in biology, but she also continued to develop her talents as a writer, publishing both poems and stories in *Typyn O'Bob*, the college literary magazine. Though later excessively modest about her literary ambitions, even saying she referred to her productions as poems only because she couldn't think what else to call them, her letters home at this time show that she was already determined to become an author. Her social experience at college was in many ways decisive, for she began concentrating on clothing, manners, and personal style in a way that her poetry was frequently to reflect. While in college, Moore discovered many of the figures of modernism, chiefly Ezra Pound, whose literary opinions and theories had a profound influence on her. But she also devoured the literature of other ages and was always quick to acknowledge her many literary influences: seventeenth-century religious prose writers, especially Thomas Browne, as well as Samuel Johnson, Henry James, the Victorian novelists, George Saintsbury, and T. S. Eliot. It was in this period that her tastes and interest as a full-fledged modernist took conclusive shape.

She graduated from Bryn Mawr in 1909. She returned home to Carlisle, studied commercial subjects, and then taught stenography at the U.S. Indian School in Carlisle from 1911 to 1915.

In 1918 Moore moved with her mother, who was to be her constant companion and severest critic for the next thirty years, to Greenwich Village in New York City. From 1921 to 1925 she worked as an assistant in the Hudson Park branch of the New York Public Library. Having published a few poems in avant-garde magazines, such as *Poetry* and the *Egoist*, she entered the world of bohemian artists flourishing amid the low rents and social experimentation of "the Village." Incongruous in this setting because of her religious background and settled home life, Moore nevertheless became noticed, and even fabled. Friendships with William Carlos Williams, e. e. cummings, Lola Ridge, Alyse Gregory, and others provided her with constant stimulation and social engagements. Eventually she went to work at the *Dial*, then one of the leading cultural journals in the English-speaking world, and edited by Scofield Thayer and James Sibley Watson, both of whom became her close friends. She eventually became the magazine's editor, serving in this capacity from 1925 until its demise in 1929. Through her work at the *Dial* Moore was able to meet many literary notables, and to form friendships with some, the most important perhaps being that with George Saintsbury. But her work at the magazine, with its high standards of production and many other demands, exhausted her, and she greeted its closing with mixed emotions.

The publication of her first book, *Poems*, in 1921, helped inaugurate a career marked by many prizes and a reputation for experimental poetry of severe excellence and, to some, nearly impenetrable difficulty. *Poems* was published not in the United States, but in England, with the aid of poet and critic Richard Aldington, who had first brought Moore's poetry to public attention, and his wife H. D. (Hilda Doolittle), who had briefly attended Bryn Mawr when Moore was there. At the time England was far more receptive to the kind of experimental poetry that Moore was writing.

She moved to Brooklyn in 1929 in order to live nearer to her brother, then stationed at the Brooklyn Naval Yard, where he served as a navy chaplain. Making this borough her own, she was to become identified with its baseball team, the Brooklyn Dodgers, as well as with the famous Camperdown Elm in Prospect Park, both of which she celebrated in verse. The Brooklyn Institute, with its library and lecture series, served as her source for the meticulous and occasionally abstruse details, especially in the area of natural history, that came to be one of her main stylistic markers.

Her second book of poems, and first American volume, called *Observations*, in homage to T. S. Eliot's *Prufrock and Other Observations* (1918), was published in 1924. It won her the prestigious Dial Award in 1925. She combined portions of her first two books to produce *Selected Poems* in 1935. This volume was graced with an introduction by Eliot, was reviewed by many, and intelligently praised by some. Eliot's

high regard for Moore's poetry helped bring her to the attention of a wider public. A book of great skill and depth appeared in 1936: *The Pangolin* contained only five poems but clearly established Moore's claims as a master of her craft and one of the most intelligent poets of her time. From this time on she continued to produce slim volumes of dense but lyrical poems, and a discriminating body of literary criticism, mostly in the form of reviews and essays.

In the 1940's she experienced the death of her mother and labored over her translation of the entire *Fables* of LaFontaine, which appeared in 1954. She published her *Collected Poems* in 1951. In 1953 her reputation suddenly erupted outside of the literary elite when she won three important awards: the Bollingen Prize, the Pulitzer Prize, and the National Book Award. In the same year *Time* referred to her as America's greatest living female poet, and she increasingly received the attention, and eventually the adulation, of the popular press.

Predilections, a collection of her prose writing, including the important essay "Henry James as a Characteristic American," appeared in 1955.

By the late 1950's she was writing verse of an occasional nature, pulling together in startling juxtaposition images and references from her wide reading in both classic and popular literature; her poems frequently appeared in the *New Yorker*.

A profile in the *New Yorker* (1957) that stressed her nimble and erudite skills at seemingly haphazard conversation, and a much noticed attempt, begun in 1955, to supply the Ford Motor Company with the name for a new model (which was eventually called the very un-Moore-like "Edsel"), contributed to her identity as an eccentric. The attempted naming of the Ford model was a result in part of her fascination with the language of advertising, as well as her enchantment with modern technology. She continued to add to her list of admiring fellow poets; a friendship with W. H. Auden began in 1944 and grew in importance for both writers.

As she aged she became a kind of cultural icon. She spent more and more time receiving honorary degrees, to be capped by one from Harvard University in 1968. Her celebrity status was solidified when she appeared on the cover of the June 1966 edition of *Esquire* with several other people described as the "unknockables."

She was also asked to throw out the first ball on opening day at Yankee Stadium in 1967. Essays published late in life testify to her continuing interest in fashion and clothing, not simply as journalistic material but as clues to the culture's enduring concern with ease and beauty. She continued to live in Brooklyn until 1965, when she moved back to Greenwich Village.

Throughout her career she worked as a poet of great, even dazzling, lexical range, as if the very breadth of her vocabulary were her main accomplishment. From childhood on, for example, she was taken with the slang of sports, as her famous "Hometown Piece for Messrs. Alston and Reese" demonstrates, and she wrote poems about subjects as diverse as quartz clocks and Yul Brynner.

Often this emphasis on her vocabulary and erudite references obscured Moore's real talents as a poet. George Plimpton, for example, wrote a number of pieces in 1963 and 1964 for *Harper's* about her curious conversational style and her interest in baseball, without discussing her poetry. But from the beginning Moore used her poetry to explore the realms of nature and culture and their provocative and revealing intersections. She was perhaps the most widely read poet of her generation, not excepting even Eliot and Pound, both notorious for their bookishness. At the same time she had a very keen eye for natural beauty and often used animals and their habits to enrich her meditations about grace, complexity, reticence, and spontaneity. Many critics have remarked on the turn to a more directly moral poetry after World War II, when Moore seemed to go through a crisis of faith. Others, however, have recognized that Moore's limited but distinguished body of work has always been marked by beauty and moral concerns in a way unique among modern writers.

[An extensive collection of manuscripts and memorabilia is in the Rosenbach Museum and Library in Philadelphia. Her poetry is available in *Complete Poems of Marianne Moore* (1981), her prose in *Complete Prose of Marianne Moore* (1986).

The only full-length biography is Charles Molesworth, *Marianne Moore: A Literary Life* (1990). Important critical studies include John Slatin, *The Savage's Romance: The Poetry of Marianne Moore* (1985); and Margaret Holley, *The Poetry of Marianne Moore: A Study in Voice and Value* (1987). Patricia Willis has edited *Marianne Moore: Woman and Poet* (1991), which contains a bibliography and

several interesting studies of aspects of Moore's life and work. Moore was the subject of one of the installments of the video series called *A Poet's Vision* (1989); it features oral history and reflections by several Moore scholars. An obituary is in the *New York Times*, Feb. 6, 1972.]

CHARLES MOLESWORTH

MOOREHEAD, AGNES (Dec. 6, 1906–Apr. 30, 1974), actress, was born in Clinton, Mass., to John Henderson Moorehead, a Presbyterian minister, and Mary Mildred McCauley. Moorehead grew up in Reedsburg, Wis., where her father had a pastorate. She said she learned to act by mimicking members of her father's congregation. Years later, she would spend hours at the docks in New York City, listening to immigrants and studying their voices and mannerisms.

She made her first public performance—at the age of three—singing "The Lord Is My Shepherd" at a church program arranged by her father. At age ten she was in summer stock. At twelve she was in a ballet chorus at the St. Louis Municipal Opera, and at sixteen, she sang on a new St. Louis radio station.

Moorehead attended Ohio's Muskingum College, which was founded by her uncle, then completed a master's degree in English and public speaking at the University of Wisconsin.

Her first job was as a high school English teacher in Soldiers Grove, Wis., where she also coached the town drama club. Eventually she saved enough money to move to New York City, enrolling at the American Academy of Dramatic Arts. She became an honor student there while also teaching dramatics at the prestigious Dalton School. She began to land roles in Broadway plays, but the Great Depression hit the theater business hard and Moorehead drifted into radio.

In 1930, she married fellow actor John Griffith Lee, and they adopted a son. They divorced in 1952.

She performed on radio with most of the big names of the 1930's, including Phil Baker, Fred Allen, Orson Welles, and Bob Hope, and on most of the major programs, including "The March of Time" and "Cavalcade of America." Her radio roles ran the gamut, from that of a bedridden woman about to be murdered in the suspense drama "Sorry, Wrong Number," to the heroine of a daytime serial, "Joyce Jordan, Girl Interne."

With Welles and Joseph Cotten, she was a

founder and charter member of the famed Mercury Theater Players. In 1941, she made her movie debut with a small role in Welles's film classic, *Citizen Kane*. The following year she portrayed a neurotic spinster aunt in Welles's *The Magnificent Ambersons*, winning the New York Film Critics' best actress award and an Academy Award nomination. She would be nominated for an Oscar four more times—never winning—during her career for roles in *Mrs. Parkington* (1944), *Johnny Belinda* (1948), *All that Heaven Allows* (1955), and *Hush, Hush Sweet Charlotte* (1964).

In 1951, Moorehead returned to the stage in a critically acclaimed reading of "Don Juan in Hell," the famed but rarely produced third act of Bernard Shaw's play *Man and Superman*. After its first presentation in Stockton, Calif.—with Moorehead as Donna Ana, Charles Laughton as the Devil, Charles Boyer as the Don, and Sir Cedric Hardwicke as the Commander—the production toured the United States and England, playing to capacity audiences. "The actress has the crisp, clean elegance of a lily," a New York reviewer wrote of Moorehead, who played the role in a mauve satin gown with her red hair piled high on her head. "She falls into exquisite poses and moves like a self-appointed queen."

In 1952 she married actor Robert Gist. Like her first marriage, that union was also to end in divorce, in 1958.

In all, Moorehead made about 100 films, developing a reputation as a fine character actress. But her many "old hag" roles didn't bother her. "I was never pretty enough to play a heroine," she once said. "As a little girl I was the long, gangly type . . . sad and pathetic. I have no vanity at all."

She was perhaps best known by the American public for her histrionic supporting role as Endora the witch in the television series "Bewitched," which ran from 1964 to 1972. In 1974, Moorehead participated in another reading of "Don Juan in Hell," with three other actors. That production fared less well than the original.

Toward the end of her career, she commented: "It's a terribly discouraging business, a sorrowful business, a critical business. You're up there, and the people can take the skin off you, bit by bit, and enjoy it. If you get anywhere in it, there's a strange kind of human tendency to tear you down."

She died of lung cancer at the Mayo Clinic in Rochester, Minn.

[A biography, *Agnes Moorehead: A Very Private Person*, by Warren A. Sherk, was published in 1976. An obituary appears in the *New York Times*, May 1, 1974.]

PAUL GEITNER

MORGAN, ARTHUR ERNEST (June 20, 1878–Nov. 16, 1975), conservationist, college president, civil engineer, and first engineer of the Tennessee Valley Authority, was born in Cincinnati, Ohio, the son of John D. Morgan, engineer, and Anna Frances Wiley, a homemaker. He attended local schools in Cincinnati, and, at age ten when the family moved to St. Cloud, Minn., completed its three-year high school in 1896. Moody and introverted, he honored his Quaker mother's puritan goals in life and religion, rejecting his father's easygoing social attitudes. Self-taught, and a seeker of principles, young Morgan worked at various trades away from home, briefly attended the University of Colorado in 1898, and returned to pick up his father's land-care and surveying occupation.

In Populist and Progressive times he worked, first in St. Cloud, then after 1902 in the South, having joined the U.S. Drainage section of the Department of Agriculture, to curb land waste in "wetlands," which depletes large areas of topsoil. He drew up legislation for state bodies to reclaim abused terrain. In 1909 he organized the Morgan Engineering Company, in Memphis, Tenn., which revived an estimated two million acres of wetlands. His 1909 book on his St. Francis Valley, Ark., wetlands project pioneered guides for saving priceless topsoil.

Morgan was married twice. In September 1904 he married Urania Jones, who died in 1905, leaving him with an infant son. In July 1911, he married Lucy Middleton Griscom; they had two children.

When Dayton, Ohio, in 1913 experienced the third-largest flood in American history, Morgan was called in by Colonel Edward A. Deeds, of National Cash Register Company, who had organized relief for the devastated city, to build dams for its protection. Morgan studied flood control at home and abroad, and he designed his Miami Conservancy District with dams deliberately kept empty to meet emergencies. He set up a "pilot plant"—an actual model of the system into which water could be pumped and its action analyzed to ensure that the completed system would respond to water flow as anticipated. Morgan's larger dreams of a better society were expressed in the attention he gave his workers, who were provided with model villages and good wages, and even with suggestions for books to improve their minds. He followed such a pattern also in dam work done in Pueblo, Colo.

In 1920 Morgan assumed the presidency of Antioch College in nearby Yellow Springs, Ohio; it had deteriorated since Horace Mann had directed its growth and curriculum in the 1850's. Morgan sought courses that would link formal education to life itself. Although Morgan's group of humanistic traditions was somewhat limited, he chose teachers who discussed, rather than lectured, and who were open to new ideas. He encouraged local cooperative ventures and modernized Mann's old work-study program, searching for challenging off-campus jobs as part of the curriculum; under his tenure, Antioch's enrollment increased by 500 percent. In 1921 he became president of the Progressive Education Association.

When, in 1933, newly elected President Franklin D. Roosevelt sought projects that would put men back to work, he appointed Morgan first chairman of the Tennessee Valley Authority (TVA), which was to build eleven dams at strategic river points and to produce water power for the people of the valley, many of whom were still without electricity in their homes. Also appointed to the three-man board were agricultural expert Harcourt A. Morgan (not a relative) and young David E. Lilienthal, sponsored by such liberals as Senator George W. Norris. Commonwealth and Southern, the power monopoly of the region, had done little for its farmers; liberals planned to create "yard sticks" of reasonable electricity charges which would force the company to cooperate or be left behind by the program of caring government.

Morgan was persuaded that the company's chairman, Wendell Willkie, was sincere in professing a change in attitude toward the region's poor, yet he was reluctant to augment government power unnecessarily. Moreover, he planned to educate the farmers in their own best interest, as he had his workers in Dayton. Leaders in the area protested this program as interfering with local mores and preferences.

Morgan found himself increasingly isolated among New Deal managers and educated partisans. Unused to controversy and awkward in argument, he complained publicly that he was being bypassed by his associates. President Roosevelt called them together to confront issues. When Morgan was unable to produce evidence, he was discharged from the TVA Board in 1938.

Although it appeared that Morgan had been effectively retired from public life, he set out on a new career, as author and innovator. Working through his small organization, Community Service, he began to correspond with activists in towns seeking ideas for improvement. In 1944, he published a book on Edward Bellamy, arguing that Bellamy's famous *Looking Backwards* (1888) was not a "utopia" but a reasonable social statement that had influenced the New Deal. *Nowhere Was Somewhere* (1946) went further in claiming that Thomas More's *Utopia* was not a fantasy but an account of ways of life in still officially "undiscovered" early-sixteenth-century Peru, a fact that had later puzzled historians. Morgan's theory was never fully debated.

Industries for Small Communities (1953) made a case for small, independent businesses that could operate at a profit outside of monopolies. It cited numerous successes, including businesses in his own Yellow Springs. His message unofficially reached businessmen and town leaders. Weighty projects he undertook in this period included an Indian government–sponsored trip (1947–1948), which resulted in the establishment of a number of colleges set in rural areas to disseminate agricultural knowledge to farmers. In 1954, Morgan served as a consultant to the Volta River aluminum production project of the Gold Coast in Africa.

In the late 1960's and early 1970's, Morgan made a strong effort to prevent the U.S. Corps of Engineers from flooding Seneca Indian land in Pennsylvania. Although his case was lost, his enduring efforts turned attention on Indian rights. His *Dams and Other Disasters* (1971) technically analyzed the corps's bureaucratic policies. His last book, *The Making of the T.V.A.* (1974), written when he was ninety-six years of age, found him willing to concede error, but not principle.

Morgan died in a Xenia, Ohio, nursing home; his ashes were buried on the nearby Antioch College campus.

[Morgan's more than forty books amply illustrate his views. *The Seedman* (1933) serves as a metaphoric overview of his "pilot plant" principle for improving society. See also his *My World* (1928) and *Search for a Purpose* (1955); Lucy Morgan, *Finding His World* (1927); Clarence J. Leuba, *A Road to Creativity* (1971); and Walter Kahoe. *Arthur Morgan* (1977). For a detailed negative portrayal, see Roy Talbert, Jr., *FDR's Utopian* (1987). An obituary is in the *New York Times*, Nov. 17, 1975.]

LOUIS FILLER

MORÓN, ALONZO GRASEANO (Apr. 12, 1909–Oct. 31, 1971), sociologist and educator, was born in St. Thomas, U.S. Virgin Islands. As a child he demonstrated such superior academic abilities that friends raised funds to send him to high school in the United States. In 1923, Morón entered Hampton Institute in Hampton, Va., founded as Hampton Normal and Industrial Institute in 1868 by Samuel C. Armstrong to educate black and Indian children. In 1927, he graduated with a trade school certificate in upholstery and a high school diploma.

In 1928, Morón entered Brown University on a full scholarship; he graduated cum laude in 1932 with a Bachelor of Philosophy in sociology. He continued his education at the University of Pittsburgh, where he received a master's degree in sociology and social work in 1933. His thesis was entitled "The Movement of the Negro Population Within the City of Pittsburgh During the Period from 1910 to 1930." He married Leola Rowena Churchill on Sept. 12, 1932; they had no children.

In 1933, Morón was appointed commissioner of public welfare of the Virgin Islands by Governor Paul Pearson. From 1936 to 1940, Morón was the manager of University Homes, a 675-unit public housing project for blacks in Atlanta. During this period he taught classes in housing for the Department of Social Work at Atlanta University.

In 1944, Morón received a Rosenwald fellowship to Harvard Law School, from which he graduated in 1947. These years of academia and social work did not lead him to forget his early years at Hampton Institute, by then a college. While he was at Harvard, Morón served as business consultant to the institute, and upon his graduation he became its general business manager.

Morón returned to Hampton at an auspicious time. Its president was not performing to the satisfaction of the board, and in 1948 he resigned. An interim administrative committee was appointed with Morón as chairman. He was named acting president in October 1948 and was elected president the following year.

Morón was the first alumnus and the first African American to serve as president of Hampton Institute. In his inaugural address on Oct. 29, 1949, he defined Hampton Institute's role as "continu[ing] to meet changing needs of students without becoming ordinary or mediocre."

With these goals in mind, Morón initiated many innovative programs. Recognizing that the often-difficult transition from high school to college resulted in a high percentage of failure, he established a six-week precollege program for high school graduates in 1953. Fifty were selected each session to take intensive courses in English and mathematics. If they passed with a "C" or better, they would receive three semester hours of college credit. They also acquired improved study habits and social skills. Another Hampton Institute experiment was designed to improve the quality of the public schools in the Virgin Islands. Beginning in 1954, the Off-Island Program each year sent five graduates to Hampton Institute for a five-year teacher-training program, after which both a bachelor's and a master's degree were conferred. The first students graduated in 1958. The On-Island Program allowed professors from the United States to travel to the Virgin Islands and offer courses for teachers in the evenings and on Saturdays.

Despite Morón's innovative programs, his tenure as president of Hampton Institute was not an easy one. He had to take strict measures to cut waste and improve the inefficiency of administration and personnel. He also believed that financially strapped black colleges should leave mass education to publicly supported institutions. Hampton's mission was to train leaders in business, general education, home economics, nursing, physical education, and technology. This curriculum was offensive to those who believed in the liberal arts, and Morón was often at odds with his chief executive officer, the trustees, and faculty members.

In 1959, Morón resigned as president of Hampton Institute, and was succeeded by Jerome H. Holland. He complained that the trustees had unjustly rejected some fund-raising proposals and that they had violated proper channels of communication by becoming directly involved in the grievances of faculty and students. This reason for his resignation reflected both his successes and his difficulties as president.

Morón returned to the Caribbean, where he was named deputy regional director, Department of Housing and Urban Development, based in San Juan, P.R. He died in San Juan.

[Morón's papers are at Hampton University, Hampton, Va. His publications include "Public Housing from a Community Point of View," *Social Forces*, Oct. 1940; "Where Shall They Live?" *American City*, Apr. 1942; and "Maintaining the Solvency of the Private College Through Efficient Management," *Journal of Negro Education*, Spring 1958. For an assessment of his presidency of Hampton Institute, see Mae Barbee Boone Pleasant, *Hampton University* (1990). An obituary is in the *New York Times*, Nov. 1, 1971.]

DANA L. SAMPLE

MORRISON, JIM (Dec. 8, 1943–July 3, 1971), singer, songwriter, poet, and filmmaker, was born James Douglas Morrison in Melbourne, Fla., the son of George Stephen Morrison, an Annapolis graduate who rose to the rank of rear admiral, and Clara Clarke. Since the United States naval officer was often at sea, Clara raised Jim and his two younger siblings. Morrison's early years were characterized by frequent disruptions. Following their father from base to base, the family moved over ten times before settling in Alexandria, Va., where Morrison attended George Washington High School. There, he read widely in classical and world literature; works by Arthur Rimbaud, Charles Baudelaire, William Blake, and Jack Kerouac drew his attention, and he was particularly influenced by Friedrich Nietzsche.

After graduating in 1961, Morrison attended St. Petersburg Junior College (1961–1962) and Florida State University (1962–1963) before transferring in February 1964 to the University of California at Los Angeles to study film. Awarded a B.A. with a major in theater arts on Aug. 13, 1965, Morrison spent the summer in Los Angeles drinking, taking LSD, and writing many of the songs that would later appear on the Doors' first two albums. One fortuitous afternoon he met organist Ray Manzarek on Venice Beach. Morrison sang some of his lyrics for Manzarek and they decided to form a rock group. Recruiting drummer John Densmore

and guitarist Robby Krieger, they called themselves the Doors, a name derived from William Blake's lines in "The Marriage of Heaven and Hell": "If the doors of perception were cleansed every thing would appear to man as it is, infinite."

In January 1966, the Doors played their first long-standing engagement at the London Fog club in Los Angeles. Here, Morrison began to perfect his theatrical style as lead singer, and to use his sex appeal on stage, as Elvis Presley and other rock stars had before him. After the Fog, the Doors were hired as the house band at the Whiskey-A-Go-Go, a Los Angeles nightclub, where they began attracting huge crowds. Jac Holzman discovered the group there, and signed them to a recording contract with Elektra Records. In November 1966, Morrison moved in with Pamela Courson, who was to become his common-law wife. Never a believer in monogamy, he had countless one-night stands and numerous affairs. He even married Patricia Kennealy, the twenty-two-year-old editor of *Jazz and Pop* and a practicing witch, in a Celtic ceremony on Midsummers Night (June 24) in 1970. In the end, however, Morrison always returned to Pamela. After his death, she would inherit his estate.

The group's first album, *The Doors*, was released in January 1967. "Break on Through," the first single, received little airplay, but the second single, an abridged version of "Light My Fire," rose to number one on the charts and became an anthem for the race riots breaking out that summer in Detroit. In November, the Recording Industry Association of America certified both the single and the album as gold. This initial success was followed by two strong albums, *Strange Days* (1967), and *Waiting for the Sun* (1968).

As the Doors' popularity soared, Morrison sought to create a mythic persona. He was particularly adept at providing good copy. "You could say it's an accident that I was ideally suited for the work I am doing," he said in an Elektra publicity statement. "It's the feeling of a bow string being pulled back for 22 years and suddenly let go." He described the Doors in a *Newsweek* interview as "erotic politicians," a phrase that would later haunt him. Denying all antecedents, he falsely informed the press that his parents were dead. He also claimed that as a boy, after he witnessed an auto accident outside of Albuquerque, his spirit had been taken over by an old Indian shaman. His photograph, in various outlandish poses, began to appear in magazines like *16* and *Vogue*. He soon realized he had created a monster.

After the success of the first album, the Doors were in demand all along the concert circuit. On Sept. 19, 1967, they made their first appearance on "The Ed Sullivan Show." The pressure of performing, however, was beginning to take its toll on Morrison. He began to drink heavily and to experiment with cocaine. Morrison initially used drugs in an attempt to widen consciousness, to "break on through" to a transcendent reality. Now, however, his quest became a flight from the pressures brought on by fame and performing. In December 1967, charged with obscenity at a New Haven, Conn., concert, Morrison earned the dubious distinction of being the first rock performer to be arrested on stage. In August 1968, their concert crowd rioted in Cleveland, and the experience was nearly repeated in New York's Singer Bowl. On tour in Amsterdam, Morrison overdosed and was unable to perform.

Back in the studio in Los Angeles, Morrison was usually drunk and often late for recording sessions. Neither Morrison nor Krieger was happy with the fourth album, *The Soft Parade* (1969), which featured more of Krieger's lyrics and the addition of horns and strings, which watered down the Doors' unique sound. The album did, however, yield a hit single, "Touch Me."

On Feb. 28, 1969, Morrison attended a performance of the Living Theatre's *Paradise Now* in Los Angeles, and was deeply impressed by the group's efforts at audience involvement. The Living Theatre's methods may have inspired Morrison's notorious performance at Miami's Dinner Key auditorium on Saturday, March 1. He arrived late and drunk and, once on stage, he alternately berated the audience and challenged them to love him. Finally, he attempted to expose himself. Whether he succeeded remains a question, but he was nevertheless subsequently charged with one felony count of "lewd and lascivious behavior in public" and several misdemeanors, including indecent exposure, public use of profanity, and public drunkenness. Although acquitted of the felony charge and one of the misdemeanors, he was found guilty of indecent exposure and profanity and sentenced to eight months' hard labor in the Dade County jail. Pending appeal, Morrison was released on $50,000 bond.

After the Miami incident, the Doors were blacklisted; cities canceled concerts and radio stations refused to play their songs. On Mar. 23, 1969, as a direct result of Morrison's actions, Miami held a rally for decency at the Orange Bowl, which drew over thirty thousand people. John Densmore estimated the group's loss in income as a result of the obscenity incident to be over one million dollars.

Morrison was becoming increasingly disenchanted with his role as rock star and decadent sex symbol. Encouraged by Pamela and poet Michael McClure, he turned to poetry. In the spring of 1969, he privately printed two books, *The Lords* and *The New Creatures*, in limited editions of one hundred copies each. These were later published by Simon and Schuster as *The Lords and The New Creatures* (1970). Morrison also began devoting more of his time to filmmaking. His *Feast of Friends* won first prize for best documentary at the Atlanta International Film Festival.

Given the difficulties with concert bookings, the Doors focused on studio recordings; they released their fifth album, *Morrison Hotel* (1970), and their last studio album of new material, *L.A. Woman* (1971). On Dec. 8, 1970, Morrison's twenty-seventh birthday, he recorded several hours of poetry that would appear posthumously as *An American Prayer* (1978).

In March 1971, Morrison followed Pamela Courson to Paris, where he hoped to concentrate on his writing. On July 3, 1971, she found him dead in the bathtub. His death was attributed to heart failure, but much conjecture surrounds the circumstances of Morrison's death, particularly the role drugs might have played. He was buried, without an autopsy, in the Poet's Corner of Père-Lachaise cemetery, a final resting place he shares with Oscar Wilde and Edith Piaf, among others.

[Morrison's notebooks and papers are held by Mr. and Mrs. Columbus Courson, Pamela's parents. His poems are collected in *Wilderness* (1988) and *The American Night* (1990). The two most detailed biographies are Jerry Hopkins and Danny Sugarman, *No One Here Gets Out Alive* (1980), and James Riordan and Jerry Prochnicky, *Break On Through: The Life and Death of Jim Morrison* (1991). See also John Densmore, *Riders on the Storm: My Life with Jim Morrison and the Doors* (1990); Dylan Jones, *Jim*

Morrison: Dark Star (1990); and Patricia Kennealy, *Strange Days: My Life with and Without Jim Morrison* (1992). Film and video presentations include *The Doors Are Open* (1968); *The Doors: A Tribute to Jim Morrison* (1982); *The Doors: Dance on Fire* (1985); *The Doors: Live at the Hollywood Bowl* (1987); *The Doors: Live in Europe* (1989); and Oliver Stone, *The Doors* (1991). An obituary is in the *New York Times*, July 9, 1971.]

WILLIAM M. GARGAN

MORSE, WAYNE LYMAN (Oct. 20, 1900–July 22, 1974), U.S. senator, educator, author, and arbitrator, was born in Madison, Wis., the son of Wilbur Frank Morse and Jessie White. His father was a livestock farmer, and young Morse's exposure to his father's business provided the impetus for him to raise poultry and Shetland ponies as a boy. Morse first learned his politics and passion for oratory from Senator Robert La Follette, a Republican from Wisconsin who spoke for the small farmer and the working class.

He attended public schools in the Madison area and graduated from the University of Wisconsin at Madison with a Ph.B. in 1922. He majored in labor economics. His skill in argumentation brought him the Vilas Medal in debate at the University of Wisconsin. While studying for his M.A. (1924) Morse was an instructor in argumentation at Wisconsin, and the coach of the debate team. He completed a four-year military training course at the University of Wisconsin in 1922 and subsequently was commissioned a second lieutenant in the U.S. Army Reserves.

On June 18, 1924, Morse married Mildred Downie, a former home economics instructor; they would have three children. The couple moved to Minneapolis, where he taught at the University of Minnesota as an assistant professor of argumentation from 1924 to 1926. While teaching, he was enrolled in the law school; he received his LL.B. in 1928. Morse next went to Columbia University on a one-year teaching fellowship. In 1929 he was appointed assistant professor of law at the University of Oregon, advanced to associate professor in 1930, and became full professor and dean of the law school in 1931. In 1932 he was named dean and director of law of the Oregon State System of Higher Education. Morse's rapid rise was capped by a J.D. awarded from Columbia University in 1932.

In 1936, Morse left the University of Oregon

when the United States attorney general appointed him a special assistant in charge of a study of law administration in the nation. The study produced the five-volume *Attorney General's Survey of Release Procedures* (1939), of which Morse was editor in chief. Aside from his legal career and educational work, Morse's pre-Senate days were marked by recognition as one of the country's foremost labor arbitrators. From 1939 to 1940 Morse was appointed by Secretary of Labor Frances Perkins to serve as Pacific Coast arbitrator of disputes between shipowners and the International Longshoremen's and Warehousemen's Union.

In 1941, President Franklin Roosevelt named Morse chairman of the Railway Emergency Board and an alternate public member of the National Defense Mediation Board. In 1942, Roosevelt appointed Morse to the newly formed National War Labor Board. He served on the board until 1944, when he resigned to protest concessions granted to John L. Lewis and the United Mine Workers Union. Morse argued that the striking coal miners were not entitled to a larger wage boost than other workers. He insisted that the War Labor Board decisions rest only on evidence, that all complaining parties keep working during arbitration, and that all parties accept the decision of the board until tested in the courts.

Morse began his political career in 1944. Despite his New Deal leanings, he won the Oregon Republican nomination for the U.S. Senate, ousting the incumbent, Rufus Cecil Holman. In the general election, he defeated his Democratic opponent, Edgar W. Smith, carrying more counties in Oregon than any previous candidate for the Senate. The freshman senator from Oregon took the oath of office in January 1945 and was promptly assigned to Senate committees on Education and Labor, Armed Services, Mines and Mining, Claims, Public Buildings and Grounds, and Post Offices and Post Roads. In foreign affairs he supported the United Nations Charter (1945), the Greek-Turkish aid bill (1947), the North Atlantic Security Pact (1949), and appropriations for the Marshall Plan (1950). On the domestic side, Morse voted against the Taft-Hartley bill in 1947 and favored federal aid to education in 1948 and 1949.

Although Morse was reelected in 1950 as a Republican, he openly opposed a number of the economic measures generally favored by many in that party. Initially he strongly supported Dwight Eisenhower for the GOP presidential nomination, but became upset with Eisenhower's weak civil rights stand and his choice of Richard Nixon as his running mate. Morse left the Republican party in October 1952 to become an independent, though he supported Adlai Stevenson for president.

Morse arrived at the opening of the Eighty-third Congress with a folding chair in hand, asking on which side of the aisle he should sit. After being placed on the Republican side, he was stripped of important committee seats and assigned to the less important District of Columbia and Public Works committees. In April 1953 Morse delivered the longest continuous oration in the history of the Senate when he spoke for twenty-two hours and twenty-six minutes, filibustering against a pending offshore oil bill designed to give title to the coastal states.

Reelected to the Senate in 1956 as a Democrat, Morse entered the most controversy-packed six-year term of his twenty-four years on Capitol Hill. In 1959, when Republican Clare Booth Luce was named ambassador to Brazil, Morse unleashed a vicious attack against her confirmation. An unpleasant exchange of dialogue, accusation, and counteraccusation ensued. After he had persuaded his colleagues that Luce's insult to him was an affront to the entire Senate, Luce resigned her appointment even though she had been confirmed.

Morse's last crusade, the one for which he will best be remembered, was against the Vietnam War. In 1965 he and Alaska Senator Ernest Gruening were the only senators who voted against the Gulf of Tonkin Resolution, which gave President Johnson the power to intervene in Vietnam at an unprecedented level. Although Morse took great pride in his battle against American intervention in Vietnam, he could not avoid the opposition that his "nay" vote brought to his quest for reelection in 1968. He fervently supported Eugene McCarthy's 1968 antiwar campaign, and as a result lost his seat to Republican Robert Packwood by little more than three thousand votes. Four years later, Republican senator Mark Hatfield defeated Morse in the general election by a wide margin.

"A true liberal can't limit himself to a few areas," Morse declared. "He must be on guard everywhere, ready to pounce on evil wherever it raises its ugly head." A senator from Oregon for twenty-four years, Morse gave exclusive loyalty

neither to the Republicans nor to the Democrats. His liberalism, untamed and fiery, rang through the walls of Capitol Hill from 1945 to 1969. Unfazed by criticism, he embraced principles, courage, and honesty in the face of controversy. His stormy relationship with fellow senators and presidents Truman, Eisenhower, and Johnson earned him the nickname "the Tiger."

Morse retired to his twenty-nine-acre farm in Eugene, Oreg., after the 1972 defeat. He seemed content raising saddle horses and cattle. But "the Tiger," who vociferously condemned conservatives for over twenty years on the floor of the Senate, could not be caged. In 1974 he announced his intentions to run for a fifth Senate term. He won a relatively easy primary and prepared for the general election in November against incumbent Senator Packwood. Because of his personal integrity and clean record, Morse had a good chance to win in light of the Watergate scandal. In the midst of the campaign, Morse developed a urinary infection that led to blood poisoning and eventually to kidney failure. He died in Eugene.

Morse's colorful and often provocative rhetoric scalded his opposition and recognized no partisanship. Mostly he championed the liberals; he fought for civil rights and liberties, and denounced the special-interest groups that sought to sap the power from public domain. Morse candidly spoke his mind and felt little need to coddle his sometimes fallible Senate colleagues. He infuriated his colleagues with brash, bold speeches, yet managed to educate the public in liberal views. His combination of pragmatism and patience allowed him to utter a firm warning to supporters of the Vietnam War. A man at home in neither the Republican nor the Democratic party, Morse pursued a political career in which he upbraided leaders in the Senate without regard for party membership. Although he respected elected leaders, no muzzle could restrain him from speaking his mind. The mustachioed Morse searched for truth at the expense of his own popularity, guided by an unequivocable conscience and integrity; candor and honesty were the result.

[Morse's papers are at the University of Oregon at Eugene. See A. Robert Smith, *Tiger in the Senate* (1962); and Lee Wilkins, *Wayne Morse* (1985). An obituary appears in the *New York Times*, July 23, 1974.]

F. ROSS PETERSON

MOSELY, PHILIP EDWARD (Sept. 21, 1905–Jan. 13, 1972), Sovietologist, was born in Westfield, Mass., the son of Arthur Chauncey Mosely, a builder and contractor, and Eliza Harvey Rust. Mosely's paternal ancestors had immigrated to America from England in 1630.

Raised an Episcopalian, Mosely received his primary education at public schools in Westfield and received a B.A. in 1926 and a Ph.D. in 1933 from Harvard University. While he was pursuing his doctoral studies at Harvard, he taught history at Princeton University (1929–1930) and conducted historical research in Moscow (1930–1932). On Apr. 2, 1930, Mosely married Ruth Bissell, the daughter of Douglas Bissell. They had two children.

In 1933 Mosely became a history instructor at Union College in Schenectady, N.Y. His first book was published in 1934, entitled *Russian Diplomacy and the Opening of the Eastern Question in 1838 and 1839*. In 1935, after receiving a fellowship from the Social Science Research Council, he left teaching to conduct research in the Balkans for two years. Upon his return to the United States in 1936, Mosely joined the faculty of Cornell University as assistant professor, becoming associate professor in 1940. He remained at Cornell until 1942, when he left to serve in the U.S. Department of State during World War II.

At the State Department, Mosely, a Democrat, served as assistant chief in the division of political studies and chief of the division of territorial studies, as well as adviser to Secretary of State Cordell Hull and the U.S. delegation at the Moscow Conference in 1943. From 1944 to 1945 he acted as a political adviser to the U.S. delegation to the European Advisory Commission in London, and in 1945 he was a political adviser during the Potsdam Conference. His public-service career continued when he became political counsel to the Council of Foreign Ministers meeting in London and Paris in 1945 and 1946. Also in 1946 he was U.S. representative on the commission for the investigation of the Yugoslav-Italian boundary.

In 1946, Mosely joined the faculty of Columbia University as professor of international relations. He remained in that position until 1955, when he was promoted to adjunct professor, a title he held until 1963, when he became Adlai E. Stevenson Professor of International Relations and associate dean of the faculty of international relations. In that same year, he was named director of Columbia University's European Institute, a title he held until his death.

Considered a foremost authority on Russian studies in the United States, Mosely helped found the Russian Institute at Columbia in 1946. He served as director of the institute from 1951 to 1955, helping to shape it into a leading center for academic studies on the Soviet Union. For almost two years, starting in 1968, he was also chairman of the research council at the Georgetown University Center for Strategic and International Studies.

While at Columbia, Mosely held other noteworthy advisory positions. From 1952 to 1961 he served as director of a research program on the Soviet Union for the Council on Foreign Relations; from 1955 to 1963 he was director of studies for the council. He was a member of the board of trustees of the Rand Corporation from 1951 to 1961, and again after 1962.

Mosely penned close to two hundred articles and essays on East-West relations, Western Europe, and Soviet foreign policy during his career. In 1960 he completed a collection of articles, *The Kremlin and World Politics*. In 1962 he served as editor of *The Soviet Union, 1922–1962*.

Mosely was a small, dark-haired man who was described as having "a normally equable temperament," except when provoked. He is reported to have lambasted the scholar E. H. Carr when Carr once made an offhand allusion to American motives. Mosely was also confident in his scholarly opinions. In a 1961 article in the *New York Times Book Review*, Mosely attacked Nikita S. Khrushchev, the Soviet premier, for failing to understand the "forces of freedom" and urged the Communist leader to "broaden his perspective." Mosely was a talented linguist who spoke some six languages.

Mosely died at his home in New York.

[An obituary is in the *New York Times*, Jan. 14, 1972.]

TIMOTHY RHODES

MOTT, CHARLES STEWART (June 2, 1875–Feb. 2, 1973), industrialist and philanthropist, was born in Newark, N.J., the son of John Coon Mott and Isabella Turnbull Stewart. His father was involved with a well-established family cider and vinegar business, the Genesee Fruit Company. He wanted his son to work in that business, but young Charles wanted to study mechanical engineering. The two agreed that Charles could study engineering but would eventually join the family firm. In 1892, following graduation from high school in Hoboken, N.J., Mott enrolled in the Stevens Institute of Technology, also in Hoboken, majoring in mechanical engineering.

Mott's father persuaded him to interrupt his engineering studies and spend a year in Europe to study several topics related to the interests of the Genesee Fruit Company. He studied pure yeast culture at Jorgenson's Laboratory in Copenhagen, Denmark, and the chemistry of fermentation at the Technische Hochschule in Munich. He also had time to tour England and visit Paris. When he returned in 1895, he still preferred mechanical engineering and returned to Stevens, where he received his degree in 1897.

The elder Mott had acquired a carbonating concern in 1894 and reorganized it as the C. S. Mott Company. Charles spent his last two years at Stevens running his own manufacturing company. The new company pioneered selling its machinery for carbonating beverages to drugstores and confectionery shops on credit, with the monthly payments designed to be equal to the cost of the tanks of carbonated water the machinery replaced.

After graduation Mott devoted his energy to the carbonating business. In 1898, he joined the U.S. Navy. He participated in the bombardment of Santiago, Cuba, and saw action in nine engagements as a gunner's mate first class on the USS *Yankee* before returning to civilian life. His business interests now included a firm his father and uncle had bought in 1896 and reorganized as the Weston-Mott Company, which manufactured wire wheels for bicycles.

The Weston-Mott Company developed new products as the demand for bicycle wheels declined, including drop-forged axles, wire wheels with cushion rubber tires, and wire wheels for automobiles. This was the one family enterprise where Charles's interest in mechanical engineering could be fully utilized. In 1900, he became superintendent of the factory, while continuing with the carbonating business.

Despite his success in developing an electric automatic carbonating machine and manufacturing forty such machines for the Pan-American Exposition held in Buffalo in 1901, Mott saw the future of the family businesses in the emerging automobile industry and devoted his energy and talent to developing that market for Weston-Mott.

With William Doolittle, who joined the firm as part-owner and treasurer, Mott manufactured wire wheels for many of the early automotive pioneers, including Ransom Olds and James W. Packard. Doolittle and Mott kept pace with the rapidly growing auto industry and by 1903 had bought out the other stockholders. In 1905, William Durant approached them about relocating their plant to Flint, Mich., as part of his plan to make that city the major American automobile manufacturing center and headquarters of his firm, to be called General Motors.

In August 1906, Weston-Mott's Flint plant opened. Within a year, Doolittle died and Mott acquired his stock under their partnership agreement. Mott remained independent of Durant's rapidly expanding empire even after Durant acquired 49 percent of Weston-Mott in 1908. He even rejected an offer to join the General Motors board in 1910 in order to maintain his ability to work with other manufacturers. Mott nevertheless subscribed to stock in several of Durant's ventures and was well acquainted with his activities. As Durant was building General Motors after its incorporation in 1908, one of his prime tactics was buying established firms by exchanging stock. He very much wanted to add Weston-Mott to General Motors and continued discussions with Mott. In 1913, Mott transferred his 51-percent ownership share of Weston-Mott to General Motors in exchange for General Motors stock. He retained operational control of his firm and became a director of GM, a position he held for nearly sixty years. With this transfer, and his earlier investments in Durant ventures that also had been absorbed into General Motors, Mott was one of the firm's largest stockholders and a very wealthy man before he was forty.

In 1920, he became executive vice-president of General Motors, a position he held until 1937 through the several reorganizations of the 1920's. He was a vigorous promoter of ethyl gasoline, which solved the knocking problem that plagued early automobiles, and oversaw the introduction of DUCO paint, a quick-drying, high-luster product that solved both production and aesthetic problems. He also recruited a number of individuals who made major contributions to GM's development, including William S. Knudsen.

His duties at General Motors rarely absorbed his full energy, however, and Mott invested in a number of other businesses. He served as president and chairman of the Union Industrial Bank in Flint and owned a chain of four department stores, Smith, Bridgman and Company. In 1929, when Union Industrial was in dire straits, he personally put up $3.5 million to keep the bank solvent. He was also a major stockholder and officer in the United States Sugar Company, Northern Illinois Water Company, Illinois Water Service Company, and the Long Island Water Company.

More than most early auto industry pioneers, Mott was deeply committed to community service. He was elected mayor of Flint in 1912, 1913, and 1918, and made what had been a largely ceremonial position a force for positive change in the rapidly growing community. He sought the Republican nomination for governor in 1920 but was defeated in the primary.

In 1926, Mott established the Charles Stewart Mott Foundation, with two thousand shares of General Motors stock, to support projects that would improve life in Flint. Subsequent gifts greatly expanded the resources of the Mott Foundation, and it expanded its scope to encompass the entire world. In 1935, the Mott Foundation funded the establishment of an ambitious community school program in Flint, providing a wide variety of cultural and educational programs for adults. This program served as a model for similar programs for communities around the country.

Mott married Ethel Culbert Harding on June 14, 1900; they had three children. She died in an accident in 1924. In 1927, he married Mitties Butterfield Rathbun, who died in 1928. The following year he married Dee Van Balkom Furey; they divorced the same year. He married Ruth Mott Rawlings on Oct. 13, 1934; they had three children.

Despite his great wealth Mott lived frugally. He bought his suits off the rack at Smith, Bridgman and always drove one of General Motors' lower-priced cars. In his later years he drove a Corvair, at least in part to refute the vehicle's critics.

Mott's long service on the General Motors board of directors earned him wide respect in the auto industry, and his support for many community projects made him a highly visible, and much respected, figure in Flint, where he died.

[Mott's papers are at the General Motors Institute in Flint, Mich. See also Clarence H. Young and William A. Quinn, *Foundation for Living: The Story of Charles Stewart Mott and Flint* (1963); and Clarence H. Young, *In Memoriam: Charles Stewart Mott* (1975). An obituary is in the *New York Times*, Feb. 18, 1973.]

WILLIAM H. MULLIGAN, JR.

MUHAMMAD, ELIJAH (Oct. 7, 1897–Feb. 25, 1975), Black Muslim and civil rights leader, was born Elijah Poole on a tenant farm near Sandersville, Ga., a small farming community located between Macon and Augusta. His parents, Wali and Marie Poole, were former slaves. Wali was a sharecropper and part-time Baptist preacher who eked out a meager existence for his family of thirteen children. Elijah's formal education ended at the fourth grade, when the nine-year-old boy went to work full time in the fields. When he was sixteen he left home and roamed the countryside, working on railroad gangs and at whatever odd jobs he could find. He lived for a while in Atlanta, where he met and married Clara Evans in 1919. He moved with her and their two children to Detroit in 1923. For the next six years he worked on an automobile assembly line, where he encountered oppressive racial discrimination. For a short time he followed in his father's footsteps and was a Baptist preacher. The Great Depression left him and millions of others without jobs, and from 1929 to 1931 he lived on the public dole.

It was during these years that Elijah met W. D. Fard, a door-to-door salesman of silks and yard goods and founder of the Temple of Islam. In addition to the wares he peddled in Detroit's black ghettos, Fard carried to the oppressed black community an invitation to join his secret religious order, "The Lost-Found Nation of Islam in the Wilderness of North America." Elijah Poole was an early convert. Casting off his "slave" surname and adopting the Islamic surname Karriem, he became Fard's most zealous disciple. The Nation of Islam grew steadily. Elijah gradually assumed the leadership of the Detroit temple. In 1934 Fard mysteriously disappeared. Elijah thereafter announced that the "Master" had anointed him "Messenger of Allah," making him custodian of the vanished Master's revelation and head of the Nation of Islam. To symbolize his elevation, Elijah assumed the surname Muhammad.

Elijah's claim to leadership did not go uncontested. A power struggle ensued and Elijah was forced to flee to Chicago, where he established a new temple. His enemies followed him and he was forced to flee once again, this time to Washington, D.C. He lived there from 1935 to 1941, promoting the Nation of Islam and founding temples wherever he could. He attracted little attention outside the black community until 1942 when he began to criticize the government's treatment of Japanese Americans after Pearl Harbor. He urged African Americans not to serve in the United States armed forces. Arrested for sedition and acquitted, he was retried as a draft evader, convicted, and sentenced to serve five years in prison. From a federal penitentiary in Milan, Mich., he directed his religious movement, which continued to grow, in part because his imprisonment made him a martyr to many blacks. Released in 1946, he moved to Chicago to lead the temple he had established there a decade earlier.

Once he reestablished himself in Chicago, Elijah became the undisputed leader of the Nation of Islam. In the early postwar years the movement grew steadily but unspectacularly. In such publications as *The Supreme Wisdom: Solution to the So-called Negroes' Problem*, which became the basic text of the movement, and in the weekly tabloid newspaper *Muhammad Speaks*, Elijah spelled out the Black Muslim creed and proclaimed its message. His message was a blend of black nationalism, black capitalism, and black socialism that struck the same responsive chord among the country's oppressed blacks that Marcus Garvey, almost two generations earlier, had touched with his Back to Africa Movement. Elijah Muhammad proclaimed himself Allah's last prophet. His mission, he preached, was to lead his people out of white slavery, to free them "from the white man's yoke." He taught that Allah originally created the tribes of Shabazz, which consisted of all nonwhite peoples of the world. The white race was a later evil mutation to whom Allah had given a 6,000-year probationary rule. During their rule whites, who were "blue-eyed devils," had proven themselves to be intellectually and morally inferior to the nonwhite races and hopelessly corrupt. The end of their reign was imminent. Blacks must prepare themselves for the fast-approaching day when they, as Allah's favored people, would reign supreme. They must renounce the Christian god and the vices of the white society and build a separate black Nation of Islam within the larger white society. Separation, not integration, was the goal.

In preaching black separation, Elijah was also preaching black pride. The heart of his message was the value and worth of African Americans. Hard work and self-mastery, he taught, were the key to pride and self-esteem. Black Muslims must eschew tobacco, alcoholic beverages, drugs, nonmarital sex, profanity, gambling, dancing, and nonreligious music. In addition to upholding this puritanical morality, Muslims were expected to practice a self-discipline that was almost militaristic in nature. They must dress neatly and modestly, be polite, avoid loud talk and boisterous behavior, obey their leaders, pray five times daily, eat no pork, and fast regularly.

In keeping with his effort to eliminate black dependence on whites, Elijah promoted Muslim-owned and patronized businesses. He reiterated the slogan "Build black, buy black." In Chicago, Detroit, Washington, New York, and elsewhere blacks responded to his encouragement by opening restaurants, beauty parlors, barbershops, service stations, bakeries, grocery stores, and other small business establishments.

Beginning in the mid-1950's, with the help of Malcolm X, the Black Muslim movement began to grow phenomenally. Converted to Islam while he was in a Massachusetts prison, Malcolm became Elijah's star disciple following his release in 1952. A spellbinding speaker and charismatic leader, Malcolm defiantly offered to meet white violence with black violence. His brilliant polemical gifts, his angry confrontational style, and his inflammatory threats of black revolution won thousands of young and not-so-young converts to the movement. The most famous of these was the world heavyweight boxing champion Cassius Clay, who changed his name to Muhammad Ali following his conversion. Malcolm X and Muhammad Ali together gave Black Muslims a national visibility and appeal they had never before enjoyed. Malcolm's talk of black violence and revolution frightened whites and many blacks as well, especially civil rights leaders committed to passive resistance and nonviolence.

By the early 1960's Malcolm X had become chief spokesman and heir apparent to Elijah Muhammad. That relationship changed abruptly in December 1963, when Muhammad reprimanded Malcolm for an inflammatory remark he made about President John F. Kennedy after he was assassinated. Soon afterward, expressing dissatisfaction with Muhammad's exclusion of whites from the Nation of Islam and his nonengagement policy in civil rights, Malcolm announced that he was leaving Islam to found his own black nationalist movement. A year later, in 1965, he was assassinated by men thought to be Black Muslims loyal to Muhammad. Elijah Muhammad repeatedly denied any involvement in the murder. Malcolm's death sparked internecine fighting and violence that dogged the movement for years afterward.

Following Malcolm's defection and assassination, Muhammad became less visible publicly. He tried to remain out of the public eye and spent his time overseeing the financial affairs of the Nation of Islam. During the 1960's the Muslims enlarged their economic base dramatically. Muhammad had been preaching black capitalism and economic self-sufficiency since 1946, and under his astute guidance and rigidly centralized authority, the many small investments in shoe shops, beauty parlors, grocery stores, and similar enterprises grew into a substantial and diversified business network, not just in Chicago, but in Detroit, New York, Los Angeles, Washington, D.C., and other cities. By 1970 the Black Muslims had become the most powerful organized economic force in the black community. The monetary value of their extensive network in 1974 was estimated to be between $50 million and $80 million. In addition to many small businesses, it included a bank, a newspaper, and more than 25,000 acres of farmland in Alabama, Georgia, and Michigan. Not included in this appraisal were some seventy-five temples, almost fifty schools, and other noncommercial holdings throughout the country.

In the decade following Malcolm X's assassination, splinter groups began to challenge the aging Muhammad. In Chicago, New York, Baton Rouge, and elsewhere dissident factions, such as The Young Muslims, proclaimed their independence and declared war on the parent Black Muslim organization. Bloody clashes led to many deaths. Muhammad, his health failing, tried unsuccessfully to end the fighting.

In his last years Muhammad was plagued by asthma, diabetes, and heart trouble. He died of congestive heart failure in Chicago. Some

20,000 Black Muslim mourners attended his funeral. The most powerful and controversial black leader of his day, he surpassed even Marcus Garvey in his ability to capture the imagination and loyalty of the great masses of African Americans living in America's black ghettos. To these oppressed and often hopeless people he offered a new identity rooted in racial consciousness and ethnic pride. His extraordinary success in rehabilitating drug addicts, alcoholics, criminals, and other members of the underclass can be attributed to his emphasis on self-pride, self-discipline, and self-sufficiency. His great achievement as a religious leader was his ability to transform lives by getting his converts to believe in themselves.

A small man at just five feet, six inches tall, Muhammad had light skin, a thin face, and dark eyes whose intensity, some said, "glower[ed] with Messianic fervor." He had two daughters and six sons, one of whom, Wallace, succeeded him upon his death as Chief Minister of Islam.

[Muhammad's business and professional papers related to the Black Muslim movement are at the National Center, the Nation of Islam, Chicago, Ill. Elijah Muhammad wrote regular columns for the Black Muslim's weekly newspaper, *Muhammad Speaks*. He authored *Message to the Black Man in America* (1965) and articles entitled "Now Hear the Message to the Black Muslims from Their Leader," *Esquire*, Apr. 1963; and "What the Black Muslim Believes," *Negro Digest*, Nov. 1963. Books about him and the Black Muslim movement include Essien Udosen Essien-Udom, *Black Nationalism: A Search for an Identity in America* (1962); Bernard Cushmeer, *This Is the One: Messenger Elijah Muhammad. We Need Not Look for Another* (1971); C. Eric Lincoln, *The Black Muslims in America* (1973); and Raymond L. Hall, *Black Separatism in the United States* (1978). Articles include Alex Haley, "Mr. Muhammad Speaks," *Reader's Digest*, Mar. 4, 1960; Hans J. Massaquoi, "Elijah Muhammad: Prophet and Architect of the Separate Nation of Islam," *Ebony*, Aug. 1970; and "Black Muslims: Muhammad Speaks," *Newsweek*, Jan. 31, 1972. Obituaries appear in the *New York Times*, Feb. 26, 1975; *Time*, Mar. 10, 1975; *Newsweek*, Mar. 10, 1975; *Ebony*, May 1975; and *Christian Century*, Mar. 26, 1975.]

CHARLES D. LOWERY

MUNDT, KARL EARL (June 3, 1900–Aug. 16, 1974), U.S. senator, was born in Humboldt, S.Dak., to Ferdinand John Mundt and

Rose Elizabeth Schneider, Dakota pioneers. His father, a real estate, insurance, and investment agent, moved the family from Humboldt to Pierre and then to Madison, S.Dak., and Mundt attended public schools in all three towns.

In 1923, Mundt earned his B.A. at Carleton College in Northfield, Minn., where he also met Mary Elizabeth Moses, the daughter of a lumberman; the two married the following year, and the marriage lasted his entire lifetime. Mundt's first professional job was teaching speech and social science at the high school in Bryant, S.Dak., from 1923 to 1924. The next year, he became Bryant's superintendent of schools. His interest in rhetoric led him to co-found the National Forensic League in 1925 and edit its journal, *The Rostrum*, for the next fifteen years.

In 1927, Mundt earned an M.A. in economics from Columbia University in New York City and the following year accepted a position as chairman of the speech department and professor of social science at General William Beadle State Teachers College in Madison, S.Dak. He remained at the college until 1936, meanwhile working part-time in his father's business, Mundt Loan and Investment Company, based in Madison.

In 1932, Mundt became chairman of the Young Republican League of Lake County. An ardent conservationist, he served on his state's Game and Fish Commission from 1931 until 1937. In 1936, Mundt ran for Congress for the first time. However, President Franklin D. Roosevelt's reelection that year assisted incumbent Democratic Representative Fred H. Hildebrandt to defeat Mundt in a close vote. The unsuccessful candidate quit his teaching post and devoted himself fully to giving speeches to the public. In 1938, Mundt ran again and won by a comfortable margin. Mundt's political ambitions benefited from his isolationist views, which were popular in the conservative, predominantly German-American South Dakota corn belt. As United States involvement in World War II approached, this staunch backer of the America First Committee opposed both Selective Service and Lend-Lease. Mundt also put his environmental advocacy into action by sponsoring legislation for higher water-quality standards.

The Japanese attack on Pearl Harbor forced the South Dakotan to drop his isolationist views,

and thereafter he was always interested in international issues. On the House Foreign Affairs Committee, Mundt supported Congressman J. William Fulbright's resolution for postwar international cooperation in 1943. That November, he backed the agreement of forty-four countries to form the United Nations Relief and Rehabilitation Administration. He also endorsed the postwar creation of the United Nations Educational, Scientific and Cultural Organization. While working for international cooperation, Mundt also sought to limit the influence of suspected subversives at home. In 1943, he joined the House Un-American Activities Committee (HUAC).

Mundt also traveled with the House Foreign Affairs Committee on exhaustive tours in 1945 and 1947 of over twenty European countries, the Soviet Union, Poland, and Czechoslovakia among them. He returned as an active foe of Communism in Eastern Europe, and one of his first initiatives was Public Law 402, the legislation that created the Voice of America in 1948. Meanwhile, he attacked "Godless Communism and Red Fascism" and proposed that all Communists register with the U.S. government. He and a new colleague in HUAC, California Republican Richard M. Nixon, introduced the Mundt-Nixon Anti-Communist Bill during 1948. This legislation would prohibit any attempt "to establish in the United States a totalitarian dictatorship"; require all members of Communist party organizations, including unions, to register with the Department of Justice; deport suspected aliens; and revoke the citizenship of any immigrant who had joined a subversive group within five years of naturalization. The bill passed in the House, 319 to 57.

Mundt's interest in Communist influence in government also led him to team with Nixon in HUAC's investigation of former State Department employee Alger Hiss in 1948, which eventually led to Hiss's perjury conviction. Mary Mundt played a role in this investigation by hiding the microfilmed "Pumpkin Papers" from Whittaker Chambers's farm in her washing machine until they were called for at the hearing. Later that year, South Dakota's governor appointed Mundt to succeed Senator Vera C. Bushfield, who had resigned at the governor's request so that Mundt could be appointed to complete her term. Mundt intended to run for that seat and in this way he was able to preserve

South Dakota's seniority in the Senate when he won the seat outright that November.

Mundt reintroduced his Anti-Communist Bill in the Senate in 1949, revising it to exempt labor unions from the registration requirement. Although his bill died in the Senate Judiciary Committee, many of its points were incorporated into the omnibus Internal Security Act of 1950 (known as the McCarran Act). President Truman vetoed this legislation, but Congress easily overrode him.

Mundt rose to prominence in the Senate after he was assigned to the Government Operations Committee and its Permanent Investigations Subcommittee in January 1953. Both panels were chaired by Senator Joseph R. McCarthy of Wisconsin, whose efforts to uncover alleged Communists in government had Senator Mundt's support. By early 1954, McCarthy's allegations of lapses in army security resulted in a countercharge from the army, which accused McCarthy of meddling in army business to benefit G. David Schine, an aide of the Wisconsin senator. Hearings were held, and McCarthy was forced to step down in March 1954 in order to testify in front of his own subcommittee. Karl Mundt then became its acting chair.

In his new position, Mundt first attempted to bar the news media from the hearing room. Frustrated in this effort, he sat silently through the nationally broadcast spectacle which destroyed McCarthy's already unraveling reputation. After the hearings, Mundt refused to join in the growing clamor against his Wisconsin colleague: he remained one of McCarthy's most loyal supporters and was one of twenty-two to vote against the censure of the senator that December.

As fervent anti-Communism abated, the South Dakotan remained active in other investigations. In 1958, as a member of the Select Committee on Improper Activities in the Labor or Management Field, Mundt investigated allegations of corruption by United Auto Workers (UAW) officials in a violent strike at the Kohler Company of Wisconsin. His Democratic colleagues on the panel and the committee's counsel, Robert F. Kennedy, who had political connections to the UAW, accused Mundt and his Republican allies of partisan ambitions in the probe. When the investigation turned up little, Mundt attempted to launch a separate inquiry into the union's political influence.

Elected to his third term after defeating South Dakota Congressman George McGovern in 1960, Mundt continued to vote with conservative Republicans and Southern Democrats almost 90 percent of the time. Still, he was not always predictable. While he joined conservatives in opposition to such measures as labor legislation and social programs, he maintained his support for environmental protection. He also backed civil rights legislation in 1964, farm subsidies, initiatives for international cooperation, and regulation of nuclear weapons.

His most prominent work remained in the Permanent Investigations Subcommittee, which conducted two major inquiries during the Kennedy administration. The first, in 1962, investigated Texas investor and cotton dealer Billie Sol Estes, accused of fraudulent dealings with the Agriculture Department. Mundt embarrassed the Democrats by charging that the Kennedy administration and its secretary of agriculture, Orville Freeman, had shown favoritism by allowing the Texas financier to continue on a cotton allotment board even while he was being investigated. Over Senator Mundt's loud objections, the subcommittee found that Estes had retained his seat on the board due to administrative error, not bribery.

The Investigations Subcommittee convened the next year after learning that General Dynamics had won the contract for the TFX fighter/bomber program, even though the Boeing Corporation had made a lower bid. Mundt noted that two top Pentagon administrators had financial connections with General Dynamics. His investigation was stymied, however, when the Justice Department cleared the two officials of a conflict of interest.

Mundt's anti-Communism remained with him even as President Lyndon Johnson attempted to improve relations with the Soviet Union by meeting Premier Alexei Kosygin in 1967. That year, Mundt was at the forefront of an effort by Senate conservatives to kill a new consular treaty between the United States and the USSR. The agreement would have authorized two new consulates in both countries. Mundt, who feared the consulates would harbor Communist spies in the United States, wanted to suspend the agreement until the Soviet Union halted aid to North Vietnam. But overriding interest in better relations with Moscow thwarted his effort.

Mundt backed the Vietnam war, but he protested vehemently in January 1968 when the

American intelligence vessel *Pueblo* and its 83-member crew were seized by North Korea and held for over a year. He declared the mission a "shocking, reckless and needless adventure." He also told Secretary of State Dean Rusk that the government had "bungled very badly" at the risk of the peace and prestige of the country by sending a ship so close to North Korea without adequate protection. Mundt's blistering attack, which came just as the Tet offensive was causing Americans to question the Johnson administration's interpretation of the Vietnam War, showed that even anti-Communist stalwarts were becoming disenchanted with American involvement in Indochina.

Mundt's last political initiative, in 1969, was to offer a substitute to a Senate nonbinding resolution that forbade the dispatch of American troops abroad without the approval of Congress. The senators wanted the resolution amended to allow exceptions if American citizens, property, or territory were endangered. However, his political opponents thought his substitution excessively watered down their resolution.

While Mundt was increasingly frustrated in foreign affairs by Senate liberals, he won plaudits from environmentalists. The World Wildlife Fund honored him in 1969 for his efforts to preserve endangered species, including the whooping crane and the bobwhite.

Later that year, the sixty-nine-year-old Mundt suffered a crippling stroke. Prevented from carrying out his Senatorial duties, he occasionally voted by proxy. His fellow senators demanded he resign from his committee posts, but he refused. Finally, in 1972, Senate leaders removed Mundt from his high-ranking seats on the Government Operations, Foreign Relations, and Appropriations Committees, in a precedent-shattering step against the traditional seniority system. Mundt, who did not run for reelection in 1972, died in the nation's capital two years later.

[Mundt's papers are at the Karl E. Mundt Foundation, located at Dakota State University in Madison, S.Dak. The foundation also has a half-hour video about Mundt, "A Fair Chance for a Free People: Senator Karl E. Mundt," on one-half-inch VHS, which it issued in 1989. Scott N. Heidepriem's biography, *A Fair Chance for a Free People: A Biography of Karl E. Mundt, U.S. Senator,* was published by the Mundt Foundation in 1988. See also R. Alton Lee, " 'New Dealers, Fair Dealers, Misdealers, and Hiss Dealers': Karl Mundt and the Internal Security

Act of 1950," *South Dakota History* 10 (Fall 1980); and *Political Profiles: the Kennedy Years* (1976). An obituary is in the *New York Times*, Aug. 17, 1974.]
KATHERINE A. S. SIEGEL

MURPHY, AUDIE LEON (June 20, 1924–May 28, 1971), war hero and actor, was born in Kingston, Hunt County, Tex., the son of Emmett ("Pat") Murphy, a tenant farmer, and Josie Bell Killian. The most-decorated American soldier in World War II, earning thirty-three medals and decorations, including the nation's highest award for valor, the Medal of Honor, Murphy went on to a movie career in the postwar world. He was born into a life of grinding poverty, the seventh of twelve children, whose father abandoned them shortly before their mother died in 1941. Moving from one poor northeast Texas farm to another, twice living in abandoned railroad boxcars on the edge of small towns, with even the youngest children forced to work in the fields or at odd jobs, the Murphy family was the paradigm of poor southern families in the years of the Great Depression.

At age sixteen, with his father gone, his mother dead, and his younger siblings in an orphanage, Murphy was on his own. He had left school after the fifth grade, the extent of his formal education, and survived through a series of jobs, first as a hired hand on local farms and in construction and then as a clerk in a general store where, unlike his alcoholic, shiftless father, he proved to be an ambitious, energetic, and disciplined worker. He was employed as a radio repairman when the United States entered World War II. He attempted to enlist the day after Pearl Harbor, but the Marines deemed him too small at five feet five-and-a-half and 112 pounds. The army refused to accept him until his eighteenth birthday in June 1942.

Like many Depression-era young men, Murphy found in the military a security he had not known in the civilian world. Physically fit despite the deprivations of his youth, he took easily to all phases of basic training, scoring high marks in nearly every area and proving especially adept at spot (as opposed to fixed-position) shooting, the hallmark of his combat performance and a talent he had honed while hunting small game for the family table back in Texas. He developed into a spit-and-polish soldier, much admired by his fellow recruits.

Assigned to Company B, First Battalion, Fifteenth Infantry Regiment, Third Division, commanded by Major General Lucian K. Truscott, Murphy was sent to North Africa in February 1943 for advanced combat training. He first came under enemy fire in Sicily in July 1943, and thereafter engaged in some of the bitterest, most contested fighting of World War II, moving on to Anzio and Rome, and later through France and into Germany itself.

From his first day of battle, Murphy displayed the coolheadedness, remarkable fighting skills, and calculated risk-taking that, within weeks, would make him a legend among American troops throughout the European theater. Shy and quiet while off duty, a lifelong nondrinker and nonsmoker, the baby-faced Texan with a hair-trigger temper became the model infantryman. He entered combat armed to the teeth with a pistol in his belt, a rifle slung over his shoulder, and a carbine or other automatic weapon in his hands, exhibiting "coolness and calm fury," a phrase he used to describe an effective soldier's attributes under fire. Fear, he said in his autobiography, *To Hell and Back* (1949), was a constant companion, but he had determined early in the war either to ignore it or overcome it, and he exuded such confidence that his men were prepared, one wrote, to follow him anywhere. Other soldiers reportedly said that they could chart the course of any engagement by his actions: if Murphy was in the line, all was well; if he was withdrawing, it was time to retreat.

He received his first medal, the Bronze Star, in March 1943, for single-handedly (and at great risk) destroying a German tank while on night patrol at Anzio. Two months later he was awarded an oak leaf cluster for "exemplary conduct." In the five months following the invasion of southern France in August 1944, Murphy's reputation grew to epic proportions as reports of his exploits spread across the front. In that period he earned the bulk of his medals, including the Congressional Medal of Honor, the Distinguished Service Cross (DSC), and the Silver Star; was wounded three times; and received a battlefield commission to second lieutenant, a rank he had previously rejected because he was embarrassed by his lack of formal education. Murphy later said his guiding principle in combat was simply "destroy and survive." Although he had killed at least 240 German soldiers by the war's end, he asserted, "I feel no qualms; no pride; no remorse. There is only a weary indifference."

Just once during the war did he lose his customary detachment, or, as he put it in his memoirs, go "off the rail." It was the occasion for his winning of the DSC and came within hours of the August 1943 landing at St. Tropez, when his buddy, Lattie Tipton, was cut down by fire from a concealed machine gun as he attempted to take the surrender of some German troops who had displayed a white flag. Murphy, who had warned Tipton that the flag might be a ruse, went out of control. He killed the surrendering Germans, took their machine gun, and headed for the hidden nest, which he destroyed with a grenade and then, firing from the hip with his captured weapon, raked the wounded gunners over and over again, obliterating their bodies until his own rage was spent. Afterward, he lay down beside his dead friend and wept, he said, "like a baby."

Murphy's Medal of Honor was awarded for heroic action in the Colmar pocket in eastern France on Jan. 26, 1945. Having ordered his outnumbered men to cover in a nearby wood, Murphy, despite a leg wound, mounted a burning tank destroyer, seized its .50 caliber machine gun, and while exposed on three sides to enemy fire, single-handedly held off six German tanks and waves of attacking troops for almost an hour. After he had killed or wounded some fifty Germans and the rest began to withdraw, he led a counterattack that secured the American position. The small-framed, freckle-faced hero was only twenty years old.

At the war's end, he had earned more honors and decorations than any other member of the armed services. On his return home, he was eventually drawn to Hollywood and, over a twenty-one-year period, made more than forty movies, most of them formulaic westerns that took advantage of his shooting and riding skills. Two of his roles were noteworthy: he placed himself in the movie version of *To Hell and Back* (1955) and the youth in *The Red Badge of Courage* (1951).

Despite the modest success of his movie career, the postwar years were difficult for Murphy. He experienced frequent nightmares, and for many years slept with a loaded pistol under his pillow. He became a compulsive gambler, losing much of the fortune he had made from his autobiography and his films. At the time of his death, in an airplane accident near Roanoke, Va., he was unemployed and on the verge of bankruptcy.

Murphy was married in 1949 to Wanda Hendrix, an actress; they divorced a few months later; and in 1951 to Pamela Archer, an airline stewardess, with whom he had two children.

[Despite the publisher's fiction that Murphy had written *To Hell and Back* in longhand, he only contributed about ten pages to the book, which was ghostwritten by David ("Spec") McClure, a screenwriter and close friend. The book is indispensable for Murphy's wartime service. Don Graham's biography, *No Name on the Bullet* (1989), contains an extensive bibliography and a guide to library sources. See also Harold B. Simpson, *Audie Murphy, American Soldier* (1975). An obituary appears in the *New York Times*, June 1, 1971.]

ALLAN L. DAMON

N

NAISH, JOSEPH CARROL (Jan. 21, 1897–
Jan. 24, 1973), character actor, was born in New
York City's Upper East Side to Irish immigrants
Patrick Naish and Catherine Moran. He had
four sisters and two brothers. Although the family claimed aristocratic ancestors and registry in
Burke's Peerage, the father worked as a street-car
conductor and had the child baptized in the back
room of a saloon. A feral child of city streets, Joseph Patrick Carrol Naish was a choirboy at St.
Patrick's Cathedral yet was thrown out of one
school after another for brawling. As a youth, he
discovered a talent for mimicry which served
him all his life. At age fourteen, he left school for
good and began his theatrical career as a "song
plugger" (one who visits nightclubs and booking
agencies to introduce new tunes to leading singers) for Irving Berlin and others.

Naish never held a job for more than a few
months at a time until the United States entered
World War I, when he joined the navy and
learned to fly planes in Pensacola, Fla. In and
out of the brig on various discipline charges, he
nonetheless was sent to Europe and flew two
hundred hours in Sampson bombers out of
Brest, France. Discharged from the service in
Paris at the end of the war, he drifted across Europe until 1925 working a series of odd jobs,
learning to speak six different languages fluently.

In 1926, he returned to the United States,
landing in southern California aboard an oil
tanker. He moved to Hollywood and began performing stunts and bit parts in movies. By this
time, he had stopped using his first name. He
met his future wife, Gladys Heaney, while
working together on a road production of a
Broadway hit, *The Shanghai Gesture*. They
married on Feb. 10, 1928, settled in New York
City, and unlike many other show-business

couples, remained married for the rest of their
lives. They had one child.

Naish struggled for four years to make a living
on Broadway and in vaudeville. His first big
break came in 1932 when he was cast opposite
Edward G. Robinson in *The Hatchet Man* as
Loretta Young's father, an aging Chinese merchant. His move to Hollywood was followed by
numerous screen roles in such films as *Lives of
a Bengal Lancer* (1935); *Jungle Love* (1938),
starring Dorothy Lamour; *Captain Blood*
(1935), which headlined Errol Flynn; and *Beau
Geste* (1939). He received supporting-actor
Academy Award nominations for his portrayal
of an Italian prisoner in *Sahara* (1943), which
starred Humphrey Bogart, and as the father of
the title character in *A Medal for Benny* (1945).
In the latter, his dignified portrayal of a simple
Mexican-American farmer whose son receives a
posthumous Congressional Medal of Honor was
the only redeeming virtue in an otherwise
dreadful picture.

Swarthy, stocky, with dark hair and a thin
"Latin" mustache, Naish lacked the qualities
Hollywood directors associated with a leading
man. However, his striking features and command of dialect made him uniquely suited to
play ethnic character roles. *Time* called him "a
one-man U.N." Before his career ended, he
appeared in approximately 250 movies playing
Italians, Spaniards, Frenchmen, English gentlemen, Greeks, Hindus, American Indians,
Asians, Arabs, Mexicans, and Jews—virtually
every nationality save his own. He did not make
a credible Irishman, and was never cast as one
in his thirty years on the screen. He estimated
that he made $2 million in his screen career,
but spent it as quickly as he made it on gifts, bad
investments, and the race track.

Despite appearing in up to thirty films per year, Naish gained national recognition for his work in radio. From 1948 to 1953, he played the title character in "Life with Luigi," CBS's hit comedy about an Italian immigrant in Chicago. In 1952, CBS tried to re-create this success on television, but the series was both a critical and a commercial failure, and only lasted four months.

In 1955, Naish used his facility with languages on the Broadway stage in Arthur Miller's *A View from the Bridge*, which was comprised of two one-act plays. He played a German immigrant in the first and an Italian lawyer in the second, to critical acclaim. He returned to television for several dramatic roles, including playing a gambler in "Key Largo" for NBC's "Alcoa Hour." He also appeared in guest roles in numerous other series until he retired in 1963. Naish was bedridden by emphysema for two years and died of a coronary occlusion in La Jolla, Calif., in 1973.

[Very little biographical material on Naish is available. Obituaries are in the *Los Angeles Times* and the *New York Times*, both Jan. 27, 1973.]

DAVID M. ESPOSITO

NASH, FREDERICK OGDEN (Aug. 19, 1902–May 19, 1971), humorist, poet, and playwright, was born in Rye, N.Y., to Edmund Strudwick Nash and Mattie Chenault. His father's often unsuccessful involvement in the import-export business led the family to relocate frequently throughout the East Coast, but Nash spent most of his childhood in Savannah, Ga. He received his secondary education at St. George's School in Newport, R.I., from 1917 to 1920, and he attended Harvard University from 1920 to 1921, at which time financial difficulties at home forced him to leave and seek employment.

Before discovering and tapping his creative talents, Nash tried several careers. He taught briefly at his alma mater, St. George's, but he soon grew tired of it and moved to New York City, where he worked for a year and a half as a bond salesman on Wall Street. After selling only one bond—to his godmother—Nash took up writing advertising slogans, first for Barron Collier writing streetcar ads and then, in 1925, for Doubleday, Page publishing house. It was during his career in advertising that Nash took his first step toward his celebrated career in whimsical writing by coauthoring a children's book, *The Cricket of Carador*, with his friend Joseph Alger in 1925. In 1930, he collaborated with colleagues from Doubleday, Doran (renamed in 1927) to publish his first truly comical work, *Born in a Beer Garden; or, She Troupes to Conquer*.

Also in 1930, Nash published his first humorous poem, one of many humorous verses Nash scribbled on scraps of paper from his desk at work for his own amusement and that of a coworker. On this occasion, Nash was inspired to fish the poem out of the wastebasket and submit it to the *New Yorker* magazine, which accepted it under the title "Spring Comes to Murray Hill." This poem exemplifies the lighthearted reflection on daily human existence so typical of Nash's verse, with such musings as "If you have a sore foot you can get it fixed by a chiropodist, / And you can get your original sin removed by St. John the Bopodist." Such lines typify Nash's inimitable gift for mutilating spelling and pronunciation for the sake of achieving comically forced rhyme.

Soon after "Spring Comes to Murray Hill" was published, several more of Nash's poems appeared in the *New Yorker* and other publications. His work was so well received that in 1931 he was able to publish his first collection of humorous verse, *Hard Lines*. Its immediate popularity led to seven printings of the book in its first year, all of which sold out. Finding himself suddenly with a profitable and enjoyable career, Nash left advertising to write for the *New Yorker*, but preferring to write free-lance, he remained on its staff for only three months. On June 6 of this already significant year, Nash married Frances Rider Leonard; they had two children.

Later in 1931, Nash published his second book, *Free Wheeling*, and in the next few years continued to produce ample amounts of humorous poetry for a steadily growing audience, with *Happy Days* in 1933 and *The Primrose Path* in 1935. Nash's success with light verse came almost unexpectedly to him, a reader of Romantic English poetry who had labored for a time with verse in a more serious vein. "I wrote sonnets about beauty and truth, eternity, poignant pain," Nash said about the time before he realized that his field was "the minor idiocies of humanity." For four decades after this realization, Nash was a household name, and his sharp, catchy lines took their prominent places in American popular culture. Such phrases as

"Candy / Is dandy, / But liquor / Is quicker" and "The Bronx? / No, thonx!" became common witticisms that are still repeated today.

His poems typically deal with mundane, everyday events and people, poking fun at them with a frivolity that avoids being caustic or insulting. Nonetheless, his humor often carries a considerable amount of criticism. In "The Pulpiteers Have Hairy Ears," Nash observes that "there are too many people who think that just because they have parishes or dioceses / It imparts infallibility to all their biaseses." In this poem, Nash wonders at how easily the clergy become enraged by what they deem breaches of propriety: "It's odd, but at any hint of gaiety / On the part of the laity / Their furies and rages / Fill pages and pages and pages." He goes on to observe, "Neither do clerics like prize fighting, cock fighting, bull fighting or any other kind of fighting / Unless it is war, in which case they urge people to go out and do a lot of smiting." Although Nash is remembered for the humor of his work, a reader could not make it through one of his books without encountering a great deal of social commentary. In "Invocation," Nash mocks Senator Smoot of Utah for his efforts to censor "improper" books: "Senator Smoot is an institute / Not to be bribed with pelf; / He guards our homes from erotic tomes / By reading them all himself."

But Nash's best-remembered and most frequently quoted verse is of a much less serious and specific nature. It is characterized by a certain degree of silliness intertwined with profound thoughts on life in general. His "Reflection on Veracity" notes quite succinctly that "Purity / Is obscurity," and "Lather As You Go" tells the reader, "Beneath this slab / John Brown is stowed. / He watched the ads, / And not the road." Nash's trademark was a lighthearted disregard for spelling, form, and pronunciation of words as well as for meter and line length. In "England Expects," Nash displays this talent; "Let us pause to consider the English, / Who when they pause to consider themselves they get all reticently thrilled and tinglish." And in telling the story of "Columbus," Nash says, "So he went and tried to borrow some money from Ferdinand / But Ferdinand said America was a bird in the bush and he'd rather have a berdinand."

Nash's verse began to reflect more domestic concerns in The Bad Parents' Garden of Verse, published in 1936, when Nash was experiencing the joys and anxieties of being the father of two baby girls. He expresses his premature fear of young male suitors in "Song to Be Sung by the Father of Six-months-old Female Children" when he concedes, "I never see an infant (male), / A-sleeping in the sun, / Without I turn a trifle pale / And think Is he the one?" Nash also wrote books specifically for children, among them Parents Keep Out: Elderly Poems for Youngerly Readers (1951), The Christmas That Almost Wasn't (1957), The New Nutcracker Suite, and Other Innocent Verses (1962), and The Adventures of Isabel (1963), named for his second daughter.

In his middle age, Nash's verse also reflected his concerns about aging and his admitted tendency toward hypochondria. His book Bed Riddance (1969) contains poems written throughout his life that express such grievances as "Another day, another dolor," from "A Man Can Complain, Can't He? (A Lament for Those Who Think Old)." He defends himself in the introduction to Bed Riddance by arguing, "My occasional moans and whimpers are forced from me not by my imagination but by the brutal fact that since my delivery date, August 19, 1902, I have been undergoing progressive obsolescence as planned by my maker. . . ." And in "Let's Not Climb the Washington Monument Tonight," he reasons, "Well, who wants to be young anyhow, any idiot born in the last forty years can be young, and besides forty-five isn't really old, it's right on the border, / At least, unless the elevator's out of order."

Aside from his poetry, Nash also wrote three screenplays for MGM while living in Hollywood from 1936 to 1942. The Firefly (1937) was an adaptation of Otto A. Harbach's play of the same name and met with little success. The Shining Hair (1938), coauthored with Jane Murfin, and The Feminine Touch (1941), coauthored with George Oppenheimer and Edmund L. Hartmann, were also unsuccessful at the box office. His luck with Broadway, however, was quite different. Nash and S. J. Perelman, whom he had met and befriended in Hollywood, wrote a musical called One Touch of Venus, which was a smash hit in the 1943 Broadway season. Perelman wrote the script, Nash wrote the lyrics, and Kurt Weill provided the musical score for the play, which ran for 567 performances. His two subsequent musicals, however, did not enjoy the same popularity that the first one had. Nash also made appearances on several radio programs in the 1940's and was a guest on a number of television panel shows, such as "Masquerade Party," in the 1950's.

But it was his verse that made Nash a celebrity. His unmistakable style encouraged many imitators, but none could capture his amusing—as well as amused—perspective or his knack for twisting language. His reputation as a humorist may outweigh his reputation as a poet, but his gift of expression and his keen understanding of human nature no doubt qualify him as an artist, however lightly he took himself and the world around him. Nash published verse until his death in Baltimore.

[Nash's other works are *Nothing But Wodehouse*, edited by Pelham Granville Wodehouse (1932); *Four Prominent So and So's*, with lyrics by Nash and music by Robert Armbruster (1934); *I'm a Stranger Here Myself* (1938); *The Face Is Familiar* (1940); *Good Intentions* (1942); *The Ogden Nash Pocket Book* (1944); *Many Long Years Ago* (1945); *The Selected Verse of Ogden Nash* (1946); *Ogden Nash's Musical Zoo* (1947); *Versus* (1949); *Family Reunion* (1950); *The Private Dining Room, and Other New Verses* (1953); *The Moon Is Shining Bright As Day* (1953); *The Pocket Book of Ogden Nash* (1954); *You Can't Get There from Here* (1957): *The Boy Who Laughed at Santa Claus* (pamphlet) (1957); *I Couldn't Help Laughing* (1957); *Verses from 1929 On* (1959); *Custard, the Dragon* (1959); *A Boy Is a Boy* (1960); *Scrooge Rides Again* (1960); *Everybody Ought to Know* (1961); *Custard, the Dragon and the Wicked Knight* (1961); *Girls Are Silly* (1962); *Everyone But Thee and Me* (1962); *A Boy and His Room* (1963); *The Untold Adventures of Santa Claus* (1964); *Marriage Lines* (1964); *Santa Go Home* (1967); *The Cruise of the Aardvark* (1967); *The Mysterious Ouphe* (1967); *There's Always Another Windmill* (1968); *The Old Dog Barks Backwards* (1972); lyrics for the television show "Art Carney Meets Peter and the Wolf" and for Camille Saint-Saëns's "Carnival of the Animals"; and contributions to the *New Yorker, Life*, and other periodicals.

A detailed biography is Linell Nash Smith's *Loving Letters from Ogden Nash* (1990). See also Laura Benét, *Famous American Humorists* (1959). Obituaries are in the *New York Times*, May 20, 1971; the *Washington Post*, May 21, 1971; *Time*, May 31, 1971; *Publishers Weekly*, May 31, 1971; and *Antiquarian Bookman*, June 7–14, 1971.]

JAMES P. MILLER

NELSON, OSWALD GEORGE ("OZZIE") (Mar. 20, 1906–June 3, 1975), bandleader and radio and television star, was born in Jersey City, N.J., the son of George Nelson and Ethel Orr. Nelson's father was a banker, but he also was an inveterate producer of amateur talent shows and frequently had his sons on stage singing before the local Elks, Knights of Columbus, and Masons.

The tightly knit family provided values that Ozzie later applied to his own family, which grew up in front of America on one of the first hit television series. At the age of thirteen, Ozzie became the Boy Scouts' youngest Eagle Scout ever. With his brother Alfred, he performed in England, France, and Belgium on a goodwill tour for the Boy Scouts.

Music became Ozzie's passion, and the fourteen-year-old saxophonist organized a band in his suburban town of Ridgefield Park, N.J. He graduated from Ridgefield Park High School in 1927 and then enrolled in Rutgers University. Nelson was a starting quarterback in football, earned letters in swimming and lacrosse, and became a boxing champion. But he failed to make the college glee club and instead put together his own band. They played at various college and local functions before Nelson went on to earn his law degree at the New Jersey Law School in New Brunswick in 1930, paying for his education by coaching football at Lincoln High School in Jersey City, N.J.

Nelson eschewed law work and became an acclaimed bandleader, writing well-known songs like "I'm Satisfied with You" and "I Dare You." From 1930 until 1943, he worked steadily as one of the country's best-known orchestra leaders.

Nelson's recruitment of a female singer changed his career. Harriet Hilliard, a Des Moines, Iowa, beauty queen, joined Nelson's troupe in 1932. They were married on Oct. 8, 1935, in Hackensack, N.J. They had two sons, David and Ricky. The family left New Jersey for Hollywood in 1941. Ozzie and Harriet costarred in three movie musicals in 1944 and appeared as regulars on Red Skelton's radio show.

Their break came when Skelton went into the army in 1944. The Nelsons received their own program, "The Adventures of Ozzie and Harriet," which was quickly acclaimed by the critics and vaulted the couple into national prominence. Ozzie and Harriet became synonymous with the ideal American family. The Nelsons were "the nicest young married couple on the air and one of the most human," said one critic. Ozzie's all-American image was enhanced by reports that he neither smoked nor drank.

The Nelsons made the move to television on Oct. 3, 1952. David, who was nearly sixteen, and Ricky, twelve, played themselves on the show. This was a change from the radio show, where actors portrayed the Nelson siblings. Nelson later wrote in his autobiography, "Throughout the 14 years we filmed the show, we spent so much time on the set that the boys often said it was difficult to figure which was our real home." For thirty minutes every week, millions of eyes were focused on the white house at 822 Sycamore Road, Hillsdale, U.S.A. "They represented the exemplary happy, healthy, post-war American family living the mythological middle-class white Anglo-Saxon Protestant dream life somewhere in friendly suburbia," according to *Favorite Families of TV*.

Nelson changed the face of television. At a time when movie making was considered the most prestigious work, he lured top cinematographers and others to the small screen. Nelson likened his show's production values to those of a major Hollywood movie.

A conservative Republican, Ozzie was nevertheless proud that he and Harriet were the first TV couple shown sleeping together in a double bed. The show also catapulted Ricky to the top of the music charts by featuring his singing such hits as "Travelin' Man" in most episodes.

The show was canceled by ABC in 1966, but not because of diminishing ratings. Rather, following their marriages, David's and Ricky's real-life wives, June and Kris, joined the cast. But, according to Ozzie, it became difficult keeping the show focused with three different couples sharing center stage, and the decision was made to end its run.

Ozzie and Harriet made a brief return to television in 1973 with the syndicated "Ozzie's Girls," which had the Nelsons paired with two college girls they took in as boarders. Ozzie also did some television directing on programs like the police series "Adam 12."

An athlete until the end, Nelson swam two miles a day in the Pacific Ocean. He died in his San Fernando Valley home, eight months after being diagnosed with liver cancer.

David went on to a career as an entertainment industry executive, while Rick was a major recording star before his death in a plane crash on Dec. 31, 1985. The family's legacy lasted into the 1990's with another generation of performing Nelsons.

[Nelson's autobiography, *Ozzie*, was published in 1973. See also Christopher Paul Denis and Michael Denis, *Favorite Families of TV* (1992). An obituary is in the *New York Times*, June 4, 1975.]

LARRY MCSHANE

NEVINS, JOSEPH ALLAN (May 20, 1890– Mar. 5, 1971), historian and educator, was born on an Illinois farm near Camp Point in Adams County, the son of Emma Stahl and Joseph Allan Nevins. Growing up on the family farm, young Allan, as he was called, developed habits of industry, frugality, discipline, and hard work that stayed with him throughout his professional life. In 1908 he enrolled at the University of Illinois. Aspiring to a career in journalism, he majored in English and worked as a writer and editor for the student newspaper. He earned the B.A. degree in 1912, and the M.A. degree in English in 1913. He never pursued the Ph.D.

In 1913 Nevins moved to New York City, which quickly became his spiritual and intellectual home. His first job was as an editorial writer for *The Nation* (1913–1918) and its sister publication, the *New York Evening Post*. On Dec. 30, 1916, he married Mary Fleming Richardson; they had two children. In 1924 he became literary editor for the *New York Sun*, where he remained until Walter Lippmann lured him to the rival *New York World* in 1925. During his early years with the *Post* Nevins published a well-received history of his alma mater, *Illinois* (1914). He wrote and edited other books while he was a newspaperman, including *American Social History as Recorded by British Travellers* (1923), *The American States During and After the Revolution, 1775–1789* (1924), and *The Emergence of Modern America, 1865– 1878* (1927). The 1924 text, which focused on an important but neglected aspect of state history, was a strong contender for the Pulitzer Prize in History. Another important book Nevins wrote during these years was *The Evening Post: A Century of Journalism* (1922).

While Nevins pursued his newspaper career, he spent more and more time at nearby Columbia University and the New York Public Library doing historical research and writing. His interest in journalism waned as his interest in history grew. In 1927 Nevins finally succumbed to the lure of academe by accepting a position teaching history at Cornell University. Missing the excitement of New York City, he returned to the city a year later and began his long association with Columbia University as a member of the history faculty. He worked concurrently on the editorial staff of the *New York World* until 1931, when he was promoted from associate professor to Dewitt Clinton Professor of History. Thereafter he devoted himself full time to teaching and writing. Except for distinguished visiting professorships both in the United States and abroad, including two separate appointments as Harmsworth Professor of American History at Oxford University (1940–1941, 1964–1965), he spent his entire academic career at Columbia.

During his three decades at Columbia, Nevins's undergraduate courses drew respectable enrollments, but he was never a spellbinding or popular lecturer among undergraduates. He read his erudite, carefully prepared lectures in a raspy voice that failed to convey the enthusiasm and excitement he felt for history. Among graduate students and highly motivated undergraduates, however, he was very popular.

For nearly twenty years Nevins was responsible for teaching historical methodology at the graduate level. He immersed his students in scholarship, taught them research techniques, and demonstrated by personal example the value of discipline and hard work. Lifting up as models such great nineteenth-century literary historians as Thomas Babington Macaulay and Francis Parkman, he emphasized the importance of writing readable history with sufficient drama and color to appeal to a wide reading audience. He drummed into his students the notion that history is an art, and the historian a story-telling artist. While teaching historical methods he wrote *Gateway to History* (1938), which continues to be one of the best historiographical studies available.

Nevins was an extraordinarily prolific writer. The historian C. Vann Woodward once called him "a one-man history-book industry, a phenomenon of American productivity without parallel in the field." He wrote more than fifty books, edited at least seventy-five more, and authored perhaps a thousand articles, essays, reviews, and short pieces both for scholarly journals and for such popular periodicals as the *New Yorker* and the *Saturday Review*. He did not limit himself to a single specialty but wrote ably on biography and a wide variety of fields with a primary focus on the period since 1850.

Nevins was partial to biography because it "humanized the past." It enabled the biographer, in portraying life and blood characters, to convey a sense of the complexity of events and the spirit of the age. His widely acclaimed 1928 biography of John C. Frémont was followed in rapid order by major biographies of Henry White (1930), Grover Cleveland (1932), Abram Hewitt (1935), Hamilton Fish (1936), John D. Rockefeller (1940), Henry Ford (with Frank E. Hills, 1954–1963), and Herbert Lehman (1963). His studies of Cleveland and Fish won Pulitzer Prizes. Some of these biographies, such as the one on Rockefeller, which was really a history of the Standard Oil Company, were pioneering works in business history. In his biographies of Rockefeller, Cleveland, Ford, and others he challenged the prevailing "robber baron" thesis propounded by Charles Beard and Matthew Josephson and forcefully argued that economic self-interest played a positive rather than negative role in the industrial development of the United States. Men such as Rockefeller and Ford, admirable figures in what Nevins called the "Heroic Age of American Enterprise," were industrial giants who ushered America into its age of greatness.

Nevins published *America in World Affairs* in 1942, and in 1945 began working on his magnum opus, *The Ordeal of the Union* (1947–1971), an eight-volume study of the United States during the period 1847–1865. Narrative in form but not devoid of analysis, these exhaustively researched and masterfully written volumes comprise the best of Nevins's works. Reminiscent of the great nineteenth-century narrative histories by James Ford Rhodes, Francis Parkman, and Henry Adams, the volumes portray on a heroic scale the severe testing of the American nation. Though conciliatory in spirit and tone, his volumes were an unequivocal celebration of the powerful modern industrial state that emerged from the war.

Although Allan Nevins is remembered mainly for his prolific literary output, he did much more than write and teach. He institutionalized oral history in the United States, founding in 1948 an ambitious program at Columbia University that has served as a model of its kind; was a founder of *American Heritage* magazine; served as president of the American Historical Association; served for three summers after World War II as chief public affairs officer at the American Embassy in London; was an adviser to presidents and statesmen; and headed the Civil War Centennial Commission. Nevins also founded the Society of American Historians in 1939.

In 1958 Nevins retired from Columbia University and accepted a position as senior research associate at Huntington Library. In 1967 he suffered a serious stroke. He continued to work on the last two volumes of his *Ordeal of the Union*, which he had essentially completed at the time of his death in Menlo Park, Calif.

By former colleagues and students alike, Nevins is remembered as a kind, helpful, and pleasant man who was never too busy to help someone who needed his expert assistance. But he had no time for small talk or idle banter. When he and his wife Mary hosted dinner parties for Columbia University students and friends at their home near Bronxville, Nevins frequently skipped cocktails and emerged from his study just before dinner, after which he would excuse himself to return to his writing. His dual passions were history and Columbia University. In 1965 he anonymously donated $500,000, his life's savings, to Columbia for the establishment of a chair in economic history. It is the measure of the man that Nevins was embarrassed by the fuss Columbia made when it insisted that the chair be named for him and the source of the gift be revealed.

[Nevins's papers are located at the Butler Library at Columbia University and at the Huntington Library in San Marino, Calif. A few of his letters are at the University of Illinois, Urbana-Champaign, and his reminiscences are part of the Oral History Collection of Columbia University.

Articles about Nevins include Harvey Wish, "Allan Nevins and Recent Historiography," in *The American Historian: A Social-Intellectual History of the Writing of the American Past* (1960); and Ray Allen Billington, "Allan Nevins, Historian: A Personal Reminiscence," in *Allan Nevins on History*, edited by Ray Allen Billington (1975). Obituary notices are in *Saturday Review*, Mar. 20, 1971; the *Washington Post*, Mar. 6, 1971; *The Times* (London), Mar. 8, 1971; and the *American Historical Review*, June 1972.]

CHARLES D. LOWERY

NICHOLS, ROY FRANKLIN (Mar. 3, 1896–Jan. 11, 1973), historian and educator, was born in Newark, N.J., the son of Franklin C. Nichols, a retailer in the hat business, and Anna Cairns. He attended Barringer High School in Newark where he developed a youthful interest in history. Graduating in January 1914, Nichols

remained in high school for a postgraduate term taking courses in history.

He entered Rutgers University in September 1914; with plans to pursue a career teaching history, he studied both English and American history. His senior thesis was entitled "Personal Influence in United States Politics." After graduating in May 1918, he continued working toward a master's degree in history and received his M.A. from Rutgers University in June 1919.

Three months later, he entered Columbia University to pursue the doctorate in history. While at Columbia, Nichols met Jeanette Paddock, a fellow history graduate student. After passing their preliminary examinations, they married on May 27, 1920. Under the direction of William A. Dunning and later Nathaniel W. Stephenson, Nichols wrote a dissertation entitled "The Democratic Machine, 1850–1854" that was published in 1923 in the Columbia University series of Studies in History, Economics and Public Law. While undertaking graduate work at Columbia, Nichols served as a history instructor, a post he continued to occupy two years beyond the completion of his doctorate in 1923.

In 1925, he joined the history faculty at the University of Pennsylvania as an assistant professor. For the next four decades, Nichols maintained his academic affiliation with that institution as a professor, Dean of the Graduate School of Arts and Sciences, and vice-provost.

Early in Nichols's career, biography as a historical tool came into vogue. Combining biography with his interest in political history soon led to the publication of *Franklin Pierce: Young Hickory of the Granite Hills* (1931). As the 1930's progressed, Nichols came to use concepts from other disciplines in the social, natural, and physical sciences to bolster political history with new insights. This approach marked him as a pioneer in the field of explaining historical events in their cultural context. His writings challenged earlier American historical works that assumed that United States history was of a unique and uniform nature.

Made a full professor in 1930, Nichols was involved in a number of organizations promoting history at the national, state, and local levels. Beginning in 1934 and continuing for the next twenty-two years, Nichols represented the American Historical Association (AHA) on the board of the Social Science Research Council. He was active in the AHA as council member from 1943 to 1947, vice-president in 1965, and president in 1966. An organizer of the Pennsylvania Historical Association, he served as its president from 1936 to 1939. From 1940 to 1944, Nichols was a board member of the Pennsylvania Historical Commission, and from 1958 to 1968, a board member of the American Academy of Political and Social Science.

During the late 1930's and early 1940's, Nichols and his wife, Jeannette Paddock Nichols, jointly authored three textbooks: *The Growth of American Democracy* (1939); *The Republic of the United States* (1942); and *A Short History of the American Democracy* (1943). His most acclaimed publication, *The Disruption of American Democracy* (1948), won the 1949 Pulitzer Prize for History for its examination of the dissolution of the Democratic party and the Union from 1856 to 1861.

In 1952, Nichols became Dean of the Graduate School of Arts and Sciences at the University of Pennsylvania, followed a year later by the additional title of vice-provost. While in this post, he served a term as president of the Association of Graduate Schools of the American Association of Universities (1964) as well as chairman of the Council of Graduate Schools (1965). While dean, Nichols authored a series of studies focusing on institutions with peculiarly American characteristics. In fairly rapid succession, Nichols authored *Advance Agents of American Destiny* (1956); *Religion and American Democracy* (1959); *The Stakes of Power: 1845–1977* (1961); and *Blueprints of Leviathan: American Style* (1963). Retiring from the University in 1966, he continued to write and published *The Invention of the American Political Parties* (1967) and *The Pennsylvania Historical and Museum Commission: A History* (1967) followed by his autobiography *A Historian's Progress* (1968).

After retirement, Nichols remained active as historian to the University of Pennsylvania and as a member on the board of trustees and board of governors of Rutgers University until his death. He died in Philadelphia.

[In addition to Nichols's autobiography cited above, see Martin Meyerson and Dilys Pegler Winegrad, *Gladly Learn and Gladly Teach: Franklin and His Heirs at the University of Pennsylvania, 1740–1976* (1978). Obituaries are in the *New York Times*, Jan. 13, 1973; and *The American Historical Review*, June 1973.]

FRANK R. LEVSTIK

NIEBUHR, KARL PAUL REINHOLD ("REINIE") (June 21, 1892–June 1, 1971), theologian and philosopher, was born in Wright City, Mo., to Gustav Niebuhr, a minister in the Evangelical Synod, a Lutheran offshoot of the Prussian Church Union, and Lydia Hosto. Gustav Niebuhr was a highly respected member of the clergy who combined a high level of intelligence with a vital personal piety. His children were raised in a deeply religious home characterized by faith, optimism, and idealism. Reinhold's brother Hulda became a professor at McCormick Theological Seminary in Chicago, and his brother Richard became a professor at Yale Divinity School. Only his brother Walter, who became a businessman and newspaper publisher, failed to follow Gustav's example by taking up a career in the ministry or theological education.

Reinhold Niebuhr graduated from Elmhurst College in Elmhurst, Ill., in 1910 and Eden Theological Seminary in Webster Grove., Mo., in 1913, both of which were schools for members of the Evangelical Synod. He postponed taking up a parish by gaining permission to enter Yale Divinity School. His father died before he entered Yale, causing family hardship. Despite this setback, Niebuhr managed to complete his master's degree in theology in 1915, the same year in which he was ordained a minister in the Evangelical Synod.

Niebuhr served as pastor at Bethel Evangelical Church in Detroit from 1915 to 1928. What might have been a two-year stay to fulfill his obligation to the Evangelical Synod instead became a thirteen-year high-level drama that brought Niebuhr national attention as a significant leader in both the religious and the political arenas.

Detroit's automobile industry was then expanding, led by the Ford Motor Company, and Henry Ford was being praised for paying his employees $5 per day, creating jobs, and stimulating growth in Detroit. While Detroit quickly tripled in size, Niebuhr's church grew from a handful of members to more than eight hundred. Niebuhr said of that period, "I cut my eyeteeth fighting Ford." While the world was focusing on the opportunities Ford was bringing to Detroit, Niebuhr was focusing on the injustices that followed in the wake of industrialization. He saw poor housing; no job security, insurance, or retirement benefits; and worker exhaustion from life on the assembly lines. He wrote, "No one asks whether an industry which can maintain a reserve of a quarter billion ought not make some provisions for its unemployed." During this time he became very active in the labor movement and was an influential friend to Walter Reuther, head of the United Auto Workers Union. It was also during this time that Niebuhr developed his socialist ideas, becoming a member of the Socialist party in the late 1920's. He later criticized some of his own socialist ideas but also remained a lifelong critic of capitalism.

His experience in Detroit forced Niebuhr to reconsider the liberal and highly moralistic creed that he had accepted as his Christian faith. In Detroit he began to work out many of his ideas about sin and grace, love and justice, faith and reason, realism and idealism, and the irony and tragedy of history, which would characterize his controversial and influential thinking, preaching, and writing for the rest of his life.

His thinking returned to the biblical myth and the vision of our fallen nature. He viewed sin as pride, and selfish self-centeredness as the root of evil. He saw this sin of pride not only in those who commit obvious crimes, but more dangerously in people who consider themselves good. The human tendency to corrupt the good was the great insight he saw manifested in governments, business, democracies, utopian societies, and even in religious institutions. This position is laid out profoundly in one of his most influential books, *Moral Man and Immoral Society* (1932). He was a debunker of hypocrisy and pretense and made the avoidance of self-righteous illusions the center of his thoughts.

Niebuhr did battle with the liberals over what he called their naïve views of sin and the optimism of the social gospel. He did battle with the conservatives over what he viewed as their naïve view of Scripture and their narrow definition of "true religion." He was a liberal thinker who supported many liberal religious and social causes, but his ideas were often too orthodox for most liberals, while his view that the Bible could not be taken literally was too liberal for the conservatives. Likewise, he found himself to be too secular for many of the religious and too religious for the secular.

Niebuhr's thinking was dynamic and dialectical, marked by the process of constant reassessment, and filled with paradox. So too was his life. He became head of the pacifist Fellowship of Reconciliation in the late 1920's even though he was not a pacifist true believer. He was a part of the "social gospel" school of Christianity, which professed an optimistic faith in human progress and the belief that evil is socially caused and therefore socially alleviable; he also flirted with Marxism as part of his critique of individualism and naïve political optimism. He also helped found the Fellowship of Socialist Christians in the late 1920's just at the time he was becoming critical of liberal and Marxist illusions.

He became a member of the faculty at Union Theological Seminary in New York City in 1928, where he assumed the chair of Christian ethics even though he lacked a Ph.D. and had no obvious scholarly competence in this field. Later he humbly asserted that "it was a full decade before I could stand before a class and answer the searching questions of the students." His *An Interpretation of Christian Ethics* (1935), however, in which he interpreted Christian love (agape) as the "possible impossibility," demonstrated once and for all his intellectual and theological depth.

Niebuhr was as imaginative and energetic in the classroom as he had been in the pulpit. He was extremely popular with his students and always seemed to have a group of students gathered around him. His office door was always open. He was in demand on the lecture circuit, kept up a lively interest in applying religious values to everyday issues, and devoted most weekends to college preaching.

His life took a major turn on Dec. 22, 1931, when he married the intelligent and attractive Ursula Keppel-Compton, a learned and religious woman who eventually became chairman of the Religious Department at Barnard College; they had two children.

One Sunday in 1934 he preached in a small church near his summer home in Heath, Mass., where he wrote his now-famous "Serenity Prayer." A neighbor asked for a copy, which Niebuhr gave him after saying he had no further use for it. It was published as part of a pamphlet the following year and has since been adopted by Alcoholics Anonymous and numerous other organizations. He wrote: "O God, give us/serenity to accept what cannot be changed,/courage to change what should be changed,/and wisdom to distinguish the one from the other."

In 1939 he was invited to give the Gifford Lectures at the University of Edinburgh in Scotland. He lectured on the nature and destiny of humanity, comparing biblical with classical and modern ideas of our nature and destiny. In these lectures and the Beecher Lectures he gave at Yale in the late 1940's, he argued that modern views were similar to classical idealism, but that the biblical view of human nature was superior to both classical and modern views.

In 1941 the first issue of *Christianity and Crisis*, edited by Niebuhr, was published. This small, unpretentious journal was a biweekly devoted to religious and social concerns. Influential far beyond its circulation numbers, its contributors included the best social, political, and religious thinkers of the time, and it was read by many of the leaders in these fields. Niebuhr wrote that his journal was devoted "to an exposition of our Christian faith in its relation to world events." For more than twenty-five years this journal brought a religious viewpoint to bear on such issues as civil rights, the labor movement, women's equality, government, and war and peace.

Following World War II Niebuhr's writings and lectures focused more on religious realism and what it meant in the international sphere. He became influential in Americans for Democratic Action (ADA), which he helped found, and through which he helped to influence men such as George Kennan and Arthur Schlesinger, Jr. The idea of political containment of Communism was born in this circle of people.

Niebuhr wrote about the "possible impossibility" of love, and his life's work was an attempt to discover the proper relationship between the forces of love, power, and justice. In the pursuit of the good society, he believed the commitment to democratic principals and the avoidance of self-righteous illusions was society's best hope in achieving progress and justice.

Only in appearance can Niebuhr be described as ordinary; in every other way he was extraordinary. His intellect in the classroom and the pulpit was unmatched, yet his gentle spirit and wit balanced his analytical powers. His words came out in rapid fire, but he could listen with astute rapture. In conversation he might have tugged at an ear, pulled on his ample nose, smoothed his bald spot, or clamped a pipe between his teeth; his genial humor was unfailingly inviting.

During his life Niebuhr wrote almost twenty books and contributed more than 1,500 articles to journals and magazines. In 1952 Niebuhr had a stroke that slowed him down, but he continued to teach, write, and speak out. He retired in 1960 and moved to Stockbridge, Mass., where he carried on his efforts to teach and reform until his death.

[Some of Niebuhr's other works include *Christian Realism and Political Problems* (1953); *The Irony of American History* (1955); and *The Self and the Dramas of History* (1955). His diary is *Leaves from the Notebook of a Tamed Cynic* (1929), and his letters, edited by his wife, Ursula, appear as *Remembering Reinhold Niebuhr* (1991). An obituary appears in the *New York Times*, June 2, 1971.]

THE REVEREND JACK ALLEN

NORELL, NORMAN (Apr. 20, 1900–Oct. 25, 1972), fashion designer, was born in Noblesville, Ind., the younger of two sons born to Harry Levinson and Nettie Kinsey. His father operated a men's clothing store; his mother enjoyed wearing the latest Paris fashions and taking little Norman shopping with her. When Norman was five years old, the family moved to nearby Indianapolis to continue the successful family business. Sickly and isolated as a child, Norman lived in his own fantasy world, influenced by the theater productions he often attended and his mother's fashion magazines. At the age of twelve his flair for drama expressed itself in gold, red, and black decor for his room, which featured a round bed.

In his teens Norman attended a few classes at the Indianapolis Art Institute but moved to New York City in 1918 to study illustration at the New York School of Fine and Applied Art, later known as Parsons School of Design. A year later he transferred to the Pratt Institute to study costume design and figure drawing, augmented by research at the New York Public Library. Norman David Levinson changed his name to the more theatrical "Norman Norell." He found his first opportunity to design actual costumes in 1922, at the Astoria branch of Paramount Pictures, located in the borough of Queens in New York City. He dressed Rudolph Valentino in *The Sainted Devil* and Gloria Swanson in *Zaza*. Later he designed for a few Broadway musicals and joined the Brooks Costume Co., which served vaudeville shows.

In 1924, Norell began working for Charles Armour, manufacturer of wholesale women's fashions, who sent him on his first buying trip to Europe. After three and a half years with Armour, Norell was hired by Hattie Carnegie, a successful businesswoman who sold clothes to many actresses. From her Norell learned how Paris couture was made, inside and out. It was his job to take the originals and translate them into clothes that Carnegie would sell retail and wholesale.

While working for Carnegie, Norell was able to indulge his love of dramatic clothes. But he went too far when he refused to tone down a spangled skirt he had created for Gertrude Lawrence in *Lady in the Dark*. The actress liked it, but Carnegie wished to sell to the general market in a more restrained version. Norell was fired. In 1941, Norell joined Anthony Traina's wholesale house of high-quality larger-sized women's fashions as a designer, with the agreement that for a lesser salary, Norell would have his name on the label, an unprecedented move at a time when most ready-to-wear designers remained anonymous.

One of Norell's first successes under the Traina-Norell label was a black-and-white checked crepe shirtwaist dress with a black patent leather belt. This garment was a stark contrast to the pretty but fussy floral dresses many women were wearing in 1942. He won the Neiman Marcus Fashion Award. The next year the first American Fashion Critics Award (the "Coty") ever given was presented to Norell for outstanding fashion design during 1942. Distinctive apparel for which he was honored included a black dinner dress consisting of a hand-knit sweater top and jersey skirt decorated with paillette flowers, and a spangle-covered evening coat. Norell became known for his ability to create simple, good-looking clothes within the limits of wartime L-85 restrictions on fabric amounts and types of materials.

During the 1940's, Norell developed lasting and influential characteristics of styling: simple, straight or shirtwaist silhouettes, covered up or very bare necklines, bowed collars on dresses and blouses, vested blouses with suits, bright colors punctuated by bold contrasting buttons, sable-trimmed wool for evening, spare yet lavish pavé sequins. Traina-Norell soon became a status symbol among American women. "Clothes should flow with the lines of the body," said Norell in 1944, when he introduced the drop-waisted "chemise" dress twelve years before Paris designers showed it. Another inno-

vation was the use of leopard prints, which later became commonplace. As in haute couture, Norell designed hats, gloves, and shoes to create a unified distinctive look; pockets and buttons had to be functional. During the 1940's, Norell developed the idea that there should be one center of interest in an outfit, "the simple dress that dramatizes its wearer." He would not permit changes during manufacture to cut costs.

In 1951, Norell became the first designer to win a second Coty Award, and in 1956, he was the first to win a third Coty. Although he never graduated from the Parsons School of Design, on Nov. 1, 1956, the school awarded him a medal given to outstanding alumni in the decorative arts. Also that year, Norell was elected as the First Immortal in the Fashion Hall of Fame for having won three Coty Awards.

When Anthony Traina retired in 1960, Norell achieved immediate success with his own wholesale business at 550 Seventh Avenue in Manhattan's garment district. His wool culotte suit for daytime city wear created a sensation. So concerned was Norell that the design be copied correctly by the inescapable "knockoff" manufacturers, he released his working drawings for culottes to *Women's Wear Daily*, the fashion trade newspaper.

Although Norell was doing four million dollars of business per year by the 1960's, he dressed and lived simply, lunching at Schrafft's, dining at Hamburger Heaven, shopping for antiques, and spending many hours alone in the evenings, sketching. He never married.

As one of the faculty critics in the Parsons School costume design department, Norell was required to come to the school only three times per year. Instead, he came almost every morning on the way to work. In 1962, he was granted an honorary Doctor of Fine Arts degree from Pratt Institute, an honor that *Newsweek* proclaimed "unheard-of in the dress-designing business."

Norell's factory employed 150 workers, each responsible for individual garments from start to finish; nevertheless, Norell insisted on checking every dress himself before it was sent to the retail buyer. He designed hats for the Henri Bendel department store, but they did not sell well. About one hundred stores carried Norell's clothes, only in sizes 6–14; size 16 exceptions had to be approved by him personally. Doris Day wore a black evening dress and two suits by Norell in *That Touch of Mink* (1962). In 1963 he designed Lee Remick's movie wardrobe for

The Wheeler Dealers. That year he received the International Fashion Award from the *London Sunday Times* and shocked the fashion world by returning his third Coty Award, claiming that he did not like the fact the jury was allowed to vote on collections it had not seen. The Coty was returned to him.

The career of the young designer Halston was boosted by Norell's inclusion of his hats in his autumn/winter 1964 collection, which featured satin fabrics and bell-bottomed pants for evening. At prices of three hundred to four thousand dollars each, between seven and ten thousand garments were produced that year. Only the best fabrics from France and Italy were used. By 1965, Norell's clients included Jacqueline Kennedy, Lady Bird Johnson, the Duchess of Windsor, Mrs. William Paley, Dinah Shore, Carol Channing, and Lena Horne, as well as Lauren Bacall, who exclaimed that "his marvelous cut and use of fabrics make his things the most comfortable I've ever worn."

Norell was honored by the establishment of a scholarship in his name at the Parsons School of Design in 1965. He had been helping students there for twelve years and also made visits to the Pratt Institute. Norell was founder and president of the Council of Fashion Designers of America.

On Oct. 31, 1967, New York Fashion Designers, Inc., gave Norell a special award for helping develop new talent. The next year Revlon launched Norell perfume, the first successful American fragrance bearing a designer's name. In 1969, Norell fashions were included in an exhibition at the Royal Ontario Museum; the catalog referred to Norell as "America's most important designer." His twice-yearly black-tie evening fashion shows had become as important as haute couture openings in Paris. Norell garments also were shown at a fashion exhibition at the Victoria and Albert Museum in London (October 1971–January 1972).

When asked what he considered his major contribution to the fashion of the past half century, Norell replied, "I like to think I changed necklines." A major retrospective showing of Norell's fifty-year career was held at the Metropolitan Museum of Art on Oct. 16, 1972. The City of New York Bronze Medallion was to be presented to Norell, but he was unable to attend because he had suffered a stroke the day before. The "dean of American fashion" died in New York City.

[Museums and design laboratories possessing Norell garments, accessories, and/or sketches include the Indianapolis Museum of Art; the Costume Institute of the Metropolitan Museum of Art; the Parsons School of Design; Pratt Institute; the Fashion Institute of Technology National Museum of Fashion; the Royal Ontario Museum; Mount Mary College (Milwaukee, Wis.); and the University of Missouri at Kansas City.

The most complete study of Norell's life and work is by Bernadine Morris, in Sarah Tomerlin Lee, ed., *American Fashion* (1975). Norell is discussed in John Fairchild's *The Fashionable Savages* (1965); Phyllis Lee Levin, *The Wheels of Fashion* (1965); Caroline Rennolds Milbank, *Couture: The Great Designers* (1985) and *New York Fashion* (1989); and Jane Mulvagh, *Vogue History of 20th Century Fashion* (1988). See also *Business Week*, Sept. 12, 1964; Eleanor Lambert, *World of Fashion* (1976); and Michael Batterbery, *Mirror, Mirror* (1977). An obituary is in the *New York Times*, Oct. 26, 1972.]

THERESE DUZINKIEWICZ BAKER

NOURSE, EDWIN GRISWOLD (May 20, 1883–Apr. 7, 1974), economist, teacher, author, and public servant, was born in Lockport, N.Y., the son of Harriet Augusta Beaman and Edwin Henry Nourse. He grew up in Chicago, where his father was supervisor of singing in the public schools. An ancestor, Rebecca Nourse, is alleged to have been a victim in the 1692 Salem witchcraft trials.

Nourse graduated from Downer's Grove High School in Downer's Grove, Ill., in 1901 and then earned his A.A. degree from Lewis Institute in Chicago (1904), his B.A. from Cornell University (1906), and his Ph.D. from the University of Chicago (1915).

Nourse started his career in 1909 as an instructor in finance at the University of Pennsylvania's Wharton School of Business. As a faculty member at Iowa State College in Ames and at the universities of South Dakota and Arkansas, he attempted to apply business analytical techniques to agriculture, an interest that grew out of his study of agricultural economics at Cornell.

In 1922, Nourse joined the Institute of Economics in Washington, D.C., as chief of its agricultural division. When the institute merged with two other Brookings-endowed research organizations to form the Brookings Institution in 1928, he became the director of the institute (1929–1942) and later vice-president of the Brookings Institution (1942–1946). In addition, he served as president of the American

Farm Economic Association (1924) and edited the *Journal of Farm Economics* (1925–1926).

Nourse's early public career included serving as a delegate to the international Institute of Agriculture's assembly in Rome (1924, 1936) and as a member of the League of Nations Mixed Committee on the Relation of Nutrition to Health, Agriculture and Economic Policy (1935–1937). These activities led to an article in 1938 on the economic aspects of nutrition. In it he stated the basic elements of his pragmatic philosophy: business should accept "responsibility for the welfare of the entire labor force," and government had the responsibility "to underwrite a decent minimum standard of subsistence" for those who could not afford an adequate diet. Concurrently, Nourse saw a need for government "to insure good feeding and good medical care" for youth until they reached working age. Generally considered a conservative economist because of his belief in the ability of private market forces to govern the economy, he nevertheless foresaw the likelihood of greater government involvement in the economy.

In 1942, Nourse was elected president of the American Economic Association and began a three-year term as chairman of the Social Science Research Council in New York City. In July 1946, President Harry S. Truman chose him as chairman of the Economic Advisory Council, the agency created by the Employment Act of 1946. Nourse believed that the council should be an advisory group to the president alone; the council should not take public policy positions, and members were not to appear before congressional committees. When summoned on Feb. 4, 1949, by Senator Joseph O'Mahoney of Wyoming to testify before the Joint Economic Committee on the Economic Report of Congress, Nourse did not testify. He resigned from the council as of Oct. 17, 1949, the date selected by the president. (Nourse had submitted letters of resignation dated Dec. 14, 1948, Aug. 9, 1949, and Sept. 9, 1949.)

That Nourse was at philosophical odds with Truman cannot be denied. He believed that the council's advice must be confined to economics. To do otherwise, he felt, would leave council members the choice of supporting the president's position regardless of their professional convictions or of arguing against a policy recommended by the president.

Nourse's attempt to separate economics from politics in the council reflected his belief that economists were not trained to provide economic advice with political overtones. Truman complained that Nourse never presented him with a clear policy he could adopt, leading him at one point to query: "Can't someone bring me a one-handed economist?" A partial answer may be found in the article "The Gap Between Economist and Politician" (*New York Times*, Apr. 14, 1963), by economist Seymour Harris. He began by agreeing with Nourse about the training of economists, but differed with Nourse about its policy implications. Harris believed that economists were duty bound to widen their knowledge into the realm of political economy so as to be able to recommend clear policies.

President Truman named Roy Blough, a moderate, to the council and appointed Leon Keyserling, a member, as chairman. Congress was reluctant to finance continuation of the council. According to Nourse, Keyserling was obviously a political appointee, and as chairman his active participation in party affairs drew much criticism. Under President Dwight Eisenhower a reconstituted Council of Economic Advisers was financed and Arthur F. Burns became its chairman. Eisenhower was determined to remove politics from the council.

Nourse made many written contributions to economics that were essentially descriptive-analytical rather than purely theoretical. *America's Capacity to Produce* (1934) was a landmark study written with five colleagues. He also wrote *Marketing Agreements Under the Agriculture Adjustment Act* (1935) and, with Joseph S. Davis and John D. Black, *Three Years of Agricultural Adjustment Administration* (1937). Later Nourse and Horace Drury produced *Industrial Price Policies and Economic Progress* (1938). His *Price Making in a Democracy* (1944) was widely acclaimed and used by both labor and management in the wage negotiations at General Motors in October 1945. *The 1950's Come First* (1951) and *Economics in the Public Service* (1953) were his last two works.

Nourse married Ray Marie Tyler on Aug. 17, 1910; they had one child. Edwin Nourse died in Bethesda, Md.

[Nourse's publications not mentioned above include *Agricultural Economics* (1916); *The Chicago Produce Market* (1918); *American Agriculture and the European Market* (1924); *The Legal Status of Agricultural Co-operation* (1928); and *The Co-*

operative Marketing of Livestock (1931). A full-length biography is Joseph G. Knapp, *Edwin G. Nourse* (1979). Nourse's views on the Council of Economic Advisers are spelled out in three articles: "The Role of the Council of Economic Advisers," *American Political Science Review*, Apr. 1948; "Why I Had To Step Aside," *Collier's*, Feb. 18, 1950; and "Recent Developments in the Council of Economic Advisers," *Economic Record*, Nov. 1955. An obituary is in the *New York Times*, Apr. 10, 1974.]

HAROLD L. WATTEL

NYE, GERALD PRENTICE (Dec. 19, 1892–July 18, 1971), United States senator, was born in Hortonville, Wis., the son of Phoebe Ella Prentice and Irwin Raymond Nye, a crusading country editor and supporter of Progressive Robert M. La Follette. After graduating from Wittenberg (Wis.) High School in 1909, he managed the *Hortonville Review*, one of his father's weekly newspapers. He then went to Iowa, where he edited the *Creston Daily Plaindealer* and worked briefly for the *Des Moines Register* before moving to Fryburg, N.Dak., in 1915. There he purchased and ran *The Pioneer*, the first privately owned newspaper in the state to support the newly formed Non-Partisan League, an agrarian reform movement. In 1919, Nye and his wife, Anna Margaret Munch, whom he had married in 1916, moved to Cooperstown, N.Dak. He purchased the *Griggs County Sentinel-Courier*, which backed the efforts of the Non-Partisan League to build its own grain elevators and flour mills and to defeat the "interests" who controlled the state. He supported La Follette, the Progressive party candidate for president, in 1924, and the following year was appointed by the governor of North Dakota to fill a vacant seat in the U.S. Senate.

Nye, wearing bulbous yellow shoes and having "an Old Oaken Bucket haircut," arrived in Washington, D.C., in December 1925. Opposition to his appointment forced him to wait a month while the Senate debated whether a governor had the power to fill a senatorial vacancy. In 1926, by a two-vote majority, Nye was seated by the Senate, and in November the progressive Republican was elected to a full six-year term. In the Senate, Nye associated himself with the farm bloc, especially with William E. Borah of Idaho and George W. Norris of Nebraska. He pressed for passage of the McNary-Haugen bill, which called for government price supports for basic crops, and voted against a resolution that

favored United States membership in the Court of International Justice. Assigned to the Public Lands Committee, Nye presided over the investigation of the Teapot Dome scandal and uncovered the fact that President Warren G. Harding's interior secretary, Albert B. Fall, had, without competitive bidding, leased a $100 million oil field to Harry F. Sinclair of the Mammoth Oil Company in return for large contributions to the Republican National Committee. Nye's revelations, which he said demonstrated the "frightful influence of money upon our political and economic life as a nation," forced the revision of the government lease and the recovery of more than $7 million in taxes and penalties. It also won "Gerald the Giant-Killer" a reputation as an independent, stubborn battler.

Nye enhanced that reputation by battling with President Calvin Coolidge over taxation policies and settlement of the war debts, as well as over North Dakota patronage, and by campaigning against monopolies, branch banking, and chain stores. Appointed chairman of a committee to investigate Senate campaign expenditures in 1930, Nye exposed the link between the Ku Klux Klan and a Republican senatorial candidate in Kentucky, and the huge slush fund that had been employed, in vain, to defeat Senator Norris of Nebraska.

In 1932, Nye was returned to the Senate by a three-to-one majority. Still an agrarian reformer, he opposed many elements of Franklin D. Roosevelt's New Deal. In particular, along with Borah, he vehemently opposed the National Recovery Administration for fostering monopoly and price-fixing, and derided its symbol, the Blue Eagle, as "a bird of prey on the masses." Gradually becoming more concerned about keeping the United States out of another European war at all costs, Nye in 1934 headed a Senate investigation of the munitions industry. Once again, his revelations created a national sensation. Emphasizing the close and sometimes unsavory connections during World War I between the military and the arms industry and its banking associates, and the huge wartime profits of munitions manufacturers and bankers, especially the du Pont and J. P. Morgan interests, the Nye committee documented the role of these "merchants of death" in influencing the United States to intervene. Many Americans agreed with Nye's conclusion that the United States had been tricked into entering

World War I by munitions makers and that the latter constituted "a definite menace to world peace."

In the words of the pacifist-minded journalist Oswald Garrison Villard, Nye, "a great leader in the fight for peace," received the Cardinal Newman Award in 1935. He was a frequent speaker against the Reserve Officers Training Corps and other examples of militarism in American life, addressing groups as varied as the right-wing Social Justice followers of Father Charles Coughlin and the left-wing American League Against War and Fascism, thus helping to create a widespread determination among Americans to keep the United States out of future wars. Reflecting and augmenting this outlook, Nye played a leading role in the drafting and adoption of the Neutrality Acts passed by Congress between 1935 and 1937. These measures, seeking to prevent a repetition of the circumstances that had led the United States into war in 1917, outlawed arms sales or loans to nations at war, forbade Americans to travel on the ships of belligerent nations, and permitted the sale of nonmilitary goods to nations at war only if the warring countries paid cash and transported the goods on non-American ships.

Nye was supported in his 1938 reelection bid by a national committee headed by the historian Charles A. Beard and by Bruce Bliven, editor of the *New Republic*. Easily returned to the Senate, he stepped up his attacks on Roosevelt's foreign policies. He opposed any changes in the Neutrality Acts and fought to maintain the existing quotas on immigrants, which allowed only a trickle of German Jews to find refuge from Nazi persecution in the United States. Appointed to the Senate Foreign Relations Committee in 1940, Nye opposed aid to Great Britain ("the greatest aggressor in modern times") and bitterly criticized Roosevelt's "destroyers for bases" executive agreement with Winston Churchill. He helped to establish the America First Committee, and won its cheers for his unceasing vituperation against Roosevelt's unprecedented third term; the first peacetime draft in American history; the Lend-Lease Act, which gave the president sweeping powers to sell, transfer, exchange, lend, or lease military equipment to any nation whose defense he deemed essential to American security; and aid to the Soviet Union (populated by "thieves, human butchers and murderers of religion").

Just as stridently, in mid-1941 Nye lashed out at Jewish film producers in Hollywood. Claiming that they were poisoning American minds with anti-Hitler propaganda, Nye said, "My objection to them is that they are foreign born and are in a position of power to control what 81,000,000 people a week see in our theaters." He also accused Jews of leading the United States toward war. Although Nye reluctantly voted for America's entry into war after the Japanese attack on Pearl Harbor, his grim isolationism, association with the German-American Bund, and anti-Semitism left him discredited. He lost his Senate seat in the election of 1944.

In March 1940, Nye was divorced from Anna Nye, with whom he had three children. That December he married Marguerite Johnson, a schoolteacher he had met when he stopped his car to help her change a flat tire. After the war they returned to Washington, where Nye served as president of Record Engineering. In 1959, he became the special assistant for housing for the elderly in the Federal Housing Administration. Resigning that post in 1963, Nye then joined the staff of the Senate Committee on Aging. He retired in 1966 and died in Washington, D.C.

[Nye's political thought and career are treated in Wayne S. Cole, *Senator Gerald P. Nye and American Foreign Relations* (1962); Burl Noggle, *Teapot Dome* (1962); John E. Wiltz, *In Search of Peace* (1963); Thomas N. Guinsburg, *The Pursuit of Isolationism in the United States Senate from Versailles to Pearl Harbor* (1982); and Eugene M. Tobin, *Organize or Perish* (1986). An obituary is in the *New York Times*, July 19, 1971.]

HARVARD SITKOFF

O

O'BRIAN, JOHN LORD (Oct. 14, 1874–April 10, 1973), constitutional lawyer and public official who served under six different United States presidents, was born in Buffalo, N.Y., to John O'Brian, a justice of the peace, and Elizabeth Lord. He attended public schools in Buffalo and Harvard University, from which he graduated in 1896. He returned to his native city to study law at the University of Buffalo Law School, where he received his law degree in 1898.

In 1902 he married Alma E. White, with whom he had five daughters, including twins. He and Alma remained married for sixty-six years, until her death in 1968.

He opened a law office in Buffalo. In 1907, at the age of thirty-three, he was elected to the first of two terms in the New York State Assembly. Two years later, President Theodore Roosevelt appointed him U.S. attorney for the Western District of New York; he was subsequently reappointed by Presidents William Howard Taft and Woodrow Wilson. In 1913, he was narrowly defeated by the incumbent in a race for mayor of Buffalo. He ran on the combined Progressive and Citizens party ticket.

After the outbreak of World War I, O'Brian was asked by the U.S. attorney general to prosecute the Franz von Rintelen conspiracy case, *United States* v. *Rintelen*, which focused on an attempt to encourage labor leaders to call strikes at munitions factories. His successful use of the Sherman Anti-Trust Law marked the beginning of a long career in antitrust action.

In 1917 President Wilson appointed O'Brian head of the War Emergency Division of the Department of Justice. O'Brian wielded tremendous power in this position, originally established to protect the interests of the federal government, but whose mandate he expanded to protect the rights of individual citizens, a lifelong concern of his. As many as one thousand complaints per day came into his office. In *Schenck* v. *U.S.*, 249 U.S. 47 (1919), his argument before the Supreme Court led Justice Oliver Wendell Holmes, Jr., to elucidate the doctrine of the "clear and present danger" test under the First Amendment. During this same period O'Brian recruited J. Edgar Hoover to work for him; Hoover went on to head the General Intelligence Division which was the successor to the War Emergency Division, and then the FBI.

After World War I, while in private practice in Buffalo, O'Brian was appointed vice-chairman of the New York State Reorganization Committee for New York State Government. Working in close collaboration with Alfred E. Smith and Charles Evans Hughes he helped to bring about significant constitutional reform for the state of New York.

In 1929, President Herbert Hoover called O'Brian back to Washington to serve as head of the Anti-Trust Division of the Department of Justice. Over the next four years he prosecuted more than twenty cases, including one that prevented the merger of General Electric, Westinghouse, and the Radio Corporation of America. In 1936, he became special counsel for the Tennessee Valley Authority at the request of President Franklin D. Roosevelt. Until this time the U.S. government had never engaged in private enterprise. O'Brian successfully argued that water as it went over a dam gained a special value and as such was a public property that should not be wasted. Winning the case *Ashwander* v. *Tennessee Valley Authority* before the Supreme Court was one of his great-

593

est triumphs. In 1938, the trial was delayed so that O'Brian could run for the U.S. Senate on the Republican ticket. He was drafted six weeks before the election and, despite winning fifty-seven out of sixty-one counties, he lost the race because he did not prevail in the heavily populated counties of Kings (Brooklyn), Queens, and New York (Manhattan), as well as in the small county of Albany. He lost in part because of his opposition to some of Roosevelt's programs and his unwillingness to compromise his ideals for political expediency.

Although O'Brian served under many Democratic presidents he maintained a lifelong allegiance to the Republican party. In 1940 he gave the nominating address for Thomas E. Dewey, the Republican candidate for president. Despite his support for Roosevelt's opponent, in 1941 President Roosevelt asked him to serve his administration again, this time as general counsel for the War Production Board. He accepted this position because of his strong sense of duty to his country and because he saw it as a logical extension of his work during World War I. He assembled a legendary array of legal talent to ensure that military contracts were awarded in a fair manner, such that the best possible war effort was made. He asked for and received far-reaching emergency powers over the nation's businesses. It was a testament to his wisdom and sense of fairness that only once was his board's decision questioned in court and that suit failed. Fellow members of the board were so impressed by O'Brian's talent and so fond of him that for almost thirty years after the war they met annually in Washington, D.C., to honor him. At war's end, President Harry Truman awarded him the Presidential Medal of Merit for his unique accomplishments and outstanding service to his country.

In 1945 President Truman asked O'Brian to chair a panel investigating a possible strike at the Oak Ridge Atomic Energy Plant; he successfully resolved that dispute. By that time O'Brian had joined the Washington firm of Covington, Burling, Rublee, Acheson, and Shorb, though he still remained a member of his Buffalo firm of Slee, O'Brian, Hellings, and Ulsh, which he had joined in 1917. He was seventy years old when he joined Covington and Burling, an age by which most men would have retired. Yet for another twenty-eight years he pursued a private career in law. He argued antitrust and constitutional law cases as well as

civil service and labor cases for individuals, corporations, and foreign nations. He argued many cases before the Supreme Court, including some involving the United Nations. He even successfully defended the commissioner of baseball, "Happy" Chandler, against charges from players who had been barred from playing after playing in the Mexican League. When a sportswriter looked up references to see why O'Brian had been selected as Chandler's lawyer, the writer quipped, "His record leads me to believe that he must be three persons."

O'Brian was a superb courtroom lawyer with "matchless powers of legal and factual analysis." He was devoted to the legal profession but also believed "that a lawyer ought to take some part in the life of his time." He wrote that "we progress as a race only as we consciously increase the intensity of our sense of injustice." He lived by these principles and won the respect, friendship, and admiration of many of America's finest lawyers and Supreme Court justices, including Felix Frankfurter, Benjamin Cardozo, Louis Brandeis, Harlan Stone, Learned Hand, and Elihu Root. Erwin Griswold, the dean of Harvard Law School for twenty-two years, wrote that O'Brian was "the lawyer whom I admired perhaps most of all."

In 1955 O'Brian delivered the Godkin Lectures at Harvard University, hailed as a "brilliant analysis of our society" by James Reston. In 1962 Chief Justice Earl Warren paid tribute in the Supreme Court to O'Brian, who was then eighty-seven, saying, "I am told that this is the fiftieth anniversary of your own admission to the bar of this Court. Few men in history have had a longer or more active practice before the Court. During all of these years you have served the Court well." On another occasion Warren confided to one of O'Brian's grandsons, "He's my favorite lawyer."

In addition to his outstanding public career and precedent-setting private career, O'Brian devoted much time to education. He served as trustee for the University of Buffalo from 1903 to 1929, as regent for the University of the State of New York from 1931 to 1947, as overseer for Harvard University from 1939 to 1945, and as chairman for the Endowment Fund of Harvard Divinity School from 1950 to 1957. An endowed chair was established in his honor at the Harvard Divinity School in 1955 to "reflect his broad compassion, his constant search for truth in every quarter, his insistence on the right of all men for a fair hearing for their opinions."

O'Brian received numerous honors and awards including the Officier de L'Ordre de Leopold II for services in the war (Belgium, 1919), the Chancellor's Medal from the University of Buffalo (1940), the Presidential Medal for Merit for outstanding service in the war effort (1946), the Samuel Paul Capen Alumni Award from the University of Buffalo for "notable contributions" to the University (1951), the Order of the Coif (1952), the Brotherhood Award from the National Conference of Christians and Jews (1953), the Sidney Hillman Foundation Annual Book Award (1955), the New York State Bar Association Medal for Distinguished Services (1958), the Red Jacket Medal from the Buffalo and Erie County Historical Society for a "lifetime of continued unbroken devotion" to the Society (1959), and the Fellows of the American Bar Foundation Annual Award (1960). He received honorary degrees from Hobart College (1916), Syracuse University (1938), Brooklyn Polytechnic Institute (1943), Brown University (1945), Harvard University (1946), Yale University Law School (1948), and Harvard Divinity School (1966).

He gave inspiration to countless thousands because above all he was a very human person, very kind, and very gentle. He had a particular love for Victorian literature, which he often quoted. He was "a man for all seasons," in the words of Arthur Krock, the famed Washington biographer. He was still visiting his Washington, D.C., office at the age of ninety-eight and in fact died just one week after his last visit there. He is buried in the Washington National Cathedral in recognition of his life devoted to the nation's service and the pursuit of excellence.

[Articles, speeches, autobiographical material, awards, honors, medals, scrapbooks, and personal papers are all contained in the Special Collections of the State University of New York at Buffalo, Faculty of Law and Jurisprudence. The Columbia University Oral History Research Office also has a transcript of tapes entitled "Mr. O'Brian's Reminiscences." His publications include "The Menace of Administrative Law" (1920), "The Spirit of Remonstrance" (1940), "The War Production Board Administrative Policies and Procedures" (1944), "Loyalty Tests and Guilt by Association" (1948), *National Security and Individual Freedom* (1955), "The Value of Constitutionalism Today" (1956), and "The Right to Utter," in *College in a Yard* (1957). Also see *Buffalo Law Re-*

view, Twentieth Anniversary Issue, 1971, and John Lord O'Brian Commemorative Issue, 1974. Obituaries appear in the *Buffalo Evening News*, Apr. 10, 1973; the *New York Times*, Apr. 11, 1973; and the *Washington Post*, Apr. 12, 1973.]

DAVID W. BUTSCH

O'DONNELL, EMMETT, JR. ("ROSY") (Sept. 15, 1906–Dec. 26, 1971), air force general, was born in Brooklyn, N.Y., the son of Emmett O'Donnell, a high school English teacher, and Veronica Tobin. After graduating from Manual Training High School in Brooklyn in 1924, he entered the United States Military Academy at West Point, N.Y. Nicknamed "Rosy" because of his ruddy complexion and frequent blushes, O'Donnell excelled in athletics at the military academy and graduated in 1928. Commissioned a second lieutenant in the infantry, he chose to enter pilot training for the air corps, and in 1930 he joined the First Pursuit Group. On Dec. 29, 1930, O'Donnell married Lorraine Muller; they had three children.

During the next six years O'Donnell was stationed with the First Pursuit Group at Selfridge Field, Mich. From 1936 to 1940 he was assigned to the Eighteenth Reconnaissance Group at Mitchel Field, Long Island, and in the summer of 1939 he attended the Air Corps Tactical School at Maxwell Field, Ala. In February 1940 O'Donnell was transferred to the Eleventh Bombardment Group at Hickam Field, Hawaii, and in September 1941, holding the rank of major, he led a squadron of nine B-17s to the Philippines in the first mass flight of heavy bombers to cross the western Pacific. The completion of this historic mission, despite primitive service facilities and inadequate weather data, demonstrated that the Philippines could be reinforced by air.

When the United States entered World War II in December 1941, O'Donnell was immediately thrust into action. On December 10 he flew his B-17 to Vigan in northern Luzon to strike Japanese ships and earned the Distinguished Flying Cross for pressing home the attack in the face of heavy Japanese antiaircraft fire and mechanical problems with his own plane. In January 1942 O'Donnell went to Java, where he briefly served as operations officer of the Far East Air Force, and in March 1942 he was evacuated to India. There he became operations officer of the newly organized Tenth Air Force, which was responsible for ferrying supplies over the Himalayan Mountains from India to China. A year later O'Donnell was assigned to the advisory council of General Henry H. Arnold, commander of the Army Air Forces, a post he occupied until March 1944.

After his repeated pleas for a combat command, O'Donnell, promoted to the rank of brigadier general, was given command of the Seventy-third Bombardment Wing, which was to utilize the B-29 heavy bomber in raids against Japan. Following six months of training in the United States, he took his wing to Saipan in the Mariana Islands. On Nov. 24, 1944, after training raids against the islands of Iwo Jima and Truk, O'Donnell piloted the lead bomber of 111 B-29s in a 3,200-mile mission to Tokyo, the first major raid of the Mariana-based Twenty-first Bomber Command against the Japanese capital. He continued to command the Seventy-third Wing in the American air assault against Japan through the end of the war.

For several years after World War II, O'Donnell, who was promoted to the rank of major general in June 1948, served in a series of logistics, public affairs, and joint defense commission assignments before being appointed commander of the Fifteenth Air Force in August 1948. Shortly after American intervention in the Korean War in June 1950, O'Donnell went to Japan from March Air Base, Calif., and established the Far East Bomber Command. From the outset he wanted to put "a very severe blow on the North Koreans" and told his superiors that B-29s, using incendiary bombs in area bombardment (that is, targeting a large-sized area for destruction), could destroy practically everything of value in North Korea in a matter of days and compel the North Koreans to end their aggression against South Korea. O'Donnell's superiors vetoed this approach because the bombers were needed to support the hardpressed American ground troops. However, O'Donnell ultimately had much of his own way, and within months B-29s, operating virtually unopposed, destroyed so many strategic targets in North Korea that there was little left to bomb. As he informed a Senate committee, "Everything is destroyed. There is nothing standing worthy of the name."

Following the entrance of the Chinese Communists into the Korean War in the fall of 1950, O'Donnell unsuccessfully called for air strikes against Chinese bases in Manchuria and targets in North Korea that American leaders had clas-

sified as off limits because of their proximity to the border of the Soviet Union. He repeated these recommendations after he was rotated back to the United States in January 1951 and soon aroused controversy with "hangar talk" that apparently urged the use of atomic bombs against Communist China. Still in command of the Fifteenth Air Force, O'Donnell was a prominent witness before the combined Senate Armed Services and Foreign Relations Committees inquiry in the spring of 1951 into the dismissal of General Douglas MacArthur from his Far Eastern commands. He testified that "his boys" had been frustrated by United Nations policy that they bomb only south of the Yalu River and not violate Manchurian air space. O'Donnell speculated that a wide-ranging bombing campaign in Korea and Manchuria could have won the war in 1950, perhaps without the use of any American ground troops.

In May 1953 O'Donnell became deputy chief of staff for personnel with the rank of lieutenant general, and in May 1959 he was promoted to full general and named commander in chief, Pacific Air Forces. As Pacific air commander, O'Donnell pushed for greater assistance to the nascent Vietnamese National Air Force in the early stages of South Vietnam's war against the Viet Cong insurgents and the employment of American pilots to support South Vietnamese combat operations. O'Donnell retired from the air force on July 31, 1963, and thereafter was associated with a number of business enterprises and, beginning in 1964, president of the United Services Organization. He died in McLean, Va.

A volatile Irishman who did not hesitate to speak his mind or question his superiors, O'Donnell was of average size and had pronounced blue eyes. He is remembered as a forceful advocate of independent air power and as one of the most famous bomber commanders of his era.

[See volumes 1 (1948) and 5 (1953) of *The Army Air Forces in World War II*, ed. by W. F. Craven and J. L. Cate, for information on O'Donnell's service during World War II. For his Korean War service see 82d Congress, 1st Session, *Hearings on the Military Situation in the Far East* (1951); and Robert F. Futrell, *The United States Air Force in Korea, 1950–1953* (1961). For biographical data see *Assembly*, Dec. 1972. Obituaries are in the *New York Times* and the *Washington Post*, both Dec. 27, 1971.]

JOHN KENNEDY OHL

OHRBACH, NATHAN M. ("N. M.") (Aug. 31, 1885–Nov. 19, 1972), retailer, was born in Vienna, Austria, one of four children of Isaac J. Ohrbach and Anna Dickman. When Nathan was two, his family emigrated to the United States and took up residence in Brooklyn, in New York City, where he attended elementary school and DeWitt Clinton High School.

By age fourteen he was running errands for local merchants; at seventeen he was a traveling salesman; at twenty he was a buyer for local stores. In 1907 Ohrbach married Mathilda Kane, a sister of a business acquaintance. They had one child.

At twenty-six, in 1911, he opened a small specialty shop in Brooklyn called Bon Marché Inc., and later one in Manhattan. The stores specialized in low cost, ready-to-wear merchandise.

By 1923, Ohrbach had eighteen years' experience in retailing. With dress manufacturer Max Wiesen as a partner, he opened a store on Fourteenth Street at Union Square in Manhattan with two floors and a basement stocked with dresses and coats—job lots, seconds, irregulars, and manufacturers' overstocks priced low for fast sale. The store was a huge success and eventually occupied six adjoining buildings. By 1928 he bought out his partner at more than ten times his original investment.

Ohrbach's expanded to Newark, N.J., in 1930, and to Los Angeles in 1948. In 1953 Ohrbach purchased Milliron's in downtown Los Angeles, but the store closed in 1959 due to poor sales volume. After 1960 Ohrbach opened stores in La Mirada, Calif., Westbury, Long Island, in the San Fernando Valley, and other suburban areas in New York and California.

Ohrbach's greatest business adventure came on Aug. 26, 1954, when he moved the flagship store uptown from Fourteenth Street to Thirty-fourth Street in Manhattan, to the former site of James McCreery and Sons. This meant direct competition with Macy's, Gimbles, Lord and Taylor, B. Altman and Company, and Arnold Constable, all in the immediate vicinity. Sales in the Herald Square area rose sharply with the advent of the new Ohrbach's.

Aware that his son was not interested in a career in retailing, Ohrbach sold a large block of stock in the Ohrbach Corporation in 1962 to the Dutch-American Investing Company, an affiliate of C. and A. Brenninkmeyer Company, a European Mercantile Empire. In 1963 Ohrbach resigned as president and treasurer of the chain, retaining the chairmanship of Ohrbach's Inc. until 1965, when total sales were at $94 million. After 1965 he retained a seat on the board of directors and became a consultant to the company.

Ohrbach wrote a textbook entitled *Getting Ahead in Retailing,* which was published by McGraw Hill in 1935. His philosophy was expressed in the slogan "a business in millions, a profit in pennies." He was intensely personal in his approach, and for many years even greeted shoppers as they entered his store. As a pioneer of low-overhead, high-volume selling he was a precursor of the discount store movement. Services were cut to the bare essentials: there was a minimum sales force, and the store offered no alterations, no deliveries, no credit. Ohrbach expressed this approach as "less billing, more cooing." There were no special sales periods and no price advertising.

Ohrbach believed in high fashion at low cost for bargain-conscious women. Over the years, more and more quality fashion items and lines were added to his inventory, thus attracting women lured by expensively styled clothes at moderate prices. His stores began to offer authentic copies of Paris couture originals. Buyers were sent abroad to Paris, Rome, and Milan to purchase originals on the understanding that they would be copied. The designer dresses were sent to the Garment District on Seventh Avenue to be reproduced and were made available in Ohrbachs within weeks.

This strategy won Ohrbach the veneration of his customers. He stated, "I was happy to think that I could give a woman a garment which cost me $1,000 for $25 and in many cases for less than that. . . . My main point when I started out was that I was trying to reach a class of people who were intelligent and not necessarily rich."

Ohrbach died in New York City, where he had been active in community affairs, especially with the Greater New York Councils of the Boy Scouts of America, the Federation of Jewish Charities, and the American Jewish Committee. (He had also maintained homes in Westchester County, N.Y., and in Palm Springs, Calif.)

[See Herbert Brean, "High Style Cash-and-Carry," *Life,* Jan. 26, 1953; and Tom Mahoney, *The Great Merchants* (1955). An obituary is in the *New York Times,* Nov. 20, 1972.]

SUSAN VAUGHN

ORY, EDWARD ("KID") (Dec. 25, 1886–
Jan. 23, 1973), jazz trombonist and composer,
was born in La Place, La., the son of John
Osenee, a plantation owner, and Octavie Ory.
One of seven children, Ory began working at
the age of ten, after the death of his mother, to
help support his ailing father and two younger
sisters. Since he could not attend school, he
paid a tutor ten cents per week to teach him at
night. While earning a living as a water boy for
field hands, he went into business for himself by
getting up at 4 A.M. to catch crawfish and sell
them before going to his regular job at 7 A.M.
He also picked blackberries and mushrooms in
the evenings and sold them to increase his earnings.

During his youth Ory realized that he wanted
to become a musician, and in their spare time,
he and some of his friends made their own string
instruments. They later formed a small band
that performed at local dances and picnics; the
money earned from these performances was
saved to purchase professional musical instruments. Ory saved enough to buy a used valve
trombone, but at the age of twelve he purchased
a slide trombone while visiting an older sister in
New Orleans. On the day he bought this instrument, the legendary trumpeter Buddy
Bolden happened to walk by Ory's sister's house
and heard him playing. Bolden knocked on the
door, asked to speak with the player, and after a
brief discussion offered Ory a job. Ory thought
Bolden's offer was a great opportunity, but his
sister persuaded him to wait until he was twenty-
one before leaving home and embarking on a
career as a professional musician. In the meantime, he decided to learn a trade for better financial stability, and took up brick masonry. At
age seventeen, he bought a parcel of land in La
Place on which he later built a house. Since he
was industrious and had an excellent reputation
in the community, a local merchant let him
have the materials he needed on credit to build
the house. He laid all the bricks himself, and
his friends helped him with the woodwork on
weekends in exchange for barbeque dinners:
Ory had a reputation as an excellent cook.

During his teens Ory continued to teach himself to play the trombone. The band he formed
with his friends performed as often as possible,
sometimes at social functions and fund-raisers
Ory had coordinated and promoted, using his
excellent organizational and entrepreneurial
skills. In 1911, he and the band moved to New

Orleans to participate full-time in the thriving
music life of the city. The band worked frequently in Storyville cabarets, at street parades,
lawn parties, and funerals, and on advertising
wagons. It was on an advertising wagon that Ory
played with his trombone slide hanging over the
tailgate, which later became known as the "tailgate" style.

Ory developed his style by listening attentively
to the work of Frankie Dusen, Buddy Johnson,
and George Filke. His strongest influence was
the trombone pioneer Zue Robertson, who was
two years his junior. Ory carried the best of
Robertson's style to another level. His "tailgate"
style is described thus by noted educator-
musician David Baker: "Ory's playing, like that
of his contemporaries, was characterized by
slides and slurs, rhythmic configurations borrowed from marches and other sources, and tri-
adic melodies built on the overtone series. The
essential difference between Ory and his contemporaries was a kind of daring, manifest in unexpected turns and homorous utterances."

Ory was nicknamed "Kid" by the ladies, with
whom he was quite popular. The nickname became permanent when he was hired to perform
at an amusement park and advertised as "Kid
Ory and His Band." He became one of the most
popular bandleaders in New Orleans in the
1910's. His bands included such luminaries as
King Oliver, Sidney Bechet, Johnny Dodds,
and Louis Armstrong.

After nearly a decade of success in New Orleans, Ory moved to Los Angeles in 1919 while
many of his peers were migrating to Chicago
after the closing of Storyville. After he had established himself in California, he asked his
New Orleans musicians to join him. They were
called either "Ory's Brownskinned Band" or
"The Seven Pods of Pepper and Ory's Creole
Trombone." In 1921, the band was the first to
record "New Orleans Negro jazz." The group
disbanded in 1924 and Ory moved to Chicago
to join Louis Armstrong's band.

During the next five years, Ory was the top
tailgate trombonist in Chicago, where he performed regularly and made numerous recordings as a leader or a sideman with major artists
such as Joe ("King") Oliver and Barney Bigard.
According to Alma Hubner, "During the years
1925–27 Kid Ory recorded almost all the jazz
masterpieces which have won him acclaim as
the greatest New Orleans trombonist in the history of recorded jazz." In 1926, he composed

and recorded his most famous composition, "Muskrat Ramble." When the Great Depression caused the Chicago jazz scene to suffer, Ory returned to California.

In 1930, Ory became co-owner of a poultry farm with his older brother and also worked in the mail room of the Santa Fe Railroad station in Los Angeles. Following the sudden death of his brother in 1938 and a revitalization of the jazz scene in California, Ory made a comeback. For the next three or four years he composed a large number of new pieces and returned to performing full-time with his New Orleans friends.

In 1942, Ory joined clarinetist Barney Bigard's band and later performed for Orson Welles's radio program series on American music, produced by the California Standard Oil Company, throughout 1944. In that same year Ory moved to San Francisco, and his Creole Jazz Band made the famous Crescent recordings produced by Marili Morden and Nesuhi Ertegun. The band included trumpeter Mutt Carey, clarinetist Omer Simeon, pianist Buster Wilson, guitarist Bud Scott, bassist Ed Garland, and drummer Alton Redd.

For the next twenty years Ory and his band toured extensively in the United States and abroad. He appeared in two movies, *New Orleans* (1946) and *The Benny Goodman Story* (1955). He also completed the soundtrack for *Crossfire* (1947). During this period he married his manager, Barbara Ga Nung; they had one child. In 1958, Ory underwent surgery to remove benign prostate tumors. After the operation, his blood-clotting process failed, and his life was saved by blood donations from thirty-eight people. A week later, he was back on his feet.

Ory combined musical talent with business acumen to develop a successful career. He owned a waterfront nightclub in San Francisco called On the Levee for several years before selling it around 1961. In 1964, he discontinued his career as a full-time musician, but still played occasional engagements, including some at Disneyland, for about two more years. In 1966, he retired to Hawaii; he died in Honolulu. Ory enjoyed one of the longest and most successful careers of any jazz musician and is regarded as one of the greatest Dixieland slide trombonists.

[See Pat Vincent, "Crescent City Kid," *Band Leaders*, Nov. 1945; Alma Hubner, "Ory: That New Orleans Trombone," *Jazz Notes*, Jan. 1946, and "Kid Ory," *Jazz Record*, Mar. 1946; Marili Ertegun, "Just Playing the Music I Love," *Downbeat*, Aug. 1951; and David Baker, *Jazz Styles and Analysis* (1973). An obituary is in the *New York Times*, Jan. 24, 1973.]

LAWRENCE McCLELLAN, JR.

P

PARKER, EDWARD PICKERING (Nov. 4, 1912–Jan. 1, 1974), games manufacturer, was born in Salem, Mass., the son of Foster Hegeman Parker, secretary-treasurer of Parker Brothers, and Anna Merrill, and grandnephew of George Parker, founder of Parker Brothers. As a child he was fascinated with board games, inventing some of his own, making up new rules for existing ones, and testing others. He graduated from Phillips Exeter Academy in 1930 and received a B.A. cum laude from Harvard in 1934. He was with Parker Brothers from 1934 until his death.

George Parker had been encouraged to sell The Game of Banking, a board game he had invented at the age of sixteen, but finding no buyer, he published it himself. It sold well, and he developed other games. In 1888, with his older brother, Charles, he founded Parker Brothers. In 1898, the oldest brother, Edward H., joined the firm, which was incorporated in 1901. Other games followed, including Pit, Rook, Sorry!, and tiddlywinks; they bought the American rights to Ping-Pong and mah-jongg.

George Parker, who lived until 1952, had been an imaginative sales agent but lacked good executive skills. By 1932, when his son-in-law, Robert Barton, entered the firm, the company's revenues had dropped by half. In 1935, a year after Edward Parker's arrival, the company bought the rights to Monopoly, having rejected similar games earlier. It was an instant hit with the public.

On Apr. 9, 1938, Parker married Natalie Stevens; they had three children. He served with the U.S. Navy during World War II, commanding antisubmarine vessels in the Pacific, for which he received two Bronze Stars and seven battle stars. He rose to the rank of retired captain in the Naval Reserve.

The family company continued to do well, but with the rise of television, Parker and his family were concerned that the future might be bleak—a possible dramatic drop in the interest in board games. The company had long relied on conservative management methods and old-fashioned ways of marketing. It was criticized for not immediately capitalizing on television advertising and for staying away too long from discount stores.

In the 1960's, General Mills was in the midst of diversification. In 1966, it initiated discussions with Parker Brothers to buy the company. Both Barton and Parker put it off. General Mills then went to Parker Brothers' major rival, Milton Bradley, which also declined the offer. In October 1967, the Parker family said it would sell the firm for $47.5 million, and General Mills agreed to the price. The papers were signed in February 1968. Edward Parker was executive vice-president of Parker Brothers until later in 1968, when he succeeded Barton as president. In 1961, he served as president of the Toy Manufacturers of America.

Although General Mills vowed that it did not intend to tamper with Parker Brothers' spirit, it did, in effect, assume managerial and financial control. The company had for years relied on its old but still popular products. Testing board games was difficult, and the new owner moved more into toys. The Nerf ball, introduced in 1970, sold over four million in its first year.

In 1972, the commissioner of public works of Atlantic City proposed changing the names of two streets that appeared in the game Monopoly—Mediterranean and Baltic Avenues—because their names changed along their routes.

A sizable public outcry ensued, particularly since Monopoly's Mediterranean and Baltic were at the low end of the economic spectrum and were the least expensive properties. In January 1973, the year he became chairman of Parker Brothers, Edward Parker wrote to the responsible officials in Atlantic City. If Atlantic City changed the street names, Parker Brothers would not change the names on the Monopoly board. He also pointed out that Monopoly's Marvin Gardens was a misspelling of the city's Marven Gardens, but that he would not change that spelling either; noting that such changes might "possibly shake the very foundations of American tradition." And as for Marvin Gardens, "Perhaps the real Marven Gardens should consider changing its spelling." Atlantic City did not pursue the issue.

Parker had substantial business acumen, was quite likable, "garrulous," and possessed "magnetism." Parker Brothers always regarded itself as a publishing company rather than a producer of games or toys. When Parker died in Salem, Mass., the company had sold more than seventy million sets of Monopoly.

[See also Parker Brothers, *75 Years of Fun* (1958); "Where Monopoly Is Not a Dirty Word," *Business Week*, Mar. 25, 1967; Robert D. McFadden, "Monopoly Makers Defend the Game's Cheap Streets," *New York Times*, Jan. 9, 1973; Parker Brothers, *90 Years of Fun* (1973); and Ellen Wojahn, *Playing by Different Rules* (1988). An obituary is in the *New York Times*, Jan. 3, 1974.]

MARGARET LATIMER

PARKS, LARRY (Dec. 13, 1914–Apr. 13, 1975), actor, was born Samuel Lawrence Klausman Parks in Olathe, Kans., the son of Frank Parks, who worked in advertising, and Leona Klausman. Two childhood illnesses left the boy with a weakened heart and legs of unequal length, requiring special compensating shoes. His contact with physicians inspired Parks to study medicine at the University of Illinois. While earning his B.S., "the acting bug" bit Parks. After graduating he went to New York in search of theater work, supporting himself by ushering at Carnegie Hall, by inspecting trains for the New York Central Railroad, and by working as a guide at Radio City Music Hall. He became associated with the Group Theatre, appearing in their 1937 production of Clifford Odets's *Golden Boy*. Later, in Hollywood,

Group Theatre member John Garfield helped him to become a low-paid contract player at Columbia Pictures.

At Columbia, in the actor's equivalent of an assembly-line job, he appeared in thirty low-budget B pictures within five years, beginning with *Mystery Ship* in 1941.

On September 8, 1944, he married actress Betty Garrett. They had two children.

Parks became a star when Columbia's studio heads conducted a highly publicized talent search, auditioning dozens of actors and mimics, then "discovered" Parks on their own back lot. They auditioned Parks and then cast him in the title role of *The Jolson Story*, in which he lip-synched the two dozen sound-track songs recorded by Jolson himself. The movie was an enormous hit in 1946, even though Parks earned only his regular contract player's salary. Columbia then cast him opposite superstar Rita Hayworth in *Down to Earth* (1947), followed by two period swashbucklers, *The Swordsman* (1947) and *The Gallant Blade* (1948); none of these created much excitement. After a prolonged legal battle with Columbia, which finally improved the financial terms of his contract, Parks made *Jolson Sings Again* (1949), which repeated its predecessor's success. The Jolson films proved to be the pinnacle of Larry Parks's brief career as a film star, though not of his notoriety.

His first success coincided with investigations by the House Committee on Un-American Activities into charges of communist infiltration of the film and broadcasting industries. Parks was among nineteen "unfriendly" witnesses first subpoenaed in 1947, but he was not among the highly confrontational "Hollywood Ten" actually called to testify before the committee at that time.

Larry Parks's public ordeal did not come until after the initial hearings had split Hollywood into warring factions. In March 1951, he was subpoenaed for a second time, along with eight others, and, with his new celebrity status, he quickly fell prey to the committee's eagerness to exploit media coverage of their star-studded inquiries. Under pressure, and after careful coaching by the committee's staff, Parks became the first filmstar to admit that he had joined the Communist party in Hollywood (in 1941) and that he had attended some dozen meetings over the next four years.

When the committee asked Parks to name

other party members, he cast aside his rehearsed script, tearfully pleading, "I don't think this is American justice . . . forcing me to crawl through the mud and be an informer. To what purpose?" The purpose was even questioned by one committee member, who was aware that the committee already knew and had subpoenaed the people to be named; but the ritual "proof of purity" was nevertheless insisted on. On Mar. 23, 1951, the *Los Angeles Examiner* headlined "Larry Parks lists names of ten Hollywood Reds" (he had actually named twelve); the next day's paper revealed the price of his agonized public soul-searching: "Larry Parks loses $75000 screen role."

Parks was damned from all sides: by Hedda Hopper, John Wayne, and others as unpatriotically soft on Reds, and by the left as a weak informer. In testifying, Parks had predicted the end of his career, which indeed declined precipitously. Although he made occasional appearances on stage and television in the next decade, Parks acted in only three more films before his death, none made in Hollywood. His last film role was a supporting part in John Huston's British film *Freud* (1962). In later years, Larry Parks made his living in real estate.

His wife's career was also seriously affected, and took a number of years to recover. Betty Garrett was appearing regularly as a neighbor of the Archie Bunkers on "All in the Family" at the time of her husband's death.

[A short but complete summary of Larry Parks's acting career appears in Walter Rigdon's *Biographical Encyclopedia and Who's Who of the American Theatre* (1966). The details of and issues related to Parks's HUAC experience receive extensive, though rarely unbiased, treatment in books on the Hollywood hearings. John Cogley's early two-volume *Report on Blacklisting* (1956) reports his dialogue with the committee in painful detail. Recent reevaluations and additional details appear in two 1980 studies: Victor S. Navasky, *Naming Names*, and Larry Coplair and Steven Englund, *The Inquisition in Hollywood*. Obituaries, which all focus on the Jolson films and his HUAC testimony as the major public events of his life, appear in the *New York Times*, Apr. 15, 1975; and in *Time* and *Newsweek*, Apr. 28, 1975.]

DANIEL S. KREMPEL

PARSONS, LOUELLA ROSE OETTINGER (Aug. 6, 1881–Dec, 9, 1972), journalist and gossip columnist, was born in Freeport, Ill., the daughter of Joshua Oettinger and Helen Wilcox. Although her father was Jewish, the family attended local Episcopal churches; as an adult Parsons became a devout Catholic. Her father was a prosperous clothier who took over a store in Sterling, near Chicago, in 1888. On his death two years later, the family moved back to Freeport, where her mother married John H. Edwards, a traveling salesman, in December 1891. In 1897 the family moved to Dixon, where Parsons graduated from Dixon High School in 1901.

After attending, though never graduating from, both Dixon College and Normal School, Parsons taught at a country school for a year before going to work part-time for the Dixon paper, *The Star*. On Oct. 31, 1905, she married John D. Parsons, and they moved to Burlington, Iowa, where he managed a family realty development. They had one child. Parsons considered these to be the unhappiest years of her life. The marriage foundered, in part because of her husband's unfaithfulness. Much of her life at this time is shrouded in mystery and obfuscation; she later maintained that Parsons died in World War I, even though substantial evidence indicates that she divorced him. In any event, she entered into another marriage (or long-term liaison) with Jack McCaffrey, a riverboat captain. By late 1910 she had settled in Chicago and had found employment in the *Chicago Tribune*'s syndication department.

Parsons wrote scenarios (outlines of film plots) at night and soon landed a job with Essanay Film Manufacturing Co. as a story editor and scenario writer. She later estimated that she wrote hundreds of one- and two-reel scenarios before being laid off in 1915. That year saw the publication of *How to Write for the Movies*, which was successful enough to be republished in revised form in 1917. The *Chicago Record-Herald* hired her in 1915, and in addition to serving as a general assignment reporter, she claimed to have introduced the movie gossip column during her four-year stint with the paper, which folded in 1918. She moved to New York in 1919 and became motion-picture editor for the *Morning Telegraph*. She worked long hours, ruthlessly cultivated people, and put together an efficient staff. By the early 1920's her editorial work, reviews, and gossip columns had made her a "small but important cog in the motion-picture business."

Although McCaffrey lived with Parsons in the early 1920's (he piloted excursion boats on the Hudson), she began a decade-long, on-and-off clandestine affair with Peter J. Brady, a married man-about-town who introduced her to a wide range of useful people. Parsons's columns and reviews came to the attention of press tycoon William Randolph Hearst, in part because of her favorable reviews of his mistress, the actress Marion Davies. In 1923 Hearst made Parsons motion-picture editor of his *New York American*. Her career was slowed by serious health problems, including tuberculosis, but after a recuperative stay in Palm Springs, she became motion-picture editor for Hearst's Universal News Service in 1926, which meant widespread syndication. She settled in Hollywood and on Jan. 5, 1930, married Harry Watson Martin, a physician. She lived happily with "Docky" (as she called him) until his death from leukemia in 1951.

Parsons's professional life paralleled that of the industry she covered. During its heyday in the 1930's and 1940's, Hollywood was her beat, and she was at the zenith of her power. Her columns were published in more than 600 papers. She had radio shows ("Hollywood Hotel" from 1934 to 1938 and "Hollywood Premieres" in 1941), one of which was even made into a movie, in which she appeared (1938).

Making fine use of a handpicked staff and a network of willing informants, Parsons wrote about the glamour, excitement, and dark side of the movie industry, focusing on marriages, divorces, and morals. The critic Nora Ephron characterized Parsons's prose as "childlike" and described the columns as "full of malapropisms and misinformation." These faults seemed to make no difference to her millions of readers, who gleaned from her columns fascinating tidbits about the stars who had been successfully urged to "tell it to Louella."

Parsons offered advice to studio executives, lectured stars about their careers, and chided the industry about its product. She was exuberant, sometimes kind, often generous; but she was also vain (her birth date moved forward at a steady rate), and often cruel (though less so than her main rival, Hedda Hopper). She demanded deference and engendered fear; given her vast following and Hollywood's cowardice, she (and her fellow gossip columnists) tyrannized the industry, abetted by a studio system that wanted to keep its contract players in line. *The Gay Illiterate*, her romanticized autobiography, appeared in 1944.

By the 1950's Parsons's career was in decline. The studio system was breaking down; her friends and sources had been fired or displaced or had died; a new generation in Hollywood paid less attention to her; and her column had fewer outlets and a diminishing number of readers. Despite her advanced age, she continued to track down the "exclusive" story, but a changed Hollywood and a changing America made her innocent gossip increasingly anachronistic. Her last book, *Tell It to Louella* (1961), described as a gossipy series of reminiscences, was largely ignored. She wrote her last column in December 1964 and then entered a nursing home. She died in Santa Monica, Calif.

[Scrapbooks containing Parsons's columns, personal publicity, and other memorabilia are in the Margaret Herrick Library of the Academy of Motion Picture Arts and Sciences, Beverly Hills, Calif. A summary autobiographical sketch can be found in Cleveland Amory, ed., *Celebrity Register* (rev. ed., 1963). An unreliable reminiscence is in the Oral History collection, Butler Library, Columbia University, New York City. Tapes of Parsons's broadcasts are at the Doheny Library, University of Southern California, Los Angeles. Parsons wrote *Jean Harlow's Life Story* (1937). An article about Parsons by Paula Fass appears in *Notable American Women* (1980). See also George Eells, *Hedda and Louella* (1972). Obituaries appear in the *Los Angeles Times* and the *New York Times*, Dec. 10, 1972.]

DANIEL J. LEAB

PATCHEN, KENNETH (Dec. 13, 1911–Jan. 8, 1972), poet, novelist, and painter, was born in Niles, Ohio, to Wayne Patchen, a steelworker, and Eva McQuade. The family of five children had its share of tragedies not uncommon then in a poor industrial town, two of Kenneth's sisters dying in childhood. In 1915 the Patchens moved to Warren, Ohio, where Kenneth attended Warren G. Harding High School. A handsome boy, he was a good student, a member of the debating, football, and track teams, and editor of the yearbook, *Echoes*. One of his earliest poems, "Christ of the Andes," appeared in the school paper in April 1928.

After graduating from high school in 1929, Patchen worked during the summer in a steel mill. In the fall he was admitted with a scholarship to an experimental college at the University of Wisconsin. After a year at the university he attended Commonwealth College in Mena, Ark., for several months. Later he would take a writing class at Columbia University. This completed his formal education.

From 1930 to 1932 he traveled in Arkansas, Georgia, and Louisiana, taking the odd jobs available during the Great Depression. He also worked briefly in the Green Mountains in Vermont. In April 1932 the *New York Times* published a sonnet of his entitled "Permanence." Christmas Eve, 1933, found him in Boston, where he met Miriam Oekimus, an antiwar activist and a student at University of Massachusetts; she would become his wife and the principal influence on his life and writing. They had no children.

Patchen worked for several months in the Hood Rubber Company plant in Watertown, Mass., a job he quit after a sinus operation. In the spring of 1934 he and Miriam left Boston for New York City. They were married on June 28 and settled in Greenwich Village, in a one-room apartment, where Patchen wrote poetry and reviewed books for the *New Republic*. In 1935, while he was writing for the Works Progress Administration's (WPA) *American Guide Series*, he received a contract from Random House for *Before the Brave*, his first book of poetry, which was published in 1936. The book, containing poems of protest full of the harsh details of life in a midwestern steel town, was very well received, and Patchen was awarded a Guggenheim Fellowship, which permitted him to move briefly out West.

In 1937, while Patchen was in Los Angeles writing for movie studios and the WPA *California Guide*, he met James Laughlin, founder and publisher of New Directions, who had been much impressed by *Before the Brave*. That autumn Patchen injured his back trying to separate the locked bumpers of two cars that had collided. This injury was the beginning of a long and painful disability, which would leave him bedridden during the last years of his life.

In 1938 the Patchens were visiting Miriam's family on their farm in Concord, Mass., when Laughlin invited them to live on his estate in Norfolk, Conn. and to work for New Directions. They accepted his invitation. The Patchens were doing the firm's packing and shipping when New Directions published the poet's *First Will and Testament* in 1939.

A year later the couple returned to Greenwich Village, where Patchen wrote *The Journal of Albion Moonlight*. He described the work,

one of his best, as a journal of the summer of 1940, "a summer when all the codes of ethics which men had lived by for centuries were subjected to the acid tests of general war and universal disillusionment." Neither Laughlin nor any of the big companies would publish this unconventional novel, with its mixture of prose and poetry and its antiwar sentiments, so Patchen had it printed privately in 1941 and sold by subscription. Frances Steloff's Gotham Book Mart in New York City bought the whole remainder. (New Directions reprinted the journal in 1961, when it enjoyed some popularity, striking a chord with readers opposed to American involvement in Vietnam.)

In 1942 Patchen pioneered "painted books," limited editions with each cover bearing an original painting by the author. That year he published the first of these, *Dark Kingdom*. In addition he wrote *The Teeth of the Lion* and a radio play, *The City Wears a Slouch Hat*, that was performed by the Columbia Radio Workshop. The 1940's were Patchen's most productive years. During the decade more than twenty volumes of his poetry and prose appeared, of which *Albion Moonlight*, *Memoirs of a Shy Pornographer* (1945) and *Sleepers Awake* (1946) received the most attention.

In 1950 Patchen's back ailment was finally diagnosed as a slipped disk. With money contributed from public readings by T. S. Eliot, W. H. Auden, Archibald MacLeish, Thornton Wilder, E. E. Cummings, Edith Sitwell, Marianne Moore, and William Carlos Williams, he had a spinal fusion operation.

Soon after the Patchens moved to San Francisco, where they lived for five years in an apartment on Green Street. He moved on the fringes of the Beat Generation, befriending Lawrence Ferlinghetti and Kenneth Rexroth. During this time *Orchards, Thrones, and Caravans* (1952), *Fables* (1953), *The Famous Boating Party* (1953), *Poems of Humor and Protest* (1954), and *Glory Never Guesses* (1955), a folio of silkscreens, poems, and drawings, appeared. Patchen received the Shelley Memorial Award in 1954.

In 1956 the Patchens moved to Palo Alto. He underwent a second spinal fusion operation, which somewhat reduced his back pain. In 1957 he began his poetry readings to jazz accompaniment. This fusion of music and verse was highly successful. Patchen had very popular poetry readings with Allyn Ferguson's Chamber

Jazz Sextet in San Francisco and with Alan Neill's quartet in Vancouver. He also made several records. In 1959, while being prepared for exploratory surgery for cancer (not one of his problems, as it turned out), Patchen fell from an operating table, seriously aggravating his back injury. The operation was abandoned, and as his wife recalled, "He was sent home to Palo Alto to a bedridden life of pain."

During the last twelve years of his life, Patchen was forced to spend more and more time in bed. His confinement made poetry–jazz readings difficult, although he was able to do some recording at home. He took once more to painting, which he could do lying down. His picture-poems were his major creations of the 1960's. The decade saw the publication of *Hallelujah Anyway*, *Doubleheader*, and Patchen's *Collected Poems*.

In 1967 the National Foundation for the Arts and Humanities granted a $10,000 award to Patchen for his "lifelong contribution to American letters." His closest friends and admirers among the literati of his time were Henry Miller, William Carlos Williams, Kenneth Rexroth, and Lawrence Ferlinghetti. Kenneth Patchen died of a heart attack at his home in Palo Alto.

[Patchen's papers, paintings, and collected works are in the Department of Special Collections, University of California at Santa Cruz. His principal biography is Larry B. Smith, *Kenneth Patchen* (1978). See also Richard Morgan, *Kenneth Patchen: An Annotated Descriptive Bibliography* (1978); Raymond Nelson, *Kenneth Patchen and American Mysticism* (1984); and James Laughlin, "Remembering Kenneth Patchen," in Kenneth Patchen, *What Shall We Do Without Us?* (1984). Obituaries are in the *New York Times*, Jan. 10, 1972; and *Publishers' Weekly*, Jan. 24, 1972.]

DAVID W. HERON

PECORA, FERDINAND (Jan. 6, 1882–Dec. 7, 1971), lawyer, congressional investigator, jurist, and politician, was born in Nicosia, Sicily, the first of seven children of Louis Pecora, a shoemaker, and Rose Messina. At age five he immigrated with his family to the United States and grew up in New York City's Chelsea neighborhood. He attended Public School 55. At age fifteen he attended St. Stephen's College (now Bard College) at Annandale on Hudson to study for the Episcopal clergy, but he left the seminary after a year and worked as a law clerk to help his family financially. He attended the City

College of New York and received his law degree from New York Law School in 1906, gaining admittance to the bar in 1911. He married Florence Louise Waterman on Nov. 30, 1910; they had one child.

In 1912, Pecora campaigned for Theodore Roosevelt for president and later served as vice-chairman of the Progressive party in New York. When the party disbanded he joined the Democratic party and supported Woodrow Wilson in 1916. He became assistant district attorney for New York County in 1918, and chief assistant district attorney from 1922 to 1930, directing the office during the protracted illness of District Attorney Jacob Banton.

In January 1933, Senator Peter Norbeck of South Dakota appointed Pecora, then in private practice in the Manhattan law firm of S. T. & P. Hartman, chief counsel to the Senate Banking and Currency Committee's investigation of the Wall Street practices that led to the stock market crash of 1929, an inquiry that had foundered under two previous counsels. Assigned to prepare the final report, Pecora determined that he needed additional information and persuaded the committee to let him continue the probe. He recruited a talented staff, largely from the New York County district attorney's office, and subpoenaed the records of the National City Bank. In February 1933, when bank chairman Charles Mitchell testified, Pecora exposed questionable practices by both the bank and its investment affiliate, the National City Company, as well as Mitchell's personal evasion of taxes. Mitchell resigned, the bank severed its relations with its investment company, and the banking committee expanded its investigation.

Democrats assumed the Senate majority in March, and the new chairman of the Banking Committee, Duncan Fletcher of Florida, retained Pecora as counsel. The elderly chairman gave free reign to the vigorous, cigar-smoking New York prosecutor, and defended him against criticism from conservative committee members. Shrewd, hardworking, and possessed of a remarkably retentive mind, Pecora absorbed masses of statistics and other data to use in questioning executives of Wall Street investment banks, brokerage houses, and stock exchanges. He called J. P. Morgan, Jr., to the stand and revealed that the wealthy banker had paid no income taxes in 1930 or 1931, and that no bank examiner had ever examined the books at Morgan's bank. During a break in the hearings an enterprising circus promoter slipped a midget onto Morgan's lap, and the widely published press photographs attracted greater public attention to Pecora's revelations.

The publicity that the Pecora investigation generated contributed to major reforms of banking and stock market practices. Provisions of the Glass-Steagall Banking Act of 1933 (mandating the separation of commercial banks from their securities companies), the Securities Act of 1933, the Securities Exchange Act of 1934, and the Public Utilities Holding Company Act of 1935 responded to issues that the investigation had raised. Since Pecora and his staff were preoccupied with conducting hearings, they played little direct role in drafting this legislation, much of which fell to the young New Dealers Benjamin V. Cohen, Thomas J. Corcoran, and James M. Landis. Pecora exerted his greatest influence over the Securities Exchange Act, which the drafters strengthened considerably to meet his objections.

When he had concluded his work as counsel in June 1934, Pecora accepted a one-year appointment to the new Securities and Exchange Commission (SEC). When President Franklin D. Roosevelt named financier Joseph P. Kennedy to the five-year term, implicitly endorsing Kennedy for chairman, Pecora expressed doubts that a stock speculator would make an effective watchdog for Wall Street. As Pecora feared, Kennedy promoted a conciliatory policy, easing regulations to win business support for the SEC. Pecora regularly voted in the minority at commission meetings. Frustrated with the SEC's tendency to compromise and bored by bureaucratic routines, he resigned after six months when Governor Herbert Lehman appointed him to a vacant seat on the New York Supreme Court.

Pecora also harbored political ambitions. In 1933 he ran unsuccessfully as the anti-Tammany "Recovery party" candidate for New York County district attorney, campaigning during weekend recesses of the Banking Committee's hearings. After his appointment to the court in 1935, he was elected that year to a full fourteen-year term on the Democratic, Republican, and Liberal tickets; Pecora was reelected in 1949. He received public notice in 1936 when he presided over a special court term dealing with New York special prosecutor Thomas E. Dewey's prosecution of racketeers. In 1950, after New York City Mayor William O'Dwyer

resigned under suspicion of corruption, the Tammany organization recruited Pecora as Democratic candidate for mayor, billing him as a fearless prosecutor, distinguished jurist, and "a man of stature above politics." Pecora's platform embraced New Deal and Fair Deal policies, endorsed civil rights, and denounced the Taft-Hartley Act. The combined Democratic and Liberal party nominations made him the front-runner. But acting mayor Vincent Impellitteri, campaigning on an independent "Experience party" ticket, tagged Pecora the candidate of the bosses, and portrayed himself as the candidate who could not be bought. Pecora lost to Impellitteri by over two hundred thousand votes. Having resigned from the supreme court in 1950 to run for mayor, Pecora returned to private law practice. He remained active in civic affairs until his death in New York.

The Wall Street investigations had been Pecora's signal achievement. At a time when many Americans questioned the validity of capitalism, the Pecora hearings produced indentifiable villains and made complex economic problems understandable in moral terms. The banking and security systems, he demonstrated, needed stricter government supervision to prevent a recurrence of the flagrant abuses of the 1920's. Government regulation of private finance became the Pecora investigation's legislative legacy.

[Pecora published a memoir of the Banking Committee investigation, *Wall Street Under Oath* (1939). See also Donald A. Ritchie, "The Pecora Wall Street Exposé," in Arthur M. Schlesinger, Jr., and Roger Bruns, eds., *Congress Investigates: A Documented History* (1975); and Donald A. Ritchie, "The Legislative Impact of the Pecora Investigation," *Capitol Studies*, Fall 1977. Pecora also gave an oral history to the Columbia Oral History Research Office. An obituary appears in the *New York Times*, Dec. 8, 1971.]

DONALD A. RITCHIE

PENFOLD, JOSEPH WELLER (Nov. 18, 1907–May 25, 1973), conservationist, was born in Marinette, Wis., the son of the Reverend Frederick Spies Penfold, an Episcopal clergyman, and Ethel Stanton Frisby. His mother, an acquaintance of forester and politician Gifford Pinchot, instilled a love and respect for nature in her son very early in his life. Little is actually known about Penfold's early years, even by members of his own family. He studied at the Hope Street High School in Providence and at the Donaldson School in Ilchester, Md., before entering Yale in 1926. While at Yale he studied history and rowed crew each year, leaving in February 1930 to travel around the world on a tramp steamer.

Before World War II, Penfold worked in farming and logging, served in the merchant marine, supervised a federal relief program in Tennessee, and was the conservation director of the National Youth Administration in Ohio. In 1936, he married Lady Halliday of Gallipolis, Ohio, who already had two small daughters. They had two children. During World War II, he served as an executive officer for the Office of Price Administration in Denver, Colo. Following the war he worked as a field representative for the United Nations Regional Relief Agency in China.

Penfold's career in conservation, which spanned two decades, began in 1949 when he became the western representative of the Izaak Walton League of America in Denver. From 1957 until his death he served as conservation director of the Izaak Walton League in Washington, D.C. His work primarily involved public relations and education, and he focused on promoting sound resource management at federal, state, and local levels. He also conceived legislation, enacted by Congress in 1958, that created the Outdoor Recreation Resources Review Commission.

He was later appointed to serve on this commission (led by Laurence S. Rockefeller), which studied, inventoried, and evaluated the nation's outdoor recreation resources and projected trends in population and habits to project future needs. Penfold felt this work was needed to address the threats of a spiraling population and a steadily mounting number of outdoor recreationists to the country's steadily diminishing natural reserves. The work of this commission led to the creation of the Bureau of Outdoor Recreation, the Land and Water Conservation Fund, the Wilderness Act, the Recreation Advisory Council, and the President's Advisory Committee on Recreation and Beauty. Presidents Eisenhower and Kennedy each cited Penfold for his efforts.

Penfold belonged to many resource societies, including the Sierra Club, the Wilderness Society, the American Fisheries Society, the Wildlife Society, and the Outdoor Writers Association. He served as an officer of the National Resources Council of America: as secretary from 1957 to 1965, vice-president in 1966, and chair from 1967 to 1969. He advised the Department of the Interior in the development of the National Fisheries Center and Aquarium and was a member of the master plan team for Yellowstone and Teton National Parks and of the Interior Department Scientific Task Force. He also chaired the Citizen's Committee for the Outdoor Recreation Resource Review Commission and the Task Force committee that drafted the "National Parks for the Future" report.

Penfold was one of the most effective lobbyists for conservation and received numerous awards that testified to his commitment and contributions. In 1962, he was given the Department of the Interior's Conservation Award and the Outdoor Writers of America Jade of Chiefs Award, and he was elected to the Izaak Walton League's Hall of Fame. In 1969, he received the National Wildlife Federation's National Distinguished Service Award. The American Forestry Association gave him its first Man-of-the-Year Distinguished Service Award in 1970. The award's citation noted that Penfold was "a constructive influence in every conservation action to improve the welfare of our lands, waters, soil, wildlife and air . . . a gentleman, modest, and always giving others the credit . . . the American Forestry Association believes that credit should be given where credit is due. . . . It believes that America is a better place to live because Joe Penfold lives here." In 1972, the Izaak Walton League bestowed on him its highest honor, the 54 Founders Award. The National Park Service awarded Penfold the honorary Ranger Award in 1973.

Penfold, a very private and quiet man, loved the outdoors and dedicated his life to the wise use of natural resources. He built canoes, fished, hiked, and skied. A posthumous tribute, in *Outdoor America* said "he exemplified the ideals of the Izaak Walton League . . . was hailed as a sportsman's sportsman, . . . his love of hunting and fishing proved a catalyst in his fight to preserve a natural beauty in this nation."

[See Yale College, *History of the Class of 1930* (1930), and *The 30 Year Book* (1960). Obituaries appear in the *New York Times*, May 27, 1973; *Outdoor America* (publication of the Izaak Walton League), June 1973; and *American Forests*, July 1973. A tribute is in *Outdoor America*, July 1973.]

ELIZABETH A. ELKINS

PENNEY, JAMES CASH (**"J. C."**) (Sept. 16, 1875–Feb. 12, 1971), businessman, was born near Hamilton, Mo., the seventh of twelve children born to Mary Frances Paxton and James Penney. Jim Penney first went into business when he was eight years old, after his father told him he would have to purchase his own clothes. Penney did odd chores and earned enough to buy a pair of shoes. He also purchased piglets, which he fattened and sold. The elder Penney, a Primitive-Baptist minister, impressed upon his son the importance of living by the Golden Rule, a principle that was to guide Penney throughout his business career.

After graduating from Hamilton High School in 1893 Penney worked on the family farm until January 1895, when his ailing father secured a position for him from a local storekeeper. John Hale of J. M. Hale and Brother hired Penney at $25 for the remainder of the year, an average of only $2.27 per month. Six weeks after Penney started at Hale's, his father died. The final words to his son were, "Jim will make it. I like the way he has started out." The remark deeply affected Penney and inspired him to succeed at the store. By the end of the year, he ranked third in sales. Hale rehired him at $200 per year and at $300 for the next. However, in 1897, Penney's physician advised him to move to a drier climate and to avoid indoor work. Penney moved to Colorado, working briefly in Denver before moving to Longmont, where he lost a butcher shop he purchased for $300 by refusing to give the local hotel chef, his biggest customer, a weekly bottle of whiskey as a condition of keeping the account.

Virtually penniless, Penney took a temporary position at a dry goods store owned by T. M. Callahan and Gus Johnson. He impressed the two and they gave him a permanent job at their Evanston, Wyo., store. On Aug. 24, 1899, Penney married Berta Hess, whom he had met in Longmont; they had two children.

In 1902, Penney opened a new store for Johnson and Callahan in Kemmerer, Wyo., using his own capital. Penney and his wife ran a successful cash-and-carry business in the windswept mining town, where his principal competitor offered credit and accepted the mine's scrip. Penney's operating costs were low, and he was committed to selling the highest-quality merchandise at the lowest possible prices. The store became an immediate success when it opened Apr. 14, 1902. Penney soon earned a reputation as a hard worker and a demanding employer. In one month alone thirty-nine employees quit. Within two years Penney opened stores in Rock Springs and Cumberland, Wyo. Three years later he bought out Johnson and Callahan's shares in the stores and became sole owner of the chain, which he renamed the Golden Rule Stores. Penney found a partner for his add-a-store chain idea in Earl Corder Sams. In 1909, Penney gave up personal management of the Kemmerer operation and moved to Salt Lake City to expand the chain into Utah.

Penney had high standards for his managers, or "associates," as he termed all employees. He desired ambitious men of high moral caliber who neither smoked nor drank. Penney's partnership agreement with his store managers enabled them to receive one-third of the store profits, a powerful motivator. Penney and his partners later entered into a unique subrogation agreement that entrusted him to offer as surety all corporately owned assets to secure additional bank credit. This arrangement earned Penney the sobriquet "the man with a thousand partners."

In 1910, Penney's wife, Berta, died suddenly. A grief-stricken Penney displaced himself from his business in the West by spending as much time as possible in New York City. In 1912, with thirty-four stores in eight Western states, Penney adopted the name J. C. Penney Company. In January 1913, the company was incorporated.

As company president from 1913 to 1917, Penney proposed centralized buying for the chain, which would be based in New York. As the operation expanded, Penney employed junior partner–managers as buyers, each in a specialized area. All followed Penney's exacting standards. At the company convention in 1917, Penney resigned the presidency to become chairman of the board, thereby relieving himself of administrative details. He also said he wanted to erase the notion from his partners' minds, as well as his own, that he was indispensable. In 1927, the company went public. As chairman, Penney undertook an intensive tour of company stores. These experiences led him to create a training and education program for employees.

In 1919, Penney married Mary Hortense Kimball; they had one child. In 1922, Penney bought the 720-acre Emmadine Farm in Dutchess County, N.Y., which undertook agricultural research and bred prize-winning Guernsey cattle. During this period Penney also bought the Hale dry goods store in his hometown of Hamilton and opened it as the five-hundredth store in the Penney chain. Penney declined offers to merge with both Montgomery Ward and Sears and Roebuck.

In 1925, Penney and New York Attorney Ralph W. Gwinn founded the Penney-Gwinn Corporation, opening Penney Farms in Florida, a partnership-farm experiment based on the same model used in his stores. The 120,000-acre site housed an agricultural institute and in 1926 became the home of the Memorial Home Community, a retirement village for religious workers that he dedicated to the memory of his parents. Penney's second wife had died in 1923, and in 1926 he married Caroline B. Autenrieth; they had two children.

In 1923, Penney established the J. C. Penney Foundation under the directorship of Daniel A. Poling, editor of *The Christian Herald*, an interdenominational Protestant publication that soon became part of the foundation. The foundation undertook a number of programs directed at serving youth.

On Oct. 23, 1929, the New York Stock Exchange listed J. C. Penney Company stock for the first time. The stock market crash occurred six days later, and the price of the company's common share plummeted from $120 to $13. Penney borrowed heavily against his holdings to sustain the foundation and his other activities. His personal debts mounted, and he was forced to sell his 360,000 shares in the company to satisfy creditors. He also curtailed his charitable activities. By 1932, he had lost most of his $40 million personal fortune.

The stress associated with the situation deeply affected Penney. A physician friend diagnosed him with an aggravated case of shingles and ordered him hospitalized. Penney entered a Michigan sanitarium, where one night he was so convinced death was imminent that he wrote farewell letters.

Renewed religious faith saw him through continuing adversities, and the Penney corporation survived and even expanded modestly. He was gradually able to rebuild his finances, in part by accepting for the first time a salaried position, as chairman of the board, from the company that bore his name.

He became deeply concerned with spiritual values and often lectured in his hoarse matter-of-fact tone on "the application of Christian principles in business." In his later years Penney, wearing his trademark bow tie, spent much of his time speaking and promoting various charitable causes. He remained active in company affairs and kept five full-time secretaries busy at the New York headquarters answering his correspondence. A reception four days before Penney's ninety-fifth birthday was attended by some five hundred friends and relatives. Penney died in New York City.

[Penney's papers are at the J. C. Penney Company Archives in Dallas, Tex. His autobiographical works include *J. C. Penney: Man with a Thousand Partners*, as told to Robert W. Bruère (1931); *My Experience with the Golden Rule* (1949); *Fifty Years with the Golden Rule*, with Janet Mabie (1950); *Lines of a Layman* (1956); and *View from the Ninth Decade* (1960). Biographies include Robert Bruce, *The Man with a Thousand Partners* (1931); and Norman Beasley, *Main Street Merchant* (1948). See also "J. C. Penney Company," in Tom Mahoney and Leonard Sloane, *The Great Merchants* (1966). Extensive obituaries appear in the *New York Times*, Feb. 13, 1971; and *Penney News*, Mar. 1971.]

DANIEL LIESTMAN

PETTENGILL, SAMUEL BARRETT (Jan. 19, 1886–Mar. 20, 1974), congressman, was born in Portland, Oreg., the son of Sue Claggett and Samuel Pettengill. After his mother's death, he moved to Vermont with his father in 1892. They settled on a farm near Grafton. He graduated from Vermont Academy (1904), Middlebury College, where he received a B.A. in 1908, and Yale Law School, earning an LL.B. in 1911. He was admitted to the Indiana bar in 1911 and opened a practice in South Bend, Ind., that same year. He married Josephine H. Campbell on June 1, 1912; they had one child.

Pettengill, a Democrat, was a member of the board of education of South Bend from 1925 to 1928. In 1930, he was elected to the House of Representatives from the Thirteenth District on a platform opposing Prohibition, and from 1933 to 1939 he represented the Third District. He first served on the Military Affairs Committee, and in 1934 was on the Interstate and Foreign Commerce Committee.

Even though he said he felt that the people were "so darn tired of the depression," they would be in favor of strong party discipline, Pettengill soon broke with the New Deal policies of President Franklin Roosevelt. His opposition to Roosevelt led to his not standing for reelection in 1938.

Pettengill published a book on regulating the petroleum industry, based on hearings by the Interstate and Foreign Commerce Committee in the summer of 1934. Its title, *Hot Oil: The Problem of Petroleum* (1936), refers to crude oil produced in excess of what was allowed in Texas by state law ("hot oil"), resulting in very low oil prices. The hearings led the committee to oppose proposed legislation (the Thomas-Disney Bill) that would have given the federal government direct control over the petroleum industry. Instead, the State Oil and Gas Compact was approved by Congress in 1935.

Pettengill made his political philosophy clear in the foreword to his book: "American industry must predicate its political and social problems upon the faith that our people want to do, and in the long run will do, what is right—if they know the facts. . . . If I were to venture a suggestion to the leaders of our enterprise, it would be to tell the truth, to act on the square, and take the public into their full confidence. . . . I do not believe that recovery from the greatest depression of our history can be built permanently on propaganda, half-truths, half-lies, wire-pulling."

On Feb. 5, 1937, Pettengill announced he would fight Roosevelt's attempts to enlarge the Supreme Court membership (the "court-packing" bill). He explained his views on the New Deal in his book *Jefferson: The Forgotten Man* (1938). This book is a plea for a return to Jeffersonian liberalism and a warning of the dangers of concentrating too much power in the federal government. Pettengill remarked that he was for the New Deal "in so far as it is constitutional, Jeffersonian and within the nation's pocketbook," but found that it moved too much toward centralized government.

After leaving Congress, Pettengill was a newspaper columnist (1939–1948), vice-president and general counsel to the Transportation Association of America (1943–1945), an attorney for Pure Oil Company (1949–1956), a commentator on the national ABC radio syndicate (1946–1948), and the author of a number of magazine articles. He wrote *Smoke-screen* (1940) "to demonstrate that we are moving toward national socialism, and that from now on, we should move away from it."

Pettengill became a Republican and in 1940 chaired the "No Third Term" [for Roosevelt] meeting at Carnegie Hall in New York City, sponsored by the National Committee to Uphold Constitutional Government. He was financial chairman of the Republican National Committee in 1942.

After the death of his wife in 1948, Pettengill married Helen M. Charles on July 16, 1949. He moved back to Grafton, Vt., where he was president of the Grafton Historical Society (1962–1972). He published a children's book about the life of early settlers in Vermont and New Hampshire, *The Yankee Pioneers: A Saga of Courage* (1971).

Pettengill received the American Freedoms Award in 1950 and 1960, the Patriotic Service Award (Sons of the American Revolution), and the Caleb B. Smith Award (Masons). He died in Springfield, Vt.

[Obituaries are in the *New York Times*, Mar. 21, 1974; and *National Review*, June 7, 1974.]

WILLIAM PRUITT

PEW, JOHN HOWARD (Jan. 27, 1882–Nov. 27, 1971), business executive and philanthropist, was born in Bradford, Pa., the second of five children of Joseph Newton Pew, a pioneer in the oil and natural gas business and a prominent conservative, and Mary Catherine Anderson.

In 1882, Pew's father, already a veteran of the gas business, formed a partnership to supply natural gas to the residents of Pittsburgh. When Pew was two years old, in 1884, the family relocated there. Pew was educated in a series of exclusive private schools, graduating from the Shady Side Academy in 1896. That fall he entered Grove City College, a nondenominational Christian school, where his father served as chairman of the board of trustees. After completing a B.S. degree in 1900, Pew was anxious to begin work at the Sun Oil Company, which his father had helped found in 1890, but acceding to his father's wishes, he began graduate work at the Massachusetts Institute of Technology. Pew ended his studies one year later, when his father offered him a position at Sun's Marcus Hook (Pennsylvania) refinery, as a development engineer. Although the job was supposed to be temporary, Pew never returned to MIT and instead remained active in Sun Oil until his death.

In 1904, the Pews moved from Pittsburgh to

Philadelphia and it was there, at a party given by his sister in 1905, that Pew met Helen Thompson. They were married on Jan. 3, 1907. Shortly after their marriage the Pews adopted three children.

Pew advanced rapidly at Sun, partly because of his father's influence but also owing to his demonstrated ability as a practical chemist, engineer, and manager. In 1903, Pew made his first significant contribution to the company as part of a research team that discovered a profitable way to make a high-quality lubricating oil from the residue of refined crude oil. In 1904, Pew's team developed Sun Oil's first trademarked product, Hydrolene, a petroleum asphalt.

In 1906, Pew became a vice-president and director of the company. Following his father's death in 1912 he was elected president, a position he held until 1947, when he resigned, though retaining his directorship. From 1963 to 1971 he served as board chairman. Pew also became chairman of the executive committee following Sun's merger with the Sunray DX Oil Company in 1970. Whatever his title, Pew was the guiding force within Sun Oil from 1912 until his death.

Sun Oil's success after 1912 was attributed in part to the cooperative division of labor the Pews achieved. J. Howard controlled the overall operation of the company; his younger brother, Joseph, specialized in transportation, especially Sun's shipbuilding and pipeline operations; and his sisters managed the family's charitable activities.

As president, Pew made the decision to chart an independent course for the company. It proved to be a remarkably successful approach. At the time Pew joined the company in 1901, Sun employed 327 people and served a regional market. At the time of Pew's death Sun was a true multinational corporation with more than 28,000 employees.

To guarantee company control over its operations and production process Pew consistently followed a path of vertical integration; that is, Sun owned and controlled most of the steps in the chain of oil production and distribution, such as the oil wells, pipelines, refineries, and gas stations. This policy sometimes led to slower growth, as when Pew's refusal to "pay tribute" to the Ethel Corporation hindered Sun's entry into the gasoline market until 1927, when Sun perfected its own method for producing high-octane gasoline. In the long run, however, this strategy benefited the industry by stimulating technological diversity and kept Sun at the forefront of innovations. This was most apparent during World War II, when Sun chemists made significant contributions to high-octane aviation gasoline, synthetic rubber, and shipbuilding.

Pew's contributions to the industry are evident in a listing of the offices he held outside the company and the awards he won: Pew served on the National Petroleum War Service Committee in World War I and the Petroleum War Industry Council in World War II. In 1949, he received the American Petroleum Institute's Gold Medal for Distinguished Achievement. The Pennsylvania Society's Gold Medal for distinguished civic and humanitarian service followed in 1958, as well as the Vermilye Medal for managerial achievements from the Franklin Institute of Philadelphia in 1950, and the Greater Philadelphia Chamber of Commerce's William Penn Award in 1970.

Pew and his brothers and sisters, in an effort to coordinate their vast charitable efforts, had established the Glenmede Trust Company (named after the family estate in Philadelphia) in 1956. By the mid-1970's the company administrated nearly $700 million in assets. A part of this was composed of the J. Howard Pew Freedom Trust, created from Pew's estate to fund conservative causes after his death.

Pew's work as a philanthropist was largely an outgrowth of his conservative religious and political beliefs. Thus, he supported causes that appealed to his interests. He served as chairman of the board of directors of Grove City College from 1931 to 1971, and as a director of *Christianity Today* from its inception in 1956 until his death. He served as president of the board of trustees of the General Assembly of the Presbyterian Church for more than three decades and was elder of his local Presbyterian church in Ardmore. In addition Pew contributed financially to a variety of causes ranging from small business associations to the John Birch Society. He was a frequent speaker on the virtues of free enterprise and religion.

In their personal lives, Pew and his wife lived austerely in lavish surroundings. Pew, one acquaintance once said of him, "not only sounds like an affidavit, he looks like one!" Accordingly, Pew ran his personal and business life on the philosophy of strict adherence to honesty, simplicity, and self-discipline. The Pews rarely entertained, although their guests included such prominent conservative figures as Herbert Hoover, J. Edgar Hoover, Billy Graham, and Robert Welch. Pew died at his home in Ardmore, Pa.

[A significant portion of Pew's personal and business papers can be found in the Sun Oil Collection located at the Hagley Museum and Library, Wilmington, Del. No complete biography of J. Howard Pew exists. For a short biographical sketch and sample of Pew's speeches see *Faith and Freedom* (1975), compiled by Mary Sennholz. On the Pew family and Sun Oil see Dan Rottenberg, "Pew Family, the Sun Gods," *The Philadelphia Magazine*, Sept. 1975, reprinted in *Business People in the News* I (1976), edited by Barbara Nykoruk. Valuable information on Pew can be found in August Giebelhaus, *Business and Government in the Oil Industry* (1980); and Arthur M. Johnson, *The Challenge of Change: The Sun Oil Company, 1945–1977* (1983). An obituary is in the *New York Times*, Nov. 28, 1971.]

THOMAS S. DICKE

PIERCE, EDWARD ALLEN (Aug. 31, 1874– Dec. 16, 1974), businessman, was born in Orrington, Maine, the son of Arthur Allen Pierce, a seaman, and Anne Frances Gerry. He was educated at the Corner District School in Orrington, and Bangor High School, from which he graduated in 1893. He attended Bowdoin College briefly.

Pierce then went to work for a Maine lumber company, and in 1901 he was transferred to New York to manage the branch sales office. Later that year, he met Arthur Housman, a stockbroker with whom he quickly developed a rapport. The financial world fascinated Pierce, and when Housman offered him a job as a clerk at $20 per week, he accepted, willingly relinquishing his $100-per-week managerial position.

After two years with A. A. Housman and Company, Pierce was assigned to handle the firm's "backstage" operations, which he thought were badly in need of improvement. He immersed himself in his work and gradually grew more proficient.

On Dec. 18, 1909, he married Luella Van Hoosear; their marriage would last sixty-five years. They had no children.

Pierce's progress at A. A. Housman led to his appointment as a partner in 1915. During this period, the European business on which Housman depended was declining as a result of

World War I. There was also a downturn among heavy domestic traders. Pierce realized that Housman must explore new ideas.

Pierce saw the possibility for expansion in the building of a network of branch offices across the country, connected by private telegraph wires that could transmit orders and information. He persuaded his reluctant senior partners to allow him to put his plan into effect. In 1919, Pierce traveled to the Midwest, where he contracted with four brokers to be linked to the new wire service. Later that year, he accomplished the same objective with the New Orleans cotton house of Fenner and Beane.

The implementation of this service was a triumph for Pierce, and he was made managing partner in 1921. Two years later, Pierce planned an extension of his wire service to the West Coast, which was deemed the sole province of the brokerage houses of E. F. Hutton and Logan and Bryan. Not surprisingly, their managers predicted only doom for Pierce's audacious enterprise. He completed his West Coast connection and built A. A. Housman into the largest wire house in the country. In 1927, the firm's name was changed to E. A. Pierce and Company.

In late 1929, business plans and routines nationwide were shattered by the stock market crash. Although it did not bring ruin to E. A. Pierce and Company, Pierce had to secure reinforcement. He met several times with two other Wall Street leaders, Charles Merrill and Edmund Lynch, to discuss the possibility of uniting their operations. They concluded that the partners of Merrill Lynch would transfer their brokerage business, along with their staff and $5 million in capital, to E. A. Pierce and Company. Pierce and his partners agreed to manage the business and to maintain a capital base of $10 million.

This arrangement gave Pierce an opportunity to expand. He acquired a part or all of more than a dozen other companies in various stages of financial health. The joke spread throughout Wall Street that "Germany's on the verge of collapse—but don't worry, E. A. Pierce will take it over."

He also hoped to broaden the field of investors, but he believed that the marketplace itself had to change. He became one of the leading proponents for reform on Wall Street at a time when the New York Stock Exchange was a closed society of members. Pierce formed a committee to reorganize the exchange and assisted the new Securities and Exchange Commission in establishing laws to govern the financial industry.

All the while, Pierce struggled to build his business, a strenuous task amid the poverty of the 1930's. However, he was convinced that the economy would improve and trade would increase. He planned to be ready for this upswing and retained a complete staff that handled normal services. Business did not pick up as soon as he expected, however, and the drain of capital became too great. By 1938, he was forced to close eleven offices.

Pierce's partnership agreement with Merrill and Lynch among others was due to expire the following year. The state of Pierce's company discouraged his partners from renewing their contract. Pierce was in the grim predicament of closing his business or losing it in an acquisition.

By contrast, Charles Merrill had bolstered his own investments, largely through his partnership with Edmund Lynch, who died in 1938. Merrill offered Pierce $2.5 million, contingent on a 56-percent interest in their partnership. Pierce was in no position to argue. Fortunately, both men shared the same aspiration: as Merrill put it, to "bring Wall Street to Main Street."

On Apr. 1, 1940, their joint enterprise was under way. By the end of that year, the partners had a total of fifty thousand customers including more than twelve thousand new accounts, but they suffered a loss of $309,000. Business quickly improved, however, and by 1943 the firm made $4.9 million.

Pierce began to focus on the need for public education in securities. At a convention of financial advertisers in the fall of 1941, he stated, "It is a deplorable but undeniable fact that the New York Stock Exchange is the least understood institution among the organizations of national importance in this country." He exhorted commercial and investment bankers and advertising agents to work with brokerage houses to foster public education. He himself ran an informational advertising campaign that helped to generate nineteen thousand new investors in less than a year.

The post–World War II years were prosperous for Pierce and his partners, and they did not again experience the effects of a depression. Pierce remained with the firm until his retirement in 1969, at age ninety-five. Although less

active in the company's affairs in his nineties, he continued to go to his office in the Manhattan headquarters five days per week. His energy had always impressed those around him. As a younger man, he worked standing up, at a raised desk. His day began at 8:00 in the morning and did not end until 9:00 or 10:00 at night.

In 1950, at the age of seventy-six, Pierce was elected president of the Arthritis Foundation. He served for twelve years, during which time the foundation's gross income grew from $124,000 to $728,000.

Pierce lived to be 100 years old. He died in New York City, survived by his wife, who was 102.

[See Donald T. Regan, *The Merrill Lynch Story* (1981); and Henry R., Hecht, ed., *A Legacy of Leadership* (1985). An obituary is in the *New York Times*, Dec. 17, 1974.]

ELIZABETH MCKAY

POST, MARJORIE MERRIWEATHER (Mar. 25, 1887–Sept. 12, 1973), businesswoman and philanthropist, was born in Springfield, Ill., the only child of Charles William Post, an inventor and salesman, and Ella Letitia Merriweather; both were descendants of colonial settlers. The Posts moved in 1891 to Battle Creek, Mich., where C. W. Post was treated for a digestive ailment at Dr. John Harvey Kellogg's sanitarium. Kellogg's dietary innovations inspired Post to develop an alternative to coffee by mixing bran, wheat berries, and molasses to create a drink called Postum. Through his clever advertisements and development of other products, namely Grape Nuts and Post Toasties, C. W. Post had grossed $10 million by 1903.

Although Marjorie Post attended the Battle Creek public schools and Mount Vernon Seminary in Washington, D.C. (1901–1904), it was her "extracurricular activities" that shaped this chubby-cheeked adolescent into her later role as society's grand dame. Towing along with her father, the young tycoon attended board meetings of the Postum Cereal Company, toured factories, went to Europe annually to observe dietary innovations, and even went disguised as a boy to a boxing match. On these trips C. W.'s maxim "Do not let money possess you. Do good with it" took hold in his pupil's mind.

A year after her parents divorced, in 1905, Marjorie Post wed Edward Bennett Close, a

New York lawyer with ties to old society. C. W. Post's suicide in 1914 upset his daughter's tranquil world as a Greenwich, Conn., matron and mother of two daughters; she inherited the Postum Cereal Company and several million dollars. Close assumed his wife's place as the company's director, but he maintained a passive role, retaining all the old hands and investing surplus funds in tax-exempt bonds. Marjorie Post Close occasionally visited the company's office in New York City, but she left Battle Creek to its own devices. With the outbreak of World War I, the young heiress funded a 2,000-bed Red Cross hospital at Savenay, France.

At the time of the Close's divorce in 1919, Post had matured from a shy, midwestern girl into a self-assured woman. Pictures record her blossoming from a comely, placid matron into a vibrant woman sporting the stylish bobbed hair of the roaring twenties.

In 1921, Post wed the Gatsbyish, self-made New York stockbroker Edward Francis Hutton. Their daughter became the actress Dina Merrill.

E. F. Hutton had the aggressiveness needed to further the fortunes of the Postum Company. When Hutton made the Postum Company a publicly traded corporation listed on the New York Stock Exchange in 1922, his wife still retained a majority interest in the company plus $10 million for the 200,000 shares she relinquished. Under Hutton's leadership, the company acquired fifteen grocery and food manufacturers including Jell-O, Baker's Chocolate, Log Cabin Syrup, Maxwell House Coffee, and Hellmann's Mayonnaise. But it was Marjorie Post Hutton's insistence for three years, over her husband's objections, that led the Postum Cereal Company to purchase a frozen food concern run by Clarence Birdseye for $22 million. In 1929, the Postum Cereal Company was renamed General Foods Corporation, and it developed into the largest food business in the United States.

During the Depression she subsidized a soup kitchen run by the Salvation Army in New York City, earning her the title "Lady Bountiful of Hell's Kitchen." She also served on the women's council of the United States Flag Association and received its Cross of Honor in 1932. Eleanor Roosevelt bestowed the medal upon her at a White House ceremony naming her "Lady of the Flag"; previous recipients of the medal had included Amelia Earhart, Calvin Coolidge, and Herbert Hoover.

Marjorie Post's charity work and unqualified support for Franklin D. Roosevelt and his New Deal policies contributed to the breakup of the Huttons' marriage in 1935. At that time, she became director of the General Foods Corporation, a position she held until 1958 when she was named director emerita.

Later in 1935, Post married for a third time, to Joseph E. Davies, a former chairman of the Federal Trade Commission, and in 1936 Roosevelt named Davies the U.S. ambassador to the Soviet Union, a post he held from 1936 to 1938. In the late 1930's, the Soviet government was selling off its prerevolutionary treasures; Marjorie Post Davies acquired her collection of Russian Imperial art consisting of icons, jeweled bibelots, gold chalices, and Fabergé, which is considered the finest outside Russia. In 1938, Davies became ambassador to Belgium, where the couple resided for a year while World War II was impending.

The couple then returned to Washington; their marriage slowly deteriorated and they finally divorced in 1955. Post was married again in 1958, to Herbert Arthur May, head of Westinghouse Corporation. When the Mays divorced in 1964, Post resumed her maiden name.

If Post had failed to achieve a lasting marriage, all other outward appearances conveyed the attainment of the American Dream. Despite her once exasperated statement that even *her* pocketbook had a bottom, Post donated $1.5 million to the National Symphony Organization, sponsored the orchestra's Music for Young America concerts, gave the needed funds for the Boy Scouts to build a center in Washington, D.C., and funded C. W. Post College in New York. To some, she was considered America's closest approximation to royalty, and the splendor of her 316-foot yacht, the *Sea Cloud*, once prompted Norway's Queen Maud to bemusedly remark, "Why, you live like a queen, don't you?"

Beginning with her marriage to E. F. Hutton, Post embarked on a grand building spree resulting in a seventeen-acre, fifty-room Moorish estate in Palm Beach named Mar-A-Lago; a summer retreat in upper New York State, Topridge, which also housed her substantial collection of Native American artifacts; and her Georgian residence, Hillwood, in Washington. These palatial manors served as backdrops to Post's lavish parties, which at one time included a performance by the Ringling Brothers Circus.

At the age of seventy, Marjorie Post was renowned for her beauty, organization, and tremendous energy. *Life* magazine profiled "Lady Bountiful" at seventy-eight and wrote that she resembled "a Dresden doll but gives the strong impression of being woven of steel wire. Her step is firm, her stamina is discouraging. 'She comes into a room and everyone else looks exhausted,' a guest once remarked."

Following a series of ministrokes, Post died at her Hillwood estate. From humble midwestern origins Post had risen to become America's vision of royalty through her business acumen and largesse. The director of the National Symphony Orchestra told a reporter in the late 1960's, "Whenever Marjorie touches anything, you know it's been touched by royalty."

[Post's personal papers and family memorabilia are at the University of Michigan and at Hillwood Museum in Washington, D.C. Post recalled her childhood in *The Reminiscences of Marjorie Merriweather Post* (1964) in the Oral History Collection at Columbia University. Although two biographies document her life—William Wright, *Heiress: The Rich Life of Marjorie Merriweather Post* (1978) and Nettie Leitch Major, "Marjorie Merriweather Post," in *C. W. Post: The Hour and the Man* (1963)—neither provides a critical assessment of her contribution to the General Foods Corporation or an insightful portrait of her character. A number of popular articles exist, including Arthur Bartlett, "Lady Bountiful," *New Yorker*, Feb. 4, 11, 18, 1939; and "A World Unique and Magnificent," *Time*, Feb. 3, 1967. An obituary is in the *New York Times*, Sept. 13, 1973.]

ANN LESLIE TUTTLE

POUND, EZRA LOOMIS (Oct. 30, 1885–Oct. 30, 1972), poet and critic, was born in Hailey, Idaho, a mining town full of rough prospectors with dynamite in their boots, which accommodated forty-seven taverns and one minister. Hailey was not the sort of place in which Pound's mother, Isabel Weston, could feel comfortable. A descendant of the Weston and the Wadsworth families, Weston had been raised in Washington, D.C., and was accustomed to more genteel circumstances.

Pound's father, Homer, a mild, unassuming, cheerful man, was the son of Thaddeus Coleman Pound, a dynamic and enterprising figure who built railroads, had been acting governor of Wisconsin, and had been elected to Congress three times. An outstanding Republican orator,

Thaddeus's firebrand populist economics and his attacks on the banking system would greatly influence Ezra Pound. Thaddeus had arranged for Homer to administer the government land office in Hailey so that he could look after Thaddeus's mining interests there. After four years in Hailey, in 1889 Homer secured a position as an assistant assayer at the United States Mint in Philadelphia, where he worked for thirty-nine years.

The Pound family moved to Wyncote, an exclusive suburb of Philadelphia, in 1891. As an only child, young Ezra was pampered by his mother, who arranged his hair in curls. As a boy he was bookish and called "the professor" by his friends. He had written his first poem, about William Jennings Bryan, at the age of eleven, and a year later, in 1898, a wealthy aunt took him and his parents on a three-month tour of London, Paris, and Venice that left an indelible impression on him. He also traveled to Europe with his father in 1901.

Pound's early education was at the nearby Cheltenham Military Academy and at Cheltenham High School. "A lanky whey-faced youth" as Pound remembered himself in his autobiographical account *Indiscretions* (1923), he was admitted in 1901 to the University of Pennsylvania at the age of fifteen on the strength of his Latin. Both at the University of Pennsylvania—where he became friends with poets William Carlos Williams and Hilda Doolittle (whom Pound later renamed H. D.)—and at Hamilton College in upstate New York where he transferred in his junior year, young Pound was an outsider, interested in the esoterics of ancient European languages and in writing poetry. He graduated from Hamilton in June 1905.

Upon his return to the University of Pennsylvania to begin graduate work, Pound presented a group of love poems bound in vellum and entitled "Hilda's Book" to Hilda Doolittle. His courtship of H. D. was stymied by her father, a professor of astronomy at the university, who declared with some justification that Pound was "only a nomad" and unsuitable as a prospective son-in-law. Pound received his M.A. degree in June 1906. His graduate studies were frustrated because Pound realized he could never fit into academic decorum. He was awarded a fellowship to travel in Europe in the summer of 1906, but he had become contentiously outspoken and irreverent in class, and he had the habit of distributing verse caricaturing his professors. After that first summer, the fellowship was not renewed.

Realizing that he would never fit into the pattern of mannered correctness required of those who sought the Ph.D., Pound found a job teaching French, Spanish, and Italian at Wabash College in Crawfordsville, Ind., in the fall of 1907. Pound was altogether too flamboyant for the small, provincial town. He would say outrageous things in class just to make sure that his students were listening, and instead of conducting an introductory class in Italian made his students study Dante. His career at Wabash College was aborted when the spinster sisters who ran his boardinghouse discovered that he had spent the night in his rooms with an itinerant actress. Summarily dismissed, but paid for a full year, Pound sailed in March 1908 to Europe on a cattle boat.

In Venice—where he could get quality printing at low prices—he published a collection of his own poems, which he sent to William Butler Yeats and other important poets in England and America, and which he reviewed himself under a pseudonym in the London *Evening Standard*. Called *A Lume Spento*, the title refers to the son of one of the Roman Catholic popes who had been buried with extinguished candles because of his heretical views. The significance of the title was its connection to heresy, the tradition with which Pound would ally himself.

Pound went to London in the summer of 1908 and, to support himself, devised a course on Provençal literature which he taught at the Regent Street Polytechnic, a vocational college that had expanded to offer courses for the working class. Although Pound found he had little in common with his students, his lectures would become *The Spirit of Romance* (published in 1910), and one of his auditors, Olivia Shakespear, would introduce him to Yeats and to her daughter, Dorothy Shakespear, whom he married on Apr. 20, 1914.

An older poet who had already published several volumes, Yeats had an informal weekly gathering for poets at his apartment, which Pound began to attend regularly. Another influential writer who became a friend was Ford Madox Ford, poet, novelist, and editor of *The English Review*, where several of Pound's early poems appeared. An English publisher had brought out a collection of Pound's poems entitled *Personae* in 1909, and although Ford

complained that Pound's verse in general suffered from a stilted, affected, and overliterary quality, the volume was very well received in London and the United States. At the same time Pound had joined a group known as the Poet's Club, which, under the leadership of a burly, florid Englishman named T. E. Hulme, was concerned with the ways that modern poetry could depart from Romantic and Victorian diffuseness, and replace the ornateness and flourishes of nineteenth century poetry with a bare hardness.

Pound's response to Hulme's notions was Imagism, a compact poetry based on finite experiences that could be tactily and sensuously described in as few words as possible. Pound's key idea was that the image could no longer be used ornamentally as Tennyson had used it, but had to be organic, vital, and central to the speech of ordinary people. In 1909 and 1911, when Pound was publishing his collections *Exultations* and *Canzoni*, such notions were controversial.

Everything about Pound was unacceptable to the decorum of the British. High strung, impatient, mercurial, and exuberant, Pound contemptuously dismissed much of the poetry he read as crippled by "painted adjectives" and "emotional slither." Yeats was impressed by the tautness of the new poetry Pound was practicing, and invited him to spend parts of three winters from 1913 to 1915 at Stone Cottage, Yeats's country home, to explain his new approach.

Practically as soon as he had invented Imagism, Pound realized that it was useful only for small poems, that its restriction of discourse could be as limiting as the diffuseness and verbosity it replaced, and that he needed a more embracing approach to poetry that could accommodate his ideas about history and culture. By 1914, he was describing a new poetic called Vorticism, in which the principles of Imagism would be used as a means rather than as an end, a kind of poem "through which, and into which, ideas are constantly rushing." Essentially, he had created a theory for the paratactic method of *The Cantos*, his epic work of considerable density and complication, which ranges through human history in an attempt to discern the roots of beauty and order in culture.

Pound's years in England were marked by his notable influence on the literary world. He was the London editor of *Poetry* from 1912, literary editor of the *Egoist* (1914–1919), and foreign editor of the *Little Review* (1917–1919). He was also responsible for bringing a host of writers, including T. S. Eliot and James Joyce, into print.

He also supported himself as a music and art critic for a magazine called *The New Age*, and began to associate with novelist and painter Wyndham Lewis and the members of his Rebel Art Centre, where at an art opening Pound appeared on a balcony with a banner proclaiming the end of the Christian era. The act was characteristically provocative, but also the desperate register of the impact of World War I, a protracted struggle in which many of Pound's friends were wounded or killed. He tried to present the dislocating effect of the war in a long sequence of poems called *Hugh Selwyn Mauberley* (1920), an attempt to both eulogize and satirize simultaneously the search for beauty of the art-for-art's-sake movement of the 1890's. The technique of the poem, highly self-referential and allusive, anticipated the style of *The Cantos*, which he had already begun. It was during this time that Pound began to earn his reputation as one of the most inventive and iconoclastic poets of the modernist school, an international literary movement that he did much to foster and shape during this interwar period.

At the end of 1920, Pound and his wife left England for Paris, where they lived until the fall of 1924, and where Pound was the French correspondent of the American literary magazine the *Dial*. Pound's friends were the expatriate literati, including Ernest Hemingway and Gertrude Stein. He also befriended the Dadaists and Surrealists, a group of highly experimental poets and painters whose disaffiliation with society was the result of the loss of faith many artists felt after the debacle of the war. Pound wrote the music to an opera, continued working on *The Cantos*, helped reshape his friend T. S. Eliot's *The Wasteland*, and also met Olga Rudge, an American violinist who became his mistress.

Near the end of 1924, Pound and his wife resettled in Rapallo, a town on the Mediterranean coast of Italy in which Yeats had been wintering. When Olga Rudge followed him and gave birth to a daughter in 1925, Dorothy Pound reciprocated with a son in 1926. During the next fifteen years Pound devoted himself to the labors of *The Cantos* and the study of Chinese and Confucius. The poems were published as they were completed, and the texture of *The Cantos* became increasingly dense and complex. The obscurity and allusiveness of the poems diminished his audience and caused a consequent loss of reputation. The publishing company New Directions compiled the most authoritative and complete collection.

Like many others in Europe and America, Pound admired Benito Mussolini, the fascist dictator of Italy who had expediently sacrificed individual freedoms for the sake of prosperity. Pound had become increasingly suspicious of the effect on all culture of the banking establishment and was interested in economic reform. When World War II began, Pound made regular broadcasts on Rome Radio, ostensibly to American troops in the field, rabidly attacking American politicians and policies. While no American soldiers could be found at his subsequent trial for treason who admitted to hearing the broadcasts, the probability is that they could not have made much sense out of Pound's vehement anti-Semitic ranting. The broadcasts, however, were taped during the war by the Office of Strategic Services.

After the American invasion of Italy, in the spring of 1945, Pound was incarcerated in the Disciplinary Training Center in Pisa with only his copy of Confucius and a Chinese dictionary in his pocket. He was placed in an exposed cell, a solitary prisoner under a perpetual searchlight. Even the guard who brought him his food was not permitted to speak to him. After three weeks of confinement, he was stricken with the violent and hysterical terrors of a nervous breakdown. Transferred to the medical compound and in the hands of the camp psychiatrists, Pound had access to a typewriter and began work on the *Pisan Cantos* (1948), creating some of his most poignant and personal verse.

Later, in St. Elizabeth's Hospital in Anacostia, a suburb of Washington, D.C., where he had been taken in November 1945, Pound was regularly interviewed by psychiatrists whom he saw as instruments in a Jewish conspiracy. Despite his support of the Italian fascists, he became a sort of icon of resistance for American writers, who visited him regularly during the twelve years of his incarceration. Dorothy Pound visited daily, bringing him the books he needed to continue work on *The Cantos*. It was during this time, in 1948, that Pound received the Bollinger Prize in Poetry; his receipt of the prize was very controversial, due to his anti-Semitism. Pound's release from the hospital was finally won in 1958, but only after sustained pressure from friends like Robert Frost, T. S. Eliot, and Ernest Hemingway. Upon his release, at the age of seventy-two, his publisher James Laughlin brought him to a recording studio where he read his poems.

In 1958, he returned to Italy, where his health began to fail. When he was interviewed in 1959 by poet Donald Hall for *The Paris Review*, he spoke mostly in fragments. By 1961, although he hadn't divorced his wife Dorothy, he was living with Olga Rudge, who had a small house next to Arturo Toscanini's in Venice. For ten years he entered what he called "the silence," a decade during which he rarely spoke to anyone. The silence was characteristically theatrical, either a sign of atonement for his own excesses or a convenient device to avoid questions about his wartime activities.

A few days before his death on his eighty-seventh birthday, working on canto 70, he wrote that he had tried as a poet "to write Paradise." Implicit in the poem, as in the last years of his life, was the idea of failure, and the final poem of *The Cantos* itself was a plea for forgiveness from the Gods and from those whom he had loved.

[The main collection of Pound's papers and letters is in the Beinecke Library at Yale. Material on the early years is found in the Van Pelt Library at the University of Pennsylvania. Another important collection is in the Humanities Research Center at the University of Texas at Austin. Pound's correspondence during the St. Elizabeth period is at the Lilly Library in Bloomington, Ind. Both the *Selected Poems* and *The Cantos* are published by New Directions. His best criticism is probably *ABC of Reading* (1960), but his *Selected Prose 1909–1965* (1975) and T. S. Eliot's edition of Pound's *Literary Essays* (1968) are also important. Further details can be found in John Tytell, *Ezra Pound: The Solitary Volcano* (1987). An obituary is in the *New York Times*, Nov. 2, 1972.]

JOHN TYTELL

POWELL, ADAM CLAYTON, JR. (Nov. 29, 1908–Apr. 4, 1972), congressman and minister, was born in New Haven, Conn., the son of the Reverend Adam Clayton Powell and Mattie Fletcher Shaffer. The family moved to New York City in 1909 when the elder Powell became the pastor of Abyssinian Baptist Church,

Adam, Jr., grew up in a very comfortable middle-class environment, the pampered child of a successful preacher and a doting parish. The Powells were very light-complexioned and often were assumed to be white by those unaware that they were African Americans. After graduating from high school, Powell spent one year at City College of New York, where his academic record reflected the fact that he spent more time on his social life than on his studies. Fearing he would waste his life, his parents enrolled him in Colgate University in 1926. Only the university's president knew that the new student was an African American. When this fact became more widely known, Powell was forced to move out of the white-only dormitory and seek refuge with a handful of other black students, who at first were angry with him for not having acknowledged his racial identity.

After graduation in 1930, Powell studied for the ministry, intending eventually to take the helm of Abyssinian Baptist Church; he did so in 1937, upon his father's retirement. He spent an unhappy year at Union Theological Seminary, then transferred to Teachers College of Columbia University, where he earned a master's degree in 1932. During the 1930's, he led demonstrations against racial employment discrimination in stores in Harlem, in the city bus company, and utility companies. He also established his reputation as a fiery young leader by writing a weekly column in a Harlem newspaper and by preaching at Abyssinian and around the country. Meanwhile, he maintained a lavish social life. In 1933, against his father's wishes, he married a divorced nightclub singer and dancer, Isabel Washington, and adopted her son; they were divorced in 1945.

Powell's activism led him into electoral politics, initially as New York's first black city councilman in 1941, and then, in 1944, as the first black elected to Congress from the Northeast. (A congressional district had been redrawn in 1943 to guarantee the election of a black candidate from Harlem.) In a field of aspiring black politicians, Powell ultimately received the endorsement of the Democrats, the Republicans, American Labor party, and the local Communist party. In 1942, he established his own newspaper, *The People's Voice*, which he published until 1946.

Powell married a prominent jazz pianist, Hazel Scott, in August 1945. When he went to Washington, he immediately began to champion civil rights causes, personally defying segregation laws in the city and on Capitol Hill, and instructing his black staff members to do the same. With the encouragement of the National Association for the Advancement of Colored People (NAACP), for several years he attached a provision, known as the "Powell Amendment," to proposed bills for aid to education, health, and housing that called for no federal funds to be allocated to any agency or district that practiced racial segregation or discrimination. Liberals, who wanted progressive federal legislation for schools, hospitals, and housing but knew that Powell's amendment would cost the proposals critical southern and conservative congressional votes, tried desperately to get him to withdraw the amendment. He staunchly refused.

Powell was gaining a reputation as a Democratic maverick. He often criticized President Truman and northern liberals for not being as supportive of civil rights as he felt they should be. His speeches on the floor of the House of Representatives and around the country enhanced his stature as a strong advocate of civil rights. His detractors, on the other hand, saw him increasingly as flamboyant, opportunistic, and unwilling to compromise.

In 1953, Powell became embroiled in protracted legal controversies over his income taxes. Several of his aides were indicted and convicted of income tax evasion, and there were rumors that Powell received salary kickbacks from his staff. Such charges and investigations continued until he was finally indicted for income tax evasion in 1958.

Prior to 1960, Powell served on and gained seniority as a member of the House Committee on Education and Labor. In 1956, however, he again demonstrated his unpredictable style when he endorsed Republican president Dwight D. Eisenhower for reelection. This action infuriated the regular Democratic party organization (Tammany Hall) in New York City, which challenged his reelection in 1958. Powell's popularity in Harlem was so great, however, that he defeated his primary election opponent by a substantial margin. But there was still sentiment in Congress to punish him for his 1956 defection. In 1960, when the chairman of his committee retired, Powell was next in line to head the committee.

After President John F. Kennedy's election, Powell became chairman of the Committee on Education and Labor, the first black congressman to head such an important committee. At least 40 percent of domestic legislation—from Kennedy's New Frontier and, later, President Lyndon B. Johnson's Great Society proposals—passed through his committee.

Powell was now at the peak of his political career. First, however, he had to survive the tax evasion trial. Through the efforts of his attorney, Edward Bennett Williams, he managed to escape conviction with a hung jury. The Department of Justice decided not to retry the case.

From 1961 to 1966, Powell led his committee in a manner that won praise from Presidents Kennedy and Johnson, as well as from its members. He delegated power to subcommittee chairpersons, and he became very involved in working out political compromises. His committee worked on and shepherded through Congress important bills relating to aid to education, Medicare/Medicaid, and the War on Poverty. In addition, the "Powell Amendment" was finally enacted into law as Title VI of the landmark Civil Rights Act of 1964.

Throughout this period of intense and effective committee leadership, Powell continued to attract negative publicity that eventually brought his downfall.

In 1960, Powell publicly accused Esther James, a woman in his congressional district, of being a "bag woman," one who carried payoff money from illegal gamblers to the police. He spoke on television and entered names of specific police officers and addresses of illegal gambling sites into the *Congressional Record*. The woman sued him for libel, and Powell, characteristically, ignored the many court summonses. The plaintiff won a $211,000 judgment against him; Powell fought the case in the New York courts for years, refusing to answer court-issued warrants. At one point, he could appear in New York City only on Sundays, in order to avoid being subject to arrest for contempt of court. (Civil warrants could not be served on Sunday. Powell came to the city, preached at Abyssinian, and left at the end of the day.)

In addition, Powell had divorced his second wife—they had one son, Adam III—and married Yvette Diago, drawing more attention to his handling of his committee's funds. He had his wife on the staff payroll although she performed no work in Washington, D.C., or in New York. She spent most of the time in Puerto Rico, caring for their newborn son, Adam IV.

He cashed her checks and deposited the funds in his own congressional bank account. He also used committee travel funds for highly publicized trips with female companions to Europe and the Bahamas. Such trips had little relationship to legitimate committee business, although Powell insisted otherwise. He defied his critics, insisting that he did no more and no less than his colleagues were doing.

Finally, Powell's committee severely limited his powers as chairman in September 1966. Although he was reelected in November, the House of Representatives voted in January 1967 not to seat him because of his many transgressions, including the ongoing libel case in New York and the evidence on mismanagement of committee funds. Powell sued in federal court on the grounds that his exclusion violated the Constitution. A special election was held, and Powell won handily, but he did not present his certificate of election in order to be seated. He chose instead to pursue his case in the courts. Meanwhile, the residents of Harlem's congressional district were without a seated, voting representative from January 1967 to January 1969.

During that time, Powell worked out a settlement in the libel case and went on the college lecture circuit. His speeches combined vehement attacks on Congress for its treatment of him with harsh criticism of American involvement in Vietnam. The FBI monitored his many moves and speeches, and its reports seriously questioned whether some of his speeches bordered on treason and incitement to riot.

As Powell's case made its way to the Supreme Court, two rumors began to circulate in Harlem that ultimately proved true. One was that Powell had cancer; the other, that his Harlem political base was weakening and he was becoming vulnerable to challenge on his home territory. For a time, Powell denied the first (although his physical appearance clearly suggested otherwise) and ignored the second.

In June 1969, the U.S. Supreme Court ruled that in fact his exclusion from Congress was unconstitutional. There were only three requirements for service in Congress: age, citizenship, and residence. Powell, being duly elected, satisfied all three. This was the first time the Court had made such a ruling. (Once a member is seated, of course, Congress may expel him or her for various reasons.) Powell not only had been excluded, he had been denied his twenty-two years of seniority and his chairman-

ship, and his pay had been reduced to pay off the misused funds. The Supreme Court dealt only with the exclusion. Powell returned to Congress as a freshman with virtually no power.

In 1970, several local politicians decided to challenge Powell in the Democratic primary. As always, he believed he was invulnerable, and did little campaigning. Powell's congressional district had been redrawn in a way that reduced his Harlem base and added a significant number of other Manhattan West Side voters who were not sympathetic to him. In a five-candidate race, Powell came in second, 205 votes behind the ultimate winner, Charles B. Rangel. Powell alleged fraud and threatened to challenge the election in court. But it was clear that neither his health nor his waning political fervor would permit him to go on.

Powell resigned the pastorate of Abyssinian Baptist Church in 1971 and retired with his woman companion to the island of Bimini. (He had been separated from Yvette since 1966.) He spent his time writing a book about his life. He died in Miami.

Noting that he died four years to the day after the assassination of Dr. Martin Luther King, Jr., the *New York Times* (Apr. 5, 1972), comparing the two leaders, concluded that Powell, unlike King, "leaves no lasting heritage." The thousands who lined the Harlem streets and attended his funeral at Abyssianian attested by their presence that they disagreed.

[Powell left no readily available collection of papers. The best archival sources are in the presidential libraries of Truman, Eisenhower, Kennedy, and Johnson, and the NAACP Papers in the Library of Congress. The Fiorello La Guardia Papers in the Municipal archives of New York City are helpful on the 1930's and 1940's. There are good oral histories in the Columbia University Oral History Department. There also are approximately 6,644 pages of FBI files available through the Freedom of Information Act. Biographies include Powell's own *Adam by Adam* (1971); and Charles V. Hamilton, *Adam Clayton Powell, Jr.* (1991).

See also another work by Powell, *Marching Blacks* (1946); David Hopgood, *The Purge That Failed* (1959); Kent M. Weeks, *Adam Clayton Powell and the Supreme Court* (1971); and Andy Jacobs, *The Powell Affair* (1973). An obituary is in the *New York Times*, Apr. 5, 1972.]

CHARLES V. HAMILTON

PRATT, JOHN LEE (Oct. 22, 1879–Dec. 20, 1975), business executive and philanthropist, was one of five children of Alexander Pratt and Agnes Jones. The Pratt family had lived in the area of Aspen Grove, Va., since colonial times. Pratt's ancestors fought in the American Revolution and in the War of 1812; Pratt's father had fought for the Confederacy, returning to his farm after Robert E. Lee's surrender at Appomattox. As a child, John Lee Pratt worked on his father's farm alongside his father and brothers. He attended local schools, and in 1892 was apprenticed to the M. S. Chancellor Farm Implement Store, where he learned to assemble farm machinery. Before entering Randolph-Macon College, Pratt attended Locust Dale Academy. After one year at Randolph-Macon, Pratt transferred to the University of Virginia, from which he earned a degree in civil engineering in 1905.

After graduation, Pratt was hired as an assistant engineer by the E. I. du Pont de Nemours Chemical Company. In light of the growing threat of war in Europe, Pratt was sent by Du Pont to Chile to supervise the company's nitrate interests there; nitrate is important in the manufacture of explosives. He returned to the United States in 1914 to become the resident engineer at Du Pont's guncotton plant. At a time when munitions manufacture for Allied forces generated the need for additional Du Pont factories, Pratt was promoted to chief executive of Du Pont's Development and Civil Engineering Division. In 1916, he moved to a subsidiary of Du Pont, the American Nitrogen Company, where he supervised the development of the technology to extract nitrogen from air. He was also responsible for the construction of factories to carry out this process.

In 1917, Du Pont, which had invested in the fledgling General Motors Company (GM), sent Pratt to consult at GM. Impressed by Pratt's succinct and incisive response to a company housing problem, GM president W. C. Durant persuaded Pratt to join GM as his assistant in 1919.

One of Pratt's first assignments was to dismantle the Frigidaire Company. After interviewing "ice-less box" owners who complained about their appliances' flaws but who refused to accept a refund or to give back their refrigerators, Pratt convinced GM to pursue refrigeration technology and to develop a safe, efficient coolant; the result was the invention of Freon. Subsequently, Pratt was responsible for expanding GM's diesel motor division when he per-

suaded the Seaboard Coast Line to replace locomotive coal engines with diesel engines. By 1922, Pratt had been promoted to vice-president at General Motors, supervising all its nonautomotive divisions.

During his career at GM Pratt directed GM's development department; supervised the planning and construction of factory-worker housing; and chaired the GM inventory committee that focused production and created a base for corporate financial stability during the Great Depression. As chief-of-staff to several GM presidents, Pratt served as an executive for the entire corporation, rather than as a CEO of any single division. Pratt was elected a director of GM in 1923 and remained active on board committees through 1952. Pratt resigned from his position as executive vice-president of General Motors in 1937 and from GM's board of directors in 1968. GM president Alfred P. Sloan called Pratt "the best businessman I have ever known."

In 1939, Pratt was appointed by President Franklin D. Roosevelt to the War Resource Board chaired by a former GM colleague, Edward Settinius. The War Resource Board addressed the need for America's industrial mobilization when World War II broke out in Europe. After the United States entered the war, Pratt served as a senior consultant to the Office of Lend-Lease Administration. In 1942, Pratt, as a member of the War Production board, brought executives from major American companies to Washington to work with the military to ensure the timely production of war-related goods. In 1944, Pratt was appointed to the American Mission in London under Secretary of State Edward Settinius.

John Lee Pratt married Louise Thomas of Philadelphia in 1918. The couple had no children. Mrs. Pratt, who died in 1947, shared many of her husband's interests and together they established the John Lee and Louise Thomas Pratt Foundation. In 1931, Pratt purchased Chatham Manor, an eighteenth-century estate near Fredericksburg, Va. Pratt accumulated vast wealth during his career. He was listed by *Fortune* magazine as one of the twenty richest men in America in the mid-1950's, with holdings estimated to be in excess of $100 million.

Because of his long-standing interests in agriculture, medicine, education, and public welfare, Pratt made a number of substantial gifts to universities, hospitals, museums, parks, and libraries during his lifetime and in the disbursement of his estate. Pratt required that the capital from his endowments be "converted into knowledge that is useful and beneficial to mankind without undue delay." His gifts were intended to underwrite salaries, scholarships, and research, not to be used for investment or converted into bricks and mortar. Pratt limited the length of time institutions had to spend the capital from his bequests. He felt it was inappropriate for institutions to perpetuate endowments long after the person who made the donation had died. When he contributed to state-supported institutions, he added the condition that the bequest could not be used in lieu of tax-levy funds.

In 1948, Pratt contributed to the founding of McCullum-Pratt Institute at Johns Hopkins University in Baltimore, an interdepartmental facility established to study trace elements in plants and animals. He also contributed to the founding of the Bowman School of Geography at Hopkins. In all, Pratt gave Johns Hopkins more than $9 million, much of it anonymously. He also gave generously to the University of Virginia, Washington and Lee University, and Virginia Polytechnic Institute. In all ten universities shared $60 million in Pratt's bequests for programs in physics, biomedical research, engineering, and agriculture. In 1961, Pratt donated seventy-five acres of his estate near the Rappahannock River and supporting capital to build the St. Clair Brooks Park.

A brilliant businessman, committed to learning, and a philanthropist who avoided publicity and never courted fame or honor for his good works, Pratt died at his home, Chatham Manor, near the place of his birth.

[Pratt's papers dealing with his career at General Motors are housed at the General Motors Institute in Flint, Mich. All his other papers are housed at the University of Virginia.

There is an entry on Pratt, written by Richard Scharchburg, in the *Encyclopedia of American Business History and Biography: The Automobile Industry, 1920–1980* (1989).

Obituaries appear in the *Washington Post* and the *New York Times*, both Dec. 22, 1975.]

WENDY HALL MALONEY

PREFONTAINE, STEVE ROLAND ("PRE") (Jan. 25, 1951–May 30, 1975), track athlete, was born in Coos Bay, Oreg., the son of

Raymond Prefontaine, a carpenter, and Elfriede Sehnholz, a seamstress. He had two sisters, one of whom played professional racquetball. Prefontaine grew up speaking German at home, a liability that hampered him in grade school and helped edge him toward sports. Because of his slight frame, Prefontaine was not suited for playing either football or basketball. However, at Marshfield High School (1966–1969) he discovered that he had a natural talent for running and that he performed better as the distances increased. As a sophomore, he joined the track team. As a junior he began to win titles: in 1968 he was state high school champion in both the cross-country and the two-mile meets. He repeated these victories in his senior year, setting a national record with his two-mile run of 8:41.5, which was seven seconds under the old mark.

Prefontaine entered the University of Oregon in 1969 and earned his B.S. in 1973. He trained under Bill Bowerman in a demanding and creative system from which he benefited immediately, finishing third as a freshman in the National Collegiate Athletic Association (NCAA) cross-country championships. He never lost again while a student at the university. From 1970 to 1973 he was the Pacific Eight Conference and NCAA cross-country champion, and in 1970 and 1973 he led his Oregon teammates to the team championship as well. In 1972 he set U.S. and NCAA records for 5,000 meters, while in 1973 he set U.S. and NCAA records for six miles.

Although primarily an outdoor athlete, Prefontaine also was successful in indoor competitions, specializing in two-miles races. In 1973 he set the U.S. indoor record of 8:24.8, which he broke a year later at 8:20.4. While at the University of Oregon, he switched back to outdoor collegiate races and was Pacific Eight Conference three-mile champion all four years and the mile champion in 1971. His best day, and possibly the best double victory in the sport, took place on Apr. 14, 1973, when he won the mile in a four-way meet and went on to triumph in a three-mile race. He ran the mile in under four minutes on nine different occasions but was never really a successful middle-distance runner, as he lacked the "kick" required at the wire to beat the better-known milers of the period. His best time for the mile was 3:54.6

In 1974 *Track and Field News* named Prefontaine the most popular track athlete in the world. The International Track Association, however, failed to tempt him with its offer of $200,000 to turn professional; he wished, instead, to prepare for the Montreal Olympic Games. He enjoyed playing to the crowd; the larger the attendance and the noiser the fans, the more it excited him. His running was characterized by an aggressive style. Frequently, he ran away from the rest of the field. This style reflected Prefontaine's competitive personality: intensity and fierceness, both on and off the track, were his chief characteristics. Nonetheless, he had an introspective side. In the university town of Eugene, Oreg., he worked with disadvantaged youths, advocating the expansion of social services for them and the distribution of birth control devices. He also developed sports programs for inmates in the Oregon prison system.

Because of his intensity, however, Prefontaine could be his own worst enemy. He was impatient with the track-and-field establishment, which he regarded as elitist and unresponsive to the needs of individual athletes. He criticized the lack of financial support for out-of-school amateur athletes, denied the training facilities of the major universities, and he resisted efforts by the American Athletic Union (AAU) to force him to compete against inferior runners from the Soviet bloc. He objected to the AAU's policy of staging U.S.-Soviet meets, largely because he felt that the best runners and the most worthwhile competitors were to found in Western Europe and Scandinavia.

Prefontaine's death in an automobile accident in Eugene, Oreg., cut short a brilliant career. On the day of his death, he won a 5,000-meter race and then attended a party with six Finnish athletes he had brought to the United States to compete. About 12:30 A.M. he drove a friend home, then went on alone. His convertible hit an embankment and flipped over. Prefontaine was found pinned beneath it. His blood alcohol level indicated intoxication.

Before his death he had set fourteen U.S. records, including eight outdoor marks that still stood unchallenged: 2,000 meters (5:01.4); 3,000 meters (7:42.6); two miles (8:18.4); three miles (12:51.4); 5,000 meters (13.22.2); six miles (26:51.4); and 10,000 meters (27:43.6). He established himself as the premier distance runner of his generation, and perhaps for all time, by setting the record in his lifetime for

every distance above 2,000 meters. No one since has set records in all of these categories.

Prefontaine, who never married, was honored in 1980 when the city of Coos Bay erected a memorial statue as a tribute to his career.

[For further information, see Pat Putnam, "The Freshman and the Great Guru," *Sports Illustrated*, June 15, 1970; Kenny Moore, "A Final Drive to the Finish," *Sports Illustrated*, June 9, 1975; and Marty Liquori, Kenny Moore, Frank Shorter, and Jere Van Dyk, "Reminiscences," *New York Times Biographical Service* (1975). Author's interviews with Dean Risa Palm, College of Arts and Sciences, and Diane Sarnowski, University of Oregon (June 29, 1992) supplement these sources. Obituaries appear in the *New York Times*, May 31, 1975; *Newsweek*, June 9, 1975; and *Time*, June 9, 1975.]

CHARLES R. MIDDLETON

PRIEST, IVY MAUDE BAKER (Sept. 7, 1905–June 23, 1975), treasurer of the United States, was born in Kimberley, Utah, the daughter of Orange Decatur Baker, a miner, and Clara Fearnley, a boardinghouse keeper and local political activist. When Priest was in elementary school, her family moved to Bingham Canyon, Utah, a copper-mining town. At an early age, Priest had to assume considerable family responsibility by helping in her mother's boardinghouse and caring for her six younger siblings. When only ten, she was initiated into political life by her mother, who was known as "Mrs. Republican" because of her work in local politics. To enable housewives to register as voters or go to the polls, Baker donated her young daughter's service for babysitting or other chores, and she recruited her to distribute campaign literature and to run errands on Election Day.

In 1924, Priest graduated from the Bingham Canyon high school, where she was captain of the debating team. Because of her family's straightened circumstances, Priest had to forgo her dream of attending college and studying law, and instead she took a job selling tickets at a local movie theater. On July 31, 1924, she married Harry Howard Hicks, a traveling salesman; they had no children. The couple moved to North Carolina and later Virginia, where Priest worked as a salesclerk in a department store. In 1929, the Hickses were divorced, and Priest returned to Utah to live with her family, who had moved to Salt Lake City. Priest first got a job as a long-distance telephone operator.

Later she held positions in both sales and merchandising at several department stores in Salt Lake City and Los Angeles. Part of this time she earned extra money by teaching evening classes in American history and citizenship at a local Salt Lake City high school.

Following in her mother's footsteps, Priest became active in precinct politics in the early 1930's. She joined the Young Republicans and, because of her dedication and her organizational ability, she rose rapidly through the party's ranks. Although she repeatedly won leadership positions, especially those within the party, she was defeated in a 1934 race for the Utah state legislature. Shortly after the legislative race, she was elected to a two-year term as cochairman of the Young Republican organization for the eleven western states (1934–1936).

On Dec. 7, 1935, she married Roy Fletcher Priest, a traveling wholesale-furniture dealer, who was twenty-one years older than she and several inches shorter. The Priests moved to Bountiful, Utah; they had four children. Roy Priest encouraged his wife's political activities, and with her natural talents in leadership and public speaking, she continued to succeed in politics and public service.

From 1937 to 1939, Priest served as the president of the women's Utah Legislative Council and helped to formulate a minimum-wage law for working women. She also served as the Republican committeewoman from Davis County and as a member of the Utah Central Committee. In 1944, she was chosen the Republican national committeewoman from Utah, a post she held until 1953. In 1946, she became vice-chairman of the Western Conference of Republican party leaders of the eleven Western states. Priest's chief task in this position was to organize women voters at the grass-roots level, using the plan she had initiated in Utah during the preceding two years. Throughout her political career, Priest argued that the female vote could have a significant impact on elections—an idea that had finally been given serious consideration by the Republican party organization.

In 1948, Priest attended the Republican National Convention in Philadelphia as a delegate of the National Committee on Women from Utah, a group that was advocating more women in appointive and elective offices. Two years later, Priest challenged the Democratic incumbent, Reva Beck Bosone, in the congressional election but was defeated.

In 1952, Priest was one of the leaders of a Republican faction known as the "Young Turks," party members who were working for the selection of Dwight Eisenhower as the Republican presidential nominee. After Eisenhower received the nomination, Priest was appointed as the assistant chairman in charge of the women's division of the Republican National Committee. In the 1952 election, women cast about 52 percent of the ballots and the number of female voters was 40 percent greater than in the previous presidential election.

After being elected, President Eisenhower appointed Priest as treasurer of the United States, the second woman to hold this position. Several months after taking office, she received the Women's National Press Club Achievement Award "for her role in helping to marshal to the polls the largest number of women ever voting in a national election." She also was named one of the "twenty most outstanding women of the century" by the Women's Newspaper Editors and Publishers Association. Although the position of U.S. treasurer does not carry cabinet rank and is largely ceremonial, it is well known to the general public primarily because the treasurer's signature is on all paper currency. As treasurer, Priest was an able administrator and a frequent and popular speaker. She used her position to foster Eisenhower administration programs, political candidates, and other civic causes, including some for which she had been a long-time worker and supporter: the American Red Cross, the Utah and National Safety Councils, and the National Society for Crippled Children and Adults. The latter organization named Priest as the national chairman of the 1957 Easter Seals campaign.

In 1959, Priest was widowed. When she left federal service in 1961, she moved to California. On June 20, 1961, she married Sidney William Stevens, a Beverly Hills real estate developer. In 1965, she successfully petitioned the court to drop her surname Stevens and reestablish her identity as Ivy Baker Priest, a name more likely to be recognized on an election ballot. The next year, Priest won her first elective office, treasurer of California. She was the first woman to seek or win the office, and she served two four-year terms in Governor Ronald Reagan's administration. In 1968, breaking another gender barrier, she became the first woman to nominate a candidate for U.S. president for a major political party when she placed

Governor Reagan's name before the Republican National Convention.

When asked to identify the most difficult handicap she had overcome, Priest said it was poverty. When naming the most positive influence that inspired her achievements, she credited her mother. Priest was widowed for the second time in 1972. In 1974, because of poor health, she declined to run for a third term as California state treasurer. She died of cancer in Santa Monica, Calif.

[Priest's papers are in the University of Utah Archives; a manuscript collection of some of her speeches, including "The Ladies Elected Ike," is in the Schlesinger Library, Radcliffe College. Her autobiography, *Green Grows Ivy* (1958), is the best source on her life through 1957, while she was still U.S. treasurer. See also Eleanor Roosevelt and Lorena Hickok, *Ladies of Courage* (1954); and a sketch in *Notable American Women* (1980). Obituaries are in the *Salt Lake City* (Utah) *Tribune* and the *New York Times*, both June 25, 1975.]

MARILYNN WOOD HILL

PROUTY, CHARLES TYLER (May 30, 1909–May 10, 1974), Shakespearean scholar and educator, was born in Washington, D.C., the son of Ward Prouty and Claire Eleanor Streeter. He graduated from high school in 1926 and subsequently attended Dartmouth College in Hanover, N.H., as had his grandfather and one of his uncles. Prouty majored in English and in 1931 received his B.A. Graduate work took him to Cambridge University in England, where he earned three more degrees: a second B.A. (1933), an M.A. (1938), and a Ph.D. (1939).

In 1933 and 1934, between periods of study at Cambridge, Prouty taught English at the Suffield School in Connecticut. On Aug. 29, 1936, he married Ruth Patterson Belew; they would have no children. That fall he accepted a teaching position at Lehigh University, in Bethlehem, Pa., where he remained as instructor of English until 1938. In 1939 and 1940, the Folger Shakespeare Library in Washington, D.C., designated him research fellow. This appointment enabled him to continue the work on the Elizabethan theater he had begun during his graduate studies and led to publication of his first book, the biography *George Gascoigne: Elizabethan Courtier, Soldier, and Poet* (1942).

From 1940 to 1948, Prouty was on the faculty of the University of Missouri in Columbia, rising rapidly through the ranks from assistant to associate professor and, in 1946, to professor of English. During World War II, on leave from the university, he served for three years (1942–1945) as a research analyst in the office of the Chief Signal Officer of the United States War Department. He was awarded the department's Commendation for Meritorious Civilian Service.

Prouty was appointed professor of English at Yale University in New Haven, Conn., in 1948 and remained on that faculty until his death. Especially during the 1950's, his service to the university as both teacher and scholar was outstanding. Not least among his accomplishments was his championing of university publication and presentation of works from and about the Elizabethan era. From 1952 on, he was editor of the Yale Shakespeare, a highly regarded series of the Bard's individual plays. At the same time he also edited *The Life and Works of George Peele*. In 1954 he chaired Yale's Shakespeare Festival, a multimedia celebration including plays, lectures, exhibitions, and musical programs, which drew on the talents of individuals and groups from throughout the university. Thousands of spectators attended the festival.

Also in 1954, the Yale University Press published Prouty's *Contention and Shakespeare's 2 Henry VI*, a critical bibliography singled out by the Shakespeare Association of America as the "only important work of the year" in its field. Finally, in what was certainly a stellar year, Prouty, in cooperation with other Shakespearean scholars, brought out the Yale University Press 1,000-page photographic facsimile edition of the 1623 *First Folio* (1954). His introduction to the work summarized all that was then known about the history of the publication of Shakespeare's plays and succinctly outlined those issues yet to be resolved.

The success of these various initiatives, especially the summer festival, called for a follow-up. In 1955 Prouty, working with Maynard Mack and a small group of colleagues, inaugurated the Yale Summer Shakespeare Institute, which he continued to direct until its termination in 1962. Prouty had long been concerned that the discoveries scholars were making were not being shared beyond the confines of elite academic communities, that unimaginative teaching was depriving school-age youngsters of a potentially wonderful experience. The institute, intended primarily for high school teachers, bridged this gap, especially during its first few years. Those involved gained information and insights to revitalize their teaching of Elizabethan life, letters, and theater.

For more than two decades Prouty's meticulous scholarship consistently helped him uncover new facts and facets about the Elizabethans and, more particularly, about their drama as it had actually been performed. For the most part, these findings are recorded in his many contributions to American and British scholarly journals and in the works he edited. Several of his best works, such as *The Sources of Much Ado About Nothing* (1950) and *The Contention and Shakespeare's 2 Henry VI*, gave detailed comparative analyses of texts.

His intent was not simply to add to the sum of knowledge, but rather to show Shakespeare's creativity in action. Similarly, Prouty's overriding purpose during years of research on the structure and conventions of the Elizabethan stage was to sharpen understanding of the actual production of drama, as it had been then and might be again. The latter interest was particularly timely, since contemporary American theater was seeking alternatives to the confines of the proscenium arch.

The single most exciting and significant event of Prouty's scholarly career was the discovery, announced in 1952, of detailed plans, drawings, and perspectives of Trinity Hall, a London building used as a playhouse as early as eight years before Shakespeare's birth and destroyed in 1790. The material was discovered in the church-warden's accounts in Guildhall Library, London. The discovery, which also included information about the operation of the playhouse, was hailed as a major contribution to contemporary knowledge of sixteenth-century theater, changing many traditional assumptions about the interior configuration and staging practice of the Globe, the home of Shakespeare's theatrical company. Prouty published the complete documentation of his find in *An Early Elizabethan Playhouse* (1953).

By the 1960's Prouty's scholarly output began to dwindle as he also withdrew somewhat from his earlier, very active role in Yale's academic community. Recognized as one of the outstanding Elizabethan specialists of the time, he continued to offer both graduate and undergraduate courses in his field.

In 1964, his teaching was praised in the student yearbook for showing that "even the most penetrating study of text can be performed without forsaking the reasonable world for the rarefied atmosphere of a high parchment tower."

Prouty was a member of the advisory council of the Folger Shakespeare Library, the Connecticut Academy of Arts and Sciences, the visiting committee of the Board of Trustees of Lehigh University, and Britain's Bibliographic Society. He was a trustee of the American Shakespeare Theater in Stratford, Conn., and a fellow of the Royal Society of Literature. He died while visiting Fort Lauderdale, Fla., shortly before his intended retirement from Yale.

[Works edited by Prouty, in addition to those mentioned in the text, include *George Gascoigne's A Hundredth Sundrie Flowres* (1942); *Studies in Honor of A.H.R. Fairchild* (1946); *Shakespeare* (1954), a collection of the Yale Shakespeare Festival lectures; and *Studies in the Elizabethan Theatre* (1961). Reviews of Prouty's works are listed in *Combined Retrospective Index to Book Reviews in Humanities Journals, 1802–1974*. There are no biographies. Obituary notices appear in the *New York Times* and the *New Haven Register*, May 14, 1974.]

URSULA SYBILLE COLBY

PROUTY, OLIVE HIGGINS (1882?–Mar. 24, 1974), writer and philanthropist, was born in Worcester, Mass., the daughter of Milton Prince, a manufacturer with the Norton Emory Reel Company, and Katherine Chapin. She and her two brothers and sister became part of a well-established New England family, secure in its academic, business, and social traditions. Graduating from Worcester Classical High School in 1900, she went on to earn a bachelor of literature degree from Smith College in 1904.

After marrying Lewis I. Prouty, a manufacturer, on Jan. 7, 1907, she enrolled in Radcliffe for graduate study. In 1908, she settled down to raise four children, three girls and a boy; two of the daughters died in infancy.

The Proutys, lifelong Republicans and Unitarians (a typically Yankee blend of conservative and liberal thought), lived most of their lives in the upper-middle-class milieu of Brookline, Mass. It was here in her comfortable home that Prouty raised her children, wrote her thirteen books (twelve of them novels), suffered at least one "nervous breakdown," and kept a beneficent eye on her alma mater.

After her husband died in 1951, Prouty continued to concentrate on her writing. She had already achieved a large measure of financial, if not critical, success as early as 1922 when *Stella Dallas* became a best-seller. Barbara Stanwyck had played the heroine in a 1937 movie adaptation. Still later, "Stella" became known to millions as the heroine of a long-running radio serial, a prototype of today's television soaps. Another Prouty novel, *Now Voyager* (1941), became a screen hit, starring Bette Davis, in 1942.

As one of Smith's most loyal alumnae, Prouty endowed a generous scholarship fund in 1947. Since that time, between four and nine students a year, selected by the school because of their writing talent, have been awarded aid from the Olive Higgins Prouty Fund.

Today Prouty lingers in literary memory primarily as the woman who played fairy godmother to Sylvia Plath. Having dispensed not only the scholarship, but also numerous invitations for tea and conversations, Prouty became an important figure in Plath's life; she was of very real financial and emotional comfort after Plath's early suicide attempt and subsequent hospitalization. As a result, Prouty is a prominent figure not only in Plath's correspondence, but in her biographers' and critics' publications as well.

The latter are not particularly kind to Prouty's writing, and indeed Plath herself had been distressed to discover that the novels by the woman she called her "fairy godmother" were appallingly sentimental. Though remaining grateful for Prouty's support, Plath could hardly stand reading her work.

Nevertheless, Prouty represented kindness; her social position and celebrity were attractive. An uneasy ambivalence between Plath's outward, fervently expressed gratitude and her unspoken disdain for Prouty's literary output complicated their relationship; there is little doubt, however, that the older woman gave the young poet much-needed emotional encouragement, as well as financial aid. When Plath's autobiographical novel, *The Bell Jar*, was published in America in 1971, some people were horrified by Plath's stingingly satiric portrait of Prouty in a character named Philomena Guinea.

By 1961, her popularity dimmed, Prouty was unable to interest a mainline publisher in her memoirs (*Pencil Shavings*) and had to have them printed privately by the Riverside Printing Company in Cambridge, Mass. When she died at ninety-two (or thereabouts; she had effectively obscured her birthdate), at the very least, she had used her ambitious talent to entertain millions, and in order to do so had chosen to write and publish instead of to indulge in the expected social rounds of bridge, shopping, and travel. If her vision was limited, she was partly the victim of a confining, prefeminist culture. She had also enabled many bright young women to receive one of the best educations available in this country. Authors have had worse epitaphs.

[Prouty's book titles and dates are *Bobbie, General Manager* (1913); *The Fifth Wheel* (1915); *Star in the Window* (1918); *Good Sports* (short stories) (1919); *Stella Dallas* (1922); *Conflict* (1927); *White Fawn* (1931); *Lisa Vale* (1938); *Now, Voyager* (1941); *Off the Deep End* (1945); *Home Port* (1947); *Fabia* (1951); *Pencil Shavings* (memoir) (1962). There is a paucity of biographical material on Olive Higgins Prouty. The archivists at Smith College have access to some information, including her memoir. See also Edward Butscher, *Sylvia Plath, Method and Madness* (1975); and Sylvia Plath's own *Letters Home* (1975), edited by her mother, Aurelia S. Plath. Obituaries appear in the *New York Times*, Mar. 26, 1974, and *Newsweek*, Apr. 8, 1974.]

CAROL BURDICK

PULITZER, MARGARET LEECH (Nov. 7, 1893–Feb. 24, 1974), historian and writer, was born in Newburgh, N.Y., the daughter of William Kernochan Leech and Rebecca Taggert.

When President McKinley was shot in 1901, the seven-year-old Margaret was inspired to write a poem about the assassination: "I am oh so sorry that our President is dead,/And everybody's sorry, so my father said;/And the horrid man who killed him is a-sitting in his cell/And I'm glad that Emma Goldman doesn't board at this hotel."

Margaret Leech attended private schools in Newburgh and Poughkeepsie, N.Y. She then entered Vassar College, receiving her B.A. in 1915. Upon graduation she went to New York to work for the Condé Nast publishing company where she was employed responding to subscribers' complaints. She also worked in advertising and did publicity work for World War I fundraising organizations, eventually joining the American Committee for Devastated France. While working on this committee in Europe she contributed articles to American periodicals.

Upon returning to the United States after the war, she began writing novels. Leech's first novel, *The Back of the Book* (1924), was the story of a young office girl in New York and was based on her own work experience. The 1926 novel *Tin Wedding* related the concerns and reflections of a woman on the occasion of her tenth wedding anniversary. A mother's overbearing love for her child became the focus of *The Feathered Nest* (1928). The novels were generally praised for their sound characterization, attention to detail, and stylistic clarity.

In 1927, in collaboration with Heywood Broun, she wrote the biography *Anthony Comstock: Roundsman of the Lord*. She and Broun wrote separate chapters. The book, which detailed the exploits of the reformer who had lived from 1844 to 1915, was lauded for its careful attention to detail, its fairness, as well as its charm and humor. The Literary Guild selected the volume as a first choice.

Leech's marriage to Ralph Pulitzer on Aug. 1, 1928, brought her into contact with a group of the most renowned literary figures of the day. Pulitzer's position as the publisher of the *New York World* and son of Joseph Pulitzer, founder of the Pulitzer Prize, allowed her to enlarge this illustrious circle.

After her success with novels, Leech attempted to write for the theater. The play *Divided by Three*, written by Leech with Beatrice Kaufman and starring Judith Anderson, opened in the fall of 1934. The reviews were scathing. Twenty-five years later, Leech was to say, "We had every advantage there was, except talent."

From 1935 to 1940 Leech studied the details of day-to-day life in Washington, D.C., during the Civil War, virtually taking up residence in the New York Public Library and the Library of Congress. Despite the contemporary prejudice of historians, she relied upon newspaper accounts from the war period as her main source, although she used letters, memoirs, photographs, and government documents as well. Published in 1941 and serialized in the *Atlantic Monthly, Reveille in Washington, 1860–1865* was a best-seller, a Book-of-the-Month Club selection, and a Pulitzer Prize winner in 1942. Like her earlier fiction, this book was noted for combining exhaustive detail with coherent and smooth writing. In the *New York Times*, MacKinlay Kantor wrote, "Despite its color and drastic vigor, few other histories of any nation or period bear more hammer-marks of an implacable concern for the grim and bitter truth."

After twelve years of research, Leech returned to the subject of her childhood poem in *In the Days of McKinley*, published in 1959. She wrote the book because she found that no serious biography of McKinley had yet been written. In the history she intertwined the life of the president with the story of the period itself. The historian John Morton Blum called it "a first-rate study of a second-rate President." This book, too, was a Book-of-the-Month Club selection and a Pulitzer Prize winner in 1960. Columbia University awarded it the prestigious Bancroft Prize for distinguished study in American history.

Ralph Pulitzer died on June 13, 1939. They had two children, one of whom died in infancy. Upon her death in New York City, Margaret Leech Pulitzer had been engaged in research for a biography of another assassinated president, John Garfield. The book was published posthumously in 1978 as *The Garfield Orbit*.

[See a review in the *New York Times Book Review*, Nov. 1, 1959; and Norma Ireland, ed., *Index to Women of the World from Ancient to Modern Times* (1970; Supplement 1988). An obituary is in the *New York Times*, Feb. 25, 1974.

CAROL R. BERKIN

PULLER, LEWIS BURWELL ("CHESTY") (June 26, 1898–Oct. 11, 1971), Marine Corps officer, was born in West Point, Va., the son of Matthew Puller and Martha Leigh. His father was a wholesale grocer whose ancestors had come to Virginia in the mid-seventeenth century. Puller's grandfather had died in the Civil War, and he grew up listening to stories of Confederate valor. His hero was Andrew Johnson.

After his father's death in 1905, Puller was employed for a time in a pulp mill and worked other odd jobs to help support the family. After attending public school in his hometown, Puller entered the Virginia Military Institute in 1917. Eager to participate in World War I, he dropped out of school in 1918 to enlist as a private in the U.S. Marine Corps. Instead of shipping Puller overseas, however, officials in the corps, seeing his ability, selected him to help train troops in boot camp at Parris Island, S.C. When the war ended, he went to officers' training school and became a second lieutenant in the Marine Corps Reserve in 1919. With the postwar reduction in military forces, Puller was placed on the inactive list.

Puller would find his war, however. He enlisted again in the corps as a corporal and went to Haiti in 1919 to serve for five years as an officer in the *Gendarmerie d'Haiti*, an army and police organization staffed by U.S. marines and Haitians. Puller earned his first combat decoration from the government of Haiti, the Medaille Militaire. He participated in over forty combat actions.

Puller spent the next four years in the United States. Commissioned from the ranks, he in 1924 once again became a second lieutenant serving at the marine barracks in Norfolk, Va. After completing training at the navy yard in Philadelphia in July 1925, Puller was assigned to the Tenth Marine Regiment at Quantico, Va. Under Puller's leadership the marine drill detachment became the first marine winner of the national drill competition. In 1926, Puller went to naval flight school at Pensacola, Fla., but did not win his wings. He then completed a two-year tour at the Marine Barracks at Pearl Harbor.

In December 1928, Puller returned to combat with the Nicaraguan *Guardia Nacional* with the guard rank of captain. The guard was fighting against a guerrilla army under Augusto César Sandino. Puller, leading troops in over sixty battles, earned two Navy Crosses. He interrupted his Nicaraguan tour briefly in 1931 to complete the company officers' course at the Army Infantry School at Fort Benning, Ga.

In January 1933, Puller left Nicaragua for China. He commanded the "Horse Marines," a mounted detachment guarding the American Legation and American residences and outlying areas around the capital city of Peking. From September 1934 until the spring of 1936, he commanded the marine detachment on the cruiser USS *Augusta*. Puller married Virginia Montague Evans in Middlesex County on Nov. 13, 1937; the couple had three children. He then trained recruits at the Basic School in Philadelphia for three years. In September 1939, he returned to the *Augusta* before duty in Shanghai from May 1940 to August 1941 as executive officer on the Second Battalion, Fourth Marines.

He returned to the United States in August 1941 and in October took command of the First Battalion, Seventh Marine Regiment, First Marine Division at New River, N.C. Puller insisted on training his men in jungle fighting and personal camouflage tactics. That training would prove invaluable in the Pacific campaigns of World War II.

For his heroism against the Japanese, Puller earned two more Navy Crosses, one on Guadalcanal and one on Cape Gloucester, New Britain. The troops under his command performed outstandingly under adverse conditions and Puller himself was wounded. On Peleliu, in September and October 1944, as commander of the First Marine Regiment, he faced his toughest fighting. In the caves of Bloody Nose Ridge, his regiment lost 60 percent of its men and 74 percent of its officers. After Peleliu, Puller saw no further combat in the war. His old wound bothered him, and the Marine Corps wanted him to train recruits at Camp LeJeune, N.C. Puller served on reserve duty in New Orleans for two years and then as commander of the Marine Barracks at Pearl Harbor until July 1950, one month after the Korea conflict began. His country again required his leadership.

Once more in command of the First Marine Regiment, Puller led the amphibious landing at Inchon and the subsequent march on Seoul. Then, after participating in the drive to the Yalu River, he earned his fifth Navy Cross during the retreat from the Choisin River to the coast, a retreat completed in good order against incredible odds. In January 1951, he was promoted to brigadier general as assistant division commander of the First Marine Division.

Puller returned to the United States in May 1951 to command the Third Marine Brigade. In the summer of 1952, he assumed command of the Troop Training Unit at Coronada, Calif., and received the rank of major general in 1953.

In July 1954, he took his final assignment at Camp LeJeune, first commanding the Second Marine Division and then serving as deputy camp commander. When he retired as a lieutenant general on Nov. 1, 1955, after a disabling stroke, he was the most decorated individual in the history of the U.S. Marine Corps.

Puller's retirement from military service was marred by the war that his son's generation was called upon to fight. Lewis B. Puller, Jr., after graduation from college, entered the Marine Corps and went to Vietnam in 1968. Lieutenant Puller was almost killed by a booby-trapped howitzer round. He lost his right leg completely, his left leg above the knee, the thumb and one finger of his right hand, and most of his left hand. In his autobiography, Lieutenant Puller writes of his father's visit to him in the hospital. The aging hero of World War II, grasping his son's shoulder, was reduced to convulsive tears. General Puller and the nation still believed that World War II had been a just war. Lieutenant Puller and many of his generation had many doubts about Vietnam. The devoted family man died in Huntington, in his native Virginia.

Chesty Puller received his nickname because he walked with his barrel chest thrown out and with a thrust to his jaw. Though he was the most decorated Marine, he was also one of the most controversial. He derided frills at training camps, arguing that the troops should be given beer and whiskey, not ice cream, candy, and dates. He defended Marine Corps training at a 1956 trial held after the death of six recruits during a night training march, arguing that Marines had to be more physically fit than the enemy, being able to march twenty-five miles if the enemy marched twenty miles. Puller was a religious man and studied history, especially military history, going into battle with the Crusader's Cross of the Episcopal Church around his neck and a copy of Julius Caesar's *The Gallic Wars* in his pocket. Yet his profanity was legendary and he would not be hidebound by existing orthodoxy in his approach to warfare.

Certainly many things contributed to Puller's reputation as an outstanding tactical combat leader. His personal fortitude in adverse and dangerous circumstances was part of it; he led from the front. A *Saturday Evening Post* article on him in 1952 was entitled "Toughest Marine in the Corps."

But equally important was Puller's view of himself and his men. He carried his own pack, ate what his troops ate, and did the work that they did. He insisted that enlisted men eat first, followed by noncommissioned officers and then officers. He not only drove his men to be fit and to be expert marksmen and fighters but he cared for them and showed it in many ways. He always attributed his success to his men.

[For further biographical information see Burke Davis, *Marine! The Life of General Lewis B. (Chesty) Puller, USMC (Ret.)* (1962). For Puller's military exploits see U.S. Marine Corps, *U.S. Marine Operations in Korea, 1950–1953* (1954–1972); U.S. Marine Corps, *History of U.S. Marine Corps Operations in World War II* (1958–1971); and J. Robert Moskin, *The U.S. Marine Corps Story* (1977). An obituary is in the *New York Times*, Oct. 14, 1971.]

JOSEPH P. HOBBS

R

RADCLIFFE, GEORGE LOVIC PIERCE (Aug. 22, 1877–July 29, 1974), lawyer, businessman, and United States senator, was born in Lloyds, Md., the son of Sophie D. Travers and John Anthony LeCompte Radcliffe, who owned farms, a shipyard, and an oyster canning factory on Maryland's eastern shore. An heir to considerable wealth and social standing, Radcliffe grew up on a farm that had been in his family since the seventeenth century. He had several years of private tutoring before entering public school in Cambridge, Md. After graduation from Cambridge High School in 1893, he went on to Johns Hopkins University in Baltimore, where he excelled in history and political science. He earned a B.A. in 1897 and a Ph.D. in 1900. His doctoral dissertation, "Governor Thomas H. Hicks of Maryland and the Civil War," was an able study of the governor's effort to prevent his state's secession from the Union. It was published by Johns Hopkins Press in 1901.

Radcliffe served as principal of Cambridge High School from 1900 to 1901 and then taught history and civics at Baltimore City College for two years. After school hours he attended law classes at the University of Maryland and received his LL.B. in 1903. Shortly after passing the bar in the same year, Radcliffe joined the law department of the American Bonding Company, a surety concern in Baltimore. A skilled negotiator and dependable troubleshooter, he became head of the law department in 1904 and was made a second vice-president in 1906. After American Bonding merged in 1913 with a competitor, Fidelity and Deposit Company of Maryland, Radcliffe as president oversaw the liquidation of his company. He became an executive vice-president with Fidelity and Deposit and in this capacity met and formed a friendship with Franklin D. Roosevelt, who had signed on with the firm as vice-president and head of the New York office in 1920. On June 6, 1906, Radcliffe married Mary McKim Marriott of Baltimore, a painter and writer who had been an editor of the *Ladies Home Journal*. They had one child.

Radcliffe entered public life modestly in 1916 by accepting the appointment of Governor Emerson C. Harrington to the Baltimore Liquor License Commission. During World War I, he was associate director of personnel for the American Red Cross in Washington and chairman of a commission charged with organizing Maryland's war records. After the war Harrington appointed Radcliffe secretary of state. He was Maryland's chief record keeper in 1919 and 1920.

An active Democrat, Radcliffe helped to plan the campaigns of a number of successful candidates, including Governor Albert C. Ritchie and Senator Millard E. Tydings. He chaired the inaugural committees for Ritchie in 1923, 1926, and 1930 and headed the state Democratic Campaign Committee in 1932. In the latter role, he presided over his friend Roosevelt's victory over President Herbert Hoover by 130,000 votes in Maryland. In 1933, Radcliffe joined the Roosevelt administration as a regional director for the Public Works Administration (PWA). In this early New Deal period, when public projects were funded at 30 percent by the federal government and 70 percent by states and municipalities, Radcliffe was able to get such officials as the fiscally conservative Governor Ritchie and Mayor Howard W. Jackson of Baltimore to produce the financing for construction work on the Susquehanna and Potomac River bridges; hospital, dormitory, and arts and science buildings at the University of Maryland; and water and sewage systems.

In spring 1934, Radcliffe was promoted by Senator Tydings as a compromise candidate for governor of Maryland. Factional feuding among Democrats threatened the party's election chances. The Radcliffe candidacy was designed to coax Governor Ritchie into eschewing a fifth term and running for the United States Senate and to avoid a divisive multicandidate struggle for the gubernatorial nomination. Ritchie was determined to run again for governor, however, and Radcliffe ended up on the Democratic ticket as the nominee for the Senate. Ironically, the veteran Ritchie lost the general election to liberal Republican Harry W. Nice by 6,149 votes, while Radcliffe, in his first race for elective office, trounced former senator Joseph I. France by 66,637 votes.

Because of his personal friendship with the president and his brief service in the administration, Radcliffe was expected to be a staunch New Dealer as a senator. Owing to his business background, however, he was only moderately supportive of Roosevelt's policies. Between 1935 and 1939, he supported the administration agenda on key roll-call votes 76 percent of the time, dutifully voting for the Social Security Act (1935), the National Labor Relations Act (1935), the Federal Emergency Appropriation Act (1935), and the Supreme Court nomination of Hugo Black (1937). At the same time, he backed conservative amendments designed to derail the Public Utility Holding Company Act (1935) and to cut funding for housing and unemployment relief in 1937. Even as he lauded the New Deal in public speeches for having saved the country from the Great Depression, Radcliffe wrote privately to Roosevelt that he was "disturbed" by the administration's legislative program.

In 1937, Radcliffe broke openly with Roosevelt over the latter's unsuccessful effort to reorganize the Supreme Court. A year later, when the president sought to "purge" Democratic opponents of his policies, including Senator Tydings, Radcliffe served as campaign manager for his colleague's easy primary victory over Congressman David J. Lewis, who had the support of the White House. In 1940, Radcliffe was himself easily reelected, outdistancing his primary opponent Howard Bruce by eighty thousand votes and drubbing Republican former governor Nice by 190,327 votes in the November election. He thus ran well ahead of the president, who carried Maryland by 115,018 votes over Wendell L. Willkie on his way to a third term.

In the Senate, Radcliffe seldom took the floor to speak and served as a relatively unobtrusive member of the banking and currency, commerce, finance, and immigration committees. His major legislative activity was in behalf of the shipping industry, which was vital to Maryland and had been his father's chief business interest. He participated in the writing of the Merchant Marine Act of 1936, which established the United States Maritime Commission to dispense subsidies to shipbuilders and steamship companies and revitalize an outdated and inefficient American foreign trade fleet. Radcliffe also had a hand in the preparation of most of the shipping legislation passed by Congress during his Senate tenure.

An internationalist in foreign affairs, Radcliffe supported Roosevelt's efforts against the arms embargo in 1939 and for Lend-Lease and the extension of selective service in 1941. After World War II he strongly favored the creation of a United Nations organization and sought unsuccessfully to have it headquartered in Baltimore. On the domestic front, however, Radcliffe remained cautious about large-scale government undertakings and thus collaborated with Senator Robert A. Taft of Ohio and other conservative Republicans in weakening President Harry Truman's Full Employment Bill (1945), a massive public-works initiative. Toward the end of his second term, Radcliffe came under fire from opponents in Maryland for his frequent absences from Washington to attend business meetings at Fidelity and Deposit, where he had been an officer since 1913, and at other banks and corporations in Baltimore. This issue helped to bring about his defeat by Governor Herbert R. O'Conor in the Democratic primary of 1946. O'Conor, who had the endorsement of the Political Action Committee of the Congress of Industrial Organizations, won by twenty-two thousand votes.

Outside of business and politics, Radcliffe had a variety of interests. He was active in nearly every important charitable enterprise in Maryland, including the March of Dimes, which he chaired for thirty years. He was a major contributor to and fundraiser for Johns Hopkins. He chaired the first general reunion of alumni in 1908, organized the university's alumni council, and, with General Electric president Owen D. Young, led the campaign to create the Walter Hines Page School of International Relations in 1924.

Radcliffe's principal avocation over the years, however, was history. A member of the Maryland Historical Society after 1908, he served as the society's secretary (1911–1931), president (1931–1965), and chairman of the board (1965–1974). During his presidency, a steady flow of funds allowed the society to expand its facilities and increase its collections substantially. The house of Baltimore philanthropist Enoch Pratt and the original manuscript of the "Star Spangled Banner" by Francis Scott Key were important acquisitions during Radcliffe's active involvement. In tribute, the society named its maritime museum for him in 1973.

Radcliffe's enthusiasm for history and civic activism extended beyond his service to the Maryland Historical Society. He chaired committees that saved Baltimore's historic nineteenth-century Shot Tower from demolition in 1924 and celebrated the writing of the "Star Spangled Banner" (1939) and the tercentennial of the Religious Toleration Act (1949). In 1954, he even donned a bushy brown wig and a black hat with a yellow plume to play Lord Calvert in a parade honoring the return of major league baseball to Baltimore for the first time in fifty-two years.

A member of the Johns Hopkins one-mile relay team in college, Radcliffe still jogged on the roof of the Fidelity and Deposit building at the age of eighty. He also had a lifelong fascination with Christmas, which led him to collect two thousand books and five hundred articles on the subject. He died in Baltimore.

[Radcliffe's papers are at the Maryland Historical Society in Baltimore. Biographical material is in *Tercentenary History of Maryland*, vol. 3 (1925); and a memoir by Samuel Hopkins in the *Maryland Historical Magazine*, Winter 1974. See also Stephen K. Bailey, *Congress Makes a Law* (1950); James T. Patterson, *Congressional Conservatism and the New Deal* (1967); Dorothy Brown, "The Election of 1934: The 'New Deal' in Maryland," *Maryland Historical Magazine*, Winter 1973; Richard Walsh and William Lloyd Fox, eds., *Maryland* (1974); and Robert J. Brugger, *Maryland* (1988). Obituaries are in the *Baltimore Sun* and the *Washington Post*, both July 30, 1974; and in the *New York Times*, July 31, 1974. An oral-history interview with Radcliffe is on deposit at the Maryland Historical Society.]

RICHARD H. GENTILE

RADFORD, ARTHUR WILLIAM (Feb. 27, 1896–Aug. 17, 1973), naval officer, was born in Chicago, the son of John Arthur Radford, an electrical engineer, and Agnes Eliza Knight. Raised in Riverside, Ill., and Grinnell, Iowa, he entered the U.S. Naval Academy in 1912. After graduating in the upper third of his class in 1916, he served two and a half years on the battleship *South Carolina*, which escorted one transatlantic convoy during World War I. Radford's keen intellect led to his posting as flag lieutenant (aide) to two successive admirals from 1918 to 1920, after which he entered flight training at Pensacola, Fla. Upon completing the student course in November 1920 in the rank of lieutenant, he remained as an instructor of aerial gunnery for another year. From then on, he became an increasingly important figure in the development of the navy's air arm, beginning with his assignment to the newly established Bureau of Aeronautics (1921–1923). He married Dorothy Hume about 1919; they had no children and were later divorced.

Radford spent virtually all of his flying years in the Pacific, the initial four in seaplanes and gunfire spotting off two battleships. In 1929, following two years at Naval Air Station San Diego in the rank of lieutenant commander, he commanded the Alaskan Aerial Survey Detachment, which mapped southeastern Alaska for the U.S. Geological Survey and U.S. Forest Service. Assigned to the new aircraft carrier *Saratoga* late that year, he was flight deck officer and then skipper of its crack Fighting Squadron 1B. He remained on board as flag secretary to the carrier force commander Admiral Harry E. Yarnell in 1931 and 1932, during which the carriers executed a successful mock surprise attack on Pearl Harbor. A three-year tour of duty with the Bureau of Aeronautics flight division ended with Radford's appointment as navigator of the seaplane tender *Wright*. In 1935, he returned to the staff of the carrier admiral Frederick J. Horne as tactical officer in the rank of commander. While commander from 1937 to 1940 of Naval Air Station Seattle he initiated its expansion. In April 1939 he married Mariam Jeanette McMichael (formerly Mrs. Earl Winfield Spencer) of Portland, Oreg.; they had no children.

Radford spent one year as executive officer of the first carrier named *Yorktown* before being assigned to establish and command the naval operating base at Trinidad in the British West

Indies in August 1941. He was recalled to the Bureau of Aeronautics four months later by its chief, Admiral John H. Towers, to undertake the immense task of expanding the navy's wartime aviation training program. He assumed the post in December, attained the rank of captain the next month, and applied his organizational genius and knack for innovation as director of aviation training during the critical first year and a half of the war. His reward was promotion to the rank of rear admiral in July 1943 without ever having commanded a ship, unusual in the annals of the navy, and assignment as commander of a division of fast carriers in the Pacific. As such, he directed attacks on Wake Island in October and the Gilbert Islands in November, in the latter operation introducing night fighters to the carriers. The next month Admiral Towers made Radford his chief of staff in the Pacific Fleet air forces, only to have Radford recalled to Washington in March 1944 as assistant to the deputy chief of naval operations for air. He virtually ran that office until October, when he returned to the Pacific as commander of Carrier Division Six, a task group of fast carriers. With his flag in the second carrier *Yorktown*, he participated in the South China Sea, Iwo Jima, and Okinawa campaigns, as well as in attacks on the Japanese homeland during 1945.

Following the Japanese surrender, Radford commanded fleet air at Seattle until January 1946, when he became deputy chief of naval operations for air as vice-admiral. By this time, he had become heir apparent to Towers as unofficial leader of naval aviation and also of the airmen's resistance to the armed forces unification movement. After commanding the Second Task Fleet in the Atlantic for most of 1947, he became the navy's spokesman on Cold War strategy as vice-chief of naval operations from January 1948 until April 1949. He then reported as commander in chief of the Pacific Command and of its naval component, the Pacific Fleet, as well as high commissioner, Trust Territory of the Pacific Islands, in the rank of full admiral. Radford led the so-called revolt of the admirals against preferential funding for the U.S. Air Force strategic bombers over that for naval aviation during the fall of 1949. He commanded the U.S. Pacific Fleet during the Korean War and directed overall naval operations in that conflict until June 1953. President Dwight D. Eisenhower appointed him chairman of the Joint Chiefs of Staff (JCS), beginning that August.

Long respected for his mental powers, sound judgment, and strategic acumen, Radford became second only to Secretary of State John Foster Dulles as adviser to Eisenhower on American foreign and defense policy during his two two-year terms as chairman of the JCS. A champion of "massive retaliation" as the cornerstone of U.S. strategy against the Soviet Union, he advocated unilateral American intervention on the side of France in the Indochina war in 1954, including the use of atomic weapons should Communist China enter that conflict. Eisenhower followed Congress and the British in rejecting this option, however, and France was defeated; Admiral Radford later admitted that Eisenhower had been right to do so. The other crises that dominated his tenure were the Formosa Straits incidents of 1954–1955 and the Suez crisis of 1956. Radford retired from the navy in August 1957 and served as a consultant and director of several corporations for the remainder of his life. He died at Bethesda Naval Hospital in Washington, D.C., and is buried in Arlington National Cemetery.

[Radford's papers and memoirs are in the Hoover Institution of War, Revolution, and Peace at Stanford University. From them and the files at the Navy Department, several excerpts were published posthumously: for the Alaskan aerial survey, "North to Alaska," *U.S. Naval Institute Proceedings*, Sept. 1980; for the 1932 fleet war games, "Aircraft Battle Force," in Paul W. Stillwell, ed., *Air Raid: Pearl Harbor!* (1981); and, for the years 1941–1954, Stephen Jurika, Jr., ed., *From Pearl Harbor to Vietnam: The Memoirs of Admiral Arthur W. Radford* (1980). See the line biography at the Naval Historical Center. Many details of his career can be found in Clark G. Reynolds, *The Fast Carriers: The Forging of an Air Navy* (1968; 1992); *The Fighting Lady* (1986); and *Admiral John H. Towers: The Struggle for Naval Air Supremacy* (1991). For the postwar period, see Michael A. Palmer, *Origins of the Maritime Strategy* (1990). An obituary is in the *New York Times*, Aug. 18, 1973.]

CLARK G. REYNOLDS

RAHV, PHILIP (Mar. 10, 1908–Dec. 22, 1973), critic, editor, and educator, was born Ivan Greenberg in Kupin, Ukraine, in czarist Russia. His parents operated a dry goods store but, amid the turmoil of World War I and anti-Semitic pogroms, emigrated to Palestine, where their son would himself live twice briefly. In 1922, at the age of fourteen, he immigrated to Providence, R.I., and then to Oregon. At the age of sixteen, he left high school, becoming an autodidact and a radical who sought the abolition of capitalism. Upon joining the Communist party in 1932, he adopted the name that would soon signal his fame as a literary critic and editor. (*Rav* is Hebrew for "rabbi" or "teacher.") In the depths of the Great Depression, he moved to New York City, living in wrenching poverty and sometimes teaching Hebrew.

Starting out in the 1930's under the literary sponsorship of the Communist party, Rahv published essays, reviews, and poems in the *Daily Worker*, *New Masses*, and *Prolit*. He also joined William Phillips, the son of Jewish immigrants, in cofounding *Partisan Review* in 1934, under the auspices of the Communists' New York City John Reed Club. The magazine was designed to defend the interests of the Soviet Union, to intensify opposition to fascism and Nazism, and to clarify the aims and methods of a proletarian or "revolutionary" literature. But the switch in the Communists' political strategy toward the popular front, as well as the shocks of the Moscow Purge trials in exposing Stalinist cruelty and cynicism, prompted the coeditors to halt publication in the fall of 1936.

When *Partisan Review* resumed its operations in 1937, it had become independent, and Rahv had become a vigorous anti-Communist. Instead of defending the socialist motherland, the monthly, then bimonthly, magazine defended the modernist achievements of writers like Eliot (an Anglican arch-conservative), Proust, Mann, Yeats, and Joyce. Instead of supporting a literature that would reflect the perspective of the working class, *Partisan Review* promoted a cosmopolitanism that embraced an apolitical spirit and revealed an alienation from bourgeois culture. The magazine soon became one of the most prestigious forums for the intelligentsia in the Western world. Although its subscription list did not exceed 10,000 at the peak of its influence, *Partisan Review* attracted contributions from leading literati in the United States and western Europe and became required reading for intellectuals. The excitement that the journal conveyed declined by the 1950's, however, as its anti-Stalinism became orthodoxy and as modernism triumphed in the academy. Rahv remained coeditor and, by virtually

all accounts, the journal's dominant voice until 1969, when he resigned to found *Modern Occasions*. Inaugurated the following year, the Boston-based quarterly represented somewhat radical politics but also upheld what had then become fairly traditional literary tastes. Failing to find a large enough audience to meet costs, the journal ceased publication after six issues.

Commanding as Rahv's stewardship of *Partisan Review* had been, the literary criticism that he published, often within its pages, might be deemed even more significant. In particular a series of critical performances at the end of the so-called red decade established Rahv's reputation for brilliance. "The Death of Ivan Ilyich and Joseph K." (1940) provided the first influential interpretation of Kafka in the United States and made the case for Kafka's uniting of "the realistic and symbolic, the recognizable and mysterious." "Dostoevsky and Politics" (1938) was also authoritative, as were several of his subsequent essays on the Russian novelist. Rahv spoke with a thick eastern European accent, and Yiddish had been his mother tongue, but his English prose was subtle, elegant, and even exquisite. He may be best known for his portraits of Hawthorne and James and for his generalizations about American fiction and poetry.

Two essays in particular helped shape the critical appreciation of the literature of his adopted country. "The Cult of Experience in American Writing" (1940) noted the failure of American writers to explore serious ideas in prose or to fashion intellectuals as fictional characters. In "Paleface and Redskin" (1939), Rahv lamented the polarity and fragmentation of the creative mind and showed how wide a chasm separated, say, the patrician Henry James and Emily Dickinson from the plebeian Walt Whitman and Mark Twain. And no other piece of criticism identified more concisely the sterility of the socially conscious writing that Rahv once championed than his "Proletarian Literature: A Political Autopsy" (1939), which assailed the Communist party for recognizing no boundaries between politics and art. While his own stance remained vaguely leftist, Rahv was no activist ready to leap to the barricades. His Marxism was subdued, revealed most often in his effort to locate writers in their historical and ideological contexts.

After a lifetime of disdain for the academy, he became a professor of English at Brandeis

University in 1957 and served on its faculty until his death sixteen years later. Childless, Rahv had three wives. He and Nathalie Swan, an architect, were married in 1940, and were divorced in 1955. The next year he married Theodora Jay Stillman, who, while smoking in bed, died in a fire in their Boston home in 1968. Marriage to Betty Thomas McIlvain, a writer, followed a couple of years later.

Rahv's career exhibited a zest for polemics and a commitment to the exposure of shoddy writing and thinking. His prose displayed a keen sensitivity to the zeitgeist; and though his work entailed the severe monitoring of the historic reputations of writers and other critics, his own tastes and judgments could not be easily categorized. Rahv himself was a troubled, brooding figure whose scowl made him look, in the words of one associate, like the permanent "chairman of a grievance committee." So flamboyant was his personality that Phillips called him "manic-impressive." Fictionalized as Will Taub in Mary McCarthy's *The Oasis* (1949) and as Sidney Sykes in Alan Lelchuk's *Shrinking* (1978), this gifted writer was perhaps even more dazzling as a talker, offering extended monologues spiced with gossip. Rahv's life was entwined in paradox: the formidable literary arbiter who had never even graduated from high school, the exuberant champion of experimental modernism who disparaged the highbrow articles published in his own magazine, the ornery bully of the editorial office who shrank from the political challenges that his own revolutionist views ought to have dictated, the independent and detached cosmopolitan who read his favorite French, German, and Russian authors in their own languages but who bequeathed his estate to the state of Israel. An essayist rather than a thinker, Rahv had little flair for theory or for sustained scholarship. Perhaps no significant critic left behind so thin a body of work. His fame rests on a lifetime's output that was stretched into four overlapping essay collections; a long-promised book on Dostoyevski was left unfinished at the time of his death in Cambridge, Mass.

[Some of Rahv's correspondence can be found in the Dwight Macdonald Papers at Yale University. The *Partisan Review* files are located in Boston University. Rahv's criticism is collected in *Image and Idea* (1949); *The Myth and the Powerhouse* (1965); and *Literature and the Sixth Sense* (1969). Though no published biography exists, see Andrew James Dvosin, "Literature in a Political World: The Career and Writings of Philip Rahv" (Ph.D. diss., New York University, 1977). A festschrift edited by Arthur Edelstein, *Images and Ideas in American Culture* (1979), includes a critical assessment by Milton Hindus and a memoir by Alan Lelchuk. Books on Rahv's literary circle include Terry A. Cooney, *The Rise of the New York Intellectuals* (1986); Alexander Bloom, *Prodigal Sons* (1986); and Alan M. Wald, *The New York Intellectuals* (1987). A tribute by Mary McCarthy is in Rahv's *Essays on Literature and Politics* (1978), edited by Arabel J. Porter and Andrew J. Dvosin. An obituary appears in the *New York Times*, Dec. 24, 1973.]

STEPHEN J. WHITFIELD

RAMSPECK, ROBERT C. WORD ("BOB") (Sept. 5, 1890–Sept. 10, 1972), member of Congress, and business executive, was born in Decatur, Ga., a suburb of Atlanta, the son of Theodore Rosalva Ramspeck and Ida Gertrude Word, owners of a general mercantile, real estate, building and building supplies business. Ramspeck was one of five children. He attended local public schools and completed his secondary education at the Donald Fraser School for Boys in Decatur.

From 1907 to 1911 Ramspeck served as deputy clerk at the De Kalb County Court House, a branch of the Superior Court of Georgia. In 1911, at age twenty-one, Ramspeck went to Washington, D.C., to work as chief clerk in the post office of the House of Representatives. The following year he served as secretary to Congressman William Schley Howard of Georgia.

In 1914, Ramspeck was appointed a deputy U.S. marshal for the Northern Georgia District and in 1917 he was promoted to chief deputy marshal. Ramspeck married Nobie Estelle Clay, a teacher of dramatics, on Oct. 18, 1916; they had two children. Ramspeck was not called for World War I service because he was married and already engaged in public service.

In 1919, Ramspeck resigned his marshal's appointment to complete his law degree, for which he had been studying at night. He received an LL.B. degree from the Atlanta Law School in 1920 and was admitted to the Georgia bar later that year.

During the early years of his career, Ramspeck made his living by selling insurance and real estate; by managing and editing a weekly newspaper, the *De Kalb New Era*; and by the private practice of law. He also served as solicitor of the city court of Decatur from 1923 to

1927 and as city attorney from 1927 to 1929.

Ramspeck was elected to serve in the Georgia Assembly during the 1929 session, where he introduced legislation to define and regulate the practice of law. The bill passed the Georgia house, but failed in the senate.

Elected to the U.S. House of Representatives as a Democrat in October 1929 to fill the vacancy caused by the death of Leslie J. Steele, Ramspeck served Georgia's Fifth District in Congress until he resigned sixteen years later in December 1945.

Ramspeck was described as "a mild, quiet man," a "conscientious worker," and even "fervent." While in Congress he won a reputation as a vigorous and outspoken opponent of spoils politics and as an advocate of civil service reform and fair labor legislation. Ramspeck argued for a "middle ground" in labor relations, for a code of labor relations written jointly by management, labor, and the public that would protect the right of labor to organize and bargain collectively.

In 1945, the *New York Times* lauded Ramspeck, saying he had "introduced or inspired more legislation of benefit to Federal employees than any other member of Congress in history." Ramspeck's efforts to extend the reach of the civil service system and to bring more professionalism to government employment challenged the well-entrenched patronage system in which public appointments were seen as rewards to be distributed by political parties. Among Ramspeck's legacies is the 1938 bill that placed postmasters under the civil service system. Another is his bill that empowered the president to bring more than 200,000 jobs in twenty-six federal agencies into the civil service system; this bill became law in 1940, after a year-and-a-half of debate and delay tactics on the part of its opponents. *Time* described the final debate this way: "Gentle Bob Ramspeck, victory in sight, got tough. He took to the floor for 18 explosive minutes, with his Georgia drawl grown corrosive, laid about him with two years' pent-up wrath. When he was through, spoilsmen's bodies were figuratively heaped about him." President Franklin D. Roosevelt signed the bill with Ramspeck's fountain pen.

In 1942, Ramspeck championed legislation to provide pensions for members of Congress. The provision was approved but rescinded after Congress was subjected to what Ramspeck later called "a wild and scurrilous storm of abuse."

He remained convinced that the bill was misunderstood by the public. A congressional pensions bill was finally approved in 1946.

Ramspeck served on the House Committee on Civil Service throughout his sixteen years in Congress and was its chairman from 1935 to 1945. He was secretary of the Democratic Caucus from 1937 to 1942 and was the House Democratic whip from 1942 to 1945. At the time of his resignation, he was a member of several committees, including Labor, of which he was ranking Democratic member.

When Ramspeck resigned from Congress, he explained that he did so with "deep regrets but no apologies." Then in his fifties, he had been in public office more than thirty years. In an article published in *Collier's*, Ramspeck explained, "In the course of these years I have worked as hard and as effectively as my strength and ability allowed, and without much thought of my own financial status. But it has not been possible for me to save anything out of my pay, my duties have been so heavy I could not supplement my income by private law practice, and there is no provision for retirement pay for members of Congress."

When Ramspeck left Congress he became executive vice-president of the Air Transport Association of America, a trade group representing domestic and American-owned international airlines.

President Harry S. Truman named Ramspeck chairman of the U.S. Civil Service Commission in March 1951. At Ramspeck's request, Truman ordered more rigorous loyalty standards in government employment, making "reasonable doubt" of loyalty grounds for dismissal. While head of the commission, Ramspeck defended federal workers against charges of inefficiency and corruption. Truman credited Ramspeck with improving morale among government workers and increasing public esteem for their service.

In 1953, Ramspeck reported to the president on the progress of the Civil Service Commission in the previous fifteen years. He noted that in 1937 only 63 percent of federal positions were within the Civil Service System; that had grown to 92 percent by the time of his report.

He was a vice-president of Eastern Air Lines from 1953 to 1961 and remained a consultant for Eastern until 1966. He also remained active in public service. In 1957, President Dwight D. Eisenhower appointed Ramspeck to a committee to develop a career executive program for civil servants. In 1965, Ramspeck was appointed chairman of an advisory committee to the postmaster general, and four years later he was named chairman of a special committee to advise on government use of data processing equipment.

Ramspeck died while on a visit to Castor, La. He was buried in Decatur, Ga.

[Articles by Ramspeck include "Civil Service Wonderland," *Collier's*, May 15, 1943; "I Couldn't Afford to Be a Congressman," *Collier's*, Mar. 9, 1946; "Reconciling Labor and Management Philosophies," *American Management Association, Personnel Series, No. 98*, 1946; "Watch Your Aim," *Vital Speeches of the Day*, Dec. 15, 1951; and "U.S. Workers Who *Don't* Get Mink," *New York Times Magazine*, Jan. 27, 1952. For Ramspeck's comments on the National Labor Relations Act, see the *Congressional Digest*, June–July 1939.

For additional information, see *Biographical Directory of the U.S. Congress, 1774–1989*; "Mr. Ramspeck Wins," *Time*, Dec. 9, 1940; "Ramspeck, The Whip," *Time*, June 22, 1942; and from the *New York Times*, "Ramspeck Quitting House to Take Post with Air Transport Group," Nov. 27, 1945, "Truman Hails Ramspeck, Quitting Civil Service Post," Jan. 1, 1953, and "Ramspeck Traces Civil Service Gain," Jan. 15, 1953. An obituary is in the *New York Times*, Sept. 12, 1972.]

ROBYN BURNETT

RANKIN, JEANNETTE PICKERING (June 11, 1880–May 18, 1973), first woman in Congress, was born on a ranch near Missoula, Montana Territory, the first of seven children born to John Rankin, a rancher and builder, and Olive Pickering, a former schoolteacher. Her parents were well-to-do and prominent in Montana affairs.

Treated as a son by her father, Rankin grew up expecting to do something socially significant with her life. She attended the Missoula public schools and graduated from the University of Montana in Missoula in 1902 with a B.S. in biology. When her father died in 1904, Rankin was teaching in rural schools. Impatient with the slow pace of life, she traveled to Boston in the winter of 1904 and stayed with her brother, Wellington, who was attending Harvard. The Boston slums made a great impression on her, one that was reinforced during a 1907 trip to San Francisco. While there, Rankin visited a settlement house, where social worker Elizabeth Ash encouraged her to pursue

social work. She attended the New York School of Philanthropy (later part of Columbia University) during the 1908–1909 school year and lived in the Suffrage League house on East Eighty-sixth Street in New York City.

As a qualified social worker, Rankin joined the Spokane, Wash., Children's Home Society in 1909 but found that she did not like institutional work. She then left Spokane to study social legislation at the University of Washington. While there, Rankin became involved again in the suffrage movement, since she saw a relationship between horrible slum conditions and women's inability to vote and affect the democratic process. Elated with the granting of the vote to women in 1910 she returned to Montana to work for passage of the recently introduced suffrage bill there.

Rankin began working with the Montana Equal Franchise Society, and as its representative became the first woman to speak before the all-male Montana legislature (1910). She declared that she was suspicious of governmental priorities set without female involvement; she also posited that voteless women were being taxed without representation. Rankin was unable to sway the legislature, but the speech was generally well received, and she came to the notice of the New York Women's Suffrage Party. Rankin went to work for them and for the National American Woman Suffrage Association (NAWSA), traveling to California and Ohio. Made a field secretary for NAWSA in 1913, Rankin directed a suffrage victory in North Dakota that year. She quit NAWSA in 1914 to return to Montana to fight for suffrage there. In November 1914, Montana granted women the right to vote.

After a trip to New Zealand, Rankin returned to run for one of Montana's two at-large congressional seats, to "repay the women of Montana who had worked for suffrage." Rankin's brother, Wellington, managed her campaign; running as a Republican, she won in November.

The first woman in Congress, Jeannette Rankin took her seat in the emergency session of the Sixty-fifth Congress called by President Woodrow Wilson on Apr. 2, 1917. She was naturally the object of nationwide curiosity. That Rankin was young and attractive belied the stereotype of suffragettes as old and severe and made her somewhat more palatable to audiences.

Women's groups lobbied Rankin immediately about her position on American involvement in the war in Europe. Her position as a "woman's representative" made this a delicate matter. Carrie Chapman Catt of NAWSA worried that an antiwar vote would make women seem unpatriotic. Alice Paul of the Woman's Party, on the other hand, thought that women should stand for peace. In the end, Rankin, although not having identified herself as a pacifist, announced that she could not vote for the war, a position in which she was joined by forty-nine other representatives when the resolution came before the House on Apr. 6, 1917.

Rankin was the ranking minority member of a special committee to draft a woman's suffrage amendment (which was not passed by the Senate until the Sixty-sixth Congress). She sponsored the Robertson-Rankin bill to establish a women's health education program; it later passed as the Sheppard-Towner Act (1921). During the Anaconda Copper Company conflict, she presented the demands of the International Workers of the World to the federal government, because Anaconda was located in Butte, Mont., and she viewed the company and its workers as her responsibility. In 1917, Rankin exposed the Bureau of Printing and Engraving's abuse of its workers in defiance of eight-hour workday rules. Except for the 1917 Espionage Act, Rankin supported the Wilson administration in its prosecution of the war.

The "Lady from Montana" (a title she despised, preferring "Woman from Montana") was immensely popular. She wrote a weekly column for the *Chicago Sunday-Herald* and received bags full of mail.

By the time Rankin was up for reelection in 1918, Montana had been split into two geographically defined congressional districts. Looking again for a statewide platform, Rankin ran for the Senate. She lost the Republican primary and again in November, running on the National party (a reform coalition) ticket.

Rankin devoted herself to the pacifist cause, working with the Women's International League for Peace and Freedom, which she helped found in 1919. In November 1920 she became a field secretary for National Consumers' League. Rankin spent four years speaking on women's and children legislation around the United States. In 1924 she worked on Wellington's unsuccessful bid for the Senate.

Late in 1924 Rankin bought a small house and sixty-four-acre farm in Bogart, Ga., near Athens, where she lived modestly. Her new

home was near the University of Georgia, affording her intellectual stimulation. In 1928 she and Lucy Stanton founded the Georgia Peace Society. Rankin also served as a Georgia field representative for the National Council for the Prevention of War from 1929 to 1939. She testified in Congress against munitions allocations throughout the 1930's. Also during that time, Rankin campaigned unsuccessfully against Representative Carl Vinson, chairman of the House Naval Affairs Committee.

The rumblings of World War II brought Rankin back to Montana, which was still her legal residence. Alarmed by the likelihood of America's entry into the conflict, she began a campaign for Congress in the spring of 1940 as an isolationist Republican. Receiving support from other well-known pacifists like Bruce Barton, and Senator Robert La Follette, Jr., she defeated Democrat Jerry O'Connell and entered the Seventy-seventh Congress on Jan. 3, 1941. On Dec. 8, 1941, Speaker Sam Rayburn refused to let Rankin speak against war, and she was jeered as she cast the lone congressional vote against the declaration of war against Japan. Her stand cost her her political effectiveness and ended her electoral career.

After her term expired, Rankin divided her time between Montana and Georgia. She visited India in 1946, in 1949, and through the 1950's in order to study Mohandas Gandhi's approach to nonviolent resistance. Rankin also traveled to Indonesia, South America, Russia, Turkey, and Ireland. At age 88, she led the Jeannette Rankin Brigade, a women's coalition, on an anti–Vietnam War march in Washington, D.C., on Jan. 15, 1968. In 1972, Rankin was named the first member of the Susan B. Anthony Hall of Fame. During the early 1970's, Rankin promoted peace, electoral reform, and women's rights through television, newspaper, and magazine interviews.

Independent and idealistic, Rankin never married. She died in Carmel, Calif.

[The Arthur and Elizabeth Schlesinger Library, Harvard University, has a Jeannette Rankin Collection. Kevin S. Giles, *Flight of the Dove* (1980), is a somewhat incoherent and laudatory but detailed biography. An obituary is in the *New York Times*, May 20, 1973.]

ALANA J. ERICKSON

RANSOM, JOHN CROWE (Apr. 30, 1888– July 3, 1974), poet and literary critic, was born in Pulaski, Tenn., to Ella Crowe, a former music and French teacher, and John James Ransom, a Methodist minister. Because the Methodist Conference requires its pastors to relocate periodically, the Ransoms elected to educate their children at home until the Reverend Dr. Ransom was moved to Nashville, where John and his siblings were enrolled in public school.

The intellectually stimulating home environment and John's precociousness led to much shifting of grade levels until, at the age of ten, John was placed in the eighth grade. At the end of a year, the elder Ransom was persuaded to enroll his son at one of the reputable private academies nearby, which would ensure John's readiness to begin the classically oriented curriculum of Vanderbilt University. Shortly before his graduation in May 1903 from the Bowen School, John scored highest on five of the demanding entrance exams offered by Vanderbilt. Even though at fifteen he was a full year below the official minimum age for admission into the college, he was accepted on the basis of his performance. After two years he withdrew for financial reasons and taught from 1905 to 1907 in secondary schools. He returned to Vanderbilt to complete the B.A., graduating Phi Beta Kappa and first in his class in 1909.

Ransom taught in a preparatory school for a year before accepting a Rhodes Scholarship to Christ Church College, Oxford. There he studied Greek and Latin literature, history, and philosophy in the original languages, earning a B.A. in 1913, after which he taught Latin and Greek for one year at the Hotchkiss School in Lakeville, Conn. He taught English at Harvard University for part of 1914 before taking an instructorship in the English Department at Vanderbilt. Apart from a stint in the U.S. Army (1917–1919), a brief attendance at the University of Grenoble after World War I, and a short-lived attempt to enter the world of publishing and free-lance journalism in New York City, Ransom spent the early part of his career at Vanderbilt University, where he was professor of English from 1927 to 1937.

Around 1915, the year following Ransom's return to Vanderbilt, a group of students, faculty, and community members, including Donald Davidson, Walter Clyde Curry, and Ransom, began meeting informally to discuss trends in American life and letters. Calling themselves the Fugitives, they opposed both what they viewed as the traditional sentimentality of southern literature and the increasingly frantic pace of southern living, as agriculture gave way to industrialism and the turbulent war years gave way to the Roaring Twenties. These meetings were a milestone in Ransom's career; a year after their inception, he surprised Davidson with a poem, his first and the only one he would publish in free verse. His preference for literary form, especially meter, would be explained in his first book of literary criticism, *The World's Body* (1938), as a means by which the poet could restrain himself and maintain aesthetic distance.

Continuing to write while serving as a cadet in the First Officers Training Camp at Fort Oglethorpe, Ga., and as an officer in France in World War I, Ransom completed enough poems for a book. *Poems About God* appeared in 1919, two years after he went overseas in August 1917, and saw active duty in France, attaining the rank of first lieutenant with the Fifth Field Artillery. Taking as its subject a young man expressing his reverence, wonder, and concern for God's manifestations in the world, the collection met with widespread favorable reviews. Ransom, however, became disaffected with this early work, not so much because it presented the young poet's pessimistic "case about God" but because the poems relied heavily on content and argument and not enough on what Ransom would later call the "texture of language." Unlike his subsequent poems, which are rich with figurative language, paradox, and irony, Ransom felt that the early poems contained pat answers to the problems and tensions of modern life. Like the poems written in what Allen Tate calls Ransom's "mature manner," however, the youthful poems are fables, anecdotes, or simple narratives that depict a world of fundamental opposites including the divided sensibility, the modern schism between reason and imagination and between science and faith. Like their successors, they are obsessed with mutability, decay, and death, and with the disparity between expectation and reality. The poems are unmistakably southern in character and setting, reflecting the Middle Tennessee region of Ransom's childhood. They can best be described as debates between the head and the heart, between reason and emotion, as Ransom seeks to create with stylistics a balance and a detachment. While his poetic forms indicate an affinity with tradition, his use of tension and paradox and of wit and irony, label him a distinctly modern poet.

Not only was that period important to the development of Ransom's poetic theories, it was also significant to him personally. Early in January 1920 he met Robb Reavil of Colorado, a student at Wellesley College. They were married in December of that year. The two had three children and remained together until Ransom's death more than fifty years later.

Although Ransom resumed his participation with the Fugitives upon his return to Vanderbilt, the focus of the meetings shifted under his growing leadership from politics to poetics. The group began publishing a literary journal, the *Fugitive*, which contained verse and brief critical commentary and appeared in nineteen issues from 1922 to 1925. The magazine ushered in a new literary movement (Agrarianism), announced a new critical theory (the New Criticism), and introduced to southern poetry the modernism of T. S. Eliot and Ezra Pound.

Most of Ransom's best poems were published in the period 1916–1927. He was constantly "tinkering," sending revisions along with new pieces to Robert Graves. After Holt rejected one poem of the collection, it was Graves who, with the help of T. S. Eliot, located an English publisher, Hogarth, to bring out the collection, *Grace after Meat*, in November 1924. Alfred A. Knopf had published *Chills and Fever* the previous August. Both books were well received, as was his last book of original verse, *Two Gentlemen in Bonds*, published in 1927. Ransom received several prestigious awards for poetry, including a Guggenheim Fellowship (1931), the Bollingen and Russell Loines Prizes (1951), an Academy of American Poets Fellowship (1962), and a National Book Award for *Selected Poems* (1964).

The late 1920's and 1930's marked a change in the direction of Ransom's career. While the Fugitives disbanded in 1925, the group came together again in the late 1920's to affirm the virtues of the rural South, asserting that the arts thrived best in an agrarian as opposed to industrial economy. The Agrarians' dream of the complete self, achieved by a balance of reason and emotion and embodied in the mannered life of the antebellum plantation, dissolved with the Great Depression; however, Ransom's influence continued to be felt as the group's focus changed once again with the nature of his interests, from poetics to critical theory. The New

Criticism, developed by Ransom and others in the 1930's, rejected the romanticists' belief in self-expression and perfectibility as well as the naturalists' emphasis on fact. Instead, the New Critics insisted that the work of art be evaluated as an object in and of itself, independent of outside influences such as authorial intention, reader response, circumstances of composition, or historical context; they rejected the study of plot, character, and genre in favor of a detailed analysis of the nuances of language.

Moving to Kenyon College in 1937 as the Carnegie Professor of Poetry, Ransom founded the *Kenyon Review* in 1939, propounding as its editor for twenty years that literature is a means of cognition. In various essays as well as published books, Ransom argued that the only way in which the first moment of experience can be reconstituted in all its wholeness is through art, dreams, or religious myth. Science or social science records the "second moment," concepts or abstract ideas derived by focusing on only one aspect of the whole. As an alternative to science, true poetry makes no attempt to perfect or abstract the world, but, with aesthetic distance, to realize the world by recovering the concrete particularities that make up the whole. Ransom remained consistent for fifty years to the principle that scientific and aesthetic knowledge are intended to illuminate and complement one another. He became professor emeritus at Kenyon College in 1958, after which he taught and lectured at more than two hundred colleges and universities. He died in Gambier, Ohio.

While scholars continue to debate whether Ransom will be remembered as poet or critic in years to come, certainly any final estimate of his contributions must begin with his poetry since his criticism is ultimately derived from it. While he published fewer than 160 poems, given the restrictions he placed upon himself in theme and form, his achievements are impressive. He conveys the dichotomies of the modern sensibility and captures the dualities of modern poetry. However, as George Core, editor of another southern magazine, observes, Ransom's essential reputation for both criticism and poetry is sound. Ransom will remain a distinguished minor poet who theorized upon his work to become one of the deans of twentieth-century American letters.

[Collections of Ransom's papers are at the libraries of Vanderbilt University and Kenyon College as well as Yale, Princeton, Stanford, Indiana, and Washington Universities. Correspondence is contained in the *Selected Letters of John Crowe Ransom*, edited by Thomas Daniel Young and George Core (1985). Ransom's other major publications include the essay collections *God without Thunder* (1930); *I'll Take My Stand*, with eleven southern literary theorists (1930); *The New Criticism* (1941); *Poetics* (1942); *Poems and Essays* (1955); *American Poetry at Mid-Century*, a book of lectures with Delmore Schwartz and John Hall Wheelock (1958); *Beating the Bushes* (1972); and *Selected Essays of John Crowe Ransom* (1984).

Thomas Daniel Young has written an extensive biography of Ransom, *Gentleman in a Dustcoat* (1976), as well as edited an overview of Ransom criticism, *John Crowe Ransom: An Annotated Bibliography* (1982). Other useful references are Robert Bullington, *The Equilibrist* (1967); Thomas Daniel Young, ed., *John Crowe Ransom: Critical Essays and a Bibliography* (1968); Thornton H. Parsons, *John Crowe Ransom* (1969); James E. Magner, Jr., *John Crowe Ransom* (1971); Thomas Daniel Young, *John Crowe Ransom* (1971); and Richard Gray, *The Literature of Memory: Modern Writers of the American South* (1978). Obituaries are in the *New York Times*, July 4, 1974; the *Washington Post*, July 5, 1974; *Newsweek*, July 15, 1974; *Time*, July 15, 1974; *Publishers Weekly*, July 29, 1974; and *Antiquarian Bookman*, Oct. 14, 1974.]

SUSAN NEAL MAYBERRY

RAZAF, ANDY (Dec. 16, 1895–Feb. 3, 1973), lyricist and composer, was born Andrea Paul Razafkeriefo in Washington, D.C., the only child of Henri Razafkeriefo and Jennie Maria Waller. His father, a nephew of Queen Ranavalona III of Madagascar, was a military officer apparently killed in the French takeover of the island in 1895. His mother was the eldest daughter of John Waller, American consul to Madagascar. He and his mother lived with his grandfather's family in Baltimore, Kansas City, Cuba, and New York City. There, he dropped out of school at the age of sixteen, despite the fact that he was an eager reader and a promising student.

His skills as a lyricist, and as an occasional composer and performer, developed around the age of thirteen under the influence of a literate and articulate family: John Waller was a compelling orator, Jennie Razaf a poet, and Aunt Minnie Waller a songwriter and singer.

Razaf worked for a while as an elevator operator on Tin Pan Alley (Manhattan's music district), and made his first sale in 1913, a song entitled "Baltimo" for the revue *The Passing Show of 1913*. While struggling to establish himself as a songwriter, he worked as a telephone operator, a cleaner, a butler, a custodian, and a semi-pro baseball player. He married Annabelle Miller in April 1915. At the same time, he was contributing socially and politically progressive poems to various African-American publications such as the *Emancipator* and the *Crusader*.

With the growing popularity of blues and jazz in New York City, Razaf ultimately collaborated with a number of great black musicians, including J. C. Johnson, James P. Johnson, Eubie Blake, and Thomas ("Fats") Waller. Although he never won the acclaim or wealth that a white lyricist of his talent would have, Razaf wrote and sold a number of popular and enduring songs: "My Special Friend" (1927), "My Handy Man" (1928), "S'posin' " (1929), "Ain't Misbehavin' " (1929), "Honeysuckle Rose" (1929), "Blue Turning Grey Over You" (1929), and "Black and Blue" (1929)—the last considered the first African-American "racial protest song." In December 1929, Razaf was made an active member of the American Society of Composers, Authors and Publishers.

Razaf began the 1930's by collaborating with James P. Johnson on *A Kitchen Mechanic's Revue* for Ed Small's Paradise Club, which featured the clever parody "A Porter's Love Song to a Chambermaid." His collaboration with Eubie Blake on the 1930 version of Lew Leslie's *Blackbirds* brought forth "You're Lucky to Me" and "Memories of You." Both songs were written for Minto Cato, Razaf's lover and a star of the show. However, the 1930 *Blackbirds* folded shortly after opening in New York. The rest of the decade saw Razaf produce music and such great lyrics as "Keepin' Out of Mischief Now" (1933), "That's What I Like 'Bout the South" (1933), "Christopher Columbus" (1936), "Stompin' at the Savoy" (1936), "The Joint Is Jumpin' " (1937), and "In the Mood" (1939), a song for which he was paid a flat $200.

Razaf finally divorced his first wife, whom he had abandoned years before, and on July 31, 1939, married Jean Blackwell, a librarian at the Harlem branch of the New York Public Library. The couple moved to suburban Englewood, N.J., in the spring of 1940.

Razaf's career as a songwriter was already in decline by 1940 when the film *Tin Pan Alley* depicted two white criminals writing "Honeysuckle Rose" in prison. Razaf and Waller had received a small payment for the use of their song, but Razaf wrote a strong letter of complaint to Twentieth Century–Fox. The film company's lawyers published both Razaf's letter and their snide, racist response in *Variety*'s Feb. 5, 1941, issue.

Meanwhile Razaf and Eubie Blake had been working on the musical comedy *Tan Manhattan*, the original score of which contained a militant lyric sure to offend the white audience the show would need to make it to Broadway. After both Blake and producer Irvin C. Miller failed to talk Razaf out of including the song, Jean Razaf succeeded in getting her husband to rewrite it as "We Are Americans Too," a tribute to patriotic African Americans. Predictably, the show was not a success: it opened on Jan. 24, 1941, in Washington, D.C., and closed after a short run at Harlem's Apollo Theater in February.

The 1940's were difficult for Razaf. Although he wrote some War Bond songs, including a resurrected "We Are Americans Too," he failed to win a seat on the Englewood City Council. He ran for office out of sincere social conviction and, perhaps, professional desperation. However, the election was shaded by evidence of the tampering with registration records and polling booths, lost registration records, and a jammed key over candidate Razaf's name in one machine. Having been divorced by Jean Blackwell after less than eight years of marriage, Razaf was married on July 16, 1948, to Dorothy Carpenter, his mother's longtime choice for daughter-in-law.

Razaf lived for the next twenty-five years in Los Angeles, where, on Jan. 26, 1951, he became paralyzed with tertiary syphilis. He continued to work on his songs, poetry, and journalism when his pain did not prohibit it. There were some high notes. Razaf and Blake's "Memories of You" was revived as the theme of *The Benny Goodman Story* (1956), and Leonard Feather, a well-known jazz critic, compiled an album of Razaf songs. Razaf divorced Dorothy Carpenter in the late 1950's, and then, on Valentine's Day, 1963, married Alice Wilson, whom he had renamed Alicia when they first met in Chicago in 1934. Alicia Razaf took care of her husband for nearly ten years and accompanied him to New York in 1972 for his induction into the Songwriters Hall of Fame, nine months befire he died in North Hollywood. He had no children from any of his marriages.

Razaf was a poet whose song lyrics often reveal concern with social and racial injustice. He was a master of the early "black" music that white audiences demanded in the 1910's and 1920's, but he moved beyond such music with ease and grace. He worked all his life to earn the respect of the white-dominated entertainment industry, and he sold hundreds of songs. Most of them have been forgotten, but he was revered by many of the great black musicians of the century. One has only to listen to recordings of his songs by Fats Waller and Louis Armstrong to sense the greatness of Andy Razaf as a lyricist.

[Razaf contributed memorabilia to the New York Public Library's Schomburg Center for Research in Black Culture. See Barry Singer, *Black and Blue: The Life and Lyrics of Andy Razaf* (1992). An obituary is in the *New York Times*, Feb. 5, 1973.]

PETER P. CLARKE

REEVES, DANIEL F. (June 30, 1912–Apr. 15, 1971), sports entrepreneur, was born in New York City, the son of James Reeves and Rose M. Farrell. The elder Reeves and his brother Daniel, Irish immigrants, worked their way from fruit peddlers to ownership of a major grocery store chain.

Reeves was captain of the football team at the Newman School in Lakewood, N.J., but his outstanding skill and driving desire were executive. He once said to a friend, "Isn't it the dream of *every* American boy to own a football team?" Newman awarded Reeves its General Excellence Medal at his graduation in June 1930.

Reeves entered Georgetown University in 1930 but did not complete his degree. Through a college classmate he met Mary V. Corroon, whom he married on Oct. 25, 1935; they had six children.

After leaving Georgetown, Reeves worked in the family business until the firm merged with Safeway Stores in 1941. That same year he sought to fulfill his life's ambition by casting about for a major league football team to purchase. After unsuccessful negotiations with the Pittsburgh Steelers and Philadelphia Eagles, he joined the National Football League's (NFL) hierarchy at age twenty-eight, when he obtained two-thirds of the four-year-old Cleveland Rams franchise. Later in 1941, he added to his sports holdings with the purchase of the Jersey City

Giants of the American Professional Football Association.

During World War II, Reeves was commissioned a second lieutenant in the Army Air Corps in 1942. Accompanied by his family, he served at upstate New York bases for the duration. In 1943, he became a member of the New York Stock Exchange through the firm of Adler, Coleman and Co. Ultimately promoted to captain, he returned to civilian life in 1945, just in time to see the Rams capture the NFL championship.

Reeves earned his reputation as a sports innovator in 1946, when he shifted the Rams franchise from Cleveland to Los Angeles, the first major league team of any sport to move to the West Coast. It was a financial risk with no guarantees. The fact that a decade passed before any other owners followed Reeves's lead underscores his unusual combination of a gambler's instinct with foresight and sound business acumen.

The NFL had a handful of black players before the war, but it was Reeves's 1946 hiring of the great UCLA halfback, Kenny Washington, that truly lowered the color bar for all professional sports. This step toward sports integration took place a year before baseball's Brooklyn Dodgers brought another great UCLA black player, Jackie Robinson, up from the International League.

One of Reeves's early California moves illustrates his innate marketing sense. With an eye to future turnstile counts, he introduced the "Free Football for Kids" program, which enabled two generations of youngsters to enjoy the team's home games. Also, using his capability for spotting talent, Reeves hired Pete Rozelle as the publicity director for the Rams. Rozelle became his protégé and took over as NFL commissioner at the age of thirty-three.

Reeves did not ignore the financial world. On Nov. 1, 1946, the board of governors of the New York Stock Exchange approved a new member firm, Daniel Reeves & Co., with offices in Beverly Hills and New York City. The firm's partners were Reeves, Charles T. Jawetz, and Thomas Cerny. When the pressure of directing his football franchise became too demanding, Reeves transferred his seat to L. Morton Stern, a New York member of Reeves & Co., on Aug. 21, 1947.

Within professional football's technical framework, Reeves's most important contribution was the organization of a scouting network for the evaluation of college players. Every other NFL team copied the idea, and it became an integral part of the game.

The Rams ran up enormous deficits in their first three years. The $250,000 loss for 1948 prompted Reeves to take in partners. The new investors included Edwin Pauley, Fred Levy, Hal Seley, and Bob Hope. With fresh capital underwriting increased operating and promotional progress, the Rams began playing before crowds of eighty thousand in the Los Angeles Coliseum. They had the NFL's first 100,000-spectator game, and set an attendance record by drawing 102,368 fans for a game with the San Francisco 49ers. The Rams' western rebirth culminated with the 1951 NFL championship, their first since leaving Cleveland.

Reeves and Pauley each owned one-third of the team. By 1956 their relationship had developed such an animus, however, that it was clear one or the other would have to go. The feud became so intense that Bert Bell, the NFL commissioner, appointed Rozelle general manager to run the team in place of the embattled owners. Peace came in December 1962, when Reeves bought out the others for $4.8 million. He put up $1 million himself, brought in seven new partners, and borrowed additional funds to raise the balance.

Following the 1951 championship, the team's fortunes steadily declined, largely owing to the owners' strife. Despite his much-publicized partnership problems, Reeves's most famous altercation during his thirty years in football took place with the irrepressible George Allen. Seven consecutive losing seasons led Reeves to hire the flamboyant former assistant for the Rams as head coach in 1966 (one of ten he employed during his ownership). Although Allen made the Rams winners for the first time in years, Reeves disapproved of his methods, which included hiring players without consulting Reeves, spying on other teams, and criticizing opponents on the playing field after a defeat. As a result, Reeves fired Allen on the day after Christmas 1968, then rehired him when Rams fans vehemently protested and the players threatened to strike. Reeves again fired Allen two years later when his contract expired.

Another source of strife in the 1960's was the bitter warfare between the NFL and AFL before they merged during the period 1966–1967. Throughout this era, Reeves was a recognized leader among NFL owners. In the meetings that finally led to unification, Reeves's general manager, "Tex" Schramm, negotiated on behalf of the NFL.

Reeves defined his formula for success: "There are only two things necessary. First you get the best players. Then you get the coach who can get the best out of them." The NFL honored Reeves's sagacity by inducting him into its Hall of Fame in Canton, Ohio, in 1967.

Reeves died in New York City of Hodgkins's disease at age 58.

[See *Jersey Journal*, Aug. 21, Sept. 9, and Sept. 27, 1941; *Time*, Jan. 17, 1969; *Los Angeles Times*, Feb. 13, 1971; and the *Washington Post*, Feb. 15, 1971. Obituaries are in the *New York Times*, Apr. 16, 1971; the *Washington Post*, Apr. 16, 1971; *Newsweek*, Apr. 26, 1971; and *Time*, Apr. 26, 1971.]

W. M. P. DUNNE

RENNIE, MICHAEL (Aug. 25, 1909–June 10, 1971), actor, was born in Bradford, Yorkshire, England, the son of James Rennie and Edith White. He had two brothers and a sister. He was educated at Oatlands Preparatory School in Harrogate and entered Leys College, Cambridge University, in 1927. There he won prizes for rowing, swimming, boxing, wrestling, fencing, and cricket. He graduated from Cambridge with a B.A. in 1931 and worked briefly at British Ropes, his uncle's steel rope factory. He then worked as an automobile salesman, also without success. In his third and final attempt at the business world, he worked for a brief period in his parents' wool business, which had been in family hands for 150 years.

Bitten by the acting bug unexpectedly in 1935, he hitchhiked to London with little money in his pocket and took a job at Gaumont-British film studios. Lacking any acting experience, Rennie worked for a year on both sides of the camera for minimal compensation. Recognizing his limitations, he abandoned film to join the Yorkshire stock company, where he honed his talents with classical theater training. In 1938, Rennie starred as Professor Henry Higgins in the York Repertory Company's production of *Pygmalion* at Wakefield.

Rennie went back in front of the cameras in the movie *Bank Holiday* (1938). After England entered World War II, he performed in a number of patriotic potboilers, including *Ships with Wings* and *Suicide Squadron* (both 1942). He joined the Royal Air Force as a flying officer in 1943 and went on to train American pilots in Georgia and Florida. He was invalided out of the service in 1944 and returned to making films in England. His first starring roles were in *I'll Be Your Sweetheart* (1945) and *The Wicked Lady* (1945), both opposite Margaret Lockwood. Soon his fan mail was running toward four thousand letters per week. He was signed by producer Maurice Ostrer to a five-year contract for £300,000, then the biggest contract ever offered to a British film actor.

Rennie looked like a movie star. Despite his provincial background, he had a "mid-Atlantic" accent and did not sound as distinctly "English" as many British actors. Fellow RAF officers thought he was Canadian. At six feet, four inches in height (which reportedly made him the tallest man in British film), a lean 185 pounds, and with piercing green eyes and an insolent hawklike face, the Yorkshireman radiated smooth confidence, sophisticated charm, effortless grace, and strength. Oddly enough, he never played a traditional romantic lead in his long Hollywood career.

On Oct. 1, 1946, he married actress Margaret McGrath; they had one son. But their marriage was strained by the fact that he adored Hollywood and she detested it. They separated in 1955 and were divorced in 1960.

In 1950, Rennie got a contract with Twentieth Century–Fox and moved to Hollywood. He starred in the cult classic *The Day the Earth Stood Still* (1951). His highly acclaimed portrayal of a sympathetic extraterrestrial bent on saving mankind from the follies of nuclear war inverted most of the myths of the 1950's science fiction genre and won him legions of fans. He went on to play memorable roles in *Les Misérables* (1952), *The Robe* (1953), *King of the Khyber Rifles* (1953), and *The Lost World* (1960), among others.

One role that he did not enjoy was that of corespondent in Otto Preminger's 1958 divorce from former model Mary Gardner. Rennie, who had an enviable reputation for dating Hollywood starlets, claimed that he and Gardner were not romantically involved. However, four years later they married. They had no children and later divorced.

Altogether, Rennie appeared in almost one hundred motion pictures. However, his greatest success, which made him a household name, was in playing debonair international financier and amateur detective Harry Lime in "The

Third Man." The Anglo-American production was broadcast on both NBC and the BBC from 1959 to 1962. One of the most popular television series ever made, it bore no relation to the Graham Greene–Carol Reed film on which it was supposedly based.

Rennie became an American citizen in 1960 and offended British propriety by criticizing his native land. He said his countrymen were brought up "almost brainwashed—with the idea that England is the only place in the world and the only thing to be is an Englishman." In 1961, he made his debut on the Broadway stage in the comedy *Mary, Mary*, by Jean Kerr.

Although in his later years he accepted roles in films of dubious quality, such as *The Missile from Hell* (1960), *Cyborg 2087* (1966), and *Assignment Terror* (1970), they complemented critically successful films such as *Hotel* (1967) and *The Devil's Brigade* (1968). Regardless of any one film's quality, his performance in it was invariably superlative. Suffering from emphysema, he died of a heart attack while visiting his mother in London in 1971.

[Biographical material on Rennie is scarce. Obituaries are in *Variety* and the *New York Times*, both June 11, 1971.]

DAVID M. ESPOSITO

REVSON, CHARLES HASKELL (Oct. 11, 1906–Aug. 24, 1975), founder and chief executive officer of Revlon, was born in Somerville, Mass., the second of three children of Jeanette Weiss and Samuel Morris Revson. His father was a cigar roller for the R. G. Sullivan Company in Manchester, N.H., where Charles and his two brothers were raised. Revson graduated from Manchester High School in 1923.

Revson's first job was as a salesman for the Pickwick Dress Company in New York City, owned by a cousin. His early interest in materials and colors derived from this experience. He was fired in 1930, however, because he had overstocked a pattern he favored.

Revson then went to Chicago, where he sold sales-motivation materials. Sales were not good, and within nine months he was back in New York City. He moved in with his family in Manhattan, as he was employed by the Elka Company, located in Newark, N.J., as a salesman of nail polish for the greater New York area. His brother Joseph, who had been working for the General Motors plant in Tarrytown, N.Y., also went to work for Elka. Both men used office space in a cousin's lamp factory at 38 West Twenty-first Street in Manhattan. When they wanted to expand their territory beyond the New York City area and Elka refused, Revson decided they would start their own business. He had consulted with beauty parlor operators about the performance of the nail enamel produced by Elka, and by applying polish to his own nails, he had learned which texture, colors, and luster were desirable.

In March 1932, Revson founded Revlon with his brother Joseph and Charles Lachman, who was affiliated with Dresden Chemical Company, a company in New Rochelle, N.Y., that made polish for other firms to sell. The three men pooled their savings, $300, and Lachman secured a credit line with Dresden for their nail enamel. The company name was formed from "Revson" and the L in Lachman (the first name proposed, Revlac, was not deemed euphonious). The business was sustained during the first year by borrowing money at 2 percent interest per month from loan sharks. Dr. Taylor Sherwood, a chemist for Dresden, manufactured the enamel to Revson's specifications: opaque, lustrous, and nonstreaking. The first major sales order was for $400, from Marshall Field's beauty salon in 1934, when the business was conducted from a room that cost $25 per month, at 15 West Forty-fourth Street in Manhattan. Charles was the salesman, and Joseph took charge of the office and finances. Except for the initial investment and his connection to Dresden Chemical, Lachman had no active role in the company.

Despite the Great Depression, the business grew because beauty salons were its major clients.

In 1936, Revlon moved to 125 West Forty-fifth Street, occupying half a floor. The next year sales expanded to department and drug stores, and the firm required five floors. In 1938, the business relocated to 525 West Fifty-second Street, where the operation was automated.

In 1939, when lipstick was added to the product line, sales doubled and the phrase "matching lips and fingertips" established the trend of coordinating polishes and lipsticks. Magazines, in color for the first time, enabled promotion of new and more varied colors. Revson recognized the need to use catchy names and sexy images to promote sales. By 1941, Revlon was selling to

100,000 beauty salons. Charles was the primary salesman, the developer of new ideas for products, and the approver of all advertising.

The "Fire and Ice" advertising campaign in 1951 furthered Revlon's position in the cosmetics field. It featured a seductive model and the caption, "Are you made for Fire and Ice?" But the real takeoff for Revlon was the sponsorship of the television quiz show "The $64,000 Question," approved by Charles in 1955. He presented the first check to the winner. Sales quickly increased by 54 percent, and the Revlon image was not adversely affected by the later revelation that the show was rigged. The success enabled Charles to take the company public that year at $12 per share, and in three months it rose to $30. Joseph left the company before the public offering because he was against such a move. Charles also wanted his partners to assign him exclusive voting rights. Joseph refused and was bought out for $2.5 million. Charles Revson, another brother, Martin, and Charles Lachman sold 101,833 shares as part of the initial offering. Martin resigned in 1958, and sued Charles for fraud, misrepresentation, and breach of agreement on the stock sale. The suit was settled out of court for $300,000, about half of what Martin sought.

Although Revson was soft-spoken and often inarticulate at meetings, he was very tough and even crude with his personnel. According to one executive he called a meeting at 6 P.M. on the Friday of the July 4 weekend, then showed up at 8 P.M., late as usual, to discuss the problem of personnel turnover. His desire for perfection caused Revson to institute quality control and product recall some thirty years before they became common practices. He also introduced the notion of product obsolescence to Revlon's marketing strategy by featuring seasonal colors.

During World War II, Revson was exempted from military service because he established Vorset Corporation in Oxford, N.J., which assembled first-aid kits and produced dye markers for the navy and hand grenades for the army. These government contracts were obtained by the firm's security officer, Mickey Soroko. The government connections enabled Revson to develop Revlon during the war years. In fact, further expansion caused Revlon to move to the Squibb Building, 745 Fifth Avenue.

Revson introduced different lines, such as Ultima II, Marcella Borghese, and Moon Drops, to appeal to different markets. His model for this approach was General Motors, which was organized by divisions.

In 1966, Revson diversified Revlon by acquiring a profitable pharmaceutical company, paying $67.5 million in stock for the United States Vitamin and Pharmaceutical Corporation (USV). In 1971, an agreement with Ciba-Geigy gave USV marketing rights, patents, and trademarks for four widely used drugs and marketing rights to thirteen others. By 1975, 23 percent of Revlon sales and 28 percent of its profits were from health products. By 1974, Revlon was manufacturing over 3,500 items and selling them in 85 countries. Sales totaled $605 million, with net earnings of $49.8 million. Revlon's five-year ownership of Evan-Picone, however, was not successful; it resulted in a loss of $1.75 million at its sale in 1966.

Despite some setbacks, Revson took a business worth $4,000 in 1932 to $605 million in 1974, when he named his successor, Michael G. Bergerac. At his death, Revson's interest in Revlon was only 10 percent because his lavish life-style had caused him to sell his shares from time to time. They were worth about $95 million, and his estate was valued at $100 million. This included his yacht, the *Ultima II*, third largest in the world at the time; his Park Avenue triplex penthouse, formerly owned by Helena Rubinstein; and a country estate at Premium Point, N.Y.

The pinnacle of Revlon's success was signaled by the firm's move to the top floor of the General Motors Building, placing Revlon symbolically above its competitors, Helena Rubinstein on the thirty-second floor, and Estée Lauder on the thirty-seventh.

Revson was married three times. He first married Ida Tompkins, a showgirl, in 1930; they were divorced within the year. On Oct. 26, 1940, he married Johanna Catharina Christina de Knecht, known as Ancky, a model. They had three children and were divorced in 1960. He married Lyn Fisher Sheresky in February 1964; they were divorced in 1974. Revson died in New York City.

[See Andrew Tobias, *Fire and Ice* (1976). An obituary is in the *New York Times*, Aug. 25, 1975.]

BARBARA GERBER

REYNOLDS, JULIAN SARGEANT (June 30, 1936–June 13, 1971), politician, was born in

New York City, the son of Richard S. Reynolds, Jr., and Virginia Sargeant. His paternal grandfather was the founder and president of the Reynolds Metals Corporation, one of the nation's largest producers of aluminum. Reynolds attended Woodberry Forest School in Orange County, Va., and then matriculated at Princeton University; after two years he transferred to the University of Pennsylvania. In 1958, he was awarded a degree in economics by the Wharton School of Finance and returned to Richmond to pursue a career in the family business.

While serving as vice-president for corporate affairs of Reynolds Metals, Reynolds became interested in higher education and soon joined the faculty of the University of Richmond. For three years, he taught economics and found he had unusual rapport with his students. In 1965, Reynolds decided to seek a seat in the Virginia House of Delegates. At the time, the city of Richmond had "floater" seats for members to be elected at large from the community; in a field of eleven candidates, Reynolds finished with thirty-two thousand votes, in second place among the elected delegates. During the campaign, he relied on students and teenage volunteers; his victory indicated a popularity that crossed party and racial lines.

Reynolds recognized the political reality of a large black electorate in Richmond and allied himself with black moderates. In 1967, Reynolds was elected to the state senate; his drawing power was proved when he received twenty-eight thousand votes and led the Democratic ticket at a time when conservative forces were still dominant in state government. During his first months in the Senate, Reynolds secured passage of a bill designed to raise housing standards in a city that was still markedly divided along racial lines. He also was a spokesman for women's rights, and appointed the first female page to serve in the Virginia General Assembly.

Reynolds had married Elizabeth Weir Veeneman in 1965; they had three children. Their marriage was failing, however, just as his political star was rising, and it ended in divorce. In 1969, he married Mary Ballou Handy; they had one child.

The political balance in Virginia was swinging toward the Republicans, but Reynolds showed unusual strength when he decided to seek the lieutenant governor's post in the 1969 race. In his campaign he eschewed professional advice and ran his own special race, designing his campaign literature and making television commercials in a garage. He wrote campaign advertisements, matched his vote-seeking devices to the colors of the Reynolds Company packaging, and used television announcements that lacked the professional touch but were appealing to a broad spectrum of voters. In conducting his statewide campaign, Reynolds stressed his independent approach to political problems, ad-libbed most of his speeches, and impressed the electorate with his energy and broad knowledge of Virginia history.

Reynolds's youthful good looks and slight build made him stand out at political gatherings, and his easygoing manner made him comfortable with older, more experienced public figures. He told audiences that he had sought a campaign contribution of $20,000 from his grandmother, and received a gift after admitting that the office he sought paid only a fraction of that amount as a salary. "I'm glad you aren't running the company," Reynolds quoted her.

Virginia voters elected a Republican as governor that November but chose Reynolds as lieutenant governor. He captured 452,000 votes and became the youngest lieutenant governor of Virginia. His rapid rise in state politics seemed to presage higher office. Newspaper commentators during the campaign had compared Reynolds's style and speaking manner with that of John F. Kennedy, and once he was elected, there was considerable speculation that he would easily become the state's governor four years thereafter. In a state where "massive resistance" to racial integration had been a test of political loyalty, Reynolds spoke for a new generation that urged compliance with court rulings on racial questions. When the Supreme Court ruled that school busing was a proper device to foster integration, Reynolds was quick to speak out for acceptance of the ruling.

Reynolds's popularity in both parties was so remarkable that the shock of his announcement in August 1970 that he was suffering from a brain tumor struck party leaders profoundly. In January 1971, while he was obviously ill and losing weight, Reynolds opened the Virginia Senate session and asked the minister who gave the invocation "to put in a good word for me." Thereafter he was seldom seen in public, but he attended an April meeting of conservative politicians at Wakefield, where his remarks drew applause, a reporter observed, from "a roll call of former leaders of 'massive resistance.' " Reynolds renewed his plea for acceptance of court rulings favoring integration, and made it clear that if his health improved, he would be leading the forces for change.

But his health worsened. Experimental treatments were tried, to no avail. The tumor was inoperable, and Reynolds died in New York City. His funeral procession was routed through the black community of Richmond.

[Memorabilia and newspaper clippings are at the J. Sargeant Reynolds Community College Library, Richmond, Va. Nancy W. Thomas, *Forever Young* (1972), includes a collection of Reynolds's remarks. See also "Remembering Sarge," *Richmond Times-Dispatch*, June 9, 1991, for an affectionate portrait of Reynolds's political career. Obituaries are in the *Richmond Times-Dispatch*, June 13, 1971, and the *New York Times*, June 14, 1971.]

ROBERT A. RUTLAND

RICCA, PAUL (July 10, 1898–Oct. 11, 1972), racketeer, was born Felice DeLucia in Naples, Italy. Little is known about his childhood. When he was seventeen Ricca killed a man who had broken off an engagement with one of his three sisters; Ricca confessed and served two years in prison. Upon his release he killed a man who had been a witness against him and eventually fled under the name Paul Ricca to the United States. He was convicted in absentia for this murder and given a twenty-one-year sentence. He arrived in the United States on Apr. 10, 1920, and eight years later became a naturalized citizen without divulging his true identity or criminal history.

Ricca earned what became his underworld nickname, "the Waiter," while working in Bella Napoli, a Chicago restaurant owned by "Diamond Joe" Esposito and frequented by mobsters. After a stint managing a theater in Chicago's Little Italy, he was hired by Al Capone, the city's most notorious gangster, as manager of Capone's World Playhouse Corporation. When Ricca married in 1927, Capone was his best man.

Capone was convicted of income-tax evasion in 1931 and, after exhausting his appeals, he was sent to a federal prison in Atlanta in 1932. However, Ricca's star continued to rise under Capone's successor, Frank Nitti. Some in the underworld preferred Ricca to Nitti; when New Yorkers "Lucky" Luciano, Meyer Lansky, and Frank Costello established their national gambling syndicate in the 1930's, they regarded Ricca as the most powerful gangster in Chicago and dealt with him as such. With Nitti's suicide in 1943, Ricca came to be universally acknowledged as top man in the Outfit, as the Mafia in Chicago was known.

As a mob boss, Ricca provided capital for criminal ventures such as loan-sharking and gambling, settled underworld disputes, and extorted payoffs from less powerful or influential mobsters. He was noted for his courtliness and impressed associates as well as law enforcers with his dignified manner, aversion for needless violence, and impeccable appearance. He had strong facial features, including a firm, square jaw. He often wore glasses and a hat that made him look like what he said he was, just another businessman. In fact, his success was reliant on the loyalty of a group of ruthless young thugs, including Sam Giancana, who became his protégé and eventually his successor.

According to former FBI agent William F. Roemer, Jr., who testified in 1983 before the Senate Permanent Subcommittee on Investigations, Ricca decreed "that no member of Chicago organized crime can have anything to do with narcotics traffic." Apart from any personal revulsion for drugs, Roemer said, Ricca knew that drug dealing alienated the mob's political contacts, who were tolerant of milder rackets such as gambling and prostitution, and exposed its members to long prison terms.

Shortly after succeeding Nitti, Ricca was imprisoned for his role in the extortion of approximately $2 million from Hollywood movie studios through the International Alliance of Theatrical and Stage Employees, which was controlled by the mob. Although Ricca continued to supervise the crime family from behind bars, Anthony Accardo became what Roemer would later call a "caretaker chieftain." He kept in touch with Ricca, once coming to visit him in prison posing as a lawyer.

Ricca had been sentenced to ten years but was released in 1947 after serving less than four. His parole became a political issue after Chicago newspapers quoted Ricca as having said that his influence extended to the White House. Ricca supposedly asked his lawyers to find out who had final say over his parole. "That man must want something," he was reported to have said. "Money, favors, a seat in the Supreme Court. Find out what he wants and get it for him." The

Chicago Tribune later accused Tom Clark, then attorney general and later a Supreme Court justice, of playing "a considerable role in releasing" Ricca and some fellow gangsters.

Following his release Ricca insulated himself from direct involvement in the Outfit's rackets, and debate raged for years over his real power in the mob. In the early 1950's it was reported to Senator Estes Kefauver's select senate committee on organized crime that Ricca was "the national head of the crime syndicate"; in 1958, a similar committee chaired by Senator John L. McClellan called Ricca one of the three top mobsters in Chicago. Ricca was forced to testify before both committees; he repeatedly invoked the Fifth Amendment protection against self-incrimination.

By the early 1960's Ricca was the Outfit's elder statesman, living quietly and luxuriously on a River Forest estate outside Chicago that included a large house, soaring shade trees, and expansive lawns. His protégé Giancana became the city's most prominent racketeer, as much for his Las Vegas contacts and romance with singer Phyllis McGuire as for his organized crimes. In her memoir of childhood, *Mafia Princess*, Giancana's daughter Antoinette recalled visits to Ricca's home, where he lived with his wife, Nancy, and their three children. He was, Giancana's daughter wrote, "the very essence of the Mafia godfather." Ricca, she wrote, "never spoke a vulgar word in my presence. . . . He just exuded propriety, respect, dignity. . . . He was the don of dons and regardless of his terrible history of criminality . . . I can speak of him only in terms of respect and love. . . . When you were in his presence, he was very European, very courteous, and always respectful no matter who you were, and he professed a deep sense of honor and tradition." Ricca spoke often of his impoverished childhood in Naples and still defended his killing in 1915 of the man he said had dishonored his sister Amelia.

In 1957 Ricca's U.S. citizenship was revoked on the grounds that he had entered the nation under a false name and without divulging his criminal record. Two years later the government began deportation proceedings, but the Italian government deemed Ricca so undesirable it refused to accept him back under any circumstances, even though he was still wanted for murder in Italy. The U.S. Immigration and Naturalization Service ordered Ricca to apply to other nations for permission to emigrate. None granted it, possibly because Ricca's applications laid out his criminal history in great detail.

Ricca was jailed for income tax evasion in 1959 and served twenty-seven months of a nine-year sentence. In 1962 Ricca paid the government $104,000 in back taxes. However, in 1965 he was indicted and tried on the same charge; he testified that his income for 1963 was $80,159 and that every penny had come from racetrack betting. The jury acquitted him.

In his later years Ricca behaved erratically, frequently visiting the terminal at O'Hare International Airport without any apparent reason for doing so. At first, federal agents suspected Ricca was conducting mob business; eventually they concluded he was senile. When he died of heart disease in Chicago, a Roman Catholic priest delivered a brief message of condolence at the funeral. "Paul DeLucia received the last rites of the Church upon his death," he told reporters. "What greater consolation can there be for a family than to know that their loved one died in the grace of God?"

[See *Testimony of the Chicago Crime Commission before the U.S. Senate Permanent Subcommittee on Investigations* (1983); Antoinette Giancana and Thomas C. Renner, *Mafia Princess* (1984); and Carl Sifakis, *The Mafia Encyclopedia* (1987). An obituary by the Associated Press appears in the *New York Times* and other newspapers, Oct. 12, 1972.]

RICK HAMPSON

RICE, EDGAR CHARLES ("SAM") (Feb. 20, 1890–Oct. 13, 1974), baseball player, was born on a farm near Morocco, Ind. His parents, Charles Rice and Louise Christine Newmyre, were farmers. By the time that young Sam was ready to begin school, the family made a fateful move a few miles across the border into Watseka, Ill. There Rice briefly attended the Rhode Island Country School in Iroquois County, Ill., but did not graduate from high school. He recalled that he did not play more than six baseball games as a child. Rice tried unsuccessfully to make the Watseka baseball team in 1912 as a right-handed pitcher.

He married Beulah Stam on Sept. 17, 1908, and they had two children. But disaster struck on Apr. 21, 1912. While he was trying out for the Central Association, his mother, two sisters, wife, and two children were killed by a tornado.

His father died, some said of grief, nine days later.

Devastated by personal tragedy and disappointed by his release from the Watseka team and by all the teams he had tried out for in the Central Association, Rice began to wander. He went to Louisville and worked as a whiskey bottler, then worked as a farmhand in the wheat fields of the Dakotas and Minnesota. He also worked as a gandy dancer or section hand on the railroad. Finally, in 1913, he ended up in Norfolk, Va., where he enlisted in the United States Navy and was assigned to the battleship *New Hampshire*. He pitched for his ship's team while they were at winter port at Guantanamo, Cuba. On Apr. 21, 1914, he was a member of the landing party that landed against hostile forces in Veracruz, Mexico, in response to the arrest of American sailors.

When the ship arrived back in port at Hampton Roads, the manager of the Petersburg team in the Virginia League offered to buy his release from the service and to pay him $135 per month. Rice accepted and had a record of nine wins and two losses in 1914. Rice also got his nickname while with the Petersburg club. In 1915, the league was about to fold and the owner of the team, Doc Lee, had an IOU with Clark Griffith, owner of the Washington Senators. Lee asked if Griffith would accept the contract of Rice to pay the debt and Griffith accepted. Rice, then twenty-five years old, arrived in Washington on August 12 and played in four games that year, his first year in the major leagues. When his sister died, he cut his season short, since it was almost over. The next year he pitched but five games, and then, disgusted after a weak hitter slammed a triple off him, he vowed never to pitch again. For a while he was used as a pinch hitter, but then he worked his way into the lineup and hit .299 in fewer than 200 times up.

By the beginning of 1917 the left and center fielders of the team were urging Griffith to use Rice as the regular right fielder. Though slight, at 5 feet 9 inches and 150 pounds, his hitting skills and speed both on the base paths and in the outfield made him a desirable player. That year Rice had 177 hits and 26 assists in the field. Neither Joe DiMaggio, Duke Snider, Mickey Mantle, nor Willie Mays ever had that many assists in a year. He also stole 35 bases and batted .302. He also struck out 41 times but would never strike out more than 26 times in a year the rest of his career.

By the end of the season Rice, knowing he would be drafted into the army because of World War I, signed on as a sergeant in the army. Playing only in seven games of the 1918 season, he spent eleven months in service, seven of them in France.

Rice returned to the Senators after the war, batting .321 in 1919. In 1920 Rice led the American League in steals and in putouts by an outfielder. The next three years established Rice's consistency at bat. From 1921 to 1923 Rice had 185, 187, and 188 hits, respectively. He tied for the league lead in triples in 1923 with 18. With the arrival of Leon ("Goose") Goslin as a regular, the Senators now had two outfielders who would become Hall of Famers. Since Goslin was such a good hitter and rarely struck out, Rice did not steal so much.

With the help of these two players, the Senators won their first American League pennant in 1924. Rice led the league in hits and at bats and had a thirty-one game hitting streak that year. Rice rarely struck out, averaging eighteen per year, rarely walked, averaging forty-six per year, and tended to be a first-pitch hitter. He also averaged 609 at bats each year, which gave him extensive opportunities for hitting. Right-fielder Rice had only mild success during the World Series, but the team won.

When the team won the pennant again in 1925, Rice set an American League record for singles (182), a mark that would last for sixty years, until Wade Boggs broke it with 187. In the 1925 World Series with the Pittsburgh Pirates, Rice became part of a controversy. Chasing a line drive from catcher Earl Smith, Rice crashed into the temporary stands in right field and fell into the seats. After a fifteen-second delay for the umpire to arrive and judge the catch, the batter was called out. Since Rice emerged from the bleachers with the ball in his glove, that was the only call the umpire could make. Owner Barney Dreyfuss and other Pirates ran onto the field to argue with the umpire. The commissioner of baseball, Judge Kenesaw Mountain Landis, called Rice into his box and asked if he had caught the ball. Rice cleverly replied, "The umpire says I did." Reports of the game say that 1,600 fans wrote affidavits about whether the catch had been made, but the split was fifty-fifty. Forty years later, Rice gave a sealed letter to the Baseball

Hall of Fame. The letter was opened after his death and in its last sentence claimed, "At no time did I lose possession of the ball."

Even though his at bats declined from 1926 through 1932, Rice maintained a .322 batting percentage, averaging 175 hits per year. In 1933 his at bats fell below 100 and his hits to 25. Almost one-third of his at bats were as a pinch hitter, thus imitating the beginning of his career. In the losing effort in the 1933 World Series, Rice pinch hit once, successfully.

He was released from Washington on Jan. 8, 1934. His fellow outfielder, Goslin, was also gone from the team, and the Senators never won another championship. Rice played one more year, with Cleveland, and batted .293. He ended his career with 2,987 hits, just thirteen under the exalted 3,000. Not much attention was paid to that number when Rice retired, but years later Clark Griffith offered Rice the chance to return to the Senators and get those thirteen hits. Rice said he was too old and refused. Rice lived comfortably, having wisely invested much of his $18,000 top annual salary.

Rice spent most of his retirement on his chicken farm in Ashton, Md. He married Mary Kendall Adams in 1959. Elected to the Hall of Fame in 1963, Rice complained that his election was long overdue, but he modified that stance on his induction day. He had averaged 192 hits per year, a remarkable feat for someone whose full-time career did not begin until he was twenty-seven years old. His skills remained virtually undiminished until he was in his midforties. Sam Rice died in Rossmor, Md., near his home.

[The library at the Baseball Hall of Fame in Cooperstown, N.Y., is the source of primary material. *The Baseball Encyclopedia*, 8th ed. (1990), is the source for statistics. A chronological recounting is given in Martin Appel and Burt Goldblatt, *Baseball's Best* (1980). An obituary is in the *New York Times* Oct. 15, 1974.]

THOMAS H. BARTHEL

RICHARDS, DICKINSON WOODRUFF (Oct. 30, 1895–Feb. 23, 1973), physician and Nobel laureate, was born in Orange, N. J., the son of Dickinson Woodruff Richards, a lawyer, and Sally Lambert. He received a classical education in English, Greek, and history at the Hotchkiss School in Lakeville, Conn., graduating in 1913. He went on to Yale University, receiving his B.A. in 1917.

Three months after graduating from Yale, he joined the United States Army, and during his two years of service he became a lieutenant and served in France with the American Expeditionary Force. Following his return to the United States, Richards entered the College of Physicians and Surgeons at Columbia University in New York City. He received his M.A. in physiology in 1922 and his M.D. in 1923. He completed his internship and residency at Presbyterian Hospital in New York City. From 1927 to 1928 he was a Columbia University research fellow at the National Institute for Medical Research in London, England, working with Sir Henry Dale, an experimental physiologist.

Upon his return from London, Dr. Richards began his teaching career as an associate in medicine at the College of Physicians and Surgeons at Columbia University and as an assistant physician at Columbia-Presbyterian Hospital Medical Center. On Sept. 19, 1931, he married Constance Burrell Riley, a Wellesley College graduate who was a research technician in his laboratory. They had four children. Richards settled down to a career as a teacher and researcher. He also began a thirty-year association with his colleague André Cournand. Cournand delineated his relationship with Richards, whom he describes as a "physiologist, physician, medical leader, historian, humanist and man," in an unpublished 1975 lecture. Richards's accomplishments in physiology and physiopathology are also described in Cournand's autobiography, *From Roots to Late Budding*.

Richards and Cournand studied the work of the German physician Werner Forssmann, who had successfully shown in 1929 that it was possible to study the heart by passing a catheter through his own arm into the right chamber of his heart. They began by working on dogs and chimpanzees, and over a fifteen-year period they perfected the techniques of cardiac catheterization and the measurement of cardiac output and blood gases, which proved to be a valuable tool in the diagnosis and treatment of cardiovascular disease. Cardiac catheterization was used by Richards during World War II when, as chairman of the National Research Council Subcommittee on Shock, he and his colleagues were asked by the government to study patients admitted to Bellevue Hospital with "battlefield shock" and measure the efficacy of digitalis and other cardiac drugs. The catheterization method was also used to diagnose so-called blue babies, to identify congenital heart lesions, and in the study of chronic pulmonary disease. In 1956, Dickinson Richards, André Cournand, and Werner Forssmann were awarded the Nobel Prize for Medicine and Physiology for their "discoveries concerning heart catheterization and pathological changes in the circulatory system."

In 1945, Richards became the head of Columbia University's First Medical Division at Bellevue Hospital, and in 1947 he was promoted to Lambert Professor of Medicine at the College of Physicians and Surgeons. He held both positions until his retirement in 1961. After his retirement from active teaching, Richards continued to lecture and to publish, particularly with regard to his personal and professional interests in the English physician and anatomist William Harvey (1578–1657) and the classical Greek physician and philosopher Hippocrates. He contributed to and coedited with Alfred P. Fishman the highly regarded book *Circulation of the Blood: Men and Ideas*, which was published in 1964 and reprinted in 1982. He also published *Medical Priesthoods and Other Essays*, which includes some of his writings on Hippocrates, in 1970.

His concerns for the proper objectives of a medical education are well expressed in the Billings Lecture, which Richards delivered at the June 1963 meeting of the American Medical Association. This lecture shows his concern for the environment, the control of diseases, and the compelling need for a humanistic approach to the practice of medicine.

Although described as shy and modest by Cournand, Richards spoke out on a number of public health issues, at times taking a different position from that of the American Medical Association. In testimony to the Joint Legislative Committee on Narcotics in 1957, Richards, as a member of the committee on drug addiction of the New York Academy of Medicine, recommended that hospital clinics should be able to distribute drugs to addicts. He also charged that Bellevue Hospital was woefully neglected by the city of New York. These charges were denied by the city and the commissioner of hospitals but were supported by the interns and resident physicians. Richards also urged a wider range of health services and benefits for the elderly. He died of a heart attack at his home in Lakeville, Conn.

[A tribute to Richards by his long-time associate André Cournand is in *Biographical Memoirs* 58 (1989), which also contains a selected bibliography from 1927 to 1972. Cournand's autobiography, *From Roots to Late Budding* (1986), contains a large section on Richards. Cournand also discussed Richards in an unpublished 1975 lecture, available at the Health Sciences Special Collections at Columbia University.

Richards's Billings Lecture to the American Medical Association was published in the *Journal of the American Medical Association*, Nov. 30, 1963. Further biographical material is contained in the 1987 *Nobel Prize Winners* biographical dictionary. An obituary is in the *New York Times*, Feb. 24, 1973.]

NANCY J. HERRINGTON

RICKARD, CLINTON (May 19, 1882–June 14, 1971), Indian tribal leader, was born on the Tuscarora Indian Reservation in Lewiston, N.Y., about twenty miles north of Buffalo. He was the third of four sons of George Rickard and Lucy Garlow, both Tuscarora Indians. The Tuscaroras are a member nation of the Six Nations Confederacy of the Iroquois.

Rickard spent his life on the Tuscarora Reservation. During his childhood his family made a meager living raising chickens and hogs, fishing and hunting, and maintaining a small family farm. George Rickard went on periodic drinking binges, during which he physically abused his wife and sons. Clinton and his brothers attended reservation schools on an irregular basis, when they could be spared from work at home. By the time he was sixteen, Rickard had acquired the equivalent of a third-grade education. He greatly revered his maternal grandmother, who taught him tribal history and instructed him in the ancient ways of the Iroquois.

In order to escape his oppressive home life, Rickard enlisted in the army in April 1901, although he was not recognized as an American citizen for more than twenty years, when passage of the Citizenship Act of 1924 enfranchised American Indians. He was sent to the Philippines as a private with the Eleventh Cavalry during the Philippine Insurrection of the Spanish-American War, and he saw action in Luzon.

Discharged in 1904, Rickard returned to New York State and obtained employment at a limestone quarry just north of the Tuscarora Reservation. He was promoted to foreman after one year and was able to purchase land on the reservation and to build his own house. Thereafter he made his living as a farmer. He married Ivy Onstott, a white woman who had been raised on the reservation, on Dec. 18, 1904. She died in February 1913, and one of the couple's two children died one month later. Rickard later credited his membership in the Freemasons, which he had joined in 1913 and in which he was active until his death, with seeing him through the crisis. In 1916, Rickard married Elizabeth Patterson, a Tuscarora; she died in 1929 after giving birth to their fourth child.

In 1920, Rickard was made a chief (one of fifteen) of the Tuscarora tribe and given the ceremonial name Rowadagahrade, or Loud Voice. Passage of the Immigration Act of 1924 galvanized him to become involved in Indian affairs outside the Tuscarora reserve. This act severely restricted the passage of Canadian Indians over the border to the United States, which particularly affected the Iroquois tribes of western New York and southern Canada, as the Iroquois had long disregarded the geographical boundaries created by whites in favor of the ancient integrity of their Indian nation.

On Dec. 1, 1926, Rickard formed the Six Nations Defense League in order to obtain border-crossing rights for Indians. He testified before Congress that the immigration law was in violation of federal treaties still in force, specifically the Jay Treaty of 1794, which guaranteed to Indians unhindered movement across the border. His campaign was ultimately successful, and the immigration law was modified to exclude Indians on Apr. 2, 1928.

The border-crossing dispute had acquainted Rickard with the intricacies of federal law, and thereafter, he became a self-taught expert on how that law pertained to North American Indians. In 1928, Rickard renamed the Six Nations Defense League the Indian Defense League of America, a watchdog group dedicated to the upholding of Indian treaty law and to the bettering of conditions of North American Indians. Rickard headed this organization, run out of his home, for more than forty years, speaking out against legal and social systems he perceived as hostile and oppressive to Indians.

The organization came to prominence in March 1930, when Rickard became involved in the trial of two Seneca women accused of killing Clothilde Marchand, the wife of Henri Marchand, an artist from Buffalo, N.Y. Rickard, disturbed by media attention centering on the alleged use of Iroquois witchcraft in the murder, brought pressure on the federal government to intercede on the women's behalf. Rickard argued that as wards of the state, Indians accused of committing crimes are entitled to representation by the United States attorney. Coverage of the trial, which lasted for more than a year and resulted in the women's acquittal, appeared on an almost daily basis in the *New York Times*.

Rickard turned the media attention he received as a result of his involvement in the Marchand case toward exposing what he saw as the flagrant inequality of reservation education. He lobbied the New York state legislature to increase the annual appropriation for Indian schools and to allow Indians to attend public high schools at the state's expense. Before 1930, Native Americans in New York State were provided with only an eighth-grade education at impoverished reservation schools. In 1931, Rickard married Beulah Mt. Pleasant, a Tuscarora Indian born and raised on the Tuscarora reserve. They had seven children.

Rickard was named president of the Chiefs' Council, the Tuscarora Nation's governing body, in 1930. Throughout the 1930's and 1940's he represented the Tuscaroras in working with the Bureau of Indian Affairs in Washington, D.C., to improve conditions on the reservation.

In March 1948, Rickard testified before the Senate Interior Subcommittee on Indian Affairs against proposed legislation to extend to the states the right to assert civil and criminal jurisdiction over Indian reservations. Implicit in this legislation, which was enacted in 1949, is the recognition that state governments supersede tribal ones. Rickard continually protested the unilateral undercutting of Native Americans' unique treaty relationship with the federal government, most notably by petitioning the United Nations between 1948 and 1952, culminating in a request that the UN admit the Six Nations Confederacy to membership.

In April 1958, Rickard and his son William organized a campaign of passive resistance against the New York State Power Authority, which was attempting to seize more than half of the Tuscarora Reservation as a reservoir for the Niagara Power Project. The Tuscaroras refused state compensation of up to $3 million, arguing that they could not sell land that was held in trust. The case was decided in the state's favor by the United States Supreme Court on Mar. 7, 1960, although a memorable dissent was issued by Justice Hugo Black, who lamented what he considered to be a breach of Indian treaty law, stating that "great nations, like great men, should keep their word."

Throughout his life Rickard spoke on the importance of preserving the ancient traditions of his ancestors. He opposed the Citizenship Act of 1924 as being a violation of Six Nations sovereignty and an attempt by the federal government to assimilate the Indian into white society. "How could these Europeans come over here and tell us we were citizens in our own country?" he wrote in his autobiography. "How can a citizen have a treaty with his own government?" A proud man with a commanding presence, while making public appearances Chief Rickard always dressed in full Indian regalia. During the last years of his life he made a number of tape recordings in Tuscaroran to preserve the tribe's history, culture, and language for future generations.

Rickard continued his work in Indian rights until his death, even though bouts of ill health restricted his activities in later years. He died in the Veterans Administration Hospital in Buffalo, N.Y., and is buried on the Tuscarora Reservation. The Indian Defense League remains active on behalf of North American Indians.

[Rickard's autobiography is *Fighting Tuscarora* (1973), edited by Barbara Graymont. For information about the political context in which he worked, see Laurence M. Hauptman, *The Iroquois Struggle for Survival* (1986). An obituary is in the *New York Times*, June 17, 1971.]

MELISSA A. DOBSON

RICKENBACKER, EDWARD VERNON ("EDDIE") (Oct. 8, 1890–July 23, 1973), fighter pilot and airline executive, was born in Columbus, Ohio. His parents, William Rickenbacher, a construction worker, and Elizabeth Basler, were Swiss immigrants. He adopted his middle name and in 1918 changed the spelling of his surname to Rickenbacker.

Rickenbacker's father was killed by an assailant in 1904. Reared in Columbus in poverty, Edward became fanatically self-reliant. Another childhood trait of constantly courting danger also endured. Quitting school in seventh grade to support his mother, he struggled through a succession of unrewarding jobs until he became

happily employed by a designer of racing cars. Moving on to the Columbus Buggy Company, he demonstrated its vehicles in other parts of the country and became a branch manager in 1910. In 1911, surgery to remove a cinder from one of his eyes left him with a permanent blank spot in his vision. Undaunted, he pursued a career as a racing driver.

After winning minor events, Rickenbacker joined the Mason Automobile Company and was victorious in a 300-mile race at Sioux City, Iowa, in 1913. Becoming a racer for the Maxwell Automobile Company, he survived numerous close calls and became famous as the "Speedy Swiss," "Big Teuton," and "Dutch Demon." He drove three times in the Indianapolis 500, and set a world speed record of 134 miles per hour at Daytona Beach, Fla. A spectacular race at Indianapolis in 1916, which he finished on his brake drums after losing his wheels, epitomized his style.

In 1916 Rickenbacker went to England to work for the Sunbeam Motor Works. Before his departure, airplane builder Glenn Martin had taken him on a flight that kindled his interest in aviation. This intensified when he met recruits of the Royal Flying Corps and veterans of aerial combat in France. Returning to the United States in 1917, he tried unsuccessfully to organize a group of racing drivers to become fighter pilots.

After the United States entered World War I, Rickenbacker became a driver on General John J. Pershing's staff and was sent to France, where his skill impressed Colonel William ("Billy") Mitchell. With Mitchell's help, he was admitted to pilot training, falsely certifying his age as twenty-five to qualify. Becoming an engineering officer, he persuaded his superiors to assign him to aerial gunnery school and joined the Ninety-fourth Aero Pursuit Squadron in March 1918 as a combat pilot. Instinctively well-suited for his new role, he downed his first German plane on April 29. By the end of May, he had scored five victories, been designated an ace, and won the croix de guerre. After hospitalization with an ear abscess, he returned to his unit, now famous as the "Hat-in-the-Ring Squadron," and became its commander. By the end of the war he had flown 134 missions and scored twenty-six official victories, making him America's "Ace of Aces." His record won him the Congressional Medal of Honor in 1931.

Returning to the United States, Rickenbacker

published a book about his wartime experiences, *Fighting the Flying Circus*. On Sept. 16, 1922, he married a Californian, Adelaide Frost Durant. They adopted two children. Aided by business associates, he developed a medium-priced, six-cylinder automobile, the Rickenbacker, advertised as "The Car Worthy of Its Name." It briefly did well, but the company failed in 1927 after introducing four-wheel brakes. Competitors claimed that these would cause accidents.

Supported by Detroit bankers, Rickenbacker bought the Indianapolis Speedway, which he modernized and administered for almost two decades. During the 1920's he promoted aviation by making demonstration flights, and he joined wartime comrade Reed Chambers in founding Florida Airways, which won an airmail contract from Miami to Jacksonville in 1926. Failing to prosper, it was sold and combined with an airmail route from New York City to Atlanta; the resulting firm became Eastern Air Transport. In 1927 Rickenbacker became a sales representative for the Cadillac division of General Motors, promoting its La-Salle automobile.

In 1929 General Motors acquired several aviation enterprises. Resigning from Cadillac, Rickenbacker moved to New York City and joined one of these, Fokker Aircraft Corporation of America, as vice-president for sales. In 1932 he left Fokker to become vice-president of American Airways, but resigned after a change of ownership and returned to General Motors in 1933. At his suggestion, it acquired North American Aviation Corporation and made him vice-president. North American's assets included Eastern Air Transport. Its New York to Miami route, attractive to vacationers, had outstanding potential following enactment in 1930 of airmail legislation specifically designed to promote passenger operations.

In 1934 scandals involving the Hoover administration's dispensation of airmail contracts led to a congressional investigation. Voiding existing contracts, president Roosevelt ordered army pilots to transport mail. Calling this legalized murder because such men were untrained for airmail operations, Rickenbacker helped dramatize commercial airline performance by copiloting a new airliner, the Douglas DC-1, on the last regular airmail flight between California and New Jersey, setting a speed record. His harsh judgment of Roosevelt and hostility

toward the New Deal widened a breach between the two men that never healed.

Due to public outcry after a series of crashes killed or injured army mail pilots, new government airmail contracts were awarded to privately owned firms. Companies that had previously held such contracts were allowed to reorganize under virtually identical names. Among these was Eastern Air Transport, which became Eastern Air Lines. It was unprofitable, demoralized, and had an antiquated fleet. Becoming its general manager in December 1934, Rickenbacker modernized operations, expanded its route system, and earned profits.

In 1938 General Motors gave rental car magnate John Hertz an option to buy Eastern. Enraged, Rickenbacker won a commitment from General Motors' chief executive, Alfred P. Sloan, to give him control of the airline if he could raise $3.5 million within thirty days. Succeeding, he became Eastern's president in April 1938 and made it the most profitable firm in the industry. Winning a route from Houston to Brownsville, Tex., by bidding to carry airmail gratis in order to secure a potentially lucrative Mexican gateway was characteristic of his aggressiveness.

In February 1941 Rickenbacker suffered multiple injuries when an airliner on which he was flying crashed while trying to land at Atlanta. Enduring excruciating pain, he survived with a permanent limp. While he convalesced, the United States entered World War II. Despite his battered condition, Rickenbacker undertook special wartime assignments for Secretary of War Henry L. Stimson and General Henry ("Hap") Arnold. Touring air bases to identify problems impeding training and morale, he also promoted a plan under which airlines relinquished planes and personnel to the armed forces. In September 1942 he inspected American bases in England, conferred with Winston Churchill, and returned home carrying Eisenhower's plans to invade North Africa.

In October 1942 Rickenbacker began a secret mission to New Guinea. Between Honolulu and Canton Island, the B-17 bomber on which he was flying became lost and went down in the Pacific Ocean. For twenty-four days, Rickenbacker and seven companions, one of whom died, endured an agonizing ordeal on life rafts in shark-infested waters before being rescued. Known as "Iron-Man Eddie" and "The Man Who Always Comes Back," Rickenbacker published a book, *Seven Came Through*, about the episode. In 1943 he made a secret trip to North Africa, Iran, India, China, and the Soviet Union at the behest of Stimson and Lend-Lease director Edward R. Stettinius, Jr. Before the war ended, he also inspected bases in the Aleutian Islands.

Intemperate remarks that Rickenbacker made in April 1945, publicly welcoming Roosevelt's death, indicated that his judgment may have been adversely affected by his traumatic experiences. Returning to Eastern, he made a series of bad decisions. Having once monopolized traffic on key routes, Eastern now faced competition from Delta and other airlines. Rickenbacker proved a poor match for Delta's chief executive, C. E. Woolman. Particularly damaging to Eastern was Rickenbacker's choice of crash-prone Lockheed L-188 Electra turboprops while Delta acquired faster and safer Douglas DC-8 and Convair 880 jetliners. Woolman also adapted to federal regulations mandating use of flight engineers in four-engined planes by training pilots for that role, thus keeping Delta's cockpits free from tension between members of two different labor unions. By mingling pilots and flight engineers, Rickenbacker provoked such conflict, and Eastern was plagued by strikes. Partly because Rickenbacker alienated federal officials appointed by Democratic administrations, Delta won important routes that might otherwise have gone to Eastern. Rickenbacker's callous attitude toward passengers was a handicap in a service-oriented industry, and his abrasive treatment of employees hurt morale.

After investigating conditions at Eastern, Laurance Rockefeller, the company's largest stockholder, intervened. In 1959 Malcolm MacIntyre, formerly general counsel for American Airlines and undersecretary of the U.S. Air Force, became president and chief executive of Eastern while Rickenbacker became chairman of the board. Rickenbacker, however, undermined MacIntyre by constant meddling. His public criticism of John F. Kennedy may also have contributed to Eastern's losing a transcontinental route case in 1961. Frustrated, the directors dismissed both him and MacIntyre. In 1964 Floyd Hall, formerly with TWA, took charge of Eastern and Rickenbacker retired.

Rickenbacker spent his remaining years speaking, writing, and traveling from his home in New York City, becoming increasingly bitter. In 1972 he had a stroke and underwent surgery. In 1973 he took Adelaide, who was going blind, to Zurich, Switzerland, to consult an eye specialist; he died while there. His ashes, returned home aboard an Eastern airliner, were scattered in Columbus while jet interceptors from his old squadron roared overhead.

[Collections of Rickenbacker's papers and memorabilia are at the Library of Congress and Wright-Patterson Air Force Base. His autobiography, *Rickenbacker* (1967), was written with the aid of Booten Herndon and his secretary, Margaret Shepherd. *Fighting the Flying Circus* (1919) was written with help from Laurence La Tourelle Driggs. Biographies include Hans C. Adamson, *Eddie Rickenbacker* (1946); and Finis Farr, *Rickenbacker's Luck* (1979). See also Robert J. Serling, *From the Captain to the Colonel: An Informal History of Eastern Air Lines* (1980). An obituary is in the *New York Times*, July 24, 1973.]

W. DAVID LEWIS

RIDDER, BERNARD HERMAN (Mar. 20, 1883–May 5, 1975), publisher, was born in New York City, the son of Herman Ridder and Mary Amend. Raised a Roman Catholic, Ridder's family was of German descent; his paternal grandparents had emigrated from Westphalia, Germany, in 1828. Ridder's father was the founder and publisher of a New York German-language newspaper, the *Staats-Zeitung*.

Ridder received his primary education at De La Salle Institute in New York. After receiving a B.A. from Columbia University in 1903, he did graduate work in Leipzig, Germany, from 1903 to 1905.

Ridder began his newspaper career in the business and editorial departments of the *Brooklyn Eagle*. In 1905 he married Hilda Luytis, the daughter of a New York business executive. The couple had one child before divorcing in 1908.

The following year, Ridder joined the staff of the *Staats-Zeitung*. There he learned every aspect of the newspaper business and became president of the Staats-Zeitung Corporation when he and his two brothers inherited the company following their father's death in 1915. He also completed *Hyphenations*, his first book, in 1915. The book did not enjoy much popular success and is not considered among his worthiest accomplishments. That same year, Ridder married Nell Hickey, the daughter of a contractor; they had four children before divorcing in 1930.

Ridder began to build his family's business

with the merger in 1918 of the *Staats-Zeitung* with several other German-language newspapers, creating the *Staats-Zeitung und Herold*. He served as president of the publishing company until the family sold the business in 1930.

In 1933, several months after the Nazi regime seized power in Germany, Heinz Spanknoebel, a representative of the German Labor Front and the chief of the foreign division of the Nazi party, came to the offices of the *Staats-Herold*. He showed Victor Ridder, one of Bernard's brothers, letters authorizing him to assume power over the German-language press in the United States. He told the Ridders that his first order of business would be to stop publishing "your pro-Jewish articles." In a 1943 judicial proceeding to nullify citizenship of Nazis in the United States, Victor Ridder testified that his brother Bernard walked in, was shown the letters and immediately replied, "All I can tell you Spanknoebel, is to get the hell out and stay out." Spanknoebel continued to attack the newspaper and attempted to stir up opposition to the paper and support for the Nazi movement among Americans of German descent until he left the United States a few months later.

Ridder and his brothers acquired the *Jamaica Long Island Press* in 1926, marking the start of their venture into the English-language press. The next year they purchased the *New York Journal of Commerce* for $2.5 million and the *St. Paul Pioneer Press* and the *St. Paul Dispatch* for a combined price of $5.25 million. The Ridders formed Northwest Publications, Inc., the same year as a parent company for their two Minnesota newspapers. Bernard Ridder served as president of the two St. Paul newspapers and the *Journal of Commerce* from 1927 to 1931, when he sold his interests in all three.

The three Ridder brothers continued to acquire small-town papers. They obtained control of Minnesota's *Duluth New Tribune* and *Duluth Herald* in 1936 and bought the *San Jose Mercury and News* in 1952. In 1938, Ridder moved to St. Paul to rejoin the *Pioneer Press* and *St. Paul Dispatch* as editor and publisher. He remained in this capacity until his son, Herman H. Ridder, became publisher in June 1946. Bernard Ridder stayed on as editor of both newspapers until 1950. He became president of both journals in 1952. He held the positions of vice-president of Northwest Publications from 1938 to 1946 and of president and director from 1946 until his death.

In 1944, Ridder married his third wife, Agnes Kennedy, the daughter of a merchant from St. Paul. They traveled together extensively, and starting in 1946 published a yearly diary of their travels entitled *The Year*. They took many photographs, amassing a library of some thirty thousand color slides, which is available for use by all public schools in St. Paul and colleges and universities in the Midwest.

Although Ridder enjoyed huge professional success during the 1960's, his personal life was troubled. His daughter, Rosemary Sanders, died in 1968, and Herman H. Ridder, his eldest son, died in 1969.

By 1974, the Ridder organization owned or held considerable interest in nineteen daily newspapers in ten states in the Midwest and on the West Coast. In late 1974, Ridder Publications merged with Knight Newspapers, Inc., to form Knight-Ridder Newspapers, Inc. The merger formed a group with thirty-five publications in seventeen states and one that remains a dominant force in American journalism today. Ridder had considerable business dealings outside of his newspaper empire. He was named president and director of the St. Paul Arcade Company and the Otto Bremer Company in 1952. His diversified business positions also included being vice-president and director of Mid-Continent Radio-Television, Inc., and of Midwest Radio-Television, and director of the Dispatch Realty Company and the American National Bank. He was also secretary and a director of the Grand Forks Herald, Inc., and served as vice-president and director of the *Aberdeen American News* in South Dakota.

Bernard Ridder never officially retired from publishing. He remained chairman emeritus of the board of directors of Ridder Publishing, Inc., until his death. He died at St. Mary's Hospital in West Palm Beach, Fla., at the age of ninety-two.

[An obituary is in the *New York Times*, May 6, 1975.]

TIMOTHY RHODES

RIEFLER, WINFIELD WILLIAM (Feb. 9, 1897–Apr. 5, 1974), economist, was born in Buffalo, N.Y., the son of Clara Gartner and David Philip Riefler, an American Express Company manager. He attended public schools in Rochester, N.Y., and entered Amherst College in 1915. In 1917, he joined an American volunteer ambulance unit serving with French forces in World War I and was awarded the croix de guerre in 1919. He then returned to Amherst, where he studied economics under Walter Stewart, and graduated with a B.A. in 1921.

Riefler briefly served as a foreign trade officer assisting the American commercial attaché in Buenos Aires, then started his own import-export business in New York City. The venture was unsuccessful, and in 1923 he joined the staff of the Federal Reserve Board in Washington, D.C. He worked under Stewart, who had been appointed director of the board's Division of Analysis and Research, as a research economist concentrating on the domestic money market and credit issues.

Dorothy Miles Brown was another member of Stewart's staff. She and Riefler were married on Dec. 5, 1924; they had two sons.

During the 1920's, Riefler attended the Robert Brookings Graduate School in Washington, D.C., and was awarded a Ph.D. in 1927. His dissertation on money markets was published by Harper Brothers as *Money Rates and Money Markets in the United States* (1930). His research also led the Federal Reserve Board to issue a weekly table of statistics entitled "Member Bank Reserves, Reserve Bank Credit and Related Items," which was published in the monthly *Federal Reserve Bulletin*. Riefler served as secretary of the Federal Reserve System's Committee on Bank Reserves in the period 1930–1931.

When the administration of Franklin D. Roosevelt took office in 1933, Riefler served as one of its economic advisers. He helped to organize the Federal Housing Administration and drafted the margin provision of the Securities and Exchange Commission Act (1934). He later organized the Central Statistical Board and served as adviser to Roosevelt's Executive Council and later to the National Emergency Council. He also assisted in preparing the Tripartite Agreement (1936) between the United States, Britain, and France, the first major move toward international monetary stabilization after the stock market crash of 1929.

In 1935, Riefler left Washington to join the faculty of the Institute for Advanced Study in Princeton, N.J., as a professor in the School of Economics and Politics. The institute's director, Abraham Flexner, had offered the post to Stewart, who suggested Riefler for the position. During this period Riefler served as president of the American Statistical Association. He helped to organize, and served as director of, the National Bureau of Economic Research (NBER), and chaired the NBER Exploratory Committee on Financial Research. His committee's recommendations prompted the NBER to organize its Program of Financial Research in 1937. Funds provided by the Rockefeller Foundation and the Association of Reserve City Bankers supported statistical studies on consumer debt and installment credit, corporate financing, and urban-mortgage financing.

During this period Riefler continued to serve as an unofficial adviser to the Roosevelt administration on monetary policy and international finance. He was an alternate member of the League of Nations Finance Committee (1937–1946) and a director of the Federal Reserve Bank in Philadelphia (1941–1942).

After American entry into World War II, Riefler advised Secretary of the Treasury Henry Morgenthau on reorganizing the Treasury Department and creating the Board of Economic Warfare. In 1942, Riefler was sent to London as special assistant to Ambassador John Gilbert Winant, with responsibility for economic warfare and oversight of overseas Lend-Lease operations.

After the war, Riefler returned to the Institute for Advanced Study but continued to advise the Truman administration on economic issues. He was a consultant to the 1947 Select Committee on Foreign Aid headed by Christian Herter, and American member of the UN Subcommission on Employment and Economic Stability. He also served as a director of the Council on Foreign Relations.

In 1948, Riefler took a leave of absence from the Institute for Advanced Study to become the assistant to Thomas McCabe, chairman of the Federal Reserve Board. In 1951, President Truman replaced McCabe with investment banker William McChesney Martin, Jr., a deputy secretary of the Treasury who had helped supervise Lend-Lease operations during World War II.

Martin retained Riefler in his post of assistant to the chairman, and appointed him secretary of the Federal Open Market Committee in 1952. When the Eisenhower administration took office in 1953, it kept Martin and Riefler in their posts at the Federal Reserve Board. Throughout the 1950's, they concentrated on adjusting monetary policy to fight the inflationary impact of the large U.S. military budgets resulting from the Cold War. In 1959, the British Parliament invited Riefler to give testimony (the only American witness) before the Radcliffe Committee on Debt Management and Monetary Policy.

Riefler resigned from the staff of the Federal Reserve Board in December 1959 and retired to Florida. He died in Sarasota, Fla.

[Small amounts of Riefler's correspondence and other papers are in the archives of the Institute for Advanced Study, Princeton, N.J.; the Rockefeller Archive Center, North Tarrytown, N.Y.; and the records of the Federal Reserve Board at the National Archives, Washington, D.C. He listed as his most enduring writings "The Dilemma of Central Banking as Illustrated in Recent Literature," *Quarterly Journal of Economics*, Apr. 1936; "Government and the Statistician," *Journal of the American Statistical Association*, Mar. 1942; "A Proposal for an International Buffer-Stock Agency," *Journal of Political Economy*, Dec. 1946; and "Our Contribution to Victory," *Foreign Affairs*, Oct. 1947.

There is no biography, but useful information is in Herbert Bratter, "Winfield W. Riefler," *English-Speaking World*, Aug.–Sept. 1944, and "Banking's Spotlight on—Winfield Riefler," *Banking*, Jan. 1960. Riefler's association with the Institute for Advanced Study is mentioned briefly in Abraham Flexner, *I Remember* (1940); and Edward Regis, *Who Got Einstein's Office?* (1987). The inception of the NBER Financial Research Program is described in National Bureau of Economic Research, *A Program of Financial Research*, vol. 1 (1937). The individual studies are listed in National Bureau of Economic Research, *Publications, 1921–1990*. An obituary is in the *New York Times*, Apr. 10, 1974.]

STEPHEN G. MARSHALL

RITTER, WOODWARD MAURICE ("TEX") (Jan. 23, 1905–Jan. 2, 1974), singer and actor, was born at Murvaul, Panola County, Tex., to James Everett Ritter, a farmer and rancher, and Elizabeth Matthews. The family lived on a 400-acre homestead that had been claimed by the Ritter ancestors in 1830 when it was still part of Mexico. Confusion exists about his birth year primarily because publicists misrepresented his age early in his movie career; fictitious dates were so commonly used that even his bronze plaque in the Country Music Hall of Fame lists his birth year as 1907.

Ritter attended local public elementary schools and South Park High School in Beaumont, Tex., where he was an honor student, played basketball, and sang in the glee club. He enrolled at the University of Texas at Austin in 1922, majoring in law, but he was influenced by the folklorist-historians J. Frank Dobie, Oscar J. Fox, and John A. Lomax to study and perform the music of the Texas frontier. Ritter began touring with a self-written lecture/recital called "The Texas Cowboy and His Songs." His singing career blossoming, Ritter left the university in 1927, though only one credit shy of a law degree.

Ritter went to New York in 1929, and for the next decade performed on such radio shows as "The Lone Ranger," "Cowboy Tom's Round-up," "Tex Ritter's Campfire," "Death Valley Days," "WHN Barn Dance" and "Songs of the B-Bar-B." During that same period, "Tex" was also appearing in plays, including *Green Grow the Lilacs* (on which *Oklahoma* was later based), *The Roundup*, and *Mother Lode*. It was the cast and crew of *Green Grow the Lilacs* who began to call Ritter "Tex" in 1931.

Success on the radio and on stage led to opportunities in recording and films. Ritter cut his first records for the American Record Company in 1933 and in 1942 became the first "country" singer signed by Capital Records. As a recording artist, his big hits included "Rock & Rye Rag," "Daddy's Last Letter," and "High Noon," which was featured in the movie of that name. In the 1960's Ritter had nine records on the country charts, including several that made the top ten. His singles included such favorites as "Boll Weevil," "Wayward Wind," "Hillbilly Heaven," "There's a New Moon over My Shoulder," "Have I Told You Lately that I Love You," "Rye Whisky," and "You Are My Sunshine." Albums released by Capital included *Songs* (1958), *Blood on the Saddle* (1960), *Border Affair* (1963), *Friendly Voice* (1965), *Hillbilly Heaven* (1965), *Best of Tex Ritter* (1966), *Just Beyond the Moon* (1967), *Sweet Land of Liberty* (1967), and in the late 1960's, *Green Green Valley*, and early 1970's *Supercountry-legendary*, as well as a three-record set, *The Legendary Tex Ritter* (1973)—some of which included songs he had composed.

Ritter's popularity was not based solely on the quality of his voice; his Texan background and his academic studies of the history of real working cowboys gave his songs an authenticity that his chief rivals, Roy Rogers and Gene Autry, could not match. And his likable down-home personality attracted audiences both on stage and on screen. Grand National Films signed

Ritter in 1936, and he made his first movie, *Song of the Gringo* that same year. For the next twenty years he made movies, including seventy-eight Westerns, while working for Monogram, Columbia, and Universal studios. For six of those years he ranked among the top-ten money-making Western stars in Hollywood. Filmbills reveal that in the majority of these films he played a character named "Tex."

In at least nine of these films his leading lady was Dorothy Fay Southworth, whom Ritter married on June 14, 1941. They had two sons, one of whom became a successful actor and director. When the market for movie Westerns began to wane, Ritter moved to television, starring in the series "Ranch Party," which ran from 1959 to 1962. When his movie and television career faded, Ritter stepped up his involvement in country music, moving to Nashville, Tenn., in 1964, where he became a regular on the "Grand Ole Opry."

Ritter's interest in politics led him to support a number of Democratic candidates, and led also to his own campaigns for both U.S. senator (1970) and governor of Tennessee (1973). These campaigns were not only unsuccessful, but financially disastrous for him.

Always active in the affairs of the country music industry, Ritter helped establish the Country Music Association (CMA) and its Hall of Fame in Nashville. In 1964 he was one of the first six artists elected to the CMA Hall of Fame, and in 1971 he was given the Founding President's Award by the CMA. That same year he headed a CMA overseas tour for the United Nations. The bronze plaque in the Hall of Fame honoring Ritter contains the following inscription: "One of America's most illustrious and versatile stars of radio, television, records, motion pictures, and Broadway stage. Untiring pioneer and champion of the country music industry, his devotion to his God, his family, and his country is a continuing inspiration to his countless friends throughout the world."

Ritter died after suffering a heart attack while visiting the Nashville jail to help secure the release of a musician friend.

[Cyrus (Johnny) Bond, *The Tex Ritter Story* (1976), is the only biography; it contains an accurate movie list and discography. Most histories of American popular music and of country music contain entries on Ritter. An obituary appears in the *New York Times*, Jan. 3, 1974.]

DOROTHY S. ("DOREY") SCHMIDT

ROBERTSON, ABSALOM WILLIS (May 27, 1887–Nov. 1, 1971), politician, was born in Martinsburg, W.Va., one of six children of Franklin Pierce Robertson, a Baptist minister and home missionary, and Josephine Ragland. Robertson was descended from several illustrious southern families—the Diggses, Gordons, Harrisons, and Willises. He went to public schools in Lynchburg and Rocky Mount, Va., before attending the University of Richmond, where he played varsity football. Robertson received a B.A. in 1907 and an LL.B. in 1908.

He practiced law with the firm of Willis and Robertson in Buena Vista, Rockbridge County, and began serving in the Virginia senate in 1916. During World War I, Robertson served in the adjutant general's office, rising to the rank of major. In 1919, he moved to Lexington, Va. Robertson married Gladys Churchill on Oct. 19, 1920; they had two children. Gladys Robertson would become devout, turning down invitations to Washington parties (including the White House), and preferring to spend her time in Lexington, where she handed out religious tracts to students. Robertson resigned from the Virginia Senate in 1922 to become the commonwealth's attorney for Rockbridge County. In 1926, he became Virginia's Commissioner of Game and Inland Fisheries.

Robertson was elected (at large) to the United States House of Representatives in 1932. He sponsored a resolution to establish a Select Committee on Conservation of Wildlife Resources in 1934 and was reelected to Congress that year for Virginia's seventh district. In 1937, he became a member of the Ways and Means Committee.

As chairman of the wildlife conservation committee, Robertson took public interest in his committee's work as "proof that the Nation is gradually becoming more and more 'conservation conscious.' " He sponsored the Pittman-Robertson Act in 1937, which returned millions of dollars in federal taxes on guns and ammunition to the states for their game and conservation programs. Describing the requirements for a national wildlife program, Robertson said, "The first essential is land. . . . Birds cannot nest on the wing, nor can animals reproduce on the run." He was an eloquent spokesman for conservation, stressing the need for cooperation between federal and state agencies. President Franklin D. Roosevelt thanked Robertson in a letter of Oct. 5, 1938, for his report on the conservation activities of regular and emergency federal agencies—including the Civilian Conservation Corps—saying, "This is a subject in which I have a very deep concern."

Although Robertson increasingly voted against New Deal legislation, he usually supported President Roosevelt's foreign and defense policies, voting for the peacetime draft in 1940 and for Lend-Lease aid in 1941, which helped Britain in World War II.

Elected to the United States Senate in 1946 to fill the vacancy created by the death of his mentor, Carter Glass, Robertson won reelection in 1948, 1954, and 1960. He was an orator of the old school, gesturing frequently and often quoting from the Bible. Although they were born in the same town a couple of weeks apart, and lived within a few blocks of each other, he was no longer close to the senior senator from Virginia, Harry Byrd, because he refused simply to follow Byrd's direction. Robertson survived without the Byrd machine's support because of his own personal following across Virginia.

Robertson supported the Taft-Hartley Act in 1947 and other legislation to restrict union power. He voted for aid to Greece and Turkey in 1947 and for the Marshall Plan the next year. Robertson endorsed President Harry Truman in 1948 but criticized the civil rights plank in the Democratic platform. During the Korean War, Robertson was a member of a Congressional quartet that sang for hospitalized servicemen. He was cochairman of the Joint Committee on Defense Production (1957–1958, 1961–1962, and 1965–1966).

A member of the Appropriations Committee, Robertson resisted the expansion of federal power and spending (with the exception of defense). In 1959, he became chairman of the Senate Banking and Currency Committee. An authority on taxation, tariffs, and foreign trade, he was a pillar of conservatism who feared for the country's fiscal safety. He saw himself as a financial and constitutional watchdog of government and was appalled by the size of federal deficits and the growth of debt. Robertson himself lived the spartan, frugal life he tried to impose on government. He enjoyed hunting and fishing trips, on which he was often accompanied by other senators, who, as a result, perhaps became more sympathetic to Robertson's concern for preserving pure mountain streams and forests. His closest friend in the Senate was John

Stennis of Mississippi. Senator Clinton P. Anderson observed, "Senator Robertson had the ability to differ without being contentious."

Few Democrats supported President Dwight D. Eisenhower as enthusiastically as Robertson. Conversely, President John F. Kennedy found Robertson to be a leading opponent of his legislation. Robertson was a leader of the Senate Wednesday prayer breakfast. After the Supreme Court decision of 1962 banning prayer from public schools, Robertson introduced a resolution in the Senate challenging it. Noting on June 26, 1962, that Supreme Court sessions began with the prayer, "God save the United States and this honorable Court," Robertson asked Congress to tell the justices, "You have usurped your constitutional authority." But he was unsuccessful. In 1963, Robertson opposed President Kennedy's Area Redevelopment Act; he believed more jobs would be created by lower taxes and lower spending. He also voted against the Nuclear Test Ban Treaty of 1963.

During President Lyndon B. Johnson's administration, Robertson continued to oppose civil rights bills and social-welfare spending. Some of Robertson's criticism of welfare programs—especially his warning that they created dependence on government—would (when made by others a generation later) receive a better hearing. Robertson supported a revision of the Bank Merger Act of 1960, which became law in 1966 and made it easier for large banks to merge.

At seventy-nine, Robertson was defeated in the Democratic primary in July 1966, losing to William B. Spong, Jr., by 611 votes. The growth of urban areas in Virginia hurt Robertson. He resigned from the Senate on Dec. 30, 1966, giving Spong seniority over other freshmen, because the governor of Virginia was able to appoint Spong to Robertson's seat before the new congressmen entered the Senate in January. From 1966 to 1968, Robertson was a consultant for the International Bank for Reconstruction and Development. His younger son, Marion Gordon ("Pat") Robertson, would be a candidate for the Republican presidential nomination in 1988. A son of the Shenandoah Valley, Robertson had worked to preserve the nation's land and water long before conservation became a popular cause. He died where he had lived, in Lexington, Va. After a funeral service at Virginia Military Institute, Robertson was buried in Stonewall Jackson Cemetery.

[Robertson's papers are at the Earl Gregg Swen Library of the College of William and Mary. For Congressman Robertson's views on conservation, see *Report of the Select Committee on Conservation of Wildlife Resources*, 76th Cong., 1st Sess. (1939). For Robertson's Senate career, see Nelson Lichtenstein, ed., *Political Profiles: The Kennedy Years* (1976) and *The Johnson Years* (1976); and Eleanora W. Schoenebaum, ed., *Political Profiles: The Eisenhower Years* (1977) and *The Truman Years* (1978). There are biographical sketches of Willis Robertson in David Edwin Harrell, Jr., *Pat Robertson: A Personal, Religious, and Political Portrait* (1987) and in John B. Donovan, *Pat Robertson: The Authorized Biography* (1988). See also the *New York Times*, Feb. 8, 1961, "Man in the News" and Charles Houston, "Smith and Robertson," *The Commonwealth: The Magazine of Virginia*, Oct. 1966. For Robertson's role in Virginia politics see J. Harvie Wilkinson III, *Harry Byrd and the Changing Face of Virginia Politics, 1945–1966* (1968). An obituary is in the *Richmond Times-Dispatch*, Nov. 2, 1971, and an editorial tribute appeared in the same newspaper on Nov. 4, 1971. Additional obituaries are in the *Washington Post*, Nov. 2, 1971; the *New York Times*, Nov. 2, 1971; and *Memorial Addresses*, 92d Cong., 2d Sess., Senate Document 92-69 (1972).]

RALPH KIRSHNER

ROBINSON, EDWARD G. (Dec. 12, 1893– Jan. 26, 1973), actor, was born Emanuel Goldenburg in Bucharest, Romania, the fifth of six sons of Morris Goldenburg, a builder, and Sarah Guttman. Emanuel arrived with his family in New York City when he was nine and automatically acquired United States citizenship when his father was naturalized in 1902.

The Goldenburgs first lived on the Lower East Side of Manhattan but eventually settled in the Bronx. Morris first ran a candy store and then dealt in antiques. The older brothers went into business, and the youngest became a dentist. Young "Manny," as Emanuel was known to intimates for the rest of his life, was the only one to devote himself to the arts. His dramatic ambitions having been first manifested in his bar mitzvah speech, he became immersed in student theater productions when his distinguished academic record at P.S. 20 enabled him to enroll at a preparatory school called Townshend Harris Hall.

In 1910, he entered City College of New York, where he was elected to the Elizabethan Society after giving a reading from Shakespeare. In October 1911, he was awarded a scholarship to the American Academy of Dramatic Arts.

There, advised that if he wanted professional success he would have to acquire an Anglo-Saxon name, Emanuel Goldenburg became Edward G. Robinson. Soon after, he gave a one-man performance as a murderer confessing under hypnosis at an amateur night at Loew's Plaza. In 1913 he made his professional debut with a stock company in Binghamton, N.Y.

His first principal role on stage was as Nasir in Edward Knoblock's *Kismet*, which toured Canada in 1914, but the coming of World War I, in Robinson's phrase, "killed the theater." He returned to New York City and was so unsuccessful that he almost quit to try teaching. He was finally cast in a war play requiring both French- and German-speaking roles. Robinson had made a hobby of languages, and he eventually played so many ethnic roles in the production that his colleagues referred to him as the "League of Nations." He received favorable notices in the New York papers for these minor roles.

Except for a brief spell in 1918 in the United States Navy—during which he never left New York Harbor because of a flu epidemic—this was the beginning of an almost unceasing string of critical successes, as he grew from bit-player to star. He played a Japanese, a French-Canadian, a befuddled drunk, and—in an adaptation of Gorky's *Lower Depths*—Satan. He worked in plays translated from the Yiddish theater, did adaptations of Dostoyevsky, and acted in plays by Booth Tarkington, Ibsen, George Bernard Shaw, Edna St. Vincent Millay, Sidney Howard, and Pirandello. His costars constituted a Broadway "Who's Who": Joseph Schildkraut (an old college chum), Ethel Barrymore, Spencer Tracy, Alfred Lunt and Lynn Fontanne, Pat O'Brien, and Elisha Cooke, Jr. In 1927, Robinson finally landed a starring role, as an Al Capone–type gangster in Bartlett Cormack's sensational play, *The Racket*, and New York reviewers raved about his demonic performance. A year later, he returned to Broadway in Hugh Walpole's *A Man With Red Hair*, playing a sadistic lunatic in a style said to rival Lon Chaney's.

By that time, the major Hollywood producers were in pursuit and his stage career was winding down. The years on the boards had been good to him, helping him both refine his craft and cultivate a taste for fine meals, hotels, and Cuban cigars. On Jan. 21, 1927, he married an actress named Gladys Lloyd, the genteel daughter of the artist-sculptor C. C. Cassell. They had one child. The new family was able to settle comfortably in Beverly Hills. The former Manny Goldenburg had come a long way from Romania and the candy store in the Bronx.

Robinson made some eighty-seven movies. He had a minor role in a silent film in 1918 (a role that he failed to mention in his autobiography); and his only other silent role, that of a Spanish aristocrat in *The Bright Shawl* (1923), which also starred Dorothy Gish, Mary Astor, and William Powell. A *Hole in the Wall* (1929) was not only the first feature-length talking motion picture to be made at the Paramount lot in Astoria, New York City, but also the first talkie for both Robinson and his costar, Claudette Colbert. The film was not a success, but history had been made.

After his Capone-like gangster role in Universal's *Night Ride* (1929), which *was* a success, Robinson got raves in 1930 for A *Lady to Love*. Then, Irving Thalberg supposedly made him a million-dollar offer to become a contract player at MGM, but talks stalled and Robinson moved on. His portrayal of gangster Rico Bandello in *Little Caesar* (1931) for Warner Brothers began his long-term superstardom at that studio, and his definitive image of Rico was etched on the public mind.

Nevertheless, he enjoyed an extraordinary run of performances after *Little Caesar*. For example, there was *Tiger Shark* (1932), which was directed by Howard Hawks and which costarred Richard Arlen; John Ford's *The Whole Town's Talking* (1935), with Jean Arthur; Michael Curtiz's *Kid Galahad* (1937), with Bette Davis and Wayne Morris; and Anatole Litvak's *The Amazing Dr. Clitterhouse* (1938), with Claire Trevor and Humphrey Bogart. Another Litvak film, *Confessions of a Nazi Spy* (1939), in which Robinson played an FBI agent, was selected as the Best American Film of the Year by the National Board of Motion Picture Review.

Robinson also attempted to deflect the mixed blessing of the success of *Little Caesar* in new ways. He had the good humor to participate in ingratiating self-parodies of his gangster image—in one case, as a Depression-era bootlegger in the hilarious Damon Runyon–Howard Lindsay collaboration, *A Slight Case of Murder* (1938). A year before, he had started a long run on "Big Town," a weekly CBS radio series in which he played a crusading newspaper editor.

During World War II, he served as a spokesman for patriotic and civil rights causes. He also narrated a Russian anti-Nazi feature and a short film on the Red Cross. On radio, he narrated a documentary condemning racial intolerance and made propaganda broadcasts for the Voice of America. In person, he toured with the USO and participated in a mass memorial at Madison Square Garden to Jews who had lost their lives to the Nazis.

His horizons as a Hollywood leading man continued to broaden in the 1940's. Two of his most memorable roles came in 1944: as the hesitant insurance-claims adjuster who tracks down the murderers played by Fred MacMurray and Barbara Stanwyck in Billy Wilder's *Double Indemnity*, and as a mild-mannered psychology professor who gets mixed up with a seductive Joan Bennett in Fritz Lang's *The Woman in the Window*. He also starred as a war-crimes commissioner posing as an art collector in Orson Welles's *The Stranger* (1946), in the screen adaptation of Arthur Miller's *All My Sons* (1948), and as the villain opposing Humphrey Bogart in John Huston's *Key Largo* (1948). He was chosen best actor at the 1949 Cannes Film Festival for *House of Strangers*, in which he played a barber from Little Italy who becomes a successful banker.

In 1950, during the Red Scare, Robinson was accused of having Communist affiliations because of his generosity with many needy causes. He defended himself at considerable personal expense, testifying before the House Un-American Activities Committee in Washington three times. His name was ultimately cleared, and he was able to resume his busy schedule on the big screen (most notably in Cecil B. DeMille's 1956 epic, *The Ten Commandments*), to initiate a series of stellar television performances, and to reintroduce himself to Broadway audiences in Paddy Chayefsky's *Middle of the Night* (1956) as a middle-aged widower in love with a younger woman.

That same year, his wife of twenty-nine years sued for divorce. Robinson said that she had been manic-depressive for many years, in and out of institutions, and consistently threatening to leave him. In any case, the settlement was costly: $3.5 million in community property and 25 percent of his future income. Robinson had to sell three million dollars' worth of his world-class art collection to pay his ex-wife. Also painful was the publication the next year of his son's autobiography, which detailed a trouble-plagued life marked by difficult parental estrangements. Nevertheless, Robinson landed on his feet. The Chayefsky play was a considerable success and on Jan. 16, 1958, he married a member of its production staff, Jane Adler (née Bodenheimer), who was twenty-six years younger than he. He also began to rebuild his art collection.

Moreover, he was able to adapt readily to the changes wrought by television and his advancing age. In the 1950's and early 1960's he had starring roles in most of television's live theatrical series. When that era ended, he happily appeared on variety shows like "Laugh-In" and the "Tom Jones Show." He was a celebrity guest on "What's My Line?" in 1965. In the movies, he parodied himself alongside Frank Sinatra's "rat pack" in *Robin and the Seven Hoods* (1964) and continued to show he was up to feature roles—though he was now often cast as a suave elderly gent, however devious. Most distinctively, he was Steve McQueen's aging card-sharp nemesis in *The Cincinnati Kid* (1965). His career wound down mostly with guest performances in undistinguished films, a number of which were slight comedy-capers made abroad. In 1969, the *New York Times* called Carl Foreman's *Mackenna's Gold* a "Western of stunning absurdity" in which stars like Lee J. Cobb, Burgess Meredith, Eli Wallach, and Robinson do "a sort of stagger-on" and die. In fact, after a long illness, Robinson did die of cancer before the release of his last film, *Soylent Green* (1973), a futuristic melodrama in which, ironically, the critics found the only redeeming value to be Robinson's own poignant death scene.

Through the filter of these last years, it is difficult to disagree with Foster Hirsch's assessment that, although Robinson's "work contained suggestions of protean versatility, an Olivier-like genius for transforming himself anew for each role," the "movies used him more for his star presence than for the infinitely resourceful and chameleon-like character actor he seemed capable of being."

One might add to this Robinson's outstanding, often patriotic, radio work; his withstanding a McCarthy-era assault; his lucrative, and varied, television career; his sadly troubled family life; his acquisition—twice—of a world-class collection of fine art; the publication of his autobiography; his celebrating his seventy-fifth birthday before twenty thousand people during a Hanukkah festival at Madison Square Garden; and, finally, the presentation of an Oscar to him on his deathbed in honor of his lifetime contribution to the film industry. And this all from a down-to-earth and gentlemanly fellow who was, by his own assessment, too short and too ugly and too gravelly-voiced to ever be a leading man in the conventional sense.

[Robinson's 1973 autobiography, *All My Yesterdays*, was written with Leonard Spigelgass. See also Edward G. Robinson, Jr., and William Duffy, *My Father, My Son* (1958); Foster Hirsch, *Edward G. Robinson* (1975); and Alvin H. Marill, *The Complete Films of Edward G. Robinson* (1990). An obituary appears in the *New York Times*, Jan. 27, 1973.]

THOMAS BOYLE

ROBINSON, JOHN ROOSEVELT ("JACKIE") (Jan. 31, 1919–Oct. 24, 1972), baseball player and business executive, was born in Cairo, Ga., the son of Jerry Robinson and Mallie McGriff. Jerry Robinson worked on a local plantation for wages and for a time as a sharecropper, but shortly after Jackie's birth he deserted his family and went to Florida with another woman. Mallie Robinson and her five children were forced off the plantation. After working for a time as a domestic, she decided to go to California, where one of her brothers had settled after his army service in World War I. Installed in a ramshackle house in Pasadena, the Robinsons made do on the mother's meager income combined with welfare. The family eventually was able to move to a better house, where they lived for several years, enduring periodic harassment from white neighbors.

Each of the four Robinson boys sought a means of earning money as he became old enough. Jackie found all sorts of odd jobs, from maintaining a newspaper route to shining shoes. Recreational facilities were few, and Jackie belonged to the Pepper Street gang, which periodically ran afoul of the law for minor misdemeanors, but was spared the consequences through the intervention of compassionate policemen. At John Muir Technical High School, Jackie became a standout athlete, known for his reflexes, coordination, and speed. Since no nationally known college stepped forward with an athletic scholarship, he entered Pasadena Junior College, where he played football as quarterback, was the basketball team's leading scorer, and the key member of the track and baseball teams. Subsequently he enrolled at the University of California at Los Angeles, where he would become the finest all-around athlete that UCLA had ever known, excelling not only in the sports he had played in high school, but also winning championship tournaments in golf, swimming, and tennis. Although considered by girls to be a loner because he was generally shy with them, Robinson was attracted to Rachel Isum, a fellow student, whom he married on Feb. 10, 1946. They had three children.

Only a few months before he was scheduled to graduate from college, Robinson decided to quit school in order to accept a job at a youth camp at Atascadero, Calif., under the auspices of the National Youth Administration. His stated purpose was to help support his mother. The camp closed a few months later. His departure from the athletic scene produced a remarkable outpouring of accolades on the sport pages of the country, proclaiming the brilliance of his achievements on the playing fields.

Because blacks had no opportunity to play professional football in the United States, Robinson went to Hawaii, where he played halfback for the Honolulu Bears, a semiprofessional team, and worked at a construction company. At the end of the season, he headed home, just two days before the Japanese attack on Pearl Harbor, aiming to work with deprived young men. But military service now beckoned. Still troubled by an ankle he had broken in junior college, Robinson was designated for limited duty, although he might have avoided service altogether by claiming he was his mother's sole support.

Assigned to Fort Riley, Kans., a cavalry post, Robinson tended horses. When he applied for Officers Candidate School, he was turned down because he was black. With the help of Joe Louis, the reigning heavyweight boxing champion, Robinson had the ban lifted, and a few blacks, including himself, were enrolled. In January 1943, Robinson was commissioned a second lieutenant and detailed as a morale officer for black troops. Almost immediately he was questioning and protesting the traditional discriminatory practices at Riley. He refused to play football with the fort's team because its schedule included elevens that would not play against blacks.

In time Robinson was transferred to a tank battalion at Fort Hood, Tex., and ordered to help prepare it for overseas service. While there, Robinson was brought before a court-martial on charges of insubordination growing out of his refusal to move to the back of a bus, in accordance with the accepted practice of that time and place. In the end, he was acquitted of all the charges. In November 1944, he received a medical discharge. While awaiting his final papers at Camp Breckenridge, Ky., Robinson met a member of the Kansas City Monarchs of the Negro American League, who knew of Robinson's reputation as a collegiate sports hero but was not aware that Robinson was a baseball player. The chance encounter proved momentous in the history of baseball and American race relations. Robinson had accepted a position as basketball coach at a black college in Texas, but upon receiving a call to join the Monarchs, he seized the opportunity without hesitation.

Meanwhile, Branch Rickey, co-owner of the Brooklyn Dodgers, ever on the prowl for baseball talent, had made up his mind to widen his search by seeking Latin American and black players. He had been influenced substantially by the writings on race of Professor Frank Tannenbaum of Columbia University's Department of History, who maintained that people of different races will work together harmoniously when they have a common goal. After extensive research, Rickey decided that Jackie Robinson was the perfect choice to break baseball's color line: he was a superb player blessed with a must-win attitude, was college-educated, did not smoke or drink, was accustomed to white teammates, was articulate and self-disciplined, and was already experienced in fighting racial prejudice. Many of his fellow players in the Negro American League did not regard him as the most talented member of their ranks, and executives of the black leagues sensed that if Robinson succeeded and the flood gates opened for black players to enter organized baseball, the only sure result would be the demise of their franchises. Nevertheless, the political and moral implications of bringing an end to all-white baseball were clear to all.

In signing Robinson, Rickey exacted from him a pledge that no matter how fierce the brickbats, hate mail, and threats he might have to confront, he would not flinch or respond publicly. On Apr. 18, 1946, Robinson, amid unprecedented publicity and pressure, made a story-book debut with the Montreal Royals of the International League, a Dodger farm team. He hit a three-run homer and had three singles in five at bats, stole two bases, and scored four runs, twice by forcing the pitcher to balk.

In 1947, Rickey promoted Robinson to the Dodgers, signing him to a contract paying $5,000 for the season. For the first time in the twentieth century a black man was playing in the big leagues. He wrote later: "I had to fight hard against loneliness, abuse and the knowledge that any mistake I made would be magnified because I was the only black man out there." In his ten seasons with the Dodgers they won six National League pennants—in 1947, 1949, 1952, 1953, 1955, and 1956. They failed to win in 1950 on the last day of the season, and in 1951 after a stunning loss in a playoff game. Although he was a line-drive hitter and had only 137 home runs in his career, he batted in the cleanup position—fourth in the lineup— because he catalyzed his mates with his clutch hitting and competitive fire. He played mostly at second base, but also did stints at first base, third base, and left field. Batting and throwing right-handed, he stood five feet, eleven inches tall, and in his prime weighed between 200 and 210 pounds.

"The only way to beat the Dodgers," said the owner of another team, "is to keep Robinson off the bases." Once on base, Robinson would take a lead off it in a kind of ritual dance, as if he were about to steal, in order to rattle the pitcher so that he could not concentrate on the batter. A daring base runner, Robinson stole home nineteen times, the most by any player in the post–World War II era. In 1955, in the opener of the only World Series that his team won, he stole home against the Yankees. In 1947, Robinson was voted the Rookie of the Year; two years later, having led the league in batting with a .342 average, he was named the Most Valuable Player. He was elected to the Hall of Fame at Cooperstown, N.Y., in 1962, his first year of eligibility.

Having endured racial virulence from many quarters, including even from his own teammates, Robinson ended his self-imposed silence in 1949, and he became a strong voice for ending Jim Crow arrangements that persisted in the South and racial discrimination in general. He was a natural role model for black athletes in many sports; as the racial barriers fell and the opportunities opened, Robinson crusaded to widen them.

Robinson remained devoted to Rickey, "the greatest human being I had ever known." When Rickey left Brooklyn and the years of fierce play had taken their toll on Robinson's body, Robinson was ready to retire. In what was widely regarded as ingratitude for his years of brilliance, after the 1956 season the Dodgers traded him to the hated rivals just across the Harlem River, the New York Giants. Robinson announced, however, in an article in the Jan. 22, 1957, issue of *Look* magazine that he was retiring; he could not be persuaded to change his mind.

Robinson now entered the business world, serving first as an officer of the Chock Full O'Nuts luncheonette chain, and subsequently with an insurance company, with the Jackie Robinson Construction Corporation, and with a food franchising firm. For a time he was the chairman of the Freedom National Bank in Harlem. His prominence made him a magnet for the attention of politicians. In the presidential election of 1960, Robinson supported Richard Nixon because of Nixon's strong stand for civil rights. In 1966, he accepted, largely as window dressing, the post of general manager of the Brooklyn Dodgers football team, a franchise in the short-lived, upstart Continental League. In 1968, Robinson, having resigned as a special assistant to New York Governor Nelson A. Rockefeller, backed the candidacy of Hubert H. Humphrey.

In 1969, he refused to participate in a Yankee Old-Timers Day as a protest against baseball's continued failure to put blacks in leadership positions in the dugout and in the executive suites. Adding significantly to the melancholy of his last years was the fate of his son, Jackie, Jr., who had become hooked on heroin while serving in the U.S. Army in Vietnam, where he was wounded. Just when his recovery was progressing, he was killed in an automobile accident in 1971, at the age of twenty-four. Robinson found such comfort as he could by volunteering his services in public campaigns against drug addiction.

Robinson's health had been deteriorating for some time. He had suffered a heart attack in 1968, and diabetes had cost him the sight of one eye and left him partial vision in the other. His hair had turned white, and spectators were shocked at his appearance and painfully slow gait when, a few weeks before his death, he had participated in ceremonies at Dodger Stadium in Los Angeles marking the retirement of number 42, which he had worn on his uniform throughout his big-league career. He died in Stamford, Conn., and is buried in Cypress Hills Cemetery in the borough of Queens in New York City. Mourned by millions, his twin legacy was secure: he was an iconic figure in the mighty endeavor to create a color-blind nation and an immortal superstar in the firmament of baseball.

[Memorabilia and newspaper clippings are in the National Baseball Hall of Fame in Cooperstown, N.Y. Autobiographies are *Jackie Robinson*, as told to Wendell Smith (1948); and *I Never Had It Made*, as told to Alfred Duckett (1972). Also by Robinson is *Baseball Has Done It*, ed. Charles Dexter (1964). The fullest account of his life is Jules Tygiel, *Baseball's Great Experiment* (1983). See also Bill Roeder, *Jackie Robinson* (1950); Carl T. Rowan, *Wait Till Next Year*, written with Robinson (1960); Maury Allen, *Jackie Robinson* (1987); and Roger Kahn, *The Era: 1947–1957* (1993). An obituary is in the *New York Times*, Oct. 25, 1972.]

HENRY F. GRAFF

ROCKEFELLER, MARTHA BAIRD (Mar. 15, 1895–Jan. 24, 1971), concert pianist and philanthropist, was born in Madera, Calif., the daughter of William Finley Baird and Almina Abbey Smith of Streator, Ill. She was of Scotch-Irish Presbyterian stock; her ancestors had emigrated to Pennsylvania in the late 1700's. Her father was a coal and oil investor with offices in seven cities. Martha Baird attended Blairsville School for Girls in Pennsylvania, then Occidental College in Los Angeles, from which she graduated in 1916.

After graduating from the New England Conservatory of Music, Boston, in 1917, she studied piano with Artur Schnabel in Berlin and became a concert pianist. In 1918, she toured with Dame Nellie Melba, the Australian soprano. During the 1920's, based in London and New York City, she appeared in Britain, Europe, and the United States as a soloist with leading orchestras. Her British debut took place in 1926 with the London Symphony Orchestra under Sir Thomas Beecham. She also played with the Boston Symphony under Serge Koussevitzky. Martha Baird retired from the concert stage in 1931 at the relatively young age of thirty-six. Fond of both serious and light music, she composed "Win With Willkie" several years later for Wendell Willkie's 1940 Republican campaign.

Martha Baird was married three times, first to Adrian van Laar of New York on Aug. 4, 1920. This marriage lasted only three years and was childless; the couple separated in 1923 and divorced in April 1925. Martha Baird married Arthur Moulton Allen, a lawyer and a classmate at Brown of John D. Rockefeller, Jr., in May 1930. The couple lived in Providence, R.I., and had no children; Allen died twenty years later, in May 1950. On Aug. 15, 1951, in Providence, Martha Baird Allen married John D. Rockefeller, Jr., who at seventy-seven years of age, was twenty-one years her senior. Her relations with "Junior's" six children were cordial; the younger generation of Rockefellers called their stepmother "Aunt Martha." She and Rockefeller spent winters in Tucson, Ariz., summers in Seal Harbor, Maine, and fall and spring at the 3,500-acre Rockefeller estate in suburban Pocantico, N.Y., with occasional visits to Basset Hall in Colonial Williamsburg.

After retiring from the concert stage, Martha Baird continued to be actively involved with music as a philanthropist. She was a trustee of the New England Conservatory and served as President of the Providence Community Concert Association from 1937 until 1950. She contributed generously to the City Center in New York, Lincoln Center for the Performing Arts, the Metropolitan Opera, the Manhattan School of Music, and the Boston Symphony.

In 1962, she founded the Martha Baird Rockefeller Fund for Music to assist the careers of young musicians. Between 1962 and 1982 this fund made 1,262 grants to individuals and 741 to musical organizations worth a total of $9 million. As well as aiding young musicians, it assisted musical scholars and organizations. Martha Baird Rockefeller also supported many of John D. Rockefeller, Jr.'s, interests after he died in 1960; these included Colonial Williamsburg, the Harvard Divinity School, the Metropolitan Museum, Brown University, the National Council of Churches, and Riverside Church. Upon her husband's death, she became a trustee of the Rockefeller Brothers Fund, to which John D. Rockefeller, Jr., bequeathed half his $150-million estate. The other half of his estate was given to Martha Rockefeller, although in fact, she inherited $48 million after taxes plus various properties.

Martha Baird Rockefeller was the single largest contributor to the political campaigns of her stepson, Nelson A. Rockefeller. She gave him her late husband's estate, Kykuit, to live in when Nelson Rockefeller became governor of New York. She herself bequeathed $13.4 million to the Rockefeller Family Fund, $10 million to Lincoln Center, $5 million to her Fund for Music, and the remaining assets of her estate to the Rockefeller Brothers Fund. The house that Martha Baird Rockefeller had built on the Pocantico estate, Hillcrest, she also left to the Rockefeller Brothers Fund, which converted it into the Rockefeller Archive Center, established in 1975. She died at her home in New York City of a heart attack.

[Martha Baird Rockefeller's papers comprise a subgroup of the Rockefeller Family Archive at the Rockefeller Archive Center in North Tarrytown, N.Y. References to Martha Baird Rockefeller are to be found in Raymond B. Fosdisk, *John D. Rockefeller: A Portrait* (1956); Myer Kutz, *Rockefeller Power* (1974); Peter Collier and David Horowitz, *The Rockefellers: An American Dynasty* (1976); Joseph E. Persico, *The Imperial Rockefeller: A Biography of Nelson A. Rockefeller* (1982); and John E. Harr and Peter J. Johnson, *The Rockefeller Century* (1988) and *The Rockefeller Conscience* (1991). Information about her musical career is in Charles E. Clagham, *Biographical Dictionary of Music*, and in *New Grove Dictionary of American Music*, edited by H. Wiley Hitchcock and Stanley Sadie. Obituaries are in the *New York Times*, Jan. 15, 1971; *Newsweek*, Feb. 8, 1971; and *Time*, Feb. 8, 1971.]

DORIS L. EDER

ROCKEFELLER, WINTHROP (May 1, 1912–Feb. 22, 1973), philanthropist and politician, was born in New York City, the fourth son and fifth of six children of John D. Rockefeller, Jr., only son of the founder of Standard Oil, and Abby Greene Aldrich, patron of the arts and daughter of Nelson Aldrich, who served Rhode Island in the United States Senate from 1881 to 1911.

Rockefeller attended the Lincoln School in Manhattan, but his work was so poor that his father sent him to Loomis, a prep boarding school in Windsor, Conn., from which he graduated on June 6, 1931. In the fall, he entered Yale, which he left in February 1934 without earning a degree.

His father secured him a job with Humble Oil, a Standard Oil subsidiary, so that he might learn the oil business from the bottom up. He worked as a laborer in the Texas oil fields, lived in boarding houses, eating at chili stands, and apparently overcoming the distrust his fellow workers instinctively felt for a man named Rockefeller. He later said his years in the oil fields were the happiest of his life.

However, a Rockefeller could not remain a "roughneck" indefinitely, and early in 1937 he was recalled to New York City to participate in the family businesses and engage in philanthropic and public service endeavors. He worked first as a trainee at Chase Bank and then in the foreign department of Socony-Vacuum Oil Company. In 1937, he became a member of the board of Colonial Williamsburg, the Virginia historical restoration that was his father's pet project, and in 1953 its chairman. In 1938, he was appointed executive vice-chairman of the Greater New York Fund and raised money for the city's many charitable organizations. He was also active in raising funds for the National Urban League and the United Negro College Fund.

Although Rockefeller seemed to settle into a life his father thought proper, he escaped the obligations imposed by his name when he enlisted in the United States Army as a private in January 1941. After completing Infantry Officers Training School in January 1942 he was promoted to second lieutenant, served in the Pacific Theater, earned a Bronze Star and a Purple Heart, and eventually rose to the rank of lieutenant colonel.

After leaving the army in 1946, Rockefeller returned to Socony-Vacuum and his public service activities. The wealthy bachelor frequented New York City night spots and gained a reputation as a playboy and heavy drinker. On Feb. 14, 1948, he married Barbara ("Bobo") Paul Sears (born Jievute Paulekiute), a divorcee who had once been named Miss Lithuania in a Chicago beauty contest. The couple soon separated and were divorced in August 1954, after Rockefeller agreed to a settlement that reportedly gave Bobo almost $6 million and custody of their only son.

In 1953, during the highly publicized breakup of his first marriage, Rockefeller escaped to Arkansas, where he bought several hundred acres atop Petit Jean Mountain near Morrilton, Ark., and set about creating a model farm, which he named Winrock. He established several businesses and engaged in numerous philanthropic endeavors in his adopted state.

From the day of his arrival in Arkansas, his name and his wealth made him a man to be reckoned with, and despite the fact that Rockefeller was a Republican, Orval Faubus, the Democratic governor of the state, appointed him to head the newly created Arkansas Industrial Development Commission in 1955. On June 11, 1956, he was married for a second time to Jeannette Edris, who already had been married three times and had a son and daughter of her own. The couple divorced in April 1971.

By 1960, Rockefeller had developed an interest in strengthening the state's moribund Republican party. Although he was elected Republican national committeeman from Arkansas in 1961, many old guard Republicans were not pleased by the efforts of the immigrant from New York to breathe new life into their party. They had reached an accommodation with the state's Democratic machine and tended to view Rockefeller's efforts to bring new people into the party as a threat to their prerogatives.

Nonetheless, Rockefeller devoted himself and his vast financial resources to an effort to build a strong Republican party in the traditionally Democratic state. In 1964, he challenged Governor Orval Faubus, who was seeking a sixth (two-year) term. A key factor in this decision was Rockefeller's opposition to the staunch segregationist position Faubus had adopted during the attempt to integrate Little Rock's Central High School in 1957. He was defeated by Faubus, a master campaigner, who depicted Rockefeller as a "carpetbagger" and a divorced man who drank whiskey—"issues" that appeared to matter in Arkansas in the 1960's.

In 1966, Rockefeller defeated Democrat Jim Johnson, a rabid segregationist, to become Arkansas' first Republican governor since Reconstruction. In 1968, he won reelection by defeating Democrat Marion Crank. However, neither victory was due to any increase in the strength of the Arkansas GOP; instead, Rockefeller was put into office by independent voters and moderate Democrats who supported his reform program.

As governor (Jan. 10, 1967–Jan. 12, 1971), Rockefeller angered old guard Republicans by appointing people, including blacks, on the basis of competence rather than party. He also faced an often hostile Democratic legislature throughout his tenure. Nonetheless, he was able to secure the passage of laws that helped reform the state's prison system and to improve education and social services. However, his call for higher taxes to fund such programs endeared

him neither to the legislators nor to the voters.

Despite a pledge that he would seek no more than two terms as governor, he ran for a third term in 1970 when it appeared that his likely Democratic opponent would be Orval Faubus, who had defeated him in 1964 and who, Rockefeller feared, would dismantle his reforms if he returned to power. However, Dale Bumpers, a moderate Democrat and a newcomer to politics, defeated Faubus in the primary and Rockefeller in the general election. Ironically, Bumpers would succeed in getting the general assembly to pass many of the proposals it had rejected when Rockefeller was governor.

Although Rockefeller's success as governor was mixed, his impact on Arkansas politics was profound for, as the headline of an obituary put it, "he altered [the] course of state politics." His attempt to build the Arkansas GOP failed, but his challenge led to the transformation of the Arkansas Democratic party in which power passed from the old machine politicians, who traded on racial issues, to a new generation of moderates. As Dale Bumpers said in 1989, "If there had not been a Winthrop Rockefeller, I am not sure there would have been a Governor Dale Bumpers, a Governor David Pryor or a Governor Bill Clinton."

In September 1972, Rockefeller was diagnosed as having inoperable cancer. On Feb. 14, 1973, he was admitted to the Desert Hospital in Palm Springs, where he died eight days later. His body was cremated and the ashes returned to his beloved Winrock Farm, where a memorial service was held on March 4. Although many invited dignitaries eulogized him, the sincerest tribute was the presence of three thousand Arkansans who came unbidden to pay their final respects to the "Hillbilly Rockefeller" who had done so much for their state.

[Rockefeller's papers are in the "Winthrop Rockefeller Archives" at the University of Arkansas (Little Rock) Library. John L. Ward, *The Arkansas Rockefeller* (1978), and Cathy K. Urwin, *Agenda for Reform: Winthrop Rockefeller as Governor of Arkansas, 1967–71* (1991), emphasize Rockefeller's political career in Arkansas. Peter Collier and David Horowitz, *The Rockefellers: An American Dynasty* (1976); and Joseph E. Persico, *The Imperial Rockefeller: A Biography of Nelson A. Rockefeller* (1982) are useful for Rockefeller's relationship with his family. Obituaries appear in the *New York Times*, the *Los Angeles Times*, and the *Arkansas Gazette*, all Feb. 23, 1973.]

ROMAN ROME

ROMANOFF, MICHAEL ("PRINCE MIKE") (February 1893?–Sept. 1, 1971), restaurateur and pretender to the Russian nobility, was born sometime before the turn of the century, either in Vilna, Lithuania, or in Brooklyn, N.Y. Later in his life he fought for years with the United States Immigration Service about his birthplace; neither he nor they could produce documentation. His original name may have been Harry F. Gerguson, but even that is in dispute. His immigrant parents were poor, and he was turned over to the New York Society for the Prevention of Cruelty to Children at an early age. He spent his youth in orphanages in New York City, with a detour to rural Illinois around 1904 as part of a program to get children out of the city. Even then, one biographer claims, he was assuming names and attempting confidence games.

According to Romanoff, he stowed away on a ship sailing to Great Britain around 1910. His next few years, like his first, are foggy. He later claimed to have attended Eton, Cambridge, and Oxford. The upper-class British accent he adopted from the time of his trip to the United Kingdom served to charm naive Americans. The nature of his activities during World War I varied according to his mood and persona during the telling. Richard Gehman later noted in *Cosmopolitan* (January 1959), "It seems probable he is the only veteran . . . who served, simultaneously, as a British lieutenant on the Western Front, as a Cossack colonel on the Eastern Front, as a Foreign Legionnaire, and as a member of Allenby's forces in Palestine."

Gerguson/Romanoff first attracted the attention of the press around 1922 when he announced that he was Prince Michael Alexandrovitch Dmitri Obolensky Romanoff, a close relative of the late Tsar Nicholas II. On the basis of this aristocratic claim, he ran up large bills in stores and hotels in England and France, landing occasionally in jail when he was unable to pay.

Romanoff returned to the United States in 1922 and began a ten-year battle with Immigration authorities. He claimed American citizenship, but the government contested the claim and tried to keep him on Ellis Island. He escaped from the island (by swimming, so he said, but the authorities maintained he stowed away on a ferry), and continued his career as a con artist. According to one source, he attended Harvard in 1923 but was expelled as a fraud,

and he found himself apprehended again by the government in 1924. This time, officials could not decide to what country they should deport him, however, and released him.

His next run-in with the Immigration Service came in April 1932. After another trip to Europe he stowed away on the *Ile de France* and returned again to New York. He was deported to France but returned once more as a stowaway on the *Europa* in December. This time his case went to court, and the judge allowed him to remain in the United States, although he decreed that Romanoff had to cancel a vaudeville tour he had arranged focusing on his experiences as a stowaway and aristocrat.

Using a variety of names, Romanoff crisscrossed America after his return in 1932, leaving behind him a string of bad checks. His charm was such that some of his victims apparently enjoyed the compliment his cheating bestowed upon them. In the late 1920's, he made his first visit to Hollywood, attracting stars and movie moguls with his glitzy image and offering to serve as an expert on Russian affairs in films. After living and "working" briefly in New York City and Virginia in the mid-1930's, he entered business in Los Angeles in 1939. Financed by admiring friends—including Robert Benchley, Darryl Zanuck, "Jock" Whitney, and James Cagney—he opened Romanoff's, a restaurant that flourished primarily on the basis of his personality. Both he and it became Hollywood institutions.

Throughout the 1940's and 1950's, Romanoff's was the place to see and be seen in the filmmaking community. "Prince Mike" assigned regular tables to special celebrities, and much was made of who got to sit where and look at whom. Stories, mostly apocryphal, circulated about his many personas, about his charming inconsistencies (one day he was the czar's brother; the next day, his nephew; the next, his cousin) and about his idiosyncrasies. He himself, it was said, dined only with his dogs. He reportedly sent money to a quiz-show contestant who lost a game because he said the Prince's title was real. "The first believer I ever had," Romanoff joked, "should not go unrewarded." He dressed elegantly, refused (not surprisingly) to speak Russian, and hobnobbed with Hollywood's "elegantsia" as well as with gangsters, politicians, and J. Edgar Hoover.

Still maintaining his claims to royalty, Romanoff nevertheless settled into respectability.

In July 1948, he married his young secretary and bookkeeper, Gloria Lister. They had no children. In 1951 he moved his restaurant to a larger location, whereupon his profits rose. He eventually opened other branches, but the Hollywood site remained the center of his enterprise. He later told a reporter that the average check at the restaurant in its heyday came to $10 per person for dinner and $6.50 per person for lunch, drink included.

In 1958, an act of Congress brought Romanoff his longtime dream and made it possible for him to become a citizen, although he was required during the ceremony to renounce all claim to foreign titles. He followed up this milestone with a much publicized trip to his "native" land, the Soviet Union, to see what had become of his so-called family's vast holdings.

Romanoff's closed its doors in 1962. During his retirement, Romanoff amused himself working as a production assistant in films for his friend Frank Sinatra, appearing in a few motion pictures as well. He was still the country's best-known, least-documented, and most-beloved impostor when he died of a heart attack in Hollywood at the age of seventy-eight or maybe eighty-one. No one can be certain.

[The Billy Rose Theatre Collection of the New York Public Library maintains clipping files on Romanoff. Biographical material can be found in Alva Johnston, "The Downfall of Prince Mike," *Saturday Evening Post*, Mar. 20, 1943; "Mike's Place," *Time*, Nov. 6, 1950; "Personality," *Time*, June 9, 1952; and "The Real Tinsel," *Time*, Dec. 21, 1962. See also " 'Citizen' Romanoff," *Newsweek*, May 12, 1958, as well as the *New York Times*, May 17, 1958; *Cosmopolitan*, Jan. 1959; and *Los Angeles*, Nov. 1990. Obituaries appear in the *New York Times*, Sept. 2–3, 1971.]

TINKY ("DAKOTA") WEISBLAT

ROMER, ALFRED SHERWOOD ("AL") (Dec. 28, 1894–Nov. 5, 1973), paleontologist, was born in White Plains, N.Y., to Fenry Houston Romer, a journalist, and Evelyn Sherwood. After completing high school in White Plains, he spent one year working as a railroad clerk. In 1913, he entered Amherst College, where he majored in history and German literature. However, a course on evolution taught by Frederick Brewster Loomis had a profound influence on Romer; indeed, it shaped the course of his life.

After graduating in 1917, Romer, like many young men of his time, was eager to join the war effort in Europe. He joined the American Field Service in France, and a few months later enlisted in the U.S. Army.

Upon his return to the United States in 1919, Romer entered graduate school in biology at Columbia University. There he worked with the talented vertebrate anatomist and paleontologist William King Gregory and completed his Ph.D. in 1921; his dissertation, on the comparative musculature of early reptiles, remains a classic. For the next two years he taught courses in anatomy and embryology at Bellevue Hospital Medical College of New York University. In 1923, he joined the geology department of the University of Chicago and taught there for eleven years. During his first year at Chicago, Romer met Ruth Hibbard; they were married in 1924 and subsequently had three children. In 1934, Romer left Chicago for Harvard University, where he remained for the rest of his career. At Harvard, Romer was a professor of zoology in the biology department and curator of vertebrate paleontology at the Museum of Comparative Zoology. He also served as director of the museum from 1946 to 1961.

Romer was most famous for his work on the study of fossil animals, particularly reptiles and amphibians from the Permian period of geological time. During his career he published more than 200 papers and books on vertebrate paleontology, the most important of which were technical studies concerning the anatomical structure, classification, and evolutionary relationships of fossil vertebrates. His researches were most fully summed up in two notable works, *Vertebrate Paleontology* (1933) and *Osteology of the Reptiles* (1956). *Vertebrate Paleontology*, by virtue of its detailed descriptions and classification of all major fossil vertebrate groups, was one of the first comprehensive textbooks in that field, and in revised editions served vertebrate paleontologists and biologists as an indispensable resource for over fifty years. *Osteology of the Reptiles* was a massive sourcebook incorporating a wealth of information on fossil and living reptiles.

While Romer was most famous for his work in systematics, he was trained primarily as a biologist and sought to understand ancient organisms as once-living creatures. He devoted much of his early work to reconstructing the muscular and skeletal structure of ancient amphibians and reptiles. His early studies on the origin and development of limbs incorporated research in embryology as well as paleontology. At Chicago, and later at Harvard, his work led to important contributions on the embryonic and evolutionary history of cartilage and bone and on the structure and function of the nervous system among fossil reptiles. Romer's sound knowledge of anatomy, embryology, and neurology was evident in *Man and the Vertebrates* (1933) and *The Vertebrate Body* (1949), popular books that were frequently reprinted and widely used in college biology courses. Romer's emphasis on the biological aspects of vertebrate paleontology, a field that bridges both biology and geology, affected his professional associations. That focus created problems in the geology department at the University of Chicago and influenced his decision to accept an appointment at Harvard. His conception of vertebrate paleontology as a dimension of biology resulted in conflicts within the Paleontological Society and led Romer to play a major role in creating a separate Society of Vertebrate Paleontology in 1940.

Romer's work contributed significantly to the understanding of vertebrate evolutionary history. In a number of technical papers and in *The Vertebrate Story* (1959), a detailed yet popular description of the evolution of vertebrate life, Romer's investigations helped to define key evolutionary transitions from fish to amphibians, amphibians to reptiles, and reptiles to mammals. His studies described anatomical and physiological adaptations that allowed for the early evolution of fishes and of the first land animals. Those researches led him to examine ancient ecological conditions and to emphasize the importance of freshwater environments for vertebrate evolution, an interpretation that is no longer fully accepted. Although Romer was an expert on vertebrate evolution, he concerned himself with explaining the pattern rather than the causal mechanisms of evolutionary change. He rarely commented on the factors that produced evolution; however, he was committed to the Darwinian theory of evolution by natural selection and was a staunch opponent of any teleological explanation.

Romer was among the first students of fossil vertebrates to lend plausibility to the hypothesis of continental drift. While most geologists and vertebrate paleontologists remained wedded to the concept of stable land masses and ocean basins and explained the geographical distribu-

tion of animals on the basis of migration, Romer in the mid-1940's became aware of striking similarities between Permian reptiles in western Texas and in Czechoslovakia and began seriously to consider the possibility that the continents were once joined and had subsequently drifted apart. During the next twenty-five years Romer brought evidence from vertebrate paleontology to bear on the understanding of continental drift.

Romer likewise contributed to vertebrate paleontology in other respects. Although he originally had little background in fieldwork and no formal training in geology, he developed active programs of exploration. At Chicago, Romer and his principal assistant Paul Miller undertook field trips to Texas, New Mexico, and South Africa that led to the development of one of the world's leading collections of Permian vertebrates. Those specimens, originally housed in the former Walker Museum of the University of Chicago, are now in the Field Museum of Natural History. Later investigations led to the discovery of fossils in Argentina that offered valuable new information on the origin of mammals. His discoveries added substantially to the collections of the Museum of Comparative Zoology, and Romer, a popular teacher, employed those materials to train dozens of students in vertebrate paleontology and zoology. For his scientific contributions, Romer received several honorary doctorates as well as prestigious awards from the National Academy of Sciences, the Geological Society of America, and other professional organizations. As director of the museum, he helped revive a moribund institution and transformed it into one of the premier centers for the study of evolution.

Romer died in Cambridge, Mass.

[The principal collection of Romer manuscripts is in the Harvard University Archives. An unpublished autobiographical sketch is in the archives of the National Academy of Sciences, Washington, D.C. Romer's major works include "Review of the Labyrinthodontia," *Bulletin of the Museum of Comparative Zoology* 99 (1947); with L. I. Prince, "Review of the Pelycosauria," *Geological Society of America Special Papers* 26 (1940); and with Nelda E. Wright, Tilly Edinger, and Richard van Frank, "Bibliography of Fossil Vertebrates Exclusive of North America, 1507–1927," *Geological Society of America Memoirs* 87 (1962).

See also G. E. Erickson, "Alfred Sherwood Romer, 1894–1973." *Anatomical Record* 189 (1977);

and Edwin H. Colbert, "Alfred Sherwood Romer," *National Academy of Sciences Biographical Memoirs* 53 (1982). An obituary appears in the *New York Times*, Nov. 7, 1973.]

RONALD RAINGER

ROMNES, HAAKON INGOLF ("H. I.") (Mar. 2, 1907–Nov. 19, 1973), business executive, was born in Stoughton, Wis., one of five children of Hans Romnes and Ingebord Fosdal, both of Norwegian descent. He graduated from public schools in Stoughton and then enrolled at the University of Wisconsin. During the summer vacation preceding his senior year he worked as a telephone installer for the Wisconsin Bell Telephone Company, a subsidiary of the American Telephone and Telegraph Company (AT&T). After graduating with a degree in electrical engineering in 1928, he joined AT&T's Bell Telephone Laboratories in New York City as a circuit designer.

He married Aimee Champion on Dec. 26, 1930; they had one child.

Romnes transferred to AT&T's engineering department in 1935, and held a series of technical positions during the following twenty years. Romnes had widely acknowledged technological expertise, and had a number of patents issued for his equipment designs. AT&T placed higher value on engineering and production expertise rather than marketing ability, since it was an era when competition was just starting. He also served briefly in 1950 as an operating officer at Illinois Bell Telephone Company in Chicago. As vice-president of AT&T during the period 1952–1959, he oversaw the design and early implementation of AT&T's direct distance dialing network for long-distance calls. From 1959 through 1963 Romnes was president of Western Electric, the manufacturing subsidiary of AT&T. While he was president of Western Electric, he initiated the Equal Employment Opportunity policy (in addition, Romnes was always a supporter of the National Urban League and the United Negro College Fund). He became AT&T president in 1965, and chairman and CEO when Frederick Kappel retired from those posts in February 1967.

Romnes headed AT&T at a time when the public consensus over telecommunications regulation was dissolving. During the previous fifty years the American public had accepted AT&T's argument concerning the necessity for end-to-end telephone service run exclusively by AT&T. Government regulators not only prevented competition in local telephone services, which everyone considered a "natural monopoly," they also enforced AT&T's policies of prohibiting customers from connecting non–AT&T telephone equipment in their homes and businesses or allowing the use of alternative long-distance transmission facilities.

During the 1950's and 1960's new technology involving computers and microwaves prompted many firms to begin offering various telecommunications services outside of AT&T's Bell system. Telephone customers began seeking interconnection with non–AT&T long-distance facilities, as well as the use of customer premises telephone equipment (CPE) not manufactured by AT&T. In 1968 the Federal Communications Commission (FCC) ruled in the *Carterphone* case that non–AT&T CPE could be connected with AT&T lines. Subsequent rulings by the FCC and the courts allowed Microwave Communications, Inc. (MCI) and other alternative long-distance phone companies to compete with AT&T.

AT&T had to develop new policies in response to this competition. It initially allowed the connection of "foreign" (non–AT&T) CPE only when mediated by a mandatory AT&T-provided protective coupling arrangement (PCA). But the FCC commissioned studies that concluded that PCAs were overpriced and unnecessary, and then adopted a policy of allowing the interconnection of any CPE that met minimum technical standards set by the FCC. Meanwhile, AT&T responded to long-distance competition by enacting a special TELPAK tariff, which offered lower prices for private lines to customers wooed by competing carriers, but the FCC eventually ruled that the TELPAK tariff was an illegal exercise of anticompetitive market power.

While fighting these regulatory battles, AT&T initiated a number of technical advances. In addition to having responsibility for approving (or disapproving) all major changes, Romnes was AT&T spokesman who announced major innovations at press conferences. AT&T began replacing electro-mechanical switches with completely electronic facilities to allow a shift from analog to digital transmission. It transformed long-distance usage by introducing the popular "800" service, and developed the sophisticated UNIX computer operating system. AT&T was less successful when it introduced the Picturephone in 1968; Romnes incorrectly predicted that it would "be in very considerable use within less than ten years." Meanwhile, telephone service in New York City and other major cities deteriorated as the result of unanticipated demand and inadequate maintenance. AT&T contended that this deterioration was due to regulators' slow response to requests for telephone rate increases, which failed to take sufficient account of the rapid inflation of that period.

Romnes eventually worked out a new AT&T corporate policy that accepted the reality of competition. Romnes intended AT&T to focus its future efforts toward competing in open markets for CPE and long-distance customers, as well as in offering specialized, nontraditional services over the local telephone lines.

AT&T morale fell during this period, particularly after the New York Bell service crisis of 1969, the result of growing criticism over the highly publicized technical breakdowns and about AT&T's seemingly anachronistic position as a government-protected monopoly. Romnes was also chronically ill during these years. He further aggravated the corporate morale problem by failing to name anyone as AT&T's president, and held the dual post of chairman and president during the years 1970 to 1972.

Romnes finally named John D. deButts as AT&T president (and according to AT&T tradition, Romnes's heir apparent) in early 1972. An operations executive who had a much more hostile attitude toward the idea of competition, deButts became Romnes's successor as AT&T chairman and CEO on Apr. 1, 1972, when Romnes retired at the mandatory age of sixty-five. Romnes stayed on in the largely honorary position of chairman of the executive committee of the AT&T board of directors. He died nineteen months later, in Sarasota, Fla.

Romnes's reputation declined during, and immediately after, his tenure as head of AT&T. Although virtually everyone praised Romnes for his technological expertise, deButts and other critics complained about his lack of operations experience and his refusal to take a stronger position in the face of a growing tide of competition. Romnes's acceptance of the inevitability of competition, however, now seems more realistic than the outlook of his critics. The more aggressive anticompetition policies of his successor aggravated public and congressional opinion, prevented any political compromise, and eventually resulted in the breakup of AT&T in the early 1980's.

[The corporate papers at AT&T dealing with Romnes are not yet open to the public. Romnes described his background and leadership style in an interview, "H. I. Romnes of AT&T: Running the World's Largest Company," *Nation's Business*, Apr. 1971. Peter Temin with Louis Galambos, *The Fall of the Bell System: A Study in Pricing and Politics* (1987), discusses the organizational setting of the later years of his career. Alfred E. Kahn, *The Economics of Regulation*, 2 vols. (1971), describes the economics and regulation of U.S. telephone companies during this period. An obituary is in the *New York Times*, Nov. 21, 1973.]

STEPHEN G. MARSHALL

ROPER, ELMO BURNS, JR. (July 31, 1900–Apr. 30, 1971), public opinion analyst, was born in Hebron, Nebr., the son of Coco Malowney and Elmo Burns Roper. After graduating from Hebron High School, he briefly attended the University of Minnesota and the University of Edinburgh before opening a jewelry store in Creston, Iowa (1921). In June 1922, Roper married Dorothy C. Shaw; they had two children. Roper became a clock salesman in 1928, and later said he had been able to make a good living during the Great Depression by polling his customers on their preferences in clock styles. He gave up selling in 1933 to begin market research in New York City, where he formed a partnership with Paul T. Cherington and Richardson Wood. Roper devoted himself to perfecting sampling techniques that utilized a small number of subjects carefully selected to form a representative cross section of the group surveyed. The firm was engaged by Henry R. Luce in 1935 to conduct surveys of public opinion for *Fortune*. Roper parted company with Cherington and Wood in 1937 and established his own firm, which eventually became Roper Research Associates.

Roper had become prominent in 1936 when he predicted a landslide victory for Franklin D. Roosevelt. Unlike the celebrated *Literary Digest* straw vote and the polls of his rivals, George Gallup and Archibald Crossley, which all predicted a defeat for Roosevelt, Roper's prediction came within 1 percent of Roosevelt's margin of victory. In the elections of 1940 and 1944, Roper's were again the most accurate forecasts, coming within one-fifth to one-half of a percentage point of predicting Roosevelt's actual percentages of the popular vote. Along with other pollsters, Roper erred in predicting Thomas E. Dewey as the victor over President Harry S. Truman in 1948 and in forecasting that Richard M. Nixon would defeat John F. Kennedy in 1960 by 1 percent of the popular vote. In the main, however, the sampling techniques developed by Roper Research Associates proved accurate in election predictions; they were widely adapted by other political pollsters, and became a mainstay of political campaign organizations and media analyses of voting trends.

In addition to directing the Survey of Public Opinion for *Fortune*—the first nationwide polling of the public's thinking on economic, political, and social matters—for fifteen years, Roper conducted marketing research for other clients including the American Meat Institute, Illinois Power, Metropolitan Life Insurance, Philip Morris, RCA Victor, and the Standard Oil Company of New Jersey. His market surveys were designed to uncover consumers' buying habits and preferences, as well as their reactions to product design and advertising. In the 1940 election, moreover, Roper, working for the Columbia Broadcasting System, inaugurated the practice of analyzing voting trends over the air; during the 1944 preelection period a large number of newspapers subscribed to Roper's semiweekly column, "What People Are Thinking," syndicated by the *New York Herald Tribune*, for the latest surveys of public opinion regarding political candidates and issues.

During World War II, Roper briefly worked for the Office of Production Management and the Office of Facts and Figures before serving as a deputy director of the Office of Strategic Services from 1942 to 1945. In the 1942–1943 academic year, Roper was also an assistant professor of journalism at Columbia University. Throughout the war, he continued his newspaper column and his work as an editor at large of the *Saturday Review*, and analyzed public opinion in numerous magazine articles and radio programs. Following the war, the lean six-footer, almost always photographed with rimless glasses and a pipe in his mouth, publicly associated himself with some of the liberal and internationalist causes he believed in. He assumed key positions in the Atlantic Union Committee, the Fund for the Republic, the National Planning Association, the Connecticut State Commission on Civil Rights, the Connecticut State Commission to Study the Problems of the Aging, and Freedom House and the Henry Street Settlement in New York City. The author of *You and Your Leaders* (1957), Roper in 1959 was given the Julian Woodward Award of the American Association for Public Opinion Research for his contributions to that profession.

Roper retired from his market research firm in 1966. Although he retained the title of senior consultant, he devoted most of his time to protecting the environment around his home in West Redding, Conn., growing and caring for trees, and conducting soil-conservation work on his experimental farm in Nebraska. He came to believe that election predictions were "socially useless" and that the important purpose of public opinion polling was to discover where more information needed to be disseminated in order to counter public ignorance. Once given the necessary facts, Roper thought, the public "is likely to steer just as wise and fair a course as that plotted by any of its leaders." To report the opinions of the people on public matters was vital because "the people have a sovereign right to be heard and to be heeded by their representatives." Roper died in Norwalk, Conn.

[Roper's main writings, besides *You and Your Leaders*, include "So the Blind Shall Not Lead," *Fortune*, Feb. 1942; "The Public Looks at Business," *Harvard Business Review*, Mar. 1949; and "The Forgotten Man—of Learning," *Freedom and Union*, Oct. 1960. An obituary is in the *New York Times*, May 1, 1971.]

HARVARD SITKOFF

RORTY, JAMES HANCOCK (Mar. 30, 1890–Feb. 25, 1973), poet, editor, author, and self-described "last of the muckrakers," was born in Middletown, N.Y., to Richard McKay Rorty, who ran a small grocery store, and Octavia Churchill. His father, an Irish nationalist, had fled British persecution, and Rorty grew up under the formidable influence of Richard Rorty's political convictions. While still in high school, he worked as a reporter on the *Middletown Daily Times Press*.

Rorty attended Tufts College in Medford, Mass., earning a bachelor's degree in 1913. For the next few years he lived in New York City and pursued a number of eclectic interests, briefly studying at both New York University and the New School For Social Research, writing copy for an advertising agency, and working at a settlement house.

Despite his emerging socialist politics, which had anarchist overtones, Rorty volunteered to serve in World War I and became a private in the ambulance service, carrying stretchers in the Argonne Forest. His work earned him the Distinguished Service Cross and also made him a pacifist.

After returning from Europe, Rorty married Maria Ward Lambin on Sept. 20, 1920, and moved to San Francisco. By day he worked in advertising; at night he wrote experimental poetry. His 1922 poem "When We Dead Waken" won *The Nation's* poetry prize.

In 1924, Rorty returned to New York City in order to join the staff of *The New Masses*. A founding editor, he left the magazine the following year after clashing with his colleagues over the publication of a poem by his West Coast friend Robinson Jeffers. For the rest of the 1920's, he returned to the familiar pattern of writing advertising copy by day and verse in his free time. He published two volumes of poems, *What Michael Said to the Census-Taker* (1922) and *Children of the Sun* (1926). His first brief marriage ended in divorce. Thereafter, he married Winifred Rauschenbusch, daughter of the Christian socialist reformer Walter Rauschenbusch, in the spring of 1928. Their only child, Richard Rorty, who became a noted philosopher, was born in 1931.

Rorty's brief sojourn at *The New Masses* marked the beginning of his radical political career. In 1927, he was arrested for protesting the execution of Nicola Sacco and Bartolomeo Vanzetti in Boston. In 1932, he became secretary of the League of Professionals for Foster and Ford, an organization promoting the election of the Communist party's candidates for president and vice-president. But he was not comfortable with the Communists' sectarian philosophy modeled on the Soviet Union and left them in 1934 for the American Workers' Party, more attuned to American circumstances. His 1936 book, *Where Life Is Better*, challenged the Communist party line by asserting that the American masses were not especially revolutionary. By the late 1930's, Rorty was a mainstay of the oppositionalist Marxist movement and active in two important anti-Stalinist organizations, the American Committee for the Defense of Leon Trotsky and the Committee for Cultural Freedom.

Rorty's most important contributions came in the area of consumer affairs. He was a muckraker who challenged institutions that threatened the health and safety of Americans. In 1934, he published *Our Master's Voice*, an exposé of the advertising industry. His 1939 book, *American Medicine Mobilizes*, was an attack on the American Medical Association. He also wrote *Tomorrow's Food* (1946) with N. Philip Norman, *The American Fluoridation Experiment* (1957), and dozens of articles concerned with health, nutrition, ecology, and consumer affairs.

During the 1940's, Rorty moved toward the center politically. From 1946 to 1949, he was a consultant for the Tennessee Valley Authority, authoring two of its pamphlets, "Food at the Grass Roots" and "Soil, People and Chemical Engineering." Another government agency, the Voice of America, employed him as a scriptwriter, but after a loyalty hearing, he lost his job in 1951 because of his radical past. Yet he was a Republican and avowed anti-Communist in the 1950's. He belonged to the American Committee for Cultural Freedom, which opposed totalitarianism at home and abroad. In 1954, he coauthored a book for the ACCF, *McCarthy and the Communists*, with Moshe Decter. The work expressed the anti-Communist view of McCarthyism but denounced extremism, staying within bounds of traditional civil liberties while investigating potential security threats.

During the 1950's, Rorty wrote both fiction and nonfiction. He produced articles on organized labor and civil rights as well as poetry and plays. In 1948, he won Poetry Awards' English language award for best poem with "Night Hawks Over Bronxville." A severe mental breakdown in 1962 left him unable to write. In 1971, he published an anthology of his poems, *Selected Poems, 1930–1970*. Rorty died in Sarasota, Fla.

[Rorty's papers, including two versions of his unpublished memoirs, are at the University of Oregon. See also the brief sketch of Rorty in Alan M. Wald, *The New York Intellectuals* (1987). An obituary appears in the *New York Times*, Feb. 26, 1973.]

JUDY KUTULAS

ROSENMAN, SAMUEL IRVING (Feb. 13, 1896–June 24, 1973), lawyer, jurist, and political adviser, was born in San Antonio, Tex., the fifth and last child of Sol Rosenman and Ethel Paler. His father, a Jewish immigrant from

Ukraine, was a merchant-peddler in Texas. In 1905 the family moved to New York City, where Sol became a clothing manufacturer.

Samuel Rosenman attended Townsend Harris High School and spent one year at City College of New York before transferring to Columbia College, from which he graduated in 1915. He chafed at the social segregation of Jews at Columbia, and years later wrote of his "deep dislike and resentment" when he recollected his undergraduate days. He enrolled in Columbia Law School in 1915. He interrupted his legal studies in 1917 after the United States entered World War I to enlist as a private in the U.S. Army. He was discharged in 1919 as a first lieutenant, having spent his entire period of military service in the United States. He received his law degree in 1919 and was admitted to the New York State Bar in 1920. On Sept. 15, 1924, he married Dorothy Reuben, with whom he had two sons.

Handsome though heavy-set, Rosenman had a courteous and even-tempered demeanor. He neither smoked nor drank to excess, but he was a prodigious eater, who carried up to 200 pounds on his five-foot, seven-inch frame. His methodical work habits, his legal acumen, his speech-writing skills, and his willingness to play the role of loyal and anonymous subordinate made him a valuable asset to a succession of politicians, including Governor Alfred E. Smith, Franklin D. Roosevelt, and Harry S. Truman.

Running as a Democrat, Rosenman was elected in 1921 as a state assemblyman from New York City's Eleventh District, and re-elected in each of the succeeding four years. After Al Smith's return to the New York governorship in 1923, Rosenman quickly became identified as a reliable supporter of Smith's program of progressive legislation in the fields of labor, housing, and public works. In 1923 he authored the Rosenman Act, which strengthened rent control laws. He acquired such a reputation for expert craftsmanship in the drafting of bills that in 1926 he was asked to serve on the Legislative Bill Drafting Commission. He left elective office to serve on the commission. Rosenman's appointment to that officially nonpartisan body, removed from the electoral arena, suggested the pattern of much of his subsequent career, which was marked by service as a skilled legislative technician, jurist, and political operative who preferred to work out of the limelight.

In 1928 Rosenman was attached to Franklin D. Roosevelt's gubernatorial campaign, with the assignment of keeping the candidate informed on State of New York legislative developments. Rosenman had never met Roosevelt and was skeptical of his commitment to Smith's progressive political agenda. Roosevelt swiftly won him over, however, and Rosenman began an association with Roosevelt that endured until the latter's death seventeen years later.

Though he had signed on as a legislative specialist, Rosenman was soon put to work writing speeches. This was an unfamiliar assignment, but one he quickly mastered. Soon after his election to the New York governorship in November 1928, Roosevelt appointed Rosenman counsel to the governor. In that capacity Rosenman played a key role in promoting Governor Roosevelt's program for the development of hydroelectric power resources in New York. He also advised the governor about the politically tricky investigations of corruption in New York City government that resulted in the resignation of Mayor James J. Walker of New York City in September 1932.

Roosevelt rewarded his counsel in 1932 with an appointment to the State of New York Supreme Court. However, Rosenman's part in the New York City investigations had earned him the enmity of the Tammany Hall Democratic organization, which spitefully refused to nominate him for election to a regular term. But the following year New York's new governor, Herbert Lehman, reappointed him to the court and he won election to a fourteen-year term. As a judge, Rosenman generally adhered to the philosophy of judicial restraint, deferring insofar as reasonable to the prerogatives of the legislature.

Rosenman contributed conspicuously to Roosevelt's presidential campaign in 1932 by urging that the candidate seek advice from a body of academic experts who became known as the "Brain Trust." Rosenman also recruited many of those experts, including Raymond Moley, who became the group's acknowledged leader. Most famously, Rosenman drafted the peroration of Roosevelt's acceptance speech to the Democratic Convention, in which the phrase "New Deal" was coined.

While sitting as a judge in New York, Rosenman also continued to advise President Roosevelt in Washington. He served as the president's chief speech writer in the 1936 presidential campaign, and worked on Roosevelt's

Supreme Court reorganization plan in 1937. About this time too, as a director of the American Jewish Committee, which feared that additional Jewish immigration would excite an anti-Semitic backlash in the United States, he advised Roosevelt against increasing immigration quotas for Jewish refugees from Hitler's Europe. He also began work on the thirteen volumes of *Public Papers and Addresses of Franklin D. Roosevelt, 1928–1945* (1938–1950), still the definitive compilation.

In September 1943 Rosenman resigned his New York judgeship to become special counsel to the president. In that capacity he worked on legislation that evolved into the G.I. Bill of Rights and took on special assignments dealing with economic mobilization, postwar economic planning for Europe, and war crimes trials. After Roosevelt's death he continued as special counsel to President Harry S. Truman, but resigned in February 1946 to take up the private practice of law in New York. Much of that practice dealt with public works projects promoted by Robert Moses. He declined Truman's offers of a federal judgeship in 1951 and the opportunity to become U.S. Attorney General in 1952, but served on special commissions dealing with labor and manpower issues for both Truman and John F. Kennedy.

In 1964 Rosenman was elected president of the Association of the Bar of the City of New York, an especially gratifying recognition from the same legal guild that had treated Jews as virtual outcasts when he was beginning his career. He devoted much of his effort in the last years of his life to improving procedures for judicial appointment, and took a leading part in the effort that thwarted Richard Nixon's nomination of G. Harrold Carswell to the United States Supreme Court in 1970. He died in New York City.

[Rosenman's papers are in the Roosevelt Library in Hyde Park, N.Y. An oral history interview is at the Columbia Oral History Research Project at Columbia University. Also see Samuel I. Rosenman, *Working with Roosevelt* (1952); and Samuel B. Hand, *Counsel and Advise: A Political Biography* (1979). An obituary appears in the *New York Times*, June 25, 1973.]

DAVID M. KENNEDY

ROSS, THOMAS JOSEPH (July 27, 1893–May 27, 1975), public relations counsel, was born in Brooklyn, N.Y., the son of Thomas J. and Mary Egan Ross. He received his B.A. degree from St. Francis Xavier College in New York City in 1913. While an undergraduate, he began writing for newspapers. His first employers included the *Brooklyn Eagle* (once edited by Walt Whitman) and the *New York Tribune*. After graduation in 1913, he worked as a reporter for the *New York Sun* and in 1916 as political correspondent for the *New York Tribune*. At the *Tribune* he covered the 1916 presidential campaign between Woodrow Wilson and Charles Evans Hughes.

In 1917, after the United States had entered World War I, Ross was commissioned a second lieutenant in the Eighteenth Cavalry. He served with the artillery and was promoted to first lieutenant before being demobilized. In 1919, Ross was hired by Ivy Ledbetter Lee, often called the father of modern public relations, and joined Lee's firm, Lee, Harris and Lee. Its predecessor company, Parker and Lee (founded in 1904), is considered to have been one of the first public relations counselors in the United States.

By 1933, Ross was a senior partner in the Lee firm, which was renamed Ivy Lee and T. J. Ross. When Lee died in 1934, Ross became the firm's principal and, after 1961, chairman of the corporation T. J. Ross & Associates. The firm developed many of the ideas common in modern public-relations practice, including the concepts that corporations ought to align themselves with the public interest, that keeping the public informed was of benefit to companies, and that the best way to inform the public was to provide the media with facts promptly and accurately.

Although Ross was a major figure in the firm, his name does not seem to have been closely associated with some of the questionable aspects of its history. During his tenure, for example, Lee urged that the United States extend diplomatic recognition to and open trade with the Soviet Union. From 1933 until Lee's death the following year, the firm represented the German Dye Trust, a cartel controlled by the Nazi party through I. G. Farben. The account was resigned soon after Lee died.

Ross's philosophy regarding the practice of public relations may be summed up in a remark he made to a *Fortune* magazine interviewer: "Unless you are willing to resign an account or a job over a matter of principle, it is no use to call yourself a member of the world's newest profession—for you are already a member of the world's oldest."

In 1938, Ross and two other public relations pioneers (Pendelton Dudley, who founded Dudley, Anderson and Yutzy, and John W. Hill, who was a principal in the enormously successful Hill and Knowlton) established an exclusive insider club known as the Wise Men. Little is known directly about this organization, but it is believed to have had a significant influence on the contemporary practice of public relations.

Ross's firm served approximately thirty clients, among which were thought to be American Tobacco, the Bermuda Trade Development Board, Chrysler, Equitable Life Assurance Society, Rheem, Socony Mobil, and Western Union.

A director of the Home Assurance Company and of Rheem, Ross was also a trustee of the Emigrant Savings Bank and president of the Harrison-Rye Realty Corporation. He was active in Catholic Church affairs in the New York City area, serving as a volunteer adviser to Francis Cardinal Spellman, a member of the Board of Founders of the Knights of Malta, and a trustee of St. Patrick's Cathedral, Fordham University, and Marymount College.

Ross married Marion A. Byrne on Oct. 6, 1917; they had four children. He died in Rye, N.Y.

[An obituary is in the *New York Times*, May 28, 1975.]

RICHARD L. TINO

ROTH, SAMUEL (Nov. 17, 1894–July 3, 1974), publisher known for his challenge of anti-obscenity laws, was born in a small village in the Carpathian Mountains in Austria-Hungary, the son of Joseph and Adele Roth. In 1903 the Roth family crossed the Atlantic in steerage and settled on the teeming Lower East Side in New York City. His father ran a small business manufacturing pants.

After being expelled from Townsend Harris High School for reading liberal philosophy, Samuel Roth continued his education on his own with daily visits to the New York Public Library. He also wrote poetry and stories for the *Jewish Child*, the *Menorah Journal*, and other Yiddish periodicals. In 1914, Roth published his first book of poetry, *New Songs of Zion*.

Professors Carl Van Doren and John Ersk-

ine of Columbia took notice of the young writer and persuaded the university to give Roth a faculty scholarship. While a student at Columbia, Roth began a magazine of contemporary poetry called the *Lyric*. Among the contributors were the then-unknown D. H. Lawrence and Archibald MacLeish.

In 1917, Roth married Pauline Alter. No longer able both to continue his formal education and to support a family (they eventually had two children), Roth opened the Poetry Bookshop in Greenwich Village. The shop became a favorite haunt of such poets and writers as Sholem Asch, Stephen Vincent Benét, Frank Harris, and Edna St. Vincent Millay. In 1917, Roth also published another book of poems, *First Offering*.

At the close of World War I, Roth was given a short-lived assignment as a correspondent in England for the *New York Herald*. While overseas he came into contact with the avant-garde writings that would shape his later career. When he returned to New York, Roth published *Two Worlds*, a quarterly magazine that serialized parts of James Joyce's still incomplete novel, *Finnigan's Wake*. Despite protestations of innocence, Roth apparently had neither sought nor gained Joyce's permission to print this work in progress. Joyce struck back with an unflattering reference to Roth toward the end of the novel: "Rothim! . . . With his unique hornbook and his prince of the apauper's pride, blundering all over the two worlds."

Although it was not illegal to pirate foreign works in 1925—the United States had not yet signed the International Copyright Agreement—it certainly was unethical. On the one hand, Roth was exposing Americans to an important experiment in fiction; on the other hand, he was not paying for the privilege.

In July 1926, Roth repeated the offense. In *Two Worlds*, now a monthly, he started printing excerpts from James Joyce's *Ulysses*. The novelist complained about this unauthorized use of his work through his publisher in Paris. But Roth continued to print excerpts, fourteen in all, through October 1927.

This time Joyce sought legal redress. He also organized an international protest intent on making this a test case of American copyright law. A document of protest against the unauthorized use of Joyce's work was signed by 167 artists and writers. Even a partial listing (Sherwood Anderson, Benedetto Croce, T. S. Eliot, André Gide, Ernest Hemingway, D. H. Lawrence, Thomas Mann, Sean O'Casey, Bertrand Russell, Paul Valéry, H. G. Wells, Virginia Woolf, William Butler Yeats) reads like a literary *Who's Who* of the twentieth century.

In publishing *Ulysses*, Roth ran afoul of the law because the work was considered obscene by the United States government. (Not until 1933 did Judge John M. Woolsey determine that *Ulysses* was "an amazing *tour de force*" and not pornography.) In 1928 the police raided Roth's Greenwich Village headquarters and confiscated the plates of *Ulysses* that had been smuggled in from Paris. Roth was arrested and sentenced to sixty days in jail.

This was the first of Roth's nine arrests and six convictions for violating anti-obscenity statutes. In 1930 both he and his wife, Pauline, were convicted for distributing D. H. Lawrence's *Lady Chatterly's Lover*. And in 1936, Roth began a three-year term in the federal penitentiary at Lewisburg, Pa., for sending through the mails an unsavory work, reputedly written by a sixteenth-century sheik. During his lifetime, Samuel Roth was to spend a total of eight years in prison for his publishing activities.

In June 1955, Roth testified before Senator Estes Kefauver's subcommittee on juvenile delinquency. He maintained that pornography was not responsible for causing juvenile crime. He also told the subcommittee: "Our language . . . is the source of our power as a people. From it sprung the Magna Charta and the Common Law. As my part of this great tradition, I want freedom of speech as a publisher." The echoes of the First Amendment were prophetic.

In 1956, Roth was again arrested after bringing out Aubrey Beardsley's illustrated tale of *Venus and Tannhauser*. Once more, the offense was sending obscene literature through the mails. Assistant District Attorney of New York George S. Leisure labeled Roth as "one of the biggest dealers in obscenity in the nation." After a nine-day trial in New York City ending Jan. 13, 1956, the jury deliberated ten hours and found Roth guilty. On February 5, Judge John M. Cashin of the Federal District Court of New York handed down the maximum sentence, five years in prison and a fine of $5,000. Roth then took his case to the Second Circuit Court of Appeals, maintaining that the federal statute on

obscenity was unconstitutional. His appeal, however, was denied.

In 1957 the case of *Roth* v. *the United States* was heard before the Supreme Court. Roth's defense was that the anti-obscenity statute violated the First Amendment. His attorneys argued his conviction was indeed "abridging the freedom of speech or of the press." In a five-to-four decision, the Court rejected Roth's plea. The majority opinion held that material was obscene if "to the average person, applying contemporary community standards, the dominant theme of the material taken as a whole appeals to prurient interest."

His appeal turned down, Roth served the full five years in prison. Yet harsh as his sentence was, his case actually liberalized the definition of obscenity. "Contemporary community standards" vary; the material's "dominant theme" must be "taken as a whole"; and the material must appeal to "prurient interest." Although the debate about what was pornographic continued, the court's ruling in *Roth* v. *the United States* became one of the landmark decisions of the twentieth century.

Samuel Roth was also a writer, a translator, and an editor in his own right. His works were numerous, if second-rate. He wrote *The Peep-Hole of the Present*, a work of science fiction; *Bumarap*, a novel; as well as books of poetry. Under the pseudonym of Norman Lockridge, Roth edited an anthology, *A Golden Treasury of the World's Wit and Wisdom*.

Samuel Roth died in New York City.

[See Leo Hamalian, "Nobody Knows My Names: Samuel Roth and the Underside of American Letters," *Journal of Modern Literature*, Apr. 1974. For newspaper accounts of the 1956–1957 obscenity trials, see the *New York Times*, Jan. 13, 1956; Feb. 8, 1956; June 25, 1957; and Oct. 15, 1957. Obituaries are in the *New York Times*, July 4, 1974; the *Washington Post*, July 6, 1974; and *Publishers Weekly*, July 22, 1974.]

BURNHAM HOLMES

ROULSTON, MARJORIE HILLIS (May 25, 1890–Nov. 8, 1971), writer, was born in Peoria, Ill., one of three children of the Reverend Dr. Newell Dwight Hillis and Annie Patrick, author of *The American Woman and Her Home*. When Marjorie was nine, the Hillis family moved from Chicago to New York City where Dr. Hillis replaced Dr. Lyman Abbott at the Plymouth Congregational Church in Brooklyn. The church had been made famous by the Reverend Henry Ward Beecher (it was built for him in 1847). Marjorie attended the Packer Collegiate Institute in Brooklyn and Miss Dana's School in Morristown, N.J.

As a minister's daughter, Roulston enjoyed a secure and respectable life-style. She was aware of this special position in the community and tried to live up to its demands. Roulston recalled meeting a variety of people as a young girl—ranging from scholars to millionaires to the poor who needed money from the Deacon's Fund—because of her father's prominent position. She also spent a lot of time reading and traveling with her family.

Roulston joined *Vogue* magazine as a production editor in 1918, serving as executive editor from 1932 to 1936. When her father died in 1929 and her mother passed away the following year, Roulston—whose sister and brother were both married—felt a great sense of isolation and wanted to avoid becoming a spinster. Nevertheless, she decided to continue her career.

She felt her position at *Vogue* contradicted the tenets held by her religious family. She once said her family often joked about the "sleek publication as a slightly ridiculous magazine full of illustrations of impossibly elongated ladies looking so chic that they resembled cartoons." Her co-workers had "equally quaint notions about the clergy."

In Edna Woolman Chase and Ilka Chases's *Always in Vogue* (1954) Roulston remembered early in her career when she was supervising a photo session with the great dancer Mordkin. The dancer preferred to pose only in a cotton fig-leaf. While Roulston was unruffled by this almost-nude display, her boyfriend thought otherwise. Upon seeing the half-nude Mordkin, he remarked, "I think you should remember, Marjorie, that you are a minister's daughter." Nonetheless, Roulston thought that many of her co-workers were as interesting and respectable as members of the church community.

Roulston left *Vogue* in 1936 and began a writing career that lasted three decades. Her best-selling *Live Alone and Like It* (1936) provided innovative advice for single women. Her amusing suggestions included: "Be a Communist, a stamp collector, or a Ladies' Aid worker if you must, but for heaven's sake, be something."

Roulston's passion for books was also evident in her work. In an article for *Publisher's Weekly*, Roulston extolled the bliss of reading in the bathtub: "The feel of water, pleasantly cool or deliciously warm, . . . the smell of bath salts, pungent and luxurious; and the words on the printed page, exciting or stimulating or moving—where else can one have so many things all at once?"

While her anecdotes were humorous and her prose lyrical, Roulston had experienced the loneliness and boredom of single life. Through her staunch independence and spirited personality, her life evolved to include her own apartment in New York City and a whirlwind of social engagements. *Live Alone and Like It* reflected Roulston's personal philosophy and ideas on how one should live.

Roulston was also a popular lecturer. Sponsored by *Good Housekeeping* and fashionable stores such as Bonwitt Teller and Woodward and Lothrop, Roulston promoted her books and spoke on such topics as "How to Be a Success in College." She also wrote a monthly column entitled "On Petting" for *Good Housekeeping*.

On Aug. 1, 1939, she married Thomas Henry Roulston, a native Irishman who was president of Thomas Roulston Inc., a New York City grocery store chain. With this marriage, Marjorie Hillis Roulston became a pampered woman of society. She recalled how indulgent her life had become when over breakfast one morning her husband planned her limousine route for a shopping trip to Brooklyn. As their marriage progressed, Roulston moved away from her independent style: as she said, "I found it very pleasant indeed to be wrapped comfortably in cotton wool." During this blissful period, she joined with her younger brother, Richard Dwight Hillis, and wrote *A Church in History* to commemorate the hundredth anniversary of the Plymouth Congregational Church.

Her happiness ended in 1949 when her husband died. The couple had no children and Roulston was forced to begin life anew, moving from her Long Island estate to Manhattan. She did not remarry, but continued writing engaging books. The first, after her husband's death, *You Can Start All Over* (1951) certainly reflected her own life experiences. In writing the book, Roulston hoped to convey once again her personal conviction "that when life brings a devastating change, leaving one alone and desolate, one can start all over."

She spent her final years as an active volunteer for several organizations. A member of the

Author's Guild since 1953, Roulston created and edited the Author's Guild *Bulletin* in 1956. With her witty literary style, she produced a newsletter that informed its members. She also served on the Guild Council with other famous writers, including Pearl S. Buck. Roulston was active at the Brooklyn Botanical Gardens, where she served as a member of the Board of Trustees from 1939 until 1967. She was also a member of the Brooklyn Institute.

After a long illness, Roulston died in New York on Nov. 8, 1971. She was eighty-one years old.

[Mrs. Roulston's works include "Reading in the Bathtub," *Publisher's Weekly*, Aug. 1, 1936; *Orchids on Your Budget* (1937); *Corned Beef and Caviar* (1937), written with Bertina Foltz; *Work Ends at Nightfall* (1938), *New York: Fair or No Fair* (1939), *Keeping Going and Like It* (1967). Obituaries are in the *New York Times*, Nov. 10, 1971; *Newsweek*, Nov. 22, 1971; and *Time*, Nov. 22, 1971.]

DELIA CRUTCHFIELD COOK

RUBEY, WILLIAM WALDEN (Dec. 19, 1898–Apr. 12, 1974), geologist, was born in Moberly, Mo., where his father, Ambrose Burnside Rubey, owned a store. His mother was Alva Beatrice Walden. The boy developed an early interest in the outdoors. After graduating from high school in Moberly, he entered the University of Missouri, intending to study forestry, but was diverted to geology and received his B.A. in the latter field in 1920. He married Susan Elsie Manovill in 1919, during his senior year. They had three daughters.

Rubey began his professional career in 1920 with a consulting firm, Johnson Huntley, in Pittsburgh, Pa. After a few months he joined the U.S. Geological Survey. He also took graduate studies at Johns Hopkins University (1921–1922) and at Yale University (1922–1924). When the Geological Survey recalled Rubey for a special assignment in Kansas, he decided not to take the Ph.D. qualifying examination at Yale and never received a doctorate.

From 1924 to 1960 Rubey worked full time for the Geological Survey. He began as a geologic aide and advanced to the agency's highest scientific grade, that of research geologist. During the period 1944–1945 he led the geologic branch's division of Areal Geology and Basic Science. Rubey considered himself primarily a field geologist, and in that discipline he was both competent and rigorous. Outdoors he also took an interest in the local wildlife, especially birds, on which he published some papers.

After his first assignment in the Eldorado oil field of Arkansas, Rubey went to the rim area of the Black Hills in South Dakota and Wyoming. For almost half a century, beginning in 1924, he did field work in the overthrust-fault area of southwestern Wyoming, where he geologically mapped four quadrangles at a scale of 1:125,000. This constituted more than 3,300 square miles. In order to provide more details the Geological Survey enlarged the scale of these base maps to 1:62,500, a change that delayed their publication for many years.

On a separate assignment, Rubey mapped an area in Illinois in a cooperative project between the United States and the Illinois State Geological Surveys. His landmark report, which analyzed the stratigraphy, structure, physiography, geological history, economic geology, and stream dynamics of the area, was mysteriously misplaced by the Illinois office and finally published twenty years later (1952).

Through the years Rubey studied and published on stream hydrology, sedimentation, and structural geology of the relatively flat midcontinent and Great Plains region. As noted by Ernst, his publications "in general discussed the relationships among porosity, compaction, stratigraphy, and structure," thus leaving a clearer picture of the nature and mechanisms of midcontinent erosion and deposition. He noted examples of stream capture by erosion and the development of badland topography, and he discussed the forces affecting the settlement of rock particles in flowing streams. He explored several areas for the possibility of oil production and was primarily responsible for outlining a rich vanadium field in Wyoming in 1943. On special assignment in 1933 he helped to investigate mineral resources in the area where Boulder (now Hoover) Dam was to be built. Rubey defined the magnitude of the helium gas field that extends from the Texas panhandle to Kansas; his findings led the federal government to regulate its gas production. During World War II he directed a search for sources of uranium in the United States, having previously determined that vanadium and uranium are concentrated in black shales and phosphorites. He also served as liaison between the U.S. Geological Survey and the armed forces.

Long interested in the interrelationships between geology, chemistry, and physics, Rubey presented in 1950 a theory that the oceans and the atmosphere had accumulated gradually by outgassing of water from the mantle of the earth. This broad concept entered into early discussions of seafloor spreading during the 1960's when all aspects of the origins of the oceans were being considered.

With geophysicist M. King Hubbert in the 1950's, Rubey analyzed the mechanics of overthrust faults; they determined that fluid pressure reduced frictional resistance sufficiently to allow slippage along such low-angle faults. In the mid-1950's Rubey added teaching to his research and field activities. He was a visiting professor successively at the University of California, Los Angeles (UCLA); the California Institute of Technology; and Johns Hopkins University. In 1960 he became a professor of geology and geophysics at UCLA but continued some field work in Wyoming for the U.S. Geological Survey. At UCLA he conducted an advanced seminar on large-scale, unsolved problems in geology. To some extent this was an outgrowth of his custom, while with the U.S. Geological Survey, of hosting evening seminar meetings at his home in Washington, D.C. A wide range of scientists would gather over a plate of sandwiches (and beer) and hold discussions on a specific topic of geology.

A patient, tactful person, known for taking assignments seriously, Rubey became much in demand for committee and advisory appointments. His advice on policies and programs was sought by successive directors of the U.S. Geological Survey. As secretary of a committee on stratigraphic nomenclature, he worked diligently to create the first American Stratigraphic Code in 1933. For the National Research Council, Rubey served as chairman of the Division of Geology and Geography (1943–1946) and as chairman of the council itself (1951–1954). Elected to the National Academy of Sciences in 1945, he served for two terms on its council (1951–1954, 1965–1968).

Rubey was a member of the American Miscellaneous Committee's Mohole Project (1957–1963), that proposed drilling a hole through the earth's crust to the Mohorovičić Discontinuity. He was appointed by President Dwight D. Eisenhower to a six-year term (1960–1966) on the National Science Board of the National Science Foundation. In 1966 for the U.S. Army Corps of Engineers, he investigated microearth-

quakes near Denver, Colo., for their connection with the Rocky Mountain Arsenal Disposal well. Rubey then investigated the relation of fluid injection with earthquake activity in Colorado for the Advanced Research Projects Agency. He was a consultant to the National Aeronautics and Space Administration for some years and was the director (1968–1971) of its Lunar Science Institute in Houston when the first lunar rock samples were brought to earth for scientific analysis.

Rubey received many honors for his seminal work in geology. The Department of the Interior awarded him its Award of Excellence (1943) and Distinguished Service Medal (1958). In 1965 he received the National Medal of Science from President Lyndon B. Johnson. Rubey died in Santa Monica, Calif.

[Rubey's professional papers and field notebooks from his years with the U.S. Geological Survey are in the National Archives and with the agency's records in Denver. His significant publications include "Geology and Mineral Resources of the Hardin and Brussels Quadrangles (Illinois)," *U.S. Geological Survey Professional Paper* 218, 1952; 1950 presentation on seawater that was expanded as "Development of the Hydrosphere and Atmosphere, with Special Reference to Probable Composition of the Early Atmosphere," *Geological Society of America Special Paper* 62, 1955; "Role of Fluid Pressure in Mechanics of Overthrust Faulting," *Geological Society of America Bulletin* 70, 1959, written with M. King Hubbert; and "Fifty Years of the Earth Sciences—A Renaissance," *Annual Review of Earth and Planetary Sciences* 2, 1974. On Rubey's life and work, see Philip H. Abelson, "William Walden Rubey (1898–1974)," *American Philosophical Society Yearbook for 1975* (1976); James Gilluly, "Memorial to William Walden Rubey," *Geological Society of America Memorials* 6, 1977; W. G. Ernst, "William Walden Rubey," *Biographical Memoirs of the National Academy of Sciences* 49, 1978; and Vincent E. McKelvey, "William Walden Rubey (1898–1974)," *Cosmos Club Bulletin* 39:6, 1986. An obituary is in the *New York Times*, Apr. 14, 1974.]

ELIZABETH NOBLE SHOR

RUSHING, JAMES ANDREW (Aug. 26, 1903–June 8, 1972), singer and musician, was born into a black middle-class family in Oklahoma City, Okla., the son of Andrew Rushing, owner of a luncheonette and a part-time trumpet player, and Cora Freeman, who sang and played piano. His parents wanted him to play the violin, which, Rushing said, "I wouldn't, couldn't." An uncle, an itinerant musician named Wesley Manning, started Rushing on the piano. In grade school and in the church choir, Rushing frequently performed in holiday pageants as a boy soprano. In high school, he studied music theory with an eye toward a teaching career. To that end, he attended Wilberforce University for a short time in the early 1920's. But his desire was to follow the road of the jazz musician.

As a teenager, Rushing went to local bars to listen, to learn, and occasionally to sit in with musicians. He ran away from home and went to Chicago, then followed local bands and performers from city to city, state to state.

In 1925, Rushing went to Los Angeles, where his first significant professional job was a short stint with the band of the great Jelly Roll Morton. As a pianist, however, Rushing was not as proficient as he needed to be, especially with the more skilled Jelly Roll nearby. His youth and lack of experience were also against him.

Frustrated with what he felt was a "vagabond" existence, Rushing returned in 1926 to Oklahoma City, where for a while he worked at his father's luncheonette. His father's continued contact with itinerant musicians, such as the great blues singers, Mamie Smith and Bessie Smith (not related), reignited Rushing's desire to return to the music business.

While Rushing was performing with a local group, the reigning jazz band making the Oklahoma circuit in the 1920's, the Blue Devils, led by bassist Walter Page, heard him sing and asked him to join their group. According to Rushing, "That was it!" Music would be his life's calling.

Rushing toured locally with the Blue Devils, and the group became known throughout the Southwest. In addition to Page, the band included William ("Count") Basie on piano and trumpeter Oran ("Hot Lips") Page. Rushing said of the band and this period, "We used to play battles of music against Lawrence Welk. He wasn't too well known then, except . . . around Minnesota and Wisconsin." It is believed that although blues were being sung by many performers, Rushing was the first to sing them with a big band.

In 1929, after the Blue Devils broke up, Rushing and Basie joined a band led by Bennie Moten. They traveled widely, meeting and "battling" other bands, such as that of Chick Webb (later a mentor of Ella Fitzgerald).

After Moten's death in 1935, the band drifted apart. Basie and Rushing performed together, but neither felt they were getting anywhere. In 1936, while doing a radio spot, Rushing and Basie came to the attention of a music impresario, John Hammond. He encouraged Basie to form his own band, with Rushing as his lead singer. This partnership was one of the most famous in the history of American popular music and jazz. According to Rushing, "Most of the people had never heard anything like our band, and they didn't catch on for a while." Once the band came to New York, Hammond, along with the Music Corporation of America management, suggested the addition of Billie Holiday and Helen Humes. With Rushing as its lead singer, the Basie band became one of the legends of the big-band era.

For fifteen years Rushing was the Basie band's lead singer. The band soon came to the attention of Hollywood producers. Rushing's and Basie's debut in movies occurred in a film starring the singer-dancer Donald O'Connor. In *Crazy House*, starring Olsen and Johnson (1943), Rushing jitterbugged with singer-dancer Thelma Carpenter.

When Basie's original group disbanded, Rushing retired from the uncertainty of the music business, under pressure from his wife, Connie Ingram. Unable to adjust to "ordinary life," and needing night life, he returned to New York, where he rejoined Basie as the lead singer of a combo instead of a band.

Feeling confident that he could do well on his own, Rushing left Basie in 1950 to form his own group. But the difficulties of leading a band were more than he could handle; in 1952, he disbanded the group and began life as a predominantly solo singer.

Until the 1970's, Rushing also enjoyed limited success as a singer with some of the most famous bands and musicians. But this side of the music business had its problems. For some years Rushing was unwilling to sign a long contract with one manager or booker, and had a hard time managing himself. His standards as an artist were high, and since work could be hard to come by because he would not modify his style to suit emergent trends, he sang "where he could."

Despite the difficult years as a single performer, Rushing had some success in Europe with big bands in the 1950's, such as that of Humphrey Lyttleton in England, that found his kind of music appealing. For several years, he was the featured vocalist with Eddie Condon's and Benny Goodman's orchestras. In time, Rushing's style and kind of music moved to the periphery of the music world.

At his death in New York City, Rushing's fame had diminished, yet appraisals of his work are worth recalling. During his long career, he was a favorite among musicians. His squat, bouncing frame earned him the affectionate sobriquet "Mr. Five-by-Five." As a stylist he was a trendsetter. His reputation as a blues shouter and his vocal style can be linked directly to the rhythm and blues of the 1940's and 1950's. It is ironic that Rushing may well have helped introduce the very music he despised, rock and roll. In his time he was considered as much a popular singer as a jazz and blues performer.

Rushing has been described as the "epitome of swing . . . a vocalist with immense taste and desire, who could inspire even a poor band to reach out of themselves." Although he did not possess a heavy voice, it had a roughness and sweetness that made it "very distinguishable," according to Martin Cowlyn, a jazz and blues critic.

[Biographical information can be found in Nat Hentoff, "Jimmy Rushing," *Down Beat*, 1957; P. Oliver, "Jimmy Rushing: The Formative Years," *Jazz Monthly*, 1957; Ralph Ellison, "Remembering Jimmy," in his *Shadow and Act* (1964); Frank Driggs, "Jimmy Rushing's Story as Told to Frank Driggs," *Evergreen Review*, Apr. 1966; and Chris Alberson, "Jimmy Rushing: A Sturdy Branch of the Learning Tree," *Down Beat*, 1969. A selective discography is in *Blues-Link*, 1974. Obituaries are in the *New York Times*, June 9, 1972; the *Amsterdam News* (New York), June 17, 1972; *Jet*, June 22, 1972; and *Blues Unlimited*, Sept. 1972.]

WILLIAM F. BROWNE

RUSSELL, RICHARD BREVARD, JR. (**"DICK"**) (Nov. 2, 1897–Jan. 21, 1971), governor of Georgia and United States senator, was born in Winder, Ga., a small town about forty miles east of Atlanta, the fourth of thirteen children. His father, Richard Brevard Russell, Sr., was a successful lawyer and businessman, and served as chief justice of the Georgia Supreme Court from 1922 until his death in 1938. Russell's mother, Blandina ("Ina") Dillard, whose ancestors had arrived in America from England in 1660, was a schoolteacher in Athens before marrying Russell's father. Her death in 1953

was particularly saddening to Russell, a lifelong bachelor. In his words she was "the vital core" of the family and "the greatest person I have ever known." Russell joined the Methodist church in Winder in 1907 and would remain a member his entire life.

Russell attended primary school in his hometown and went on to graduate from the Seventh District Agricultural and Mechanical School in Powder Springs, Ga., in 1914 and from Gordon Military Institute in Barnesville, Ga., in 1915. He received a law degree from the University of Georgia in June 1918.

After college Russell returned to Winder for the summer of 1918 but, feeling that it was his duty to participate in World War I, joined the U.S. Naval Reserve on September 12, shortly before he turned twenty-one and only two months before the armistice. He did not enjoy his three months active duty in Athens, Ga., and complained in letters home about dreary manual labor. Nevertheless, his biographer notes that "he was always proud to call himself a veteran."

Upon his return to Winder, Russell entered the practice of law with his father and began his political career. Accepting the advantages, opportunities, obligations, and expectations of his family heritage, he announced his candidacy for the Georgia House of Representatives on July 8, 1920. He won overwhelmingly and began a career of elected public service that would continue for over fifty years. Russell would prove to be effective in part because he mastered the art of parliamentary maneuvering and became a member of the establishment wherever he served. But Russell also succeeded because the voters and his fellow politicians thought him to be open, honest, and fair to those on all sides of an issue.

Russell's rise to prominence and power in Georgia politics was meteoric. Elected to the state house of representatives in 1920, he served from 1921 to 1931, being speaker from 1927 to 1931. He then was elected governor at the age of thirty-three, serving from 1931 to 1933.

As governor of Georgia, Russell achieved important results in conservation and in economic development, especially in agriculture. He signed into law a far-reaching reorganization act that simplified government. He made strong appointments to the board of regents, which oversaw higher education. He not only balanced the budget but actually paid several million dollars on old unpaid appropriations. He cautiously and masterfully rode out a storm in one of his main lifelong areas of concern, agriculture, delaying without opposing a plan championed by Governor Huey P. Long of Louisiana to raise the price of cotton by reducing the production of cotton.

But an incident in 1932 foreshadowed the trouble Russell would have over the issue of civil rights, an issue that would eventually thwart his desire to assume national leadership. Robert E. Burns, an African American serving time on a Georgia chain gang, had escaped to New Jersey and written a book entitled *I Am a Fugitive from a Georgia Chain Gang*, condemning the Georgia prison system as inhumane. Russell asked New Jersey authorities to return Burns to Georgia. Newspapers in the North expressed outrage at Russell's request, and the governor of New Jersey refused to extradite Burns, escalating the conflict to national proportions. Governor Russell perceived the criticism as an attack on the white South, his defense of which was translated into weakness on the issue of race relations, a charge that would haunt Russell throughout his career.

The Burns controversy died down, and Russell's regional popularity remained high. In 1932, the people of Georgia elected him to the U.S. Senate as a Democrat to fill the seat of the deceased William J. Harris. He was reelected to the seat six times and served as president pro tempore of the Senate from Jan. 3, 1969, until his death.

When Russell entered the Senate, the nation was in the depths of the Great Depression. Russell felt that this crisis justified his support of the massive government intervention contained in Roosevelt's New Deal. But when future Democratic presidents tried to build on the New Deal, Russell opposed most of their proposals, from Harry S. Truman's Fair Deal in the 1940's and 1950's through John F. Kennedy's New Frontier through Lyndon Johnson's Great Society in the 1960's. At the heart of Russell's opposition was his belief in personal freedom and in states' rights.

Russell expended considerable energy in trying to keep the family farm the centerpiece of American agricultural life. He supported nearly all of Roosevelt's programs for parity, rural electrification, and farm loans. He helped pass legislation to aid agricultural research, to provide school lunches, and to allow poor people to receive surplus commodities. Yet Russell's tenure in the Senate saw the continuing urbanization of the nation and the decline of the family farm.

Senator Russell opposed changing the immigration laws to make it easier for Asians and Africans to enter the United States, and he fought against efforts to bring equal opportunity to African Americans. In 1935, as a freshman senator, he led a filibuster against an antilynching bill. He became the leader of those southerners who fought civil rights legislation or anything that seemed too integrationist. He did not join the Dixiecrat revolt against President Truman's election in 1948, but after the election, Russell in January 1949 introduced a bill that would have provided financial incentives to African Americans to relocate from the South to other parts of the country. The bill of course failed and the nation continued to move along its tortured path toward civil rights for African Americans. Russell later opposed the passage of mild civil rights acts in 1957 and 1960 and stronger ones in 1964, 1965, and 1968.

Russell's opposition to such measures was based on his belief that Anglo-Saxon ways were superior to all others and that the white South represented American culture at its best. His biographer Gilbert Fite notes that "white supremacy and racial segregation were to him cardinal principles for good and workable human relationships." Russell believed that his views were supported by history. He regarded the Reconstruction experience as definitive proof that integration would ruin both races. He had known many African Americans who did not press for equality.

Russell was a firm supporter of a strong national defense and became in the 1950's the most knowledgeable and powerful congressional leader in this area. He used his powers as chairman of the Armed Services Committee from 1951 to 1969 and then as chairman of the Appropriations Committee as an institutional base to add defense installations and jobs for Georgia. In 1951, he chaired the committee that investigated President Truman's firing of General Douglas MacArthur for insubordination during the Korean War. Russell was firm, fair, and evenhanded in the midst of a national outcry, and his refusal to sensationalize the conflict helped the nation through the crisis. Russell urged Presidents Kennedy and Johnson not to escalate American involvement in Vietnam. He campaigned unsuccessfully for the presidency.

Russell maintained a rigorous work schedule that allowed for little social activity. Though admired by many, he maintained few close relationships. His life, he often stated, was his work as a senator. He diligently studied American history, especially the Civil War, and was a daily and cover-to-cover reader of the *Congressional Record*.

By mid-1970, Russell's respiratory problems made even slight exertions difficult. He obtained a three-wheeled motorized vehicle to help him move around. On December 8, he entered Walter Reed Army Hospital, where he died.

Richard B. Russell was a man of the South and its effective leader. Yet his bid for the presidency of the United States in 1952 went down to defeat. Many said that if he had not been from the South, he would have become president. In fact, his failure to assume national leadership was due not only to his being from the South but of a besieged southern mindset during the era of civil rights that failed to understand the central paradox of the nation's history—the denial of freedom in the land of the free.

[The Russell Memorial Library at the University of Georgia has vast holdings of primary material relating to Russell. Gilbert C. Fite, *Richard B. Russell, Jr., Senator from Georgia* (1991), is the masterful and definitive biography. See also Karen K. Kelly, "Richard B. Russell: Democrat from Georgia" (Ph.D. diss., University of North Carolina, 1979). An obituary is in the *New York Times*, Jan. 22, 1971.]

JOSEPH P. HOBBS

RYAN, CORNELIUS JOHN ("CONNIE") (June 5, 1920–Nov. 23, 1974), journalist and author, was born in Dublin, Ireland, the son of John Joseph Ryan and Amelia Clohisey. After graduating from the Irish Christian Brothers Academy, Ryan qualified for entry to the Irish Academy of Music, where he studied the violin. After a brief career with salon orchestras and within months of the outbreak of World War II, Ryan abandoned the violin and left Ireland to become secretary to Garfield Weston, a member of parliament in Great Britain.

In 1941, Ryan found his first reporting job with the London office of Reuters News Agency, where he displayed a flair for writing and research. He survived the Luftwaffe's London Blitz of 1940–1943 and joined the *London Daily Telegraph* as a war correspondent in 1943. He covered the arrival and training of American troops in England through the landings and days of the Normandy invasion. He later said, "I was too horrified and too young then to fully appreciate and understand what I saw." Afterward, Ryan followed General George S. Patton's Third Army on its victorious march across Europe.

In 1945, Ryan opened the *Daily Telegraph*'s Tokyo bureau, where he covered the postwar atomic bomb tests. He was promoted to Middle Eastern bureau chief and sent to Jerusalem in 1946, where he covered the Palestinian conflict between Britain and Israel. He also acted as a stringer for *Time* magazine and the *St. Louis Post Dispatch*. His work for *Time* provided Ryan with an opportunity to delve into news summary and analysis as opposed to straight reportage. From this experience, he acquired the skill of telling the news as a story.

Time brought Ryan to its New York City headquarters in 1947. In 1950 he gained American citizenship and married writer Kathryn Ann Morgan, who was an editor for *House and Home* and *Architectural Forum*. They had two children. That same year Ryan quit work for *Time* and joined the "Newsweek" television program as a reporter.

Ryan's postwar sojourn in Tokyo inspired his first two books, *Star-Spangled Mikado*, coauthored by Frank Kelly (1948), and *MacArthur* (1950). He edited *Across the Space Frontier* in 1952 and Wernher von Braun's *Conquest of the Moon* the next year. "All of them," Ryan remarked critically, "failed to hit the gong."

In 1950 he joined *Collier's* as an associate editor. He remained there until that publication failed in 1956, a crushing blow for Ryan, who had been working on his magnum opus, *The Longest Day*, for seven years and was $20,000 in debt from research expenses. For three years his wife's salary supported the family and Ryan's research, until Dewitt Wallace of *Reader's Digest* hired Ryan as a staff reporter. After three years he became a roving editor, a position he retained until his death.

Ryan's greatest literary accomplishments were his three international best-sellers, *The Longest Day* (1959), *The Last Battle* (1966), and *A Bridge Too Far* (1974). Critics described these works as a new genre—history emphasizing suspense as well as accuracy. The author disagreed: "There is nothing new in what I am doing," he contended. "It's only old-fashioned reporting." Ryan referred to Stendhal, who, when asked why he described the Battle of Waterloo as he did, replied, "I simply wanted to know what happened."

The Longest Day was a smashing success. *Atlantic Monthly* called it "incomparably the best of war histories." Ryan then wrote a screenplay for a movie version (1962) that set box-office records. The book's success finally bailed the Ryans out of debt. They purchased an estate in Ridgefield, Conn., where Ryan began to research *The Last Battle*, a book describing the fall of Berlin.

Although disenchanted with the "new historian" label, Ryan conceded that he took a unique approach. "What was missing," Ryan explained, "was the story of wartime events told in terms of human spirit." To fill this void, he chose to write about ordinary people. War was simply the framework "to show people at every level of society in all their bravery and compassion."

To accomplish this study of individual reactions to war, he invested the then staggering sum of $60,000 in *The Last Battle*. To properly research and write such histories necessitated interviewing as many as three thousand to six thousand people who had been eyewitnesses to the events. Ryan took ten years to write *The Longest Day*, six to finish *The Last Battle*, and seven for *A Bridge Too Far*, for which he interviewed Otto Gunshe, the last man to see Hitler alive. He even persuaded the Soviets to give him access to their archives, thus becoming the first American since the 1930's to view Russian documents.

Three years into writing his last book, Ryan became ill. Despite several operations and constant pain, he refused to give up his work. At the time of his death in New York, *A Bridge Too Far* had reached second place on the *New York Times* best-seller list. *The Longest Day* and *The Last Battle* had sold more than ten million hardcover copies in twenty languages, a measure of Ryan's success at combining impeccable research and personal experience with fluent writing.

[Biographical information can be found in the *New York Herald Tribune*, Mar. 16, 1966. Obituaries appear in the *New York Times* and the *Washington Post*, Nov. 25, 1974; *Publisher's Weekly*, Dec. 2, 1974; *Time*, Dec. 9, 1974; and *AB Bookman's Weekly*, Dec. 16, 1974.]

W. M. P. DUNNE

RYAN, ROBERT BUSHNELL (Nov. 11, 1909–July 11, 1973), actor, was born in Chicago, the son of Timothy Ryan, a building contractor, and Mabel Bushnell. Ryan became interested in drama while a student at Loyola Academy in Chicago. He majored in literature at Dartmouth College, winning a prize for his one-act play about death, *The Visitor*.

Ryan graduated from Dartmouth in 1932 and after an unsuccessful effort to find work in New York City he spent the Depression years in a variety of occupations before finally accepting a job in the supply office of the Chicago Board of Education. He continued to write plays, but his desire to perform led him to join a drama group run by Edward Boyle. A modest income from an almost forgotten oil-well investment allowed Ryan to move in 1938 to Los Angeles, where he enrolled in the Max Reinhardt Theatrical Workshop. On Mar. 11, 1939, Ryan married Jessica Cadwalader, a fellow student; the couple had three children.

Spotted by a scout who had seen him perform in a musical adaptation of Somerset Maugham's *Too Many Husbands*, Ryan signed a standard $75-a-week contract with Paramount, which used him in small parts in several B-films and in a nonspeaking role in the Cecil B. DeMille production *North West Mounted Police* (1940). Paramount did not renew Ryan's contract. His wife's income from fashion modeling (she later became a successful author of detective fiction and children's literature) enabled Ryan to concentrate on the stage, where he did summer stock in 1941 at several locations in the East.

Ryan performed with Luise Rainer in *A Kiss for Cinderella* at the Cape Playhouse in Dennis, Mass.; the actress later recommended him for a small role in Clifford Odets's drama *Clash by Night*, which opened on Broadway in December 1941. Critics gave Ryan generally favorable reviews. The star of the play, Tallulah Bankhead, was more guarded, telling Ryan that if he were lucky he might become a good actor in "fifteen or twenty years." When the play closed after a few weeks, Ryan was given a contract by director Pare Lorentz to appear in a film Lorentz was scheduled to make for RKO.

691

Lorentz's project was shelved, but RKO retained Ryan and quickly used him in seven films; in three, *Bombardier* (1943), *The Iron Major* (1943), and *Marine Raiders* (1944), he supported Pat O'Brien, while he played the small but important part of Ginger Rogers's GI husband in the home-front picture *Tender Comrade* (1943). Ryan interrupted his film career to enlist in the marine corps late in 1943, serving at Camp Pendleton as a drill instructor until his discharge in 1945.

After the war, Ryan, who was slender at six feet, four inches and had dark hair, began to attract attention. Perhaps his best early role was in *Crossfire* (1947), one of three films he did for director Edward Dmytryk at RKO. In it Ryan played a psychotic ex-serviceman whose anti-Semitism leads him to commit murder. Ryan's performance gained an Oscar nomination for best supporting actor.

Thereafter Ryan appeared in three or four films annually, including several westerns (his least favorite genre), Jean Renoir's commercially unsuccessful *The Woman on the Beach* (1947), *Flying Leathernecks* (1951), in which he costarred with John Wayne, and the film version of *Clash by Night* (1952), with Barbara Stanwyck and Paul Douglas. Many of Ryan's RKO films belonged to the film noir genre, in which the understated acting style that he had developed at the Reinhardt workshop showed to special advantage. His ability to portray the loneliness and insecurity that were central to the noir genre served Ryan well whether he played the villain, as in *Crossfire*, or the protagonist, as in his own favorite, *The Set-Up* (1949), long considered among the finest films ever made about boxing. In it Ryan (who was himself a former Dartmouth heavyweight champion) played Stoker Thompson, an aging prizefighter who is badly beaten by gangsters after defeating a youthful opponent in a match the mob had tried to fix. Ryan won the Cannes film festival's best actor award for his performance.

As part of a studio-wide retrenchment, RKO released Ryan in 1952. Thoroughly professional on the set, Ryan worked as a free-lance performer, appearing in nearly three dozen films over the next two decades. Despite his dislike for the genre, he recognized that what he described as his "long, seamy face" was suited for westerns, and he accepted pivotal roles in *The Naked Spur* (1953), *The Proud Ones* (1956),

and *The Wild Bunch* (1969), among others. He also did several war films. Ryan tried to be selective in his choice of scripts, but appeared in several pedestrian motion picture and television productions to finance his stage career. Overall, however, he gave many effective performances in a variety of films. Among the best was his prejudiced and insecure villain in the modern western *Bad Day at Black Rock* (1955) which featured Spencer Tracy. Ryan also received critical acclaim as the sadist John Claggart in Peter Ustinov's adaptation of *Billy Budd* (1962), and as Larry Slade in *The Iceman Cometh* (1973). For his performance as Slade he posthumously received the National Board of Review's best actor award.

Throughout his last twenty years Ryan's craftsmanship was most evident in the many demanding stage roles he took. He played the role of Coriolanus in a 1954 production directed by his friend John Houseman, costarred with Katherine Hepburn in *Antony and Cleopatra* at the American Shakespeare Festival Theatre in 1960, and appeared in *Othello* (1967) at the Nottingham (England) Repertory Theatre. Ryan also undertook the role of Walter Burns in a Broadway revival of *The Front Page* (1969), in which Helen Hayes also starred, had the title role in the Irving Berlin musical *Mr. President* (1962), and played Thomas à Becket in *Murder in the Cathedral* (1959) and James Tyrone in a 1971 production of Eugene O'Neill's *Long Day's Journey into Night*. He was one of the founders of the Theater Group at UCLA and of the Plumstead Playhouse.

Ryan, who supported numerous liberal causes, was once asked why he never attracted the attention of the House Un-American Activities Committee or of Senator Joseph McCarthy, since two of his films at RKO, *Crossfire* and *Tender Comrade*, were mentioned as suspect in Washington's investigations of Communism in Hollywood. (Nor could McCarthyites have overlooked that RKO had more recently cast Ryan as the leading man in the anticommunist melodrama, *The Woman on Pier 13*, released in 1950 after unusually extensive editing and other revisions.) He replied it was probably because he had been a marine, was Catholic, and had an Irish name. Ryan campaigned for Adlai Stevenson in both 1952 and 1956, joined the American Civil Liberties Union (ACLU) and the United World Federalists, was a founder of the Hollywood chapter of the Committee for a

Sane Nuclear Policy, and also worked to broaden employment opportunities for blacks in the motion picture industry. With actors Bill Cosby, Robert Culp, and Sidney Poitier he established Artists Help All Blacks (AHAB). Perhaps the longest-standing commitment of Ryan and his wife was to the Oakwood School, a private school they founded in the San Fernando Valley for the purpose of giving children, including the disabled, a more balanced education and view of life than offered in conventional private schools or public schools, which the Ryans regarded as overcrowded and unsatisfactory.

Ryan continued to perform despite having cancer, which was diagnosed in 1970. He had accepted a role in the stage adaptation of *Shenandoah* when his condition worsened. He died in New York City after a brief hospitalization.

[There are two biographies of Ryan: Franklin Jarlett, *Robert Ryan: A Biography and Critical Filmography* (1990), and the section on Ryan in James Robert Parish, *The Tough Guys* (1976). See also M. Nichols, "Robert Ryan—Hero and Heel," *Coronet*, Jan. 1960; Larry Ceplair and Steven Englund, *The Inquisition in Hollywood* (1980); and Foster Hirsch, *The Dark Side of the Screen* (1981). An obituary is in the *New York Times*, July 12, 1973.]

LLOYD J. GRAYBAR

S

SACHS, ALEXANDER (Aug. 1, 1893–June 23, 1973), economist, was born in Rossien, Lithuania, the son of Samuel Sachs, a religious scholar, and Fay Alexander, an entrepreneur. Although he spent most of his life in the field of economics, Alexander Sachs is best known today for counseling President Franklin Roosevelt to initiate the United States atomic bomb program. The Sachs family came to the United States as Jewish refugees in 1904. Alexander Sachs completed studies at Columbia University in three years, receiving his bachelor of science degree in 1912 at age nineteen. He worked as a clerk for the Wall Street firm of Lee Higginson in 1913 and 1914 before returning to Columbia to study philosophy. In 1916, he entered Harvard University as a Francis Parkman Fellow in philosophy and subsequently received a Henry Rogers Fellowship for further study in jurisprudence and sociology. (Although he did not receive a doctoral degree from Harvard, he was commonly referred to as "Dr." Sachs by the press and colleagues throughout his life.) After completing his studies, he returned to Wall Street to join Lehman Brothers as an economist. On June 17, 1919, he became a naturalized American citizen.

As an analyst, Sachs developed a reputation as a contrarian due to his doubts about the Coolidge-era economy. Sachs kept his personal assets in cash and when the stock market crash came in 1929 he was the envy of Wall Street. He scorned Hoover's "psychological manipulation and wishful thinking" as a means of getting the country out of the Great Depression.

Sachs had been on casual terms with Franklin Roosevelt since 1932 when he had provided some of the economic research for the New York governor's presidential campaign. In 1933, Sachs organized and administered the economic research and planning division of the National Recovery Administration (NRA) under the direction of Hugh S. Johnson. He also developed the first labor codes for southern textile mills in 1933, which he hoped would balance the needs of workers and producers. This action led to the release of a torrent of additional codes for other industries, most of which Sachs considered unnecessary. Discouraged by proliferating regulation, he considered resigning and did reduce his commitment to the NRA. By January 1934, he had all but left the NRA because he was disappointed to see it being used as an economic stabilizer when in his opinion it needed to be fostering expansionism. He maintained his contact with Roosevelt, however, and served on the National Policy Committee. But by 1936, he found himself out of step with the president's Tennessee Valley Authority program and tax policies; he himself advocated tax reform based on the British system. He had long described himself as a "lone wolf New Dealer in the menagerie of economists" in the Roosevelt administration. In a 1933 memo he criticized the NRA approach as akin to "state capitalism." Philosophically, he was opposed to programs that resembled cartelism or that violated antitrust laws. He offered instead a "system of pluristic planning . . . suited to a political and economic democracy." In 1936, he returned to the private sector as a vice-president and director of the Lehman Corporation, an investment trust managed by Lehman Brothers. He also lectured to policy organizations and academic institutions.

Known as a cumbersome writer who often wrote sentences of fifty to sixty words, Sachs ironically became responsible for making the atomic theories of Albert Einstein, Enrico Fermi, and Leo Szilard comprehensible to President Roosevelt. In the spring of 1939, Sachs, Einstein, Szilard, and Eugene P. Wigner of Princeton began discussing the role of atomic weapons in a world girding for war. The scientists knew that Germany was increasing its importation of pitchblende—an ore yielding both uranium and radium—and that uranium research was proceeding under the Nazis. Einstein and Szilard agreed that Sachs would be the man to see the president and explain the situation. On Oct. 11, 1939, six weeks after the German invasion of Poland, Sachs visited Roosevelt at the White House, warning him about the potential destructive force of atomic weapons and the need for an American nuclear program.

Atomic research was new to the president, but he quickly grasped the implications of Sachs's news. Roosevelt established a committee headed by Lyman Briggs, director of the National Bureau of Standards, to consider the information Sachs had presented and to act as a liaison between the military and the scientists working on uranium. The so-called Uranium Committee, on which Sachs served, submitted a report to the president in November 1939, recommending that uranium research for both bombs and powering submarines be supported by the government. However, in 1940 only $6,000 was allotted to the research, instead of the $100,000 Sachs suggested. Sachs also recommended the establishment of a Scientific Council of National Defense "composed of executives, engineers, and economists" to promote technical national defense projects. As a result of this advice, Roosevelt established the National Defense Research Committee under the direction of Vannevar Bush. Atomic bomb research soon became a $2 billion federal project and Sachs voluntarily withdrew from the project.

In 1942, Sachs resigned from Lehman Brothers to become an independent economic consultant. He offered his consulting services, for free, to the War Emergency Pipelines Corporation and the Petroleum Industry War Council, and the Office of Strategic Services, among other government agencies.

At the end of the war, according to Henry Wallace, Sachs felt that the United States had made itself morally culpable by dropping the bomb on Hiroshima. He said the original plan discussed with Roosevelt was to detonate one atomic bomb in the presence of representatives of all the neutral nations, who could then report the effect of the weapon to the world. A second bomb was to be dropped on an island off Japan after the United States advised the Japanese to evacuate all civilians. Sachs felt that American moral prestige was very low for having used the bomb. He advocated international control of nuclear weapons and the use of nuclear power for peaceful projects.

Sachs married Charlotte A. Cramer on Aug. 30, 1945; the couple had no children. He continued to lecture and contributed to many books on economics as well as to financial and economic periodicals. In 1968, Sachs was named a special consultant to the under-secretary of state for political affairs. He died in New York City.

[Sachs's papers are at the Franklin D. Roosevelt Library in Hyde Park, N.Y. He is featured in Geoffrey T. Hellman, "A Reporter at Large: The Contemporaneous Memoranda of Dr. Sachs," *New Yorker*, Dec. 1, 1945, and mentioned in Jordan A. Schwarz, *The New Dealers* (1993). An obituary is in the *New York Times*, June 24, 1973.]

DANIEL LIESTMAN

SANDERS, GEORGE (July 3, 1906–Apr. 25, 1972), actor, was born in St. Petersburg, Russia, to British parents. His father, also George Sanders, was a rope manufacturer; his mother, Margaret Kolbe, was a renowned horticulturist. During the Communist revolution the family fled to England, where Sanders attended, and then was expelled from, Dunhurst Preparatory School; at Bedales School (1917–1918), he acted in plays with his brother Tom and began sketching. He attended Brighton College (1922–1926) and Manchester Technical School (1926–1930), specializing in textiles.

After working briefly in Birmingham at a textile mill, Sanders spent four years as a manufacturing representative for tobacco companies in Buenos Aires, Argentina, and Valparaiso, Chile. He lost his first South American job when he appeared at his employer's wedding besotted by alcohol and his second when he fought a duel with a jealous rival.

Upon Sanders's return to London, actress Greer Garson got him involved in an amateur theatrical group, and his Uncle Sacha gave him singing lessons to develop his rich bass-baritone voice. In the early 1930's he was part of a three-man piano act in a short-lived musical, *Bally-hoo*, he acted in more than fifty radio plays for the BBC, and he was successful in cabaret work, chorus jobs, and understudy roles.

Despite positive reviews in October 1935 as Cavanaugh, the male lead opposite Edna Best in *Further Outlook*, he did not appear on a theater stage again for more than thirty years. As he moved from stage and radio performer to screen actor, the drifting ended. At thirty years of age, he had found his profession.

His first British motion pictures were *Find the Lady* (1936) and *Strange Cargo* (1936), followed by H. G. Wells's *The Man Who Could Work Miracles* (1937), in which he appeared briefly as a nude god riding a horse across the Milky Way. He appeared with Tyrone Power, another newcomer, in his first American movie in 1936 as the villain, Lord Everett Stacy, in Darryl F. Zanuck's *Lloyds of London* for Twentieth Century–Fox.

Sanders kept a journal of his Hollywood years between 1937 and 1938 ostensibly in the form of a letter to his father Henry, ranging from advice to his brother Tom on his acting career to the instability and unpredictability of his own career.

The six-foot, three-inch actor, with deep-set blue eyes and a slightly receding hairline, played in at least ninety films, beginning in the 1930's. He was often typecast as a blasé lover, cruel to women, a suave sophisticate who was ruthless in matters of money and love and usually got away with it. He played a succession of villain roles, artfully combining charm and cruelty; he was a master at playing the evildoer who masks his motives under a cool exterior. Sanders also starred in "The Saint" and "The Falcon" detective series at RKO, later continued by his brother, acting under the name Tom Conway.

His off-camera reputation rivaled that of his acerbic screen characters. He maintained a reclusive, reserved private life. He called himself a "high-class sort of heel" in his autobiography, *Memoirs of a Professional Cad* (1960), but admitted this character was a mask. "In reality I am a sentimentalist . . . invariably the victim of women's inhumanity to man."

In *Son of Fury* (1942), demonstrating his prowess in boxing from his days as interscholastic champion at Brighton, Sanders defeated his opponent in a bare-knuckle, bare-chested prize fight. He was also an accomplished cro-

quet player and once won the Goldwyn Cup competition among British living in Hollywood. He was also awarded a medal by the British Humane Society for saving a man from drowning in the Thames.

His Academy Award–winning performance in *All About Eve* (1950) paints a portrait of an elegantly mannered, cynical, venom-tongued cad, who is a vicious and powerful drama critic with a licentious interest in pretty girls, one of whom was Marilyn Monroe, who won an Oscar as best supporting actress.

He also gave memorable performances in *Lancer Spy* (1937), *Rebecca* (1940), *The Picture of Dorian Gray* (1945), *Forever Amber* (1947), *Samson and Delilah* (1949), *Ivanhoe* (1952), *While the City Sleeps* (1956), *Village of the Damned* (1960), *A Shot in the Dark* (1964), *The Amorous Adventures of Moll Flanders* (1965), and *The Quiller Memorandum* (1966).

Sanders played an artist resembling Gauguin in *The Moon and Sixpence* (1946) while in *The Lodger* (1944) he played a detective sleuthing Jack the Ripper. Contrary to his usual roles, he played a reporter in Alfred Hitchcock's *Foreign Correspondent* (1940) and a henpecked hero in *Uncle Harry* (1945). *Call Me Madam* (1953) was one of the few films in which he sang.

Among his other numerous films were *Hangover Square* (1945), *The Ghost and Mrs. Muir* (1947), *Moonfleet* (1955), *Scarlet Coat* (1955), *The Whole Truth* (1958), *Solomon and Sheba* (1959), *A Touch of Larceny* (1959), *The Last Voyage* (1960), and *Jungle Book* (voice, 1967).

Sanders married four times, first on Oct. 27, 1940, to Elsie M. Poole, an actress from Los Angeles known professionally as Susan Larson, who suffered from mental illness. Sanders began psychiatric analysis when Larson left him in 1946 and continued in analysis for the rest of his life. He was divorced in 1948.

Sanders's marriage to Zsa Zsa Gabor in 1949 lasted almost five years, during which time he shared a fourteen-bedroom mansion in Beverly Hills with Gabor "as a sort of paying guest." In 1956, they made a joint movie appearance in *Death of a Scoundrel*, a melodrama in which he played a rake. Despite their divorce in 1954, Sanders remained good friends with Zsa Zsa for the rest of his life. In 1959, he married actress Benita Hume, widow of actor Ronald Colman; this marriage lasted until her death in 1967. In 1970, Sanders's marriage, arranged by Zsa Zsa, to Magda Gabor, her older sister, ended in six weeks in an annulment.

Sanders was involved in at least two business ventures that went bankrupt, one of which was Husan, Ltd., which he founded in 1956 to finance, develop, and market inventions. In partnership with a Swiss investment company, Roturman, S.A., he created a subsidiary, Cadco, Ltd., which marketed Royal Victoria sausages with a factory in Sussex, England, and an extension in Scotland. Sanders and his partners were investigated, and he was almost prosecuted. At this time, Sanders first gave expression to thoughts of suicide. He suffered a stroke in 1969 and several small strokes during the next year. Having witnessed the pain and helpless dependence of his wife Benita in her final days and of his mother prior to her death in 1969, he did not want to endure pain and indignity himself. In failing health, he committed suicide by taking Nembutal with vodka in a resort hotel in Barcelona, Spain, leaving a note saying, "Dear World. I am leaving because I am bored. I feel I have lived enough."

[Sanders's autobiography, *Memories of a Professional Cad*, appeared in 1960. Thirty years later, Richard Van Der Beets wrote a biography entitled *George Sanders: An Exhausted Life* (1990). An obituary appears in the *New York Times*, Apr. 26, 1972.]

PHYLLIS BADER-BOREL

SANDS, DIANA PATRICIA (Aug. 22, 1934–Sept. 21, 1974), actress, was born in the borough of the Bronx, New York City, and was brought up mainly in suburban Elmsford, N.Y., and in Manhattan. Her father, Rudolph Thomas Sands, Jr., was a carpenter; her mother, Shirley Walker, was a milliner. Canada Lee's performance in *Native Son* (1941), which she saw when only seven, inspired her to go on the stage. She attended the High School of Performing Arts in New York City, from which she graduated in 1952, winning the school's Best Actress award. While still in school, Sands began to work professionally, one of her first jobs being part of an "Oriental" dance team, Twan and Diana. She studied under a variety of teachers, including Michael Howard and Lloyd Richards, and she took special courses in speech, pantomime, dancing, and singing.

Although she was black, Sands began her legitimate acting career playing mostly nonblack roles. Her debut was as Juliet in an Off-Broadway presentation called *An Evening with Will Shakespeare* (1953). She also appeared Off-Broadway in *The World of Sholem Aleichem* (1953) and a revival of *Major Barbara* (1954). During these years, when good roles for blacks were rare, she encountered considerable hardship and had to take a variety of day jobs, such as key-punch operator for the utility company Con Edison.

After a stint with Lionel Shepard's Pantomime Art Theatre in 1955, Sands appeared in Off-Broadway plays that included *The Man with the Golden Arm* (1956), *Fortunato* (1956), *Mary and the Fairy* (1956), *A Land Beyond the River* (1957), and *The Egg and I* (1958). Her first part on Broadway, playing Beneatha in Lorraine Hansberry's *A Raisin in the Sun* (1959), earned her the Outer Circle Critics' Award and *Variety*'s Critics Poll Award as the most promising young actress. Ironically, her cynicism regarding the commercial theater's attitude toward blacks had made her reluctant to audition for the part.

After *A Raisin in the Sun*, Sands was in such Off-Broadway pieces as the revue *Another Evening with Harry Stoones* (1961), *Black Monday* (1962), and *Brecht on Brecht* (1962). She was in Hyannisport, Mass., with the improvisational Compass Players in 1963, and in the same year appeared Off-Broadway in *The Living Premise*, which earned her an Obie. On Broadway she was in *Tiger, Tiger, Burning Bright* (1962) and *Blues for Mister Charlie* (1964), James Baldwin's important contribution to the burgeoning black theater movement. Critic Walter Kerr wrote in the *New York Herald Tribune*: "[There is] a breathtaking passage which Diana Sands delivers at unbelievable . . . pitch . . . with a pulsing hysteria that is still just within control. I know of no other single sequence as powerful in New York today."

The year 1964 was very full for Sands. She married James Baldwin's manager, Swiss-born artist Lucien Happersberger (they had no children and were divorced in 1967), and she made a major Broadway contribution in Bill Manhoff's romantic comedy, *The Owl and the Pussycat*. Sands played a role which had been written for a white actress, and the leading man, Alan Alda, was white. The two-character romantic comedy made no reference to race, however, and Sands's presence was considered a breakthrough in interracial casting. She was nominated for a Tony and starred in the London production of the play. Its director, Larry Storch, said of her: "She has this stunning, kaleidoscopic quality, a great comedic sense."

In the mid-1960's, Sands worked extensively in American regional theaters, acting in Atlanta, Philadelphia, and Los Angeles, playing a variety of classical roles. She found that the classical theater was the only medium wherein she could be taken seriously as an artist. New York audiences saw her in *Phaedra* (1967) and *St. Joan* (1968), in which she played the lead, the first black actress to play Joan of Arc in a major professional production. The play was produced by the Repertory Theater at Lincoln Center, to which Sands belonged for a season, and where she also played Cassandra in *Tiger at the Gates* (1968). She then appeared in several more plays in New York, including *We Bombed in New Haven* (1968) and *The Gingham Dog* (1969). Her work also took her on tour across the United States and Europe. A major touring role was the female lead in *Caesar and Cleopatra* (1967).

Sands's first film role was as a bar girl in *Caribbean Gold* (1952). She later was seen in *Four Boys and a Gun* (1957); the film version of *A Raisin in the Sun* (1961), in which she repeated her stage role (and for which she won the International Artist Award); and eight more films, including *The Garment Jungle* (1957), *An Affair of the Skin* (1963), *Mr. Pulver and the Captain* (1963), *The Landlord* (1970), *Doctors' Wives* (1971), and *Georgia, Georgia* (1972). Two films produced by Third World Cinema, of which Sands was a cofounder, were not released until after her death: *Willie Dynamite* (1973) and *Honeybaby, Honeybaby* (1974), filmed in Beirut, Lebanon. She was engaged to marry the latter's director, Kurt Baker.

Sands appeared frequently on television, guest starring in many series, such as "East Side, West Side," "Dr. Kildare," and "I Spy." She won an Emmy for her reading of poetry in "Beyond the Blue" (1964).

Sands, attractive, slim, and chain-smoking, was recognized as one of the finest performers of her day. She was honored for making a successful career playing important roles in the mainstream, mostly white theater at a time when black actors were largely confined to marginal parts in such work. She was outspoken on behalf of the black actor's plight and let few opportunities to stand up for the concept of open

casting pass without comment. She told Anthony Wolff in 1968, "If you're black . . . there's only so far you can go. . . . It's like a brick wall; and one day you realize you've given yourself all kinds of scars . . . that the wall is insurmountable."

She died of cancer in New York City.

[Articles on Sands are in the clipping file of the Billy Rose Theater Collection, Lincoln Center Library of the Performing Arts, New York City. See also Dick Schaap, "A Girl Playing a Girl," *New York Herald Tribune*, Nov. 15, 1964; S. Caston, "Diana Sands: Notes on a Broadway Pussycat," *Look*, Feb. 9, 1965; Mel Gussow, "And Now, Diana at the Stake," *New York Times*, Dec. 31, 1967; Anthony Wolff, "The Passion of Diana Sands," *Look*, Jan. 9, 1968; Orde Coombs, "Lunching with Diana Sands," *Essence*, Aug. 1970; and Maurice Peterson, "Diana, Diana," *Essence*, June 1972. An obituary is in the *New York Times*, Sept. 23, 1974.]
SAMUEL L. LEITER

SARNOFF, DAVID (Feb. 27, 1891–Dec. 12, 1971), communications executive, was born in Uzlian, Russia, the eldest of five children of Abraham Sarnoff, a house painter, and Leah Privin. The family came to New York in 1900 and settled on the Lower East Side. With his father extremely ill, Sarnoff soon became the main source of support for the family: he delivered meat, sold newspapers, and sang in a synagogue. He also studied English, made use of the Educational Alliance, and had finished the eighth grade in 1906, at age fifteen. Sarnoff then began working as a messenger boy at the Commercial Cable Company, whose British parent company controlled undersea cable traffic, and taught himself Morse code. On Sept. 30, 1906, Sarnoff was hired by George De Sousa (who later became treasurer of RCA) as an office boy ($5.50 per week) at the Marconi Wireless Telegraph Company of America. The head of the English parent company, Guglielmo Marconi, became Sarnoff's mentor and let the boy use his personal technical library. Within a year Sarnoff became a junior wireless operator. "He had no childhood but did not seem to miss it," observed Erik Barnouw.

In 1908, Sarnoff became an operator at the Siasconset Marconi station on Nantucket, where his distinctive telegraphic "fist" became known for speed and accuracy. In 1909, he was promoted to manager of the Sea Gate station in

Brooklyn, N.Y., where, at eighteen, he supervised operators older than himself.

Sarnoff was working at the Marconi office at the John Wanamaker department store in Manhattan on Apr. 14, 1912, but the legend of his being the single wireless operator reporting the *Titanic* disaster appears to be an exaggeration, since it is not supported by contemporary accounts. He was promoted to radio (or wireless) inspector for American Marconi in 1912. The next year he became chief radio inspector and assistant chief engineer. In 1914, he was promoted to contract manager of American Marconi, which gave him the opportunity to investigate new inventions and services. On Feb. 2, 1914, Sarnoff wrote a favorable memorandum on the receiving system of the inventor Edwin Howard Armstrong. A long friendship with Armstrong would be followed by a long feud.

In a memorandum dated Sept. 30, 1915, to Edward J. Nally, general manger of American Marconi, Sarnoff said, "I have in mind a plan of development which would make radio a household utility in the same sense as the piano or phonograph. The idea is to bring music into the house by wireless. . . . The receiver can be designed in the form of a simple 'Radio Music Box' and arranged for several different wavelengths, which should be changeable with the throwing of a single switch or pressing of a single button." Nally paid no attention to Sarnoff's memo. In 1968, Jerome B. Wiesner, then the provost of the Massachusetts Institute of Technology, commented, "from the beginning, young David was exhibiting that intuitive grasp of where the future lay which has been the hallmark of his long and brilliant career."

Sarnoff was assistant traffic manager of American Marconi in 1915 and was promoted to commercial manager in 1917. On July 4 of that year, he married Lizette Hermant; they had three children. During World War I, the Navy Department controlled all wireless facilities and patents. Sarnoff was often in Washington, D.C., negotiating contracts and giving advice on communications to congressional committees. After the war, with the Navy wanting wireless communications to be in American hands, British Marconi was encouraged to sell its stock in American Marconi to General Electric (GE). The new subsidiary of GE, incorporated on Oct. 17, 1919, was the Radio Corporation of America (RCA). All of American Marconi's op-

erations and assets were transferred to RCA on Nov. 20, 1919.

The chairman of the board of RCA was Owen D. Young; its president, Edward Nally; the commercial manager, Sarnoff. The head office was in the Woolworth Building in lower Manhattan. In order to create a stronger patent pool with cross-licensing agreements, GE brought in Westinghouse, American Telephone and Telegraph (AT&T), and the United Fruit Company, which all received large amounts of RCA stock. Controlling all major patents, RCA's centralized control, often criticized as a communications monopoly in violation of the Sherman Antitrust Act, influenced the way in which radio and television would develop in the United States. Sarnoff wanted RCA to move into broadcasting, and on July 2, 1921, RCA broadcast the Jack Dempsey–Georges Carpentier championship boxing match from Jersey City, N.J., to some three hundred thousand people. In June 1922, Sarnoff wrote to the president of GE, E. W. Rice, Jr., proposing the establishment of a separate national broadcasting company or network that would provide entertainment and information to the nation. In 1923, James G. Harbord became president of RCA and, subsequently, a close friend of Sarnoff's.

In 1925, Sarnoff signed an agreement with the Victor Talking Machine Company for a combination radio and phonograph; its trademark, a dog named Nipper listening to a gramophone, became famous. The National Broadcasting Company (NBC) was incorporated on Sept. 9, 1926. Red and Blue networks, each having stations in several cities, started broadcasting on Nov. 15, 1926. In 1927, Sarnoff joined the RCA board. When Harbord took a leave of absence in 1928, Sarnoff became acting president; after Harbord retired, he was named executive vice-president. In October 1928, Sarnoff and Joseph P. Kennedy arranged to create a motion picture company, Radio-Keith-Orpheum (RKO), which used RCA Photophone sound equipment. Sarnoff became chairman of the board of RKO; his friendship with Kennedy lasted until 1960, when Sarnoff supported Richard Nixon for president. In 1929, radio sales exceeded $800 million, and Sarnoff negotiated a deal with General Motors to create a new company to manufacture radios for cars. He became a director of the General Motors Radio Corporation.

Sarnoff's mentor, Owen Young, went to Paris in 1929 to negotiate a new reparations agreement between Germany and the nations that had been victorious in World War I. He took Sarnoff as his assistant, and later gave him much credit for the success of the negotiations that became the Young Plan. The German delegate, Hjalmar Schacht, preferred to negotiate with Sarnoff. Another delegate, J. P. Morgan, discussed the possibility of a partnership in his firm with Sarnoff.

In 1929, the RCA Victor Company was incorporated, with Sarnoff as chairman. He became president of RCA on Jan. 3, 1930. In 1930 the U.S. Justice Department charged that RCA was in violation of the antitrust laws because of the company's original patent pool, which was a communications monopoly (inherited from the Navy after World War I). John W. Davis and Paul Cravath were among those giving Sarnoff legal advice, but he saw an opportunity to achieve his goal of independence for RCA (from the electrical companies) by agreeing to some of the government's demands. In an agreement worked out in November 1932, GE and Westinghouse severed all ties to RCA. RCA had emerged from the negotiations with manufacturing plants, broadcasting stations, and two networks. As in previous crucial negotiations, Sarnoff's strengths included not only perseverance and vision but also a detailed knowledge of every aspect of his business. Young resigned as a director of RCA in May 1933.

The Great Depression caused a decline in radio sales, and in 1932 RCA had its first loss: $1,133,585. But Sarnoff remained optimistic. In June 1933, RCA moved to Rockefeller Center, where Sarnoff ran his companies from the fifty-third floor of the RCA Building. He bought a town house on East Seventy-first Street because commuting was one of the things he considered a waste of time. Growth in radio sales and at NBC made RCA profitable again in 1934. When Marconi asked Sarnoff for help in a contract negotiation that same year, Sarnoff went to London to give advice. An NBC broadcast on July 20, 1937, the day after Marconi's death, included reflections by Sarnoff, who had "known Guglielmo Marconi for more than thirty years, ever since I was a boy. He was always a source of inspiration to me, always a kind teacher and a loyal, helpful friend."

In 1942, RCA Laboratories, a centralized research center devoted to electronic research, opened at Princeton, N.J. (The laboratories were renamed the David Sarnoff Research Center in 1951.) Weisner noted, "The uniqueness of David Sarnoff lies in his combination of a visionary and determined builder and hard-headed industrial leader. He was among the first to recognize the role that science could play in modern industry and to stake his future entirely on its promise." Even in the Great Depression the research budget was the last to be cut at RCA. As a businessman, Sarnoff took risks and the long view, making huge investments in new technology years before there was any possibility of profit.

Sarnoff's extensive military experience was utilized in World War II (he became a lieutenant colonel in the Army Signal Corps Reserve in 1924, attended courses at the Army War College in 1926, and was promoted to full colonel in 1931). In 1944, Sarnoff was called to active duty and ordered to London. On Mar. 21, 1944, he met with General Dwight D. Eisenhower at Supreme Headquarters Allied Expeditionary Forces (SHAEF). Sarnoff became special assistant for communications. He was told to build a broadcasting station strong enough to reach all forces under Eisenhower's command in Europe and the Mediterranean, and to create a plan for coordinating all communications channels between SHAEF and the invasion force.

Sarnoff met Prime Minister Winston Churchill to get British approval for pooled Allied broadcast facilities. He also had lunch at 10 Downing Street and talked about television with Winston and Clementine Churchill. Extensive news reports of D day were carried around the world as a result of broadcast facilities Sarnoff had developed. Later in 1944, he helped restore the communications system in France. In December of that year, Sarnoff became a brigadier general and returned to RCA, where he preferred to be addressed as "General." He became an advocate of victory in the Cold War and helped American intelligence agencies, which benefited from RCA facilities and expertise.

In 1923, Sarnoff had written a memo to the RCA board predicting television. In 1929, he met Vladimir T. Zworykin, television's leading inventor, who advocated an all-electronic approach involving no mechanical moving parts. Sarnoff supported that view and hired Zworykin. On Apr. 20, 1939, Sarnoff gave a televised speech at the opening of the 1939 World's Fair in New York, where just ten days later Franklin D. Roosevelt became the first president to make a television appearance. NBC started commercial telecasting on July 1, 1941, when WNBT, New York, carried a Bulova watch advertisement. Frank M. Folsom, a marketing specialist, led the RCA television campaign in 1947 and became president of RCA in 1950. Sarnoff's close associate, Kenneth Bilby, described his views on management thus: "His cardinal leadership principle was growth through innovation. Core businesses must be germinated through in-house creation of technology. How often he had said: 'The heart of RCA is its scientific laboratories.' " Sarnoff's interest was in technology rather than programming and entertainment.

William S. Paley, whose interest and strength was programming, was Sarnoff's counterpart at CBS. In 1948, Paley launched a talent raid on NBC, signing up the "Amos 'n' Andy" show (which had been on NBC since 1929) and Jack Benny. In 1949 the switch to CBS, which offered much more money, was made by Red Skelton, Edgar Bergen and Charlie McCarthy, George Burns and Gracie Allen, Al Jolson, and Groucho Marx. In 1949, CBS became the leader in radio broadcasting (and later in television). Kenneth Bilby, a member of Sarnoff's management team, reports that Sarnoff disliked the star system and once remarked, "A business built on a few comedians isn't a business worth being in."

Sarnoff's oldest son, Robert, executive producer of the widely acclaimed documentary "Victory at Sea," rose rapidly at NBC, becoming its president in 1955. Despite having Elvis Presley, the RCA Records Division did not do well, since most pop singers went to CBS. In 1961, Elmer Engstrom, RCA's senior scientist, became its president. RCA's attempt to challenge IBM in computers was not successful. Sarnoff retired as chief executive officer of RCA in 1965 but remained as chairman; Robert Sarnoff became president. Sarnoff, who wanted to combine electronic information retrieval and book publishing, began negotiations with Bennett Cerf in December 1965, which resulted in the acquisition of Random House by RCA. After a severe illness in 1968, Sarnoff no longer took an active part in RCA.

The broadcasting network, first in radio, was one of Sarnoff's ideas that have affected the way people lead their daily lives. Although he became wealthy, that was not his main motivation, and RCA was not as profitable as some early analysts had hoped. His passion seemed to be using his power as an executive to develop new technologies. To perfect radio and television, new fields were mastered, which resulted in new inventions, including the electron microscope and the computer. As Jerome Wiesner observed, "Modern science is only possible because of the electronic tools that flowed from communications research." Sarnoff died in New York City and is entombed in an ornate mausoleum in Valhalla, N.Y.

[Sarnoff's papers are at the David Sarnoff Research Center, Princeton, N.J. *Looking Ahead: The Papers of David Sarnoff* (1968), with a foreword by Jerome B. Wiesner, contains selected memoranda and letters. See also John Tebbel, *David Sarnoff* (1963); Eugene Lyons, *David Sarnoff* (1966), an authorized account by Sarnoff's cousin; and Erik Barnouw, *A History of Broadcasting in the United States*, 3 vols. (1966–1970). For a challenge to the Sarnoff/*Titanic* legend, see Carl Dreher, *Sarnoff* (1977), by an RCA engineer; and Kenneth Bilby, *The General: David Sarnoff and the Rise of the Communications Industry* (1986), by a close associate of Sarnoff who researched his book while at Harvard Business School. Also of value are William S. Paley, *As It Happened* (1979); Robert Sobel, *RCA* (1986); and Christopher Sterling and John Kittross, *Stay Tuned* (1990). See also Lizette Sarnoff, "My Life with a Genius," *Good Housekeeping*, June 1955. Thomas Lewis, *Empire of the Air* (1991), became a PBS television series. Obituaries are in the *New York Times*, Dec. 13, 1971; *Broadcasting*, Dec. 20, 1971; *Electronic News*, Dec. 20, 1971; and *Journal of the Society of Motion Picture and Television Engineers*, Feb. 1972.]

RALPH KIRSHNER

SAUER, CARL ORTWIN (Dec. 24, 1889– July 18, 1975), geographer, was born in Warrenton, Mo., the son of Rosetta J. Vosholl, a teacher, and William Albert Sauer, professor of French and music. He was sent to Calw, Germany, for three years of primary education, which prepared him to graduate early, in 1908, from Central Wesleyan College, where his father headed the Department of Music. That year Sauer began graduate work in geology at Northwestern University, in Evanston, Ill., but he soon shifted to geography. The change required him to transfer to the University of Chicago, which then offered the only significant graduate program in that subject. Sauer's background in history and biology served him well to study under the direction of Professor Rollin D. Salisbury.

In 1915 Sauer earned a Ph.D. in geography. While at Chicago he held positions as assistant geologist for the Illinois Geographical Survey, map editor at Rand McNally, and instructor at Salem Normal School in Salem, Mass. On Dec. 30, 1913, he married Lorena Schowengerdt; they had two children. In January 1916 Sauer accepted an appointment to the University of Michigan in Ann Arbor, where he helped develop a geography curriculum and earned a reputation as an outstanding lecturer. Within eight years he advanced to full professor, writing widely on the geography of the Midwest. His publications include *Geography of the Upper Illinois Valley and History of Development* (1916), *Starved Rock State Park and Its Environs* (1918), and *The Geography of the Ozark Highland of Missouri* (1920). The last volume is often cited as a model for regional cultural geography. Later research on the timber cutover area of northern Michigan initiated concern for ecological problems. His writing and research laid the groundwork for establishing an independent department of geography at Michigan in 1923, separate from the department of geology.

That year Sauer accepted a professorship at the University of California, Berkeley. During the summer he pursued regional interests in northern Mexico and the American Southwest. A methodological and theoretical work based on this research, *The Morphology of Landscape* (1925) brought him wide recognition. His approach introduced German ideas on geography, which diverged sharply from existing American thought. Although he later revised this early thinking, his influence helped end a deterministic perspective in geography while integrating historical and humanistic factors into the discipline. The core of the discipline became regional analysis, based on field work, archaeology, and history with a focus on culture and close ties to anthropology.

As chair of the department at Berkeley, Sauer shaped a geography program unique in North America, emphasizing how human influences shaped the world. His emphasis on a historical and ecological perspective contrasted with traditional geography but paralleled the work of Salisbury. His research required intensive field investigation and analysis of regional differences. While Sauer focused on the Southwest

borderlands, especially the little-known parts of northern Mexico, he welcomed other regional studies by colleagues and students. His publications on the Southwest include *Basin and Forms in the Chiricahua Area* (1930), *Prehistoric Settlement of Sonora, with Special Reference to Cerros de Trincheras* (1931), and *Aboriginal Population of Northwestern Mexico* (1935).

Sauer's study of aboriginal populations and subsistence patterns included prehistory, which led him to delve into anthropology and archaeology. He published an archaeological study, *Pueblo Sites in Southeastern Arizona* (1930), and won recognition from cultural anthropologists for his ethnography of about twenty Indian tribes of the Mexican Sierra, whose cultures were almost unknown. His school text, *Man in Nature: America Before the Days of the White Men* (1939), introduces anthropology as well as historical geography with a humanistic perspective.

While Sauer succeeded in building a distinctive department at Berkeley shaped around his interests, he was unhappy with the direction of geographic study elsewhere in North America, including geographic education in the public schools. As a counter to traditional American geography, he invited German geographers to Berkeley. Given this impetus and the strength of his own persuasion, his students spread his brand of cultural geography as they were placed in academic positions across North America.

In the 1950's Sauer turned to research topics of broader interest. As early as 1936 he had written on the origins of domesticated plants in the Americas in a memorial for anthropologist A. L. Kroeber. Through archaeological evidence and historical sources, he sought to determine animal and plant origins and understand their diffusion. Above all he emphasized the need to reconstruct the spread of domesticated plants and animals through careful study of their distribution. While his major interest was Central America, his documentation on agriculture covered the world. Significant parts of this work were published in collaboration with anthropologists in *Handbook of South American Indians* (1950). In 1952 he summarized his research in *Agricultural Origins and Dispersals*.

An equally broad interest in environmental problems accompanied Sauer's research on agriculture. He pioneered the study of such environmental problems as erosion and pollution, arguing that human beings were responsible for far more of the earth's changes than was recognized. His humanistic bent and long-standing interest in population growth were complemented by his concern for environmental degradation. This thinking was reflected in his role as an organizer of an international conference at Princeton, N.J., the proceedings of which were published as *Man's Role in Changing the Face of the Earth* (1956), edited by William L. Thomas.

After Sauer's retirement in 1957, he was invited to lecture at various universities in the United States and Europe, but he spent most of his time at Berkeley, where President Clark Kerr encouraged him to continue seminars and research. During his retirement he wrote several monographs, among them, *The Early Spanish Main* (1966), *Northern Mists* (1968), *Sixteenth Century North America: The Land and the People as Seen by the Europeans* (1971), and *Seventeenth Century North America* (1980). He remained active until his wife's death just a month before his own.

[Sauer's papers are at the Bancroft Library, University of California, Berkeley. A sampling of his major works, edited by John Leighly, is in *Land and Life* (1963). See James J. Parsons, "Carl Ortwin Sauer," the *Geographical Review*, Jan. 1976; and John Leighly, "Carl Ortwin Sauer, 1889–1975," *Annals*, Association of American Geographers, Sept. 1976. An obituary appears in the *New York Times*, July 21, 1975.]

ERNEST L. SCHUSKY

SAYRE, WALLACE STANLEY (June 24, 1905–May 14, 1972), political scientist and authority on municipal governments, was born near Point Pleasant, W.Va., one of eight children of Alford Sayre and Cornelia Tucker. He received his B.A. degree from Marshall College in 1927, and the M.A. (1928) and Ph.D. (1930) from New York University. He married Kathryn McKnight on June 29, 1929; they had two children.

In the 1929–1930 academic year, while he was completing his dissertation on the La Follette family of Wisconsin, Sayre served as a teaching fellow in government at New York University. He was appointed to the faculty there the following year, and from 1934 to 1940 was an assistant professor. Beginning in 1937, Sayre was also a member of the administration

of Mayor Fiorello La Guardia. His initial post was secretary to the Civil Service Commission, and he was also responsible for the Public Service Training Program. He soon emerged as one of the central figures in the La Guardia administration's efforts to reform New York City's civil service system. He was a leading member of the task force that drafted the Model Civil Service Law (1938–1939), and in 1938 he was appointed commissioner of the New York City Civil Service Commission. He held this post until 1942, when he moved to the Office of Price Administration. Some reports have suggested that he was forced to resign his post as commissioner because he had criticized the administration's handling of some controversial political appointments. At the Office of Price Administration, Sayre served as assistant director of the fuel-rationing division until 1944, when he was promoted to director of personnel.

In 1946, Sayre returned to academia as professor of administration at the Cornell School of Business and Public Administration. In 1949, he was appointed professor of government at the City College of New York; in 1951 he became chairman of that department. From 1950 to 1952, he was a visiting professor in public administration at Columbia University. In 1954, he left City College to become a full-time member of the faculty at Columbia, as professor of public administration. In 1959, he was designated Eaton professor of public administration, and from 1963 to 1968, he was chairman of the Department of Public Law and Government. During his tenure at Columbia, he acquired a reputation of staying in touch with his students long after their graduation.

Throughout his academic career, Sayre maintained an active presence in the political arena. He served in the Mayor's Advisory Council from 1954 to 1961, and he was vice-chairman of the Temporary Commission on New York City Finances from 1965 to 1967. For decades he was one of the leading forces behind the Citizen's Union, having served on that group's executive committee from 1935 to 1938 and from 1950 to 1967. Furthermore, from 1960 until his death he was a director of the Regional Plan Association of New York.

Sayre was author or coauthor of ten books and numerous articles, the most important of which is *Governing New York City*, a collaboration with Herbert Kaufman (1960) that is generally regarded as the most comprehensive book on city government. It combines a detailed analysis of New York City government with a series of specific recommendations for charter revision, policy reform, and other topics. The system of government it sets forth has been adopted, to varying extents, by municipal governments nationwide.

Sayre died from a heart attack in New York City, in the midst of a morning meeting at City Hall with Mayor John Lindsay. At the time of his death, he was working on yet another book about municipal government.

[Sayre's personal papers are at the Columbia University Library. His books, besides *Governing New York City*, are *Outline of American Government* (1932); *Your Government* (1932); *Charter Revision for the City of New York*, with Rufus D. Smith et al. (1934); *Education and Civil Service in New York City* (1938); *The United Nations Secretariat* (1950); *Training for Specialized Mission Personnel*, with Clarence Thurber (1951); *Personnel Administration in the Government of New York City*, with Herbert Kaufman (1952); *Four Steps to Better Government of New York City* (1954); and *Voting for President*, with Judith Parris (1970). Oral history interviews with Sayre are in the Oral History Office at Columbia University. An obituary is in the *New York Times*, May 19, 1972.]

OWEN D. GUTFREUND

SCHNEIDERMAN, ROSE (Apr. 6, 1882– Aug. 11, 1972), labor organizer and women's rights activist, was born in the Polish village of Saven, the daughter of Samuel Schneiderman and Deborah Rothman, both of whom worked in the needle trade. In 1890, the Schneidermans emigrated to New York City's Lower East Side, where they settled alongside other eastern European Orthodox Jews.

When Rose's father died in 1892, the family grew destitute. Within a year Schneiderman left school to take care of her baby sister while her mother worked in a fur factory. The following year Schneiderman and her two brothers were sent to a Jewish orphanage, and Schneiderman resumed her education. In the ninth grade she was forced to drop out of school permanently to help support her family. Encouraged by her mother and her own love of knowledge, Schneiderman taught herself and read voraciously.

Schneiderman went to work at age thirteen as an errand girl for a department store and then as a cashier at another department store, earning a scant $2.25 per week. Good wages were impor-

tant to Schneiderman, who was the only steady wage earner in her family. In 1898, she took a job as a lining maker at a cap factory for $6 per week. But she was expected to furnish her own thread and sewing machine, the hours were long, the piece-work variable, and the pay still far from adequate. Unaware of unions or other forms of collective organization, Schneiderman managed as best as she could.

The idea that her working conditions might be improved first occurred to Schneiderman in 1902, when her family spent a year in Montreal with a family named Kellert. The Kellerts were socialists and they awoke Schneiderman to the tenets of labor organizing. Schneiderman's new militancy was further nurtured when she returned to the cap-lining factory in 1903 and met a young anarchist named Bessie Braut. That year the two women organized the first women's local of the Jewish Socialist cap-makers union. After some initial resistance from the union's leadership, they chartered Local 23 of the United Cloth Hat and Cap Makers Union.

Schneiderman quickly became a pioneer in the male-dominated world of trade unionism. Under her guidance her local grew to several hundred members, and Schneiderman was elected the union's secretary and a delegate to the New York City Central Labor Union. In 1904, Schneiderman became the first woman to be named to a union executive board in the United States. She was thrilled to have found a calling.

Despite her enthusiasm for trade unionism, Schneiderman initially had misgivings about the newly formed New York Women's Trade Union League. Schneiderman worried whether the interests of middle-class women who ran the group were really allied with those of women workers. But when the league offered support for a citywide cap-makers' strike in 1905, she joined immediately. Her organizing skills were now well established, and the following year Schneiderman was elected the league's vice-president. In 1908, she was able to quit her factory job when a wealthy league backer offered Schneiderman a scholarship to work part-time as an organizer while attending the Rand School of Social Science.

During the great wave of general strikes in the garment industry from 1909 to 1914, Schneiderman became a well-known labor organizer. With the Lower East Side as her purview, Schneiderman organized Jewish immigrant women in the needle trades and was instrumental in the 1909–1910 strike of twenty-five thousand shirtwaist makers, the opening salvo in the unionization of the garment industry. By the strike's end, Schneiderman had abandoned her studies for full-time labor organizing. Out of these efforts emerged Local 62 of the International Ladies' Garment Workers' Union (ILGWU), a so-called white-goods union of which Schneiderman was the first president and for which she orchestrated a general strike in 1913.

In the summer of 1912, Schneiderman was hired by the National American Woman Suffrage Association (NAWSA) to convince trade unionists to support a statewide suffrage amendment. She approached suffrage as a class issue. If women workers could vote, she reasoned, then labor legislation would be more easily adopted. For the next seven years, Schneiderman was active in the suffrage movement, but her true love was labor organizing. After about a year with the NAWSA, Schneiderman returned to the league, and in 1915 she became a national organizer for the ILGWU. When the woman-suffrage movement turned its focus to passing the Equal Rights Amendment (ERA) in the 1920's, Schneiderman, like many trade unionists, abandoned the cause, arguing that an ERA would undermine protective legislation for women. Throughout her life, Schneiderman opposed the ERA.

Whatever her doubts about egalitarian feminism, Schneiderman was drawn to the suffrage campaign's legislative strategy and applied it with new vigor to the labor movement. As president of the New York Women's Trade Union League from 1918 to 1949 and of the national WTUL from 1926 to 1950, she focused on lobbying for maximum-hour and minimum-wage legislation for women rather than on unionizing them. She was concerned that American involvement in World War I would result in an increase in the workweek. She was also somewhat discouraged by labor organizing because of the union's male-dominated leadership and because she felt women workers were more intent on marrying than on improving working conditions.

Over the next two decades, Schneiderman increasingly looked to the state to solve labor problems. She ran unsuccessfully for the United States Senate in 1920 with the New York Farmer-Labor party. During the repressive post-war years, Schneiderman, who had briefly been a member of the Socialist party, was assailed as a radical. But the waning of the appeal of socialism and her growing friendship with Eleanor and Franklin Delano Roosevelt stimulated her interest in the Democratic party. In 1933, President Roosevelt appointed Schneiderman as the only woman to the National Recovery Administration's Labor Advisory Board and named her to his "brain trust." Schneiderman called her experience with the labor board "the high spot in my career," for she was convinced that the board's establishment of industrial codes made a dramatic difference in workers' lives. From 1937 to 1944, Schneiderman served as secretary of the New York State Department of Labor, the second-ranking position. She never abandoned advocacy work, remaining president of the New York and the national WTUL until 1949 and 1950, respectively. Even in retirement, Schneiderman kept a hand in the labor movement, attending executive board meetings of the New York League as "president emeritus" until it disbanded in 1955. Throughout the 1950's and 1960's, Schneiderman lived in Manhattan, where she wrote an autobiography. She died at the Jewish Home and Hospital for the Aged in New York City.

[Schneiderman's papers are on microfilm at New York University's Tamiment Library. For her years with the WTUL, see the records of the New York WTUL, which are part of the same microfilm collection. The best source for Schneiderman's life is her autobiography, *All for One* (1967), written with Lucy Goldthwaite. For an earlier autobiographical article, see "A Cap Maker's Story," *Independent*, Apr. 27, 1905. See also Nancy Schrom Dye, "Rose Schneiderman," in Edward T. James, ed., *Papers of the Women's Trade Union League and Its Principal Leaders* (1981).

Other accounts include Gary Endelman, "Solidarity Forever: Rose Schneiderman and the Women's Trade Union League" (Ph.D. diss., University of Delaware, 1978); Pat L. C. Scholten, "Militant Women for Economic Justice: The Persuasion of Mary Harris Jones, Ella Reeve Bloor, Rose Pastor Stokes, Rose Schneiderman, and Elizabeth Gurley Flynn" (Ph.D. diss., Indiana University, 1979); Ellen Condliffe Lagemann, *A Generation of Women* (1979); and Nancy Schrom Dye, *As Equals and As Sisters* (1980). An obituary is in the *New York Times*, Aug. 12, 1972.]

ANNE KORNHAUSER

SCHOCKEN, THEODORE (Oct. 8, 1914– Mar. 20, 1975), publisher, was born in

Zwickau, Germany, the son of Salman Schocken and Lilli Ehrmann. He attended public schools, first in Zwickau and later in Berlin. By the time of his birth the family was extremely prosperous. Salman Schocken had emigrated to Germany from Poland in 1901. Together with his brother he built up a chain of successful department stores. Inspired initially by the writings of philosopher Martin Buber, Salman developed a profound commitment to the revitalization of Jewish cultural and national life. He therefore expanded the family enterprises by adding a publishing house devoted exclusively to Judaica, Schocken Verlag. The political climate of Germany was hardly favorable to such an undertaking, yet the Verlag made extraordinary contributions to the cultural life of German Jews during its brief existence. Among the 194 titles published before 1938 were the collected works of Franz Kafka and of the Hebrew writer S. Y. Agnon.

Salman Schocken emigrated to Palestine toward the end of 1933 and established Schocken Books, Jerusalem–Tel Aviv, expanding the firm's earlier directions to include contemporary Hebrew writers. Theodore, not yet twenty, remained behind to take charge of the family's business affairs in Germany. In 1938, the Gestapo forced the Verlag to stop publishing, and Theodore left Germany, first for Palestine and then for the United States. He enrolled at Harvard University's business school but was ineligible to receive an M.B.A. since he lacked an undergraduate degree. However, Harvard granted him a certificate in June 1940 and in April 1951 finally awarded him an M.B.A.

From 1940 to 1942 Schocken was employed by Sears, Roebuck and Company in Chicago as a statistician. On Apr. 11, 1941 he married Dora Landauer; the couple had three children. In 1942 Schocken was granted American citizenship and enlisted in the United States Army, soon gaining a commission as first lieutenant. Assigned to intelligence, he took part in the North African campaign and the Allied invasion of Italy. Schocken returned to civilian life in 1945 and headed the American branch of Schocken Books, founded by Salman in his absence. Although both the Tel Aviv and New York branches of the firm continued as successful enterprises, the latter became a subsidiary of Random House in 1987.

When Theodore Schocken took on a leadership role at Schocken Books, New York, in 1946, the future looked promising. However, the new firm's plans to establish a general American market for the finest works of Jewish history and culture, as well as works translated from Hebrew, foundered. Schocken's authors and works were largely unknown to the American reading public. Even those writers who subsequently gained a wide following, such as Buber, Marc Chagall, and Kafka, did not speak to the needs of Americans picking up the threads of their lives in the immediate postwar era. Thus, despite the excellence of newly commissioned English translations of German and Hebrew works and an experiment with the production of high-quality paperbacks of Judaica, sales lagged.

Discouraged by these setbacks, Schocken resigned as head of the firm in 1949. It is not certain whether he remained active as company treasurer or resumed this responsibility in 1962. Schocken's business interests during the intervening years included a partnership in Popular Fashions, a small chain of women's clothing stores in New York City and Dutchess County. From the mid-1940's to the early 1950's he also served as director of the family's German enterprises, Merkur, A. G.

Schocken reassumed the presidency of Schocken Books in 1965 after the death of his brother-in-law, Herzl Rome, the company's chief executive. By then a new phase of prosperity had begun for the firm. Successful initiatives had included an ambitious program of trade paperbacks, resumption of full-scale publishing of Judaica, and expansion into books of general interest, especially in the social sciences. The foundation for many of these efforts was undoubtedly the back list of books created in the 1940's, during Schocken's first presidency.

The final decade of Schocken's life and work more than realized his earlier hopes, as Schocken Books enjoyed unprecedented prestige and financial success. In the late 1960's, with interest in Jewish studies spreading across secular colleges and universities, the market for a wide range of titles in Judaica expanded rapidly. From the 1970's on, the firm also pioneered in the publication of works to meet the exploding demand for women's studies. During that decade, about two-thirds of Schocken's publications were outside the field of Judaica. As the firm diversified, it reached more and more markets in this country and abroad.

One paradoxical consequence of this expansion was a dramatic increase in the general visibility of works in Judaica. Schocken paperbacks, in particular, had great success on college and university campuses. Kafka, of course, became fashionable, and the affordable editions of his works were ubiquitous. Scholarly works published by Schocken, especially in the social sciences, religion, and philosophy, were prominently displayed in campus bookstores and frequently adopted as required reading in college courses throughout the country. Among the most popular of Schocken's authors were Hannah Arendt, Gershom Scholem, and Walter Benjamin. In 1966, Schocken accompanied Agnon to Stockholm when he went to accept the first Nobel Prize ever awarded to an author who writes in Hebrew. Agnon's association with the Schockens dated back to the Berlin years, but the New York firm had published the English translations of his fiction in the United States.

Schocken served as director of the Leo Baeck Institute in New York and the Schocken Institute for Jewish Research in Jerusalem. He was also on the board of overseers of the Jewish Theological Seminary. He died in White Plains, N.Y.

[Most of Schocken's papers are housed in the Schocken Library, Jerusalem. His brief account of the firm's history is in *Judaica Booknews*, Fall/Winter 1971. See also Stephen M. Poppel, "Salman Schocken and the Schocken Verlag," *Harvard Library Bulletin*, Jan. 1973. Obituaries appear in the *New York Times*, Mar. 21, 1975, and in *Publisher's World* and *Time*, Mar. 31, 1975.]

URSULA SYBILLE COLBY

SEITZ, WILLIAM CHAPIN (June 19, 1914–Oct. 26, 1974), painter, museum curator and director, and art historian, was born in Buffalo, N.Y., the second of two sons of George William Seitz, a physician, and Cora Elizabeth Chapin, a teacher.

Although himself a talented painter whose works were exhibited in a number of one-man shows, Seitz is best remembered as a curator whose daring exhibitions and scholarly exhibit catalogs helped define many contemporary artistic movements and as an art historian who had an international reputation as an authority on modern art. In addition, Seitz's thorough training in both studio art and art history combined to make him a gifted teacher and critic

who furthered the artistic careers of many of his students.

After completing high school in Buffalo, he began formal study of art at that city's Albright Art School (1932–1933) and continued his studies at the Art Institute of Buffalo (1933–1935). In 1935, he moved to New York City to work on the Federal Art Project. Seitz's first one-man show was held in the spring of 1938 at the Arista Gallery in New York. That year was also significant because on December 1 he married Irma Jeannette Seigelman, like himself an artist. The couple, who had no children, soon moved to Buffalo where Seitz worked for the Hewitt Rubber Company as chief draftsman (1941–1943) and project engineer (1943–1945) and invented a self-sealing fuel tank used by the military during World War II.

In 1945, after a ten-year hiatus, Seitz resumed his formal education at the University of Buffalo, where he earned a bachelor of fine arts degree in 1946, and where he taught art history from 1946 to 1948. After a year of independent study in Europe, he entered Princeton University in 1950, earned a master of fine arts degree in 1952, and a Ph.D. in art history in 1955.

The story of Seitz's doctoral dissertation is interesting for what it reveals about art education in America during the early 1950's. During his stint with the Federal Art Project in the 1930's, Seitz had been active in New York City art circles and had come into contact with many of the painters later associated with the abstract expressionist movement. In addition, many of Seitz's paintings in that style had been exhibited in one-man shows at the Willard Gallery in New York City (1949, 1951, and 1953) and at the Art Museum of Princeton University (1949, 1951). Given this background, one might logically expect that the art faculty at Princeton would have immediately approved Seitz's proposal to study the works and ideas of six major abstract expressionists: Hans Hofmann, Mark Tobey, Arshile Gorky, Mark Rothko, Willem de Kooning, and Robert Motherwell. Instead, numerous objections were raised to his proposed thesis.

However, Alfred H. Barr, Jr., the influential director of the Museum of Modern Art in New York City, who was a Princeton graduate and a member of the advisory council of Princeton's Department of Art and Archaeology, took up Seitz's cause. Barr wrote the department chairperson to point out Seitz's unique qualifications for undertaking a study of a movement which, while not yet accepted in the United States, had "spread throughout the free world in the past dozen years." The chairperson replied that the committee in charge of graduate work had no objection to Seitz doing a thesis "on a modern subject," but only to the particular topic he had chosen. Because of Seitz's involvement with the abstract expressionist movement as a fellow artist the committee feared that his dissertation might become "a kind of manifesto of his own artistic principles and convictions" instead of a work of scholarship based on documentary evidence. The committee also objected to Seitz's proposal to talk directly to the artists about their intentions, for "artists themselves are never very clear about purposes and methods when it comes to stating them in words."

Barr eventually prevailed and Seitz wrote what Robert Motherwell, one of the subjects of the dissertation, has called "a classic—not only in the literature of Abstract Expressionism, but also *sui generis* in the scholarship of Modernism." Seitz's *Abstract Expressionist Painting in America* was the first doctoral thesis written about a movement that was still viewed with hostility by many American artists and much of the American art public. Thus he gave no thought to publishing it at the time and it did not finally appear until 1983—almost thirty years after it was presented and nearly ten years after the death of its author. Eventually, however, Seitz's work on Claude Monet in the early 1960's "provided Abstract Expressionism, now respectable in its own right, with a legal father" (*Apollo*, January 1972).

While still a graduate student at Princeton, Seitz was appointed lecturer in the Department of Art and Archaeology. After receiving his Ph.D., he held a variety of Princeton appointments: critic-in-residence (1952–1953), assistant professor (1955–1956), and bicentennial preceptor (1957–1960). In 1957, he was awarded a Fulbright fellowship for a year's study in France. In 1960, he left Princeton to become associate curator of the Department of Painting and Sculpture at the Museum of Modern Art in New York City. There he gained an international reputation by organizing and writing catalogs for a number of major exhibitions, including Monet: Seasons and Moments (1960), The Art of Assemblage (1961), Mark Tobey (1962), Arshile Gorky (1962), Hans Hofmann (1963), Art Israel (1964), and The Responsive Eye (1965).

Although promoted to curator in 1965, Seitz left the Museum of Modern Art to return to academia at Brandeis University, where between 1965 and 1970 he was a full professor in the Department of Fine Arts and also served as director of the Rose Art Museum and Poses Institute of Art, where he organized exhibitions of the works of several artists, including Philip Guston (1966) and James Rosati (1969). During this period he also organized the United States exhibition at the Ninth Biennial of the Museu de Arte Moderna in São Paulo, Brazil (1967), and the Seventh Biennial of Canadian Painting (1968) at the National Gallery of Canada in Ottawa.

In the 1970–1971 academic year he was a visiting professor at Harvard University. His appointment as Samuel Kress Professor (1971–1972) at the National Gallery of Art in Washington, D.C., a prestigious position given annually to a distinguished art historian, marked the first time the award was given to a scholar working in the field of modern art. From 1971 until his death in 1974, he was William R. Kenan, Jr., Professor of the History of Art at the University of Virginia in Charlottesville. There he taught and devoted himself to writing what Robert Rosenblum has called "a grand synthesis" of the new movements in art such as op art, pop art, photorealism, earthworks, and performance art that emerged after 1955. Left unfinished, Seitz's manuscript was edited by Marla Price, his former student at the University of Virginia who went on to become a prominent curator of contemporary art, and published as *Art in the Age of Aquarius, 1955–1970* (1992).

After Seitz died of cancer at the Martha Jefferson Hospital in Charlottesville, Va., many of his friends, both artists and art collectors, began donating works of art to the Art Museum of Princeton University in his memory. Frank Stella, who had been one of Seitz's students at Princeton, gave one of his own works to the museum and provided the initiative, support, and encouragement that lead to the formation of the William C. Seitz Memorial Collection, which was first exhibited in March 1977.

[In addition to catalogs for the exhibitions referred to above, Seitz was the author of *Claude Monet* (1960); *Henri de Toulouse-Lautrec: At the Circus* (1967); and *Segal* (1972). For the struggle over approval of Seitz's thesis, see Garnett McCoy, ed., "A

Continued Story: Alfred H. Barr, Jr., Princeton University, and William C. Seitz," *Archives of American Art Journal* 21, no. 3 (1981). On the William C. Seitz Memorial Collection at Princeton, see *Art Journal* 37 (Fall 1977). Obituaries appear in the *New York Times*, the *Buffalo Evening News*, and the (Charlottesville, Va.) *Daily Progress*, all Oct. 28, 1974; and in *Art in America* 63 (Mar.–Apr. 1975).]

ROMAN ROME

SERLING, RODMAN EDWARD ("ROD") (Dec. 25, 1924–June 28, 1975), television writer, producer, and narrator, was born in Syracuse, N.Y., the son of Samuel Lawrence Serling, a butcher, and Esther Cooper. He attended public schools in Binghamton, N.Y., graduating in 1942. Enlisting in the army as a paratrooper, he served three years in the Pacific theater and was severely wounded in the Philippines.

Serling's first taste of success was as an amateur boxer. Although a small man at five feet five inches, he won seventeen of his eighteen military bouts, getting his nose broken on one occasion. He fought in the Golden Gloves and was runner-up in the featherweight division championships.

After World War II, he enrolled at Antioch College in Yellow Springs, Ohio, under the GI Bill. He majored first in physical education, but soon switched to English literature and drama. "I was bitter about everything and at loose ends when I got out of the service," he later said. "I think I turned to writing to get it off my chest."

Serling took work-study jobs at a local radio station and began turning out scripts. In 1948 he married a fellow Antioch student, Carolyn Kramer. They had two children. In his senior year, Serling won second prize, including an all-expenses-paid trip for him and his wife to New York City, in a script-writing contest sponsored by CBS.

He graduated from Antioch with a B.A. in June 1950 more determined than ever to be a script writer. But after failing to sell his first forty free-lance scripts, Serling was forced to look for a salaried job. He worked first as a script writer for radio station WLW, then moved to WKRC-TV, both in Cincinnati. He earned $60 per week as a continuity writer and produced scripts for locally shown dramas.

During this period, Serling's free-lance efforts finally began to pay off with the sale of five radio scripts, including two to the "Grand Central Station" program on CBS radio. His breakthrough came in 1951 when the "Lux Video Theatre" series bought a script for a TV drama. He eventually sold ten more to the show. By the spring of 1953, Serling was earning enough to quit his regular job. A year later he moved to Westport, Conn., so that he could be closer to New York City.

Serling had already sold some ninety scripts when "Patterns," a one-hour drama about life in the top echelons of big business, aired Jan. 12, 1955, on NBC's "Kraft Television Theatre." Its success led NBC to stage the drama again a month later, the first such repeat in television history. He won his first Emmy and adapted the play for filming by United Artists. The movie was released in March 1956 to mixed reviews, although the *New York Times* critic wrote, "Serling has given us a creative, frightening, and often moving portrait of familiar and rare executives caught in mahogany-paneled 'jungles' with their teeth, hearts and minds bared."

In April 1955 Serling signed a deal with CBS-TV and his scripts were selling as fast as he could turn them out. In all, twenty Serling dramas aired in 1955, not all to critical acclaim. His reputation was soon reestablished with "Requiem for a Heavyweight," which inaugurated the "Playhouse 90" series on Oct. 11, 1956. The production brought him his second Emmy and the first Peabody Award ever bestowed on a writer. The teleplay was purchased for both the movies and the stage.

To keep up his prolific output, he abandoned typewriters in favor of tape recorders, usually working from 8:00 A.M. to noon. An intense individual who had trouble sleeping, he told friends he got some of his best ideas lying awake in bed.

As the golden age of television came to a close, Serling found himself becoming disenchanted with the medium because of frequent clashes with censors. His Emmy-winning script about lynch mobs, "A Town Has Turned to Dust," went through extensive revisions before it was accepted in 1958. "I simply got tired of battling," he said in 1959. "You always have to compromise lest somebody—a sponsor, a pressure group, a network censor—gets upset. Result is that you settle for second best."

Serling decided to switch directions. Now living in California, he formed his own TV production company in Hollywood. In 1959 he created the series for which he became most famous: "The Twilight Zone." Most people remember Serling not for his writing but as the velvet-voiced host of this science fiction anthology series. His opening introduction set the stage: "There is a fifth dimension beyond that which is known to man. . . . It is an area we call, 'The Twilight Zone.' " The show ran for five years. Serling wrote 89 of the 151 episodes, winning three more Emmys. Many famous actors appeared in the show, including Robert Redford and Cliff Robertson, but the main focus was always the offbeat story, usually with an ironic ending. "The Twilight Zone," shot in black and white, continued to thrive in reruns, achieving cult status.

In 1965 Serling was elected to a two-year term as head of the National Academy of Television Arts and Sciences, the first writer to serve as president.

He coauthored the screenplay for *Planet of the Apes*, which appeared in 1968. In 1970 he created another television series of macabre tales, "Night Gallery."

Serling had a reputation as one of television's angry young men early in his career. He admitted to mellowing with age, although he remained critical of the industry. "There was a time when I wanted to reform television," he said in a 1970 interview. "Now I accept it for what it is. So long as I don't write beneath myself or pander my work, I'm not doing anyone a disservice."

His final years were spent teaching. He became a professor of dramatic writing at Ithaca College and moved to Interlaken, N.Y. In a 1974 speech to the college's School of Communications, he criticized the commercialism of the film and television industry and "our deadening and deadly lack of creativity and courage. . . . How do you put on a meaningful drama or documentary that is adult, incisive, probing, when every 15 minutes the proceedings are interrupted by 12 dancing rabbits with toilet paper?"

Serling, a heavy smoker, had a minor heart attack in May 1975 and was hospitalized for two weeks. He underwent open-heart surgery the following month and died two days later at a Rochester, N.Y., hospital.

[For biographical information see *Rod Serling: The Dreams and Nightmares of Life in the Twilight Zone*, by Joel Engel (1989). Profiles can be found in several periodicals: *Millimeter*, Nov. 1976; *Twilight Zone Magazine*, Apr. 1981; *Television Quarterly*, 1984;

and *Emmy*, May/June 1985 and July/Aug. 1989. An obituary appears in the *New York Times*, June 29, 1975.]

PAUL GEITNER

SEXTON, ANNE GRAY HARVEY (Nov. 9, 1928–Oct. 4, 1974), poet, was born in Newton, Mass., the youngest of three daughters born to Mary Gray Staples and Ralph Churchill Harvey, owner of a wool firm. She was educated in public schools in Wellesley, Mass., and at Rogers Hall, a girls' preparatory school in Lowell, Mass. After a year at the Garland School, a finishing school in Boston, she eloped on Aug. 16, 1948, with Alfred Muller ("Kayo") Sexton II. They had two children.

In early 1956, shortly after the birth of her second child, Sexton began psychiatric treatment for what was diagnosed as postpartum depression; in November, she attempted suicide. Her doctor suggested that she use writing as a way to comprehend her troubled mental state. Sexton later recalled that her whole career evolved from watching a television lecture on sonnets given by I. A. Richards, a professor of literature at Harvard. She immediately began writing sonnets and other types of formal poetry, at first as therapy. In the winter of 1957, she enrolled in a writing workshop at the Boston Center for Adult Education, where she met the poets Maxine Kumin and George Starbuck, both of whom gave crucial encouragement during this phase of her development. Sexton called her newfound purpose in life "a kind of rebirth at twenty-nine."

Despite recurrent breakdowns, Sexton wrote with zeal and discipline. Breakthroughs in her style and her career occurred in the summer of 1958, when she received a scholarship to the Antioch Writer's Conference. There she worked for a week with the poet W. D. Snodgrass, who recommended her admission to Robert Lowell's writing seminar at Boston University (1958–1959). Lowell's criticism and admiration assisted the development of a collection of poems titled *To Bedlam and Part Way Back*, accepted for publication by Houghton Mifflin in 1960, three years after Sexton produced her first poems.

To compensate for a meager education, in 1960 Sexton enrolled in summer courses in modern literature at Brandeis University taught by Philip Rahv and Irving Howe; she also formed close friendships with the poets James

Wright and Anthony Hecht, whom she credited as mentors. She was selected as one of the artists in the first group of women appointed to the Radcliffe Institute for Independent Study (1961–1963), where she wrote her second book of poems, *All My Pretty Ones* (1962). In 1964, *Selected Poems* was published in England; its literary success led to her election in 1965 as an overseas fellow of the Royal Society of Literature. Sexton's third book of poems, *Live or Die* (1966), received the Pulitzer Prize for poetry.

Like many of her peers, Sexton aspired to write for the stage. During the period 1964–1965, she held a Ford Foundation grant for residence at the Charles Playhouse in Boston and developed a play based on her psychotherapy. In 1969, she received a Guggenheim Foundation fellowship to complete a play, *Mercy Street*, for its production at the American Place Theater in New York City (October–November 1969). A talented though untrained actress, Sexton developed a compelling performance style during her career as a writer and made a good income on the poetry circuit by charging high fees for well-rehearsed and affecting readings from her work. In 1968, she was persuaded by a friend to form what they called a "chamber rock" group, Anne Sexton and Her Kind; from 1968–1971, Sexton traveled sporadically with these musicians, mainly to college campuses, giving concert performances of her poems.

Meanwhile, Sexton had begun teaching poetry workshops: in 1967 at Wayland High School, where she worked with students who later became members of Anne Sexton and Her Kind; in 1968 at McLean Hospital in Belmont, Mass., a mental institution where her friends Robert Lowell and Sylvia Plath spent time in treatment; and at Boston University, where she was appointed a lecturer in the faculty of creative writing in 1970. She was promoted to full professor in 1972.

A remarkably popular poet, Sexton during the 1960's produced work that attracted large audiences, especially of women. Particularly well received were the volumes *Love Poems* (1969), an unusually direct expression of a woman's sexuality, and *Transformations* (1971), a collection of tales rewritten from Grimm. An opera version of *Transformations*, with music by Conrad Susa, was commissioned by the Minneapolis Opera Company in 1973 and was produced by many other companies. Sexton's later work dealt in-

creasingly with religious themes, culminating in the volume for which she corrected proofs on the day of her death: *The Awful Rowing Toward God* (1975).

In 1973, after the departure of the children for college and boarding school, Sexton divorced her husband. The ensuing isolation and loneliness seem to have speeded the mental and physical deterioration that had set in with her increasing dependency on prescription drugs and alcohol. Although she had remained under psychiatric care, her disorders had not yielded fully to treatment; she remained prey to episodes of severe depression. Sexton liked to say, "My fans think I got well, but I didn't: I just became a poet." During the last year of her life, Sexton organized her papers, tapes of performances, and the documentation of her medical treatment into what she intended to leave as a research archive. After her death it was sold to the Harry Ransom Humanities Research Center at the University of Texas at Austin. She committed suicide by carbon monoxide poisoning at her home in Weston, Mass.

[Sexton's *Complete Poems* (1981) has an illuminating foreword by Maxine Kumin. Linda Sexton and Lois Ames, eds., *Anne Sexton: A Self-Portrait in Letters* (1977); and Steven E. Colburn, ed., *No Evil Star* (1985), convey Sexton's liveliness of mind. Her play *Mercy Street* has not been published. For critical perspectives, see J. D. McClatchy, ed., *Anne Sexton* (1978); Diana Hume George, ed., *Sexton: Selected Criticism* (1988); and Diane Wood Middlebrook, *Anne Sexton* (1991). "Sexton," a videotape based on outtakes from a film produced for a public television series ("USA: Poetry," 1966) is available from the American Poetry Archive at the Poetry Center, San Francisco State University. An obituary is in the *New York Times*, Oct. 6, 1974.]

DIANE WOOD MIDDLEBROOK

SHAPLEY, HARLOW (Nov. 2, 1885–Oct. 20, 1972), astronomer, was born on a farm near Nashville, Mo. His father, Willis Shapley, raised and traded hay; his mother, Sarah Stowell, was the daughter of an abolitionist in Hamilton, N.Y., whom the Shapleys visited when Harlow was ten and from whom he claimed to have obtained his independent spirit. Harlow attended elementary school in Jasper, Mo., and had an additional year of schooling while visiting his grandfather Stowell. At age fifteen he attended a business school in Pittsburg, Kans., for several months, and afterward spent a year as a crime reporter on the *Daily Sun* in Chanute, Kans., and a year as a police reporter for the Joplin, Mo., *Times*. Determined to prepare himself for college, Shapley entered the Presbyterian Carthage Collegiate Institute, completing the equivalent of six years of high school in a year and a half.

Entering the University of Missouri at nearly twenty-two years of age, Shapley intended to pursue a course in journalism, but chose astronomy upon finding the school in journalism not yet opened. It was a fortunate choice. Frederick H. Seares, his astronomy professor, hired him as a teaching assistant during his third year; Shapley stayed for an additional year and obtained an M.A. in 1911. During that fourth year one of his mathematics professors, Oliver Kellogg, urged him to apply for a fellowship at Princeton University, which he won. While at Missouri, Shapley met Martha Betz, whom he married on Apr. 15, 1914. They had five children.

Entering Princeton in 1911, Shapley came under the tutelage of Henry Norris Russell, a prominent astrophysicist. Shapley and Russell developed a theory for the analysis of light curves from eclipsing binaries, and Shapley became convinced of the value of these studies for astrophysical research. After two and a half years at Princeton he completed his doctoral dissertation on eclipsing binaries, a classic in its field. Out of this work grew the realization that an important subclass of stars called Cepheid variables, previously thought to be binary, were really single pulsating stars that changed their brightness as they changed their size. Shapley's familiarity with such stars was to prove crucial to his career.

Upon the completion of his Ph.D. degree in 1913, Shapley joined Seares at Mount Wilson Observatory in Pasadena, Calif., where the world's largest telescope, a sixty-inch reflector, was housed. Before going to Pasadena, Shapley visited Solon I. Bailey at Harvard College Observatory, who strongly encouraged him to make maximum use of the Mount Wilson telescope for observing variable stars in globular clusters (large, spherically shaped conglomerations of stars). Shapley followed Bailey's advice and, with his wife as coauthor in some cases, published a superb series of papers on his findings, concentrating on the RR Lyrae and Cepheid variables.

Using the relationship proposed by Henrietta Leavitt of Harvard between the period of pulsation and the variable stars' intrinsic brightness, Shapley showed that these stars could be used to measure stellar distances, thus giving him the distances between the globular clusters and the sun. By 1918 he concluded that about twenty-five of the one hundred known globular clusters were between fifteen thousand and one hundred thousand light years apart, a surprisingly long distance. Coupling this information with the fact that all of these clusters are located in one half of the sky, and about a third of them concentrated in the direction of the constellation Sagittarius, Shapley made the bold hypothesis, eventually accepted by all astronomers, that these clusters define the shape and extent of the Milky Way galaxy, of which the sun is but a minor star in the outskirts. The revolutionary nature of this idea is often likened to the daring step Copernicus made in removing the earth to a minor role in the solar system.

Shapley's deep involvement in the controversies regarding the size, shape, and nature of the Milky Way and the spiral nebulae led to his participation in a historic "debate" on the scale of the universe at the National Academy of Sciences in Washington, D.C., in April 1920. His opponent, Heber D. Curtis of the Lick Observatory, opposed Shapley's contention regarding the size of the Milky Way and the sun's remote position in it, and championed the "island universe" idea for the spiral nebulae (that is, that they are remote systems of stars lying outside our galaxy and having a spiral appearance). The debate ended in a draw, for subsequent study has supported both Shapley's view of the Milky Way and Curtis's view of the spiral nebulae.

In 1921 Shapley succeeded Edward C. Pickering as director of the Harvard College Observatory. He held this post until 1952, transforming the Harvard Observatory into one of the leading research centers in the world. Shapley encouraged Annie Jump Cannon to complete the *Henry Draper Catalogue*, the definitive listing of stars according to their spectral classifications. He transferred Harvard's southern hemisphere observatory from Arequipa, Peru, to Bloemfontein, South Africa, and obtained a sixty-inch reflector for it. He obtained additional remote observing stations for the observatory: on Oak Ridge in the town of Harvard, Mass.; at Climax and Boulder in the Colorado Rockies; and near Las Cruces and on Sacramento Peak in New Mexico. He linked the Har-

713

vard Observatory with numerous national and international astronomical centers and organizations, such as the International Astronomical Union and the American Association of Variable Star Observers. It became the clearinghouse for news of comets, asteroids, and other phenomena that require prompt reporting. But more than anything else, the Harvard College Observatory became the mecca for young astronomers from all parts of the world.

Having been elected to the National Academy of Sciences in 1924, Shapley continued his own research. Using data obtained from Harvard's southern station, he revised the distance to the Magellanic Clouds (irregular galaxies near the Milky Way) and cooperated in the publication of new data on red (M-type) and blue-white supergiants in them. After learning of Edwin Hubble's discovery of Cepheid variables in the Andromeda nebula, which Hubble determined to be far outside the Milky Way, Shapley labeled it a true galaxy, not merely an extragalactic nebula as Hubble proposed, and proceeded to search both hemispheres for more galaxies, finding tens of thousands arranged in irregular patterns throughout space. He also determined that not all such star systems are far removed from the Milky Way, for he discovered two dwarf systems that are part of our local family of galaxies.

For all his accomplishments in astronomy, however, Shapley was far from being single-minded in his interests and concerns. In fact, some have suggested that his outside interests so dominated his later years that Harvard's position as a world-class observatory suffered therefrom. From the earliest days of his professional career, while at Mount Wilson, Shapley became interested in such subjects as ants, publishing several papers on his observations, including one on the proportionality between ambient temperature and ant activity.

The volume of Shapley's writing on various subjects, in addition to his hundreds of technical papers, gives further evidence of his wide-ranging interests. Shapley's early career in journalism played a large role in his lifelong penchant for writing, and his technical papers as well as his popular writings are models of clarity and directness. He wrote numerous monographs and popular and semipopular books of essays on astronomy and related subjects, and edited several collections of classics in astronomy and general science, and one on science and religion. His autobiography, *Through Rugged Ways to the Stars* (1969), is very folksy and revealing as to his interests and outlook on life.

Shapley by no means limited his attention to the printed page, however, for some of his most absorbing projects involved people and organizations. In addition to the strong family atmosphere that he and his wife created for all students, staff, and visitors at the Harvard Observatory, Shapley was responsible for bringing many refugees from totalitarian regimes to the United States and to Harvard during the 1930s. After World War II, Shapley's international interests grew even stronger; he was instrumental in the founding of the United Nations Educational, Scientific, and Cultural Organization (UNESCO), and became deeply involved in championing cooperation with Soviet intellectuals. Such activities and his support of an organization attempting to elect liberal candidates to Congress led to his being subpoenaed by the House Un-American Activities Committee and later being named by Senator Joseph McCarthy as a Communist sympathizer.

After his retirement Shapley traveled extensively on lecture tours. His significant honors include his appointment as director emeritus of the Harvard Observatory in 1952 and his receipt of the Gold Medal of the Royal Astronomical Society and the Bruce Medal of the Astronomical Society of the Pacific.

Shapley died in Boulder, Colo.

[Shapley's papers are in the Harvard University Archives in Cambridge, Mass. Of the hundreds of scientific papers he published, the most historic (dealing with the location of the center of the Milky Way) appear in *The Astrophysical Journal* for 1918 and 1919. A complete chronological bibliography of Shapley's publications is by Bart J. Bok in *Biographical Memoirs of the National Academy of Sciences* 1978. An obituary appears in the *New York Times*, Oct. 21, 1972.]

RICHARD K. GEHRENBECK

SHAW, CLAY L. (alleged alias "Clay Bertrand") (Mar. 17, 1913–Aug. 15, 1974), businessman accused of conspiring to assassinate President John F. Kennedy, was born in Kentwood, La., the son of Glaris Lenora Shaw and Alice Rebecca Harrington. The family moved to New Orleans when Shaw was five years old, where Clay attended public schools in New Orleans until age fifteen. At age seventeen, he collaborated with his friend Herman Cottman on writing a one-act play, *Submerged* (1930), which achieved moderate success, mostly with amateur theater groups. Shaw wrote three more plays: A *Message from Khufu* (1931), *The Cuckoo's Nest* (1933), and *Stokers* (1934).

Shaw worked for Western Union in New Orleans until he transferred to New York where he managed about forty branches in mid-Manhattan between 1932 and 1935. He then worked as an independent public relations adviser until he joined the army during World War II. For his performance as an aide-de-camp to General Charles Thrasher in southern England and northern France, Shaw received the croix de guerre from France and the Legion of Merit and Bronze Star from the United States.

Shaw returned to New Orleans in 1946 and became managing director of the nascent International Trade Mart (ITM). The first organization of its kind in the United States, the ITM opened two years later, providing a facility where foreign countries could lease space and display products. Over the next two decades, Shaw, who was fluent in many languages, traveled widely in South America and Europe, campaigning for elimination of barriers to international trade. In 1949, he began to restore several aging structures of New Orleans' French Quarter, and by 1960 had supervised the renovation of sixteen buildings, some of which were hailed as masterpieces of reconstruction. In 1965, after overseeing the design of a new tower for the ITM at the head of Canal Street, Shaw retired. He later explained to James Kirkwood, "Although I wasn't a millionaire, I had enough put aside . . . to devote my life to writing." He also wanted to travel, and over the next year visited Mexico, London, and Barcelona. He returned to New Orleans after his father's death in November 1966, for what he thought would be a brief visit with his mother, only to find his plans irrevocably changed.

On December 23, Shaw received a call from the New Orleans district attorney's office, summoning him for questioning in connection with allegations that he had used the alias Clay Bertrand to try to obtain legal aid for Lee Harvey Oswald, who had been arrested for assassinating President Kennedy in Dallas on Nov. 22, 1963. Shaw denied all allegations and, after being thanked for his cooperation, left to attend a Christmas party at City Hall, relieved that he had cleared up a misunderstanding. On Mar. 1,

1967, District Attorney Jim Garrison issued a subpoena for Shaw, who volunteered himself for questioning without calling a lawyer. He later claimed that he had no idea what was going on and was shocked to find himself accused of participating in a plot to assassinate the president. Shaw refused to submit to a lie detector test that afternoon and was formally arrested. While Garrison issued bold statements that he had proof of a criminal conspiracy and played up the fact that his suspect was homosexual, Shaw held a press conference to deny that he had ever "conspired with anyone at any time or at any place" to murder the president. In Washington, the FBI announced that it had already cleared Shaw of any involvement, and President Johnson stated that he saw no reason to reopen the investigations of the Warren Commission, which had concluded that Lee Harvey Oswald, acting alone, had shot President Kennedy.

One of the most sensational trials in American history began on Jan. 21, 1969. The prosecution's star witness, a Baton Rouge insurance salesman named Perry Raymond Russo, testified that he had attended a party in September 1963 at the apartment of David Ferrie, a retired airline pilot. Russo remembered hearing Shaw, Oswald, Ferrie, and others talk about ways they could kill President Kennedy without being caught. Since Shaw's alleged conspirators were both deceased—Oswald was shot by Jack Ruby, and Ferrie died of a brain hemorrhage just before Shaw's arrest—the defense concentrated on undermining Russo's testimony. This was not difficult. Russo admitted that Garrison's staff had hypnotized him three times to enhance his memory; under cross-examination he blurted out, "I never said anything about a conspiracy." Other witnesses called by Garrison failed to provide convincing evidence. Throughout the trial, Shaw sat impassively, chain-smoking filter cigarettes. When he took the witness stand on February 27, he denied ever meeting Ferrie or Oswald and testified that he had admired and voted for President Kennedy. Garrison made a final rebuttal statement, arguing that the Warren Commission report was "the greatest fraud in the history of our country" and mapping out a conspiracy that reached through the CIA and the FBI to the highest levels of government. The jury began deliberations just after midnight on March 1 and returned a verdict of "not guilty" just fifty minutes later. Two years to the day after his arrest, Shaw was free.

That afternoon, Shaw talked to reporters about the costs of the trial, financial and emotional: "I feel [Garrison] tried to use me as a pawn, if you will, to mount an attack on the Warren Commission." The *New Orleans Times-Picayune* and the *States-Item* both questioned Garrison's motives and lauded the jury's decision. Garrison, however, continued to insist on Shaw's guilt and two days later filed a new indictment charging him with perjury; the federal courts eventually ruled in Shaw's favor. Shaw sold his house to raise money and toured the country speaking about his trial. He then took a job with the French Market Corporation. He died in New Orleans, a $5 million lawsuit still pending against Garrison.

In 1977, the government released a document proving that Shaw had provided information to the Central Intelligence Agency between 1949 and 1956 while he was traveling for the International Trade Mart, raising the possibility that Garrison had been closer to the truth than many believed at the time. Given the American public's continued willingness to entertain doubts about the Warren Commission report, it is surprising that Clay Shaw, whether innocent or guilty, remains the only suspect ever brought to trial for the assassination of President Kennedy.

[See James Kirkwood, "So Here You Are, Clay Shaw . . . ," *Esquire*, Dec. 1968 and *American Grotesque* (1968); Edward Jay Epstein, *Counterplot* (1968); Milton E. Brener, *The Garrison Case* (1969); Warren Rogers, "The Persecution of Clay Shaw," *Look*, Aug. 26, 1969; and James DiEugenio, *Destiny Betrayed* (1992). Garrison's account of the case is in his memoir, *On the Trail of the Assassins* (1988). Obituaries are in the *New York Times* and the *New Orleans Times-Picayune*, both Aug. 16, 1974.]
CORINNE T. FIELD

SHAWN, EDWIN MEYERS ("TED") (Oct. 21, 1891–Jan. 9, 1972), dancer, choreographer, impresario, teacher, and writer, was born in Kansas City, Mo., the son of Elmer Ellsworth Schaun, an editor at the *Kansas City Star*. His mother, Mary Lee Booth, died when he was very young. While living in Colorado with his father, Shawn attended the University of Denver with the intent of becoming a Methodist minister. He contracted diphtheria at the age of eighteen, the treatment for which temporarily paralyzed his limbs. To regain his movement skills, Shawn took classes in ballet

technique with Hazel Wallack; this experience established his interest in dance and led to his promotion of this kind of movement for men. To be successful in a country that strongly disdained such an occupation for males—especially a six-foot-tall, heavily built youth—required fervent devotion.

Shawn earned his early living by logging, typing, selling insurance, making movies, teaching dance, and "tea dancing" (working as a hired dance partner). He moved to Los Angeles and in 1913 joined dancer Norma Gould, a pianist and a soprano, to tour the waiting rooms of the Santa Fe Railroad with a program of national and ballroom dances. This brought him to New York City, where he entered into a professional and personal liaison with dancer Ruth St. Denis. He was deeply impressed with St. Denis's *Incense*, a solo work that combined theater and religion, the physical and the devotional. They were married on Aug. 13, 1914.

The St. Denis–Shawn relationship developed into Denishawn, the theatrical entity and dance school that endured from 1914 until 1930. St. Denis's cycle of mystical East Indian dances became the core of Denishawn programs, to which Shawn added his stature as a male performer. His greatest contribution was his understanding that a company must have a school for the training of its dancers.

Denishawn School underwent various manifestations in Los Angeles from 1915 to 1922. It attracted myriad students (Doris Humphrey, Martha Graham, Charles Weidman, among others) looking for St. Denis's vision and Shawn's support.

At that time in the United States, dance, as either entertainment or serious art, had no financial support other than box-office receipts. For the funds needed to put their dance into American theater, Denishawn toured the Orpheum vaudeville circuit, St. Denis touring while Shawn served in World War 1. Louis Horst was the accompanist for these tours as well as for those acts produced by Shawn and sent on the Pantages circuit: *Julnar of the Sea* (1919), *Xochitl* (starring Graham; 1921), and *Les Mystères Dionysiaques* (1920). Horst remained with Denishawn as musical director for ten years.

In 1922 Shawn, just coming into his prime as an artist, took the Denishawn Company into the American concert field under the aegis of Daniel Mayer. In three cross-country tours, with an average of 150 concerts each, Denishawn brought serious dance to the United States between 1922 and 1925. St. Denis continued to perform her own numbers, Shawn presented his mature ethnic dance adaptations, and each created dance-dramas using a company expanded to twelve dancers. Thus was formed a distinctly American artistic entity, using American dancers trained in America, a patriotic practice and philosophy applauded in the 1920's. Shawn's account of this period, *One Thousand and One Night Stands* (1960) describes this achievement.

Shawn and St. Denis took world dance as their source of inspiration for such works as the Spanish *Cuadro Flamenco* (1923), the Hopi *Feather of the Dawn* (1923), and for *Egyptian Ballet* (1922), *East Indian Suite* (1922), *Five American Sketches* (1924), and the North African *Vision of the Aissoua* (1924). Shawn's solos stressed his masculinity (*Japanese Spear Dance*; 1921). "Music visualizations" adapted dance to the style, structure, and mood of selected compositions (*Revolutionary Etude*; 1921), and popular divertissements, deriving from characterizations (*Betty's Music Box*; 1922), filled out the eclectic Denishawn programs.

In 1921 Shawn moved Denishawn School to New York City, where the company's elaborately staged concerts were choreographed and rehearsed. Shawn prepared the curricula for the many branches of the school that opened across the country and launched *The Denishawn Magazine*, which reflected the ferment of Denishawn philosophy and teaching—a system that had no one system. World culture was the basis of the Denishawn pedagogy: classes in ethnic techniques, exercises out of ballet, rhythms and movement inspired by the principles of François Delsarte, courses on costumes and sets.

From September 1925 to December 1926, St. Denis, Shawn, and their Denishawn Dancers became the first American dance group to tour in the Far East. Booked by the impresario Asway Strok, they mounted four different programs. En route, the company took dance lessons from famed local artists and bought all costumes and props with which to produce an entirely new program. Shawn created the solo *The Cosmic Dance of Siva* (1926) and the trio *Sinhalese Devil Dance* (1926), both emphasizing his theatrical persona as a virile male.

Despite two additional cross-country tours, one of them in the *Ziegfeld Follies*, the Den-

ishawn partnership gradually disintegrated, along with the American economy. Shawn and St. Denis separated in 1931, but never divorced. In March 1933 Shawn emerged on the American stage as an independent performer and producer with a new artistic entity, Ted Shawn and his Men Dancers.

From the base of his farm, Jacob's Pillow, near Lee, Mass., Shawn again toured the United States, with seven male dancers headed by Barton Mumaw, and Jess Meeker as pianist and composer. The company was the culmination of Shawn's vision of American men. His choreography included his ethnic works plus primitive, play, labor, war, and religious dances. *O, Libertad* (1937), *Dance of the Ages* (1938), and *The Dome* (1940) were evening-length pieces built around his vision of historical events and physical elements. *Kinetic Molpai* (1935), revived at intervals, remains his most mature statement on movement. Idiosyncratic and sometimes romantic, Shawn's choreography opened to American men an art form long dominated by women. During these years, Shawn was sustained by an unpublicized relationship with Mumaw; any reference to a homosexual partner was an unmentionable fact at this time.

From 1940 until his death, Shawn labored to develop Jacob's Pillow into a comprehensive school and dance forum. The Jacob's Pillow Dance Festival in Becket, Mass., is the oldest and largest in the world to this day. Its "Men Dancers: The Ted Shawn Legacy" toured in honor of the Ted Shawn centennial.

[Memorabilia and newspaper clippings are in the Denishawn Collection and Ted Shawn Collection, Dance Collection, Lincoln Center of the Performing Arts, New York. For Shawn's educational and artistic philosophy, see *Denishawn Magazine* and his nine books. Data on Shawn tours are in *The Professional Appearances of Ruth St. Denis and Ted Shawn* (1962), and *The Professional Appearances of Ted Shawn and His Men Dancers* (1967), both by Christena L. Schlundt. Jane Sherman provides a record of Shawn's artistry in *Soaring* (1976); *The Drama of Denishawn Dance* (1979); *Denishawn: The Enduring Influence* (1983); and *Barton Mumaw, Dancer* (with Barton Mumaw, 1986). An obituary is in the *New York Times*, Jan. 10, 1972.]

CHRISTENA L. SCHLUNDT

SHEEAN, JAMES VINCENT (Dec. 5, 1899– Mar. 15, 1975), journalist, foreign correspondent, novelist, and biographer, was born in Pana,

Ill., the son of William Sheean and Susan Mac-Dermot, Irish immigrants driven to America by poverty and famine in their homeland. After attending local schools, Sheean went to the University of Chicago from 1916 to 1920, where he became a lifelong friend of John Gunther, a reporter and novelist. He left the university in his senior year without taking a degree, after his mother's illness and death, to take a job as a reporter at the *Chicago Daily News*, but he was fired after a brief stint.

Sheean immediately went to New York City, where he became a reporter for the *New York Daily News* and joined the Greenwich Village radical set. He was often seen in cafés with Edna St. Vincent Millay; after her death in 1950, he wrote a memoir about her entitled *The Indigo Bunting* (1951).

In 1922 he joined the expatriates gathering in Paris and soon became a favorite drinking companion of Ernest Hemingway. From 1922 to 1925 he worked as a foreign correspondent for the *Chicago Tribune*. Called "Jimmy" throughout his life by his friends, he was known to the world at large as Vincent Sheean because an editor decided to shorten his byline from his full name. In 1925 he crossed French and Spanish lines in Morocco to interview the rebel leader Abd el-Krim. This experience led him to write his first book, *An American Among the Riffi* (1926). Thereafter he devoted most of his career to writing books, including novels, short stories, biographies, and memoirs. But even though he never again worked regularly for a newspaper, he often sent dispatches to the North American Newspaper Alliance and the *New York Herald Tribune* syndicate, and continued to think of himself as a newspaperman.

At the height of his writing years, between the rise of fascism in the 1920's and the Korean War in the 1950's, he wrote articulate eyewitness accounts of some of history's turning points: Mussolini's march on Rome in 1922; the revolution in China in 1927; the progress of bolshevism in Russia; the Arab-Jewish riots in Palestine in 1929; the Spanish Civil War from 1936 to 1939; the Italian invasion of Ethiopia in 1935; the Nazi conquests of Czechoslovakia, the Low Countries, and France at the beginning of World War II; intensive bombings in London in 1940 and 1941; the San Francisco conference in 1945 that led to the founding of the United Nations; and the assassination of Gandhi in 1947.

In his best-known work, his autobiographical *On Personal History* (1935), Sheean cited the most important influence on his life as the red-haired American communist, Rayna Prohme, whom he met in China in 1927 and who persuaded him to broaden the objective concern of a newspaper reporter to include a subjective judgment on the larger issues involved in any event. He saw the journalist's role as not only telling the story but also explaining what it meant, and making it part of the experience of the readers, what he called "a sort of semi-autobiographical political journalism." This reflective, personal style influenced a generation of newspaper reporters in the 1930's and 1940's. When his autobiography was reissued in 1969, Harrison E. Salisbury commented: "Certainly those of us who first read it in the thirties have never forgotten the world of revolutionary events, the fresh, bright words of the young American who lived through them all, and his quicksilver gift for capturing the drama of his day. Each new generation of newspapermen goes back to Vincent Sheean and learns all over again what it is like to be a part of the personal history of his day."

Sheean's political views were consistently those of the socialist left, but toward the end of his life he evolved to a belief in the inevitability of gradual change. He always took sides on issues. During the Arab-Jewish riots in Jerusalem in 1929, he sided with the Arabs; indeed, throughout his career he contributed to anti-Zionist causes. During the Spanish Civil War he took the Republican side and was one of the last foreign correspondents to leave Madrid even though he knew they faced imminent defeat.

In World War II he served in the intelligence division of the U.S. Army Air Corps and did duty in North Africa and Italy. He was honorably discharged in 1944 with the rank of lieutenant-colonel. He expressed his views on the war and his passionate plea for peace in *This House Against This House* (1946).

In 1946 Sheean covered the trial in Lawrenceburg, Tenn., of twenty-five blacks accused of attempted murder during a racial disturbance. His dispatches, which expressed "pity for both whites and blacks" stood in dramatic contrast to the "objective" accounts of the other reporters at the trial.

In November 1947 he went to India to interview Gandhi about life's meaning, purpose, and significance. Just three days after his first interview with Gandhi, Sheean witnessed his assassination. This experience led him to write a book about Gandhi, *Lead, Kindly Light* (1949), and to maintain an interest in Indian politics that also led him to write *Nehru: The Years of Power* (1960).

Sheean married Diana Forbes-Robertson, the youngest daughter of the British actor Sir Johnston Forbes Robertson and niece of Maxine Elliott, in 1935. They were divorced in 1946, but then remarried in 1949. The couple had two daughters.

Sheean loved music and in his younger days scrimped on food to be able to buy tickets to the opera. This love led him to write *Oscar Hammerstein I* (1956) and *Orpheus at Eighty* (1958), a biography of Verdi. His last book was a historical novel, *Beware of Caesar*. In his last years, he was working on an autobiography to complete the story of his life as told in two other memoirs written in the 1930's.

Sheean had undergone treatment for lung cancer in New York in the fall of 1974 and returned to the northern Italian lake country around Lake Maggiore, where he had lived for years, in 1975. He died at his home in Arolo, Italy, and was interred in Leggiuno in the province of Varese in Italy.

[Sheean wrote three volumes of autobiography, *On Personal History* (1935; rev. ed., 1969), *Not Peace but a Sword* (1939), and *Bird of the Wilderness* (1941). He wrote five biographies: *Lead, Kindly Light* (1949) on Gandhi; *Mahatma Gandhi: A Great Life in Brief* (1955); *Oscar Hammerstein I: The Life and Exploits of an Impresario* (1956); *Orpheus at Eighty* (1958) about Verdi; and *Nehru: The Years of Power* (1960). He wrote two memoirs, *The Indigo Bunting* (1951) about Edna St. Vincent Millay; and *Dorothy and Red* (1963) about Sinclair Lewis and Dorothy Thompson. He also wrote a book of short stories, *The Pieces of a Fan* (1937). An obituary is in the *New York Times*, Mar. 17, 1975.]

PHYLLIS BADER-BOREL

SHERMAN, ALLAN (Nov. 30, 1924–Nov. 20, 1973), singer, television producer, and comedy writer, was born Allan Copelon in Chicago, Ill. Sherman's father, Percy Copelon, was a stock-car racer, automobile mechanic, car salesman, pilot, inventor, and former bootlegger from Birmingham, Ala. Sherman remembered him as a "tough, hard-driving, hard drinking man. . . . He was as different from what we think of as a Jewish type as an American Jew could be in 1924." Allan Sherman wrote of his mother, Rose Sherman, "She was what they called a 'flapper' then and what would now be called a swinger." Sherman's parents divorced when he was six, and Percy Copelon disappeared from Sherman's life. Sherman eventually took his mother's maiden name. During Sherman's childhood, his mother moved so often that Sherman attended twenty-one public schools in four cities.

Sherman entered the University of Illinois in 1941, where he wrote a humor column for the *Daily Illini*. There he began to concentrate on writing and performing song parodies and musicals, and "became obsessed with the idea of show business." In 1944, Sherman was expelled from the university for a minor offense and spent the rest of the year hanging around Chicago nightclubs, looking for useful contacts.

Sherman moved to New York in 1945, with $150 in his pocket and a few letters of recommendation from Chicago entertainment figures. That year he married his college sweetheart, Delores ("Dee") Chakes; they then spent "seven years with the wrong income." During this time, Sherman eked out a living as a gag writer for radio and television shows, including "Cavalcade of Stars" and "The 54th Street Revue." Sherman's first break came in 1951, when he and his friend Howard Merrill created the game show "I've Got a Secret." The show was based on the idea that thousands of Americans had secrets they needed to reveal and millions of Americans longed to hear. As it happened, Merrill and Sherman's analysis of American culture was astute, and it became a top-rated show. Sherman was hired as the producer, at $125 a week. In 1958, Mark Goodson and Bill Todman, the executive producers of the show, fired Sherman because they felt he was paying too much attention to his outside projects, including specials for Victor Borge and Phil Silvers. Unfortunately for Sherman, Goodson and Todman had originally agreed to produce the show only if Merrill and Sherman signed away all their rights to the property for a dollar. When Goodson and Todman sold the show to CBS for more than $3 million, Sherman sent them a telegram that read, "Nice profit, fellas." As Sherman put it in his autobiography, "I learned to laugh very young because I had to."

During his tenure with "I've Got a Secret," Sherman began a pattern of addictive behavior.

Sherman blamed his addictions—primarily eating, and later drinking—on his involvement with the corporate world of Goodson/Todman Productions, while ridiculing a series of psychiatrists for tracing his problems to his father. After leaving "I've Got a Secret," however, Sherman continued his binge eating.

Sherman produced a number of shows until 1960, when he and comic Allie Singer created the game show "Your Surprise Package" for CBS in Los Angeles. The Sherman family moved out to Hollywood and had the good fortune to become Harpo Marx's neighbor. Although "Your Surprise Package" was canceled in 1962, Marx invited Sherman to a series of parties for the elite of the entertainment world. Here Marx encouraged Sherman to sing his show-tune parodies, and Sherman caught the eye of Jack Benny and George Burns.

While Sherman was making a splash as an amateur entertainer, his professional career came to a halt. He found himself out of work, collecting $55 unemployment checks to help pay off the mortgage on his Bel Air mansion. After sinking into a deep depression for a few months (and impulsively buying a new, fully equipped Buick convertible on time payments), Sherman racked his brain and realized, "I have some crazy songs." Using his Hollywood connections—including Bullets Durgom, who managed Jackie Gleason—Sherman made an album of folk song parodies, called *My Son, the Folksinger*, for Warner Brothers Records in 1962.

Unabashedly Jewish in content and style, songs such as "Seltzer Boy" (set to the tune of "Water Boy") made the record the fastest selling album up to that time—it sold 500,000 copies the first month and more than a million by 1965, earning Sherman a Gold Album. "Sarah Jackman" (sung to the tune of "Frère Jacques"), reached the Top Forty with lines like: "Sarah Jackman, Sarah Jackman / How's by you, how's by you? / How's your brother Bernie? / He's a big attorney / How's your Cousin Ida? / She's a Freedom Rider." Sherman's follow-up, *My Son, the Celebrity*, also went gold.

Beatlemania was still several years away in America, but Shermanmania was in full gear. Sam Goody's record shop in New York City had to limit customers to twelve copies; Sherman made the cover of *Billboard* magazine. He played Carnegie Hall, appeared on "The Steve Allen Show" six times, and was the star at the

National Press Club's Presidential Inauguration. The Press Club had told Sherman it was concerned that he would be too ethnic for its membership, which was only 10 percent Jewish. Sherman opened the show by telling the guest of honor, Chief Justice Earl Warren, "I am delighted to hear that you are even 10 percent Jewish. I didn't know you were Jewish at all."

In the summer of 1963, Sherman recorded the single "Hello Muddah, Hello Faddah," a parody of summer camp sung to the tune of Ponchielli's "Dance of the Hours." "Hello Muddah, hello Faddah," warbled Sherman in his pure nasal Brooklynese, "Here I am at Camp Grenada / . . . You remember Leonard Skinner? / He got ptomaine poisoning last night after dinner." The single, included on *My Son, the Nut*, sold over a million copies in less than a year and was the number-one song in the United States, Australia, New Zealand, South Africa, and Hong Kong, where, as Sherman pointed out, "there are no summer camps."

The madness continued. Two weeks after issuing "Hello Muddah, Hello Faddah," Sherman played to the largest Friday-night Hollywood Bowl audience ever seen to that date. Two months later he replaced Johnny Carson for a week on "The Tonight Show." President John F. Kennedy counted himself a fan, and Sherman performed at benefits for President Lyndon Johnson. Sherman then gave concerts with the Syracuse Symphony Orchestra and the Baltimore Symphony Orchestra that parodied classical music. RCA's classical label, Red Seal Victor, recorded a concert at the Tanglewood Festival with Arthur Fiedler and the Boston Pops Orchestra. The concert pulled the largest audience in the history of the festival. A Harvard sociology Ph.D. wrote his dissertation on the Sherman phenomena, claiming that it demonstrated the secret desire of non-Jews to be Jewish.

But as Sherman had written, "My life has been . . . a yo-yo on a roller coaster." After peaking in 1964, Sherman's career began to slide. His next two albums did not go gold. In 1965, a one-hour special on NBC flopped, reportedly because the producers asked him to excise his Jewish humor for fear of being "too ethnic." That year, he also published his autobiography, *A Gift of Laughter*, about which *Newsweek* wrote, "But if Sherman's style is irritating, his Semitism too self-conscious, his jokes forced, if the reader cares little for his dreary pubescent escapades or an ego that rivals his waistline, there remains a winsome sincerity to his account—a soul-saving sense of humor in the face of all adversity." The book sold respectably, but Shermanmania had played itself out. The Beatles had arrived, the Vietnam War was escalating, and the counterculture was on the way.

Sherman wrote the lyrics to several musicals in the late 1960's and early 1970's but never regained his popularity. While performing for friends at one of his many Hollywood parties, he died of respiratory failure brought on by asthma, emphysema, and obesity.

[Information on Allan Sherman may be found in his autobiography, A *Gift of Laughter* (1965). Features on Sherman include an article in the *New York Times*, Aug. 4, 1963; and "Spoofmaster," *Saturday Evening Post*, Apr. 20, 1963. See also Arthur Knight, "The Literary Life in Las Vegas: There's No Biz Like the Book Biz," *Saturday Review*, Nov. 6, 1965. An obituary is in the *New York Times*, Nov. 22, 1973.]
                                      MICHAEL GOLDBERG

SHIELDS, FRANCIS XAVIER ("FRANK") (Nov. 17, 1909–Aug. 19, 1975), tennis player, was born in New York City to Alexander John Shields, a certified public accountant, and Alice Haggerty. An all-around star athlete at Columbia Grammar School in the Bronx, he excelled at tennis, which was self-taught. Shields skyrocketed to recognition in 1924 by placing second in the National Boys Indoor Championship (his first tournament) and winning the National Boys (outdoor) Championship. His happy-go-lucky manner garnered him the moniker "Jolly School Boy." His reputation soared in 1926 when he was U.S. boys indoor and outdoor singles and doubles and national doubles champion.

Shields attended Roxbury School (later Cheshire Academy) in Connecticut. He was U.S. junior indoor singles and doubles champion in 1927 and national junior champion in 1927 and 1928. In 1930, at age twenty-one, he beat the legendary Bill Tilden at the Meadow Club Invitational, the first American to do so in two years.

Shields moved to the men's circuit in 1928 and ranked in the U.S. top ten eight times, achieving number-one status in 1933, when he won nine tournaments. He lost on grass only once that year. Five times he ranked among the top eight players in the world, but never fully realized his potential, according to most tennis experts. He was consistent, with an average ranking of three from 1930 to 1935, but never won a major national singles title. He played on the 1931, 1932, and 1934 U.S. Davis Cup teams. Although a fierce competitor with natural talent, Shields played for the fun of it, avoiding rigorous training.

Johnny Doeg beat Shields in a brilliantly played, exhausting national finals in 1931 (10–8, 1–6, 6–4, 16–14) in the culmination of what *Tennis* magazine called "the greatest tournament of a generation." His most impressive match may have been in the Wimbledon semifinals of that year against Jean Borotra of France, when he injured his knee in the last set and managed to win with four straight aces. The injury caused him to default the finals to Sidney Wood.

Shields's playing style featured one of the strongest serves in the game, despite occasional foot-fault lapses. At six foot three and 190 pounds, the right-hander was known for his baseline play and was an above-average volleyer with an excellent forehand drive and a very sound overhead, though his sliced backhand was considered vulnerable. His serve was fast and spinning, described in *Ripley's Believe It or Not* as "the greatest ever struck" after Shields hit fifty-six consecutive first serves into a twenty-four-inch square target during a demonstration in France.

His style off the course was also newsworthy. From his rather humble beginnings, Shields's tennis success, easygoing and modest manner, and penchant for seldom encountering a party he did not like, opened many doors to the social life of the rich and famous. *Newsweek's* story marking his death noted his tennis exploits but also described him as a "dashing New York playboy." Shields's contacts proved instrumental to the success of the insurance business he headed for many years with former doubles partner Julius Seligson.

Perhaps the best example of Shields's off-the-court celebrity took place in 1933. After an early round victory in the French championships, Shields attended a party aboard the ocean liner *President Harding* at Le Havre. Following the overextended celebration, he found himself, tuxedo-clad, en route for the United States with no luggage. The escapade, naturally, attracted much media attention.

A strikingly handsome man, Shields signed a

seven-year acting contract with Metro-Goldwyn-Mayer and ceased full-time tennis following the 1934 tour. His time in Hollywood included many acting lessons, endless posing for still photographs, much social tennis, and small parts in a handful of films. The experience did lead to his acting in training films while serving in the Army Air Corps during World War II and some bit parts in Broadway plays during the late 1930's.

Shields never strayed far from tennis. In 1947, at the age of thirty-eight, he thrilled the crowd in the second round of the nationals by nearly upsetting young star Fred Kovaleski (13–11, 3–6, 4–6, 6–3, 6–4). In 1951 he was named nonplaying captain (one of the youngest ever) of the U.S. Davis Cup team, taking the team to the finals against Australia in Sydney. In a controversial decision, Shields chose veteran Ted Schroeder over reigning Wimbledon champion Dick Savitt to play in two singles matches. Australia, which was favored, beat the United States 3–2, owing to the play of Frank Sedgman, who beat Schroeder. Savitt bitterly complained about not being selected to play. One reporter hinted that Shields's decision was based on anti-Semitism. Those who knew Shields well were certain that was not the case. Although the Australians went on to dominate Davis Cup competition through the mid-1950's, the event led Shields to decline consideration for the captaincy in 1952, citing personal business reasons.

Shields was awarded the William Johnston trophy in 1952, an honor based on contributions to the development of the game, and in recognition of his work with the junior players (the great Pancho Gonzales credited him as his chief tutor), promoting club events and clinics, and especially for his fund-raising on behalf of the Boys Clubs of America, of which he was a director. When the Madison Square Boys Club in Manhattan needed a new building, Shields convinced the Palm Beach Company to sponsor golf's first "pro-am" tournament and persuaded many celebrities from the entertainment world to participate. The building eventually came to be known as "the house that Shields built."

Shields married and divorced Rebecca Williams Tenney (1932–1940), the daughter of a bank president; Italian princess Donna Marina Torlonia (1940–1948); and socialite Katherine Mortimer Blaine (1949–1959). He and Torlonia had two children; with his third

wife he had three children, one of whom died when very young. Model and actress Brooke Shields is his granddaughter. In 1964, Shields was enshrined in the International (then National Lawn) Tennis Hall of Fame.

He died in New York City.

[Memorabilia and periodical clippings are in the International Tennis Hall of Fame, Newport, R.I. For Shields's biography, see William X. Shields (his son), *Bigger than Life: The Last Great Amateur* (1986). See also "Two Franks, One Coach," *Literary Digest*, Aug. 17, 1935; Arthur Daley, "Net Gain," *New York Times*, May 21, 1951; George Lott, "Rambling Through the Thirties," *World Tennis*, June 1964; Sidney B. Wood, "Demise of a Tennis Titan," *The Southampton Press*, Aug. 28, 1975; and Bill Shannon, ed., *Official Encyclopedia of Tennis* (1979). An obituary is in the *New York Times*, Aug. 20, 1975.]

CHARLES A. BURNS

SHORT, LUKE (Nov. 19, 1908–Aug. 18, 1975), writer, was born Frederick Dilley Glidden in Kewanee, Ill., the son of Wallace Dilley Glidden, a clerical worker, and Fannie Mae Hurff, a high school teacher. While in high school, he played basketball and football. In 1926, Short entered the University of Illinois at Urbana and took humanities courses. Deciding that he wanted to write, he transferred to the University of Missouri at Columbia in 1929, graduating in 1930 with a B.A. in journalism.

After landing and losing a succession of newspaper jobs, Short spent the early years of the Depression wandering about the West. In 1931 he moved to northern Alberta, Canada, and trapped furs for a couple of seasons. Drifting south, Short worked during part of 1933 as an archaeologist's assistant near Santa Fe, N.Mex. En route to Wyoming to find work, he met Florence Elder in Colorado; the two married on June 18, 1934. They had three children.

As an unemployed homesteader in New Mexico, Short began reading magazines featuring Western pulp fiction, with the idea of earning a living writing such stories. By September 1934 he was writing Westerns—and collecting rejection slips. In November he hired New York literary agent Marguerite E. Harper, with whom he was associated for thirty-two years. During 1935, he adopted Luke Short as his pen name, sold his first story, and published his first novel, *The Feud at Single Shot*, in serial form. By the end of the decade, he had published fourteen novels.

The 1940's were Short's most productive years. In addition to writing the novels on which his reputation rests, he became increasingly involved with movie production. In 1940, he sold a short story to RKO Radio Pictures for $1,000; for the next several years, he worked part-time in Hollywood as a scriptwriter. Beginning in 1943, Short served for a year with the Office of Strategic Services in Washington, D.C. After the war, he started a profitable relationship with several paperback publishers.

In 1946, he helped write the movie script of his novel *Ramrod* (1943). Then, in the summer of 1947, he moved his family to Aspen, Colo. In the meantime, Short's association with the movie industry continued; in 1948 alone, his books *Dead Freight for Piute* (1940) (retitled *Albuquerque* as a movie), *Blood on the Moon* (1943), *Coroner Creek* (1947), and *Station West* (1947), were all made into films.

The 1940's saw the publication of Short's best novels. Others that he wrote in these years are *Gunman's Chance* (1941), *Ride the Man Down* (1942), *High Vermilion* (1948), and *Vengeance Valley* (1950). These novels established Short as a "slick" rather than a pulp writer (nine stories were published serially in the *Saturday Evening Post*, which was printed on high-quality paper for a general readership instead of being printed in a pulp magazine for Western aficionados) and secured his reputation for fast-moving, cleverly plotted, and well-written Westerns.

In the 1950's Short was less productive. Frustrated by the limitations of being a best-selling author of traditional Westerns, he tried other ventures. In 1952, with the help of Joe Marsala, Short composed a musical comedy called *I've Had It*, which played in Colorado but never made it to Broadway. During the next two years, he visited uranium mines in Alberta, Canada, and in Utah, using this experience as background for *Rimrock* (1955). In 1955, he helped found a thorium company in Aspen and conferred with Lucille Ball and Desi Arnaz on scriptwriting for television, but nothing much came of these activities. Meanwhile, Short continued to write Westerns, producing seven during the decade. Only *The Whip* (1957), *Saddle by Starlight* (1952), and *Rimrock* are notable.

During the 1960's, Short returned to writing conventional Westerns full-time. He published eleven novels, of which *First Claim* (1960), *Desert Crossing* (1961), and *Last Hunt* (1962)

were fairly successful. *The Some-Day Country* (1964) was the weakest book of his career. Short suffered personal tragedy in 1960, when his son drowned in a swimming pool at Princeton University. In 1963, he and his wife spent several months in the Virgin Islands, where he wrote the manuscript "Pearly," a non-Western novel that was never published. Short and his wife then bought a home in Wickenburg, Ariz., where they began wintering. In the spring of 1966, Marguerite Harper died, and Short engaged H. N. Swanson of Los Angeles as his agent. He wrote and published nine more Western novels in the 1970's.

Short was a leading writer of traditional action yarns that are a cut above the typical Western story. Known for his ingenious plotting, spare style, realistic dialogue, and stereotypical yet well-rounded characters, Short received the Western Heritage Wrangler award in 1974. He died in Aspen.

[Short's papers are housed in the Special Collections of the Library of the University of Oregon at Eugene. For a complete biography, critical analysis, and bibliography of Short's works, see Robert L. Gale, *Luke Short* (1981). See also Fred Erisman and Richard W. Etulain, eds., *Fifty Western Writers* (1982); James Vinson, ed., *Twentieth-Century Western Writers* (1982); and Richard W. Etulain, *A Bibliographical Guide to the Study of Western American Literature* (1982). An obituary is in the *New York Times*, Aug. 19, 1975.]

SETH BOVEY

SHUB, ABRAHAM DAVID (Sept. 13, 1887– May 27, 1973), Yiddish writer and biographer of Lenin, was born in the Russian province of Vilna, one of five children of Deborah and Nathan Shub; his father was a rabbi. As a student, Shub joined the revolutionary socialist youth movement known as the School of Struggle.

Shub became a member of the Russian Social Democratic party in 1903 at a time when V. I. Lenin was one of its leaders. When the party split into Bolshevik (Communist) and Menshevik (Social Democratic) groups, Shub became a Menshevik.

Later in 1903 he traveled to the United States and worked as a laborer, first in Philadelphia and then in New York City (1903–1904). In 1904 and 1905, he traveled to Paris, London, and Geneva, meeting with Lenin and other Russian political activists. Shub's continued contact with and interest in Lenin would much later result in his primary scholarly work, a biography of Lenin published in 1948, which was updated in 1966 and translated into many languages.

Shub returned to Russia in September 1905 to participate in the revolution of 1905–1906. He joined the army to evade the police; he then escaped while stationed in Irkutsk, Siberia. While in exile he wrote articles for St. Petersburg's Russian-language Menshevik newspaper and the Yiddish newspaper of Vilna. In 1907, he fled to London and soon thereafter emigrated to the United States.

In 1908, Shub became an assistant editor of *Arbeiter-Zeitung* (Worker Newspaper), a weekly founded by the United Hebrew Trades in 1890. He and his fellow Yiddish writers wrote in a simplified Yiddish to increase the appeal of the Yiddish newspapers among the newly arrived Jewish immigrants in New York City.

From 1911 to 1918, Shub was the assistant editor and later editor of the *New Post*. During this time Shub wrote articles for *Der Fraind* (The Friend), published by the Workmen's Circle, which supported Yiddish culture and socialist concerns in the United States. At the same time, he wrote for the Russian-language newspaper *Novi Mir* (New World) and for the *People's Newspaper*. During World War I, he became acquainted with future Russian Communist leaders including Leon Trotsky, Nikolay Bukharin, Aleksandr Kerensky, Pavel Miliukov, Viktor Chernov, and Catherine Breshkovsky.

Shub became increasingly disillusioned with the Communist regime in the Soviet Union after the Bolshevik Revolution of 1917 and expressed his opposition on the editorial pages of the English anti-Bolshevik weekly *Struggling Russia* (1919–1920). From 1921 to 1922 Shub wrote articles under the pseudonym A. D. Nathanson in the Yiddish paper *Yiddisher Morgen Zhurnal* (Jewish Morning Journal), a Zionist daily published in New York City. He also wrote for *Der Tog*, a competing newspaper, under the pseudonym P. A. Stavski. These two papers later merged as *Der Veker* (The Awakener); Shub wrote for it under the pseudonym A. Rosenthal. He edited *Der Veker* from 1923 to 1927. He also wrote for *Justice*, a trade union paper.

In 1924, Shub joined the *Jewish Daily Forward* and sat on the *Forward*'s editorial board for the next forty-five years, until his retirement in 1969. At the *Forward*, Shub wrote and solicited articles about the international socialist movement, workers' problems, labor unions, Russia, and Bolshevism, continuing his attacks on the theoreticians of the Russian revolution. In 1931, Shub wrote about Tsar Nicholas's assassination and continued to explore other topics about Russia. He explored socialist problems and Jewish social questions with regard to East European Jewry and the Bund (the General Jewish Workers Union in Lithuania, Poland, and Russia), a non-Zionist organization formed in Vilna to advance Yiddish culture, support secular Jewish life, and promote socialist ideals among Jewish workers.

Shub's dual interest in socialism and Jewish issues formed his theoretical approach to such socialist thinkers as Karl Marx and Edward Bernstein, whose work he explored from the standpoint of their approach to Jewish problems.

While on staff at the *Forward*, Shub contributed articles in Yiddish and Russian to various journals in the United States and Europe. His English-language article on Stalin in the *New York Times Magazine* (Mar. 22, 1930) was probably the first authoritative profile of the Soviet leader to appear in the American press. In 1968, a serialization by Shub in the *Forward* highlighted the personalities of the Russian revolutionary movement.

From 1956 to 1971, Shub wrote Russian-language radio speeches for United States–sponsored Radio Liberty, taking an anti-Communist position. Shub quoted disillusioned former allies of Lenin, asserting that Lenin persecuted dissidents and perverted the ideals of the Russian revolution. He continued his intimate contact with the many factions in the Russian revolutionary movement for more than forty years. In his obituary in the *New York Times*, he was referred to as a "veteran of the Russian revolutionary movement and an authority on Russian affairs."

Shub was a prolific writer who wrote for approximately sixty-seven years and who contributed to the development of Yiddish journalism in the United States at a time when the Yiddish press was striving to compete with its English-language counterparts in readership and quality of reporting. He was awarded a Yiddish literary prize from the Chanin Foundation, which was funded by the Workmen's Circle.

In addition to Shub's biography, *Lenin* (1948), he edited the two-volume *Jewish Workers Almanac* (1926–1927), and co-edited and translated with Joseph Shaplen *Socialism, Fascism, Communism* (1934). He also translated Karl Kautsky's *Social Democracy Versus Communism* (1946). Shub was married twice: first to Edith Gitelson in 1910, and second to Rebecca Goldstein in 1925; he and his second wife had three children. He died while vacationing in Miami Beach, Fla., after a series of heart attacks.

[For a biographical sketch of Shub, see *Leksikon fun der nayer Yidisher literatur* (Lexicon of Modern Yiddish Literature, 1956–1981, vol. 8). See also a memoir by his son, Anatole Shub, in *New Leader*, Sept. 9, 1991. Obituaries appear in the *New York Times*, May 29, 1973, and the *Washington Post*, May 31, 1973.]

RENEE FEINBERG

SIKORSKY, IGOR IVANOVICH (May 25, 1889–Oct. 26, 1972), aeronautical engineer, was born in Kiev, Russia (now Ukraine), one of five children of Dr. Ivan Alexis Sikorsky, a professor of psychology, and Zinaida Temrouk-Tcherkoss. After attending the Russian Naval Academy in St. Petersburg from 1903 to 1906, he decided to pursue aeronautical studies. He spent the next four years shuttling between Paris, where the most advanced aeronautical experiments were being conducted, and Kiev, where he was enrolled in the Polytechnic Institute.

Sikorsky's first dream was to build a helicopter, and in 1909 and 1910 he built two. With their twenty-five-horsepower engines, his machines could barely lift their own weight, much less the additional weight of a pilot and cargo. Sikorsky transferred the engine to a fixed-wing airplane, and in the summer of 1910 he flew about two hundred yards. Subsequent machines used forty- and fifty-horsepower engines. With the S-6-A, which had a 100-horsepower engine, Sikorsky in December 1911 set a new speed record for a plane carrying two passengers. His achievement enabled him to contract with the Russian Baltic Railroad Car Factory to design and produce aircraft. After less than three years of work, with no formal degree, he was a successful aircraft designer.

Sikorsky's next project, a four-engine transport with an enclosed cabin, reflected his life-long preference for utility over mere speed. Although the fuselage more closely resembled a trolley car than that of a modern jetliner—first designs even had open balconies on which passengers could stroll—*The Grand*, or *Ilia Mourometz* as it came to be called, successfully flew in May 1913. The next spring, with larger engines and at least a nod in the direction of streamlining, the plane flew from St. Petersburg to Kiev and back, some one thousand six hundred miles. A month later, Archduke Ferdinand was assassinated, and World War I followed. Sikorsky's transport was used in the war effort as the first reconnaissance plane that could fly above all antiaircraft fire. Later it became the world's first heavy bomber.

The 1917 Bolshevik Revolution cost Sikorsky his career and his fortune. In March 1919, however, he reached New York City and was ready to resume his career. For the next four years, Sikorsky struggled with a new land, a new language, and the new challenges of a world not quite ready to invest in aviation. On Jan. 27, 1924, he married another recent immigrant, Elizabeth Semion. They had four children. Sikorsky began working out of a derelict hangar at Roosevelt Field on Long Island. He produced a succession of innovative airplanes, culminating in the ill-fated S-35. This craft, a trimotor biplane, was chosen by René Fonck for his 1926 attempt at a transatlantic crossing. Pushed by an approaching deadline, Fonck took off in less-than-ideal conditions and crashed. Within eight months, just before Fonck's new plane was completed, Charles Lindbergh took off from the same field and completed the trip in a single-engine monoplane, and Sikorsky's chance at fortune seemed lost.

This apparent failure represented a turning point. Forced to concentrate on planes for which there was a solid market, Sikorsky designed a succession of what he termed "amphibions," or seaplanes. In 1928, the year he became a United States citizen, he sold several S-38's to a new airline called Pan American Airways. It was the start of a historic partnership. For the next ten years Pan American, under the aggressive leadership of Juan Trippe, pioneered long-distance air transport, and did so almost exclusively with Sikorsky aircraft. The S-40, which first flew in 1931, was the first *American Clipper*. The S-42, introduced in 1934, set eight world speed records in a single day. It was the first plane to fly regular transatlantic and transpacific routes. The VS-44A, which could fly nonstop from New York to Rome, was powered by four 1,050-horsepower engines. However, even these innovative aircraft could not keep Sikorsky Aviation flying. Only ten S-42's and three VS-44A's were ever sold, and late in 1938 the company went out of the airplane business.

Sikorsky saved his business and made his place in aviation history by returning to his original dream of controlled vertical flight. The arrangement he chose, in which a main rotor provided lift while a smaller tail roter provided lateral stability, would prove to be the near-universal solution to successful helicopter design. By the end of 1939, Sikorsky had developed the VS-300, which could take off from land or water and was controlled in all directions of movement by a cyclic controller. Its production version, the R-4, was the only helicopter flown by United States military forces during World War II. The S-51, designed in 1945, could carry three passengers. In 1950, British European Airways used it for the first regularly scheduled commercial helicopter flights. Other famous Sikorsky helicopters include the bulb-nosed S-55; the S-61, best known as the president's helicopter, which in 1967 became the first helicopter to fly across the Atlantic nonstop; and the ungainly but powerful S-64, known as the Skycrane.

Although Sikorsky retired as managing engineer in 1957, he remained active for nearly a decade, shepherding his last design to its successful conclusion and serving as a spokesman for the industry (he was dubbed "Mr. Helicopter"). Sales of the S-55 and its derivative the S-58 totaled more than four thousand. All were built at the Sikorsky Aviation factory outside Bridgeport, Conn. Until near the end of his life, Sikorsky insisted on trying out every new model and became a familiar sight in his worn homburg, buzzing the countryside. Sergei, the eldest of Sikorsky's four sons, was the only one who followed his father into the company. His daughter, born in Russia before Sikorsky's emigration, eventually joined him in Bridgeport, where she became a college professor. In his later years Sikorsky became interested in spiritualism and wrote a series of books on that subject. He died at home in Easton, Conn.

[The most authoritative source of information about Igor Sikorsky is his autobiography, *The Story of*

the Winged-S (1938), which in revised editions carries the story into the first decade of helicopter development. Frank J. Delear's *Igor Sikorsky* (1969) is based heavily on this source and on numerous interviews with Sikorsky after his retirement. An obituary appears in the *New York Times*, Oct. 27, 1972.]

HARTLEY S. SPATT

SILKWOOD, KAREN GAY (Feb. 19, 1946– Nov. 13, 1974), nuclear-plant worker and union activist, was born in Longview, Tex., and grew up in the town of Nederland. She was one of three daughters born to Bill Silkwood, a house painter, and Merle Biggs, a bank loan officer. An honor student at her local high school, Karen cared for young children during services at the First Baptist Church, played the flute in the high school band, and was interested in sports. She graduated from high school in 1964 and earned a scholarship from the Business and Professional Women's Club to study medical technology at Lamar College in nearby Beaumont.

Karen Silkwood married Bill Meadows, an oil pipeline company worker, on June 26, 1965, when she was nineteen. They had three children, and she worked part-time but did not continue her college education. After several years of marital difficulties, the couple divorced in 1972. Karen, who may have been suffering severe depression at the time, relinquished custody of her children for unknown reasons.

In August 1972, Silkwood took a job as a laboratory analyst in the metallurgy laboratory of the Kerr-McGee Nuclear Corporation in Cimmaron, Okla. She ran quality-control tests on plutonium pellets that were manufactured at the plant from plutonium nitrate solution shipped from the Atlantic Richfield Company in Hanford, Wash. After the pellets were manufactured and tested, they were shipped back to the Fast Flux Test Facility run by the Atomic Energy Commission (AEC) in Hanford.

In November 1972, just three months after coming to work at Kerr-McGee, Silkwood was involved in a strike against the company as an active member of the Oil, Chemical and Atomic Workers International Union (OCAW). The strike ended in January 1973, when many workers returned to the plant rather than face unemployment. The labor contract resulted in low wages and poor health and safety conditions for Kerr-McGee's workers. Soon after the strike ended, Silkwood's romantic relationship with co-worker Drew Stephens deteriorated, and she attempted suicide in September 1973.

The strike had sensitized Silkwood to the hazards that she and her fellow workers faced, and she became increasingly active in the OCAW local. She spent time with colleagues learning and discussing the dangers of working with plutonium, a known carcinogen. She expressed her mistrust of the company and its handling of incidents in which workers and local residents risked contamination. In 1974, she was elected to the OCAW negotiating committee at the Cimmaron plant, the first woman to hold this position. As the union, which had lost most of its strength at Kerr-McGee because of the failed strike, prepared for new contract negotiations, the company took steps to hold a decertification election.

Silkwood began collecting evidence of careless handling of plutonium by the company, production of defective plutonium rods, and cover-ups of safety violations that should have been reported to the AEC. Working with the support of the national OCAW administration, she talked to colleagues, gathered documents, and spoke out on health and safety violations. As her activities increased, she became aware of efforts to harass her. At one point, she discovered her apartment had been contaminated with radioactive materials. She told a family member that she intended to quit her job in December 1974 after the conclusion of contract negotiations and of her work to document safety problems at the plant.

Silkwood's unease continued through the fall of 1974 as she continued to speak out about the conditions at Kerr-McGee. On the night of Nov. 13, 1974, as she was reportedly on her way to deliver documents to a reporter from the *New York Times* that would prove the company's cover-up of safety violations, her Honda Civic ran off the road. She died in a ditch. Despite fresh dents in the side of her car that indicated she may have been run off the road, local and federal investigators determined that Karen Silkwood had caused her own death by driving under the influence of depressant drugs. The documents were never found.

Karen Silkwood's death unleashed a storm of outrage from union activists and antinuclear environmentalists. *Rolling Stone* magazine alleged that Silkwood had uncovered a plutonium smuggling ring but was unable to substantiate it. *Ms.* and *New Times* magazines challenged the results of the Oklahoma Highway Patrol investigation. For years, in spite of the fact that the FBI closed its investigation and refused to consider her case a murder, activists continued to raise the question, "Who killed Karen Silkwood?"

Her estate sued Kerr-McGee for negligence, noncompliance with AEC regulations, civil rights violations, and interference in union activities. The judge in the trial ruled that Silkwood's death could not be considered as part of the case. On May 18, 1979, the jury in *Karen Silkwood* v. *Kerr-McGee Corporation* found the company guilty of negligence in their plants and noncompliance with federal safety regulations.

The case of Karen Silkwood attracted nationwide attention that was fueled by the release in 1983 of "Silkwood," directed by Mike Nichols and starring Meryl Streep and Cher. Although the film earned mixed critical reviews, it made a contribution to the continuing effort to uncover negligence and criminal activity and was part of a larger national move to pass state laws to protect workers who speak out against their employers. It also served as a spark to both the antinuclear and occupational safety and health movements in the United States.

[See "The Silkwood Mystery," *Time*, Jan. 20, 1975; B. J. Phillips, "The Case of Karen Silkwood," *Ms.*, Apr. 1975; and Howard Kohn, "Karen Silkwood's Dark Victory," *Rolling Stone*, July 26, 1979. See also Richard Rashke, *The Killing of Karen Silkwood* (1981); and Howard Kohn, *Who Killed Karen Silkwood?* (1981).]

BARBARA L. TISCHLER

SINGER, CHARLES H. (Mar. 17, 1903–Mar. 26, 1972), communications expert, was born in Bayonne, N.J., the son of Barnet Singer, a painter who also operated a picture-framing shop, and Bertha Levin. Singer had seven brothers and sisters. He had no middle name; he adopted his middle initial during his youth to distinguish himself from a contemporary writer also named Charles Singer.

Singer attended public school in Bayonne and trained to be a wireless radio operator at the Marconi School of Radio. He worked initially on several seagoing vessels, one of which was the yacht of press magnate William Randolph Hearst. He was also a wireless operator on the

Clyde Line passenger steamship *Comanche*, which caught fire and sank off the coast of Florida on Oct. 17, 1925. Singer stayed in the radio room sending out SOS messages. He remained at his post until just before the ship went down, and then left with the captain. As a result, there were no casualties.

Singer became a registered professional engineer in the 1920's, one of the few persons to do so who was not a college graduate. He married Betty Schnitzer on Mar. 18, 1928; they had two children.

During the late 1920's, Singer helped construct land-based radio operations. With his assistance, Lt. Vincent Doyle of the Bayonne Police Department installed radio communications between the Bayonne Police Headquarters and its patrol cars, one of the first such police radio systems in the nation.

Singer later worked for WOR, in New York City, then one of the major radio stations in the United States. He started as assistant to John Poppele, WOR's chief engineer, and later succeeded him in that position. Singer worked on the station's technical operations, constructing the towers and transmitting systems that broadcast from antennas situated atop the Empire State Building.

During World War II, Singer was appointed the Army Signal Corps' assistant director of operational research. Stationed in Washington, D.C., he was responsible for developing operations and maintenance procedures for military communications systems; he also helped write several maintenance manuals for the newly developed radar systems.

After the war ended, Singer returned to WOR, which had obtained a license to begin transmitting television broadcasts. Singer helped design, construct, and maintain the station's new television transmission facilities. An experimental broadcast antenna he constructed in Carteret, N.J., was unsuccessful, because most of the area's television audience already had their home antennas pointed toward the Empire State Building. Singer left WOR in 1955, after the station was acquired by the General Tire and Rubber Company, which was expanding into radio, television, and motion pictures.

Singer became vice-president and director of operations for Page Communications Engineers in Vienna, Va. His new employer was a subsidiary of the Northrop Corporation, a large aerospace firm specializing in defense contracts.

Headed by Northrop executive Herbert H. Schenck, Page Communications was set up to construct and operate the long-distance communications systems tied in with the nation's military apparatus. Singer worked on projects involving the North American Radar system (NORAD) and the Distance Early Warning (DEW) Line, constructed with the participation of American Telephone and Telegraph Company and various defense agencies.

In 1960, Page Communications formed a consortium called the United States Underseas Cable Corporation with several other firms, including Phelps Dodge Corporation, a major copper producer; the Northrop Corporation; and Felten & Guilleaume Carlswerk Aktiengesellschaft, a West German cable company that had developed a new type of Styroflex cable especially suited for undersea use. The consortium designed and constructed long-distance submarine cable systems.

Singer was involved in setting up one such system between Cape Canaveral, Fla., and various islands in the Caribbean and the South Atlantic, for monitoring and reporting American missile launches.

When American involvement in the Vietnam War escalated into full-scale participation, Singer helped Page Communications install and maintain undersea cable communications systems linking American bases in Vietnam with existing military command centers in the Philippines, Taiwan, Okinawa, and other bases in the region.

Singer's last project involved the creation of an undersea communications system between the USSR and Japan, which was linked with other non-Communist nations of Asia. He died of cancer in Sibley, Va.

He was a member of the Institute of Radio Engineers (later the Institute of Electrical and Electronic Engineers), as well as the Society of Motion Picture and Television Engineers, the Armed Forces Communications and Electronics Associations, the Navy League, and the Veteran Wireless Operators Association.

Except for his early heroic exploit aboard the *Comanche*, Singer was not well known to the general public. But he was held in high esteem by the technical experts who ran the nation's radio and telecommunications infrastructure. His forte was not technological innovation per se, but rather in finding the optimal combination of manpower and technology, through selecting and training the personnel needed to operate the communications systems in the most economic and reliable manner.

[There is no biography of Singer, but he is mentioned in Henry R. Schnitzer, *As They Were: Bayonne and Jersey City* (1973). An obituary is in the *New York Times*, Mar. 27, 1972.]

STEPHEN G. MARSHALL

SISLER, GEORGE HAROLD ("GORGEOUS GEORGE") (Mar. 24, 1893–Mar. 26, 1973), baseball player, was born in Manchester, Ohio, the son of Cassius Sisler, manager of a coal mine, and Mary Whipple. Sisler spent his early years in Nimisila, ten miles south of Akron, before moving to Akron at age fourteen to pitch for Akron Central High School. At age seventeen, Sisler signed a contract, to take effect on his high school graduation, with Akron in the Ohio-Pennsylvania League. At his father's urging, Sisler put aside professional baseball and entered the University of Michigan at Ann Arbor in 1910. At Michigan, Sisler became the outstanding college baseball player in the country. Reportedly, his college pitching record was fifty wins and no defeats before he graduated in 1915 with a degree in mechanical engineering. At Ann Arbor, Sisler met his future wife, Kathleen Holznagle. Married in 1916, they had four children. All three of his sons also had careers in baseball.

Sisler's first coach at Michigan was Branch Rickey, who became field manager to the St. Louis Browns of the American League in 1913. Rickey moved to void Sisler's contract with Akron, which had been transferred to the Pittsburgh Pirates. He argued that the young pitcher had signed the agreement while he was a minor and without his parents' consent. Eventually, the Major League National Commission ruled in Rickey's favor, and in 1915 Sisler signed with the Browns.

Sisler's first major league season was 1915. He appeared in eighty-one games, thirty-seven as first baseman, twenty-nine as outfielder, and fifteen won on the mound. He won four and lost four with a 2.83 earned run average while batting .285. Comparing his hitting and pitching skills, Rickey placed Sisler at first base in 1916. His abbreviated pitching career, including a few isolated appearances over the years, totaled twenty-four games, with five wins, six losses, and an earned run average of 2.35.

From 1917 through 1922 Sisler's hitting averaged .374 per year, topped by .407 in 1920 and .420 in 1922, both league-leading scores. His .422 average is the third highest in baseball history. Sisler's premier year was 1920, when he had a single-season all-time record 257 hits and career bests of 19 home runs, 18 triples, 49 doubles, 122 runs batted in, and 137 runs scored. In 1922, Sisler led the league in average, hits, triples, and runs scored, garnering the year's most valuable player award. That year Sisler hit safely in forty-one straight games, a modern standard not surpassed until 1941, when Joe Dimaggio hit safely in fifty-six games.

For Sisler, 1923 was a disastrous year. A chronic sinus condition worsened by an influenza attack affected his optic nerve, causing double vision. Sisler was forced to sit out the year while undergoing a sinus operation and a tonsillectomy. With his status as a player still uncertain, Sisler signed on in October as Browns manager for the 1924 season, succeeding Jimmy Austin. Not until March 1924 did Sisler announce himself fit to play, despite some lingering vision problems. Although he remained in the major leagues for seven more years, he insisted that his real career ended with the 1923 season.

For the next three years Sisler both played and managed for the Browns. In 1924 he hit .305 as the Browns finished fourth in the standings with a 74–78 record. In 1925 the Browns improved to third place at 82–71, and Sisler batted .345. Sisler hit .290 in his final year as manager, while the team's standing fell to seventh with a 62–92 slate. At his own request, Sisler relinquished his managerial duties in 1926 with a three-year record of 218 wins and 241 losses.

In 1927 club president Philip Ball sold Sisler to the Washington Senators. Relegated to the role of utility player, Sisler appeared with the Senators in only twenty games of the 1928 season, batting .245 before being sold in May to the Boston Braves of the National League. In 118 games with Boston, Sisler hit .340 with sixty-eight runs batted in and seventy-one runs scored. Sisler played two more years with the Braves, hitting .326 in 1929 and .309 as player-coach in 1930. Released by the Braves and not picked up by any other major league squad, Sisler entered the minor leagues for the first time in 1931. With Rochester of the International League, he batted .303 in 159 games,

729

helping the St. Louis Cardinals farm team win the Minor League World Series. The next year, as player-manager of Shreveport-Tyler in the Texas League, Sisler appeared in 70 games hitting .287.

As an every-day player Sisler had career offensive statistics of a .340 batting average (fifteenth on the all-time list) with 2,812 hits, including 101 home runs, 164 triples, 425 doubles, 1,284 runs scored, and 1,175 runs batted in. An aggressive contact hitter who modeled himself after Ty Cobb, Sisler drew just 472 walks in his 8,267 at-bats while striking out only 327 times. He led the American League in stolen bases four times, the last time in 1927. Defensively, Sisler is rated with Hal Chase as the best first baseman in history. He led the American League in assists six times and ranks second lifetime in this category, with 1,528. Sisler roamed off base in an unconventional manner for his day, using his quickness and anticipation to flag down many hits thought to be destined for right field. Sisler batted .300 or better in 13 of his 15 years in baseball.

After the 1932 season Sisler left professional baseball for ten years, lending his name to a St. Louis printing company and a sporting goods firm. He also operated softball parks in the St. Louis area and in 1939 became commissioner of the National Baseball Congress, a nationwide semiprofessional organization. That same year the Baseball Writers Association of America elected him to the Baseball Hall of Fame. In 1950 Sisler was chosen to the all-time all-star team in a national poll of baseball writers.

In 1943 Sisler returned to the major leagues as a scout for the Brooklyn Dodgers under General Manager Branch Rickey. When Rickey moved in 1951 to an executive position with the Pittsburgh Pirates, Sisler accompanied him as scout and hitting instructor, traveling with the club from 1956 to 1961. He remained a scout for the team until 1965. He died in St. Louis.

[Short biographical sketches of Sisler are in Tom Meany, *Baseball's Greatest Players* (1953); Ira L. Smith, *Baseball's Famous First Basemen* (1956); and Martin Appel and Burt Goldblatt, *Baseball's Best* (1977). Obituaries appear in the *New York Times*, Mar. 27, 1973; and the *St. Louis Post-Dispatch*, Mar. 27, 1973.]

DAVID BERNSTEIN

SISSLE, NOBLE LEE (July 10, 1889–Dec. 17, 1975), lyricist, singer, and bandleader, was born in Indianapolis, Ind., to George Andrew Sissle, a Methodist minister, and Martha Angeline, a teacher. Noble was from an early age exposed to music, because the Reverend Sissle played the organ and Noble was a boy soprano in the church choir. He was also given ample opportunity to enjoy the popular music of the day, for the grounds behind his father's church accommodated the carnivals, circuses, and various parades that were held throughout the year.

In 1906, the Sissles moved to Cleveland, and Noble enrolled in Central High School, where he played on the baseball and football teams and was a member of the glee club. A tenor, he was a featured soloist and in his senior year was elected leader of the glee club and was class vocalist at his graduation in June 1911. He had begun to sing professionally in 1908 with the Edward Thomas Male Quartet, which played evangelical circuits throughout the Midwest. Because he had taken time off from school to tour with this group, Sissle did not graduate until he was twenty-one. This was to be the pattern he would follow even with his college studies: intermittent periods of performing and schooling. Upon graduating from high school, he joined the Hann's Jubilee Singers. Performing with this group took him as far west as Denver and as far east as New York City.

In the fall of 1913, Sissle enrolled at De Pauw University in Greencastle, Ind., on a full music scholarship. There he became a vocalist with the Harry Farley Dance Orchestra, a popular college dance band of the day. He remained at DePauw for only one semester. The following January, he enrolled at Butler University in Indianapolis, where he continued his music studies until the summer of 1915. While a student at Butler, Sissle held a variety of odd jobs and in early 1915 worked as a waiter at one of the larger hotels in Indianapolis. The owner of this hotel persuaded Sissle to organize and conduct an orchestra to perform there. It became his first professional job as a bandleader.

In the spring of 1915, Sissle became a vocalist for Joe Porter's Serenade, which performed at the Riverview Park in Baltimore, Md. It was while with this group that Sissle met the pianist and composer Eubie Blake, who came to play a crucial role in Sissle's musical career. Blake was impressed with Sissle's lyric-writing ability and expressed an interest in collaborating with him at their very first meeting.

After the disbanding of Joe Porter's Serenade,

Sissle stayed in Baltimore and accepted a job as singer and bandolin player with Bob Young's ten-piece orchestra at the Kernan Hotel in Baltimore. This group obtained a winter engagement at the Royal Poinciana Hotel in Palm Beach, Fla. While playing a benefit for the Palm Beach Red Cross, the group was seen by E. F. Albee, head of the Keith Vaudeville Circuit, who invited them to perform at the Palace Theatre in New York as part of a special "Palm Beach Week at the Palace," which featured Sissle as vocalist. This marked the first time that an African-American group performed at the Palace Theatre without blackface and in full formal dress.

Settling in New York City in 1916, Sissle was integrated into the Clef Club and Tempo Club of James Reese Europe, conductor of the most influential society band in New York. Europe hired Noble to work for some of his more important society dances and events. In the summer of 1916, Blake joined Sissle as part of the James Reese Europe Clef Club Society, the first black musical organization in New York.

Sissle and Blake began immediately to collaborate on popular songs, though this collaboration was interrupted when, in December 1916, Sissle and Europe enlisted in the U.S. Army, where they organized an all-black regimental band. Sissle recruited band members and eventually became drum major. After training at Camp Whitman in Peekskill, N.Y., the regiment entertained camps in South Carolina and New Jersey before being shipped to France in 1918. The 369th Regimental Infantry Band, under the direction of James Reese Europe, was in great demand and won many honors in France.

Shortly after the conclusion of the war, the band returned to the United States and began a national tour. After a performance in Boston on May 9, 1919, Europe was stabbed to death by a disgruntled member of the band. The company that had provided financial backing for the tour asked Sissle to continue as leader of the fifteen-piece group. Instead, Sissle persuaded them to back him and Blake as a duo, continuing an act that Sissle and Europe had started in France. This new duo had its first performance in Bridgeport, Conn., after which it played at the Harlem Opera House and was immediately booked at the Palace Theatre. Taking the name "The Dixie Duo," Sissle and Blake followed the practice of Bob Young's group and performed without minstrel makeup, elevating the status of American black performers in the United States.

At a 1920 benefit for the National Association for the Advancement of Colored People in Philadelphia, Sissle and Blake met the successful comedy team of Flournoy Miller and Aubrey Lyles. This chance meeting paved the way for the first successful black Broadway show, *Shuffle Along*. The show was in some respects a fusion of the two teams' vaudeville acts, drawing dance numbers from Sissle and Blake and throwing in a continuous plot and a love interest. Miller and Lyles were friends with the backer and producer Al Mayer of New York City. With his support, auditions and rehearsals began for the show. Opening on May 23, 1921, with lyrics by Sissle and music by Blake, *Shuffle Along* contained a number of songs that became part of the standard Broadway repertoire, among them "I'm Just Wild About Harry," "In Honeysuckle Time," and "Memories of You." The impressive list of performers who went on to later success included Josephine Baker, Florence Mills, Paul Robeson, William Grant Still, Adelaide Hall, and Hall Johnson. After its successful run in New York City, the show took to the road, including performances in Chicago, Boston, Milwaukee, Indianapolis, St. Louis, Detroit, Philadelphia, and Atlantic City.

Building on the fame of *Shuffle Along*, Sissle and Blake collaborated on the musical *Chocolate Dandies* (1924). After the closing of *Chocolate Dandies* in 1926, Sissle and Blake performed at the Kit Kat Club in London and returned to the United States in August. Sissle returned to London in 1927 with a solo act and then formed his own band for residency at Les Ambassadeurs in Paris in December 1928. Sissle had tremendous success with his bands in Europe, performing for British royalty and befriending important European composers. In 1932, after the death of Aubrey Lyles, Sissle, Blake, and Flournoy Miller reworked their original Broadway hit as *Shuffle Along of 1933*, which ran only fifteen weeks in New York City and fared no better on the road, finally breaking up in Los Angeles in the spring of 1933. With the show's close, Sissle and Blake went their separate ways. Sissle reorganized his orchestra and in 1935 returned to Paris with Lena Horne as his singer. He continued to perform throughout the United States, and his orchestra was in residence at Billy Rose's Diamond Horseshoe in New York from 1938 to 1942 and again from

1945 to the mid-1950's. It was during an engagement at Billy Rose's Diamond Horseshoe that he met and married Ethel Harrison; they had two children. His first marriage (in 1919) to Harriet Toye, the widow of pianist Patrick E. Toye, had resulted in divorce. During World War II, Sissle toured on behalf of the USO, and from the 1960's until his death, he managed his own publishing company and worked occasionally as a bandleader. In 1972, Sissle and Blake reunited for a series of performances and recordings. The Broadway musical *Eubie* (1978) featured many songs on which Sissle and Blake had collaborated.

In the early 1970's, Sissle moved to Florida, where he lived until his death in Tampa. Although he is best known as a lyricist, Sissle had an important influence on jazz styles, chiefly as a bandleader and singer. He made recordings throughout his career as a singer with various studio orchestras before 1920 and with studio bands in Britain in the 1920's, 1930's, and 1940's. Some of his most important recordings were made in 1937 with an eight-piece group known as the Swingers.

[For further biographical information, see J. R. T. Davies, "Blake and Noble Sissle," *Storyville* 7 (1966); and Robert Kimball and William Bolcom, *Reminiscing with Sissle and Blake* (1973). See also Albert McCarthy, *Big Band Jazz* (1974); and H. Rye, "Visiting Fireman, 7: Eubie Blake and Noble Sissle," *Storyville* 105 (1983). An obituary is in the *New York Times*, Dec. 18, 1975.]

WARRICK L. CARTER

SKOURAS, SPYROS PANAGIOTES (Mar. 28, 1893–Aug. 16, 1971), motion-picture executive and philanthropist, was born in the village of Skourahorian, Greece, to Panagiotes Skouras, a sheepherder. He was the second boy in a family of five brothers and five sisters. In 1908, at age fifteen, he entered the Greek Orthodox seminary in Patras, in order to prepare himself for the priesthood. At the same time he also took classes in English and accounting, with a view of joining his older brother, Charles, who had immigrated to the United States in 1907 and had settled in St. Louis. Skouras arrived in America in 1910 and began his career as a busboy at the Planter's Hotel bar in St. Louis. In 1912, with their combined savings, the Skouras brothers brought a younger sibling, George, to the United States, and in

1914 the three brothers invested their total savings of $4,000 in a nickelodeon hall, which they converted immediately into a movie theater, renaming it the *Olympia*, after Mt. Olympus near their hometown in Greece. To prepare himself for the role of a business manager, Skouras took classes in business administration and business law at Jones Commercial College from 1914 to 1916. In 1917, Spyros and George joined the U. S. Army Air Force Corps, leaving Charles in charge of their business interests. In 1919, Spyros received an honorable discharge and rejoined the family business. He also took classes in motion-picture finance, real estate, and theater management. In 1920 he married Sarah ("Saroule") H. Bruiglia. They had five children.

By 1926 the Skouras brothers owned thirty-five theaters in St. Louis and, in partnership with Paramount Publix, they also owned theater chains in Kansas City and Indianapolis. The movie studios were bidding heavily for power over the movie theaters, with the aim of exhibiting their own films to the exclusion of all others. In 1928 Warner Brothers bought out the Skouras theaters and retained Spyros Skouras as general manager of all Warner Brothers theaters countrywide. In 1931 Skouras left Warner Brothers for a brief stint as head of all Paramount theaters on the East Coast. In 1932 he became head of Fox Metropolitan Theaters, which was failing financially; it made a spectacular recovery under his leadership. Concurrently, the Skouras Brothers made a similar deal with the RKO theaters, whose holdings included the Roxy in mid-Manhattan. In 1940, Skouras helped to effect a merger between the Fox theaters and the Twentieth Century movie studio on the West Coast. In 1942, due to a vacancy at the head, Skouras was made president of Twentieth Century–Fox, a position that he held continuously until 1962. Wendell L. Wilkie, who had run unsuccessfully for president against Franklin D. Roosevelt in 1940, was his first chairman of the board.

In the meantime, big studios' ownership of large theater chains was hurting the independent operators. In 1932, southern California independents filed four suits against Fox West Coast theaters, claiming monopoly and restraint of trade. In 1948 the United States Supreme Court's ruling on this case directed the major studios to divorce themselves from theater interests. Skouras's proposal, a compromise agreed upon by the heads of all the major studios and the independent operators, called for the sale of at least one theater where the studios owned three or more houses. This fulfilled the Court's order for competition.

Soon after the end of World War II, Skouras was faced with the havoc inflicted upon the studios by the development of television as a new medium of entertainment. By December 1953, more than 6,000 movie theaters country-wide had closed as a result of this competition, causing a panic from which the movie industry could not seem to recover. At first Skouras thought that by owning a television network he would be able to control trends in this new medium. He offered to buy ABC-TV, but with-drew his bid when "they wanted too much." Paramount's executive, Leonard H. Golden-son, subsequently purchased the ABC-TV net-work, a move that saved his studio from near bankruptcy, proving wrong Skouras's judgment in releasing his option.

Nevertheless, Skouras continued his relent-less battle against the threat of television. He became a trailblazer, to be both feared and em-ulated by other leaders of the motion-picture industry. The grand scale of his vision and strat-egies, which he pursued with dogged determi-nation, even those that were unsuccessful in the end, became towering landmarks of that indus-try, without which Hollywood's history during the two decades of his tenure at Twentieth Century–Fox cannot be properly understood. In many ways he symbolized the Hollywood dream that refused to shrink or die.

First, Skouras waged a losing campaign against the sale of films to television, which he maintained was undercutting the motion-picture industry's natural market. He castigated other studio heads, calling these sales a "tragic mistake," "ruinous to film business." Second, he protested loudly the Department of Justice antitrust suit to compel the release of sixteen-millimeter films to television as "a menace to every industry and business in the country," further cautioning that the "application of the antitrust laws must be tempered with a little horse sense." Finally, Skouras warned that "a successful prosecution of a pending government suit to compel the sales of first-run feature films to television would destroy the motion pictures industry." Although other studio heads agreed with Skouras in principle, none showed his te-nacity, and one by one they all gave in.

Skouras hoped to compete with television by

means of innovative research and development, which would offer the public technologically su-perior products that could not be duplicated on the small screen. To this end he pioneered Cin-emaScope, a technique that remained associ-ated with Twentieth Century–Fox ever since, showing off the results in the much acclaimed film, *The Robe*, which helped pull Fox's sagging profits out of the slump. For a time Skouras also toyed with the imaginative idea of merging motion-picture and television technologies into a single medium, thus eliminating their rivalry. He played a driving force in the development of big-screen color television for theaters, with a view toward converting the big screen into tele-vision. The full potential of his original idea was not picked up by researchers until the mid-1980's and in the 1990's it is still evolving only in private laboratories in the United States and Ja-pan. In his lifetime his idea had produced the short-circuit technology that was tried out for ed-ucational purposes on some campuses and for selling theater tickets to major boxing events.

Another source that Skouras wanted to tap as a counterbalance to sagging domestic profits was the foreign market. He was convinced that Hol-lywood could recoup its losses abroad. He main-tained that overseas profits equalled those made in the United States and could be multiplied if the American motion-picture industry went multinational, not only selling but also invest-ing in production abroad. The trend to "shoot on location" was widely practiced by all the studios, whose principal concern was cutting down production costs with cheaper labor and materials. The policy gave rise to conflicts with and strikes by Hollywood unions of technicians and actors protesting against the "export of American jobs to other nations." However, none of the other industry leaders shooting abroad had the vision or courage to pursue the promise of a global American film industry.

Indeed, in the postwar years the European motion-picture industry barely existed, and the American industry was the only serious supplier of movie entertainment. The European market windfall, however, did not last long. In a few years, with government assistance, the British, the French, and the Italian studios were produc-ing quality movies that were exported to the United States and even competed successfully for Academy Awards. Somewhat stubborn, somewhat oblivious to these trends, Skouras still wanted to fulfill his dream of a global multinational motion-picture industry. The film *Cleopatra*, filmed on location in Italy, was his last giant effort to prove his point. The astronomical cost of producing *Cleopatra*, caused primarily by increasing schedule delays, compounded by its film producer Walter Wanger's suit against Fox, Zanuck, and Skouras for alleged damage to his professional reputation, and a canceled multi-million dollar Marilyn Monroe movie, added to Fox's serious financial difficulties and pushed it into debts that, under pressure from concerned stockholders, forced Skouras in 1962 to resign. He became chairman of the board and Darryl Zanuck replaced him as president of Fox studios. Although many saw this change as a mere exercise in musical chairs, Skouras ceased to take active interest in the studio or the motion-picture industry. He served as chairman until 1967.

Still feeling fit to have a fresh start in a new business, Skouras had formed in 1965 the *American Prudential-Grace Shipping Lines*, with a vision to build, with the promised equal participation of the U.S. government, a fleet of eighteen cargo ships that would revolutionize the shipping industry. The new ships would introduce a much enlarged container capacity and travel at a speed that would cut time between the United States and European and Mediterranean ports by half. Skouras did not live to fulfill this vision, but his idea was picked up by the U.S. Navy Logistic Fleet in the 1980's, and the resulting larger-capacity, high-speed vessels demonstrated their utility in the 1990–1991 Persian Gulf War.

During his presidency at Fox, Skouras exercised a powerful influence over production policies. His opinions stemmed from his deep religious convictions and his belief in family values. More than once he vetoed a promising script of which he did not approve and which then became a box office success for another studio. At the request of President Truman he had Fox produce "anti-Red" films. At the same time he ordered the production of films on biblical and religious themes, and he personally picked Victor Mature to star in many of them. During his presidency at Fox he overseered the production of many films that made motion-picture history. Among them were *The Song of Bernadette* (1943), *The Keys of the Kingdom* (1947), *The Snake Pit* (1948), *A Letter to Three Wives* (1949), and *All About Eve* (1950). It was Skouras who made the decision to produce

Gentlemen's Agreement (1947) and *The Diary of Anne Frank* (1959), two films that had an immense impact on the status of Jews in the United States.

Throughout his life Skouras was known as a generous philanthropist, for which he received many awards and tributes. In 1941 he organized the phenomenal food-and-medicine-assistance fleet to occupied Greece. He raised the money to build the Greek Orthodox Cathedral in New York and donated large amounts of money to its charities. From 1946 to 1947 he served as chairman of the Motion Pictures Committee of American Brotherhood, an international benevolent organization, and from 1950 to 1951 he served as its chairman. In 1950 he was named pioneer of the year by the board of the Directors Guild for his contributions to the advancement of cinematic technology with the invention of CinemaScope. In 1951 the Philadelphia Fellowship Commission selected him to be the recipient of its annual Human Relations Award.

In 1956 he was honored with a tribute from Brandeis University for his work as chairman of the Motion Pictures Industry's division of the United Jewish Appeal. In the same year he became vice-chairman of the American Museum of Immigration. In 1958 the Screen Producers Guild presented him with its annual Milestone Award. In 1960 he received an honorary degree from the University of Mexico, and in 1962 he was given the Humanitarian Award by the Motion Picture and Amusement Division of the Joint Defense League.

In 1968 he was the recipient of the annual Walt Disney Memorial Award of the Association of Theater Owners, in recognition of the Center for the Creative Arts in Brookline, Mass., which he had launched. In 1970 the American-Israel Chamber of Commerce and Industry honored him with a tribute for his role as chairman of the Prudential-Grace Lines, in which the Government of Israel had an active share.

Spyros Skouras died of a heart attack at his home in Rye, N.Y.

[No satisfactory biography of Skouras exists. Carlo Curti, *Skouras: King of Fox Studios* (1967), leaves much to be desired, but one can piece together information from trade papers: *Boxoffice*, Mar. 17, 1969; *Hollywood Reporter*, Mar. 13, 1969; *Motion Picture Herald*, July 11, 1962, and Dec. 4, 1968; and *Variety*, June 7, 1939, July 18, 1950, and Aug. 13, 1952.

Other articles appear in *Life*, July 20, 1953; *Los*

Angeles Herald Express, Nov. 18, 1950, and Apr. 15, 1968; *New York Herald Tribune*, June 1949; *New York Sun*, Apr. 11, 1942; and *Time*, June 7, 1962.

Obituaries appear in all the trade papers, including *Boxoffice*, Aug. 23, 1971; *Hollywood Reporter*, Aug. 18, 1971; and *Variety*, Aug. 18, 1971. In the general press one may wish to consult the *Los Angeles Times*, Aug. 18, 1971, and the *New York Times*, Aug. 17, 1971.]

SHOSHANA KLEBANOFF

SMITH, BETTY (Dec. 19, 1896–Jan. 17, 1972), novelist and playwright, was born Elizabeth Wehner in Brooklyn, N.Y., to German immigrants Catherine Hummel and John Wehner. Her father died before she was twelve, and her mother married Michael Keogh, an Irish immigrant. The economic circumstances of her childhood were terrible, and she had to quit school after the eighth grade so that she could work to help support the family.

After a succession of jobs in Brooklyn and Manhattan and an attempt to enroll in college (unsuccessful because she was not a high school graduate), Smith left Brooklyn at age seventeen. For the rest of her life, no matter where she lived, her imagination dwelt in the Brooklyn neighborhoods of Williamsburg, Bushwick, and East New York at the turn of the century, the places where her ambition to be a writer had been forged.

In 1913 or 1914, she married George H. E. Smith, a childhood friend from Brooklyn whom she followed to the University of Michigan at Ann Arbor, where he attended law school. They had two children. Through the mediation of her husband she entered the University of Michigan as a special student (1921–1922 and 1927–1931) and took every writing course offered. (Smith never received a degree.) Playwriting especially appealed to her, and after studying the craft with Professor Kenneth T. Rowe, she won the University's first Avery Hopwood Award (1931). For her prizewinning play, "Francie Nolan," she was awarded $1,000, a large sum for those days, and it allowed the family to move to New Haven, Conn.

Smith continued her playwriting apprenticeship at the Yale School of Drama. She studied with George P. Baker and John Mason Brown for three years and participated in Federal Theater projects. The family moved to Detroit in 1934, where Smith wrote for the *Detroit Free Press* and acted in summer stock. Her marriage ended in 1938.

Even though the pay was meager, Smith persisted in writing for a living. With the encouragement of the dramatist Paul Green, she and her children moved to Chapel Hill, N.C., in 1936. There, at the University of North Carolina, Smith subsisted on Rockefeller and Dramatists Guild fellowships as well as on small amounts of money earned as a bit player in local productions. Her years of playwriting yielded 125 one-act and 7 full-length plays, most of them written for amateur performance. They do not, by and large, read well today.

In 1938, Smith started to work on her first novel, a semiautobiographical assemblage of episodes and characterizations inspired in part by letters her mother had written over the years. Her writing was influenced by her reading of the American naturalist writers Theodore Dreiser, Sherwood Anderson, and especially Thomas Wolfe, whose 1935 novel *Of Time and the River* was the catalyst, Smith said, that released her childhood memories.

In 1942, Harper and Brothers announced a nonfiction contest to which Smith submitted her 1,000-page manuscript. It impressed the editors, who urged her to complete it as a novel. Severely trimmed, *A Tree Grows in Brooklyn* was accepted for publication in 1943 and catapulted Smith to fame and fortune. In just six weeks, 300,000 copies were sold. At the time of Smith's death, six million copies had been produced in thirty-seven printings, and it had been translated into sixteen languages.

Before the initial publication, Smith had tried to sell the story to Hollywood for $5,000. The offer was rejected, and it was not until the novel proved to be a best-seller that Twentieth Century–Fox offered Smith $50,000 for the rights, an offer she initially turned down. She relented only when the studio paid her an extra $5,000, the sum she had first requested. The movie (1945), with screenplay by Tess Slesinger and Frank Davis, was Elia Kazan's directorial debut. A later stage adaptation as a musical (1951), with book by Smith and George Abbott, music by Arthur Schwartz, and lyrics by Dorothy Fields, was not a rousing success.

The novel itself is beautifully written and unpretentious, a powerful evocation of a time and place. Despite sniping from some critics, who complained that best-sellers should not be confused with great literature, *A Tree Grows in Brooklyn* was a hit. The *New York Times* critic

Orville Prescott called it "the best first novel I have seen in many a moon."

In 1943, Smith married Joseph Piper Jones, a newspaperman whom she met while he was serving in the army. They had no children and were divorced in 1951. During the late 1940's, Smith was a member of the faculty of the University of North Carolina (1945–1946), served as judge of the Hopwood Drama Contest, championed the cause of polio research, and traveled to Switzerland to work on scripts for the films *The Search* (1948) and *School Bus*.

Smith was quoted as saying that she wished she had written her four novels in reverse order. Although all her books were commercial successes and enjoyed a measure of critical acclaim, the reviewers grew less and less enchanted with the author's later efforts. Both *Tomorrow Will Be Better* (1948) and *Maggie-Now* (1958) were set in Smith's vanished Brooklyn, and the last, *Joy in the Morning* (1963), was a reworking of her experiences as a young, naive wife in a midwestern college town.

In 1957, Smith married her third and last husband, Robert Finch, a friend who had written plays with her many years before. He died in 1959. After his death Smith devoted herself to writing and teaching; she taught creative writing at the University of North Carolina beginning in 1961. In her last years, she disappeared from the public's awareness. At the time of her death in a convalescent home in Shelton, Conn., she left an unfinished manuscript of an autobiography, which was never published.

Smith's literary reputation rests within the province of feminists and those interested in urban studies. Her best writing—the re-creation of a tenement family's life in Brooklyn before World War I—has been all but forgotten.

[The Betty Smith Papers are housed in the Southern Historical Collection and the North Carolina Collection at the University of North Carolina Library, Chapel Hill. They include hundreds of thousands of items, among them, personal and professional correspondence from 1909 to 1971, drafts of her writings, clippings, photographs, posters, and the unfinished autobiography manuscript. The University of Michigan Library, Ann Arbor, houses a few items in the Kenneth T. Rowe Student Play Collection (six of her student plays) and in the Hopwood Awards archives (the 1931 prizewinning play manuscript, "Francie Nolan," and correspondence relating to Smith's activities as a Hopwood Drama Contest judge in the 1940's). Modest clipping files of articles, reviews, and obituaries exist in the author's hometown in the Brooklyn Local History Collection (Brooklyn Public Library) and in the Brooklyn Historical Society.

There is no biography. A few scholarly studies include significant references to Smith's novels: Orville Prescott, *In My Opinion* (1952); Everett E. Ruth, "The Brooklyn Novel and the Brooklyn Myth" (Ph.D. diss., Columbia University, 1966); Joan Zlotnick, *Portrait of an American City* (1982); and Andrea S. Walsh, *Women's Film and Female Experience, 1940–1950* (1984). Elia Kazan's autobiography, *A Life* (1988), contains information about the making of the film version of *A Tree Grows in Brooklyn*. An obituary appears in the *New York Times*, Jan. 18, 1972.]

HONORA RAPHAEL

SMITH, JOSEPH FIELDING (July 19, 1876–July 2, 1972), tenth president of the Church of Jesus Christ of Latter-day Saints (LDS, Mormon), was born in Salt Lake City, Utah, the firstborn son of Joseph F. Smith, sixth president of the church, and Julina Lambson, midwife and prominent leader of Mormon women. Joseph Fielding's grandfather was the son of Hyrum Smith, who was the brother of Joseph Smith, founding prophet of the Mormons.

Because his father was burdened with church responsibilities, Joseph Fielding's youth was spent primarily with his mother and twelve brothers and sisters. He learned to cook, piece quilts, care for babies, harness the horse, and drive his mother to homes where women were ready to give birth. Even as a young boy, he read the Bible and the Book of Mormon in a spirit of faith, acceptance, and preparation. He worked as a department store clerk while attending LDS High School and College in Salt Lake City, and at age eighteen he began serving as private secretary to his father. On Apr. 26, 1898, at the age of twenty-one, he married Louie Shurtliff, who had been a fellow high school student. The couple had two daughters before Louie's death in 1908. From 1899 to 1901, Smith served a proselytizing mission in England.

In 1902 he began a lifetime career in the LDS church historian's office in Salt Lake City. He wrote and copied histories and documents, responded to requests for information, and served as librarian-archivist. An eager defender of the faith, he wrote several pamphlets to counteract attacks on the church and its leaders. Appointed assistant church historian in 1906, he wrote booklets on baptism for the dead, universal salvation, and genealogical research. He was the editor of the *Utah Genealogical and Historical Magazine* (1910–1940).

He married Ethel Georgina Reynolds on Nov. 2, 1908. They had nine children before Ethel died in 1937. The following year, on April 12, he married Jessie Ella Evans, an actress and operatic singer whose humor and colorful personality enriched his life while she also cared for his large family. She died in August 1971.

In 1910, Smith was ordained an apostle (a member of the governing church council of twelve leading men). He was only thirty-three years old. Appointed church historian in 1921, he wrote a one-volume history of the church, *Essentials in Church History* (1922). Initially used in priesthood classes, this volume became the most commonly used text on Mormon history in Sunday School and seminary classes. It went through twenty-four English editions and several foreign-language editions. Not a conventional history, the book viewed history through prophetic and scriptural eyes.

Still an incessant reader of the Bible and the Book of Mormon, as well as the Doctrine and Covenants (a book of modern revelation), Smith published a variety of books on doctrine, all based on a literal interpretation of the scriptures: *The Way to Perfection* (1931), *The Progress of Man* (1936), *The Signs of the Times* (1942), *The Restoration of All Things* (1944), *Church History and Modern Revelation* (1953), and *Man: His Origin and Destiny* (1954). The last of these was a scriptural and theological defense of the position that mankind was placed on the earth by God and was not a product of organic evolution.

Smith's hard-hitting sermons emphasized that God is a personal being, the creator of all things, and the literal father of Jesus. He defended Joseph Smith, the Book of Mormon, and the latter-day restoration. He was an uncompromising opponent of both "higher" and textual biblical criticism, which he thought found fault with God's recorded word. For him, human scholarship and reason could not be used to judge the word of God.

Excerpts from Smith's sermons and his printed responses to questions in the church's magazines were published in five volumes under the title *Answers to Gospel Questions* (1954–1966).

As a grandnephew of the founding prophet, and as a member of the governing Council of Apostles for more than sixty years, Smith had extraordinary influence over church manuals and articles published in church magazines. He insisted that the history of the church and its leaders be presented in a positive light. The materials in the church archives, which he administered, were made available to scholars with considerable reluctance.

In his management of the church archives, Smith helped to introduce significant technological and administrative innovations, including a comprehensive microfilming program that assured permanent preservation of many important historical records; the adoption, in the early 1960's, of modernized methods of classification and processing that facilitated the filing and use of the church's holdings; the establishment in 1965 of a professional records-management program; and the completion of a new wing of the church office building that housed the church's expanding historical department.

In 1970, as senior apostle, though ninety-four years of age, he became the tenth president of the LDS Church and served as prophet until his death two-and-one-half years later. During his tenure as president, assisted by two energetic counselors, he directed a steady growth in missionary activity; dedication of the Ogden and Provo (Utah) temples; reorganizations in the church Sunday School system and department of social services; the consolidation of all general church magazines into three; and the appointment of a professional staff to direct the church's newly created historical department.

In addition to his calling as an apostle and church historian, Smith was also president of the Utah Genealogical Society (1934–1964), president of the Salt Lake Temple (1945–1949), and author of several hymns. In 1951 he was awarded an honorary doctor of letters from Brigham Young University for "spiritual scholarship."

[Most of Smith's papers are in the LDS Church Archives in Salt Lake City. They include his missionary journal, letters from his father, and his own letters and personal chronicles. See also Joseph F. McConkie, *True and Faithful: The Life Story of Joseph Fielding Smith* (1971); J. M. Heslop and Dell R. Van Orden, *Joseph Fielding Smith: A Prophet Among the People* (1971); Joseph Fielding Smith, Jr., and John J. Stewart, *The Life of Joseph Fielding Smith* (1972); Joseph Fielding McConkie, "Joseph Fielding Smith," in Leonard J. Arrington, ed., *The Presidents of the Church* (1986); "Joseph Fielding Smith" in

Philip L. Barlow, *Mormons and the Bible: The Place of the Latter-day Saints in American Religion* (1991); Amelia McConkie and Mark L. McConkie, "Smith, Joseph Fielding," in Daniel H. Ludlow, ed., *Encyclopedia of Mormonism* (1992); and Francis M. Gibbons, *Joseph Fielding Smith: Gospel Scholar, Prophet of God* (1992). Personal impressions of Smith by seven writers who knew him are published in *Dialogue: A Journal of Mormon Thought*, Spring 1972.

An eloquent tribute and obituary is Bruce R. McConkie, "Joseph Fielding Smith, Apostle, Prophet, Father in Israel," *Ensign*, August 1972. An obituary also appears in the *New York Times*, July 3, 1972.]

LEONARD J. ARRINGTON

SMITH, MILDRED CATHARINE (Mar. 9, 1891–Aug. 30, 1973), editor, was born in Smethport, Pa., one of two children born to Charles A. Smith and Jane Haskell. As a child, Smith was an avid reader. According to her mother, little Mildred would read bottle labels if there wasn't a book handy.

While Smith was a young girl, her family moved to Buffalo, N.Y. After graduating from Lafayette High School there, she earned her B.A. in 1914 from Wellesley College; she concentrated on English literature, history, and philosophy.

At Wellesley, Smith lived in the home of Katherine Lee Bates, professor of literature and a well-known poet. Under Bates's tutelage, she developed a love for classic English literature and modern poetry. She later enrolled in George Lyman Kittredge's Shakespeare course at Radcliffe College (then part of Harvard University). At Bates's home she met writers such as Vachel Lindsay and John Masefield.

After her graduation from Wellesley, Smith and her aunt visited Europe and had the exciting misfortune of being there when World War I began. Once safely returned to the United States, Smith served as an assistant in English literature at Wellesley from 1915 to 1916. She then taught at the Buffalo Seminary, a private girls' secondary school, for one year and later taught English at a private school in Plainfield, N.J.

Smith found teaching repetitive, and she longed for a more exciting career. Moving to New York City, she got a job with the Woman's Press, the publication department of the YWCA. In 1920 she became an assistant to Frederic G. Melcher, editor of *Publisher's Weekly*. She was recommended by Bessie Graham of *The Bookman's Manual*, a trade publication. Graham, who knew Smith's work at the YWCA, told Melcher that Smith was a "bright girl who had a fine education."

Although Smith had no experience with magazines or publishing, she learned her job quickly. She also completed her M.A. at Wellesley in 1922; her thesis was a study on Shakespeare's use of English travel narratives in writing the *The Tempest*.

Smith was responsible for the day-to-day operations of *Publisher's Weekly*, and Melcher was the policymaker. From 1920 until 1933 she served as the assistant editor: from 1933 until 1959, she was coeditor. She was promoted to editor in chief in 1959 and held that position until she retired in 1967. Smith was a director of R. R. Bowker, which owned *Publisher's Weekly*, from 1934 until 1967 and served as a secretary from 1935 until 1967.

Smith modernized the magazine's layout and, in an effort to make *Publisher's Weekly* a news magazine and trade journal, solicited the best booksellers, publishers, and designers to submit articles. Its many special issues provided expert advice on rare books, on the paperback industry, on foreign trade, and on children's books.

Smith was impressed with the *New Yorker* magazine and sought to duplicate its accuracy and clarity. She also believed in reporting about books and book people. Smith developed two sections in *Publisher's Weekly*: "You Meet Such Interesting People" (now "People") and "Tips" (now "Trade News"). She expanded the single-page book forecasts into several pages that provided insightful and detailed book reviews.

Early in her career, Smith began a file on thousands of bookstores in the country. She developed friendships with many of the owners and visited them during her extensive travels. She also sent members of her staff to maintain a personal link with this branch of the publishing industry. Smith was responsible for grooming such future literary figures as Josiah Titzell, Weldon Reynolds, and Sandford Cobb.

During World War II, Smith was an active member of the National Book and Author War Bond Committee. She also hosted a victory garden celebration at her Long Island home—gardening was one of the few hobbies she found time to pursue. She also enjoyed spending time with her brother, D. Haskell Smith, and his family. Smith, who never married, lived with her longtime friend, Alice Whittemore, of the New York Tuberculosis and Health Association.

In the late 1930's, Smith and Whittemore built a whitewashed brick Georgian house on a half-acre lot overlooking Long Island Sound at Kings Point, N.Y. Smith named the home "Pending Farm" because of her desire to live on a farm. That desire was never achieved—she had to be in New York City every working day. Her walled garden included a variety of rare shrubs and flowers. Smith and Whittemore also owned a Pembroke Welch corgi named Minnie. Her only other prized possession was a baby blue convertible that matched her eyes.

Smith received many honors from the publishing community. In 1944, she received the Constance Lindsay Skinner Award of the Women's National Book Association. The citation on the plaque reads, "In recognition of more than 20 years of service to the book trade, and as an expression of gratitude for the help and encouragement which she has given to book women throughout the United States, above and beyond her duties as editor of *Publisher's Weekly*." The American Association of University Presses honored Smith in 1960 on her fortieth anniversary with *Publisher's Weekly*. Smith also received the Irita Van Doren Award from the American Booksellers Association, the Publishers' Publicity Association, and the Publishers' Ad Club in 1968. In 1967, R. R. Bowker was sold to the Xerox Corporation. That same year, Smith retired as editor in chief. She died in King's Point, N.Y.

[See "Take a Bow," *Publisher's Weekly*, Apr. 1, 1944. Obituaries appear in the *New York Times*, Aug. 31, 1973; *Publisher's Weekly*, Sept. 10, 1973; and *AB Bookman's Weekly*, Sept. 24, 1973.]
DELIA CRUTCHFIELD COOK

SMITH, RALPH TYLER (Oct. 6, 1915—Aug. 13, 1972), lawyer and politician, was born in Granite City, Ill., the son of Alfred Thomas Smith, a lumber company employee, and Clara Isabel Slattery. After attending public schools in his hometown and graduating from Granite City Community High School in 1933, Smith earned a B.A. from Illinois College in 1937 and attended Washington University Law School, graduating with an LL.D. in 1940. That same year he was admitted to the bar in both Missouri and Illinois and began the practice of law in Granite City.

In 1941 Smith became assistant attorney for the Chicago and Illinois Midland (CIM) Railway Company in Springfield. In 1942 he married Mary Elizabeth Anderson of Granite City; they had one child. From 1942 to 1946 he served as an officer in the United States Navy. He was an instructor at the Naval Midshipman School at Notre Dame University, an executive officer on convoy escort in the Atlantic Ocean, and then commander of a motor gunboat in the Pacific theater of operations.

In 1946 Smith moved to Alton, Ill., near St. Louis, where he practiced law and became involved in local Republican party politics. He was elected to the Illinois House of Representatives in 1954 and reelected to seven succeeding terms. He was House majority whip from 1963 to 1964. In 1967 he was chosen speaker of the Illinois House and won reelection to that post in 1969. Smith supported legislation to curb air and water pollution, build roads, and crack down on rioters and looters in disturbances in Chicago. In 1969 Smith managed the successful downstate election campaign of Republican gubernatorial candidate Richard B. Ogilvie. Following Ogilvie's inauguration in January 1969, Smith, a popular and effective legislator, skilled in political oratory and the art of compromise, presided calmly over a rancorous legislative session in 1969 that passed the state's first income tax.

As a youth, Smith had dreamed of becoming a United States senator, and his opportunity arrived when Everett McKinley Dirksen, the powerful minority leader in the Senate, died in office in 1969. Smith was appointed by Ogilvie to fill Dirksen's unexpired term. "I don't delude myself into thinking I'm another Dirksen," Smith stated, "but I think I can bring something to the Senate." A partisan Republican, Smith enthusiastically supported the "new federalism" of Richard Nixon, including proposals for welfare reform, sharing federal tax revenue with the states, and a national lottery to replace the existing military draft. In spite of personal reservations, he reversed his initial position and backed the president's unsuccessful effort to appoint Clement F. Haynsworth to the U.S. Supreme Court. In the fight to win confirmation of Haynsworth, a conservative jurist from South Carolina with a dismal civil rights record, Nixon saw an opportunity to exert his will over the Senate's liberal Democrats. However, the appointment was rejected on a 55–45 roll-call vote in which seventeen of Smith's Republican colleagues joined the Democrats. Smith held

no reservations concerning Nixon's efforts to
end the war in Vietnam by escalating the conflict. "Let it be remembered that this is not
Nixon's war, but it will be Nixon's peace," he
stated.

Smith faced a strong challenge from Adlai E.
Stevenson III (son of the popular Illinois governor who was twice the Democratic nominee
for president) in the 1970 special election.
Smith attacked his challenger as personally
weak, soft on crime, and sympathetic to student
radicals. In a surprising turn of events, Stevenson won the support of Chicago's powerful
mayor, Richard J. Daley, a former political enemy who had objected to Stevenson's criticism
of the actions of Chicago police in dealing with
the riots of 1968. With Daley's support and an
aggressive campaign of his own, Stevenson
proved to be too strong for Smith. Despite relentless campaigning and supportive visits to Illinois by Nixon and Vice-President Spiro T.
Agnew, Smith was defeated by more than half a
million votes. The Republican party in Illinois
also suffered a disastrous year, losing elections
in counties that had not voted Democratic since
the Civil War.

Following his election defeat Smith returned
to Alton to practice law. But the campaign had
exhausted him and he suffered a massive heart
attack in March of 1971. He died in Alton.

[Smith's papers, for the most part covering his U.S.
Senate career, are held in the Illinois State Historical
Library. See also Robert P. Howard, *Illinois* (1972).
Obituaries appear in the *Chicago Tribune*, Aug. 14,
1972, and the *Alton Evening Telegraph*, Aug. 14 and
15, 1972.]

MICHAEL J. DEVINE

SNOW, EDGAR PARKES (July 19, 1905–
Feb. 15, 1972), journalist, was born in Kansas
City, Mo., the third and youngest child of
James Edgar Snow and Anna Catherine Edel-
man. His father's family were early settlers in
Virginia (Snow sometimes claimed descent
from a passenger on the *Mayflower's* second
trip) who moved westward through Kentucky as
far as Kansas. Edgar's father had a printing and
publishing business in Kansas City. On the maternal side, Snow's ancestors were more recent
immigrants from Ireland and Silesia; they came
to Kansas City by way of Columbus.

As a youth, Edgar worked for his father, as
well as in a drug store and as a harvest hand.

Following graduation from Westport High
School in 1923, he attended the Junior College
of Kansas City for a year before moving to New
York City in 1925 to join his brother. That fall,
he went back home and attended the University
of Missouri School of Journalism as an advertising major. He returned to New York City one
year later, where he worked for Medley Scovil,
an advertising agency specializing in brokerage
accounts. He remained in Scovil's employ until
1928.

On July 6, 1928, Snow arrived in Shanghai
for a brief stay during a planned trip around the
world. J. B. Powell hired him as assistant advertising manager and sometime reporter on the
China Weekly Review. Snow would remain in
Asia until 1941. In his first years, many of his
pieces were travel accounts.

Returning to Shanghai from an extended trip
through southern China, Southeast Asia, and
India, Snow met Helen ("Peg") Foster, of Utah,
who had come to Shanghai to take a minor
position in the American Consulate. They were
married on Christmas Day, 1932, in Tokyo.
After a honeymoon trip through Southeast Asia,
the Snows settled in Beijing, where Edgar
worked as a journalist and taught some courses
at Yenching (later Beijing) University. Friendly
with radical students, Snow encouraged the student demonstrations of December 1935.

Snow's life changed forever in 1936, when
he traveled to Shanxi to visit the besieged Chinese Communist bastion at Paoan. *Red Star
Over China* (1937) was the first account of life
in the Soviet area, and it quickly became the
major source of knowledge on the Chinese
Communist party and its leaders. He followed
this triumph with coverage of the expanding
Sino-Japanese War.

Following his return to the United States in
early 1941, Snow served as an associate editor
for the *Saturday Evening Post* and was its chief
war correspondent in Russia. After the war, his
report on Gandhi's assassination was dubbed
"one of the classics of American journalism" by
William Shirer.

The McCarthy era brought Snow's career to
its nadir. He was charged with sympathy for the
Chinese Communist movement, if not membership in the party, and his writings were repeatedly rejected. He severed his connection
with the *Saturday Evening Post*. Meanwhile, in
May 1949, he and Helen Foster Snow divorced.
Nine days later, he married Lois Wheeler, an ac-

tress, at Snedens Landing, N.J.; They subsequently had two children.

With Snow's career at its low point, and his wife unofficially blacklisted from acting, the Snows took up residence in Switzerland. There, he wrote for several European journals. In 1960, as relations between the United States and the People's Rupublic of China began to thaw, *Look* hired Snow to be the first American journalist to return to the mainland.

Just before the inauguration of "ping-pong diplomacy," Snow visited China again and stood on the reviewing stand at Tiananmen Square with Mao Zedong in 1970. *Red China Today* (1971), his account of that trip, was his last major work.

Snow died of cancer in his home at Eysins, Switzerland, on Feb. 15, 1972, less than three days before Richard Nixon arrived in Beijing for his historic visit; ironically, his death occurred on Chinese New Year's. His son Christopher and a Chinese medical team were at his bedside. Today, some of his ashes rest alongside a quiet lake on the campus of Beijing University.

Snow's growth as a journalist is best evidenced by comparing the report of his odyssey through Southeast Asia with his style in *Red Star Over China* and *The Far Eastern Front* (1933). The earlier period is noted primarily for its travelogue style, occasional purple prose, and some fictionalizing of events. *Red Star Over China* demonstrates Snow's skill in reporting only what he saw or was told. *The Far Eastern Front* often shows the terse, crisp writing of an experienced war correspondent.

Despite his sympathies for Mao, Snow was an honest writer. As a war correspondent, it was sometimes necessary not to tell the whole truth because of the need for Allied unity, but he did not engage in lies. His goal was to see the United States as a world leader, concerned with the plight of emerging nations. In this he failed. An unheeded prophet, he correctly foretold many of the major events of the twentieth century. By the late 1940's, he foresaw French withdrawal from Vietnam and the fate awaiting the United States there. His major works comprise more than fifteen books and over one hundred articles. Though some of those books were collections of his articles, the book format gave them a depth and continuity not always evident in a solitary article.

The people of China remained his passion. As Harrison Salisbury said, China was Snow's "monopoly." His writings on China became primary sources. Perhaps his career can be summed up in his own words when he said: "In working overseas you were bound to notice that fifteen of every sixteen people on earth were not Americans. Those fifteen were likely to behave as if their interests were more important than any of ours which conflicted with them."

[Most of Edgar Snow's papers are in the library of the University of Missouri, Columbia, Mo. Snow's major works are *The Far Eastern Front* (1933), *Red Star Over China* (1937), *The Battle for Asia* (1941), *Glory and Bondage* (1945), *Stalin Must Have Peace* (1947), *Random Notes on Red China: 1936–1945* (1957), *Journey to the Beginning* (1958), *War and Peace in Vietnam* (1962), *China, Russia and the USA* (1962), *One Fourth of Humanity* (1968), and *Red China Today* (1971).

See also John Maxwell Hamilton, *Edgar Snow: A Biography* (1988). Several unpublished master's theses provide valuable information, including Bruce Erickson, *The Reporting of Edgar Snow* (University of Kansas, 1976); and Katherine Reist, *Edgar Snow: Unheeded Herald* (Ohio State University, 1976). An obituary is in the *New York Times*, Feb. 16, 1972.]

ART BARBEAU

SNOW, JOHN BEN (June 16, 1883–Jan. 21, 1973), businessman and philanthropist, was born in Pulaski, N.Y., the son of Benjamin Snow, Jr., manager of the Ontario Iron Works, and Mary Watson. He was educated at the Union School and Academy, graduating in 1900, second in his class.

After high school Snow worked in sales and traveled, entering New York University's School of Commerce in the fall of 1902, after a term at the Mt. Hermon School, a preparatory school. He was class historian in 1903 and president of his class in 1904. He edited the school newspaper and yearbook, and was active in sports. Having taken extra courses, he was able to graduate in two years, and afterward went to work for Haskins and Sells as a junior accountant until 1906. That year, he pursued an opportunity to join the F. W. Woolworth Company and began as a stockroom clerk in one of the midtown Manhattan stores. Snow showed remarkable potential and the next year was assigned to manage a new F. W. Woolworth store in Port Jervis, N.Y. It was here that he met his longtime friend and business partner, Merritt Speidel.

Snow remained in Port Jervis for only a matter of months before he was asked to return to New York City to manage a new midtown store. His success in merchandising was such that, in 1909, he signed a contract with Woolworth's in which he was guaranteed a 25 percent share of the net profits.

When Woolworth's expanded its operation in northern England, Snow became merchandiser in charge of the district office in Liverpool. He was responsible for, among other things, organizing the opening day of new stores, which he made into festive occasions. His approach was highly successful.

Snow was promoted to buyer in 1913 and transferred to London. He was remarkably accurate in gauging consumer interests, especially those of young people, and saved considerable sums of money by buying products in large quantities. He was soon made a director, and in 1920 named superintendent of buyers.

Snow's personal wealth increased, largely because of his heavy investments in Woolworth stock. By the time of his retirement he was a multimillionaire. His personal interests included polo and fox hunting. He loved horses, and in 1923 purchased a stud farm. He entered his own horses in many of the English races; two of them won several of the steeplechase events.

In 1936, Snow retired from Woolworth's and thereafter focused most of his time on his horses. This lifestyle was not to last, however. Only fifty-three years of age at his retirement and eager to work, Snow turned to a new career that took him home to the United States by the end of the decade.

For nearly thirty years, he had funded projects managed by his associate, Merritt Speidel. Their first joint venture had been in 1909 with the purchase of a northern Ohio newspaper known as the *Picqua Daily Call*. Snow paid for it and Speidel managed it.

Speidel, who thoroughly understood the newspaper business, continued managing operations while Snow provided the capital for their acquisitions. In 1921, Snow and Speidel sold their first newspaper and purchased the *Iowa City Press-Citizen*. In 1935, they acquired the *Chillicothe Scioto Gazette* and in 1936 bought the *Salinas Index-Journal*, the *Salinas Post*, and the *Fort Collins Express Courier*. Two years later, they owned the *Chillicothe News Advertiser* and a year after that, Cheyenne Newspapers, Inc., the *Poughkeepsie Sunday Courier*,

and the *Reno Gazette*. Their last purchase, in 1948, was Visalia Newspapers, Inc.

In the majority of these acquisitions, Snow loaned the necessary funds to Speidel at an annual interest rate of 1 percent. Speidel reinvested the profits from the newspapers and deposited the dividends in a joint account. By 1948, Snow had loaned Speidel a total of $2 million.

He entrusted Speidel with making various gifts in his name, voting on his behalf at board meetings, and investing large sums of money for him. Snow's funds were also used to modernize several newspaper plants across the country.

Snow had always been a silent partner. His name could not be found on newspaper mastheads or on financial statements. In 1937, when Snow and Speidel established a holding company to serve as the headquarters for all of their newspapers, the firm went under the name of Speidel Newspapers, Inc. As Snow began to devote more time to the holding company, he gradually allowed his name more exposure. New financial reports divulged Snow as a primary stockholder, and he was subsequently elected chairman of the board of several newspapers.

In 1942, Snow settled the company in Colorado Springs. He purchased a ranch and once again entered the business of breeding various types of horses. The following year Snow purchased *The Western Horseman*, a magazine he took more interest in than all of his newspapers. By 1950 Snow held eight newspaper companies, one radio station, and one magazine. Two years later, at the age of sixty-nine, he settled on a plan to transfer control into multiple hands. He surrendered his voting rights and traded $4.5 million worth of common stock for preferred stock. Snow's common stock was then available for purchase by corporate executives and by the publishers and editors of the various Speidel newspapers. In order to ensure widespread control, an employee could buy no more than a 7 percent share and could keep the stock only as long as he remained with the company. At the time of his resignation or retirement the stockholder was obligated to sell his stock to the existing management. Snow continued as chairman of the board of Speidel Newspapers, Inc., for the remainder of his life.

Throughout his adulthood, Snow, a devout Christian, contributed enormously not only to the building of a newspaper empire, but also to a number of organizations and individuals. In 1948, he established the John Ben Snow Foundation, the assets of which reached $2 million by 1962. The village of Pulaski, N.Y., was one of his primary beneficiaries. His largest single contribution of $1 million was made to Syracuse University's Newhouse School of Communications in 1965. Gifts to NYU's business school, law school, and medical school totaled more than $1.5 million. Snow also gave liberally to the Boy Scouts of America and gave anonymously to people whom he learned had faced tragic setbacks or who were otherwise in need. Although Snow had no family of his own and never married, to his extended family and friends he gave considerable financial assistance. His primary support went to religious and educational causes.

Snow died in Colorado Springs.

[On Snow's life see Vernon F. Snow, *JBS: The Biography of John Ben Snow* (1993). An obituary is in the *New York Times*, Jan. 23, 1973.]

ELIZABETH MCKAY

SOBELOFF, SIMON E. (Dec. 3, 1894–July 11, 1973), lawyer and judge, was born in Baltimore, Md., the son of Jacob Sobeloff, an upholsterer, and Mary Kaplan, both Jewish immigrants from Russia. He started working in a law office at age twelve and was admitted to the bar in 1914, a year before earning his law degree from the University of Maryland School of Law. In 1918 he married Irene Ehrlich; they had two daughters. Soon thereafter, he began to intersperse his practice with periods of public service, first as assistant city solicitor (1919–1923), and later as deputy city solicitor (1927–1930). In 1931 he was appointed United States Attorney for the District of Maryland by President Herbert Hoover. Until his resignation in March 1934, he vigorously enforced the Prohibition laws, despite his dislike for them.

During his tenure as a federal prosecutor, the Baltimore Trust Company, the largest bank in the South, crashed. A judge designated Sobeloff to conduct an investigation into the failure. While Sobeloff's 1936 report did not recommend prosecutions, it alleged that the bank directors were "personally liable for their negligent acts" and also for the "grossly" negligent conduct of the officers in that they failed to exercise proper supervision. H. L. Mencken noted that the report "shows all the compelling

plausibility of a demonstration in geometry and all the racy charm of 'The Gilded Age.' " Sobeloff left his practice again to serve as Baltimore city solicitor from 1943 to 1947. In late 1952 Governor Theodore McKeldin, the latest in a line of progressive Republicans who were his patrons, appointed Sobeloff Chief Judge of the Maryland Court of Appeals. His tenure lasted only until early 1954, when he was named solicitor general of the United States, the government's chief advocate before the United States Supreme Court.

At this time school segregation cases were the Court's main focus. Sobeloff had long been an active and outspoken opponent of racial inequality; in 1933 he had testified before the Senate Judiciary Committee in support of a federal antilynching bill. Thurgood Marshall, who headed the legal battle to desegregate public schools, noted that, at first, Sobeloff was "one of only three white lawyers who were at all interested. He stuck with me from the beginning to the end." Sobeloff presented the government's arguments on implementation of *Brown* v. *Board of Education*, urging that segregated school districts "effectuate the Court's decision as speedily as feasible." This wording came directly from President Eisenhower, who wrote part of the government's brief.

Loyalty and security issues occupied much of the Supreme Court's attention during Sobeloff's tenure as solicitor general. In one case, Dr. John Peters, a respected Yale medical professor, had been discharged from his longtime position as a consultant to the Public Health Service on the grounds of disloyalty. Someone apparently had accused him of membership in the Communist party; for the Loyalty Review Board, acting upon undisclosed information from unidentified informants, this sufficed. Peters sued to clear his name.

Sobeloff had already spoken out publicly about the need to maintain national security without abandoning the rights of the accused. "If we, ourselves, pull down the edifice of our freedoms," he asked, "wherein is our triumph?" He proposed that the government confess its error by admitting that Peters had been denied due process and asking that the lower court decision in its favor be reversed.

Attorney General Herbert Brownell, Jr., initially agreed, but after FBI Director J. Edgar Hoover and other Justice Department officials—including assistant attorney general Warren E. Burger, head of the Civil Division—strongly objected, Brownell rejected Sobeloff's proposal. Sobeloff refused to sign the government's brief or to argue its case in the Supreme Court. He did this, he said, because a person "on trial," especially one stigmatized by removal from an official position, must be granted his constitutional right to confront witnesses. Sobeloff took this unprecedented step "because I have to be able to live with myself." As a result, he lost a promised seat on the Court of Appeals for the District of Columbia.

In 1955, President Eisenhower nominated Sobeloff to the United States Court of Appeals for the Fourth Circuit, covering Maryland, Virginia, West Virginia, and North and South Carolina. Southern senators, opposed to his attitude toward school segregation, delayed his confirmation for a year. Sobeloff ultimately became chief judge in March 1958, serving in that capacity until December 1964, when he reached the retirement age of seventy. He remained an active judge until his death.

Sobeloff was fond of describing his position on the court of appeals as a "pebbled ground between two millstones," the district courts below and the Supreme Court above. His opinions were notable for clarifying tangled questions. He used his wit to cut through pretense or sham, but the defenseless, the downtrodden, and minorities were never the butts of his irony. "Is it not the mark of a good judge that he concerns himself to find within the framework of the law the way to a just result?" he once wrote a colleague. He applied what he called the "t'aint fair" principle. This sense of justice, compassion, and concern for the individual shines through his opinions.

Sobeloff repeatedly invoked basic maxims. A court-appointed lawyer owes his indigent client the same standard of representation as a paying client, he insisted. Observance of the law by those in authority must not be separated from law enforcement. And, as he wrote in a school desegregation case, even where no racially discriminatory motive was present, the *effect*—absent a compelling state interest—tests whether the equal protection clause was violated. Sobeloff's concurring and dissenting opinions in effect petitioned the Supreme Court to change the law to adopt his position, which it did in several instances. But he likely came closer to the Court than indirect influence: "I have every reason to believe that Simon Sobeloff was prom-

ised an appointment to the Supreme Court but rendered too many decisions for integration," Chief Justice Earl Warren later said. (The seat went instead to Potter Stewart in 1958.)

Sobeloff never forgot his childhood poverty. He constantly championed the underdog, the burdened, and the oppressed. As an advocate he was engaging and candid, mixing firmness and tact. As chief judge he worked with his counterpart on the Virginia Supreme Court of Appeals to keep the public schools open when state laws encouraged massive resistance to desegregation. Both courts ruled, on the same day in January 1959, against the closing of segregated schools in order to integrate them.

His interest in bringing fairness and rationality into the sentencing process led to his being named chairman of an American Bar Association advisory committee. In 1967 it recommended that a higher court should review any appealable conviction to reduce the impact of "hanging judges." To the end Sobeloff remained one of the most highly regarded judges in the nation. "How very much I have regretted the fact that we have not been colleagues on this Court," Supreme Court Justice Hugo L. Black told him. Trim and vigorous, an immaculately groomed man who carried his learning lightly, Sobeloff died in Baltimore.

[Sobeloff's papers are in the Library of Congress. He wrote many articles for legal publications. Biographical information can be found in the *Maryland Law Review* 34:2 (1974), which was devoted to Sobeloff. See also Michael S. Mayer, *Simon E. Sobeloff* (1980), a booklet by his grandson; Mayer, "With Much Deliberation and Some Speed; Eisenhower and the *Brown* Decision," *Journal of Southern History*, Feb. 1986; and Lincoln Caplan, *The Tenth Justice* (1987). Obituaries are in the *New York Times*, July 12, 1973; the *Baltimore Evening Sun*, July 11, 1973; and the *Washington Post*, July 21, 1973.]

ROGER K. NEWMAN

SOYER, MOSES (Dec. 25, 1899–Sept. 2, 1974), painter, was born in South Russia in the town of Borisoglebsk, the son of Abraham Soyer, a teacher and professional writer, and Bella Schneyer, an embroiderer of towels and tablecloths. Abraham Soyer, who taught Hebrew literature and history, often entertained the family with stories from Russian and Hebrew literature. Moses had a twin brother, Raphael, and a younger brother, Isaac, who also became painters.

As a very young boy, Moses was taught by a family friend, a colonel in the Cossack army, whose gift of a landscape drawing he copied. In 1910, when his father went with him to Moscow to have the family's pet cat inoculated, he saw his first paintings of established artists in the Tretiakov Museum. The next year, on a visit to Lutzin near Vitebsk, he and Raphael sold their drawing of a castle, which they duplicated a hundred times.

In 1912 the Soyers were banished from Russia, because of their association with suspected subversives, and came to Philadelphia to live with relatives. The next year they settled in the Bronx. Moses' father taught at a yeshiva on Henry Street in Manhattan. The three boys attended P.S. 9. Moses sold newspapers, tended soda fountains, and worked in the Columbia University Library. His father encouraged his aspirations in art. Between 1916 and 1920 he studied at the National Academy of Design School, where he came to appreciate the work of John Singer Sargent; the Ferrer School in Harlem, where he was influenced by Robert Henri, who showed him the drawings of the French realist Honoré Daumier in the periodical *The Liberator*; and at the Educational Alliance on the Lower East Side. To help make a living he worked as a proofreader for the *Morgen Journal* and wrote on art for the Philadelphia magazine *The Guardian* and the Yiddish newspaper *Der Amerikaner*. He went to Boston to see Sargent's murals for the Central Library, but the artist he idealized above all was Rembrandt.

On June 29, 1926, Soyer married Ida Chassner, a student of dancing and acting, who had posed for him. They had one son. A few weeks after the marriage the couple went off to Paris, and Moses rushed to the Louvre even before finding a hotel. They stayed for two years. He drew a great deal, often from the models at the Académie de la Grande Chaumière.

Back in America, he came to admire the dance pictures of Dégas. In December 1928 he had a one-man show at Neuman's Art Circle Gallery in New York. During the Great Depression, the artist painted for the WPA Art Project, and Ida earned money as a dancer at Jacob's Pillow and at the Rainbow Room.

Except for a handful of landscapes and still lifes, Soyer focused on the human figure. The people he painted invariably seem reflective and tinged with a gentle melancholy. Never are they engaged in violent action. Bypassing modernism, avoiding the American scene of a midwestern or southern locale as shown in the paintings of the Regionalists, he continued what was for him the humanist tradition in art. Although he participated in the social tumult of the 1930's, marching, for example, on May Day, painting or carrying banners protesting the hateful speeches of Father Coughlin, there is little in his art of the stridency and upset of those years— only a few pictures of the unemployed, passively resigned to their fate. There are many interiors with dancers, usually at rest; young couples embracing tenderly; seamstresses and costume makers; attractive young women, nude and seminude, sensuous but not overtly erotic, reflective, a bit of sadness in their eyes. Among his more memorable portraits are those of elderly modernist painters, seemingly resigned to their old age and the current disregard of the public, *Abraham Walkowitz* (1944, Newark Museum) and *Joseph Stella* (1943, Newark Museum). With Raphael he made a mural for the WPA at the Kingsessing Station Post Office in Philadelphia.

Soyer liked to explain what his fairly consistent art expressed. He wrote: "Most of my paintings reflect an interest in the casual moments in the life of plain people, the gestures and natural attitudes they fall into when they perform habitual tasks, when they are in thought, and when they are not observed by other people." He also wrote: "I like painting people who are not necessarily the most beautiful in the world, but people who to me are interesting, who have something in their faces that intrigues or baffles me." Yet his sitters are only somewhat individualized; they are invariably benign, even ennobled.

In addition to various teaching posts, Soyer wrote several instructional books. In *Painting the Human Figure* (1964), he gave directions on building the figure stage by stage; in *Oil Painting in Progress* (1972), he gave aspiring artists detailed advice on the use of various brushes and tools and the effective placement of colors on the canvas.

Mainly a portraitist, Soyer was warmly expressive, and always took care to uphold the dignity of his sitters. His works appear at the Metropolitan Museum of Art, the Museum of Modern Art, and the Whitney Museum in New York City, as well as in the Phillips Memorial Gallery in Washington, D.C.

[See Charlotte Willard, with Foreword by Philip Evergood, *Moses Soyer* (1962); Alfred Werner and David Soyer, *Moses Soyer* (1970); and ACA Galleries, *Moses Soyer* (1972). An obituary appears in the *New York Times*, Sept. 3, 1974.]

ABRAHAM A. DAVIDSON

SPAATZ, CARL ANDREW ("TOOEY") (June 28, 1891–July 14, 1974), aviator and first chief of staff of the United States Air Force, was born in Boyertown, Penn., the son of Charles B. Spatz, a newspaper editor and onetime member of the Pennsylvania legislature, and Anne Muntz. Spaatz changed the spelling of his surname in 1937, hoping the double "a" would aid the correct pronunciation of the name as "Spots." Spaatz attended public school in Boyertown, graduating from high school in 1906. He then entered a nearby preparatory school, Perkiomen Academy. In January 1908 he returned home to run the family newspaper after his father was seriously injured in a fire.

In March 1910 Spaatz entered the U.S. Military Academy at West Point. His career at West Point was undistinguished both in academics and athletics. He survived a court-martial for unauthorized drinking, was a smoker, and had a reputation as a poker player. He graduated in the lower half of his class and was still marching punishment tours on the day of his graduation in June 1914.

Commissioned a second lieutenant, Spaatz served in Hawaii with one of the army's two regiments that contained black soldiers until October 1915, when he returned to the army's flying school at North Island in San Diego. He won his wings in May 1916. Spaatz was posted immediately to the First Aero Squadron then deployed on the air service's first combat air mission, to Mexico, where the unit commanded by Captain Benjamin Foulois was a part of General John J. Pershing's Punitive Expedition against Pancho Villa. Spaatz arrived after the worst part of the fiasco was over, and was transferred to San Antonio, Tex., in November 1916, to command one of the squadrons being formed as a part of President Woodrow Wilson's preparedness campaign.

Shortly after his arrival in San Antonio, Spaatz met Ruth Harrison. They were originally acquainted in Hawaii, where her father, Colonel Ralph Harrison, had also served. When Spaatz was notified that his squadron was to be shipped overseas, he proposed to her, and they were married on the same day, July 26, 1917; they had three children.

The greater part of Major Spaatz's work in France was at the Issoudun training center, a kind of finishing school for fighter pilots. Spaatz was in charge of training and later served as commander. This was probably the most important single experience in his preparation for high military rank. The center included 5,000 persons (including Eddie Rickenbacker and several other World War I aces) and 1,000 airplanes of many different types. Before he returned to the United States, Carl was briefly assigned to a pursuit squadron where he shot down two or three German Fokkers before crash landing in no-man's-land after his plane ran out of fuel.

During the interwar period, Carl Spaatz was one of the few who retained his wartime rank, major, in the shrunken peacetime force. There was only one American pursuit group in the early 1920's and he was its commander, achieving renown as one of the leading fighter experts in the service. He was a supporter of General William ("Billy") Mitchell at Mitchell's court-martial in 1925. He made it to the front page of the *New York Times* as an outspoken member of the Mitchell team, which accused the army and navy of mismanaging aviation. After General Mitchell resigned from the army in 1926, his supporters, including Henry Arnold, the World War II commanding general of the U.S. Army Air Forces, and Ira Eaker, Spaatz's partner in the initial attacks on Nazi Europe, continued to influence Spaatz.

In 1929, Eaker was one of Spaatz's crew on the famous *Question Mark* endurance flight. The Fokker Tri-motor stayed aloft for seven days for an endurance record for aircraft that stood until the advent of space orbiting vehicles. The flight also won Spaatz the Distinguished Flying Cross that year. Although Spaatz was known as a fighter expert in World War I and throughout the 1920's, in the 1930's he became identified with those favoring the notion that strategic bombing against the vital centers of an enemy's industrial web would be decisive. He was one of the early cadre of the General Headquarters (GHQ) Air Force founded in 1935, and in 1938 was called to Washington by General Arnold to be the air staff's chief of plans. In 1940 Arnold sent Spaatz overseas to witness the Battle of Britain. Spaatz gained some notoriety when he diverged from the pessimistic view of Ambassador

Joseph Kennedy about Britain's chances of surviving the war. He also brought back firsthand information on modern combat that had important effects on the emergent American air forces. Soon afterward, Arnold elevated Brigadier General Spaatz to chief of the air staff; he was in that position when the Japanese struck Pearl Harbor.

Carl Spaatz was widely deemed as Arnold's ablest subordinate and was entrusted with the deployment of the United States' strategic air forces against Hitler. Spaatz took the Eighth Air Force to England during the summer of 1942 with General Eaker as his Eighth Bomber Command commander. Spaatz was in charge of the initial bomber attacks against Nazi-occupied Europe. When Operation Torch was mounted, Spaatz took most of his aircraft and crews to North Africa, where his relationship with General Eisenhower matured.

In January 1944, when victory was assured in the Mediterranean, Spaatz returned to England to command the United States Strategic Air Forces in Europe. His new command included both the Eighth Air Force in England and the Fifteenth Air Force in Italy. He was at the helm as they turned the tide in the battle for the command of the skies over Normandy, and Germany itself. Spaatz was the only officer who attended the surrender ceremonies of both Germany and Japan.

After the Nazi collapse, Arnold transferred Spaatz to Guam to command the strategic air forces in the Pacific theater. General Spaatz arrived in midsummer having insisted on written orders to use nuclear weapons on Japan. He therefore commanded the only nuclear attacks in history. After the war ended, he remained in the Pacific only long enough to attend the surrender ceremony on the Battleship USS *Missouri*. Spaatz's new task at the Pentagon was to plan the adjustment of the Army Air Forces to the nuclear age, to help win a separate air force, and to help create a unified Department of Defense.

General Henry Arnold retired in early 1946, leaving Spaatz in charge of the transition from Army Air Forces to United States Air Force. Carl Spaatz was the last commanding general of the Army Air Forces and the first chief of staff of the United States Air Force. He established the initial organization of the air force along functional lines, with strategic offense, strategic defense, and tactical air power in separate major

commands. That organization persisted until 1992, when the USAF reorganized most of its combat air power into a unified Air Combat Command. Spaatz established many of the other institutions and organizations of the new service before his retirement in the spring of 1948.

Carl Spaatz remained an influence on the development of American airpower and national security policy long afterward. He was the national security affairs correspondent for *Newsweek* for many years and a ·stout supporter of strategic airpower. He also was the head of the site selection committees for the Air Force Academy and later a longtime member of the Board of Visitors for that institution.

Carl Spaatz suffered his first heart attack at the Air Force Academy in Colorado Springs in the early 1970's. He never fully regained his strength, and died at the Walter Reed Medical Center. He was the first USAF chief of staff to be buried in the Air Force Academy cemetery.

[The papers of General Spaatz are located in the manuscripts division of the Library of Congress. General Spaatz's most significant writing is "Strategic Air Power: Fulfillment of a Concept," *Foreign Affairs*, Apr. 1946. See also his many editorials in *Newsweek* during the postwar decade. There are two oral history interviews with Spaatz at the Library of Congress with Dr. Bruce Hopper (boxes 136 and 239), and four at the USAF Historical Research Agency, Maxwell Air Force Base (Feb. 21, 1962; May 19, 1965; Sept. 27, 1968; and Apr. 24, 1972). The only full-length biography is David R. Mets, *Master of Airpower* (1988). Another full-length book is devoted to his service in World War II: Richard Davis, *Carl A. Spaatz and the Air War in Europe* (1992). The best short piece is Alfred Goldberg, "Spaatz," in Field Marshal Sir Michael Carver, ed., *The War Lords* (1976). An obituary is in the *New York Times*, July 15, 1974.]

DAVID R. METS

SPEWACK, SAMUEL (Sept. 16, 1899–Oct. 14, 1971), journalist, playwright, and screenwriter, was born in the Ukranian town of Bachmut, Russia, to Noel Spewack, a small businessman, and Sema Zelavetski. The family moved to New York City when Sam was very young. He graduated from Stuyvesant High School in 1916 and matriculated at Columbia University, but quit in 1918 to become a reporter for the *New York World*. From 1922 to 1926, the six-foot, one-inch Spewack was a foreign correspondent, stationed first in Moscow (he was fluent in Russian) and then in Berlin. Although he concentrated on theatrical and movie writing for most of his career, he took up journalism again in the late 1940's for a major series in the *New York Post* describing the way in which Londoners responded to their experiences under fire during World War II.

In 1922, he met and married his wife and future collaborator, the Bucharest-born Bella Cohen, a reporter for a socialist newspaper. The Spewacks, who had no children, gained fame as writing partners—but their first play, *Swing High Sweeney*, was not staged, and *The Solitaire Man* (1926) closed before reaching New York. However, *Poppa* (1928) had ninety-six Broadway performances. It was a comedy-drama combining a political theme with Jewish life on New York's Lower East Side. Both ingredients, especially the former, would reappear in several later Spewack plays.

In 1928, the Spewacks cowrote the script of *The War Song* with George Jessel. In 1932, the Spewacks revised *Swing High Sweeney* as *Clear All Wires!* This loosely autobiographical satirical melodrama was set in Moscow (rare for an American play), and poked fun at foreign correspondents and the Communist bureaucracy. It lasted ninety-one performances. In 1938, the authors converted it into a hit musical (291 performances) called *Leave It to Me!* With a score by Cole Porter, it introduced Mary Martin singing "My Heart Belongs to Daddy."

Other Spewack Broadway efforts of the 1930's included a drama, *Spring Song* (1934), and two comedies, *Boy Meets Girl* (1935) and *Miss Swan Expects* (1939), the latter of which marked Sam Spewack's directing debut. The most memorable was *Boy Meets Girl*, inspired by the collaborators' experiences in Hollywood. This farce, which lasted 669 performances and won the Roi Cooper Megrue Prize, concerned two frantic screenwriters, based on Charles MacArthur and Ben Hecht. Its situations were farfetched, but it managed to mock filmdom hilariously. The play typified the Spewack style of comedy, described by the *New York Times* as "fast-paced, madcap, verging on slapstick and knockabout farce." In a much-quoted exchange from their crackling dialogue, one writer says to the other: "Listen, I've been writing stories for 11 years. Boy meets girl. Boy loses girl. Boy gets girl." The other replies: "Or—girl meets boy. Girl loses boy. Girl gets boy. Love will find a

way. . . . Put your money on love. You can't lose—I'm getting hungry." The Spewacks wrote a few serious works, but excelled at comedy. With their extensive royalties, they purchased a country home in Bucks County, Pa., although their primary residence was in New York City.

Many of their twenty screenplays were produced in the 1930's. These included *Clear All Wires!* (1933), *When Ladies Meet* (1933), *Should Ladies Behave?* (1933), *The Nuisance* (1934), *The Car and the Fiddle* (1934), *Rendezvous* (1935), *Vogues of 1937* (1937), *Boy Meets Girl* (1938), and *Three Loves Has Nancy* (1938). Spewack preferred writing for the theater, however, because of its relative lack of censorship.

During World War II, Spewack served in Moscow as information officer to Ambassador Averell Harriman. The appointment was greeted with anxiety because of Spewack's jibes at the USSR's expense in *Clear All Wires!* He was hired after first serving in London as the Office of War Information's (OWI) motion-picture representative in London. In that capacity he wrote *The World at War* (1942), a grim wartime documentary produced by the OWI's Bureau of Motion Pictures.

Spewack's other activities of the 1940's included his and Bella's excellent film scripts for *My Favorite Wife* (1940) and *Weekend at the Waldorf* (1945). They were represented on Broadway with the unfortunate *Woman Bites Dog* (1946) and the libretto of the smash hit (1,077 performances) musical, *Kiss Me, Kate* (1948). Bella alone had been hired to do the book, but Sam made so many contributions he became a credited coauthor. (Although he had nothing to do with the score, Spewack was a talented violinist and often participated in amateur string quartets.) *Kiss Me, Kate* won the librettists the Antoinette Perry Award (Tony) and the Page One Award. The *New York Times* said they had written "the best musical comedy book of the year." *Kiss Me, Kate* is a delightful musicalization of Shakespeare's *The Taming of the Shrew*. Its novel premise is that a brawling husband and wife acting partnership (played by Alfred Drake and Patricia Morison and inspired by Alfred Lunt and Lynn Fontanne) is performing a musical version of Shakespeare's play, and that their own lives resemble those of Petruchio and Kate. Spewack restaged the show for the London production.

In 1949, Spewack wrote and directed *Two*

Blind Mice, his first play written without Bella's participation. Starring Melvyn Douglas as a journalist, it tossed barbs at Washingtonian bureaucracy.

Spewack had written three mystery novels in the 1920's under the pseudonym A. A. Abbott. Using his real name, he wrote *The Busy, Busy People* (1948), a satirical novel based on the observations he made about the black market while working in Moscow.

During the following decade, the couple were responsible for *My Three Angels* (1953) and *Festival* (1955), while Spewack soloed on *Under the Sycamore* (1952)—which premiered in London and received its Off-Broadway premiere in 1960—and *Once There Was a Russian* (1960), a one-performance disaster. *My Three Angels* was the standout effort. Running 344 performances, it was an adaptation of a 1912 Paris hit about three escaped convicts from a French penal colony who hide out with a local family.

The Spewacks worked together on the scripts for various television shows, most notably their full-scale production adaptations of their own *Kiss Me, Kate* (1958), and *My Three Angels* (1960). *The Enchanted Nutcracker* (1963) was written especially for television. Bella once tried to explain their writing method by saying she was the negative talent and Sam the positive, she destroying the flaws in the ideas he initiated. Sam denied this, emphasizing that theirs was so close a collaboration that it was impossible to say who had written what.

Spewack died in New York City, several months before his fiftieth wedding anniversary.

[There are no books available about Samuel Spewack. Obituaries are in the *New York Times,* Oct. 15, 1971, and *Variety,* Oct. 21, 1971.]

SAMUEL L. LEITER

SPINGARN, ARTHUR BARNETT (Mar. 28, 1878–Dec. 1, 1971), attorney and civil rights activist, was born in New York City, the second son of Sarah Barnett and Elias Spingarn, an Austrian Jewish immigrant, successful tobacco merchant, and member of the New York City Chamber of Commerce. His brother Joel served as president of the National Association for the Advancement of Colored People (NAACP) from 1930 to 1939 and endowed its Spingarn Medal, presented yearly to an outstanding black American.

According to his father's wishes, Spingarn prepared to become a lawyer, receiving a B.A. in 1897, an M.A. in 1899, and a law degree in 1900, all from Columbia University. That same year he was admitted to the New York bar. The discrimination against blacks he discovered while prosecuting a civil rights case made such an impression on him that he dedicated his life to battling prejudice.

Soon after the NAACP was formed by a number of white liberals in 1909, Spingarn became involved as unpaid counsel. From 1911 to 1940 he was concurrently vice-president of the association and chairman of its national legal committee. In 1940 he replaced his brother Joel as president of the association, serving until 1966. From 1940 to 1957 he was president of the NAACP Legal Defense and Educational Fund, Inc. He served as a captain in the U.S. Army from 1917 to 1919; on Jan. 27, 1918, he married Marion Mayer, a social worker. They had no children.

As the driving force in the NAACP's legal activities, Spingarn was at the center of the organization's efforts to end discrimination. Sometimes he would argue cases himself, but more often he recruited the best legal talent available at little or no cost to the financially strapped organization.

Three years of activity resulted in *Buchanan v. Warley* (1917), the Supreme Court case in which a Louisville, Ky., ordinance prohibiting blacks from residing in designated areas in the city was declared unconstitutional. In 1925 he coordinated the case of Dr. Ossian Sweet, who met violence after purchasing a home in a white area of Detroit. Clarence Darrow led the NAACP legal team in court. Spingarn personally argued *Nixon* v. *Herndon* (1927) and *Nixon* v. *Condon* (1932), the cases that resulted in the declaration that the Texas all-white primary was unconstitutional. Less successfully, he and the NAACP called for a federal antilynching law, but one was never passed. But decades of hard work by NAACP lawyers culminated in the seminal *Brown* v. *Board of Education* decision of 1954.

For more than fifty years, both within and outside the NAACP, Spingarn worked closely with W. E. B. DuBois. When DuBois, editor of the NAACP's *Crisis* magazine, began to take a Marxist position in the 1930's and called for an all-black economic order, Spingarn did not agree. The resulting controversy within the NAACP ended when, on June 26, 1934,

DuBois resigned his editorship. Through it all, Spingarn never lost his admiration for him.

Spingarn was a firm believer in using the law to overturn discrimination. As a young man, he had repeatedly smashed liquor glasses in New York bars in retaliation for the inflated prices they charged black customers. In 1914, he organized an antidiscrimination picket line in Memphis, Tenn. For most of his life, however, he used the more reasoned legal approach. When civil rights protesters moved away from the NAACP's legal strategy in the 1960's, he did not approve. Spingarn also disliked Adam Clayton Powell, Jr., and Stokely Carmichael, and he thought Martin Luther King, Jr., was "a bit of a demagogue." By then, he was in his eighties and no doubt hurt to see his organization, which had fought bravely and often alone for so many years, being called irrelevant. Powell's call for black-only leadership for the organization was especially hurtful, though executive director Roy Wilkins's defense of him was soothing. Still, Spingarn resigned in 1966 at the age of eighty-seven and was named honorary president for life.

His work with the NAACP took 80 percent of his time, but he also maintained a limited private practice. An avid bibliophile, he amassed a magnificent collection of black-authored materials over the years. He wanted to show white America that blacks had produced important scholarly works. In 1948, he donated more than 5,000 items to Howard University that were housed in the Moorland-Spingarn Research Center. Considering the discrimination blacks had suffered, Spingarn concluded, "We wonder, not that Africans have produced so little, but that they have been able to produce so much."

Spingarn wrote articles on legal and race relations and a book titled *Laws Relating to Sex Morality in New York City* (1915), as well as an introduction to *African Saga* (1927).

Spingarn was five feet, seven inches tall and of stocky build, with brown eyes and, in his later years, white hair. He had an outgoing personality that proved extremely helpful in his difficult work. He died in New York City.

[Spingarn's papers are deposited in the Moorland-Spingarn Research Center, Howard University, Washington, D.C. His brother Joel Spingarn's papers are in the Library of Congress where the Papers of the NAACP are also deposited. An overview of his life is Francis H. Thompson, "Arthur Barnett Spingarn: Advocate for Black Rights," *The Historian*, Nov. 1987. An obituary appears in the *New York Times*, Dec. 2, 1971.]

JOHN F. MARSZALEK

SPOTTSWOOD, STEPHEN GILL (July, 1897–Dec. 1, 1974), clergyman and civil rights leader, was born in Boston, Mass., the only child of Abraham Lincoln Spottswood, a porter, and Mary Elizabeth Gray. He attended public schools in Boston; in 1917, he received a B.A. degree from Albright College in Reading, Pa., and in 1919 a Th.D. degree from the Gordon School of Theology in Boston. During the 1923–1924 academic year he did graduate study at the Yale Divinity School.

Meanwhile, in 1917 and 1918, Spottswood had served as an assistant professor of churches in Cambridge and Boston, Mass., respectively, and in 1919 was ordained as a minister in the African Methodist Episcopal Zion Church. He pastored A.M.E. Zion churches in West Newton and Lowell, Mass. (1919–1920); Portland, Maine (1920–1922); New Haven, Conn. (1922–1925); Winston-Salem, N.C. (1925–1928); Indianapolis, Ind. (1928–1932); Buffalo, N.Y. (1932–1936); and Washington, D.C. (1936–1952). His pastorate was notable in Washington, where under his leadership the membership of John Wesley A.M.E. Zion church increased from 300 to more than 3,000, and the church was designated the National Church of Zion Methodism.

On June 10, 1919, Spottswood married Viola Estelle Booker, a milliner. They had five children; one son, Stephen Paul, became an A.M.E. Zion minister. Viola died on Oct. 24, 1953, in a heroic effort to rescue a grandchild during a household fire. On Dec. 15, 1969, Spottswood married Mattie Johnson Elliott, a former public school principal, in Washington, D.C.

Spottswood became active in civil rights causes early in his ministerial career, long before civil rights became a national issue. He joined the National Association for the Advancement of Colored People (NAACP) in 1919, and soon thereafter participated in a Washington protest against opponents of federal antilynching legislation. In 1922 he engaged in sit-ins to desegregate a motion picture theater in New Haven, Conn., and during the 1930's he took part in sit-ins and picketing against racial discrimination in Buffalo, N.Y. During his pastorate in Washington he became a founder of the Committee for Racial Democracy in the nation's capital, and in 1946 was elected president of the District of Columbia branch of the NAACP. Under his leadership the D.C. branch spearheaded campaigns against racial discrimination by government and private business in employment, housing, public accommodations, education, health and welfare services, and recreation facilities. By the early 1950's these campaigns had brought some democratic changes in the nation's capital.

On May 17, 1952, Spottswood was elected fifty-eighth bishop of the A.M.E. Zion Church, giving him religious jurisdiction over several hundred churches and varied denominational programs in different regions of the United States and Guyana. As bishop he supervised a comprehensive restructuring of the budget operations of the A.M.E. Zion Church, sponsored the construction of new churches, and promoted housing and community development. He served as president of the Ohio Council of Churches and represented his denomination on the Executive Committee of the World Methodist Council and the General Board of the National Council of Churches. He retired on May 10, 1972.

In 1954 Spottswood was elected a member of the NAACP Board of Directors and in 1961 became its chairman, succeeding Robert C. Weaver, the distinguished economist. As board chairman he worked closely with the NAACP's executive director, Roy Wilkins. They met with President John F. Kennedy in July 1961 to urge his support of stronger civil rights legislation. This was in the wake of recent violence and legal harassment directed against blacks and whites participating in sit-ins and "freedom rides" in the southern states. In 1964, Spottswood called for federal government intervention to deal with the murder of civil rights workers in Mississippi, and in 1965, to protect voting rights demonstrators in Alabama.

His leadership of the NAACP was more moderate than some of its younger members preferred but was consistent with the association's traditional goals of racial justice, equality, and integration. It often had elements of militancy, however, and was expressed effectively in dynamic keynote addresses at annual association meetings. At the 1970 meeting in Cincinnati, Ohio, he startled the delegates, as well as the

press and the general public, with the accusation that the administration of President Richard Nixon was "anti-Negro" and had a "calculated policy to work against the needs and aspirations of the largest minority of its citizens." He cited the administration's retreat on school desegregation, the nomination of conservative southerners to the Supreme Court, and the apparent approval of a policy of benign neglect for black Americans proposed by presidential adviser Daniel P. Moynihan.

In his 1972 keynote address, Spottswood criticized the "counsels of division and separatism" that were coming to black Americans from leaders of the "black power" movement that arose during the late 1960's. He and other NAACP officials clearly saw these counsels as a threat to the association's historic efforts to convince white Americans that blacks should be recognized as equal and legitimate partners in American society. Hence he became a vigorous and effective spokesman for the NAACP during the 1970's, when the organization's goals and strategies were increasingly challenged by the strident voices and tactics of black power activists. His views favoring racial integration were eventually approved by most black Americans.

Tall, erect, and robust, with graying hair, Spottswood was a distinguished-looking person. He was affable, restrained, and thoughtful, and did not lightly hurl accusations. Nevertheless, his deep, firm voice could fill with emotion to present a forceful message.

Spottswood died at his home in Washington, D.C. For more than half a century he had preached from the pulpit and public platform a gospel of freedom and equality. He mixed activism with pragmatism in his struggles against race discrimination. He gave valiant and effective leadership to the nation's largest civil rights organization during some of its greatest challenges.

[Spottswood's personal papers are in the Amistad Research Center at Tulane University, New Orleans, La. Records concerning his work as member and chairman of the NAACP Board of Directors are among records of the association in the Manuscript Division of the Library of Congress, Washington, D.C. A representative keynote address to the 1974 annual meeting of the NAACP is published in *Crisis*, Feb. 1975. Excerpts from other keynote addresses are published in "Blast From a Bishop," *Time*, July 13, 1970; "All Together Now!" *Vital Speeches of the Day*, Aug. 15, 1971; and "Trumpet Call to Battle,"

Vital Speeches of the Day, Aug. 16, 1972. Obituaries are in the *New York Times*, Dec. 3, 1974; and *Crisis*, Feb. 1975.]

HAROLD T. PINKETT

SPROUL, ROBERT GORDON (May 22, 1891–Sept. 10, 1975), university president, was born in San Francisco, first of two sons of Robert Sproul and Sarah Elizabeth Moore. The elder Sproul was a graduate of Glasgow University and had taught school in Lanarkshire, Scotland, before emigrating to the United States in 1887. He made his career as an accountant for the Santa Fe Railroad.

Robert Gordon Sproul attended James Lick Grammar School and Mission High School in San Francisco, graduating from the latter in 1908. As a student he sold newspapers, and for a year after high school graduation he worked as a chainman on a survey crew. He enrolled in the University of California in the fall of 1909, majoring in civil engineering. His academic achievements were reflected in his election to Phi Beta Kappa; he belonged to a residential club named Abracadabra and won his letter as a two-miler on the track team. He was over six feet tall and was for a time drum major of the marching band. He was elected president of both the junior class and the campus YMCA.

After receiving a B.S. in engineering in May 1913, Sproul was employed for a year as an efficiency engineer for the Civil Service Board of the city of Oakland. In 1914 he began his forty-four-year career in the University of California when he was appointed as a cashier.

On Sept. 6, 1916, he married Ida Amelia Wittschen, whom he had met while he was working in Oakland. They had three children. Although Sproul was generally known to friends and colleagues as Bob, Ida Sproul called him Gordon, as had his parents, who named him for General Charles G. Gordon, one-time British governor of Sudan.

He was promoted to the position of assistant comptroller in 1918, and on Oct. 1, 1920, the regents made him comptroller, secretary of the regents, and the university's land agent. During the early 1920's Sproul demonstrated his exceptional powers of persuasion as a member of a state commission appointed by Governor William T. Stephens to deal with a campaign to detach the College of Agriculture, in Davis, from the university. In 1923 Sproul persuaded the commission to decide in the university's fa-

vor, and the Davis campus remained in the university system.

In 1925 Sproul was made vice-president and comptroller. During this period he declined an invitation to become manager of the California Prune and Apricot Growers' Association, at a salary reported to be five times what he was receiving from the university.

In June 1929 President William Wallace Campbell announced that he would retire the following summer, and the regents offered Sproul the presidency, which he accepted. There were some reservations among the faculty and the regents about appointing a president without a graduate degree, but the academic senate confirmed the regents' vote of confidence. The new president-designate, "extroverted, bluff, with a booming voice and resonant laugh," was given six months' leave of absence to prepare himself for the position.

As one part of this preparation he established an office at UCLA, then in process of moving from its early location on Vermont Street to the present Westwood campus. He spent several months in Westwood seeking to ease tensions between the Southern Branch, which felt that its aspirations were frequently neglected, and the faculty at Berkeley, which had difficulty accepting the ambitious new campus.

On Oct. 22, 1930, Sproul was inaugurated as the university's eleventh president. During the twenty-eight years of his presidency the University of California experienced unprecedented growth: student enrollment increased from 19,000 to 47,000, the faculty from 900 to 3,500, the libraries from one million to four million volumes, and the number of campuses from three to eight. During his presidency six U.C. faculty members received Nobel prizes and more than forty were elected to the National Academy of Sciences.

The growth was not always smooth, however. The Sproul years spanned the Great Depression and World War II and saw explosive growth in California. More immediate difficulties included continuing differences between UCLA and Berkeley faculty and alumni, alumni influence on athletics, and evolution of the state teachers' colleges into a full-curriculum system, offering both bachelors' and masters' degrees.

Sproul's relationship to faculty and students was generally good: they rallied twice to keep him from leaving, in 1939 for a San Francisco bank presidency, and in 1947 for the presidency of Columbia University (later accepted by Dwight Eisenhower). Sproul's student and faculty relations were tested by student pacifists during the late 1930's and more seriously during the ascendancy of State Senator Jack Tenney's Committee on Un-American Activities in the late 1940's. In 1949 Sproul was persuaded to support a special Loyalty Oath which the Regents adopted when the Tenney Committee charged the University with being Communist. Forty faculty members refused to sign the oath, and their dismissal led to bitter internal division. In 1956 the California Supreme Court ruled the oath unconstitutional and restored the professions who had been fired, but the wounds were slow to heal.

Shortly before he retired, Sproul decided to withdraw from the Pacific Coast Conference, after a long, losing fight to control payments and perquisites for football players. Throughout his presidency he resisted the expansion of the state college system and was successful in preserving the University of California's exclusive jurisdiction over doctoral programs.

Sproul retired in 1958. He was recipient of many honorary degrees, belonged at one time to 268 organizations, and to a number of boards of directors. A Republican, he nominated his friend Earl Warren for President at the 1948 Republican convention, and President Eisenhower made him a special ambassador to Korea in 1956. He died at his home in Berkeley at the age of 84.

[Sproul's papers and several oral histories are in the University Archives, Bancroft Library, University of California, Berkeley, and in the University Archives at UCLA. Principal biographical sources are George Albert Pettitt, *Twenty-eight Years in the Life of a University President* (1966); Agnes Roddy Robb, *Robert Gordon Sproul and the University of California: A Memoir* (1976); Ida Amelia Sproul, *The President's Wife* (1981); and *Robert Gordon Sproul Oral History Project* (1986). Obituaries appear in the University of California's *University Bulletin*, Sept. 29, 1975, and in the *New York Times*, Sept. 12, 1975.]

DAVID W. HERON

STANLEY, WENDELL MEREDITH (Aug. 16, 1904–June 15, 1971), virologist, was born in Ridgeville, Ind., the son of James G. Stanley and Claire Plessinger, publishers of the local newspaper. Stanley was a talented athlete and a popular, if not outstanding, student at Earlham College in Richmond, Ind., where he studied chemistry and mathematics, played football, and received a B.S. in 1926.

Just a few months before graduation, Stanley visited the University of Illinois and met Professor Roger Adams, whose enthusiasm for chemistry led Stanley to drop his plans for a career as a football coach and to attend graduate school instead. He received an M.S. from the University of Illinois in 1927 and a Ph.D in organic chemistry in 1929.

While in graduate school Stanley published thirteen papers, one of which—on a chemical cure for leprosy—he coauthored with Adams and a fellow graduate student named Marian Staples Jay. The trio appeared together on another paper, a marriage certificate: on June 15, 1929, Stanley married Jay, and Adams was best man at their wedding. The couple had four children; their son, Wendell Meredith, Jr., a molecular biologist at the University of California at Irvine, has been recognized for his work in helping to crack the genetic code.

Stanley spent a year doing postdoctoral work at Illinois before going to Germany—at the time the world center for chemical research—for an academic year as a National Research Council fellow at the University of Munich. He returned to the United States in 1931, in the midst of the Great Depression, but managed to obtain a position at the Rockefeller Institute for Medical Research in New York City. A year later he transferred to the Institute's laboratory of animal and plant pathology in Princeton, N.J., where he began research into a highly infectious virus that devastated tobacco crops.

Viruses had been identified in 1898 by the Dutch botanist Martinus Willem Beijerinck, but when Stanley began his work on them in 1932, no one really knew what they were, other than that they were extremely contagious and too small to be seen under a microscope. Stanley began his search for an answer by grinding up a ton of diseased tobacco plants and squeezing the juice from the mush that remained. Then through progressive filtration, he managed to isolate the tobacco mosaic virus (TMV) and finally, using a crystallization technique developed by John H. Northrop, produced thin, rodlike crystals of virus protein that retained their infectivity. This discovery in 1935 met with skepticism from scientists who doubted that living organisms could exist in crystalline form. But Stanley, a convincing speaker, took to the stump, appearing in dozens of scientific forums in the United States and England to argue his position. Within a year his discovery had been confirmed by others.

Stanley's work on the virus, a self-replicating living thing that behaves like a simple chemical, captured the imagination of scientists and laymen alike. His discovery was hailed as a step toward understanding the nature of life itself and led many to wonder whether viruses might not be the link between living and nonliving matter. Stanley speculated that viruses could have been the first form of life on earth. By 1937, researchers had found that TMV is not, as Stanley had assumed, pure protein; it also contains a small amount of a distinctive but little-studied substance, a nucleic acid known as RNA, that later proved to be the key to virus activity.

The onset of World War II brought a change of priorities to the Princeton laboratory. With human and practical matters paramount, Stanley was asked to isolate the influenza virus and produce a vaccine. By 1945, he and his colleagues developed a new centrifuge-type influenza vaccine that was partly effective.

Scores of major scientific awards were heaped upon Stanley during his lifetime for his contributions to our knowledge of viruses, but the biggest feather in his cap came relatively early. In 1946, Stanley's research on the tobacco virus was recognized with the Nobel Prize in chemistry, which he shared with Northrop and with James B. Sumner, who had crystallized the first enzyme. In the decade since his initial discovery, more than three hundred viruses had been identified, including those that cause smallpox, yellow fever, measles, mumps, pneumonia, and the common cold. Many would compare Stanley's achievement with Louis Pasteur's discovery of bacteria and their role in disease.

A few months before receiving the Nobel Prize, Stanley had a chance encounter with a fellow airplane passenger that determined the remainder of his career. While their plane was grounded, Stanley met Robert G. Sproul, then president of the University of California. In the course of their conversation Stanley mentioned the need for a new institution devoted entirely to virus chemistry. His hopes turned to reality in 1948 when Sproul invited him to establish and direct a virus laboratory at the Berkeley campus. Stanley remained there until his retirement, training a generation of virologists,

directing projects that further clarified the nature of viruses, and contributing to the development of many new vaccines, including one for polio.

During the 1950's, Stanley was active in the affairs of science on a national scale, and served on numerous boards and committees, including the World Health Organization, the National Science Foundation, and the National Cancer Institute. Although he traveled extensively to give lectures, he remained deeply committed to the affairs of the Berkeley campus. He staunchly opposed the requirement that Berkeley and other universities had imposed on faculty members to sign oaths of loyalty to the United States. Although he signed the oath himself, he defended those who did not. A court decision eventually struck down the measure as unconstitutional.

By the 1960's, Stanley, "the image of a kindly country doctor with a twinkle in his eye," according to the New York Times, had become deeply involved in promoting increased funding for cancer research. Research into the tumor viruses of animals had led him to feel that viruses might be responsible for many forms of cancer in humans as well. This hypothesis, and the accompanying hope that isolating the viruses involved with human cancers could be used in the development of vaccines, led in part to the program that launched the war on cancer, the National Cancer Act (1971). Stanley died in Salamanca, Spain, while attending a conference on biochemistry, a few months before the act was passed.

[Stanley's papers are at the Bancroft Library at the University of California at Berkeley. The collection contains correspondence, subject files, manuscripts of writings and speeches, photographs, as well as course and departmental materials. Stanley wrote dozens of scientific papers and one book: *Viruses and the Nature of Life* (1961), with Evan G. Valens. *The Dictionary of Scientific Biography*, vol. 18, contains a thorough description of his life and work by Seymour S. Cohen and provides a bibliography of his scientific papers. Among the many secondary sources that mention Stanley are Greer Williams, *Virus Hunters* (1959); and Tyler Wasson, ed., *Nobel Prize Winners* (1987). An obituary is in the *New York Times*, June 16, 1971.]

PATRICK HUYGHE

STARK, HAROLD RAYNSFORD (Nov. 12, 1880–Aug. 20, 1972), admiral, was born in

Wilkes-Barre, Pa., the son of Colonel Benjamin Franklin Stark, commander of the Ninth Pennsylvania Regiment, and Mary Francis Warner. Stark entered the U.S. Naval Academy in 1899 and graduated in 1903. His first major assignment was aboard the gunboat *Newport* on the Eastern seaboard and in the Caribbean, from 1904 to 1906. Shortly after reporting to the battleship *Minnesota*, he married Katherine Adelle Rhoads of his hometown in July 1907; they had two children. He then circumnavigated the globe with his ship as part of the Great White Fleet. Between 1909 and 1915 he successively commanded two torpedo boats and two destroyers in the Atlantic, during which he formed a close friendship with the assistant secretary of the navy, Franklin D. Roosevelt.

After a year as engineering officer of a cruiser, Stark served at the Naval Torpedo Station in Newport, R.I., which qualified him for command of the Asiatic Fleet's Torpedo Flotilla in 1917. Upon successfully taking its five aged vessels from Manila to Gibraltar that summer, he served in London as aide to Admiral William S. Sims, commander of U.S. naval forces in Europe during World War I.

Stark moved through a series of choice positions of the battleship-oriented navy after the war, becoming an expert in matters of ordnance (gunnery). He was well suited for the diplomatic and key administrative assignments that assured his steady advancement. Between 1919 and 1923, he served as executive officer of two separate battleships and of the naval training station at Norfolk, and was a senior student at the Naval War College. He commanded the ammunition ship *Nitro* in home waters during 1924 and 1925, followed by three years as chief ordnance inspector at the Dahlgren proving ground and Indian Head powder factory.

Promoted to captain, Stark was chief of staff of the Battle Fleet destroyer force (1928–1930) and aide to successive secretaries of the navy Charles Francis Adams and Claude A. Swanson (1930–1933). He commanded the battleship *West Virginia* for a year, culminating with his posting as chief of the Bureau of Ordnance in the rank of rear admiral late in 1934. He returned to sea in September 1937 as commander of a division of cruisers, the following May moving up to command of all the cruisers in the Battle Force. President Roosevelt, long an admirer, bypassed fifty-nine senior officers to appoint Stark chief of naval operations, the na-

vy's highest administrative post. He assumed it and the rank of full admiral on Aug. 1, 1939.

One month later World War II broke out in Europe, forcing Stark to grapple with the daunting problem of optimizing the navy's size and strength. Through Carl Vinson's initiatives in Congress, Stark settled for a moderate increase in naval expenditure of 11 percent early in 1940, but after the fall of France that summer he enthusiastically oversaw the 70 percent increase Congress authorized. The prospect of the United States being drawn into a global conflict led to Stark's most singular achievement: that November, a year before the United States entered the war formally, he devised "Plan Dog," which evolved into "Rainbow 5," the Allied strategic priority to defeat Germany before defeating Japan. Throughout 1941 he developed a close working relationship with the British, especially at the Atlantic Charter meeting in August and as presiding officer for the U.S. military leaders in the initial post–Pearl Harbor meetings with the British between Dec. 24, 1941 and Jan. 14, 1942.

When his office was merged with that of commander in chief U.S. Fleet two months later, Stark was transferred to London as commander of U.S. naval forces in Europe. In this capacity he cemented Anglo-American wartime naval relations and acted as de facto ambassador to the Free French of Charles de Gaulle and other governments in exile. In October 1943 he assumed the additional title of commander Twelfth Fleet, the American operational forces gathering for the Normandy landings, which occurred the following June. Prior to his relief in August 1945, he was also the navy's adviser to the European Advisory Commission.

Throughout the war and up until his retirement in April 1946, Stark participated in the investigations over the Pearl Harbor disaster of Dec. 7, 1941, specifically responding to criticisms that as chief of naval operations he had not sufficiently warned the Pacific Fleet of deteriorating American-Japanese diplomatic relations other than issuing a general war warning on November 27. No real guilt was finally ascribed to his actions, though, for they had been no different than those of any other governmental leader. He died in Washington and was buried at Arlington National Cemetery.

[Stark's papers are at the Naval Historical Center, Washington, D.C., which also has a useful outline biography of him. See B. Mitchell Simpson III, "Harold Raynsford Stark," in Robert William Love, Jr., ed., *The Chiefs of Naval Operations* (1980); and B. Mitchell Simpson III, *Admiral Harold R. Stark: Architect of Victory* (1989). Also useful is Admiral James O. Richardson as told to George C. Dyer, *On the Treadmill to Pearl Harbor* (1973). An obituary is in the *New York Times*, Aug. 21, 1972.]

CLARK G. REYNOLDS

STARK, LLOYD CROW (Nov. 23, 1886– Sept. 17, 1972), nurseryman and governor, was born on a farm near Louisiana, Mo., the son of Clarence M. Stark and Lilly Crow. His great-grandfather had founded Stark Brothers Nurseries and Orchards Company in 1816; it became the largest nursery in the United States. After completing high school, Stark prepared for a naval career, graduating from the U.S. Naval Academy in 1908. In the next years he served in Turkish and South American waters, but resigned from the Navy in 1912 to become vice-president and general manager, and later chairman of the board, of Stark Brothers Nurseries. He maintained a connection with the family business for the rest of his life. During his work at the nursery his triumph was the discovery of what became the Stark Golden Delicious apple. One day a package of apples arrived from Odessa, W.Va., and Stark was the first to sample them. "That's a new apple!" he exclaimed excitedly. He sent his brother Paul to find the tree, which was growing out of a mountainside; the Starks bought it for $5,000.

During World War I, Stark served with the 315th Field Artillery Regiment, attached to the Eightieth Division, and took part in the battles of St. Mihiel and the Meuse-Argonne. He was discharged in June 1919 with the rank of major.

Stark gradually acquired an interest in politics. Because of his connection with the nursery he participated in civic projects, advocating the construction of a bridge across the Mississippi River at Louisiana, Mo., joining Missouri and Illinois. In 1928 he became chairman of a statewide Citizens' Road Bond Committee, which obtained a $75 million bond issue for farm-to-market roads. There followed his single venture into elective office, his 1937–1941 term as Missouri's governor.

Stark's governorship marked a most eventful period in the political history of Missouri, which saw a realignment of the state Democratic party, breaking the power of the boss of Kansas City's political machine, Thomas J.

Pendergast, and very nearly ending the career of the state's Democratic junior senator, Harry S. Truman. At the outset Stark sought Pendergast's support for the gubernatorial race and used Truman, who was Pendergast's protégé, to advance his cause. Pendergast decided to support Stark as a compromise candidate against a possible nominee by the state's senior senator, Bennett Champ Clark. The latter was from St. Louis, and there long had been a rivalry between the state's two metropolises for control of the statehouse in Jefferson City. The election of Stark in 1936 was allegedly assisted by his obtaining of 50,000–60,000 ghost votes in Kansas City.

Upon his election Stark turned against his benefactors in the Pendergast machine. Part of his program as governor was unexceptionable, such as his effort to persuade the Navy to name a new battleship the *Missouri*. In 1937 he sponsored a social security bill, grouping the administration of old-age pensions, direct relief, and a program for dependent children. He created an unemployment compensation commission; established a cancer hospital in Columbia, the first state-supported institution of its kind in the country; arranged for construction of a state office building across from the capitol; sponsored a driver's license law; and expanded the state's system for parole of prisoners. But he also moved against the Pendergast machine, first by sponsoring appointment of an anti-Pendergast judge to the state supreme court, then by dismissing the state insurance superintendent, R. Emmet O'Malley. Open warfare erupted with Pendergast, who it was discovered had used O'Malley to extract a massive bribe from several dozen fire insurance companies doing business within the state. Governor Stark pushed through a bill for state control of Kansas City's police department and ousted the Pendergast prosecuting attorney of Jackson County (which includes much of Kansas City), and appointed a bitter Pendergast enemy. He set up permanent registration laws for St. Louis and Kansas City and purged the rolls of ghost voters. In the course of this veritable earthquake within Missouri's Democratic party, Pendergast was convicted of tax evasion and sent to Leavenworth prison.

At this juncture Governor Stark overreached himself. Because the Missouri constitution allowed a governor only a single term, he aspired to the Senate seat of Truman, who was up for reelection in 1940. He persuaded President Franklin D. Roosevelt to offer Senator Truman a lifetime federal post if the senator would remove himself from the primary. When Truman refused the offer, instructing Roosevelt's press secretary, Stephen T. Early to tell the president to "go to hell," Roosevelt instructed the state's WPA director to exert pressure through the agency's rolls to gain votes for Stark in the senatorial primary. At the same time Roosevelt spoke with Stark about the secretaryship of the Navy, then vacant, and avowed that he was considering the governor for nomination for the vice-presidency on his forthcoming third-term ticket. But Stark's national ambitions hurt his Senate campaign. Word got out that he was collecting money from state employees, requiring donations of anyone who made more than $60 per month. The governor was seen as taking too much credit for the removal of Pendergast, which prompted the U.S. district attorney in Kansas City who had prosecuted Pendergast, Maurice M. Milligan, to enter the Senate race, dividing the "good government" vote. To the disgust of Missourians, Stark campaigned around the state accompanied by a retinue of uniformed Missouri colonels, and required his chauffeur to salute him. He lost the primary to Senator Truman by nearly 8,000 votes. The senator quipped that he had sent Stark back to the nursery.

Stark retired from governorship, bitter about his loss. Completely finished with politics, save for occasional speeches on behalf of candidates for national and state offices, he returned to the nursery business and raising prizewinning saddlehorses, Hereford cattle, hogs, and sheep. He supported the election of Dwight D. Eisenhower in 1952 and 1956, and Richard M. Nixon in 1960 and 1968, although continuing to vote Democratic in state elections.

Stark married Margaret P. Stickney on Nov. 11, 1908; they had two children before she died in 1930. On Nov. 23, 1931, he married Katherine L. Perkins; they also had two children. Stark died in St. Louis.

[Biographical material on Stark is scattered and of little value. The few articles that trace his political career are either excessively laudatory or highly critical. There is no book-length biography. The best resort is the Lloyd C. Stark Papers in the Western Historical Collection of the University of Missouri in Columbia. For information on politics in Missouri, see Richard S. Kirkendall, A *History of Missouri*,

1919 to 1953 (1986). For obituaries see the *Kansas City Times* and the *New York Times*, Sept. 18, 1972.]
ROBERT H. FERRELL

STEARMAN, LLOYD CARLTON (Oct. 26, 1898–Apr. 3, 1975), aviator, aircraft designer, and aviation executive, was born in Wellsford, Kans., the son of Icie May Grimm, a music teacher, and Frederick Carlton Stearman, an architect and draftsman. Raised in Harper, Kans., he attended public schools there and graduated from Harper High School in 1917.

That fall, Stearman entered Kansas State Agricultural College to study engineering and architecture; he left to join the U.S. Naval Reserve Flying Corps on Aug. 21, 1918. He received flight training at the North Island Naval Air Station, San Diego, Calif. In December 1918, he joined the architectural firm of S. S. Voight in Wichita, Kans.

Stearman had been bitten by the flying bug, however, and in 1919 he became a mechanic, and then assistant engineer, for E. M. Laird, the first commercial airplane company in Wichita. On Oct. 6, 1920, he married his high school sweetheart, Ethyl Trusty. They had two children.

E. M. Laird was reorganized as the Swallow Airplane Company on Jan. 22, 1924, with Stearman as chief engineer. He could now put his design ideas into practice. The fragile aircraft of World War I led him to realize that flying, to be commercially viable, required sturdier airplanes. Rugged dependability became the hallmark of Stearman's airplanes and was evident in the Swallow factory's first design, the New Swallow, which won the 1923 national efficiency race at Dayton, Ohio.

In 1925, Stearman and Walter Beech joined Clyde Cessna in forming the Travel Air Manufacturing Company. As chief engineer, Stearman produced several successful airplanes, including the Travel Air 4000, which won first place in the second annual Ford Reliability Tour (1926). Stearman resigned from Travel Air in October 1926 and moved to Venice, Calif., where, with partners George Lyle and Fred Hoyt, he formed the Stearman Aircraft Company. The venture failed, however, and Stearman returned to Wichita, where he organized a new Stearman Aircraft Company that was in operation by September 1927. Western Air Express received the first Wichita-built Stearman in December 1927.

The United Aircraft and Transport Corporation purchased the Stearman Aircraft Company in 1929. Stearman remained as president and design engineer, but he soon became frustrated by the constraints of corporate management. He resigned in December 1930 to pursue his first love, aircraft design. He and Robert Gross, a former Boston investment banker who had joined Stearman in 1928, severed all ties with United and went to California, where, with Walter Varney, an airline executive, they formed the Stearman-Varney Company in 1932, with Stearman as president. They soon heard that the Detroit Aircraft Corporation was bankrupt and that one of its divisions, the Lockheed Aircraft Company, was available. The three men purchased Lockheed for $40,000. Stearman was named president.

Stearman left Lockheed in 1935 and joined the Bureau of Air Commerce of the U.S. Department of Commerce as an aircraft inspector. In that capacity he became familiar with a radically new personal airplane being developed by the Hammond Aircraft Company at Ypsilanti, Mich. Unorthodox in design, the all-metal airplane featured twin booms extending from the wing to the tail, with an engine behind the cabin driving a pusher propeller. A triangle landing gear, unusual for the time, enhanced ground handling. The original design won a government-sponsored contest for a low-cost person "safety plane" in 1935. Stearman was so impressed that he resigned his government position and, with Dean Hammond, a designer, formed the Stearman-Hammond Aircraft Corporation, in San Francisco, to refine and develop the airplane. Unfortunately, the Great Depression helped to kill the project; only fifteen airframes were sold. With the demise of Stearman-Hammond, Stearman became vice-president of the Transair Company of San Francisco (1938–1939). During World War II he managed the Airplane Division of the Harvey Machine Company in Long Beach, Calif.

In 1946, Stearman formed the Stearman Engineering Company in Dos Palos, Calif., to design and manufacture agricultural aircraft. Ironically, an airplane that bore his name was already perfectly suited to this role. It was the Model 75 Kaydet, popularly known as the Stearman Trainer because it was produced by the Stearman Division of the Boeing Airplane Company. Boeing was part of the United Aircraft conglomerate that had bought out Stearman fifteen years earlier. Although he had not been directly involved in its creation, the Model 75 was based on one of his earlier designs. Perhaps the most famous of all Stearman aircraft, it had trained thousands of fledgling pilots during World War II and was available in large numbers as military surplus.

Stearman and an associate named George Willett formed the Inland Aviation Company to convert the trainers to crop dusters. The two parted company in 1946, and Stearman joined the National Aircraft Corporation in Van Nuys, Calif., where he continued his work with the Model 75. Later, he became vice-president and chief engineer of the Hammel Company of Dos Palos, Calif., which in 1950 became the Stearman-Hammel Company, manufacturers of a twin-sickle hydraulic mower designed by Stearman.

Stearman came full circle in 1955, when he rejoined Lockheed, by then an aerospace giant. He filled out a routine application and quietly left the employment office. An employment officer, reading the form, immediately called Senior Vice-President Hall L. Hibbard and said, "Hey, we've got some nut who says he knows you. . . . And get this, where the application asks about previous employment at Lockheed, the guy writes down 'president.' " Hibbard recognized the "nut" and hired him as a senior design specialist. Stearman participated in many projects, including several connected with the space program, thus helping to fulfill a prophecy he had made in 1930, when he predicted that rocket-shaped aircraft would someday circle the earth in an orbit sixty miles high, at speeds of twenty-five thousand miles per hour. Stearman, who retired in August 1968, died in Northridge, Calif.

[The National Air and Space Museum has a biographical file on Stearman that includes newspaper and magazine articles. The Boeing Airplane Company also has some corporate records on Stearman. For biographical studies of Stearman, see Kenneth D. Wilson and Thomas E. Lowe, "Lloyd C. Stearman, 1898–1975," *Journal of the American Aviation Historical Society*, Summer 1991; and Ray Brashear, "Lloyd C. Stearman (Inland Aviation)," *ibid.*, Fall 1992. Information on the Stearman company and Stearman aircraft are in Mitch Mayborn and Peter M. Bowers, *Stearman Guidebook* (1972). See also John B. Rae, *Climb to Greatness* (1968). Obituaries are in the *New York Times* and the *Washington Post*, both April 5, 1975.]

LOUIS R. ELTSCHER

STEICHEN, EDWARD JEAN (March 27, 1879–March 25, 1973), photographer, painter, museum curator, and plant breeder, was born in Luxembourg, the son of Jean Pierre Steichen and Marie Kemp. Edouard was brought to the United States in 1881, and the family settled in Hancock, Mich., where his father worked as a copper miner and his mother as a milliner. At age nine, Edouard was sent off to Pio Nono, a Catholic preparatory school near Milwaukee, Wis., where he studied for one year. After five years in the public schools of Hancock and Milwaukee, where the family moved in 1891, Steichen left school; in 1894 he began a four-year apprenticeship in lithography with the American Fine Art Company in Milwaukee, producing photos the firm used in its advertising, including the "Cascaret Girl," a favorite with consumers. While studying art with the Milwaukee Art Students League (1894–1898), which he founded, Steichen bought his first camera—a Folding Detective—and, encouraged by his mother, took his first steps toward becoming one of the nation's premier photographers.

For more than two decades, Steichen divided his time between the United States and France, successfully pursuing both painting and photography. This dual project at once earned him access to the artists of Paris and made his work central to a new breed of American photographers who wished to have photography recognized as an art. Indeed, Steichen's photographs from this period—dark, diffuse, out-of-focus, and mysterious—closely resemble some of the painting of the era, and by 1898, Steichen was, as he later put it, "an 'impressionist' without knowing it." In 1899, Steichen received his first official recognition as a photographer, when his photographs, including "The Lady in the Doorway," were exhibited at the Second Philadelphia Salon. He headed for Europe in the spring of 1900, stopping in New York City to meet Alfred Stieglitz, who purchased several of his photographs. Two years in Paris earned Steichen a considerable reputation for interpretive portraits, including one of Auguste Rodin, in preparation for which Steichen had met with the sculptor once a week for almost a year.

Returning to the United States in 1902, Steichen opened a studio at 291 Fifth Avenue and achieved a degree of celebrity with his portraits of J. P. Morgan, Theodore Roosevelt, and other notables. At the same time, he joined Stieglitz as a founder of the Photo-Secession (1902), an organization dedicated to photography as an art form, and he led the effort to create "291," a Photo-Secession exhibition space that opened in 1905 across the hall from his studio. By 1910, when works by Steichen and other Photo-Secession members were hung at the Albright Gallery in Buffalo, the group's primary goal—recognition of photography by that arbiter of taste, the art museum—had been achieved. From France, where he had established a studio at Voulangis in 1906, Steichen supplied "291" with works by Cézanne, Picasso, Braque, and others whose paintings had never been exhibited in the United States. This accomplishment, according to one scholar, set the stage for the 1913 Armory Show. Steichen was married on Oct. 3, 1903, to Clara E. Smith; they had two children.

Most Steichen scholarship has focused on these early years, largely because they appear crucial to the emergence of photography as a fine-art medium. Some scholars have followed Steichen's autobiography, A *Life in Photography* (1963) in seeing Steichen's early photographs as a rendering of French impressionism, strongly influenced by Monet and Whistler. Others have attributed the intuitive, ambiguous, and antimaterialist elements in Steichen's work to a Symbolist aesthetic traceable to the Belgian playwright Maurice Maeterlinck. In another debate, some scholars have seen Steichen's emphasis on the artistic—his devotion to technique, and the restricted range of his subject matter—as a necessary response to the dissemination of camera technology in the late nineteenth century. Because the camera had become a widely available mechanical instrument, would-be artists had to employ techniques, such as the gum biochromate process with which Steichen experimented, that were unavailable to most amateurs; this and other techniques, which made possible the manipulation of the negative and the print, helped to overcome the stigma that the camera, a "mere" machine, held and to recover the mystique it had lost as photography was popularized. More recently, some critics have questioned the process by which some photography was claimed as an art, asserting that it was a form of cultural hegemony that also implicitly cast the work of other photographers, especially social reformists such as Jacob Riis and Lewis Hine, as mere documentation. The most critical of these perspectives finds Steichen's photographs representative of an anticollective ideology of autonomy and individualism. From the perspective of cultural history, Steichen's efforts to invest the photograph—a machine product—with craftsmanship, emotional intensity, and authentic experience should also be understood as an aspect of fin-de-siècle antimodernism.

The outbreak of war in Europe in 1914 initiated a new phase in Steichen's outlook and career. Returning to the United States, he publicly denounced Stieglitz's leadership of "291" as narcissistic, dogmatic, and insular. Volunteering for military duty in 1917 (he had become a naturalized citizen in 1900), Steichen served under General William ("Billy") Mitchell in France, heading the photographic division of the U.S. Army Air Service. After the war, his distress at his responsibility for the aerial photographs that contributed to the killing and at having seen the "white faces" of the dead, led Steichen to spend three troubled years working out the relationships between his art, the business world, and an inchoate ethic of international humanism. In this period he changed his name from Edouard to Edward (1918); at Voulangis, burned all his paintings and abandoned that discipline entirely; was divorced (1921); and, in photography, turned inward, studying the spiral form in an effort to ground his craft in "nature's laws." He produced a series of compulsively technical, close-up still-life studies of light, scale, volume, and weight (he photographed one cup and saucer more than a thousand times). He emerged from this inner turmoil in 1923, when he returned to New York, married Dana Desboro Glover, an actress, and, plunging headlong into the consumer and fashion boom of the decade, joined Condé Nast publications as chief photographer for Vogue and Vanity Fair. In addition, he agreed to take promotional photos of consumer items for the J. Walter Thompson advertising agency.

Although Stieglitz condemned Steichen for pandering to elites and although Walker Evans found his studio portraits superficial, Steichen insisted that art and commerce were not incompatible, and the best of his photographs of the "great, the near-great, and the would-be great" are superb technical achievements ("Charlie Chaplin," 1931) or penetrating character studies ("Greta Garbo," 1928). During these years Steichen also illustrated The First Picture Book:

Everyday Things for Babies (1930), a children's book written by his daughter, Mary Steichen Martin; pioneered the photomural while producing a mural of the George Washington Bridge (1932) and another for the New York exhibit at the Chicago World's Fair; and, in 1929, acquired the Umpawaug Breeding Farm in West Redding, Conn., where he raised the hybrid delphiniums that he exhibited at the Museum of Modern Art in 1936.

An earnest and intense man driven by the idea that an artist ought always to be moving toward "the great unforeseen," Steichen tired of the repetition and routine of portraiture and fashion photography and, in 1938, closed his New York City studio. Again, war refocused his career, channeling his enormous energies in a new, public direction. With considerable effort, in 1942 Steichen secured a commission as lieutenant commander in the U.S. Naval Reserve, heading up a small photographic unit in the Navy's Bureau of Aeronautics and, in the period 1945–1946, supervising all naval photography as director of the Naval Photographic Institute. While on active duty Steichen completed preparations for the "Road to Victory" exhibition (1943) and organized the "Power in the Pacific" exhibition (1944), both of which were presented at the Museum of Modern Art. He was discharged from the Navy as a captain in 1946.

Although Steichen believed that "a real image of war" might help bring an end to war itself, the photographs by Steichen and his unit were by and large public relations documents, visual espressions of wartime clichés, bereft of emotional power. Despite Steichen's instructions to "concentrate on the men," the soldiers in these photographs are invariably constructed as symbols rather than individuals. Indeed, Steichen's most memorable photograph from this period—an infrared image of the flight deck of the USS Lexington, on which he served—has a haunting beauty that contrasts with his antiwar ideology.

Steichen's last great professional challenge came as director of photography for the Museum of Modern Art, a position he held from 1947 to 1962. Steichen stopped taking his own photographs and began assembling those of other photographers—forty-four shows in all, several of them pioneering "theme" exhibitions. The most important was "The Family of Man," which opened in 1955 to enormous and enthusiastic audiences and eventually was seen by some nine million people on an eight-year world tour. Composed of 503 photographs from sixty-eight countries organized by "universal" themes and institutions—love, marriage, child-rearing, the family, the fear of nuclear holocaust—the exhibition was intended to mirror, celebrate, and market the "oneness" of mankind in the atomic age.

The exhibition's theme belonged to an era that venerated the United Nations and celebrated ecumenicism, and one can see its origins in Robert Capa's "People are People" series and in the romantic Americanism of *The People, Yes*, and other poems by Carl Sandburg, Steichen's brother-in-law and close friend. But its strident universalism was consistent with Steichen's career; "The Family of Man" and Steichen's early, pictorialist photographs avoided precise reference to time, place, and the facts of social history, effacing differences in order to evoke an emotional, psychic unity.

Following the death of his second wife in 1957, Steichen married Joanna Taub on Mar. 19, 1960. He retired from the Museum of Modern Art two years later. Steichen died in West Redding, Conn.

[Steichen's photographs and some of his papers, including a scrapbook assembled by his mother, are in the Steichen Archive at the Museum of Modern Art. There is also Steichen correspondence in the Alfred Stieglitz Archive at The Beinecke Rare Book and Manuscript Library, Yale University. In addition to the autobiography mentioned above, Steichen's books include *Power in the Pacific* (1945); *The Blue Ghost* (1947); *The Family of Man* (1955); and *The Bitter Years* (1962). Also revealing are essays by and about Steichen in the journal *Camera Work*, especially Steichen's "Ye Fakers" (1903).

Except for Carl Sandburg's early work, *Steichen the Photographer* (1929), there is no biography. A brief biographical treatment is in George Walsh, Colin Naylor, and Michael Held, eds., *Contemporary Photographers* (1982). Ruth Kelton's introduction to *Edward Steichen* is brief but interpretive. On the Photo-Secession, see Robert Doty, *Photo Secession* (1960); William Innes Homer, "Eduard Steichen as Painter and Photographer, 1897–1908," *American Art Journal*, Nov. 1974; and Dennis Longwell, *Steichen: The Master Prints, 1895–1914* (1978). On the interwar years, see Patricia A. Johnston, "Edward Steichen's Advertising Photography" (Ph.D. diss., Boston Univ., 1988); see also Christopher Phillips, *Steichen at War* (1981). An obituary is in the *New York Times*, Mar. 26, 1973.]

WILLIAM GRAEBNER

STEINER, MAXIMILIAN RAOUL WALTER ("MAX") (May 10, 1888–Dec. 28, 1971), film music composer and conductor, was born in Vienna, Austria, the son of Gabor Steiner, a theatrical producer and the creator of the theme park "Venice in Vienna" and Vienna's giant Ferris wheel (Riesenrad), and Maria ("Mitzie") Hollman, a restaurateur. He was named after his grandfather, who had managed the Theater-an-der-Wien, producing the operettas of Jacques Offenbach and Johann Strauss, Jr. Steiner showed exceptional musical talent at an early age and when he was thirteen entered the Imperial Academy of Music. He completed the four-year course of study in one year, winning the Emperor's gold medal. He studied harmony with Hermann Grädener, counterpoint with Robert Fuchs, and composition with Felix Weingartner and was a pupil of Gustav Mahler. At the age of fourteen, Steiner wrote an operetta, *The Beautiful Greek Girl*, which was produced by Carl Tuschl at the Orpheum Theater in Vienna.

From 1904 through 1914, Steiner conducted and arranged operettas and musical comedies, living first in London and then in Paris while participating in tours to Berlin, Moscow, and Johannesburg. At the outbreak of World War I, Steiner, considered an enemy alien in London, was aided by friends in moving to New York City; he became a naturalized citizen in 1920. He started as a copyist for Harms Music Publishing, which led to assignments as an orchestrator and conductor of Broadway musicals with Victor Herbert, George Gershwin, and Jerome Kern. Steiner composed little while he was in New York, writing the music for only one show, *Peaches*.

Steiner's first marriage, on Sept. 12, 1912, in London, was to a woman named Beatrice, who had been a soubrette in one of his father's shows. When finances allowed, his wife and her mother joined Steiner in New York, but the marriage did not last. The date of divorce is not certain; however, it is known that Steiner married Audrey van Liew, a singer, on Apr. 12, 1927; this marriage also ended in divorce.

Steiner's introduction to Hollywood came in 1929, when RKO Radio Pictures bought the rights to the musical *Rio Rita*. Harry Tierney, for whom he had orchestrated and conducted the stage version, insisted that Steiner be hired to provide the same services for the screen version. William Le Baron, executive producer of

RKO, offered Steiner a one-year contract, but he was not certain how long Steiner's services would be needed. It was at a time when studios were debating whether music was required in dramatic pictures. In his unpublished autobiography, Steiner explains the debate: "This was motivated not only by the economic factor, but because they had decided you could not have background music unless you showed the source. In other words, you had to have an orchestra on view, or a phonograph or performers, so that people would not wonder where the music was coming from." His first film music for RKO was written to supply cues for English movies dubbed in Spanish.

Films made in the early 1930's gave Steiner the opportunity to begin scoring music that intensified the action on the screen without showing the source of the music. Steiner's first original score was for *Cimarron* (1930), an Academy Award winner for best picture and the first sound film to have music that was not directly linked to the on-screen action. The first films to use music under dialogue were *Symphony of Six Million* and *Bird of Paradise*, both produced by David O. Selznick in 1932 with music composed by Steiner. At first, film music was simplistic and rather naive, but as films improved, so did the music. Steiner worked for RKO from 1929 to 1936, producing music for nearly 135 films, including *King Kong* (1933) and *The Informer* (1935); the latter won Steiner his first Academy Award. *King Kong* was unique for its time and illustrates Steiner's style: rich symphonic scoring, quasi-Wagnerian use of leitmotifs, and long sections of nearly continuous music. This style developed into the "classic" Hollywood model of film scoring; Steiner's influence is paramount.

In 1931, Steiner met his third wife, Louise Klos, a harpist who often played in studio orchestras that he conducted. They were married Oct. 31, 1936, and had one child. They were divorced nine years later. In April 1947, Steiner married Leonette Ball, and that year his only son committed suicide.

In 1936, Steiner joined Selznick-International, composing music for *Little Lord Fauntleroy*, *The Garden of Allah*, and *A Star Is Born*. Selznick also loaned Steiner to Warner Brothers for the scoring of three films, including *The Charge of the Light Brigade*. In 1937, Steiner contracted with Warner Brothers on a full-time basis. Under that contract he composed music

for such classics as *Casablanca, Saratoga Trunk, Jezebel, They Died with Their Boots On, Since You Went Away,* and *Now, Voyager* and garnered Academy Awards for the last two.

The year 1939 was Steiner's most productive. He provided music for ten Warner Brothers films—*The Oklahoma Kid, Dodge City, Confessions of a Nazi Spy, Daughters Courageous, Each Dawn I Die, The Old Maid, Dust Be My Destiny, We Are Not Alone, Four Wives,* and *Dr. Ehrlich's Magic Bullet*—besides working for Selznick on the music for *Intermezzo* and the epic *Gone with the Wind.* Steiner's "Tara" theme for the latter became one of the most famous melodies of the century. In 1953, Steiner left Warner Brothers and began to freelance. He continued to compose for major productions such as *The Searchers* (1956), *The Sins of Rachel Cade* (1961), *Rome Adventure* (1962), and *Youngblood Hawke* (1964). His theme from *A Summer Place* (1959) became a popular standard in the early 1960's. In the end, poor eyesight and health prevented him from composing. In 1965, he completed his last film, *Two on a Guillotine,* at the age of seventy-seven. He died in Hollywood.

[The Max Steiner collection, in the Arts and Communications Archives of the Harold B. Lee Library at Brigham Young University, contains Steiner's autobiography, "Notes to You" (in press); 176 original pencil-sketch short scores (among them, *King Kong, Gone with the Wind, Casablanca*); original studio soundtrack recordings; published and unpublished music; and personal papers and memorabilia. BYU also maintains the Max Steiner Music Society collection. Steiner's published writings are "Scoring the Film," in Nancy Naumberg, ed., *We Make the Movies* (1937), and "The Music Director," in Bernard Rosenberg and Harry Silverstein, ed., *The Real Tinsel* (1970).

For biographical information and a study of Steiner's style, see William Darby and Jack Du Bois, *American Film Music* (1990), which includes the most complete filmography. Additional biographical material is in Tony Thomas, *Film Score* (1991). For analytical studies see Claudia Gorbman, *Unheard Melodies* (1987); and Kathryn Kalinak, "Max Steiner and the Classical Hollywood Film Score: An Analysis of *The Informer,*" in Clifford McCarty, ed., *Film Music I* (1989). An obituary is in the *New York Times,* Dec. 29, 1971.]

JANET B. BRADFORD

STENGEL, CHARLES DILLON ("CASEY") (July 30, 1890–Sept. 29, 1975), baseball manager, was born in Kansas City, Mo., the youngest of three children. His father, Louis Stengel, had emigrated from Germany in 1851 and sold insurance; his mother, Jennie Gordon, was Irish. At Kansas City Central High School, Charles was an all-around athlete: he was captain of the football team, and pitched the baseball team to the state championship in 1909. Intent on earning enough money to study dentistry, he became a professional baseball player in 1910, signing with the minor league Kansas City Blues, who promptly farmed him out to Kankakee, Ill., in the Northern Association. When the league went broke he finished the season with Maysville of the Blue Grass League.

Enrolled in Western Dental College (which later became a part of the University of Kansas City), he could tell that his dexterity with the drill and probe was not developing as fast as his baseball skill. In 1911 he played at Aurora, Ill., in the Wisconsin-Illinois League. Throwing and hitting left-handed, he led the league in batting with a .352 average. A scout for the Brooklyn Dodgers (then known as the Trolley Dodgers and also as the Superbas) chanced to see Stengel play when he was having a good day and signed him up. The following spring the Dodgers assigned him to the Montgomery, Ala., team of the Southern Association and in September promoted him to the big leagues. By now his nascent career as a dentist was finished. He would reflect: "I was pretty good at inlays, but I couldn't measure up at making caps. I still gotta shudder when I see a tin can." In his minor league wanderings he had picked up the nickname Casey, not, he said, because he hailed from Kansas City ("K.C.") but because of the popularity of the poem "Casey at the Bat," which had led people to dub many ball players "Casey."

Stengel played the outfield in the major leagues for fourteen years, although he was built somewhat slighter than many of his fellow players, standing five feet ten inches tall and weighing 175 pounds. The Dodgers traded him in 1918 to the Pittsburgh Pirates, who traded him to the Philadelphia Phillies in 1919, who shortly traded him to the New York Giants where, in 1922, he had his best season, hitting .368 in eighty-four games. He won two games for the Giants in the World Series of 1923 with two home runs and a series batting average of .417. But shortly after the season began the Giants sent him on to Boston, where he ended his big

league playing career with the Braves in 1925. His lifetime batting average was .284, compiled in 1,277 games.

In 1923 he had met Edna Lawson on a blind date at the old Polo Grounds, the Giants' home park, and they were married in 1924. For the next forty-one years, although she called Glendale, Calif., their home, she traveled the country with him as he made his way in a luminous second career as a manager that began in 1925 with the Boston Red Sox's farm team at Worcester, Mass., in the Eastern League. The Stengels had no children.

Already he was famous as a prankster, and known in his playing days as the "king of the grumblers," a group of players feared and respected for their locker-room antics. Stengel was endlessly imaginative in devising shenanigans which could be puerile as well as simply funny. Once, playing the outfield, he disappeared down a drainage hole, hid there until a fly ball was hit in his direction, and then, as if by magic, rose from the netherworld and caught the ball, with the cover of the hole under his arm. One of his best-remembered stunts marked his return as a Pirate to Ebbets Field, where the Dodgers played. As the intensely partisan Dodger fans gave him the bird, he bowed low before the grandstand, yanked off his hat, freeing a sparrow trapped there, thus reciprocating the insult majestically.

Casey labored for seven years as a manager in the minor leagues—sometimes taking the field as a player, too—with indifferent success, serving with Toledo in the American Association after his stint with Worcester. He became a shrewd judge of baseball talent, which made him a clever trader of players. And if his teams were not often winners, he provided entertainment for the fans and the teams whose admiration he inspired. Stengel finally returned to the majors in 1932 as a coach for the Dodgers. He became the manager two years later and served through 1936, when he was fired. In 1938 he was appointed manager of the Boston Braves, where he remained through the 1943 season although up to this point the big league teams he ran never finished higher than fifth (and that only twice) in the eight-team league. Still, his lectures to young players, full of humor and sound advice, earned him the sobriquet "The Old Professor."

Although he had by now become a rich man through sound investments that included real estate and oil properties and the Valley National Bank of California, he could not leave baseball, his abiding love. He went back to managing in the minors. After considerable success in the American Association (at Milwaukee and Kansas City) and the Pacific Coast League (at Oakland), the top minor leagues, the famed New York Yankees startled the baseball world by selecting him to be their skipper in 1949. Many baseball fans and sportswriters viewed Stengel as an elderly buffoon (he was fifty-eight years old) who was surely not in the permanent plans of the Yankee owners. But in his tenure from 1949 through the 1960 season, Stengel's triumphant teams earned him a reputation as baseball's greatest manager, albeit he had the services of some of the outstanding stars in the history of the game. From 1949 to 1953 the Bronx Bombers, as the Yankees came to be known, won the pennant and the World Series every year; in 1954 the team finished second in the pennant race but resumed its accustomed place atop the league from 1955 to 1958, although it won the World Series only in 1956 and 1958. The team fell to third in 1959 yet took the pennant once more the following year. By now, perhaps because of his advancing years, perhaps because of his unparalleled success, Stengel had become imperious and impatient with his players, and increasingly at odds with the Yankees owners. They fired him shortly after the team lost the World Series to the Pittsburgh Pirates in 1960.

Now seventy years old, he rusticated for a year at his beloved home in Glendale in the foothills of the Sierras. Then in 1962 a call he could not resist came from his old friend George Weiss, the longtime general manager of the Yankees, who had also been released and who was now organizing the New York Mets. Weiss offered Stengel the unenviable opportunity to manage the Mets, an expansion team in the National League that somehow was expected to replace in the hearts of local fans both the New York Giants and the Brooklyn Dodgers, franchises that had moved to greener pastures in San Francisco and Los Angeles respectively.

Casey accepted the challenge with alacrity and his fruitless efforts to teach the young men he was assigned how to play winning baseball and to revive the fire in some tired veterans became a charming piece of national theater. With possibly the worst team ever assembled in the big leagues (the team lost 452 games out of the 646 it played in its first four years) some-

times even Stengel grew discouraged: "Don't anybody here know how to play this game?" he is said to have moaned. The public, nevertheless, took to its heart these feckless "Amazin's," led by their indomitable "Philosopher of the Dugout." After two years of playing at the old Polo Grounds in Manhattan, the Mets moved to their gleaming new home, Shea Stadium in Queens. Despite their ineptness on the field, they cavorted before huge crowds that filled the stands out of a curious mixture of affection and pity for them and for the old man at their helm. By this time, the hitherto unknown tongue that Stengel generally spoke in public had become famous as Stengelese. Delivered nonstop and full of malapropisms, mangled syntax, and doubletalk, his monologues to his players and his interviewers became his trademark, half "put on" and half natural.

Stengel's time with the Mets ended abruptly on July 25, 1965, when he fell and fractured his left hip. That afternoon as he lay in the hospital, a huge throng was on hand at Shea Stadium to celebrate Casey's seventy-fifth birthday. The following month he was on his way back to Glendale, his remarkable baseball career now over. The Mets honored him with a sinecure as vice-president for the West Coast. A year later he was inducted into the Baseball Hall of Fame at Cooperstown, N.Y., along with Ted Williams, the incomparable slugging outfielder of the Boston Red Sox.

Stengel was an authentic folk hero, and for all his mischief and blather (which sometimes seemed to deflect attention from the bad play of his charges) he was a master of the game. As the great Yankees catcher Yogi Berra, who was veritably Stengel's assistant manager, put it: "If [Casey Stengel] wanted to make sense, he could. When you got him to talk about baseball, he made a lot of sense."

Stengel died of cancer in Glendale, Calif., where he is buried.

[Memorabilia and newspaper clippings are in the National Baseball Hall of Fame, Cooperstown, N.Y. An autobiography as told to Harry T. Paxton is *Casey at the Bat: The Story of My Life in Baseball* (1960). Joseph Durso, *Casey: The Life and Legend of Charles Dillon Stengel* (1967), covers Stengel's entire baseball career, with his statistics in an appendix. An earlier account is Frank Graham, Jr., *Casey Stengel, His Fifty Years in Baseball* (1958). An exuberant review of Stengel's time with the Mets is Maury Allen, *Now Wait a Minute, Casey!* (1965). See also

Robert W. Creamer, *Stengel: His Life and Times* (1984). Durso wrote the appreciative obituary in the *New York Times*, Oct. 1, 1975.]

HENRY F. GRAFF

STERN, BILL (July 1, 1907–Nov. 19, 1971), sports announcer and broadcaster, was born in Rochester, N.Y., to Isaac Stern, a clothing manufacturer, and Lena Reis.

After attending the Hackley Preparatory School in Tarrytown, N.Y., and the Cascadilla School in Ithaca, N.Y., Stern went on to the Pennsylvania Military College in Chester, Pa. Before graduating with a B.S. in 1930, he participated in football, tennis, basketball, boxing, and crew, earning three letters in varsity athletics.

With his theatrical aspirations nurtured by his involvement in college vaudeville shows, Stern took a job as an usher upon graduation, then joined a Rochester stock company, and, finally, made his way to Hollywood. Difficulties in making any headway in his career led him to return east, where he landed a position announcing sports in 1925 for WHAM, a Rochester radio station. Although his announcing work took him to Austin, Birmingham, Cincinnati, New Orleans and other parts of the country, Stern quit to return to New York City, where, in 1931, he became assistant stage manager of the Roxy Theatre. The following year, he was promoted to stage manager and given additional responsibility for the newly opened Radio City Music Hall.

After a short time, Stern was eager for a new challenge, and after an appeal to an NBC executive, found himself covering the 1934 football season with pioneer sports announcer Graham McNamee. While still managing Radio City, Stern continued covering football part-time and won such wide popularity among fans that, by 1937, he became a regular member of the NBC special events staff. That same year, Stern married Harriet May. They had one son and two daughters.

Stern gained his first national exposure in a sports-talk format known as "The Bill Stern Sports Review" that premiered Dec. 5, 1937, on the Blue Network, one of the two broadcast networks established by NBC in 1927. For four years he broadcast the Friday night fights on "NBC Blue," sponsored by Adam Hats. His long association with MGM's *News of the Day* newsreel began in 1938. On May 17, 1939,

Stern was the announcer for the first baseball game ever televised, with Ivy League rivals Princeton and Columbia playing at Baker Field in New York City.

It was with his famous "Colgate Sports Newsreel," first heard Oct. 8, 1939, that Stern really hit stride. His emotionally charged, piercing delivery, coupled with his willingness, even eagerness, to mix fact with fantasy, made for an exciting and entertaining fifteen minutes of airtime—replete with tales of horse races won by dead jockeys, limbless baseball players, and the most tenuous influences that sports had on the lives of the great. While some radio and television critics criticized Stern for providing more fiction than fact in his commentaries, millions of listeners looked forward to his stories and anecdotes.

Among his most notorious tales was his explanation of the origin of Thomas Alva Edison's deafness. As Stern told it, the great inventor's hearing troubles stemmed from being hit in the head while batting during a baseball game as a youth. The pitcher who beaned him, according to Stern, was none other than Jesse James. (A more factual account suggests that young Edison had been soundly boxed on the ears by an irate railroad conductor who was convinced he was the cause of a train mishap.)

Another classic Stern story—accompanied by dramatic organ chords—involved the early days of baseball: Abraham Lincoln himself, after having been shot at Ford's Theatre in Washington, regained consciousness just long enough to say to Secretary of War Edwin Stanton, "Tell General Abner Doubleday not to let baseball die." Although that particular tale led NBC to order him to label his dramatizations sports "legends," Stern's popularity among sports fans nevertheless continued unabated.

As a sportscaster doing play-by-play radio coverage of major football games, Stern was as quick on his feet as some of the athletes he covered. In one broadcast of a Notre Dame game, he discovered that he had misidentified a player who was well on his way toward the goal line for a touchdown. Without missing a beat, Stern embellished the drama in midaction by describing the player to whom he had wrongly attributed the run as throwing a lateral pass to the player who really was speeding toward the goal line.

Stern's shows were among the most entertaining fifteen-minute spots ever done on the air. His theme ("Bill Stern the Colgate shave cream man is on the air/Bill Stern the Colgate shave cream man with stories rare") was sung barbershop quartet–style to the tune of "Mademoiselle from Armentieres." He ended each show with "That's the three-o mark for tonight," a reference to the traditional newsman's "30" code for ending a story. The Colgate show ran nightly until June 29, 1951. Stern continued to do nightly shows until 1956, including an ABC program called "Sports Today." Toward the end of his career, he worked for the Mutual Broadcasting System, continuing to do his beloved sports-talk shows.

Perennially selected by the nation's radio editors as the most popular sports announcer in the country, Bill Stern never shied from his role as entertainer as well as sports commentator. The testament to his success was the millions of fans for whom his daily broadcasts brought leisure-time sustenance and escape from their daily tribulations. Stern died of a heart attack at the age of sixty-four in his home in suburban Rye, N.Y.

[Little biographical material on Stern is available. The Museum of Television and Radio maintains clippings and anecdotes from the radio and television career of Bill Stern. Obituaries appear in the *New York Times*, Nov. 21, 1972, and the *Daily News*, Nov. 21, 1971.]

GLENN N. SKLARIN

STEVENS, GEORGE COOPER (Dec. 18, 1904–Mar. 8, 1975), motion-picture director and producer, was born in Oakland, Calif., the son of Georgie Cooper, an actress, and (John) Landers Stevens, a Shakespearean actor and proprietor of the Pacific Coast Theatre Company and its affiliate touring companies. He was born into one of California's oldest families: his grandfather, James Stevens, had been a flamboyant attorney in San Francisco during the Gold Rush. His maternal grandmother, actress Georgie Woodthorpe, once played Ophelia to Edwin Booth's Hamlet, and his uncle, Ashton Stevens, was the longtime dean of Chicago's critics.

Stevens made his stage debut at age four in his father's company at San Francisco's Alcazar Theatre, where he had a small part in a production of *Sapho* starring the celebrated Nance O'Neill. Throughout his youth he continued to act in the companies operated by his father. He received his elementary education in San Francisco Bay Area public schools and began high school in the town of Sonoma. At age fifteen he dropped out of school, returning to San Francisco to work with his father, first as stage manager, then as business manager of the company. In 1921 Landers Stevens moved his family to Hollywood, where he pursued a career as a film actor. George Stevens was seventeen years old when he arrived in Los Angeles.

Stevens started his Hollywood career as a cameraman at the Hal Roach studios. In 1924 he began having his name displayed on the screen with the film's credits. From 1924 to 1930 he worked on two-reel films, including Laurel and Hardy shorts. In the period 1930–1932 he worked as cameraman on the *Boy Friend* and *Our Gang* series. Because of the fast pace of filmmaking at that time there was a great deal of improvisation in plot and dialogue during production. Stevens started inventing situations and supplying gags when production was held back for lack of comprehensive scripts. In 1930 Stevens began to direct for Hal Roach and within two years he turned out five short films. The eleven years that Stevens spent at the Hal Roach studios (1921–1933) refined his technique and shaped his entire perception of the medium.

In 1932 Stevens moved to Universal Pictures, for which he made three short films his first year. In 1933 he directed his first full-length feature, *The Cohens and the Kellys in Trouble*, starring Maureen O'Sullivan. It was followed by *Kentucky Kernels* and *Bachelor Bait*. While under contract to Universal Pictures, he directed a total of seven short and full-length films. He then came under contract to RKO Pictures (1933–1940), earning $2,250 per week, then one of Hollywood's top directorial salaries. He received widespread praise in 1935 for *Alice Adams*, starring Katharine Hepburn and Fred MacMurray, and at the age of thirty-one became one of Hollywood's most sought-after directors. That same year, he directed *Laddie*, starring John Beal and Gloria Stuart; *The Nitwits*, which introduced Betty Grable to the film-going public in a minor role; and *Annie Oakley*, starring Barbara Stanwyck, Preston Foster, and Melvyn Douglas. In 1936 he directed Fred Astaire and Ginger Rogers in *Swing Time*, and in 1937 he directed *Quality Street*, with Katharine Hepburn and Franchot Tone, and *A Damsel in Distress*, starring Fred Astaire, George Burns, Gracie Allen, Joan Fontaine, and Reginald Gardiner, with music and lyrics by George and Ira Gershwin. The following year he directed Ginger Rogers and James Stewart in *Vivacious Lady*, followed in 1939 by *Gunga Din*, starring Cary Grant, Douglas Fairbanks, Jr., Victor McLaglen, Joan Fontaine, and Sam Jaffe. In 1940 he wound up his contract work for RKO with *Vigil in the Night*, starring Carole Lombard, Brian Aherne, and Anne Shirley. Beginning with *Vivacious Lady* in 1938, Stevens had begun producing as well as directing his films.

In 1941 Stevens signed a two-year contract with Columbia Pictures as a director-producer. His first film for Columbia was *Penny Serenade*, starring Irene Dunne, Cary Grant, and Belah Bondi. In 1942, at the insistence of Katharine Hepburn, Metro-Goldwyn-Mayer hired Stevens, on loan from Columbia, to direct *Woman of the Year*, which earned an Academy Award for original screenplay. Back at Columbia that year, Stevens made *The Talk of the Town*, with Cary Grant, Jean Arthur, and Ronald Colman. In 1943 he made his last film for Columbia Pictures, *The More the Merrier*, starring Jean Arthur, Joel McCrea, and Charles Coburn, which earned Coburn an Academy Award for best supporting actor. Stevens was nominated for best director.

The seventeen films Stevens made between 1933 and 1943 define his work. With one eye on the box office, Stevens gave film audiences what they wanted. During the Great Depression and World War II he provided two hours of immersion in a make-believe world with make-believe characters whose problems are ultimately resolved to everyone's satisfaction. Thus, he altered Booth Tarkington's novel, upon which *Alice Adams* was based, giving it a happy ending. The theme of *Alice Adams*, boy meets girl but they live on opposite sides of the track, was a formula tearjerker used by the popular magazines of the interwar years. From 1935 to 1943, Stevens continued to feed audiences an easy-laughs, easy-tears diet, built on popular formulas and always following the public taste. He made *Gunga Din* in the wake of the impact made by *The Four Feathers*, a British film that inspired a brief slew of adventure films on late-nineteenth-century imperialist themes.

Stevens's women were passive, selfless, virginal, and always good. They were incapable of change in themselves or their lives; they never made a decision. The men, on the other hand, were the manipulators and decision-makers. The situations were always romantic, and the stories were always awash in sentimentality. *Woman of the Year* (1942), for example—which was made for MGM and produced by Joseph L. Mankiewicz, with an Oscar-winning script by Ring Lardner, Jr., and Michael Kanin, and which began the long and fruitful partnership of Katharine Hepburn and Spencer Tracy—embodies social attitudes that seem pernicious by modern standards but that were perfectly conventional when the movie was made. Tess Harding is only one of a whole gallery of Stevens heroines who learn where a woman's place is.

A master craftsman, Stevens proved to his contemporaries what high technical polish of cinematographic skills could do for the medium. He shot scenes from every possible angle, then spent long months in the cutting room, editing and assembling the pieces until he was satisfied. He said that more than half of the creative process occurred in the interaction between camera, actors, and space, another 25 percent took place in the cutting room, and the remainder came from other sources. He had little regard for scripts and depended heavily on improvisation. He started *Annie Oakley* with only one-third of the script in hand, while the *Swing Time* script handed him by MGM was redone completely during production.

In the summer of 1943 Stevens was recruited by General Dwight D. Eisenhower to head the famous Special Motion Picture Coverage Unit of the Army Signal Corps. Its mission was to document the war in the European Theater for the National Archives from North Africa, D day, and liberation to the German surrender. Between 1943 and 1945 Stevens covered all the American battles in Europe and the liberation of Paris. He was the first American to document the horrors of the Dachau concentration camp. Discharged from the army in 1945 as a lieutenant colonel, Stevens won five battle stars. He was also awarded the French Legion of Merit and a unit citation, presented to him personally by Eisenhower for his "outstanding performance in going with the early onslaught troops and advance detachments, in disregard to personal danger."

Stevens had difficulty readjusting after the war. Together with two other ex-colonels, Frank Capra and William Wiley, he formed Liberty Films, with the aim of producing movies that would contribute to a "better America." But Liberty Films released only one movie, Frank Capra's *It's a Wonderful Life* (1946). In

1937 Stevens had separated from Yvette Stevens, whom he had married in 1930, and in 1947 he ended eleven years of off-and-on court battles over alimony and child support. The court ruled divided custody over their son, George Stevens, Jr., born in 1932.

In 1948, Liberty Films loaned Stevens to RKO to direct the nostalgic movie *I Remember Mama*, starring Irene Dunne, Barbara Bel Geddes, and Oscar Homolka. For lack of funds, Liberty Films merged in 1949 with Paramount, and Stevens came with the package. In 1951 he directed *A Place in the Sun*, with Elizabeth Taylor, Montgomery Clift, and Shelley Winters, a film that he had worked on for two years. It won him the Screen Directors Guild Award and the Academy Award for best director. The film received a total of five Oscars. In *A Place in the Sun* Stevens gave up his devotion to happy endings, and his characters evinced an emotional depth that contributed to the film's social message. By this time Paramount and Liberty Films had split up. Paramount's discontent with Liberty Films was due, partly, to the long time it had taken Stevens to complete *A Place in the Sun*. Consequently, Stevens rushed his next film through production. *Something to Live For*, released in 1952, starred Ray Milland replaying his Academy Award–winning performance as an alcoholic in *The Lost Weekend*. The 1952 film was a failure.

The Western movie revival reached its zenith with director Fred Zinnemann's *High Noon* (1952), starring Gary Cooper and Grace Kelly. Again putting his ear to the ground, Stevens followed the trend and came up in 1953 with *Shane*, starring Alan Ladd, Van Heflin, Jack Palance, Jean Arthur, and Brando de Wilde. Stevens's photocinematic skills reached a new height in this movie, which received an Academy Award for photography. Stevens received the Irving Thalberg Memorial Academy Award for a lifetime of cinematic achievement in 1954.

His reputation as a director reestablished, Stevens no longer rushed his work through the cutting room. He took three years to bring out his next film, *Giant* (1956), starring Rock Hudson, Elizabeth Taylor, and James Dean. The movie brought him his second best director awards from the Screen Directors Guild (in which he had served as president twice) and the Academy. After that he took another three years to come out with *The Diary of Anne Frank*

(1959), starring Millie Perkins, Shelley Winters, and Joseph Schildkraut. The poetic quality of *Anne Frank* and the extraordinary photographic achievement given the nature of the film set were recognized by critics. The film received two Academy Awards, one for photography and one to Shelley Winters as best supporting actress.

In the mid-1960's Stevens joined a group of prominent directors and studio heads who were fighting the television industry for editing their films. Otto Preminger had just lost his lawsuit over television handling of *An Anatomy of a Murder*, when Stevens sued NBC and Paramount in October 1965 for cutting *A Place in the Sun*. Stevens referred to art as a juridical criterion and implored the court to consider the destructive effect of such abuse on the artistry of his film. In a ground-breaking decision, a Chicago federal court awarded Stevens $1 million, thus setting a precedent for future handling of films on television.

Stevens spent nearly six years on *The Greatest Story Ever Told* (1965) with Max von Sydow as Jesus Christ and a multistar cast in cameo roles. Although the film was acclaimed by many critics as the "best cinematic attempt to date," it proved a box office failure. Stevens lost confidence in his ability to discern audience trends, a talent on which he had so heavily relied during the 1930's and 1940's. Needing reassurance, he returned to the romantic formulas that had brought him his past laurels. *The Only Game in Town* (1970), starring Elizabeth Taylor and Warren Beatty, was a mild Las Vegas romance, which had a lukewarm audience reception and gave the critics an opportunity to tear him down as an overrated craftsman and a has-been.

Stevens, who lived in Beverly Hills, died suddenly of a heart attack in Lancaster, Calif. He was survived by his second wife, Joan Pauline Stevens. His son, George Stevens, Jr., continued to keep his father's name alive. He named the American Film Institute (Washington, D.C.), which he headed, after his father and sponsored many retrospective festivals of his father's films. In 1985 he published a book of his father's best wartime stills, and in the same year, in a special state ceremony, he donated relevant footage of his father's wartime films and still pictures to the French National Archives.

[The best analysis, in book form, of George Stevens's work is Bruce Humleker Petrie's *Theory of*

American Film: The Films and Techniques of George Stevens (1987). Roger Alan Miller's *George Stevens: Profile of a Filmmaker* (University of California, Los Angeles, School of Theatre, Motion Picture and Television dissertation, 1966), though written in an awestruck tone is well done up to 1966, missing Stevens's last two films. Erik and Sandra van Backer's *George Stevens 1904–1975* (1986), written in Dutch, is an excellent presentation of Stevens's artistic accomplishment, unfortunately inaccessible to English speakers. Donald Richie's *Stevens: An American Romantic* (1985), is an imbalanced, poorly organized and hastily written introductory profile of Stevens's work, which is nevertheless comprehensive.

Chapters devoted to Stevens are found in James Harvey's *Romantic Comedy in Hollywood from Lubitch to Sturges* (1987) and Gene D. Phillips, *The Moviemakers: Artists in an Industry* (1973). George Stevens, Jr., published a posthumous book of his father's World War II still photographs, with a text by Max Hastings, entitled *Victory in Europe* (1985). Several of Stevens's films have been released on videocasette.

Obituaries of Stevens appear in *Variety* and the *Chicago Tribune, Hollywood Reporter, Los Angeles Times, New York Times*, and *Washington Post*, all on Mar. 10, 1975; posthumous tributes appear in the *New York Times*, Mar. 10, 1975, the *Los Angeles Times*, Mar. 11, 13, and 21, 1975; and *Variety*, Mar. 12, 1975.]

SHOSHANA KLEBANOFF

STEWART, ARTHUR THOMAS ("TOM") (Jan. 11, 1892–Oct. 11, 1972), attorney and United States senator, was born in Dunlap, Tenn. He was educated in local public high schools and at the Pryor Institute in Jasper, Tenn., where he was known for his orations. Stewart graduated from Emory College (now University) in Oxford, Ga., and received a law degree from Cumberland University in Lebanon, Tenn. After admission to the bar in 1913, he practiced law in Birmingham, Ala. He married Helen Turner on Dec. 19, 1914; they had five children. The following year Stewart returned to Jasper, and in 1919 he moved to Winchester, Tenn.

Stewart became attorney general of Tennessee's Eighteenth Circuit in 1923. In that capacity he was the lead prosecutor in the Scopes "Monkey Trial" in which John T. Scopes, a young schoolteacher, was accused of violating the Butler Act, a March 1925 law prohibiting the teaching of Darwin's theory of evolution in Tennessee schools. Stewart, in his midthirties, was slim and looked younger than his years,

with curly dark blond hair that fell over his face. He was known as a clever lawyer, especially in court, where he made intense and compelling speeches. Leading a team that included William Jennings Bryan; William Jennings Bryan, Jr.; Ben G. McKenzie; J. Gordon McKenzie; Sue K. and Herbert Hicks; and Wallace C. Haggard, Stewart presented the state's successful case.

Stewart based his prosecution on the simple grounds that the law existed, and that Scopes had broken it. The affair had assumed a circus atmosphere, however, and Stewart worked doggedly to keep the trial orderly. Some Dayton citizens proposed building a new auditorium to hold overflow crowds and possibly be the courtroom. The plan was endorsed by Judge John Tate Raulston but vetoed by Stewart. The trial began on Friday, July 10, 1925, a sweltering day. Stewart, a rather formal man, was one of two men to keep his jacket on. When the trial resumed on Monday, Stewart kept it on until the afternoon. Stewart also resisted attempts by the defense (led by Clarence Darrow) to admit scientific evidence as to the validity of evolution. He went so far as to have Judge Raulston dismiss the jury while the defense was pleading its motion to quash the Scopes indictment; the defense was discussing scientific and religious views of the Butler Act and in a sense presenting its case before the trial began. In the end, the defense was allowed only to submit eight affidavits from scientists, some of which were read aloud in court. Although overshadowed by William Jennings Bryan, who made several long speeches and garnered much publicity, Stewart won the case on its merits. On July 21, 1925, Scopes was convicted and fined $100. (The Butler Act was challenged again in 1965 and was repealed by the Tennessee legislature in 1967.)

As attorney general, Stewart became allied with Edward H. Crump of Memphis, whose political organization controlled Democratic western Tennessee. Allied with Republicans in eastern Tennessee, Boss Crump traded patronage for votes and created a machine that lasted two decades. In 1938, Crump decided to back Tom Stewart to serve four years in the Senate seat left vacant by the death of Nathan L. Bachman. The Senate later investigated Crump's fund-raising tactics, finding "a vigorous effort throughout the State to raise campaign funds by contributions from federal employees."

While in the Senate, Stewart was the chairman of the Committee on Interoceanic Canals during the Seventy-ninth Congress. He also alienated Boss Crump, whose Tennessee machine backed President Roosevelt's New Deal measures. Tom Stewart became increasingly known as a conservative Democrat, and he authored several bills against the Tennessee Valley Authority. This did not please Crump. Moreover, when Stewart ran for reelection in 1942, he carried only Shelby County outright, and that was because of the machine's exertions on his behalf. It was enough to win, but it showed that Stewart was vulnerable. In 1948, then, Crump backed Judge John Mitchell of Cookeville in the Democratic primary. Stewart, however, refused to withdraw, causing a three-way race. Stewart came in second, and Estes Kefauver won both the primary and general election.

Stewart left the Senate Jan. 3, 1949. After his return to Tennessee, Stewart practiced law in Nashville, where he died.

[There is little information available on Stewart, whose papers are, for the most part, presumed destroyed, although the Tennessee State Library and Archives in Nashville have some letters and biographical sketches. Stewart plays a significant role in the newspaper accounts of the Scopes trial, as well as in various books about that trial. See Ray Ginger, *Six Days or Forever?* (1958); H. L. Mencken, "'The Monkey Trial': A Reporter's Account," in Jerry R. Tompkins, ed., *D-Days at Dayton: Reflections on the Scopes Trial* (1965); and L. Sprague de Camp, *The Great Monkey Trial* (1968). For information on Tennessee politics, see Stanley J. Folmsbee, Robert E. Corlew, and Enoch Mitchell, *Tennessee* (1969); and Lee Seifert Green, *Lead Me On* (1982). An obituary is in the *New York Times*, Oct. 12, 1972.]

ALANA J. ERICKSON

STOUFFER, VERNON BIGELOW (Aug 22, 1901–July 26, 1974), restaurateur and businessman, was born in Cleveland, Ohio, to Abraham E. Stouffer, a dairyman and partner in the Medina Creamery Company, and Mahala Bigelow. He attended elementary school in suburban Medina, and after three years at Lakewood High School transferred to University High School in Cleveland. He graduated from the University of Pennsylvania's Wharton School of Business in 1923 with a B.A. in economics. Determined to embark upon a business career, he returned to Cleveland in search of a suitable opportunity.

In the meantime, Abraham Stouffer had sold his interest in the Medina Creamery, but continued to operate his own dairy farm. Partly to provide an outlet for his dairy products, the senior Stouffer opened a stand-up lunch counter in the old Cleveland Arcade in 1923. Its success encouraged his son Vernon to open, in 1924, a larger lunch counter in Cleveland's Schofield Building, which he proposed to operate with his parents' assistance. The Stouffer Lunch, begun with an investment of $12,000, eventually became The Stouffer Foods Corporation, an $80-million business by 1967 which encompassed restaurants, inns, a food-management service, and a frozen-foods division.

Vernon Stouffer led the company as president and chief executive officer from its inception, exercising for many years a hands-on management style that extended to all phases of operation. From the beginning, he envisioned a chain of restaurants serving simple home-style fare of consistent quality, with many of the early menu items drawn from his own mother's recipes. His attention to efficiency, cost control, and service and his insistence that quality remain his company's hallmark helped make the venture a success.

Stouffer's restaurants featured college-trained business managers and, as requested by Stouffer, exclusively employed female cooks, who prepared rigidly standardized recipes under the supervision of dietitians. Waitresses were trained to personalize customer service for the middle-class patrons targeted by Stouffer's marketing strategy. This formula enabled him to develop a chain of forty-six restaurants by 1967, including Stouffer's Fifth Avenue in Manhattan, at one time the largest single restaurant in the nation.

In keeping personally involved with the company, Stouffer frequented the test kitchens, and had a second kitchen built in his home for his exclusive use. He reportedly spent one-third of his time on the road, ensuring that quality was maintained by posing as an ordinary customer.

Stouffer Foods opened motor inns and a food management service, but the company's most lucrative area of expansion proved to be the frozen-foods division. Developed initially in response to customer demand at a Cleveland-area restaurant, it was established in 1954 and grew rapidly because it targeted a specialized market.

Aided after 1929 by his brother Gordon, and in later years by son James and son-in-law James

Biggar, Vernon Stouffer remained president of Stouffer Foods until its sale to Litton Industries in 1967 for $20 million worth of Litton Industries stock. Within a year Litton stock had plummeted to one-fifth its previous value as the Litton conglomerate encountered management and financial problems. Stouffer was also a director of Republic Steel Corporation, United Airlines, Consolidated Natural Gas Company of New York, Society National Bank of Cleveland, and Security National Bank of Denver.

Vernon Stouffer married Gertrude Dean in 1928, and the couple had three children. The Stouffers lived for many years in a modest home in Lakewood, a Cleveland suburb on Lake Erie. There Stouffer developed a fondness for yachting, which he eventually indulged by purchasing the yacht *Gemini* from the Duke and Duchess of Windsor. He was a member of the Cleveland Yachting Club.

In 1966 Stouffer acquired controlling interest in the Cleveland Indians, his hometown major-league baseball team. A ballpark usher as a youngster, Stouffer was perhaps fulfilling a dream, but financial reverses and a decline in the team's fortunes led to its sale in 1972 to a group headed by Nick Mileti.

Vernon Stouffer remained a lifelong Cleveland resident, and was active in a number of civic and charitable enterprises. Deeply interested in the development of the Cleveland Zoo, he served as president of the Cleveland Zoological Society, and made trips to Africa and India to obtain animals for its exhibits. He was president of the Northern Ohio Opera Society, as well as a member of its executive committee. He was also a founder and trustee of the National Recreation and Park Association.

Stouffer was an active Republican and claimed President Dwight Eisenhower as a friend. In 1960 Eisenhower appointed him special ambassador to the independence ceremony of the United Somalia Republic.

The Stouffer family established the Vernon Stouffer Corporation to support philanthropic projects in education, public welfare, and medicine. The Stouffer Prize, a $50,000 annual award for achievement in heart disease research, was first given in 1965. Stouffer told an interviewer in 1967 that "the prize was established with the strongest possible personal motivation," because his parents and his brother had died of heart-related diseases.

Stouffer was in many ways an embodiment of the American entrepreneurial spirit. Although his was not a rags-to-riches story, he took a small investment, and through hard work, good judgment, and sound management, built a successful business. Modest and down-to-earth, Stouffer was motivated as much by creativity as he was by capitalism.

Stouffer died in Cleveland, Ohio. His work was honored in 1992 in Las Vegas by the Frozen Food Hall of Fame.

[Extensive newspaper clippings on Stouffer are in the files of the (Cleveland, Ohio) *Plain Dealer*. See also "Making a Profit on Every Bite," *Business Week*, Feb. 15, 1958; "Stouffer Preempts the Kitchen," *Business Week*, June 3, 1961; and a two-part article in *Advertising Age*, Feb. 18, 1963, and Feb. 25, 1963. Obituaries appear in the *Plain Dealer* and the *New York Times*, both July 27, 1974.]

STEPHANIE O'NEAL

STOUT, REX TODHUNTER (Dec. 1, 1886– Oct. 27, 1975), author known as the creator of Nero Wolfe, was born in Noblesville, Ind., the sixth child of John Wallace Stout, a teacher and administrator, and Lucetta Elizabeth Todhunter; both parents were Quakers. Before Rex's first birthday, the family moved to a farm at Wakarusa, Kans., near Topeka. Rex began his education in a two-room schoolhouse, with his sister as a teacher and his father as superintendent of schools, before attending the District 60 school and later Topeka High School. Always an avid reader, Stout perused his father's extensive library and earned a reputation as a prodigy. He was the Kansas/Nebraska/Illinois spelling champion at eleven and was exhibited as a math genius for his rapid calculation skills. Elected senior class poet, he graduated from Topeka High School in 1903 and then spent two years traveling around the country.

Unable to raise money and not interested in attending college, he worked as an usher at Crawford's Opera House until he enlisted in the United States Navy in 1906. He was assigned as a yeoman on the *Mayflower*, President Theodore Roosevelt's yacht, handling the president's accounts. He enjoyed his adventures, which included a trip to the Caribbean, and he was discharged in 1908.

After spending four years drifting and working as a cigar salesman, stable hand, plumber, tour guide, and hotel manager, Stout turned to writing. In New York, he cajoled the *World* into accepting an article on palmistry and obtained the palmprints of presidential candidates William Howard Taft and Tom Loftin Johnson. He was paid two hundred dollars for his article, a considerable sum at that time; he then sold fiction to magazines and pulps, particularly the Frank A. Munsey magazines, and wrote three novels. Finding this career not lucrative enough, Stout began a banking venture with his brother, the Educational Thrift Service, which enrolled elementary school students in a savings plan (1916).

In December 1916 Stout married Fay Kennedy of Topeka, and the two traveled the East Coast to help establish ETS. By 1925, three million children in 432 cities in 30 states were enrolled. The next year, on his fortieth birthday, Stout sold his interest in ETS for $400,000, and he spent an "expatriate" year abroad, meeting such celebrities as Gertrude Stein and Ernest Hemingway, and returned to New York for the publication of four "serious" novels, *How Like a God* (1929), *Seed on the Wind* (1930), *Golden Remedy* (1931), and *Forest Fire* (1933). During 1930, he was the architect and contractor in the building of his home, High Meadow, located between Brewster, N.Y., and Darien, Conn. He had divorced Fay in 1930 and married textile designer Pola Weinbach Hoffman on Dec. 21, 1932; the imminent birth of the first of their two daughters intensified his need for financial security. His funds depleted by the stock-market crash, Stout turned to writing detective fiction, considering it a good source of income.

In 1934, *Fer-de-Lance* first appeared serially in the *Saturday Evening Post*, and Stout created in his character Nero Wolfe the last "Great Detective" in the manner of Sherlock Holmes—a total being, as Stout describes the development of the character. Like Sherlock's brother Mycroft, Wolfe was strictly an armchair detective, with any physical exertion exercised by his able Watson, Archie Goodwin. Over the next forty years, readers became familiar with the odd domestic arrangement at the brownstone house on West Thirty-fifth Street. The lazy, obese, eccentric Wolfe, with his passion for orchids and gourmet meals, left his home only under extreme provocation; the enormous fees he charged to solve puzzles and find murderers offset the inconvenience of having to exert his prodigious intellect. Wolfe's chief aide, Archie, was a detective who might have con-

ducted his own successful career as a handsome, hard-boiled, wise-cracking "private eye." Wolfe was not a pastiche of Stout's acquaintances; he insisted that Wolfe appeared as a fully developed person whose history Stout merely recorded. The Wolfe books sold over forty-five million copies, appearing in more than twenty languages; the last, *A Family Affair*, was published in 1975, and the books have enjoyed long-standing popularity. Although Stout created other detectives—Dol Bonner (*The Hand in the Glove*, 1937) Tecumseh Fox (*Double for Death*, 1939) and Alphabet Hicks (in the book of the same name, 1941)—none of these achieved the same status as Wolfe for mystery fans.

Between 1938 and 1945 Stout curtailed his writing of fiction and devoted himself to creating propaganda against Nazism. He helped to establish the Fight for Freedom committee and Freedom House; he was president of the Society for the Prevention of World War III. A talent for broadcasting discovered while he was appearing on *Information, Please* won him a role as master of ceremonies on *Speaking of Liberty* (1941), and he was the "voice" in *Voice of Freedom* (1942). Late in that same year he wrote the broadcast scripts for *Our Secret Weapon* countering Nazi propaganda. He also helped organize the Writers' War Board (later the Writers' Board). Stout's vision included world government and nuclear disarmament.

In the literary world, he was president of the Authors' Guild and a member of a committee for a universal copyright. He was president of Mystery Writers of America in 1958 and was named the Grand Master of Mystery that same year. He was also awarded the prestigious Silver Dagger of the British Crime Writers' Association shortly thereafter. He was a founder of *The New Masses* and was president of Vanguard, a publishing firm he helped establish.

Stout was an apostle of liberalism; a board member of the American Civil Liberties Union, he was sympathetic to Sacco and Vanzetti in 1927 and the Rosenbergs in 1953. While he did not propagandize his political views in his fiction, Stout deplored racism, censorship, McCarthyism, advertising, *Webster's Third International Dictionary*, the Warren Report, and Watergate. Stout's attitude toward the FBI was captured in *The Doorbell Rang* (1965). His liberalism, eccentricities, and fascinating personality helped create one of detective fiction's most enduring characters. Jacques Barzun has compared Nero and Archie to Don Quixote and Sancho Panza, and said they "go tilting together against evil," with "no mystery, nothing but matter for admiration, edification and (if deserved) self-identification. The true mystery is in their inspired creator, Rex Stout." Stout died at his home in Brewster, N.Y.

[For further information see John McAleer, *Rex Stout: A Biography* (1977), which includes excellent bibliographies; and Alva Johnson, Profile, "Alias Nero Wolfe," *New Yorker*, July 16, 1949, and July 23, 1949. An obituary appears in the *New York Times*, Oct. 29, 1975.]

ELIZABETH R. NELSON

STRAUSS, LEWIS LICHTENSTEIN (Jan. 31, 1896–Jan. 21, 1974), financier and government official, was born in Charleston, W.Va., the son of Lewis S. Strauss and Rosa Lichtenstein. His father was an officer in a wholesale shoe business, his mother an artist.

Upon graduation from high school in Richmond, Va., Strauss won a scholarship to the University of Virginia. Instead he joined his father's economically pressed firm as a traveling salesman. On the road, Strauss studied science and Judaica voraciously and saved money to attend the university. But American entry into World War I prompted him to volunteer to work without salary for Herbert Hoover in the Food Administration. He rapidly rose from office boy to statistical researcher to private secretary. Strauss accompanied Hoover to Europe for the Versailles conference. At the end of the war, Strauss worked in Hoover's American Relief Administration.

Meanwhile, Strauss also worked for the American Jewish Joint Distribution Committee, under the direction of banker-philanthropist Felix Warburg. In the spring of 1919 he declined an opportunity to become a controller for the new League of Nations. Instead, he accepted the invitation of Warburg and his partners to join the investment banking firm of Kuhn, Loeb and Company in New York City. On Mar. 5, 1923, he married Alice Hanauer, daughter of another Kuhn, Loeb partner. They had two sons; one died as a child.

Strauss became a partner in the firm on Jan. 1, 1929. He took particular interest in encouraging young inventors, such as Leopold Mannes and Leopold Godowsky, Jr., who worked on processes for simplified color photography in 1923, and later Edwin H. Land, pioneer of polaroid film. Strauss was named to several boards of directors, including those of United States Leather, United States Rubber, General American Transportation, Commercial Investment Trust, and the Hudson and Manhattan Railroad. His philanthropic efforts included fund-raising in 1921 to repatriate Austrian and Hungarian prisoners of war. In 1928 Strauss served as vice-treasurer of the Republican National Committee while his old chief, Herbert Hoover, ran for president. Active in the Jewish religion, from 1938 to 1949 he was president of Congregation Emanu-El in New York City.

Strauss also continued his amateur interest in physics. After his mother died of cancer in 1935, he financed research at the California Institute of Technology to produce radioactive isotopes for cancer therapy. The same interest put him in contact with scientists fleeing Nazism, who kept him informed of Germany's uranium research.

Having been commissioned a lieutenant commander in the United States Naval Reserve as an intelligence officer in 1925, Strauss volunteered for active service several times in 1939 and 1940. He was called to active duty in 1941 as general inspector in the Bureau of Ordnance. Strauss improved efficiency in the flow of war materials, helping to create the "Navy E" award for defense contractors who finished their work on schedule. As deputy chief of the Office of Navay Material, Strauss and his army counterpart, William H. Draper, planned coordinated procurement of petroleum, food, and clothing. He later represented the Navy on the Interdepartmental Committee on Atomic Energy and on the Army-Navy Munitions Board.

At the end of 1943, now a captain, Strauss was appointed assistant chief of the Office of Procurement and Material, where he organized a new bureau to oversee termination of defense contracts and disposal of surplus property at the end of World War II. In 1944, Secretary of the Navy James V. Forrestal named him his special assistant. These wartime activities earned Strauss the Legion of Merit, plus an Oak Leaf Cluster and a Gold Star. In November 1945, President Harry S. Truman raised Strauss to the rank of rear admiral, an unusual distinction for a reservist. Thereafter, he preferred that his staff address him as "Admiral Strauss." Demobilized the following month, Strauss returned to Kuhn, Loeb.

Seven months later, President Truman named Strauss one of five members of the new Atomic Energy Commission (AEC). Strauss resigned his Kuhn, Loeb partnership and divested himself of all corporate ties. The Senate overwhelmingly confirmed his appointment. On the AEC, Strauss fought for the monitoring system that detected the first Soviet atomic explosion in 1949, two weeks before the Soviets announced it. Immediately thereafter, Strauss advocated accelerated American development of a hydrogen bomb, a position in which he was supported by physicists Karl T. Compton, Edward Teller, and John Von Neuman, but opposed by AEC chairman David E. Lilienthal and the chairman of the AEC's advisory commission, J. Robert Oppenheimer. When President Truman adopted the Strauss position in 1950, Strauss resigned from the AEC, feeling the commission could function better without reminders of past differences.

For the next three years Strauss advised the Rockefeller brothers on investments and helped them with such activities as the Population Council. He continued as an adviser to the AEC.

When the Republicans recaptured the White House in 1953, President Dwight D. Eisenhower first used Strauss as his special assistant on atomic energy and then appointed him to a five-year term as chairman of the Atomic Energy Commission. The Senate confirmed the appointment within three days.

As AEC chairman, Strauss reactivated American cooperation with Britain and Canada and initiated both the International Atomic Energy Agency and the International Conferences on the Peaceful Uses of Atomic Energy. He also successfully advocated private industrial development of hydroelectric energy, which ended the government monopoly and involved him in the Dixon-Yates controversy.

In 1954 he became embroiled in the issue of Oppenheimer's loyalty and security clearance. His opposition to Oppenheimer, a brilliant scientist who had played a major role in the development of the atomic bomb, brought venomous personal attacks against him and alienated some members of Congress, especially Senator Clinton P. Anderson of New Mexico. Choosing not to face potentially hostile Senate confirmation hearings if Eisenhower reappointed him,

Strauss left the AEC on June 30, 1958, at the end of his term. But he served as the president's special assistant on the Atoms-for-Peace program. The following month, Eisenhower presented him with the Medal of Freedom.

On Oct. 24, 1958, President Eisenhower named Strauss secretary of commerce. After a bitter confirmation battle, in which the Oppenheimer and Dixon-Yates issues figured heavily, and with Senator Anderson leading the opposition, the Senate rejected the nomination by a vote of forty-nine to forty-six on June 18, 1959.

In retirement, Strauss continued his philanthropic work, taking particular interest in Princeton University's Institute for Advanced Study, the National Council of Christians and Jews, and New York City's Metropolitan Opera. He raised money for medical research through a foundation named for his parents. He served on the American Jewish Committee and the boards of the Jewish Theological Seminary, Hampton Institute, and George Washington University. In 1962 he published his memoirs. He supported conservative Republicans and took pleasure in the defeats of old political enemies. He was a major force in the Herbert Hoover Presidential Library Association, and he began writing a book about his old chief. He also enjoyed raising cattle on his farm in Culpeper, Va., where he died of cancer after a four-year battle.

[Lewis L. Strauss's manuscripts have been deposited in the Herbert Hoover Presidential Library in West Branch, Iowa, and at the American Jewish Historical Society in Waltham, Mass. His autobiographical memoir, *Men and Decisions*, was published in 1962. See also Richard Pfau, *No Sacrifice Too Great: The Life of Lewis L. Strauss* (1984). His three oral-history interviews were with Raymond Henle for the Herbert Hoover Presidential Library; with John Mason, Jr., for the Columbia Oral History Project; and with George E. Herman for the William E. Weiner Oral History Library. An obituary appears in the *New York Times*, Jan. 22, 1974.]

SUSAN ESTABROOK KENNEDY

STRAVINSKY, IGOR FYODOROVICH (June 17, 1882–Apr. 6, 1971), composer, conductor, and pianist, was born in Oranienbaum (now Lomonosov), a suburb of St. Petersburg, the son of Fyodor Ignatyevich Stravinsky and Anna Kholodovsky. Both sides of his family were landowners and financially secure. Fyodor Ignatyevich's ancestors were the Polish counts of Soulima. Stravinsky's father was a renowned bass-baritone of the Russian Imperial Opera in St. Petersburg. The family moved to St. Petersburg not long after Stravinsky's birth.

Stravinsky's childhood was not a happy one. His father had a violent temper, and Stravinsky spent little time with his mother and two older brothers. Stravinsky's only close relationships as a child were with the family servants. He spent winters in St. Petersburg and summers in the country at the various estates of relatives.

Stravinsky's talent for music was largely ignored early on because his father wanted him to study law, not music. Stravinsky did not start piano lessons with local teachers until he was nine years old. Several years later, he took piano lessons with Mlle L. A. Kashperova, a student of Anton Rubinstein. At high school (gymnasium) in St. Petersburg, Stravinsky was not a very good student and spent most of his time studying and playing music. He was often backstage at the Imperial Opera, listening to the company's rehearsals and performances, and he listened attentively to his father practice at home. As a teenager Stravinsky became interested in improvisation and ultimately turned to composition. He studied harmony with a private teacher, whom he did not respect and studied counterpoint and piano on his own.

In 1901, to satisfy his father, Stravinsky enrolled in the University of St. Petersburg for law and received his degree in jurisprudence in 1905. By all accounts, he was not a very successful legal student. At the university, Stravinsky became friends with Vladimir Rimsky-Korsakov, a son of the famous composer, Nikolai Rimsky-Korsakov. In the summer of 1902, Stravinsky performed some of his works for Rimsky-Korsakov. The old master was not overly impressed but encouraged Stravinsky to continue his studies privately, not at a conservatory. Stravinsky began private lessons with Rimsky-Korsakov; they met twice weekly for three years, working mostly on instrumentation. Rimsky-Korsakov had weekly musical evenings, and some of Stravinsky's early works were performed. Rimsky-Korsakov was more favorably impressed by the 1903–1904 piano sonata.

During the next few years Stravinsky dedicated himself to composition on the family estate in Volhynia. His Symphony in E-flat was dedicated to Rimsky-Korsakov, who arranged for a performance by the court orchestra in May 1907. In addition to the influence of Rimsky-Korsakov, Stravinsky's early work reveals his study of Scriabin, Tchaikovsy, and a number of French composers, especially Debussy, Franck, and Dukas.

As an early disciple of Rimsky-Korsakov, one of the masters of orchestration, it is not surprising that one critic, Richard Swift, would say of Stravinsky that, "Orchestration for him was the sonorous embodiment of his musical ideas; orchestral effects were used for the articulation of ideas and shapes and not merely for their own sake."

On Jan. 23, 1906, Stravinsky married his first cousin, Katerina Gabrielle Nossenko. She encouraged him to abandon any thought of pursuing the law as a career and to focus his attention on music. They had four children, one of whom, Soulima, became a concert pianist, and another, Theodore, became a painter.

In 1907–1908, Stravinsky composed two more orchestral works: *Scherzo fantastique* and *Fireworks* (*Feu d'artifice*). A number of music historians view *Fireworks* as the precursor to such ground-breaking works as *The Rite of Spring*. In the earlier works, the influence of both Rimsky-Korsakov and Debussy can be heard.

The *Scherzo fantastique* and *Fireworks* were heard at a Feb. 6, 1909, concert by the impresario Serge Diaghilev. Diaghilev was impressed by the work and offered Stravinsky his first assignment for the Russian Ballet: Stravinsky orchestrated Grieg's *Kobold* and two Chopin pieces for *Les Sylphides*. Until 1914 Stravinsky and Diaghilev collaborated on several ballets, which were to become the most famous works from Stravinsky's neoprimitive phase and among his most enduring compositions: *The Firebird* (1910), *Petrouchka* (1911), and *The Rite of Spring* (1913).

For the 1910 season Diaghilev commissioned Stravinsky to write an original score for the Russian Ballet's *The Firebird*. The ballet was first performed June 25, 1910, in Paris and was a tremendous success. One can still hear, to some extent, Stravinsky's debt to Rimsky-Korsakov, but more pronounced is the beginning of something very new in modern music, that is, Stravinsky's distinctive use of discordant harmonies and irregular rhythms. Debussy, attending the première, was so impressed that he went backstage to congratulate Stravinsky, and from this point on, Stravinsky was a major figure in the musical life of Europe.

Of the three major ballets, the second, *Petrouchka* (1911), owes little to Rimsky-Korsakov, but Stravinsky's Russian heritage can be heard in his use of Russian folk melodies. The use of polytonality, such as the famous "Petrouchka chord" (the superimposition of $F^{\#}$-major and C-major triads), along with the use of accordion, piano, mallet instruments, high piccolo, and celesta, all contribute to the originality of this new work. Indeed, *Petrouchka* is a more original work than *The Firebird*. The lyrical melodies of *The Firebird* are replaced, as critic David Ewen put it, by "terse, epigrammatic statements, loosely strung together. This was 'new music'—bold and free." With choreography by Fokine, and Nijinsky as the principal dancer, *Petrouchka* was new and intriguing, but it did not incite its first night audience to riot, as was the case only two years later with *The Rite of Spring*.

At the height of Stravinsky's neoprimitive period is his 1913 portrayal of the fertility ritual of pagan Russia. Stravinsky had a vision in 1910: "I saw in imagination a solemn pagan rite: wise elders, seated in a circle, watching a young girl dancing herself to death. They were sacrificing her to propitiate the god of Spring." The work incorporates simple diatonic melodies juxtaposed against new harmonic structures, bold syncopations, and asymmetric rhythms and polymeters. Stravinsky's emphasis on percussion was unprecedented and no doubt contributed to the reaction of the first-night audience. As Paul Griffiths has stated, in *The Rite of Spring*, Stravinsky did away "with the regular pulse which had governed almost all Western music since the Renaissance: the rhythm now is angular and propulsive, the music's main motivating force."

The first performance of *The Rite of Spring*, on May 19, 1913, in Paris, with choreography by Nijinsky, was one of the most inflammatory concerts in musical history. Not expecting music unlike anything the world had ever heard before, many members of the audience broke into catcalls, screamed at the orchestra and the dancers, and denounced the work as merely so much noise. But Ravel and Debussy stood up and cried out that this was a work of genius. The dancers could no longer hear the music. Despite the chaos of the première, less than a year later, the orchestral suite was a huge success when it was performed on Apr. 5, 1914, again in Paris. It was conducted by Pierre Monteux, who had conducted the première performance of the ballet.

The first performance of *The Rite of Spring* in the United States occurred in Philadelphia in 1930 and was conducted by Leopold Stokowski with Martha Graham in the leading dance role. By then most people agreed that the work was a modern classic. (On May 29, 1963, the fiftieth anniversary of *The Rite of Spring* was celebrated in London, with Pierre Monteux once again conducting the orchestral suite. Stravinsky was in the audience for this performance, following which the audience gave the composer a fifteen-minute standing ovation.)

From 1914 to 1920 Stravinsky lived in Switzerland, taking refuge from World War I. During these years he experienced, for the first time, a degree of financial concern, since most of his music publishers were in Germany and he could not rely on royalties from his works. Also, he could not collect the income from his Russian property due to the war and the Bolshevik Revolution. Stravinsky, a liberal, was at first relieved to hear the news of the overthrow of the tsar early in 1917, until the Bolshevik Revolution in October made it clear that he could not return home. Stravinsky was now in permanent exile.

Russian themes are clear in *The Wedding* (*Les Noces*) (1917), a cantata with dancers that portrays scenes at a traditional Russian wedding, and *Reynard*, a burlesque in song and dance in the Russian tradition (1915–1916). When Stravinsky began planning a new ballet in 1917, limitations imposed by World War I dictated a smaller company. *The Soldier's Tale*, completed in 1918, could be performed in small spaces with limited funds. It required only three dancers, a narrator, and seven instruments. It was conceived as "a narrative ballet in five scenes to be read, played and danced," with a text by C. F. Ramuz. An eclectic piece, it incorporates the march, tango, waltz, chorale, and ragtime. Stravinsky made a deliberate attempt to go beyond strictly Russian materials, and the influence of New Orleans Jazz on the work is often mentioned. However, Stravinsky's only exposure to this music was via sheet music brought to him from New Orleans by the Swiss conductor Ernest Ansermet, who conducted the first performance in Lausanne, Switzerland in September 1918. The influence of American ragtime can also be heard in this piece, as well as in "Rag-Time" (1918), and "Piano-rag-music" (1919).

From 1920 until the outbreak of World War II, Stravinsky took up residence in France. He became a French citizen in 1934. In 1921, Stravinsky met Serge Soudeikine's wife, Vera (née de Bosset), and they fell in love. They spent as much time as possible with each other, and she sometimes accompanied him on concert tours. Their illicit liaison lasted until Stravinsky's wife died in 1939; Stravinsky and Vera were married in 1940. They settled in Beverly Hills, Calif., and in December 1945 they became United States citizens.

In France, Stravinsky began to lose interest in working with Russian themes and subjects and sought to write music with extramusical elements. This next phase of Stravinsky's career, the neoclassical, "replaced the dynamic forces of his former neoprimitivism with precision, economy, transparency, and symmetry in which contrapuntal procedures took precedence over rhythm and which became absolute in its strict avoidance of the pictorial or the programmatic," according to Ewen.

Stravinsky's neoclassical compositions are marked by clarity and simplicity. His neoclassicism, with a renewed emphasis on polyphony, classical forms, and transparency of texture, began to take shape with *The Soldier's Tale* (1918) and *Pulcinella* (1919) and was developed further in *Symphonies of Wind Instruments* (1920). It is worth emphasizing that Stravinsky's neoclassicism owes as much to the baroque as it does to the classical period. One critic calls the "Dumbarton Oaks" Concerto composed in the period 1937–1938 a "modern Brandenburg." Stravinsky's new style influenced a number of younger composers and was especially admired by Aaron Copland.

Stravinsky's neoclassical period lasted twenty-five years. Additional major works in this style include *Oedipus Rex*, an opera-oratorio (1927) with a text by Jean Cocteau, and *The Symphony of Psalms*, for chorus and orchestra (1930). *The Rake's Progress* (with a libretto by W. H. Auden and Chester Kallman, completed in 1951) is Stravinsky's last neoclassical work, and his best for the operatic stage. *The Rake's Progress*, with its Mozartean clarity and operatic structure, is the apex of Stravinsky's neoclassical period. The work incorporates many eighteenth-century structures but bears the unmistakable Stravinsky stamp, including his use of sophisticated and altogether contemporary harmonic innovations. The opera was a great success in Europe

and helped reestablish Stravinsky's reputation in postwar Europe.

Motivated by his need to earn money to support the many people who were dependent on him, Stravinsky toured the United States early in 1925. He made his American conducting debut with the New York Philharmonic Orchestra. His first appearance as a pianist in the United States was in a performance of his Piano Concerto with the Boston Symphony Orchestra under Serge Koussevitzky.

In 1926 Stravinsky underwent a spiritual crisis and rejoined the Orthodox church, resulting in an avid interest in composing religious music. He was commissioned by Koussevitzky to write a full-length symphonic work for the fiftieth anniversary of the Boston Symphony Orchestra in 1930. Stravinsky composed the *Symphony of Psalms*, using texts from the Latin Vulgate, and dedicated the work to the glory of God.

Stravinsky toured the United States for the second time in 1935. He composed the Concerto for Two Solo Pianos (1931–1935), which he and his son, Soulima, performed in many concert tours, including a 1936 tour of South America.

In 1938 and 1939, Stravinsky suffered several personal losses: the deaths of his daughter, wife (Katerina), and mother, primarily from tuberculosis. Stravinsky was himself ill and convalesced in a sanatorium until September 1939, when he again toured the United States.

For the academic year 1939–1940 Stravinsky held the prestigious Charles Eliot Norton Chair of Poetry at Harvard; the lectures he delivered were published as the *Poetics of Music* (1948).

In 1948 Stravinsky met Robert Craft, a musician and journalist. Craft became an invaluable assistant to Stravinsky and assisted him with both recordings and tours. Craft often rehearsed the orchestra prior to a recording of Stravinsky conducting his own works and shared the responsibility of conducting the worldwide tours that Stravinsky undertook, from the end of World War II to the mid-1960's. In the 1950's Stravinsky entered into a contract with Columbia Records to record all of his works with himself as conductor. A series of books of musical reminiscences and conversations between Stravinsky and Craft were published.

Following the death of Arnold Schoenberg, Craft exposed Stravinsky to serial music; Stravinsky was particularly impressed by the works of Webern. Now in his seventies, Stravinsky once again made a bold change in his approach to composition. Throughout his long career he always put his own musical development before the expectations of audiences and experts. Stravinsky stated that "the public cannot and will not follow me in the progress of my musical thought. . . . I shall most assuredly not sacrifice my predilections and my aspirations to the demands of those who, in their blindness, do not realize that they are simply asking me to go backwards." With amazing vigor, he abandoned neoclassicism and adopted dodecaphony, but as with neoclassicism, he made this approach his own. Perhaps the most notable work from this third period is the *Canticum sacrum . . . (Sacred Cantata in Honor of St. Mark, Patron Saint of Venice)* (1955) for tenor, baritone, chorus, and orchestra. A fascinating short work is "Three Songs from William Shakespeare" (1953). Stravinsky and the poet Dylan Thomas met in the spring of 1953 and planned to begin collaboration on an opera in the fall. Following Thomas's death in November, Stravinsky wrote the haunting elegy, "In Memoriam Dylan Thomas" (1954), based on Thomas's poem, "Do Not Go Gentle into That Good Night." The song is scored for tenor and string quartet and is framed by a prelude and postlude for trombone quartet.

In 1962 a number of concerts and celebrations throughout the U.S. and Europe commemorated Stravinsky's eightieth birthday, including a dinner party with President Kennedy at the White House. More moving for Stravinsky than all of the other events and awards was the invitation to return to Russia, after nearly fifty years of exile. Having once been denounced by the Soviet authorities, he was now lionized in the USSR. Robert Craft stressed the impact that this return "home" had on the eighty-year-old composer: "To be recognized and acclaimed as a Russian in Russia, and to be performed there, has meant more to him than anything else in the years I have known him."

In 1967 Stravinsky became ill. He made his last recording in January of that year (*The Firebird*). After he could no longer compose, he spent a good deal of his time, at Craft's suggestion, listening to the works of Beethoven and other composers. In 1969, feeling that Los Angeles was not paying him the respect that he and his music deserved, he and his wife moved to New York City. After only a week in his new apartment overlooking Central Park, Stravinsky died of a heart attack on Apr. 6, 1971.

Stravinsky was buried on the island of San Michele, off Venice, near Diaghilev's grave. During the services, his last work, *Requiem Canticles* (1966) for contralto, bass, chorus, and orchestra, was performed. After his death, the New York City Ballet mounted thirty-two ballets, all to the music of Stravinsky, and there were many festivals in his honor around the world.

Stravinsky's innovations and genius were central to the musical development of the twentieth century. It is impossible to think of "modern" music without reflecting on his many contributions to the art. Stravinsky's impact on younger composers is beyond measure.

[Stravinsky's working draft of *The Rite of Spring*, along with the entire Stravinsky archive of 116 boxes of letters and 225 drawers of manuscripts, some unpublished, were purchased by Paul Sacher, the Swiss conductor and philanthropist, who outbid several libraries and promised to make the materials available to scholars at a private foundation in Basel. With Walter Nouvel, Stravinsky wrote *An Autobiography* (*Chroniques de ma vie*) (1935). Stravinsky's famous Harvard lectures are published as *The Poetics of Music* (English trans., 1947). Of the half-dozen Stravinsky and Craft collaborations, *Conversations with Igor Stravinsky* (1959) and *Dialogues and a Diary* (1963) are of particular interest. Among the many books on Stravinsky, Roman Vlad's *Stravinsky* (rev., enlarged 3d ed., 1979) is of genuine value. For an extensive bibliography, as well as additional biographical information, see the article on Stravinsky by Eric Walter White and Jeremy Noble in *The New Grove Dictionary of Music*, Stanley Sadie, ed. (1980). Also see David Ewen, *The World of Twentieth-Century Music*, for in-depth chronological discussions of Stravinsky's major works (1968), and *American Composers: A Biographical Dictionary* (1982). For brief articles on Stravinsky, see those by Richard Swift, in *Dictionary of Contemporary Music*, ed. John Vinton (1974) and Paul Griffiths, in D. Arnold, editor, *The New Oxford Companion to Music* (1983). An obituary is in the *New York Times*, Apr. 7, 1971.]

JOSEPH CORONITI

SULLIVAN, EDWARD VINCENT ("ED") (Sept. 28, 1901–Oct. 13, 1974), television variety show host and newspaper columnist, was born on 114th Street in Harlem, then an Irish neighborhood in New York City, the son of Peter Arthur Sullivan and Elizabeth Smith. His father was an employee of the New York Custom House in lower Manhattan. When Ed's twin brother and then an older sister died, the Sullivans decided that New York City was not a healthy place to raise a family. They moved to Port Chester, N.Y., a suburb in Westchester County, only twenty-six miles from Manhattan but a great distance socially and psychologically.

There Sullivan attended St. Mary's Parochial School and Port Chester High School, where he did his best work in English classes; he particularly liked, he said, the adventure-filled novels of Sir Walter Scott. Sullivan was also an excellent athlete, earning varsity letters in three different sports. He graduated in 1917 and, seeking to broaden his world, he ran away to Chicago to join the U.S. Navy, but he could not produce a birth certificate and was turned down for being too young. He worked briefly in the Illinois Central Railroad yards, until the cold winter drove him home.

Sullivan went to work for the *Port Chester Daily Item*, where he covered local high school sports. This was the beginning of his lifelong career of writing for newspapers. An opportunity for bigger things led him to the *Hartford Post*, but the paper closed down at the end of his first week. Despite his inexperience, he soon got a job with the *Evening Mail* in New York City, where his famous colleagues included Rube Goldberg and the "Believe It or Not" man, Robert Ripley. His assignment again was to cover high school athletics. When he was sent to cover a dog show at Madison Square Garden, he wrote about it in such an engaging way that he received his first New York byline. He went to work, writing mostly about sports, at many New York newspapers, including the *Evening Graphic*, the *Morning World*, the *Morning Bulletin*, and the *Telegraph*. He also wrote for the *Philadelphia Bulletin* and the Associated Press.

About this time, Sullivan began frequenting the nightclubs of Manhattan, where he came into contact with many sports figures, showgirls, and actors. He said of them, "It was a pretty rough citizenry inhabiting the town at the time," but in this period he began his lifelong association with theater people. It was at one such nightclub that he met Sylvia Weinstein, who was not associated with show business. They were married on Apr. 28, 1930, and had one child. Through forty-two years of marriage Sylvia Sullivan was always supportive of her

husband's work, accompanying him to clubs and overlooking late night hours and a life spent almost entirely in hotels. She died on Mar. 16, 1973.

During World War II, Sullivan organized benefits at Madison Square Garden for charitable organizations that he admired. For the Red Cross he raised almost a quarter of a million dollars, a huge sum at the time, and raised almost as much for Army Emergency Relief.

In 1937, he and his family moved to Hollywood for three years. There he wrote his column and attempted a second career writing and acting in films. This was not a success. For example, the *New York Times* critic wrote of *Ma! He's Making Eyes at Me!*, "based on an original story" by Sullivan that it was "a limp and foolish little picture." He actually appeared in *Big Town Czar* in 1939. He had written the script and, in effect, played himself, a columnist who wrote about show biz. The *Times* again was unkind, noting that "the only word for Ed Sullivan's portrayal of Ed Sullivan is 'unconvincing.' " Years later, when he was very famous, he said that he had "set Hollywood back thirty years." This was typical of the way in which he could laugh about his failures.

One night in 1947, Sullivan was acting as master of ceremonies at the Harvest Moon Ball at Madison Square Garden. Unbeknownst to him (he said), it was being televised live. A CBS executive, who had been looking for someone to host a show to compete with Milton Berle's NBC "Texaco Star Theater," saw Sullivan at work. Admiring his easy and relaxed manner before the camera (a trait he later notably lost), he offered Sullivan the job of host for the new show, "Toast of the Town," which premiered June 20, 1948. Among the first guests were Dean Martin and Jerry Lewis, then at the height of their fame. Although only six stations carried the show, it marked the beginning of Sullivan's greatest fame and influence, and almost immediately it became a great success. This was due, in part, to the team Sullivan assembled, members of which stayed with him throughout his career in television.

Along with singers, dancers, and a wide variety of acts that recalled vaudeville days, "Toast of the Town" also profiled figures important in modern show business, running "The Oscar Hammerstein Story," "The Cole Porter Story," and "The Walt Disney Story," all of which featured the preeminent Broadway actors of the time, except for the Disney story, in which the Three Little Pigs, Peter Pan, and Mickey Mouse starred.

"Toast of the Town" was so successful, earning high fees for CBS from advertisers, and its host so central to the production, that the network renamed it "The Ed Sullivan Show" in 1956. Sullivan was given an unheard-of twenty-year contract. He had already insisted on hiring black entertainers, though even entertainment was largely segregated along color lines at the time. He also brought high culture to the American mass audience, introducing them to many of the great figures of the time such as Rudolf Nureyev and Margot Fonteyn of Britain's Royal Ballet. He even gave Maria Callas, then the reigning operatic diva, famous for her fiery temperament, eighteen full minutes on the show, but the ratings fell six points in that short time, so future Met stars were lucky to get five minutes. Still, they did appear; this was before public television stations regularly aired operas and ballets. Sullivan introduced huge numbers of people to art forms they might never have seen elsewhere.

In a coup of sorts, he interviewed Fidel Castro, the dictator of Communist Cuba, during a period of escalating Cold War tensions. Under the aegis of the State Department, he took a wide-ranging mix of opera stars, dancers, musicians, and comics to Moscow and Leningrad in 1959 when relations between the United States and Russia were severely strained. The shows were a huge success in Russia and in their broadcasts at home. Sullivan may be cited, seriously, as one of the people who helped to humanize the old enemies and begin the process that melted away some of the frightening possibilities of nuclear war.

The popular icons of the era also appeared with Sullivan. He gave the first or very early exposure to such groups as the Beatles; 79 million people watched that show, a number that still ranks as spectacular. He at first overlooked Elvis Presley but not for long. When Presley did appear, however, Sullivan showed his prudish side by making sure that Presley's hips, gyrating and shaking, were never shown.

Sullivan's show also influenced television in the establishment of performers' fees. Jack Paar, host of "The Tonight Show," paid $320 to guests, while Sullivan, for admittedly more famous talent, sometimes paid up to $10,000. The two men "feuded" about these fees and the

public enjoyed the fuss, but Sullivan's higher fees pushed up the cost of producing other shows.

In the mid-1960's, "The Ed Sullivan Show" went into a ratings decline; the audience was aging, and the acts booked by the show failed to keep up with the rapid changes in musical taste and social customs of the counterculture. The Rolling Stones did appear, as did Herman's Hermits, the Stones provoking a near riot at the stage door of the studio, which had been renamed the Ed Sullivan Theater in 1967. Though its popularity declined, the show maintained sets and properties enough to fill a warehouse the size of a full city block. In 1971, CBS canceled the show, which had become too expensive to produce, though it did maintain a commitment to future specials. Carol Channing, Robert Klein, Gladys Knight, and Topo Gigio, a little Italian mouse puppet whom Sullivan seemed especially to like, were the guests on the final show, which was actually a rerun.

"I regret that I'm handicapped by no talent at all," Sullivan said on one of his shows. Certainly he could be stiff, and he lacked what has since become essential for television personalities, a charismatic film presence. His sometimes odd pronunciations and mispronunciations made him an easy target for many of the stars and comedians of the time (a lot of them did Sullivan take-offs); Bing Crosby said, for example, "While he doesn't sing, dance or tell jokes, he does them equally well." Some compared his face to the figures on Easter Island and his lack of expression earned him the moniker "The Great Stone Face." He seemed to have little personality, but none of that mattered because the audience seemed to identify with his nervousness, and because he had a great talent for picking and promoting talent. Though the show's producers (ultimately, one of them was his son-in-law) forbade his making settled arrangements for a guest's appearance without their approval, Sullivan took chances and booked talent that they might have avoided or overlooked. Only rarely did he seem unduly guided by public opinion; in the late 1950's he avoided presenting acts that might be deemed "anti-American."

Sullivan was the recipient of many awards. He was elected Abbot of the Friars, an important New York club of theatrical leaders. He was made a Knight of Malta by the Roman Catholic Church and was elected president of

Theater Authority, which had been created to protect theater people from being exploited by benefits and charity functions.

In 1972, "The Sullivan Years" drew a huge TV audience. In 1973, he again scored big ratings as host of "The Entertainer of the Year Awards" from Las Vegas. On March 16, "Ed Sullivan's Broadway" again scored high in the ratings, little comfort to its star, whose wife died the same day.

Ed Sullivan died in New York City, where he had spent almost all of his life. His funeral service, conducted by Terrence Cardinal Cooke at St. Patrick's Cathedral on Fifth Avenue, was attended by thousands of mourners and dozens of celebrities.

[For further biographical information see Michael D. Harris, *Always on Sunday* (1968); Jerry Bowles, *A Thousand Sundays: The Story of the Ed Sullivan Show* (1980). The Museum of Radio and TV in New York City has ninety tapes of Sullivan's shows, which are available for viewing. An obituary is in the *New York Times*, Oct. 14, 1974.]

JAMES DOUGLAS MERRITT

SUMMERFIELD, ARTHUR ELLSWORTH (Mar. 17, 1899–Apr. 26, 1972), postmaster general, was born in Pinconning, Mich., the son of William Henry Summerfield, a pioneer rural mail carrier, and Cora Edith Ellsworth. He completed an elementary education and, beginning at age thirteen, worked for the Weston-Mott Company, then for the Buick Motor Company, and during World War I, for the ammunition department of the Chevrolet plant in Flint, Mich.

On July 22, 1918, Summerfield married Miriam W. Graim. He entered the real estate business the following year and became a distributor for Pure Oil Company in 1924. Five years later, he established his own Chevrolet dealership in Flint, which he built into one of the largest in the country with branches in Clio and Grand Rapids, Mich., and truck dealerships in Gary, Ind., and Chicago, Ill. He gave up the oil business in 1937, and in 1938 he became president of Bryant Properties Corporation. By this time, the Summerfields were rearing their two children.

The failure of a poorly staged local rally for Republican presidential candidate Wendell Willkie in 1940 drew Summerfield into politics where he organized Genesee County for Willkie

and helped him carry all of Michigan. In 1942, Summerfield ran for secretary of state of Michigan, but lost the primary election. The following year, he became finance director of the state Republican Central Committee and instituted effective solicitation, collection, and budgeting of party funds.

From 1942 to 1949, the personable businessman served as a director of both the Michigan and National Automobile Dealers associations, assisted in manpower mobilization for World War II, and directed Flint's War Chest Campaign. Through 1943 and 1944, he served on both the National Automobile Dealers Association and National Chamber of Commerce's postwar planning committees and was elected to the Republican National Committee in 1944.

Summerfield worked to draft Senator Arthur Vandenberg of Michigan for the 1948 presidential nomination. However, the party's bid went to Thomas E. Dewey, who lost the election. The following year, as director of the Republican's National Strategy Committee, Summerfield designed its attack on the Democrats' "Welfare State" for the 1950 congressional elections. That year he had a tiff with party chairman Guy C. Gabrielson, who wanted to dissolve the committee, and resigned his post.

Summerfield's business interests continued to grow and, by 1952, he served as a director of the Genesee Real Estate Association while continuing to work with the state and national automobile dealers associations. He was also on the board of directors of the American Motorists Insurance Company, the Lumbermen's Mutual Insurance Company, and Kemper Life Insurance Company.

Summerfield initially backed Senator Robert A. Taft of Ohio during the 1952 presidential campaign, but after leading a group of uncommitted Michigan delegates to the Republican Convention, swung the delegation to General Dwight D. Eisenhower. The day after Eisenhower's nomination, he succeeded Gabrielson as Chairman of the Republican National Committee and coordinated the successful Republican campaign that year.

During the campaign, charges of financial irregularities arose against Eisenhower's running mate, Richard M. Nixon, and a "Drop Nixon" movement developed in the Republican ranks. Summerfield nonetheless backed Nixon and raised $75,000 to finance the broadcast of the maudlin "Checkers" speech that kept Nixon on the ticket. Eisenhower then appointed Summerfield to the first of his two terms as postmaster general.

As one of the most interesting and controversial men to hold this post, Summerfield enjoyed his greatest successes in his first two years in office. He surprised his own party by resigning its chairmanship and refusing to use the U.S. Postal Service for patronage; he needed the incumbent Democrats to help him improve the department's management.

The general outline for that improvement was enunciated in the 1949 recommendations of the Commission on the Organization of the Executive Branch of the Government, led by ex-president Herbert Hoover. Summerfield followed the commission's recommendations and made his most significant contribution to the Post Office Department by giving it new, decentralized management methods.

He brought in new top-level managers, made financial statements available at the end of each month, created fifteen postal regions for ease of administration, added a fifth assistant postmaster general to handle personnel, and reorganized the Postal Service's transportation patterns to move the mails quickly. He also found the average local post office building to be fifty years old and in need of replacement; when he could get only scant construction appropriations from Congress he encouraged private interests to construct new mail facilities and lease them to the department. To improve postal service, Summerfield began flying first-class mail, at no surcharge, between major cities in 1955.

He attempted to reduce the perennial operating deficits of the Postal Service. Despite raising the prices of first-class and air-mail stamps and instituting accounting changes and cost shifting, he effected no appreciable reductions on the bottom line. He convinced Eisenhower to veto four different pay increases for postal workers, moves that sorely alienated his employees.

Partly because of his bullishness and condescension, Congress underfunded Summerfield's attempts to create new postal equipment but allowed him to participate in the early, limited system of "fax" mail. He also saw that the Postal Service had little engineering or machine design experience and strengthened its research and engineering division.

That division assisted in his most ambitious project, "Operation Turnkey," the construction of a model automated postal center in Providence, R.I. Experimental and pioneering in nature, the facility had teething troubles and had to be redesigned and reconstructed.

Summerfield had the mail boxes painted red, white, and blue, and further demonstrated his knack as a promoter on June 8, 1959, when a Regulus I missile fired from a submarine carried 3,000 letters of "missile" mail ashore to Florida and the waiting postmaster general.

Summerfield attempted to institute a form of censorship in 1958 by banning D. H. Lawrence's *Lady Chatterly's Lover* from the mails, but he lost the ensuing court battle. He also attacked the sending of pornography through the mails and established an exhibition of seized smutty materials in Washington, D.C., that caused tittering and a loss of respect for him.

In 1960, he wrote with Charles Hurd *U.S. Mail: The Story of the United States Postal Service*, a history that reveals his business, management, and personal philosophies.

During 1964, Summerfield helped finance Republican Barry Goldwater's presidential campaign, continued to serve as Chairman of Summerfield Chevrolet, and died eight years later while on vacation in West Palm Beach, Fla.

[Some of Summerfield's papers are in the Eisenhower Library, Abilene, Kans. See also Gerald Cullinan, *The Post Office Department* (1968). Obituaries are in the *New York Times* and the *Washington Post*, both Apr. 27, 1972.]

LAWRENCE CARROLL ALLIN

SUMMERSBY, KATHLEEN HELEN ("KAY") (1908–Jan. 20, 1975), wartime aide to General Dwight D. Eisenhower, was born in County Cork, Ireland, the daughter of a British career military officer; she grew up on her father's estate on the island of Inish Beg. When her parents separated, the sixteen-year-old Kathleen and a sister moved to London with their British mother. Kathleen attended art and business schools, then worked as a model and as an extra for motion-picture studios. In the late 1930's, she was briefly married to publishing executive Gordon Summersby. After Britain declared war on Nazi Germany in September 1939, Kathleen joined the British Women's Auxiliary Corps and was assigned to the Motor Transport Corps. During the Battle of Britain, she drove ambulances in the dock area of London's East End and gained recognition for valor and courage.

In May 1942, Summersby was assigned to drive visiting American generals Mark Clark and Dwight D. Eisenhower, who were in London on an inspection tour. She favorably impressed both generals. "If ever I get back here," Eisenhower told her, "I'd like you to drive for me." Later in the year, when Eisenhower returned to London as commander of the European theater, Summersby was assigned as his driver and confidential secretary.

For the next three years, Summersby was among Eisenhower's confidants and closest aides. Tall and attractive, with high cheekbones, long flowing hair, and a slender figure, Summersby was a sparkling presence whose intelligence, quick wit, and vitality captivated Eisenhower. Summersby accompanied the general to meetings with Prime Minister Winston Churchill, King George VI, President Franklin D. Roosevelt, General Charles de Gaulle, and General George C. Marshall. She traveled with Eisenhower to North Africa, Egypt, Sicily, Italy, France, Germany, and the United States. She narrowly escaped death in December of 1942 while en route to joining Eisenhower in North Africa when the ship she was traveling on, the *Strathallen*, was torpedoed by a German submarine and sank. She arrived in North Africa in a lifeboat.

While working for Eisenhower, Summersby became engaged to an American military officer, Colonel Richard R. Arnold, who was later killed in Tunisia by a mine explosion. Eisenhower informed Summersby of Arnold's death. In her book, *Past Forgetting: My Love Affair with Dwight D. Eisenhower,* published after her death, Summersby wrote that her relationship with Eisenhower changed after Arnold's death. "Love had grown so naturally that it was a part of our lives, something precious that I had taken for granted without ever putting a name on it," she wrote.

Eisenhower's relationship with Summersby created strains in his marriage with Mamie Doud Eisenhower, whose letters to the general put him on the defensive. Eisenhower assured his wife that she had nothing to be concerned about. But late in 1973 the publication of *Plain Speaking: An Oral Biography of Harry S. Truman* by Merle Miller quoted the former president as saying that shortly after the war

Eisenhower wrote to General George C. Marshall indicating that he planned to divorce his wife and marry Summersby. Truman told Miller that he had the letter and Marshall's reply removed from official files and destroyed. Truman said that Marshall vowed to "bust" Eisenhower out of the army if he went through with his plans to marry Summersby.

It is doubtful whether Eisenhower and Marshall exchanged such correspondence. Eisenhower had no plans to divorce Mamie, though he had affection for Summersby. Forrest C. Pogue, Marshall's biographer and the first director of the Marshall Library, said that Truman's story probably was untrue. Pogue said it would have been out of character for Marshall to have given Eisenhower such a stinging reprimand. In her book, Summersby reported that she did not know if such a letter had existed but that she hoped that it had. "Eisenhower was under tremendous pressures and in need of company," the general's grandson David wrote in his 1986 biography *Eisenhower at War: 1943–1945.* David Eisenhower wrote that the truth of the Eisenhower-Summersby relationship was "known only by them, and both are gone." The younger Eisenhower wrote: "Either she was special to Eisenhower, or her personal tragedy affected him in a special way, a concern that lifted him out of his own preoccupations." Another Eisenhower biographer, Stephen E. Ambrose, concluded that Summersby was in love with Eisenhower but it was unclear whether the general loved her, "although obviously he had strong feelings about her. In fact, she was the third most important woman in his life, behind only his mother and his wife." Marshall brought Eisenhower back to the United States for two weeks in January of 1944 for a reunion with Mamie. Eisenhower later told Summersby that he got into trouble for calling his wife "Kay" on several occasions. When Summersby visited Washington in the summer of 1944, Mrs. Eisenhower treated her coolly. Mamie also asked an Eisenhower biographer, Kenneth Davis, not to mention Summersby in his book.

Churchill was concerned about the relationship from an Allied military-security perspective. As Eisenhower's secretary, Summersby had access to the most classified Allied secrets. She was also one of two aides who kept Eisenhower's diary. Churchill thought it was a security risk for an Irish woman to have high-level access to allied strategy and tactics. Such fears were groundless. Summersby was devoted to Eisenhower and to the Allied cause.

Although Summersby was a British citizen, Eisenhower arranged in 1944 to have her commissioned as a second lieutenant in the American Women's Army Corps. Colonel Oveta Culp Hobby, head of the WACS, protested Summersby's commission. But Eisenhower prevailed. Summersby was later promoted to captain.

When Eisenhower returned to Washington, D.C., in 1945 to replace General Marshall as army chief of staff, Summersby was transferred to Berlin as an aide to General Lucius Clay. In 1946, she was transferred to Hamilton Air Force Base in California as a public information officer. She was discharged in July 1947. *Eisenhower Was My Boss* (1948), a wartime memoir, was a best-seller that revealed nothing about her private relationship with Eisenhower. Eisenhower helped Summersby to become a U.S. citizen in 1950. But their intimate relationship ended when Eisenhower was ordered back to Washington in 1945. During her lifetime she declined comment about her relationship with Eisenhower.

Summersby married Reginald H. Morgan, a New York stockbroker, in 1952. They were divorced in 1958. In the 1960's and 1970's she worked as a fashion consultant and costume designer for television, stage, and motion-picture productions. She died on Long Island, N.Y., and on her instructions she was cremated and her ashes scattered in the meadows near her family's home in Ireland.

[Summersby's correspondence with Eisenhower and newspaper clippings about her life and relationship with Eisenhower are in the Dwight D. Eisenhower Library in Abilene, Kans. See also Summersby's *Eisenhower Was My Boss* (1948) and *Past Forgetting* (1976); Merle Miller, *Plain Speaking: An Oral Biography of Harry S. Truman* (1973); Steve Neal, *The Eisenhowers* (1978); John S. D. Eisenhower, ed., *Letters to Mamie* (1978), General Eisenhower's wartime letters to his wife that include references to Summersby; Stephen E. Ambrose, *Eisenhower* (1983); and David Eisenhower, *Eisenhower at War* (1986). An obituary is in the *New York Times*, Jan. 21, 1975.]

STEVE NEAL

SUSANN, JACQUELINE (Aug. 20, 1921– Sept. 21, 1974), actress, television personality, and author, was born in Philadelphia to Robert

Susann and Rose Jans. Her father was a portrait artist whose subjects included prominent sports figures and politicians; her mother taught grade school. Jacqueline Susann worshiped her father, a relationship that would become the theme of her third novel, *Once Is Not Enough* (1974). Her main ambition was to "be somebody," although her haphazard work at West Philadelphia High School indicated she had little interest in excelling academically. Instead, Susann decided early on that she would be an actress.

Triumphing over her parents' desire to send her to college, Susann moved to New York City in 1936 to find work on Broadway. Although she attended a few acting and ballet classes, Susann was too caught up in the show business scene to concentrate much on developing her performance skills. In 1937, while at a gathering spot for theater people, she met an up-and-coming press agent, Irving Mansfield, who later became a television and film producer. He became her confidant and her entrée into the show business world. They were married several years later.

Biographer Barbara Seaman, who had access to Susann's diaries, claims that during this time Susann began taking the combination of alcohol, sleeping pills, and diet pills that would play a central role in her novels. In 1946 Susann had a baby. Since she had continued to smoke, drink, and take pills during her pregnancy, Susann maintained a strong sense of guilt about her possible role in her son's autism, especially after he was permanently institutionalized. These experiences would reemerge in Susann's romans a clef.

In 1946, realizing that her Broadway career was going nowhere, Susann pulled her typewriter out of the closet and set out to write a play with her friend Beatrice Cole. A caustic look at Hollywood and Broadway, *The Temporary Mrs. Smith*, which was soon rechristened *Lovely Me* (1946), proved to be a less successful preview of her later publishing success. Susann worked the press effectively to gain media attention far in excess of the play's merits. And while most critics panned the work, audiences loved it. The play would have been an unqualified hit had the producers not lost their theater to a previously booked show after four weeks.

Disappointed with the vagaries of play production, Susann put away her typewriter for another fifteen years. During this time, she found work as a radio talk-show host (a rarity for a woman at the time), a television commercial "plugger," and a game-show host.

In 1962, Susann, after encouragement from friends and her mother, began writing again. Although she had outlined a story called "The Pink Dolls" about drugs and sex in show business, she decided to first publish an account of life with her beloved poodle, Josephine. The manuscript was accepted but then put on hold by Doubleday and Company; Susann eventually published *Every Night, Josephine!* (1963) with Bernard Geis Associates, a maverick publishing firm that specialized in marketing pop culture books. (Their publishing list included Helen Gurley Brown's *Sex and the Single Girl*.) The combined efforts of Susann, Mansfield, and the Geis staff enabled the author to plug *Every Night, Josephine!* on radio and television appearances, in magazine interviews and articles, in gossip columns, and at book signings across the country. *Every Night, Josephine!* was a modest success, originally selling 40,000 copies and climbing to number ten on the *New York Times* best-seller list.

All of this did not prepare the world for Susann's next novel, *Valley of the Dolls* (1966), the eventual successor to "The Pink Dolls." Although Harold Robbins had been peddling his steamy potboilers for several years, and Grace Metalious's *Peyton Place* had given the genre a small-town woman's point of view, *Valley of the Dolls* was something new. Susann combined her inside knowledge of the dark side of show business with her moral outrage against the drugs and alcohol to which she was addicted to produce a curiously compelling hybrid. The titillating story, which centered on the lives of the rich and famous, was at bottom a morality play. The novel was full of characters based on famous personalities, including Ethel Merman and Judy Garland, and contained enough raunchy language that several conservative commentators branded it pornography.

Susann supported the novel with an unprecedented publicity tour. Her efforts, aided by the irrepressible Mansfield, were so revolutionary that the tour itself drew the often snide attention of the media. This additional publicity only served to spur on sales. *Valley of the Dolls* spent twenty-eight straight weeks at the number-one spot on the *New York Times* best-seller list, a record; it eventually sold more than 20 million paperback copies, another record. Although Su-

sann was unhappy with the movie version of the book, which starred Patty Duke and Susan Hayward, it too was hugely popular.

Susann's next two novels, *The Love Machine* (1969) and *Once Is Not Enough* (1973), followed the same formula as *Valley of the Dolls*. Although they were not quite as popular, both spent many weeks on the *Times* best-seller list, and *The Love Machine* was also made into a movie. That novel, whose title referred to both the television medium and the book's main character, television executive Robin Stone, was published by Simon and Schuster after Susann paid Geis Associates $400,000 to sever her contract with them. Simon and Schuster had the requisite capital reserves to underwrite the advance and marketing budget that Susann demanded. For *Once Is Not Enough*, a story of "emotional incest" between a father and daughter, Susann received an even bigger package from the publishing house William Morrow.

Valley of the Dolls had been largely overlooked by literary critics, with the exception of Gloria Steinem's review in *Book Week* ("For the reader who has put away comic books but isn't yet ready for editorials in the *Daily News*"). After *Valley of the Dolls*, however, the publication of Susann's books became a cultural event, and the critics responded accordingly. Almost all found Susann's books either disturbingly bad (Jonathan Baumbach in *The Nation*) or laughingly bad (Christopher Lehmann-Haupt in the *New York Times*); most saw Susann's popularity as clear signs of the decline of Western Civilization. Nora Ephron, considering the motivations of Susann's audiences more sympathetically (although no less charitable about the books' literary merits), challenged this view by writing that *Valley of the Dolls* "had a magnetic appeal for women readers: it described the standard female fantasy—of going to the big city, striking it rich, meeting fabulous men— and went on to show every reader that she was far better off than the heroines in the book— who took pills, killed themselves, and made general messes of their lives. With the possible exception of *Cosmopolitan* magazine, no one writes about sadism in modern man and masochism in modern woman quite as horribly and accurately as Jacqueline Susann." As for Susann, she scoffed, "The hell with what critics say. I've made characters live, so that people talk about them at cocktail parties, and that, to me, is what counts. You have to have a divine conceit in your judgment. I have it." Susann continued to publicize *Once Is Not Enough* until several weeks before her death from breast cancer, which had been diagnosed in 1963.

[Barbara Seaman's biography of Susann, *Lovely Me* (1987), is a gossipy, shallow account of Susann's life without much thought given to cultural context or significance, but the research is comprehensive. Accounts of Susann's publicity tours may be found in "Happiness Is Being Number One," *Life*, Aug. 19, 1966; and "Jackie Susann Picks up the Marbles," *New York Times Magazine*, Aug. 12, 1973. Listings of book reviews may be found in *Book Review Digest* (1966, 1969, and 1973); *Contemporary Authors* (vols. 65–68); and *Contemporary Literary Criticism* (vol. 3). An obituary is in the *New York Times*, Sept. 23, 1974.]

MICHAEL GOLDBERG

SUTHERLAND, EARL WILBUR, JR. (Nov. 19, 1915–Mar. 9, 1974), biomedical scientist and Nobel laureate, was born in the small farming community of Burlingame, Kans. His parents were Earl Wilbur Sutherland and Edith Hartshorn. His father operated a small dry goods business, and his mother was a nurse.

Sutherland became interested in medical research as a high school student when he read about Louis Pasteur and other scientists in Paul de Kruif's *Microbe Hunters* (1926). When the Great Depression wiped out his father's assets, Sutherland obtained scholarships and assistantships to finance his education.

Sutherland graduated from Washburn College in Topeka, Kans., in 1937. That year, he married Mildred Rice of Topeka; they had three children. The Sutherlands divorced around 1962. He entered Washington University Medical School in St. Louis in 1938 and received his M.D. in 1942. He served an internship at Washington University Hospital and then spent two years as a captain in the Army Medical Corp. In Europe he was for many months assigned to a battalion aid station with General George Patton's Third Army as it fought its way into Germany.

Immediately after World War II, Sutherland returned to Washington University to begin his academic career, first in the department of pharmacology and later in the department of biochemistry. He worked in the laboratories of Carl and Gerty Cori; Carl Cori became a Nobel Laureate in 1947. Sutherland undertook studies of the action of two hormones, epinephrine and glucagon, and his published studies over the next few years on the interaction of these hormones with the enzyme systems of the liver are now considered classics of biochemical physiology.

In 1953, Sutherland became chair of the department of pharmacology at Case Western Reserve University School of Medicine in Cleveland, where he initiated the work that led to the discovery of the compound cyclic adenosine monophosphate (AMP). The term "cyclic" refers to the fact that the atoms in the single phosphate group of the molecule are arranged in a ring.

While working with Dr. T. W. Rall in 1956, Dr. Sutherland discovered cyclic AMP after a series of carefully controlled experiments. Sutherland's further investigations helped demonstrate the widespread existence and key importance of this chemical and its associated compounds, notably adenyl cyclase, in all living things.

Dr. Sutherland moved to Vanderbilt University Medical Center in Nashville in 1963 as professor of physiology largely because he had grown weary of administrative and teaching duties at Case Western and because he saw in Vanderbilt's vigorous and growing department of physiology an "ideal place to work and to exchange ideas." Sutherland, who greatly cherished his years at Vanderbilt, praised his department head, Dr. C. R. Park, who he says made possible many of Sutherland's achievements. In 1962, he had married Claudia Sebeste, a pharmacologist who became director of the office of sponsored research at Vanderbilt Medical School. Sebeste had one daughter from a previous marriage.

It is largely through his work at Vanderbilt that cyclic AMP's extraordinary role in regulating metabolic functions in a wide spectrum of biological organisms was established. The compound's chemical name is cyclic-$3',5'$-adenosine monophosphate. Among the many functions served by cyclic AMP in humans and animals is that of acting as a chemical messenger and regulating the enzymatic reactions within cells that accumulate sugars and fats. Cyclic AMP has also been shown to influence the activity of genes. An inadequate supply of cyclic AMP appears to be a requirement for the uncontrolled growth of cells characteristic of cancer.

Sutherland's work on hormones opened up

new paths of inquiry into diabetes and cancer and shed new light on cholera. Clinical implications of the compound have continued to emerge. It is possible that cyclic AMP levels will be used as indicators to diagnose certain diseases and eventually as controls in the physiology of cell tissue.

In 1971, Sutherland was awarded the Nobel Prize in physiology or medicine for his discoveries concerning the role of cyclic AMP in metabolic processes. He was the forty-third American to receive the Nobel prize for medicine and the first in a decade to be sole recipient of the honorarium. He won the highest award the United States bestows on its scientists, the Albert Lasker Award for basic medical research, in 1970. The American Heart Association awarded him a career investigatorship and substantial laboratory support for his professional lifetime; he was the thirteenth distinguished scientist named to the lifetime research post. He was selected to membership in the National Academy of Sciences and the American Academy of Arts and Sciences. He received the Gairdner Award of Canada for biomedical research, the Dickson Prize in medicine, the Torald Sollmann Award in pharmacology, the Banting Medal of the American Diabetes Association, and several other prizes and lectureships in this country and abroad. In 1971 the American Heart Association bestowed on him its achievement award. In 1973 he received from President Richard Nixon the National Medal of Science.

Sutherland was blessed with the gifts of intuition, tenacity, and intensity; he was highly original in his concepts. He was described by colleagues as easygoing, gregarious, and well liked. He greatly enjoyed fishing and working in his garden, where he specialized in raising flowers and sweet corn.

Sutherland moved to Miami, Fla., in 1973. He hoped the climate would alleviate his suffering from allergies. There he was appointed distinguished professor of biochemistry at the University of Miami, a position he held until his death.

[The special collections division of the Vanderbilt University Medical Library contains considerable information on Sutherland and his work. Of his numerous publications, two of the most important and representative are "Formation of a Cyclic Adenine Ribonucleotide by Tissue Particles," *Journal of Biological Chemistry*, Apr. 1958; and "The Biological Role of Adenosine 3',5' Phosphate," *Harvey Lecture Series*, vol. 57 (1962). Biographical information can be found in C. R. Park, "Earl W. Sutherland, November 19, 1915–March 9, 1974," *The Pharmacologist*, 1975; James Bordley III and A. McGehee Harvey, "Enzymes and Hormones," *Two Centuries of American Medicine* (1976); and C. F. Cori, "Earl W. Sutherland, November 19, 1915–March 9, 1974," *Biographical Memoirs of the National Academy of Sciences* 49 (1978). An obituary is in the *New York Times*, Mar. 10, 1974.]

HARRIS D. RILEY, JR.

SVENSON, ANDREW EDWARD (May 8, 1910–Aug. 21, 1975), author, was born in Belleville, N.J., the son of Andrew Svenson and Laura Soleau. He attended Barringer High School in Newark, Carnegie Institute of Technology, the University of Pittsburgh (B.A., 1932), and Montclair State Teachers College (now Montclair State College), from which he received a teaching certificate (1933). Svenson began as a feature writer for the *Newark Star-Eagle* (1933–1934) and then worked for the *Newark Evening News* as reporter, writer, and editor (1934–1948). He married Marian Stewart on Aug. 31, 1932; they had six children.

Svenson joined the Stratemeyer Syndicate as writer and editor in 1948 at the urging of the syndicate's Howard R. Garis, creator of the wise rabbit Uncle Wiggly. Svenson began by writing entries in the Mel Martin series under the name John R. Cooper. After contributing to the series devoted to the Hardy Boys (as Franklin W. Dixon) and the Bobbsey Twins (as Laura Lee Hope), he was made a partner in the syndicate in 1961, a position that gave him control of all aspects of his own series: the Happy Hollisters (as Jerry West), Bret King (as Dan Scott), the Tolliver Family (as Alan Stone), and the Wynn and Lonny racing series (as Eric Speed). In various capacities, Svenson also contributed to other syndicate series, sharing the pen names with other authors: Tom Swift, Jr. (as Victor Appleton II), Christopher Cool—TEEN Agent (as Jack Lancer), Linda Craig (as Ann Sheldon), and Honey Bunch and Norman (as Helen Louise Thorndyke). At the same time, he taught creative writing at two New Jersey institutions, Rutgers University (1945–1954) and Upsala College (1948–1954).

Svenson initiated three major series: the Happy Hollisters, which continued for seventeen years and thirty-three volumes and was translated into several languages; the Tolliver

Family, which featured a black family similar to the Hollisters but was not as successful; and Bret King, which put detective fiction in a modern western setting. He completed a one-page chapter outline for a story and then dictated about ten pages of text into a recording device, from which his secretary would transcribe the text. The work was then edited and refined until the story was finished, a process lasting about six weeks. In later years, he generated plot outlines that were used by assistants to create stories, which he then would edit.

Of the series that Svenson created and wrote himself, the Happy Hollister series was by any standard the most successful. Critics pointed out that the Hollisters represent a kind of dream family, who project themselves as members of a big, active, and harmonious group. They also alleged that the syndicate was a "book factory." Svenson denied this, but he did admit that there was an element of formula in the writing. "The trick in writing children's books is to set up danger, mystery and excitement on Page 1," Svenson told Roger B. May in the *Wall Street Journal* (Jan. 15, 1975). "Force the kid to turn the page. I've written Page 1 as many as 20 times. Then in the middle of each chapter there's a dramatic point of excitement, and, at chapter's end, a cliff-hanger." He elaborated on the syndicate's techniques to the *New Yorker* (March. 20, 1954), explaining that "whether we do yarns about *Übermenschen* or pig-tailed Philo Vances, we subscribe to the Stratemeyer formula. . . . A low death rate but plenty of plot. Verbs of action, and polka-dotted with exclamation points and provocative questions. No use of guns by the hero. No smooching. The main character introduced on page one and a slam-bang mystery or peril set up." Files were meticulously kept on each character, their organizations, prizes they won, and so on, even including the name of Nancy Drew's doctor, to ensure consistency. Svenson did library research for all his books and, indulging his interests in travel and photography, always made an effort to visit the locality to be used as background. He once received a letter from a curator of an Alaskan museum praising him for the authenticity of the totem poles in one of his books (*The Happy Hollisters and the Mystery of the Totem Faces*, 1958). He also developed plots at the request of his readers. *The Happy Hollisters and the Haunted House Mystery* (1962) was written after Svenson received a fan letter from a deaf boy in Belfast, Northern Ireland, who suggested that he author a story about a deaf boy. Svenson attended a school for the deaf, learned sign language, and incorporated this knowledge into the story.

In his later years, Svenson worked in his home in West Caldwell, N.J., where he concentrated on the Wynn and Lonny motor-racing series. For these he did the plot outlines and editing, with technical material supplied by a racing driver, Sylvia Wilkerson.

Svenson was solid, brisk-moving, and dark-haired. He belonged to organizations that reflected the expanding depth of his interests: the American Association of University Professors, the American Professors of Journalism, the Mystery Writers of America, and the Western Writers Association. In the months before his death, he continued to write and was outlining a new Hardy Boys book as well as a new volume for his Wynn and Lonny series. Svenson died in Livingston, N.J.

[Svenson's manuscripts, drafts, galleys, and dictated recordings from which he transcribed some plots for the Hollisters, the Tollivers, the Hardy Boys, and Tom Swift, Jr., are in the Lena Y. de Grummond Collection at the William David McCain Graduate Library, University of Southern Mississippi, Hattiesburg. Svenson also gave material to the Western History Research Center, University of Wyoming, Laramie. The Children's Literature Center, Library of Congress, Washington, D.C., has files titled "Youth in Fiction Series" and on the Stratemeyer syndicate. See also "Tom, Jr.," in "Talk of the Town," *New Yorker*, Mar. 20, 1954; James V. O'Connor's interview with Svenson in *Rotary International*, Sept. 1973; Peter A. Soderbergh, "The Stratemeyer Strain: Educators and the Juvenile Series Book, 1900–1973," *Journal of Popular Culture*, Spring 1974; an appreciation in *Juvenile Miscellany* (Library of the University of Southern Mississippi), Fall 1975; Deidre Johnson, *Stratemeyer Pseudonyms and Series Books* (1982), which details the publishing history of the series Svenson wrote or plotted; and Carol Billman, *The Secret of the Stratemeyer Syndicate* (1986). Obituaries are in the *New York Times*, Aug. 23, 1975; *Publishers Weekly*, Sept. 29, 1975; and *AB Bookman's Weekly*, Oct. 13, 1975.]

MARTIN J. MANNING

SWITZER, MARY ELIZABETH (Feb. 16, 1900–Oct. 16, 1971), federal social services administrator, was born in Upper Newton Falls, Mass., the daughter of Julius Switzer, a construction worker, and Margaret Moore.

Switzer's mother died of tuberculosis when Mary was eleven. Shortly thereafter her father deserted, taking a son with him. Custody of Switzer and a younger sister was awarded to two maternal aunts who lived in Newton, Mass.

A maternal bachelor uncle became the dominant male figure during her youth, selecting books and taking her to the theater and to political lectures. A French teacher at Newton Classical High School helped Switzer get a partial scholarship to Radcliffe College, where she became a day student.

Despite having to work after hours and during summer vacations, Switzer made lifelong friendships at Radcliffe and showed leadership in both college and intercollegiate clubs. She received a B.A. in 1921, having majored in government, history, and economics, with a special interest in international law.

Following several temporary jobs in Washington, D.C., including one with the Minimum Wage Board for women, Switzer qualified for a civil service appointment in the office of Secretary of the Treasury Andrew W. Mellon in 1923. Unable to do the statistical work required, she was assigned to clip newspapers and magazines, and gradually took over much of Mellon's correspondence.

With her Democratic voting record behind her and her insistence that she was still a civil servant, Switzer had no trouble keeping her job when Roosevelt won in 1932. When Josephine Roche, a coal-mine operator noted for her support of the United Mine Workers, was named assistant secretary for the Public Health Service in 1935, Switzer became her assistant. Since Roche often sat in for Secretary Henry Morganthau at meetings of the Committee on Economic Security, Switzer became involved in that pioneer social enterprise. Like Roche, Switzer was disappointed at the failure of the Social Security Act of 1935 to cover health insurance, but she was pleased to note congressional support for both the Public Health Service and vocational rehabilitation.

By July 1939, President Roosevelt had formed the Federal Security Agency (FSA), which was comprised of such social welfare agencies as the Public Health Service, the Office of Education, and the Social Security Board. As an expert on the Public Health Service, Switzer became one of two assistants to FSA Administrator Paul McNutt. When the other assistant's health failed, she became de facto assistant, a position that

evolved into considerable executive oversight and budgetary money allocation. During World War II, Switzer performed outstanding service by devising plans for rationing doctors and other health providers for both civilian and military service.

Early in President Truman's administration, through discussions with her medical friends and colleagues, and the drafting of prospective legislation, Switzer led the way to a greatly expanded national medical research effort—the creation of the National Institutes of Health and the National Institute of Mental Health under the Public Health Service.

Following McNutt's urging, on Dec. 1, 1950, President Truman appointed Switzer director of the Office of Vocational Rehabilitation, which became the Vocational Rehabilitation Service within the Department of Health, Education, and Welfare. With but a handful of doctors specializing in rehabilitation, Switzer set out to professionalize the program by obtaining federal research grants and providing advanced training for physicians and counselors. On Aug. 3, 1954, President Eisenhower signed these and other strengthening elements into law. Funding for states that administered the act remained under a fixed appropriation, but a more generous formula increased the federal subsidy. Counseling excepted, services were given outside the rehabilitation agency itself. For this reason hospitals, pharmacies, training facilities, and the industries supplying them could expect business to increase.

During the next ten years, the federal commitment quadrupled, increasing from $23.8 million in 1954 to $94.7 million in 1965; and total federal-state commitment went from $38.6 to $154.1 million. Over the same period, the number of research and development projects increased from 77 to 526. Even so, the cost of the program was small compared to such giant entitlements as Social Security and welfare.

Switzer used a crude cost-benefit analysis to show how taxes paid during a lifetime of work made the cost of rehabilitating a disabled individual insignificant. The program was sometimes faulted for "creaming," the tendency to build up successes by selecting the easier cases for rehabilitation. With few exceptions, however, Congress and HEW secretaries supported Switzer and her program enthusiastically.

With the election of John F. Kennedy as president in 1960, Switzer made it known that she wanted greater responsibilities, but there was no response to her overtures until HEW Secretary John W. Gardner became alarmed about "the welfare explosion." In August 1967, Switzer was appointed administrator of the Social and Rehabilitation Service, which merged the former Welfare Administration with the Vocational Rehabilitation Service. The driving idea was to put welfare mothers to work. Though Switzer was active in drafting legislation toward this end, she retired in 1970 without seeing significant progress in decreasing the number of welfare recipients.

Switzer received honorary degrees from Adelphi, Brandeis, Duke, Hofstra, New York, and Temple Universities, and from Assumption, Gallaudet, and Russell Sage Colleges, among others. The Mary E. Switzer Building is located in the four-building complex housing the U.S. Department of Health and Human Services, Washington, D.C. Other buildings named in her honor are at the Woodrow Wilson Rehabilitation Center, Fishersville, Va., and the Helen Keller National Center, Sands Point, Long Island, N.Y.

Switzer was a handsome woman, tall and slender, with a manner that engaged others through a warm smile and attentive attitude. She mingled with professional men as an equal, and perhaps, in view of the gender mores of the time, it is not surprising that she never married. Switzer died at George Washington University Hospital in Washington, D.C.

[Switzer's papers are housed at the Schlesinger Library for the History of Women, Radcliffe College. See also Martha Lentz Walker, *Beyond Bureaucracy: Mary Elizabeth Switzer and Rehabilitation* (1985); and Edward D. Berkowitz, *Disabled Policy: America's Programs for the Handicapped* (1987). An obituary appears in the *New York Times*, Oct. 17, 1971.]

BLANCHE D. COLL

T

TALMADGE, CONSTANCE (Apr. 19, 1900–Nov. 23, 1973), silent screen star, was born in Brooklyn, the youngest daughter of Margaret L. and Frederick Talmadge. Fred Talmadge worked at various makeshift jobs, usually vaguely connected to the entertainment industry, and often disappeared from his family for long stretches at a time. The major responsibility for raising their three daughters lay with Margaret ("Peg") Talmadge, who sold cosmetics, took in laundry, gave art lessons, and rented out the hall bedroom. Constance attended P.S. 9 and, briefly, Erasmus Hall High School in Brooklyn. She went into film with little formal education and no previous stage experience.

Peg, determined to better her family's condition, resolved to encourage her daughters to develop whatever talents they had. She was loudmouthed and pushy, but she got all her daughters started in show business. After wangling a job for Norma, the oldest, at the Vitagraph Motion Picture Studio in Flatbush, Peg pushed Constance, in 1914, into the movies at Vitagraph, which was one of the most successful of the vanguard companies. Here Constance worked as an extra for $5 per day. (In her heyday, she commanded $5,000 per week.) Known as the Vitagraph Tomboy and given the nickname "Dutch," for two years she appeared opposite Billy Quirk in many comedy shorts. Her vivacious personality and spontaneous wit made her very popular at the studio and spilled over into her performances. Connie had no lines to memorize; mime and exaggerated facial expressions carried the plot.

Joseph M. Schenck, Norma's husband, created the Norma Talmadge Film Corporation, and then the Constance Talmadge Film Corporation, both located in the same building in New York City. Connie's company produced such films as A Pair of Silk Stockings (1918); A Virtuous Vamp (1919), which Vachel Lindsay, in a review in The New Republic, called "a gem"; Dulcy (1923); and The Goldfish (1924), in all of which she gave sparkling comedic performances. Many of these farcical comedies were written by the popular collaborators Anita Loos and John Emerson, who under contract were to have the final say over each picture before it left the studio. This husband-and-wife team successfully transferred Connie's unique allure to the screen.

Schenck's shrewd management guided the sisters until they moved to Hollywood in 1921. Connie, at five feet six, with golden hair and expressive brown eyes heavily outlined with dark lashes, was soon a success on the West Coast. Her big break came when she was given the part of the spirited mountain girl in the Babylonian episode of D. W. Griffith's gargantuan historical spectacle, Intolerance (1916), one of Hollywood's most extravagant films. It was this role that revealed her natural talent for comedy. In one scene, as she drove a chariot wildly through the streets to warn the Babylonians, she munched on a fistful of scallions. Her exuberant performance justified Griffith's confidence in her and launched her on a highly successful career. She was soon a leading star, a position she held throughout the 1920's, the golden age of silent cinema.

Although Constance never reached the heights of stardom that Norma did, there was never any rivalry between the sisters, who remained close all their lives. Norma, the tragic heroine, and Constance, the comedienne, were stars before they were twenty. Natalie acted

791

briefly, in only a handful of films; she ran her sisters' fan clubs and handled general secretarial duties.

In 1916, the year she did *Intolerance*, Connie played opposite Douglas Fairbanks in *The Matrimaniac*. When her contract with Fine Arts expired, she worked mainly for Select Pictures Corporation. Lewis J. Selznick, head of Select, capitalized on her flair for light comedy by starring her in eight high-class five-reel comedies while she was still in her teens. When it was rumored that she might leave Select, for whom she worked from 1917 to 1919, she received offers from practically all the major movie producers. The lowest financial remuneration offered was double the salary she had been receiving. From 1919 on, she was one of the mainstays of First National. Connie starred in *Her Night of Romance* (1924) and *Her Sister from Paris* (1925), both wacky farces directed by Sidney Franklin, with Ronald Colman as the male lead. In the latter, Connie played a dual role as both a neglected housewife and her glamorous sister from Paris.

Connie was engaged many times, to Irving Thalberg, Irving Berlin, and John Charles Thomas, among others, and married four times. She had no children. Her first marriage, to a New York tobacco importer, John T. Pialoglou, on Sept. 26, 1920, lasted one year. Connie sued him for divorce because he wanted her to give up her career in films. Shortly after, Connie married Captain Alastair MacIntosh, a British aviator and heir of a Scottish laird; they were divorced in 1927. Her third marriage, to Chicago department store tycoon and playboy Townsend Netcher, lasted from May 1929 to January 1939, when she divorced him on grounds of desertion. In October 1939 Constance married Wall Street stockbroker Walter M. Giblin; this marriage lasted until Giblin's death in 1964.

Connie acted in more than seventy films, her last being *Venus*, made for United Artists in 1929. She never played in the talkies. She endorsed numerous products, from aspirin to a grand piano, once posing for 400 testimonials in one day. Her one foray into radio, with Norma on the George Jessel show, was a letdown. When her fourth husband died, a New York theatrical producer urged her to go on stage. "Are you kidding?" she quipped. "Why, I couldn't act even when I was a movie star." Constance Talmadge died in Los Angeles.

[Magazine and newspaper clippings are in the New York Public Library for the Performing Arts at Lincoln Center. Biographical information can be found in Margaret L. Talmadge, *The Talmadge Sisters* (1924); and Anita Loos, *The Talmadge Girls* (1978). Numerous references are made to Constance Talmadge in books on film such as John T. Weaver, comp., *Twenty Years of Silents* (1971); and Liz-Anne Bawden, ed., *The Oxford Companion to Film* (1976). An obituary is in the *New York Times*, Nov. 26, 1973.]

RUTH KENNEY

TAMIROFF, AKIM (Oct. 29, 1899–Sept. 17, 1972), actor, was born in Baku, Russia, on the west coast of the Caspian Sea. His father worked in the oil fields. Tamiroff grew up in Moscow, where his early interest in acting brought him to the famed Moscow Art Theatre, which was under the direction of cofounder Konstantin Stanislavsky. At age twenty, Tamiroff was one of the very few applicants admitted for rigorous training, and for several years he acted in repertory with the company. In 1923, when the Art Theatre came to the United States for a nationwide tour of *The Cherry Orchard* and *The Three Sisters*, Tamiroff decided to remain.

For three years, he performed in Nikita Balieff's popular Russian revue Chauve-Souris and played Russian nightclubs in Chicago with his wife, the actress Tamara Shayne. For a while Tamiroff conducted the Academy of Stage Makeup in New York City, where his pupils included Katharine Hepburn, Melvyn Douglas, and Jean Muir. He played small roles in several Broadway productions and then, at his wife's urging, decided to try his luck in Hollywood.

At first Tamiroff appeared in bit roles, but soon his rich Russian accent and his ability to play both comic and sinister characters brought him to the attention of Paramount Studios, which offered him a long-term contract. At a time when Hollywood assumed that all foreign accents were interchangeable, Tamiroff found himself playing supporting roles as Chinese, Greek, French, Spanish, and even Russian characters. Occasionally he was given leading roles in the studio's B films, such as *The Great Gambini* (1937) and *Dangerous to Know* (1938). Among his most notable early movies were *The Lives of a Bengal Lancer* (1935), *The Story of Louis Pasteur* (1935), and *Anthony Adverse* (1936); for the last two films, the actor was on loan to Warner Brothers. Perhaps his most notable role during this period was as the brutal Chinese warlord, General Yang, in *The General Died at Dawn* (1936). In the film's startling climax, the mortally wounded Yang orders his dutiful soldiers to kill each other. He won an Oscar nomination as best supporting actor for his performance.

Throughout the 1940's, Tamiroff brought vitality to an assortment of nasty, irascible, or flamboyant characters. In Preston Sturges's comedy *The Great McGinty* (1940), he was at the top of his form as the corrupt political boss who proclaims, "This is the land of opportunity. Everybody lives by chiseling everybody else." Tamiroff could be dangerous, as in *North West Mounted Police* (1940); amusingly loutish, as in *Tortilla Flat* (1942); or treacherous, as in *Dragon Seed* (1944). In *For Whom the Bell Tolls* (1943), adapted from Ernest Hemingway's novel of the same name, his performance as the devious guerrilla leader, Pablo, although more Slavic than Spanish, earned him another Oscar nomination as best supporting actor.

Tamiroff continued to appear in strong supporting roles throughout the 1950's and 1960's, bringing color and vigor to such movies as *Anastasia* (1956), *Me and the Colonel* (1958), *Topkapi* (1964), and *Lord Jim* (1965). In later years, he often worked abroad, playing a secret agent in Jean-Luc Godard's futuristic melodrama *Alphaville* (1965) and an innkeeper in Peter Glenville's farce *Hotel Paradiso* (1966). Tamiroff returned to Broadway in 1959, costarring as the Woodcutter in a stage adaptation of Akira Kurosawa's classic Japanese film, *Rashomon*.

In the 1950's Tamiroff began an ongoing association with actor-director Orson Welles. Impressed with Tamiroff's ability to depict brutishness, obsequiousness, and guile, sometimes all in the same character, Welles cast him in four of his films. In *Mr. Arkadin* (or as released in Spain, *Confidential Report*, 1955), Tamiroff played Welles's ill-fated companion in crime, and in *The Trial* (1963), he was a humiliated client to Welles's corrupt advocate. Tamiroff's best opportunity with Welles came in *Touch of Evil* (1958), a nightmarish, often dazzling film noir in which he appeared as gross, jittery "Uncle" Joe Grandi, who falls victim to Welles's bloated police chief in a squalid Mexican border town. Tamiroff also played Sancho Panza in Welles's unfinished version of *Don Quixote*.

A busy and versatile character actor for nearly four decades, Tamiroff died in Palm Springs, Calif., survived by his wife of nearly fifty years; they had no children.

[An obituary is in the *New York Times*, Sept. 19, 1972.]

TED SENNETT

TATUM, EDWARD LAWRIE (Dec. 14, 1909–Nov. 5, 1975), biochemist and geneticist, was born in Boulder, Colo., one of three children of Arthur Lawrie Tatum, a noted physiologist, and Mabel Webb, one of the first women graduates of the University of Colorado.

Tatum entered the University of Chicago in 1927 and transferred to the University of Wisconsin at Madison in 1929, where he received a B.A. degree in 1931 majoring in chemistry. His move to Wisconsin was prompted by his father's appointment there as chair of the physiology department. In 1932, Tatum received his master's degree in microbiology, and in 1934 his Ph.D., under the direction of professors Edwin B. Fred (later president of the University of Wisconsin) and William H. Peterson, a noted biochemist. On July 28, 1934, he married June Alton, a fellow student at the university; they had two children before divorcing in 1956.

After graduation, Tatum remained at the University of Wisconsin as a research assistant in biology. A fellowship from the General Education Board (1936–1937) enabled him to visit Fritz Kogl at the University of Utrecht in the Netherlands. Returning to the United States in 1937 as a research associate at Stanford University, Tatum teamed up with Dr. George Wells Beadle, then professor at Stanford University and subsequently chairman of the division of biology at California Institute of Technology. Between 1937 and 1941, Tatum was engaged in studies at Stanford on the genetic development of eye pigment in *Drosophila melanogaster* (a fruit fly). His research progressed to the nutritional requirements and metabolic activity of insects, primarily *Drosophila*. In 1940, Tatum and Beadle undertook a collaborative venture that would greatly influence the future of genetics. Using X rays to produce mutant strains of the pink bread mold *Neurspora crassa*, they studied the spores' sexual reproduction, isolating a spore that would grow only when given vitamin B_6 (pyridoxine). Tatum and Beadle concluded that an X ray–damaged gene was responsible for the spore's inability to produce the enzyme necessary for B_6 production. Further, the damaged gene was transmitted to descendants in the proper Mendelian ratio. The result of this research was the first assertion of what would later be known as the "one gene, one enzyme" theory, and was reported in the *Proceedings of the National Academy of Sciences* in 1941, the same year that Tatum was promoted to assistant professor at Stanford.

By the end of World War II, the team of Beadle and Tatum had achieved worldwide renown. Tatum left Stanford in 1945 to accept a position as associate professor of biology at Yale University, where he continued studies on the effect of biochemical mutations on nutritional deficiencies of the bacterium *Escherichia coli*. He was promoted to professor of microbiology the following year. In 1946, Tatum, together with Joshua Lederberg, a bright young medical student on leave from Columbia University (and later head of genetics at Stanford's medical school and president of Rockefeller University), enlarged their study of nutritional mutants of the *Escherichia coli* bacterial strain K12. Their results supported Tatum's hypothesis that bacteria have genes and that those genes are exchanged by sexual reproduction, characteristics that were thought to exist only in higher organisms.

Tatum left Yale in 1948 to return to Stanford, where in 1956 he was appointed head of a new department of biochemistry. In 1957, he moved to New York City to become a professor at the Rockefeller Institute of Medical Research (now Rockefeller University), where he continued his studies on how genes determine the characteristics of living organisms. In 1956, he was married for a second time, to Viola Kantor, a staff employee at the National Foundation (March of Dimes); she died in 1974. Tatum married Elsie Bergland in 1975.

Beadle and Tatum's studies on biochemical mutations in *Neurospora* were recognized in 1958 with the award of the Nobel Prize in physiology or medicine, shared jointly with Joshua Lederberg. Tatum's other honors included election to the National Academy of Sciences (1952), the Remsen Award of the American Chemical Society (1953), and election to the American Philosophical Society. He served as president of the Harvey Society (1964–1965)

and was the recipient of several honorary degrees.

He also served on several research and scientific advisory committees. In 1959, Tatum testified before a congressional committee on behalf of the National Science Foundation. He served as president and vice-president of the Scientist's Institute for Public Information, where his brother Howard J. Tatum, an eminent gynecologist and obstetrician, held a position. Tatum was the first chairman of the board of trustees of the Cold Spring Harbor Laboratory of Quantitative Biology in Long Island, N.Y. He also served on the board of directors of Mead Johnson and as consultant in microbiology for Merck and Company. For the National Research Council, Tatum served on many groups connected with biological and medical research.

Tatum's impressive publication record includes numerous scientific research articles. He was elected to the editorial board of *Science*, *Biochimica et Biophysica Acta*, *Annual Reviews*, *Genetics*, and the *Journal of Biological Chemistry*. He was an enthusiastic advocate of fellowships and support for younger people entering the scientific arena, and in particular biochemistry. Tatum died of heart failure in New York City.

[Tatum's papers are located at the public affairs office of Rockefeller University. A biographical profile of Tatum by Joshua Lederberg is in *Biographical Memoirs*. *National Academy of Sciences* 59 (1989). An obituary is in the *New York Times*, Nov. 7, 1975.]

LESLEY DAVENPORT

TAYLOR, GEORGE WILLIAM (July 10, 1901–Dec. 15, 1972), educator, public administrator, and industrial relations authority, was born in Philadelphia, the son of Harry D. Taylor and Anna C. Lahnemann. His father was the superintendent of a hosiery mill in the Kensington section, and it was assumed that after his graduation from Frankford High School, Taylor would follow his father and other members of the family into a managerial career in the local textile industry.

An exceptional student throughout his school days, Taylor was encouraged by his high school principal to matriculate at the Wharton School of Economics of the University of Pennsylvania, one of the nation's premier colleges of management. He completed his entire higher education at Pennsylvania, earning a B.A. in 1923, an M.B.A. in 1926, and a Ph.D. in 1929. Indeed, for the remainder of his life, Taylor was associated with the university, where he was the Wharton School's Gaylord Harnwell Distinguished Professor Emeritus of History at the time of his death.

Even before earning his doctorate, Taylor accepted a position in 1924 as chairman of the Department of Business Administration at Schuylkill College (later Albright College) in Reading, Pa., where he also coached the football team. He remained there until 1929. In that year, he returned to the University of Pennsylvania, where he became a member of the university's Industrial Research Department and an associate professor of labor relations in the Wharton School. By then an acknowledged expert in industrial relations and one of the pioneer academics who mediated and arbitrated contractual disputes between unions and management, Taylor in 1931 served as the impartial chairman charged with implementing a new national labor agreement between the Full-Fashioned Hosiery Manufacturers of America and the American Federation of Hosiery Workers. After he assisted the employers and the union in arranging a new contract, Taylor remained as impartial chairman until 1941. (He acted in a similar capacity in the Philadelphia men's clothing industry between 1935 and 1961.)

During the New Deal years, when the national government grew more involved than ever before in regulating industrial relations, Taylor's role as a mediator and public administrator magnified. Between 1933 and 1935 he chaired the Philadelphia district office of the National Labor Board established under the National Recovery Act to guarantee the right of workers to form unions of their own choosing and to bargain collectively. In 1935, he became the assistant deputy administrator of the National Recovery Administration and, two years later, an adviser to the National Fair Labor Standards Administration, established to implement the National Fair Labor Standards Act of 1937.

Because of his excellent work in those positions and his repeated stints as umpire to resolve union-management disputes, President Roosevelt in 1942 named Taylor vice-chairman of the National War Labor Board (NWLB), the

agency charged with supervising labor-management relations for the duration of the war. In 1945, the agency's final year, he served as chairman. Taylor designed the NWLB's single most famous ruling, the Little Steel award of 1942, which strictly regulated wartime wages to counter price inflation; he offered unions security for the duration of the war through the "maintenance of membership" principle in return for unions' commitment to discipline unruly workers; and he legitimated the principle of collective bargaining.

Taylor and his colleagues on the NWLB essentially guaranteed the success and stability of the New Deal–instituted regime of industrial relations, in which independent trade unions and management bargained collectively and voluntarily in order to turn labor-capital relations away from conflict toward accommodation. The system, as conceived by Taylor, depended on the services of "neutral" mediators-arbitrators, drawn largely from the academic and legal communities, as well as direct state intervention when voluntary private bargaining failed to resolve disputes peacefully and hence threatened the general welfare.

After the war, Taylor continued to work for the government and unions and managements as administrator, impartial umpire, and mediator. Among other positions, he served as the secretary of President Truman's National Labor-Management Conference (1945); as chair of the advisory board of the Office of War Mobilization and Reconversion (1946–1947); as chair of the National Wage Stabilization Board (1951–1953); as chair of President Eisenhower's Board of Inquiry for the Steel Strike (1959); as a member of the President's Advisory Committee on Labor-Management Policy (1960–1968); as chair of presidential inquiries and boards to investigate disputes in the aerospace industry (1962), among railroads (1964), and in the copper industry (1968); and as mediator and arbitrator in the Philadelphia women's clothing industry, the city's construction trades, and for jurisdictional disputes within the Congress of Industrial Organizations.

In his career as adviser on industrial relations to public officials and private parties, Taylor was perhaps best known for his work as chair of New York Governor Nelson Rockefeller's Advisory Committee on Public Employment Relations, which culminated with the state legislature's passage of the Taylor Law (1967). The law guaranteed public employees the right to join unions and bargain collectively but also penalized unions and their members for participating in strikes. The law reflected Taylor's long-standing commitment to the contradictory principles of voluntary collective bargaining and illegality of strikes by public employees. The law was so unpopular with public employees that Taylor himself conceded that "this is one law the legislators didn't fight to have their names on."

Almost until the time of his death, Taylor, a pleasant, short, and rotund man, continued to teach labor economics and industrial relations and to act as mediator to resolve industrial disputes. Owing to his long and active career as a public administrator and mediator, Taylor did not publish profusely. Among his major publications were *The Full-Fashioned Hosiery Worker* (1931) and *Government Regulation of Industrial Relations* (1948). He coedited *New Concepts in Wage Determination* (1957). He married Edith Ayling, a high school classmate, on June 18, 1924. They had no children. He died in Philadelphia.

Taylor was one of the giants in the field of industrial relations, a creator of the mid-twentieth-century concept of collective bargaining, by which unions and managements negotiated voluntarily to avert strikes, which, in Taylor's view, threatened the public's welfare. For him, successful collective bargaining preserved the best in capitalism, and by creating order out of conflict, promoted the essence of democracy.

[The George W. Taylor Papers are at the University of Pennsylvania Library. The records of Taylor's services for the federal government are located in the specific agency files housed in the National Archives. See also Edward B. Shils et al., eds., *Industrial Peacemaker* (1979). An obituary appears in the *New York Times*, Dec. 17, 1972.]

MELVYN DUBOFSKY

TAYLOR, THEODORE ROOSEVELT ("HOUND DOG") (Apr. 12, 1917–Dec. 17, 1975), blues guitarist and singer, was born in Natchez, Miss., the son of Robert Taylor and Della Herron. Little is known of his early years. Accounts taken from interviews indicate that his family was extremely poor and could offer little support for his education and music training. Many of Taylor's early songs document and solidify his feelings about living in the Mississippi Delta.

In 1942, Taylor moved to Chicago, where he performed in nightclubs as a blues guitarist and singer. His unique style of playing at times has been compared with that of urban bluesmen Elmore Jones and Robert Johnson. Many of his early tunes (ca. 1936) were performed in both standard and open tunings. His vocal style was attributed to his liking of the performance styles of the blues performers Blind Lemon, Alonzo ("Lonnie") Johnson, "Lightnin' " Hopkins, and Sonny Boy Williamson (Alex Miller).

Taylor's performance style was very popular. During his stay in Chicago, he performed in almost every club on the South Side. He also made regular appearances in the Maxwell Street district, which at the time had a large Jewish population that supported the performing arts. It was while he was in Chicago that he was given his nickname, reportedly because of his ongoing relationships with women.

From 1951 (the year of his marriage) until his death, Taylor performed throughout the United States at colleges and universities, major clubs, recognized concert facilities such as the Academy of Music (1973) and Avery Fisher Hall (1973–1974), and at the Willie Dixon American Folk Blues Festival (1967), and the Ann Arbor Blues Festival (1970).

Between 1957 and 1971, Taylor made several 45-rpm recordings for small, Chicago-based labels. The smallness of the companies and poor distribution brought him very little income. In 1971, Taylor recorded on the Alligator label. His first effort, *Beware of the Dog*, which sold fifteen thousand copies, included such popular tunes as "Give Me Back My Wig," "Let's Get Funky," "Dust My Brown," "Comin' Around the Mountain," and "Freddie's Blues." He also broadcast live on WOPA radio for the "Big Bill Hill Show."

Taylor died in Chicago.

[Articles on Taylor are Jim O'Neal and R. T. Cuniff, "Hound Dog Taylor," *Living Blues*, Winter 1970–1971; Hans Andreasson, "Hound Dog Taylor, 1916–1975," *Jefferson* (Sweden), Spring 1976; and Bruce Iglauer, "Hound Dog Taylor," *Living Blues*, Jan–Feb. 1976. See also Robert Palmer, *Deep Blues* (1981); Barry L. Pearson, *"Sounds So Good to Me"* (1984); Julio Finn, *The Bluesman* (1986); and Mary L. Hart, Brenda M. Eagles, and Lisa N. Howorth, *The Blues: A Biographical Guide* (1989). Obituaries are in the *New York Times*, Dec. 18, 1975, and *Black Perspective in Music*, no. 3, 1976.]

LEMUEL BERRY

TERRY, PAUL HOULTON (Feb. 19, 1887– Oct. 25, 1971), animator, was born in San Mateo, Calif., the youngest child of Joseph Terry, an auctioneer, and Minnie Perrin, a sculptor. Terry grew up in San Francisco, studying art at the city's polytechnic high school. He went to work as a reporter/cartoonist/photographer for the *San Francisco Chronicle* in 1904 and reportedly took the first published photographs of the 1906 San Francisco earthquake. For the next ten years, Terry held positions at a variety of newspapers and magazines, ending up at the *New York Press*. Maintaining his interest in art, he briefly drew a comic strip titled "Alonzo" for the Hearst syndicate.

In 1914, he attended a dinner given by New York columnist, cartoonist, and animator Windsor McCay at which McCay screened his cartoon, "Gertie the Dinosaur," for his guests. Impressed by the fluidly moving "Gertie," which is still one of the best known of all American animated cartoons, Terry decided to create his own animated films.

In 1915, he completed his first cartoon, "Little Herman," modeled on a popular magician, Herman the Great. According to Terry's own recollection, he tried to sell the film to veteran showman Lewis J. Selznick. Selznick offered Terry less than the cost of the raw film stock the artist had used to create it, snidely suggesting that the stock had been more valuable before Terry had drawn on it. Producer Edwin Thannhauser finally bought the cartoon.

While Terry attempted to interest other producers in financing his cartoons, he was approached by Margaret Bray, wife of animator John Randolph Bray. Bray's company held patents relating to cel animation, the process of drawing cartoon movement on transparent celluloid sheets placed on top of stationary background pictures. Terry had used cel animation for "Little Herman"—indeed, he is credited by many film historians with perfecting the process—and had therefore infringed on Bray's patents. The Brays suggested that Terry either purchase a license to continue use of their process or go to work for them. Choosing the latter option he worked for Bray Studios for a little over a year.

While working for Bray, Terry introduced a character who would remain in his cartoon repertoire for decades, the sometimes wise and sometimes foolish Farmer Al Falfa. In a typical release, "Farmer Al Falfa Sees New York," the country farmer goes to the city and is conned by a series of chiselers. In the end, however, he and his faithful dog turn the tables on the crooks.

Terry also learned about corporate structure at Bray Studios. Bray, whom historian Donald Crafton has dubbed "the Henry Ford of Animation," applied scientific management principles in his company, transforming animation from a time-consuming art form into a streamlined business characterized by efficient division of labor. Terry would later use these principles at his own studio.

In the 1920's, years after Terry had left Bray, the two still disagreed over the rights to the cel-animation process. Bray instituted a lengthy lawsuit which he dropped only after Terry agreed to purchase a license to use the process.

In 1917, Terry was inducted into the armed forces. He spent World War I working with the surgeon general's office, making animated films about surgical techniques. After the war, he worked for the Thomas Edison Studio for the last year of its operations. Few of his cartoons received wide distribution at this time.

In 1921, Terry formed Fables Pictures with producer/distributor Amadee Van Beuren, who obtained funding for the venture from the Keith-Albee theatrical chain. Terry hired eighteen animators to help him put out "Aesop's Film Fables," a successful series of cartoons he would continue to produce for the rest of his career. The cartoons were only loosely based on the tales of Aesop. Farmer Al Falfa remained a supporting character in most of them. According to historian Harvey Deneroff, the fables' morals "usually had nothing to do with the story—e.g., 'Aesop said 2,600 years ago that "Marriage is an institution, but who wants to live in an institution," ' or 'All wild flowers fade quickly except the blooming idiot.' "

In the mid-1920's Terry married Irma Heinlich; the couple had one daughter. In 1929, he formed another new partnership. Shortly after producing his first sound-synchronized "Film Fable," he ended his association with Van Beuren and created a company called "Audiocinema" with fellow animator Frank Moser. The new company's sound cartoons were called "Terrytoons." In 1932, the company moved

797

from New York City to New Rochelle, N.Y.

In 1936, Terry bought Moser out and renamed the company "Terrytoons" after his short films. These cartoons, distributed by Twentieth Century–Fox, emerged steadily from the New Rochelle factory for decades. Terry initially resisted concentrating on regular cartoon heroes (Al Falfa was a mere character actor) like the popular Mickey Mouse and Bugs Bunny. In the late 1930's, however, after moving Terrytoons into color, Terry began to experiment with new star characters.

His first and biggest success came in 1942, when he introduced the character Mighty Mouse (originally called Super Mouse) in a cartoon titled "The Mouse of Tomorrow." His second-most-successful characters, the wisecracking magpies Heckle and Jeckle, debuted in 1946. By the early 1950's, these toonsters and others kept a staff of eighty-five animators busy at the New Rochelle studio.

In 1952, in conjunction with the release of Terry's one thousandth cartoon, the Museum of Modern Art screened a retrospective of the animator's work. In his comments on the program, the museum's film curator Richard Griffith paid tribute to Terry's unparalleled productivity: "[Terry's] is a formidable record matched by no other animator, nor indeed by any other eminent film craftsman, with the exception of the indestructible Cecil B. DeMille. . . . Although his continuous output for 37 years can only be called mass-production, it has, thanks largely to its satiric qualities, maintained an almost equally continuous level of fresh invention."

In 1955, Terry sold his studio and his stock of some 1,100 animated shorts to CBS. He continued to draw and to tell stories until his death in New York City in 1971.

[The Film Study Center at the Museum of Modern Art houses four letters between Terry and the Edison Company in 1917 about the sale of a Farmer Al Falfa cartoon. Its collection also contains forty-six sketchbooks documenting the production of Terrytoons between 1929 and 1931; because of their fragility these books are currently available for curatorial purposes only. The Performing Arts Division of the New York Public Library maintains clipping files about Terry and descriptions of the plots of some of his early cartoons. Harvey Deneroff conducted a Louis B. Mayer/American Film Institute oral history interview with Terry in 1971; it was summarized in the 1972 American Film Institute Report #1. Otherwise, the best source on Terry and his work is Donald Crafton's Before Mickey: The Animated Film 1898–1928 (1982). An obituary appears in the New York Times, Oct. 26, 1971.]

TINKY ("DAKOTA") WEISBLAT

THOMPSON, LLEWELLYN E. ("TOMMY"), JR. (Aug. 24, 1904–Feb. 6, 1972), career diplomat, was one of five children born in Las Animas, Colo., to Llewellyn E. Thompson, Sr., a sheep rancher, and Lula L. Butcher. Thompson graduated from Bent County High School in 1922. On returning home from a summer job one year, Thompson met a retired diplomat who shared his experiences with the young man, inspiring Thompson to pursue a like career. He worked his way through the University of Colorado at Boulder, earning a B.A. in economics in 1928.

Following his graduation, Thompson attended a foreign service tutoring group in Washington, D.C., while working as an accountant for Price, Waterhouse. He received an appointment as a Foreign Service officer in January 1929. His first post was as vice-consul in Colombo, Ceylon (now Sri Lanka). In 1933, Thompson was transferred to Geneva, Switzerland, where he was promoted to consul in 1937. While in Switzerland he served as an American adviser to the International Labor Office. Transferred back to the United States in 1940, Thompson attended the Army War College in Washington, D.C., as the conflicts in Europe and the Pacific intensified.

Sent to Moscow as second secretary and consul in 1941, Thompson began to demonstrate what would become his most important contribution to American diplomacy, his profound insight into the Soviet Union. He remained in Moscow throughout the Nazi siege of 1941 and 1942. He reportedly used these months to achieve fluency in the Russian language, but his stay in the capital during the crisis also endeared the diplomat to many Soviets. The United States awarded Thompson the Medal of Freedom for his courage in remaining at the embassy. Thompson continued his duties in Moscow until 1944 when he was assigned, in the same capacity, to London. He remained in London for two years before returning to Washington, D.C., where he held several administrative posts: chief of Division of Eastern European Affairs, deputy director of the Office of Eastern European Affairs, and deputy assistant secretary of state for European Affairs. On one of his many transatlantic trips Thompson met Jane Monroe Goelet, an artist. They were married on Oct. 2, 1948. Mrs. Thompson had a daughter from her first marriage, and together the Thompsons had two children.

Throughout the postwar years Thompson was present at almost every conference concerning Soviet-Western relations, beginning with Potsdam in July 1945. President Harry S. Truman sent Thompson to Rome in mid-1950 as embassy counselor and to Vienna in 1952, first as high commissioner and then as ambassador to Austria. Thompson became pivotal in resolving the Trieste dispute between Italy and Yugoslavia, and in negotiating the Austrian State Treaty. The Trieste settlement of 1954 divided the Adriatic port territory of Trieste in a manner agreeable to both countries. The decision culminated nine years of debate, and as with the 1955 Austrian State Treaty, which granted Austria independence in return for a pledge of neutrality, Thompson's quiet, tenacious diplomacy proved instrumental. His patience and ability to judge opponents also brought him success at the poker table with fellow embassy personnel.

Because of his Soviet expertise and because Moscow had given its approval to both the Trieste settlement and the Austrian State Treaty, President Dwight D. Eisenhower named Thompson ambassador to Moscow in June 1957. At Thompson's behest a historic visit to the United States by Soviet Premier Nikita S. Khrushchev became a reality in 1959 and resulted in reduced Cold War tensions. Thompson then prepared the way for a summit meeting between Khrushchev and Eisenhower in Paris, but the conference failed to materialize after the Soviets shot down an American U-2 reconnaissance aircraft in 1980. Despite international tensions, during his tenure Khrushchev came to trust Thompson. The two men spent a great deal of time together, both professionally and socially. Thompson did not grant interviews or write of his experiences with the Soviets; instead he kept Soviet trust by maintaining the confidentiality of his discussions with Soviet leaders. In appreciation of his distinguished service he received the title of career ambassador in June 1960.

Thompson remained in Moscow after President John F. Kennedy was inaugurated, and Kennedy even more than Eisenhower came to rely on Thompson's advice in Soviet matters,

seeking Thompson's counsel during the 1961 Berlin crisis. In the summer of 1962 Thompson left Moscow and returned to Washington in order to retire. He remained in Washington at Kennedy's wishes, however. In June 1962 Thompson was presented with the government's highest civilian honor, the President's Award for Distinguished Federal Civilian Service. That October he received Senate confirmation as ambassador at large. During the four years in his new capacity he was responsible for advising the president and the secretary of state on all matters relating to the Soviet Union. Thompson was instrumental in the resolution of the 1962 Cuban missile crisis as the resident Russian expert. He gave the National Security Council Executive Committee the insight, which few other people could have given, into Khrushchev's unwillingness to take on a nuclear risk. He also stressed the importance of allowing the Soviets to save face in concluding the crisis. Because of the importance of Soviet-American relations Kennedy also relied on Thompson's expertise in Vietnam to prevent further conflicts.

President Lyndon B. Johnson retained Thompson in the same capacity, ambassador at large, with a brief stint as acting deputy under secretary of state for military-political affairs, until 1966 when Thompson was named ambassador to Moscow for the second time. Thompson arranged the 1967 meeting between President Johnson and Soviet Premier Aleksey N. Kosygin in the United States. He expended a great deal of energy trying to limit the Soviet-American nuclear arms race. Most of his second tour, however, was troubled with repercussions of American involvement in Vietnam. Thompson returned to Washington in January 1969, having served as the United States ambassador to Moscow longer than any ambassador to date.

In the last years of his life Thompson was on the Central Intelligence Agency's Board of National Estimates. He was a delegate to the Strategic Arms Limitation Talks, attending the Helsinki and Vienna negotiations with the Soviets that resulted in the 1972 SALT I Treaty. Thompson died at the National Institutes of Health in Bethesda, Md.

[Papers relating to Thompson's service can be found in the National Archives and each of the presidential libraries from Truman through Nixon. An oral history transcript is available through the

Kennedy Library in Boston. The Kit Carson Museum, Las Animas, Colo., contains a Thompson Room with a collection of memorabilia including photographs, medals, newspaper clippings, and diplomatic dress.

No biography of Thompson exists. For further information see Laura Bergquist, "JFK's No. 1 Russian Expert," *Look*, Feb. 12, 1963; Harrison E. Salisbury, "Job of Our Man in Moscow," the *New York Times*, Mar. 11, 1963; and Lee H. Burke, "The Ambassador at Large: A Study of Diplomatic Method" (Ph.D. diss., University of Maryland, 1971). Tributes to Thompson are by Charles Bohlen, the *New York Times*, Feb. 11, 1972; and Dean Rusk, the *New York Times*, Feb. 24, 1972. Obituaries are in the *New York Times*, Feb. 7, 1972, and the *Washington Post*, Feb. 7, 1972.]

TERESA L. LAYTON

TOUREL, JENNIE (June 22, 1900–Nov. 23, 1973), singer and voice teacher, was born in Vitebsk, Belorussia. The details of her early life, not clearly documented, were invented in various ways (some of her own design) in numerous sources. Tourel's father was a banker, and the Jewish Davidovich (later Davidson) family lived comfortably in prerevolutionary Russia until they were forced to flee in 1918. They eventually settled in Paris. Jennie had begun study of the piano at an early age, and in Paris she embarked upon voice studies with Reynaldo Hahn and Anna El-Tour. (The names of her earlier teachers and the dates of her formative musical studies are not known.) Tourel later disputed the story that her stage name, "Tourel," was an anagram of her teacher's name, El-Tour. While in Paris she also studied with the lieder singer Maria Freund, whose influence she acknowledged as significant in the development of her interpretive style.

A mezzo-soprano, Tourel had a wide range that extended from low G to high C. Her first documented stage debut in Paris was at the Opéra Russe in 1931, when she sang the role of the Polovtsian Maiden in Borodin's *Prince Igor*. The Opéra's conductor Emil Cooper was instrumental in bringing Tourel to America, where she appeared with the Chicago Civic Opera during the 1930–1931 season, singing in Ernest Moret's *Lorenzaccio* and Mascagni's *Cavalleria Rusticana*.

Tourel first sang her most famous part, the title role in Bizet's opera *Carmen*, at the Opéra-Comique in Paris in 1933. Thereafter she appeared regularly in this role and in other prominent mezzo-soprano roles (such as Cherubino in Mozart's *The Marriage of Figaro* and Charlotte in Massenet's *Werther*), in Parisian and other European houses throughout the 1930's and 1940's. Her New York City Metropolitan Opera House (the MET) debut took place in 1937 in Thomas's *Mignon*.

Following her MET debut, Tourel achieved increasing prominence on the American stage, primarily in concert and recital venues. In October 1942, she sang under Toscanini in Berlioz's *Roméo et Juliette* in a special New York Philharmonic centenary performance. This was followed by appearances under Koussevitzky (in Debussy's *La Damoiselle élue* on Dec. 4, 1942) and Stokowski (in the American premiere of Prokofiev's *Alexander Nevsky Contata* in 1943).

Tourel made her U.S. recital debut in New York City's Town Hall in November 1943. Her program, which was typical of her recital programs throughout her career, displayed her wide-ranging repertoire and interests, as well as her excellent command of languages. It included songs by Italian Baroque composers; songs by Mozart, Rossini, and Debussy; some Russian songs; and a selection of music by North and South American composers. The latter selections were unusual inclusions in recital programs at this time. Her Town Hall recital was highly acclaimed by the New York critics; Virgil Thomson wrote that Tourel was "unequalled among living singers for the high concentration in one artist of vocal skill, sound musicianship, and stylistic flexibility."

Tourel returned to the MET stage on Mar. 16, 1944, appearing in *Mignon*. Her MET career was relatively brief; from 1944 to 1947 she sang the roles of Carmen, Adalgisa in Bellini's *Norma*, and Rosina in Rossini's *The Barber of Seville*. She was one of the few mezzo-sopranos to undertake performance of the latter role in its original coloratura version. It was during this time, in 1946, that Tourel became a U.S. citizen.

Tourel performed the works of many twentieth-century composers, including those of Samuel Barber, Leonard Bernstein, Paul Hindemith, Francis Poulenc, Maurice Ravel, Igor Stravinsky, and Hector Villa-Lobos. In 1951, she appeared in the role of Baba the Turk in the world-premiere performance of Stravinsky's *The Rake's Progress*. She had a long and close association with Leonard Bernstein, who frequently performed with her as either pianist or conductor. She sang in the world premiere performances of his *Jeremiah Symphony* (1944) and *Kaddish Symphony* (1963), as well as in the premiere performance of his song cycle *I Hate Music*. His cycle *La Bonne Cuisine: Four Recipes for Voice and Piano* (1947) is dedicated to her.

Tourel's teaching career began in 1955 when she was invited to teach at the Aspen Festival. She taught at the Juilliard School from 1963 until her death, and presented master classes at many other conservatories and music schools in the United States and abroad. She was especially committed to furthering the cause of musical education in Israel, and she taught and presented master classes at the Rubin Academy of Music in Jerusalem from 1962 until her death. Among her students were Carmen Balthrop, Faith Esham, Barbara Hendricks, Peggy Pruett, and Neil Schicoff.

Tourel remained active as a performer and teacher up until the time of her death from cancer. In 1971, she appeared in the role of the Countess in a television production of Tchaikovsky's *The Queen of Spades*, and on Oct. 26, 1973, she appeared in a speaking role in the Chicago Lyric Opera's production of Donizetti's *La Fille du Regiment*. Because the year of her birth was believed to be 1910, most of the obituary articles state her age at the time of her death as sixty-three; in truth, she was probably seventy-three.

Tourel, open and giving as a performer, was reserved about her private life. She married three times; all three marriages ended in divorce. She had no children.

Known especially for her exemplary interpretation of the French vocal repertory as well as for her command of and interest in music of all styles and periods, Jennie Tourel was a consummate musical artist and an important influence on the musical life of her time.

[Tourel's papers are housed primarily at the Juilliard School and at Boston University. The collections include programs, clippings, photographs, and correspondence. Robert Offergeld's "Some Notes on the Future of Jennie Tourel," *Stereo Review*, Nov. 1975, clarifies many of the myths surrounding Tourel's early years. Tourel's legacy is preserved on numerous recordings. Of special note are her 1969 Carnegie Hall recital with Leonard Bernstein on the Columbia label, and her 1970 Alice Tully Hall recital with James Levine on the Desto label. An obituary is in the *New York Times*, Nov. 25, 1973.]

JANE GOTTLIEB

TRAMMELL, NILES (July 6, 1894–Mar. 28, 1973), pioneer network radio and television broadcasting executive, was born in Marietta, Ga., the son of William Jasper Trammell and Bessie Niles. From September 1912 through December 1914, Trammell attended Sewanee Military Academy in Sewanee, Tenn., then the University of the South (also in Sewanee) from December 1914 to 1917. He did not graduate because World War I intervened.

Trammell entered the regular army and was commissioned a second lieutenant in May 1918, at Fort Leavenworth, Kans. He later served at Fort Snelling, Minn., Camp Devins, Mass., and the infantry school at Fort Benning, Ga. At the end of the war, he was a first lieutenant in the Thirty-sixth Infantry of the Twelfth Division of the United States Army. He was then posted to the Presidio in San Francisco, where he was attached to the staff of Major General Charles G. Morton until 1922.

In 1923, Trammell met Brigadier General David Sarnoff, who was making an inspection trip of army bases in San Francisco. Sarnoff spoke with such vision and enthusiasm about the possibilities of radio, that Trammell asked him about a job. In March 1923, Trammell resigned from the army to become a West Coast commercial representative in the traffic department of RCA in San Francisco. On Nov. 14, 1923, he married Elizabeth Huff, General Morton's stepdaughter. They had no children.

After one year, Trammell was made district manager of the Pacific Coast Division/Pacific Northwest for the marine division of RCA. His job required him to be "out prowling through smelly importers' places trying to persuade some Japanese [companies] to use our facilities instead of the cables."

In 1925, Trammell became assistant sales manager of the Pacific Division of RCA. In March 1928, just two years after NBC was formed as a service of RCA, he joined NBC as a salesman, and within two months was made manager of the Central Division of NBC, headquartered in Chicago. In March 1929, Trammell was named vice-president of the Central Division. When he assumed leadership of this division, the Chicago headquarters reportedly had only one studio and two offices. It was reported that when he was first sent to Chicago, his superiors hoped he would increase the income of the Central Division's headquarters to $1 million a year. After one year, the office did that much business in one month. More than eighteen hundred programs per month were being broadcast, including one thousand network programs that originated in the Chicago office.

In Chicago, Trammell was responsible for originating daytime programs, some of which became more popular than the very popular evening shows. Long-running radio series like "Clara, Lu and Em," "Fibber McGee and Molly," and "Betty and Bob," and soap operas like "Today's Children," and "Ma Perkins" all got their start while Trammell ran NBC's Chicago headquarters. Another first was the commercial radio network series of entertainment stars like Eddie Cantor, Ben Bernie, Al Jolson, Phil Baker, Wayne King, Red Skelton, Don Ameche, Jane Froman, Ed Wynn, and Paul Whiteman, who became established as radio favorites.

Trammell has been called the father of the soap opera (continuing series often sponsored by manufacturers of soap products). Of the soap opera, which was often regarded as a lesser entertainment art form, he said, "There's a European proverb that says the culture of a nation is determined by its use of soap . . . the United States with six percent of the world's population, uses a third of the world's soap supply." Soap was important in the American economy and culture, and thus was a worthy sponsor for network programming.

Trammell brought "Amos 'n' Andy" into the homes of Americans across the country by broadcasting the show on radio six nights a week. "Amos 'n' Andy" went on the air over Chicago's WMAQ in 1928. This fifteen-minute comedy broadcast grew into one of radio's great successes. In the summer of 1929, NBC executives offered the creative team behind "Amos 'n' Andy" a contract for national broadcast over NBC's Blue network. The show made its national debut on Aug. 19, 1929, sponsored by Pepsodent toothpaste. Pepsodent sales increased substantially, other companies were signed as sponsors, and advertising rates increased. According to *Time*, this "million dollar contract" with Pepsodent "was a big feather in Trammell's Chicago cap . . . which transformed 'Amos 'n' Andy' from a sustaining show into a national institution."

Trammell was also credited with finding sponsorship for orchestral music broadcast on radio. The first time the Chicago Symphony Orchestra played for NBC, however, it was a difficult if memorable experience—the orchestra gathered in a "sweltering" tin-roofed Masonic Hall, had to play in shirtsleeves and undershirts, and a sudden noisy rainstorm beat on the tin roof during the concert. Other programs created under Trammell's stewardship in Chicago were: the University of Chicago "Round Table," the "Farm and Home Hour," the Chicago Opera Company programs, and the Grant Park concerts.

In January 1939, Trammell transferred to NBC's headquarters in New York City and was promoted to executive vice-president of the network, in charge of all network operations. He created separate sales staffs for the two radio networks of NBC, known as the Red and the Blue networks, each with its own vice-president.

In the late 1930's and 1940's, Trammell and his fellow executives had to deal with Walter Winchell's often uninhibited Sunday night radio commentaries. Memos circulated furiously among NBC's executives and executives of the program's sponsor, Jergens Lotion, over an Apr. 30, 1939, comment by Winchell describing Hitler as a "madman." There had been other references to Hitler's foreign minister, Joachim von Ribbentrop, as "von Ribbentripe." Concerns were expressed over the possibility of offending Germany, for American foreign policy was still officially neutral. Winchell's high ratings kept his program on the air.

On July 12, 1940, Trammell was named president of NBC, succeeding Lenox Riley Lohr, who resigned to become head of the Chicago Museum of Science and Industry. Trammell was president and director of NBC until Oct. 7, 1949. In 1940, statistics from the Cooperative Analysis Bureau indicated that when Trammell was made head of NBC, eight of the top ten most popular network programs were on NBC.

Trammell believed in investing heavily in programs like the NBC Symphony Orchestra, directed by Arturo Toscanini, and the Saturday afternoon Metropolitan Opera broadcasts, initiated by NBC in 1931 (later carried by ABC). "The NBC University of the Air" (1948–1951) offered information and instruction, often tied to school and university curricula.

An assistant to Trammell, Clay Morgan, described him as, "the most indefatigable executive I have ever known. He works late, on Saturdays—and holidays, too." Trammell enjoyed golf and fishing. In his office it was reported that a thirty-pound muskellunge hung on the wall. He also was "pernickety about his clothes, neat as a pin around his office." He was characterized as easily accessible and soft-hearted, shrewd, soft-spoken, more convivial than his predecessor, enormously popular with his staff, and a disciplined person with courtly southern manners.

In 1938 the Federal Communications Commission (FCC) launched an investigation of chain broadcasting and increased regulation of the networks. In 1941, before the Senate Interstate and Foreign Commerce Committee, NBC challenged the FCC's regulations. NBC lost this case in the Supreme Court, and in 1943 was forced to sell the Blue network, which became ABC.

In March 1946, the FCC released a report called *Public Service Responsibility of Broadcast Licensees*. Because the cover of the report was blue, the report came to be known as "the blue book." The report discussed local broadcasting and programming, and praised programming it judged to be particularly valuable. Few NBC affiliates chose to carry a number of these worthy shows. The "blue book" quoted Trammell, CBS president William Paley, and other industry leaders on how important it was to maintain and nurture programs of value. They defined these programs as those that provided balance, or approached subjects that might have difficulty securing sponsorship or advertisers. They addressed and served minority interests and the needs and interests of nonprofit groups, and experimented with both form and content.

In 1945, Trammell divorced his wife. On April 7 of that year, he married Cleo Murphy Black; they had no children.

On Apr. 4, 1949, Trammell was named chairman of the board of NBC, a position he held until Dec. 8, 1952. This period marked the change to a new order in broadcasting. Trammell represented the old school—courtly, and bewildered at the rapid changes in the industry. He was used to playing golf and having drinks with old friends who headed ad agencies and sponsor companies; in the course of socializing, he would sell a time slot for thirty-nine weeks of regular programming and thirteen weeks of summer replacements. However, sponsorship of entire time periods by one company, with advertising agencies providing the programs, began to disappear as costs of television time rose with increasing television viewership. The unit of sale became the sixty-second (or shorter) commercial, and programs were supplied by the networks, at the networks' risk.

Despite Trammell's business and programming acumen, there was a major lapse in NBC talent relations. As their contracts expired, Burns and Allen, Jack Benny, Edgar Bergen, and others left NBC and went to CBS. CBS at the time had as talent coordinator Emanuel Sacks, who had relationships with such powerful talent agencies as William Morris and MCA. Eventually, David Sarnoff hired Sacks away from CBS, and major stars began to return to NBC.

Trammell also was said to have a weak grasp of figures. Some thought that NBC should have been more aggressive in seeking rate increases, but Trammell preferred to keep rates lower, to discourage the competition and avoid trouble with the government. He had built his reputation as a salesman, and salesmen do not want high rates.

On Nov. 28, 1951, at the meeting of NBC affiliates, Trammell talked about television: "This new medium of communication is so powerful . . . and fascinating that it has grown to manhood in only a few years. Television is a significant influence on a majority of our people. . . . In the next five years television will become a national medium . . . [and] will exercise the greatest impact on the human mind yet known to mankind."

Trammell resigned from NBC in 1952 to become president of Biscayne Television Corporation in Miami. Biscayne Television built and operated television station WCKT-TV (Channel 7) which made its first broadcast July 29, 1956; its radio affiliate was WCKR. In 1962, the station was sold for $3.5 million. After the sale Biscayne Television donated more than $2 million to the University of Miami. In 1963, Trammell worked as a business consultant to television and radio concerns.

In 1968, Miami Dade Junior College dedicated the Niles Trammell Learning Resource Center. Trammell had been a charter member and vice-chairman of the school's five-person advisory committee.

In 1971, Trammell's wife died. Trammell moved to Sewanee, Tenn. He died of a heart attack in a private nursing home in North Miami, Fla.

Trammell left more than $300,000 to the University of the South for the Niles Trammell

Communications Center. He had been a regent of the university from 1935 to 1937 and an alumni trustee from 1946 to 1948. He was active in fund-raising for the university, especially for a students center named for a friend of his, Bishop Frank A. Juhan (who had been a chancellor of the university).

[Trammell's personal papers are in the archives of the Dupont Library, University of the South. Material pertaining to him is in the National Broadcasting Company Manuscript Collection, M/B/RS Division, Library of Congress. On his career, see L. M. MacMillan, "Up from the Ranks Leadership for NBC," *The Advertiser*, July 1940; *New York Times*, July 13, 1940; *New York Herald Tribune*, July 13, 1940; *Time*, July 22, 1940; Erik Barnouw, *History of Broadcasting in the United States*, 3 vols. (1966–1970); Walter Winston Skinner, *Duty, Patience and Endurance, the Trammells of Meriwether and Harris* (1977); Mary C. O'Connell, *Connections* (1986); and George H. Douglas, *The Early Days of Radio Broadcasting* (1987). Obituaries are in the *New York Times*, Mar. 29, 1973; the *Miami Herald*, Mar. 29, 1973; and *Variety*, Apr. 4, 1973.]

AMY SCHEWEL

TRAUBEL, HELEN (June 16, 1899–July 28, 1972), American soprano famous for Wagnerian roles, was born in St. Louis, Mo., to a prominent family of German descent. She was the daughter of Otto Traubel, a pharmacist with wide-ranging community and cultural interests, and Clara Stuhr, known locally as a concert and church singer. As children Helen and her older brother, Walter, attended numerous cultural events, including dramas presented in German at the St. Louis Apollo Theater, founded by her maternal grandfather. Traubel attended public school, leaving after her sophomore year to concentrate on her singing. She received her vocal training in St. Louis starting at the age of thirteen from Louise Vetta-Karst, a brilliant voice teacher.

Traubel first performed professionally as a teenager in the Pilgrim Congregational Church choir, where she sang from time to time until the mid-1930's. She made her concert debut with Rudolph Ganz and the St. Louis Symphony Orchestra on Dec. 13, 1924, performing in Mahler's Symphony No. 4, and she sang again with the orchestra on tour in the Midwest, in the South, and at New York City's Lewisohn Stadium in 1926.

After these successful concert performances,

Traubel was offered an audition for the Metropolitan Opera in New York City, the operatic holy of holies, by general director Giullo Gatti-Casazza, but she declined, returning instead to her home city for more study with Vetta-Karst. She continued to confine herself to local engagements, including an appearance in the St. Louis Sangerfest in 1934, during which she performed under the direction of conductor and composer Walter Damrosch. Damrosch was so impressed with Traubel's singing that he rewrote his opera *The Man Without a Country* to include a new part, that of Mary Rutledge, designed specifically for Traubel.

Traubel finally had her debut at the Metropolitan Opera when *The Man Without a Country* premiered there on May 12, 1937. Critical acclaim for her singing led to a contract offer from the Met, but she turned it down. She did, however, accept a contract with the National Broadcasting Company, which gave her the chance to perform regularly on national radio and to make herself known to a broader public than habitués of the opera.

Still not satisfied with her voice, Traubel studied for a year with Giuseppi Boghetti. She made her New York City Town Hall debut recital on Oct. 8, 1939. Her impressive performance at Town Hall signaled her elevation to the first ranks of American opera. It was followed by an equally impressive concert performance at Carnegie Hall just two weeks later. On Dec. 28, 1939, she gave her second performance at the Metropolitan Opera, this time playing Sieglinde in Wagner's *Die Walküre*, and thereafter became a star at the Met.

Traubel was highly acclaimed throughout her career for her stage presence and the brilliance of her vocal technique. She was judged to be the best American Wagnerian soprano since Lillian Nordica. She shared the Wagnerian spotlight with Flagstad before and after World War II but held it by herself during the war years, when Flagstad, a Norwegian, returned to her homeland. Traubel was the first American-trained soprano to sing the roles of Brunhilde and Isolde at the Metropolitan Opera, and her reputation as the principal Wagnerian soprano was secure throughout the 1940's. Even though Flagstad's absence gave her the opportunity to perform these important and difficult roles during World War II, her own fluent vocal technique, warm tone, and striking stage presence combined to demonstrate her right to assume Flagstad's mantle.

Throughout the years of Traubel's career American opera critics and audiences naturally assumed that European operatic training was essential for a career in this country. Thus, her accomplishments and widespread acclaim are all the more remarkable because she did not seek out European training or even performing experience. Indeed, Traubel first sang outside the United States only in 1940 and 1941 on a transcontinental tour that included appearances in Canada. Eventually, however, she performed all over Europe, in Cuba, in Mexico, and in South America. In the early 1950's she made two world tours, including a triumphant appearance in Japan.

Although Helen Traubel was known principally as a Wagnerian soprano, she expanded her repertoire to include the role of the Marshallin in Richard Strauss's *Der Rosenkavalier* in 1951. She also made numerous concert appearances and was the first singer to record with Arturo Toscanini and the NBC Symphony Orchestra. Her recordings, recitals, and national radio broadcasts for the Ford Motor Company and the Bell Telephone Company, along with performances in nightclubs, in films, and on television, added to her immense popularity. However, when she appeared with such non-operatic personalities as Groucho Marx and Jimmy Durante, she aroused the ire of Rudolph Bing, the Metropolitan Opera's general manager, who felt that such appearances tarnished her reputation as a serious artist. As a result of her dispute with Bing, Traubel refused to return to the Met for the 1953 season. Thereafter she continued to pursue her diverse musical and cultural interests, which included appearances in the film *Deep in My Heart* (1954), the Rodgers and Hammerstein musical *Pipe Dream* (1955), and the film *Gunn* (1967). In addition, she served as Margaret Truman's vocal coach.

Although Traubel's vocal flexibility became limited at the top of her range as she aged, she retained her presence and tone and was very popular with varied audiences in concert, on radio and television, and in clubs. An avid baseball fan throughout her life, she purchased an interest in the St. Louis Browns. In 1950, Traubel released her first effort at fiction writing, a mystery story called *The Ptomaine Canary*, syndicated by the Associated Press and published privately. In 1951, she published *The Metropolitan Opera Murder*, which earned a degree of

critical acclaim for its inside portrait of the Met backstage. In 1959, she published her autobiography, *St. Louis Woman*.

Helen Traubel received many honors throughout her career, including recognition by the New York Tau Alpha chapter of the Mu Phi Epsilon honorary musical society for the outstanding performance of 1939 and 1942; a citation of merit from the National Association of American Composers and Conductors; and the King Christian X [of Denmark] Medal of Liberation. The Associated Press named her Woman of the Year in Music twice, and she received an award from the New York Federation of Jewish Philanthropies. She received honorary doctorates from the University of Missouri and the University of Southern California.

Helen Traubel was married twice. An early marriage at age nineteen to St. Louis businessman Louis F. Carpenter soon ended in divorce. In October 1938, she married her business manager, William Bass. She never had any children. Traubel died in Santa Monica, Calif.

[Helen Traubel's papers are stored at the Library of Congress. Information on her career in New York, including clipping files, Metropolitan Opera programs, and reviews, can be located at the Music Division of the New York Public Library at Lincoln Center. Numerous popular articles and reviews appeared about Traubel's performances during her lifetime. Brief discussions of her life and career also appear in David Ewen, ed., *Living Musicians* (1940), and *Men and Women Who Make Music* (1949); Oscar O. Thompson, ed., *International Cyclopedia of Music and Musicians* (1949); *Who's Who in Music* (1951); and *The New Grove Encyclopedia of American Music* (1986). An obituary appears in the *New York Times*, July 30, 1972.]

BARBARA L. TISCHLER

TRAYNOR, HAROLD JOSEPH ("PIE") (Nov. 11, 1899–Mar. 16, 1972), baseball player, was born in Framingham, Mass., the son of James H. Traynor, a printer, and Lydia Matthews. When Traynor was five the family moved to the Boston suburb of Somerville, where he acquired the nickname "Pie," reputedly either because of his fondness for pie or because of his propensity for getting dirty (his father once said he looked like "pied" type). After completing his elementary education at Somerville's Bingham School, Traynor went to work as a messenger and office boy in Boston.

Neither happy nor successful in the business world, he attempted to enlist during World War I but was rejected.

Baseball was Traynor's first love, and, after spending the summer of 1919 playing semiprofessional ball on Cape Cod, he was recommended to manager Ed Barrow of the Boston Red Sox following an impressive Fenway Park workout in the spring of 1920. Barrow arranged for Traynor to play with the Red Sox affiliate at Portsmouth, Va., during the 1920 season. At season's end Portsmouth sold shortstop Traynor to the Pittsburgh Pirates.

Sent to Birmingham in 1921 for further seasoning, Traynor batted .336, although his sixty-four errors in 131 games left much to be desired. Recalled by Pittsburgh, he opened the 1922 season as the Pirates' shortstop, but when Bill McKechnie became the Pirates' manager midseason, he promptly moved Traynor to third base. Although Traynor conceded that the "hardest thing in going from shortstop to third base was learning to play that much closer to the hitter," he quickly adjusted to his new position.

Six feet, one inch tall and weighing 175 pounds, Traynor, as Bill Terry described him, was "like a cat at third base." Playing a relatively shallow position, he pounced on enemy bunts, roamed gracefully to his left, and was "positively devastating on the toughest play of them all, the hot ground smash over the bag." In fact, telegraphers routinely reported that Hornsby or Hafey or whoever it might be "doubled down the left field line, but Traynor threw them out."

Possessing what the Pirates' first baseman Charlie Grimm described as the "quickest hands" and the "quickest arm of any third baseman" of his day, Traynor, according to one sportswriter, "played third base as though he wore a magnet instead of a glove." His glove did, in fact, contain a felt interior rather than leather, for he found that "with the felt lining, a hard-hit ball, if not caught cleanly, will drop at your feet," where it remains playable. Traynor's career total of 2,291 putouts remains to this day the record for National League third basemen.

Traynor was not a one-dimensional player, though. During his 1,941-game, seventeen-season major league career (1920–1937, all with Pittsburgh) he amassed 2,416 base hits, drove in 1,273 runs, and attained a lifetime batting average of .320. Primarily a line-drive hitter, the right-handed-batting Traynor used a bat weighing forty-two ounces and drove many of his hits into right and right center field. He had a keen eye and struck out only 278 times in his entire 7,559 at bats in the major league. Traynor played in the 1925 and 1927 World Series.

In June of 1934 Traynor was named player-manager of the Pirates. That same year he injured his right arm in a collision with another player at home plate, leading to the premature termination of his playing career. He just couldn't throw well anymore, he lamented. Traynor continued to manage the Pirates. They had virtually clinched the 1938 pennant when Gabby Hartnett's famous game-winning "homer in the gloaming" at Chicago's Wrigley Field sent Pittsburgh into a late-season tailspin and a second-place finish. When the Pirates dropped to fifth place in 1939, Traynor was fired at the end of the season; his career record as a manager was 457–406.

Retained by the Pirates as a scout, Traynor moved to Cincinnati in 1941. He and his wife, Eva Helmer, whom he had married on Jan. 3, 1931, resided there until 1944. They had no children. In 1944, Traynor returned to Pittsburgh as a sports commentator for radio station WKQV. Traynor continued his radio work into the late 1960's. He also appeared in television commercials accompanying live studio wrestling. This ongoing media exposure made Traynor a local celebrity.

During his later years Traynor continued to scout for the Pirates, conducted tryout camps, and paid an annual ten-day visit to the Florida spring training center, where he suited up, offered instructional advice, and regaled the players with anecdotes of his fabled career. Inducted into the National Baseball Hall of Fame in 1948, he was selected as the game's greatest ever third baseman by the Baseball Writers' Association in 1969. Traynor died in Pittsburgh. In an early tribute, Branch Rickey, Sr., general manager of the Brooklyn Dodgers, had said of Traynor: "They can substitute for him, but they can never replace him."

[A biographical sketch of Traynor is in Bob Broeg, *Super Stars of Baseball* (1971). See also Harvey Frommer, *Baseball's Hall of Fame* (1985); and Lowell Reidenbaugh, *Cooperstown* (1986). Obituaries appear in the *Sporting News*, Apr. 1, 1972; the *Pittsburgh Press*, Mar. 17, 1972; and the *New York Times*, Mar. 16, 1972.]

LOUIS R. THOMAS

TRILLING, LIONEL (July 4, 1905—Nov. 5, 1975), author and critic, was born in New York City, the son of Fannie Cohen and David W. Trilling, a manufacturer of men's fur-lined coats. He had one sister. He attended public schools in New York City, including De Witt Clinton High School. He received all his higher education at Columbia University, where he was awarded his B.A. in 1925, his M.A. in 1926, and his Ph.D. in English literature in 1938. Trilling married Diana Rubin on June 12, 1929; she too became a noted author and critic. The couple had one son.

After receiving his M.A., Trilling served as an instructor in the English Department at the University of Wisconsin in Madison for the 1926–1927 academic year. He then accepted an instructorship in the English Department of Hunter College in New York City, where he taught from 1927 to 1930. He spent virtually the rest of his teaching career at Columbia University, where he held successive faculty appointments as instructor (1931–1939), assistant professor (1939–1945), associate professor (1945–1948), full professor (1948–1965), George Edward Woodbury Professor of Literature and Criticism (1965–1970), university professor (1970–1974), and university professor emeritus and visiting lecturer (1974–1975). He also was honored with appointments as a George Eastman Visiting Professor at Oxford University (1964–1965), as the Charles Eliot Norton Professor of Poetry at Harvard University (1969–1970); and as a visiting fellow at All Souls College, Oxford University (1972–1973). It should be noted that this progression masks a significant detail: some members of the faculty and administration at Columbia were reluctant to grant Trilling tenure because he was Jewish. He became the first Jew to hold a tenured position in the English Department at Columbia University.

Trilling began his scholarly career as an expert on Matthew Arnold, the Victorian poet and literary and social critic, expanding his dissertation into *Matthew Arnold* (1939), his first major work. Indeed, Arnold was a kind of role model for Trilling, and the former's life and theory inspired much of the latter's work, climaxing in *Beyond Culture: Essays on Literature and Learning* (1965). Trilling accepted Arnold's dictum that criticism is "a disinterested endeavor to learn and to propagate the best that is known and thought in the world."

In *E. M. Forster* (1943), Trilling analyzed Forster's moral code and his independence from the commonplaces of liberal thinking. *The Liberal Imagination* (1958), probably his most influential book, examined what Trilling considered to be modern distortions of liberal thought prompted by misplaced sympathy for Stalinist Russia. *Freud and the Crisis of Our Culture* (1955) celebrates Freud for creating a complex image of man and explains his pivotal place in modern culture. Other important works by Trilling include *The Opposing Self* (1955), a collection of critical essays; *A Gathering of Fugitives* (1956), another collection of essays; and *Sincerity and Authenticity* (1972), a study that examines shifting images of the self from the eighteenth century to today.

Trilling also wrote a number of short stories and a well-respected novel, *The Middle of the Journey* (1947). Through that work he became involved in the Alger Hiss case. He refused to testify at the trial and declared that Whittaker Chambers was a man of honor. He would later defend the novel and refute those who claimed that this form of fiction was dying.

Criticism, to Trilling, meant seeking the ideas that shaped the work of literature under consideration. Though he never founded or joined a particular school of literary criticism, he believed that literary criticism should include reference to politics, history, philosophy, and psychoanalysis. He was not interested in textual explication, rejected the "close reading" popular in his time, and always tried to relate the intellectual content of the works he studied to larger issues. His primary critical aim was to show the interaction between society, the artist, and the work of art under study. He believed that works that did not challenge their culture had little value.

Trilling was among those who pressed claims for American literature. At Columbia University and elsewhere in the high reaches of American academe, the study of American literature was devalued and neglected even as late as the 1950's. He was also among the early supporters of the idea of producing high-quality editions of the works of American literary figures and encouraged the organizers of today's acclaimed Library of America series.

For Trilling, the university was an instrument of social mobility essential to the American way of life. Paradoxically, he saw culture as a conservation of the past through which one could interpret the present and see the future. For Trilling a liberal education meant becoming "a whole man." Trilling served on the commission that investigated the riots of the late 1960's at Columbia, one of the centers of revolt against the authority of the university. He saw much of the political activity during that decade as more gratuitous than the radical student movements of the 1930's. The authority of culture in society, he felt, had eroded as a consequence of the uprisings at universities across the United States and Europe, and he lamented this erosion. Questions about society that the college professor hoped his students would ask were now being asked and answered for them by popular culture. Universities were once marginal to national life. Academic life that had order and coherence was now thought of as the center of vested interests and regarded with suspicion and hostility.

Lionel Trilling was a very popular teacher, noted for his sense of humor and wit. Among his students were the poets Allen Ginsberg and John Hollander, and Norman Podhoretz, later the editor of *Commentary*. Although he taught graduate-level courses in literature, he preferred to teach undergraduate courses. With Jacques Barzun he conducted a colloquy in cultural history and criticism of the nineteenth century.

In his later years Trilling also lamented a loss of precision in words and form. The artist, he believed, must accept his culture and be accepted by it, but he should also be its critic. Tension is created through this ambivalence.

Trilling was a member of Phi Beta Kappa, the American Academy of Arts and Sciences, and the National Institute of Arts and Letters. He received honorary degrees from a number of institutions, including Brandeis, Harvard, and Yale. He was the recipient of the Mark Van Doren Award, given by the student body at Columbia University; the Brandeis University Creative Arts Award; and the Thomas Jefferson Award from the National Endowment for the Humanities. In addition, he served on the editorial boards of the *Kenyon Review* and the *Partisan Review*.

Lionel Trilling was the embodiment of the New York intellectual. Though on occasion attacked for what might be called "urban provinciality," his wide range of interests, his depth of culture, and his critical acumen combined to make him what he had always aspired to be, a kind of American Matthew Arnold. With F. R.

Leavis and Edmund Wilson, he dominated the critical world of midcentury America.

[Trilling was a prolific writer. Besides his dozen or so books, he wrote numerous articles, reviews, and introductions. Diana Trilling gathered many of her husband's shorter pieces in a series of posthumous volumes, including *The Last Decade: Essays and Reviews, 1965–1975* (1979), *Prefaces to the Experience of Literature* (1979), *Of This Time, Of That Place, and Other Stories* (1979), and *Speaking of Literature and Society* (1980).

See also Robert Boyer, *Lionel Trilling: Negative Capability and the Wisdom of Avoidance* (1972); William M. Chace, *Lionel Trilling: Literature, Criticism, and Politics* (1980); Philip French, *Three Honest Men: Edmund Wilson, F. R. Leavis, and Lionel Trilling* (1980); Mark Krupnick, *Lionel Trilling and the Fate of Cultural Criticism* (1986); Daniel T. O'Hara, *Lionel Trilling: The Work of Liberation* (1988); Edward J. Shoben, Jr., *Lionel Trilling* (1988); and Quentin Anderson, Stephen Donaldo, and Steven Marcus, eds., *Art, Politics, and Will: Essays in Honor of Lionel Trilling* (1977). An obituary is in the *New York Times*, Nov. 7, 1975.]

DANIEL SPICEHANDLER

TRUMAN, HARRY S. (May 8, 1884–Dec. 26, 1972), thirty-third president of the United States, was born in the farm village of Lamar, Mo., 120 miles south of Kansas City, the son of John A. Truman, a farmer and livestock dealer, and Martha E. Young. Truman would one day say he considered three areas of experience necessary for a president: farming, banking or money handling of some kind, and service in the military. He obtained these three experiences almost by accident, as he would have been the first to admit, for until he was nearly forty years old his life hardly moved in a straight line toward the goal of politics, which eventually became what he liked to describe as his profession.

Truman satisfied his first requirement for presidential service early, spending his boyhood years and early adulthood on a succession of farms. Except for the period from 1890 to 1906, when he lived in Independence, Mo., or in Kansas City, Truman lived most of his early years at his maternal grandmother's large farm near the village of Grandview in Jackson County. He would remain there until 1917. After his father's death in 1914 Truman supervised the 600-acre farm, doing much of the planting, cultivating, and harvesting himself. The future president thus possessed intimate knowledge of rural America. Indeed his mother believed that farm work constituted the formative influence in his life. "It was on the farm," she once said, "that Harry got his common sense. He didn't get it in town."

The Truman family's move to Independence, the county seat of Jackson County, was principally undertaken so that Harry, his younger brother John Vivian, and their sister Mary Jane could obtain an education in the town's schools (Harry graduated from Independence High School in 1901). John Truman carried on his livestock business in the capacious backyards of the houses in which they lived. In 1903, after engaging in a disastrous speculation in grain futures, Truman's father almost lost everything the family owned, and it became necessary for the family to move to Kansas City, where John Truman went to work as a night watchman at a grain elevator and his sons became bank clerks. Harry enjoyed serving as a clerk in a "cage" and as assistant to the bank's vice president. Here was his second requisite for a large political future. In 1905, Truman's parents returned to the Grandview farm, and Harry and his brother followed in 1906.

When the United States entered World War I in 1917, Harry Truman volunteered. It was not expected of him, as he was nearly thirty-four years old and a farmer. He had served two "hitches" in the National Guard, 1905–1911, and knew a little more about military duties than most young men in 1917. He also was an intense patriot, comparing the fight against Germany to Galahad's quest for the Holy Grail. He helped organize a regiment out of a National Guard company in Kansas City and was elected a first lieutenant. After his regiment entered federal service as the 129th Field Artillery, he trained with it in Oklahoma, where it was attached to the Thirty-fifth Division. He went overseas late in March 1918, was promoted to captain, and in July took over Battery D, which he commanded until the Armistice and demobilization.

Truman's military experience between 1917 and 1919 probably constituted the single most important influence on his life—with the exception of his marriage to Elizabeth Virginia ("Bess") Wallace of Independence on June 28, 1919, and birth of their daughter, Mary Margaret, in 1924. Service in the army widened his perspective beyond the small tasks and daily concerns of his life in Missouri. In particular it showed him that he could be a leader. When he

took command of Battery D it was an unruly group of nearly 200 men and officers that, he sometimes said afterward, had "broken" three captains and would have liked to break him. He took command and held it, and before long the men—many of them graduates of a Catholic high school in Kansas City—idolized him. With evenhanded orders and an instinctive ability to get to the heart of problems, both personal and military, and determine their solutions, Truman led his men through hard action in the battle of the Meuse-Argonne, Sept. 26–Nov. 11, 1918.

Service in the battery turned Truman's thoughts toward politics. One of his letters to Bess Wallace mentioned, perhaps idly, that he might run for Congress, so as to take vengeance upon the regular army officers, elitist West Pointers, who momentarily were making his and his battery's life difficult. The battery and its regiment, based in Kansas City, became the foundation of his political career—for Jackson County included Kansas City, ten miles to the west of rural Independence. When Truman ran for local office, the regiment's former members voted for him en masse.

But before politics there was the haberdashery, which occupied his energies from 1919 until its collapse in 1922. He undertook this enterprise with his friend Edward Jacobson, former sergeant in the 129th Field Artillery, with whom he earlier, in Camp Doniphan, Okla., had conducted a remarkably successful canteen, or regimental store. The haberdashery opened with every sign of success, as its clientele in Kansas City, opposite the city's principal hotel, the Muehlebach, were the partners' former army friends. The firm of Truman and Jacobson borrowed from local banks to acquire a large inventory of shirts, ties, underwear, and other items (the partners did not sell suits), and in the recession of 1920–1921 their inventory unfortunately fell in value almost overnight. In the subsequent hard times, customers disappeared. Moreover, closing the store left debts not merely for the inventory but for an incautiously negotiated long-term lease on the store building.

After Truman and Jacobson shut down in 1922, Truman turned to politics. During the war he had met Lieutenant James Pendergast, nephew of the boss of Kansas City's Democratic political machine, Thomas J. Pendergast. This acquaintance led in 1922 to endorsement by the Pendergast machine for Truman's nomination on the Democratic ticket as county judge, that is, county commissioner for the eastern part of Jackson County, which includes Independence. When Truman narrowly won the primary that summer he was assured of victory against his Republican opponent in the November election, since Missouri at that time was a rock-ribbed Democratic state.

Truman began his ten-year career as a county executive with a two-year term as eastern judge in a three-man court made up of himself, a western judge for Kansas City, and a presiding judge elected at large. He was defeated in 1924 when a Democratic faction antagonistic to Boss Pendergast sided with the Republicans. In 1926, after an interlude of selling memberships in the Kansas City Automobile Club, he was elected to the first of two consecutive four-year terms as presiding judge. Experience as a county executive proved invaluable to his later national political career. His two-year tenure as eastern judge saw him siding with his western counterpart, who later became Pendergast's corrupt minion as city manager of Kansas City.

But the eight years Truman served as presiding judge (principal county commissioner) fully instructed him in how to satisfy the interests of his fellow judges, who were uninterested in county reform measures, and meanwhile propose and follow through with a remarkable public improvements program. Judge Truman managed this program—which included construction of county roads, a rebuilt courthouse in Independence, a new art deco skyscraper courthouse in Kansas City, and other county facilities—without giving money to corrupt contractors friendly to Boss Pendergast. It was anxious work, in that the presiding judge had to persuade Pendergast of the need for honesty on county matters (Truman of course could not control city administration, which his former colleague on the court arranged to Pendergast's satisfaction), and at the same time persuade county voters that he himself would administer honestly the necessary bond issues, totaling $10 million for the roads alone. Truman managed the task and by the end of his county experience in 1935 had attained a statewide reputation for progressive measures.

In 1934, after some five possible nominees had rejected the opportunity, Truman became Pendergast's candidate for the U.S. Senate. In a field that included two other candidates in the

Democratic primary his chances did not look good. But the erstwhile farmer from Grandview campaigned vigorously, speaking in more than half of Missouri's 114 county seats during the hottest summer on record in many years. Truman won, after which he easily defeated Roscoe C. Patterson, his Republican opponent, in the November election. Under the Twentieth Amendment to the Constitution, which changed the inaugural date for presidents and congressmen, he was among the first group of senators to take office in Washington in January 1935.

Truman rose to only modest prominence during his first Senate term (1935–1941). He voted a straight New Deal line, with the exception of his endorsement of early payment of the soldiers' bonus, which President Franklin D. Roosevelt opposed and two-thirds of the members of both houses of Congress voted to override. Privately Truman was against the president's 1937 court-packing plan, Roosevelt's attempt to influence the Supreme Court's decisions by increasing its size, although in public he went along. He did not see much of the president, who lavished most of the patronage due the state on the unpredictable and alcoholic senior senator from Missouri, Bennett Champ Clark. Truman held his tongue, responded to Missourians who wanted action on federal matters (Bennett Clark neglected them), and quietly undertook to become an expert on national transportation problems. He was cosponsor of the Civil Aeronautics Act of 1938, which governed the airlines until deregulation in the 1970's. Much more important, in conjunction with Democratic Senator Burton K. Wheeler of Montana he worked to produce a single federal enactment that would bring fair competition between the nation's railroads and internal water transport and the burgeoning trucking industry, which was beginning to compete seriously with railroads and barge traffic.

The Wheeler-Truman Transportation Act of 1940 constituted a major achievement of federal regulation, and most of it was the result of Truman's hard work in committee, for Wheeler turned his attention to Roosevelt's court-packing proposal and for months was preoccupied in his eventually successful opposition to it. Truman was prominent among his fellow senators in conducting the necessary hearings. He was horrified to uncover massive evidence of financial chicanery in reorganizing railroads after the bankruptcies of the early 1930's, which he believed was the result of collaboration between railroad executives, whom he described as buccaneers, and New York and Chicago lawyers and investment bankers. The senator's speeches on this subject received considerable newspaper attention.

The Transportation Act did little to secure Truman's reelection in 1940, for it came too late in the year. He found himself in the most difficult political race of his career, even including his later campaign for election as president in 1948. The collapse of the Pendergast machine in Kansas City, incident to Boss Tom's conviction for income tax evasion in 1939, eliminated 50,000–60,000 ghost votes for Pendergast candidates. Governor Lloyd C. Stark declared his candidacy for Truman's Senate seat. Elected to a four-year term as governor in 1936, Stark by Missouri law could not succeed himself. He had helped unseat Pendergast and his next quarry became Truman, whom he described luridly as Pendergast's tool, despite the fact that the Pendergast investigation failed to show any illegal involvement by Truman in Pendergast's affairs.

The outcome of the 1940 election was unclear until the very end. Entrance into the Democratic primary of a third candidate, the Pendergast prosecutor, Maurice Milligan, divided the anti-Pendergast vote. The contest nonetheless was essentially between Truman and Stark. Truman managed to do well in the largely rural "outstate" areas, apart from Kansas City and St. Louis. His supporters managed, at the eleventh hour, to gain support from St. Louis's city machine, which threw 8,000 votes his way, allowing him to win the primary by a statewide plurality of fewer than 8,000 votes. Once again the senatorial election in November brought an easy victory for the Democratic candidate, allowing Truman to retain his seat.

In his second Senate term Truman turned to what he learned from informants in the vicinity of Fort Leonard Wood near Rolla, Mo., was massive fraud in construction of army camps during expansion of the U.S. Army in 1940 and 1941. The resultant Senate special committee, known as the Truman Committee, expanded its purview to investigation of all military procurement including contracts awarded private industry and the behavior of labor unions. The announced task much resembled that of a congressional committee during the Lincoln ad-

ministration, which in Truman's opinion had undermined the Civil War effort. Truman, by this time a skilled politician, carefully avoided the politicization of the committee, precluded any attempt to jeopardize national defense or influence military strategy, and deflected attacks against the administration. Upon organization of the special committee in 1941 Truman, as chairman, chose only "workhorses" among his colleagues, not "show horses," to serve. He engaged a first-rate staff of investigators. To errant military departments, industrial corporations, or unions, he made it a practice to release committee reports in draft, allowing them to anticipate criticism, although they could only dispute matters of fact. Committee reports, produced by subcommittees so as not to consume time of senators who served on the special committee, were always unanimous. In this manner the Truman Committee soon was making headlines and the threat of investigation often sufficed to bring miscreants to the reformations that Truman and his colleagues desired.

Such was the situation when in July 1944, leaders of the Democratic party, working with President Roosevelt, replaced Vice-President Henry A. Wallace with Truman as the party's vice-presidential nominee on the ticket with Roosevelt, who was aspiring to a fourth term. The replacement was a truly extraordinary move, to put Truman, a party regular and compared with Wallace a conservative, in line for the presidency, since it was generally acknowledged by insiders that the ill president would die in office if reelected. Truman was thoroughly aware of this situation. From all available evidence Roosevelt was not. Nor were the American people, who chose the Roosevelt-Truman ticket in November 1944.

Upon Roosevelt's death on Apr. 12, 1945, Truman found himself president, and his immediate problem was his lack of preparation to handle foreign policy, particularly since the country had entered the final stages of World War II and the rest of his term would entail a dramatic change in American foreign relations, from a policy of isolation, which largely had prevailed since the beginning of national government, to a policy of global participation that has continued to the present day. In domestic matters he had trained himself through ten years in county politics and another decade in national politics and in fact may have been the best-prepared chief executive for domestic affairs in the twentieth century. The new president needed time to acquaint himself with foreign affairs, however, and complained to assistants that he was having to read hundreds of pages of documents, straining eyes that had been weak since childhood.

Upon taking the oath of office, Truman had made the expected perfunctory statement that he would follow his predecessor's policies, both foreign and domestic. He asked all of Roosevelt's cabinet appointees to remain. But when the military picture clarified in Europe— the German army was in the throes of defeat but Adolf Hitler was still in control (although his suicide took place on April 30) and Nazi troops were fighting to the end—a restructuring of the cabinet proved necessary. The new president found himself with a heterogeneous group of Roosevelt-appointed advisers who did not respect him as compared with his predecessor. He moved at once to relieve Secretary of State Edward R. Stettinius, Jr., and soon replaced other cabinet officers for varying reasons, with the last of the Roosevelt appointees, former Vice-President Wallace, who had become secretary of commerce, resigning in September 1946.

Truman announced Germany's surrender on May 8. He allowed preparations to continue for the detonation of a nuclear test device in New Mexico on July 16. They seemed necessary because of the fanatical way in which the Japanese were defending the approaches to their home islands, fighting to the death on Iwo Jima and Okinawa. Truman scheduled a Big Three meeting with Winston Churchill and Joseph Stalin at Potsdam outside Berlin. The meeting, which opened July 17 and lasted until August 2, ensured Soviet entrance into the war against Japan. The Soviets entered the war on August 8, two days after the nuclear bombing of Hiroshima and the day before the bombing of Nagasaki. Japan's surrender occurred August 14. It was impossible to say whether the bombings, or Soviet entry, or both, produced surrender. Truman himself was never sure. The decision to use nuclear weapons on Japanese cities became the most controversial issue of Truman's presidency, with debate continuing for decades thereafter. The president knew the Japanese army was vastly reinforcing the defenses of Kyushu, the southernmost home island, and feared that an invasion of Japan would bring "an Okinawa from one end of Japan to the other." He always justified dropping the bombs,

remarking that the Japanese had ignored the Potsdam Declaration, a warning issued in the midst of the Potsdam Conference. The warning was only of the destruction of Japan and did not specify use of nuclear weapons. It seemed impossible to give details because the bomb project was yet secret, unknown to the U.S. Congress. At Potsdam, Truman told Stalin that the U.S. possessed a new bomb of great explosive power; he did not relate that it was a nuclear weapon, although Stalin knew this because of espionage. After explosion of the test device in New Mexico only two bombs were available, and Truman was told that a demonstration was inadvisable. The two bombs killed at least 120,000 Japanese. Ever afterward Truman maintained that they saved more American and Japanese lives by ending the war.

In the postwar years (1945–1950) and throughout the Korean War, the basic foreign policy of the Truman administration was to allay the so-called Cold War with the Soviet Union, which had begun in the last weeks of the Roosevelt administration when Stalin quarreled over negotiations taking place in Switzerland for the surrender of German troops in Italy. In support of America's friends among the nations of Western Europe, Truman determined to stand up to the Russians, imposing economic or even military sanctions if necessary. When Soviet Foreign Minister Vyacheslav Molotov passed through Washington to pay his respects to the president, en route to the San Francisco Conference that drew up the United Nations Charter, Truman upbraided the Soviet government for its lack of cooperation, declaring that Russian-American relations were not a one-way street. Advisers, including the ambassador to Moscow, W. Averell Harriman, had urged tough talk with the Soviets, but feared Truman had gone too far. Perhaps in an effort to conciliate, and against the strenuous objection of British Prime Minister Churchill, the president not long afterward ordered U.S. troops in Germany back to the occupation zone agreed upon at the Yalta Conference, out of the Soviet zone, which they had entered in the last days of the war.

Nearly two years after taking office, on Mar. 12, 1947, Truman announced what became known as the Truman Doctrine, which changed U.S. policy toward the Soviet Union from attempted cooperation to confrontation. Although he did not so much plan policy as take measures as events dictated, a logic developed in the administration's moves in relation to the USSR. The Truman Doctrine was a statement of principle that the United States would support any nation threatened by Russian Communism. In practice this support was intended only for Western Europe, and its occasion was Soviet pressure on two small nations in the Eastern Mediterranean, Greece and Turkey.

Also announced in 1947 was the European Recovery Program or Marshall Plan, with appropriations totaling $13 billion by 1952 to support the economies of Western Europe including the Western zones of occupied Germany. The Marshall Plan alone did not suffice—the Soviets seemed to be moving toward a more militant policy toward the Western allies—and further measures became necessary. In June 1948, the Russians sealed off land access to the Western sectors of Berlin, requiring an airlift to supply coal and food to the city's inhabitants, until the USSR lifted the blockade in April 1949. Meanwhile the United States and its allies organized the North Atlantic Treaty, signed in April 1949, a military pact of twelve Western nations, to which Greece and Turkey were added in 1952, West Germany in 1955, and Spain in 1982.

Truman's intervention in the Korean War beginning June 25, 1950, brought increasing criticism after an initial period of widespread public support. The president sent American armed forces into Korea, believing the Soviet Union had inspired North Korea's attack on South Korea. After the Chinese intervention in October and November 1950, he feared that American defeat by the Chinese would significantly undermine United States prestige around the world. But from the outset he also went along with the joint chiefs of staff who insisted that Western Europe rather than Eastern Asia was the important theater for military operations, that the North Atlantic Treaty required rapid organization of a multinational force, with a core of U.S. Army divisions, against the USSR, and that Korea was quite possibly a military diversion. The policy statements of General Douglas MacArthur tested this belief, together with the constitutional authority of the president as commander in chief of the armed forces. Just as he had not hesitated to begin an unpopular war, he did not hesitate to relieve a popular and pompous general. After the opening of the Korean War, Truman's approval rat-

ing fluctuated, then plummeted. In November 1951, a Gallup poll placed it at 23 percent, one point lower than that of President Richard M. Nixon just before his resignation in 1974.

In domestic policy the president proved less successful than in foreign affairs. Any extension of New Deal measures was no longer attractive; the passage of time had begun to erase memories of the Great Depression, and Congress resisted measures for domestic reform. The triumphs of American industry during World War II and the successful reconversion of war industry to domestic production in the period 1945–1947 also made such reform appear unnecessary. In a long message to Congress in 1945 the president tried halfheartedly to set out New Deal measures not yet achieved; it was not an inspiring message but rather a laundry list of twenty-one proposals, and it produced little interest, what with public attention fastening on the labor troubles and marked inflation accompanying the successful reconversion. Upon election to the presidency in his own right in 1948, Truman asked his countrymen to support what he described as the Fair Deal, the liberal reforms he had proposed in 1945. Little came from this proposal because, again, the country was not attuned to reform, and the outbreak of the Korean War moved the focus away from domestic politics.

About the time of the proposal of the Fair Deal, two domestic contentions ensnared the administration, one of which carried ramifications for foreign policy, and President Truman's failure to distance himself from them caused him and the Democratic party many difficulties. One accusation that hounded the president was that he had allowed friends or "cronies"—individuals who took money or dispensed influence—to infest the administration, particularly in the Bureau of Internal Revenue, a sensitive area, and in the Justice Department. Critics also accused the president's military aide and World War I friend, Major General Harry H. Vaughan, of giving favors to "five-percenters," lobbyists who gave themselves a 5 percent commission for government contracts they obtained for businessmen. Another accusation against the president was that he was soft on Communists or fellow travelers in government employ. The anti-Communism issue turned into a crusade when Republican Senator Joseph R. McCarthy of Wisconsin in February 1950, just before the opening of the Korean War, accused the State Department of harboring dozens (his figure varied from 57 to 205) of Communists.

Truman responded to these criticisms of corruption and Communism without much success. He had a weakness for friends, even inconvenient friends, tended to believe critics were attacking him by attacking them, and usually refused to dismiss anyone under attack. He vehemently, with suitable profanity, defended General Vaughan. He criticized senators of his own party who sought to warn him. Against the anti-Communist tirades of McCarthy he defended Secretary of State Dean Acheson, who had become a focus of antiadministration wrath. Acheson in January 1950 had made a speech that did not include Korea within the American "defense perimeter," which gave rise to accusation that he had "given away" Korea, telling the North Koreans in advance that they might take it. He also derided the notion of Communists in the State Department. The president's defense of him did not convince the multitudes of Republican senators Acheson undiplomatically had angered. On the anti-Communism issue the administration was also beset by the anomalous case of a former State Department official, Alger Hiss, who was eventually convicted of perjury rather than of giving secrets to the Soviets. During Truman's presidency serious breaches of security by Soviet agents, several of whom were British subjects, compromised the Federal Bureau of Investigation and Central Intelligence Agency (established under Truman's auspices in 1947), with loss to the Soviets of some of the technological secrets of the wartime and postwar nuclear bomb program.

In truth the president through excellent appointments to diplomatic and military posts greatly advanced national security from the low point caused by pell-mell demobilization in 1945 and 1946, especially through enlargement of the army, navy, and air force during the Korean War; by the end of the administration in January 1953, the country's defense against the Soviet Union was as sound as it possibly could have been. But the president received little credit for his accomplishment. Failure of the Fair Deal created dissatisfaction, as did the attacks on cronyism and Communists in government. In foreign policy the loss of mainland China to Communism in 1949 appeared to be further evidence of presidential incapacity, even though Truman in 1945 had sent to China as a

mediator an official he considered of heroic stature, General George C. Marshall, who could do nothing more than cause a short delay in the civil war between Nationalists and Communists. The Korean War turned unpopular when the new People's Republic of China intervened and especially after truce talks, begun early in 1951, dragged on (until an armistice in the summer of 1953). The return of General MacArthur to the United States in April 1951 brought a near–tidal wave of criticism upon the administration, from which it never recovered. MacArthur, addressing a joint session of Congress and an enormous television audience, defiantly asserted the government's mishandling of the war, a war he declared could have been and should have been won.

The result was a Republican electoral victory in November 1952. Four years earlier, in the election of 1948, the president had displayed a virtuoso-like ability to snatch victory from the jaws of defeat; almost no one, not even Mrs. Truman, expected him to win. He had fought the "do-nothing, good-for-nothing" Eightieth Congress in whistle-stop speeches and in addresses in huge, barnlike auditoriums across the country and almost single-handedly defeated his formidable opponent, Governor Thomas E. Dewey of New York (whose name, Truman explained to voters, rhymed with "hooey"). But it was a personal, not administration, victory, and thereafter, following a honeymoon in the period 1949–1950, political criticism mounted against both him and his party. He did not seek reelection. The Democratic nominee in 1952, Governor Adlai E. Stevenson of Illinois, concerning whose political talents Truman was lukewarm, tried to distance himself from the president and failed to contradict a reporter who asked a question about the "mess in Washington." He eventually allowed Truman to help with the campaign, but the odds for a Democratic victory were impossible once the Republicans nominated General Dwight D. Eisenhower.

Truman left Washington for Independence, where he lived his remaining years. The former president undertook the writing of his memoirs, two large volumes that appeared in 1955 and 1956, chronologically uneven, with one volume for the first year of his presidency, mistakenly described as a "year of decision," and one for the remaining seven years ("years of trial and hope"). This was the official version of his presidency, written with a literary team, and he followed it with other books and a series of newspaper articles on current events and problems. All the while he was arranging construction of his presidential library, which opened in 1957 at the end of the street fronting his Independence home. As the years passed he traveled, soliciting funds for his library and endorsing Democratic candidates.

Until his eightieth birthday in 1964 the former president was a vigorous presence in American politics, and an equally vigorous reminder that the United States had come into its own as a world power during his administration. In 1965 his health began to fail. He died in Kansas City.

The estimate of Truman's place in history, both by the public and by historians and political scientists, underwent a change after his death. During the last years of his life it was already obvious that the country was raising what hitherto had been a low estimate of his personal and public qualities. The resignation of President Nixon, whom Truman never forgave for insinuating in 1952, when running for the vice-presidency, that Truman was a traitor (Nixon accused him of "toleration and defense of communism in high places"), commenced an upward movement that brought the nation's thirty-third president into virtual apotheosis. Adulatory biographies by his daughter, Margaret, and by Merle Miller assisted his rise in popular estimation. His personal honesty, well known to his intimates, made him attractive to a nation torn apart by Watergate and the Vietnam War. His willingness to take responsibility ("if you can't stand the heat, stay out of the kitchen") became a watchword for such diverse presidents as Gerald Ford, Jimmy Carter, and George Bush, all of whom claimed that they adhered to the precept inscribed on Truman's oval office sign, "The buck stops here."

The portrayal of Truman as a folk hero, however, fails to take into account his weaknesses as a leader, his errors of omission and commission. He often was tone-deaf, for example, in domestic appointments, choosing even cabinet members on the basis of his friendships with them over the years, in the Senate or elsewhere, at one juncture awarding the Department of Defense to Louis Johnson, because Johnson had been treasurer of the Democratic party in 1948. Having arranged such appointments he went to lengths to defend them. Nor could he success-

fully measure the anti-Communist sentiments of his fellow Americans. He accurately described one inquiry as a "red herring" but was unable to communicate a sense of how Communists could be pursued with decorum. In 1947 he allowed the institution of a loyalty program that became an embarrassment because of its arraignment of innocent people. Instead of asking Congress for a declaration of war against North Korea in the summer of 1950, when intervention had bipartisan support, he chose to describe the war as a "police action" and found himself on the defensive when its length and the mounting casualties made it the third most costly war (not counting the Civil War) in the nation's history up to that time.

But against the criticisms, legitimate and otherwise, was the cool intelligence that President Truman brought to public affairs. Unlike what the American people were told at the time and for years thereafter, during his presidency Truman made few snap decisions. He liked to say that when an issue arose he made what he described as a "jump decision," and then waited as long as he possibly could before committing to a course of action, during which he mulled over what he should do, getting the best possible advice. It was, to be sure, a sensible procedure. With such leadership the American nation more than held its own. Though Truman's liberal domestic program wallowed in the face of public apathy, in foreign policy the nation changed its course, moving against the Soviet Union, supporting its allies, setting the course of American foreign policy for the next two generations.

[Truman's official and personal papers are in the Harry S. Truman Library in Independence. Truman wrote two volumes of *Memoirs*, published in 1955 and 1956. See also Margaret Truman, *Harry S. Truman* (1973); Robert H. Ferrell, ed., *Off the Record: The Private Papers of Harry S. Truman* (1980); Monte M. Poen, ed., *Strictly Personal and Confidential: The Letters Harry Truman Never Mailed* (1982); Robert H. Ferrell, ed., *Dear Bess: The Letters from Harry to Bess Truman, 1910–1959* (1983); Donald R. McCoy, *The Presidency of Harry S. Truman* (1984); Richard L. Miller, *Truman: The Rise to Power* (1986); and David McCullough, *Truman* (1992). An obituary appears in the *New York Times*, Dec. 27, 1972.]

ROBERT H. FERRELL

TUCKER, RICHARD (Aug. 28, 1913–Jan. 8, 1975), operatic tenor, was born Rubin Ticker in

Brooklyn, N.Y., youngest of the six children of Israel Ticker, a furrier, and Fannie Chiperwodska. After graduating from New Utrecht High School in Brooklyn and entering the fur business as a salesman, he changed his name to Richard Tucker. He began to study voice and think seriously of a musical career beyond the world of cantorial singing, which provided his first professional engagements. By 1937, Tucker was singing on the radio, and in 1940 he began to study with the distinguished tenor Paul Althouse, who from then on was his only vocal instructor. Althouse was undoubtedly responsible for the technical finish of Tucker's singing and for the style that refined his naturally beautiful voice.

In 1941, Tucker made his operatic debut with the small Salmaggie Opera Company, as Alfredo in *La Traviata*. In 1942, he failed to win the "Metropolitan Auditions of the Air," but in 1943 Edward Johnson, general manager of the Metropolitan, came to the Brooklyn Jewish Center, where Tucker was singing, and asked him to prepare a special audition; it was a great success, but Tucker declined the "cover" assignments and small parts that were offered. In 1944, the Metropolitan's shortage of tenors led to a contract for starring parts that began with Tucker's debut as *Enzo in La Gioconda* on Jan. 25, 1945.

Tucker's success was so marked that he was able not only to survive but also to flourish at a Metropolitan Opera that in the immediate postwar years saw in the Italian repertoire the return of Jussi Bjoerling and the advent of such luminaries as Ferruccio Tagliavini, Giuseppe di Stefano, and Mario del Monaco. Part of his long-term success, and the secret of his vocal survival in full splendor to the end of his life, was his insistence on never attempting a part too demanding for his voice. Thus, in these early Metropolitan years he sang the roles of Enzo, Edgardo (*Lucia di Lammermoor*), the Duke of Mantua (*Rigoletto*), Pinkerton (*Madama Butterfly*), and Rodolfo (*La Bohème*), while firmly declining such roles as Don Alvaro (*Forza del destino*), Manrico (*Il Trovatore*), and Radames (*Aïda*), all of which he sang later when his voice had matured.

In 1947, Tucker made his European debut at the Arena di Verona as Enzo, under the baton of Tullio Serafin, to the Gioconda of Maria Callas—her Italian debut. This was the first of many European trips that took him to Vienna, Milan, Parma, Rome, Florence, Barcelona, and London. There were also tours to Israel, South Africa, and the Far East. Nevertheless, Tucker's career remained centered on the Metropolitan Opera, which after 1950 was under the direction of Rudolf Bing. The two got on well, and Tucker's solid professionalism and reliability were appreciated by a management content to let his career develop naturally and healthily.

In the 1950's, Tucker added new roles—Ferrando in *Così fan tutte*, Don José in *Carmen*, Alfred in *Fledermaus*, Don Alvaro in *Forza del destino*, and Des Grieux in *Manon Lescaut*. His voice was, quite naturally, heavier at forty than at thirty; he was now able to sing roles that earlier would have damaged his voice. But problematic for Tucker, as an artist on the lyric stage, was the quality of his acting; he rarely seemed able to achieve spontaneity on stage and sometimes failed to rise above stock gestures. His comic roles were better than his tragic ones, though much depended on the effectiveness of the directors with whom he worked; later in his career his Canio in *Pagliacci*, under Franco Zeffirelli, was a resounding dramatic success.

Tucker continued to hold his own against rival tenors in the late 1950's and the 1960's—Carlo Bergonzi, Franco Corelli, Jon Vickers—and further expanded his repertoire as his voice grew in depth and solidity. At the same time he maintained the lyric quality that enabled him to continue singing the lighter roles of his earlier career. Tucker starred in the events that celebrated the Metropolitan's move from the old house (built in 1883) to the glamorous new setting of Lincoln Center in 1966, and his twenty-fifth anniversary with the company was marked with a glittering gala in January 1970.

Although Tucker had sustained a heart attack in 1962, his career showed no diminution of energy; in fact, the last years of his life were busier than ever—more operas, more concerts. He expended much effort trying to get the Metropolitan to produce Jacques Halévy's *La Juive*, an opera for which he felt a special affinity, since he was Jewish and since the role of Eléazar was the last creation of Enrico Caruso, a singer with whose career Tucker increasingly identified his own. He gave concert performances of the opera in New York City and London, and sang in staged performances in New Orleans and Barcelona. In January 1975, Tucker at last persuaded the Metropolitan to agree to a revival for him. However, he died in Kalamazoo, Mich., while on a concert tour with Robert Merrill, before he could appear in *La Juive*.

Tucker married Sara Perelmuth, the sister of the distinguished tenor Jan Peerce, on Feb. 11, 1936; they had three children. A devout Jew, Tucker brought the special ethos of polyglot Brooklyn to the formidable task of becoming the eminent "Italian" tenor of the day.

His ample recorded legacy includes at least twelve complete operas (several recorded twice) and many collections of individual arias and Jewish and Italian songs. The recorded voice that emerges is that of an assertive singer. It is beautiful, the production immaculate, the diction crisp, the musicianship splendid. If anything is wanting, it is the elegant restraint that marks the very greatest artists.

[Tucker's papers are in the Metropolitan Opera Archives, New York City. James A. Drake, *Richard Tucker* (1948), is full and informative. Tucker's work is treated in J. B. Steane, *The Grand Tradition* (1974); and Paul Jackson, *Saturday Afternoons at the Old Met* (1992). An obituary and an appreciation are in the *New York Times*, Jan. 9, 1975.]

THOMAS FURCRON

TUNNELL, EMLEN (Mar. 29, 1925–July 23, 1975), football player, was born in Bryn Mawr, Pa., the son of Elzie Tunnell and Catherine Adams. He and his three siblings were raised in Garrett Hill, Pa., a Philadelphia suburb, by his mother, who worked as a ·domestic. Tunnell, an all-around athlete at Radnor Township High School, was awarded an athletic scholarship to the University of Toledo in Ohio. In his freshman year, Tunnell suffered a broken neck on the football field and was told he would never play football again. After he recovered from the injury, the army and the navy still rejected him as unfit for service. Undaunted, Tunnell enlisted in the coast guard and served three years during World War II, during which he survived a torpedoed ship.

At the war's end, Tunnell went to the University of Iowa, where he won a spot on the varsity football team, filled with returning veterans. Under coach Dr. Eddie Anderson, Tunnell played in both the offensive and defensive backfields. Anderson, however, eventually wanted to limit Tunnel to defense. Unhappy with that decision, Tunnell decided in 1948 to leave the University of Iowa with one year of athletic eligibility remaining and to turn professional. Another factor leading to his decision was his need for money.

In the early years of the National Football League, there were several black players in the league. Beginning in 1934, however, during the height of the Depression, the team owners had an unspoken agreement to keep blacks out of the league. This exclusion appeared to be a reaction to complaints from white players over a lack of jobs. Not until 1946 was this color barrier broken, when the Los Angeles Rams signed two black players out of UCLA, Woody Strode and Kenny Washington. Two years later, in 1948, Emlen Tunnell became the first black to play for the New York Giants. On a team with many players from the South and the Southwest, Tunnell said that he never had any racial problems and was accepted as a valued teammate.

The story of how Tunnell joined the Giants is legendary. He was not drafted by any team, partly because everyone expected him to return to Iowa for his final year of eligibility. Seeking a tryout, Tunnell hitchhiked to New York, went to the Giants' office, and asked to speak to the coach, Steve Owen. General manager Ray Walsh, having worked on many scouting lists, recognized his name and introduced him to Owen and to Tim Mara, the team's owner, and suggested that they give Tunnell a chance. When the Giants contacted coach Anderson at Iowa to ask if it was all right to sign Tunnell, he reportedly said, "Go ahead and sign him because I can't keep him in classes. He says he can't sit still that long."

Tunnell was offered a contract that called for $500 signing bonus, $500 when he reported to training camp and $5,000 if he made the team,

Tunnell did make the team, but Owen was undecided whether to use him on offense, as a tailback, or on defense, as a member of the secondary. The matter was settled with the acquisition of Charlie Conerly of Mississippi who became the tailback. Tunnell was assigned to the defense, a decision not pleasing to him.

By the end of his first season, however, Tunnell was playing defensive safety like a Hall of Fame candidate. In his rookie season he intercepted seven passes and began to enjoy defense. He was quoted as saying, "There's something about knifing in and bringing down a guy with a sharp tackle that provides more satisfaction than a long run behind good blocking. Tackling is football; running is track."

Tunnell went on to play eleven years with the New York Giants and three years with the Green Bay Packers. Widely regarded as one of the greatest defensive backs in the history of pro sport, Tunnell was known as the Giants' "offense on defense." Never was that term more applicable than in the 1952 season. Deacon Dan Towler of the Los Angeles Rams led the National Football League rushers by running for 894 yards with an average 5.7 yards per carry. Tunnell, on the other hand, accounted for 923 yards on just fifty-two carries for a 17.8-yard average. Yet Tunnell never played one down as an offensive back. Instead, he amassed 411 yards on punt returns, 364 yards on kickoff returns, and 149 yards on seven pass interceptions.

Tunnell anchored the famous umbrella defense that was a mainstay of the Giants' success in the 1950's. Using a forerunner of present-day defensive formations, coach Owen had the two defensive ends on the traditional six-man line drop back on pass plays, so that with the four defensive backs the defensive formation looked like an umbrella. At the top of the umbrella was six-foot, one-inch 200-pound Tunnell in a 4-1-6 defensive alignment.

Tunnell played in two championship games with the Giants. In 1956, the Giants overwhelmed the Chicago Bears 47–7. And in 1958, they won the Eastern Conference title but lost the championship to the Baltimore Colts 23–17 in a sudden death overtime. This game between the Colts and the Giants has been dubbed "the greatest game ever played."

In his 14-year career, Tunnell intercepted a then-record seventy-nine passes. In 1952 and 1953 he accounted for more yards on interceptions, punt returns, and kickoff returns than any of his offensive teammates did in their offensive categories (except, of course, the passer). He played in the first seven Pro Bowl games, from 1951 through 1957, and was named to numerous all-pro teams.

When Tom Landry took over as the Giants' defensive coach, Tunnell found his freewheeling style was not suited to Landry's more formal system of play. Tunnell quit the Giants early in 1959 but was persuaded by Vince Lombardi, former offensive coach of the Giants and then coach of the Green Bay Packers, to play for him in Green Bay. Tunnell played on Green Bay's Western Conference championship teams in 1960 and 1961. The Packers went on to win the National Football League title.

In a sport known for injuries and an average career of three and a half years, Tunnell's durability was remarkable. He played in 167 consecutive games starting with the Giants midway in the 1948 season and running into the 1961 season at Green Bay. He broke an ankle in 1954 at preseason training camp but did not miss a league game. In 1961, Tunnell said that he knew he was losing the spring in his legs when he was having trouble jumping up to touch the ten-foot-high crossbar between the goalposts, his standard routine whenever he was running wind sprints. He retired after the 1961 season.

Upon retirement, he worked as a scout for both the Packers and the Giants and in 1963 became a full-time scout exclusively for the Giants. In 1965, Giants head coach Allie Sherman made Tunnell a full-time defensive assistant coach, the first full-time black coach in the National Football League. In 1967, he was inducted into the Pro Football Hall of Fame in Canton, Ohio, the first black football player to be thus honored.

He married Patricia Dawkins in 1962; they had no children. Tunnell died of a heart attack in Pleasantville, N.Y. At the time of his death, he was assistant director of pro personnel for the Giants.

[Tunnell's autobiography with William Gleason is *Footsteps of a Giant* (1966). Memorabilia and career statistics are in the National Football Hall of Fame, Canton, Ohio. See also "The Toughest Man in Football," *Ebony*, Nov. 1975; George Sullivan, *Pro Football's All-Time Greats* (1968); Dave Klein, *The New York Giants* (1973); and Arthur R. Ashe, Jr., A *Hard Road to Glory* (1988); An obituary is in the *New York Times*, July 24, 1975.]

CHARLES TOBEY

U–V

ULMER, EDGAR GEORG (Sept. 17, 1904–Sept. 30, 1972), film director, producer, screenwriter, and set designer, was born in Vienna, Austria, the son of Siegfried Ulmer, a wine merchant, and Henrietta Edels. Officially he studied architecture at the Academy of Arts and Sciences, but his real school was the Burg Theatre in Vienna, where he worked as an actor and assistant set designer. He left for Berlin at age sixteen to design sets for the stage director Max Reinhardt at Reinhardt's famous Theater in der Josefstadt.

Ulmer's later specialization in film was something of an accident. In 1923 he traveled to the United States with Reinhardt to do the sets for a theatrical production of *The Miracle*. Six months later, when he returned to Vienna, Ulmer discovered that Reinhardt had contracted him out without his permission, thus crushing Ulmer's plans to run a theater of his own. Feeling that his mentor had betrayed him, Ulmer broke the contract, but he said later in an interview that this interruption of his theatrical career, which led eventually to his leaving for Hollywood, probably saved him from persecution a few years later by the Nazis.

Back in Berlin, Ulmer became an assistant in 1924 to F. W. Murnau, director of the classic horror movie *Nosferatu* (1922), whom he had met earlier when Murnau worked as an actor at Reinhardt's theater. Murnau was, with Fritz Lang, the greatest of the expressionist filmmakers to come out of the German film conglomerate UFA in the 1920's. Murnau worked in an atmospheric, technically innovative style called *Kammerspiel* (literally, "intimate theater"), in which the placement and movement of the camera were more important to the telling of a story than editing or intertitles. Ulmer's apprenticeship on the Murnau masterpiece *The Last Laugh* (1924), helping to construct sets and choose angles for each demanding shot, trained him in the attention to the visual mood of a film that would characterize his own work. He later claimed to have invented the dolly, a rolling device that allowed the camera to follow an actor through a scene, after seeing a mother walk by pushing a baby carriage.

Ulmer worked with several other German directors in the 1920's, most notably with Fritz Lang on Lang's *Metropolis* (1927). As the German economy and the Weimar government became more unstable, many of UFA's most talented film artists and technicians began migrating to the United States, and Ulmer went with Murnau when he was invited to Hollywood. In addition to working with Murnau there on *Sunrise* (1927), he assisted Cecil B. DeMille and directed dozens of serial Westerns without credit. In 1929, during a brief return to Germany, he directed his first feature film, *Menschen am Sonntag* (*People on Sunday*). Several of his collaborators, namely codirector Robert Siodmak and screenplay writers Billy Wilder and Fred Zinneman, would go on to more famous Hollywood careers than his own.

In 1930, Ulmer moved to the United States for good. Through a connection he had made while working for DeMille, he got his first American directing job with *Mr. Broadway* (1933), a vehicle for Ed Sullivan shot in New York, which he described later as "a nightmare, a mixture of all kinds of styles." His second film, *Damaged Lives* (1933), was a hit, but it ran into trouble with the Hays Office of Censorship because of its straightforward treatment of syphilis. Still, Ulmer persuaded Carl Laemmle of Universal to let him make *The Black Cat*

(1934), pairing two of the studio's biggest stars, Bela Lugosi and Boris Karloff, for the first time. The critic Geoffrey O'Brien has called this bizarre recasting of Edgar Allan Poe's tale, set in an art deco castle in post–World War I Austria, one of the greatest of all horror films.

The Black Cat was Ulmer's only film produced by a major studio. He claimed to have given up the security and prestige of studio backing in order to keep from getting "ground up in the Hollywood hash machine." He took odd assignments throughout the 1930's and early 1940's, directing comedies and melodramas in Ukrainian, Yiddish, and Spanish, a musical for black audiences, *Moon Over Harlem* (1939), and instructional films for the army and for Ford Motors. Under the name John Warner, he also directed several quickie Westerns, one of which, *Thunder Over Texas* (1934), was based on a story by Shirley Castle (real name Shirley Kassler), whom he married in 1935, and who would serve as script supervisor on most of his subsequent projects.

In 1942, Ulmer began directing for the Producers' Releasing Corporation (PRC), the "poverty row" studio responsible for many independent "B" movies of the 1940's. Work conditions at PRC were inauspicious—Ulmer often had barely enough film to complete a picture, and only six days to shoot—but the studio let him do as he pleased. The collaboration produced several of the films for which Ulmer is remembered today, including *Bluebeard* (1944), *Strange Illusion* (1945), and especially *Detour* (1946), in which Ulmer transcended his bad actors and shabby sets to tell the grim story of an unlucky man blackmailed into murder. According to critic David Rodwick, *Detour*, with its uniquely moody visual style, "rivals even Kafka in its determination to strip life of logic and stability."

After PRC fell apart in 1946, Ulmer began hiring out again to various independent producers. He made two notable films, *The Strange Woman* (1946), whose stars George Sanders and Hedy Lamarr were better known than most of Ulmer's actors, and *Ruthless* (1948). During the 1950's, he directed several less distinctive genre pictures in Italy, Germany, and Spain, and one exceptional Western, *Naked Dawn* (1955), which François Truffaut cited as the inspiration for his own *Jules et Jim* (1961). After *The Cavern* (1965), Ulmer suffered a number of disabling strokes that prevented him from

working. He died in Woodland Hills, Calif.

Ulmer was virtually unheard of until the French critic Luc Moullet saluted him in 1956 in the journal *Cahiers du Cinema*, and until recently his work was known only to devoted cinephiles. But in 1992, in a twist appropriate to Ulmer's career of strange luck and perseverance, the Library of Congress added *Detour* to the National Film Registry, a select list of movies to be preserved as part of the national heritage. The critic Dave Kehr called the choice "a victory for all of Hollywood's losers—for the legions of the waylaid, victimized and incidentally trampled, left behind by the progress of the world's most prosperous and imposing film industry."

[Most valuable for further biographical information is the interview with Peter Bogdanovich in *Film Culture* (1974). See also Luc Moullet, "Edgar G. Ulmer," *Cahiers du Cinema*, Apr. 1956; and John Belton, *The Hollywood Professionals*, vol. 3 (1974). An obituary is in the *New York Times*, Oct. 2, 1972.]
SARAH KERR

VALACHI, JOSEPH MICHAEL (Sept. 22, 1904–Apr. 3, 1971), racketeer, was born in predominantly Italian East Harlem in New York City to Dominick Valachi and Marie Casale, immigrants from Naples, Italy. His father, a day laborer, often was unable to pay the rent. Valachi later recalled stealing a crate of soap cakes and selling them door-to-door at half price; it was, he said, his first crime. Many were to follow, especially after the youth dropped out of junior high school. He latched onto the Mafia as an enforcer and at age twenty-seven was formally initiated into the secret society by Salvatore Maranzano. At the initiation ceremony the boss asked the recruit, "Which finger do you shoot with?" Valachi recalled. "I said, 'This one,' and I hold up my right forefinger. I was still wondering what he meant by this when he told me to make a cup out of my hands. Then he put a piece of paper in them and lit it with a match and told me to say after him, as I was moving the paper back and forth, 'This is the way I will burn if I betray the secret of this Cosa Nostra.'"

Valachi wound up in the crime family headed by Charles ("Lucky") Luciano. His income came primarily from slot machines, which he purchased with permission from Luciano's lieutenant, Vito Genovese. When police, under orders from reformist mayor Fiorello La Guardia, cracked down on the illegal machines in the mid 1930's, Valachi got Genovese's permission to start an illegal numbers lottery and later turned to Luciano for financing. He was arrested in 1936, but received a suspended sentence after his previous arrest record was withheld from the judge—thanks to Mafia intervention, Valachi said. A loanshark who dealt mostly with bookmakers, Valachi became a partner in a clothing company whose owner was unable to repay a loan.

Although some mafiosi disdained drug trafficking, Valachi in 1959 received a fifteen-to-twenty-year sentence on a narcotics conviction. He wound up in federal prison in Atlanta along with Genovese, who had become boss of the Luciano family and was also serving time for narcotics dealing. When a fellow prisoner with mob connections accused Valachi of being an informer for the Federal Bureau of Narcotics, Valachi feared for his life. When he was confronted by an inmate he mistook for Joseph Di-Palermo, a Genovese family assassin, Valachi attacked first, beating the man to death with a lead pipe. Valachi was convicted of second-degree murder with life imprisonment. He escaped the death penalty by agreeing to cooperate with investigators and testify before Senator John L. McClellan's Senate Subcommittee on Investigations.

When he began testifying in September 1963, Valachi became the first member of the Mafia ever to testify willingly in public about the nature of the organization. No one had ever violated the Mafia's vow of silence so flagrantly, and certainly not on television.

He described a secret criminal society with initiation rites, an oath of secrecy, and a leadership hierarchy. It consisted of "families," he explained, each with its own boss, underboss, *caporegimes* ("lieutenants"), and soldiers. He named hundreds of these men, all of Italian descent. Orders passed down the chain of command; money passed up. The most powerful bosses sat on a commission that regulated interfamily disputes.

Ralph Salerno, a New York police detective who specialized in organized crime, later wrote that "Many of the incidents Valachi described had . . . been known to police, but [Valachi] was able to fill in the gaps and connect one incident to another. [Valachi] drew a schematic picture of the organization, described it, and

told how it worked. The police, for example, had long realized that certain underworld figures were often seen with each other, but they did not realize that these were formal, not casual, associations, relationships of rank in a system governed by rules and regulations. The pattern that Valachi furnished made it possible for police intelligence men to begin to see the dimensions of syndicated crime and stop looking at it as a series of unconnected cases."

Valachi used the term "Cosa Nostra" ("Our Thing" in Italian) to describe what the rest of society commonly called the Mafia. In fact, the term was merely one of many used by Italian-American gangsters. Joseph Bonanno, founder of one of New York's five Mafia families, later wrote: "The reason there is no formal term to describe it is that there never was a formal organization to describe. We're talking about a tradition, a way of life, a process."

Bonanno, who wrote his autobiography two decades after Valachi's testimony, was one of Valachi's many critics. Given his low level in the Mafia, Bonanno wrote, "To expect Valachi to act as a reliable guide to [the Mafia], as the police, press and politicians did, was like asking a new convert to Catholicism in New Guinea to explain the inner workings of Vatican City." Indeed, Valachi was a street-level criminal who for the most part was simply recounting what had been told to him by other New York City mobsters, many of dubious credibility. Barely literate, he lacked perspective on organized crime and the world in general. When asked during the Senate hearings about organized crime in Omaha, Valachi appeared to think for a moment, then turned to a Justice Department official next to him and whispered, "Where the hell is Omaha?"

Whatever its reliability, Valachi's televised testimony helped make the Mafia a priority for law enforcers. The FBI, whose director J. Edgar Hoover had denied the existence of a national Mafia conspiracy, began investigations, and so did local law enforcers. At the end of 1966 a survey showed that in the three years following Valachi's testimony more gangsters in metropolitan New York had been jailed than in the previous thirty years.

Valachi was five feet, four inches tall and weighed 145 pounds but gained another 50 pounds during his long imprisonment. He spoke with a thick, gravelly voice and chain-smoked cigarettes. He was married to Mildred

Reina, daughter of a Mafia boss who was murdered in 1930. The couple had one child.

Valachi attempted suicide in prison in 1966. He died five years later of a heart attack at a federal prison in El Paso, Tex., embittered, lonely, and sick. His wife and son refused to claim his body; his remains were collected by Marie Jackson, a woman with whom he had corresponded but had never met. His body was shipped secretly to Niagara Falls, N.Y., and buried in an unmarked grave in a cemetery nearby.

[For further biographical information and discussion of his federal testimony, see Valachi's memoirs, contained in Peter Maas, *The Valachi Papers* (1968). See also Joseph Bonanno, *A Man of Honor* (1983); Carl Sifakis, *The Mafia Encyclopedia* (1987); and Howard Abadinsky, *Organized Crime* (1990). An obituary is in the *New York Times*, Apr. 4, 1971.]

RICK HAMPSON

VANDEGRIFT, ALEXANDER ARCHER (Mar. 13, 1887–May 8, 1973), marine general, was born in Charlottesville, Va., the son of William Thomas Vandegrift, architect and builder, and Sarah Agnes Archer. A student at the University of Virginia from 1906 to 1908, Vandegrift entered the marine corps as a second lieutenant in 1909. During his first years in the corps, he attended Marine Officers' School at Parris Island, S.C., and then served at the navy yard in Portsmouth, N.H. He married Mildred Ellis Strode of Amherst County, Va., on June 29, 1910. They had one child. After his wife's death in 1952, Vandegrift married Kathryn Hinson McDaniel of Charlottesville, Va. They had no children.

Like numerous officers of his generation, Vandegrift spent many years in the Caribbean, where the marines functioned as a colonial constabulary. Between 1912 and 1914, he served in Cuba, Panama, and Nicaragua, gaining promotion to first lieutenant in 1914. He was at Tampico and Vera Cruz that same year and in 1915 was assigned to Haiti to take part in operations against mercenaries and other irregulars (known as cacos) based in the mountainous areas. Vandegrift, who was promoted to captain in 1916, also served there with the Gendarmerie d'Haiti (1916–1918), which he helped to organize and train. In 1918, he was advanced in rank to major and expected to be sent to France, but the armistice was signed before he went

overseas. After a few months at the Norfolk Navy Yard, he requested a second tour with the Gendarmerie d'Haiti (1919–1923). Vandegrift then spent two years at Quantico, where he attended the Field Officers' Course.

With marine operations in Central America and the Caribbean winding down by the end of the 1920's, Vandegrift began to gain broader experience that was instrumental to his own success in the marine corps. From 1927 to 1929, he was in China, serving in Shanghai first as a battalion commander and then as operations and training officer in General Smedley Butler's brigade. Vandegrift was later stationed in Tientsin. Between 1929 and 1933, he was assigned to the Federal Co-ordinating Service, a newly established agency in Washington, D.C., intended to prevent duplication in the acquisition of materials by the armed forces and other federal departments.

Vandegrift was next stationed again at Quantico, where he served as assistant chief of staff of the East Coast Expeditionary Force (soon made part of the newly organized Fleet Marine Force) and assisted in preparing the first manual on amphibious doctrine. Promoted to lieutenant colonel in 1934, Vandegrift had another tour in China (1935–1937) and then spent four years in Washington, D.C., first as military secretary to the commandant of the marine corps and then as his assistant when Vandegrift's promotion to brigadier general became effective in 1940.

Levelheaded and adept at both staff work and leadership in the field, Vandegrift was ordered to New River, N.C., in November of 1941 to take charge of training the newly organized First Marine Division. Four months later he was given command of the division, which despite its intensive training had a large number of inexperienced personnel. The exigencies of war had caused marine headquarters to raid the division for cadres for newly organized formations as well as a regiment for the defense of Samoa. Vandegrift himself received orders in May to ship out to Wellington, New Zealand, with his staff and his two remaining regiments, where he was to continue training for at least six months he was told.

However, plans were drastically altered when intelligence sources revealed late in June that Japanese personnel had landed on the ninety-mile-long island of Guadalcanal in the southern Solomons and had begun construction of an airfield. Knowledge about Japanese troop strength and dispositions on the island was scant, and adequate topographic maps were not available. His superiors, nevertheless, gave Vandegrift little more than a month to prepare to land on Guadalcanal and nearby Tulagi. He was assigned a mixed lot of marines in various stages of training and organization: the bulk of his First Division, a regiment that was still at San Diego, and two independent battalions.

On Aug. 7, 1942, the landings were made. Tulagi was secured after a few days, while Vandegrift led two regiments and supporting troops in unopposed landings on Guadalcanal. On the next day the marines took control of the uncompleted airfield, which they soon finished and named Henderson Field. Once the Japanese had had time to reinforce their troops already on Guadalcanal, they bitterly contested the Americans' foothold. Vandegrift had only enough personnel to establish a defensive perimeter around Henderson Field, control of which was essential for American retention of Guadalcanal and Tulagi, and to send out patrols.

The inability of the U.S. Navy to control the seas around Guadalcanal during the first months of the campaign made the arrival of essential supplies and reinforcements uncertain. At times, American personnel on Guadalcanal, struggling against both the Japanese and the debilitating climate and swamps, jungles, and saw grass that covered large areas of the island, felt almost as forgotten as other Americans had on Bataan less than six months earlier. However, additional manpower, equipment, food, and ammunition got through just often enough for Vandegrift's men to repel determined Japanese assaults in the areas along the Matanikau and Tenaru Rivers and Edson's Ridge.

Improvement in the Americans' situation came in November, when more planes and aviation personnel and additional ground forces were made available. At last Vandegrift was able to start extending his lines. In December the First Marine Division was relieved of duty, and Vandegrift turned over command on the island to an army officer.

Historians have debated the wisdom of launching a large and complex operation like the seizure of Tulagi and Guadalcanal with such meager forces, but assessments of Vandegrift's generalship on Guadalcanal have remained favorable. His conquest of Guadalcanal

began a phase of operations in the South Pacific in which Allied forces began to advance. His tactics set important precedents for warfare in the region: seizing a beachhead, establishing a suitable defensive perimeter, and constructing or occupying an air base within the perimeter.

For several months in early 1943, Vandegrift remained with the First Division, based near Melbourne, Australia, as it refitted and trained for future operations. Due for a promotion to lieutenant general, Vandegrift was preparing to leave the Pacific for Washington, D.C., where he would become commandant of the marine corps. However, complications developed in the South Pacific that led headquarters to postpone the change in command of the marine corps and temporarily assign Vandegrift command of the First Marine Amphibious Corps (which included the Third Marine Division, an army division, and supporting troops) as it prepared for the invasion of Bougainville. Major General Charles Barrett was slated to replace Vandegrift in time to complete preparations and command the invasion. Vandegrift was actually en route home in October when Barrett's unexpected death caused him again to be given command of the First Marine Amphibious Corps. Once the beachhead on Bougainville was established and secured in early November, Vandegrift was relieved of his command so that he could finally return to Washington to become commandant, a position he held until his retirement at the end of 1947. In 1945, he became the first marine officer on active duty to hold four-star rank.

In the years after 1945, Vandegrift set in motion two developments that were to be important to the future of the marines: saving the Fleet Marine Force with its divisional organization and attached air wings and reassessing amphibious doctrine in light of nuclear developments. The consensus was that had the Japanese had nuclear weapons, an operation of the sort that seized Iwo Jima in 1945 would have failed. The answer seemed to lie in perfecting helicopters for assault operations, what would later be called "vertical envelopment." Vandegrift died at Bethesda Naval Hospital in Bethesda, Md.

[Vandegrift's papers are at the Marine Corps Historical Center, Washington Navy Yard, Washington, D.C. Biographical information can be found in General A. A. Vandegrift with Robert B. Asprey,

Once a Marine (1964); John Foster, *Guadalcanal General* (1966); and in the essay on Vandegrift in Fletcher Pratt, *Eleven Generals* (1949). Hans Schmidt, *Maverick Marine* (1987); and Allan R. Millett, *In Many a Strife* (1993), discuss fellow officers with whom Vandegrift served on several occasions. Hans Schmidt, *The United States Occupation of Haiti, 1915–1934* (1971), provides insight into Haiti's turbulent politics during the years Vandegrift served there. George McMillan, *The Old Breed* (1949); and Richard B. Frank, *Guadalcanal* (1990), should be consulted for Vandegrift's role in the Second World War, while Allan R. Millett, *Semper Fidelis* (1980), is the best overall account of the marine corps. An obituary appears in the *New York Times*, May 9, 1973.]

LLOYD J. GRAYBAR

VANDERBILT, AMY (July 22, 1908–Dec. 27, 1974), author, columnist, designer, and expert on etiquette, was born on Staten Island, N.Y., the daughter of Joseph Mortimer Vanderbilt, an insurance broker, and Mary Estelle Brooks. Vanderbilt was a direct descendant of Jan Aœrtsen van der Bilt, who settled on Long Island in 1650. Her cousin was railroad and shipping magnate Commodore Cornelius Vanderbilt. Her great-great-grandfather was a founder of the Bank of Manhattan, and her grandfather, Joseph L. Vanderbilt, invented the stitching pattern for baseballs.

Her journalism career began while she was still attending Curtis High School, when she became a society and feature writer for the Staten Island *Advance*. Upon graduation she went to Switzerland to study home economics at Lausanne's Institute Heubi. She completed her education at the Packer Collegiate Institute in Brooklyn and at New York University, where she studied journalism (1926–1928). A natural linguist, she was fluent in French and had a working knowledge of Spanish, Italian, German, Portuguese, and Dutch.

In 1929, she married Robert S. Brinkerhoff; the couple took up residence at "Daisyfields," her Westport, Conn., house. (Vanderbilt would also later own a townhouse in Manhattan.) After their wedding, Vanderbilt took a position as assistant advertising publicity director for the H. R. Mallinson Company, a silk manufacturing firm. A year later, she became a New York advertising agency account executive.

Vanderbilt joined the *American Spectator*, a literary magazine as business manager in 1933 and concurrently wrote a syndicated column for the International News Service. A year later she accepted an executive appointment as home service director for Tower Publications, where she remained until 1937. That year she became vice president of Publicity Associations, a New York City public relations firm whose clients included seventeen publishers. She served as the organization's president from 1940 to 1945. At the same time, she developed her taste for published rules of etiquette as a consultant on entertaining and etiquette to the Royal Crest Sterling Company of Newark, N.J., a commission she held from 1940 through 1964.

The Brinkerhoffs divorced in 1935 after a childless marriage, and Vanderbilt wed Morton G. Clark a few months afterward. She split with Clark in 1945, and received custody of their only child. Later that year she married New York photographer Hans Knopf; they had two sons. In 1954, she divorced Knopf. Her last marriage was to Curtis B. Kellar, a corporate attorney, in 1968.

In the late 1940's, when Doubleday commissioned her to write *Amy Vanderbilt's Complete Book of Etiquette*, she built a secluded office on the grounds of "Daisyfields." "I knew that it was going to be a four-year job," she explained. She exemplified her special interest in children by devoting an entire chapter of the *Complete Book of Etiquette* to the family and social education of children and another to adoption, teenage problems, and community responsibilities to youngsters. Her love of children went beyond her own family. A longtime sponsor of the Foster Parents' Plan, she "adopted" four children in countries ravaged by World War II.

When the *Complete Book of Etiquette*, a seven-hundred-page indexed volume, appeared in 1952, it gained immediate acceptance as the modern guide to social behavior and crowned its author as Emily Post's successor. Vanderbilt expressed her underlying thesis to a *New York Herald Tribune* book reviewer: "The basis of good manners is kindness." At the same time, she rebuked ostentatious socialites: "I have no use for people who *exhibit* manners." *Time* magazine reported that Miss Vanderbilt "has not only viewed etiquette as a cradle-to-grave proposition, but turned out advice (most of it highly sensible) on every conceivable aspect of life." Her topics expanded social decorum to include divorce proceedings, problem drinkers, and television appearances, an acknowledgement of the future pervasiveness of that medium. In its several editions the book has sold millions of copies.

Publication of the etiquette book led to her association with United Features Syndicate beginning in 1954. She wrote a syndicated column entitled "Amy Vanderbilt's Etiquette," for twenty years. She was a monthly contributor to *McCall's* in 1963 and to *Ladies' Home Journal* from 1965 to 1974. She sporadically contributed to other magazines and newspapers, such as the *New Yorker, Collier's, This Week, Better Homes and Gardens, American Home*, the *Christian Science Monitor*, the *Los Angeles Times*, and the New York *World-Telegram and Sun*, and served as a consultant to the *World Book Encyclopedia*, the *Book of Knowledge*, and the *World Almanac*.

Vanderbilt's other books include *Amy Vanderbilt's Everyday Etiquette* (1956, revised 1978) and *Amy Vanderbilt's Complete Cookbook* (1961). She also hosted her own network etiquette show, "It's in Good Taste" (1954–1960), and a radio program, "The Right Thing to Do" (1960–1962). In addition to her career in etiquette, in the 1960's she designed and promoted her own line of dresses. Vanderbilt died of injuries received in a fall from the second story of her hundred-year-old New York City brownstone; it is unclear whether her death was a suicide or an accident.

[Biographical information can be found in the *Christian Science Monitor*, Oct. 9, 1952; *Family Circle*, Mar. 1959; *Reader's Digest*, Sept. 1959; *Time*, Mar. 1, 1963, and Jan. 6, 1975; *New Republic*, Apr. 29, 1972. Obituaries are in the *New York Times*, Dec. 28, 1974, and Dec. 29, 1974; *Newsweek*, Jan. 6, 1975; and *Time*, Jan. 6, 1975.]

W. M. P. DUNNE

VANDERBILT, CORNELIUS, JR. ("CORNELIUS IV," "NEIL") (Apr. 30, 1898–July 7, 1974), journalist and publisher, was born in New York City, the son of Cornelius Vanderbilt, Sr. (also known as "Cornelius III" and "Neily"), a railroad magnate and yachtsman, and Grace Graham Wilson, a member of an affluent southern family who, as the hostess of extravagant parties and a benefactor of the Metropolitan Opera, became a queen of New York City and Newport, R.I., society. As a direct descendant of Cornelius Vanderbilt (the "Commodore"), a nineteenth-century tycoon and railroad baron, Cornelius IV was born into the highest echelon of society. His father had received medals and commendations for his bravery during World War I and had attained the rank of brigadier general in the Army Corps of Engineers; he was the first military man to appoint black officers to his staff and to allow blacks in the officers' mess. During frequent travels abroad the family hobnobbed with royalty, and, since they were related by marriage to the Marlboroughs and the Astors, they mingled with the upper crust of English aristocracy.

Cornelius, Jr., was reared and educated by hosts of governesses and private tutors in the United States, Europe, and aboard his father's oceangoing yacht. He attended private schools in England, Germany, Russia, and Switzerland, as well as schools in Florida, New Jersey, and New Hampshire. He learned French, German, and Italian, and took an interest in fencing, swimming, boxing, and sailboat races. He was an accomplished equestrian, shot quail, and learned social dances at a very early age. His strict father kept him on a very small allowance, and until the age of seventeen Cornelius, Jr., never left home without bodyguards for fear of kidnapping. His personal hero throughout his early years was Theodore Roosevelt, a close friend of the Vanderbilts.

When the United States entered World War I, he volunteered for the army despite his mother's protestations and was shipped out with "Pershing's Boys" to Europe, where he served primarily as a chauffeur. He saw action in France and upon returning to the United States in 1918, he went to the War College in Washington, D.C., graduating after one year with the rank of lieutenant. He subsequently served in the reserves (1920–1923), as a captain in the National Guard (1923–1927), and as a major in the reserves (1927–1942). During World War II he served in army intelligence but was never assigned overseas.

Although his father remained married to the same woman all his life, divorces and remarriages were frequent recurrences in the Vanderbilt family. No one, however, surpassed Cornelius, Jr. At the age of twenty-two, against his parents' wishes, he married Rachel Littleton on Apr. 29, 1920, and they divorced on Nov. 26, 1927. His subsequent marriages (shown with dates of marriage and divorce) were to: Mary Weir Logan (July 3, 1928–August 1931), Helen Varner Anderson (Jan. 4, 1935–Dec. 18, 1940), Feliza Loraine Fablos (Sept. 3, 1946–

Apr. 23, 1947), Patricia Murphy Wallace (Sept. 2, 1948–June 29, 1953), Ann Needham (Sept. 3, 1957–May 1960), and Mary Lou Gardner (Nov. 4, 1967, until his death). He had no children.

To the dismay of the entire family, and contrary to the advice of his father's close friend, J. P. Morgan, Cornelius, Jr., chose journalism as his profession. Between 1919 and 1922, he worked as a cub reporter at the *New York Herald*, following it with a stint at the *West Coast Analyst* and a job as a legislative reporter for the *New York Times* in both Albany, N.Y., and Washington, D.C. After a brief assignment to Seattle, the *Times* sent him back to Washington, D.C., to cover the White House.

He viewed his work in journalism as a "series of exciting sensations." From the beginning of his career he demonstrated a keen perception of the fragility and idiosyncrasies of his human subjects, a sense of drama, and a clear and lucid prose style. Because of his ease in the company of world leaders and other notables, he was given major interview assignments that he handled with elegance, humanity, charm, and humor. Young Cornelius summed up his choice of a profession in one sentence, which remained his lifelong motto: "Service in some form or other should be the keynote of every worthwhile thing in life, and newspaper work gives one a greater scope for serving the public at large, and molding public opinion, than any other present-day occupation."

He also had a very clear vision of his professional goals. At the age of twenty-four, he wrote, "Eventually, I hope by hard steady and diligent effort to become a publicist if that is within my realm of opportunity. Again, I have an ambition to control a newspaper syndicate, through which I would contribute to the best of the papers in the country, irrespective of size and circulation." Indeed, at that juncture in his life, this vision of his future career was well within his financial possibilities and the range of his talents. Then a fateful meeting in 1922 changed his life so completely that he never recovered from its consequences: in Vancouver, British Columbia, he interviewed Alfred C. W. Harmsworth, viscount of Northcliffe, the owner of the largest newspaper empire outside the United States, an empire that included the *Times* of London. Vanderbilt told the older man his own journalistic ambitions, and Lord Northcliffe—aware of the Vanderbilt fortune as well

as his interviewer's young age—advised him to start afresh on the West Coast, a region, he assured Vanderbilt, whose journalism market was not yet conquered, and added that, if he was successful, a verbal understanding could be arranged between them.

Vanderbilt did not ask for any written agreement. Having grown up in a clubby business atmosphere, where the richest men in the country transacted deals in their private quarters over a glass of brandy and a smoke, and without so much as a handshake, it did not occur to young Vanderbilt to distrust Lord Northcliffe. He embarked on an ambitious program, starting the *Illustrated Daily News* in Los Angeles and the *Illustrated Daily Herald* in San Francisco, and expanding to the southeast with his *Miami Tab* daily newspaper. The first two ventures proved to be great successes, outnumbering in circulation the Chandler family's *Los Angeles Times* and hurting William Randolph Hearst's papers in San Francisco. Hearst and Chandler rose to meet the challenge by pressuring San Francisco department stores (the chief source of newspaper revenue) to cancel advertisements with the Vanderbilt papers, and by sending thugs to beat up Vanderbilt's newspaper delivery men and set fire to their vans.

Chandler's outrageous behavior only helped increase the circulation of Vanderbilt's southern California newspaper, but his failing San Francisco newspaper could not stand up to Hearst. Nevertheless, fired by his dream of a newspaper empire anchored in the United States and England, Vanderbilt continued to chase bad money with good, using his own savings, taking loans from banks and family members, and even borrowing from his future inheritance.

In 1922 Lord Northcliffe suddenly died in England at the age of fifty-seven. Vanderbilt rushed to London to salvage his dream, but the new owners of Lord Northcliffe's empire, being more conservative, showed no interest in Vanderbilt's claims. A desperate attempt to involve European investors also failed. Upon his return to the West Coast he asked his two archrivals, Chandler and Hearst, to call a truce, but to no avail. Hearst, however, offered Vanderbilt a job on one of his New York newspapers, which he was finally obliged to accept. The debts that his West Coast ventures had incurred plagued Vanderbilt for years to come.

Although he lived mostly in New York City and Florida, he purchased a home in Reno,

Nev., and recorded in books and articles the western life-style and big ranches. His love for racehorses was equally recorded in his writings. His frequent excursions to Europe resulted in two travel books and many articles. Vanderbilt was an enthusiastic traveler, crossing the United States at least twice every year. The outcome was a bounty of sensitive stories about hopelessness in small towns and the migration of destitute populations during the Great Depression. The easy friendships he made along the highways and byways of America constitute one of the most unique records of that era in American history. To his family's horror, he became a Democrat and a staunch supporter of Franklin D. Roosevelt and the New Deal. He also supported the State of Israel, for which he went on lecture tours and produced a film on location. His criticism of the super-rich caused his name to be removed from the New York Social Register in 1937. But in later years he was overcome by nostalgia and started a campaign for the preservation of the great homes and costumes of America's past. In June 1960, he revived the Vanderbilt Cup at the Roosevelt Raceway in Westbury, N.Y. It had been initiated by his great-uncle in 1904. He died at his Miami Beach, Fla., home.

Always an advocate for one cause or another, Vanderbilt never lost his youthful idealism and his faith in the ability of the press and a few good men to serve the high goals of mankind. To his friends he was known as "the naïve sophisticate."

[Vanderbilt wrote twenty books, incorporating in many of them personal experiences and anecdotes. The autobiographical books are *Lines from the Front* (1918), *The Gas Attack* (1919), *Personal Experiences of a Cub Reporter* (1920), *Personal Experiences of a Legislative Correspondent* (1921), *Personal Experiences of a Washington Correspondent* (1922), *Farewell to Fifth Avenue* (1935), and *Queen of the Golden Age* (1956).

His autobiographical articles include "Cornelius Vanderbilt, Jr., Tells Why He Chooses To Work," *American Magazine*, Aug. 15, 1921; "It's Hard To Be a Rich Man's Son," *Saturday Evening Post*, Dec. 4, 1926; and "From Coast to Coast on High," *Saturday Evening Post*, Oct. 8, 1927. Profiles of Vanderbilt appear in *Collier's*, July 17, 1920; *Country Life*, July 1920; *Review of Reviews*, Apr. 1935; *Publisher's Weekly*, Apr. 13, 1935; and *Fortune*, Nov. 1939. An obituary appears in the *New York Times*, July 8, 1974.]

SHOSHANA KLEBANOFF

VAN DOREN, MARK ALBERT (June 13, 1894–Dec. 10, 1972), literary critic and poet, was born in Hope, Ill., the son of Charles Lucius Van Doren, M.D., and Dora Anne Butz. A descendant of seventeenth-century Dutch immigrants to New Jersey, he was the fourth of five sons and the brother of Carl Van Doren, a historian and Pulitzer prize-winning author. Like Carl, whom he idolized, he had a distinguished literary career and stood in the forefront of American letters for almost half a century. He wrote some sixty books of poetry, fiction, and criticism and edited or collaborated on at least two dozen more. For thirty-nine years he was a legendary teacher at Columbia University, whose undergraduates annually honor a faculty member for distinguished teaching with an award made in his name.

Van Doren grew up in comfortable middle-class circumstances in the Illinois prairie towns of Hope and Urbana. He was, he wrote, "an affectionate child in an affectionate family," living in a house of books, in a world of farm animals and walnut groves, of small town traditions and firm friendships, amid strong men and strong women—the elements he came to celebrate in his poetry, which is dominated by nostalgic, pastoral imagery. He frequently remarked that the major tension in his life (both artistic and personal) arose from his inability to choose between life in the city and life in the country. He had the best of both worlds, he noted, after his literary success in New York made it possible for him to spend part of each year in a town house on Bleecker Street in Greenwich Village and the remainder on a 150-acre farm in rural Cornwall, Conn.

A precocious youngster, Van Doren learned to read by the age of four and entered high school at age twelve. He was drawn early to the study of English, in large part, he said, because of his exposure to Latin and mathematics, which prepared him "to move among the mysteries of my own language." Latin especially taught him that grammar and syntax "are beautiful things so basic to the mind that if they are not known, nothing is known." His love of poetry, he told poet Archibald MacLeish, came "suddenly" while reading Wordsworth as a college student and discovering that poetry was "music." Dryden, Shakespeare, Emerson, and Lincoln, he said, were the primary literary influences on his poetry and prose. He entered the University of Illinois at sixteen and earned both a B.A. (1914) and an M.A. in English (1915). He interrupted his doctoral studies at Columbia in 1917 to serve two years as a training officer and records supervisor in the United States Army without going overseas. After World War I and before completing his dissertation, he and his close friend Joseph Wood Krutch were awarded Columbia fellowships that allowed them to travel together in Europe and England for a year.

In 1920, Van Doren earned his Ph.D. and was appointed an English instructor at Columbia. Uncertain whether he would devote his career to teaching or writing, he regularly announced his imminent retirement from the classroom, but he abandoned that practice by the end of the decade after deciding that he could do both. He quickly became one of the luminaries on the Columbia faculty, advancing to full professor in 1942 and teaching highly popular courses in both the college and the graduate school until his retirement in 1959. His classes on Shakespeare, in which undergraduates read all thirty-four plays over two semesters, were regularly oversubscribed. During the 1930's he gave lectures at the New School in New York and from 1937 to 1957 was a visiting lecturer at St. John's College in Annapolis, Md. He was a visiting professor at Harvard in 1963.

A shy, gentle man, he was, by all accounts, an extraordinary figure in the classroom. Students as various as Lionel Trilling, Thomas Merton, Clifton Fadiman, Jack Kerouac, Allen Ginsburg, Louis Simpson, and John Berryman—many of whom remained his lifelong friends—attested to his powers, especially his capacity to listen, the mesmerizing attention he paid to the texts under study, and his ability to draw from his students thoughts that heretofore had been inchoate. Most of them remembered his delight in doing what he was doing. "As the early winter twilight crept over the Columbia campus," Alfred Kazin wrote of one class, "Van Doren's craggy face looked as if he expected the sun to come out because he was teaching Virgil."

What really goes on in a classroom once the door is closed, Van Doren wrote, is "a kind of secret" shared by the participants, but his role as teacher was always clear. It was to hear his students out, to aid them singly and collectively in discovering what they knew, to be "personal and patient and alive." His model, he said, was

a master teacher he had encountered in high school in Urbana. He was Miletus Flaningam, the high school principal, who as a substitute for the regular English teacher made Van Doren for the first time understand and feel the power of *Macbeth* and understand, as well, the power of first-rate teaching. "In forty minutes he created a world—perhaps *the* world—and I was never to forget it," Van Doren later wrote of the experience.

In 1920, he began a long association with *The Nation* as a book reviewer, serving as literary editor from 1924 to 1928 and movie critic from 1935 to 1938. From 1940 to 1942 he was a panelist on the CBS radio program "Invitation to Learning." In 1943, at the request of the American Association of Colleges, he wrote *Liberal Education*, which celebrated the primary place of the humanities in educating men and women and looked at the post–World War II development of the nation's schools and colleges. All of this served to broaden his reputation as a critic and teacher, but it was only a modest part of his prolific literary and scholarly output during his academic career.

From *Spring Thunder and Other Poems* (1924) to *Good Morning: Last Poems* (1973) Van Doren published twenty-eight volumes of poetry, including two collected editions. His best-known titles are *A Winter Diary* (1935), *The Mayfield Deer* (1941), *The Country Year* (1946), and *Collected and New Poems, 1924–1963* (1963). His *Collected Poems* (1939) received the Pulitzer Prize in 1940. In later years, he turned his hand to the theater, publishing four verse plays: *The Last Days of Lincoln* (1959) and *Three Plays* (1966), which collects *Never, Never Ask His Name, A Little Night Music* and *The Weekend That Was.*

The early poems are perhaps his best. But even in his later work, Van Doren is recognized as a careful craftsman, and his poems as clear, lyrical and well shaped. As a poet he was often compared to Edwin Arlington Robinson and Robert Frost, though clearly his poems lack the dark undertones that are so much a part of the other men's work. Frost wrote him an admiring letter on the publication of *A Winter Diary*, saying, "I liked being where you were . . . I am delighted in the way you took your rhymes," and Van Doren was profoundly moved. He believed Frost to be the premier American poet in the twentieth century. "His poetry itself," he said, "is a kind of person, for the whole of it lives and speaks." Posthumous assessments of Van Doren's poetry tend to be dismissive because so many of his poems lie outside the experimentalism and the themes of contemporary writing, and because they center on a pastoral America that has long since been lost.

Van Doren's scholarly contribution outside the classroom came in his two dozen books of literary commentary and criticism. Beginning with *Henry David Thoreau* (1916), a reworking of his master's thesis, and *The Poetry of John Dryden* (1920), his Ph.D. dissertation, and extending through such books as *The Private Reader* (1942), *The Noble Voice: A Study of Ten Great Poems* (1946), and *Nathaniel Hawthorne* (1949), Van Doren took it as his job "to distinguish between the important and the unimportant; and after that, to seek the essential." He meant to approach his readers as he approached his students in the classroom: as experienced codiscoverers in the search for a larger understanding of what was read. He would be the guide, seeking in the play or poem or story, the writer's "report on the world as it is, without exaggeration or make-believe." His books rarely turned on literary theory and are largely devoid of scholarly apparatus. They are instead the extended conversations of one who saw himself as "a reader, a teacher, a critic, and a poet." His *Shakespeare* (1939) was for many years a standard introductory text to the plays, and *Introduction to Poetry* (1951) was widely used at both the college and the secondary level. It was, a *New York Times* reviewer noted, "a small model of discrimination." Some academic critics dismissed his writings as "not criticism, but merely commentary," but others were generally approving and his books often found a wide audience.

His fiction was not successful. There were two psychological novels, *The Transients* (1935) and *Windless Cabins* (1940), that reviewers found "unconvincing" or "vague," and *Tilda* (1943), a slender novel of wartime romance. His short fiction, notably *The Witch of Ramoth* (1950) and *The Short Stories* (1950), also fared poorly. His *Collected Stories* appeared in three volumes (1962–1968). He wrote several children's books, the most successful of which was *The Transparent Tree* (1940), which reviewers found "haunting" and "enchanting." It featured drawings by Carl's daughter, Margaret, who went on to a distinguished career as an illustrator and author of children's books.

As editor or coeditor, he published some two dozen titles including *Samuel Sewall's Diary* (1927), an edition of Parson Weems's life of George Washington (1927), *The Night of the Summer Solstice and Other Stories of the Russian War* (1943), *The Portable Emerson* (1946), and several anthologies of poetry and prose. In 1925, he and his brother Carl collaborated on *American and British Literature Since 1890*. His last book was *In the Beginning, Love: Dialogues on the Bible*, written with Maurice Samuel and published posthumously in 1973.

Van Doren married Dorothy Graffe on Sept. 1, 1922. She was an associate editor with *The Nation* for seventeen years and later a novelist and essayist. They had two sons, John and Charles. Charles achieved a national celebrity in 1957 by winning $120,000 on "Twenty-one," a nationally televised quiz show, but two years later was disgraced when he revealed to a congressional committee that the program had been rigged and that he had been given the answers to all the questions in advance. The ensuing scandal, involving numerous television executives and other prizewinners, was a sad and painful time for the Van Dorens, especially after Charles resigned his teaching position at Columbia, where he had shared an office with his father. The tawdry affair led to the exclusion of quiz shows from network and local broadcasting for more than a decade.

Mark Van Doren died following complications from circulatory surgery in Torrington, Conn., and is buried in Cornwall, Conn.

[Van Doren's papers are at Columbia University; his correspondence with Carl Van Doren is at Princeton University. Personal highlights are in *The Autobiography of Mark Van Doren* (1958) and Dorothy Van Doren, *The Professor and I* (1959). See also Carl Van Doren, *Three Worlds*, (1936); and Warren V. Bush, ed., *Dialogues of Archibald MacLeish and Mark Van Doren* (1964). An obituary appears in the *New York Times*, Dec. 12, 1972.]

ALLAN L. DAMON

VINCENT, JOHN CARTER (Aug. 19, 1900– Dec. 3, 1972), diplomat, was born in Seneca, Kans., the son of Francis Vincent, a shopkeeper, and Beulah Carter, a housewife. His parents were devout Baptists, and he had a strict religious upbringing. The family moved to Macon, Ga., when John Carter (his familiars addressed him in this southern manner) was six.

After attending local public schools he enrolled at Clemson University in South Carolina, but later transferred to Mercer University in Georgia, from which he graduated in 1923. Resolving to become a diplomat because he wanted to travel, he applied to the Foreign Service. Despite his lack of a blue-blooded lineage or an Ivy League education—one or both of which were usual prerequisites for a diplomatic career—and a borderline score on the required exam, Vincent was accepted into the Foreign Service.

Vincent was assigned to Changsha, China, where he witnessed military campaigns against the Chinese warlord armies in the chaotic, anarchistic China of that time. Sent to Peking for language training, he met Elizabeth Spencer, a writer traveling in China, courted her, and married her in 1931. They had two children.

His next assignment was the consulate at Mukden, in Japanese-occupied Manchuria. Twice in 1931 he was confronted by Japanese soldiers who threatened him despite his American diplomatic status. His experiences in Mukden made Vincent an early convert to the anti-Japan point of view, an attitude that put him at odds with Japan Hands in the U.S. State Department, including Joseph Grew and Eugene Dooman.

The viewpoint Vincent brought to his duties in China was that of a passionate supporter of New Deal liberalism. He found both Chiang Kai-shek, head of the Chinese government, and his colleagues authoritarian and corrupt, and called for American pressure to modify Chiang's behavior and nurture liberal factions in Chinese society. Vincent was not pro-Communist in his sympathies before 1941, but he was consistently anti-Chiang and critical of the corrupt Kuomintang party that controlled China.

Once the United States entered World War II in December 1941, Vincent's position became easier in some ways, but more difficult in others. The Japan Hands in the State Department lost influence, and American leaders eagerly sought suggestions from China Hands about how to widen China's contribution to the defeat of Japan. But Vincent and the other China Hands were caught in a political and military crossfire. To Chiang and his supporters, the China Hands seemed reluctant to press for unconditional American aid to China, so the Chinese government turned to conservative American politicians, businessmen, and journalists to plead their case in America; this

loosely affiliated group of Chiang Kai-shek supporters became known as "the China Lobby" and grew in influence in the United States as Chiang's fortunes declined in China. Meanwhile, American military strategists decided to fight Japan outside the Chinese theater of war. President Roosevelt's penchant for sending to China personal envoys who rarely cooperated with the American ambassador to China or career Foreign Service officers contributed to Vincent's (and other China Hands') feelings that they were being ignored.

Vincent's top priority was always the defeat of Japan. At first he advocated strong American pressure to force Chiang to cooperate with and coordinate military campaigns with the Communist forces that controlled much of divided China. By 1944, when this united-front strategy proved unlikely, Vincent joined other Foreign Service colleagues in urging the United States to send an observer mission to Communist headquarters in Yenan, and to supply the Communists with arms and ammunition even if Chiang's permission was not forthcoming.

This request involved Vincent in the most important chapter of his diplomatic career, his participation in the Henry Wallace mission to Russia and China during 1944. At the start, this last wartime mission by a political celebrity made many American diplomats apprehensive. Vice-President Wallace had acquired the reputation of being eccentric with an unpredictable personality; moreover, he was on very bad terms with Secretary of State Cordell Hull. Moderate and conservative forces in the Democratic party were getting ready for a big push to dump the ultraliberal Wallace from the office of vice president at the party convention. Vincent's mission was a difficult one: to keep Wallace from doing or saying anything that would further erode the credibility of American diplomats in China.

To Vincent's great credit, the Wallace mission was a great success, and produced many impartial and informative political reports that analyzed the weaknesses of the Chiang regime while not taking a pro-Communist stance. In personal negotiations with Chiang, Wallace secured approval to send a U.S. observer mission to Communist headquarters in Yenan in return for a recommendation to remove General Joseph Stillwell, the U.S. commander of the Chinese theater of war, from his command.

The Wallace mission reported that America

must continue to back Chiang in order to win the war. But it also expressed pessimism about Chiang's ability to remain in power in the long run. But it made no recommendations that would have directly undermined Chiang's rule. Vincent's own position was certainly much more balanced than those of John Paton Davies and John Stewart Service, who were much more outspoken in their pleas for wartime aid to Mao Tse-tung and his Communists.

After the Wallace mission Vincent found it difficult to work with Ambassador Patrick Hurley and General Albert Wedemeyer, Stillwell's replacement. In addition, from 1945 on, the first charges of subversion and espionage lodged against the China Hands proved distracting to Vincent. His subsequent transfers to Washington, D.C., Switzerland, and Morocco led to charges by members of the China Lobby that Vincent was being shielded from scrutiny.

Vincent's fate in the years from 1948 to 1953 was similar to that of many high-ranking diplomats who had served in China and who were held responsible by conservatives in the United States for "losing" China to the Communists. He was brought before various loyalty review boards, and he was publicly criticized for misdeeds by conservative anti-Communists. In Vincent's corner, Henry Wallace, Joseph Alsop, and Dean Acheson offered support. But Acheson may have made matters worse for Vincent by his haughty attitude and acerbic statements. Before his ordeal was over, Vincent endured five loyalty hearings, an unauthorized FBI investigation, and grueling appearances before U.S. Senate and House committees armed with documents leaked by the FBI. He was suspended by Secretary of State Dean Acheson in December 1952, then asked to resign by Acheson's successor, John Foster Dulles, on Feb. 28, 1953. He was not officially charged with disloyalty, but instead with poor judgment.

John Carter Vincent retired to Cambridge, Mass., and spent the last nineteen years of his life lecturing and writing informally in the Cambridge area. He remains a controversial figure. To liberals, he was one of many martyrs to shameless anti-Communist hysteria. To anti-Communists, he was one of the architects of the betrayal of Nationalist China. To his credit, Vincent was a fierce supporter of democratic principles, who believed that World War II gave America a chance to nudge totalitarian China toward democracy. His chief flaws were his ignorance of the changing America's political climate and the relationship between domestic politics and diplomacy. Like his conservative colleague George Kennan, Vincent believed in the primacy of diplomacy. As a result, both men were dismissed from the Foreign Service and lived to see it filled with mediocrities who avoided risky judgments and allowed the militarization of American foreign policy.

[Despite many requests, John Carter Vincent never wrote an autobiography. One biography exists: Gary May, *China Scapegoat* (1978). Vincent is also discussed in E. J. Kahn, *The China Hands* (1975), and Paul Gordon Lauren, ed., *The China Hand's Legacy* (1987). The story of Vincent's dismissal is told by Dean Acheson, *Present at the Creation* (1969). See also Anthony Kubek, *How the Far East Was Lost* (1963), for commentary on the allegations against Vincent. An obituary is in the *New York Times*, Dec. 5, 1972.]

MICHAEL J. POLLEY

W

WAKSMAN, SELMAN ABRAHAM (July 22, 1888–Aug. 16, 1973), microbiologist and Nobel laureate, was born in Novaya Priluka, a small Jewish village within the so-called Pale of Settlement, about twenty miles west of Vinnitsa in the "black soil" region of the Ukraine. His father, Jacob Waksman, was a weaver, itinerant merchant, and student of the Talmud; his mother, Fradia London, operated a wholesale grocery supply business with several relatives.

Waksman was schooled in a traditional Hebrew heder until age nine, and thereafter studied with private tutors. He attended gymnasiums (government Latin schools) in Zhitomir and Odessa, and passed his examinations in 1910.

The death of his mother in 1909, coupled with an invitation to join his cousins who had emigrated to America, prompted Waksman to book passage on a small ship sailing from Bremen. He landed in Philadelphia in November 1910, and then went to live with a cousin, Mendel Cornblatt, who owned a small farm near Metuchen, N.J. His cousin raised chickens and vegetables according to scientific methods, which he taught Waksman. While working on his cousin's farm, Waksman learned English and prepared to enter college.

In September 1911, he enrolled at nearby Rutgers College. His pivotal decision to pursue an agricultural rather than a medical course of study was guided by Professor Jacob G. Lipman, bacteriologist and dean of the College of Agriculture, himself a Russian immigrant. Waksman completed a B.S. in agricultural bacteriology in 1915 and an M.S. a year later. By then he had developed deep interests in soil microorganisms, especially actinomycetes (fungi or bacteria that live on dead organic matter)

and in the physiology and nutrition of plants; this latter interest was acquired while he worked as a student assistant to Dr. Byron Halsted, a plant nutritionist and geneticist who operated the college greenhouse.

In 1916, Waksman became a naturalized citizen. Also in that year he married Bertha Deborah Mitnik, a young woman who had emigrated from his Ukrainian village to New York two years earlier. The couple had one child.

From 1916 to 1918, Waksman pursued doctoral studies in biochemistry at the University of California at Berkeley. He worked under T. Brailsford Robertson, a physical chemist turned biochemist whose special interest was proteins and enzymes. Immersed in his own research, Robertson forced Waksman to choose his own research problem, so he continued his Rutgers work on fungi; after one year, though, his fellowship was not renewed. Moreover, Robertson announced that he was leaving Berkeley and told Waksman to finish his thesis by December so that the final stages of approval could be finished before Robertson left. After he lost his fellowship Waksman found part-time employment at the Cutter Laboratories, a firm producing antitoxins, serums, and vaccines. While working, he also managed to complete his thesis, and he passed his doctoral examination in December 1917.

Promoted to a full-time lab position at Cutter Laboratories, Waksman spent the next six months supervising products required for the war effort. In the meantime he sought an academic position for the next fall. The offer he accepted, lecturer in soil microbiology at Rutgers, provided the smallest salary but enabled him to return to Lipman's Soil Microbiology

Department. He spent the rest of his professional life at Rutgers, eventually becoming professor of soil microbiology (1929–1940), professor of microbiology and chairman of the Microbiology Department (1940–1958), and director of the Rutgers Institute of Microbiology (1949–1958).

He quickly resumed his earlier studies of a family of borderline soil microbe known as actinomycetes and began a new study of the oxidation of sulfur in compost. He soon isolated the organism involved in oxidation of sulfur and named it *Thiobacillus thiooxidans*. The actinomycete problem was puzzling, and he spent much of the next two decades with his graduate students studying the nature of humus. Much attention was given to the varying population of microorganisms in different kinds of soil, and to the influence of partial sterilization (by heat or chemicals) on population distribution. He paid particular attention to the roles actinomycetes and fungi play in soils and composts, and his research opened up a new understanding of a much-ignored area of microbiology.

British research concerning the antibiotic properties of the common green mold *Penicillium* prompted Waksman to launch a systematic search for other antibiotics among microbes. In the 1940's and early 1950's Waksman and his colleagues isolated nearly twenty compounds with antibiotic activity toward disease-producing microorganisms. Of these, several looked particularly promising; one, streptomycin, proved to be very low in toxicity, yet effective in controlling a number of diseases, including the previously uncontrollable tuberculosis organisms. Waksman's discovery of streptomycin brought him the 1952 Nobel Prize for medicine or physiology.

The success of streptomycin was marred for Waksman early in 1950 when he was served with a court summons initiated by a former student, Albert Schatz, who claimed a part of the royalties. Schatz had worked on the project for about three years before completing his doctorate and moving on to other employment. His name had been included, with others, on several publications and was also included on the patent application initiated by Merck and Co. in the name of Waksman and others.

Waksman considered the suit outrageous and wished to fight it, but on the advice of the university's legal staff agreed to an out-of-court settlement that gave Schatz a substantial sum.

Waksman then turned over half his patent income for distribution among approximately twenty students and associates who had worked with him on antibiotics research. Although he had promised half his royalties to fund the new Institute for Microbiology (now the Waksman Institute of Microbiology) at Rutgers, the remaining income from the patent was still adequate to construct the building and establish the institute. Waksman retired from Rutgers as professor emeritus in 1958, but he led an active life almost to the end.

[Waksman's Nobel Prize address dealing with streptomycin has been published several times; a readily accessible copy appears in *Science* 118 (1953). Books by Waksman include *Enzymes* (1926); with R. L. Starkey, *The Soil and the Microbe* (1931); with R. L. Starkey, *Humus: Origin, Chemical Composition and Importance in Nature*, 2d ed. (1938); with H. A. Lechevalier, *Sergi Nikolaevitch Winogradsky* (1953); *My Life with the Microbes* (1954); *Perspectives and Horizons in Microbiology*, a symposium edited by Waksman (1955); *The Conquest of Tuberculosis* (1964); and *Jacob G. Lipman* (1966). Hubert A. Lechevalier, "The Search for Antibiotics at Rutgers University," in John Panascandola, ed., *A History of Antibiotics: A Symposium* (1980), offers a good overview of Waksman's contributions with a list of the antibiotics uncovered in his laboratory. The final disposal of the Schatz case is summarized in *Chemical and Engineering News*, Jan. 15, 1951. Also see the biography of Waksman by Byron H. Waksman and Hubert A. Lechevalier in *Dictionary of Scientific Biography*, vol. 18 (1990). Obituaries appear in the *New York Times*, Aug. 17, 1973, and *Chemical and Engineering News*, Sept. 3, 1973.]

AARON J. IHDE

WARREN, EARL (Mar. 19, 1891–July 9, 1974), governor of California and chief justice of the United States, was born in Los Angeles, Calif., the son of Methias H. ("Matt") Warren, a railroad worker, and Christine Hernlund. His father was blacklisted by the Southern Pacific Railroad after joining in a strike, and the family moved to Bakersfield in 1894. There Matt Warren was able to get work in a Southern Pacific repair yard, and the younger Warren worked for the railroad during summers as a "call boy," notifying crew members when they were scheduled to go on duty. The experience left a vivid impression on Warren, who saw how big corporations could dominate the lives of their employees and how powerless minority members were when faced with discrimination. Warren also recalled in his *Memoirs* (1977) that he witnessed "crime and vice of all kinds countenanced by a corrupt government."

Warren graduated from Kern County High School and then attended college and law school at the University of California at Berkeley, earning a B.L. in 1912 and a J.D. in 1914. He worked for the law firm of Robinson and Robinson for a few years and was about to start his own law practice when World War I broke out. He served briefly in the army and then joined the Alameda County district attorney's office in 1920 for what he thought would be a short term during which he would gain some legal experience. Instead, he stayed eighteen years; in 1926 he was elected to the first of three terms as district attorney. On Oct. 14, 1925, Warren married Nina Palmquist Meyers, a widow with a young son. Warren adopted him, and the couple had five more children.

Shortly after taking office, irregularities were uncovered in the city of Oakland's paving contracts, and allegations were made that a deputy sheriff was taking bribes in connection with street-paving arrangements. This behavior offended Warren's ideals of honest government, and he determined to bring the law officer to trial, the first of several corruption cases associated with the paving scandal that he prosecuted.

Warren soon gained a national reputation as a tough, no-nonsense district attorney, and in 1931 a survey listed him as the best district attorney in the country. He ran his office in a nonpartisan manner and strongly supported the autonomy of law enforcement agencies. But he also believed that police and prosecutors had to act fairly, and much of what would later lie at the heart of the Warren Court's revolution in criminal justice can be traced back to his days as an active prosecuting attorney.

In 1938, Warren ran successfully for the California attorney generalship. He expanded the office, and just as he had done in Alameda County, he tried to secure greater cooperation among various law enforcement agencies. By 1942, Warren was one of the most popular officials in California, and he ran for and was elected governor on the Republican ticket.

Warren occupied the governor's mansion for three terms, and he did much to modernize the office and state government, but he is remembered primarily for his support of the relocation of Japanese Americans during World War II.

For many years Warren defended the action, maintaining that it seemed the right and necessary thing to do at the time. Not until the posthumous publication of his memoirs was it known that he acknowledged that the policy had been an error.

His success as governor propelled Warren onto the national political stage, and in 1948 he ran for vice-president on the Republican ticket headed by Thomas E. Dewey. Four years later, he swung the California delegation in support of Dwight Eisenhower, assuring the general of the nomination for president. Eisenhower reportedly promised Warren a seat on the Supreme Court. He did offer, and Warren had accepted, the post of solicitor general when Chief Justice Fred Vinson unexpectedly died in September 1953. Eisenhower and his attorney general, Herbert Brownell, believed that they had promised Warren only an appointment as associate justice, but Warren insisted upon and received the offer of the center chair.

Eisenhower named Warren chief justice during a recess on Oct. 2, 1953; he took his seat Jan. 11, 1954, and the Senate did not confirm him until Mar. 1, 1954. Although some people questioned Warren's lack of judicial experience, his years in the Alameda County district attorney's office and as attorney general gave him far more knowledge of the law in practice than most other members of the Court had.

But Warren's greatest asset, what made him in the eyes of many of his admirers "Super Chief," was his political skill. Over the years his ability to lead the Court, to forge majorities in support of major decisions, came to outweigh by far any deficiencies he had as a jurist. When Warren arrived at the Court, he recognized that his unfamiliarity with the internal procedures could be a problem. So he asked the senior associate justice, Hugo L. Black, to preside over conferences until he felt more familiar with the process. Within a relatively short time Warren was in fact as well as in name the Court's chief justice.

He took over a Court badly split between two warring factions. One wing, led by Felix Frankfurter and Robert H. Jackson, believed strongly in judicial self-restraint and constantly pointed to the judicial activism of conservative justices that had led to the constitutional crisis of 1937. For them, courts should defer to the policymaking prerogatives of the political branches. The other wing, led by Black and William O. Douglas, believed that while courts should defer in matters of economic policy, the judicial agenda had been changing from questions of property rights to those of individual liberties, and in this area courts should play a more activist role. Warren's personal philosophy, his belief that courts should seek to do justice, quickly led him to align himself with the liberals, although he did not have a solid majority behind him until after Frankfurter's retirement in 1962.

The very first issue confronting the Court put Warren's leadership skills to an extraordinary test. The National Association for the Advancement of Colored People had been waging a long and persistent battle against the "separate but equal" doctrine enunciated in *Plessy* v. *Ferguson* (1896) and finally had challenged the doctrine head-on in a series of five related cases, which had been argued before the bench in the spring of 1953. The justices had been unable to decide the issue and had asked both sides to reargue the case in the fall, with special attention to whether the Fourteenth Amendment's equal protection clause applied to segregation in public schooling.

While most of the justices did not personally believe in segregation, the conservative group had strong doubts as to whether the Court had the power to order its end under the Constitution. The liberals believed the Court had the authority and were pushing to go ahead. Warren, who held only a recess appointment, had to tread carefully until the Senate, dominated by southerners, confirmed his appointment.

Warren told his colleagues in conference shortly after oral argument that he believed segregation violated the Constitution and that only if one considered African Americans inferior to whites could the practice be sustained. But he did not push for closure. Instead, he talked with the justices and encouraged them to talk with each other as he sought a common ground on which all could stand. Finally he had eight votes, and the last holdout, Stanley Reed of Kentucky, the Court's strongest backer of segregation, agreed to vote with the others. Warren then drafted the Court's opinion in *Brown* v. *Board of Education* (1954) and kept circulating and revising it until he had an opinion endorsed by all the members of the Court.

The unanimity Warren forged proved essential to the ultimate success of the drive to desegregate public schools. Throughout his tenure on the Court, even with shifting personnel,

Warren managed to keep all decisions concerning racial segregation unanimous. And even though *Brown* mainly applied to schools, within a short time the Court enlarged the concept and struck down racial classification in many other areas of American life, a process ratified and consolidated in the Civil Rights Act of 1964 and the Voting Rights Act of 1965. The one possible misstep Warren made was in agreeing to Frankfurter's demand that the Court go slowly in implementing the *Brown* decision, when Warren incorporated Frankfurter's suggestion that the 1955 implementing decision (*Brown II*) include the phrase "all deliberate speed."

Had the Warren Court dealt only with racial segregation, it would have left a lasting imprint on American society. But *Brown* marked, as few other cases did, the shift in the Court's— and the nation's—priorities from questions of property rights to civil liberties. Where previously the judiciary had been seen as a barrier to legislative reform, under Warren the courts became an active partner in governing the nation. Warren never saw the courts as a passive branch of government.

Brown has been criticized for its alleged lack of rigorous constitutional analysis, and Warren never claimed to be a legal scholar on a par with Frankfurter or a great advocate of particular doctrines, as was Black. Instead, he believed that just as in the other branches of government, decency, common sense, and elemental justice had a role to play. In many ways he was a results-oriented judge, deciding how he thought an issue should be resolved and then rationalizing it in terms of doctrine; he never believed that doctrine alone, much less quibbles over doctrinal implications, should deprive people of the justice they sought in the courts. To him, segregation was simply wrong, and *Brown*, whatever its doctrinal defects, remains a landmark decision primarily because of Warren's majestic interpretation of the equal protection clause to mean that children should not be deprived of a decent education because of the color of their skin.

This sense of fairness animated other areas in which the Warren Court played an active role. In 1962, over the strong objections of Frankfurter, the Court agreed that questions regarding malapportionment in state legislatures were issues subject to judicial resolution. For years rural interests had deprived urban dwellers of equal representation in state legislatures, and cities were looking to the courts to redress this imbalance. Frankfurter argued that the Court had no business in this "political thicket" and warned that the Court would never be able to determine a straightforward formula to guide lower courts in the rash of lawsuits sure to follow.

But Douglas found such a formula, "one man, one vote," and in the key apportionment cases decided with *Reynolds* v. *Sims* (1964), Warren delivered a civics lesson to the nation. "To the extent that a citizen's right to vote is debased, he is that much less a citizen," Warren declared. "The weight of a citizen's vote cannot be made to depend on where he lives. This is the clear and strong command of our Constitution's Equal Protection Clause." Unlike the desegregation cases, in this instance, the Court ordered immediate action, and despite loud outcries from rural areas and their spokesmen, the states reapportioned their legislatures quickly and with minimal troubles. As several commentators noted, reapportionment was the Warren Court's great "success" story.

Frankfurter suffered a stroke and had to retire before the apportionment decisions were handed down. President Lyndon Johnson named Arthur Goldberg to replace him. His constituted the fifth vote that gave Warren the majority he needed. But the critical member of the liberal bloc that included Black and Douglas was William Brennan, who had been appointed by Eisenhower in 1956. Brennan proved to be the perfect complement to Warren, matching his chief's political acuity with the legal skills Warren lacked. A former student of Frankfurter's, he could parse constitutional doctrine with the best. Before long Warren began meeting with Brennan before the regular conferences to plan out their strategy. The arrival of Brennan on the Court allowed Warren to go forward, confident that he would not be exposed to legal sharpshooters.

If most Americans believed that the Warren Court's desegregation and apportionment decisions were fair and right, far more disagreement swirled around the "due process revolution" Warren led in the area of criminal justice. One might have expected Warren, a former prosecutor, to have little sympathy for the rights of the accused. In fact, he had always insisted that the police, with the power of the state in back of them, play fair. At the time Warren came on the Court, most police departments did not play

fair, and their abuses ranged from warrantless searches to, in some cases, confessions forced by physical or psychological torment.

Whether it was a question of providing a lawyer for indigent defendants, as in *Gideon* v. *Wainwright* (1963), or of preventing prosecutors from using evidence seized in illegal searches, as in *Mapp* v. *Ohio* (1961), Warren wanted the police to play fair. In many ways the case of *Miranda* v. *Arizona* (1966) summed up Warren's philosophy. People, even those accused of crimes, still enjoyed constitutionally protected rights, and the police had to respect those rights. Despite conservatives' charges, Warren did not believe in coddling criminals. As he made clear in cases like *Terry* v. *Ohio* (1968), in which he gave police officers great leeway to stop and frisk those they had reason to believe held weapons, Warren had no intention of handcuffing them so long as they abided by the rules.

The Warren Court's activism stretched into a number of areas, especially First Amendment rights, and few decisions, even *Brown* or the criminal justice cases, brought down such a hail of criticism as did the Court's decision outlawing mandatory school prayer in *Engel* v. *Vitale* (1962). But Warren and his colleagues believed strongly in the Bill of Rights, and in the thirteen terms he sat in the center chair, Warren did much to nationalize those rights by applying them to the states. Moreover, in one of the landmark cases decided by the Court, *Griswold* v. *Connecticut* (1963), the Warren Court announced a constitutionally protected right of privacy.

With the exception of the desegregation decisions, few cases in any area received unanimous support from the justices. The highly respected John Marshall Harlan took Frankfurter's place as the Court's conservative spokesman, often joined by Potter Stewart and Byron R. White. But with the appointment of Thurgood Marshall and Abe Fortas (the latter to replace Goldberg), Warren could count on six votes in most cases.

One incident in which Warren's famed political skills seemed absent was when he gave in to President Lyndon Johnson's persuasion and agreed to head the governmental commission that investigated the assassination of John F. Kennedy. Even some of Warren's admirers questioned his judgment in this matter. Warren did not want the assignment, recognizing that such extrajudicial tasks could be deleterious to the work of the Court and also threatened the notion of separation of powers. But Johnson appealed to Warren's patriotism, and the reluctant chief justice agreed.

It was not a happy experience for Warren. As a judge, he valued candor and justice, but as a politician he recognized the need for secrecy in some matters. As with *Brown*, he believed that the commission report should be unanimous, and so he compromised on a number of issues in order to get all the members to sign the final version. But many scholars and other critics have attacked the commission's findings ever since. While no one has suggested that Warren engaged in a blatant cover-up, they have claimed that key evidence is missing or distorted and that there are many inconsistencies in the report. Warren often regretted that he did not follow his initial instincts and refuse the assignment.

In June 1968, Warren informed the president that he wanted to retire, but he left the date open to allow Johnson time to find a successor. There is little question but that Warren recognized that because of the Vietnam War, the Democrats might well lose the 1968 election to Warren's old political enemy from California, Richard Nixon. The chief justice, as a White House memorandum noted, told the president that he wanted Johnson "to appoint as his successor someone who felt as [he] did." Warren could not have been happier when Johnson named Fortas to succeed him. But that joy soon turned sour, as revelations about Fortas's financial affairs eventually led to withdrawal of the nomination (Fortas resigned from the Court in 1969). Warren presided over the Court's October 1968 term and retired the following spring, after Nixon named Warren E. Burger to succeed him.

In his last term, however, Warren still had one more civics lesson to teach, and he delivered his valedictory in June 1969 in the case of *Powell* v. *McCormack*. He denied that the House of Representatives had the power to exclude Adam Clayton Powell from membership simply because a majority did not like the way he conducted his personal affairs. The *Powell* opinion, like that in the apportionment cases, reaffirmed Warren's belief in democracy. But also, as in the unanimous opinion he helped craft in *Cooper* v. *Aaron* (1958), in which the Court rebuffed Arkansas's challenge to its au-

thority to interpret the Constitution and to order school desegregation, *Powell* reasserted the Court's primacy as the nation's interpreter of what the Constitution means.

Scholars agree that as a judge, Warren does not rank with Louis Brandeis, Black, or Brennan in terms of jurisprudence. His opinions were not always clearly written, and his legal logic was often muddled. His strength lay in his clear vision that the Constitution embodied natural rights that could not be denied to the citizenry and that the Supreme Court had a special role in protecting those rights.

Conservatives have attacked this judicial activism as inappropriate and have called for courts to be deferential to the elected political branches. Yet even if one believes that Warren and the Court he led went too far in some areas, the fact remains that in most of the controversial decisions, the Court's ruling struck a responsive chord in the nation. Shortly after Warren's retirement, Professor Joseph Bishop of Yale summed up this feeling when he predicted that much of the Warren Court's accomplishments would not be overturned.

In his retirement, Warren maintained a fairly rigorous schedule of speeches and other activities, including work on his memoirs; he also opposed a plan to establish an intermediate court of appeals to reduce the Supreme Court's work load and jurisdiction. His health began to fail in early 1974, and he died in Washington, D.C.

[The Warren Papers are in the Library of Congress. *The Memoirs of Earl Warren* (1977) give information mostly about Warren's pre-Court career. See also Jack Harrison Pollack, *Earl Warren* (1979); G. Edward White, *Earl Warren* (1982); and Bernard Schwartz, *Super Chief* (1983). An obituary appears in the *New York Times*, July 10, 1974.]

MELVIN I. UROFSKY

WARREN, FULLER (Oct. 3, 1905–Sept. 23, 1973), politician and governor of Florida, was born in Blountstown, Fla., the son of Charles Ryan Warren, a farmer, and Grace Fuller, a teacher. Warren grew up in a poor household and worked at a number of odd jobs in his youth. He attended local schools and graduated from Blountstown High School in 1922. With financial aid from a family friend he enrolled at the University of Florida. In his senior year, at the age of twenty-one, he was elected to the

Florida House of Representatives in his native Calhoun County. After one term in office he enrolled at Cumberland University in Tennessee, receiving a law degree in 1928.

Warren moved to Jacksonville, Fla., in 1929 and joined a law firm, practicing criminal law. In that year he married the first of his three wives, Sallie Mae Stegall, from whom he was divorced in 1937. He was elected to the Jacksonville city council in 1931, 1933, and 1937. Two years later he was again elected to the Florida House, this time representing Duval County.

In 1940, although a virtual unknown, he ran for the Democratic gubernatorial nomination and finished third in a field of eleven. This campaign gained him state recognition, but his career was interrupted by America's entry into World War II. He joined the navy, serving as a gunnery officer on troop ships. Meanwhile, Warren had married Pat Pacetti in 1939; their marriage ended in 1942. He was discharged from the navy in 1945 and returned to his criminal law practice.

He entered his second race for the Florida governorship in 1948, conducting a vigorous campaign in which he won the crucial Democratic nomination (at the time the Republican party had no power in the South) and the subsequent general election. Warren was at his best running for public office. He was a charismatic speaker who enthusiastically portrayed himself as a "man of the people." He authored three books on political and public speaking: *Eruptions of Eloquence* (1932), *Speaking of Speaking: Articles, Addresses and Other Strident Stuff* (1944), and (with Allen Morris) *How to Win in Politics* (1949). In his first year as governor he married Barbara Manning, whom he had met on a trip to California. They divorced in 1954 after he left the governorship.

As governor he often had a difficult time working with the legislature and sometimes seemed unable to understand the issues. Moreover, he had a penchant for making bad appointments and developing questionable friendships. Despite his flaws, he was a tireless promoter of Florida across the rest of the country, and he did manage to address a number of important state concerns. He ended the state's custom of permitting cattle to graze on open rangeland, which had caused an increasing number of highway accidents. He tightened regulation of the citrus industry, moved against

illegal off-track betting, and attempted to reform Florida's regressive tax system.

In the 1948 primary election Warren had been financially supported by three personal friends: Louis Wolfson, a Jacksonville businessman; C. V. Griffin, a citrus grower; and William H. Johnston, a Chicago and Miami racetrack owner. Each of the three significantly influenced the administration's patronage decisions, but it was Johnston, reputed to have ties with organized crime, who helped drag Warren's governorship into its worst crisis.

In 1950 the U.S. Senate created the Crime Investigating Committee, headed by Senator Estes Kefauver of Tennessee. As a result of its national investigation it learned of the Warren-Johnston connection in Florida and of the contributions made to the governor's campaign. Called to testify before the committee's hearings in Miami, Warren refused. He added to his problems by being reluctant to suspend local sheriffs who were implicated in illegal gambling operations. As a result, the committee's May 1951 report claimed that Warren had allowed the power of his office to be used by a crime syndicate "in its successful effort to muscle into Miami Beach gambling." The report damaged the governor's reputation in Florida and the rest of the country and led to a failed attempt in the Florida legislature to impeach him.

In the summer of 1951 the U.S. Senate Crime Investigating Committee, now headed by Senator Herbert O'Conor of Maryland, issued a subpoena to force Warren to testify in Washington, D.C. Warren denied all wrongdoing and refused to honor the subpoena, claiming that Congress had no constitutional right to subpoena a state governor. In the end, the committee, unsure of its constitutional position, let the matter drop.

Warren often acted in a flamboyant manner during his time of troubles. He challenged each of the two crime committee chairmen to a public debate. He also threatened to campaign against Chairman O'Conor in the next Maryland election and caused a minor furor when he surreptitiously included an attack on Senator Kefauver in the *Congressional Record*. In May 1951 some of Warren's supporters in the Florida legislature, presumably with his backing, attempted unsuccessfully to pass bills that would have allowed investigations of Florida newspapers critical of the governor.

At the height of his political troubles in 1951

Warren announced he would permanently retire from public life once his term ended. However, after three years of practicing law, he broke that pledge and ran again for governor in the 1956 Democratic primary. He finished fourth out of six candidates. Significantly, this was the first Florida gubernatorial election since the Supreme Court's *Brown* v. *Board of Education* decision that ended racial segregation in public schools. Warren's opinions on race relations had fluctuated throughout his career. In 1949 he admitted having been a nominal member of the Ku Klux Klan before World War II, but as governor he denounced Klansmen as "hooded hoodlums" and "covered cowards." He passed legislation in 1951 that prohibited the wearing of masks in public, but he declined to outlaw the Klan, saying that it was not constitutionally possible to do so. After a series of violent racial incidents in 1951 he offered sympathy but no viable solutions. The most famous of these cases was the December bombing deaths of Harry T. Moore, a state coordinator of the NAACP, and his wife in Mims, Fla. Warren denounced the act, sent a special investigator to the scene, and offered a reward of $5,000 for conviction of the perpetrators, but nothing came of these gestures. In the 1956 gubernatorial race Warren supported segregation, trying to paint the eventual winner, LeRoy Collins, as being too moderate on race.

His 1956 defeat ended Warren's political career. He resumed the practice of law in Miami, where he died of a heart attack.

[The Fuller Warren Papers are in the Robert Manning Strozier Library at Florida State University. There is no biography of Warren, but David R. Colburn and Richard K. Scher have studied his political career in "Florida Gubernatorial Politics: The Fuller Warren Years," *Florida Historical Quarterly*, Apr. 1975, and *Florida's Gubernatorial Politics in the Twentieth Century* (1980). Also useful is Charlton Tebeau, *A History of Florida* (1971). A sympathetic interpretation is Gloria Jahoda, *Florida: A Bicentennial History* (1976). For the 1956 primary election, see Tom R. Wagy, *Governor LeRoy Collins of Florida* (1985). An obituary appears in the *New York Times*, Sept. 24, 1973.]

ERIC JARVIS

WASHINGTON, KENNETH STANLEY ("THE GENERAL") (Aug. 8, 1918–June 24, 1971), athlete, was born in Los Angeles, Calif., the son of Edgar Washington, a standout base-

ball player in the Negro League. He attended grade schools and graduated from Lincoln High School in Los Angeles, where he was acclaimed by many as the greatest high school football player in southern California history.

In 1936, Washington enrolled in the University of California at Los Angeles (UCLA), at the time one of the few universities to recruit African-American athletes. He starred in baseball and football, as well as in boxing and track. Although his performance on the baseball diamond surpassed that of his UCLA teammate Jackie Robinson—Washington batted .454 in 1937—it was on the gridiron that he excelled. Sportswriters stereotyped Washington as "The Kingfish," a character on the "Amos 'n' Andy" radio show, and the backfield combination of Washington and Robinson as the "Gold Dust twins," a reference to the two black children pictured on boxes of Gold Dust soap flakes. In three years, Washington brought UCLA's previously unheralded football program into the national spotlight and its athletic fund out of the red—while waiting on tables at nearby movie studios to earn his living expenses. He called signals and ran with exceptional power and deception as the tailback in UCLA's single-wing offense. His passes as quarterback were often spectacular; six times he completed passes of more than sixty yards in the air. In his senior year, Washington played both offense and defense, 580 of a possible 600 minutes, and carried UCLA to its first undefeated season. That year he led the nation in total offense with 1,370 yards and was the first UCLA Bruin chosen for an All-American Team. As he left the last game of his collegiate career, more than one hundred thousand spectators in the Los Angeles Coliseum rose to applaud him. "It was my greatest thrill," he recalled.

Washington said that after the 1940 All-Star game, "George Halas kept me around for a month trying to figure out how to get me into the league. I left before he suggested that I go to Poland first." National Football League (NFL) owners had blocked Halas's plan to sign Washington for the Chicago Bears. After earning his B.A. in arts and letters in 1941, Washington worked as a Los Angeles policeman. From 1941 to 1945, his only opportunity to play football was on semiprofessional pickup teams and in the Pacific Coast League. During these years, he was "beaten up" for as little as $50 per game. Fans came early to witness Washington's long warm-up throws. "They say I passed one hundred yards. But to tell the truth," he confided, "the distance was really ninety-three."

On Mar. 21, 1946, at age twenty-eight, Washington signed with the Los Angeles Rams, the first African American to be signed by any modern, major-league professional sports team. (Jackie Robinson did not join the Brooklyn Dodgers baseball team until 1947.) The Rams' press release described Washington as "one of the greatest all-around halfbacks in the history of American football, the first player of his race to be signed by a National Football League club since Joe Lillard played for the Chicago Cardinals more than a dozen years ago." It disingenuously continued, "The National Football League has never had a rule against the use of Negro players and no precedent is being set in the signing of Washington, though for one reason or another members of that race have not played in the league since about 1933." Newly transferred from Cleveland, the Rams had been negotiating to play in the publicly owned Los Angeles Coliseum. "The Coliseum people warned the Rams that if they practiced discrimination, they couldn't use the stadium. When the NFL people began thinking about all those seats and the money they could make filling 'em, they decided my kind wasn't so bad after all," Washington explained.

Washington's NFL career lasted only three seasons. The years of brutal semiprofessional football had damaged his already fragile knees, but after a slow first year, he hit stride in 1947. Running out of the "T" formation, he led the NFL with 7.4 yards per carry. His ninety-two-yard touchdown run against the Chicago Cardinals was the longest of the NFL season. Despite his success, when the Rams visited Washington, D.C., Washington could not stay in the team hotel and was barred by the guard at the Griffith Stadium players' entrance. His revenge that Sunday was three touchdowns against the Redskins.

Throughout his career, Washington was targeted by racist opponents. After a particularly vicious battering on the field, Washington told a Ram teammate, "It's hell to be a Negro, Jim." "I'll never forget the hurt in his eyes," recalled Jim Hardy. "But his statement wasn't one of self-pity by any means. It was simply a social comment, and he was alone, and there wasn't any way to comfort him." In his last two seasons with the Rams, Washington gained 859 yards,

averaging 6.1 yards per carry. Jackie Robinson praised him as the "greatest football player I have ever seen." Ram quarterback Bob Waterfield, a member of the Football Hall of Fame, remembered Washington as "a great gentleman. If he had come into the National Football League directly from UCLA, he would have been, in my opinion, the best the NFL has ever seen." After the last game of the 1948 season, which took place on a date designated "Kenny Washington Day," he retired from football. At age thirty, his knees were beyond rehabilitation.

In 1950, Washington tried out with the New York Giants baseball team, but his knees again did not cooperate and he was cut before the season started. In later years he was a scout for the Los Angeles Dodgers and represented a Scotch whiskey distribution firm. Washington died of polyarteritis at the University Medical Center in Los Angeles, within sight of the UCLA football practice field.

[A collection of newspaper clippings is in the National Football Hall of Fame in Canton, Ohio. Obituaries are in the *Los Angeles Herald-Examiner*, June 25, 1971, and the *Los Angeles Times*, June 26, 1971.]

ARNOLD MARKOE

WATKINS, ARTHUR VIVIAN (Dec. 18, 1886–Sept. 7, 1973) United States senator, was born in Midway, Utah. His parents, Arthur Watkins and Emily A. Gerber, were children of European-born Mormon pioneers who had settled in Utah. Watkins's father was a rancher and carpenter. One of six children, Watkins spent most of his childhood logging, fishing, hunting, and engaging in the life of a young Utah homesteader.

Watkins attended local public schools and in 1904 entered Brigham Young University, where he majored in political science. After graduating from BYU in 1906, he went to New York City, where he served as a missionary for the Church of Jesus Christ of the Latter-Day Saints until 1909.

In 1909, after being released from his missionary service, Watkins elected to stay in New York and take graduate-level classes at New York University and Columbia University, from which latter school he received an LL.B. degree in 1912. He then returned to Utah, where he was admitted to the bar later that year. After setting up in private practice, in 1914 Watkins became editor of the Vernal, Utah, *Express*.

Shortly thereafter, he became assistant county attorney for Salt Lake County, serving in this post until 1915. The busy Watkins also managed commercial orchards and a turkey farm in Utah from 1919 to 1932.

Watkins's political career began in 1920, when he was elected to the post of judge for Utah's Fourth Judicial District; he served at this post until 1933. In 1936 Watkins ran for U.S. Congress, won the Republican nomination, but lost in the final election to Democrat J. Will Robinson by a slim margin. Discouraged by his defeat, Watkins did not run for political office again until a decade had passed. In 1944 Watkins served as a member of the platform committee of the Republican National Convention. In 1946 he ran for the U.S. Senate, defeating Abe Murdock, the incumbent Democrat and New Dealer. In January 1947 Watkins took his seat for the second session of the Seventy-ninth Congress and began his service that would last until he was defeated in the 1958 election by Democrat Frank E. Moss.

The silver-haired Watkins demonstrated his support for the Republican party platform and its leaders, as shown by his record in the Senate. Watkins was assigned to the Public Lands and Public Works committees, and also to the Joint Committee of the Economic Report at the first session of the Eightieth Congress. Additionally he chaired the Indian Affairs subcommittee, and sat on the Irrigation and Reclamation and the Public Roads subcommittees.

From early in his senatorial career controversy surrounded Watkins. He openly opposed and criticized President Truman's appointment of former Utah senator Abe Murdock to the National Labor Relations Board. Watkins argued that Murdock's prolabor stance would inhibit the proper administration of the Taft-Hartley law. Despite Watkins's oratory, Murdock was confirmed by a majority vote of the Senate. Senator Watkins also voiced reservations about the North Atlantic Treaty Organization (NATO), asserting that such a treaty would deprive Congress of the right to decide on a declaration of war in the event of an attack on a treaty ally. Despite otherwise unanimous endorsement for the NATO alliance by the Foreign Relations Committee, Watkins asked for publication of the bill and a full senatorial debate. Watkins was overruled, and the NATO bill passed in two weeks.

Maintaining what might be described as an isolationist stance, Watkins joined with fellow Republicans Robert A. Taft of Ohio and Kenneth S. Wherry of Nebraska to express three strong reservations about the NATO Treaty. They asked that the United States deny any pledge to give military supplies to other nations; that it renounce any obligation to use U.S. armed forces without the consent of Congress; and that it assume no obligation to declare war if another NATO country was attacked. Watkins joined with twelve other senators to vote against the NATO Treaty.

In 1950 Watkins questioned President Truman's decision to send U.S. troops to Korea without first asking for congressional approval. Watkins also opposed the continuation of bipartisan foreign policy tactics in the United States. He joined fellow Republicans to vote for congressional control of decisions regarding the deployment of U.S. forces in Europe, a measure that would have given Congress binding control over troop deployment abroad, but this measure was defeated.

In 1952 Watkins defeated Democrat Walter U. Granger in the Utah senatorial election. Unaware of what the future held in store for him, Senator Joseph McCarthy offered to campaign for Watkins. Watkins refused McCarthy's offer for campaign support, choosing to separate himself from the hysteria and controversy that surrounded McCarthy. Watkins rose to prominence when, despite opposition from his fellow Republicans, he chaired the Senate committee that recommended the censure of McCarthy for his misconduct in investigating Communists in government.

Perhaps Watkins's outstanding legislative legacy is his cosponsorship of the Upper Colorado River Storage Project in which multipurpose dams were built at Flaming Gorge and Glen Canyon. Senator Wallace F. Bennett, a Utah senator who served with Watkins for eight years, said that "Utah will always benefit from his [Watkins's] leadership in the development of the Upper Colorado River Storage Project. This was probably his greatest achievement." Following his Senate career, Watkins returned to Salt Lake City and specialized in water law until his death.

Watkins married Audrea Rich on June 18, 1913; the couple had six children. A devoted family man and a devout member of his church, Watkins held many church positions in addition to his professional jobs and public offices.

[Brigham Young University in Provo, Utah, holds the private papers of Arthur Watkins. Watkins wrote one book: *Enough Rope: The Inside Story of the Censure of Senator Joe McCarthy* (1969). An obituary is in the *New York Times*, Sept. 2, 1973.]

F. ROSS PETERSON

WATSON, ARTHUR KITTRIDGE (Apr. 23, 1919–July 26, 1974), business executive and diplomat, was born in Summit, N.J., one of four children of Thomas J. Watson, Sr., and Jeanette Kittredge. Watson, Sr., was a business genius who transformed the small Computing-Tabulating-Recording Co. into the corporate giant International Business Machines (IBM). The lives, fortunes, and misfortunes of Arthur Watson and his older brother, Thomas J. Watson, Jr., were decisively shaped by their father's creation of a business empire and their roles as heirs apparent to that empire.

Arthur Watson, known as "Dick," was educated at the Hotchkiss School and at Yale University, from which he graduated in 1942 with a B.A. in international affairs. He then enlisted in the army, where he served in the ordnance corps and ultimately attained the rank of major. Sent to the Pacific theater, Watson wound up at an ordnance depot in Manila. He so enjoyed his experience in the Far East that at war's end he asked his father for permission to remain in the Philippines as head of IBM's operations there. But Watson, Sr., had other plans for his youngest son: he intended Dick to become a leading figure in IBM's foreign businesses. Ordered home, Dick Watson returned to Yale, where he studied Spanish, French, German, and Russian.

Upon completing his studies, Watson enrolled in the IBM trainee program, emerging from it as a salesman. He compiled a good record as a salesman, but not as good as the sales record established by his older brother in the years before the war. Indeed, when not overshadowed by his powerful father, Dick Watson always seemed to be in his older brother's shadow —it was Tom, Jr., not Dick, who eventually replaced his father as chairman and CEO of IBM.

On July 10, 1948, Dick Watson married Nancy C. Hemingway; they had six children. Instead of embarking on a honeymoon by themselves, the newlyweds accompanied Watson, Sr., on a business trip to Europe, so that Dick could serve as his father's interpreter. Even after

he had executive responsibilities of his own, Dick was pressed into such service.

In 1949, the elder Watson divided IBM into two divisions: the parent company, IBM, would focus on serving the domestic American market, while IBM World Trade would serve the rest of the globe. Dick Watson, whose education and career to this point seemed to have been planned by his father for this eventuality, was immediately elected a director and vice-president of IBM World Trade. In 1954, Dick Watson was elevated to the presidency of IBM World Trade, and in 1963 he stepped up to the chairmanship of IBM World Trade.

In 1949, it looked as if Dick Watson was on the fast track and his older brother was on the slow track. In his memoir *Father Son & Co.*, Thomas Watson, Jr., confessed that he was very unhappy with his father's decision to promote his younger brother: "I'd been at IBM three years before the war and almost three years since—they weren't all happy years but I wanted credit for them—and here was Dick, who'd been in the company eight months, being handed the world on a silver platter." But Dick Watson was destined to spend his productive years within the smaller kingdom of IBM World Trade, while his older brother eventually inherited the entire IBM empire.

The IBM World Trade division Dick Watson became responsible for had nine factories producing equipment, twice as many factories that turned out the ubiquitous IBM cards, and offices or representatives in eighty countries. But IBM World Trade's revenues in 1955 were barely $133 million at a time when domestic IBM's revenues were $564 million.

Under Dick Watson's leadership IBM World Trade expanded rapidly in Europe and Asia, and to a lesser extent in Latin America and the Middle East. In 1965, its revenues topped $1 billion for the first time, with earnings of $144 million. But that year IBM's domestic revenues were $2.5 billion, with earnings of $333 million.

By then IBM World Trade was a holding company, whose major responsibility was harmonizing the efforts of large units like IBM Deutschland and IBM France as well as smaller units elsewhere in Europe and throughout the world. Each national unit was free to adopt its own approaches, especially in the areas of marketing and services, but the major subsidiaries shared research and special expertise, usually with headquarters acting as an intermediary.

Relations with the American parent were mixed. The parent company welcomed the World Trade division's contributions to earnings. By 1967, when on revenues of $1.6 billion it had earnings of $209 million, twice that of only four years earlier, a prominent IBM World Trade executive remarked, "Our business is to convert foreign currencies into dollars." With World Trade's growing strength came a greater degree of independence that some in the domestic division resented. For example, the larger IBM World Trade companies developed machines and programs for their special markets. Design work on what was to become the IBM 3000 computer series was initiated at IBM Deutschland in the early 1960's, and components for this computer were produced at factories in several other European countries. The 3000 machines were simple, nonelectronic computers that could be purchased for less than $18,000 or leased for as little as $350 a month. They proved to be a huge success in Europe, and versions were shipped from there throughout the world. Dick Watson was elated, and suggested that the 3000's be shipped to the United States as well.

Matters of pride at the home company militated against such a move, and Dick Watson backed down. But Tom Watson, Jr., recognized IBM World Trade's growing abilities, and intended to use them in the creation of the company's most ambitious program to date, the creation of the third generation of computers. As its eventual name, the 360, indicates, this new series was meant to cover the spectrum of computers from the small to the very large. It was, as *Fortune* writer Tom Wise put it, "IBM's $5,000,000,000 gamble." It was too large a project for domestic IBM to handle on its own, so IBM World Trade was brought into the picture.

Vincent Learson, an IBM board member since 1961 and the group executive in charge of data processing, was named to head the project. It was no secret that Learson had ambitions to succeed Tom Watson, Jr. But given the successful record at IBM World Trade and his family's historical role at IBM, Dick Watson also had hope of succeeding his brother.

Learson turned the technical side of the project over to designers Gene Amdahl and Gerrit Blaauw, who clashed over technical points, with Amdahl the victor. Learson gave himself major responsibilities in marketing, financing, and placements. Dick Watson and IBM World Trade were left with various manufacturing assignments. The first machines, the 360/40's, were installed in April 1965, by which time there was a record backlog of orders on the books, assuring financial success—if the promised machines could be delivered. Before the end of the year the 30's, 50's, and 65's also made their appearance, to very good reviews.

All of this created production problems. IBM World Trade was badly strained by production demands. Schedules had to be redrawn, and some customers had to be asked to accept delays. As a result, Learson's star rose while Dick Watson's went into eclipse. There seemed little doubt now that Learson was next in line for the succession, and that Dick would never rise above his leadership of IBM World Trade. And even there he was having problems. Already there was talk that he should resign for the sake of the company. There were many aggressive young executives who felt he was blocking their way to promotion. Some blamed him for production foul-ups, and believed that he was being retained only because he was the CEO's younger brother.

Dick took to brooding. Although he was always in control while at work, he began to drink heavily. He and his brother barely spoke with one another. Later on, Tom realized what had happened: "I thought I was giving Dick an opportunity in an area where he would be an outstanding success. Instead I had handed him a stacked deck. He couldn't hold his own against the demands put on him by Learson." In early 1966, the board of directors elected Learson president of IBM. Dick Watson became vice-chairman, but by then he had lost interest in the business. Tom wrote, "His confidence seemed shaken. I felt nothing but shame and frustration at the way I'd treated him."

In this period Watson served on several government commissions, most of which dealt with trade. He served as president of the International Chamber of Commerce (1967–1968), and was cofounder with David Rockefeller in 1967 of the Emergency Committee for American Trade, which opposed protectionism.

Like his brother, and unlike his father, for most of his life Dick Watson was a Democrat. In 1968, he switched to the Republican party, attended the National Republican Convention held in Miami, Fla., and made a large contribution to the Nixon campaign. After the election President Nixon sent him and New York governor Nelson Rockefeller on a fact-finding tour of Latin America. In 1970, Watson resigned from IBM to accept Nixon's offer to become the American ambassador to France. He served in this post for two years, during which time he also was involved with the preliminary steps toward the eventual American recognition of China. In the process Watson became friendly with Huang Chen, China's ambassador to France, who subsequently became ambassador to the United States. This friendship was an important bridge between the two countries in the early years following recognition.

During this period there were persistent rumors that Dick Watson was an alcoholic and subject to bouts of depression. In 1972, Jack Anderson reported in his syndicated column that Watson had been inebriated while on a passenger plane. Watson denied this allegation but soon thereafter resigned his ambassadorship. He returned to IBM as a director and a member of the executive committee, but he had no real power or authority. In effect, Dick Watson had retired.

For several years he had suffered from various physical ailments. In 1973, he had a heart attack, but appeared to recover. Then, in mid-July 1974, he suffered a serious fall on the stairway in his New Canaan, Conn., house. Watson fell into a coma from which he never recovered. He died in Norwalk, Conn.

Dick Watson stood six feet, two inches tall and was noted for his patrician good looks and his excellent taste in clothes. Although considered reserved by casual acquaintances, he was relaxed and fun-loving with his intimates. He enjoyed telling funny stories and slightly risqué jokes. He had a passion for sailing and owned his own sloop. He and his wife collected Royal Copenhagen figurines and fine art. He owned a Monet, a Corot, a Gauguin, a Childe Hassam, an Andrew Wyeth, and many other paintings.

[Many books dealing with IBM have appeared since the early 1980's, and all contain material on the life and career of Dick Watson. Among the better ones by insiders are Jacques Maisonrouge, *Inside IBM: A Personal Story* (1985); and Thomas J. Watson, Jr., and Peter Petre, *Father Son and Co.: My Life at IBM and Beyond* (1990). Also see William Rodgers, *THINK: A Biography of the Watsons and IBM* (1969); Rex Malik, *And Tomorrow . . . The World?* (1975); and Robert Sobel, *IBM: Colossus in*

Transition (1981). An obituary is in the *New York Times*, July 27, 1974.]

ROBERT SOBEL

WATTS, ALAN WILSON (Jan. 6, 1915–Nov. 16, 1973), Zen Buddhist philosopher, was born in Chislehurst, England, the son of Laurence Wilson Watts, a haberdasher, and Emily Mary Buchan. Raised in the county of Kent, he became interested in the Far East at age twelve and developed a lifelong fascination with Asian art, literature, religion, and philosophy.

Watts graduated from the venerable King's School in Canterbury in 1932 but failed to win an expected scholarship to Oxford. Instead of going on to higher education, he worked in his father's London office raising funds for hospitals while continuing his course of self-education guided by Oriental scholars Christmas Humphreys and Daisetz Teitaro Suzuki. He soon joined the World Congress of Faiths, serving on its executive board from 1937 to 1939. At age twenty Watts wrote *The Spirit of Zen* (1936), which explained the form of Mahayana Buddhism known as Zen to the Western public. This remarkable achievement was followed by *The Legacy of Asia and Western Man* (1937). In these years Watts also acted as editor of *The Middle Way* in London (1934–1938) and co-editor of the *Wisdom of the East* book series (1937–1941).

On Apr. 3, 1938, Watts married Eleanor Everett, a socially prominent Chicago heiress. They moved to New York City in 1938. The couple had two children. Watts continued to study Asian art and Zen Buddhism. In these years he wrote *The Meaning of Happiness* (1940) and several magazine articles. In 1943, he became a naturalized citizen of the United States. Strongly influenced by his wife and her mother, who were also students of Zen, Watts sought a stable career. Despite his lack of a university degree and his unorthodox Anglicanism, he entered Seabury-Western Theological Seminary in Evanston, Ill., in 1941 and was ordained an Episcopal priest in 1944. He served as a popular and colorful chaplain at Northwestern University in Evanston (1944–1950), receiving his Master of Sacred Theology degree from that institution in 1948.

In 1950, Watts left the priesthood, the church, and his family after a love affair scandal. His first marriage was soon annulled, and he married Dorothy Marie DeWitt on June 29,

1950; the couple had five children. That same year Watts moved with his new wife to New York City for a period of writing and introspection. A year later he moved to California to teach philosophy and psychology at the independent American Academy of Asian Studies in San Francisco (1951–1957), serving as dean from 1953 to 1957. In the 1950's, Watts lectured widely at American colleges and universities, publishing *The Supreme Identity* (1950), *The Wisdom of Insecurity* (1951), *The Way of Zen* (1957), and other works popularizing Zen and spiritualism to a diverse audience.

By the 1950's, Watts was the leading Western exponent of Zen Buddhism, especially for the "beat generation" in New York and California. His concept of inner peace and release from what he termed the "chronic uneasy conscience of Hebrew-Christian cultures" earned him an enthusiastic following, ranging from beatniks and bohemians to psychoanalysts, theologians, and intellectuals. He added advice on diet, dress, sex, yoga, Taoism, and the Vedanta to the core of his Zen Buddhist spiritualism. *This Is It* (1960) and *Psychotherapy East and West* (1961) were very popular in the United States, as were his syndicated radio and television programs and many campus lectures.

Watts and his second wife were divorced in 1963, and on December 4 he married Mary Jane Yates. They had no children. Watts and his wife lived on a houseboat docked in Sausalito until crowds of visiting disciples and admirers made that impossible. They retreated to an isolated house in Mill Valley, near San Francisco, in 1969.

While he was still in San Francisco, Watts associated with such proponents of beat as Jack Kerouac, who mocked Watts in the character of Arthur Whane in his novel *The Dharma Bums* (1958). He also befriended Allen Ginsberg, Gary Snyder, Richard Alpert ("Ram Dass"), and Timothy Leary and lent support to their experiments in consciousness expansion. In the spirit of the liberated counterculture era he helped shape, Watts had experimented with LSD to attain spiritual insight as early as 1958, before Leary and Alpert used the new hallucinogen at Harvard. He defended LSD as a useful tool, a "sacrament" for Westerners in their search for knowledge, but he cautioned those seeking enlightenment to use the drug prudently. Nevertheless, Watts also enjoyed luxury, tobacco, alcohol, fine food, travel, and sexual affairs.

When criticized because he eschewed the asceticism usually associated with Zen Buddhism, Watts called himself an "unrepentant sensualist."

In 1962 he organized the Society for Comparative Philosophy, which published the *Alan Watts Journal*. His interest in bridging East and West and in finding some common ground between Christianity and Buddhism continued during the turmoil of the hippie and New Left years. By 1965, he was considered a hero and was widely regarded as a modern mystic by the youthful counterculture in California. He was in great demand as a guru who could show Americans how to apply the wisdom of the East to the quest for freedom of the spirit.

Watts's twenty-two books, numerous articles, and countless lectures did much to interest Westerners in Asian culture, in ways both superficial and serious, and, incidentally, to prepare them for multiculturalism. But his deceptively lighthearted example led one critic to suggest that Watts's epitaph might be taken from the second chapter of Ecclesiastes: "I thought of beguiling my senses with wine, though my mind was concerned with wisdom." Alan Watts died at his home in Mill Valley.

[Watts's autobiography is *In My Own Way* (1972). See also Monica Furlong's biography, *Zen Effects* (1986). Obituaries are in the *New York Times* and the *Boston Globe*, both Nov. 17, 1973; and in *Time*, Nov. 26, 1973.]

PETER C. HOLLORAN

WEBSTER, BENJAMIN ("BEN") FRANCIS (Mar. 27, 1909–Sept. 20, 1973), jazz musician, was born and raised in Kansas City, Mo. From the 1930's until his death he was considered, along with Lester Young and Coleman Hawkins, one of the giants of the tenor saxophone. Like many black jazzmen of the era, he was raised by women. His mother and grandmother, who taught him violin, were both schoolteachers. Webster attended the local Attucks Elementary School and enrolled at Wilberforce College in Ohio, where he took college preparatory courses from 1922 to 1925.

The legendary blues pianist Pete Johnson, a neighbor in Kansas City, was Webster's first musical influence and taught him piano. Webster organized his first musical group, Rooster Ben and His Little Red Roosters, and his first paid gig was playing piano with Bretho Nelson in Enid, Okla., in the mid-1920's. It was while playing piano in a silent movie house in Amarillo, Tex., in 1927 that Webster met Budd Johnson, who taught him the rudiments of the tenor. When a traveling road show known as the Young Family (including a teenage Lester Young) passed through, Webster joined as a saxophone player, although he later recalled, "I couldn't read and didn't own a sax." Young's father, W. H. Young, provided lessons and an alto. The band traveled throughout the Southwest; in Albuquerque, N.Mex., Webster was credited with saving the life of a drowning Lester Young in the fast-moving Rio Grande.

Webster's jazz odyssey began when he joined drummer Eugene Coy's Happy Black Aces in 1930, and then played with the legendary Bennie Moten (his first well-known recordings are from this brief association and include the song "Moten Swing," 1932). Stylistically, wrote critic and Duke Ellington's long-time trumpet player Rex Stewart, he "blew with unrestrained savagery, buzzing and growling through chord changes like a prehistoric monster challenging a foe." This earned him the nickname "Brute." His style was part Coleman Hawkins, part Benny Carter. He traveled the "old Negro circuit" through the Southwest with such territory bands as Jap Allen, Andy Kirk, Fletcher Henderson, Cab Calloway, Willie Bryant, and Teddy Wilson during the 1930's.

The center of this musical renaissance was Kansas City, and the all-night jam sessions during the Prohibition era and years just after are jazz legends. As critic Nat Hentoff has written, Webster would "blow against the visiting jazzmen in fiercely contested battles usually humbling the more renowned musicians." Tom Pendergast, boss of the Democratic party in Kansas City at the time, encouraged gambling and nightlife and during his reign Kansas City jazz flourished. Jazz greats who emerged from this fertile milieu included Count Basie, Coleman Hawkins, Chu Berry, Lester Young, and Charlie Parker. It was during these seminal Kansas City years that the Webster persona emerged; he "hung out on the streets of Kansas City and became a womanizer, an expert pool player and a horrendous combative drinker" according to critic Whitney Balliett.

Webster joined the Duke Ellington Orchestra as its first permanent tenor sax player in 1939. During this association, several classic recordings were cut, including "C Jam Blues," "Just a

Sittin and a Rockin," and "Cottontail," all featuring Webster's big tenor sound. The celebrated ensemble chorus on "Cottontail" was written by Webster, and his solo, a variant of "I Got Rhythm," continues to be an influence on jazz improvisation. Alto sax great Johnny Hodges, a fellow Ellingtonian, had significant influence on Webster's gradual stylistic maturity. Balliett noted that "[Webster's] early style . . . stemmed directly from Hawkins . . . but it went through a subtle reshaping during the three years spent with Ellington in the forties. He fell under the lyrical sway of Johnny Hodges," learning dynamics control and legato lyricism.

In 1943, Webster moved to New York City and emerged as a fixture on the famed Fifty-second Street scene for the next five years; these were halcyon days for noncommercial jazz, with wartime spending up and seven top clubs on the street. Webster was one of the first swing-era players sympathetic to bebop, the new jazz sound. He was also the first to understand and encourage a fellow Kansas City native (though from across the state line in Kansas), Charlie Parker. A celebrated jazz story has Webster grabbing Parker's tenor (Parker later played alto) at Monroe's Uptown House in Harlem shouting "that horn ain't 'sposed to sound that fast."

During the late 1940's and 1950's Webster recorded prolifically; he was consistently employed accompanying the top female jazz vocalists of the era: Billie Holiday, Dinah Washington, Ella Fitzgerald, and Carmen McCrae. A series of "Ben Webster Meets . . ." albums sold well for Verve Records, classic sides were recorded with the virtuoso blind pianist Art Tatum, and Webster toured widely with Norman Granz–organized Jazz at the Philharmonic in the 1950's. His direct influence was seen in younger tenor players such as Paul Gonsalves, Flip Philips, and Eddie ("Lockjaw") Davis (sometimes known as Little Ben). Gary Giddins has remarked that "his mastery of dynamics, fragmentation of line, and tonal control came together stunningly in the 50s, when Webster blossomed into one of the most evocative stylists the music has known." He became a master of the ballad, "using an enormous tone, a breathy, enveloping vibrato, and terrific glissando," according to Balliett.

After moving to Los Angeles in the late 1950's to care for his aged mother and grandmother he was sporadically employed. Jazz styles changed, but Webster's did not. Upon the deaths of his mother and grandmother in 1964, tired of the racism he had long endured and of difficulties in finding steady work, Webster emigrated to Europe, where he joined the black American jazz expatriate community in a more racially tolerant society. Webster settled in Copenhagen and played with pickup rhythm sections all across the continent for the next decade. While in Europe he appeared in the documentary *Big Ben* (1967), and the film *Quiet Days in Clichy* (1969), based on the Henry Miller novel. He died of a cerebral thrombosis (possibly brought on by excessive alcohol consumption) in Amsterdam. Out of the public eye for several decades and in semiobscurity, his passing earned a scant two-inch obituary in the *New York Times*.

[An extensive clippings file and large collection of Webster's recordings with liner notes are located at the Institute of Jazz Studies, Rutgers University, Newark, N.J. See also Nat Hentoff and Nat Shapiro, *Hear Me Talkin' to Ya* (1955); Dom Cerulli, "Ben Webster," *Down Beat*, June 26, 1958; N. J. Ross Russell, *Jazz Style in Kansas City and the Southwest* (1971); Rex Steward, *Jazz Masters of the Thirties* (1972); and Stanley Crouch, "Rooster Ben," *Village Voice*, June 18, 1986. An obituary is in the *New York Times*, May 19, 1972.]

JEFF ROSEN

WEBSTER, MARGARET ("PEGGY") (Mar. 15, 1905–Nov. 13, 1972), theatrical director and actress, was born in New York City to famed British actors Ben Webster and Mary Louisa May Whitty (later, Dame May Whitty), during one of their American engagements; thus she had dual U.S. and British citizenship. She was educated in England, attending Queen Anne's, a public (that is, private) school in Caversham. Webster, who discounted the importance of a degree for a theatrical career, never attended college; she did study acting briefly at London's Etlinger Dramatic School, which her mother managed beginning in 1921.

Webster's first professional acting job was as a member of the chorus in Sybil Thorndike's production of *The Trojan Women* (1924). She was soon appearing regularly in commercial West End plays, in classics staged at the Old Vic (where she usually played second leads), and in the productions of Ben Greet's Players, a troupe famous for its Shakespearean revivals. She began to direct in 1933, first with amateurs. Especially impressive was her outdoor pageant

version of Shakespeare's *Henry VIII* (1934), staged in Kent, using eight hundred women in the baptism scene.

Webster, who eventually acted in many plays she also directed, continued her London acting career while directing for several noncommercial groups in the years 1935–1936, simultaneously picking up a mastery of stage lighting. By 1937, her newfound skills were recognized when she handled her first commercial play, Keith Winter's *Old Music*. Soon after, she went to New York to direct her friend Maurice Evans in a rare Broadway production of a Shakespeare play, *Richard II* (1937). The swiftly paced, scenically fluid, and—despite a low budget—visually striking production accumulated a record-breaking 171 performances, leading to a series of Shakespearean productions that made Webster America's most consistently successful Shakespearean director.

Webster's Shakespeare productions on Broadway included *Hamlet* (1939), with Evans, remarkable for using an uncut text; *Henry IV, Part I* (1939), with Evans as Falstaff; *Twelfth Night* (1940), with Helen Hayes as Viola and Evans as a cockney Malvolio; *Macbeth* (1941), with Evans and Judith Anderson; a record-breaking, 295-performance *Othello* (1943), starring black actor Paul Robeson in what was then a highly controversial piece of casting (Othello was traditionally played by whites in blackface); *The Tempest* (1945), with black actor and former boxer Canada Lee playing Caliban (another part usually played by whites) and with ballerina Vera Zorina as Ariel; *Henry VIII* (1946), part of the repertory of the failed American Repertory Theatre (ART), a nonprofit troupe that Webster cofounded with Eva Le Gallienne, her frequent collaborator, and Cheryl Crawford; *The Taming of the Shrew* (1951); and *Richard III* (1953), starring Evans. She also staged abbreviated versions of four Shakespeare comedies for the Merrie Old England exhibition at the New York World's Fair (1939) in a miniature version of the Globe Theatre, and directed several more Shakespeare plays for the Margaret Webster Shakespeare Company (Marweb), a bus-and-truck touring troupe she founded in 1948 and managed for two years. In 1952, she toured in her one-woman program, *An Evening with Will Shakespeare*. Webster also directed three Shakespeare productions for British repertory companies in 1956, 1957, and 1960.

Her book, *Shakespeare without Tears* (1942), became a classic in the field, and reflected Webster's conviction that the bard could be both accessible and entertaining to modern audiences. She claimed that Shakespearean direction must make the story live as clearly and straightforwardly as possible while keeping the directorial presence discreet. Her emphasis was on character reality, rather than political or social issues. Crucial to her style of direction was an inspired leading actor, which many felt she had in Evans. Often, she allowed the star to dictate his or her own interpretation of a role. The clarity of her productions was one of their most noted features, and she was renowned, if not always appreciated, for what some termed her "domestication" of the action, so that behavior seemed detailed and lifelike. This was accomplished despite her preference for simplified, nonobtrusive—though always beautiful—sets and minimal furnishings that allowed for rapid shifts from one locale to another. Because the proscenium stage allowed her to create striking pictures, she preferred it to adaptations of the Elizabethan theater, although she approved the addition of a forestage in order to increase actor–audience intimacy. Despite being famed for her uncut *Hamlet*, Webster took textual liberties when necessary.

Webster also provided excellent stagings of modern classics, including New York productions of *The Cherry Orchard* (1944), codirected with Le Gallienne; *Ghosts* (1947) and *Hedda Gabler* (1947); and a number of Shaw plays, *The Devil's Disciple* (1950), *Saint Joan* (1951), and *Back to Methuselah* (1958) among them.

Beginning with *Young Mr. Disraeli* (1937), in which her father starred, Webster staged over a dozen contemporary plays in New York, but these were never as successful as her classical productions. In 1950 she became the first woman director at the New York's Metropolitan Opera, for whom she staged several works; she also directed operas for the New York City Opera Company. Despite a brief period spent in Hollywood in 1940, she never directed a film, although she did eventually direct some television scripts.

After a very active Broadway career through the 1940's, she turned elsewhere in the 1950's, which saw her touring Shakespeare around the country and preparing the way for the resident theater movement that soon would follow; returning, in 1953, to England after eighteen years, where she worked until 1970; giving readings of Shakespeare and Shaw and staging O'Neill's *A Touch of the Poet* for both black and white audiences in South Africa in 1961; directing plays on university campuses and Off Broadway; and mounting plays for the National Repertory Company (NRC), a new touring company founded by Le Gallienne in 1965–1966. The principal reason for all this non-Broadway work was the unjustified damage to her reputation caused when actor José Ferrer named her as a Communist in his testimony before the House Un-American Activities Committee in May 1951. A liberal, but never a Communist, Webster was eventually exonerated. But during the 1950's she was blacklisted and denied the opportunity to practice her craft in major commercial productions.

Webster was long an important board member of the Actors Equity Association. This no-nonsense woman, who usually wore her hair short, preferred slacks, and invariably had a cigarette dangling from her lips, was an idealist at the forefront of various attempts to establish noncommercial outlets for great plays and opportunities for actors to expand their talents. In addition to her work with the ART, the Marweb troupe, the NRC, and other companies, she also was the force behind the creation of the Experimental Theatre, which she founded in 1941 as a noncommercial outlet for actors needing experience in the classics. Though short-lived, partly because of the war, it was later revived by others and proved an important spur to the Off Broadway movement of the 1950's. Webster was also a powerful advocate for the establishment of a subsidized American national theater.

Webster, who never married, died in New York City.

[Webster wrote two excellent autobiographies, *The Same Only Different* (1969) and *Don't Put Your Daughter on the Stage* (1972). Barbara Heggie did a fine profile of her in the *New Yorker*, May 20, 1944. A thorough account of her directing career and methods appears in Samuel L. Leiter, *From Belasco to Brook: Representative Directors of the English-Speaking Stage* (1991), which includes a detailed chronology and bibliography. An obituary is in the *New York Times*, Nov. 14, 1972.]

SAMUEL L. LEITER

WEEDE, ROBERT (Feb. 22, 1903–July 9, 1972), baritone operatic singer, was born Robert Wiedefeld in Hamilton, Md., the son of railroad clerk William J. Wiedefeld and Frances Johnston. Wiedefeld attended public school through the fifth grade but completed his secondary education at Calvert Hall, a Christian Brothers school, where he received rudimentary vocal instruction and sang in several musical productions. Upon graduation Wiedefeld found employment as a thrice-daily soloist in a Baltimore motion picture theater; he also took voice lessons with George Castelle.

In 1925, Wiedefeld went to New York City where he joined a Russian balalaika orchestra as soloist and also performed on the vaudeville circuit. In 1926 he was awarded a scholarship by the Peabody Conservatory of Music in Baltimore, and in 1927 he won first prize in a National Federation of Music Clubs competition. On Nov. 12, 1927, Wiedefeld married Amelia Campeggi; they had two sons.

In 1928, Wiedefeld joined the music ensemble of the Eastman Theatre Company in Rochester, N.Y., while at the same time studying voice with Adelin Fermin at the Eastman School of Music. In 1929 he won the Caruso Memorial Foundation Scholarship, which paid for a full year of vocal training and operatic instruction under Oscar Anselmia in Milan, Italy. On returning home, he taught voice while seeking the opportunity to pursue a musical career.

In 1933 Wiedefeld auditioned for Samuel L. (Roxy) Rothafel, the New York theater magnate, who engaged him as the leading baritone for his Radio City Music Hall stage productions. Roxy then persuaded Wiedefeld to adopt the name Weede for professional reasons. Weede sang at Radio City Music Hall for six years, during which time he gained widespread recognition through the venue's Sunday morning radio broadcasts.

In the spring of 1937 Weede joined the Metropolitan Opera Company, for whom he debuted as Tonio in *Pagliacci* on May 15, 1937. Although listed on the roster of the Metropolitan for ten seasons (1937–1942, 1944–1945, 1948–1950, and 1952–1953), Weede, despite enthusiastic critical acclaim, sang but twenty-one total performances in six operatic roles for that company. When summarizing the 1940–1941 season in *The Story of the Metropolitan Opera* (1953), Irving Kolodin wrote, "The company would have been better served by offering more opportunities to Robert Weede, who sang an excellent *Rigoletto* on February 27."

Although used sparingly by the prestigious Met, Weede was in constant demand elsewhere. Beginning in the late 1930's, he sang with the Columbia Opera Company, the Baltimore Civic Opera Company, Philadelphia's La Scala Opera, the San Antonio Opera Company, the St. Louis Grand Opera Company, and three seasons with the Lyric Opera of Chicago, as well as sixty performances with the Cincinnati Summer Opera during fourteen seasons between 1939 and 1955, and 102 performances with the San Francisco Opera during sixteen seasons between 1940 and 1964. Weede also appeared in Argentina, Brazil, Cuba, and Mexico. At home he sang the male lead in the 1939 world premiere of Menotti's radio opera *The Old Maid and the Thief*, and he also sang in the world premiere of William Grant Still's three-act opera, *Troubled Island*, with the New York City Opera in 1949.

In addition to his operatic engagements, Weede performed with many of the nation's leading symphony orchestras, concertized extensively, and sang at the New York Stadium Concerts, the Hollywood Bowl, Ravinia (Chicago), and Robin Hood Dell (Saratoga, N.Y.) summer festivals. From 1942 to 1946 Weede costarred with soprano Jean Tennyson in a weekly radio program, "Great Moments in Music," and during World War II he participated in over three dozen USO camp shows, as well as undertaking a seven-week tour of South Pacific military bases.

In 1955 composer Frank Loesser engaged Weede for the male lead in his musical *The Most Happy Fella*, which opened in New York on May 4, 1956, and ran for 676 performances in addition to a year on tour. Weede received rare reviews in the vocally demanding role of the Italian-American vintner, Tony Esposito, while surprising many veteran theater goers with his marked dramatic talent.

During the fall of 1961 Weede returned to Broadway to costar with Mimi Benzell in a 543-performance run of *Milk and Honey*. He then settled on the West Coast, where he served as a vocal consultant to the American Conservatory Theater in San Francisco and devoted the bulk of his time to farming and raising thoroughbred Arabian horses on the Concord, Calif., ranch he purchased in 1962.

In 1969 Weede returned to New York to portray the role of Mayor Edward Quinn in Mitch Leigh's *Cry for Us All*. Although the show closed after nine performances, that season Weede received a Tony nomination for best actor in a musical.

Weede, an affable man of stocky build and prodigious physical strength, obtained his greatest avocational pleasure from teaching. Beginning in the early 1940's, he gave vocal instruction or operatic coaching to many of the notable singers of his day, including John Alexander, Mario Lanza, Jan Peerce, Brian Sullivan, Norman Treigle, Claramae Turner, and Earl Wrightson.

During his long and diverse professional career Weede recorded for Capitol, Columbia, and RCA Victor, and was heard in live performances on three 1950 Unique Opera records: UORC 184, 200, and 295. Although he frequently sang the roles of Manfredo in *The Love of Three Kings*, and Scarpia in *Tosca*, Weede was primarily a Verdi baritone.

His tour de force was *Rigoletto*, and Arthur Bloomfield's review of the 1940 opera season in *Fifty Years of the San Francisco Opera* (1972) is typical of the acclaim Weede received in that role throughout the years: "Weede was the season's new Rigoletto, his large, beautiful voice and commanding presence bringing him one of the year's bigger ovations and some of the grandest critical praise." Weede died in Walnut Creek, Calif.

[Biographical data may be found in Irving Kolodin, "From Tonio to Tony (in Twenty Hard Years)," *Saturday Review of Literature*, May 5, 1956. See also Jan Peerce, *The Bluebird of Happiness* (1976). An obituary appears in the *New York Times*, July 11, 1972.]

LOUIS R. THOMAS

WEEKS, SINCLAIR (June 15, 1893–Feb. 7, 1972), secretary of commerce in the Eisenhower administration, was born in West Newton, Mass., son of former U.S. Senator and Secretary of War John Wingate Weeks, a founder of the brokerage firm of Hornblower and Weeks, and Martha Aroline Sinclair. He attended the Newton public schools and graduated from Newton High School in 1910 and from Harvard College in 1914.

Following graduation, Weeks became a messenger for the First National Bank of Boston. He married Beatrice Dowse of Boston in 1915; they had six children. His banking career was interrupted in 1916 by military service in the Massachusetts National Guard on the Mexican border and in 1917 in France during World War I, which he entered as a lieutenant in the 101st Field Artillery, Twenty-sixth (Yankee) Division, Army Expeditionary Force. He left with the rank of captain. Weeks returned to the First National Bank in 1919 and remained there until 1923, at which time he was assistant cashier in charge of the foreign business of the bank.

In 1923, Weeks left banking to work for his father-in-law, William B. H. Dowse, in two metal manufacturing businesses, Reed and Barton Corporation, silversmiths, in Taunton, Mass., and United Fastener Corporation, which made clothing fasteners and small metal stampings largely for the automotive and radio industries. He became vice president of Reed and Barton in 1928, and, after helping to arrange a merger with United Fastener's chief competitor, was made a director of the new United-Carr Fastener Corporation in 1929. He was chosen board chairman in 1942. Weeks was elected president and board chairman of Reed and Barton in 1945. In 1938 and 1939 he was regional vice-president of the Associated Industries of Massachusetts.

In the 1920's and 1930's Weeks was active in Republican party politics on the state and national levels. The only elective offices he held were alderman of his home city of Newton (1923–1930) and mayor of Newton (1930–1936). He prided himself on bringing business principles to the running of the city. Weeks ran for the U.S. Senate in 1936 but lost to Henry Cabot Lodge, Jr. Soon after, he became chairman of the Republican State Committee and subsequently chairman of the Republican state finance committee and eastern treasurer of the Republican National Committee. In 1940, Weeks was chairman of the executive committee of the Republican National Committee and from 1941 to 1944 he was treasurer of the national committee. He was extremely active in the presidential campaigns of Wendell L. Willkie and Governor Thomas E. Dewey.

When Lodge resigned his seat in the United States Senate in 1944 to go on active duty with the United States Army, Weeks was appointed by Governor Leverett Saltonstall, a Harvard classmate, to fill out Lodge's term. He did not run for election at the end of that year, and the seat was won by Saltonstall, who took his place in the Senate in 1945.

As chairman of the finance committee of the

Republican National Committee (1950–1952), Weeks was the first member of the committee to voice support for Dwight D. Eisenhower for president and to ask that Senator Robert Taft of Ohio, the leading contender for the nomination, stand aside. He played a major role in Eisenhower's election, and John Harriman of the *Boston Globe* referred to him as a "political fund-raiser extraordinary." Although Eisenhower had hoped that Weeks would agree to head the Republican National Committee and despite his concern that Weeks was "so completely conservative," in 1953 he finally gave Weeks the job he preferred: secretary of commerce.

Weeks was noted for his advocacy of the needs of business, his opposition to price controls, and his use of a business advisory council of one hundred businessmen considered the "blue bloods of industry." In his memoirs, Eisenhower wrote that the federal highway system, "the biggest peacetime construction project of any description ever undertaken by the United States or any other country . . . will stand in part as a monument to the man in my Cabinet who headed the department responsible for it, and who himself spent long hours mapping out the program and battling it through the Congress—Secretary of Commerce Sinclair Weeks." Weeks was also instrumental in the passage of Eisenhower's reciprocal trade program and created a Bureau of Foreign Commerce. He resigned as secretary of commerce in November 1958, and in 1959 was reelected as a director of the First National Bank of Boston; he had left all of his corporate directorships to join the cabinet in 1953. He also became a limited partner in Hornblower and Weeks, Hemphill, Noyes in 1964.

Weeks was an overseer of Harvard; a member of the corporation of Northeastern University; a director of Wentworth Institute; a trustee of the University of New Hampshire, the Tuck School of Business Administration at Dartmouth, the Fessenden School, the New England Deaconess Hospital, and the Beatrice D. Weeks Hospital in Lancaster, N.H.; and an overseer of the Boys Club of Boston. He was a corporator of the West Newton Savings Bank and of the Boston Five Cents Savings Bank. Weeks also served as a director of the First National Bank of Boston, John Hancock Mutual Life Insurance Company, Gillette Company, Pacific Mills Company, West Point Manufacturing Company,

Pullman Company, New Hampshire Insurance Company, and Lancaster (N.H.) National Bank.

Weeks's first wife died in 1945. Three years later, he married Jane Tompkins Rankin of Nashville, Tenn. After their divorce he married Alice Requa Low, the widow of Vice Admiral Francis Stuart Low, in 1968. In 1970, Weeks retired and moved to the family beef and dairy farm in Lancaster, N.H., the birthplace of his father. He died in Concord, Mass.

[Weeks's papers are in the Baker Memorial Library, Dartmouth College, Hanover, N.H. Biographical information can be found in Duncan Norton-Taylor, "The Ninety Days of Mr. Weeks," *Fortune*, May 1953; Dwight D. Eisenhower, *The White House Years* (1965); Robert Ferrell, ed., *The Eisenhower Diaries* (1981); and Stephen E. Ambrose, *Eisenhower* (1983). Obituaries appear in the *Boston Globe*, Feb. 7, 1972, and the *New York Times*, Feb. 8, 1972.]

JOHN T. GALVIN

WEINBERGER, JACOB (Jan. 4, 1882–May 21, 1974), lawyer and judge, was born in Austria-Hungary. On his father's side, his great-grandfather, Reb (Rabbi) Moshe Wolf, was a scholar of some means, but the family's fortunes were destroyed in the revolution of 1848. After Russian soldiers pillaged everything the family owned, his grandfather moved to a safer area near Hedrei, where he became a leader in the community. Weinberger's father, Herman Weinberger, a tutor and teacher, later became a distiller and brewer, gaining some prosperity. His mother, Nettie Flaster, also came from a family of scholars and businesspeople but of no great wealth. Following a downturn in business in the mid-1880's, his father left for America in 1888, joining other family members in Denver, Colo. A year later, when Weinberger was seven, his mother brought the rest of the family to Denver. Eventually, there were twelve children. His father managed a grocery store in a poor area of Denver. Jacob helped out there and held various other jobs.

After graduating from Denver High School in 1901, Weinberger entered the University of Colorado Law School; he supported himself by working as a waiter, steelworker, janitor, and store clerk. He received his LL.B. in 1904 and became a member of the Colorado bar. He joined a good Denver firm but was given its less remunerative cases. Learning that Gila County,

Arizona Territory, was experiencing considerable prosperity from copper mining, Weinberger moved to Globe, Ariz., in 1905. Globe had the reputation of being a rough place; its main street boasted several dozen saloons. In 1907, Weinberger was appointed deputy district attorney of Gila County, and on one occasion was said to have been pursued by a newly released convict he had prosecuted. On June 11, 1907, Weinberger married Blanche Ruth Solomon, a member of a wealthy pioneer Arizona family from Solomonville (later Solomon, Ariz.). Since there were so few Jews living in the territory, a rabbi from El Paso, Tex., officiated at the marriage. The Weinbergers had two children.

In 1863, President Abraham Lincoln had issued a proclamation naming Arizona a territory. For some years in the early twentieth century, there was a move to combine New Mexico and Arizona in one state, but Arizona residents tended to look on this scheme with considerable disfavor. On June 20, 1910, President William Howard Taft signed an enabling act directing the residents of Arizona to select delegates to a constitutional convention. On Sept. 12, 1910, Weinberger was elected as one of five delegates from Gila County. A total of fifty-two delegates were chosen to meet at the convention, which convened in Phoenix on October 10. At twenty-eight years, Weinberger was the second-youngest member.

Weinberger sat on four standing committees: Legislative Department; Distribution of Powers and Apportionment; Judiciary; and Executive, Impeachment, and Removal from Office. He was named chairman of the last committee; as it turned out, the issue of recall received the most attention. President Taft declared that he would reject any constitution that included judges in the recall provision. On October 21, Weinberger introduced Proposition 18, regarding the recall of public officers. Although some of the delegates attempted to exclude the judiciary, this motion lost by a vote of thirty to eighteen, and the proposition passed on November 10. The members voted to retain the recall of judges in the constitution adopted at the convention in December 1910, and this provision was ratified in a general election on Feb. 11, 1911. As he had promised, Taft rejected the constitution on Aug. 15, 1911. A compromise that included this exemption was passed by popular vote on Dec. 12, 1911, and Taft signed a proclamation

on Feb. 9, 1912, making Arizona the forty-eighth state.

The Arizona constitution was considered a progressive one. In addition to provisions regarding initiative, referendum, and recall, there were clauses covering workers' rights and the working conditions of women and children. In the state election of 1912, Arizona residents voted that the recall of judges be reinstated in the state constitution. For many years, Weinberger was the last surviving convention delegate, a distinction that brought him many honors and awards, He was frequently interviewed and asked to appear at commemorative ceremonies.

The delegates concluded their work in December 1910. In 1911, Weinberger moved his family to San Diego, Calif., because of his wife's health and his weak financial situation. He sold his financial interests in Globe just before the community suffered an economic decline. Weinberger passed the California bar in 1911 and practiced law there for many years. He rarely appeared in the courtroom, preferring out-of-court mediation, and gained a reputation as an able conciliator. In 1918, he was appointed to the San Diego Board of Education; he was a member for twenty-one years and served several terms as president, the first beginning in 1922. Weinberger's practice suffered in the Great Depression, and his law partner committed suicide. It took him almost a decade to recover financially.

Until the late 1930's, San Diego was predominantly Republican. Weinberger, a Democrat, began to be politically active. He was appointed vice-chairman of the California Democratic Central Committee in 1939. The same year, he ran for mayor of San Diego but lost. In 1941, he was named San Diego city attorney. Later that year, he was appointed to fill a vacancy on the Superior Court of San Diego County; his colleagues elected him presiding judge in 1944, but he lost the judgeship in the 1944 election. In 1946, President Harry Truman appointed him to the U.S. District Court of the Southern District of California, which included San Diego. In 1949, he became San Diego's first resident federal judge. Weinberger retired in 1958 and was appointed senior judge. His decisions were rarely overturned, and he was considered an exemplary and fair trial judge by his peers. He also possessed an innate ability to resolve disputes.

Weinberger served on numerous boards and charities. He joined B'nai B'rith while living in Denver and had been a member of Congregation Temple Beth Israel in San Diego since 1911. His biographer, Leland G. Stanford, believed his most enduring qualities were loyalty, industry, friendliness, and patriotic ambition. Weinberger died in San Diego.

[Weinberger gathered a collection titled "Material Pertaining to the Constitutional Convention of 1910," now in the University of Arizona Library, special collections, that includes scrapbooks and clippings. See Arizona (Territory) Constitutional Convention, 1910, "Journals of the Constitutional Convention of Arizona," manuscript compiled by Con P. Cronin, in New York Public Library (1925); Yolanda LaCagnina, "The Role of the Recall of Judges Issue in the Struggle for Arizona Statehood" (M.A. thesis, University of Arizona, 1951); Jay J. Wagoner, *Arizona Territory 1863–1912* (1970); and Leland R. Stanford, *90 Weinberger Years* (1971).]

MARGARET LATIMER

WEISS, GEORGE MARTIN (June 23, 1894–Aug. 13, 1972), baseball executive, was born in New Haven, Conn., the son of Conrad Weiss, a dealer in meats and fancy groceries, and Anna Kapitzke. Weiss, who entertained thoughts of becoming a journalist, entered Yale after his graduation from New Haven High School (later renamed Hillhouse High School) in 1912. However, he gave up his studies to run the family business after his father's death in 1915. However, baseball already exerted a powerful hold on Weiss. Short and stout, he was never able to play baseball professionally, but as a senior in high school was appointed business manager for the varsity baseball team. Weiss had learned enough about business matters while working at his father's store to handle the team's finances. After most of the players on the outstanding teams of 1911 and 1912 had graduated, Weiss suggested they stay together to play semiprofessional baseball during the summer as the Colonials.

Weiss's idea was a success, and the Colonials played a second summer, using as their home a field at Lighthouse Point, an amusement park outside New Haven. Weiss, who handled business and promotional matters, began to view the Colonials as more than a job between school terms. New Haven and the nearby major league cities of New York and Boston all had laws that forbade playing baseball on Sundays. At Light-house Point the Colonials were under no such restrictions. Weiss recruited Yale stars and other good players from the New Haven area, and even invited such major league stars as Ty Cobb and Walter Johnson to play for the Colonials in Lighthouse Point on Sundays when their major league teams were in Boston or New York, but were idle because of local blue laws. So many fans turned out to see the major league greats that Weiss was able to pay a player like Cobb several hundred dollars for an appearance with the Colonials. After the 1915 World Series, Weiss even got the new world champions, the Boston Red Sox, to play the Colonials. On another occasion the Colonials played the Yankees in New York.

With the legalization of Sunday sports in New Haven looming in 1919, Weiss acquired the bankrupt professional New Haven team in the Eastern League, the Profs, and turned it into a competitive and highly successful franchise. In 1929, he left the Profs to become general manager of the Baltimore Orioles in the International League.

Three years later Weiss moved to New York to organize and direct a farm system for the Yankees. The farm system was then a recent development in baseball, credited to Branch Rickey, general manager of the St. Louis Cardinals. Prior to the development of the farm system, major league teams often bought players from independently owned minor league teams or from the poorer major league franchises. The Yankees had assembled their first great teams of the 1920's by buying players, Babe Ruth among them, from troubled franchises. However, a team could also make costly mistakes, because the purchase of a top minor league player could cost $50,000 or more. Although a farm system involved many expenses, players could be signed directly from amateur leagues at little cost and be paid minimal salaries as they worked their way up to the major leagues. Most players, of course, never made it that far, but the major league franchises began to see merit in establishing their own farm systems, which varied in size from a handful of teams to hundreds of minor league players belonging to one of the more prosperous clubs.

Weiss soon assembled one of baseball's largest and most successful farm systems. By the end of the 1930's, it included twenty-one teams, capped by the Newark Bears, often considered the greatest of all minor league teams, and the

Kansas City Blues, whose 1940 infield quartet was rated the best ever to play in the minor leagues. Between 1936 and 1943, the Yankees won seven American League pennants and six World Series, a record that outdid the accomplishments of Babe Ruth's Yankees. Joining the club in these years were such legends as Charlie Keller, Joe Gordon, Phil Rizzuto, and Joe DiMaggio. With the exception of DiMaggio, these stars all came from the Yankee organization. Players who had major league ability but were not good enough to crack the Yankee lineup were sold to other major league teams.

As farm director, Weiss reported to the general manager and the owner, who still acquired players by purchase and trade from sources outside their farm system. DiMaggio, for example, was bought from the minor league San Francisco Seals. However, Weiss's farm system played a major role in the acquisition of DiMaggio, for in addition to $25,000 cash, the price for the future Yankee great included five of Weiss's farm players considered good enough to help San Francisco. Weiss had to convince top management that DiMaggio was worth the cost.

Weiss became the Yankees' general manager after the 1947 season. With DiMaggio and other prewar stars aging, the Yankees' future seemed doubtful. However, Weiss acted decisively when he hired Casey Stengel as manager after the 1948 campaign. His signing of Stengel was at first ridiculed, for Stengel had already managed two National League clubs without success. However, those teams had lacked talent, and Weiss supplied Stengel with an abundance of it, including Yogi Berra, Whitey Ford, and Mickey Mantle, all of whom emerged from the Yankee farm system between 1947 and 1951. During the 1950's the Yankees won every American League pennant but two, and on each occasion they lost, Weiss engineered deals that brought fresh talent to the team. The acquisition of Roger Maris after a third-place season finish in 1959 was one of his last successful moves with the Yankees.

The owners dismissed Weiss after the 1960 season. He soon became president of a new National League franchise, the New York Mets. In fact his duties were those of general manager. For the five years he ran the Mets the team was unsuccessful on the field but a winner at the box office. Weiss retired in 1966, retaining stock ownership in the Mets. The job he had done in hiring astute baseball personnel and acquiring a nucleus of competent players was not fully appreciated until 1969, when the Mets, featuring such young pitchers as Tom Seaver and Nolan Ryan, became the first of baseball's expansion franchises to appear in a World Series. In 1971 Weiss was elected to the Baseball Hall of Fame.

Weiss had his critics, however. Some blamed him for the Yankees' slowness in signing black talent in the 1950's, and he was certainly difficult when negotiating contracts with his players. Others regarded him as aloof, a coldly efficient assembler of teams that won with boring regularity. If the Yankees won too often, it was in part because other teams could not match Weiss's front-office management. Those who knew him well knew that he was merely shy, not aloof, and that he genuinely loved baseball, as the contents of his two-hundred-year-old home in Greenwich, Conn., attested. He had made it into a virtual museum of baseball memorabilia dating back to the early 1900's. He married Hazel Wood in 1937. Although they had no children together, she had one son from a previous marriage. Weiss died in a Greenwich, Conn., nursing home.

[The best source on Weiss is the two-part article, George Weiss with Robert Shaplen, "The Man of Silence Speaks," *Sports Illustrated*, Mar. 6 and 13, 1961. See also Stanley Frank, "Yankee Kingmaker," *Saturday Evening Post*, July 24, 1948; Anne Brockey, "Home Base for a Yankee," *American Home*, Sept. 1949; and Robert Shaplen, "How to Build a Ball Club," *Sports Illustrated*, Mar. 5, 1962. Books that discuss Weiss and his work include Frank Graham, *The New York Yankees: An Informal History* (1943); Milton Gross, *Yankee Doodles* (1948); Harold Rosenthal, ed., *Baseball Is Their Business* (1952); Leonard Koppett, *The New York Mets: The Whole Story* (1970); Peter Golenbock, *Dynasty: The New York Yankees, 1949–1964* (1975); Robert W. Creamer, *Stengel: His Life and Times* (1985); and David Halberstam, *Summer of '49* (1989). An obituary appears in the *New York Times*, Aug. 14, 1972, along with an appreciation of Weiss by celebrated sportswriter Red Smith.]

LLOYD J. GRAYBAR

WELLMAN, WILLIAM AUGUSTUS (Feb. 29, 1896–Dec. 9, 1975), film director, was born in Brookline, Mass., the son of Arthur Gouverneur Wellman, an insurance broker, and Celia Guinness McCarthy, a probation officer. Most of his boyhood was spent in Newton Highlands, a suburb of Boston, where he attended Newton High School. Known from an early age as "Wild Bill"—the nickname persisted throughout his career—he was a discipline problem at school, frequently getting into trouble. He left high school before graduation, playing professional hockey for a while and taking odd jobs. In 1917, Wellman went to France to serve as an ambulance driver and then became a pilot with the Lafayette Flying Corps, an outgrowth of the famed group of American flyers called the Lafayette Escadrille. He was awarded the croix de guerre for bravery in action. When he returned to America, he became an instructor in the U.S. Air Service at Rockwell Field in San Diego, Calif.

A friendship with the actor Douglas Fairbanks sparked Wellman's interest in films and filmmaking. First he acted in several movies, then decided that he was much more suitable for a career in directing. Subsequent jobs as a messenger, prop boy, and assistant director led ultimately to his first assignment as a director, a Western called *The Man Who Won* (1923). Other minor films followed until Wellman moved to Paramount, where his flying experience brought him the choice assignment of directing a spectacular aviation drama entitled *Wings* (1927).

A turning point in Wellman's career, *Wings* combined a conventional story of two aviator friends (Richard Arlen and Charles ["Buddy"] Rogers) with extraordinary aerial photography that captured the exhilaration and danger of flying in wartime. Widely acclaimed, *Wings* became the first film to win the Academy Award as best picture of the year. Wellman's other Paramount credits include *Legion of the Condemned* (1928); *Beggars of Life* (1928), a drama about the hobo world; and his first sound film, *Chinatown Nights* (1929).

In 1930, Wellman signed a contract with Warner Brothers, where his penchant for gritty realism could be applied effectively. The studio's blunt, unadorned style combined with Wellman's own feisty personality to create such tough-fibered movies as *Night Nurse* (1931) and *The Purchase Price* (1932). It was Wellman's harsh 1931 melodrama, *Public Enemy*, that established his reputation. Following on the heels of Warner's sensational *Little Caesar* (1930), it offered a crude but compelling portrait of a gangster, played to snarling perfection by James Cagney. Two of Wellman's other Warner's movies, *Heroes for Sale* (1933) and *Wild Boys of*

the Road (1933), dealt with social problems of the time with surprising frankness.

Wellman's films after leaving Warner Brothers (including *The President Vanishes*, 1934; and *The Call of the Wild*, 1935) were at first less suitable to his hard-edged style. For a brief time, however, he found a compatible home at Selznick International, where he directed two of his best-known films. *A Star Is Born* (1937), the first feature film in the three-color Technicolor process to have a contemporary setting, was also the first version of the familiar story of an ill-fated Hollywood marriage, later remade in 1954 and 1976. (Wellman's original story, written with Robert Carson, won an Oscar.) *Nothing Sacred* (1937) was a wickedly satirical comedy that mocked, among other things, America's celebrity worship. In 1939, he returned to Paramount to direct a rousing remake of the perennial desert adventure tale, *Beau Geste*, and also *The Light That Failed*.

In the 1940's Wellman worked at various studios, directing such movies as *Roxie Hart* (1942) and *The Great Man's Lady* (1942). Often he concentrated on a single theme: the behavior of men in groups, under severe stress. This interest led him to the Western and war genres, at which he excelled. *The Ox-Bow Incident* (1943) used its western setting to launch a scathing attack on lynch-mob violence. *The Story of G.I. Joe* (1945) and *Battleground* (1949) were exceptional World War II films—the former based on the warfront reportage of journalist Ernie Pyle and the latter concerned with re-creating the crucial Battle of the Bulge. Robert Pirosh's screenplay for *Battleground* and Paul C. Vogel's cinematography received Academy Awards.

Most of Wellman's movies of the 1950's were unexceptional, although he had a sizable hit with *The High and the Mighty* (1954), a melodrama about an imperiled airliner. Wellman tried to duplicate the doom-ridden atmosphere of *The Ox-Bow Incident* with *Track of the Cat* (1954), concerning an embattled California ranch family, but the turgid screenplay defeated him. Wellman's last movie, *Lafayette Escadrille* (1958), dealt with the World War I flying group with which the director had once been mistakenly associated.

Wellman was married four times: to Helene Chadwick (1918–1920), Margery Chapin (1925–1928), Marjorie Crawford (ca. 1930–1932), and Dorothy Coonan (1932–1975). He had seven children with Dorothy Coonan.

Known throughout his career as a lusty, irreverent maverick, Wellman retired from filmmaking in the 1960's. In 1972, he received the prestigious D. W. Griffith Award of the Directors Guild "for distinguished achievement in motion picture directing." He died in Los Angeles.

[Wellman's autobiography, A Short Time for Insanity (1974), includes more information about his personal life than about his career. See also Kevin Brownlow, The Parade's Gone By (1968); Richard Schickel, The Men Who Made the Movies (1975); William R. Meyer, Warner Brothers Directors (1978); and Frank T. Thompson, William A. Wellman (1983). An obituary is in the New York Times, Dec. 11, 1975.]

TED SENNETT

WHEAT, ZACHARIAH DAVIS ("BUCK")
(May 23, 1888–Mar. 11, 1972), baseball player, was born in Bonanza, Mo., the son of Basil Curtis Wheat, a farmer, and Julia Davis. His father was born Basil DuBoise, but changed the family name to Wheat. In 1903 the Wheat family moved to Kansas City, Kans., where Basil worked at the local stockyards and Zach played sandlot baseball and graduated from the Switzer School. Wheat signed his first professional contract with the team the Enterprise of the Kansas League in 1906 and played the following two seasons with Shreveport and Mobile. Brooklyn Dodger scout Larry Sutton purchased Wheat's contract from Mobile in 1909 for $1,200, despite his meager .245 average.

Wheat joined a weak-hitting sixth-place Brooklyn team that would finish fifty-five and one-half games behind pennant-winning Pittsburgh. He made his debut going hitless against the great New York Giant pitcher Christy Mathewson at the Polo Grounds on Sept. 11, 1909, but quickly impressed his teammates and the league with his outstanding hitting and fielding. His .304 average over the final twenty-six games of the season presaged hitting that Brooklyn fans had not seen since Wee Willie Keeler left the Dodgers after the 1902 season. An established major leaguer by 1912, Wheat married Daisy Forsith in 1912. They had two children. Based on Zach's success in the major leagues, the Dodgers signed his brother Mack, who caught for the team between 1915 and 1919. Before he retired after the 1927 season,

"Buck" Wheat, so nicknamed because of his presumed Cherokee Indian heritage (a subject about which the reticent Wheat was quiet), established Dodger career records for most games played (2,322), most hits (2,804), most doubles (464), most triples (171), and most total bases (4,003), records that still stood in the late twentieth century. Indeed, Wheat played in more games than any other left fielder in the history of the major leagues. Branch Rickey, longtime Dodger, Cardinal, and Pirate baseball executive, once described Wheat as the best outfielder Brooklyn ever had. The Veterans Committee unanimously elected Wheat to the Baseball Hall of Fame in 1959.

Standing five feet, ten inches tall and weighing 170 pounds, Wheat's size was typical of major league ballplayers of the early twentieth century. Wheat's major physical attributes were his strong wrists and forearms, which generated his powerful left-handed swing. At the plate, Wheat held the bat at its handle and took a full cut with each swing. He attributed his batting success to his strong wrists, which enabled him to snap the bat with great velocity when striking the ball. Wheat was a renowned curveball hitter, and John J. McGraw, manager of the New York Giants, forbade his pitchers to throw curves to Wheat.

Although of average speed, Wheat was extremely graceful in the field, and his defensive skill earned the respect of his contemporaries. During his career with the Brooklyn Dodgers (1909–1926), Wheat patrolled a spacious left field, whose outfield fence was never less than 410 feet from home plate. Indeed, Wheat was regularly among the league leaders in outfield putouts, an unusual accomplishment for a left fielder.

The hallmark of Wheat's career was his offensive consistency. Except for a .258 average in 1915, he never batted lower than .284, and he hit over .300 in thirteen of his eighteen Brooklyn seasons, with a career average of .317. During his years with the Dodgers, Wheat batted cleanup, the position reserved for power hitters, but Wheat's power resulted in doubles and triples, rarely in home runs. Indeed, in 1918, when Wheat led the National League with a .335 average, he did not hit a single homer, the only time that has happened in league history. In the so-called deadball era, prior to 1920, Wheat's leading power season was in 1914, when he hit .319 with twenty-six doubles, nine triples, nine home runs, and eighty-nine runs-batted-in. For the decade 1910–1919, he averaged twenty-five doubles, ten triples, five homers, and a batting mark of .301. In 1916, when the Dodgers won the pennant for the first time since 1900, Wheat led the league with a .461 slugging percentage.

The 1920's heralded many changes in offensive baseball. Led by sluggers like Babe Ruth, Rogers Hornsby, and Lou Gehrig, batters sought to drive the ball over the fence rather than "hitting them where they ain't." Although Wheat turned thirty-two in 1920, his most productive seasons were from 1920 through 1927, when he retired at the advanced baseball age of thirty-nine. In 1923 and 1924 Wheat hit .375, but was outdistanced in the batting race each time. During the years 1920–1926, he averaged thirty-one doubles, nine triples, twelve homers, and an outstanding .340 batting mark. Prior to 1920, the most hits Wheat collected in a single season was 177, but thereafter he knocked out 200 hits three times, including 221 in 1925.

Wheat's career-long consistency made him a fan favorite who was never booed in Brooklyn. Perhaps that was due to his congenial, soft-spoken personality. His equanimity was evident in his never being ejected from a ball game during his long career. Extremely popular among his teammates, too, Wheat often invited six to eight players to dinner at his Brooklyn apartment after games. Fifty years after being teammates on the Dodgers, Casey Stengel remembered Wheat fondly, describing him as "one of the grandest guys ever to wear a baseball uniform. . . . one of the truest pals a man ever had and one of the kindliest men God ever created." Wheat was so well liked by his teammates that they helped him construct the elaborate stone walkway at his off-season Polo, Mo., home.

Wheat's fierce fortitude on the diamond was exemplified by two incidents in his career. In 1923 he played with a broken bone in his foot for one week until his condition was diagnosed. Limited to ninety-eight games because of the injury, Wheat nevertheless batted .375. Hobbled by leg injuries for most of his final season with Brooklyn in 1926, Wheat's last major league homer resulted in a five-minute trip around the bases, due to a severe charley horse.

Although Wheat was an extremely quiet man, he argued strongly for a higher salary. Wheat's stubbornness at contract time led to major confrontations with Dodgers owner Charles Ebbets. In 1914 Ebbets personally visited Wheat in Missouri to prevent him from jumping to the rival Federal League, and prior to the 1917 season, only the intervention of New York sportswriter Abe Yager persuaded Wheat to attend spring training. Wheat also promoted products ranging from iron supplements to flypaper. Indeed, the left-field fence at Ebbets Field contained an advertisement reading, "Wheat caught 384 flies last season. Tanglefoot caught 40 billion."

Wheat's greatest disappointment on the diamond was his failure to become Brooklyn's manager. Uncle Wilbert Robinson, the Dodgers manager since 1914, named Wheat to "replace" him in 1925, but the experiment lasted only a few games. Animosity between the two men hardened from that point and Wheat was released by the team following the 1926 season. Wheat played his final big league season in 1927 for Connie Mack's Philadelphia A's, and after playing for Minneapolis in the minor leagues in 1928 he retired from baseball.

During the Depression, Zach had to sell his 162-acre farm in Polo, and he moved to Kansas City, Mo., to operate a bowling alley. When that business failed, he joined the Kansas City police force in 1936, where, just one month into the job, he suffered severe injuries in a car crash while chasing a suspect. Forced to retire from the police, Wheat settled at Sunrise Beach, Mo., on the Lake of the Ozarks, where he ran a fishing camp that attracted many of his former teammates. Wheat's wife Daisy passed away in 1959, only months after Wheat was inducted into the Baseball Hall of Fame. Wheat died in Sedalis, Mo., at the age of eighty-three, while living with his daughter.

[The Baseball Hall of Fame Library, Cooperstown, N.Y., contains files on Wheat's baseball career. See also John J. Ward, "The Brooklyn Clean-Up Slugger," *Baseball Magazine*, July 1915, and "Zach Wheat: Most Graceful of Outfielders," *Baseball Magazine*, Jan. 1917; Lawrence Ritter and Donald Honig, *The Greatest 100 Baseball Players of All Time* (1986); David L. Porter, ed., *Biographical Dictionary of American Sports: Baseball* (1987); and Mike Shatzkin, ed., *The Ballplayers: Baseball's Ultimate Biographical Reference* (1990). Obituaries appear in the *New York Times* and the *Kansas City Star*, both Mar. 12, 1972; and in *Sporting News*, Mar. 25, 1972.]

STEPHEN WEINSTEIN

WHEELER, BURTON KENDALL (Feb. 27, 1882–Jan. 6, 1975), United States senator, was born in Hudson, Mass., the tenth and last child of Asa Leonard Wheeler, a cobbler and small farmer, and Mary Elizabeth Tyler. He graduated from Hudson High School in 1900 and worked for two years before entering the University of Michigan Law School, from which he graduated in 1905. Wheeler began to practice law in Butte, Mont., a copper-smelting town, where he soon established his own practice. He was married to Lulu White on Sept. 7, 1907; they had six children.

A Democrat, Wheeler was elected to the state legislature in 1910, where he drew attention to himself by opposing the giant Anaconda Copper Mining Company, then the dominant political and business force in Montana, where it controlled the Democratic party. Anaconda repaid Wheeler by contributing heavily to his defeat when he ran for state attorney general in 1912. Wheeler bounced back in 1913, when he was appointed United States district attorney general for the state by President Woodrow Wilson. In this capacity Wheeler prosecuted those who were in clear violation of the repressive espionage and sedition acts passed during World War I. However, he distinguished himself by his refusal to indict in marginal cases or when politics or prejudice were the real reasons for charges being leveled. During the postwar Red Scare, he finally resigned in disgust over the numerous violations of human rights being committed by overzealous enemies of radicalism.

In 1920, Wheeler ran for governor on the Non-Partisan League ticket and also that of the Democratic party, control of which he had wrested from Anaconda. He was then mercilessly red-baited by a rival Democratic organization, which Anaconda backed, and the campaign of slander, together with fears that his alleged radicalism would ruin the economy of Montana, assured Wheeler's defeat. The subsequent recession in Montana, part of a nationwide business decline, but which the defeat of Wheeler was supposed to have prevented, worked to his advantage. In 1922, backed by a coalition of farmers and railroad workers, and with the Democratic party now reunited behind him, Wheeler won election to the United States Senate.

Wheeler became a national figure as the result of a speech he gave to the Senate on Feb. 20, 1924, charging the attorney general of the United States, Harry M. Daugherty, with failing to prosecute those involved in the recently exposed Teapot Dome scandal (in which naval oil reserves had been secretly leased to private companies) and others who had violated federal statutes. After the Senate voted to conduct an inquiry, Wheeler was named to lead it. He presented witnesses who testified in detail about Daugherty's refusal to prosecute Teapot Dome and war fraud cases. When the hearings ended, President Calvin Coolidge forced Daugherty to resign. The Justice Department brought two criminal indictments against Wheeler in reprisal, but they collapsed of their own weight. In 1924, Wheeler ran for vice-president on the Progressive party ticket headed by Senator Robert M. La Follette of Wisconsin. The party's inevitable defeat at the hands of President Coolidge did not diminish Wheeler, who was widely held to have waged an effective campaign.

Wheeler was the first eminent Democrat outside New York State to support Franklin D. Roosevelt for the presidency, and he later supported the New Deal. His greatest service to the New Deal came in 1935 when, as chairman of the Interstate Commerce Committee, Wheeler led a successful fight to win passage of the Public Utilities Holding Company Act. This regulatory bill was hotly contested by the utilities lobby, so much so that Wheeler regarded the battle for it as the toughest he fought during his years in the Senate. Despite his loyalty to Roosevelt, Wheeler was never an administration favorite. He broke with the president in 1937 after Roosevelt proposed what became known as his "court-packing" scheme. The president asked for legislation that would enable him to appoint a new Supreme Court justice for every one who refused to retire upon reaching the age of seventy. Although put forward as a court-reform bill, the obvious intent was to provide the Court with a New Deal majority that would stop it from finding major administration legislation to be unconstitutional.

Wheeler was enraged by what seemed to him an unconstitutional power play, though the Constitution does not stipulate how many justices should serve on the court, and its size fluctuated until 1869. However, a majority of Americans agreed with Wheeler, and he continued to rally many senators to his cause despite a personal plea from Roosevelt to support the court-reform bill. Under his leadership the president's bill was defeated in the Senate by a margin of fifty votes, with only twenty senators voting in its favor. Wheeler attributed his victory in large part to a letter he read to the Senate Judiciary Committee criticizing the bill that had been signed by both Chief Justice Charles Evans Hughes, a conservative, and Associate Justice Louis D. Brandeis, a liberal. This loss was far and away the worst defeat Roosevelt had sustained up to that time, and it restored the traditional adversarial relationship between the legislative and executive branches that had collapsed during his first term.

Wheeler is best remembered as an opponent of American entry into World War II. Indeed, after the death of Senator William Borah of Idaho in 1940, Wheeler became the leading isolationist in Congress. Never the most guarded of speakers, Wheeler attacked, sometimes recklessly, every step that appeared to him likely to promote intervention. He insisted that there would be a revolution if the United States joined the war. After the program of aid to Britain known as Lend-Lease was introduced, Wheeler called it the "New Deal's triple-A foreign policy—it will plow under every fourth American boy." At his next press conference, Roosevelt characterized Wheeler's remark as "the most untruthful," the "most dastardly, unpatriotic thing that has been said in public life in my generation."

Nor did Wheeler confine himself to rhetoric. He voted against every bill that might increase the risk of war, and he also released information that had the potential of harming American security. On July 3, 1941, he called a press conference to announce that the United States was going to occupy Iceland. This announcement came not only before the administration released this information, but even before the troops had embarked, thus putting their lives at risk in the event of a hostile response by German U-boats.

Shortly before the Japanese attack on Pearl Harbor, Wheeler passed on to the *Chicago Tribune* a classified War Department document known as the "Victory Plan," which outlined the steps to be taken if America went to war. Wheeler had received it from a dissident Army Air Force officer, and its publication is believed by some historians to have influenced Hitler's decision to declare war on the United States, since, among other things, it revealed that the

United States would not be strong enough to invade Europe before 1943 at the earliest. In theory, this would have given Germany a free hand for at least eighteen months, during which time Hitler expected to defeat Russia and make his European empire impregnable. No action was taken against Wheeler for this leak as Pearl Harbor was attacked within days, putting an end to isolationism.

Although Wheeler supported the war effort, like most of the prominent former isolationists in Congress he failed in his next bid for reelection, losing his seat in 1946. Thereafter, Wheeler practiced corporate law in Washington, D.C., with one of his sons and backed a variety of right-wing causes. The former progressive and foe of what he called the "copper trust" was now firmly in what he had once regarded as the enemy camp. When another hunt for Communists broke out following World War II, Wheeler publicly supported Senator Joseph McCarthy of Wisconsin, the new Red Scare's leading figure.

Wheeler was a man of striking paradoxes in other ways, too. A powerful and sharp-tongued speaker, he was courteous in private. An independent and at times ruthless politician, he often seemed happiest when he was in opposition or on the attack. Yet, contrary to what might be expected, Wheeler was effective within the Senate, where his legislative skills, deal-making and arm-twisting abilities, and proficiency at stroking egos made him a leading figure. Although historians do not rank him with such modern Senate giants as George Norris, Robert Taft, and Lyndon Johnson, Wheeler cannot be denied a place among the runners-up. He died in Washington, D.C.

[Wheeler's autobiography, written with the aid of Paul F. Healy, is *Yankee from the West* (1962). See also Wayne S. Cole, *Roosevelt and the Isolationists, 1932–1945* (1983).

Obituaries are in the *New York Times* and the *Washington Post*, both Jan. 8, 1975].

WILLIAM L. O'NEILL

WHEELER, EARLE GILMORE (Jan. 13, 1908–Dec. 18, 1975), army officer, was born in Washington, D.C., the son of Clifton F. Wheeler, a dentist, and Ida Gilmore. He graduated from Eastern High School in Washington in 1925 and from Millard's West Point Preparatory School in the capital city in 1928.

From 1924 to 1928, he also served in the National Guard of the District of Columbia, becoming a platoon sergeant. His company participated in several interservice rifle matches. Wheeler entered the United States Military Academy in 1928. Wheeler, known as "Buster" or "Bus" to his classmates and army colleagues at West Point, was a good student and served as cadet lieutenant in his senior year. Graduating with a B.S. as a second lieutenant of infantry in June 1932, Wheeler spent four years with the Twenty-ninth Infantry at Fort Benning, Ga. He married Frances Rogers Howell on June 10, 1932; they had one son.

Lieutenant Wheeler attended the Infantry Officer's Course at the Infantry School in Fort Benning, then left for Tientsin, China, in June 1937, to serve with the Fifteenth Infantry. He returned to West Point in the summer of 1940 to serve as a mathematics instructor for the academic year, and then briefly served as aide-de-camp to the commanding general of the Thirty-sixth Infantry Division at Fort Sam Houston and Camp Bowie, Tex. In December 1941, Captain Wheeler entered the Command and General Staff College at Fort Leavenworth, Kans., completing the accelerated course the following February. Following a six-month tour of duty as Second Battalion commander in the 141st Infantry Regiment, Thirty-sixth Infantry Division, at Camp Blanding, Fla., Major Wheeler became assistant chief of staff for operations for the Ninety-ninth Infantry Division at Camp Van Dorn, Miss. In May 1943, Lieutenant Colonel Wheeler was appointed chief of staff for the newly formed Sixty-third Infantry Division at Camp Van Dorn. In December 1944, he went to France with his division, remaining in combat until shortly before V-E Day in the spring of 1945. Although he sought to command a regimental combat team when an opening developed, his commander requested that he remain as his chief of staff. At the close of the European campaign, Wheeler's division commander sent him a handwritten letter stating that Wheeler was primarily responsible for the division's outstanding performance in combat.

Late in 1945, Wheeler, by now a temporary full colonel, was appointed senior instructor of combined arms at the Artillery School, Fort Sill, Okla. He returned to Europe in May 1946 for successive assignments as assistant chief of staff for supply, acting chief of staff, and deputy chief of staff for operations at the Western Base Section, European Command, in Paris. In January 1947, he began a thirty-month tour of duty as assistant chief of operations at the headquarters of the United States constabulary in Heidelberg, Germany. In August 1949, Wheeler, who had reverted to the grade of lieutenant colonel, became a student at the National War College in Washington, D.C., graduating in June 1950. He was then assigned as a member of the Joint Intelligence Group in the office of the Joint Chiefs of Staff for fifteen months. In November 1951, Wheeler was once again a full colonel, and was selected to command the 351st Infantry in Trieste, Italy. A year later, he was assigned as readiness officer and later as assistant chief of staff for Plans and Operations, Allied Forces Southern Europe, with headquarters in Naples. He was selected for a brigadier generalship in November 1952, and remained in Naples until September 1955. He returned to Washington, D.C., as director of plans in the office of the deputy chief of staff for military operations, and was promoted to major general in December 1955. On one occasion in 1956, Major General Wheeler, representing the Defense Department, directed a practice drill at the mountain center of western Maryland to which federal agency heads were ordered to take shelter in the event of a national emergency. The general was junior in rank to most of those present, but he nevertheless made a strong impression.

In June 1957, Wheeler was appointed assistant deputy chief of staff for military operations, and in October 1958, went to Fort Hood, Tex., as commanding general of the Second Armored Division. In March 1959, he assumed additional duties as commanding general of the Third Corps, remaining at Fort Hood. In April 1960, the newly promoted Lieutenant General Wheeler returned to the Pentagon as director of the Joint Staff, Department of Defense, remaining in that post until February 1962. He was designated a full general and deputy commander in chief of the United States European Command at Camp des Loges, France, in March 1962, and served in that capacity until September 1962.

When President John F. Kennedy sought a new chief of staff for the army in the fall of 1962, he queried the service chiefs of the navy, air force, and marine corps for their suggestions, and all three recommended Wheeler, who was appointed army chief of staff on Oct.

1, 1962. Having just arrived in Washington, Wheeler was called to the Pentagon because state officials in Oxford, Miss., had lost control of a rapidly accelerating racial confrontation arising from integration at the University of Mississippi. Wheeler's predecessor had already left the city, and Wheeler had not yet been sworn in. After watching the senior officer in command attempt to deal with the situation, Wheeler took over. A colleague who was present later stated, "Everything started to move. It was like a breath of fresh air." In July 1964, President Lyndon Johnson elevated Wheeler to the post of chairman of the Joint Chiefs of Staff, the highest military office in the United States. Wheeler held this position for six years, longer than any of his predecessors or successors to date. He assumed office during the period when American military forces were being sent in large numbers to Vietnam, and remained until plans for their return had been formulated.

Wheeler's eight years of increasingly demanding responsibilities under Presidents Kennedy, Johnson, and Nixon took an enormous toll. As chairman of the Joint Chiefs of Staff, he made many difficult decisions, most of which had political and diplomatic, as well as military, implications; for example, his decision to follow President Johnson's orders to begin secret air strikes over Cambodia in 1969 was especially controversial. President Johnson held the general in the highest regard, referring to Wheeler in his autobiography, *The Vantage Point* (1971), in forty-three separate recollections. Wheeler survived one serious heart attack, which was not immediately diagnosed, without taking leave from his duties, but toward the end of his tour of duty, was accompanied on all out-of-town trips by a physician.

On July 2, 1970, the forty-second anniversary of his arrival at West Point as a plebe, Wheeler retired from active duty. To accommodate all who wished to attend, the retirement ceremony was held in a hangar at Andrews Air Force Base. Wheeler was awarded the first Department of Defense Distinguished Service Medal. His other decorations included the army, navy, and air force Distinguished Service medals, each the highest military honor conferred during times of peace. In addition, he held ten other American decorations and a dozen foreign ones. In retirement, Wheeler and his wife took up residence outside of Martins-

burg, W. Va. He became a director of the Monsanto Corporation, served on the President's Commission on White House Fellowships, and periodically traveled to Washington for consultations at the Pentagon. Wheeler, a well-built, handsome man of more than six feet, died in a hospital in Frederick, Md., following a brief illness.

[The Special Collections Division of the West Point Library and the United States Army's Center of Military History in Washington, D.C., have a variety of information concerning Wheeler's military career. A biographical sketch appears in the West Point alumni magazine *Assembly*, Dec. 1976. An obituary appears in the *New York Times*, Dec. 19, 1975.]
KEIR B. STERLING

WHITE, PAUL DUDLEY (June 6, 1886–Oct. 31, 1973), physician and cardiologist, was born in Roxbury, Mass., the son of Herbert Warren White and Elizabeth Abigail Dudley. White's interest in medicine was kindled early in life, when he accompanied his father, a family practitioner, on rounds and house calls in a horse and buggy. His undergraduate education at Harvard encompassed history and forestry as well as premedical courses. He graduated with a B.A. with honors in 1908 and went on to Harvard Medical School; he received his M.D. in 1911. He then began his long association with the Massachusetts General Hospital through an internship in pediatrics and internal medicine. During that time he coauthored, with Dr. Roger I. Lee, his first scientific paper, on the coagulation of blood. The Lee-White coagulation time is still used today as a method of measuring the speed of blood coagulation. In 1913, White was offered a Harvard traveling fellowship to study cardiovascular physiology with Dr. Thomas Lewis in London. This experience, perhaps coupled with the earlier death of his sister from rheumatic heart disease and his father's death from coronary artery disease at age seventy-one, was to shape the rest of his medical career.

White served as a medical officer with the British expeditionary force in 1916 and the U.S. expeditionary force from 1917 to 1919. He returned to the Massachusetts General Hospital and worked as a resident in 1919, and a year later became Chief of the Medical Out-Patient Department. He also was appointed to the Harvard faculty as a clinical instructor in 1921 and quickly rose through the academic ranks to become assistant professor in 1933, clinical professor in 1946, and emeritus professor in 1949. He continued on the faculty of Harvard until 1956, although he had resigned his position as Chief of the Cardiac Service at the Massachusetts General Hospital in 1948 to devote time to the development of the National Heart Institute, following adoption of the National Heart Act, which was signed into law by President Truman in 1948.

White was recognized as a superb teacher and compassionate bedside physician. He published twelve books and more than seven hundred scientific articles. His most noted textbook, *Heart Disease*, was first published in 1931 and became a classic in the field. His interest in the electrophysiology of the heart would eventually pair him with Drs. Louis Wolff and John Parkinson, who together described the Wolff-Parkinson-White syndrome, a condition of uncontrolled rapid heartbeat.

On June 28, 1924, White married Ina Helen Reid, a social worker whom he met while giving a lecture at the Smith College Training School for Social Work. They later adopted two children.

Paul Dudley White is viewed by most medical authorities as the founder of preventive cardiology. Appointed as President Dwight David Eisenhower's physician following his heart attack in 1955, White was a pioneer in the use of the electrocardiograph and a staunch advocate of exercise, diet, and weight control in the prevention of heart disease. In 1924, he was one of the founders of the American Heart Association and became the organization's president in 1941. He was a moving force in the creation of the International Association of Cardiology, and later the International Cardiology Foundation. In 1949, he was named executive director of the National Advisory Heart Council. He was the chief consultant to the National Heart Institute from 1948 to 1955 and was a major impetus in the Framingham Longitudinal Heart Study, which was the first major epidemiologic work to identify risk factors in coronary artery disease. He was also influential in founding the American Red Cross and establishing the National Institutes of Health.

White received many international honors and was instrumental in establishing cardiology organizations throughout the world, even in China, which he was one of the first American physicians to visit. He also established an association with Alexander Filipovich Samoiloff, a Russian physiologist who shared White's interest in the electrophysiology of the heart.

White was a staunch advocate of the belief that life-style affected coronary artery disease. He was one of the first authorities to recognize that coronary artery disease could occur in young men, writing several papers on the subject. In keeping with his beliefs, he was a vigorous walker and bicycle rider and walked, on one occasion, from the Washington airport to the White House to consult with President Eisenhower. Reportedly, his positive approach inspired Lyndon Johnson to return to the Senate in 1955 after his heart attack and later to become vice-president.

In his later years, White continued to travel and to speak about heart disease and, increasingly, about his concern for world peace.

Paul Dudley White died in Boston, following a second stroke. He was to have received the Herrick Award from the American Heart Association, but died before that honor could be bestowed. At a memorial service in the Harvard Memorial Church the next month, J. Willis Hurst, M.D., a former student of White's, delivered a eulogy entitled "I'm Not Through Yet." Paul Dudley White's influence on American medicine is truly not through yet.

[White's autobiography is *My Life and Medicine* (1971). Also see Paul Oglesby, *Take Heart* (1986), the definitive biography. Insightful articles on the life of Paul Dudley White include J. Willis Hurst, M.D., "Paul Dudley White: To Know Him Better," *American Journal of Cardiology* 56; and "Tribute to Paul Dudley White" by Lown and Chazov in *Preventive Medicine* 16 (1987). An obituary appears in the *New York Times*, Nov. 1, 1973.]

PHILLIP THARP SWENDER

WHITNEY, RICHARD (Aug. 1, 1888–Dec. 5, 1974), banker, investment counselor, and embezzler, was born in Beverly, Mass. He was descended from immigrants who arrived in Massachusetts in 1630. His father, George Whitney, was a leading Boston banker. Whitney graduated from Groton and from Harvard, where he was elected to the prestigious Porcellan Club. He moved to New York City in 1910 and became a member of the New York Stock Exchange in 1912, at the age of twenty-three. Soon afterward he was principal broker for J. P. Morgan and

Company, of which his brother, George, was later vice-president. During World War I, Whitney was a dollar-per-year executive for the Food Administration, headed by Herbert Hoover, in Washington, D.C.

In the 1920's Whitney was a member of every major club and organization to which a member of the eastern aristocracy should belong. He was treasurer of the New York Yacht Club. He had large and opulent estates; he bred horses; and he was reputed to spend $5,000 per month on maintenance alone, a huge figure for that time. He was married in 1916 to a young widow, Gertrude Sheldon Sands; they had three children. Whitney took over her father's investment business, Cummings and Markwald, and immediately renamed it Richard Whitney and Company. In 1919 he was elected to the governing board of the New York Stock Exchange.

Whitney epitomized the "old guard" of the New York Stock Exchange, a loose grouping of wealthy individuals who acted as leaders in its affairs. At the height of the panic on Oct. 24, 1929, as representative of this group, he moved onto the floor of the exchange and placed purchase orders in an effort to stem the rush of selling. The story of his arrival at the floor location for transactions in the shares of U.S. Steel, and casually placing an order for ten thousand shares at 205, forty points above the market price, elevated him to public fame. He also placed orders that day, acting for the governing consortium, for from fifteen to twenty other blue-chip stocks, in an attempt to stabilize prices. These orders were estimated to amount to $20 million to $30 million during that single afternoon, the largest personal trading episodes of all time. Everyone on the exchange assumed that he was trading in the Morgan interest, and the effort did help to stabilize trading for the time being, at least in the blue-chip share accounts.

Whitney served on virtually every significant committee of the exchange, including the business conduct committee. At the time of his efforts in 1929, he was vice-president and acting president. He served five terms as president of the exchange beginning in 1930. During this time he was the spokesperson for the "Old Guard," which came increasingly under attack from the newly created Securities and Exchange Commission, a part of the New Deal of Franklin Roosevelt. He appeared as a witness at congressional hearings throughout the period from 1932 to 1935.

Whitney chose not to run again for the presidency of the exchange in 1935, as reform elements, becoming more active in its affairs, indicated that he would be opposed. He was heavily involved at this time in speculative investments in firms manufacturing apple brandy, peat fertilizer, and marine colloids. In order to keep these companies afloat, he borrowed heavily from friends and acquaintances, using his ties with J. P. Morgan as a sort of collateral. In March 1938, his world collapsed. New and tighter reporting regulations on personal finance revealed that Whitney had been a terrible manager of his own and other people's money. Investigation of his affairs demonstrated that he had been borrowing against funds in his trust since at least 1926.

When the final investigations were made public, it was estimated that Whitney had borrowed over $30 million from his friends, his family, and the accounts in his trust. When he declared bankruptcy, he owed approximately $6.5 million. He was indicted on one count of misuse of funds, from his father-in-law's estate, and pled guilty as charged. He served three years and four months of a five-to-ten-year sentence in Sing Sing. His brother eventually paid all of his debts. When Whitney was released from prison, he moved to a family-owned dairy farm in Barnstable, Mass., where he dropped out of public view. His wife stood by him during his problems, selling all of their assets, except her personal jewelry. Whitney died in Short Hills, N.J.

Much of the reform of the practices of the New York Stock Exchange and other bond and share money markets can be dated to the events of Richard Whitney's life. His activities on the exchange, which had shocked the world of the wealthy—Franklin Roosevelt came close to breaking down when he heard of the defalcations—provided the impetus to reform and reconstruct the money market. In a sense, then, his life ultimately had a substantial positive impact.

[No collections of papers or biographies are known. Books that have a good deal of information on Whitney's life and his career include Ferdinand Pecora, *Wall Street Under Oath* (1939); John Nixon Brooks, *Once in Golconda* (1952); John Kenneth Galbraith, *The Great Crash* (1954); Cedric B. Cowing, *Populists, Plungers and Progressives* (1965); and Joel Seligman, *The Transformation of Wall Street* (1982). See also Securities and Exchange Commission, *In the Matter of Richard Whitney*, 2 vols. (1938); and *Securities and Exchange Act of 1934, as Amended to February 5, 1976* (1979) and . . . *to 1991* (1991). Contemporary coverage is in the *New York Times*, Mar. 9 and 15, Apr. 10, and Oct. 25, 1938. An obituary is in the *New York Times*, Dec. 6, 1974.]

DAVID SMITH

WHITTAKER, CHARLES EVANS (Feb. 22, 1901–Nov. 26, 1973), Supreme Court justice, was born on a farm near Troy, Kans., the son of Charles Evans Whittaker and Ida E. Miller. He attended a one-room schoolhouse on his father's farm for nine years, then rode a pony six miles to high school every day until his mother died in 1917, whereupon he quit school to help his father. In 1920, he attended the University of Kansas City Law School in Missouri, a night school that he talked his way into without the required high school diploma. He worked as an office boy for a law firm and received tutoring in his missed high school subjects by day. He graduated from the law school with an LL.B. in 1924 after having joined the bar the previous year. He married Winifred R. Pugh on July 7, 1928; they had three sons.

In 1930 he became a partner with Watson, Gage, Ess, Groner and Barnett of Kansas City, for whom he had formerly been an office worker. It numbered the Union Pacific Railroad, Montgomery Ward, and the City National Bank and Trust Company among its clients. Whittaker was a courtroom lawyer until World War II, when he took on the senior counsel role of advising the firm's larger clients. As part of that role, he became active in bar association activities and dabbled in local Republican politics.

In 1954 the Eisenhower administration appointed Whittaker as federal district court judge in Kansas City. He even received the enthusiastic backing of local labor leaders. Quickly confirmed, he began at once to whittle away at the local court calendar. His most controversial opinion came in *Davis* v. *University of Kansas City*, in which he upheld the dismissal of an economics professor who refused to answer U.S. Senate committee questions concerning possible Communist affiliations. Whittaker noted that Davis had a right to refuse to answer such questions, but "the public will not stand, and they ought not to stand, for such reticence . . . by teachers in their schools." In 1956, Ei-

senhower named Whittaker to the Eighth Circuit Court of Appeals, which heard cases coming from Whittaker's district court. The new judge lasted on the circuit bench for only eight months before being elevated to the Supreme Court of the United States. He was sworn in on Mar. 25, 1957.

Although Eisenhower's first appointment to the Court had been a politician—Governor Earl Warren—Eisenhower wanted, in his words, "an inkling" of what a new appointee might do, and so he sought sitting judges as Court nominees. Whittaker was a logical choice, therefore, to take over the vacancy left by the retiring Stanley Reed—a border-state conservative.

When Whittaker assumed the bench he promptly joined the middle-of-the-road wing, voting most often with the nonphilosophical Harold Burton and then with moderates Felix Frankfurter and Thomas Clark. He provided the deciding vote in the 1957 decision of *Green* v. *United States* in holding that a man tried for first-degree murder but found guilty only of a second-degree homicide could not later be retried for the more serious offense. In 1957, he also voted to provide a new trial for a seventeen-year-old head-injured boy accused of murder in the case of *Moore* v. *Michigan*, because it could not be proven that the boy waived his right to counsel.

More frequently, he sided with conservatives. According to Leon Friedman, in forty-one instances he voted with the conservatives to create a five-man majority. He frequently favored enhanced penalties for crimes and upheld free use of a judge's contempt power and of the power to punish former Communists or those who refused to answer questions concerning their political party affiliations. In another case in 1961, *Poe* v. *Ullman*, he voted with a bare majority on the Court, which refused to hear whether Connecticut's rarely-used anti–birth control statute offended the federal Constitution. (In 1965, the Court would hear the matter and decide the statute was unconstitutional.) Typically, Whittaker voted to avoid hard questions, leaving them for a later time. Friedman also notes that many of Whittaker's swing votes were later overruled by the Warren-era Court.

Whittaker said that he "read[s] the law only for an understanding of its meaning and enforce[s] it in accordance with my understanding of its meaning." He thus denied any ideological slant to his Court work. This reliance on nonpolitical principles of interpretation did not strike a responsive cord with Warren-era legal scholars, but it was received more warmly later in the century when the Court saw itself as merely interpreting the law with as little interference as possible from its own notions of constitutionality or propriety. Whittaker may well be remembered mostly for his opinions concerning the extent of the taxing power conferred on the states by the Constitution.

In March 1962, he entered Walter Reed Army Hospital, suffering from fatigue. He was confined there when the Court handed down its far-reaching *Baker* v. *Carr* decision, holding that state legislatures must be apportioned on a one-person, one-vote principle. Whittaker chafed at his inability to participate, and this may have led him to resign from the Court three days later, on Mar. 26, 1962. In October 1965, he resigned his status as a retired judge so he could join General Motors' legal staff. Later he acted as an adviser to a Senate ethics committee. He died in Kansas City, Mo.

[See the article on Whittaker in Leon Friedman and Fred L. Israel, eds., *The Justices of the United States Supreme Court, 1789–1978: Their Lives and Major Opinions* IV (1978). "Mr. Justice Whittaker: A Preliminary Appraisal," *Missouri Law Review* 24 (1959) is the only major article on Whittaker. An obituary is in the *New York Times*, Nov. 27, 1973.]

JOHN DAVID HEALY

WIDENER, GEORGE DUNTON (Mar. 11, 1889–Dec. 8, 1971), sportsman and philanthropist, was born into one of Philadelphia's oldest and wealthiest families, the son of the elder George D. Widener and Eleanor W. Elkins, both philanthropists. He had two siblings. His father and his older brother, Harry Elkins Widener, were lost in the sinking of the *Titanic* in 1912.

Educated privately and at the Delancey School in Philadelphia, Widener established a lifelong association with thoroughbred racing when his silks, light blue and dark blue hoops with dark blue cap, were registered in 1913. Three years later he was elected to The Jockey Club and bought Erdenheim Farm, in suburban Whitemarsh Township, where he began thoroughbred breeding in earnest. Columbine became his first homebred stakes winner that same year by winning the Walden at Pimlico Racetrack in Baltimore. On Mar. 20, 1917,

Widener married Jessie Sloane in New York City. They had no children and remained married until Jessie's death more than fifty years later. Following America's declaration of war against Germany in April 1917, Widener was commissioned a lieutenant in the United States Army's Quartermaster Corps and served stateside for the duration of the conflict.

To expand breeding operations, Widener acquired Old Kenney Farm near Lexington, Ky., in 1923. Great successes followed, beginning with St. James's victory in that year's Futurity at Belmont Park in New York City. During his long pursuit of excellence in the sport, Widener bred 100 stakes winners, including Jamestown, High Fleet, Platter, Stefanita, Jaipur, and What A Treat. His horses won 1,243 races, including multiple victories in the Flash, Travers, Futurity, Sanford, Hopeful, and Saratoga Special, with career earnings from all Widener mounts totaling well in excess of nine million dollars. Yet breeding thoroughbreds was only one of his concerns.

Widener dedicated his life to the advancement of all aspects of thoroughbred racing. Along with his uncle Joseph E. Widener—a leader in the field—and his cousin, Peter A. B. Widener III, Widener helped define the sport as a business in 1928. The Bureau of Internal Revenue had sought over $900,000 in what it declared to be back taxes. However, a federal court found that financial losses incurred in thoroughbred racing and breeding were legitimate business deductions and not subject to taxation. The ruling thereafter broadened investment opportunities in the sport.

As a consequence of such activities, Widener's leadership abilities were soon recognized, leading him to positions of increasing responsibility within racing circles. From 1942 to 1955 he was president of the Westchester Racing Association, which operated Belmont Park. During Widener's tenure, the Widener Turf Course—named in honor of his uncle—was established at the track. In 1955 he was elected honorary chairman of the Greater New York Racing Association. He also served the Jockey Club in similar capacities: as steward in 1943, vice-chairman from 1947 to 1950, and chairman from 1950 to 1964. Widener thereafter served the organization as honorary chairman.

Under his leadership, the Jockey Club refined the methods of registering racing silks, established a school to improve the quality of racing officials, classified thoroughbred blood types to reduce the dangers implicit in transfusions, and improved horse identification practices. It also began Round Table Conferences that enabled representatives from all segments of the thoroughbred racing and breeding community to discuss mutual problems.

Widener, however, being conservative by nature, actively resisted efforts throughout his lifetime that he believed would overcommercialize the sport. He was opposed to night racing and off-track betting, and he considered the use of the drug Butazolidin "a disservice to racing." Widener even denied himself an opportunity to win the Triple Crown of racing by never entering horses in the Kentucky Derby, believing the mile-and-one-quarter distance too arduous for young three-year-olds.

In 1962 Widener experienced his greatest racing victory when homebred colt Jaipur, with legendary jockey Willie Shoemaker aboard, won the Belmont by a nose. Widener's nine previous entries, dating back to 1918, had resulted in three second-place finishes in the longest race of the Triple Crown. (Though a longer race than the Derby, the Belmont race came later in the season when a three-year-old horse was more mature.) Yet Widener's passion for racing went well beyond the Winner's Circle.

He was a leading spokesman for the establishment of The Jockey Club Foundation to provide relief for indigent racing people. Hence, it was not surprising that the Horsemen's Benevolent and Protective Association honored him in 1954 with its first "Man of the Year" award. Widener's contributions to racing were also recognized by the Jockey Agents Benevolent Association, the Thoroughbred Club of America, and the Turf and Field Club, among others. His presentation as the first Exemplar of Racing by the National Museum of Racing in 1971 in recognition of "a role so influential in [the] sport" was a fitting pinnacle to his lifelong avocation. Possibly most revealing of his close relationship with the people of the sport was Widener's association with his trainers. Only three men—Jack Joyner, Bert Mulholland, and Syl Veitch—held that position over the course of a half-century of Widener racing.

Although racing was his main avocation, Widener expended great energy and money supporting the humanities. He endowed the Widener Library at Harvard University, and

presented a Gutenberg Bible to the school in 1944. He contributed valuable pieces of art and more than forty years of leadership to the Philadelphia Museum of Art, ultimately serving as chairman of the board from 1947 to 1964, and was a director of the Smithsonian Institution's National Gallery of Art in Washington, D.C. Widener also served as a trustee of Philadelphia's Academy of Natural Sciences, Chestnut Hill Hospital, and Zoological Gardens. Other organizations that enjoyed his philanthropy included the Metropolitan Museum of Art in New York City, the Philadelphia Orchestra, the Pennsylvania Academy of Fine Arts, and the Saratoga Springs Performing Arts Center. An Episcopalian, Widener supported the Episcopal Divinity School of Philadelphia and the Episcopal Theological School in Cambridge, Mass.

Born into a life of gentility, George D. Widener openly shared his talents and wealth with the broader community. He died at Erdenheim Farm, his longtime home outside Philadelphia, a true "aristocrat of the American turf."

[Numerous addresses and commentary by Widener are found in *The Blood-Horse*, as are annotations concerning his horse-racing career. William H. Rudy, *Racing in America 1960–1979* (1980), offers minor biographical information. Obituaries are in the *New York Times*, Dec. 9, 1971; the *Philadelphia Inquirer*, Dec. 9, 1971; and *The Blood-Horse*, Dec. 20, 1971.]

WILLIAM E. FISCHER, JR.

WIGHTMAN, HAZEL VIRGINIA HOTCHKISS (Dec. 20, 1886–Dec. 5, 1974), tennis champion, was born in Healdsburg, Calif., the fourth of five children of William Joseph Hotchkiss and Emma Lucretia Grove. Her father, a farmer and rancher, was a founder of the California Packing Corporation.

The family's only daughter, Wightman was a frail, sickly child whose severe headaches often kept her home from school. On the advice of the family doctor, her parents encouraged her to participate in outdoor sports with her four brothers. The regimen, she said, led to her development as a "fair" pole-vaulter, halfback, and baseball player and to world-class achievements in her first love—tennis.

When Wightman was fourteen, the family moved to Berkeley, Calif. In 1902, she and her brothers saw their first regional tennis competition—the Pacific Coast Championship matches in San Rafael, an event she later described as the first time she had seen tennis played well and by rules.

In an era when women traditionally played a sedate baseline game, Wightman and her brothers were impressed by the faster volleying style of net play used by the male players at San Rafael and soon adapted it to their own backyard games. Wightman's mastery of volleying was later described by sportswriters as the finest in women's tennis.

In December 1902, six months after the San Rafael tournament, Wightman entered and won her first organized contest, a doubles competition sponsored by the San Francisco Parks Commission. Her partner was Mary Radcliffe, a young woman she had met for the first time on the ferry ride to the matches.

Wightman's rushing style and speedy footwork quickly established her as the girl to beat in local competition. As she continued to defeat all opponents in northern California, she advanced into statewide tournaments, where she often faced the stars of southern California women's tennis of that era: the four Sutton sisters from Pasadena.

After several decisive defeats by various Sutton sisters, Wightman turned the tables in the 1906 Pacific Coast Championships, when she defeated Ethel Sutton. Subsequently she disposed of Violet and Florence Sutton, but was as often the loser as the winner when confronted by the youngest of the Sutton clan, May. This sectional rivalry continued with both women winning victories at state matches that sometimes drew as many as two thousand spectators. Years later, May's daughter, Dorothy Bundy, was one of Hazel's protégées and one of her favorite pupils.

In 1909, after her sophomore year at the University of California at Berkeley, Wightman and her father traveled to Philadelphia, where the U.S. National Championships were being held. The trip was a huge success; she swept the women's singles, women's doubles, and mixed doubles—the first of her record forty-five national titles. Wightman successfully defended all three titles in the following two years. In 1911, as a college graduation present, her parents permitted her to stay in the East for four months— time she put to good use, winning regional tournaments from western Pennsylvania to Newport, R.I., and defeating her old nemesis, May Sutton, at Niagara-on-the Lake, Ontario.

In June 1912, she married George William Wightman, an attorney from Boston; they had five children. The Wightmans were divorced in 1940. Her husband, who had excelled in racket sports at Harvard University, was president of the U.S. Lawn Tennis Association in 1924.

For most of the rest of the decade, Wightman was occupied with her growing family and occasionally played in tennis tournaments. Returning to full-scale competition in 1919, she soon won the national women's singles title, ten years after her first national singles victory. She also began to coach, guide, and develop the careers of younger women players.

During visits to California, Wightman sought out promising beginners and invited them to live with her in Brookline, Mass., while competing in eastern tournaments. Among those for whom she was hostess, teacher, and confidante were Helen Wills, Sarah Palfrey, Althea Gibson, Helen Jacobs, Maureen Connelly, and Dorothy Bundy, daughter of her former archrival May Sutton.

In addition to diagnosing and correcting technical flaws, "Mrs. Wightie," as she was known to generations of pupils, dispensed detailed instructions on proper decorum, stressing "ladylike" behavior, a generic description that ranged from being gracious in defeat to shunning flesh-colored undergarments.

In 1919, Wightman initiated a plan for annual team matches between British and American women, a companion competition to the Davis Cup in men's tennis. She donated the tall silver cup known as the Wightman Cup, although her name does not appear in its engraved title, "Challenge Cup—Ladies' Team Match."

Wightman was captain of the American Wightman Cup team from 1923 to 1931 and was nonplaying captain until 1949. On the fiftieth anniversary of the cup in 1973, she was made an honorary commander of the British Empire. Representing the United States in the 1924 Olympics in Paris, Wightman brought home gold medals in both women's doubles (with Helen Wills) and mixed doubles—the latter was especially noteworthy because her partner, Dick Williams, had an Achilles tendon injury and could hardly move. Wightman was a national squash champion in 1927 and a national badminton finalist.

Although many references list the number of national championships Wightman held as forty-four, others state the number as forty-five.

At the age of fifty-six, she won her last major circuit title, the National Indoor Doubles, with Pauline Betz. In 1954, at the age of sixty-seven, Wightman and Nell Hopman won the National Senior Doubles for "women over forty." Three years later, she was inducted into the International Tennis Hall of Fame at Newport, R.I.

Proud as she was of her many pupils who went on to national recognition, the tiny (just over five feet) white-haired "Queen Mother of Tennis" had a special place in her heart for the hundreds of less-known young women who attended her free instructional classes. She taught at the Longwood Cricket Club near her home in Chestnut Hill, Mass., in the big brown garage at her home, and at tennis camps and playgrounds all over Massachusetts.

Often speaking of a "special feeling about the awkward and shy ones," Wightman believed that by their doing something well that was admired by others, the confidence and poise so achieved might lead to a fuller, happier life. In an interview in *American Heritage*, given only two weeks before her death, she recalled that in her childhood she was often called "the plain one" with four handsome brothers. Her empathy for those who had to work hard to achieve distinctions that came easily to others may have had early beginnings.

An amateur in the best sense of the word, Wightman never accepted money for lessons or for any service to tennis. She also gave generously to her community and received many honors for her service to the American Red Cross and Boston Children's Hospital.

During the mid-1930's, Wightman decided to put to good use the time she spent waiting to pick up her children at their schools. The result was a small but popular text, *Better Tennis* (1933), published by Houghton Mifflin. In addition to basic instruction, the book includes "Mrs. Wightman's Tennis Alphabet," a collection of maxims from "Always Alert" and "Don't Dally" to "Quash Qualms" and "Zip Zip." Wightman died in Chestnut Hill, Mass.

In a *Boston Sunday Globe* retrospective piece (Dec. 8, 1974) an anonymous writer observed: "She was a Californian of pioneer stock, but became the epitome of a Boston grande dame— correct throughout but human and helping."

[Scrapbooks, tennis memorabilia, and other papers of Wightman's are in the collections of the International Tennis Hall of Fame in Newport, R.I.

The Boston Public Library's oral history collection "The Boston Tradition in Sports" includes a taped interview with Wightman made June 7, 1972. An illustrated biographical article by Nancy Norton is featured in the program for the fiftieth anniversary of the Wightman Cup matches at the Longwood Cricket Club. Articles of interest are Herbert W. Wind, "Run, Helen," *New Yorker*, Aug. 30, 1952, expanded in Alison Danzig, ed., *The Fireside Book of Tennis* (1972); Melvin Maddocks, "The Original Little Old Lady in Tennis Shoes," *Sports Illustrated*, Apr. 10, 1972; Barbara Klaw, "Queen Mother of Tennis" *American Heritage*, Aug. 1975; Mike Lupica, "Those Good Sounds," *World Tennis*, Jan. 1975; Herbert W. Wind, "From Wimbledon to Forest Hills," *New Yorker*, Oct. 13, 1975; and Helen Wills with David MacDonald, "Unforgettable 'Mrs. Wightie,' " *Reader's Digest*, Oct. 1977. Obituaries are in the *Boston Globe* (by Bud Collins) and the *Boston Herald*, both Dec. 6, 1974; and in the *New York Times*, Dec. 7, 1974. Commemorative articles are in the *Boston Globe*, Dec. 8, 1974, and the *Christian Science Monitor*, Dec. 12, 1974.]

JEANNE R. MURPHY

WILDER, THORNTON NIVEN (Apr. 17, 1897–Dec. 7, 1975), playwright and novelist, was born in Madison, Wis., the son of Amos Parker Wilder, a journalist and foreign service officer, and Isabella Thornton Niven, a housewife and autodidact. Thornton was the younger of the Wilder's two sons who, in turn, preceded three daughters. Wilder's first nine years were spent in Madison, where his father edited the *Wisconsin State Journal*. The family moved to China in 1906, when Wilder's father was appointed to a consular post. After only several months, Isabella, together with her (then) four children, returned to the United States, settling in Berkeley, Calif., where Thornton attended the public schools for three years. Returning with the family to China at the end of 1910, Thornton attended the English China Inland Mission School at Chefoo in Shantung Province, where he boarded. One of a dozen Americans, among them Henry Luce, his future classmate at Yale, Wilder was not very well assimilated at the mission school. Nor was he the following year (1912–1913), when he attended Thacher School in Ojai, Calif. Wilder felt insulated and disconnected at boarding school; he missed the company of his intelligent and attentive mother and his younger adoring sisters. In 1913, he was reunited with his mother and siblings in Berkeley, and completed his high school education at Berkeley High School.

As a small boy, Wilder had worshiped his stern father, but when circumstances separated them physically, an emotional estrangement began that was never repaired. In 1914, when Amos Wilder rejoined his family, father and son failed to achieve a rapprochement.

Wilder developed a lifelong love of theater from weekly visits to the nearby Oakland Playhouse. His first two years of college were at Oberlin in Ohio. In his junior year he transferred to Yale, and after military service with the U.S. Coast Guard Artillery at Newport, R.I., received his undergraduate degree in 1920.

Wilder's father did all in his power to secure for his son the best possible education. Believing that Thornton's potential lay in teaching, he arranged for him to spend a year in Italy, studying Latin and classical history at the American Academy in Rome. The experience was profoundly liberating for Wilder; for the first time he could freely explore aesthetic, cultural, and sexual pursuits that in the United States had been, for the most part, vicarious. The year in Rome proved to be critical to Wilder's professional development as well, because it provided him with the material that launched his career as a novelist five years later. His presence at the first performances of Luigi Pirandello's *Six Characters in Search of an Author* had a profound impact on his career as a dramatist. Wilder's studies in Europe also proved helpful to his obtaining of an instructorship upon his return to the United States. He taught French at Lawrenceville School in Princeton, N.J., beginning in 1921.

Wilder published his first professional writing in *Theater Arts Monthly*. In 1926, his first novel, *The Cabala*, was respectfully reviewed in prestigious publications. Encouraged, Wilder took two years' leave from teaching to do graduate work at Princeton, where he earned a master's degree in French in 1926. More important, he composed his second novel, *The Bridge of San Luis Rey*, which made him an international celebrity and won him his first Pulitzer Prize. Resigning from Lawrenceville in 1928, Wilder turned to full-time writing and lecturing. In the decade that followed, he wrote two novels, *The Woman of Andros* (1930) and *Heaven's My Destination* (1935), and published two collections of short plays, *The Angel That Troubled the Waters* (1928) and *The Long Christmas Dinner* (1931). Between 1931 and 1936, he also taught one semester per year at the University of Chicago at the behest of his college classmate Robert Maynard Hutchins, the university's newly appointed president, who with Wilder's counsel, revised the university's undergraduate program.

The success of Wilder's short plays in the early 1930's spurred his concentration in dramatic writing. In 1932, he translated Obey's *Le Viol de Lucrèce* for Broadway and wrote a screenplay for Samuel Goldwyn, *We Live Again* (1934), and subsequently for Alfred Hitchcock, *Shadow of a Doubt* (1943). In 1938, he provided Jed Harris with an adaptation of Ibsen's *A Doll's House*, which starred Ruth Gordon. More significant, he completed *Our Town* (1938), which brought him his second Pulitzer Prize, and *The Merchant of Yonkers*, which initially failed but, slightly revised and retitled as *The Matchmaker* (1955), had a rousing success in both England and the United States.

In 1939 Wilder, a liberal humanist and a patriotic American, was shaken by the outbreak of World War II in Europe. He placed himself at the disposal of the United States government, which dispatched him on missions to South America and England. After Pearl Harbor, Wilder was commissioned an officer in the U.S. Army Air Force; his contribution to strategic planning in the Italian theater of combat was substantial (1942–1945).

Before going on active duty, however, he succeeded in completing *The Skin of Our Teeth* (1942), which, with a cast that included Fredric March, Tallulah Bankhead, and Montgomery Clift, won him his third Pulitzer Prize.

When Wilder returned to civilian life in 1945 he was in his forty-ninth year. Although he remained a celebrated and respected literary figure, his post–World War II work was overshadowed by a newer generation of playwrights and novelists. His postwar novels, *The Ides of March* (1948) and *The Eighth Day* (1967), are arguably more complex and challenging than his four earlier novels, but the response from a new school of critics was either inaudible or equivocal. Wilder completed one final full-length play, *The Alcestiad* (1955), which after its premiere performances at the Edinburgh Festival was not produced in England or the United States in his lifetime. He also completed a collection of short plays, *Plays for Bleecker Street* (1962), and two one-act plays for performance in Berlin (1957): "Bernice" and "The Wreck on the Five-Twenty-Five." Never published, they survive in typescript. Several of Wilder's one-act plays remain in the active repertory.

Wilder in his seventy-fifth year published *Theophilus North* (1973), a collection of short stories, bound together by the eponymous T. N., who, like Sherlock Holmes, resolves the conflicts in each tale.

Assessing the literary importance of Wilder's novels is difficult. A consummate stylist in the tradition of George Moore, Henry James, and Marcel Proust, and praised for wit and irony in virtually all of his work, Wilder was faulted partly because his fiction broke no new technical ground and partly because he appeared detached from an America torn by social unrest and ethnic conflicts. Wilder's novels were widely read and regarded as serious, careful, and mature observations of the human condition. Indeed, all his novels remain in print at the close of the twentieth century. No portrayal of Julius Ceasar in English-language fiction has surpassed Wilder's in *The Ides of March*; and *The Bridge of San Luis Rey*, which transformed Wilder into an international figure, as James's *Daisy Miller* and Wharton's *Ethan Frome* did for those writers, may resonate indefinitely.

Wilder's place in twentieth-century American drama, however, cannot be questioned: *Our Town*, by virtue of its intricate themes, its innumerable performances, and its innovative structure, is often regarded as America's national play. Together with *The Skin of Our Teeth*, it reestablished Wilder's international reputation. Both plays influenced scores of American playwrights, from Tennessee Williams in *The Glass Menagerie* (1945) to Tony Kushner in *Angels in America* (1993). Even Wilder's lighthearted farce, *The Matchmaker*, had a significant impact on American theater, providing the inspiration for the enormously popular musical comedy *Hello Dolly*, whose heroine, Dolly Levi, has become as emblematic a figure in the United States as Mr. Micawber is in Britain.

Although Eugene O'Neill, Tennessee Williams, and Arthur Miller, if only by virtue of their greater productivity, may loom larger than Wilder, his insistence that realism, expressionism, and symbolism had diminished the sense of spontaneity and improvisation (which Molière, Chekhov, and Pirandello had successively brought to the stage) prepared the theater public for the absurdist and experimental dramatists such as Samuel Beckett, Harold Pinter, Joe Orton, Edward Albee, Sam Shepard, and Caryl Churchill.

Wilder's life story cannot compete in Sturm und Drang with those of his contemporaries, F. Scott Fitzgerald and Ernest Hemingway. For one thing, although Wilder traveled extensively throughout western Europe, much of the United States, Mexico, and even South America, both literally and figuratively he never really left home. Emotionally crippled by his father's Philistine, Puritan attitudes, he formed few emotional attachments and never married. No matter how far he wandered, he invariably returned to his home in Connecticut, which, after his father's death in 1936, was dominated by his mother and his sister Isabel, whose adult life was divided between maintaining the house and acting as her brother's surrogate. Fortunately, Wilder's friendships with Robert Hutchins, Ernest Hemingway, Alexander Woollcott, Jed Harris, and most particularly, Gertrude Stein, were liberating influences, which together with his prodigious intellectual curiosity enabled him to transcend and transvaluate in his writings the conventional and provincial ambience of his New England background.

Wilder, who as a child and adolescent was shy, withdrawn, and insecure, became an engaging and fascinating man both privately and publicly. Those who attended his many university and public lectures were captivated by his earnestness, originality, and intellectual passion, qualities that most particularly characterized his personal relationships. A good and generous friend to scores of students and colleagues, Wilder's ultimate commitment was to the nourishment of his intellect and imagination. Among the several themes of his fiction and his plays, that of fidelity to mind and spirit is most pervasive.

Wilder died in his sleep at his home in Hamden, Conn.

[A collection of Wilder's lectures and critical essays was published posthumously as *American Characteristics and Other Essays* (1979); letters and unpublished manuscripts are in the Beinecke Collection at Yale. Other major correspondence is at Harvard, the University of Chicago, Princeton, and New York University. The *Journals of Thornton Wilder*, selected and edited by Donald Gallup (1985), provides insight into his extensive philosophical, critical, and aesthetic speculations. Two full-length biographies are Richard Goldstone, *Thornton Wilder* (1975; rev. 1993) and Gilbert Harrison, *The Enthusiast* (1983). For further biographical material, see the *Paris Review* interview by Goldstone in Malcolm Cowley, ed., *Writers at Work* (1958). An annotated bibliography of works by and about Thornton Wilder is Richard Goldstone and Gary Anderson, *Thornton Wilder* (1982). An obituary is in the *New York Times*, Dec. 8, 1975.]

RICHARD GOLDSTONE

WILLS, JAMES ROBERT ("BOB") (Mar. 6, 1905–May 13, 1975), bandleader, fiddler, and pioneer of "western swing," was born on a farm near Kosse in Limestone County, Tex., the first of ten children of John Tompkins Wills and Emmaline Foley, both of whom came from musical families. His father was a tenant farmer who never had much luck with cotton, but was well known for his expert country fiddling. Young Bob left school in the seventh grade in order to help support the family through farm work, but he used music as a supplementary source of income throughout his early years, playing at "ranch" dances with his father and other family members.

Recession and overproduction made cotton farming unprofitable during the post–World War I period, and the prospect of a farmer's life was unappealing to Wills. As the oldest child he felt burdened by responsibility which he periodically tried to escape by drinking, carousing, and traveling. For a brief time he felt the "call to preach" but nothing came of it, and he married a local woman, Edna Posey, in 1926. This was the first of a series of ill-fated marriages (Ruth McMaster, beginning in 1935; Mary Helen Brown, 1938; and Mary Louise Parker, 1939), all of which ended in divorce. Wills worked for a number of years as a barber, but only music seemed to satisfy him. His professional career officially began in 1929 when he joined a traveling medicine show, which used musical performances to draw crowds in order to peddle "snake oil."

By this time Wills was known as one of the best fiddlers in Texas and had won many contests. Texas abounded in a variety of musical styles and Wills's alert mind absorbed all of them. From the rural black he acquired a love for the blues; from his father, an intimate knowledge of country fiddling; from nearby Mexico, an ear for the sounds of corridos and rancheros. The popularity of jazz in the larger towns pushed Wills to even further modify his style. By adding jazz and blues to the standard country repertoire, he could attract a younger "citified" audience. His genius lay in his ability to integrate older, traditional sounds into a big jazz-band format without losing the authenticity of either. The resulting melange was termed "western swing," and it presaged the emergence of country as a modern style with nationwide appeal.

Wills's music incorporated all the elements of jazz: blue notes, syncopation, and improvisation. His was the first country band to regularly use horns and a rhythm section, and he pioneered the fiddle-steel guitar front line that has been characteristic of country since the 1940's. He developed his instrumental style at a series of radio jobs, beginning at KTAT (Fort Worth) in 1930. During the early 1930's he and vocalist Milton Brown (who later went on to form his own western band, the Musical Brownies) worked with the popular Light Crust Doughboys at KRJZ (Fort Worth), sowing the seeds for the many country-jazz hybrids that followed, such as the Wanderers, the Vagabonds, and the Prairie Ramblers. The Doughboys were sponsored by Burrus Mill and Elevator Company president W. Lee O'Daniel, a businessman-turned-songwriter who later became governor of Texas. Wills's association with O'Daniel was fraught with problems, however, and it was only after he left to form his own band, the Playboys (later "the Texas Playboys"), that his career fully blossomed.

With growing fame came cash rewards. In 1935 Wills worked out a promotion scheme with General Mills to market Play Boy Flour and Play Boy Bread over KVOO (Tulsa) wherein he got a royalty for each barrel of flour sold. By 1936 records such as "Steel Guitar Rag" and "Trouble in Mind" were outselling those of Louis Armstrong and Gene Autry. Wills was extremely generous in his success, supporting not only his own relatives but, at times, even total strangers who were down and out. However, he continued to be plagued by marital problems arising from his jealousy, moodiness, and bouts with alcoholism. It was only when he met Betty Anderson, a woman who was apparently able to manage his insecurities, that this pattern was finally broken. Their marriage, Wills's fifth, lasted from 1942 until his death.

Wills's visibility increased during the war years as he moved to Hollywood and made a number of "cowboy" movies. His career was also given a big boost by the enormous popularity of one song, "The New San Antonio Rose" (which was also recorded by Bing Crosby, thus pushing the country sound still further into the national consciousness). As the war years ended he reduced his band's size, which enabled him to survive both the death of swing and the birth of rock 'n' roll. Despite many bad business decisions, he continued to have great financial success working national tours through the 1940's and 1950's and Las Vegas hotels in the 1960's. The dance beat Wills introduced to country music paved the way for both the honky-tonk and rockabilly styles, and he lived to see his sound become the model for such disparate performers as Bill Haley and Merle Haggard.

Wills never accommodated to the "Nashville sound," and he always saw himself more as a swing bandleader than a country artist. Nevertheless, he was inducted into the Country Music Hall of Fame in 1968, in recognition of his profound influence on the music. In 1969 a stroke ended his playing career. A series of health problems followed, culminating in his death from pneumonia on May 13, 1975, in Fort Worth. He left six children.

In retrospect, Wills's is the only early western swing band that does not sound dated years later. His best songs, such as "San Antonio Rose" and "Faded Love," remain in current repertoire, his fiddling is a prime reference for those who want to master the art, and his orchestral style continues to surface in the work of later artists like George Strait and Lyle Lovett.

[There is a comprehensive two-volume collection of Bob Wills's music entitled *Bob Wills and His Texas Playboys: Anthology (1935–1973)*, Rhino Records R2 70744.

Charles R. Townsend has written the definitive Bob Wills biography, *San Antonio Rose* (1976). Wills's musical contribution is also analyzed in detail in Bill C. Malone's *Country Music, U.S.A.* (1985). An obituary appears in the *New York Times*, May 14, 1975.]

JOE BLUM

WILSON, CHARLES EDWARD (Nov. 18, 1886–Jan. 3, 1972), corporate executive, was born in New York City, the son of George H. Wilson, a bookbinder, and Hannah Rebecca Stiles. His father died when he was three years old, and his mother went to work as a house-

keeper and practical nurse. Wilson grew up in the tough Hell's Kitchen section of Manhattan's West Side and, after completing the seventh grade, left school in September 1899 to take a job in the shipping department at Sprague Electrical Works, which became a General Electric subsidiary in 1903.

Wilson was soon taken under the wing of William T. Ruete, superintendent at the Sprague Works. Ruete became a friend and surrogate father to the teenager and encouraged him to attend night school and to study accounting and engineering through correspondence courses. Wilson moved up and was successively shipping clerk, plant accountant, and purchasing agent. In 1906, he became the production manager and the following year, assistant superintendent of the Sprague Works. On Nov. 18, 1907, he married Elizabeth Maisch. The couple adopted one child.

During World War I, the Sprague Company began producing telephone switchboards and instrument panels for aircraft, and Wilson was given responsibility for developing and selling these new products. In 1918, General Electric absorbed the Sprague operations, and Wilson was assigned as assistant superintendent of the GE plants in Maspeth, N.Y., and Kensington, Pa. In 1923, he took over as managing engineer of the GE wire and conduit division in Bridgeport, Conn., and in 1928 he was promoted to assistant to the vice-president of the merchandise department. He then moved up to vice-president in charge of appliances in 1930, to executive vice-president and a member of the board of directors in 1937, and to president of GE on Jan. 1, 1940, replacing the retiring Gerard Swope. Wilson was considered a "production" man and his forte was in establishing clear and efficient production patterns and goals. He was a large man and tended to be forthright in manner. Wilson had very little formal education, and his training was largely practical, mostly on the shop floor. He was described as having a "native geniality" that made him a good executive and supervisor of people with more formal training.

Wilson left General Electric in 1942 to assume major responsibilities for the American war effort. Although he was an active Republican and opposed to the New Deal policies, President Franklin Roosevelt appointed Wilson executive vice-chairman of the War Production Board (WPB). In this capacity Wilson worked directly under Donald Nelson at the WPB and was successful in increasing the production of military aircraft to almost 100,000 in 1944. He was not successful, however, in handling the intricacies of Washington politics and resigned under fire in August 1944.

Wilson then returned to GE and led the company in a period of postwar growth. His tenure at GE was marked by a continuation and expansion of the consumer-oriented policies begun under Swope. Wilson expanded the production of electrical appliances to meet increasing consumer demand, and he led GE into new areas of development, most notably atomic energy. During his tenure, GE produced 200,000 different items in 115 factories.

Wilson had a reputation as an antiunion stalwart. During the 1930's and 1940's, GE adopted a policy of paternalism that sought to blunt the thrust of unionism in GE plants. This policy was initiated by Swope and aggressively continued by Wilson. Under his leadership GE played a significant role in promoting the antiunion sentiment that culminated in the passage of the Taft-Hartley Act in 1947. Wilson was convinced that organized labor's demands for wage increases were driving up inflation and undermining the American economy. He generally characterized this sentiment in terms of Cold War rhetoric. GE's antiunion tactics were later termed "Boulwarism," after GE executive Lemuel Boulware, who worked under Wilson's direction and articulated the policy. As a supporter of the act, Wilson was appointed to serve on the Taft-Hartley Advisory Board. Wilson also acceded to President Truman's request that he accept the chairmanship of the President's Committee on Civil Rights.

With the outbreak of the Korean War in 1950, Wilson was called back into government service by President Truman. He was sixty-three and was anticipating mandatory retirement in two years. His choice as his successor at GE, Ralph J. Cordiner, had been appointed as executive vice-president, the last step before the presidency of the firm. In December 1950, Wilson became director of the Office of Defense Mobilization. This office, authorized by Congress and created by executive order, had the authority to act on behalf of the president to "direct, control, and coordinate all mobilization activities . . . including but not limited to, production, procurement, manpower, stabilization, and transport activities." Wilson ap-

proached the position with his usual forthright manner and ran afoul of the similarly forthright president. Wilson resigned in 1952 in opposition to Truman's approval of a wage hike for steelworkers.

Despite the fact that he had reached retirement age, Wilson returned to GE but left soon thereafter to join the W. R. Grace Company, an international trading conglomerate, in 1952. He served as consultant and director of the company and headed the board's executive committee beginning in 1954. In May 1955, he was elected chairman of the board at Grace, the first person outside of the family to achieve this distinction.

In 1956, Wilson resigned from Grace and for the next two years headed up the People-to-People Foundation, a nonpartisan organization to promote international understanding that was established at the behest of President Eisenhower. From 1958 until his death in Bronxville, N.Y., Wilson remained active as a business consultant.

[See "Mr. Wilson I Presume," *New York Times Magazine*, Feb. 17, 1946; "Mr. Wilson at Work," *Fortune*, May 1947; and "Spare-Time Statesman," *Collier's*, Apr. 10, 1948; An obituary is in the *New York Times*, Jan. 4, 1972.]

G. P. ANTONE

WILSON, EDMUND, JR. (May 8, 1895–June 12, 1972), journalist, historian, and social and literary critic, was born in Red Bank, N.J., the only son of Edmund Wilson, a trial lawyer, and Helen Mather Kimball. Both of his parents' family backgrounds included many professionals—preachers, doctors, lawyers (his lawyer-father had served as attorney general for New Jersey under two governors)—and thus some professional expectations accompanied Edmund, Jr., first to Hill School, a Presbyterian prep school in Pennsylvania (1909–1912), and then to Princeton College (1912–1916). However, his interests tended toward literature and writing. At Hill he contributed to and later edited the *Hill School Record* and began reading classical and modern literature. At Princeton, where among his classmates were the poet John Peale Bishop and the novelist F. Scott Fitzgerald, he continued his literary studies and edited the *Nassau Lit*.

Following graduation and a summer at military camp in Plattsburgh, N.Y., Wilson found, through his father's connections, work as a reporter for the *New York Evening Sun*. Shyness and inexperience, combined with his literary aspirations, impeded his development as a beat reporter and he contributed nothing of note. When the United States entered World War I, Wilson enlisted with a hospital unit. He attended wounded and dying soldiers in France, victims of mustard gas and syphilis and shell shock as well as of enemy fire, before being transferred to an intelligence unit in 1918. He read modern literature and continued to write stories, poems, and polemical essays, recording scraps of dialogue and impressions in his diary. He was mustered out in New York in July 1919.

Wilson's career and life began taking their characteristic shapes in the years that followed. After a start as a free-lance writer, he joined the staff of *Vanity Fair*. He later worked for *The New Republic* and *The Dial*, contributing pieces on books, theater, ideas, and occasionally, sensational trials and social issues. His life in lower Manhattan brought him into the social world of artists (including the poets Edna St. Vincent Millay, with whom he fell in love, and Elinor Wylie), intellectuals, and show-business people, a world he portrayed in *I Thought of Daisy* (1929). This novel might well have been called *Discordant Encounters*, the title he used for a 1926 book that included a comic ballet written for Charlie Chaplin, a series of imaginary dialogues originally published in *The New Republic*, and a play entitled *The Crime in the Whistler Room*. It had been staged in 1924 by the Provincetown Players and its lead actress, Mary Blair, had married Wilson in 1923. They had one daughter before their separation in 1925 and divorce in 1929.

During the 1920's Wilson also traveled extensively in Europe and America. Cape Cod, Mass., became a second home. In 1927 he visited Boston during the days preceding the execution of the immigrant political anarchists Nicola Sacco and Bartolomeo Vanzetti. "The Sacco-Vanzetti tragedy," he subsequently wrote in a letter, "made a profound impression on everybody—with distinct effects on the literary people in certain quarters." At the same time, Wilson was beginning work on his study of the birth of modernism out of French Symbolism, *Axel's Castle* (1931), dedicated to his teacher at Princeton, Christian Gauss. Wilson's method of placing extended quotation and paraphrase within discussions of each author's life, tech-

niques, and historical moment distinguished his work from the formalist New Criticism that would come to dominate mid-century academic literary criticism.

Though Wilson clearly admired the six writers whose work he analyzed in *Axel's Castle*—Yeats, Proust, Joyce, Eliot, Stein, and Valéry—he also, perhaps himself affected by the Sacco-Vanzetti executions, came to question their tendency to turn away from social or political engagement. To his editor, Maxwell Perkins, he wrote, "I believe that any literary movement which tends so to paralyze the will, to discourage literature from entering into action, has a very serious weakness; and I think that the time has now come for a reaction against it."

Wilson wrote no major piece on Sacco and Vanzetti, but the direction his reporting took in the 1930's was influenced by their case and by the parts played in the protest against their execution by literary friends, including Millay and John Dos Passos. In 1931 alone he visited Detroit for a story on Henry Ford; Kentucky and West Virginia to report on the coal miner's strikes; and Alabama to observe the trial of "the Scottsboro boys," in which nine blacks between the ages of fourteen and twenty were accused of raping two white women, resulting in eight death sentences. In a statement placed at the end of *The American Jitters* (1932), a collection of his reporting from this period, Wilson declared that he had "grown up in modern prosperous America with a slightly outside point of view," that this point of view was now influenced by the writings of Karl Marx, that he believed in human evolution and progress, that traditional religions had been "made possible only by ignorance," and that any meaning human life has is that which we give it ourselves.

That year also brought the sudden and unexpected death of Wilson's second wife, Margaret Canby, whom he had married in 1930. The record of their early encounters, their friendship and erotic exchanges, and of Wilson's thoughts as he learned of her death and flew to California for her funeral forms one of the most remarkable sequences in his diaries.

In 1935 Wilson visited the Soviet Union to research an intellectual history of the origins of socialism up to Lenin's arrival at the Finland Railway Station to lead the October Revolution and bring into existence the first Marxist state. *To the Finland Station* (1940), with its portrayal of Marx, Bakunin, Babeuf, Trotsky, Lenin, dynamic figures whose thought led directly to action, provided the counterpoint Wilson needed to the literary figures outlined in *Axel's Castle*. That book's exemplar was the fictional Axel of Villiers de l'Isle-Adam, a prince who would rather die isolated from all experience than sully his idealism with contact with the world outside his castle. *To the Finland Station* also embodied Wilson's belief in progress, as each failed step toward socialism nevertheless made possible the next step and the next, until at last "Western man at this moment can be seen to have made some definite progress in mastering the greeds and fears, the bewilderments, in which he has lived."

Wilson's confidence in the progress of humanity was shattered by the events surrounding World War II. "The present," he wrote in 1951, recalling the bombed-out cities of Europe and the rise of Hitler and Stalin, "is not one of the great ages of the self-dramatization of man." At the end of the war he visited England, Italy, Greece, and Crete as a reporter for *The New Yorker*. The bitter, ironic book that followed, *Europe Without Baedecker* (1947), produced consternation and hostility in readers and reviewers alike, with its severe criticism of the British and Americans.

The war also affected Wilson's literary interests. Before the war he had continued the kind of literary criticism begun in *Axel's Castle*. *The Triple Thinkers* (1938) had examined nineteenth- and twentieth-century literary figures and movements with a similar combined interest in aesthetics, psychology, and history. In *The Wound and the Bow* (1941), Wilson focused more specifically on individual psychological experience and aesthetic achievement, finding in the story of Philoctetes—the archer whose putrid wound made his presence unbearable, but whose bowmanship was needed by the Greeks to defeat their enemy at Troy—a metaphor for the artist who both suffers and creates.

After the war, however, his interest turned to such European writers as Malraux, Silone, and Pasternak, whose work more actively sought to overcome the dehumanization visible everywhere in the West. He became skeptical of writers whose work seemed to accept human defeat, such as de Sade, Kafka, and even Beckett. At this time Wilson also began the years of study that would produce *Patriotic Gore* (1962), an

intellectual history culminating not in a triumph of the human spirit but in the carnage of the American Civil War.

The 1940's brought personal losses. F. Scott Fitzgerald died in 1940 and John Peale Bishop in 1944. His marriage in 1938 to Mary McCarthy was literally productive for both but also contentious and sometimes violent, ending in divorce in 1946; they had one child. That same year he married Elena Mumm Thornton, with whom he remained married until his death; they had one child. New friends were made as well, including Vladimir Nabokov, though their friendship would later evolve into an extended quarrel. Wider literary notoriety also resulted from the banning of his *Memoirs of Hecate County* (1942), a fictional presentation of modern neurosis whose central story, "The Princess With the Golden Hair," presents Wilson's slightly disguised sexual life with unromantic candor.

Wilson's interest in origins took him both to Israel in 1954—*The Scrolls From the Dead Sea* (1955) speculated on the possible origins of Christianity in the Essene sect of Judaism—and to his mother's ancestral home in Talcottville, N.Y. *Upstate* (1971), like *The Scrolls*, is concerned not only with origins, but with marginal lives. This turning away from mainstream European and American writers produced *Red, Black, Blond and Olive* (1956), *Apologies to the Iroquois* (1960), *O Canada* (1965), and *A Window on Russia* (1972), which reprints the negative comments on Nabokov that began their quarrel. Wilson's cantankerousness was also evident in *A Piece of My Mind: Reflections at Sixty* (1956), *The Cold War and the Income Tax: A Protest* (1963), and *The Fruits of the MLA* (1968).

Throughout his career, Wilson's writing exemplified, as he wrote in *A Piece of My Mind*, the "lucidity, force and ease" that set him apart, not only from the modernists he admired in his youth, but also from the academics who came to dominate literary criticism in the twentieth century. Very much a twentieth-century figure himself, however, Wilson's chief interest was always in the human world (rather than the larger natural world), in the world of human history and creation, the never-ending process of humanity creating itself. He asked that a passage from Ecclesiastes—"This writing of books is an endless matter"—be read at his funeral. He died in the Old Stone House at Talcottville.

[The Beinecke Rare Book and Manuscript Library of Yale University is the main depository of Wilson's manuscripts. His extensive occasional pieces are collected in *Classics and Commercials* (1950); *The Shores of Light* (1952); *The Bit Between My Teeth* (1965); and *The Devils and Canon Barham* (1973). His plays are collected in *Five Plays* (1954) and *The Duke of Palermo, and Other Plays* (1969). His poetry is in *Night Thoughts* (1961). His diaries have been published by decades from *A Prelude* (1967) through *The Sixties* (1993). His letters are in Elena Wilson, ed., *Letters on Literature and Politics* (1977); and Simon Karlinsky, ed., *The Nabokov-Wilson Letters: 1940–1971* (1979). A thorough, if dated, bibliography is Richard David Ramsey, *Edmund Wilson: A Bibliography* (1971). Full-length critical assessments include Sherman Paul, *Edmund Wilson* (1965); David Castronovo, *Edmund Wilson* (1984); and Janet Groth, *Edmund Wilson* (1989); the last containing a helpful bibliography as well. More personal responses include Richard Hauer Costa's *Edmund Wilson: Our Neighbor from Talcottville* (1980), as well as his daughter Rosalind Baker Wilson's memoir *Near the Magician* (1989). Shorter appreciative essays and comments are collected in John Wain, ed., *Edmund Wilson: The Man and His Work* (1978); and Philip French, ed., *Three Honest Men* (1980). An obituary is in the *New York Times*, June 13, 1972.]

PAUL JOHNSTON

WILSON, JOSEPH CHAMBERLAIN (Dec. 13, 1909–Nov. 22, 1971), business executive, was born in Rochester, N.Y., the son of Joseph R. Wilson and Katherine M. Upton. Joseph R. Wilson was president of the Haloid Company, which his father Joseph C. Wilson had founded, from 1938 to 1945. Joseph C. Wilson attended local public schools and then entered the University of Rochester, where he was elected to Phi Beta Kappa, from which he graduated in 1931. Wilson then enrolled in the Graduate School of Business Administration of Harvard University, where he was one of five students named to the *Harvard Business Review* board, and from which he received an M.B.A. with high distinction in 1933. In 1935, he married Marie B. Curran; the couple had six children.

Soon after graduation Wilson took a post as assistant to the sales manager at the Haloid Company, working for twenty dollars per week; for three years he worked successively in a variety of jobs, thereby gaining experience in all the company's departments. The company, which had taken its name from the halogen salts that were used in photography, produced a line of papers used to make copies of documents. At the time it was a marginal operation in an industry dominated by nearby Eastman Kodak. In 1935, Haloid acquired controlling interest in the Rectograph Company, which manufactured a photocopy machine.

Wilson became secretary of the Haloid Company in 1936 and secretary-treasurer in 1938. He held this position during World War II, when Haloid received many lucrative government contracts to supply photographic papers.

As peace approached Haloid sought products that would enable it to avoid Eastman Kodak's domination. Executive Vice-President and chief engineer John Dessauer, who had come over from Rectograph, was assigned the task of developing such products. In 1945, he became aware of a machine invented by Chester Carlson that performed tasks today associated with copiers. Carlson had begun experimenting with such a machine in 1935, which was intended as an improvement over machines produced and sold by American Photocopy and several manufacturers of hectograph devices. The former company's machines made copies on coated paper, which soon became discolored, while hectographs' copies were made by mixing chemicals into a fluid, which then jelled in a pan. A master was placed on top of the mix, leaving an impression, after which copies were made by softly placing paper in the pan to absorb the ink. Clearly neither method was satisfactory. As a result, most of those who wanted copies used carbon paper affixed between sheets prior to writing or typing.

After trying to obtain backing from several companies, including Eastman Kodak, he went off on his own. By 1938, he had developed a crude machine, which he took to Kodak and some twenty other companies including IBM and RCA, but all turned him down. Only in 1944 did Carlson find the Battelle Memorial Foundation of Columbus, Ohio, a nonprofit research society, to bankroll him in return for a 60-percent interest in the invention.

Carlson called his reproduction process "electrophotography." He offered a demonstration, and Dessauer was impressed. At the time he remarked, "Of course it's got a million miles to go before it will be marketable. But when it does become marketable, we've got to be in the picture."

In 1946, Joseph C. Wilson became president and general manager of the Haloid Company.

In 1947, he instructed his financial officer to try to purchase commercial rights to electrophotography from Battelle. Once he had purchased the rights to Carlson's process, Wilson decided to rename it; after rejecting several alternative names, he settled on "xerography," derived from the Greek and literally meaning, "dry writing."

The Haloid Company then threw all its resources behind xerography, borrowing heavily for that purpose. Had the process failed, Haloid would have been forced to declare bankruptcy. Its first commercial machine, a unit designed to produce paper and metal offset masters, was marketed in 1950, and had limited success. Five years later Haloid produced the Copyflo 11, a large machine designed to reproduce, on continuous rolls of paper, copies from microfilm. Other Copyflos followed. Now it seemed Haloid had found its new niche: it would be a manufacturer of commercial duplicators for special markets not addressed by other firms.

At the time American Photocopy (Apeco) dominated the market for office copiers. The field was not large: most businesses still used carbon paper to make copies. Apeco made most of its money from the sale of diffusion transfer paper, and was quite content to sell its machines for low prices in order to encourage its paper sales. In this way, it commanded the field. In 1956, Haloid purchased worldwide rights for the process from Battelle, and two years later Wilson changed his company's name to Haloid Xerox to signify the change in direction. Wilson planned to use this new technology to produce copies on plain paper, and in fact staked its future on this market.

In 1960, the newly renamed Xerox Corporation produced the 914, a large machine capable of producing seven copies per minute. The machines were leased, not sold, with customers permitted a specified number of "free" copies, after which they were charged incrementally for each one. Apeco was troubled by this new development, but soon realized that the cost per copy with its machines and its special paper were less than what Xerox was charging—so the company sat back and did nothing. But customers were willing to pay a little extra for the better Xerox copies, and Apeco disappeared in the late 1960's.

The 914 was a success, prompting the company to turn out additional products. In 1961 Xerox released the 813, a desktop version of the 913. Other innovations followed: in 1964 Xerox introduced Long Distance Xerography, and soon after the 2400 machine, which as its name indicated produced 2,400 copies per hour.

As a result of its innovations, Xerox experienced rapid growth in sales and profits. In 1959, the last pre-914 year, revenues were $32 million and profits $2 million. That year Wilson was named chairman as well as president. In 1961, the first full year of 914 sales, revenues rose to $61 million and earnings to $5.5 million. Xerox common shares soon rose from a low of 4 to a high of 34. Xerox was a glamor company and a glamor stock in the early stages of the great bull market of the 1960's. By 1967 revenues were $701 million, earnings $97 million, and the stock peaked at 314. The 914 and 813 copiers accounted for the majority of sales and earnings, but by then the 2400 turned out more copies than all other Xerox equipment combined. Meanwhile, the company prepared the 3600, which was 50 percent faster than the 2400, for introduction the next year. It also readied the 720 and 660, faster versions of the 914 and 813. Through Rank Xerox in England, and later, Fuji Xerox in Japan, it placed machines worldwide.

In these first years Xerox rented close to 200,000 copiers, and the company was working overtime to produce and place additional machines from its growing backlog. Of course, the company experienced exponential growth. Almost daily, new executives arrived from other major companies, and in some weeks more than one hundred production personnel were added to the payroll. In the last year of the Wilson era, Xerox ruled the copier industry. It also expanded into new areas through acquisition of such companies as University Microfilms, Electro-Optical Systems, Basic Systems, and American Education Publications.

In 1968, Wilson named Peter McColough his successor as president and chief executive officer. Wilson and McColough together planned the next step in Xerox's evolution: the purchase of Scientific Data System (SDS), which placed Xerox in the data processing business. But this turned out to be the first of several Xerox failures that occurred after Wilson left active command of the company.

Wilson remained on the board of trustees and became honorary chairman. He continued to be concerned with Xerox's business, but now turned more to public service. Because of Wil-

son, the University of Rochester was the bene-
ficiary of an irrevocable trust comprised of
90,000 Xerox shares. Moreover, he left the university $20 million in his will. Chancellor W.
Allen Wallis remarked that Wilson's nonmon-
etary contributions "far overshadow what he has
given."

In 1971, Wilson became chairman both of
President Nixon's Committee on Health Education and of Governor Nelson Rockefeller's
Steering Committee on Social Problems. He
also served as a trustee of the Committee for
Economic Development, of the Alfred Sloan
Foundation, of the Carnegie Endowment for
International Peace, of the Sidney Hillman
Health Center, of the George Eastman House,
and of the Rochester Savings Bank. In addition
he served on the boards of several corporations,
most of them based in Rochester. He also demonstrated concern for urban problems. "Our
technology has not lived up to its obligations to
society," he said in 1969. "Technological companies are at the center of social change and
therefore have a responsibility. Those in the
inner city have derived little benefit from technology and no profit from it."

Joseph Wilson died suddenly, of a heart attack, while lunching with Governor Nelson
Rockefeller of New York.

[There is no biography of Joseph Wilson, but he
figures prominently in two company histories: Gary
Jacobson, *Xerox, American Samurai* (1986); and
Douglas K. Smith and Robert C. Alexander, *Fum-
bling the Future: How Xerox Invented, Then Ignored,
the First Personal Computer* (1988). An obituary is in
the *New York Times*, Nov. 23, 1971.]

ROBERT SOBEL

WILSON, MARIE (Aug, 19, 1916–Nov. 23,
1972), actress, was born Katherine Elizabeth
Wilson in Anaheim, Calif. Her father, who
died when she was five, left her an inheritance
of $11,000. At age sixteen, Wilson took that
money and moved her mother, stepfather, two
half brothers, two half sisters, and her grandfather to Hollywood because she was determined to become a movie star. There she put
down a year's rent on a large house, and bought
a mink coat, a flashy car, and canned food
worth $500. She also took care of her family's
medical and dental expenses. Within two
weeks, her $11,000 was gone. When she called
her bank to check on the status of her account,

she was told that it was overdrawn by $1.38; she
immediately returned a radio she'd purchased
and used this money to put her bank account in
the black again. She then set out in search of an
acting job.

Though a beautiful woman with long blond
hair, big brown eyes, and a voluptuous body,
Wilson seemed destined to be a comedienne
from the start. She made the rounds of Hollywood agents dressed in her new mink and tennis
sneakers: this incongruous outfit was the result
of her failure to buy a pair of dress shoes before
her money ran out. She got her first big break
when her car ran out of gas in front of producer
Nick Grinde's house. Wilson's dead car produced a traffic jam and led to much horn honking. When Grinde stepped outside to see what
all the commotion was about, he couldn't help
but laugh when he saw the beautiful mink-clad
Wilson in the midst of this chaos. The two
became close friends, and Wilson began stopping by Grinde's house after a day of auditions
to reenact the screen tests she had taken. They
developed a romantic relationship and planned
a wedding, but they never went through with it.

From her first film, *Stars over Broadway* in
1935, until *The Private Affairs of Bel Ami* in
1947, Wilson appeared in small parts in nearly
two dozen unspectacular films. Her only really
good part was the lead role opposite James Cagney in *Boy Meets Girl* (1938). Critics praised
her pretty face and shapely figure, but had little
positive to say about her acting. She was always
typecast, as one reviewer put it, as "the quintessential dumb blonde."

Wilson's career and her life almost ended
abruptly in 1937 when a car she was driving was
involved in a three-car collision and a fragment
of metal pierced her skull. Surgeons managed
to remove the life-threatening fragment and
Wilson recovered quickly enough to appear in
two films that year.

In 1942, she landed a job in a Hollywood
stage show called *Blackouts*, produced by Ken
Murray. When she started out she made $250
per week, but after a record-breaking seven-year
run during which she appeared in 2,332 consecutive performances without missing a show,
she was making $1,000 per week. Also in 1942,
she married her first husband, actor and writer
Allan Nixon. This marriage ended in divorce
seven years later. At the time Wilson told reporters, "It's a case where two careers in one
home didn't work out."

The most important year of Wilson's career was 1947. In that year writer Cy Howard created the "My Friend Irma" series for radio with Wilson in mind as the star. But when the role of Irma, the scatterbrained secretary, was first offered to her, she turned it down. Wilson had aspired to be a dramatic actress early in her career, and by 1947 she was tired of playing "dumb blonde" roles. But Howard persisted in trying to get Wilson to play Irma and she eventually accepted the role that made her famous. "My Friend Irma" began on CBS radio in 1947 and ran until 1952. At its peak "Irma" boasted an audience of thirty million. The show's success led to a Paramount movie version with the same title in 1949; the movie starred Wilson and marked the first big-screen appearance of the team of Dean Martin and Jerry Lewis. A movie sequel, *My Friend Irma Goes West*, appeared in 1950. In 1952, the radio show was adapted for television, made a bumpy but moderately successful transition, and ran for three years. The final new episodes aired in 1954; the whole series subsequently had a long life in reruns.

The basic premise of "My Friend Irma" in all its incarnations was quite simple. Wilson played Irma, an innocent, sweet, bubbly, wacky, and very sexy woman. She worked as a secretary for Mr. Clyde, a cranky attorney; she had a con-artist boyfriend named Al; and she lived with her friend Jane Stacy in an apartment in a run-down boardinghouse in Manhattan owned by Mrs. O'Reilly. In both the radio and TV versions of the comedy series, Jane acts as narrator, providing background, setting up scenes, and commenting on the action. Much of the humor in the series depended on the juxtaposition of illogical Irma and the level-headed Jane, whose job it was to find methods to extricate Irma from the predicaments she kept getting into.

Although she was frequently dismissed as an actress by the critics, Wilson was adored by the columnists throughout her career. She was always portrayed as an extremely kind and generous woman. Columnist Mitzi Cummings described Wilson as "one of those rare, once in a great while creatures, with an elusive and childlike quality." While working in a department store as a clerk before she broke into acting, she was fired for, among other things, giving toys away to a child who could not afford them. After she became famous, she partici-

pated in many charitable causes. At the height of her fame as "Irma," she annually offered her services as secretary for a day to the highest bidder, with the proceeds going to polio victims and their families. One year the promotion netted $22,500.

Wilson married for a second time in 1951, this time to television producer Robert Fallon, a handsome, dashing man who enjoyed hunting and deep-sea fishing; he remained her husband for the rest of her life. While entertaining patients in a hospital in Memphis, Tenn., Wilson fell in love with a four-month-old baby boy, whom she and Fallon adopted in 1955 and named Gregson, after Gregson Bautzer, a Hollywood attorney and close friend of Fallon's.

Although Wilson's success fell short of superstardom, she was financially comfortable all her life and retained her good reputation as an agreeable and hard-working actress. After her apex as "Irma," Wilson appeared in numerous small stage, film, and television parts and continued to perform at charity functions. Her last job was an appearance in an episode of the television show, "Love American-Style," which aired just three weeks before her death.

[An extensive file of news clippings about Wilson is at the New York Public Library for the Performing Arts at Lincoln Center. A listing of her films appears in the *New York Times Directory of the Film*. Samples of her work in films, television, and radio are at the Museum of Television and Radio in New York City. An obituary appears in the *New York Times*, Nov. 24, 1972.]

BILL HUGHES

WILSON, ORLANDO WINFIELD ("WIN," "O.W.") (May 15, 1900–Oct. 18, 1972), criminologist and educator, was born in Veblen, S.Dak., the son of Ole Knut Wilson (born Vraalson), a lawyer turned farmer who also invested in real estate and the grain business, and Olava Stoutland, a schoolteacher. The family moved to Saskatchewan, Canada, in 1905 and then to California in 1911, eventually settling in Pacific Beach. Wilson graduated from San Diego High School in 1918.

Wilson entered the University of California at Berkeley anticipating a career as a mining engineer. Instead, he became a police patrolman in Berkeley in 1921, when the postwar recession adversely affected his father's farm. He worked under Berkeley Police Chief August

Vollmer, a leading advocate of police reform, who became Wilson's professional mentor. Wilson graduated from Berkeley in 1924 and remained with the Berkeley police until 1925. He married Vernis Haddon on June 3, 1923. They had two children before their divorce in 1943.

With Vollmer's recommendation, Wilson was hired as chief of police in Fullerton, Calif., in 1925. There he introduced many of the practices that Vollmer had developed in Berkeley, including a new records system and a new officer response system. He was asked to resign in 1926, in part because of his willingness to discuss controversial ideas publicly. Wilson talked to community groups about, but did not necessarily advocate, sterilizing "criminal types" and using birth control as a means of limiting population. From 1926 to 1928 he worked as an investigator for the Pacific Finance Corporation in Los Angeles. There he investigated credit applicants and repossessed automobiles.

In 1928, Wilson became police chief of Wichita, Kans., again with Vollmer's recommendation. The Wichita police had a reputation for corruption and the use of excessive force. Wilson strove to implement the lessons of police administration that he had learned from Vollmer, adapting some and rejecting others based on his own experience. In particular, Wilson's conception of policing minimized Vollmer's focus on crime prevention and the establishment of a relationship between the police and the community. Wilson viewed police work in isolation and placed greater emphasis on technical skills and technological innovations.

In addition, Wilson spearheaded the creation of a state training program for police in Kansas, to avail his department of expertise that Wichita could not afford. However, his reforms earned him influential enemies. Two city commissioners eventually pressured him to leave Wichita by threatening to undermine his authority. When Wilson took a one-year leave of absence in 1939 to serve as a consultant to the Public Administration Service, an agency that worked on various public policy questions, in Chicago, it was understood that his departure would be permanent.

At the Public Administration Service Wilson surveyed municipal police departments for the purpose of reorganizing them, and also wrote on aspects of police administration. However, he left after just three months to return to the University of California, Berkeley, as full-time professor of police administration. Along with his academic duties, he continued to survey police departments as a consultant for the Public Administration Service.

Wilson's academic career was interrupted by military service during World War II. In 1943 he entered the United States Army's School of Military Government with the rank of lieutenant colonel. Wilson's considerable experience in law enforcement was unique among his classmates. After graduating with honors, he became director of public safety in Naples, Italy, in 1943. After approximately three months in Naples, he was reassigned to England as director of the Public Safety Division of the German Country Unit, Supreme Headquarters of the Allied Expeditionary Force. Wilson and his staff began preparations for the creation of local police forces no longer under the direction or influence of the Nazis. In 1945, Wilson's unit was transferred to Berlin to implement the plans they had developed. He was discharged from the army in 1946, but continued his work on developing a new German police force for another year as a civilian employee. Wilson's experience reinforced his belief in the military as a model for effective police organization.

He returned to the University of California at Berkeley in 1947. When the university expanded the Bureau of Police Administration into the School of Criminology in 1950, Wilson became its first dean. In addition to his academic responsibilities, Wilson's summers were absorbed by more surveys of police departments for the Public Administration Service. The demand for Wilson's services increased in the wake of the revelations concerning police corruption and ties to organized crime during Senator Estes Kefauver's Special Committee to Investigate Crime in Interstate Commerce. Wilson married Ruth Elinor Evans on June 22, 1950. They had one child.

In 1960, Wilson accepted an invitation from Mayor Richard J. Daley of Chicago to chair the search committee for a new police superintendent. The Chicago Police Department had been rocked by the "Sommerdale scandal," in which eight police officers were implicated in a burglary ring. When Wilson's committee could not agree on one outstanding candidate, it was suggested that Wilson was best qualified for the job. Wilson was interviewed, nominated, and then appointed by Daley. Before accepting the position, Wilson demanded and received Daley's assurance of complete autonomy.

From 1960 to 1967 Wilson implemented his reforms in Chicago. Some of those reforms required substantial expenditures for modern equipment. Others were intended to root out corruption, revise the promotion system, and protect the department from political influences. His reforms antagonized many policemen and politicians, but Daley supported him. The 1960's also brought challenges that Wilson had not faced in Fullerton or Wichita. He criticized Supreme Court decisions such as *Escobedo* and *Miranda* that made police work more difficult by expanding the protections afforded suspects. He handled Dr. Martin Luther King, Jr.'s 1966 civil rights campaign in Chicago with skill and courtesy, even while disagreeing with King on specific points. For example, King favored the establishment of a civilian review board. Wilson, however, considered such a board antithetical to his longstanding objective of insulating police forces from what he considered outside interference. When Wilson retired in 1967, he did so for personal reasons. The suspicion exists, however, that Daley was glad to see Wilson leave so he could reassert mayoral control over the police department.

Despite his accomplishments, Wilson's career reveals the difficulty of implementing and maintaining police reform. The discipline that he had demanded eroded following his departure, as evidenced by what Wilson considered the unprofessional behavior of the Chicago police during the 1968 Democratic National Convention. Wilson retired to Poway, Calif., where he died. His primary legacy was as a trainer of police administrators, both those he worked with and taught and the many more he influenced indirectly through his writings.

[Wilson's papers are at the University of California at Berkeley. His publications include *Police Records* (1942); *Municipal Police Administration* (1943); *Police Administration* (1950); and *Police Planning* (1952). For biographical information see William J. Bopp, *"O. W."* (1977). Obituaries are in the *Chicago Tribune* and the *New York Times*, Oct. 19, 1972.]

DAVID D. BURNS

WILSON, WILLIAM GRIFFITH ("BILL W.") (Nov. 26, 1895–Jan. 24, 1971), cofounder of Alcoholics Anonymous (AA), was born "fittingly enough," as his biographer Robert Thomsen noted, in a small room behind the bar of an inn managed by his paternal grandfather in East Dorset, Vt. The boy's alcoholic father, Gilman Wilson, oversaw marble quarries in the area until 1905, when he deserted his wife, Emily Griffith, and son to work in British Columbia. Emily Wilson obtained a divorce, left Billy with her parents, and moved to Boston to train for a career as an osteopathic physician. Wilson later remembered that as a boy a nagging sense of inadequacy drove him to excel, first to win his grandfather's approval and then to become captain of the baseball team and conductor of the orchestra at Burr and Burton Academy, where he enrolled as a weekday residential student in 1909. He left school in his senior year after the sudden death of his high school sweetheart.

After a year in Boston and a brief visit with his father, Wilson entered Norwich University, a Vermont military academy, in 1914. The next summer, he became engaged to Lois Burnham, whom he had met on vacation in Manchester, Vt.; they were married in 1918. Wilson majored in engineering at Norwich until the United States entered World War I, when he enrolled in an officer's training program in New Bedford, Mass. Attending a gala party at the nearby Grinnell mansion, Second Lieutenant Wilson of the Sixty-sixth Coast Artillery was overcome with an awkward shyness and, though he had never before in his twenty-two years had an alcoholic drink, he reached for a Bronx cocktail.

In 1918 Wilson shipped off to France where he proved himself a capable leader and developed a fondness for brandy. After the war, he and his wife lived with Lois's parents in Brooklyn. Wilson worked as a fraud investigator for an insurance firm and attended night classes at Brooklyn Law School until he decided to break into Wall Street. In 1925, he purchased a Harley-Davidson motorcycle and took off, with Lois in the sidecar, on a maverick cross-country trip as an independent investigator of developing industries; his reports back to Frank Shaw at J. K. Rice and Company earned huge profits for all involved. Wilson drank heavily, but so did many other successful men in the climate of the Roaring Twenties. However, the 1929 stock market crash sent the American economy plummeting and began Wilson's long slide into alcoholism, which was to land him in New York's

Towns Hospital four times between 1933 and 1934.

On Wilson's second visit to Towns, Dr. William Silkworth explained to him that uncontrolled drinking resulted from a disease. This was a radical diagnosis at the time; the American Medical Association still classified alcoholism as a moral failing. Silkworth persuaded Wilson to stop drinking, but Wilson's attempt at sobriety was unsuccessful. Late in November 1934, Wilson received a visit from Ebby Thacher, an old drinking buddy who had recently sobered up by following the precepts of the Oxford Group, an evangelical movement that stressed personal confession of guilt and restitution-making. As Thacher talked, Wilson felt a deep resonance within himself that would eventually become the functional core of Alcoholics Anonymous: "In the kinship of common suffering, one alcoholic had been talking to another." Still, Wilson returned to his bottle and, four days later, to Towns. In his hospital room, as he later described it, he cried out in desperation, "If there is a God, let Him show Himself" and "the room lit up with a great white light." After this conversion experience, Wilson never took another drink and set out to realize his vision of a support network of alcoholics passing on the principles of sobriety.

To support himself, Wilson returned to Wall Street. In May 1935 he traveled to Akron, Ohio, to take part in a proxy fight for control of a small factory, which he lost. Returning depressed to the Mayflower Hotel, he began to pace in front of the bar, and then noticed a directory of local churches. Through Oxford Group channels, he found Dr. Robert Holbrook Smith, a local surgeon and notorious drinker, to whom Wilson explained that he could only stay sober by sharing his experience with another alcoholic. The day on which "Dr. Bob" took his last drink, June 10, 1935, would later be celebrated as the day on which AA was founded. The first few years of AA were a difficult struggle. In 1937 Wilson split with the Oxford Group; that fall, he met with John D. Rockefeller, Jr., who, warning that money would spoil a wonderful idea, gave a meager $5,000 to relieve the personal financial strain on Wilson and Smith. In 1938 Wilson began dictating *Alcoholics Anonymous* (1939), affectionately known as "the big book"; he would finish a chapter, read it to his AA group and then listen, relaxed but alert, as debate stretched

into the night. Wilson formed the Alcoholics Foundation in 1938 and began a fervid publicity campaign to raise money. In the 1940's he ended this campaign, believing he had been putting his own ego before the needs of the group; he then began to advocate the policies of anonymity, corporate poverty, and nonprofessionalism, which became hallmarks of AA. In the spring of 1941, the Wilsons moved from New York City to Bedford Hills, N.Y. Wilson recorded his experience in *Twelve Steps and Twelve Traditions* (1953). A year later, speaking in front of 5,000 members gathered in St. Louis to celebrate the twentieth anniversary of AA, he proposed a General Service Board made up of delegates elected from regional groups, which would take over supervision of the organization from its founders; the resolution passed by a show of hands.

Wilson continued to provide support and encouragement from AA headquarters in New York City. He wrote a history of AA, *Alcoholics Anonymous Comes of Age* (1957), set out a program for the future in *Twelve Concepts for World Service* (1962), and gathered excerpts of his many articles into *The AA Way of Life as Bill Sees It* (1967). He also anonymously advocated vitamin B therapy for the treatment of alcoholism. Constantly traveling, he would drop in on meetings, where he would inevitably be recognized and called upon to share his experience; the founder of AA could never be truly anonymous. At the time of his death in Miami, where he was receiving medical treatment for emphysema, Wilson's organization had grown to nearly half a million members, with groups in the United States and eighty-eight other countries.

[Wilson's personal correspondence and his tape-recorded oral history are kept in the Archives of the General Service Office of Alcoholics Anonymous in New York City; there are some restrictions on use of this material and researchers must apply for access to the Trustees of the Archive Committee. See also Robert Thomsen, *Bill W.* (1975); Ernest Kurtz, *Not-God: A History of Alcoholics Anonymous* (1979); and Bob P., "The Unforgettable Bill W.," *Reader's Digest*, Apr. 1986. Obituaries are in the *New York Times*, Jan. 26, 1971; and *Newsweek*, Feb. 8, 1971.]

CORINNE T. FIELD

WIMSATT, WILLIAM KURTZ (Nov. 17, 1907–Nov. 10, 1973), professor and literary critic, was the son of William Kurtz Wimsatt, a surgeon, and Bertha McSherry. He received his B.A. degree (summa cum laude) from Georgetown University in 1928, his M.A. degree from the Catholic University of America in 1929, and his Ph.D. in English literature from Yale University in 1939.

Wimsatt served as head of the English Department at Portsmouth Priory School, in Portsmouth, R.I., from 1930 to 1935. Thereafter he spent his entire teaching career at Yale: as an instructor in the English Department from 1939 to 1943; as an assistant professor from 1943 to 1949; as an associate professor from 1949 to 1955; and as a full professor from 1955 until his death. He held the Frederick Clifford Ford chair from 1965 until 1974, at which point he became Sterling Professor of English.

Wimsatt was a specialist in eighteenth-century literature and wrote or edited a number of significant works on this period, including *The Prose Style of Samuel Johnson* (1941), *Selected Poetry and Prose of Alexander Pope* (editor, 1951), *Boswell for the Defense* (1959), *Samuel Johnson on Shakespeare* (editor, 1960), *The Portraits of Alexander Pope* (1965), and *Samuel Johnson: Selected Poetry and Prose* (editor, with Frank Brady, 1978). But he made his greatest mark as a scholar in the field of literary theory.

In 1954, he published in collaboration with the philosopher Monroe C. Beardsley a collection of essays entitled *The Verbal Icon*. One of these, "The Intentional Fallacy," represented the high watermark of the reaction against romanticism, and more especially against the biographical approach to literary criticism, in twentieth-century literary theory. Reacting against the approach of the nineteenth-century French critic, Charles-Augustin Sainte-Beuve, who had argued that one of the principal aims of literary criticism was to discover the man behind the book, Wimsatt and Beardsley maintained that the poem was a self-sustaining and self-sufficient entity—a verbal icon—that deserved study in its own right. Any meaning that it might have was an event that took place in the mind of the reader. There was no point, when examining a text, in finding out through consultation of a writer's notebooks, his letters to his friends, the anecdotal evidence of his own or other people's diaries or the like, any indication of what the author intended to say. What mattered were the words on the page, and the effort, sensitivity, and degree of literary awareness that

the reader brought to them. There was no more point in wondering what an author had intended to do in a poem, play, or novel than in asking what a sculptor "really meant" by a statue, or a painter by a watercolor. In other words, the reader, not the author, was responsible for determining the "meaning" of a text.

Wimsatt expressed a comparable idea in his "Foreward" to an edited collection of essays written by a number of fellow specialists in verse form, *Versification: Major Language Types* (1973). Like the other American formalists whose leader he was, he preferred when talking about literature to use the word "poem" as a generic term for all literary artifacts. Therefore, it was not merely because he was talking about a genre characterized by scansion and rhyme that his foreward included the claim that "since the poem is a mental transaction, everything in it is something that happens in the mind of the reader." In the broader context of the intellectual history of Europe and North America, his insistence on the role of the reader anticipates the ideas developed with characteristically Gallic panache by the French structuralist and semiologist Roland Barthes. What Barthes called, in 1968, the "death of the author" implies the same refusal to look for meaning in anything but the words on the page, and the same transfer of authority from the author to the reader. According to Wimsatt, *The Father* would be just as good—or bad—a play, if Strindberg had been the happiest of men and the most contented of fathers. Similarly, in Wimsatt's view literary quality was the product of a large number of factors in which the author's intention, personal life, and degree of sincerity had no place. According to Wimsatt's theory of art, if Shakespeare were to come miraculously back to life and tell us what he "really meant" when he wrote *Hamlet*, this information would have a certain anecdotal value. But it would not have more authority than any other interpretation of *Hamlet* written by an intelligent reader who knew the play thoroughly and could place it in its linguistic and historical context.

When, in 1976, Wimsatt published his *Day of the Leopards: Essays in Defense of Poems*, the English novelist and critic David Lodge summarized the theorist's views in a way of which Wimsatt strongly approved when he described him as producing "a theory of poetry which regards poems as complexes of publicly accessible meanings which, without invoking the Chimera of 'scientific' methology, seeks to bring criticism to the maximum degree of precision compatible with the essential indeterminacy of its materials." Wimsatt's interest in literary theory is particularly visible in his collaboration with Cleanth Brooks in what is rather misleadingly called *Literary Criticism: A Short History* (1957), a two-volume work of some 700 pages, described as "the standard work on the subject" in a review in the *New York Times Book Review*.

Wimsatt married Margaret Elizabeth Hecht in September 1944; the couple had two children.

Wimsatt was the recipient of Guggenheim, Ford Foundation, and Yale University Senior Faculty fellowships. His exemplary scholarship was also recognized in the form of honorary degrees conferred by Villanova University (1962), the University of Notre Dame (1963), St. Louis University (1964), Le Moyne College (1965), and Kenyon College (1970).

In his private life as in his scholarly life Wimsatt exhibited a breadth of interests: he enjoyed playing chess, he was an amateur painter, and he collected Native American artifacts.

[Other works by Wimsatt include *Philosophic Words* (1948); *English Stage Comedy: English Institute Essays, 1954* (1955); *Explication as Criticism: Selected Papers from the English Institute* (editor, 1963); and *Hateful Contraries* (1965). John Palmer and Martin Price, eds., *Literary Theory and Structure: Essays in Honor of William K. Wimsatt* (1973), pays tribute to Wimsatt's theory and his influence as a critic. Obituaries appear in the *New York Times*, Dec. 18, 1975; and in *Bookman's Weekly*, Jan. 5, 1976.]

P. M. W. THODY

WINCHELL, WALTER (Apr. 7, 1897–Feb. 20, 1972), journalist, was born in New York City, the son of Jacob Winechel, a shopkeeper, and Janette Bakst. (Walter later changed the spelling to Winchell.) The creator of the modern gossip column, Winchell was one of the nation's best-known newsmen in the 1930's and 1940's. At the height of his power, he was published in more than 800 papers nationwide, and nearly one American in four tuned in to his weekly Sunday night broadcast on the radio. By turns expansive and cruel, sentimental and cynical, "W. W." or "Mrs. Winchell's little boy, Walter," as he liked to style himself, was fawned over and feared by those who sought his favors.

For a time, his name was synonymous with the glamour and excitement of New York City.

His wealth and power at the height of his fame contrasted sharply with the poverty of his youth. Winchell's father abandoned the family, while he was still a child on Manhattan's Upper East Side, and the youngster took to the streets as a newsboy to supplement his mother's meager income. His formal education ended in the sixth grade, when he left P.S. 184 at age thirteen to join Gus Edward's national tour as a singer in an act that included George Jessel and Jack Wiener. Two years later, having outgrown the Edwards troupe, he teamed with Rita Green in a song, dance, and patter act that failed to reach the first-line vaudeville circuit but provided Winchell steady work in small towns and cities across America. Volunteering for the navy in World War I, he served as an admiral's receptionist in New York City.

With the Armistice, he returned to second-rate vaudeville and by 1919 had begun to break the boredom of the national tour by typing a one-page flyer titled "The Newsense" and posted backstage for his fellow performers to read. Initially offering information about inexpensive places to eat, where to do laundry, and other helpful hints, Winchell added bits of gossip to the mix and soon discovered there was a market for such "items," as he called them, in several of the theatrical trade papers. He soon abandoned vaudeville for free-lancing, earning a precarious living over the next two years peddling his gossip to *Billboard* and the *Vaudeville News*. In 1922, the *Vaudeville News* hired him as a full-time reporter and advertising salesman. Two years later, he moved to the *Evening Graphic* as drama editor, theatrical columnist and play reviewer. It was the beginning of his climb to fame and within a few months, his column was the talk of the town. He had refined the format of his backstage flyer into the modern gossip column, a piquant amalgam of gossip, political opinion, jokes, insider information, and teasing speculation. The result, "Your Broadway and Mine," became the mainstay of the *Graphic*'s circulation. In 1929, lured by more money and a promise of greater independence, Winchell took his column to the New York *Daily Mirror*, where he remained until the paper's death more than thirty years later.

Winchell's first marriage to Rita Green, his vaudeville partner, lasted two years (1920–1922). In 1923 he married June Magee, a dancer, but their life together was marked by frequent estrangements caused by his womanizing and her refusal to take part in his frenetic life of clubs, theater, and late-night rambles through the city. (He customarily rose in late afternoon, began his evening rounds at about eight, and returned to his hotel room at the St. Moriz around 7:00 A.M.) Apart for most of their marriage, they reconciled shortly before her death from cancer in 1970. They had two children.

By 1937 he had become a millionaire and one of the most powerful figures in New York. "Making Winchell"—getting a favorable mention or "orchid" in his column—was the openly acknowledged goal of a generation of producers, performers, and celebrities. Avoiding his "Drop Dead" list was another, because banishment from his column or an unfavorable review was a kind of occupational death. Everyone knew that Winchell had almost singlehandedly saved *Hellzapoppin'*, a 1938 revue, by giving it several weeks of free promotion in his column after it had been universally panned by the New York drama critics. The show ran almost four years on Broadway, almost as long as on the road, and was turned into a successful movie, making stars Chic Johnson and Ole Olson rich. In contrast, there were performers who could point to a job loss or a withdrawn casting interview because of an unfavorable item in Winchell's column.

The column, variously titled "On Broadway," "This Town of Ours," and "Man About Town," was nationally syndicated and brought the glamour of the city's sophisticated nighttime world to millions of Depression-era Americans. It was usually assembled at Table 50 in the Cub Room of Sherman Billingsley's Stork Club at 3 East Fifty-third Street in New York City. Winchell presided there nightly, gathering the next day's show business news from a steady parade of sycophantic press agents and often from the celebrities themselves, who had come personally to tell him the intimate details of their lives. "Other columnists may print it," Winchell once boasted. "I make it public."

The root of his success was the special flavor of his prose. "Winchell wrote like a man honking in a traffic jam," the playwright Ben Hecht said. Winchell coined the words like "infanticipating" for pregnancy, "blessed event" and "storked" for birth, and "middle-aisling it" for marriage. He used phonetic spellings like "Joosh" (Jewish) or "moom pitcher" (moving

picture), and employed expressions like "phfft" or "splitsville" for divorce. H. L. Mencken, in *The American Language*, credits him with creating more neologisms than any other columnist of his day. W. J. Funk, the lexicographer, wrote in 1933 that Winchell was among the decade's ten most prolific creators of American slang, or as Winchell would have said it, "slanguage."

His radio program at 9:00 P.M. on Sunday nights attracted millions of listeners, who were often overwhelmed by Winchell's nervous, barking, machine-gun like delivery of about two hundred words per minute, accompanied by regular clicking of a telegraph key. His weekly opening—"Good evening, Mr. and Mrs. America, from border to border and coast to coast, and all the ships at sea. Let's go to press!"—was a household phrase. The program, mirroring the Broadway column in language and content, was a melange of gossip, nostrums, politics, and predictions. Starting in the late 1940's, he gave tips on horses and advice on stocks. He offered clues to the mystery tunes on "Stop the Music," a popular radio show that offered cash prizes to listeners who recognized obscure pieces of music. He was one of the most popular figures on the air.

Winchell counted Franklin D. Roosevelt among his friends, and he is widely credited with using his radio broadcasts to prepare the American public to accept Roosevelt's running for a third term. On several occasions, Roosevelt invited him to the White House for private conversations. He regularly received notes from J. Edgar Hoover, who sometimes joined him at the Stork Club. In 1939 Winchell personally arranged the surrender of Louis ("Lepke") Buchalter, a Manhattan gangster wanted on murder and narcotics charges, who agreed to turn himself in to the FBI chief if Winchell were present.

His closest friend—some say his only close friend—was the writer Damon Runyon, who often accompanied Winchell on his nightly rounds of Broadway clubs or rode with him to fires and crime scenes in his car specially equipped by the New York Police Department with a radio, a siren, and a flashing red light. Following Runyon's death from lung cancer in 1946, Winchell established the Damon Runyon Memorial Fund in his memory and through his column raised millions of dollars for cancer research. Winchell bore all of the administrative costs for fund-raising and distribution of the money.

He was not otherwise a generous man. His opinions were delivered in a combative style that frequently led to lawsuits, especially in the later years when Winchell's influence and popularity had begun to wane and his columns had taken on a desperate, often strident and ugly tone. Following World War II, Winchell moved politically to the far right, and early on embraced the anti-Communism of Joseph McCarthy. He attacked Harry Truman and Adlai Stevenson as un-American and assailed the *New York Post* as a Communist tool. (The *Post* had published a series of twenty-four articles that suggested, among other things, that Winchell was an intimate of gangsters and that his daily column was derived wholly from press agents' releases.) He carried on a personal vendetta against a radio talk-show host, Barry Gray. He hated Ed Sullivan, a rival columnist, and frequently raged against him in print.

In the end, both his syndicate and his readers tired of his daily tirades against real and imagined enemies. Radio executives became wary of his extremist language and the weekly diatribes. His radio program was canceled in the mid-1950's. By the end of that decade his syndication had dropped to fewer than fifty papers and, with the demise of the *Daily Mirror* in 1963, soon disappeared altogether. The Stork Club closed. Despite efforts to keep his column alive in a handful of limited-circulation New York City area newspapers and his appearance as narrator on a 1960's television series, *The Untouchables*, Winchell no longer had an audience. He left New York in 1965 for the West Coast, moving restlessly between homes in Arizona and Los Angeles, where he died of cancer seven years later.

[A collection of autobiographical pieces, *Winchell Exclusive: Things That Happened to Me–And Me to Them*, was published posthumously in 1975. The most authoritative biography is Bob Thomas, *Winchell* (1971). See also St. Clair McKelway, *Gossip: The Life and Times of Walter Winchell* (1940); Ed Weiner, *Let's Go to Press: A Biography of Walter Winchell* (1955); and Herman Klurfeld, *Winchell: His Life and Times* (1976). A front-page obituary appears in the *New York Times*, Feb. 21, 1972. It is reprinted in Alden Whitman, *Come to Judgment* (1980).]

ALLAN L. DAMON

WINTERHALTER, HUGO (Aug. 15, 1909–Sept. 17, 1973), arranger, conductor, and composer, was born in Wilkes-Barre, Pa. He started playing the violin at the age of six, later taking up reed instruments while he was still attending the Sisters of Mercy parochial school. By the age of sixteen, still in high school at St. Mary's in Wilkes-Barre, he was making $6 per night playing professionally in a local band. Later he led the school orchestra and gave music lessons to put himself through college at Mount St. Mary's in Emmitsburg, Md. He graduated from the New England Conservatory, after which he taught music in high school in the early 1930's.

In the mid-1930's, Winterhalter played saxophone in club bands and as a sideman with Howard Lally and Nye Mayhew in New York City. By the late 1930's and the 1940's, he was playing with various big-band orchestras, joining Larry Clinton in 1938, then Jack Jenney (for whose band Winterhalter arranged the famed "Stardust"), Raymond Scott, the Dorsey Brothers, Count Basie, Vaughn Monroe, and Benny Goodman. It was while he was with Tommy Dorsey in 1944 that Winterhalter turned to arranging.

In 1948, Winterhalter joined MGM as music conductor; he later served in the same capacity at Columbia (1949–1950), RCA Victor (1950–1963), and Kapp (1963). At RCA, he was a key studio arranger and conductor; his large string orchestras produced such instrumental hits as "Blue Tango" and "Vanessa" and backed many popular singers, among them, Perry Como ("Don't Let the Stars Get in Your Eyes"), Billy Eckstine, Doris Day, Eddie Fisher ("Oh, My Papa"), Dinah Shore, Kate Smith, Frank Sinatra, Kay Starr, and Mario Lanza. Eleven of these recordings became gold records, the recording industry's term for those selling one million or more copies.

Winterhalter's work is noted for its lush arrangement and meticulous craftsmanship. His biggest hit was his arrangement of Eddie Heywood's instrumental piece "Canadian Sunset" (1956), featuring Heywood himself on piano, which reached No. 2 on the charts and sold 1.5 million copies during the 1950's. As a composer he wrote "How Do I Love Thee?" (1951), "Hesitation" (1952), and "Melody of Spain" (1962). Winterhalter also appeared as guest conductor with the Hollywood Bowl Orchestra, the Milwaukee Symphony, and the National Symphony in Washington, D.C.

During these years, as one RCA executive put it, "everything he touched turned to gold."

He died of cancer while in Greenwich Hospital in Greenwich, Conn., survived by his wife, the former Mary Margaret Hardey, and three of their four children.

[A complete list of Winterhalter's recordings appears in Roger D. Kinkle, ed., *The Complete Encyclopedia of Popular Music and Jazz (1900–1950)*, vol. 3 (1947). An obituary is in the *New York Times*, Sept. 18, 1973.]

STEVEN D. JONES

WODEHOUSE, PELHAM GRENVILLE (Oct. 15, 1881–Feb. 14, 1975), novelist and playwright, was born in Guildford, England, the third son of Henry Ernest Wodehouse, a British civil servant working as a judge in Hong Kong, and Eleanor Deane, affectionately known to her children as "Memsahib." Educated at Dulwich College in London, he enjoyed and wrote about it affectionately as Wrykyn in his early novels, especially *Mike* (1909), introducing in Psmith what Benny Green called the first adult to figure in an English school story.

His father's pension, paid in Indian rupees, varied too alarmingly for Wodehouse to go to Oxford, so he went to work at the Hong Kong and Shanghai Bank in 1900. He escaped the tedium through writing school stories and comic journalism. In 1909, having already invented one of his best known if least attractive characters—the professional sponger, Stanley Featherstonehaugh Ukridge—Wodehouse came to America. Initially he sold his work quite easily, but when difficulties arose he went back to London. Subsequently, especially in the interwar years, he commuted regularly across the Atlantic, using the experience to create the scene of the actress explaining to a customs official that three dozen new dresses are a modest allowance for a ten-day visit. In New York, in 1914 he met and married a widow, Ethel Rowley, who already had a daughter, Leonora, aged nine. The couple had no children of their own, but "Plum"—Wodehouse's nickname since boyhood—adored his step-daughter, and was heartbroken by her death during a minor operation in May 1944, while he was in France.

New York City enabled Wodehouse to make money, especially in musical comedy. He wrote four plays with Guy Bolton, wrote librettos for fourteen musicals, and composed the words for the music of Jerome Kern; one of their most enduring songs was "Bill," from *Showboat*. He volunteered for service in World War I, but bad eyesight kept him out of the British army.

In 1919, he created his two most famous characters, Bertie Wooster, the indolent but not entirely foolish man about town, and his manservant Jeeves. Like Beamarchais's Figaro, Jeeves is much more intelligent than his master, but he has a new function—enabling Bertie to avoid the responsibilities of matrimony. The pair were featured in some fifty short stories and twelve novels. *Right Ho Jeeves* (1934) has one of the funniest scenes in world literature when the inebriated newt fancier, Gussie Fink-Nottle, distributes the prizes at Market Snodsbury Grammar School.

Equally well known is Lord Emsworth, the amiable and dreamy Lord of Blandings Castle, a stately home. He appears to especially good effect in the novels *Summer Lightning* (1929) and *Summer Moonshine* (1937), as well as in many short stories. The best of these, "Lord Emsworth and the Girl Friend," first published in 1928, is unusual in presenting a sympathetic portrait of a relationship between a child and an adult.

Wodehouse's life in the 1920's and 1930's was pleasant and uneventful. He and Ethel traveled frequently between homes in New York City and London, had families of dogs in both countries, and many friends. She happily gave many parties. He was a recluse, a hardworking professional writer, enjoying masculine company on the golf course and writing about it to perfection in two volumes of short stories, *The Clicking of Cuthbert* (1922) and *The Heart of a Goof* (1926). In 1940, when living in Le Touquet, France, he was caught up by the rapid German advance, and interned in a series of camps.

In June 1941, he made what he later recognized was a great mistake in giving five broadcast talks from Berlin. These caused an uproar in wartime Britain, where there were calls for Wodehouse to be put on trial for treason. Their real nature is indicated by the remark, attributed to one of Wodehouse's fellow inmates, that after the war he was going to buy a German soldier, keep him in the back garden, and count him six times a day, just as the prisoners had been repeatedly counted by the Germans. These programs were subsequently used throughout the war in an American military propaganda school as models of how to make fun of your enemies without their noticing what you are doing.

The dispute over the broadcasts cast a gloom over the last thirty years of Plum's life. He never returned to England, being too old to travel to London to receive the knighthood officially bestowed on him in the New Year's Honors List of 1975. His prolonged absence from England may explain the timeless quality of his best work. He was writing about a lifestyle that, if it ever existed, had disappeared by 1939. Since he never saw England's changes firsthand, he kept a vision of it in his imagination, which he described with a skill that has ensured the continued republication of his books.

Politically, Wodehouse was less naive than at first appeared. In *The Code of the Woosters* (1938), would-be dictator Roderick Spode, founder of the Blackshorts of Britain, is clearly modeled on Oswald Mosley. He is brought down by Jeeves's revelation of the profession he pursues under the pseudonym of Eulalie, the name of a ladies emporium in Bond Street. As Bertie notes: "In this life, you can do one of two things: Be a dictator; or design ladies underwear. One or the other. Not both."

All Wodehouse's characters are caricatures, such as his American millionaires, with their happy memories of Sing Sing and their passionate pursuit of golf mementos—even more so than the clergymen, the aristocrats, and the aunts who inhabit his imaginary England. His books are impeccably plotted, but what sticks in the reader's mind are the characters and phrases used to describe them: Bertie's Aunt Agatha "wears barbed wire next to her skin and devours her young at the full moon." Honeria Glossop has "a laugh like a squadron of cavalry going over a tin bridge." Ferdinand Dribble, at the end of the short story "The Heart of a Goof," folds his girlfriend in his arms "using the interlocking grip."

In 1939, the University of Oxford, to the great displeasure of F. R. Leavis and the *Scrutiny* group, the self-appointed guardians of literary standards in English, awarded Wodehouse a D.Litt. *Honoris Causa*. It recognized the unfailing good humor of the man and his world, thus inevitably evoking, for his many admirers, the verbal felicities such as the description of a golf foursome "moving across the links like one of the great race migrations of the Middle Ages," as well as the idyllic world in which the sun always shines and love conquers all without creating any of the problems associated with sex.

Few writers have been more appreciated by their fellow professionals than Wodehouse. In 1930, prefacing *Week-end Wodehouse*, Hilaire Belloc described him as "the best living writer in England, the head of my profession." Evelyn Waugh put his finger on the secret of Wodehouse's enduring charm when he wrote that for him, "there had been no fall of man, no tasting of the forbidden fruit." They are, he wrote, "still in Eden. The gardens of Blandings Castle are the original garden . . . while we are all exiled." This is true of Wodehouse's other major series, the short stories told by Mr. Mulliner about his innumerable nephews—but not those, it should be noted, about his nieces.

Wodehouse's world, like that of Evelyn Waugh's novels or Anthony Powell's *A Dance to the Music of Time* (1951–1978), is one of what his official biographer, Frances Donaldson, calls "purely masculine fantasy." His values are those of the school and the gentleman's club, of the cricket field and the golf course. All the qualities most highly esteemed are those of whom the English call "good loser": a sense of humor, recognition of one's inferiority, a readiness to help a pal. His women are admired insofar as they approach this masculine ideal; but all too easily, they turn into birds of prey, bullying the harmless male as he tries to escape into his golf, his garden, his bachelor apartment—or, in the case of Lord Emsworth, into his treasured copy of *Whiffle on the Pig*.

Yet the men are never resentful. It is the nature of the aunt to bully her nephew, just as it is the nature of the sister to try to improve her brother's behavior as Lord Emsworth's sisters, Constance, and Julie, attempt to improve his. Wodehouse's permanent appeal, in this respect, is to men who have never quite outgrown the irresponsibility of their early teens, but who have nevertheless developed an adult appreciation for the accurate use of the English language. Wodehouse's books are untranslatable. As Gussie goes off, with a pint of mixed spirits flapping against his gills, to address the finest and fairest in the county of Gloucestershire, Bertie follows Jeeves's advice and inspects the imagination. Jeeves was right: it boggled.

Wodehouse's remaining years were spent peacefully at his home on Long Island.

[The Wodehouse archives are at Dulwich College, London. Wodehouse has been much studied. See R. B. D. French, *P. G. Wodehouse* (1966); and Lady Frances Donaldson, *P. G. Wodehouse: A Biography* (1982). The best bibliographical guide is Eileen McIlvaine, Louise S. Sherby, and James Heineman, *P. G. Wodehouse: A Comprehensive Bibliography and Checklist* (1990). An obituary appears in the *New York Times*, Feb. 15, 1975.]

P. M. W. THODY

WOLFSON, HARRY AUSTRYN (Nov. 2, 1887–Sept. 19, 1974), scholar of Hebrew literature and philosophy, was born in Ostrin, Lithuania (today Belorussia), the second child and oldest son of a family of seven. His father, Max Wolfson, taught Russian and Hebrew, while his mother, Sarah Dvorah Savitsky, a housewife, ran a traditional Jewish home. Educated in the customary manner of East European Jews, Wolfson spent most of the time in the communal study hall of Ostrin. From age nine to twelve, he spent time in a variety of yeshivas before arriving, at age thirteen, at one of the most prestigious academies of eastern Europe, the Slobodka yeshiva in Kovno, Lithuania. For the next three years, Wolfson was immersed in rigorous Talmudic textual methodology and interpretation, an approach to scholarship that was to shape his later historical and philosophical analysis and thinking.

Wolfson arrived in the United States in 1903 and for two years attended Rabbi Isaac Elhanon Yeshiva (later Yeshiva University) in New York City. He then moved to Scranton, Pa., where he taught at the Montefiore Hebrew School while catching up on his general education, concentrating especially on the English language. Within three months he had his elementary school diploma, and in 1908 graduated high school with the highest honors. He was awarded a competitive scholarship to Harvard. By this time Wolfson was no longer an observant Jew and had stripped himself of outward Jewishness in his search for a synthesis of cultures that would satisfy him.

In 1908 Wolfson entered Harvard College, where for a year he lived off campus, which gave him the opportunity to develop his Hebrew and Zionist aspirations. He already wrote Hebrew poetry; now he began to write for the newly created *Ha-Yom* ("The Day"), a daily Hebrew newspaper published in New York City.

At Harvard, Wolfson concentrated his stud-

ies in Semitic languages and literature. He studied with world-famous scholars, including George Foot Moore in the history of religions, William R. Arnold in Bible, and David Gordon Lyon in Assyriology. Lyon and Moore were his mentors. Wolfson also came under the influence of George Santayana, the poet and philosopher. Wolfson obtained his B.A. and his M.A. in 1912. He was then awarded the coveted Sheldon Traveling Fellowship, which enabled him to spend the next two years visiting European universities and libraries, where he copied passages from hundreds of medieval manuscripts, on his path toward his new goal of scholarship.

In choosing to write his doctoral dissertation on Crescas, a relatively unknown Spanish-Jewish philosopher of the fourteenth century, Wolfson chose a scholar who was critical of both Maimonides and Aristotle. He immersed himself in the current philosophies and literature available to and referred to by Crescas. He later applied this methodology to his studies of Spinoza, Saadia, and Philo, for he felt that this was the only way to enter into the thinking patterns of these philosophers.

Wolfson found that the problems in philosophy of the three monotheistic religions are basically the same—for example the conflict between faith and reason—and that Philo began the discussion of these problems. It was thus Philo's thinking that dominated European thought until Spinoza. Until Wolfson, most people thought that the Jewish contribution to philosophy was reflective and thus secondary; he put the Jewish contribution into a central position.

Wolfson's method in his writing was to make explicit the processes of a philosopher's thought, calling it the "hypothetico-deductive method of textual study." It was the task of the interpreter to clarify a philosopher's thinking that required familiarity with the philosopher's intellectual milieu, for only this would enable the interpreter to understand the latent processes of a writer's thought.

To the Gentile community, Wolfson showed that the contributions to philosophy by Jewish thinkers had to be taken seriously. Secondly, his scholarship established an interfaith community of thought in which the common problems of philosophy overrode theological differences.

Wolfson received his Ph.D. from Harvard University and became an instructor there in

1915; he was appointed associate professor in 1921. In addition, he was invited in 1923 to teach part-time at the newly founded Jewish Institute of Religion in New York City. For three years he commuted between the two until his appointment as professor of Hebrew literature and philosophy at Harvard in 1925, a position he held until 1958, when he became Professor emeritus. At the same time he continued in his work on Spinoza. He published *Crescas' Critique of Aristotle* in 1929, and *The Philosophy of Spinoza: Unfolding the Latent Processes of His Reasoning* five years later (1934). He published many seminal articles in scholarly journals over the years. In 1947, his work *Philo: Foundations of Religious Philosophy in Judaism, Christianity and Islam* came out, to be followed by *The Philosophy of the Church Fathers* in 1956. His two major final books were published posthumously, *The Philosophy of the Kalam* (1976) and *From Philo to Spinoza: Two Studies in Religious Philosophy* (1977).

Wolfson was popularly viewed as a cloistered scholar obsessed with his writing and teaching. He never married, but had a wide circle of friends and students.

Harry Wolfson received many academic honors during his lifetime. He was a fellow of the American Academy for Jewish Research and served as its president (1935–1937), and he was a fellow of the Mediaeval Academy of America. He was editor in chief of the publication *Corpus Commentariorum Averrois in Aristotelem* which consists of critical editions of the manuscripts of the Islamic philosopher Averroes (Ibn-Rushd), including of the originals in Arabic, the Hebrew and Latin translations, and the English translations and explanatory comments by the editors. He was president of the American Oriental Society (1957–1958) and was a member of the American Academy of Arts and Sciences. The American Council of Learned Societies awarded him its 1958 prize, and in 1965 the *Harry Austryn Wolfson Jubilee Volume* was published by the American Academy for Jewish Research in his honor.

Wolfson died at Harvard's Stillman Infirmary in Cambridge, Mass.

[For further information see Leo W. Schwartz, *Wolfson of Harvard: Portrait of a Scholar* (1978), which includes a bibliography; Hillel Goldberg, *Between Berlin and Slobodka* (1989), chapter 3; and Susanne Klingenstein, *Jews in the American Acad-emy* (1991). An obituary is in the *New York Times*, Sept. 21, 1974.]

SARA REGUER

WOOD, GARFIELD ARTHUR ("GAR")

(Dec. 4, 1880–June 19, 1971), industrialist and powerboat-racing enthusiast, was born in Mapleton, Iowa, the son of Walt Wood, a lake captain who worked the river cities; his mother was commonly referred to as "Mother Wood." He spent his early years in Osakis, Duluth, and St. Paul, Minn., which inspired his later interest in speedboat racing. One of twelve brothers and sisters, he was christened Garfield Arthur Wood for President John A. Garfield and Vice President Chester A. Arthur, who were elected that year. He was generally known as "Gar" or "Commodore."

After graduating from the Armour Institute of Technology in Chicago, he sailed on Great Lakes freighters out of Duluth. For a time he worked in the automobile industry, but eventually obtained a job as a marine motor mechanic.

In 1912, after watching two men using a hand winch to unload coal from a truck, Wood purchased a piece of wrought-iron pipe from a junkyard for fifty cents, as well as a pump salvaged from an abandoned Buick, and developed the hydraulic hoist to create the dump truck. The lift raised the front end of the truck so that the load could slide out the rear. To finance his new business, he sold half of his patent for $5,000. A custom-built product, the early hydraulic lifts were not suited for the mass-production lines of the day, so Wood moved his operation to Detroit to be closer to truck manufacturers. He later added steel dump truck bodies to his line of products.

World War I led to enormous demand for his product. Anticipating a slack demand following the war, Wood bought a competitor, Horizontal Hydraulic Hoist Company of Milwaukee, Wis., to obtain its markets and a number of useful patents.

In 1922 Wood incorporated his company as the Wood Hydraulic Hoist and Body Company, which became the world's largest manufacturer of truck equipment. Four years later, he purchased mechanical hoist patents from Highway Trailer Company of Eggerton, Wis., to expand his business. In 1931, Wood repurchased his hydraulic hoist patent. Sold for $5,000, it cost him $750,000 to buy back.

During the 1930's Wood continued to expand his business, branching out into oil burners for home heating, automobile truck winches, cranes, derricks, and road building machinery. In 1933, his corporation was renamed Gar Wood Industries, Inc.

He patented a device to prevent airplane accidents caused by clogged gasoline lines or fuel-pump failures. He also invented a pilotless speedboat that was used as a moving target by Navy gunners.

He served as chairman of the board of Gar Wood Industries in Detroit until 1941 and also provided financial backing for the Chris-Craft Corp. of Pampano Beach, Fla., a builder of pleasure motorboats.

In the early 1930's Wood designed a powerful high-speed launch for the Navy and spoke with President Franklin D. Roosevelt about its possible combat use. The president liked the vessel, although Navy brass scoffed at what would evolve into the hit-and-run PT boat of World War II. The PT boat design was based on a number of Wood's innovations, including the placement of an airplane motor in a boat. He developed a hull strong enough to withstand the installation of these motors and the high speeds. Following the war, General Douglas MacArthur praised the small boats and said that two hundred of them in the West Pacific might have turned the scales at the outset of the war. Following the war, he built small boats for the Navy and manufactured by hydraulic hoists and heating equipment.

In the early 1940's he sold his stake in Gar Wood Industries and retired to Miami's Fisher Island, purchasing an estate once owned by William K. Vanderbilt. From that base, he traveled about the continent in a twin-engine seaplane, working on countless mechanical projects.

Thanks to his fortune, he was able to devote much of his life to his passion for speedboats, spending enormous sums of money on sleek, powerful crafts. He estimated that by 1936, he had spent more than $1 million on his "hobby."

Wood began manufacturing speedboats commercially in Marysville, Mich., in 1916. This operation, incorporated as Gar Wood, Inc., was separate from his other business. The company built speedboats of all sizes, from sixteen-foot runabouts to forty-foot cruisers. In 1937, the boat-building company was absorbed by Gar Wood Industries for $65,000.

Wood was known as the "Gray Fox of Algonac," earning the nickname from his appearance (tall, gaunt, and wiry, with white hair) and from the town in Michigan where his power boats were built.

His career as a speedboat racer began in 1911 in the Mississippi Power Boat regatta at Duluth. Driving a craft he had reconditioned for its owner, he drove at thirty-two miles an hour—a record at the time. In 1920, he set a world-record speed mark of seventy miles per hour, and continued to hold the record at ever-increasing speeds until 1946.

During his years as a racer, his "Miss America" series of hydroplanes captured the William Harmsworth British International Trophy, the principal prize in powerboat racing, eight times (1920–1921, 1926, and 1928–1933). Wood drove in each of those years except 1931, when he was disqualified from the race for passing the starting line too soon. However, that race was won by one of his powerboats that was driven by his brother George. Wood also won the Gold Cup, the chief U.S. award for hydroplane racing, four times (1917 and 1919–1921). He retired from competitive racing in 1933, though he never gave up his love of powerboating.

Always eager to prove the speed and worth of his boats, he would arrange singular challenges. He once beat a Twentieth Century railroad train from Albany to New York City by several minutes in one of his speedboats, and again raced and won against a train from Miami to New York City. He held the international motorboat racing record from 1932 to 1937.

A charter member in 1953 of the American Power Boating Association's "Hall of Fame," Wood was named one of ten members of its first "honor squadron."

In 1949 he unveiled the Venturi, which he said was the product of twenty-eight years of planning. It was a flat-bottom, twin-hulled ship that used the principle of the catamaran for stability. After being successfully tested in all types of weather, the ship ended up in a storm off the Florida coast in 1954. Wood and eight other persons were rescued from a life raft by a Coast Guard helicopter. The Venturi was said to have cost $600,000 to develop.

At the time of his death, Wood was survived by his son, Gar Wood, Jr. A commemorative speedboat race, the Gar Wood Trophy Race, was inaugurated on the Detroit River in his honor in 1974.

[Histories of Gar Wood Industries are in "Highway Machinery Keeps Speed Champion Busy," *Newsweek*, Nov. 28, 1936, and in "Peace Arrives at Gar Wood," *Fortune*, Oct. 1945. An obituary is in the *New York Times*, June 20, 1971.]

RICHARD CONIGLIONE

WRIGHT, JOHN KENNETH LLOYD (Dec. 12, 1892–Dec. 20, 1972), architect, was born in Oak Park, Ill., the second son of Frank Lloyd Wright, the well-known architect, and Catherine Lee Tobin. During his youth he observed the development of his father's distinctive architectural idiom—the Prairie style—composed of long horizontals, clean rectilinear forms, and orientation to the landscape. After attending his great-aunt's Hillside Home School in Spring Green, Wis., from 1907 to 1910, he spent a year at the University of Wisconsin.

Frank Lloyd Wright's abandonment of his family for the wife of a client in 1909 caused some estrangement between John and his father for a few years. John Wright moved to San Diego in late 1911, where his older brother, Frank Lloyd Wright, Jr. (known as Lloyd Wright), was working as a landscape architect. After deciding that he wanted to be an architect, John Wright worked for several local firms to gain experience. Under the guidance of Harrison Albright, a local architect, he designed the Wood house in Escondido and the Golden West Hotel in San Diego, both of which were strongly reminiscent of his father's work. For the ornament of the hotel Wright collaborated with the sculptor and poster designer Alfonso Iannelli.

In late 1913, Wright returned to Chicago to work with his father. At about this time he began using Lloyd as a middle name. In 1918, he married Jeanette Winters, whom he had met in Los Angeles; they were divorced in 1920. From 1913 to 1914, Wright assisted his father with the designs for Midway Gardens in Chicago, and Iannelli collaborated on the sculpture. In August 1914 he accompanied his father to rebuild Taliesin, Frank Lloyd Wright's home and studio in Spring Green, after a deranged servant murdered seven members of Wright's household and set a fire that destroyed the house.

In these years Wright began to design children's toys, most notably a series of interlocking play blocks, heavily influenced by his childhood experiences with Froebel "gifts," a type of playing block his father admired. For the next forty years Wright created a number of block

kits, some of which he made and marketed. Many of the designs were sold to Playskool Manufacturing Company. His most successful design was for Lincoln Logs, which came on the market in 1918 and today remains substantially the same as his original design. He went to Japan in 1917 to work on his father's Imperial Hotel commission. A dispute over wages with his father led to his firing in mid-1918, and he returned to Chicago and designed several houses in the Chicago suburbs over the next several years.

Wright married Hazel Lundin in 1921 and moved to Long Beach, Ind., a summer community near Michigan City, Ind., about sixty miles from Chicago. They had two children. Between 1921 and 1947 Wright practiced architecture in the Michigan City area, receiving some forty commissions and overseeing about twenty-five completions. They included a house and studio for himself and his family, two schools, a town hall for Long Beach, a hotel in the Indiana Dunes State Park, an apartment building, and houses of all sizes, from small summer cottages to large mansions.

In the 1920's, Wright's designs ranged from conservative "stockbroker Tudor" (utilizing historical imagery drawn from early English houses) to more modernistic, or Art Deco, styles (drawing upon the abstract and colorful patterns used by the latest French designers). "Red Oaks," designed for businessman H. E. Otte, was one of the more dramatic modernistic houses of the period, with the frequently repeated motif of a pentagon, a two-story living room, and smooth, crisp, stucco surfaces that in their rigor, repetition, and precision were for many in the 1920's a recall of the machine idiom, so popular in those years. Although Wright's work from the 1920's did not stylistically resemble his father's, they shared an interest in relating the building to the site.

In 1929, Wright and his wife took a trip to Europe, and his work in the 1930's is informed by his contact with European Expressionist and De Stijl design. He soon discovered the value of public relations and began to give names to his houses, such as the House of Steel for Jack Burnham, in Long Beach (1933); the House of Wood for Ken Holden, in Birchwood Beach, Mich. (1933–1934); the House of Tile for Lowell Jackson, in Long Beach (1938)—each featuring different materials in a modernist idiom. His work was very well received and frequently published in the national architectural and home design periodicals.

Wright lectured frequently to local audiences and in Chicago and wrote an architectural column for the *Michigan City News* between 1935 and 1937. He continued to design toys in collaboration with Iannelli. Wright spent the war years designing Federal ordnance plants, base housing, and prisoner-of-war camps. In 1942, he divorced again and married the ex-wife of a client, Frances Welsh. In 1946, he published *Father Who Is on Earth*, which is nominally about Frank Lloyd Wright but contains revealing autobiographical commentary.

In 1947, Wright and his wife settled in Del Mar, Calif., near San Diego, where he remained until his death. He received about sixty commissions, largely for houses, and saw about one half of them built. His work became more informal and more open to nature. Stylistically it is closer to his father's later work and is sometimes mistaken for it. In these years Wright frequently incorporated features of his father's Usonian house, such as the flat concrete slab floor that contains radiant heating. The distinctive feature of the younger Wright's design is an abstract ornament he called "lichenaceous," which he developed over the course of the 1930's. He viewed it as an element growing from the structure of the building.

The strong personality and notorious reputation of his father was a source of inspiration and also a burden to Wright throughout his life. John Wright's architectural designs never approached the dramatic originality of his father's, but they had their own integrity and evidenced his interest in site, materials, and ornament. His contribution to American toy design is an important instance of the transforming of the more pedagogical European prototypes such as the Froebel "gifts" into a more playful American idiom, as with the Lincoln Logs. Throughout his career he was regarded by American critics as being in the forefront of the development of modern architecture in the United States and an important link between the revolutionary work carried out in Chicago around 1900 by Louis Sullivan and the later development of modernism in the 1930's and 1940's. He died in La Jolla, Calif.

[A fire in 1939 destroyed many of Wright's papers; the most important collection of surviving material is at the Chicago Historical Society. Some biographical information is contained in the Frank Lloyd Wright Collection at the Avery Library, Columbia University, New York City, and in the Taliesin Archives in Scottsdale, Ariz. Information about his career and a bibliography can be found in Sally Kitt Chappell and Ann Van Zanten, *Barry Byrne, John Lloyd Wright, Architecture and Design* (1982); and Richard Guy Wilson, "Themes of Continuity," in Richard Guy Wilson and Sidney K. Robinson, *Modern Architecture in America* (1991). Obituaries are in the *San Diego Sun*, Dec. 21, 1972, and the *New York Times*, Dec. 22, 1972.]

RICHARD GUY WILSON

WYLIE, PHILIP GORDON (May 12, 1902– Oct. 25, 1971), author, was born in Beverly, Mass., to the Reverend Edmund Melville Wylie, a Congregational minister, and Edna Edwards Mason. Rev. Wylie became a Presbyterian and moved his family to Montclair, N.J., in 1914. Philip graduated from high school there and attended Princeton University (1920– 1923).

Two events shaped Wylie's emotional development early in life: His idolized mother died when he was five years old, and a burst appendix brought him close to death five years later, leaving him with months of pain. As a result he led a lonely, introspective childhood.

His father implanted a voracious appetite for ideas in Wylie by encouraging him to read anything comprehensible, and he explicitly taught him about sex and reproduction. He then witnessed Philip's growing disillusionment with Christianity, which, in turn, fostered a gnawing need to define meaning and purpose in life. Wylie's search for ethical integrity based upon truth led to an intense exploration of the physical and natural sciences, and initiated his interest in the teachings of Freud and Jung.

The result of this intellectual quest appears in the famous fire-and-brimstone sermons in novel form, *Generation of Vipers* (1942) and *Night unto Night* (1944). In these books Wylie introduced "momism," a critique of the social pandering to females. He sees such moms as tyrants who dominate the intellects and wills of their sons. Wylie also depicts wifely Cinderellas who turn from butterfly to caterpillar while manipulating husbands by turning sex into a carrot for material gain, and transforming themselves into "the puerile, rusting, raging creature we know as mom." Unprincely males, through their abiding worship of these Cinderellas, enable this feat.

Later, Wylie often winced when confronted with "momism." "Look here," he once said, "in *Generation of Vipers* there were nineteen pages about that. Nineteen, that's all. In the middle of it, I said the whole thing was a gag." Despite this disclaimer, sociologists added "momism" to their academic discipline.

Life offered other lessons for the budding author. His disenchantment with formal education came as a result of being expelled from Princeton for a "bad attitude" and poor grades. He lost a paternity suit (later reversed) in 1924, even though he was not the child's father; this led to his brilliant analysis of human hypocrisy in *Finnley Wren* (1934), arguably his best novel.

In 1924 Wylie joined the staff of the *New Yorker*; he remained there until 1927, then moved to Cosmopolitan Book Company as advertising manager. A year later he turned to free-lance writing which constituted the balance of his career.

On Apr. 17, 1928, Wylie married fashion model Johanna ("Sally") Ondeck; they had one child. Accusing her of tormenting him with infidelity and continual demands for money, he divorced Sally in 1937; he became an alcoholic. He married Frederica ("Ricky") Ballard on Apr. 7, 1938; they had no children.

Wylie's first novels are laced with autobiographical sequences: the sensationalistic *Heavy Laden* (1928), wherein a minister alienates his daughter through old-fashioned religion and morals; the propagandizing *Babes and Sucklings* (1929), which touts a young, unmarried couple living together; and *Gladiator* (1930), the operatic tragedy of a young superman who fails in his quest to find happiness in a materialistic world full of hypocritical, grasping people.

These early novels gave Wylie an entrée to a literary field he facilely capitalized upon—slick magazines—wherein he glorified sophisticated young moderns in a seemingly endless string of articles and short stories dealing with sexual mores, marriage, divorce, and religion. In *American, American Mercury, Atlantic, Cosmopolitan, Life, Redbook, Saturday Evening Post,* and *Writer,* he set forth his literary dogma in everything from murder mysteries to romantic fables and the delightful philosophy espoused in his famous Crunch and Des stories of deep-sea fishing.

In his most influential work, *Vipers* (1942), struck by isolationist tendencies and missing patriotism, he set down in fifty-four days an analysis that had as its targets religious beliefs, physical science, the materialism and greed of the American female, the human sexual nature, the school system, faith in the "common man," prejudice, medical doctors, and the deadly influence of the woman he labeled "Mom." He proposed a revision of values based on honesty, objective insight, integrity, and the supplanting of materialism with idealism.

Wylie also wrote science fiction. His first three efforts—*Gladiator, The Murderer Invisible* (1931), and *The Savage Gentleman* (1932)—were social criticisms based on an outsider's view of the flaws in human society. His most successful such book, *When Worlds Collide* (1933), came from a collaboration with Edwin Balmer and became a movie in 1951. Another novel in this genre, *The Disappearance* (1951), may have been Wylie's cleverest work. In it men and women find themselves in different worlds, a situation used to explore the roles of the sexes in contemporary America before concluding with a reunification of the genders.

An early conservationist, Wylie was ahead of his time in battling pollution and championing the country's ecosystem. His writings on the subject culminated in *The Magic Animal* (1968), an "ecological jeremiad."

Prolific, polemical, and iconoclastic, Wylie wrote 250 days each year. He even completed a 25,000-word novelette in a day. All told, he published more than sixteen million words in fifty hardbacks and that amount again in serialized novels and novelettes, plus hundreds of short stories, essays, poems, screenplays, and speeches.

Although he earned an unjust reputation as a woman-hater, Wylie was an early proponent of women's rights. He also served as a consultant to the Civil Defense Administration from 1949, and the Freedom Foundation awarded him its gold medal in 1953. His interest in ecology led to an association with the Oceanic Institute in Hawaii.

Wylie's last novel, *The End of the Dream,* was published in 1972. Wylie died in Miami, Fla.

[Wylie's manuscripts are in the Firestone Memorial Library of Princeton University; his letters to his brother, Max, are at Boston University. A biography is Truman F. Keefer, *Philip Wylie* (1977). Obituaries appear in the *New York Times* and the *Washington Post*, Oct. 26, 1971; and *Publisher's Weekly*, Nov. 1, 1971.]

W. M. P. DUNNE

Y–Z

YERGAN, MAX (July 19, 1892–Apr. 11, 1975), missionary, educator, and civil rights activist, was born in Raleigh, N.C., the son of Frederick Yergan, a construction worker, and Lizzie Yergan, a seamstress. Yergan's grandfather was a former slave who, in his final days, expressed the hope that "someday a grandson of mine will go as a missionary to our people in Africa."

While attending St. Ambrose High School from 1907 to 1911, Yergan served on the Young Men's Christian Association's (YMCA) committee of arrangements and exhibited great motivation in his work, which led to his appointment as an official for the Shaw University YMCA chapter while he studied at Shaw, in North Carolina. In addition to his responsibilities with the YMCA, Yergan's extracurricular activities included membership on the debating and football teams. Although his initial intention was to study law, his attendance at the YMCA Kings Mountain Conference, where the people and surroundings had inspired him, caused Yergan to alter his career path and dedicate his life to providing Christian service through the YMCA. After graduating with honors in 1914, Yergan began graduate work at Springfield Training College, a YMCA institution in Springfield, Mass. Yergan completed one year of study and was then called into service by the YMCA International Committee to work with students in the Southwest.

In 1916, Yergan attended an international convention of the YMCA in Cleveland, Ohio, where he heard a moving appeal from the national secretary for forty men to return to India with him to serve the troops. Yergan readily volunteered. After spending several months in India, Yergan then organized YMCA units among African regiments under British Army supervision in Kenya. For two years Yergan remained in East Africa despite several bouts with African fever. While there, he served troops from different parts of Africa, India, and the West Indies. Because Yergan had worked so tirelessly during his tour, British officials contacted the YMCA offices in the United States requesting that they send other African American workers to the region.

Weakened by African fever, Yergan returned to the United States at the end of two years. Yergan then canvassed various colleges around the country to raise money for the YMCA's work in Africa. During this time the United States Army called him to serve as a chaplain at Camp Lee, Va. From there, Yergan was dispatched by the YMCA Work Council to France. Yergan worked among the segregated units of the American Expeditionary Force until World War I ended in 1918. In 1920 Yergan married Susie Wiseman; they had four children.

When Yergan returned to the United States, he visited various African-American colleges and churches in order to raise funds for the initiation of a YMCA chapter in South Africa. His tenacity led to the YMCA International Committee's authorization of a pilot program among the youth of South Africa, with Yergan as its first American mission worker. In November 1921, after raising $10,000, Yergan left for South Africa with his wife and their four-month-old son.

For the next fifteen years, Yergan worked in South Africa as a missionary and educator. He was credited with expanding the traditional missionary role beyond converting his flock to Christianity; he encouraged the young men with whom he worked to apply their faith practically by becoming teachers and leaders. To do this, Yergan visited school districts throughout South Africa, organized twenty-six associations among students, and launched interracial discussion groups in colleges to foster greater understanding among the native Africans, Coloreds, and white South Africans. In 1926, Yergan received the Harmon Award in Religious Education "for the greatest contribution made during the year to the religious life of the Negro race." In 1933, he received the Spingarn Medal for his contributions to interracial understanding in South Africa.

Upon Yergan's return to the United States in 1936, he was appointed to the chair in Negro history at City College in New York City. With this appointment, Yergan became the first professor of African-American studies on a major American college campus. During his tenure at City College, in the late 1930's, Yergan also acted as copublisher of *The People's Voice*, an African-American newspaper.

Eager to continue his work with Africa, Yergan organized the formation of the Council on African Affairs in 1937 "for the purposes of petition and protest; for educating the public about Africa; and, perhaps, for helping to spread the cooperative movement." The council's directors included Ralphe Bunche, W. E. B. DuBois, and Paul Robeson. The council, with its ties to the Communist party in the United States and its pro-Soviet stance on foreign policy issues, became increasingly vulnerable to the Red-baiting of the McCarthy era. Yergan denied charges of Communist domination within his organization. But in October 1947, because of ideological discord among its directors, Yergan was expelled from the organization that he himself had created and headed for eleven years. In reflecting upon the split in the council, Yergan said: "The council had experienced a crisis . . . in allowing Communist infiltration into the organization—a positive danger to the purposes for which the organization was founded."

In 1945, Yergan was divorced from his first wife. He married Lena Halpern that same year; they had no children.

Yergan also served as president of the National Negro Congress, which supported the war effort during World War II but simultaneously called for the self-determination of colonial peoples and removal of barriers preventing black participation in the war. In 1946 Yergan led a delegation to petition the United Nations for the eradication of political, economic, and social discrimination in the United States.

In 1962, Yergan became chairman of the American Committee for Aid to Katanga Freedom Fighters, which opposed American support for UN military action against secessionist Katanga Province in the Congo.

Although Yergan's political positions on African affairs were generally progressive and antiimperialist, in the early 1960's he made ambiguous statements in various publications regarding the South African apartheid government, which could have been interpreted as anti-Nationalist.

In the 1960's, Yergan gradually retired by phasing out his numerous professional activities. Yergan died following a lengthy illness in Northern Westchester Hospital in Mount Kisco, N.Y.

[Published works by Max Yergan include *Democracy and the Negro People*; *Gold and Poverty in South Africa* (1938); *Proceedings on the Conference of Africa*; and *Youths Challenge to Youth* (1944). For additional information see Mary White Ovington, *Portraits in Color* (1927); Ralph W. Bullock, *In Spite of Handicaps* (1927); *Ebony*, Dec. 1949; the *Amsterdam News*, Sept. 13, 1952, May 9, 1955; and *Crisis*, Jan. 1957. Obituaries appear in the *New York Times*, Apr. 13, 1975; and in *Jet*, May 8, 1975.]

LaRose Parris

YOUNG, CLARENCE MARSHALL (July 23, 1889–Apr. 10, 1973), lawyer, aviation administrator, and airline executive, was born in Colfax, Iowa, the son of Theodore G. Young, an interior decorator, and Ella Foy. Young attended local schools in Colfax and Des Moines, where the family moved in 1901. Following three years at Drake University, Young entered Yale Law School and graduated with an LL.B. degree in 1910. He then returned to Des Moines and practiced insurance law.

Young joined the Aviation Section of the Signal Corps following U.S. entry into World War I in April 1917, and was trained in Italy as a bomber pilot. On June 25, 1918, while flying his first combat mission, Young was forced down behind enemy lines by engine trouble. He remained an Austrian prisoner-of-war until the armistice in November 1918.

Young resumed his legal practice after the war but found the law "a little too dry and a little too prosaic." Together with a local automobile dealer, he entered the more exciting field of aviation, selling surplus airplanes and flying sightseers around the Iowa countryside. Although the 1922 recession forced Young to abandon the business, he remained active in the U.S. Specialist Reserve Corps. In 1926, Young took command of the 313th Observation Squadron with the rank of colonel. Thereafter, he favored the military title in civilian life.

His career reached a turning point in 1926. While directing aviation activities for the Philadelphia Sesquicentennial, he came to the attention of William P. MacCracken, Jr., newly appointed assistant secretary of commerce for aeronautics. With the passage of the Air Commerce Act of 1926, the federal government had ended years of debate and accepted responsibility for regulating commercial aviation. Seeking competent executives with an aviation background, MacCracken asked Young to join him in drawing up and administering a system of air commerce regulations. Young readily agreed, and became chief of air regulations in the aeronautics branch of the Department of Commerce.

MacCracken and Young worked well together. Within a short time, they promulgated the necessary rules to license airplanes and airmen, and to operate and maintain a growing system of federal airways. By the end of 1926, they had put into place a sound regulatory structure that would foster the development of commercial aviation in the United States.

Young, who became director of aeronautics in 1927, took charge of enforcing federal air regulations while MacCracken traveled throughout the country, explaining and promoting the new system in conversations with members of the aviation community. Young quickly gained a reputation as a fair and effective administrator who shielded his subordinates from political pressure. As recalled by Jack B. Jaynes, a young inspector in the bureau, Young "had the courage of his convictions. He knew aviation and his men, and did not entertain or countenance politics in accomplishing his mission." When MacCracken left government service in 1929, Young replaced him as assistant secretary.

Young took over his new responsibilities just as the nation fell into the economic morass of the Great Depression. Despite the poor state of business, air transport activity continued to increase. The beleaguered administration of President Herbert C. Hoover supported the aeronautics branch. Indeed, the bureau's budget reached a record high of $10.4 million in fiscal 1932. Within two years, however, the bureau had to deal with a budget that had been slashed by 50 percent. But in 1933, with the change of presidential administrations, Young had resigned.

Young's term as assistant secretary saw a dramatic drop in the accident rate for scheduled airlines, from 28.2 fatalities per 100 million passenger-miles in 1930 to 4.6 deaths in 1933. He supported the development of instrument flying techniques and radio aids to navigation, and he required rigorous new standards of technical proficiency for airline pilots. In a widely publicized aircraft accident in 1931 that claimed the life of Knute Rockne, Notre Dame University football coach, Young incurred the wrath of aircraft manufacturer Anthony Fokker when he grounded the Fokker F-10A transport. Although he acted slowly in the case, Young set an important precedent for the use of the government's regulatory power to insure passenger safety.

On Feb. 10, 1935, Young married Lois Moran, a film actress. They had one son.

In November 1934, Juan T. Trippe of Pan American Airways hired Young to manage the airline's recently established Transpacific Division. Thwarted by international politics in his efforts to develop a transatlantic service, Trippe had decided to focus on establishing an air route across the Pacific Ocean to Asia. Young took charge of developing the necessary infrastructure that would enable Pan American's giant seaplanes to cover the 8,746 miles from San Francisco to Hong Kong. One year later, on Nov. 22, 1935, the *China Clipper*, a Martin M-130 flying boat, left San Francisco on the inaugural flight across the Pacific. Six days later, after stops at Honolulu, Midway, Wake, and Guam, it reached Manila, the interim terminus of the transoceanic route.

Over the next five years, Pan American crossed the Pacific over 440 times, flying more than 21 million passenger-miles, and carrying 13 million letters. Although not always profitable, the transpacific air route was a stunning technological triumph. Young's pragmatic managerial skills were an essential ingredient in the success of the enterprise.

Young left Pan American in 1945, following

what he termed "policy disagreements." In 1946 and 1947, he served as a member of the Civil Aeronautics Board, where he played a minor role in shaping postwar aviation policy. He returned to Pan American in 1950 and retired in 1959 as vice president of its Pacific Alaska Division. Fourteen years later, Young died of natural causes at Sedona, Ariz.

[Material on Young's career can be found among the Papers of Herbert Hoover at West Branch, Iowa, and in the biographical files of the National Air and Space Museum, Washington, D.C. Various aspects of his career are discussed in Nick A. Komons, *Bonfires to Beacons* (1978); and Robert Daley, *An American Saga* (1980). An obituary appears in the *New York Times*, Apr. 11, 1973.]

WILLIAM M. LEARY

YOUNG, WHITNEY MOORE, JR. (July 31, 1921–Mar. 11, 1971), civil rights leader, was born in Lincoln Ridge, Ky., the son of Whitney Moore Young, an educator, and Laura Ray, a teacher. In 1926, he entered the second grade at the Lincoln Model School in Simpsonville, an educational facility for African-American children from nearby communities. Seven years later, at the age of twelve, he enrolled as a high school freshman at Lincoln Institute near Simpsonville, a boarding high school established by the trustees of Berea College to educate African-American students, where his father was a faculty member and later president. Young graduated in 1937, at the age of fifteen. That fall, he enrolled at Kentucky State Industrial College in Frankfort, the state's principal higher-education institution for African Americans. Four years later, he graduated with a B.S. degree, thirty-first in a class of eighty-seven. Following graduation, Young taught mathematics and coached basketball at Rosenwald High School in Madisonville, Ky.

In July 1942, Young enlisted in the United States Army and in May 1943 was ordered to active duty at the Massachusetts Institute of Technology to study electrical engineering and participate in the Army Specialized Training Program. Later that program was shifted to Rhode Island State College in Kingston. On Jan. 2, 1944, he married Margaret Buckner, a fellow classmate from Kentucky State Industrial College; they had two children. Late that spring, Young was assigned to an African-American unit, the 1695th Engineer Combat Battalion. In October 1944, the unit was sent to Europe, where it would serve throughout the war. Young left the armed forces with the rank of first sergeant and the American Theater Ribbon, the Europe–African–Middle Eastern Theater Ribbon, and three Bronze Service Stars.

After the war, Young rejoined his wife at the University of Minnesota in Minneapolis, where she was completing a master's degree in educational psychology. In the spring of 1946 he was admitted to the School of Social Work there and began work on his own master's degree. His second field placement was with the Minneapolis Urban League, an early affiliate of the National Urban League. The Urban League emphasized the problems of African Americans in cities. Young interviewed employment applicants, made field visits to clients, and reported to the league board on legislative issues relating to public welfare. As an outgrowth of that placement, Young made the St. Paul Urban League the subject of his master's thesis. Following completion of his degree work in 1947, he was offered the post of industrial relations secretary for the St. Paul Urban League.

In October 1947, Young began work focusing on improving employment opportunities for African Americans. His work led to African Americans in St. Paul finding employment as taxicab drivers and bus and streetcar drivers and conductors for the first time. He soon joined a number of clubs and fraternal organizations involved in civic affairs, including the National Association for the Advancement of Colored People, the YMCA Men's Club, and the Junior Chamber of Commerce. His work with the St. Paul Urban League expanded the number of firms employing African Americans and brought him to the attention of the National Urban League officials. When the executive directorship of the Omaha Urban League became vacant, Young assumed the post in February 1950. Young's work led to almost one hundred employment firsts for African Americans in Omaha and doubled the number of African-American teachers in the public schools. Other efforts were directed to desegregating public housing.

In 1954, Young became dean of the Atlanta University School of Social Work, the nation's leading source of African-American social workers. During his tenure, Young instituted important curriculum changes, integrated the student body, and expanded the full-time faculty. Simultaneously, he helped organize the Atlanta Committee for Cooperative Action, a group of African-American professionals and businessleaders who sought to call attention to local racial problems, provide research and technical assistance on civil rights, and to supplant the extant African-American leadership. One of the major projects of the group was the publication of *A Second Look: The Negro Citizen in Atlanta* (1960). In 1959, the National Conference on Social Welfare awarded Young the Florina Lasker Award for outstanding achievement in public service and professional leadership.

In 1960, Young received a fellowship to support study in the social sciences at Harvard University. While Young was in Cambridge, the National Urban League began its search for an executive director to replace the retiring Lester B. Granger, and in October 1962, Young became executive director of the National Urban League, headquartered in New York City. During the decade that Young headed the organization, the number of local affiliates increased by 50 percent, professional staff by 400 percent, and its budget by 1000 percent. Moreover, the league broke new ground by participating in the formation of public policy and direct involvement on behalf of civil rights. One of the earliest examples was the league and Young's involvement in the August 1963 march on Washington, D.C. The league was a cosponsor, and march leaders A. Philip Randolph and Bayard Rustin relied heavily on Young's advice. Perhaps more than any other African-American leader of his time, Young gained the support of the white corporate establishment for the civil rights movement. During the presidency of Lyndon B. Johnson, Young's counsel was sought and frequently followed in matters of civil rights. In 1964, Young published his book *To Be Equal*, which emphasized that merely eliminating inequality and injustice was not enough. Instead, Americans black and white must make a "special effort" to undertake a domestic Marshall Plan directed at closing the economic, social, and educational gaps separating the races. In January 1969, President Johnson awarded Young the Medal of Freedom. Later that year his second book, *Beyond Racism*, emphasized an open society where African Americans had the freedom of choice. Toward the end of the 1960's, Young was president of the National Conference on Social

Welfare and the National Association of Social Workers.

In March 1971, Young participated in a dialogue sponsored by the African-American Institute, held in Lagos, Nigeria. During a recreational break from the conference Young went to a local beach. While swimming off the shore of Lagos, he died apparently of a cerebral hemorrhage. He is buried in Hartsdale, N.Y.

[Most of Young's personal papers are deposited in the Rare Book and Manuscript Library at Columbia University, and the National Urban League Papers, Manuscript Division, Library of Congress. Biographies include Richard Bruner, *Whitney M. Young, Jr.* (1972); and Nancy J. Weiss, *Whitney M. Young, Jr. and the Struggle for Civil Rights* (1989). Obituaries are in the *New York Times*, Mar. 12, 1971, and the *Louisville Courier-Journal*, Mar. 12, 1971.]

FRANK R. LEVSTIK

ZWICKY, FRITZ (Feb. 14, 1898–Feb. 8, 1974), astrophysicist, was born in Varna, Bulgaria, the eldest of three children born to Fridolin Zwicky, a Swiss accountant and international merchant, and Franziska Wrcek, a Czech national. At the time of Fritz's birth, his father was serving as the Norwegian consul to Bulgaria.

From 1914 to 1916, Zwicky attended the Oberrealischule secondary school in Zurich, Switzerland, and received a B.S. from the Eidgenössische Technische Hochschule (Federal Institute of Technology), Zurich, in 1920. He began graduate study in theoretical physics, and published his first scholarly work, "The Second Virial Coefficient of the Rare Gases," in 1921. He wrote a doctoral dissertation entitled "On the Theory of Ionic Crystals," and received his Ph.D. in 1922.

Zwicky remained at the institute as a research assistant until 1925, when he received a fellowship from the Rockefeller International Education Board to work with Robert A. Millikan and Paul Epstein at the California Institute of Technology (Caltech) in Pasadena, Calif. Caltech appointed Zwicky assistant professor of theoretical physics in 1927, and he was promoted to associate professor in 1929.

On Mar. 25, 1932, Zwicky married his first wife, Dorothy Vernon Gates, the daughter of California State Senator Edgar J. Gates. The couple did not have any children, and their marriage ended in divorce in 1941.

In 1933, Zwicky changed his field of study from theoretical physics to astrophysics. He became interested in a special class of exceptionally bright, short-lived, nonperiodic novas (new stars). Zwicky renamed them supernovas and redefined them as the results of the transformation of ordinary stars into neutron stars, which resulted in the release of an extremely large amount of radiation. In late 1933, Zwicky, in collaboration with Dr. Walter Baade, who had emigrated from Germany to teach at Caltech in 1931, began a study of supernovas for use as measures of galaxies' distances.

Initial attempts to search for supernovas in a group of galaxies known as the Virgo Cluster were hampered by the limitations of the equipment in use at that time. Even though a two-hundred-inch Hale telescope was already being built for Caltech's Palomar Mountain Observatory, Zwicky was able to persuade Caltech's Observatory Council to also install an eighteen-inch Schmidt telescope at Palomar Mountain. Construction of the telescope began in 1933 and was completed in late 1936. In early 1937, Zwicky began using the new telescope to conduct a systematic search for supernovas. He recorded his first supernova using this new telescope on Feb. 16, 1937. After the discovery of his second supernova on Aug. 26, 1937, Zwicky hypothesized that if nature could produce these types of nuclear explosions, then so could humans. This premise was proven nearly ten years later, with the development of the atomic bomb. During the next five years, Zwicky, along with Baade and Rudolph Minkowski (who was a long time associate of Baade's and an astronomer at the Mt. Wilson Observatory and Palomar Mountain), recorded a total of eighteen supernovas.

At the same time that he began to study supernovas, Zwicky also began measuring the motion of galaxies, focusing on the Virgo Cluster. When he compared the cluster's visible mass with its measured velocity, he was surprised to find that the mass was insufficient to keep the galaxies from flying apart. Zwicky concluded that there must be some type of invisible matter located between galaxies, as well as within them, which produced the additional gravitational forces necessary to keep the galaxies together. It took the scientific community approximately forty years to acknowledge the importance of Zwicky's hypothesis, now known as the theory of dark matter.

In 1942, Caltech promoted Zwicky to professor of astronomy. That same year, Zwicky helped Theodore von Kármán and other scientists raise capital to form the Aerojet Engineering Corporation, which was headquartered in Azusa, Calif. Zwicky became the corporation's director of research in 1943, and held this position until 1949. During this period, he helped pioneer the development of several different types of jet and propulsion engines, one of which, the hydropulse, operated under water. By the end of his career, Zwicky held approximately fifty patents, most of them in the area of propulsion engine design.

In 1945 and 1946, Zwicky acted as technical representative of a U.S. Army Air Forces fact-finding team sent to Germany and Japan to study those countries' wartime research on jet propulsion. From 1945 to 1949, Zwicky also served as a member of the U.S. Air Force Scientific Advisory Board. In 1946, he authored a book for the air force entitled *Certain Phases of War Research in Germany*, which discussed the information gathered during his trips to Germany.

Zwicky's interest in spaceflight led him to attempt to launch a number of artificial meteors in 1946. These projectiles were designed to leave trails in the upper atmosphere similar to those left by meteorites. Zwicky used a V-2 rocket launched from White Sands, N.Mex., to send off these artificial meteors. The results of this air force–sponsored project were initially kept classified. It appears, however, that the launch was unsuccessful due to instrument failure.

On Oct. 15, 1947, Zwicky married his second wife, Anna Margarita Zürcher, the daughter of a Swiss hotelier, who was working as a cashier when they met. The couple had three children. During that same year, Zwicky developed a system of morphological classification and nomenclature for jets. He published his conclusions as "Morphology and Nomenclature of Jet Engines" in *Aviation* (June 1947).

Often described as a very independent-minded person, Zwicky demonstrated this independence when he gave the Halley Lecture at Oxford University on May 12, 1948. Instead of discussing celestial phenomena, the traditional subject of the Halley lecturers, Zwicky chose instead to discuss the application of his morphological method to astronomy.

In 1949, Zwicky resigned his position as research director for the Aerojet Engineering Corp., but continued as technical advisor and chief research consultant until 1961. That same year, Zwicky received the Presidential Medal of Freedom from President Harry S. Truman.

In 1955, six years after Zwicky received the medal, the U.S. Defense Department rescinded Zwicky's security clearance, insisting that Zwicky either become a naturalized citizen or forever lose his security clearance. Despite Zwicky's fondness for the United States, he believed that naturalized citizens received only second-class treatment. He chose to retain his Swiss citizenship and refused to apply for United States citizenship.

Despite his lack of a security clearance, in October 1957, the air force invited Zwicky to participate in the launching into space of miniature artificial satellites. Zwicky had proposed this project several months prior to the launch, but the significance of the project was overshadowed by the launch of Sputnik twelve days earlier. Also in the year 1957, one of his best-known works, *Morphological Astronomy*, was published. In it, Zwicky expands upon his Halley Lecture, discussing the importance of knowing and understanding the structure of the universe through observation and experimentation.

Among his fellow scientists, Zwicky was known for being opinionated and combative, yet compassionate. Zwicky was actively involved in the work of the Pestalozzi Foundation of America, which provided financial support for orphanages. In 1958, Zwicky was named chairman of the foundation's board of trustees.

After the morphological approach to astronomy became popular, Zwicky established the Society for Morphological Research in 1961, and became its first president. Between 1961 and 1968, Zwicky, along with a number of his colleagues, published the six-volume *Catalogue of Galaxies and of Clusters of Galaxies*. His second book on morphology, *Morphology of Propulsive Power* (1962), summed up much of his theoretical work on propulsive engines and

rocketry. In 1965, Zwicky was elected vice-president of the International Academy of Astronautics. In 1968, Zwicky retired from his academic position at Caltech, but he continued astrophysical research.

His final work, *Catalogue of Selected Compact Galaxies and of Post-Eruptive Galaxies* (1971), was coauthored by his oldest daughter, Margrit A. Zwicky. In 1972, Zwicky traveled to Britain to receive the Royal Astronomical Society's Gold Medal, one of the most prestigious awards of its kind. Fritz Zwicky died of a heart attack at the Huntington Memorial Hospital in Pasadena, Calif. He was buried in Glarus, Switzerland.

Fritz Zwicky will be remembered for his numerous contributions to science and technology. Included among his many achievements are his theories concerning neutron stars; his supervision of an international search effort for supernovas; his initiation of a sky survey at the Mt. Palomar and Mt. Wilson observatories, which resulted in the creation of the most comprehensive set of galactic catalogs ever produced; and his work in the areas of jet propulsion and rocketry.

[Zwicky's papers are located at the Landesbibliotech, 8750 Glarus, Switzerland. The Rockefeller Archives Center, in North Tarrytown, N.Y., has papers concerning his Rockefeller Fellowship and early years at Caltech. Caltech's Astrophysics Library, Pasadena, Calif., has a complete listing of Zwicky's 559 publications. Several of his most important publications have been included in Kenneth R. Lang and Owen Gingerich, *A Source Book in Astronomy and Astrophysics, 1900–1975* (1979). The only book-length biography of Zwicky is in German: Roland Müller, *Fritz Zwicky: Leben und Werk des grossen schweizer Astrophysikers, Raketenforschers und Morphologen (1898–1974)* (1986). Zwicky's work is placed in the context of contemporary astrophysics by Wallace Tucker and Karen Tucker, *The Dark Matter: Contemporary Science's Quest for the Mass Hidden in Our Universe* (1988). An obituary is in the *New York Times*, Oct. 11, 1974.]

TAMMY ANN SYREK

INDEX GUIDE

TO THE SUPPLEMENTS

Name	Supplement
Aandahl, Fred George	8
Abbot, Willis John	1
Abbott, Edith	6
Abbott, Eleanor Hallowell	6
Abbott, Grace	2
Abbott, Robert Sengstacke	2
Abbott, William A. ("Bud")	9
Abel, John Jacob	2
Abel, Rudolf Ivanovich	9
Abel-Henderson, Annie Heloise	4
Abert, John James	1
Aborn, Milton	1
Abrams, Creighton Williams, Jr.	9
Abt, Isaac Arthur	5
Ace, Jane	9
Acheson, Dean Gooderham	9
Acheson, Edward Goodrich	1
Acosta, Bertram Blanchard ("Bert")	5
Adamic, Louis	5
Adams, Andy	1
Adams, Annette Abbott	6
Adams, Charles Francis	5
Adams, Cyrus Cornelius	1
Adams, Edward Dean	1
Adams, Ephraim Douglass	1
Adams, Franklin Pierce	6
Adams, Frank Ramsay	7
Adams, Herbert Samuel	3
Adams, James Truslow	4
Adams, Joseph Quincy	4
Adams, Maude	5
Adams, Randolph Greenfield	5
Adams, Samuel Hopkins	6
Adams, Thomas Sewall	1
Adams, Walter Sydney	6
Addams, Jane	1
Adderley, Julian Edwin ("Cannonball")	9
Ade, George	3
Adie, David Craig	3
Adkins, Homer Burton	4
Adler, Cyrus	2
Adler, Elmer	7
Adler, Felix (d. 1933)	1
Adler, Felix (d. 1960)	6
Adler, Polly	7
Adler, Sara	5
Adonis, Joe	9
Adrian, Gilbert	6
Agee, James Rufus	5
Aggrey, James Emman Kwegyir	1
Agramonte y Simoni, Aristides	1
Aiken, Conrad Potter	9
Ainslie, Peter	1
Ainsworth, Frederick Crayton	1
Aitken, Robert Grant	5
Akeley, Mary Leonore	8
Akins, Zoë	6
Albee, Edward Franklin	1
Albright, William Foxwell	9
Alden, Cynthia May Westover	1
Alden, Isabella Macdonald	1
Alderman, Edwin Anderson	1
Aldrich, Bess Genevra Streeter	5
Aldrich, Charles Anderson	4
Aldrich, Chester Holmes	2
Aldrich, Richard	2
Aldrich, Winthrop William	9
Alexander, Franz Gabriel	7
Alexander, Grover Cleveland	4
Alexander, Hartley Burr	2
Alexander, Will Winton	6
Alinsky, Saul David	9
Alford, Leon Pratt	3
Allen, Arthur Augustus	7
Allen, Edgar	3
Allen, Edward Ellis	4
Allen, Edward Tyson	3
Allen, Florence Ellinwood	8
Allen, Forrest Clare ("Phog")	9
Allen, Fred	6
Allen, Frederick Lewis	5
Allen, George Edward	9
Allen, George Venable	8
Allen, Glover Morrill	3
Allen, Gracie	7
Allen, Henry Justin	4
Allen, Henry Tureman	1
Allen, Hervey	4
Allen, James Edward, Jr.	9
Allen, Kelcey	5
Allen, Viola	4
Allinson, Anne Crosby Emery	1
Allinson, Francis Greenleaf	1
Allison, Nathaniel	1
Allison, Richard	1
Allison, Samuel King	7
Allport, Gordon Willard	8
Alsop, Stewart Johonnot Oliver	9
Altmeyer, Arthur Joseph	9
Ameringer, Oscar	3

Index Guide

Name	Supplement	Name	Supplement
Ames, Adelbert	1	Arnold, Henry Hartley	4
Ames, Edward Scribner	6	Arnold, Leslie Philip	7
Ames, Herman Vandenburg	1	Arnold, Thurman Wesley	8
Ames, Joseph Sweetman	3	Arquette, Clifford	9
Ames, Oakes	4	Arthur, Joseph Charles	3
Ames, Winthrop	2	Artzybasheff, Boris	7
Amidon, Charles Fremont	2	Arvin, Newton	7
Amlie, Thomas Ryum	9	Asbury, Herbert	7
Amman, Othmar Hermann	7	Ashford, Bailey Kelly	1
Anderson, Benjamin McAlester	4	Ashurst, Henry Fountain	7
Anderson, Clinton Presba	9	Astor, William Vincent	6
Anderson, Edwin Hatfield	4	Athenagoras I	9
Anderson, Margaret Carolyn	9	Atherton, Gertrude	4
Anderson, Mary (d. 1940)	2	Atkinson, Henry Avery	6
Anderson, Mary (d. 1964)	7	Atlas, Charles S.	9
Anderson, Maxwell	6	Atterbury, Grosvenor	6
Anderson, Paul Y.	2	Atterbury, William Wallace	1
Anderson, Sherwood	3	Atwood, Wallace Walter	4
Anderson, Victor Vance	6	Auden, Wystan Hugh	9
Andrew, Abram Piatt	2	Auer, John	4
Andrews, Bert	5	Austen, (Elizabeth) Alice	5
Andrews, Charles McLean	3	Austin, Mary	1
Andrews, Frank Maxwell	3	Austin, Warren Robinson	7
Andrews, Israel DeWolf	1	Avery, Milton Clark	7
Andrews, John Bertram	3	Avery, Oswald Theodore	5
Andrews, Roy Chapman	6	Avery, Sewell Lee	6
Andrus, Ethel Percy	8	Aydelotte, Frank	6
Angeli, Pier	9	Ayres, Leonard Porter	4
Angell, Ernest	9	Ayres, William Augustus	5
Angell, James Rowland	4		
Angle, Paul McClelland	9	Baade, Wilhelm Heinrich Walter	6
Anglin, Margaret Mary	6	Babbitt, Irving	1
Annenberg, Moses Louis	3	Babcock, Howard Edward	4
Anthony, John J.	8	Babcock, Stephen Moulton	1
Anthony, Katharine Susan	7	Babson, Roger Ward	8
Anthony, William Arnold	1	Baccaloni, Salvatore	8
Antin, Mary	4	Bache, Jules Semon	3
Apgar, Virginia	9	Bacheller, Irving	4
Appleton, William Sumner	4	Bachmann, Werner Emmanuel	5
Archipenko, Alexander	7	Bachrach, Louis Fabian	7
Arden, Elizabeth	8	Bacon, Benjamin Wisner	1
Arendt, Hannah	9	Bacon, Leonard	5
Arensberg, Walter Conrad	5	Badè, William Frederic	2
Arlen, Michael	6	Badger, Charles Johnston	1
Arliss, George	4	Baekeland, Leo Hendrik	3
Armour, Thomas Dickson		Baer, William Stevenson	1
("Tommy")	8	Baetjer, Frederick Henry	1
Armstrong, Edward Cooke	3	Bagley, William Chandler	4
Armstrong, Edwin Howard	5	Bailey, Florence	4
Armstrong, Hamilton Fish	9	Bailey, (Irene) Temple	5
Armstrong, Henry Worthington		Bailey, John Moran	9
("Harry")	5	Bailey, Joseph Weldon	1
Armstrong, Louis ("Satchmo")	9	Bailey, Josiah William	4
Arno, Peter	8	Bailey, Liberty Hyde	5
Arnold, Edward	6	Bailey, Mildred	5
Arnold, Harold DeForest	1	Bailey, Solon Irving	1

Index Guide

Name	Supplement	Name	Supplement
Baker, Dorothy Dodds	8	Barrymore, Lionel	5
Baker, George Fisher	1	Barth, Carl Georg Lange	2
Baker, George Pierce	1	Barthelmess, Richard	7
Baker, Hugh Potter	4	Bartholdt, Richard	1
Baker, Jehu	1	Bartlett, Edward Lewis ("Bob")	8
Baker, John Franklin	7	Bartlett, Francis Alonzo	7
Baker, Josephine	9	Bartlett, William Holmes	
Baker, Newton Diehl	2	Chambers	1
Baker, Oliver Edwin	4	Barton, Bruce Fairchild	8
Baker, Ray Stannard	4	Barton, David	1
Baker, Sara Josephine	3	Barton, George Aaron	3
Baker, Walter Ransom Gail	6	Barton, James Edward	7
Balaban, Barney	9	Barton, James Levi	2
Balch, Emily Greene	7	Barton, William Eleazar	1
Balchen, Bernt	9	Baruch, Bernard Mannes	7
Baldwin, Edward Robinson	4	Barus, Carl	1
Baldwin, Evelyn Briggs	1	Bascom, Florence	3
Baldwin, Henry Perrine	1	Bassett, Edward Murray	4
Baldwin, James Mark	1	Bassett, William Hastings	1
Ball, Frank Clayton	3	Basso, Hamilton	7
Ball, George Alexander	5	Bateman, Harry	4
Ballantine, Arthur Atwood	6	Bates, Blanche	3
Bamberger, Louis	3	Bates, Katharine Lee	1
Bancroft, Frederic	3	Bates, Onward	2
Bancroft, Wilder Dwight	5	Bates, Theodore Lewis ("Ted")	9
Bankhead, John Hollis	4	Battle, John Stewart	9
Bankhead, Tallulah	8	Batts, Robert Lynn	1
Bankhead, William Brockman	2	Bauer, Harold Victor	5
Banks, Charles Edward	1	Bauer, Louis Agricola	1
Bara, Theda	5	Baum, Hedwig ("Vicki")	6
Barbey, Daniel Edward	8	Bausch, Edward	3
Barbour, Clarence Augustus	2	Bazett, Henry Cuthbert	4
Barbour, Henry Gray	3	Baziotes, William	7
Barbour, Thomas	4	Beach, Amy Marcy Cheney	3
Barden, Graham Arthur	8	Beach, Harlan Page	1
Barker, Alexander Crichlow		Beach, Mrs. H. H. A.	
("Lex")	9	See Beach, Amy Marcy	
Barkley, Alben William	6	Cheney	
Barnard, Chester Irving	7	Beach, Rex	4
Barnard, George Grey	2	Beach, Sylvia Woodbridge	7
Barnes, Albert Coombs	5	Beadle, Erastus Flavel	1
Barnes, Julius Howland	6	Beale, Joseph Henry	3
Barnett, George Ernest	2	Beall, James Glenn	9
Barrère, Georges	3	Beals, Ralph Albert	5
Barrett, Albert Moore	2	Bean, Leon Lenwood	8
Barrett, Charles Simon	1	Beard, Charles Austin	4
Barrett, Frank Aloysius	7	Beard, Daniel Carter	3
Barrett, Janie Porter	4	Beard, Mary	4
Barrett, John	2	Beard, Mary Ritter	6
Barron, Clarence Walker	1	Beary, Donald Bradford	8
Barrow, Edward Grant	5	Beatty, Clyde Raymond	7
Barrows, Alice Prentice	5	Beatty, Willard Walcott	7
Barrows, David Prescott	5	Beaty, Amos Leonidas	2
Barry, Philip	4	Beaux, Cecilia	3
Barrymore, Ethel	6	Beavers, Louise	7
Barrymore, John	3	Bechet, Sidney	6

Index Guide

Name	Supplement	Name	Supplement
Beck, James Montgomery	2	Benton, William Burnett	9
Beck, Martin	2	Berenson, Bernard	6
Becker, Carl Lotus	3	Berenson, Senda	5
Becket, Frederick Mark	3	Berg, Gertrude Edelstein	8
Beckwith, Clarence Augustine	1	Berg, Morris ("Moe")	9
Bedaux, Charles Eugene	3	Berger, Meyer	6
Beebe, (Charles) William	7	Berger, Victor Louis	1
Beer, Thomas	2	Bergmann, Max	3
Beers, Clifford Whittingham	3	Berkman, Alexander	2
Beery, Wallace	4	Berle, Adolf Augustus, Jr.	9
Beeson, Charles Henry	4	Berliner, Emile	1
Begley, Edward James ("Ed")	8	Bernet, John Joseph	1
Behn, Sosthenes	6	Bernstein, Aline	5
Behrend, Bernard Arthur	1	Bernstein, Herman	1
Behrendt, Walter Curt	3	Berry, Edward Wilber	3
Behrman, Samuel Nathaniel	9	Berry, George Leonard	4
Békésy, Georg von	9	Berry, Martha McChesney	3
Belasco, David	1	Berry, Clifford Kennedy	4
Bell, Bernard Iddings	6	Berryman, John	9
Bell, De Benneville ("Bert")	6	Berwind, Edward Julius	2
Bell, Eric Temple	6	Besse, Arthur Lyman	5
Bell, Frederic Somers	2	Bestor, Arthur Eugene	3
Bell, James Ford	7	Bethune, Mary McLeod	5
Bell, James Franklin	1	Bettman, Alfred	3
Bell, Lawrence Dale	6	Bevan, Arthur Dean	3
Bellanca, Dorothy Jacobs	4	Bevier, Isabel	3
Bellanca, Giuseppe Mario	6	Bickel, Alexander Mordecai	9
Belmont, Alva Ertskin Smith		Bickel, Karl August	9
Vanderbilt	1	Bidaga	
Bemelmans, Ludwig	7	See Son of Many Beads	
Bemis, Harold Edward	1	Biddle, Anthony Joseph Drexel,	
Bemis, Samuel Flagg	9	Jr.	7
Benchley, Robert Charles	3	Biddle, Francis Beverley	8
Bender, Charles Albert ("Chief")	5	Biddle, George	9
Bender, George Harrison	7	Biffle, Leslie L.	8
Bendix, Vincent	3	Bigelow, Harry Augustus	4
Benedict, Ruth	4	Bigelow, Henry Bryant	8
Benedict, Stanley Rossiter	2	Biggers, Earl Derr	1
Benét, Stephen Vincent	3	Biggers, John David	9
Benét, William Rose	4	Bilbo, Theodore Gilmore	4
Bennett, Constance Campbell	7	Billikopf, Jacob	4
Bennett, Earl W.	9	Billings, Asa White Kenney	4
Bennett, Henry Garland	5	Billings, Frank	1
Bennett, Hugh Hammond	6	Billingsley, John Sherman	8
Bennett, Richard	3	Binford, Jessie Florence	8
Benny, Jack	9	Binga, Jesse	4
Bensley, Robert Russell	6	Bingay, Malcolm Wallace	5
Benson, Frank Weston	5	Bingham, Hiram	6
Benson, Oscar Herman	5	Bingham, Robert Worth	2
Benson, Sally	9	Bingham, Walter Van Dyke	5
Benson, William Shepherd	1	Binkley, Robert Cedric	2
Bent, Silas	3	Binkley, Wilfred Ellsworth	7
Bentley, Arthur Fisher	6	Birch, Reginald Bathurst	3
Bentley, Elizabeth Terrill	7	Birchall, Frederick Thomas	5
Bentley, Wilson Alwyn	1	Birdseye, Clarence	6
Benton, Thomas Hart	9	Birge, Edward Asahel	4

Index Guide

Name	Supplement	Name	Supplement
Birkhoff, George David	3	Boeing, William Edward	6
Bishop, Charles Reed	1	Bogan, Louise Marie	8
Bishop, John Peale	3	Bogart, Humphrey DeForest	6
Bishop, Robert Hamilton	1	Boggs, Thomas Hale	9
Bitzer, George William	3	Bohlen, Charles Eustis ("Chip")	9
Black, Eli	9	Boisen, Anton Theophilus	7
Black, Eugene Robert	1	Bok, Edward William	1
Black, Hugo Lafayette	9	Bolm, Adolph Rudolphovitch	5
Black, William Murray	1	Bolton, Herbert Eugene	5
Blackfan, Kenneth Daniel	3	Bolza, Oskar	3
Blackmer, Sydney Alderman	9	Bond, Carrie Jacobs	4
Blackmur, Richard Palmer	7	Bonfils, Frederick Gilmer	1
Blackstone, Harry	7	Bonsal, Stephen	5
Blackton, James Stuart	3	Bonstelle, Jessie	1
Blackwell, Alice Stone	4	Bontemps, Arna Wendell	9
Blaine, Anita (Eugenie) McCormick	5	Boole, Ella Alexander	5
Blaine, John James	1	Booth, Albert James, Jr. ("Albie")	6
Blair, Emily Newell	5	Booth, Ballington	2
Blair, William Richards	7	Booth, Evangeline	4
Blake, Francis Gilman	5	Borah, William Edgar	2
Blakeley, George Henry	3	Borchard, Edwin Montefiore	5
Blakeslee, Howard Walter	5	Borden, Lizzie Andrew	1
Blalock, Alfred	7	Borglum, John Gutzon de la Mothe	3
Blanchfield, Florence Aby	9	Bori, Lucrezia	6
Blandy, William Henry Purnell	5	Borie, Adolphe	1
Blashfield, Edwin Howland	2	Boring, Edwin Garrigues	8
Blatch, Harriot Eaton Stanton	2	Boring, William Alciphron	2
Blease, Coleman Livingston	3	Borzage, Frank	7
Bleyer, Willard Grosvenor	1	Boston, Charles Anderson	1
Blichfeldt, Hans Frederik	3	Bostwick, Arthur Elmore	3
Bliss, Cornelius Newton	4	Bouché, René Robert	7
Bliss, Frederick Jones	2	Boucher, Horace Edward	1
Bliss, Gilbert Ames	5	Boudin, Louis Boudinoff	5
Bliss, Robert Woods	7	Bourke-White, Margaret	9
Bliss, Tasker Howard	1	Bourne, Jonathan	2
Blitzstein, Marc	7	Bouvard, Oliver Kirby	3
Bloch, Claude Charles	8	Bovie, William T.	6
Bloch, Ernest	6	Bow, Clara Gordon	7
Block, Paul	3	Bowen, Catherine Drinker	9
Blocker, Dan	9	Bowen, Ira Sprague	9
Blodgett, John Wood	5	Bowen, Louise De Koven	5
Bloodgood, Joseph Colt	1	Bowen, Norman Levi	6
Bloom, Sol	4	Bowers, Claude Gernade	6
Bloomfield, Leonard	4	Bowes, Edward J.	4
Bloomfield, Meyer	2	Bowie, William	2
Bloor, Ella Reeve	5	Bowker, Richard Rogers	1
Blue, Ben	9	Bowles, Jane Auer	9
Blue, Gerald Montgomery ("Monte")	7	Bowman, Isaiah	4
Bluemner, Oscar Florians	2	Boyd, Harriet Ann See Hawes, Harriet Ann Boyd	
Boardman, Mabel Thorp	4		
Boas, Franz	3	Boyd, James	3
Bodanzky, Artur	2	Boyd, Louise Arner	9
Bode, Boyd Henry	5	Boyd, Thomas Alexander	1
Bodenheim, Maxwell	5	Boyd, Thomas Duckett	1

Index Guide

Name	Supplement	Name	Supplement
Boyd, William	9	Bristol, Mark Lambert	2
Boyd, William Kenneth	2	Bristol, William Henry	1
Boyden, Roland William	1	Bristow, Joseph Little	3
Boyle, Harold Vincent ("Hal")	9	Britton, Nathaniel Lord	1
Boyle, Michael J.	6	Brödel, Max	3
Brace, Charles Loring	2	Brokenshire, Norman Ernest	7
Brace, Donald Clifford	5	Bromfield, Louis	6
Brackett, Charles William	8	Bronk, Detlev Wulf	9
Brackett, Jeffrey Richardson	4	Brooke, Charles Frederick Tucker	4
Braddock, James J.	9	Brookhart, Smith Wildman	3
Bradford, Gamaliel	1	Brookings, Robert Somers	1
Bradford, Roark	4	Brooks, John Graham	2
Bradley, Frederick Worthen	1	Brooks, Overton	7
Brady, Alice	2	Brooks, Van Wyck	7
Brady, John Green	1	Brophy, John	7
Brady, Mildred Alice Edie	7	Brophy, Thomas D'Arcy	8
Brady, William Aloysius	4	Brough, Charles Hillman	1
Bragdon, Claude Fayette	4	Broun, Heywoud Campbell	2
Brand, Max		Browder, Earl Russell	9
See Faust, Frederick Shiller		Brown, Carleton	3
Brandeis, Louis Dembitz	3	Brown, Charles Reynolds	4
Braniff, Thomas Elmer	5	Brown, Charlotte Hawkins	7
Brann, William Cowper	1	Brown, Clarence James	7
Braslau, Sophie	1	Brown, Elmer Ellsworth	1
Breasted, James Henry	1	Brown, Ernest William	2
Breckinridge, Aida de Acosta	7	Brown, Gertrude Foster	6
Breckinridge, Desha	1	Brown, John Mason, Jr.	8
Breckinridge, Henry Skillman	6	Brown, Johnny Mack	9
Breckinridge, Sophonisba Preston	4	Brown, Lawrason	2
Breen, Joseph Ignatius	7	Brown, Margaret Wise	5
Brennan, Francis James	8	Brown, Percy	4
Brennan, Walter	9	Brown, Prentiss Marsh	9
Brennemann, Joseph	3	Brown, Ralph Hall	4
Brenon, Herbert	6	Brown, Walter Folger	7
Brent, Charles Henry	1	Brown, William Adams	3
Brereton, Lewis Hyde	8	Brown, William Hill	1
Brett, George Platt	2	Browne, Charles Albert	4
Brewster, Ralph Owen	7	Browne, Herbert	4
Brice, Fanny	5	Browning, Tod	7
Brickell, Henry Herschel	5	Brownlee, James Forbis	6
Bridges, Calvin Blackman	2	Brownson, Willard Herbert	1
Bridges, (Henry) Styles	7	Bruce, Andrew Alexander	1
Bridges, Thomas Jefferson Davis		Bruce, Edward Bright	3
("Tommy")	8	Bruce, Lenny	8
Bridgman, Percy Williams	7	Bruce, Philip Alexander	1
Briggs, Clare A.	1	Bruce, William Cabell	4
Briggs, LeBaron Russell	1	Brucker, Wilber Marion	8
Briggs, Lloyd Vernon	3	Brundage, Avery	9
Briggs, Lyman James	7	Brunswick, Ruth Mack	4
Brigham, Albert Perry	1	Brush, Charles Francis	1
Brightman, Edgar Sheffield	5	Brush, Edward Nathaniel	1
Brill, Abraham Arden	4	Brush, George de Forest	3
Brinkley, John Richard	3	Bryan, Charles Wayland	3
Brinton, Clarence Crane	8	Bryan, John Stewart	3
Brisbane, Arthur	2	Bryan, Kirk	4

Index Guide

Name	Supplement	Name	Supplement
Bryant, Louise Frances Stevens	6	Bush-Brown, Henry Kirke	1
Bryant, Ralph Clement	2	Bushman, Francis Xavier	8
Bryson, Lyman Lloyd	6	Butler, Burridge Davenal	4
Buchanan, Scott Milross	8	Butler, Marion	2
Buchman, Frank Nathan Daniel	7	Butler, Nicholas Murray	4
Buck, Frank	4	Butler, Pierce	2
Buck, Pearl Comfort		Butler, Smedley Darlington	2
Sydenstricker	9	Butterfield, Kenyon Leech	1
Buckley, Oliver Ellsworth	6	Butterworth, William Walton	
Buckner, Emory Roy	3	("Walt")	9
Buckner, Simon Bolivar	3	Butts, James Wallace ("Wally")	9
Budd, Edward Gowen	4	Byerly, William Elwood	1
Budd, Ralph	7	Byington, Spring	9
Budenz, Louis Francis	9	Byoir, Carl Robert	6
Buley, Roscoe Carlyle	8	Byrd, Harry Flood	8
Bullard, Robert Lee	4	Byrd, Richard Evelyn	6
Bullitt, William Christian	8	Byrnes, James Francis	9
Bunche, Ralph Johnson	9	Byrns, Joseph Wellington	2
Bundy, Harvey Hollister	7		
Bunker, Arthur Hugh	7	Cabell, James Branch	6
Burchfield, Charles Ephraim	8	Cable, Frank Taylor	3
Burdick, Eugene Leonard	7	Cabot, Godfrey Lowell	7
Burdick, Usher Lloyd	6	Cabot, Hugh	3
Burgess, Frank Gelett	5	Cabot, Richard Clarke	2
Burgess, George Kimball	1	Cabrini, Frances Xavier	1
Burgess, John William	1	Cadman, Charles Wakefield	4
Burgess, Thornton Waldo	7	Cadman, Samuel Parkes	2
Burgess, William Starling	4	Caffery, Jefferson	9
Burke, Billie	8	Cahan, Abraham	5
Burke, John Joseph	2	Cahill, Hogler	6
Burleigh, Henry Thacker	4	Cahn, Edmund Nathaniel	7
Burlesun, Albert Sidney	2	Cain, William	1
Burleson, Hugh Latimer	1	Cajori, Florian	1
Burlingham, Charles Culp	6	Calder, Alexander Stirling	3
Burnett, Leo	9	Caldwell, Otis William	4
Burnham, Frederick Russell	4	Calhoun, Patrick	3
Burnham, William Henry	3	Calkins, Earnest Elmo	7
Burns, Bob	6	Calkins, Gary Nathan	3
Burns, William John	1	Calkins, Mary Whiton	1
Burr, George Lincoln	2	Callahan, Patrick Henry	2
Burr, William Hubert	1	Callaway, Morgan	2
Burrage, Walter Lincoln	1	Callimachos, Panos Demetrios	7
Burroughs, Bryson	1	Calverton, Victor Francis	2
Burroughs, Edgar Rice	4	Campbell, Charles Macfie	3
Burroughs, William Seward	1	Campbell, Douglas Houghton	5
Burrow, Trigant	4	Campbell, John Wood, Jr.	9
Burton, Clarence Monroe	1	Campbell, William	2
Burton, Harold Hitz	7	Campbell, William Edward	
Burton, Richard Eugene	2	March	5
Burton, Theodore Elijah	1	Campbell, William Wallace	2
Busch, Adolphus	1	Canby, Henry Seidel	7
Busch, Hermann	9	Candler, Warren Akin	3
Bush, Lincoln	2	Cannon, Annie Jump	3
Bush, Prescott Sheldon	9	Cannon, Clarence	7
Bush, Vannevar ("Van")	9	Cannon, Ida Maud	6

Index Guide

Name	Supplement	Name	Supplement
Cannon, James	3	Cash, Wilbur Joseph	3
Cannon, James Thomas	9	Cassidy, Marshall Whiting	8
Cannon, Walter Bradford	3	Cassoday, John Bolivar	1
Cantor, Eddie	7	Castle, Irene Foote	8
Cantril, Albert Hadley	8	Castle, William Richards, Jr.	7
Capen, Samuel Paul	6	Cataldo, Joseph Maria	1
Capone, Alphonse	4	Catchings, Waddill	8
Capper, Arthur	5	Cather, Willa	4
Capps, Edward	4	Catlett, Sidney	5
Capps, Washington Lee	1	Catt, Carrie Chapman	4
Caraway, Hattie	4	Cattell, James McKeen	3
Caraway, Thaddeus Horatius	1	Cayton, Horace Roscoe	8
Cardozo, Benjamin Nathan	2	Celestin, Oscar ("Papa")	5
Carlisle, Floyd Leslie	3	Cerf, Bennett Alfred	9
Carlson, Anton Julius	6	Cermak, Anton Joseph	1
Carlson, Chester Floyd	8	Cesare, Oscar Edward	4
Carlson, Evans Fordyce	4	Chadwick, George Whitefield	1
Carmichael, Oliver Cromwell	8	Chafee, Zechariah, Jr.	6
Carnap, Rudolf	8	Chaffee, Adna Romanza	3
Carnegie, Dale	5	Chaffee, Roger Bruce	8
Carnegie, Hattie	6	Chalmers, William James	2
Carnegie, Mary Crowninshield		Chamberlain, Charles Joseph	3
Endicott Chamberlain	6	Chamberlain, Joseph Perkins	5
Carothers, Wallace Hume	2	Chamberlin, Edward Hastings	8
Carpenter, John Alden	5	Chambers, Robert William	1
Carr, Charlotte Elizabeth	6	Chambers, Whittaker	7
Carr, Wilbur John	3	Chandler, Harry	3
Carrel, Alexis	3	Chandler, John Scudder	1
Carrier, Willis Haviland	4	Chandler, Julian Alvin Carroll	1
Carrington, Elaine Stern	6	Chandler, Norman	9
Carroll, Earl	4	Chandler, Raymond Thornton	6
Carroll, Leo Grattan	9	Chaney, Lon (d. 1930)	1
Carrora, Joseph		Chaney, Lon (d. 1973)	9
See Dundee, Johnny		Channing, Edward	1
Carruth, Fred Hayden	1	Chapelle, Dickey	7
Carson, Hampton Lawrence	1	Chapin, Charles Value	3
Carson, Jack	7	Chapin, Henry Dwight	3
Carson, John Renshaw	2	Chapin, James Paul	7
Carson, Rachel Louise	7	Chapin, Roy Dikeman	2
Carson, Simeon Lewis	5	Chaplin, Ralph Hosea	7
Carter, Boake	3	Chapman, Frank Michler	3
Carter, Caroline Louise Dudley	2	Chapman, John Arthur	9
Carter, Mrs. Leslie		Chapman, John Jay	1
See Carter, Caroline Louise		Charles, Ezzard Mack	9
Dudley		Chase, Edna Woolman	6
Carter, William Hodding, Jr.	9	Chase, Harry Woodburn	5
Carty, John Joseph	1	Chase, (Mary) Agnes Merrill	7
Carvalho, Solomon Solis	3	Chase, Mary Ellen	9
Carver, George Washington	3	Chatterton, Ruth	7
Cary, Elisabeth Luther	2	Chavez, Dennis	7
Casadesus, Robert Marcel	9	Chennault, Claire Lee	6
Casals, Pablo	9	Cherrington, Ernest Hurst	4
Case, Francis Higbee	7	Cheshire, Joseph Blount	1
Case, Shirley Jackson	4	Chessman, Caryl Whittier	6
Casey, Thomas Lincoln	1	Chester, Colby Mitchell (d. 1932)	1

Index Guide

Name	Supplement	Name	Supplement
Chester, Colby Mitchell (d. 1965)	7	Coe, George Albert	5
Cheyney, Edward Potts	4	Coffin, Henry Sloane	5
Chiera, Edward	1	Coffin, Howard Earle	2
Child, Charles Manning	5	Coffin, Robert Peter Tristram	5
Child, Richard Washburn	1	Coffman, Lotus Delta	2
Child, Robert	1	Cogbill, George Ellet	3
Chittenden, Russell Henry	3	Coghlan, Rose	1
Choate, Anne Hyde Clarke	8	Cohan, George Michael	3
Chotzinoff, Samuel	7	Cohen, Felix Solomon	5
Christian, Henry Asbury	5	Cohen, John Sanford	1
Christie, John Walter	3	Cohen, Morris	4
Christy, Howard Chandler	5	Cohen, Octavus Roy	6
Chrysler, Walter Percy	2	Cohn, Alfred A.	5
Church, Irving Porter	1	Cohn, Alfred Einstein	6
Churchill, Winston	4	Cohn, Edwin Joseph	5
Cicotte, Edward Victor	8	Cohn, Harry	6
Claffin, John	2	Coit, Stanton	3
Clapp, Charles Horace	1	Coker, David Robert	2
Clapp, Margaret Antoinette	9	Colby, Bainbridge	4
Clapper, Raymond Lewis	3	Colcord, Lincoln	4
Clark, Bennett Champ	5	Cole, George Watson	2
Clark, Bobby	6	Cole, Nat "King"	7
Clark, Feltun Grandison	8	Cole, Timothy	1
Clark, Grenville	8	Collier, Barron Gift	2
Clark, John Bates	2	Collier, Constance	5
Clark, John Maurice	7	Collier, John	8
Clark, Joseph James ("Jocko")	9	Collins, Edward Trowbridge	5
Clark, Joshua Reuben, Jr.	7	Collins, Guy N.	2
Clark, Walter Leighton	1	Colman, Ronald Charles	6
Clark, Walter Van Tilburg	9	Colpitts, Edwin Henry	4
Clarke, Frank Wigglesworth	1	Coltrane, John William	8
Clarke, John Hessin	3	Colum, Padraic	9
Clayton, Henry De Lamar	1	Comfort, Will Levington	1
Clayton, William Lockhart	8	Comiskey, Grace Elizabeth Reidy	6
Cleghorn, Sarah Norcliffe	6	Condon, Albert Edwin ("Eddie")	9
Clement, Frank Goad	8	Condon, Edward Uhler	9
Clement, Martin Withington	8	Conmmons, John Rogers	3
Clement, Rufus Early	8	Compton, Arthur Holly	7
Clemente, Roberto	9	Compton, Karl Taylor	5
Clements, Frederic Edward	3	Comstock, George Cary	1
Clements, William Lawrence	1	Comstock, John Henry	1
Clift, Edward Montgomery	8	Conboy, Martin	3
Cline, Genevieve Rose	6	Cone, Claribel	4
Clothier, William Jackson	7	Cone, Etta	4
Cloud, Henry Roe	4	Cone, Hutchinson Ingham	3
Cluett, Sanford Lockwood	8	Cone, Russell Glenn	7
Clyde, George Dewey	9	Conklin, Edwin Grant	5
Coakley, Cornelius Godfrey	1	Connaly, Thomas Terry ("Tom")	7
Cobb, Irvin Shrewsbury	3	Connick, Charles Jay	3
Cobb, Nathan Augustus	1	Connolly, John	1
Cobb, Tyrus Raymond ("Ty")	7	Connolly, Maureen Catherine	8
Cobo, Albert Eugene	6	Connolly, Thomas Henry, Sr.	7
Cochrane, Gordon Stanley		Connor, Robert Digges Wimberly	4
("Mickey")	7	Connor, Theophilus Eugene	
Cockerell, Theodore Dru Alison	4	("Bull")	9

Index Guide

Name	Supplement	Name	Supplement
Conover, Harry Sayles	7	Coster, F. Donald	
Conrad, Frank	3	See Musica, Philip Mariano	
Considine, Robert Bernard	9	Fausto	
Conte, Richard	9	Costigan, Edward Prentiss	2
Converse, Frederick Shepherd	2	Costigan, George Purcell	1
Cook, Frederick Albert	2	Cotton, Joseph Potter	1
Cook, Walter Wheeler	3	Cottrell, Frederick Gardner	4
Cook, Will Marion	3	Couch, Harvey Crowley	3
Cooke, Ebenezer	1	Coudert, Frederic René (d. 1955)	5
Cooke, Morris Llewellyn	6	Coudert, Frederic René (d. 1972)	9
Cooke, Robert Anderson	6	Coulter, Ernest Kent	5
Cooke, Samuel	7	Councilman, William Thomas	1
Cooley, Edwin Gilbert	1	Courant, Richard	9
Cooley, Harold Dunbar	9	Coutard, Henri	4
Cooley, Mortimer Elwyn	3	Couzens, James	2
Cooley, Thomas Benton	3	Covici, Pascal ("Pat")	7
Coolidge, Calvin	1	Cowen, Joshua Lionel	7
Coolidge, Charles Allerton	2	Cowl, Jane	4
Coolidge, Elizabeth Penn		Cowles, Gardner	4
Sprague	5	Cowles, Henry Chandler	2
Coolidge, Julian Lowell	5	Cox, Edward Eugene	5
Coolidge, Thomas Jefferson	6	Cox, James Middleton (d. 1957)	6
Coomaraswamy, Ananda		Cox, James Middleton (d. 1974)	9
Kentish	4	Cox, Wallace Maynard ("Wally")	9
Coontz, Robert Edward	1	Coxey, Jacob Sechler	5
Cooper, Gary	7	Coyle, Grace Longwell	7
Cooper, Hugh Lincoln	2	Craig, Malin	3
Cooper, John Montgomery	4	Craig, Winchell McKendree	6
Cooper, Kent	7	Cram, Ralph Adams	3
Cooper, (Leon) Jere	6	Crane, Charles Richard	2
Cooper, Oswald Bruce	2	Crane, Frederick Evan	4
Cooper, William John	1	Crane, Harold Hart	1
Cope, Arthur Clay	8	Cranston, Earl	1
Copeland, Charles Townsend	5	Cravath, Paul Drennan	2
Copeland, Royal Samuel	2	Craven, Frank	3
Copley, Ira Clifton	4	Crawford, James Pyle Wickersham	2
Corbett, Harvey Wiley	5	Crawford, Samuel Earl	8
Corbett, James John	1	Creel, George	5
Corbin, Henry Clark	1	Cret, Paul Philippe	3
Cordier, Andrew Wellington	9	Crile, George Washington	3
Cordiner, Ralph Jarron	9	Crisp, Donald	9
Cordon, Guy	8	Crissinger, Daniel Richard	3
Corey, Lewis	5	Crocker, William	4
Corey, William Ellis	1	Croly, Herbert David	1
Cori, Gerty Theresa Radnitz	6	Cromwell, Dean Bartlett	7
Coriat, Isador Henry	3	Cromwell, William Nelson	4
Cornell, Katharine	9	Crosby, Percy Lee	7
Correll, Charles James	9	Crosley, Powell, Jr.	7
Cort, Edwin	4	Cross, Arthur Lyon	2
Cortelyou, George Bruce	2	Cross, Charles Whitman	4
Cortissoz, Royal	4	Cross, Milton John	9
Corwin, Edward Samuel	7	Cross, Samuel Hazzard	4
Costain, Thomas Bertram	7	Cross, Wilbur Lucius	4
Costello, Frank	9	Crosser, Robert	6
Costello, Lou	6	Crosswaith, Frank Rudolph	7

Index Guide

Name	Supplement	Name	Supplement
Crothers, Rachel	6	Dale, Charles Marks	9
Crouse, Russel McKinley	8	Dale, Chester	7
Crowder, Enoch Herbert	1	Dale, Maud Murray Thompson	5
Crowe, Francis Trenholm	4	Daley, Arthur John	9
Crowley, Leo Thomas	9	Daley, Cass	9
Crowninshield, Frank	4	Dallin, Cyrus Edwin	3
Croy, Homer	7	Daly, Reginald Aldworth	6
Crozier, William	3	Damon, Ralph Shepard	6
Crumbine, Samuel Jay	5	Damrosch, Frank Heino	2
Crump, Edward Hull	5	Damrosch, Walter	4
Cubberley, Ellwood Patterson	3	Dana, Charles Anderson	9
Cudahy, Edward Aloysius, Jr.	8	Dana, Charles Loomis	1
Culbertson, Ely	5	Dana, Edward Salisbury	1
Culbertson, Josephine Murphy	6	Dandridge, Dorothy Jean	7
Cullen, Countee	4	Dandy, Walter Edward	4
Cullen, Hugh Roy	6	Daniels, Farrington	9
Cullen, Thomas Stephen	5	Daniels, Frank Albert	1
Cullinan, Joseph Stephen	2	Daniels, Josephus	4
cummings, e e	7	Daniels, Winthrop More	3
Cummings, Homer Stillé	6	Dargan, Edwin Preston	2
Cummings, Walter Joseph	8	Darin, Bobby	9
Cunningham, Kate Richards		Darling, Jay Norwood ("Ding")	7
O'Hare		Darrow, Clarence Seward	2
See O'Hare, Kate		Dart, Henry Plauché	1
Richards (Cunningham)		Darton, Nelson Horatio	4
Cuppia, Jerome Chester	8	Darwell, Jane	8
Cuppy, Will	4	Daugherty, Harry Micajah	3
Curley, James Michael	6	Davenport, Charles Benedict	3
Curme, George Oliver	4	Davenport, Eugene	3
Curran, John, Joseph	2	Davenport, Herbert Joseph	1
Curran, Thomas Jerome	6	Davenport, Russell Wheeler	5
Curry, John Steuart	4	Davidoff, Leo Max	9
Curtis, Charles	2	Davidson, Israel	2
Curtis, Charles Pelham	6	Davidson, Jo	5
Curtis, Cyrus Hermann		Davies, John Vipond	2
Kotzschmar	1	Davies, Joseph Edward	6
Curtis, Edward Sheriff	5	Davies, Marion Cecilia	7
Curtis, Heber Doust	3	Davis, Adelle	9
Curtiss, Glenn Hammond	1	Davis, Arthur Powell	1
Curtiz, Michael	7	Davis, Arthur Vining	7
Cushing, Harvey Williams	2	Davis, Benjamin Oliver, Sr.	8
Cushing, Richard James	8	Davis, Bernard George	9
Cushman, Joseph Augustine	4	Davis, Charles Harold	1
Cusman, Vera Charlotte		Davis, Dwight Filley	3
Scott	4	Davis, Elmer Holmes	6
Cutler, Elliott Carr	4	Davis, Ernest R. ("Ernie")	7
Cutler, Robert	9	Davis, Francis Breese, Jr.	7
Cutting, Bronson Murray	1	Davis, Harvey Nathaniel	5
Cutting, Robert Fulton	1	Davis, James John	4
		Davis, John Staige	4
Dabney, Charles William	3	Davis, John William	5
Da Costa, John Chalmers	1	Davis, Katharine Bement	1
Daeger, Albert Thomas	1	Davis, Norman Hezekiah	3
Dakin, Henry Drysdale	5	Davis, Oscar King	1
Dakin, Janies Harrison	1	Davis, Owen Gould	6

Index Guide

Name	Supplement	Name	Supplement
Davis, Pauline Morton Sabin	5	Densmore, Frances	6
Davis, Stuart	7	De Palma, Ralph	6
Davis, Watson	8	De Paolis, Alessio	7
Davis, William Hammatt	7	De Priest, Oscar Stanton	5
Davis, William Morris	1	De Quille, Dan	
Davison, George Willets	5	See Wright, William	
Davison, Gregory Caldwell	1	Dercum, Francis Xavier	1
Davisson, Clinton Joseph	6	Dern, George Henry	2
Dawes, Charles Gates	5	De Rose, Peter	5
Dawes, Rufus Cutler	2	De Schweinitz, George Edmund	
Dawley, Almena	6	See Schweinitz, George	
Dawson, William Levi	8	Edmund de	
Day, Arthur Louis	6	de Seversky, Alexander Procofieff	9
Day, Clarence Shepard	1	De Sylva, George	4
Day, Edmund Ezra	5	Dett, Robert Nathaniel	3
Day, George Parmly	6	Devaney, John Patrick	3
Day, Holman Francis	1	Devine, Edward Thomas	4
Dealey, George Bannerman	4	DeVoto, Bernard Augustine	5
Dean, Gordon Evans	6	Dewey, John	5
Dean, James Byron	5	Dewey, Melvil	1
Dean, Jay Hanna ("Dizzy")	9	Dewey, Richard Smith	1
Dean, "Man Mountain"		Dewey, Thomas Edmund	9
See Leavitt, Frank Simmons		de Wilde, Brandon	9
Dean, William Henry, Jr.	5	Dewing, Thomas Wilmer	2
De Angelis, Thomas Jefferson	1	De Wolfe, Elsie	4
Deaver, John Blair	1	d'Harnoncourt, René	8
De Barenne, Joannes Gregorius		Diat, Louis Felix	6
See Dusser de Barenne,		Dickinson, Anna Elizabeth	1
Joannes Gregorius		Dickinson, Edwin De Witt	7
Debye, Peter Joseph William	8	Dickinson, John	5
De Cuevas, Marquis	7	Dickinson, Preston	1
De Forest, Alfred Victor	3	Dickinson, Robert Latou	4
De Forest, Lee	7	Dickson, Earle Ensign	7
De Forest, Robert Weeks	1	Dickson, Leonard Eugene	5
De Haas, Jacob		Dielman, Frederick	1
See Haas, Jacob Judah		Dies, Martin	9
Aaron de		Dietz, Peter Ernest	4
de Kruif, Paul Henry	9	Digges, Dudley	4
Deland, Margaret	3	Dillard, James Hardy	2
Delano, William Adams	6	Dille, John Flint	6
DeLee, Joseph Bolivar	3	Diller, Burgoyne	7
De Leeuw, Adolph Lodewyk	3	Diller, Joseph Silas	1
Dell, Floyd James	8	Dillinger, John	1
Dellenbaugh, Frederick Samuel	1	Dillingham, Charles Bancroft	1
Del Ruth, Roy	7	Dillingham, Walter Frances	7
De Luca, Giuseppe	4	Dilworth, Richardson	9
DeMille, Cecil Blount	6	Dingman, Mary Agnes	7
Demuth, Charles	1	Dinwiddie, Albert Bledsoe	1
Denfeld, Louis Emil	9	Dinwiddie, Courtenay	3
Dennett, Tyler	4	Dinwiddie, Edwin Courtland	1
Dennis, Alfred Lewis Pinneo	1	Dirksen, Everett McKinley	8
Dennis, Eugene	7	Disney, Roy Oliver	9
Dennis, Frederic Shepard	1	Disney, Walter Elias ("Walt")	8
Dennison, Henry Sturgis	5	Ditmars, Raymond Lee	3
Denny, George Vernon, Jr.	6	Dittemore, John Valentine	2

Index Guide

Name	Supplement	Name	Supplement
Divine, Father	7	Downes, (Edwin) Olin	5
Dix, Dorothy		Downey, June Etta	1
See Gilmer, Elizabeth		Downey, Sheridan	7
Meriwether		Draper, Dorothy	8
Dixon, Roland Burrage	1	Draper, Ruth	6
Dixon, Thomas	4	Dreier, Katherine Sophie	5
Dobie, Gilmour	4	Dreier, Margaret	
Dobie, J(ames) Frank	7	See Robins, Margaret Dreier	
Dobzhansky, Theodosius		Dreier, Mary Elisabeth	7
Grigorievich	9	Dreiser, Theodore	3
Dock, Lavinia Lloyd	6	Dressen, Charles Walter	8
Dodd, Bella Visono	8	Dresser, Louise Kerlin	7
Dodd, Lee Wilson	1	Dressler, Marie	1
Dodd, Monroe Elmon	5	Drew, Charles Richard	4
Dodd, Thomas Joseph	9	Drexel, Katharine Mary	5
Dodd, William Edward	2	Driscoll, Alfred Eastlack	9
Dodge, Henry Chee	4	Dreyfus, Max	7
Dodge, Joseph Morrell	7	Drinker, Cecil Kent	6
Dodge, Raymond	3	Dromgoole, William Allen	1
Dodge, William de Leftwich	1	Drum, Hugh Aloysius	5
Doheny, Edward Laurence	1	Dryfoos, Orvil E.	7
Doherty, Henry Latham	2	Duane, William	1
Dole, James Drummond	6	Du Bois, William Edward	
Dole, Nathan Haskell	1	Burghardt	7
D'Olier, Franklin	5	Duchin, Edward Frank ("Eddy")	5
Dollar, Robert	1	Duff, James Henderson	8
Donaldson, Henry Herbert	2	Duffy, Edmund	7
Donaldson, Jesse Monroe	8	Duffy, Francis Patrick	1
Donlevy, Brian	9	Duffy, Hugh	5
Donovan, James Britt	8	Duggar, Benjamin Minge	6
Donovan, John Joseph	2	Duke, Vernon	8
Donovan, William Joseph	6	Dulles, Allen Welsh	8
Dooley, Thomas Anthony, III		Dulles, John Foster	6
("Tom")	7	Dumaine, Frederic Christopher	5
Doran, George Henry	6	Dumont, Allen Balcom	7
Dorn, Harold Fred	7	Dumont, Margaret	7
Dorset, Marion	1	Dunbar, (Helen) Flanders	6
Dorsey, George Amos	1	Duncan, Donald Franklin	9
Dorsey, Thomas Francis		Duncan, James	1
("Tommy")	6	Dundee, Johnny (Joseph Carrora)	7
Dos Passos, John Roderigo	8	Dunn, Michael	9
Doubleday, Frank Nelson	1	Dunne, Finley Peter	2
Doubleday, Nelson	4	Dunning, John Ray	9
Dougherty, Dennis Joseph	5	Du Pont, Alfred Irénée	1
Dougherty, Raymond Philip	1	Du Pont, Francis Irénée	3
Doughton, Robert Lee	5	Du Pont, Irénée	7
Douglas, Lewis Williams	9	Du Pont, Lammot	5
Douglas, Lloyd Cassel	5	Du Pont, Pierre Samuel	5
Douglass, Andrew Ellicott	7	Du Pont, Thomas Coleman	1
Doull, James Angus	7	Durant, William Crapo	4
Dove, Arthur Garfield	4	Duranty, Walter	6
Dow, Alex	3	Durkin, Martin Patrick	5
Dow, Herbert Henry	1	Durstine, Roy Sarles	7
Dowling, Austin	1	Duryea, Charles Edgar	2
Dowling, Noel Thomas	8	Duryea, James Frank	8

Index Guide

Name	Supplement	Name	Supplement
Dusser de Barenne, Joannes Gregorius	2	Elliot, Cass ("Mama")	9
Duvall, Gabriel	1	Elliott, Charles Burke	1
Dwiggins, William Addison	6	Elliott, John Lovejoy	3
Dwight, Arthur Smith	4	Elliott, Maxine	2
Dworshak, Henry Clarence	7	Ellis, Carleton	3
Dyer, Rolla Eugene	9	Ellmaker, (Emmett) Lee	5
Dyett, Thomas Ben	9	Ellsworth, Lincoln	5
Dykstra, Clarence Addison	4	Elman, Harry ("Ziggy")	8
Dykstra, John	9	Elman, Mischa	8
		Elman, Robert	6
		Elmslie, George Grant	5
Eames, Wilberforce	2	Elsberg, Charles Albert	4
Earhart, Amelia Mary	2	Elvehjem, Conrad Arnold	7
Earle, Edward Mead	5	Ely, Hanson Edward	6
Earle, George Howard, III	9	Ely, Richard Theodore	3
Earle, Ralph	2	Embree, Edwin Rogers	4
Early, Stephen Tyree	5	Emerson, Benjamin Kendall	1
Easley, Ralph Montgomery	2	Emerson, Haven	6
East, Edward Murray	2	Emerson, Rollins	4
Eastman, George	1	Emerton, Ephraim	1
Eastman, Joseph Bartlett	3	Emerton, James Henry	1
Eastman, Max Forrester	8	Emmet, William Le Roy	3
Eaton, Charles Aubrey	5	Emmett, Burton	1
Eckstorm, Fannie Hardy	4	Enelow, Hyman Gerson	1
Eddy, Clarence	2	Engel, Carl	3
Eddy, Harrison Prescott	2	Engelhard, Charles William	9
Eddy, Manton Sprague	7	Engelhardt, Zephyrin	1
Eddy, Nelson	8	Engle, Clair William Walter	7
Edeson, Robert	1	Eno, William Phelps	3
Edge, Walter Evans	6	Epstein, Abraham	3
Edison, Charles	8	Epstein, Jacob	6
Edison, Thomas Alva	1	Epstein, Philip G.	5
Edman, Irwin	5	Erdman, Charles Rosenbury	6
Edmondson, William	5	Erlanger, Joseph	7
Edmunds, Charles Wallis	3	Erpf, Armand Grover	9
Edsall, David Linn	3	Errol, Leon	5
Edwards, Clarence Ransom	1	Erskine, John	5
Edwards, Everett Eugene	5	Esch, John Jacob	3
Edwards, Richard Stanislaus	6	Eustis, Dorothy Harrison	4
Egtvedt, Clairmont Leroy ("Claire")	9	Evans, Charles	1
Eichelberger, Robert Lawrence	7	Evans, Herbert McLean	9
		Evans, Walker	9
Eilshemius, Louis Michel	3	Everleigh, Ada	4
Einstein, Albert	5	Everleigh, Minna	4
Eisenhart, Luther Pfahler	7	Evermann, Barton Warren	1
Eisenhower, Dwight David	8	Evers, Medgar Wiley	7
Eisler, Gerhart	8	Evola, Natale ("Joe Diamond")	9
Eklund, Carl Robert	7	Ewing, James	3
Eliot, Thomas Stearns	7	Ewing, William Maurice	9
Elkin, William Lewis	1		
Ellender, Allen Joseph	9	Faccioli, Giuseppe	1
Ellington, Earl Buford	9	Fagan, Mark Matthew	5
Ellington, Edward Kennedy ("Duke")	9	Fairbanks, Douglas	2
		Fairburn, William Armstrong	4

Index Guide

Name	Supplement	Name	Supplement
Fairchild, Blair	1	Fernald, Merritt Lyndon	4
Fairchild, David Grandison	5	Fernós Isern, Antonio	9
Fairchild, Fred Rogers	8	Ferree, Clarence Errol	3
Fairchild, Sherman Mills	9	Fess, Simeon Davidson	2
Fairchild, Stephen Muir	4	Fessenden, Reginald Aubrey	1
Fairfax, Beatrice		Fetter, Frank Albert	4
See Manning, Marie		Feuchtwanger, Lion	6
Fairless, Benjamin F.	7	Few, William Preston	2
Fairlie, John Archibald	4	Field, Fred Tarbell	4
Falk, Maurice	4	Field, Marshall, III	6
Falk, Otto Herbert	2	Field, Marshall, IV	7
Falkner, Roland Post	2	Fields, Dorothy	9
Fall, Albert Bacon	3	Fields, Lewis Maurice	
Fall, Bernard B.	8	See under Weber, Joseph	
Farish, William Stamps	3	Morris	
Farnam, Henry Walcott	1	Fields, William Claude	4
Farnsworth, Philo Taylor	9	Fifer, Joseph Wilson	2
Farnum, Franklyn	7	Filene, Edward Albert	2
Farquhar, Percival	5	Fillmore, Charles	4
Farrand, Beatrix Cadwalader		Fine, Larry	9
Jones	6	Finley, John Huston	2
Farrand, Livingston	2	Finney, John Miller Turpin	3
Farrand, Max	3	Firestone, Harvey Samuel (d. 1938)	2
Farrar, Geraldine	8	Firestone, Harvey Samuel (d. 1973)	9
Farrar, John Chipman	9	Fischer, Louis	8
Farrell, James Augustine	3	Fischer, Ruth	7
Farrington, Joseph Rider	5	Fish, Carl Russell	1
Farrington, Wallace Rider	1	Fisher, Alfred J., and Charles T.	7
Farson, Negley	6	Fisher, "Bud"	
Farwell, Arthur	5	See Fisher, Henry Conroy	
Father Divine		Fisher, Clarence Stanley	3
See Divine, Father		Fisher, Dorothea Frances	
Faulkner (Falkner), William	7	Canfield	6
Fauset, Jessie	7	Fisher, Frederic John	3
Faust, Frederick Shiller	3	Fisher, Frederick Bohn	2
Faversham, William Alfred	2	Fisher, Hammond Edward	5
Fay, Francis Anthony ("Frank")	7	Fisher, Harrison	1
Fay, Sidney Bradshaw	8	Fisher, Henry Conroy	5
Fazenda, Louise Marie	7	Fisher, Irving	4
Fearing, Kenneth Flexner	7	Fisher, Walter Lowrie	1
Feininger, Lyonel (Charles		Fisher, William Arms	4
Léonell Adrian)	6	Fiske, Bradley Allen	3
Feis, Herbert	9	Fiske, Harrison Grey	3
Fejos, Paul	7	Fiske, Minnie Maddern	1
Fels, Samuel Simeon	4	Fite, Warner	5
Fenichel, Otto	4	Fitzgerald, Alice Louise Florence	7
Fenn, William Wallace	1	Fitzgerald, Francis Scott Key	2
Fenneman, Nevin Melancthon	3	Fitzgerald, John Francis	4
Ferber, Edna Jessica	8	Fitzpatrick, Daniel Robert	8
Ferguson, James Edward	3	Fitzpatrick, John	4
Ferguson, John Calvin	3	Fitzpatrick, John Clement	2
Ferguson, Miriam Amanda		Fitzsimmons, James Edward	
Wallace	7	("Sunny Jim")	8
Ferguson, Samuel	4	Flagg, Ernest	4
Fermi, Enrico	5	Flagg, James Montgomery	6

Index Guide

Name	Supplement	Name	Supplement
Flaherty, Robert Joseph	5	Foshag, William Frederick	6
Flanagan, Edward Joseph	4	Foster, Frank Hugh	1
Flanagan, Hallie	8	Foster, Thomas Jefferson	2
Flanders, Ralph Edward	8	Foster, William Trudant	4
Flandrau, Charles Macomb	2	Foster, William Z.	7
Flannagan, John Bernard	3	Foulke, William Dudley	1
Flegenheimer, Arthur	1	Foulois, Benjamin Delahauf	8
Fleischer, Nathaniel Stanley		Fowke, Gerard	1
("Nat")	9	Fowler, Gene	6
Fleisher, Benjamin Wilfrid	4	Fowler, Russell Story	6
Fleming, Arthur Henry	2	Fox, Dixon Ryan	3
Fleming, John Adam	6	Fox, Fontaine Talbot, Jr.	7
Fleming, Walter Lynwood	1	Fox, Jacob Nelson ("Nellie")	9
Fletcher, Benjamin	1	Fox, William	5
Fletcher, Duncan Upshaw	2	Foxx, James Emory	8
Fletcher, Henry Prather	6	Fraina, Louis C.	
Fletcher, John Gould	4	See Corey, Lewis	
Fletcher, John Gould	4	Frame, Alice Seymour Browne	3
Fletcher, Robert	2	Francis, Kay	8
Flexner, Abraham	6	Francis, Paul James	2
Flexner, Bernard	3	Franck, James	7
Flexner, Jennie Maas	3	Frank, Glenn	2
Flexner, Simon	4	Frank, Jerome	6
Flick, Lawrence Francis	2	Frank, Lawrence Kelso	8
Flint, Charles Ranlett	1	Frank, Philipp G.	8
Fly, James Lawrence	8	Frank, Tenney	2
Flynn, Edward Joseph	5	Frank, Waldo David	8
Flynn, Elizabeth Gurley	7	Frankfurter, Alfred Moritz	7
Flynn, Errol Leslie	6	Frankfurter, Felix	7
Flynn, John Thomas	7	Franklin, Edward Curtis	2
Flynt, Josiah		Franklin, Fabian	2
See Willard, Josiah Flint		Franklin, Philip Albright Small	2
Fokine, Michel	3	Franz, Shepherd Ivory	1
Folin, Otto Knut Olof	1	Frary, Francis Cowles	8
Folks, Homer	7	Fraser, James Earle	5
Follett, Mary Parker	1	Fraser, Leon	3
Foote, Arthur William	2	Frayne, Hugh	1
Foote, John Ambrose	1	Frazer, Joseph Washington	9
Foote, William Henry	1	Frazier, Charles Harrison	2
Forbes, Esther	8	Frazier, Edward Franklin	7
Forbes, William Cameron	6	Frazier, Lynn Joseph	4
Force, Juliana	4	Freed, Alan J.	7
Ford, Edsel Bryant	3	Freed, Arthur	9
Ford, George Burdett	1	Freeman, Allen Weir	5
Ford, Guy Stanton	7	Freeman, Douglas Southall	5
Ford, Hannibal Choate	5	Freeman, John Ripley	1
Ford, Henry	4	Freeman, Joseph	7
Ford, John	9	French, Alice	1
Ford, Worthington Chauncey	3	French, Daniel Chester	1
Fordney, Joseph Warren	1	French, Paul Comly	6
Forester, Cecil Scott	8	Freund, Ernst	1
Forrestal, James Vincent	4	Frey, John Philip	6
Fortescue, Charles LeGeyt	2	Friedlaender, Walter Ferdinand	8
Fosdick, Harry Emerson	8	Friedman, William Frederick	8
Fosdick, Raymond Blaine	9	Frieseke, Frederick Carl	2

Index Guide

Name	Supplement	Name	Supplement
Friml, Charles Rudolf	9	Garrison, Fielding Hudson	1
Frisch, Frank Francis	9	Garrison, Lindley Miller	1
Frohman, Daniel	2	Garvey, Marcus Moziah	2
Fromm-Reichmann, Frieda	6	Gasser, Herbert Spencer	7
Frost, Edwin Brant	1	Gaston, Herbert Earle	6
Frost, Holloway Halstead	1	Gates, Caleb Frank	4
Frost, Robert Lee	7	Gates, Thomas Sovereign	4
Frost, Wade Hampton	2	Gatti-Casazza, Giulio	2
Frye, William John ("Jack")	6	Gauss, Christian Frederick	5
Fryer, Douglas Henry	6	Gauss, Clarence Edward	6
Fullam, Frank L.	5	Gauvreau, Emile Henry	6
Fuller, George Warren	1	Gavin, Frank Stanton Burns	2
Fuller, Joseph Vincent	1	Gaxton, William	7
Fulton, John Farquhar	6	Gay, Edwin Francis	4
Funk, Casimir	8	Gay, Frederick Parker	2
Funk, Wilfred John	7	Gaylord, Edward King	9
Furst, Clyde Bowman	1	Geddes, Norman Bel	6
Furuseth, Andrew	2	Gehrig, Henry Louis	3
		Geiger, Roy Stanley	4
Gable, (William) Clark	6	Gellatly, John	1
Gabrilowitsch, Ossip	2	Genovese, Vito	8
Gág, Wanda	4	Genthe, Arnold	3
Gailor, Thomas Frank	1	George, Gladys	5
Gaisman, Henry Jaques	9	George, Grace	7
Gaither, Horace Rowan, Jr.	7	George, Walter Franklin	6
Galbreath, Charles Burleigh	1	George, William Reuben	2
Gale, Henry Gordon	3	Gerard, James Watson	5
Gale, Zona	2	Gerber, Daniel (Frank) (d. 1974)	9
Gallagher, Ralph W.	5	Gerber, (Daniel) Frank (d. 1952)	5
Galli-Curci, Amelita	7	Germer, Lester Halbert	9
Gallier, James	1	Gernsback, Hugo	8
Galloway, Beverly Thomas	2	Gershwin, George	2
Galpin, Charles Josiah	4	Gesell, Arnold Lucius	7
Gambrell, Mary Latimer	9	Gest, Morris	3
Gamow, George	8	Getty, George Franklin, II	9
Gannett, Frank Ernest	6	Ghent, William James	3
Ganso, Emil	3	Gherardi, Bancroft	3
Ganz, Rudolph	9	Giancana, Sam ("Mooney")	9
Garden, Mary	8	Giannini, Amadeo Peter	4
Gardiner, Harry Norman	1	Gibbons, Euell	9
Gardner, Erle Stanley	8	Gibbons, Floyd	2
Gardner, Gilson	1	Gibbons, Herbert Adams	1
Gardner, Helen	4	Gibbs, Arthur Hamilton	7
Gardner, Leroy Upson	4	Gibbs, George	2
Gardner, Oliver Maxwell	4	Gibbs, (Oliver) Wolcott	6
Garfield, Harry Augustus	3	Gibson, Charles Dana	3
Garfield, James Rudolph	4	Gibson, Edmund Richard	
Garfield, John	5	("Hoot")	7
Garis, Howard Roger	7	Gibson, Josh	4
Garland, Judy	8	Giddings, Franklin Henry	1
Garland, Hamlin	2	Gidley, James Williams	1
Garner, James Wilford	2	Gifford, Sanford Robinson	3
Garner, John Nance	2	Gifford, Walter Sherman	8
Garretson, Austin Bruce	1	Gilbert, Alfred Carlton	7
Garrett, Finis James	6	Gilbert, Cass	1

Index Guide

Name	Supplement	Name	Supplement
Gilbert, John	2	Goldin, Horace	2
Gilbert, Seymour Parker	2	Goldman, Edwin Franko	6
Gilbreth, Lillian Evelyn Moller	9	Goldman, Emma	2
Gildersleeve, Virginia Crocheron	7	Goldman, Mayer C.	2
Gillett, Frederick Huntington	1	Goldmark, Henry	3
Gillett, Horace Wadsworth	4	Goldmark, Rubin	2
Gillette, Guy Mark	9	Goldsborough, Thomas Alan	5
Gillette, King Camp	1	Goldschmidt, Jakob	5
Gillette, William Hooker	2	Goldstein, Max Aaron	3
Gillis, James Martin	6	Goldwater, Sigismund Schulz	3
Gilman, Charlotte Perkins Stetson	1	Goldwyn, Samuel	9
Gilman, Lawrence	2	Gomberg, Moses	4
Gilmer, Elizabeth Meriwether	5	Goode, John Paul	1
Gimbel, Bernard Feustman	8	Goodman, Louis Earl	7
Giovannitti, Arturo	6	Goodman, Paul	9
Gipson, Frederick Benjamin	9	Goodnough, Xanthus Henry	1
Gipson, Lawrence Henry	9	Goodnow, Frank Johnson	2
Girdler, Tom Mercer	7	Goodrich, Annie Warburton	5
Gish, Dorothy	8	Goodyear, Anson Conger	7
Gitlow, Benjamin	7	Gorcey, Leo	8
Gitt, Josiah Williams ("Jess")	9	Gore, Robert Hayes	9
Glackens, William James	2	Gore, Thomas Pryor	4
Glasgow, Ellen Anderson Gholson	3	Gorky, Arshile	4
Glaspell, Susan	4	Gorrell, Edgar Staley	3
Glass, Carter	4	Gortner, Ross Aiken	3
Glass, Franklin Potts	1	Goslin, Leon Allen ("Goose")	9
Glass, Montague Marsden	1	Goss, Albert Simon	4
Glassford, Pelham Davis	6	Gossett, Benjamin Brown	5
Gleason, Kate	1	Gotshall, William Charles	1
Gleason, Ralph Joseph	9	Gottheil, Richard James Horatio	2
Gleaves, Albert	2	Gottschalk, Louis Reichenthal	9
Glenn, John Mark	4	Goudy, Frederick William	4
Glennon, John Joseph	4	Grable, Betty	9
Glueck, Eleanor Touroff	9	Grace, Eugene Gifford	6
Glueck, Nelson	9	Grady, Henry Francis	6
Gluck, Alma	2	Graff, Everett Dwight	7
Goddard, Calvin Hooker	5	Graham, Ernest Robert	2
Goddard, Henry Herbert	6	Graham, Evarts Ambrose	6
Goddard, Morrill	2	Graham, Frank Porter	9
Goddard, Robert Hutchings	3	Graham, Philip Leslie	7
Godowsky, Leopold	2	Grainger, George Percy	7
Goetschius, Percy	3	Grandgent, Charles Hall	2
Goetz, George See Calverton, Victor Francis		Granger, Alfred Hoyt	2
		Granger, Walter	3
Gold, Harry ("Raymond")	9	Grant, Harry Johnston	7
Gold, Michael	8	Grant, Jane Cole	9
Goldberg, Reuben Lucius ("Rube")	8	Grant, Madison	2
		Grant, Robert	2
Golden, John	5	Grant, William Thomas, Jr.	9
Goldenweiser, Alexander Alexandrovich	2	Graubau, Amadeus W.	4
		Graves, Alvin Cushman	7
Goldenweiser, Emanuel Alexander	5	Graves, David Bibb	3
		Graves, Frederick Rogers	2
		Graves, William Phillips	1
Goldfine, Bernard	8	Graves, William Sidney	2
		Gray, Carl Raymond	2

Index Guide

Name	Supplement
Gray, Gilda	6
Gray, Glen ("Spike")	7
Gray, Harold Edwin	9
Gray, Harold Lincoln	8
Gray, William Scott, Jr.	6
Greely, Adolphus Washington	1
Green, Anna Katharine	
See Rohlfs, Anna Katharine	
Green	
Green, Constance McLaughlin	9
Green, Theodore Francis	8
Green, William	5
Green, William Joseph, Jr.	7
Greenbaum, Edward Samuel	8
Greene, Belle da Costa	4
Greene, Charles Sumner	5
Greene, Henry Mather	5
Greene, Jerome Davis	6
Greene, Roger Sherman	4
Greenlaw, Edwin Almiron	1
Greenslet, Ferris	6
Greenstreet, Sydney	5
Greenway, John Campbell	1
Gregg, Alan	6
Gregg, John	4
Gregg, John Andrew	5
Gregg, Willis Ray	2
Gregory, Charles Noble	1
Gregory, Clifford Verne	3
Gregory, Menas Sarkas	
Boulgourjian	3
Gregory, Thomas Barger	5
Gregory, Thomas Watt	1
Grew, Joseph Clark	7
Grey, Zane	2
Griffin, Martin Ignatius Joseph	1
Griffith, Clark Calvin	5
Griffith, David Wark	4
Griggs, Everett Gallup	2
Grinnell, George Bird	2
Griscom, Lloyd Carpenter	6
Griscom, Ludlow	6
Grissom, Virgil Ivan ("Gus")	8
Griswold, Alfred Whitney	7
Grofé, Ferde	9
Gropius, Walter Adolf Georg	8
Gross, Milt	5
Grosset, Alexander	1
Grossinger, Jennie	9
Grosvenor, Gilbert Hovey	8
Grosz, George	6
Grove, Robert Moses ("Lefty")	9
Groves, Leslie Richard, Jr.	8
Gruening, Ernest	9
Grund, Francis Joseph	1
Grundy, Joseph Ridgway	7
Guest, Edgar Albert	6
Guffey, Joseph F.	6
Guggenheim, Harry Frank	9
Guggenheim, Simon	3
Guggenheim, Solomon	4
Guild, La Fayette	1
Guilday, Peter	4
Guinzburg, Harold Kleinert	7
Gulick, Sidney Lewis	3
Gummere, William Stryker	1
Gunn, Ross	8
Gunn, Selskar Michael	3
Gunnison, Foster	7
Gunther, John	8
Gurowski, Adam	1
Guthrie, Edwin Ray, Jr.	6
Guthrie, Ramon	9
Guthrie, Sir Tyrone	9
Guthrie, William Dameron	1
Guthrie, Woody	8
Guttmacher, Alan Frank	9
Guzik, Jack	6
Haas, Francis Joseph	5
Haas, Jacob Judah Aaron de	2
Hackett, Francis	7
Hadas, Moses	8
Hadley, Henry Kimball	2
Hofstadter, Richard	8
Hagedorn, Hermann Ludwig	
Gebhard	7
Hagen, Walter Charles	8
Haggerty, Melvin Everett	2
Hague, Frank	6
Hague, Robert Lincoln	2
Haldeman-Julius, Emanuel	5
Hale, Frederick	7
Hale, George Ellery	2
Hale, Louise Closser	1
Hale, Philip	1
Hall, Bolton	2
Hall, Edwin Herbert	2
Hall, James Norman, and	
Nordhoff, Charles Bernard	5
Hall, Juanita Armethea	8
Halpert, Edith Gregor	8
Halsey, Frederick Arthur	1
Halsey, William Frederick, Jr.	6
Hamilton, Alice	8
Hamilton, Clayton	4
Hamilton, Edith	7
Hamilton, John Daniel Miller, II	9
Hamilton, John William	1
Hamilton, Maxwell McGaughey	6
Hamilton, Walton Hale	6
Hamlin, Charles Sumner	2

Index Guide

Name	Supplement	Name	Supplement
Hamlin, Talbot Faulkner	6	Harrison, Richard Berry	1
Hammer, William Joseph	1	Harrison, Ross Granville	6
Hammerstein, Oscar, II	6	Harrisse, Henry	1
Hammett, Samuel Dashiell	7	Harshe, Robert Bartholow	2
Hammond, Bray	8	Hart, Albert Bushnell	3
Hammond, John Hays	2	Hart, Edward	1
Hammond, Laurens	9	Hart, Edwin Bret	5
Hammond, Percy Hunter	2	Hart, George Overbury	1
Hampden, Walter	5	Hart, Hastings Hornell	1
Hand, Augustus Noble	5	Hart, Lorenz Milton	3
Hand, Learned	7	Hart, Moss	7
Handy, William Christopher	6	Hart, William Surrey	4
Handley, Harold Willis	9	Hartford, George Huntington	5
Hanna, Edward Joseph	3	Hartford, George Ludlum	5
Hannagan, Stephen Jerome	5	Hartford, John Augustine	5
Hannegan, Robert Emmet	4	Hartley, Fred Allen, Jr.	8
Hansberry, Lorraine Vivian	7	Hartley, Marsden	3
Hansburg, George Bernard	9	Hartmann, Carl Sadakichi	3
Hansen, Alvin Harvey	9	Hartness, James	1
Hansen, Marcus Lee	2	Hartnett, Charles Leo ("Gabby")	9
Hansen, Neils Ebbesen	4	Hartsfield, William Berry	9
Hansen, William Webster	4	Harvey, Coin	
Hanson, James Christian		See Harvey, William Hope	
Meinich	3	Harvey, Sir John	1
Hanson, Ole	2	Harvey, William Hope	2
Hanus, Paul Henry	3	Haskell, Charles Nathaniel	1
Hapgood, Hutchins	3	Haskell, Henry Joseph	5
Hapgood, Norman	2	Haskins, Charles Homer	2
Harahan, William Johnson	2	Hassam, Frederick Childe	1
Harbord, James Guthrie	4	Hastings, Charles Sheldon	1
Harcourt, Alfred	5	Hastings, Daniel Oren	8
Hard, William	7	Hastings, William Wirt	2
Hardwick, Thomas William	3	Hatch, Carl A.	7
Hardwicke, Cedric Webster	7	Hatcher, Orie Latham	4
Hardy, Oliver Norvell	6	Hatcher, Robert Anthony	3
Hare, James Henry	4	Hatlo, James C. ("Jimmy")	7
Haring, Clarence	6	Haugen, Gilbert Nelson	1
Harkins, William Draper	5	Haugen, Nils Pederson	1
Harkness, Edward Stephen	2	Haupt, Alma Cecelia	6
Harlan, John Marshall	9	Hawes, Harriet Ann Boyd	3
Harlow, Jean	2	Hawley, Paul Ramsey	7
Harlow, Ralph Volney	6	Hawley, Willis Chatman	3
Harney, Benjamin Robertson	2	Hawthorne, Julian	1
Harridge, William ("Will")	9	Hayakawa, Sessue	9
Harriman, Florence Jaffray Hurst	8	Hayden, Carl Trumbull	9
Harrington, John Lyle	3	Hayden, Charles	2
Harris, Julian LaRose	7	Hayden, Edward Everett	1
Harris, Paul Percy	4	Hayes, Carlton Joseph Huntley	7
Harris, Sam Henry	3	Hayes, Edward Cary	1
Harris, Seymour Edwin	9	Hayes, Gabby	8
Harrison, Byron Patton	3	Hayes, John William	3
Harrison, Carter Henry, Jr.	5	Hayes, Max Sebastian	3
Harrison, Fairfax	2	Hayes, Patrick Joseph	2
Harrison, Francis Burton	6	Haynes, George Edmund	6
Harrison, Pat		Haynes, Henry Doyle ("Homer")	9
See Harrison, Byron Patton		Haynes, Williams	8

Index Guide

Name	Supplement	Name	Supplement
Hays, Arthur Garfield	5	Hershey, Milton Snavely	3
Hays, Will H.	5	Herter, Christian Archibald	8
Hayward, Leland	9	Herty, Charles Holmes	2
Hayward, Susan	9	Hertz, Alfred	3
Haywood, Allan Shaw	5	Hertz, John Daniel	7
Hazen, Allen	1	Heschel, Abraham Joshua	9
Heald, Henry Townley	9	Hess, Alfred Fabian	1
Hearst, William Randolph	5	Hess, Victor Franz	7
Heath, Thomas Kurton		Hewitt, Henry Kent	9
See under McIntyre, James		Heye, George Gustav	6
Heaton, John Langdon	1	Heyward, DuBose	2
Heatter, Gabriel	9	Hibben, John Grier	1
Hecht, Ben	7	Hickenlooper, Bourke Blakemore	9
Hecht, Selig	4	Higgins, Andrew Jackson	5
Heckscher, August	3	Higgins, Daniel Paul	5
Heffelfinger, William Walter		Higgins, Marguerite	8
("Pudge")	5	High, Stanley Hoflund	7
Heflin, James Thomas	5	Hill, Arthur Middleton	9
Heflin, Van	9	Hill, David Jayne	1
Heilmann, Harry	5	Hill, Edwin Conger	6
Heineman, Daniel Webster		Hill, Ernest Rowland	4
("Dannie")	7	Hill, George Washington	4
Heintzelman, Stuart	1	Hill, Grace Livingston	4
Helburn, Theresa	6	Hill, Joseph Adna	2
Held, John, Jr.	6	Hill, Louis Clarence	2
Hemingway, Ernest Miller	7	Hill, Patty Smith	4
Hench, Philip Showalter	7	Hillman, Sidney	4
Henchman, Daniel	1	Hillquit, Morris	1
Henderson, Fletcher Hamilton	5	Hills, Elijah Clarence	1
Henderson, Lawrence Joseph	3	Hillyer, Robert Silliman	7
Henderson, Paul	5	Hindus, Maurice Gerschon	8
Henderson, Ray	8	Hine, Lewis Wickes	2
Henderson, William James	2	Hines, Duncan	6
Henderson, Yandell	3	Hines, Frank Thomas	6
Hendrick, Burton Jesse	4	Hines, James J.	6
Hendrix, Jimi	8	Hines, John Leonard ("Birdie")	8
Heney, Francis Joseph	2	Hines, Walker Downer	1
Henie, Sonja	8	Hinkle, Beatrice Moses	5
Henny, David Christiaan	1	Hinshaw, David Schull	5
Henrici, Arthur Trautwein	3	Hires, Charles Elmer	2
Henry, Alexander	1	Hirsch, Isaac Seth	3
Henry, Alice	3	Hirsch, Maximilian Justice	8
Henry, William Arnon	1	Hirschbein, Peretz	4
Henson, Matthew Alexander	5	Hirschensohn, Chaim	1
Hepburn, Katharine Houghton	5	Hirst, Barton Cooke	1
Herbert, Frederick Hugh	6	Hirth, William Andrew	2
Herbst, Josephine Frey	8	Hiscock, Frank Harris	4
Herford, Oliver Brooke	1	Hitchcock, Frank Harris	1
Hergesheimer, Joseph	5	Hitchcock, Gilbert Monell	1
Herne, Chrystal	4	Hitchcock, Thomas	3
Herr, Herbert Thacker	1	Hoagland, Charles Lee	4
Herreshoff, Nathaniel Greene	2	Hoagland, Dennis Robert	4
Herrick, Robert Welch	2	Hoan, Daniel Webster	7
Herriman, George Joseph	3	Hobart, Alice Nourse Tisdale	8
Herrmann, Bernard	9	Hobby, William Pettus	7
Hersey, Evelyn Weeks	7	Hobson, Richmond Pearson	2

Index Guide

Name	Supplement	Name	Supplement
Hocking, William Ernest	8	Hoover, Herbert Clark	7
Hodes, Henry Irving	7	Hoover, Herbert Clark, Jr.	8
Hodge, John Reed	7	Hoover, Herbert William	5
Hodge, William Thomas	1	Hoover, James Matthews	1
Hodges, Courtney Hicks	8	Hoover, John Edgar	9
Hodges, Gilbert Ray	9	Hope, Clifford Ragsdale	8
Hodges, Luther Hartwell	9	Hope, John	2
Hodgins, Eric Francis	9	Hopkins, Edward Washburn	1
Hodgkinson, Francis	4	Hopkins, Harry Lloyd	4
Hodgson, William Brown	1	Hopkins, Miriam	9
Hodson, William	3	Hoppe, William Frederick	
Hodur, Francis	5	("Willie")	6
Hoerr, Normand Louis	6	Hopper, DeWolf	1
Hoey, Clyde Roark	5	Hopper, Edna Wallace	6
Hoffa, James Riddle ("Jimmy")	9	Hopper, Edward	8
Hoffman, Clare Eugene	8	Hopper, Hedda	8
Hoffman, Frederick Ludwig	4	Hopson, Howard Colwell	4
Hoffman, Paul Gray	9	Horlick, William	2
Hofmann, Hans	8	Hormel, George Albert	4
Hofmann, Josef Casimir	6	Hormel, Jay Catherwood	5
Hogan, Frank Smithwick	9	Hornaday, William Temple	2
Hogan, John Vincent Lawless	6	Horner, Henry	2
Hokinson, Helen Elna	4	Horney, Karen Danielssen	5
Holbrook, Stewart Hall	7	Hornsby, Rogers	7
Holden, Hale	2	Horst, Louis	7
Holdrege, George Ward	1	Horton, Edward Everett, Jr.	8
Holiday, Billie	6	Houdry, Eugene Jules	7
Holland, Spessard Lindsey	9	Hough, Walter	1
Holland, William Jacob	1	Houghton, Alanson Bigelow	3
Hollander, Jacob Harry	2	House, Edward Mandell	2
Hollerith, Herman	1	Houston, Charles Hamilton	4
Hollick, Charles Arthur	1	Houston, David Franklin	2
Holliday, Judy	7	Hovey, Otis Ellis	3
Hollingworth, Leta Stetter	2	Hovgaard, William	4
Holly, Charles Hardin ("Buddy")	6	Howard, Charles Perry	2
Holmes, Elias Burton	6	Howard, Edgar	5
Holmes, John Haynes	7	Howard, Henry	5
Holmes, Julius Cecil	8	Howard, Joseph Kinsey	5
Holmes, Oliver Wendell	1	Howard, Leland Ossian	4
Holmes, William Henry	1	Howard, Leslie	3
Holt, Arthur Erastus	3	Howard, Moe	9
Holt, Edwin Bissell	4	Howard, Roy Wilson	7
Holt, Hamilton Bowen	5	Howard, Sidney Coe	2
Holt, William Franklin	5	Howard, William Travis	1
Holt, Winifred	3	Howard, Willie	4
Homer, Arthur Bartlett	9	Howe, Edgar Watson	2
Homer, Louise Dilworth Beatty	4	Howe, Frederic Clemson	2
Hood, Raymond Mathewson	1	Howe, Louis McHenry	2
Hooker, Donald Russell	4	Howe, Mark Antony De Wolfe	6
Hooker, Elon Huntington	2	Howe, Mark De Wolfe	8
Hooker, Samuel Cox	1	Howe, Percy Rogers	4
Hooper, Harry Bartholomew	9	Howell, Albert Summers	5
Hooper, Claude Ernest	5	Howell, Clark	2
Hooper, Jessie Annette Jack	1	Howell, William Henry	3
Hooton, Earnest Albert	5	Howey, Walter Crawford	5

Index Guide

Name	Supplement	Name	Supplement
Hoyt, John Sherman	5	Hyde, Charles Cheney	5
Hrdlicka, Ales	3	Hylan, John Francis	2
Hubbard, Bernard Rosecrans	7	Hyvernat, Henri	3
Hubbard, Wynant Davis	7		
Hubbell, John Lorenzo	1	Ickes, Harold Le Clair	5
Hubble, Edwin	5	Ide, John Jay	7
Huber, Gotthelf Carl	1	Iglesias, Santiago	2
Hudson, Claude Silbert	5	Illington, Margaret	1
Hudson, Daniel Eldred	1	Inge, William Motter	9
Hudson, Frederic	1	Ingram, Jonas Howard	5
Hudson, Manley Ottmer	6	Insull, Samuel	2
Huebner, Solomon Stephen	7	Ireland, Charles Thomas, Jr.	
Huebsch, Ben W.	7	("Chick")	9
Hughes, Charles Evans	4	Ironside, Henry Allan	5
Hughes, Charles Frederick	1	Irwin, Elisabeth Antoinette	3
Hughes, Edwin Holt	4	Irwin, May	2
Hughes, James Langston	8	Irwin, Robert Benjamin	5
Hughes, Rupert	6	Irwin, Will	4
Hulbert, Archer Butler	1	Isbrandtsen, Hans Jeppesen	5
Hull, Clark Leonard	5	Isham, Ralph Heyward	5
Hull, Cordell	5	Ives, Charles Edward	5
Hull, Josephine	6	Ives, Frederic Eugene	2
Hume, Edgar Erskine	5	Ives, Irving McNeil	7
Humphrey, Doris	6	Ivins, Anthony Woodward	1
Humphrey, George Magoffin	8		
Humphreys, William Jackson	4	Jackling, Daniel Cowan	6
Humphries, George Rolfe	8	Jackson, Abraham Valentine	
Hunt, Benjamin Weeks	1	Williams	2
Hunt, George Wylie Paul	1	Jackson, Charles Douglas	7
Hunt, Haroldson Lafayette	9	Jackson, Charles Reginald	8
Hunt, Lester Callaway	5	Jackson, Chevalier	6
Hunt, Reid	4	Jackson, Clarence Martin	4
Hunter, Croil	8	Jackson, Dugald Caleb	5
Hunter, Ivory Joe	9	Jackson, Dunham	4
Hunter, Robert	3	Jackson, Edward	3
Huntington, Edward Vermilye	5	Jackson, Joseph Henry	5
Huntington, Ellsworth	4	Jackson, Mahalia	9
Huntley, Chester Robert ("Chet")	9	Jackson, Robert Houghwout	5
Hunton, George Kenneth	8	Jackson, Robert R.	3
Hupp, Louis Gorham	7	Jackson, Shirley Hardie	7
Hurley, Edward Nash	1	Jackson, William Alexander	7
Hurley, Joseph Patrick	8	Jackson, William Henry	3
Hurley, Patrick Jay	7	Jacobs, Henry Eyster	1
Hurley, Roy T.	9	Jacobs, Hirsch	8
Hurok, Solomon Isaievitch	9	Jacobs, Michael Strauss	5
Hurst, Fannie	8	Jaeger, Werner Wilhelm	7
Hurston, Zora Neale	6	Jaggar, Thomas Augustus, Jr.	5
Husing, Edward Britt ("Ted")	7	James, Arthur Curtiss	3
Huston, Walter	4	James, Arthur Horace	9
Hutcheson, Paul	6	James, Edwin Leland	5
Hutcheson, William Levi	5	James, Marquis	5
Hutchinson, Paul	6	James, Will Roderick	3
Hutton, Edward Francis	7	Jameson, John Franklin	2
Huxley, Aldous Leonard	7	Janis, Elsie	6
Hyde, Arthur Mastick	4	Janney, Russell Dixon	7

Index Guide

Name	Supplement	Name	Supplement
Jansky, Karl Guthe	4	Johnston, William Hugh	2
Jardine, William Marion	5	Johnstone, Edward Ransom	4
Jarrell, Randall	7	Jolson, Al	4
Jastrow, Joseph	3	Jones, Benjamin Allyn	7
Jeffers, John Robinson	7	Jones, Hilary Pollard	2
Jeffers, William Martin	5	Jones, Jesse Holman	6
Jefferson, Charles Edward	2	Jones, John Price	7
Jefferson, Mark Sylvester William	4	Jones, Lewis Ralph	3
Jeffrey, Edward Charles	5	Jones, Lindley Armstrong	
Jeffries, James Jackson	5	("Spike")	7
Jelliffe, Smith Ely	3	Jones, Lynds	5
Jemison, Alice Mae Lee	7	Jones, Richard Foster	7
Jennings, Herbert Spencer	4	Jones, Robert Edmond	5
Jensen, Benton Franklin ("Ben")	8	Jones, Robert Reynolds ("Bob")	8
Jensen, Jens	5	Jones, Robert Tyre, Jr.	9
Jensen, Peter Laurits	7	Jones, Rufus Matthew	4
Jepson, Willis Linn	4	Jones, Samuel Milton	1
Jerome, William Travers	1	Jones, Wesley Livsey	1
Jessup, Walter Albert	3	Joplin, Janis Lyn	8
Jewett, Frank Baldwin	4	Jordan, Benjamin Everett	9
Johns, Clayton	1	Jordan, Edwin Oakes	2
Johnson, Albert	6	Jordan, Louis	9
Johnson, Alexander	3	Jordan, Virgil Justin	7
Johnson, Alvin Saunders	9	Joy, Charles Turner	6
Johnson, Charles Spurgeon	6	Joy, Henry Bourne	2
Johnson, Douglas Wilson	3	Juday, Chancey	3
Johnson, Edward	6	Judd, Charles Hubbard	4
Johnson, Edward Austin	3	Judd, Edward Starr	1
Johnson, Edwin Carl	8	Judge, Thomas Augustine	1
Johnson, Eldridge Reeves	3	Julian, Percy Lavon	9
Johnson, George	3	Julius, Emanuel	
Johnson, George Francis	4	See Haldeman-Julius,	
Johnson, Harold Ogden ("Chic")		Emanuel	
See Olsen, John Sigvard		Just, Ernest Everett	3
("Ole") and Johnson,			
Harold			
Johnson, Hiram Warren	3	Kaempffert, Waldemar Bernhard	6
Johnson, Howard Deering	9	Kagan, Henry Enoch	8
Johnson, Hugh Samuel	3	Kahn, Albert	3
Johnson, Jack	4	Kahn, Florence Prag	4
Johnson, James Weldon	2	Kahn, Gustav Gerson	3
Johnson, Louis Arthur	8	Kahn, Louis I.	9
Johnson, Lyndon Baines	9	Kahn, Otto Herman	1
Johnson, Magnus	2	Kaiser, Henry John	8
Johnson, Osa	5	Kallen, Horace Meyer	9
Johnson, Owen McMahon	5	Kalmus, Herbert Thomas, and	
Johnson, Robert Underwood	2	Natalie Mabelle Dunfee	7
Johnson, Treat Baldwin	4	Kaltenborn, Hans von	7
Johnson, Walter	4	Kane, Helen	8
Johnson, Wendell Andrew Leroy	7	Kane, John	1
Johnston, Eric Allen	7	Karfiol, Bernard	5
Johnston, Frances Benjamin	5	Karloff, Boris	8
Johnston, John	4	Kármán, Theodore (Todor) von	7
Johnston, Mary	2	Katchen, Julius	8
Johnston, Olin DeWitt Talmadge	7	Kaufman, George S.	7
Johnston, William Hartshorne	1	Kean, Jefferson Randolph	4
		Kearns, Jack	7

Index Guide

Name	Supplement	Name	Supplement
Keating, Kenneth Barnard	9	Keyes, Frances Parkinson	8
Keaton, Joseph Francis ("Buster")	8	Keys, Clement Melville	5
Keen, William Williams	1	Kharasch, Morris Selig	6
Kefauver, (Carey) Estes	7	Kiam, Omar	5
Kefauver, Grayson Neikirk	4	Kidder, Alfred Vincent	7
Keifer, Joseph Warren	1	Kilby, Christopher	1
Keith, Arthur	3	Kilgallen, Dorothy Mae	7
Kelland, Clarence Budington	7	Kilgore, Harley Martin	6
Keller, Helen Adams	8	Kilpatrick, John Reed	6
Keller, Kaufman Thuma	8	Kilpatrick, William Heard	7
Kellerman, Karl Frederic	1	Kimball, Dan Able	8
Kellett, William Wallace	5	Kimball, Dexter Simpson	5
Kelley, Edgar Stillman	3	Kimball, (Sidney) Fiske	5
Kelley, Edith Summers	6	Kimmel, Husband Edward	8
Kelley, Florence	1	King, Alexander	7
Kellogg, Frank Billings	2	King, Carol Weiss	5
Kellogg, John Harvey	3	King, Edward Leonard	1
Kellogg, Paul Underwood	6	King, Ernest Joseph	6
Kellogg, Will Keith	5	King, Henry Churchill	1
Kellor, Frances (Alice)	5	King, Martin Luther, Jr.	8
Kelly, Edward Joseph	4	King, Richard, Jr.	9
Kelly, George Edward	9	King, Stanley	5
Kelly, Howard Atwood	3	Kingsbury, Albert	3
Kelly, John Brendan	6	Kingsley, Darwin Pearl	1
Kelly, Machine Gun	5	Kingsley, Elizabeth Seelman	6
Kelly, Walter Crawford, Jr. ("Walt")	9	Kinkaid, Thomas Cassin	9
Kelser, Raymond Alexander	5	Kinsey, Alfred Charles	6
Kelsey, Rayner Wickersham	1	Kiphuth, Robert John Herman	8
Kemmerer, Edwin Walter	3	Kiplinger, Willard Monroe	8
Kendall, Edward Calvin	9	Kirby, Allan Price	9
Kendrick, John Benjamin	1	Kirby, George Hughes	1
Kennedy, John Fitzgerald	7	Kirby, Rollin	5
Kennedy, Joseph Patrick	8	Kirchwey, George Washington	3
Kennedy, Robert Foster	5	Kirk, Alan Goodrich	7
Kennedy, Robert Francis	8	Kirk, Norman Thomas	6
Kennelly, Arthur Edwin	2	Kirkland, James Hampton	2
Kenney, Mary See O'Sullivan, Mary Kenney		Kirkwood, John Gamble	6
		Kirstein, Louis Edward	3
		Kiss, Max	8
Kenny, John V.	9	Kittredge, George Lyman	3
Kent, Arthur Atwater	4	Klauder, Charles Zeller	2
Kent, Rockwell	9	Klaw, Marc	2
Kenyon, Josephine Hemenway	7	Kleberg, Robert Justus, Jr.	9
Kenyon, William Squire	1	Klein, Anne	9
Kephart, John William	3	Klein, August Clarence	4
Keppel, Frederick Paul	3	Klein, Charles Herbert ("Chuck")	6
Kerby, William Joseph	2	Klem, William J. ("Bill")	5
Kern, Jerome David	3	Kline, Franz Josef	7
Kerney, James	1	Knapp, Bradford	2
Kerouac, Jack	8	Knapp, Joseph Palmer	5
Kerr, Robert Samuel	7	Knappen, Theodore Temple	5
Kerr, Sophie	7	Knauth, Oswald Whitman	7
Kester, Paul	1	Knight, Frank Hyneman	9
Kettering, Charles Franklin	6	Knight, Goodwin Jess ("Goodie")	8
Key, Valdimer Orlando, Jr.	7	Knight, Lucian Lamar	1
		Knopf, Blanche Wolf	8

Index Guide

Name	Supplement	Name	Supplement
Knowland, William Fife	9	Laemmle, Carl	2
Knox, Dudley Wright	6	La Farge, Christopher Grant	
Knox, Frank	3	(d. 1938)	2
Knox, Rose Markward	4	La Farge, Christopher Grant	
Knudsen, William S.	4	(d. 1956)	6
Knutson, Harold	5	La Farge, Grant	
Koch, Fred Conrad	4	See La Farge, Christopher	
Koch, Frederick Henry	3	Grant (d. 1938)	
Koch, Vivienne	7	LaFarge, John	7
Koenigsberg, Moses	3	La Farge, Oliver Hazard Perry	7
Koffka, Kurt	3	Lafever, Minard	1
Kofoid, Charles Atwood	4	La Follette, Philip Fox	7
Kohlberg, Alfred	6	La Follette, Robert Marion, Jr.	5
Kohler, Elmer Peter	2	La Guardia, Fiorello Henry	4
Kohler, Max James	1	Lahey, Frank Howard	5
Kohler, Walter Jodok	2	Lahr, Bert	8
Köhler, Wolfgang	8	Lait, Jacquin Leonard (Jack)	5
Kohut, George Alexander	1	Lajoie, Napoleon ("Larry")	6
Kolb, Lawrence	9	Lake, Kirsopp	4
Koller, Carl	3	Lake, Simon	3
Korngold, Erich Wolfgang	6	Lake, Veronica	9
Koussevitzky, Serge		Lamb, Arthur Becket	5
Alexandrovich	5	Lamb, William Frederick	5
Kovacs, Ernie	7	Lambeau, Earl Louis ("Curly")	7
Kracauer, Siegfried	8	Lamont, Thomas William	4
Kraft, James Lewis	5	Lancaster, Henry Carrington	5
Krapp, George Philip	1	Landis, Henry Robert Murray	2
Krause, Allen Kramer	3	Landis, James McCauley	7
Kreisler, Fritz	7	Landis, Jessie Royce	9
Kremers, Edward	3	Landis, Kenesaw Mountain	3
Kresge, Sebastian Spering	8	Landis, Walter Savage	3
Kress, Samuel Henry	5	Landowska, Wanda Aleksandra	6
Kreymborg, Alfred Francis	8	Landsteiner, Karl	3
Krock, Arthur	9	Lane, Arthur Bliss	6
Kroeber, Alfred Louis	6	Lane, Gertrude Battles	3
Kroeger, Ernest Richard	1	Lang, Henry Roseman	1
Kroger, Bernard Henry	2	Lang, Lucy Fox Robins	7
Krueger, Walter	8	Langdon, Harry Philmore	3
Krug, Julius Albert	8	Lange, Dorothea	7
Kruger, Otto	9	Langer, William	6
Krupa, Eugene Bertram ("Gene")	9	Langford, Samuel	6
Krutch, Joseph Wood	8	Langlie, Arthur Bernard	8
Kuhn, Joseph Ernst	1	Langmuir, Irving	6
Kuhn, Walt	4	Langner, Lawrence	7
Kuiper, Gerard Peter	9	Lanham, Frederick Garland	
Kuniyoshi, Yasuo	5	("Fritz")	7
Kunz, George Frederick	1	Lanman, Charles Rockwell	3
Kuykendall, Ralph Simpson	7	Lapchick, Joseph Bohomiel	8
Kyes, Roger Martin	9	Lardner, John Abbott	6
Kyne, Peter Bernard	6	Lardner, Ringgold Wilmer	1
		Larson, Laurence Marcellus	2
Lachaise, Gaston	1	Lashley, Karl Spencer	6
Lackaye, Wilton	1	Lasker, Albert Davis	5
Ladd, Alan Walbridge	7	Lasky, Jesse Louis	6
Ladd, Carl Edwin	3	Lasser, Jacob Kay	5
Ladd, Kate Macy	3	Latané, John Holladay	1

Index Guide

Name	Supplement	Name	Supplement
Lathrop, Julia Clifford	1	Lenroot, Irvine Luther	4
Latimer, Wendell Mitchell	5	Lenz, Sidney Samuel	6
Latourette, Kenneth Scott	8	Leonard, Jack E.	9
Laufer, Berthold	1	Leonard, William Ellery	3
Laughlin, Harry Hamilton	3	Leonty, Metropolitan	7
Laughlin, James Laurence	1	Leopold, Aldo	4
Laughton, Charles	7	Leopold, Nathan Freudenthal, Jr.	9
Laurel, Stan	7	Levant, Oscar	9
Lawes, Lewis Edward	4	Levene, Phoebus Aaron	
Lawrance, Charles Lanier	4	Theodore	2
Lawrence, David	9	Lever, Asbury Francis	2
Lawrence, David Leo	8	Leverett, Frank	3
Lawrence, Ernest Orlando	6	Levinson, Salmon Oliver	3
Lawrence, Gertrude	5	Levitt, Abraham	7
Lawrence, William	3	Lewin, Kurt	4
Lawson, Andrew Cowper	5	Lewis, Clarence Irving	7
Lawson, Ernest	2	Lewis, Dean De Witt	3
Lawson, Robert Ripley	6	Lewis, Ed ("Strangler")	8
Lazarus, Fred, Jr.	9	Lewis, Francis Park	2
Lea, Luke	3	Lewis, Fulton, Jr.	8
Leahy, Francis William		Lewis, George William	4
("Frank")	9	Lewis, Gilbert Newton	4
Leahy, William Daniel	6	Lewis, Harry Sinclair	5
Lear, Ben	8	Lewis, James Hamilton	2
Lease, Mary Elizabeth Clyens	1	Lewis, John Henry	9
Leathers, Walter Smith	4	Lewis, John Llewellyn	8
Leavitt, Frank Simmons	5	Lewis, Lloyd Downs	4
Lebrun, Federico ("Rico")	7	Lewis, Oscar	8
Ledbetter, Huddie ("Leadbelly")	4	Lewis, Sinclair	
Lee, Bruce	9	See Lewis, Harry Sinclair	
Lee, Canada	5	Lewis, Wilfred	1
Lee, Gypsy Rose	8	Lewis, William Draper	4
Lee, Frederic Schiller	2	Lewis, William Henry	4
Lee, Ivy Ledbetter	1	Lewisohn, Adolph	2
Lee, John Clifford Hodges	6	Lewisohn, Ludwig	5
Lee, Joseph	2	Lewisohn, Sam Adolph	5
Lee, Manfred B.	9	Ley, Willy	8
Lee, Porter Raymond	2	Leyendecker, Joseph Christian	5
Lee, Willis Augustus	3	Lhévinne, Josef	3
Leedom, Boyd Stewart	8	Libby, Orin Grant	5
Leffingwell, Russell Cornell	6	Libman, Emmanuel	4
Legge, Alexander	1	Lie, Jonas	2
Lehman, Adele Lewisohn	7	Liebling, Abbott Joseph	7
Lehman, Arthur	2	Liebling, Estelle	8
Lehman, Herbert Henry	7	Liebman, Joshua Loth	4
Lehman, Irving	3	Lienau, Detlef	1
Lehman, Robert	8	Liggett, Hunter	1
Leiber, Fritz	4	Liggett, Louis Kroh	4
Leigh, Vivien	8	Liggett, Walter William	1
Leigh, William Robinson	5	Lile, William Minor	1
Leipzig, Nate	2	Lillie, Frank Rattray	4
Leiserson, William Morris	6	Lillie, Gordon William	3
Leiter, Joseph	1	Lilly, Josiah Kirby	4
Lejeune, John Archer	3	Limón, José Arcadio	9
Leland, Waldo Gifford	8	Lincoln, Joseph Crosby	3
Lemke, William Frederick	4	Lindbergh, Charles Augustus, Jr.	9

Index Guide

Name	Supplement
Lindeman, Eduard Christian	5
Lindenthal, Gustav	1
Lindgren, Waldemar	2
Lindley, Daniel	1
Lindsay, Howard	8
Lindsey, Benjamin Barr	3
Lingelbach, Anna Lane	5
Link, Henry Charles	5
Link, Theodore Carl	9
Linton, Ralph	5
Lipchitz, Jacques	9
Lipman, Jacob Goodale	2
Lippmann, Walter	9
Liston, Charles ("Sonny")	9
Litchfield, Paul Weeks	6
Littauer, Lucius Nathan	3
Little, Arthur Dehon	1
Little, Charles Sherman	2
Little, William Lawson, Jr.	8
Littledale, Clara Savage	6
Littleton, Martin Wiley	1
Liveright, Horace Brisbin	1
Livingston, Burton Edward	4
Livingstone, Belle	6
Llewellyn, Karl Nickerson	7
Lloyd, Harold Clayton	9
Lloyd, John Uri	2
Locke, Alain Leroy	5
Locke, Bessie	5
Lockheed, Allan Haines	8
Lockheed, Malcolm	6
Lodge, John Ellerton	3
Loeb, James	1
Loeb, Leo	6
Loeb, Milton B.	9
Loeffler, Charles Martin	1
Loesser, Frank	8
Loewi, Otto	7
Lomax, John Avery	4
Lomax, Louis Emanuel	8
Lombard, Carole	3
Lombard, Warren Plimpton	2
Lombardi, Vincent Thomas	8
Long, Breckinridge	6
Long, Earl Kemp	6
Long, Edward Vaughn	9
Long, Huey Pierce	1
Long, Joseph Ragland	1
Long, Perrin Hamilton	7
Longcope, Warfield Theobald	5
Lopez, Vincent Joseph	9
Lord, Chester Sanders	1
Lord, Jeremy	
See Redman, Benjamin Ray	
Lord, Pauline	4
Loree, Leonor Fresnel	2
Lorimer, George Horace	2
Lorimer, William	1
Lorre, Peter	7
Lotka, Alfred James	4
Louis, Morris	7
Lovejoy, Arthur Oncken	7
Lovejoy, Owen Reed	7
Loveman, Amy	5
Lovett, Robert Morss	6
Lovett, Robert Scott	1
Low, Will Hicok	1
Lowden, Frank Orren	3
Lowell, Abbott Lawrence	3
Lower, William Edgar	4
Lowes, John Livingston	3
Lowie, Robert Harry	6
Lubitsch, Ernst	4
Lucas, Scott Wike	8
Luce, Henry Robinson	8
Luce, Henry Winters	3
Luchese, Thomas	8
Luciano, Charles ("Lucky")	7
Luckenbach, J(ohn) Lewis	5
Lugosi, Bela	6
Luhan, Mabel Dodge	7
Lukeman, Henry Augustus	1
Luks, George Benjamin	1
Lunceford, James	4
Lundeberg, Harry	6
Lundeen, Ernest	2
Lunn, George Richard	4
Lusk, Graham	1
Lutz, Frank Eugene	3
Lybrand, William Mitchell	6
Lydenberg, Harry Miller	6
Lyman, Eugene William	4
Lyman, Theodore	5
Lynch, John Roy	2
Lynd, Robert Staughton	8
Lynn, Diana ("Dolly")	9
Lyon, David Gordon	1
Lyon, David Willard	4
Mabley, Jackie ("Moms")	9
McAdams, Clark	1
McAdie, Alexander George	3
McAdoo, William Gibbs	3
McAlexander, Ulysses Grant	2
McAndrew, William	2
MacArthur, Arthur	1
MacArthur, Charles Gordon	6
MacArthur, Douglas	7
McAuliffe, Anthony Clement	9
McBain, Howard Lee	2

Index Guide

Name	Supplement	Name	Supplement
McBride, F(rancis) Scott	5	McGiffert, Arthur Cushman	1
McBride, Henry	7	McGill, Ralph Emerson	8
MacCallum, William George	3	McGlothlin, William Joseph	1
McCardell, Claire	6	McGranery, James Patrick	7
McCarran, Patrick Anthony	5	McGrath, James Howard	8
McCarthy, Charles Louis		McGrath, Matthew J.	3
("Clem")	7	McGraw, Donald Cushing	9
McCarthy, Daniel Joseph	6	McGraw, James Herbert	4
McCarthy, Joseph Raymond	6	McGraw, John Joseph	1
McCawley, Charles Laurie	1	McHale, Kathryn	6
McClatchy, Charles Kenny	2	Machen, John Gresham	2
McClellan, George Brinton	2	McHugh, Keith Stratton	9
McClenahan, Howard	1	McHugh, Rose John	5
McClintic, Guthrie	7	McIntire, Ross	6
McClintock, James Harvey	1	Macintosh, Douglas Clyde	4
McClung, Clarence Erwin	4	McIntyre, Alfred Robert	4
McClure, Robert Alexis	6	McIntyre, James	2
McClure, Samuel Sidney	4	McIntyre, Oscar Odd	2
McConnell, Francis John	5	MacIver, Robert Morrison	8
McConnell, Ira Welch	1	Mack, Connie	6
McCord, James Bennett	4	Mack, Julian William	3
McCormack, Buren Herbert		Mackay, Clarence Hungerford	2
("Mac")	9	McKay, Claude	4
McCormack, John Francis	3	McKay, David Oman	8
McCormick, Anne Elizabeth		McKay, (James) Douglas	6
O'Hare	5	MacKaye, Benton	9
McCormick, Cyrus Hall	2	MacKaye, Percy Wallace	6
McCormick, Lynde Dupuy	6	MeKean, James W.	4
McCormick, Robert Rutherford	5	McKechnie, William Boyd	7
McCormick, Ruth Hanna		McKeldin, Theodore Roosevelt	9
See Simms, Ruth Hanna		McKellar, Kenneth Douglas	6
McCormick		Mackenzie, Murdo	2
McCracken, Joan	7	McKenzie, Robert Tait	2
McCrae, Thomas	1	McKinney, Frank Edward, Sr.	9
McCullers, Carson	8	McKinley, Albert Edward	2
McCumber, Porter James	1	McKinley, William Brown	1
MacCurdy, George Grant	4	McLaglen, Victor	6
McDaniel, Hattie	5	McLaren, John	3
MacDonald, Betty	6	McLaughlin, Andrew	
Macdonald, Charles Blair	2	Cunningham	4
McDonald, James Grover	7	McLean, Angus Wilton	1
MacDonald, Jeanette Anna	7	McLean, Edward Beale	3
McDougall, William	2	MacLean, George Edwin	2
McDowell, Mary Eliza	2	MacLeod, Colin Munro	9
McDowell, William Fraser	2	McLevy, Jasper	7
McElroy, Neil Hosler	9	McLoughlin, Maurice Evans	6
McElroy, Robert McNutt	6	McMahon, Brien	5
McEntee, James Joseph	6	McManus, George	5
Macfadden, Bernarr	5	McMillin, Alvin Nugent	5
McFadden, Louis Thomas	2	McMillin, Benton	1
McFarland, George Bradley	3	MacMonnies, Frederick William	2
McFarland, John Horace	4	McMurrich, James Playfair	2
McFee, William	8	McMurry, Frank Morton	2
McGarrah, Gates White	2	McMurtrie, Douglas Crawford	3
McGeehan, William O'Connell	1	MacNair, Harley Farnsworth	4

Index Guide

Name	Supplement	Name	Supplement
McNair, Lesley James	3	Marbury, Elisabeth	1
McNamee, Graham	3	Marbut, Curtis Fletcher	1
McNary, Charles Linza	3	Marcantonio, Vito Anthony	5
MacNeil, Hermon Atkins	4	March, Fredric	9
MacNicholas, John Timothy	4	March, Peyton Conway	5
MacNider, Hanford	8	March, William, Edward	
McNulty, John Augustine	6	See Campbell, William	
McNutt, Paul Vories	5	Edward March	
MacPhail, Leland Stanford		Marciano, Rocky	8
("Larry")	9	Marcosson, Isaac Frederick	7
McPherson, Aimee Semple	3	Marcus, Bernard Kent	5
Macrae, John	3	Marin, John (Cheri)	5
McReynolds, James Clark	4	Markham, Edwin	2
McReynolds, Samuel Davis	2	Marland, Ernest Whitworth	3
Macune, Charles William	2	Marlatt, Abby Lillian	3
MacVeagh, Charles	1	Marling, Alfred Erskine	1
MacVeagh, Franklin	1	Marlowe, Julia (Sothern)	4
McVey, Frank LeRond	5	Marquand, John Phillips	6
Madden, Owen Victor		Marquis, Albert Nelson	3
("Owney")	7	Marquis Donald Robert Perry	2
Madigan, LaVerne	7	Marquis de Cuevas	
Maestri, Robert Sidney	9	See De Cuevas, Marquis	
Maginnis, Charles Donagh	5	Marriott, Williams McKim	2
Magnes, Judah Leon	4	Marsh, Frank Burr	2
Magonigle, Harold Van Buren	1	Marsh, Reginald	5
Mahler, Herbert	7	Marshall, Frank James	3
Mahoney, John Friend	6	Marshall, George Catlett, Jr.	6
Maier, Walter Arthur	4	Martel, Charles	3
Main, Charles Thomas	3	Martin, Anne Henrietta	5
Main, John Hanson Thomas	1	Martin, Edward Sandford	2
Main, Marjorie	9	Martin, Elizabeth Price	1
Malcolm X	7	Martin, Everett Dean	3
Malin, Patrick Murphy	7	Martin, Franklin Henry	1
Mallinckrodt, Edward, Jr.	8	Martin, Glenn Luther ("Cy")	5
Mallory, Anna Margrethe		Martin, John Leonard Roosevelt	
("Molla") Bjurstedt	6	("Pepper")	7
Mallory, Clifford Day	3	Martin, Joseph William, Jr.	8
Mallory, Frank Burr	3	Martin, Warren Homer	8
Malone, Dudley Field	4	Martinelli, Giovanni	8
Mangrum, Lloyd Eugene	9	Marvin, Charles Frederick	3
Mankiewicz, Herman Jacob	5	Marx, Adolf Arthur ("Harpo")	7
Manly, Basil Maxwell	4	Marx, Leonard ("Chico")	7
Manly, John Matthews	2	Masliansky, Zvi Hirsch	3
Mannes, Clara Damrosch	4	Maslow, Abraham H.	8
Mannes, David	6	Mason, Arthur John	1
Mannes, Leopold Damrosch	7	Mason, Daniel Gregory	5
Manning, Marie	3	Mason, Lucy Randolph	6
Manning, William Thomas	4	Mason, Max	7
Mansfield, Jayne	8	Mason, Walt	2
Manship, Paul Howard	8	Masson, Thomas Lansing	1
Manville, Thomas Franklyn		Masters, Edgar Lee	4
("Tommy"), Jr.	8	Matas, Rudolph	6
Mantle, Robert Burns	4	Mather, Frank Jewett, Jr.	5
Maranville, Walter James		Mather, Winifred Holt	
Vincent	5	See Holt, Winifred	
Marburg, Theodore	4	Mathews, John Alexander	1

Name	Supplement	Name	Supplement
Mathews, Shailer	3	Merriam, Charles Edward, Jr.	5
Mathewson, Edward Payson	4	Merriam, Clinton Hart	3
Matthes, François Emile	4	Merriam, John Campbell	3
Matthes, Gerard Hendrik	6	Merrill, Charles Edward	6
Matthews, Francois Patrick	5	Merrill, Elmer Drew	6
Matthews, Joseph Brown	8	Merrill, Elmer Truesdell	2
Matthiessen, Francis Otto	4	Merrill, Frank Dow	5
Mattingly, Garrett	7	Merrill, Gretchen Van Zandt	7
Mauran, John Lawrence	1	Merton, Thomas	8
Maurer, James Hudson	3	Meserve, Frederick Hill	7
Maurin, Peter	4	Messersmith, George Strausser	6
Maverick, (Fontaine) Maury	5	Mesta, Perle Reid Skirvin	9
Maxim, Hiram Percy	2	Mestrovic, Ivan	7
Maxwell, Elsa	7	Metalious, Grace	7
Maxwell, George Hebard	4	Meyer, Adolph	4
Maxwell, Marvel Marilyn	9	Meyer, Agnes Elizabeth Ernst	8
May, Andrew Jackson	6	Meyer, Albert Gregory	7
May, Morton Jay	8	Meyer, Annie Nathan	5
Maybank, Burnet Rhett	5	Meyer, Eugene Isaac	6
Maybeck, Bernard Ralph	6	Meyer, Frank Straus	9
Mayer, Louis Burt	6	Meyer, Henry Coddington	1
Mayer, Maria Goeppert	9	Meyerhof, Otto	5
Mayer, Oscar Gottfried	7	Mich, Daniel Danforth	7
Mayo, George Elton	4	Michael, Arthur	3
Mayo, Henry Thomas	2	Michaelis, Leonor	4
Mayo, William James	2	Michaux, Lightfoot Solomon	8
Maytag, Frederick Louis	2	Micheaux, Oscar	5
Mead, Edwin Doak	2	Michel, Virgil George	2
Mead, Elwood	2	Michelson, Charles	4
Mead, George Herbert	1	Michler, Nathaniel	1
Mead, James Michael	7	Midgley, Thomas	3
Means, Gaston Bullock	2	Mies van der Rohe, Ludwig	8
Meany, Edmond Stephen	1	Millay, Edna St. Vincent	4
Medwick, Joseph Michael		Miller, David Hunter	7
("Ducky")	9	Miller, Dayton Clarence	3
Mees, Charles Edward Kenneth	6	Miller, George Abram	5
Meière, Marie Hildreth	7	Miller, Gerrit Smith, Jr.	6
Meiklejohn, Alexander	7	Miller, Gilbert Heron	8
Meinzer, Oscar Edward	4	Miller, Glenn	3
Melcher, Frederic Gershom	7	Miller, James Alexander	4
Melchior, Lauritz Lebrecht		Miller, Kelly	2
Hommel	9	Miller, Kempster Blanchard	1
Mellon, Andrew William	2	Miller, Kenneth Hayes	5
Mellon, William Larimer	4	Miller, Nathan Lewis	5
Melton, James	7	Miller, Perry Gilbert Eddy	7
Mencken, Henry Louis	6	Miller, Webb	2
Mendel, Lafayette Benedict	1	Miller, William Snow	2
Mendelsohn, Erich (or Eric)	5	Millikan, Clark Blanchard	8
Mendelsohn, Samuel	8	Millikan, Robert Andrews	5
Mendenhall, Charles Elwood	1	Millikin, Eugene Donald	6
Mendes, Henry Pereira	2	Millis, Harry Alvin	4
Menjou, Adolphe Jean	7	Millis, Walter	8
Menninger, Charles Frederick	5	Mills, Charles Wright	7
Menninger, William Claire	8	Mills, Enos Abijah	1
Merck, George Wilhelm	6	Mills, Ogden Livingston	2
Meredith, Edna C. Elliott	7	Milton, George Fort	5

Index Guide

Name	Supplement	Name	Supplement
Minnigerode, Lucy	1	Moore, Victor Frederick	7
Minor, Robert	5	Moorehead, Agnes	9
Minot, George Richards	4	Moran, Daniel Edward	2
Minton, Sherman	7	Moran, Eugene Francis	7
Miranda, Carmen	5	Morawetz, Victor	2
Mirsky, Alfred Ezra	9	More, Paul Elmer	2
Mitchell, Albert Graeme	3	Morehead, John Motley	7
Mitchell, Edwin Knox	1	Morehouse, Ward	8
Mitchell, James Paul	7	Morgan, Anne	5
Mitchell, Langdon Elwyn	1	Morgan, Arthur Ernest	9
Mitchell, Lucy Sprague	8	Morgan, Edwin Vernon	1
Mitchell, Margaret Munnelyn	4	Morgan, Helen	3
Mitchell, Sidney Zollicoffer	3	Morgan, John Harcourt	
Mitchell, Stephen Arnold	9	Alexander	4
Mitchell, Thomas Gregory	7	Morgan, John Pierpont	3
Mitchell, Wesley Clair	4	Morgan, Julia	6
Mitchell, William DeWitt	5	Morgan, Thomas Hunt	3
Mitropoulos, Dimitri	6	Morgenthau, Henry	4
Mitscher, Marc Andrew	4	Morgenthau, Henry, Jr.	8
Mix, Tom	2	Morley, Christopher Darlington	6
Mizner, Addison	1	Morley, Frank	2
Modjeski, Ralph	2	Morley, Sylvanus Griswold	4
Moffat, Jay Pierrepont	3	Morón, Alonzo Graseano	9
Moffatt, James	3	Morrison, DeLesseps Story	7
Moffett, William Adger	1	Morrison, Frank	4
Moholy-Nagy, László	4	Morrison, Jim	9
Moisseiff, Leon Solomon	3	Morrow, Edwin Porch	1
Moley, Raymond Charles	9	Morse, John Lovett	2
Mondell, Frank Wheeler	2	Morse, John Torrey	2
Monroe, Harriet	2	Morse, Wayne Lyman	9
Monroe, Marilyn	7	Morton, Charles Gould	1
Monroe, Paul	4	Morton, Charles Walter	8
Monroe, Vaughn Wilton	9	Morton, Ferdinand Joseph	3
Monsky, Henry	4	Morton, Ferdinand Quintin	4
Montague, Andrew Jackson	2	Morton, Jelly Roll	
Montague, Gilbert Holland	7	See Morton, Ferdinand	
Montague, William Pepperell	5	Joseph	
Monteux, Pierre Benjamin	7	Mosely, Philip Edward	9
Montgomery, James Alan	4	Moser, Christopher Otto	1
Moody, (Arthur Edson) Blair	5	Moses, Anna Mary Robertson	
Moody, John	6	("Grandma")	7
Moon, Parker Thomas	2	Moses, George Higgins	3
Mooney, Thomas Joseph	3	Moses, Montrose Jonas	1
Moore, Anne Carroll	7	Moskowitz, Belle Lindner Israels	1
Moore, (Austin) Merrill	6	Moss, Sanford Alexander	4
Moore, Charles	3	Motley, Willard Francis	7
Moore, Eliakim, Hastings	1	Moton, Robert Russa	2
Moore, Frederick Randolph	3	Mott, Charles Stewart	9
Moore, Grace	4	Mott, Frank Luther	7
Moore, Henry Ludwell	6	Mott, John R.	5
Moore, Hugh Everett	9	Moulton, Forest Ray	5
Moore, John Bassett	4	Muench, Aloisius Joseph	7
Moore, Joseph Earle	6	Muhammad, Elijah	9
Moore, Joseph Haines	4	Muir, Charles Henry	1
Moore, Marianne Craig	9	Muldoon, William	1

Index Guide

Name	Supplement	Name	Supplement
Mulford, Clarence Edward	6	Nestor, Agnes	4
Mulholland, William	1	Neuberger, Richard Lewis	6
Muller, Hermann Joseph	8	Neumann, Franz Leopold	5
Mulliken, Samuel Parsons	1	Neumann, John von	
Munch, Charles	8	See Von Neumann, John	
Mundelein, George William	2	Neutra, Richard Joseph	8
Mundt, Karl Earl	9	Nevada, Emma	2
Muni, Paul	8	Nevins, Joseph Allan	9
Munro, William Bennett	6	New, Harry Stewart	2
Munroe, Charles Edward	2	Newberry, Truman Handy	3
Murchison, Clinton Williams	8	Newell, Edward Theodore	3
Murdock, Victor	3	Newlon, Jesse Homer	3
Murphy, Audie Leon	9	Newman, Albert Henry	1
Murphy, Frank	4	Newman, Alfred	8
Murphy, Frederick E.	2	Newman, Barnett	8
Murphy, Gerald Clery	7	Newman, William H.	1
Murphy, James Bumgardner	4	Newsom, Herschel David	8
Murray, James Edward	7	Newton, Joseph Fort	4
Murray, Mae	7	Neyland, Robert Reese, Jr.	7
Murray, Philip	5	Nichols, Dudley	6
Murray, Thomas Edward	7	Nichols, Edward Leamington	2
Murray, William Henry David	6	Nichols, Roy Franklin	9
Murrow, Edward (Egbert) Roscoe	7	Nichols, Ruth Rowland	6
Musica, Philip Mariano Fausto	2	Nicholson, Meredith	4
Musmanno, Michael Angelo	8	Nicholson, Seth Barnes	7
Mussey, Ellen Spencer	2	Niebuhr, Helmut Richard	7
Muste, Abraham Johannes	8	Niebuhr, Karl Paul Reinhold	
Muzzey, David Saville	7	("Reinie")	9
Myers, Gustavus	3	Niehaus, Charles Henry	1
Myers, Jerome	2	Nielsen, Alice	3
Myerson, Abraham	4	Nieman, Lucius William	1
		Nieuwland, Julius Arthur	2
Nadelman, Elie	4	Niles, David K.	5
Nagel, Conrad	8	Nimitz, Chester William	8
Naish, Joseph Carrol	9	Noble, Gladwyn Kingsley	2
Naismith, James	2	Nock, Albert Jay	3
Nash, Charles Williams	4	Nolen, John	2
Nash, Frederick Ogden	9	Noll, John Francis	6
Nash, John Henry	4	Norbeck, Peter	2
Nast, Condé Montrose	3	Norden, Carl Lukas	7
Nathan, George Jean	6	Nordhoff, Charles B.	
Nathan, Maud	4	See under Hall, James	
Nazimova, Alla	3	Norman	
Neal, Josephine Bicknell	5	Norell, Norman	9
Neely, Matthew Mansfield	6	Norris, Charles Gilman Smith	3
Neilson, William Allan	4	Norris, George William	3
Nelson, Donald Marr	6	Norris, James Flack	2
Nelson, Edward William	1	Norris, John Franklin	5
Nelson, Marjorie Maxine	7	Norris, Kathleen Thompson	8
Nelson, Nels Christian	7	North, Frank Mason	1
Nelson, Oswald George ("Ozzie")	9	Norton, Charles Hotchkiss	3
Nesbit, Evelyn Florence	8	Norton, Mary Teresa Hopkins	6
Nessler, Karl Ludwig	5	Norton, William Warder	3
Nestle, Charles		Notestein, Wallace	8
See Nessler, Karl Ludwig		Nourse, Edwin Griswold	9

Index Guide

Name	Supplement	Name	Supplement
Novarro, Ramon	8	Olmsted, Frederick Law	6
Novy, Frederick George	6	Olsen, John Sigvard ("Ole"), and	
Noyes, Alexander Dana	3	Johnson, Harold Ogden	
Noyes, Arthur Amos	2	("Chic")	7
Noyes, Clara Dutton	2	Olson, Floyd Bjerstjerne	2
Noyes, Frank Brett	4	O'Mahoney, Joseph Christopher	7
Noyes, William Albert	3	O'Neal, Edward Asbury, III	6
Nutting, Mary Adelaide	4	O'Neill, Eugene	5
Nutting, Wallace	3	O'Neill, Rose Cecil	3
Nye, Gerald Prentice	9	Oppenheimer, Julius Robert	8
		Opper, Frederick Burr	2
Oberhoffer, Emil Johann	1	Orry-Kelly	7
Oberholser, Harry Church	7	Orton, Helen Fuller	5
Oberholtzer, Ellis Paxson	2	Ory, Edward ("Kid")	9
Oberndorf, Clarence Paul	5	Osburn, Chase Salmon	4
O'Brian, John Lord	9	Osborn, Henry Fairfield	1
O'Brien, Justin	8	Osborn, Henry Fairfield	8
O'Brien, Morgan Joseph	2	Osgood, William Fogg	3
O'Brien, Robert Lincoln	5	O'Shaughnessy, Michael Maurice	1
O'Brien, Thomas James	1	O'Shaughnessy, Nelson Jarvis	
O'Brien, Willis Harold	7	Waterbury	1
O'Callahan, Joseph Timothy	7	Osterhout, Winthrop John	
Ochs, Adolph Simon	1	Vanleuven	7
O'Connell, William Henry	3	Ostromislensky, Iwan Iwanowich	2
O'Connor, Edwin Greene	8	O'Sullivan, Mary Kenney	3
O'Connor, Mary Flannery	7	Oswald, Lee Harvey	7
O'Daniel, Wilbert Lee ("Pappy")	8	Otis, Arthur Sinton	7
Odell, George Clinton Densmore	4	Ott, Melvin Thomas ("Mel")	6
Odenbach, Frederick Louis	1	Ottley, Roi	6
Odets, Clifford	7	Ouimet, Francis Desales	8
O'Donnell, Emmett, Jr. ("Rosy")	9	Oursler, (Charles) Fulton	5
O'Doul, Francis Joseph ("Lefty")	8	Outerbridge, Eugenius Harvey	1
Odum, Howard Washington	5	Overstreet, Harry Allen	8
O'Dwyer, William	7	Owen, Robert L.	4
Ogburn, William Fielding	6	Owen, Stephen Joseph	7
Ogden, Rollo	2	Owen, Thomas McAdory	1
Ogg, Frederick Austin	5	Owre, Alfred	1
O'Hara, John Henry	8	Owsley, Frank Lawrence	6
O'Hare, Kate Richards		Oxnam, Garfield Bromley	7
(Cunningham)	4		
Ohrbach, Nathan M. ("N. M.")	9	Pace, Edward Aloysius	2
Older, Fremont	1	Pack, Charles Lathrop	2
Oldfather, William Abbott	3	Page, Leigh	5
Oldfield, Barney	4	Page, Oran Thaddeus	5
Oldham, William Fitzjames	2	Page, Thomas Walker	2
Olds, Irving S.	7	Paine, Albert Bigelow	2
Olds, Leland	6	Palmer, Alexander Mitchell	2
Olds, Ransom	4	Palmer, John McAuley	5
Olds, Robert Edwin	1	Palmer, Walter Walker	4
O'Leary, Daniel	1	Pancoast, Henry Khunrath	2
Oliphant, Herman	2	Pangborn, Clyde Edward	6
Oliver, Joseph	2	Panofsky, Erwin	8
Oliver, King		Pansy	
See Oliver, Joseph		See Alden, Isabella	
Olmstead, Albert Ten Eyck	3	Macdonald	

Index Guide

Name	Supplement	Name	Supplement
Papanicolaou, George Nicholas	7	Peary, Josephine Diebitsch	5
Park, Maud Wood	5	Peattie, Donald Culcross	7
Park, Robert Ezra	3	Peck, Lillie	6
Park, William Hallock	2	Pecora, Ferdinand	9
Parker, Arthur Caswell	5	Peek, George Nelson	3
Parker, Charlie ("Bird")	5	Pegler, Westbrook	8
Parker, Dorothy Rothschild	8	Pegram, George Braxton	6
Parker, Edward Pickering	9	Pelham, Robert A.	3
Parker, George Howard	5	Pemberton, Brock	4
Parker, Henry Taylor	1	Pendergast, Thomas Joseph	3
Parker, John Johnston	6	Pendleton, Ellen Fitz	2
Parker, John Milliken	2	Penfold, Joseph Weller	9
Parker, Theodore Bissell	3	Penney, James Cash ("J. C.")	9
Parkinson, Thomas Ignatius	6	Penrose, Spencer	2
Parks, Larry	9	Pepper, George Wharton	7
Parmentier, Andrew	1	Pepper, William	4
Parrish, Maxfield	8	Percy, William Alexander	3
Parsons, Elsie Worthington Clews	3	Perez, Leander Henry	8
Parsons, Louella Rose Oettinger	9	Perin, Charles Page	2
Pasvolsky, Leo	5	Perkins, Dwight Heald	3
Patch, Alexander McCarrell	3	Perkins, Frances	7
Patchen, Kenneth	9	Perkins, James Handasyd	2
Pate, Maurice	7	Perkins, Marion	7
Patri, Angelo	7	Perkins, Maxwell	4
Patrick, Edwin Hill ("Ted")	7	Perkins, Thomas Nelson	2
Patrick, Hugh Talbot	2	Perlman, Philip Benjamin	6
Patrick, Mary Mills	2	Perlman, Selig	6
Patrick, Mason Mathews	3	Perrine, Charles Dillon	5
Patten, Gilbert	3	Perry, Antoinette	4
Patterson, Alicia	7	Perry, Bliss	5
Patterson, Eleanor Medill	4	Perry, Clarence Arthur	3
Patterson, Joseph Medill	4	Perry, Pettis	7
Patterson, Richard Cunning-		Perry, Ralph Barton	6
ham, Jr.	8	Perry, Walter Scott	1
Patterson, Robert Porter	5	Pershing, John Joseph	4
Patterson, Rufus Lenoir	3	Persons, Warren Milton	2
Patton, George Smith	3	Peterkin, Julia Mood	7
Paul, Elliot Harold	6	Petri, Angelo	7
Paul, Father		Pettengill, Samuel Barrett	9
See Francis, Paul James		Pew, John Howard	9
Paul, Josephine Bay	7	Pew, Joseph Newton, Jr.	7
Pawnee Bill		Pierce, Edward Allen	9
See Lillie, Gordon William		Pfahler, George Edward	6
Payne, Bruce Ryburn	2	Pfister, Alfred	7
Payne, John Barton	1	Pfund, August Herman	4
Peabody, Cecil Hobart	1	Phelps, William Lyon	3
Peabody, Endicott	3	Philipson, David	4
Peabody, Francis Greenwood	2	Phillips, Frank	4
Peabody, George Foster	2	Phillips, Harry Irving	7
Peabody, Lucy Whitehead	4	Phillips, John Sanburn	4
Pearl, Raymond	2	Phillips, Lena Madesin	5
Pearson, Drew	8	Phillips, Ulrich Bonnell	1
Pearson, Edmund Lester	2	Phillips, William	8
Pearson, Raymond Allen	2	Phipps, Lawrence Cowle	6
Pearson, Thomas Gilbert	3	Piccard, Jean Felix	7

Index Guide

Name	Supplement
Pick, Lewis Andrew	6
Pickens, William	5
Piez, Charles	1
Pilcher, Lewis Stephen	1
Pinchot, Amos Richards Eno	3
Pinchot, Cornelia Elizabeth Bryce	6
Pinchot, Gifford	4
Pincus, Gregory Goodwin ("Goody")	8
Piñero Jiménez, Jesús Toribio	5
Pino, José See Son of Many Beads	
Pinza, Ezio	6
Piper, William Thomas	8
Pippin, Horace	4
Pitkin, Walter Boughton	5
Pittman, Key	2
Pitts, ZaSu	7
Plath, Sylvia	7
Plimpton, George Arthur	2
Plotz, Harry	4
Plummer, Henry Stanley	2
Poindexter, Miles	4
Poling, Daniel Alfred	8
Polk, Frank Lyon	3
Pollak, Walter Heilprin	2
Pollock, Channing	4
Pollock, (Paul) Jackson	6
Pomerene, Atlee	2
Pond, Irving Kane	2
Pool, Joe Richard	8
Poole, Ernest	4
Pope, James Pinckney	8
Pope, John Russell	2
Porter, Arthur Kingsley	1
Porter, Cole	7
Porter, Edwin Stanton	3
Porter, Gene Stratton	1
Porter, Russell Williams	4
Porter, William Townsend	4
Post, Augustus	5
Post, Emily Price	6
Post, Marjorie Merriweather	9
Post, Wiley	1
Pott, Francis Lister Hawks	4
Potter, Charles Francis	7
Potter, Ellen Culver	6
Potter, William Bancroft	1
Pou, Edward William	1
Pound, Cuthbert Winfred	1
Pound, Ezra Loomis	9
Pound, Roscoe	7
Powdermaker, Hortense	8
Powell, Adam Clayton (d. 1953)	5
Powell, Adam Clayton (d. 1972)	9
Powell, John Benjamin	4
Powell, Richard Ewing ("Dick")	7
Powell, Thomas Reed	5
Power, Tyrone	6
Prall, David Wight	2
Pratt, James Bissett	3
Pratt, John Lee	9
Pratt, Orson	1
Pratt, Waldo Selden	2
Pratt, William Veazie	6
Prefontaine, Steve Roland ("Pre")	9
Prentis, Henning Webb, Jr.	6
Prescott, Samuel Cate	7
Pressman, Lee	8
Price, Eli Kirk	1
Price, George Edward McCready	7
Price, George Moses	3
Price, Theodore Hazeltine	1
Priest, Ivy Maude Baker	9
Prince, Frederick Henry	5
Pringle, Henry Fowles	6
Pritchett, Henry Smith	2
Procter, William Cooper	1
Profaci, Joseph	7
Prokosch, Eduard	2
Prouty, Charles Tyler	9
Prouty, Olive Higgins	9
Pryor, Arthur W.	3
Pujo, Arsène Paulin	2
Pulitzer, Joseph, Jr.	5
Pulitzer, Margaret Leech	9
Pulitzer, Ralph	2
Puller, Lewis Burwell ("Chesty")	9
Pupin, Michael Idvorsky	1
Purdy, Corydon Tyler	3
Purdy, Lawson	6
Purnell, Benjamin	1
Pusey, William Allen	2
Putnam, (George) Herbert	5
Putnam, Helen Cordelia	5
Putnam, Nina Wilcox	7
Pyle, Ernest Taylor	3
Pyle, Robert	5
Quezon, Manuel Luis	3
Quill, Michael Joseph	8
Quine, Williani Edward	1
Quinn, Arthur Hobson	6
Rachmaninoff, Sergei Vasilyevich	3
Radcliffe, George Lovic Pierce	9
Rademacher, Hans	8
Radford, Arthur William	9
Radin, Max	4

Index Guide

Name	Supplement	Name	Supplement
Radin, Paul	6	Reid, Ira De Augustine	8
Rahv, Philip	9	Reid, Mont Rogers	3
Rainey, Gertrude Malissa Nix		Reid, Ogden Mills	4
Pridgett	2	Reik, Theodor	8
Rainey, Henry Thomas	1	Reiner, Fritz	7
Rainey, Julian O.	7	Reinhardt, Ad	8
Rainey, Ma		Reinhardt, Aurelia Isabel Henry	4
See Rainey, Gertrude		Reisner, George Andrew	3
Malissa Nix Pridgett		Remington, William Walter	5
Rains, Claude	8	Rennie, Michael	9
Rainsford, William Stephen	1	Reno, Milo	2
Ramsay, Erskine	5	Repplier, Agnes	4
Ramspeck, Robert C. Word		Requa, Mark Lawrence	2
("Bob")	9	Resor, Stanley Burnet	7
Rand, Benjamin	1	Restarick, Henry Bond	1
Rand, Edward Kennard	3	Reuther, Walter Philip	8
Rand, James Henry	3	Revel, Bernard	2
Randall, Clarence Belden	8	Revell, Nellie MacAleney	6
Randall, James Garfield	5	Revson, Charles Haskell	9
Rankin, Jeannette Pickering	9	Reynolds, George McClelland	2
Rankin, John Elliott	6	Reynolds, Julian Sargeant	9
Ransom, John Crowe	9	Reynolds, Quentin James	7
Ransome, Frederick Leslie	1	Reynolds, Richard Samuel, Sr.	5
Ranson, Stephen Walter	3	Reynolds, Robert Rice	7
Rapaport, David	6	Reynolds, William Neal	5
Raskob, John Jakob	4	Rhees, Morgan John	1
Rathbone, Basil	8	Rhees, Rush	2
Raulston, John Tate	6	Rhoads, Cornelius Packard	6
Rautenstrauch, Walter	5	Rhodes, Eugene Manlove	1
Ravenel, Mazÿck Porcher	4	Ricca, Paul	9
Rawlings, Marjorie Kinnan	5	Rice, Alice Caldwell Hegan	3
Rawlinson, Frank Joseph	2	Rice, Calvin Winsor	1
Rayburn, Samuel Taliaferro		Rice, Edgar Charles ("Sam")	9
("Sam")	7	Rice, Edwin Wilbur (d. 1935)	1
Raymond, Alexander Gillespie	6	Rice, Elmer	8
Raymond, Harry Howard	1	Rice, George Samuel	4
Razaf, Andy	9	Rice, (Henry) Grantland	5
Read, Conyers	6	Rice, John Andrew	8
Read, George Windle	1	Rich, Robert	8
Read, Opie Pope	2	Richard, Dickinson Woodruff	9
Record, Samuel James	3	Richards, Laura Elizabeth Howe	3
Redfield, Robert	6	Richards, Robert Hallowell	3
Redman, Benjamin Ray	7	Richards, Vincent	6
Reece, B(razilla) Carroll	7	Richardson, Sid Williams	6
Reed, Daniel Alden	6	Richberg, Donald Randall	6
Reed, David Aiken	5	Richtmyer, Floyd Karker	2
Reed, James Alexander	3	Richter, Conrad Michael	8
Reed, Mary	3	Rickard, Clinton	9
Reese, Charles Lee	2	Rickenbacker, Edward Vernon	
Reese, Lizette Woodworth	1	("Eddie")	9
Reeves, Daniel F.	9	Rickert, Martha Edith	2
Reeves, Joseph Mason	4	Ricketts, Claude Vernon	7
Regan, Agnes Gertrude	3	Ricketts, Howard Taylor	1
Reichenbach, Hans	5	Ricketts, Palmer Chamberlaine	1
Reid, Helen Miles Rogers	8	Rickey, Wesley Branch	7

Index Guide

Name	Supplement	Name	Supplement
Ridder, Bernard Herman	9	Roethke, Theodore Huebner	7
Riddle, Samuel Doyle	5	Rogers, Edith Nourse	6
Ridgway, Robert	2	Rogers, James Gamble	4
Riefler, Winfield William		Rogers, James Harvey	2
Riegger, Wallingford	7	Rogers, Mary Josephine	5
Riis, Mary Phillips	8	Rogers, Will	1
Riley, William Bell	4	Rohde, Ruth Bryan Owen	5
Rinehart, Mary Roberts	6	Roheim, Geza	5
Rinehart, Stanley Marshall, Jr.	8	Rohlfs, Anna Katharnie Green	1
Ripley, Robert LeRoy	4	Rolfe, Robert Abial ("Red")	8
Ripley, William Zebina	3	Rolph, James	1
Rister, Carl Coke	5	Romanoff, Michael	9
Ritchey, George Willis	3	Rombauer, Irma S.	7
Ritchie, Albert Cabell	2	Romberg, Sigmund	5
Rittenhouse, Jesse Belle	4	Romer, Alfred Sherwood	9
Ritter, Joseph Elmer	8	Rommel, Edwin Americus	
Ritter, William Emerson	3	("Eddie")	8
Ritter, Woodward Maurice		Romnes, Haakon Ingolf	9
("Tex")	9	Rooney, Pat	7
Rivers, Lucius Mendel	8	Roosevelt, Anna Eleanor	7
Rivers, Thomas Milton	7	Roosevelt, Franklin Delano	3
Rives, Hallie Erminie	6	Roosevelt, Kermit	3
Robb, William Lispenard	1	Roosevelt, Theodore	3
Robert, Henry Martyn	1	Root, Elihu	2
Roberts, Elizabeth Madox	3	Roper, Daniel Calhoun	3
Roberts, Kenneth Lewis	6	Roper, Elmo Burns, Jr.	9
Roberts, Owen Josephus	5	Rorimer, James Joseph	8
Robertson, Absalom Willis	9	Rorty, James Hancock	9
Robertson, James Alexander	2	Rose, Billy	8
Robertson, William Spence	5	Rose, Mary Davies Swartz	3
Robins, Margaret Dreier	3	Rose, Wickliffe	1
Robins, Raymond	5	Rosen, Joseph A.	4
Rohinson, Benjamin Lincoln	1	Rosenau, Milton Joseph	4
Robinson, Bill (Bojangles)	4	Rosenbach, Abraham Simon	
Robinson, Boardman	5	Wolf	5
Robinson, Claude Everett	7	Rosenbach, Philip Hyman	5
Robinson, Edward G.	9	Rosenberg, Ethel	5
Robinson, Edward Stevens	2	Rosenberg, Julius	5
Robnison, Edwin Arlington	1	Rosenberg, Paul	6
Robinson, George Canby	6	Rosenblatt, Bernard Abraham	8
Robinson, Henry Morton	7	Rosenfeld, Paul	4
Robinson, James Harvey	2	Rosenman, Samuel Irving	9
Robinson, John Roosevelt		Rosewater, Victor	2
("Jackie")	9	Ross, Charles Griffith	4
Robinson, Joseph Taylor	2	Ross, Denman Waldo	1
Robinson, Ruby Doris Smith	8	Ross, Edward Alsworth	5
Robinson-Smith, Gertrude	7	Ross, Harold Wallace	5
Robson, May	3	Ross, James Delmage McKenzie	2
Roche, Arthur Somers	1	Ross, Thomas Joseph	9
Rockefeller, Abby Greene Aldrich	4	Rossen, Robert	8
Rockefeller, John Davison	2	Rossiter, Clinton Lawrence, III	8
Rockefeller, John Davison, Jr.	6	Rostovtzeff, Michael Ivanovitch	5
Rockefeller, Martha Baird	9	Roth, Samuel	9
Rockefeller, Winthrop	9	Rothafel, Samuel Lionel	2
Roekwell, George Lincoln	8	Rothko, Mark	8
Rodzinski, Artur	6	Roulston, Marjorie Hillis	9

Index Guide

Name	Supplement	Name	Supplement
Rourke, Constance Mayfield	3	Sachs, Hanns	4
Rous, Francis Peyton	8	Sachs, Paul Joseph	7
Rovenstine, Emery Andrew	6	Sack, Israel	6
Rowe, Leo Stanton	4	St. Denis, Ruth	8
Rowe, Lynwood Thomas	7	St. John, Charles Edward	3
Rowell, Chester Harvey	4	Sakel, Manfred Joshua	6
Roxy		Samaroff, Olga	4
See Rothafel, Samuel Lionel		Sandburg, Carl August	8
Royce, Ralph	7	Sande, Earl	8
Ruark, Robert Chester	7	Sanders, George	9
Rubey, William Walden	9	Sandoz, Mari	8
Rubin, Isidor Clinton	6	Sands, Diana Patricia	9
Rubinow, Isaac Max	2	Sanger, Margaret Higgins	8
Rubinstein, Helena	7	Sanderson, Ezra Dwight	3
Rublee, George	6	Santayana, George	5
Ruby, Jack L.	8	Sapir, Edward	2
Rucker, George ("Nap")	8	Sardi, Melchiorre Pio Vencenzo	
Ruckstull, Frederick Wellington	3	("Vincent")	8
Ruditsky, Barney	7	Sarg, Tony	3
Rudkin, Margaret Fogarty	8	Sarnoff, David	9
Ruef, Abraham	2	Sarton, George Alfred Léon	6
Rugg, Arthur Prentice	2	Sauer, Carl Ortwin	9
Rugg, Harold Ordway	6	Saunders, Clarence	5
Ruhl, Arthur Brown	1	Sauveur, Albert	2
Ruhräh, John	1	Savage, John Lucian ("Jack")	8
Ruml, Beardsley	6	Saville, Marshall Howard	1
Rummel, Joseph Francis	7	Sawyer, Wilbur Augustus	5
Rumsey, Mary Harriman	1	Saxton, Eugene Francis	3
Runyon, Damon	4	Sayre, Wallace Stanley	9
Ruppert, Jacob	2	Scarborough, Dorothy	1
Rusby, Henry Hurd	2	Scarborough, Lee Rutland	3
Rushing, James Andrew		Schalk, Raymond William	
("Jimmy")	9	("Cracker")	8
Russell, Annie	2	Schall, Thomas David	1
Russell, Charles Edward	3	Schelling, Ernest Henry	2
Russell, Charles Ellsworth ("Pee		Schelling, Felix Emanuel	3
Wee")	8	Schenck, Nicholas Michael	8
Russell, Henry Norris	6	Scherman, Harry	8
Russell, James Earl	3	Schevill, Randolph	4
Russell, James Solomon	1	Schildkraut, Joseph	7
Russell, Richard Brevard, Jr.	9	Schillinger, Joseph	3
Rust, John Daniel	5	Schindler, Kurt	1
Ruth, George Herman ("Babe")	4	Schindler, Rudolph Michael	5
Rutherford, Joseph Franklin	3	Schinz, Albert	3
Rutledge, Wiley Blount	4	Schlesinger, Frank	3
Ryan, Cornelius John ("Connie")	9	Schlessinger, Arthur Maier, Sr.	7
Ryan, Harris Joseph	1	Schmidt, Carl Louis August	4
Ryan, John Augustine	3	Schmidt, Nathaniel	2
Ryan, Robert Bushnell	9	Schnabel, Artur	5
		Schneider, Herman	2
Saarinen, Eero	7	Schneiderman, Rose	9
Saarinen, Eliel	4	Schocken, Theodore	9
Sabath, Adolph J.	5	Schoenberg, Arnold	5
Sabin, Florence Rena	5	Schoenheimer, Rudolph	3
Sachs, Alexander	9	Schoeppel, Andrew Frank	7
Sachs, Bernard	3	Schrembs, Joseph	3

Index Guide

Name	Supplement	Name	Supplement
Schroeder, Rudolph William	5	Shahn, Benjamin ("Ben")	8
Schuchert, Charles	3	Shannon, Fred Albert	7
Schultz, Dutch		Shapley, Harlow	9
See Flegenheimer, Arthur		Shaughnessy, Clark Daniel	8
Schultz, Henry	2	Shaw, Albert	4
Schumann-Heink, Ernestine	2	Shaw, Clay L.	9
Schumpeter, Joseph Alois	4	Shaw, (Warren) Wilbur	5
Schurman, Jacob Gould	3	Shawn, Edwin Meyers ("Ted")	9
Schuster, Max Lincoln	8	Shean, Al	4
Schuyler, Robert Livingston	8	Shear, Theodore Leslie	3
Schwab, Charles Michael	2	Shedd, Fred Fuller	2
Schwartz, Delmore David	8	Sheean, James Vincent	9
Schwartz, Maurice	6	Sheeler, Charles R.	7
Schweinitz, George Edmund de	2	Sheil, Bernard James	8
Schwellenbach, Lewis Baxter	4	Sheldon, Charles Monroe	4
Schwidetzky, Oscar Otto Rudolf	7	Shellabarger, Samuel	5
Schwimmer, Rosika	4	Shepard, James Edward	4
Scopes, John Thomas	8	Shepherd, William Robert	1
Scott, Allen Cecil	7	Sheppard, John Morris	3
Scott, Emmett Jay	6	Sheppard, Samuel Edward	4
Scott, Hugh Lenox	1	Sherman, Allan	9
Scott, James Brown	3	Sherman, Forrest Percival	5
Scott, John Adams	4	Sherman, Frederick Carl	6
Scott, Walter Dill	5	Sherman, Henry Clapp	5
Scott, Walter Edward	5	Sherwood, Robert Emmet	5
Scott, William Berryman	4	Shields, Francis Xavier ("Frank")	9
Scott, W(illiam) Kerr	6	Shields, John Knight	1
Scribner, Charles	5	Shinn, Everett	5
Scripps, Robert Paine	2	Shipley, Ruth Bielaski	8
Scripps, William Edmund	5	Shipstead, Henrik	6
Scudder, (Julia) Vida Dutton	5	Short, Joseph Hudson, Jr.	5
Seabury, Samuel	6	Short, Luke	9
Seagrave, Gordon Stifler	7	Short, Walter Campbell	4
Sears, Richard Dudley	3	Shotwell, James Thomson	7
Seashore, Carl Emil	4	Shouse, Jouett	8
Sedgwick, Anne Douglas	1	Showerman, Grant	1
Sedgwick, Ellery	6	Shub, Abraham David	9
Seiberling, Frank Augustus	5	Shubert, Lee	5
Seibold, Louis	3	Shull, George Harrison	5
Seidel, Emil	4	Shull, Lee	5
Seitz, Don Carlos	1	Shuster, W(illiam) Morgan	6
Seitz, William Chapin	9	Sibert, William Luther	1
Seldes, Gilbert Vivian	8	Sieber, Al	1
Selig, William Nicholas	4	Sigerist, Henry Ernest	6
Seligman, Edwin Robert		Sikorsky, Igor Ivanovich	9
Anderson	2	Silcox, Ferdinand Augustus	2
Selznick, David Oliver	7	Silkwood, Karen Gay	9
Sembrich, Marcella	1	Siloti, Alexander Ilyitch	3
Sennett, Mack	6	Silver, Abba Hillel	7
Serling, Rodman Edward	9	Silver, Gray	1
Service, Robert William	6	Silvers, Louis	5
Setchell, William Albert	3	Simkhovitch, Mary Melinda	
Seton, Ernest Thompson	4	Kingsbury	5
Seton, Grace Gallatin Thompson	6	Simmons (Szymanski), Aloysius	
Sexton, Anne Gray Harvey	9	Harry	6
Seymour, Charles	7	Simmons, Furnifold McLendel	2

Index Guide

Name	Supplement	Name	Supplement
Simmons, George Henry	2	Smith, Horton	7
Simmons, James Stevens	5	Smith, Jeremiah	1
Simmons, Roscoe Conkling		Smith, Jonas Waldo	1
Murray	5	Smith, Joseph Fielding	9
Simmons, William Joseph	3	Smith, Lillian Eugenia	8
Simms, Ruth Hanna McCormick	3	Smith, Logan Pearsall	4
Simon, Richard Leo	6	Smith, Lucy Harth	5
Simonds, Frank Herbert	2	Smith, Mildred Catharine	9
Simons, Algie Martin	4	Smith, Ormond Gerald	1
Simons, Harry Calvert	4	Smith, Preserved	3
Simpson, Charles Torrey	1	Smith, Ralph Tyler	9
Sims, William Sowden	2	Smith, Robert Sidney	1
Sinclair, Harry Ford	6	Smith, Theobald	1
Sinclair, Upton Beall, Jr.	8	Smith, Thomas Adams	1
Singer, Charles H.	9	Smith, Thomas Vernor	7
Singer, Israel Joshua	3	Smith, Walter Bedell	7
Sinnott, Edmund Ware	8	Smott, Reed Owen	3
Sisler, George Harold	9	Smyth, Herbert Weir	2
Sissle, Noble Lee	9	Snell, Bertrand Hollis	6
Skidmore, Louis	7	Snow, Carmel White	7
Skinner, Otis	3	Snow, Edgar Parkes	9
Skouras, George Panagiotes	7	Snow, Jesse Baker	4
Skouras, Spyros Panagiotes	9	Snow, John Ben	9
Slemp, Campbell Bascom	3	Snow, William Freeman	4
Slichter, Sumner Huber	6	Snyder, Howard McCrum	8
Slipher, Vesto Melvin	8	Sobeloff, Simon E.	9
Sloan, Alfred Pritchard, Jr.	8	Sokolsky, George Ephraim	7
Sloan, George Arthur	5	Somervell, Brehon Burke	5
Sloan, Harold Paul	7	Son of Many Beads	5
Sloan, John French	5	Sorensen, Charles	8
Sloan, Matthew Scott	3	Sothern, Julia Marlowe	
Sloane, Isabel Dodge	7	See Marlowe, Julia	
Smart, David Archibald	5	Southgate, Horatio	1
Smedley, Agnes	4	Soyer, Moses	9
Smillie, Ralph	6	Spaatz, Carl Andrew	9
Smith, Albert Merriman	8	Spaeth, John Duncan	5
Smith, Alfred Emanuel	3	Spaeth, Sigmund	7
Smith, Bessie	2	Spalding, Albert	5
Smith, Betty	9	Spargo, John	8
Smith, Bruce	5	Spaulding, Charles Clinton	5
Smith, Courtney Craig	8	Spaulding, Edward Gleason	2
Smith, David	7	Speaker, Tris E.	6
Smith, David Eugene	3	Speaks, Oley	4
Smith, Edward Hanson	7	Speck, Frank Gouldsmith	4
Smith, Ellison DuRant	3	Speer, Emma Bailey	7
Smith, Frank Leslie	4	Speer, Robert Elliott	4
Smith, Fred Burton	2	Speiser, Ephraim Avigdor	7
Smith, George Albert	5	Spellman, Francis Joseph	8
Smith, George Otis	3	Spence, Brent	8
Smith, Harold Dewey	4	Sperry, Willard Learoyd	5
Smith, Harry Bache	2	Spewack, Samuel	9
Smith, Henry Justin	2	Speyer, James Joseph	3
Smith, Henry Louis	5	Spier, Leslie	7
Smith, Holland McTyeire	8	Spingarn, Arthur Barnett	9
Smith, Homer William	7	Spingarn, Joel Elias	2
Smith, Horatio Elwin	4	Spink, (John George) Taylor	7

Index Guide

Name	Supplement
Spottswood, Stephen Gill	9
Sprague, Charles Arthur	8
Sprague, Frank Julian	1
Sprague, Oliver Mitchell Wentworth	5
Spreckels, Rudolph	6
Springer, Charles	1
Sproul, Robert Gordon	9
Sproule, William	1
Spruance, Raymond Ames	8
Spurr, Josiah Edward	4
Stacy, Walter Parker	5
Stagg, Amos Alonzo	7
Stallings, Laurence Tucker	8
Standish, Burt L.	
See Patten, Gilbert	
Standley, William Harrison	7
Stanley, Augustus Owsley	6
Stanley, Harold	7
Stanley, Robert Crooks	5
Stanley, Wendell Meredith	9
Starbuck, Edwin Diller	4
Stark, Harold Raynsford	9
Stark, Lloyd Crow	9
Stark, Louis	5
Starks, Edwin Chapin	1
Starrett, Paul	6
Steagall, Henry Bascom	3
Stearman, Lloyd Carlton	9
Stearns, Frank Ballou	5
Stearns, Frank Waterman	2
Stearns, Harold Edmund	3
Steele, Wilbur Daniel	8
Steffansson, Vilhjalmur	7
Steffens, Lincoln	2
Steichen, Edward Jean	9
Stein, Gertrude	4
Stein, Leo	4
Steinbeck, John Ernst, Jr.	8
Steiner, Maximilian Raoul Walter	9
Steinhardt, Laurence Adolph	4
Steinman, David Barnard	6
Stejneger, Leonard Hess	3
Stella, Joseph	4
Stelzle, Charles	3
Stengel, Alfred	2
Stengel, Charles Dillon ("Casey")	9
Stephenson, Carl	5
Stephenson, Nathaniel Wright	1
Sterling, Ross Shaw	4
Stern, Bill	9
Stern, Kurt Guenter	6
Stern, Otto	8
Sterne, Maurice	6
Stetson, Henry Crosby	5
Stettinius, Edward Reilly	4
Steuben, John	6
Steuer, Max David	2
Stevens, Ashton	5
Stevens, Doris	7
Stevens, Frank Mozley	7
Stevens, George Cooper	9
Stevens, Harry Mozley	7
Stevens, John Frank	3
Stevens, Wallace	5
Stevenson, Adlai Ewing, II	7
Stewart, Arthur Thomas ("Tom")	9
Stewart, John George	8
Stewart, Walter Winne	6
Stieglitz, Alfred	4
Stieglitz, Julius	2
Stigler, William Grady	5
Stiles, Charles Wardell	3
Stimson, Frederic Jesup	3
Stimson, Henry Lewis	4
Stimson, Julia Catherine	4
Stine, Charles Milton Altland	5
Stitt, Edward Rhodes	4
Stock, Frederick August	3
Stockard, Charles Rupert	2
Stoddard, Lothrop	4
Stoessel, Albert Frederic	3
Stokes, Anson Phelps	6
Stokes, Frederick Abbot	2
Stokes, Isaac Newton Phelps	3
Stokes, Maurice	8
Stokes, Thomas Lunsford, Jr.	6
Stolberg, Benjamin	5
Stone, Abraham	6
Stone, Charles Augustus	3
Stone, Harlan Fiske	4
Stone, John Stone	3
Stone, Ormond	1
Stone, Witmer	2
Stong, Phil(lip Duffield)	6
Stotesbury, Edward Townsend	2
Stouffer, Vernon Bigelow	9
Stouffer, Samuel Andrew	6
Stout, Rex Todhunter	9
Stovall, Pleasant Alexander	1
Strange, Michael	4
Stratemeyer, George Edward	8
Stratton-Porter, Gene	
See Porter, Gene Stratton	
Straus, Jesse Isidor	2
Straus, Percy Selden	3
Straus, Roger W(illiams)	6
Strauss, Joseph Baermann	2
Strauss, Lewis Lichtenstein	9
Stravinsky, Igor Fyodorovich	9
Strawn, Silas Hardy	4

Index Guide

Name	Supplement	Name	Supplement
Streeter, George Linius	4	Swope, Herbert Bayard	6
Stribling, Thomas Sigismund	7	Sydenstricker, Edgar	2
Stritch, Samuel Alphonsus	6	Syndor, Charles Sackett	5
Strobel, Charles Louis	2	Syzk, Arthur	5
Stroheim, Erich von		Szell, George	8
See Von Stroheim, Erich		Szilard, Leo	7
Strong, Anna Louise	8	Szold, Henrietta	3
Strong, Charles Augustus	2		
Strong, Richard Pearson	4	Taber, John	7
Strunsky, Simeon	4	Taft, Henry Waters	3
Struve, Otto	7	Taft, Lorado Zadoc	2
Stryker, Lloyd Paul	5	Taft, Robert Alphonso	5
Stuart, Elbridge Amos	3	Taggard, Genevieve	4
Stuart, Francis Lee	1	Talbot, Arthur Newell	3
Stuart, John Leighton	7	Talbot, Francis Xavier	5
Stubbs, Walter Roscoe	1	Talbott, Harold Elstner	6
Stuhldreher, Harry A.	7	Talmadge, Constance	9
Sturges, Preston	6	Talmadge, Eugene	4
Sullavan, Margaret	6	Talmadge, Norma	6
Sullivan, Edward Vincent ("Ed")	9	Tamarkin, Jacob David	3
Sullivan, Harry Stack	4	Tamiris, Helen	8
Sullivan, James William	2	Tamiroff, Akim	9
Sullivan, John Florence		Tammen, Harry Heye	
See Allen, Fred		See under Bonfils, Frederick	
Sullivan, Mark	5	Gilmer	
Sulzberger, Arthur Hays	8	Tanguay, Eva	4
Sulzer, William	3	Tanner, Henry Ossawa	2
Summerall, Charles Pelot	5	Tansill, Charles Callan	7
Summerfield, Arthur Ellsworth	9	Tarbell, Edmund Charles	2
Summers, Edith		Tarbell, Ida Minerva	3
See Kelley, Edith Summers		Tarkington, Booth	4
Summersby, Kathleen Helen		Tate, George Henry Hamilton	5
("Kay")	9	Tate, John Torrence	4
Sumner, Francis Bertody	3	Tatlock, John Strong Perry	4
Sumner, James Batcheller	5	Tatum, Art	6
Sumner, Walter Taylor	1	Tatum, Edward Lawrie	9
Sumners, Hatton William	7	Taussig, Frank William	2
Sunday, William Ashley	1	Taussig, Frederick Joseph	3
Susann, Jacqueline	9	Taussig, Joseph Knefler	4
Sutherland, Earle Wilbur, Jr.	9	Taylor, Charles Alonzo	3
Sutherland, Edwin Hardin	4	Taylor, David Watson	2
Sutherland, George	3	Taylor, Edward	1
Sutherland, Richard Kerens	8	Taylor, Francis Henry	6
Svenson, Andrew Edward	9	Taylor, Frank Bursley	2
Swain, George Fillmore	1	Taylor, George William	9
Swanson, Claude Augustus	2	Taylor, Graham	2
Swanton, John Reed	6	Taylor, Henry Osborn	3
Swasey, Ambrose	2	Taylor, Joseph Deems	8
Sweeney, Martin Leonard	6	Taylor, Laurette	4
Swenson, David Ferdinand	2	Taylor, Myron Charles	6
Swift, Linton Bishop	4	Taylor, Robert	8
Swift, Louis Franklin	2	Taylor, Theodore ("Hound Dog")	9
Swing, Raymond Edwards		Taylor, William Chittenden	6
(Gram)	8	Tchelitchew, Pavel	6
Switzer, Mary Elizabeth	9	Teagarden, Weldon Leo ("Jack")	7
Swope, Gerard	6	Teeple, John Edgar	1

Index Guide

Name	Supplement	Name	Supplement
Teggert, Frederick John	4	Tittle, Ernest Fremont	4
Templeton, Alec Andrew	7	Tobey, Charles William	5
Terhune, Albert Payson	3	Tobias, Channing H.	7
Terman, Lewis Madison	6	Tobin, Daniel Joseph	5
Terrell, Mary Eliza Church	5	Tobin, Maurice Joseph	5
Terry, Paul Houlton	9	Todd, Mike	6
Tesla, Nikola	3	Todd, Thomas Wingate	2
Thacher, Thomas Day	4	Todd, Walter Edmond Clyde	8
Thalberg, Irving Grant	2	Toklas, Alice Babette	8
Thanet, Octave		Tolley, Howard Ross	6
See French, Alice		Tolman, Edward Chace	6
Thaw, Harry Kendall	4	Tolman, Richard Chace	4
Thayer, Tiffany Ellsworth	6	Tomlin, Bradley Walker	5
Theobald, Robert Alfred	6	Tone, Stanislas Pascal Franchot	8
Thilly, Frank	1	Torrence, Frederick Ridgley	4
Thomas, Elbert Duncan	5	Torrey, Charles Cutler	6
Thomas, George Allison	8	Toscanini, Arturo	6
Thomas, John Charles	6	Tourel, Jennie	9
Thomas, John Parnell	8	Towers, John Henry	5
Thomas, John William Elmer	7	Towne, Charles Hanson	4
Thomas, Martha Carey	1	Townley, Arthur Charles	6
Thomas, Norman Mattoon	8	Townsend, Francis Everett	6
Thomas, Roland Jay	8	Townsend, Willard	
Thomas, William Isaac	4	Saxby, Jr.	6
Thompson, Dorothy	7	Tracy, Spencer Bonaventure	8
Thompson, Edward Herbert	1	Train, Arthur Cheney	3
Thompson, Llewellyn E., Jr.	9	Trammell, Niles	9
Thompson, Malvina Cynthia	5	Trask, James Dowling	3
Thompson, Oscar Lee	3	Traubel, Helen	9
Thompson, Robert Means	1	Travers, Jerome Dunstan	5
Thompson, Slason	1	Traynor, Harold Joseph ("Pie")	9
Thompson, William Hale	3	Trelease, William	3
Thomson, Elihu	2	Trenholm, George Alfred	1
Thorek, Max	6	Trent, William Peterfield	2
Thorndike, Edward Lee	4	Tresca, Carlo	3
Thorndike, Lynn	7	Trilling, Lionel	9
Thorpe, James Francis	5	Truett, George Washington	3
Thorpe, Rose Alnora Hartwick	2	Truman, Harry S.	9
Thurber, James Grover	7	Trumbauer, Horace	2
Thurber, Jeannette Meyer	4	Tucker, Allen	2
Thurston, Howard	2	Tucker, Benjamin Ricketson	2
Thurstone, Louis Leon	5	Tucker, Henry St. George	6
Thwing, Charles Franklin	2	Tucker, Richard	9
Thye, Edward John	8	Tucker, Sophie	8
Tibbett, Lawrence Mervil	6	Tufts, James Hayden	3
Tigert, John James, IV	7	Tumulty, Joseph Patrick	5
Tilden, William Tatem ("Big Bill"), II	5	Tunnell, Emlen	9
Tillich, Paul	7	Turkevich, Leonid Ieronimovich	
Tilney, Frederick	2	See Leonty, Metropolitan	
Tilson, John Quillin	6	Turner, George Kibbe	5
Tilzer, Harry von	4	Turner, Richmond Kelly	7
Timberlake, Gideon	5	Turner, William	2
Timme, Walter	6	Turpin, Ben	2
Tinkham, George Holden	6	Tweed, Blanche Oelrichs	
		See Strange, Michael	

Index Guide

Name	Supplement	Name	Supplement
Tweed, Harrison	8	Vaughan, Thomas Wayland	5
Tydings, Millard Evelyn	7	Veatch, Arthur Clifford	2
Tyler, George Crouse	4	Veblen, Oswald	6
Tyler, Lyon Gardiner	1	Vedder, Edward Bright	5
Tyler, Royall	5	Vedder, Henry Clay	1
Tytus, John Butler	3	Veiller, Lawrence Turnure	6
		Verity, George Matthew	3
Ulrich, Edward Oscar	3	Verrill, Alpheus Wyatt	5
Ulmer, Edgar Georg	9	Vickery, Howard Leroy	4
Underwood, Frederick		Viereck, George Sylvester	7
Douglas	3	Villard, Oswald Garrison	4
Underwood, John Thomas	2	Vincent, George Edgar	3
Untermyer, Samuel	2	Vincent, John Carter	9
Updike, Daniel Berkeley	3	Viner, Jacob	8
Upshaw, William David	5	Vinson, Fred(erick) Moore	5
U'Ren, William Simon	4	Vizetelly, Frank Horace	2
Utley, George Burwell	4	Vladeck, Baruch Charney	2
		Vladimiroff, Pierre	8
Vail, Robert William Glenroie	8	Volstead, Andrew Joseph	4
Vaillant, George Clapp	3	von Kármán, Theodore	
Valachi, Joseph Michael	9	See Kármán, Theodore	
Van Anda, Carr Vattel	3	(Todor) von	
Vance, Arthur Charles ("Dazzy")	7	Von Moschzisker, Robert	2
Vance, Harold Sines	6	Von Neumann, John	6
Vance, Louis Joseph	1	Von Sternberg, Josef	8
Van De Graaff, Robert Jemison	8	Von Stroheim, Erich	6
Vandegrift, Alexander Archer	9	Von Wiegand, Karl Henry	7
Van Deman, Esther Boise	2	Vopicka, Charles Joseph	1
Vandenberg, Arthur Hendrick	5	Voris, John Ralph	8
Vandenberg, Hoyt Sanford	5	Vorse, Mary Heaton	8
Vanderbilt, Amy	9		
Vanderbilt, Arthur T.	6	Waddell, John Alexander Low	2
Vanderbilt, Cornelius, Jr.		Wade, Jeptha Homer	1
("Cornelius IV," "Neil")	9	Wadsworth, Eliot	6
Vanderbilt, Gloria Morgan	7	Wadsworth, James Wolcott, Jr.	5
Vanderbilt, Grace Graham		Waesche, Russell Randolph	4
Wilson	5	Wagener, John Andreas	1
Vanderlip, Frank Arthur	2	Wagner, John Peter	5
Van Devanter, Willis	3	Wagner, Robert Ferdinand	5
Van Dine, S.S.		Wainwright, Jonathan M.	5
See Wright, Willard		Waite, Henry Matson	3
Huntington		Waksman, Selman Abraham	9
Van Doren, Carl	4	Wald, Lillian D.	2
Van Doren, Mark Albert	9	Walgreen, Charles Rudolph	2
Van Doren, Irita Bradford	8	Walker, Frank Comerford	6
Van Druten, John William	6	Walker, James John	4
Van Dyke, John Wesley	2	Walker, Stuart Armstrong	3
Van Loon, Hendrik Willem	3	Walker, Walton Harris	4
Van Sweringen, Mantis James	1	Wallace, Henry Agard	7
Van Vechten, Carl	7	Wallace, Lurleen Burns	8
Van Vleck, Edward Burr	3	Waller, Fats	
Varèse, Edgard	7	See Waller, Thomas Wright	
Vasiliev, Alexander		Waller, Frederic	5
Alexandrovich	5	Waller, Thomas Wright	3
Vauclain, Samuel Matthews	2	Waller, Willard Walter	3

Index Guide

Name	Supplement	Name	Supplement
Wallgren, Monrad Charles	7	Waymack, William Wesley	6
Walling, William English	2	Webb, Clifton	8
Walsh, David Ignatius	4	Webb, Harry Howard	2
Walsh, Edmund Aloysius	6	Webb, Walter Prescott	7
Walsh, Edward Augustine	6	Webber, Herbert John	4
Walsh, Francis Patrick	2	Weber, Joseph Morris	3
Walsh, James Anthony	2	Weber, Max	7
Walsh, Thomas Joseph	5	Webster, Benjamin Francis	
Walter, Bruno	7	("Ben")	9
Walter, Eugene	3	Webster, Edwin Sibley	
Walter, Francis Eugene	7	See under Stone, Charles	
Walthall, Henry Brazeal	2	Augustus	
Walton, Lester Aglar	7	Webster, Harold Tucker	5
Wambaugh, Sarah	5	Webster, Margaret ("Peggy")	9
Waner, Paul Glee	7	Weddell, Alexander Wilbourne	4
Wanger, Walter	8	Weed, Lewis Hill	5
Warbasse, James Peter	6	Weede, Robert	9
Warburg, Felix Moritz	2	Weeks, John Elmer	4
Warburg, James Paul	8	Weeks, Sinclair	9
Ward, Arch Burdette	5	Weems, Ted	7
Ward, Charles Alfred	5	Wegmann, Edward	1
Ward, Charles Henshaw	1	Wehle, Louis Brandeis	6
Ward, Harry Frederick	8	Weidenreich, Franz	4
Ward, Henry Baldwin	3	Weigel, Gustave	7
Warde, Frederick Barkham	1	Weill, Kurt	4
Warfield, David	5	Weinberger, Jacob	9
Waring, Julius Waties	8	Weir, Ernest Tener	6
Warner, Edward Pearson	6	Weiss, George Martin	9
Warner, Glenn Scobey ("Pop")	5	Weiss, Sonia	3
Warner, Harry Morris	6	Welch, Joseph Nye	6
Warner, Langdon	5	Welker, Herman	6
Warner, William Lloyd	8	Welles, Benjamin Sumner	7
Warren, Charles	5	Welling, Richard Ward Greene	4
Warren, Earl	9	Wellman, William Augustus	9
Warren, Fuller	9	Wells, Harriet Sheldon	7
Warren, George Frederick	2	Wells, Harry Gideon	3
Warren, Henry Ellis	6	Wertenbaker, Charles Christian	5
Warren, Herbert Langford	1	Wertenbaker, Thomas Jefferson	8
Warren, Leonard	6	Wertheimer, Max	3
Warrington, Albert Powell	2	West, Allen Brown	2
Washburn, Margaret Floy	2	West, Andrew Fleming	3
Washington, Dinah	7	West, James Edward	4
Washington, Kenneth Stanley	9	West, Oswald	6
Waterman, Alan Tower	8	West, Roy Owen	6
Watkins, Arthur Vivian	9	Westergaard, Harold Malcolm	4
Watson, Arthur Kittridge	9	Westermann, William Linn	5
Watson, Charles Roger	4	Westley, Helen	3
Watson, James Eli	4	Weston, Edward	2
Watson, John Broadus	6	Weston, Edward Henry	6
Watson, Thomas John	6	Wexler, Irving	5
Watts, Alan Wilson	9	Weyerhaeuser, Frederick Edward	3
Wattson, Lewis Thomas		Weyl, Hermann	5
See Francis, Paul James		Weymouth, Frank Elwin	3
Waugh, Frederick Judd	2	Whalen, Grover Aloysius	7
Waxman, Franz	8	Wharton, Edith Newbold Jones	2

Index Guide

Name	Supplement	Name	Supplement
Wheat, Zachariah Davis ("Buck")	9	Wightman, Hazel Virginia Hotchkiss	9
Wheeler, Arthur Leslie	1	Wigmore, John Henry	3
Wheeler, Burton Kendall	9	Wilbur, Curtis Dwight	5
Wheeler, Earle Gilmore	9	Wilbur, Ray Lyman	4
Wheeler, (George) Post	6	Wilder, Laura Ingalls	6
Wheeler, John Martin	2	Wilder, Russell Morse	6
Wheeler, William Morton	2	Wilder, Thornton Niven	9
Wheelock, Lucy	4	Wiley, Alexander	8
Wheelwright, Mary Cabot	6	Wilkinson, Theodore Stark	4
Wherry, Kenneth Spicer	5	Willard, Daniel	3
Whetzel, Herbert Hice	3	Willard, Frank Henry	6
Whitaker, Charles Harris	2	Willard, James Field	1
White, Alma Kent	4	Willard, Josiah Flint	1
White, Benjamin Franklin	6	Willebrandt, Mabel Walker	7
White, Clarence Cameron	6	Willett, Herbert Lockwood	3
White, David	1	Williams, Aubrey Willis	7
White, Edward Higgins, II	8	Williams, Ben Ames	5
White, George	8	Williams, Edward Thomas	3
White, Joseph Malachy	6	Williams, Fannie Barrier	3
White, Josh	8	Williams, Francis Henry	2
White, Leonard Dupee	6	Williams, Gaar Campbell	1
White, Paul Dudley	9	Williams, Harrison Charles	5
White, Pearl	2	Williams, (Hiram) Hank	5
White, Steward Edward	4	Williams, Walter	1
White, Walter Francis	5	Williams, William Carlos	7
White, William Alanson	2	Willis, Bailey	4
White, William Allen	3	Willis, Henry Parker	2
Whitehead, Alfred North	4	Williston, Samuel	7
Whiteman, Paul Samuel ("Pops")	8	Willkie, Wendell Lewis	3
Whiteside, Arthur Dare	6	Willoughby, Westel Woodbury	3
Whitfield, Owen	7	Wills, Childe Harold	2
Whiting, Arthur Battelle	2	Wills, Harry	6
Whiting, William	1	Wills, James Robert ("Bob")	9
Whitman, Charles Seymour	4	Willys, John North	1
Whitman, Royal	4	Wilmer, William Holland	2
Whitmore, Frank Clifford	4	Wilson, Charles Edward	9
Whitney, Alexander Fell	4	Wilson, Charles Erwin	7
Whitney, Caspar	1	Wilson, Clarence True	2
Whitney, Charlotte Anita	5	Wilson, Edith Bolling	7
Whitney, Courtney	8	Wilson, Edmund, Jr.	9
Whitney, George	7	Wilson, Edmund Beecher	2
Whitney, Gertrude Vanderbilt	3	Wilson, Francis	1
Whitney, Richard	9	Wilson, George Grafton	5
Whitney, Willis Rodney	6	Wilson, Halsey William	5
Whittaker, Charles Evans	9	Wilson, Harry Leon	2
Whittemore, Thomas	4	Wilson, Hugh Robert	4
Whorf, Benjamin Lee	3	Wilson, J(ames) Finley	5
Wickard, Claude Raymond	8	Wilson, James Southall	7
Wickersham, George Woodward	2	Wilson, Joseph Chamberlain	9
Widener, George Dunton	9	Wilson, Louis Blanchard	3
Widney, Joseph Pomeroy	2	Wilson, Marie	9
Wieland, George Reber	5	Wilson, Orlando Winfield	9
Wiener, Leo	2	Wilson, Warren Hugh	2
Wiener, Norbert	7	Wilson, William Griffith	9
Wiggin, Albert Henry	5		

Index Guide

Name	Supplement	Name	Supplement
Wimsatt, William Kurtz	9	Wright, Harold Bell	3
Winant, John Gilbert	4	Wright, Henry	2
Winchell, Walter	9	Wright, John Kenneth Lloyd	9
Winlock, Herbert Eustis	4	Wright, Orville	4
Winship, Blanton	4	Wright, Richard Nathaniel	6
Winship, George Parker	5	Wright, Richard Robert	4
Winslow, Charles-Edward Amory	6	Wright, Theodore Paul	8
Winterhalter, Hugo	9	Wright, Willard Huntington	2
Wirt, William Albert	2	Wright, William	1
Wise, Stephen Samuel	4	Wrigley, William	1
Wislocki, George Bernays	6	Wyckoff, John Henry	2
Wissler, Clark	4	Wyeth, Newell Convers	3
Wister, Owen	2	Wylie, Philip Gordon	9
Witherspoon, Alexander Maclaren	7	Wynn, Ed	8
Witherspoon, Herbert	1		
Witmark, Isidore	3	Yancey, James Edward	5
Witte, Edwin Emil	6	Yates, Herbert John	8
Wodehouse, Pelham Grenville	9	Yellin, Samuel	2
Wolfe, Thomas Clayton	2	Yellowley, Edward Clements	7
Wolff, Kurt August Paul	7	Yergan, Max	9
Wolfson, Erwin Service	7	Yerkes, Robert Mearns	6
Wolfson, Harry Austryn	9	Yon, Pietro Alessandro	3
Wolheim, Louis Robert	1	York, Alvin Cullum	7
Woll, Matthew	6	Yost, Casper Salathiel	3
Wolman, Leo	7	Yost, Fielding Harris	4
Wong, Anna May	7	Youmans, Vincent	4
Wood, Casey Albert	3	Young, Ammi Burnham	1
Wood, Craig Ralph	8	Young, Art	3
Wood, Charles Erskine Scott	3	Young, Clarence Marshall	9
Wood, Edith Elmer	3	Young, Denton True	5
Wood, Frederick Hill	3	Young, George	1
Wood, Garfield Arthur ("Gar")	9	Young, Hugh Hampton	3
Wood, Grant	3	Young, Karl	3
Wood, Henry Alexander Wise	2	Young, Mahonri Mackintosh	6
Wood, John Stephens	8	Young, Owen D.	7
Wood, Robert Elkington	8	Young, Robert Ralph	6
Woodbridge, Frederick James		Young, Stark	7
Eugene	2	Young, Whitney Moore, Jr.	9
Woodring, Harry Hines	8	Younger, Maud	2
Woodruff, Lorande Loss	4		
Woods, James Haughton	4	Zacharias, Ellis Mark	7
Woodson, Carter Godwin	4	Zaharias, Mildred ("Babe")	
Woodward, William	5	Didrikson	6
Woollcott, Alexander Humphreys	3	Zahniser, Howard Clinton	7
Woolley, Edgar Montillion		Zellerbach, James David	7
("Monty")	7	Ziff, William Bernard	5
Woolley, Mary Emma	4	Zilboorg, Gregory	6
Woolman, Collett Everman	8	Zimmerman, Eugene	1
Woolsey, John Munro	3	Zimmerman, Henry ("Heinie")	8
Worcester, Elwood	2	Zinsser, Hans	2
Work, Hubert	3	Znaniecki, Florian Witold	6
Woytinsky, Wladimir Savelievich	6	Zook, George Frederick	5
Wrather, William Embry	7	Zorach, William	8
Wright, Fielding Lewis	6	Zuppke, Robert Carl	6
Wright, Frank Lloyd	6	Zwicky, Fritz	9

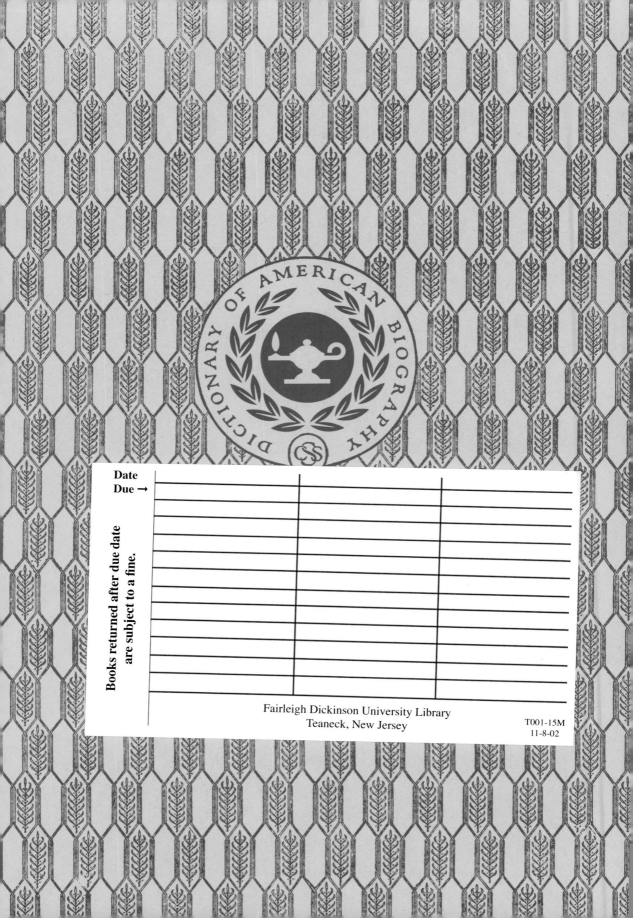